October 15–19, 2016
Amsterdam, The Netherlands

Association for
Computing Machinery

Advancing Computing as a Science & Profession

MM'16

Proceedings of the 2016 ACM
Multimedia Conference

Sponsored by:

ACM SIGMM

Supported by:

Qualcomm Research, FXPal, COMMIT, IBM, Facebook, Microsoft Research, Google, Unified Streaming Platform, & ViSENZE

Association for
Computing Machinery

Advancing Computing as a Science & Profession

The Association for Computing Machinery
2 Penn Plaza, Suite 701
New York, New York 10121-0701

ISBN: 978-1-4503-3603-1 (Digital)

ISBN: 978-1-4503-4687-0 (Print)

Additional copies may be ordered prepaid from:

ACM Order Department
PO Box 30777
New York, NY 10087-0777, USA

Phone: 1-800-342-6626 (USA and Canada)
+1-212-626-0500 (Global)
Fax: +1-212-944-1318
E-mail: acmhelp@acm.org
Hours of Operation: 8:30 am – 4:30 pm ET

Printed in the USA

ACM Multimedia 2016 Chairs' Welcome

We warmheartedly welcome you to the 24th ACM Multimedia conference, which is hosted for the first time in the Netherlands, in the wonderful city of Amsterdam. ACM Multimedia 2016 brings an extensive program consisting of technical sessions covering all aspects of the multimedia field in the form of oral and poster presentations, tutorials, panels, exhibits, demonstrations and workshops, bringing into focus the principal subjects of investigation, competitions of research teams on challenging problems, and an interactive art program stimulating artists and computer scientists to meet and discover together the frontiers of artistic communication. The call for contributions attracted submissions from all over the world, which were all thoroughly reviewed for their merit in terms of scientific quality, innovation, and match to the conference. In summary, the various dedicated program committees reviewed and accepted the following:

Track	*Reviewed*	*Accepted*	
Long papers	237	52	22%
Short papers	413	127	31%
Brave new idea papers	14	4	29%
Demos	54	31	57%
Doctoral symposium papers	14	9	64%
Multimedia grand challenge submissions	20	12	60%
Video demonstrations	3	3	100%
Open source competition submissions	22	16	73%
Interactive art papers	23	10	43%

In addition to these, the main program has two exciting keynote presentations, by **Dirk Helbing** from ETH Zurich, Switzerland, titled "A digital world to thrive in – How the Internet of Things can make the ‚invisible hand‘ work" and by **Jack van Wijk** from Eindhoven University of Technology, the Netherlands, titled "Visual Analytics for Multimedia: Challenges and Opportunities". Furthermore, a visionary presentation will be given by the winner of the SIGMM Award for Outstanding Technical Contributions to Multimedia Computing, Communications and Applications 2016, **Alberto del Bimbo**, from the University of Florence, Italy**.** The main program will conclude with the SIGMM Rising Stars Symposium, highlighting the scientific results and vision of the invited young researchers, who demonstrated great potential in multimedia research and who are considered to become future leaders in the multimedia field.

The main program is accompanied by eight workshops to discuss challenging topics and six tutorials to bring you up to speed on important foundations of our multimedia field. The unique co-location of ACM Multimedia 2016 with the European Conference on Computer Vision (ECCV 2016) has brought the opportunity to have additional twelve invited tutorials from world leaders covering both multimedia and computer vision.

Putting together a conference like ACM Multimedia is a team effort with many people volunteering their precious time. We would like to thank all who contributed to making this year's conference a success: the authors for submitting their latest work, the chairs and reviewers of the various tracks and activities for realizing a high quality program, and all others who assured smooth organization and realization of the conference. Finally, we would like to thank our sponsors and supporters, SIGMM, University of Amsterdam, Delft University of Technology, Qualcomm Research, FxPal, COMMIT, Facebook, Microsoft, Google, Unified Streaming, IBM and ViSenze for allowing us to bring you more than just the scientific program.

ACM Multimedia 2016 General Chairs

Alan Hanjalic
Delft University of Technology

Cees Snoek
Qualcomm Research &
University of Amsterdam

Marcel Worring
University of Amsterdam

Message from the Program Coordinator

I am very happy to welcome you to Amsterdam for Multimedia 2016. This is the 24th edition of what can be considered as the premier academic conference on multimedia systems, content and applications.

The conference general and technical program chairs have given a wealth of information on the nature, structure and process used to assemble the program that will unfold this week. I, too, would like to add a few comments to help participants better understand the nature of the sessions and the combination of program elements that we hope will serve as the basis of an inspiring visit.

There are always two broad audiences for the collections of papers presented as part of the ACM Multimedia series. First are researchers who access individual papers via the ACM Digital Library. Over the coming years, this is where the greatest impact of the contributions presented here is likely to manifest itself. The Technical Program Committee has done an excellent job in providing a corpus of research that reflects the current state of the various sub-disciplines covered at the conference. As a Program Coordinator, I have little influence on the selection of these papers: this is the work of the reviewers, various area chairs and the technical program committee chairs.

The second audience for this year's papers, posters and presentations are the attendees of the conference in Amsterdam. These people come to the conference not only to hear the latest individual research results – this is something that they can do more quickly and cheaply via the ACM DL! – but also to be inspired by work that is perhaps (just) outside their own areas of expertise. Here, the Program Coordinator has the responsibility to 'package' the papers at the conference in a way that makes new work available to as many people as possible while also maintaining the community bonds within our various historical and emerging interests groups.

This year, the conference program has been architected so that each session block contains a *Topics in Multimedia* session, along with three more specialized special-interest sessions. The *Topics* session contains a collection of papers from different disciplines but often on (somewhat) related topics. The specialized sessions allow members of particular groups to interact more directly. In this way, there should always be a session of interest (either in breadth or depth) to capture the imagination of the participant. We hope that you find this approach useful and inspiring.

Another responsibility of the Program Coordinator is to coordinate the selection of the best paper at the conference. This year, the program committee nominated eight candidate papers. A second committee was formed (using recommendations from the technical program chairs) that selected four of these papers as candidates for the award at the conference. This was a particularly difficult task, as the quality of each of the candidates was very high. Since ACM Multimedia is a generalist conference, we used this as a guide in the ultimate selection. I encourage you to attend the best paper session to see this broad sampling of first-class research in our community.

Coming to a conference is an expense and time-consuming venture, but I hope that the work of all of the members of our community who volunteered to put together ACM Multimedia 2016 will inspire your own research, allow you to make new contacts and help us all advance the quality of our fields.

Dick C.A. Bulterman, *CWI and Vrije Universiteit Amsterdam*

Message from the Technical Program Chairs

We are pleased to introduce to you to the Technical Program for the ACM International Conference on Multimedia (ACM Multimedia) 2016, which will take place in Amsterdam in October 2016. While adopting the best practices from previous ACM Multimedia conferences, this year we also introduced new approaches and guidelines in the review process to ensure an efficient and fair evaluation of all submissions in providing a high quality conference.

Following last year's structure, fifteen areas of interest were grouped into four research themes, including a System Theme (covering Multimedia Transport and Delivery, Multimedia Systems and Middleware, Multimedia Telepresence and Virtual/Augmented Reality, Multimedia Scalability and Management, Mobile Multimedia), an Experience Theme (covering Multimedia HCI and Quality of Experience, Music, Speech and Audio Processing in Multimedia, Multimedia Art, Entertainment and Culture, Multimedia for Collaboration in Education & Distributed Environments), an Understanding Theme (covering Deep Learning for Multimedia, Multimodal Analysis and Description, Multimedia and Vision), and an Engagement Theme (covering Emotional and Social Signals In Multimedia, Social Multimedia, Multimedia Search and Recommendation). Minor changes compared to last year's structure included moving the Multimedia Art area from the Engagement to the Experience theme and the addition of the Multimedia Scalability and Management area within the System's theme.

Among the noticeable changes for ACM Multimedia 2016 is the addition of a fifth page (reserved for citations) for the short papers, demos, grand challenge and open source software competitions, doctoral symposium, and interactive art submissions. Additionally, long paper submissions can range from 8 to 10 pages, with the minimum page length introduced this year.

Each research theme was overseen by one of this year's Technical Program Chairs. For each area of interest, a team of Area Chairs (ACs), ranging from one to eight members, was recruited to handle the paper review process. In total, 46 ACs were appointed. A new contribution this year was the preparation of detailed instructions for ACs and reviewers, describing each step of the process and an accompanying time schedule. Organizationally, we believe it helped ACs and reviewers with overall planning logistics and time management. It is suggested that this process should be updated and used as a standard practice in future conferences. The second innovation this year was the use of the Toronto Paper Matching System (TPMS) for paper-reviewer assignment. This system has gained adoption in both machine learning and computer vision conferences and is being used, for example by CVPR, ICCV and ECCV. The TPMS worked in conjunction with the conference management system (CMT), whereby invited reviewers uploaded their own papers for analysis as part of the automatic assignment process. Overall, the matching system provided reasonably reliable results in most cases, but required close supervision and tweaking by the technical program chairs, to avoid issues such as reviewers from one area being allocated papers from another. The conference ACs played an important role here also in

The paper review and submission is described in detail below:

- Submission of full (abstract pre-submission was allowed for better review planning) and short papers were separated from each other, with the short paper submission deadline one month later than the deadline for full paper submissions.
- Following the previous year's approach, a two-stage review process for full paper submissions was applied. Authors were invited to submit a rebuttal based on the first round of reviews. The reviewers were then asked to consider the rebuttal, to revise their reviews accordingly, and to enter discussion with other reviewers with the aim of improving review consensus on each paper. The results of the second round reviews and discussions were then summarized by the ACs into meta-reviews, which included tentative recommendations, to be discussed and finalized during the TPC meeting.
- In the second review stage, authors had the opportunity to communicate with the Author's Advocate if they believed there were issues or anomalies with the reviews. During this year's review cycle, the Author's Advocate was utilized in several cases to ensure a more equitable and satisfying review procedure.

- Submissions from any authors who also acted as ACs/TPCs were handled personally by non-conflicting Technical Program Chairs.
- Deadlines were predominantly adhered to, with minor delays on occasion.

In total, 248 full and 425 short paper submissions were received by their respective deadlines and entered into the regular review process.

The table below gives the exact submission numbers across the various research areas

Area	Full	Short
Emotional and Social Signals In Multimedia	7	26
Multimedia Search and Recommendation	41	52
Social Multimedia	16	19
Multimedia Art, Entertainment and Culture	9	7
Multimedia for Collaboration in Education & Distributed Environments	2	3
Multimedia HCI and Quality of Experience	12	21
Music, Speech and Audio Processing in Multimedia	8	17
Mobile Multimedia	6	12
Multimedia Scalability and Management	5	5
Multimedia Systems and Middleware	13	12
Multimedia Telepresence and Virtual/Augmented Reality	10	12
Multimedia Transport and Delivery	17	10
Deep Learning for Multimedia	20	57
Multimedia and Vision	45	125
Multimodal Analysis and Description	26	35

Decisions on full and short paper acceptances were made at the one-day TPC meeting held at Columbia University on June 10, 2016. All four Technical Program Chairs attended the meeting and handled their assigned themes in different allocated rooms. The emphasis of the TPC meeting was on high-score, borderline, and controversial paper submissions. The discussions were detailed and intensive, taking into account all the available data, including reviews, the authors' rebuttals, the post-rebuttal discussions, the initial recommendations by the ACs (in the form of a meta-review) and any subsequent reviews performed by other ACs during the meeting itself. For some papers that span across multiple themes, the TPC/AC Chairs collaborate across theme to reach a consensus on the decision. Technical Program Chairs and ACs were requested to leave the room when a conflicting submission was discussed.

After the separate meetings, a plenary session coordinated by the TPCs took place to make final decisions, where the overall quality and balance of different tracks was taken into consideration. By the end of the day, the participants accepted 52 full and 127 short papers, leading to acceptance rates of 22.2% and 30.3% for full and short papers, respectively. Five high quality full paper submissions were also recommended for acceptance as short papers.

The TPC meeting was organized in conjunction with a supporting workshop as per previous years. This years' workshop (http://acmmmtpcws16.eurecom.fr/) was integrated with the ICMR conference which also took place in New York in June. Workshop participants had the chance to listen to 13 enlightening talks about recent research developments from the entire spectrum of topics covered by ACM Multimedia.

The Technical Program Committee has worked diligently over the last year to ensure that the technical program of this year's conference is of the highest possible quality. We would like to recognize the great effort and hard work from the volunteer team of ACs and reviewers who helped shape an exciting technical program.

We look forward to seeing you this autumn, in Amsterdam, Netherlands for a compelling ACM Multimedia technical program.

Benoit Huet, *EURECOM (FR)*

Yiannis Kompatsiaris, *CERTH-ITI (GR)*

Aisling Kelliher, *Virginia Tech (USA)*

Jin Li, *Microsoft (USA)*

Table of Contents

Session: Video Program

Demonstrations

Session: Art Exhibition

Session: Topics in Multimedia I

Session: Analysis & Search

Session: Video Analysis & Streaming

Session: Topics in Multimedia II

Session: Brave News Topic

Session: Deep Learning

Session: Events and Context

Session: Multimedia Grand Challenge

Session: Keynote 2

Session: Topics in Multimedia III

Session: Open Source Software Competition

Session: Learning & Hashing

Session: Transport & Experience

Session: Topics in Multimedia IV

Session: Analysis & Middleware

Session: Emotions, People and Faces

Session: Doctoral Symposium

Session: Tutorials

Session: Workshops

MM 2016 Conference Organization

General Chairs: Alan Hanjalic *(Delft University of Technology)*
Cees Snoek *(Qualcomm Research Netherlands / University of Amsterdam)*
Marcel Worring *(University of Amsterdam)*

Honorary Chair: Arnold Smeulders *(University of Amsterdam)*

Program Coordinator: Dick Bulterman *(CWI / VU University Amsterdam)*

Program Chairs: Benoit Huet *(EURECOM)*
Aisling Kelliher *(Virginia Tech)*
Yiannis Kompatsiaris *(CERTH-ITI)*
Jin Li *(Microsoft)*

Local Arrangements Chairs: Hayley Hung *(Delft University of Technology)*
Cynthia Liem *(Delft University of Technology)*

Author's Advocate: Shervin Shirmohammadi *(University of Ottawa)*

Workshop Chairs: Lexing Xie *(Australian National University)*
Alan Smeaton *(Dublin City University)*

Brave New Idea Chairs: Martha Larson *(Delft University of Technology / Radboud University Nijmegen)*
Hari Sundaram *(University of Illinois)*

Tutorial Chairs: Rita Cucchiara *(University of Modena)*
Susanne Boll *(University of Oldenburg)*

Doctoral Symposium Chairs: Winston Hsu *(National Taiwan University & IBM TJ Watson)*
Eckehard Steinbach *(Technische Universität München)*

Panel Chairs: Alberto Del Bimbo *(University of Florence)*
David Shamma *(Yahoo Labs)*

Multimedia Grand Challenge Chairs: Xavier Anguera *(ELSA Corp.)*
Shuicheng Yan *(Qihoo 360 & NUS)*

Demo Chairs: Pablo Cesar *(CWI)*
Max Mühlhäuser *(Technische Universität Darmstadt)*

Open Source Competition Chairs: Tao Mei *(Microsoft Research Asia)*
Christian Timmerer *(Alpen-Adria-Universität Klagenfurt)*

Travel Grant Chairs: Wessel Kraaij *(Radboud University Nijmegen / TNO)*
Remco Veltkamp *(Utrecht University)*

Video Chairs: Marco Bertini *(University of Florence)*
Shin'ichi Satoh *(University of Tokyo)*

Interactive Arts Chairs: Lucas Evers *(Waag Society)*
Frank Nack *(University of Amsterdam)*

Sponsor Chairs: Touradj Ebrahimi *(EPFL)*
Gerald Friedland *(ICSI)*

Publicity Chairs: Carsten Griwodz *(University of Oslo)*
Meng Wang *(Hefei University of Technology)*

Publication Chairs: Chong-Wah Ngo *(City University of Hong Kong)*
Balakrishnan Prabhakaran *(University of Texas at Dallas)*

Web Chairs: Stevan Rudinac *(University of Amsterdam)*
Pascal Mettes *(University of Amsterdam)*

History Preservation Chairs: Yong Rui *(Microsoft Research Asia)*
Heng Tao Shen *(University of Queensland)*

MM 2016 Area Chairs

Emotional and Social Signals in Multimedia:	Julien Epps *(University of New South Wales)* Mohammad Soleymani *(University of Geneva)* Jean-Marc Odobez *(IDIAP)*
Multimedia Search and Recommendation:	Joemon Jose *(Glasgow)* Stéphane Marchand-Maillet *(UNIGE)* Michele Merler *(IBM TJ Watson Research Center)* Muriel Visani *(University of La Rochelle)* Zheng-Jun Zha *(University of Science and Technology of China)*
Social Multimedia:	Luca Maria Aiello *(Yahoo Labs, London, UK)* Symeon Papadopoulos *(CERTH-ITI)* Jonathon Hare *(University of Southampton)*
Multimedia Art, Entertainment and Culture:	Jinsil Hwaryoung Seo *(Simon Fraser)* David Ayman Shamma *(Yahoo)*
Multimedia for Collaboration in Education & Distributed Environments:	Matt Cooper *(FXPAL)*
Multimedia HCI and Quality of Experience:	Teresa Chambel *(Lisbon University)* Judith Redi *(Delft)* Bart Thomee *(Yahoo)*
Music, Speech and Audio Processing in Multimedia:	Brian Pardo *(Northwestern)*
Mobile Multimedia:	Winston Hsu *(National Taiwan University, Taiwan)* Jochen Huber *(MIT Media Lab, USA)*
Multimedia Scalability and Management System:	Xiansheng Hua *(Alibaba, China)* Lei Zhang *(Microsoft, USA)*
Multimedia Systems and Middleware:	Jiangchuan Liu *(Simon Fraser University, Canada)* Wenwu Zhu *(Tsinghua University, China)* Roger Zimmerman *(NUS, Singapore)*
Multimedia Telepresence and Virtual/Augmented Reality:	Pablo Cesar *(CWI)* Zicheng Liu *(Microsoft, USA)*
Multimedia Transport and Delivery:	Ali Begen *(CISCO, USA)* Christian Timmerer *(Alpen-Adria-Universität Klagenfurt, Austria)*

MM 2016 Program Committee

Luca Maria Aiello
Ergun Akleman
Xavier Alameda Pineda
Kevin Almeroth
Jose M Alvarez
Joseph Antony
Ahsan Arefin
Grenville Armitage
Yannis Avrithis
Slawomir Bak
Saeideh Bakhshi
Prabhakaran Balakrishnan
Lamberto Ballan
Tadas Baltrusaitis
Jean-Charles Bazin
Alejandro Bellogin
Jenny Benois-Pineau
Marco Bertini
Laurent Besacier
Chidansh Bhatt
Piotr Bilinski
Arijit Biswas
Isabelle Bloch
Tom Blount
Giulia Boato
Marc Bolanos
Egor Bondarev
Fernando Boronat Seguí
Damian Borth
Alessandro Bozzon
Herve Bredin
Andrei Bursuc
Junjie Cai
Jianfei Cai
Simone Calderara
Cristian Canton
Liangliang Cao
Kristin Carlson
Mark Cartwright
Carlos Castellanos
Andrea Cavallaro
Shayok Chakraborty
Houssem Chatbri
Faouzi Cheikh
Huizhong Chen
Kuan-Ta Chen
KuanTing Chen
Shu-Ching Chen
Songqing Chen
Yung-Yao Chen
Gong Chen
Jia Chen
Jun-Cheng Chen
Yan-Ying Chen
Hsu-Yung Cheng
Jian Cheng
Mohamed Chetouani
Liang-Tien Chia
Jason Chou
Wei-Ta Chu
Yung-Yu Chuang
Adrian Clark
Cyril Concolato
Greg Corness
Nuno Correia
Marco Cristani
Peng Cui
Yong Cui
Dubravko Culibrk
Ricardo da Silva Torres
Petros Daras
Claire-Helene Demarty
Cheng Deng
Om Deshmukh
Niloo Dezfuli
Mariella Dimiccoli
Keisuke Doman
Jean-Philippe Domenger
Zhiyao Duan
Carlos Duarte
Stefan Duffner
Jean-Claude Dufourd
Pinar Duygulu-Sahin
Sebastian Egger
Peter Eisert
Tahra Eissa
Abdulmotaleb El Saddik
Sebastian Ewert
Philipp Fechteler
Jie Feng
Wu-Chi Feng
Marcio Ferreira Moreno
Robert Fisher
Manuel Fonseca
Jason Freeman
Gerald Friedland
Pascal Frossard
Takuya Funatomi
Philip Galanter
Andrew Gallagher
Chuang Gan
Debasis Ganguly
Marie-Neige Garcia
Antonis Gasteratos
Kirill Gavrilyuk
George Ghinea
Andreas Girgensohn
Roland Goecke
Mar Gonzalez-Franco
Jordi Gonzàlez
Fabien Gouyon
Costantino Grana
Carsten Griwodz
Zhouye Gu
Ling Guan
Charlie Gullström
Yandong Guo

Michael Gurevich
Cathal Gurrin
Michael Gygli
Martin Halvey
Pal Halvorsen
Bill Hamilton
Yahong Han
Frank Hartung
Mohamed Hefeeda
Hermann Hellwagner
Niels Henze
Keita Higuchi
Keiichiro Hoashi
Richang Hong
Frank Hopfgartner
Ehsan Hoque
Timothy Hospedales
Tobias Hossfeld
Cheng-Hsin Hsu
Min-Chun Hu
Qinghua Hu
Kai-Lung Hua
Zixia Huang
LiangKang Huang
Noureldien Hussein
Wolfgang Hürst
James Ivory
Ebroul Izquierdo
Jack Jansen
Iveel Jargalsaikhan
Morgan Jenks
I-Hong Jhuo
Rongrong Ji
Lu Jiang
shuqiang Jiang
Cheng Jin
Alexis Joly
Dhiraj Joshi
Bhautik Joshi
Brendan Jou
Rene Kaiser
Yannis Kalantidis
Sebastian Kaltwang
Eunsu Kang
Li-Wei Kang
Rafal Kapela
Svebor Karaman
Marie Katsurai
Isaak Kavasidis
Ian Kegel
Christian Keimel
Aisling Kelliher
John Kender
Sara Kepplinger
Hua Kien
Ewa Kijak
Yelin Kim
Bongjun Kim
Akisato Kimura
Hill Kobayashi
Dorothea Kolossa
Stephan Kopf
Pavel Korshunov
Joke Kort
Dimitrios Kosmopoulos
Iaroslav Kryvyi
Fons Kuijk
Gauthier Lafruit
Rodrigo Laiola Guimaraes
Agata Lapedriza
Duy-Dinh Le
Thi-Lan Le
Jonathan Le Roux
Gwénolé Lecorvé
Hyun Jean Lee
Jin Ha Lee
Vincent Lemaire
Baochun Li
Xinchao Li
Zhu Li
Kai Li
Bochen Li
Haojie Li
Xi Li
Yen Liang
Miao Liao
Cynthia Liem
Weisi Lin
Georges Linares
Rhema Linder
Dimitris Liparas
Suzanne Little
Dong Liu
Fangming Liu
Xueliang Liu
Hantao Liu
Jing Liu
Si Liu
Xiang Liu
Zhen Liu
Xiaobai Liu
Antoine Liutkus
Josep Llados
Joan Llobera
Yijuan Lu
Jiwen Lu
Hanqing Lu
Jiebo Luo
Minnan Luo
Mathias Lux
Kevin Ma
Joao Magalhaes
Marwa Mahmoud
Diego Maranan
Mark Marsden
Jean Martinet
Maria Martini
Saverio Mascolo
Masoud Mazloom
Chris McCool
Philip McParlane
Andrew McPherson
Tao Mei

Britta Meixner
Rufael Mekuria
Angeliki Metallinou
Vasileios Mezaris
Eva Mohedano
Mario Montagud
Sean Moran
Francesc Moreno-Noguer
Vicki Moulder
Emily Mower Provost
Francesca Murabito
Niall Murray
Klara Nahrstedt
Yuta Nakashima
Ryohei Nakatsu
Manish Narwaria
Edith Ngai
Laurent Nguyen
Rongrong Ni
Eric Nichols
Liqiang Nie
Marcos Nieto
Nikolaos Nikolaidis
Kuo Nini
Masafumi Nishida
Naoko Nitta
Neil O'Hare
Jean-Marc Ogier
Hiroaki Ohshima
Wei Tsang Ooi
Jörg Ott
Simone Palazzo
Pan Pan
Ioannis Panagakis
Nikolaos Papamarkos
Frederic Parke
Omkar Parkhi
Jose Luis Patino Vilchis
Ioannis Patras
Amy Pavel
George Pavlidis
Yuxin Peng
Giorgos Petkos
Stavros Petridis
Julien Pinquier
Hamed Pirsiavash
Fatemeh Pishdadian
Adrian Popescu
Ronald Poppe
Gerasimos Potamianos
Ioannis Pratikakis
Nicholas Race
Zafar Rafii
Benjamin Rainer
Miriam Redi
Gael Richard
Fabien Ringeval
George Rizos
Edgar Roman-Rangel
Samuel Rota-Bulò
Ognjen Rudovic
Javier Ruiz
Enrico Rukzio
Tom Runia
Andreas Sackl
Diego Saez Trumper
Alan Said
Albert Salah
Amaia Salvador
Juan-Carlos SanMiguel
Nabil Sarhan
Shin'ichi Satoh
Peter Schelkens
Manos Schinas
Marwin Schmitt
Klaus Schoeffmann
Bjoern Schuller
Florence Sedes
Prem Seetharaman
Shiguang Shan
Ling Shao
James She
Koichi Shinoda
Frank Shipman
Shervin Shirmohammadi
Hong-Han Shuai
Behjat Siddiquie
Stefan Siersdorfer
Gwendal Simon
Vivek Singh
Sudipta Sinha
Mats Sjoberg
Malcolm Slaney
Nasim Souly
Eleftherios Spyromitros-Xioufis
Ryan Stables
Jacopo Staiano
Vladimir Stankovic
Eckehard Steinbach
Thomas Steiner
Ralf Steinmetz
Ramanathan Subramanian
Chen Sun
Lifeng Sun
Jinhui Tang
Anastasios Tefas
Jelena Tesic
Xinmei Tian
Yonghong Tian
Steve Tjoa
Michele Trevisiol
Remi Trichet
Andrew Tryba
Chun-Yu Tsai
Sam Tsai
Jeremy Turner
Rosario Uceda-Sosa
Jasper Uijlings
Luis Unzueta
Thierry Urruty
Yoshitaka Ushiku
Peter Vajda
Michel Valstar

Radu Vatavu
Vladan Velisavljevic
Carles Ventura
Tuomas Virtanen
Stefanos Vrochidis
Feng Wang
Meng Wang
Yang Wang
Yao Wang
Zhangyang Wang
Zhi Wang
Xialong Wang
Chen Wang
Ye Wang
Zhaowen Wang
Yonggang Wen
Bo Wu
Chuan Wu
Xiao Wu
Gangshan Wu
Hui Wu
Yue Wu
Zuxuan Wu
Tao Xiang
Lingxi Xie
Toshihiko Yamasaki
Junchi Yan
Yan Yan
Keiji Yanai
Kuiyuan Yang
Lu Yang
Ting Yao
Dengpan Ye
Guangnan Ye
Jun Ye
Mei-Chen Yeh
Lijun Yin
Felix Yu
Jun Yu
Yi Yu
Shoou-I Yu
Stefanos Zafeiriou
Maia Zaharieva
Markos Zampoglou
Gloria Zen
Matthias Zeppelzauer
Biqiao Zhang
Cha Zhang
Jian Zhang
Jing Zhang
Shiliang Zhang
Wei Zhang
Yimin Zhang
Luming Zhang
Weinan Zhang
Hanwang Zhang
Tianzhu Zhang
Yongdong Zhang
Liang Zheng
Changtao Zhong
Shenghua Zhong
Wengang Zhou
Ce Zhu
Shiai Zhu
Michael Zink
Marcos Zuniga
Wangmeng Zuo

MM 2016 Brave New Idea Committee

Chairs: Martha Larson *(Delft University of Technology / Radboud University Nijmegen)*
Hari Sundaram *(University of Illinois at Urbana-Champaign)*

Program Committee: Giulia Boato *(University of Trento)*
Ramesh Jain *(University of California, Irvine)*
Gareth Jones *(Dublin City University)*
Klara Nahrstedt *(University of Illinois)*
Jasminko Novak *(European Institute for Participatory Media e.V.)*

MM 2016 Doctoral Symposium Committee

Chairs: Winston Hsu *(National Taiwan University & IBM TJ Watson)*
Eckehard Steinbach *(Technische Universität München)*

Program Committee: Kiyoharu Aizawa *(University of Tokyo)*
Ali Begen *(Ozyegin University)*
Yan-Ying Chen *(FX Palo Alto Laboratory)*
Hermann Hellwagner *(Klagenfurt University)*
Cheng-Hsin Hsu *(National Tsing Hua University)*
Rainer Lienhart *(University of Augsburg)*
Hari Sundaram *(University of Illinois at Urbana-Champaign)*
Bart Thomee *(Yahoo Labs)*

MM 2016 Grand Challenge Committee

Chairs: Xavier Anguera *(ELSA Corp.)*
Shuicheng Yan *(Qihoo 360 & NUS)*

Program Committee:

MSR Image Recognition Challenge
Yuxiao Hu *(Microsoft Research)*
Lei Zhang *(Microsoft Research)*
Shiguang Shan *(Chinese Academy of Sciences)*

Additional reviewers:
Cheng Cheng *(Chongqing Institute of Green and Intelligent Technology, Chinese Academy of Sciences)*
Jianshu Li *(National University of Singapore)*
Shilun Lin *(Beijing University of Posts and Telecommunications)*
Jie Shao *(Beijing University of Posts and Telecommunications)*
Yue Wu *(Northeastern University, Boston, US)*
Yingbin Zheng *(Shanghai Advanced Research Institute, Chinese Academy of Sciences)*
Xiang-Dong Zhou *(Chongqing Institute of Green and Intelligent Technology, Chinese Academy of Sciences)*

Flickr Grand Challenge on Tag and Caption Prediction
Bart Thomee *(Yahoo Labs)*
Pierre Guarrigues *(Yahoo Labs)*
Liangliang Cao *(Yahoo Labs)*
David A. Shamma *(Yahoo Labs)*

Additional reviewers:
Yuncheng Li *(University of Rochester)*
Stacey Svetlichnaya *(Flickr)*

MSR Video to Language Challenge
Tao Mei *(Microsoft Research Asia)*
Ting Yao *(Microsoft Research Asia)*
Yong Rui *(Microsoft Research Asia)*

Additional reviewers
Jianlong Fu *(Microsoft Research Asia)*
Yingwei Pan *(University of Science and Technology of China)*

Sky and the Social Eye: Enriching Remote-Sensed Events

Alan Woodley *(Queensland University of Technology)*
Shlomo Geva *(Queensland University of Technology)*

Additional reviewers

Timothy Chappell *(Queensland University of Technology)*
Lance De Vine *(Queensland University of Technology)*
Roman Fedorov *(Politecnico di Milano)*
Alan Woodley *(Queensland University of Technology)*

MM 2016 Demo Committee

Chairs: Pablo Cesar *(CWI)*
Max Mühlhäuser *(Technische Universität Darmstadt)*

Program Committee: Marco Bertini *(University of Florence)*
Dick Bulterman *(CWI / VU University Amsterdam)*
Teresa Chambel *(University of Lisbon)*
Raimund Dachselt *(Technische Universität Dresden)*
Niloo Dezfuli *(TU Darmstadt)*
Gerald Friedland *(ICSI)*
Andreas Girgensohn *(FX Palo Alto Laboratory)*
Mar Gonzalez Franco *(Microsoft Research)*
Wolfgang Hürst *(Utrecht University)*
Ichiro Ide *(Nagoya university)*
Rene Kaiser *(JOANNEUM RESEARCH)*
Ian Kegel *(BT)*
Joke Kort *(TNO)*
Rodrigo Laiola Guimaraes *(IBM Research)*
Cynthia Liem *(Delft University of Technology)*
Artur Lugmayr *(Curtin University)*
Kris Luyten *(Hasselt University)*
Britta Meixner *(FX Palo Alto Laboratory)*
Vasileios Mezaris *(Information Technologies Institute / Centre for Research and Technology Hellas (ITI/CERTH)*)
Mario Montagud *(Universitat Politècnica de València)*
Frank Nack *(University of Amsterdam)*
Suranga Nanayakkara *(Singapore University of Technology and Design)*
Shin'ichi Satoh *(University of Tokyo)*
Christian Timmerer *(Alpen-Adria-Universität Klagenfurt)*
Doug Williams *(BT)*
Roger Zimmermann *(National University of Singapore)*

MM 2016 Open Source Competition Committee

Chairs: Tao Mei *(Microsoft Research Asia)*
Christian Timmerer *(Alpen-Adria-Universität Klagenfurt)*

Program Committee: Marco Bertini *(University of Florence)*
Pablo Cesar *(CWI, The Netherlands)*
Kuan-Ta Chen *(Academia Sinica)*
Yan-Yin Chen *(FXPAL)*
Wen-Huang Cheng *(SINICA)*
Jianlong Fu *(Microsoft Research)*
Steven Hoi *(SMU)*
Yu-Gang Jiang *(Fudan University)*
Chia-Wen Lin *(National Tsing Hua University)*
Mathias Lux *(University of Klagenfurt)*
Michael Riegler *(Simula)*
Klaus Schoffmann *(University of Klagenfurt)*
Gwendal Simon *(Telecom Bretagne)*
Jingdong Wang *(Microsoft Research)*
Yonggang Wen *(Nanyang Technological University)*
Kuiyuan Yang *(Microsoft Reasearch)*
Yi Yang *(UTS)*
Ting Yao *(Microsoft Research)*
Lei Zhang *(Microsoft Research)*
Yimin Zhang *(Intel)*
H. Vicky Zhao *(Tsinghua University)*
Roger Zimmermann *(NUS)*

ACM Multimedia 2016 Sponsor & Supporters

Sponsor

acm SIGMM

Platinum Supporter

Qualcomm Research

Silver Supporters

FX PAL

COMMIT/ A public- private research community

IBM®

Bronze Supporters

Data Aesthetics – The Ethics and Aesthetics of Big Data Gathering seen from the Artists Eye

Lucas Evers
Waag Society
Amsterdam
lucas@waag.org

Frank Nack
Informatics Institute
University of Amsterdam
Amsterdam
nack@uva.nl

ABSTRACT
Art can reflect in depth about data (vertical) and at the same time has an aesthetical, ontological, intentional, and conscious realm (horizontal) that can communicate cross-dimensionally to the general public. In that way data can be contextualized in its being, can be made palpable and hence facilitate the communication of data into communication about data.

The art exhibition of the 24th ACM MM conference will be presented at the Amsterdam Public Library (http://www.oba.nl/oba/english.html) and aims to provide art works that critically reflect on the use of data in procedural contexts. The presented art works were established in collaborations between artists and researchers that, in cases, have access to large data volumes. The presented art works make use of non-motivated and motivated functions art is valued for, as it is art in its act of resembling, expression and the presentation of the self that facilitates the representation of reality.

CCS Concepts
• Applied computing~Media arts

Keywords
ACM multimedia conference exhibition; big data aesthetics; media arts;

1. INTRODUCTION
The social, cultural, ecological, and economic processes of the current world are so complex that it is difficult to fully comprehend their construction and inherent dynamics. The collected data from very different (scientific) fields allows science new glimpses into the world as it is and facilitates more accurate models for speculating about how it might become. Data becomes the medium that will essentially influence our perception of reality – stronger than any other medium in the history of human sign gathering or manipulation. Yet, the process of data accumulation, which increases the understanding of the world's complexity, also challenges established ontological and epistemological classification.

MM '16, October 15-19, 2016, Amsterdam, Netherlands.
ACM 978-1-4503-3603-1/16/10.
http://dx.doi.org/10.1145/2964284.2993205

Thus, this potential garnet of knowledge remains difficult to be grasped as the analysis of normalized search terms reflects more what we know now but does not facilitate us to investigate the hidden and yet not visible [1, 2]

Though big data changes the scientific view of the world it remains rather unknown, suspicious and inaccessible to the general public. The influence of daily gathered data on the individual life becomes apparent due to biofeedback data that allows to optimize the individual body but also inform of unauthorized collection of potentially intimate data the individual generates through use of convenient technologies that so enhance everyday life. The questions remains – what is it we intend to see in the data, which directions of data development do we wish to foster, and what types of data do we wish to use?

2. ART AND BIG DATA
The connection between media art and big data is significant and hence it can be found that data scientists and artists often work collaboratively. With the exhibition and related events we wish to further stimulate this fruitful cooperation.

However, our coupling of the terms **data** and **aesthetics** should not leave the visitor of the exhibition with the expectation that he or she will be presented with a collection of beautiful, exceptional, and spectacular scientific visualizations that explain the world. This might be understandable as the term aesthetics is connotated since Kant with the concept of beauty [3]. Over the first decade of the 21st century the term aesthetics gained a wider conceptualization, as in 'relational aesthetics' (Nicolas Bourriaud [4]), 'accelerationist aesthetics' (Gean Moreno [5]), or 'info aesthetics' (Lev Manovich [6).

In this exhibition we consider the term "data aesthetics" in a similar line of thought, namely that it poses questions about the perception and representation of big data, where research on and with big data tries to analyze large data volumes (such as the works of Lev Manovich [7] and Übermorgen [8]), produce data volumes (the work of Edit Kaldor [9] and the Nervousnet intiative [10]) and critically reflect on who has access to data volumes (such as works of Paulo Cirio [11]), to establish patterns that help us to understand the world we live in.

The means are visualizations of the data in a way that patterns reveal themselves. This rational view on data can be aligned with Kant's conceptualization of the Beautiful, which is connected with the form and the boundaries of an object. He considers the Beautiful as an "indefinite" concept, where beauty relates to the "Understanding". On the other hand Kant establishes in his theory of aesthetics the concept of the Sublime [5, 12]. The sublime is for Kant the absolute great, distinguished from the Beautiful, by the sublime's boundlessness, its mathematical (aesthetical comprehension and understanding) and dynamical conceptualization, where the dynamical sublime refers to the notion of absolute greatness not inhibited with ideas of limitations. The dynamically sublime is "nature considered in an aesthetic judgment as might that has no dominion over us", and thus shows a faculty of the mind surpassing every standard of Sense.

Big data in form of large amount of mediated representations represents the sublime, matter that fascinates and overwhelms the human spirit. Both scientists and artists gain pleasure in finding and extracting the beautiful, the formal in this indefinite stream of data. The way that artists and scientists select data streams, how they experience and reflect on them, might differ, mainly because artists do not necessarily have to explore with the aim of determining fundamentals in reality. Artists might be interested in rather idiosyncratic reasons to approach big data, they might be interested in data to reveal hidden realities or taboos in society, they might be interested in power structures, try to reveal still unlocked structures in communication, or might consider data as the goldmine that facilitates the deciphering of the meaning of representation: in what way does data represent objectivity of reality, what does data tells us about abstraction and simplification in respect to reducing reality to information and sign collections? Technology has blurred public and private spaces, aimed to make all measurable and hence every pattern traceable and naturally interpretable. It is therefore a justifiable question who then should have access to that data to perform which sort of algorithmic search and has the right to present the inferred information or knowledge in which perceptional form.

3. THE EXHIBITION

The exhibition will be presented at the Amsterdam Central Public Library (http://www.oba.nl/oba/english.html) by providing art works that critically reflect on the use of data in procedural contexts. The exhibition location not only integrates the core functionality of a library with the topic of the exhibition but also facilitates an interaction between the general public with this timely topic of societal discourse.

For the first time the ACM MM art exhibition will be open to the public for a continuously run of 4 weeks, and hence be visible longer than the duration of the actual conference. The exhibition links works presented in the conference with selected art works that were established in collaborations between artists and researchers that have access to large data volumes. The presented art works make use of non-motivated and motivated functions art is valued for, as it is art in its act of resembling, expression and the presentation of the self that facilitates the representation of reality. The aim of the exhibition is to create a discursive space between us, the data poor citizens and us, the data rich researchers and technologists by means of artistic research into the form and societal impact of big data.

The exhibition additionally provides a supporting programme, which includes 3 panels on questions related to big data and art, as well as a 3-day Hackathon at the eve of the exhibition. The Hackathon "Building a Citizen Webb: The Internet of Things network meets Blockchain" aims at developing new forms of visualization aesthetics that allow citizens to gain control over the data they generate in various forms within city landscapes. The winning solutions of the hackathon will be integrated into the exhibition.

4. ACKNOWLEDGMENTS

Our thanks to The Mondriaan Fund for the generous provision of funds that made this exhibition possible in the first place. We also wish to the thank the ACM MM conference, Waag Society, and the Institute of Informatics of the University of Amsterdam for their generous financial and material assistance. We also wish to thank the Public Library Amsterdam OBA for hosting and presenting the exhibition and its events. We finally wish to express our gratitude to the TU Delft and the ETH Zürich for their support, which allowed us to organize the hackathon.

5. REFERENCES

[1] DeLanda, M. 2011. Philosophy and Simulation: The Emergence of Synthetic Reason. Bloomsbury Academic

[2] Yuval Noah Harari, Y. N. 2016. Homo Deus: A Brief History of Tomorrow. Harvill Secker

[3] Kant, I 1951. *Critique of Judgment*. Trans. J.H. Bernard. Macmillan.

[4] Bourriaud, N. 2002. *Relational Aesthetics*. Dijon: Les presses du réel, p. 113.

[5] Moreno, G. 2013. *Editorial – "Accelerationist Aesthetics"*. E-flux journal #46, 06/2013 last accessed at 30.08.2016: http://www.e-flux.com/issues/46-june-2013/

[6] Manovich, L. 2001. *Info Aesthetics*. A semi-open source book/Web site in progress. Project started 8/00, last update 10/27/01. Last accessed at 30.08.2016: http://manovich.net/index.php/projects/info-aesthetics

[7] Manovich: http://manovich.net/index.php/exhibitions

[8] Ubermorgen: http://www.ubermorgen.com/manifesto/

[9] Kaldor: http://www.editkaldor.com/en/index.html

[10] Nervousnet: http://www.coss.ethz.ch/research/nervousnet.html

[11] Cirio: https://www.paolocirio.net/

[12] Kant, I. 1961. *Observations on the Feeling of the Beautiful and Sublime*. Trans. John T. Goldthwait. University of California Press.

Play and Rewind: Optimizing Binary Representations of Videos by Self-Supervised Temporal Hashing

Hanwang Zhang[†] Meng Wang[‡] Richang Hong[‡] Tat-Seng Chua[†]
[†]National University of Singapore [‡]Hefei University of Technology
{hanwangzhang,eric.mengwang,hongrc.hfut}@gmail.com; dcscts@nus.edu.sg

ABSTRACT

We focus on hashing videos into short binary codes for efficient Content-based Video Retrieval (CBVR), which is a fundamental technique that supports access to the ever-growing abundance of videos on the Web. Existing video hash functions are built on three isolated stages: frame pooling, relaxed learning, and binarization, which have not adequately explored the temporal order of video frames in a joint binary optimization model, resulting in severe information loss. In this paper, we propose a novel unsupervised video hashing framework called Self-Supervised Temporal Hashing (SSTH) that is able to capture the temporal nature of videos in an end-to-end learning-to-hash fashion. Specifically, the hash function of SSTH is an encoder RNN equipped with the proposed Binary LSTM (BLSTM) that generates binary codes for videos. The hash function is learned in a self-supervised fashion, where a decoder RNN is proposed to reconstruct the original video frames in both forward and reverse orders. For binary code optimization, we develop a backpropagation rule that tackles the non-differentiability of BLSTM. This rule allows efficient deep network training without suffering from the binarization loss. Through extensive CBVR experiments on two real-world consumer video datasets of Youtube and Flickr, we show that SSTH consistently outperforms state-of-the-art video hashing methods, *e.g.*, in terms of mAP@20, SSTH using only 128 bits can still outperform others using 256 bits by at least 9% to 15% on both datasets.

Keywords

Temporal Hashing;Binary LSTM;Sequence Learning;Video Retrieval

1. INTRODUCTION

Content-based retrieval—a technique focusing on the indexing and querying of a large data collection based on visual content—is the key to many multimedia applications [17]. Unlike Content-based Image Retrieval (CBIR) that has been extensively studied in the past decades [24, 5, 42], Content-based Video Retrieval (CBVR) has not received sufficient attention in Multimedia community [25, 14]. However, due to the popularity of mobile video capturing devices and high-speed network transmission, we are witnessing the rapid growth of videos and video-related Web services such as Vine and Snapchat. Indeed, during the time of reading this paragraph, around 50 thousand video snippets are shared and 2.4 million videos are viewed on Snaptchat[1]. Without a doubt, the ever-growing abundance of videos on the Web has brought about an urgent need for more advanced CBVR technologies [18, 39, 40, 37].

Video is beyond a set of frames. However, most current works on video analytics generally resort to pooling frame-level features into a single video-level feature by discarding the temporal order of the frame sequence[2]. Such bag-of-frames degeneration works well when high-dimensional frame-level features such as CNN responses [35] and motion trajectories [31] are used, as certain temporal information encoded in a high dimension can be preserved after pooling. However, for large-scale CBVR, where hashing (or indexing) of these high-dimensional features as short binary codes is necessary, the temporal information loss caused by frame pooling will inevitably result in suboptimal binary codes of videos. The loss usually takes place in the process of hash function learning [33], which is a post-step after pooling; as compared to dominant video appearances (*e.g.*, objects, scenes and short-term motions), nuanced video dynamics (*e.g.*, long-term event evolution) are more likely to be discarded as noise in the drastic feature dimensionality reduction during hashing [7].

We argue that the key reason to the above defect is that both the temporal pooling and the hash code learning steps have not adequately addressed the temporal nature of videos. To this end, we propose a novel video hashing method for CBVR called **S**elf-**S**upervised **T**emporal **H**ashing (SSTH), which especially tackles this defect. In a nutshell, SSTH is an end-to-end system that encodes an m-frame video into a single k-bit binary code. We highlight three key characteristics that make SSTH effective and distinguishable from other state-of-the-art video hashing methods [26, 3, 38]:

Self-Supervision. Most existing unsupervised hashing methods are not temporal-aware and hence will lose long-

[1]https://www.snapchat.com/ads

[2]Though some approaches represent videos as a set of frame features (*e.g.*, TRECVID Instance Search Task [20]), they essentially fall into the pooling approach since the ultimate similarity calculation is temporal-independent

MM '16, October 15-19, 2016, Amsterdam, Netherlands

DOI: http://dx.doi.org/10.1145/2964284.2964308

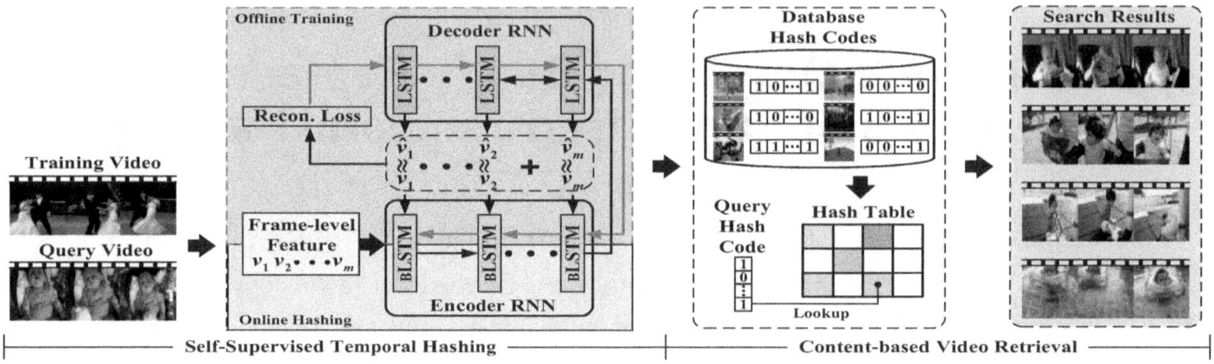

Figure 1: The overview of the proposed Self-Supervised Temporal Hashing for Content-based Video Retrieval. In offline training, the black and red arrows denote forward and back propagation, respectively. In particular, the two-way black arrow in Decoder RNN denotes the forward and reverse reconstruction.

term video dynamics. So, we explore an alternative unsupervised hashing: how can we exploit the frame order of a video to *self-supervise* the binary code learning? To this end, we propose a strategy dubbed **Play** and **Rewind** within an encoder-decoder Recurrent Neural Network (RNN) framework [27, 28]—after the RNN hash function encodes a video (*i.e.*, "play"), the output hash code should be able to decode the viewed frames in a certain order (*i.e.*, "rewind"), only if the code successfully encodes both video appearances and dynamics. In this way, SSTH is able to continuously refine itself by playing and rewinding the inexhaustible amount of videos on the Web.

Temporal Awareness. The hash function of SSTH explicitly encodes the temporal order of frames by using an RNN, which has shown to be especially effective in sequence modeling [27]. In particular, we propose a novel recurrent unit called **B**inary **L**ong-**S**hort **T**erm **M**emory (BLSTM), where the video binary code at time t is a function of the code at time $t-1$. RNN equipped with BLSTM unifies temporal modeling and video hashing in a principled way, where the binary codes are expected to capture the long-term dynamics of the entire video.

Optimized Video Binary Representation. Since the problem of binary code learning is essentially NP-hard [13], existing video hashing methods generally follow a three-stage process: pooling, relaxation, and binarization. The isolated steps make the approach suboptimal. In the proposed SSTH framework, we cast the temporal modeling and binary code learning into a joint model. Specifically, we develop a binary backpropagation rule which tackles the binary nature of SSTH without any relaxation. In this way, SSTH can be considered as an end-to-end unsupervised learning framework for optimizing the transformation from videos to binary codes.

The overview of the proposed SSTH framework for CBVR is illustrated in Figure 1. In the offline training stage, a training video is represented by a sequence of frame-level features (*e.g.*, by deep CNN [23]). The encoder RNN with BLSTM runs through the sequence, generating a set of hash codes and then the decoder RNN decodes it to reconstruct the frame-level feature sequence in both forward and reverse orders. During optimization, the reconstruction error is back propagated through the entire encoder-decoder RNNs. In the online retrieval stage, the encoder RNN can be considered as a temporal-aware hash function, which generates binary hash codes for both database videos and query videos. Finally, the database hash codes are indexed into a hash table for practical retrieval. The effectiveness of SSTH is demonstrated on two real-world consumer video datasets from Youtube and Flickr.

The contributions of this paper are as follows:

1) We propose a novel unsupervised video hashing framework called Self-Supervised Temporal Hashing (SSTH). To the best of our knowledge, SSTH is the first principled deep framework for video hashing. It is an optimized end-to-end approach that addresses a variety of weakness in conventional video hashing approaches, such as the ignorance of temporal nature and the isolation of pooling, relaxation and binarization.

2) We develop a novel LSTM variant dubbed Binary LSTM (BLSTM), which serves as the building block of the temporal-aware hash function. We also develop an efficient backpropagation rule that directly tackles the challenging problem of binary optimization for BLSTM without any relaxation.

3) We improve the conventional one-order encoder-decoder RNN [27, 28] by incorporating forward and reverse order frame reconstruction. Our strategy is a novel unsupervised learning objective that better models the temporal nature of data.

It is also worth mentioning that, although SSTH is developed for video hashing, it is actually a flexible and generic framework that can be easily extended to deal with the hashing of other signal sequences such as music and text.

2. RELATED WORK

By hashing data into short binary codes, efficient storage and search can be achieved due to the fast bit XOR operations in Hamming space. Today's hashing methods have evolved from hand-crafted hash functions [9] to data-driven learning-to-hash [33], which either requires pairwise data similarities for unsupervised learning [34, 11, 41] or data labels for supervised learning [32, 22]. However, due the challenging temporal nature of videos—to our best knowledge—limited video hashing studies have been carried out. For example, the hash functions proposed by Song *et al.* [26] and Cao *et al.* [3] are unaware of the temporal order of video frames. Ye *et al.* [38] exploited the pairwise frame order but their method requires video labels and only generates frame-level codes. Although Revaud *et al.* [21] exploited the short-term temporal order, their video quantization codes are not binary. In sharp contrast to the above methods, our SSTH is an unsupervised binary code learning framework that explicitly exploits the long-term video temporal information.

The encoder-decoder RNN framework used in SSTH is inspired by recent advances in sequence learning, where RNN has shown great success in machine translation [28] and image/video caption generation [30]. In particular, our architecture is most related to the unsupervised video representation learning work by Srivastava *et al.* [27]. However, we distant from them by developing Binary LSTM (BLSTM) in place of the original LSTM [12] for binary code learning and a forward/reverse reconstruction strategy for self-supervised learning. By viewing SSTH as a deep network for hashing, our work also relates to recent studies on deep learning-to-hash [8, 43, 6]. However, besides the fact that none of the existing methods considers the temporal nature of videos, they also resort to relax the binary optimization to real-valued optimization or merely append a quantization loss minimizer at the top layer [8]. In contrast, our deep hashing architecture is re-designed with BLSTM for direct binary optimization by efficient backpropagation without relaxation.

3. SELF-SUPERVISED TEMPORAL HASHING

In this section, we formulate the proposed Self-Supervised Temporal Hashing (SSTH) framework. First, we introduce the proposed temporal-aware hash function that yields a single compact binary code for a video sequence. Then, we present a novel recurrent unit called Binary LSTM (BLSTM), which is the building block for the hash function. Finally, we introduce the proposed self-supervised strategy for learning to hash and its deep architecture.

3.1 Temporal-aware Hash Function

Suppose a video sequence of m frames is denoted as a matrix $\mathbf{V} = (\mathbf{v}_1, ..., \mathbf{v}_m) \in \mathbb{R}^{d\times m}$, where the t-th frame is represented by a feature vector $\mathbf{v}_t \in \mathbb{R}^d$. Our goal is to find a hash function $H : \mathbb{R}^{d\times m} \rightarrow \{\pm 1\}^k$ that encodes $\mathbf{V}$ into a k-bit binary code[3] $\mathbf{b}_m \in \{\pm 1\}^k$, where $k \ll d$. In order to capture the temporal nature of videos, we require the hash function to be temporal-aware, *i.e.*, if $\mathbf{V}'$ is a matrix that is column-permuted from $\mathbf{V}$, $\mathbf{b}'_m$ is not necessarily equal to $\mathbf{b}_m$. In other words, rather than assuming $\Pr(\mathbf{b}_m|\mathbf{V}) = \Pr(\mathbf{b}_m|\mathbf{V}')$ (*e.g.*, pooling-based hashing [3]) or $\Pr(\mathbf{b}_m|\mathbf{V}) = \prod_{t=1}^{m} \Pr(\mathbf{b}_t|\mathbf{v}_t)$ (*e.g.*, frame-level hashing [26, 38]), a temporal-aware hash function models $\Pr(\mathbf{b}_t|\mathbf{v}_1, ..., \mathbf{v}_t) = \Pr(\mathbf{b}_t|\mathbf{b}_{t-1}, \mathbf{v}_t)$, where we assume that the previous code $\mathbf{b}_{t-1}$ is statistically sufficient to represent the previous frames $\mathbf{V}_{t-1}$. So, the hash code $\mathbf{b}_t$ of a t-length frame sequence is dependent on the code $\mathbf{b}_{t-1}$ of the last viewed $(t-1)$ frames and the current frame $\mathbf{v}_t$.

It is natural to use a Recurrent Neural Network (RNN) [12] to fit the temporal-aware requirement. In particular, the output $\mathbf{b}_t$ of a recurrent unit (or layer) at t-th time is expressed by a non-linear function f, whose input includes the last output $\mathbf{b}_{t-1}$ and the current frame $\mathbf{v}_t$:

$$\mathbf{b}_t = f(\mathbf{b}_{t-1}, \mathbf{v}_t). \tag{1}$$

[3]It is trivial to transform binary code $b \in \{\pm 1\}$ to $b \in \{0, 1\}$ by $b \leftarrow (1 + b)/2$.

Therefore, the resultant binary code $\mathbf{b}_m$ for video $\mathbf{V}$ can be generated recurrently by:

$$\mathbf{b}_m = H(\mathbf{V}) = f(\mathbf{b}_{m-1}, \mathbf{v}_m). \tag{2}$$

The design of f is crucial to the hash function in an RNN style. Recently, Long-Short Term Memory (LSTM) has shown state-of-the-art performance on sequence learning tasks, due to its capability in dealing with the vanishing and exploding gradient issues of deep RNN (*i.e.*, long sequence) [12]. However, original LSTM can only generate a real-valued hidden variable rather than a binary code, *e.g.*, $\mathbf{h}_t = f(\mathbf{h}_{t-1}, \mathbf{v}_t)$, where $\mathbf{h}_t \in \mathbb{R}^k$. In order to modify LSTM to generate binary codes, a straightforward approach, which is similar to some hashing deep networks [8, 43], is to use sgn function to binarize the resultant hidden variable, *e.g.*, $\mathbf{b}_m = \mathrm{sgn}(\mathbf{h}_m)$, where $\mathrm{sgn}(x) = 1$, if $x \geq 0$; and $\mathrm{sgn}(x) = -1$ otherwise. However, we argue that it is essentially based on frame pooling, where the pooling function is an RNN: even though the pooling is temporal-aware, the hash codes *per se* do not directly capture the temporal nature of videos.

3.2 Binary LSTM

In order to design a hash function that not only inherits the numerical stability of LSTM but also generates binary codes, we propose a novel variant of LSTM named Binary LSTM (BLSTM). As illustrated in Figure 2(a), BLSTM follows a similar data flow as LSTM. First, the input variable $\mathbf{z}_t$ is calculated by tanh-squashing the linear combination of the current feature $\mathbf{v}_t$ and the last binary code $\mathbf{b}_{t-1}$. Then, the memory variable $\mathbf{c}_t$ is updated by adding how much the "old knowledge" $\mathbf{c}_{t-1}$ should forget and how much the "new knowledge" $\mathbf{z}_t$ should memorize. Note that this additive memory update design enables the derivatives distribute over sums and hence the error does not vanish quickly when performing backpropagation over time [12]. Then, the memory is batch normalized (BN). Finally, the hash code $\mathbf{b}_t$ is a binarization (sgn) of how much the "current knowledge" $\mathbf{h}_t$ should be output. The behaviors of "forget", "memorize", and "output" are respectively controlled by three gate variables: forget gate $\mathbf{F}$, input gate $\mathbf{I}$, and output gate $\mathbf{O}$. They are applied element-wise multiplicatively and thus can either keep a value from the gated variable if the gate is 1 or discard a value if the gate is 0. In particular, all of the gate variables: $\mathbf{i}_t$, $\mathbf{f}_t$, and $\mathbf{o}_t$, use sigmoid function σ as an estimation of the pass-through probability. The detailed implementation of BLSTM in Eq. (1) is given as follows:

$$\mathbf{z}_t \leftarrow \tanh\left(\mathbf{W}_{vz}\mathbf{v}_t + \mathbf{w}_{bz} \circ \mathbf{b}_{t-1} + \mathbf{a}_z\right) \tag{3a}$$
$$\mathbf{f}_t \leftarrow \sigma\left(\mathbf{W}_{vf}\mathbf{v}_t + \mathbf{W}_{bf}\mathbf{b}_{t-1} + \mathbf{w}_{cf} \circ \mathbf{c}_{t-1} + \mathbf{a}_f\right) \tag{3b}$$
$$\mathbf{i}_t \leftarrow \sigma\left(\mathbf{W}_{vi}\mathbf{v}_t + \mathbf{w}_{bi}\mathbf{b}_{t-1} + \mathbf{w}_{ci} \circ \mathbf{c}_{t-1} + \mathbf{a}_i\right) \tag{3c}$$
$$\mathbf{c}_t \leftarrow \mathbf{f}_t \circ \mathbf{c}_{t-1} + \mathbf{i}_t \circ \mathbf{z}_t \tag{3d}$$
$$\mathbf{c}_t \leftarrow \mathrm{BatchNorm}(\mathbf{c}_t) \tag{3e}$$
$$\mathbf{o}_t \leftarrow \sigma\left(\mathbf{W}_{vo}\mathbf{v}_t + \mathbf{W}_{bo}\mathbf{b}_{t-1} + \mathbf{w}_{co} \circ \mathbf{c}_t + \mathbf{a}_o\right) \tag{3f}$$
$$\mathbf{h}_t \leftarrow \mathbf{o}_t \circ \mathbf{c}_t \tag{3g}$$
$$\mathbf{b}_t \leftarrow \mathrm{sgn}\left(\mathbf{h}_t\right) \tag{3h}$$

where $\circ$ denotes the element-wise multiplication.

Now we discuss the motivation behind the two novel designs of the proposed BLSTM as compared to LSTM:

Binarization (sgn). This allows BLSTM yielding $\{\pm 1\}$ binary output. Different from the popular vanilla LSTM [12],

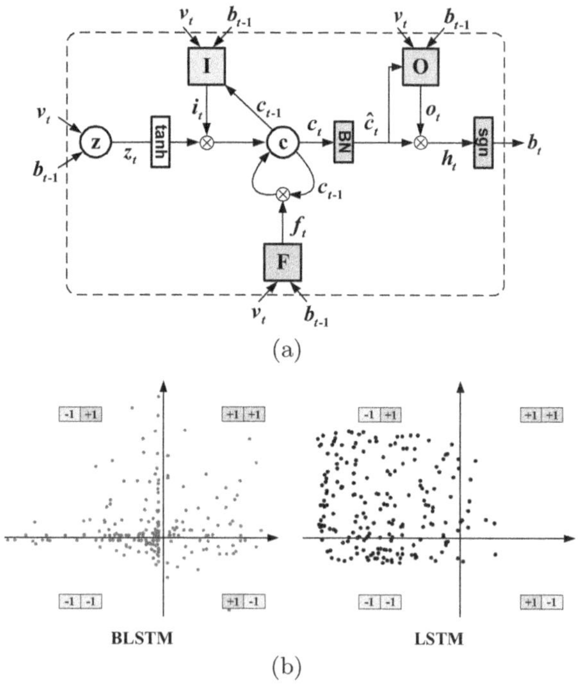

(a)

(b)

Figure 2: (a) The data flow of the proposed Binary LSTM (bLSTM) at the t-th time. (b) Two dimensions of $\mathbf{h}_t$ of the proposed BLSTM (left) and LSTM (right). We can see that BLSTM yields more decorrelated and balanced binary codes as compared to LSTM.

where $\mathbf{h}_t \leftarrow \mathbf{o}_t \circ \tanh(\mathbf{c}_t)$, we remove the tanh squash $\mathbf{c}_t$ before entering the sgn function as in Eq. (3g). Intuitively, as sgn only cares for the sign of $\mathbf{h}_t$, squashing the input to $[-1, +1]$ is unnecessary. In fact, since the gradient of tanh is always nonzero, any small change in the input modifies most of the entries in memory $\mathbf{c}_t$. Therefore, as we will discuss later in Section 4.1, when the tanh before $\mathbf{c}_t$ is removed, small input changes will not modify the memory values if they are already definitive on its sign, *e.g.*, $|\mathbf{c}_t| > \mathbf{1}$. In this way, BLSTM can be considered as a sparse model that contributes better disentangling ability for data variance and efficient training [10].

Batch Normalization (BN). It has shown to be effective in removing layer-wise covariance shift in deep neural networks [15]. It normalizes $\mathbf{c}_t$ to zero-mean unit-variance Gaussian distribution and then a linear transformation: $c_t \leftarrow \frac{c_t - \mu_t}{\sigma_t}$, $c_t \leftarrow \gamma_1 c_t + \gamma_2$, where c_t is any entry of $\mathbf{c}_t$, μ_t and σ_t are the mean and unbiased variance of the training minibatch at time t, γ_1 and γ_2 are trainable transformation parameters. Note that in testing, μ_t and σ_t are estimated from the whole training data. By denoting matrix $\mathbf{C}_t$ as the memory variables of a minibatch, BN approximates the constraints $\mathbf{C}_t^T\mathbf{C}_t = \mathbf{I}$ and $\mathbf{C}_t^T\mathbf{1} = \mathbf{0}$, which respectively impose decorrelation (*i.e.*, bits should be as independent as possible) and balance (*i.e.*, each bit should split the data as balanced as possible) on the resultant codes $\mathbf{B}_t = \text{sgn}(\mathbf{O}_t \circ \mathbf{C}_t)$. In fact, these constraints are shown to maximize the information entropy in binary codes [34], *i.e.*, BN helps BLSTM yielding informative binary codes (cf. Figure 2(b)).

3.3 Learning Objective

We use the temporal order of the video sequence as a self-supervision for learning to hash. Essentially, our learning objective falls in the RNN encoder-decoder framework for unsupervised sequence learning [28, 27]. In particular, we propose to implement the framework as follows. First, an encoder RNN with BLSTM first runs through a video sequence $(\mathbf{v}_1, \mathbf{v}_2, ..., \mathbf{v}_m)$ to come up with a hash code $\mathbf{b}_m$. Then, a decoder composed of two independent RNNs with LSTM: forward and reverse reconstruction RNNs, decodes the hash code to features that reconstruct the input frames in the forward order $(\tilde{\mathbf{v}}_1, \tilde{\mathbf{v}}_2, ..., \tilde{\mathbf{v}}_m)$ and reverse order $(\hat{\mathbf{v}}_m, \hat{\mathbf{v}}_{m-1}, ..., \hat{\mathbf{v}}_1)$, respectively. Specifically, we adopt linear reconstructions for the output of the decoder LSTMs:

$$\begin{cases} \tilde{\mathbf{v}}_t = \tilde{\mathbf{W}}\tilde{\mathbf{h}}_t + \tilde{\mathbf{a}}, \ \tilde{\mathbf{h}}_t = \tilde{f}(\tilde{\mathbf{h}}_{t-1}, \mathbf{0}), \\ \hat{\mathbf{v}}_t = \hat{\mathbf{W}}\hat{\mathbf{h}}_t + \hat{\mathbf{a}}_r, \ \hat{\mathbf{h}}_t = \hat{f}(\hat{\mathbf{h}}_{t+1}, \mathbf{0}), \end{cases} \tag{4}$$

where $\{\tilde{\mathbf{W}}, \tilde{\mathbf{a}}\}$ and $\{\hat{\mathbf{W}}, \hat{\mathbf{a}}\}$ are the parameters of the forward and reverse reconstruction; $\tilde{f}$ and $\hat{f}$ are the functions of the forward and reverse LSTMs. Particularly, $\tilde{\mathbf{h}}_0 = \mathbf{b}_m$ or $\hat{\mathbf{h}}_m = \mathbf{b}_m$ denotes that the decoder starts from the hash code and the $\mathbf{0}$ input highlights that the decoder RNNs do not take any input features. The missing input feature $\mathbf{0}$ prevents the decoder from learning trivial reconstruction that is directly from the input. As a result, the encoder is encouraged to generate hash codes that retain sufficient information for valid reconstructions.

The proposed forward and reverse RNNs focus on learning different aspects of video dynamics. On one hand, the forward RNN attempts to memorize long-term event evolution since the reconstruction starting from the first frame will encourage the memory not to forget too much about the early frames; on the other hand, reverse RNN is more likely to capture short-term temporal relations among video semantics, *e.g.*, objects and motion changes, since the reconstruction from the last frame, which has been just viewed, is a relatively easy task if the memory holds sufficient information about recent frames. Based on the above analysis, the overall loss function for our SSTH can be formulated as:

$$L = \underbrace{\sum_{t=1}^{m} \|\tilde{\mathbf{v}}_t - \mathbf{v}_t\|_2^2}_{\text{forward order}} + \underbrace{\sum_{t=m}^{1} \|\hat{\mathbf{v}}_t - \mathbf{v}_t\|_2^2}_{\text{reverse order}}. \tag{5}$$

However, minimizing the above loss function is challenging since the deeply nested binary codes $(\mathbf{b}_1, ..., \mathbf{b}_m)$ are non-differentiable. Later, we will introduce an efficient binary optimization method based on backpropagation of the binary codes.

3.4 Architecture Details

The detailed architecture of the proposed SSTH is illustrated in Figure 3. Both the encoder and two decoders adopt a two-layer structure in order to enhance the expressive power of the model. On the encoder side, the first-layer is a conventional vanilla LSTM [12], where the output hidden variable $\mathbf{h}$ is used as the input to the second-layer BLSTM and the next LSTM. Specifically, the dimensions of $\mathbf{h}$ is $2k$, *i.e.*, two times as the bit size of the binary code. By doing this, the first-layer LSTMs of the encoder can be viewed as higher-level feature extractors for the frames. After the hash code $\mathbf{b}_m$ being encoded, *i.e.*, the BLSTM output of the last frame, we directly feed it to the first layer of the two decoder RNNs. On the decoder side, the dimension of the first and second layer are k and $2k$, respectively. In particular,

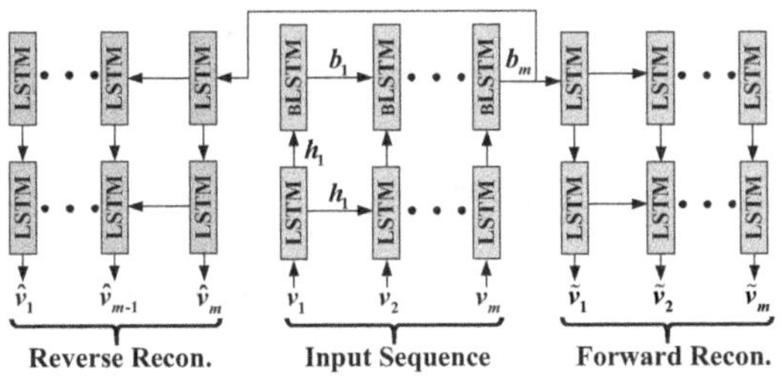

Figure 3: The encoder-decoder architecture used in SSTH learning. Both encoder and decoder are two-layer RNNs. Red: encoder RNN. Green: forward decoder RNN. Blue: reverse decoder RNN.

the linear transformation reconstructs the $2k$-D hidden variables of the second layer to d-D frame-level features. Note that this is different from [27] which aligns the two-layer encoder outputs to the two-layer decoder inputs. The reason is that we want to limit the decoder to access information from other source, *e.g.*, the first hidden layer of the encoder, in order to encourage the hash code retaining more higher-level video dynamics. One should also note that the trainable parameters of the encoder LSTM-BLSTM, forward and reverse decoder LSTM-LSTM are independent with each other since the three RNNs are responsible for different purposes.

4. BINARY OPTIMIZATION

Training SSTH equipped with BLSTM is essentially NP-hard as it involves binary optimization of the hash codes that requires combinatorial search space [13]. However, approximated solution by discarding the binary constraints will lead to large quantization loss [11]. In this section, we propose to directly tackle the challenging binary optimization. We first introduce how to take the derivative of the sgn binarization and then detail the learning algorithm.

4.1 Derivative of Binarization

As the derivative of the sgn function in BLSTM is zero almost everywhere, it is impossible to apply exact backpropagation for BLSTM. Here, we propose an approximation by estimating the derivative of the sgn function.

In fact, the binary code generated by sgn can be viewed as binary classification results, where the classifier responses are $\mathbf{h}_t$. So, $\text{sgn}(\mathbf{h}_t)$ is a set of hidden classifiers that collaboratively make predictions for a final objective [2], *e.g.*, the reconstruction loss in our case. Based on this view, our key idea is to design a delegate classifier d that approximates the original classifier sgn by allowing a certain loss. Without loss of generality, we only consider a single entry h of $\mathbf{h}_t$ in Eq. (3h):

- When $h \geq 0$, we use $d(h)$ to approximate $\text{sgn}(h) = 1$ by allowing some classification loss as:

$$\text{sgn}(h) \approx d(h) = \text{sgn}(h) - \ell(h), \ h \geq 0, \tag{6}$$

where $\ell(\cdot) \geq 0$ is the loss function. Since $h \geq 0$, we can view it as a score for the positive label $+1$. In fact, $d(h)$ is equivalent to $\text{sgn}(h)$ when $\ell(h) = \mathbb{1}(1 \cdot h \leq 0)$, *i.e.*, the loss is 0 if the response h is consistent with the label $+1$; and 1 otherwise. However, such 0–1 loss is useless since we constrain $h \geq 0$. A popular way to soften the "hard" 0–1 loss is to use the hinge loss with a margin: $\ell(h) = \max(0, 1 - 1 \cdot h)$, which is widely used in penalizing large-margin classifiers such as SVM. Specifically, it allows a certain violation $1 - (+1) \cdot h$ to the ideal response $+1$ when $0 \leq h \leq 1$. Thus, Eq. (6) can be rewritten as:

$$d(h) = 1 - \max(0, 1 - 1 \cdot h), h \geq 0, \tag{7}$$

- When $h < 0$, similar to the above analysis, we can view it as a score for the negative label -1. By allowing a hinge loss to the ideal binary response -1, $\text{sgn}(h) = -1$ can be approximated as:

$$d(h) = -1 + \max(0, 1 - (-1) \cdot h), h < 0, \tag{8}$$

where a violation as $1 + h$ is allowed when $-1 \leq h < 0$.

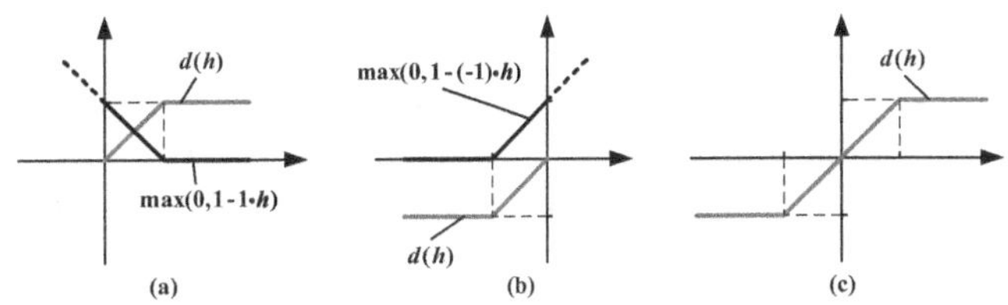

Figure 4: Illustrative process of how $d(\cdot)$ (red line) approximates $\text{sgn}(\cdot)$ using a hinge loss function (black line). (a) when $h \geq 0$, $d(h) = \text{sgn}(h) - \max(0, 1 - 1 \cdot h)$; (b) when $h < 0$, $d(h) = \text{sgn}(h) + \max(0, 1 - (-1) \cdot h)$; (c) $d(h)$.

Combining Eq. (7) and Eq. (8), the resultant approximation of $\text{sgn}(h)$ can be written as:

$$\text{sgn}(h) \approx d(h) = \begin{cases} -1, & h < -1, \\ h, & -1 \leq h \leq 1, \\ 1, & h > 1. \end{cases} \tag{9}$$

So far, we are ready to define the derivative of $\text{sgn}(h)$ as:

$$\text{sgn}'(h) := d'(h) = \mathbb{1}(|h| \leq 1). \tag{10}$$

Figure 4 illustrates how we use the hinge loss to approximate the sgn function.

The derivative $d'(h)$ states a simple backpropagation rule for BLSTM: when the gradients back propagate to the sgn function, we only allow gradients, whose neural responses are between $[-1, +1]$, to pass through. Intuitively, this rule encourages BLSTM to update if the hidden value h is not well separated with respect to a margin, resulting in hash functions that are more certain about binarization. In fact, d' can be considered as a "straight-through estimator" which has been used in SGD for discrete neurons [4]. Though d' is not an exact gradient for sgn, the convergence of SGD can be achieved [1].

4.2 Algorithmic Details

Thanks to the derivative of the sgn function introduced in Eq. (10), we are now ready to develop forward propagation (FP) and back propagation (BP) for training the deep RNNs. Due to space limit, we only summarize FP and BP for the key component: the proposed BLSTM.

The FP for BLSTM is illustrated in Algorithm 1. For notational simplicity, we divide BLSTM into four steps: 1) subroutine BLSTMHEAD, parameterized by α, runs from Eq. (3a) to Eq. (3d). Note that the input $\mathbf{v}_t$ can be video feature or the output of the first layer LSTM; 2) subroutine BATCHNORM, parameterized by γ, runs for the batch normalization in Eq. (3e); 3) subroutine BLSTMTAIL, pa-

Table 1: Time expense (millisecond) of LSTM and BLSTM on TITAN X. Batch size $B = 50$, frame length $l = 25$, feature dimension $d = 4096$, bit size $k = 128$.

	FP	BP	BATCHNORM	BATCHNORMBP	Hashing
LSTM	23.6	93.4	N.A.	N.A.	17.1
BLSTM	23.7	144	$3.03e^{-2}$	50.6	17.3

rameterized by β, runs from Eq. (3f) to Eq. (3g); and 4) binarization in Eq. (3h). The BP for BLSTM is detailed in Algorithm 2. The input $\nabla \mathbf{b}_m = \frac{\partial L}{\partial \mathbf{b}_m}$ is the derivative of the loss function L in Eq. (5) with respect to hash code $\mathbf{b}_m$. Line 2 is the binarization BP according to Eq. (10). Then, from Line 3 to Line 9, we assume that the three gradient subroutines are available: BLSTMHEADBP, BLSTMTAILBP and BATCHNORMBP. Note that Line 4, 6, and 9 are the gradients of the model parameters updated using chain rules.

After applying FP and BP over a minibatch of training videos, we use SGD to update the model parameters $\{\alpha, \beta, \gamma\}$ with momentum and dynamic learning rate. Denote frame length as l, frame-level feature dimension as d, bit size as k, and the SGD batch size as B, it is easy to see that it takes $\mathcal{O}(Bdkl)$ for FP and BP, and $\mathcal{O}(\frac{1}{2}Bdkl))$ for generating hash codes. Thus, the training and testing time is linear to the frame length, bit size and sample size. In particular, Table 1 lists the training/testing time expense comparison between LSTM and BLSTM on a TITAN X GPU. We only need to pay off a little overhead for BLSTM due to the introduction of batch normalization.

Algorithm 1: Forward Propagation for BLSTM

Input : $(\mathbf{v}_1, ..., \mathbf{v}_m)$: frame-level feature sequence
α, β: BLSTMHEAD,TAIL parameters
γ: BATCHNORM parameters
Output: $\mathbf{b}_m$: the binary code
Init : $\mathbf{c}_0 \leftarrow \mathbf{0}$, $\mathbf{b}_0 \leftarrow \mathbf{0}$
for $t = 1$ **to** m **do**
  $\mathbf{c}_t \leftarrow$ BLSTMHEAD $(\mathbf{c}_{t-1}, \mathbf{b}_{t-1}, \mathbf{v}_t; \alpha)$
  $\mathbf{c}_t \leftarrow$ BATCHNORM $(\mathbf{c}_t; \gamma)$
  $\mathbf{h}_t \leftarrow$ BLSTMTAIL $(\mathbf{c}_t, \mathbf{b}_{t-1}, \mathbf{v}_t; \beta)$
  $\mathbf{b}_t \leftarrow \mathrm{sgn}(\mathbf{h}_t)$
end
return $\mathbf{b}_t$

5. EXPERIMENTS

As the proposed SSTH is a novel unsupervised video hashing framework, the goal of our experiments is to answer the following three research questions:

RQ1. Why is SSTH designed to what we have proposed? How do different components of it affect the performance?

RQ2. How does SSTH perform as compared to other state-of-the-art video hashing methods?

RQ3. What is the generalization ability of SSTH, *e.g.*, less training data and cross-dataset performance?

5.1 Datasets

We used two challenging large-scale video datasets for unsupervised training and retrieval[4]:

[4]Details of the two datasets are in the supplementary material.

Algorithm 2: Back Propagation for BLSTM

Input : $\nabla \mathbf{b}_m$: gradient of $\mathbf{b}_m$ propagated from the decoder
$\nabla \mathbf{c}_m$: gradient of $\mathbf{c}_m$ propagated from the decoder
Output: $\nabla\alpha$, $\nabla\beta$: gradients of BLSTMHEAD,TAIL parameters
$\nabla\gamma$: gradient of BATCHNORM parameters
Init : $\nabla\alpha_{m+1} \leftarrow \mathbf{0}$, $\nabla\beta_{m+1} \leftarrow \mathbf{0}$, $\nabla\gamma_{m+1} \leftarrow \mathbf{0}$
// Backpropagation through time
1 **for** $t = m$ **to** 1 **do**
2 $\nabla \mathbf{h}_t \leftarrow \nabla \mathbf{b}_t \circ \mathbb{1}(|\mathbf{h}_t| \leq 1)$
3 $\left(\nabla \hat{\mathbf{c}}_t, \nabla \hat{\mathbf{b}}_{t-1}, \nabla \alpha_t\right) \leftarrow$ BLSTMTAILBP$(\nabla \mathbf{h}_t, \nabla \mathbf{c}_t)$
4 $\nabla\alpha_t \leftarrow \nabla\alpha_{t+1} + \nabla\alpha_t$
5 $(\nabla \mathbf{c}_t, \nabla\gamma_t) \leftarrow$ BATCHNORMBP$(\nabla \hat{\mathbf{c}}_t)$
6 $\nabla\gamma_t \leftarrow \nabla\gamma_{t+1} + \nabla\gamma_t$
7 $(\nabla \mathbf{c}_{t-1}, \nabla \mathbf{b}_{t-1}, \nabla\beta_t) \leftarrow$ BLSTMHEADBP$(\nabla \mathbf{c}_t)$
8 $\nabla \mathbf{b}_{t-1} \leftarrow \nabla \hat{\mathbf{b}}_{t-1} + \nabla \mathbf{b}_{t-1}$
9 $\nabla\beta_t \leftarrow \nabla\beta_{t+1} + \nabla\beta_t$
10 **end**
11 **return** $\nabla\alpha_1$,$\nabla\beta_1$,$\nabla\gamma_1$

FCVID. It is Fudan-Columbia Video Dataset [16]. FCVID is one of the largest datasets for video categorization with accurate manual annotations in generic domain. This dataset contains 91,223 Youtube videos annotated manually according to 239 categories, covering a wide range of topics like events (*e.g.*, "Tailgate Party"), objects (*e.g.*, "Panda") and scenes (*e.g.*, "Beach"). The average video length is about 167 seconds. Its train/test split is 45,611/45,612. We used the train split for unsupervised learning and the test split for retrieval.

YFCC. It is Yahoo Flickr Creative Common dataset [29], the largest public multimedia collection that has ever been released. It is officially announced with 0.8M videos from Flickr, however, we only collected 700,882 videos by filtering out invalid urls and corrupted video files. The average video length is about 37 seconds. Particularly, we also contributed to the community a large video scene dataset of 100,000 videos selected from YFCC, manually annotated according to the most popular 80 scenes from the third level of MIT SUN secene hierarchy [36], such as indoor (*e.g.*, "Coffee Shop") and outdoor (*e.g.*, "Golf Court"). We used the unlabeled 600,882 videos for unsupervised learning and the rest 100,000 labeled videos for retrieval.

Note that unlike FCVID where a considerable amount of the Youtube videos are taken by professionals, YFCC videos are mostly taken by the mobile phones of Flickr casual users. Therefore, the visual quality of YFCC videos is much lower and hence it is more challenging for video content understanding. For each video, we uniformly sampled 25 frames as video sequences. As a result, our SSTH is a very deep RNN that has 75 layers after unfolding (*i.e.*, 25-layer encoder, 25-layer forward decoder and 25-layer reverse decoder). Though we set the frame number to 25 as a comprise for training time and GPU memory, we believe that higher frame rate will lead to stronger models. For frames, we used VGG-fc19 [23] to extract 4,096-D CNN features as the frame-level representations. Note that we did not use motion features such as dense trajectories [31] for all the methods, since we intended to investigate whether they can capture video dynamics by modeling sequences.

5.2 Experimental Setup

5.2.1 Evaluation Metrics

We adopted Average Precision at top K retrieved videos (AP@K) for retrieval performance evaluation [20]. Denote R as the number of relevant videos in the database. At any ranked position j ($1 \leq j \leq K$), let R_j be the number of relevant videos in the top j results and let $I_j = 1$ if the j-th video is relevant and 0 otherwise, then AP@K is defined as $\frac{1}{min(R,K)} \sum_{j=1}^{K} \frac{R_j}{j} \times I_j$. For each class label, we considered every test video that belongs to the label as query and the rest of test data as the database; then, we used the mean of AP@K of the queries (mAP@K) as the performance metric for the label. We also slightly abused mAP@K to be the mean of all the label-specific mAP@K as an overall metric.

5.2.2 Search Protocols

We adopted two search protocols which are widely used in search with binary codes. We evaluated code length $k \in \{8, 16, 32, 64, 128, 256\}$.

Hamming Ranking: Videos are ranked according to their Hamming distance (or similarity) from the query user. Although the search complexity of Hamming ranking is still linear, it is very fast in practice since the Hamming distance calculation can be done by fast bit XOR operations and the sorting is constant time due to integer distance.

Hashtable Lookup: A lookup table is constructed using the video hash codes and all the items in the buckets that fall within a small Hamming radius (*e.g.*, 2) of the query are returned. Therefore, search is performed in constant time. However, a single table would be insufficient when the code length is larger than 32 since it would require over $\mathcal{O}(2^{32})$ space to store the table in memory. We adopted Multi-Index Hashing (MIH) table [19], which builds one table for each code subsegment. Items are aggregated by all the tables and then conducted Hamming ranking for the items. By doing this, the search time is significantly reduced to sublinear. We empirically set the substring length as $\{1, 1, 1, 2, 4, 8\}$ for bit size $\{8, 16, 32, 64, 128, 256\}$ as suggested in [19].

It is worth mentioning that the above two search protocols focus on different characteristics of hash codes. Ranking provides a better measurement of the learned Hamming space, *i.e.*, the accuracy upper bound that the codes can achieve since it linearly scans the whole data. Lookup, on the other hand, emphasizes the practical speed of large-scale search. However, a common issue in this protocol is that it may not return sufficient items for recommendation, as a query lookup may miss items due to the sparse Hamming space. In our experiments, if a query returns no videos, we treated it as a failed query with an AP of zero.

5.2.3 Compared Methods

To validate the architecture design of the proposed **SSTH**, we compared the following possible architectures that can also be viewed as temporal-aware hashing methods:

LSTM. We used the conventional vanilla LSTMs [12] for both the encoder and decoder. After training, the real-valued output of the encoder is binarized as the hash code. Note that this setting can be considered as a relaxed deep hashing model.

LSTM-sgn. We directly added a sgn function to the output of every LSTM in the encoder. This method includes the tanh function for the memory cell and does not use batch normalization. Its optimization adopts the same binary backpropagation as BLSTM.

Enc-sgn. The encoder consists of LSTM with batch normalization for the memory. Moreover, we added a sgn function at the end of the encoder to generate binary codes. This method is mentioned at the end of Section 3.1. Its optimization adopts the same binary backpropagation as the proposed BLSTM.

SSTH-F/R. This is SSTH without the reverse (SSTH-F) or the forward reconstruction decoder (SSTH-R).

SSTH-1/2. This is SSTH with one or two layer architecture. Note that all the aforementioned methods are one-layer except SSTH-2.

As we will show that the two-layer SSTH-2 introduced in Section 3.4 performs better, we use SSTH instead of SSTH-2 when the context is clear. To compare with the state-of-the-art unsupervised hashing methods, we have:

ITQ. This is perhaps the most popular unsupervised hashing method called Iterative Quantization [11]. It first uses average pooling for video data representations, then applies PCA to reduce the dimensionality of the data to the target bit size (*i.e.*, k), and finally iteratively learns a rotation that minimizes the quantization loss.

SubMod. This is Submodular video hashing [3]. It first uses average pooling for video data representations, then it applies traditional hashing methods such as LSH to hash the videos into long codes (*e.g.*, we used 1024), and then it greedily selects k most informative hash functions, where the informativeness is measured using the training data.

MFH. This is Multi-Feature Hashing for videos [26]. It learns hash functions based on the similarity graph of the frames. Since the hash function is learned on frame-level, it uses average pooling to pool the real-valued outputs of hash functions and then binarizes them for hash codes.

DH. This is a Deep Hashing framework [8]. Its key idea for binary code learning is to add a binarization loss function at the top layer of a neural network. For fair comparison, we used the original encoder-decoder RNN [27] with the loss function imposing at the end of the encoder RNN. By doing this, DH is able to hash temporal data like videos.

Although there are other video hashing methods, they are either based on supervised hashing [38] or specialized non-binary hash codes [21], hence do not apply in our comparable experiments. For deep models such as DH and SSTH, we used a TITAN X GPU with Theano implementation. The minibatch size of all the deep models was set to 50, training for 30 epochs.

5.3 Result Analysis

5.3.1 Architecture Investigation (RQ1)

Figure 5 shows how the possible designs of SSTH affect the overall performances. Due to space limit, we only report the results of 128-bit codes. From the results on both datasets, we can arrive at the following observations: 1) only LSTM leads to considerable performance drop when using table lookup since it is the only two-stage method with large quantization loss. On the contrary, we do not observe significant performance drop of the other models using binary backpropagation, which is a joint framework; 2) by naively adding sgn function for LSTM, LSTM-sgn achieves the worst

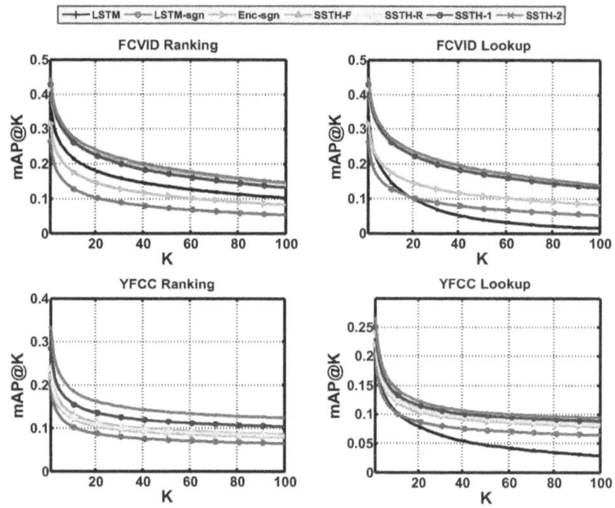

Figure 5: Performances (mAP@K) of 128-bit hash codes learned from various RNN architectures.

Table 2: Cross-dataset mAP@20 gain (%) by Hamming ranking of various methods using different bit sizes.

Dataset	Training: FCVID, Testing: YFCC					
Bits	8	16	32	64	128	256
SubMod	**-2.13**↓	-3.64↓	**-7.32**↓	-14.8↓	-15.1↓	-33.8↓
MFH	-23.8↓	-7.29↓	-16.5↓	-34.3↓	-30.0↓	-24.7↓
ITQ	-14.7↓	-10.1↓	-22.7↓	**-5.76**↓	**-2.47**↓	-4.76↓
DH	-7.03↓	**-3.16**↓	-10.0↓	-12.9↓	-13.8↓	**-2.04**↓
SSTH	-8.71↓	-5.03↓	-12.5↓	-11.4↓	-10.0↓	-11.6↓
Dataset	Training: YFCC, Testing: FCVID					
SubMod	-1.78↓	-3.54↓	-5.07↓	-12.5↓	-12.1↓	-20.3↓
MFH	12.6↑	13.6↑	-7.28↓	5.03↑	3.64↑	2.38↑
ITQ	14.5↑	15.9↑	-8.83↓	-7.62↓	5.17↑	-8.26↓
DH	11.3↑	11.6↑	13.8↑	-8.02↓	-9.70↓	-3.93↓
SSTH	**28.1**↑	**27.7**↑	**22.9**↑	**10.1**↑	**8.64**↑	**7.58**↑

results. This is because of the absence of batch normalization as discussed in Section 3.2: without batch normalization, the hidden variables are likely to be imbalanced and correlated, *e.g.*, some of the hidden variables may be out of the range $[-1, 1]$. Thus, the zero gradients will result in premature hash codes; 3) the temporal hashing models such as SSTH-F/R/1/2 are better than Enc-sgn that only deploys binarization at the end of the encoder. This demonstrates the effectiveness of the temporal-aware design as defined in Eq. (1); 4) by combining both forward and reverse reconstruction, SSTH-1 is better than SSTH-F and SSTH-R; 5) by adding more layers, SSTH-2 can enhance the expressive power of SSTH. Therefore, based on the above observations, we have demonstrated the effectiveness of our particular design for SSTH.

5.3.2 *Comparison with State-of-The-Arts (RQ2)*

Figure 8 shows how SSTH performs as compared to state-of-the-art video hashing methods. We can see that SSTH consistently performs the best on both datasets. Specifically, we have the following observations:
1) Compared to pooling based hashing methods such SubMod, MFH and ITQ, SSTH explicitly models the temporal information of videos. For example, on FCVID, by using only 128 bits, SSTH achieves 24.5% mAP@20, which is

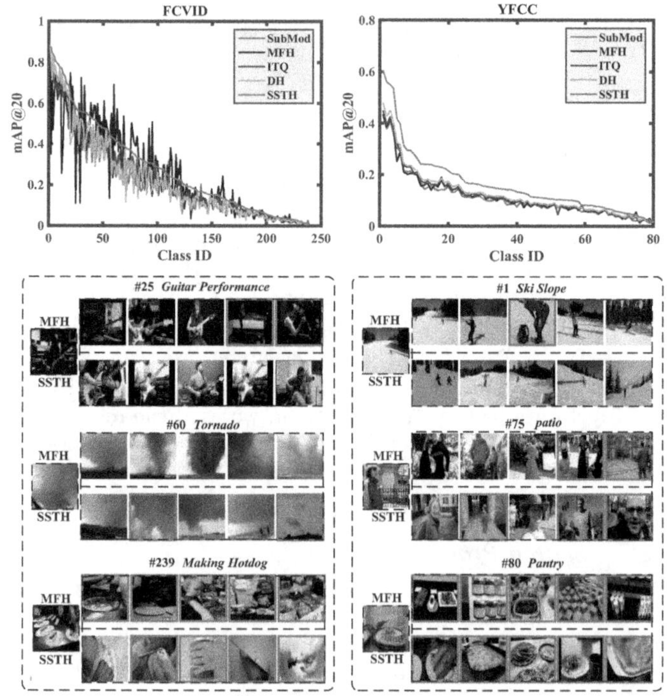

Figure 6: Detailed performance (mAP@20 of 256 bits) of all the methods on both datasets. The Class ID is sorted according to the descending order of performances of SSTH. The illustrative examples are the top 5 retrieval results of SSTH and the most competitive MFH queried by three categories of different performances. Red borders denote wrong results. Left: FCVID; Right: YFCC.

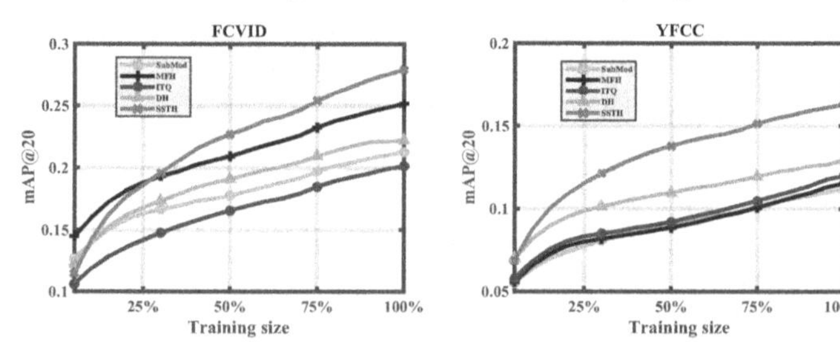

Figure 7: Performance (mAP@20 of 256 bits) on two datasets using various percentages of training data.

comparable to 25.1% of the most competitive MFH using 256 bits. Figure 6 detailed the mAP@20 of various methods using 256 bits on both datasets. We can see that modeling temporal information is beneficial to discriminate concepts that involves human actions like "Guitar Performance" in FCVID. More interestingly, we can observe that SSTH consistently outperforms the pooling-based methods on the scene retrieval task on YFCC. This demonstrates that the temporal information of videos are not only crucial for events but also indispensable for recognizing scenes. For the example of YFCC "Ski Slope" in Figure 6, pooling-based methods like MFH will inevitably mis-classify frames of "Snow" as "Ski Slope" while SSTH successfully captures the informative "Ski" motion.
2) However, we should note that pooling-based methods such as MFH are also powerful, especially for video categories that are not likely to be distinguished by temporal information. As illustrated in Figure 6, MFH that only

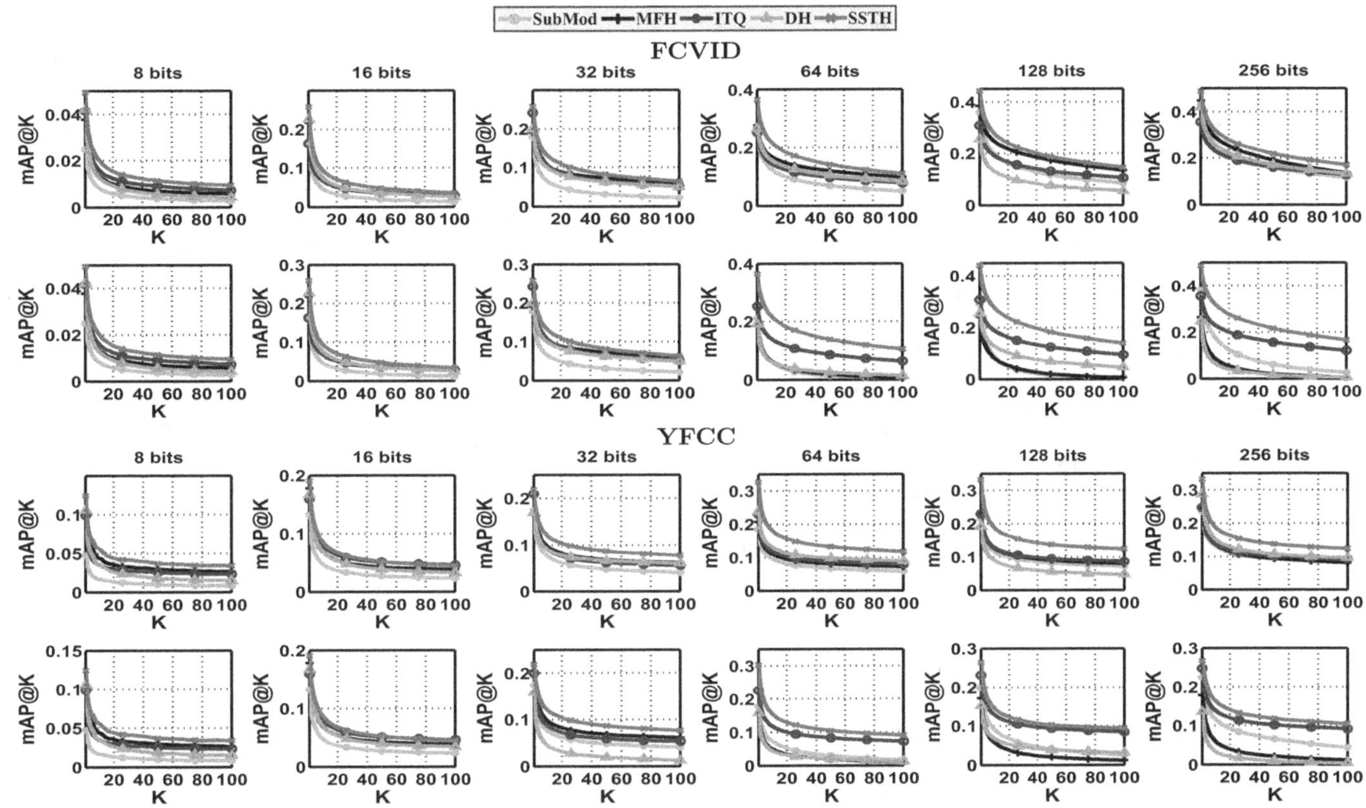

Figure 8: Performance (mAP@K) of various video hashing methods at different bit sizes. For each dataset, the top row is the performance by Hamming ranking and the bottom row is by table lookup.

captures visual appearances seems sufficient for the "Tornado" category in FCVID; while SSTH over-emphasizes on the cloud motion. As another example, SSTH overfits to the motion of individual selfies in YFCC "Patio", and thus performs worse than MFH. We also find some hard cases for all the methods. One example is the food related events like FCVID "Making Hotdog", where MFH is biased to the general concepts of "Food", and SSTH is more likely favored the motion of "Making" like "Nail Painting" and "Cutting Potatoes". Another example is the YFCC "Pantry", where MFH and SSTH are both biased to the appearance of "Waffle".
3) DH, which also attempts to capture temporal information, performs much worse than SSTH and even some pooling-based methods such as MFH and ITQ. The reason is similar to why Enc-sgn in the previous experiment performed worse than SSTH: although DH exploits RNN to model the temporal order of frames, it is essentially a pooling-based hashing method since the hash codes are not temporal-aware as defined in Eq. (1).
4) As shown in Figure 8, when retrieval is performed by using hash table lookup, relaxed methods—SubMod, MFH and DH—show significant performance drop using longer hash codes, *e.g.*, 128 and 256 bits. This demonstrates the effectiveness of binary optimization adopted in ITQ and SSTH, for the minimization of the binarization loss.

5.3.3 Generalization Ability (RQ3)

Generalization ability is especially crucial for learning-to-hash methods since the queries provided by users are usually out-of-domain as compared to the training data. Therefore, it is important to investigate how SSTH performs given limited training data and how SSTH generalizes to cross-dataset retrieval tasks, *e.g.*, training on FCVID but testing on YFCC and vice versa.

Figure 7 shows the mAP@20 of all the methods using 256 bits on two datasets trained by various percentages of training data. Obviously, all the methods gain better performance when using more training data. In particular, the generalization ability of the proposed SSTH is significantly better than others. For example, by using only the half training data, SSTH achieves similar performance to the most competitive MFH on FCVID and outperforms all the methods on YFCC. We believe that this is due to the strong expressive ability of the deep architecture of SSTH. Table 2 lists the cross-dataset performance of all the hashing methods. We can see that all of them suffer a considerable performance drop when training on FCVID but testing on YFCC. This demonstrates that when training data are relatively small, *e.g.*, around 50 thousands of FCVID, the practical use of data-driven hash models is limited due to the train/test dataset discrepancy. However, if the training data are sufficient, *e.g.*, around 600 thousands of YFCC, we can observe that all the methods, except SubMod, achieves much better performance gain as compared to that of training on FCVID; in particular, SSTH achieves consistently increasing gain when using all the bit sizes. This demonstrates that the expressive power of the SSTH architecture is strong. The reason why SubMod achieves the worst generalization is perhaps that the binary code selection procedure is heavily biased to particular datasets. In summary, based on the above observations, we believe that SSTH has a great potential in real-world CBVR due to its generalization ability in unsupervised learning from the inexhaustible videos on the Web.

6. CONCLUSIONS

In this paper, we proposed a novel video hashing framework called Self-Supervised Temporal Hashing (SSTH). In sharp contrast to existing video hashing methods that are generally based on frame pooling, SSTH explicitly models video temporal information and directly optimizes the binary code learning problem without relaxation. Through extensive experiments on two large consumer video datasets, we have demonstrated that the effectiveness of SSTH is due to its three distinguished designs: Binary Long-Short Term Memory, Self-Supervision Learning Strategy and Binary Backpropagation. To the best of our knowledge, SSTH is the first unsupervised deep video hashing model.

SSTH is essentially a generic end-to-end framework for binary representation learning of any sequential multimedia data. In this view, a possible future direction is to apply SSTH to other temporal multimedia applications where images and texts can be traced by time, such as multimedia user profiling and news event prediction. Further, we can also extend SSTH to supervised and semi-supervised hashing framework if labels are available.

Acknowledgements

NExT research is supported by the National Research Foundation, Prime Minister's Office, Singapore under its IRC@SG Funding Initiative.

7. REFERENCES

[1] Y. Bengio, N. Léonard, and A. Courville. Estimating or propagating gradients through stochastic neurons for conditional computation. *arXiv preprint arXiv:1308.3432*, 2013.

[2] A. Bergamo, L. Torresani, and A. W. Fitzgibbon. Picodes: Learning a compact code for novel-category recognition. In *NIPS*, 2011.

[3] L. Cao, Z. Li, Y. Mu, and S.-F. Chang. Submodular video hashing: a unified framework towards video pooling and indexing. In *MM*, 2012.

[4] M. Courbariaux and Y. Bengio. Binarynet: Training deep neural networks with weights and activations constrained to+ 1 or-1. *arXiv preprint arXiv:1602.02830*, 2016.

[5] R. Datta, D. Joshi, J. Li, and J. Z. Wang. Image retrieval: Ideas, influences, and trends of the new age. *ACM Computing Surveys*, 2008.

[6] T.-T. Do, A.-D. Doan, and N.-M. Cheung. Learning to hash with binary deep neural network. In *ECCV*, 2016.

[7] J. Donahue, L. Anne Hendricks, S. Guadarrama, M. Rohrbach, S. Venugopalan, K. Saenko, and T. Darrell. Long-term recurrent convolutional networks for visual recognition and description. In *CVPR*, 2015.

[8] V. Erin Liong, J. Lu, G. Wang, P. Moulin, and J. Zhou. Deep hashing for compact binary codes learning. In *CVPR*, 2015.

[9] A. Gionis, P. Indyk, R. Motwani, et al. Similarity search in high dimensions via hashing. In *VLDB*, 1999.

[10] X. Glorot, A. Bordes, and Y. Bengio. Deep sparse rectifier neural networks. In *ICAIS*, 2011.

[11] Y. Gong, S. Lazebnik, A. Gordo, and F. Perronnin. Iterative quantization: A procrustean approach to learning binary codes for large-scale image retrieval. *TPAMI*, 2013.

[12] A. Graves and J. Schmidhuber. Framewise phoneme classification with bidirectional lstm and other neural network architectures. *Neural Networks*, 2005.

[13] J. Håstad. Some optimal inapproximability results. *JACM*, 2001.

[14] W. Hu, N. Xie, L. Li, X. Zeng, and S. Maybank. A survey on visual content-based video indexing and retrieval. *TSMC Part C*, 2011.

[15] S. Ioffe and C. Szegedy. Batch normalization: Accelerating deep network training by reducing internal covariate shift. *arXiv preprint arXiv:1502.03167*, 2015.

[16] Y.-G. Jiang, Z. Wu, J. Wang, X. Xue, and S.-F. Chang. Exploiting feature and class relationships in video categorization with regularized deep neural networks. *arXiv preprint arXiv:1502.07209*, 2015.

[17] M. S. Lew, N. Sebe, C. Djeraba, and R. Jain. Content-based multimedia information retrieval: State of the art and challenges. *TOMM*, 2006.

[18] H. Li. Multimodal visual pattern mining with convolutional neural networks. In *ICMR*, 2016.

[19] M. Norouzi, A. Punjani, and D. J. Fleet. Fast search in hamming space with multi-index hashing. In *CVPR*, 2012.

[20] P. Over, J. Fiscus, G. Sanders, D. Joy, M. Michel, G. Awad, A. Smeaton, W. Kraaij, and G. Quénot. Trecvid 2014–an overview of the goals, tasks, data, evaluation mechanisms and metrics. In *Proceedings of TRECVID*, page 52, 2014.

[21] J. Revaud, M. Douze, C. Schmid, and H. Jégou. Event retrieval in large video collections with circulant temporal encoding. In *CVPR*, 2013.

[22] F. Shen, C. Shen, W. Liu, and H. Tao Shen. Supervised discrete hashing. In *CVPR*, 2015.

[23] K. Simonyan and A. Zisserman. Very deep convolutional networks for large-scale image recognition. *arXiv preprint arXiv:1409.1556*, 2014.

[24] A. W. Smeulders, M. Worring, S. Santini, A. Gupta, and R. Jain. Content-based image retrieval at the end of the early years. *TPAMI*, 2000.

[25] C. G. Snoek and M. Worring. Concept-based video retrieval. *FTIR*, 2008.

[26] J. Song, Y. Yang, Z. Huang, H. T. Shen, and R. Hong. Multiple feature hashing for real-time large scale near-duplicate video retrieval. In *MM*, 2011.

[27] N. Srivastava, E. Mansimov, and R. Salakhudinov. Unsupervised learning of video representations using lstms. In *ICML*, 2015.

[28] I. Sutskever, O. Vinyals, and Q. V. Le. Sequence to sequence learning with neural networks. In *NIPS*, 2014.

[29] B. Thomee, D. A. Shamma, G. Friedland, B. Elizalde, K. Ni, D. Poland, D. Borth, and L.-J. Li. The new data and new challenges in multimedia research. *arXiv preprint arXiv:1503.01817*, 2015.

[30] O. Vinyals, A. Toshev, S. Bengio, and D. Erhan. Show and tell: A neural image caption generator. In *CVPR*, 2015.

[31] H. Wang and C. Schmid. Action recognition with improved trajectories. In *ICCV*, 2013.

[32] J. Wang, S. Kumar, and S.-F. Chang. Semi-supervised hashing for large-scale search. *TPAMI*, 2012.

[33] J. Wang, W. Liu, S. Kumar, and S.-F. Chang. Learning to hash for indexing big data: A survey. *Proceedings of the IEEE*, 2016.

[34] Y. Weiss, A. Torralba, and R. Fergus. Spectral hashing. In *NIPS*, 2009.

[35] Z. Wu, Y. Fu, Y.-G. Jiang, and L. Sigal. Harnessing object and scene semantics for large-scale video understanding. In *CVPR*, 2016.

[36] J. Xiao, J. Hays, K. A. Ehinger, A. Oliva, and A. Torralba. Sun database: Large-scale scene recognition from abbey to zoo. In *CVPR*, 2010.

[37] Y. Yang, Z.-J. Zha, Y. Gao, X. Zhu, and T.-S. Chua. Exploiting web images for semantic video indexing via robust sample-specific loss. *TMM*, 2014.

[38] G. Ye, D. Liu, J. Wang, and S.-F. Chang. Large-scale video hashing via structure learning. In *CVPR*, 2013.

[39] Z.-J. Zha, M. Wang, Y.-T. Zheng, Y. Yang, R. Hong, and T.-S. Chua. Interactive video indexing with statistical active learning. *TMM*, 2012.

[40] Z.-J. Zha, H. Zhang, M. Wang, H. Luan, and T.-S. Chua. Detecting group activities with multi-camera context. *TCSVT*, 2013.

[41] H. Zhang, F. Shen, W. Liu, X. He, H. Luan, and T.-S. Chua. Discrete collaborative filtering. In *SIGIR*, 2016.

[42] H. Zhang, Z.-J. Zha, Y. Yang, S. Yan, Y. Gao, and T.-S. Chua. Attribute-augmented semantic hierarchy: towards bridging semantic gap and intention gap in image retrieval. In *MM*, 2013.

[43] F. Zhao, Y. Huang, L. Wang, and T. Tan. Deep semantic ranking based hashing for multi-label image retrieval. In *CVPR*, 2015.

Multi-Stream Multi-Class Fusion of Deep Networks for Video Classification

Zuxuan Wu, Yu-Gang Jiang*, Xi Wang, Hao Ye, Xiangyang Xue
School of Computer Science, Shanghai Key Lab of Intelligent Information Processing,
Fudan University, Shanghai, China
{zxwu, ygj, xwang10, haoye10, xyxue}@fudan.edu.cn

ABSTRACT

This paper studies deep network architectures to address the problem of video classification. A multi-stream framework is proposed to fully utilize the rich multimodal information in videos. Specifically, we first train three Convolutional Neural Networks to model spatial, short-term motion and audio clues respectively. Long Short Term Memory networks are then adopted to explore long-term temporal dynamics. With the outputs of the individual streams on multiple classes, we propose to mine class relationships hidden in the data from the trained models. The automatically discovered relationships are then leveraged in the multi-stream multi-class fusion process as a *prior*, indicating *which* and *how much* information is needed from the remaining classes, to adaptively determine the optimal fusion weights for generating the final scores of each class. Our contributions are two-fold. First, the multi-stream framework is able to exploit multimodal features that are more comprehensive than those previously attempted. Second, our proposed fusion method not only learns the best weights of the multiple network streams for each class, but also takes class relationship into account, which is known as a helpful clue in multi-class visual classification tasks. Our framework produces significantly better results than the state of the arts on two popular benchmarks, 92.2% on UCF-101 (without using audio) and 84.9% on Columbia Consumer Videos.

Keywords

Video Classification; CNN; LSTM; Fusion.

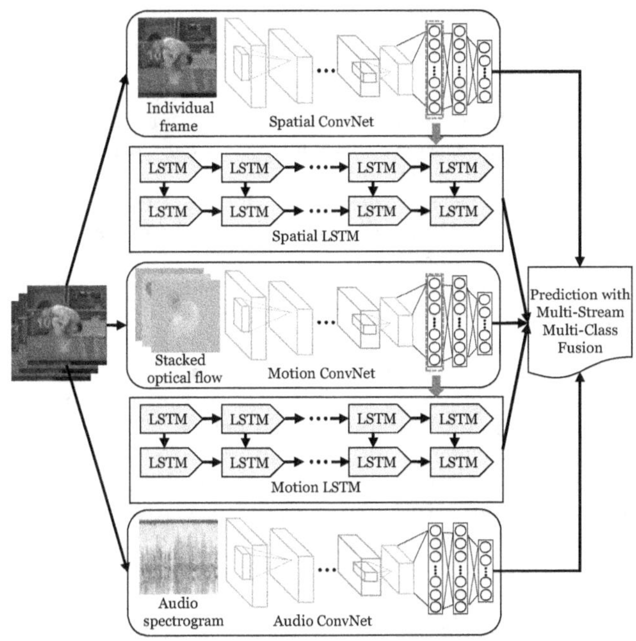

Figure 1: Illustration of the proposed framework.

1. INTRODUCTION

The sheer volume of video data nowadays demands robust video classification techniques that can effectively recognize human actions and complex events for applications like video search, summarization, intelligent surveillance and *etc.* However, it is a particularly challenging problem due to the complicated nature of videos, including large intra-class variations caused by different viewing conditions and multiple view points, noisy contents unrelated to the video topic, and complex temporal structures incurring understanding and computational difficulties. The fact that videos are intrinsically multimodal requires solutions that can explore not only static visual information, but also motion and auditory clues. Key to the development of video classification systems is the design of good features. Popular feature descriptors include the SIFT [33], the Mel-Frequency Cepstral Coefficients (MFCC) [66], the STIP [31] and the dense trajectories [56], which can be encoded into video-level representations by bag-of-words (BoW) [50, 68, 37] or Fisher vectors (FV) [40, 43, 30, 70].

In contrast to the hand-engineered descriptors, the deep neural networks that can learn features automatically from raw data have demonstrated strong performance in various domains. In particular, the convolutional neural networks (ConvNets) are very successful on image analysis tasks like object detection [14], object recognition [46, 51] and image segmentation [11]. However, for video classification,

*Corresponding author.

MM '16, October 15-19, 2016, Amsterdam, Netherlands

DOI: http://dx.doi.org/10.1145/2964284.2964328

most deep network based approaches [22, 26, 45, 62] demonstrated worse or similar results to the hand-engineered features [56]. This is largely due to the high complexity of the video data. Unlike images that only have static visual appearance information, videos also contain temporal motions and auditory soundtracks. For example, a "diving" action video usually involves a sequence of atoms, such as "jumping from a platform", "rotating in the air" and "falling into water", accompanied by cheering or clapping sounds. Some approaches [22, 26, 45] only focused on the static frames and short-term motion clues captured by a few adjacent frames, which are apparently not sufficient. A few very recent studies attempted to use recurrent neural networks (RNN) to model long-term temporal information and achieved competitive performance [39, 64]. Nevertheless, the audio information has rarely been exploited. Furthermore, most existing approaches fused the outputs of multiple networks in a very straightforward way using simple classifiers like logistic regression, which could lead to sub-optimal performance.

In addition, existing works for video categorization often assign single or multiple class labels to a video sample independently without considering the relationships among video semantics. However, humans do not recognize an object (concept) separately but rely on the interconnections of objects (concepts). The presence of related classes could help better categorize the class of interest. For example, "marathon" and "marching band" contain similar human motion patterns (at least when compared with unrelated class pairs like "marathon" and "fishing"), and the confidence of a video containing "marathon" could potentially help recognize "marching band". In other words, if a video receives extremely low score of "marathon", it is also unlikely to be "marching band". To leverage semantic relationships (*i.e.*, context knowledge), many existing methods rely on computational expensive models (*e.g.*, CRF), which are not feasible for large-scale applications.

Realizing the above limitations, in this paper, we propose a multi-stream framework of deep neural networks to exploit the multimodal clues for video classification. Figure 1 illustrates the diagram of our approach. Three ConvNets are trained to model the static spatial information, short-term motion and auditory clues, respectively. The motion stream is computed on stacked optical flows over a short temporal windows and thus can only capture short-term motion. In order to model the long-term temporal clues, we employ a Recurrent Neural Network (RNN) model, namely the Long Short Term Memory (LSTM), on the frame-level spatial and motion features extracted by the ConvNets. The LSTM encodes history information in memory units regulated with non-linear gates to discover temporal dependencies. To combine the outputs from different networks, we develop a simple yet effective fusion method to learn the optimal fusion weights adaptively for each class. Note that the deep models are trained using state-of-the-art networks, they possess high discriminative power and hence contain valuable knowledge on how classes are correlated. Therefore, we propose to leverage the class relationships hidden in the data to constrain the learning process, by informing the classifier *which* classes are related and *how much* information is needed from the each of these related classes. In other words, to generate the final prediction of a class of interest, the classifier also considers the predictions of other correlated classes.

Our contributions are summarized as follows:

1. We introduce a multi-stream framework that integrates spatial, short-term motion, long-term temporal and auditory clues in videos. We demonstrate the multi-stream networks are able to digest complementary clues to receive significantly improved performance.

2. We propose a multi-stream multi-class fusion method to combine the outputs of the individual networks. The method not only learns the weights of individual network streams adaptively for each class, but also harnesses class relationships that can further improve the performance.

3. We conduct extensive experiments to validate the performance of the proposed framework, and we achieved superior performance on two popular datasets.

The rest of this paper is organized as follows. Section 2 reviews and discusses related works. Section 3 describes the proposed multi-stream multi-class framework in detail. Experimental results and comparisons are discussed in Section 4, followed by conclusions in Section 5.

2. RELATED WORKS

As aforementioned, video classification has been extensively studied and significant efforts have been paid to design discriminative features or robust classifiers. We focus the review on recent works related to our proposed approach.

Hand-crafted Representations. There have been numerous works focusing on developing effective features that are expected to be robust to withstand intra-class variations and discriminative to separate different categories. For example, one can utilize image-based shape features, such as HOG and SIFT [33], to capture appearance information on individual frames. Different from frame-based features, motion features are designed to take the object movements into account, which is appealing since motion information is critical for understanding video contents. A popular way to obtain motion features is by extending frame-based local features into 3D space. For instance, Laptev *et al.* [31] extended the Harris detector into 3D space to find space-time interest points. Instead of locating interest points using 3D detectors, Wang *et al.* obtained better performance on video classification tasks by sampling patches densely [58]. In a later work, Wang *et al.* adopted the dense point trajectories, upon which several features are extracted from regions that are tracked with optical flow [56]. In addition, audio features are also adopted as a complement of the visual channel, among which the Mel-frequency cepstral coefficients (MFCC) is the most popular one.

CNN Representations. Motived by the promising results of deep networks (particularly the ConvNets) on image analysis tasks [51, 46, 14], several works have exploited deep architectures for video classification. Ji *et al.* extended CNN models into spatial-temporal space by operating on stacked video frames [22]. Karparthy *et al.* compared several architectures for action recognition [26]. Tran *et al.* proposed to learn generic spatial-temporal features which can be computed efficiently [53]. Xu *et al.* adopted advanced feature encoding strategies (*i.e.*, VLAD) to promote the generalization ability of CNN representations [65]. Zha *et al.* evaluated several options of using CNNs for event detection [70].

Simonyan and Zisserman [45] introduced an interesting two-stream approach, where two ConvNets are trained to explicitly capture spatial and short-term motion information using frames and stacked optical flows as inputs, respectively. Final predictions can be obtained by linearly averaging the prediction scores of the two ConvNets. A recent work by Wang *et al.* [59] combined the two-stream approach with the traditional dense trajectories [56] and reported strong results. In this paper, we also adopt two similar ConvNets as [45]. However, as the two-stream approach is not able to model the auditory and the long-term temporal clues, we adopt additional networks to build a more comprehensive framework. A novel fusion method is also proposed to combine the multi-stream outputs, which is better than the simple linear fusion used in [45].

Temporal Structure. Extensive works have been conducted to explore the temporal dynamics in videos. For example, Tang *et al.* introduced a HMM model to capture the changes of states for videos with variable durations [52]. Wang *et al.* combined feature templates with parts in a max-margin hidden CRF framework [61]. In addition to using graphical models, Fernando *et al.* proposed to train a linear ranking machine on the frames of a video, whose parameters will then be used to obtain a video-level representation [12]. Ramanathan introduced an unsupervised way to learn temporal embeddings using context information like word vectors [42]. More recently, RNN has been shown to be effective on many sequential modeling tasks, such as speech recognition [15] and image/video analysis [9, 67, 71]. For long-term temporal modeling of the video data, Srivastava *et al.* proposed an LSTM encoder-decoder framework to learn video representations in an unsupervised manner [48]. Donahua *et al.* [9] and Wu *et al.* [64] trained a two-layer LSTM network for action classification. Ng *et al.* [39] further demonstrated that a five-layer LSTM network is slightly better. Veeriah *et al.* proposed a differential gating scheme for LSTM to emphasize on the change in information gain [55]. More recently, Sharma *et al.* incorporated the attention mechanism into LSTM to identify the most relevant information (*e.g.*, objects) for recognizing actions [44].

Fusion. Videos naturally contain abundant clues, and hence a decent video categorization system often fuses multiple sources of information for improved recognition performance [69, 20]. The simplest fusion strategy is linear weighted fusion, which has been adopted in many recent approaches like [45]. Nandakumar *et al.* performed score fusion using a method called likelihood ratio test [36]. More recently, Xu *et al.* [66] and Ye *et al.* [68] proposed robust late fusion methods by seeking a low rank matrix to remove the noise of individually trained classifiers. Liu *et al.* [32] proposed to predict sample-specific weights in the fusion process. There are also a few works attempting to fuse multiple features with deep neural networks. Srivastava *et al.* proposed to combine features using deep Boltzmann Machines [49]. Neverova formulated the fusion problem as a modality dropping process [38]. Our paper relies on state-of-the-art deep models to characterize videos from different perspectives, and then performs a simple late fusion approach to further combine scores from multiple streams for final predictions.

Class Relationships. There are many studies using class relationships (a.k.a. context) to improve multi-class visual recognition performance. For instance, Rabinovich *et al.* utilized a Conditional Random Field (CRF) model to maximize object label agreement based on contextual relevance [41]. Jiang *et al.* used a semantic diffusion algorithm to incorporate class relationships [24]. Deng *et al.* proposed to jointly train a hierarchy and exclusion graph model with a ConvNet to learn class relations for image classification [8]. Assari *et al.* exploited class co-occurrences for improved video classification [2]. Wu *et al.* [63] proposed a regularized neural network to fuse features and explore class relationships, but used traditional hand-engineered features as inputs. Recently, Chen and Gupta utilized the class correlations in the form of confusion matrix to refine the classification scores from the softmax layer [6]. Note that Multi-Task Learning (MTL) also attempts to improve recognition performance by enforcing similar zero/nonzero patterns in the weight matrix through structural norms, which enables knowledge sharing among highly related tasks (classes). In our work, we adopt a data-driven approach, mining the knowledge learned by the models themselves, to borrow useful information from classes with relatedness.

3. THE PROPOSED APPROACH

In this section, we first describe the individual network streams and then introduce the proposed fusion method.

3.1 Multi-Stream ConvNets

Carrying abundant multimodal information, videos normally show the movements and interactions of objects under certain scenes over time, accompanied by human voices or background sounds. Therefore, video data can be naturally decomposed into spatial, motion and audio streams. The spatial stream consisting of individual frames depicts the static appearance information, while the motion stream captures object or scene movements demonstrated by continuous frames. In addition, sounds in the audio stream provide crucial clues that are often complementary to the visual counterpart. Motivated by the recent two-stream approach [45], we train three ConvNets to exploit the multimodal information, as described below.

In brief, the spatial ConvNet uses the raw frames as inputs, where we adopt a deep architecture with superior performance on image recognition tasks [46]. It can effectively recognize certain video semantics that have clear and discriminative appearance characteristics. For the motion stream, we train a ConvNet model operating on stacked optical flows following [45]. More specifically, through computing displacement vectors in both horizontal and vertical ways, the optical flows encode subtle motion patterns of objects between each pair of adjacent frames, which can be converted into two flow images as the inputs of the motion stream ConvNet. Previous studies have shown that further improvements can be obtained by stacking consecutive optical flow images in a short time window, owing to the inclusion of relatively more compact movements [45]. In order to leverage the audio information, we first apply the Short-Time Fourier Transformation to convert the 1-d soundtrack into a 2-D image (namely spectrogram) with the horizontal axis and vertical axis being time-scale and frequency-scale respectively. Then we employ a ConvNet to operate on the spectrograms as suggested in [54]. Notice that the ConvNet is well suited for modeling audio signals based on spectrograms with the weight sharing and max pooling mechanism to strive invariance of small frequency shifts [1].

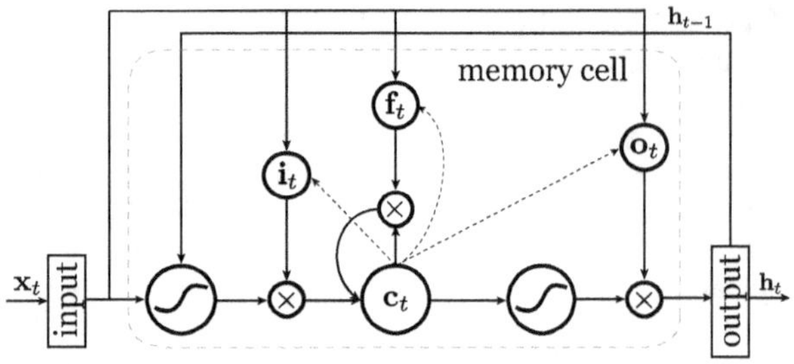

Figure 2: The structure of an LSTM unit.

3.2 Long Term Temporal Modeling

As the motion stream ConvNet only captures short-term motion patterns, we further employ LSTM [18] to model long-term temporal clues in the visual channel. LSTM is able to exploit temporal information of a data sequence with arbitrary length through recursively mapping the input sequence to output labels with hidden units. Each of the units maintains a built-in memory cell, which stores information over time guarded by several non-linear gate units to control the amount of changes and influence of the memory contents. To keep this paper self-contained, we briefly introduce LSTM as follows.

Figure 2 illustrates the typical structure of a hidden LSTM unit. In our framework, we denote $\mathbf{x}_t$ as the feature representation of a video frame or a stacked optical flow image at the t-th time step. Generally, an LSTM maps an input sequence $(\mathbf{x}_1, \mathbf{x}_2, \ldots, \mathbf{x}_T)$ to output labels $(\mathbf{y}_1, \mathbf{y}_2, \ldots, \mathbf{y}_T)$ through computing activations of the units in the network recursively from $t = 1$ to $t = T$. At time t, the activation vectors of memory cell $\mathbf{c}_t$, output gate $\mathbf{o}_t$ and hidden state $\mathbf{h}_t$ are computed as:

$$\begin{aligned} \mathbf{c}_t &= \mathbf{f}_t \odot \mathbf{c}_{t-1} + \mathbf{i}_t \odot \tanh(\mathbf{W}_{xc}\mathbf{x}_t + \mathbf{W}_{hc}\mathbf{h}_{t-1} + \mathbf{b}_c), \\ \mathbf{o}_t &= \sigma(\mathbf{W}_{xo}\mathbf{x}_t + \mathbf{W}_{ho}\mathbf{h}_{t-1} + \mathbf{W}_{co}\mathbf{c}_t + \mathbf{b}_o), \\ \mathbf{h}_t &= \mathbf{o}_t \odot \tanh(\mathbf{c}_t), \end{aligned} \tag{1}$$

where $\mathbf{W}_{xc}, \mathbf{W}_{hc}, \mathbf{W}_{xo}, \mathbf{W}_{ho}, \mathbf{W}_{co}$ are the weight matrices connecting two different units. $\mathbf{b}_c, \mathbf{b}_o$ are the bias terms, σ is the sigmoid function, and $\odot$ is an element-wise product operator. Notice that $\mathbf{i}_t$ and $\mathbf{f}_t$ are the activation vectors of input and forget gates, which are calculated with weight matrices as:

$$\begin{aligned} \mathbf{i}_t &= \sigma(\mathbf{W}_{xi}\mathbf{x}_t + \mathbf{W}_{hi}\mathbf{h}_{t-1} + \mathbf{W}_{ci}\mathbf{c}_{t-1} + \mathbf{b}_i), \\ \mathbf{f}_t &= \sigma(\mathbf{W}_{xf}\mathbf{x}_t + \mathbf{W}_{hf}\mathbf{h}_{t-1} + \mathbf{W}_{cf}\mathbf{c}_{t-1} + \mathbf{b}_f). \end{aligned} \tag{2}$$

From the above equations, the contents of the memory cell at the t-th time step $\mathbf{c}_t$ is computed as the weighted sum of the current inputs and the previous memory contents $\mathbf{c}_{t-1}$. The input and forget gates (*i.e.*, $\mathbf{i}_t$ and $\mathbf{f}_t$) impose regularization to determine whether to consider new information or forget old information. In addition, the output gate $\mathbf{o}_t$ controls the amount of information from the memory contents that is passed to the hidden state $\mathbf{h}_t$ to influence the computation in the next time step.

As a neural network, the LSTM model can be easily deepened by stacking the hidden states from a layer $l-1$ as inputs of the next layer l. In order to obtain the prediction scores for a total of C classes at a time step t, a softmax layer is placed on top of the last LSTM layer L to estimate the posterior probability p_c of the c-th class as:

$$p_c = \text{softmax}(\mathbf{h}_t^L) = \frac{\exp(\mathbf{u}_c{}^T\mathbf{h}_t^L + b_c)}{\sum_{c' \in C} \exp(\mathbf{u}_{c'}{}^T\mathbf{h}_t^L + b_{c'})}, \tag{3}$$

where $\mathbf{u}_c$ and b_c represent the corresponding weight vector and the bias term of the c-th class. Such an LSTM network can be trained using the Back-Propagation Through Time (BPTT) algorithm [16], which "unrolls" the model into a feed forward neural net and back-propagates to determine the optimal network parameters. We adopt the output from the last layer as the video-level prediction scores since this output is computed based on the information from the entire sequence. Our empirical results show that using the output of the last time step is better than pooling the predictions at all the time steps.

3.3 Multi-Stream Fusion

Given the prediction scores of the multiple deep network streams (each stream outputs scores of multiple classes), we are able to capture the video characteristics from different aspects. It is critical to effectively fuse the scores to generate the final predictions. Different semantic classes associate with the multiple streams with different strength. For example, some classes are strongly associated with particular objects which could be effectively recognized with the spatial stream, while others may contain dramatic movements so the short-term motion and the long-term temporal clues can contribute more significantly. Traditional fusion methods are usually performed in a uniform way without considering the class-specific preferences.

More formally, we denote the prediction scores from the m-th stream as $\mathbf{s}^m \in \mathbb{R}^C$ $(m = 1, \cdots, M)$ with C being the number of classes, and let $\hat{\mathbf{y}}$ be the final predicted labels. A straightforward way of late fusion is to compute the final prediction as $\hat{\mathbf{y}} = f(\mathbf{s}^1, \cdots, \mathbf{s}^M)$. Here f is a transition function, which can be a linear function, a logistic function, *etc.* However, such a late fusion approach treats all the classes uniformly and relies on the assumption that scores from multiple networks are explicitly complementary.

Different from the uniform fusion methods, we attempt to adaptively integrate the predictions from multiple streams to determine the optimal fusion weights for each class. To this end, we first stack the multiple score vectors of a training sample n as a coefficient vector:

$$\mathbf{s}_n = \left[\mathbf{s}_n^{1\,T}, \cdots, \mathbf{s}_n^{m\,T}, \cdots, \mathbf{s}_n^{M\,T}\right]^T \in \mathbb{R}^{CM} \tag{4}$$

Then the best class-specific fusion weights can be learned with simple classifiers like logistic regression:

$$\mathbf{W} = \arg\min_{\mathbf{w}, \cdots, \mathbf{w}_C} \sum_{n,c} \log\left(1 + \exp\left[(1 - 2y_{n,c})\mathbf{s}_n^T\mathbf{w}_c\right]\right), \tag{5}$$

where $y_{n,c}$ is the ground-truth label of the n-th sample for class c, and $\mathbf{W} = [\mathbf{w}_1, \cdots, \mathbf{w}_c, \cdots, \mathbf{w}_C] \in \mathbb{R}^{CM \times C}$. However, the final prediction score of class c in this process not only comes from its own scores of different streams, but also utilizes knowledge from other classes, which incurs extra parameters that will often lead to over-fitting.

3.4 Utilizing Class Relationships

To alleviate the over-fitting effect, one may use sparsity constraints (*e.g.*, ℓ_1 or ℓ_{21} norm) to force entries to be zero in the weight matrix as a means of feature selection. For example, ℓ_1 norm penalizes non-zero weights, which will lead to the parameter vector to be sparse ignoring certain information in the input data. Nevertheless, instead of recognizing objects/concepts independently, humans can utilize the relations among concepts to derive a better understanding of the object of interest. Researchers also confirm that class relationships (a.k.a. semantic context) are known as helpful clues in multi-class visual recognition tasks and have been popularly used for improved performance [41, 4, 8]. Therefore, we believe that injecting such intrinsic class relationships in the learning process can improve the result.

Different from enforcing zero patterns in the weight matrix, in this paper, we tackle this problem by resorting to existing knowledge to determine the information from which classes and to what extent will be needed, and hence the parameters do not need to be learned from scratch. For example, we can adopt off-the-shelf WordNet/ConceptNet to obtain the relations among multiple concepts. However, these relations are handcrafted, which might be semantically similar but ignore the visual patterns. Note that each stream is a well-trained deep network, consisting of valuable information on data distribution. Therefore, we propose to mine knowledge (*i.e.*, class relationships) from the models themselves using the confusion matrix, which is a good indicator on how classes are related. More formally, we denote $\mathbf{V}^m \in \mathbb{R}^{C\times C}$ to be the similarity matrix of different classes for the m-th stream, and hence $\mathbf{V}^m_{ij}$ indicates the correlation between class C_i and C_j.

Confusion Matrix. We simply test the network on the validation set and adopt the confusion matrix to measure similarity among video classes:

$$\mathbf{V}^m_{ij} = \frac{1}{|C_i|}\sum_{n\in C_i} \mathbf{1}_{\arg\max_c(s^m_n)==C_j}. \quad (6)$$

where $\mathbf{1}(\cdot)$ is the indicator function, C_i is the collection of training samples that belongs to class i, and $|\cdot|$ is the cardinality function. Here each entry $\mathbf{V}_{ij}$ indicates the percentage of the samples with the ground-truth label of class i being wrongly classified into class j. We visualize the confusion matrix generated by the spatial ConvNet on CCV in Figure 3, which demonstrates how classes are correlated.

The reason of using a separate correlation matrix for each stream is that the captured class relationships in different streams are likely to be quite different. For instance, some classes are similar visually and some may share certain audio clues.

After obtaining the class relationship matrices of all the streams using the above equation, we stack the matrices $\mathbf{V} = [\mathbf{V}^1, \cdots, \mathbf{V}^m, \cdots, \mathbf{V}^M]^\top$ to constrain the weight learning process as:

$$\min_{\mathbf{W}} \; L(\mathbf{S},\mathbf{Y};\mathbf{W}) + \lambda_1 \|\mathbf{W}-\mathbf{V}\|_F^2, \quad (7)$$

where the first term is the empirical loss defined in Equation 5. The second term constrains the fusion weights using the class correlation as a prior, with "F" indicating the Frobenius norm. For each similarity matrix $\mathbf{V}^m$, the non-diagonal entries demonstrate the similarities among different classes, which can be used to guide the weight learning process through borrowing information from highly related classes. Since the class relationship matrix $\mathbf{V}$ constrains which classes to be used and how much is needed, the best

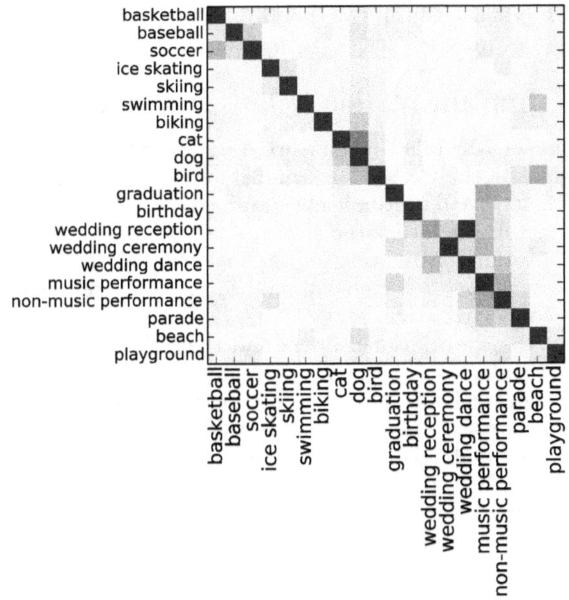

Figure 3: The confusion matrix of the spatial ConvNet on CCV.

optimal weights could be learned easier without suffering over-fitting. In addition, we also incorporate an ℓ_1 norm term to impose sparsity on the weight matrix, which, to some extent, can help avoid information sharing across irrelevant classes. Integrating all the terms, we have the following optimization problem:

$$\min_{\mathbf{W}} \; L(\mathbf{S},\mathbf{Y};\mathbf{W}) + \lambda_1 \|\mathbf{W}-\mathbf{V}\|_F^2 + \lambda_2 \|\mathbf{W}\|_1. \quad (8)$$

Different from enforcing sparsity patterns as in standard MTL:

$$\min_{\mathbf{W}} \; L(\mathbf{S},\mathbf{Y};\mathbf{W}) + \lambda_1 \|\mathbf{W}\|_p, \quad (9)$$

where the second term could be ℓ_1-norm, ℓ_2-norm or $\ell_{2,1}$-norm, our fusion approach relies on the class relationship matrix to constrain the weights for improved performance. As our approach not only fuses the multiple network streams but also utilizes class relationship, we name it as *multi-stream multi-class fusion*. The contribution from each component of the objective function will be evaluated later.

Although the loss function in Equation 8 is convex, it is non-trivial to solve it due to the non-smooth term. To tackle the optimization problem efficiently, we adopt the proximal gradient descent method that splits the objective function into a smooth part and a non-smooth part:

$$g = L(\mathbf{S},\mathbf{Y};\mathbf{W}) + \lambda_1 \|\mathbf{W}-\mathbf{V}\|_F^2, \quad (10)$$

$$h = \lambda_2 \|\mathbf{W}\|_1. \quad (11)$$

The update of $\mathbf{W}$ at the $k+1$ iteration can be simply computed as:

$$\mathbf{W}^{k+1} = \mathrm{Prox}_h(\mathbf{W}^k - \nabla g(\mathbf{W}^k)),$$

where Prox_h denotes the soft-thresholding operator for the ℓ_1 norm [10].

Note that the additional computational cost lies in the estimation of the proximal operator. Since it can be analytically solved in linear time [3], the above optimization process is fairly efficient.

3.5 Implementation Details and Discussions

ConvNet Models. In this work, we adopt two ConvNet architectures, the CNN_M [45] model for capturing the short-term motion and the audio clues and a recent deeper VGG_19 architecture for the spatial stream [46]. The CNN_M is basically a variant of the AlexNet [28] with more filters included, which contains five convolutional layers followed by three fully connected layers. The VGG_19 not only reduces the size of the convolutional filters and the stride, but also extends the depth of the network to a total of 19 layers, equipping the architecture with the capacity of learning more robust representations. These two deep networks achieved 13.5% [45] and 7.5% [46] top-5 error rates on the ImageNet ILSVRC-2012 validation set, respectively. All the ConvNet models are trained using mini-batch stochastic gradient descent with a momentum fixed to 0.9. Our implementation is based on the publicly available Caffe toolbox [23] with some modifications. The input video frame is uniformly fixed to the size of 224×224. In addition, we also perform simple data augmentations like cropping and flipping following [45].

The spatial and the audio ConvNets are first pre-trained using the ILSVRC-2012 training set with 1.2 million images and then fine-tuned using the training video data. This strategy has been observed effective in [45] for the spatial stream, and we have observed it also helpful for the audio stream. To fine-tune the spatial and the audio ConvNets, we gradually decrease the learning rate from 10^{-3} to 10^{-4} after 14K iterations, then to 10^{-5} after 20K iterations. In addition, dropout is applied to the fully connected layers with a ratio of 0.5 to avoid over-fitting.

To train the motion ConvNet, we first compute optical flow using the GPU implementation of [5] and stack the optical flows in each 10-frame window to receive a 20-channel optical flow image as the input (one horizontal channel and one vertical channel for each frame pair). Unlike the spatial and the audio ConvNets, we train the motion ConvNet from scratch by adopting 0.7 dropout ratio and setting the learning rate to 10^{-2} initially, which is reduced to 10^{-3} after 100K iterations and then to 10^{-4} after 200K iterations. Note that we also tried to use the VGG_19 network to train the motion ConvNet, but observed worse results as the network contains much more parameters that cannot be well-tuned using the limited training video data.

LSTM. We adopt the two-layer LSTM model proposed by Graves [16] for temporal modeling. Two models are trained with features extracted from the first fully-connected layer of the spatial and the motion ConvNets respectively as inputs. Each LSTM has 1,024 hidden units in the first layer and 512 hidden units in the second layer. We utilize a parallel implementation of the BPTT algorithm with a mini-batch size of 10 to train the network weights, where the learning rate and momentum are set as 10^{-4} and 0.9. In addition, we set the maximal training iterations to be 150K. Note that, in this paper, we focus on a multi-stream framework by utilizing the audio signal as a single stream for video classification. Further decomposing the audio track into multiple segments to extract more detailed temporal audio dynamics is feasible.

Fusion. As shown in Equation 8, the proposed fusion method seeks a tradeoff among the three terms. We uniformly fix λ_2 to be 10^{-3} to encourage sparsity in the learned weight matrix. The parameter λ_1 is selected among $\{10^{-5}, 10^{-4}, 10^{-3}, 10^{-2}\}$ using cross-validation.

Discussions. Our proposed framework has the capability of modeling video data comprehensively by adaptively fusing audio, static spatial, short-term motion and long-term temporal clues. As described above, such a framework consists of multiple separately trained deep networks. Although being feasible to jointly train the entire framework, it is complicated and computationally demanding. A recent work performing joint training of the LSTM with a ConvNet improves the results on the UCF-101 benchmark from 70.5% (separate network training) to 71.1% [9], which is not very significant. In addition, training multiple deep networks separately makes the approach more flexible, where a component may be replaced without the need of re-training the entire framework. For instance, one can utilize more discriminative ConvNet models like the GoogLeNet [51] and deeper RNN models [7] to replace the current ConvNet and LSTM parts respectively for better performance. Therefore, in this work, we focus on presenting a general framework for video classification. With the proposed multi-stream multi-class fusion method, the framework is empirically proved to be effective for the video classification task, as discussed in the following section.

4. EXPERIMENTS

In this section, we report results on two popular datasets. Experiments are designed to study the effectiveness of each individual stream and the proposed fusion method.

4.1 Experimental Setup

Datasets and Evaluation Measures. UCF-101 [47] is a widely adopted dataset for human action recognition, containing 13,320 video clips annotated into 101 action classes. All the video clips have a fixed frame rate of 25 fps with a spatial resolution of 320 × 240 pixels. This dataset is challenging because most videos were captured under uncontrolled environments with camera motion, cluttered backgrounds and large intra-class variations. We follow the suggested experimental protocol and report mean accuracy over the three training and test splits [19].

The Columbia Consumer Videos (CCV) dataset [25] contains 9,317 YouTube videos and 20 classes. Most of the classes are events like "basketball", "graduation ceremony" and "wedding dance". A few are scenes and objects like "beach" and "dog". Following [25], we adopt the suggested training and test split and compute the average precision (AP) for each class. Mean AP (mAP) is used to measure the overall performance on this dataset.

The two datasets possess very different characteristics. Besides the difference of the defined semantic classes, the average video duration of CCV is 80 seconds, which is around ten times longer than that of UCF-101. Testing on these two datasets is helpful for evaluating the effectiveness and the generalization capability of our multi-stream classification approach.

Compared Methods. To validate the effectiveness of our multi-stream multi-class fusion method, we compare with the following alternatives: (1) Average Fusion, where the mean scores of multiple network streams are used as the final prediction; (2) Weighted Fusion, where the scores are fused linearly with weights estimated by cross-validation; (3) Kernel Average Fusion, where the scores are used as features and kernels computed from different network scores are averaged to train an SVM classifier; (4) Multiple Kernel Learning (MKL) Fusion, where the kernels are combined using the ℓ_p-norm MKL algorithm [27]; (5) Logistic Regression Fusion, where a logistic regression model is trained to estimate the fusion weights; (6) Domain Adaptive Semantic Diffusion (DASD) [24], which uses a graph diffusion formulation for context-based multi-class score fusion.

4.2 Results and Discussions

4.2.1 Multi-Stream Networks

We first report the performance of each individual stream on both datasets. After that, average fusion is adopted to study whether two or more streams are complementary. The proposed fusion method will be evaluated later.

Table 1 reports the results. Comparing the top two cells of results on UCF-101, it is interesting to observe that the spatial LSTM outperforms the spatial ConvNet and the motion LSTM is also comparable to the motion ConvNet. This is largely due to the fact that the long-term temporal clues are fully discarded in the ConvNet based classification, which can be exploited by the LSTM.

On the CCV dataset, the ConvNet achieves significantly better results than the LSTM on both spatial and motion streams. This is because the classes in CCV are either high-level events or objects/scenes. Compared with human actions, the temporal clues of these classes are more obscure and thus difficult to be captured. Also, the CCV videos are temporally untrimmed, which may contain significant portions of contents irrelevant to the classes, making the temporal modeling task even more difficult.

One may notice that our motion networks perform worse than spatial networks, which is not consistent with the observations in dense trajectory features [56]. We would like to underline that motion information extracted from optical flow images tends to be noisy, especially on temporally untrimmed long videos, as reported in [39]. In addition, the dense trajectory features are hand-crafted without the need of training, while the motion stream networks demand extensive training. Unfortunately, labeled training data in the video domain is still quite limited. We expect to obtain better results from the motion stream network once sufficient training data is available.

The audio ConvNets operated on spectrograms produce 16.2% on UCF-101 and 21.5% on CCV. Note that only 51 classes in UCF-101 have audio signals, and the performance on the 51-class subset is actually 32.1%. The audio stream is much worse than the spatial and the motion streams on both datasets, confirming that the visual channel are more informative than the audio counterpart.

Next, we evaluate the combinations of multiple networks to study whether fusion can compensate the limitations of a single stream in describing complex video data. The simple average fusion is adopted. Results are summarized in the bottom three groups of Table 1. We first assess the gain from integrating the spatial and the motion information modeled by ConvNet and LSTM respectively. On UCF-101, significant improvements (about 6% for ConvNet and 3% for LSTM) are observed over the best single stream results. The gain on CCV is consistent but not as significant

	UCF-101	CCV
Spatial ConvNet	80.1	75.0
Motion ConvNet	77.5	58.9
Spatial LSTM	83.3	43.3
Motion LSTM	76.6	54.7
Audio ConvNet	16.2*	21.5
ConvNet (spatial+motion)	86.2	75.8
LSTM (spatial+motion)	86.3	61.9
ConvNet+LSTM (spatial)	84.0	77.9
ConvNet+LSTM (motion)	81.4	70.9
ConvNet+LSTM (spatial+motion)	90.1	81.7
All the streams	90.3	82.4

Table 1: Performance of each individual stream and their average fusion (indicated by "+"). *Note that the videos of only 51 classes in UCF-101 contain audio soundtracks. The audio ConvNet can produce an accuracy of 32.1% on the 51-class subset.

as that on UCF-101, indicating that the short-term motion is more critical for human action analysis. Note that the average fusion of the spatial and the motion ConvNets follows the same idea of the two-stream approach proposed in [45]. Our implementation of this approach produces slightly worse performance than that originally reported in [45] (86.2% vs. 88.0%).

We also fuse ConvNet with LSTM separately on both streams to investigate the contribution of the long-term temporal modeling. Overall, we observe very consistent improvements on both datasets. In particular, on CCV, although the individual LSTM model is worse than ConvNet, the combination of them leads to significant improvements. Especially, a gain of nearly 12% is obtained on the motion stream. These results show that the long-term temporal clues are highly complementary to the ConvNet-based predictions, even in the case of modeling complex contents in the long CCV videos.

Finally, the combination of ConvNet and LSTM on both streams, indicated by "ConvNet+LSTM (spatial+motion)", achieves 90.1% and 81.7% on UCF-101 and CCV respectively. Further adding the audio ConvNet ("all the streams") can improve the results particularly on CCV which contains many classes that can be partly revealed by auditory clues (*e.g.*, cheering sounds in the sports events). In summary, the fusion results clearly demonstrate that all the multimodal clues in our approach are useful and should be adopted in a successful video classification system.

4.2.2 Multi-Stream Multi-Class Fusion

In this subsection, we evaluate the proposed fusion method and compare it with the alternative methods. Table 2 gives the results. We see that all the methods produce better results than the individual streams. The simple average fusion and weighted fusion are slightly better than the learning based kernel fusion and logistic regression fusion, indicating that the learning based methods are prone to overfitting. Kernel average fusion shows slightly better results than MKL, which is consistent with the observations in several previous studies like [13]. DASD produces similar results to weighted fusion as it is essentially an iterative weighted fusion method.

	UCF-101	CCV
Average fusion	90.3	82.4
Weighted fusion	90.6	82.7
Kernel average fusion	90.2	82.1
MKL fusion	89.6	81.8
Logistic regression fusion	89.8	82.0
DASD	90.4	82.9
Multi-stream fusion (λ_1=0)	90.9	82.8
Multi-stream multi-class fusion (λ_2=0)	91.6	83.7
Multi-stream multi-class fusion (-A)	92.2	84.0
Multi-stream multi-class fusion	92.6	84.9

Table 2: Comparison of fusion methods. "-A" indicates that the audio stream ConvNet is not adopted. See texts for discussions.

Our proposed multi-stream multi-class fusion (the bottom group of results) outperforms all the alternatives with clear margins. To investigate the contributions of the class relationship term and the sparsity term in our approach, we set λ_1 and λ_2 to be zero respectively. As can be seen, both terms are very useful. Relatively, the class relationship (λ_1) plays a more important role than the sparsity term (λ_2). This corroborates the effectiveness of using the class relationship, even when it is roughly estimated based on prediction score correlations (see Section 3.3), which is very appealing. The two terms are complementary as the sparsity inducing norm further enhances robustness by alleviating incorrect information sharing. Note that when eliminating both terms, our fusion approach degenerates to the standard logistic regression fusion. In summary, these results show that it is helpful to fuse the outputs of both multiple network streams and multiple classes.

The contribution of the audio clues is similar on both datasets ("-A" indicates the same approach without using the audio ConvNet). Audio improves just 0.4% on UCF-101 because only half of the video clips contain soundtracks. Figure 4 further shows the per-class performance on CCV, where we can see that fusion leads to very consistent and significant improvements for all the classes.

Comparisons with different regularizers. Since sparsity regularizers are popular constraints to improve generalization ability as in standard MTL, we also compare the proposed approach with this line of work by replacing the proposed regularizers with alternative ones (see Eq. 9). The results are summarized in Table 3. As we can see from the table, the proposed regularization norm that utilizes class relationship as contextual information outperforms the competing regularizers. Different from forcing entries to be zero (*i.e.*, ℓ_1 norm) or selecting the same set of parameters for related tasks (*i.e.*, ℓ_{21} norm), the proposed norm leverages the class relationships in the models to guide the fusion process, through constraining which and how much information is required from other classes. This corroborates the fact the scores from the softmax layer contain meaningful information rather than simply indicating the predicted label [17].

4.2.3 Computational Efficiency

The proposed approach can achieve effective recognition efficiently. For a CCV video clip with an average duration of 80 seconds, extracting the improved dense trajectories requires 850 seconds, while it only takes 131 seconds for our method to finish the entire process, which is evaluated on a single NVIDIA Telsa K40 GPU.

	UCF-101	CCV
Fusion with ℓ_1 norm	90.9	82.8
Fusion with ℓ_{21} norm	91.0	82.4
Fusion with ($\ell_{21}+\ell_1$) norm	91.4	83.2
Multi-stream multi-class fusion	92.6	84.9

Table 3: Comparison with different regularization strategies.

4.2.4 Comparison with State of the Arts

UCF-101		CCV	
Donahue *et al.* [9]	82.9	Lai *et al.* [29]	43.6
Srivastava *et al.* [48]	84.3	Jiang *et al.* [25]	59.5
Wang *et al.* [57]	85.9	Xu *et al.* [66]	60.3
Tran *et al.* [53]	86.7	Ma *et al.* [34]	63.4
Simonyan *et al.* [45]	88.0	Jhuo *et al.* [21]	64.0
Ng *et al.* [39]	88.6	Ye *et al.* [68]	64.0
Lan *et al.* [30]	89.1	Liu *et al.* [32]	68.2
Zha *et al.* [70]	89.6	Wu *et al.* [64]	83.5
Wang *et al.* [59]	91.5	Nagel *et al.* [35]	71.7
Wang *et al.* [60]	92.4		
Ours (-A)	92.2	Ours (-A)	84.0
Ours	**92.6**	Ours	**84.9**

Table 4: Comparison with state-of-the-art results. Our approach produces to-date the highest reported results on both datasets. "Ours (-A)" indicates the same framework without using the audio stream ConvNet.

We compare our approach with the state of the arts on both datasets. Results are listed in Table 4. Our proposed multi-stream approach achieves the highest performance on both datasets. On UCF-101, many works with competitive results are based on the hand-engineered dense trajectory features [57, 30], while our approach fully relies on the deep networks. Compared with the original result of the two-stream approach [45], our approach captures a more comprehensive set of useful clues with a more effective fusion method. Zha *et al.* [70] combined the ConvNet features with the dense trajectories [56] to achieve competitive results. The previous best performance on UCF-101 is from Wang *et al.* [59], who combined the two-stream approach [45] and the dense trajectories. Note that a gain of 1% on the widely adopted UCF-101 dataset is generally considered as a significant progress.

In addition, the recent works in [9, 48, 64, 39] also adopted the LSTM to model the temporal clues for video classification and reported promising performance, but did not explore the audio stream nor employ advanced fusion strategies.

On the CCV dataset, all the recent approaches were developed based on multiple features, either the hand-engineered descriptors or the ConvNet-based representations. Our approach produces better results than all of them.

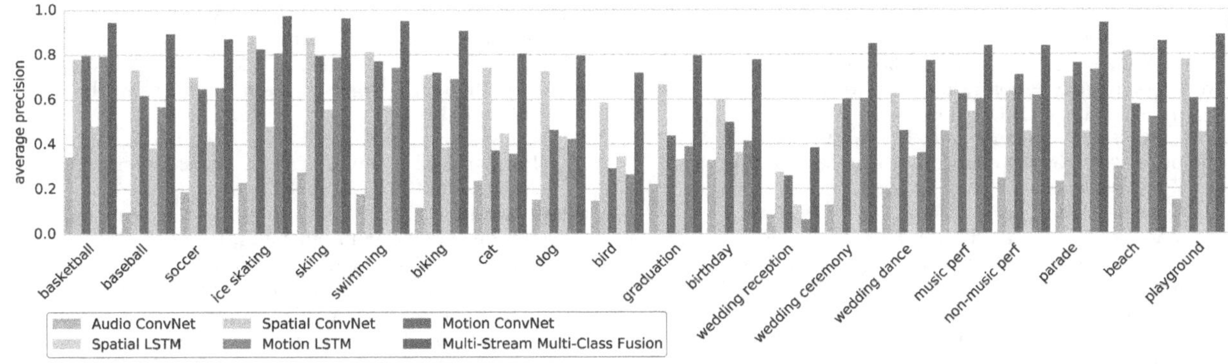

Figure 4: Per-class performance on CCV. Multi-stream multi-class fusion of the deep network outputs produces consistently better results than the individual streams on all the classes.

5. CONCLUSIONS

We have presented a multi-stream framework of deep networks for video classification. The framework harnesses multimodal features that are more comprehensive than those previously adopted. Specifically, standard ConvNets are applied to audio spectrograms, visual frames and stacked optical flows to exploit the audio, spatial and short-term motion clues in videos, respectively. LSTM is further adopted on the spatial and the short-term motion features from the ConvNets for long-term temporal modeling. The outputs from the different streams are then combined using a novel method called multi-stream multi-class fusion, which not only learns the best weights of the multi-stream networks for each class, but also considers class relationships for improved performance. Our results confirm that all the adopted streams are effective for modeling both simple human actions in short clips and complex events in temporally untrimmed Internet videos. Combining the multi-stream multi-class predictions by our proposed fusion method consistently outperforms peer approaches on two popular benchmarks.

This paper is among the limited number of studies showing strong video classification performance using deep networks. As aforementioned, unlike the spatial ConvNet that can be trained by fine-tuning a model pre-trained on the ImageNet dataset, the motion ConvNet has to be trained from scratch on videos. Therefore, one promising future direction is to pre-train the motion ConvNet using large video datasets like the Sports-1M [26], which may lead to much better results.

Acknowledgment

This work was supported by a China's National 863 Program (#2014AA015101), and two grants from National Natural Science Foundation of China (#61572138 and #U1509206).

6. REFERENCES

[1] O. Abdel-Hamid, L. Deng, and D. Yu. Exploring convolutional neural network structures and optimization techniques for speech recognition. In *INTERSPEECH*, 2013.

[2] S. M. Assari, A. R. Zamir, and M. Shah. Video classification using semantic concept co-occurrences. In *CVPR*, 2014.

[3] F. Bach, R. Jenatton, J. Mairal, G. Obozinski, et al. Convex optimization with sparsity-inducing norms. *Optimization for Machine Learning*, 2011.

[4] S. Bengio, J. Dean, D. Erhan, E. Ie, Q. Le, A. Rabinovich, J. Shlens, and Y. Singer. Using web co-occurrence statistics for improving image categorization. *CoRR*, 2013.

[5] T. Brox, A. Bruhn, N. Papenberg, and J. Weickert. High accuracy optical flow estimation based on a theory for warping. In *ECCV*. 2004.

[6] X. Chen and A. Gupta. Webly supervised learning of convolutional networks. In *ICCV*, 2015.

[7] J. Chung, Ç. Gülçehre, K. Cho, and Y. Bengio. Gated feedback recurrent neural networks. *CoRR*, 2015.

[8] J. Deng, N. Ding, Y. Jia, A. Frome, K. Murphy, S. Bengio, Y. Li, H. Neven, and H. Adam. Large-scale object classification using label relation graphs. In *ECCV*, 2014.

[9] J. Donahue, L. A. Hendricks, S. Guadarrama, M. Rohrbach, S. Venugopalan, K. Saenko, and T. Darrell. Long-term recurrent convolutional networks for visual recognition and description. In *CVPR*, 2015.

[10] D. L. Donoho and I. M. Johnstone. Adapting to unknown smoothness via wavelet shrinkage. *Journal of the american statistical association*, 1995.

[11] C. Farabet, C. Couprie, L. Najman, and Y. LeCun. Learning hierarchical features for scene labeling. *IEEE TPAMI*, 2013.

[12] B. Fernando, E. Gavves, J. M. Oramas, A. Ghodrati, and T. Tuytelaars. Modeling video evolution for action recognition. In *CVPR*, 2015.

[13] P. Gehler and S. Nowozin. On feature combination for multiclass object classification. In *ICCV*, 2009.

[14] R. Girshick, J. Donahue, T. Darrell, and J. Malik. Rich feature hierarchies for accurate object detection and semantic segmentation. In *CVPR*, 2014.

[15] A. Graves, A. Mohamed, and G. E. Hinton. Speech recognition with deep recurrent neural networks. In *ICASSP*, 2013.

[16] A. Graves and J. Schmidhuber. Framewise phoneme classification with bidirectional lstm and other neural network architectures. *Neural Networks*, 2005.

[17] G. Hinton, O. Vinyals, and J. Dean. Distilling the knowledge in a neural network. *CoRR*, 2015.

[18] S. Hochreiter and J. Schmidhuber. Long short-term memory. *Neural Computation*, 1997.

[19] H. Idrees, A. R. Zamir, Y.-G. Jiang, A. Gorban, I. Laptev, R. Sukthankar, and M. Shah. The thumos challenge on action recognition for videos" in the wild". *arXiv preprint arXiv:1604.06182*, 2016.

[20] M. Jain and et al. University of amsterdam at thumos 2015. In *CVPR THUMOS Workshop*, 2015.

[21] I.-H. Jhuo, G. Ye, S. Gao, D. Liu, Y.-G. Jiang, D. T. Lee, and S.-F. Chang. Discovering joint audio-visual codewords

for video event detection. *Machine Vision and Applications*, 2014.

[22] S. Ji, W. Xu, M. Yang, and K. Yu. 3d convolutional neural networks for human action recognition. In *ICML*, 2010.

[23] Y. Jia, E. Shelhamer, J. Donahue, S. Karayev, J. Long, R. Girshick, S. Guadarrama, and T. Darrell. Caffe: Convolutional architecture for fast feature embedding. In *ACM Multimedia*, 2014.

[24] Y.-G. Jiang, J. Wang, S.-F. Chang, and C.-W. Ngo. Domain adaptive semantic diffusion for large scale context-based video annotation. In *ICCV*, 2009.

[25] Y.-G. Jiang, G. Ye, S.-F. Chang, D. Ellis, and A. C. Loui. Consumer video understanding: A benchmark database and an evaluation of human and machine performance. In *ACM ICMR*, 2011.

[26] A. Karpathy, G. Toderici, S. Shetty, T. Leung, R. Sukthankar, and L. Fei-Fei. Large-scale video classification with convolutional neural networks. In *CVPR*, 2014.

[27] M. Kloft, U. Brefeld, S. Sonnenburg, and A. Zien. Lp-norm multiple kernel learning. *The Journal of Machine Learning Research*, 2011.

[28] A. Krizhevsky, I. Sutskever, and G. E. Hinton. Imagenet classification with deep convolutional neural networks. In *NIPS*, 2012.

[29] K.-T. Lai, F. X. Yu, M.-S. Chen, and S.-F. Chang. Video event detection by inferring temporal instance labels. In *CVPR*, 2014.

[30] Z. Lan, M. Lin, X. Li, A. G. Hauptmann, and B. Raj. Beyond gaussian pyramid: Multi-skip feature stacking for action recognition. *CoRR*, 2014.

[31] I. Laptev. On space-time interest points. *IJCV*, 2007.

[32] D. Liu, K.-T. Lai, G. Ye, M.-S. Chen, and S.-F. Chang. Sample-specific late fusion for visual category recognition. In *CVPR*, 2013.

[33] D. G. Lowe. Distinctive image features from scale-invariant keypoints. *IJCV*, 2004.

[34] A. J. Ma and P. C. Yuen. Reduced analytic dependency modeling: Robust fusion for visual recognition. *IJCV*, 2014.

[35] M. Nagel, T. Mensink, and C. G. M. Snoek. Event fisher vectors: Robust encoding visual diversity of visual streams. In *BMVC*, 2015.

[36] K. Nandakumar, Y. Chen, S. C. Dass, and A. K. Jain. Likelihood ratio-based biometric score fusion. *IEEE TPAMI*, 2008.

[37] P. Natarajan, S. Wu, S. Vitaladevuni, X. Zhuang, S. Tsakalidis, U. Park, and R. Prasad. Multimodal feature fusion for robust event detection in web videos. In *CVPR*, 2012.

[38] N. Neverova, C. Wolf, G. Taylor, and F. Nebout. Moddrop: adaptive multi-modal gesture recognition. *IEEE TPAMI*, 2014.

[39] J. Y.-H. Ng, M. Hausknecht, S. Vijayanarasimhan, O. Vinyals, R. Monga, and G. Toderici. Beyond short snippets: Deep networks for video classification. In *CVPR*, 2015.

[40] D. Oneata, J. Verbeek, C. Schmid, et al. Action and event recognition with fisher vectors on a compact feature set. In *ICCV*, 2013.

[41] A. Rabinovich, A. Vedaldi, C. Galleguillos, E. Wiewiora, and S. Belongie. Objects in context. In *ICCV*, 2007.

[42] V. Ramanathan, K. Tang, G. Mori, and L. Fei-Fei. Learning temporal embeddings for complex video analysis. In *ICCV*, 2015.

[43] J. Sánchez, F. Perronnin, T. Mensink, and J. Verbeek. Image classification with the fisher vector: Theory and practice. *IJCV*, 2013.

[44] S. Sharma, R. Kiros, and R. Salakhutdinov. Action recognition using visual attention. *CoRR*, 2015.

[45] K. Simonyan and A. Zisserman. Two-stream convolutional networks for action recognition in videos. In *NIPS*, 2014.

[46] K. Simonyan and A. Zisserman. Very deep convolutional networks for large-scale image recognition. In *ICLR*, 2015.

[47] K. Soomro, A. R. Zamir, and M. Shah. UCF101: A dataset of 101 human actions classes from videos in the wild. *CoRR*, 2012.

[48] N. Srivastava, E. Mansimov, and R. Salakhutdinov. Unsupervised learning of video representations using LSTMs. In *ICML*, 2015.

[49] N. Srivastava and R. Salakhutdinov. Multimodal learning with deep boltzmann machines. In *NIPS*, 2012.

[50] X. Sun, M. Chen, and A. Hauptmann. Action recognition via local descriptors and holistic features. In *CVPR*, 2009.

[51] C. Szegedy, W. Liu, Y. Jia, P. Sermanet, S. Reed, D. Anguelov, D. Erhan, V. Vanhoucke, and A. Rabinovich. Going Deeper with Convolutions. In *CVPR*, 2015.

[52] K. Tang, L. Fei-Fei, and D. Koller. Learning latent temporal structure for complex event detection. In *CVPR*, 2012.

[53] D. Tran, L. Bourdev, R. Fergus, L. Torresani, and M. Paluri. C3d: Generic features for video analysis. *CoRR*, 2014.

[54] A. Van den Oord, S. Dieleman, and B. Schrauwen. Deep content-based music recommendation. In *NIPS*, 2013.

[55] V. Veeriah, N. Zhuang, and G.-J. Qi. Differential recurrent neural networks for action recognition. In *ICCV*, 2015.

[56] H. Wang and C. Schmid. Action recognition with improved trajectories. In *ICCV*, 2013.

[57] H. Wang and C. Schmid. Lear-inria submission for the thumos workshop. In *ICCV THUMOS Workshop*, 2013.

[58] H. Wang, M. M. Ullah, A. Klaser, I. Laptev, and C. Schmid. Evaluation of local spatio-temporal features for action recognition. In *BMVC*, 2009.

[59] L. Wang, Y. Qiao, and X. Tang. Action recognition with trajectory-pooled deep-convolutional descriptors. In *CVPR*, 2015.

[60] X. Wang, A. Farhadi, and A. Gupta. Actions ~ transformations. In *CVPR*, 2016.

[61] Y. Wang and G. Mori. Max-margin hidden conditional random fields for human action recognition. In *CVPR*, 2009.

[62] Z. Wu, Y. Fu, Y.-G. Jiang, and L. Sigal. Harnessing object and scene semantics for large-scale video understanding. In *CVPR*, 2016.

[63] Z. Wu, Y.-G. Jiang, J. Wang, J. Pu, and X. Xue. Exploring inter-feature and inter-class relationships with deep neural networks for video classification. In *ACM Multimedia*, 2014.

[64] Z. Wu, X. Wang, Y.-G. Jiang, H. Ye, and X. Xue. Modeling spatial-temporal clues in a hybrid deep learning framework for video classification. In *ACM Multimedia*, 2015.

[65] Z. Xu, Y. Yang, and A. G. Hauptmann. A discriminative cnn video representation for event detection. In *CVPR*, 2015.

[66] Z. Xu, Y. Yang, I. Tsang, N. Sebe, and A. Hauptmann. Feature weighting via optimal thresholding for video analysis. In *ICCV*, 2013.

[67] L. Yao, A. Torabi, K. Cho, N. Ballas, C. Pal, H. Larochelle, and A. Courville. Describing videos by exploiting temporal structure. In *ICCV*, 2015.

[68] G. Ye, D. Liu, I.-H. Jhuo, and S.-F. Chang. Robust late fusion with rank minimization. In *CVPR*, 2012.

[69] S.-I. Yu, L. Jiang, and et al. Informedia@ trecvid 2014 med and mer. In *NIST TRECVID Video Retrieval Evaluation Workshop*, 2014.

[70] S. Zha, F. Luisier, W. Andrews, N. Srivastava, and R. Salakhutdinov. Exploiting image-trained cnn architectures for unconstrained video classification. In *BMVC*, 2015.

[71] H. Zhang, M. Mang, R. Hong, L. Nie, and T.-S. Chua. Play and rewind: Optimizing binary representations of videos by self-supervised temporal hashing. In *ACM Multimedia*, 2016.

QoE Prediction for Enriched Assessment of Individual Video Viewing Experience

Yi Zhu
TU Delft
Delft, the Netherlands
Y.Zhu-1@tudelft.nl

Alan Hanjalic
TU Delft
Delft, the Netherlands
A.Hanjalic@tudelft.nl

Judith A. Redi
TU Delft
Delft, the Netherlands
J.A.Redi@tudelft.nl

ABSTRACT

Most automatic Quality of Experience (QoE) assessment models have so far aimed at predicting the QoE of a video as experienced by an average user, and solely based on perceptual characteristics of the video being viewed. The importance of other characteristics, such as those related to the video content being watched, or those related to an individual user have been largely neglected. This is suboptimal in view of the fact that video viewing experience is individual and multifaceted, considering the perceived quality (related to coding or network-induced artifacts), but also other – more hedonic - aspects, like enjoyment. In this paper, we propose an expanded model which aims to assess QoE of a given video, not only in terms of perceived quality but also of enjoyment, as experienced by a specific user. To do so, we feed the model not only with information extracted from the video (related to both perceived quality and content), but also with individual user characteristics, such as interest, personality and gender. We assess our expanded QoE model based on two publicly available QoE datasets, namely i_QoE and CP-QAE-I. The results show that combining various types of characteristics enables better QoE prediction performance as compared to only considering perceptual characteristics of the video, both when targeting perceived quality and enjoyment.

Keywords

QoE; User Factors; Objective Quality Assessment.

1. INTRODUCTION

With the increasing volume of online video consumption, users' expectations in terms of Quality of Experience (QoE) are growing rapidly. According to its most widespread definition [18], "*Quality of Experience (QoE) is the degree of delight or annoyance of the user of an application or service. It results from the fulfillment of his or her expectations with respect to the utility and / or enjoyment of the application or service in the light of the user's personality and current state*". As such, QoE has been established as the main indicator of the user satisfaction with the video viewing experience. Insufficient QoE will be less and less accepted by users, leading them to quit the experience or even change the delivering service/application altogether [23]. Intelligent mechanisms to assess, in real time, the quality of the viewing experience of a user, and to enhance it when possible are, therefore, critical for the adoption of future video delivery services.

MM '16, October 15-19, 2016, Amsterdam, Netherlands

DOI: http://dx.doi.org/10.1145/2964284.2964330

The definition given above indicates that QoE is an abstract concept, which is difficult to quantify. Because of this, in the context of video consumption, QoE has been mostly identified with the more easily quantifiable concept of perceived (visual) quality (PQ) [3]. PQ refers to the perceptual impact of the presence of network-related impairments in video, such as buffering events or transmission errors, and/or visible artifacts resulting from e.g. video coding (e.g., blockiness or blur). Consequently, automatic QoE assessment efforts have focused on estimating the annoyance that artifacts and impairments cause to users [5]. This process has relied mostly on video and/or network condition analysis [3], extracting perceptual characteristics of the video to serve as input to the QoE assessment model. The latter has generally targeted the prediction of one PQ value per video (or service or application), in a user–agnostic way. That is, PQ predictions are the same for all users, mimicking the perception of an "average user", typically measured subjectively through Mean Opinion Scores (MOS) [32].

On the other hand, the QoE definition suggests, just as the recent evidence provided in [20], that QoE is a multifaceted concept, of which PQ is only one aspect. This points to the need to complement PQ by measuring other aspects of QoE, such as the level of enjoyment of the experience [11, 40]. Users tend to be willing to repeat and share enjoyable experiences, thus offering enjoyable experiences can enhance user's loyalty to services and applications [22]. Enjoyment reflects the hedonic part of QoE, being a pleasurable response to media use [33]. As such, it can be considered complementary to PQ (with which it has been shown to be only poorly correlated [40]) in properly characterizing QoE.

In order to predict enjoyment, the perceptual characteristics mentioned above may not be informative enough. Better results could be achieved by also taking into account content characteristics [41], providing clues about the video content being watched, and user characteristics, such as personal interest [40], personality [29], or cultural background [21]. Especially the inclusion of user characteristics would enable us to consider individual differences when assessing QoE, resulting in more fine-grained predictions than those expressed in MOS or similar "one-fits-all" measures. In addition, since user and content characteristics [7] have been shown to have influence on viewing experience in general [26, 40], feeding QoE assessment models with this type of information could result in better predictions of various QoE aspects, thus not only enjoyment, but also PQ.

In view of the rationale given above, we define the contribution of this paper as specified in the following items:

Contribution 1: We expand the traditional QoE assessment paradigm (Figure 1a) to take as input not only the perceptual characteristics, but also the user characteristics and content characteristics. Specifically regarding the content characteristics, we focus on the extraction of information on the affective charge of a video [12, 34]. Regarding user characteristics, we consider personality, gender, interest and cultural background of the specific user for which the QoE needs to be assessed.

Contribution 2: We also expand the traditional QoE assessment paradigm in terms of the output: we predict not only the PQ but also the level of enjoyment that a user experiences with a video. The predictions of both PQ and enjoyment are based on the expanded set of characteristics, as explained in the previous item.

Contribution 3: In contrast to the current practice of targeting the QoE prediction for an average user via MOS, we produce individual PQ and enjoyment predictions reflecting the opinion that a specific user has of a specific video.

The contributions with respect to the traditional video QoE assessment paradigm (Figure 1.a) are illustrated in Figure 1.b. We note that we are not interested in delivering a new, fully functional QoE model at this stage, but rather in answering the following research questions:

RQ1: Does the expanded set of characteristics help improve the prediction of PQ and enjoyment for individual users?

RQ2: If so, which of these characteristics are most informative for which QoE aspect?

In the following section, we review the literature on perceived quality and enjoyment prediction in the domain of video consumption, as well as knowledge on individual differences in QoE assessment. We then present our proposed expanded QoE prediction paradigm in Section 3 and the experimental setup for its validation in Section 4. The results are presented in Section 5, while the discussion in Section 6 summarizes the main insights and sets targets for future research.

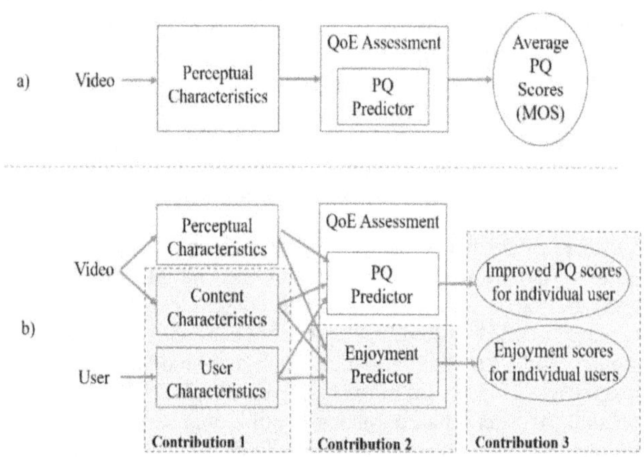

Figure 1 a) The traditional approach to assessing video QoE, b) The proposed expanded QoE assessment model targeting individual scores representing two selected QoE aspects, PQ and enjoyment.

2. RELATED WORK

2.1 Perceived video quality assessment

Methods for the automatic PQ assessment are also known as video quality metrics and rely mainly on the analysis of the decoded bitstream (i.e., accessing pixel values), the encoded bitstream (i.e., at a packet level) or both. Metrics that analyze the decoded bitstream use information on the (audio-) visual signal to compute the PQ. Hence, they do not need any information about the video delivery system under testing and are fully unobstrusive [3, 5]. Beside the so-called "data metrics" (e.g. MSE and PSNR), which are known to correlate poorly with user perceptions, "picture metrics" [37] have been developed based on the analysis of video content and distortion types. Within this family, metrics either predict PQ by directly modeling mechanisms of the Human Vision System (HVS) deemed relevant to video quality (e.g., color perception or contrast sensitivity, as in the case of VQM [24]) or by inferring artifact visibility from statistical properties and/or visual features of the video (e.g., blockiness or blur, as in the case of e.g. MOVIE [30]). Albeit accurate in their predictions, these metrics usually rely on the availability of a lossless source video as reference. As a result, they are not applicable to optimize the quality of multimedia delivery in real time [5]. Recently, many *no-reference* metrics [13, 28] have also been proposed, which work only on the degraded video and do not need a reference, yet with room for improving performance.

In practice, up until now, the most reliable way to measure PQ is to perform subjective experiments. According to [32], subjective PQ can be quantified in terms of Mean Opinion Scores (MOS), i.e. the average of the (numerical) judgments expressed by users relative to their perceptual satisfaction with respect to a video [5, 32]. The MOS measure is popular since it can express the perceived quality of videos in a commonly understandable way [32]. Therefore, most objective QoE metrics, as listed above, are designed to predict MOS, and most QoE (video) datasets report, along with the tested sequences, only the corresponding MOS, rather than the individual PQ scores [17], leaving little space for investigating individual differences in PQ perception. As indicated by our *Contribution 3*, in this paper we abandon the MOS-based PQ assessment paradigm and explore possibilities for individual PQ assessment.

2.2 Video enjoyment assessment

Video enjoyment has been tied closely to the amount of positive emotional pleasure (i.e., high arousal, positive valence) that a video presents [41]. Lately, however, evidence has been brought that video enjoyment doesn't only relate to videos with positive valence. Users may also enjoy videos portraying events with negative valence, such as horror or dramatic scenes [6]. A broad range of research has been carried out in order to measure/estimate affective content automatically [4]. For instance, several studies investigated the influence that different types of segments or shots, the use of color and audio characteristics (extensive review in [4, 39]) have in determining the video affective content. Others modeled affective content by combining multiple audio-visual characteristics extracted from the video [12].

Since the analysis of affective video content relies on features that are extracted from video data, it enables one to obtain insights about the level of enjoyment only in general, for an average user, similarly as in the case of PQ. Here, again, the challenge remains to learn about the individual enjoyment while watching a video, which can be seen as an outcome of the dynamic interaction between the affective content of the video, user characteristics (e.g., personality, personal interest), and user's current mood [7]. We pursue this challenge in this paper.

2.3 User characteristics influencing QoE

According to [18], a number of user characteristics (human factors) influence QoE, including demographics (e.g., age, gender), interest, personality and cultural background. With respect to demographics, males are reported to get more easily immersed in the content of a video than females [40], and older users were shown to have higher requirements for QoE as compared to younger users [26]. Interest in video content also counts, as users have been shown to be more tolerant to visual impairments when they are interested in the content of the video [26]. Regarding personality, extraversion (a personality trait describing enthusiastic and talkative individuals [2]) has been found to have a positive impact on users' video enjoyment [36]. Furthermore, cultural background was shown to capture individual differences in rating the QoE for a given video content [40]. Finally, user's mood is another influencing factor of QoE, and specifically when related to the user's intent to seek pleasant experiences [7]. For example, if a user is tense and eager to relax, he/she may enjoy a comedy show more than an intense action movie, even if he/she would normally prefer watching such movie.

To the best of the authors' knowledge, hardly any attempt has been made at incorporating user characteristics into automatic QoE assessment, mostly due to the complexity of retrieving personal user information in an unobtrusive fashion. We witness, however, rapidly emerging channels for collecting information about users via the services they subscribe to, e.g., movie preferences on Netflix (http://netflix.com), and large advances in user modeling (e.g. natural language processing to infer user personality from textual contributions to social media [10]). Therefore, the time when user information will be easily attainable in real time for automatic QoE assessment is not far, and it is worthwhile starting looking into how to incorporate this type of information in QoE assessment models. Making a substantial step in this direction is one of the objectives and contributions of this paper.

3. THE PROPOSED QoE MODEL

As illustrated in Figure 1a, the prediction of QoE in a video viewing scenario has been approached so far according to the following three principles:

- QoE was simplified to PQ only,
- PQ was assessed using a limited set of perceptual characteristics related to the visibility of artifacts and other video impairments,
- QoE was expressed in terms of MOS, neglecting individual differences among users.

QoE is, however, more than PQ alone, and the set of factors potentially influencing QoE is much broader than the perceptual characteristics considered so far. Especially the user characteristics, if taken into account, could not only help improve the prediction of various QoE aspects, but could also bring differentiation in QoE predictions across individual users.

In this paper, we propose a new QoE prediction model in which we overcome the three limitations mentioned above, targeting QoE prediction for individual users and broadening the prediction scope by producing the scores not only for PQ, but also for enjoyment. The model consists of the modules depicted in Figure 1b. In the following subsections, we elaborate on the realization of each of the modules, starting with the model input, i.e., the experience characteristics. Each type of experience characteristics considered in this paper, thus either the perceptual, content or user characteristics, is represented by a set of numerical indicators that feed the prediction module. We note that the set of characteristics deployed in this paper is not intended to be exhaustive. Instead, as indicated by the research questions posed in Section 1, we aim at discovering whether combining characteristics of different types brings improvement in predicting different QoE aspects, and which types of characteristics are more informative in this respect. Based on these insights, a more elaborate analysis of characteristics per type can be performed in a future work.

3.1 Perceptual characteristics

A great number of perceptual characteristics has been proposed so far, mainly targeting the prediction of the PQ of videos [3, 5]. In our study, we decided to use characteristics from a well-known no-reference model working at the decoded-bitstream level [19, 28]. We chose to go for off-the-shelf indicators rather than designing new ones because the focus of this work is to unveil the role of different types of influencing factors in predicting QoE, rather than to improve the performance of PQ models according to the traditional approach (Figure 1a). Also note that we have not considered temporal impairments (e.g., re-buffering or packet-loss) at this stage, although this is of great interest for future study.

We consider 44 perceptual characteristics (hereafter referred to as *PCs*). Thirty-six of those are computed based on the Natural Scene Statistics (NSS) model [19] at each frame m ($m = 1, \dots M$) and are denoted as $PC_k(m)$, where $k = 1,2,\dots 36$. The NSS features are parameters describing the shape of the distribution of (transformed) pixel values in distorted images. Depending on the level of distortion in an image, the distribution changes, and so do the parameters describing it, revealing the perceptual impact of image distortions. They are computed as follows. First, each frame m is partitioned into squared patches of n × n pixels. The sharpness of each patch is computed as specified in [19], and only those patches whose sharpness value is higher than a certain threshold (0.75 in this study) are selected. Within the selected patches at frame m, intensity values are transformed by applying mean removal and divisive normalization. The transformed values are then used to fit a Generalized Gaussian Distribution (GGD), which is known to represent the distribution of such values in unimpaired images:

$$f_m(x;\ \alpha,\beta) = \frac{\alpha}{2\beta\Gamma(\frac{1}{\alpha})}\exp\left(-\left(\frac{|x|}{\beta}\right)^{\alpha}\right) \tag{1}$$

where the gamma function is defined as $\Gamma(a) = \int_0^{\infty} t^{a-1}e^{-t}dt,\ a > 0$ and x are the transformed patch intensity values. To evaluate the impact of distortions at each frame, the products of adjacent transformed values (in the horizontal, vertical, and diagonal orientations) are used to fit an Asymmetric Generalized Gaussian Distribution, described by the parameters γ, β_l, β_r:

$$f(x;\ \gamma,\beta_l,\beta_r) = \begin{cases} \frac{\gamma}{(\beta_l+\beta_r)\Gamma(\frac{1}{\gamma})}\exp\left(-\left(\frac{-x}{\beta_l}\right)^{\gamma}\right) & \forall x < 0 \\ \frac{\gamma}{(\beta_l+\beta_r)\Gamma(\frac{1}{\gamma})}\exp\left(-\left(\frac{-x}{\beta_r}\right)^{\gamma}\right) & \forall x \geq 0 \end{cases} \tag{2}$$

Finally, the mean of the distribution is computed as well:

$$\eta = (\beta_r - \beta_l)\frac{\Gamma(\frac{2}{\gamma})}{\Gamma(\frac{1}{\gamma})} \tag{3}$$

The parameters $\alpha, \beta, \gamma, \beta_l, \beta_r, \eta$ that shape these distributions are known to capture the differences between lossless and distorted images, as well as the severity of these distortions [19]. In order to capture multi-scale behavior, the set of 18 parameters ($\gamma, \beta_l, \beta_r, \eta$ being calculated for 4 orientations, plus α, β) is computed for two patch sizes (i.e., 96x96 and 48x48 in this case). Thus, eventually, 36 NSS *PCs* are computed for each frame. We then average their values across the M video frames to obtain the values PC_k, $k = 1,2,\dots 36$, that feed out model. The temporal variation of the frame mean DC coefficients is the PC_{37}. This *PC* represents sudden local changes in a video, which may arise from various temporal distortions. Six statistical DCT *PCs* (represented as PC_{38} to PC_{43}) are also computed from each frame difference using the spatio-temporal model described in [28]. These *PCs* describe the distribution of DCT coefficients across the frame differences of the video, and have been shown to be able to reflect the perceptual impact brought about by spatio-temporal artifacts in video. Finally, the PC_{44} relates to motion estimation, and is computed based on the coherence of motion vectors in strength and direction (the predefined window size is 10). PC_{44} denotes variations in local motion due to temporal distortions. Details regarding its implementation can be found in [28].

3.2 Content characteristics

As described in Section 2.2, an insight in the enjoyment elicited in a user while watching a video could be obtained from the affective aspects of the video content being watched [41]. The underlying assumption is, however, based more on psychological studies than on empirical measurements. It is therefore unclear (a) to which extent enjoyment is indeed related to affective video content and (b) which aspects of the video related to eliciting affective reactions are most informative for drawing conclusions about the enjoyment. In this paper we aim at providing some answers to these questions.

Due to the complexity of the problem, we focus only on one affective dimension, *arousal* (i.e., from excited to calm), and build on a set of proven arousal-related audiovisual features, namely *motion activity*, *sound energy*, *hue ratio* and *shot change rate* [12, 34]. Hereafter we refer to these features as content characteristics (*CC*). Again, we rely on existing work, as the improvement of the affective video content representation is not the goal of this paper.

The *motion activity* [12] is computed as:

$$MA = \frac{1}{M}\sum_{m=0}^{M-1}\frac{100}{N_m|\vec{v}_{MAX}(m)|}\left(\sum_{i=1}^{N_m}|\vec{v}_i\,(m)|\right) \tag{4}$$

In (4), the overall magnitude of all (N_m) motion vectors $\vec{v_i}(m)$ between two adjacent frames m and m+1 is normalized by the length of the longest motion vector $\vec{v}_{MAX}(m)$ at frame m. The obtained values are then averaged across all M frames to yield the motion activity (*MA*) value.

The *sound energy* [12] is computed from the audio track of the videos. The sound energy E_m at frame m is defined as the sum of the power spectrum of the audio samples corresponding to frame m. The overall *sound energy* E is then computed as the mean of E_m across all frames.

The *hue ratio* [31] is computed as:

$$\text{HR} = \sum_{m=1}^{M}\frac{G_m}{H_m}/M \tag{5}$$

where H_m is the total number of pixels in frame m while G_m is the number of green pixels in frame m.

The *shot change rate* [12] represents the level of dynamics in the video content and is defined as

$$\text{S} = \frac{\sum_{m=1}^{M} 100e\text{^}((1-(m_n-m_p))/\delta)}{M} \tag{6}$$

where m_n and m_p are the frame indexes of the two closest shot boundaries to the left and right of frame m. δ is a constant value, set as recommended in [12].

3.3 User characteristics

We make use of the information provided directly (through self-report) from the users that judged their video experience. Specifically, we rely on the user information collected in [40] and [29] capturing the *interest, immersive tendency*, *personality*, *cultural background* and demographics, as described in more detail below.

Personal *interest* is defined as the level of prior interest in the (genre of) the video that the user is about to experience and judge. Similarly, we include values that quantify the user's *Immersive Tendency* (*IT*), which reflects how easily a user gets involved in a particular task [38], in this case specifically in the content of the video. It is argued that a high level of involvement may result in high satisfaction [22].

The *personality* characteristics included in this study represent the "the big five" personality traits i.e., *openness, conscientiousness, extraversion, agreeableness*, and *neuroticism* [2]. *Cultural background* is also represented through a set of six characteristics, namely *power distance, individualism, uncertainty, masculinity, pragmatism*, and *indulgence*. Finally, we include some user demographics information as well, i.e., *gender* and *origin*. The *origin* was defined based on the user's nationality.

3.4 The Prediction modules

The proposed model, depicted in Figure 1b, targets the prediction of both PQ and enjoyment based on the same, broadened set of characteristics. The decision to predict PQ and enjoyment independently is due to the fact that, although these two aspects of QoE are not necessarily uncorrelated (they have been found to be poorly although significantly positively correlated [40]), the nature of their relationship remains mostly vague. Hence, in this exploratory study we target their prediction separately, and leave the investigation of their interdependencies to the future work. The prediction module per QoE aspect can be implemented in many ways, from a linear combination of the input characteristics to more complex non-linear models. In addition, a feature selection step before prediction process may be needed depending on the selected model [8]. In this paper, we choose for a simple implementation using a linear classifier, and a more complex Support Vector Machine, as explained and justified in more detail in Section 4.2.

4. EXPERIMENTAL SETUP

In this section we describe the experimental setup through which we implemented and evaluated the proposed QoE prediction model. The section covers dataset description (Section 4.1), predictor implementation (Section 4.2), and the evaluation procedure (Section 4.3).

4.1 Dataset description

To the best of our knowledge, only two public datasets, namely i_QoE (available at http://ii.tudelft.nl/iqlab/iQOE.html) and CP-QAE-I (Available at: 1drv.ms/1M1bnwU), meet our requirements, i.e., include user characteristics and individual QoE (PQ and enjoyment) ratings. These two datasets were derived from two independent user studies conducted in [40] and [29], respectively.

4.1.1 i_QoE

As shown in table 1, the i_QoE dataset uses 6 high resolution (i.e., 1280*720) videos as sources, covering three genres, i.e., sports, comedy and education. All six videos last for about 5 minutes, and are further encoded with H.264/AVC at two bitrate levels, i.e., 600kbps and 2000kbps. The two resulting versions of each video present clear differences in PQ. 59 participants evaluated the videos, split into two disjoint groups: 30 participants viewed the test sequences themselves, the remaining 29 viewed the sequences in the company of two friends (so, in groups of three; interaction among them was allowed). After a short training session in which users became acquainted to the type of artifacts they would see during the experiment, each participant viewed only one version (either 600 kbps or 2000 kbps, in random and counterbalanced order) of all six videos. For each video, participants scored their level of enjoyment through 4 questions (each to be answered on a 7-point Likert scale) [40]. They were also asked to score their perceived video quality on a 5-point ACR scale, according to [16]. In total, 354 ratings (59x6 videos) on these two QoE aspects were collected.

Before starting the experiment, participants were asked to fill in a questionnaire investigating personal information, such as the level of *interest* they had (a priori) in the video genres they were about to see, their *immersive tendency*, *nationality*, *gender* as well as their *personality*. *Interest* in the video genre was quantified on a 7-point Likert scale (with 7 being the highest possible level of interest in the video content). The *Immersive Tendency* was quantified via the questionnaire [38], returning an IT score on a scale ranging from 18 to 126 (the higher the score, the higher the immersive tendency). *Personality* traits were quantified via the 10-items TIPI questionnaire (also known as BFI-10), where each item is assessed on a 7-point Likert scale, and each trait is measured by a pair of opposite items [9]. For example, the trait "*Agreeableness*" was quantified by adding up the self-assessment of the user on the positive item *Sympathetic & Warm* and the inverse of the self-assessment on the negative item *Critical & Quarrelsome*.

Table 1 Description of the core characteristics of the i_QoE and CP-QAE-I datasets (F = female, M = male)

Video material		
	i_QoE [40]	CP-QAE-I [29]
Num. source sequences	6	12
video format	h.264/AVC	h.264/AVC
Bitrate (kbps)	600, 2000	384, 768
Resolution	1280*720	1280*720, 854*480
Framerate (fps)	30	5, 15,25
User Characteristics		
	i_QoE [40]	CP-QAE-I [29]
Participants	59	114
Gender	27 F, 32 M	33 F, 81 M
Interest	Yes	No
Nationality	Yes	Yes
Personality	Yes	Yes
Immersive tendency	Yes	No
Cultural Background	No	Yes

4.1.2 CP-QAE-I

The CP-QAE-I dataset uses 12 short videos (i.e., around 2 minutes long) selected to cover different affective categories (i.e., sadness, anger and disgust). 12 versions of each video are included in the dataset, resulting from a combination of three system factors: bitrate, resolution and frame rate (see table 1 for the specific settings). 114 participants from three universities were involved in this study. They were first asked to report personal information, being *age*, *gender*, *cultural background* and *personality*. *Cultural background* was measured via the VSM-2013 questionnaire [14] on 7-point Likert scale. *Personality* was quantified through the BFI-10 [9].

Participants were encouraged (but not forced) to evaluate one of the 12 versions of each short video (i.e., they evaluated only one of the 12 combinations of system factors for specific video content). Participants were asked to report their level of enjoyment and PQ immediately after watching each video. Both QoE aspects were rated on a five-point scale. In total, 84 participants managed to finish all 12 videos. The minimum number of clips that one participant evaluated was 3. Eventually, 1232 individual ratings were recorded for both enjoyment and PQ.

4.1.3 Common and exclusive characteristics

For both datasets, *PC*s and *CC*s (48 in total) were extracted from all test videos in an identical way. With respect to *UC*, the information in the two datasets is only partially overlapping. Both datasets report information on the user's *gender* and *personality*, based on the big five model (one score per trait, normalized between 0 and 1). Those six characteristics are used as *UC*s for both datasets, leading to a total of 54 common characteristics for the two datasets.

With respect to the exclusive characteristics, as shown in Table 1, the i_QoE dataset presents the individual ratings on *interest* (one value) as well as on *immersive tendency* (one value). CP-QAE-I reports information on *cultural background* (one value per each of six traits) which is not given in i_QoE. Those *UC*s are considered as exclusive of each dataset in our study, with values being normalized between 0 and 1. In addition, as shown in Table 1, both datasets have information about user's *nationality*. However, because the majority of participants in i_QoE was from either the Netherlands or China, the nationality information for i_QoE is reported as a binary value (i.e., either Westerner or Asian [40]). The CP-QAE-I, on the other hand, assumes five categorical values for nationality, being British, Chinese, Singaporean, Indian and the rest of the world. Due to the mismatch in encoding of the nationality variable for the two datasets, the latter is considered as an exclusive indicator for the two datasets. Finally, both datasets measure *personality* by using the same questionnaire [9]. As mentioned earlier, each personality trait (five in total) was measured by adding up the self-reported scores on two opposite items, a positive and a negative one. i_QoE reports the values of each item as well as the aggregated trait scores. CP-QAE-I dataset reports only the latter. We include the scores of the 10 items (2x5 traits) as exclusive *UC* for i_QoE. Hence, there are 7 exclusive characteristics for CP-QAE-I and 13 for i_QoE.

4.2 Prediction module implementation

Both datasets report discrete (ordinal) ratings of enjoyment and PQ. The rating distributions are shown in Figure 2. For i_QoE, enjoyment ratings range between 4 and 28, while for CP-QAE-I, they range between 1 and 5. For both datasets, perceived quality ratings are expressed on an ACR scale, ranging between poor and excellent.

According to [16], a score of 'fair' on an ACR scale (middle point in the 5-point scale) or less indicates "Unacceptable Quality" (UQ), whereas a score of 'good' or 'excellent' (4 and 5) indicates "Acceptable Quality" (AQ). Although this distinction was originally conceived for acceptability of perceptual quality [16], we extend it to the enjoyment ratings as well. For CP-QAE-I, videos rated between 1 and 3 on the enjoyment Likert scale are considered as "Not Enjoyed" (NE) by the user, whereas scores of 4 and 5 indicate that the video was "Enjoyed" (E) by the user. In line with these settings, the threshold for identifying enjoyed video experiences for i_QoE is set at 17, i.e., experiences scored 17 or less are considered not enjoyed, whereas experiences with score above 17 are considered as enjoyed.

As shown in Table 2, the i_QoE has 154 and 200 instances in which a user found the video to be not enjoyable and enjoyable, respectively. In 130 of the 354 instances the user deemed the perceived quality of the video unacceptable. The CP-QAE-I dataset

Table 2. Overview of class distribution for the two datasets. In the parentheses we indicate the percentage of instances of the majority class across the dataset

	Enjoyment	PQ
i_QoE	154UE, 200E(56.4%)	130UQ, 224AQ (63.28%)
CP-QAE-I	771NE, 461E(62.58%)	788UQ, 444AQ (63.96%)

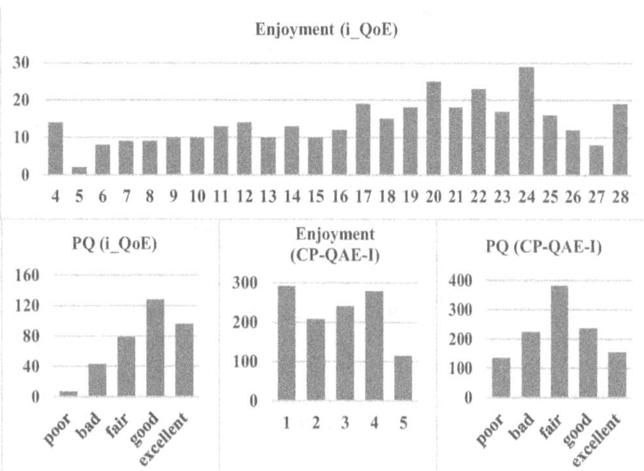

Figure 2. Histograms showing the distribution of individual ratings for the two datasets considered in the experiments. Here, the X-axis represents points on the rating scale, whereas the Y-axis represents the number of instances for each score

includes 771 instances of not enjoyed experiences, and 461 of enjoyed experiences. Similarly, in 788 cases videos were deemed by a user to be of unacceptable quality and in 444 cases the quality was considered acceptable. Each dataset contains a percentage of instances (i.e., a specific video evaluated by a specific user) for which the user enjoyed the video, and a complementary percentage of instances for which the user did not (the same goes for perceptual quality).

The prediction module is implemented by using classification algorithms, targeting the prediction of acceptable versus unacceptable quality (AQ vs UQ) for PQ and enjoyed vs not enjoyed (E or NE) for enjoyment. Due to the exploratory nature of this study, it is still early for deploying complex machine learning algorithms to learn the relationships between *PCs*, *CCs* and *UCs* and QoE aspects to optimize the prediction. This is justified only after we have learned more about which characteristics influence what QoE aspect and to which extent. We therefore use a modeling tool that is easily interpretable (i.e, with a limited number of parameters to fit), and specifically, a Linear Discriminant Classifier (LDC). LDC can reduce the dimensionality of the input while preserving as much of the class discriminatory information as possible, and has been used to predict QoE in [1]. In addition to the LDC, we use a Support Vector Machine (SVM) to verify the added value of non-linear modeling in the prediction [15]. The advantage of SVM is that, when using a linear kernel, every input indicator gets a weigh, which indicates its importance in the classification process, hence allowing intelligibility of the trained model.

4.3 Evaluation procedure

The LDC and SVM are trained independently on the two datasets for each QoE aspect. That is, each classifier is trained to predict either PQ or enjoyment. An *R*-fold cross-validation is performed in order to estimate the predictor performance in a robust way, especially considering the relatively small size of the datasets. Thus, data is split in *R* folds depending on the size of dataset. Then, *R* runs are performed where samples from one fold are used as test data whereas samples from the remaining folds are used as training data. Each run returns a misclassification rate (*MisRate*) on the test data. The final accuracy of the model is then defined as:

$$\text{Accuracy} = 1 - \sum_{r=1}^{R} MisRate_r / R \qquad (13)$$

The prior probability of correctly predicting QoE (or more specifically, of correctly predicting whether a user described by *UC* would experience a video described by *CC* and *PC* as of being enjoyable, or having acceptable PQ), is defined as the percentage of the accumulation of the majority class in the total number of the ratings. For example, based on the numbers listed in Table II, the prior probability for a user to find a video enjoyable in i_QoE is calculated as:

$$Enjoyment_{i\_QoE} = \frac{200E}{154UE + 200E} \times 100 = 56.4\%$$

The prior probabilities per QoE aspect and dataset are indicated in Table 2. Since these percentages are unbalanced, we use the prior probability to the majority class as baseline, rather than even chance (50% accuracy). In addition, we compute the Matthews Correlation Coefficient (MCC) to indicate the performance of our model [25]. The MCC is a value between -1 and 1 (i.e., -1 means total inverse prediction, 0 means no better than prior probability, 1 means perfect prediction) and is considered as a reliable measure of assessing the quality of binary classification [25].

5. RESULTS

Our evaluation is carried out through two different experiments. The first experiment analyzes each dataset separately (i.e., either i_QoE or CP-QAE-I) towards 1) evaluating the performance of the proposed model when all the available characteristics are used (i.e., all common characteristics and the exclusive ones) and 2) understanding which (types of) characteristics are most informative for the prediction of PQ and enjoyment. In the second experiment, the two datasets are merged. The aim of this second experiment is to check the generalization potential of our approach, that is, what performance can be achieved across datasets.

5.1 Experiment 1: Model performance

The first experiment consists of three parts. Part I evaluates the overall performance when using all characteristics, Part II evaluates the performance for a specific type of characteristics (*PC*, *CC*, *UC*) and Part III investigates the key influencing characteristics in predicting PQ and/or enjoyment.

5.1.1 Part I: Overall performance

First, the LDC and the SVM were trained separately for the prediction of PQ and enjoyment, based on all available characteristics for each dataset. A 10-fold cross validation was performed for each model and dataset. For the SVM-based model, a Radial Basis Function (RBF) kernel was chosen.

The resulting accuracy for i_QoE and CP-QAE-I is reported, under the column labeled "All", in Tables 3 and 4 respectively, whereas the MCC values and the confusion matrices are reported in Table 5. Note that each fold in the cross-validation returned a partial confusion matrix, and that the final confusion matrices were composed of the resulting ten partial matrices. In general, SVM gives better overall accuracy than LDC, as also confirmed by the MCC values. With regard to i_QoE, better accuracy is achieved in PQ prediction (around 17% above the baseline) than in enjoyment prediction (around 13% above the baseline). For CP-QAE-I, on the

Table 3. i_QoE: The performance of LDC and SVM on Enjoyment and Perceived Quality, based on all characteristics, the three characteristic categories and selected indicators

	Enjoyment (Baseline 56.4%)					Perceived Quality (Baseline 63.28%)				
Predictor	All	CC	PC	UC	Selected	All	CC	PC	UC	Selected
LDC	67.79%	63.02%	59.59%	66.11%	69.51%	78.24%	64.94%	80.22%	60.14%	78.48%
SVM	69.51%	63.02%	60.15%	65.30%	69.51%	80.22%	64.94%	80.22%	63.27%	80.22%

Table 4. CP-QAE-I: The performance of LDC and SVM on Enjoyment and Perceived Quality, based on all characteristics, the three characteristic categories and selected indicators

	Enjoyment (Baseline 62.58%)					Perceived Quality (Baseline 63.96%)				
Predictor	All	CC	PC	UC	Selected	All	CC	PC	UC	Selected
LDC	71.27%	70.45%	65.42%	61.85%	63.80%	65.50%	64.44%	66.07%	63.96%	64.77%
SVM	73.13%	70.37%	68.67%	65.75%	68.53%	68.18%	65.42%	67.20%	69.57%	66.23%

Table 5. The confusion matrices and MCC of LDC and SVM for Enjoyment and Perceived Quality prediction based on all characteristics. The dataset the results refer to is indicated in parenthesis: i_QoE (iQ) or CP-QAE-I (CP)

	Enjoyment							
	LDC (iQ) MCC:0.35		SVM (iQ) MCC:0.39		LDC (CP) MCC:0.37		SVM (CP) MCC:0.42	
Pred./ Truth	NE	E	NE	E	NE	E	NE	E
NE	103	51	110	44	633	138	626	145
E	63	137	64	136	216	245	186	275

	Perceived Quality							
	LDC (iQ) MCC:0.52		SVM (iQ) MCC:0.57		LDC (CP) MCC:0.19		SVM (CP) MCC:0.26	
Pred./ Truth	UQ	AQ	UQ	AQ	UQ	AQ	UQ	AQ
UQ	84	46	89	41	672	116	691	97
AQ	31	193	29	195	309	135	295	149

Table 6. Key influencing characteristics for LDC on i_QoE

QoE aspect	CC	PC	UC
Enjoyment	-	PC_{16}(2) PC_{12}(3)	*Interest*(1) *Conscientiousness*(4)
Perceived Quality	-	PC_{28}(1) PC_{41}(2)	*Gender*(3)

Table 7. Key influencing characteristics for LDC on CP-QAE-I

QoE aspect	CC	PC	UC
Enjoyment	*Motion Activity* (1)	PC_{41}(2) PC_{34}(4)	*Uncertainty*(3)
Perceived Quality	-	PC_1(1) PC_{22}(2) PC_{41}(4) PC_5(5)	*Indulgence(2), Agreeableness (3) Neuroticism (7)*

other hand, the models perform better in predicting enjoyment (around 10% above the baseline) than for PQ (around 5% above the baseline). In the latter case, MCC indicates a relatively weak prediction power of the model, highlighting how PQ prediction may be more difficult when multiple system factors impair a video, as it is the case for CP-QAE-I (whereas only bitrate is manipulated in i-QoE).

5.1.2 Part II: Performance per characteristic type

To investigate whether a specific type of characteristics is informative for the prediction of either enjoyment or PQ, we trained the classifiers by feeding them only one type of characteristics at the time (i.e., *UC*, *CC* or *PC*). The rest of the setup was kept the same as in Part I.

The results are reported in Tables 3 and 4 under the column labeled *UC*, *CC* and *PC*. For i_QoE, *UC*s perform best in predicting enjoyment (achieving an accuracy around 66%). In contrast, *PC*s perform best in predicting PQ, achieving an accuracy of 80.22% regardless of the classifier used. For enjoyment prediction in CP-QAE-I, only using *CC*s achieved better performance than only using *UC*s or *PC*s, leading to an accuracy of around 70.45%. For PQ prediction in CP-QAE-I, only considering *PC*s gave slightly better accuracy compared to only using any of the other two types of characteristics. Nevertheless, in general we can observe that using a single type of characteristics is suboptimal with respect to using all three types of information together.

5.1.3 Key influencing characteristics

In this section, we check to which extent specific subsets of characteristics, possibly mixtures from different types, are suitable for individual QoE prediction. To this end, we performed feature selection to identify the optimal set of key characteristics. Here, data from each dataset was randomly split into two equally sized sets. We used the first set for feature selection, and the second for model training and testing, based on the selected characteristics.

We used Sequential Forward Feature Selection (SFS) for the LDC. Characteristics were selected starting from an empty pool, to which they were sequentially added until there was no improvement in reducing the number of misclassified observations. For SVM, we exploited its intrinsic capability to identify key characteristics in the prediction when using a linear kernel. All input characteristics were assigned a relevance weight [15], based on which only the top 25 were considered to be key characteristics.

In order to evaluate the prediction accuracy on the second half of the dataset, the data was first randomized and then the QoE models were trained (and tested) by using only the key characteristics selected for each classifier. A 5-fold cross-validation was performed due to the smaller data size as compared to Part I. The rest of the setup was kept identical.

To verify whether the feature selection influenced accuracy, the procedure above was performed 100 times, and the same was repeated using all characteristics as input. Then, a series of independent sample t-tests were performed between corresponding values from using either the key or all characteristics in order to

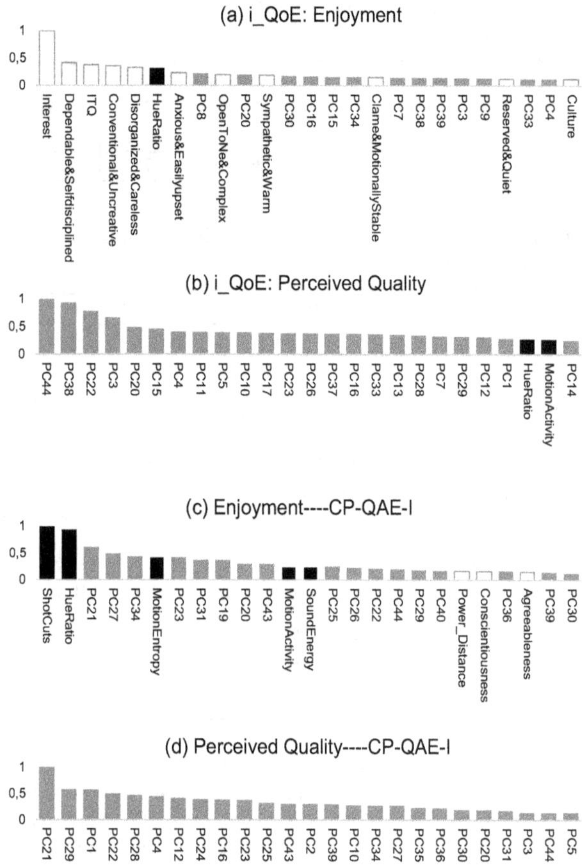

Figure 3. Relevance (y-axis) of the key influencing indicators per QoE aspect and dataset, by using SVM. Yellow bars indicate perceptual characteristics, black bars indicate content characteristics, and white bars concern user characteristics

check whether there is a statistically significant difference between the performances in both cases. Tables 6 and 7 report the key characteristics for the prediction of enjoyment and PQ, respectively, selected for the LDC. The corresponding results for SVM are presented in Figure 3. With regard to enjoyment prediction for i_QoE, *Interest* was selected as the most relevant characteristic for both SVM and LDC, supporting the finding of previous studies [40]. Thus, collecting information on user personal preferences on video content and genres (e.g., possibly via social media by tracking user watching history, like the most watched genres) may be a key requirement when designing systems able to predict user enjoyment. With respect to *personality*, *conscientiousness* and its sub-characteristic *dependable & self-disciplined* were found to be the key influencing indicators by both LDC and SVM in enjoyment prediction of i_QoE. This resonates with findings in psychological literature that *conscientious* individuals are more likely to have enjoyable experience [35]. Two perceptual characteristics (i.e., PC_{12} and PC_{16}) were selected by LDC as well. In the case of SVM, as shown in Figure 3.a, the top 5 key influencing characteristics of SVM were *UC*s and one *CC* (i.e., *Hue Ratio*).

For enjoyment prediction in CP-QAE-I, *Motion Activity* was found to be the most relevant characteristic by LDC. Together with two *PCs* (PC_{34} and PC_{41}), one characteristic related to *cultural background* (i.e., *uncertainty*) was also considered to be among the key ones for LDC. As shown in Figure 3.c, two content characteristic (i.e., *Shot cuts* and *Hue ratio*) were among the top 25 key influencing characteristics of enjoyment prediction selected by SVM. The dominance of *CC* with respect to *UC* in enjoyment prediction for CP-QAE-I (which was already suggested by the experiment reported in Section 5.1.2) may be due to the fact that videos in this dataset were purposely selected to vary in terms of their affective charge. This may explain more variance in the data than individual user characteristics.

With regard to PQ prediction in i_QoE, two *PCs* were selected by LDC, PC_{28} and PC_{41}. These two characteristics describe both spatial (i.e., PC_{28}) and temporal (i.e., PC_{41}) aspects of distortions in the videos. Moreover, *gender* was also identified as a key influencing characteristic in PQ prediction by LDC. For SVM, instead, as shown in Figure 3.b, two *CCs* (i.e., *Hue ratio* and *Motion Activity*) were found as the key influencing characteristics. The rest of the key influencing characteristics relate to *PCs*. Finally, for PQ prediction of CP-QAE-I, SVM selected only *PCs* as top 25 key influencing characteristics. One characteristic related to *cultural background* (i.e., *indulgence*) and two *personality* traits (i.e, *agreeableness* and *neuroticism*) were considered relevant by LDC.

Finally, the resulting accuracy for i_QoE and CP-QAE-I based on the selected characteristics is reported in Table 3 and 4, under the column labeled "Selected". No significant difference was found in the performance accuracy on the test fold of both i_QoE and CP-QAE-I, suggesting that the performance of using the key influencing characteristics was comparable to the one when using all characteristics, despite the reduced amount of input information and with the advantage of working with substantially reduced complexity of the QoE assessment process.

5.2 Experiment 2: Generalization

In the second experiment, only the common characteristics available for both datasets were used as input for training the predictors. In order to make the characteristics values of the two datasets compatible with each other, the set of joint values of each characteristic from both datasets was normalized in [0,1].

First, we attempted a cross-dataset evaluation, using the data of one dataset (e.g., i_QoE) for training the models, and those of the other dataset (e.g., CP-QAE-I) for testing. In these experiments, we only used SVM (with RBF kernel), as it was giving the best performance on both datasets and for both enjoyment and PQ. The resulting accuracy, MCC values and confusion matrix are shown in Table 8. In general, the accuracy was found to be only around (or even lower than) the baseline, with MCC values close to 0. This might be due to the fact that each dataset uses different test videos with different media configuration (e.g., different resolution, bitrate) and content, resulting in different ranges of *PC* and *CC*. For example, the high bitrate of test videos in i_QoE (i.e., 2000kbps) is much higher than that of (test) videos in CP-QAE-I (i.e., 768kbps). In this way, videos (and users) from one dataset seem to sample an area of the video (and user) space different from that covered by the videos (and users) in the other dataset. As a result, a model trained on one dataset may be unable to extrapolate and predict PQ and enjoyment for the data in the second dataset.

In order to compensate for the differences between the datasets, we decided to merge the two datasets into a single one, possibly achieving a better coverage of the video and user space in the training phase. Enjoyment and PQ again were set as two separate targets. A 10-fold cross validation was performed by using again SVMs as predictors. Table 9 presents the accuracy of the SVM trained on the merged dataset as well as the corresponding MCC values and confusion matrices. The baseline for enjoyment and

Table 8. The confusion matrices, Accuracy (Acc) and MCC values of SVM for cross-dataset validation: results on the left columns refer to experiments using i_QoE as training and CP-QAE-I as test data; the rightmost columns refers to experiments using CP-QAE-I as training data and i_QoE as test data

	Enjoyment (i_QoE) Acc:61.12%, MCC:-0.04		Enjoyment (CP-QAE-I) Acc:55.37%, MCC:0.03	
Pred./ Truth	NE	E	NE	E
NE	743	28	31	123
E	451	10	35	165

	PQ (I-QoE) Acc:61.28%, MCC:0.12		PQ (CP-QAE-I) Acc:59.89% MCC:0.07	
Pred./ Truth	UQ	AQ	UQ	AQ
UQ	600	188	35	95
AQ	289	155	47	177

Table 9. The confusion matrices, Accuracy (Acc) and MCC values of SVM for validation on merged datasets

	Enjoyment Acc:67.91%, MCC:0.33	
Pred./ Truth	NE	E
NE	731	194
E	315	346

	Perceived Quality Acc:68.91% MCC:0.35	
Pred./ Truth	UQ	AQ
UQ	805	113
AQ	380	288

perceived quality prediction in this experiment was 58.32% and 57.8%, respectively. As the table shows, the best accuracy that SVM achieved was around 10% above the baseline. The MCC values were higher as compared to only considering one dataset as training set, but still lower than the performance achieved for both enjoyment and PQ prediction in the Experiment 1 by using all characteristics (except for PQ prediction of CP-QAE-I). This lower performance might be due to the fact that the model here were trained on a smaller number of common indicators (especially *UC* characteristics), missing essential characteristics (such as, e.g., *interest*) and possibly under-fitting the data.

6. DISCUSSION AND CONCLUSION

In this section we highlight a number of main conclusions that can be drawn from the results reported in the previous section and related to the research questions posed in Section 1.

Regarding the RQ1, the results show that for accurate prediction of different aspects of individual QoE, combining the information describing different types of characteristics (perceptual, content and user) is more effective in than using only one type of characteristics. As a result, we not only reached a promising performance in predicting enjoyment using multi-type characteristics, but we also managed to reach an improvement in PQ prediction compared to the traditional approaches where only PCs are deployed, e.g. in the case of CP-QAE-I.

Enjoyment was shown to be influenced by all three types of characteristics used, indicating that perceptual and affective characteristics of the video content as well as the characteristics of the user watching are all relevant in this respect. More in depth, and also touching upon RQ2, *Interest* and several *personality* traits were selected as key characteristics for the prediction of enjoyment. Additionally, a set of *PC* was selected, suggesting that *PC* also matters in influencing more hedonic aspects of QoE (i.e., enjoyment). However, since no consistent set of *PC*s has been identified across different datasets, we note that more studies are needed to identify an optimal set of *PCs* for enjoyment prediction in a general case.

With regard to perceived quality (PQ) prediction, *PCs*, as expected, are dominant. Our feature selection returned the ones describing both spatial and temporal characteristics of distortions in the videos. In addition, it is interesting to point out that *gender* was identified as a key influencing characteristic in predicting PQ of i_QoE, suggesting that gender differences should be further investigated when it comes to PQ prediction in a general case. Up till now, *gender*, as one core user characteristic, is hardly investigated in the context of QoE. Most existing QoE datasets do not report the gender information of the users, and the ones that have such information, are usually imbalanced, neglecting gender differences in QoE as noted in [27].

In general, the performance of our individual PQ and enjoyment predictors is satisfactory, and maximized when *UC*, *CC* and *PC*, are used. However, room for improvement exists, and some limitations of our setup should be taken into account in future studies. First, our model only considered a limited number of *UC*s, and more could be included in future models. For example, the more dynamic (varying) *UC*s, like skills or affective state, may potentially benefit QoE prediction. Therefore, collecting more, and more diverse *UC* information is crucial for creating a future individual QoE dataset. Expanding the set of *UC*s may be also beneficial for extending the model to predict other QoE aspects, such as endurability or immersiveness, which may be influenced by other user individual traits as well as video characteristics. Secondly, our model should be trained on a larger range of videos (with different content and system configurations) covering various ranges of *PC* and *CC*. Finally, our results show that SVM in general has better performance as compared to LDC. This result may imply that the QoE prediction can be further improved if we implement the prediction module with non-linear models (e.g., random forests or neural networks).

7. REFERENCE

[1] Agboma, F. and Liotta, A. 2012. Quality of experience management in mobile content delivery systems. Telecommunication Systems, 49, 1, 85-98.

[2] Atkinson, R. L. 1996. Hilgard's introduction to psychology. Harcourt Brace College Publishers Philadelphia, PA.

[3] Barkowsky, M., Sedano, I., Brunnström, K., Leszczuk, M. and Staelens, N. 2014. Hybrid video quality prediction: reviewing video quality measurement for widening application scope. Multimedia Tools and Applications, 74, 2, 323-343.

[4] Calvo, R. and D'Mello, S. 2010. Affect detection: An interdisciplinary review of models, methods, and their applications. Affective Computing, IEEE Transactions on, 1, 1, 18-37.

[5] Chikkerur, S., Sundaram, V., Reisslein, M. and Karam, L. J. 2011. Objective video quality assessment methods: A classification, review, and performance comparison. Broadcasting, IEEE Transactions on, 57, 2, 165-182.

[6] De Wied, M., Zillmann, D. and Ordman, V. 1995. The role of empathic distress in the enjoyment of cinematic tragedy. Poetics, 23, 1, 91-106.

[7] Eliashberg, J. and Sawhney, M. S. 1994. Modeling goes to Hollywood: Predicting individual differences in movie enjoyment. *Management Science*, 40, 9, 1151-1173.

[8] Gastaldo, P., Zunino, R. and Redi, J. 2013. Supporting visual quality assessment with machine learning. EURASIP Journal on Image and Video Processing, 2013, 1, 1-15.

[9] Gosling, S. D., Rentfrow, P. J. and Swann, W. B. 2003. A very brief measure of the Big-Five personality domains. Journal of Research in personality, 37, 6, 504-528.

[10] Gou, L., Zhou, M. X. and Yang, H. 2014. Knowme and shareme: Understanding automatically discovered personality traits from social media and user sharing preferences. In Proceedings of the SIGCHI Conference on Human Factors in Computing Systems (Toronto, 2014). ACM.

[11] Gulliver, S. R. and Ghinea, G. 2006. Defining user perception of distributed multimedia quality. ACM Transactions on Multimedia Computing, Communications, and Applications (TOMCCAP), 2, 4, 241-257.

[12] Hanjalic, A. and Xu, L.-Q. 2005. Affective video content representation and modeling. Multimedia, IEEE Transactions on, 7, 1, 143-154.

[13] Hemami, S. S. and Reibman, A. R. 2010. No-reference image and video quality estimation: Applications and human-motivated design. Signal processing: Image communication, 25, 7, 469-481.

[14] Hofstede, G., Hofstede, G. J., Minkov, M. and Vinken, H. 2008. Values survey module 2008 manual. Maastricht: Institute for Research on Intercultural Cooperation.

[15] Hoßfeld, T., Keimel, C., Hirth, M., Gardlo, B., Habigt, J., Diepold, K. and Tran-Gia, P. 2014. Best practices for QoE crowdtesting: QoE assessment with crowdsourcing. Multimedia, IEEE Transactions on, 16, 2, 541-558.

[16] ITU-R. 2002. BT.500-11, Methodology for the subjective assessment of the quality of television pictures. International Telecommunication Union, Geneva, Switzerland, 4, 2.

[17] Le Callet, P. and Autrusseau, F. 2005. Subjective quality assessment IRCCyN/IVC database.

[18] Le Callet, P., Möller, S. and Perkis, A. 2012. Qualinet white paper on definitions of quality of experience. European Network on Quality of Experience in Multimedia Systems and Services (COST Action IC 1003).

[19] Mittal, A., Soundararajan, R. and Bovik, A. C. 2013. Making a "completely blind" image quality analyzer. Signal Processing Letters, IEEE, 20, 3, 209-212.

[20] Möller, S. and Raake, A. 2014. Quality of Experience. Springer.

[21] Nisbett, R. E. and Miyamoto, Y. 2005. The influence of culture: holistic versus analytic perception. Trends in cognitive sciences, 9, 10, 467-473.

[22] O'Brien, H. L. and Toms, E. G. 2008. What is user engagement? A conceptual framework for defining user engagement with technology. Journal of the American Society for Information Science and Technology, 59, 6, 938-955.

[23] Pérez, P., Macías, J., Ruiz, J. J. and García, N. 2011. Effect of packet loss in video quality of experience. Bell Labs Technical Journal, 16, 1, 91-104.

[24] Pinson, M. H. and Wolf, S. 2004. A new standardized method for objectively measuring video quality. Broadcasting, IEEE Transactions on, 50, 3, 312-322.

[25] Powers, D. M. 2011. Evaluation: from precision, recall and F-measure to ROC, informedness, markedness and correlation.

[26] Redi, J. A., Zhu, Y., de Ridder, H. and Heynderickx, I. 2015. How Passive Image Viewers Became Active Multimedia Users. Springer.

[27] Redi, J. A. a. l. C., P. 2015. Revisiting QoE for future media.www.qualinet.eu/images/stories/Qualinet-Newslet-Vol%2004.pdf

[28] Saad, M. A., Bovik, A. C. and Charrier, C. 2014. Blind prediction of natural video quality. Image Processing, IEEE Transactions on, 23, 3, 1352-1365.

[29] Scott, M. J., Guntuku, S. C., Huan, Y., Lin, W. and Ghinea, G. 2015. Modelling human factors in perceptual multimedia quality: On the role of personality and culture. ACM.

[30] Seshadrinathan, K. and Bovik, A. C. 2009. Motion-based perceptual quality assessment of video. In Proceedings of the IS&T/SPIE Electronic Imaging (2009). International Society for Optics and Photonics.

[31] Smits, E. and Hanjalic, A. 2010. A system concept for socially enriched access to soccer video collections. IEEE MultiMedia, 17, 4, 0026-0035.

[32] Streijl, R. C., Winkler, S. and Hands, D. S. 2014. Mean opinion score (MOS) revisited: methods and applications, limitations and alternatives. Multimedia Systems, 1-15.

[33] Tamborini, R., Bowman, N. D., Eden, A., Grizzard, M. and Organ, A. 2010. Defining media enjoyment as the satisfaction of intrinsic needs. Journal of communication, 60, 4, 758-777.

[34] Wang, H. L. and Cheong, L.-F. 2006. Affective understanding in film. Circuits and Systems for Video Technology, IEEE Transactions on, 16, 6, 689-704.

[35] Wang, W. 2010. How Personality Affects Continuance Intention: An Empirical Investigation of Instant Messaging. In Proceedings of the PACIS (Taipei, 2010).

[36] Wang, Y.-S., Lin, H.-H. and Liao, Y.-W. 2010. Investigating the individual difference antecedents of perceived enjoyment in the acceptance of blogging. World Academy of Science, Engineering and Technology, 67, 1, 1014-1023.

[37] Winkler, S. and Mohandas, P. 2008. The evolution of video quality measurement: from PSNR to hybrid metrics. Broadcasting, IEEE Transactions on, 54, 3, 660-668.

[38] Witmer, B. G. and Singer, M. J. 1998. Measuring presence in virtual environments: A presence questionnaire. Presence: Teleoperators and virtual environments, 7, 3, 225-240.

[39] Zeng, Z., Pantic, M., Roisman, G. and Huang, T. S. 2009. A survey of affect recognition methods: Audio, visual, and spontaneous expressions. Pattern Analysis and Machine Intelligence, IEEE Transactions on, 31, 1, 39-58.

[40] Zhu, Y., Heynderickx, I. and Redi, J. A. 2015. Understanding the role of social context and user factors in video Quality of Experience. Computers in Human Behavior, 49, 412-426.

[41] Zillmann, D. and Bryant, J. 2002. Entertainment as media effect. McQuail's reader in mass communication theory, 406.

Deep CTR Prediction in Display Advertising

Junxuan Chen[1,2]*, Baigui Sun[2], Hao Li[2], Hongtao Lu[1]†, Xian-Sheng Hua[2]‡
[1]Department of Computer Science and Engineering, Shanghai Jiao Tong University
[2]Alibaba Group, Hangzhou, China
{chenjunxuan, htlu}@sjtu.edu.cn {baigui.sbg, lihao.lh, xiansheng.hxs}@alibaba-inc.com

ABSTRACT

Click through rate (CTR) prediction of image ads is the core task of online display advertising systems, and logistic regression (LR) has been frequently applied as the prediction model. However, LR model lacks the ability of extracting complex and intrinsic nonlinear features from handcrafted high-dimensional image features, which limits its effectiveness. To solve this issue, in this paper, we introduce a novel deep neural network (DNN) based model that directly predicts the CTR of an image ad based on raw image pixels and other basic features in one step. The DNN model employs convolution layers to automatically extract representative visual features from images, and nonlinear CTR features are then learned from visual features and other contextual features by using fully-connected layers. Empirical evaluations on a real world dataset with over 50 million records demonstrate the effectiveness and efficiency of this method.

Keywords

DNN, CNN, Click through rate, Image Ads, Display Advertising

1. INTRODUCTION

Online display advertising generates a significant amount of revenue by showing textual or image ads on various web pages [3]. The ad publishers like Google and Yahoo sell ad zones on different web pages to advertisers who want to show their ads to users. And then Publishers get paid by advertisers every time the ad display leads to some desired action such as clicking or purchasing according to the payment options such as cost-per-click (CPC) or cost-per-conversion (CPA) [15]. The expected revenue for publishers is the product of the bid price and click-through rate (CTR) or conversion rate (CVR).

Figure 1: Display ads on an e-commerce web page.

Recently, more and more advertisers prefer displaying image ads [17] (Figure 1) because they are more attractive and comprehensible compared with textual ads. To maximize the revenue of publishers, this has led to a huge demand on approaches that are able to choose the most proper image ad to show for a particular user when he or she is visiting a web page so that to maximize the CTR or CVR.

Therefore, in most online advertising systems, predicting the CTR or CVR is the core task of ads allocation. In this paper, we focus on CPC and predict the CTR of display ads. Typically an ads system predicts and ranks the CTR of available ads based on contextual information, and then shows the top K ads to the users. In general, prediction models are learned from past click data based on machine learning techniques [3, 24, 9, 5, 32, 16].

Features that are used to represent an ad are extremely important in a machine learning model. In recent years, to make the CTR prediction model more accurate, many researchers use millions of features to describe a user's response record (we call it an ad impression). Typically, an image ad impression has basic features and visual features. The basic features are information about users, products and ad positions in a web page, etc. Visual features describe the visual appearance of an image ad at different levels. For example, color and texture are low level features, while face and other contextual objects are high level features. Low level and high level features may both have the power to influence the CTR of an image ad (Figure 2). Traditionally, researchers lack effective method to extract high-level visual features. The importance of visual features is also usually under estimated. However, as we can see from Figure 2, ads with same basic features may have largely different CTRs due to different ad images. As a consequence, How to use

*The work is done while the author was an intern at Alibaba Group.

†Corresponding author.

‡Corresponding author.

MM '16, October 15-19, 2016, Amsterdam, Netherlands
© 2016 ACM. ISBN 978-1-4503-3603-1/16/10...$15.00
DOI: http://dx.doi.org/10.1145/2964284.2964325

the visual features in machine learning models effectively becomes an urgent task.

Among different machine learning models that have been applied to predict ads CTR using the above features, Logistic regression (LR) is the mostly well-known and widely-used one due to its simplicity and effectiveness. Also, LR is easy to be parallelized on a distributed computing system thus it is not challenging to make it work on billions of samples [3]. Being able to handle big data efficiently is necessary for a typical advertising system especially when the prediction model needs to be updated frequently to deal with new ads. However, LR is a linear model which is inferior in extracting complex and effective nonlinear features from handcrafted feature pools. Though one can mitigate this issue by computing the second-order conjunctions of the features, it still can not extract higher-order nonlinear representative features and may cause feature explosion if we continue increasing the conjunction order.

To address these problems, other methods such as factorization machine [22], decision tree [9], neural network [32] are widely used. Though these methods can extract non-linear features, they only deal with basic features and handcrafted visual features, which are inferior in describing images. In this paper, we propose a deep neural network (DNN) to directly predict the CTR of an image ad from raw pixels and other basic features. Our DNN model contains convolution layers to extract representative visual features and then fully-connected layers that can learn the complex and effective nonlinear features among basic and visual features. The main contributions of this work can be summarized as follows:

1. This paper proposed a DNN model which not only directly takes both high-dimensional sparse feature and image as input, but also can be trained from end to end. To our best knowledge, this is the first DNN based CTR model which can do such things.

2. Efficient methods are introduced to tackle the challenge of high-dimensionality and huge data amount in the model training stage. The proposed methods reduce the training time significantly and make it feasible to train on a normal PC with GPUs even with large-scale real world training data.

3. We conduct extensive experiments on a real-world dataset with more than 50 million user response records to illustrate the improvement provided by our DNN model. The impacts of several deep learning techniques have also been discussed. We further visualize the saliency map of image ads to show our model can learn effective visual features.

The paper is organized as follows. Section 2 introduces the related work, followed by an overview of our scheme in Section 3. In Section 4, we describe the proposed DNN model in detail, and we show the challenges in the training stage as well as our solutions in Section 5. Section 6 presents the experimental results and discussion, and then Section 7 is the conclusion.

2. RELATED WORK

We consider display advertising CTR prediction and deep neural network are two mostly related areas to our work.

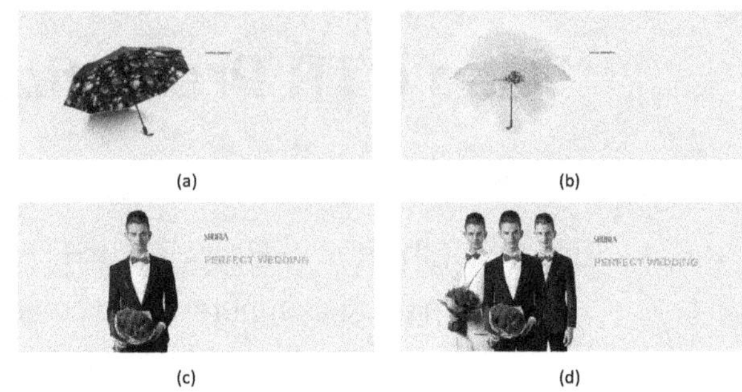

Figure 2: Two groups of image ads in each row. The two ads in each group have completely same ad group id, ad zone and target people. CTRs of image ads (a) and (b) are 1.27% and 0.83%. (b) suffers from low contrast between product and background obviously. CTRs of (c) and (d) are 2.40% and 2.23%. We find too many subjects in an men's clothing ad may bring negative effect. (the number of impressions of each ad is sufficiently high to make the CTR meaningful).

2.1 Display Advertising CTR prediction

Since the display advertising has taken a large share of online advertising market, many works addressing the CTR prediction problem have been published. In [24, 2], authors handcraft many features from raw data and use logistic regression (LR) to predict the click-through rate. [3] also uses LR to deal with the CTR problem and scales it to billions of samples and millions of parameters on a distributed learning system. In [20], a Hierarchical Importance-aware Factorization Machine (FM) [23] is introduced, which provides a generic latent factor framework that incorporates importance weights and hierarchical learning. In [5], boosted decision trees have been used to build a prediction model. In [9], a model which combines decision trees with logistic regression has been proposed, and outperforms either of the above two models. [32] combines deep neural networks with FM and also brings an improvement. All of these methods are very effective when deal with ads without images. However, when it comes to the image ads, they can only use pre-extracted image features, which is less flexible to take account of the unique properties of different datasets.

Therefore, the image features in display advertisement have received more and more attention. In [1, 4], the impact of visual appearance on user's response in online display advertising is considered for the first time. They extract over 30 handcrafted features from ad images and build a CTR prediction model using image and basic features. The experiment result shows that their method achieves better performance than models without visual features. [18] is the most related work in literature with us, in which a decapitated convolutional neural network (CNN) is used to extract image features from ads. However, there are two important differences between their method and ours. First, they do not consider basic features when extracting image features using CNN. Second, when predicting the CTR they use logistic regression which lacks the ability in exploring the complex relations between image and basic features. Most of the information in their image features is redundant such as product category which is included in basic features. As a result, their model only achieves limited improvements when combining both kinds of features. Worse still, when the dataset contains too many categories of products, it can hardly converge when training. Our model uses an end to end model to predict the CTR of image ads using basic features and raw images in one step, in which image features can be seen as supplementary to the basic features.

2.2 Deep Neural Network

In recent years, deep neural network has achieved big breakthroughs in many fields. In computer vision field, convolutional neural network (CNN) [13] is one of the most efficient tools to extract effective image features from raw image pixels. In speech recognition, deep belief network (DBN) [10] is used and much better performance is obtained comparing with Gaussian mixture models. Comparing with traditional models that have shallow structure, deep learning can model the underlying patterns from massive and complex data. With such learning ability, deep learning can be used as a good feature extractor and applied into many other applications [21, 26].

In CTR prediction field, besides [32] that is mentioned in Section 2.1, DNN has also been used in some public CTR prediction competitions[1,2] recently. In these two competitions, only basic features are available for participants. An ensemble of four-layer DNNs which use fully-connected layers and different kinds of non-linear activations achieves better or comparable performance than LR with feature conjunction, factorization machines, decision trees, etc. Comparing with this method, our model can extract more powerful features by taking consideration of the visual features in image ads.

3. METHOD OVERVIEW

As aforementioned, in this paper, each record of user's behavior on an ad is called an impression. denoted by x. Each impression has an image u with a resolution of around 120×200. Besides the image, the basic feature vector is denoted by $v \in \mathbf{R}^d$ such as the user's gender, product's category, ad position in the web page, and usually d can be very large, say, from a few thousand to many million. Our goal is to predict the probability that a user clicks on an image ad given these features. We will still use logistic regression to map our predicted CTR value $\hat{y}$ to 0 to 1, thus the CTR prediction problem can be written as:

$$\hat{y} = \frac{1}{1+e^{-z}} \tag{1}$$

$$z = f(x) \tag{2}$$

where $f(.)$ is what we are going to learn from training data, that is, the embedding function that maps an impression to a real value z. Suppose we have N impressions $\mathbf{X} = [x_1, x_2...x_N]$ and each with a label $y_i \in \{0, 1\}$ depends on the user's feedback, 0 means *not clicked* while 1 means *clicked*. Then the learning problem is defined as minimizing a Logarithmic Loss (Logloss):

$$L(\mathbf{W}) = -\frac{1}{N}\sum_i (y_i \log \hat{y}_i + (1-y_i)\log(1-\hat{y}_i)) + \lambda||\mathbf{W}||^2 \tag{3}$$

where $\mathbf{W}$ is the parameters of the embedding function $f(.)$ and λ is a regularization parameter that controls the model complexity.

In this model, what we need to learn is the embedding function $f(.)$. Conventional methods extract handcrafted visual features from raw image u and concatenate them with basic features v, then learn linear or nonlinear transformations to obtain the embedding function. In this paper we learn this function directly from raw pixels of an image ad and the basic features using one integrated deep neural network.

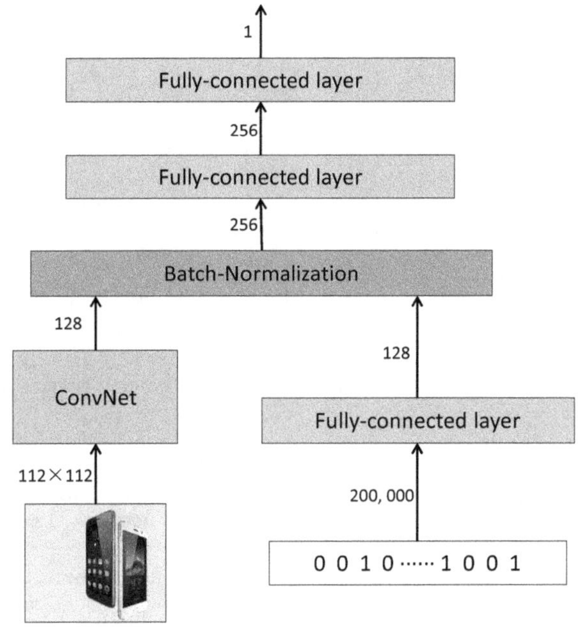

Figure 3: The overall architecture of the network. The output of each fully-connected layer is then pass through a ReLU nonlinear activation function.

4. NETWORK ARCHITECTURE

Considering basic features and raw images come from two different domains, we cannot simply concatenate them together directly in the network. Training two separate networks is also inferior since it cannot take into account the correlations between the two features. As a result, our network adopts two different sub-networks to deal with basic features and raw images, respectively, and then uses multiple fully-connected layers to capture their correlations.

As illustrated in Figure 3, a deep neural network called DeepCTR is designed which contains three parts. One part, *Convnet*, takes raw image u as input and follows with a convolutional network. The output of the *Convnet* is a feature vector of the raw image. The second part which is called *Basicnet*, takes basic features v as input and applies a fully-connected layer to reduce the dimensionality. Subsequently, outputs of *Convnet* and *Basicnet* are concatenated into one

[1]https://www.kaggle.com/c/avazu-ctr-prediction
[2]https://www.kaggle.com/c/criteo-display-ad-challenge

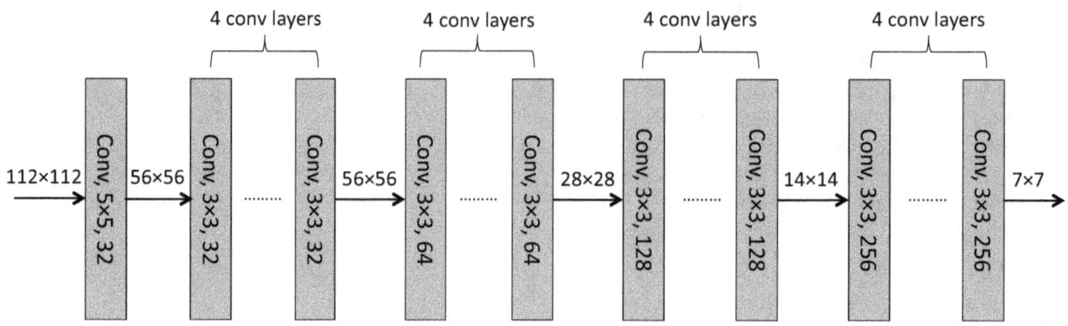

Figure 4: The architecture of the 17-layer *Convnet* in our model.

vector and fed to two fully-connected layers. The output of the last fully-connected layer is a real value z. This part is called *Combnet*. On the top of the whole network, Logloss is computed as described in Section 3.

The design of *Convnet* is inspired by the network in [7, 27], as shown in Figure 4. The network consists of 17 convolution layers. The first convolution layer uses 5×5 convolution kernels. Following first layer, there are four groups and each has four layers with 3×3 kernels. We do not build a very deep network such as more than 50 layers in consideration of the trade off between performance and training time. We pre-train the *Convnet* on the images in training dataset with category labels. We use two fully-connected layers with 1024 hidden nodes (we call them *fc18* and *fc19*), a fully-connected layer with 96-way outputs (we call it *fc20*) and a softmax after the *Convnet* in pre-training period. Since our unique images set is smaller (to be detailed in Section 6) than ImageNet [6], we use half the number of outputs in each group comparing with [7]. After pre-training, a 128-way fully-connected layer is connected behind the last convolution layer. Then we train the whole DeepCTR using Logloss from end to end.

5. SPEED UP TRAINING

An online advertising system has a large number of new user response records everyday. It is necessary for ad systems to update as frequently as possible to adapt new tendency. An LR model with distributed system requires several hours to train with billions of samples, which makes it popular in industry.

Typically a deep neural network has millions of parameters which makes it impossible to train quickly. With the development of GPUs, one can train a deep CNN with 1 million training images in two days on a single machine. However, it is not time feasible for our network since we have more than 50 million samples. Moreover, the dimensionality of basic features is nearly 200,000 which leads to much more parameters in our network than a normal deep neural network. Directly training our network on a single machine may take hundreds of days to converge according to a rough estimation. Even using multi-machine can hardly resolve the training problem. We must largely speed up the training if we want to deploy our DeepCTR on a real online system.

To make it feasible to train our model with less than one day, we adopt two techniques: using sparse fully-connected layer and a new data sampling scheme. The use of these two techniques makes the training time of our DeepCTR suitable for a real online system.

5.1 Sparse Fully-Connected Layer

In CTR prediction, the basic feature of an ad impression includes user information like gender, age, purchasing power, and ad information like ad ID, ad category, ad zone, etc. This information is usually encoded by one-hot encoding or feature hashing [29] which makes the feature dimension very large. For example, it is nearly 200,000 in our dataset. Consequently, in *Basicnet*, the first fully-connected layer using the basic feature as input has around 60 million parameters, which is similar to the number of all the parameters in AlexNet [13]. However, the basic feature is extremely sparse due to the one-hot encoding. Using sparse matrix in first fully-connected layer can largely reduce the computing complexity and GPU memory usage.

In our model, we use compressed sparse row (CSR) format to represent a batch of basic features V. When computing network forward

$$Y_{fc1} = VW, \tag{4}$$

sparse matrix operations can be used in the first fully-connected layer. When backward pass, we only need to update the weights that link to a small number of nonzero dimensions according to the gradient

$$\nabla(W) = V. \tag{5}$$

Both of the forward pass and backward pass only need a time complexity of $O(nd')$ where d' is the number of non-zero elements in basic features and $d' \ll d$. An experiment result that compares the usages of time and GPU memory with/out sparse fully-connected layer can be found in Section 6.2.

5.2 Data Sampling

Another crucial issue in training is that *Convnet* limits the batch-size of Stochastic Gradient Descent (SGD). To train a robust CTR prediction model, we usually need millions of ad samples. However, the *Convnet* requires lots of GPU memory, which makes our batch-size very small, say, a few hundred. For a smaller batch-size, the parallel computing of GPU can not maximize the effect in the multiplication of large matrix. And the number of iterations of each epoch will be very large. We need much more time to run over an epoch of iterations. Though the sparse fully-connected

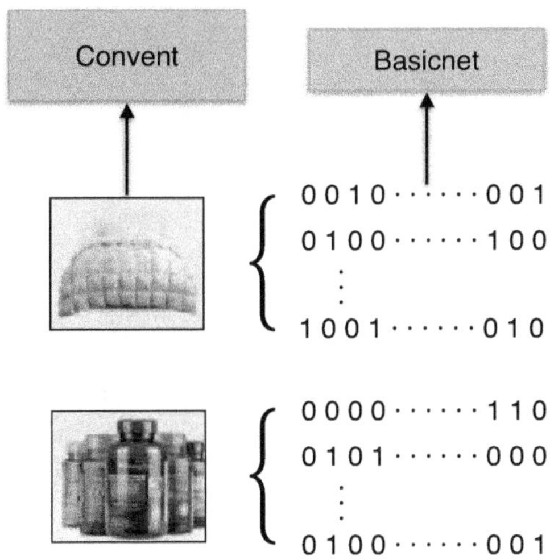

Figure 5: Originally, the image and the basic feature vector are one to one correspondence. In our data sampling method, we group basic features of an image together, so that we can deal with much more basic features per batch.

layer can largely reduce the forward-backward time in *Basicnet*, training the whole net on such a large dataset still requires infeasible time. Also, the gradient of each iteration is unstable in the case of smaller batch-size, which makes the convergence harder. In CTR prediction, this problem is even more serious because the training data is full of noise.

In this paper, we propose a simple but effective training method based on an intrinsic property of the image ads click records, that is, many impressions share a same image ad. Though the total size of the dataset is very large, the number of unique images is relatively smaller. Since a good many of basic features can be processed quickly by sparse fully-connected layer, we can set a larger batch-size for *Basicnet* and a smaller one for *Convnet*. In this paper we employ a data sampling method that groups basic features of a same image ad together to achieve that (Figure 5), which is detailed as follows.

Suppose the unique images set in our dataset is $\mathbf{U}$, the set of impressions related to an image u are $\mathbf{X}_u$ and basic features are $\mathbf{V}_u$. At each iteration, suppose the training batch size is n, we sample n different images U from $\mathbf{U}$. Together with each image $u \in U$, we sample k basic features V_u from $\mathbf{V}_u$ with replacement. Thus we have n images and kn basic features in each batch. After *Convnet*, we have n image features. For each feature vector $conv_u$ we copy it k times to have C_u and send them forward to *Combnet* along with V_u. In backward time, the gradient of each image feature vector can be computed as:

$$\nabla(conv_u) = \frac{1}{k}\sum_{c \in C_u} \nabla(c) \tag{6}$$

The training method is summarized in Alg. 1 and Alg. 2. In fact, this strategy makes us able to deal with kn samples in a batch. Since the sparse fully-connected layer requires very small GPU memory, we can set k a very big value according to the overall average number of basic feature vectors of

Algorithm 1 Training a DeepCTR network

Input: : Network Net with parameter $\mathbf{W}$, unique images set $\mathbf{U}$, basic features set $\mathbf{V}$, labels $\mathbf{Y}$, batch size n, basic feature sample number k.
Output: : Network for CTR prediction, Net

Initialize Net.
Compute the sample probability $p(u)$ of each image u,

$$p(u) = \frac{\#\mathbf{V}_u}{\sum_{u' \in \mathbf{U}} \#\mathbf{V}_{u'}} \tag{7}$$

repeat
  Sample n images U according to $p(u)$.
  For each u in U, sample k basic features V_u from $\mathbf{V}_u$ with labels Y_u uniformly with replacement.
  $forward\_backward(Net, U, V, Y)$.
until Net converges

Algorithm 2 *forward_backward*

Input: : Network Net with parameters $\mathbf{W}$ which contains a *Convnet*, *Basicnet* and *Combnet*, image samples U, basic features V, labels Y, basic feature sample number k.

Compute the feature vector $conv_u$ of each image u: $conv = net\_foward(Convnet, U)$
Copy each feature vector k times so we have C.
$loss = net\_forward(Basicnet \text{ and } Combnet, V, C)$.
$\nabla(C) = net\_backward(Combnet \text{ and } Basicnet, loss)$.
Compute $\nabla(conv_u)$ of each image u according to Eq. 6.
$net\_backward(Convnet, \nabla(conv))$.
Update network Net.

image ads. This strategy reduces the number of iterations of an epoch to several thousand and largely speeds up training. A larger batch-size also makes the gradient of each batch much more stable which leads to the model easy to converge. We also conduct an experiment to evaluate whether this sampling method influences the performance of DeepCTR comparing a throughly shuffle strategy in Section 6.2.

6. EXPERIMENT

In this section, a series of experiments are conducted to verify the superiority of our DeepCTR model.

6.1 Experimental Setting

6.1.1 Dataset

The experiment data comes from a commercial advertising platform (will expose it in the final version) in an arbitrary week of year 2015. We use the data from first six days as our training data and the data from last day (which is a Friday) as testing data. As described in Section 3, each impression consists of an ad x and a label y. An impression has an image u (Figure 2) and a basic feature vector v. The size of training data is 50 million while testing set is 9 million. The ratio of positive samples and negative samples is around 1:30. We do not perform any sub-sampling of negative events on the dataset. We have 101,232 unique images in training data and 17,728 unique images in testing data. 3,090 images in testing set are never shown in training set. Though the image data of training set and test data are highly overlapped, they follow the distribution of the real-world data. To make our experiment more convincing, we also conduct a experiment on a sub test set that only contains new images data that never been used in training. The basic feature v is one-hot encoded and has a dimensionality of 153,231. Following information is consisted by basic features:

1. Ad zone. The display zone of an ad on the web page. We have around 700 different ad zones in web pages.
2. Ad group. The ad group is a small set of ads. The ads in an ad group share almost same products but different ad images (in Figure 2, (a) and (b) belong to an ad group while (c) and (d) belong to another group). We have over 150,000 different ad groups in our dataset. Each ad group consists less than 20 different ads.
3. Ad target. The groups of target people of the ad. We have 10 target groups in total.
4. Ad category. The category of the product in ads. We have 96 different categories, like clothing, food, household appliances.
5. User. The user information includes user's gender, age, purchasing power, etc.

Besides above basic features, we do not use any handcrafted conjunction features. We hope that our model can learn effective non-linear features automatically from feature pools.

6.1.2 Baselines

We use LR only with basic features as our first baseline. We call this method *lr basic* in following experiments. To verify that our DNN model has the ability of extracting effective high-order features, a Factorization Machine implemented by LibFM [23] only with basic features is our second baseline. We call it *FM basic*. We use 8 factors for 2-way interactions and MCMC for parameter learning in *FM basic*. Then we evaluate a two hidden layers DNN model only using basic features. The numbers of outputs of two hidden layers are 128 and 256 respectively. The model can be seen as our DeepCTR net without the *Convnet* part. This method is called *dnn basic*. We further replace the *Convnet* in our DeepCTR net with pre-extracted features, SIFT [14] with bag of words and the outputs of different layers of the pre-trained *Convnet*. We call these two methods *dnn sift* and *dnn layername* (for example *dnn conv17*).

6.1.3 Evaluation Metric

We use two popular metrics to evaluate the experiment result, Logloss and the area under receiver operator curve (AUC). Logloss can quantify the accuracy of the predicted click probability. AUC measures the ranking quality of the prediction. Our dataset comes from a real commercial platform, so both of these metrics use relative numbers comparing with *lr basic*.

Since the AUC value is always larger than 0.5, we remove this constant part (0.5) from the AUC value and then compute the relative numbers as in [30]:

$$\text{relative AUC} = \left(\frac{AUC(method) - 0.5}{AUC(lr\ basic) - 0.5} - 1\right) \times 100\% \quad (8)$$

6.1.4 Network Configuration

In our *Convnet*, a 112×112 random crop and horizontal mirror for the input image are used for data augmentation.

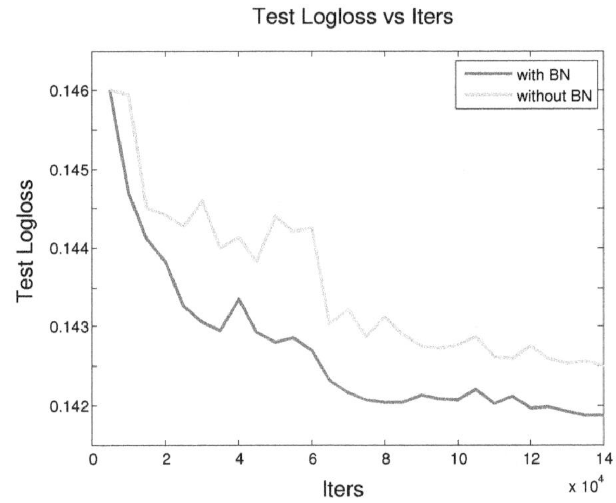

Figure 6: Test Logloss of the DeepCTR net with/without batch normalization in *Combnet*.

Each group has four convolution layers followed by a batch normalization [11] and a ReLU [19] activation. The stride of the first convolution layer is 2 if the output size of a group halves. We initialize the layer weights as in [8]. When pre-training the *Convnet* on our image dataset with category labels, we use SGD with a mini-batch size of 128. The learning rate starts from 0.01 and is divided by 10 when test loss plateaus. The pre-trained model converges after around 120 epochs. The weight decay of the net is set as 0.0001 and momentum is 0.9.

After pre-training *Convnet*, we train our DeepCTR model from end to end. Other parts of our net use the same initialization method as *Convnet*. We choose the size of mini-batch n as 20, and $k = 500$. That is to say, we deal with 10,000 impressions per batch. We start with the learning rate 0.1, and divided it by 10 after 6×10^4, 1×10^5 and 1.4×10^5 iterations. The *Convnet* uses a smaller initial learning rate 0.001 in case of destroying the pre-trained model. The weight decay of the whole net is set as 5×10^{-5}. The *dnn basic*, *dnn sift* and *dnn layername* use the same learning strategy.

We implement our deep network on C++ Caffe toolbox [12] with some modifications like sparse fully-connected layer.

6.2 Results and Discussion

In this section we compare the results of various methods and the effects of some network structures. First we compare the results of models with deep features in different levels. We plot the two metrics of *dnn conv13*, *dnn conv17*, *dnn fc18*, *dnn fc19*, and *dnn fc20* in the middle of Table 1. From the results, we find that *dnn conv17* and *dnn fc18* achieve best performance. Image features in these layers are of relatively high level but not highly group invariant [31]. Comparing with following fully-connected layers, they have more discriminations in same category. Comparing with previous layers, they contain features in a sufficiently high-level which are superior in describing the objects in images. Consequently, we connect *conv17* layer in our DeepCTR model. We do not choose *fc18* because it needs higher computations. We have also tried to compare our DeepCTR with the approach in [18]. However the model in [18] does not

Table 1: relative AUC and Logloss. All the numbers are best resuts achieved in three repeated experiments. We omit *dnn* of methods using deep neural network with pre-extracted features.

method	lr basic	FM basic	basic	sift	conv13	conv17	fc18	fc19	fc20	DeepCTR	3 DeepCTRs
AUC(%)	-	1.47	1.41	1.69	3.92	4.13	4.10	3.48	3.04	5.07	**5.92**
Logloss(%)	-	-0.40	-0.39	-0.45	-0.79	-0.86	-0.86	-0.74	-0.69	-1.11	**-1.30**

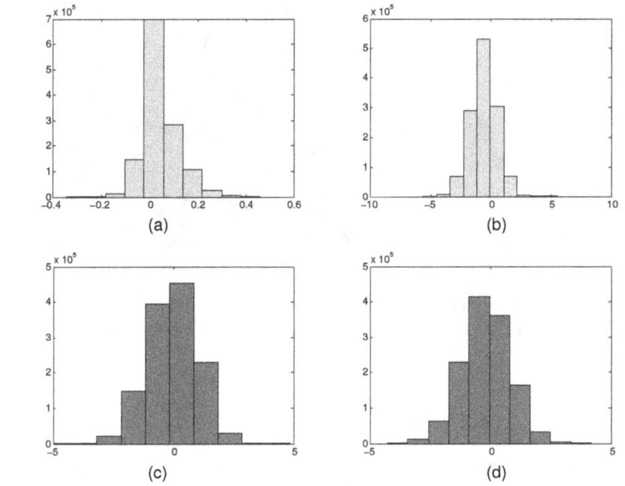

Figure 7: (a) and (b) are the histograms of outputs of *Basicnet* and *Convnet* without batch normalization while (c) and (d) with batch normalization.

converge on our dataset. We think the reason is that our dataset consists of too many categories of products while in their datasets only 5 different categories are available.

Comparison between other baselines is shown in Table 1 too. From the result, it can be seen that a deep neural network and image features can both improve the CTR prediction accuracy. *FM basic* and *dnn basic* achieve almost same improvements comparing with *lr basic*, which indicates that these two models both have strong power in extracting effective non-linear basic features. For the image part, comparing with handcrafted features, like SIFT, deep features have stronger power in describing the image, which leads to a significant improvement in the prediction accuracy. Our DeepCTR model goes one step further by using an end to end learning scheme. Ensemble of multiple deep networks usually brings better performance, so we train 3 DeepCTR models and average their predictions, and it gives the best AUC and Logloss. Compared with *lr basic*, the AUC increase will bring us 1~2 percent CTR increase in the advertising system (according to online experiments), which will lead to over 1 million earnings growth per day for an 100 million ads business.

To make our results more convincing, we also conduct an experiment on the sub test set that only contains 3,090 images that are never shown in training set. The relative AUC and Logloss of three representative methods *dnn basic*, *dnn sift* and a single DeepCTR are in Table 2. Clearly, our DeepCTR wins by a large margin consistently. We also notice that while the AUC of *dnn basic* decreases, *dnn sift* and our DeepCTR have an even higher relative AUC than the result on the full test set. Ad images in 3K sub test

Table 2: relative AUC and Logloss of the sub test set that only contains images never shown in the training set.

	AUC (%)	Logloss (%)
lr basic	-	-
dnn basic	1.07	-0.21
dnn sift	2.14	-0.48
DeepCTR	**5.54**	**-0.85**

set are all new ads added into the ad system and the ad groups have not appeared in the training set. This lead to the prediction worse in 3K sub test set because the ad group feature does not exist in the training set. However, though we lack some basic features, visual features bring much more supplementary information. This is the reason that *dnn sift* and DeepCTR have more improvements over the baseline methods (which only have basic features) in 3K sub test set comparing with the full test set. This experiment shows that visual features can be used to identify ads with similar characteristics and thus to predict the CTR of new image ads more accurately. It also verifies that our model indeed has strong generalization ability but not memories the image id rigidly.

For different real-world problems, different techniques may be needed due to the intrinsic characteristics of the problem, network design and data distribution. Therefore, solutions based on deep learning typically will compare and analyze the impact and effectiveness of those techniques to find the best practices for a particular problem. Therefore, we further explore the influence of different deep learning techniques in our DeepCTR model empirically.

First we find that the batch normalization in the *Combnet* can speed up training and largely improve performance (Figure 6). To investigate the reason, we show the histogram (Figure 7) of the outputs of *Convnet* and *BasicNet*. We can see from the histogram that two outputs have significant difference in scale and variance. Simply concatenating these two different kinds of data stream makes the following fully-connected layer hard to converge.

Dropout [28] is an efficient way to prevent over-fitting problem in deep neural network. Most deep convolution networks remove the dropout because batch normalization can regularize the models [7, 11]. However, in our DeepCTR model, we find it still suffers from over-fitting without dropout. We compare the loss curves of the model with/without dropout in the last two fully-connected layers. We can see that the model with dropout achieves lower testing Logloss, though we need more time to reach the lowest test loss.

We also evaluate the performance of the sparse fully-connected layer and our data sampling method. We plot computing time and memory overhead (Table 3) of the sparse fully-connected layer comparing with dense layer. Loss curves of training and testing are exactly the same since sparse fully-

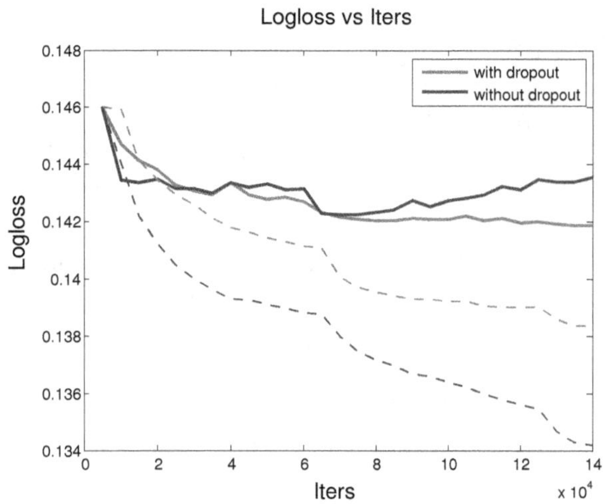

Figure 8: Logloss of the DeepCTR net with/without dropout in *Combnet.* Dashed lines denote training loss, and bold lines denote test loss.

Table 3: forward-backward time and GPU memory overhead of first fully-connected layer with a batch size of 1,000.

	time (ms)	memory (MB)
sparse layer	6.67	397
dense layer	189.56	4667

connected layer does not change any computing results in the net, so we do not plot them. From this table we can find dense layer requires much more computing time and memory than sparse one. Using sparse layer allows a lager batch size when training, which speeds up the training and makes the net much easier to converge.

Finally, we investigate whether the performance of our model descends using our data sampling method comparing a throughly shuffle. We only evaluate the sampling method on *dnn conv17* model, that is, we conduct experiments on a model where the *Convnet* is frozen. Ideally, we should use an unfrozen *Convnet* without data sampling as the contrast experiment. However, as mentioned in Section 5.2, training an unfrozen *Convnet* limits our batch-size less than 200 because the *Convnet* needs much more GPU memory, while a model with frozen *Convnet* can deal with more than 10000 samples in a batch. It will takes too much time to training our model on such a small batch-size. Also, the main difference between with/out sampling is whether the samples were thoroughly shuffled, while freezing the *Convnet* or not does not influence the order of samples. Therefore, we believe that our DeepCTR model performs similarly with *dnn conv17* model. From Table 4 we can see the performance of the model is not influenced by the data sampling method. At the same time, our method costs far less training time comparing with the approach without data sampling. Using this data sampling method, training our DeepCTR model from end to end only takes around 12 hours to converge on a NVIDIA TESLA k20m GPU with 5 GB memory, which is acceptable for an online advertising system requiring daily update.

Table 4: AUC and Logloss of *dnn conv17* model with our data sampling and a throughly shuffle.

	AUC(%)	Logloss(%)
data sampling	4.13	-0.86
throughly shuffle	4.12	-0.86

Figure 9: Saliency map of an image ad. We can see that cats, texture, and characters all have effect on the CTR.

6.3 Visualizing the Convnet

Visualizing the CNN can help us better understand exactly what we have learned. In this section, we follow the saliency map visualization method used in [25]. We use a linear score model to approximate our DeepCTR for *clicked* or *not clicked*:

$$z(U) \approx w^T U + b, \tag{9}$$

where image U is in the vectorized (one-dimension) form, and w and b are weight and bias of the model. Indeed, Eq 9 can be seen as the first order Taylor expansion of our DeepCTR model. We use the magnitude of elements of w to show the importance of the corresponding pixels of U for the *clicked* probability. where w is the derivative of z with respect to the image U at the point (image) U_0:

$$w = \frac{\partial z}{\partial U}\Big|_{U_0} \tag{10}$$

In our case, the image U is in RGB format and has three channels at pixel $U_{i,j}$. To derive a single class saliency value $M_{i,j}$ of each pixel, we take the maximum absolute value of $w_{i,j}$ across RGB channels c:

$$M_{i,j} = \max_c |w_{i,j}(c)| \tag{11}$$

Some of the typical visualization examples are shown as heat maps in Figure 10. In these examples, brighter area plays a more important role in impacting the CTR of the ad. We can see main objects in ads are generally more important. However, some low level features like texture, characters, and even background can have effect on the CTR of the ad. In another example (Figure 9), it is more clearly to see that visual features in both high level and low level have effectiveness. From the visualization of the *Convnet*, we can find that the task of display ads CTR prediction is quite different from object classification where high level features dominate in the top layers. It also gives an explanation why an end-to-end training can improve the model. Apparently, the *Convnet* can be trained to extract features that are more particularly useful for CTR prediction.

The visualization provides us an intuitive understanding

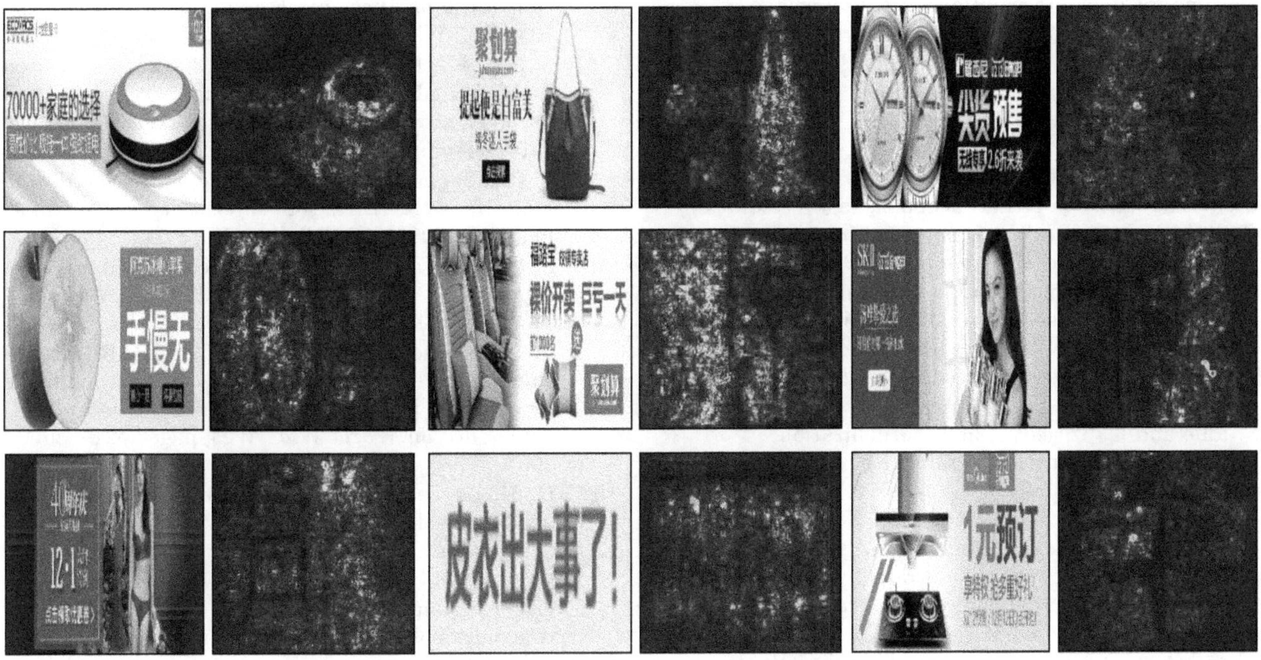

Figure 10: Saliency map of the image ads. Brighter area plays a more important role in effecting the CTR of ads.

of the impact of visual features in ad images which may be useful for designers to make design choices. For example, we can decide whether add another model or not in an ad according to the saliency map of this model.

7. CONCLUSIONS

CTR prediction plays an important role in online display advertising business. Accurate prediction of the CTR of ads not only increases the revenue of web publishers, also improves the user experience. In this paper we propose an end to end integrated deep network to predict the CTR of image ads. It consists of *Convnet*, *Basicnet* and *Combnet*. *Convnet* is used to extract image features automatically while *Basicnet* is used to reduce the dimensionality of basic features. *Combnet* can learn complex and effective non-linear features from these two kinds of features. The usage of sparse fully-connected layer and data sampling techniques speeds up the training process significantly. We evaluate DeepCTR model on a 50 million real world dataset. The empirical result demonstrates the effectiveness and efficiency of our DeepCTR model.

8. ACKNOWLEDGMENTS

This paper is partially supported by NSFC (No. 61272247, 61533012, 61472075), the 863 National High Technology Research and Development Program of China (SS2015AA020501), the Basic Research Project of Innovation Action Plan (16JC1402800) and the Major Basic Research Program (15JC1400103) of Shanghai Science and Technology Committee.

9. REFERENCES

[1] J. Azimi, R. Zhang, Y. Zhou, V. Navalpakkam, J. Mao, and X. Fern. The impact of visual appearance on user response in online display advertising. In *Proceedings of the 21st international conference companion on World Wide Web*, pages 457–458. ACM, 2012.

[2] D. Chakrabarti, D. Agarwal, and V. Josifovski. Contextual advertising by combining relevance with click feedback. In *Proceedings of the 17th international conference on World Wide Web*, pages 417–426. ACM, 2008.

[3] O. Chapelle, E. Manavoglu, and R. Rosales. Simple and scalable response prediction for display advertising. *ACM Transactions on Intelligent Systems and Technology (TIST)*, 5(4):61, 2014.

[4] H. Cheng, R. v. Zwol, J. Azimi, E. Manavoglu, R. Zhang, Y. Zhou, and V. Navalpakkam. Multimedia features for click prediction of new ads in display advertising. In *Proceedings of the 18th ACM SIGKDD international conference on Knowledge discovery and data mining*, pages 777–785. ACM, 2012.

[5] K. S. Dave and V. Varma. Learning the click-through rate for rare/new ads from similar ads. In *Proceedings of the 33rd international ACM SIGIR conference on Research and development in information retrieval*, pages 897–898. ACM, 2010.

[6] J. Deng, W. Dong, R. Socher, L.-J. Li, K. Li, and L. Fei-Fei. Imagenet: A large-scale hierarchical image database. In *Computer Vision and Pattern Recognition, 2009. CVPR 2009. IEEE Conference on*, pages 248–255. IEEE, 2009.

[7] K. He, X. Zhang, S. Ren, and J. Sun. Deep residual

learning for image recognition. *arXiv preprint arXiv:1512.03385*, 2015.

[8] K. He, X. Zhang, S. Ren, and J. Sun. Delving deep into rectifiers: Surpassing human-level performance on imagenet classification. *arXiv preprint arXiv:1502.01852*, 2015.

[9] X. He, J. Pan, O. Jin, Xu, et al. Practical lessons from predicting clicks on ads at facebook. In *Proceedings of 20th ACM SIGKDD Conference on Knowledge Discovery and Data Mining*, pages 1–9. ACM, 2014.

[10] G. Hinton, L. Deng, D. Yu, G. E. Dahl, Mohamed, et al. Deep neural networks for acoustic modeling in speech recognition: The shared views of four research groups. *Signal Processing Magazine, IEEE*, 29(6):82–97, 2012.

[11] S. Ioffe and C. Szegedy. Batch normalization: Accelerating deep network training by reducing internal covariate shift. *arXiv preprint arXiv:1502.03167*, 2015.

[12] Y. Jia, E. Shelhamer, J. Donahue, S. Karayev, J. Long, R. Girshick, S. Guadarrama, and T. Darrell. Caffe: Convolutional architecture for fast feature embedding. In *Proceedings of the ACM International Conference on Multimedia*, pages 675–678. ACM, 2014.

[13] A. Krizhevsky, I. Sutskever, and G. E. Hinton. Imagenet classification with deep convolutional neural networks. In F. Pereira, C. Burges, L. Bottou, and K. Weinberger, editors, *Advances in Neural Information Processing Systems 25*, pages 1097–1105. Curran Associates, Inc., 2012.

[14] D. G. Lowe. Object recognition from local scale-invariant features. In *Computer vision, 1999. The proceedings of the seventh IEEE international conference on*, volume 2, pages 1150–1157. Ieee, 1999.

[15] M. Mahdian and K. Tomak. Pay-per-action model for online advertising. In *Proceedings of the 1st international workshop on Data mining and audience intelligence for advertising*, pages 1–6. ACM, 2007.

[16] H. B. McMahan, G. Holt, D. Sculley, M. Young, D. Ebner, J. Grady, L. Nie, T. Phillips, E. Davydov, D. Golovin, et al. Ad click prediction: a view from the trenches. In *Proceedings of the 19th ACM SIGKDD international conference on Knowledge discovery and data mining*, pages 1222–1230. ACM, 2013.

[17] T. Mei, R. Zhang, and X.-S. Hua. Internet multimedia advertising: techniques and technologies. In *Proceedings of the 19th ACM international conference on Multimedia*, pages 627–628. ACM, 2011.

[18] K. Mo, B. Liu, L. Xiao, Y. Li, and J. Jiang. Image feature learning for cold start problem in display advertising. In *Proceedings of the 24th International Conference on Artificial Intelligence*, IJCAI'15, pages 3728–3734. AAAI Press, 2015.

[19] V. Nair and G. E. Hinton. Rectified linear units improve restricted boltzmann machines. In *Proceedings of the 27th International Conference on Machine Learning (ICML-10)*, pages 807–814, 2010.

[20] R. J. Oentaryo, E.-P. Lim, J.-W. Low, D. Lo, and M. Finegold. Predicting response in mobile advertising with hierarchical importance-aware factorization machine. In *Proceedings of the 7th ACM international conference on Web search and data mining*, pages 123–132. ACM, 2014.

[21] S. Ren, K. He, R. Girshick, and J. Sun. Faster r-cnn: Towards real-time object detection with region proposal networks. In *Advances in Neural Information Processing Systems*, pages 91–99, 2015.

[22] S. Rendle. Factorization machines. In *Data Mining (ICDM), 2010 IEEE 10th International Conference on*, pages 995–1000. IEEE, 2010.

[23] S. Rendle. Factorization machines with libfm. *ACM Transactions on Intelligent Systems and Technology (TIST)*, 3(3):57, 2012.

[24] M. Richardson, E. Dominowska, and R. Ragno. Predicting clicks: estimating the click-through rate for new ads. In *Proceedings of the 16th international conference on World Wide Web*, pages 521–530. ACM, 2007.

[25] K. Simonyan, A. Vedaldi, and A. Zisserman. Deep inside convolutional networks: Visualising image classification models and saliency maps. *arXiv preprint arXiv:1312.6034*, 2013.

[26] K. Simonyan and A. Zisserman. Two-stream convolutional networks for action recognition in videos. In *Advances in Neural Information Processing Systems*, pages 568–576, 2014.

[27] K. Simonyan and A. Zisserman. Very deep convolutional networks for large-scale image recognition. *arXiv preprint arXiv:1409.1556*, 2014.

[28] N. Srivastava, G. Hinton, A. Krizhevsky, I. Sutskever, and R. Salakhutdinov. Dropout: A simple way to prevent neural networks from overfitting. *The Journal of Machine Learning Research*, 15(1):1929–1958, 2014.

[29] K. Weinberger, A. Dasgupta, J. Langford, A. Smola, and J. Attenberg. Feature hashing for large scale multitask learning. In *Proceedings of the 26th Annual International Conference on Machine Learning*, pages 1113–1120. ACM, 2009.

[30] L. Yan, W.-j. Li, G.-R. Xue, and D. Han. Coupled group lasso for web-scale ctr prediction in display advertising. In *Proceedings of the 31st International Conference on Machine Learning (ICML-14)*, pages 802–810, 2014.

[31] M. D. Zeiler and R. Fergus. Visualizing and understanding convolutional networks. In *Computer Vision–ECCV 2014*, pages 818–833. Springer, 2014.

[32] W. Zhang, T. Du, and J. Wang. Deep learning over multi-field categorical data: A case study on user response prediction. *arXiv preprint arXiv:1601.02376*, 2016.

Event Specific Multimodal Pattern Mining for Knowledge Base Construction

Hongzhi Li *†, Joseph G. Ellis *†, Heng Ji ‡ and Shih-Fu Chang †

†Columbia Univeristy, New York, NY 10027, USA
‡Rensselaer Polytechnic Institute,Troy, NY 12180, USA
{hongzhi.li, jge2105, shih.fu.chang}@columbia.edu, jih@rpi.edu

ABSTRACT

Knowledge bases, which consist of a collection of entities, attributes, and the relations between them are widely used and important for many information retrieval tasks. Knowledge base schemas are often constructed manually using experts with specific domain knowledge for the field of interest. Once the knowledge base is generated then many tasks such as automatic content extraction and knowledge base population can be performed, which have so far been robustly studied by the Natural Language Processing community. However, the current approaches ignore visual information that could be used to build or populate these structured ontologies. Preliminary work on visual knowledge base construction only explores limited basic objects and scene relations. In this paper, we propose a novel multimodal pattern mining approach towards constructing a high-level "event" schema semi-automatically, which has the capability to extend text only methods for schema construction. We utilize a large unconstrained corpus of weakly-supervised image-caption pairs related to high-level events such as "attack" and "demonstration" to both discover visual aspects of an event, and name these visual components automatically. We compare our method with several state-of-the-art visual pattern mining approaches and demonstrate that our proposed method can achieve dramatic improvements in terms of the number of concepts discovered (33% gain), semantic consistence of visual patterns (52% gain), and correctness of pattern naming (150% gain).

CCS Concepts

•**Information systems** → *Clustering;* •**Computing methodologies** → *Machine learning algorithms;*

Keywords

Multimodal, Pattern Mining, Convolutional Neural Network, Event Schema, Multimodal Knowledge Base

*Denotes equal contribution.

ACMMM '16 Amsterdam, The Netherlands

ISBN 978-1-4503-3603-1/16/10...$15.00

DOI: http://dx.doi.org/10.1145/2964284.2964287

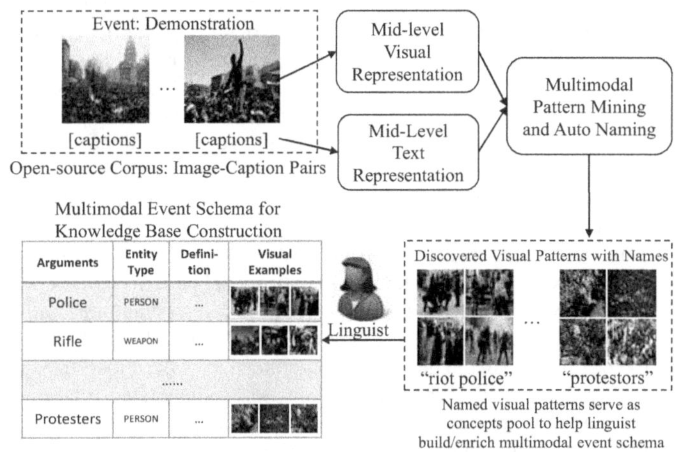

Figure 1: We propose a novel system to automatically discover and name visual patterns specific to each high-level event which helps experts construct event schema and related knowledge bases.

1. INTRODUCTION

With recent advances in computer vision, researchers have been able to demonstrate impressive performance at near-human level capabilities in difficult tasks such as image recognition. For example, computer vision systems now have the ability to recognize if a dog, cat, or car appears in an image. These advances are made possible by utilizing the massive amount of image datasets and label annotations, sometimes also with bounding boxes around the objects of interest within the image. However, the difficulty with the current systems is that every time when we want to learn a new visual concept, users must be looped in to manually define the target class and label the training data. Also, it is unclear how we can know apriori for a particular domain what the most important concepts we want to focus on and train corresponding detectors. For example, if an ontology expert is asked to construct a schema to describe high-level events like "attack", what visual classes or concepts are most relevant and can be automatically detected? Can we use data mining to discover such relevant classes directly from data available from the domain and use the discovered concepts to help the expert to build the new schema? Our intuition tells us that "gun", "knife", or "explosion", could be important things to try to detect from the images. However without inspecting the content of the images our preconceived notions of what is important may only tell part of the story of a given event. We will show later that other concepts such as "smoke", "air strike", and "police" might actu-

Figure 2: Examples of the localized patterns automatically discovered and named by the proposed multimodal approach.

ally appear much more frequently in the specific data corpus in the domain, but it would be difficult to know these concepts appear frequently without first inspecting a portion of the images. Situations like this can arise in many application domains (like sports, security, and open source content). Thus, there are great needs for automatically discovering concepts relevant to events of interest from data corpora in various specific domains.

In response to the challenge mentioned above, in this work we attempt to answer the following question: given a specific target domain and associated data corpora, how do we develop automatic methods to rapidly discover salient multimodal patterns that are semantically coherent, visually consistent, and can be automatically named with semantic concepts relevant to the high-level events in the target domains. The proposed architecture is described in Fig. 1. We use artifical neural network models to generate visual and text representation for image-caption pairs, and apply the association rule mining algorithm to discover multimodal visual patterns. In this work, we use news as an example domain and image caption pairs as example multimodal corpora to demonstrate the effectiveness of the proposed methods. But the overall proposed framework is general and can be easily extended to other domains.

In many applications like personalized news or social media tracking, it's often necessary to process information at the high-level event level (such as "Baltimore Riot" or "Syria Bombing"). Using knowledge bases to improve event-level processing has been a major research topic. In this work, we specifically focus on discovery of named multimodal patterns related to events in a specific domain. We use such patterns as candidate concepts that can be used to assist knowledge experts to construct new event knowledge bases.

As shown in Fig. 1 and 2, a pattern is formed by a collection of localized instances within images (referred to as image patches later in the paper) and their associated text captions. We specifically focus on patterns that are represented by both text and image modalities. We also emphasize the importance of the automatic naming process in order to assign semantic concepts relevant to high-level events (such as "explosion", "vigil" concepts for "attack" event). Such automatic discovery and naming processes will produce a pool of high-quality multimodal concepts that are semantically coherent, visually consistent, and semantically relevant to specific events of interest.

The proposed discovery and naming methods for multimodal patterns are distinct from the existing work in mining of visual patterns. Recently, [21] and [12] proposed discovery of representative and discriminative visual patterns as mid-level image representation in order to improve image classification performance, compared to the traditional representations using low-level features (such as visual bags of words). Visual patterns have also been used to summarize image collections by [31] [18]. Although such visual patterns capture unique visual characteristics that can be used to separate image classes, they often do not correspond to clear semantic concepts that are at a level suitable for defining entities included in high-level events. For example, visual patterns discovered in [12] from the MIT scene dataset are often at the lower level like chairs, windows, or furniture parts that do not meet the needs of high-level knowledge base construction.

Evaluation of pattern mining and naming is challenging due to the novelty of the problem and the subjectiveness of the task. It's important to note the goal is not to improve image classification tasks like what has been done in past works [12] [7]. Instead, our focus is on semantic naming of the discovered patterns and their relatedness to high-level events as mentioned earlier. In this work, we propose expert evaluation methods to compare the proposed approaches with several state-of-the-art baselines for visual discovery and naming procedures. The contributions of this paper can be summarized as follows:

- We develop a novel multimodal mining framework for discovering visual patterns from a collection of image-caption pairs and automatically naming the discovered patterns, producing a large pool of semantic concepts specifically relevant to a high-level event. The named visual patterns can be used to construct event schema needed in the knowledge base construction process.
- The proposed system can discover many novel semantic concepts not covered by existing visual ontologies such as ImageNet. This helps break the aforementioned bottleneck in extending existing visual classifiers to new domains.
- Our system exploits the joint multimodal representations in discovering unique patterns, which are shown to be more visually coherent and semantically correct, compared to baselines using separate processing of individual media modalities.

2. RELATED WORK

Low-level image features such as SIFT [15] and Bag-of-Words methods were widely used as a representation for image retrieval and classification. However, researchers have proven that these low-level features are insufficient for representing the semantic meaning of images. Mid-level image feature representations are often used to achieve better performance in a variety of computer vision tasks. Some frameworks for using middle level feature representations, such as [11, 28, 29, 30], have achieved excellent performance in object recognition and image retrieval. ImageNet [5], was introduced and has led to breakthroughs in tasks such as object recognition and image classification due to the availability of a massive amount of well-labeled data. Each of the images within ImageNet is manually labeled. Thus, it is a very expensive and time-consuming task. Other similar datasets, including SUN[25], MSCOCO [13], and UCF101 [22] are created for object/scene/concept classification tasks. However, the manually defined ontologies are quite limited and oftentimes do not extend to real-world data, and therefore may not cover the concepts needed to build an event schema for high-level events. This work looks beyond a manually defined ontology, and instead focuses on mining multimodal patterns automatically from weakly supervised data to attempt to unbind researchers from the need for costly supervised datasets. We approach this problem from a multi-modal perspective (using the image and caption together), which allows us to name and discover higher-level image concepts.

Visual pattern mining is an important task since it is the foundation of many middle-level feature representation frameworks. [9] and [31] use low-level features and a hashing approach to mine visual patterns from image collections. [26] utilizes a spatial random partition to develop a fast image matching approach to discover visual patterns. All of these methods obtain image patches from the original image collection either by random sampling or salient object proposal and utilize image matching or clustering to discover similar patches to create visual patterns. These methods are computationally intense, because they have to examine possibly hundreds or thousands of image patches from each image. These methods rely heavily on low-level image features, and therefore do not often produce image patches that exhibit high-level semantic meaning. The generated image patterns are typically visually duplicated or near-duplicated image patches.

Convolutional neural networks (CNN) have achieved great success in many research areas [20], [10]. Recently, [12] combined the image representation from a CNN and the association rule mining technique to effectively mine visual patterns. They first uniformly sampled image patches from the original image and extracted the fully connected layer response as features for each image patch utilized in an association rule mining framework. This approach is able to find consistent visual patterns, but cannot guarantee the discovered visual patterns are relevant to specific events and can be used in event schema construction. Most of the existing visual pattern mining work focuses on how to find visually consistent patterns.

Other related works focus on visual knowledge mining. [6] propose a visual instance mining system to find the unique visual elements that are the most distinctive for a certain geo-spatial area. They attempt to answer the question "What makes Paris looks like Paris?", which is answered by the visual patterns discovered by their system. They first collect images from Google Street View. Then the images are sampled to obtain image patches at different scales. A discriminative clustering approach is proposed to take into account the weak geographic supervision and discover the visual patterns with the unique character of a specific city. This idea is very inspiring, as the visual patterns discovered are used not only as a mid-level representation, but as valuable knowledge by themselves.

The NEIL system [3] is another example of visual knowledge mining work. NEIL automatically discovers common sense relationships and labels instances of given visual categories. In NEIL, the discovered knowledge consists of relationships between predefined objects and concepts. The NEIL system is also able to find new visual instances of given categories. However, while NEIL is limited to a predefined ontology, our proposed multimodal pattern mining method aims to discover and name new objects/concepts from an unstructured set of image-caption pairs.

Another category of related works is image captioning. In recent years, many researchers have focused on teaching machines to understand images and captions jointly. Image caption generation focuses on automatically generating a caption that directly describes the content in an image using a language model. Multimodal CNN [8] is often used to generate sentences for the images. All the existing works use supervised approaches to learn a language generation model based on carefully constructed image captions created for this task. The datasets used in caption generation, such as the MSCoco dataset [13] consist of much simpler sentences than appear in news image-caption pairs. We differ from these approaches in that we do not try to generate a caption for images, but instead use them jointly to mine and name the patterns that appear throughout the images.

3. MULTIMODAL PATTERN MINING

In this section, we discuss our multimodal pattern mining (MMPM) framework. In particular, we will describe how we collect a large-scale dataset, generate feature-based transactions from the images and captions, and discover and name semantic visual patterns.

3.1 Weakly Supervised Event Dataset Collection

We believe that by using weakly supervised image data from target categories that are sufficiently broad, we can automatically discover meaningful and easily nameable image patch patterns for structured ontology generation. To accomplish this task, we collect a set of image caption pairs from a variety of types of news event categories.

We begin by crawling the complete Twitter feeds of four prominent news agencies, the Associated Press, Al Jazeera, Reuters, and CNN. Each of these agencies has a prominent Twitter presence, and tweet links to their articles multiple times a day. We collect the links to the articles and then download the HTML file from each extracted link. The articles span the time frame from 2007-2015, and cover a variety of different topics. We then parse the raw HTML files and find the image and caption pairs from the downloaded news articles. Through this process, we were able to collect approximately 280k image-caption pairs.

Once we have collected the dataset, we want to find image-caption pairs that are related to different events covered in news. We utilized the event ontology that was defined for the Knowledge Base Population (KBP) task in the National Institute for Standards and Technology Text Analysis Conference in 2014 to provide supervision to our dataset. Within this task, there is an event track with the stated goal to "extract information such that the information would be suitable as input to a knowledge base." This track goal closely models the goals of learning patterns that are easily nameable with semantic concepts and hence could be used in knowledge base population. This makes this ontology a perfect fit for our task.

The KBP event task utilizes the ontology defined by the Lingustic Data Consortium in 2005 [24]. This event ontology contains 34 distinct event types; the events are broad actions that appear commonly throughout news documents, such as *demonstrate*, *divorce*, and *convict*. Provided in the training data with these event ontologies is a list of trigger words for each of the events that are used to detect when an event appears in text data. An example of some of the trigger words used for the *demonstrate* event are: protest, riot, insurrection, and rally. We search each of the captions for a trigger word from the event category, and if an image caption contains that trigger word, we assign that image caption pair to the given event category. An example of the number of images for some representative events can be seen in Table 1.

Table 1: Number of images per event category for some of the most popular event categories in our dataset.

Event	# of Images	Event	# of Image
Attack	52649	Injure	5853
Demonstrate	20933	Transport	51187
Elect	9265	Convict	1473
Die	26475	Meet	32787

3.1.1 *Review of Pattern Mining*

In this section, we will review the basic ideas and definitions necessary for pattern mining. Assume that we are given a set of n

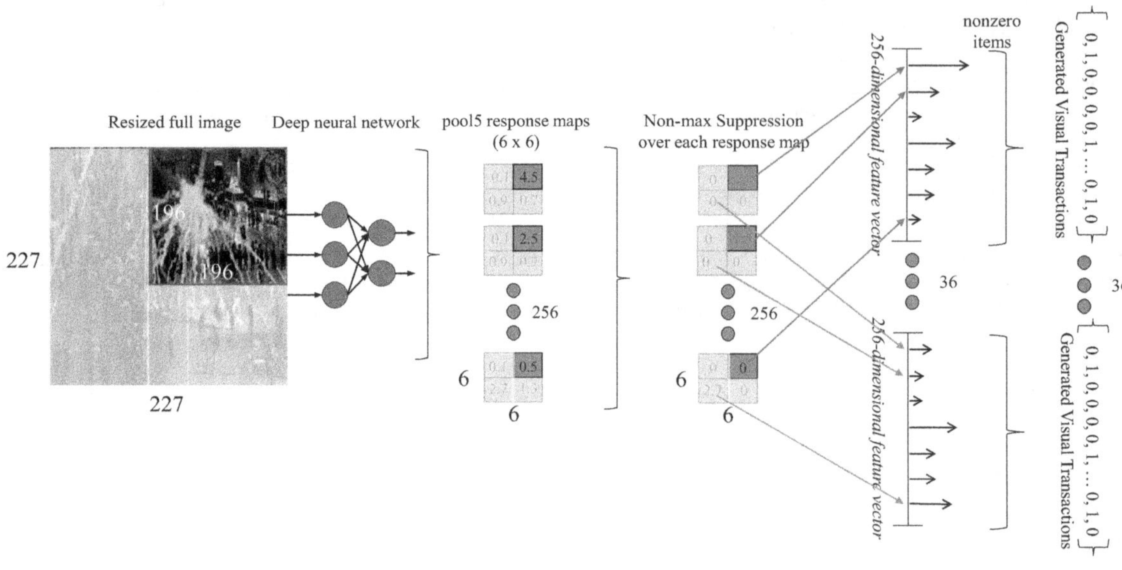

Figure 3: The visual transaction generation pipeline utilizing the last convolutional layer of a convolutional neural network. Using this pipeline, we are able to obtain representations of each image that can localize the presence of a pattern within the image. We use convolutional layers from AlexNet as an example.

possible observations $X = \{x_1, x_2, ...x_n\}$; a *transaction*, T, is a set of observations such that $T \subseteq X$. Given a set of transactions $S = \{T_1, T_2, ...T_m\}$ containing m transactions, our goal is to find a particular subset of X, say t^*, which can accurately predict the presence of some target element $y \in T_a$, given that $t^* \subset T_a$ and $y \cap t^* = \emptyset$. t^* is referred to as a *frequent itemset* in the pattern mining literature. The relationship from $t^* \rightarrow y$ is known as an *association rule*. The support of t^* reflects how often t^* appears in S and is defined as,

$$s(t^*) = \frac{|\{T_a | t^* \subseteq T_a, T_a \in S\}|}{m} \quad (1)$$

Our goal is to find association rules that accurately predict the correct event category for the image-caption pairs. Therefore, we want to find patterns such that if t^* appears in a transaction there is a high likelihood that y, which represents an event category, appears in that transaction as well. We define the *confidence* as the likelihood that if $t* \subseteq T$ then $y \in T$, or,

$$c(t^* \rightarrow y) = \frac{s(t^* \cup y)}{s(t^*)}. \quad (2)$$

3.1.2 Transaction Generation from Images

Certain portions of a CNN are only activated by a smaller region of interest (ROI) within the original image. Throughout this paper, we will utilize the CNN defined in [10], which is a common CNN structure that is often used for computer vision tasks. The last layer in which the neurons in that layer do not correspond to the entire image is the output of the final convolutional and pooling layer. Based on this observation, for each image we find the maximum magnitude response from a particular feature map from this layer of the CNN. The last pooling layer of [10] is commonly known as "pool5". This layer consists of 256 filters; and the response of each of the filters over a 6×6 mapping of the image. The corresponding ROI from the original image in which all the pixels in that region contribute to the response of a particular neuron in the pool5 layer is a 196×196 image patch from the 227×227 resized image. These 196×196 image patches come from a zero-padded representation of the image with zero-padding around the image edges of 64 pixels and a stride of 32. Namely, from a 227×227 scaled input image, a total of 6×6 (36) patch areas are covered from all the stride positions, resulting in a 6×6 feature map for each filter in this layer. Using this approach, we are able to leverage the existing architecture to compute the filter responses for all patches at once without actually changing the network structure. This idea allows us to extract image patch patterns in a way that is much more efficient than many current pattern mining methods, which utilize a sampling approach.

We use the pre-trained CNN model from [10], trained on the ImageNet dataset for extracting the pool5 features for the news event images. For each image, we keep the maximum response over the 6×6 feature map and set other non-maximal values to zero for all 256 filters, which is similar to non-maximum suppression that appears throughout the CNN literature. This operation finds the patch triggering the highest response in each filter and helps avoid redundant patches in the surrounding neighborhood in the image that may also generate high responses. The above process results in a 256-dimensional feature vector representation for each image patch. We then set the nonzero items in this feature vector to 1. This creates a binary representation of which filters are activated for each image patch. We use these sparse binarized features to build *transactions* for each image patch as discussed in Sec. 3.1.1, where the nonzero dimensions are the items in our transaction.

By utilizing the architecture of the CNN directly, we are able to efficiently extract image features that come from specific ROI that are suitable for pattern mining. The current state-of-the-art pattern mining technique proposed by [12] requires a sampling of the image patches within each image and then operating the entire CNN over this sampled and resized image patch. This procedure is very costly, because the CNN must be used to extract features from a number of sampled images that can be orders of magnitude larger than the dataset size. For example, for the MIT indoor

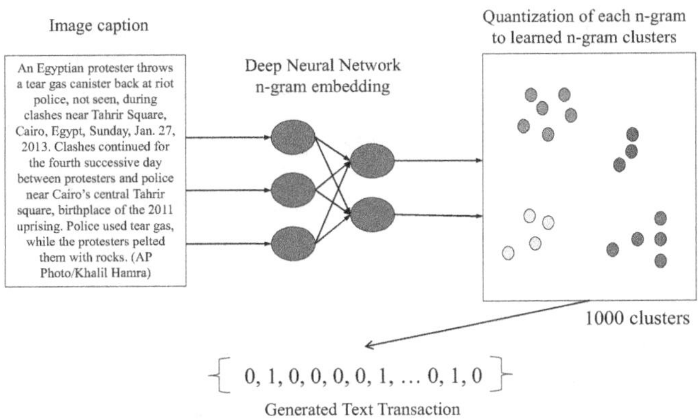

Figure 4: The text transaction generation pipeline.

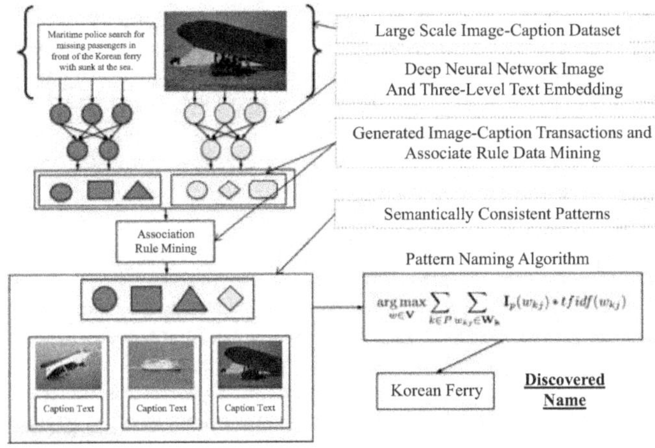

Figure 5: Our full multimodal pattern discovery and naming pipeline

dataset, the authors of [12] sample 128×128 size image patches with a stride of 32 from images that have been resized such that their smallest dimension is of size 256. Thus, the number of image samples that are taken for each image is greater than or equal to $(\frac{256-128}{32}+1)^2 = 25$. The full CNN must operate on all of these sampled images. In contrast, our method works directly on the images themselves without any sampling, but still has the ability to localize images within the dataset. We are able to extract representations for 36 image patches from an image while only having the CNN operate on the image once. By leveraging the structure of the CNN during test or deployment, our method is *at least* 25 times less computationally intensive than the current state of the art. We will discuss the speed-up we have in deploying our event-specific pattern mining compared with other approaches in our experiment section. Fig. 3 shows our visual transaction generation pipeline in detail.

In this paper, we choose to use the response map of the pooling layer after the last convolutional layer to build the image transactions. This choice is inspired by the research on visualizing the convolutional neural network [27] and the recent success of using convolutional layers for object semantic segmentation [14] [19]. Those works have proved that the filters in the last convolutional layers have strong capability to capture the semantic objects in the input images. Thus, we use this particular setup in our model. However, it is important to note that our proposed multimodal framework is very flexible so that the image transaction generation model or the text transaction generation model can be replaced by other advanced models to achieve even better results.

3.1.3 Transaction Generation from Captions

We have discussed how we generated transactions by binarizing and thresholding the CNN features that are extracted from the images. Similarly, we require an analogous algorithm for generating transactions from image captions.

We begin by cleaning each of the image captions by removing stopwords and other ancillary words that are not relevant (HTML tags or URLs). We then tokenize each of the captions and find all of the words that appear in at least 10 captions in our dataset. Once we find these words, we use the skip-gram model proposed in [16] that was trained on a corpus of Google News articles to map each word to a 300-dimensional embedded space. This model works well in our setting, because the structure of image captions is similar to that of news article text, which this model was trained on. The skip-gram model works well in our context because words with similar uses end up being embedded close to each other in the feature space. Words such as "religious clergy", "priest", and "pastor" all end up close in Euclidean distance after embedding and far away from words that are not similar. We cluster the words using K-means clustering to generate 1,000 word clusters.

To generate transactions for each caption, we map each word back to its corresponding cluster, then include that cluster index in the transaction set. We remove patterns that contain cluster indices that are associated with commonly used words by having a high confidence score threshold as defined in Eq. 2. The cluster indices that frequently appear in captions from a particular event category but rarely for other categories are found through our association rule mining framework.

We require our discovered patterns to contain items from both the visual and text transactions. By requiring words with similar meaning to appear in all captions of a visual pattern, we are able to discard patterns that may be visually similar but semantically incoherent. The skip-gram-based algorithm is able to handle differences in word choice and structure between captions to effectively encode meaning into our multimodal transactions.

3.2 Mining the Patterns

We add the event category of each image as an additional item in the generated transaction for each of the image caption pairs. Inspired by [12], we use the popular apriori algorithm [1] to find patterns within the transactions that predict which event category the image belongs to. We only find the association rules that have a confidence higher than 0.8, and calculate the support threshold that ensures that at least 30 image patches exhibit a found pattern. Finally, we also remove any rules that only contain items generated from the image or caption transactions, ensuring that we only retain truly multimodal patterns. Therefore, our pattern requirements can be described mathematically as,

$$\begin{aligned} &c(t^* \rightarrow y) \geq c_{min} \\ &s(t^*) \geq s_{min} \\ &t^* \cap \mathbf{I} \neq \emptyset \\ &t^* \cap \mathbf{C} \neq \emptyset. \end{aligned} \tag{3}$$

where as defined in Eq 1 and Eq 2, y is the event category of the image-caption pair, c_{min} is the minimum confidence threshold, s_{min} is our minimum support threshold, **I** represents the items generated from the image transaction pipeline, and **C** are those generated from the caption pipeline. At the end, each multimodal pattern t* contains a set of visual items (fired filter responses in pool5 in CNN model) and a set of text patterns (clusters in the skip-gram embedded space).

3.3 Naming the Patterns

We name the generated patterns so that they can be used for higher-level information extraction tasks, such as event schema generation. We leverage the fact that we have captions associated with each of the images to generate names for each pattern.

We begin the process of name generation by removing the words that are not generally useful for naming but appear often in captions. The words that are removed include standard English language stop words (or, I, etc.), the name of each month, day, and directional words such as "left" and "right". After cleaning the caption words, we then encode both unigram and bigrams into a vector using tf-idf encoding. We ignore any unigrams or bigram that does not appear at least 10 times across our caption dataset.

Once these words are removed we then sum the TF-IDF vector representations of each word in all of the captions associated with a particular pattern. We then take the argument max over the summed TF-IDF representations to obtain the name for this pattern. The word embedding described in Sec. 3.1.3 ensures that words with semantically similar usages and meanings will be clustered together, and the TF-IDF naming algorithm chooses the most appropriate word from the associated clusters for a particular pattern. This procedure is explained mathematically in the following way: Let p be a found multimodal itemset (pattern), and T_k is the multimodal transaction for the k'th generated transaction in our dataset. We define the set P as all the indices of transactions that contain p, or $P = \{i | p \subseteq T_i, \forall i\}$. In Eq. 4, $\mathbf{V}$ is our vocabulary, W_k is the set of words from the k'th caption, $\mathbf{I}_p(w)$ is an indicator function on whether w corresponds to a word cluster in the itemset of p, and w_{kj} is the j'th word in the k'th caption,

$$w_{name} = \arg\max_{w \in \mathbf{V}} \sum_{k \in P} \sum_{w_{kj} \in W_k} \mathbf{I}_p(w_{kj}) * tfidf(w_{kj}) \quad (4)$$

Once the names are found, we remove any name that appears in more than 10% of the captions of a particular event. This is important because for particular events like "injure", words such as *injure* and *wounded* appear across many captions, and may lead to poor naming. Some examples of discovered patterns and the names that we have assigned to them can be seen in Fig 6. Our full pattern naming algorithm and pipeline can be seen in Fig 5.

4. EVALUATION

4.1 Baseline Methods

In this paper, we propose a complete end-to-end pipeline for discovering and naming visual patterns from large-scale image-text datasets, in particular news event-related content. The discovered visual patterns with names are used to help linguists build the multimodal event schema. To the best of our knowledge, there is no existing research that attempts to solve the specific problem that we have addressed. However, some existing techniques can be modified and then used to address this problem. We propose 3 different baseline approaches based on some state-of-the-art pattern mining techniques and then compare our approach with those baselines.

4.1.1 Baseline 1: Object Proposal and Clustering (OPC)

We follow the commonly used pipeline that is widely used in the visual pattern mining literature [6] [4] for this baseline approach. We first sample the images at multiple scales to obtain image patches, and then image features are extracted from each patch. The patches are then clustered using K-Means clustering to group the image patches into visual patterns. We use existing state-of-the-art methods in each component to implement this baseline. Selective Search [23] is used to propose multi-scale image patches. The response from second to last fully connected layer of the CNN, VGG19 [20], is used as the feature representation of each image patch. We attempted different cluster numbers for the K-Means algorithm and report the best performance in the following section. The selection of parameters is discussed in Sec. 4.4.

To name the discovered visual patterns, we utilize topics discovered by Latent Dirichlet Allocation (LDA) [2] to find pattern names from the associated caption text for each visual pattern. We first collect all the image captions from one visual pattern, and this collection of captions represents a document in our LDA framework. Then we discover n topics over all the documents, in this work, n was set to be 1,000. Each document is then assigned to be generated from some distribution over the topics. We first take the intersection of the set of all the words from its document and the set of the topic words from the topic. The words in this intersection are then ranked based on the corresponding topic score for each word. The word ranking score can be seen in Eq. 5 where w_i is the word being ranked, W_k is the set of words that appear in the captions of a pattern, T_j is the set of words from the jth topic, and t_{ij} is topic score for word w_i in relation to topic j. In this equation, T_j represents the topic that is chosen by LDA to be most representative of this document.

$$w_{score}(w_i) = \sum_{w_i \in W_k \cap T_j} t_{ij} \quad (5)$$

We choose the top 3 words based on our above ranking algorithm to name each visual pattern.

4.1.2 Baseline 2: Mid-level Deep Pattern Mining (MDPM)

MDPM is proposed by Li et al. in [12]. They use the response of a fully connected layer of a pre-trained CNN to build transactions and apply association rule mining to find visual patterns. Their method is the most similar current approach to ours, but they only use visual information in their approach, while we use both visual and text modalities to build the multimodal transactions. This method is a state-of-the-art approach for visual pattern mining, and we will demonstrate the performance gains that can be achieved using multimodal information as opposed to visual only. We use the code provided by the authors of [12] in our experiments. As their method is designed for finding visual patterns only, we use the same LDA naming algorithm introduced in section 4.1.1 to name the discovered visual patterns.

4.1.3 Baseline 3: Object Detection to Find Concepts from Image Dataset (OD)

With the recent rapid development of artificial neural networks for image classification, researchers can accurately detect objects and concepts from images. We use a pre-trained convolutional neural network model [20] to detect concepts and objects from our dataset. We select the top k frequently detected objects/concepts in each event as k visual patterns. We set k to be 50 in our experiment. Naturally, all the images with the same detected concept are

Figure 6: Some examples of named visual patterns discovered by our MMPM. These examples are discovered for the "attack" event. Although each pattern may contain more images, we only show the first six images for each pattern.

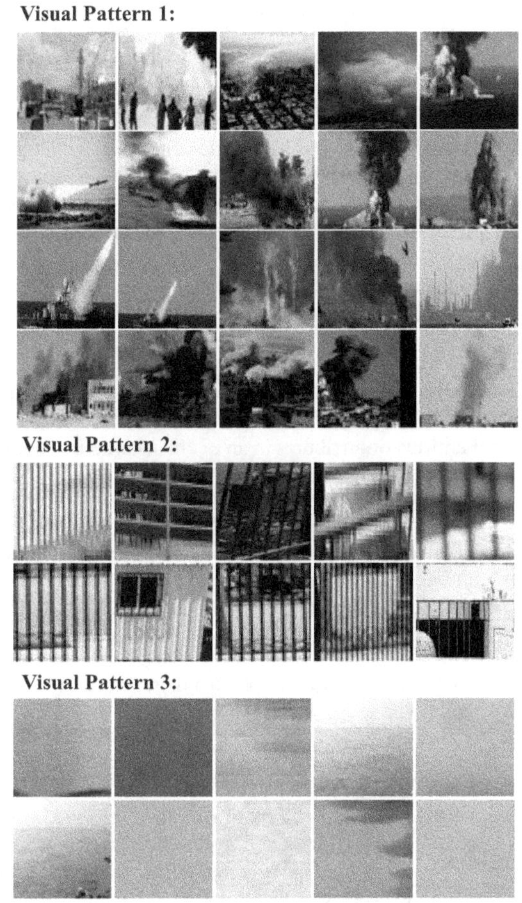

Figure 7: Some examples of visual patterns discovered by baseline 1: object proposal and clustering (OPC) approach. It is important to note that OPC is also capable of finding meaningful concepts. We selectively show these examples to demonstrate the common problem with OPC. For example, the partial object in "visual pattern 2" and the solid color pattern in "visual pattern 3". These types of patterns are not useful for multimodal event schema construction.

grouped as a visual pattern, and the name of the synset corresponding to the detected visual pattern is used as the pattern name.

4.2 Subjective Evaluation

We first show some examples of visual patterns discovered by our method and the baseline approaches in Fig. 6 and 7. Some subjective conclusions can be drawn from the illustration. These conclusions are representative of the algorithms and the patterns that are generated by all of the methods.

Image patch sampling-based approaches (OPC and MDPM) have a tendency to find low-level visual patterns. Examples of this are solid color patches and partial objects (Visual Pattern 2 and 3 in Fig. 7). This is due to the fact that these methods sample image patches at the beginning of their pipeline, which is necessary for discovering visual patterns at different scales. However, the solid color patches and partial object patches are often produced using these approaches. Unfortunately, it is very difficult and expensive to avoid generating such patches by either a random/uniform image patch sampling approach or using object proposals. It is, therefore, not a surprise to find meaningless or very low-level conceptual image patterns, such as color similarity or "bars", as can be seen in "Visual Pattern 2" in Fig. 7. In our MMPM method, we use the response map of the last convolutional layer of a CNN to generate visual transactions and localize the image patches. It has been shown in [27] and [32] that the filters in the last convolutional layer of a CNN are particularly useful in capturing high-level semantic concepts/objects from local regions in an image. This high-level semantic nature of the filters we use in conjunction with the text information that we extract from the captions naturally leads to higher-level semantically meaningful patterns than the baseline approaches. Another issue with visual-only approaches is that the visual clustering based approach (OPC) fails to distinguish different semantic concepts if they have the similar visual appearances. For example, "Visual Pattern 1" in Fig. 7 shows a mix of patches that were generated from images containing "rocket", "smoke", and "air strike" concepts. It is an obvious drawback of a visual-only approach and particularly difficult to overcome since those concepts are indeed visually similar. Our MMPM approach can overcome this problem by involving the semantically relevant text information from image captions to distinguish between visually similar patterns. Examples of "air strike", "burns", "smoke", and "rockets" and the differences can be seen in Fig. 6.

4.3 Quantitative Evaluation

We evaluate the quality of multimodal visual patterns by evaluating whether the named visual patterns generated by each method can be used to construct an event schema. The names of visual patterns are usually used as entities or arguments in the multimodal event schema. The images from the visual pattern are used as visual examples and can be further used to train visual classifiers to expand the visual example set. To obtain this annotation, we have hired linguists and others who have experience in designing structured event schemas and ontologies. We give the annotators a set of named visual patterns for each event. The task they complete is to build a multimodal event schema using the concepts provided by the pattern mining methods. The linguist is asked to determine if the pattern name, which is a unigram or bigram, and the associated images can be used to construct an event schema based on the following three criteria:

1. **Event relatedness:** The discovered concepts (pattern names and related images) are relevant to the event, and would be useful entities or attributes in an event schema for that event.
2. **Visual semantic coherence:** The visual pattern associated with the name is semantically consistent. Namely, the images shown under the pattern depict a coherent semantic concept, and not a mix of many different concepts. If the majority of images in a pattern are consistent, with few outliers, the pattern is considered to exhibit this property.
3. **Text-visual matching:** The pattern name correctly describes the semantic concept of the visual pattern.

In our experiment, three experts [1] examine the event relatedness of approximately 2,500 unique pattern names discovered from the dataset we described in Sec. 3.1 by our method and the baselines. We also check the visual semantic coherence and name quality (text-visual matching) of 10,000 visual patterns. Each pattern name is checked by three experts to determine the event relatedness independently. To avoid bias, the discovered pattern names from all the methods are mixed and then presented to the experts without the information of which method discovers the pattern name. Similarly, the semantic coherence and name quality of each pattern are also checked by three experts independently without bias. The final results reported in the following sections are determined using majority vote of all the examiners.

4.3.1 *Coverage of the Discovered Concepts*

We want to measure how many concepts are correctly discovered by each method and how many unique concepts each method is responsible for. This experiment does not aim to prove which method is better, but we make the point that the proposed MMPM can find additional concepts that cannot be discovered by the baseline visual pattern mining plus a naming algorithm and do not currently exist in the current concept/object ontologies defined by computer vision researchers, such as ImageNet[5], Places[33], MIT Indoor[17], and others. Table 2 shows the coverage of discovered concepts for each method. The metrics shown are averaged across each of the events tested for each method. We show two metrics for each method: 1. the number of detected concepts by each method relevant to a particular event, and 2. The number of unique concepts that a method detects relevant to the event and that are not found by other methods.

The MMPM method finds many more event relevant concepts than other approaches, with at least 33% increase. Among the discovered concepts in each event, there are approximately 58 unique concepts that cannot be found by any other baseline methods. Compared with the commonly used visual ontology ImageNet, over 95% of the concepts discovered by MMPM are not covered by the ImageNet ontology. We find that there are only around 5 related concepts discovered by the visual ontology ImageNet for each event. This demonstrates the narrowness of current state-of-the-art visual ontologies. Those visual concepts do not meet the needs of high-level knowledge base construction, particularly for events. It is therefore important to adopt a multimodal approach to concept discovery.

[1]The evaluators include a linguist and two CS PhD students.

Table 2: Average number of relevant concepts discovered by each method (per event), and number of unique concepts that are only discovered by each method

Method	# concepts discovered (per event)	# unique concepts
OPC	73	29
OD	5	3
MDPM	50	25
MMPM	97	58

Table 3: Number of found patterns in news events.

Event	# of Patterns	Event	# of Patterns
Attack	573	Convict	0
Demonstrate	1247	Die	146
Elect	42	Injure	45
Meet	5159	Transport	509

4.3.2 *Visual Semantic Coherence*

A pattern is judged to be semantically coherent if the majority of annotators judge patches associated with the patter have consistent semantic concepts. As shown in Table 5, all the methods achieve reasonable results in finding visual patterns that exhibit semantic coherence. We can see that our method outperforms the competing baselines by a large margin, and exhibits a 52% performance improvement over the current state-of-the-art approach. The ability to leverage the text information in our algorithm for discovering patterns tends to lead to patterns that exhibit this semantic coherence, because we ensure that not only is the visual content similar in appearance, but the corresponding text content also has similar meaning. The other approaches that utilize only visual information can be misled by image patches that are visually similar but share little to no semantic similarity, as shown in Fig. 7. The added visual semantic coherence of our patterns allows them to be leveraged in event schema construction, which demonstrates why we are able to find more patterns suitable for this task as shown in Fig. 6.

4.3.3 *Correctness of Visual Pattern Names*

We show the accuracy of attempting to name the visual patterns in Table 6. MMPM significantly outperforms the other methods for visual pattern naming, with approximately 150% improvement in naming accuracy. This is because MMPM combines information from both visual and textual modalities to build the image caption representations, and therefore the discovered patterns tend to be more semantically consistent, and are discovered based on the appearance of semantically similar words in the captions. MMPM can distinguish different semantic concepts even if they are visually similar, as shown in the naming results. The baseline approaches first find the visual patterns and then use the LDA naming model to name the visual patterns. In this approach, text is not leveraged in the pattern discovery process. In such cases, the naming

Table 4: Concepts (visual pattern names) discovered in "attack" event using our multimodal pattern mining method

air strike	damage	rockets
aggravated assault	dead	security forces
army	destroyed	shot
arrested	explosion	strike
bomb	fighting	tank
bomb attack	forces	tear gas
bomber	gun	terrorist
burns	helicopter	troops
confrontation	riot police	

Table 5: Semantic coherence of the visual patterns. We show the percent of semantically coherent visual patterns among all the patterns discovered by each method.

Method	Semantically Coherent Visual Patterns (%)
OPC	33.76
OD	31.25
MDPM	50.15
MMPM	**76.32**

algorithm cannot find correct names for these patterns, because the patterns may be visually similar, but semantically different. We noticed that the performance of baseline 3, object detection, does not achieve good performance in pattern semantic coherence and name quality evaluation. The cross-domain issue is the reason why baseline using object detectors trained in a different domain could not achieve high performance. However, the comparison is still appropriate since our method and other baselines also use the same network architecture and pretrained model without fine-tuning using the target dataset (although we only use the top five convolutional layers). This demonstrates again the deficiency of existing visual ontology and object detectors in extracting knowledge in a new target domain, and importantly why we require a multimodal approach to find visual patterns for event schema construction, particularly when naming them is important.

4.4 Discussion of Parameters

We discuss some parameters of MMPM and baseline methods in this section. As is natural in clustering methods, the number of clusters is an important tunable parameter. In baseline 1, OPC, we tried different numbers of clusters in the experiments. The clusters are formed over each event. Instead of setting a unique cluster number for all the events, we calculated the number of clusters as the number of patches in each event divided by the expected number of patches in each cluster. We tried $\{20, 30, 50\}$ as the expected number of patches in each cluster. We only report the best performance in the experiment section. Since we use the apriori algorithm [1] for association rule mining in our MMPM method and baseline 2 MDPM method, there are two tunable parameters within the algorithm: support rate and confidence rate; we discussed them in Section 3.2. In general, our performance is not sensitive to those two parameters. However, we do note that a small support rate may lead to finding many duplicate visual patterns for both methods. The number of selected concepts in baseline 3 (object detection) is not sensitive to parameters. In our experiment, the top 50 concepts are able to cover all the potential discovered concepts in the ImageNet ontology. We examined the top 100 concepts, but we found

Table 6: Evaluation of naming the discovered patterns. The accuracy of each method is shown.

Method	Pattern Naming Accuracy (%)
OPC	15.0
OD	21.4
MDPM	23.0
MMPM	**57.4**

that there were no "relevant concepts" discovered after the top 50 concepts for each event.

4.5 Complexity and Efficiency

MMPM is not only effective for finding and naming multimodal visual patterns, but it is also quite efficient when compared with the baseline approaches. Most current state-of-the-art pattern mining methods work on the image patch level. The complexity of the algorithm can be roughly estimated by the number of patches. Since the value of the response map of the last convolutional layer is usually sparse, on average, we only select about $3-5$ patches per image after non-max suppression. (We ignore the transactions that only contain "0" in each dimension of the feature vector.) Compared with the other baselines, object proposal usually generates hundreds of image patches per image and MDMP generates approximately one hundred patches per image. Therefore, our method is faster by more than an order of magnitude than competing approaches, because as discussed in Sec. 3.1.2 our method works on an image level, unlike other approaches. It is important to note that although our method takes the whole image as input, it is still able to localize the visual patterns, similar to the other image patch based methods. The actual running time of our experiments demonstrates what we have described here. We run our experiments on the same workstation with two Intel Xeon E5 CPUs, 64GB memory, and Nvidia TITAN X GPU. The dataset used in our experiments has about 100,000 images. MMPM takes about 2 hours to finish the entire pipeline, including feature extraction, transaction generation, pattern mining, and naming. OPC takes about 18 hours, and MDPM requires approximately 36 hours. It is necessary to mention that MDPM is implemented in MATLAB by the original authors of [12]. The actual running time may be improved by using a more efficient implementation.

5. CONCLUSIONS

We have developed a novel dataset and algorithm for mining and naming multimodal visual patterns from a corpus of high-level news event image caption pairs. Our multimodal pattern mining method is able to discover patterns that are more informative than the state-of-the-art vision-only approaches, and accurately name those patterns. These patterns are then leveraged to build multimodal event schemas for each particular news event. We demonstrate that our method discovered patterns that greatly outperform other competing methods for this task. This work represents the first approach for using multimodal pattern mining to discover and name high-level semantically meaningful image patterns for event schema construction. The combination of our ability to find meaningful patterns and name them allows for many applications in high-level information extraction tasks, such as knowledge base population using multimodal documents and automatic event ontology creation. Our work can be leveraged as a bridge between structured information extraction tasks in the Computer Vision and Natural Language Processing communities.

6. ACKNOWLEDGMENTS

This work was supported in part by the National Science Foundation Graduate Research Fellowship under Grant No. DGE-11-44155 and a multimedia seedling grant through the DARPA DEFT Program #FA8750-12-2-0347. The views and conclusions contained in this document are those of the authors and should not be interpreted as representing the official policies, either expressed or implied, of the U.S. Government. The U.S. Government is authorized to reproduce and distribute reprints for Government purposes notwithstanding any copyright notation here on.

7. REFERENCES

[1] R. Agrawal and R. Srikant. Fast algorithms for mining association rules in large databases. In *20th International Conference on Very Large Data Bases*, pages 487–499, 1994.

[2] D. M. Blei, A. Y. Ng, and M. I. Jordan. Latent dirichlet allocation. *the Journal of machine Learning research*, 3:993–1022, 2003.

[3] X. Chen, A. Shrivastava, and A. Gupta. Neil: Extracting visual knowledge from web data. In *Proceedings of the IEEE International Conference on Computer Vision*, pages 1409–1416, 2013.

[4] A. Cruz-Roa, J. C. Caicedo, and F. A. González. Visual pattern mining in histology image collections using bag of features. *Artificial intelligence in medicine*, 2011.

[5] J. Deng, W. Dong, R. Socher, L.-J. Li, K. Li, and L. Fei-Fei. Imagenet: A large-scale hierarchical image database. In *IEEE Conference on Computer Vision and Pattern Recognition (CVPR)*, pages 248–255, 2009.

[6] C. Doersch, S. Singh, A. Gupta, J. Sivic, and A. Efros. What makes paris look like paris? *ACM Transactions on Graphics*, 31(4), 2012.

[7] B. Fernando, E. Fromont, and T. Tuytelaars. Mining mid-level features for image classification. *International Journal of Computer Vision*, 108(3):186–203, 2014.

[8] A. Frome, G. S. Corrado, J. Shlens, S. Bengio, J. Dean, T. Mikolov, et al. Devise: A deep visual-semantic embedding model. In *NIPS*, pages 2121–2129, 2013.

[9] J. Han, J. Pei, and Y. Yin. Mining frequent patterns without candidate generation. In *ACM SIGMOD Record*, 2000.

[10] A. Krizhevsky, I. Sutskever, and G. E. Hinton. Imagenet classification with deep convolutional neural networks. In *Advances in Neural Information Processing Systems (NIPS)*, pages 1097–1105. 2012.

[11] L.-J. Li, H. Su, L. Fei-Fei, and E. P. Xing. Object bank: A high-level image representation for scene classification & semantic feature sparsification. In *NIPS*, 2010.

[12] Y. Li, L. Liu, C. Shen, and A. van den Hengel. Mid-level deep pattern mining. *IEEE Conference on Computer Vision and Pattern Recognition (CVPR)*, pages 971–980, 2015.

[13] T.-Y. Lin, M. Maire, S. Belongie, J. Hays, P. Perona, D. Ramanan, P. Dollár, and C. L. Zitnick. Microsoft coco: Common objects in context. In *European Conference on Computer Vision (ECCV)*, 2014.

[14] J. Long, E. Shelhamer, and T. Darrell. Fully convolutional networks for semantic segmentation. In *Proceedings of the IEEE Conference on Computer Vision and Pattern Recognition (CVPR)*, pages 3431–3440, 2015.

[15] D. G. Lowe. Distinctive image features from scale-invariant keypoints. *Int. J. Comput. Vision*, 60(2):91–110, Nov. 2004.

[16] T. Mikolov, I. Sutskever, K. Chen, G. Corrado, and J. Dean. Distributed representations of words and phrases and their compositionality. *Computing Research Repository (CoRR)*, abs/1310.4546, 2013.

[17] A. Quattoni and A. Torralba. Recognizing indoor scenes. In *Computer Vision and Pattern Recognition, 2009. CVPR 2009. IEEE Conference on*, pages 413–420. IEEE, 2009.

[18] K. Rematas, B. Fernando, F. Dellaert, and T. Tuytelaars. Dataset fingerprints: Exploring image collections through data mining. In *Proceedings of the IEEE Conference on Computer Vision and Pattern Recognition*, pages 4867–4875, 2015.

[19] H. Schulz and S. Behnke. Learning object-class segmentation with convolutional neural networks. In *ESANN*, 2012.

[20] K. Simonyan and A. Zisserman. Very deep convolutional networks for large-scale image recognition. *Computing Research Repository (CoRR)*, abs/1409.1556, 2014.

[21] S. Singh, A. Gupta, and A. Efros. Unsupervised discovery of mid-level discriminative patches. *European Conference on Computer Vision (ECCV)*, pages 73–86, 2012.

[22] K. Soomro, A. R. Zamir, and M. Shah. Ucf101: A dataset of 101 human actions classes from videos in the wild. *arXiv preprint arXiv:1212.0402*, 2012.

[23] J. R. Uijlings, K. E. van de Sande, T. Gevers, and A. W. Smeulders. Selective search for object recognition. *International journal of computer vision*, 2013.

[24] C. Walker, S. Strassel, J. Medero, and K. Maeda. Ace 2005 multilingual training corpus. *Linguistic Data Consortium, Philadelphia*, 2006.

[25] J. Xiao, J. Hays, K. A. Ehinger, A. Oliva, and A. Torralba. Sun database: Large-scale scene recognition from abbey to zoo. In *Computer vision and pattern recognition (CVPR), 2010 IEEE conference on*, pages 3485–3492. IEEE, 2010.

[26] J. Yuan and Y. Wu. Spatial random partition for common visual pattern discovery. In *IEEE International Conference on Computer Vision (ICCV)*, pages 1–8, 2007.

[27] M. D. Zeiler and R. Fergus. Visualizing and understanding convolutional networks. In *European Conference on Computer Vision (ECCV)*, pages 818–833. 2014.

[28] H. Zhang, X. Shang, W. Yang, H. Xu, H. Luan, and T.-S. Chua. Online collaborative learning for open-vocabulary visual classifiers. In *CVPR*, 2016.

[29] H. Zhang, Y. Yang, H. Luan, S. Yang, and T.-S. Chua. Start from scratch: Towards automatically identifying, modeling, and naming visual attributes. In *Proceedings of the 22nd ACM international conference on Multimedia*, pages 187–196. ACM, 2014.

[30] T. Zhang, H. Li, H. Ji, and S.-F. Chang. Cross-document event coreference resolution based on cross-media features. In *Proc. Conference on Empirical Methods in Natural Language Processing (EMNLP2015)*, 2015.

[31] W. Zhang, H. Li, C.-W. Ngo, and S.-F. Chang. Scalable visual instance mining with threads of features. In *ACM International Conference on Multimedia*, pages 297–306, 2014.

[32] B. Zhou, A. Khosla, A. Lapedriza, A. Oliva, and A. Torralba. Object detectors emerge in deep scene cnns. *arXiv preprint arXiv:1412.6856*, 2014.

[33] B. Zhou, A. Lapedriza, J. Xiao, A. Torralba, and A. Oliva. Learning deep features for scene recognition using places database. In *Advances in neural information processing systems*, pages 487–495, 2014.

Joint Graph Learning and Video Segmentation via Multiple Cues and Topology Calibration

Jingkuan Song
University of Trento
Trento, Italy
jingkuan.song@unitn.it

Lianli Gao
University of Electronic Science and Technology of China, Chengdu, China
lianli.gao@uestc.edu.cn

Mihai Marian Puscas
University of Trento
Trento, Italy
mihaimarian.puscas@unitn.it

Feiping Nie
Northwestern Polytechnical University
Xi'an, China
feipingnie@gmail.com

Fumin Shen
University of Electronic Science and Technology of China, Chengdu, China
fshen@uestc.edu.cn

Nicu Sebe
University of Trento
Trento, Italy
niculae.sebe@unitn.it

ABSTRACT

Video segmentation has become an important and active research area with a large diversity of proposed approaches. Graph-based methods, enabling top performance on recent benchmarks, usually focus on either obtaining a precise similarity graph or designing efficient graph cutting strategies. However, these two components are often conducted in two separated steps, and thus the obtained similarity graph may not be the optimal one for segmentation and this may lead to suboptimal results. In this paper, we propose a novel framework, *joint graph learning and video segmentation (JGLVS)*, which learns the similarity graph and video segmentation simultaneously. JGLVS learns the similarity graph by assigning adaptive neighbors for each vertex based on multiple cues (appearance, motion, boundary and spatial information). Meanwhile, the new rank constraint is imposed to the Laplacian matrix of the similarity graph, such that the connected components in the resulted similarity graph are exactly equal to the number of segmentations. Furthermore, JGLVS can automatically weigh multiple cues and calibrate the pairwise distance of superpixels based on their topology structures. Most noticeably, empirical results on the challenging dataset VSB100 show that JGLVS achieves promising performance on the benchmark dataset which outperforms the state-of-the-art by up to 11% for the BPR metric.

CCS Concepts

•**Computing methodologies** → **Video segmentation;**

Keywords

Video segmentation; Graph-based method; multiple cues; Topology

MM '16, October 15-19, 2016, Amsterdam, Netherlands

© 2016 ACM. ISBN 978-1-4503-3603-1/16/10...$15.00

DOI: http://dx.doi.org/10.1145/2964284.2964295

1. INTRODUCTION

Video segmentation can be defined as partitioning a video into several disjoint spatial-temporal regions such that each region has consistent appearance and motion. In the last few years, it has achieved an extraordinary success and has become a fundamental problem in a wide range of applications, such as object tracking, activity recognition and video summarization [15, 34, 31, 17]. Segmenting general and unconstrained videos is a challenging research problem due to existent scene and scale ambiguities of the segments [40] as well as the temporal-consistency constraints [14]. Different types of video segmentation algorithms have been recently introduced, from ones based on clustering [30, 9], to graph-based processing [14, 19, 10, 41] and tracking [3, 32, 34].

Among the existing video segmentation techniques, many successful ones benefit from mapping the video elements onto a graph which pixels/superpixels are nodes and edge weights measure the similarity between nodes. Cutting or merging is then applied on this graph to generate the video segments. Most of the existing graph-based methods focus on (i) what features to extract from each node; (ii) how to define a precise similarity graph and (iii) how to cut/merge the nodes effectively.

Meaningful features are necessary for good video segmentation. Previous work has extracted a variety of features [9, 40] from superpixels. To get the similarity graph, a graph topology is firstly designed according to the spatio-temporal neighborhood of the superpixels and the extracted features are used to weigh their edges. While standard similarity measures on the extracted features provide the basic way to calculate the similarity graph [30, 9], more recent work introduces learning a more precise similarity graph in either a supervised [19] or an unsupervised manner [20]. While supervised video segmentation methods [19, 40] can generally achieve better performance, the human annotation is time-consuming and the inherent video object hierarchy may be highly subjective. In contrast, a group of methods improve on cutting techniques [41, 10, 30, 14], which explicitly organize the image elements into mathematically sound structures based on the optimization of the predefined cutting loss function. One representative criterion is the normalized cut [14]. By minimizing a cutting cost objective function, the best segmentation can be obtained. This objective function is further proved to be equivalent to the generalized eigenvalue decomposition problem and a number of follow-ups proposed efficient solutions for this problem [23]. To reduce the computational cost, in [41, 10], fast partitioning methods that identify and remove between-cluster edges to form node clusters are proposed.

Graph cut methods provide well-defined relationships between the segments, but the problem of finding a cut in an arbitrary graph may be NP-hard. More importantly, because the graph similarity learning [13, 33, 35, 12, 25, 26] and the graph cutting are conducted in two separated steps, the learned graph similarity matrix may not be the optimal one for cutting, leading to suboptimal results. To tackle this problem, in this paper we propose a novel video segmentation framework: *Joint Graph Learning and Video Segmentation* (JGLVS), which learns the similarity graph and segmentations simultaneously. To summarize, the main contributions of this paper are:

- Our unsupervised video segmentation framework learns the similarity graph and cutting structure simultaneously to achieve the optimal segmentation results. We derive a novel and efficient algorithm to solve this challenging problem.
- We utilized multiple cues of the superpixels and the weights of different cues are automatically learned. Furthermore, we calibrate the similarity of different superpixels based on their topology structures to make them comparable.
- The proposed JGLVS achieves up to 11% improvement over the state-of-the-art baselines on the largest public dataset VSB100, which validates the effectiveness and efficiency of our approach.

The remainder of this paper is organized as follows. Section 2 discusses some related works. The details of JGLVS are introduced in section 3. Section 4 illustrates the experiments results and we draw a conclusion in section 5.

2. RELATED WORK

The relevant state-of-the-art methods on video segmentation are reviewed in this section. The problem definitions for video segmentation have been diverse.

Motion segmentation focuses on separating point trajectories from an image sequence with respect to their motion [24, 18, 29, 4]. In [29, 4], the segmentation is based on pairwise affinities, while in [28] third order terms are employed to explain not only translational motion but also in-plane rotation and scaling, and [42] models even more general 3D motions using group invariants. The actual grouping in these methods is done using spectral clustering. Differently, in [18], they formulate the segmentation of a video sequence based on point trajectories as a minimum cost multicut problem. Unlike the commonly used spectral clustering formulation, the minimum cost multicut formulation gives natural rise to optimize not only for a cluster assignment but also for the number of clusters while allowing for varying cluster sizes. Similarly, in [5], they utilize improved point trajectories to segment moving object in video by a graph-based segmentation method. And in [8], motion trajectory grouping in a setup similar to [4] is used to perform tracking. Although the grouping in [8] is computed using spectral clustering, repulsive weights computed from segmentation topology are used in the affinity matrix. In [24], they introduced minimal supervision, which is shown to be helpful to improve the performance of motion segmentations. In [22], they propose a framework to segment the objects in relative video shots, while discarding the irrelative video shots.

On the other hand, [41, 20, 9, 10] seek to construct full pixelwise segmentation, where every pixel (not only the moving objects) is assigned one of several labels. They can generally be divided into unsupervised and supervised methods.

A large body of literature exists on unsupervised video segmentation, with methods that leverage appearance [3, 14, 32, 38], motion [3, 16], or multiple cues [41, 20, 9, 10]. Unsupervised supervoxel generation [9, 2] has been widely accepted as a valuable preprocessing step for various techniques, such as graph-based methods [10, 9, 41, 14], hierarchical methods [14, 27, 38] and streaming methods [10, 38, 20]. Graph-based methods map the video elements onto a graph in which pixels/superpixels are nodes, and edge weights measure the similarity between them. Galasso *et al.* [9] proposed a frame-based superpixel segmentation approach (VSS) by extending the ultra-metric contour map [1] to combine with motion-cues and appearance-based affinities for obtaining better video segmentation performance. To deal with the high computational costs of spectral techniques, Galasso *et al.* [10] proposed a spectral graph reduction (SGR) method for video segmentation. They assumed that all pixels within a superpixel are connected by must-link constraints, and then reduced the original graph to a relative small graph such that a density-normalized-cut was preserved. Yu *et al.* [41] proposed an efficient and robust video segmentation framework based on parametric graph partitioning, resulting in a fast and almost parameter free method. On the other hand, hierarchical video segmentation provides a rich multi-scale decomposition of a given video. Grundmann *et al.* [14] proposed a hierarchical graph-based (HGB) video segmentation approach by firstly over-segmenting a volumetric video graph into space-time regions grouped by appearance, and then constructing a "region graph" over the obtained segmentation. Iteratively repeating this process over multiple levels results in a a tree of spatio-temporal segmentations. In order to process long videos, Xu *et al.* [38] proposed a streaming hierarchical video segmentation framework by integrating a graph-based hierarchical segmentation method with a data streaming algorithm (SHGB). This method leveraged ideas from data streams and enforced a Markovian assumption on the video stream to approximate full video segmentation. Li *et al.* [20] proposed a Sub-Optimal Low-rank Decomposition (SOLD) method, which defines a low-rank model based on very generic assumption that the intra-class supervoxels are drawn from one identical low rank feature subspace, and all supervoxels in a period lie on a union of multiple subspaces, which can be justified by natural statistic and observations of videos. In addition, this method adopts the Normalized-Cut (NCut) algorithm with a solved low-rank representation to segment a video into several spatio-temporal regions. To tackle the lack of a common dataset with sufficient annotation and the lack of an evaluation metric, a united video segmentation benchmark was provided by Galasso *et al.* [11] to effectively evaluate the over- and under-segmentation performance of video segmentation methods.

Supervised video segmentations [19, 21] can achieve better performance, but the human annotation is time-consuming and the inherent video object hierarchy may be highly subjective. In [21], they address the problem of integrating object reasoning with supervoxel labeling in multiclass semantic video segmentation. They first propose an object augmented dense CRF in spatio-temporal domain, which captures long-range dependency between supervoxels, and imposes consistency between object and supervoxel labels. Then, they develop an efficient mean field inference algorithm to jointly infer the supervoxel labels, object activations and their occlusion relations for a moderate number of object hypotheses. While in [19], they propose to combine features by means of a classifier, use calibrated classifier outputs as edge weights and define the graph topology by edge selection. Learning the topology provides larger performance gains and benefits efficiency due to a sparser structure of the constructed graph. On the other hand, lots of supervised image segmentations have been proposed [37]. In [39], they propose a novel discriminative deep feature learning framework based on stacked autoencoders (SAE) to tackle the problem of weakly supervised semantic segmentation. In [37], they use CNN to train images most only with image-level labels and very few with pixel-level labels for semantic segmentation.

Unsupervised full pixelwise segmentation is the research focus of this paper. A substantial difference between our approach and previous unsupervised work is that, instead of separately obtaining a graph and finding a cut in it, we propose a joint graph learning and video segmentation method by assigning adaptive neighbors for each superpixel and imposing a rank constraint on the Laplacian matrix of the similarity graph, such that the learned graph has exactly K connected components, representing K segmentations.

3. OUR APPROACH

In this section, we first introduce our JGLVS framework, and then elaborate on the details of each component.

3.1 The framework

In our JGLVS framework (see Fig. 1), we propose a novel perspective in solving the graph-based video segmentation problem. Our model makes use of superpixels instead of pixels for two reasons: a great decrease in the number of graph nodes that need to be processed, and an initial, accurate frame-level segmentation.

Firstly, in each temporal sliding window of the video, we extract N superpixels from M successive frames by setting a specific hierarchical level of an image segmentation algorithm [2]. Note that a too small value of N leads to large superpixels, and more under-segmentation errors, while a large value of N is computationally expensive. Then, for each superpixle, a set of features (e.g., appearance, motion and shape features) are extracted. Using these features and the predefined topology structure, our JGLVS framework can learn a similarity graph of superpixels which has exactly K connected components.

3.2 Feature extraction and graph topology construction

For each superpixel, we follow [2, 9] to extract *LAB*, *boundary*, *motion* and *shape* features, and use them to calculate the distance between two superpixels. However, not all of the superpixels are connected. By allowing different edge connections between neighbors, different graph topologies are constructed. Following [14, 19], edges may connect neighbors: *within frame* (if two superpixels share a common part of their contour or are close by in the spatial domain of the frame); *across 1 frame* (connected by coordinate correspondences over time); *across 2 frames* (connected by across-1 correspondences, further propagated over one more frame) and *across > 2 frames* (linked if overlapping with common long-term point trajectories).

We refer to these four types of neighbours as different topological structures $(1, 2, 3, 4)$ and record the topological structure of each pair of superpixels in a $N \times N$ matrix $\mathbf{W}$. Based on these features and topological structures, we can have the following pairwise distances between superpixels: common boundary strength (*cbs*), LAB (*lab*), boundary optical flow (*bof*), superpixel optical flow (*sof*), superpixel shape distance (*ssd*) and superpixel trajectory intersection (*sti*) (See Section 4 for details).

As shown in Table 1, different topological types have different distances. We further define a set of most-likely-linked superpixels $\mathbb{M}^1, \mathbb{M}^2, \mathbb{M}^3$ and $\mathbb{M}^4$ for each topological structure. More specifically, for the case of within frame, we decrease the number of superpixels by changing the threshold of superpixel generation algorithm, and some similar superpixels will merge into one superpixel. These similar superpixels will be selected as the within frame most-likely-linked superpixels. For the case of across 1 or 2 frame, if two superpixels' *ssd* distance is less than a threshold, they will be selected as a pair of across 1 or 2 frame most-likely-linked superpixels. Similarly, if two superpixels' *sti* distance is less than a threshold in the case of across > 2 frame, they will be selected as a pair of across > 2 frame most-likely-linked superpixels.

Table 1: The corresponding distances for different topological structures

Topology type	Distances
Within frame	lab, sof, cbs, bof
Across 1 frame	lab, sof, ssd, sti
Across 2 frames	ssd, sti
Across > 2 frames	sti

3.3 Joint graph learning and video segmentation

Let $\mathbf{D}^t = \{\mathbf{D}_{ij}^t\}_{i,j=1}^N$ denote the t-th distance matrix of a set of N superpixels, where $t \in \{1, ..., T\}$. $\mathbf{Y} = \{\mathbf{y}_1, \mathbf{y}_2, ..., \mathbf{y}_N\}$ is the average location information for the superpixels. The goal is to learn the similarity matrix $\mathbf{S}$ between superpixels by using different distances as well as existent spatial information, and that all the superpixels have exact K connected components.

An optimal graph $\mathbf{S}$ should be smooth on different features as well as on the spatial information distribution, which can be formulated as:

$$\min_{\mathbf{S},\alpha} \mathbf{g}\left(\mathbf{Y},\mathbf{S}\right) + \mu \sum_{t=1}^{T} \alpha^t \mathbf{h}\left(\mathbf{D}^t,\mathbf{S}\right) + \beta \mathbf{r}\left(\mathbf{S},\alpha\right) \tag{1}$$

where $\mathbf{g}\left(\mathbf{Y},\mathbf{S}\right)$ is the penalty function that measures the smoothness of $\mathbf{S}$ on the spatial information $\mathbf{Y}$ and $\mathbf{h}\left(\mathbf{D}^t,\mathbf{S}\right)$ is the loss function that measures the smoothness of $\mathbf{S}$ on the feature $\mathbf{D}^t$. $\mathbf{r}\left(\mathbf{S},\alpha\right)$ is a regularizer defined on the target $\mathbf{S}$ and α. μ and β are balancing parameters, and α^t determines the importance of each feature.

The penalty function $\mathbf{g}\left(\mathbf{F},\mathbf{S}\right)$ should be defined in a way such that close superpixels have high similarity and vice versa. In this paper, we define it as follows:

$$\mathbf{g}\left(\mathbf{Y},\mathbf{S}\right) = \sum_{ij} \left\|\mathbf{y}_i - \mathbf{y}_j\right\|_2^2 s_{ij} \tag{2}$$

where $\mathbf{y}_i$ and $\mathbf{y}_j$ are the locations of the superpixels $\mathbf{x}_i$ and $\mathbf{x}_j$. Similarly, $\mathbf{h}\left(\mathbf{D}^t,\mathbf{S}\right)$ is defined as:

$$\mathbf{h}\left(\mathbf{D}^t,\mathbf{S}\right) = \sum_{ij} d_{ij}^t s_{ij} \tag{3}$$

The regularizer term $\mathbf{r}\left(\mathbf{S},\alpha\right)$ is defined as:

$$\mathbf{r}\left(\mathbf{S},\alpha\right) = \left\|\mathbf{S}\right\|_F^2 + \gamma \left\|\alpha\right\|_2^2 \tag{4}$$

If there is no regularizer on $\mathbf{S}$ (same for α), $\mathbf{S}$ has a trivial solution. Only the nearest data point can be the neighbor of $\mathbf{x}_i$ with the probability of 1. We further introduce the following constraints: $\mathbf{S} \geq 0$, $\mathbf{S1} = \mathbf{1}$, $\alpha \geq 0$ and $\alpha^T \mathbf{1} = 1$, where $\mathbf{1}$ is a column vector with all 1s. This is because that the similarity and weights should be positive, and the sum of similarity and weights is set to be 1.

We can then obtain the objective function for learning the optimal graph by replacing $\mathbf{g}\left(\mathbf{Y},\mathbf{S}\right)$, $\mathbf{h}\left(\mathbf{D}^t,\mathbf{S}\right)$ and $\mathbf{r}\left(\mathbf{S},\alpha\right)$ in (1) using

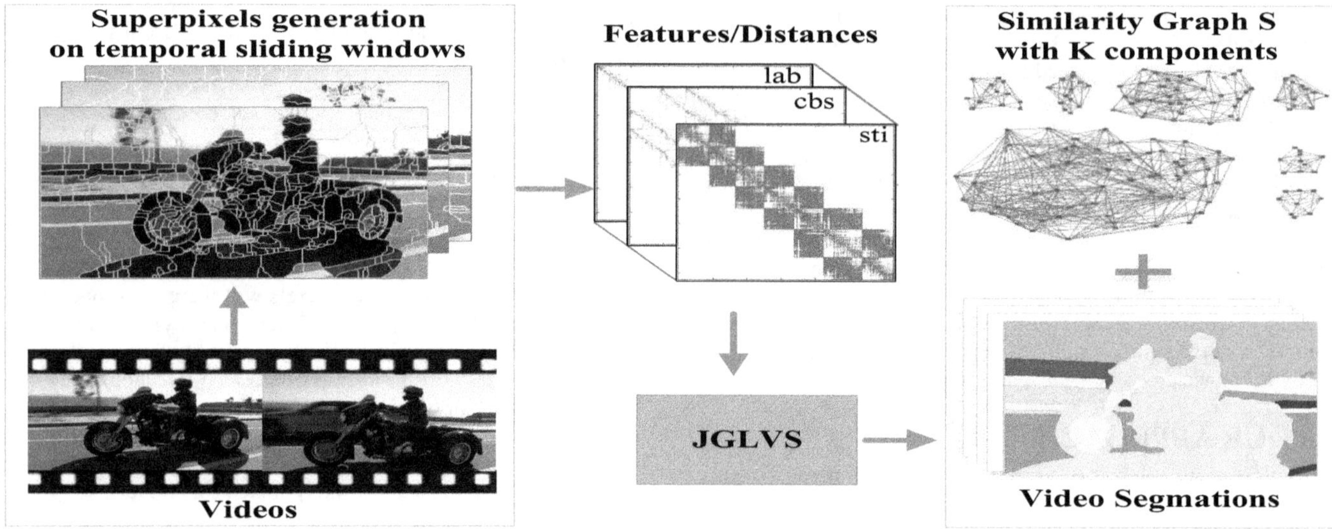

Figure 1: The overview of JGLVS. Superpixels are firstly generated from the overlapping sliding windows, based on which the features and distances are computed. Then, JGLVS is applied to learn the similarity matrix and video segmentations.

(2), (3) and (4), as follows:

$$\begin{aligned} &\min_{\mathbf{S},\alpha} \sum_{ij} \|\mathbf{y}_i - \mathbf{y}_j\|_2^2 s_{ij} + \mu \sum_{tij} (\alpha^t d_{ij}^t s_{ij}) \\ &+\beta \|\mathbf{S}\|_F^2 + \beta\gamma \|\alpha\|_2^2 \\ &s.t., \ \mathbf{S} \geq 0, \mathbf{S1} = \mathbf{1}, \alpha \geq 0, \alpha^T \mathbf{1} = 1 \end{aligned} \tag{5}$$

One limitation for this model is that it assumes that all the superpixels have the same types of distances, which conflicts with the video segmentation application where different topologies have different distances. For example, if superpixels $(i,\ k)$ are across > 2 frames neighbors and $(i,\ j)$ are within frame neighbors, the similarity between $(i,\ k)$ are determined by *sti* but the similarity between $(i,\ j)$ are determined by *lab, sof, cbs* and *bof*. Their distances are not comparable to each other, and we need to calibrate them. Based on the topology type $w_{ij} \in [1,2,3,4]$ of superpixels i and j, we define a calibration function

$$\mathbf{c}^z(x) = (x - \tau^z)/(max^z - \tau^z), z \in [1,2,3,4], \tag{6}$$

where τ^z is the threshold for z-th topology type determined by the mean distance of the set $\mathbb{M}^z$. Then, the objective function becomes:

$$\begin{aligned} &\min_{\mathbf{S},\alpha} \sum_{ij} \|y_i - y_j\|_2^2 s_{ij} + \mu \sum_{ij} \mathbf{c}^{w_{ij}} \left(\sum_t \alpha^t d_{ij}^t \right) s_{ij} \\ &+\beta \|\mathbf{S}\|_F^2 + \beta\gamma \|\alpha\|_2^2 \\ &s.t., \ \mathbf{S} \geq 0, \mathbf{S1} = \mathbf{1}, \alpha \geq 0, \alpha^T \mathbf{1} = 1 \end{aligned} \tag{7}$$

Forcing the number of connected components to be exactly K seems like an impossible goal since this kind of structured constraint on the similarities is fundamental but also very difficult to handle. In this paper, we will propose a novel but very simple method to achieve this goal.

The matrix $\mathbf{S} \in \mathbb{R}^{N \times N}$ obtained in the neighbor assignment can be seen as a similarity matrix of the graph with the N data points as the nodes. For a nonnegative similarity matrix **S**, there is a Laplacian matrix **L** associated with it. According to the definition of Laplacian matrix, for any values of $\mathbf{f}_i \in \mathbb{R}^{K \times 1}$, **L** of a similarity matrix **S** can be calculated as:

$$\sum\nolimits_{ij} \|\mathbf{f}_i - \mathbf{f}_j\|_2^2 s_{ij} = 2tr\left(\mathbf{F}^T \mathbf{L} \mathbf{F}\right) \tag{8}$$

where $\mathbf{F} \in \mathbb{R}^{N \times K}$ with the i-th row formed by $\mathbf{f}_i$, $\mathbf{L} = \mathbf{D} - \frac{\mathbf{S}^T + \mathbf{S}}{2}$ is called the Laplacian matrix in graph theory, the degree matrix $\mathbf{D} \in \mathbb{R}^{N \times N}$ is defined as a diagonal matrix where the i-th diagonal element is $\sum_j (s_{ji} + s_{ij})/2$. The Laplacian matrix **L** has the following property.

THEOREM 1. *The number K of the eigenvalue 0 of the Laplacian matrix **L** is equal to the number of connected components in the graph with the similarity matrix **S** if **S** is nonnegative.*

Theorem 1 indicates that if $rank(\mathbf{L}) = N - K$, then the superpixels have K connected components based on S. Motivated by Theorem 1, we add an additional constraint $rank(\mathbf{L}) = N - K$ into the (7). Thus, our new similarity graph learning model is to solve:

$$\begin{aligned} &\min_{\mathbf{S},\alpha} \sum_{ij} \|\mathbf{y}_i - \mathbf{y}_j\|_2^2 s_{ij} + \mu \sum_{ij} \mathbf{c}^{w_{ij}} \left(\sum_t \alpha^t d_{ij}^t \right) s_{ij} \\ &+\beta \|\mathbf{S}\|_F^2 + \beta\gamma \|\alpha\|_2^2 \\ &s.t. \begin{cases} \mathbf{S} \geq 0, \mathbf{S1} = \mathbf{1}, \alpha \geq 0, \alpha^T \mathbf{1} = 1 \\ rank(\mathbf{L}) = N - K \end{cases} \end{aligned} \tag{9}$$

It is difficult to solve the problem (9). Because $\mathbf{L} = \mathbf{D} - (\mathbf{S}^T + \mathbf{S})/2$ and **D** also depends on **S**, the constraint $rank(\mathbf{L}) = N - K$ is not easy to tackle. In the next subsection, we will propose a novel and efficient algorithm to solve this challenging problem.

3.4 Iterative optimization

Suppose e_i is the i-th smallest eigenvalue of **L**, we know $e_i \geq 0$ since **L** is positive semi-definite. It can be seen that the problem (9) is equivalent to the following problem for a large enough value of ρ:

$$\begin{aligned} &\min_{\mathbf{S},\alpha} \sum_{ij} \|\mathbf{y}_i - \mathbf{y}_j\|_2^2 s_{ij} + \mu \sum_{ij} \mathbf{c}^{w_{ij}} \left(\sum_t \alpha^t d_{ij}^t \right) s_{ij} \\ &+\beta \|\mathbf{S}\|_F^2 + \beta\gamma \|\alpha\|_2^2 + 2\rho \sum_{i=1}^{K} e_i \\ &s.t., \ \mathbf{S} \geq 0, \mathbf{S1} = \mathbf{1}, \alpha \geq 0, \alpha^T \mathbf{1} = 1 \end{aligned} \tag{10}$$

When ρ is set to a large enough value [1], $\sum_i^K e_i$ will be imposed to be close to 0, which results in $rank(\mathbf{L}) = N - K$.

According to the Ky Fan's Theorem [7], we have:

$$\sum_{i=1}^{K} e_i = \min_{\mathbf{F}\in\mathbb{R}^{N\times K}, \mathbf{F}^T\mathbf{F}=\mathbf{I}} tr\left(\mathbf{F}^T\mathbf{L}\mathbf{F}\right) \tag{11}$$

Therefore, the problem (10) is further equivalent to the following problem:

$$\begin{aligned} &\min_{\mathbf{S},\mathbf{F},\alpha} \sum_{ij} \left\|\mathbf{y}_i - \mathbf{y}_j\right\|_2^2 s_{ij} + \mu \sum_{ij} \mathbf{c}^{w_{ij}} \left(\sum_t \alpha^t d_{ij}^t\right) s_{ij} \\ &+\beta \left\|\mathbf{S}\right\|_F^2 + \beta\gamma \left\|\alpha\right\|_2^2 + 2\rho tr\left(\mathbf{F}^T\mathbf{L}\mathbf{F}\right) \\ &s.t., \begin{cases} \mathbf{S} \geq 0, \mathbf{S}\mathbf{1} = \mathbf{1}, \alpha \geq 0, \alpha^T\mathbf{1} = 1 \\ \mathbf{F} \in R^{N\times K}, \mathbf{F}^T\mathbf{F} = \mathbf{I} \end{cases} \end{aligned} \tag{12}$$

Compared with the original problem (9), (12) is much easier to solve. We propose an iterative method to minimize the above objective function (12).

Firstly, we initialize $\alpha^t = 1/T$ and then $\mathbf{S}$ by the optimal solution to the problem (7). Once these initial values are given, in each iteration, we first update $\mathbf{F}$ given $\mathbf{S}$ and α, and then update $\mathbf{S}$ and α by fixing the other parameters. These steps are described below:

Update F: By fixing $\mathbf{S}$ and α, the problem (12) is equivalent to optimizing the following objective function:

$$\min_{\mathbf{F}\in R^{N\times K}, \mathbf{F}^T\mathbf{F}=\mathbf{I}} tr\left(\mathbf{F}^T\mathbf{L}\mathbf{F}\right) \tag{13}$$

The optimal solution $\mathbf{F}$ to the problem (13) is formed by the K eigenvectors of $\mathbf{L}$ corresponding to the K smallest eigenvalues.

Update S: By fixing $\mathbf{F}$ and α, we can obtain $\mathbf{S}$ by optimizing (12). It is equivalent to optimize the following objective function:

$$\begin{aligned} &\min_{\mathbf{S}\geq 0, \mathbf{S}\mathbf{1}=\mathbf{1}} \sum_{ij} \left\|\mathbf{y}_i - \mathbf{y}_j\right\|_2^2 s_{ij} + \rho \sum_{ij} \left\|\mathbf{f}_i - \mathbf{f}_j\right\|_2^2 s_{ij} \\ &+\beta \left\|\mathbf{S}\right\|_F^2 + \mu \sum_{ij} \mathbf{c}^{w_{ij}} \left(\sum_t \alpha^t d_{ij}^t\right) s_{ij} \end{aligned} \tag{14}$$

It can be reformulated as:

$$\begin{aligned} &\min_{\mathbf{S}\geq 0, \mathbf{S}\mathbf{1}=\mathbf{1}} \sum_i \left(\beta \mathbf{s}_i \mathbf{s}_i{}^T + \left(\mathbf{a}_i + \mu\mathbf{b}_i + \rho\mathbf{c}_i\right) \mathbf{s}_i{}^T\right) \\ &\Rightarrow \min_{\mathbf{S}\geq 0, \mathbf{S}\mathbf{1}=\mathbf{1}} \sum_i \left(\mathbf{s}_i \mathbf{s}_i{}^T + \tfrac{\mathbf{a}_i + \mu\mathbf{b}_i + \rho\mathbf{c}_i}{\beta} \mathbf{s}_i{}^T\right) \end{aligned} \tag{15}$$

where $\mathbf{a}_i = \{a_{ij}, 1 \leq j \leq n\}$ with $a_{ij} = \left\|\mathbf{y}_i - \mathbf{y}_j\right\|_2^2$, $\mathbf{b}_i = \{b_{ij}, 1 \leq j \leq n\}$ with $b_{ij} = \sum_t \alpha^t d_{ij}^t$ and $\mathbf{c}_i = \{c_{ij}, 1 \leq j \leq n\} \in \mathbb{R}^{1\times n}$ with $c_{ij} = \left\|\mathbf{f}_i - \mathbf{f}_j\right\|_2^2$. It is further equivalent to:

$$\min_{\mathbf{S}\geq 0, \mathbf{S}\mathbf{1}=\mathbf{1}} \sum_i \left(\mathbf{s}_i + \tfrac{\mathbf{a}_i + \mu\mathbf{b}_i + \rho\mathbf{c}_i}{2\beta}\right)_2^2 \tag{16}$$

Then each $\mathbf{s}_i$ can be efficiently solved by using a quadratic programming solver, which will be introduced in the next subsection (solution for problem (16)).

Update α: By fixing $\mathbf{F}$ and $\mathbf{S}$, we can obtain α by optimizing (12). It is equivalent to optimize the following objective function:

$$\begin{aligned} &\min_{\alpha\geq 0, \alpha^T\mathbf{1}=1} \mu \sum_{ij} \mathbf{c}^{w_{ij}} \left(\sum_t \alpha^t d_{ij}^t\right) s_{ij} + \beta\gamma \left\|\alpha\right\|_2^2 \\ &\Rightarrow \min_{\alpha\geq 0, \alpha^T\mathbf{1}=1} \mu \sum_t \alpha^t \sum_{ij} d_{ij}^t s_{ij} / (\max{}^{w_{ij}} - \tau^{w_{ij}}) + \beta\gamma \left\|\alpha\right\|_2^2 \\ &\Rightarrow \min_{\alpha\geq 0, \alpha^T\mathbf{1}=1} \mu d\alpha + \beta\gamma \left\|\alpha\right\|_2^2 \end{aligned} \tag{17}$$

[1] In the real implementation, we initialize ρ with 1000, and increase ρ to $\rho \times 2$ if the current number of connected components is less than K, and decrease rho to $\rho/2$ if the current number of connected components is larger than K

where $d = \left\{d^t\right\}_{t=1}^T$, $d^t = \sum_{ij} d_{ij}^t s_{ij} / (\max{}^{w_{ij}} - \tau^{w_{ij}})$ and $\max{}^{w_{ij}}$ is the max value of $\mathbf{S}$ with the topological structure w_{ij}. Then we can use a quadratic programming solver to obtain α.

We update $\mathbf{F}, \mathbf{S}$ and α iteratively until the objective function (7) converges, as shown in Algorithm 1.

Algorithm 1 Solution for JGLVS

Input: Initialized α, segmentation number K, topology structure matrix $\mathbf{W}$, most-likely-linked sets $\mathbb{M}$, parameters β, γ, μ, a large enough ρ;

Output: $\mathbf{S} \in \mathbb{R}^{N\times N}$ with exact K connected components, α;

```
Initialize c^z(x) using α, W and M;
Initialize S by the optimal solution of 7;
repeat
    Fix S and α, calculate F according to the solution of problem (13);
    Fix F and α, update S by solving the problem (16);
    Fix F and S, update α by solving the problem (17);
    Update c^z(x) using α, W and M;
until convergence or max iteration is reached.
return S, α;
```

3.4.1 *Solution for problem (16)*

In this subsection, we introduce an efficient solution for problem (16) for determining the regularization parameter β, so that we have fewer parameters to tune. The Lagrangian function of problem (16) is:

$$\begin{aligned} \ell\left(\mathbf{s}_i, \eta, \varepsilon_i\right) = \tfrac{1}{2} \sum_i \left\|\mathbf{s}_i + \tfrac{\mathbf{a}_i + \mu\mathbf{b}_i + \rho\mathbf{c}_i}{2\beta}\right\|_2^2 \\ -\eta(\mathbf{s}_i^T\mathbf{1} - 1) - \mathbf{s}_i^T \varepsilon_i \end{aligned} \tag{18}$$

where η, $\varepsilon_i \geq 0$ are the Lagrangian multipliers, and β is the regularization parameter for each $\mathbf{s}_i$. Let $d_{ij} = a_{ij} + \mu b_{ij} + \rho c_{ij}$. According to the KKT condition, it can be verified that the optimal solution $\mathbf{s}_i$ should be:

$$s_{ij} = \left(-\frac{a_{ij} + \mu b_{ij} + \rho c_{ij}}{2\beta} + \eta\right)_+ \tag{19}$$

By replacing η and ε_i according to the KKT condition, we obtain the optimal $\mathbf{s}_i$. However, in practice, we usually could achieve better performance if $\mathbf{s}_i$ is sparse, i.e., only the P nearest neighbors of $\mathbf{x}_i$ could have chance to connect to $\mathbf{x}_i$. Another benefit of learning a sparse similarity matrix $\mathbf{S}$ is that the computational burden can be largely alleviated for subsequent processing. With this motivation, we determine the parameter β.

Without loss of generality, suppose $d_{i1}, d_{i2}, ..., d_{iN}$ are ordered from small to large. If the optimal $\mathbf{s}_i$ has only P nonzero elements, then according to (19), we know $s_{iP} > 0$ and $s_{i,P+1} = 0$. Therefore, we have:

$$-\tfrac{d_{iP}}{2\beta_P} + \eta > 0, \; -\tfrac{d_{i,P+1}}{2\beta_{P+1}} + \eta \leq 0 \tag{20}$$

and

$$\begin{aligned} &\mathbf{s}_i^T 1 = \sum_{j=1}^{P} \left(-\tfrac{d_{ij}}{2\beta_i} + \eta\right) = 1 \\ &\Rightarrow \eta = \tfrac{1}{P} + \tfrac{1}{2P\beta_i} \sum_{j=1}^{P} d_{ij} \end{aligned} \tag{21}$$

By replacing η in (20) using (21), we have the following inequality for β_i:

$$\frac{P}{2}d_{ip} - \frac{1}{2}\sum_{j=1}^{P} d_{ij} < \beta_i \leq \frac{P}{2}d_{i,P+1} - \frac{1}{2}\sum_{j=1}^{P} d_{ij} \tag{22}$$

Therefore, in order to obtain an optimal solution $\mathbf{s}_i$ to the problem (16) that has exact P nonzero values, we set

$$\beta_i = \frac{P}{2}d_{i,P+1} - \frac{1}{2}\sum\nolimits_{j=1}^{P} d_{ij} \tag{23}$$

The overall β is set to the mean of $\beta_1, \beta_2, ..., \beta_n$. That is, we set β to be

$$\beta = \frac{1}{N}\sum\nolimits_{i=1}^{N}\left(\frac{P}{2}d_{i,P+1} - \frac{1}{2}\sum\nolimits_{j=1}^{P} d_{ij}\right) \tag{24}$$

The number of neighbors P is much easier to tune than the regularization parameter β since P is an integer and has explicit meaning.

3.5 Streaming video segmentation

An effective streaming algorithm can enable us to process an arbitrary long video with limited memory and computational resources, and thus is essential in video segmentation. We propose a simple yet effective clip-based segmentation method that scales well while maintaining temporal coherence, without processing the entire volume at once.

Figure 2: The segmentation labels L_1, L_2 of the overlapping frame f. L_1 denotes the segmentation of the overlapping in the previous clip, and provides some constraints to the segmentation of L_2, which is the segmentation in the current clip.

We start by partitioning the video into equally sized clips of n frames (n = 6 in our experiments), and one frame f is overlapped between neighboring clips. The temporal consistent constraints are introduced by properly propagating solutions from previous temporal window to the current window. Given the previous and current segmentation labels L_1, L_2 of the overlapping frame f, we first compute the similarity matrix O of different segments. The similarity of the i-th segment i_{L_1} in the previous segmentation and the j-th segment j_{L_2} in the current segmentation is defined as:

$$o(i_{L_1}, j_{L_2}) = |m_{i_{L_1}} \cap m_{j_{L_2}}| / min\left(|m_{i_{L_1}}|, |m_{j_{L_2}}|\right), \tag{25}$$

where $m_{i_{L_1}}$ and $m_{j_{L_2}}$ are masks to indicate which pixels belong to the segments i_{L_1} and j_{L_2}. After obtaining the similarity matrix O, we can assign new segmentation ids to the segments in L_2. Intuitively, two segments with the highest similarity should have the same segment id. However, there are three special cases to consider, which are illustrated in Fig. 2. The first case is that a segment (e.g., 3_{L_2}) has no overlapping in the previous segment. Then a new segment id should be assigned to 3_{L_2}. The second case is that two segments (e.g., 1_{L_2} and 2_{L_2}) are included by one previous segment (1_{L_1}). Then the one (2_{L_2}) with larger size will be assigned the id (1) of overlapping segment (1_{L_1}), and the one (1_{L_2}) with smaller size will be assigned a new id. Lastly, if one segment (e.g., 4_{L_2}) includes two previous segments (2_{L_1} and 3_{L_1}), this segment will be assigned the id (2) of a larger segment (2_{L_1}). The algorithm for generating temporal consistent constraints is given in Algorithm 2. It takes previous and current segmentation labels L_1 and L_2, and similarity threshold $threshold$ as input. And it calculates which segment id in L_1 corresponds to each segment in L_2. Algorithm 2 outputs the refined segmentation labels L_2' as well as the segment id mapping $mapping$.

Algorithm 2 The algorithm for generation of the temporal consistent constraints between previous and current segmentation labels L_1, L_2 of the overlapping frame f.

Input: Previous and current segmentation labels L_1 and L_2, threshold $threshold$;
Output: Refined segmentation labels L_2', $mapping$;

```
Get number of segments num1 and num2 in L1 and L2;
Computer O by Eq.(25);
Assign mapping the ids with the largest similarity to L2 by
  [value, mapping] = max(O);
for i = 1 : num2 do
  if value(i) is smaller than threshold, then
    Updating mapping(i) with a new id;
  end if
  if mapping(i) is used by a previous segment, then
    Assign a new id to the segment with a smaller size;
  end if
  if Another segment in L1 has the same similarity to segment
    i as mapping(i), then
    Updating mapping(i) with the id of a larger segment;
  end if
  Refine L2 to L2' based on mapping;
end for
return L2', mapping;
```

4. EXPERIMENTS

In this section, we evaluate our JGLVS on the standard benchmark VSB100 [11]. First, we compare our method with other state-of-the-art methods. Then, we further analyze the effectiveness of our main components. Finally, we report the efficiency of our method.

4.1 Experimental Settings

We give the details of dataset selection, feature extraction and evaluation metrics in this subsection.

4.1.1 Dataset:

The selected VSB100 [11] is a very challenging dataset used for empirical evaluation. It is the largest video segmentation dataset with high definition frames, and consists of four difficult sub-datasets: general, motion segmentation, non-rigid motion segmentation and camera motion segmentation. Following the setting in [11, 20], we regard the general sub-dataset (60 video sequences) as our test set for all the approaches.

To make the comparison comprehensive, we set $\{\mu, \gamma\} = \{1000, 1\}$, $\{\rho\} = \{1000\}$ and $\{iteration\} = \{30\}$ in the experiment. β is automatically determined by the algorithm. In addition, the number of frames per window is set to be 6, and 1 frame is overlapped between neighboring windows.

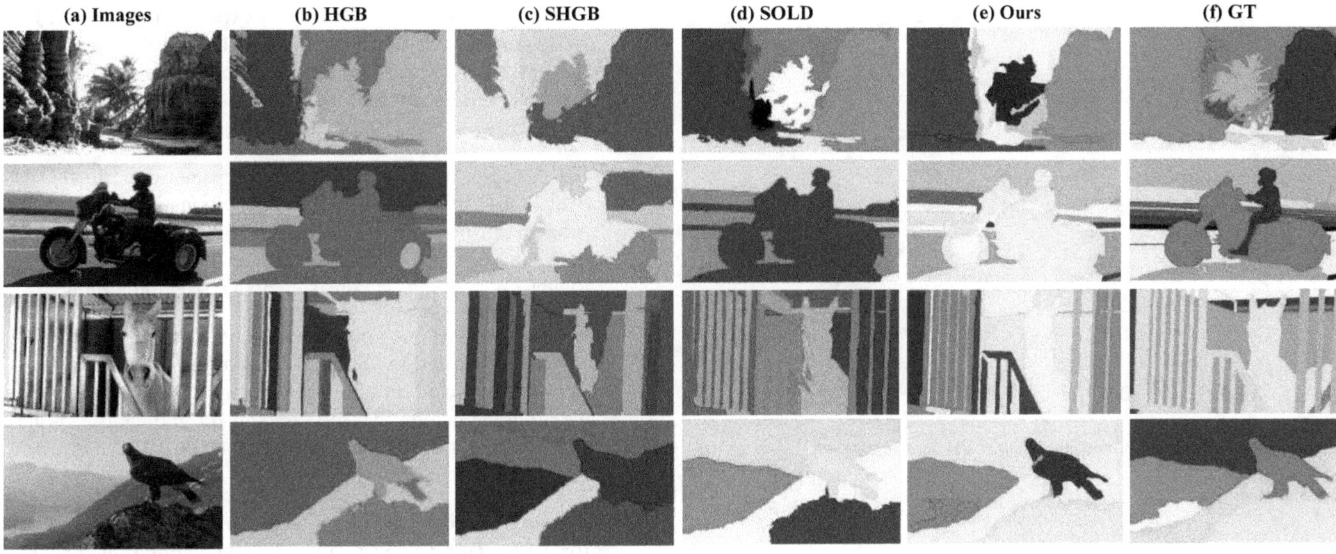

Figure 3: Qualitative comparisons with the state-of-the-art video segmentation methods HGB, SHGB and SOLD. We can see that our method substantially outperforms the algorithms of HGB, SHGB and SOLD.

Table 2: Comparison of state-of-the-art video segmentation algorithms with our proposed method on the test set of VSB100.

	BPR			**VPR**		
Algorithm	**ODS**	**OSS**	**AP**	**ODS**	**OSS**	**AP**
BMC [6]	0.47	0.48	0.32	0.51	0.52	0.38
VSS [9]	0.51	0.56	0.45	0.45	0.51	0.42
HGB [14]	0.47	0.54	0.41	0.52	0.55	**0.52**
SHGB[38]	0.38	0.46	0.32	0.45	0.48	0.44
SOLD [20]	0.54	0.58	0.40	0.53	0.60	0.46
Ours$_{-calibration}$	0.64	0.64	0.45	0.53	0.58	0.49
Ours$_{-consistency}$	0.65	0.65	**0.50**	0.51	0.53	0.47
Ours	**0.65**	**0.65**	0.48	**0.55**	**0.61**	0.51
Human	0.81	0.81	0.67	0.83	0.83	0.70

4.1.2 *Features and Distances:*

Common boundary strength [*cbs*]. This measures distance in the close vicinity of the common boundary between two superpixels i_f and j_f by averaging the common boundary strength. We take $\overline{\mathbf{v}}_f^{ij}$ the average UCM of [2] as a measure of the boundary strength between i and j and define: $cbs(i_f, j_f) = \overline{\mathbf{v}}_f^{ij}$.
Lab [*lab*]. This uses the distance between the median brightness and color of a superpixel in Lab-color-space as a measure of the overall distance among two superpixels i and j, from the same or different frames f and f': $lab(i_f, j_{f'}) = \|\overline{LAB}_{i_f} - \overline{LAB}_{j_{f'}}\|_2$.
Boundary optical flow [*bof*]. We consider an optical flow estimation [9]. The resulting $u_f(x)$ allows to compute the motion distance in the vicinity of the boundary between two superpixels by averaging their u_f across the common boundary φ_f^{ij}: $bof(i_f, j_f)= \left(\sum_{(x_i^m, x_i^m)\in\varphi_f^{ij}} \|\overline{u}^f\left(x_i^m\right) - \overline{u}^f\left(x_j^m\right)\|_2\right)/|\varphi_f^{ij}|$.
Superpixel optical flow [*sof*]. This measures the overall motion distance between two superpixels i_f and $j_{f'}$ based on their median optical flow u: $sof(i_f, j_{f'}) = \|\overline{u}_{i_f} - \overline{u}_{j_{f'}}\|_2$.
Superpixel shape distance [*ssd*]. We measure the shape distance by comparing $m_{j_{f'}}$ the shape of a superpixel j at frame f' with the shape of i_f propagated with optical flow to frame f' (its projected mask $m_{i_f}^{f'}$). *ssd* is given by the Dice coefficient between the true $m_{j_{f'}}$ and optical-flow-projected $m_{i_f}^{f'}$ binary mask: $ssd(i_f, j_{f'}) = 1 - 2|m_{i_f}^{f'} \cap m_{j_{f'}}|/\left(|m_{i_f}^{f'}| + |m_{j_{f'}}|\right)$.
Superpixel trajectories intersection [*sti*]. It measures the distance between superpixels i_f and $j_{f'}$ which belongs to frames potentially further in time from each other $f' = f + m, m > 2$. We consider the dense point trajectories of [36] as a measure of the shape (binary mask) projection. Let $\phi(i_f)$ be the subset of trajectories intersecting superpixel i_f. The distance is the Dice measure between the intersection sets $\phi(i_f)$ and $\phi(j'_f)$: $sti(i_f, j_{f'}) = 1 - 2|\phi(i_f) \cap \phi(j'_f)|/\left(|\phi(i_f)| + |\phi(j'_f)|\right)$.

4.1.3 *Evaluation Metrics:*

Following [11, 20], we use two evaluation metrics: 1) Boundary Precision-Recall (BPR), which casts the boundary detection problem as one of classifying boundary from nonboundary pixels and measures the quality of a segmentation boundary map in the precision-recall framework; and 2) Volume Precision-Recall (VPR), which optimally assigns spatio-temporal volumes between the computer generated segmentation and the human annotated segmentations and then measures their overlap. For both BPR and VPR, we report average precision (AP), optimal dataset scale (ODS), and optimal segmentation scale (OSS).

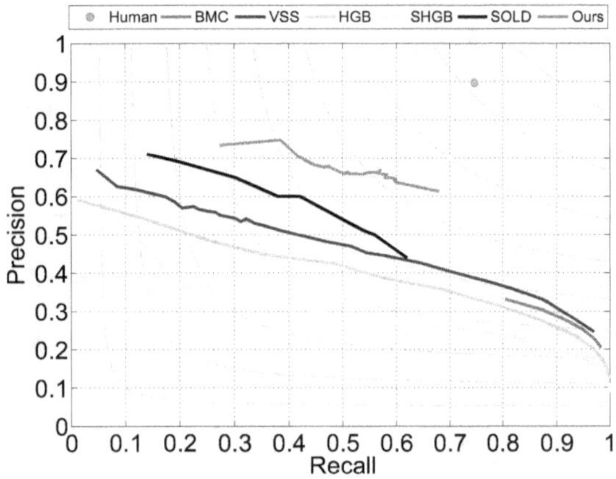

(a) Bourndary Global PR Curve

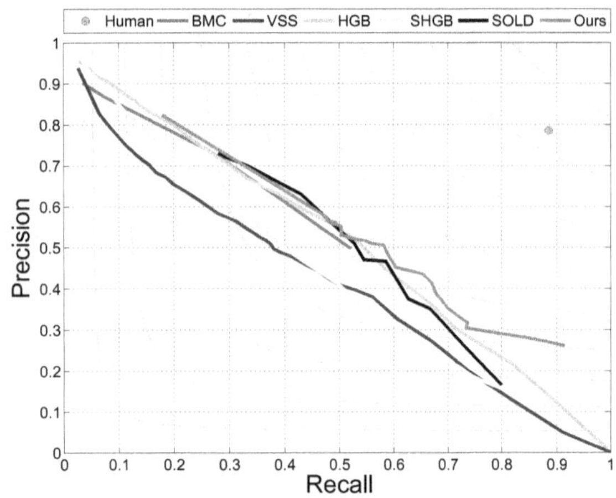

(b) Volume Global PR Curve

Figure 4: Comparison curves of our framework with the state-of-the-art video segmentation approaches BMC [6], VSS [9], HGB [14], SHGB [38] and SOLD [20].

4.2 Comparison with state-of-the-art video segmentation methods

We compare our approach with the following five state-of-the-art video segmentation algorithms: BMC [6], VSS [9], HGB [14], SHGB [38] and SOLD [20]. We also report our method without calibration (Ours$_{-calibration}$) and our method without temporal consistency (Ours$_{-consistency}$). Table 2 illustrates a summary of the aggregate evaluation performance, including ODS, OSS and AP of both BPR and VPR. Fig.4 shows the BPR and VPR curves of the comparisons on the VSB100 dataset. From Table 2 and Fig.4, we have the following observations:

- Our approach outperforms the state-of-the-art methods (BMC, VSS, HGB, SHGB and SOLD) in both BPR and VPR on the VSB100 dataset. Specifically, our proposed method outperforms the currently best performance (SOLD [20]) on both BPR and VPR by a large margin, as it appears both in the Table 2 and Fig.4 (11%, 7% and 8% in BPR, 2%, 1% and 5% in VPR). Our AP in VPR is slightly lower than HGB. But we can alleviate it by simply increasing the superpixels number, as shown in Table 3.
- Though VSS [9] and SOLD [20] exploits multiple cues as well, our method performs better. This probably owes to the proposed joint graph learning and video segmentation framework, and the automatically learned weights for different cues.
- SOLD [20] is a strong competitor. The superior performances over SOLD in both BPR and VPR demonstrate that our approach can not only effectively infer the spatial similarity between superpixels within a frame, but also preserve the longer-range temporal consistency in a streaming mode.
- Temporal consistency processing plays an important role for VPR, as indicated in Table 2. An example is given in Fig.5 to illustrate the effect of temporal consistency processing. If we do not constrain that the same object in the close frames to have the same label, the performance on VPR metric will decrease.
- Topology calibration improves the performance, especially for VPR. This is due to that without calibration, the distances of different topological structures (especially for cross frame) are not comparable.

We illustrate qualitative results in Fig.3, comparing our proposed method to the state-of-the-art video segmentation algorithms including HGB, SHGB and SOLD. Fig.3 shows consistent results to the quantitative results. Our method is able to provide better distinguished visual objects with well-localized boundaries and limited label leakage.

4.3 Component analysis

In this subsection, we study the effect of *level* and the different types of *distances* on our proposed method.

As described in Section 3, our proposed algorithm is imposed on the superpixels which are extracted from [2]. The number of superpixels is determined by the value of *level*. From the Table 3, we can see that the *level* is important to the performance. In general, when $level = 75$, the overall best performance is achieved for both BPR (65%, 65% and 48%) and VPR (55%, 61% and 51%). In addition, when $level = 25$, the AP for both BPR and VPR reaches the peak values: 54% and 56% respectively. This is due to that when $level = 25$, more superpixels are generated and over-segmentation improves the precision but decreases the recall [2].

The effect of different distances is analyzed and the results are shown in Table 4. As described in Section 3, our method uses different types of pairwise distance between superpxiels for video segmentation. From Table 4, we can see that *distances* have different impact on the performance, hence it is important to learn the weights for different distances. Using a combined distances with learned weight achieves better performance than using a single distance.

Table 3: The effect of *level* on our proposed method.

	BPR			VPR		
Algorithm	**ODS**	**OSS**	**AP**	**ODS**	**OSS**	**AP**
$Level = 25$	0.59	0.59	**0.54**	0.54	0.58	**0.56**
$Level = 50$	0.64	0.65	0.53	**0.55**	0.57	0.51
$Level = 75$	**0.65**	**0.65**	0.48	**0.55**	**0.61**	0.51
$Level = 95$	0.64	0.64	0.47	**0.55**	0.59	0.46
$Level = 125$	0.61	0.61	0.41	0.53	0.58	0.40
Human	0.81	0.81	0.67	0.83	0.83	0.70

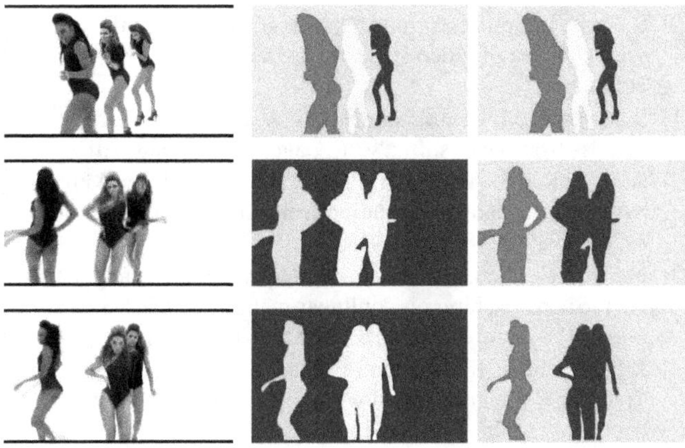

Figure 5: Segmentations of a given sequence of video frames. The left are the original frames, the middle lines are the segmentations without temporal consistency, and the right lines are the segmentations with temporal consistency processing. It is clear that if no temporal consistency processing is applied, the same object in the successive frames cannot be guaranteed to have the same segment id (i.e., label). In this case, the VPR will degrade.

Table 4: The effect of *distances* on our proposed method.

	BPR			VPR		
Algorithm	**ODS**	**OSS**	**AP**	**ODS**	**OSS**	**AP**
CBS	0.64	0.64	0.46	0.43	0.46	0.38
BOF	0.64	0.64	0.44	0.43	0.44	0.37
LAB	0.64	0.65	0.45	0.51	0.53	0.43
SOF	0.64	0.64	0.47	0.42	0.45	0.37
SSD	0.64	0.64	0.44	0.51	0.56	0.45
STI	0.64	0.64	0.45	0.46	0.49	0.42
All	0.65	0.65	0.48	0.55	0.61	0.51
Human	0.81	0.81	0.67	0.83	0.83	0.70

4.4 Efficiency Analysis

In this subsection, we evaluate the time efficiency of our proposed method. These experiments are carried out on a desktop with an Intel(R) Core (TM)2 Duo CPU and 8GB RAM. Our method is conducted on the features of the generated superpixels, which are obtained in the preprocessing step. The computational cost for our algorithm is $O(N^2) + O(N^3)$. However, we do segmentation on the N superpixels, which is usually 10-100s. Therefore, our method can segment 1 frame within 0.2s on average, as indicated in Fig. 6. Fig. 6 reports the running time corresponding to the number of segmentations. In average, it costs 0.1895 seconds per frame for our proposed method. Large number of segmentations does not necessarily consume more time, because the optimization may terminate in less iterations.

5. CONCLUSIONS

This paper proposes the JGLVS framework that simultaneously learns the graph similarity matrix and video segmentation, instead of first organizing the superpixels into graphs and then cutting the generated graph for segmentation. Based on the spatial and visual information, each vertex is assigned with adaptive and optimal neighbors for graph similarity learning. By imposing rank constraints on the Laplacian matrix, the number of connected components in the generated similarity graph are equal to the number of segmentations, sidestepping the need for separate steps in similarity computation and graph cutting. Experimental results show that the proposed unsupervised JGLVS outperforms state-of-the-art video segmentation algorithms by a large margin on the VSB100 dataset.

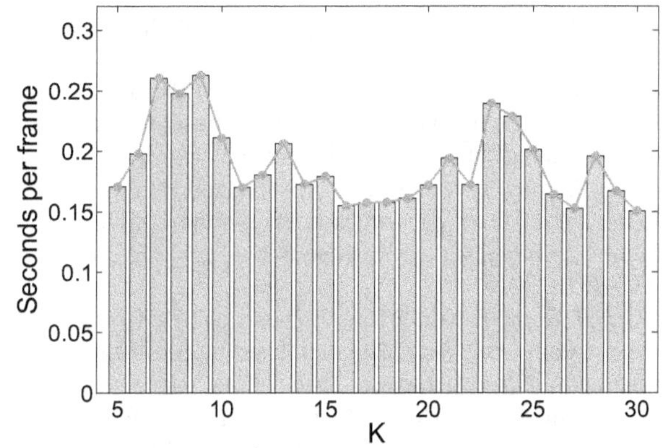

Figure 6: The running time (seconds per frame) *vs.* number of segmentations (K) of our proposed method.

6. ACKNOWLEDGMENTS

The work of Jingkuan Song and Nicu Sebe has been partially supported by the FP7 EC project xLiMe. The work of Lianli Gao is partially supported by the Fundamental Research Funds for the Central Universities (Grant No.ZYGX2014J063) and the National Natural Science Foundation of China (Grant No. 61502080).

7. REFERENCES

[1] P. Arbelaez, M. Maire, C. Fowlkes, and J. Malik. From contours to regions: An empirical evaluation. In *CVPR*, pages 2294–2301, 2009.

[2] P. Arbelaez, M. Maire, C. Fowlkes, and J. Malik. Contour detection and hierarchical image segmentation. *IEEE Trans. Pattern Anal. Mach. Intell.*, 33(5):898–916, 2011.

[3] W. Brendel and S. Todorovic. Video object segmentation by tracking regions. In *ICCV*, pages 833–840, 2009.

[4] T. Brox and J. Malik. Object segmentation by long term analysis of point trajectories. In *ECCV*, pages 282–295, 2010.

[5] L. Chen, J. Shen, W. Wang, and B. Ni. Video object segmentation via dense trajectories. *IEEE Trans. Multimedia*, 17(12):2225–2234, 2015.

[6] J. Corso, E. Sharon, S. Dube, S. El-Saden, U. Sinha, and A. Yuille. Efficient multilevel brain tumor segmentation with integrated bayesian model classification. *Medical Imaging, IEEE Transactions on*, 27(5):629–640, 2008.

[7] K. Fan. On a Theorem of Weyl Concerning Eigenvalues of Linear Transformations. I. *Proceedings of the National Academy of Science*, 35:652–655, Nov. 1949.

[8] K. Fragkiadaki and J. Shi. Detection free tracking: Exploiting motion and topology for segmenting and tracking under entanglement. In *CVPR*, pages 2073–2080, 2011.

[9] F. Galasso, R. Cipolla, and B. Schiele. Video segmentation with superpixels. In *ACCV*, 2012.

[10] F. Galasso, M. Keuper, T. Brox, and B. Schiele. Spectral graph reduction for efficient image and streaming video segmentation. In *CVPR*, 2014.

[11] F. Galasso, N. S. Nagaraja, T. J. Cardenas, T. Brox, and B. Schiele. A unified video segmentation benchmark: Annotation, metrics and analysis. In *ICCV*, 2013.

[12] L. Gao, J. Song, F. Nie, Y. Yan, N. Sebe, and H. T. Shen. Optimal graph learning with partial tags and multiple features for image and video annotation. In *CVPR*, pages 4371–4379, 2015.

[13] L. Gao, J. Song, F. Nie, F. Zou, N. Sebe, and H. T. Shen. Graph-without-cut: An ideal graph learning for image segmentation. In *AAAI*, pages 1188–1194, 2016.

[14] M. Grundmann, V. Kwatra, M. Han, and I. Essa. Efficient hierarchical graph-based video segmentation. In *CVPR*, pages 2141–2148, 2010.

[15] A. Jain, S. Chatterjee, and R. Vidal. Coarse-to-fine semantic video segmentation using supervoxel trees. In *ICCV*, pages 1865–1872, 2013.

[16] H. Jiang, G. Zhang, H. Wang, and H. Bao. Spatio-temporal video segmentation of static scenes and its applications. *IEEE Trans. Multimedia*, 17(1):3–15, 2015.

[17] M. Keuper, B. Andres, and T. Brox. Motion trajectory segmentation via minimum cost multicuts. In *ICCV*, 2015.

[18] M. Keuper, B. Andres, and T. Brox. Motion trajectory segmentation via minimum cost multicuts. In *ICCV*, pages 3271–3279, 2015.

[19] A. Khoreva, F. Galasso, M. Hein, and B. Schiele. Classifier based graph construction for video segmentation. In *CVPR*, 2015.

[20] C. Li, L. Lin, W. Zuo, S. Yan, and J. Tang. Sold: Sub-optimal low-rank decomposition for efficient video segmentation. In *CVPR*, 2015.

[21] B. Liu and X. He. Multiclass semantic video segmentation with object-level active inference. In *CVPR*, pages 4286–4294, 2015.

[22] B. Luo, H. Li, T. Song, and C. Huang. Object segmentation from long video sequences. In *ACM Multimedia*, pages 1187–1190, 2015.

[23] T. Ma and L. J. Latecki. Maximum weight cliques with mutex constraints for video object segmentation. In *CVPR*, pages 670–677, 2012.

[24] N. S. Nagaraja, F. R. Schmidt, and T. Brox. Video segmentation with just a few strokes. In *ICCV*, pages 3235–3243, 2015.

[25] F. Nie, X. Wang, and H. Huang. Clustering and projected clustering with adaptive neighbors. In *SIGKDD*, pages 977–986, 2014.

[26] F. Nie, X. Wang, M. I. Jordan, and H. Huang. The constrained laplacian rank algorithm for graph-based clustering. In *AAAI*, pages 1969–1976, 2016.

[27] P. Ochs and T. Brox. Object segmentation in video: A hierarchical variational approach for turning point trajectories into dense regions. In *ICCV*, pages 1583–1590, 2011.

[28] P. Ochs and T. Brox. Higher order motion models and spectral clustering. In *CVPR*, pages 614–621, 2012.

[29] P. Ochs, J. Malik, and T. Brox. Segmentation of moving objects by long term video analysis. *IEEE Trans. Pattern Anal. Mach. Intell.*, 36(6):1187–1200, 2014.

[30] S. Paris. Edge-preserving smoothing and mean-shift segmentation of video streams. In *ECCV*, pages 460–473, 2008.

[31] S. H. Raza, M. Grundmann, and I. A. Essa. Geometric context from videos. In *CVPR*, pages 3081–3088, 2013.

[32] A. V. Reina, S. Avidan, H. Pfister, and E. L. Miller. Multiple hypothesis video segmentation from superpixel flows. In *ECCV*, pages 268–281, 2010.

[33] F. Shen, C. Shen, Q. Shi, A. van den Hengel, Z. Tang, and H. T. Shen. Hashing on nonlinear manifolds. *IEEE Trans. Image Processing*, 24(6):1839–1851, 2015.

[34] J. Son, I. Jung, K. Park, and B. Han. Tracking-by-segmentation with online gradient boosting decision tree. In *ICCV*, 2015.

[35] J. Song, Y. Yang, Z. Huang, H. T. Shen, and J. Luo. Effective multiple feature hashing for large-scale near-duplicate video retrieval. *IEEE Trans. Multimedia*, 15(8):1997–2008, 2013.

[36] H. Wang and C. Schmid. Action recognition with improved trajectories. In *ICCV*, 2013.

[37] Y. Wang, J. Liu, Y. Li, and H. Lu. Semi- and weakly-supervised semantic segmentation with deep convolutional neural networks. In *ACM Multimedia*, pages 1223–1226, 2015.

[38] C. Xu, C. Xiong, and J. J. Corso. Streaming hierarchical video segmentation. In *ECCV*, pages 626–639, 2012.

[39] X. Yao, J. Han, G. Cheng, and L. Guo. Semantic segmentation based on stacked discriminative autoencoders and context-constrained weakly supervised learning. In *ACM Multimedia*, pages 1211–1214, 2015.

[40] S. Yi and V. Pavlovic. Multi-cue structure preserving MRF for unconstrained video segmentation. In *ICCV*, 2015.

[41] C.-P. Yu, H. Le, G. Zelinsky, and D. Samaras. Efficient video segmentation using parametric graph partitioning. In *ICCV*, 2015.

[42] V. Zografos, R. Lenz, E. Ringaby, M. Felsberg, and K. Nordberg. Fast segmentation of sparse 3d point trajectories using group theoretical invariants. In *ACCV*, pages 675–691, 2014.

Parsimonious Mixed-Effects HodgeRank for Crowdsourced Preference Aggregation

Qianqian Xu
State Key Laboratory of Information Security, Institute of Information Engineering, Chinese Academy of Sciences, Beijing 100093 & BICMR, Peking University, Beijing 100871, China
xuqianqian@iie.ac.cn

Jiechao Xiong
School of Mathematical Sciences, BICMR-LMAM-LMEQF-LMP, Peking University, Beijing 100871, China
xiongjiechao@pku.edu.cn

Xiaochun Cao *
State Key Laboratory of Information Security, Institute of Information Engineering, Chinese Academy of Sciences, Beijing 100093
caoxiaochun@iie.ac.cn

Yuan Yao *
School of Mathematical Sciences, BICMR-LMAM-LMEQF-LMP, Peking University, Beijing 100871, China
yuany@math.pku.edu.cn

ABSTRACT

In crowdsourced preference aggregation, it is often assumed that all the annotators are subject to a common preference or utility function which generates their comparison behaviors in experiments. However, in reality annotators are subject to variations due to multi-criteria, abnormal, or a mixture of such behaviors. In this paper, we propose a parsimonious mixed-effects model based on HodgeRank, which takes into account both the fixed effect that the majority of annotators follows a common linear utility model, and the random effect that a small subset of annotators might deviate from the common significantly and exhibits strongly personalized preferences. HodgeRank has been successfully applied to subjective quality evaluation of multimedia and resolves pairwise crowdsourced ranking data into a global consensus ranking and cyclic conflicts of interests. As an extension, our proposed methodology further explores the conflicts of interests through the random effect in annotator specific variations. The key algorithm in this paper establishes a dynamic path from the common utility to individual variations, with different levels of parsimony or sparsity on personalization, based on newly developed Linearized Bregman Algorithms with Inverse Scale Space method. Finally the validity of the methodology are supported by experiments with both simulated examples and three real-world crowdsourcing datasets, which shows that our proposed method exhibits better performance (i.e. smaller test error) compared with HodgeRank due to its parsimonious property.

*Corresponding author.

MM '16, October 15-19, 2016, Amsterdam, Netherlands
© 2016 ACM. ISBN 978-1-4503-3603-1/16/10...$15.00
DOI: http://dx.doi.org/10.1145/2964284.2964298

Keywords

Preference Aggregation; HodgeRank; Mixed-Effects Models; Linearized Bregman Iterations; Personalized Ranking; Position Bias

1. INTRODUCTION

With the Internet and its associated explosive growth of information, individuals today in the world are facing with the rapid expansion of multiple choices (e.g., which book to buy, which hotel to book, etc.). Inferring user's preference or utility over a set of alternatives has thus become an important issue. Among various methods to infer user viewpoint/preference, crowdsourcing technology is becoming a new paradigm, which collects voting data from a large crowd or population on Internet and pursue some statistical preference aggregations. For example, the following platforms are frequently used by researchers to crowdsource voting data of participants: MTurk, InnoCentive, CrowdFlower, CrowdRank, and AllOurIdeas, etc. A typical and perhaps the simplest scenario is the pairwise comparison experiment. Specifically, there are a set of items to rank, and participants are asked to choose between various pairs among these items; the goal is to aggregate these pairwise comparisons into a global consensus ranking that summarizes the preference of all users. We have seen that researchers exploit such a paradigm to evaluate the quality of multimedia content [4, 27], predict image/video interestingness [10], estimate ages from face pictures [11], and rank taste of food [12] etc.

However, different individuals might very well have distinct preferences, such that participants of the crowdsourced

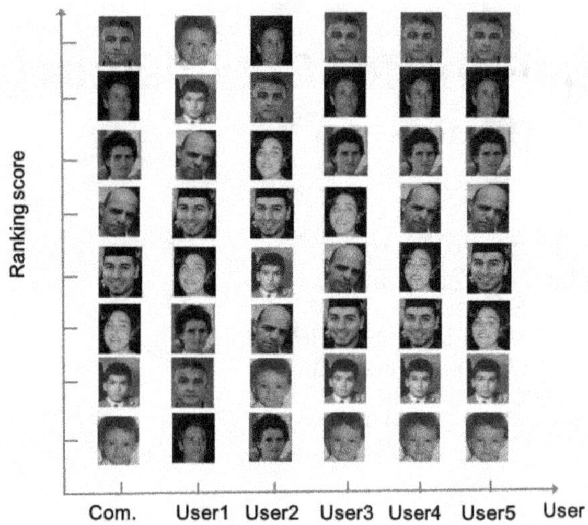

Figure 1: An illustrative example on estimation of human ages, with the fixed effect of common ranking and random effects of user's personalized ranking. The faces in the first column are ordered according to a common ranking score aggregated from crowdsourced pairwise comparisons, while other columns are according to personalized rankings of different users. The ground truth ages in the first column, in a top-down order, are 46, 51, 36, 30, 25, 23, 10, and 2, respectively.

experiments might vote under different criteria or conditions. It might be misleading to merely look at a global consensus while ignoring personal diversity. For example Fig.1 shows an age estimation from photos that will be discussed in detail later in this paper. The majority is not always correct, as the common ranking by mistake thinks 46 older than 51! Moreover, even though `User2` is largely deviated from the common ranking, it is noticeable that he/she makes correct judgements between the faces of year 46 and 51. So if one is looking for features that correctly predict the ages of these two particular faces, `User2` is a better consultant than the majority. Particularly, `User1` is clearly an adversarial voter, whose personalized ranking is largely against the common ranking reflecting the majority, so should be removed from a preference aggregation procedure.

Moreover, in crowdsourcing experiments, the participants are distributed over the Internet with a diverse environment. Even they might share the same preference or utility function in making choices, they might suffer various disturbances during the experiments. For example, i) one typically clicks one side more often than another. As some pairs are highly confusing or annotators get too tired, in these cases, some annotators tend to click one side hoping to simply raise their record to receive more payment; while for pairs with substantial differences, they click as usual. ii) some extremely careless annotators, or robots pretending to be human annotators, actually do not look at the instances and click one side all the time to quickly receive payment for work. Such a kind of behavior is called the annotator's position bias which has been studied in [6, 26].

These examples above suggest us that we have to take into account of user or annotator specific variations in a crowdsourced preference aggregation task. As the classical social choice theory [1] points out, preference aggregation toward a global consensus is doomed to meet the conflicts of interests. *What is a suitable way to quantitatively analyze the conflicts of interests?*

In this paper, we pursue the Hodge-theoretic approach by [13] which decomposes the pairwise comparison data into three orthogonal components: the global consensus ranking, the local inconsistency as triangular cycles, and the global inconsistency as harmonic cycles. The latter two are both cycles, collectively decoding all the conflicts of interests in the data. Instead of the merely extracting from the data the global ranking component, often called *HodgeRank* which has been introduced into the quality assessment of multimedia by [25], we extend it here by including some annotator-specific random effects to further decompose the cycles. To decipher the sources of the conflicts of interests, we mainly consider two types of annotator-specific variations: annotator's personalized preference deviations from the common ranking which characterize multi-criteria in data, and annotator's position bias which deteriorates the quality of data. This results in a linear mixed-effects extension of HodgeRank, called Mixed-Effects HodgeRank here.

To initiate a task of crowdsourced preference aggregation, we usually assume the majority of participants share a common preference interest and behave rationally, while deviations from that exist but are sparse. So a parsimonious model is assumed in this paper, with sparsity structure on personalized preference deviations and position biases. Due to the unknown amount of such sparse random effects in reality, it is natural to pursue a family of parsimonious models at a variety levels of sparsity. Algorithmically we adopt the Linearized Bregman Iteration, which is a simple iterative procedure generating a sequence of parsimonious models, evolving from the common global ranking in HodgeRank, to annotator's personalized ranking till a full model. Fig.1 is in fact a result of our algorithm. As the algorithm iterates, typically the abnormal annotators with large preference deviations and/or position biases appear early, and the annotators who behave normally appear at a later stage. In practice when the number of participants is large and sample size is relatively small, early stopping regularization is needed to prevent the overfitting in full model.

Equipped with such a new scheme, given a set of entities, we choose a set of entity pairs and ask Internet crowds which entity is more preferable in each pair. Based on the feedback we not only can derive the common preference on population-level, but also can estimate rapidly an annotator's large preference/utility deviation in an individual-level, and an abnormal annotator's position bias. Individual preference deviations from the population common ranking are helpful to understand different criteria among annotators when they judges, and especially to monitor the adversarial users. On the other hand, annotator's position bias is a helpful tool to monitor the quality of his/her voting data, through the mixing behavior that the annotator simply clicks one side of the pair in comparisons without paying attention to their contents. Such a statistical mixed-effects framework simultaneously considers both the fixed effect of common ranking as the HodgeRank and the random effects of annotator-specific variations, which, up to the author's knowledge, has not been seen in literature.

As a summary, our main contributions in this new framework are highlighted as follows:

(A) A linear mixed-effects extension of HodgeRank including both the fixed effect of common ranking, and the random effects of annotator's preference deviation with position bias;

(B) A path of parsimonious estimates of the preference deviation and position bias at different sparsity levels, based on Linearized Bregman Iterations.

The remainder of this paper is organized as follows. Sec.2 contains a review of related works. Then we systematically introduce the methodology for parsimonious mixed-effects HodgeRank estimation in Sec.3. Extensive experimental validation based on one simulated and three real-world crowdsourced datasets are demonstrated in Sec.4. Finally, Sec.5 presents the conclusive remarks.

2. RELATED WORK

2.1 Statistic Ranking Aggregation

Statistical preference aggregation, in particular ranking or rating from pairwise comparisons, is a classical problem which can be traced back to the 18th century. Various algorithms have been studied for this problem, including maximum likelihood under a Bradley-Terry model assumption, rank centrality (PageRank/MC3) [5, 15], HodgeRank [13] , and a pairwise variant of Borda count [7] among others. In [21], it shows that under a natural statistical model, where pairwise comparisons are drawn randomly and independently from some underlying probability distribution, the rank centrality (PageRank) and HodgeRank algorithms both converge to an optimal ranking under a "time-reversibility" condition. However, PageRank is only able to aggregate the pairwise comparisons into a global ranking over the items. HodgeRank not only provides us a mean to determine a global ranking under various statistical models, but also measures the inconsistency of the global ranking obtained.

HodgeRank, as an application of combinatorial Hodge theory to the preference or rank aggregation problem from pairwise comparison data, was first introduced in [13], inspiring a series of studies in statistical ranking [18–20], game theory [3], and computer vision [30], etc. It is a general framework to decompose paired comparison data on graphs, possibly imbalanced (where different video pairs may receive different number of comparisons) and incomplete (where every participant may only give partial comparisons), into three orthogonal components. In these components HodgeRank not only provides us a mean to determine a global ranking from paired comparison data under various statistical models (e.g., Uniform, Thurstone-Mosteller, Bradley-Terry, and Angular Transform), but also measures the inconsistency of the global ranking obtained. The inconsistency shows the validity of the ranking obtained and can be further studied in terms of its geometric scale, namely whether the inconsistency in the ranking data arises locally or globally. Local inconsistency can be fully characterized by triangular cycles, while global inconsistency involves cycles consisting nodes more than three, which may arise due to data incompleteness and once presented with a large component indicates some serious conflicts in ranking data. However through random graphs, we can efficiently control global inconsistency.

However, all of these methods have a major drawback: they aim to find one ranking thus cannot model the discrepancies across users. Therefore, in recent years, personalized ranking methods arise to fill in this gap. This task can be seen as rank aggregation analog to the standard collaborative filtering (CF) problem. There have been many CF algorithms, including Bayesian networks, clustering models, and latent semantic models, etc. Recent algorithms for collaborative filtering are mostly based on matrix factorization [22, 23]. The key idea behind them is to find a low rank user rating matrix that best approximates the observed ratings. Most recently, the application of the nuclear norm approach to CF was first proposed by [28], which shows good empirical evidence for using such a nuclear norm regularized based approach. The key difference between our study and the low rank matrix collaborative filtering algorithms is that we assume the majority of voters share a fixed effect of common ranking while some annotators might deviate from that significantly. Such parsimonious model from population to individual is a natural fit for crowdsourcing scenarios.

2.2 Linearized Bregman Iteration (LBI)

Linearized Bregman Iteration (LBI) was firstly introduced in [29] in the literature of variational imaging and compressive sensing. It is well-known that LASSO estimators are always biased [9]. On the other hand, [16] notices that Bregman iteration may reduce bias, also known as contrast loss, in the context of Total Variation image denoising. Now LBI can be viewed as a discretization of differential equations (inclusions), called *Inverse Scale Spaces*, which may produce unbiased estimators under nearly the same model selection consistency conditions as LASSO [17].

Beyond such a theoretical attraction, LBI is an extremely simple algorithm which combines an iterative gradient descent algorithm together with a soft thresholding. It is different to the well-known iterative soft-thresholding algorithm (ISTA) (e.g., [2, 8] and references therein) which converges to the biased LASSO solution. To tune the regularization parameter in noisy settings, one needs to run ISTA with many different thresholding parameters and chooses the best among them; in contrast, LBI only runs in a single path and regularization is achieved by early stopping like boosting algorithms [17], which may save the computational cost greatly and thus suitable for large scale implementation, e.g., distributive computation [31].

3. METHODOLOGY

In this section, we systematically introduce the methodology for parsimonious mixed-effects HodgeRank estimation. Specifically, we first start from extending the HodgeRank to a linear mixed-effect model. Then we present a simple iterative algorithm called Linearized Bregman Iterations to generate paths of parsimonious models at different sparsity levels. Early stopping regularization is discussed in the end.

3.1 Mixed-Effects HodgeRank on Graphs

In crowdsourced pairwise comparison experiments, Let $V = \{1, 2, \ldots, n\}$ be the set of nodes and $E = \{(u, i, j) : i, j \in V, u \in U\}$ be the set of edges, where U is the set of all annotators. Suppose the pairwise ranking data is given as $y : E \to R$. $y^u_{ij} > 0$ means u prefers i to j and $y^u_{ij} \leq 0$

otherwise. The magnitude of y_{ij}^u can represent the degree of preference and it varies in applications. The simplest setting is the binary choice, where

$$y_{ij}^u = \begin{cases} 1 & \text{if } u \text{ prefers } i \text{ to } j, \\ -1 & \text{otherwise.} \end{cases} \quad (1)$$

The general purpose of preference aggregation is to look for a global score $\theta\colon V \to \mathbb{R}$ such that

$$\min_{\theta \in \mathbb{R}^{|V|}} \sum_{i,j,u} \omega_{ij}^u l(\theta_i - \theta_j, y_{ij}^u), \quad (2)$$

where $l(x,y)\colon \mathbb{R}\times\mathbb{R}\to\mathbb{R}$ is a loss function, ω_{ij}^u denotes the confidence weights on $\{i,j\}$ made by rater u (for simplicity, assumed to be $\omega_{ij}^u = 1$ for the existing voting data), and θ_i (θ_j) represents the global ranking score of item i (j, respectively). In HodgeRank, one benefits from the use of square loss $l(x,y) = (x-y)^2$ which leads to fast algorithms to find optimal global ranking θ, which becomes one component of a general orthogonal decomposition of paired comparison data [13], i.e.

$$y = \textit{global ranking} \oplus \textit{cycles},$$

where the component *cycles* can be further decomposed into

$$\textit{cycles} = \textit{local cycles} \oplus \textit{global cycles}.$$

Local cycles are triangular cycles, e.g. $i \succ j \succ k \succ i$; while global cycles, also called harmonic cycles, are loops involving nodes more than three (e.g. $i \succ j \succ k \succ \ldots \succ i$) and typically traversing all nodes in the graph. These cycles may arise due to conflicts of interests in ranking data. Therefore to analyze the statistical models of cycles is crucial to understand the conflicts of interests.

In crowdsourcing scenarios, the conflicts of interests are mainly due to two kinds of sources: the multi-criteria adopted by different annotators when they compare items in V; the abnormal behavior of annotators in the experiments, e.g. simply clicking one side of the pair when they got bored, tired, or distracted. To quantitatively characterize these effects, we propose the following model of cycles

$$\textit{cycles} = \textit{personalized ranking} + \textit{position bias} + \textit{noise}.$$

To be specific, together with the global ranking component in HodgeRank, we consider the following linear mixed effects model for annotator's pairwise ranking:

$$y_{ij}^u = (\theta_i + \delta_i^u) - (\theta_j + \delta_j^u) + \gamma^u + \varepsilon_{ij}^u, \quad (3)$$

where

- θ_i is the common global ranking score, as a fixed effect;
- δ_i^u is the annotator's preference deviation from the common ranking θ_i such that $\theta_i^u := \theta_i + \delta_i^u$ becomes annotator u's personalized ranking score, as a random effect;
- γ^u is an annotator's position bias, which captures the careless behavior by clicking one side during the comparisons;
- ε_{ij}^u is the random noise which is assumed to be independent and identically distributed with zero mean and being bounded.

Putting in matrix form, (3) becomes

$$y = d\theta + X\beta + \varepsilon, \quad (4)$$

where $d \in \mathbb{R}^{|E|\times|V|}$ satisfies $d\theta(u,i,j) = \theta_i - \theta_j$, $\beta = [\delta, \gamma] \in R^{(|V|+1)|U|}$ and $X = [D, A]$, where $D \in \mathbb{R}^{|E|\times|V||U|}$ satisfies $D\delta(u,i,j) = \delta_i^u - \delta_j^u$ and $A \in \mathbb{R}^{|E|\times|U|}$ satisfies $\gamma(u,i,j) = \gamma^u$.

Here θ is population-level parameter which indicates some common score on V. In crowdsourcing studies, as the data vary greatly across individual annotators, we thus allow each annotator to have personalized parameters θ^u. These personalized parameters can be obtained by adding some random effects δ^u to the population parameter θ, representing individual deviations from the population behavior. Besides, γ^u measures an annotator's position bias, i.e. the tendency of u always clicking one side in paired comparison experiments. Under the random design of pairwise comparison experiments, a candidate should be placed on the left or the right randomly, so the position should not affect the choice of a careful annotator. However, some annotator might get confused, tired or distracted in experiments, such that he/she always clicks one side during some periods in experiments. Such a type of position bias captures a kind of noise in data not included in the zero mean ε and may severely deteriorates the quality of data. The remainder ε_{ij}^u measures the random noise in sampling which is of zero mean and bounded (hence subgaussian).

3.2 Parsimonious Paths with Linearized Bregman Iteration

In crowdsourced preference aggregation scenarios with good controls, it is natural to assume a parsimonious model. In such a model, the majority of annotators carefully follows the common behavior governed by the fixed effect parameter θ, while only a small set of annotators might have nonzero personalized deviations and abnormal behavior in position bias. This amounts to assume that parameter δ^u to be group sparse, i.e. δ_i^u vanishes for all i simultaneously, and γ^u to be sparse as well, i.e. zero for most of careful annotators. Such a sparsity pattern motivates us to consider the following penalty function with a mixture of LASSO (L_1) penalty on γ and group LASSO penalty on δ:

$$P(\beta) = \|\gamma\|_1 + \sum_u \|\delta^u\|_2, \beta = (\delta, \gamma). \quad (5)$$

Remark 1. *Usually a normalization factor $\sqrt{n}$ is used before a group lasso penalty $\|\delta^u\|_2$, where n is the group size of δ^u. But here all the δ^u have the same group size, and $\|D^u\|_F = \sqrt{2}\|A^u\|_F$, so the column norm of D^u is on average $\frac{\sqrt{2}}{\sqrt{n}}$ times of $\|A^u\|_F$, this basically cancels out the factor $\sqrt{n}$. So here we just use this simple formula.*

Following the square loss in HodgeRank, the Euclidean distance (mean square error) in R^E can be used for the total loss function:

$$L(\theta,\beta) = \frac{1}{2m}\|y - d\theta - X\beta\|_2^2. \quad (6)$$

The following Linearized Bregman Iterations (LBI) give

rise to a sequence of parsimonious (sparse) models:

$$\theta^{k+1} = \theta^k - \alpha\kappa\nabla_\theta L(\theta^k, \beta^k) \quad (7a)$$

$$z^{k+1} = z^k - \alpha\nabla_\beta L(\theta^k, \beta^k), \quad (7b)$$

$$\beta^{k+1} = \kappa \cdot \mathrm{prox}_P(z^{k+1}), \quad (7c)$$

where $\beta^0 = 0$, $\theta^0 = \arg\min_\theta L(\theta, 0)$, and variable z is an auxiliary parameter used for gradient descent, $z = \rho + \beta/\kappa, \rho \in \partial P(\beta)$. Besides, the proximal map associated with the penalty function P is given by

$$\mathrm{prox}_P(z) = \arg \min_{v \in R^{(|V|+1)|U|}} \left(\frac{1}{2}\|v - z\|^2 + P(z)\right).$$

The Linearized Bregman Iteration (7) generates a path of global ranking score estimators θ^k and sparse estimators for preference deviation and position bias, $\beta^k = (\delta^k, \gamma^k)$. It starts from the common HodgeRank as $\theta^0 = \arg\min_\theta L(\theta, 0)$, and evolves into parsimonious mixed effect models with different levels of sparsity until the full model, often overfitted. To avoid the overfitting, early stopping regularization is required to find an optimal tradeoff between the model complexity and in-sample error. For more details, we refer the readers to see [17] and references therein. In this paper, we find that cross validation works to find the early stopping time that will be discussed in Sec.3.3.

The Linearized Bregman algorithm was firstly introduced in [29] extended from Bregman iteration [16] as a scalable algorithm for large scale image restoration and compressed sensing. It has several advantages than the widely used LASSO-type convex regularizations. First of all, it is simpler than LASSO in generating the sparse regularization paths: instead of a parallel run of several optimization problem over a grid of regularization parameters, a single run of LBI generates the whole regularization path. LBI is thus desired in dealing with big problems. Moreover, it can be less biased than LASSO as if nonconvex regularizations [9]. In fact, it is shown recently in [17] that as $\kappa \to \infty$ and $\alpha \to 0$, the limit dynamics of Linearized Bregman Iterations in sparse linear regression with LASSO (L_1) penalty may achieve the model selection consistency under nearly the same condition as LASSO yet return the unbiased Oracle estimator, while the LASSO estimator is well-known biased.

Here we give some remarks on the implementation details of the Linearized Bregman Iterations (7).

- The parameter κ determines the bias of the sparse estimators, a bigger κ leading to the less biased ones. The parameter α is the step size which determines the precise of the path, with a large α rapidly traversing a coarse grained path. However one has to keep $\alpha\kappa$ small to avoid possible oscillations of the paths, e.g. $\alpha\kappa\|X^TX\|_2/m < 2$. The default choice in this paper is $\alpha = \frac{m}{\kappa\|X^TX\|_2}$ as a tradeoff between performance and computation cost.

- The step (7a) can also be replaced by

$$\theta^{k+1} = \arg\min_\theta L(\theta, \beta^k)$$

if it is easy to solve.

- Now we turn to simplify the third step (7c) with an explicit formula for the proximal map with the particular penalty function defined in Eq. (5). Recovering β^{k+1} from z^{k+1} is equivalent to the following group shrinkage on each group component of β, i.e. γ^u and δ^u:

$$\beta^{k+1} = \kappa\mathbf{Shrinkage}(z^{k+1}) \quad (8)$$
$$\triangleq \begin{cases} \delta^{u,k+1} = \kappa \max(0, 1 - 1/\|z_{\delta^u}\|_2) z_{\delta^u} \\ \gamma^{u,k+1} = \kappa \max(0, 1 - 1/|z_{\gamma^u}|) z_{\gamma^u} \end{cases}$$

Now we are ready to give the following Linearized Bregman Algorithm for our Mixed-Effects HodgeRank as

Algorithm 1 LBI for ME-HodgeRank

Input: Data (d, X, y), damping factor κ, step size α.
Initialize: $\beta^0 = 0, \theta^0 = (d^Td)^{-1}d^Ty, z^0 = 0, t^0 = 0$.
for $k = 0, \ldots, K$ **do**

1. $\theta^{k+1} = (d^Td)^{-1}d^T(y - X\beta^k)$.
2. $z^{k+1} = z^k + \frac{\alpha}{m}X^T(y - d\theta^k - X\beta^k)$.
3. $\beta^{k+1} = \kappa\mathbf{Shrinkage}(z^{k+1})$
4. $t^{k+1} = (k+1)\alpha$.

end for
Output: Solution path $\{t^k, \theta^k, \beta^k\}_{k=0,1,\ldots,K}$.

3.3 Early Stopping Regularization

The Alg.1 actually returns a solution path with many estimators of different sparsity. So we need to find an optimal stopping time among $t^k = \alpha k$ to choose some best estimators and avoid overfitting. Here we sketch the procedure of cross-validation to choose the optimal stopping time:

- Given the training data, fix κ and α, then split the data into K folds. Then choose a list of parameter t.
- **for** $k = 1, \ldots, K$ **do**
  1. Run Alg.1 on the training data except k-th fold to get the solution path.
  2. For pre-decided parameter list of t, use a linear interpolation to get $(\theta(t), \beta(t))$.
  3. On the k-th fold of training data, use the estimator $(\theta(t), \beta(t))$ to predict, and then compute prediction error.

  end for
- Return the optimal t_{cv} with minimal average prediction error.

Remark: Because the Alg.1 only returns the estimator at discrete $\{t^k\}$ and may not contain the pre-decided parameter t, so we use a linear interpolation of the nearest two estimator (θ^k, z^k) and (θ^{k+1}, z^{k+1}) to approximate $(\theta(t), z(t))$. $\beta(t)$ is further obtained by using $\mathbf{Shrinkage}(z(t))$.

4. EXPERIMENTS

In this section, four examples are exhibited with both simulated and real-world data to illustrate the validity of the analysis above and applications of the methodology proposed. The first example is with simulated data while the latter three exploit real-world data collected by crowdsourcing.

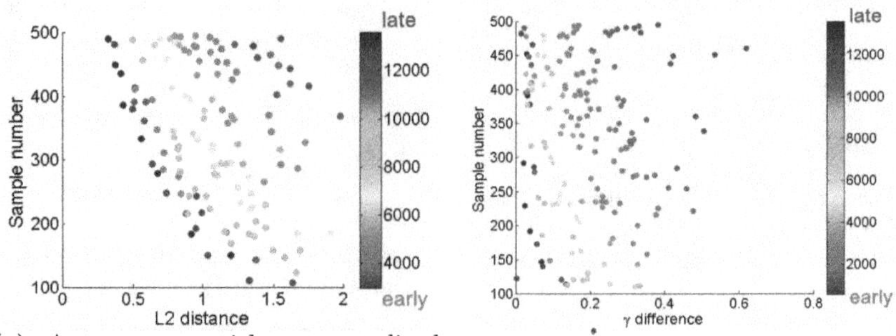

(a) Annotators with personalized ranking

(b) Position-biased annotators

Figure 2: Annotators with personalized ranking and position bias detected in simulated data.

4.1 Simulated Study

Settings We validate the proposed algorithm on simulated data labeled by 500 annotators. Specifically, we first generate the true $\theta_i \sim \mathbb{N}(0,1)$. Then each annotator has a probability $p_1 = 0.4$ having a nonzero γ^u and a probability $p_2 = 0.4$ having a nonzero δ^u. Those nonzero γ^u is drawn randomly from $\mathbb{N}(0, 0.2^2)$. And each entry δ_i^u of nonzero δ^u is drawn randomly from $\mathbb{N}(0, s^2)$ with $s \sim \mathbb{U}(0, 0.3)$. The noise ε_{ij}^u is i.i.d. $\mathbb{N}(0, 0.3^2)$. At last, we draw N^u samples for each user randomly following the model (3). The sample number N^u uniformly spans in $[N_1, N_2] = [100, 500]$. Here we choose $n = |V| = 30$, which is consistent with the first real-world dataset. Finally, we obtain a multi-edge graph with 150,494 pairwise comparisons annotated by 500 annotators.

Results Fig.2(a) shows the annotators exhibiting personalized preferences selected via cross-validation, where each color dot represents one annotator. The optimal t obtained via cross-validation is shown in Fig.3. The scores derived from each user are denoted as $\hat{\theta}^u$ and the common ranking as $\hat{\theta}$. Here the scores are the least squares solution of Eq.(3). The X-axis represents the L_2-distance between each user's personalized ranking and the common ranking, $\|\hat{\theta}^u - \hat{\theta}\|$. The Y-axis counts the number of pairwise comparisons each user provides. Clearly one can see the larger the L_2-distance and sample size, the more earlier this user is treated as one with personalized ranking (from color red to blue). This indicates that users jumped out earlier are those with large deviation from the population's opinion and a big sample size indicating a high confidence. Similar results of position-biased user is illustrated in Fig.2(b), in which the X-axis (γ difference) represents the absolute difference of γ between each user and the population.

Finally, to see whether our proposed method could provide more precise preference function for users by introducing individual-specific parameters (i.e., δ and γ), we split the data into training set (70% of the total pairwise comparisons) and testing set (the remaining 30%). To ensure the statistical stability, we repeat this procedure 20 times. Tab.1 shows the experimental results of the proposed mixed-effects model compared with HodgeRank, which indicates that our method exhibits smaller test error with an average of 0.0948 ± 0.0008 (in contrast to 0.1298 ± 0.0008 in HodgeRank) due to its parsimonious property.

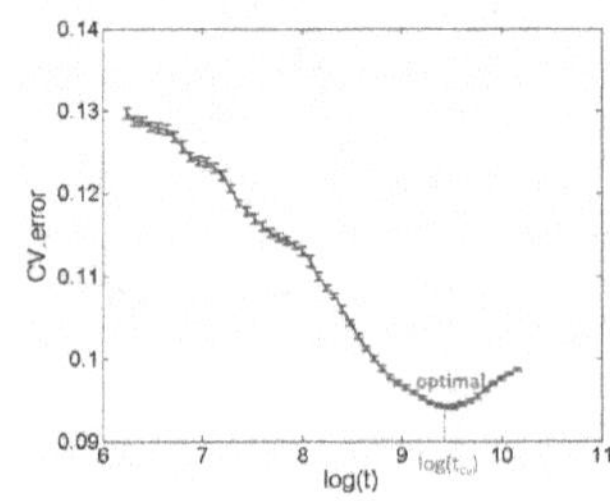

Figure 3: Optimal t with minimal average prediction error in simulated data.

Table 1: HodgeRank vs. Mixed-effects model in simulated data.

	min	mean	max	std
HodgeRank	0.1282	0.1298	0.1315	0.0008
Mixed effects model	0.0934	0.0948	0.0961	0.0008

4.2 Human Age

Figure 4: Images in Human age dataset.

Settings In this dataset, 30 images from human age dataset FG-NET [1] are annotated by a group of volunteer users on ChinaCrowds platform, as is illustrated in Fig.4. The annotator is presented with two images and given a binary choice of which one is older. Totally, we obtain 14,011 pairwise comparisons from 94 annotators.

Results Tab.2 shows the mean test error (70% data for training, 30% for testing) results of 20 times achieved by this scheme. It is shown that this mixed-effects model could

[1] http://www.fgnet.rsunit.com/

Table 2: HodgeRank vs. Mixed-effects model in Human age dataset.

	min	mean	max	std
HodgeRank	0.5542	0.5716	0.5907	0.0101
Mixed effects model	0.4199	0.4455	0.4680	0.0111

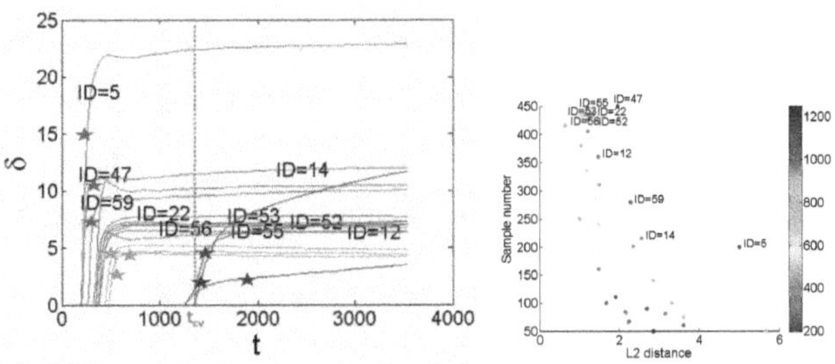

(a) LBI regularization path of δ. (Red: top 10) (b) Jumping out order.

Figure 5: Top 10 annotators with personalized ranking in Human age dataset.

provide better approximate results of the annotators' preference than the HodgeRank estimator, with an average test error of 0.4455 ± 0.0111 (in contrast to 0.5716 ± 0.0101 in HodgeRank).

To further investigate the characteristics of annotators with personalized ranking, Fig.5(a) illustrates annotator's LBI regularization paths of preference deviations with optimal t (i.e., t_{cv}) returned by cross-validation, while Fig.5(b) shows the relationships among L_2-distance to the common ranking, sample number and jumping out order of each annotator. The red curves in Fig.5(a) represent the top 10 annotators who jumped out early which are also marked in Fig.5(b). Similar to the simulated data, annotators jumped out earlier are those with a large deviation (L_2-distance) from the common ranking and a big sample size showing high confidence of such deviations. Moreover, Fig.6 shows the order comparisons of common ranking (i.e., com.) and personalized ranking of 9 representative annotators at t_{cv}. The X-axis represents user index: user = 2, 3, 4 jumped out early corresponding to paths labeled with red stars in Fig.5(a); user = 5, 6, 7 jumped out in the middle time corresponding to green stars; user = 8, 9, 10 jumped out late corresponding to blue stars. The order of faces in Y-axis is arranged from lower to higher (i.e., from color blue to red) according to the common ranking score calculated by our method. The color represents the ranking position returned by the corresponding user. It is easy to see users jumped

Table 3: Top 10 position-biased annotators in Human age dataset, together with the click counts of each side (i.e., Left and Right).

Order	ID	Left	Right	Order	ID	Left	Right
1	**12**	90	270	6	**91**	79	5
2	**70**	191	9	7	51	63	0
3	**59**	213	66	8	**50**	60	3
4	**38**	110	15	9	**18**	74	25
5	**43**	79	1	10	40	40	0

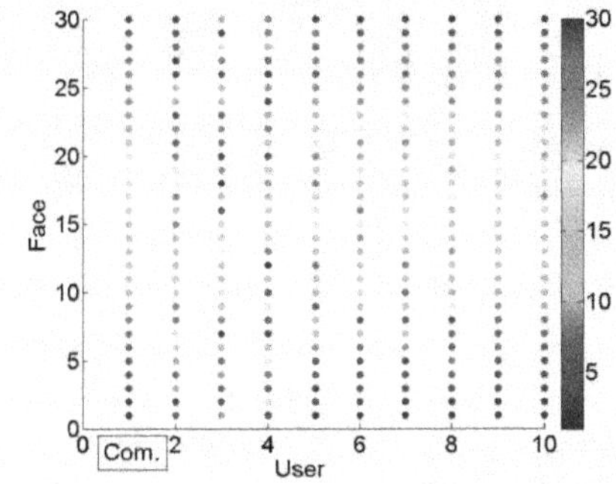

Figure 6: Comparison of common vs. personalized rankings of 9 representative annotators in Human age dataset.

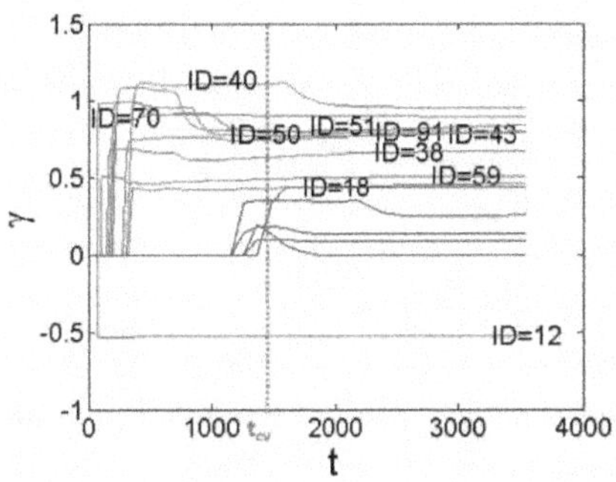

Figure 7: LBI regularization path of γ in Human age dataset. (Red: top 10 position-biased annotators; Blue: bottom 5 position-biased annotators)

out late exhibit almost consistent ranking order with the common ranking, while the earlier ones are almost the adversarial against the common. A subset of this has been shown in Fig.1 in introduction.

Moreover, Fig.7 illustrates the LBI regularization paths of annotator's position bias with red lines represent the top 10 annotators. Tab.3 further shows the click counts of each side (i.e., Left and Right) for these top 10 position-biased annotators. It is easy to see that these annotators can be divided into two types: (1) click one side all the time (with ID in blue); (2) click one side with high probability (others). Although it might be relatively easy to identify the annotators of type (1) above by inspecting their inputs, it is impossible for eye inspection to pick up those annotators of type (2) with mixed rational and abnormal behaviors. Therefore it is essential to design such a statistical methodology to quantitatively detect these kind of position-biased annotators for crowdsourcing platforms in market.

4.3 Image Quality Assessment (IQA)

Settings Two publicly available datasets, LIVE [24] and IVC [14], are used in this work. The LIVE dataset contains 29 reference images and 779 distorted images. Considering the resolution limit of most test computers, we only choose 6 different reference images (480 × 720) and 15 distorted versions of each reference, for a total of 96 images. The second dataset, IVC, which is also a broadly adopted dataset in the community of multimedia quality evaluation, includes 10

Figure 8: Images in LIVE and IVC dataset.

Table 4: HodgeRank vs. Mixed-effects model in IQA dataset (reference image 1).

	min	mean	max	std
HodgeRank	0.4918	0.5135	0.5429	0.0134
Mixed effects model	0.2922	0.3241	0.3576	0.0158

reference images and 185 distorted images derived from four distortion types–JPEG2000, JPEG, LAR Coding, and Blurring. Following the collection strategy in LIVE, we further select 9 different reference images (512×512) and 15 distorted images of each reference. Totally, we obtain a medium-sized image set that contains a total of 240 images from 15 references, as illustrated in Fig.8. Finally, 342 observers of different cultural background, each of whom performs a varied number of comparisons via Internet, provide 52,043 paired comparisons in total. The number of responses each reference image receives is different.

Table 5: Top 10 position-biased annotators in IQA dataset (reference image 1).

Order	ID	Left	Right	Order	ID	Left	Right
1	259	96	0	6	2	55	0
2	334	90	0	7	**260**	49	2
3	177	77	0	8	23	42	0
4	**103**	74	4	9	**207**	46	2
5	29	58	0	10	287	34	0

To validate whether the annotators' preference function we estimated is good enough, we randomly take reference image 1 as an illustrative example while other reference images exhibit similar results.

Results In terms of prediction performance, it can be seen that the mixed-effects model is more accurate than HodgeRank by significantly reducing the mean test error, as is shown in Tab.4.

Besides, Fig.9(a) and 9(b) shows the regularization paths of personalized ranking with top 10 annotators (red curves) selected early in the paths, as well as comparisons in order of jumping, sample size, and common ranking. It is easy to see that among these 10 annotators, 9 of them (except annotator with ID = 133) exhibit almost the same L_2-distance with the common ranking. The reason behind this is these 9 annotators click one side all the time (i.e., position-biased annotators), thus inducing a large γ. In this case, each image quality scores estimated from each annotator are close to 0 (though have differences), thus deriving the almost the same L_2-distance with the common ranking scores. Similar to the Age dataset, the common ranking vs. personalized ranking results of 9 representative users is shown in Fig.10, corresponding to the red/green/blue stars in Fig.9(a).

Moreover, the LBI regularization paths of position bias γ and click counts of top 10 annotators in this dataset are shown in Fig.11 and Tab.5. It is easy to see that annotators

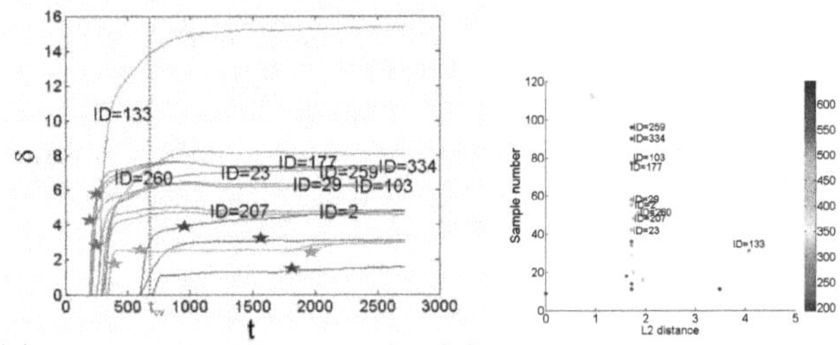

(a) LBI regularization path of δ. (Red: top 10) (b) Jumping out order.

Figure 9: Top 10 annotators exhibiting personalized ranking in IQA dataset (reference image 1).

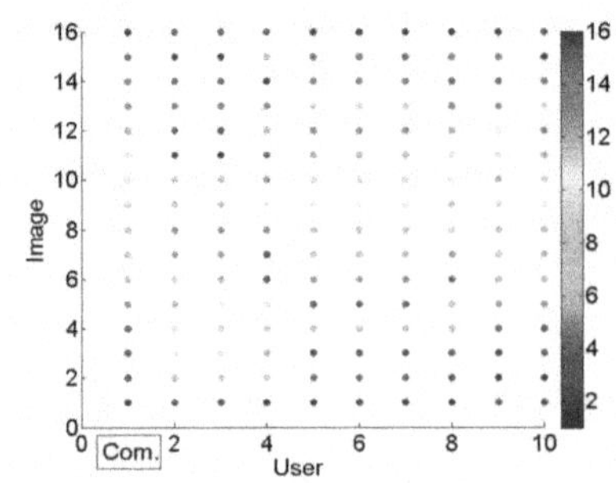

Figure 10: Comparison of common vs. personalized rankings of 9 representative annotators in IQA dataset (reference image 1).

picked out are mainly those clicking on one side almost all the time. Besides, it is interesting to see that all these annotators highlighted with blue color in Tab.5 click the left side all the time. We then go back to the crowdsourcing platform and find out that the reason behind this is a *default choice* on the left button, which induces some lazy annotators to cheat for the task.

4.4 WorldCollege Ranking

Settings We now apply the proposed method to the WorldCollege dataset, which is composed of 261 colleges. Using the Allourideas crowdsourcing platform, a total of 340 distinct annotators from various countries (e.g., USA, Canada, Spain, France, Japan) are shown randomly with pairs of these colleges, and asked to decide which of the two universities is more attractive to attend. Finally, we obtain a total of 8,823 pairwise comparisons.

Results We apply the proposed method to the resulting dataset and find out that, similar to the simulation and other two real-world datasets, the mixed-effects model could produce better performance than Hodgerank with smaller mean test error, shown in Tab.6. Noting that in this dataset, only 7 annotators are treated as annotators with distinct personalized rankings at optimal t (i.e., t_{cv}) selected via cross-validation, as is shown in Fig.12(a) and 12(b). The reason why others with relative big δ are not detected out lies in the small sample size they provide indicating high variances. The common ranking vs. personalized ranking of these 7 users is shown in Fig.13 with a similar observation

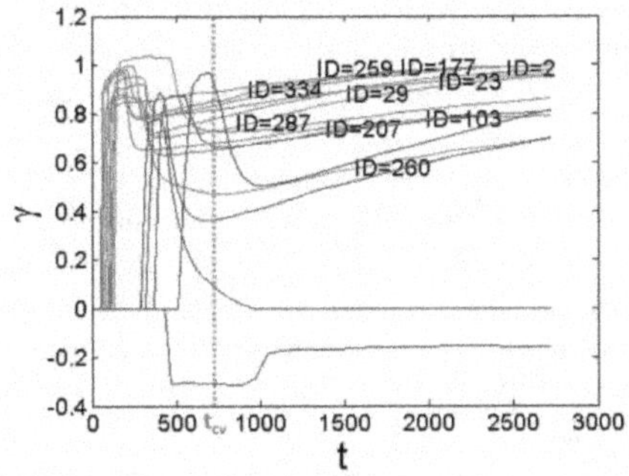

Figure 11: LBI regularization path of γ in IQA dataset (reference image 1). (Red: top 10 position-biased annotators; Blue: bottom 5 position-biased annotators).

to the other datasets. Besides, the regularization paths of position bias and click counts of top 10 annotators in this dataset are shown in Fig.14 and Tab.7. It is easy to see that similar to the human age dataset, these annotators are either clicking one side all the time, or clicking one side with high probability in mixed behaviors.

Table 6: HodgeRank vs. Mixed-effects model in WorldCollege ranking dataset.

	min	mean	max	std
HodgeRank	0.8089	0.8217	0.8406	0.0078
Mixed effects model	0.7066	0.7199	0.7398	0.0088

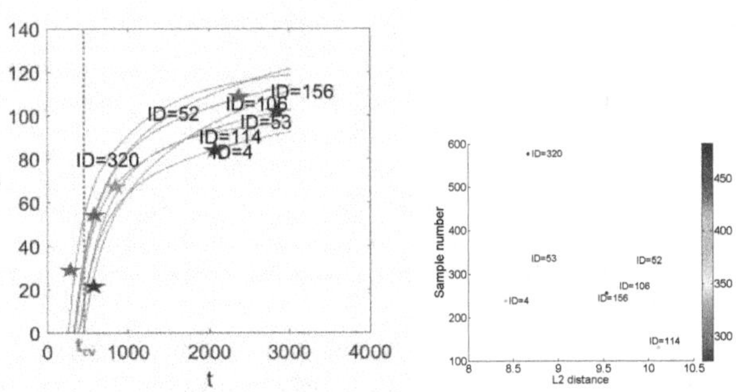

(a) LBI regularization path of δ. (Red: top 7; Blue: others)

(b) Jumping out order.

Figure 12: The 7 annotators with personalized ranking in WorldCollege ranking dataset.

5. CONCLUSIONS

In this paper, we propose a parsimonious mixed-effects model based on HodgeRank to learn user's preference or utility function in crowdsourced ranking, which takes into account both the personalized preference deviations from the common and position biases of the annotators. To be specific, common preference scores indicate the consistent ranking on population-level which approximates the behavior of all users, while a small set of annotators might have nonzero personalized deviations and abnormal behavior in position bias. Equipped with the newly developed Linearized Bregman Iteration, which is a simple iterative procedure generating a sequence of parsimonious models, we establish a dynamic path from the common utility to individual variations, with different levels of parsimony or sparsity on personalization. Experimental studies are conducted with both simulated examples and real-world datasets. Our results suggest that the proposed methodology is an effective tool to investigate the diversity in annotator's behavior in modern crowdsourcing data.

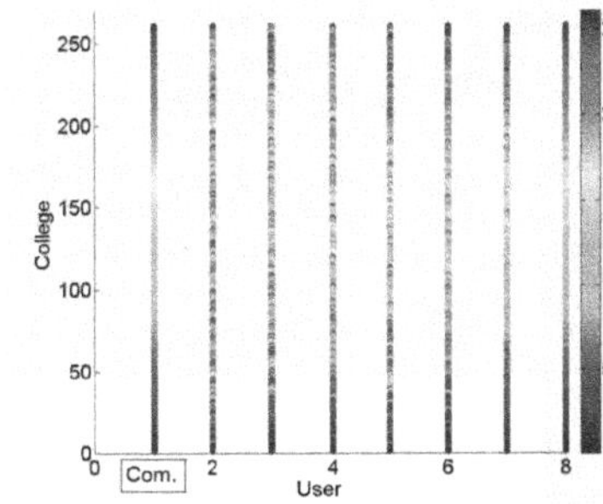

Figure 13: Comparison of common vs. personalized rankings of 7 annotators in WorldCollege ranking dataset.

Table 7: Top 10 position-biased annotators in WorldCollege ranking dataset.

Order	ID	Left	Right	Order	ID	Left	Right
1	268	148	0	6	**270**	20	70
2	209	127	0	7	267	45	0
3	**156**	189	67	8	**276**	16	54
4	**320**	253	324	9	166	35	0
5	**87**	11	62	10	115	34	0

Acknowledgements

The research of Qianqian Xu was supported by National Key Research and Development Plan (No. 2016YFB0800603), National Natural Science Foundation of China (No. 61422213, 61402019, 61390514, 61572042), "Strategic Priority Research Program" of the Chinese Academy of Sciences (XDA06010701), National Program for Support of Top-notch Young Professionals, and China Postdoctoral Science Foundation (2015T-80025). The research of Jiechao Xiong and Yuan Yao was supported in part by National Basic Research Program of China under grant 2015CB85600, 2012CB825501, and NSFC grant 61370004, 11421110001 (A3 project), as well as grants from Baidu and Microsoft Research-Asia. We would like to thank anonymous reviewers who gave valuable suggestions to help improve the manuscript.

6. REFERENCES

[1] K. Arrow. *Social Choice and Individual Values, 2nd Ed.* Yale University Press, New Haven, CT, 1963.

[2] A. Beck and M. Teboulle. A fast iterative shrinkage-thresholding algorithm for linear inverse problems. *SIAM Journal on Imaging Sciences*, 2(1):183–202, 2009.

[3] O. Candogan, I. Menache, A. Ozdaglar, and P. A. Parrilo. Flows and decompositions of games: Harmonic and potential games. *Mathematics of Operations Research*, 36(3):474–503, 2011.

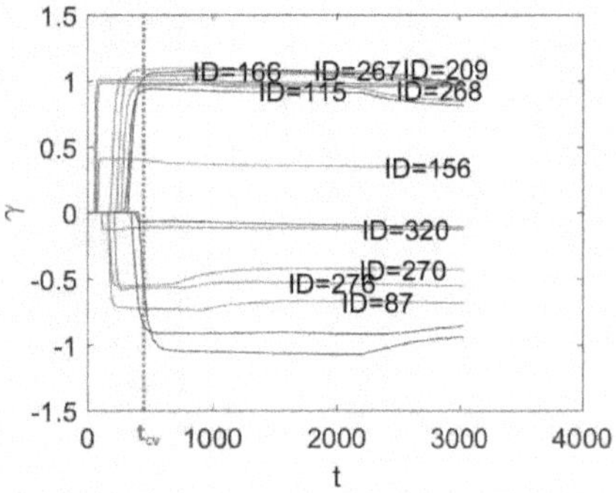

Figure 14: LBI regularization path of γ in WorldCollege ranking dataset. (Red: top 10 position-biased annotators; Blue: bottom 5 position-biased annotators).

[4] K.-T. Chen, C.-C. Wu, Y.-C. Chang, and C.-L. Lei. A crowdsourceable QoE evaluation framework for multimedia content. pages 491–500. ACM Multimedia, 2009.

[5] D. Cynthia, K. Ravi, N. Moni, and S. Dandapani. Rank aggregation methods for the web. In *International Conference on World Wide Web*, pages 613–622, 2001.

[6] R. L. Day. Position bias in paired product tests. *Journal of Marketing Research*, 6(1):98–100, 1969.

[7] J. de Borda. *Mémoire sur les Elections au Scrutin.* Histoire de l'Académie Royale des Sciences, 1781.

[8] D. L. Donoho. De-noising by soft-thresholding. *IEEE Transactions on Information Theory*, 41(3):613–627, 1995.

[9] J. Fan and R. L. Variable selection via nonconcave penalized likelihood and its oracle properties. *Journal of American Statistical Association*, 96(456):1348–1360, 2001.

[10] Y. Fu, T. M. Hospedales, T. Xiang, S. Gong, and Y. Yao. Interestingness prediction by robust learning to rank. In *Europeon Conference on Computer Vision*, volume 8690, pages 488–503. 2014.

[11] Y. Fu, T. M. Hospedales, T. Xiang, J. Xiong, S. Gong, Y. Wang, and Y. Yao. Robust subjective visual property prediction from crowdsourced pairwise labels. *IEEE transactions on pattern analysis and machine intelligence*, 38(3):563–577, 2016.

[12] K. G. Jamieson and R. D. Nowak. Active ranking using pairwise comparisons. *Annual Conference on Neural Information Processing Systems*, pages 2240–2248, 2011.

[13] X. Jiang, L.-H. Lim, Y. Yao, and Y. Ye. Statistical ranking and combinatorial Hodge theory. *Mathematical Programming*, 127(6):203–244, 2011.

[14] P. Le Callet and F. Autrusseau. Subjective quality assessment irccyn/ivc database, 2005. http://www.irccyn.ec-nantes.fr/ivcdb/.

[15] S. Negahban, S. Oh, and D. Shah. Iterative ranking from pair-wise comparisons. In *Annual Conference on Neural Information Processing Systems*, pages 2483–2491, 2012.

[16] S. Osher, M. Burger, D. Goldfarb, J. Xu, and W. Yin. An iterative regularization method for total variation-based image restoration. *SIAM Journal on Multiscale Modeling and Simulation*, 4(2):460–489, 2005.

[17] S. Osher, F. Ruan, J. Xiong, Y. Yao, and W. Yin. Sparse recovery via differential inclusions. *Applied and Computational Harmonic Analysis*, 2016.

[18] B. Osting, C. Brune, and S. Osher. Enhanced statistical rankings via targeted data collection. In *International Conference on Machine Learning*, pages 489–497, 2013.

[19] B. Osting, J. Darbon, and S. Osher. Statistical ranking using the l_1-norm on graphs. *Inverse Problems & Imaging*, 7(3), 2013.

[20] B. Osting, J. Xiong, Q. Xu, and Y. Yao. Analysis of crowdsourced sampling strategies for hodgerank with sparse random graphs. *Applied and Computational Harmonic Analysis*, 2016.

[21] A. Rajkumar and S. Agarwal. A statistical convergence perspective of algorithms for rank aggregation from pairwise data. In *International Conference on Machine Learning*, pages 118–126, 2014.

[22] J. D. Rennie and N. Srebro. Fast maximum margin matrix factorization for collaborative prediction. In *International conference on Machine learning*, pages 713–719, 2005.

[23] R. Salakhutdinov and A. Mnih. Bayesian probabilistic matrix factorization using markov chain monte carlo. In *International conference on Machine learning*, pages 880–887, 2008.

[24] H. Sheikh, Z. Wang, L. Cormack, and A. Bovik. LIVE image & video quality assessment database, 2008.

[25] Q. Xu, Q. Huang, T. Jiang, B. Yan, W. Lin, and Y. Yao. HodgeRank on random graphs for subjective video quality assessment. *IEEE Transactions on Multimedia*, 14(3):844–857, 2012.

[26] Q. Xu, J. Xiong, X. Cao, and Y. Yao. False discovery rate control and statistical quality assessment of annotators in crowdsourced ranking. In *International Conference on Machine Learning*, pages 1282–1291, 2016.

[27] Q. Xu, J. Xiong, Q. Huang, and Y. Yao. Robust evaluation for quality of experience in crowdsourcing. In *ACM Multimedia*, pages 43–52, 2013.

[28] J. Yi, R. Jin, S. Jain, and A. Jain. Inferring users' preferences from crowdsourced pairwise comparisons: A matrix completion approach. In *AAAI Conference on Human Computation and Crowdsourcing*, 2013.

[29] W. Yin, S. Osher, J. Darbon, and D. Goldfarb. Bregman iterative algorithms for compressed sensing and related problems. *SIAM Journal on Imaging Sciences*, 1(1):143–168, 2008.

[30] J. Yuan, G. Steidl, and C. Schnorr. Convex Hodge decomposition and regularization of image flows. *Journal of Mathematical Imaging and Vision*, 33(2):169–177, 2009.

[31] K. Yuan, Q. Ling, W. Yin, and A. Ribeiro. A Linearized Bregman algorithm for decentralized basis pursuit. *European Signal Processing Conference*, pages 1–5, 2013.

without exploiting any particular properties of different functions ϕ_i or observations $\mathbf{x}_i$. A common one pervasively used in the literature is weighted linear fusion which can be expressed as follows:

$$\Phi(\mathbf{x}_1, \ldots, \mathbf{x}_n; \phi_1, \ldots, \phi_n, w_1, \ldots, w_n) = \sum_{i=1}^{n} [w_i \times \phi_i(\mathbf{x}_i)], \tag{1}$$

where:

$$\forall i = 1, \ldots, n.\ w_i \geq 0, \quad \text{and} \quad \sum_{i=1}^{n} w_i = 1. \tag{2}$$

Here $\Phi(\mathbf{x}_1, \ldots, \mathbf{x}_n; \phi_1, \ldots, \phi_n, w_1, \ldots, w_n)$ is the fused matching score which is derived by simply combining different $\phi_i(\mathbf{x}_i)$, and (2) ensures that the condition $0 \leq \phi_i(\mathbf{x}_i) < \infty$ is maintained for $\Phi(\mathbf{x}_1, \ldots, \mathbf{x}_n; \phi_1, \ldots, \phi_n, w_1, \ldots, w_n)$ as well, i.e. that it is the case that $0 \leq \Phi(\mathbf{x}_1, \ldots, \mathbf{x}_n; \phi_1, \ldots, \phi_n, w_1, \ldots, w_n) < \infty$.

The fusion approach described by (1) can also be rewritten more simply as:

$$\Phi(\mathbf{x}_1, \ldots, \mathbf{x}_n; \phi_1, \ldots, \phi_n, w_1, \ldots, w_n) = \tag{3}$$

$$\hat{\Phi}(\mathbf{x}_1, \ldots, \mathbf{x}_n; \phi_1, \ldots, \phi_n, w_1, \ldots, w_n) = \tag{4}$$

$$\sum_{i=1}^{n} \left[\frac{1}{n} \times \hat{\phi}_i(\mathbf{x}_i, w_i, n)\right], \tag{5}$$

where:

$$\hat{\phi}_i(\mathbf{x}_i, w_i, n) = n \times w_i \times \phi_i(\mathbf{x}_i). \tag{6}$$

Here the original weighted linear fusion of the contributing terms $\phi_i(\mathbf{x}_i)$ in (1) has been replaced by unweighted linear fusion of terms $\hat{\phi}_i(\mathbf{x}_i, w_i, n)$ which adjust the magnitudes of the fused scores directly. This can be achieved simply by considering the statistics of the distributions of different $\phi_i(\mathbf{x}_i)$ and the corresponding prediction, and without any knowledge of what different features $\mathbf{x}_i$ represent or what form different ϕ_i have, i.e. while maintaining the premise of uninformed fusion.

It can be readily seen that the described fusion approach fits the conditions specified in the preceding section – namely, simplicity (both methodological and that of implementation) and broad applicability. Although simple, uninformed fusion demonstrates remarkably good performance across a wide span of different data types and domains, ranging from dementia screening [17] to multimodal biometric identification [14, 5, 12].

$$\Phi_o(\mathbf{x}_1, \ldots, \mathbf{x}_n; \phi_1, \ldots, \phi_n, \omega_1, \ldots, \omega_n) = \tag{7}$$

$$\sqrt{\sum_{i=1}^{n} [\omega_i \times \phi_i(\mathbf{x}_i)^2]}, \tag{8}$$

where as before:

$$\forall i = 1, \ldots, n.\ \omega_i \geq 0, \quad \text{and} \quad \sum_{i=1}^{n} \omega_i = 1. \tag{9}$$

$$\Phi_o(\mathbf{x}_1, \ldots, \mathbf{x}_n; \phi_1, \ldots, \phi_n, \omega_1, \ldots, \omega_n) = \tag{10}$$

$$\hat{\Phi}_o(\mathbf{x}_1, \ldots, \mathbf{x}_n; \phi_1, \ldots, \phi_n, \omega_1, \ldots, \omega_n) = \tag{11}$$

$$\sqrt{\sum_{i=1}^{n} \left[\frac{1}{n} \times \widetilde{\phi}_i(\mathbf{x}_i, \omega_i, n)^2\right]}, \tag{12}$$

where, analogously to (6), the adjusted fusion scores can be expressed as:

$$\widetilde{\phi}_i(\mathbf{x}_i, \omega_i, n) = \sqrt{n} \times \omega_i \times \phi_i(\mathbf{x}_i). \tag{13}$$

The formulation in (12) can be readily recognized as the quadratic mean, in engineering also commonly referred to as the root mean square (RMS), of the n terms $\widetilde{\phi}_i(\mathbf{x}_i, \omega_i, n)$.

Before proceeding with a formal analysis of the two fusion approaches, it is insightful to gain an intuitive understanding of the difference between them. Note that simple linear fusion described in (5) treats different scores as effectively interchangeable – a decrease in one score is exactly compensated by an increase in another score by the same amount. This is sensible when the scores correspond to the same measurement which is merely repeated. The described fusion can then be seen as a way of reducing measurement error, assuming that measurement is unbiased and that errors are identically and independently distributed [9]. However this is a rather trivial case of fusion and in practice one is more commonly interested in fusion of different types of data modalities. Indeed, in practice it is often the explicit aim to try to use information sources which vary independently, and attempt to exploit best their complementary natures [5]. In such instances different scores are best treated as describing a source in orthogonal directions, thereby giving rise to a feature vector $\left[\widetilde{\phi}_1(\mathbf{x}_1), \ldots, \widetilde{\phi}_n(\mathbf{x}_n)\right]^T \in \mathbb{R}^n$. The quadratic mean-based fusion of (12) can then be thought of as emerging from a normalized distance measure between such feature vectors in the corresponding ambient embedding space $\mathbb{R}^n$.

Let us now consider the effects of the two fusion approaches in more detail. Firstly, note that scoring measures $\hat{\phi}_i(\mathbf{x}_i, w_i, n)$ and $\widetilde{\phi}_i(\mathbf{x}_i, \omega_i, n)$ are inevitably imperfect – neither can be expected to produce universally the perfect matching score of 0 when the query correctly matches a source and ∞ when it does not. Even the weaker requirement of universally smaller pseudo-distances for correct matches is unrealistic. Indeed, it is precisely this practical challenge that motivates multimodal fusion. Consequently, they are appropriately modelled as resulting from draws from random variables:

$$\hat{\phi}_i(\mathbf{x}_i), \widetilde{\phi}_i(\mathbf{x}_i) \sim X_i. \tag{14}$$

Let us examine the effects of the two fusion approaches in detail. Specifically, for clarity consider the fusion of two sources, say i and j, while observing that the derived results are readily applicable to the fusion of an arbitrary number of sources through the use of an inductive argument. Following (5) and (12), applying linear and quadratic mean-based fusion results in scores described respectively by random variables $\hat{Y}_{ij}$ and $\widetilde{Y}_{ij}$, where:

$$\frac{\hat{\phi}_i(\mathbf{x}_i) + \hat{\phi}_j(\mathbf{x}_j)}{2} \sim \frac{X_i + X_j}{2} = \hat{Y}_{ij}, \tag{15}$$

and:

$$\sqrt{\frac{\widetilde{\phi}_i(\mathbf{x}_i)^2 + \widetilde{\phi}_j(\mathbf{x}_j)^2}{2}} \sim \sqrt{\frac{X_i^2 + X_j^2}{2}} = \widetilde{Y}_{ij}. \tag{16}$$

The former can be further expanded as:

$$E\left[\hat{Y}_{ij}^2\right] = E\left[\left(\frac{X_i + X_j}{2}\right)^2\right] \tag{17}$$

$$= \frac{1}{4}\left\{E\left[X_i^2\right] + E\left[X_j^2\right] + E\left[X_i X_j\right]\right\}, \tag{18}$$

$$e_k(0) = \frac{P3_k}{P_a(1-P3_k)} \left\{ \frac{1}{(1-P2_k)} \left[A_1 P3_k - kr^{T_2+1}\left(\frac{1-r^{T_1}}{1-r}\right) + P_a(P1_k+P2_k)e_k(0) - e_k(T_1)\right] + A_1 r^{T_1+1}\left(\frac{1-r^{T_2-T_1}}{1-r}\right)\right\}, \quad (24)$$

$$e_k(T_1) = \frac{A_1}{P2_k} r^{T_1+1} - P1_k P_a e_k(0) - \frac{P1_k P3_k}{P2_k} A_1 r^{T_2+1} - \frac{P3_k}{P2_k} A_1 r^{T_1+T_2+1}, \quad (25)$$

$$1 = \left[1 + \frac{P_a(1-P3_k)}{P3_k}\right] e_k(0) + \frac{Ar^{T_2+1}}{1-r}. \quad (26)$$

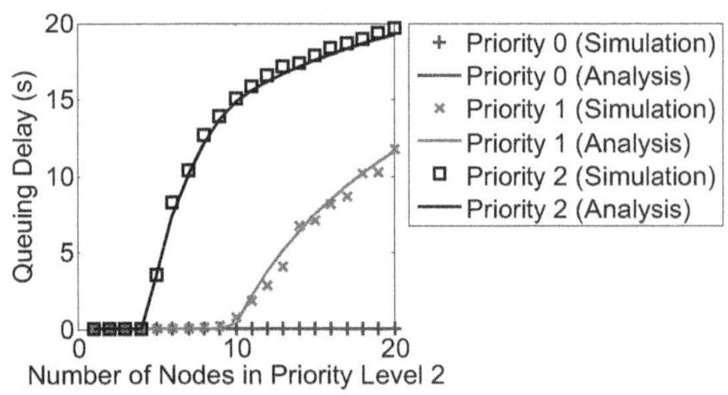

Figure 6: The model validation result.

(32) and Eq. (33), we have

$$\overline{D}_k(T) = \sigma \mathbf{E}\left[\frac{\sum_{i=1}^{N_T} i \cdot \frac{\lambda_k^2 - \mu_k^2}{\lambda_k \mu_k}}{N_T}\right]$$
$$\xrightarrow{a.s.} \sigma \cdot \frac{\mathbf{E}[N_T]+1}{2} \cdot \frac{\lambda_k^2 - \mu_k^2}{\lambda_k \mu_k}$$
$$\xrightarrow{a.s.} \frac{\sigma T}{2} \cdot \frac{\lambda_k - \mu_k}{\lambda_k}.$$

□

5.6 Model Validation

In our model validation, there are 3 priority levels, i.e., $k = 0, 1, 2$. The minimum CW sizes are $W_{0,0} = 3$, $W_{0,1} = 7$, and $W_{0,2} = 15$, respectively. To present the validation results clearly, we fix the numbers of nodes in priority levels 0 and 1, and change the number of nodes in priority level 2. Concretely, we fix $N_0 = 2$ and $N_1 = 2$, and change N_2 from 1 to 20. The packet size is set to $500B$. For all the nodes, the packet arrival rate is $1Mbps$, which matches the standard bit rate of YouTube 360p videos. Each run of simulations lasts for a duration of 50 seconds, i.e., $T = 50$. All the queues are empty at the beginning of this 50-second duration. We use a date rate of $24Mbps$ as an example.

We validate our models with queueing delay in Fig. 6. Generally, it is shown that the queueing delays are well captured by our two-level models. One interesting observation is that the average queueing delay of nodes in priority level 2 increases suddenly at the point of $N_2 = 5$. This sudden increase of queueing delay also happens for nodes in priority level 1 at the point of $N_2 = 11$. When $\lambda_k < \mu_k$, packets are transmitted rapidly by nodes in priority level k. The queue length stays as a constant even if time goes to infinity. When $\lambda_k > \mu_k$, packets begin to accumulate in queues of nodes in priority level k, and the lengths of these queues keep increasing as time goes by. Therefore, instead of having a constant value, the average queueing delay becomes an increasing function of time, and will approach infinity if time approaches infinity. Note that this is captured by our queue level models.

Table 1: Candidate delay sets for DRIVING.

Setting	β_2	β_1	β_0
1	$[0,1)$	$[1,2)$	$[2,+\infty)$
2	$[0,1)$	$[1,4)$	$[4,+\infty)$
3	$[0,2)$	$[2,4)$	$[4,+\infty)$
4	$[0,2)$	$[2,10)$	$[10,+\infty)$
5	$[0,4)$	$[4,10)$	$[10,+\infty)$

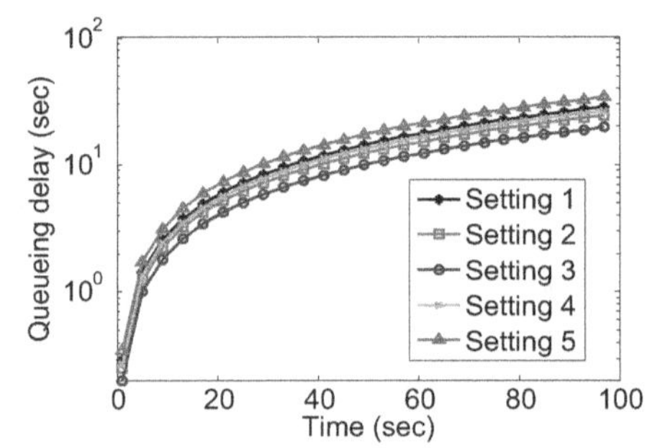

Figure 7: The evolution of queueing delays under different settings of DRIVING.

5.7 Tuning DRIVING with the Models

One important application of our analytical models is to tune the DRIVING for better performance before real deployment. There are three kinds of parameters to be tuned, i.e., the number of priority levels, their corresponding delay sets, and their corresponding minimum CW sizes. Due to the limited space, we only present the tuning of the delay sets while fixing the number of priority levels and the corresponding minimum CW sizes. Concretely, we use 3 priority levels, and set their minimum CW sizes as 3, 7, and 15, respectively. We compare five candidate delay sets as presented in Table 1, and select the best one from them.

Based on our two-level models, we calculate the evolution of queueing delays under these five settings. As an example, we set set packet size as $500B$, and the packet arrival rate as $1Mbps$. Fig. 7 illustrate how the queueing delays increase with time. It is shown that Setting 3, which is neither the most aggressive nor the most conservative, achieves the lowest queueing delay at all time. The reason is two-fold. On ond hand, an aggressive setting tends to push all nodes to the highest priority level quickly. As a result, the CW sizes of all nodes become too small to avoid packet collisions. On the other hand, a conservative setting tends to retain all nodes in at the lowest priority level. Consequently, the CW sizes of all nodes remain too large, and thus the channel utilization remains low.

6. PERFORMANCE EVALUATION

In this section, we conduct comprehensive simulation studies to illustrate the improvements brought by DRIVING. We

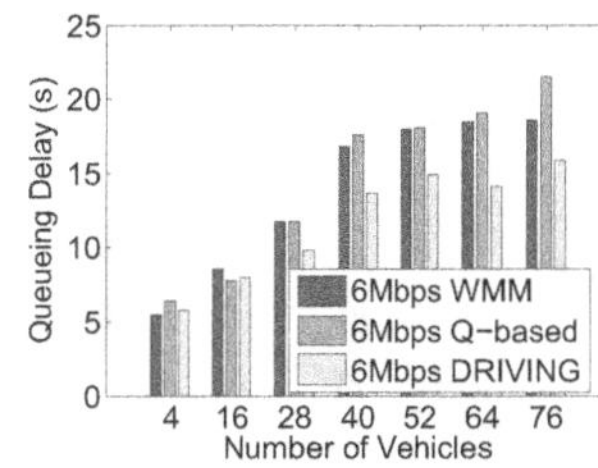

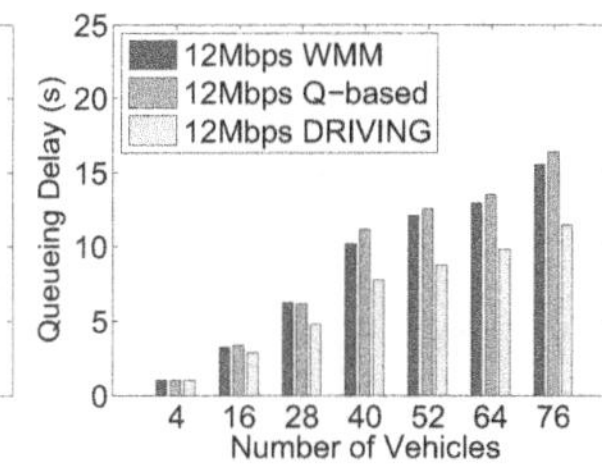

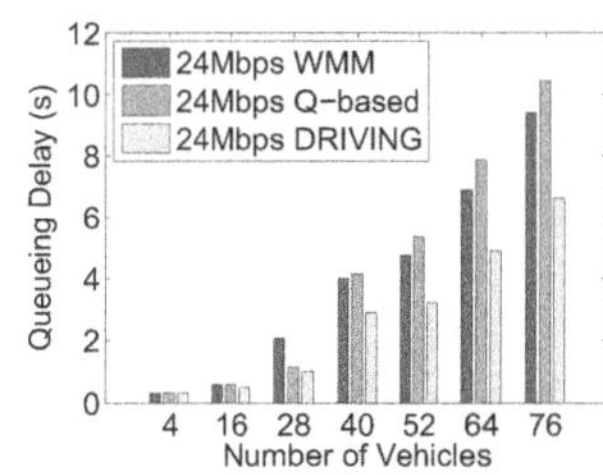

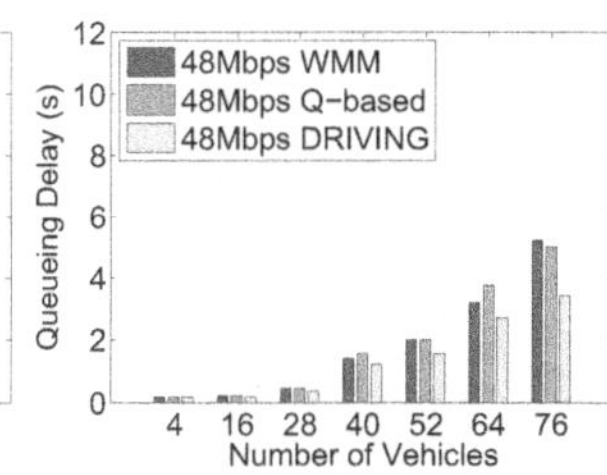

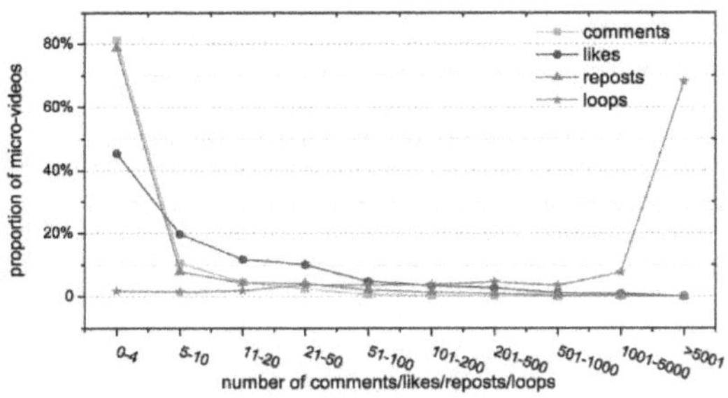

Figure 3: Distribution of the number of comments, likes, reposts and loops of micro-videos in our dataset.

all the videos are denoted by $\mathbf{y} = \{y_1, y_2, \cdots, y_N\}^T \in \mathbb{R}^N$. Let $\mathbf{f} = \{f_1, f_2, \cdots, f_N, f_{N+1}, f_{N+2}, \cdots, f_{N+M}\}^T \in \mathbb{R}^{N+M}$ stand for the predicted results regarding popularity for all samples, including the labeled and unlabeled ones. We aim to jointly learn the common space $\mathbf{X_0} \in \mathbb{R}^{(N+M)\times Z_0}$ shared by multiple modalities and the popularity for the M unlabeled micro-videos.

Our proposed model targets at reasoning from observed training micro-videos to testing ones. Such prediction belongs to transductive learning, in which both labeled samples as well as unlabeled samples are available for training. It hence obtains better performance. In contrast, inductive model is reasoning from observed training cases to general rules, which are then applied to the test cases.

4.2 Problem Formulation

It is apparent that different modalities may contribute distinctive and complementary information about micro-videos. For example, textual modality gives us hints about the topics of the given micro-video; acoustic and visual modalities may respectively convey location and situation of micro-videos, and user modality demonstrates the influence of the micro-video publisher. These clues jointly contribute to the popularity of a micro-video. Obviously, due to the noise and information insufficiency of each modality, it may be suboptimal to conduct learning directly from each single modality separately. In contrast, we assume that there exists an optimal latent space, in which micro-videos can be better described. Moreover, the optimal latent space should maintain the original intrinsic characteristics conveyed by multi-modalities of the given micro-videos. Therefore, we penalize the disagreement of the normalized Laplacian matrix between the latent space and each modality. In particular, we formalize this assumption as follows. Let $\mathbf{S}_k \in \mathbb{R}^{(N+M)\times(N+M)}$ be the similarity matrix[10], which is computed by the Gaussian similarity function as follows,

$$S_k(i,j) = \begin{cases} exp\Big(-\frac{\left\|\mathbf{x}_k^i - \mathbf{x}_k^j\right\|^2}{2\sigma_k^2}\Big) & , \text{ if } i \neq j; \\ 0 & , \text{ if } i = j. \end{cases} \tag{2}$$

where $\mathbf{x}_k^i$ and $\mathbf{x}_k^j$ are the micro-video pairs in the k-th modality space. Thereinto, the radius parameter σ_k is simply set as the median of the Euclidean distances over all video pairs in the k-th modality. We then derive the corresponding normalized Laplacian matrix as follows,

$$\mathbf{L}(\mathbf{S_k}) = \mathbf{I} - \mathbf{D}_k^{-\frac{1}{2}}\mathbf{S}_k\mathbf{D}_k^{-\frac{1}{2}}, \tag{3}$$

[10]To facilitate the illustration, k ranges from 0 to K.

where $\mathbf{I}$ is a $(N+M)\times(N+M)$ identity matrix and $\mathbf{D}_k \in \mathbb{R}^{(N+M)\times(N+M)}$ is the diagonal degree matrix, whose (u,u)-th entry is the sum of the u-th row of $\mathbf{S}_k$. Since $S_k(i,j) > 0$, we can derive that $tr(\mathbf{L}(\mathbf{S_k})) > 0$. We thus can formulate the disagreement penalty between the latent space and the original modalities as,

$$\sum_{k=1}^{K} \| \frac{1}{tr(\mathbf{L}(\mathbf{S_0}))}\mathbf{L}(\mathbf{S_0}) - \frac{1}{tr(\mathbf{L}(\mathbf{S_k}))}\mathbf{L}(\mathbf{S_k}) \|_F^2, \tag{4}$$

where $tr(\mathbf{A})$ is the trace of matrix $\mathbf{A}$ and $\|\cdot\|_F$ denotes the Frobenius norm of matrix. In addition, inspired by [32], considering that similar micro-videos attempt to have similar popularity in the latent common space, we adopt the following regularizer,

$$\begin{aligned} &\frac{1}{2}\sum_{m=1}^{N+M}\sum_{n=1}^{N+M}\Big(\frac{f(\mathbf{x}_0^m)}{\sqrt{D_0(\mathbf{x}_0^m)}} - \frac{f(\mathbf{x}_0^n)}{\sqrt{D_0(\mathbf{x}_0^n)}}\Big)^2 S_0(m,n) \\ &= \mathbf{f}^T\mathbf{L}(\mathbf{S_0})\mathbf{f}. \end{aligned} \tag{5}$$

Based upon these formulations, we can define the loss function that measures the empirical error on the training samples. As reported in [22], the squared loss usually yields good performance as other complex ones. We thus adopt the squared loss in our algorithm for simplicity and efficiency. In particular, since we do not have the labels for testing samples, we only consider the squared loss regarding the N unlabeled samples to guarantee the learning performance. We ultimately reach our objective function as,

$$\begin{aligned} &\min_{\mathbf{f},\mathbf{L}(\mathbf{S_0})} \sum_{i=1}^{N}(y_i - f_i)^2 + \mu\mathbf{f}^T\mathbf{L}(\mathbf{S_0})\mathbf{f} \\ &+ \lambda\sum_{k=1}^{K} \| \frac{1}{tr(\mathbf{L}(\mathbf{S_0}))}\mathbf{L}(\mathbf{S_0}) - \frac{1}{tr(\mathbf{L}(\mathbf{S_k}))}\mathbf{L}(\mathbf{S_k}) \|_F^2, \end{aligned} \tag{6}$$

where λ and μ are both nonnegative regularization parameters. To be more specific, λ penalizes the disagreement among the latent space and modalities, and μ encourages that similar popularity will be assigned to similar micro-videos.

4.3 Alternative Optimization

To simplify the representation, we first define that,

$$\begin{cases} \tilde{\mathbf{L}} = \frac{1}{tr(\mathbf{L}(\mathbf{S_0}))}\mathbf{L}(\mathbf{S_0}), \\ \tilde{\mathbf{L}}_\mathbf{k} = \frac{1}{tr(\mathbf{L}(\mathbf{S_k}))}\mathbf{L}(\mathbf{S_k}). \end{cases} \tag{7}$$

Therefore, the objective function can be transformed to,

$$\begin{aligned} &\min_{\mathbf{f}} \sum_{i=1}^{N}(y_i - f_i)^2 + \lambda\sum_{k=1}^{K}\left\|\tilde{\mathbf{L}} - \tilde{\mathbf{L}}_\mathbf{k}\right\|_F^2 + \mu\mathbf{f}^T\tilde{\mathbf{L}}\mathbf{f}, \\ &\text{subject to} \quad tr(\mathbf{L}(\mathbf{S_0})) = 1. \end{aligned} \tag{8}$$

Furthermore, to optimize $\tilde{\mathbf{L}}$ more efficiently, inspired by the property that $tr(\tilde{\mathbf{L}}_\mathbf{k}) = 1$, we let,

$$\mathbf{L}(\mathbf{S_0}) = \sum_{k=1}^{K}\beta_k\tilde{\mathbf{L}}_\mathbf{k}, \quad \text{subject to} \quad \sum_{k=1}^{K}\beta_k = 1. \tag{9}$$

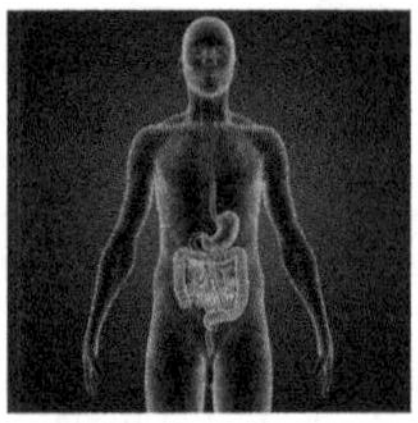

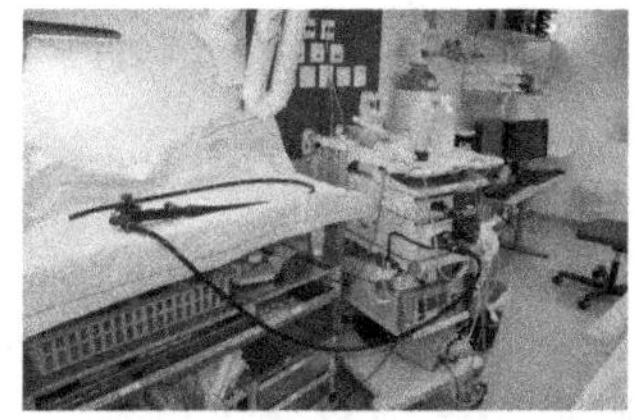

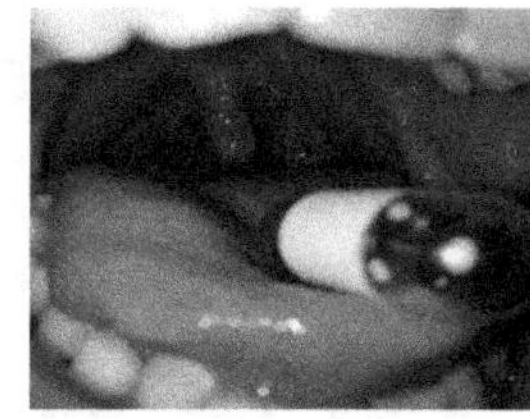

Weighted Linear Fusion of Multimodal Data – A Reasonable Baseline?

Ognjen Arandjelović
School of Computer Science
University of St Andrews
St Andrews KY16 9SX
United Kingdom
ognjen.arandjelovic@gmail.com

ABSTRACT

The ever-increasing demand for reliable inference capable of handling unpredictable challenges of practical application in the real world, has made research on information fusion of major importance. There are few fields of application and research where this is more evident than in the sphere of multimedia which by its very nature inherently involves the use of multiple modalities, be it for learning, prediction, or human-computer interaction, say. In the development of the most common type, score-level fusion algorithms, it is virtually without an exception desirable to have as a reference starting point a simple and universally sound baseline benchmark which newly developed approaches can be compared to. One of the most pervasively used methods is that of weighted linear fusion. It has cemented itself as the default off-the-shelf baseline owing to its simplicity of implementation, interpretability, and surprisingly competitive performance across a wide range of application domains and information source types. In this paper I argue that despite this track record, weighted linear fusion is not a good baseline on the grounds that there is an equally simple and interpretable alternative – namely quadratic mean-based fusion – which is theoretically more principled and which is more successful in practice. I argue the former from first principles and demonstrate the latter using a series of experiments on a diverse set of fusion problems: computer vision-based object recognition, arrhythmia detection, and fatality prediction in motor vehicle accidents.

Keywords

Prediction; arrhythmia; object recognition; computer vision; car accident.

1. INTRODUCTION

Score-level fusion of information is pervasive in algorithms addressing a wide variety of problems. From predictions of the price of French vintage wine using the fusion of predictions based on rainfall and temperature data [13] or more robust estimates of a person's gaze through the fusion of estimates obtained by considering each of the eyes in isolation [10], to sophisticated biometric algorithms which fuse similarity measures based on visual and infrared face appearance [11, 6] or gait characteristics [14], the fundamental premise underlying information fusion is the same: the use of multiple information sources facilitates the making of better decisions, be they in the form of classification, regression, or any of a number of others.

Whatever the specific problem, the effectiveness of a specific information fusion methodology needs to be demonstrated. If possible this should be done by comparing its performance against the current state-of-the-art. However this is often prohibitively difficult in practice. For example, in some cases the state-of-the-art may not be readily available for evaluation – the original code may not have been released and re-implementation may be overly time-consuming, the algorithm may not have been described in sufficient detail, the technology may be proprietary and costly to purchase, etc. In other cases there may not be a clear state-of-the-art because the particular problem at hand has not been addressed before. In such circumstances it is useful to compare the novel methodology with a simple yet sensible baseline.

Probably the simplest choices for the baseline would be the performances achieved using individual information sources which are being fused. However this is an excessively low bar for comparison. Instead what is widely done by authors across the research spectrum is to use simple weighted fusion of individual scores as a reference.

2. UNINFORMED INFORMATION FUSION

Let us start by formalizing the problem considered in this paper. I adopt the broad paradigm of so-called data source identification and matching. In particular, I assume that the available data comprises a set of n sensed observations, $\mathbf{X} = \{\mathbf{x}_i\} = \{\mathbf{x}_1, \ldots, \mathbf{x}_n\}$, which correspond to different modalities sensing the same data source. Furthermore, I assume that there are functions (i.e. algorithms) $\phi_1, \ldots, \phi_n$ which quantify how well a particular observation $\mathbf{x}_i$ matches a specific data source. Without loss of generality I assume $0 \leq \phi_i(\mathbf{x}_i) < \infty$, where 0 indicates the best possible match, and ∞ the worst i.e. $\phi_i(\mathbf{x}_i)$ can be thought of a quasi-distance – 'quasi-' to emphasise that it is not required that $\phi_i(\mathbf{x}_i)$ meets the strict conditions required of a metric. Note that the aforestated setting describes observations in the most general sense, e.g. these may be feature vectors (such as rasterized appearance images or SIFT descriptors in computer vision), sets of vectors, and so on, and they do not need to be of the same type (for example, some may be vectors, others sequences) or dimensionalities.

As noted in the previous section, we are looking for a simple way of fusing different matching decisions $\phi_i(\mathbf{x}_i)$ in a manner which provides a reasonable baseline in an uninformed setting, that is,

MM '16, October 15–19, 2016, Amsterdam, The Netherlands.

ISBN 978-1-4503-3603-1/16/10...$15.00

DOI: http://dx.doi.org/10.1145/2964284.2964304

without exploiting any particular properties of different functions ϕ_i or observations $\mathbf{x}_i$. A common one pervasively used in the literature is weighted linear fusion which can be expressed as follows:

$$\Phi(\mathbf{x}_1,\dots,\mathbf{x}_n;\phi_1,\dots,\phi_n,w_1,\dots,w_n) = \sum_{i=1}^{n} \left[w_i \times \phi_i(\mathbf{x}_i) \right], \tag{1}$$

where:

$$\forall i = 1,\dots,n.\; w_i \geq 0, \qquad \text{and} \qquad \sum_{i=1}^{n} w_i = 1. \tag{2}$$

Here $\Phi(\mathbf{x}_1,\dots,\mathbf{x}_n;\phi_1,\dots,\phi_n,w_1,\dots,w_n)$ is the fused matching score which is derived by simply combining different $\phi_i(\mathbf{x}_i)$, and (2) ensures that the condition $0 \leq \phi_i(\mathbf{x}_i) < \infty$ is maintained for $\Phi(\mathbf{x}_1,\dots,\mathbf{x}_n;\phi_1,\dots,\phi_n,w_1,\dots,w_n)$ as well, i.e. that it is the case that $0 \leq \Phi(\mathbf{x}_1,\dots,\mathbf{x}_n;\phi_1,\dots,\phi_n,w_1,\dots,w_n) < \infty$.

The fusion approach described by (1) can also be rewritten more simply as:

$$\Phi(\mathbf{x}_1,\dots,\mathbf{x}_n;\phi_1,\dots,\phi_n,w_1,\dots,w_n) = \tag{3}$$

$$\hat{\Phi}(\mathbf{x}_1,\dots,\mathbf{x}_n;\phi_1,\dots,\phi_n,w_1,\dots,w_n) = \tag{4}$$

$$\sum_{i=1}^{n} \left[\frac{1}{n} \times \hat{\phi}_i(\mathbf{x}_i, w_i, n) \right], \tag{5}$$

where:

$$\hat{\phi}_i(\mathbf{x}_i, w_i, n) = n \times w_i \times \phi_i(\mathbf{x}_i). \tag{6}$$

Here the original weighted linear fusion of the contributing terms $\phi_i(\mathbf{x}_i)$ in (1) has been replaced by unweighted linear fusion of terms $\hat{\phi}_i(\mathbf{x}_i, w_i, n)$ which adjust the magnitudes of the fused scores directly. This can be achieved simply by considering the statistics of the distributions of different $\phi_i(\mathbf{x}_i)$ and the corresponding prediction, and without any knowledge of what different features $\mathbf{x}_i$ represent or what form different ϕ_i have, i.e. while maintaining the premise of uninformed fusion.

It can be readily seen that the described fusion approach fits the conditions specified in the preceding section – namely, simplicity (both methodological and that of implementation) and broad applicability. Although simple, uninformed fusion demonstrates remarkably good performance across a wide span of different data types and domains, ranging from dementia screening [17] to multimodal biometric identification [14, 5, 12].

$$\Phi_o(\mathbf{x}_1,\dots,\mathbf{x}_n;\phi_1,\dots,\phi_n,\omega_1,\dots,\omega_n) = \tag{7}$$

$$\sqrt{\sum_{i=1}^{n} \left[\omega_i \times \phi_i(\mathbf{x}_i)^2 \right]}, \tag{8}$$

where as before:

$$\forall i = 1,\dots,n.\; \omega_i \geq 0, \qquad \text{and} \qquad \sum_{i=1}^{n} \omega_i = 1. \tag{9}$$

$$\Phi_o(\mathbf{x}_1,\dots,\mathbf{x}_n;\phi_1,\dots,\phi_n,\omega_1,\dots,\omega_n) = \tag{10}$$

$$\tilde{\Phi}_o(\mathbf{x}_1,\dots,\mathbf{x}_n;\phi_1,\dots,\phi_n,\omega_1,\dots,\omega_n) = \tag{11}$$

$$\sqrt{\sum_{i=1}^{n} \left[\frac{1}{n} \times \tilde{\phi}_i(\mathbf{x}_i, \omega_i, n)^2 \right]}, \tag{12}$$

where, analogously to (6), the adjusted fusion scores can be expressed as:

$$\tilde{\phi}_i(\mathbf{x}_i, \omega_i, n) = \sqrt{n} \times \omega_i \times \phi_i(\mathbf{x}_i). \tag{13}$$

The formulation in (12) can be readily recognized as the quadratic mean, in engineering also commonly referred to as the root mean square (RMS), of the n terms $\tilde{\phi}_i(\mathbf{x}_i, \omega_i, n)$.

Before proceeding with a formal analysis of the two fusion approaches, it is insightful to gain an intuitive understanding of the difference between them. Note that simple linear fusion described in (5) treats different scores as effectively interchangeable – a decrease in one score is exactly compensated by an increase in another score by the same amount. This is sensible when the scores correspond to the same measurement which is merely repeated. The described fusion can then be seen as a way of reducing measurement error, assuming that measurement is unbiased and that errors are identically and independently distributed [9]. However this is a rather trivial case of fusion and in practice one is more commonly interested in fusion of different types of data modalities. Indeed, in practice it is often the explicit aim to try to use information sources which vary independently, and attempt to exploit best their complementary natures [5]. In such instances different scores are best treated as describing a source in orthogonal directions, thereby giving rise to a feature vector $\left[\tilde{\phi}_1(\mathbf{x}_1),\dots,\tilde{\phi}_n(\mathbf{x}_n)\right]^T \in \mathbb{R}^n$. The quadratic mean-based fusion of (12) can then be thought of as emerging from a normalized distance measure between such feature vectors in the corresponding ambient embedding space $\mathbb{R}^n$.

Let us now consider the effects of the two fusion approaches in more detail. Firstly, note that scoring measures $\hat{\phi}_i(\mathbf{x}_i, w_i, n)$ and $\tilde{\phi}_i(\mathbf{x}_i, \omega_i, n)$ are inevitably imperfect – neither can be expected to produce universally the perfect matching score of 0 when the query correctly matches a source and ∞ when it does not. Even the weaker requirement of universally smaller pseudo-distances for correct matches is unrealistic. Indeed, it is precisely this practical challenge that motivates multimodal fusion. Consequently, they are appropriately modelled as resulting from draws from random variables:

$$\hat{\phi}_i(\mathbf{x}_i), \tilde{\phi}_i(\mathbf{x}_i) \sim X_i. \tag{14}$$

Let us examine the effects of the two fusion approaches in detail. Specifically, for clarity consider the fusion of two sources, say i and j, while observing that the derived results are readily applicable to the fusion of an arbitrary number of sources through the use of an inductive argument. Following (5) and (12), applying linear and quadratic mean-based fusion results in scores described respectively by random variables $\hat{Y}_{ij}$ and $\tilde{Y}_{ij}$, where:

$$\frac{\hat{\phi}_i(\mathbf{x}_i) + \hat{\phi}_j(\mathbf{x}_j)}{2} \sim \frac{X_i + X_j}{2} = \hat{Y}_{ij}, \tag{15}$$

and:

$$\sqrt{\frac{\tilde{\phi}_i(\mathbf{x}_i)^2 + \tilde{\phi}_j(\mathbf{x}_j)^2}{2}} \sim \sqrt{\frac{X_i^2 + X_j^2}{2}} = \tilde{Y}_{ij}. \tag{16}$$

The former can be further expanded as:

$$E\left[\hat{Y_{ij}}^2\right] = E\left[\left(\frac{X_i + X_j}{2}\right)^2\right] \tag{17}$$

$$= \frac{1}{4}\left\{E\left[X_i^2\right] + E\left[X_j^2\right] + E\left[X_i X_j\right]\right\}, \tag{18}$$

and the latter as:

$$E\left[\widetilde{Y}_{ij}^2\right] = E\left[\sqrt{\frac{{X_i}^2 + {X_j}^2}{2}}^2\right] \tag{19}$$

$$= \frac{1}{2}\left\{E\left[{X_i}^2\right] + E\left[{X_j}^2\right]\right\} \tag{20}$$

$$= \frac{1}{4}\left\{2E\left[{X_i}^2\right] + 2E\left[{X_j}^2\right]\right\}. \tag{21}$$

Writing:

$$\mu_i \equiv E\left[X_i\right], \tag{22}$$

and

$$\mu_j \equiv E\left[X_j\right], \tag{23}$$

as well as:

$$\sigma_i \equiv E\left[(X_i - \mu_i)^2\right], \tag{24}$$

and

$$\sigma_j \equiv E\left[(X_j - \mu_j)^2\right], \tag{25}$$

and using the standard definition of Pearson's correlation coefficient ρ:

$$\rho = \frac{E[(X_i - \mu_i)(X_j - \mu_j)]}{\sigma_i\, \sigma_j}, \tag{26}$$

we can write:

$$E\left[\hat{Y_{ij}}^2\right] - E\left[\widetilde{Y}_{ij}^2\right] = \tag{27}$$

$${\sigma_i}^2 + {\mu_i}^2 + {\sigma_j}^2 + {\mu_j}^2 - 2\left(\rho\sigma_i\sigma_j - \mu_i\mu_j\right) = \tag{28}$$

$${\sigma_i}^2 + {\sigma_j}^2 - 2\rho\sigma_i\sigma_j + (\mu_i + \mu_j)^2 \geq \tag{29}$$

$${\sigma_i}^2 + {\sigma_j}^2 - 2\sigma_i\sigma_j + (\mu_i + \mu_j)^2 = \tag{30}$$

$$(\sigma_i + \sigma_j)^2 + (\mu_i + \mu_j)^2 \geq 0. \tag{31}$$

Therefore: $E\left[\hat{Y_{ij}}^2\right] \geq E\left[\widetilde{Y_{ij}}^2\right]$. In other words, following the fusion of the same scores the proposed quadratic mean-based fusion results in lower fused matching scores (quasi-distances described by the random variable $\widetilde{Y_{ij}}$) than those obtained by employing linear fusion (described by the random variable $\hat{Y}_{ij}$).

At first sight, the significance of the finding in (31) is not clear, given that it applies equally to the fusion of scores which result from matching and non-matching sources – quadratic mean-based fusion produces lower fusion scores in both cases. For the proposed fusion strategy to be advantageous it has to exhibit a differential effect and reduce matching scores more than non-matching ones. To see why there are indeed sound reasons to expect this to be the case, consider the intermediate result in (29). From this expression it can be readily seen that the reduction in the magnitude of the fused score effected by the proposed quadratic mean-based fusion in comparison with the linear baseline is dependent on Pearson's correlation ρ between random variables X_i and X_j which capture the stochastic properties of the original non-fused scores. Specifically, the greater the correlation between them the greater the corresponding reduction in the fused score becomes. The reason why this observation is key lies in the nature of the problem at hand: though imperfect, by their very design sensible matching functions which produce different $\hat{\phi}_i$ and $\widetilde{\phi}_i$ $(i = 1 \ldots n)$ should be expected preferentially and systematically to produce lower scores for correctly matching sources and higher scores for incorrectly matching sources. Therefore, while non-matching comparisons may result in some of the fused scores erroneously to be low, on average such errors should exhibit a lower degree of correlation than low scores across different modalities do for correct matches. In the next section I will demonstrate that this indeed is the case in practice.

3. EXPERIMENTS

Having laid out the theoretical argument against simple weighted combination as the default baseline for uninformed fusion, in favour of the quadratic mean, in this section the two are compared empirically on three real, challenging data sets of vastly different types. In particular, the popular computer vision problem of image-based object recognition is used as a case study in Section 3.2, arrhythmia prediction in Section 3.3, and finally fatality prediction in road vehicle accidents in Section 3.4.

3.1 Performance evaluation

I compared the performance of the two fusion approaches discussed in Section 2 by computing fused quasi-similarities between the ground truth data and the two information sources. Specifically, the linearly fused quasi-similarity of $\hat{\phi}_1^{(1)}(x_{i,1})$ and $\hat{\phi}_1^{(1)}(x_{i,2})$ was computed as:

$$\frac{1}{2}\left(\hat{\phi}_1^{(1)}(x_{i,1}) + \hat{\phi}_1^{(1)}(x_{i,2})\right), \tag{32}$$

and similarly of of $\hat{\phi}_1^{(2)}(x_{i,1})$ and $\hat{\phi}_1^{(2)}(x_{i,2})$ was computed as:

$$\frac{1}{2}\left(\hat{\phi}_1^{(2)}(x_{i,1}) + \hat{\phi}_1^{(2)}(x_{i,2})\right). \tag{33}$$

The proposed quadratic-mean-based fusions were computed as respectively:

$$\sqrt{\frac{1}{2}\left[\left(\hat{\phi}_1^{(1)}(x_{i,1})\right)^2 + \left(\hat{\phi}_1^{(1)}(x_{i,2})\right)^2\right]}. \tag{34}$$

and:

$$\sqrt{\frac{1}{2}\left[\left(\hat{\phi}_1^{(2)}(x_{i,1})\right)^2 + \left(\hat{\phi}_1^{(2)}(x_{i,2})\right)^2\right]}. \tag{35}$$

To evaluate and compare the two methods I examined the corresponding differential matching scores computed for the correct and incorrect information sources, that is:

$$\partial_1 = \hat{\phi}_1^{(1)}(x_{i,1}) - \hat{\phi}_1^{(2)}(x_{i,1}) = \|x_{i,1}\| - \|1 - x_{i,1}\|, \tag{36}$$

for the linear fusion, and

$$\partial_2 = \hat{\phi}_2^{(1)}(x_{i,2}) - \hat{\phi}_2^{(2)}(x_{i,2}) = \|x_{i,2}\| - \|1 - x_{i,2}\|. \tag{37}$$

for the proposed quadratic mean-based fusion where, without loss of generality, the correct prediction target for the first information source is taken to be 0 and for the second 1. It can be readily seen that a positive differential score corresponds to the correct source attribution (and a more confident decision for greater magnitudes thereof), a negative one to incorrect attribution (and a more mistaken confidence for greater magnitudes thereof), and a vanishing score to uncertain attribution.

3.2 Object recognition

My first case-study involves computer-based object recognition. This is an important problem in the spheres of computer vision and pattern recognition which has potential for use in a wide spectrum of practical applications. Examples range from motorway toll booths that automatically verify that the car type and its licence plate match the registration database, to online querying and searching for an object of interest that was captured using a mobile phone camera. Object recognition has attracted much research attention [1, 2, 7, 8] and this interest has particularly intensified in recent years after significant advances towards practically viable systems have been made [20, 7, 8].

Here I consider fusion of texture-based and shape-based object descriptors. The former group has dominated research efforts to date [20] and has been highly successful in the matching of textured objects. However, it fails when applied on untextured objects (sometimes referred to as 'smooth') [7] Considering that their texture is not informative, characteristic discriminative information of smooth objects must be extracted from shape instead. Following the method described in [3] I extract and process the representations of the two modalities (texture and shape) independently. An object's texture is captured using a histogram computed over a vocabulary of textural words, learnt by clustering local texture descriptors extracted from the training data set. Similarly, a histogram over a vocabulary of elementary shapes, learnt by clustering local shape descriptors, is used to capture the object's shape. I adopt the standard SIFT descriptor as the basic building block of the texture representation and an analogous descriptor of local shape for the characterization of shape [4]. In both cases descriptors are matched using the Euclidean distance.

3.2.1 *Results, analysis, and discussion*

As explained in Section 3.1, the performances of the two fusion approaches was assessed by analysing the corresponding differential matching scores computed for the correct and incorrect information sources as summarized by (36) and (37).

My findings are summarized in Figure 1 which shows a plot of the cumulative density distribution of the relative improvement achieved by the proposed method (as before please note that the abscissa scale is logarithmic and that it is increasing in the leftward direction). Firstly let us make the remarkable observation that in *all* cases the proposed fusion strategy did at least as well as the simple weighted fusion. In approximately 66% of the cases the proposed quadratic fusion exhibited superior performance, performing on par in the remaining 34% of the cases. A further examination of the plot reveals an even stronger case for the proposed method – not only does it outperform simple weighted fusion in 66% of the cases but it does so with a great margin. For example in 30% of the cases the inter-class separation is increased 10-fold (i.e. by an order of magnitude).

3.3 Arrhythmia prediction

My second real-world case-study concerns automatic arrhythmia prediction from demographic data and physiological measurements. This is a challenging task of enormous importance in the provision of timely and informed health care provision to the population at risk of cardiac complications. This primarily includes individuals with preexisting cardiac problems or congenital factors, which are further modulated by various environmental factors such as high physical exertion [16] or the use of certain classes of drugs.

A normally functioning human heart maintains a remarkably well controlled heartbeat rhythm. Arrhythmias are abnormalities of this rhythm and are caused by physiological factors pertaining to electrical impulse generation or propagation. Arrhythmia types can be grouped under the umbrellas of three broad categories: tachycardias (overly high heartbeat rate), bradycardias (overly low heartbeat rate), and arrhythmias with an irregular heartbeat rate. While most arrhythmias are transient in nature and do not pose a serious health risk, some arrhythmias (particularly in high risk populations) can have serious consequences such as stroke, cardiac arrest, or heart failure and death [18].

Arrhythmias can be diagnosed using nonspecific means, e.g. using a stethoscope or a tactile detection of pulse, or specific methods and in particular the electrocardiogram (ECG). Moreover, the rich information provided by the latter can be used to predict and detect the onset of arrhythmias by analysing electric impulse patterns [15]. In the present study I evaluate the proposed fusion methodology in the context of this prediction.

I used the dataset collected by Guvenir *et al.* [15] which is freely available[1]. The dataset comprises a rich set of demographic and anthropometric variables, such as each person's age, sex, height, and bodyweight, as well as a variety of features extracted from the person's ECG, including the heart rate and a series of characteristics of the corresponding signal deflections (the duration of the QRS interval, amplitudes of Q, R, and S waves etc); please refer to the original publication for full detail [15]. The target variable for the purpose of the present experiment can be considered to be binary valued, taking on the value 0 when arrhythmia is not present and 1 when it is; please see Table 1.

I consider two baseline classifiers. The first of these takes height, bodyweight, and the duration of the QRS interval as input variables (i.e. independent variables). The second one makes the prediction based on what are effectively integrals of Q, R, and S deflections (i.e. referred to as QRSA in the dataset description; please see the original reference for detail [15]), and the Q, R, S, and T deflections (i.e. referred to as QRSTA in the dataset description). Each classifier is built upon a generalized linear model (GLM) [19]. Recall that in a GLM the mean $E[Y]$ of the target, outcome variable Y is related to a linear predictor based on the independent variables through a link function $\mathcal{L}$:

$$E[Y] \equiv \mu = \mathcal{L}^{-1}(1+\alpha x). \tag{38}$$

The variance Var$[Y]$ of Y is modelled as a function $\mathcal{V}$ of this mean:

$$\text{Var}[Y] = \mathcal{V}(\mu) = \mathcal{V}(\mathcal{L}^{-1}(1+\alpha x)). \tag{39}$$

In my experiment the continuous output of a GLM is used to detect the presence of arrhythmia using what is effectively the nearest neighbour criterion: if the output is closer to 0 the prediction is taken to be negative, and if it is closer to 1 positive. The dataset contains 452 diagnosis cases of which 100 were used for training the classifiers; the remaining 352 were used for testing.

3.3.1 *Results, analysis, and discussion*

As in the previous experiment, the performances of the two fusion approaches was assessed by analysing the corresponding differential matching scores computed for the correct and incorrect information sources as summarized by (36) and (37).

My findings are summarized in Figure 2 which shows a plot of the cumulative density distribution of the relative improvement achieved by the proposed method (as before please note that the abscissa scale is logarithmic and that it is increasing in the leftward direction). We can again start with the observation which can be made by comparing the characteristics of the plot in Figure 2 with those of the plot in Figure 1 and observing that again the same qualitative behaviour is exhibited on this data too. In all cases the proposed fusion strategy did at least as well as the simple weighted fusion, with approximately 65% of the cases resulting in superior performance of the proposed quadratic fusion and the remaining 35% in on a par performance. As in the previous experiments when

[1]The dataset can be downloaded from http://archive.ics.uci.edu/ml/datasets/Arrhythmia.

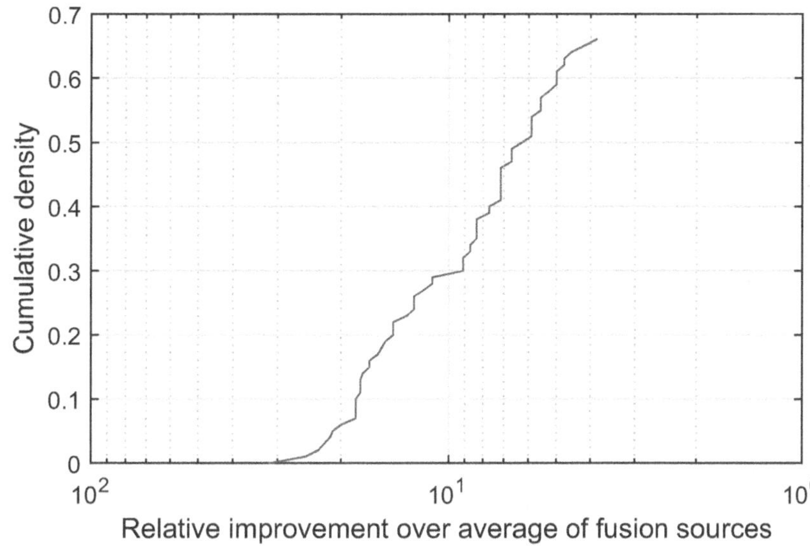

Figure 1: General object recognition: relative improvement in the correct information source identification of the proposed quadratic mean-based fusion over linear fusion, as the corresponding cumulative distribution function.

Table 1: An illustration of the adopted arrhythmia dataset, originally collected and described in detail by Guvenir *et al.* [15]. It comprises 279 input variables, of which only a small selection is shown here, and the corresponding target variable which for the purpose of the present experiment can be considered to be binary valued, taking on the value 0 when arrhythmia is not diagnosed and 1 when it is.

Age (years)	Gender	Height (cm)	Body weight (kg)	QRS duration (ms)	...	Arrythmia (yes/no)
75	Male	190	80	91	...	Yes
56	Female	165	64	81	...	Yes
...	...	...	...	...	...	...
55	Male	175	94	100	...	No
...	...	...	...	...	...	

my method outperforms simple weighted fusion it does so with a significant margin with an over doubled separation increase in approximately 16% of the cases. Moreover I found that while simple weighted fusion failed to improve the prediction of the better performing baseline classifier in 15% of the cases, the same was the case with the proposed method in fewer than 7.8% of the cases.

3.4 Car accident fatality prediction

My third and final experiment herein concerns the inference of risk factors for car accident fatalities. In particular in this experiment I was interested in discovering what aspects of the context of an accident predict best if a fatality will occur. For this purpose I used the official statistics released by the government of the USA through the Fatality Analysis Reporting System (FARS) for the year 2011. These are freely publicly available[2]. The dataset comprises a number of person specific variables, such as age, sex, race, blood alcohol level, and drug use status, as well as a variety of variables pertaining to the context of the accident, including the type of the road and the state where the accident took place, and the weather conditions at the time (please see http://www-fars.nhtsa.dot.gov/Main/index.aspx for full description). The target variable for the purpose of the present experiment can be considered to be binary valued, taking on the value 1 when there has been a fatality and 0 otherwise; please see Table 2.

As in the previous experiment I consider two baseline classifiers, each built upon a generalized linear model. The first of these takes the person's age and blood alcohol level as input variables (i.e. independent variables). The second one makes the prediction based on atmospheric conditions and the road type. Following the same framework as described in the previous section, the continuous output of a GLM is used to predict the occurrence of a fatality using what is effectively the nearest neighbour criterion: if the output is closer to 0 the prediction is taken to be negative, and if it is closer to 1 positive. The dataset contains 5000 accidents of which 1000 ran-

[2]The dataset can be downloaded from http://www-fars.nhtsa.dot.gov/Main/index.aspx.

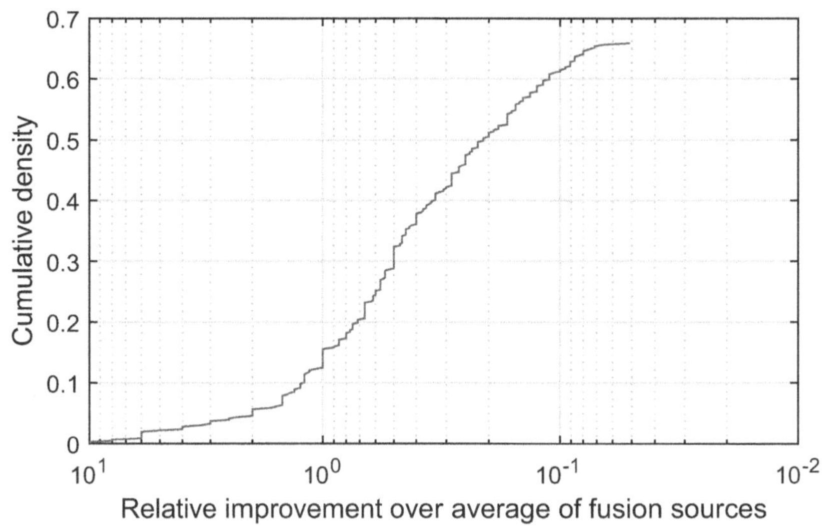

Figure 2: Arrhythmia prediction: relative improvement in the correct information source identification of the proposed quadratic mean-based fusion over linear fusion, as the corresponding cumulative distribution function.

Table 2: An illustration of the adopted car accidents dataset released by the government of the USA through the Fatality Analysis Reporting System (FARS) for the year 2011. It comprises 15 input variables, of which only a selection is shown here, and the corresponding target variable which for the purpose of the present experiment can be considered to be binary valued, taking on the value 1 when there has been a fatality and 0 when not.

Clear atmospheric conditions (yes/no)	Driver age	Alcohol blood level	Driver gender	...	Fatalities (yes/no)
Yes	27	0	Male	...	No
Yes	60	0	Female	...	Yes
...	...	...	...	...	...
No	20	0.21	Male		Yes
...	...	...	...	...	...

domly selected cases were used for training the baseline classifiers with the remainder employed for performance evaluation.

3.4.1 Results, analysis, and discussion

I followed the same evaluation methodology as in the preceding experiments. In the same vein I display my findings in Figure 3 which shows a plot of the cumulative density distribution of the relative improvement achieved by the proposed method (as before please note that the abscissa scale is logarithmic and that it is increasing in the leftward direction). Yet again, in agreement with the results obtained in all experiments I conducted, we can observe the same functional characteristics in the plot of Figure 3 and of those in Figures 1 and 2. In further agreement with the previous experiments is my finding that in all instances of car accidents used for evaluation, the proposed fusion strategy did at least as well as the simple weighted fusion in terms of its predictive ability. With regard to this point, it is interesting to note that notwithstanding the remarkable qualitative similarity of the CDFs corresponding to different experiments, there are some quantitative differences. For example, note that in the present experiment approximately 73% of the cases resulted in superior performance of the proposed quadratic fusion and the remaining 27% in on a par performance. The proportion of evaluation instances yielding superior performance is thus higher than e.g. in the object recognition experiment described in Section 3.2. However, the resulting benefit is smaller. For example, while in the object recognition experiment about 30% of the evaluation cases result in at least 10-fold class separation increase, in the present experiment in no case is the benefit as large. This is most likely a consequence of the inherent information content in the data itself, rather than of some algorithmic aspect of the proposed method. In other words, the lesser advantage (though still consistent and observed in an overwhelming number of cases) of using the proposed method stems from greater redundancy across the fused information sources.

4. REFERENCES

[1] G. Aggarwal and D. Roth. Learning a sparse representation

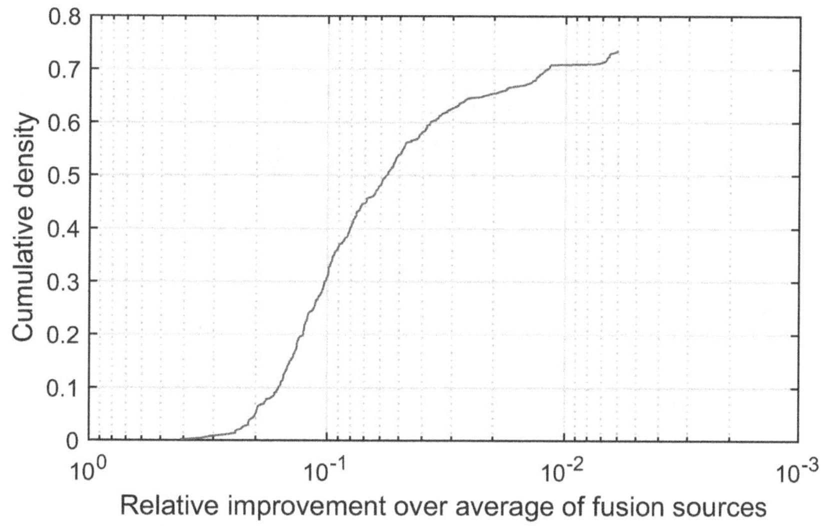

Figure 3: Fatalities in car accidents prediction: relative improvement in the correct information source identification of the proposed quadratic mean-based fusion over linear fusion, as the corresponding cumulative distribution function.

for object detection. *In Proc. European Conference on Computer Vision*, 2002.

[2] A. Ahmadyfard and J. Kittler. A comparative study of two object recognition methods. *In Proc. British Machine Vision Conference*, pages 1–10, 2002.

[3] O. Arandjelović. Matching objects across the textured–smooth continuum. *In Proc. Australasian Conference on Robotics and Automation*, pages 354–361, 2012.

[4] O. Arandjelović. Object matching using boundary descriptors. *In Proc. British Machine Vision Conference*, 2012. DOI: 10.5244/C.26.85.

[5] O. Arandjelović and R. Cipolla. A new look at filtering techniques for illumination invariance in automatic face recognition. *In Proc. IEEE International Conference on Automatic Face and Gesture Recognition*, pages 449–454, 2006.

[6] O. Arandjelović, R. I. Hammoud, and R. Cipolla. Thermal and reflectance based personal identification methodology in challenging variable illuminations. *Pattern Recognition*, 43(5):1801–1813, 2010.

[7] R. Arandjelović and A. Zisserman. Smooth object retrieval using a bag of boundaries. *In Proc. IEEE International Conference on Computer Vision*, pages 375–382, 2011.

[8] P. N. Belhumeur and D. J. Kriegman. What is the set of images of an object under all possible illumination conditions? *International Journal of Computer Vision*, 28(3):245–260, 1998.

[9] C. M. Bishop. *Pattern Recognition and Machine Learning*. Springer-Verlag, New York, USA, 2007.

[10] R. S. Ghiass and O. Arandjelović. Highly accurate gaze estimation using a consumer RGB-depth sensor. *In Proc. International Joint Conference on Artificial Intelligence*, pages 3368–3374, 2016.

[11] R. S. Ghiass, O. Arandjelović, A. Bendada, and X. Maldague. Infrared face recognition: a literature review. *In Proc. IEEE International Joint Conference on Neural Networks*, pages 2791–2800, 2013.

[12] R. S. Ghiass, O. Arandjelović, A. Bendada, and X. Maldague. Infrared face recognition: a comprehensive review of methodologies and databases. *Pattern Recognition*, 47(9):2807–2824, 2014.

[13] V. Ginsburgh, M. Monzak, and A. Monzak. Red wines of médoc: What is wine tasting worth? *Journal of Wine Economics*, 8(2):159–188, 2013.

[14] Y. Guan, X. Wei, C. T. Li, and Y. Keller. People identification and tracking through fusion of facial and gait features. *Biometric Authentication*, pages 209–221, 2014.

[15] H. A. Guvenir, B. Acar, G. Demiroz, and A. Cekin. A supervised machine learning algorithm for arrhythmia analysis. *In Proc. Computers in Cardiology Conference*, pages 433–436, 1997.

[16] C. Lengyel, A. Orosz, P. Hegyi, Z. Komka, A. Udvardy, E. Bosnyák, E. Trájer, G. Pavlik, M. Tóth, T. Wittmann, J. G. Papp, A. Varró, and I. Baczkó. Increased short-term variability of the qt interval in professional soccer players: Possible implications for arrhythmia prediction. *PLOS ONE*, 6(4):e18751, 2011.

[17] A. Mackinnon and R. Mulligan. Combining cognitive testing and informant report to increase accuracy in screening for dementia. *The American Journal of Psychiatry*, 155:1529–1535, 1998.

[18] R. J. Myerburg, A. J. Interian, R. M. Mitrani, K. M. Kessler, and A. Castellanos. Frequency of sudden cardiac death and profiles of risk. *The American Journal of Cardiology*, 80(5):10F–19F, 1997. (supplement 2).

[19] J. Nelder and R. Wedderburn. Generalized linear models. *Proceedings of the Royal Society, Series A*, 135(3):370–384, 1972.

[20] J. Sivic, B. Russell, A. Efros, A. Zisserman, and W. Freeman. Discovering object categories in image collections. *In Proc. IEEE International Conference on Computer Vision*, pages 370–377, 2005.

DRIVING: Distributed Scheduling for Video Streaming in Vehicular Wi-Fi Systems

Xi Chen
McGill University
xi.chen11@mail.mcgill.ca

Lei Rao
General Motors Company
lei.rao@gm.com

Qiao Xiang
Yale University
qiao.xiang@cs.yale.edu

Xue Liu
McGill University
xueliu@cs.mcgill.ca

Fan Bai
General Motors Company
fan.bai@gm.com

ABSTRACT

Video streaming has been dominating the mobile bandwidth, and is still expanding drastically. Its tremendous economic benefits have driven the automobile industry to equip vehicles with video streaming capacity. As a result, the new in-cabin Wi-Fi systems have been deployed, enabling each vehicle as a streaming hotspot on the wheels. A built-in Access Point (AP) bridges the communications between Wi-Fi devices inside and cellular networks outside. Distinct advantages offered by this system include a more powerful antenna array to improve multimedia quality, a constant energy source to power the streaming, etc. However, there exist two challenging features that may jeopardize the system performance. (1) The in-cabin Wi-Fi hotspots are mostly deployed on private vehicles, and thus are completely decentralized. (2) Video packets need to be delivered before their deadlines with small delays. Due to these features, existing algorithms may fail to efficiently schedule the in-cabin Wi-Fi video streaming. To fill the gap, we propose the Delay-awaRe dIstributed Video schedulING (DRIVING) framework. Being fully distributed and delay-aware, DRIVING not only increases the streaming goodput, but also reduces the delivery latency and deadline missing ratio. In a typical scenario, DRIVING increases the goodput by up to 27.0%, while reducing the queueing delay and the deadline missing ratio by up to 40.0% and 38.4%, respectively.

1. INTRODUCTION

Mobile multimedia services have been expanding significantly. Among them, video streaming is and will be the dominating one, accounting for over 75% of mobile data traffic by 2020 [1]. This leads to a huge and fast-growing market, which drives car manufacturers to actively deploy video streaming capacity to their vehicles. The new in-cabin Wi-Fi systems are thus developed to power all the Wi-Fi devices inside the cabin, bridging the communication gap between these devices and 3G/4G cellular networks [2]. A built-in Wi-Fi hotspot (we call it an in-cabin Wi-Fi AP in the rest of this paper) provides drivers and passengers a variety of multimedia services including the most popular video streaming. Comparing with LTE connected smart phones and tablets, the built-in Wi-Fi connection offers distinct advantages including a more powerful antenna array to improve signal quality, a constant energy source to power this connection, and an integrated design that is optimized for in-vehicle use.

Considering the high popularity and large bandwidth consumption of video streaming, in-cabin Wi-Fi APs on different vehicles must be efficiently scheduled. The design of a scheduling algorithm needs to consider two challenging features. (1) The in-cabin Wi-Fi APs are mainly deployed on private vehicles, serving different individuals in a non-cooperative manner. (2) The video streaming requires small delays and jitters, and low deadline missing ratio.

Existing scheduling algorithms may fail to handle the coexistence of these two features. (1) Centralized algorithms (e.g., those proposed in [3, 4, 5, 6]) could be inefficient for the non-cooperative and distributed in-cabin Wi-Fi APs. Meanwhile, distributed scheduling algorithms designed for stationary networks (e.g., those proposed in [7, 8, 9, 10]) may degrade largely in a vehicular scenario, where the topology of APs is fast-varying. Hence, a candidate scheduling scheme should be fully distributed and robust to the rapid changes in AP topology. (2) Existing distributed scheduling criteria, such as queue length [11], historical throughput [12] or energy efficiency [9, 13], could fail in fulfilling delay requirements of video streaming.Thus, the delay sensitive feature should be integrated into the distributed scheduling. To sum up, we are still in need of a scheduling scheme that is both **fully distributed** and **delay-sensitive**.

In this paper, we develop the **D**elay-awa**R**e d**I**stributed **V**ideo schedul**ING** (DRIVING) framework for in-cabin Wi-Fi systems. DRIVING carefully retrofits existing distributed Carrier Sense Multiple Access (CSMA) schemes to prioritize packets with large queueing delays. In this way, it addresses the unawareness of delays in existing distributed schemes (e.g., those proposed in [11, 12]), and reduces delays and jitters in video streaming. At the same time, DRIVING is lightweight, requiring only a software upgrade for deployment on commodity Wi-Fi APs.

The **main contribution** of this paper is twofold.

• We study the important problem of scheduling video streaming in in-cabin Wi-Fi systems. We develop a fully dis-

MM '16, October 15-19, 2016, Amsterdam, Netherlands

DOI: http://dx.doi.org/10.1145/2964284.2964290

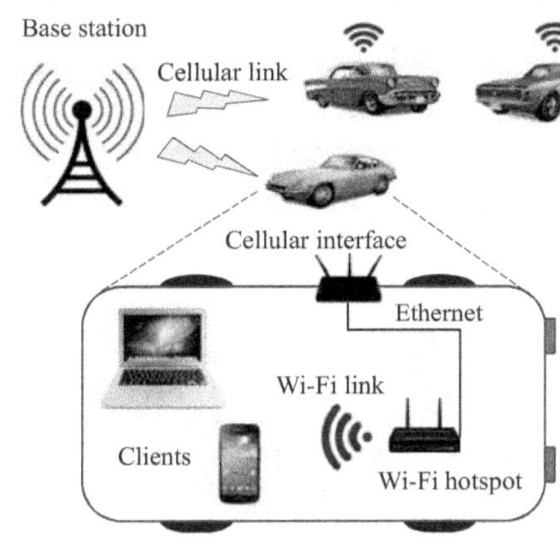

Figure 1: An example of In-cabin Wi-Fi systems.

tributed and delay-aware framework DRIVING to embrace the distinct features of in-cabin Wi-Fi video streaming.

• We characterize DRIVING with advanced cross-layer analytical models, which serve as the guidelines to tune this new framework for better performance.

In a typical scenario, DRIVING increases the average goodput by up to 27.0% while reducing the average queueing delay and the average deadline missing ratio by up to 40.0% and 38.4%, respectively.

2. PROBLEM AND CHALLENGES

In this section, we describe the in-cabin Wi-Fi systems, and present the problem definition and the challenges.

2.1 System Overview

2.1.1 In-cabin Wi-Fi System

An example of in-cabin Wi-Fi systems is shown in Fig. 1. The in-cabin Wi-Fi services are delivered via two kinds of wireless links - the long range cellular links and the short range Wi-Fi links. A long range cellular link is in charge of delivering data from cellular networks to in-cabin Wi-Fi APs, while a short range Wi-Fi link serves the in-vehicle Wi-Fi devices directly. An Ethernet is used to relay the data between these two links. While the cellular links are well controlled and scheduled by the cellular base station (BS), there is still much room for improvement on the performance of the Wi-Fi links. In the rest of this paper, we focus on the short range Wi-Fi transmissions, which are the bottleneck of the whole system. Note that the joint scheduling of the Wi-Fi links and the cellular links is also an important research topic, and will be considered in our future work.

The in-cabin Wi-Fi system is very attractive for multimedia streaming services due to the following unique advantages. First of all, an antenna array tailored for moving environments improves the cellular signal quality. Also, a constant energy source is offered by the vehicle to power the in-cabin Wi-Fi AP. In addition, off-the-shelf Wi-Fi devices can enjoy in-vehicle multimedia services without an expensive cellular module.

However, in-cabin Wi-Fi video streaming has several features, making it more difficult to schedule than conventional communications and multimedia services.

(1) The in-cabin Wi-Fi APs are deployed on private vehicles and moving rapidly. The cellular BS has no control of them. Also, there are few coordination message exchanges among the APs. Hence, these APs are fully distributed and non-cooperative with a frequently varying topology.

(2) Video packets require to be delivered before deadline with low delays and small jitters.

(3) Most client-side devices are off-the-shelf Wi-Fi devices. Any practical attempt to upgrade the system must be compatible with existing Wi-Fi protocols.

2.1.2 MAC Access in Wi-Fi

Wi-Fi communications are based on IEEE 802.11 standards, and adopt the Distributed Coordination Function (DCF) as its fundamental MAC technique. The DCF requires a Wi-Fi node to listen to the channel for a period of time equal to a Distributed Interframe Space (DIFS) before transmission. If the channel is idle, then the node can transmission. Otherwise, the node keeps listening until the channel is idle for a DIFS. Upon this, the node generates a random backoff interval and waits for it before transmission, so as to minimize collisions in the wireless channel. This backoff interval is a number randomly selected from a range called Contention Window (CW), of which the size determines the average waiting time. The CW size will be doubled (until a maximum value is reached), if the channel is sensed busy during the random backoff interval. By setting different CW sizes, one can adjust the priorities of different Wi-Fi packets.

2.2 Problem Statement and Metrics

In this paper, we aim to improve the performance of video streaming in the in-cabin Wi-Fi system by developing an advanced scheduling scheme. The performance metrics to be improved are defined as follows.

The average queueing delay and delay jitter: The queueing delay $D^{(p)}$ of a packet p is defined as

$$D^{(p)} = \begin{cases} t_{end} - t_{arr}, & p \text{ is received or dropped,} \\ t_{cur} - t_{arr}, & p \text{ is waiting for transmission,} \end{cases} \tag{1}$$

where t_{arr} is the time that packet p arrives at an in-cabin Wi-Fi AP, t_{end} is the time that packet p is received by a client or is dropped by the AP, and t_{cur} is the current time. Then the average queueing delay $\overline{D}$ is defined as the expected value of the queueing delay, i.e., $\overline{D} = \mathbf{E}\{D^{(p)}\}$.

There are different definitions of delay jitter (we call it jitter for short) in the literature. In this paper, we use the definition of jitter in the IP network [14], and define the jitter J as the average deviation of delays from the average delay, i.e.,

$$J = \Sigma_p |D^{(p)} - \overline{D}| / \Sigma_{i=1}^{N} \eta_i, \tag{2}$$

where N is the total number of clients, η_i is the number of video packets received by client i.

The deadline missing ratio: Suppose video buffer of a client device is going to drain at time t_{pre}, and the next packet p is going to arrive at t_{arr}. If $t_{arr} > t_{pre}$, then packet p misses its deadline. The deadline missing ratio ξ is then defined as the portion of packets that miss their deadlines, i.e.,

$$\xi = \Sigma_{i=1}^{N} \theta_i / \Sigma_{i=1}^{N} \eta_i, \tag{3}$$

where θ_i is the number of packets that arrive at client i and miss their deadlines.

The average goodput: The average goodput S is defined as the average streaming rate of all clients, i.e.,

$$S = \Sigma_{i=1}^{N}(\eta_i - \theta_i)\phi/NT, \quad (4)$$

where T is the time period we are interested in, and ϕ is the average size of video packets.

2.3 Challenges

The design of an advanced scheduling scheme for in-cabin Wi-Fi video streaming faces the following challenges.

Challenge 1: *The scheduling decisions must be made and executed in a fully distributed manner.* Due to the large communication delay, a cellular BS is not suitable to control the dynamic in-cabin Wi-Fi transmissions. Meanwhile, it is inefficient to select a centralized controller from all the constantly moving in-cabin Wi-Fi APs.

Challenge 2: *Meanwhile, the distributed scheduling must be delay-aware.* Existing delay-aware scheduling algorithms are mainly designed for centralized networks, and thus are not suitable for in-cabin Wi-Fi systems.

Challenge 3: *The scheduling scheme must be compatible with the commodity client and AP devices.* For the ease of deployment, the scheduling scheme should introduce little modification to the off-the-shelf devices.

3. RELATED WORK

Due to the limited space, we only discuss the most pertinent work on the distributed scheduling in a mobile scenario.

3.1 Scheduling of Video Streaming

A wealth of work exists on the scheduling of video streaming over wireless networks. Approaches for stationary networks (e.g., those proposed by Pahalawatta et al. [6] and Dua et al. [5]) are not suitable for the fully distributed in-cabin Wi-Fi APs. A number of distributed video scheduling algorithms have been proposed. For instance, Chuah et al. [9] designed an energy-efficient scheduling wireless mesh networks (WMNs). However, the assumption that no packet is lost due to delay is invalid in a vehicular scenario. Zhang et al. [10] jointly considered content priority, delay and channel condition in their model, which would consume much time in estimating the dynamic parameters. To sum up, these scheduling algorithms fail to address **Challenge 1**.

3.2 Adaptive CSMA

The basic idea of adaptive CSMA algorithms is to adjust the channel access probabilities of wireless nodes according to local and/or neighbouring information. A number of these algorithms, such as Q-SCHED proposed by Gupta et al. in [15], MIMO-pipe proposed by Qian et al. in [16] and DMDS proposed by Zhou et al. in [17], are based on message exchanges. However, message passing introduces large communication overhead, especially in a dense vehicular network. As a result, these adaptive CSMA algorithms cannot address **Challenge 1**.

Another line of research develops adaptive CSMA without message exchanges. Examples include, but are not limited to, the transmission length control algorithm proposed by Jiang et al. in [12], the Network Utility Maximization (NUM) based algorithm proposed by Rad et al. in [18] and the Q-CSMA algorithms proposed by Ni et al. in [11]. However, the delay and deadline of video streaming have not yet been considered explicitly, and thus fail to address **Challenge 2**.

3.3 Delay/Deadline-Aware Scheduling

To support delay sensitive services, such as video streaming in VANETs, a delay/deadline-aware scheduling algorithm is a must. A number of delay/deadline-aware scheduling algorithms have been proposed in the literature. Centralized algorithms, such as those proposed by Hou et al. in [3] and by Wu et al. in [4], are not suitable for a fully distributed vehicular network. Caccamo et al. in [7] proposed a distributed implicit Earliest Deadline First (EDF) scheduling, which establishes the scheduling pattern with a long initiation stage. Kanodia et al. in [8] designed a distributed algorithm, which exchanges the EDF priorities among nodes. These algorithms require either an initiation stage, message exchanges or prior knowledge of topology. They are impractical in highly dynamic scenarios, and are not able to tackle **Challenge 1**.

3.4 Distributed TDMA

A number of distributed TDMA algorithms, such as VeMAC [19] and SUV [20], have been proposed for 802.11p based communications. A considerable portion of time resource could be wasted when the vehicle density is low. Moreover, most of today's commercial Wi-Fi devices (e.g. phones and laptops) do not support the 802.11p protocol. Consequently, these distributed TDMA algorithms cannot address **Challenge 3**.

4. THE DRIVING FRAMEWORK

To address all the challenges, we propose the delay-aware distributed video scheduling framework.

4.1 Overall Design

The core idea of DRIVING is to assign high transmission priorities to packets with large queueing delays. DRIVING supports K levels of priorities. Level 0 represents the highest priority while level $K-1$ denotes the lowest priority. To realize the priorities, a small Contention Window (CW) size is assigned to a high-priority packet. DRIVING consists of three modules, and is summarized as follows.

The DRIVING framework

---

1. **The delay measurement** module measures the queueing delay of the head-of-line packet, and saves this delay as D_{head}. D_{head} is set to 0 for an empty queue.
2. **The priority evaluation** module evaluates the priority level of the head-of-line packet according to D_{head}, and set the corresponding priority as k, where $k = 0, 1, \cdots, K-1$.
3. **The scheduling decision** module sets the CW size of the upcoming backoff procedure as $W_{i,k}$, according to the priority level k and a number i. This number i denotes the number of transmission attempts that have been made for the current head-of-line packet. The scheduling decision module then instructs the backoff handler of the selected CW size $W_{i,k}$.

Note that the priority level k only determines the minimum CW size $W_{0,k}$. The final CW size is then determined by $W_{0,k}$ and retransmission times as $W_{i,k} = (W_{0,k}+1)2^i$, where i is the number of transmission attempts (and $i-1$ is the retransmission times).

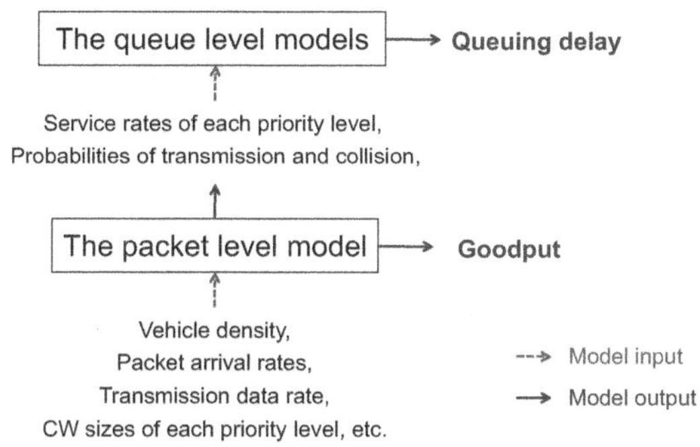

Figure 2: The two-level models.

4.2 Solving the Challenges with DRIVING

The delay measurement module measures the queueing delay D_{head} of the head-of-line packet. This information is measured locally by APs (while acquiring the deadline information requires extra message exchanges). This delay serves as a fully distributed criterion of scheduling. In this way, DRIVING solves **Challenge 1**.

The priority evaluation module evaluates the transmission priority level of each head-of-line packet, according to the queueing delay D_{head}. A large queueing delay indicates an approaching deadline. Thus, a high transmission priority is assigned to the packet. In this way, transmissions are scheduled by delay-aware priorities. Hence, DRIVING is delay-aware and solves **Challenge 2**.

The detailed implementation of the priority evaluation module is summarized as follows. Each priority level k corresponds to a continuous set β_k of the queueing delay. The queueing delay of a packet with a higher priority is always larger than the queueing delay of a packet with a lower priority. Let D_k denotes the queueing delay of a packet in priority level k. For two priority levels i and j, we have

$$\max(D_j|D_j \in \beta_j) < \min(D_i|D_i \in \beta_i), 0 \leq i < j \leq K-1. \tag{5}$$

Further, the union of all the delay sets covers all the non-negative real numbers, i.e., $\bigcup_{k=0}^{K} \beta_k = \mathbf{R}^+ \cup \{0\}$. Note that the DRIVING framework generalize different designs of the delay sets.

The scheduling decision module realizes the scheduling decision based on the priority passed down from the priority evaluation module. To achieve this, this module sets the minimum CW size of the upcoming backoff procedure as $W_{0,k}$ according to the priority k. A packet with a high priority has a small minimum CW size, i.e.,

$$W_{0,0} \leq W_{0,1} \leq \cdots \leq W_{0,K-1}. \tag{6}$$

For a packet that has been transmitted i times, this module further sets the CW size as $W_{0,k}2^i$, and informs the backoff handler of this number. In this way, DRIVING utilizes the CSMA backoff procedures to realize its scheduling decisions. It only requires a software upgrade to integrate the updated backoff procedure into commodity APs, and thus solves **Challenge 3**.

5. MODELING

To apply the DRIVING framework in practice, the number of priority levels K and the design of each delay set β_k should determined. This requires us to theoretically analyze the DRIVING framework.

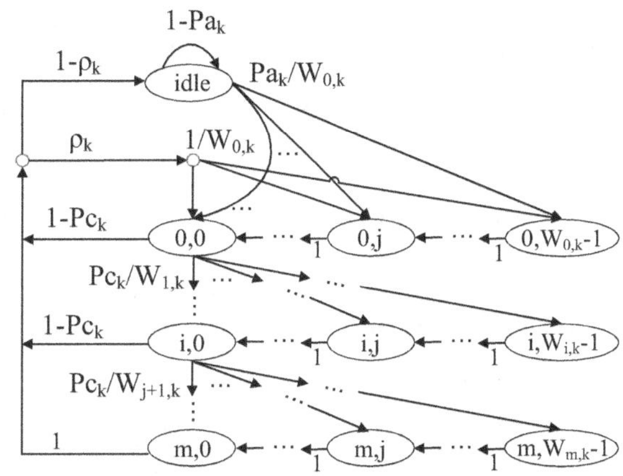

Figure 3: The DTMC for the backoff process of a node in priority level k, extended from [21][22].

5.1 Analytical Models in Two Levels

We establish one packet level model for the backoff process and two queue level models for the queueing process. These two levels of models are correlated through their inputs and outputs, as presented in Fig. 2.

5.2 The Packet Level Model

5.2.1 The Markov Chain of Priority Level k

A discrete-time Markov chain (DTMC) is used to model the backoff process of each node in priority level k. This DTMC is presented in Fig. 3. This DTMC is extended from the models in [21][22]. Denote each state in the DTMC as $\{s[t], b[t]\}$. Here, $s[t]$ denotes the backoff stage, i.e., the number of re-transmissions made by the head-of-line packet. Each packet will be dropped after m unsuccessful re-transmission attempts. $b[t]$ denotes the backoff time counter, which decrements by one if the channel is idle. To characterize unsaturated packet arrival, we introduce an idle state $\{idle\}$. We divide time into **virtual slots** of length E_S, which denotes the average time that the backoff process spends in each state. Such a time division allows us to achieve more accurate results than those in [21][22].

Denote the average packet arrival rate and the average service rate of a node in priority level k as λ_k and μ_k, respectively. Then at current virtual slot, the probability ρ_k that the node has at least one packet to transmit is [21]

$$\rho_k = \min[1, \lambda_k/\mu_k]. \tag{7}$$

Assume packets arrive according to a Poisson process, then the probability Pa_k that at least one packet arrives during the current virtual slot is calculated as

$$Pa_k = 1 - e^{-\lambda_k E_S}. \tag{8}$$

5.2.2 Interactions among Markov Chains in the Packet Level Model

Denote the number of nodes with priority k as N_k. In real deployment, an indicator can be appended to the packet header to indicate the priority k of the packet. Then, N_k can be estimated by monitoring this indicator and the distinct MAC addresses encapsulated in headers of received packets [23]. The total number of nodes is then $N = \sum_{k=0}^{K-1} N_k$. We assume that all these N nodes are within the carrier sensing range of each other. For a node in priority level k, it not only contends with other $N_k - 1$ nodes in the same priority level, but also experiences collisions from $N - N_k$ nodes in other priority levels. Let τ_k denote the probability that a node in priority level k attempts to transmit in the current virtual slot. Then, the probability Pc_k that the channel is busy is

$$Pc_k = 1-(1-\tau_k)^{N_k-1}\prod_{i\neq k}(1-\tau_i)^{N_i}, k = 0,\cdots,K-1. \quad (9)$$

The probability Ps_k that a node in priority level k successfully transmits a packet in the current virtual slot is [24]

$$Ps_k = \tau_k(1-Pc_k), k = 0,1,\cdots,K-1. \quad (10)$$

Further, the probability P_{tr} that at least one of the nodes is transmitting at current virtual slot is defined as [24]

$$P_{tr} = 1-\prod_{k=0}^{K}(1-\tau_k)^{N_k}. \quad (11)$$

5.3 Average Service Rate and Goodput

In this section, we derive the average service rate μ_k and the average goodput S_k based on the packet level model. We denote the average time the channel is sensed busy because of a successful transmission as T_S, and denote the average time the channel is sensed busy by each node during a collision as T_C. As discussed in Section 2.1.2, Wi-Fi adopts the DCF as the default MAC access technique. For transmissions with the DCF mechanism, we have

$$T_S = T_{DIFS}+T_H+T_P+\delta+T_{SIFS}+T_{ACK}+\delta, \quad (12)$$
$$T_C = T_{DIFS}+T_H+T_P+\delta, \quad (13)$$

where T_H is the duration of a packet header, T_P is the duration of data section of each packet, T_{DIFS} is the duration of DIFS, T_{SIFS} is the duration of Short Interframe Space (SIFS), T_{ACK} is the duration of an ACK packet, and δ is the prorogation delay. To capture the RTS/CTS mechanism, T_S and T_C can be further modified as those in [24]. Then the mean state duration E_S is estimated as

$$E_S = \sigma(1-P_{tr})+T_S\sum_{k=0}^{k}N_kPs_k+T_C(P_{tr}-\sum_{k=0}^{k}N_kPs_k), \quad (14)$$

where σ is the time unit defined by the IEEE 802.11 g/n standards.

We then employ transfer-function approach to evaluate the Probability Generating Function (PGF) of the MAC access delay. The average MAC access delay d_k is then estimated by Eq. (15). Then the average service rate μ_k is

$$\mu_k = 1/d_k. \quad (16)$$

The average goodput of a node in priority level k is

$$S_k = \min[Ps_kT_PR/E_S,\ \lambda_k], \quad (17)$$

where R is the Wi-Fi data rate selected for transmission.

5.4 The Queue Level Models

The queue level model consists of another set of DTMCs. We establish one DTMC to model the queueing process of one node in each priority level. We notice that queues with $\lambda_k \le \mu_k$ evolve differently from queues with $\lambda_k > \mu_k$.

5.4.1 The Queue Level Model of $\lambda_k \le \mu_k$

The DTMC for this case is presented in Fig. 4. Each state represents the queueing delay of the current head-of-line packet, which is measured by number of **time units** of length σ. We denote the expected interval between two consecutive packet arrivals as T_a, where $T_a = 1/\lambda_k$. We further define $T_1 = T_C/\sigma$ and $T_2 = (T_a - T_S)/\sigma$. When $\lambda_k \le \mu_k$, we have $T_2 = (T_a - T_S)/\sigma \ge 0$.

There are three one-step transition probabilities for each state except state 0. (a) Let $P1_k$ denote the probability that the channel is busy and the head-of-line packet does not reach its re-transmission limit (thus is not dropped). In this case, the queueing delay increases by T_1 time units. (b) Let $P2_k$ denote the probability that the channel is idle. In this case, the queueing delay increases by 1 time unit. (c) Let $P3_k$ denote the probability that the head packet is successfully transmitted or is dropped after $m+1$ transmission attempts. In this case, the queueing delay of the head packet decreases by $\min[D, T_2]$ time units, where D is the current queueing delay.

For the special case of state 0, we have the following rules. From state 0, the DTMC stays in state 0 with probability $(1 - Pa_k) + Pa_kP3_k$, transits to state 1 with probability Pa_kP2_k, and transits to state T_1 with probability Pa_kP1_k.

Taking the outputs from the packet level model, we determine $P1_k$, $P2_k$, and $P3_k$ as follows

$$P1_k = Pc_k(1-Pc_k^m\pi_{0,0,k}), \quad (18)$$
$$P2_k = (1-\tau_k)(1-Pc_k), \quad (19)$$
$$P3_k = \tau_k(1-Pc_k)+Pc_k\cdot Pc_k^m\pi_{0,0,k}, \quad (20)$$

where $\pi_{0,0,k}$ is the stationary probability of the state (0,0) in the DTMC of priority k from the packet level.

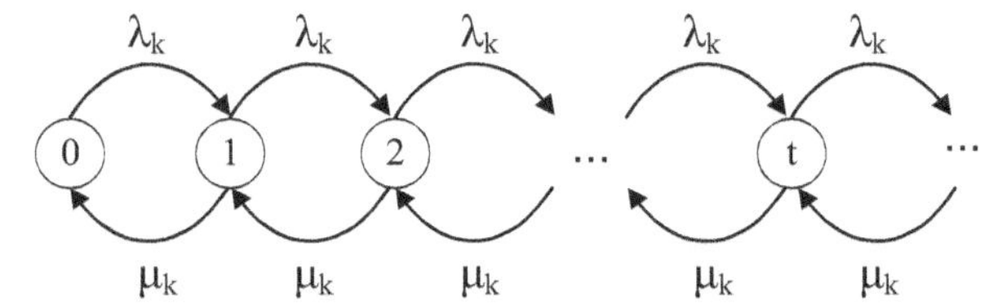

Figure 5: The DTMC for the queueing process of each node in priority level k when $\lambda_k > \mu_k$.

5.4.2 The Queue Level Model of $\lambda_k > \mu_k$

To model the queueing process of this case, we use a M/M/1 queue with an arrival rate of λ_k and a service rate of μ_k, as shown in Fig. 5. Each state in the DTMC in Fig. 5 represents a queue length. M/M/1 queues have been extensively studied. However, we still need a ready-to-use queueing delay analytical model for the case of $\lambda_k > \mu_k$.

5.5 Average Queueing Delay

Given the queue level model, λ_k and μ_k, we next derive the average queueing delay $\overline{D}$. Note that μ_k is derived in Section 5.3.

5.5.1 The Average Queueing Delay of $\lambda_k \le \mu_k$

We focus on the DTMC shown in Fig. 4. Let $e_k(t)$ denote the stationary distribution of this DTMC, where t is the index of state. Then we have the following recurrence

$$d_k = T_S[1-(Pc_k)^{m+1}] + T_C(Pc_k)^{m+1} + \frac{E_S(Pc_k)^{m+1}}{2}[W_{0,k}(2^{m+1}-1)-(m+1)]$$
$$+ E_S\left\{W_{0,k}(1-Pc_k)\left[\frac{1-(2Pc_k)^{m+1}}{1-2Pc_k} - \frac{1-(Pc_k)^{m+1}}{2(1-Pc_k)}\right] - \frac{1-(m+2)(Pc_k)^{m+1}+(m+1)(Pc_k)^{m+2}}{2(1-Pc_k)}\right\}. \quad (15)$$

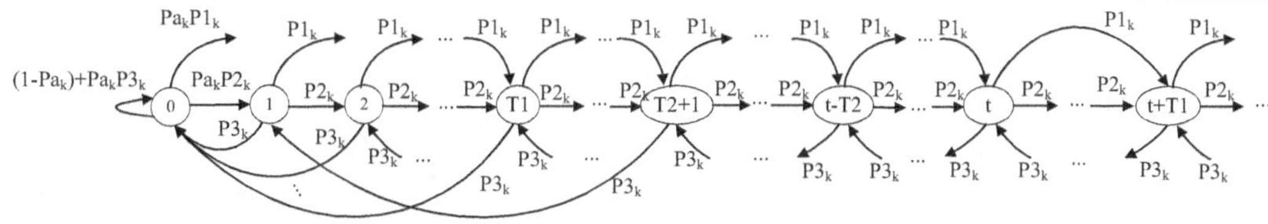

Figure 4: The DTMC for the queueing process of each node in priority level k when $\lambda_k \leq \mu_k$

equations

$$e_k(t) = \begin{cases} P1_k e_k(t-T_1) + P2_k e_k(t-1) \\ \quad + P3_k e_k(t+T_2), t \geq T_1+1, \\ P_a P1_k e_k(t-T_1) + P2_k e_k(t-1) \\ \quad + P3_k e_k(t+T_2), t = T_1, \\ P2_k e_k(t-1) + +P3_k e_k(t+T_2), 2 \leq t \leq T_1 - 1, \\ P_a P2_k e_k(t-1) + +P3_k e_k(t+T_2), t = 1, \\ \dfrac{P3_k}{Pa_k(1-P3_k)} \displaystyle\sum_{i=1}^{T_2} e_k(i), t = 0. \end{cases} \quad (21)$$

The next lemma characterizes $e_k(t)$ when $t \geq T_1 + 1$.

Lemma 1. *The stationary distribution of the DTMC shown in Fig. 4 satisfies*

$$e_k(t) = A_1 r^t, \; t \geq T_1 + 1, \quad (22)$$

where A_1 is a constant, $0 < r < 1$, and r is a root of the following characteristic function

$$P1_k u + P2_k u^{T_1} + P3_k u^{T_1+T_2+1} - u^{T_1+1} = 0. \quad (23)$$

We skip the detailed proof of this lemma, due to limited space.

With *Lemma 1* and Eq. 21, we can further derive equations (24), (25) and (26). By solving Eq. (24), (25) and (26), we obtain the values of $e_k(0)$, $e_k(T_1)$, and the constant A_1. All the $e_k(t), t = 0, 1, \cdots$, can be explicitly expressed by $e_k(0)$, $e_k(T_1)$, and A_1. Thus, the stationary distribution of the DTMC in Fig. 4 is achieved.

Denote the average queueing delay of packets transmitted by any node in priority level k as $\overline{D}_k$. Given the stationary distribution, $\overline{D}_k$ is estimated as

$$\overline{D}_k = \sigma \cdot \sum_{t=0}^{\infty} t \cdot e_k(t). \quad (27)$$

5.5.2 The Average Queueing Delay of $\lambda_k > \mu_k$

We focus on the DTMC shown in Fig. 5. We number the arrival packets by $1, 2, \cdots$, in the order of their arrival time. Denote the arrival time of the nth packet as a_n, and the departure time of the nth packet as c_n. We focus on the case where the queue begins to evolve with no packet. (An initially non-empty queue can be easily modeled by changing the initial conditions of our model.) Then we have the following lemma on the expectations of a_n and c_n.

Lemma 2. *Let $\mathbf{E}(a_n)$ and $\mathbf{E}(c_n)$ be the expectations of arrival and departure time of the nth packet, respectively. When $\lambda_k > \mu_k$, we have the following equations for the queueing process presented in Fig. 5*

$$\lim_{n\to\infty} \mathbf{E}(a_n)/n = (\lambda_k + \mu_k)/\lambda_k, \quad (28)$$
$$\lim_{n\to\infty} \mathbf{E}(c_n)/n = (\lambda_k + \mu_k)/\mu_k. \quad (29)$$

The proof of this lemma is skipped due to limited space.

When $\lambda_k > \mu_k$, the average queueing delay keeps increasing as time goes by. Therefore, we focus on the average queueing delay of packets that are transmitted before a constant time unit T ($T < \infty$). To capture the delay up to T, we first need to calculate the number of clients transmitted before T. We have the following lemma for the average number of transmitted packets before time unit T.

Lemma 3. *Let N_T be the number of packets that are transmitted before T. When $\lambda_k > \mu_k$, we have the following equation for the queueing process presented in Fig. 5*

$$\lim_{T\to\infty} N_T/T = \mu_k/(\lambda_k + \mu_k). \quad (30)$$

We skip the proof because of the limited space.

Given *Lemma 2* and *Lemma 3*, we can characterize the average queueing delay for the case of $\lambda_k > \mu_k$ with the following theorem.

Theorem 1. *Let $\overline{D}_k(T)$ denote the average queueing delay (in seconds) of packets transmitted by a priority k node before time slot T. When $\lambda_k > \mu_k$, we have the following equation for the queueing process presented in Fig. 5*

$$\overline{D}_k(T) \xrightarrow{a.s.} \frac{\sigma T}{2} \cdot \frac{\lambda_k - \mu_k}{\lambda_k}, \quad (31)$$

where $\xrightarrow{a.s.}$ means "converges almost surely".

Proof. By *Lemma 2*, we have the following equation for the queueing delay $c_n - a_n$ of the nth packet

$$\mathbf{E}[c_n - a_n] = \mathbf{E}[c_n] - \mathbf{E}[a_n]$$
$$\xrightarrow{a.s.} \frac{\lambda_k + \mu_k}{\mu_k} n - \frac{\lambda_k + \mu_k}{\lambda_k} n = \frac{\lambda_k^2 - \mu_k^2}{\lambda_k \mu_k} n. \quad (32)$$

And by *Lemma 3*, we have the following equation for the number of packets transmitted before T

$$\mathbf{E}[N_T] \xrightarrow{a.s.} \frac{\mu_k}{\lambda_k + \mu_k} T. \quad (33)$$

Take the length of each time slot as σ. Then combining Eq.

$$e_k(0) = \frac{P3_k}{P_a(1-P3_k)}\left\{\frac{1}{(1-P2_k)}\left[A_1P3_k - kr^{T_2+1}\left(\frac{1-r^{T_1}}{1-r}\right) + P_a(P1_k+P2_k)e_k(0) - e_k(T_1)\right] + A_1r^{T_1+1}\left(\frac{1-r^{T_2-T_1}}{1-r}\right)\right\}, \quad (24)$$

$$e_k(T_1) = \frac{A_1}{P2_k}r^{T_1+1} - P1_kP_ae_k(0) - \frac{P1_kP3_k}{P2_k}A_1r^{T_2+1} - \frac{P3_k}{P2_k}A_1r^{T_1+T_2+1}, \quad (25)$$

$$1 = \left[1 + \frac{P_a(1-P3_k)}{P3_k}\right]e_k(0) + \frac{Ar^{T_2+1}}{1-r}. \quad (26)$$

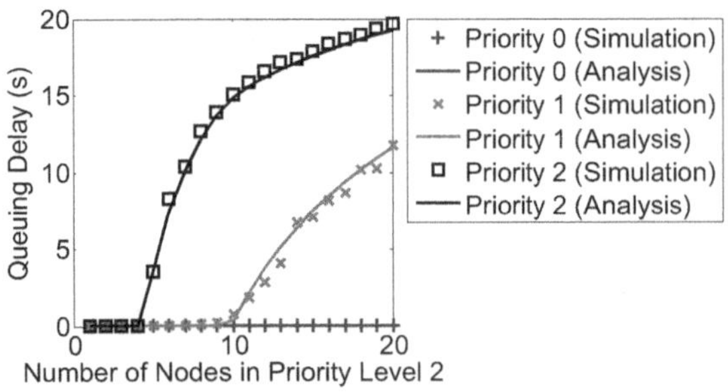

Figure 6: The model validation result.

(32) and Eq. (33), we have

$$\overline{D}_k(T) = \sigma\mathbf{E}\left[\frac{\sum_{i=1}^{N_T} i \cdot \frac{\lambda_k^2-\mu_k^2}{\lambda_k\mu_k}}{N_T}\right]$$

$$\xrightarrow{a.s.} \sigma \cdot \frac{\mathbf{E}[N_T]+1}{2} \cdot \frac{\lambda_k^2-\mu_k^2}{\lambda_k\mu_k}$$

$$\xrightarrow{a.s.} \frac{\sigma T}{2} \cdot \frac{\lambda_k-\mu_k}{\lambda_k}.$$

□

5.6 Model Validation

In our model validation, there are 3 priority levels, i.e., $k = 0, 1, 2$. The minimum CW sizes are $W_{0,0} = 3$, $W_{0,1} = 7$, and $W_{0,2} = 15$, respectively. To present the validation results clearly, we fix the numbers of nodes in priority levels 0 and 1, and change the number of nodes in priority level 2. Concretely, we fix $N_0 = 2$ and $N_1 = 2$, and change N_2 from 1 to 20. The packet size is set to $500B$. For all the nodes, the packet arrival rate is $1Mbps$, which matches the standard bit rate of YouTube 360p videos. Each run of simulations lasts for a duration of 50 seconds, i.e., $T = 50$. All the queues are empty at the beginning of this 50-second duration. We use a date rate of $24Mbps$ as an example.

We validate our models with queueing delay in Fig. 6. Generally, it is shown that the queueing delays are well captured by our two-level models. One interesting observation is that the average queueing delay of nodes in priority level 2 increases suddenly at the point of $N_2 = 5$. This sudden increase of queueing delay also happens for nodes in priority level 1 at the point of $N_2 = 11$. When $\lambda_k < \mu_k$, packets are transmitted rapidly by nodes in priority level k. The queue length stays as a constant even if time goes to infinity. When $\lambda_k > \mu_k$, packets begin to accumulate in queues of nodes in priority level k, and the lengths of these queues keep increasing as time goes by. Therefore, instead of having a constant value, the average queueing delay becomes an increasing function of time, and will approach infinity if time approaches infinity. Note that this is captured by our queue level models.

Table 1: Candidate delay sets for DRIVING.

Setting	β_2	β_1	β_0
1	$[0, 1)$	$[1, 2)$	$[2, +\infty)$
2	$[0, 1)$	$[1, 4)$	$[4, +\infty)$
3	$[0, 2)$	$[2, 4)$	$[4, +\infty)$
4	$[0, 2)$	$[2, 10)$	$[10, +\infty)$
5	$[0, 4)$	$[4, 10)$	$[10, +\infty)$

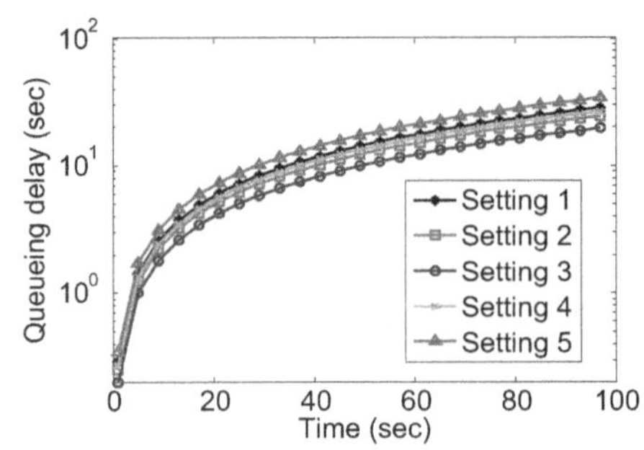

Figure 7: The evolution of queueing delays under different settings of DRIVING.

5.7 Tuning DRIVING with the Models

One important application of our analytical models is to tune the DRIVING for better performance before real deployment. There are three kinds of parameters to be tuned, i.e., the number of priority levels, their corresponding delay sets, and their corresponding minimum CW sizes. Due to the limited space, we only present the tuning of the delay sets while fixing the number of priority levels and the corresponding minimum CW sizes. Concretely, we use 3 priority levels, and set their minimum CW sizes as 3, 7, and 15, respectively. We compare five candidate delay sets as presented in Table 1, and select the best one from them.

Based on our two-level models, we calculate the evolution of queueing delays under these five settings. As an example, we set set packet size as $500B$, and the packet arrival rate as $1Mbps$. Fig. 7 illustrate how the queueing delays increase with time. It is shown that Setting 3, which is neither the most aggressive nor the most conservative, achieves the lowest queueing delay at all time. The reason is two-fold. On ond hand, an aggressive setting tends to push all nodes to the highest priority level quickly. As a result, the CW sizes of all nodes become too small to avoid packet collisions. On the other hand, a conservative setting tends to retain all nodes in at the lowest priority level. Consequently, the CW sizes of all nodes remain too large, and thus the channel utilization remains low.

6. PERFORMANCE EVALUATION

In this section, we conduct comprehensive simulation studies to illustrate the improvements brought by DRIVING. We first present the setup of our ns-2 evaluation platform. We then evaluate the performance of DRIVING in terms of delay, jitter, deadline missing ratio and goodput.

6.1 Evaluation Setup

The evaluation is conducted in our ns-2 based platform, and its setup is described as follows.

6.1.1 *The Highway Scenario*

We conduct our simulations in an urban bidirectional highway section. This highway section is of $3000m$ long. It has 2 lanes in each direction and an isolation zone in the middle. The vehicle number varies from 4 to 80. The movement traces of vehicles are generated using the tool of Simulation of Urban MObility (SUMO).

6.1.2 *In-cabin Wi-Fi Settings*

Each vehicle on the highway is equipped with an in-cabin Wi-Fi AP, which runs on the 2.4GHz band. We assume that all APs are working in the same 20MHz Wi-Fi channel. The transmission power of the APs is set to 20dBm. Each in-cabin Wi-Fi AP has a $16MB$ buffer for video streaming. We focus on the case where each Wi-Fi AP serves one client. We apply the two-slope vehicular prorogation model presented in [25]. The path loss factor introduced by the vehicle cabin is $-10dB$.

6.1.3 *Wireless Traffic Settings*

The video bit-rate in our simulations is $3.3Mbps$ (High-Definition video streaming). Each video packet carries 500 bytes of video data. Multiple packets are grouped into one large video chunk [26], which represents around 10 seconds of video. Video chunks arrive at in-cabin Wi-Fi APs periodically [27]. Besides the video streaming traffic, there are other kinds of data traffic in the wireless channel, including web browsing traffic, audio traffic and file sharing traffic. The percentages of video, web browsing, audio and file sharing in the whole traffic are 75%, 17%, 6% and 2%, respectively [1].

6.1.4 *Scheduling Algorithms*

In the simulations, we compare the following three distributed algorithms.

The **DRIVING** algorithm is an implementation of the DRIVING framework, which adopts the tuning result from Section 5.7. It supports 3 levels of priorities (in consistence with the industrial practice, e.g., 802.11 EDCA.). It assigns priority 0 to the head-of-line packets with delays larger than 4 seconds, and allocate priority 2 to the head-of-line packets with delays smaller than 2 seconds. The rest of the head-of-line packets are with priority 1. The minimum CW sizes corresponding to priorities 0, 1 and 2 are $W_{0,0} = 3$, $W_{0,1} = 7$ and $W_{0,2} = 15$, respectively.

The **Q-based** algorithm is an extension from the queue-length based CSMA algorithms in [12, 18, 11]. To compare with the DRIVING algorithms, we update existing queue-length based CSMA algorithms into the Q-based algorithm as follows. The Q-based algorithm also supports 3 levels of priorities. The minimum CW sizes of transmissions in priorities 0, 1 and 2 are $W_{0,0} = 3$, $W_{0,1} = 7$ and $W_{0,2} = 15$, respectively. If the length of a queue is larger than $8MB$ (i.e., 50% of the AP's buffer size), the Q-based algorithm assigns the highest priority (i.e., priority 0) to the head-of-line packet in this queue. If the length of a queue is between $3.2MB$ and $8MB$ (i.e., $20 - 50\%$ of the AP's buffer size), the Q-based algorithm assigns priority 1 to the head-of-line packet in this queue. Otherwise, the head-of-line packet is with priority 2.

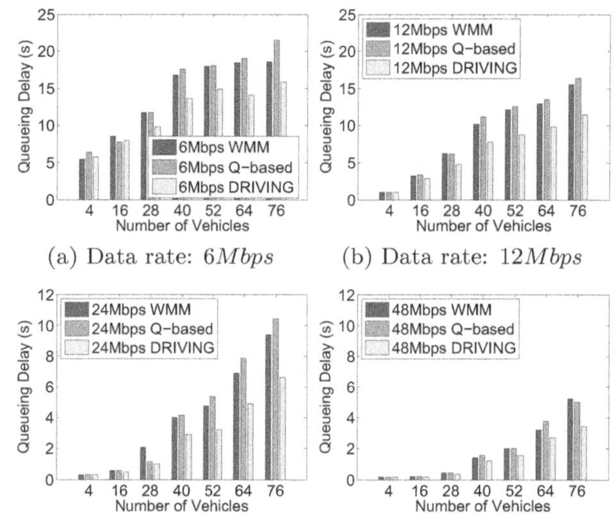

(a) Data rate: $6Mbps$ (b) Data rate: $12Mbps$

(c) Data rate: $24Mbps$ (d) Data rate: $48Mbps$

Figure 8: The average queueing delays.

The **WMM** algorithm follows the Wi-Fi Multimedia protocol, which is a Wi-Fi Alliance certification based on IEEE 802.11e standard. This algorithm prioritizes traffic according to four Access Categories (AC) - voice, video, best effort, and background.

6.2 Delay and Jitter Performance

Fig. 8 compares the average queueing delays of the three algorithms. Compared to the second best algorithm, the DRIVING algorithm reduces the average queueing delay by up to 26.1%, 31.1%, 40.0% and 31.8% for transmission data rates of $6Mbps$, $12Mbps$, $24Mbps$ and $48Mbps$, respectively. Furthermore, even with the highest traffic density, DRIVING still results in the lowest queueing delay. This demonstrates that DRIVING is robust to the changes of traffic.

Another observation from Fig. 8 (b) and Fig. 8 (c) is worth noticing. The Q-based algorithm yields the largest average queueing delay when the number of vehicles is larger than 40. This indicates that the Q-based algorithm is not suitable for the delay sensitive service of video streaming in high traffic scenarios. The reason is as follows. When the scheduling decision is made based on the queue length, the packets in a large queue always has a higher priority than those in a small queue. Upon the arrival of a new video chunk to an AP Z_1, the queue length of this AP soars. Suppose there is another AP Z_2, who has only one largely delayed packet p. By the Q-based algorithm, packet p in AP Z_2 has a lower priority than those of the newly arrived packets in AP Z_1. Therefore, the largely delayed packet p has to wait for almost all the newly arrived packets in AP Z_1. Consequently, the delay of packet p becomes really large. On the contrary, the DRIVING algorithm avoids this problem by assigning higher priorities to packets with larger delays, and thus outperforms the other two algorithms, especially in high-density scenarios.

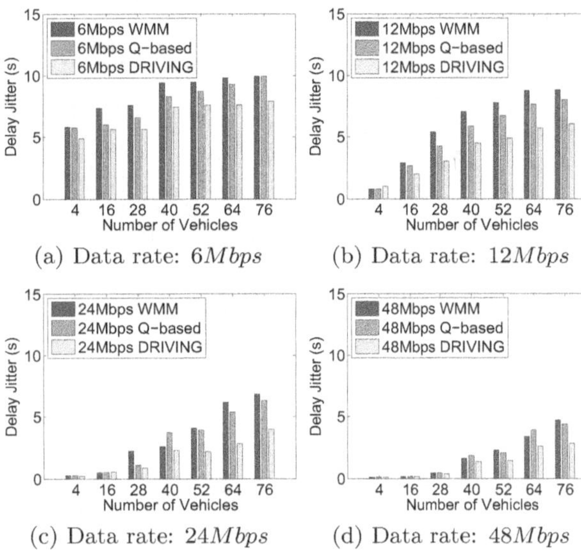

(a) Data rate: $6Mbps$ (b) Data rate: $12Mbps$

(c) Data rate: $24Mbps$ (d) Data rate: $48Mbps$

Figure 9: The delay jitters.

Fig. 9 compares the three algorithms in terms of the jitter. A smaller jitter of the queueing delay indicates a smoother video streaming, thus a better video viewing experience. Compared to the second best algorithm, the DRIVING algorithm reduces jitter by up to 20.3%, 28.8%, 47.4% and 35.6% for the transmission data rates of $6Mbps$, $12Mbps$, $24Mbps$ and $48Mbps$, respectively. Therefore, the DRIVING algorithm provides the most stable video streaming.

6.3 Deadline Missing Ratio Performance

In this section, we evaluate the performance of in-cabin Wi-Fi video streaming in terms of the deadline missing ratio.

Fig. 10 compares the Cumulative Distribution Functions (CDFs) of the deadline missing ratios, when there are 80 vehicles. It is illustrated that, with the support of the DRIVING algorithm, the deadline missing ratio of in-cabin Wi-Fi video streaming is largely reduced. Compared to the second best algorithm, the DRIVING algorithm reduces the average deadline missing ratio by 19.0%, 29.4%, 38.4% and 37.9% for transmission data rates of $6Mbps$, $12Mbps$, $24Mbps$ and $48Mbps$, respectively. By using the queueing delay as the criterion of scheduling, the DRIVING algorithm is able to assign smaller CW sizes to packets that are approaching their deadlines. On average, these deadline-approaching packets are transmitted faster than others. In this way, the DRIVING algorithm reduces the deadline missing ratio.

6.4 Goodput Performance

Fig. 11 compares the average goodputs of the three algorithms. It is shown that the DRIVING algorithm achieves the highest average goodput. Compared to the default algorithm, the DRIVING algorithm enlarges the average goodput by up to 27.0%, 25.1%, 26.1% and 22.1% (for the transmission data rates of $6Mbps$, $12Mbps$, $24Mbps$ and $48Mbps$, respectively. More importantly, the gap between DRIVING's average goodput and those of the other two algorithms increases with traffic density. Take the data rate of $24Mbps$ for example: DRIVING increases the goodput by 13.5% when there are 16 vehicles. The improvement increases to 26.1% when there are 76 vehicles. This suggests that, compared to the other two algorithms, the DRIVING algorithm is more capable of effective scheduling video streaming service in high-density traffic conditions.

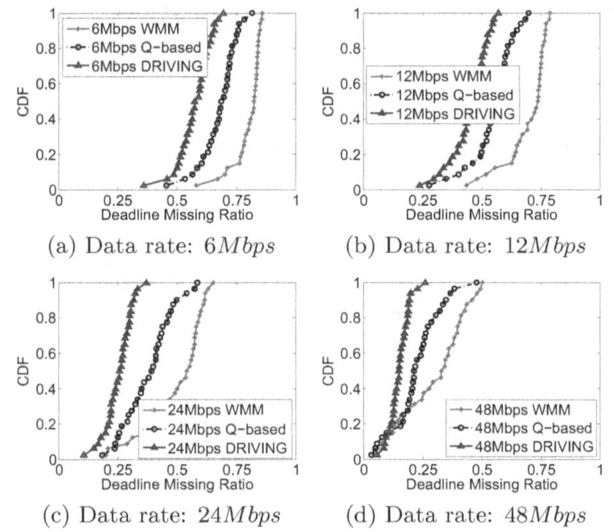

(a) Data rate: $6Mbps$ (b) Data rate: $12Mbps$

(c) Data rate: $24Mbps$ (d) Data rate: $48Mbps$

Figure 10: The CDFs of deadline missing ratios when the vehicle number is 80.

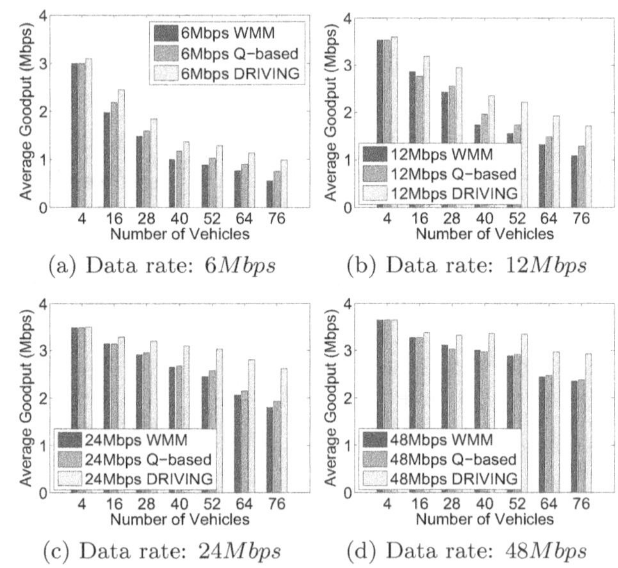

(a) Data rate: $6Mbps$ (b) Data rate: $12Mbps$

(c) Data rate: $24Mbps$ (d) Data rate: $48Mbps$

Figure 11: The average goodputs.

7. CONCLUSION

This paper studies the problem of scheduling video streaming in the new in-cabin Wi-Fi systems. Considering the completely decentralized in-cabin Wi-Fi APs and the delay-sensitive video packets, we propose the fully distributed and delay-aware DRIVING framework. To reduce latency and minimize deadline missing ratio, DRIVING prioritizes packets with large queueing delays. We conduct extensive theoretical and simulation studies to evaluate and optimize DRIVING. In a typical scenario, DRIVING enlarges the average video streaming goodput by up to 27.0%, and at the same time lowers the average queueing delay and deadline missing ratio by up to 40.0% and 38.4%, respectively.

Acknowledgements

This work was supported in part by the NSERC Collaborative Research and Development Grant (CRDJP 418713). We also thank the anonymous reviewers and editors for their constructive comments.

8. REFERENCES

[1] *Cisco Visual Networking Index: Global Mobile Data Traffic Forecast Update, 2015 - 2020.* Cisco Systems Inc, Feb, 2016.

[2] X. Chen, L. Rao, Y. Yao, X. Liu, and F. Bai, "The answer is rolling on wheels: Modeling and performance evaluation of in-cabin Wi-Fi communications," *Vehicular Communications*, vol. 2, no. 1, pp. 13 – 26, 2015.

[3] I.-H. Hou and P. R. Kumar, "Utility-optimal scheduling in time-varying wireless networks with delay constraints," in *Proc. of ACM MobiHoc*, 2010.

[4] H. Wu, X. Lin, X. Liuz, and Y. Zhang, "Application-level scheduling with deadline constraints," *in Proc. of IEEE INFOCOM*, pp. 1–9, 2014.

[5] A. Dua, C. Chan, N. Bambos, and J. Apostolopoulos, "Channel, deadline, and distortion (CD^2) aware scheduling for video streams over wireless," *IEEE Trans. on Wireless Communications*, vol. 9, no. 3, pp. 1001–1011, 2010.

[6] P. Pahalawatta, R. Berry, T. Pappas, and A. Katsaggelos, "Content-aware resource allocation and packet scheduling for video transmission over wireless networks," *IEEE Journal on Selected Areas in Communications*, vol. 25, no. 4, pp. 749–759, 2007.

[7] M. Caccamo, L. Zhang, L. Sha, and G. Buttazzo, "An implicit prioritized access protocol for wireless sensor networks," in *Proc. of IEEE RTSS*, 2002, pp. 39–48.

[8] V. Kanodia, C. Li, A. Sabharwal, B. Sadeghi, and E. Knightly, "Distributed priority scheduling and medium access in ad hoc networks," *Springer Journal of Wireless Networks*, vol. 8, no. 5, pp. 455–466, 2002.

[9] S.-P. Chuah, Z. Chen, and Y.-P. Tan, "Energy-efficient resource allocation and scheduling for multicast of scalable video over wireless networks," *IEEE Trans. on Multimedia*, vol. 14, no. 4, pp. 1324–1336, 2012.

[10] Y. Zhang, S. Qin, and Z. He, "Fine-granularity transmission distortion modeling for video packet scheduling over mesh networks," *IEEE Trans. on Multimedia*, vol. 12, no. 1, pp. 1–12, 2010.

[11] J. Ni, B. Tan, and R. Srikant, "Q-CSMA: Queue-length based CSMA/CA algorithms for achieving maximum throughput and low delay in wireless networks," in *Proc. of IEEE INFOCOM*, 2010.

[12] L. Jiang and J. Walrand, "Approaching throughput-optimality in distributed CSMA scheduling algorithms with collisions," *IEEE/ACM Trans. on Networking*, vol. 19, no. 3, pp. 816–829, 2011.

[13] P. Si, F. Yu, H. Ji, and V. Leung, "Distributed sender scheduling for multimedia transmission in wireless mobile peer-to-peer networks," *IEEE Trans. on Wireless Communications*, vol. 8, no. 9, pp. 4594–4603, 2009.

[14] C. Demichelis and P. Chimento, "IP packet delay variation metric for IP performance metrics (IPPM)," 2002.

[15] A. Gupta, X. Lin, and R. Srikant, "Low-complexity distributed scheduling algorithms for wireless networks," in *Proc. of IEEE INFOCOM*, 2007, pp. 1631–1639.

[16] D. Qian, D. Zheng, J. Zhang, N. Shroff, and C. Joo, "Distributed csma algorithms for link scheduling in multihop mimo networks under sinr model," *IEEE/ACM Trans. on Networking*, vol. 21, no. 3, pp. 746–759, 2013.

[17] L. Zhou, X. Wang, W. Tu, G. Muntean, and B. Geller, "Distributed scheduling scheme for video streaming over multi-channel multi-radio multi-hop wireless networks," *IEEE Journal on Selected Areas in Communications*, vol. 28, no. 3, pp. 409–419, 2010.

[18] A. Rad, J. Huang, M. Chiang, and V. Wong, "Utility-optimal random access without message passing," *IEEE Trans. on Wireless Communications*, vol. 8, no. 3, pp. 1073–1079, 2009.

[19] H. Omar, W. Zhuang, and L. Li, "Vemac: A tdma-based mac protocol for reliable broadcast in VANETs," *IEEE Trans. on Mobile Computing*, vol. 12, no. 9, pp. 1724–1736, 2013.

[20] F. Soldo, C. Casetti, C. Chiasserini, and P. Chaparro, "Video streaming distribution in VANETs," *IEEE Trans. on Parallel and Distributed Systems*, vol. 22, no. 7, pp. 1085–1091, 2011.

[21] Y. Yao, L. Rao, X. Liu, and X. Zhou, "Delay analysis and study of IEEE 802.11p based DSRC safety communication in a highway environment," in *Proc. of IEEE INFOCOM*, 2013.

[22] D. Malone, K. Duffy, and D. Leith, "Modeling the 802.11 distributed coordination function in nonsaturated heterogeneous conditions," *IEEE/ACM Trans. on Networking*, vol. 15, no. 1, pp. 159–172, Feb 2007.

[23] D. Rawat, D. Popescu, G. Yan, and S. Olariu, "Enhancing vanet performance by joint adaptation of transmission power and contention window size," *IEEE Trans. on Parallel and Distributed Systems*, vol. 22, no. 9, pp. 1528–1535, 2011.

[24] G. Bianchi, "Performance analysis of the IEEE 802.11 distributed coordination function," *IEEE Journal on Selected Areas in Communications*, vol. 18, no. 3, pp. 535–547, 2000.

[25] L. Cheng, B. Henty, D. Stancil, F. Bai, and P. Mudalige, "Mobile vehicle-to-vehicle narrow-band channel measurement and characterization of the 5.9 GHz Dedicated Short Range Communication (DSRC) frequency band," *IEEE Journal on Selected Areas in Communications*, vol. 25, no. 8, pp. 1501–1516, 2007.

[26] *ISO/IEC 23009-1: Information technology âĂŤ Dynamic adaptive streaming over HTTP (DASH)*, 2014.

[27] P. Ameigeiras, J. J. Ramos-Munoz, J. Navarro-Ortiz, and J. Lopez-Soler, "Analysis and modelling of YouTube traffic," *Trans. on Emerging Telecommunications Technologies*, vol. 23, no. 4, pp. 360–377, 2012.

Dynamic Resource Provisioning with QoS Guarantee for Video Transcoding in Online Video Sharing Service

Guanyu Gao
School of Computer Science and Engineering
Nanyang Technological University
ggao001@e.ntu.edu.sg

Yonggang Wen
School of Computer Science and Engineering
Nanyang Technological University
ygwen@ntu.edu.sg

Cedric Westphal
Huawei Innovation Center &
University of California, Santa Cruz
cedric.westphal@huawei.com
cedric@soe.ucsc.edu

ABSTRACT

Video transcoding is widely adopted in online video sharing services to encode video content into multiple representations. This solution, however, could consume huge amount of computing resource and incur excessive processing delays. Moreover, content has heterogeneous QoS requirements for transcoding. Some content must be transcoded in real time, while some are deferrable for transcoding. It needs to determine the strategy for intelligently provisioning the right amount of resource under dynamic workload to meet the heterogeneous QoS requirements. To this end, this paper develops a robust dynamic resource provisioning scheme for transcoding with heterogeneous QoS criteria. We adopt the *Preemptive Resume Priority* discipline for scheduling, so that the transcoding-deferrable content can utilize idle resources for transcoding to maximize resource utilization while remain transparent to delay-sensitive content. We leverage *Model Predictive Control* to design the online algorithm for dynamic resource provisioning using predictions to accommodate time-varying workload. To seek robustness of system performance against prediction noises, we improve our online algorithm through *Robust Design*. The experiment results in a real environment demonstrate that our proposed framework can achieve the QoS requirements while reducing 50% of resource consumption on average.

Keywords

Video transcoding, cloud computing, resource provisioning, quality of service, model predictive control, online algorithm

1. INTRODUCTION

Nowadays online video sharing service has become enormously popular, it has become an important medium for people to have entertainment and obtain information [15]. The online video sharing and social network websites (e.g., Youtube, Facebook, and Twitter) allow users and professional video content producers to upload and publish video content online. It has shown an explosive growing trend of the online video content [24]. For instances, as of 2015, the estimated amount of new videos uploaded to Youtube during one minute is 300 hours [2]. In the live streaming platform Twitch, the peak number of concurrent live streams for broadcasting the live events is above 12000 [23]. These newly uploaded video content, however, cannot be published and delivered to the viewers directly due to the heterogeneous devices and diverse network conditions at the viewer side. To cope with such problems, adaptive bitrate (ABR) streaming [19] has been widely adopted.

With ABR, each video file (or stream) needs to be encoded into multiple representations. When the viewers request the online video content, the streaming server can always deliver the best possible quality representation to the viewers according to their device capacities and network conditions. Nevertheless, video transcoding [21] is very computing intensive and time consuming, it would consume a huge amount of computing resource for transcoding the user uploaded video content into the target representations [16]. The online video sharing service providers need to deploy a large number of servers for transcoding the video content. This greatly increases the service operating cost [17].

The dynamic of transcoding workload and the heterogeneous QoS criteria in online video sharing service make it a great challenge for provisioning the computing resource. First, the arrival rate of the user uploaded content is time-varying [14]. And thus, provisioning a fixed number of dedicated transcoding servers would incur resource wastage when the arrival rate is low, and would incur large latency when the arrival rate is high. Second, video content has heterogeneous QoS requirements for transcoding. For instances, the live content is very sensitive to delay, and must be transcoded in real time. The video-on-demand (VoD) content does not need to be transcoded and delivered in real time, and the transcoding can be finished within a specified deadline. For the seldom requested content, the transcoding is deferrable and can be performed when resources are sufficient or using the idle resources. The QoS requirements for transcoding can also be categorized according to the service level agreement (SLA). For instance, the transcoding for premium service is real-time or guaranteed to finish within a deadline, while the transcoding time for free service may not be guaranteed. Thus, it is necessary to consider the dynamic workload and the heterogeneous QoS requirements of content for provisioning resources for transcoding.

Many recent research works have studied the resource pro-

MM '16, October 15-19, 2016, Amsterdam, Netherlands

DOI: http://dx.doi.org/10.1145/2964284.2964296

visioning and QoS management for video transcoding. Most of the previous works, however, considered one class of QoS criteria [25, 13, 7] or the system with known workload [18, 10]. There still lacks of some efforts on the problem of resource provisioning for transcoding with heterogeneous QoS criteria under dynamic workload. The challenges in this scenario are twofold: 1) The deterministic QoS requirements of delay-sensitive content may lead to limitations on system processing capacity, resulting in low resource utilization. The transcoding-deferrable content can utilize these idle resources for transcoding. Thus, it needs to investigate how to schedule the transcoding with heterogeneous QoS criteria to minimize overall resource consumption. 2) The performance of the transcoding system is affected by the uncertainty of time-varying workload, it needs to assess how to provision resource under the uncertainty of dynamic workload.

To address the challenges, we design a robust dynamic resource provisioning scheme for transcoding with heterogeneous QoS requirements in online video sharing services. We aim to achieve the heterogeneous QoS requirements while reducing the resource consumption. We first consider three fundamental QoS criteria for transcoding, namely:

1) *Real-time transcoding*, the QoS cost for transcoding increases with any possible processing delays.

2) *Deadline-sensitive transcoding*, the QoS cost increases if the processing time exceeds the specified deadline.

3) *Deferrable transcoding*, the QoS cost is not directly impacted by the processing time.

We adopt the *preemptive-resume priority* discipline for scheduling the content that has heterogeneous QoS requirements in each transcoding server. The transcoding for the delay-sensitive content (namely, the real-time and deadline-sensitive content) is performed in high priority to guarantee the QoS requirements, while the transcoding for the deferrable content is performed in low priority using idle resources and remain transparent to delay-sensitive content.

We formulate the system management as a problem of minimizing the overall system cost over time, including the computing cost, QoS cost, and switching cost. We design the online algorithm by leveraging *Model Predictive Control* (MPC) for dynamic resource provisioning. We improve the performance of our proposed online algorithm through *Robust Design* against the prediction noises. The experiments in a real environment demonstrate that our proposed framework can improve resource utilization for transcoding while maintaining the required QoS with reduced resource consumption. Our contributions in this paper are as follows:

- We design a preemptive-resume priority scheduling for transcoding the content with heterogeneous QoS criteria. It can greatly improve the resource utilization. To the best of our knowledge, our work is the first to utilize the preemptive-resume priority to implement the multiple-priority transcoding mechanism.

- We propose a robust dynamic resource provisioning scheme for transcoding. It can intelligently provision the right amount of resources using prediction to guarantee QoS, while keeping robust to prediction noise.

- We implement and evaluate the system performance in a real environment. The system can achieve the QoS requirements while reducing 50% of resource consumption on average compared with the *AlwaysOn* policy.

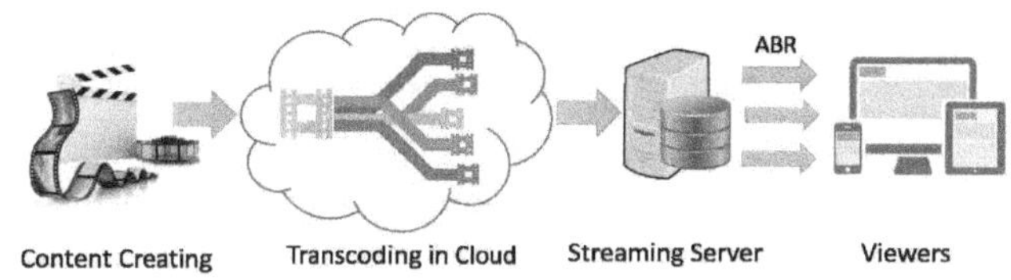

Figure 1: Video delivery flow for online sharing.

The rest of this paper is organized as follows. Section 2 introduces the background and related work. Section 3 presents the system design. Section 4 describes our system models and problem formulation. Section 5 designs the online algorithm. Section 6 introduces our system implementation. Section 7 presents the performance evaluations. Section 8 concludes the paper and presents the future work.

2. BACKGROUND AND RELATED WORK

We first start with a high-level overview of the video delivery flow in an online video sharing service, and then we introduce the related work on the cloud video transcoding.

2.1 Video Delivery Flow

We illustrate the video delivery flow in an online video sharing service in Fig. 1. It consists of the following steps for delivering the video content to the online viewers.

Content Creating: The users and the professional video content producers create the video files or streams by encoding the raw video data into compressed high-definition video using video and audio codecs (e.g., H.264 and AAC). The high-definition video files or streams will be uploaded onto the online video sharing website for publishing.

Video Transcoding: The user uploaded video content will be transcoded into multiple representations in different bitrates, resolutions, and formats. Transcoding is computing intensive. It consumes huge amounts of computing resource for transcoding the large volume of user uploaded video content. A new approach for transcoding is to use the scalable cloud infrastructure for dynamic resource provisioning.

Adaptive Bitrate Streaming: To deliver the video content in high availability and quality, the multiple representations of the video content will be cached in the streaming servers of the content delivery network (CDN). The viewers have varying network connection speeds with the streaming servers. With adaptive bitrate streaming (ABR), the viewers can dynamically adjust the requested quality of the video content by detecting the current bandwidth.

2.2 Cloud Video Transcoding

Numerous algorithms have been designed for reducing the resource consumption or achieving the target QoS. We investigate some related research, and discuss the differences between our method and the previous works.

The current research in this field mainly focuses on reducing the resource consumption and achieving the specified QoS. For reducing the resource consumption, [25] proposed a Lyapunov-based energy-efficient transcoding task dispatching algorithm to manage the tradeoff between energy consumption and processing delay. [18] proposed a dynamic voltage and frequency scaling (DVFS) scheme for adjusting the frequency and workload of each server to minimize power consumption and meet transcoding task deadlines. [7] used

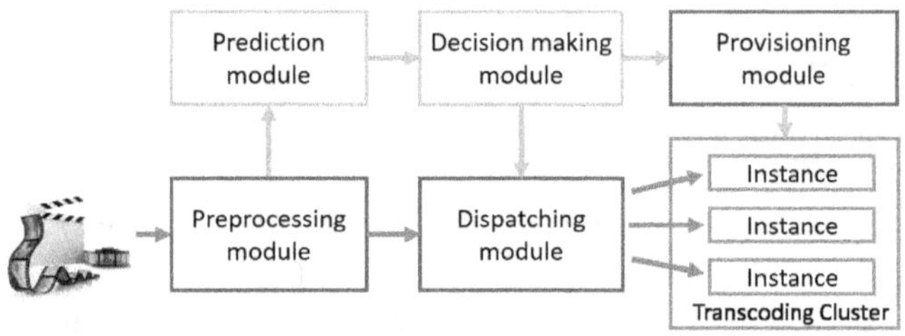

Figure 2: System design of transcoding system.

the prediction-based method for dynamic resource allocation to scale video transcoding service. [9, 12] proposed resource provisioning and performance management frameworks in cloud and data center using the predicted workload. [6] implemented a scalable open source cloud transcoding system that can dynamically provision resource. For achieving the target QoS or reducing the processing delay, [13] presented a dynamic task scheduling method to minimize the transcoding delay. [10] used the parallel video transcoding framework for reducing the transcoding time. [11] leveraged the video popularity information for prediction to pre-transcode video content to reduce the transcoding latency. [20] presented Bitcodin, which enabled transcoding and streaming as a service for live video streaming. [4] studied the transcoding settings for live streaming to maximize the QoE. [8] studied the impact of computing resource and cache size on the performance of the transcoding system.

The main difference between our work and the previous research is that we consider the heterogeneous QoS requirements of different types of content. The first-order goal of this work is to design the resource provisioning scheme under dynamic workload for transcoding with heterogeneous QoS requirements. The aim is to achieve the different QoS targets while reducing the resource consumption. The addressed challenges are twofold: 1) provisioning resource under the uncertainty of dynamic workload and 2) scheduling the transcoding with heterogeneous QoS criteria.

3. SYSTEM DESIGN AND WORKFLOW

3.1 Design

Our system leverage the elasticity of cloud infrastructure for video transcoding in the online video sharing service. We present the system design in Fig. 2. The functionalities of each module are detailed as follows.

Preprocessing module: The users and professional video content producers upload their content for online video sharing. The preprocessing module uses the media stream segmenter to segment content into a series of equal-duration (e.g., 10s) chunks, which are suitable for HTTP streaming.

Prediction module: It monitors the arrival rates of the different types of video chunks, and makes the prediction for the future arrival rate of each type of video chunk.

Decision making module: It uses the system information (e.g., available transcoding instances, QoS requirements, and future video chunk arrival rate) to make control decisions for resource provisioning and content dispatching.

Provisioning module: It dynamically adjusts the number of active transcoding instances to accommodate the time-varying workload and to satisfy the QoS requirements for

Table 1: Key Parameters

Parameter	Meaning
t	discrete time slot, $t = 0, 1, 2, ...$
r, l, d	**r**eal-time, dead**l**ine-sensitive, and **d**eferrable
N	maximum number of available instances
$b_i(t)$	state of the i-th transcoding instance at t
$b_i^m(t)$	type of content transcoded by instance i
$C(t)$, $E(t)$	computing cost, QoS cost
$q(t)$	queue length for deferrable content
$\lambda^m(t)$	arrival rate of type m at t, $m \in \{r, l, d\}$
$\lambda_i^m(t)$	dispatched rate of type m to instance i at t
V_1, V_2	weights of QoS cost and switching cost
μ,γ	expectation and second moment
$w_i(t)$	processing time of high priority video chunks

transcoding. To elastically allocate the computing resource, our system can adopt Virtual Machines (VM) or Containers as transcoding servers. We refer to a VM instance or a Container provisioned for transcoding as a transcoding instance. The performance of the instances is homogeneous.

Dispatching module: The video chunks are dispatched to the active transcoding instances to be encoded into a predefined set of target representations. The dispatching module determines how to dispatch the video chunks to meet the QoS requirements for transcoding while not exceeding the processing capacity of each transcoding instance.

3.2 Workflow

The real-time and deadline-sensitive content has deterministic QoS requirements and are sensitive to the processing time, they will be directly dispatched to the active instances for transcoding after arriving. In contrast, the deferrable content has no strict processing time requirements, and can be dispatched for transcoding when idle resource is available. In our system, the dispatching module maintains a FIFO queue for the deferrable content, and the deferrable content can be cached in the queue if the capacity allows. For making the system modeling trackable and deriving the closed-form solution, one active instance will only transcode one type of the delay-sensitive content (i.e., either real-time or deadline-sensitive content) during each time slot. However, the transcoding for deferrable content can be performed on any active instance.

We adopt the *Preemptive Resume Priority* discipline in each active instance for transcoding different types of content. Specifically, the transcoding for real-time and deadline-sensitive content is performed in high priority, while the transcoding for deferrable content is performed in low priority. The new arrival of content in high priority can immediately preempt the low priority transcoding operation which is currently being performed, and start the high priority transcoding operation. When computing resource is available, the previously preempted low priority transcoding operations can be resumed from the point where it was interrupted earlier. We adopt *POSIX Signal* [1] for the preemptive resume priority implementation.

4. SYSTEM MODELS

We adopt a discrete time model, where the time slot is denoted as $t = 0, 1, 2, ...$ The duration of one time slot could be from 10 minutes to an hour.

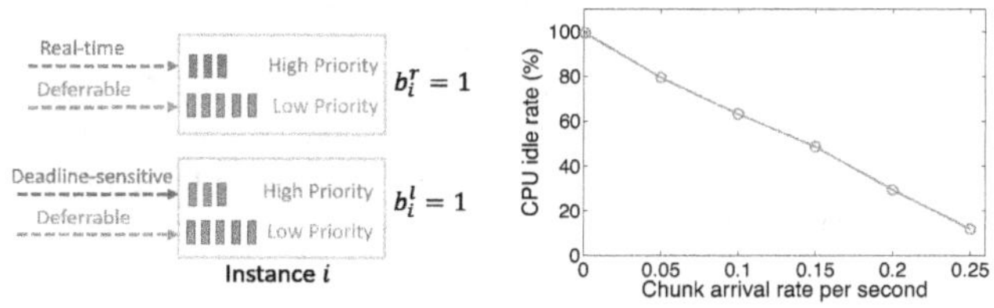

(a) Instance provisioning for different types of content. (b) CPU idle rates under varying chunk arrival rates.

Figure 3: Instance provisioning model.

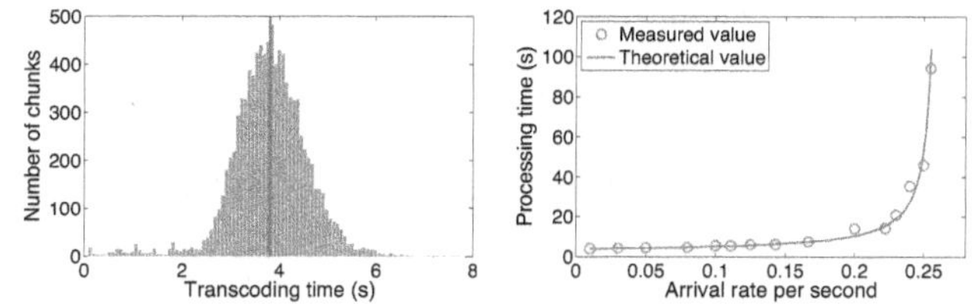

(a) Video chunk transcoding time distribution (b) Processing time under varying arrival rates

Figure 4: Video chunk processing time model.

4.1 Video Chunk Arrival Model

We consider three fundamental QoS criteria for transcoding, and correspondingly categorize the content into three types, namely, **r**eal-time, dead**l**ine-sensitive, and **d**eferrable content, represented as r, l, d, respectively. We assume that the video chunks of each type of content arrive according to the Poisson process during each time slot. The arrival rate for the video chunks of type m during the time slot t is denoted as $\lambda^m(t)$, where $m \in \{r, l, d\}$.

4.2 Computing Cost Model

The computing cost is incurred by provisioning VM instances or Containers. The system has N transcoding instances, and performance is homogeneous. At the beginning of each time slot, the system determines whether an instance should be activated according to the workload and QoS requirement. We denote the computing cost for an active instance during one time slot as B^c. The overall computing cost incurred at time t can be calculated as:

$$C(t) = \sum_{i=1}^{N} b_i(t) B^c, \tag{1}$$

where $b_i(t)$ is a binary variable to indicate that whether the transcoding instance i is active at time t.

4.3 Instance Provisioning Model

In our design, each active instance only transcodes one type of delay-sensitive content during each time slot, either real-time or deadline-sensitive content. A more sophisticated design would be mingling the three types of content in an active instance using three priority classes. This, however, would bring great difficulties for both practical implementation and deriving the solutions. To make the modeling trackable, we simplify it in this work: one active instance can transcode deferrable content in low priority, and transcode one type of delay-sensitive content in high priority.

As shown in Fig. 3(a), we adopt binary variables $b_i^m(t)$, $m \in \{r, l\}$, to denote which type of delay-sensitive content will be transcoded by instance i at time t; if $b_i^r(t)$ equals one, it transcodes real-time content; if $b_i^l(t)$ equals one, it transcodes deadline-sensitive content. If an active instance only transcodes delay-sensitive content, the deterministic QoS requirements would limit the video chunk dispatched rate to the instance. As shown in Fig. 3(b), the low chunk dispatched rate to an instance would lead to high CPU idle rate. Thus, deferrable content can be transcoded in low priority in an instance to improve resource utilization when no delay-sensitive content is being transcoded.

4.4 Dispatching Model

The arriving video chunks are dispatched to the active instances for transcoding. Each of the video chunks will be transcoded into a set of pre-defined representations, e.g., 240p, 360p, and 720p. We denote the dispatched rate of the chunks of type m to instance i at time t as $\lambda_i^m(t)$, where $m \in \{r, l, d\}$. The deferrable content can be temporally cached in the queue, and dispatched for transcoding at some later time. The queue dynamic for deferrable content is

$$q(t+1) = q(t) + \lambda^d(t) - \sum_{i=1}^{N} \lambda_i^d(t), \tag{2}$$

where $q(t)$ is the queue length for deferrable content at the beginning of each time t.

4.5 Video Chunk Processing Time Model

Each video chunk has the same duration, however, the transcoding time for video chunks is varying based on many factors, e.g., bitrate, resolution, and server performance. We adopt the empirical method to measure the distribution of the transcoding time for video chunks. We denote the transcoding time for a video chunk as x, and the expectation and second moment of x are represented as

$$E(x) = \frac{1}{\mu}, E(x^2) = \gamma, \tag{3}$$

where μ and γ can be measured in the system offline. In practice, we measure the time for transcoding 9800 video chunks into three target resolutions[1] for determining μ and γ. The distribution of the transcoding time for the video chunks is illustrated in Fig. 4(a). Further, we determine the values of μ and γ as 0.2632 and 15.1, respectively.

4.6 Video Chunk Queueing Model

The queueing for video chunks in each instance can be modelled as a *M/G/1* system with *preemptive resume priority*. The delay-sensitive (real-time or deadline-sensitive) content is transcoded in high priority to guarantee the QoS requirements. The deferrable content is transcoded in low priority when no delay-sensitive content is being transcoded. The transcoding of deferrable content can be interrupted on arrival of delay-sensitive content, and will be resumed from the point of interruption when idle resource is available again. Thus, deferrable content can use the idle resource in an active instance for transcoding, while remain transparent to delay-sensitive content.

[1]The target resolutions are 240p, 360p, and 480p.

Given the chunk dispatched rate $\lambda_i^m(t)$, $m \in \{r, l\}$, of delay-sensitive content to instance i, the average processing time for video chunks of delay-sensitive content is

$$w_i(t) = \frac{1}{\mu} + \frac{\mu\gamma\lambda_i^m(t)}{2(\mu - \lambda_i^m(t))}, m \in \{r, l\}. \quad (4)$$

Using μ and γ derived from Fig. 4(a), we measure the average chunk processing time of delay-sensitive content under varying dispatched rate to an instance, with deferrable content is transcoded in low priority when CPU is idle. As shown in Fig. 4(b), the average chunk processing time of delay-sensitive content fits with Eq. (4).

4.7 QoS Cost Model

The QoS cost for delay-sensitive content is incurred by the video chunk processing delay. Specifically, the QoS cost for real-time content incurred on instance i at time t is

$$F_i^r(t) = \lambda_i^r(t)\mathcal{G}(w_i(t)), \quad (5)$$

where $\mathcal{G}(\cdot)$ is QoS function for real-time content. We let the deadline for average chunk processing time be u. The deadline-sensitive content will incur QoS cost if the average processing time exceeds the deadline. The QoS cost for deadline-sensitive content incurred on instance i at t is

$$F_i^l(t) = \lambda_i^l(t)\mathcal{H}(\max(w_i(t) - u, 0)), \quad (6)$$

where $\mathcal{H}(\cdot)$ is QoS function for deadline-sensitive content. The overall QoS cost for delay-sensitive content incurred on all active instances at time t is

$$E(t) = \sum_{i=1}^{N}(F_i^r(t) + F_i^l(t)). \quad (7)$$

Our formulation requires $E(t)$ to be convex for λ_i^r and λ_i^l for deriving the closed-form solution. Examples for $\mathcal{G}(\cdot)$ and $\mathcal{H}(\cdot)$ are the increasing linear function or the logarithmic function. We only consider the queue capacity constraint for deferrable content in our system. Our framework, however, can also add the QoS cost for deferrable content into consideration. For instance, the QoS cost incurred for deferrable content in each time slot is an non-decreasing convex function with related to the queue length; more QoS cost would be incurred with more content is deferred.

4.8 Switching Cost Model

Frequently toggling the instances back and forth between the active and sleep mode will increase the risk of system failure. We adopt the switching cost to represent the operation cost and risk associated with activating an instance from the sleep mode. The overall switching cost for activating the instances from the sleep mode at time t is

$$S(t) = \sum_{i=1}^{N} B^s \max(b_i(t) - b_i(t-1), 0), \quad (8)$$

where B^s is the marginal switching cost for activating an instance from sleep mode.

4.9 System Cost Minimization Problem

We aim to minimize the overall system cost over time under dynamic workload. We consider three costs, namely, the computing cost, QoS cost, and switching cost. If more instances are provisioned, the QoS cost will be low, but it would incur more computing cost. On the contrary, if fewer instances are provisioned, it can save the computing cost, but the QoS cost may be high. Meanwhile, frequently switching the instances between the sleep mode and active mode would increase the switching cost. The control decisions are the provisioning of the instances and the scheduling of dispatching the content for transcoding. The system cost minimization problem is presented as:

$$\begin{aligned}
\mathcal{P}1: \min \quad & \sum_{t=1}^{T}\{C(t) + V_1E(t) + V_2S(t)\}, && (9)\\
\text{s.t.} \quad & \lambda_i^m(t) \geq 0, \forall i, t, m, && (10)\\
& \sum_{i=1}^{N}\lambda_i^m(t) = \lambda^m(t), \forall t, m \in \{r, l\}, && (11)\\
& b_i(t) = \{0, 1\}, \forall i, t, && (12)\\
& b_i^m(t) = \{0, 1\}, \forall i, t, m \in \{r, l\}, && (13)\\
& b_i(t) = b_i^r(t) + b_i^l(t), \forall i, t, && (14)\\
& \lambda_i^m(t) \leq b_i^m(t)\mu, \forall i, t, m \in \{r, l\}, && (15)\\
& \lambda_i^r(t) + \lambda_i^l(t) + \lambda_i^d(t) \leq b_i(t)\mu, && (16)\\
& 0 \leq q(t) \leq L, \ \forall t, && (17)
\end{aligned}$$

where V_1 and V_2 are the tunable parameters to adjust the weight of each cost, and L is the maximum capacity of the queue for the deferrable content.

Constraint (10) and (11) ensure that the delay-sensitive content can be dispatched directly. Constraint (12) - (14) ensure that one active instance can only transcode one type of delay-sensitive content during each time slot. Constraint (15) ensures that the delay-sensitive content is only dispatched to the active instances provisioned for this type of content. Constraint (16) ensures that the overall amount of video chunks dispatched to an active instance will not exceed its processing capacity. Constraint (17) validates the queue capacity constraint for deferrable content .

5. ALGORITHM DESIGN

This section presents methods for deriving the offline solution of the cost minimization problem, and introduces the online algorithm design with the MPC and robust design.

5.1 Offline Solution

The chunk arrival rates are random processes and cannot be known in advance. Given the access to the precise chunk arrival information for the next T time slots, we can derive the offline solution by solving $\mathcal{P}1$. While $\mathcal{P}1$ is a *mixed boolean-convex problem* [5], it is NP-hard and cannot be solved in polynomial time. However, we can solve it optimally with *Branch-and-Bound* via convex relaxation when the number of binary variables is small [5]. In practice, we can also obtain the optimal solution with the CVX solver (e.g., Gurobi, MOSEK, and GLPK). In a real production environment, the number of provisioned instances could be several thousands. It may take many hours to derive the optimal solution with Branch-and-Bound or CVX solvers. Next, we discuss how to obtain the approximate solution when the number of provisioned instances is large.

We let the number of instances provisioned for the real-time and deadline-sensitive content at time t be $n^r(t)$, $n^l(t)$, respectively, while deferrable content can be transcoded on these instances in low priority. Given the numbers of active

Table 2: Multiple-Step Prediction

Step	Inputs of Neural Network	Output
1	$\lambda^m(t-h)$, ... , $\lambda^m(t-1)$	$\hat{\lambda}^m(t)$
2	$\lambda^m(t-h+1)$, ... , $\hat{\lambda}^m(t)$	$\hat{\lambda}^m(t+1)$
3	$\lambda^m(t-h+2)$, ... , $\hat{\lambda}^m(t+1)$	$\hat{\lambda}^m(t+2)$
4	$\lambda^m(t-h+3)$, ... , $\hat{\lambda}^m(t+2)$	$\hat{\lambda}^m(t+3)$

instances $n^m(t)$, $m \in \{r, l\}$, we can use the KKT condition to prove that the optimal dispatching pattern for each type of content is to equally dispatch the video chunks among the $n^m(t)$ active instances. Let $\lambda_*^m(t)$, $m \in \{r, l\}$, be the dispatched rates of real-time or deadline-sensitive content to each of the $n^m(t)$ active instances, and we have $\lambda_*^m(t) = \lambda^m(t)/n^m(t)$ for delay-sensitive content. Let $\lambda_*^d(t)$ be the amount of deferrable content dispatched for transcoding at time t. We can rewrite $\mathcal{P}1$ as follow for deriving $\lambda_*^d(t)$, $n^m(t)$,

$$\min \quad \sum_{t=1}^{T}\{C(t) + V_1E(t) + V_2S(t)\}, \qquad (18)$$

$$\begin{aligned} \text{s.t.} \quad & \lambda^m(t) \leq n^m(t)\mu, \forall t, m \in \{r, l\}, \\ & \lambda^r(t) + \lambda^l(t) + \lambda_*^d(t) \leq n(t)\mu, \forall t, \\ & q(t+1) = q(t) + \lambda^d(t) - \lambda_*^d(t), \\ & 0 \leq q(t) \leq L, \ \forall t, \\ & n(t) \leq N, \end{aligned}$$

where $n(t)$ is the total number of active instances at time t, and $n(t) = n^r(t) + n^l(t)$. The computing cost $C(t)$ can be rewritten as $n(t)B^c$, and the switching cost $S(t)$ can be rewritten as $\max(n(t) - n(t-1), 0)B^s$. When the number of provisioned instances is large, it is acceptable to allow $n^m(t)$ to be fractional. We can relax the integral variables $n^m(t)$ to be $n^m(t) \geq 0$, allowing fractional values for $n^m(t)$. The problem after relaxing is convex, and we can derive the solution by Lagrange method, and it can also be solved efficiently by CVX solvers.

5.2 Online Algorithm

The future video chunk arrival information cannot be known in advance, and thus it is infeasible to obtain the offline optimal decisions. We design the online algorithm with MPC, which makes decisions taking into account of predictions.

5.2.1 Arrival Rate Prediction

We adopt *neural network* method for predicting the future video chunk arrival rates based on historical arrival information. We assume that the video chunk arrival rates of different types of content are independent. The neural network method for prediction is to train a nonlinear function $f : \mathcal{R}^h \to \mathcal{R}$, which can estimate $\lambda^m(t)$ using the last h observations, i.e., $\lambda^m(t-1)$, ..., $\lambda^m(t-h)$. The nonlinear relation among the past observations and the prediction is

$$\hat{\lambda}^m(t) = f(\lambda^m(t-1), ..., \lambda^m(t-h)),$$

where $f(\cdot)$ is determined by the parameters of the neural network and can be learnt offline using the training data. Using the last h observations and the trained neural network, we can predict the arrival rate for one time slot ahead.

The cost minimization problem takes into account of the video chunk arrival information for the next T time slots. To make the prediction for the next T time slots, we can iteratively use the predicted arrival rates as the inputs of the neural network, and get the prediction for the next time slot. We illustrate the case of making four-step prediction at time $t-1$ in Table 2. At $t-1$, we first use the last h observations, $\lambda^m(t-1)$, ..., $\lambda^m(t-h)$, as the inputs of the neural network to get the prediction for $\hat{\lambda}^m(t)$. Next, we can use $\hat{\lambda}^m(t)$, ..., $\lambda^m(t-h+1)$ as the inputs for predicting $\hat{\lambda}^m(t+1)$. This can be iteratively done until we get the predictions for the next T time slots.

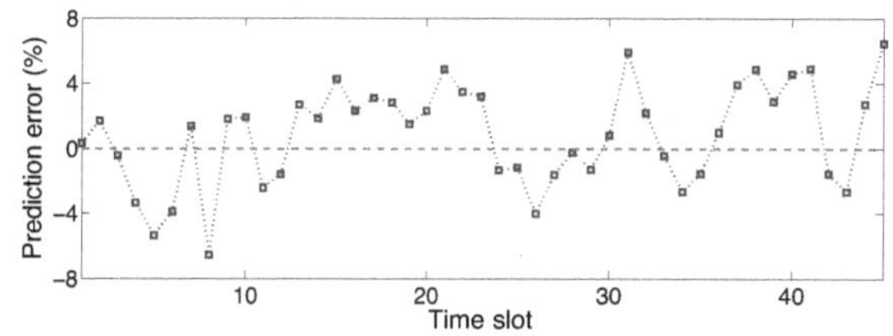

Figure 5: Fluctuation of prediction error over time.

5.2.2 Online Algorithm Design

We design the online algorithm with MPC using predictions for making control decisions. The control decisions are affected by the video chunk arrival rates, and thus the prediction accuracy affects the performance of the online algorithm. The predictions always have noise, and the noise may increase as one looks more steps ahead. If the noise for multiple-step ahead prediction is too large, it would be better to ignore the predicted information. The MPC is an online method by looking ahead for T time slots, and it makes decisions in each time slot in the following steps.

Predict: the arrival rate predictor predicts the video chunk arrival rates for the next T time slots.

Optimize: use the prediction to derive the solution of $\mathcal{P}1$ for minimizing the cost over the next T time slots.

Apply: apply the derived control decisions for the next time slot in the system.

The predictions always have noise. We illustrate the prediction error distribution for neural network method in Fig. 5, we can observe that the prediction error fluctuates in an range over time. The prediction error may lead to bad decisions and deteriorate the system performance, especially when the workload is underestimated and the provisioned resource cannot satisfy the QoS requirements. To seek the robustness of the performance against the uncertainty of the prediction error, we adopt *Robust Design* to minimize the worst-case of the system cost for deriving control decisions.

The predicted arrival rates lie around the actual values within an error bound. Instead of predicting a specified value for $\lambda^m(t)$, we estimate the possible range of $\lambda^m(t)$. We let $\underline{\lambda}^m(t)$ be the lower bound of $\lambda^m(t)$, and $\overline{\lambda}^m(t)$ be the upper bound, i.e., $\lambda^m(t) \in [\underline{\lambda}^m(t), \overline{\lambda}^m(t)]$. Given the possible range of the arrival rates, we first need to determine the arrival rates which would incur the largest system cost, and then derive control decisions for the worst-case system cost. We can use the contradiction method to prove that the worst-case system cost takes place when the video chunk arrival rates are at the upper bound of $[\underline{\lambda}^m(t), \overline{\lambda}^m(t)]$, i.e., at $\overline{\lambda}^m(t)$. As such, the minimization of the worst-case system cost is equivalent to take upper bounds of the predicted chunk arrival rates as inputs of $\mathcal{P}1$ to derive the solution.

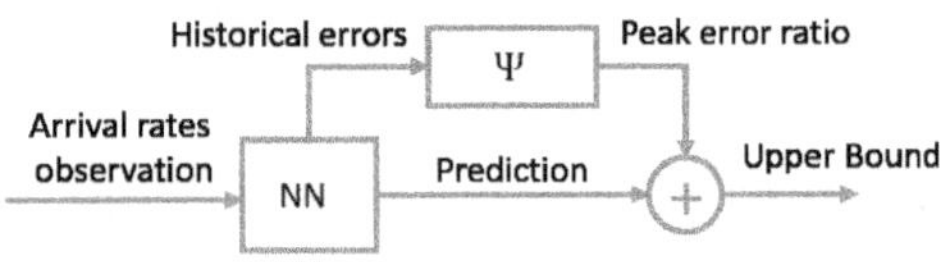

Figure 6: Robust prediction framework.

Instead of directly using the predicted arrival rates as inputs of $\mathcal{P}1$ in MPC method, our online algorithm takes upper bounds as inputs for deriving solutions. The prediction for the arrival rates are optimal in the sense of mean-square-error, and provides the best average performances. The underlying noise, however, often conflicts with the prediction models, making system unstable and leading to poor performance. The aim of obtaining the upper bound for the prediction (also known as robust prediction) is to accommodate uncertainties against prediction noise. We illustrate the procedure for making the robust prediction for the arrival rates in Fig. 6. The neural network predictor estimates the arrival rates, and the noise analyzer determines the peak error ratio using observed historical prediction errors. The upper bound for the predicted arrival rate is calculated as $\overline{\lambda}^m(t) = \hat{\lambda}^m(t)/(1+\Psi)$, where$\Psi \leq 0$ is the peak error ratio [22]. In our system, we set the peak error ratio as the minimum of the last 10 prediction errors and the training errors. The prediction error and training error are calculated as $e_t = (\hat{\lambda}^m(t) - \lambda^m(t))/\lambda^m(t)$, and $\Psi = \min(e_{t-10}, .., e_{t-1}, e_T)$, where e_T is the minimum in the training set. We illustrate the details of the online algorithm in Algorithm 1.

Algorithm 1 Online algorithm for dynamic system control

Set t as the current time.
while the system is in service **do**
    Predict video chunk arrival rates for the next T time slots, namely, $\hat{\lambda}^m(t)$, $\hat{\lambda}^m(t+1)$, ..., $\hat{\lambda}^m(t+T-1)$.
    Calculate upper bounds of the predicted arrival rates, namely, $\overline{\lambda}^m(t)$, $\overline{\lambda}^m(t+1)$, ..., $\overline{\lambda}^m(t+T-1)$.
    Optimize $\mathcal{P}1$ using the upper bounds of the predicted arrival rates as inputs.
    Apply control decisions for time slot t in the system.
    $t \leftarrow t+1$
end while

The algorithm running time is dominated by the time for solving $\mathcal{P}1$. We can apply the method discussed in Section 5.1 to solve the problem in an acceptable time.

6. SYSTEM IMPLEMENTATION

We build the cloud environment with *Docker* and implement our proposed system with *Python*. The main components of our system are illustrated in Fig. 7.

Portal: It segments video files and streams into a series of 10-second chunks. The chunk data is stored into the storage system, and the chunk information is stored in *MySQL*. The arrivals of the chunks will be informed to the dispatcher.

Controller: It makes predictions by neural network and control decisions by performing the online algorithm.

Dispatcher: It sends the arriving chunk information to the distributed queue implement with *RabbitMQ*. Each instance has one queue for delay-sensitive content and one queue for deferrable content. The transcoding procedure in the worker will be invoked when new chunk enters the queue. The worker will fetch the chunk information and download chunk data from storage system for transcoding.

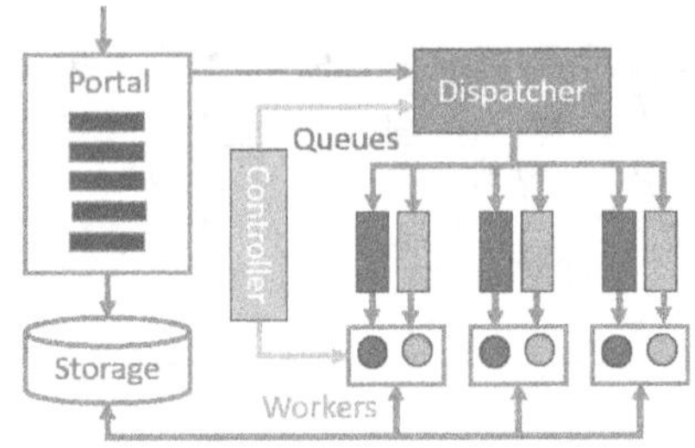

Figure 7: Implementation of the system

Worker: Each worker in an instance has two processes for transcoding, namely, background process and foreground process, corresponding to the two queues. The background process transcodes deferrable content. The foreground process transcodes delay-sensitive content. The workers use *avconv* for transcoding, and the preemptive resume mechanism is implemented with *POSIX Signals*. When the transcoding procedure of foreground process is invoked by incoming delay-sensitive chunks, it first send a *SIGSTOP signal* to suspend background process and start its own transcoding. It will resume background process by sending a *SIGCONT signal* when finishing and no chunk left in its queue.

7. PERFORMANCE EVALUATION

We first introduce the dataset and experiment settings. We then evaluate the performance of our system under different settings, and compare it with the baseline schemes.

7.1 Dataset and Experiment Setting

We obtain the number of concurrent online video channels in Twitch during each minute through *Twitch* API [3]. In our experiment, we assume that the video chunk arrival rate is proportional to the number of online channels. Each time slot lasts for 10 minutes. To speed up the experiment, each time slot corresponds to one hour in the dataset. The arrival rates for each time slot are averaged over 60 minute intervals in the dataset. We use the arrival rates in different days as the arrival rates for the three types of content.

Each container in our system has 4 CPU cores. The containers are connected with Gigabit Ethernet. We adopt the Amazon EC2-based pricing mechanism to calculate the computing cost, and the price for an instance is \$0.0398 per time slot. The online algorithm looks ahead for 4 time slots. The QoS cost functions $\mathcal{G}(\cdot)$ and $\mathcal{H}(\cdot)$ are linear, and the coefficient terms are 1 and constant terms are 0. The default values for the other parameters are summarized in Table 3.

Table 3: Default values of parameters

V_1	=	10^{-4}	V_2	=	1	B^s	=	0.0040
u	=	20	μ	=	0.2632	B^c	=	0.0398
L	=	1000	γ	=	15.1	N	=	20

7.2 Prediction Performance

We evaluate the prediction performance of the neural network. We use a 3-layer feed-forward neural network with

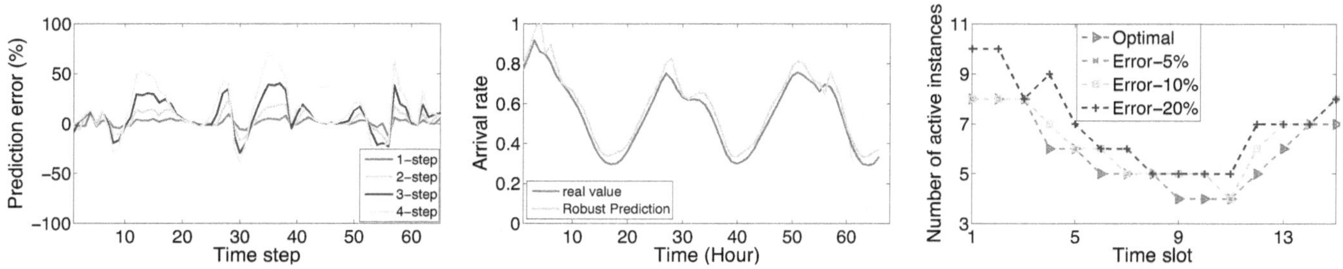

(a) The prediction error for the test data using different prediction steps. (b) The robust prediction for arrival rates. (c) The number of active instances under different prediction errors.

Figure 8: Prediction performance and impact of prediction error.

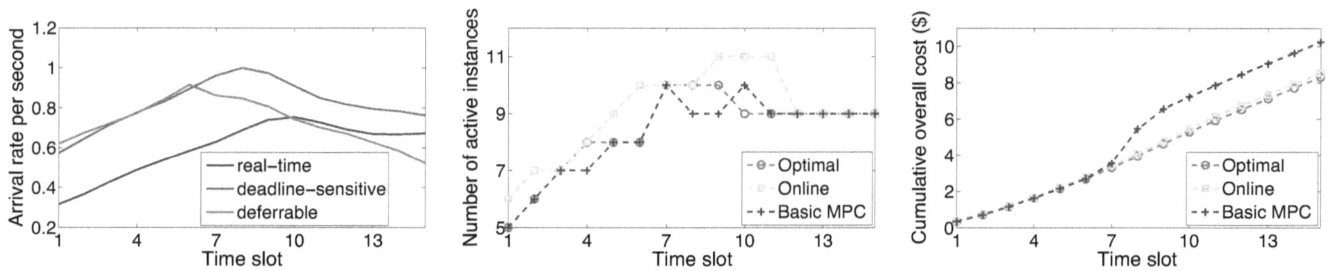

(a) The video chunk arrival rates of the three types of content. (b) The number of active transcoding instances during each time slot. (c) The cumulative overall system cost.

Figure 9: Effectiveness of the online algorithm.

sigmoid hidden neurons and linear output neurons. The neural network has two inputs (i.e., the arrival rates in the past two time slots), and the hidden layer consists of 10 neurons. The network is trained with Levenberg-Marquardt backpropagation algorithm. We select the data of 100 continuous time steps for training. The data point in each time step is the arrival rate in each hour of the real dataset. We evaluate the performance for predicting the arrival rates of another 65 time slots. The prediction errors of using different prediction steps are illustrated in Fig. 8(a). The mean prediction error is 2.5% for 1-step prediction, 6.4% for 2-step prediction, 11.0% for 3-step prediction, and 16.0% for 4-step prediction. The prediction noise increases with more time steps to look ahead. We illustrate the performance of the robust prediction in Fig. 8(b). The predicted arrival rates by the robust prediction are slightly higher than the real value to avoid resource under-provisioning.

We evaluate the performance of our online algorithm under different prediction errors. To generate different prediction errors, we add uniform distributed random noise to the real arrival rates, and use the synthetic data as the prediction, and thus the prediction is independent of the specified predictor. We illustrate the number of provisioned instances over 15 time slots under different prediction errors in Fig. 8(c). The optimal policy, knowing the precise future arrival rates, provisions the minimum number of instances to meet the QoS requirements. When the prediction error is within 5%, our online algorithm can achieve the near-optimal performance. With larger prediction errors, our online algorithm provisions more instances against the larger uncertainty. Compared with the optimal policy, however, the system cost only increases 2.3% when prediction error is within 10%, and increases 5.8% when prediction error is within 20%.

7.3 Effectiveness of the online algorithm

We evaluate the effectiveness of our proposed online algorithm, and compare its performance with the offline optimal solution and the *Basic MPC method*. The Basic MPC method is the same as our online algorithm, but without the robust design. The video chunk arrival rates for the three types of content over 15 time slots are illustrated in Fig. 9(a). We can observe in Fig. 9(b) that the number of instances provisioned by our online algorithm is always no less than offline optimal solution. This is due to the robust design of our online algorithm, which makes decisions according to the maximum possible arrival rates. In contrast, the Basic MPC method makes decisions directly according to the predictions of the neural network. As such, the number of provisioned transcoding instances may be lower than required, if the predictor underestimates the video chunk arrival rates. In this case, it will deteriorate the system performance and incur more QoS cost. As described in Fig. 9(c), the cumulative cost of our online algorithm is only slightly higher than the offline optimal solution, which is incurred by the resource over-provisioning. While the Basic MPC method has the near-optimal average performance in most of the time slots, but would incurs more cost when the provisioned resource cannot meet the QoS requirements.

7.4 Impact of Tunable Parameters

We illustrate the computing cost and the average processing time for real-time content over 5 time slots under different values of V_1 in Fig. 10(a). The computing cost for real-time content increases with V_1, while the average processing time for the video chunks decreases with it. Intuitively, the QoS cost takes more weights with the larger values of V_1, and the system will provision more computing resource to reduce the processing time. One can select

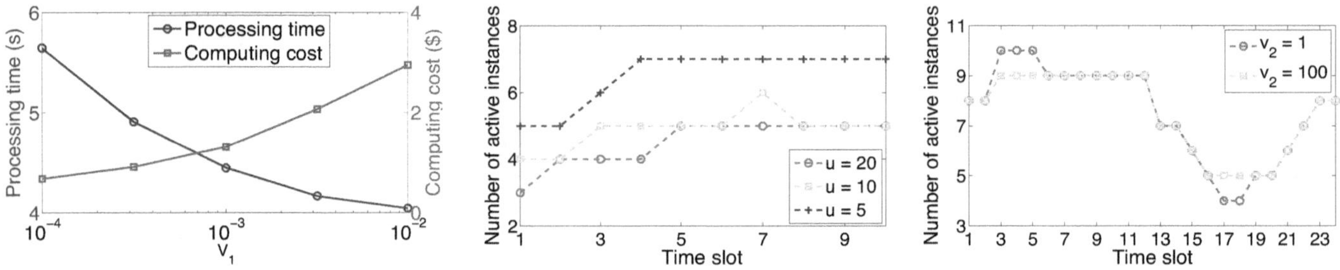

(a) The computing cost and processing time under different values of V_1. (b) The number of active instances in each time slot under different values of u. (c) The number of active instances in each time slot under different values of V_2.

Figure 10: Impact of Tunable Parameters.

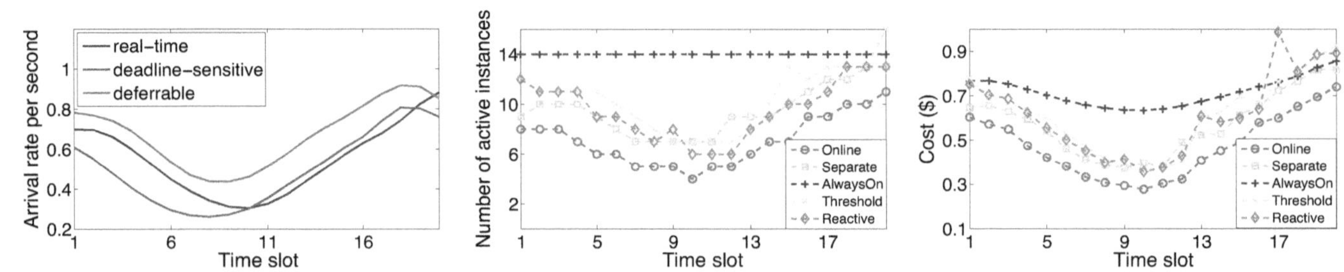

(a) The arrival rates for different types of video content. (b) The number of active instances in each time slot under different policies. (c) The overall cost in each time slot under different policies.

Figure 11: Comparison with baseline policies.

Table 4: Cost and resource consumption reduction percentage compared with AlwaysOn

	Online	Separate	Threshold	Reactive
Cost	34%	20%	14%	14%
Resource	50%	32%	25%	31%

the suitable value of V_1 for managing the QoS for real-time content. We illustrate the number of provisioned transcoding instances for deadline-sensitive content over time under different values of u in Fig. 10(b). With the smaller values of u, the system needs to provision more instances to reduce the dispatched rates of deadline-sensitive content to each active instance for achieving the average processing time deadline. We illustrate the impact of the switching cost in Fig. 10(c). With the larger weight of the switching cost, there will be less switching of the states of the transcoding instances. This is because switching the state of the transcoding instance frequently will incur more cost than keeping the transcoding instances active for a few more time slots.

7.5 Comparison with Baseline Methods

We compare the performance of our online algorithm with the following baselines: 1) *AlwaysOn*: It provisions a fixed number of instances for each type of content according to the peak workloads. 2) *Separate*: It uses the same dynamic resource provisioning policy with our online algorithm, however, each active instance only transcodes one type of content during each time slot. The queue in each instance is M/G/1 with FIFO discipline. 3) *Threshold*: It uses a minimum number of active instances for transcoding to guarantee QoS, keeping the over-provisioned instances idle. When an instance is idle for two time slots, it would be shut down. If the workload exceeds the current capacity, it will increase the capacity by 30% above the requested workload. 4) *Reactive*: It provisions the computing resource based on the observed arrival rates in the past time slot.

The arrival rates for the three types of content are shown in Fig. 11(a). We illustrate the number of provisioned instances and the incurred cost in each time slot under different policies in Fig. 11(b) and 11(c), respectively. The overall cost for the AlwaysOn policy decreases when the arrival rates are low, because less QoS cost is incurred. Our online algorithm provisions fewer instances and incurs less overall cost than the baseline policies. The performance gains are from two parts. First, our system can utilize the idle computing resource for transcoding deferrable content to improve resource utilization. This can be verified by comparison with *Separate* policy. If each type of content is transcoded using separate instances, it needs to provision more active instances. Meanwhile, the computing resource of the instances transcoding delay-sensitive content cannot be fully utilized, due to the deterministic QoS requirements. Adopting the preemptive resume priority for transcoding multiple types of content can improve the resource utilization without affecting the QoS of the delay-sensitive content.

The second part for the performance gain is that our online algorithm can intelligently provision resource under dynamic workload using prediction. We verify this by comparing with the *Reactive* policy and the *Threshold* policy. The *Reactive* policy attempts to keep the exact number of instances reacting to the past observed workload. By comparing it with the *Separate* policy, we can find that the *Reactive* policy may lag behind the changing workload, because it only uses the past workloads for decision. This, without considering changing trends, may induce over- or under-provisioning under dynamic workload. The *Threshold* policy is more conservative, keeping idle instances active for 2 more time slots and provisioning an extra capacity to avoid resource under-provisioning. However, without future workload information, this still may lead to over-provisioning if the extra capacity is large, and under-provisioning if the extra capacity is small. We summarize the overall cost and resource consumption reduction percentage of different policies compared with the *AlwaysOn* policy in Table 4. Our online policy can on average reduce the overall cost by 34%, and reduce the resource consumption by 50%, which shows a great performance gain compared with the baseline policies.

8. CONCLUSION

This paper designs and implements a video transcoding system for dynamic resource provisioning with QoS guarantee in online video sharing service. We propose a framework for transcoding with heterogeneous QoS criteria. We adopt the preemptive resume priority for processing different types of content to improve resource utilization without affecting QoS for delay-sensitive content. We design an online algorithm which can intelligently provision the right amount of resource using prediction to guarantee QoS, while keeping robust to prediction noise. The experiment results demonstrates that our online algorithm can achieve the QoS requirements while reducing 50% of resource consumption. As future work, we may consider the resource provisioning for hardware-accelerated (e.g. GPU) video transcoding.

9. REFERENCES

[1] POSIX-style signals. https://en.wikipedia.org/wiki/Unix_signal.

[2] Statistics and facts about YouTube. http://www.statista.com/topics/2019/youtube/.

[3] Twitch. https://github.com/justintv/Twitch-API.

[4] R. Aparicio-Pardo, K. Pires, A. Blanc, and G. Simon. Transcoding live adaptive video streams at a massive scale in the cloud. In *Proceedings of the 6th ACM Multimedia Systems Conference*, pages 49–60, 2015.

[5] S. Boyd and J. Mattingley. Branch and bound methods. *Notes for EE364b, Stanford University.*

[6] G. Gao and Y. Wen. Morph: A fast and scalable cloud transcoding system. In *Proceedings of the 24th ACM international conference on Multimedia.*

[7] F. Jokhio, A. Ashraf, S. Lafond, I. Porres, and J. Lilius. Prediction-based dynamic resource allocation for video transcoding in cloud computing. In *Parallel, Distributed and Network-Based Processing, 21st Euromicro International Conference on.* IEEE, 2013.

[8] S. Ko, S. Park, and H. Han. Design analysis for real-time video transcoding on cloud systems. In *Proceedings of the 28th Annual ACM Symposium on Applied Computing*, pages 1610–1615. ACM, 2013.

[9] D. Kusic, J. O. Kephart, J. E. Hanson, N. Kandasamy, and G. Jiang. Power and performance management of virtualized computing environments via lookahead control. *Cluster computing*, 12(1):1–15, 2009.

[10] F. Lao, X. Zhang, and Z. Guo. Parallelizing video transcoding using map-reduce-based cloud computing. In *Circuits and Systems (ISCAS), 2012 IEEE International Symposium on*, pages 2905–2908, 2012.

[11] Z. Li, Y. Huang, G. Liu, F. Wang, Z.-L. Zhang, and Y. Dai. Cloud transcoder: Bridging the format and resolution gap between internet videos and mobile devices. In *NOSSDAV '12.*

[12] M. Lin, A. Wierman, L. L. Andrew, and E. Thereska. Dynamic right-sizing for power-proportional data centers. *IEEE/ACM Transactions on Networking (TON)*, 21(5):1378–1391, 2013.

[13] H. Ma, B. Seo, and R. Zimmermann. Dynamic scheduling on video transcoding for mpeg dash in the cloud environment. In *Proceedings of the 5th ACM Multimedia Systems Conference.* ACM, 2014.

[14] R. Mehrotra and P. Bhattacharya. Modeling the evolution of user-generated content on a large video sharing platform. In *Proceedings of the 24th International Conference on World Wide Web Companion*, pages 365–366. International World Wide Web Conferences Steering Committee, 2015.

[15] S. Mitra, M. Agrawal, A. Yadav, N. Carlsson, D. Eager, and A. Mahanti. Characterizing web-based video sharing workloads. *ACM Transactions on the Web (TWEB)*, 5(2):8, 2011.

[16] J. Ostermann, J. Bormans, P. List, D. Marpe, M. Narroschke, F. Pereira, T. Stockhammer, and T. Wedi. Video coding with h. 264/avc: tools, performance, and complexity. *Circuits and Systems magazine, IEEE*, 4(1):7–28, 2004.

[17] K. Pires and G. Simon. Dash in twitch: Adaptive bitrate streaming in live game streaming platforms. In *Workshop on Design, Quality and Deployment of Adaptive Video Streaming*, pages 13–18. ACM, 2014.

[18] M. Song, Y. Lee, and J. Park. Scheduling a video transcoding server to save energy. *ACM Trans. Multimedia Comput. Commun. Appl.*, Feb. 2015.

[19] T. Stockhammer. Dynamic adaptive streaming over http: standards and design principles. In *Proceedings of the second annual ACM conference on Multimedia systems*, pages 133–144. ACM, 2011.

[20] C. Timmerer, D. Weinberger, M. Smole, R. Grandl, C. Müller, and S. Lederer. Cloud-based transcoding and adaptive video streaming-as-a-service. *E-Letter.*

[21] A. Vetro, C. Christopoulos, and H. Sun. Video transcoding architectures and techniques: an overview. *Signal Processing Magazine, IEEE*, 20(2):18–29, 2003.

[22] X. Yin, A. Jindal, V. Sekar, and B. Sinopoli. A control-theoretic approach for dynamic adaptive video streaming over http. *ACM SIGCOMM Computer Communication Review*, 45(4):325–338, 2015.

[23] C. Zhang and J. Liu. On crowdsourced interactive live streaming: a twitch. tv-based measurement study. In *Proceedings of the 25th ACM Workshop on Network and Operating Systems Support for Digital Audio and Video*, pages 55–60. ACM, 2015.

[24] L. Zhang, F. Wang, and J. Liu. Understand instant video clip sharing on mobile platforms: Twitter's vine as a case study. In *Proceedings of Network and Operating System Support on Digital Audio and Video Workshop*, page 85. ACM, 2014.

[25] W. Zhang, Y. Wen, J. Cai, and D. O. Wu. Toward transcoding as a service in a multimedia cloud: energy-efficient job-dispatching algorithm. *Vehicular Technology, IEEE Transactions on*, 2014.

High-speed Depth Stream Generation from a Hybrid Camera

Xinxin Zuo[†,‡] Sen Wang[†,‡] Jiangbin Zheng[†] Ruigang Yang[‡]
[†]Northwestern Polytechnical University, Xi'an, P.R.China
[‡]University of Kentucky, Lexington, KY, USA
{xinxinzuo2353,wangsen1312}@gmail.com, zhengjb@nwpu.edu.cn, ryang@cs.uky.edu

ABSTRACT

High-speed video has been commonly adopted in consumer-grade cameras, augmenting these videos with a corresponding depth stream will enable new multimedia applications, such as 3D slow-motion video. In this paper, we present a hybrid camera system that combines a high-speed color camera with a depth sensor, e.g. Kinect depth sensor, to generate a depth stream that can produce both high-speed and high-resolution RGB+depth stream. Simply interpolating the low-speed depth frames is not satisfactory, where interpolation artifacts and lose in surface details are often visible. We have developed a novel framework that utilizes both shading constraints within each frame and optical flow constraints between neighboring frames. More specifically we present (a) an effective method to find the intrinsics images to allow more accurate normal estimation; and (b) an optimization-based framework to estimate the high-resolution/high-speed depth stream, taking into consideration temporal smoothness and shading/depth consistency. We evaluated our holistic framework with both synthetic and real sequences, it showed superior performance than previous state-of-the-art.

Keywords

High-speed imaging; depth stream; Intrinisic decomposition; shape from shading

1. INTRODUCTION

With the recent advances in depth sensing, active depth sensors have become to be widely used in many multimedia applications, from 3D TV, gaming, to virtual reality. Nevertheless depth sensors still suffer from limited resolution and refresh rate. There are some previous works that focus on improving the spatial resolution of the depth map (e.g., [25, 27, 2, 33]). These methods have shown good performance in resolution enhancement. In this paper we pay our attention to the temporal resolution, i.e., the frame rate of depth sensing. High-speed video has been commonly adopted in consumer-grade cameras and even cellphones. They allow the capture of high-speed motion that is difficult to observe with naked eyes. Augmenting these videos with a corresponding depth stream will enable new applications, such as high-speed motion analysis or sports video playback and high-quality gait analysis for medical purpose.

Among all the publicly available commodity depth sensors, the SwissRanger™ and PMD™ can capture the depth at higher speed than 30Hz, but with a much lower resolution at about 100 × 200. For the well known Kinect depth sensor, it has depth resolution at 640×480 for Kinect version 1 and 512 × 424 for Kinect version 2. Both have a refresh rate of 30Hz. No single active depth sensor can provide both reasonable depth resolution and fast update rate of at least 60Hz. To overcome this limitation, we present a hybrid camera system that combines a high-speed color camera with a Kinect depth sensor that, with our novel post-processing algorithm, can generate the depth stream that has the same frequency and resolution as the color camera.

Given our hybrid camera setup, one straightforward way to generate high-speed depth stream is to apply bi-directional interpolation based on the optical flow. This is easy to implement. However, it is not always sufficient, since the linear motion assumption is not always true. In fact, usually it is the non-linear motion between frames that makes high-speed video interesting.

In addition to the flow field, shading information also provides useful cues for depth stream generation. We present a novel algorithm that enforces the shading constraints with the flow guidance in a unified framework. Instead of recovering the depth sequence frame by frame, we formulate an objective function with the shading constraints within frames and optical flow constraints between frames. The objective function is solved in a hierarchical manner with coarse-to-fine strategy to generate all the unknown depth maps at once.

We are certainly not the first to explore the shading cue for depth recovery. In addition to classic shape-from-shading (SfS) work [4, 12], there are several sensor fusion papers (e.g. [24, 32]) that combine the raw noisy depth with shading constraints to enhance the initial depth, which can resolve the ambiguity in traditional SfS to some extent. But in our case, we do not even have a depth map to start the refinement process. The interpolated depth map from the flow information can be far away from the real surface. We are dealing with a more challenging sensor fusion problem here.

One of the prerequisites to apply SfS techniques is the

MM '16, October 15-19, 2016, Amsterdam, Netherlands

DOI: http://dx.doi.org/10.1145/2964284.2964305

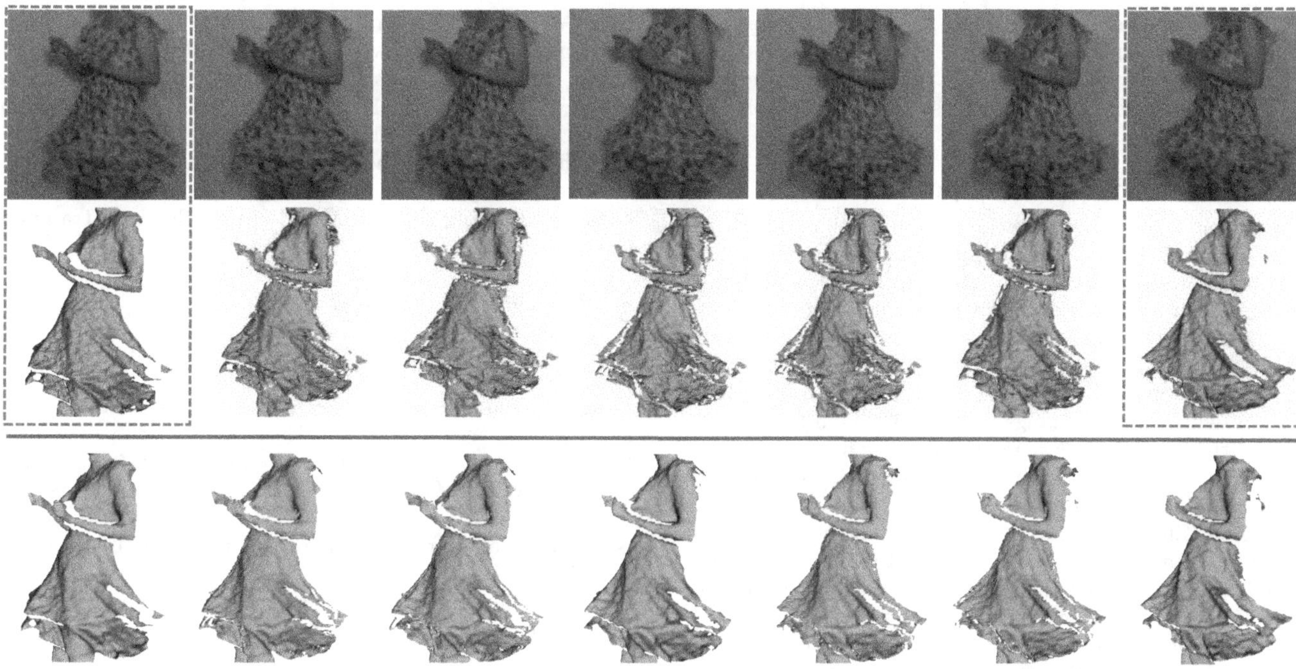

Figure 1: Depth stream results. (top) high-speed color images. (middle) interpolated depth maps based on optical/scene flow. The first and the last depth map are input. (bottom) corresponding depth generated with our algorithm.

known surface albedo. In our setup, we do not assume a known or uniform albedo. Therefore we must recover the surface albedo from captured images. This is the *intrinsic image* decomposition problem in computer vision, which is known to be ill-posed. We therefore develop a novel method that takes advantage of the fact that we do have depth maps for some of the color images. Our method compares favorably to previous state of the art in intrinsic image decomposition.

In summary the major contributions of this paper are:

- We identify a new problem that has not been studied, which is the low temporal refresh rate of currently available commodity depth sensors. Given the computational cost and their principles of operations, this limitation is unlikely to be addressed in hardware in the foreseeable future. We present a low-cost hybrid-camera setup to overcome this limitation.
- **Intrinsic image decomposition**: SfS performs best when the surface albedo is uniform or known. We propose a new intrinsic decomposition method (Section 4.2) Compared to existing intrinsic images decomposition techniques, we have a few frames with known depth maps, but not all of them. We take advantages of these depth maps and provide a sequence-based optimization framework to estimate surface albedo, making the problem more tractable.
- **Global optimization-based depth map interpolation**: We formulate a novel optimization-based framework (Section 4.3), which combines the shading constraints in each frame and motion field constraints to generate the missing depth maps between know depth maps that are captured at low speed. An effective coarse-to-fine strategy is developed to make the optimization efficient and effective.

Our algorithm is validated with both synthetic and real datasets. In both cases satisfactory results have been obtained. Some examples are shown in Figure 1.

2. RELATED WORK

In this section, we will review the previous works in three related topics: hybrid camera setup, intrinsic image decomposition, and depth enhancement using shading information.

2.1 Hybrid camera

A single image system often cannot satisfy the diverse, sometime even contradictory, requirements of many imaging applications. Various types of hybrid camera setups have been developed to combine multiple image sensors to achieve better performance, such as high resolution, high speed, or high dynamic range. A high-speed color camera with low resolution (HSLR) and a low-speed color camera with high resolution (LSHR) is a common setup to deal with the motion blur in color images and recover high-speed color images with high resolution [29].

With the availability of video-rate depth cameras, researchers have developed techniques for depth image enhancement and super-resolution using a hybrid of depth camera and color cameras. For example, Zhu et al. [38] demonstrated improved accuracy and robustness on depth sensing with adaptive fusion of time-of-flight sensor and a pair of stereo cameras. Alternatively, the combination of high quality or high resolution color camera with a depth sensor is also a popular setup for depth map enhancement [33, 13]. For the most of these methods, they rely on the co-occurrence of depth and intensity discontinuities or they try to exploit the statistical relationship between these two modal images. In this paper, we present a novel hybrid setup with high-speed color camera and a depth sensor, e.g. Kinect depth sensor, to recover depth frames at the same frequency as the high-speed camera.

2.2 Intrinsic image decomposition

The problem of intrinsic image decomposition, which is to separate reflectance and illumination from a single image, is introduced by Barrow [6]. It is an ill-posed problem since there are two unknowns for every observation, additional constraints must be adopted to make the problem solvable. The Retinex theory [22] is widely used for this purpose. It assumes that shading variations are mostly low frequency while albedo changes are mostly high-frequency. Based on this assumption, many approaches have been proposed. For example, Tappen et al. [30] train a classifier from reflectance and shading datasets to separate these two components. Zhao [37] added non-local smoothness term on reflectance to preserve global shading and reflectance structure. Global priors, such the reflectance sparsity, are developed [14] and they perform clustering on image reflectance. Bi [7] also exploits the global sparsity cues by enforcing an L1 smoothness term. Barron [4] obtain strong priors by training from reflectance and shading exemplers and they try to recover the reflectance, shape and illumination in a unified framework.

All of these above-mentioned methods focus on a single-image input. To reduce the ambiguity, other additional information are adopted. For example, image sequences [20, 21] are used under different lighting conditions. Also, depth images are important cues to at least reduce the ambiguities [11, 19, 5]. Lee et al. [23] simply adjusted the weight of shading constraints based on pixel normals, while they employed temporal constraints for RGBD video. Some researchers [9, 34, 8] perform the decomposition in an interactive way with manual annotation as guidance. In our setup we have a video sequence with depth maps in some key frames. Therefore we have developed a new method to handle our unique input.

2.3 Shape-from-shading and sensor fusion

The SfS problem has long been studied since the pioneering work by Horn [18]. There are various regularization terms or prior assumptions [3, 4] that have been enforced to deal with the inherently ill-posed problem in traditional SfS. As it is really hard to solve this inverse rendering optimization, this has led to the work on photometric stereo [16, 36] that uses multiple images of a scene taken under different controlled illumination to compute the surface normal as a well-defined problem.

Recent methods have shown that SfS can be used to refine the noisy depth map captured from RGB-D cameras under uncontrolled lighting [15, 35]. The rough normal computed from initial depth map provides the information to estimate the light source and also recover the multiple albedos from the color image [24, 32], which eliminates the need for assumptions and constraints on shape or the use of several images. This type of depth refinement has worked very well to provide more surface details. There are also previous works that adopt the shading constraints to refine the coarse 3D shape reconstructed using multi-view stereo [31].

All existing shading-refinement schemes assume that the initial depth is given for every image and the shading information is incorporated with the depth information to recover subtle surface details and remove noise. In our setup we do not have the initial depth map to start with. We also demonstrated that simply combining depth interpolation and shading refinement is unable to yield satisfactory results. Therefore we develop a new global optimization framework that considers shading constrains and optical flow constraints at the same time.

3. SYSTEM SETUP

We now briefly introduce our system setup and the overall processing pipeline. Our hybrid camera uses a PointGrey™ Dragonfly camera as the high-speed color camera. It captures images with resolution 640 × 480 at 180fps. We put the depth camera, for which we use the Kinect depth sensor, next to the PointGrey camera (see section 1 in supplementary material for more details). The original depth stream is captured at 30fps. The two cameras are calibrated and synchronized with system timestamps.

An overview of our high-speed depth map generation framework is shown in Figure 2. First, we will obtain the flow in-

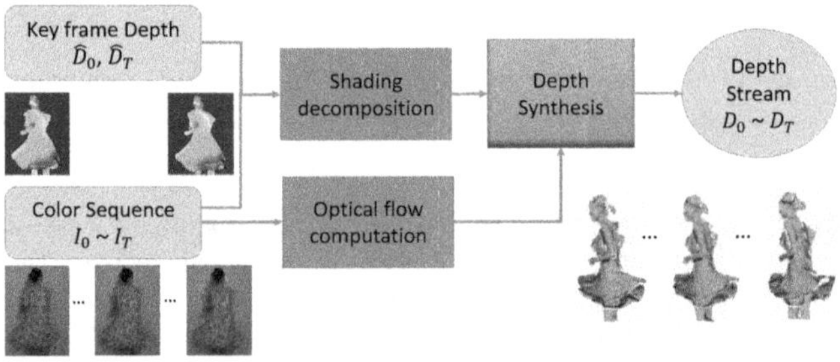

Figure 2: System Pipeline.

formation between color images. In the meantime the lighting condition is estimated in these key frames, which is assumed to be changing slowly over time. Then the albedo and shading images for the whole sequence are estimated with a novel decomposition algorithm. It uses the depth cues in key frames and temporal constrains (Section 4.2). Finally, the shading cues and flow information are combined together into our proposed global optimization framework, from which we can generate the depth stream ($D_0 \sim D_T$) between any two key frames (Section 4.3), leading to an output RGB-plus-depth stream at 180Hz (the same rate as the high-speed color camera). Notice that we do not attempt to increase the spatial resolution of the depth map. Existing algorithms can be adopted if desired.

4. OUR APPROACH

Suppose we have two depth frames $\hat{D}_0$ and $\hat{D}_T$, which are denoted as the depth key frames, and color frames $I_0 \sim I_T$, where I_0 and I_T correspond to the depth frame $\hat{D}_0$ and $\hat{D}_T$ respectively. Our goal is to estimate or refine the depth frames $D_0 \sim D_T$.

4.1 Preprocessing

First, we will describe some pre-processing steps and clarify some notations.

Depth warp The two cameras are calibrated and we warp

the key frame depth maps into color coordinates using the calibrated intrinsic and extrinsic parameters.

3D point Suppose we have a pixel $p = (i, j)$ with depth $D(p)$, then with the depth camera intrinsic K we can get its 3D point position as

$$X(p) = D(p)K^{-1}(i, j, 1)^T, \tag{1}$$

$$K = \begin{pmatrix} f_x & 0 & \mu \\ 0 & f_y & \nu \\ 0 & 0 & 1 \end{pmatrix} \tag{2}$$

where f_x and f_y are the focal length in x and y direction, μ and ν are the camera's principal point.

Normal In this paper, we use the perspective camera projection model, and the unnormalized normal $\tilde{\boldsymbol{n}}_p$ for pixel p can be computed as,

$$\tilde{\boldsymbol{n}}(p) = (X(i, j+1) - X(p)) \times (X(i+1, j) - X(p)) \tag{3}$$

Then substitute the 3D points in Eq. 3 with Eq. 2 and Eq. 1, the normal can be written as

$$\tilde{\boldsymbol{n}}(p) = \frac{D(i+1,j)\cdot D(i,j+1)}{f_x \cdot f_y} \begin{pmatrix} \frac{f_x \cdot (D(i,j+1) - D(p))}{D(i+1,j)} \\ \frac{f_y \cdot (D(i+1,j) - D(p))}{D(i,j+1)} \\ \frac{(\mu - j)\cdot(D(i,j+1) - D(p))}{D(i+1,j)} + \frac{(\nu - i)\cdot(D(i+1,j) - D(p))}{D(i,j+1)} - 1 \end{pmatrix} \tag{4}$$

Finally, we can normalize it to $\boldsymbol{n}(p)$.

Optical flow We have the color sequence $\mathbf{I} = [I_0, I_1, \cdots I_T]$ and the corresponding mapping between any two neighboring frames can be obtained from optical flow [10]. $W_t(p)$ maps the pixel p in frame t to next frame $t + 1$.

4.2 Intrinsic decomposition

Before enforcing the shading constraints for generating high-speed depth stream, we need to perform the intrinsic image decomposition to separate the shading effect from albedo and estimate the lighting condition using the depth key frames.

4.2.1 Lighting estimation

Similar to the majority of prior work on lighting estimation, we assume the object surfaces to be Lambertian, based on which Spherical Harmonics (SH) can be used to represent the incident lighting L efficiently. We use the first nine SH basis functions (up to second order), which is a good approximation for Lambertian reflectance [26]. Then the reflected irradiance I for each pixel p can represented as

$$I(p) = A(p) \cdot S(p), \tag{5}$$

$$S(p) = \sum_{m=1}^{9} l_m H_m(\boldsymbol{n}(p)), \tag{6}$$

where $A(p)$ is represented as albedo vectors for pixel p which contains three channels, and $S(p)$ donates the scalar shading vaule for p. l_m are the corresponding SH coefficients of incident lighting, $H_m(\boldsymbol{n}_p)$ represent the SH basis functions (see section 2 in supplementary material for more details).

Similar to [28], we assume that the pixels within the same super-pixel share the same albedo value, therefore we cluster the color image to SN segments with super-pixel algorithm [1].

For every two neighboring key depth maps with their color images, we can get the l_m by minimizing the energy function,

$$E_L = \sum_{t \in \{0,T\}} \sum_{sn=1}^{SN} \sum_{p} ||A_t^{sn}(p) \sum_{m=1}^{9} l_m H_m(\boldsymbol{n}_t(p)) - I_t(p)||^2, \tag{7}$$

where SN is the number of superpixels segments of color images, $A_t^{sn}(p)$ means the albedo in frame t for pixel $p \in$ snth segments, which is approximated by the mean color of the superpixel.

We can solve this minimization by computing the mean albedo of the superpixels and lighting coefficients in an iterative way and the iteration starts by setting the albedo as mean color of pixels inside each superpixels. Since we assume that the lighting is changing slowly during the data capture, we use the same lighting coefficients l_m for the sequence between two key frames.

4.2.2 Shading and albedo computation

The goal of shading computation is recovering the albedo $A(p)$ and shading $S(p)$ that best match the image $I(p)$. This is an essential step before SfS can be used. Different from the previous works on shading decomposition using RGBD images, we do not have depth images in every frame but only some key frames. On the other hand, the depth information in key frames provides us the valuable cues to resolve the ambiguity for single image decomposition. Therefore, we propose to compute the shading images for the sequence between any two key frames in a unified optimization making use of the depth cues in key frames and albedo consistency constraints along the sequence. The objective function is described below.

First, we have the data terms. The first is to match the image input. We operate in the logarithmic domain and $\hat{A}$, $\hat{S}$ and $\hat{I}$ stand for the logarithm of albedo, shading and color image, respectively.

$$E_{d\_im} = \sum_{t=0}^{T} \sum_{c \in \{R,G,B\}} \sum_{p} \omega_t^{lum}(p)||\hat{A}_t(p,c) + \hat{S}_t(p) - \hat{I}_t(p,c)||^2, \tag{8}$$

where

$$\omega_t^{lum}(p) = lum(p) + \epsilon \tag{9}$$

This term is weighted by the luminance of the input intensity image to prevent disproportionably strong affect of dark pixels.

The second data term is to preserve the initial shading images in key frames, which can be computed with the lighting vector(Section 4.2.1) and coarse surface normals. The generated shading images may not be accurate but they are good approximations.

$$E_{d\_s} = \sum_{t \in \{0,T\}} \sum_{p} ||log(\sum_{m=1}^{9} l_m H_m(\boldsymbol{n}_p)) - \hat{S}_t(p)||^2 \tag{10}$$

Regularization terms Next, we have the spatial priors for shading and albedo in each frame, as well as the temporal consistency priors of albedo between neighboring frames.

The albedo smoothness term for each frame with adaptive weighting is

$$E_{s\_a} = \sum_{t=0}^{T} \sum_{p,q \in \mathcal{N}} \omega_t^a(p,q)||\hat{A}_t(p) - \hat{A}_t(q)||_2^2 \tag{11}$$

The adaptive weight is computed with the differences of intensity and chromaticity between adjacent pixels

$$\omega_t^a(p,q) = \begin{cases} 0 & if \nabla ch_t > \tau_{ch} \\ 0 & if \nabla lum_t > \tau_{lum} \\ exp(-\frac{\nabla ch_t^2}{\sigma_{ch}^2}) \cdot exp(-\frac{\nabla lum_t^2}{\sigma_{lum}^2}) & otherwise \end{cases} \quad (12)$$

where

$$\nabla ch_t = ||ch(I_t(p)) - ch(I_t(q))||_2 \quad (13)$$

$$\nabla lum_t = ||lum(I_t(p)) - lum(I_t(q))|| \quad (14)$$

The shading smoothness term is formulated as below

$$E_{s\_s} = \sum_{t=0}^{T} \sum_{p,q \in \mathcal{N}} \omega_t^n(p,q)||\hat{S}_t(p) - \hat{S}_t(p)||^2, \quad (15)$$

For key frame 0 and T, we have coarse depth from which we can compute the surface normal $\boldsymbol{n}$, and then the smooth weight $\omega_t^n(p,q)$ is set as

$$\omega_t^n(p,q) = 1 - exp(-\frac{(\boldsymbol{n}_p^T \boldsymbol{n}_q)^2}{\sigma_n^2}) \quad (16)$$

It means that we will favor smooth shading for adjacent pixels that have similar normal orientations. For other frames $1 \sim T-1$ that only have color images, the smooth weight may be set as a constant value. However, the weight is not easy to choose. As shown in figure 3 , the texture is not separated clearly from shading image if the weight is small (figure 3(b)), while the shading is over-smoothed when the weight is large (figure 3(c)).

To deal with this problem, we decide to propagate the adaptive weighting terms computed in key frames into other frames. In more detail, the weight term in frame 0 is propagated forward to next frames using the following equation

$$\omega_t^{n,f}(p,q) = \begin{cases} \omega_{t-1}^{n,f}(p_{t-1}, q_{t-1}) & p_{t-1}, q_{t-1} \in \mathcal{N} for \quad 1 < t < T \\ \omega_0^n(p_0, q_0) & p_0, q_0 \in \mathcal{N} for \quad t = 1 \\ 0.1 & otherwise \quad for \quad t \in [1, T-1] \end{cases} \quad (17)$$

In the above formula, for adjacent pixels p and q in frame t, the corresponding pixels p_{t-1} and q_{t-1} in previous frame $t-1$ can be found with optical flow. The smooth weight is propagated from previous frames when the adjacent pixels stay connected as neighbours, otherwise is set to 0.1. In this way, the smooth shading is propagated and shading details will still get preserved. We can compute the weight $\omega_t^{n,b}$ using backward propagation from frame T. The weight is blended as

$$\omega_t^n(p,q) = max\{\omega_t^{n,f}(p,q), \omega_t^{n,b}(p,q)\} \quad (18)$$

The temporal albedo consistency is defined as

$$E_{t\_a} = \sum_{t=0}^{T-1} \sum_{p} \omega_t^{fb}(p)\omega_t^{ta}(p)||\hat{A}_t(p) - \hat{A}_{t+1}(W_t(p))||^2, \quad (19)$$

The weight terms are necessary as we need to prevent the artifacts caused by occlusion between frames and the inaccuracy in flow computation. The weighting term $\omega_t^{fb}(p)$ is used to discard the occluded regions and is set to 0 if the froward-backward flow consistency check fails, otherwise it is set to 1. We set the weighting term ω_t^{ta} as

$$\omega_t^{ta}(p) = \begin{cases} 0 & ||I_t(p) - I_{t+1}(W_t(p))||_2 > \tau_{ta} \\ 1 & otherwise \end{cases} \quad (20)$$

The final objective function is the weighted sum of all terms, that is

$$E_l = E_{d\_im} + \lambda_{d\_s} \cdot E_{d\_s} + \lambda_{s\_a} \cdot E_{s\_a} + \lambda_{s\_s} \cdot E_{s\_s} + \lambda_{t\_a} \cdot E_{t\_a} \quad (21)$$

The objective function can be solved with linear optimization.

With the above propagation framework, for middle frames that do not have depth images, we are still able to decompose the texture from color images while preserving shading details, as shown in figure 3(d).

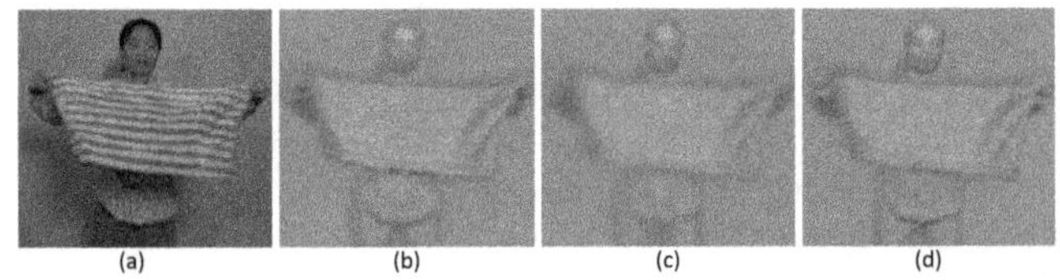

Figure 3: Results on intrinsic decomposition. (a) a sampled middle frame; (b) decomposed shading image when constant shading smooth weight ω_t^n set as 1.0; (c) shading image computed when ω_t^n is set as 6.0; (d) our shading image with adpative smooth shading weight.

4.3 Depth stream generation framework

Now we have all the albedo and shading images for each frame ($A_0 \sim A_T$ and $S_0 \sim S_T$), and the key frame depth images ($\tilde{D}_0$ and $\tilde{D}_T$), we can recover the in-between depth frames.

Given equally sampled temporal frames indexed by t, the 3D scene velocity , $U_t(D(p))$ at pixel p, is computed as (for simplicity, we omit p here),

$$U_t(\mathbf{D}) = X_{W_t}(D_{t+1}(W_t)) - X(D_t) \quad (22)$$

where $\mathbf{D} = [D_0, D_1, \cdots D_{T-1}]$. The above function is the velocity field for the sequence.

It is assumed that the motion between neighboring color frames should not be too fast and will prefer small velocities that are spatially smooth. Our first term is denoted as the velocity term,

$$E_v = \sum_{t=0}^{T-1} \sum_{p} (||U_t(D)||^2 + \lambda_v \psi(||\nabla U_t(D)||^2)) \quad (23)$$

where

$$\psi(a^2) = \sqrt{a^2 + \varepsilon^2} \quad (24)$$

The first term in Eq. 23 has the similar effect as bi-linear interpolation that will spread the spatial movement in 3D between the two key frames into the whole sequence. The second term in Eq. 23 is exploited here to preserve the smooth scene flow field [17]. We do not enforce any linear constraints for this term while only spatial smoothness is favored for the 3d flow field. Therefore, the velocity term will try to preserve the smooth transition along the depth sequence while allowing for non-linear motion.

Secondly, with the albedo images computed from the previous section, we have the shading constraint that penalizes the differences between rendered images and the captured color images. We use the Charbonnier penalty function(Eq. 24), which is more robust to the outliers in the shading image,

$$E_s = \sum_{t=0}^{T} \sum_{p} \psi(||A_t(p) \sum_{m=1}^{9} l_m H_m(\boldsymbol{n}(p)) - I_t(p)||_2^2) \quad (25)$$

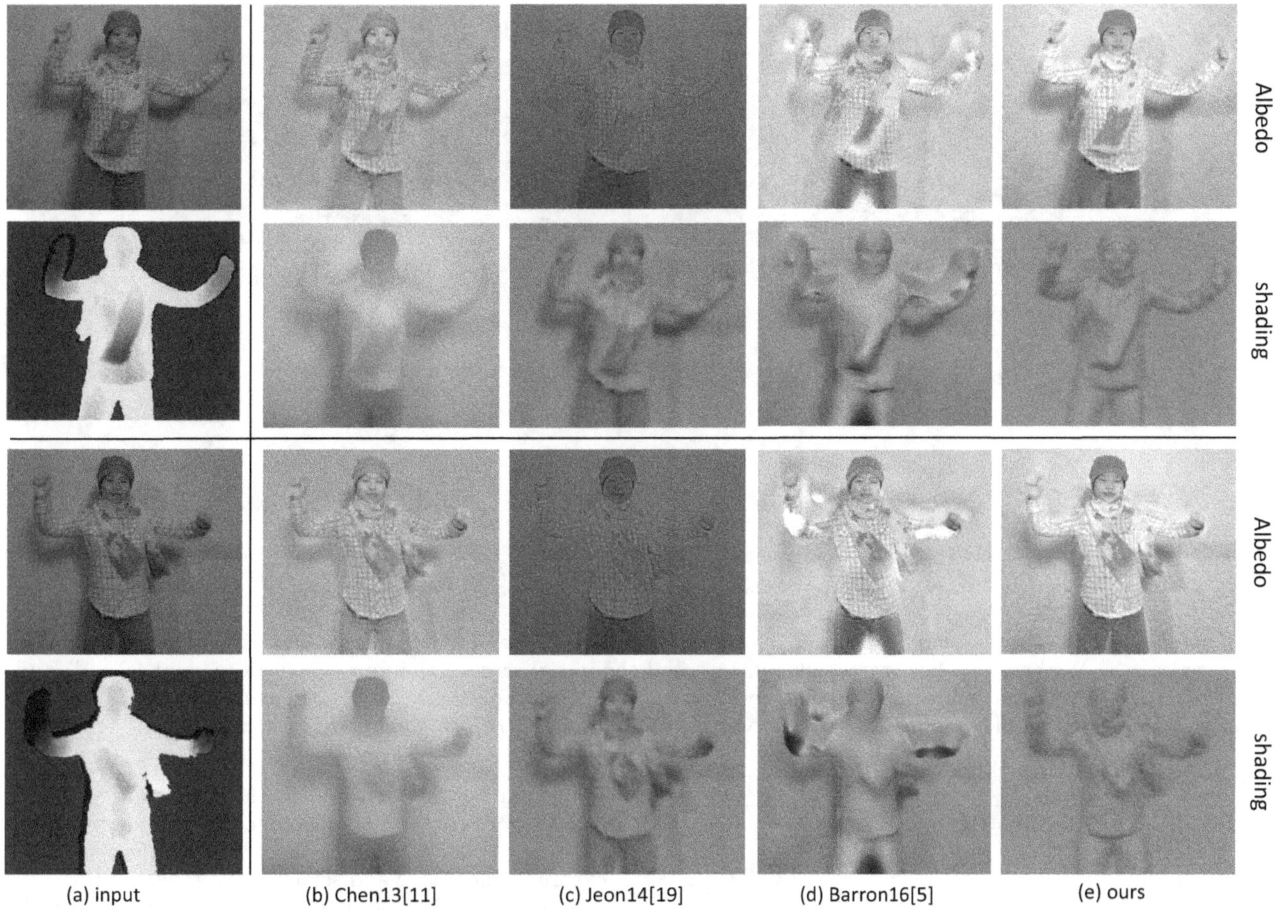

Figure 4: Results on sampled images from hand waving stream. (a) Input color image and depth map. (b-e) Albedo and Shading images estimated by three recent approaches for intrinsic decomposition and by our approach.

For the above formula, $\boldsymbol{n}(p)$ can be substituted with depth D based on the normal computation equation (Eq. 4). Therefore, the shading constraints are directly enforced on depth streams.

Next, in order to have the smooth surface, we utilize a Laplacian smoothness term for each frame. We use the adaptive weighting again to preserve the surface boundary.

$$E_{lap} = \sum_{t=0}^{T} \sum_{p} \Big(D_t(p) - \frac{\sum_{q \in \mathcal{N}_p} \omega_t(p,q) \cdot D_t(q)}{\sum_{q \in \mathcal{N}_p} \omega_t(p,q)} \Big)^2 \quad (26)$$

In the above formula, the weighting term is computed using the Gaussian filter as,

$$\omega_t(p,q) = exp(-\frac{||D_t(p) - D_t(q)||^2}{\sigma_{lap}^2}) \quad (27)$$

Finally, the data term enforces the constraint provided by two depth key frames $\tilde{D_0}$ and $\tilde{D_T}$, which can be regarded as the boundary condition.

$$E_d = \sum_{t \in \{0,T\}} \sum_{p} (D_t(p) - \tilde{D}_t(p))^2 \quad (28)$$

In summary, our energy function for depth map generation is formulated as

$$E = E_v + \lambda_s \cdot E_s + \lambda_{lap} \cdot E_{lap} + \lambda_d \cdot E_d \quad (29)$$

The formulation for generating the depth stream is a non-linear minimization problem. We use the Levenberg-Marquard (LM) method to solve this optimization problem. We have found out that it is difficult to achieve convergence directly since the solution space could have many local minimums. We instead develop a coarse-to-fine refinement strategy. First, we build up the pyramid for shading sequence and two key depth frames. In our implementation, we have four layers for the pyramid. In the first two coarsest levels, the energy function Eq. 29 is minimized and we can get the initial rough depth sequence. Then we will refine the depth with shading constraints separately for each frame. In this step, the initial depth propagated from the coarser level will be enhanced with the shading constraints together with Laplacian smoothness with the Eq. 25 and Eq. 26.

5. EXPERIMENTS

We have captured some real data sets with the prototype of our hybrid camera setup described in Section 3 and tested our method on these datasets. Also, we have generated some synthetic datasets to validate the method quantitatively. In this section, we will show quantitative and qualitative comparison results. All the parameters in our algorithms are showed on Table 1, these values are tuned empirically and remain fixed for all the experiments.

We have also implemented two baseline algorithms. The

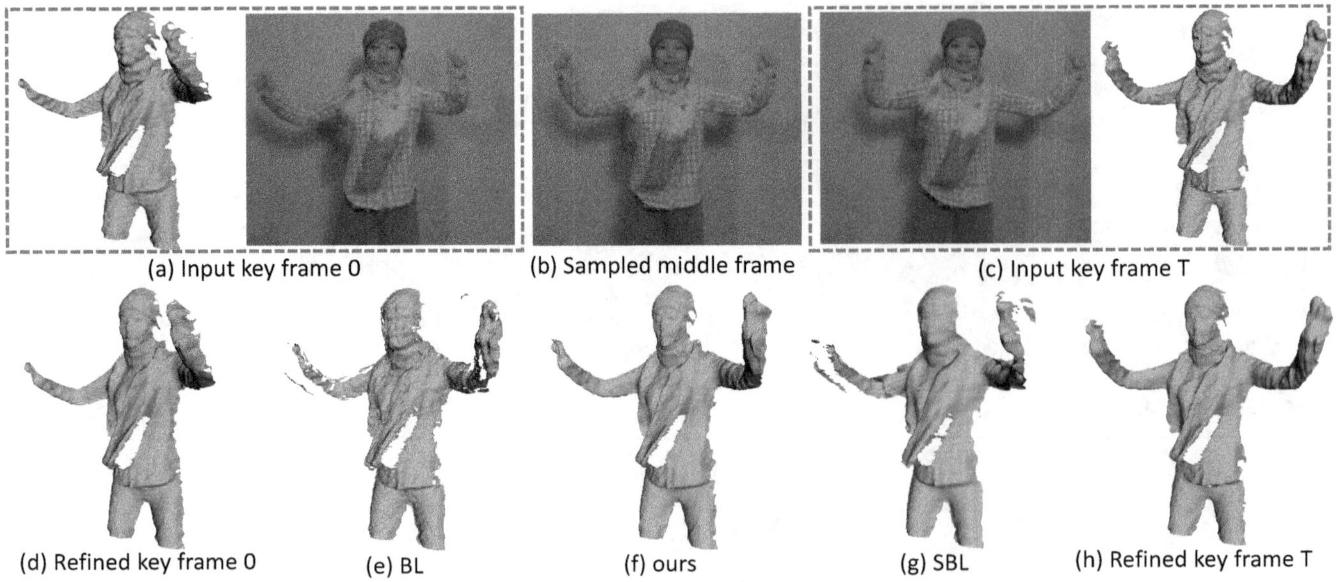

Figure 5: Results on the hand waving sequence. To better show the shape of the hands, we adjust the perpective angle of the generated mesh. We have two key frame color images and the initial meshes as input shown in (a) and (c). (d) and (h) are the key frame meshes after refinement. The second row shows the interpolation result of one sampled frame shown in (b). (e)-(g) are the recovered meshes using BL, our proposed method and SBL, respectively.

Eq. 7	Eq. 9	Eq. 12				Eq. 16	Eq. 20
SN	ϵ	τ_{ch}	τ_{lum}	σ_{ch}	σ_{lum}	σ_n	τ_{ta}
30	0.001	0.06	0.10	0.01	0.05	0.1	0.08
Eq. 24	Eq. 27	Eq. 21			Eq. 29		
ε	σ_{lap}	λ_{s_a}	λ_{s_s}	λ_{t_a}	λ_s	λ_{lap}	λ_d
0.001	5mm	2.0	3.0	5.0	0.1	0.01	10

Table 1: The parameter settings for our experiments.

first is to use the optical flow information to interpolate the in-between frames. We denote this baseline method as the BL (bi-directional interpolation) method. The second is to refine the interpolated depth map with shading information. More specifically, we first apply a low-pass filter to smooth out the interpolated depth maps and then do the refinement with shading constraints, e.g., using method [24], to recover more surface details. We denote this method as the SBL method.

5.1 Intrinsic image decomposition

We have compared our method with three previous works on intrinsic image decomposition with single RGB-D image as input. As shown in figure 4, the upper rows demonstrate the decomposition for key frame images that have captured depth frames as input. For the lower row, it corresponds to a sampled middle frame that has no captured depth as input. For this middle frame, the interpolated depth from the BL method is taken as the input depth for all these comparison methods; for our method the interpolated depth is not needed, since the decomposition is performed using global optimization with key frames and middle frames computed all together.

Chen et al. [11] performs the decomposition without taking surface details into account and tends to get shading image that is quite smooth, as shown in figure 4(b). This method performs better on scene level decomposition not on surface details. Jeon et al. [19] explicitly deal with the texture in the image and separate the repeated texture patterns before shading decomposition. Therefore, the grid patterns can be separated into albedo image correctly, while the texture on the scarf stays at the shading image, as shown in figure 4(c). Figure 4(d) displays the results using the method [5] which takes as input a single RGB-D image and produces as output an improved depth map, albedo image, shading image and illumination model. This approach is sensitive to the outliers in input depth map, especially along the surface boundary, as the zero depth value is not handled explicitly. It will fail in our case where the depth round the moving hands and arms is quite noisy caused by motion blur and also the interpolated depth is wrong around the arms. Figure 4(e) shows the results from our method where the texture is successfully decomposed into albedo image while real surface details, i.e. on the hat and the around the arms, can be seen in the shading image. More comparison results are shown in the supplementary material.

5.2 Qualitative evaluation for depth frame generation

In Figure 5, we demonstrate the recovered depth of the relative simple case, where the human subject is waving her arms and hands quite fast. For this relative simple case, since the 3D motion can be approximated by the linear motion, the bi-directional interpolation(BL) result is acceptable in most of the parts except for some artifacts along the hands. After the shading refinement(SBL), the depth becomes more smooth and the surface details can be recovered. However, the artifacts have got passed from the interpolation result and the shading refinement could not handle this properly. In comparison with these two methods, our

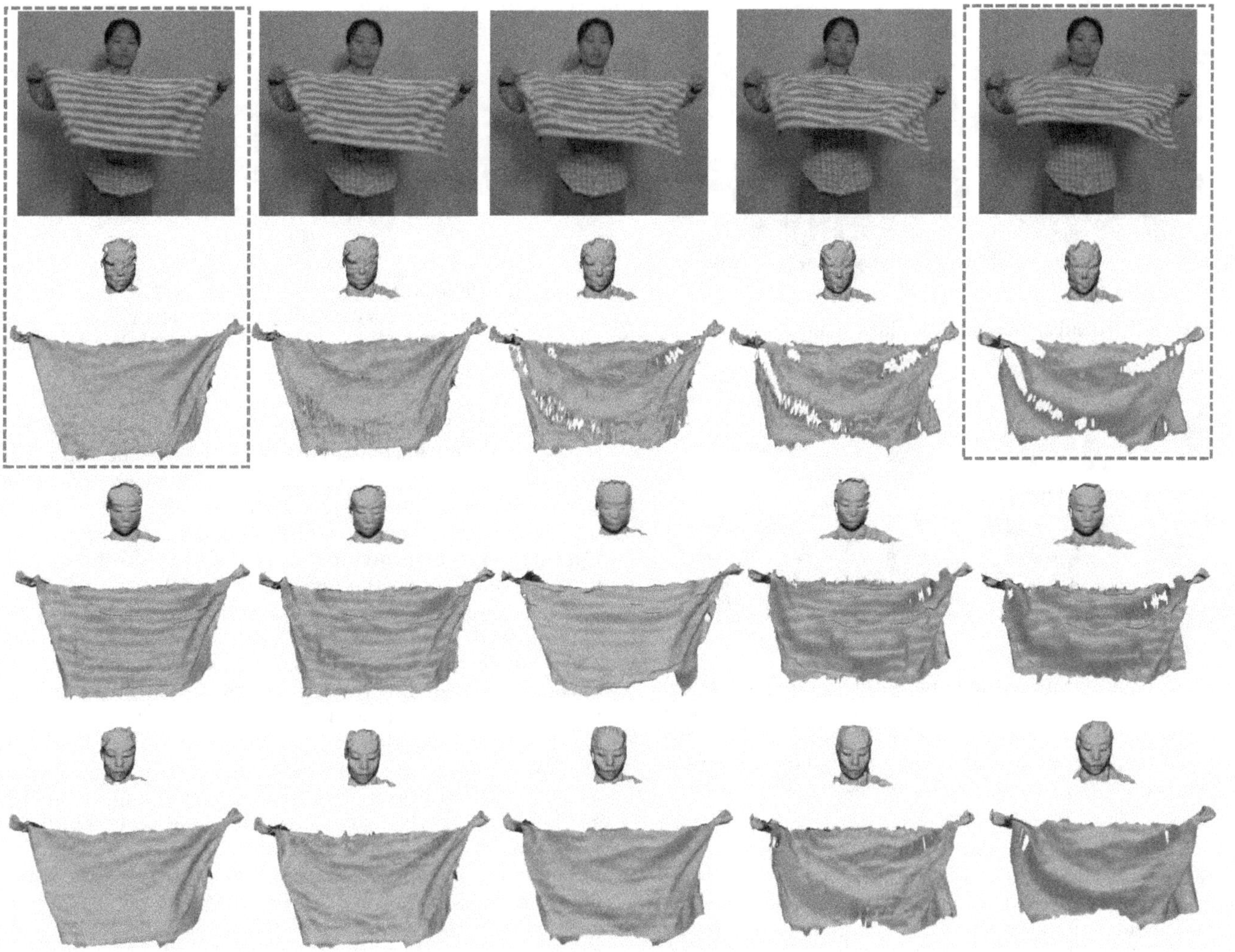

Figure 6: Results on the towel shaking sequence. To better demonstrate the shape of the towel, we adjust the perpective angle of the generated mesh which differs from the color image. First row shows the input color sequence with left most and right most have the corresponding input depth frame, while the middle ones are sampled frames between these two frames. Second row gives the input depth on the left and right, and interpolated depth with BL method for the middle frames. Third row displays the shading refinement result using SBL method. The last row shows the recovered depth from our method.

method yield better results thanks to the smooth velocity field constraints in the whole sequence and our bundle optimization approach. Also, considering the motion blur effect along the moving boundary, for the key frame depth, we detect the object boundaries with both depth and color contrast and enforce the gradient smoothness in the boundary area along with shading refinement. The refined key frame meshes are shown in (d) and (h).

Figure 6 shows the sequence where a towel is waved in front of the hybrid camera. For this case, the towel is experiencing both global translation and local deformations, which are more challenging to recover. Similar to the above case, the error in the interpolated depth will pass to the shading refinement. Also, the texture-copy problem has not been handled properly for the SBL method, as the stripe patterns on the towel are visible as hallucinated surface details. As most of the texture details have been separated clearly with our intrinsic decomposition, the recovered depth from our method is more faithful with the real surface details preserved.

More results can be seen in the supplementary material.

5.3 Quantitative evaluation

Quantitative evaluation for Synthetic data We use synthetic data to demonstrate the effectiveness of the global optimization framework for depth map generation compared to frame-by-frame method. The shading images are supposed to be given for the optimization framework, therefore we ignore the influence of albedo or texture.

We have generated two cases of synthetic data displayed in Figure 7 and Figure 8. For each sequence, it consists of seven depth frames with resolution of 64×64. We have the ground-truth lighting condition, therefore we can render the shading images for each frame. The optical flow between any frames are all set to zeros for simplicity, which means that the motion is purely in the z-direction. Given the first and last depth frame as two key frames and the shading

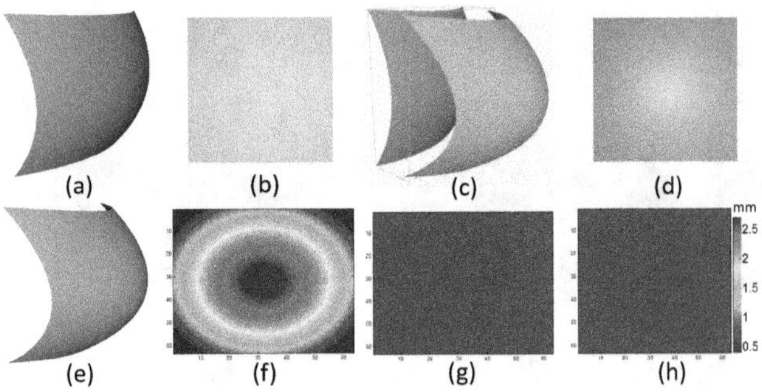

Figure 7: Results on synthetic data (simple case).

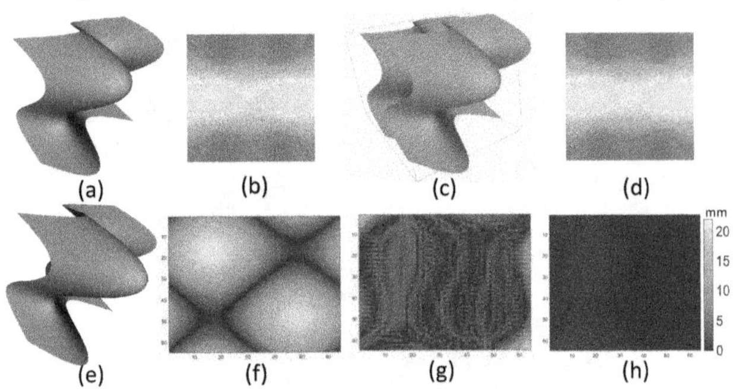

Figure 8: Results on synthetic data (more complex case). The two shading images (b) and (d) are the same to each other as we set the sequence to have half period of sine wave and these two key frames have the same shape, but they have the global displacement in depth, as shown in (c).

sequence, we present the result computed with BL, SBL, and also our method.

The first case (Figure 7) displays a simple case where the surface is bending forward along with the global linear translation. As illustrated in Figure 7, both SBL and our approach can recover the depth with quite small error.

For the second case (Figure 8), we have generated the depth sequence that has the sine wave in the shape deformation and also the global translation, which is the complex combination of linear and non-linear motion. For this more complex motion, our method will get smaller error than the BL and SBL method. The regularization terms and the global optimization will make our method converge to a better local minimum that is closer to the real depth.

For Figure 7 (Figure 8), the first row shows the mesh and shading image, which are the key frames as our input. Figure 7a (Figure 8a) is the mesh for the first frame with the shading image shown in Figure 7b (Figure 8b). We put the meshes of the key frames together in Figure 7c (Figure 8c). The second row shows one sampled frame, where the first column Figure 7e (Figure 8e) is the groundtruth mesh and the next three columns present the error map for the depth maps recovered with BL, SBL and also our method respectively.

To better illustrate the results, we compute the relative depth error with the formula below, where the error is evaluated using the difference between recovered depth and the ground-truth depth divided by the displacement from the first frame,

$$err = \frac{1}{T-1}\sum_{t=1}^{T-1}\frac{\sum_p |D^t(p) - R^t(p)|}{\sum_p |D^t(p) - D^0(p)|} \tag{30}$$

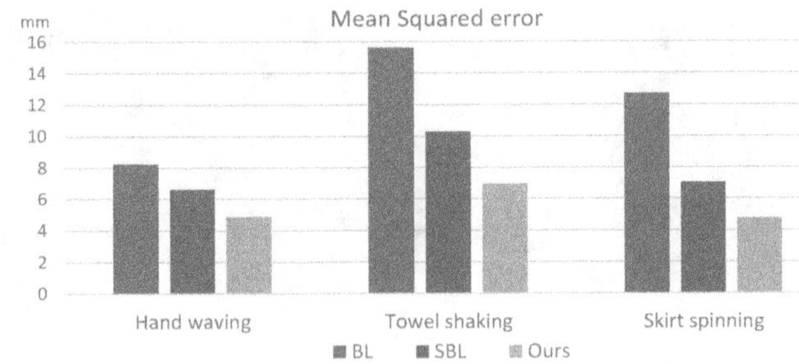

Figure 9: Quantitative results for real datasets. All the results are computed with squared mean error. We discard the extreme outliers around the surface boundaries during the evaluation.

For the BL method, the relative error is 0.1962 for the simple case and 0.3788 for complex case. The error will decrease to 0.0012 after the shading refinement (SBL) for the simple case and 0.0837 for the complex one. For our proposed method, the error is 0.0012 and 0.0569 respectively.

Quantitative evaluation for real data To better validate our method on the real datasets with some quantitative measurement, we sample several frames from our real datasets and down-sample the captured depth frames into 15Hz and then use these frames to recover all the depth sequences corresponding to color frames (180Hz), which means for every two key frame depth maps, we will get thirteen depth frames interpolated from the interpolation methods. The middle frame corresponds to the original depth frames in 30Hz. The captured depth frames can be approximated as the groundtruth depth to measure the accuracy of the interpolated depth maps. We evaluate the BL method, SBL method and our approach using this strategy on three real datasets we have captured. We evaluate the performance of each method by measuring the mean value of the depth error compared to ground-truth depth. The results are shown in Fig. 9. Again our method is the best one.

Limitations During our experiments we have found a few limitations of our method. First, there are still some artifacts at the discontinuous boundary of the recovered depth which is caused by the motion blur effect of the captured depth sequence. This might be resolved using the normal constraints along the contours on the boundary. Secondly, we have not dealt with the occlusions and topology changes explicitly in our formulation, the artifacts exist in our recovered depth caused by the occlusions and topology changes. In future work, we plan to detect the occlusions via bi-directional matching and track the pixel or 3D point in the whole sequence and try to deal with the occlusions and topology changes.

6. CONCLUSION

In this paper, we present our novel hybrid camera setup, which is composed of a high-speed color camera and a depth sensor. Using this hybrid camera, we propose a framework to recover the depth sequence of the scene with high-speed motion. Considering that the bi-directional interpolation method will fail when there exists non-linear motion in the scene, we exploit the shading constraints in each color frame to overcome this limitation. In our formulation, we use the depth information captured from low-speed depth camera as the boundary constraints for the whole sequence and enforce the SfS constraints in each frame. Also, the depth maps of neighboring frames are associated with our proposed velocity term that preserves smooth motion field. Therefore, we can recovery the depth sequence in a single optimization. Finally, we present the comparison results for real datasets captured with our hybrid camera and also for synthetic datasets. Our high-speed and high-quality RGB-D sequence can be used in many areas where the motion is fast, such as sport event, gait analysis, etc.

Acknowledgments

The work is supported in part by US National Science Foundation grants IIS-1231545 and IIP-1543172, Natural Science Foundation of China (No.61332017, 61572243), Key Industrial Innovation Chain of Shaanxi Province Industrial Area (2015KTZDGY04-01), Chinese Scholarship Council, and Zhejiang Provincial Natural Science Foundation grant LY13F020019. Jiangbin Zheng and Ruigang Yang are the co-corresponding authors for this paper.

7. REFERENCES

[1] R. Achanta, A. Shaji, K. Smith, A. Lucchi, P. Fua, and S. Susstrunk. Slic superpixels compared to state-of-the-art superpixel methods. *IEEE TPAMI*, 34(11):2274–2282, 2012.

[2] O. M. Aodha, N. D. Campbell, A. Nair, and G. J. Brostow. Patch based synthesis for single depth image super-resolution. In *ECCV*, pages 71–84, 2012.

[3] J. T. Barron and J. Malik. High-frequency shape and albedo from shading using natural image statistics. In *CVPR*, pages 2521–2528, 2011.

[4] J. T. Barron and J. Malik. Shape, illumination, and reflectance from shading. *IEEE TPAMI*, 37(8):1670–1687, 2015.

[5] J. T. Barron and J. Malik. Intrinsic scene properties from a single rgb-d image. *IEEE TPAMI*, 38(4):690–703, 2016.

[6] H. G. Barrow and J. M. Tenenbaum. Recovering intrinsic scene characteristics from images. *Comput. Vis. Syst.*, 1978.

[7] S. Bi, X. Han, and Y. Yu. An l1 image transform for edge-preserving smoothing and scene-level intrinsic decomposition. *ACM Trans. Graph.*, 34(4):78, 2015.

[8] N. Bonneel, K. Sunkavalli, J. Tompkin, D. Sun, S. Paris, and H. Pfister. Interactive intrinsic video editing. *ACM Trans. Graph.*, 33(6):197, 2014.

[9] A. Bousseau, S. Paris, and F. Durand. User-assisted intrinsic images. *ACM Trans. Graph.*, 28(5):130, 2009.

[10] T. Brox and J. Malik. Large displacement optical flow: descriptor matching in variational motion estimation. *IEEE TPAMI*, 33(3):500–513, 2011.

[11] Q. Chen and V. Koltun. A simple model for intrinsic image decomposition with depth cues. In *ICCV*, pages 241–248, 2013.

[12] J. Durou, M. Falcone, and M. Sagona. Numerical methods for shape-from-shading: A new survey with benchmarks. *CVIU*, 109(1):22–43, 2008.

[13] D. Ferstl, C. Reinbacher, R. Ranftl, M. RÃijther, and H. Bischof. Image guided depth upsampling using anisotropic total generalized variation. In *ICCV*, pages 993–1000, 2013.

[14] E. Garces, A. Munoz, J. Lopez-Moreno, and D. D. Gutierrez. Intrinsic images by clustering. In *Computer Graphics Forum*, volume 31, pages 1415–1424, 2012.

[15] Y. Han, J. Lee, and I. Kweon. High quality shape from a single rgb-d image under uncalibrated natural illumination. In *ICCV*, pages 1617–1624, 2013.

[16] S. M. Haque, A. Chatterjee, and V. M. Govindu. High quality photometric reconstruction using a depth camera. In *CVPR*, pages 2283–2290, 2014.

[17] E. Herbst, X. Ren, and D. Fox. Rgb-d flow: Dense 3-d motion estimation using color and depth. In *ICRA*, pages 2276–2282, 2013.

[18] B. K. P. Horn. *Shape from Shading: A Method for Obtaining the Shape of a Smooth Opaque Object from One View*. PhD thesis, MIT, 1970.

[19] J. Jeon, S. Cho, X. Tong, and S. Lee. Intrinsic image decomposition using structure-texture separation and surface normals. In *ECCV*, pages 218–233, 2014.

[20] N. Kong, P. Gehler, and M. Black. Intrinsic video. In *ECCV*, pages 360–375. 2014.

[21] P. Laffont, A. Bousseau, S. Paris, F. Durand, and G. Drettakis. Coherent intrinsic images from photo collections. *ACM Trans. Graph.*, 31(6), 2012.

[22] E. H. Land and J. J. McCann. Lightness and retinex theory. *JOSA*, 1971.

[23] K. J. Lee, Q. Zhao, X. Tong, M. Gong, S. Izadi, S. U. Lee, P. Tan, and S. Lin. Estimation of intrinsic image sequences from image+ depth video. In *ECCV*, pages 327–340. 2012.

[24] R. Or-El, G. Rosman, A. Wetzler, R. Kimmel, and A. M. Bruckstein. Rgbd-fusion: Real-time high precision depth recovery. In *CVPR*, pages 5407–5416, 2015.

[25] J. Park, H. Kim, Y. Tai, M. S. Brown, and I. Kweon. High quality depth map upsampling for 3d-tof cameras. In *ICCV*, pages 1623–1630, 2011.

[26] R. Ramamoorthi and P. Hanrahan. An efficient representation for irradiance environment maps. In *ACM SIGGRAPH*, pages 497–500, 2001.

[27] C. Richardt, C. Stoll, N. A. Dodgson, H. Seidel, and C. Theobalt. Coherent spatiotemporal filtering, upsampling and rendering of rgbz videos. In *Computer Graphics Forum*, volume 31, pages 247–256, 2012.

[28] J. Shi, Y. Dong, X. Tong, and Y. Chen. Efficient intrinsic image decomposition for rgbd images. In *ACM VRST*, pages 17–25, 2015.

[29] Y. Tai, H. Du, M. S. Brown, and L. Stephen. Correction of spatially varying image and video motion blur using a hybrid camera. *IEEE TPAMI*, 32(6):1012–1028, 2010.

[30] M. F. Tappen, W. T. Freeman, and E. H. Adelson. Recovering intrinsic images from a single image. *IEEE TPAMI*, 27(9):1459–1472, 2005.

[31] C. Wu, K. Varanasi, Y. Liu, H. Seidel, and C. Theobalt. Shading-based dynamic shape refinement from multi-view video under general illumination. In *ICCV*, pages 1108–1115, 2011.

[32] C. Wu, M. Zollhöfer, M. NieÃ§ner, M. Stamminger, S. Izadi, and C. Theobalt. Real-time shading-based refinement for consumer depth cameras. *ACM Trans. Graph.*, 33(3), 2014.

[33] Q. Yang, R. Yang, J. Davis, and D. Nistér. Spatial-depth super resolution for range images. In *CVPR*, 2007.

[34] G. Ye, E. Garces, Y. Liu, Q. Dai, and D. Gutierrez. Intrinsic video and applications. *ACM Trans. Graph.*, 33(4):80, 2014.

[35] L. Yu, S. Yeung, Y. Tai, and S. Lin. Shading-based shape refinement of rgb-d images. In *CVPR*, pages 1415–1422, 2013.

[36] Q. Zhang, M. Ye, R. Yang, Y. Matsushita, B. Wilburn, and H. Yu. Edge-preserving photometric stereo via depth fusion. In *CVPR*, pages 2472–2479, 2012.

[37] Q. Zhao, P. Tan, Q. Dai, L. Shen, E. Wu, and S. Lin. A closed-form solution to retinex with nonlocal texture constraints. *IEEE TPAMI*, 34(7):1437–1444, 2012.

[38] J. Zhu, L. Wang, R. Yang, J. Davis, and Z. Pan. Reliability fusion of time-of-flight depth and stereo geometry for high quality depth maps. *IEEE TPAMI*, 33(7):1400–1414, 2011.

Spatio-Temporal Analysis of Bandwidth Maps for Geo-Predictive Video Streaming in Mobile Environments

Bayan Taani
School of Computing
National University of Singapore
Singapore 117417
bayan@comp.nus.edu.sg

Roger Zimmermann
School of Computing
National University of Singapore
Singapore 117417
rogerz@comp.nus.edu.sg

ABSTRACT

High quality video streaming is increasingly popular among mobile users especially with the rise of high speed LTE networks. But despite the high network capacity of LTE, streaming videos may suffer from disruptions since the quality of the video depends on the network bandwidth, which in turn depends on the location of the user with respect to their cell tower, crowd levels, and objects like buildings and trees. Maintaining a good video playback experience becomes even more challenging if the user is moving fast in a vehicle, the location is changing rapidly and the available bandwidth fluctuates. In this paper we introduce *GeoStream*, a video streaming system that relies on the use of geostatistics to analyze spatio-temporal bandwidth. Data measured from users' streaming videos while they are commuting is collected in order to predict future bandwidth availability in unknown locations. Our approach investigates and leverages the relationship between the separation distance between sample bandwidth points, the time they were captured, and the semivariance, expressed by a variogram plot, to finally predict the future bandwidth at unknown locations. Using the datasets from GTube our experimental results show an improved performance.

CCS Concepts

•**Networks → Wide area networks; Mobile networks;** *Network measurement;*

Keywords

Mobile video; DASH; adaptive streaming; spatio-temporal geostatistics; geo-prediction; kriging

1. INTRODUCTION

Media streaming has been growing as a fraction of the Internet traffic in the last decade to become the majority traffic, as video dissemination is converging around various services such as so-called over-the-top IPTV, Video-on-Demand (VoD) and e-learning. Further driving this trend is the common use of handheld devices, which enable increasing amounts of video content to be uploaded and downloaded to and from video hosting sites, which often leverage Content Distribution Networks (CDNs). According to the Visual Networking Index forecast produced by Cisco Inc., 55% of the total mobile data traffic in 2015 was video and this is expected to reach 75% by 2020 [5]. The increasing number of users and video traffic poses a challenge in delivering these videos in a manner that complies with what best pleases the viewers, *i.e.*, watching the videos at a high quality and providing a very satisfactory end user experience. Additionally, as users' expectations are rising and high resolution content is increasingly available, it will become even more challenging to deliver videos in the best possible quality while there exists significant competition over the available bandwidth, especially in wireless environments.

Since mobile devices are the dominant entertainment devices for people on the go, users prefer to spend their time watching online videos on their phones or tablets while commuting. In a study conducted in the US and Europe, the percentage of time that viewers spend streaming videos while commuting ranges from 14–27% on smartphones and 28–47% on tablets [7]. However, streaming in wireless environments is a challenging task considering the varying behavior of radio frequency signals that depend on many factors including the location, crowd levels and the surrounding obstructions such as objects. Thus the viewing experience may suffer from disruptions, such as a dramatic change in quality or discontinuous playback. It has been shown that rapid change between video representations has a negative impact on the quality of the video watching experience, which is also known as the Quality of Experience (QoE) [6, 12, 18]. Moreover, a previous study has shown that video stalls account for the largest impact on the viewing experience [8]. These challenges make it crucial for a video client to plan for buffering, quality switching, and estimating future network conditions in order to achieve a high QoE.

The study conducted in this paper has been inspired by GTube [13], a video streaming system based on Dynamic Adaptive Streaming over HTTP (DASH), that leverages receivers equipped with GPS location sensors. The key components of the GTube architecture are (1) the collection of measured bandwidth values in different locations, (2) the execution of bandwidth estimation queries by the streaming clients at some locations, and (3) the planning of quality adaptations by the clients based on the retrieved and predicted bandwidth values. The first step aims to gather as

MM '16, October 15-19, 2016, Amsterdam, Netherlands
© 2016 ACM. ISBN 978-1-4503-3603-1/16/10...$15.00
DOI: http://dx.doi.org/10.1145/2964284.2964333

many bandwidth measurements as possible in different locations to be able to describe the network conditions with respect to location and time to establish a bandwidth map. We have collected data from different areas across Singapore while using public transportation to enable us to analyze and model the bandwidth distribution and leverage it to predict future values in unknown locations.

This paper introduces *GeoStream*, a video streaming application that is best suited for mobile DASH clients. The novelty of this work centers on the use of *spatio-temporal geostatistics* to model and predict future bandwidth in unknown locations as the user moves while watching a video. The mobile user communicates with a geo-server that provides it with bandwidth predictions, as well as a video server for fetching video segments. We developed a testbed that consists of a GeoStream Android client, a geo-server equipped with the appropriate bandwidth prediction module and a media streaming server to be able to experiment with and observe the effects of geo-spatial bandwidth predictions on the user's video streaming experience.

The rest of this paper is organized as follows. Section 2 presents a literature review of existing geo-predictive systems. Section 3 provides a brief background on geostatistics. The methodology used in estimating the available bandwidth is described in Section 4. The experimental setup and results are then evaluated in Section 5. Next we present a discussion about real-world scenarios in Section 6. Finally, we conclude our work in Section 7.

2. RELATED WORK

With the increasing deployment of wireless and mobile networks in recent decades, it became imperative to consider the varying network conditions while streaming videos. In HTTP Adaptive bitrate Streaming (HAS), the video is divided into a number of small chunks of appropriate duration, each one encoded at different bitrates (and hence qualities) and stored on a web server. The client can then ask for the appropriate quality according to the network conditions. Numerous adaptive streaming approaches have been developed and are widely used by content providers nowadays, such as Apple's HTTP Live Streaming (HLS) [16], Microsoft's Smooth Streaming [26], and Adobe's HTTP Dynamic Streaming [2]. Each one of these commercial solutions uses slightly different container formats and organizes the chunks into playlists somewhat differently. Because of these differences, there has been a movement to standardize HAS streaming technologies. The result, Dynamic Adaptive Streaming over HTTP (DASH) [21] has been gaining attention from the research community as an open specification for a single standard that unifies adaptive streaming over HTTP. It was developed as part of MPEG and standardized as MPEG-DASH in 2012 [1]. It offers the support for client-based adaptation, but leaves the implementation of the adaptation logic up to third-party developers, depending on the application needs. DASH clients try to match the delivery rate of a video to the available bandwidth by fetching *segments* at appropriate encoding-levels from the streaming server. These segments are maintained through an XML-based manifest file, also called the Media Presentation Description (MPD), which lists the video segment presentation details (like URL, timing, resolution, and bitrates). The client implements the adaptation logic. The adaptation algorithm attempts to minimize the buffering time by estimating the network conditions to be able to fetch the suitable segments from the server. Other functions can help to improve the QoE, such as rate stabilization for smooth switching between qualities, and initial buffering to avoid a lengthy start-up delay.

2.1 Geo-Predictive Video Streaming

Cellular signal strength varies based on the location, crowd level, and large objects like buildings and trees. This section reviews some of the work focused on delivering video content to mobile users depending on their geographical location. The challenges lie with both the varying network conditions and the movements of the users, so both factors should be taken into account while planning for proper rate adaptation schemes. Singh *et al.* [20] introduced a streaming system over RTP with a Network Coverage Map Server that contains bandwidth and location information, and it is used to help the client pre-buffer and switch video rates. Related to adaptive streaming, Yao *et al.* evaluated the performance of HTTP adaptive streaming in 3G vehicular environments compared to non-adaptive streaming [25]. The bandwidth traces used in their study were collected in a previous study of theirs [23] by driving a car on daily commuting routes in Sydney, where one bandwidth sample was measured for every 200 m section of the route. The experimental setup used a bandwidth shaper to emulate the bandwidth changes in the network link according to their trace files. The results showed that the adaptive scheme experiences less and shorter buffering and a condensed glitch duration compared to a non-adaptive approach. In a previous work of the same authors [24], they utilized the same datasets to construct bandwidth maps to infer the relationship between bandwidth and location so that it could be used in adaptive streaming applications. In their method, when the client needs to fetch a new segment, the predicted bandwidth value is the mean of the past measured values at the same location. When the mobile device changes its location, it informs the server which in turn does a look-up of the mean bandwidth at the new point and returns it back to the client. The server then updates the mean including the most recent measurement value. Riiser *et al.* [17] introduced a video streaming system for users commuting along known paths. A central service maintains a bandwidth map of measurements collected from users together with their corresponding GPS coordinates, and computes the mean of bandwidth values in each location. Hence, when a user queries for a bandwidth value using the coordinates, the mean is returned. However, the client must already specify the route it will be taking, and instruct the server of that information.

The work most closely related to our proposed approach is GTube [13]. This system introduces the use of bandwidth maps with path prediction along commute routes. The system consists of a geo-predictive server and streaming clients. The server maintains a bandwidth map of previously measured values with GPS coordinates and can be updated by streaming clients in real time (via crowd sourcing). Furthermore, since GPS sensors can sometimes be inaccurate, the server performs map matching using an enhanced HMM-based model [9] to match locations to the road network. Once a client sends a query using its location, the server predicts the trajectory using their proposed path prediction method. The resulting estimated bandwidth is derived from the interpolation of the k-nearest locations around the queried point. The authors also propose two quality adaptation algorithms, 1-predict and N-predict, and compare them to existing well-known quality adaptation algorithms.

Incorporating a bandwidth map into a system is useful in describing the available bandwidth distribution. In this paper we utilize the datasets from GTube to model and predict bandwidth using more sophisticated *spatio-temporal geostatistics.* The focus of the approach is on obtaining the most accurate, predicted bandwidth values in unknown locations, given a relatively sparse dataset. Geostatistical algorithms can model several types of spatially distributed random variables while taking into account other dependent variables, resulting in the production of smoothed maps of previously measured discrete samples.

3. BACKGROUND

Geostatistics is a branch of statistics that is concerned with spatial or spatio-temporal data. It was originally developed for mining operations where the probability distributions of ore grades was needed [15]. It is widely used in many branches of geography in cases where extensive amounts of data representing random variables are observed over wide spatial regions that need to be analyzed and modeled. The method is also currently gaining attention in the field of spatial networks, such as transportation and mobility networks, cellular networks and power grids. Geostatistical algorithms are incorporated in geographic information systems (GIS) and the R statistical programming language and software environment, which are used in this study.

Data scientists approach geostatistical algorithms for the purpose of identifying the ways in which natural phenomena are subject to both spatial and temporal variations. Although geostatistics has not been extensively used in computer science research, we found it to be an applicable tool that is useful in modeling and predicting bandwidth values in mobile networks. Moreover, we found that it outperforms other state-of-the-art geo-prediction techniques in both accuracy and robustness.

The main requirement for geostatistical analysis to be applicable is the availability of data that are spatially distributed over a region, along with any other dependent variables (*e.g.*, the time when the measurements were obtained or any other variables that affect the measurements). Using these methods we are able to model and predict values in unknown locations. Likewise, from a temporal perspective, if sufficient information is available, we can model and predict *future* values at unknown locations.

3.1 Estimating Spatial Correlation: The Variogram

Geostatistics are concerned with random fields B measured at locations s_i. Typically, a limited number of occurrences of B is observed at sample locations, and the prediction (B^*) of B is required at non-observed locations. Geostatistical analysis involves the estimation and modeling of spatial correlations, represented by the covariance or semivariance. When analyzing geo-spatial data, describing the spatial pattern of a measured variable is of great importance. A common way of visualizing the spatial correlation of a variable is the variogram plot, which is a representation of the relationship between the semivariance and distance [3]. The basic idea of the variogram plot is to represent how the measurements vary with distance. Generally the x-axis of the plot represents the lag distances in which values are observed, while the y-axis is the semivariance, which is computed from the squared differences in the sample values as a function of the distances between all of the known points, as shown in Equation (1).

$$\gamma(h) = \frac{\sum_{i=1}^{N(h)} (B(s_i) - B(s_i + h))^2}{2N(h)}, \quad (1)$$

where the variables represent the following quantities

- s_i: the vector of spatial coordinates,
- h: the lag vector representing the distance between two spatial locations,
- $B(s_i)$: the sample value at location s_i,
- $B(s_i + h)$: the sample value at location $s_i + h$, and
- $N(h)$: the number of samples at distance h from s_i.

Plotting $\gamma(h)$ will result in the variogram graph that shows the relationship between the lag distance and the semivariance of the sample data. Finding an appropriate model that fits the variogram plot is the key to the efficient prediction of unknown values. A number of variogram models are commonly used in geostatistics and also available in the R statistical environment [4], which can be used to estimate the parameters needed for prediction.

To take the temporal factor into account, Equation (1) can be extended with a time component. In this case, each sample point s_i will be associated with a time t_i, and the separation is both spatial (by the vector h) and temporal, expressed by the vector u. Thus, the *spatio-temporal variogram* is computed as shown in Equation (2) below [19], where s_j and t_j indicate the sample point at spatio-temporal distance (h, u) from point s_i, and $N(h)$ is the number of samples at distance (h, u) from s_i, t_i.

$$\gamma(h, u) = \frac{\sum_{i=1}^{N(h,u)} (B(s_i, t_i) - B(s_j, t_j))^2}{2N(h, u)} \quad (2)$$

3.2 Interpolation Using Kriging

Kriging is similar to the technique of Inverse Distance Weighting (IDW) in that it weights the surrounding measured values to derive an estimate B^* for an unmeasured location. The general formula for both interpolators is formed as shown in Equation (3):

$$B^*(s_0) = \sum_{i=1}^{N} \lambda_i B(s_i), \quad (3)$$

where the variables represent the following quantities

- $B(s_i)$: the measured value at location s_i,
- λ_i: the unknown kriging weights,
- s_0: the prediction location, and
- N: number of samples at distance h from s_i.

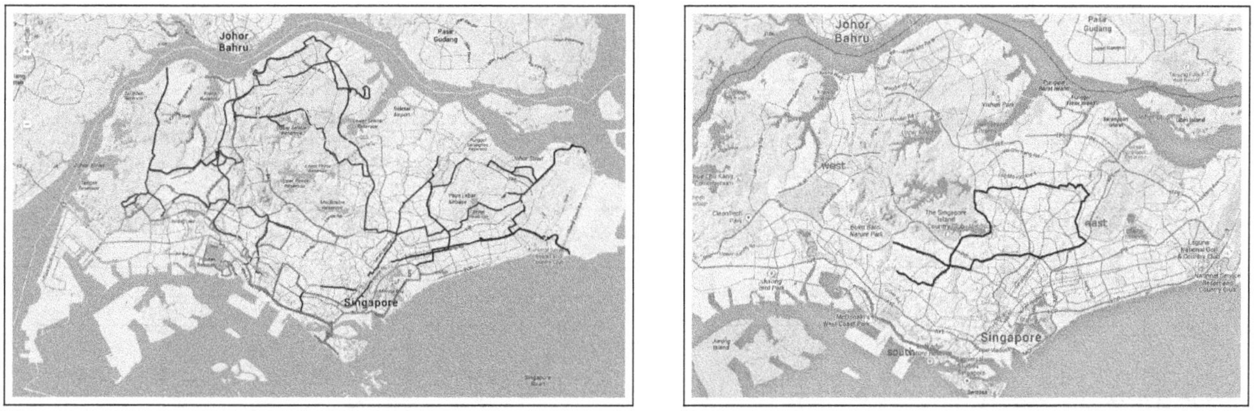

(a) The 2D map covers most of the Singapore island with measurements collected once on difference days.

(b) The 3D map covers three major routes (east, west, and south), each containing measurements performed three times a day over 7 days.

Figure 1: (a) Spatial (*2D map*) and (b) spatio-temporal (*3D map*) subsets of Dataset 1 used in this study.

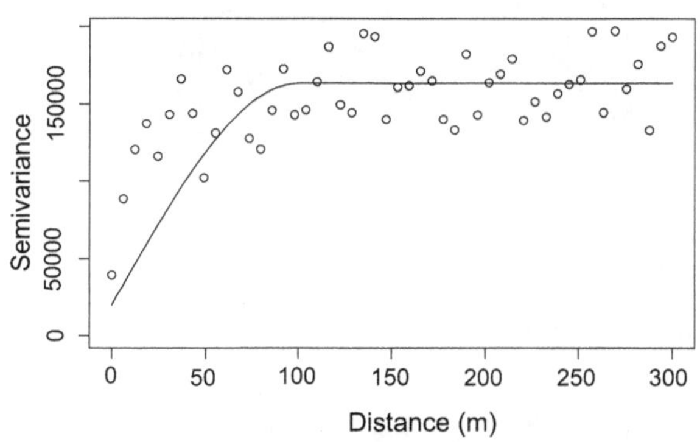

Figure 2: Spatial variogram applied to one day of the west route of the 3D map. The scattered points are the semivariance between samples separated by the corresponding distance on the horizontal axis, and the regression line is the variogram model (spherical) fit to the sample variogram.

In IDW, the weights depend only on the distances between sample points. The disadvantage of IDW is that it treats all points that fall within the search radius the same way, which in the case of cellular signals can be inadequate since the signal strength decays with respect to distance plus other factors. Kriging, on the other hand, is an unbiased estimator that uses different weighting functions that depend on the distance that separates the sample points, and the spatial arrangement expressed by the variogram model. Kriging weights are determined by minimizing the variance of the estimated bandwidth $E[(B - B^*)^2]$ using an optimization function like Lagrange multipliers. More details about kriging and its algorithms in R can be found in the documents by Bohling [4] and Gräler *et al.* [11].

4. GEO-PREDICTED BANDWIDTH

4.1 Datasets

In order to evaluate our proposed approach, we collected two datasets in an urban area along bus routes in Singapore. The details of each dataset are as follows.

Dataset 1 was collected in 2014 by a group of students that used public transportation buses and recorded a large set of bandwidth values every 10 seconds, associated with the corresponding location, instantaneous speed and time of day. An Android smartphone was used to collect GPS trajectories via an app called *GPS Essentials*, while bandwidth measurements were made via the *AdapComm* app [22]. Each GPS location was then related to the corresponding bandwidth measurement using the timestamps. We refer to the combined dataset as *bandwidth map*, which consists of data tuples of $\langle nid, t, s, P, bw \rangle$, where *nid* is the ID of the device, t is time at which the data was recorded, s represents the speed of the device, P is the location, and bw is the measured bandwidth. This dataset was collected during two separate periods for two different purposes. (a) The first period contains samples that cover most of Singapore and are measured only once each. This dataset is used to model the bandwidth map for spatial analysis only since it lacks temporal repetition. We refer to this subset as the *2D map*. (b) The second period contains samples that were measured along 3 major bus routes over 7 consecutive days and is used by our study for modeling the bandwidth to find the relationship between the separation distance, time and the sample points, and we refer to it as *3D map*. A visual representation of Dataset 1 is shown in Figure 1. Table 1 provides some statistics on Dataset 1.

Dataset 2 was collected more recently prior to the experiments conducted for this study and is not a subset of Dataset 1. It is a 3D map that has the time of day as an attribute. The samples were measured every 4 seconds on each route. This set covers a bus route inside our university campus and we have used it as input for the prediction module in the streaming experiments to evaluate the streaming quality based on the predicted bandwidth values. More details about Dataset 2 are described in Section 5

4.2 Spatial Analysis

The existing implementation of the bandwidth map in GTube consists of a database of bandwidth-location pairs. To obtain a future value of the bandwidth, a kNN-IDW interpolation method is performed. This step uses the position sent by the client as input, finds the k-nearest neighbors,

Table 1: Summary of Dataset 1, consisting of two subsets.

Dataset subset	1 (*2D map*)	2 (*3D map*)
Collection period	22 April to 4 May 2014	26 May to 5 August 2014
Measurement description	One-time measurement of each sample	Repeated measurements over 7 days, 3 times per day for each sample in one location
Total duration of collection (hh:mm:ss)	67:49:15	246:50:26
Number of measurements	12,801	32,896
Average bandwidth (Kbps)	5,375.7	2,763.4
Percentage of 4G data connection	86.30%	94.10%

and then performs inverse distance weighting (IDW) interpolation to estimate the bandwidth at the requested point. However, as mentioned in Section 3, the weights in IDW only depend on the distance between the sample points. In this study, we investigate the correlation between sample points and its effect on the predicted values through the concept of a variogram. Pure spatial variograms are 2D tables that match the lag distance h to the semivariance γ. A sample spatial variogram calculated from our 3D map is shown in Figure 2. The scattered points represent the semivariance between points separated by the corresponding distances on the x-axis, and the regression curve is the fitted variogram model (spherical) that describes the sample variogram.

4.3 Spatio-Temporal Analysis

In spatial variograms, the relationship between the distance between samples and the semivariance is the goal and time is rarely taken into consideration due to either its unavailability in the data, or that the spatial correlation is sufficient. However, there are cases and datasets in which performing spatio-temporal variograms is appropriate and reveals interesting information about the correlation between the measured variable and space and time. In our case, the measured bandwidth varies significantly during different times of a day even in a single location because of variations in user activities. Thus, we use spatio-temporal modeling and interpolation in order to estimate the future bandwidth.

In our 3D dataset, each bandwidth sample is associated with the GPS location and the Universal Coordinated Time (UTC). The variogram calculated can be either represented as a 3D surface or a levelplot instead of a set of scattered points in 2D and is termed a *spatio-temporal variogram*, which is a collection of spatial variograms at different time lags. Our dataset is collected during 7 days, three times in each day, *i.e.*, morning, afternoon, and evening. Figure 3a depicts the correlation between the bandwidth and both location and time as a levelplot. The color scale ranges from dark blue, which indicates a strong correlation, to yellow as a weak correlation. Seven spatial variograms are calculated and shown as rows, the first one (the lowest in the plot) represents the spatial variogram of the measurements separated by zero days (measured on the same day), the second one shows the correlation between the set of points that are one day apart, and so on. The further we deviate in time, as expected the less correlated the measurements are (*e.g.*, those separated by two days are more correlated than those separated by 7 days). This is useful in the prediction part where we can reduce and optimize the amount of data to be stored on the server to a few days worth of measurements.

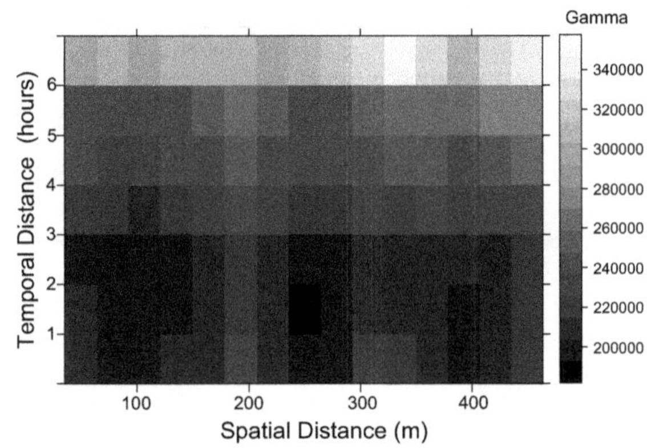

(a) Spatio-temporal variogram depicting the correlation between the bandwidth measurements separated by a series of distances (the x-axis) and 7 days of temporal distance.

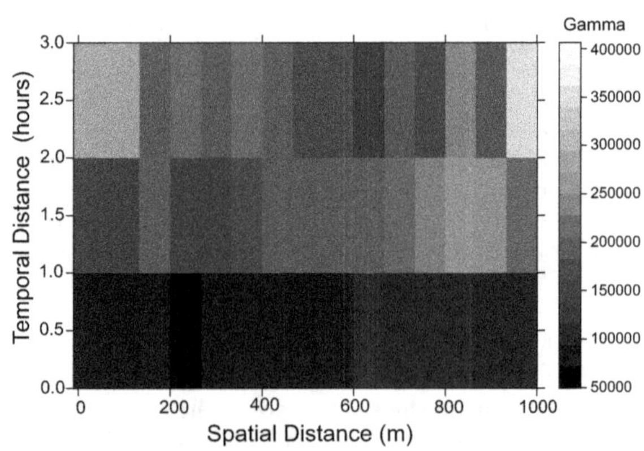

(b) Spatio-temporal variogram of the east route, with temporal separation of 1, 2, and 3 hours.

Figure 3: Spatio-temporal variograms with different temporal lags.

On a smaller temporal scale, the behavior of the bandwidth in one day varies dramatically during the day in the same location as the study in GTube [13] revealed. Plotting a spatio-temporal variogram to represent the correlation, but in hours instead of days, would be helpful. However, our data is collected during three times of the day, three hours in the morning, afternoon and evening. That is why we determined the maximum temporal separation distance of the spatio-temporal variogram to be 3 hours. That is, 3 spatial variograms are generated, each separated by a temporal distance of 1, 2, and 3 hours, respectively. Fig-

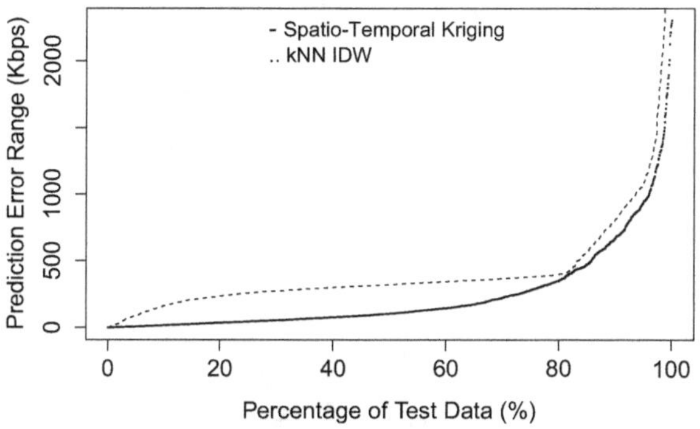

Figure 4: Prediction results of spatio-temporal kriging compared with the kNN IDW approach with $k = 10$ (lower is better).

ure 3b shows a sample spatio-temporal variogram from the east route with a maximum temporal separation of 3 hours.

4.3.1 Kriging Interpolation

Simple approaches like inverse distance weighted predictions are well known and have been applied for many years. Nowadays, modern sensors allow the observation of different variables at an increasing temporal resolution, producing rich spatio-temporal data sets. This calls for theory and methods to handle these datasets to gain a better understanding of the observed variables. Kriging is applicable and can be used in spatio-temporal prediction as well as in pure spatial prediction.

For spatio-temporal interpolation using kriging, the same dataset is partitioned for training and testing. The training dataset is used to compute the variogram, fit an appropriate model and to be used to derive the weights for kriging. The model that describes the spatio-temporal variogram is the product-sum model. For the interested reader, all the theory behind spatio-temporal covariance models and the methods of fitting are explained in Gräler *et al.* [11].

We implemented two algorithms to compare their prediction results with those of spatio-temporal kriging, kNN IDW from Hao *et al.* [13] and the Mean of past Samples that are in the same location (with a granularity of a 100m radius around the queried location) from Riiser *et al.* [17]. Table 2 summarizes the prediction results of these three methods. It is worth mentioning here that the same training and testing datasets were used for the three methods. However, the mean of past values takes each measurement in the testing dataset and looks for those that are within a 100 meters vicinity from it in the training dataset, which is not applicable for all points in the testing dataset due to the sparsity of the collected data.

Figure 4 shows the CDF of the prediction results using kriging compared with kNN IDW (with $k = 10$). The reason for not including the pure spatial predictions in the comparison is because the data set contains many duplicate spatial points that have different timestamps, and this creates errors in computing the spatial variogram where all the measurements should be taken at unique locations. The prediction error range (x-axis) is the absolute value of the difference between the predicted and observed value at that point and time. It shows that 50% of the test data achieves an error of 105 Kbps or less. The mean absolute error (calculated through Equation (4)) is 239.26 Kbps. Table 2 summarizes the prediction results for both spatio-temporal kriging and the kNN method with $k = 10$.

$$MeanError = \frac{1}{n}\sum_{i=1}^{n} |predicted_i - real_i|, \qquad (4)$$

where $observed_i$ and $real_i$ are the predicted and true values, respectively.

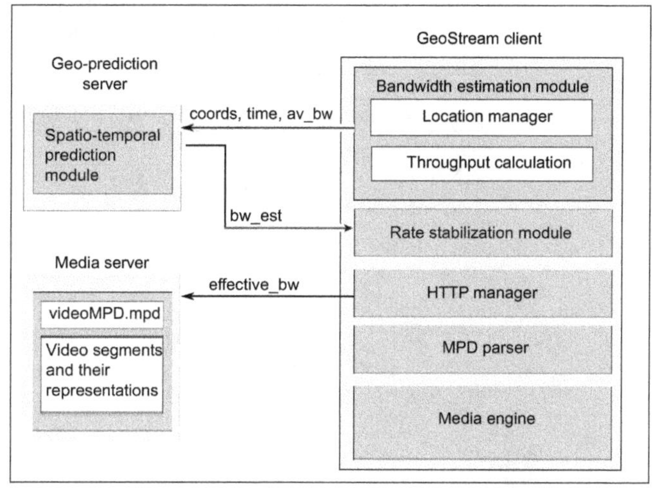

Figure 5: Detailed GeoStream architecture.

5. STREAMING EXPERIMENTS

The detailed GeoStream architecture is depicted in Figure 5. It consists of a geo-prediction server that implements the module which uses spatio-temporal geostatistics to model and interpolate the values in the bandwidth map. The underlying map database is frequently updated depending on the users' activities and changes in network conditions. The module sends the clients the estimated bandwidth (*bw_estimate*) as a response to incoming requests and at the same time collects their currently measured, available bandwidth (*av_bw*). The clients implement DASH-compatible video players. Whenever a video session starts, a player asks the geo-prediction server for the bandwidth estimate at its current location and time (*gps_coords, timestamp, av_bw*) and this estimate is input into a rate stabilization module to calculate the effective bandwidth (*effective_bw*) that is used to fetch the appropriate segment from the media server. The download time of the video segment is measured and used to calculate the instantaneous available bandwidth (*av_bw*) which is sent to the geo-prediction server to update its database. The media server is implemented in a conventional, DASH-compliant web server that manages the video files which are segmented into a number of chunks, each transcoded into different qualities.

To observe the effects of the geo-predicted bandwidth on the user-perceived quality, we conducted real-time experiments using the architecture shown in Figure 6a. We extended ExoPlayer[1], which is Google developed Android media player that supports DASH-compliant video playback, to include fetching the estimated available bandwidth from

[1]https://google.github.io/ExoPlayer/

Table 2: Statistics of prediction error of three different approaches: spatio-temporal kriging (Kriging), kNN IDW with $k = 10$, and Mean of past Samples. All measurements are in Kbps.

	Prediction error (Kbps)					
Prediction method	Minimum	1st Quantile	Median	Mean	3rd Quantile	Maximum
Kriging	1.35	158.3	217.6	239.3	271.0	1,422
kNN IDW	1.00	259.0	322.0	417.0	382.0	3,190
Mean of past Samples	1.00	78.0	196.0	362.0	419.0	2,270

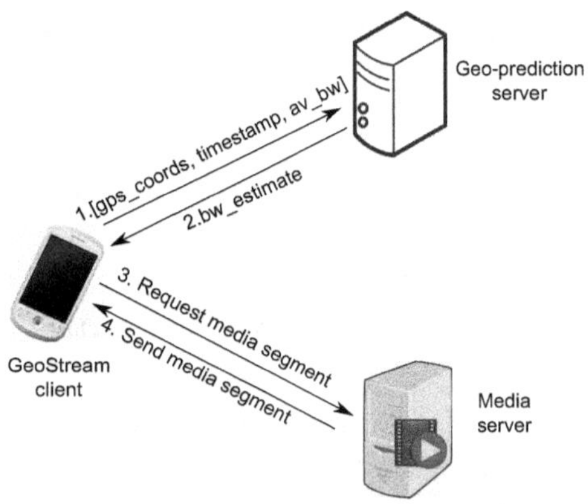

(a) Request and response flow in the architecture of GeoStream.

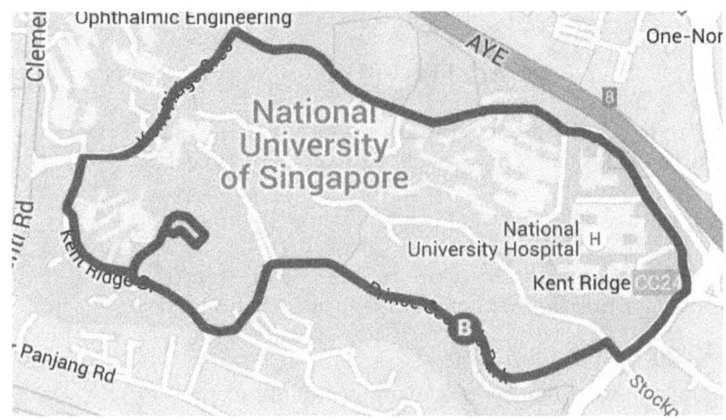

(b) Bus route of Dataset 2 used for the streaming experiments.

Figure 6: Data flow in the experimental setup and the bus route that was used to collect Dataset 2 for the experiments.

the geo-prediction server and use this value as input into the ExoPlayer's rate stabilization function for smooth playback (see details in Section 5.2). The geo-prediction server consists of a web server that is connected via the geo-prediction module to an SQL database storing the bandwidth measurements which were collected using crowdsourcing. When the server receives location and time information from streaming clients it provides them with the correct bandwidth estimates in return.

For comparison purposes, in addition to our geo-prediction module, we further implemented the kNN IDW method and the *Mean of past Samples* approach from Hao *et al.* [13] and Riiser *et al.* [17], respectively. To ensure the same network conditions for all streaming sessions, we first conducted a test for the geo-prediction module and recorded the raw bandwidth samples along with the GPS coordinates in a trace file while the video was being played. Subsequently we used a network emulator to constrain the available bandwidth for the other sessions to the trace data recorded in the first test. Additionally, instead of measuring the real location coordinates, the recorded GPS coordinates were fed into the player and used to query for the estimated bandwidth.

5.1 Data Collection

To measure the bandwidth GeoStream uses ExoPlayer's native bandwidth estimation technique which divides the number of bytes transmitted in each stream by the elapsed time it took for the data to reach the client. We measured the available bandwidth under real world mobile network conditions by traveling on the NUS campus bus at different times of the day for three consecutive days. The Android device used was a Sony model Xperia Z3 Compact D5833 with the GeoStream app installed. Figure 6b illustrates the route of the data collection of Dataset 2 which was used later by the streaming clients to evaluate the QoE.

5.2 Rate Stabilization

In the GeoStream player, the predicted bandwidth estimate from the server is not directly used in determining which quality of the next video segment to fetch. Rather, the player makes use of the ExoPlayer's built-in stabilization function, which is fed with the bandwidth estimates instead of the usual bandwidth measurements. The rate stabilization ensures that segment video qualities change gradually, even if the bandwidth changes abruptly, which results in a better QoE [10]. The rate stabilization algorithm works as follows. Before fetching each segment, the player retrieves the bandwidth estimate from the geo-prediction server and uses it in a function which calculates a desired percentile over a sliding window of weighted values of past bandwidth estimates. A maximum total weight is configured, such that when it is reached, the oldest value in the window receives less weight until it reaches zero and is removed from the window. We term the output of the rate stabilization function the *effective bandwidth*. This value is used when determining which video quality segment to fetch next, which is described in Section 5.3.

Note that rate stabilization has both advantages and disadvantages. While it will smooth out abrupt changes in quality, it may also be slow to adapt in highly fluctuating wireless networks. Improving this part of the adaptation framework is part of our future work.

5.3 Quality Switching

During playback, if the calculated effective bandwidth of the next segment is lower (higher) than the actual bitrate value of the current segment, then the client requests a segment with a lower (higher) bitrate that still does not exceed the effective bandwidth. In GeoStream, the quality is increased if the buffered content represents at least 1 second worth of playback duration. On the other hand, it is decreased when the buffered content represents less than 5 seconds of playback time. The values of these thresholds play an important role in reducing rebuffering time as was shown by Huang *et al.* [14]. However, we choose these specific values empirically to observe how the switching reacts with respect to the predicted bandwidth.

5.4 Evaluation Metrics

To evaluate the spatio-temporal prediction method, we used the collected bandwidth measurements as input data for all three methods for comparison. We streamed the Big Buck Bunny[2] movie using the GeoStream app to see how closely the predicted and the measured values would match.

Per-segment metrics: GeoStream records data representing three metrics alongside each fetched segment for evaluation:

- **Available bandwidth**: The raw estimate of the instantaneous bandwidth, which is the size of the fetched segment(s) divided by the transfer time.
- **Effective bandwidth**: The smoothed value of the predicted bandwidth along with the past values.
- **Video bitrate**: The representation of the video segment that is fetched according to the effective bandwidth.

Per-streaming session metrics: we also record data for four other metrics at the end of each streaming session, that describe the overall quality of the video streaming experience:

- **Average bitrate**: the average of all fetched video segment bitrates:

$$BR_{avg} = \frac{\sum_{i=0}^{N} BR_i}{N}$$

  where i is the segment index and N is the total number of segments.
- **Number of quality switches**: which corresponds to how many times the player fetches a segment of a different representation than the previous one. High values indicate very frequent switching which leads to poor QoE.
- **Total buffer stall count**: the number of video stalls during playback.
- **Average buffer delay**: the total buffering time (including the start-up delay) divided by the session length.

5.5 Streaming Results of Geo-Predicted Bandwidth

We streamed the Big Buck Bunny video to see how well the predicted values match the real measured bandwidth trace. Figure 7 shows the raw captured bandwidth compared to the effective bandwidth and the video bitrate for the video session with the kriging-predicted bandwidth module. At the beginning of the session, the effective bandwidth is the geo-predicted bandwidth alone with no smoothing (due to no past measurements), and as the playback progresses, it starts adapting to the available bandwidth by taking into account the recently observed raw bandwidth values. If the bandwidth is over-estimated, buffer stalls will occur due to fetching a high quality segments during a low-bandwidth period. As Figure 7 illustrates, the video bitrate varies between 800 Kbps and 1.5 Mbps with an average of around 1 Mbps. However, there are frequent switches in the bitrate due to bandwidth fluctuations, but overall the video experienced a total of 9 buffer stalls with an average length of just 0.106 seconds each.

To take the temporal factor into account for both algorithms by Hao *et al.* [13] and Riiser *et al.* [17], we set a time window when querying for a new bandwidth value from the server. A 3-hour window was centered around the queried sample timestamp. Figure 8 shows the streaming results for kNN IDW from GTube [13] with the mentioned time window. The effective bandwidth is over-estimated at several points during playback (around 100 s and 300–400 s of the video), which leads to frequent and long buffer stalls. A total of 11 stalls occurred with an average length of 1.1 seconds each. The session achieved an average bitrate of around 1 Mbps, ranging from 500 Kbps to 1.5 Mbps, with 25 quality switches. Notably, the video playback suffers from large fluctuations in quality, which has a negative effect on QoE.

Lastly, Figure 9 shows the streaming results for bandwidth predicted by calculating the mean of past values that are in the same location, with a granularity of 100 m around the point [17], and a time window of 3 hours. Since this method is straightforward and considers all the points that fall into the specified diameter, we observed an average video bitrate of 923.058 Kbps, ranging from 577 Kbps to 1,207 Kbps, and we experienced switching in quality 21 times throughout the video. The playback also suffered from more frequent buffer stalls with an average duration of 0.6 seconds each since the bandwidth was overestimated many times during playback.

5.6 Comparison

Table 3 summarizes the measurement data of the four quality metrics collected during the streaming experiments with three different bandwidth prediction methods. We observe that the kriging approach outperforms the other two methods in all four of the metrics, albeit only slightly in three of them. It achieves a marginally higher average video bitrate compared to kNN IDW and results in fewer quality switches and buffer stalls over both the other methods. However, a compelling difference is observable in the buffering delay, where kriging achieves a significantly lower value. Due to kNN IDW's less accurate predictions, the playback suffers from long freezing periods which likely leads to a poorer overall video experience. Notably, while the average bitrate of the kriging and the kNN IDW methods are similar, the latter results in significantly more quality fluctuations (illustrated in the bitrate curve in Figure 8). The third method that calculates the Mean of past Samples clearly achieves results that indicate a worse user-perceived quality. The experienced video bitrates are lower and the video has more quality switches compared to kriging. Overall the kriging approach shows that it has merit and beneficially impacts four of the factors that contribute to a user's perceived QoE.

[2]https://www.bigbuckbunny.org/

Table 3: Video quality statistics of video sessions for the three geo-prediction methods.

Prediction method	Average bitrate (Kbps)	Number of quality switches	Buffer stall count	Average buffering delay (sec)
Kriging	1,035.735	22	9	0.106
kNN IDW	1,033.432	25	11	1.100
Mean of past Samples	923.058	29	21	0.647

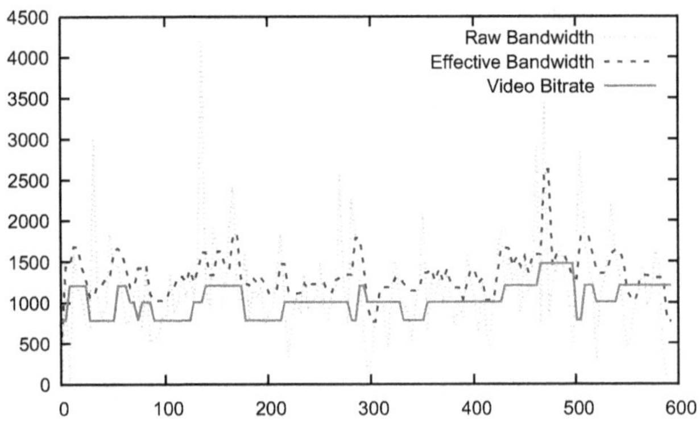

Figure 7: Kriging bandwidth prediction: The raw and effective bandwidth plotted together with the video bitrate for a streaming session.

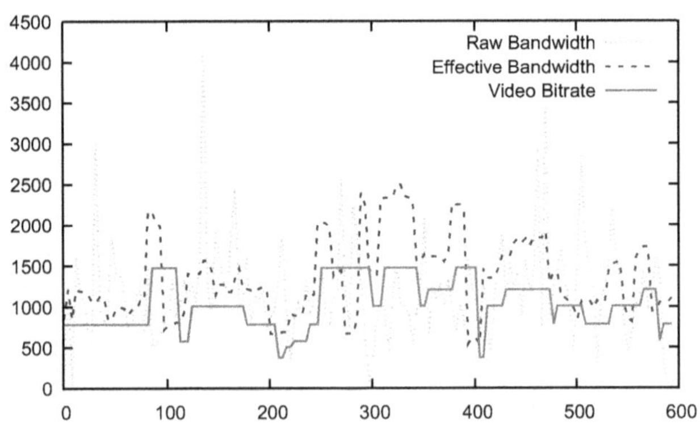

Figure 8: kNN IDW bandwidth prediction: The raw and effective bandwidth plotted together with the video bitrate for a streaming session. While the average video bitrate is similar to the case with kriging bandwidth prediction (see Figure 7 and Table 3), the fluctuations are much larger.

6. REAL-WORLD SCENARIOS

In this section we discuss two main aspects regarding the method we used to model our data. The first point elaborates on the issues related to maintaining the consistency of the data in the server while the second concerns scenarios which include handovers between cell carriers.

6.1 Maintaining the Bandwidth Map

As mentioned in Section 4, when the users query for bandwidth provided their location and timestamp, the server stores these values and adds them to the bandwidth map. However, the size of the map will grow dramatically if we keep all measurements. Having a proper replacement technique is necessary. Plus, having too many samples in the

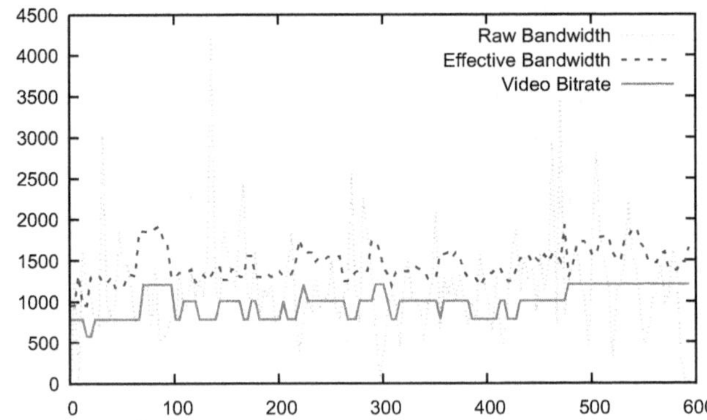

Figure 9: Mean of past Samples bandwidth prediction: The raw and effective bandwidth plotted together with the video bitrate for a streaming session. The Mean of past Samples results are computed in the same location with a granularity of 100 m radius around each point and a time window of 3 hours.

modeling part can result in over-fitting. This is an open issue and is beyond the scope of this paper.

6.2 Handover Scenarios

In practice, a vehicle moves in a speed that results in changing the cell tower that each mobile device is associated with. Handover frequencies depends on the speed of the vehicle which is available in our collected Dataset1, but handover issues are not explicitly addressed since they occur seamlessly. Having such factors implicit in the measurements may be considered an advantage of our model. It can also be applied to datasets from other cellphone carriers.

7. CONCLUSIONS

In this study we introduce and describe GeoStream, a video streaming system that uses geostatistics to analyze spatio-temporal bandwidth measurements and then provide location-based bandwidth predictions. A bandwidth map is maintained by a central server and the streaming clients both provide measurements and perform queries to obtain bandwidth predictions. Using datasets that were crowd-sourced by the clients we were able to find a relationship between the distance among samples, the time of their capture and the semivariance, such that the higher the deviation in space and time, the less correlated the bandwidth values are. This relationship is expressed through a statistical variogram. We leverage this relationship to predict future bandwidth values at unknown locations using kriging interpolation, resulting in a better accuracy than previous methods. We further conducted real world streaming experiments to demonstrate the effectiveness of such geo-predicted bandwidth values. The proposed method outperforms existing algorithms especially in terms of buffering delay. However, the rate adaptation and smoothing algorithms that are part of the adaptation logic in any client are crucial to obtain a high QoE, and further investigation is needed to discover the optimal combination of these algorithms and their parameter settings. Moreover, our currently implemented system does not take multiple, concurrent streaming users into account, which can significantly impact the available bandwidth estimates. Incorporating methods to improve the fairness in streaming systems over wireless networks is part of our future work.

Acknowledgments

This research has been supported in part by Singapore's Ministry of Education Academic Research Fund Tier 1, grant number T1 251RES1415, by the National Natural Science Foundation of China under Grant no. 61472266, and by the National University of Singapore (Suzhou) Research Institute, 377 Lin Quan Street, Suzhou Industrial Park, Jiang Su, People's Republic of China, 215123.

8. REFERENCES

[1] MPEG-DASH Specification. ISO/IEC 23009-1:2012 Information technology – Dynamic adaptive streaming over HTTP (DASH) – Part 1: Media presentation description and segment formats, April 2012.

[2] Adobe Systems. Adobe HTTP Dynamic Streaming. www.adobe.com/products/httpdynamicstreaming. Retrieved 26 July 2016.

[3] R. S. Bivand, E. Pebesma, and V. Gómez-Rubio. Interpolation and Geostatistics. In *Applied Spatial Data Analysis with R*, pages 213–261. Springer, 2013.

[4] G. Bohling. Kriging. Technical report, 2005.

[5] Cisco Systems, Inc. Cisco Visual Networking Index: Global Mobile Data Traffic Forecast Update, 2014-2019. White Paper, 2014.

[6] N. Cranley, P. Perry, and L. Murphy. User Perception of Adapting Video Quality. *International Journal of Human-Computer Studies*, 64(8):637–647, 2006.

[7] Digital Strategy Consulting. Mobile Streaming Trends: How are Consumers Using Their Smartphones and Tablets? Infographic, 2013.

[8] F. Dobrian, V. Sekar, A. Awan, I. Stoica, D. Joseph, A. Ganjam, J. Zhan, and H. Zhang. Understanding the Impact of Video Quality on User Engagement. *ACM SIGCOMM Computer Communication Review*, 41(4):362–373, 2011.

[9] S. Fang and R. Zimmermann. EnAcq: Energy-Efficient GPS Trajectory Data Acquisition Based on Improved Map Matching. In *Proceedings of the* 19th *ACM SIGSPATIAL International Conference on Advances in Geographic Information Systems*, pages 221–230, 2011.

[10] M. Grafl and C. Timmerer. Representation Switch Smoothing for Adaptive HTTP Streaming. In *Proceedings of the* 4th *International Workshop Perceptual Quality of Systems (PQS)*, pages 178–183, 2013.

[11] B. Gräler, E. Pebesma, and G. Heuvelink. Spatio-Temporal Geostatistics using gstat. 2015.

[12] R. Hamberg and H. de Ridder. Time-Varying Image Quality: Modeling the Relation Between Instantaneous and Overall Quality. *SMPTE journal*, 108(11):802–811, 1999.

[13] J. Hao, R. Zimmermann, and H. Ma. GTube: Geo-predictive Video Streaming over HTTP in Mobile Environments. In *Proceedings of the* 5th *ACM Multimedia Systems Conference*, pages 259–270, 2014.

[14] T.-Y. Huang, R. Johari, N. McKeown, M. Trunnell, and M. Watson. A Buffer-Based Approach to Rate Adaptation: Evidence from a Large Video Streaming Service. *ACM SIGCOMM Computer Communication Review*, 44(4):187–198, 2015.

[15] D. Kbiob. A Statistical Approach to Some Basic Mine Valuation Problems on the Witwatersrand. *Journal of Chemical, Metallurgical, and Mining Society of South Africa*, 1951.

[16] R. Pantos and W. May. HTTP Live Streaming. *IETF Internet-Draft*, April 2016.

[17] H. Riiser, H. S. Bergsaker, P. Vigmostad, P. Halvorsen, and C. Griwodz. A Comparison of Quality Scheduling in Commercial Adaptive HTTP Streaming Solutions on a 3G Network. In *Proceedings of the* 4th *Workshop on Mobile Video*, pages 25–30, 2012.

[18] D. C. Robinson, Y. Jutras, and V. Craciun. Subjective Video Quality Assessment of HTTP Adaptive Streaming Technologies. *Bell Labs Technical Journal*, 16(4):5–23, 2012.

[19] M. Sherman. *Spatial Statistics and Spatio-Temporal Data: Covariance Functions and Directional Properties*. John Wiley & Sons, 2011.

[20] V. Singh, J. Ott, and I. D. Curcio. Predictive Buffering for Streaming Video in 3G Networks. In *IEEE International Symposium on a World of Wireless, Mobile and Multimedia Networks (WoWMoM)*, pages 1–10, 2012.

[21] T. Stockhammer. Dynamic Adaptive Streaming over HTTP–: Standards and Design Principles. In *Proceedings of the Second Annual ACM Conference on Multimedia Systems*, pages 133–144, 2011.

[22] R. Thapliya and C. Hu. AdapComm: A Bandwidth Allocation Methodology for Multimedia Applications in Wireless Networks. In *Proceedings of the 2013 ACM SIGCOMM Workshop on Future Human-Centric Multimedia Networking*, pages 27–32, 2013.

[23] J. Yao, S. S. Kanhere, and M. Hassan. An Empirical Study of Bandwidth Predictability in Mobile Computing. In *Proceedings of the third ACM International Workshop on Wireless Network Testbeds, Experimental Evaluation and Characterization*, pages 11–18, 2008.

[24] J. Yao, S. S. Kanhere, and M. Hassan. Improving QoS in High-Speed Mobility Using Bandwidth Maps. *IEEE Transactions on Mobile Computing*, 11(4):603–617, 2012.

[25] J. Yao, S. S. Kanhere, I. Hossain, and M. Hassan. Empirical Evaluation of HTTP Adaptive Streaming Under Vehicular Mobility. In *International Conference on Research in Networking*, pages 92–105. Springer, 2011.

[26] A. Zambelli. IIS Smooth Streaming Technical Overview. *Microsoft Corporation*, 3:40, 2009.

Micro Tells Macro: Predicting the Popularity of Micro-Videos via a Transductive Model

Jingyuan Chen[†], Xuemeng Song[‡,†*], Liqiang Nie[‡,†], Xiang Wang[†], Hanwang Zhang[†], Tat-Seng Chua[†]
[†] National University of Singapore, [‡] Shandong University
{jingyuanchen91, sxmustc, nieliqiang, xiangwang.nus, hanwangzhang}@gmail.com,
dcscts@nus.edu.sg

ABSTRACT

Micro-videos, a new form of user generated contents (UGCs), are gaining increasing enthusiasm. Popular micro-videos have enormous commercial potential in many ways, such as online marketing and brand tracking. In fact, the popularity prediction of traditional UGCs including tweets, web images, and long videos, has achieved good theoretical underpinnings and great practical success. However, little research has thus far been conducted to predict the popularity of the bite-sized videos. This task is non-trivial due to three reasons: 1) micro-videos are short in duration and of low quality; 2) they can be described by multiple heterogeneous channels, spanning from social, visual, acoustic to textual modalities; and 3) there are no available benchmark dataset and discriminant features that are suitable for this task. Towards this end, we present a transductive multi-modal learning model. The proposed model is designed to find the optimal latent common space, unifying and preserving information from different modalities, whereby micro-videos can be better represented. This latent space can be used to alleviate the information insufficiency problem caused by the brief nature of micro-videos. In addition, we built a benchmark dataset and extracted a rich set of popularity-oriented features to characterize the popular micro-videos. Extensive experiments have demonstrated the effectiveness of the proposed model. As a side contribution, we have released the dataset, codes and parameters to facilitate other researchers.

Keywords

Micro-Videos; Popularity Prediction; Multi-View Learning

1. INTRODUCTION

The last couple of years have witnessed the unprecedented growth of smart mobile devices, enabling users to record life stories vividly with short videos and then instantly upload them to social media websites, such as Snapchat[1] and Vine[2]. Since micro-videos, acting more like 'live action photographs', are usually short in length, they need little bandwidth and hence gain tremendous user enthusiasm. The limits regarding the maximum length of micro-videos on Snapchat and Vine, are set as 10 and 6 seconds, respectively. Considering Vine as an example, its video length distribution over our collected 303,242 Vine videos is illustrated in Figure 1. Micro-videos, representing a new form of user generated contents (UGCs), can be viewed, discussed and even reposted by users once they are uploaded, which leads to their rapid rise. It is reported that Vine hit 1.5 billion daily loops[3] in 2015[4] and Snapchat hit 7 billion daily views in 2016[5]. As a video messaging platform, it is hard to crawl micro-videos from Snapchat. Hence, we focus on Vine here, which can be gathered more easily for research.

Interestingly, among the tremendous volume of micro-videos, some popular ones will be widely viewed and spread by users, while many only gain little attention. This phenomena is similar to many existing social media sites, such as Twitter[6]. For example, the micro-video about the explosion that interrupted during the France-Germany soccer match in 2015 has been successfully looped by over 330 million times. Obviously, if we can identify the hot and popular micro-videos in advance, it will benefit many applications, such as online marketing and network reservation. Regarding online marketing, the accurate early prediction of popular micro-videos can facilitate companies' planning of advertising campaigns and thus maximizing their revenues. For network service providers, they can timely reserve adequate distributed storage and bandwidth for popular ones, based on the prediction. Therefore, it is highly desirable to develop an effective scheme to accurately predict the popularity of micro-videos.

However, the popularity prediction of micro-videos is non-trivial due to the following challenges. First of all, due to the short duration of micro-videos, each modality can only provide limited information, the so-called modality limitation. Fortunately, micro-videos always involve multiple modalities, namely, social, visual, acoustic

*Xuemeng Song is the corresponding author.

MM '16, October 15-19, 2016, Amsterdam, Netherlands

DOI: http://dx.doi.org/10.1145/2964284.2964314

[1] https://snapchat.com.
[2] https://vine.co.
[3] Loops refer to the times a micro-video has been viewed.
[4] http://blog.vine.co.
[5] http://goo.gl/YYnBbd.
[6] https://twitter.com.

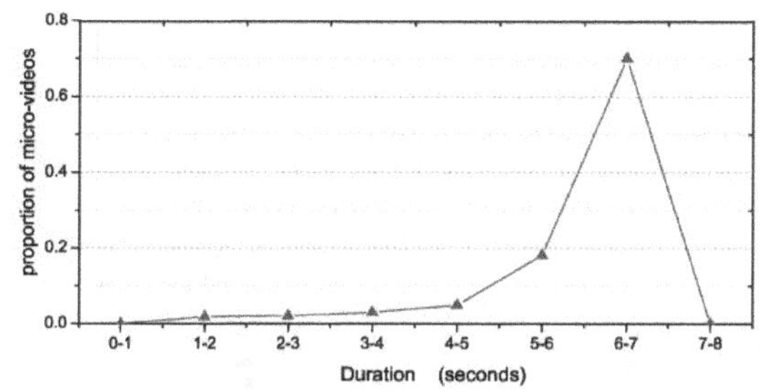

Figure 1: Duration distribution over our collected 303, 242 micro-videos.

and textual[7] modalities. In a sense, these modalities are co-related rather than independent and essentially characterize the same micro-videos. Therefore, the major challenge lies on how to effectively fuse micro-videos' heterogeneous clues from multiple modalities [31, 30, 36]. The most naive strategies are early fusion and late fusion [27]. They, however, fail to account for the relatedness among multiple modalities. Therefore, it is important to take modality relatedness into consideration. Secondly, due to certain external factors, such as camera shaking and lighting condition, some modalities of the micro-videos, such as visual or acoustic ones, may be of poor quality, which is another kind of modality limitation. Hence, learning directly from the original feature spaces of modalities, which was adopted by most multi-modal learning methods may be imprecise. Consequently, to improve the learning performance, how to compensate the noisy modality with reliable ones poses a crucial challenge for us. The last challenge we are facing is the lack of benchmark dataset to support our research. We found that both the contents and social influence of micro-video publishers would account for their popularity. As far as we know, the only available micro-video dataset [24] does not contain the important textual and social modalities and is lack of popularity indicators as the ground truth, which makes it unsuitable for our research. It is thus necessary to build a comprehensive micro-video dataset and further extract a rich set of discriminant features to enhance the learning performance.

To address the aforementioned challenges, we present a novel **T**ransductive **M**ulti-mod**AL** **L**earning approach, TMALL for short, to predicting the popularity of micro-videos. As illustrated in Figure 2, we first crawl a representative micro-video dataset from Vine and develop a rich set of popularity-oriented features from multi-modalities. We then perform multi-modal learning to predict the popularity of micro-videos, which seamlessly takes the modality relatedness and modality limitation into account by utilizing a common space shared by all modalities. We assume that there exists an optimal common space, which maintains the original intrinsic characteristics of micro-videos in the original spaces. In the light of this, all modalities are forced to be correlated. Meanwhile, micro-videos with different popularity can be better separated in such optimal common space, as compared to that of each single modality. In a sense, we alleviate the modality limitation problem. Extensive experiments on this real-world dataset have well-validated our work.

Our main contributions can be summarized in threefold:

- We approached the popularity prediction of micro-videos by proposing a TMALL model, which is able to simultaneously model the modality relatedness and handle the modality limitations by introducing a common space shared among all modalities. Moreover, we have derived its closed-form solution rigorously.
- We developed a rich set of popularity-oriented features from multiple modalities to comprehensively characterize the popular micro-videos. Apart from numerical results, we also provided several deep insights based on the experimental results.
- We constructed a large-scale micro-video dataset, comprising of 303, 242 micro-videos, 98, 166 users and 120, 324 following relationships. We have released our compiled dataset, codes and parameters[8] to facilitate other researchers to repeat our experiments and verify their proposed approaches.

The remainder of this paper is structured as follows. Section 2 reviews the related work. Data preparation is introduced in Section 3. Sections 4 and 5 detail the proposed TMALL model and the feature extraction, respectively. Section 6 presents the experimental results and analysis, followed by our concluding remarks in Section 7.

2. RELATED WORK

Popularity predication and multi-view learning are both related to this work.

2.1 Popularity Prediction

Due to its enormous commercial potential, popularity prediction of UGCs has attracted great attention from both the industry and academia [12, 20, 5, 29, 11]. Hong et al. [12] explored the popularity prediction of tweets, which is measured by the number of future retweets, by introducing a rich set of features, such as topological features, temporal features and meta features. Beyond the text popularity prediction, McParlane et al. [20] focused on the popularity of images. They extracted some sophisticated features and cast the task of image popularity prediction as a problem of binary classification, where the given image would be classified as popular or not. Later, Cappallo et al. [5] proposed a latent ranking method for the image popularity prediction solely based on the visual content. The proposed method was evaluated on several image datasets collected from micro-blogging and photo-sharing websites. Although huge success has been achieved by these approaches, limited efforts have thus far been dedicated to the problem of video popularity prediction, where multiple modalities coexist. Noting this gap, Trzcinski et al. [29] shifted from images to videos, and studied the problem of video popularity prediction utilizing both the visual clues and the early popularity pattern of the video once it is released. However, this approach suffered from two limitations. First, the proposed approach can only work on videos that have been published over a certain period. Second, the authors only used the traditional machine learning method—Support Vector Regression (SVR), which failed to make full use of the relationship among modalities. As a complement, we aim to timely predict the popularity of a given micro-video even before it get published by proposing a novel multi-modal learning scheme.

[7] Micro-videos are usually associated with certain textual data, such as video descriptions given by the video owners.

[8] The dataset can be accessible via http://acmmm2016.wix.com/micro-videos.

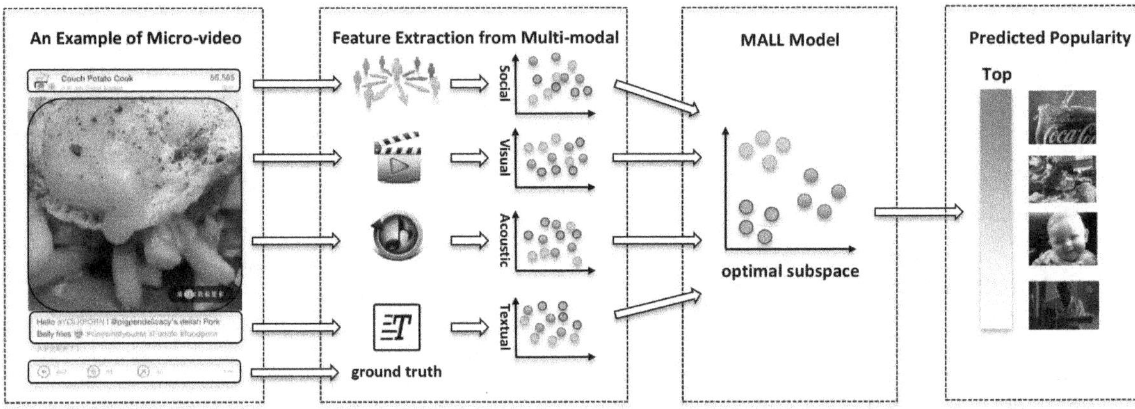

Figure 2: Micro-video popularity prediction via our proposed TMALL model.

2.2 Multi-View Learning

To deal with data containing multiple modalities, multi-view learning is a highly feasible paradigm. Multi-view learning is designed to improve the learning performance by introducing a function to model each view and jointly optimizing all functions. Existing work follows this line can be roughly classified into two categories: co-training and subspace learning. Co-training algorithms usually train separate learners on distinct views, which are then imposed to be consistent across views. Sindhwani et. al. [26] introduced a co-regularization framework for multi-view semi-supervised learning, as an extension of supervised regularization algorithms. Noticing that corruption may exist among different views, Christoudias et al. [7] proposed an approach for multi-view learning taking the view disagreement into consideration. In contrast, subspace learning approaches hold the general assumption that different views are generated from a latent view. Chaudhuri et al. [6] first employed canonical correlation analysis (CCA) to learn an efficient subspace, on which traditional machine learning algorithms can be applied. Gao et al. [9] later introduced a novel multi-view subspace clustering method, which is able to simultaneously perform clustering on the subspace of each view and guarantee the consistency among multiple views by a common clustering structure.

Overall, compelling success has been achieved by multi-view learning models on various problems, such as categorization [26, 28], clustering [6, 9] and multimedia retrieval [18, 19]. However, to the best of our knowledge, limited efforts have been dedicated to applying multi-view learning in the context of micro-video popularity prediction, which is the major concern of our work.

3. DATA COLLECTION

This section details the dataset setup, which covers the crawling strategy, and ground truth construction.

3.1 Crawling Strategy

Our micro-video dataset was crawled from one of the most prominent micro-video sharing social networks, Vine. Beside the historical uploaded micro-videos, Vine also archives users' profiles and their social connections.

In particular, we first randomly selected 10 active Vine users from Rankzoo[9], which provides the top 1,000 active users on Vine, as the seed users. We then adopted the breadth-first crawling strategy to expand the seed users by crawling their followers. Considering that these seed users may have millions of followers, we practically only retained the first 1,000 returned followers for each seed user to improve the crawling efficiency. After three layers of crawling, we harvested a densely connected user set consisting of 98,166 users as well as 120,324 following relationships among users. For each user, his/her brief profile was crawled, containing full name, description, location, follower count, followee count, like count, post count and loop count of all post videos. Besides, we also collected the timeline (the micro-video posting history, including the repostings from others.) of each user between July 1st and October 1st, 2015. Finally, we obtained 1.6 million video postings, including a total number of 303,242 unique micro-videos with a total duration of 499.8 hours.

[9]https://rankzoo.com.

3.2 Ground Truth Construction

We employed four popularity-related indicators, namely, the number of comments (n_comments), the number of likes (n_likes), the number of reposts (n_reposts), and the number of loops/views (n_loops) to measure the popularity of micro-videos. Figure 3 illustrates the proportion of micro-videos regarding each of the four indicators in our dataset. It is noticed that the distributions of them are different, and each of them measure one aspect of the popularity. In order to comprehensively and precisely measure the popularity of each micro-video, y_i, we linearly fuse all the four indicators:

$$y_i = \frac{(n\_reposts + n\_comments + n\_likes + n\_loops)}{4}. \quad (1)$$

4. OUR PROPOSED TMALL MODEL

4.1 Notation

We first declare several notations. We employ bold capital letters (e.g., $\mathbf{X}$) and bold lowercase letters (e.g., $\mathbf{x}$) to denote matrices and vectors, respectively. We use non-bold letters (e.g., x) to represent scalars, and Greek letters (e.g., β) as parameters. If not clarified, all vectors are in column form.

Without loss of generality, suppose we have N labeled samples and M unlabeled samples with $K \geqslant 2$ modalities. It is worth noting that the unlabeled samples also serve as testing samples. Z_k stands for the number of features generated from the k-th modality. Then the k-th modality can be represented as $\mathbf{X_k} \in \mathbb{R}^{(N+M) \times Z_k}$. The popularity of

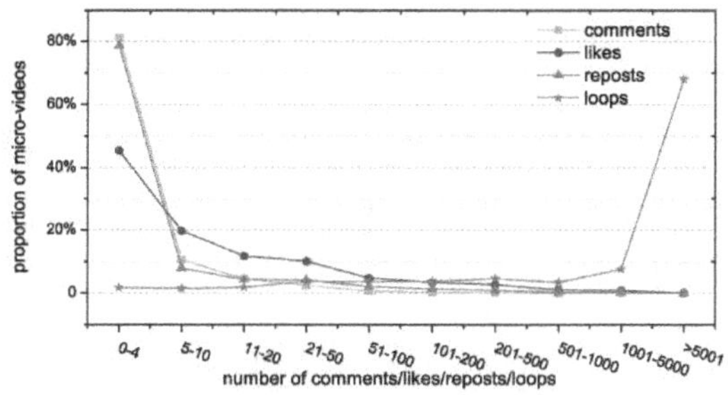

Figure 3: Distribution of the number of comments, likes, reposts and loops of micro-videos in our dataset.

all the videos are denoted by $\mathbf{y} = \{y_1, y_2, \cdots, y_N\}^T \in \mathbb{R}^N$. Let $\mathbf{f} = \{f_1, f_2, \cdots, f_N, f_{N+1}, f_{N+2}, \cdots, f_{N+M}\}^T \in \mathbb{R}^{N+M}$ stand for the predicted results regarding popularity for all samples, including the labeled and unlabeled ones. We aim to jointly learn the common space $\mathbf{X_0} \in \mathbb{R}^{(N+M)\times Z_0}$ shared by multiple modalities and the popularity for the M unlabeled micro-videos.

Our proposed model targets at reasoning from observed training micro-videos to testing ones. Such prediction belongs to transductive learning, in which both labeled samples as well as unlabeled samples are available for training. It hence obtains better performance. In contrast, inductive model is reasoning from observed training cases to general rules, which are then applied to the test cases.

4.2 Problem Formulation

It is apparent that different modalities may contribute distinctive and complementary information about micro-videos. For example, textual modality gives us hints about the topics of the given micro-video; acoustic and visual modalities may respectively convey location and situation of micro-videos, and user modality demonstrates the influence of the micro-video publisher. These clues jointly contribute to the popularity of a micro-video. Obviously, due to the noise and information insufficiency of each modality, it may be suboptimal to conduct learning directly from each single modality separately. In contrast, we assume that there exists an optimal latent space, in which micro-videos can be better described. Moreover, the optimal latent space should maintain the original intrinsic characteristics conveyed by multi-modalities of the given micro-videos. Therefore, we penalize the disagreement of the normalized Laplacian matrix between the latent space and each modality. In particular, we formalize this assumption as follows. Let $\mathbf{S}_k \in \mathbb{R}^{(N+M)\times(N+M)}$ be the similarity matrix[10], which is computed by the Gaussian similarity function as follows,

$$S_k(i,j) = \begin{cases} exp\Big(-\frac{\left\|\mathbf{x}_k^i - \mathbf{x}_k^j\right\|^2}{2\sigma_k^2}\Big) & , \text{ if } i \neq j; \\ 0 & , \text{ if } i = j. \end{cases} \quad (2)$$

where $\mathbf{x}_k^i$ and $\mathbf{x}_k^j$ are the micro-video pairs in the k-th modality space. Thereinto, the radius parameter σ_k is simply set as the median of the Euclidean distances over all video pairs in the k-th modality. We then derive the corresponding normalized Laplacian matrix as follows,

$$\mathbf{L(S_k)} = \mathbf{I} - \mathbf{D}_k^{-\frac{1}{2}}\mathbf{S}_k\mathbf{D}_k^{-\frac{1}{2}}, \quad (3)$$

[10]To facilitate the illustration, k ranges from 0 to K.

where $\mathbf{I}$ is a $(N+M)\times(N+M)$ identity matrix and $\mathbf{D}_k \in \mathbb{R}^{(N+M)\times(N+M)}$ is the diagonal degree matrix, whose (u,u)-th entry is the sum of the u-th row of $\mathbf{S}_k$. Since $S_k(i,j) > 0$, we can derive that $tr(\mathbf{L(S_k)}) > 0$. We thus can formulate the disagreement penalty between the latent space and the original modalities as,

$$\sum_{k=1}^{K} \| \frac{1}{tr(\mathbf{L(S_0)})}\mathbf{L(S_0)} - \frac{1}{tr(\mathbf{L(S_k)})}\mathbf{L(S_k)} \|_F^2, \quad (4)$$

where $tr(\mathbf{A})$ is the trace of matrix $\mathbf{A}$ and $\|\cdot\|_F$ denotes the Frobenius norm of matrix. In addition, inspired by [32], considering that similar micro-videos attempt to have similar popularity in the latent common space, we adopt the following regularizer,

$$\frac{1}{2}\sum_{m=1}^{N+M}\sum_{n=1}^{N+M}\Big(\frac{f(\mathbf{x}_0^m)}{\sqrt{D_0(\mathbf{x}_0^m)}} - \frac{f(\mathbf{x}_0^n)}{\sqrt{D_0(\mathbf{x}_0^n)}}\Big)^2 S_0(m,n) = \mathbf{f}^T\mathbf{L(S_0)}\mathbf{f}. \quad (5)$$

Based upon these formulations, we can define the loss function that measures the empirical error on the training samples. As reported in [22], the squared loss usually yields good performance as other complex ones. We thus adopt the squared loss in our algorithm for simplicity and efficiency. In particular, since we do not have the labels for testing samples, we only consider the squared loss regarding the N unlabeled samples to guarantee the learning performance. We ultimately reach our objective function as,

$$\min_{\mathbf{f},\mathbf{L(S_0)}} \sum_{i=1}^{N}(y_i - f_i)^2 + \mu\mathbf{f}^T\mathbf{L(S_0)}\mathbf{f} + \lambda\sum_{k=1}^{K} \| \frac{1}{tr(\mathbf{L(S_0)})}\mathbf{L(S_0)} - \frac{1}{tr(\mathbf{L(S_k)})}\mathbf{L(S_k)} \|_F^2, \quad (6)$$

where λ and μ are both nonnegative regularization parameters. To be more specific, λ penalizes the disagreement among the latent space and modalities, and μ encourages that similar popularity will be assigned to similar micro-videos.

4.3 Alternative Optimization

To simplify the representation, we first define that,

$$\begin{cases} \tilde{\mathbf{L}} = \frac{1}{tr(\mathbf{L(S_0)})}\mathbf{L(S_0)}, \\ \tilde{\mathbf{L}}_\mathbf{k} = \frac{1}{tr(\mathbf{L(S_k)})}\mathbf{L(S_k)}. \end{cases} \quad (7)$$

Therefore, the objective function can be transformed to,

$$\min_{\mathbf{f}} \sum_{i=1}^{N}(y_i - f_i)^2 + \lambda\sum_{k=1}^{K}\left\|\tilde{\mathbf{L}} - \tilde{\mathbf{L}}_\mathbf{k}\right\|_F^2 + \mu\mathbf{f}^T\tilde{\mathbf{L}}\mathbf{f}, \quad \text{subject to} \quad tr(\mathbf{L(S_0)}) = 1. \quad (8)$$

Furthermore, to optimize $\tilde{\mathbf{L}}$ more efficiently, inspired by the property that $tr(\tilde{\mathbf{L}}_\mathbf{k}) = 1$, we let,

$$\mathbf{L(S_0)} = \sum_{k=1}^{K}\beta_k\tilde{\mathbf{L}}_\mathbf{k}, \qquad \text{subject to} \quad \sum_{k=1}^{K}\beta_k = 1. \quad (9)$$

Consequently, we have,

$$\tilde{\mathbf{L}} = \frac{1}{tr(\mathbf{L}(\mathbf{S_0}))}\mathbf{L}(\mathbf{S_0}) = \sum_{k=1}^{K} \beta_k \tilde{\mathbf{L_k}},$$

$$\text{subject to} \quad \sum_{k=1}^{K} \beta_k = 1. \tag{10}$$

Interestingly, we find that β_k can be treated as the co-related degree between the latent common space and each modality. It is worth noting that we do not impose the constraint of $\beta \geq 0$, since we want to keep both positive and negative co-relations. A positive coefficient indicates the positive correlation between the modality space and the latent common space, while a negative coefficient reflects the negative correlation, which may be due to the noisy data of the modality. The larger the β_k is, the higher correlation between the latent space and the k-th modality will be. In the end, the final objective function can be written as,

$$\min_{\mathbf{f},\boldsymbol{\beta}} \sum_{i=1}^{N}(y_i - f_i)^2 + \lambda \sum_{k=1}^{K} \left\|\sum_{i=1}^{K} \beta_i \tilde{\mathbf{L}_\mathbf{i}} - \tilde{\mathbf{L}_\mathbf{k}}\right\|_F^2 +$$

$$\mu \mathbf{f}^T \sum_{k=1}^{K} \beta_k \tilde{\mathbf{L}}_\mathbf{k}\mathbf{f} + \theta \left\|\boldsymbol{\beta}\right\|^2, \text{ subject to } \mathbf{e}^T\boldsymbol{\beta} = 1, \tag{11}$$

where $\boldsymbol{\beta} = [\beta_1, \beta_2, \cdots, \beta_K]^T \in \mathbb{R}^K$ and $\mathbf{e} = [1, 1, \cdots, 1]^T \in \mathbb{R}^K$. θ is the regularization parameter, introduced to avoid the overfitting problem. We denote the objective function of Eqn.(11) as $\boldsymbol{\Gamma}$. We adopt the alternating optimization strategy to solve the two variables $\mathbf{f}$ and $\boldsymbol{\beta}$ in $\boldsymbol{\Gamma}$. In particular, we optimize one variable while fixing the other one in each iteration. We keep this iterative procedure until the $\boldsymbol{\Gamma}$ converges.

4.3.1 *Computing β_j with $\mathbf{f}$ fixed*

We first fix $\mathbf{f}$ and transform the objective function $\boldsymbol{\Gamma}$ as,

$$\min_{\boldsymbol{\beta}} \lambda \sum_{k=1}^{K} \sum_{t=1}^{N+M} \left\|\mathbf{M}^{(t)}\boldsymbol{\beta} - \tilde{\mathbf{l}}_\mathbf{k}^{(t)}\right\|_F^2 + \mu \mathbf{g}^T\boldsymbol{\beta} + \theta\left\|\boldsymbol{\beta}\right\|^2,$$

$$\text{subject to} \quad \mathbf{e}^T\boldsymbol{\beta} = 1, \tag{12}$$

where $\mathbf{g} = [\mathbf{f}^T\tilde{\mathbf{L}}_1\mathbf{f}, \mathbf{f}^T\tilde{\mathbf{L}}_2\mathbf{f}, \cdots, \mathbf{f}^T\tilde{\mathbf{L}}_K\mathbf{f}]^T \in \mathbb{R}^K$, $\mathbf{M}^{(t)} = [\tilde{\mathbf{l}}_\mathbf{1}^{(t)}, \tilde{\mathbf{l}}_\mathbf{2}^{(t)}, \cdots, \tilde{\mathbf{l}}_\mathbf{K}^{(t)}] \in \mathbb{R}^{(N+M)\times K}$ and $\tilde{\mathbf{l}}_\mathbf{k}^{(t)} \in \mathbb{R}^{N+M}$ denotes the t-th column of $\tilde{\mathbf{L}}_\mathbf{k}$. For simplicity, we replace $\tilde{\mathbf{l}}_\mathbf{K}^{(t)}$ with $\tilde{\mathbf{l}}_\mathbf{k}^{(t)}\mathbf{e}^T\boldsymbol{\beta}$, as $\mathbf{e}^T\boldsymbol{\beta} = 1$. With the help of Lagrangian, $\boldsymbol{\Gamma}$ can be rewritten as follows.

$$\min_{\boldsymbol{\beta}} \lambda \sum_{k=1}^{K} \sum_{t=1}^{N+M} \left\|(\mathbf{M}^{(t)} - \tilde{\mathbf{l}}_\mathbf{k}^{(t)}\mathbf{e}^T)\boldsymbol{\beta}\right\|_F^2 + \mu \mathbf{g}^T\boldsymbol{\beta} + \delta(1 - \mathbf{e}^T\boldsymbol{\beta})$$

$$+ \theta\left\|\boldsymbol{\beta}\right\|^2, \tag{13}$$

where δ is a nonnegative Lagrange multiplier. Taking derivative of Eqn.(13) with respect to $\boldsymbol{\beta}$, we have,

$$\frac{\partial \boldsymbol{\Gamma}}{\partial \boldsymbol{\beta}} = \mathbf{H}\boldsymbol{\beta} + \mu\mathbf{g} - \delta\mathbf{e}, \tag{14}$$

where,

$$\mathbf{H} = 2\Big[\Big(\lambda \sum_{k=1}^{K} \sum_{t=1}^{N+M} (\mathbf{M}^{(t)} - \tilde{\mathbf{l}}_\mathbf{k}^{(t)}\mathbf{e}^T)^T(\mathbf{M}^{(t)} - \tilde{\mathbf{l}}_\mathbf{k}^{(t)}\mathbf{e}^T)\Big) + \theta\mathbf{I}\Big], \tag{15}$$

and $\mathbf{I}$ is a $K \times K$ identity matrix. Setting Eqn.(14) to zero, we have,

$$\boldsymbol{\beta} = \mathbf{H}^{-1}(\delta\mathbf{e} - \mu\mathbf{g}). \tag{16}$$

Substituting Eqn.(16) into $\mathbf{e}^T\boldsymbol{\beta} = 1$, we have,

$$\begin{cases} \delta & = \dfrac{1 + \mu\mathbf{e}^T\mathbf{H}^{-1}\mathbf{g}}{\mathbf{e}^T\mathbf{H}^{-1}\mathbf{e}}, \\ \boldsymbol{\beta} & = \mathbf{H}^{-1}\Big[\dfrac{\mathbf{e} + \mu\mathbf{e}^T\mathbf{H}^{-1}\mathbf{g}\mathbf{e}}{\mathbf{e}^T\mathbf{H}^{-1}\mathbf{e}} - \mu\mathbf{g}\Big]. \end{cases} \tag{17}$$

According to the definition of positive-definite matrix, $\mathbf{H}$ is always positive definite and hence invertible. Therefore, $\mathbf{H}^{-1}$ is also positive definite, which ensures $\mathbf{e}^T\mathbf{H}^{-1}\mathbf{e} > 0$.

4.3.2 *Computing $\mathbf{f}$ with β_j fixed*

With fixed β_j, taking derivative of $\boldsymbol{\Gamma}$ with respect to f_i, where $1 \leq i \leq N$, we have,

$$\frac{\partial \boldsymbol{\Gamma}}{\partial f_i} = 2(f_i - y_i) + 2\mu \sum_{j=1}^{N+M} \tilde{L}(i,j)f_j. \tag{18}$$

We then take derivative of the $\boldsymbol{\Gamma}$ with respect to f_i, where $N + 1 \leq i \leq N + M$. We reach,

$$\frac{\partial \boldsymbol{\Gamma}}{\partial f_i} = 2\mu \sum_{j=1}^{N+M} \tilde{L}(i,j)f_j. \tag{19}$$

In a vector-wise form, we restate the solution of $\mathbf{f}$ as follows,

$$\mathbf{f} = \mathbf{G}^{-1}\hat{\mathbf{y}}, \tag{20}$$

where $\mathbf{G} = \hat{\mathbf{I}} + \mu\sum_{k=1}^{K} \beta_k\tilde{\mathbf{L}}_\mathbf{k}$, $\hat{\mathbf{y}} = \{y_1, y_2, \cdots, y_N, 0, 0, \cdots, 0\}$ and $\hat{\mathbf{I}} \in \mathbb{R}^{(N+M)\times(N+M)}$ is defined as follows,

$$\hat{I}(i,j) = \begin{cases} 1 & \text{if } i = j, \text{ and } 1 \leq i \leq N, \\ 0 & \text{otherwise.} \end{cases} \tag{21}$$

5. FEATURE EXTRACTION

It is apparent that both the publisher influence and content influence contribute to the popularity of UGCs. In particular, we characterized the publisher influence via the social modality, and the content influence via visual, acoustic and textual modalities. For content influence, we first examined the popular micro-videos in our dataset and propose three common characteristics of online micro-videos. For each characteristic, we then explained the insights, and transformed it into a set of features for video representation. Finally, we developed a rich set of popularity-oriented features from each modality.

5.1 Observations

Universal Appeal. The subjects of widely popular micro-videos cannot be something that can only be appreciated by a small group of people. Therefore, the topics and objects contained in micro-videos should be something common so that to be interpreted the same way across people and cultures. To capture this characteristic, we extracted Sentence2Vector feature from the textual modality and deep object feature from the visual one.

Emotional Content. People are naturally drawn to things that arouse their emotions. Micro-videos showing funny animals or lovely babies make people feel urge to share them to express the same emotions. As a result, micro-videos that are highly emotional are more likely to be shared. Therefore, we extracted textual sentiment, visual sentiment features for each video as well as several acoustic features, which is widely used in emotion recognition in music [33].

High Quality and Aesthetic Design. When people share information on social networks, people are actually showing a little piece of themselves to their audience. Therefore, high quality and aesthetic design of the content, which could reflect the taste of people, is another important characteristic of popular micro-videos. Color histogram, aesthetic feature and visual quality feature were thus extracted to encode such characteristic. In addition, the acoustic features we extracted are frequently used in music modeling, which could help to detect music in the audio track of micro-videos [17].

5.2 Social Modality

It is intuitive that micro-videos posted by users, who has more followers or has a verified account, are more likely to be propagated, and thus tend to receive a higher number of audiences. To characterize the influence of micro-video publishers, we developed the following publisher-centric features for micro-videos.

- **Follower/Followee Count**. The number of followers and followees of the given micro-video publisher.
- **Loop Count**. The total number of loops received by all the posts of the publisher.
- **Post Count**. The number of posts generated by the publisher.
- **Twitter Verification**. A binary value indicating whether the publisher has been verified by Twitter[11].

5.3 Visual Modality

Due to the short-length of micro-videos, the visual content is usually highly related to a single theme, which enables us to only employ a few key frames to represent the whole micro-video. Inspired by this, we extracted the visual features from certain key frames. The mean pooling was performed across all the key frames to create a fixed-length vector representation of each micro-video.

5.3.1 Color Histogram

It has been found that most basic visual features (i.e., intensity and the mean value of different color channels in HSV space) except color histogram, have little correlation with popularity [15]. Color histogram has outstanding correlation due to the fact that striking colors tend to catch users' eyes. Therefore, we only extracted color histogram as the basic visual feature to characterize popular micro-videos. To reduce the size of color space, we grouped the color space into 50 distinct colors, which results in a 50-D vector for each frame.

5.3.2 Object Features

It has been studied that popular UGCs are strongly correlated with the objects contained in the videos [10]. We believe that the presence of certain objects affect micro-videos' popularity. For example, micro-videos with 'cute dogs' or 'beautiful girls' are more likely to be popular than those with 'desks' and 'stones'. We thus employed the deep convolutional neural networks (CNNs) [16], a powerful model for image recognition problems [35], to detect objects in micro-videos. Specifically, we applied the well-trained AlexNet DNN provided by the Caffe software package [13] to the input key frames. The output of the fc7 layer and the final $1,000$-way softmax layer in AlexNet is a probability distribution over the $1,000$ class labels predefined in ImageNet. We treat them as our feature representation of each frame. In the end, a mean pooling was performed over the frames to generate a single $4,096$-D vector and $1,000$-D vector for each micro-video.

5.3.3 SentiBank Features

We performed the sentiment analysis of the visual modality due to that the sentiment of UGCs has been proven to be strongly correlated with their popularity [10]. In particular, we extracted the visual sentiment features based on the deep CNNs model which was trained on the SentiBank dataset[4]. SentiBank contains $2,089$ concepts and each of them invokes specific sentiments such as 'cute girls' and 'funny animals'. Therefore, after mean pooling among keyframes, each micro-video is represented by a $2,089$-D vector.

5.3.4 Aesthetic Features

Aesthetic features are a set of handful selected features related to the principles of the nature and appreciation of beauty, which have been studied and found to be effective in popularity prediction [8]. Intuitively, micro-videos that are objectively aesthetic are more likely to be popular. We employed the released tool[12] [3] to extract the following aesthetic features: a) dark channel feature; b) luminosity feature; c) s3 sharpness; d) symmetry; e) low depth of field; f) white balance; g) colorfulness; h) color harmony, and i) eye sensitivity, at 3×3 grids over each key frame. We then calculated: a) normalized area of dominant object; and b) normalized distances of centroid of dominant objects with respect to four stress points at frame level. In the end, we obtained 149-D aesthetic features for each micro-video.

5.3.5 Visual Quality Assessment Features

It is important that the visual quality of popular contents are maintained at an acceptable level, given rising consumer expectations of the quality of multimedia content delivered to them [25]. In particular, we employed the released tool[13] to extract the micro-videos quality features based on the motion and spatio-temporal information, which have been proven to correlate highly with human visual judgments of quality. This results in a 46-D features.

5.4 Acoustic Modality

Acoustic modality usually works as an important complement to visual modality in many video-related tasks, such as video classification [34]. In fact, audio channels embedded in the micro-videos may also contribute to the popularity of micro-videos to a large extent. For example, the audio channel may indicate the quality of a given micro-video and convey rich background information about the emotion as well as the scene contained in the

[11] A Vine account can be verified by Twitter, if it is linked to a verified Twitter account.

[12] http://www.ee.columbia.edu/~subh/Software.php.

[13] http://live.ece.utexas.edu/.

micro-video, which significantly affects the popularity of a micro-video. The acoustic information is especially useful for the cases where the visual features could not carry enough information. Therefore, we adopted the following widely-used acoustic features, i.e., Mel-Frequency Cepstral Coefficients (MFCC) [17] and Audio-Six (i.e., Energy Entropy, Signal Energy, Zero Crossing Rate, Spectral Rolloff, Spectral Centroid, and Spectral Flux [33]). These features are frequently used in different audio-related tasks, such as emotion detection and music recognition. We finally obtained a 36-D acoustic feature vector for each micro-video.

5.5 Textual Modality

Micro-videos are usually associated with textual modality in the form of descriptions, such as "when Leo finally gets the Oscar" and "Puppy dog dreams", which may precisely summarize the micro-videos. Such summarization may depict the topics and sentiment information regarding the micro-videos, which has been proven to be of significance in online article popularity prediction [2].

5.5.1 *Sentence2Vector*

We found that the popular micro-videos are sometimes related to the topics of the textual descriptions. This observation propels us to conduct content analysis over the textual descriptions of micro-videos. Considering the short-length of descriptions, to perform content analysis, we employed the state-of-the-art textual feature extraction tool Sentence2Vector[14], which was developed on the basis of work embedding algorithm Word2Vector [21]. In this way, we extracted 100-D features for video descriptions.

5.5.2 *Textual Sentiment*

We also analyze the sentiments over texts, which has been proven to play an important role in popularity prediction [1]. With the help of the Sentiment Analysis tool in Stanford CoreNLP tools[15], we assigned each micro-video a sentiment score ranging from 0 to 4 and they correspond to *very negative*, *negative*, *neutral*, *positive*, and *very positive*, respectively.

6. EXPERIMENT

In this section, we conducted extensive experiments to comparatively verify our model.

6.1 Experiment Settings

The remaining experiments were conducted over a cluster of 50 servers equipped with Intel Xeon(2x) CPU E5-2620 v3 at 2.40 GHz on 64 GB RAM, 24 cores and 64-bit Linux operating system. Regarding the deep feature extraction, we deployed Caffe framework [13] on a server equipped with a NVIDIA Titan Z GPU. The experimental results reported in this paper were based on 10-fold cross-validation. In each round of the 10-fold cross-validation, we split our dataset into two chunks: 90% of the micro-videos were used for training, 10% were used for testing. We report performance in terms of normalised Mean Square Error (nMSE) [22] between the predicted popularity and the actual popularity. The nMSE is an estimator of the overall deviations between predicted and measured values. It is defined as,

$$nMSE = \frac{\sum_{i=1}(p_i - r_i)^2}{\sum_{i=1} r_i^2}, \qquad (22)$$

where p_i is the predicted value and r_i is the target value in ground truth.

We have three key parameters as shown in Eqn.(8). The optimal values of these parameters were carefully tuned with the training data in each of the 10 fold. We employed the grid search strategy to obtain the optimal parameters between 10^{-5} to 10^2 with small but adaptive step sizes. In particular, the step sizes were 0.00001, 0.0001, 0.001, 0.01, 0.1, 1 and 10 for the range of [0.00001,0.0001], [0.0001,0.001], [0.001,0.01], [0.01,0.1], [0.1,1], [1,10] and [10,100], respectively. The parameters corresponding to the best nMSE were used to report the final results. For other compared systems, the procedures to tune the parameters are analogous to ensure the fair comparison. Considering one fold as an example, we observed that our model reached the optimal performance at $\lambda = 1$, $\mu = 0.01$ and $\theta = 100$.

6.2 On Model Comparison

To demonstrate the effectiveness of our proposed TMALL model, we carried out experiments with several state-of-the-art multi-view learning approaches:

- **Early_Fusion**. The first baseline concatenates the features extracted from the four modalities into a single joint feature vector, on which traditional machine learning models can be applied. In this work, we adopted the widely used regression model—SVR, and implemented it with the help of scikit-learn [23].
- **Late_Fusion**. The second baseline first separately predicts the popularity of micro-videos from each modality via SVR model, and then linearly integrates them to obtain the final results.
- **regMVMT**. The third baseline is the regularized multi-view learning model [37]. This model only regulates the relationships among different views within the original space.
- **MSNL**. The fourth one is the multiple social network learning (MSNL) model proposed in [27]. This model takes the source confidence and source consistency into consideration.
- **MvDA**. The fifth baseline is a multi-view discriminant analysis (MvDA) model [14], which aims to learn a single unified discriminant common space for multiple views by jointly optimizing multiple view-specific transforms, one for each view. The model exploits both the intra-view and inter-view correlations.

Table 1 shows the performance comparison among different models. From this table, we have the following observations: 1) TMALL outperforms the Early_Fusion and Late_Fusion. Regarding the Early_Fusion, features extracted from various sources may not fall into the same semantic space. Simply appending all features actually brings in a certain amount of noise and ambiguity. Besides, Early_Fusion may lead to the curse of dimensionality since the final feature vector would be of very high dimension. For the Late_Fusion, the fused result however might not be reasonably accurate due to two reasons. First, a single modality might not be sufficiently descriptive to represent

[14]https://github.com/klb3713/sentence2vec.

[15]http://stanfordnlp.github.io/CoreNLP/.

Table 1: Performance comparison between our proposed TMALL model and several state-of-the-art baselines in terms of nMSE.

Methods	nMSE	p-value
Early Fusion	59.931 ± 41.09	9.91E-04
Late Fusion	8.461 ± 5.34	3.25E-03
regMVMT	1.058 ± 0.05	1.88E-03
MSNL	1.098 ± 0.13	1.42E-02
MvDA	0.982 ± 7.00E-03	9.91E-04
TMALL	0.979 ± 9.42E-03	–

the complex semantics of the videos. Separate results would be thus suboptimal and the integration may not result in a desired outcome. Second, it is labor-intensive to tune the fusion weights for different modalities. Even worse, the optimal parameters for one application cannot be directly applied to another one. 2) TMALL achieves better performance, as compared with regMVMT and MSNL. This could be explained that linking different modalities via a unified latent space is better than imposing disagreement penalty directly over original spaces. 3) The less satisfactory performance of MvDA indicates that it is necessary to explore the consistency among different modalities when building the latent space. And 4) as compared to the multi-view learning baselines, such as regMVMT, MSNL, and MvDA, our model stably demonstrates its advantage. This signals that the proposed transductive models can achieve higher performance than inductive models under the same experimental settings. This can be explained by the fact that TMALL leverages the knowledge of testing samples.

Moreover, we performed the paired t-test between TMALL and each baseline on 10-fold cross validation. We found that all the p-values are much smaller than 0.05, which shows that the performance improvements of our proposed model over other baselines are statistically significant.

6.3 On Modality Comparison

To verify the effectiveness of multi-modal integration, we also conducted experiments over different modality combinations of the four modalities. Table 2 summarizes the multi-modal analysis and the paired t-test results. It is obvious that the more modalities we incorporated, the better performance we can obtain. This implies the complementary relationships rather than mutual conflicting relationships among the different modalities. Moreover, we found that removing features from any of these four modalities suffers from a decrease in performance. In a sense, this is consensus with the old saying "two heads are better than one". Additionally, as the performance obtained from different combinations are not the same, this validates that incorporating β which controls the confidence of different modalities is reasonable. Interestingly, we observed that the combination without social modality obtains the worst result which indicates that the social modality plays a pivotal role in micro-video propagation, as compared to visual, textual or acoustic modality. This also validates that the features developed from social modality are much discriminative, even though they are with low-dimensions. On the other hand, the textual modality contributes the least among all modalities, as the performance of our model without textual modality still achieves good performance. This may be caused by the sparse textual description, which is usually given in one short sentence.

Table 2: Performance comparison among different modality combinations with respect to nMSE. We denote T, V, A and S as textual, visual, acoustic and social modality, respectively.

View combinations	nMSE	p-value
T+V+A	0.996 ± 4.20E-03	2.62E-05
T+A+S	0.982 ± 4.27E-03	2.59E-05
T+V+S	0.982 ± 4.13E-03	3.05E-04
V+A+S	0.981 ± 5.16E-03	2.16E-05
T+V+A+S	0.979 ± 9.42E-03	–

Table 3: Performance comparison among different visual features with respect to nMSE.

Features	nMSE	p-value
Color Histogram	0.996 ± 6.88E-03	1.94E-04
Object Feature	0.994 ± 6.71E-03	2.47E-04
Visual Sentiment	0.994 ± 6.72E-03	2.49E-04
Aesthetic Feature	0.984 ± 6.95E-03	4.44E-01
ALL	0.979 ± 9.42E-03	–

6.4 On Visual Feature Comparison

To further examine the discriminative visual features we extracted, we conducted experiments over different kinds of visual features using TMALL. We also performed significant test to validate the advantage of combining multiple features. Table 3 comparatively shows the performance of TMALL in terms of different visual feature configurations. It can be seen that the object, visual sentiment and aesthetic features achieve similar improvement in performance, as compared to color histogram features. This reveals that micro-videos' popularity is better reflected by their content, sentiment and design, including what objects they contain, which emotion they convey and what design standards they follow. This is highly consistent with our oberservations and also implies that micro-videos which aim to gain high popularity need to be well designed and considered more from the visual content.

6.5 Illustrative Examples

To gain the insights of the influential factors in the task of popularity prediction of micro-videos, we comparatively illustrate a few representative examples in Figure 4. From this figure, we have the following observations: 1) Figure 4(a) shows three micro-video pairs. Each of the three micro-video pairs describes the similar semantics, i.e., animals, football game and sunset, respectively, but they were published by different users. The publishers of the videos in top row are much more famous than those of the bottom. We found that the corresponding popularity of micro-videos in the second row are much lower than those in the first row, although they have no significant difference from the perspective of video contents, which clearly justifies the importance of social modality. 2) Figure 4(b) illustrates three micro-video pairs, where each pair of micro-videos were published by the same user. However, the micro-videos in the first row achieve much higher popularity than those in the second row, which demonstrates that the contents of micro-videos also contribute to their popularity. In

(a) Illustration of three micro-video pairs, and each pair was published by two distinct users. The publishers of the videos in top row are much more famous than those of the bottom.

(b) Illustration of three micro-video pairs, and each pair was published by the same user. The videos in the first row are much more acoustically comfortable, visually joyful, and aesthetically beautiful than those in the second row.

(c) Illustration of three popular micro-videos with different textual descriptions, which contains superstar names, hot events, and detail information, respectively.

Figure 4: Comparative illustration of video examples. They respectively justify the importance of social, acoustic as well as visual, and textual modalities. We use three key frames to represent each video.

particular, the comparisons in Figure 4(b), from left to right, are i) the existence of 'skillful pianolude' compared with 'noisy dance music', ii) 'funny animals' compared with 'motionless dog', and iii) 'beautiful flowers' compared with 'gloomy sky'. These examples indicate the necessity of developing acoustic features, visual sentiment and visual aesthetic features for the task of micro-video popularity. And 3) Figure 4(c) shows a group of micro-videos, whose textual descriptions contain either superstar names, hot hashtags, or informative descriptions. These micro-videos received a lot of loops, comments, likes and reposts. These examples thus reflect the value of textual modality.

6.6 Complexity Analysis

To theoretically analyze the computational cost of our proposed TMALL model, we first compute the complexity in the construction of $\mathbf{H}$ and $\mathbf{g}$, as well as the inverse of matrices $\mathbf{H}$ and $\mathbf{G}$. The construction of $\mathbf{H}$ has the time complexity of $\mathbf{O}(K^2(N+M))$. Fortunately, $\mathbf{H}$ keeps the same in each iteration, and thus can be computed by offline. The computation of $\mathbf{g}$ needs the time cost $\mathbf{O}(K(N+M)^2)$. In addition, computing the inverse of $\mathbf{H}$ and $\mathbf{G}$ has the complexity of $\mathbf{O}(K^3)$ and $\mathbf{O}((N+M)^3)$, respectively. The computation cost of $\boldsymbol{\beta}$ in Eqn.(17) is $\mathbf{O}(K^2)$. Therefore, the speed bottleneck lies in the computation of the inverse of $\mathbf{G}$. In practice, the proposed TMALL model converges very fast, which on average takes less than 10 iterations. Overall, the learning process over 9,720 micro-videos can be accomplished within 50 seconds.

7. CONCLUSION AND FUTURE WORK

This paper presents a novel transductive multi-modal learning method (TMALL), to predict the popularity of micro-videos. In particular, TMALL works by learning an optimal latent common space from multi-modalities of the given micro-videos, in which the popularity of micro-videos are much more distinguishable. The latent common space is capable of unifying and preserving information from different modalities, and it helps to alleviate the modality limitation problem. To verify our model, we built a benchmark dataset and extracted a rich set of popularity-oriented features to characterize micro-videos from multiple perspectives. By conducting extensive experiments, we draw the following conclusions: 1) the optimal latent common space exists and works; 2) the more modalities we incorporate to learn the common space, the more discriminant it is; and 3) the features extracted to describe the social and content influence are representative. As a side research contribution, we have released the dataset, codes and parameters to facilitate other researchers. In the future, we plan to incorporate the cross-domain knowledge, such as the hot topics on Twitter, to enhance the performance of popularity prediction.

8. ACKNOWLEDGMENTS

This research is supported by the National Research Foundation, Prime Minister's Office, Singapore under its IRC@SG Funding Initiative.

9. REFERENCES

[1] J. Berger. Arousal increases social transmission of information. *Psychological science*, 22(7):891–893, 2011.

[2] J. Berger and K. L. Milkman. What makes online content viral? *Journal of Marketing Research*, 49(2):192–205, 2012.

[3] S. Bhattacharya, B. Nojavanasghari, T. Chen, D. Liu, S.-F. Chang, and M. Shah. Towards a comprehensive computational model foraesthetic assessment of videos. In *Proceedings of the ACM Multimedia Conference*, pages 361–364. ACM, 2013.

[4] D. Borth, R. Ji, T. Chen, T. M. Breuel, and S. Chang. Large-scale visual sentiment ontology and detectors using adjective noun pairs. In *Proceedings of the ACM Multimedia Conference*, pages 223–232. ACM, 2013.

[5] S. Cappallo, T. Mensink, and C. G. M. Snoek. Latent factors of visual popularity prediction. In *Proceedings of the ACM on International Conference on Multimedia Retrieval*, pages 195–202. ACM, 2015.

[6] K. Chaudhuri, S. M. Kakade, K. Livescu, and K. Sridharan. Multi-view clustering via canonical correlation analysis. In *Proceedings of the International Conference on Machine Learning*, pages 129–136. ACM, 2009.

[7] C. M. Christoudias, R. Urtasun, and T. Darrell. Multi-view learning in the presence of view disagreement. *CoRR*, abs/1206.3242, 2012.

[8] S. Dhar, V. Ordonez, and T. L. Berg. High level describable attributes for predicting aesthetics and interestingness. In *Proceedings of the IEEE Conference on Computer Vision and Pattern Recognition*, pages 1657–1664. IEEE, 2011.

[9] H. Gao, F. Nie, X. Li, and H. Huang. Multi-view subspace clustering. In *IEEE International Conference on Computer Vision*, pages 4238–4246. IEEE, 2015.

[10] F. Gelli, T. Uricchio, M. Bertini, A. D. Bimbo, and S. Chang. Image popularity prediction in social media using sentiment and context features. In *Proceedings of the ACM Multimedia Conference*, pages 907–910. ACM, 2015.

[11] X. He, M. Gao, M. Kan, Y. Liu, and K. Sugiyama. Predicting the popularity of web 2.0 items based on user comments. In *Proceedings of the International ACM SIGIR Conference on Research and Development in Information Retrieval*, pages 233–242. ACM, 2014.

[12] L. Hong, O. Dan, and B. D. Davison. Predicting popular messages in twitter. In *Proceedings of the ACM International Conference on World Wide Web*, pages 57–58. ACM, 2011.

[13] Y. Jia, E. Shelhamer, J. Donahue, S. Karayev, J. Long, R. B. Girshick, S. Guadarrama, and T. Darrell. Caffe: Convolutional architecture for fast feature embedding. In *Proceedings of the ACM Multimedia Conference*, pages 675–678. ACM, 2014.

[14] M. Kan, S. Shan, H. Zhang, S. Lao, and X. Chen. Multi-view discriminant analysis. *IEEE Transactions on Pattern Analysis and Machine Intelligence*, 38(1):188–194, 2016.

[15] A. Khosla, A. D. Sarma, and R. Hamid. What makes an image popular? In *Proceedings of the ACM International Conference on World Wide Web*, pages 867–876, 2014.

[16] A. Krizhevsky, I. Sutskever, and G. E. Hinton. Imagenet classification with deep convolutional neural networks. In *Proceedings of the Annual Conference on Neural Information Processing Systems*, pages 1106–1114. NIPS Foundation, 2012.

[17] Z. Li, J. Wang, J. Cai, Z. Duan, H. Wang, and Y. Wang. Non-reference audio quality assessment for online live music recordings. In *Proceedings of the ACM Multimedia Conference*, pages 63–72. ACM, 2013.

[18] A. Liu, W. Nie, Y. Gao, and Y. Su. Multi-modal clique-graph matching for view-based 3d model retrieval. *IEEE Transactions on Image Processing*, 25(5):2103–2116, 2016.

[19] A. Liu, Z. Wang, W. Nie, and Y. Su. Graph-based characteristic view set extraction and matching for 3d model retrieval. *Information Sciences*, 320:429–442, 2015.

[20] P. J. McParlane, Y. Moshfeghi, and J. M. Jose. "nobody comes here anymore, it's too crowded"; predicting image popularity on flickr. In *Proceedings of the ACM International Conference on Multimedia Retrieval*, page 385. ACM, 2014.

[21] T. Mikolov, I. Sutskever, K. Chen, G. S. Corrado, and J. Dean. Distributed representations of words and phrases and their compositionality. In *Proceedings of the Annual Conference on Neural Information Processing Systems*, pages 3111–3119. NIPS Foundation, 2013.

[22] L. Nie, L. Zhang, Y. Yang, M. Wang, R. Hong, and T.-S. Chua. Beyond doctors: future health prediction from multimedia and multimodal observations. In *Proceedings of the ACM Multimedia Conference*, pages 591–600. ACM, 2015.

[23] F. Pedregosa, G. Varoquaux, A. Gramfort, V. Michel, B. Thirion, O. Grisel, M. Blondel, P. Prettenhofer, R. Weiss, V. Dubourg, J. Vanderplas, A. Passos, D. Cournapeau, M. Brucher, M. Perrot, and E. Duchesnay. Scikit-learn: Machine learning in Python. *Journal of Machine Learning Research*, 12:2825–2830, 2011.

[24] M. Redi, N. O'Hare, R. Schifanella, M. Trevisiol, and A. Jaimes. 6 seconds of sound and vision: Creativity in micro-videos. In *Proceedings of the IEEE Conference on Computer Vision and Pattern Recognition*, pages 4272–4279. IEEE, 2014.

[25] M. A. Saad, A. C. Bovik, and C. Charrier. Blind prediction of natural video quality. *IEEE Transactions on Image Processing*, 23(3):1352–1365, 2014.

[26] V. Sindhwani, P. Niyogi, and M. Belkin. A co-regularization approach to semi-supervised learning with multiple views. In *Proceedings of the International Conference on Machine Learning*, pages 74–79. ACM, 2005.

[27] X. Song, L. Nie, L. Zhang, M. Akbari, and T. Chua. Multiple social network learning and its application in volunteerism tendency prediction. In *Proceedings of the International ACM SIGIR Conference on Research and Development in Information Retrieval*, pages 213–222, 2015.

[28] X. Song, L. Nie, L. Zhang, M. Liu, and T. Chua. Interest inference via structure-constrained multi-source multi-task learning. In *Proceedings of the International Joint Conference on Artificial Intelligence*, pages 2371–2377. AAAI Press, 2015.

[29] T. Trzcinski and P. Rokita. Predicting popularity of online videos using support vector regression. *CoRR*, abs/1510.06223, 2015.

[30] M. Wang, X. Hua, R. Hong, J. Tang, G. Qi, and Y. Song. Unified video annotation via multigraph learning. *IEEE Transactions on Circuits and Systems for Video Technology*, 19(5):733–746, 2009.

[31] M. Wang, H. Li, D. Tao, K. Lu, and X. Wu. Multimodal graph-based reranking for web image search. *IEEE Transactions on Image Processing*, 21(11):4649–4661, 2012.

[32] M. Wang, X. Liu, and X. Wu. Visual classification by $_1$-hypergraph modeling. *IEEE Transactions on Knowledge and Data Engineering*, 27(9):2564–2574, 2015.

[33] B. Wu, E. Zhong, A. Horner, and Q. Yang. Music emotion recognition by multi-label multi-layer multi-instance multi-view learning. In *Proceedings of the ACM Multimedia Conference*, pages 117–126. ACM, 2014.

[34] Z. Wu, Y. Jiang, J. Wang, J. Pu, and X. Xue. Exploring inter-feature and inter-class relationships with deep neural networks for video classification. In *Proceedings of the ACM Multimedia Conference*, pages 167–176. ACM, 2014.

[35] H. Zhang, X. Shang, W. Yang, H. Xu, H. Luan, and T. Chua. Online collaborative learning for open-vocabulary visual classifiers. In *Proceedings of the IEEE Conference on Computer Vision and Pattern Recognition*. IEEE, 2016.

[36] H. Zhang, M. Wang, R. Hong, and T. Chua. Play and rewind: optimizing binary representations of videos by self-supervised temporal hashing. In *Proceedings of the ACM Multimedia Conference*. ACM, 2016.

[37] J. Zhang and J. Huan. Inductive multi-task learning with multiple view data. In *Proceedings of the ACM SIGKDD International Conference on Knowledge Discovery and Data Mining*, pages 543–551. ACM, 2012.

Leveraging Contextual Cues for Generating Basketball Highlights

Vinay Bettadapura
Google Inc.
Mountain View, CA
vinaykb@google.com

Caroline Pantofaru
Google Inc.
Mountain View, CA
cpantofaru@google.com

Irfan Essa
Georgia Institute of Technology
Atlanta, GA
irfan@cc.gatech.edu

http://www.vbettadapura.com/highlights/basketball

ABSTRACT

The massive growth of sports videos has resulted in a need for automatic generation of sports highlights that are comparable in quality to the hand-edited highlights produced by broadcasters such as ESPN. Unlike previous works that mostly use audio-visual cues derived from the video, we propose an approach that additionally leverages contextual cues derived from the environment that the game is being played in. The contextual cues provide information about the excitement levels in the game, which can be ranked and selected to automatically produce high-quality basketball highlights. We introduce a new dataset of 25 NCAA games along with their play-by-play stats and the ground-truth excitement data for each basket. We explore the informativeness of five different cues derived from the video and from the environment through user studies. Our experiments show that for our study participants, the highlights produced by our system are comparable to the ones produced by ESPN for the same games.

CCS Concepts

•**Computing methodologies** → **Scene understanding; Activity recognition and understanding; Video summarization; Visual content-based indexing and retrieval;** •**Information systems** → *Multimedia and multimodal retrieval;*

Keywords

Basketball Video, Video Highlights, Content Analysis, Highlight Ranking.

1. INTRODUCTION

In recent years, there has been a proliferation in sports broadcasting due to the large number of games played across college and professional leagues throughout the year. Due to time limitations and regional differences, sports fans have a hard time watching the games live and keeping up with their favorite teams and players. This necessitates the need for high-quality sports highlights that allow the viewers to watch the interesting and exciting moments of the games at their own convenience. However, hand-editing the videos to generate the highlights is a time-consuming process and is not scalable, especially when we want to generate highlights of various lengths for all the different games depending on the needs of the viewers.

Previously published works that automatically produce sports highlights have mostly focused on audio-visual cues that can be derived from the videos. However, the environment within which the game is taking place provides us with rich contextual information that can be leveraged to produce better quality highlights. The players are active within the environment and the audience reacts to their actions with a range of emotions ranging from excitement to frustration. Sensors such as cameras and microphones are setup by the broadcasters which capture the player activity and the audience reaction (both audio and video). There are also several expert third party observers within the environment such as referees, coaches, commentators, and on-court statisticians. The data from these observers coupled with the video data from the broadcast videos provides rich contextual cues that can be leveraged to better understand the sporting scene.

In this paper, we focus on basketball, which is the third most popular sport in the US (after Football and Baseball) [1]. Basketball games are typically held in the indoor stadiums and gymnasiums of schools and colleges and provides us with a representative test-bed to develop our methodology and evaluate it. However, the system presented here is general and can be applied to any sport. Generating the highlights for an entire sports game involves understanding the salient moments of the game, generating an excitement-based rank-ordering of the plays, segmenting and extracting them from the broadcast video, and selecting the top clips to generate the game highlights. In the context of this study, we define a sports highlight as a "highlight reel" that showcases the top n exciting moments of the game in a chronological order.

The contextual cues used in our approach are derived from two sources within the basketball environment: (1) microphones that capture the audience and commentator audio, and (2) the play-by-play stats data from the on-court statisticians. From these two environmental sources, we extract four different cues: "Audio", "Score Differential", "Player

MM '16 October 15-19, 2016, Amsterdam, Netherlands

ACM ISBN 978-1-4503-3603-1/16/10.
DOI: http://dx.doi.org/10.1145/2964284.2964286

Ranking" and "Basket Type". Finally, a fifth cue "Motion" is extracted from the broadcast video which captures the magnitude of player and camera motion. For each basket within a given game, the data from these five cues is combined to generate an "excitement score" for the basket. Once all the baskets have been scored, we can then rank them by their excitement scores and pick the top n exciting clips and use them to generate the game highlights.

In order to conduct this study, we built a database of 25 NCAA games (played between February and March of 2015) totaling 35.44 hours of basketball footage along with the corresponding play-by-play stats data. There are a total of 1,173 baskets across these 25 games. We conducted extensive user-studies using Amazon's Mechanical Turk in order to obtain ground-truth on the excitement levels for each of these 1,173 baskets. The ground-truth data was then used to study the effectiveness of each of the cues as an indicator of how exciting a basket is. Finally, the five cues are combined using a weighted sum wherein the weights are learned from the data using 25-fold cross-validation (where we train using 24 games and test on the held-out game and repeat). We conducted a second round of user-studies for evaluation purposes, wherein we show (1) the effectiveness of cue-combination over each of the individual cues, and (2) that the highlights that we generate with our cue-combination are comparable to the highlights produced by ESPN for those games, wherein the ESPN highlights were regenerated using the same video pipeline that was used to generate our highlights (in order to make our highlights and ESPN highlights look visually similar in the user studies).

Contributions: Our contributions are as follows: (1) We present a method to leverage contextual cues from the environment to understand the excitement levels within a basketball game and automatically produce basketball highlights, (2) We introduce a new dataset of 25 NCAA games (35.44 hours of video with 1,173 baskets) along with the play-by-play stats and the ground-truth excitement data for each basket (we will make this dataset public to the research community), (3) We explore five different cues and study their effectiveness in determining the excitement of baskets through an extensive user study, and (4) We conduct user studies and show that the final highlights that we produce are comparable to the ESPN-ranked highlights.

2. RELATED WORK

Sports analytics and summarization has been an active area of research for the past two decades. Most of the work has been on analyzing broadcast videos from sports such as soccer, basketball, hockey, football and tennis. Professional broadcast videos (such as videos from ESPN) contain replays which can be extracted by detecting the logo-sweeps (shown before and after the replays) and the "arousal" level of the replays can be computed using the audience's audio energy and the amount of camera motion in order to rank the replays in terms of their excitement level [22]. Slow-motion replays can also be detected using Hidden Markov Models (HMMs) and Support Vector Regressors [18] and summaries can be generated by concatenating the detected replays. When replays are not available in the broadcast video, baskets can be detected by detecting breaks in the game and using object detectors to detect the referee and the penalty boxes to make informed choices about the importance of different plays during the games [2]. However, these approaches are limiting since detecting replays and slow motions and using those clips in the highlights will give us a highlight reel that has only those baskets for which replays or slow motions were shown. There could be many other exciting baskets that are missed because the broadcast director chose not to show the replays or slow motions for those baskets.

Audio plays a crucial role in detecting highlights in sports. The energy of the crowd and the excitement in the commentator's voice provides useful cues that can be used to pick exciting moments in the game. Audio-based architectures for sports summarization have been developed that extract audio features and classify the audio segments as applause, cheering, music, speech, etc. and also perform background noise modeling to further refine the results [20]. Along with audio, the amount of motion within the broadcast footage also helps identify exciting moments. The motion content of videos is encoded into the MPEG-7 motion activity descriptors. These motion vectors can be quantized and combined with the audio features to generate cumulative rankings of exciting moments [19, 9]. Audio and motion curves can also be combined to generate excitement time curves wherein the maximas represent the game highlights [4, 5] and the minimas around the maximas can be used to determine the segment boundaries of the highlight clips [11]. Motivated by these approaches, we investigate the use of audio and motion in our system.

An interesting area of research in sports summarization involves studying the problem from a affective rather than a cognitive point-of-view. The cognitive point-of-view is fact-based, wherein the features used for highlight detection are facts such as audio energy, amount of motion, position of ball, etc. In contrast, the affective point-of-view is emotion-based and tries to understand the human emotions within the game. Affect has three underlying dimensions: valence (ranging from pleasant to unpleasant), arousal (ranging from excited to peaceful) and control (no-control to full-control). All of human emotions can be mapped in as a set of points in this 3D VAC space. Computational methods have been developed to compute the valence and arousal using video and audio features and using them to find highlights in both sports and movies, thereby generating summaries from an affective point-of-view [6].

In the past few years, with the proliferation of social media and blogging websites, researchers have turned their attention to "crowd-sourced" sports summarization techniques. People watching broadcast games use Twitter to tweet their reactions. Mining the Twitter data for relevant tweets and looking for times when there is a spike in the volume of tweets gives us the moments in time that the crowd deems to be interesting [12, 7]. Crowd-sourced summaries have several differences over traditional summaries generated by sports professionals. In crowd-sourced summaries the highlights that get selected include interesting plays that require high degree of skill (expected and easy plays are ignored), controversial plays and unusual occurrences (like fights and stunts) and "lowlights" which are moments in time when the fans are frustrated and angry at their favorite teams [16]. Other methods include analyzing web-casting text and social media blogs, aligning them with the broadcast videos and looking for highlights using player popularity and crowd sentiments [17, 21].

While most of these published works use cues derived only

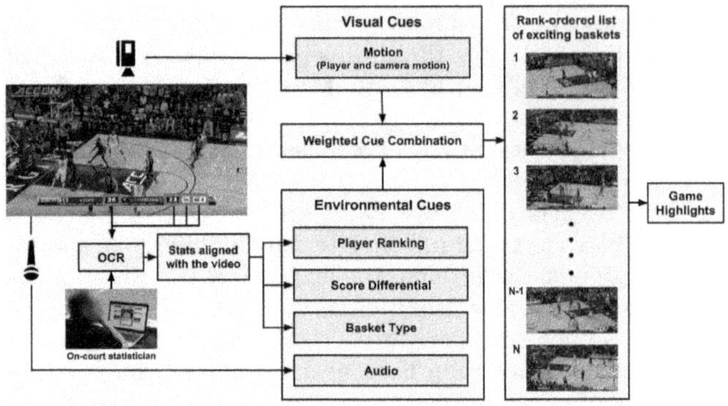

Figure 1: An overview of our system that uses visual and environmental contextual cues for automatically producing basketball highlights.

from the video data, the only other environmental contextual cue that is used is the commentator and audience audio. In the proposed work, we look at the play-by-play stats that is obtained from the on-court statisticians, a source of data that has largely been ignored by the research community. We show that the play-by-play stats contain a wealth of information that can be leveraged to generate highlights that are comparable to the ESPN-ranked highlights.

3. METHODOLOGY

An overview of our system is given in figure 1. The five different cues (four environmental and one visual) form the core component of our system. Let us look at each of these five cues in detail:

3.1 Cue 1: Audio

Gymnasiums and stadiums are equipped with microphones that capture the commentator and audience audio. Exciting baskets typically draw loud cheers from the audience and result in an elevation in the loudness and pitch in the commentator's voice. The changes in their audio levels are important contextual cues that are indicative of how exciting a basket is [4, 5, 11, 20].

In our study, the audience and commentator audio are obtained from the broadcast video and thus unavailable on two separate channels for analysis. Let us denote this signal as a. Before we can compute statistics on a, it has to be pre-processed in order to obtain the true audio loudness, a_l, based on human perception of loudness. We perform this pre-processing by following the audio filtering guidelines provided by the International Telecommunications Union (ITU) [8]. The first stage of pre-processing applies a pre-filtering of the audio signal prior to the Leq(RLB) measure. The pre-filtering accounts for the acoustic effects of the head, where the head is modeled as a rigid sphere. The second stage of the algorithm applies the RLB weighting curve, which consists of a single high-pass filter. With the pre-filter and the RLB filtering applied, the mean square energy in the measurement interval T is then measured. Once the weighted mean square level has been computed for each channel, the final step is to sum the N audio channels. The audio loudness levels obtained using this approach is shown for two sample baskets in figure 2.

The true audio level, a_l, obtained using the ITU's guidelines has been shown to be effective for use on audio programs *that are typical of broadcast content* which makes it the ideal audio pre-processing step for our system. Once the audio signal has been pre-processed, the measure of excitement for a given basket b is computed as

$$A_b = \sum_{i=1}^{m} p_i(a_l), \tag{1}$$

where $p_i(a_l)$ is the ith highest loudness peak in a 4 second window around the basket (3 seconds before the basket and 1 second after the basket). The overall audio loudness level for each basket, A_b, is obtained by summing the top m peaks. Empirically, for our NCAA dataset, m was determined to be 7. Finally, for each game, the A_b values for all the baskets are normalized between 0 and 1 by computing the min and max values across all baskets for that game.

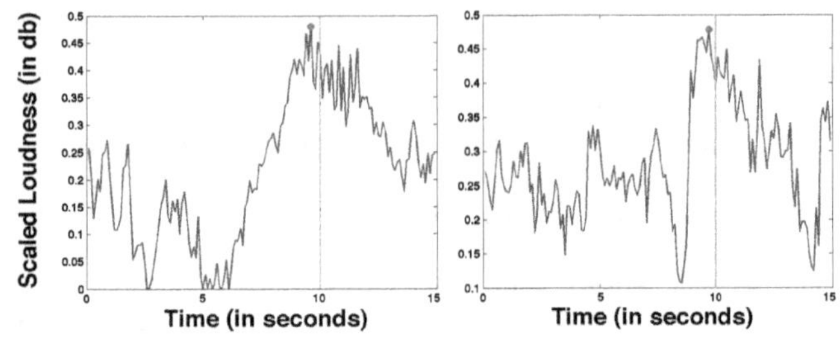

Figure 2: Audio loudness plots for two sample baskets. The red dot represents the time when the basket was scored and the green line (at the 10 second mark) represents the time when the scoreboard was updated to reflect the new scores. We can see that (1) the audio excitement peaks when the basket occurs, and (2) there is a slight delay of a few milliseconds between when the basket occurs and the scoreboard updates (the time difference between the red dot and the green line). The audio excitement drops soon after as the game continues.

Figure 3: A typical graphics overlay shown in basketball broadcasts. They contain four key pieces of information (shown highlighted using red boxes): (1) home team score, (2) visiting team score, (3) game period, and (4) game clock.

3.2 OCR: Aligning the Stats With the Videos

A main source of environmental context in our approach, is the play-by-play stats data that is generated by the on-court statisticians. The play-by-play data can be available in near-real-time or it can be available post-game. In either case, the stats need to be aligned with the broadcast video in order to determine when the particular play mentioned in the play-by-play stats actually occurred in the video. Unfortunately, the play-by-play stats are specific to a game and not specific to any particular broadcast video of the game. Hence they do not contain the video time-stamp of when the play occurred in the broadcast video.

In order to align the stats with the video, we introduce a novel Optical Character Recognition (OCR) based tech-

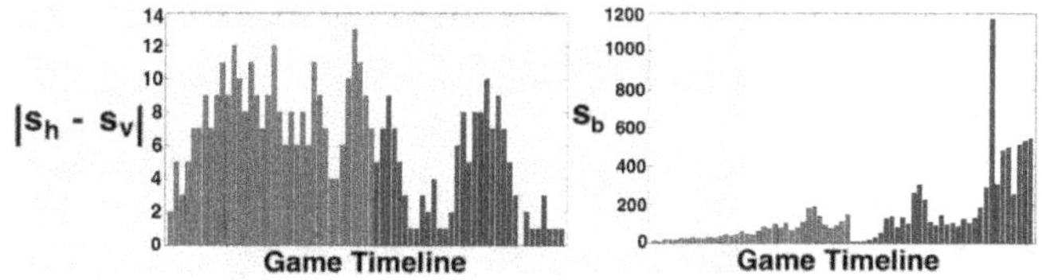

Figure 4: Score differential plots for a sample game. The x-axis represents the game timeline and the red and blue sections of the plots represent the 1st half and 2nd half of the game respectively. Left: $|s_h - s_v|$, the absolute score differential. Right: S_b, the inverted score differential weighted by the game-clock for each period of the game (see equation 2).

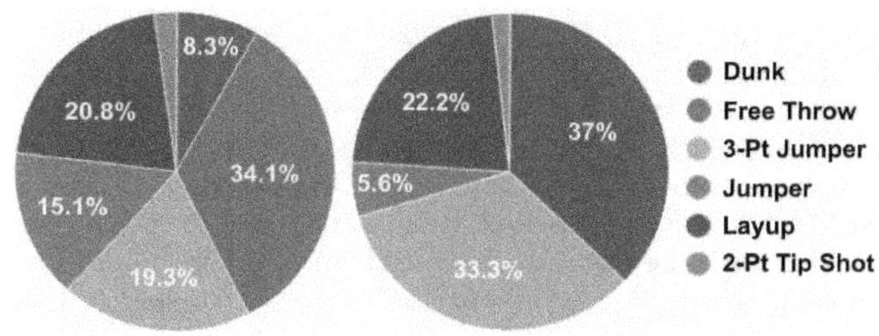

Figure 5: This figure shows the preference in baskets shown in the highlights generated by ESPN based on the basket type. Left: The distribution of baskets based on basket type across 10 full-length NCAA games. Right: The distribution of baskets based on basket type across the 10 highlights produced by ESPN for the same 10 NCAA games.

nique. The broadcast videos have a graphics overlay which contain four key pieces of information: (1) home team score, (2) visiting team score, (3) game period, and (4) game clock. An example is shown in Figure 3. Using the Tesseract OCR system [15], these four values are read for each frame of the video and are stored along with the corresponding video time-stamp. Next, we parse the play-by-play stats file and match the stored OCR info with each of the stats. This results in a mapping of the stats to the broadcast video. *Example:* Say for a particular game, for a particular frame of the video, using OCR on the graphics overlay, we know that the home team score changed from "35" to "38" while the visiting team score was "29" during the "1st half" of the game at game clock "12:22" and when the video timestamp was "28:34". While parsing the play-by-play stats, we see an entry "Player: Jahlil Okafor, Basket Type: 3-Pt Jump Shot, Game Period: 1st Half, Home Score: 38, Visiting Score: 29, Game Clock: 12:22". By matching this entry with the OCR data, we can see that this particular 3-Pt Jump Shot basket by Jahlil Okafor took place at time-stamp "28:34" in the video. This allows us to align the rich contextual info from the stats with the corresponding basket within the video.

Next, we extract three different cues from the stats data that are indicative of the excitement levels within the game: "Player Ranking", "Score Differential" and "Basket Type" . Each of these cues are described below.

3.3 Cue 2: Player Ranking

Baskets by "star" (top-ranked) players tend to be generate more excitement among basketball fans than baskets by other lower ranked players. Also, our analysis of ESPN highlights of 10 NCAA games showed that ESPN tends to favor baskets by the star athletes and showcases them more in the highlights. The game stats may or may not contain the player ranking, but they almost always have the data on each player's Points-Per-Game average (PPG). PPG has very strong correlation with player ranking and can be used as a proxy when player ranking data is not available. For each game, we normalize each player's PPG between the *min* and *max* PPG of all the players in that game (across both the teams). For each basket b, the scaled PPG value, P_b, of the player who made the basket gives us the "player ranking" excitement score for that basket.

3.4 Cue 3: Score Differential

People tend to find a game to be more exciting when the game is close ("neck-to-neck") and less exciting when one team has a huge lead over the other. Furthermore, the game tends to be more exciting if the scores of the two teams are close towards the end of the game period. For a given basket b, if the home team score is s_h and the visiting team score is s_v, then the "score differential" excitement, S_b, for that basket is computed as

$$S_b = \frac{1}{(|s_h - s_v| + 1)} * (1200 - g_s), \tag{2}$$

where g_s is the game clock in seconds. As the score differential gets smaller, the excitement score S_b increases. Each game period is 20 minutes long and the game clock counts down from 20:00 (1200 seconds) to 00:00 (0 seconds). So, the score differential is weighed by the amount of time remaining in the game period. Lower score differentials towards the end of the game period will get higher weights, and in-turn, higher excitement scores. The score differential plots for a sample game are shown in figure 4. The first half of the game is shown in red and the second half of the game is shown in blue. We can see the absolute score differential on the left and our "score differential" excitement, S_b, on the right. As with the other cues, the S_b scores are normalized between 0 and 1 for each game.

3.5 Cue 4: Basket Type

There are five types of baskets that are shown in basketball highlights: "Dunk", "Jumper", "Layup", "Two Point Tip Shot", and "Three Point Jumper" ("Free Throws" are typically not featured in the highlights). Each of these five baskets require different techniques and skills. Basketball fans tend to find some basket types more exciting than others. For example, the dunk shot is universally considered to be one of the most exciting basketball plays and is prominently featured in the highlights produced by ESPN. This is illustrated in figure 5. On the left, we can see the distribution of baskets based on the basket type across 10 full-length NCAA games. On the right, we can see the distribution of baskets based on the basket type across the 10 highlights produced by ESPN for the same 10 NCAA games. We can clearly see that ESPN favors certain basket type over others. Although "Free Throw" occurs 34.1% of the time, they are almost never featured in the highlights due to the fact that a "Free Throw" is not very exciting to watch. However, "Dunk" occurs only 8.3% of the time, but is featured in 37% of the highlights. This is due to the fact that the viewers love watching a "Dunk" and consider it to be much more exciting than the other basket types.

These 5 baskets can be rank-ordered in $5! = 120$ different ways. Each of these 120 different basket rankings were evaluated on our NCAA dataset and the ranking that best matched the user-generated ground-truth was chosen. The ranking with the best match was: "Dunk" >"Two Point Tip Shot" >"Three Point Jumper" >"Layup" >"Jumper". Using this ranking, for each basket b, the corresponding basket type's rank position, B_b, gives us the "basket type" excitement score for that basket. The B_b scores are normalized between 0 and 1 for each game.

3.6 Cue 5: Motion

The amount of player motion during a given play is usually an indication of how exciting the play is. For example, a "Free Throw" which has minimal player motion is less exciting than a "Dunk" wherein all the players are in rapid motion. The amount of camera motion is also indicative of the excitement levels of the game. For example, a large panning motion is involved when something exciting happens, such as a player running from one end of the court to another with the ball. In contrast, a free-throw has almost no camera movement and is less exciting than the other types of plays.

For each basket, we computed the optical flow using KLT tracking [14] across all the frames. Camera motion was determined by computing the dominant optical flow and player motion was computed by subtracting the camera motion from the overall flow. For each basket b, the corresponding camera motion magnitude M_b^c, player motion magnitude M_b^p, and the overall motion M_b, gives us the "motion" excitement scores for that basket. Our experiments showed that M_b was a better indicator of excitement when compared against M_b^c and M_b^p individually. The M_b scores are normalized between 0 and 1 for each game.

3.7 Cue Combination

Once all the 5 cues have been extracted for all the baskets and have been normalized for each game so that they have the same scale, we can combine them using a weighted sum. The final score, C_b, for each basket b is given by

$$C_b = \omega_1 * A_b + \omega_2 * P_b + \omega_3 * S_b + \omega_4 * B_b + \omega_5 * M_b, \quad (3)$$

where $\sum_{i=1}^{5} w_i = 1$. For our 25 game NCAA dataset, the weights are learned using 25-fold cross-validation. One of the games is held out as test and the weights are learned using the ground-truth excitement data from the other 24 games. The process is repeated 25 times, each time holding out a different game for testing. The final cues weights are computed by averaging the weights across all the 25 runs.

3.8 Generating Highlights

With the final cue combination score for all the baskets of a game, we can rank-order them in terms of their excitement scores. The next step is to put them together to form the game highlights. The top n exciting baskets are selected from the rank-ordered list, extracted from the broadcast video, sorted by time-stamp (so that the baskets appear in chronological order), and put together to form the game highlights. The value of n depends on the length of the desired summary.

Each of the n clips that were extracted from the broadcast video were 7 seconds long and had 1.5 second duration between when the basket occurred and the clip ended. These numbers were learned from the data by studying ESPN highlights. Figure 6 shows the histogram of durations of the baskets shown across 10 ESPN highlights and the time elapsed between when the basket occurred and the clip ended. We can see that ESPN prefers to have basket clips that are 6-7 seconds long with 1-2 seconds between the basket and the end of the clip.

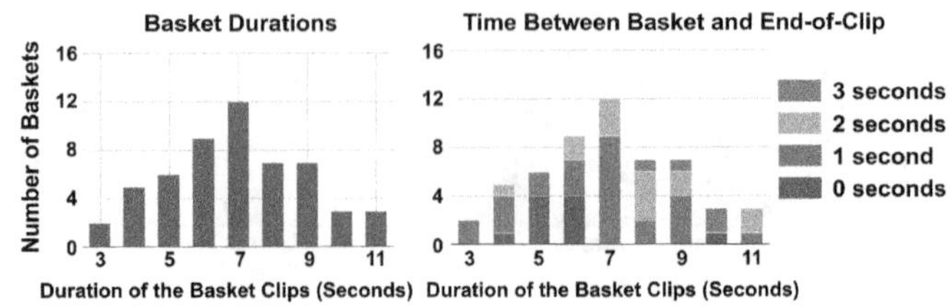

Figure 6: Left: Histogram of duration of the baskets shown across 10 ESPN highlights. We can see that ESPN prefers to show basket clips that are 6 to 7 seconds long. Right: Within each duration, we can see the time elapsed between when the basket occurred and the clip ended. For example, there are 12 baskets which were 7 seconds long. Out of these 12 baskets, 9 baskets had 1 second duration between when the basket happens and the clip ends and the other 3 baskets had 2 seconds duration.

4. EVALUATION

In this section, we describe our NCAA dataset and the process by which we collected ground-truth pairwise excitement for each of the baskets. This is followed by the evaluation of each of our cues and a demonstration of the effectiveness of weighted cue combination as a predictor of excitement. Finally, we evaluate the highlights generated using cue combination against highlights generated using each individual cue and also compare against the highlights produced by ESPN.

4.1 Dataset Description

In order to gather ground-truth excitement data and evaluate our approach, we built a new basketball dataset. This dataset will be made public.

We collected 25 full-length broadcast videos of NCAA games from 2015 (March Madness) from YouTube. This is a total of 2,126.5 minutes (35.44 hours) of basketball videos. All the videos are 720p HD at 30fps.

For each of these games, we also collected the play-by-play stats data. Next, using the OCR technique described above, we aligned the play-by-play stats with the corresponding videos and extracted all the baskets such that each basket clip was 8 seconds long (5.5 seconds before the basket and 2.5 seconds after the basket). Free Throws were ignored since Free Throws are typically not shown in highlight reels (see Figure 5). This gave us a total of 1,173 baskets across all the 25 NCAA games with the corresponding stats data for each basket. The stats data contains the following information: (1) player name, (2) basket type, (3) home team score, (4) visiting team score, (5) game clock, and (6) game period.

For 10 out of the 25 games, we also have the game highlights produced by ESPN. The videos were collected from

Table 1: The inter-rater reliability metrics for our A/B tests on assessing the pairwise excitement of the baskets in our NCAA dataset.

Agreement between N or more users	Number of baskets	Average pairwise agreement percentage	Average pairwise Cohen's kappa	Fleiss' kappa	Interpretation
8	1173	54.26%	0.067	0.067	Slight agreement
9	880	56.79%	0.105	0.105	Slight agreement
10	625	60.14%	0.154	0.154	Slight agreement
11	384	65.01%	0.212	0.213	Fair agreement
12	203	71.18%	0.270	0.270	Fair agreement
13	92	77.76%	0.304	0.305	Fair agreement
14	18	88.15%	0.416	0.382	Fair agreement

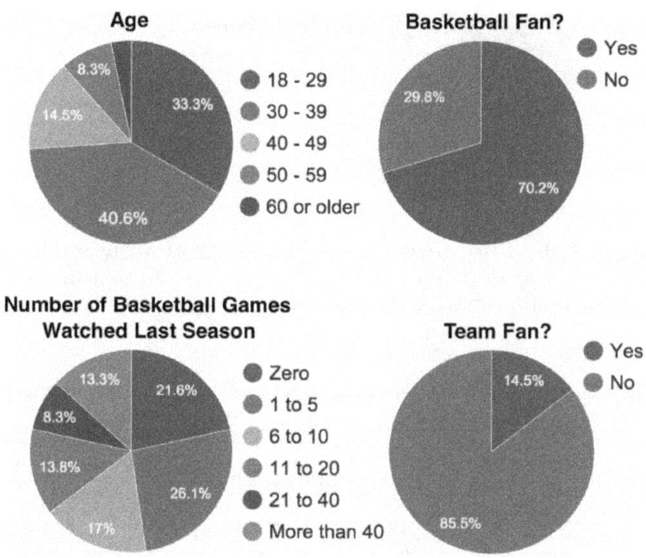

Figure 7: The distribution of 399 users across the different A/B tests for capturing the ground-truth pairwise excitement levels of the baskets. Top Left: Distribution across age groups. Top Right: Distribution on whether basketball fan or not. Bottom-Left: Distribution based on the number of games watched last season. Bottom Right: Distribution on whether team fan or not.

YouTube and are 720p HD at 30fps.

4.2 Ground-Truth Pairwise Excitement

Getting ground-truth excitement data on all the 1,173 baskets in our dataset lets us analyze each of our five cues individually and the effectiveness of cue combination. However, collecting this ground-truth is non-trivial. Users find it hard to subjectively rank a bunch of clips based on how exciting the clips are. The more the number of clips, the harder the task becomes. However, users find it fairly easy to pick the exciting clip given only two choices. Thus, in order to gather the ground-truth data, we conducted A/B test user studies on Amazon's Mechanical Turk where users were shown a basket from one of the games and another random basket from the same game and were asked the question "Which of these two clips is more exciting to watch?". We took several steps to ensure the quality of these user studies:

- Each A/B pair was shown to 15 different users in order to get good data and reduce the likelihood of selection based on chance. This resulted in 17,595 A/B tests (15 studies for each of the 1,173 baskets).
- We required all Mechanical Turk users to have atleast 95% approval rating and a minimum of atleast 1,000 previously approved tasks. The A/B tests took an average of 1 minute and 29 seconds and the users were paid $0.03 per study.
- The order in which the clips were shown in each A/B test was randomized. This further decreased the likelihood of user bias towards any one choice.
- The users were asked additional questions as a part of each A/B test in order for us to gain more insight into who our users were. These additional questions were:
  - "Are you a basketball fan?" [options "Yes, "No"].
  - "Are you a fan (or alumnus) of one of the teams in the clips?" [options "Yes, "No"].
  - "How many basketball games did you watch last season?" [options: "None", "1 to 5", "6 to 10", "11 to 20", "21 to 40", "Greater than 40"].
  - "What's your age?" [options: "18 to 29", "30 to 39", "40 to 49", "50 to 59", "60 or older"].

After all the A/B test user studies were completed, we analyzed the data and found that there were 399 unique users who had participated in our studies. The distribution of the users based on the questions we asked is as shown in Figure 7. We can see that the majority of our users are between the age range of 18 to 39, are mostly basketball fans, and mostly not fans of any of the two teams shown in the clips.

4.3 Inter-Rater Reliability

In order to compute the overall consensus across our 15 A/B tests for each of the 1,173 baskets, we compute two inter-rater reliability metrics – the Fleiss' kappa and the average pairwise Cohen's kappa [3]. These statistical measures take into account the amount of agreement that could be expected to occur through chance. Table 1 shows the inter-rater reliability metrics for different values of N, where N is the number of users who agreed that one basket was more exciting than the other. For example, from Table 1 we can see that there are 384 baskets for which 11 or more users

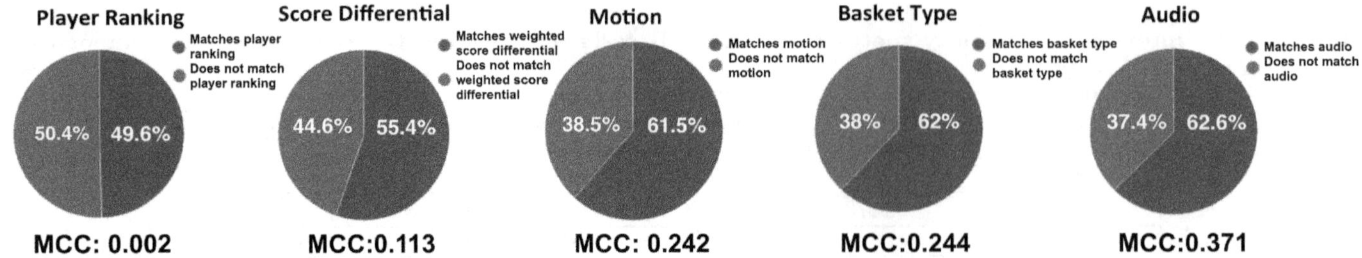

Figure 8: The performance of each cue as a predictor of the excitement levels of baskets.

(out of the total 15) agreed that one basket was more exciting than the other in the randomized A/B tests. This has a Fleiss' kappa of 0.213 which is interpreted as "Fair Agreement".

4.4 Evaluating Individual Cues

The pairwise excitement ground-truth data allows us to study the effectiveness of each of our five cues in predicting how exciting a basket is. For our evaluations, we ignore the baskets which were hard to decide and focus only those baskets which had atleast 2/3rd agreement among the users, i.e. atleast 10 out of 15 must agree that one basket is more exciting that the other. This lets us study the effectiveness of our cues in the absence of noise from the hard-to-decide baskets. From Table 1, we can see that this gives us 625 baskets for evaluations.

For this evaluation, each of the 625 A/B pairs that was shown to the users, is given as input to our system. For each individual cue, the system decides which basket is more exciting. The output of our system for each cue is then compared against the majority decision made by the users for that basket. If the system decision is same as the user decision, then we have a match. For each cue, we also compute the Matthews Correlation Coefficient (MCC) that gives the amount of agreement or disagreement between the system decision and the user decision [10, 13]. If MCC is -1, it means that the system decision and the user decision are in total disagreement. If MCC is +1, it means that the system decision and the user decision are in total agreement. If the MCC is 0, it means that the match is decision is no better than random.

The performance of each individual cue is shown in figure 8. We can see that "Motion", "Basket Type" and "Audio" are relatively strong indicators of how exciting a basket is while "Score Differential" and "Player Ranking" are very close to being no better than random. Out of the five cues, "Audio" is the strongest indicator with a MCC score of 0.371.

4.5 Evaluating Weighted Cue Combination

To learn the weights of the various cues, we perform 25-fold cross-validation where we hold out all the baskets from 1 game for testing while using all the baskets from the other 24 games for learning the weights. The process is repeated 25 times, with a different game being held out for testing in each run. In each run, all combinations of weights are tried and the combination that results in the most matches with the user decision on the held out test game is deemed as the winning set of weights for that run. After all the runs are complete, we average the weights across the 25 runs to get the final set of weights.

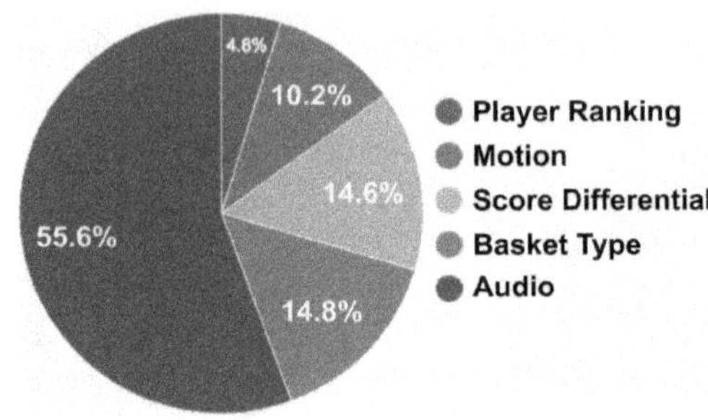

Figure 9: The percentage of the total weight that each cue gets during weighted cue combination (after running 25-fold cross-validation).

Table 2: McNemar's tests on statistical significance between each individual cue vs. cue combination.

	χ^2	p-value
Player Ranking vs. Cue Combination	86.98	<0.0001
Score Differential vs. Cue Combination	63.00	<0.0001
Motion vs. Cue Combination	31.74	<0.0001
Basket Type vs. Cue Combination	57.34	<0.0001
Audio vs. Cue Combination	32.48	<0.0001

The average percentage of baskets that matched user decision across 25 runs was 75.33%. The lowest average percentage was 52.81% with the highest was 91.90%. When the weights are averaged across all the 25 runs and normalized to add upto one, as shown in figure 9, we see that **Player Ranking** gets **4.8%** of the total weight, while **Motion** gets **10.2%**, **Score Differential** gets **14.6%**, **Basket Type** gets **14.8%**, and Audio gets **55.6%** of the total weight respectively.

It is interesting to see that after combining all the cues, Audio makes up 55.6% of the total share. This shows that the audience cheers and the loudness and pitch of the commentator does indeed drive the excitement levels during a basketball game. It is also interesting to note that the top three dominant cues, Audio, Basket Type, and Score Differential, which make up 85% of the total weight are all contextual cues derived from the environment. This highlights the importance of the use of contextual cues in our approach.

When the final average weights are used in cue combination and the system output is compared with the user decision, the percentage of baskets that match the user decision is **76.4%**. This is a significant improvement over the best percentage obtained by any single cue (62.6% with Audio,

Table 3: A/B test results with all users: Cue combination highlights vs highlights generated using the individual cues.

Cue Combination vs.	Num games for which cue combination highlights was selected by user majority	Median user agreement percentage
Player Ranking	22 / 25	61.29%
Score Differential	17 / 25	54.84%
Motion	17 / 25	58.06%
Basket Type	16 / 25	58.06%
Audio	16 / 25	61.29%

Table 4: A/B test results with basketball fans: Cue combination highlights vs highlights generated using the individual cues.

Cue Combination vs.	Num games for which cue combination highlights was selected by user majority	Median user agreement percentage
Player Ranking	20 / 25	60.00%
Score Differential	14 / 25	60.00%
Motion	18 / 25	60.00%
Basket Type	16 / 25	60.00%
Audio	15 / 25	60.00%

see 8). Furthermore, the MCC score goes up to **0.528** (from the previous best of 0.371 with only Audio). In order to ensure that the improvement we see from cue combination over each of the individual cues is statistically significant, we ran the McNemar's chi-square test (with Yates' continuity correction). The *null* hypothesis says that the improvements we see after cue combination are due to chance., However as shown in Table 2, the χ^2 values are greater than the critical value (at 95% significance level) of 3.84 and the p-values are less than the significance level (α) of 0.05. Thus the *null* hypothesis can be rejected allowing us to conclude that the improvements seen after cue combination are *not* due to chance.

4.6 Evaluating Highlights

With the final weights for each cue, we can now rank order all the baskets in a game by their excitement score, pick the top N baskets, order them by the game clock (so that they are in chronological order), and generate the highlight video. For the 10 games for which we have ESPN highlights to compare against, we pick N as the number of baskets that ESPN put in their highlights for each of those 10 games. For the other 15 games, we pick N to be 10 (the average number of baskets that ESPN shows in their highlights).

Cue Combination vs. Individual Cues: We generated highlights for all the 25 games using cue combination and also using each of the five individual cues. This gave us 6 highlight videos for each game. Figure 10 shows 4 sample frames from the highlights generated for the Louisville vs. North Carolina NCAA game. Highlights generated using only Player Ranking mostly featured baskets by Terry Rozier (circled in red) who was Louisville Cardinals' star player (now a NBA draft pick for the Boston Celtics). The highlights generated using only Score Differential featured "neck-to-neck" baskets (for example, a score of 58-57 can be seen in the figure) while the highlights generated using only Motion featured baskets with lots of player and camera motion (as seen in the figure). Finally, the highlights generated using only Basket Type featured mostly Dunk shots (a sample shot is shown in the figure).

In order to see if users prefer cue combination highlights over the highlights generated by individual cues, we ran another A/B test user study. Given the harder nature of this study where users have to watch two minute-long clips, we doubled the number of users per test from 15 to 31. For each game, the users were asked to pick the highlight that they preferred. Similar to the previous study, sufficient care was taken to randomize the A/B pairs and the users were asked to fill in a similar questionnaire mentioning their age, if they are a basketball fan, if they are a fan of one of the teams, and the number of games they watched last season.

This study had 335 unique users out of which 245 are basketball fans. The results of the study with all 335 users are shown in Table 3 and the results with only the 245 basketball fans is shown in Table 4. We can see that highlights generated using cue combination were preferred over the highlights generated using the individual cues by both regular users and basketball fans. However, it is interesting to note that basketball fans seem to prefer score differential highlights slightly more than regular users. This could be due to the fact that basketball fans watch the game more closely and pay more attention to the scores shown on the graphics overlay.

Cue Combination vs. ESPN: Our dataset contains the highlights produced by ESPN for 10 out of the 25 games. We ran a similar A/B test study with 31 users where users were shown the ESPN highlight and our cue combination highlight and were asked to pick the highlight that they preferred. To make the comparison fair, we regenerated the ESPN highlights using the same video production pipeline that we used to produce our highlights. This ensured that both the highlights shown in the A/B tests are visually similar.

The results of the A/B tests showed that among all users, our highlights were preferred in 5/10 games and the ESPN-ranked highlights were preferred in the other **5/10** games. The median agreement percentage was 51.61%. Among basketball fans, our highlights were preferred in **7/10** games while the ESPN-ranked highlights were preferred in 3/10 games. The median agreement percentage was 53.33%. Although basketball fans showed a slight preference to our highlights, the median agreement percentage shows that the decision was really hard to make. This shows that the users had a tough time picking between our highlights and ESPN-ranked highlights which in-turn indicates that we are performing as well as ESPN in picking baskets for producing basketball highlights.

Comparing the individual baskets that were picked for the highlights across all the 10 games, we noticed 67.4% overlap in the baskets that we picked and the baskets that ESPN picked. This is illustrated in figure 11 where we show the basket picks for a sample game (Duke vs. Florida State, 9th Feb 2015). We can see that across both the game periods,

Figure 10: Sample frames from highlights generated using individual cues. From left to right: Player Ranking, Score Differential, Motion, and Basket Type.

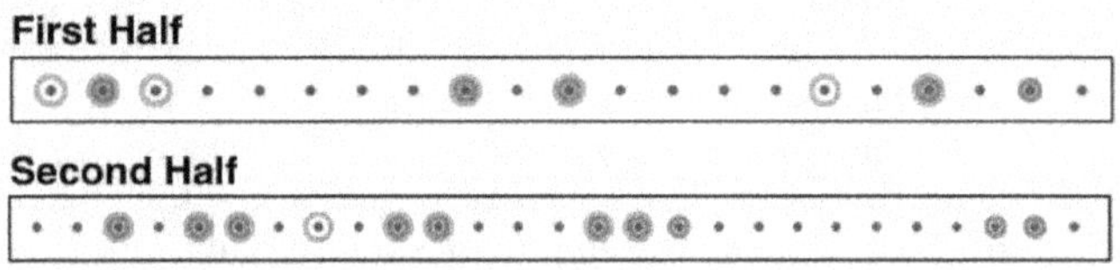

Figure 11: Basket picks for a sample game (Duke vs. Florida State, 9th Feb 2015). Each blue dot represents a basket that occurred during the game play. Baskets with red circles were picked by ESPN for their highlights and baskets with green circles were picked by our method for our highlights. We can see that 11 out of the 15 baskets were commonly picked (4 overlaps in the first half and 7 overlaps in the second half).

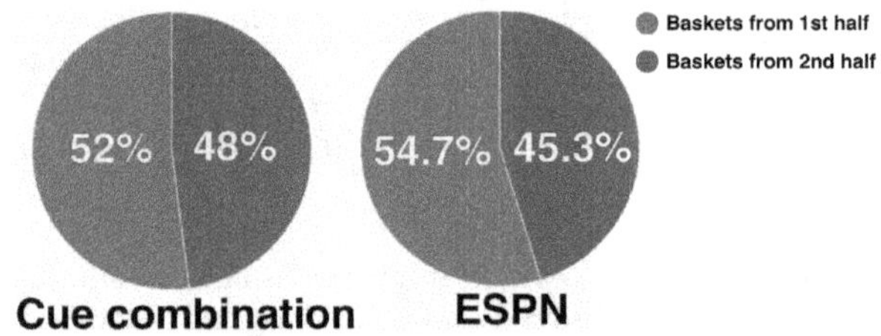

Figure 12: The distribution of baskets across the two halves of the game for 10 games. Left: The basket distribution for our cue combination highlights. Right: The basket distribution for ESPN highlights. We can see that our approach isn't biased towards any particular half of the game and closely follows ESPN's distribution across the two halves.

out of the 15 baskets, 11 baskets were commonly picked by our cue-combination approach and by ESPN. The probability of these 11 baskets being picked in common, by chance, is 0.00005.

Another factor to consider is the distribution of the baskets shown in the highlights across the two halves of the game. As shown in figure 12, for the 10 games, our cue combination picks 48% of the baskets from the first half of the game and 52% of the baskets from the second half of the game. Looking at the ESPN highlights for those 10 games, we can see that ESPN has a very similar distribution. They pick 45.3% of the baskets from the first half and 54.7% of the games from the second half. This shows that our approach isn't biased towards baskets from any single period of the game and closely follows ESPN's distribution.

Figure 11 and figure 12 further highlights the practicality of our approach and the similarity of our highlights to the ESPN-ranked highlights. Also, this gives us an insight into why the users had a hard time deciding between our highlights and ESPN-ranked highlights in the A/B test user studies.

5. DISCUSSION

Our comprehensive user studies and analysis have shown the effectiveness of leveraging contextual cues derived from the environment in determining the exciting baskets of a game and automatically producing the game highlights.

However, there are some limitations of our work. The ground-truth data that we used for evaluations is the pairwise excitement gathered using our A/B tests. Pairwise excitement scores are inherently different from true excitement scores wherein the users look at all the baskets in a game and rank orders them from least exciting to most exciting. While this kind of data would be more useful than pairwise excitement scores, it is practically impossible to get the true excitement scores through user studies. A typical basketball game has 50 or more baskets and it is very hard for humans to look at so many baskets, remember their excitement levels, and rank order them. Another limitation is that our method does not adaptively change the weights of the cues based on changes in the environment. For example, if the audience start leaving after the first half, we should be able to detect this and adaptively decrease the weight given to the audio cue. This is a good direction for our future work.

While running the A/B tests where users are shown two basket clips and asked to pick the one that is more exciting, we wondered how the results would change if users were shown the same A/B pair, but with only the audio and only the video. To answer this question, we picked the top 203 baskets that had 80% (12/15) agreement between the users (i.e. baskets for which most users had a strong consensus in deciding between choice A and choice B), and generated two more A/B tests with the same pairs as before. But this time one of the A/B tests had just the audio of the game and the other A/B test had clips with just the video (with the audio stripped out). We ran these new A/B tests for the 203 baskets with 15 users per test (as before) and analyzed the results. It is interesting to note that for the audio-only case, the agreement fell from 80% to **59.70%** and the Fleiss' kappa value dropped from 0.270 (fair agreement) to **0.177** (slight agreement), and for the video-only case, the average pairwise agreement fell to **59.82%** and the Fleiss' kappa value dropped to **0.116** (slight agreement). This shows that the strong consensus between the users broke down when they had to pick between clips that had either only the audio or only the video.

Another interesting question is "how would a highlight

generated using randomly selected baskets compare against our cue combination highlights and against ESPN-ranked highlights?". To answer this question, we generated 10 highlights using random baskets selected from 10 of the games (and placed in chronological order) and ran additional A/B tests for evaluating these random highlights against our cue combination highlights and also against the ESPN-ranked highlights. As before, we ran the tests with 31 users per A/B test. The results showed that among all users our cue-combination highlights were preferred over random highlights in **7/10** games with **61.29%** median user agreement. Basketball fans preferred our highlights in **8/10** games with **53.33%** median user agreement. The A/B test results against ESPN-ranked highlights showed that among all users ESPN highlights were preferred over random highlights in **7/10** games with a median user agreement of **54.84%**. Basketball fans preferred ESPN-ranked highlights in **9/10** games with a median user agreement of **60.00%**. These results tell us that while users prefer our highlights and ESPN-ranked highlights over random highlights, the random highlights still do get picked in some of the games. This further highlights the subjective and complex nature of the problem domain.

6. CONCLUSION

In this paper, we explored the use of context derived from the environment along with the visual cues to automatically produce basketball highlights. We explored 5 cues that are indicative of excitement levels in basketball games. We introduced a new dataset of 25 NCAA games with 1,173 baskets with ground-truth pair-wise excitement scores for evaluating our approach. We conducted comprehensive user studies with multiple participants which showed the effectiveness of our cues and our cue combination method that can produce highlights that are comparable to those produced by ESPN. Interesting directions for future work include exploring methods to collect more ground-truth excitement data in a way that maximizes inter-rater reliability, exploring more cues that are indicative of excitement levels, and dynamically adapting the weights of the cues as the game proceeds based on the changes in the environment.

7. REFERENCES

[1] Gallup sports popularity survey. http://www.gallup.com/poll/4735/sports.aspx.

[2] A. Ekin, A. M. Tekalp, and R. Mehrotra. Automatic soccer video analysis and summarization. *IEEE Transactions on Image Processing*, 12(7):796–807, 2003.

[3] J. L. Fleiss and J. Cohen. The equivalence of weighted kappa and the intraclass correlation coefficient as measures of reliability. *Educational and psychological measurement*, 1973.

[4] A. Hanjalic. Generic approach to highlights extraction from a sport video. In *International Conference on Image Processing (ICIP)*, volume 1. IEEE, 2003.

[5] A. Hanjalic. Multimodal approach to measuring excitement in video. In *ICME*, volume 2. IEEE, 2003.

[6] A. Hanjalic and L.-Q. Xu. Affective video content representation and modeling. *IEEE Trans. on Multimedia*, 7(1):143–154, 2005.

[7] J. Hannon, K. McCarthy, J. Lynch, and B. Smyth. Personalized and automatic social summarization of events in video. In *Proc. 16th Int. Conf. on Intelligent User Interfaces*, pages 335–338. ACM, 2011.

[8] R. ITU-R. Itu-r bs. 1770-2, algorithms to measure audio programme loudness and true-peak audio level. *International Telecommunications Union, Genewa*, 2011.

[9] C. Liu, Q. Huang, S. Jiang, L. Xing, Q. Ye, and W. Gao. A framework for flexible summarization of racquet sports video using multiple modalities. *CVIU*, 113(3):415–424, 2009.

[10] B. W. Matthews. Comparison of the predicted and observed secondary structure of t4 phage lysozyme. *Biochimica et Biophysica Acta (BBA)-Protein Structure*, 405(2):442–451, 1975.

[11] E. Mendi, H. B. Clemente, and C. Bayrak. Sports video summarization based on motion analysis. *Computers & Electrical Engineering*, 39(3):790–796, 2013.

[12] J. Nichols, J. Mahmud, and C. Drews. Summarizing sporting events using twitter. In *Proc. ACM Int. Conf. on Intelligent User Interfaces*, pages 189–198. ACM, 2012.

[13] D. M. Powers. Evaluation: from precision, recall and f-measure to roc, informedness, markedness and correlation. 2011.

[14] J. Shi and C. Tomasi. Good features to track. In *IEEE CVPR*, pages 593–600. IEEE, 1994.

[15] R. Smith. An overview of the tesseract ocr engine. In *icdar*, pages 629–633. IEEE, 2007.

[16] A. Tang and S. Boring. # epicplay: crowd-sourcing sports video highlights. In *Proceedings of the SIGCHI Conference on Human Factors in Computing Systems*, pages 1569–1572. ACM, 2012.

[17] D. Tjondronegoro, X. Tao, J. Sasongko, and C. H. Lau. Multi-modal summarization of key events and top players in sports tournament videos. In *IEEE WACV*, pages 471–478. IEEE, 2011.

[18] X. Tong, Q. Liu, Y. Zhang, and H. Lu. Highlight ranking for sports video browsing. In *Proceedings of the 13th annual ACM international conference on Multimedia*, pages 519–522. ACM, 2005.

[19] Z. Xiong, R. Radhakrishnan, and A. Divakaran. Generation of sports highlights using motion activity in combination with a common audio feature extraction framework. In *ICIP*. IEEE, 2003.

[20] Z. Xiong, R. Radhakrishnan, A. Divakaran, and T. S. Huang. Audio events detection based highlights extraction from baseball, golf and soccer games in a unified framework. In *ICASSP)*, volume 5. IEEE, 2003.

[21] C. Xu, J. Wang, H. Lu, and Y. Zhang. A novel framework for semantic annotation and personalized retrieval of sports video. *IEEE Trans. on Multimedia*, 10(3):421–436, 2008.

[22] Z. Zhao, S. Jiang, Q. Huang, and G. Zhu. Highlight summarization in sports video based on replay detection. In *International Conference on Multimedia and Expo*, pages 1613–1616. IEEE, 2006.

Server Allocation for Multiplayer Cloud Gaming

Yunhua Deng[‡] Yusen Li[§] Xueyan Tang[‡] Wentong Cai[‡]
[‡]School of Computer Science and Engineering, Nanyang Technological University, Singapore
[§]Department of Computer Science and Information Security, Nankai University, China
{yhdeng, asxytang, aswtcai}@ntu.edu.sg liyusen@nbjl.nankai.edu.cn

ABSTRACT

Advances in cloud computing and GPU virtualization are allowing the game industry to move into a cloud gaming era. While shifting standalone video games to the cloud gaming mode is straightforward, adapting multiplayer online games to the cloud gaming paradigm faces unique challenges. In this paper, we consider multiplayer cloud gaming (MCG), which is the natural integration of multiplayer online gaming and cloud gaming paradigms. We formulate an MCG server allocation problem with the objective of minimizing the total server rental and bandwidth cost charged by the cloud to support an MCG session. We propose several efficient heuristics to address the MCG server allocation problem which is hard to solve optimally. We conduct extensive experiments using real Internet latency and cloud pricing data to evaluate the effectiveness of our proposed algorithms as well as several alternatives. Experimental results show that our best algorithm can achieve near-optimal cost under real-time latency constraints.

Keywords

Cloud gaming; multiplayer online games; server allocation

1. INTRODUCTION

Cloud computing has been undergoing rapid expansion in recent years. Nowadays, many clouds such as Amazon EC2 [1] provide abundant, elastic and geo-distributed computation, storage and bandwidth resources for running various online services. Most recently, the maturity of cloud computing and recent advances in GPU virtualization have brought forth a new application – *cloud gaming* [13, 9, 19, 46]. In cloud gaming, a video game is hosted on a cloud server and virtually all the graphics required for the game are processed by the server. An end user's machine only needs to display/play the game screen/audio captured and streamed by the server, as well as to relay the user's game input commands (e.g., mouse clicks or keystrokes) to the server for game controls. With cloud gaming, users can play resource-intensive video games on less powerful devices anywhere and anytime over the Internet.

In this paper, we consider *multiplayer cloud gaming (MCG)*, a new form of multiplayer online gaming in the cloud gaming era.

MM '16, October 15-19, 2016, Amsterdam, Netherlands
© 2016 ACM. ISBN 978-1-4503-3603-1/16/10. . . $15.00
DOI: http://dx.doi.org/10.1145/2964284.2964301

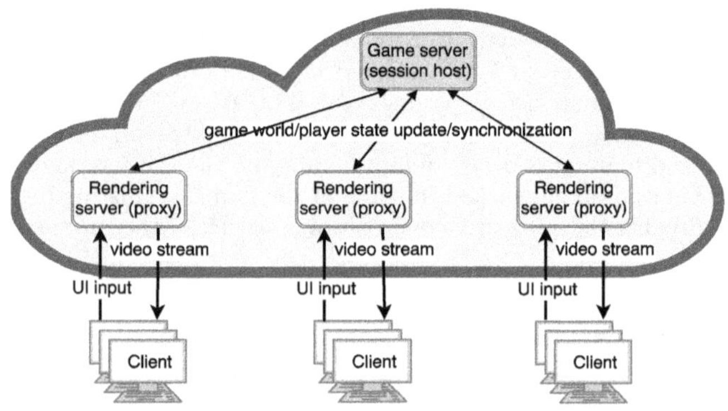

Figure 1: An MCG architecture.

In conventional multiplayer online gaming, a game server, which is the authoritative source of game events, disseminates state updates about the game session to its connected clients, allowing them to maintain their own versions of the game world. Meanwhile, the games are also required to run on clients' devices. Therefore, clients not only need sufficient hardware resources to render the games, but also require the games to be installed locally on their devices. By contrast, in MCG, clients can enjoy multiplayer online gaming without these hassles thanks to the advantages brought by cloud gaming. Figure 1 depicts the architecture of MCG. The game server is identical to that in traditional multiplayer online gaming. The rendering servers, on the one hand, act as the "clients" that are connected to the game server in traditional multiplayer online gaming to receive/exchange state updates, and on the other hand, function as the servers which host the game application instances for their connected clients in cloud gaming. The rendering servers process game graphics and logics and capture the game scenes for the clients to display. The clients are known as "thin-clients" which merely transit user interaction (UI) input to the rendering servers. A number of cloud gaming systems supporting MCG have emerged in recent years [24, 33, 29, 39, 10].

With MCG, a game server and a set of rendering servers for the players need to be located and launched in the clouds for each game session. In this paper, we focus on the provisioning and acquisition of these servers from available data centers with the minimum cost. Heterogeneous server and bandwidth prices from different datacenters together with the real-time interaction requirements of gaming applications present unique opportunities and challenges for MCG server allocation. The main contributions of this paper are:

- We formulate an MCG server allocation problem, with the objective of minimizing the total server rental and bandwidth cost charged by the cloud to support an MCG session. This problem can be viewed as a natural extension to the traditional game server selection problem, with several distinctive characteristics related to the cloud gaming paradigm.

- We propose a set of efficient heuristic algorithms to address the MCG server allocation problem, and conduct extensive experiments using real-world data to evaluate the performance of the proposed algorithms as well as several alternatives. Our best algorithm can achieve near-optimal cost while satisfying the latency constraints.

The rest of this paper is organized as follows. Section 2 presents a summary of the related work. Section 3 discusses the requirements of MCG. Section 4 formulates the MCG server allocation problem. Section 5 proposes a set of cost-aware client-to-datacenter assignment algorithms to efficiently address the MCG server allocation problem. The experimental setup and results are shown and discussed in Section 6. Section 7 discusses some possible extensions and future work. Finally, Section 8 concludes the paper.

2. RELATED WORK

Cloud computing provides a scalable and cost-effective way for hosting and delivering large-scale services over the Internet to geo-distributed end users. The problem of how to place services in multiple data centers is a key challenge and has been extensively studied. Existing work on this problem generally targeted at minimizing energy consumption (or electricity cost) while guaranteeing some performance requirement such as response time [34, 37]. In more complicated scenarios, the demand and resource price fluctuations were also considered [38, 49]. However, these service placement models are quite different from our problem in which we aim to minimize the total cost of cloud server rental and bandwidth usage while satisfying the real-time delay constraint among clients in a multiplayer cloud gaming session.

Our work is also relevant to the game server selection problems for online gaming or Distributed Interactive Applications (DIAs) in general. In DIAs, given a set of clients and a set of candidate server locations, the objective is to choose one or more servers to minimize the interaction delay among the clients [22, 47, 48, 50, 51], or to place the minimum number of servers while satisfying some QoS requirements [17, 18, 28, 40]. However, cloud gaming is quite different from traditional online gaming. In addition to the game servers, the rendering servers for the clients also need to be deployed in cloud gaming, which makes the problem much more challenging. There is also some work [45] focusing on exploiting well-provisioned inter-datacenter connections to reduce the communication latency from clients to servers. In contrast, the purpose of cloud gaming is to leverage the rich computing resources in the clouds for clients to play high-quality games without dedicated hardware equipped.

Some server provisioning issues in cloud gaming have been studied recently. Hong *et al.* [23] considered the problem of how to consolidate multiple rendering servers (virtual machines) on a physical machine in order to provide high gaming Quality of Experience (QoE) in a cost-effective way. The request dispatching and admission control issues were studied in [43] with the goal of cutting down the provisioning cost while guaranteeing the queuing delay requirement. However, all of the above work has focused on cloud gaming operators with their own private datacenters, and monetary cost issues for hosting cloud gaming in public clouds were not considered. A server rented from the public cloud is normally charged at a fixed rate regardless of whether it is fully or partially utilized. Many cloud gaming systems have acquired resources (virtual machines) from public clouds to serve as rendering and game servers [39, 29]. The problem of how to allocate cloud resources to minimize the interaction delay among clients was studied in [42]. However, the rental cost of servers was not considered either. Very recently, Tian *et al.* [41] studied the cost for running single-player games in cloud gaming where each player is assigned to a separate and dedicated server. In contrast, we focus on multiplayer cloud gaming where server sharing among clients plays an important role in optimizing the server cost.

3. REQUIREMENTS OF MCG

In an MCG session, each player connects to a cloud server that captures and streams the game screen to the player. This cloud server is called the *rendering server* or *R-server* for that player. A single R-server may be shared by multiple players in the same session, if the server has sufficient capacity to process all the rendering and streaming workloads of these players. All the R-servers communicate with a *game server* or *G-server* which manages and updates the game state during the session.

In conventional multiplayer online gaming, *matchmaking* is the process of setting up game sessions with the goal of finding a required number of players for each game session subject to some constraint on the network latency between any player and the game server [22, 35]. In MCG, matchmaking becomes more complicated due to the presence of R-servers in-between the players and the G-server. Consider the scenario where we are given a set of clients C that form the player group, a set of datacenters D, and the G-server located at a network location g which may either be one of the datacenters or outside all datacenters. An MCG session is called *feasible* if we can find at least one datacenter to place an R-server for each player such that, 1) the connection latency from each player to the G-server through his R-server is below a threshold L_G, and 2) the connection latency from each player to his R-server is below another threshold L_R. That is, for each client $c \in C$, there exists at least one datacenter $d_c \in D$ to satisfy the following constraints:

$$l(c, d_c) + l(d_c, g) \leq L_G \text{ and } l(c, d_c) \leq L_R, \qquad (1)$$

where $l(c, d_c)$ is the network latency from c to d_c, and $l(d_c, g)$ is the network latency from d_c to g, while L_G and L_R are the latency thresholds.

The first latency threshold L_G is related to the maximum tolerable network latency for traditional online gaming. Note that, in traditional online gaming, the actual game is stored, executed and rendered on the player's computer locally and the player's global in-game actions such as firing at the enemies are sent to the G-server. The consequences of an in-game action such as an enemy being killed are only seen by the player after the lag caused by the time taken for the action to reach the G-server and the time taken for the update to come back to the player's computer over the Internet. The second latency threshold L_R is related to the maximum tolerable network latency for cloud gaming. Note that, in cloud gaming, the actual game is stored, executed, and rendered on the R-server remotely and the player's raw input commands such as keystrokes are sent to the R-server for controlling the game. The consequences of an input command such as "moving forward", can only be displayed on the player's computer screen after a time lag. This lag is caused by the time taken for the input command to reach the R-server for rendering and the time taken for the game scene updates to be streamed back to the player's computer over the Internet. The network latency is the major source of lag for traditional online gaming [16]. The delay caused by video coding (i.e., server-side encoding and client-side decoding) adds another source of lag for cloud gaming [15]. In addition, in traditional online gaming, lag can often be hidden to some extent using client-side compensation techniques such as dead-reckoning [36, 14], but in cloud gaming, lag is far more difficult to hide as the client does not maintain any game state locally [27]. Moreover, the smoothness of live video streaming in cloud gaming is heavily dependent on the network quality which is likely to degrade as the network latency (distance) increases. Therefore, L_R is often required to be smaller than L_G. Several empirical studies [20, 25] have been conducted for traditional online gaming and cloud gaming, respectively. These studies confirmed that the network latency requirement in cloud gaming is generally more stringent than that in traditional online gaming.

Both latency thresholds L_G and L_R are dependent on the game genre [20, 25]. In general, fast-paced games such as first-person shooter or car racing games, have more stringent latency requirements (i.e., lower latency thresholds) than moderate-paced games such as third-person role-playing or strategy/simulation games (e.g., L_G = 150 ms and L_R = 100 ms for fast-paced games, and L_G = 300 ms and L_R = 200 ms for moderate-paced games according to [20, 25]). Once the connection latencies are below the corresponding thresholds, any further reduction of them would not necessarily bring along easily-noticeable improvement in the player's perceived playability [20, 25]. Thus, our objective of MCG server allocation is not to minimize the above two connection latencies, but to optimize the server allocation cost subject to the latency thresholds. Specifically, our objective is to minimize the total monetary cost of server and network resources charged by the cloud to support an MCG session, from the perspective of the game host that can be either the player who initiates the session or a cloud gaming service provider.

4. PROBLEM FORMULATION

Once a feasible MCG session is set up after matchmaking, we need to allocate servers to ensure that each client can be served by an R-server launched at one of the datacenters. For each client $c \in C$, all the datacenters that satisfy constraints (1) are called the *eligible* datacenters for c. Let $E_c \subseteq D$ denote the set of eligible datacenters for each client c. For each datacenter $d \in D$, let $s(d)$ denote the price for renting one server from d to act as an R-server. Multiplayer online game sessions usually span some tens of minutes [4, 26], which matches the billing interval of on-demand servers offered by most public cloud providers. For simplicity of billing and management, we assume that servers are not shared across game sessions. That is, for each session, a set of dedicated servers are launched to support it and these servers can be destroyed once the session ends. Since cloud gaming is bandwidth-intensive due to the need of high-definition video streaming, we also take bandwidth cost into account in the problem formulation. Let $b(d)$ denote the price for the expected outbound data transfer[1] (i.e., video streaming) of a game session from each datacenter d. To facilitate exposition, we assume that each client incurs the same amount of outbound bandwidth from its assigned datacenter during the MCG session. We formulate the MCG server allocation problem with the goal of finding the number of servers to be opened at each datacenter such that each client can be assigned to one R-server located at one of its eligible datacenters and the total server and bandwidth cost is minimized.

For each client c and each of its eligible datacenters $d \in E_c$, we define a binary variable $X_c^d \in \{0, 1\}$ to describe whether c is assigned to d. For each datacenter $d \in D$, we further define a variable Y_d to indicate the total number of clients assigned to d. For simplicity, we assume that the servers rented from different datacenters have the same capacity k ($k \in \mathbb{Z}^+$). That is, each server rented can handle the rendering and streaming workloads of up to k clients. Prevalent cloud billing schemes normally charge each server rented at a fixed rate regardless of its utilization [1]. Thus, the MCG server allocation problem can be written as follows:

$$\min \sum_{d \in D} \left(s(d) \cdot \left\lceil \frac{Y_d}{k} \right\rceil + b(d) \cdot Y_d \right), \tag{2}$$

subject to

$$Y_d = \sum_{c \in C} X_c^d, \quad \forall d \in D \tag{3}$$

$$\sum_{d \in E_c} X_c^d = 1, \quad \forall c \in C \tag{4}$$

$$X_c^d \in \{0, 1\}, \quad \forall c \in C,\, d \in E_c \tag{5}$$

The term $\lceil Y_d/k \rceil$ in objective (2) calculates the number of servers opened at datacenter d to run games for all the clients assigned to it. Constraint (3) derives the total number of clients assigned to each datacenter. Constraint (4) ensures that each client is assigned to exactly one of its eligible datacenters. It is easy to add extra constraints such as the capacity of each datacenter, and to consider heterogeneous clients with different requirements on aspects such as the screen resolution and video streaming bitrate. We leave these extensions to future work which will be discussed in Section 7.

In general, the server capacity k is dependent on the server's resource volume and the rendering workload of the particular game. In the special case where k = 1, objective (2) can be minimized by simply opening a server to serve as the R-server for each client c at its eligible datacenter in E_c with the minimum value of $\big(s(d) + b(d)\big)$. When $k \geq 2$, this may not minimize the total cost, since it does not consider server sharing among clients. If a datacenter is assigned less than k clients, the server opened at the datacenter cannot be fully utilized, leading to capacity wastage and unnecessary cost. It is easy to see that the server allocation problem is tightly coupled with the assignment of clients to datacenters.

The MCG server allocation problem defined so far assumes that the G-server is given whose location is fixed prior to the allocation of R-servers. We call it the *basic problem.* A typical scenario for the basic problem is that G-servers are offered and hosted by some multiplayer game server providers [8, 5] and cloud gaming providers only need to set up the R-servers in an on-demand manner for game sessions. Besides the basic problem, we further consider a more general problem where the G-server did not exist and needs to be launched in one of the datacenters to support a game session as well. Nowadays, public clouds such as Amazon EC2 have already offered a comprehensive suite of services and products for game hosting [2], so that one can easily set up multiplayer game servers similar to those offered by game server providers. This motivates us to study the above variation of the problem in which the G-server location also needs to be determined along with R-servers. We call it the *general problem.* In the general problem, changing the G-server's location may result in different sets of eligible datacenters E_c for each client $c \in C$. Thus, an MCG session is feasible only if there exists at least one datacenter $d_g \in D$ for running the G-server such that for all clients $c \in C$, $E_c \neq \emptyset$. We call such a datacenter *eligible* for placing the G-server. Let $D_G \subseteq D$ denote the set of eligible datacenters for placing the G-server. Apparently, choosing different G-server locations in D_G may lead to different

[1]In major public clouds, only the outbound data transfer is charged while the inbound data transfer is for free [1, 7].

assignments of clients to datacenters, which consequently may give rise to different total costs of the server allocation solutions for the same set of clients. Note that the basic problem can be viewed as a special case of the general problem when there is only one eligible datacenter for placing the G-server.

It is easy to establish polynomial reductions from the set cover problem to show that both our basic and general problems are NP-hard. Specifically, the basic MCG server allocation problem degenerates to the classic set cover problem when all datacenters have the same server/bandwidth cost and the server capacity k is larger than the number of clients in a session. In such a case, at most one server is needed at each datacenter and the objective is equivalent to minimizing the number of datacenters chosen to cover all clients of a session subject to the latency constraints.

In the next section, we propose a set of greedy heuristic algorithms to efficiently address MCG server allocation problems.

5. GREEDY HEURISTICS

We first present the algorithms for the basic problem and then we extend them for the general problem. All these algorithms assume that a feasible MCG session is already set up by matchmaking.

5.1 Price-based Assignment

We begin with three simple algorithms that determine the assigned datacenter d_c for each client $c \in C$ individually based on different priorities of price consideration.

Lowest-Server-Price (LSP) Assignment: Every client is assigned to the datacenter with the minimum *server price* among all of its eligible datacenters.

Lowest-Bandwidth-Price (LBP) Assignment: Every client is assigned to the datacenter with the minimum *bandwidth price* among all of its eligible datacenters.

Lowest-Combined-Price (LCP) Assignment: Every client is assigned to the datacenter with the minimum *combined price* among all of its eligible datacenters. The combined price associated with each datacenter d is defined as $s(d)/k + b(d)$, which assumes that the servers can be "partially" rented to serve individual clients.

In the above three algorithms, if a client has more than one eligible datacenters offering the same lowest price, the client is assigned to the nearest one in terms of network latency. The time complexities of the three algorithms are all $O(|C||D|)$. Once the *client-to-datacenter assignment* is determined using any of the above algorithms, the next procedure is to open servers at each datacenter to serve as R-servers for clients. We call this procedure *client-to-server assignment* which proceeds as follows:

1. At each datacenter $d \in D$, open $\lceil Y_d/k \rceil$ servers where Y_d is the number of clients assigned to d, and k is the capacity of each server.
2. Assign each client $c \in C$ to a server opened at d_c which has spare capacity, that is, it has been assigned less than k clients so far.

In the above client-to-server assignment procedure, there is at most a capacity of $k - 1$ wasted at each datacenter. It is intuitive that the LCP algorithm would produce an optimal server allocation for the case of $k = 1$, since there is no wasted capacity at any datacenter and each client incurs the lowest total server and bandwidth cost. For the cases of $k \geq 2$, however, it is possible for the LSP, LBP and LCP algorithms to result in significant capacity wastage at some datacenters. For instance, if the clients' eligible datacenters with the lowest server prices are very diverse, most clients may be assigned to distinct datacenters when using the LSP algorithm, which loses the opportunity of server sharing, especially when the number of clients are small or the number of datacenters available are large. The next algorithm we present determines the client-to-datacenter assignment on a datacenter or server basis instead of on an individual client basis in order to promote server sharing among clients.

5.2 Wastage-aware Assignment

For convenience of presentation, we give the following definitions. Let $S_d \subseteq C$ be the set of clients that can be covered by datacenter $d \in D$ (i.e., d is an eligible datacenter for each of these clients) and have not been assigned to any datacenter. Let $p(d)$ be the projected capacity wastage if all the clients in S_d are assigned to d, which is given below based on the aforementioned client-to-server assignment procedure:

$$p(d) = \begin{cases} 0 & \text{if } |S_d| \bmod k = 0, \\ k - (|S_d| \bmod k) & \text{if } |S_d| \bmod k > 0. \end{cases}$$

Intuitively, the server cost, the bandwidth cost and the capacity wastage are major factors to consider for minimizing the total cost of server allocation. While the LSP, LBP and LCP algorithms consider one or both of the first two factors, the next heuristic called *Lowest-Capacity-Wastage* attempts to improve the cost-effectiveness of server allocation by explicitly avoiding the projected capacity wastage at each datacenter in the server allocation.

Lowest-Capacity-Wastage (LCW) Assignment:

1. For each datacenter $d \in D$, initialize S_d as the set of all the clients that can be covered by d.
2. Let $d^* = \arg\min_{d \in D, S_d \neq \emptyset} p(d)$ be the datacenter with the lowest projected capacity wastage whose S_d is not empty. If more than one datacenter is found with the same lowest projected capacity wastage, let d^* be the one with the lowest server price. If there are still ties, break them arbitrarily.
3. Assign all clients in S_{d^*} to d^*. That is, for each client $c \in S_{d^*}$, set $d_c = d^*$.
4. For each datacenter $d \in D$, set $S_d \leftarrow S_d \setminus S_{d^*}$.
5. If all the clients in C have been assigned, the algorithm terminates. Otherwise, loop back to Step 2.

The LCW algorithm explicitly considers minimizing the projected capacity wastage at each datacenter by trading off the chance to assign each individual client to its cheapest datacenter in terms of server, bandwidth or combined price.

In the LCW algorithm, the number of iterations is at most $|D|$. In each iteration, finding d^* can be done in $O(|D|)$ time. For each datacenter d, the set S_d can only shrink over iterations, and therefore the time complexity for updating S_d over all iterations is bounded by $O(|C|)$. Hence, the overall time complexity of the LCW algorithm is $O(|C||D| + |D|^2)$. After determining d_c for each client $c \in C$, the aforementioned client-to-server assignment procedure is executed to finalize the server allocation for an MCG session.

5.3 Extension for the General Problem

For the general problem where there are a set of eligible datacenters D_G for placing the G-server, we extend each of the above algorithms by examining every possible choice of the G-server location d_g in D_G and choosing the one which results in the minimum server allocation cost. For example, the extended LSP algorithm works as follows:

1. For each choice of d_g in D_G, find the set of eligible datacenters E_c for each client c, apply the LSP algorithm to determine the client-to-datacenter assignment, and calculate the total cost[2] of all servers opened after the client-to-server assignment procedure.

2. Find the lowest cost among all the costs calculated in Step 1 and then return the corresponding d_g and client-to-datacenter assignment solution.

Since we need to iterate through all the choices of d_g in D_G and $D_G \subseteq D$, the time complexity of the extended LSP algorithm for the general problem is $O(|C||D|^2)$, so are those of the extended LBP and LCP algorithms. Likewise, the time complexity of the extended LCW algorithm for the general problem is $O(|C||D|^2 + |D|^3)$. In practice, the number of datacenters $|D|$ offered by public clouds is typically in the order of tens. For example, Amazon and Microsoft currently operate 30 datacenters globally in total. Normally, the number of clients $|C|$ is also in the order of tens in a multiplayer online game session [11, 3]. Therefore, all the above algorithms should be efficient enough to instantly solve the MCG server allocation problem so that players will not suffer from undesirable waiting times. In fact, according to our experiments, the running times of our algorithms are typically less than a few milliseconds on a commodity computer, which are negligible compared to the cloud server startup times.[3]

6. EXPERIMENTAL EVALUATION

We evaluate the performance of our proposed algorithms by making use of real-world Internet latency data [44, 21] and cloud pricing models [1, 7] of two public clouds (Amazon EC2 and Microsoft Azure).

6.1 Evaluation Methodology

Network latency datasets. We make use of two network latency datasets to set up trace-driven experiments. The first dataset collected by Wu *et al.* [44] contains latency (RTT) measurements between PlanetLab nodes and datacenters from Amazon and Microsoft. The second dataset collected by Garcia-Dorado *et al.* [21] contains latency (RTT) measurements between all pairs of datacenters from Amazon and Microsoft. By integrating these two datasets, we simulate a network that is formed by 253 PlanetLab nodes and 13 datacenters with 7 from Amazon and 6 from Microsoft. Assuming that a client is located at each PlanetLab node, we have a total number of 253 clients which is sufficiently large for setting up MCG sessions.

Cloud pricing dataset. Since an R-server handles the game rendering workload for its assigned clients, it is necessary to use cloud servers equipped with GPUs to serve as the R-servers. GPU servers are available in Amazon EC2 (we choose the *g2.8xlarge* model as the GPU server [1]), but this is not the case in Microsoft Azure. To deal with this, we derive the prices of GPU servers in Microsoft's datacenters (assuming that they will be available in the future) based on the prices of GPU servers in Amazon's datacenters as follows. First, we find two non-GPU baseline server types from Amazon and Microsoft respectively which are best-matched in terms of CPU core count and memory size: the *m3.2xlarge* model from EC2 and the *D4* model from Azure. Then, for each Azure datacenter, we approximate its GPU server's price via multiplying its non-GPU baseline server's price by the ratio between the GPU server's price and the non-GPU baseline server's price in the nearest EC2 datacenter to this Azure datacenter. Table 1 shows the rental price per server[4] used in our experimental evaluation. Also shown in Table 1 is the data transfer price per client, which is estimated by assuming that each client will consume 2GB outbound data transfer from its assigned datacenter in a game session.[5]

Table 1: Server rental and data tranfser prices (in dollars).

Datacenter	Baseline server price	GPU server price	Data transfer price
EC2-Virginia	0.532	2.600	0.180
EC2-Oregon	0.532	2.600	0.180
EC2-California	0.616	2.808	0.180
EC2-Ireland	0.585	2.808	0.180
EC2-Singapore	0.784	4.000	0.240
EC2-Tokyo	0.770	3.592	0.280
EC2-Sao Paulo	0.761	3.720	0.500
Azure-Hong Kong	0.902	4.604	0.276
Azure-Virginia	0.616	3.012	0.174
Azure-Ireland	0.584	2.804	0.174
Azure-Singapore	0.784	4.000	0.276
Azure-Amsterdam	0.672	3.224	0.174
Azure-California	0.616	2.808	0.174

Table 2: L_G and L_R settings according to [20, 25].

(L_G, L_R)	Game Genre	Game Pace
(150, 100)	first-person shooter, etc.	fast
(300, 200)	third-person role-playing, etc.	moderate

Latency thresholds. The thresholds for the latencies from the clients to the G-server (L_G) and the R-servers (L_R) are set according to the empirical data provided by [20] and [25], respectively. Table 2 summarizes the settings of L_G and L_R for different game genres (all are round-trip delay times in milliseconds). Having the latencies below such thresholds offers satisfactory playability according to the above studies.

Session size. In general, the number of clients $|C|$ in a multiplayer game session is in the order of tens, thereby we let $|C| \in \{10, 20, 30, 40, 50\}$ in our experiments. For each setting of $|C|$ and each setting of (L_G, L_R), we generate 100 feasible MCG sessions where the clients are randomly chosen from the 253 PlanetLab nodes subject to the latency thresholds. Note that, for simplicity, we use the median latency provided by the aforementioned dataset in all the matchmaking processes that generate the feasible sessions. The latency between client-server pairs is expected to be relatively stable during a game session period since each session typically lasts for just a few tens of minutes [4, 26]. If this is not the case, a higher percentile (e.g., 90th percentile) of network latency can be compared against the latency thresholds in the matchmaking process to cater for the latency variation. In the experimental results, we compute and plot the average server allocation cost and standard deviation of these 100 sessions resulting from each algorithm for performance comparison.

Server capacity. The server capacity k is dependent on the R-server's resource volume and the game's rendering workload. To

[2]The total cost in the general problem also includes the cost for renting the G-server which can be much cheaper than that for renting an R-server because the R-server requires GPU resources for game rendering and video encoding.

[3]The startup times of cloud servers are normally within one minute based on our measurements on Amazon EC2.

[4]The GPU servers are not available in the EC2 Sao Paulo datacenter, thereby we derive the price for this datacenter according to its non-GPU server's price ratio to the EC2 Virginia datacenter.

[5]This is an estimated amount of data transfer for 1-hour HD (720p) live video streaming at the bitrate of 4000 Kbps [6].

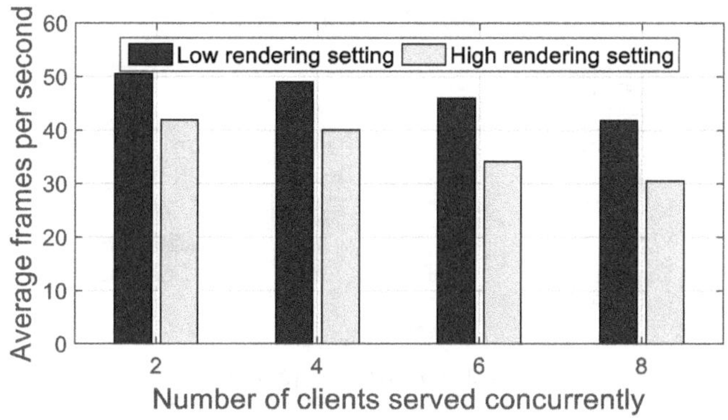

Figure 2: Heaven Benchmark's average frame rate against the number of clients served by an R-server concurrently.

emulate a range of workload intensities imposed on each R-server (i.e., a *g2.8xlarge* instance), we set $k \in \{2, 4, 6, 8\}$. We have conducted a set of measurements to verify the feasibility of these settings of k, based on the Unigine Heaven Benchmark [12] and a cloud gaming system prototype developed by ourselves [29]. With this prototype, a single cloud server can serve as the R-servers for multiple clients concurrently. Figure 2 shows the frame rate (i.e., frames per second) of the Unigine Heaven Benchmark running at 1280x720 resolution and different rendering quality levels for each setting of k. From Figure 2 we can see that even for $k = 8$, the frame rate of the Unigine Heaven Benchmark is still above 30 frames per second (the threshold for an acceptable frame rate for most video games). Since the Heaven Benchmark is a widely used tool for determining the gaming performance of a computer under extremely stressful conditions, we believe that our measurements are representative and the settings of k are reasonable.

Theoretical lower bound. To benchmark the performance of our algorithms, we calculate a theoretical lower bound on the total server rental and bandwidth cost for an MCG session as follows:

$$\sum_{d \in D} \left(\frac{s(d)}{k} + b(d) \right) \cdot Y_d \qquad (6)$$

where Y_d (the number of clients assigned to each datacenter d) is obtained via the LCP algorithm that assigns each client to the datacenter with the minimum combined price. The above calculation assumes that the number of servers to be opened at datacenter d is Y_d/k which can be a fraction just enough to serve all of its clients. Thus, this lower bound is a super-optimum and may not be achievable by any real server allocation when $k \geq 2$. To quantify the relative performance, we normalize the server allocation cost produced by each algorithm with respect to the above lower bound.

Alternative algorithms. We also evaluate the following alternatives which are neither aware of the server/bandwidth price nor aware of the projected capacity wastage when assigning clients to datacenters:

- ***Random Assignment***: Every client is assigned to a random datacenter from the set of its eligible datacenters. This algorithm serves as a baseline.
- ***Nearest Assignment***: Every client is assigned to the nearest datacenter in terms of network latency among all of its eligible datacenters. If a client has more than one eligible datacenters with the same lowest network latency to it, the client is assigned to the one with the minimum server price.

6.2 Results and Analysis

Figure 3 shows the normalized cost of each algorithm for the basic problem (we only show the results for $|C| = 10$ and $|C| = 50$ due to the space limit). In all these experiments, the G-server location for each session is randomly picked from the 13 datacenters. In general, the LSP, LCP, and LCW algorithms consistently produce significantly lower normalized costs than other algorithms, with the LCW algorithm being closest to the super-optimum lower bound. This reveals the importance of being aware of the server/bandwidth price or the projected capacity wastage in assigning clients to datacenters. The poorer performance of the LBP algorithm compared with the LSP and LCP algorithms indicates that the bandwidth cost is not as important as the server cost or the projected capacity wastage in optimizing the total cost. The superior of the LCW algorithm over the LSP and LCP algorithms reflects that it is rational to trade the chance of assigning each individual client to its eligible datacenter with the minimum server or combined price for the chance of reducing the capacity wastage.

Figure 3 also shows that, for the same session size $|C|$, as the latency thresholds (L_G, L_R) get larger (i.e., from faster-paced games to slower-paced games), the Random, Nearest, and LBP algorithms deteriorate significantly, while the LSP, LCP, and LCW algorithms remain stable. For instance, the normalized cost produced by the Random algorithm is 2.6 for (L_G = 150, L_R = 100) with $|C| = 10$ and $k = 8$, and it increases to 3.7 (nearly a 40% increase) for (L_G = 300, L_R = 200) with the same $|C|$ and k. This can be explained using Figure 5 which shows the cumulative distribution of the number of eligible datacenters per client of all the sessions. As seen from Figure 5, the clients tend to have more eligible datacenters for larger latency thresholds (L_G, L_R). For instance, for (L_G = 300, L_R = 200), over 50% of the clients have at least 6 eligible datacenters which are almost half of all 13 datacenters. In this case, clients are more likely to be scattered over different datacenters if we apply the Random algorithm. This is also true for the Nearest algorithm, since the nearest datacenters for clients may be more dispersed, so is for the LBP algorithm which may act like the Nearest algorithm as the bandwidth prices are likely identical across a large portion of datacenters (e.g., Azure has the same bandwidth price for all datacenters located at US and EU as shown in Table 1). Hence, these three algorithms generate more capacity wastage for larger (L_G, L_R) (as we can see from Figure 4) and produce higher total costs eventually. This is confirmed by the capacity wastage ratios shown in Figure 4, where the capacity wastage ratio is defined as the excessive capacity (i.e., the total allocated server capacity minus the requested capacity) normalized by the requested capacity (i.e., the session size $|C|$).

From Figure 3, we can also see that, as the server capacity k gets larger (from 2 to 8), all algorithms produce increasingly higher normalized costs. This is mainly due to the increasing capacity wastage generated by every algorithm as k gets larger, which can be again observed from Figure 4. Apparently it would be more difficult to fill up a larger server with clients than fulling up a smaller one. On the other hand, the theoretical lower bound assumes that a server can be "partially" rented to perfectly fit to the number of assigned clients with no capacity wastage at all. Thus, the normalized cost increases with the server capacity. Moreover, we can see from Figure 3 that, as the session size $|C|$ gets larger (from 10 to 50), the normalized cost produced by every algorithm decreases. This is mainly due to the decreasing capacity wastage generated by every algorithm as $|C|$ gets larger (see Figure 4).

In short, the LCW algorithm which considers the capacity wastage rather than the server or bandwidth price as the dominating factor in

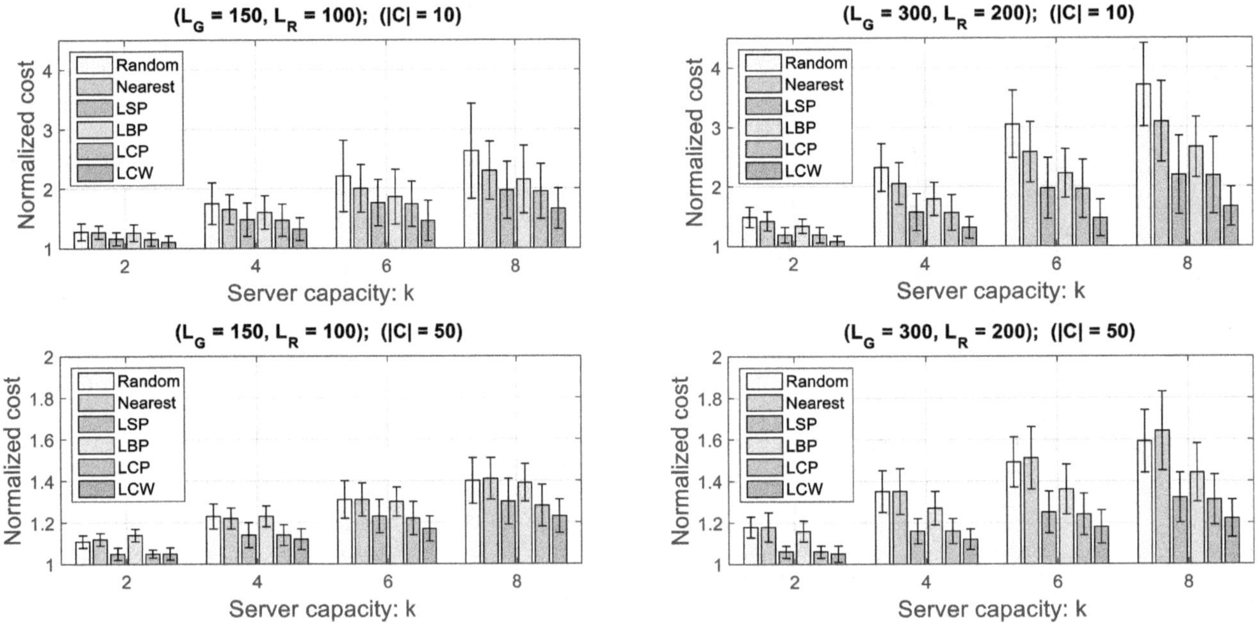

Figure 3: Normalized costs of different algorithms for the basic problem.

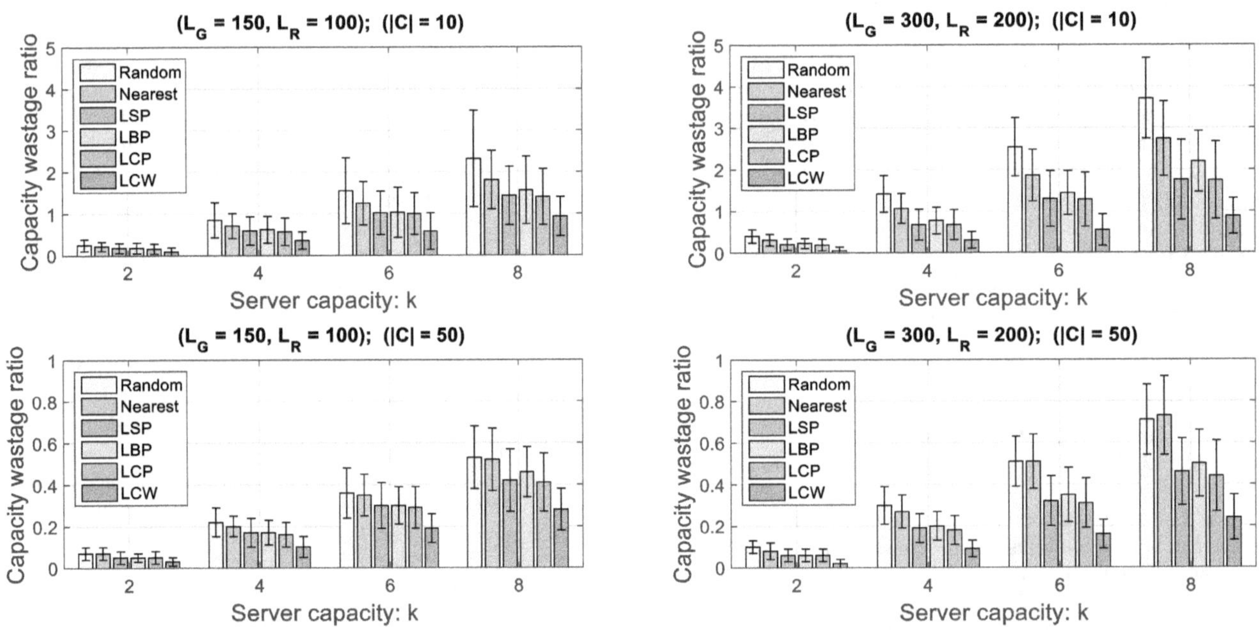

Figure 4: Capacity wastage ratios of different algorithms for the basic problem.

assigning clients to datacenters, is the most cost-effective solution for the basic problem of MCG server allocation.

The results for the general problem as shown in Figure 6 have similar performance trends to the results for the basic problem, with the LSP, LCP, and LCW algorithms significantly outperforming the Random, Nearest, and LBP algorithms. The main difference is that the advantage of the LCW algorithm over the LSP and LCP algorithms becomes less substantial. This can be explained by comparing the results of capacity wastage ratios in Figure 7 and Figure 4. From the comparison we can see that the capacity wastages generated by the LSP and LCP algorithms are much closer to that generated by the LCW algorithm for the general problem. For instance, the capacity wastage ratios of the LSP and LCP algorithms are nearly 2x of that generated by the LCW algorithm when ($L_G = 300$, $L_R = 200$), $|C| = 10$ and $k = 8$ for the basic problem. These capacity wastage ratios are just about 1.4x of that generated by the LCW algorithm under the same experimental settings for the general problem. This is mainly because having the chance to choose the G-server location from a list of eligible datacenters indirectly makes the LSP and LCP algorithms assign clients to datacenters with relatively low capacity wastages as they compare the costs of different G-server locations. This is even more likely to happen for

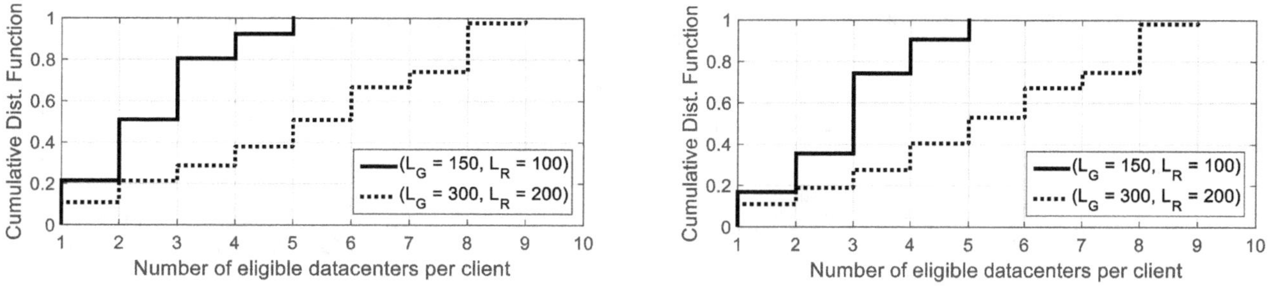

Figure 5: CDF of the number of eligible datacenters per client in sessions of $|C| = 10$ (left) and $|C| = 50$ (right).

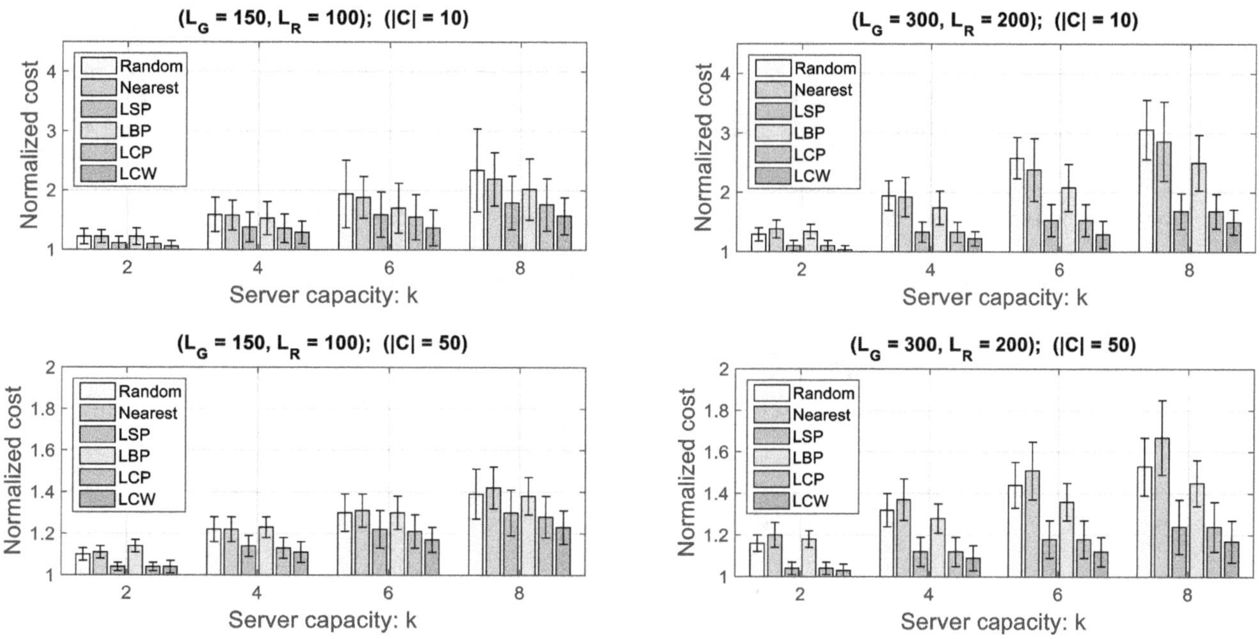

Figure 6: Normalized costs of different algorithms for the general problem.

larger latency thresholds since there are more eligible datacenters for placing the G-server as shown in Figure 8.

7. DISCUSSIONS

In our current model, we assume that servers are not shared across sessions for simplicity of billing and management. However, if an MCG session runs for a duration that is significantly shorter than the minimum billing interval of the servers offered by a public cloud provider, some revenue loss may occur in the MCG service provider. Hence, it is beneficial to keep its servers alive when the session finishes prior to the end of the charged period so that they can be reused to support a new session. Another possibility is to share servers across concurrently ongoing sessions. If the sessions with very different ending times are assigned to share the same servers, the servers may be left running at low utilizations after the sessions with early ending times finish [31]. Thus, the server cost might not be guaranteed to be reduced compared to allocating each session to dedicated servers in which all players depart together. The server allocation and assignment of players to servers here can be mapped to a dynamic bin packing problem [30, 32] which is a hard combinatorial optimization problem and hence requires further investigation.

In addition, our model can be extended to consider more general situations where clients belonging to the same session may entail different rendering or streaming qualities, due to heterogeneous thin-client devices or personal preferences. This can be achieved through modifying the cost calculation in the objective function (2). Specifically, we can consider the server capacity k and data transfer price $b(d)$ as variables of each individual client rather than constants. Our algorithms can easily be applied to this scenario.

8. CONCLUSION

In this paper, we have investigated the server allocation problem for MCG with the objective of reducing the total server and bandwidth cost to support an MCG session. We have discussed two versions of the problem and proposed several efficient algorithms to address both of them. Extensive trace-driven experiments show that simply assigning clients to some random, the nearest, or the cheapest eligible datacenters can make the total cost far worse than optimum. It is important to consider the server capacity wastage in order to achieve cost-effective MCG server allocation.

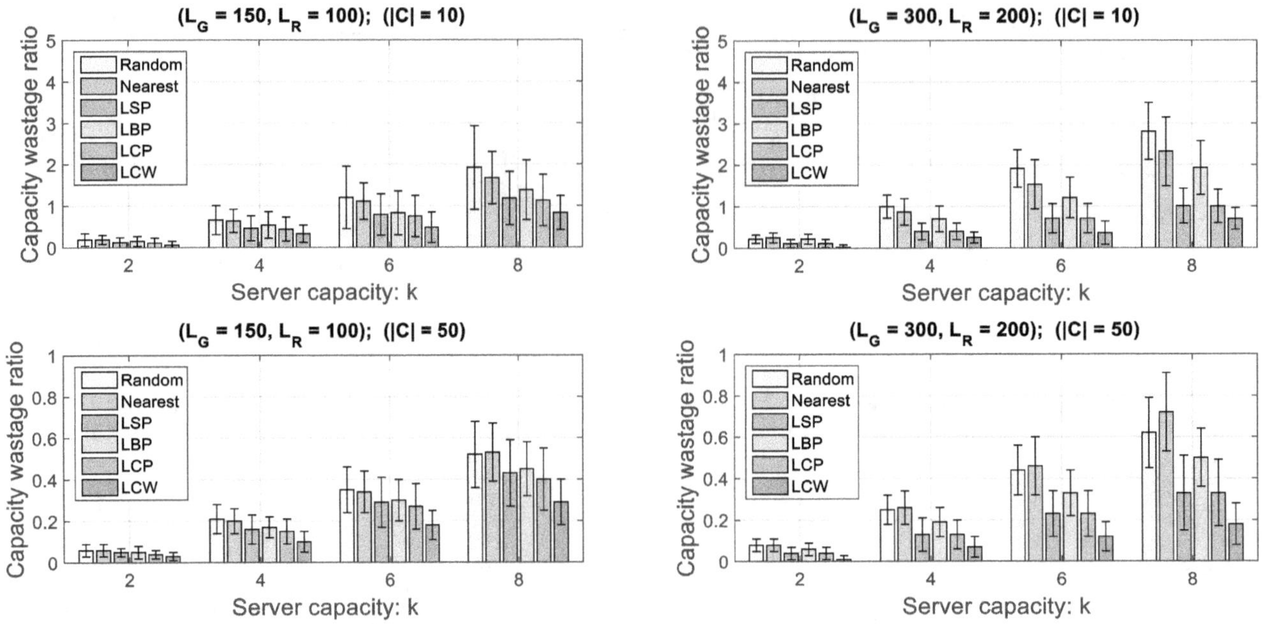

Figure 7: Capacity wastage ratios of different algorithms for the general problem.

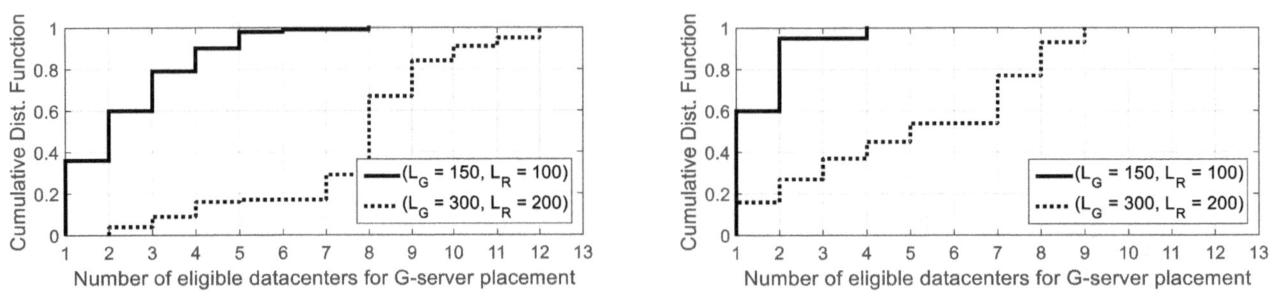

Figure 8: CDF of the number of eligible datacenters for G-server placement in sessions of $|C|$ = 10 (left) and $|C|$ = 50 (right).

9. ACKNOWLEDGMENTS

This research is supported by the National Research Foundation, Prime Minister's Office, Singapore under its IDM Futures Funding Initiative, and by Singapore Ministry of Education Academic Research Fund Tier 2 under Grant MOE2013-T2-2-067. We would like to thank Ronald Seet for his help on the Unigine Heaven Benchmark tests. Dr. Yusen Li is one of the corresponding authors.

10. REFERENCES

[1] Amazon EC2. https://aws.amazon.com/ec2/.

[2] AWS gaming. https://aws.amazon.com/gaming/.

[3] Counter-Strike servers. http://goo.gl/Cecrxk.

[4] Dota2 session length. http://goo.gl/FjKvqf.

[5] Game Servers. https://www.gameservers.com/.

[6] Live streaming bitrates. https://goo.gl/pmK4ql.

[7] Microsoft Azure. https://azure.microsoft.com/.

[8] Multiplay. http://multiplay.com/.

[9] Nvidia Cloud Gaming. http://goo.gl/Edpwbd.

[10] Nvidia GeForce NOW. https://goo.gl/xZ6D9I.

[11] Star Wars: Battlefront has 40-player cap. http://goo.gl/ThIL4W.

[12] Unigine Heaven Benchmark. http://goo.gl/sWqG7k.

[13] Why cloud hosting is the future of online gaming. http://goo.gl/9YHfCK.

[14] J. Brun, F. Safaei, and P. Boustead. Managing latency and fairness in networked games. *Communications of the ACM*, 49(11):46–51, 2006.

[15] K.-T. Chen, Y.-C. Chang, P.-H. Tseng, C.-Y. Huang, and C.-L. Lei. Measuring the latency of cloud gaming systems. In *Proc. ACM MM*, pages 1269–1272, 2011.

[16] K.-T. Chen, P. Huang, and C.-L. Lei. How sensitive are online gamers to network quality? *Communications of the ACM*, 49(11):34–38, 2006.

[17] Y.-R. Chen, S. Radhakrishnan, S. K. Dhall, and S. Karabuk. Server selection with delay constraints for online games. In *Proc. IEEE GLOBECOM Workshops*, pages 882–887, 2010.

[18] Y.-R. Chen, S. Radhakrishnan, S. K. Dhall, and S. Karabuk. On the game server network selection with delay and delay variation constraints. In *Proc. IEEE COMSNETS*, pages 1–10, 2011.

[19] S. Choy, B. Wong, G. Simon, and C. Rosenberg. The brewing storm in cloud gaming: A measurement study on cloud to end-user latency. In *Proc. ACM NetGames*, pages 2:1–2:6, 2012.

[20] M. Claypool and K. Claypool. Latency and player actions in online games. *Communications of the ACM*, 49(11):40–45, 2006.

[21] J. Garcia-Dorado and S. Rao. Cost-aware multi data-center bulk transfers in the cloud from a customer-side perspective. *IEEE Transactions on Cloud Computing*, PP(99), 2015.

[22] S. Gargolinski, C. St Pierre, and M. Claypool. Game server selection for multiple players. In *Proc. ACM NetGames*, pages 1–6, 2005.

[23] H.-J. Hong, D.-Y. Chen, C.-Y. Huang, K.-T. Chen, and C.-H. Hsu. Placing virtual machines to optimize cloud gaming experience. *IEEE Transactions on Cloud Computing*, 3(1):42–53, 2015.

[24] C.-Y. Huang, K.-T. Chen, D.-Y. Chen, H.-J. Hsu, and C.-H. Hsu. GamingAnywhere: the first open source cloud gaming system. *ACM Transactions on Multimedia Computing, Communications, and Applications*, 10(1s):10:1–10:25, 2014.

[25] M. Jarschel, D. Schlosser, S. Scheuring, and T. Hoßfeld. Gaming in the clouds: QoE and the users' perspective. *Mathematical and Computer Modelling*, 57(11):2883–2894, 2013.

[26] A. L. Jia, S. Shen, R. V. D. Bovenkamp, A. Iosup, F. Kuipers, and D. H. J. Epema. Socializing by gaming: Revealing social relationships in multiplayer online games. *ACM Transactions on Knowledge Discovery from Data*, 10(2):11:1–11:29, Oct. 2015.

[27] K. Lee, D. Chu, E. Cuervo, Y. Degtyarev, S. Grizan, J. Kopf, A. Wolman, and J. Flinn. Outatime: Using speculation to enable low-latency continuous interaction for mobile cloud gaming. In *Proc. ACM MobiSys*, pages 151–165, 2015.

[28] K.-W. Lee, B.-J. Ko, and S. Calo. Adaptive server selection for large scale interactive online games. *Computer Networks*, 49(1):84–102, 2005.

[29] Y. Li, Y. Deng, R. Seet, X. Tang, and W. Cai. MASTER: Multi-platform Application Streaming Toolkits for Elastic Resources. In *Proc. ACM MM*, pages 805–806, 2015.

[30] Y. Li, X. Tang, and W. Cai. On dynamic bin packing for resource allocation in the cloud. In *Proc. ACM SPAA*, pages 2–11, 2014.

[31] Y. Li, X. Tang, and W. Cai. Play request dispatching for efficient virtual machine usage in cloud gaming. *IEEE Transactions on Circuits and Systems for Video Technology*, 25(12):2052–2063, Dec 2015.

[32] Y. Li, X. Tang, and W. Cai. Dynamic bin packing for on-demand cloud resource allocation. *IEEE Transactions on Parallel and Distributed Systems*, 27(1):157–170, 2016.

[33] L. Lin, X. Liao, G. Tan, H. Jin, X. Yang, W. Zhang, and B. Li. Liverender: A cloud gaming system based on compressed graphics streaming. In *Proc. ACM MM*, pages 347–356, 2014.

[34] Z. Liu, M. Lin, A. Wierman, S. H. Low, and L. L. Andrew. Greening geographical load balancing. In *Proc. ACM SIGMETRICS*, pages 233–244, 2011.

[35] J. Manweiler, S. Agarwal, M. Zhang, R. Roy Choudhury, and P. Bahl. Switchboard: a matchmaking system for multiplayer mobile games. In *Proc. ACM MobiSys*, pages 71–84, 2011.

[36] L. Pantel and L. C. Wolf. On the suitability of dead reckoning schemes for games. In *Proc. ACM NetGames*, pages 79–84, 2002.

[37] L. Rao, X. Liu, L. Xie, and W. Liu. Minimizing electricity cost: optimization of distributed internet data centers in a multi-electricity-market environment. In *Proc. IEEE INFOCOM*, pages 1–9, 2010.

[38] Y. Rochman, H. Levy, and E. Brosh. Efficient resource placement in cloud computing and network applications. *ACM SIGMETRICS Performance Evaluation Review*, 42(2):49–51, 2014.

[39] R. Shea, D. Fu, and J. Liu. Rhizome: utilizing the public cloud to provide 3d gaming infrastructure. In *Proc. ACM MMSys*, pages 97–100, 2015.

[40] D.-N.-B. Ta, T. Nguyen, S. Zhou, X. Tang, W. Cai, and R. Ayani. Interactivity-constrained server provisioning in large-scale distributed virtual environments. *IEEE Transactions on Parallel and Distributed Systems*, 23(2):304–312, 2012.

[41] H. Tian, D. Wu, J. He, Y. Xu, and M. Chen. On achieving cost-effective adaptive cloud gaming in geo-distributed data centers. *IEEE Transactions on Circuits and Systems for Video Technology*, 25(12):2064–2077, Dec 2015.

[42] H. Wang, R. Shea, X. Ma, F. Wang, and J. Liu. On design and performance of cloud-based distributed interactive applications. In *Proc. IEEE ICNP*, pages 37–46, 2014.

[43] D. Wu, Z. Xue, and J. He. iCloudaccess: Cost-effective streaming of video games from the cloud with low latency. *IEEE Transactions on Circuits and Systems for Video Technology*, 24(8):1405–1416, 2014.

[44] Z. Wu and H. V. Madhyastha. Understanding the latency benefits of multi-cloud webservice deployments. *ACM SIGCOMM Computer Communication Review*, 43(2):13–20, Apr 2013.

[45] S. Yaw, E. Howard, B. Mumey, and M. P. Wittie. Cooperative group provisioning with latency guarantees in multi-cloud deployments. *ACM SIGCOMM Computer Communication Review*, 45(3):4–11, Jul 2015.

[46] M. Yu, C. Zhang, Z. Qi, J. Yao, Y. Wang, and H. Guan. Vgris: virtualized gpu resource isolation and scheduling in cloud gaming. In *Proc. ACM HPDC*, pages 203–214, 2013.

[47] L. Zhang and X. Tang. Optimizing client assignment for enhancing interactivity in distributed interactive applications. *IEEE/ACM Transactions on Networking*, 20(6):1707–1720, 2012.

[48] L. Zhang and X. Tang. The client assignment problem for continuous distributed interactive applications: analysis, algorithms, and evaluation. *IEEE Transactions on Parallel and Distributed Systems*, 25(3):785–795, 2014.

[49] Q. Zhang, Q. Zhu, M. F. Zhani, R. Boutaba, and J. L. Hellerstein. Dynamic service placement in geographically distributed clouds. *IEEE Journal on Selected Areas in Communications,*, 31(12):762–772, 2013.

[50] H. Zheng and X. Tang. Analysis of server provisioning for distributed interactive applications. *IEEE Transactions on Computers*, 64(10):2752–2766, Oct 2015.

[51] H. Zheng and X. Tang. The server provisioning problem for continuous distributed interactive applications. *IEEE Transactions on Parallel and Distributed Systems*, 27(1):271–285, Jan 2016.

Share-and-Chat: Achieving Human-Level Video Commenting by Search and Multi-View Embedding*

Yehao Li †, Ting Yao ‡, Tao Mei ‡, Hongyang Chao †, Yong Rui ‡
† Sun Yat-Sen University, Guangzhou, China
‡ Microsoft Research, Beijing, China
yehaoli.sysu@gmail.com; {tiyao, tmei, yongrui}@microsoft.com; isschhy@mail.sysu.edu.cn

ABSTRACT

Video has become a predominant social media for the booming live interactions. Automatic generation of emotional comments to a video has great potential to significantly increase user engagement in many socio-video applications (e.g., chat bot). Nevertheless, the problem of video commenting has been overlooked by the research community. The major challenges are that the generated comments are to be not only as natural as those from human beings, but also relevant to the video content. We present in this paper a novel two-stage deep learning-based approach to automatic video commenting. Our approach consists of two components. The first component, similar video search, efficiently finds the visually similar videos w.r.t. a given video using approximate nearest-neighbor search based on the learned deep video representations, while the second dynamic ranking effectively ranks the comments associated with the searched similar videos by learning a deep multi-view embedding space. For modeling the emotional view of videos, we incorporate visual sentiment, video content, and text comments into the learning of the embedding space. On a newly collected dataset with over 102K videos and 10.6M comments, we demonstrate that our approach outperforms several state-of-the-art methods and achieves human-level video commenting.

Keywords

Video Commenting; Multi-View Embedding; Deep Convolutional Neural Networks; Visual Sentiment Analysis.

1. INTRODUCTION

The advent of video sharing sites and rapid development of video technologies have led to the unprecedented delivery of online video content. Nowadays, millions of daily users are broadcasting, consuming and communicating via videos. Video has become a predominant media for the booming live social interactions, e.g., Vine, Instagram, and Periscope. Automatic generation of emotional comments to a video has great potential to significantly increase user engagement in many socio-video applications (e.g., chat bot). Therefore, video commenting has become a crucial technique yet a challenge for real-world applications.

Input Video:

Output Comment:
- Motivated me to go beyond my limits in skateboarding!!!

Human Made Comment:
- He should be a new character in the next skateboarding game.

Output Sentence:
- A man is doing a trick on a skateboarding.

Figure 1: Examples of video comment and caption (sentence). The input is a short video, while the output of comment is a text response to this video, usually a natural sentence expressing emotional views of the video.

Although there have already been emerging research on video tagging [24][36], video captioning [8][20][33], and visual question answering [1], video comments have their own characteristics and thus are different from tags, captions and answers. A video tag is usually the name of a specific object, action, or event in a video (e.g., "man," "skateboarding" in Figure 1). A caption goes beyond tags by describing a video with a natural sentence, where the basic structure is a triplet of (subject, verb, object). An answer could be a response to a specific question related to a video (e.g., "skateboard" to the question of "what is the man playing with" in Figure 1). Nevertheless, a comment is a text response to a video for the purpose of social engagement. Usually, a comment is a natural sentence with emotional perspective yet relevant to the video content. Figure 1 shows the examples of comment and caption (description) of a video. To our best knowledge, there has been little research on automatic video commenting in both vision and multimedia communities.

The problem of automatic generation of video comments provides challenges to the research communities. The need to understand not only video content but also emotional reaction makes the task very challenging. Moreover, the generated comments should be as natural as those from human beings, in other words, the comments are in the form of natural sentences. Despite the difficulty of this problem, there are two possible solutions: by generation and by

* This work was performed when Yehao Li was visiting Microsoft Research Asia as a research intern.

MM '16, October 15-19, 2016, Amsterdam, Netherlands
© 2016 ACM. ISBN 978-1-4503-3603-1/16/10...$15.00
DOI: http://dx.doi.org/10.1145/2964284.2964320

search. The former attempts to generate a sentence that describes video content, which are mainly inspired by recent advances in machine translation using Recurrent Neural Networks (RNNs) [2][27]. Among these successful works, most of them use Long Short-Term Memory (LSTM) [13], a variant of RNN, which can capture sequential information by mapping sequences to sequences. Nevertheless, this category of approaches, either explicitly or implicitly, assumes the existence of a translatable mapping between the input sequence and the output one. However, video commenting, which expresses an emotional state on a video, often responds with diverse reactions from varying angles. In other words, there are multiple possible outputs with very various statements to a given video, making it difficult to train RNN models. Commenting by search, in contrast, solves this problem by leveraging "crowdsourcing" human intelligence which is the underlying user-generated comments in online interactions. More specifically, the idea is to search visually similar videos on social platform and then exploit the real user comments associated with these similar videos to respond to the given video. A fundamental issue that underlies the success of search is video representation learning, which recently achieves promising progresses thanks to the development of deep convolutional neural networks. Therefore, we follow this elegant recipe to produce video comments by search.

In the direction of video commenting by search, there is also the need to measure the relevance between comment and video. As textual comment and video content are of different views, they cannot be directly compared. Inspired by the success of multi-view embedding, this paper studies the problem by learning a common embedding space that allows direct comparison of text comments and videos.

By consolidating the idea of search and multi-view embedding, we propose a novel framework for video commenting as illustrated in Figure 2, which is composed out of two major components: similar video search (VS) and comment dynamic ranking (DR). Given a video, a 2-D and/or 3-D convolution neural networks is utilized to extract visual features of selected video frames/clips, while the video representations are produced by mean pooling over these visual features. Then, approximate nearest neighbors (ANNs) of the given video are identified from the pool of social videos based on the video representations by using neighborhood graph search. The comments associated with ANNs are regarded as candidates to express the feelings on the given video. Next, a deep multi-view embedding model learnt on three views of video content, visual sentiment and textual comment is exploited to measure the relevance between these candidate comments and the given video. Finally, the comments are ranked by sorting their relevance scores and the top-K comments will be selected as responses to the video.

In summary, this paper makes the following contributions:

- We study the problem of automatic video commenting to express emotional response to a video. It has great potential for increasing social interaction and enhancing user engagement in many socio-video applications. To the best of our knowledge, this paper represents the first effort towards this target in the multimedia research community.
- We propose a novel two-stage framework for achieving human-level video commenting. The framework is grounded on the similar video search paradigm by using approximate nearest-neighbor search. Additionally, the framework also tackles the problem of relevance measurement between textual comment and video by learning an embedding space between three views of video content, visual sentiment and textual comment.
- The proposed methods are evaluated on a newly created dataset including about 102K videos and 10.6 million comments crawled from Vine, which is so far the first dataset for video commenting.

The remaining sections are organized as follows. Section 2 describes the related work. Section 3 presents our proposed two-stage approach including similar video search and comment dynamic ranking, while Section 4 introduces our newly created dataset for video commenting. In Section 5, we provide empirical evaluations, followed by the discussions and conclusions in Section 6.

2. RELATED WORK

We briefly group the related works into two categories: video tagging and vision to sentence. The former draws upon research in automatically assigning tags (annotations) to videos, and the later mainly focuses on sentence generation of visual content.

2.1 Video Tagging

Video tagging problem has received intensive research attention and the significance of the topic can be partly reflected from the huge volume of published papers. The research in this direction has proceeded along two different dimensions: model-based methods [6][21][37] and data driven approaches [24][32][36].

Model-based methods assume that a training set of videos along with keyword annotations is provided for developing concept classifiers. Cristianini *et al.* employed SVM with one-against-the-other strategy to learn a set of detectors, each of which independently models the presence/absence of a certain concept in [6]. Later in [21], Qi *et al.* proposed correlative multi-label method to simultaneously model both the individual concepts and their correlations in a unifying formulation and the principle of least commitment was obeyed. Recently, EventNet [37], a large scale structural concept library, is proposed for video tagging by utilizing large margin concept classifiers trained with deep representations on YouTube videos.

Different from model-based methods, data-driven approaches construct video similarity for annotation. In [24], the overlapping or duplicated content of videos was exploited for measuring video similarity. With this, tags associated with similar videos were exchanged for generating new tag assignments. In another work by Wang [32], both distance between samples and the difference of their surrounding neighborhood sample distributions were taken into account for video similarity estimation. Recently, Yao *et al.* [36] combined click-through and video document features for deriving a latent subspace, in which the dot product of the mapping can be taken as the video similarity. The learnt video similarity is then applied for video tagging tasks.

In short, the target of video tagging is to annotate video content by individual semantic tags (words). Our work in this paper contributes by not only extending the natural

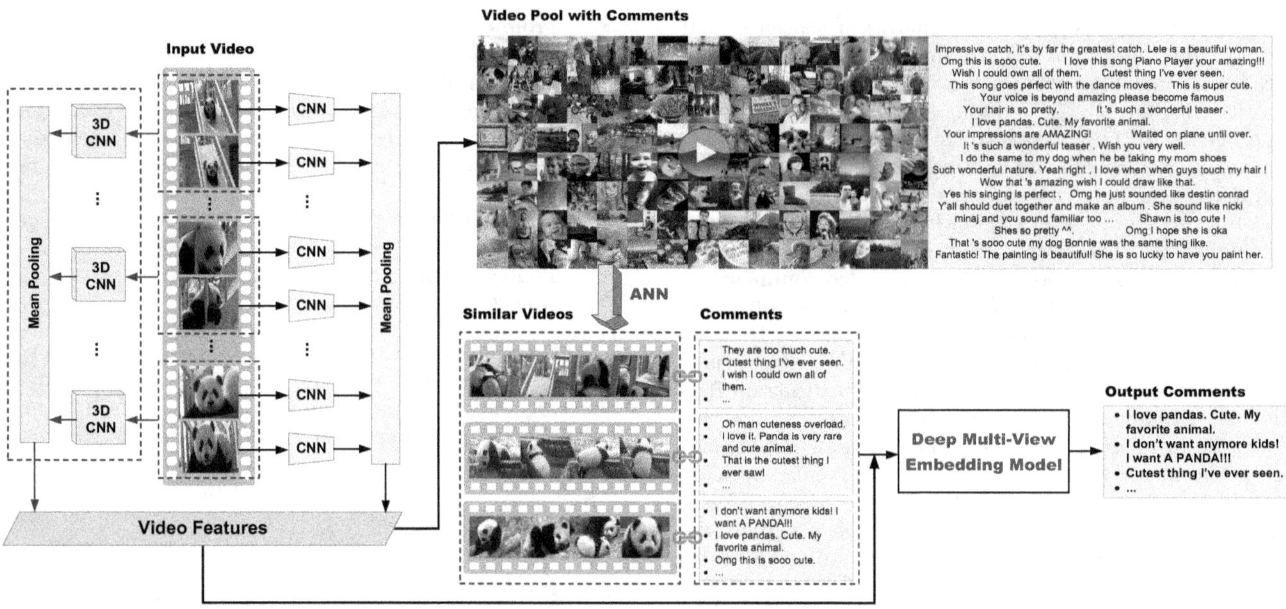

Figure 2: An overview of our video commenting framework mainly including similar video search (VS) and comment dynamic ranking (DR) (better viewed in color). In VS, the video representations are first produced by mean pooling over the visual features of frames/clips, extracted by a 2-D/3-D CNN. Next, approximate nearest neighbor (ANN) search is employed to search the visually similar videos in our video pool and the comments associated with these similar videos are regarded as candidates. In DR, a deep multi-view embedding model is exploited to measure the relevance between comment candidates and the input video. The comments with highest relevance scores are finally presented to the input video.

descriptions from individual tags to complete sentences, but also experiencing the emotions and feelings on videos.

2.2 Vision to Sentence

Image to sentence. For image sentence generation task, there have been several techniques [7][9], being proposed to generate image captions through utilizing captions from visually similar images. Farhadi *et al.* [9] annotated images with sentences by using nearest neighbors in an intermediate meaning space. Later in [7], Devlin *et al.* provided a detailed exploration on nearest neighbors approaches based on different representations and caption selection through different similarity functions. In another work by Chen *et al.* [5], viewer affect after viewing an image is predicted based on sentiment concepts defined in SentiBank [3]. An alternative scheme on image to sentence was recently proposed in [8][30], which utilize RNN to generate more flexible captions inspired by recent advances in machine translation. The basic idea is to model the probability of generating a word given previous words and image in RNN architecture.

Video to sentence. There are also two major directions for translation from videos. One is template-based methods [11][28], which first identify semantic content (subject, verb, object) in the video and then produce sentences on the predefined templates. This direction is highly depended on the sentence templates and can only generate sentences with syntactical structure. Similar to recent breakthroughs in image to sentence, another direction on video to sentence is to utilize RNN model to generate sentences for videos in [8][20][33].

The aforementioned vision to sentence approaches focus on generating sentence, which describes video content objectively. Our work is different in the way that we do not explicitly describe video content, but instead express the emotional reaction and feelings after viewing the video like a human being.

3. VIDEO COMMENTING APPROACH

The basic idea of this work is to automatic comment on videos by searching visually similar videos and ranking the comments associated with the searched similar videos. The similar video search is performed by using ANN search on powerful spatio-temporal video representations learnt by 2-D and 3-D CNN, while dynamic ranking ranks the candidate comments by learning a deep multi-view embedding model. In this way, the original incomparable views of video content, visual sentiment and textual comment could be directly compared in this embedding space. Moreover, the learning of the embedding space is integrated into an optimization to better reflect the preference relations in the training triplets. The approach overview is demonstrated in Figure 2.

In this section, we first present our adopted ANN search in VS stage, followed by three views for video commenting and our proposed deep multi-view embedding model in DR.

3.1 Notation

Let $\mathcal{V}$ and $\mathcal{C}$ denote the collections of videos and comments respectively. For each video $v_k \in \mathcal{V}$, its n associated comments are denoted as $\{c_{k1}, c_{k2}, ..., c_{kn}\} \in \mathcal{C}$. The goal of our deep multi-view embedding model is to construct three mappings $f_v : v \rightarrow \mathbb{R}^d$, $f_s : v \rightarrow \mathbb{R}^d$ and $f_c : c \rightarrow \mathbb{R}^d$ for video content view, visual sentiment view and textual comment view, such that all the three views can be mapped into a d-

Algorithm 1 Query-driven iterated neighborhood graph search

$P_0 \leftarrow$ GenerateInitialSolution(q, Tr)
$R^* \leftarrow$ LocalNGSearch(P_0, G)
repeat
  $P^{'} \leftarrow$ Perturbation(R^*, q, Tr, *history*)
  $R^{*'} \leftarrow$ LocalNGSearch($P^{'}$, G, *history*)
  $R^* \leftarrow$ AcceptanceCriterion(R^*, $R^{*'}$)
until termination condition met

dimensional embedding space, which are represented as F_1, F_2 and F_3, respectively.

3.2 ANN Search Model

Nearest neighbor (NN) search has been a fundamental research topic and widely applied in computer vision, machine learning, and information retrieval. Given a query q, one straightforward solution to the NN search is linear scan. Unfortunately, such NN search is often impractical for the large-scale high-dimensional database. To deal with the problem, we follow [31] and apply the query-driven iterated neighborhood graph search model for ANN search.

The ANN search model contains two stages. A video neighborhood graph on video visual representations is firstly built and then a query-driven iterated neighborhood graph search approach is exploited to locate the ANNs. The basic procedure is outlined in Algorithm 1.

GenerateInitialSolution(q, Tr) searches over trees Tr, which are constructed to index the reference videos. The initial solution contains a small amount of initial NN candidates that have high probabilities to be near true NNs. Following the implementation in [31], we use kd-trees in our experiments. LocalNGSearch(P_0, G) starts from a set of seeds P_0 and searches over G by conducting neighborhood expansions in a best-first manner. Perturbation(R^*, q, Tr, *history*) generates new seeds from trees Tr according to the search history and previously selected NNs (R^*), to avoid unnecessary neighborhood expansions. LocalNGSearch($P^{'}$, G, *history*) is slightly different from LocalNGSearch(P_0, G) as the search history, i.e., the NNs discovered up to the current iteration are considered in neighborhood expansion. Readers can refer to [31] for technical details.

3.3 Three Views for Video Commenting

Video can be naturally decomposed into spatial, temporal and emotional components, which are related to ventral, dorsal and limbic system for human perception respectively [16][25]. The ventral and dorsal systems play the major roles in the recognition of objects and visually guided actions which are both focusing on the video content, while the limbic view mainly supports for the neurological regulation of emotion about the visual sentiment to the given video. In addition, human-generated textual comment on shared video can be regarded as another view in natural language for video. Therefore, we input all the three views of video content, visual sentiment and textual comment into a following deep multi-view embedding model for video commenting, as shown in Figure 3. The video content view depicts objects and temporal dynamics by frame appearance and video clip consisting of multiple frames, while the visual sentiment view conveys the emotion of the whole video and the textual comment view expresses the observation and feelings from users' viewpoint.

Video content view. The video content view consists of both spatial and temporal structures underlying video. For the spatial component, VGG-19 [26], which is the recent superior 2-D CNN architecture for image classification, is exploited for extracting frame-level spatial representation. The VGG-19 is pre-trained on 1.2 million images of ImageNet challenge dataset [23] and its 4,096-way fc6 layer output is taken as frame representation. Then, mean pooling is performed over all the sampled frames to get a 4,096 dimensional video-level spatial representation (VGG). For the temporal component, to capture the temporal dynamics between multiple frames, 3-D CNN is utilized for each video clip consisting of continuous frames. Different from traditional 2-D CNN, 3-D CNN architecture takes video clip as the input and consists of alternating 3-D convolutional and 3-D pooling layers, which are further topped by a few fully connected layers. Specifically, C3D [29], which is pre-trained on Sports-1M video dataset [15], is used and we regard the output of the 4,096-way fc6 fully-connected layer as representation for each video clip. Similar to spatial component, we adopt mean pooling over all the C3D outputs of sampled clips to generate video-level temporal representation (C3D). The final representation for video content view is the concatenation of C3D and VGG (C3D+VGG) which models both spatial and temporal information in video.

Visual sentiment view. To represent the visual emotions evoked on video, we use ANP-Net [4], which is a CNN architecture pre-trained with 867,919 images from Visual Sentiment Ontology [3] to classify images into 2,089 Adjective Noun Pairs (ANPs). The 2,089-dimensional softmax scores of ANP-Net is adopted as the visual sentiment representation for each frame. Then, max pooling is performed over all the visual sentiment representations of sampled frames to generate the video-level representation from visual sentiment view.

Textual comment view. For the representations of textual comment, we utilize two popular methods: (1) Term Frequency (tf). Each comment is represented as a vector of words, and each word is weighed by term frequency. (2) Word2vec ($w2v$). We represent each word with 300-dimensional vector generated from word2vector neural network [17] pre-trained on Google News dataset (about 100 billion words) and then the sentence-level representation for textual comment view is generated by mean pooling over all the word vectors in the comment.

It is worth noticing that although the three views used here are video content, visual sentiment and textual comment, our approach is applicable to include any other view, e.g., audio view.

3.4 Deep Multi-View Embedding Model

To learn the whole architecture of our deep multi-view embedding, the objective is to maximize the correlations among video content, visual sentiment and textual comment. One natural choice is to minimize the distances between each pair of views in the embedding space. However, without any carefully designed constraints, the optimization will easily result in meaningless solution that all three views map to the identical representation in the embedding space.

Deriving from the idea of exploring relative relationship through ranking [19][34][35], we develop a triplet deep rank-

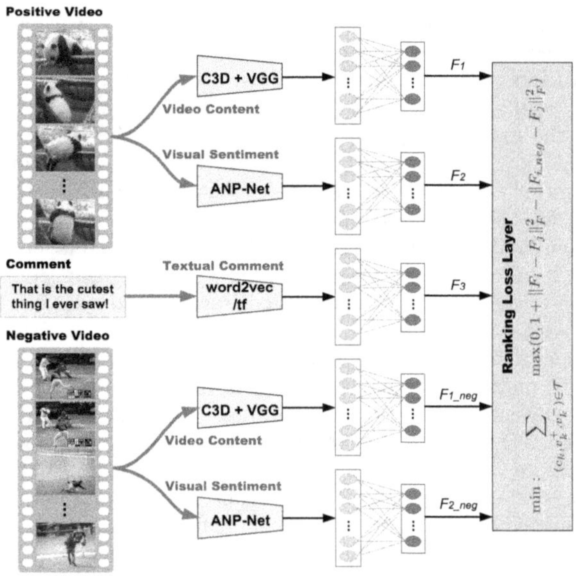

Figure 3: The training of deep multi-view embedding model. The inputs are a set of triplets: textual comment, positive video and negative video. For both videos, video representations are learnt by C3D plus VGG architectures while visual sentiment is modeled by ANP-Net, followed by an embedding layer for each of the two views, respectively. Note that the embedding layers of positive and negative videos share parameters. For textual comment, word2vec ($w2v$) or term frequency (tf) is extracted and then feed into a textual embedding layer. A loss layer is on the top to evaluate the ranking loss of the triplet.

ing model to learn our deep multi-view embedding model (DE) for dynamic ranking. Figure 3 shows the training of DE architecture with triplet deep ranking model. Given a triplet of textual comment, positive video which is associated with the textual comment and negative video which is irrelevant to the textual comment, we aim to optimize our DE architecture, which makes the mapping of textual comment closer to positive video than negative video in the embedding space. Formally, suppose we have a set of triplets $\mathcal{T}$, where each triplet $(c_i, {v_i}^+, {v_i}^-)$ consists of a textual comment c_i, a positive video ${v_i}^+$ and a negative video ${v_i}^-$. Note that c_i is selected from textual comments associated with positive video ${v_i}^+$ while the negative video ${v_i}^-$ is randomly sampled from a different category and does not contain comment c_i. The positive and negative videos in the triplet are fed separately into two identical embedding layers with shared architecture and parameters. Our goal is to learn the DE architecture that makes one view F_j in the embedding space is closer to another view F_i of positive video than that view F_{i_neg} of negative video, which can be expressed as

$$\begin{aligned} &\|F_i - F_j\|_F^2 \prec \|F_{i\_neg} - F_j\|_F^2, \quad \forall (c_k, v_k^+, v_k^-) \in \mathcal{T} \\ &s.t. \quad i,j = 1,...,3, \quad i \neq j, \quad i \neq 3 \; . \end{aligned} \tag{1}$$

As the distances between two views in embedding space exhibit a relative ranking order, a ranking loss layer on the top is employed to evaluate the margin ranking loss of each triplet, which is a convex approximation to the 0-1 ranking error loss and has been used in several information retrieval methods. Specifically, it can be given by

$$\begin{aligned} \min : &\sum_{(c_k, v_k^+, v_k^-) \in \mathcal{T}} \max(0, 1 + \|F_i - F_j\|_F^2 - \|F_{i\_neg} - F_j\|_F^2) \\ &s.t. \quad i,j = 1,...,3, \quad i \neq j, \quad i \neq 3 \; . \end{aligned} \tag{2}$$

The ranking loss layer does not have any parameters. During learning, it evaluates the model's violation of the ranking order, and back-propagates the gradients to the lower layers so that the lower layers can adjust their parameters to minimize the ranking loss. Please also note that each view is equipped with a hyperbolic tangent function plus a L_2 normalization before fed into the ranking loss layer.

After optimization, we can obtain the mappings f_v, f_s and f_c for the three views, respectively. Next, given a test video and candidate comment pair $(\hat{v}, \hat{c})$, we compute the distance value between the pair as

$$r(\hat{v}, \hat{c}) = \|F_1(\hat{v}) - F_3(\hat{c})\|_F^2 + \|F_2(\hat{v}) - F_3(\hat{c})\|_F^2 \; . \tag{3}$$

This value reflects how relevant the candidate comment could be presented for the given video, with lower numbers indicating higher relevance. Thus, given a test video, a rank list of candidate comments is produced by sorting the values of video-comment pairs.

4. VIDEO COMMENTING DATASET

To the best of our knowledge, our work is the first attempt to automatically generate comments for videos. To substantially evaluate our approach, we collect a new dataset for video commenting. The dataset is characterized by the unique properties including the large scale video-comment pairs, comprehensive video categories, diverse video content and comments. We next describe how we collect representative videos, select high-quality comments, and split the dataset.

4.1 Collection of Videos

Our dataset focuses on general videos in our life and is collected from Vine[1]. Vine is the entertainment network where the world's stories are captured, created, remixed and shared. The users can follow your favorite creators, watch their stories and post your comments as well.

To collect representative videos, we obtain 2,278 popular tags from TagsForLikes website[2], corresponding to 12 categories[3]. Then we crawl the top 100 video search results for each tag and collect at most 500 comments for each video. We remove duplication, as well as the videos with low-quality comments, to maintain the data quality. As a result, we have 101,752 representative videos. All the videos were downloaded with high quality and audio channel.

4.2 Selection of High Quality Comments

The original comments associated with each video contain too much noise, e.g., random responses, bad words and negative induced emotion. In order to make the comments in our dataset clean and high quality, we select the comments from three aspects: 1) length, 2) relevance, and 3) sentiment. In between, the length of comment is generally an important

[1] https://vine.co/

[2] http://vine.tagsforlikes.com/

[3] The categories include animal, art, celebration, entertainment, family, fashion, food, sports, urban, vehicle, weather, other.

factor based on the observation that very short comments are always general-purpose while long comments are often too specific. Furthermore, the use of relevance measurement between comment and video is to filter out the random responses. As the comments are posted as social interactions, those with very negative sentiment should be also removed. In addition, the comments containing bad or dirty words are removed directly from our dataset. Specifically, the quality measurement on each criterion is as below.

Length. Let *min_len* and *max_len* denote the expected minimal and maximal length of comment, respectively. Denote *length* as the length of comment after removing punctuation and emoji. Then, the quality score of comment in terms of length is defined as

$$S_{len} = \omega_1 * max((min\_len - length), 0) + \omega_2 * max((length - max\_len), 0) \quad , \tag{4}$$

where ω_1 and ω_2 are tradeoff parameters between punishing very short and too long comments.

Relevance. We estimate the relevance between video and comment by measuring the semantic similarity between the tag submitted for searching this video and words in the comment. Specifically, each comment c is represented as a sequence of words. Words are stemmed and stop words are removed. Then, the similarity $sim(tag, w_i)$ between the tag and each word w_i in the comment is computed by WordNet [18]. Finally, the quality score of the comment on relevance is given by

$$S_{rel} = \max_{w_i \in c} sim(tag, w_i) \quad . \tag{5}$$

Sentiment. Following [14], we apply VADER for comment sentiment analysis. VADER (Valence Aware Dictionary for Sentiment Reasoning) is a rule-based model for general-purpose sentiment analysis, which is shown to be powerful and outperforms individual human raters on some specific social media text, e.g., tweets. For each comment c, the sentiment score $senti(c)$ is taken as its quality score and is formally computed as

$$S_{senti} = senti(c) \quad . \tag{6}$$

The final quality score of each comment is obtained by linearly fusing the three scores as

$$S_{qua} = \alpha_1 * S_{rel} + \alpha_2 * S_{senti} - \alpha_3 * S_{len} \quad , \tag{7}$$

where α_1, α_2 and α_3 are tradeoff parameters, which weight the importance of the three criteria. If the final quality score is smaller than a threshold, the comment will be regarded as a low-quality one and thus removed from our dataset. After selection, there are about 10.6 millions of comments.

4.3 Statistics and Dataset Splits

Our dataset consists of 185 hours videos and 10.6 millions comments (corresponding to 90 millions words and one million unique words). It is derived from a wide variety of video categories (101,752 videos from 12 general categories) and thus this can benefit the generalization capability of model learning on this dataset. Figure 4 further details the category distribution of all the videos. Moreover, there are more than 100 comments for each video on average, leading to a better chance of finding more natural and diverse comments. In summary, we present a comprehensive, diverse, and complex dataset for video commenting.

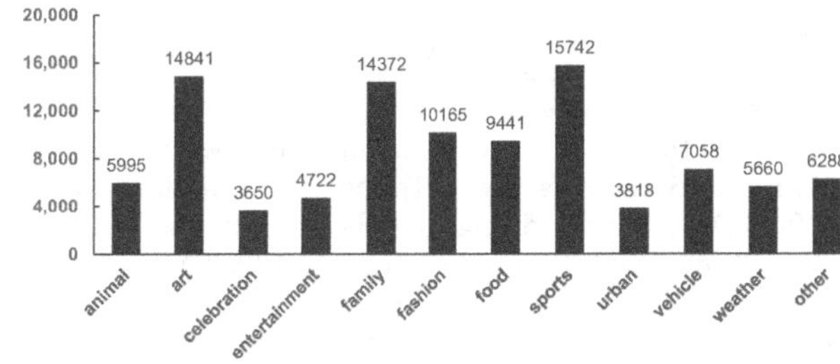

Figure 4: The distribution of video categories in our dataset. This distribution well aligns with the real data statistics in a social video platform.

To split the dataset to training, validation and testing set, we separate the videos according to the corresponding categories. The videos from the same category will appear in all the three sets to avoid overfitting. Finally, we sample 96,752, 4,000, 1,000 videos in the training, validation, and testing set, respectively.

5. EXPERIMENTS

We conducted our experiments on the aforementioned newly crawled video commenting data and evaluated our proposed framework on video commenting task.

5.1 Experimental Settings

Compared Approaches: We compare the following approaches for performance evaluation:

- Random Selection (RS). We search visually similar videos of the input video by utilizing ANN search, and then randomly select the comments from all the associated comments of these searched similar videos as the final output comments. No comment ranking model is learned in this baseline. We name this run as *RS*.
- Canonical Correlation Analysis (CCA) [10][12]. CCA is a popular and successful approach for mapping two or more input views into a latent embedding space where the correlation between different views are maximized. We employ the classical CCA method in DR stage to build a multi-view embedding space based on video content (V), textual comment (T) and/or visual sentiment (S) to measure the relevance between textual comment and video. Two slightly different variants of this run are named as *CCA-VT* and *CCA-VST*, which rank the candidate comments for the input video in the learnt two-view (V and T) embedding space and three-view (V, S and T) embedding space, respectively.
- Deep Multi-view Embedding model (DE). We design two runs, *DE-VT* and *DE-VST*, for our proposed two-stage framework. For the dynamic ranking of candidate comments, *DE-VT* learns the embedding space based on two views of video content and textual comment (V and T), while *DE-VST* exploits all the three views by additionally incorporating the view of visual sentiment (V, S and T) to learn the embedding space.

Parameter Settings: In the VS stage, the k nearest neighbors for ANN search is chosen within {1, 5, 10, 15, 20}. For each nearest neighbor video, we randomly sample at most 50 associated comments to generate the candidate comments. In the next stage, for each input view, the sample rate is set as 1 frame/clip per second. Specifically, for the tf representation in textual comment view, we use the top 35,000 most frequent words as the word vocabulary. Moreover, for the four embedding models, the dimensionality of the embedding space is in the range of {32, 64, 128, 256}. Please note that for each compared method, top 5 comments are finally presented to the input video. We set the parameters in high quality comment selection as $min\_len = 3$, $max\_len = 30$, $\omega_1 = 10$, $\omega_2 = 1$, $\alpha_1 = 0.5$, $\alpha_2 = 0.3$ and $\alpha_3 = 0.01$ empirically.

Ground Truth: To facilitate the evaluation and comparison with other approaches, we randomly selected 1,000 videos as testing samples. For each testing video, the top 5 comments obtained by different methods are annotated during the final evaluation. Eight evaluators from different education backgrounds, including linguistics, business, information management, international news, electrical engineering, and computer science are invited. All evaluators are familiar with video sharing sites. Each comment was annotated on a five point ordinal scale: 5-Very Good; 4-Good; 3-Normal; 2-Bad; 1-Very Bad. Note that only the comments with their scores more than 3 points are regarded as ground truth relevant ones for evaluation. The evaluators are requested to watch the whole video before evaluating comments.

Evaluation Metrics: For the evaluation of video commenting, we adopted average precision (AP) as the performance metric and mean Average Precision (mAP) over all the videos in testing set is finally reported. Given a comment ranked list, the AP score at the depth of m in the ranked list is defined by:

$$AP@m = \frac{1}{m}\sum\nolimits_{j=1}^{m} \frac{R_j}{j} \times I_j, \tag{8}$$

where R_j is the total number of relevant comments in the top-j list, I_j is set as 1 if the jth comment is relevant and 0 otherwise.

5.2 Performance Comparison

Table 1 shows the mAP performances of five runs averaged over 1,000 test videos. It is worth noting that *RS* selects comments randomly from candidates without learning any ranking model and for other four runs, the performances are given by choosing 64 as the dimensionality of the latent embedding space and taking tf as comment representations.

Overall, our proposed *DE-VST* consistently outperforms the other runs across different depths of mAP. In particular, the mAP@1 of *DE-VST* can achieve 0.549, making the relative improvements over *CCA-VST* by 9.6%. Though both *DE-VST* and *CCA-VST* involve utilization of multi-view embedding, different strategies are used for learning the embedding space. *CCA-VST* aims to learn an embedding space which maximizes the correlations between the heterogeneous representations across three original views, while *DE-VST* additionally incorporates the preference relations in the training triplets to further adjust the embedding space. The results indicate that our *DE-VST* is benefited from the utilization of relative preference, and capable of finding more desired comments in response to the video. *RS*, which even selects the comments randomly from the comments associated with visually similar videos, still shows encouraging performance. This somewhat reveals the effectiveness of ANN search on our powerful spatio-temporal video representations. Compared to *DE-VT* (*CCA-VT*), *DE-VST* (*CCA-VST*) exhibits better performance by considering visual sentiment as another view of video representations for multi-view embedding learning. This is expected, as for video commenting the emotions or feelings on videos are highly related to visual sentiment reflected in videos.

Table 1: Performance comparison of different approaches for video commenting.

App.	mAP@1	mAP@2	mAP@3	mAP@4	mAP@5
RS	0.259	0.244	0.219	0.203	0.191
CCA-VT[12]	0.458	0.421	0.399	0.389	0.382
CCA-VST[10]	0.501	0.465	0.439	0.429	0.419
DE-VT	0.504	0.469	0.447	0.433	0.422
DE-VST	0.549	0.513	0.486	0.471	0.459

To verify that the performance of different approaches is not by chance, we conducted significance test using the randomization test [22]. The number of iterations used in the randomization is 100,000 and at 0.05 significance level. *DE-VST* is found to be significantly better than others.

Figure 5 further details the mAP@1 performance for all the 12 categories. Among all the categories, *DE-VST* achieves the best performance for 10 categories, followed by *DE-VT* and *CCA-VST* for one category, respectively. The improvements can be generally expected by further taking the view of visual sentiment into account in both CCA and our deep multi-view embedding model learning on all the categories except "food" category. That is not surprise because the perceived sentiment or emotion signals from videos in "food" category are often neutral and thus not easy to be predicted precisely.

Figure 6 shows a few comment examples produced by different approaches. From these exemplar results, it is easy to see that all of these automatic methods can find somewhat relevant comments. With embedding model, the ranks of more precise comments are likely to be moved up and responded to the videos. Moreover, our *DE-VST* can offer more accurate emotional comments. For instance, the returned comment "wow this is amazing! I love to draw and to photograph." to the first video experiences the video content more desirably.

5.3 Search vs Generation

To empirically verify the merit of video commenting by search, we further conducted the experiments to examine how it works when the task is treated as a problem of sentence generation. Following [8], an end-to-end LSTM based model is learnt over all the video-comment pairs in training set. When we apply the model to our testing set, most of the predicted comments to the videos are very general-purpose phrases, e.g., "cute," "cool," and "it is amazing." This is arisen from the fact that these phrases often appear in the comments of different videos, making the predicted probabilities of these phrases very high for any input videos. On the other hand, for each video, the comments exploited in training are very diverse with various subjective descriptions. Therefore, it is very difficult to establish a translatable mapping from video to comment for generation. This comparison basically validates our analysis and proposal of video commenting by search.

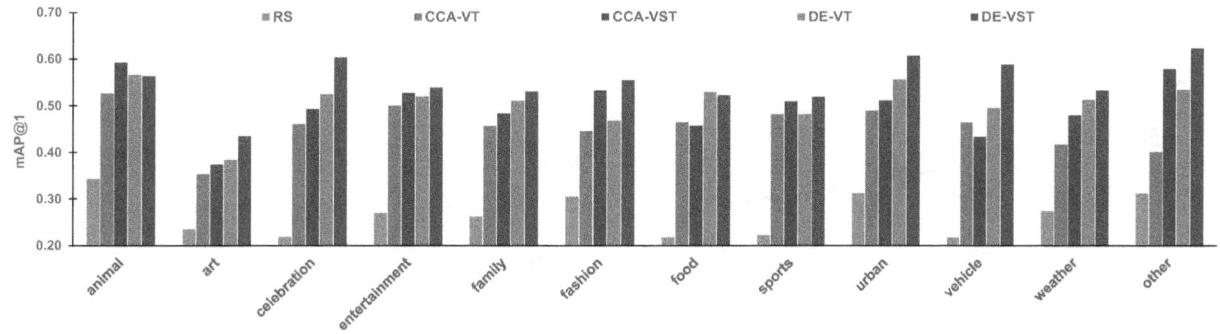

Figure 5: Per-category mAP@1 of different approaches for all the 12 categories.

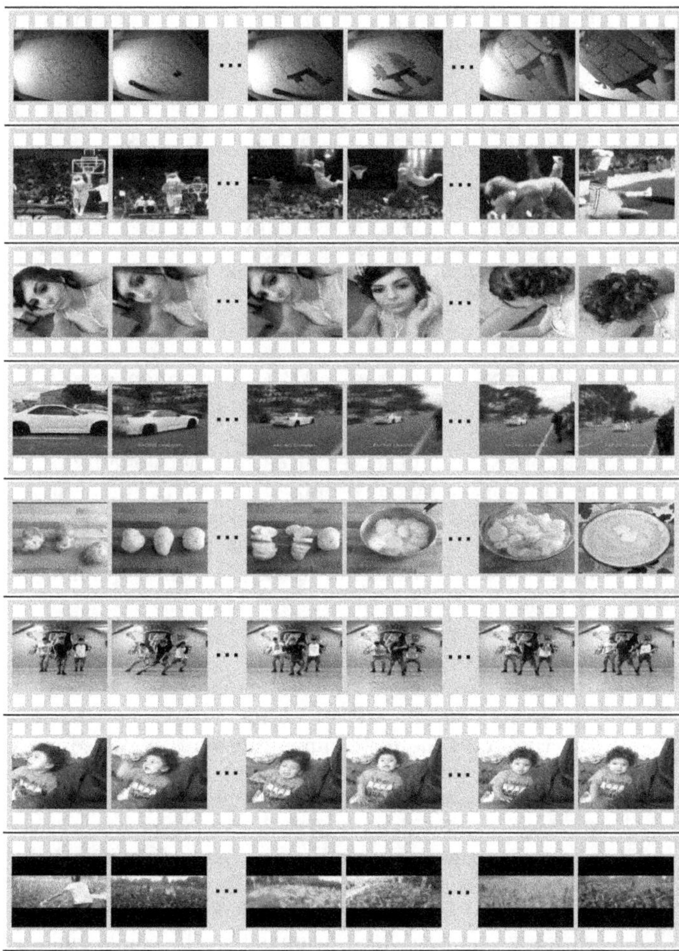

RS: Haha, you are too cute!
CCA-VT: how did u draw like that?
CCA-VST: let me know that how can make a draw like this.
DE-VT: really creative, awesome job bro.
DE-VST: wow this is amazing ! I love to draw and to photograph.

RS: steph can dunk?
CCA-VT: that is a dunk.
CCA-VST: the dunk is my all time favorite!
DE-VT: cool! A guy dunked! So surprising!
DE-VST: he will finally have a dunk package in 2K16.

RS: a beautiful lady.
CCA-VT: you are very beautiful.
CCA-VST: OMG! Your beautiful absolutely gorgeous.
DE-VT: Omg!!! I want your hair!
DE-VST: your are beautiful, pretty is for little girls, beautiful hair.

RS: what is that car?
CCA-VT: it is a lambo.
CCA-VST: lambo definitely had the right of way!
DE-VT: hahahah the lambo went flying.
DE-VST: I love lambo. It has strong power and speed.

RS: let's make it.
CCA-VT: this is fancy dinner?
CCA-VST: looks so yummy!!
DE-VT: Oh looks delicious make these please.
DE-VST: that looks very good! I just wanted to eat that food.

RS: I don't like phoenix
CCA-VT: the middle is dominic, left is phoenix and right is max
CCA-VST: phoenix is the best ever. Just saying.
DE-VT: just stalk them. They are really good.
DE-VST: crying bc song and this dance is actually really good.

RS: omg that's so funny.
CCA-VT: you are so cute.
CCA-VST: love this kid.
DE-VT: he is literally the cutest ever.
DE-VST: he is so cute and his cheeks are adorable !!

RS: look at this.
CCA-VT: song name please.
CCA-VST: what song is this? I love it !!
DE-VT: is this the festival you on about?
DE-VST: life is color festival, we are going to this one too.

Figure 6: Examples of top-1 ranked comment on each video produced by different approaches. The videos are represented by sampled frames.

5.4 Comparison on Different Representations

We designed six runs to compare the performances of our multi-view embedding model as a result of exploiting different video and comment representations, while the representations of visual sentiment are always extracted by ANP-Net. The results are shown in Figure 7.

There is a performance gap between using $w2v$ and tf representations. Though both representations are learnt on a large corpus, $w2v$ is predicted by Skip-gram models which are pre-trained on news articles, and tf vector of each comment is weighted by term frequency of each word in the vocabulary built on our created video commenting dataset. As indicated by our results, tf representations can constantly lead to better performance. We speculate that this may be caused by the big difference of wording between news (formal) and comments (social). Moreover, video representations learnt by C3D which has a better ability in encapsulating temporal information leads to better performance

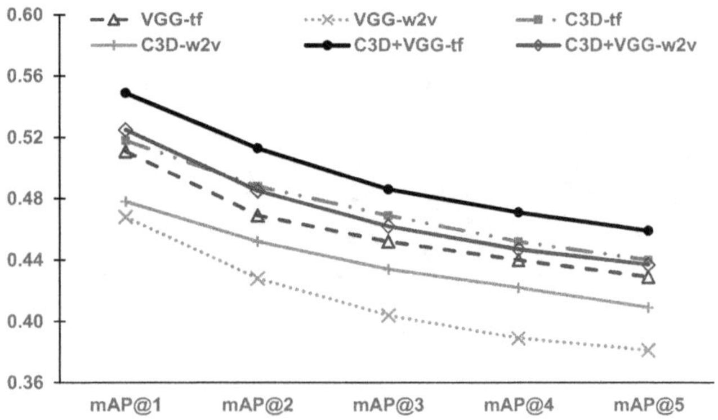

Figure 7: Performance comparison on different representations of video and comment.

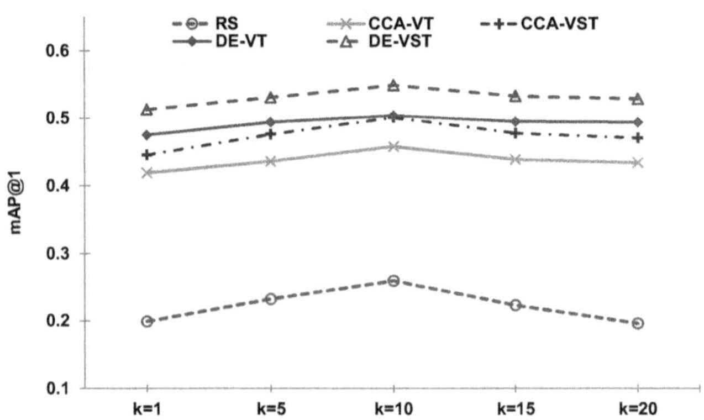

Figure 8: The mAP@1 performance curve with different number of nearest neighbors.

than those by VGG. When combining the representations from VGG and C3D, C3D+VGG further increases the performance gains.

5.5 Effect of the Number of Nearest Neighbors

The number of nearest neighbors is an important parameter in similar video search. In the previous experiments, the number was fixed to 10. Next, we conducted experiments to evaluate the performances of all the compared approaches with the number of nearest neighbors in range of {1, 5, 10, 15, 20}.

The mAP@1 of all the approaches with different number of nearest neighbors are shown in Figure 8. As illustrated in the figure, the proposed $DE-VST$ consistently outperforms others when returning each number of nearest neighbors and the optimal k is happened at 10 for all the compared methods on our dataset. This is also expected, as for few neighbors their associate comments may not be enough to find right ones while too many neighbors will include imperfect similar videos.

5.6 Effect of the Dimensionality of the Embedding Space

In order to show the relationship between the performance and the dimensionality of the embedding space, we compared the results of the dimension in the range of 32, 64, 128, and 256. Note that only the four runs with embedding space learning are included in this comparison.

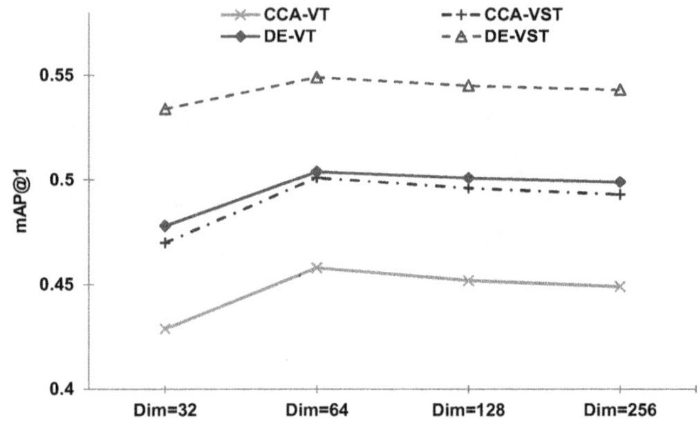

Figure 9: The mAP@1 performance curve with different dimensionality of the embedding space.

Table 2: Speed efficiency of our proposed framework for commenting on a five seconds' video.

Key step	Speed
Representation extraction by VGG	3.6 sec
Representation extraction by C3D	4.3 sec
Representation extraction by ANP-Net	0.62 sec
Similar video search	0.02 sec
Comment dynamic ranking	0.5 sec

Figure 9 shows the mAP@1 performance with respect to different dimensionality of the embedding space. Compared to the other three runs, performance improvements are consistently observed at each dimensionality of the embedding space by our proposed *DE-VST*. Furthermore, *DE-VST* achieves the best result at the dimensionality of 64 and the results at other dimensionality higher than 64 are close to the best one. In addition, the performance trends of mAP at other depths are similar with that of mAP@1.

5.7 Run Time

The experiments were conducted on a regular PC (Intel dual-core 3.39GHz CPU and 16GB RAM). Table 2 details the running time for commenting on a five seconds' video. The major portion of the processing time is consumed by video representation extraction, which takes 3.60, 4.30 and 0.62 seconds by VGG, C3D and ANP-Net, respectively. As we can run each representation extraction in parallel, the total extraction time can be very close to 4.3 sec. Similar video search basically completes a search within 0.02 sec which is very fast. By processing all the comments associated with the top-10 ranked similar videos, dynamic ranking takes about 0.50 sec. Overall, the current implementation finishes in 4.82 sec, which is less than the duration of the video. The run time will be further reduced to 1.20 sec when testing on a single NVIDIA K40 GPU.

6. CONCLUSIONS

We have presented our framework for automatic commenting videos, along with the proposal of techniques for spatio-temporal video representation learning, similar video search and dynamic ranking of candidate comments. Particularly, we analyze the advantages of addressing the commenting problem, from the viewpoint of search rather than generation, by leveraging huge amounts of real user-generated comments on the social platforms. To verify our claim, we have presented approaches based on the existing works in the literature for searching visually similar videos to obtain the comments associated with these similar videos as candidates. In comment dynamic ranking, our deep multi-view embedding model, which projects video content, visual sentiment and textual comment into a common space, offers apparent improvements over other methods, in terms of boosting the chance of finding the right comment from candidates. Experimental results demonstrate that, by searching from a newly created dataset of over 0.1 million videos and 10.6 million comments, top-K comments can be returned to an input video within the duration of that video, with a good chance of finding the desired comments.

Our work can still be improved on several aspects. First, more spatio-temporal video representations will be explored especially for modeling temporal dynamics, e.g., by using alternative solution like recurrent neural networks. Second, our multi-view embedding model can be enhanced by further considering audio information. The audio features can be exploited together with video content and visual sentiment for a more comprehensive manner of characterizing videos.

7. REFERENCES

[1] S. Antol, A. Agrawal, J. Lu, M. Mitchell, , D. Batra, C. Lawrence Zitnick, and D. Parikh. Vqa: Visual question answering. In *ICCV*, 2015.

[2] D. Bahdanau, K. Cho, and Y. Bengio. Neural machine translation by jointly learning to align and translate. In *ICLR*, 2015.

[3] D. Borth, R. Ji, T. Chen, T. Breuel, and S.-F. Chang. Large-scale visual sentiment ontology and detectors using adjective noun pairs. In *ACM MM*, 2013.

[4] T. Chen, D. Borth, T. Darrell, and S.-F. Chang. Deepsentibank: Visual sentiment concept classification with deep convolutional neural networks. *arXiv preprint arXiv:1410.8586*, 2014.

[5] Y.-Y. Chen, T. Chen, W. H. Hsu, H.-Y. M. Liao, and S.-F. Chang. Predicting viewer affective comments based on image content in social media. In *ICMR*, 2014.

[6] N. Cristianini and J. Shawe-Taylor. *An introduction to support vector machines and other kernel-based learning methods*. Cambridge university press, 2000.

[7] J. Devlin, S. Gupta, R. Girshick, M. Mitchell, and C. L. Zitnick. Exploring nearest neighbor approaches for image captioning. *arXiv preprint arXiv:1505.04467*, 2015.

[8] J. Donahue, L. A. Hendricks, S. Guadarrama, M. Rohrbach, S. Venugopalan, K. Saenko, and T. Darrell. Long-term recurrent convolutional networks for visual recognition and description. In *CVPR*, 2015.

[9] A. Farhadi, M. Hejrati, M. A. Sadeghi, P. Young, C. Rashtchian, J. Hockenmaier, and D. Forsyth. Every picture tells a story: Generating sentences from images. In *ECCV*. 2010.

[10] Y. Gong, Q. Ke, M. Isard, and S. Lazebnik. A multi-view embedding space for modeling internet images, tags, and their semantics. *IJCV*, 106(2):210–233, 2014.

[11] S. Guadarrama, N. Krishnamoorthy, G. Malkarnenkar, S. Venugopalan, R. Mooney, T. Darrell, and K. Saenko. Youtube2text: Recognizing and describing arbitrary activities using semantic hierarchies and zero-shot recognition. In *ICCV*, 2013.

[12] D. R. Hardoon, S. Szedmak, and J. Shawe-Taylor. Canonical correlation analysis: An overview with application to learning methods. *Neural Computation*, 16(12):2639–2664, 2004.

[13] S. Hochreiter and J. Schmidhuber. Long short-term memory. *Neural Computation*, 9(8):1735–1780, 1997.

[14] C. J. Hutto and E. Gilbert. Vader: A parsimonious rule-based model for sentiment analysis of social media text. In *AAAI Conference on Weblogs and Social Media*, 2014.

[15] A. Karpathy, G. Toderici, S. Shetty, T. Leung, R. Sukthankar, and L. Fei-Fei. Large-scale video classification with convolutional neural networks. In *CVPR*, 2014.

[16] M. A. Kheirbek and R. Hen. Dorsal vs ventral hippocampal neurogenesis: implications for cognition and mood. *Neuropsychopharmacology*, 36(1):373, 2011.

[17] T. Mikolov, I. Sutskever, K. Chen, G. S. Corrado, and J. Dean. Distributed representations of words and phrases and their compositionality. In *NIPS*, 2013.

[18] G. A. Miller. Wordnet: a lexical database for english. *Communications of the ACM*, 38(11):39–41, 1995.

[19] Y. Pan, Y. Li, T. Yao, T. Mei, H. Li, and Y. Rui. Learning deep intrinsic video representation by exploring temporal coherence and graph structure. In *IJCAI*, 2016.

[20] Y. Pan, T. Mei, T. Yao, H. Li, and Y. Rui. Jointly modeling embedding and translation to bridge video and language. In *CVPR*, 2016.

[21] G.-J. Qi, X.-S. Hua, Y. Rui, J. Tang, T. Mei, and H.-J. Zhang. Correlative multi-label video annotation. In *ACM MM*, 2007.

[22] J. P. Romano. On the behavior of randomization tests without a group invariance assumption. *Journal of the American Statistical Association*, 85(411):686–692, 1990.

[23] O. Russakovsky, J. Deng, H. Su, J. Krause, S. Satheesh, S. Ma, Z. Huang, A. Karpathy, A. Khosla, M. Bernstein, et al. Imagenet large scale visual recognition challenge. *IJCV*, 115(3):211–252, 2015.

[24] S. Siersdorfer, J. S. Pedro, and M. Sanderson. Automatic video tagging using content redundancy. In *SIGIR*, 2009.

[25] K. Simonyan and A. Zisserman. Two-stream convolutional networks for action recognition in videos. In *NIPS*, 2014.

[26] K. Simonyan and A. Zisserman. Very deep convolutional networks for large-scale image recognition. In *ICLR*, 2015.

[27] I. Sutskever, O. Vinyals, and Q. V. Le. Sequence to sequence learning with neural networks. In *NIPS*, 2014.

[28] J. Thomason, S. Venugopalan, S. Guadarrama, K. Saenko, and R. J. Mooney. Integrating language and vision to generate natural language descriptions of videos in the wild. In *COLING*, volume 2, page 9, 2014.

[29] D. Tran, L. D. Bourdev, R. Fergus, L. Torresani, and M. Paluri. C3d: generic features for video analysis. In *ICCV*, 2015.

[30] O. Vinyals, A. Toshev, S. Bengio, and D. Erhan. Show and tell: A neural image caption generator. In *CVPR*, 2015.

[31] J. Wang and S. Li. Query-driven iterated neighborhood graph search for large scale indexing. In *ACM MM*, 2012.

[32] M. Wang, X.-S. Hua, J. Tang, and R. Hong. Beyond distance measurement: constructing neighborhood similarity for video annotation. *IEEE Trans. on MM*, 11(3):465–476, 2009.

[33] J. Xu, T. Mei, T. Yao, and Y. Rui. MSR-VTT: A large video description dataset for bridging video and language. In *CVPR*, 2016.

[34] T. Yao, F. Long, T. Mei, and Y. Rui. Deep semantic-preserving and ranking-based hashing for image retrieval. In *IJCAI*, 2016.

[35] T. Yao, T. Mei, and C.-W. Ngo. Learning query and image similarities with ranking canonical correlation analysis. In *ICCV*, 2015.

[36] T. Yao, T. Mei, C.-W. Ngo, and S. Li. Annotation for free: Video tagging by mining user search behavior. In *ACM MM*, 2013.

[37] G. Ye, Y. Li, H. Xu, D. Liu, and S.-F. Chang. Eventnet: A large scale structured concept library for complex event detection in video. In *ACM MM*, 2015.

Research Challenges in Developing Multimedia Systems for Managing Emergency Situations

Mengfan Tang
Department of Computer Science
University of California, Irvine
mengfant@uci.edu

Siripen Pongpaichet
Department of Computer Science
University of California, Irvine
spongpai@ics.uci.edu

Ramesh Jain
Department of Computer Science
University of California, Irvine
jain@ics.uci.edu

ABSTRACT

With an increasing amount of diverse heterogeneous data and information, the methodology of multimedia analysis has become increasingly relevant in solving challenging societal problems such as managing emergency situations during disasters. Using cybernetic principles combined with multimedia technology, researchers can develop effective frameworks for using diverse multimedia (including traditional multimedia as well as diverse multimodal) data for situation recognition, and determining and communicating appropriate actions to people stranded during disasters. We present known issues in disaster management and then focus on emergency situations. We show that an emergency management problem is fundamentally a multimedia information assimilation problem for situation recognition and for connecting people's needs to available resources effectively, efficiently, and promptly. Major research challenges for managing emergency situations are identified and discussed. We also present a platform to assimilate heterogeneous data streams for intelligently detecting evolving environmental situations, and discuss the role of *multimedia micro-reports* as spontaneous participatory sensing data streams in emergency responses. Given enormous progress in concept recognition using machine learning in the last few years, situation recognition may be the next major challenge for learning approaches in multimedia contextual big data. The data needed for developing such approaches is now easily available on the Web and many challenging research problems in this area are ripe for exploration in order to positively impact our society during its most difficult times.

Keywords

Disaster; Situation recognition; Situation prediction; EventShop; Micro-reports;

1. INTRODUCTION

Disasters happen. And Disasters will always happen. We have to be ready for them, respond to them *efficiently*, *effectively*, and *promptly*, and then manage their long term consequences. Disasters such as floods, earthquakes, landslides, forest fires, tsunamis, hurricanes, terrorist bombings, Zika or similar epidemics, global warming, and air quality crisis cause huge damage in both human lives and property across the globe. Furthermore, a disaster sometimes reaches the stage when it becomes an *emergency*. During an emergency, lives are lost and property may be damaged. The right information, at the right time, at the right place, and to the right people minimizes the loss of life, property, and misery.

In this paper, we propose the use of multimedia for predicting emerging disastrous situations, identifying people's needs during disasters, and helping them during disasters. We believe that multimedia computing and communication systems have a pivotal role to play in disaster preparedness, help during disasters, and then in recovery afterward. Multimedia computing has evolved from basic audio and video applications in business and entertainment to using information from different multimodal sources for understanding and helping people and organizations. Researchers started paying attention to situation recognition and appropriate actions to help people in different novel applications [32]. Disaster management may benefit significantly from multimedia (including multimodal) information. More importantly, for the emerging broader multimedia community, disaster management in general and emergency response in particular may be a transformative research area.

Researchers from environmental science, social science, public health, computer science, and various disciplines put a lot of effort into better predicting the space, time, and severity of disasters for improving response and mitigation. Governments, NGOs, and other organizations concentrate on disaster management, appropriate information sharing and communication, analysis of citizens' needs, and disaster recovery planning. Large volumes of diverse data are being collected regularly by sensors, IoTs, social media, governmental reports, and citizen reports. The data is essentially multimedia big data, because of the volume, variety, and velocity [19].

We believe that people are the best sensors, people are the best responders, and people are the best actuators. Our approach to using multimedia for emergency response is based on using people equipped with mobile phones connected to multimedia disaster management systems, both for collecting real time in-situ information and receiving instructions for action at the right place. In this approach, multimedia data resulting in timely actionable information is the key.

MM '16, October 15-19, 2016, Amsterdam, Netherlands
© 2016 ACM. ISBN 978-1-4503-3603-1/16/10...$15.00
DOI: http://dx.doi.org/10.1145/2964284.2976761

In 2011, Thailand witnessed its worst flooding in more than half a century, causing severe damage to the country's economy, industrial sector, and society. Two-thirds of the country was declared as a disaster zone. This flood started in June and lasted until December. More than 4 million households and 13 million people were affected for over 6 months. The World Bank ranked it as the world's fourth costliest disaster as of 2011 [1]. People, companies, and disaster relief agencies could not make proper decisions in time because they received little information from authorities and any other sources. Even though there were lots of international movements, the aid was slow in reaching affected people because of the communication deficiencies. There was no good mechanism to identify where the needs were and where affected people were.

In this paper, we will use floods as a running example for emergency situations because of their common occurrence and disruptive effect on societies. Most issues discussed for floods are easily generalizable and adaptable to other emergency situations. We will discuss in more detail our multimodal approach that we apply to the Thai flood example in the above box.

A multimedia community has already developed powerful tools for personal media management, commerce, and entertainment. These were good research areas for early multimedia because the problems were not life critical, time sensitive, or inherently complex, but sill required intricate relationships among many heterogeneous media types. The multimedia community is now ready for new challenges. In this paper, we present research challenges in developing multimedia systems for predicting situations, projecting needed resources and its dissemination through people at the scene of disasters. Our goal is to introduce emergency responses to the multimedia community as the next challenging frontier for research and development in order to address life-critical problems our societies face. Many challenging problems that are central to multimedia computing are central to emergency response, but with different requirements. Moreover, emergent responses require a general framework that could be easily instantiated for specific applications. Also, though emergency response systems pull together many components, the research is well compartmentalized in many sub areas. It is easy to explore and evaluate subsystems using easily available past data. We explicitly list ten challenges for the multimedia research community.

We demonstrate our early ideas for building a multimedia emergency response as a Cyber-Physical-Social multimedia computing system. This system uses the EventShop platform [32], which allows heterogeneous geospatial data stream integration and assimilation for situation recognition by combining diverse data sources. In the proposed framework, disaster situation awareness can be enhanced using diverse data streams from sensors, IoTs, social media, and citizen reports. Improved situational awareness allows for applying contextually sensitive control actions. Participatory citizen reporting using micro-reports from emerging systems like Krumbs[1] provides a straightforward and effective way to report situations without citizens having to identify potential contacts for report sharing. This type of reporting also facilitates information sharing and collaboration between organizations and citizens to maintain and enhance their communications. We introduce what-if scenarios to aid decision makers in understanding the current and future state of disaster situations.

[1]www.krumbs.net

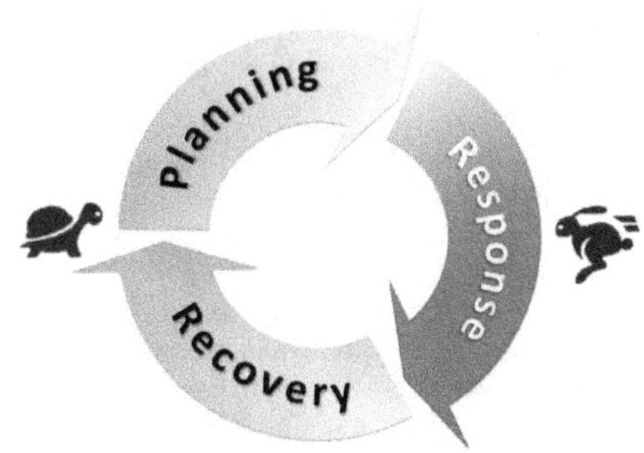

Figure 1: Three stages in the disaster management. Planning and recovery have different level of urgency than response.

2. CURRENT DISASTER MANAGEMENT RESEARCH

The term "Disaster Management" is commonly used to represent different phases of a disaster: planning, response, mitigation, and recovery. These phases were identified based on different operations that needed to be considered for dealing with disasters. From the perspective of multimedia technology, a disaster management system may comprise three phases as shown in Figure 1 and as discussed below.

- **Planning**: Planning includes preparations made to stop disasters from happening, and to plan response and rescue when they do happen. For example, evacuation plans in disasters are made and life supply necessities, such as food and water, are stocked. An important part of the planning is to send proper guidance to people during the disaster response stage. This guidance must be prepared such that it is delivered to people using the right media at the right time. During a flood, the system should inform and warn people before the flood hits them using their phones as well as public broadcast systems.
- **Response**: This is the most catastrophic stage, usually called emergency. In emergency response, actions are taken to save lives and prevent further damages. It puts prepared plans into action. Life saving responses usually require timely action. People should have access to the latest information in their vicinity. The best mechanism today is a dashboard on their smartphone that gives flood situations, road conditions, shelters, food availability, and even their friend and family situation. All this information should be prepared using various multimodal data sources including people reports. This may be one of the most challenging areas for multimedia, where semantics of different data streams, multi-granularity, and uncertainty

of data must be overcome to build current and predictive situation maps. This phase is the main theme of this paper.

- **Recovery**: Recovery includes actions taken to get back to normal or safe situations after disasters. It may require months until public facilities such as roads, schools and hospitals can function well. Recovery of human health conditions may take even longer. During this phase, the system has to assimilate information from sensors as well as from people about the state of the infrastructure that needs to be rebuilt or is being rebuilt. More importantly, information about both the material and emotional impact on people needs to be managed properly. This will also involve not only gathering information from various sensors, databases, and people, but also building current recovery situation maps that could be used for planning and prioritizing future planning, response, and recovery efforts.

Sensor networks, camera networks, and IoTs are increasingly used for collecting data, monitoring, and predicting natural disasters. Data is continuously used by geospatial models to predict time and locations of happenings or movements of disasters. There have been a lot of studies focused on developing more accurate models, and various efforts in building sensor networks for data collection [18]. The damage of disasters depends on the distance from the disaster and the potential area. To estimate the damage accurately, historical data needs to be efficiently stored, mined, and studied. [23] and [35] propose a tree-based model and use hydrological data, remote sensing data, meteorological data, and rainfall data to assess the damage from floods. [8] uses time series volcano observation data to monitor the state of volcanoes and predict potential hazards. [26] builds a seismological data warehouse for earthquake prediction. Many early warning systems have been set up for tsunamis [33]. In addition, disasters often cause other kinds of disasters, becoming multi-hazards. Floods are a multi-hazard example because they can lead to landslides and spread of diseases. A single sensor stream for flood is insufficient for detecting flood levels or diseases. Multiple sensors have to be combined. In this scenario, humidity, water level, wind velocity, rainfall, landscape, and water quality data are such data sources and thus can be integrated for flood and successive hazard responses. Despite the development of both models and sensor technology, the technology to utilize all these data sources currently exists in silos. A multimedia system can help assimilate and communicate this information.

As information sources complementary to the above sensors, social media and sensors in smartphones are becoming powerful mobile sensors in disaster management. In particular, Twitter data has been used in various disasters, such as a hurricane [16], an earthquake [10], a flood [36] and a tsunami [3]. Another commonly used social media data for disaster management is Foursquare. Foursquare has a 'check-in' feature to show where the users are. By aggregating the occurrences of 'check-in', the density of population can be estimated. When Hurricane Sandy happened, comparisons of the densities of 'check-in' before, during and after disasters showed how the disaster affected the functioning of different zones in the city [13]. A simple feature in Facebook now allows people to declare that they are safe during disasters. In addition, [40] proposes a mobile data computing framework consisting of data collection, data processing, and data representation. However, this framework considers only images and documents from social media and the web. [21] develops a visual analytics system and multimedia enabled mobile application for access to relevant disaster situation information. [39] designs a multimedia-aided disaster information integration system, which utilizes data mining techniques to analyze situation reports as well as pictures and text captured in the fields, and automatically links the reports directly to relevant multimedia content. However, all these frameworks limit themselves to social media data, and thus fail to assess the disaster situation with a comprehensive understanding of the environment because they do not combine this user-generated content with other sensory information.

Integration of physical sensors and social media is starting to get attention in disaster management. [25] proposes a landslide detection system to combine physical and social information and provide services for citizens. However, there is a growing consensus that social media provides useful but insufficient data for accurate event or situation recognition.

3. CLASSIFICATION OF DISASTERS

Disasters have varying magnitude, temporal and spatial dimensions, and varying social and economic consequences. They range from predictable to unpredictable, from intense to diffuse, and from those caused by natural factors to those caused by humans. A detailed taxonomy of disasters has been developed [9] and may be useful while developing systems for dealing with specific disasters. In this section, we classify disasters based on their technology requirements and spatio-temporal nature of multimedia information processing.

We categorize disasters into two main categories and illustrate how multimedia can contribute to disaster management research in both areas. The first category includes 'sudden' natural hazards such as floods, hurricanes, and earthquakes. The second addresses a slower 'creeping' crisis [6] which builds up gradually, often over many years, and includes a climate change, global warming, land degradation and air pollution. For the three stages of disaster management, on one hand, a prompt *response* is more critical for saving lives during a sudden crisis; on the other hand, the efficient and effective collection and use of data is more important for the *planning* and *recovery* phases in a creeping crisis.

3.1 Sudden Impact Disaster

Some disasters happen suddenly and may occur for a limited time. For these disasters, planning time is short. Their impact on people is severe and needs time sensitive responses. We consider these to be sudden impact disasters which lead to an immediate emergency response situation.

The response to these disasters includes help for finding a safe place, medicine, food, and information about friends and families. Real-time and prompt decisions are crucial. For example, during floods people in affected areas panic about what action they should take: should they stay home or evacuate to a shelter? In the past, this information was usually broadcasted to the whole community, but now we can do better and provide personalized instructions to an individual or a small group of people using their smartphones. To help people, data from physical sensors (like flood level monitors), and from governmental or other sources (like available shelters) may be obtained and used. In cases where the above data sources are not available, people in the flooded area themselves can still provide accurate and rich information including texts, images, and videos for the benefits of individuals and societies.

The goal of multimedia emergency response platforms should be not only recognizing the current emergency situation like flood severity, but also providing actionable information such as the location of the nearest accessible shelter. In this case, end users could be flood victims trapped in their homes or in their cars on flooded roads, or volunteers/organizations who provide help and resources. In general, the requests are collected from citizens, and organizations may take actions, share information, and coordinate with each other through different communication channels.

3.2 Creeping Disaster: Air Pollution

The other kind of disaster is the one that builds up slowly. Initially, their effect may not be felt. It is only after some time that their effect creeps into the life of people.

The *planning* and *recovery* stages play the most crucial roles in the long-term effects of such disasters. We use air pollution as an example. Air pollution is increasingly becoming a serious world-wide problem which attracts a lot of attention from disparate sectors. This problem is difficult to solve because of various emission factors, such as meteorological phenomena, road networks, traffic flows, point of interests, land uses, power plants, and emergent events (e.g., forest fires). These data are usually stored at multi-agency databases and in different formats. Governments need powerful tools to effectively handle and process these seemingly incompatible but often highly correlated streams in order to create proper emergency plans.

On the other hand, citizens can only rely on sparse situational reports from a few media sources to accurately assess air quality information. As a result, both governments and citizens often make plans and decisions based on incomplete information. Instead of relying on noisy data from social media, the governments can benefit from specific participatory citizen reporting, which provides a straightforward and accurate way for citizens to report situations. Environmental situations and people's feelings can be reported using photos and texts. Given photos of a sky, computer vision techniques can be employed to compute the haze level [20].

Major challenges in this area are related to accurately assessing slowly evolving situations, before they become severe. Once the situation becomes a crisis, the *response* phase becomes more important, similar to the sudden impact disaster.

4. MULTIMEDIA INFORMATION IN EMERGENCY SITUATIONS

Emergency response and situation recognition have always been a subject of interest to many disciplines and have been an active area of research. Many aspects of computing technology have been used in different forms in disaster management. GISs, databases, mobile computing, and sensor networks have all play different roles in rescuing people during disasters. All these technologies, however, have been used in isolated manners and in different silos. We believe that multimedia computing can bring them together for the purpose of building a unified framework for this important aspect of our society.

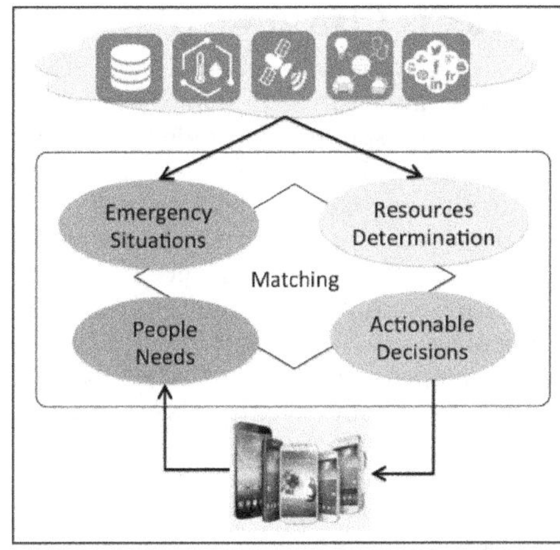

Figure 2: Multimedia systems for managing emergency situations

An obvious fact needs to be mentioned here, however. During disasters, many commonly used systems may not work due to power failures and other breakdowns in essential services. That is usually a serious problem. A multimedia technology used through smartphones is a safer option than physically connected components. But, if even wireless networks are not working, then we are back to the worst situation without help from any technology.

Norbert Wiener introduced the concept of cybernetics in 1948 [38]. Recent progress in sensors, IoTs, social networks, actuators, and information systems makes his ideas very relevant in today's societal systems. Given today's sensors, mobile framework, processing power, and participatory sensing, real time emergency response systems can now be designed using cybernetics.

Cybernetic principles - building models, measuring parameters, estimating states, and controlling the system - may play a key role in addressing problems at a societal level in many complex applications. We have diverse sensors that are inexpensive and already being used to collect observation streams at diverse locations. This motivated us [17] to explore solutions for critical problems in societal systems.

Situation recognition is crucial for closing the loop by sending an actuation or actionable information to match appropriate needs and resources. A basic architecture for an emergency response system is shown in Figure 2. These systems have the following major components: emergency situation recognition, determining resource locations, personal needs determination, and taking action to match needs and resources. For designing emergency response systems, we must use all available sensors, and all data and information sources.

In the following, we first discuss challenging research issues and then present some approaches to address them, including a prototype system. We must mention that what we present is an early prototype. The field of emergency situation recognition and appropriate response using multimedia information needs serious research in all the issues, and possibly many more, mentioned in the following section.

5. RESEARCH CHALLENGES

In this section, we address ten essential research challenges in building multimedia systems to manage emergency situations. Our goal is to inspire and provide high-level guidance to researchers in a multimedia community. We also aim to build a multimedia emergency response community. Each of these challenges is really a well defined research area that will evolve as the requirements are better identified in the process of building complete emergency response systems. These multimedia research problems could be addressed by researchers as independent research problems. Of course, some researchers may build complete systems by combining several of these.

1 **Data Identification:** In dealing with emergency response, the first question that one faces is: *how to gather all related data to evaluate and assess this emergency situation?* In the last few years, access to public data from both governmental sources, such as NASA, as well as non-governmental sources, such as Google, has become much easier. Many emerging applications and social media systems also make their data publicly available through APIs. As shown in Section (6), it is possible to build a very useful application by using data streams available on the Web from popular sources. Of course, it will be very useful to provide an environment to discover relevant data sources of different media types and to do research for assessing the quality of data sources so that appropriate sources can be selected at relevant locations. The research challenge is to define a measure for the quality of data sources in the context of specific types of emergencies.

2 **Data Processing:** Increasingly, data is heterogeneous streams. Data is collected by sensors with geo-spatial attributes and meta-data. People with their smartphones are smart sensors. The values obtained directly from sensors may range from measured facts(i.e. traffic flow) to reporting by people. The challenge is to deal with these values taken from disparate sensors and reconstruct the state by mapping sensors to attributes that are relevant in the context of computing the particular situation. A system needs to deal with the synthesis of spatio-temporal data collected at different spatial scales and temporal frequencies. For decades, GISs combine spatial data of different resolutions. However, grid resolution is usually selected without any application-specific justification. Creation of methodological guides to select a suitable grid resolution when designing a model to combine heterogeneous spatial data sets for a specific application is a new research problem. At this resolution, the model should assure that the uncertainty in the results is acceptable and the processing cost is minimal or reasonable.

3 **Multimedia Participatory Sensing:** Participatory sensing utilizes the eyes and ears of citizens to collect information about a situation. Twitter introduced micro-blogging that has been widely used as participatory sensing. However, Twitter is too broad and subjective for most emergency applications [4]. Crowdsourcing on disaster assistance has been widely studied and considered useful for tracking the latest status of emergency situations [11, 12]. For the changing demographics of the society and now significantly more powerful smartphones, it is possible to create more powerful multimedia participatory sensing approaches using multiple sensors and other contextual information. A very interesting and potentially transformative research challenge is to use computer vision and contextual reasoning to capture powerful micro-reports that will rapidly identify people's need in given situations and help them get to resources. Participant sensing is valuable, but it also raises privacy issues. Some information related to a reporter's context may reveal information that she may not normally want to divulge, for example a report from a gay bar may reveal sexual orientation. Due to the time sensitivity of reports, traditional ways of preserving privacy are unlikely to work. Solving privacy related issues for emergency situations are open and challenging problems.

4 **Heterogeneous Data Quality:** In the real world, sensors are spatially sparse, preferentially located and often lack complete measurements in targeted temporal resolution. Reliance on these measurements not only restricts the geographical region of situation recognition, but can also result in temporal uncertainty. There is a great need for spatial and temporal interpolation to increase the availability of these data across space and time. One of the challenges is to combine data sources that are at different resolutions. For example, one data stream is provided as grid cells, while other data streams are only available at point locations. One data stream is available in hours, while the other data stream is in days. Complex missing data and misalignment problems offer another research challenge. The research challenge here is to develop approaches to allow the effective associations between data at different spatial and temporal resolutions and to use them to create dense representations as needed.

5 **Situation Recognition based on Historical Data:** Cameras and sensors are deployed at different locations to continuously monitor target conditions, for example, traffic flow, air pollution, and temperature. When such data streams are combined to provide actionable information, discovering the spatially correlated and frequently evolving patterns is challenging: First, informative patterns are often flooded by trivial fluctuations. Second, the pattern search space is extremely large. A pattern can contain an arbitrary number of sensors, and the matching time intervals are at different scales. This results in an exponential pattern search space, calling for novel and efficient pattern search methods. This data may offer a novel challenge for current machine learning techniques. Situation recognition may very well be the next major research challenge for machine learning after recent great progress in concept recognition in images.

6 **Real-time Situation Recognition:** During disasters, response time is critical. The computation or processing time of large volumes of data can take too much time to be useful. For example, reporting about flooding risk every hour during a normal day is acceptable, but during the heavy raining seasons the hourly

reports of flooding risk areas may not be sufficient. A real-time visualization can serve as a first step to build a real-time situation recognition engine. The engine must have the capability to do real time visual analytics for evolving disaster situations. Communication disruption is an important factor in recognizing the severity of a sudden crisis. Total disruption suggests an extreme situation. In case of a partial disruption, the system needs to adjust for sampling bias of the severity of the situation, using prior knowledge such as population density, as well as estimate of the severity from prior situations. The research challenges here are to develop new architectures for real time processing of massive volumes of heterogeneous streaming data.

7 **Predictive Analytics:** Recognition of situations in real-time is good, but it is much better if the disaster situations are predictable. One example is the use of multimodal data and multimedia modeling tools to predict an area that might face future flooding [2]. An accurate prediction of the severity and disastrous flooding will significantly reduce the damages. The major problem making prediction difficult is the complexity of disaster behaviors . One interesting approach is to use high resolution 3D technologies to simulate and visualize realistic catastrophe behavior. Spatio-temporal dimensions also have to be considered in the predictive analytics.

8 **Communication Technology:** Rapid deployment of personalized communication systems during emergencies is a primary challenge. When disaster strikes, whole geographic regions may suffer loss of power, a high volume of telephone calls, and disruption in road services and other infrastructure. By relying on multiple information communication approaches, one may increase robustness during difficult times. Moreover, generally power based land connections usually fail first; wireless connectivity based on batteries is more reliable. Thus information collection and communication based on smartphones is likely to be more reliable than traditional infrastructure. In the case of severe disruptions in communication infrastructure, peer-to-peer networks may be useful for exchanging information. [22] presented a reliable ad-hoc network, called CalMesh, to restore the communication fabric at the site of the crisis. Even in the case of total infrastructure failure, multimedia data collected by people will still be the most powerful mechanism for documenting the situation. Once these data are available for analysis following the crisis, we will be able to understand the situation better for future planning.

In addition to physical mediums, trust and focus also play a very important role. How could one determine whether information may be trusted? How could one send information only to relevant people rather than sending everything to everybody, which results in an overload of information and which is associated with the tendency to consider it irrelevant. The challenge is to develop technology that can be quickly deployed to create 'altruistic communities' in which people can trust and assist fellow community members and the right information can be sent to the right person at the right time.

9 **What-If-Scenario Analysis:** Decision makers may not have a clear idea of what is the best action in an emergency situation. It is common to experiment and deploy strategies. In many complex situations, decision makers are provided tools for what-if analysis. These tools include doing rapid simulations to evaluate which strategy may work better. Since each emergency situation may be unique, it is important to do simulations using the situation under consideration. As far as we know, this problem remains unaddressed because until recently neither sufficient data nor computational tools were available. Now all these are available and hence this may be a research challenge that may become a very valuable decision analysis and support tool.

10 **Decision Support and Recommendation System:** In order to connect needs and resources, as well as optimize the need matching, the first challenge is to recognize where the citizens actually are and what they are doing. During disasters, citizens might be guided by disparate and perhaps inconsistent information sources and different decision making models. Thus, the locations and behaviors might be continuously changing. Tracking the locations and behaviors of citizens are important for allocating resources to aid them. Using multimedia data like photos, audio, and signals from wearable devices to detect activity and emotion [15] can be critical for personalized responses. The research challenge here is to develop multimodal recommendation engines that are not only multi-dimensional but also sensitive to time and location.

6. MANAGING EMERGENCY SITUATIONS: A PRELIMINARY SYSTEM

We present our ideas and demonstrate our early attempts to deal with the issues discussed above. The system described below is meant to demonstrate the feasibility and potential of a multimedia system for managing emergency situations. This multimedia system is a more holistic approach for disaster managements. Our idea consists of four main components. The first three components are developed and made available as open-source tools for researchers to use. We expect to continuously improve these early versions with the help of the multimedia research community. The last component is an ongoing project.

6.1 EventShop

The fundamental nature of data streams observing real-world events measured by either physical or human initiated sensors is almost always associated with time and geospatial meta-data. This commonality between different streams motivated us to develop an open-source EventShop system [32] to solve some problems in Research Challenges (**1**), (**2**), (**4**) and (**6**).

There are several approaches to modeling spatio-temporal and thematic data [27, 31, 37]. A spatial grid structure is natural for representing various geospatial data, where each cell of the grid stores a value of observations and attributes at the corresponding geo-location, at a given time. Other structures can be superimposed on this and corresponding attributes could be derived. We adopted the grid

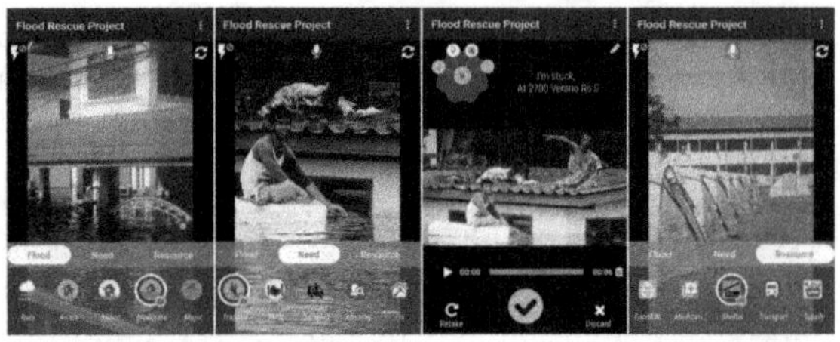

Figure 3: Flood multimedia micro-reports using Krumbs intents

structure in EventShop, and called it an Emage [29]. Techniques like [5] enable efficient processing of multiple streams. This generic data model can be used to efficiently and effectively integrate heterogeneous data coming from spatio-temporally distributed disparate data streams. Several applications have used the EventShop framework to recognize real world situations. For example, hurricane and flood detection, disaster mitigation, demand hot-spots of business products identification, flu outbreaks, wildfire detection, and allergy risk estimation and patient recommendations [28, 34].

In its current form, EventShop has:

- A data ingestor to obtain data from disparate sources, and transform it to the Emage format.
- A set of operators to select, segment, aggregate, characterize, spatially and temporally filter, and cluster spatio-temporal data streams.
- A query processing engine to process 'standing queries'[28] created using stream processing operators.
- Map visualizations of input and output streams.
- A rule based action engine that can execute tasks depending on detected situations.

Overall, EventShop accepts diverse data streams, provides appropriate mappings to obtain relevant attributes, converts this data to information events, and then assimilates these event streams into evolving situations.

6.2 Multimedia Micro-reports

In today's data-rich environment, a lot of data is readily available from many public sources, proprietary sources, IoTs, and databases. Increasingly, participatory citizen sensing and crowdsourcing are playing more important roles in understanding current trends and evolving situations. Non-people sources are combined with people sources by weighting them according to the situational context.

Citizen contributed data comes in the form of streams from mobile devices carried by people. In EventShop, persistent location sensor data, air pollution data, and pollen data were combined with citizen-contributed Twitter data to study an asthma risk situation. The accuracy of situation detection depends on the quality of data. However, micro-blogs from systems like Twitter are very noisy and subjective [4, 7]. Most applications may benefit from objective and factual citizen contributed data. Waze is a mobile app that uses GPS data from its users as micro-reports to estimate the real-time road traffic, and provides an actionable guidance such as the best route.

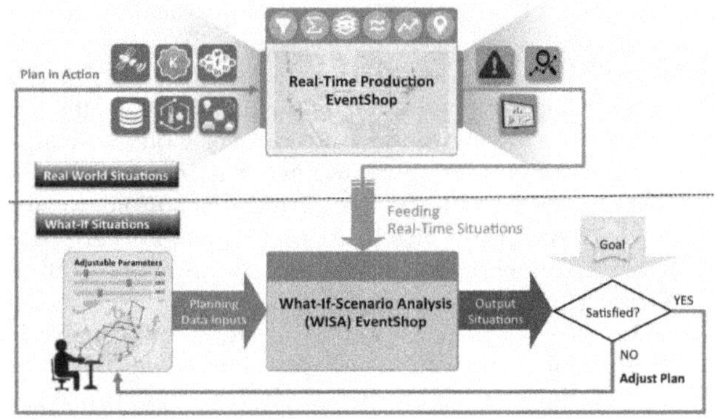

Figure 4: WISA architecture using EventShop for city plan decision making

We are exploring **multimedia micro-reports** [29], compared to **micro-blogs**, for radical improvement in the quality of participatory sensing data as in (**3**) and (**8**). Initially, we are using Krumbs from a young company championing micro-reports; later we will extend our approach to include other sources also in this paradigm. Krumbs is a platform for reporting specific situations. Krumbs uses an **Intent Camera** that combines contextual reasoning with the intent of the reporter. This camera also allows people to express opinions and contribute other information. Krumbs maintains the distinction between objective (from sensors), derived (using computational approaches and reasoning), and subjective information (from a user's opinion). A report is represented in media-JSON format. The use of media-JSON allows linking, search, and analysis using different existing platforms. An example of multimedia micro-report for a flood situation using Krumbs SDK is shown in Figure 3. We classify types of multimedia micro-reports into three categories:

- **reporting current flood situation**: heavy rain, low/ medium/ high water level, submerged vehicles, flood risk, crime report.
- **requesting needs**: medical needs, trapped in the house, trapped in the car, missing person, missing animal, needs food and water, needs sandbag.
- **offering aid and resources**: opening shelter, availability of existing shelter, safe parking spots, serving meals, distributing supplies.

6.3 Situation Recognition and Prediction

Situation recognition based on the latest observations alone could be too late for taking appropriate actions for critical events. Accurate predictions of situations can allow adequate time to take appropriate actions by connecting people to the resources they need, especially in life threatening situations. Typically, predictions in specific fields are derived from numerical models and data. By utilizing large scale data integration, machine learning models can be used in conjunction with scientific theory based models to obtain more accurate predictions and contribute to solving problems in Research Challenges (**5**) and (**7**).

Common methods for a time series prediction are auto-regressive, moving average, and auto-regressive moving average models [14]. Multivariate spatio-temporal auto-regressive

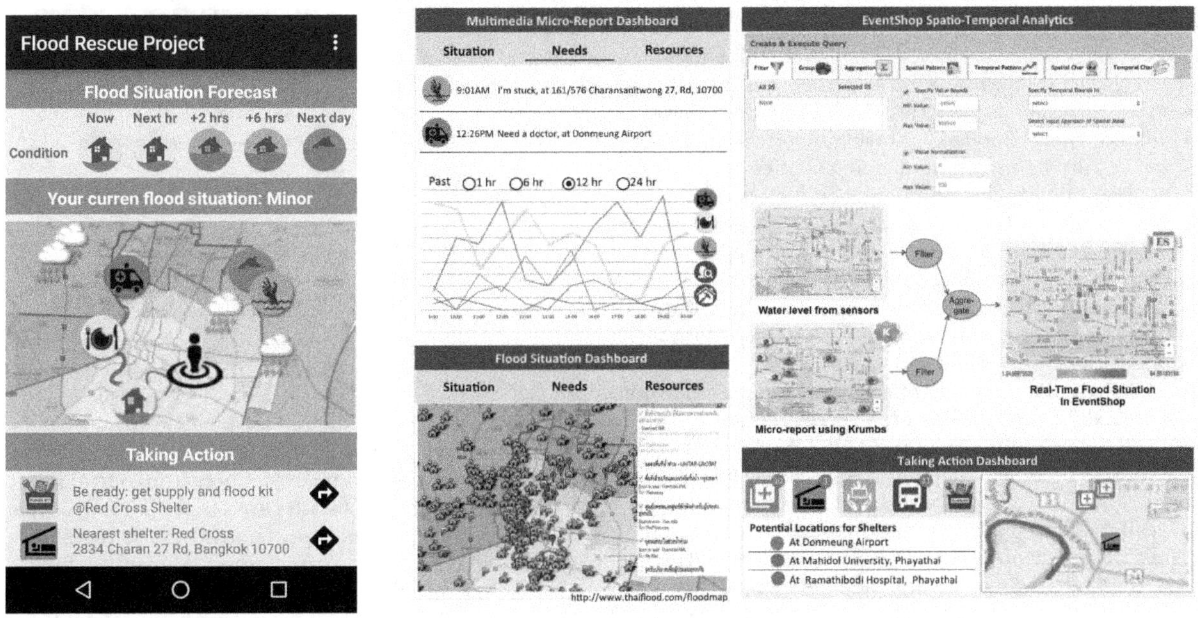

(a) Managing flood situation mobile app

(b) Flood Situation Dashboard

Figure 5: Dashboard for citizens and city planners

models take into account both spatial and temporal correlations but require an estimation of a large number of parameters. In order to reduce the number of estimated parameters, models can be developed which consider the spatial and temporal correlation in neighbors similar to [24]. Models can also be designed to incorporate spatio-temporal correlation by using tensor time series [30]. Those models can manifest hidden and evolving trends in the multidimensional data by preserving the sensor structure. Deep neural networks have become the state of the art in audio and vision, and have extended their applications to more fields. We aim to implement machine learning models in EventShop with a built-in ability to cope with STT (Space-Time-Theme) data.

6.4 What-If Scenarios Analysis

In many complex planning tasks, a planner uses his situational awareness to perform What-If-Scenario Analysis (WISA) to anticipate changes for deciding the action plan. The goal of WISA is to consider the current situation and simulate possible actions to project the results. By considering many alternative action scenarios, a decision for the optimal actions for deployment emerges. A very simple example of WISA is the use of spreadsheets to decide optimal actions. In the case of complex systems like the disaster management, this action planning needs powerful scenario analysis tools. As far as we know, this has not been tried thus far in disaster management planning using big data sets (**9**) and (**10**).

To implement such an approach, one needs to run two versions of EventShop in parallel. One version is the production version and the other is for experimenting. At any given instant the experimental version can copy the situation outputs from the production version. The experimental version can then apply proposed inputs to see their effect on the system by running the system starting with the current state and using simulated inputs and prediction operators at a faster speed. This will help in understanding how the situation evolves if particular decisions were implemented.

Figure 4 presents this architecture. The top part is the operational EventShop where real-time input data from various sources are used for situational awareness. The current state is continuously fed into the WISA EventShop as shown in the bottom of the figure. The city planners working with the WISA EventShop explore What-If scenarios by varying their planning data inputs. The WISA EventShop will combine both the real-time situation and planning input to generate a 'to be' situation. If this situation satisfies their goal, the plan will be executed, otherwise new configurations will be explored.

In summary, the multimedia systems for disaster management must deal with some new requirements. Our proposed framework is related to some of challenges discussed and accomplishes some essential functionality; specifically, it:

1. Enables effective and efficient citizen reporting and combines that with other data streams.
2. Predicts evolving situations by combining current situations with historical data as well as data related to prior planned actions. This step is essential for disaster management implementations.
3. Use of What-If scenarios for enabling decisions by planners and decision makers. This will provide a platform to help in enabling time-sensitive data based decisions using different planning and action scenarios.

7. PROOF OF CONCEPT: REAL SCENARIO

We demonstrated, and successfully used, EventShop and related systems during several disasters [28].

Managing Flood: Yesterday and Tomorrow

When the second co-author joined University of California, Irvine in 2011, there was a catastrophic event in her home country. Several major cities, including the capital city of Thailand, were flooded. During flood situations, it is very important to understand and enhance the ways in which the dynamic aspects of emergency affects citizens. Organizations should make quick plans for evacuations and provide shelters. She decided to use her knowledge and the EventShop system to manage this emergency situation. Within a day, she and her lab-mates began to collect data, recognize flood situations, and provide actionable information to citizens who were in affected areas [28].

To build this flood management application using EventShop, they first searched for any public data sources related to the Thai flood from both professional and social media sources. The former sources included flood affected areas across Thailand[2], Bangkok risk areas and water barriers, shelters' locations and availability[3], parking areas, satellite images, and flood extents. On the other hand, citizens reported their concern via text messaging and uploaded photos or video through a variety of social media sources. Since the multimedia micro-reports component was not yet available at that time, tweets associated to specific hashtags such as "#น้ำท่วม", "#ThaiFlood", and "#Flood" across the center part of Thailand were continuously harvested.

After identifying available data sources, several situation models were created to detect and recognize flood situations. The flood areas were classified into three categories based on flood conditions and shelter sufficiency. Then, for those people who tweeted about flood from the dangerous zones, the EventShop system automatically sent tweets to them and directed them to the nearest shelter in the safe areas. Some of the tweets were being re-tweeted by tweet receivers showing that they received and possibly found them useful.

This project was conducted five years ago. Several components were limited and the multimedia micro-reports did not exist. Now, advanced technologies may bring many new opportunities such as visual concepts detection using deep learning technologies in micro-reports for much better situation assessment and communication. The following is our vision for building the next generation multimedia system for managing flood situations. We design and implement a mobile app that allows users to report current flood situations, request help, and provide information about resources' availability as shown in Figure 3. The users can effortlessly submit their reports using predefined categories. Figure 5(a) shows the mobile dashboard with up-to-date information such as a flood situation forecast, a current situation around a user, and a personalized actionable recommendation. This dashboard acts as the first line of communication between citizens and authorized organizations. To forecast the flood situation, the water level flood model is created based on the historical flood events. We use data from water sensors, precipitation, and satellite images to create the flood model. Then, we used real-time flood levels detected by EventShop to adjust the model and improve the accuracy of the flood prediction model as show in Figure 6.

The first goal is to identify affected areas where people need help the most. Furthermore, we can use this information to find optimal shelter locations during evolving flood situations. We propose a city planners' dashboard in Figure 5(b). The multimedia micro-reports from our mobile app are located on the top left with three tabs that corresponding to the three categories of reports. All reports are shown in the list and line chart over time. In the bottom left, data from authorized resources are represented in the map view. On the top right, EventShop provides an experimental environment where analysts can plug in different types of operators onto any data sources to create a complex situation recognition model. For example, water physical sensors and flood situations from multimedia micro-reports are aggregated to create a finer and more complete water situation. The bottom right is where need-resource matching takes place.

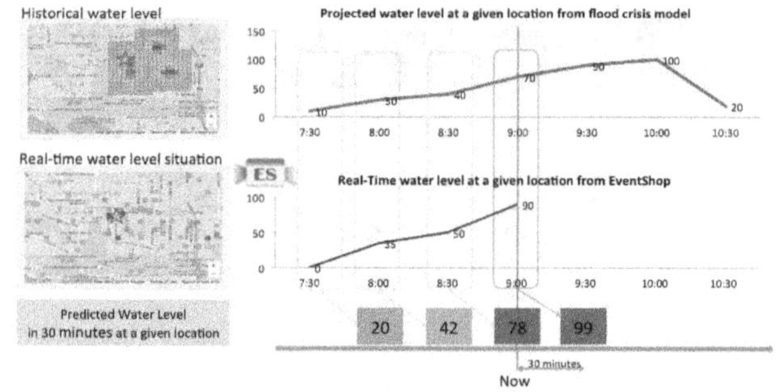

Figure 6: Predicted flood level

[2]www.thaiflood.com/floodmap

[3]www.shelters.thaiflood.com

8. CONCLUSION

Effective disaster management can potentially save lots of lives and resources. However, to build such a system, currently many technologies such as GIS, sensor networks and mobile computing are used in different silos. We believe that multimedia computing can bring them together to create a unified framework for managing complex emergency situations. Ten major research challenges in building multimedia systems for managing emergency situations are addressed and discussed. We also present one example approach that has been implemented in our laboratory using EventShop and multimedia micro-reports. Given enormous progress in concept and activity recognition using machine learning in the past few years, we foresee a great opportunity for emergency situation recognition using multimedia technologies. The time is right and ripe for the multimedia community to address challenges in managing this important societal problem.

9. REFERENCES

[1] 2011 thailand floods. https://en.wikipedia.org/wiki/2011_Thailand_floods.

[2] Modelling better flood responses in port phillip bay. http://www.csiro.au/en/Research/D61/Areas/Data-for-decisions/Disaster-management/Flood-modelling. Accessed: 2016-07-23.

[3] A. Acar and Y. Muraki. Twitter for crisis communication: lessons learned from japan's tsunami disaster. *International Journal of Web Based Communities*, 7(3):392–402, 2011.

[4] L. Barbosa and J. Feng. Robust sentiment detection on twitter from biased and noisy data. In *ICCL*. Association for Computational Linguistics, 2010.

[5] D. Carney, U. ÃĞetintemel, M. Cherniack, C. Convey, S. Lee, G. Seidman, M. Stonebraker, N. Tatbul, and S. Zdonik. Monitoring streams: a new class of data management applications. VLDB 2002.

[6] S. De Paratesi and E. Barrett. Hazards and disasters: concepts and challenges. *Remote sensing for hazard monitoring and disaster assessment: marine and coastal applications in the Mediterranean region*, pages 1–17, 1989.

[7] L. Derczynski, A. Ritter, S. Clark, and K. Bontcheva. Twitter part-of-speech tagging for all: Overcoming sparse and noisy data. In *RANLP*, 2013.

[8] R. Di Salvo, P. Montalto, G. Nunnari, M. Neri, and G. Puglisi. Multivariate time series clustering on geophysical data recorded at mt. etna from 1996 to 2003. *Journal of Volcanology and Geothermal Research*, 251:65–74, 2013.

[9] T. E. Drabek. *Human system responses to disaster: An inventory of sociological findings*. Springer Science & Business Media, 2012.

[10] P. S. Earle, D. C. Bowden, and M. Guy. Twitter earthquake detection: earthquake monitoring in a social world. *Annals of Geophysics*, 54(6), 2012.

[11] H. Gao, G. Barbier, R. Goolsby, and D. Zeng. Harnessing the crowdsourcing power of social media for disaster relief. Technical report, DTIC, 2011.

[12] M. F. Goodchild and J. A. Glennon. Crowdsourcing geographic information for disaster response: a research frontier. *International Journal of Digital Earth*, 3(3):231–241, 2010.

[13] N. Grinberg, M. Naaman, B. Shaw, and G. Lotan. Extracting diurnal patterns of real world activity from social media. In *ICWSM*, 2013.

[14] J. D. Hamilton. *Time series analysis*, volume 2. Princeton university press Princeton, 1994.

[15] R. Hegde, B. Manoj, B. Rao, and R. Rao. Emotion detection from speech signals and its applications in supporting enhanced qos in emergency response. In *Proceedings of the 3rd International ISCRAM Conference*, 2006.

[16] A. L. Hughes and L. Palen. Twitter adoption and use in mass convergence and emergency events. *International Journal of Emergency Management*, 6(3-4):248–260, 2009.

[17] R. Jain and D. Sonnen. Social life networks. *IT Professional Magazine*, 13(5):8, 2011.

[18] S. Jain, R. C. Shah, W. Brunette, G. Borriello, and S. Roy. Exploiting mobility for energy efficient data collection in wireless sensor networks. *Mobile Networks and Applications*, 11(3):327–339, 2006.

[19] G.-H. Kim, S. Trimi, and J.-H. Chung. Big-data applications in the government sector. *Communications of the ACM*, 57(3):78–85, 2014.

[20] Y. Li, J. Huang, and J. Luo. Using user generated online photos to estimate and monitor air pollution in major cities. In *ICMCS*, page 79. ACM, 2015.

[21] S. Luis, F. C. Fleites, Y. Yang, H.-Y. Ha, and S.-C. Chen. A visual analytics multimedia mobile system for emergency response. In *IEEE International Symposium on Multimedia*. IEEE, 2011.

[22] B. Manoj and A. H. Baker. Communication challenges in emergency response. *Commun. ACM*, 50(3):51–53, Mar. 2007.

[23] B. Merz, H. Kreibich, and U. Lall. Multi-variate flood damage assessment: a tree-based data-mining approach. *Natural Hazards and Earth System Sciences*, 13(1):53–64, 2013.

[24] W. Min and L. Wynter. Real-time road traffic prediction with spatio-temporal correlations. *Transportation Research Part C: Emerging Technologies*, 19(4):606–616, Aug. 2011.

[25] A. Musaev, D. Wang, and C. Pu. Multi-hazard detection by integrating social media and physical sensors. In *Social Media for Government Services*, pages 395–409. Springer, 2015.

[26] S. L. Nimmagadda and H. Dreher. Ontology based data warehouse modeling and mining of earthquake data: prediction analysis along eurasian-australian continental plates. In *IEEE ICII*, 2007.

[27] M. S. Perry. *A framework to support spatial, temporal and thematic analytics over semantic web data*. PhD thesis, Wright State University, 2008.

[28] S. Pongpaichet, V. K. Singh, M. Gao, and R. Jain. EventShop: Recognizing Situations in Web Data Streams. In *WWW*, 2013.

[29] S. Pongpaichet, M. Tang, L. Jalali, and R. Jain. Using photos as micro-reports of events. In *ICMR*, 2016.

[30] M. Rogers, L. Li, and S. J. Russell. Multilinear Dynamical Systems for Tensor Time Series. In *NIPS 2013*.

[31] A. Sheth and M. Perry. Traveling the Semantic Web through Space, Time, and Theme. *IEEE Internet Computing*, 12(2):81–86, Mar. 2008.

[32] V. K. Singh and R. Jain. *Situation Recognition using EventShop*. Springer; Auflage: 1st ed. 2016, 2016.

[33] J. H. Sorensen. Hazard warning systems: Review of 20 years of progress. *Natural Hazards Review*, 1(2):119–125, 2000.

[34] M. Tang, P. Agrawal, S. Pongpaichet, and R. Jain. Geospatial interpolation analytics for data streams in eventshop. In *ICME*. IEEE, 2015.

[35] M. S. Tehrany, B. Pradhan, and M. N. Jebur. Spatial prediction of flood susceptible areas using rule based decision tree (dt) and a novel ensemble bivariate and multivariate statistical models in gis. *Journal of Hydrology*, 504:69–79, 2013.

[36] S. Vieweg, A. L. Hughes, K. Starbird, and L. Palen. Microblogging during two natural hazards events: what twitter may contribute to situational awareness. In *CHI*, pages 1079–1088. ACM, 2010.

[37] X. Wang, X. Zhou, and S. Lu. Spatiotemporal data modelling and management: a survey. In *ICTOOLS*. IEEE, 2000.

[38] N. Wiener et al. *Cybernetics*. JSTOR, 1948.

[39] Y. Yang and S.-C. Chen. Multimedia big mobile data analytics for emergency management. *E-LETTER*, 2015.

[40] Y. Yang, W. Lu, J. Domack, T. Li, S.-C. Chen, S. Luis, and J. K. Navlakha. Madis: A multimedia-aided disaster information integration system for emergency management. In *CollaborateCom*. IEEE, 2012.

Multimedia on the Mountaintop: Using Public Snow Images to Improve Water Systems Operation

Andrea Castelletti, Roman Fedorov, Piero Fraternali, Matteo Giuliani
Politecnico di Milano, Dipartimento di Elettronica, Informazione e Bioingegneria, Milan, Italy
first.last@polimi.it

ABSTRACT

This paper merges multimedia and environmental research to verify the utility of public web images for improving water management in periods of water scarcity, an increasingly critical event due to climate change. A multimedia processing pipeline fetches mountain images from multiple sources and extracts virtual snow indexes correlated to the amount of water accumulated in the snow pack. Such indexes are used to predict water availability and design the operating policy of Lake Como, Italy. The performance of this informed policy is contrasted, via simulation, with the current operation, which depends only on lake water level and day of the year, and with a policy that exploits official Snow Water Equivalent (SWE) estimated from ground stations data and satellite imagery. Virtual snow indexes allow improving the system performance by 11.6% w.r.t. the baseline operation, and yield further improvement when coupled with official SWE information, showing that the two data sources are complementary. The proposed approach exemplifies the opportunities and challenges of applying multimedia content analysis methods to complex environmental problems.

Keywords

Image processing, crowdsourcing, snow, environment monitoring, water management

1. INTRODUCTION

Water scarcity resulting from climate change has entered the global agenda due to its impact on society and economy and is recognized as a global risk already in the short term [10]. Re-solving the uneven spatio-temporal distribution of water requires storing it when it is naturally available (e.g. when snow is melting) and delivering when required by users (e.g. agriculture, hydropower). Dam operators must hence balance the amount of water to release for short term needs with the amount to store for future demands, particularly during the dry season, possibly based on predicted water availability. The Snow Water Equivalent (SWE), i.e., the water content of the snow pack, is an important hydrological variable used to predict future water availability. State-of-practice SWE monitoring applications rely on mathematical models often based on physical laws, ad hoc campaigns, and dedicated observations from ground stations or remote sensing (specialized satellite products), which cannot be easily validated against ground truth given the high spatial heterogeneity of SWE and the few SWE point measurements available.

The public visual content generated by users or by low cost and widely available ground sensors, such as webcams, raises the question of whether it is possible to use such data, albeit collected for completely different purposes and with lower quality, as a replacement or complement to the high quality, but also more restricted and costly, data traditionally employed by environmental models, and specifically by water management models. Recently, as discussed in [2], various authors have shown the potential of using public content for monitoring natural processes [25], hazards [5], and more. However the claim that web media provides an effective input for environmental models, usable to deliver reliable management decisions, has still to be demonstrated. In this work, we build an automatic data processing architecture and apply it to investigate the operational value of public web images, either produced by users or generated by touristic webcams, as an input to an environmental model; as a case study, we focus on a management problem that entails the daily water release decisions for a sub-alpine regulated lake. Traditionally, the decision of how much water to re-

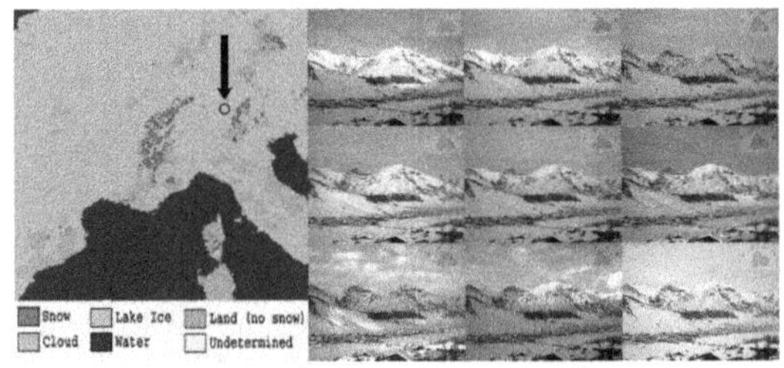

Figure 1: left: MODIS daily snow cover map on Jan. 9 2014; right: images acquired the same day by a webcam in the position shown by the black circle.

This work was partially funded by the CHEST FP7 project of the European Commission.

MM '16, October 15-19, 2016, Amsterdam, Netherlands
© 2016 ACM. ISBN 978-1-4503-3603-1/16/10... $15.00
DOI: http://dx.doi.org/10.1145/2964284.2976759

lease, which influences the level of the lake, is taken in two ways: by a limited information policy considering only the current lake level and the day of the year; or by a more sophisticated policy relying on a hydrological predictive model of the future water availability, which exploits snow information (typically, SWE). In our case study, a SWE time series is estimated weekly by the Regional Environmental Protection Agency (ARPA) through a hybrid of satellite retrieved information, ground observation, and model outputs. Ground stations and satellite data, however, have limits when used to predict snow processes, which exhibit high spatio-temporal variability [7, 25]. Ground stations are few and coarsely distributed, especially in high altitude regions. Satellite snow products have limitations in alpine contexts [7]: space-board passive microwave radiometers (e.g., AMSR-E) penetrate clouds and provide accurate snow cover estimation, but have coarse spatial resolution (25 km); active microwave systems (e.g., RADARSAT) detect the presence of liquid water content, but require additional ground observations to make accurate estimates, whereas optical sensors (e.g., MODIS) generate high spatial and temporal resolution maps, yet cannot see the earth surface when clouds are present. As an example, Figure 1 shows how clouds can occlude the satellite view, but not the ground view: the left part shows the "MODIS/Terra Snow Cover Daily L3" snow map on Jan. 9, 2014, where most of the Alps area is covered by clouds and provides no snow information; the right part shows images taken the same day by a webcam placed in Livigno, Italy (its position is denoted by the black circle in the satellite map). High clouds prevent satellite snow estimation, but do not occlude the ground view, which gives complementary information.

The research question addressed in this paper is whether visual content acquired from the web can bring a quantifiable contribution as a replacement or supplement to traditional input for environmental models. The case study used to verify the hypothesis focuses on snow information for informing water system operation and exploits an architecture that automatically crawls content from multiple web data sources, retains only geo-tagged images containing a mountain skyline with high probability, identifies the visible peaks in each image using a public online digital terrain model, classifies the image pixels as snow or no-snow to obtain a *snow mask* per image, and, finally, extracts time series of *virtual snow indexes* usable as a proxy of the snow covered area. To assess the operational value of such indexes, a simulation is performed of alternative control policies that decide the daily operations (i.e., how much water to release) for Lake Como, based on different inputs. As a criterion for defining performance, a multi-objective tradeoff function is used, which pursues two competing objectives: avoiding floods on the lake shores due to excessive water storage and delivering sufficient water to the downstream agricultural districts. Several control policies are contrasted, and the results prove that virtual snow indexes improve the system performance, and can be combined with the official ARPA SWE data.

Beside the specific impact in the snow monitoring and water management fields, the described approach can stimulate a **whole new branch of public web media exploitation** in many environmental monitoring problems. Previous work has applied multimedia processing techniques to extract environment-related data from public media, but struggled to convince environmental scientists that such data are useful. This work demonstrates that it is possible to extract environment-related information from public media, automatically and at scale, and that the extracted data are improving the performance of an environmental model. Such deep integration between multimedia and environment research can have **radical impact on environment monitoring as done today, and on environmental and societal objectives at large**; this goal challenges multimedia research to measure the impact of data extraction techniques on the performance of practical environmental models, going beyond evaluation of mere algorithm accuracy.

The original contributions of the paper are:

- A web multimedia content processing pipeline that automatically extracts environmental meta-data from users' mountain photos and touristic webcam streams. The pipeline employs a mountain image classifier (with 94% precision, 96.3% recall), a weather condition filter, with 87.4% True Positive Rate at 3.5% False Positive Rate, a peak detection algorithm (with 75% overall accuracy, 81% in good meteorological conditions) based on a matching procedure between an image and a virtual panorama generated from an online Digital Elevation Model (with 1″ resolution), and a snow/no-snow pixel-level classifier (with 90% accuracy).
- An algorithm that transforms mountain camera position, peak metadata, and snow masks into data series of virtual snow indexes for a mountain viewpoint, previously introduced in [8, 9]. Such indexes, albeit not directly comparable to available ground measures, exhibit a strong correlation with meteorological data series.
- A multi-objective water management model and simulation framework for the design and evaluation of optimal operating policies conditioned on multiple variables such as the day of the year, the lake level, the SWE, the virtual snow indexes, and more, which can be used to assess the operational value of virtual snow indexes.
- As byproducts of the content processing pipeline, we have produced a very large public data set of Alpine mountain images and a gamified web portal, where users can cooperatively access and enrich content[1].

2. RELATED WORK

Web media mining for environment studies A growing body of research studies the potential of low cost, user generated content in environmental applications, with different content types, including text, images, videos, GPS tags, and cellular phone traces. Zhang et al. [25] predict snow and vegetation cover using geo-tagged Flickr photos. The analysis is based on the tags associated with the photos and on the image visual features. Daume et al. [4] approach forest monitoring with social media data (tweets), analyzed to extract various ecosystem information types, trends, predictions and alerts. Social media are also exploited for disaster management: De Longueville et al. [5] report a study of fire propagation monitored through tweet distributions. None of these approaches evaluates the contribution of web content to the performance of environmental models. In [18], the authors manually monitor YouTube videos to derive a water level time series for a Saudi Arabian cave, which helped locate the water source. In our work, media monitoring and information extraction are completely automated.

Mountain image analysis. Traditionally, snow is moni-

[1]http://snowwatch.polimi.it

tored through manual measurement campaigns, permanent measurement stations, satellite photography, and, recently, also with terrestrial photography. Although several approaches monitor snow processes by means of short-range visual content analysis, all approaches (e.g., [20, 19]) rely on cameras designed and positioned ad hoc by researchers, and are not applicable to user-generated web content created in uncontrolled conditions. Other work addressed mountain peak identification in public photos (a key problem to retrieve snow information from public images) [1] and the segmentation of the image region corresponding to a certain mountain in snow covered areas [20, 19]. All these approaches do not provide an environmental evaluation of the utility of the data extracted with the proposed techniques. In this paper, we evaluate the utility of virtual snow indexes computed from web content collected with such pipelines, on a case study of water availability prediction and multi-objective allocation.

Water management with hydrologic information. The availability of data at increasingly higher temporal and spatial resolution creates an opportunity to enhance real-time understanding of water systems and to improve prediction of their future evolution, ultimately increasing quality of the decisions. Yet, many large water projects worldwide had their operations designed in prior decades, with rules based on very simple data, such as current inflow and previous release volumes [16]. Numerous studies have attempted to improve water reservoirs operations by using information selected on the basis of operators' experience, such as observations of the previous period's inflows [22], simplified models of hydrologic variables [6], or streamflow forecasts [21]. As for the latter, the use of reliable inflow forecasts is beneficial in most situations. Yet, its real value is often problem-specific and depends on the system's dominant dynamics and the objectives considered [24]. For example, using short-term inflow forecasts generally improves reservoir operations for flood control; for other objectives, such as water supply, medium and long term streamflow forecasts are required.

3. OVERVIEW OF THE APPROACH

The goal of this work is to experimentally assess the operational value of information derived from public web media content, specifically from mountain images contributed by users and existing webcams, to support environmental decision making in a snow dominated context. An automatic system crawls geo-located images from heterogeneous sources at scale, checks the presence of mountains in each photo, identifies individual peaks, and extracts a snow mask from the portion of the image denoting a mountain. The assessment requires a water management problem where snow information is a determinant input to the system operation and performance can be quantified. We use a water management model for Lake Como, and evaluate the impact of snow-related data extracted from web content as additional input to the lake operating policy.

The study site. Lake Como is a regulated lake in Northern Italy with an active storage capacity of 254 Mm^3 and fed by a 3,500 km^2 catchment. The hydro-meteorological regime is the typical Alpine one, with scarce discharge in winter and summer, and peaks in late spring and autumn due to snowmelt and rainfall, respectively. Snowmelt from May to July is the most important contribution to seasonal lake storage, but the operations of a number of hydropower reservoirs in the upstream lake catchment alter the natural hydrologic regime. The water stored in the lake can be used in different ways according to two main competing objectives. Farmers downstream would like to save it for the summer, when the natural inflow is not sufficient for irrigation. Yet, storing water increases the lake level and, consequently, the flood risks, which would be instead minimized by keeping the lake level low. The ability to predict future water availability, particularly from snow melt, is key for an optimal water management strategy. The competing interests of flooding and irrigation can be modeled using the following quantitative objectives:

Flooding: the average annual number of flooding days, defined as days when the lake level h_t is higher that the flooding threshold ($\bar{h}$=1.24 m), i.e.,

$$J^{flood} = \frac{1}{N_y}\sum_{t=1}^{t_{fin}} \Lambda(h_t) \quad \text{where } \Lambda(h_t) = \begin{cases} 1 & \text{if } h_t > \bar{h} \\ 0 & \text{otherwise} \end{cases}$$

Irrigation: the daily average squared water deficit w.r.t. the daily downstream demand w_t, subject to the minimum flow constraint q_t^{MEF} to ensure adequate environmental conditions in the Adda River, i.e.,

$$J^{irr} = \frac{1}{t_{fin}}\sum_{t=1}^{t_{fin}} \max\left(w_t - \max(r_{t+1} - q_t^{MEF}, 0), 0\right)^2$$

where r_{t+1} is the water volume released in the time interval $[t, t+1)$. The release r_{t+1} coincides with the release decision u_t unless a correction is needed in order to take into account the legal and physical constraints on the reservoir level and release. The quadratic formulation aims to penalize severe deficits in a single time period, while tolerating more frequent, small shortages.

4. WEB CONTENT PROCESSING

Two image sources are used: we crawl ∽2k touristic webcams in the Alpine area and search Flickr for geo-tagged user-generated mountain photos in a 300 × 160km Alpine region. Both image types carry information about the location where the image is taken, but require estimating the orientation of the camera during the shot, identifying the visible mountain peaks, and filtering out images not suitable for snow analysis (e.g., due to fog, rain etc.). The two multimedia processing pipelines, shown in Figure 2, share common steps but also have differences: webcams produce a temporal series of images of the same view, so that *only one webcam image* needs to go through the relevance classification and peak identification steps, whose results apply to the entire time series. Instead, *all crawled user-generated photos* need pre-filtering, for discarding irrelevant content before processing them for orientation and peak detection.

4.1 Webcam processing

The registered webcams capture images every 1 to 60 minutes, thus ensuring temporal density incomparably higher than any remote sensed data. On the other hand, their spatial density is lower than that of user-generated photos, because they concentrate near popular touristic destinations. We identified more than 3500 candidate webcams in the Alpine area from touristic, meteorological, and skiing webcam directories, and manually filtered them, removing those that were not framing significant mountain slopes, retaining

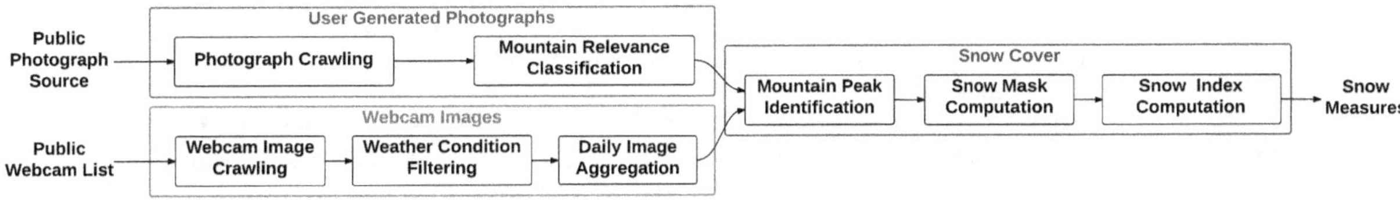

Figure 2: Schema of the web media content processing pipelines.

nearly $2k$ webcams. A web crawler checks each webcam at $1'$ frequency and processes all new images. In this way, we obtain, for each camera, from 10 to $1.5k$ images per day, depending on update frequency and working hours. Due to bad weather conditions, not all images can be exploited for estimating snow cover. A manual screening of 1000 images crawled from 4 webcams revealed that 67% were not suitable for snow analysis To retain only processable images, a *weather conditions filter* automatically discards images acquired during bad weather conditions, which are identified by checking for occlusions of the mountain skyline, as follows: *For each webcam*, we manually annotate its skyline, and a binary skyline neighborhood mask L identifies all the pixels which are distant less than a certain value (in our case empirically set to 4% of the image height) from at least one skyline point. Then, *for each webcam image*, we apply standard edge detection and compute its binary edge map E, which identifies pixels belonging to the skyline. To check for occlusions, a skyline visibility score is defined as $v = f(E \cdot L) \,/\, f(L)$, where $\cdot$ denotes the pixel-wise product between two images of the same size and $f(\cdot)$ is a function that, given an image, returns the number of columns that contain at least one non-zero entry. The value of v is in the interval $[0, 1]$ and can be intuitively interpreted as the fraction of the skyline that is visible in a given image. We retain only those images for which $v \geq \bar{v}$, where $\bar{v}$ is a threshold (empirically set to 0.75). The filtering method retains images with good skyline visibility, although clouds might still be present and interfere with the estimation of the snow cover. The effect of such transient clouds is mitigated by the next webcam image processing step.

Daily image aggregation. Good weather images might suffer from challenging light conditions (solar glares and shadows) and moving obstacles (clouds and persons in front of the webcam). At the same time, snow cover changes slowly over time, so that one (good) measurement per day is sufficient. Therefore, it is possible to aggregate all images collected in a day, to obtain a single daily image, which is both robust to transient occlusions and sufficiently representative for analysis. A simple median aggregation proved able to effectively remove transient occlusions and glares. Given a daily sample of N images $I_1, \ldots, I_N$, the Daily Median Image (DMI) is defined as

$$DMI(x, y) = med\{I_1(x, y), I_2(x, y), \ldots, I_N(x, y)\},$$

where $med\{\cdot\}$ is the median operator applied to the image pixel values. Figure 3 shows a DMI obtained from 11 daily images, which attenuates transient illuminations and removes the persons standing in front of the webcam. A challenge in the creation of DMIs lies in strong winds, which may produce a blurry aggregated image. To overcome this issue, image registration is performed w.r.t. a reference frame (the first image of the day). A global offset

Figure 3: An example of a Daily Median Image (right) performed on 11 daily images (left).

is computed by means of the cross-correlation between the two skyline edge maps and each image is compensated by this offset before computing the DMI.

Identifying mountain peaks. A DMI per webcam is processed to identify peaks, with a procedure based on the alignment between the image and a virtual terrain model[2]. Given a photo and the metadata extracted from the EXIF container (geo-tag, focal length, camera model and manufacturer), it is possible to perform a matching with a 360° panoramic view of the terrain synthesized from a Digital Elevation Model (DEM). The method proceeds in steps: *Preprocessing* - estimation of the horizontal Field Of View (FOV), edge extraction, noise edge filtering; *Global alignment* - estimation of the best overlap between the photograph and the panoramic view through Vector Cross Correlation (VCC) applied to the respective edge maps; *Local Alignment* - improving the precision of the position of each peak with a separate VCC procedure. If a webcam image does not contain EXIF data, its FOV cannot be estimated, and the alignment cannot be performed. In this case, the image is posted to an ad-hoc developed crowdsourcing web platform, where volunteers can help find the correct FOV and alignment manually. This step does not induce a significant overhead, because it is executed only once per webcam.

4.2 User generated photograph processing

Webcams are relevant data sources, with high temporal resolution but invariable positioning. Tourists are another valuable source of images, with a potentially more uniform spatial distribution. Also, if properly activated, crowds can engage in specific campaigns and act as a collective webcam that could be pointed virtually to the desired target. Differently from webcams, user generated photos are mined from sharing sites by geo-search, whose results may contain completely irrelevant images. Search outputs must be filtered, to retain only mountain pictures. Analogously to webcam images, once a photograph is classified as relevant, it must be subjected to peak labeling, to identify the mountain view it portrays and extract snow information. Flickr was selected, because it contains a large number of public images, many with the geo-tag in their EXIF container. A

[2]The procedure is the same applied to crowdsourced images.

continuous search system was built, which queries images within a 300 × 160 km region in the Alps; as of now, the Flickr search pipeline has examined ∽600k candidate photos. To train the relevance classifier, we collected ground truth labels: 6940 randomly selected photos taken above an altitude of 500 meters were processed in a crowdsourcing experiment, in which workers had to label images based on the presence of a mountain skyline. The aggregated label was obtained by majority voting. Approximately 23% of the images were classified as positive. Then, the automatic mountain classifier was built as follows. From each training image a fixed-length feature vector representing its visual content was constructed. To create a balanced dataset, we retained all the positive samples and randomly selected the same number of negative samples. Then, we used ~70% of the samples for training and validation and ~30% for testing. The encoded feature vectors were fed to a SVM classifier using a χ^2 kernel. To learn the optimal values of the C and γ kernel parameters of the SVM classifier, we adopted k-fold cross validation, with $k = 5$ for the grid search. The mountain photos classified as relevant are then subjected to the same mountain peak identification procedure as webcam images.

4.3 Experimental evaluation

The content processing pipeline has been evaluated experimentally. This required us to assess 3 components: the weather condition filter (used for webcams), the mountain relevance classifier (used for UGC) and the peak alignment algorithm (used for both webcams and UGC).

Weather condition filter. We manually labeled 1000 images collected from 4 webcams, with the tag "good weather", if the mountain area was completely visible, or "bad weather" otherwise. Due to the high temporal frequency of webcam image acquisition, many images are available; thus, the threshold parameter $\bar{v}$ was set to a value ensuring low FPR (0.75), obtaining a TPR equal to **87.4%** at FPR **3.5%**.

Mountain relevance classifier. Evaluation compared 8 configurations, by pairing 4 local and global image feature descriptors (Dense SIFT, HOG2x2, SSIM and GIST) and 2 vector encodings: Bag-of-Visual-Word (BoVW) and Fisher vector encoding. The best configuration proved to be: Dense SIFT, BoVW encoding, SVM with paramaters values $C = 3.3$, $\gamma = 0.66$; this configuration obtained **95.1%** accuracy, **94.0%** precision, and **96.3%** recall on the test set.

Peak identification. We manually inspected 200 photographs and the virtual panoramas generated from the EXIF metadata and DEM, to make sure that a plausible match existed (e.g. a match could be impossible due to bad GPS tag), obtaining 162 good photos. Ground truth peak alignment data were generated by an ad-hoc developed alignment tool, which allows users to define the correct orientation of the image and fix the position for each peak mentioned in the virtual panorama. Considering a tolerance of 3deg, **75%** of the image orientations were correctly estimated; this percentage grows to **77.6%** and **81.6%** in absence of clouds and nearby mountain slopes, respectively. The average positioning error of peaks resulted to be **0.78** deg.

Execution times. The automatic alignment procedure dominates the entire image processing time. The generation of $1500px \times 12000px$ panoramic view requires approximately 1s with a GeForce GTX 850M graphic card. The alignment of an image to the virtual panorama requires approximately 30s on an OpenStack virtual instance with 4 $2.5GHz$ VCPUs and $8Gb$ of RAM.

4.4 Snow index computation

Once an image is classified as relevant and its peak identified, snow information can be extracted and associated with the mountain(s) that appear in it, at the time the image was taken (or at the day, in case of a DMI). A *virtual snow index* is defined as a real value representing the snow information extracted from the photo or from the DMI. When used as input to environmental models, these indexes do not necessarily need a physical interpretation (e.g., like snow depth), as long as they reflect the dynamics of snow distribution. The snow indexes used in the case study are determined as follows. Let I denote an image and M a binary mask having the same size as I, where $M(x, y) = 1$ indicates that the pixel $I(x, y)$ of the image belongs to the mountain area, or $M(x, y) = 0$ otherwise. A *snow mask* is defined as the output of a pixel-level binary classifier that, given I and M as input, produces a mask S that assigns each pixel a binary label denoting the presence of snow. We computed snow masks using the Random Forest supervised learning classifier with spatio-temporal median smoothing of the output. The classifier achieves 90.0% precision at 91.1% recall, outperforming existing methods for pixel level snow detection. From the snow mask S, the snow indexes are computed as follows. Let H denote a real value map having the same size as I, where $H(x, y)$ denotes the altitude of the terrain in the point that corresponds to $I(x, y)$ (e.g., altitude in meters, that can be estimated from the projection of the pixel the on DEM), for each (x, y) such that $M(x, y) = 1$ (i.e., for pixels representing points within the mountain region of the image). M and H can be obtained during the mountain peak identification phase, because each pixel of the photo gets aligned with a pixel of the virtual panorama; the latter carries information not only about the edges of the mountains, but also about the type (terrain/sky) and altitude of each DEM pixel. Let $\hat{H}$ denote the linearly normalized version of H, where the minimum (maximum) altitude corresponds to 0 (1). Then, a *virtual snow index* for an image I is defined as $\sum_{(x,y)|S(x,y)=1} vsi(x, y)$, where vsi is a virtual snow index function that transforms a pixel position into a snow relevance coefficient. We tested three different snow feature functions:

$$vsi^1(x, y) = \hat{H}(x, y)^2, vsi^2(x, y) = \frac{\hat{H}(x, y)}{N_{x,y}}, vsi^3(x, y) = 1$$

where N is the number of horizontal bands in which we split the mountain area of the image and $N_{x,y}$ denotes the number of mountain pixels belonging to the same band of a pixel $I(x, y)$. The first snow index weights each snow-covered pixel quadratically w.r.t. its altitude, the second one weights each snow-covered pixel linearly w.r.t. its altitude and normalizes the score w.r.t. the number of pixels contained in the same band, and the third one weights each snow-covered pixel uniformly regardless of its altitude. The values for the three indexes are computed for each day and their operational value is assessed in Section 6.

4.5 Content selection for the case study

The dataset contains more than $2.5M$ mountains images located across the Lake Como catchment; such images are produced by 62 webcams and include also more than $100k$

photos produced by users. However, not all relevant images are directly exploitable for the assessment; environmental models require a very long observation period: a statistically significant evaluation *requires observations spanning multiple years*, to cope with seasonal effects. We started collecting images in Dec. 2014, and therefore most sources lack a long enough time series to be usable as input. A manual search found historical images of a few webcams and aggregated them to the dataset. Specifically, we found one webcam with enough historical data, which was chosen for the experiments. The webcam is placed in Livigno and the observation period comprises 818 days, from Jan 1, 2013 to Mar 29, 2015. The mountain framed by the webcam is positioned inside the Como lake catchment and its snow level is known to affect the lake water dynamics. Even with a single webcam, the experimental results described in Section 6 demonstrate a significant utility of the snow-related data. We plan to carry out experiments at larger scale in the lake catchments of the entire Alpine arc, as the dataset will grow thanks to continued crawling and the crowdsourcing campaigns performed with the mobile photo collection application described in Section 8.

5. WATER MANAGEMENT OPTIMIZATION

The assessment of the operational value of snow information is done by comparing the performance of alternative operating policies for the regulation of Lake Como. A *policy* is a function returning the quantity of water to be released u_t at each time instant $t = [0 \dots T-1]$, as dependent upon an information vector $\mathbf{z}_t$, i.e., $u_t = p(\mathbf{z}_t)$. Based on the input information, different policies are employed: 1) A *perfect* control policy, an ideal policy used as an upper bound of the system performance, which makes always the optimal decision based on perfect knowledge of current and future system conditions. 2) A *baseline* control policy, which considers only limited information (day of the year and current lake level). 3) An *informed* control policy, which exploits additional information, including snow-related data. Specifically, two informed policies are contrasted, one exploiting official snow data from ARPA (*official data policy*) and one using the virtual snow indexes computed from web content (*web data policy*). The assessment quantifies how closer the informed control policies get to the perfect one, in comparison to the baseline.

This evaluation methodology, called Information Selection and Assessment (ISA) framework [14], consists of 3 steps: (*i*) Quantification of the expected value of perfect information, i.e., the potential for improving operations under the assumption of perfect knowledge of future conditions; (*ii*) Automatic selection of the most valuable information to improve current operations; (*iii*) Evaluation of the selected information on the resulting control policy performance.

5.1 Expected Value of Perfect Information

The Expected Value of Perfect Information (EVPI) is the performance gain that can be achieved under the assumption of perfect foresight on the future [23]. If the value of EVPI is small, a limited information policy already performs close to the best strategy and thus the benefit of additional input data approximating future system conditions is limited. The availability of perfect knowledge of the future external drivers (e.g., lake inflows) is equivalent to assume that the operator is an omniscient oracle implementing a Perfect Control Policy (PCP), consisting of an optimal sequence of release decisions $u^{PCP}_{[0,T-1]}$, conditioned on the current system status (i.e., the time instant t and the current lake level l_t), and on the perfect knowledge of the future inflows. In the experiments illustrated in Section 6, the PCP is built by solving the control policy design problem over a 2-year horizon in which the sequence of inflows is known. This is a standard nonlinear optimization problem and can be solved by either a local optimization method (e.g., gradient-based) or a global optimization method (e.g., direct search). Alternatively, since the objective functions in our application are time-separable, we use deterministic dynamic programming (DDP), which is more efficient and provides an almost exact solution.

PCP performance ($\mathbf{J}^{PCP}$) has a relative value, because it depends on the physical characteristics of the system, e.g., the ratio between the lake capacity and its inflow. The EVPI has hence to be estimated as the distance between $\mathbf{J}^{PCP}$ and the performance of a Baseline Control Policy (BCP), defined as a simple closed-loop control policy, where $\mathbf{z}_t$ includes the time index t and the current lake level l_t.

In a single-objective scenario, the EVPI is simply the difference between the (scalar) performance of the PCP and BCP. In a multi-objective case, the evaluation is more complex; the performance objectives $\mathbf{J}^{PCP}$ and $\mathbf{J}^{BCP}$ are vector functions and the solution is not unique, but rather a set of Pareto optimal solutions (Pareto Front). Among the commonly used metrics (see [17]), the ISA framework adopts the hypervolume indicator (HV), which captures both the proximity of the Pareto Front $\mathbf{J}^{BCP}$ to the ideal one $\mathbf{J}^{PCP}$ as well as the distribution of the BCP solutions in the objective space. The hypervolume measures the volume of objective space dominated ($\preceq$) by the considered set of solutions (S). Then, the HV indicator is defined as the ratio of the hypervolumes of the solutions produced by BCP and PCP:

$$HV(BCP, PCP) = \frac{\int \alpha(\mathbf{s}_{BCP}) d s_{BCP}}{\int \alpha(\mathbf{s}_{PCP}) d s_{PCP}}$$

$$\alpha(\mathbf{s}) = \begin{cases} 1 & \text{if } \exists s' \in S \text{ such that } s' \preceq s \\ 0 & \text{otherwise} \end{cases}$$

If policy A has a value of HV greater than a policy B, the solutions produced by A dominate a larger fraction of the objective space, which means that A is better than B in pursuing the multiple objectives of the system. The EVPI can then be computed as the difference between the HV of PCP (i.e., 1 by definition) and the HV of BCP.

5.2 Most Valuable Information Selection

A large value of EVPI indicates that a control policy endowed with more information can approach the performance of the ideal, omniscient one. The ISA methodology helps identify the input information that enables the informed policy to approximate as much as possible the optimal sequence of decisions $u^{PCP}_{[0,T-1]}$. The set Ξ_t of candidate inputs may comprise *exogenous variables*, i.e., variables that are observed in the time interval $[0, T-1]$ but are not part of the problem formulation; examples are rainfall, temperature, snow presence, etc. Since Ξ_t can comprise redundant and collinear variables, its smallest subset $\mathbf{I}_t \in \Xi_t$ that carries the most valuable information must be identified, as the one that best explains the optimal sequence of decisions.

Algorithm 1 Iterative Input Selection

Inputs: a dataset $\mathcal{F}$ of candidate inputs $\mathbf{v}^i$ and the output variable to explain v^o.
Initialization:
Set $\mathcal{V} \leftarrow 0, \hat{v}^o \leftarrow v^o, D_{old} \leftarrow 0$
Iterations: repeat until stopping conditions are met
- select the most relevant input $v^* \in \mathbf{v}^i$ to explain $\hat{v}^o$
- **if** $v^* \in \mathcal{V}$, **return** $\mathcal{V}$ **endif**
- $\mathcal{V} \leftarrow \mathcal{V} \cup v^*$
- $\hat{m}(\cdot) \leftarrow$ Extra-Trees$(\mathcal{F}, v^o, \mathcal{V})$
- $\hat{v}^o \leftarrow v^o - \hat{m}(\cdot)$
- $\Delta D \leftarrow D(v^o, \hat{m}(\cdot)) - D_{old}$
- $D_{old} \leftarrow D(v^o, \hat{m}(\cdot))$
- **until** $\Delta D < \varepsilon_D$
return $\mathcal{V}$

Several techniques can be used to solve this feature selection problem [11], such as cross-correlation analysis, mutual information analysis, or input variable selection methods. We use the hybrid model-based/model-free Iterative Input Selection (IIS) algorithm (Algorithm 1), which can approximate strongly non-linear functions and scale to large datasets made of long time series and many candidate variables [11]. Given a generic output variable v^o and the set of candidate inputs $\mathbf{v}^i$, IIS first ranks the inputs w.r.t. a statistical measure of significance and adds the best performing input v^* to the current set of selected variables $\mathcal{V}$. This step avoids the inclusion of redundant variables: after an input is selected, all the other inputs highly correlated with it will rank low in the next iterations. Then, the algorithm estimates a model of v^o with input $\mathcal{V}$, such that $v^0 = \hat{m}(\mathcal{V})$, and estimates the model performance with a distance metric D (e.g., the coefficient of determination) as well as the model residuals $(v^o - \hat{m}(\mathcal{V}))$, which become the new output at the next iteration. The algorithm stops when the next best input variable selected is already in the set $\mathcal{V}$, or when over-fitting conditions are reached. Among the many alternative model classes, IIS relies on extremely randomized trees (Extra-Trees), a tree-based method proposed by [12] that was empirically demonstrated to outperform other models in terms of modeling flexibility, efficiency, and scalability with respect to the input dimensionality. Moreover, Extra-Trees structures can be exploited to infer the relative importance of variables, as required for their ranking [3].

5.3 Expected Value of Sample Information

After selecting the most valuable information $\mathbf{I}_t \subset \Xi_t$, the next step is to design the Informed Control Policy (ICP) that exploits such information to make decisions. The ICP is defined by extending the input $\mathbf{z}_t$ of the baseline control policy with the selected information, i.e., $\mathbf{z}_t = (t, l_t, \mathbf{I}_t)$, and searching the optimal control policy with approximate dynamic programming methods. We use the evolutionary multi-objective direct policy search (EMODPS), a simulation-based technique that combines direct policy search, nonlinear approximating networks, and multi-objective evolutionary algorithms [13]. EMODPS exploits the parameterization of the control policies p_θ and explores the parameter space Θ to find a policy (p^*_θ) that optimizes the expected system performance (J_θ, conventionally assumed to be a cost), i.e., $p^*_\theta = \arg\min_{p_\theta} J_\theta$ where the policy p_θ is parameterized by parameters $\theta \in \Theta$ and the problem is constrained by the dynamics of the system. Finding p^*_θ is equivalent to finding the corresponding optimal policy parameters θ^*. A tabular version of the EMODPS method is illustrated in Algorithm 2.

Algorithm 2 Evolutionary Multi-Objective Direct Policy Search.

Initialization:
Generate a random parameter values population $\{\theta^1, \dots, \theta^P\}$
Iterations: repeat until stopping conditions are met
- generate a trajectory τ^i via model simulation according to the stochastic transition function $\mathbf{x}_{t+1} = f(\mathbf{x}_t, \mathbf{u}_t, \varepsilon_{t+1})$ and following the policy p_{θ^i} (with $i = 1, \dots, P$)
- compute performance $J^1_{\theta^i}, \dots, J^q_{\theta^i}$, with $i = 1, \dots, P$
- generate new population by selection, crossover and mutation w.r.t. the best individuals (i.e., non Pareto-dominated solutions)

In general, we expect the ICP to fill the performance gap between the upper and lower bound solutions (i.e., the PCP and BCP), and to produce a performance $\mathbf{J}^{ICP}$ as close as possible to $\mathbf{J}^{PCP}$. The benefit associated to the use of the selected information is called *Expected Value of Sample Information* (EVSI) and can be quantified by means of the same metrics used for the evaluating the EVPI (see Section 5.1).

6. EXPERIMENTS AND RESULTS

The experimental setting is characterized as follows.
Perfect Control Policies: PCPs are designed via Deterministic Dynamic Programming over 2 years of historical data (2013-2014). The weighting method is used to convert the 2-objective problem (flooding and irrigation) into a single objective, via convex combination. The PCPs are designed under the assumption of perfect foresight on the future at the moment when decisions are taken, i.e., we assume perfect knowledge on the lake inflows over the evaluation period.
Baseline Control Policies: BCPs are defined as traditional control policies conditioned on the day of the year t and on the lake level l_t. These policies are designed via EMODPS.
Candidate exogenous variables and automatic selection of information: to build the informed control policies ICP, we evaluate the contribution of adding exogenous variables from the official monitoring network: previous day spatial precipitation in the Lake Como catchment (P_t), previous day freezing level (FL_t), upstream hydropower storage (sHP_t), previous day release from hydro-power reservoirs (rHP_t), and weekly estimate of snow water equivalent (SWE_t), elaborated by ARPA from ground stations and MODIS data. In addition to official variables, we consider the three virtual snow indexes computed from web images. The most valuable information is identified with the IIS algorithm.
Informed Control Policies: ICPs are designed via EMODPS, with the control policies parameterized as Gaussian Radial Basis Functions, which have been proved effective in multi-objective control problems with exogenous input [13, 14]. For the optimization, the self-adaptive Borg Multi-Objective Evolutionary Algorithm [15] is used, which is robust and efficient across diverse multi-objective problems. Each optimization is run for 2 million function evaluations, with the simulation step performed over the same 2-years horizon. To improve solution diversity and avoid dependence on randomness, the solution set from each formulation is the result of 30 random trials. The final set of Pareto optimal policies

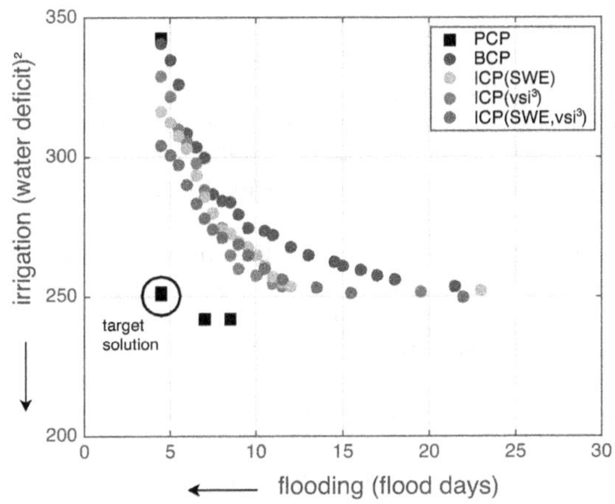

Figure 4: Performance of PCP (black squares), BCP (blue circles), and alternative ICPs with different information (SWE in cyan, $vsi3$ in red, SWE and $vsi3$ in green).

for each experiment is defined as the set of non-dominated solutions from the results of all the optimization trials.

6.1 Quantifying the EVPI

The first step of the ISA framework (Section 5) estimates the Expected Value of Perfect Information by contrasting PCPs and BCPs. Figure 4 shows the performance of the PCPs (represented by black squares) evaluated over the horizon 2013-2014. The blue circles represent the performance of the BCPs (traditional control policies conditioned on the day of the year and the lake level). The performance of the ICPs (red, cyan, and green circles) is discussed later on in Section 6.3. The arrows on the axes point in the direction of increasing preference, with the best solution located in the bottom-left corner of the figure. Visual comparison of the Pareto Fronts shows that the potential for improvement over BCPs is large: the gap between basic information and the perfect knowledge is substantial in terms of both operating objectives, as represented by the area between the black squares and the blue points. A first qualitative analysis can be done focusing on a specific target PCP solution (circled in the figure), which represents a potentially good compromise between flood control and irrigation supply. However, it seems to be difficult to turn this solution into an actual regulation of the lake with BCP: while the extreme solutions in the PCP and BCP fronts, representing the independent optima for flooding and irrigation, are almost equivalent, the maximum distance between the two fronts is in correspondence with the selected target solution. This motivates searching for ICPs that can fill the gap. Quantitative EVPI assessment is provided by the HV indicator in Table 2, where the difference between BCP and PCP is equal to 0.29, confirming the gap between Perfect and Baseline Control Policies.

6.2 Exogenous Variables Selection

The question whether snow information can help making more informed decisions is addressed by using the ISA framework to identify the most informative exogenous variables $\mathbf{I}_t \subset \Xi_t$. We first evaluate the day of the year and the lake level together will all the exogenous variables except our virtual snow indexes, to check if the official snow information is relevant. The rationale for retaining the day of the year and the lake level is to extend the BCP and avoid selecting exogenous variables correlated with t or l_t. Then, we contrast official snow information with virtual snow indexes in Section 6.3 and 6.4. We perform 20 runs of the IIS algorithm to filter the randomness associated to the construction of the Extra-Trees models. Despite the limited length of the time series (only 2 years), which introduces some variability across the runs, the best result consistently selects as most valuable information the day of the year (t), the lake level (l_t), and the official ARPA estimates (SWE_t). This confirms the key role of snow dynamics in the Lake Como system. Using the 3 variables selected, the Extra-Trees model approximates the optimal sequence of release decisions $u^{PCP}_{[0,T-1]}$ attaining a model performance, evaluated using the coefficient of determination (D), equal to 0.639. Table 1 shows the contributions of variables and statistics over the 20 repetitions.

Table 1: Variables selected by the IIS algorithm.

Variable	Best-run	Selection frequency, 20 runs	Average contribution (R2), 20 runs
t	0.231	100%	0.334
l_t	0.348	85%	0.194
SWE_t	0.060	45%	0.108

6.3 Benefits of official snow information

To quantify the value of the official ARPA snow water equivalent, we assess the performance of the ICPs conditioned on the information vector $\mathbf{z}_t = (t, l_t, SWE_t)$. The resulting policies ICP(SWE) are represented by cyan points in Figure 4. The comparison of the performance of BCP and ICP(SWE) shows a relevant contribution of the official snow information: this is due to an improved medium-long term foresight, as snow information provides useful insight about the expected water availability during the next summer, when the irrigation demand is high and the conflict between flooding and irrigation is critical. A quantitative evaluation of the EVSI associated to this variable is given by HV reported in Table 2: HV increases from 0.7079 to 0.7848 (i.e., +10.9%) when moving from BCP to ICP(SWE).

6.4 Benefits of web snow information

The question of whether the virtual snow indexes (vsi^k) defined in Section 4.4 can complement the official ARPA SWE data is addressed through the following experiments: first, we replace the ARPA SWE variable with each virtual snow index vsi^k and analyze the performance of the corresponding policies ICPs(vsi^k). Second, we explore the possibility of complementing, instead of replacing, the ARPA SWE variable with the virtual snow indexes, by evaluating the performance of ICPs conditioned on the information vector $\mathbf{z}_t = (t, l_t, SWE_t, vsi^k_t)$. We report only the results obtained using the third snow index vsi^3, because it consistently outperforms the other two indexes. The comparison of ICP(SWE) and ICP(vsi^3), represented by red points in Figure 4, shows that the value of the virtual snow index is comparable to, and sometimes higher than, the one of the ARPA SWE. In fact, the red Pareto Front intersects the cyan one, with some red solutions outperforming the cyan ones in the compromise region of the front, close to the target PCP. This observation is confirmed by the corresponding values of HV, with ICP(vsi^3) attaining a higher value than ICP(SWE), which corresponds to a 11.6% improvement with respect to the BCPs. Finally, the performance of the ICPs conditioned on both SWE_t and vsi^3 (green points in Figure 4) outperforms both BCPs and ICPs(SWE). Such superiority is certified by the values of HV: ICPs(SWE, vsi^3) attains a value equal to 0.816, which corresponds to a 15.2% improvement with respect to the BCPs and a 4% improvement with respect to ICPs(SWE). These results suggest a significant potential for complementing the official ARPA SWE estimate with virtual snow indexes derived from public web media.

Table 2: Quantification of Expected Value of Perfect and Sample Information in terms of hypervolume indicator.

Policy	HV	ΔHV
BCP	0.7079	–
ICP(SWE)	0.7848	+10.9%
ICP(vsi^3)	0.7898	+11.6%
ICP(SWE, vsi^3)	0.816	+15.2%
PCP	1.0	–

7. DISCUSSION

In this paper we have presented the results of an integration effort of multimedia and environment research, proving that low-quality, low-cost, yet widely available, public content can provide input that improves the performance of a practical environmental model in a quantifiable manner. The proposed approach exemplifies the opportunities, but also the challenges, of applying multimedia processing techniques to real-world environmental problems.

Opportunities Multimedia research has attained robust methods and high accuracy in many knowledge extraction tasks that could radically change the way in which environment monitoring is performed. The interplay of three factors makes the integration of multimedia and environment research particularly relevant and timely: 1) the increase of user generated content, which is now turning also to real-time video; 2) the deployment of IoT infrastructures and low-cost cameras, which makes ground sensing affordable for novel applications, including e.g., environment and agriculture monitoring; 3) the impact of climate change, which is increasing the frequency and severity of extreme events, putting traditional monitoring networks under stress.

Open Challenges Traditional environment research generally relies on complex models, which encode the properties of the investigated system and thus require input data endowed with a precise physical interpretation, often collected with manual procedures and dedicated equipment. On the other hand, the information that can be extracted, automatically, accurately, and at scale, from public content is much more noisy and simpler in format and meaning than that employed by many state-of-practice models. The fundamental challenge is to identify the "overlap region" where the knowledge extracted with multimedia processing methods can improve the performance of practical environmental models. The problem addressed in this paper is an almost ideal one, where several factors concur to make the case tractable: public mountain images are abundant and with sufficient spatio-temporal coverage, can be processed (offline) with high accuracy, and contain a signal (snow presence) that, albeit simpler than the parameters used by snow process models based on physical laws, is relevant for a specific environmental problem. However, future research can generalize the proposed framework to more challenging scenarios, along a number of directions, including: the type of input data (e.g., video), the processing requirements (e.g., online and real-time), the spatio-temporal dynamics, and the environmental problem addressed. For example, river basin occlusion is a relevant problem for hydrogeological risk prevention, because excessive sediment and vegetation can cause overflow: multimedia research could exploit (already existing) webcams deployed for human-assisted river bed surveillance, possibly complemented by user generated, crowdsourced images, and help estimate the river flow, which is connected to the risk of flooding during heavy rainfall. This scenario generalizes the research agenda towards another type of image processing and the analysis of the spatio-temporal dynamics of a different environment phenomenon. An even more challenging case of fast-dynamics, real-time scenario is exploiting real-time user generated video content for addressing event-based environmental monitoring. For example, flood level and water speed information extracted from user-generated video could be used in input to flood propagation prediction models based on DEM data, to forecast the reach and impact of flood, so to alert citizens and adjust evacuation plans. This scenario generalizes the research agenda towards more complex input, quasi-realtime constraints, and the analysis of the fast spatio-temporal dynamics of an environment phenomenon. Furthermore, multimedia analysis for environmental data should move from "extract already available environmental data from new media sources" paradigm to "extract novel environmental data and prove that it is complementary to existing one". We believe that this impact-focused approach will decrease the reluctance of the environmental science community to adopt novel multimedia analysis techniques.

8. CONCLUSIONS AND FUTURE WORK

In this paper we tested the hypothesis that public web content, either crowdsourced or gathered from ground sensors, can be effectively used in input to environmental decision models. The experiments, although conditioned by the limited duration of the time series available, show that it is possible to use virtual snow indexes computed from mountain images to design more informed, and thus improved, water management strategies. Preliminary results show that even a single webcam stream is capable of providing valuable information to the management policy of Lake Como and improves the system performance w.r.t. the conflicting objectives of irrigation water supply and flood risk minimization. Using simulation, we demonstrated that the virtual snow indexes obtained from public web media content can replace official snow measurements derived from permanent ground stations and satellite imagery without performance loss; also, they can complement official snow information yielding further performance improvement, which shows that the two data sources are not redundant.
As time passes and we acquire longer time series for more relevant mountains and more user generated photos, the per-

formance of the policies conditioned on web content inputs is expected to increase. In parallel, we are building an augmented reality mobile app for mountain photo sharing. The app overlays in real time peak names over photo and videos, with high accuracy. The user can save her photos, with the mountain landscape nicely adorned with peak names, in our mountain photo portal, correct the automatic alignment, and share the result on popular social networks, inviting more people to do the same. As a last objective, we are porting the architecture to different environmental problems where the same approach applies: sediment monitoring in river beds and vegetation monitoring in mountain regions.

9. REFERENCES

[1] L. Baboud, M. Cadik, E. Eisemann, and H.-P. Seidel. Automatic photo-to-terrain alignment for the annotation of mountain pictures. In *Computer Vision and Pattern Recognition (CVPR), 2011 IEEE Conference on*, pages 41–48. IEEE, 2011.

[2] E. S. Bradley and K. C. Clarke. Outdoor webcams as geospatial sensor networks: Challenges, issues and opportunities. *Cartography and Geographic Information Science*, 38(1):3–19, 2011.

[3] A. Castelletti, S. Galelli, M. Restelli, and R. Soncini-Sessa. Tree-based feature selection for dimensionality reduction of large-scale control systems. In *Proceedings of the IEEE Symposium on Adaptive Dynamic Programming and Reinforcement Learning*, Paris, France, 11–15 April 2011.

[4] S. Daume, M. Albert, and K. von Gadow. Forest monitoring and social media–complementary data sources for ecosystem surveillance? *Forest Ecology and Management*, 316:9–20, 2014.

[5] B. De Longueville, R. S. Smith, and G. Luraschi. OMG, from here, I can see the flames!: a use case of mining location based social networks to acquire spatio-temporal data on forest fires. In *Proceedings of the 2009 international workshop on location based social networks*, pages 73–80. ACM, 2009.

[6] Q. Desreumaux, P. Côté, and R. Leconte. Role of hydrologic information in stochastic dynamic programming: a case study of the Kemano hydropower system in British Columbia. *Canadian Journal of Civil Engineering*, 41(9):839–844, 2014.

[7] A. J. Dietz, C. Kuenzer, U. Gessner, and S. Dech. Remote sensing of snow–a review of available methods. *International Journal of Remote Sensing*, 33(13):4094–4134, 2012.

[8] R. Fedorov, A. Camerada, P. Fraternali, and M. Tagliasacchi. Estimating snow cover from publicly available images. *IEEE Transactions on Multimedia*, 18(6):1187–1200, 2016.

[9] R. Fedorov, P. Fraternali, and M. Tagliasacchi. Mountain peak identification in visual content based on coarse digital elevation models. In *Proceedings of the 3rd ACM International Workshop on Multimedia Analysis for Ecological Data*, pages 7–11. ACM, 2014.

[10] W. E. Forum. Global risks 2015 report (10th edition).

[11] S. Galelli, G. Humphrey, H. Maier, and et al. An evaluation framework for input variable selection algorithms for environmental data-driven models. *Environmental Modelling & Software*, 62:33–51, 2014.

[12] P. Geurts, D. Ernst, and L. Wehenkel. Extremely randomized trees. *Machine Learning*, 63(1):3–42, 2006.

[13] M. Giuliani, A. Castelletti, F. Pianosi, E. Mason, and P. Reed. Curses, tradeoffs, and scalable management: advancing evolutionary multi-objective direct policy search to improve water reservoir operations. *Journal of Water Resources Planning and Management*, 142(2), 2016.

[14] M. Giuliani, F. Pianosi, and A. Castelletti. Making the most of data: an information selection and assessment framework to improve water systems operations. *Water Resources Research*, 51(11):9073–9093, 2015.

[15] D. Hadka and P. Reed. Borg: An Auto–Adaptive Many–Objective Evolutionary Computing Framework. *Evolutionary Computation*, 21(2):231–259, 2013.

[16] M. Hejazi, X. Cai, and B. Ruddell. The role of hydrologic information in reservoir operation– learning from historical releases. *Advances in Water Resources*, 31(12):1636–1650, 2008.

[17] H. Maier, Z. Kapelan, J. Kasprzyk, and et al. Evolutionary algorithms and other metaheuristics in water resources: Current status, research challenges and future directions . *Environmental Modelling & Software*, 62(0):271–299, 2014.

[18] N. Michelsen, H. Dirks, S. Schulz, S. Kempe, M. Al-Saud, and C. SchÃijth. Youtube as a crowd-generated water level archive. *Science of the Total Environment*, 568:189–195, 2016.

[19] D. Rüfenacht, M. Brown, J. Beutel, and S. Süsstrunk. Temporally consistent snow cover estimation from noisy, irregularly sampled measurements. In *Proc. 9th International Conference on Computer Vision Theory and Applications (VISAPP)*, 2014.

[20] R. Salvatori, P. Plini, M. Giusto, and et al. Snow cover monitoring with images from digital camera systems. *Italian Journal of Remote Sensing*, 43:137–145, 2011.

[21] S. Shukla, N. Voisin, and D. P. Lettenmaier. Value of medium range weather forecasts in the improvement of seasonal hydrologic prediction skill. *Hydrol. Earth Syst. Sci. Discuss.*, 9(2):1827–1857, 2012.

[22] J. Tejada-Guibert, S. Johnson, and J. Stedinger. The value of hydrologic information in stochastic dynamic programming models of a multireservoir system. *Water Resources Research*, 31(10):2571–2579, 1995.

[23] F. Yokota and K. Thompson. Value of information analysis in environmental health risk management decisions: past, present, and future. *Risk analysis*, 24(3):635–650, 2004.

[24] J.-Y. You and X. Cai. Determining forecast and decision horizons for reservoir operations under hedging policies. *Water resources research*, 44(11), 2008.

[25] H. Zhang, M. Korayem, D. J. Crandall, and G. LeBuhn. Mining photo-sharing websites to study ecological phenomena. In *Proceedings of the 21st international conference on World Wide Web*, pages 749–758. ACM, 2012.

Crowdsourcing Biodiversity Monitoring: How Sharing your Photo Stream can Sustain our Planet

Alexis Joly
Inria, ZENITH team, LIRMM
34095 Montpellier, France

Hervé Goëau
IRD, UMR AMAP
Montpellier, France

Julien Champ
Inria, ZENITH team, LIRMM
34095 Montpellier, France

Samuel Dufour-Kowalski
INRA, UMR AMAP
Montpellier, France

Henning Müller
HES-SO
3960 Sierre, Switzerland

Pierre Bonnet
CIRAD, UMR AMAP
Montpellier, France

ABSTRACT

Large scale biodiversity monitoring is essential for sustainable development (earth stewardship). With the recent advances in computer vision, we see the emergence of more and more effective identification tools allowing to set-up large-scale data collection platforms such as the popular Pl@ntNet initiative that allow to reuse interaction data. Although it covers only a fraction of the world flora, this platform is already being used by more than 300K people who produce tens of thousands of validated plant observations each year. This explicitly shared and validated data is only the tip of the iceberg. The real potential relies on the millions of raw image queries submitted by the users of the mobile application for which there is no human validation. People make such requests to get information on a plant along a hike or something they find in their garden but not know anything about. Allowing the exploitation of such contents in a fully automatic way could scale up the world-wide collection of implicit plant observations by several orders of magnitude, which can complement the explicit monitoring efforts. In this paper, we first survey existing automated plant identification systems through a five-year synthesis of the PlantCLEF benchmark and an impact study of the Pl@ntNet platform. We then focus on the implicit monitoring scenario and discuss related research challenges at the frontier of computer science and biodiversity studies. Finally, we discuss the results of a preliminary study focused on implicit monitoring of invasive species in mobile search logs. We show that the results are promising but that there is room for improvement before being able to automatically share implicit observations within international platforms.

1. INTRODUCTION

Identifying organisms is a key step in accessing information related to the ecology of species. This is essential in recording any specimen on earth to be used in ecological studies. Unfortunately, this is difficult to achieve due to the level of expertise necessary to correctly identify and record living organisms (in particular plants that are one of the most difficult group to identify with more than 350,000 species on earth). The required knowledge makes crowdsourcing of plant identification hard, similar to other specific domains such as medical data analysis [10]. This *taxonomic gap* has been recognized since the Rio Conference of 1992 as a major obstacle to the global implementation of the Convention on Biological Diversity. Among the divers methods used for species identification, Gaston et al.[11] discussed in 2004 the potential of automated approaches typically based on machine learning and multimedia data analysis methods. They suggested that, if the scientific community is able to (i) overcome the production of large training datasets, (ii) more precisely identify and evaluate the error rates, (iii) scale up automated approaches, and (iv) detect novel species, it will then be possible to initiate the development of a generic automated species identification system that could open opportunities for work in biological and related fields.

Since the question raised by Gaston in 2004 ("automated species identification: why not?"), enormous work has been done on the development of automated approaches for plant species identification, mostly based on computer vision techniques (*e.g.* [16, 42, 22]). Some of these results were integrated in effective web or mobile tools and have initiated close interactions between computer scientists and end-users such as ecologists, botanists, educators, land managers and the general public. One remarkable system in this domain was the LeafSnap application [25], focused on a few hundred tree species of North America. This was followed a few years later by other applications such as Pl@ntNet [20] or Folia [4] more specifically dedicated to the European flora, or LikeThat garden[1] more focused on garden plants. These productions were perceived as innovative tools and have received a good support of a large part of the society. These tools are at an early stage of development according to the large number of plant species on earth, the large diversity of end-users interested in such an accessible approach and the limits of today's performance.

In parallel to the emergence of automated identification

MM '16, October 15 - 19, 2016, Amsterdam, Netherlands

ISBN 978-1-4503-3603-1/16/10...$15.00

DOI: http://dx.doi.org/10.1145/2964284.2976762

[1]https://www.likethatapps.com/LikeThatGarden/

tools, large social networks dedicated to the production, sharing and identification of biodiversity records have increased in recent years. Some of the most active ones in the botanical domain like iNaturalist[2], iSpot [32], Tela Botanica[3], federate tens of thousands of members, producing hundreds of thousands of observations. As a proof of their increasing reliability, some of these networks started to contribute to global initiatives in biodiversity such as the Global Biodiversity Information Facility (GBIF[4]) which is the largest and most recognized one.

Noticeably, the Pl@ntNet initiative was the first one attempting to combine the force of social networks with that of automated identification tools [21]. It was launched in 2009 by a consortium involving research institutes in computer sciences, ecology and agriculture in collaboration with the Tela Botanica social network. This was the starting point of several scientific and technological productions [12] which finally led to the first release of the Pl@ntNet app (iOS in February 2013 [15] and Android [14] the following year). It was the first system allowing the use of a combination of different visual features (such as leaf, stem, fruit and flower) and the first one relying on a continuously enriched collaborative training set. This app was initially based on 800 species and was progressively enlarged to thousands of plant species of the European region (6 180 species up to now). Nowadays, the platform is being used by about 300K people who produce tens of thousands of validated plant observations each year thanks to collaborative validation tools (IdentiPlante[5] and PictoFlora[6]).

Nevertheless, this explicitly shared and validated data is only the tip of the iceberg. The real potential relies on the millions of raw image queries submitted by the users of the mobile application for which there is no human validation at all. As an illustration, in 2015, 2,328,502 queries were submitted by the users of the Pl@ntNet mobile apps but only less than 1 % of them were finally shared and collaboratively validated. Allowing the exploitation of the unvalidated observations in a fully automatic way could scale up the world-wide collection of plant records by several orders of magnitude. The idea of implicitly monitoring living organisms from any kind of User Generated Content data streams has the potential to revolutionize biodiversity monitoring at a limited cost. The images are submitted by hikers who want to know about plants along the way or people who find an unknown species in their garden. Allowing to include these observations into implicit monitoring could allow to get large amounts of monitoring data with GPS coordinates, altitude, time of the year to allow for monitoring changes between years and over longer periods of time. This can not replace explicit efforts but can complement them in ways that are otherwise impossible. Whereas occlusion is a common problem in computer vision and view points or color changes are as well, there are specific challenges to plants. Plants evolve strongly over the year, from color changes to blossoms, flowering and then fruits and non-professional photographers will get these incomplete or missing out potentially important detail. This creates interesting challenges of missing information and also changing information over the year as well as diversity also within species. Long term changes as in global warming require observations over a longer period of time. Only with implicit monitoring such challenges can really be tackled.

[2]http://www.inaturalist.org/

[3]http://www.tela-botanica.org/

[4]http://www.gbif.org/

[5]http://www.tela-botanica.org/appli:identiplante

[6]http://www.tela-botanica.org/appli:pictoflora

2. THE PLANTCLEF CHALLENGE: A FIVE-YEAR OVERVIEW

In order to evaluate the performance of automated plant identification technologies in a sustainable and repeatable way, a dedicated system-oriented benchmark was setup in 2011 in the context of ImageCLEF[7]. In 2011, 2012 and 2013 respectively 8, 11 and 12 research groups participated in this large collaborative evaluation by benchmarking their image-based plant identification systems (see [17, 18, 16] for more details). In 2014, the LifeCLEF research platform was created in the continuity of this effort so as to enlarge the evaluated challenges by considering birds and fishes in addition to plants, and audio and video contents in addition to images.

Within this context, the plant identification benchmark continued to be run yearly offering today a five-year follow-up of the progress in image-based plant identification. A particularity of the benchmark is that it always focused on real-world collaborative data contrary to most other testbeds that were created through well controlled laboratory conditions. Additionally, the evaluation protocol was defined in collaboration with biologists so as to reflect realistic usage scenarios. Notably particular attention was accorded to the notion of observation rather than considering standalone images. In practice, the same individual plant is actually often photographed several times by the same observer resulting in contextually similar pictures and/or near-duplicates. To avoid bias, it is crucial to consider such image sets as a single plant observation that should not be split across the training and test set. Besides this, the use of contextual and social data was also authorized when they were judged as potentially useful and accessible in a real-world usage scenario. This includes geo-tags or location names, time information, author names, collaborative ratings, vernacular names (common names), picture type tags, etc. It is however important to note that the visual modality remained largely predominant in all the best systems along the years and that the use of metadata was shown to provide only slight additional improvements.

Tables 1 and 2 give a year-to-year overview of the shared data and of the best performing systems (detailed descriptions of the results and systems can be found in the technical overview papers of each year [17, 13] and participant working notes). To allow a comprehensive comparison along the years, we isolated in Table 1 the *leaf scans* and *white background* image categories that were part of the evaluation of the three first years but that were abandoned afterwards. Table 2 focuses on photographs of plants in their natural environment (only leaves in 2011-2012, diverse organs and plant views in the following years). For a fair comparison, we also removed from the overview, the submissions that were humanly assisted in some point (*e.g.* involving a manual segmentation of the leaves). The evaluation metric that was used from 2011 to 2015 was *i.e.* an extension of the mean reciprocal rank [38] classically used in information retrieval.

[7]www.imageclef.org

Table 1: Three-year synthesis of the PlantCLEF challenge restricted to *leaf scans* and *pseudo-scans*

Year	#Species	#Images	#Evaluated systems	Score of best system	Brief description of best system
2011	71	3,967	20	0.574	. Various local features (around Harris points) . Hash-based indexing . RANSAC based matching
2012	126	9,356	30	0.565	. Shape and texture global features . SVM classifier
2013	250	11,031	33	0.607	. Shape and texture global features . SVM classifier

The difference is that it is based on a two-stage averaging rather than a flat averaging such as:

$$S = \frac{1}{U}\sum_{u=1}^{U}\frac{1}{P_u}\sum_{p=1}^{P_u}\frac{1}{r_{u,p}} \tag{1}$$

where U is the number of image authors within the test set, P_u the number of individual plants observed by the u-th author (within the test set), $r_{u,p}$ is the rank of the correct species within the ranked list of species returned by the evaluated system (for the p-th observation of the u-th author). Note that if the correct species does not appear in the returned list, its rank $r_{u,p}$ is considered as infinite. Overall, the proposed metric makes it possible to compensate the long-tail distribution effects of social data. As in any social network, few people actually produce huge quantities of data whereas a vast majority of contributors (the long tail) produce much less data.

The main conclusion we can derive from the results of Table 1 is that the classical approach to plant identification consisting of analyzing the morphology of the leaves reached its limit. Leaf shape boundary features and shape matching techniques have been studied during 30 years and can be considered as sufficiently mature for capturing shape information in a robust and invariant way. The limited performance is thus rather due to the intrinsic limitation of using only the leaf morphology for discriminating a large number of species. The phenomenon that scientists focused on leaf-based identification during years is more related to the fact that the leaf was easier to scan and to process with state-of-the-art computer vision techniques of that period (segmentation, shape matching, etc.). With the arrival of more advanced computer vision techniques, we were progressively able to make use of other parts of the plant such as flowers or fruits. For this reason, metrics on leaf scans were abandoned from the PlantCLEF evaluation after 2013.

Table 2 gives the five-year synthesis of this approach to plant identification that we promoted through PlantCLEF. The most interesting conclusion we can derive is that we observed considerable improvements of the scores along the years whereas the difficulty of the task was increasing. The number of classes almost doubled every year between 2011 and 2015, starting from 71 species in 2011 and reaching 1000 species in 2015. The increase of the performance can be explained by two major technological breakthroughs. The first was the use of *aggregation-based* or *coding-based* image representation methods such as the Fisher Vector representation [29], that was used by the best performing system of Nakayama *et al.* [26] in 2013 and Chen *et al.* [6] in 2014. These methods consist of producing high-dimensional representations of the images by aggregating previously extracted sets of hand-crafted local features into a global vector representation. They rely on a two step process: (i) the learning of a set of latent variables that explain the distribution of the local features in the training set (denoted as the codebook or vocabulary), and (ii) the encoding of the relationship between the local features of a given image and the latent variables. Overall, this allows to embed the fine-grained visual content of each image into a single representation space in which classes are easily separable even with linear classifiers.

The second technological step explaining the last increase of performance is the use of deep learning methods, in particular convolutional neural networks (CNN) such as GoogLeNet [35]. In 2015, the 10 best evaluated systems were based on CNN. The difference of performance is mainly due to particular system design improvements such as the use of bagging in the best run of Choi [7]. CNNs recently received a high amount of attention caused by the impressive performance they achieved in the ImageNet classification task [24]. The force of these technologies relies on their ability to learn discriminant visual features directly from the raw pixels of the images without falling in the trap of the curse of dimensionality. This is achieved by stacking multiple *convolutional layers*, *i.e.* the core building blocks of a CNN. A convolutional layer basically takes images as input and produces as output *feature maps* corresponding to different convolution kernels, *i.e* looking for different visual patterns. Looking at the impressive results achieved by CNN's in the 2015 edition of PlantCLEF there is absolutely no doubt that they are able to capture discriminant visual patterns of the plants in a much more effective way than previously engineered visual features.

Besides purely visual concerns, we present in Table 3 the results obtained by the participants who attempted to use of the metadata associated to each image, specifically the one related to geography and seasonality. One can first see that among the large number of teams involved during the five years of the challenge, only few actually used the geolocation and date information. None of them obtained the best performance (the best identification methods were always based on visual content only). The best improvement was achieved by the Inria team in 2013. It was obtained by post-filtering the list of candidate species based on a flowering period histogram of each species constructed from the training set (at the week level). This difficulty of successfully using geography and seasonality is quite surprising. It is actually obvious that the habitat of a given species is highly correlated with its ecological profile. Several reasons

Table 2: Five-year synthesis of the PlantCLEF challenge (plants in their natural environment)

Year	#Species	#Images	#Evaluated systems	Score of best system	Brief description of best system
2011	71	1,469	20	0.251	. Model-driven segmentation Shape features . Random forests
2012	126	2,216	30	0.320	. Multi-scale local (color) texture SIFT + Sparse coding Spatial Pyramidal Matching . Linear SVM
2013	250	11,046	33	0.393	. Dense-SIFT, C-SIFT, Opponent SIFT HSV-SIF, self-similarity SSIM . Fisher Vectors . Linear Logistic Regression . Late fusion
2014	500	60,962	28	0.471	. ROI segmentation dense-SIFT + Color Moment . Fisher Vectors . SVM on FVs
2015	1000	113,2051	18	0.667	. GoogLeNet CNN . 5-fold bagging + Borda fusion

explain this paradox. The first one is that the occurrence data of the training set is too sparse to accurately model the distribution of the species. The second reason is that the used machine learning techniques were too straightforward to well address the problem. As discussed in section 4, species distribution modeling from occurrence data is actually still a hard problem in ecology, in particular in the context of uncontrolled observations such as the one used in the PlantCLEF challenge.

3. PL@NTNET IMPACT STUDY

Pl@ntNet is among the most advanced infrastructures in the world making use of automated identification tools for monitoring biodiversity. To measure the impact of the initiative, we did survey by email a large panel of authenticated Pl@ntnet users, *i.e.* users who created a user profile on the Pl@ntNet apps. Among the authenticated 20 859 users, and 20 003 successfully sent emails, we received a total of 719 responses within 2 weeks. The survey included a first part, common to all users, that was dedicated to the collection of personal information (place of residence, age, email and usage frequency of Pl@ntNet). The second part was specific to the two main types of use of the application: *professional* vs. *recreational*. The part related to *professionals* included 22 questions, such as their job, in which sector are they working (private or public), how often they use the application, to what extent this app has allowed to improve their botanical skills, etc. The part related to *recreational* included 22 questions too, such as the description of the situation that made them download the app (curiosity, gardening, hiking, etc.), if the application has changed their practices, their attention to nature, what is their interest for new functions. The survey was completed by several focus groups and interviews organised with representatives of different domains: (i) scientific domain (ecology, computer science) and citizen science, (ii) agriculture, (iii) biodiversity management, (iv) education.

The vast majority of respondents in the survey were located in France (85.7%) and the rest was mostly divided between Belgium (4.9%), Switzerland, Spain (1.8%) and North America (Canada 1% USA and 0.8%). This is surprising as only 30% of Pl@ntNet users are actually in France (662,295 vs. 1,490,646 outside of France). The most likely reason of this bias is that the sent email was written in French and English only, and that the English translation was provided below the French one. It appears that more than 65% of users are over 40 years old. This illustrates that even if the transfer of knowledge to young people on mobile devices seems to be facilitated by the use of this device, a greater effort is needed if we want to enlarge their attractiveness to this type of initiative.

A majority of users exploit Pl@ntNet for their recreation (88 %). This can explain the peaks of use noticed since 2013, during weekends. Most of the users in this category used Pl@ntNet in a garden or during a trekking. The horticultural and trekking domains are probably the two most important in which this kind of application can have a strong impact. Gardens are becoming more urban with the recent evolution of our societies. This recreational activity is motivated by a variety of factors from a stronger immersion in nature to gastronomy.

Based on this survey, the proportion of Pl@ntNet use for professional purposes is about 12% (which represents a volume of 1,200,000 sessions mobilized for professional activities considering the total number of sessions of over 10M). The most frequently represented professional activity is landscape management (34.6%). It includes landscape workers, managers and architects, as well as foresters. The second category is more concerned with the production and/or transfer of knowledge (23.5%), that is to say, teachers (in botany, biology, horticulture), students (in horticultural production for example), trainers (landscape management, aromatherapy, herbal medicine, etc.), facilitators (botanists, nature guides) and scientists (biologists mainly). The category of ground workers represents 16% of profes-

Table 3: **Impact of the use of geography and seasonality for plant species identification**

Year	Teams	Metadata type	Run type	Score	Improvement
2011	UAIC	GPS, Date, Author Id	. Visual . Visual + metadata	. 0.156 . 0.1	-0.056
2012	IFSC USP [3]	GPS	. Visual + metadata	. 0.16	Unknown
2012	BTU DBIS [2]	GPS	. Visual . Visual + metadata	. 0.21 . 0.2	-0.01
2013	SCG USP	GPS	. Textual	. 0.025	Unknown
2013	LIRIS [5]	GPS	. Visual + metadata	. 0.092	Unknown
2013	UAIC [31]	GPS, Author Id	. Visual + metadata	. 0.127	Unknown
2013	SABANCI-OKAN [44]	Date	. Visual + metadata	. 0.181	Unknown
2013	Inria [1]	Date	. Visual . Visual + metadata	. 0.353 . 0.385	+0.032
2014	SABANCI-OKAN [43]	Date	. Visual + metadata	. 0.127	Unknown

sional respondents. This category includes farmers, nurserymen, horticulturists and gardeners.

To further illustrate the potential future impact of Pl@ntNet, Figure 1 provides a cartography of the number of identification sessions performed through the Pl@ntNet Android version in April 2016. For the countries accounting for the most users, we provide the number of sessions as well as its increase in percentage compared to the same period in 2015 (so as to illustrate the dynamic). It first shows a strong increase in the countries neighboring France (in Italy and Spain the number of sessions was actually multiplied by respectively 35 and 22). This is not surprising since there is a high intersection between the floras of those countries and the one of France, which was the starting point in the first release of the Android application in March 2014. We thus observe a geographic diffusion of the usage of the application that is related to the increasing coverage of the related species in the database as well as to the media coverage. We also observe a very strong progression in South America that is related to the release of a version of Pl@ntNet working on the Guyana flora in October 2015. Finally, we can also observe a relatively lower but still strong increase in North America whereas no specific version of Pl@ntNet was released there.

Whatever the future of the Pl@ntNet initiative in itself is, this impact study clearly shows that domain-specific mobile search technologies are attracting strong interest. We can thus hypothesize that such new practices of questioning our environment will bring a lasting production of plant and animal observations. The implicit biodiversity monitoring scenario introduced in this paper is thus realistic from a societal point of view. Now it still raises brave new research challenges.

4. FROM EXPLICIT TO IMPLICIT PLANT BIODIVERSITY MONITORING

Whereas previous approaches to monitor plant biodiversity were based on the explicit sharing of plant observations (be they partially automated or not), the new concept we introduce in this paper is the implicit detection of plant occurrences in *mobile search logs* (or more generally in any stream of geo-localized user generated pictures). In recent years, we actually saw the arrival of more and more *mobile search* applications such as LikeThat, Goggles or CamFind,

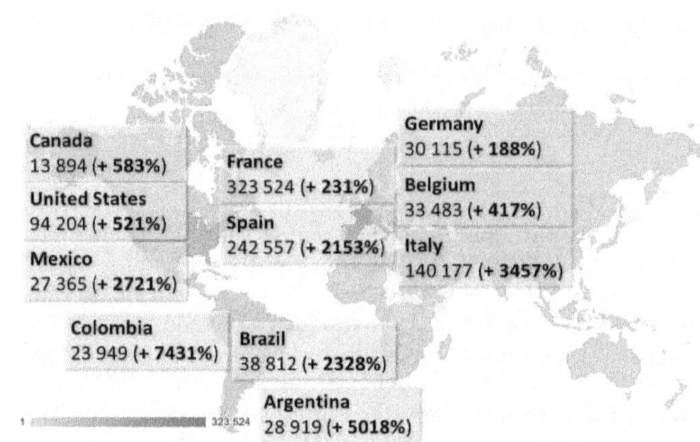

Figure 1: Cartography of the number of Pl@ntNet Android sessions in April 2016 (increase over April 2015 in parenthesis).

that allow users to get information about surrounding objects by simply photographing them These applications are still far from well recognizing any domain-specific object, but on the other side their search logs capture the user's interest about the world's objects at a very large scale and high rate. They generate quantities of geo-localized visual data that are noisy but might be used to monitor our environment and enrich its visual knowledge. In this paper, we focus on the search logs of the Pl@ntNet *mobile search* application, but in essence, the challenges we discuss could apply to any other mobile search application. As a concrete illustration, Figure 2 provides a small sample of geo-localized and dated image queries that were submitted to the Pl@ntNet application.

Challenge 1 - Dealing with novelty and uncertainty. Knowing how much automatically predicted labels can be trusted is essential for further data processing such as human validation or direct statistical analysis. A good knowledge of the uncertainty of the automatic predictions is actually required to select the most beneficial ones (for a given scenario) or to devise robust statistical inference methods. In our implicit biodiversity monitoring scenario, any automated species detection should thus be systematically associated to a confidence score in $[0, 1]$ quantifying the prob-

Figure 2: A sample of the geo-localized image search logs of Pl@ntNet mobile application

ability that this prediction is true, independently from the other predictions. Doing so in the context of a noisy visual data stream such as Pl@ntNet search logs is a hard problem for two main reasons: (i) the massive presence of unknown classes in the stream (because it works in an open world) and (ii), the heavily imbalanced training set (that is inevitable when dealing with biodiversity data). When launching a new country-specific instance of Pl@ntNet, the proportion of images belonging to unknown classes can for instance be very high, up to 80%. It can remain high even in the long term because of the continuous emergence of new classes. Estimating the probability of the membership to an open set of unknown classes is thus a crucial preliminary step before being able to model the ambiguity over the known classes. This is in essence a *novelty detection* problem (see e.g. [28] for a comprehensive review) but the fact that the data set is highly imbalanced increases the difficulty of the problem. Indeed, as the majority of the known classes in the long tail only contains few training samples, they are likely to be confused with the unknown classes when using classical novelty detection algorithms. To deal with this problem, it is required to detect the novelty at the image level, for instance by estimating the uncertainty of the visual representation of each image during the learning process.

Challenge 2 - Enriching the training set in a collaborative way. One of the main sources of uncertainty when trying to recognize plants in image search logs, is the lack of training data in sufficient quantity and quality. The majority of the images in the search logs do belong to either unknown classes, *i.e.* with no training samples in the training set, or to weakly supervised classes, *i.e.* with very few training samples. A straightforward solution to reduce the uncertainty of the predictions is thus to enrich the training set. Actually, recent deep learning models, such as convolutional neural networks [24], are capable of learning very effective visual features directly from the raw image pixels but to outperform the previous methods based on hand-crafted visual features, they still need to be trained on rich visual data with diverse enough visual patterns and accurate class labels. Such ideal content is unfortunately missing for the vast majority of plant species that lie in the long tail of existing data distribution Large domain-specific collections such as Encyclopedia of Life (EOL) archives include quantities of well structured tags across many plant groups but they are not aimed at labeling precise domain-specific elements (e.g. spine, latex, buds, etc.), nor at covering their diversity. On the other side, computer-vision oriented data sets such as ImageNet [9] are only focused on the most popular species of the web and are too noisy from a taxonomic perspective (mix of common, species and genus names, confusions across species, etc.).

In the end, the most beneficial way to enrich the training set (and reduce the uncertainty of the predictions) is to directly annotate a fraction of the search logs themselves. Applying state-of-the-art crowdsourcing approaches in this regard is however impossible (*e.g.* [23, 34, 37]). First, the brute-force approach consisting of a quiz across the full list of species would only be tractable for the few specialists of a given flora, thus drastically limiting the potential number of annotators. Second, the very high number of classes (*i.e.* species), makes it impossible to train a complete confusion matrix for each annotator as it would require to answer to a large number of queries (typically quadratic in the number of classes). A much more promising approach is thus to devise effective *collaborative active learning* algorithms, *i.e.* learning algorithms that actively select samples to be annotated as well as annotators in a joint objective. The main underlying assumption is that even non-specialists are capable of recognizing a few tens of species (if we teach them), so that in the end, they might collectively solve complex classification tasks with thousands of classes. As in crowdsourcing algorithms, this paradigm supposes that we can model the imperfection of the annotators typically by inferring their confusion based on the labels they provide. Additionally, it requires inventing *active training* strategies aimed at training the annotators on confusions that exist within the data. Overall, *collaborative active learning* poses several fundamental questions: (i) how to optimize the selection and assignment of the unvalidated samples? (ii) how to model the learning process of the annotators to train them effectively and complementary? (iii) how to design new machine learning algorithms and/or statistical inference methods that deal with the partial knowledge of the annotators?

Challenge 3 - Using the taxonomy to reduce uncertainty. Graph-based knowledge representations such as taxonomies or ontologies are available for many domains, in particular those with high expertise such as botany. When such a rich organization of the visual class labels exists, it is likely to facilitate the estimation and reduction of the uncertainty. More precisely, it allows restricting our general problem to the case where the unknown classes occurring in an uncertain visual data stream are supposed to have at least one parent in the taxonomy of the known classes. Thanks to this relaxation, challenges 1 and 2 can be revisited in a radically different manner. We can actually now have a hierarchical representation of the uncertainty, typically through hierarchical conditional probabilities. Such hierarchical structuring of the uncertainty is likely to be very effective for breaking the complexity due to an extremely large number of classes. The automatic prediction of the uncertainty of the unlabeled visual data might for instance benefit from the knowledge of the label structure by using it as a way of post-checking the veracity of a given prediction a posteriori. Concerning the collaborative active learning framework, both the active training of the annotators, the task assignment and the inference methods could be revised. For instance novices should start on easy to discriminate nodes of the taxonomy whereas the most advanced contributors should tackle the leaves of the taxonomy that are the most difficult to disambiguate.

Challenge 4 - Using environmental data to reduce taxonomic uncertainty. As discussed in section 2, using occurrence information (*i.e.* the geo-location and the date of the observation) did not conduct to significant identification improvement in the past PlantCLEF evaluation campaigns because of the sparsity of the occurrence in the training set. Thus, a first naive solution could be to use much larger occurrence data such as the one collected through the world-scale GBIF initiative. However, even with such big data, sparsity would still be a challenge, in particular for the vast majority of species lying in the long tail distribution. Actually, producing masses of occurrences, timely and globally, is precisely the objective of the implicit biodiversity monitoring scenario proposed in this paper. So that, it is somehow a chicken-egg problem. Improving plant identification systems thanks to geography would require accurate species distribution models but, on the other side, building such models requires large amounts of occurrence data and would clearly benefit from automated identification tools. A solution to that problem might rely in the use of external environmental data such as habitat maps[8], climate maps, soil characteristic maps, topographical maps, etc. Such data do actually less suffer from the sparsity problem and many regions of the world are well covered with such information. Thus, it might be possible to learn the ecological profile of each species by correlating its occurrences with the environmental variables and then predict the likelihood of its presence in other regions. Several challenges remain. Human impact does notably alter the correlation between plant habitats and environmental variables. In cities and other highly frequented places, the presence of a species is for instance rather correlated to its usage by humans (e.g. potted plants, parks, etc.). Human equipments such as roads or railways as well as human activities such as agriculture or forestry tend to quickly and deeply modify species distribution and to fragment the habitats.

Challenge 5 - Controlling observer and detection bias in species distribution models As for any presence-only data (*i.e* where information is available concerning species presence but not species absence), Pl@ntNet search logs are subject to bias due to observers being more likely to visit and record sightings at some locations than others. Such *observer bias* has already been studied in some recent work on species distribution models (SDM) [39, 36]. The goal is typically to model species occurrence data through a distribution N_{ij} $p(A_{ij}, B_{ij})$ where Aij is the relative abundance of species i in place j (to be estimated), and B_{ij} is a more or less complex observer bias. In the context of the implicit monitoring scenario developed in this paper, modeling the bias is even more challenging. It actually depends on both *observer bias* and *detection bias* as illustrated by the probabilistic graphical model of Figure 3 that we built as a first attempt to model the problem. Incorporating taxonomic confusion in the species distribution models has in particular never been addressed before and offers brave new research perspectives at the frontier of ecological modeling and machine learning. This approach might lay the foundation to a new data-driven research field, *probabilistic taxonomy*, that has the real potential to scale up biodiversity and phenological studies to several orders of magnitude. Actually, the presence of determination errors, even with low ratios, often makes biodiversity researchers skeptical on the usefulness of crowdsourced or machine-learning based data for conducting trustable biodiversity studies. Incorporating the taxonomic uncertainty in the models and analyzing the extent to which this uncertainty yields error in SDM predictions, is thus a crucial step towards automatizing biodiversity monitoring.

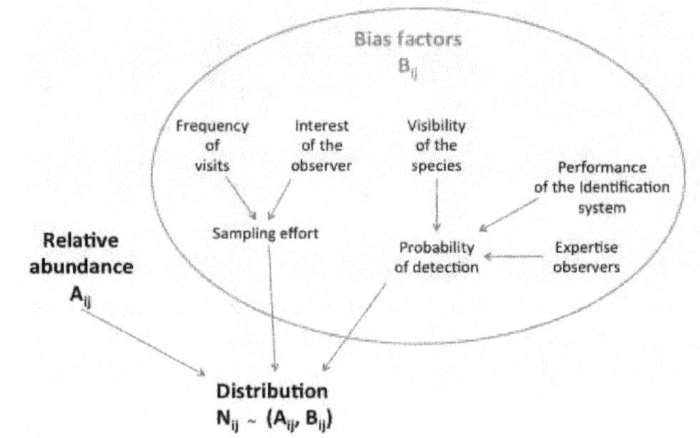

Figure 3: Probabilistic graphical model of observer and detection bias

5. IMPLICIT MONITORING OF INVASIVE SPECIES FROM MOBILE SEARCH LOGS

As a first step towards evaluating the feasibility of the implicit biodiversity monitoring paradigm, we conducted an experimental study in the context of the plant task of the LifeCLEF 2016 evaluation campaign. Therefore, we created and shared a new testbed entirely composed of image search logs of the Pl@ntNet mobile application (in contrast to the previous editions of the benchmark that were based on explicitly shared and validated plant observations). We expect that data availability will increase in the coming years, allowing to make even larger sets available to the research community.

5.1 Usage scenario

As a concrete scenario, we focused on the monitoring of invasive exotic plant species. These species represent a major economic cost to our society (estimated at nearly 12 billion euros a year in Europe) and one of the main threats to biodiversity conservation [40]. This cost can be even more important at the country level, such as in China where it is evaluated to about 15 billion US dollars annually [41], and more than 34 billion US dollars in the US [27]. The early detection of the appearance of these species, are key elements to manage them, and reduce the cost of their management. The analysis of Pl@ntNet search logs can provide a highly valuable response to this problem because the presence of these species is highly correlated with that of humans More generally, the Pl@ntNet platform has a high potential for the monitoring and early detection of threats to biodiversity related to human activities.

5.2 Data

We used the PlantCLEF 2015 dataset enriched with the groundtruth annotations of the test images (that were kept secret during the 2015 campaign). This data set contains 113,205 pictures of herb, tree and fern specimens belonging to 1,000 species (living in France and neighboring countries). Each image is associated with an xml file containing the taxonomic groundtruth (and in particular the species level ClassId), as well as other meta-data such as the type of view (fruit, flower, entire plant, etc.), the quality rating (social-based), the author name, the observation Id, the date and the geo-loc (for some of the observations).

For the test set, we started with a randomized selection of 30K image queries that were submitted by authenticated users of the Pl@ntNet mobile application. Among this set, 3049 images had already been shared by their authors within the collaborative validation tools and were thus associated with a valid species name. The remaining pictures were distributed to three botanists in charge of manually annotating them either with a valid species name from the France flora repository or with newly created tags of their choice (and shared between them). In the period of time devoted to this process, they were able to manually annotate 4951 pictures (so as to reach 8000 images in total). Therefore, 82 new tags were created to qualify the unknown classes such as for instance *non-plant objects*, *legs* or *hands*, *UVO* (Unidentified Vegetal Object), *artificial plants*, *cactaceae*, *mushrooms*, *animals*, *food*, *vegetables* or more precise names of horticultural plants such as roses, geraniums, ficus, etc. For privacy reasons, we removed from the test set all images tagged as *people* (although they represented about 1.1% of the queries). In the end, the test set of 8,000 pictures included 3482 tagged with the newly created classes (i.e. the ones not in the training set of 1,000 species). Moreover it included 366 images belonging to a selected list of 26 potentially invasive species. This list was defined by aggregating several sources (such as the National Botanical conservatory, and the Global Invasive Species Programme) and computing the intersection with the 1000 species of the training set. The final number of invasive specimens in the test set might appear rather low (366). However, it represents 1.22 % of the sample of Pl@ntNet queries used to create the test set. If we confront this statistic with the millions of queries collected each year through Pl@ntNet, we could hope monitoring critical species at an unprecedented rate without any additional cost or effort for the society.

5.3 Evaluation protocol

Based on the testbed, we conducted a system-oriented evaluation involving 8 research groups who downloaded the data and ran their system. To prevent participants from tuning their algorithms on the invasive species scenario and keep our evaluation generalizable, we did not provide the list of species to be detected. Participants only knew that the targeted species were included in a larger set of 1000 species for which we provided a large training set (actually the full dataset used in PlantCLEF 2015). Participants were also aware that (i) most of the test data does not belong to the targeted list of species (ii) a large fraction does not belong to the training set of the 1000 species, and (iii) a fraction of them might not even be plants. In essence, the task to be addressed is related to what is sometimes called *open-set* or *open-world* recognition problems [30], i.e. problems in which the recognition system has to be robust to unknown and never seen categories. Beyond the brute-force classification across the known classes of the training set, a big challenge is thus to automatically reject the false positive classification hits that are caused by the unknown classes (i.e. by the distractors). To measure this ability of the evaluated systems, each prediction had to be associated with a confidence score in $[0, 1]$ quantifying the probability that this prediction is true (independently from the other predictions).

5.4 Overview of the evaluated systems

The 8 participating research groups submitted 29 *runs* corresponding to different configurations of their systems. 26 were based on CNNs and the different systems mainly differed in (i) the architecture of the used CNN, (ii) the way in which the rejection of the unknown classes was managed and (iii), various system design improvements. We give hereafter a few more details of the 3 systems that performed the best (on the invasive species). A more detailed description of these systems can be found in the working notes written by the participants and published in the CLEF working notes.

Bluefield system: A VGGNet [33] based system with the addition of Spatial Pyramid Pooling, Parametric ReLU and unknown class rejection based on the minimal prediction score of training data (Run 1). Run 2 is the same as run 1 but with a slightly different rejection making use of a validation set. Run 3 and 4 are respectively the same as Run 1 and 2 but the scores of the images belonging to the same observation were summed and normalised.

Sabanci system: A CNN based system with 2 main configurations. Run 1: An ensemble of GoogleLeNet [35] and VGGNet [33] fine-tuned on both LifeCLEF 2015 data (for recognizing the targeted species) and on 70K images of the ILSCVR dataset (for rejecting unknown classes). Run 2 is the same than Run 1 but without rejection.

CMP system: A ResNet [19] based system with the use of bagging in Run 1 (3 networks) and without bagging (in Run 2).

5.5 Results

Figure 4 provides the mean Average Precision (mAP) of the best fully automated systems considering only the selected list of 26 invasive species as queries (only the best 2 runs of each team were kept). The mAP is computed either in open-world (*i.e.* by considering all images of the test set) or in closed-world (*i.e.* by considering only the images of the test set belonging to the 1000 species of the training set). The figure shows that the presence of the unknown classes degrades the performance of all systems in a roughly similar way. This difficulty of rejecting the unknown classes is confirmed by the very low difference between the runs of the participants who experimented their system with or without reject (*e.g.* Sabanci Run 1 vs. Run 2 or FlorisTic Run 1 vs. Run 2). On the other side, it is noticeable that all systems are quite robust to the presence of unknown classes since the drop in performance is not so high. Actually, as the CNNs were pre-trained on a large generalist data set beforehand, it is likely that they have learned a diverse enough set of visual patterns to avoid underfitting.

To better fit the implicit biodiversity monitoring scenario addressed in this paper, we completed this experiment by additional measurements more focused on high-precision operating points. If we would like the automatic predictions of the evaluated systems to be automatically integrated in an international biodiversity records database (such as GBIF), it is essential to guaranty a very high quality of the identification. Therefore, Figure 5 provides a precision/recall plot of the two best systems (in two configurations). The plot was obtained by varying the threshold of the confidence score t

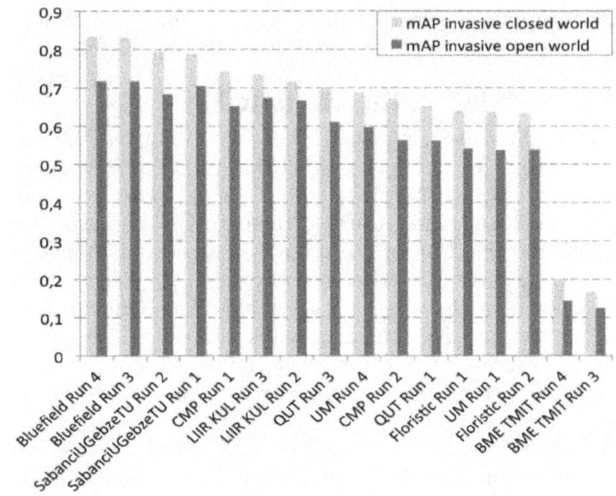

Figure 4: mean Average Precision (mAP) on the 26 invasive species in open- and closed-world

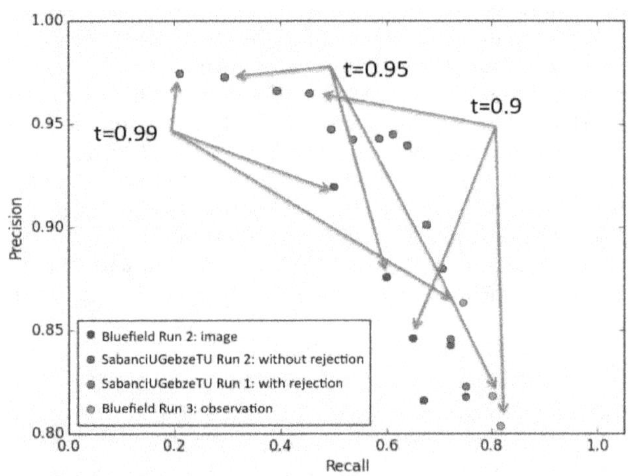

Figure 5: Precision-recall values of best systems for highly confident operating points (probability threshold $t \in [0.9, 0.99]$)

of each system and by measuring the recall and precision at each operating point. This experiment shows that for high precision values such as 0.99 or 0.95 only the Sabanci system evaluated in Run 1 is able to return results. However, this high precision at the price of low recall values, around 40% on average (and much lower for some of the species). In all other systems, the trust in false positives is too high and prevents reaching high precision values acceptable for biologists. This shows that the strategy of Sabanci consisting of adding a supervised rejection class is effective for managing unknown classes although it is theoretically less elegant than devising new novelty detection algorithms. Interestingly, the run of Bluefield averaging the predictions of the images belonging to the same observation provided significant improvements in recall but failed to reach high precision operating points. This does not mean that the multi-view information should not be considered as a way to deal with novelty. It rather indicates that the averaging of the predictions of the different views in not an adapted fusion scheme. Other fusion strategies should thus be explored so as to improve specificity.

6. CONCLUSIONS

The new concept we explored in this paper is the automated detection of plant occurrences in *mobile search logs* as a way to monitor biodiversity without asking the users to explicitly share and validate their observations. We showed through an impact study of the Pl@ntNet initiative that this concept is realistic from a societal point of view and that it could scale-up the world-wide collection of plant observations by several orders of magnitude. To assess the technical feasibility of such an implicit biodiversity monitoring, we summarized five years of the PlantCLEF evaluation benchmark and organized a new dedicated evaluation task within the 2016 campaign. Results show that automated plant identification systems considerably progressed during the last years thanks to successive technological advances (aggregation-based image representations and convolutional neural networks). However, in the context of very noisy content such as mobile search logs, reaching high precision is still challenging. Jointly dealing with novelty, uncertainty and highly imbalanced training data is actually a hard problem for which we suggested some new research directions. In the end, our study shows that there is still some room of improvement before being able to automatically share implicit observations within international biodiversity platforms.

7. ADDITIONAL AUTHORS

Timothée Morin (Cirad, Umr AMAP), Antoine Affouard (Inria, ZENITH team, LIRMM), Jean-François Molino (IRD, Umr AMAP), Daniel Barthélémy (Dir-BIOS, CIRAD) and Nozha Boujemaa (Dir-Inria).

8. ACKNOWLEDGMENTS

This work has been done throughout the Pl@ntNet project, supported by Agropolis Fondation, the French foundation for Agricultural Sciences and Sustainable Development.

9. REFERENCES

[1] V. Bakic, S. Mouine, S. Ouertani-Litayem, A. Verroust-Blondet, I. Yahiaoui, H. Goëau, and A. Joly. Inria's participation at imageclef 2013 plant identification task. In *CLEF (Online Working Notes/Labs/Workshop) 2013*, 2013.

[2] T. Böttcher, C. Schmidt, D. Zellhöfer, and I. Schmitt. Btu dbis'plant identification runs at imageclef 2012. In *CLEF (Online Working Notes/Labs/Workshop)*, 2012.

[3] D. Casanova, J. B. Florindo, W. N. Gonçalves, and O. M. Bruno. Ifsc/usp at imageclef 2012: Plant identification task. In *CLEF (Online Working Notes/Labs/Workshop)*, 2012.

[4] G. Cerutti, L. Tougne, J. Mille, A. Vacavant, and D. Coquin. Understanding leaves in natural images–a model-based approach for tree species identification. *Computer Vision and Image Understanding*, 117(10):1482–1501, 2013.

[5] G. Cerutti, L. Tougne, C. Sacca, T. Joliveau, P.-O. Mazagol, D. Coquin, and A. Vacavant. Late information fusion for multi-modality plant species identification. In *Conference and Labs of the Evaluation Forum*, pages Working–Notes, 2013.

[6] Q. Chen, M. Abedini, R. Garnavi, and X. Liang. Ibm research australia at lifeclef2014: Plant identification task. In *CLEF (Working Notes)*, pages 693–704, 2014.

[7] S. Choi. Plant identification with deep convolutional neural network: Snumedinfo at lifeclef plant identification task 2015. In *Working notes of CLEF 2015 conference*, 2015.

[8] C. E. Davies, D. Moss, and M. O. Hill. Eunis habitat classification revised 2004. *Report to: European Environment Agency-European Topic Centre on Nature Protection and Biodiversity*, pages 127–143, 2004.

[9] J. Deng, W. Dong, R. Socher, L.-J. Li, K. Li, and L. Fei-Fei. Imagenet: A large-scale hierarchical image database. In *Computer Vision and Pattern Recognition, 2009. CVPR 2009. IEEE Conference on*, pages 248–255. IEEE, 2009.

[10] A. Foncubierta-Rodríguez and H. Müller. Ground Truth Generation in Medical Imaging: A Crowdsourcing Based Iterative Approach. In *Workshop on Crowdsourcing for Multimedia, ACM Multimedia*, oct 2012.

[11] K. J. Gaston and M. A. O'Neill. Automated species identification: why not? *Philosophical Transactions of the Royal Society of London B: Biological Sciences*, 359(1444):655–667, 2004.

[12] H. Goëau, P. Bonnet, J. Barbe, V. Bakic, A. Joly, J.-F. Molino, D. Barthelemy, and N. Boujemaa. Multi-organ plant identification. In *Proceedings of the 1st ACM international workshop on Multimedia analysis for ecological data*, pages 41–44. ACM, 2012.

[13] H. Goëau, P. Bonnet, and A. Joly. The lifeclef plant identification task 2016. In CEUR-WS, editor, *CLEF*, CLEF2016 working notes, Evora, Portugal, 2016.

[14] H. Goëau, P. Bonnet, A. Joly, A. Affouard, V. Bakic, J. Barbe, S. Dufour, S. Selmi, I. Yahiaoui, C. Vignau, et al. Pl@ntnet mobile 2014: Android port and new features. In *Proceedings of international conference on multimedia retrieval*, page 527. ACM, 2014.

[15] H. Goëau, P. Bonnet, A. Joly, V. Bakić, J. Barbe, I. Yahiaoui, S. Selmi, J. Carré, D. Barthélémy, N. Boujemaa, et al. Pl@ tnet mobile app. In *Proceedings of the 21st ACM international conference on Multimedia*, pages 423–424. ACM, 2013.

[16] H. Goëau, P. Bonnet, A. Joly, V. Bakic, D. Barthélémy, N. Boujemaa, and J.-F. Molino. The imageclef 2013 plant identification task. In *CLEF*, Valencia, Spain, 2013.

[17] H. Goëau, P. Bonnet, A. Joly, N. Boujemaa, D. Barthélémy, J.-F. Molino, P. Birnbaum, E. Mouysset, and M. Picard. The imageclef 2011 plant images classification task. In *CLEF 2011*, 2011.

[18] H. Goëau, P. Bonnet, A. Joly, I. Yahiaoui, D. Barthélémy, N. Boujemaa, and J.-F. Molino. The imageclef 2012 plant images identification task. In *CLEF*, Rome, Italy, 2012.

[19] K. He, X. Zhang, S. Ren, and J. Sun. Deep residual learning for image recognition. *arXiv preprint arXiv:1512.03385*, 2015.

[20] A. Joly, P. Bonnet, H. Goëau, J. Barbe, S. Selmi, J. Champ, S. Dufour-Kowalski, A. Affouard, J. Carré, J.-F. Molino, et al. A look inside the pl@ ntnet experience. *Multimedia Systems*, pages 1–16, 2015.

[21] A. Joly, H. Goëau, P. Bonnet, V. Bakić, J. Barbe, S. Selmi, I. Yahiaoui, J. Carré, E. Mouysset, J.-F. Molino, et al. Interactive plant identification based on social image data. *Ecological Informatics*, 23:22–34, 2014.

[22] A. Joly, H. Goëau, H. Glotin, C. Spampinato, P. Bonnet, W.-P. Vellinga, R. Planqué, A. Rauber, S. Palazzo, B. Fisher, et al. Lifeclef 2015: multimedia life species identification challenges. In *Experimental IR Meets Multilinguality, Multimodality, and Interaction*, pages 462–483. Springer, 2015.

[23] H.-C. Kim and Z. Ghahramani. Bayesian classifier combination. In *International conference on artificial intelligence and statistics*, pages 619–627, 2012.

[24] A. Krizhevsky, I. Sutskever, and G. E. Hinton. Imagenet classification with deep convolutional neural networks. In *Advances in neural information processing systems*, pages 1097–1105, 2012.

[25] N. Kumar, P. N. Belhumeur, A. Biswas, D. W. Jacobs, W. J. Kress, I. C. Lopez, and J. V. Soares. Leafsnap: A computer vision system for automatic plant species identification. In *Computer Vision–ECCV 2012*, pages 502–516. Springer, 2012.

[26] H. Nakayama. Nlab-utokyo at imageclef 2013 plant identification task. In *CLEF (Working Notes)*, 2013.

[27] D. Pimentel, R. Zuniga, and D. Morrison. Update on the environmental and economic costs associated with alien-invasive species in the united states. *Ecological economics*, 52(3):273–288, 2005.

[28] M. A. Pimentel, D. A. Clifton, L. Clifton, and L. Tarassenko. A review of novelty detection. *Signal Processing*, 99:215–249, 2014.

[29] J. Sánchez, F. Perronnin, T. Mensink, and J. Verbeek. Image classification with the fisher vector: Theory and practice. *International journal of computer vision*, 105(3):222–245, 2013.

[30] W. J. Scheirer, L. P. Jain, and T. E. Boult. Probability models for open set recognition. *IEEE Transactions on Pattern Analysis and Machine Intelligence (T-PAMI)*, 36, November 2014.

[31] C. Şerban, A. Siriţeanu, C. Gheorghiu, A. Iftene, L. Alboaie, and M. Breabăn. Combining image retrieval, metadata processing and naive bayes classification at plant identification 2013. 2013.

[32] J. Silvertown, M. Harvey, R. Greenwood, M. Dodd, J. Rosewell, T. Rebelo, J. Ansine, and K. McConway. Crowdsourcing the identification of organisms: A case-study of ispot. *ZooKeys*, (480):125, 2015.

[33] K. Simonyan and A. Zisserman. Very deep convolutional networks for large-scale image recognition. *CoRR*, abs/1409.1556, 2014.

[34] E. Simpson, S. Roberts, I. Psorakis, and A. Smith. Dynamic bayesian combination of multiple imperfect classifiers. In *Decision Making and Imperfection*, pages 1–35. Springer, 2013.

[35] C. Szegedy, W. Liu, Y. Jia, P. Sermanet, S. Reed, D. Anguelov, D. Erhan, V. Vanhoucke, and A. Rabinovich. Going deeper with convolutions. In *Proceedings of the IEEE Conference on Computer Vision and Pattern Recognition*, pages 1–9, 2015.

[36] J. Velásquez-Tibatá, C. H. Graham, and S. B. Munch. Using measurement error models to account for georeferencing error in species distribution models. *Ecography*, 2015.

[37] M. Venanzi, J. Guiver, G. Kazai, P. Kohli, and M. Shokouhi. Community-based bayesian aggregation models for crowdsourcing. In *Proceedings of the 23rd international conference on World wide web*, pages 155–164. ACM, 2014.

[38] E. M. Voorhees et al. The trec-8 question answering track report. In *Trec*, volume 99, pages 77–82, 1999.

[39] D. I. Warton, I. W. Renner, and D. Ramp. Model-based control of observer bias for the analysis of presence-only data in ecology. *PloS one*, 8(11):e79168, 2013.

[40] E. Weber and D. Gut. Assessing the risk of potentially invasive plant species in central europe. *Journal for Nature Conservation*, 12(3):171–179, 2004.

[41] E. Weber, S.-G. Sun, and B. Li. Invasive alien plants in china: diversity and ecological insights. *Biological Invasions*, 10(8):1411–1429, 2008.

[42] B. Yanikoglu, E. Aptoula, and C. Tirkaz. Automatic plant identification from photographs. *Machine Vision and Applications*, 25(6):1369–1383, 2014.

[43] B. Yanikoglu, Y. Tolga, C. Tirkaz, and E. FuenCaglartes. Sabanci-okan system at lifeclef 2014 plant identification competition. In *Working notes of CLEF 2014 conference*, 2014.

[44] B. A. Yanikoglu, E. Aptoula, and S. T. Yildiran. Sabanci-okan system at imageclef 2013 plant identification competition. In *CLEF (Working Notes)*. Citeseer, 2013.

Multimedia and Medicine: Teammates for Better Disease Detection and Survival

Michael Riegler[†§], Mathias Lux[⊗], Carsten Griwodz[†§],Concetto Spampinato[▷], Thomas de Lange[*◇], Sigrun L. Eskeland[◇], Konstantin Pogorelov[†§], Wallapak Tavanapong[⊕], Peter T. Schmidt[•‡], Cathal Gurrin[◁], Dag Johansen[∘], Håvard Johansen[∘], Pål Halvorsen[†§]

[†]Simula Research Laboratory, Norway [§]University of Oslo, Norway [*]Cancer Registry of Norway
[⊗]Klagenfurt University, Austria [◇]Vestre Viken Hospital Trust, Norway [∘]UiT - The Artic University of Norway
[⊕]Iowa State University, USA [▷]University of Catania, Italy [◁]Dublin City University, Ireland
[•]Karolinska Institute, Sweden [‡]Center for Digestive Diseases, Solna & Karolinska University Hospital, Sweden

ABSTRACT

Health care has a long history of adopting technology to save lives and improve the quality of living. Visual information is frequently applied for disease detection and assessment, and the established fields of computer vision and medical imaging provide essential tools. It is, however, a misconception that disease detection and assessment are provided exclusively by these fields and that they provide the solution for all challenges. Integration and analysis of data from several sources, real-time processing, and the assessment of usefulness for end-users are core competences of the multimedia community and are required for the successful improvement of health care systems. For the benefit of society, the multimedia community should recognize the challenges of the medical world that they are uniquely qualified to address. We have conducted initial investigations into two use cases surrounding diseases of the gastrointestinal (GI) tract, where the detection of abnormalities provides the largest chance of successful treatment if the initial observation of disease indicators occurs before the patient notices any symptoms. Although such detection is typically provided visually by applying an endoscope, we are facing a multitude of new multimedia challenges that differ between use cases. In real-time assistance for colonoscopy, we combine sensor information about camera position and direction to aid in detecting, investigate means for providing support to doctors in unobtrusive ways, and assist in reporting. In the area of large-scale capsular endoscopy, we investigate questions of scalability, performance and energy efficiency for the recording phase, and combine video summarization and retrieval questions for analysis.

CCS Concepts

•Information systems → Multimedia information systems; •Applied computing → Health care information systems;

Keywords

Multimedia; Medical; Multimedia System

MM '16, October 15 - 19, 2016, Amsterdam, Netherlands

ISBN 978-1-4503-3603-1/16/10...$15.00

DOI: http://dx.doi.org/10.1145/2964284.2976760

1. INTRODUCTION

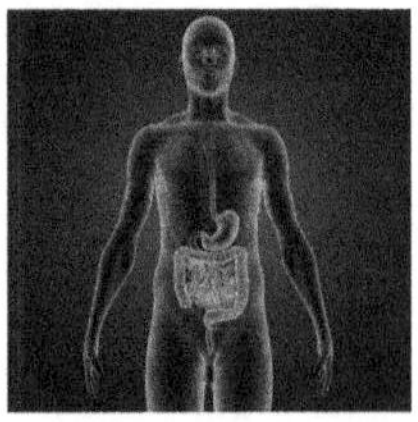

Figure 1: GI tract (shutterstock.com)

It is a typical assumption that visual analysis as it is already provided by the computer vision and medical image processing communities today is sufficient to solve health care multimedia challenges. Although we concede that computer vision and medical imaging methods are indeed essential contributors to promising approaches, we have come to the understanding that analyzing images and videos alone do not solve the challenges in medical fields such as endoscopy or ultrasound. Existing computer vision approaches do not make serious use of the multitude of additional information sources including sensors, temporal and users information.

Multimedia approaches are able to go beyond visual signals and also make use of heterogeneous sources including, e.g., the position sensors or fiber length measurement. Instead of considering the potential weakness of such signals as a nuisance, multimedia researchers are able to find ways to exploit them in combination to achieve the best possible results given the information available. Last but not least, multimedia cares first and foremost about the human user and assesses the feasibility of the resulting system. Correct and accurate diagnosis, efficient examinations and scalability are all critical for a health care system.

On the basis of these considerations, it is clear that we need to work on the challenge of realizing medical multimedia systems, which we define as follows: *a medical multimedia system is an interactive system, which provides support for diagnostics, examination, surgery, reporting and teaching in a medical setting by combining all available information sources and putting them in the hands of medical professionals or patients.* We note that some medical information systems may be fully automatic, but we still consider them to be at some level interactive, since a medical professional and/or a patient must be in the loop to interpret and act on the results.

In some areas of the human body, such as the gastrointestinal (GI) tract – our focus in this paper – the detection of abnormalities and diseases directly improves the chance of successful treatment, if the initial observation of disease indicators can be made visually, and also *before* the patient notices any symptoms. The GI tract is important since it is the site of many common diseases with high mortality rates. For example, three of the six most common cancer types are located in the GI tract (Figure 1), with a large number of cancers detected yearly and with a high mortality rate [41]. Section 2 provides more details about diseases of the GI tract and their relevance, but clearly, early detection is important for patient survival. Currently, the recommended procedure for disease detection is gastrointestinal flexible endoscopy, i.e., the use of a flexible tube containing a lens system (cf. Figure 2(a).) Early detection and removal of cancer precursors to reduce cancer incidence makes regular screening of defined cohorts of the population necessary. Its implementation is obstructed by low willingness to undertake the unpleasant procedure, but also by inhibitive resource consumptions, and particular in terms of time required from the limited number of qualified medical staff. Alleviating these two limitations is essential and demands research into less intrusive detection procedures and an increased automatization of both detection and analysis of abnormalities.

There is a multitude of different use cases for automated diagnosis support, even within the limited field of GI tract inspection, which provide different opportunities beyond image analysis, and which require different kinds of assistance for medical experts. In our case, the use cases range from training support through archival, retrieval, and summarization for offline analysis to real-time annotation during endoscopy. The following quote from one of our discussions with medical specialists in endoscopy is bound to trigger the imagination of multimedia researchers with its hints for potential use cases:

"I am performing thousands of endoscopies, but I still miss abnormalities and have difficulties to analyze what I see. I would have liked more assisted examinations, and there is no possibilities to share these data with my colleagues or retrieve them when needed. It is just stored on a computer somewhere. I don't know where, and I don't think the IT support knows either... Sadly, we are collecting a lot of data, but we do not benefit from it at all. Do you have any idea what we can do with such data? I would be for example really nice if I could search for similar cases in our image database or use it to create automatic report. Reporting steals a lot of our time every day." – A Norwegian doctor, September 2015.

This quote directly reveals the need for real-time video analysis, storage, indexing, sharing and retrieval, audio transcripts, automatic annotation, action recognition, and probably more. After listening to this and many similar statements about insufficient time for manual analysis and unused multimedia data, we teamed up with specialists in the area of GI diseases to investigate how multimedia research can improve medical systems and patient treatment.

To aid and expand GI tract examinations, we have started the development of a multimedia system, which is called EIR after the Norse goddess of medical skills. It supports endoscopists in the detection and interpretation of diseases in the entire GI tract. Our aim is to develop both, (i) a live system assisting the detection and analysis of irregularities during colonoscopies and (ii) a future fully automated screening for the GI tract using a wireless video capsule endoscope (VCE).

In the **first use case**, we consider the provision of live assistance during classical colonoscopy. To support live colonoscopy while the procedure is running, the live-assisted system must process the input video stream from the endoscope (shown in Figure 2(a)) in real-time, and indicate automatically detected polyp candidates on a live video feed from the endoscope.

This approach is not meant to reduce the attention that medical doctors (endoscopists) performing a colonoscopy have to pay to the endoscopic video. It is rather meant to reduce the number of overlooked abnormalities and assist in the assessment of abnormalities, for example by providing size estimates and surface structure analysis to ease the distinction of polyps and regions that should raise concern from those that are better ignored. Obviously, live assistance has in the past been inhibited by excessive hardware costs, which prevented the creation and deployment of system that could perform in real-time. Our experimental prototype described in Section 4 makes use of modern parallel hardware, and shows very promising results, although we have only scratched the surface of the problem.

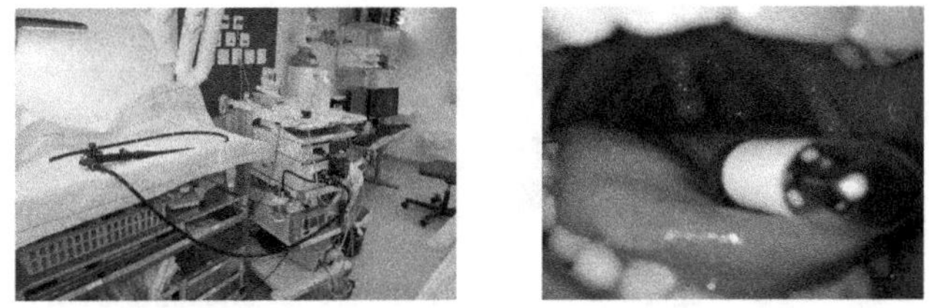

(a) Colonoscopy equipment (b) VCE capsule (camera pill)

Figure 2: Endoscopy vs. wireless capsule endoscopy (VCE).

Our **second use case** is relevant in scaling GI tract examination to population-wide screening. This use case imposes strict requirements on the accuracy of the detection to avoid false negative findings (overlooking a disease). It is also challenging in terms of resource consumption, but the most precious resource in this case is the time required of endoscopists.

We believe that screening can become feasible through the use of VCEs (shown in Figure 2(b)), which can reduce several of the inconveniences and burdens of flexible endoscopy, although its current technical restrictions limit its usefulness. Nevertheless, while VCEs that could provide sufficient information were out of reach just a few years ago, it is now up to us to investigate the appropriate trade-off decisions on the recording side, which must consider frame rate, frame rate variability, scene lighting, storage space, resolution, quantization, energy consumption, detection rate and more. When we solve this challenge, VCEs become useful for the physician if the six to eight hours long video of the VCE's travel through the human GI tract can be summarized automatically in less than an hour. Such summarization is dominated by the challenges of unsupervised recording and the subsequent need to avoid false negatives.

We hope that our paper encourages the multimedia community to help improving the health care system by applying their knowledge and methods to reach the next level of computer and multimedia assisted diagnosis, detection and interpretation of abnormalities. In this area, computer vision and medical imaging have created visual representations of the interior of a body. To automatically detect and locate abnormalities, visual representations are not sufficient. There is a need for image and video processing, analysis, information search and retrieval, combination with other sensor data, assistance by medical experts, etc. – clearly multimedia – and it all needs integration and efficient processing. Therefore, in this paper, we look beyond computer vision and medical imaging and show the potential of multimedia research and that it goes far beyond well-known scenarios like analysis of content on YouTube and Flickr.

The paper is structured as follows. First we give an overview of health care multimedia challenges focusing on the field of GI endoscopy as an example of a medical field. That is followed by an overview of related work and current technologies. After that we present a showcase for a multimedia system for GI endoscopies to discuss the complexity and possibilities of medicine teamed up with multimedia. This part is underlined by a preliminary results section that should give an idea how such a multimedia application can be evaluated and what is important. Finally and most important we give an outlook and a summary including detailed description of how multimedia can be applied and what is needed.

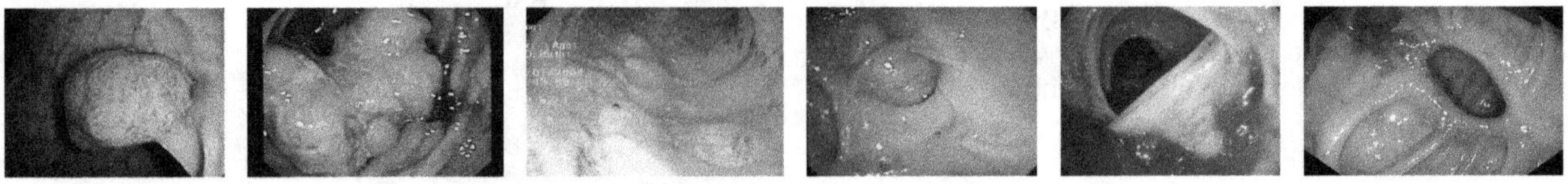

(a) Colon polyp (b) Colorectal cancer (c) Crohn's disease (d) Diverticulosis (e) Bleeding (f) Anastomosis

Figure 3: A non-exhaustive set of examples of abnormalities that can be diagnosed using colonoscopy.

2. HEALTH MULTIMEDIA CHALLENGES

There are large societal challenges in the health care systems worldwide. If we look at our GI tract case study, about 2.8 millions of new luminal GI cancers (esophagus, stomach, colorectal) are detected yearly in the world, and the mortality is about 65% [41]. In addition to these cancers, numerous other chronic diseases (see Figure 3) affect the human GI tract. The most common ones include gastroesophageal reflux disease, peptic ulcer disease, inflammatory bowel disease, celiac disease and chronic infections. All have a significant impact on the patients' health-related quality of life [7] and gastroenterology is one of the largest medical branches.

Nevertheless, there are unmet needs and potentials for improvements, which can be remedied by introducing better and more efficient digital medical systems. For colorectal cancer (CRC), which has one of the highest incidences and mortality of the diseases in the GI tract, early detection is essential for a good prognosis and treatment. Minimally invasive endoscopic and surgical treatment is most often curative in early stages (I-II) with a 5-year survival probability of more than 90%, but in advanced stages (III-IV), radiation and/or chemotherapy is often required, and it has a 5-year survival of only 10-30% [6].

The current European Union guidelines therefore recommend screening for CRC [36]. Several screening methods exist, e.g., fecal immunochemical tests (FITs), sigmoidoscopy screening, computed tomography (CT) scans and colonoscopy. However, in randomized trials, only endoscopic methods have shown a reduced CRC incidence. However, it is not the ideal screening test, for a number of reasons. Each examination demands a significant amount of time from a medical professional and the procedure is unpleasant and can cause great discomfort for the patient [35] (Figure 2(a)). Moreover, on average, 20% of polyps, precursors of CRC, are missed or incompletely removed, i.e., the risk of getting CRC depends largely on the endoscopist's ability to detect polyps [15].

Furthermore, there are high costs related to these procedures. In the US, colonoscopy is the most expensive cancer screening process with an annual cost of $10 billion dollars, i.e., an average of $1,100 per examination (up to $6,000 in New York) [32, 33]. In the United Kingdom, the costs are around $2,700 per examination [29]. To meet the need for cost-effectiveness, improved diagnostics and enhanced efficiency in health care systems, the proposed technical solution targets ground-breaking research and innovation for global major health issues like colorectal, gastric and stomach cancer worldwide. By developing and studying an automatic system for a VCE (Figure 2(b)), the aim is to make these examinations more easily accessible for patients and participants in screening programs, i.e., making the public health care system more scalable and cost-effective. It is also important that multimedia researchers address some of the challenges identified in the EU health policy, implemented through the Health Strategy, specially in the topics of prevention, health care access equalization, maintaining health into old age, and dynamic health systems incorporating new technologies. The optimal goal is to contribute in the area of medical multimedia for analysis as well as storage and processing of this type of data. Such next-generation big data applications, especially in the area of medicine, are frontiers for innovation, competition and productivity [20], where there are large initiatives both in the EU [1] and the US [21, 2].

3. RELATED WORK AND NEW TRENDS

To the best of our knowledge, currently, no start-to-end interactive medical multimedia system for annotating and analyzing data and computer aided diagnosis for the medical field exists. If one takes a closer look into the work of computer vision or medical image processing, it becomes clear that the complete loop is not their main research interest. A complete medical multimedia system including different multimedia applications that can fulfill the visions and objectives of the medical field must (i) have high detection accuracy (sensitivity, recall, precision), (ii) have an extensible and adaptable processing pipeline, (iv) support real-time processing to provide live feedback during for example endoscopy examinations, (v) support large-scale batch processing of, for example, VCE videos, (vi) be privacy-preserving, and (vii) visualize detection feedback to medical personnel. Several generally relevant systems fulfilling parts of the requirement list exist, but very few target medical scenarios, and no existing multimedia system matches all these requirements.

3.1 GI Tract Endoscopy Technology

There are several providers of endoscopy systems and VCE devices. Last generation equipment for manual procedures like colonoscopy and gastroscopy provides video with high resolution and high frame rates. There is, however, no computer-aided diagnostic feedback. In this respect, Polyp-Alert [40] is the most promising with polyp detection capabilities, but with the main purpose of evaluating how well the procedures are performed. For live analysis of endoscopy videos, our target system aims to go far beyond the currently existing systems. The other approach to record videos of the GI tract is VCEs using a small capsule type device (a 11mm×25mm pill), which has at least one image sensor, antenna, battery, light source and wireless transceiver. The capsule is swallowed to record the GI tract. There are several vendors providing such capsules, like IntroMedic, CapsoVision, Medtronic (Given) and Olympus. The current VCEs often have a variable framerate (increasing the framerate to about 30-35 FPS when entering the small intestine), but a rather low resolution ranging from 256×256 to 400×600. One of the main challenges for use of VCEs is man-hours of medical staff required for analysis. There are about 216,000 images per examination, and a very experienced endoscopist needs at least 30 to 60 minutes to process the video and possible sensor data. Therefore, it is important to develop automatic methods that can reduce the burden on medical staff and speed up the analysis of the videos. Currently, the software can segment the videos and can allow endoscopists to fast forward and look at multiple videos at the same time (probably affecting the detection accuracy). Moreover, some software includes small detection components that provides only vague "hints", for example about the detection of the color red, which may indicate bleeding. Other main limitations with VCEs are that the lack of means for cleaning particles (food/stool) in the bowels, and their uncontrolled forward movement through the bowel that cannot be guided to take a close-up picture or a tissue sample from detected lesions.

Compared to traditional endoscopy examinations, with VCE, patient discomfort is decreased, and the size of the examined cohort may be increased. However, the analysis still requires a huge amount of manual labor and the image quality is substantially lower. Our research targets a system providing a far more advanced computer-assisted disease detection in general, detecting endoscopic findings with high accuracy, with reduced compute-resource consumption, to increase the number of screened people without spending huge amounts of time on manual analysis.

Current systems use mainly video and images for analysis. However, there is a large potential for adding more information. For example, knowing the position of the camera (either VCE or endoscope may narrow down the search for endoscopic findings). Furthermore, the VCEs and endoscopes will in the future be equipped with new sensors for biomarkers (bacteria, DNA, RNA...) and pH-meters (acid) [12], and research introduces the idea of VCEs with "legs" for controlled movement and "arms" for taking samples and injecting medication locally [34].

3.2 Abnormality Detection

As described above, we target detection of abnormalities in the entire GI tract. Currently, most existing systems mainly aim for detection of polyps in the colon. The main reason is the high clinical relevance and prevalence of CRC. Several studies have been published, e.g., [10, 11, 14, 19, 22, 23, 24, 25, 37, 38]. These related papers address polyp detection in several different ways. For example by using neural networks or handcrafted features like detection of round or ellipse shapes [14, 19], and by detecting the circular content areas [22, 23]. In Table 1, we compare the most promising and relevant systems according to reported performance (though not tested on the same dataset, and not all report the same metrics). The most recent and complete system for polyp detection is Polyp-Alert [40], which is able to give near real-time feedback during colonoscopies (10 FPS) with a very high accuracy. However, not many complete multimedia systems exist, and none of them is able to do real-time detection for use as a live support system during procedures. This means that endoscopists have to re-visit the videos after procedures, adding to the typically already crowded schedule of medical experts. Furthermore, all of them are limited to a very specific use case, and they all fail in one or more of the requirements of a future automatic system. Thus, there are a lot of open challenges that can be addressed by the multimedia community. With EIR, as a first step, we already perform at the level of state-of-the-art systems (last row of Table 1). Our ambitions are (i) to extend and improve our prototype far beyond both the current version of EIR and state-of-the-art, but more importantly, (ii) to inspire other multimedia researchers to explore the medical field.

4. SHOWCASE FOR HOW-TO MULTIMEDIA IN MEDICINE

To show how complex the medical field is and why multimedia research is needed, we developed the EIR multimedia system for automatic disease detection in the GI tract. We target the entire GI tract because not just the colon (the focus of most of the computer vision and medical image processing community) can contain diseases that should be detected. Figure 4 gives an overview of this system. The main requirements of such a system are (i) ease of use, (ii) ease of extending to different diseases, (iii) efficient real-time handling of multimedia content for both scale (VCEs) and support

Publication/ System	What/ Detection Types	Recall/ Sensitivity	Precision	Specificity	Accuracy	FPS	Dataset Size
Wang et al. [40]	polyp/edge, texture	97.7%*	–	95.7%	–	10	1.8m frames
Wang et al. [39]	polyp/shape,color,texture	81.4%	–	–	–	0.14	1, 513 images
Mamonov et al. [19]	polyp/shape	47%	–	90%	–	–	18, 738 frames
Hwang et al. [14]	polyp/shape	96%	83%	–	–	15	8, 621 frames
Li and Meng [17]	tumor/textural pattern	88.6%	–	96.3%	92.4%	–	–
Zhou et al. [42]	polyp/intensity	75%	–	95.92%	90.8%	–	–
Alexandre et al. [4]	polyp/color pattern	93.7%	–	76.9%	–	–	35 images
Kang et al. [16]	polyp/shape,color	–	–	–	–	1	–
Cheng et al. [9]	polyp/texture,color	86.2%	–	–	–	0.08	74 images
Ameling et al. [5]	polyp/texture	AUC=95%	–	–	–	–	1, 736 images
EIR	extendible/multiple	98.5%	93.88%	72.5%	87.7%	~300	18, 781 frames

* The sensitivity is based on the number of detected polyps, other papers use per frame detection.

Table 1: Performance comparison of polyp detection approaches of state-of-the-art systems. Not all performance measurements are available ("–").

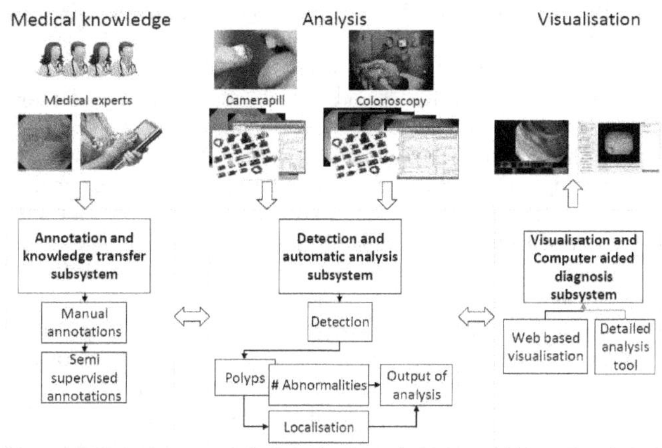

Figure 4: EIR system: annotation and knowledge transfer, detection and automatic analysis and computer aided diagnosis.

for live examinations, and (iv) high classification performance with minimal false negative classification results. To satisfy these requirements, the system has three main parts: The annotation and knowledge transfer sub-system, the detection and automatic analysis sub-system, and the visualization and computer aided diagnosis sub-system.

4.1 Annotation and Knowledge Transfer

The purpose of the annotation and knowledge transfer sub-system is to efficiently collect training data for the detection and automatic analysis sub-system. It is well known that training data is very important to make a good classification system. Additionally, in the medical field, the time of experts and annotated data are two very scarce resources. This is primarily because of high every-day workload for physicians, but also due to medical-legal issues. In terms of colonoscopy videos, the objective would be training a classifier for automatically detecting CRC, or its precursor lesions, colorectal polyps in multimedia data such as videos, sensor data and images. In our example system, we therefore developed an efficient semi-automatic annotation and knowledge transfer sub-system [3]. With a focus on ease of use and the minimal time requirements for annotation, our prototype was designed with a minimal level of required interaction.

The specialist's knowledge is only needed for the first identification of abnormalities and to tag them accordingly. This step is done manually by selecting any regions of interest in a video or image sequence and by annotation, i.e., providing information about importance and indicators for sensor data and patient records. After the manual annotation our prototype application uses object tracking to suggest annotations in further video frames by adjusting position and size of regions of interest as well as by automatically extending the annotation throughout a videos timeline. This data is then used in the analysis and detection sub-system. What we also have to learn from the medical doctors is how to interpret the various different data input sources, e.g., how to interpret the sensor data in the future, the significance of different pH (acidity) or biomarkers. It is important that multimedia researchers work hand in hand with the medical experts to gain this knowledge. Without efficient data collection tools, this will be an impossible task because of the time restrictions of medical personnel.

4.2 Detection and Automatic Analysis

The sub-system for detection and automatic analysis is designed in a modular way, making it possible to easily extend it to support different disease detectors, as well as other tasks like size determination and recognition of anatomical landmarks. Currently, it consists of two parts: (i) the detection sub-system that detects irregularities in video frames and images, and (ii) the localization sub-system that localizes the exact position of an abnormality in the frame. This part of the system is designed to detect whether there is something abnormal in a frame of the video (or image) or not. All the data that we process can be separated into two disjoint sets. These two sets contain example images, sensor data (temperature, blood, etc.) and other information that is useful for endoscopic findings, and images without any abnormality. It is important to point out, that the content based information images must be extended with other data like sensor output or information extracted from patient records to reach optimal results which makes it not a pure computer vision task. Each of these sets can be seen as the model for a specific disease. The modularity makes it possible to create a pipeline to for example first detect a polyp and then distinguish between a polyp with low or high risk of becoming a CRC by using for example the NICE classification[1]. To compare and determine the endoscopic findings in a given video frame, we use as a first approach global image features, i.e., because they are easy and fast to calculate, and at this stage, we do not need the exact position.

The basic idea is based on an improved version of a search-based method for image classification [27]. We chose this method because it is easy to implement and understand, and it gives us a first insight of the problem. Our experiments show that the detection needs good training data. However, the number of examples needed is rather low compared to other methods like deep learning. This is an important advantage at this point since there is not much data available. The classifier[2] tries to identify the frames that most probably contain a certain abnormality. Based on the classification of the results, the detection sub-system decides which endoscopic finding the input frame belongs to. This is done using late fusion of different classifiers. At the moment, we have one classifier for each global image feature. It is important to point out that the system will be expanded with other classifiers for sensor and audio data.

In contrast to other classifiers that are commonly used, this classifier is not trained in a separate learning step. Instead, the classifier searches previously generated Lucene indexes, which can be seen as the model, for similar visual features. The output is weighted based on the ranked list of the search results. Lucene indexes can contain all the information for one data point in one record (global features, sensor data, patient data, etc.). The system also includes a benchmarking function that will output evaluation information, and an HTML page with a visual representation of the results. For all video frames, we also can perform a localization. This is a pure computer vision problem and therefore we will not go in detail. It uses the information from the detection sub-system as a starting point, which means that it only processes frames that are already classified to contain an endoscopic finding. The processing of the images is implemented as a sequence of intra-frame pre- and main-filters. The output of this system can then further be used in for example a computer aided diagnosis program to help the doctor determining the size of a polyp or for reporting purposes.

4.3 Visualization and Diagnosis

One of the critical parts of each examination is the process of analyzing, reporting, facilitating and using multimedia to prepare the final result, i.e., the diagnosis and the report on the procedure. Medical doctors invest a significant part of their time on this task, and they are therefore in need of multimedia systems that help minimizing errors and increase the efficiency in this process.

For our experiments, we developed a web based visualization and annotation application to support medical experts with the goal of creating software that is easy to use and where it is easy to share data amongst participating medical experts. Our prototype facilitates the output of systems detection and localization part and creates a web based visualization which will be combined with a video sharing platform [13] where doctors are able to watch, archive, annotate and share information. We chose to use a centralized system based on web technologies to (i) minimize the necessary installs on client computers (with the current approach, a modern web browser is the only requirement), (ii) to allow for comfortable sharing of results and content with other experts, and (iii) to not duplicate data but use a centralized storage for multimedia data and annotations. This of course opens up questions about serving sensitive patient data over IP networks and leads to interesting research and organizational questions how to solve the data security problem, which is also an emerging field for the multimedia community, but data security is for now beyond the scope of the first EIR prototype.

While our first prototype is working as intended, the interplay between manually created content and automatically created content can still be improved. For example, applying object tracking algorithms is very difficult and often requires manual corrections. Most of the work in this step is done by the software end-users still need to navigate to the previously marked irregularities and playback the video from that point for the software to track the marked region on subsequent frames. Depending on the quality of the video and the speed of camera movement, user intervention is needed to assure a high quality of tracking. One can see, that there is still a fair amount of manual work involved, which makes it not really useful for medical experts. However, using a specialized – yet to be improved – tracking algorithm substantially reduces the time needed to, for example, create training videos or even datasets. Moreover, medical expert skills are maybe no longer necessarily required as the task of annotation correction is about tracking regions and adjusting rectangular dimensions rather than actually detecting or recognizing irregularities. This task could for example be outsourced using crowdsourcing. Our prototype visualization and annotation tool might be considered very basic, and there are tools resulting from multimedia research in existence that can be utilized for being a computer aided diagnosis system, but our approach already led to a benefit for the medical experts, allowing them to annotate and share data with other experts. Another area of multimedia, namely text-to-speech and text processing, could lead to great improvements in the reporting. When the endoscopic examination is completed the doctors have to transcribe what they visually observed into a written report following a standard proto-

[1] http://www.wipo.int/classifications/nice/en/

[2] To invite others to the area, we have released the basic algorithm as open source: *OpenSea*: https://bitbucket.org/mpg_projects/opensea.

col and using an internationally defined minimal standard terminology. This is a time consuming task and important information is sometimes forgotten or omitted. Consequently, computer based automatic transcription of audio information and combination of it with visual information in to a written patient record will probably increase the quality of the report and would substantially reduce the doctors workload. This will also make it possible to translate difficult medical terms into a report for the patient. Finally, not just the applications are important but also an understanding of how humans perceive multimedia content and how different aspects of the content influence them differently.

5. PRELIMINARY RESULTS

If multimedia researchers decide to work in the field of medicine we also have to make sure that our systems and applications are useful and accurate enough and achieve the required performance. Therefore, we tested our preliminary prototype in terms of accuracy and system performance. We used a computer with a dual 2.40GHz Intel Xeon CPUs (E5-2630), 16 physical CPU cores (32 with hyper-threading), 32GB of RAM, dual NVIDIA Corporation GM200 GeForce GTX TITAN X GPUs, a 256GB SSD and Ubuntu Linux. Moreover, we used the ASU-Mayo Clinic polyp database[3] which currently is the largest publicly available dataset consisting of 20 videos with a total of 18, 781 frames and different resolutions up to full HD [31]. In these experiments, we implemented the system in Java, C++ and CUDA (for GPUs). We did not include any other data apart from the visual information, such as sensor data, etc., but this will be an important step for the future. For example, using results from a fecal blood test or temperature data will most probably increase the classification performance.

1) Detection Accuracy. To evaluate detection accuracy, we used the common standard metrics precision, recall and F1 score. We conducted a leave-one-out cross-validation to evaluate the system which is a method that assesses the generalization of a predictive model.

The system that we have developed allows us to use several different global image features for the classification. The more image features we use, the more computationally expensive the classification becomes. Also, not all image features are equally important or provide equally good results for our purpose. As a first step, we therefore need to find out which image features we want to use for classification. In order to understand which image features provide the best results, we generated indexes containing all possible features provided by LIRE [18]. These indexes were used for several different measurements and also for the leave-one-out cross-validation. Using our detection system, the built-in metrics functionality can provide information on the performance of different image features for benchmarking. Further, it provides us with separate information for every single image feature, as well as the late fusion of all the selected image features.

For our first test, we ran the detection with all possible image features selected. We then combined the reported values for true-positives, true-negatives, false-positives and false-negatives for all the runs, and calculated the metrics for the combined values. The single image feature that generally achieves the best score is CEDD, which is discussed in detail in [8]. Further, also the image features JCD, Edge Histogram, Rotation Invariant Local Binary Patterns, Tamura and Joint Histogram achieve very good values. The late fusion of all the image features even achieves slightly better results. However, it is impractical to do a late fusion of all these image features as the calculation, indexing and searching of all image features is computationally expensive. Therefore, we want to find a small subset of two image features, which provides optimal results despite minimizing the computational effort.

Based on the evaluation of different combinations of image features the image features JCD and Tamura seemed to be the best ones for our performance measurements. To assess the actual performance of the classifier combining these two image features, we ran the leave-one-out cross-validation over all available video sequences. With these settings, we achieve an average precision of 0.889, an average recall of 0.964 and an average F1 score value of 0.916. The problem with this average calculation is that different video sequences contribute values based on different numbers of video frames. If we weight the values contributed by every single video sequence with the number of frames in the sequence, we achieved an average precision of 0.9388, an average recall of 0.9850, and an average F1 score value of 0.9613. In other words, these results mean that we can detect polyps with a precision of almost 94%, and we detect almost 99% of all frames containing polyps. The detailed results compared to state-of-the-art systems are presented in Table 1. Furthermore, for the localization of the polyps in the frames, we reached an average precision of 0.3207, a recall of 0.3183 and a F1 score of 0.3195. These values are low in absolute terms and show how complex and difficult it is to make a multimedia system that is really useful for the medical doctors.

Obviously, more research is needed such as neural networks, more data, different classifiers, include humans in the loop, and methods have to be developed that can help to measure if performance is sufficient compared to the user needs. However, the multimedia community has to be aware that we cannot just apply our methods that we are used to use in this new field. Stated plainly, detecting cars or cats is not the same as detecting polyps or bleedings. For example, neural networks are conceptually easy to understand and lately large amount of academic research has been done on them. Results recently reported on for example the ImageNet dataset look quite promising [11]. Nevertheless, they have some negative aspects that make them less useful for the medical field [10]. First, training is very complicated and takes a long time. Our system has to be fast and understandable since we deal with patient data, and the outcome can differentiate between life and death. Therefore, a *black box* approach, that has difficulties to explain certain decision made, seems to be the second best way to solve a problem that has to be understood very well by all users. This can lead to serious problems in the medical field since it is not possible to evaluate them properly, and there will always be a chance that they completely fail without being aware of it [26]. The best way is still to understand the problem and then solve it. This of course comes with a challenge for the multimedia community. We have to test our current methods and most probably develop new, handcrafted algorithms and tools from scratch for this new field. A further problem of neural networks is that they require a lot of training data. In the medical field, this is a very important issue since it is hard to get data due to the lack of experts time (doctors have a very high workload) and legal and ethical issues for being able to share data among countries or even hospitals in the same country. Some common conditions, like colon polyps, may reach the required amount of training data for a neural network while other endoscopic findings, like for example tattoos from previous endoscopic procedures (black colored parts of the mucosa), are not that well documented, but still important to detect [28]. Finally, neural networks are not easy to design for probabilistic results. In a multi class decision based system, that is built to support medical doctors in decision making, the probability is an important information. Approaches with a better understanding of the problem will

[3] http://polyp.grand-challenge.org/site/Polyp/AsuMayo/

give a much more accurate probabilistic score that can be directly translated to the real world scenario [30].

2) Real-Time System Performance. One further requirement for the system and the medical field in general is scalability and execution performance. This requirement comes with some challenges like for example lack of actual hardware (it is in general hard to replace hardware or operating systems in hospitals due to security and system restrictions), not being able to use distributed systems and lack of funding for new hardware (e.g., Norwegian hospitals in 2016 still use Windows XP and Internet Explorer 6 even though funding is good). These restrictions makes it very challenging for researchers to develop efficient algorithms that are also scale able on the large amount of data that they will have to process. Therefore sophisticated methods are needed that run efficient in terms of speed and hardware need but at the same time achieve good performance. Based on our example system we present a experiment that shows how this challenges can be solved using multimedia systems knowledge and methods. For the experiments, we decided to use the configuration of the system that performed best in the accuracy experiment. In our use case of supporting doctors during live colonoscopies, it is important to reach real-time performance in terms of processing a video and several other input signal at the same time and reach a frame rate of not less than 30 FPS (output rate of current endoscopes). The performance of the *detection* is important, since the system should provide a result as fast as possible and not slower than 30 FPS making it usable for live applications. Figure 5(a) shows the detection sub-system performance in terms of FPS for the highest video resolution of 1920×1080. It depicts performance for all different detection algorithm implementations (Java, C++ and GPU) and different combinations of utilized hardware resources (from 1 to 32 CPU cores and none, 1 or 2 GPUs). For the full HD videos, the required frame rate of 30 FPS is reached using 8, 5 and 1 CPU cores in parallel for the Java, the C++ and the GPU implementations, respectively. Increasing the number of used CPU cores also increases the performance for all implementations, and the system reaches the maximum performance of 330 FPS with 2 GPUs and 25 CPU cores. A slight decrease of the performance can be observed for a high number of used CPU cores. This is caused by an increased overhead for context switching and competition for resource. Figures 5(b) and 5(c) show the detection sub-system performance in terms of FPS for the videos with smaller resolution. The maximum performance of 430 (for 856×480 resolution) and 453 (for 712×480 resolution) FPS is reached using 2 GPUs and 18 and 16 CPU cores. For localization which is more computationally expensive (plots not shown), the maximum performances observed are 129, 246 and 283 FPS for 1920×1080, 856×480 and 712×480 resolutions, respectively.

The outcome of these experiments clearly shows that our system can reach real-time requirements for the video processing and still has processing power left which can be used to process other input data at the same time, for example, sensor or patient records data, etc. A number of complex features can be added into the detection and the localization sub-systems. This will increase the system's detection and localization accuracy, and at the same time, keep its ability to perform in real-time. Moreover, it can also be used to process several data streams simultaneously in real-time and significantly reduce the examination time of the VCE videos for the medical experts. The time reduction lies around 5-10 times depending on type of input data like for example video resolution, frame rate and sensors used. Our evaluation also shows, that this is a very complex topic and requires methods and technologies from several different multimedia research directions, e.g., signal processing, multimedia systems, information retrieval, etc.

6. OUTLOOK AND CHALLENGES

With 2.8 million cancer cases diagnosed in the GI system per year with a mortality rate of about 65%, we have the best motivation to perform research in the proposed area. The GI example that we used in this paper is only the tip of the iceberg of unsolved problems in the health care sector. By exposing more unexplored multimedia research questions, researchers can reveal a huge potential to save lives by combining the medical and multimedia research areas. Our aim is to raise awareness that (i) multimedia research can do a lot for and learn a lot from the field of minimally invasive medicine, (ii) interdisciplinary research in this field leads to immediate benefits, and (iii) we have only scratched the surface with our efforts.

In our experience, medical experts are open to new multimedia applications in their fields. We experienced that doctors are willing to spend a lot of time and effort into supporting such research, as it ultimately has the potential to make their daily routine more efficient, and they will have more time to focus on the patients themselves. Especially, since we live in a time where handling multimedia is part of everyone's lives, medical experts wonder why the same functionality that they can use in YouTube, Flickr and Twitter cannot be applied to their own medical field. The main reasons that we identified are that first of all the computer vision and medical imaging community that work mainly on this problems is not interested in the *whole multimedia life cycle from start to end*, i.e., from the content creation, analysis to content usage by the actual users. Second and most important, it is a problem within our own community. It is much more convenient to download pictures from Flickr or videos from YouTube and categorize and use them in research, especially as many can identify themselves as social media users. However, working with medical data involves organizational challenges like *seeking and maintaining contact with medical experts*, understanding their problems, as well as getting used to often unpleasant or even content that causes a disgust response until a researcher is habituated in working in the area. Nevertheless, if we – the multimedia community as a whole – would be more brave to tackle these problems, we could actually help to save lives, make patient examinations less uncomfortable and help to save money and time spent in the health care system for daily routines instead of research. These are possibilities for societal impact that surely are appealing for both, researchers as well as global citizens. Last but not least, being able to look back seeing that our multimedia research helped to save lives is bearing more weight than being able to say we can classify cats, cars or beautiful holiday pictures.

6.1 Open Challenges

Our EIR system has preliminarily shown how multimedia tools can impact greatly health care systems. Nevertheless, there are still many open challenges that need to be faced through a multidisciplinary approach where multimedia methods will have to play a key role. Challenges include but are not limited to:

1) Exploiting domain expert knowledge to improve automated methods performance. Most of the methods (including the ones described in this paper) devised for supporting medical investigations in analysing visual data content are still predominantly based on learning distributions of low-level and middle-level (recently using deep learning approaches) visual features. While this has proved to achieve good performance in many computer vision applications, there are cases, especially in the medical domain, where relying on visual appearance might fail since processing visual data content requires specific expertise. This is the case of endoscopy videos where the reliability of the outcome mainly depends on the examiner's expertise. Our hypothesis is that, for a real break-

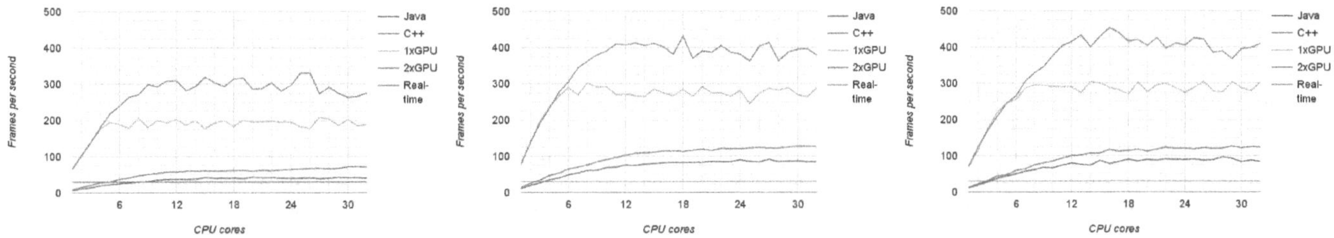

(a) Videos with a resolution of 1920×1080.

(b) Videos with a resolution of 856×480.

(c) Videos with a resolution of 712×480.

Figure 5: The performance of the detection sub-system in terms of FPS varying the number of CPU cores, the resolution of the videos and the detection algorithm. The maximum performances observed are 330, 430 and 453 FPS for 1920×1080, 856×480 and 712×480 resolutions.

through in medical image analysis, automated methods need to exploit jointly perceptive elements (visual features) and semantic factors (domain knowledge). This explains why in the medical domain relying only on image processing and computer vision methods will lead to a dead end. Instead, a multidisciplinary approach operating on multimodal data is necessary. Nevertheless, exploiting high level knowledge in computer vision methods poses several challenges from how to extract and model effectively domain expert knowledge to how to include such semantics into machine learning methods.

2) Automated report systems. A significant part of a medical professional's time is spent for preparing reports after procedures and examinations. Multimedia research can significantly support this phase by collecting all patient and examination data and by providing automatically summaries able to convey key information of the performed procedures including media fragments, e.g., video frames with detected objects, audio speeches describing colon visual features, etc. Such distilled media needs also to be interlinked with detailed information on treatments, medication for a holistic view of patients. These report will also be extremely useful for training medical experts: through multimedia enriched reports, medical doctors in training can learn based on real data according to case-based teaching and problem-based learning strategies. The multimedia field has tackled over the years, the problem of multimedia summarization for automated report generation, but such research is still at its infancy since methods developed so far are able to process only one type of media at a time (hence do not take full advantages from the richness of multimodal data). However, the most important limitation of multimedia research in this direction is the lack of generalization capabilities; in fact, most approaches cannot be applied to domains different from the ones they were devised for. To overcome these limitations, one solution we believe is worthwhile to investigate is to build automated multimedia summarization methods with a semantic nature exploiting domain ontologies, which can play an important role in the medical multimedia analysis where the data complexity and heterogeneity make the task very challenging.

3) Integration and fusion of unstructured and heterogeneous data. Beside visual data, other (equally important) information (e.g., blood pressure, temperature, breathing, oxygen levels) are recorded during examinations, which, if suitably fused to visual data content may significantly enhance procedures' outcome. An additional, and semantically rich, data source that can be exploited is recordings of medical experts spoken comments during examinations. Indeed, surgeons often describe verbally the procedure by giving details on what they see to other doctors and to issue commands and requests to the medical team. Although audio generated during procedures is a valuable source of information to train both automated methods and young doctors, it is rather unstructured and noisy and, as such, it demands for specific text mining methods approaches to distill the key information and to map it to a structured data form. Under this scenario, the semantic web may be a powerful tool for integration of such heterogeneous multimedia data. Once, heterogeneous data are all modeled using a shared formalism, visualization approaches are envisaged to present fused information in order to support medical staff, by enhancing the examination experience, for diagnosis.

4) Patient context information. Typically, health issues affect patients beyond their immediate treatment, and there are very often preceding correlated events before treatment is necessary or a health related issue is diagnosed. Therefore, health issues do not appear suddenly or as isolated events, but come in a rich context, which is largely exploited by medical doctors for diagnosis and treatment. Such context includes patients' mobility, eating habits and changes, etc. To this end, multimedia research can play an important part in developing smart wearable body sensors (and algorithms to analyze their data) that can collect routinely all such information and share with medical staff.

5) Building a knowledge base. A large collection of multimedia including videos, audio streams, sensor readings and patient records will represent a priceless knowledge base for approaches like case based reasoning and/or large empirical studies on treatments. Nevertheless, sharing such knowledge base opens up issues in privacy and data security, that, if successfully addressed, will enable the increase of such knowledge base (since many medical people will share their data), thus leading to large scale benefits in health care. To effectively address protection and reliability issues, multimedia researchers should investigate secure communications and processing through a deep interaction between signal processing, networking, and cryptography.

6) Interlinking information from different modalities. Besides endoscopic and minimally invasive surgery, there are other diagnosis systems like X-Ray, ultrasonic or MRT data from patients. Surgeons would greatly benefit from synchronized spatial information on multiple modalities to be able to investigate abnormalities from different angles. Now, all interlinking of diagnostic data from multiple modalities has to be done manually. This shows that there exists a huge need for algorithms and applications that can combine these different types of media automatically and efficient. For example, the information collected from a standard colonoscopy with a video from a capsular colonoscopy and CT colonography (virtual colonoscopy that uses special X-ray equipment) could lead to a higher detection rates and better patient survival probabilities.

7) Simplifying handling of multimedia. With today's tools, everyone is used to access multimedia everywhere and manipulate and share multimedia data with the tip of a finger. In the medical domain, software systems have a comparably long life span, and it has to be thoroughly tested before they can be applied in a hospital setting. Therefore, we need sustainable interactive tools and ways of interactivity that do not wear off as fast as they did in the last decade. Multimedia researchers have the knowledge and are needed to help creating such systems that fulfill the user needs but also to develop the algorithms that are the basis of such systems such as content retrieval, etc. This is especially important since most of the standard algorithms for object or concept detection will most probably not work in the medical field, which we experienced in the begin of our research when we tested a lot of state-of-the-art methods like for example histogram of oriented gradients or structured output tracking with kernels, etc. We believe that this is mainly caused by differences in the multimedia data provided (videos and images show completely different content, quality of the data, needs of the users, etc.).

8) Test data sets and challenges. There are already workshops, challenges and whole conferences dedicated to the topics of medical information and multimedia systems. However, just like in the multimedia community, we have to move forward to build and maintain an over-critical mass of test data including ground truth and annotations, and usage scenarios that are recent enough, i.e., recorded with up-to-date sensors and annotated thoroughly based on current medical standards and state-of-the-art. This is not only a research, but also a legal and societal, challenge as medical data is always personal and especially if it includes a patient context or long term records it is hard to anonymize. This requires not only sophisticated annotation systems, but also algorithms for unsupervised and semi-supervised learning. Furthermore, algorithms that can help to anonymize or watermark content to protect data are needed. Apart from the algorithms to analyze the data this part also needs motivated and dedicated people that contact hospital key personnel and doctors, and play a pioneering role in establishing a good data basis by collecting, annotate and make data public available.

9) Acting in concert. The greatest challenge of all, however, is to act in concert, as an interdisciplinary community. Medical experts bring in the data as well as the domain knowledge. Legal experts find ways how to deal with privacy and data security aspects from a legal and societal point of view. Companies supplying medical equipment must open up for collaboration and research beyond their own research departments. Last but not least, the multimedia community must bring in its knowledge as a core discipline, but also as a research field which historically involved other disciplines like computer vision, machine learning, interactive systems, networking, data warehousing, speech recognition, information retrieval, data mining and software engineering. The biggest task that the multimedia community faces is most probably to break the ice. Medical experts often do not know what is even possible with the data they have. Therefore, the responsibility lies in the hands of the multimedia researchers to build bridges. For example, we went to hospitals and asked for meetings with doctors to show them what we can do. Once they saw the possibilities, they were willing and very motivated to contribute with knowledge, data and new ideas. To address all these challenges, an interdisciplinary team is necessary as the problems goes far beyond visual analysis, information retrieval and annotation. It is also a multimedia area where it is essential to involve researchers from different areas like interactive system, multimedia systems and speech recognition in a specialized domain, ontologies, data mining and machine learning, sensor fusion, and synchronization of data from different modalities.

6.1.1 Possible Research Projects

We encourage the multimedia community to be open minded and help to tackle the challenges in this new field. It is important to be aware that we cannot just keep on annotating social videos, and then expect that medical technology companies can transfer these technologies to the medical use case. Therefore we need specific approaches for the field of medical multimedia.

In the sense of getting more into detail, we want to point out the more immediate and concrete challenges in this field by proposing three different research project topics and relevant research questions making for multiple challenging and interesting PhDs.

1) How can we identify and track abnormalities in a live endoscopic video? While our prototype did experiments on doing exactly that, there are fields beyond polyps as well as an opportunity to reduce manual input. Going beyond polyps would mean to identify cancerous tissue, inner injuries, bleeding, scars, fractures, and so on. This goes well with finding the current position and rotation of the camera within a patients body, i.e., by sensor fusion and asks for new and multimodal tracking algorithms taking camera movement into account. Medicine needs very high recall, but false alarms can be very costly not to mention extremely upsetting for the patients. Multimedia that detects concepts or events in YouTube videos is just not held to these kinds of standards.

2) How can we pre-prepare the final report on the surgery? As reporting takes a lot of a surgeons time, any step in this direction would be immediately beneficial for medical experts and patients alike. This actually involves several multimedia disciplines. Many surgeons direct and inform their team during a surgery by short, spoken announcements like *"Here, we've got the first polyp."*, *"Electro scalpel!"* or *"This one looks particularly odd."*. With speech recognition and synchronization with a video stream, the video can be segmented, relevant parts can be found and media for a final report can be suggested in addition with recommending relevant text passages from earlier reports of similar cases. The systems need to be able to optimize not for correct predictions, but for what humans need to know in order to make decisions. One approach is to fuse many slightly different algorithms so that the typical mistakes of one algorithm do not accidentally dominate.

3) How can we share, annotate and educate? While of course many would like to see a YouTube or Flickr like social media network for medical experts, it is simple not possible as the number of experts is limited and not everyone can be expected to be an active contributor to such a network. However, especially senior surgeons are skilled in creating videos, books or training materials and communicating them to trainees or colleagues to exchange knowledge. Still they lack tools for that. Critical for such a venture would be interdisciplinary work in (i) interactive multimedia like annotation, share, and interlinking of content, (ii) security and encryption for making sure the data stays safe, (iii) knowledge based systems as ontologies and structured knowledge plays a huge part in that, and (iv) multimedia systems, as all the data has to be handled, transferred, streamed, encoded etc.

6.1.2 First Steps

While we stressed the fact that working with medical data and medical experts is crucial for moving forward with research in the medical domain, we also acknowledge that interdisciplinary work is hard to start. What we found most important in our project is to build a working relationship with medical doctors who are personally interested in *making things better*. The VIPs for such interdisciplinary projects are senior surgeons, who are actively training new surgeons, as they (i) have experience in sharing knowledge, (ii) have access to a lot of data, (iii) are extremely good in specifying problems and very competent in working out solutions, and (iv) have influence in terms of the hospital organization.

In our experience, it takes some time for PhD students to build awareness of the field to a level, where we could work efficiently on the problem. At the begin, we organized that the PhD students attended live surgeries, watched and discussed surgery videos and reports with senior surgeons as well as trainees, and participated in regular meetings for questions and answers that were raised in this learning period. Within this starting period, in parallel with building up the knowledge, it is in general a good idea to expand the data available throughout the research project. Besides building on public data sets like the ASU-Mayo Clinic polyp database [31], we suggest to work out a scheme to obtain recent multimedia data from the before mentioned necessary contacts. This typically involves legal and organizational issues including but not limited to (i) a mutually agreed upon anonymization routine for the data, (ii) a non disclosure agreement of the participating organizations and involved people, as well as (iii) a specialized setup to make sure the data stays safe and protected during transport and in storage at the research institution.

7. REFERENCES

[1] European Commission forms EUR2.5bn big data partnership. http://www.pmlive.com/blogs/digital_intelligence/archive/2014/-november/european_commission_forms_2.5bn_big_data_partnership.

[2] Obama's big data plans: Lots of cash and lots of open data. http://gigaom.com/cloud/obamas-big-data-plans-lots-of-cash-and-lots-of-open-data/.

[3] Z. Albisser, M. Riegler, P. Halvorsen, J. Zhou, C. Griwodz, I. Balasingham, and C. Gurrin. Expert driven semi-supervised elucidation tool for medical endoscopic videos. In *Proc. of MMSYS*, 2015.

[4] L. A. Alexandre, J. Casteleiro, and N. Nobreinst. Polyp detection in endoscopic video using svms. In *Proc. of PKDD*. Springer, 2007.

[5] S. Ameling, S. Wirth, D. Paulus, G. Lacey, and F. Vilarino. Texture-based polyp detection in colonoscopy. In *BFM*. 2009.

[6] H. Brenner, M. Kloor, and C. P. Pox. Colorectal cancer. *Lancet*, 2014.

[7] S. K. Chambers, X. Meng, P. Youl, J. Aitken, J. Dunn, and P. Baade. A five-year prospective study of quality of life after colorectal cancer. *Quality of Life Research*, 21(9), 2012.

[8] S. A. Chatzichristofis and Y. S. Boutalis. CEDD: Color and edge directivity descriptor. a compact descriptor for image indexing and retrieval. In *Proc. of ICVS*, 2008.

[9] D.-C. Cheng, W.-C. Ting, Y.-F. Chen, Q. Pu, and X. Jiang. Colorectal polyps detection using texture features and support vector machine. In *MDAIS*. Springer, 2008.

[10] C. Chin and D. E. Brown. Learning in science: A comparison of deep and surface approaches. *Research in science teaching*, 37(2), 2000.

[11] J. Deng, W. Dong, R. Socher, L.-J. Li, K. Li, and L. Fei-Fei. Imagenet: A large-scale hierarchical image database. In *Proc. of CVPR*. IEEE, 2009.

[12] M. M. Francisco, B. S. Terry, J. A. Schoen, and M. E. Rentschler. Intestinal manometry force sensor for robotic capsule endoscopy: An acute, multipatient in vivo animal and human study. *Trans. on Biomedical Engineering*, 63(5), 2015.

[13] P. Halvorsen, S. Sægrov, A. Mortensen, D. K. Kristensen, A. Eichhorn, M. Stenhaug, S. Dahl, H. K. Stensland, V. R. Gaddam, C. Griwodz, and D. Johansen. Bagadus: An integrated system for arena sports analytics – a soccer case study. In *Proc. of MMSys*, 2013.

[14] S. Hwang, J. Oh, W. Tavanapong, J. Wong, and P. de Groen. Polyp detection in colonoscopy video using elliptical shape feature. In *Proc. of ICIP*, 2007.

[15] M. F. Kaminski, J. Regula, E. Kraszewska, M. Polkowski, U. Wojciechowska, J. Didkowska, M. Zwierko, M. Rupinski, M. P. Nowacki, and E. Butruk. Quality indicators for colonoscopy and the risk of interval cancer. *NE Journal of Medicine*, 362(19), 2010.

[16] J. Kang and R. Doraiswami. Real-time image processing system for endoscopic applications. In *Proc. of CCECE*, 2003.

[17] B. Li and M.-H. Meng. Tumor recognition in wireless capsule endoscopy images using textural features and svm-based feature selection. *ITBM*, 16(3), 2012.

[18] M. Lux. LIRE: open source image retrieval in java. In *Proc. of MM*. ACM, 2013.

[19] A. Mamonov, I. Figueiredo, P. Figueiredo, and Y.-H. Tsai. Automated polyp detection in colon capsule endoscopy. *MI*, 33(7), 2014.

[20] McKinsey Global Institute. Big data: The next frontier for innovation, competition, and productivity. http://www.mckinsey.com/Insights/MGI/Research/Technology_and_-Innovation/Big_data_The_next_frontier_for_innovation.

[21] McKinsey Global Institute. The big-data revolution in US health care: Accelerating value and innovation. http://www.mckinsey.com/insights/health_systems_and_services/the_big-data_revolution_in_us_health_care.

[22] B. Münzer, K. Schoeffmann, and L. Böszörmenyi. Detection of circular content area in endoscopic videos. In *Proc. of CBMS*, 2013.

[23] B. Münzer, K. Schoeffmann, and L. Böszörmenyi. Improving encoding efficiency of endoscopic videos by using circle detection based border overlays. In *Proc. of ICME*, 2013.

[24] B. Münzer, K. Schoeffmann, and L. Böszörmenyi. Relevance segmentation of laparoscopic videos. In *Proc. of ISM*, 2013.

[25] R. Nawarathna, J. Oh, J. Muthukudage, W. Tavanapong, J. Wong, P. C. De Groen, and S. J. Tang. Abnormal image detection in endoscopy videos using a filter bank and local binary patterns. *Neurocomputing*, 144, 2014.

[26] A. Nguyen, J. Yosinski, and J. Clune. Deep neural networks are easily fooled: High confidence predictions for unrecognizable images. *arXiv preprint arXiv:1412.1897*, 2014.

[27] M. Riegler, M. Larson, M. Lux, and C. Kofler. How 'how' reflects what's what: Content-based exploitation of how users frame social images. In *Proc. of ACM MM*, 2014.

[28] J. Schmidhuber. Deep learning in neural networks: An overview. *NN*, 61, 2015.

[29] L. Sharp, L. Tilson, S. Whyte, A. O'Ceilleachair, C. Walsh, C. Usher, P. Tappenden, J. Chilcott, A. Staines, M. Barry, et al. Cost-effectiveness of population-based screening for colorectal cancer: a comparison of guaiac-based faecal occult blood testing, faecal immunochemical testing and flexible sigmoidoscopy. *BJOC*, 106(5), 2012.

[30] D. F. Specht. Probabilistic neural networks. *NN*, 3(1), 1990.

[31] N. Tajbakhsh, S. Gurudu, and J. Liang. Automated polyp detection in colonoscopy videos using shape and context information. *Trans. on MI*, 35(2), 2015.

[32] The New York Times. The $2.7 Trillion Medical Bill, 01, Jun, 2013.

[33] The New York Times. The Weird World of Colonoscopy Costs, 06, Sept, 2013.

[34] The Telegraph. 'spider pill' offers new way to scan for diseases including colon cancer, 11, Oct, 2009.

[35] J. C. van Rijn, J. B. Reitsma, J. Stoker, P. M. Bossuyt, S. J. van Deventer, and E. Dekker. Polyp miss rate determined by tandem colonoscopy: a systematic review. *JOG*, 101(2), 2006.

[36] L. von Karsa, J. Patnick, and N. Segnan. European guidelines for quality assurance in colorectal cancer screening and diagnosis. first edition–executive summary. *Endoscopy*, 44(S 03), 2012.

[37] Y. Wang, W. Tavanapong, J. Wong, J. Oh, and P. C. de Groen. Computer-aided detection of retroflexion in colonoscopy. In *Proc. of CBMS*, 2011.

[38] Y. Wang, W. Tavanapong, J. Wong, J. Oh, and P. C. de Groen. Near real-time retroflexion detection in colonoscopy. *JBHI*, 17(1), 2013.

[39] Y. Wang, W. Tavanapong, J. Wong, J. Oh, and P. C. de Groen. Part-based multiderivative edge cross-sectional profiles for polyp detection in colonoscopy. *JBHI*, 18(4), 2014.

[40] Y. Wang, W. Tavanapong, J. Wong, J. H. Oh, and P. C. de Groen. Polyp-alert: Near real-time feedback during colonoscopy. *Computer methods and programs in biomedicine*, 120(3), 2015.

[41] World Health Organization - International Agency for Research on Cancer. Estimated Cancer Incidence, Mortality and Prevalence Worldwide in 2012. http://globocan.iarc.fr/Pages/fact_sheets_population.aspx, 2012.

[42] M. Zhou, G. Bao, Y. Geng, B. Alkandari, and X. Li. Polyp detection and radius measurement in small intestine using video capsule endoscopy. In *Proc. of BMEI*, 2014.

Multilayer and Multimodal Fusion of Deep Neural Networks for Video Classification

Xiaodong Yang Pavlo Molchanov Jan Kautz
NVIDIA
{xiaodongy, pmolchanov, jkautz}@nvidia.com

ABSTRACT

This paper presents a novel framework to combine multiple layers and modalities of deep neural networks for video classification. We first propose a multilayer strategy to simultaneously capture a variety of levels of abstraction and invariance in a network, where the convolutional and fully connected layers are effectively represented by our proposed feature aggregation methods. We further introduce a multimodal scheme that includes four highly complementary modalities to extract diverse static and dynamic cues at multiple temporal scales. In particular, for modeling the long-term temporal information, we propose a new structure, FC-RNN, to effectively transform pre-trained fully connected layers into recurrent layers. A robust boosting model is then introduced to optimize the fusion of multiple layers and modalities in a unified way. In the extensive experiments, we achieve state-of-the-art results on two public benchmark datasets: UCF101 and HMDB51.

CCS Concepts

•Information systems → Multimedia and multimodal retrieval; •Computing methodologies → Video summarization;

Keywords

Video Classification; Deep Neural Networks; Boosting; Fusion; CNN; RNN;

1. INTRODUCTION

Content-based video classification is fundamental to intelligent video analytics including automatic categorizing, searching, indexing, segmentation, and retrieval of videos. It has been applied to a wide range of real-word applications, for instance, surveillance event detection [49], semantic indexing [1], gesture control [11], and so forth. It is a challenging task to recognize unconstrained videos because 1) an appropriate video representation can be task-dependent, e.g., coarse ("swim" vs. "run") or fine-grained ("walk" vs. "run") categorizations; 2) there may be multiple streams of information that need to be taken into account, such as actions, objects, scenes, etc.; 3) there are large intra-class variations, which arise from diverse viewpoints, occlusions and backgrounds. As the core information of videos, visual cues provide the most significant information for video classification. Most traditional methods rely on the bag-of-visual-words (BOV) representation which consists of computing and aggregating visual features [13]. A variety of local and global visual features have been proposed, for instance, GIST [31] and SIFT [27] can be used to capture static information in spatial frames, while STIP [23] and improved dense trajectories (iDT) [44] are widely employed to compute both appearance and motion cues in videos.

There is a growing trend to learn robust feature representations with deep neural networks for various tasks such as image classification [20], object detection [35], natural language processing [40], and speech recognition [6]. As one of the most successful network architectures, the recent surge of convolutional neural networks (CNN) has given rise to a number of methods to employ CNN for video classification. Karparthy et al. [19] made the first attempt to use a buffer of video frames as input to networks, however, the results were inferior to those of the best hand-engineered features [44]. Tran et al. [42] proposed C3D using 3D-CNN over short video clips to learn appearance and micro-motion features simultaneously. However, these methods focus on short or mid-term information as feature representations are learned in short-time windows. This is insufficient for video classification since complex events are better described by leveraging the temporal evolution of short-term contents. In order to capture long-term temporal clues in videos, recurrent neural networks (RNN) were applied to explicitly model videos as an ordered sequence of frames [8, 29].

CNN-based video classification algorithms typically make predictions using the softmax scores or, alternatively, they use the last fully connected layer as a feature representation [36, 42], because CNN hierarchically compute abstract and invariant representations of the inputs. However, leveraging information across multiple levels in a network has proven beneficial for several tasks such as natural scene recognition [48], object segmentation [26] and optical flow computation [10]. This is somewhat expected since convolutional layers retain spatial information as opposed to fully connected layers. For video classification, we argue that appropriate levels of abstraction and invariance in CNN for video representation are also task- and class-dependent. For example,

MM '16, October 15–19, 2016, Amsterdam, The Netherlands.

ISBN 978-1-4503-3603-1/16/10...$15.00

DOI: http://dx.doi.org/10.1145/2964284.2964297

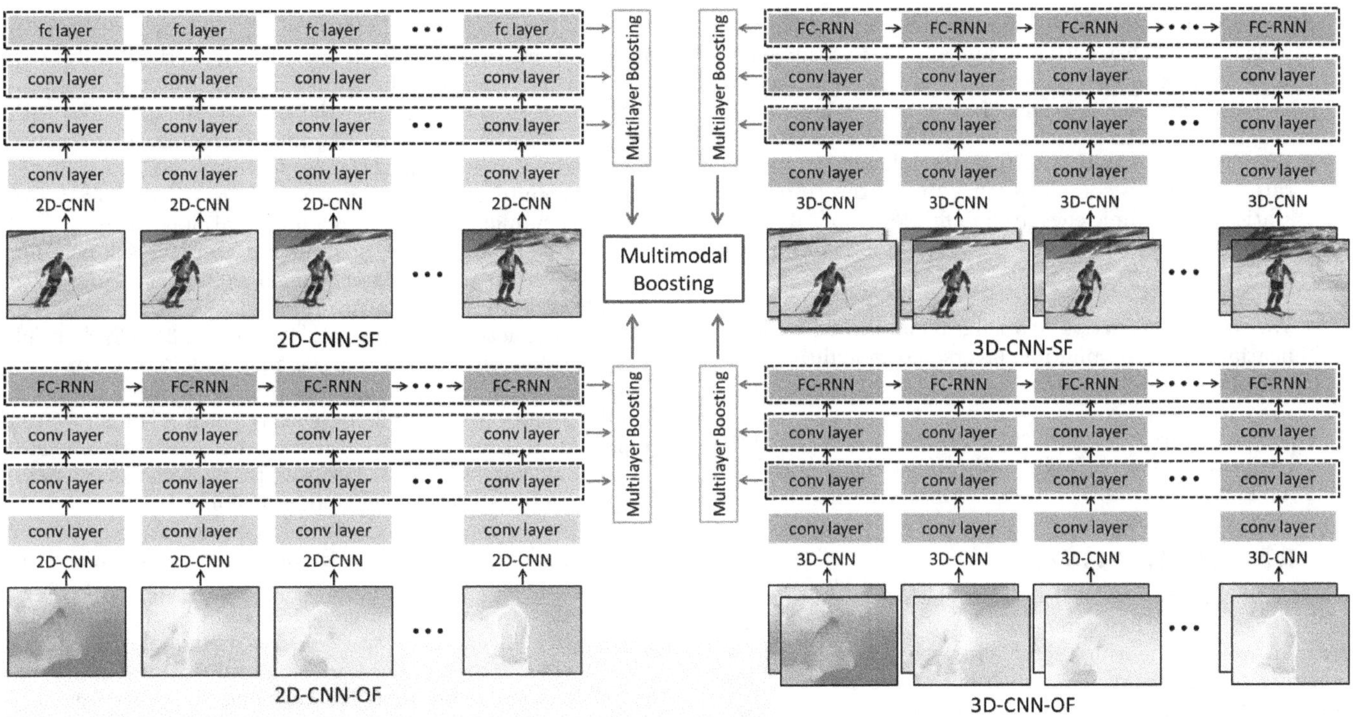

Figure 1: An overview of the proposed multilayer and multimodal fusion framework for video classification. We use four modalities to extract highly complementary information across multiple temporal scales. For each single modality, discriminative representations are computed for convolutional and fully connected layers. We employ an effective boosting model to fuse the multiple layers and modalities. Box colors are encoded according to different networks: 2D-CNN and 3D-CNN with and without RNN. We propose FC-RNN to model long-term temporal information rather than using the standard RNN structure.

distinguishing "soccer game" and "basketball game" requires high-level representations to model global scene statistics. However, classification of "playing guitar" and "playing violin" demands fine-scale features to capture subtle appearance and motion features. Therefore, leveraging the multilayer abstractions is expected to simplify video classification.

Although a significant progress in recent years has been achieved in the development of feature learning by deep neural networks [15, 20, 37], it is clear that none of the features have the same discriminative capability over all classes. For example, videos of "wedding ceremony" are strongly associated with static scenes and objects, while "kissing" is more related to dynamic motions. It is therefore widely accepted to adaptively combine a set of complementary features rather than using a single feature for all classes. Simonyan et al. [36] proposed the two-stream networks based on 2D-CNN to explicitly incorporate motion information from optical flow to complement the static per-frame information. Simple late fusion was adopted to combine the softmax scores of two networks by either averaging or with a linear classifier. This method has been widely utilized for video analysis [8, 46] thanks to the two complementary modalities and outstanding performance. Nevertheless, the question of which robust modalities to exploit and how to effectively perform multimodal fusion still remains open for video classification.

In this paper, we propose a multilayer and multimodal fusion framework of deep neural networks for video classification. The multilayer strategy can simultaneously capture a variety of levels of abstractions, thus is able to adapt from coarse- to fine-grained categorizations. Instead of using only two modalities as in the two-stream networks [36], we propose to use four complementary modalities in our multimodal scheme, i.e., 2D-CNN on a single spatial (color) frame and optical flow image as well as 3D-CNN on a short clip of spatial (color) frames and optical flow images. They not only effectively harness cues about static objects and dynamic motions in videos but also effectively exploit across temporal scales. As for the fusion of multiple layers and modalities, we adopt a powerful boosting model to learn their optimal combination.

Fig. 1 illustrates the overview of our proposed multilayer and multimodal fusion framework. Given an input video, the four modalities are used to extract complementary information at short and mid-term temporal scales. Instead of using the standard RNN structure, we propose FC-RNN to model the long-term temporal evolution across a whole video. FC-RNN takes advantage of pre-trained networks to transform the pre-trained fully-connected (`fc`) layers into recurrent layers. In the following, we use 2D-CNN-SF, 2D-CNN-OF, 3D-CNN-SF, 3D-CNN-OF to indicate 2D-CNN and 3D-CNN on spatial (color) frames and optical flow, respectively. For each individual network, an improved Fisher vector (iFV) is proposed to represent convolutional (`conv`) layers and an explicit feature map is used to represent the `fc` layers. We then employ a robust boosting model to learn the optimal combination of multiple layers and modalities. The main contributions of this paper are summarized as follows:

- We present a multilayer fusion strategy to capture multiple levels of abstraction and invariance in a single network. We propose to use the iFV and explicit feature maps to represent features of `conv` and `fc` layers.
- We introduce a multimodal fusion scheme to incorporate four highly complementary modalities to extract static and dynamic cues from multiple temporal scales. In particular, we propose FC-RNN to preserve the generalization properties of pre-trained networks.
- We adopt an effective boosting model for video classification by fusing multiple layers and modalities in an optimal and unified way.
- In the extensive experiments, our method achieves superior results on the well-known UCF101 and HMDB51 benchmarks.

2. RELATED WORK

Videos have been studied by the multimedia community for decades. Over the years a variety of problems like multimedia event recounting, surveillance event detection, action search, and many more have been proposed. A large family of these studies is about video classification. Conventional video classification systems hinge on extraction of local features, which have been largely advanced in both detection and description. Local features can be densely sampled or selected by maximizing specific saliency functions. Laptev [23] proposed STIP to detect sparse space-time interest points by extending the 2D Harris corner detector into 3D. Wang et al. [44] introduced the improved dense trajectories (iDT) to densely sample and track interest points from multiple spatial scales, where each tracked interest point generates a set of descriptors to represent shape and motion. Many successful video classification systems use iDT together with the motion boundary histogram (MBH) descriptor, which comprises the gradient of horizontal and vertical components of optical flow. It is widely recognized as the state-of-the-art feature for video analysis.

After local feature extraction, a number of coding techniques have been proposed for feature quantization, e.g., sparse coding [28] and locality-constrained linear coding [45]. Then average pooling and max pooling are normally used to aggregate statistics from local features. Several more advanced coding methods, e.g., Fisher vector (FV) [34] and vector of locally aggregated descriptors (VLAD) [16], have emerged to reserve high order statistics of local features and achieve noticeably better performance. However, these methods obviously incur the loss of spatio-temporal order of local features. Extensions to the completely orderless aggregation methods include spatio-temporal pyramids [24] and super sparse coding vectors [50]. Graphical models, such as hidden Markov models (HMM) and conditional random fields (CRF), are also popular methods to explore the long-term temporal information in videos.

Many improvements of video classification are motivated by advances in the image domain. The breakthrough on image classification [20] also rekindled the interest in deep neural networks for video classification. The pioneering work of Karpathy et al. [19] trained 2D-CNN on various forms of stacked video frames from Sports-1M. However, these deep networks are quite inferior to the shallow model based on the best hand-engineered features [44]. This is because complex motions and long-term temporal patterns are difficult to learn only through the simply stacked video frames. Simonyan et al. [36] designed the two-stream networks with two 2D-CNNs on spatial and temporal streams. This method takes advantage of the large-scale ImageNet [20] dataset for pre-training and significantly reduces the complexity to model dynamic motions through optical flow. Ji et al. [17] employed a head tracker and human detector to segment human regions in videos. The segmented regions are stacked as video volumes and used as inputs for 3D-CNN to recognize human actions. Tran et al. [42] applied 3D-CNN on full video frames to avoid pre-processing and jointly captures appearance and motion information. With these methods, similar results to the hand-engineered features [44] have been reported. In contrast to the previous methods with only single or dual modalities, we propose to use four complementary modalities during multimodal fusion.

The aforementioned models only concentrate on motions during short period and lack considerations of long-term temporal clues that are vital for video classification. Several methods have been proposed to address this limitation. Ng et al. [29] explored two schemes to handle full-length videos. They proposed various temporal feature pooling architectures and explored RNN with long short-term memory (LSTM) cells. The trajectory-pooled deep convolutional descriptor (TDD) was presented in [46] to incorporate temporal nature by trajectory constrained sampling and pooling. TDD shares the advantages of both hand-engineered features and deep-learned representations. While the improved networks using RNN can model long-term temporal order, our proposed multimodal method provides multi-temporal scales with short, mid, and long-term time contexts.

Recent work has investigated reasoning across multiple hierarchical levels in a network, which was shown to be advantageous for several tasks. Hariharan et al. [14] proposed hypercolumns for image segmentation and fine-grained localization. A hypercolumn at a given location is the vector containing all the values above that location at all layers of the CNN. DAG-CNN [48] introduced a multi-scale architecture to learn scale-specific features for natural scene recognition. FlowNet [10] preserved feature maps of both coarser and lower layers for optical flow estimation. We propose to extract feature representations from multiple layers to reason at multi-scale abstraction and invariance for video classification.

Combining multiple complementary feature representations is often effective to improve classification. Tamrakar et al. [41] evaluated various early and late fusion strategies in the context of multimedia event detection. Zhang et al. [52] computed non-linear kernels for each feature type and summed up the kernels for SVM training. Multiple kernel learning (MKL) [22] is a popular approach to estimate feature combination weights. However, it was observed [12] that simple averaging and geometric mean were highly competitive to MKL. Jiang et al. [18] proposed to jointly compute a codebook of audio and visual features for video classification with the intention to model correlations between the two modalities. Ngiam et al. [30] proposed a deep autoencoder to enforce cross modality learning between audio and video inputs. Our fusion method differs in combining robust boosting model with deep-learned representations from multiple layers and modalities.

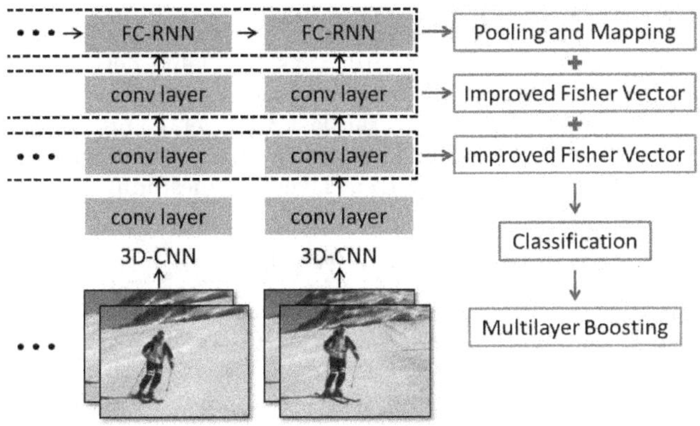

Figure 2: Illustration of multilayer representation and fusion. The proposed feature aggregation methods are used to represent fully connected and convolutional layers over time. The introduced boosting algorithm is applied to combine the representations from multiple layers.

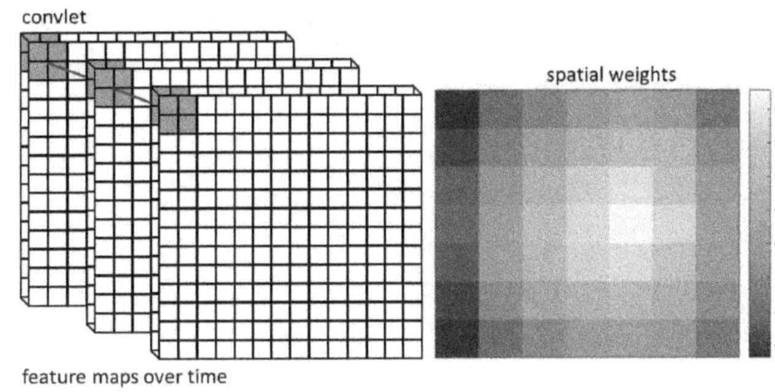

Figure 3: Learning spatial discriminative weights of a convolutional layer by convlets. A spatial weight indicates how discriminative or important that local spatial region is in a convolutional layer.

3. MULTILAYER REPRESENTATIONS

As a hierarchical feed-forward architecture, CNN progressively compute abstract and invariant representations of inputs. Recognition algorithms based on CNN often make predictions based on softmax scores or the last layer which is the summary of variables in the preceding layers. However, we argue that various abstractions such as pose, articulation, parts, objects, etc., learned in the intermediate layers can provide a complete description, from fine-scale to global scale, for video classification. Moreover, we propose a concept of convlet to utilize the spatial information reserved in conv layers to refine the final feature representation. In this section, we describe the detailed procedures to compute multilayer representations as illustrated in Fig. 2.

3.1 Improved Fisher Vector with the Convlet

Recent work on visualizing and understanding CNN reveals that conv layers demonstrate many intuitively desirable properties such as strong grouping within each feature map and exaggeration of discriminative parts of objects [51]. Therefore, a set of appropriate levels of compositionality in conv layers are able to supply plenty of fine-scale information to the category-level semantics. Meanwhile, the features from the layers come for free because they are already extracted during the forward pass. Furthermore, compared to fc layers, conv layers contain the spatial information, which can be applied to adaptive pooling and feature refinement because the discriminative information for video classification is often unevenly distributed in spatial domain.

We start from defining the convlet which is used to measure the spatial discriminability of activations at a conv layer. Assume s_l is the size (height and width) of a feature map and d_l denotes the total number of feature maps. We represent a set of conv layers extracted from a video by $\mathcal{C} = \{\mathbf{c}_{t,l};\quad t = 1, \ldots, T;\ l = 1, \ldots, L_c\}$, where T is the number of frames or short clips, L_c is the number of selected conv layers, and $\mathbf{c}_{t,l} \in \mathbb{R}^{s_l \times s_l \times d_l}$ indicates the l-th conv layer computed at the t-th timestamp. Since each convolutional kernel can be treated as a latent concept detector [47], we convert $\mathbf{c}_{t,l}$ to $s_l \times s_l$ feature descriptors, each of which is with the responses of d_l concept detectors. Thus a video can generate $n_l = s_l \times s_l \times T$ feature descriptors $\boldsymbol{x}_i \in \mathbb{R}^{d_l}$ at the l-th convolutional level, where $i = 1, \ldots, n_l$. Let R indicate the pre-defined spatial neighboring cells over a conv layer and R_j denote the j-th cell. We obtain the convlet corresponding to a spatial cell by

$$\boldsymbol{q}_j = \mathcal{G}\left(\{\boldsymbol{x}_i\}_{i \in R_j}\right), \quad j = 1, \ldots, |R|, \tag{1}$$

where $\mathcal{G}$ is a general coding and pooling operator and we employ FV [34] as $\mathcal{G}$ in our experiments. The convlet $\boldsymbol{q}_j$ is a representation that aggregates $\boldsymbol{x}_i$ in a local spatial region across the entire video, as shown in Fig. 3. We then use each convlet $\boldsymbol{q}_j$ to make video classification and the accuracy α_j associated with R_j indicates how discriminative this local spatial cell is in a conv layer. We transform the classification accuracy α_j to a spatial discriminative weight w_j with softmax function $w_j = \exp(\alpha_j) / \sum_{k=1}^{|R|} \exp(\alpha_k)$ or sigmoid function $w_j = 1 / [1 + \exp(\alpha' - \alpha_j)]$, where α' is a parameter to control the relative weight. All features $\boldsymbol{x}_i$ of spatial cell R_j have the same associated weight w_j.

The heat map in Fig. 3 demonstrates the spatial weights learned by convlets of conv5 in VGG16 [37] on the UCF101 dataset [38]. The features close to boundary regions are much less discriminative than those in the middle, in particular for the left two corner regions. It is also interesting to observe that the hot regions are not exactly centered but a bit shifted towards the right. In addition, spatial weights of different conv layers in the same network often exhibit slightly different spatial distributions. Since the weight w_i of $\boldsymbol{x}_i$ represents how discriminative or important $\boldsymbol{x}_i$ is for classification, we can take advantage of this property to improve a general feature aggregation method. We demonstrate the improvement to FV [34] in this paper.

As assumed in FV, the feature descriptors $\boldsymbol{x}_i$ have a Gaussian mixture model (GMM) distribution characterized by parameters $\{\pi_k, \boldsymbol{\mu}_k, \boldsymbol{\sigma}_k\}$ with $k = 1, \ldots, K$, where π_k, $\boldsymbol{\mu}_k$, and $\boldsymbol{\sigma}_k$ are the prior mode probability, mean, and covariance (diagonal) of the k-th Gaussian component φ_k. To better fit the diagonal covariance assumption, we apply PCA to decorrelate $\boldsymbol{x}_i$ and reduce feature dimensions. Each feature $\boldsymbol{x}_i$ is then encoded by the deviations with respect to the parameters of GMM. Let $\gamma_{i,k}$ be the soft assignment of $\boldsymbol{x}_i$ to the k-th Gaussian component:

$$\gamma_{i,k} = \frac{\pi_k \varphi_k(\boldsymbol{x}_i)}{\sum_{j=1}^{K} \pi_j \varphi_j(\boldsymbol{x}_i)}. \tag{2}$$

We obtain the improved Fisher vector (iFV) representation of a video at a convolutional layer by concatenating the following derivative vectors from K Gaussian components:

$$\boldsymbol{\rho}_k = \frac{1}{n_l\sqrt{\pi_k}} \sum_{i=1}^{n_l} \gamma_{i,k} w_i \left(\frac{\boldsymbol{x}_i - \boldsymbol{\mu}_k}{\boldsymbol{\sigma}_k}\right), \tag{3}$$

$$\boldsymbol{\tau}_k = \frac{1}{n_l\sqrt{2\pi_k}} \sum_{i=1}^{n_l} \gamma_{i,k} w_i \left[\frac{(\boldsymbol{x}_i - \boldsymbol{\mu}_k)^2}{\boldsymbol{\sigma}_k^2} - 1\right], \tag{4}$$

where $\boldsymbol{\rho}_k$ and $\boldsymbol{\tau}_k$ are the d_l-dimensional derivatives with respect to $\boldsymbol{\mu}_k$ and $\boldsymbol{\sigma}_k$ of the k-th Gaussian component. We apply the spatial discriminative factor w_i to weight the relative displacements of $\boldsymbol{x}_i$ to the mean and covariance in Eq. (3–4). In this way, more informative features gain higher contributions to the final representation, while background or noisy features are suppressed. We use iFV to compute the video representations of selected `conv` layers over time.

3.2 Feature Pooling and Mapping

We represent a set of `fc` layers computed from a video by $\mathcal{F} = \{\boldsymbol{f}_{t,l};\ t = 1,\ldots,T;\ l = 1,\ldots,L_f\}$, where $\boldsymbol{f}_{t,l} \in \mathbb{R}^{d_l}$ denotes the l-th `fc` layer computed at timestamp t. The `fc` vector is more sensitive to the category-level semantic information and usually has high dimensions (e.g., $d_l = 4096$ in VGG16). Compared to $\boldsymbol{c}_{t,l}$, which can generate $s_l \times s_l$ features at each timestamp, $\boldsymbol{f}_{t,l}$ is far more sparse as spatial information is lost. Considering these properties, we first apply temporal max pooling to aggregate $\boldsymbol{f}_{t,l}$ across time to obtain $\boldsymbol{f}_l$, which is the initial representation of a video at the l-th `fc` level.

While the last fully-connected layer in a network performs linear classification, it is flexible to inject additional non-linearity to $\boldsymbol{f}_l$ by using non-linear kernels in SVM. However, non-linear SVM is generally much slower than linear one in terms of both learning and prediction. In particular, we are able to train linear SVM in time linear with the number of training samples. This favorably extends the applicability of linear SVM algorithms to large-scale data, which is usually the case for video classification. We thus employ the explicit feature map [43] to approximate large-scale non-linear SVM by the linear one. In explicit feature map, the initial representation $\boldsymbol{f}_l$ is lifted to a Hilbert space with moderately higher feature dimensions through $\psi : \mathbb{R}^{d_l} \to \mathbb{R}^{d_l(2z+1)}$ such that the inner product in this space can reasonably well approximate a non-linear kernel κ, i.e., $\langle\psi(\boldsymbol{f}_l), \psi(\boldsymbol{f}_l')\rangle \approx \kappa(\boldsymbol{f}_l, \boldsymbol{f}_l')$. Therefore the final representation $\psi(\boldsymbol{f}_l)$ of a `fc` layer makes use of not only the discriminative power of non-linear kernels but also the efficient training and evaluation of the linear one.

4. FC-RNN STRUCTURE

Most networks hinge on short or mid-term contents such as a single frame [36] or a buffer of frames [42], where features are independently extracted for video classification. We believe that there are important connections between frames of the entire video and that the order of frames matters. To address this intuition, we propose a simple and effective structure, FC-RNN, to transform a network pre-trained on separate frames or clips to deal with video as a whole sequence.

4.1 Initialization of Recurrent Layers

One of the straightforward ways to enable networks to work with video as a sequence is to introduce a stack of recurrent layers on top of the last `fc` layer. This method is common [8, 29] and shows improvement in performance. The output of such a recurrent layer at timestamp t is computed as:

$$\boldsymbol{h}_t = \mathcal{H}(\boldsymbol{W}_{ih}\boldsymbol{f}_t + \boldsymbol{W}_{hh}\boldsymbol{h}_{t-1} + b_h), \tag{5}$$

where $\mathcal{H}$ is an activation function, $\boldsymbol{W}_{ih}$ is the input-to-hidden matrix, $\boldsymbol{f}_t$ is the input to this layer, $\boldsymbol{W}_{hh}$ is the hidden-to-hidden matrix, $\boldsymbol{h}_{t-1}$ is a hidden state vector from previous timestamp, and b_h is an optional bias. Both $\boldsymbol{W}_{ih}$ and $\boldsymbol{W}_{hh}$ are randomly initialized. We refer to this as the standard initialization.

One drawback of the standard initialization is that it requires to train an entire layer (or a stack of layers) from scratch even if a pre-trained network is used for feature extraction. This would result in reducing important generalization properties of a network that is fine-tuned on a relatively small dataset. In this paper, we propose to transform `fc` layers of a pre-trained CNN into recurrent layers. In this way, we preserve the structure of a pre-trained network as much as possible. Assume that a pre-trained `fc` layer at timestamp t has the structure:

$$\boldsymbol{f}_t = \mathcal{H}(\boldsymbol{W}_{io}\boldsymbol{y}_t + b_f), \tag{6}$$

where $\boldsymbol{W}_{io}$ is the pre-trained input-to-output matrix, $\boldsymbol{y}_t$ is output of the previous layer and b_f is bias. We suggest to transform it into a recurrent layer as:

$$\boldsymbol{f}_t = \mathcal{H}(\boldsymbol{W}_{io}\boldsymbol{y}_t + \boldsymbol{W}_{hh}\boldsymbol{f}_{t-1} + b_f). \tag{7}$$

This `fc` initialized recurrent structure is referred as FC-RNN. Fig. 4 illustrates the difference between our proposed FC-RNN and the standard RNN. Our method only introduces a single weight matrix that needs training from scratch, i.e., the hidden-to-hidden matrix $\boldsymbol{W}_{hh}$. Other weight matrices have been already pre-trained and can be just fine-tuned. We observe that this design is effective to reduce over-fitting and expedite convergence. LSTM is not used in our networks because 1) the complicated cell structure in LSTM is not well-adapted to our design; 2) the sequence of clips processed by 3D-CNN in a video is not long as each clip covers a number of non-overlapping frames; 3) LSTM has comparable results to standard RNN in our experiments.

4.2 Regularization

We apply a number of regularization techniques in the training of FC-RNN. The recurrent connection is prone to learn the specific order of videos in the training set, therefore we randomly permute the order of training videos for each epoch. This operation slows down convergence but improves generalization. The regularization term which forces to learn weights with smaller ℓ_2-norm also helps generalization. With intention of preventing the gradients from exploding in recurrent layers, we employ soft gradient clipping in the following way. For each computed gradient g during stochastic gradient descent (SGD), we check if its ℓ_2-norm $\|g\|$ is greater than a pre-defined threshold $\delta = 10$. If that is the case, we rescale the gradient to $g \leftarrow g\delta/\|g\|$. We find that without gradient clipping the explosion of gradient values is a critical barrier to successfully training the networks. To further improve generalization, we train networks with

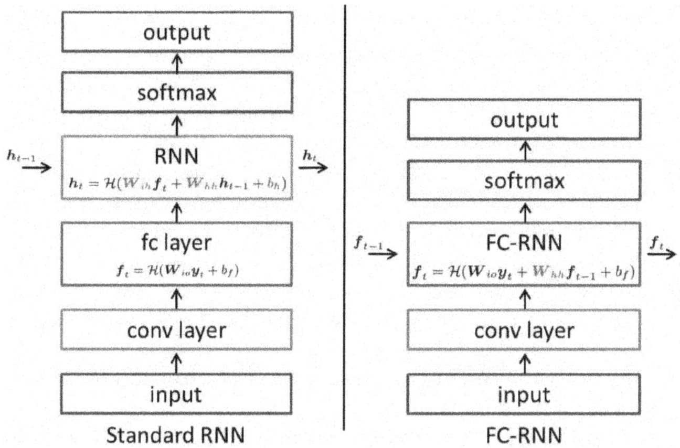

Figure 4: Comparison of standard RNN and FC-RNN. The variables in red correspond to the parameters that need to be trained from scratch.

drop-out on the outputs of recurrent layers. During training, we set the outputs of the recurrent layers to 0 with a probability of $p = 0.5$, and scale the activations of other neurons by a factor of $1/(1-p)$.

5. MULTIMODAL REPRESENTATIONS

Since the visual information in videos is a juxtaposition of not only scenes and objects but also atomic actions evolving over the whole video sequence, it is favorable to capture and combine both static appearances and dynamic motions. To address this challenge we use a multimodal approach to model a variety of semantic clues in multi-temporal scales. Fig. 1 demonstrates our proposed four modalities, which provide mutually complementary information in short, mid, and long-term temporal contexts.

The two networks operating on spatial frames (single frame in 2D-CNN-SF and short clip of frames in 3D-CNN-SF) can capture objects and scenes that are strongly correlated to certain video categories, e.g., snow and mountains in Fig. 1 indicate skiing. 2D-CNN-SF is essentially an image classification network which can be built upon the recent advances in large-scale image recognition methods and datasets. 3D-CNN-SF selectively attends to both motion and appearance cues through spatio-temporal convolution and pooling operations. It encapsulates the mid-term temporal information as the network's input is a short video clip (e.g., 16 spatial frames). We utilize the proposed FC-RNN for 3D-CNN-SF to learn the long-term temporal order. The recurrent structure is not used for 2D-CNN-SF due to very limited improvement (0.1%). This is probably because the static information such as objects and scenes modeled by 2D-CNN-SF is not very correlated with the temporal evolution.

Since optical flow [2] explicitly captures dynamic motions, the two networks running on optical flow images (single image in 2D-CNN-OF and short clip of images in 3D-CNN-OF) provide vital clues to recognize actions. Moreover, optical flow also conveys rough shape cues of moving objects, e.g., the skier and ski poles in Fig. 1. Note, in contrast to the temporal stream [36] used in most previous methods, which work on the stacked optical flow maps, we input a single *colorized optical flow image* to 2D-CNN-OF. As illustrated in Fig. 1, a colorized optical flow image contains 3 channels with RGB values, while an optical flow map includes 2 channels with the raw values of horizontal and vertical displacements. The hue and saturation of an colorized optical flow image indicate flow's orientation and magnitude. This enables us to reduce over-fitting and training time by leveraging pre-trained models from large-scale image datasets. Since the input is a single colorized image, 2D-CNN-OF captures the fine-scale and short-term temporal information between a pair of adjacent frames. 3D-CNN-OF models the high order motion cues such as spatial and temporal derivatives of optical flow, which has been successfully applied to hand-engineered features [44]. This modality also encapsulates the mid-term temporal clues. Similar to 3D-CNN-SF, FC-RNN is also employed to learn the long-term temporal order of 2D-CNN-OF and 3D-CNN-OF.

To obtain the final multimodal representation of a video, we use the aforementioned iFV as well as temporal max pooling and explicit feature map to compute the representations of selected `conv` and `fc` layers (respectively for each modality).

6. FUSION BY BOOSTING

Given the above representations of multiple layers and modalities, in this section, we focus on how to effectively utilize correlations across different representations. We formulate the multilayer and multimodal fusion as a boosting task to maximize the classification accuracy.

We represent a training set by $\{(v_i, y_i)\}_{i=1}^N$ which contains N instance pairs of a video $v_i \in \mathcal{V}$ and a class label $y_i \in \{1, \ldots, C\}$. Let $\{\boldsymbol{r}_m : \mathcal{V} \to \mathbb{R}^{d_m}\}_{m=1}^M$ indicate M video representations extracted by the proposed feature aggregation methods from `conv` and `fc` layers of multiple modalities. We use a general kernel function κ to measure the similarity between instances by the m-th video representation: $\kappa_m(v, v') = \kappa(\boldsymbol{r}_m(v), \boldsymbol{r}_m(v'))$. So the kernel response of a given instance $v \in \mathcal{V}$ to the whole training samples is defined as $\boldsymbol{\mathcal{K}}_m(v) = [\kappa_m(v, v_1), \ldots, \kappa_m(v, v_N)]^T$. We focus on the binary classification problem in the following derivation, which extends straightforwardly to multiple classes. Here the objective is to optimize a linear combination of the predictions using M representations: $U(v) = \sum_{m=1}^M \theta_m u_m(v)$, where θ_m is a mixing coefficient and u_m is a decision function. In this paper, we use SVM with the decision function $u_m(v) = \boldsymbol{\mathcal{K}}_m(v)^T \boldsymbol{a}_m + b_m$, but the weak learner u_m is not necessarily SVM. All parameters of the fusion model can be solved by training u_m based on each individual video representation and subsequently optimizing θ_m through:

$$\arg\max_{\theta,\xi,\epsilon} \quad \epsilon - \frac{1}{\nu N} \sum_{i=1}^N \xi_i \tag{8}$$
$$\text{s.t.} \quad y_i \sum_{m=1}^M \theta_m u_m(v_i) + \xi_i \geq \epsilon, \quad i = 1, \ldots, N$$
$$\sum_{m=1}^M \theta_m = 1, \quad \theta_m \geq 0, \quad m = 1, \ldots, M,$$

where ξ_i is a slack variable and ν is a regularization parameter to control the smoothness of the resulting function. This is essentially a linear programming problem and can be solved by the column generation approach [7]. Similar to image classification [12], in the multiclass case with C categories we have two variations of the mixing coefficients. We call the first variant boost-u which jointly learns a uniform coefficient vector $\theta \in \mathbb{R}^M$ for all classes. The alternative one boost-c learns a coefficient vector for each class resulting in a coefficient matrix $\Theta \in \mathbb{R}^{M\times C}$. So the final decision functions for the fusion of multiple layers and modalities with the two boosting variants are:

$$y(v) = \arg\max_{c=1,\ldots,C} \sum_{m=1}^{M} \theta_m \left(\mathcal{K}_m(v)^T \boldsymbol{a}_{c,m} + b_{c,m}\right), \quad (9)$$

$$y(v) = \arg\max_{c=1,\ldots,C} \sum_{m=1}^{M} \Theta_m^c \left(\mathcal{K}_m(v)^T \boldsymbol{a}_{c,m} + b_{c,m}\right). \quad (10)$$

This boosting algorithm is a unified method for both multilayer and multimodal fusion. It can be used by multilayer fusion to combine the video representations $\boldsymbol{r}_m$ from multiple layers in a single modality. If the set of representations is extracted over multiple modalities, it then performs as multimodal fusion. We observe that the joint fusion of multiple layers over all modalities is slightly better than the separate fusion of individual modality first then across all modalities. This is probably because the joint fusion allows different modalities to explore better correlations at different levels.

7. EXPERIMENTS

In this section, we extensively evaluate the proposed multilayer and multimodal fusion method on two public benchmark datasets for video classification: UCF101 [38] and HMDB51 [21]. In all experiments, we use LIBLINEAR [9] as the linear SVM solver. Experimental results show that our algorithm achieves the state-of-the-art results on the two benchmarks.

7.1 Experimental Setup

7.1.1 Datasets

The UCF101 [38] dataset contains 101 action classes with large variations in scale, viewpoint, illumination, camera motion, and cluttered background. It consists of 13,320 videos in total. We follow the standard experimental setting as in [38] and use three training and testing splits. In each split, 20% of training data is randomly selected as validation set for the boosting model selection. The first split of UCF101 (denoted as UCF101*) is also used to evaluate and understand the contribution of each individual component. We report the average accuracy over the three splits as the overall measurement.

The HMDB51 dataset [21] is collected from a wide range of sources from digitized movies to online videos. It contains 51 categories and 6,766 videos in total. This dataset includes original videos and stabilized ones. Our evaluations are based on the original version. There are 70 videos for training and 30 videos for testing in each class. We use 40% of training data as validation set to perform model selection for boosting. We follow the evaluation protocol defined in [21] and use three training and testing splits and report the mean accuracy over the three splits.

7.1.2 Implementations

We implement the networks of four modalities in Theano with cuDNN4 on an NVIDIA DIGITS DevBox with four Titan X GPUs. 2D-CNN and 3D-CNN in the experiments are initialized with VGG16 [37] pre-trained on ImageNet and C3D [42] pre-trained on Sports-1M, respectively. Outputs of the last four layers of each network are used to represent videos. Special attention is paid to assembling mini-batches in order to deal with varying video length. We fill all frames of a video into a mini-batch and use another video if there is still space in the mini-batch. When the limit of a mini-batch is reached and there are frames left, we use them in the next one. When there are no more frames to fill a mini-batch, we fill it with zeros and these examples are not used in computation. We shuffle video instances after each epoch to prevent learning a specific sequence of examples. The last hidden state vector of each mini-batch is propagated to the next batch.

We apply data augmentations to increase the diversity of videos. For 2D-CNN we skip every second frame and operate on a single frame resized to 320×240 and cropped to 224×224. 3D-CNN works on a clip of 16 frames resized to 160×120 and cropped to 112×112. Training frames are generated by random cropping and flipping video frames, while for testing, only a central crop with no flipping is evaluated. Since the two datasets are of quite different sizes, we apply different learning rate schedules. For UCF101, we fine-tune 9 epochs with an initial learning rate of $\lambda = 3 \times 10^{-4}$ and divide it by 10 after each 4 epochs. For HMDB51, we perform fine-tuning for 30 epochs with the same initial learning rate and divide it by 10 after every 10 epochs. All network parameters that do not have pre-trained weights are initialized with random samples drawn from a zero-mean normal distribution ($\sigma = 0.01$).We use the frame-wise negative log-likelihood of a mini-batch as the cost function, which is optimized using SGD with a momentum of 0.9.

7.2 Experimental Results

7.2.1 Evaluation of Feature Aggregations

We first evaluate the performance of iFV to represent `conv` layers in different modalities. Compared to the traditional aggregation methods, iFV retains high-order statistics; in particular, it adaptively weights the features of a `conv` layer according to the associated spatial weights learned by the proposed convlet. We keep 300 out of 512 components in PCA. For computing the spatial discriminative weights, we find the sigmoid is more discriminative than softmax, e.g., iFV with sigmoid outperforms that with softmax by 0.6% for `conv5` layer in 2D-CNN-SF. The sigmoid function is therefore used in the following experiments. We set $K = 128$ Gaussian components for both methods so the final feature dimensionality is 76.8K. We compare iFV with the conventional FV [34] in Table 1, where iFV consistently outperforms FV for `conv` layers in all modalities with the improvements ranging from 0.6% to 2.5%. A larger improvement is observed for `conv4` than `conv5`, probably because of the finer spatial information preserved in the lower layer. These improvements clearly show the advantages of utilizing the spatial discriminability learned by convlets to enhance the feature representation.

We employ temporal max pooling to aggregate `fc` layers, which are further extended with an explicit feature map to approximate non-linear kernels. This representation also benefits from the same efficiency of learning and prediction as linear SVM. We demonstrate the results of `fc` layers in 3D-CNN-SF with approximated non-linearities in Table 2.

Modality	Layer	FV [34]	iFV
2D-CNN-SF	conv4	74.2%	**76.7%**
	conv5	79.6%	**80.6%**
2D-CNN-OF	conv4	75.6%	**78.1%**
	conv5	81.9%	**82.6%**
3D-CNN-SF	conv4	83.6%	**84.8%**
	conv5	83.3%	**84.6%**
3D-CNN-OF	conv4	78.2%	**78.8%**
	conv5	78.1%	**78.7%**

Table 1: Comparison of FV and the proposed iFV to represent convolutional layers of different modalities on UCF101*.

Layer	Linear	χ^2	Jensen-Shannon	Intersection
fc6	84.1%	84.8%	84.6%	**84.9%**
fc7	82.4%	82.9%	83.0%	**83.2%**

Table 2: Comparison of different non-linear approximations to represent fully connected layers in 3D-CNN-SF on UCF101*.

Both fc6 and fc7 are transformed to recurrent layers by FC-RNN. We use the ℓ_2-norm and $z = 3$ in the explicit feature map, so the extended feature dimension is 28,672. The baseline method is the linear representation by temporal max pooling without feature mapping. We evaluate three additive non-linear kernels: χ^2, Jensen-Shannon and intersection kernels, which are widely used in machine learning and computer vision. All non-linear representations outperform the linear one, especially the representation with intersection kernel achieves the best results. We thus use the intersection non-linearity approximation to represent fc layers in the following experiments.

7.2.2 Evaluation of FC-RNN

Our method extracts static and dynamic information at multiple temporal scales. 2D-CNN and 3D-CNN on spatial frames and optical flow images compute features from short-term and mid-term temporal contexts. FC-RNN is then employed to model each video as an ordered sequence of frames or clips to capture the long-term temporal order. Since FC-RNN maintains the structure of a pre-trained network to the greatest extent, it is therefore effective at preserving important generalization properties of the network, when fine-tuned on a smaller target dataset. Moreover, FC-RNN achieves higher accuracy and is faster to converge compared to the standard RNN. We compare the training and testing performances of our proposed FC-RNN and the standard RNN in Fig. 5. To avoid clutter, we only show this comparison for 3D-CNN modalities—a similar phenomena is observed on 2D-CNN-OF as well. FC-RNN is generally able to alleviate over-fitting and converge faster, e.g., FC-RNN outperforms standard RNN and LSTM by 3.0% and 2.9% on 3D-CNN-SF. In comparison to the networks without recurrent connections, FC-RNN significantly improves the modalities of 2D-CNN-OF, 3D-CNN-SF and 3D-CNN-OF by 3.3%, 3.2% and 5.1%, respectively. This demonstrates the benefits of FC-RNN in modeling the long-term temporal clues.

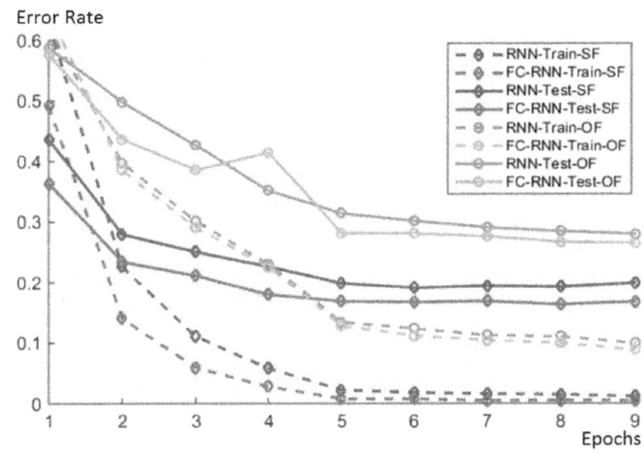

Figure 5: Comparison of the proposed FC-RNN and the standard RNN in training and testing of 3D-CNN-SF and 3D-CNN-OF on UCF101*.

7.2.3 Evaluation of Multilayer Fusion

Here we evaluate the multilayer fusion on combining various layers for individual modalities. Table 3 shows the performance of each single layer across different modalities and the fusion results on the two datasets. Although the last layer in a network is the most sensitive to category-level semantics, it is not unusual for lower layers to have on par or superior results, e.g., conv5 of 2D-CNN-OF on UCF101 and conv5 of 2D-CNN-SF on HMDB51. So it is of great potential to exploit the intermediate abstractions such as parts, objects, poses, articulations and so on for video classification. It is also of interest to observe that most layers produce accuracies better than the baseline of softmax, i.e., the prediction outputs of a network. This again validates the merit of the proposed feature aggregation methods to represent conv and fc layers.

If we use the boosting algorithm to combine multiple layers, the fusion result significantly outperforms the baseline for all modalities, especially for 3D-CNN-OF with 7.2% and 7.9% gains on UCF101 and HMDB51. This demonstrates that various abstractions extracted in multiple layers are of rich complementarity. Although boost-c is more flexible to have class-specific mixing coefficients, its results are inferior to those of boost-u. This is because the model of boost-c tends to over-fit, since the $C \times M$ parameters to fit in boost-c require more training data than the M parameters in boost-u. We thus use boost-u in the following fusion experiments. 3D-CNN-SF is the best modality before fusion as it jointly models appearance and motion information. After multilayer fusion the other two modalities involving dynamic cues are enhanced to a similar performance level, which shows that the boosting method successfully maximizes the capability of a network.

7.2.4 Evaluation of Multimodal Fusion

We now demonstrate multimodal fusion, combining the proposed four modalities. Our networks are initialized by models pre-trained on large-scale image and video datasets so it is natural to fine-tune these networks for the two modalities of spatial frames. However, for the other two modalities involving optical flow, they are distant from the source if we

	UCF101 (%)				HMDB51 (%)			
	2D-CNN-SF	2D-CNN-OF	3D-CNN-SF	3D-CNN-OF	2D-CNN-SF	2D-CNN-OF	3D-CNN-SF	3D-CNN-OF
`conv4`	75.0	79.7	83.1	80.2	37.0	41.7	49.1	48.9
`conv5`	79.9	83.9	83.7	80.6	42.0	47.0	49.9	48.6
`fc6`	81.0	81.1	84.0	80.3	42.7	48.3	51.8	51.5
`fc7`	80.5	82.7	83.7	79.9	41.6	47.3	52.1	50.0
softmax	79.5	80.9	82.9	75.3	40.2	47.9	51.2	45.1
boost-c	82.1(+2.6)	84.4(+3.5)	84.5(+1.6)	81.4(+6.1)	43.8(+3.6)	50.6(+2.7)	52.2(+1.0)	52.8(+7.7)
boost-u	**82.6**(+3.1)	**85.9**(+5.0)	**85.4**(+2.5)	**82.5**(+7.2)	**44.5**(+4.3)	**51.4**(+3.5)	**53.1**(+1.9)	**53.0**(+7.9)

Table 3: Performances of individual layers over different modalities and multilayer fusion results.

Initialized by 3D-CNN-SF			✓	✓
Using FC-RNN		✓		✓
Accuracy of 3D-CNN-OF	68.4%	70.4%	72.5%	**73.5%**

Table 4: Comparison of the initialization methods for 3D-CNN-OF on UCF101*.

Modality	Accuracy	Combinations						
2D-CNN-SF	83.2	✓		✓	✓	✓		✓
2D-CNN-OF	84.8	✓	✓			✓	✓	✓
3D-CNN-SF	85.9		✓	✓		✓	✓	✓
3D-CNN-OF	81.4				✓		✓	✓
Fusion Accuracy		90.3	90.8	87.1	90.4	91.2	91.3	**91.9**

Table 5: Classification accuracies (%) of different modalities and various combinations on UCF101*.

UCF101 (%)		HMDB51 (%)	
STIP + BOVW [21]	43.9	STIP + BOVW [21]	23.0
DT + MVSV [4]	83.5	DT + MVSV [4]	55.9
iDT + HSV [33]	87.9	iDT + HSV [33]	61.1
C3D [42]	85.2	iDT + FV [44]	57.2
LRCN [8]	82.9	Motionlets [3]	42.1
TDD [46]	90.3	TDD [46]	**63.2**
RNN-FV [25]	88.0	RNN-FV [25]	54.3
Two-Stream [36]	88.0	Two-Stream [36]	59.4
MultiSource CNN [32]	89.1	MultiSource CNN [32]	54.9
Composite LSTM [39]	84.3	Composite LSTM [39]	44.1
Ours	**91.6**	Ours	**61.8**

Table 6: Comparison of the multimodal fusion to the state-of-the-art results.

regard fine-tuning as a way of domain transformation. We introduce a simple but effective method to bridge the two domains—initialize optical flow networks by spatial frame models that have been fine-tuned on the target domain. As shown in Table 4, compared to the networks directly fine-tuned on the source model (i.e., not initialized by 3D-CNN-SF), our initialization remarkably improves the results.

Table 5 contains the accuracies for various combinations of the four modalities. Observe that fusing any pair of modalities improves the individual results. The best classification accuracy of 91.9% is obtained by the combination of all modalities. In the end, we achieve an accuracy of 91.6% on UCF101 and 61.8% on HMDB51 through combining the four modalites by boost-u. In comparison to the results in Table 3, the multimodal fusion produces much higher accuracy than any individual modality. This indicates the strong complementarity between the four modalities that capture diverse static and dynamic features at multiple temporal scales. In comparison to the baseline fusion methods, boost-u improves the result by 2.3% over geometric mean [41], 4.3% over SVM-based fusion [36], and 7.9% over AdaBoost [5] on UCF101*. This demonstrates that boost-u is more effective to exploit and fuse the complementary relationship of multiple modalities.

We finally compare our results with the most recent state-of-the-art methods in Table 6. Our method produces the best accuracy on UCF101 with a clear margin over other competing algorithms. It is more challenging to fine-tune networks and train boost-u on HMDB51, where each training split is 2.6 times smaller than UCF101. Our method still achieves superior performance on HMDB51. Other competitive results [33, 46] are based on the improved dense trajectories, which require quite a few hand-crafted processes such as dense point tracking, human detection, camera motion estimation, etc. As shown on UCF101, large training data is beneficial for training networks and boosting, so we are planing to explore techniques such as multi-task learning and temporal elastic deformation to increase the effective training size of HMDB51.

8. CONCLUSION

In this paper, we have presented a novel framework to fuse deep neural networks in multiple layers and modalities for video classification. A multilayer strategy is proposed to incorporate various levels of semantics in each single network. We employ effective feature aggregation methods, i.e., iFV and explicit feature maps to represent `conv` and `fc` layers. We further introduce a multimodal approach to capture diverse static and dynamic cues from four highly complementary modalities at multiple temporal scales. FC-RNN is then proposed to effectively model long-term temporal order by leveraging the generalization properties of pre-trained networks. A powerful boosting model is used for the optimal combination of multilayer and multimodal representations. We evaluate our approach extensively on two public benchmark datasets and achieve superior results compared to a number of recent methods.

9. REFERENCES

[1] D. Borth, T. Chen, R. Ji, and S. Chang. Sentibank: large-scale ontology and classifiers for detecting sentiment and emotions in visual content. In *ACM Multimedia*, 2013.

[2] T. Brox, A. Bruhn, N. Papenberg, and J. Weickert. High accuracy optical flow estimation based on a theory for warping. In *ECCV*, 2004.

[3] Z. Cai, L. Wang, X. Peng, and Y. Qiao. Motionlets: mid-level 3D parts for human motion recognition. In *CVPR*, 2013.

[4] Z. Cai, L. Wang, X. Peng, and Y. Qiao. Multi-view super vector for action recognition. In *CVPR*, 2014.

[5] S. Chen, J. Wang, Y. Liu, C. Xu, and H. Lu. Fast feature selection and training for AdaBoost-based concept detection with large scale datasets. In *ACM Multimedia*, 2010.

[6] G. Dahl, D. Yu, L. Deng, and A. Acero. Context-dependent pre-trained deep neural networks for large vocabulary speech recognition. *TASLP*, 2012.

[7] A. Demiriz, K. Bennett, and J. Taylor. Linear programming boosting via column generation. *JMLR*, 2000.

[8] J. Donahue, L. Hendricks, S. Guadarrama, and M. Rohrbach. Long-term recurrent convolutional networks for visual recognition and description. In *CVPR*, 2015.

[9] R. Fan, K. Chang, C. Hsieh, X. Wang, and C. Lin. LIBLINEAR: A library for large linear classification. *JMLR*, 2008.

[10] P. Fischer, A. Dosovitskiy, E. Ilg, P. Hausser, C. Hazirbas, V. Golkov, P. Smagt, D. Cremers, and T. Brox. FlowNet: learning optical flow with convolutional networks. In *ICCV*, 2015.

[11] J. Francoise, N. Schnell, and F. Bevilacqua. A multimodal probabilistic model for gesture based control of sound synthesis. In *ACM Multimedia*, 2011.

[12] P. Gehler and S. Nowozin. On feature combination for multiclass object classification. In *ICCV*, 2009.

[13] J. Gemert, C. Veenman, A. Smeulders, and J. Geusebroek. Visual word ambiguity. *TPAMI*, 2009.

[14] B. Hariharan, P. Arbelaez, R. Girshick, and J. Malik. Hypercolumns for object segmentation and fine-grained localization. In *CVPR*, 2015.

[15] K. He, X. Zhang, S. Ren, and J. Sun. Deep residual learning for image recognition. In *CoRR*, 2015.

[16] H. Jegou, M. Douze, C. Schmid, and P. Perez. Aggregating local descriptors into a compact image representation. In *CVPR*, 2010.

[17] S. Ji, W. Xu, M. Yang, and K. Yu. 3D convolutional neural networks for human action recognition. *TPAMI*, 2013.

[18] W. Jiang, C. Cotton, S.-F. Chang, D. Ellis, and A. Loui. Short-term audio-visual atoms for generic video concept classification. In *ACM Multimedia*, 2009.

[19] A. Karpathy, G. Toderici, S. Shetty, T. Leung, R. Sukthankar, and L. Fei-Fei. Large-scale video classification with convolutional neural networks. In *CVPR*, 2014.

[20] A. Krizhevsky, I. Sutskever, and G. Hinton. ImageNet classification with deep convolutional neural networks. In *NIPS*, 2012.

[21] H. Kuehne, H. Jhuang, E. Garrote, T. Poggio, and T. Serre. HMDB: a large video database for human motion recognition. In *ICCV*, 2011.

[22] G. Lanckriet, N. Cristianini, P. Bartlett, L. Ghaoui, and M. Jordan. Learning the kernel matrix with semidefinite programming. *JMLR*, 2004.

[23] I. Laptev. On space-time interest points. *IJCV*, 2005.

[24] I. Laptev, M. Marszalek, C. Schmid, and B. Rozenfeld. Learning realistic human actions from movies. In *CVPR*, 2008.

[25] G. Lev, G. Sadeh, B. Klein, and L. Wolf. RNN Fisher vectors for action recognition and image annotation. In *CoRR*, 2015.

[26] J. Long, E. Shelhamer, and T. Darrell. Fully convolutional networks for semantic segmentation. In *CVPR*, 2015.

[27] D. Lowe. Scale invariant feature transform. *IJCV*, 2004.

[28] J. Mairal, F. Bach, J. Ponce, and G. Sapiro. Online dictionary learning for sparse coding. In *ICML*, 2009.

[29] J. Ng, M. Hausknecht, S. Vijayanarasimhan, O. Vinyals, R. Monga, and G. Toderici. Beyond short snippets: deep networks for video classification. In *CVPR*, 2015.

[30] J. Ngiam, A. Khosla, M. Kim, J. Nam, H. Lee, and A. Ng. Multimodal deep learning. In *ICML*, 2011.

[31] A. Oliva and A. Torralba. Modeling the shape of the scene: a holistic representation of the spatial envelope. *IJCV*, 2001.

[32] E. Park, X. Han, T. Berg, and A. Berg. Combining multiple sources of knowledge in deep CNNs for action recognition. In *WACV*, 2016.

[33] X. Peng, L. Wang, X. Wang, and Y. Qiao. Bag of visual words and fusion methods for action recognition: comprehensive study and good practice. *CVIU*, 2016.

[34] F. Perronnin, J. Sanchez, and T. Mensink. Improving the Fisher kernel for large-scale image classification. In *ECCV*, 2010.

[35] S. Ren, K. He, R. Girshick, and J. Sun. Faster R-CNN: towards real-time object detection with region proposal networks. In *NIPS*, 2015.

[36] K. Simonyan and A. Zisserman. Two-stream convolutional networks for action recognition in videos. In *NIPS*, 2014.

[37] K. Simonyan and A. Zisserman. Very deep convolutional networks for large-scale visual recognition. In *ICLR*, 2015.

[38] K. Soomro, A. Zamir, and M. Shah. UCF101: a dataset of 101 human actions classes from videos in the wild. In *CoRR*, 2012.

[39] N. Srivastava, E. Mansimov, and R. Salakhutdinov. Unsupervised learning of video representations using LSTMs. In *ICML*, 2015.

[40] K. Tai, R. Socher, and C. Manning. Improved semantic representations from tree-structured long short-term memory networks. In *ACL*, 2015.

[41] A. Tamrakar, S. Ali, Q. Yu, J. Liu, O. Javed, A. Divakaran, H. Cheng, and H. Sawhney. Evaluation of low-level features and their combinations for complex event detection in open source videos. In *CVPR*, 2012.

[42] D. Tran, L. Bourdev, R. Fergus, L. Torresani, and M. Paluri. C3D: generic features for video analysis. In *ICCV*, 2015.

[43] A. Vedaldi and A. Zisserman. Efficient additive kernels via explicit feature maps. *TPAMI*, 2012.

[44] H. Wang, D. Oneata, J. Verbeek, and C. Schmid. A robust and efficient video representation for action recognition. *IJCV*, 2015.

[45] J. Wang, J. Yang, K. Yu, F. Lv, T. Huang, and Y. Gong. Locality-constrained linear coding for image classification. In *CVPR*, 2010.

[46] L. Wang, Y. Qiao, and X. Tang. Action recognition with trajectory-pooled deep-convolutional descriptors. In *CVPR*, 2015.

[47] Z. Xu, Y. Yang, and A. Hauptmann. A discriminative CNN video representation for event detection. In *CVPR*, 2015.

[48] S. Yang and D. Ramanan. Multi-scale recognition with DAG-CNNs. In *ICCV*, 2015.

[49] X. Yang, Z. Liu, E. Zavesky, D. Gibbon, B. Shahraray, and Y. Tian. AT&T Research at TRECVID 2013: surveillance event detection. In *NIST TRECVID Workshop*, 2013.

[50] X. Yang and Y. Tian. Action recognition using super sparse coding vector with spatio-temporal awareness. In *ECCV*, 2014.

[51] M. Zeiler and R. Fergus. Visualizing and understanding convolutional networks. In *ECCV*, 2014.

[52] J. Zhang, M. Marszalek, S. Lazebnik, and C. Schmid. Local features and kernels for classification of texture and object categories: a comprehensive study. *IJCV*, 2007.

Image Captioning with Deep Bidirectional LSTMs

Cheng Wang, Haojin Yang, Christian Bartz, Christoph Meinel
Hasso Plattner Institute, University of Potsdam
Prof.-Dr.-Helmert-Str. 2-3, 14482 Potsdam, Germany
{cheng.wang, haojin.yang,christoph.meinel}@hpi.de
christian.bartz@student.hpi.uni-potsdam.de

ABSTRACT

This work presents an end-to-end trainable deep bidirectional LSTM (Long-Short Term Memory) model for image captioning. Our model builds on a deep convolutional neural network (CNN) and two separate LSTM networks. It is capable of learning long term visual-language interactions by making use of history and future context information at high level semantic space. Two novel deep bidirectional variant models, in which we increase the depth of nonlinearity transition in different way, are proposed to learn hierarchical visual-language embeddings. Data augmentation techniques such as multi-crop, multi-scale and vertical mirror are proposed to prevent overfitting in training deep models. We visualize the evolution of bidirectional LSTM internal states over time and qualitatively analyze how our models "translate" image to sentence. Our proposed models are evaluated on caption generation and image-sentence retrieval tasks with three benchmark datasets: Flickr8K, Flickr30K and MSCOCO datasets. We demonstrate that bidirectional LSTM models achieve highly competitive performance to the state-of-the-art results on caption generation even without integrating additional mechanism (e.g. object detection, attention model etc.) and significantly outperform recent methods on retrieval task.

CCS Concepts

•**Computing methodologies** → **Natural language generation; Neural networks;** *Computer vision representations;*

Keywords

deep learning, LSTM, image captioning, visual-language

1. INTRODUCTION

Automatically describe an image using sentence-level captions has been receiving much attention recent years [10, 11, 13, 16, 17, 23, 34, 39]. It is a challenging task integrating visual and language understanding. It requires not only the recognition of visual objects in an image and the semantic interactions between objects, but the ability to capture visual-language interactions and learn how to "translate" the visual understanding to sensible sentence descriptions. The most important part of this visual-language modeling is to capture the semantic correlations across image and sentence by learning a multimodal joint model. While some previous models [15, 16, 17, 20, 26] have been proposed to address the problem of image captioning, they rely on either use sentence templates, or treat it as retrieval task through ranking the best matching sentence in database as caption. Those approaches usually suffer difficulty in generating variable-length and novel sentences. Recent work [10, 11, 13, 23, 34, 39] has indicated that embedding visual and language to common semantic space with relatively shallow recurrent neural network (RNN) can yield promising results.

In this work, we propose novel architectures to the problem of image captioning. Different to previous models, we learn a visual-language space where sentence embeddings are encoded using bidirectional Long-Short Term Memory (Bi-LSTM) and visual embeddings are encoded with CNN. Bi-LSTM is able to summarize long range visual-language interactions from forward and backward directions. Inspired by the architectural depth of human brain, we also explore the deep bidirectional LSTM architectures to learn higher level visual-language embeddings. All proposed models can be trained in end-to-end by optimizing a joint loss.

Why bidirectional LSTMs? In unidirectional sentence generation, one general way of predicting next word w_t with visual context I and history textual context $w_{1:t-1}$ is maximize $\log P(w_t|I, w_{1:t-1})$. While unidirectional model includes past context, it is still limited to retain future context $w_{t+1:T}$ that can be used for reasoning previous word w_t by maximizing $\log P(w_t|I, w_{t+1:T})$. Bidirectional model tries to overcome the shortcomings that each unidirectional (forward and backward direction) model suffers on its own and exploits the past and future dependence to give a prediction. As shown in Figure 1, two example images with bidirectionally generated sentences intuitively support our assumption that bidirectional captions are complementary, combining them can generate more sensible captions.

Why deeper LSTMs? The recent success of deep CNN in image classification and object detection [14, 33] demonstrates that deep, hierarchical models can be more efficient at learning representation than shallower ones. This motivated our work to explore deeper LSTM architectures in the context of learning bidirectional visual-language embed-

MM '16, October 15-19, 2016, Amsterdam, Netherlands
© 2016 ACM. ISBN 978-1-4503-3603-1/16/10... $15.00
DOI: http://dx.doi.org/10.1145/2964284.2964299

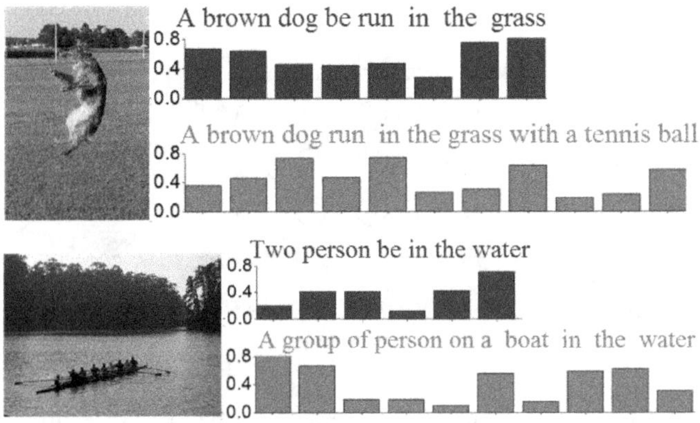

Figure 1: Illustration of generated captions. Two example images from Flickr8K dataset and their best matching captions that generated in forward order (blue) and backward order (red). Bidirectional models capture different levels of visual-language interactions (more evidence see Sec.4.4). The final caption is the sentence with higher probabilities (histogram under sentence). In both examples, backward caption is selected as final caption for corresponding image.

dings. As claimed in [29], if we consider LSTM as a composition of multiple hidden layers that unfolded in time, LSTM is already deep network. But this is the way of increasing "horizontal depth" in which network weights W are reused at each time step and limited to learn more representative features as increasing the "vertical depth" of network. To design deep LSTM, one straightforward way is to stack multiple LSTM layers as hidden to hidden transition. Alternatively, instead of stacking multiple LSTM layers, we propose to add multilayer perception (MLP) as intermediate transition between LSTM layers. This can not only increase LSTM network depth, but can also prevent the parameter size from growing dramatically.

The core contributions of this work are threefold:

- We propose an end-to-end trainable multimodal bidirectional LSTM (see Sec.3.2) and its deeper variant models (see Sec.3.3) that embed image and sentence into a high level semantic space by exploiting both long term history and future context.
- We visualize the evolution of hidden states of bidirectional LSTM units to qualitatively analyze and understand how to generate sentence that conditioned by visual context information over time (see Sec.4.4).
- We demonstrate the effectiveness of proposed models on three benchmark datasets: Flickr8K, Flickr30K and MSCOCO. Our experimental results show that bidirectional LSTM models achieve highly competitive performance to the state-of-the-art on caption generation (see Sec.4.5) and perform significantly better than recent methods on retrieval task (see Sec.4.6).

2. RELATED WORK

Multimodal representation learning [27, 35] has significant value in multimedia understanding and retrieval. The shared concept across modalities plays an important role in bridging the "semantic gap" of multimodal data. Image captioning falls into this general category of learning multimodal representations.

Recently, several approaches have been proposed for image captioning. We can roughly classify those methods into three categories. The first category is template based approaches that generate caption templates based on detecting objects and discovering attributes within image. For example, the work [20] was proposed to parse a whole sentence into several phrases, and learn the relationships between phrases and objects within an image. In [15], conditional random field (CRF) was used to correspond objects, attributes and prepositions of image content and predict the best label. Other similar methods were presented in [26, 17, 16]. These methods are typically hard-designed and rely on fixed template, which mostly lead to poor performance in generating variable-length sentences. The second category is retrieval based approach, this sort of methods treat image captioning as retrieval task. By leveraging distance metric to retrieve similar captioned images, then modify and combine retrieved captions to generate caption [17]. But these approaches generally need additional procedures such as modification and generalization process to fit image query.

Inspired by the success use of CNN [14, 45] and Recurrent Neural Network [1, 24, 25]. The third category is emerged as neural network based methods [10, 11, 13, 39, 42]. Our work also belongs to this category. Among those work, Kiro *et al.*[12] can been as pioneer work to use neural network for image captioning with multimodal neural language model. In their follow up work [13], Kiro *et al.* introduced an encoder-decoder pipeline where sentence was encoded by LSTM and decoded with structure-content neural language model (SC-NLM). Socher *et al.*[34] presented a DT-RNN (Dependency Tree-Recursive Neural Network) to embed sentence into a vector space in order to retrieve images. Later on, Mao *et al.*[23] proposed m-RNN which replaces feed-forward neural language model in [13]. Similar architectures were introduced in NIC [39] and LRCN [4], both approaches use LSTM to learn text context. But NIC only feed visual information at first time step while Mao *et al.*[23] and LRCN [4]'s model consider image context at each time step. Another group of neural network based approaches has been introduced in [10, 11] where image captions generated by integrating object detection with R-CNN (region-CNN) and inferring the alignment between image regions and descriptions.

Most recently, Fang *et al.*[5] used multi-instance learning and traditional maximum-entropy language model for description generation. Chen *et al.*[2] proposed to learn visual representation with RNN for generating image caption. In [42], Xu *et al.* introduced attention mechanism of human visual system into encoder-decoder framework. It is shown that attention model can visualize what the model "see" and yields significant improvements on image caption generation. Unlike those models, our deep LSTM model directly assumes the mapping relationship between visual-language is antisymmetric and dynamically learns long term bidirectional and hierarchical visual-language interactions. This is proved to be very effective in generation and retrieval tasks as we demonstrate in Sec.4.5 and Sec.4.6.

3. MODEL

In this section, we describe our multimodal bidirectional LSTM model (Bi-LSTM for short) and explore its deeper

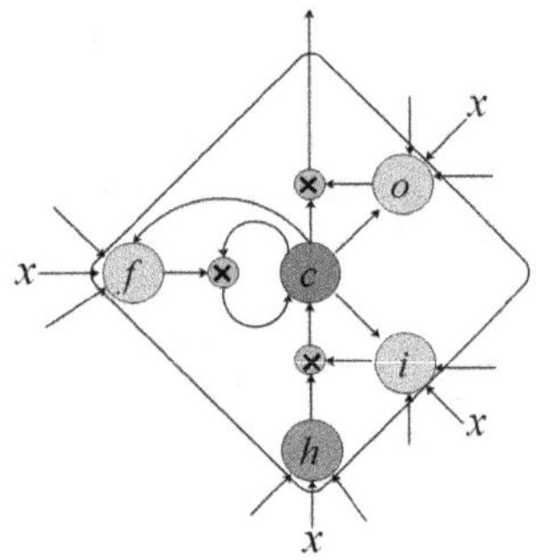

Figure 2: Long Short Term Memory (LSTM) cell. It is consist of an input gate i, a forget gate f, a memory cell c and an output gate o. The input gate decides let incoming signal go through to memory cell or block it. The output gate can allow new output or prevent it. The forget gate decides to remember or forget cell's previous state. Updating cell states is performed by feeding previous cell output to itself by recurrent connections in two consecutive time steps.

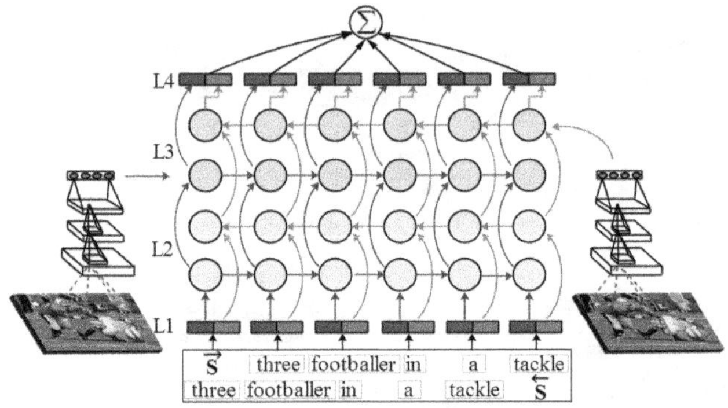

Figure 3: Multimodal Bidirectional LSTM. L1: sentence embedding layer. L2: T-LSTM layer. L3: M-LSTM layer. L4: Softmax layer. We feed sentence in both forward (blue arrows) and backward (red arrows) order which allows our model summarizes context information from both left and right side for generating sentence word by word over time. Our model is end-to-end trainable by minimize a joint loss.

variants. We first briefly introduce LSTM which is at the center of model. The LSTM we used is described in [44].

3.1 Long Short Term Memory

Our model builds on LSTM cell, which is a particular form of traditional recurrent neural network (RNN). It has been successfully applied to machine translation [3], speech recognition [8] and sequence learning [36]. As shown in Figure 2, the reading and writing memory cell c is controlled by a group of sigmoid gates. At given time step t, LSTM receives inputs from different sources: current input $\mathbf{x}_t$, the previous hidden state of all LSTM units $\mathbf{h}_{t-1}$ as well as previous memory cell state $\mathbf{c}_{t-1}$. The updating of those gates at time step t for given inputs $\mathbf{x}_t$, $\mathbf{h}_{t-1}$ and $\mathbf{c}_{t-1}$ as follows.

$$\mathbf{i}_t = \sigma(\mathbf{W}_{xi}\mathbf{x}_t + \mathbf{W}_{hi}\mathbf{h}_{t-1} + \mathbf{b}_i) \tag{1}$$

$$\mathbf{f}_t = \sigma(\mathbf{W}_{xf}\mathbf{x}_t + \mathbf{W}_{hf}\mathbf{h}_{t-1} + \mathbf{b}_f) \tag{2}$$

$$\mathbf{o}_t = \sigma(\mathbf{W}_{xo}\mathbf{x}_t + \mathbf{W}_{ho}\mathbf{h}_{t-1} + \mathbf{b}_o) \tag{3}$$

$$\mathbf{g}_t = \phi(\mathbf{W}_{xc}\mathbf{x}_t + \mathbf{W}_{hc}\mathbf{h}_{t-1} + \mathbf{b}_c) \tag{4}$$

$$\mathbf{c}_t = \mathbf{f}_t \odot \mathbf{c}_{t-1} + \mathbf{i}_t \odot \mathbf{g}_t \tag{5}$$

$$\mathbf{h}_t = \mathbf{o}_t \odot \phi(\mathbf{c}_t) \tag{6}$$

where $\mathbf{W}$ are the weight matrices learned from the network and $\mathbf{b}$ are bias vectors. σ is the sigmoid activation function $\sigma(x) = 1/(1+\exp(-x))$ and ϕ presents hyperbolic tangent $\phi(x) = (\exp(x) - \exp(-x))/(\exp(x) + \exp(-x))$. $\odot$ denotes the products with a gate value. The LSTM hidden output $\mathbf{h}_t$=$\{\mathbf{h}_{tk}\}_{k=0}^{K}$, $\mathbf{h}_t \in \mathbf{R}^K$ will be used to predict the next word by Softmax function with parameters $\mathbf{W}_s$ and $\mathbf{b}_s$:

$$\mathcal{F}(\mathbf{p}_{ti};\mathbf{W}_s,\mathbf{b}_s) = \frac{\exp(\mathbf{W}_s\mathbf{h}_{ti} + \mathbf{b}_s)}{\sum_{j=1}^{K}\exp(\mathbf{W}_s\mathbf{h}_{tj} + \mathbf{b}_s)} \tag{7}$$

where $\mathbf{p}_{ti}$ is the probability distribution for predicted word.

Our key motivation of chosen LSTM is that it can learn long-term temporal activities and avoid quick exploding and vanishing problems that traditional RNN suffers from during back propagation optimization.

3.2 Bidirectional LSTM

In order to make use of both the past and future context information of a sentence in predicting word, we propose a bidirectional model by feeding sentence to LSTM from forward and backward order. Figure 3 presents the overview of our model, it is comprised of three modules: a CNN for encoding image inputs, a Text-LSTM (T-LSTM) for encoding sentence inputs, a Multimodal LSTM (M-LSTM) for embedding visual and textual vectors to a common semantic space and decoding to sentence. The bidirectional LSTM is implemented with two separate LSTM layers for computing forward hidden sequences $\overrightarrow{\mathbf{h}}$ and backward hidden sequences $\overleftarrow{\mathbf{h}}$. The forward LSTM starts at time $t=1$ and the backward LSTM starts at time $t=T$. Formally, our model works as follows, for raw image input $\widetilde{I}$, forward order sentence $\overrightarrow{S}$ and backward order sentence $\overleftarrow{S}$, the encoding performs as

$$\mathbf{I}_t = \mathcal{C}(\widetilde{I};\mathbf{\Theta}_v)\quad \overrightarrow{\mathbf{h}}_t^1 = \mathcal{T}(\overrightarrow{\mathbf{E}}\,\overrightarrow{\mathbf{S}};\overrightarrow{\mathbf{\Theta}}_l)\quad \overleftarrow{\mathbf{h}}_t^1 = \mathcal{T}(\overleftarrow{\mathbf{E}}\,\overleftarrow{\mathbf{S}};\overleftarrow{\mathbf{\Theta}}_l) \tag{8}$$

where $\mathcal{C}$, $\mathcal{T}$ represent CNN, T-LSTM respectively and $\mathbf{\Theta}_v$, $\mathbf{\Theta}_l$ are their corresponding weights. $\overrightarrow{\mathbf{E}}$ and $\overleftarrow{\mathbf{E}}$ are bidirectional embedding matrices learned from network. Encoded visual and textual representations are then embedded to multimodal LSTM by:

$$\overrightarrow{\mathbf{h}}_t^2 = \mathcal{M}(\overrightarrow{\mathbf{h}}_t^1,\mathbf{I}_t;\overrightarrow{\mathbf{\Theta}}_m)\quad \overleftarrow{\mathbf{h}}_t^2 = \mathcal{M}(\overleftarrow{\mathbf{h}}_t^1,\mathbf{I}_t;\overleftarrow{\mathbf{\Theta}}_m) \tag{9}$$

where $\mathcal{M}$ presents M-LSTM and its weight $\mathbf{\Theta}_m$. $\mathcal{M}$ aims to capture the correlation of visual context and words at different time steps. We feed visual vector $\mathbf{I}$ to model at each time step for capturing strong visual-word correlation. On the top of M-LSTM are Softmax layers which compute the probability distribution of next predicted word by

$$\overrightarrow{\mathbf{p}}_{t+1} = \mathcal{F}(\overrightarrow{\mathbf{h}}_t^2;\mathbf{W}_s,\mathbf{b}_s)\quad \overleftarrow{\mathbf{p}}_{t+1} = \mathcal{F}(\overleftarrow{\mathbf{h}}_t^2;\mathbf{W}_s,\mathbf{b}_s) \tag{10}$$

where $\mathbf{p} \in \mathbf{R}^K$ and K is the vocabulary size.

3.3 Deeper LSTM architecture

To design deeper LSTM architectures, in addition to directly stack multiple LSTMs on each other that we named as Bi-S-LSTM (Figure 4(c)), we propose to use a fully connected layer as intermediate transition layer. Our motivation comes from the finding of [29], in which DT(S)-RNN (deep transition RNN with shortcut) is designed by adding hidden to hidden multilayer perception (MLP) transition. It

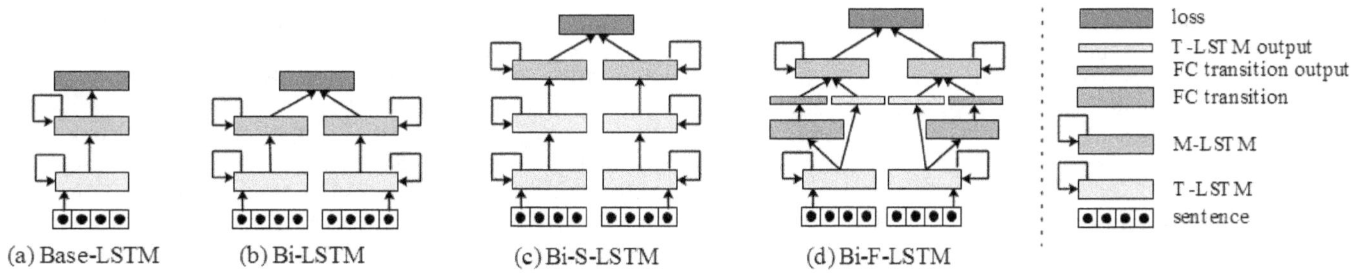

Figure 4: Illustrations of proposed deep architectures for image captioning. The network in (a) is commonly used in previous work, e.g. [4, 23]. (b) Our proposed Bidirectional LSTM (Bi-LSTM). (c) Our proposed Bidirectional Stacked LSTM (Bi-S-LSTM). (d) Our proposed Bidirectional LSTM with fully connected (FC) transition layer (Bi-F-LSTM).

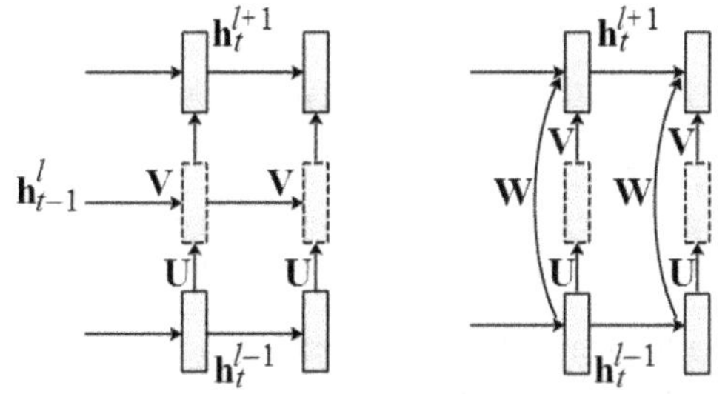

Figure 5: Transition for Bi-S-LSTM(L) and Bi-F-LSTM(R)

is arguably easier to train such network. Inspired by this, we extend Bi-LSTM (Figure 4(b)) with a fully connected layer that we called Bi-F-LSTM (Figure 4(d)), shortcut connection between input and hidden states is introduced to make it easier to train model. The aim of extension models is to learn an extra hidden transition function F_h. In Bi-S-LSTM

$$\mathbf{h}_t^{l+1} = F_h(\mathbf{h}_t^{l-1}, \mathbf{h}_{t-1}^{l}) = \mathbf{U}\mathbf{h}_t^{l-1} + \mathbf{V}\mathbf{h}_{t-1}^{l} \quad (11)$$

where $\mathbf{h}_t^l$ presents the hidden states of l-th layer at time t, $\mathbf{U}$ and $\mathbf{V}$ are matrices connect to transition layer (also see Figure 5(L)). For readability, we consider one direction training and suppress bias terms. Similarly, in Bi-F-LSTM, to learn a hidden transition function F_h by

$$\mathbf{h}_t^{l+1} = F_h(\mathbf{h}_t^{l-1}) = \phi_r(\mathbf{W}\mathbf{h}_t^{l-1} \oplus (\mathbf{V}(\mathbf{U}\mathbf{h}_t^{l-1}))) \quad (12)$$

where $\oplus$ is the operator that concatenates $\mathbf{h}_t^{l-1}$ and its abstractions to a long hidden states (also see Figure 5(R)). ϕ_r presents rectified linear unit (ReLu) activation function for transition layer, which performs $\phi_r(x) = \max(0, x)$.

3.4 Data Augmentation

One of the most challenging aspects of training deep bidirectional LSTM models is preventing overfitting. Since our largest dataset has only 80K images [21] which might cause overfitting easily, we adopted several techniques such as fine-tuning on pre-trained visual model, weight decay, dropout and early stopping that commonly used in the literature. Additionally, it has been proved that data augmentation such as randomly cropping and horizontal mirror [22, 32], adding noise, blur and rotation [40] can effectively alleviate over-fitting and other. Inspired by this, we designed new data augmentation techniques to increase the number of image-sentence pairs. Our implementation performs on visual model, as follows:

- **Multi-Corp**: Instead of randomly cropping on input image, we crop at the four corners and center region. Because we found random cropping is more tend to select center region and cause overfitting easily. By cropping four corners and center, the variations of network input can be increased to alleviate overfitting.
- **Multi-Scale**: To further increase the number of image-sentence pairs, we rescale input image to multiple scales. For each input image $\widetilde{I}$ with size $H \times W$, it is resized to 256×256, then we randomly select a region with size of $s{*}H \times s{*}W$, where $s \in [1, 0.925, 0.875, 0.85]$ is scale ratio. $s = 1$ means we do not multi-scale operation on given image. Finally we resize it to AlexNet input size 227×227 or VggNet input size 224×224.
- **Vertical Mirror**: Motivated by the effectiveness of widely used horizontal mirror, it is natural to also consider the vertical mirror of image for same purpose.

Those augmentation techniques are implemented in real-time fashion. Each input image is randomly transformed using one of augmentations to network input for training. In principle, our data augmentation can increase image-sentence training pairs by roughly 40 times (5×4×2).

3.5 Training and Inference

Our model is end-to-end trainable by using Stochastic Gradient Descent (SGD). The joint loss function $L = \overrightarrow{L} + \overleftarrow{L}$ is computed by accumulating the Softmax losses of forward and backward directions. Our objective is to minimize L, which is equivalent to maximize the probabilities of correctly generated sentences. We compute the gradient ∇L with Back-Propagation Through Time (BPTT) algorithm.

The trained model is used to predict a word w_t with given image context I and previous word context $w_{1:t-1}$ by $P(w_t|w_{1:t-1}, I)$ in forward order, or by $P(w_t|w_{t+1:T}, I)$ in backward order. We set $w_1{=}w_T{=}\mathbf{0}$ at start point respectively for forward and backward directions. Ultimately, with generated sentences from two directions, we decide the final sentence for given image $p(w_{1:T}|I)$ according to the summation of word probability within sentence

$$p(w_{1:T}|I) = \max\left(\sum_{t=1}^{T}(\overrightarrow{p}(w_t|I)), \sum_{t=1}^{T}(\overleftarrow{p}(w_t|I))\right) \quad (13)$$

$$\overrightarrow{p}(w_t|I) = \prod_{t=1}^{T} p(w_t|w_1, w_2, ..., w_{t-1}, I) \quad (14)$$

$$\overleftarrow{p}(w_t|I) = \prod_{t=1}^{T} p(w_t|w_{t+1}, w_{t+2}, ..., w_T, I) \quad (15)$$

Follow previous work, we adopted beam search to consider the best k candidate sentences at time t to infer the sentence at next time step. In our work, we fix $k = 1$ in all experiments although the average of 2 BLEU [28] points better results can be achieved with $k = 20$ compare to $k = 1$ as reported in [39].

4. EXPERIMENTS

In this section, we design several groups of experiments to accomplish following objectives:

- Qualitatively analyze and understand how bidirectional multimodal LSTM learns to generate sentence conditioned by visual context information over time.
- Measure the benefits and performance of proposed bidirectional model and its deeper variant models that we increase their nonlinearity depth from different ways.
- Compare our approach with state-of-the-art methods in terms of sentence generation and image-sentence retrieval tasks on popular benchmark datasets.

4.1 Datasets

To validate the effectiveness, generality and robustness of our models, we conduct experiments on three benchmark datasets: Flickr8K [31], Flickr30K [43] and MSCOCO [21].

Flickr8K. It consists of 8,000 images and each of them has 5 sentence-level captions. We follow the standard dataset divisions provided by authors, 6,000/1,000/1,000 images for training/validation/testing respectively.

Flickr30K. An extension version of Flickr8K. It has 31,783 images and each of them has 5 captions. We follow the public accessible[1] dataset divisions by Karpathy *et al.* [11]. In this dataset splits, 29,000/1,000/1,000 images are used for training/validation/testing respectively.

MSCOCO. This is a recent released dataset that covers 82,783 images for training and 40,504 images for validation. Each of images has 5 sentence annotations. Since there is lack of standard splits, we also follow the splits provided by Karpathy *et al.* [11]. Namely, 80,000 training images and 5,000 images for both validation and testing.

4.2 Implementation Details

Visual feature. We use two visual models for encoding image: Caffe [9] reference model which is pre-trained with AlexNet [14] and 16-layer VggNet model [33]. We extract features from last fully connected layer and feed to train visual-language model with LSTM. Previous work [23, 39] have demonstrated that with more powerful image models such as GoogleNet [37] and VggNet [33] can achieve promising improvements. To make a fair comparison with recent works, we select the widely used two models for experiments.

Textual feature. We first represent each word w within sentence as one-hot vector, $w \in \mathbf{R}^K$, K is vocabulary size built on training sentences and different for different datasets. By performing basic tokenization and removing the words that occurs less than 5 times in the training set, we have 2028, 7400 and 8801 words for Flickr8K, Flickr30K and MSCOCO dataset vocabularies respectively.

Our work uses the LSTM implementation of [4] on Caffe framework. All of our experiments were conducted on Ubuntu 14.04, 16G RAM and single Titan X GPU with 12G memory. Our LSTMs use 1000 hidden units and weights initialized uniformly from [-0.08, 0.08]. The batch sizes are 150, 100, 100, 32 for Bi-LSTM, Bi-S-LSTM, Bi-F-LSTM and Bi-LSTM (VGG) models respectively. Models were trained with learning rate $\eta = 0.01$ (except $\eta = 0.005$ for Bi-LSTM (VGG)), weight decay λ is 0.0005 and we used momentum 0.9. Each model is trained for 18~35 epochs with early stopping. The code for this work can be found at *https://github.com/deepsemantic/image_captioning*.

4.3 Evaluation Metrics

We evaluate our models on two tasks: caption generation and image-sentence retrieval. In caption generation, we follow previous work to use BLEU-N (N=1,2,3,4) scores [28]:

$$B_N = \min(1, e^{1-\frac{r}{c}}) \cdot e^{\frac{1}{N}\sum_{n=1}^{N}\log p_n} \quad (16)$$

where r, c are the length of reference sentence and generated sentence, p_n is the modified *n-gram* precisions. We also report METETOR [18] and CIDEr [38] scores for further comparison. In image-sentence retrieval (image query sentence and vice versa), we adopt R@K (K=1,5,10) and Med r as evaluation metrics. R@K is the recall rate R at top K candidates and Med r is the median rank of the first retrieved ground-truth image and sentence. All mentioned metric scores are computed by MSCOCO caption evaluation server[2], which is commonly used for image captioning challenge[3].

4.4 Visualization and Qualitative Analysis

The aim of this set experiment is to visualize the properties of proposed bidirectional LSTM model and explain how it works in generating sentence word by word over time.

First, we examine the temporal evolution of internal gate states and understand how bidirectional LSTM units retain valuable context information and attenuate unimportant information. Figure 6 shows input and output data, the pattern of three sigmoid gates (input, forget and output) as well as cell states. We can clearly see that dynamic states are periodically distilled to units from time step $t = 0$ to $t = 11$. At $t = 0$, the input data are sigmoid modulated to input gate $\mathbf{i}(t)$ where values lie within in [0,1]. At this step, the values of forget gates $\mathbf{f}(t)$ of different LSTM units are zeros. Along with the increasing of time step, forget gate starts to decide which unimportant information should be forgotten, meanwhile, to retain those useful information. Then the memory cell states $\mathbf{c}(t)$ and output gate $\mathbf{o}(t)$ gradually absorb the valuable context information over time and make a rich representation $\mathbf{h}(t)$ of the output data.

Next, we examine how visual and textual features are embedded to common semantic space and used to predict word over time. Figure 7 shows the evolution of hidden units at different layers. For T-LSTM layer, units are conditioned by textual context from the past and future. It performs as the encoder of forward and backward sentences. At M-LSTM layer, LSTM units are conditioned by both visual and textual context. It learns the correlations between input word sequence and visual information that encoded by CNN. At given time step, by removing unimportant information that make less contribution to correlate input word and visual context, the units tend to appear sparsity pattern

[1]http://cs.stanford.edu/people/karpathy/deepimagesent/

[2]https://github.com/tylin/coco-caption

[3]http://mscoco.org/home/

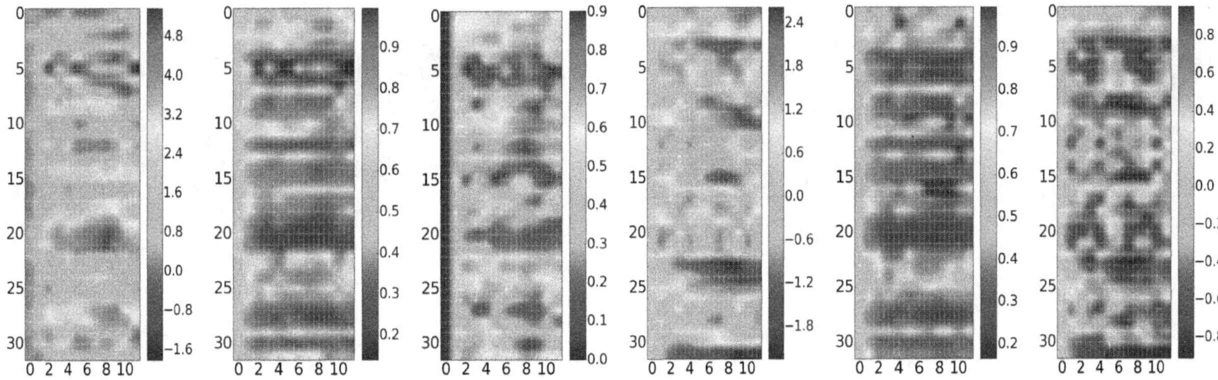

(a) input (b) input gate (c) forget gate (d) cell state (e) output gate (f) output

Figure 6: Visualization of LSTM cell. The horizontal axis corresponds to time steps. The vertical axis is cell index. Here we visualize the gates and cell states of the first 32 Bi-LSTM units of T-LSTM in forward direction over 11 time steps.

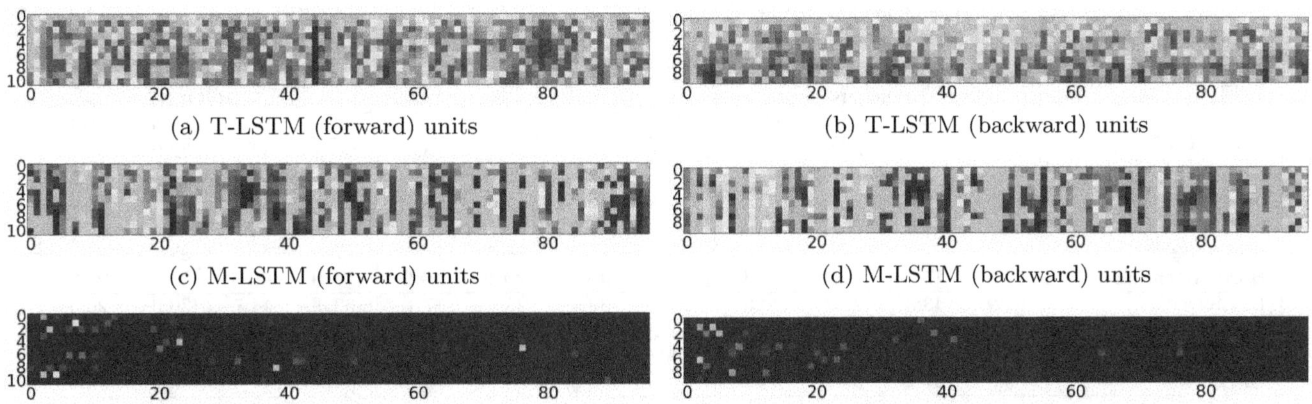

(a) T-LSTM (forward) units (b) T-LSTM (backward) units

(c) M-LSTM (forward) units (d) M-LSTM (backward) units

(e) probability (forward) units (f) probability (backward) units

A	man	in	a	black	jacket	is	walking	down	the	street
2	7	3	2	23	76	8	41	38	4	36

Street	the	on	walking	is	suit	a	in	man	a
36	4	5	41	8	193	2	3	7	2

(g) Generated words and corresponding word index in vocabulary

Figure 7: Pattern of the first 96 hidden units chosen at each layer of Bi-LSTM in both forward and backward directions. The vertical axis presents time steps. The horizontal axis corresponds to different LSTM units. In this example, we visualize the T-LSTM layer for text only, the M-LSTM layer for both text and image and Softmax layer for computing word probability distribution. The model was trained on Flickr 30K dataset for generating sentence word by word at each time step. In (g), we provide the predicted words at different time steps and their corresponding index in vocabulary where we can also read from (e) and (f) (the highlight point at each row). Word with highest probability is selected as the predicted word.

and learn more discriminative representations from inputs. At higher layer, embedded multimodal representations are used to compute the probability distribution of next predict word with Softmax. It should be noted, for given image, the number of words in generated sentence from forward and backward direction can be different.

Figure 8 presents some example images with generated captions. From it we found some interesting patterns of bidirectional captions: (1) **Cover different semantics**, for example, in (b) forward sentence captures "*couch*" and "*table*" while backward one describes "*chairs*" and "*table*". (2) **Describe static scenario and infer dynamics**, in (a) and (d), one caption describes the static scene, and the other one presents the potential action or motion that possibly happen in the next time step. (3) **Generate novel sentences**, from generated captions, we found that a significant proportion (88% by randomly select 1000 images on MSCOCO validation set) of generated sentences are novel (not appear in training set). But generated sentences are highly similar to ground-truth captions, for example in (d), forward caption is similar to one of ground-truth captions (*"A passenger train that is pulling into a station"*) and backward caption is similar to ground-truth caption (*"a train is in a tunnel by a station"*). It illustrates that our model has strong capability in learning visual-language correlation and generating novel sentences.

4.5 Results on Caption Generation

Now, we compare with state-of-the-art methods. Table 1 presents the comparison results in terms of BLEU-N. Our

(a) (b) (c) (d)

A woman in a tennis court holding a tennis racket.
A woman getting ready to hit a tennis ball.

A living room with a couch and a table.
Two chairs and a table in a living room.

A giraffe standing in a zoo enclosure with a baby in the background.
A couple of giraffes are standing at a zoo.

A train is pulling into a train station.
A train on the tracks at a train station.

Figure 8: Examples of generated captions for given query image on MSCOCO validation set. Blue-colored captions are generated in forward direction and red-colored captions are generated in backward direction. The final caption is selected according to equation (13) which selects the sentence with the higher probability. The final captions are marked in **bold**.

Table 1: Performance comparison on BLEU-N(high score is good). The superscript "A" means the visual model is AlexNet (or similar network), "V" is VggNet, "G" is GoogleNet, "-" indicates unknown value, "‡" means different data splits[4]. The best results are marked in **bold** and the second best results with <u>underline</u>. The superscripts are also applicable to Table 2.

	Flickr8K				**Flickr30K**				**MSCOCO**			
Models	**B-1**	**B-2**	**B-3**	**B-4**	**B-1**	**B-2**	**B-3**	**B-4**	**B-1**	**B-2**	**B-3**	**B-4**
NIC[39]^{G,‡}	63	41	27.2	-	<u>66.3</u>	42.3	27.7	18.3	66.6	46.1	32.9	<u>24.6</u>
LRCN[4]^{A,‡}	-	-	-	-	58.8	39.1	25.1	16.5	62.8	44.2	30.4	-
DeepVS[11]^{V}	57.9	38.3	24.5	16	57.3	36.9	24.0	15.7	62.5	45	32.1	23
m-RNN[23]^{A,‡}	56.5	38.6	25.6	17.0	54	36	23	15	-	-	-	-
m-RNN[23]^{V,‡}	-	-	-	-	60	41	28	19	67	49	35	**25**
Hard-Attention[42]^{V}	**67**	<u>45.7</u>	<u>31.4</u>	<u>21.3</u>	**66.9**	**43.9**	**29.6**	**19.9**	**71.8**	**50.4**	**35.7**	**25**
Bi-LSTM^{A}	61.9	43.3	29.7	20.0	58.9	39.3	25.9	17.1	63.4	44.7	30.6	20.6
Bi-S-LSTM^{A}	64.2	44.3	29.2	18.6	59.5	40.3	26.9	17.9	63.7	45.7	31.8	21.9
Bi-F-LSTM^{A}	63.0	43.7	29.2	19.1	58.6	39.2	26.0	17.4	63.5	44.8	30.7	20.6
Bi-LSTM^{V}	<u>65.5</u>	**46.8**	**32.0**	**21.5**	62.1	<u>42.6</u>	<u>28.1</u>	<u>19.3</u>	<u>67.2</u>	<u>49.2</u>	<u>35.2</u>	24.4

approach achieves very competitive performance on evaluated datasets although with less powerful AlexNet visual model. We can see that increase the depth of LSTM is beneficial on generation task. Deeper variant models mostly obtain better performance compare to Bi-LSTM, but they are inferior to latter one in B-3 and B-4 on Flickr8K. We conjecture it should be the reason that Flick8K is a relatively small dataset which suffers difficulty in training deep models with limited data. One of interesting facts we found is that by stacking multiple LSTM layers is generally superior to LSTM with fully connected transition layer although Bi-S-LSTM needs more training time. By replacing AlexNet with VggNet brings significant improvements on all BLEU evaluation metrics. We should be aware of that a recent interesting work [42] achieves the best results by integrating attention mechanism [19, 42] on this task. Although we believe incorporating such powerful mechanism into our framework can make further improvements, note that our current model Bi-LSTM^{V} achieves the best or second best results on most of metrics while the small gap in performance between our model and Hard-Attention^{V} [42] is existed.

The further comparison on METEOR and CIDEr scores is plotted in Figure 9. Without integrating object detection and more powerful vision model, our model (Bi-LSTM^{A}) outperforms DeepVS^{V}[11] in a certain margin. It achieves 19.4/49.6 on Flickr 8K (compare to 16.7/31.8 of DeepVS^{V}) and 16.2/28.2 on Flickr30K (15.3/24.7 of DeepVS^{V}). On MSCOCO, our Bi-S-LSTM^{A} obtains 20.8/66.6 for METEOR/CIDEr, which exceeds 19.5/66.0 in DeepVS^{V}.

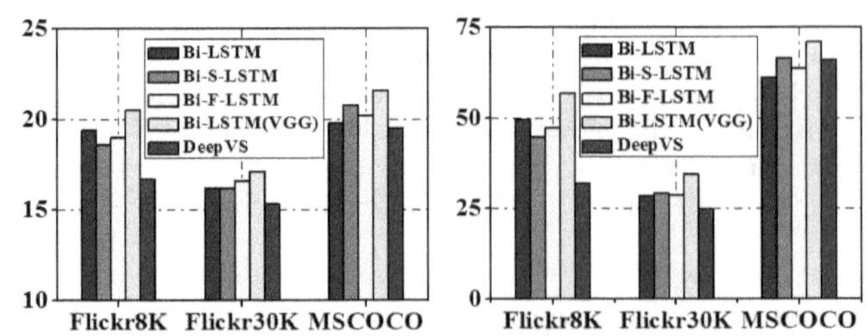

(a) METEOR score (b) CIDEr score

Figure 9: METEOR/CIDEr scores on different datasets.

4.6 Results on Image-Sentence Retrieval

For retrieval evaluation, we focus on image to sentence retrieval and vice versa. This is an instance of cross-modal retrieval [6, 30, 41] which has been a hot research subject in multimedia field. Table 2 illustrates our results on different datasets. The performance of our models exceeds those compared methods on most of metrics or matching existing results. In a few metrics, our model didn't show better result than Mind's Eye [2] which combined image and text features in ranking (it makes this task more like multimodal retrieval) and NIC [39] which employed more powerful vision

[4]On MSCOCO dataset, NIC uses 4K images for validation and test. LRCN randomly selects 5K images from MSCOCO validation set for validation and test. m-RNN uses 4K images for validation and 1K as test.

Table 2: Comparison with state-of-the-art methods on R@K (high is good) and Med r (low is good). All scores are computed by averaging the results of forward and backward results. "+O" means the approach with additional object detection.

Datasets	Methods	Image to Sentence				Sentence to Image			
		R@1	R@5	R@10	Med r	R@1	R@5	R@10	Med r
Flickr 8K	DeViSE[7]	4.8	16.5	27.3	28	5.9	20.1	29.6	29
	SDT-RNN[34]	4.5	18.0	28.6	32	6.1	18.5	29.0	29
	DeFrag[10]$^{+O}$	12.6	32.9	44.0	14	9.7	29.6	42.5	15
	Kiros et al. [13]^{A}	13.5	36.2	45.7	13	10.4	31.0	43.7	14
	Kiros et al. [13]^{V}	18	40.9	55	8	12.5	37	51.5	10
	m-RNN[23]^{A}	14.5	37.2	48.5	11	11.5	31.0	42.4	15
	Mind's Eye[2]^{V}	17.3	42.5	57.4	7	15.4	40.6	50.1	8
	DeepVS[11]$^{+O,V}$	16.5	40.6	54.2	7.6	11.8	32.1	44.7	12.4
	NIC[39]^{G}	20	-	60	6	19	-	**64**	5
	Bi-LSTM^{A}	21.3	44.7	56.5	6.5	15.1	37.8	50.1	9
	Bi-S-LSTM^{A}	19.6	43.7	55.7	7	14.5	36.4	48.3	10.5
	Bi-F-LSTM^{A}	19.9	44.0	56.0	7	14.9	37.4	49.8	10
	Bi-LSTM^{V}	**29.3**	**58.2**	**69.6**	**3**	**19.7**	**47.0**	60.6	**5**
Flickr 30K	DeViSE[7]	4.5	18.1	29.2	26	6.7	21.9	32.7	25
	SDT-RNN[34]	9.6	29.8	41.1	16	8.9	29.8	41.1	16
	Kiros et al. [13]^{A}	14.8	39.2	50.9	10	11.8	34.0	46.3	13
	Kiros et al. [13]^{V}	23.0	50.7	62.9	5	16.8	42.0	56.5	8
	LRCN[4]^{A}	14	34.9	47	11	-	-	-	-
	NIC[39]^{G}	17	-	56	7	17	-	57	8
	m-RNN[23]^{A}	18.4	40.2	50.9	10	12.6	31.2	41.5	16
	Mind's Eye[2]^{V}	18.5	45.7	58.1	7	16.6	42.5	**58.9**	8
	DeFrag [10]$^{+O}$	16.4	40.2	54.7	8	10.3	31.4	44.5	13
	DeepVS[11]$^{+O,V}$	22.2	48.2	61.4	4.8	15.2	37.7	50.5	9.2
	Bi-LSTM^{A}	18.7	41.2	52.6	8	14.0	34.0	44.0	14
	Bi-S-LSTM^{A}	21	43.0	54.1	7	15.1	35.3	46.0	12
	Bi-F-LSTM^{A}	20	44.4	55.2	7	15.1	35.8	46.8	12
	Bi-LSTM^{V}	**28.1**	**53.1**	**64.2**	**4**	**19.6**	**43.8**	55.8	**7**
MSCOCO	DeepVS[11]$^{+O,V}$	16.5	39.2	52.0	9	10.7	29.6	42.2	14.0
	Bi-LSTM^{A}	10.8	28.1	38.9	18	7.8	22.4	32.8	24
	Bi-S-LSTM^{A}	13.4	33.1	44.7	13	9.4	26.5	37.7	19
	Bi-F-LSTM^{A}	11.2	30	41.2	16	8.3	24.9	35.1	22
	Bi-LSTM^{V}	**16.6**	**39.4**	**52.4**	**9**	**11.6**	**30.9**	**43.4**	**13**

model, large beam size and model ensemble. While adopting more powerful visual model VggNet results in significant improvements across all metrics, with less powerful AlexNet model, our results are still competitive on some metrics, e.g. R@1, R@5 on Flickr8K and Flickr30K. We also note that on relatively small dataset Filckr8K, shallow model performs slightly better than deeper ones on retrieval task, which in contrast with the results on the other two datasets. As we explained before, we think deeper LSTM architectures are better suited for ranking task on large datasets which provides enough training data for more complicate model training, otherwise, overfitting occurs. By increasing data variations with our implemented data augmentation techniques can alleviate it in a certain degree. But we foresee further significant improvement gains as training example grows, by reducing reliance on augmentation with fresh data. Figure 10 presents some examples of retrieval experiments. For each caption (image) query, sensible images and descriptive captions are retrieved. It shows our models captured the visual-textual correlation for image and sentence ranking.

4.7 Discussion

Efficiency. In addition to showing superior performance, our models also possess high computational efficiency. Table 3 presents the computational costs of proposed models. We randomly select 10 images from Flickr8K validation set, and perform caption generation and image to sentence retrieval test for 5 times respectively. The table shows the averaged time costs across 5 test results. The time cost of network initialization is excluded. The costs of caption generation includes: computing image feature, sampling bidirectional captions, computing the final caption. The time costs for retrieval considers: computing image-sentence pair scores (totally 10 $\times$ 50 pairs), ranking sentences for each image query. As can be seen from Table 1, 2 and 3, deep models have only slightly higher time consumption but yield significant improvements and our proposed Bi-F-LSTM can strike the balance between performance and efficiency.

Table 3: Time costs for testing 10 images on Flickr8K

	Bi-LSTM	Bi-S-LSTM	Bi-F-LSTM
Generation	0.93s	1.1s	0.97s
Retrieval	5.62s	7.46s	5.69s

Challenges in exact comparison. It is challenging to make a direct, extract comparison with related methods due to the differences in dataset division on MSCOCO. In principle, testing on smaller validation set can lead to better results, particularly in retrieval task. Since we strictly follow dataset splits as in [11], we compare to it in most cases. Another challenge is the visual model that utilized for encoding image inputs. Different models are employed in different works, to make a fair and comprehensive comparison, we select commonly used AlexNet and VggNet in our work.

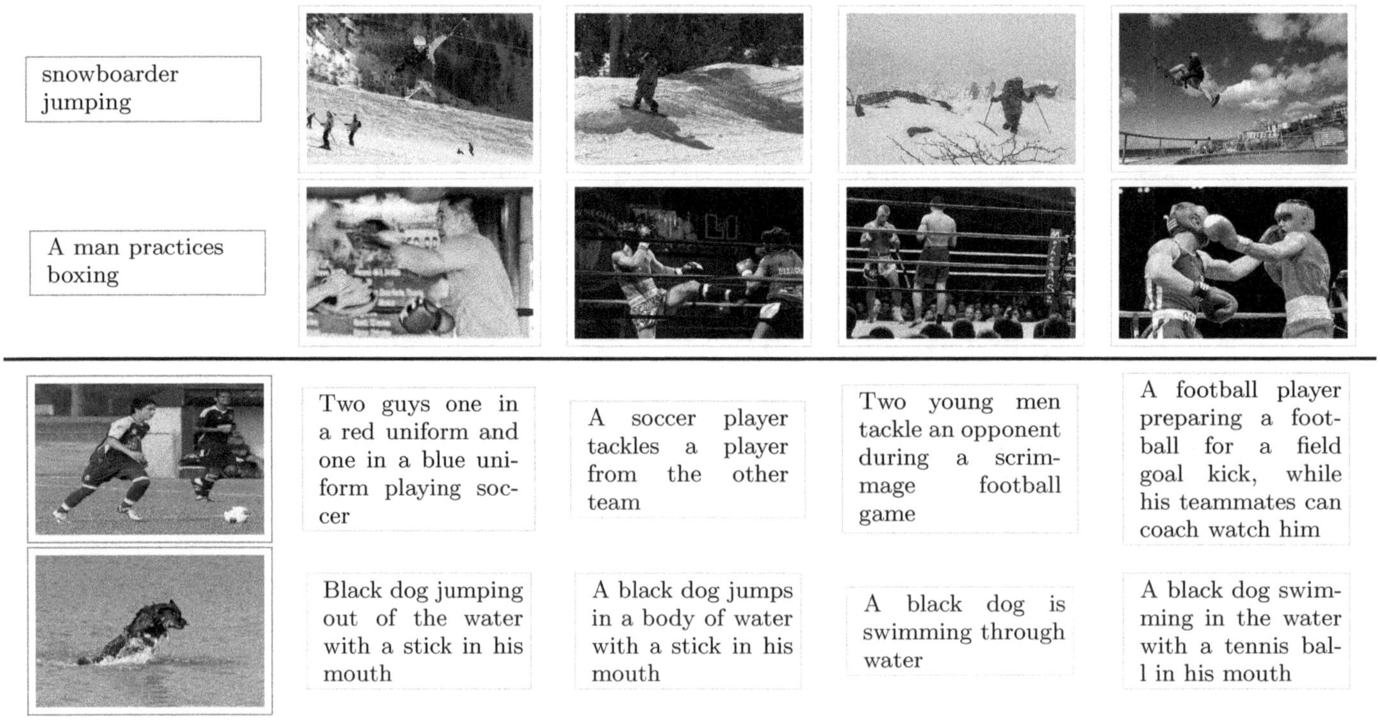

Figure 10: Examples of image retrieval (top) and caption retrieval (bottom) with Bi-S-LSTM on Flickr30K validation set. Queries are marked with red color and top-4 retrieved results are marked with green color.

5. CONCLUSIONS

We proposed a bidirectional LSTM model that generates descriptive sentence for image by taking both history and future context into account. We further designed deep bidirectional LSTM architectures to embed image and sentence at high semantic space for learning visual-language models. We also qualitatively visualized internal states of proposed model to understand how multimodal LSTM generates word at consecutive time steps. The effectiveness, generality and robustness of proposed models were evaluated on numerous datasets. Our models achieve highly completive or state-of-the-art results on both generation and retrieval tasks. Our future work will focus on exploring more sophisticated language representation (e.g. word2vec) and incorporating multitask learning and attention mechanism into our model. We also plan to apply our model to other sequence learning tasks such as text recognition and video captioning.

6. REFERENCES

[1] D. Bahdanau, K. Cho, and Y. Bengio. Neural machine translation by jointly learning to align and translate. *ICLR*, 2015.

[2] X. Chen and C. Lawrence Zitnick. Mind's eye: A recurrent visual representation for image caption generation. In *CVPR*, pages 2422–2431, 2015.

[3] K. Cho, B. Van Merriënboer, C. Gulcehre, D. Bahdanau, F. Bougares, H. Schwenk, and Y. Bengio. Learning phrase representations using rnn encoder-decoder for statistical machine translation. *EMNLP*, 2014.

[4] J. Donahue, L. A. Hendricks, S. Guadarrama, M. Rohrbach, S. Venugopalan, K. Saenko, and T. Darrell. Long-term recurrent convolutional networks for visual recognition and description. In *CVPR*, pages 2625–2634, 2015.

[5] H. Fang, S. Gupta, F. Iandola, R. Srivastava, L. Deng, P. Dollár, J. Gao, X. He, M. Mitchell, and J. Platt. From captions to visual concepts and back. In *CVPR*, pages 1473–1482, 2015.

[6] F. Feng, X. Wang, and R. Li. Cross-modal retrieval with correspondence autoencoder. In *ACMMM*, pages 7–16. ACM, 2014.

[7] A. Frome, G. Corrado, J. Shlens, S. Bengio, J. Dean, and T. Mikolov. Devise: A deep visual-semantic embedding model. In *NIPS*, pages 2121–2129, 2013.

[8] A. Graves, A. Mohamed, and G. E. Hinton. Speech recognition with deep recurrent neural networks. In *ICASSP*, pages 6645–6649. IEEE, 2013.

[9] Y. Jia, E. Shelhamer, J. Donahue, S. Karayev, J. Long, R. Girshick, S. Guadarrama, and T. Darrell. Caffe: Convolutional architecture for fast feature embedding. In *ACMMM*, pages 675–678. ACM, 2014.

[10] A. Karpathy, A. Joulin, and F-F. Li. Deep fragment embeddings for bidirectional image sentence mapping. In *NIPS*, pages 1889–1897, 2014.

[11] A. Karpathy and F-F. Li. Deep visual-semantic alignments for generating image descriptions. In *CVPR*, pages 3128–3137, 2015.

[12] R. Kiros, R. Salakhutdinov, and R. Zemel. Multimodal neural language models. In *ICML*, pages 595–603, 2014.

[13] R. Kiros, R. Salakhutdinov, and R. Zemel. Unifying visual-semantic embeddings with multimodal neural language models. *arXiv preprint arXiv:1411.2539*, 2014.

[14] A. Krizhevsky, I. Sutskever, and G. E. Hinton. Imagenet classification with deep convolutional neural networks. In *NIPS*, pages 1097–1105, 2012.

[15] G. Kulkarni, V. Premraj, V. Ordonez, S. Dhar, S. Li, Y. Choi, A. C. Berg, and T. Berg. Babytalk: Understanding and generating simple image descriptions. *IEEE Trans. on Pattern Analysis and Machine Intelligence(PAMI)*, 35(12):2891–2903, 2013.

[16] P. Kuznetsova, V. Ordonez, A. C. Berg, T. Berg, and Y. Choi. Collective generation of natural image descriptions. In *ACL*, volume 1, pages 359–368. ACL, 2012.

[17] P. Kuznetsova, V. Ordonez, T. Berg, and Y. Choi. Treetalk: Composition and compression of trees for image descriptions. *Trans. of the Association for Computational Linguistics(TACL)*, 2(10):351–362, 2014.

[18] M. Lavie. Meteor universal: language specific translation evaluation for any target language. *ACL*, page 376, 2014.

[19] Y. LeCun, Y. Bengio, and G. E. Hinton. Deep learning. *Nature*, 521(7553):436–444, 2015.

[20] S. Li, G. Kulkarni, T. L. Berg, A. C. Berg, and Y. Choi. Composing simple image descriptions using web-scale n-grams. In *CoNLL*, pages 220–228. ACL, 2011.

[21] T-Y. Lin, M. Maire, S. Belongie, J. Hays, P. Perona, D. Ramanan, P. Dollár, and C. Zitnick. Microsoft coco: Common objects in context. In *ECCV*, pages 740–755. Springer, 2014.

[22] Xin Lu, Zhe Lin, Hailin Jin, Jianchao Yang, and James Z Wang. Rapid: Rating pictorial aesthetics using deep learning. In *ACMMM*, pages 457–466. ACM, 2014.

[23] J. H. Mao, W. Xu, Y. Yang, J. Wang, Z. H. Huang, and A. Yuille. Deep captioning with multimodal recurrent neural networks (m-rnn). *ICLR*, 2015.

[24] T. Mikolov, M. Karafiát, L. Burget, J. Cernockỳ, and S. Khudanpur. Recurrent neural network based language model. In *INTERSPEECH*, volume 2, page 3, 2010.

[25] T. Mikolov, S. Kombrink, L. Burget, J. H. Černockỳ, and S. Khudanpur. Extensions of recurrent neural network language model. In *ICASSP*, pages 5528–5531. IEEE, 2011.

[26] M. Mitchell, X. Han, J. Dodge, A. Mensch, A. Goyal, A. Berg, K. Yamaguchi, T. Berg, K. Stratos, and H. Daumé III. Midge: Generating image descriptions from computer vision detections. In *ACL*, pages 747–756. ACL, 2012.

[27] J. Ngiam, A. Khosla, M. Kim, J. Nam, H. Lee, and A. Ng. Multimodal deep learning. In *ICML*, pages 689–696, 2011.

[28] K. Papineni, S. Roukos, T. Ward, and W. Zhu. Bleu: a method for automatic evaluation of machine translation. In *ACL*, pages 311–318. ACL, 2002.

[29] R. Pascanu, C. Gulcehre, K. Cho, and Y. Bengio. How to construct deep recurrent neural networks. *arXiv preprint arXiv:1312.6026*, 2013.

[30] J. C. Pereira, E. Coviello, G. Doyle, N. Rasiwasia, G. Lanckriet, R. Levy, and N. Vasconcelos. On the role of correlation and abstraction in cross-modal multimedia retrieval. *IEEE Trans. on Pattern Analysis and Machine Intelligence(PAMI)*, 36(3):521–535, 2014.

[31] C. Rashtchian, P. Young, M. Hodosh, and J. Hockenmaier. Collecting image annotations using amazon's mechanical turk. In *NAACL HLT Workshop*, pages 139–147. Association for Computational Linguistics, 2010.

[32] K. Simonyan and A. Zisserman. Two-stream convolutional networks for action recognition in videos. In *NIPS*, pages 568–576, 2014.

[33] K. Simonyan and A. Zisserman. Very deep convolutional networks for large-scale image recognition. *arXiv preprint arXiv:1409.1556*, 2014.

[34] R. Socher, A. Karpathy, Q. V. Le, C. D. Manning, and A. Y. Ng. Grounded compositional semantics for finding and describing images with sentences. *Trans. of the Association for Computational Linguistics(TACL)*, 2:207–218, 2014.

[35] N. Srivastava and R. Salakhutdinov. Multimodal learning with deep boltzmann machines. In *NIPS*, pages 2222–2230, 2012.

[36] I. Sutskever, O. Vinyals, and Q. V. Le. Sequence to sequence learning with neural networks. In *NIPS*, pages 3104–3112, 2014.

[37] C. Szegedy, W. Liu, Y. Jia, P. Sermanet, S. Reed, D. Anguelov, D. Erhan, V. Vanhoucke, and A. Rabinovich. Going deeper with convolutions. In *CVPR*, pages 1–9, 2015.

[38] R. Vedantam, Z. Lawrence, and D. Parikh. Cider: Consensus-based image description evaluation. In *CVPR*, pages 4566–4575, 2015.

[39] O. Vinyals, A. Toshev, S. Bengio, and D. Erhan. Show and tell: A neural image caption generator. In *CVPR*, pages 3156–3164, 2015.

[40] Zhangyang Wang, Jianchao Yang, Hailin Jin, Eli Shechtman, Aseem Agarwala, Jonathan Brandt, and Thomas S. Huang. Deepfont: Identify your font from an image. In *ACMMM*, pages 451–459. ACM, 2015.

[41] X.Jiang, F. Wu, X. Li, Z. Zhao, W. Lu, S. Tang, and Y. Zhuang. Deep compositional cross-modal learning to rank via local-global alignment. In *ACMMM*, pages 69–78. ACM, 2015.

[42] K. Xu, J. Ba, R. Kiros, A. Courville, R. Salakhutdinov, R. Zemel, and Y. Bengio. Show, attend and tell: Neural image caption generation with visual attention. *ICML*, 2015.

[43] P. Young, A. Lai, M. Hodosh, and J. Hockenmaier. From image descriptions to visual denotations: New similarity metrics for semantic inference over event descriptions. *Trans. of the Association for Computational Linguistics(TACL)*, 2:67–78, 2014.

[44] W. Zaremba and I. Sutskever. Learning to execute. *arXiv preprint arXiv:1410.4615*, 2014.

[45] M. D. Zeiler and R. Fergus. Visualizing and understanding convolutional networks. In *ECCV*, pages 818–833. Springer, 2014.

Deep Cross Residual Learning for Multitask Visual Recognition

Brendan Jou
Electrical Engineering
Columbia University
New York, NY 10027
bjou@ee.columbia.edu

Shih-Fu Chang
Electrical Engineering
Columbia University
New York, NY 10027
sfchang@ee.columbia.edu

ABSTRACT

Residual learning has recently surfaced as an effective means of constructing very deep neural networks for object recognition. However, current incarnations of residual networks do not allow for the modeling and integration of complex relations between closely coupled recognition tasks or across domains. Such problems are often encountered in multimedia applications involving large-scale content recognition. We propose a novel extension of residual learning for deep networks that enables intuitive learning across multiple related tasks using cross-connections called cross-residuals. These cross-residuals connections can be viewed as a form of in-network regularization and enables greater network generalization. We show how cross-residual learning (CRL) can be integrated in multitask networks to jointly train and detect visual concepts across several tasks. We present a single multitask cross-residual network with >40% less parameters that is able to achieve competitive, or even better, detection performance on a visual sentiment concept detection problem normally requiring multiple specialized single-task networks. The resulting multitask cross-residual network also achieves better detection performance by about 10.4% over a standard multitask residual network without cross-residuals with even a small amount of cross-task weighting.

Keywords

residual learning; deep networks; multitask learning; concept detection; generalization; regularization

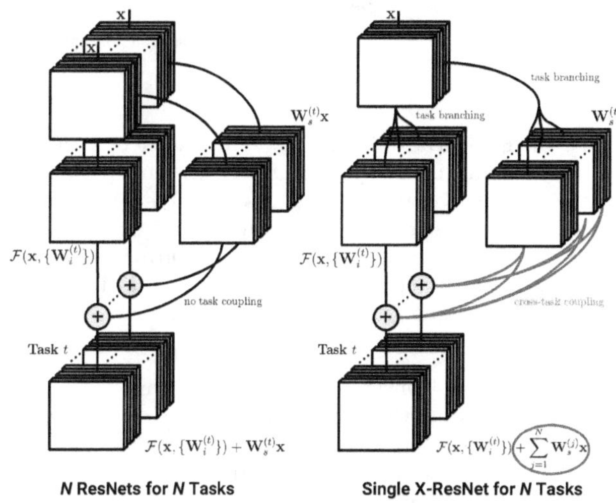

Figure 1: Feature Map Illustration of Residual Network (ResNet) and Cross-residual Network (X-ResNet) Layers. X-ResNet extends ResNet to enable structures like multitask networks where a single network can jointly perform multiple related tasks, as often encountered in multimedia applications, instead of requiring one network per task. Our network uses cross-task connections indicated in red to simultaneously enable specialization per task and overall generalization.

1. INTRODUCTION

In concept detection, leveraging the complex relationships between learning tasks remains an open challenge in the construction of many multimedia systems. While some recent approaches have begun to model these relationships in deep architectures [8, 42], still many multimedia solutions tend to have multiple parts that specialize rather than a more versatile, general solution that leverages cross-task dependencies. As an illustration, visual sentiment prediction is a rising topic of interest in multimedia and vision. In [2], a semantic construct called adjective-noun pairs (ANPs) was proposed wherein there are visual concept pairs like 'happy girl', 'misty woods' and 'good food'. These semantic concepts serve as a bridge between vision-based tasks that are focused on object (or "noun") recognition and affective computing tasks that are focused on qualifying the affective capacity or strength of multimedia, e.g. through the "adjective" in the ANP. However, even though the tasks of object recognition, affect prediction and ANP detection all have some relation to each other, the construction of classifiers for each is treated independently. In this work, we propose a novel method for jointly learning and generalizing across tasks which can be easily and very efficiently integrated into a deep residual network and as a proof-of-concept show how it can be used for visual sentiment concept detection.

To understand how "relatedness" is both important and applicable to visual concept detection, consider several ex-

MM '16, October 15-19, 2016, Amsterdam, Netherlands

DOI: http://dx.doi.org/10.1145/2964284.2964309

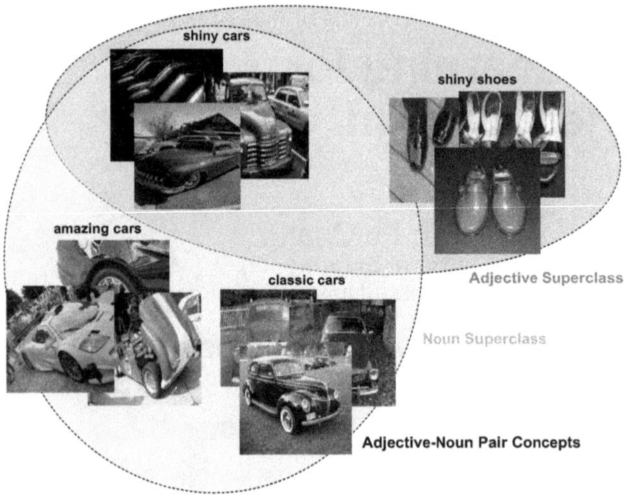

Figure 2: Example of related visual concept detection tasks that directly benefit from our proposed cross-residual learning (CRL). Adjective-noun pairs can be superclassed by their noun or adjective components. Exploitable visual and semantic similarities exist within (intra-relatedness) as well as between superclasses (inter-relatedness).

ample images and concepts from [2] in Figure 2. In the example, we observe that the ANP 'shiny cars' can be superclassed by both the 'shiny' adjective category and 'cars' noun category. Within the 'shiny' adjective category, there are other concepts like 'shiny shoes' that bear both semantic and visual similarities to the 'shiny cars' ANP, e.g. gloss or surface luster. This *intra-relatedness* also exists within the noun superclass which includes ANPs like 'amazing cars' and 'classic cars'. In addition to relatedness within the same (super)class, we observe that there are visual similarities also present between classes of different superclasses, e.g. 'classic cars' and 'shiny shoes'. This *inter-relatedness* between (super)classes illustrates how in settings like concept detection, classifiers can benefit from exploiting representational similarities across related tasks. Both of these senses of *relatedness* show that visual representations across related tasks can be shared to a degree. We develop a multitask learning problem for visual concept detection to illustrate a setting in which our proposed method can be applied. We design a deep neural network with a stack of shared low-level representations and then higher level representations that both specialize and mix information across related tasks during learning. We then show how such a multitask network architecture with cross-task exchanges can be used to simultaneously learn classifiers to detect adjective, noun and adjective-noun pair visual concepts.

In [14], residual learning is proposed as an approach for enabling much deeper networks while addressing the *degradation* problem where very deep networks have a tendency to *underfit* compared to shallower counterpart networks [40]. In residual learning, an identity mapping through the use of shortcut connections [34] is proposed where an underlying mapping $\mathcal{H}(\mathbf{x}) = \mathcal{F}(\mathbf{x}) + \mathbf{x}$ is learned given that $\mathcal{F}(\mathbf{x}) = \mathcal{H}(\mathbf{x}) - \mathbf{x}$ represents another mapping fit by several stacked layers. One interpretation is that $\mathcal{F}(\mathbf{x})$ represents a noise term and the model is fitting the input plus some additive nonlinear noise. Thus, if we were performing reconstruction, a trivial solution to the residual learning problem is that an identity mapping is optimal, i.e. $\mathcal{F}(\mathbf{x}) = 0$. However, in [14], it is argued that optimization software may actually have difficulty with approximating identity mappings with a stack of nonlinear layers, and also that for prediction problems, it is unlikely that the strict identity is optimal. They also argue that fitting residual mappings can enable deeper networks given the information boost achieved via the shortcut connection and thus reduces the likelihood of model degradation. Our work extends residual learning [14] to also integrate information from other related tasks enabling cross-task representations. Specifically, we hypothesize and experimentally show that reference components from correlated tasks can be synergistically fused in a residual deep learning network for *cross-residual learning*.

Our contributions include (1) the proposal of a novel extension of residual learning [14] using cross-connections for coupling multiple related tasks in a setting called cross-residual learning (CRL), (2) the development of a multitask network with a fan-out architecture using cross-residual layers, and (3) an evaluation of cross-residual networks on a multitask visual sentiment concept detection problem yielding a single network with very competitive or even better accuracy compared to individual networks on three classification tasks (noun, adjective, and adjective-noun pair detection) but uses >40% less model memory via branching, while also outperforming the predictive performance of a standard multitask configuration without cross-residuals by about 10.4%.

2. RELATED WORK

Our work broadly intersects three major lines of research areas: transfer learning, deep neural architectures for vision, and affective computing. In traditional data mining and machine learning tasks, we often seek to statistically model a collection of labeled or unlabeled data and apply them to other collections. In general, the distributions of these sets of data collections are assumed to be the *same*. In transfer learning [32], the domain, tasks and distributions are allowed to be *different* in both training/source and testing/target. In this work, we specifically focus on a subset of transfer learning problems that assume some *relatedness* between these collections. Specifically, in multimedia and vision contexts, *relatedness* may refer to settings where groups of tasks have semantic correlation, e.g. classifying dog breeds and bird species, or visual similarity, e.g. jointly classifying and reconstructing objects, and is often referred to as multitask learning [3]. Likewise, relatedness may also refer to the same source task but applied in different domains, e.g. classifying clothing style across cultures, and is sometimes called cross-domain learning [20] or domain transfer/adaptation [11, 21]. Nonetheless, the hypothesis of explicitly learning from related tasks is that we can learn more generalized representations with minimal performance cost or in some cases, leading to gains from learning jointly.

Multitask networks are recently becoming a popular approach to multitask learning, riding on successes in deep neural networks. One early work in [5] showed how a single network could be trained to solve multiple natural language processing tasks simultaneously like part-of-speech tagging, named entity recognition, etc. Multitask networks have since proven effective for automated drug discovery [6, 35],

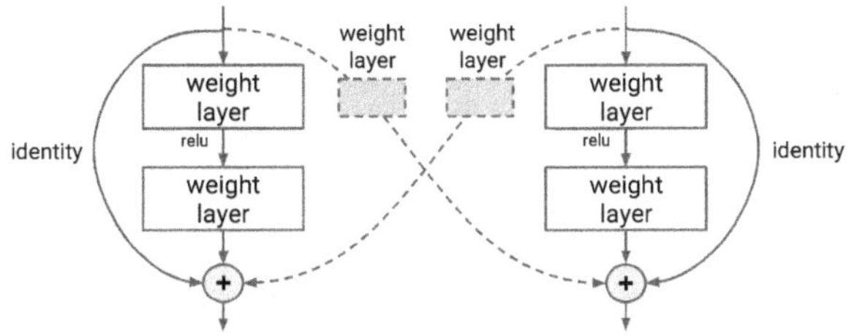

Figure 3: Cross-residual Building Block (with two tasks). Cross-residual weight layers and cross-skip connections are dashed and allow for network-level flexibility for task specialization.

query classification and retrieval [28], and semantic segmentation [7]. Recently, [10] proposed multitask auto-encoders for generalizing object detectors across domains; and in [29], multitask sequence-to-sequence learning is proposed for text translation. Also, architectures like [36, 44] can be categorized as multitask networks since they reconstruct and classify simultaneously. Unlike other multitask networks but similar to ladder networks [36], instead of a single branching point in our network that creates forked paths to only specialize to individual tasks, we continue mixing information even after branching via our cross-skip connections.

Whereas multitask learning can generally be understood as a fan-out approach where a (usually, single) shared representation is learned to solve multiple tasks, an analogous complement is a fan-in approach where multiple either features or decision scores are fused together to solve a single-task. For example, graph diffusion can be used smooth decision scores for leveraging intra-relatedness between categories [21]. In [8], instead of an undirected graph, explicit directed edges were used to model class relationships like exclusion and subsumption. And with some semblance to our work, in [42], a multimodal neural network structure is developed where inter-class (but still intra-task) relationships are integrated as an explicit regularizer. Although inspired from multitask learning, the network design in [42] still operates in a single-task context as there is only a single output network head. Additionally, because the network integrates multiple input feature towers, the overall memory and training burden of the image-to-decision pipeline is much greater than that of a fan-out network alternative.

Since we use visual sentiment concept detection to illustrate the efficacy of our proposed cross-residual learning approach, it is worth also briefly noting several advances in visual affect. In visual affective computing, a longstanding goal is to bridge the *affective gap*, a conceptual disconnect between low-level multimedia features and high-level affective states like emotions or sentiment. In [43], a codebook over local color histogram and Gabor features were proposed for image-based sentiment prediction; and in [30], psychology and art theory inspired features were proposed. Again, in [2], adjective-noun pairs were proposed as a mid-level semantic construct and an ontology was mined from a popular social multimedia platform using psychology-grounded seed queries [33]. Other problems related to affect detection include quality assessment [25], memorability [18], interestingness [12] and popularity [26]. In this work, we develop a single deep multitask cross-residual network able to simultaneously predict noun, adjective and adjective-noun visual concepts.

3. CROSS RESIDUAL LEARNING

Given an input $\mathbf{x}$ and output $\mathbf{y}$ vector to a residual learning layer and the mapping function $\mathcal{F}(\mathbf{x}, \{\mathbf{W}_i\})$ to fit, where for vision problems this might represent, for example, a stack of convolutional operations with batch normalization [17] and ReLU activation [31], we have the following in residual learning [14]:

$$\mathbf{y} = \mathcal{F}(\mathbf{x}, \{\mathbf{W}_i\}) + \mathbf{W}_s\mathbf{x}, \tag{1}$$

where $\mathbf{W}_s$ is an optional linear projection, but required when matching dimensions, on the shortcut connection. For identity shortcut connections, $\mathbf{W}_s = \mathbf{I}$.

Here, we propose a simple and efficient extension of [14] when fitting across multiple related learning tasks which we refer to as *cross-residual learning* (CRL). Given a task t and $N-1$ other related tasks, we define the task output of the cross-residual module as:

$$\mathbf{y}^{(t)} = \mathcal{F}(\mathbf{x}, \{\mathbf{W}_i^{(t)}\}) + \sum_{j=1}^{N} \mathbf{W}_s^{(j)}\mathbf{x}, \tag{2}$$

where the superscript $(\cdot)$ indexes the target task and a normalization factor is omitted for simplicity and can be lumped with the shortcut weights $\mathbf{W}_s^{(j)}$. As also illustrated in Figure 3, the other target tasks additively contribute to the current target task t by $\sum_{j\neq t}\mathbf{W}_s^{(j)}\mathbf{x}$. The cross-residual contributions can also more generally be stacks of operations $\mathcal{C}(\mathbf{x}, \{\mathbf{W}_{s,m}^{(j)}\})$, but here, we only illustrate the simple weighted once case $\mathbf{W}_s^{(j)}\mathbf{x}$.

"Early" Regularization Interpretation. In optimization, when minimizing a loss $\mathcal{L}(f(\mathbf{x}), \mathbf{y})$, we often add a regularization term $\mathcal{R}(f(\mathbf{x}))$ to constrain the "badness" of the solution, factor in assumptions of our system, and reduce overfitting. For example, in solving deep networks, the squared 2-norm is a common choice to penalize large parameter values and smooth network mappings. Cross-residual units can be viewed as a way of regularizing the solution of a specific task by other related tasks, i.e. we do not want the learned mapping $\mathcal{F}(\mathbf{x}, \{\mathbf{W}_i^{(t)}\})$ to be too far from a weighted combination of task-specialized transformations of the input $\sum_j \mathbf{W}_s^{(j)}\mathbf{x}$. For example, when learning to visually recognize species of birds, we may want to introduce regularization to ensure the mapping fit is not too far from the separate, but related task of recognizing types of mammals. While such a regularization usually takes place in the loss layer of a neural network, using cross-residual layers we can introduce this task conditioning "earlier" in the network and also stack them for additional information mixing. Unlike typical "regularization," a cross-residual layer introduces regularization by biasing at the layer-level, i.e. with respect to a given task's residual rather than with respect to the penultimate loss. Cross-residual layers thus serve as a type of in-network regularization somewhat similar to dropout [39], though with less stochasticity.

Connection to Highway Networks [40] **& LSTM** [16]**.** As also discussed in [14], residual networks can be seen as highway networks [40] that do not have transform or carry gates. In highway networks, an output highway layer is defined as

$$\mathbf{y} = \mathcal{H}(\mathbf{x}, \mathbf{W}_{\mathcal{H}})\mathcal{T}(\mathbf{x}, \mathbf{W}_{\mathcal{T}}) + \mathbf{x}\cdot\mathcal{C}(\mathbf{x}, \mathbf{W}_{\mathcal{C}}), \tag{3}$$

where $\mathcal{T}$ and $\mathcal{C}$ are the transform and carry gates, respectively. Clearly, when both gates are on, this is precisely the same as a residual layer. By extension, a cross-residual layer can be thought of as an ungated highway layer with multiple "highways" merging onto the same information path. Cross-residual weighting layers then are carry gates which govern the amount of cross-task pollination.

Similarly, it has been argued (though somewhat reductionist) that residual layers can also be viewed as a feed-forward long short-term memory (LSTM) [16] units without gates. Specifically, consider the LSTM version from [9]:

$$\left.\begin{aligned} \mathbf{i}_k &= \sigma(\mathbf{W_{xi}}\mathbf{x}_k + \mathbf{W_{hi}}\mathbf{h}_{k-1} + \mathbf{b_i}) \\ \mathbf{f}_k &= \sigma(\mathbf{W_{xf}}\mathbf{x}_k + \mathbf{W_{hf}}\mathbf{h}_{k-1} + \mathbf{b_f}) \\ \mathbf{c}_k &= \mathbf{f}_k\mathbf{c}_{k-1} + \mathbf{i}_k \tanh(\mathbf{W_{xc}}\mathbf{x}_k + \mathbf{W_{hc}}\mathbf{h}_{k-1} + \mathbf{b_c}) \\ \mathbf{o}_k &= \sigma(\mathbf{W_{xo}}\mathbf{x}_k + \mathbf{W_{ho}}\mathbf{h}_{k-1} + \mathbf{b_o}) \\ \mathbf{h}_k &= \mathbf{o}_k \tanh(\mathbf{c}_k) \end{aligned}\right\}, \quad (4)$$

where k indexes the timestep, $\mathbf{i}$, $\mathbf{f}$ and $\mathbf{o}$ are the input, forget and output gates, $\mathbf{c}$ and $\mathbf{h}$ are the cell and output states, all respectively, and peephole connections and some bias terms are omitted for simplicity. By ignoring recurrent connections $k-1$ for the feed-forward case and making the LSTM completely ungated, i.e. $\mathbf{i} = \mathbf{f} = \mathbf{o} = \mathbf{I}$, and initializing the cell state to the input $\mathbf{c}_{k-1} = \mathbf{x}$, we are left with a residual layer. Again by extension then, cross-residual layers can be thought of as feed-forward, ungated LSTMs whose cell states are additively coupled. LSTM forget gates then are analogous to cross-residual weight layers. And indeed, this is much like highway networks' carry gate, since highway layers can be viewed as feed-forward LSTMs with only forget gates [40]. A major difference to note though is that cross-residual layers couple the transformed input $\mathcal{H}$ with *multiple* and usually *different* prior cell states $\mathbf{c}_{k-1}^{(t)}$ or information highways $\mathbf{x}^{(t)}$.

Similarities to Ladder Networks [36]. Structurally, the building blocks of cross-residual learning bears some resemblance to the layout in ladder networks [36]. In ladder networks, two encoders and one decoder joined via lateral connections are used to jointly optimize a weighted sum over a cross-entropy and reconstruction loss and have thus proven successful in semi-supervised learning. As part of the reconstruction process, a Gaussian noise term is injected in one of the encoders and the decoder receives a combination of this noisy signal via a lateral connection and a vertical "feedback" connection to reconstruct the original input into the noisy encoder. Since the mapping term $\mathcal{F}(\mathbf{x})$ in residual learning can be viewed as perturbation term, albeit learned unlike in ladder networks, both models essentially are trying to fit the input subject to some additive nonlinear perturbation. For cross-residual learning, although we use shortcut connections instead of lateral connections as in ladder networks, both designs operate on the principle that combining channels of information at the same structural level in the network can ultimately result in a model with higher learning capacity under less constraints, e.g. for ladder networks, less labeled data requirements since it is semi-supervised.

4. MULTITASK CROSS RESIDUAL NETS

While there may be a number of settings that would benefit from cross-residual learning, we illustrate one natural setting here in multitask learning [3]. To implement a multitask network, a common approach [5, 10, 28, 35] is to

Output Size	Adjective	Adj-Noun Pair	Noun
112×112		7×7, 60 /2	
56×56		3×3 max pool /2	
56×56		$\begin{bmatrix} 1\times 1, 64 \\ 3\times 3, 64 \\ 1\times 1, 256 \end{bmatrix} \times 3$	
28×28		$\begin{bmatrix} 1\times 1, 128 \\ 3\times 3, 128 \\ 1\times 1, 512 \end{bmatrix} \times 4$	
14×14		$\begin{bmatrix} 1\times 1, 256 \\ 3\times 3, 256 \\ 1\times 1, 1024 \end{bmatrix} \times 6$	
7×7	$\begin{bmatrix} 1\times 1, 512 \\ 3\times 3, 512 \\ 1\times 1, 2048 \end{bmatrix} \times 3$	$\begin{bmatrix} 1\times 1, 512 \\ 3\times 3, 512 \\ 1\times 1, 2048 \end{bmatrix} \times 3$	$\begin{bmatrix} 1\times 1, 512 \\ 3\times 3, 512 \\ 1\times 1, 2048 \end{bmatrix} \times 3$
1×1	avg pool 117-d fc softmax	avg pool 553-d fc softmax	avg pool 167-d fc softmax

Table 1: Multitask Residual Network with 50 layers (without cross-residuals). Bracketed blocks are stacked residual building blocks. Downsampling is performed by stride 2 after stacked residual blocks.

introduce a branching point in the architecture that leads to one network head per task, e.g. see Figure 1. In Table 1 and Figure 4, we show 50-layer multitask residual networks with a branching point at the last input size reduction. The earlier in the network this branching point is introduced the larger the input feature map size is to the individual network heads, often resulting in multitask networks with a large memory footprint. On the other hand, if the branching point begins deeper in the network, the representational specialization available for each task is limited to a small space of high-level abstract features. In our design of a multitask cross-residual network (X-ResNet), we address this latter problem by allowing additional cross-task mixing via cross-residual weights which cheaply increases late-layer representational power without requiring large input feature spaces. While it is possible to completely forego a branching point in the network design and simply couple multiple network towers using cross-residual skip connections, this results in a composite network that is very memory intensive and only feasible in a multi-GPU environment (though this could be somewhat alleviated by freezing weights, e.g. in combination with greedy layerwise training).

In addition, to introduce some task specialization, at the branching point in our multitask network design and before the cross-residual layers, we move the last ReLU activation and batch normalization canonically present inside the residual building block outside, placing it after the elementwise addition such that there is one per task. This helps to produce a slightly different normalization for each task branch and in practice, slightly improves performance. As in most multitask networks with a branching point, the total network loss is taken to be a combination of each of the individual network head losses. While some tune the loss weight for each of these network heads, we simply use the unweighted sum over all the network head losses.

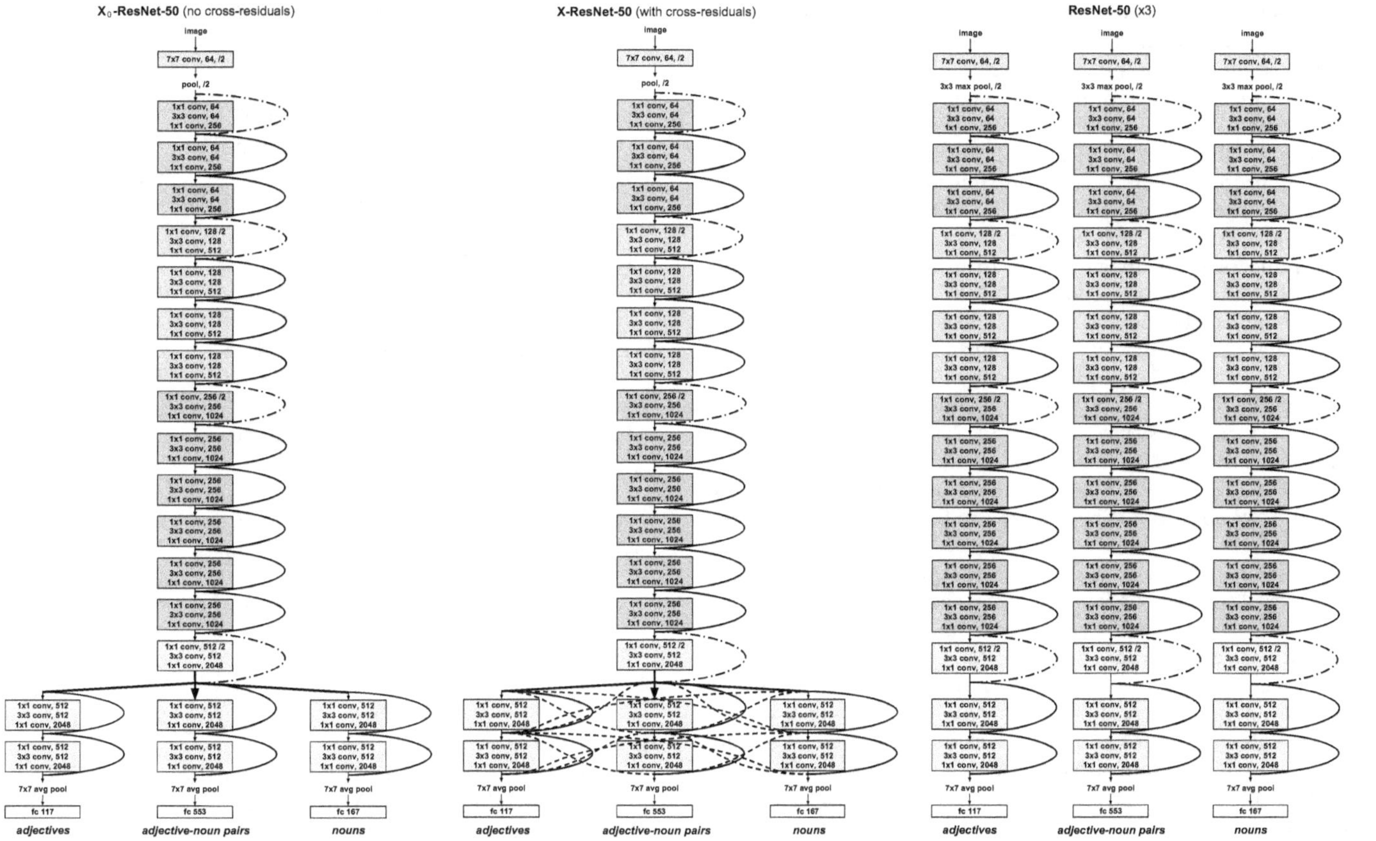

Figure 4: Example network architecture layouts for a standard multitask residual network, a multitask cross-residual network, and single-task residual networks, respectively, with 50 layers. Solid shortcuts (—) indicate identity, dash-dotted (-·-·-) shortcuts indicate 1×1 projections, and dashed (- - -) shortcuts indicate cross-residual weighted connections. Residual weight blocks show three convolutions grouped for space.

5. MULTITASK VISUAL SENTIMENT

In order to illustrate the utility and effectiveness of cross-residual layers when used in multitask networks, we re-frame visual sentiment concept detection in a multitask context. In particular, we use the Visual Sentiment Ontology (VSO)[1] [2] and cast affective mid-level concept detection as a multitask learning problem. We chose the VSO dataset for our preliminary experiments because it presents a visual affect challenge currently of rising interest in the multimedia community as VSO has since had multilingual extensions [24] and been applied in aesthetics understanding [1], emotion prediction [22, 23], popularity modeling [26], and more. While similar problems could have been created from other datasets, e.g. CIFAR-100 where we might choose to predict classes and superclasses simultaneously, the adjective-noun pair detection problem can be recast to naturally fit the multitask setting with a sufficiently large accompanying image corpus over three tasks, i.e. adjective, noun and adjective-noun pair, while other image datasets are often smaller and/or only consist of two learning tasks which yield a small number of task interactions.

Given the diversity of adjective-noun pairs, including concepts like 'cute dress', 'gentle smile', 'scary skull', 'wild rose' and 'yummy cake', there is both a considerable amount of semantic variance in VSO as well as inter-class visual variance due to the image data being gathered from social media streams. As a result, to cope with this diversity and variance, we believe that exploiting cross-task correlations as part of the network design is important, especially when the tasks are tightly related as they are with noun, adjective, and adjective-noun pair concept detection.

We additionally note that even though VSO [2] argues that the noun component of the ANP serves to visually ground the mid-level concept, no experiments were actually ever run to determine the performance of detecting adjective (or even, noun) concepts separately[2]. Our evaluation thus also serves as the first evaluation on the VSO dataset to benchmark noun-only and adjective-only detection performance.

5.1 Multitask-structured VSO

Briefly, the data in VSO [2] was originally collected from the social multimedia platform, Flickr[3], using psychology-grounded seed queries from *Plutchik's Wheel of Emotions* [33] which consists of 24 basic emotions, such as *joy*, *terror*, and *anticipation*. The query results yielded images with user-entered image tags which were annotated using a part-

[1]https://visual-sentiment-ontology.appspot.com

[2]From independent communication with the authors.

[3]https://www.flickr.com

of-speech tagger for identifying adjective and noun components and parsed for sentiment strength. The identified adjective and noun components were combined, checked for semantic consistency and filtered based on sentiment strength then used to feed back as queries to Flickr to filter based on frequency of usage. A subsampling of adjective-noun pair combinations is then done to prevent many adjective variations on any one noun, resulting in the final visual sentiment ontology. The adjective-noun pairs were then used to query and pull down an image corpus from Flickr, limiting to at most 1,000 images per concept.

The image dataset in VSO [2] has a long tail distribution where some adjective-noun pair concepts are singletons and do not share any adjectives or nouns with other concept pairs. As a result, we use a subset of VSO and use it to perform adjective, noun, and ANP concept detection in social images, specifically, as a multitask learning problem. The original VSO dataset [2] consists of a refined set of 1,200 ANP concepts. Since there are far less adjectives that serve to compose these adjective-noun pairs, and also some nouns that are massively over-represented in the ontology, we filtered to keep concepts that matched the following criteria: (1) adjectives with ≥3 paired nouns, (2) nouns that are not overwhelmingly biasing, v.s. *face* or *flowers*, and non-abstract, unlike *loss*, *adventure* or *history*, and (3) ANPs with ≥500 images. It is helpful to think of ANPs as a bipartite graph with nouns and adjectives on either side and valid ANPs as edges. From these conditions, we obtained a visual sentiment sub-ontology, suitable for multitask learning, that normalized the number of adjective and noun nodes while ensuring maximal ANP edge coverage. The final multitask-flavored VSO contains 167 nouns and 117 adjectives which form 553 adjective-noun pairs over 384,258 social images collected from Flickr.

5.2 Experiments & Discussion

In our experiments, we use a 80/20 partition of the multitask VSO data stratified by adjective-noun pairs resulting in 307,185 images for training and 77,073 for test at 224×224. All our residual layers use "B option" shortcut connections as detailed in [14] where projections are only used when matching dimensions (stride 2) and other shortcuts are identity. Except for cross-residual weight layers, projections are performed with a 1×1 convolution with ReLU activation and batch normalization as in [14]. For our cross-residual weight layers $\mathbf{W}_s^{(j)}$, we use the identity on self-shortcut connections $\mathbf{W}_s^{(t)} = \mathbf{I}$ and a cheap channelwise scaling layer for cross-task connections $\mathbf{a} \odot \mathbf{x}$, $\forall\ j \neq t$ which adds no more than 2,048 parameters each, i.e. so in our case, after branching we have $\mathbf{x} \in \mathbb{R}^{7\times7\times2048}$ and so $\mathbf{a} \in \mathbb{R}^{1\times1\times2048}$ for scaling.

For training multitask networks, we initialized most layers using weights from a residual network (ResNet) model trained on ILSVRC-2015 [37], but done such that for layers *after* the branching point in our network we initialize them to the *same* corresponding layer weights in the original ResNet model. For cross-residual weight layers, we follow [14] and initialize them as in [13], i.e. zero mean random Gaussian with a $\sqrt{2/n_l}$ standard deviation where we set n_l to be the average of input and output units layerwise. No dropout [39] was used in residual or cross-residual networks. We use random flips of the input at training. We trained our cross-residual networks with stochastic gradient descent using a batch size of 24, momentum of 0.9 and weight decay

	Task	#Params	Top-1	Top-5
Chance	Noun	–	0.60	2.96
	Adj	–	0.86	4.20
	ANP	–	0.18	0.90
DeepSentiBank [4]	ANP	65.43	7.86	11.96
CaffeNet [19]	Noun	57.55	36.11	63.48
	Adj	57.35	23.84	51.20
	ANP	59.13	18.84	41.57
Inception-v1 [41]	Noun	10.82	39.93	67.98
	Adj	10.66	26.32	55.57
	ANP	12.00	20.48	45.01
VggNet-16 [38]	Noun	134.94	41.64	69.51
	Adj	134.74	28.45	57.77
	ANP	136.53	22.68	47.70
ResNet-50 [14]	Noun	23.90	41.64	69.81
	Adj	23.80	28.41	57.87
	ANP	24.69	22.79	47.82
$\mathbf{X_O}$-ResNet-50	Noun	43.16	40.06	68.06
	Adj		26.81	56.09
	ANP		20.74	45.46
$\mathbf{X_I}$-ResNet-50	Noun	43.16	28.61	56.52
	Adj		17.98	43.10
	ANP		12.56	31.49
$\mathbf{X_S}$-ResNet-50	Noun	43.18	**42.18**	**70.04**
	Adj		**28.88**	**58.50**
	ANP		**22.89**	**48.54**

Table 2: Number of Parameters (millions) and Top-k Accuracy (%) on the Multitask VSO dataset. Note that X-ResNet-50 are multitask networks so classifiers are trained jointly in a single network while other methods train one specialized network per classification task.

of 0.0001. We used a starting fixed learning rate of 0.001 and decreased it by a factor of ten whenever the loss plateaued until convergence. All networks and experiments were run using a single NVIDIA GeForce GTX Titan X GPU and implemented with Caffe [19].

We baseline against four single-task architectures: a variant of AlexNet [27] swapping pooling and normalization layers called CaffeNet [19], the first iteration of the GoogLeNet architecture [41] denoted as Inception-v1 which uses a bottlenecked 5×5 convolution in the sub-modules, the 16-layer version of VggNet [38] (VggNet-16), and the ResNet architecture [14] with 50-layers (ResNet-50). Each of these single-task architectures were fine-tuned from an ImageNet-trained model and represent competitive baselines that achieved top ranks in ILSVRC tasks in the past. In addition, we also evaluated against DeepSentiBank [4], also an AlexNet-styled model trained on the full, unrestricted VSO data [2] to detect 2,089 ANPs. We did not retrain [4] but rather re-evaluated their model on the subset of 553 ANP concepts we focus on here; however, since we do not know the train and test image splits that they used, the result provided for DeepSentiBank [4] could still be an over-estimate. In Figure 4 (rightmost), we show the learning and inference paradigm represented by these single-task architectures with residual networks (ResNet) used as an example. Each of these baselines treat the adjective, noun and adjective-noun recognition tasks as independent targets.

We summarize network parameter costs and top-k accuracy on the multitask VSO tasks in Table 2. For network parameter costs, note that for Inception-v1 [41] we did not count the parameters from auxiliary heads although they are used during training. Top-k accuracy denotes the percentage of correct predictions within the top k ranked decision outputs.

5.2.1 *Adjective* vs. *Noun* vs. *ANP Detection*

In general, as originally posited by the VSO work [2], in terms of problem difficulty ordering, noun prediction is indeed "easier" as visual recognition task than adjective prediction. However, though not in stark contrast to [2], and although there are indeed more ANP classes than nouns and adjectives, we still did expect to observe higher accuracy rates for ANP concept detection than we did, expecting that the rates would be much closer to that of noun detection and not lower than adjective detection since [2] argues that adjectives lack visual grounding. We suspect that this difference by almost a half at top-1 between noun and ANP detection may point to the difficulty of the ANP detection problem in a slightly different sense than difficulty for the adjective detection problem. For adjective detection, visual recognition difficulty is likely to arise from visual variance, e.g. there may be a wide range of visual features required to describe the concept 'pretty'. However, for ANP detection, we believe that visual recognition difficulty is more likely due to visual nuances than overall visual variance. Much like fine-grained classification, this may imply that in ANP concept detection, concepts like 'sad dog' and 'happy dog' may share many visual characteristics but differ on few but highly distinguishing traits. The hope then is that by using a scaling layer, which acts as a soft gating mechanism in cross-residual connections, these few but distinguishable characteristics are accentuated.

5.2.2 *Effects of Cross-residual Weighting*

In Table 2, we also show results for multitask cross-residual networks with different types of weighting: no cross-residual weighting (X_0-ResNet-50), with all identity cross-residual weights (X_I-ResNet-50) and with identity on the self-task connections and channelwise scaling on just cross-residuals as described earlier (X_s-ResNet-50). The multitask cross-residual networks without and with cross-residuals are illustrated in Figure 4 (leftmost and center, respectively), and all of these multitask networks use a residual network with 50-layers (ResNet-50) as the basis and branch as described in Section 4. As we might expect, when *all* cross-residual weights are identity (X_I-ResNet-50), the accuracy of the multitask network across all tasks drastically reduces since the "amount" of cross-task mixing is forced to be equally weighted. Even as related as tasks might be forcing cross-residual weights equal across all tasks makes it difficult during learning for any single task to specialize and determine discriminative patterns useful for that specific task. It may be tempting to then assume that the other extreme of making the cross-residual weights zero where $\mathbf{W}_s^{(j)} = \mathbf{0}, \forall j \neq t$, i.e. equivalent to a multitask network without cross-residuals (X_0-ResNet-50), allows more specialization and would naturally achieve the best discriminative performance. However, we found that this actually consistently achieves lower accuracy across all tasks compared to its single-task equivalents (ResNet-50), e.g. ~9% worse relative on ANP detection. We hypothesize that without cross-residuals the performance

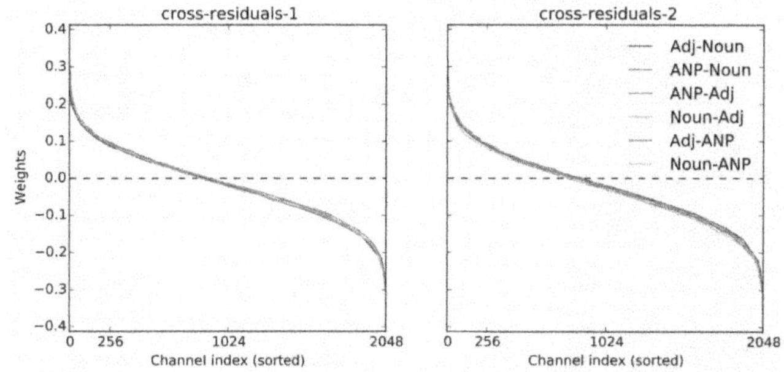

Figure 5: Example learned unnormalized cross-residual weights (sorted). Legend notation refer to cross-residual connections as `SourceTask-TargetTask`. Left and right plots show cross-residual weights of the first and second (feed-forward direction) cross-residual layers as in Figure 4 (center), respectively.

case becomes upper-bounded by the shared representation learned before the branching the multitask network.

Once we allow for even some simple learned weighting on the cross-residuals, like a channelwise scaling (X_s-ResNet-50), the predictive performance of the multitask network improves, outperforming both the case when no cross-residuals are used as well as equally weighted cross-residuals. In general, we observed that multitask networks achieved comparable performance to the three specialized single-task networks with just a single network while requiring less than 60% of the combined parameters of the three single-task networks (~43.2M vs. ~72.4M). This confirms our original hypothesis that the low-level representations can be shared across these related tasks and can be generalized to perform well across all tasks. However, in order to ensure that we do not take a hit in accuracy by generalizing, weighted cross-residuals layers can be used which, at a very marginal parameter cost, enable the multitask network to match the performance of specialized single-task networks. Notably, as we had hoped, the highest gain from using cross-residuals was on the most difficult of the three tasks: ANP detection. We observe that adding scaling cross-residual weights improves the concept detection performance by as much as ~10.37% relative on the ANP detection task compared to without any weighting.

Though we do not claim that our cross-residual multitask network (X_s-ResNet-50) definitively achieves a significantly higher accuracy over the single-task networks, we do note that we observed marginally better concept detection rates with our network across all tasks. Since we only used two cross-residual layers in our multitask network (c.f. Figure 4), it is possible that increasing the number of stacked cross-residual layers or beginning the branching in the network earlier could improve the overall cross-task performance; however, doing so would naturally come at increased parameter cost. Nonetheless, we believe that all of these observations show that jointly learning across related tasks with cross-task information mixing even at the late layers of a network can simultaneously improve the network's capacity to discriminate and generalize.

To further reinforce that the optimal weightings for cross-residual connections are unlikely to be zero or identity, in Figure 5, we show the unnormalized weight magnitudes of a learned multitask cross-residual network sorted by channel

Adjectives	*Adj-Noun Pairs*	*Nouns*
tiny	dry forest	leaves
dead	creepy eyes	forest
abandoned	dry leaves	tree
dry	dying rose	autumn
colorful	natural reserve	spider
cloudy	pretty sky	clouds
colorful	natural wonder	sky
beautiful	tasty cake	sunset
pretty	little flower	night
dark	empty train	evening
lonely	lonely boat	boat
calm	derelict factory	clouds
cloudy	heavy clouds	view
peaceful	calm sea	water
traditional	cloudy evening	evening
colorful	colorful bird	bird
curious	dry forest	forest
dry	curious bird	rain
lost	sexy lips	beauty
heavy	dangerous road	pond

Figure 6: Example top-5 classification results of adjective, noun, and adjective-noun pair concepts using our multitask cross-residual network.

index for two cross-residual layers in a network structured as in Figure 4 (center). If an all zero or identity cross-residual connection were to be optimal, we would expect to see a plateau with many weights near zero or one. Instead, we observe that mostly non-negative cross-task weights were learned across all shortcut connections such that the overall network objective was optimized. Additionally, we note that though the weight magnitudes are indeed small, this also follows from intuition in the original residual network work [14] that these small, but non-zero weights are precisely what enable residual networks to be made very deep.

5.2.3 Example Multitask Detection Results

In Figure 6, we show example classification results from our multitask cross-residual network. Note the presence of both intra- and inter-relatedness between tasks in the top detected concepts. In many cases, the cross-residual network is able to surface concepts not visually present but intuitively related; for example, in the first image, 'spider' is a detected noun which may be a result of either the branches in the image or the visual co-occurrence of the 'spider' concept in the training set with other top ranked concepts like 'tiny' (adjective) and 'leaves' (noun). As a potential failure case, in the last image, the ANP 'sexy lips' was ranked highly possibly due to relatedness learned with the 'colorful' adjective concept. In these cases, just as with over regularization in other learning settings, the network may have indeed have learned a more general representation, but as a result is unable to decouple certain learned relationships. Such cases may be easily addressed in cross-residual networks by giving cross-task weighting layers more computational budget, e.g. convolutional projections, to model more complicated task relationships. Overall, we observe here that the multitask cross-residual network is able to successfully co-detect concepts across multiple related visual recognition tasks.

6. CONCLUSIONS & FUTURE WORK

We presented an extension of residual learning enabling information mixing between related tasks called *cross-residual learning* (CRL) achieved by coupling the residual to other related tasks to ensure the learned mapping is not too far from other task representations. This enables more generalized representations to be learned in a deep network that are useful for multiple related tasks while preserving their discriminative power. We also showed how cross-residuals can be used for multitask learning by integrating cross-residual layers in a fan-out multitask network. We illustrated how such a multitask cross-residual network can achieve competitive, or even better, predictive performance on a visual sentiment concept detection problem as compared to specialized single-task networks but with $>40\%$ less parameters, while also outperforming a standard multitask residual network with no cross-residuals by about 10.4% relative on adjective-noun pair detection, the hardest of the three related target tasks. Without cross-residual connections, we observed a $\sim 9\%$ drop in accuracy on ANP detection, indicating the importance of using cross-residuals. In addition, we showed the importance of cross-residual weighting over simply forcing identity cross-residual connections since equally weighting cross-task connections bottlenecks the information flow in the network.

We believe cross-residual networks are also applicable to other learning settings and domains, and can be extended in several ways. Cross-residual networks can be applied to other multitask learning settings where we are not only interested in classification but also other tasks like reconstruction, object segmentation, etc. Likewise, cross-residual networks are likely to be useful in domain transfer and adaptation problems where, for example, network tower weights are frozen but cross-residual weights are learned. Architecturally, while we only explored the canonical shortcut connections of [14] and used a channelwise scaling layer for the cross-residual, there is recent work exploring different types of transforms and gating on shortcuts [15] that can also be extended to the self- and cross-connections in cross-residual networks. We plan to explore these learning settings and network architectures in the future.

Acknowledgements

We thank our reviewers for their helpful and constructive feedback. We also thank Rogerio Feris for insightful discussions on the network design and Tao Chen for support with the Visual Sentiment Ontology (VSO) dataset as well as discussions on prior VSO experiments.

7. REFERENCES

[1] S. Bhattacharya, B. Nojavanasghari, T. Chen, D. Liu, S.-F. Chang, and M. Shah. Towards a comprehensive computational model for aesthetic assessment of videos. In *ACM MM*, 2013.

[2] D. Borth, R. Ji, T. Chen, T. Breuel, and S.-F. Chang. Large-scale visual sentiment ontology and detectors using adjective noun pairs. In *ACM MM*, 2013.

[3] R. Caruana. Multitask learning. *Machine Learning*, 28(1), 1997.

[4] T. Chen, D. Borth, T. Darrell, and S.-F. Chang. DeepSentiBank: Visual sentiment concept classification with deep convolutional neural networks. *arXiv preprint arXiv:1410.8586*, 2014.

[5] R. Collobert and J. Weston. A unified architecture for natural language processing: Deep neural networks with multitask learning. In *ICML*, 2008.

[6] G. E. Dahl, N. Jaitly, and R. Salakhutdinov. Multi-task neural networks for QSAR predictions. *arXiv preprint arXiv:1406.1231*, 2014.

[7] J. Dai, K. He, and J. Sun. Instance-aware semantic segmentation via multi-task network cascades. In *CVPR*, 2016.

[8] J. Deng, N. Ding, Y. Jia, A. Frome, K. Murphy, S. Bengio, Y. Li, H. Neven, and H. Adam. Large-scale object classification using label relation graphs. In *ECCV*, 2014.

[9] F. A. Gers, N. N. Schraudolph, and J. Schmidhuber. Learning precise timing with LSTM recurrent networks. *JMLR*, 3, 2002.

[10] M. Ghifary, W. B. Kleijn, M. Zhang, and D. Balduzzi. Domain generalization for object recognition with multi-task autoencoders. In *ICCV*, 2015.

[11] X. Glorot, A. Bordes, and Y. Bengio. Domain adaptation for large-scale sentiment classification: A deep learning approach. In *ICML*, 2011.

[12] M. Gygli, H. Grabner, H. Riemenschneider, F. Nater, and L. V. Gool. The interestingness of images. In *ICCV*, 2013.

[13] K. He, X. Zhang, S. Ren, and J. Sun. Delving deep into rectifiers: Surpassing human-level performance on ImageNet classification. In *ICCV*, 2015.

[14] K. He, X. Zhang, S. Ren, and J. Sun. Deep residual learning for image recognition. In *CVPR*, 2016.

[15] K. He, X. Zhang, S. Ren, and J. Sun. Identity mappings in deep residual networks. *arXiv preprint arXiv:1603.05027*, 2016.

[16] S. Hochreiter and J. Schmidhuber. Long short-term memory. *Neural Computation*, 9(8), 1997.

[17] S. Ioffe and C. Szegedy. Batch Normalization: Accelerating deep network training by reducing internal covariate shift. In *ICML*, 2015.

[18] P. Isola, J. Xiao, A. Torralba, and A. Oliva. What makes an image memorable? In *CVPR*, 2011.

[19] Y. Jia, E. Shelhamer, J. Donahue, S. Karayev, J. Long, R. Girshick, S. Guadarrama, and T. Darrell. Caffe: Convolutional architecture for fast feature embedding. In *ACM MM*, 2014.

[20] W. Jiang, E. Zavesky, S.-F. Chang, and A. Loui. Cross-domain learning methods for high-level visual concept classification. In *ICIP*, 2008.

[21] Y.-G. Jiang, J. Wang, S.-F. Chang, and C.-W. Ngo. Domain adaptive semantic diffusion for large scale context-based video annotation. In *ICCV*, 2009.

[22] Y.-G. Jiang, B. Xu, and X. Xue. Predicting emotions in user-generated videos. In *AAAI*, 2014.

[23] B. Jou, S. Bhattacharya, and S.-F. Chang. Predicting viewer perceived emotions in animated GIFs. In *ACM MM*, 2014.

[24] B. Jou, T. Chen, N. Pappas, M. Redi, M. Topkara, and S.-F. Chang. Visual affect around the world: A large-scale multilingual visual sentiment ontology. In *ACM MM*, 2015.

[25] Y. Ke, X. Tang, and F. Jing. The design of high-level features for photo quality assessment. In *CVPR*, 2006.

[26] A. Khosla, A. Das Sarma, and R. Hamid. What makes an image popular? In *WWW*, 2014.

[27] A. Krizhevsky, I. Sutskever, and G. E. Hinton. ImageNet classification with deep convolutional neural networks. In *NIPS*, 2012.

[28] X. Liu, J. Gao, X. He, L. Deng, K. Duh, and Y.-Y. Wang. Representation learning using multi-task deep neural networks for semantic classification and information retrieval. In *NAACL*, 2015.

[29] M.-T. Luong, Q. V. Le, I. Sutskever, O. Vinyals, and L. Kaiser. Multi-task sequence to sequence learning. In *ICLR*, 2016.

[30] J. Machajdik and A. Hanbury. Affective image classification using features inspired by psychology and art theory. In *ACM MM*, 2010.

[31] V. Nair and G. E. Hinton. Rectified linear units improve restricted boltzmann machines. In *ICML*, 2010.

[32] S. J. Pan and Q. Yang. A survey on transfer learning. *IEEE TKDE*, 22(10), 2010.

[33] R. Plutchik. *Emotion: A Psychoevolutionary Synthesis*. Harper & Row, 1980.

[34] T. Raiko, H. Valpola, and Y. LeCun. Deep learning made easier by linear transformations in perceptrons. In *AISTATS*, 2012.

[35] B. Ramsundar, S. Kearnes, P. Riley, D. Webster, D. Konerding, and V. Pande. Massively multitask networks for drug discovery. *arXiv preprint arXiv:1502.02072*, 2015.

[36] A. Rasmus, H. Valpola, M. Honkala, M. Berglund, and T. Raiko. Semi-supervised learning with ladder networks. *arXiv preprint arXiv:1507.02672*, 2015.

[37] O. Russakovsky, J. Deng, H. Su, J. Krause, S. Satheesh, S. Ma, Z. Huang, A. Karpathy, A. Khosla, M. Bernstein, A. C. Berg, and L. Fei-Fei. ImageNet Large Scale Visual Recognition Challenge. *IJCV*, 115(3), 2015.

[38] K. Simonyan and A. Zisserman. Very deep convolutional networks for large-scale image recognition. In *ICLR*, 2015.

[39] N. Srivastava, G. Hinton, A. Krizhevsky, I. Sutskever, and R. Salakhutdinov. Dropout: A simple way to prevent neural networks from overfitting. *JMLR*, 15(1), 2014.

[40] R. K. Srivastava, K. Greff, and J. Schmidhuber. Highway networks. In *ICMLW*, 2015.

[41] C. Szegedy, W. Liu, Y. Jia, P. Sermanet, S. Reed, D. Anguelov, D. Erhan, V. Vanhoucke, and A. Rabinovich. Going deeper with convolutions. In *CVPR*, 2015.

[42] Z. Wu, Y.-G. Jiang, J. Wang, J. Pu, and X. Xue. Exploring inter-feature and inter-class relationships with deep neural networks for video classification. In *ACM MM*, 2014.

[43] V. Yanulevskaya, J. van Gemert, K. Roth, A. Herbold, N. Sebe, and J. M. Geusebroek. Emotional valence categorization using holistic image features. In *ICIP*, 2008.

[44] J. Yim, H. Jung, B.-I. Yoo, C. Choi, D. Park, and J. Kim. Rotating your face using multi-task deep neural network. In *CVPR*, 2015.

Robust Visual-Textual Sentiment Analysis: When Attention meets Tree-structured Recursive Neural Networks

Quanzeng You[1], Liangliang Cao[2], Hailin Jin[3], Jiebo Luo[1]
[1]University of Rochester, Buffalo, NY USA
[2]Yahoo Labs, New York, NY USA
[3]Adobe Research, San Jose, CA USA
{qyou, jluo}@cs.rochester.edu, liangliang@yahoo-inc.com, hljin@adobe.com

ABSTRACT

Sentiment analysis is crucial for extracting social signals from social media content. Due to huge variation in social media, the performance of sentiment classifiers using single modality (visual or textual) still lags behind satisfaction. In this paper, we propose a new framework that integrates textual and visual information for robust sentiment analysis. Different from previous work, we believe visual and textual information should be treated jointly in a structural fashion. Our system first builds a semantic tree structure based on sentence parsing, aimed at aligning textual words and image regions for accurate analysis. Next, our system learns a robust joint visual-textual semantic representation by incorporating 1) an attention mechanism with LSTM (long short term memory) and 2) an auxiliary semantic learning task. Extensive experimental results on several known data sets show that our method outperforms existing the state-of-the-art joint models in sentiment analysis. We also investigate different tree-structured LSTM (T-LSTM) variants and analyze the effect of the attention mechanism in order to provide deeper insight on how the attention mechanism helps the learning of the joint visual-textual sentiment classifier.

CCS Concepts

•Information systems → Multimedia information systems; Information systems applications; •Computing methodologies → Computer vision; •General and reference → *Measurement;*

Keywords

joint visual-textual sentiment analysis; tree-structured joint model; multimodality analysis; attention mechanism

1. INTRODUCTION

Many classical studies [7, 15, 14, 19, 42] in integrating visual and textural features follow similar procedures. First, image information and text information are treated separately using different domain-specific knowledge and techniques in computer vision and natural language processing. Next, the individual representations of two moralities will be integrated to build the final classifier. Very few studies have considered models that can explore deeper correlation between the visual and textural representations.

Figure 1: An example image tweet about a car accident, where the associated text significantly helps learning an effective visual representation for sentiment analysis. Words related to the objects and visual attributes are closely related to regions with matching colors.

Figure 1 shows an example that suggest an image and the associated text should be treated in a closely knit fashion. There are a number of objects and attribute descriptors in the text, including "people", "car", "bus", and "accident", which are associated with specific regions in the image. If we are to parse such correlated text and image content accurately, these words and image regions should be modeled jointly in an intimate fashion.

The recent progress in sentence parsing suggests that the semantic features of sentences can be well modeled by a tree-structured model with semantic dependency [28, 15]. We propose to utilize such a structured model for multimodal visual-textual analysis. To model the visual features with the semantic parsing tree, we employ deep neural networks to model both textual and visual semantics. In particular, we generalize the standard Recurrent Neural Networks [31] by considering the regions of attention in the image, and build a unified model to leverage the information from the two modalities.

In this work, we intend to bridge the gap between vision and language using a tree-structured model on both image and text for joint visual-textual sentiment analysis. Figure 1 includes one image and sentence pair to illustrate our motivation. Generally, sentiment or opinion related words can be aligned to certain image regions. We are interested in discovering such kinds of alignments and subsequently building a robust joint model for sentiment analysis. Following previous studies on tree-structured Long Short-Term Memory (LSTM) over text [33, 44], we integrate image regions into the model using an attention mechanism. In particular, we propose a

MM '16, October 15-19, 2016, Amsterdam, Netherlands
© 2016 ACM. ISBN 978-1-4503-3603-1/16/10...$15.00
DOI: http://dx.doi.org/10.1145/2964284.2964288

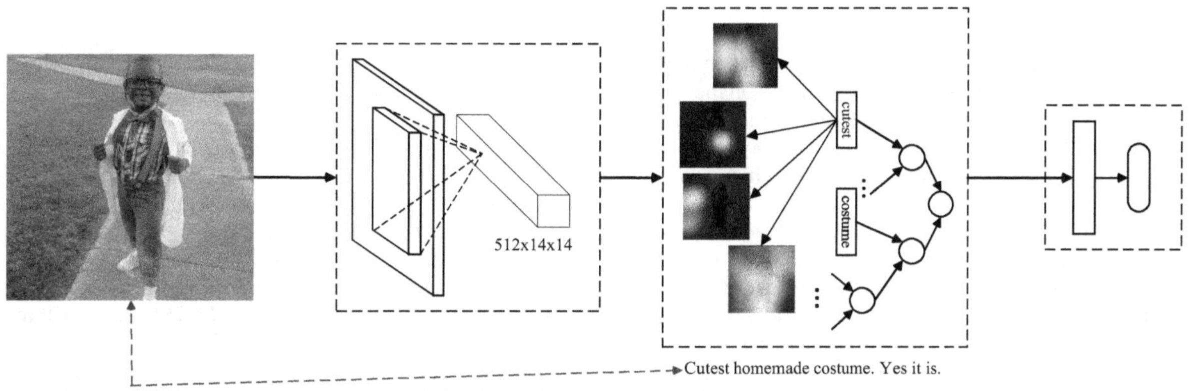

a) Input image and sentence pair b) Convolutional layer features c) T-LSTM on parsing trees d) Sentiment classifier

Figure 2: Steps of building a tree-structured LSTM (T-LSTM) model for joint sentiment analysis given a pair of sentence and image.

bilinear attention model to learn the relatedness between words and image regions. Consequently, the model is capable of structurally encoding both local vision and language features into a global semantic embedding feature space. Figure 2 shows the main steps of the proposed framework for joint sentiment analysis. The inputs to our model are pairs of image and its description. We employ CNN (convolutional neural network) for visual feature extraction. Next, we build a tree-structured Long Short-Term Memory (T-LSTM) model on top of the parsing trees to learn the joint feature representations. The attention mechanism is employed to learn the alignment between image regions and descriptive words. The hidden responses at the root node of the tree are provided as inputs to build a sentiment classifier in the end.

We apply our proposed model to the specific problem of analyzing sentiment from associated text and image. The problem of sentiment understanding of images has become popular in recent years [35, 4, 2, 42]. In particular, You *et al.* [42] proposed a cross-modality consistent regression (CCR) scheme for joint textual-visual sentiment analysis. Their approach employs deep visual and textual features to learn a regression model. By encouraging a consistent prediction between different modalities, their model achieved better performance over other different fusion models. However, almost all the previous work use simple early fusion or late fusion to combine two moralities, overlooking structured information coupling between the text and image. In contrast, our system introduces: 1) the use of an attention mechanism on local image regions and 2) joint visual-textual representation learning through tree-structured LSTM. Our system is capable of learning the semantic mapping between image regions and the words in the associated sentence. In addition, tree-structured LSTM facilitates the encoding of structured information into the joint semantic embedding. We compare the proposed model with several state-of-the-art baselines extensively on several data sets. The experimental results demonstrate the superiority of the proposed model.

We make the following contributions in this work:

- We employ tree-structured LSTM (T-LSTM) for joint textual-visual sentiment analysis, which leads to better mapping between textual words and image regions,
- We introduce a bilinear attention model to facilitate a robust joint textual-visual feature representation, and prevent the model from being dominated by single modality.
- We adopt a Siamese network as an auxiliary task to learn the semantic embedding between text and image, helping the attention mechanism to achieve high effectiveness.
- Our proposed framework outperforms the state-of-arts in three existing datasets and one new collected dataset.

In the following sections, we first briefly introduce LSTM and tree-structured LSTM. Next, we present the details of the components of the proposed framework. Finally, we describe the design of the experiments and analyze the results.

2. RELATED WORK

Computer vision and natural language processing are important application domains of machine learning. Recently, deep learning has made significant advances in tasks related to both vision and language [16]. Conseuquently, the task of higher-level semantic understanding, such as machine translation [1], image aesthetic analysis [18], and visual sentiment analysis [3, 41] have become tractable. A more interesting and challenging task is to bridge the semantic gap between vision and language, and thus help solve more challenging problem.

The successes of deep learning make the understanding and jointly modeling vision and language content a feasible and attractive research topic. In the context of deep learning, many related publications have proposed novel models that address image and text simultaneously. Starting with matching images with word-level concepts [7] and recently onto sentence-level descriptions [15, 28, 19, 20, 14], deep neural networks exhibit significant performance improvements on these tasks. Despite of the fact that there are no semantic and syntactic structures, these models have inspired the idea of joint feature learning [30], semantic transfer [7] and design of margin ranking loss [38].

Notably, automatic image captioning is widely studied [20, 6, 5, 34, 14], which more intimately connects visual content and language semantics. Instead of learning a semantic mapping space for image and sentence pairs, automatic image captioning systems are expected to generate a sentence describing the given image. Image features are commonly integrated into the generation of the captions, which is typically modeled by a neural language model.

In general, these models handle two primary tasks: 1) how to represent image and text, and 2) how to learn the model on top of visual and textual features. Indeed, Convolutional Neural Networks (CNNs) [16, 27, 32] become the common approaches for extracting visual features. Meanwhile, multimodal semantic mapping following a pairwise ranking loss is widely adopted for optimizing joint visual and textual models. Recently, different approaches, including sequential [15, 20, 14] and tree-structured models [28, 19], are selected to encode the text, among which Recurrent Neural Networks [31] and Recursive Neural Networks [29] are particularly popular. Indeed, both sequential and recursive models are closely related to the language and semantic attributes of text. On the other hand, visual content also have spatial and semantic structures [22]. Tree-structured models can benefit vision tasks in many ways [29, 40]. However, there have been few previous studies which connect the tree structures in both vision and text.

In this work, we focus on joint visual-textual sentiment analysis, which is an important task of bridging vision and language semantics. Different from the widely studied textual sentiment analysis [23], visual sentiment analysis is quite new and challenging. There are several recent works on visual sentiment analysis using initially pixel-level features [26], then mid-level attributes [2, 43], more recently deep visual features [41] and soical contextual information [37, 36]. These approaches have achieved acceptable performance on visual sentiment analysis. However, due to the complex nature of visual content, the performance of visual sentiment analysis still lags behind textual sentiment analysis.

There are also several publications on analyzing sentiment using multi-modalities, such as text and image. Both [35] and [4] employed text and images for sentiment analysis, where late fusion is employed to combine the prediction results of using n-gram textual features and mid-level visual features [2]. More recently, You *et al.* [42] proposed a cross-modality consistent regression (CCR) scheme for joint textual-visual sentiment analysis. Their approach employed deep visual and textual features to learn a regression model. Their model achieved the best performance over other fusion models, however, overlook the structured mapping between image regions and words. Our work is built on the long short-term memory (LSTM) model. In the next section, we will first introduce some basics of LSTM and then discuss our new model.

3. LONG SHORT-TERM MEMORY (LSTM) NETWORKS

For completeness, we present a brief introduction of the sequential LSTM model. With a Recurrent Neural Network (RNN), we are trying to predict the output sequence $\{y_1, y_2, \ldots, y_T\}$ given the input sequence $\{x_1, x_2, \ldots, x_T\}$. Between the input layer and the output layer, there is a hidden layer, and the current hidden state h_t is estimated using a recurrent unit (Eq.(1)):

$$h_t = f(h_{t-1}, x_t) \tag{1}$$

where x_t is the current input, h_{t-1} is the previous hidden state, $f(\cdot)$ accepts both x_t and h_{t-1} as inputs and produces the current output h_t. $f(\cdot)$ can be an activation function or other unit, such as long short-memory cell, which is one of the most widely deployed architectures [8]. Long short-memory cell can overcome the gradient *vanishing* issue [24]. Each LSTM cell c is controlled by an input gate i, an output gate o and an forget gate f, which is able to *remember* the error during the error propagation [12]. Subsequently, LSTM is capable of modeling long-range dependencies [14].

Let W^i, W^f, W^o represent the parameters of the input, forget and output gate respectively. $\odot$ denotes the element-wise multiplication between two vectors. σ is the logistic sigmoid function. The precise form of LSTM cell is described in the following equations [9, 11, 10]. For conciseness, we omit all the bias terms of linear transformations in the paper.

$$\begin{aligned}
i_t &= \sigma(W_x^i x_t + W_h^i h_{t-1}) && (2)\\
f_t &= \sigma(W_x^f x_t + W_h^f h_{t-1}) && (3)\\
o_t &= \sigma(W_x^o x_t + W_h^o h_{t-1}) && (4)\\
c_t &= f_t \odot c_{t-1} + i_t \odot \tanh(W_x^c x_t + W_h^c h_{t-1}) && (5)\\
h_t &= o_t \odot \tanh(c_t) && (6)
\end{aligned}$$

LSTM cells can also be used in non-sequential models. Recently, it has been utilized within tree structured models [33, 44]. Information is no longer propagated sequentially from current node to the next node as in sequential LSTM architectures. In tree-structured LSTM (T-LSTM) model, each internal node of the tree collects information from all of its child nodes and propagates the processed information to its parent node. In such a way, the hidden state obtained at the root node of the tree is considered to be the joint representation of the inputs at the leaf nodes of the tree. Each non-leaf node i in the tree is modeled using a LSTM cell. It will receive the hidden state of its j-th child as the j-th input. To accept multiple inputs, we use the following equations [33] to define the forward computation for a node i from all of its child nodes.

$$i_i = \sigma(W_x^i x_i + \sum_{n=1}^{N_i} W_n^i h_n^i) \tag{7}$$

$$f_k^i = \sigma(W_x^f x_i + \sum_{n=1}^{N_i} W_n^f h_n^i) \tag{8}$$

$$o_i = \sigma(W_x^o x_i + \sum_{n=1}^{N_i} W_n^h h_n^i) \tag{9}$$

$$c_i = \sum_{n=1}^{N_i} f_n^i \odot c_n^i + i_i \odot \phi(W_x^c x_i + \sum_{n=1}^{N_i} W_n^c h_n^i) \tag{10}$$

$$h_i = o_t \odot \psi(c_t) \tag{11}$$

where N_i is the number of child nodes for node i and h_n^i is the hidden state from its n-th child. Each leaf node is sequentially mapped to the words of the input sentence according to the parsing tree. During the backward propagation, the errors are back propagated from parent node to all of its child nodes[1]. Existing work of using T-LSTM for sentiment analysis are limited to textual analysis only. We will explain in the next section on how to generalize it to multimedia context.

A key challenge of using both image and text in T-LSTM is that one modality will dominate the model so that the resulted model's performance will be similar to the one with single modality. To solve this problem, we extend the attention model [1] using bilinear attention model. Different from the previous works in attention model [39] for image captioning. However, The model in [39] is based on sequential LSTM while this work is based on tree-structure LSTM. Another main difference between [39] and this work is that we use a bilinear model for attention, which is more effective in practice. Last but not the least, this paper studies the problem in a discriminative setting, while the method in [39] is based on a generative model, which is not applicable for sentiment estimation. The next section will explain our model in details.

4. PROPOSED SCHEME FOR SENTIMENT ANALYSIS

In this section, we present how to apply the tree-structured T-LSTM model for joint visual-textual sentiment analysis. Our approach is mainly motivated by the findings that tree-structured models can benefit vision tasks [29, 40]. Our system incorporates both the attention mechanism and an auxiliary semantic learning task to learn a robust joint visual-textual semantic representation. Consequently, we are able to learn a more accurate and robust sentiment classifier.

[1]We refer the readers to [44] for the detailed formulas of back propagation.

4.1 T-LSTM for Joint Sentiment Analysis

T-LSTM relies on tree-structures for learning and testing. Inspired by both [33] and [44], we also learn the T-LSTM over a parsing tree, which encodes the syntactic structure of a given sentence.

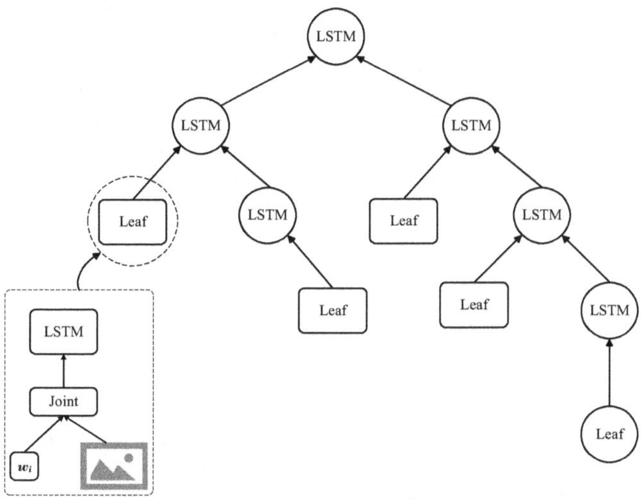

Figure 3: The scheme of the joint visual-textual tree-structured LSTM. We produce each *leaf* node (rectangle node) from a joint module. The joint module has two inputs, a word and regions of an image. Each internal node can receive information from multiple children nodes. The information is processed using a LSTM cell. The output of each node is forwarded to its parent node.

Most of previous works on T-LSTM are based on text (single modality). Next, we will explain how to generalize it to multi-modality scenario where a pair of sentence and image (t^m, v^m) are taken into account jointly. We take the hidden state at the root node of the T-LSTM as the representation for the sentence and image pair. Next, this representation can be supplied as input to build a softmax classifier for sentiment analysis. In such a way, we can solve the problem of joint visual-textual sentiment analysis. We employ the negative log-likelihood (NLL) to define the cost:

$$p(h[t^m, v^m]) = \text{softmax}\left(W_s h[t^m, v^m]\right) \tag{12}$$

$$L(t^m, v^m) = -\log\left(p(h[t^m, v^m]), l_m\right) \tag{13}$$

where $h[t^m, v^m]$ is the hidden state at the root node of a T-LSTM, W_s is the parameters for a linear model, and l_m is the sentiment label for the m-th image and sentence pair. The overall network can be trained using back propagation.

To learn and establish the joint representation $h[t^m, v^m]$ of a given pair of sentence and image (t^m, v^m), we focus on the leaf nodes, which directly accept textual words and visual representations as inputs. In particular, we want the *leaf* nodes of T-LSTM to jointly accept both individual words and image regions and produce its output based on both inputs. Eventually, the root node of the parsing tree will learn a joint embedding by receiving both the visual and the textual information propagated structurally from the *leaf* nodes. In such a way, we are able to integrate the visual information into the tree-structures. Figure 3 shows the overall framework of the proposed scheme. Each internal node is an LSTM memory cell. Meanwhile, each leaf node is a joint model, which tries to produce outputs from the input word and the input image regions.

A key challenge of introducing both image and text into T-LSTM is that one modality will dominate so that the resulted model's performance will be similar to the one with single modality. In the following subsection, we use a bilinear attention model as the joint module to learn the alignments and produce the outputs of leaf nodes simultaneously.

4.2 Bilinear Attention Model

Given a image and one descriptive sentence of the image, we assume that words of the sentence are likely associated with some regions in the image. Our goal is to automatically find such kind of connections between the words and the image regions. Let $T = \{t_1, t_2, \ldots, t_m\}$ denote a sentence with m words and let $V = \{v_1, v_2, \ldots, v_n\}$ denote the regions of an image, and n is the number of image regions. In attention model, for each word t_i, a score α_{ij} $(1 \leq j \leq n)$ is assigned to each image region v_j based on its relevance with the content of v_j. As a common approach to model relevance in vector space, a bilinear function is used to evaluate α_{ij}:

$$\alpha_{ij} \propto \varphi\left(t_i^T U v_j\right), \tag{14}$$

where the $\alpha_{i \cdot}$s are taken to normalize over all the $\{v_j\}$, $\varphi(\cdot)$ is a smooth function, and U is the weight matrix to be learned. One popular choice for $\varphi(\cdot)$ is the $\exp(\cdot)$ as in the softmax function.

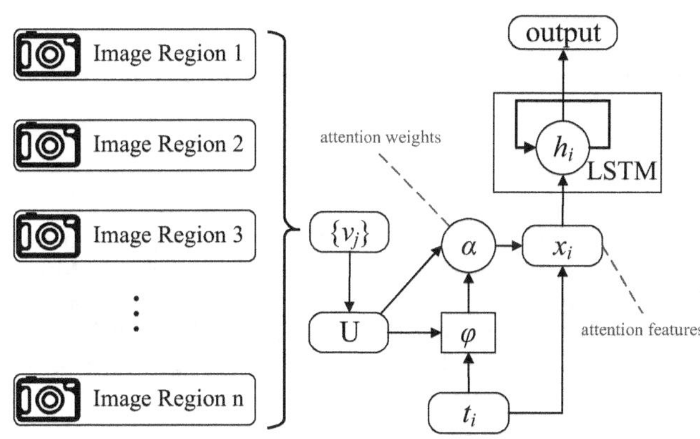

Figure 4: The bilinear attention model architecture for the leaf node. The attention model produces x_i, which is the concatenation of t_i and weighted sum of mappings of $\{v_j\}$. x_i is provided to a LSTM cell to produce the output for its parent node.

Once calculated, the attention scores are used to modulate the strength of attention on different image regions. The weighted sum of all candidate regions is mapped from visual feature space to the input word space of t_i:

$$v^i = \sum_{k=1}^{n} \alpha_{ik}(U v_k). \tag{15}$$

We obtain a weighted visual feature mapping v^i for the current word t_i. Let $x_i = [v^i; t_i]$ be the concatenation of v^i and t_i, which is the output produced by the attention model and supplied as the input to an LSTM memory cell (see Eq. (2) to Eq. (6)). In this way, we are able to integrate the visual information into the T-LSTM model. The whole bilinear attention model architecture for each leaf node is illustrated in Figure 4.

4.3 Semantic Embedding Learning

We hope that the attention model is able to assign *correct* attention weights between the input words and the feature regions for a given image and sentence pair. However, a sentiment analysis classifier mainly focuses on the performance of the joint features on sentiment analysis. There is no mechanism that explicitly helps the learning of alignments or correspondences between words and image regions. In other words, the attention model may not learn to assign semantically similar image regions to the corresponding words by optimizing on the gradients passed down from a sentiment classifier. Instead, a more secure approach is to explicitly utilize another task which will semantically learn the mapping or correspondence between words and image regions.

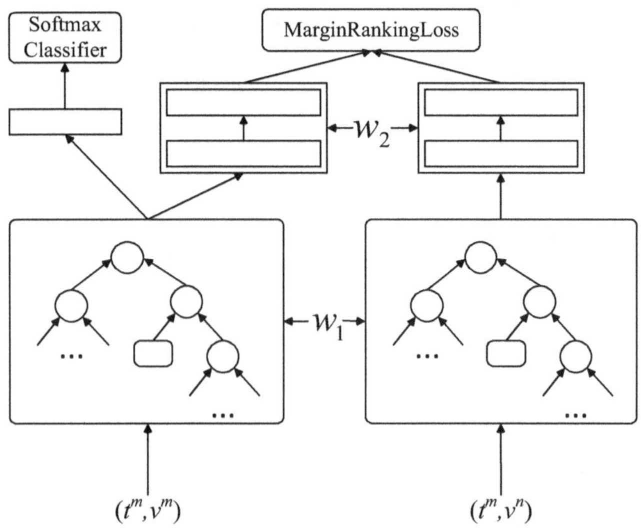

Figure 5: A multi-task learning framework for jointly training the sentiment classifier as well as the semantic embedding. (t^m, v^m) is the correct sentence and image pair and v^n is a randomly picked image from the training set. W_1 and W_2 are shared parameters for T-LSTM and the scoring MLP, respectively.

Inspired by the recent successes of deep visual-textual semantic embedding learning [14, 15, 19], we incorporate semantic learning task to pilot the learning of attention model. Let (t^m, v^m) be a sentence and image pair, and v^n (randomly picked from the training set) be a contrasting image of t^m. We then use the previously introduced T-LSTM model with the bilinear attention mechanism to encode both (t^m, v^m) and (t^m, v^n). Next, the pairwise margin ranking function is optimized to learn the semantic embedding:

$$L'(t^m, v^m, v^n) = \max\left(0, \mu - g(h[t^m, v^m]) + g(h[t^m, v^n])\right) \tag{16}$$

where $g(\cdot)$ learns the embedding score given the hidden features $h[t^m, v^m]$ and $h[t^m, v^n]$ from T-LSTM. This objective function tries to make sure that the score defined by $g(\cdot)$ is at least greater than μ for correct pair (t^m, v^m) compared to the contrastive pair (t^m, v^n).

Similar to [19], we use a multi-layer perceptron (MLP) to learn the score of each sentence and image pair given their hidden state. In particular, we define $g(\cdot)$ as follows:

$$g(h_i) = W_2^e(\delta(W_1^e h_i)) \tag{17}$$

where W_2^e and W_1^e are the parameters of the MLP and $\delta(\cdot)$ is the activation function for the hidden state. In our implementation, we use $\tanh(\cdot)$ as the activation function.

Another observation is that the calculation of attention weights α in Eq.(14) is inappropriate for learning semantic embedding. Recall the attention weights α are non-negative. It is assumed that the sentence t^m is supposed to describe the content of the image v^m. With this assumption, the attention model tries to discover the correspondence between the text words of t_i^m and the image regions of v_j^m. Therefore, softmax function is chosen as the smooth function for $\varphi(\cdot)$ (Eq.(14)). However, in the semantic learning task, we have randomly picked a negative image v^n, whose content may be totally irrelevant of t^m. Therefore, the attention weights defined in Eq.(14) could mislead the attention model given an unrelated image and sentence pair v^n and t^m as training data. To avoid this kind of *misleading or false* attention, we introduce the following way to calculate the attention weights (for simplicity, we ignore the superscript):

$$\beta_{ij} = \max(0, t_i^T U v_j) \tag{18}$$

$$\alpha_{ij} = \phi(\beta_{ij}) \tag{19}$$

where ϕ is the smoothing function. We use $\tanh(\cdot)$ to smooth α instead of $\exp(\cdot)$ as in Eq.(14). In such a way, we intend to achieve the following: 1) negative correspondences are ignored (Eq.(18)) and 2) α falls into reasonable value ranges (Eq.(19)).

4.4 Multi-task Learning for Joint Sentiment Analysis

Our model can be trained by a simultaneous optimization of both the sentiment analysis and the embedding tasks. Figure 5 shows the overall structure of the proposed model with the two tasks. The semantic embedding learning task is implemented using a Siamese network, where the parameters of T-LSTM (W_1 in Figure 5) and the parameters of the scoring MLP (W_2 in Figure 5) are shared. The loss of one training image-sentence pair is the summation of the sentiment classifier loss (Eq. (13)) and the margin ranking loss (Eq.(16)). For each training pair (t^m, v^m), we randomly choose one image v^n to make a contrasting pair (t^m, v^n), which is also given as the input to the semantic embedding module. The overall loss function is

$$L_{mt} = L(t^m, v^m) + L'(t^m, v^m, v^n). \tag{20}$$

All the parameters are automatically learned by minimizing the two loss functions over a training set. We use a mini-batch gradient descent algorithm with an adaptive learning rate to optimize the loss functions.

5. EXPERIMENTS

To the best of our knowledge, the work in [42] was the first study on joint textual-visual sentiment analysis using deep neural features. They also collected three data sets from GettyImage and Twitter, respectively, to evaluate their cross-modality consistent regression (CCR) model. We focus on comparing our proposed models with the baselines in [42]. In addition, we also add two baselines 1) T-LSTM on text only, and 2) T-LSTM on both text and image but without the semantic embedding task. Table 1 summarizes the different joint models for sentiment analysis. We also provide a short description for each model.

5.1 Data Sets

To test our proposed algorithms, we include the three datasets from previous work [42] and additionally build a new dataset for

Table 1: Summary of the models included in our evaluation. The first five models are from [42]. The last three models are our proposed models.

Model	Description
Single Visual Model	Logistic regression on deep visual features from pre-trained CaffeNet model.
Single Textual Model	Logistic regression on paragraph feature vectors [17] of text.
Early Fusion	Logistic regression on concatenated visual (CaffeNet) and textual features.
Late Fusion	Average of logistic regression sentiment score on both visual and textual features.
CCR	Cross-modality consistent regression (CCR) [42]
T-LSTM	Using T-LSTM model on the text only without attention.
T-LSTM Attention	Using T-LSTM model with attention model between text words and image regions.
T-LSTM Embedding	Learn the T-LSTM model and the semantic embedding simultaneously.

Table 2: Statistics of the four data sets.

Data Set	Positive	Negative	Total
Getty	311,940	276,281	588,221
Twitter	16,884	14,700	31,584
Twitter AMT	389	224	613
VSO-VT	129,524	124,993	254,517

joint textual-visual sentiment analysis . We will briefly describe the several data sets. Next, we will compare the performance results of the proposed approach with other state-of-the-art approaches.

The first data set is from Getty Image. It was built by querying the Getty image search engine with different sentiment keywords. The authors were able to collect a large data set containing about $588,000$ sentence-image pairs. Possibly, the data sets is noisy. However, the noise is tolerable due to the relatively formal and clean descriptions of images as argued in [42]. Meanwhile, since we use the same dataset, the noise is fair to all the candidate algorithms.

The second data set is from Twitter. More specifically, it contains image tweets (tweet messages that contain images). The dataset is relatively small after pre-processing. In total, it has $31,584$ *weakly* labeled image tweets. This dataset is also considered *weakly* labeled in that all the labels were generated by a predefined rule-based sentiment classifier. The last one is a small image-tweet dataset labeled by Amazon Mechanical Turk. In total, there are only 613 image tweets.

In addition, we build another weakly labeled dataset for evaluation. This new dataset is built on top of the visual sentiment ontology (VSO) [3], which consists of millions of images collected by querying Flickr with thousands of adjective and noun pairs (ANPs). Each ANP has hundreds of images collected from Flickr. However, this dataset only has the URLs of the images. There is no description for each image. Fortunately, Flickr has provided the API[2], which enables us to obtain the metadata (descriptions, upload date, tags, and so on) of an image by supplying its unique ID. Therefore, we are able to build a dataset for joint textual-visual sentiment analysis by collecting their Flickr descriptions using the provided API. After removing the invalid images that no longer exist, and eliminating images with too long (more than 100 words) and too short (less than 5 words) descriptions, we obtain $254,517$ images. Table 2 summarizes the statistics of the four datasets, where VSO-VT is the newly built dataset by us on top of the visual sentiment ontology.

5.2 Experimental Settings

To build a T-LSTM model, first we need to build a tree structure. In this work, we use the semantic constituency parsing tree, which was employed in [33] to build a tree-structured LSTM. We also employ the Stanford Parser[3], which is one of the state-of-the-art parsers, to build the parsing tree for each sentence.

Next, we need to choose feature representations for textual words and images. For word representation, there are two popular approaches. The first is one-hot representation with an embedding layer. In particular, the goal is to map a word w_i with representation $w_i = [0, \ldots, 1_i, \ldots, 0] \in R^{|V|}$ (only the i-th position is one in the one-hot representation) to $e_i \in R^m$, where $|V|$ is the size of the vocabulary and m is the size of embedding layer. The second approach is to directly employ the pre-trained distributed representations of words, such as Word2Vec [21] and GloVe [25]. Similar to [33], we use the pre-trained 300-dimensional GloVe features to represent words. This is particular helpful when the vocabulary size is too large, where insufficient text data may not lead to well learned word features in the one-hot representation setting.

In the visual part, Convolutional Neural Networks (CNN) have been widely used for robust visual feature extraction. In particular, features extracted from the pre-trained models on the ImageNet (http://www.image-net.org) dataset have succeeded in many visual related tasks. More recently, convolutional layer features are being studied for visual representations as well. Following [39], which employed convolutional layer features to learn an attention model for image caption generation, we use the same convolutional layer (conv5_4) in pre-trained VGG-19 model [27] to extract visual features for an input image. The feature size of the convolutional layer is 196×512. In other words, for each image, we have a total of 196 image candidate regions for the attention model.

The model is trained on GPU machines. We use the same split of [42] to make a fair comparison[4]. A separate validation dataset is used to select hyper-parameters and to control the stopping criteria. We train the model in a mini-batch mode, where 100 text-image pairs are randomly selected per batch. The hidden layer size is 512. All the source codes of the T-LSTM models will be released upon the publication of this work.

5.3 Experimental Results

5.3.1 *Results on the Getty testing dataset*

For all the T-LSTM variants, we use the same parameter settings. Table 3 shows the experimental results on the testing data set from Getty Images. T-LSTM model has significantly improve the performance using textual features only. This also coincides with the results in [33]. Indeed, the work in [42] mainly focus on the

[2]https://www.flickr.com/services/api/

[3]http://nlp.stanford.edu/software/lex-parser.shtml

[4]The splits are not publicly available. We obtain the splits by personal communication with the authors.

Table 3: **Results of different T-LSTM variants and previously reported results on the Getty testing dataset. The first five models are from [42]. The last three models are the newly proposed models (see Table 1 for the details of the models).**

Model	Precision	Recall	F1	Accuracy
Textual	0.806	0.544	0.655	0.696
Visual	0.747	0.745	0.746	0.732
Early Fusion	0.778	0.769	0.774	0.763
Late Fusion	0.785	0.775	0.780	0.769
CCR	0.846	0.759	0.800	0.800
T-LSTM	0.872	0.884	0.872	0.878
T-LSTM Attention	0.872	0.886	0.874	0.879
T-LSTM Embedding	**0.895**	**0.919**	**0.907**	**0.902**

Table 4: Results of different T-LSTM variants and previously reported results on the Twitter testing dataset.

Model	Precision	Recall	F1	Accuracy
Textual	0.746	0.693	0.727	0.722
Visual	0.584	0.561	0.573	0.553
Early Fusion	0.730	0.744	0.737	0.717
Late Fusion	0.634	0.610	0.622	0.604
CCR	0.831	0.805	0.818	0.809
T-LSTM	0.955	0.971	0.963	0.960
T-LSTM Attention	0.952	0.968	0.960	0.956
T-LSTM Embedding	**0.958**	**0.977**	**0.967**	**0.964**

learning of a robust classifier. The textual features are learned in an unsupervised way and the visual features are extracted from pre-trained CaffeNet models. Both of them are fixed in the learning of a sentiment classifier. This explains why T-LSTM can significantly improve the performance, where feature mappings and structures are also part of the model to learn.

T-LSTM with the attention model on images slightly improve the performance compared with T-LSTM. However, its peer model T-LSTM Embedding shows the best performance on all metrics. We attribute the difference to the attention model. It suggests that an auxiliary semantic learning task could lead to a better attention mechanism and thus a better sentiment classifier. We will quantitatively analyze the effect of attention in Section 5.4.

5.3.2 *Results on two Twitter datasets*

In addition, we test the proposed models on the Twitter dataset. Table 4 summarizes the results. Similarly, all the T-LSTM variants have shown significant improvements over previously reported algorithms. The accuracies of all the models are over 95%. Since T-LSTM has achieved much better results alone, the performance gain of adding visual features seems marginal. In fact, using the attention mechanism without the embedding learning task leads to slight degradation of the performance. We believe this performance is highly related to the way how ground truth labels are collected for this Twitter dataset. The authors [42] have indicated that they collect the weak or noisy sentiment labels of the image tweets by analyzing the Tweets text only using VADER [13]. Because VADER is a rule-based classifier for Tweets, it is acceptable to analyze the performance of sentiment classifiers, which is built on top of content-based features [42]. In contrast, T-LSTM tries to employ the dependency tree structures, which may have unobserved information overlap with the rules in VADER [13]. This explains the significant performance improvements of T-LSTM over previous models on this dataset.

There is another small Twitter AMT dataset, which was labeled by Amazon Mechanical Turk (AMT). This can reduce the bias induced by using another classifier to collect weak labels. This dataset is pretty small, with only 613 image tweets. We only use it as testing data to further evaluate the generability of the three T-LSTM models. In particular, we evaluate the previously trained models on the weakly labeled Twitter dataset on this small dataset without further training or fine-tuning. All the results are shown in Table 5. Both T-LSTM Attention and T-LSTM Embedding have shown better performance than T-LSTM, which indicates that the inclusion of visual features could lead to a more general model. In particular, joint embedding learning also promotes the performance of the learned model. All three T-LSTM models have shown better performance than the previous approaches, where the models trained on the weakly labeled Twitter dataset are further fine-tuned on this small dataset. Since this dataset is labeled by AMT workers, the performance is relatively worse than the performance on the weakly labeled Twitter testing dataset in Table 4.

Table 5: Results of different T-LSTM variants and previously reported results on the Twitter testing dataset labeled by Amazon Mechanical Turk workers.

Model	Precision	Recall	F1	Accuracy
Textual	0.832	0.638	0.722	0.688
Visual	0.762	0.715	0.737	0.677
Early Fusion	0.776	0.740	0.758	0.700
Late Fusion	0.799	0.738	0.767	0.716
CCR	0.846	0.759	0.800	0.800
T-LSTM	**1.000**	0.807	0.893	0.878
T-LSTM Attention	**1.000**	**0.830**	0.907	0.892
T-LSTM Embedding	**1.000**	**0.848**	**0.918**	**0.904**

Table 6: Results of different T-LSTM variants and previously reported results on the newly collected VSO-VT dataset.

Model	Precision	Recall	F1	Accuracy
Textual	0.626	0.622	0.624	0.624
Visual	0.625	0.586	0.605	0.616
Early Fusion	0.616	0.646	0.631	0.621
Late Fusion	0.660	0.629	0.645	0.650
CCR	0.672	0.678	0.675	0.672
T-LSTM	0.806	0.803	0.805	0.804
T-LSTM Attention	0.816	0.810	0.813	0.813
T-LSTM Embedding	**0.821**	**0.833**	**0.833**	**0.833**

5.3.3 *Results on VSO-VT*

Table 6 shows the performances of different algorithms on the constructed VSO-VT dataset. In particular, we implement and configure the first five models following the descriptions in [42]. Because this newly build dataset is pretty noisy[5], all of the models have relatively worse performance compared with the results on Getty and Twitter test datasets. However, T-LSTM variants still shows better performance over CCR and other baseline algorithms. Meanwhile, T-LSTM Emb has consistently demonstrated the best performance by all metrics.

[5]Recall we use the sentiment of an ANP to label all the images belonging to that ANP.

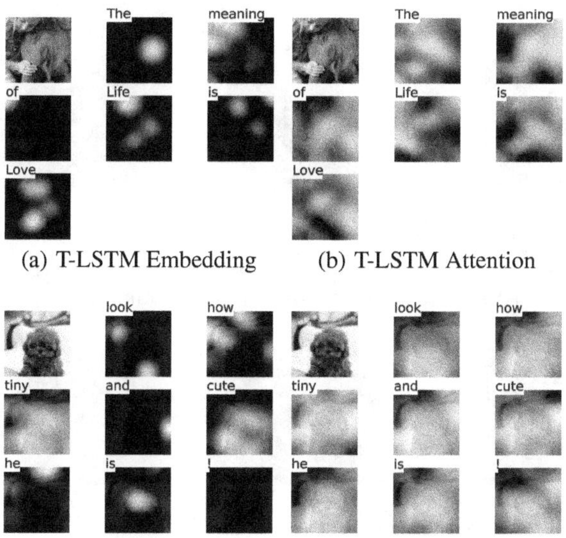

(a) T-LSTM Embedding (b) T-LSTM Attention

(c) T-LSTM Embedding (d) T-LSTM Attention

Figure 6: Visualization of *attention* on two examples with positive sentiment.

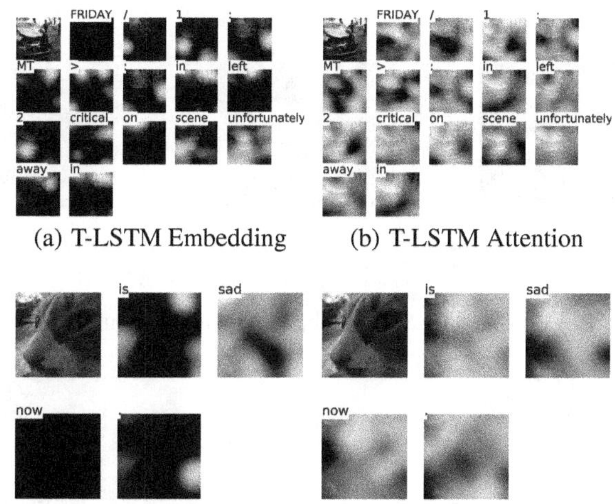

(a) T-LSTM Embedding (b) T-LSTM Attention

(c) T-LSTM Embedding (d) T-LSTM Attention

Figure 7: Visualization of *attention* on two examples with negative sentiment.

5.4 Qualitative Attention Analysis

We also try to visualize the attention weights at the leaf nodes of both T-LSTM Attention and T-LSTM Embedding. In particular, Xu *et al.* [39] have employed upsampling and Gaussian filtering to visualize attention weights. In this section, we follow the same steps to visualize the attention weights of both models. Recall that the Twitter AMT dataset is labeled by humans (Amazon Mechanical Turk workers). Therefore, we choose examples from these 613 image Tweets for illustration.

Figure 6 and Figure 7 show several positive and negative examples for T-LSTM Attention and T-LSTM Embedding, respectively. Overall, the T-LSTM Embedding model tends to learn more accurate attention than T-LSTM Attention. This indicates that the auxiliary embedding learning task helps the model to align words and image regions. Furthermore, the sentiment analysis task allows the attention mechanism to focus more on sentiment related regions. For instance, positive words *love* in Figure 6(a), *tiny* and *cute* in Figure 6(c) have all attended on the most related image regions. This is also true for *unfortunately* in Figure 7(a) and *sad* in Figure 7(c) of the two negative examples.

Another qualitative analysis is to check the top-confidence examples by different models [41, 42]. Even though the dataset is noisily labeled, Figure 8 shows the top ranked examples (according to the prediction score) of all the evaluated models on the VSO-VT dataset. Top ranked examples are quite different from model to model. For top ranked positives, T-LSTM Embedding favors images including people, while T-LSTM Attention model prefers more colorful objects, such as flowers and yummy food. T-LSTM's top ranked examples are more likely to include strong emotional words, such as "well", "amazing", "stunning" and "super", which also retrieves content-related images. Overall, CCR prefers images with long descriptions. This may be due to the fact that long sentences could lead to better learned textual representations in unsupervised distributed learning. For top ranked negative examples, both T-LSTM Embedding and CCR try to return abandoned and depressed scenes. Overall, T-LSTM Embedding provides the most reasonable top ranked examples.

6. CONCLUSIONS

In this study, we present a new end-to-end framework for joint visual-textual sentiment analysis. Our system tries to integrate textual and visual information in a structured fashion. Our model also incorporates an attention mechanism in a tree-structured LSTM to learn the alignments or correspondences between image regions and descriptive words. Therefore, the tree-structured model is capable of propagating the information from children nodes to their parents nodes in a bottom-up fashion. Later, joint features are obtained at the root nodes of the trees and supplied to a multi-layer perceptron for training a sentiment classifier. Meanwhile, we also introduce an auxiliary task, visual-textual semantic embedding, to help the learning of the attention model. Extensive experimental results have demonstrated that the proposed joint models have significantly improved the performance of joint textual-visual sentiment analysis on several datasets. In particular, the visual-textual semantic embedding task leads to better attention and in turn a better joint sentiment classifier.

Acknowledgment

This work was generously supported in part by Adobe Research and New York State through the Goergen Institute for Data Science at the University of Rochester.

7. REFERENCES

[1] D. Bahdanau, K. Cho, and Y. Bengio. Neural machine translation by jointly learning to align and translate. *arXiv preprint arXiv:1409.0473*, 2014.

[2] D. Borth, T. Chen, R. Ji, and S.-F. Chang. Sentibank: large-scale ontology and classifiers for detecting sentiment and emotions in visual content. In *Proceedings of the ACM International Conference on Multimedia (ACM MM)*, pages 459–460. ACM, 2013.

[3] D. Borth, R. Ji, T. Chen, T. M. Breuel, and S. Chang. Large-scale visual sentiment ontology and detectors using adjective noun pairs. In *Proceedings of the ACM International Conference on Multimedia (ACM MM)*, pages 223–232, 2013.

[4] D. Cao, R. Ji, D. Lin, and S. Li. A cross-media public

1) Model : Jacq Yu (Amazing Race Asia 1) Makeup : May Francisco Swimwear and Style : Fashion Fruit
2) Oryun Church Young Adult Group 2010 Summer Retreat
3) Power to the Peaceful festival in Golden Gate Park , San Francisco (Sept. 25 , 2005)

(a) Top T-LSTM Embedding positive examples

1) The Scream child's drawing Someone's kid drew this screaming face on the steps to their house. Drawings of the same face were inside one of the bedroom closets
2) Derelict building in downtown St Louis
3) Insane murderer reaches up with his bloody hand in a padded cell with bloody walls

(b) Top T-LSTM Embedding negative examples

1) Mothers Day Fresh Flowers - great gift for mom 's
2) Fresh Vegetable Salad , Healthy Food
3) Simple Wild Flowers - Pretty Bokeh

(c) Top T-LSTM Attention positive examples

1) Dry Dry River @ The Rosemount - Perth
2) Dead Earth Politics @ Dirty Dog Bar in Austin , Texas .
3) Severely damaged home ; NJ beach ; Hurricane Sandy aftermath

(d) Top T-LSTM Attention negative examples

1) Colorful paintings and well-designed decorations are always part of the traditional buildings in Beijing
2) A spectacular sunset followed 30 mins later by an amazing sky reflected in the absolutely flat calm lake . Stunning !
3) Gia Skova Super model pictures actress , Girl the blonde , Beautiful figure , Super sexual

(e) Top T-LSTM positive examples

1) Dead Earth Politics @ Dirty Dog Bar in Austin , Texas .
2) Dry Dry River @ The Rosemount - Perth
3) Photos from the Fat Face Night Air 20 Photos from the Fat Face Night Air 2008 at Bugsboarding

(f) Top T-LSTM negative examples

1) The body-con orchid dress at styleshake. Sensational jersey fabric orchid dress is perfect for romantic dinner date and special occasions.
2) Thank you Big Mama, Grandpa Gordo, Aunt Kay, Aunt Claire, and Aunt Suellen for the adorable angel teddy bear and lovely flowers!
3) This little girl visited us on her fifth birthday. She was wearing the special traditional costume. When I asked her to pose for a photo she stood near the litle flowers and smiled. She looked like a pretty little flower to me.

(g) Top CCR positive examples

1) The remains of former LMS BG abandoned and partially burned in the station. It was scrapped less than a year later when the redevelopment of the station site commenced.
2) We stayed in the smoking section so everything had that smell of death. The sheets always feel smaller in the smoking section too. There was some nasty blood stains on the side of the other bed.
3) This one was right above our front door on the soffits. Good positioning to nab some houseguests and slurp up their innards. I can't say I had thought about it until now.

(h) Top CCR negative examples

Figure 8: Top three ranked examples on the VSO-VT dataset by different approaches according to the prediction scores. The three descriptions corresponds to the three images from left to right in the same group.

sentiment analysis system for microblog. *Multimedia Systems*, pages 1–8, 2014.

[5] X. Chen and C. Lawrence Zitnick. Mind's eye: A recurrent visual representation for image caption generation. In *IEEE Conference on Computer Vision and Pattern Recognition (CVPR)*, June 2015.

[6] H. Fang, S. Gupta, F. Iandola, R. K. Srivastava, L. Deng, P. Dollar, J. Gao, X. He, M. Mitchell, J. C. Platt, C. Lawrence Zitnick, and G. Zweig. From captions to visual concepts and back. In *IEEE Conference on Computer Vision and Pattern Recognition (CVPR)*, June 2015.

[7] A. Frome, G. S. Corrado, J. Shlens, S. Bengio, J. Dean, M. Ranzato, and T. Mikolov. Devise: A deep visual-semantic embedding model. In *Advances in Neural Information Processing Systems (NIPS)*, pages 2121–2129, 2013.

[8] F. Gers. Long short-term memory in recurrent neural networks. *Unpublished PhD dissertation, École Polytechnique Fédérale de Lausanne, Lausanne, Switzerland*, 2001.

[9] F. A. Gers, N. N. Schraudolph, and J. Schmidhuber. Learning precise timing with lstm recurrent networks. *The Journal of Machine Learning Research*, 3:115–143, 2003.

[10] A. Graves, N. Jaitly, and A.-R. Mohamed. Hybrid speech recognition with deep bidirectional lstm. In *Workshop on*

Automatic Speech Recognition and Understanding (ASRU), pages 273–278. IEEE, 2013.

[11] A. Graves, A.-r. Mohamed, and G. Hinton. Speech recognition with deep recurrent neural networks. In *ICASSP*, pages 6645–6649. IEEE, 2013.

[12] S. Hochreiter and J. Schmidhuber. Long short-term memory. *Neural computation*, 9(8):1735–1780, 1997.

[13] C. J. Hutto and E. Gilbert. VADER: A parsimonious rule-based model for sentiment analysis of social media text. In *ICWSM*, 2014.

[14] A. Karpathy and F. Li. Deep visual-semantic alignments for generating image descriptions. In *IEEE Conference on Computer Vision and Pattern Recognition (CVPR)*, pages 3128–3137, 2015.

[15] R. Kiros, R. Salakhutdinov, and R. S. Zemel. Unifying visual-semantic embeddings with multimodal neural language models. *CoRR*, abs/1411.2539, 2014.

[16] A. Krizhevsky, I. Sutskever, and G. E. Hinton. Imagenet classification with deep convolutional neural networks. In *Advances in Neural Information Processing Systems (NIPS)*, pages 1106–1114, 2012.

[17] Q. V. Le and T. Mikolov. Distributed representations of sentences and documents. In *Proceedings of the 28th International Conference on Machine Learning (ICML)*, pages 1188–1196, 2014.

[18] X. Lu, Z. Lin, H. Jin, J. Yang, and J. Z. Wang. Rapid: Rating pictorial aesthetics using deep learning. In *Proceedings of the ACM International Conference on Multimedia (ACM MM)*, pages 457–466. ACM, 2014.

[19] L. Ma, Z. Lu, L. Shang, and H. Li. Multimodal convolutional neural networks for matching image and sentence. In *ICCV*, December 2015.

[20] J. Mao, W. Xu, Y. Yang, J. Wang, Z. Huang, and A. Yuille. Deep captioning with multimodal recurrent neural networks (m-rnn). *ICLR*, 2015.

[21] T. Mikolov, I. Sutskever, K. Chen, G. S. Corrado, and J. Dean. Distributed representations of words and phrases and their compositionality. In *Advances in Neural Information Processing Systems 26 (NIPS)*, pages 3111–3119, 2013.

[22] S. Nowozin and C. H. Lampert. Structured learning and prediction in computer vision. *Foundations and Trends in Computer Graphics and Vision*, 6(3-4):185–365, 2011.

[23] B. Pang and L. Lee. Opinion mining and sentiment analysis. *Foundations and trends in information retrieval*, 2(1-2):1–135, 2008.

[24] R. Pascanu, T. Mikolov, and Y. Bengio. On the difficulty of training recurrent neural networks. In *Proceedings of the 28th International Conference on Machine Learning (ICML)*, pages 1310–1318, 2013.

[25] J. Pennington, R. Socher, and C. D. Manning. Glove: Global vectors for word representation. In *Proceedings of the 2014 Conference on Empirical Methods in Natural Language Processing (EMNLP)*, pages 1532–1543, 2014.

[26] S. Siersdorfer, E. Minack, F. Deng, and J. S. Hare. Analyzing and predicting sentiment of images on the social web. In *Proceedings of the 18th International Conference on Multimedia (ACM MM)*, pages 715–718, 2010.

[27] K. Simonyan and A. Zisserman. Very deep convolutional networks for large-scale image recognition. *CoRR*, abs/1409.1556, 2014.

[28] R. Socher, A. Karpathy, Q. V. Le, C. D. Manning, and A. Y. Ng. Grounded compositional semantics for finding and describing images with sentences. *TACL*, 2:207–218, 2014.

[29] R. Socher, C. C. Lin, A. Y. Ng, and C. D. Manning. Parsing natural scenes and natural language with recursive neural networks. In *Proceedings of the 28th International Conference on Machine Learning (ICML)*, pages 129–136, 2011.

[30] N. Srivastava and R. Salakhutdinov. Multimodal learning with deep boltzmann machines. *Journal of Machine Learning Research*, 15(1):2949–2980, 2014.

[31] I. Sutskever. *Training recurrent neural networks*. PhD thesis, University of Toronto, 2013.

[32] C. Szegedy, W. Liu, Y. Jia, P. Sermanet, S. Reed, D. Anguelov, D. Erhan, V. Vanhoucke, and A. Rabinovich. Going deeper with convolutions. In *IEEE Conference on Computer Vision and Pattern Recognition (CVPR)*, pages 1–9, 2015.

[33] K. S. Tai, R. Socher, and C. D. Manning. Improved semantic representations from tree-structured long short-term memory networks. In *Proceedings of the Annual Meeting of the Association for Computational Linguistics (ACL)*, pages 1556–1566, July 2015.

[34] O. Vinyals, A. Toshev, S. Bengio, and D. Erhan. Show and tell: A neural image caption generator. In *CVPR*, June 2015.

[35] M. Wang, D. Cao, L. Li, S. Li, and R. Ji. Microblog sentiment analysis based on cross-media bag-of-words model. In *ICIMCS*, pages 76:76–76:80. ACM, 2014.

[36] Y. Wang, Y. Hu, S. Kambhampati, and B. Li. Inferring sentiment from web images with joint inference on visual and social cues: A regulated matrix factorization approach. In *ICWSM*, pages 473–482, 2015.

[37] Y. Wang, S. Wang, J. Tang, H. Liu, and B. Li. Unsupervised sentiment analysis for social media images. In *Proceedings of the Twenty-Fourth International Joint Conference on Artificial Intelligence (IJCAI)*, pages 2378–2379, 2015.

[38] J. Weston, S. Bengio, and N. Usunier. WSABIE: scaling up to large vocabulary image annotation. In *Proceedings of the Twenty-Fourth International Joint Conference on Artificial Intelligence (IJCAI)*, pages 2764–2770, 2011.

[39] K. Xu, J. Ba, R. Kiros, K. Cho, A. C. Courville, R. Salakhutdinov, R. S. Zemel, and Y. Bengio. Show, attend and tell: Neural image caption generation with visual attention. In *ICML*, pages 2048–2057, 2015.

[40] Y. Yang and D. Ramanan. Articulated pose estimation with flexible mixtures-of-parts. In *CVPR*, pages 1385–1392, June 2011.

[41] Q. You, J. Luo, H. Jin, and J. Yang. Robust image sentiment analysis using progressively trained and domain transferred deep networks. In *AAAI*, pages 381–388, 2015.

[42] Q. You, J. Luo, H. Jin, and J. Yang. Cross-modality consistent regression for joint visual-textual sentiment analysis of social multimedia. In *ACM International Conference on Web Search and Data Ming (WSDM)*, pages 13–22, 2016.

[43] J. Yuan, S. Mcdonough, Q. You, and J. Luo. Sentribute: image sentiment analysis from a mid-level perspective. In *WISDOM*, page 10, 2013.

[44] X. Zhu, P. Sobhani, and H. Guo. Long short-term memory over recursive structures. In *ICML*, pages 1604–1612, 2015.

Context-aware Image Tweet Modelling and Recommendation

Tao Chen[1,2] Xiangnan He[1] Min-Yen Kan[1,2]
[1]School of Computing, National University of Singapore
[2]NUS Interactive and Digital Media Institute
{taochen, xiangnan, kanmy}@comp.nus.edu.sg

ABSTRACT

While efforts have been made on bridging the semantic gap in image understanding, the *in situ* understanding of social media images is arguably more important but has had less progress. In this work, we enrich the representation of images in *image tweets* by considering their social context. We argue that in the microblog context, traditional image features, *e.g.*, low-level SIFT or high-level detected objects, are far from adequate in interpreting the necessary semantics latent in image tweets.

To bridge this gap, we move from the images' pixels to their context and propose a **c**ontext-aware **i**mage **t**weet modell**ing** (CITING) framework to mine and fuse contextual text to model such social media images' semantics. We start with tweet's intrinsic contexts, namely, 1) text within the image itself and 2) its accompanying text; and then we turn to the extrinsic contexts: 3) the external web page linked to by the tweet's embedded URL, and 4) the Web as a whole. These contexts can be leveraged to benefit many fundamental applications. To demonstrate the effectiveness our framework, we focus on the task of personalized image tweet recommendation, developing a feature-aware matrix factorization framework that encodes the contexts as a part of user interest modelling. Extensive experiments on a large Twitter dataset show that our proposed method significantly improves performance. Finally, to spur future studies, we have released both the code of our recommendation model and our image tweet dataset.

Keywords

image tweets; Twitter; context; recommendation; image semantics; microblog

1. INTRODUCTION

In the mobile Internet era, people now effortlessly snap pictures and share the events in their daily lives on social media. As a result, usage of social media platforms has soared, especially in terms of user-generated images. For example in Twitter, about 17.2% of tweets have associated images (which we term **image tweets**) according to our dataset collected in December 2014 (detailed in Section 5). The trend is even more evident in Sina Weibo — the largest microblog service in China — where over 45% of tweets are image tweets [8]. Being able to understand the images in image tweets is beneficial for many downstream applications, such as event detection, image tweet retrieval and recommendation [35]. For example in tweet recommendation, the widely-used collaborative filtering technique does not work well [7, 10, 15], due to the short life span of tweets. Therefore, it is crucial to look into the content of image tweets.

Figure 1: Example images affiliated with two tweets: (left) China ends the one-child policy, and (right) the movie *Fast and Furious 6*. For such microblog images, understanding their context is the key to its semantics.

Understanding image tweets, however, is non-trivial for machines. This is partially due to the technical difficulties in mining semantics from images, but more importantly, is because of the special **context** in social media. A picture is worth a thousand words, while the ever-evolving property of social media induces the full story of an image is far beyond itself and the contexts (*e.g.*, event and intent) are critical for image tweets understanding. Figure 1 shows two examples. For the left picture, image recognition algorithms tag it with words like "child, cute, girl, little, indoor"[1]. However, these visual tags can not capture the background and real intent of the picture — this image was the poster child for the story of China abandoning its controversial one-child policy. Similarly, for the right picture, the annotated tags "car, asphalt, road, people, transportation system" fail to tell the origin and objective of the picture — this is a promotional poster for the movie *Fast and Furious 6*.

In this work, we propose to exploit the contexts to tackle the challenges in understanding image tweets. We devise a **c**ontext-aware **i**mage **t**weet modell**ing** (CITING) framework (illustrated in Figure 2) to enrich the representation of im-

[1]These are the actual top five tags from Clarifai (https://www.clarifai.com), a commercial visual recognition system.

MM '16, October 15–19, 2016, Amsterdam, The Netherlands.
 ISBN 978-1-4503-3603-1/16/10...$15.00
DOI: http://dx.doi.org/10.1145/2964284.2964291

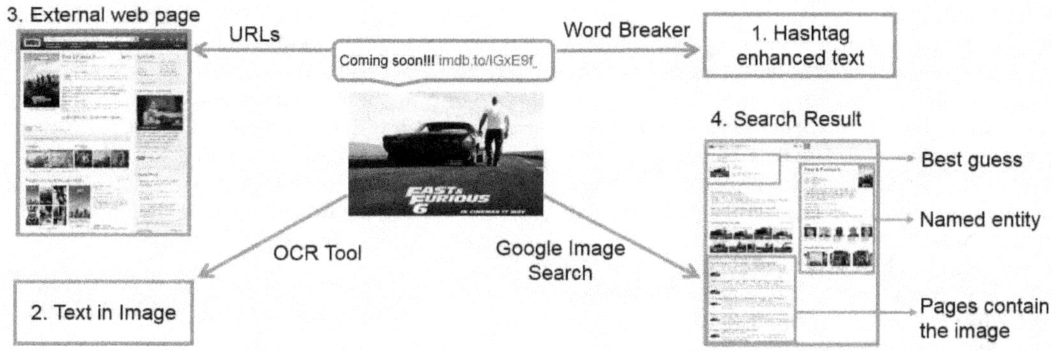

Figure 2: An image tweet's four sources of contextual text in our CITING framework. Blue outlines denote evidence frome text; orange from the image.

age tweets from both intrinsic and extrinsic contexts. We start with the intrinsic contexts: 1) for the text, we enhance hashtags to better represent the topics of images, and 2) for the image, we apply optical character recognition (OCR) to extract text from images. Then we turn to extrinsic contexts, which are especially important to understand the full story of image tweets: 3) parsing the external webpage(s) hyperlinked within the tweet; and 4) querying image search engines with the image as query. Our assessment reveals that the contextual text from each source differs in quality and coverage. As such, we further devise a series of heuristics to fuse text when multiple channels are triggered. This fusion makes the modelling more accurate and also reduces the acquisition cost of the contexts.

Our proposed framework extracts contexts in the form of textual words, which are easy to interpret and integrate with other image/visual feature inventories. To demonstrate the efficacy of the extracted contexts, we apply them to the personalized image tweet recommendation task, for which the key is to accurately model users' interests. We develop a generic feature-aware Matrix Factorization (MF) framework to model users' preference on features. As users do not explicitly express their dislikes, there is no explict negative data, which can adversely affect the learning of user interests [13]. To resolve this, we propose a time-aware negative sampling strategy that samples negative tweets for a user based on how likely the user may see the tweet but has not retweeted it. Lastly, we adopt a pair-wise learning to ranking method to infer users' interests based on our enhanced contexts. We conduct experiments on a large Twitter dataset, showing that our proposed contexts are more effective for users' interests modelling than the tweet's text and visual images themselves, which validates our recommendation methodology.

We summarize the main contributions as follows:

- We propose the CITING framework to mine and fuse contexts to better represent image tweets. Such study is fundamental and can benefit many applications such as event detection, image tweet retrieval and recommendation (Section 3).
- We develop a feature-aware recommendation model together with a featured negative sampling method for tweets, so as to effectively integrate contextual features for user interest modelling (Section 4).
- We conduct extensive experiments on Twitter image tweets that show the effectiveness of our CITING framework and the recommendation model. We have made the dataset and the model publicly available to facilitate future research (Section 5).

2. RELATED WORK

Unlike their textual counterparts, images in microblogs have only started attracting academic attention recently. We review the existing studies on image tweets, focusing on how the semantics of images are exploited for downstream applications. As there is no previous work on personalized recommendation of image tweets (to the best of our knowledge), we then review works about general tweet recommendation in the microblog setting.

2.1 Images in Microblog

As an image tweet consists of both text and image components, most existing works leverage both modalities to interpret the semantics of an image tweet [2, 3, 6, 30, 31, 34]. For text part, it is widely accepted that pre-processing — such as tokenization, lowercasing and stopword removal — is important to combat noise in the text. For the image part, existing work has followed a multimedia paradigm; that is, attempting to mine the semantics of an image from both low-level and high-level features. In terms of low-level features, works [30, 31, 16, 2, 3, 26] have considered pixels, color histograms, SIFT descriptors and Speeded Up Robust Features (SURF), among others. To be specific, SIFT descriptors and SURF are quantized by means of a visual codebook learned by k-means. However, the gap between the low-level features and the real semantics limits the model fidelity. The other works leveraged higher-level features, such as visual objects [6], human faces [8], and the output from the upper layers of convolutional neural networks (CNNs) trained for object recognition (hereafter, CNN features) [4, 34, 5]. For the CNN features, two papers [4, 5] used them directly (*e.g.*, 4096 dimensional visual features), while Zhang *et al.* [34] carried additional steps to quantize them into discrete features, which shares a similar spirit to the quantization of SIFT and SURF.

Due to the heterogeneous nature of image tweets, features extracted from the text and image lie in different spaces, which are non-trivial to integrate. To resolve this, multi-modal topic models [30, 31, 2, 4, 34, 9] have been developed to project images and the text of tweets to a shared latent topic space. As such, an image tweet is represented as a multinomial topic distribution; however, the dimensions of such latent representation are difficult to interpret semantically. One solution is to assign labels or categories to image tweets through human labelling or transfer learning [3]. However, the limited number of labels can seriously restrict the method's generalizability and coverage in practice. For example, in Bian *et al*'s work [3], only 20 categories were considered to label image tweets, which significantly limited the representation of semantics.

Although the above works have exploited image tweets in various ways, we argue that there are two key limitations of the previous work. First, concerning the tweet's text, only the textual words have been investigated; but microblog-specific textual features (*e.g.*, hashtags, external URLs) that contain known, rich contextual information have not been utilized. Second, images are leveraged only at a shallow level; that is, the community has limited itself to only using image features commonly used in general domain research. Microblog images exhibit unique characteristics, such that modelling these images using conventional manners confines an understanding to a superficial level (see the examples in Figure 1). It is thus critical to turn to external knowledge to gain a comprehensive understanding of an image tweet. In this work, we aim to fill this research gap by mining the rich contexts of image tweets.

2.2 Tweet Recommendation

With the vast amount of tweets, microblog users are now overwhelmed with many uninteresting posts. It is of great necessity to understand users' interest and recommend interesting tweet feeds for users. One line of research [14, 23, 22, 29] attempted to predict the general interestingness (or equivalently, "popularity") of a tweet, in regardless of the identity of an audience. Such prediction task is usually formulated as a classification problem (*e.g.*, popular or not). To this end, various features have been exploited, such as the explicit features from tweet's textual content (*e.g.*, words, topics and sentiments), contextual meta-data (*e.g.*, posting time), and the author's profile (*e.g.*, the number of followers and followees). The only work that has paid attention to image tweets is done by Can *et al.* [6], which also utilized shallow image features to build a classifier.

However, a generally popular tweet does not necessarily mean it will be interesting to a particular user, since interestingness is subjective and relevant to user's own taste [1]. To generate better recommendations for users, researchers have turned to build personalized models to predict tweet's interestingness. An early work by [28] built a classifier similar to general popularity predictor but with additional features from the target user, such as user's retweeting regularity and user–author relations. Later work casted it as a typical recommendation problem [7, 15, 10, 33], for which collaborative filtering (CF) is known to be the most effective technique. In the microblog platform, however, CF does not work well for tweet recommendation because of the ubiquitous cold-start problem: most live tweets are newly generated and have never been seen in the training data. To tackle this, existing works incorporate tweet's textual content into collaborative filtering models. Specifically, Chen *et al.* [7] transformed the traditional user–tweet interaction matrix to a user–word matrix before applying matrix factorization. Following the same idea, Feng *et al.* [10] additionally modelled the user–hashtag interaction, since hashtags are good topic indicators. Hong *et al.* [15] extended the Factorization Machines to jointly model user–tweet relations and the textual tweet generation process.

Despite the fact that many works have studied the tweet recommendation problem, they have primarily focused on the textual tweets. The rich signals in images and their contexts have been ignored. To the best of our knowledge, our work is the first to specifically consider the personalized recommendation task with image tweets.

3. CONTEXT-AWARE IMAGE TWEET MODELLING

In this section, we present our CITING framework for image tweets modelling. We first describe the four strategies that construct contexts from different data sources (*cf.* Figure 2), and then discuss the rules to fuse the contexts which help to improve text quality and save the acquisition cost. Unless otherwise stated, the descriptive statistics in this section are drawn from our 1.3 million Twitter image tweets dataset (detailed in Section 5).

3.1 Four Strategies to Construct Contexts

We start with the intrinsic context in image tweets: 1) the textual tweet, and 2) the image itself. Then we turn to the extrinsic context: 3) the external web pages hyperlinked in the tweet, and 4) the whole Web based on search engine.

1. Hashtag Enhanced Text. The most obvious context for a microblog image is its accompanying text. Here we focus on hashtags, which have relatively high coverage due to their prevalence in image tweets — 26.8% have hashtags in our Twitter dataset. Compared to the textual words of a tweet, hashtags exhibit stronger semantic ties to the post [21]. For example, we observe that a few hashtags (*e.g.*, #dogphoto) annotate objects present in an image, while the majority describe the topic or event of the image (*e.g.*, #itsyourbirthday). In both cases, hashtags are helpful in capturing the semantics of the image. However, a challenge in utilizing hashtags is that they do not exhibit the regularity of controlled vocabulary due to the user-generated nature. More specifically, people usually use different variant hashtags to refer to the same (series of) events (*e.g.*, #icebucket, #ALSIceBucketChallenge; #NewYears2013, #NewYears2014). Gathering hashtags variants can thus help conflate images with common semantics. Observing these variants are often composed with common keywords, we break up hashtags into component words by Microsoft's Word Breaker API[2], *e.g.*, #icebucket will be broken up as "ice" and "bucket"; we found that 14.3% of image tweets utilize multiword hashtags. We then combine such component words with post's text (including the original hashtags with their hash symbol) to form the hashtag enhanced text.

2. Text in the Image. Images in microblogs are not solely captured by camera, and many of them are software-generated or edited images, *e.g.*, graphics, memes, cartoons and screenshots. We observe that text is often embedded in images: our own manual annotation[3] of 500 randomly-sampled images (hereafter, *Twitter-500*) from our Twitter dataset identified 174 (34.8%) that fall in this category. We

[2]https://www.projectoxford.ai/weblm
[3]Annotated by the first author.

Table 1: Demographics of the 5 subtypes of text-images and associated Tesseract OCR performance.

Category	Manual	Tesseract	
	# (%)	Miss Rate	Recall
Text-style	38 (21.8%)	10.5%	0.984
Meme-style	64 (36.8%)	42.1%	0.572
Tweet screenshot	14 (8.0%)	7.1%	0.843
Other synthetic	43 (24.7%)	30.2%	0.500
Natural scene w/ text	15 (8.6%)	66.7%	0.467
Total	174	119	

Table 2: Categories of the 100 most frequent domains in URLs and Google Image indexed pages. *YT* is YouTube and *IA* is image aggregator. For the 66.0% SNS indexed by Google, 48.0% are from Twitter, 40.1% are from Pinterest.

%	News	SNS	Shop	Article	YT	IA	Music
URLs	**51.7**	15.3	11.9	10.9	3.9	2.3	1.8
Google	5.7	**66.0**	3.6	0.3	2.8	18.3	1.0

term such images as *text-images*, which we further categorize into five subtypes as shown in Table 1.

First, from the second column, we see that one-third of text-images are meme-styled: *i.e.*, a (viral Internet) image overlaid with text (as in Figure 3, left). It is impossible to differentiate the semantics of meme-style images from a visual perspective, as many originate from an identical source picture. Figure 4 shows two example images. In contrast, the embedded captions all but give away the context. In even more text-heavy cases, images can consist purely of text (Figure 3, right), accounting for roughly a fifth of text-images. Twitter users sometimes post such pure text-style images possibly to circumvent the 140 character restriction. Screenshots of tweets (8.0%) are also common; we conjecture that the primary intention of such posts is to achieve the "retweet with comment" feature before Twitter officially supported this function in April 2015[4]. For such tweets that have a strong textual nature, object detectors are close to useless. For the remaining text-images, 16.7% are other synthetic images, and 8.5% are natural photos that contain text in the scene (*e.g.*, road signs). Our findings lead to two key implications: 1) that a large proportion of social media images have a textual aspect, and for posts feature in such images, that 2) the embedded text is an important carrier of its semantics.

As such, we apply the *Tesseract* open source OCR software (version 3.02.02)[5] to recognize text from these images. After further using the vocabulary built by our Twitter posts to filter out noise, 26.4% of the images in our dataset have at least one recognized textual word. As Tesseract is designed for printed text, a natural question to ask is how well does it work for Twitter images? Using our manual annotation as a reference, we evaluate Tesseract's performance on our Twitter-500 sample set. Table 1's rightmost two columns show its miss rate and the average recall for recognized text. Overall, Tesseract detected text from 119 images, missing 55 images that actually did contain some text. The majority of the misses come from text present in the scene (missed two-thirds) and meme-style text (missed 42.1%). Tesseract performs well on pure-text style images (detected 89.5% of images with some text, and recognized 98.4% of the actual words) and tweet screenshots. The cause of the discrepancy is simple: the more similar the image is to scanned text, the better the performance.

[4]It is likely that the number of such screenshots is decreasing, while we believe the overall coverage of text-images has not change much.

[5]https://github.com/tesseract-ocr/tesseract

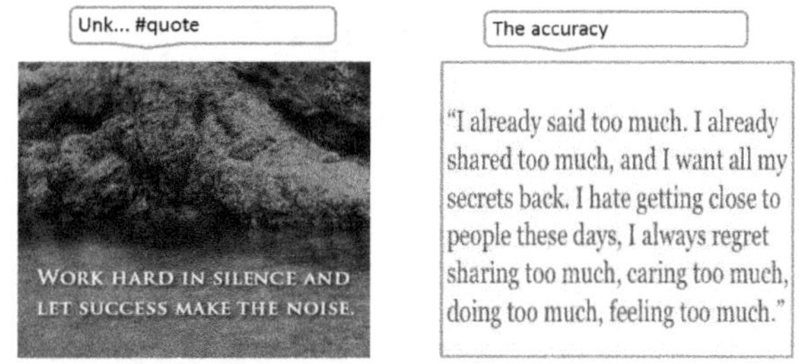

Figure 3: (left) Meme-styled and (right) text-styled image tweets. The callouts are the tweets' text.

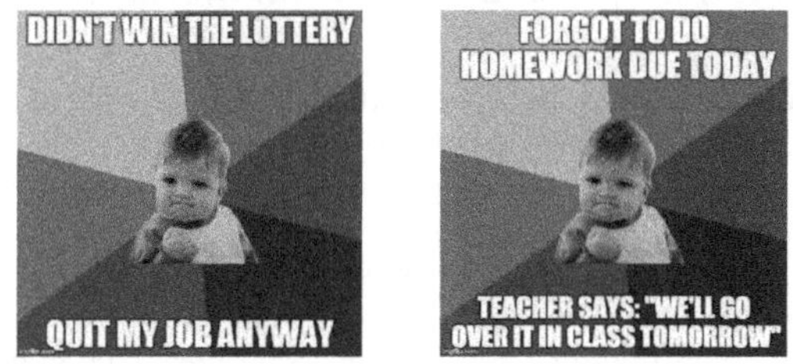

Figure 4: Two meme-styled images have similar visual properties but different embedded captions.

3. External Webpages. To provide context as well as to circumvent length limitations, microblog users also embed shortened hyperlinks in their tweets. In our dataset, 22.7% of image tweets contain at least one external URL. To the best of our knowledge, URLs in image tweets have not been studied in prior work. What are the external web pages about? How do they correlate to the images?

To answer these questions, we first resolved the hyperlinked shortened URLs and stored the redirected original URLs[6]. We then aggregated the resolved URLs by domain, manually categorizing the top 100 most frequent domains (accounting for 51.8% of URLs) into seven types. Table 2 shows the category distribution of the external resources. The majority are news reports, while three other prominent sources are online social networks (15.3%), e-commerce shops (11.9%), and articles (10.9%, *e.g.*, WordPress blogs). YouTube, image aggregators and music links account for the remaining minority (3.9%, 2.3% and 1.8%, respectively).

Interestingly, we also discover that the tweet image often originates from the external resource (82.1% of URL image tweets in our Twitter-500 set). Often, the image is a key scene in a news event, an item to be sold for online shops, or a portrait of the musician in music links. This suggests the external resource is the original, unsummarized context for such tweets, and thus a reliable source for capturing the image's semantics. We thus apply Boilerpipe [18] to extract the main textual content, then filter out stopwords, and finally use standard *tf.idf* term weighting to select the top k textual words as features. Considering some pages consist only of the title text (no main text), we use the page's title as another descriptor.

[6]Over half were still accessible, as of 30 September 2015.

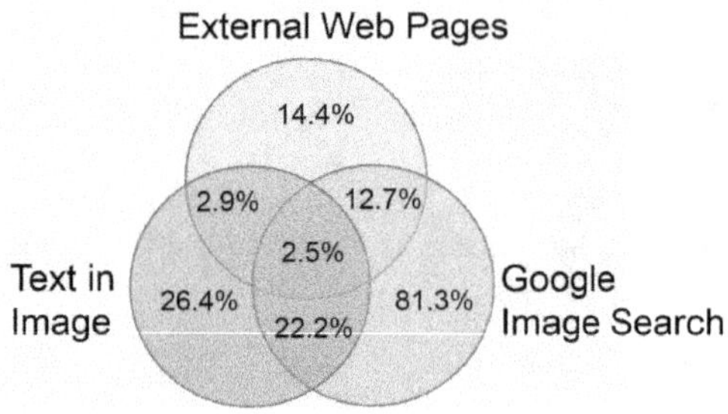

Figure 5: Percentage of image tweets that benefit from three major sources and the overlaps.

4. Search Engine as Context Miner. As 85% of Twitter trending topics are news [20] and Internet viral images are popular, many such tweet images have been previously used in other places on the Web, in similar contexts. To obtain these external contexts, we leverage Web search engines, which represent an up-to-date repository for the Web. We send each image in our dataset as a query to Google Image Search (done during the last week of August 2015), then parse the first search engine result page (SERP) to obtain a list of pages that contain the image (including URL and title). We then follow the links to crawl the actual content of the external pages. In our dataset, a surprisingly large proportion (76.0%) of Twitter images were already been indexed by Google.

Following our workflow for tweets' embedded URLs, we also categorize the top 100 domains for such SERP-listed web pages, which accounted for 54.6% of pages. From Table 2, we see 66.0% of pages are social network posts, of which 48.0% originate from Twitter itself. This implies images are re-purposed even in Twitter, and that image reuse is not limited to retweeting. The photo-based Pinterest social network takes up another 40.1% of such posts. The second largest category represents photo aggregators (18.3%, *e.g.*, imgur.com), which host images for social networks. The remaining 15.7% is distributed among the other site types (news sites, e-commerce, YouTube, music sites and blog sites, representing 5.7%, 3.6%, 2.8%, 1.0% and 0.3%, respectively).

For the query image, Google Image Search occasionally also offers a "best guess" at a short text description. Unlike the tags from traditional visual recognizer, the "best guess" can be seen as translating from a visual description to a semantic description — technically implemented as the best keyword for discovering the query image. For Figure 1 (right), the best guess is "fast and furious 6" which is spot-on. When the query image is identified as a named entity (*e.g.*, celebrity, movie or landmark), Google also sometimes shows a detailed named entity description in a knowledge graph box (functionality introduced in Google around July 2012). We additionally utilize these sources — the best guess (57.9% of Twitter images) and named entity (8.1%) as image's semantic description when available. In sum, 81.3% of images in our dataset have obtainable contextual text from Google Image Search.

3.2 Fusing the Contexts

Image tweets have rich contexts that can be exploited. In our dataset, 89.1% of images have at least one applicable strategy and 39.9% can leverage multiple ones. We survey the overlap among the contextual text sources of external URLs, OCR-ed text and Google Image Search for our dataset in Figure 5. As we can see, Google Image Search has large overlaps with external URLs and OCR text. For these overlaps, the other two sources are direct context indicated by image tweet's author, and we believe provide more accurate semantics for the image tweet than the SERP-extracted text. Take the two meme-styled images in Figure 4 as an example. The best guess description from Google Image Search is "no adulting meme" and "india pakistan match troll", respectively. Neither reveals the correct semantics which the OCR text does.

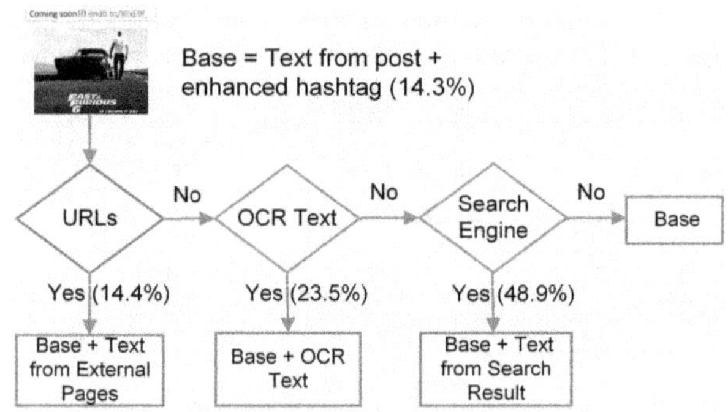

Figure 6: Our filtered rule for fusing text from context sources. The % denotes the coverage of each source alone after fusion.

As such, instead of merely polling all four sources of contextual text, we can fuse them more opportunistically to improve text quality. We feel that this cascading approach is a better option than a weighted sum, as it also cuts down computation costs. The tweet's original textual post and enhanced hashtags form the basis for fusion, as they are the most obvious context created directly by the author. We then propose a filtered fusion approach (illustrated in Figure 6) to use text obtainable from the other three sources: 1) for an image tweet with an embedded URL, we fuse only the text from its external web page, since the external page is the most accurate and accessible semantic context for the image; 2) for the remainder, we apply OCR on the image and if it contains embedded text, we fuse its OCR text recognized by Tesseract; 3) but if no embedded text is found, we obtain and fuse the SERP-extracted text from Google Image Search. It is worth noting that the fusion strategy helps to reduce the acquisition cost of contexts by 18.0% in our dataset (when treating all API calls as a unit cost), and provides better semantic modelling for image tweets (demonstrated in Section 5.2).

4. PERSONALIZED IMAGE TWEET RECOMMENDATION

We now apply the CITING contexts that encode image tweets' semantics for personalized image tweet recommendation. To the best of our knowledge, this is the first study that learns user's interest from image tweets. To be specific, for a particular user, we aim to model her interest from her previous history, and predict her interest in incoming new image tweets. A direct application is to reorder the image tweets in user's feeds according to their interestingness.

We first discuss traditional collaborative filtering tech-

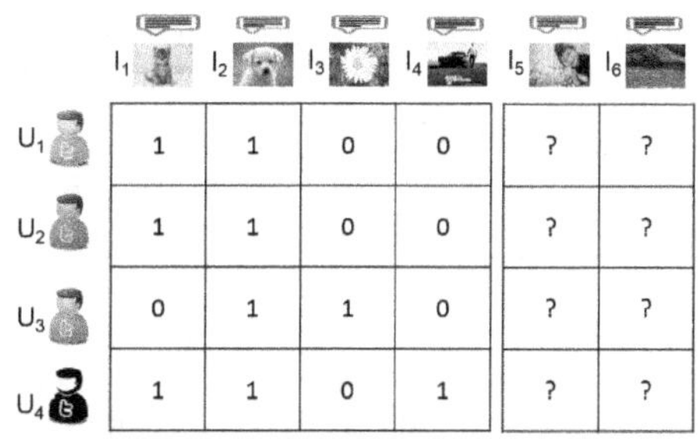

Figure 7: An example of user–item matrix, where 1 denotes the user has retweeted the image tweet and 0 otherwise. The rightmost two columns denote two new items that cause the cold-start problem.

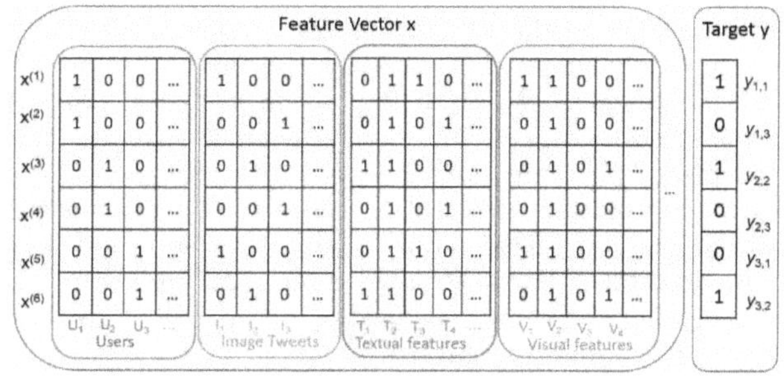

Figure 8: Example feature vectors for the user–item matrix in Figure 7. Each row consists of user ID, item ID, and the various features of the item. The rightmost column is the prediction target.

niques for tweet recommendation, then detail our proposed feature-aware Matrix Factorization model, a generic method that can incorporate various features for image tweet recommendation.

4.1 Drawbacks of Collaborative Filtering

Collaborative filtering (CF) is acknowledged to be the most effective and generalizable technique for recommender system [25]. The basic idea is to predict a user's preference based on the histories of other similar users. For example, Matrix Factorization (MF) [19], the most popular CF method, projects users and items into latent space to encode the preference similarity. As CF is designed to operate on the user–item interaction matrix, it represents an item as an ID and thus learns user's preference on item IDs.

We highlight that a key weakness of CF is its inapplicability to new items that have not yet attracted any interaction, which is known as the *cold start* problem. We show an illustrative example in Figure 7, where the rightmost two columns denote two new image tweets, which have never been seen in the training set. In this case, CF will fail to infer users' interest on the new items, and the prediction on new items is no better than random. This phenomenon is even exacerbated in social media like Twitter, due to the medium's strong timeliness and dynamicity. Said differently, old tweets (that are in training set) can quickly become dated and unattractive, while new tweets can be interesting but never appear in training. This makes the traditional CF technique unsuitable for the tweet recommendation task.

4.2 Feature-aware MF Framework

To overcome the defect of CF, a common solution is to go beyond modelling the interaction of user and item IDs which are sparse for new items, and to model more dense interactions by examining the properties of the content itself as features. As a consequence, although the ID of a new item has not been seen before, we can still infer a user's preference on new items based on their features (whose preferences have been learned during training). This motivates us to develop a generic model that can capture the interaction with various features for recommendation.

Following the paradigm of factorization machines (FM) [24], in our framework, we transform the user–item interaction matrix to a set of feature vectors (model input) and a vector of interactions (target). As illustrated in Figure 8, each row denotes an interaction consisting of user ID, item ID, and the various types of contextual features of the item. In our feature-aware MF model, we learn a low-dimensional representation (also termed as "latent vector") for each user and feature. Suppose we have N types of features that represent image tweets, then our model estimates the preference of user u on image tweet i as:

$$\hat{y}_{u,i} = \mathbf{v}_u^T (\sum_{n=1}^{N} \frac{1}{Z_{n,i}} \sum_{f \in \mathbb{F}_{n,i}} \mathbf{q}_f), \tag{1}$$

where $\mathbf{v_u}$ and $\mathbf{q_f}$ denote the latent vector for user u and feature f, respectively. $\mathbb{F}_{n,i}$ denotes the feature set of the nth feature type for item i, and $Z_{n,i}$ is the normalizer for features (setting $Z_i = \sqrt{|\mathbb{F}_{n,i}|}$ leads to good results).

This model is generic that it can incorporate any type of features (and their combinations). In the case of image tweets, they can be image features (*e.g.*, visual objects), textual words in tweets and our proposed contexts[7]. We hypothesize that incorporating our proposed contextual features will better capture the rich semantics in image tweets, leading to better personalized tweet recommendation.

We point out that the key difference with FM is in the feature interactions considered — FM models the interactions between all pairs of features (including feature pairs of the same feature type), while we only model the interactions between user and item's features. Our design choice is for the model's interpretability. By modelling only the interaction between user and feature, we can interpret user u's preference on feature f as the inner product $\mathbf{v}_u^T \mathbf{q}_f$, which benefits the explainability [12] of our recommendation model.

4.3 Learning from Implicit Feedback

The objective of tweet recommendation is to provide a user with a personalized ranked list of tweets. From a user's observed behaviors (*e.g.*, retweets), we naturally have the positive feedback that represents which tweets users are interested in. These positive tweets should be ranked higher than other negative tweets for the user. Since the idea naturally fits the framework of pairwise Learning to Rank, we adopt the *Bayesian Personalized Ranking* [25], which learns the model to maximize the probability that the positives should be given a higher score than the negatives for users:

$$p(.|\mathbf{V}, \mathbf{Q}) = \prod_{u \in \mathbb{U}} \prod_{i \in \mathbb{P}_u} \prod_{j \notin \mathbb{P}_u} \sigma(\hat{y}_{u,i} - \hat{y}_{u,j}), \tag{2}$$

[7]Note that we do not insert item IDs into the feature vector (in gray in Figure 8), since most items in test set are not observed in training. Excluding item IDs lessens the bias to recommend only tweets seem in training, and favors the prediction of new cold-start items, leading to better results.

where $\mathbb{P}_u$ denotes the positive tweets for user u, and σ is the sigmoid function that projects the margin value into probability space. We note that aside from the pairwise function, another option for learning from implicit feedback is the pointwise regression that treats the target value of negative feedback as zero [13]. Here we opt for the pairwise way that directly encodes our ranking intuition, and leave the exploration of pointwise regression as future work.

Maximizing the objective function is equivalent to minimize the following loss function:

$$\mathcal{L} = \sum_{u \in \mathbb{U}} \sum_{i \in \mathbb{P}_u} \sum_{j \notin \mathbb{P}_u} \log \sigma(\hat{y}_{u,i} - \hat{y}_{u,j}) + \lambda_1 \left\| \mathbf{v}_u \right\|^2 + \lambda_2 \left\| \mathbf{q}_f \right\|^2, \tag{3}$$

where $\|\cdot\|$ denotes the L_2 norm for preventing model overfitting, and λ_1 and λ_2 are tunable hyper-parameters that control the extent of regularization.

As the number of training instances is very large (all user–item pairs) and there does not exist a closed form solution for model's parameters, learning is usually done by stochastic gradient descent (SGD). In each descent step, the localized optimization is performed on a tuple (u, i, j). The gradients with respect to each parameter are given as follows:

$$\begin{aligned} \frac{\partial \mathcal{L}}{\partial \mathbf{v}_u} &= -\hat{e}_{u,i,j} \sum_{n=1}^{N} \left(\frac{1}{Z_{n,i}} \sum_{f \in F_{n,i}} \mathbf{q}_f - \frac{1}{Z_{n,j}} \sum_{f \in F_{n,j}} \mathbf{q}_f\right) + \lambda_1 \mathbf{v}_u, \\ \frac{\partial \mathcal{L}}{\partial \mathbf{q}^i_{n,f}} &= -\frac{1}{Z_{n,i}} \hat{e}_{u,i,j} \mathbf{v}_u + \lambda_2 \mathbf{q}^i_{n,f}, \\ \frac{\partial \mathcal{L}}{\partial \mathbf{q}^j_{n,f}} &= \frac{1}{Z_{n,j}} \hat{e}_{u,i,j} \mathbf{v}_u + \lambda_2 \mathbf{q}^j_{n,f}, \end{aligned} \tag{4}$$

where $\hat{e}_{u,i,j} = e^{-(\hat{y}_{u,i} - \hat{y}_{u,j})} / (1 + e^{-(y_{\hat{u},i} - y_{\hat{u},j})})$.

Then we iteratively loop over all the (u, i, j) tuples in the training set, and update the parameters to new values in the direction of negative gradient weighted by the learning rate until convergence. Learning rate is a key hyper-parameter for SGD that determines the speed of moving towards the optimal values — setting it too large we will skip the optimal solution, while too small a setting requires many iterations to converge. As such, we adopt *Bold Driver* [11], a technique that adjusts learning rate adaptively in each iteration. To be specific, it increases the learning rate by 5% if error rate is reduced since the last iteration; otherwise, resets the parameters to the values of the previous iteration and decreases the learning rate by 50%.

4.3.1 Time-aware Negative Sampling

In the literature of general recommender systems, uniform sampling is most widely used for sampling nagative instances due to its simplicity and acceptable performance [25]. Such sampling strategy assumes that all non-retweeted posts are equally weighted as negative instances (tweets disliked by user u). However, we believe this is invalid as: 1) many non-retweeted posts may simply be missed (never viewed) by user u, and 2) tweets may not be uniformly likely to have been seen by u. Previous works on tweet recommendation [33, 7, 15, 28] sampled negative instances from the tweets of the target user's followees only, assuming that the non-retweeted posts by the followees are more likely to be seen but disliked by the user. However, these previous efforts did not consider the effect of time, another important factor that determines whether the user may have seen the tweet.

To address this, we propose a time-aware negative sampling strategy. Our key assumption is that if a user has retweeted a post, she should also have read other tweets (of her followees) that were posted in close temporal proximity to the retweeted post. Such tweets are then more likely to be true negatives. Given a known image tweet interaction rt, we sample the non-retweeted image tweets (posted by her followees) in proportion to the time interval between the post and rt; *i.e.*, posts closer to rt have a higher chance of being selected. Our featured negative sampling method improves pairwise learning. We study its efficacy in Section 5.3.

Table 3: Image tweet training and test set demographics.

	Users	Retweets	All Tweets	Ratings
Training	926	174,765	1,316,645	1,592,837
Test		9,021	77,061	82,743

5. EXPERIMENT

We now evaluate CITING, our framework for context-aware image tweets modelling in the task of personalized image tweets recommendation. The goal of our experiment is to answer the following research questions:

RQ 1: How well do the four proposed contexts perform?

RQ 2: Do the filtered fusion improve model quality?

RQ 3: Can time-aware negative sampling strategy create better training set than uniform sampling?

RQ 4: Are visual objects sufficient to capture Twitter images' semantics?

Dataset. As there is no publicly available image tweet dataset, we constructed our own by gathering image tweets from Twitter in a user-centric manner. We first crawled one week of public timeline tweets (8–14 December 2014) which resulted in a set of 5,919,307 tweets, of which 17.2% contained images. From this collection, we randomly sampled 926 users who had at least 100 followees and 100–3000 followers, and posted at least 100 tweets. These requirements were used to select ordinary but active users, as has been done similarly by [28]. These 926 users are regarded as target users for our recommendation task.

We then crawled their latest tweets (up to 3,200 — limited by the Twitter API), their followee list and further crawled the image tweets published by their followees. In particular, given a user and her retweet rt, we sample 10 non-retweeted image tweets according to the time-aware negative sampling strategy described in Section 4.3.1. This process results in a dataset of 1,369,133 image tweets, summarized in Table 3. To simulate the real recommendation scenario, we adopt a time-based evaluation. For each user, we use her most recent 10 retweets as the test set, with the rest for training. Note that the user–tweet interaction is extremely sparse: each image tweet is retweeted by 1.22 users on average, and only 31% of the testing tweets have previously been observed in the training set. This validates the sparsity observations in previous works [7, 10].

Evaluation Metrics. The objective of tweet recommendation is to rank the candidate tweets such that the interesting tweets are placed at top for the target user. In our case, we mix the testing retweets (*i.e.*, ground-truth) and their negative samples as the candidate tweets for each user. To assess ranking quality, we adopt the average precision at

Table 4: Performance of each context source and its coverage (short for Cvr.). The best single context is the title of Google image search pages.

	P@1	P@3	P@5	MAP	Cvr.
P: Post	0.359	0.325	0.287	0.275	
P + Hashtag	0.360	0.324	0.293	0.277	14.3%
P + OCR text	0.366	0.332	0.301	0.283	26.4%
P + URL (title)	0.374	0.326	0.294	0.278	14.2%
P + URL (content)	0.381	0.330	0.300	0.279	13.2%
P + G (content)	0.369	0.319	0.289	0.275	57.2%
P + G (title)	**0.388**	**0.344**	**0.308**	**0.288**	76.0%
P + G (guess+NE)	0.381	0.330	0.296	0.280	58.1%

rank k (P@k) and Mean Average Precision (MAP) as evaluation metrics, which have been widely used for the tweet recommendation task [7, 10, 15]. Since users are usually most interested in only the few top recommendations, we report P@k at the top ranks (k=1, 3 and 5).

Parameter Settings. We tune two regularization parameters (λ_1 and λ_2) and the number of latent factors K. We first vary the regularizers until the results are generally stable, and then carefully tune K in a grid search manner (from 10 to 200). We report the performance at $\lambda_1 = 0.05$, $\lambda_1 = 0.01$ and $K = 160$, which shows good results. Similarly, we tune the parameters for other methods, and report their optimal results accordingly. For all the experiments, we set the initial learning rate as 0.01.

5.1 Utility of Proposed Contexts (RQ 1)

We first examine the efficacy of our proposed four strategies for context mining. To this end, we add the obtained text from each source to the post's original text separately, and assess performance using each combined text. For webpages, we separate the title and page content in evaluation, since we find some pages only have titles while lacking the main content and vice versa. Observing that some webpages can be very long and only the top few words (measured by *tf*idf*) are most relevant, we use the top 20 words[8] as the page content.

Table 4 shows the performance of each source with its coverage. In general, all context sources show a positive impact on the recommendation performance[9]. We find that the gains from the two external sources (external URL and Google Image Search) are more significant than the two internal sources (hashtag and OCR text). This validates the usefulness of external knowledge for interpreting images' semantics in social media. The largest improvement is obtained by integrating the titles of Google indexed pages, with a relative 8.1% and 4.7% improvement over using post's text only, in terms of P@1 and MAP, respectively. This improvement is partially due to the high coverage of Google Image Search over social media images. However, using the actual page content of the Google indexed pages neither improves over titles, nor betters the post's text — even degrading the performance for P@3 and MAP. Upon our deeper analysis, we find this might be caused by the noise introduced by Boilerpipe when extracting the main text from SNS pages and image aggregator sites. These sites make up a large portion in Google's indexed pages (84.3%) but their layouts significantly differ from news and blogs that Boilerpipe was trained on. As a result, Boilerpipe suffers from a high error rate. Thus in our subsequent experiments, we use all contextual text except the actual content of Google indexed pages.

[8]We experimented with a few settings (*e.g.*, 10, 20, 30) and found 20 works best.

[9] Although the P@3 slightly degrades for the source hashtag, other metrics still reveal it as a helpful feature.

Table 5: Context fusion performance comparison. '' denotes statistically significant difference vs. CITING with $p < 0.01$; '*' with $p < 0.05$.**

	P@1	P@3	P@5	MAP
(1): Random	0.114**	0.115	0.115	0.156**
(2): Length	0.176**	0.158	0.150	0.173**
(3): Profiling	0.336**	0.227	0.197	0.202**
(4): Post	0.359*	0.325	0.287	0.275**
(5): Non-filtered	0.413	0.352	0.319	0.296
(6): **CITING**	**0.419**	**0.355**	**0.319**	**0.298**

5.2 Effectiveness of Context Fusion (RQ 2)

We now evaluate the effectiveness of filtered fusion approach. For comparison purpose, we report the performance of our feature-aware MF model using all context without the filtered fusion (**Non-filtered**) and Post's text only (**Post**). The latter is equivalent to the results obtainable from two state-of-the-art models [7, 10] on text tweet recommendation, as the two are special cases of our model when only post's text is considered. To benchmark the performance, we also consider three baselines: 1) **Random**: ranking image tweets randomly; 2) **Length**: rank image tweets by the number of words in post's text, and the intuition is that longer tweets tend to be more informative and possibly to be more popular [32]; 3) **Profiling**: rank image tweets by the similarity of tweets' text and user's profile, which is constructed from the words of user's historical posts and retweets. To be specific, given a user u and an image tweet t, we compute the profile-based similarity score as follows:

$$S_{u,t} = (1 - w) \times cos(posts(u), t) + w \times cos(retweets(u), t),$$

where cos denotes the cosine similarity and w is a tunable parameter to balance the importance of the posting and retweeting history.

Table 5 shows the results. First, our proposed filtered fusion (CITING, R6) outperforms the three baselines (random, length, profiling) by a large margin. The filtered fusion method also significantly betters the strong baseline of using post's text by 0.06 (16.9% relative improvement) and 0.023 (8.3%) in terms of P@1 and MAP, respectively. When adopting non-filtered fusion approach, the performance slightly drops, *e.g.*, the P@1 drops from 0.419 to 0.413. Although not statistically significant, it indicates that our heuristic filtered fusion approach achieves comparable results while saving acquisition costs of the contextual text by 18.0%. These experimental results evidence the effectiveness of our fusion approach and the feature-aware MF model.

5.3 Importance of Negative Sampling (RQ 3)

We now assess the effect of the negative sampling strategy. We compare with the uniform sampling strategy, which is a commonly used strategy by previous works in tweet recommendation [33, 7, 28]. To this end, we constructed a new dataset by uniformly sampling negative image tweets from our training set and pair with the positive image tweets. We then trained our feature-aware MF on this new dataset, us-

Table 6: Performance using visual objects.

	P@1	P@3	P@5	MAP
(1): CITING	0.419	0.355	0.319	0.298
(2): Visual objects (V)	0.221	0.205	0.192	0.211
(3): Post's text + V	0.379	0.325	0.293	0.280
(4): CITING + V	0.425	0.350	0.313	0.298

ing our proposed filtered contexts, and evaluated the method in the same way. Experimental result shows the time-aware sampling strategy significantly betters the random sampling by 0.017 (4.2% relative improvement) and 0.006 (2.1%), for P@1 and MAP, respectively. Both one-tailed paired t-test for P@1 and MAP show $p < 0.05$. This validates our time-aware negative sampling strategy is effective in constructing a higher quality training set, aiding better user interest modelling.

5.4 Insufficiency of Visual Objects (RQ 4)

We now validate our claim at the outset that annotating visual objects without context does not fare well for social media interpretation. First, we applied *GoogLeNet* [27], the winning system in ILSVRC 2014, to classify the visual objects for our Twitter images. GoogLeNet is trained on 1.2 million Flickr images with 1000 object categories, where each category corresponds to a node in ImageNet/WordNet. The pre-trained model is provided by Caffe [17]. We take the top five labels as the description for each image and conduct the same experiment. We see that prediction using just visual objects does perform worse (P@1= 0.221, MAP= 0.211; Table 6, R2), due to the largely literal image descriptions. Our CITING context significantly outperforms visual objects by 89.2% of relative improvement and 40.9% in terms of P@1 and MAP, respectively. This shows the contextual text does capture image tweets' semantics much better.

For comprehensiveness, we further experiment with the combination of text and visual objects (*i.e.*, model the two as two types of features), to see whether the incorporation of visual cues could further boost the recommendation performance. As shown in Table 6 (R3), the integration of visual objects with post's text slightly improves over post's text 5.6% (relative improvement) and 1.8%, for P@1 and MAP, respectively, while our CITING context still significantly betters such combination by relatively 10.5% and 6.2%. This further validates our contextual text is able to capture semantics of image tweets better. Unlike the previous combination, the incorporation of visual objects does not lead to a stable improvement for contextual text: P@1 is slightly improved by 0.006 (1.4%), and MAP remains the same, while the other two metrics drop. This suggests the descriptors brought about by using visual objects is limited in modelling usefulness, and such visual cues might have already been largely captured by our contextual text (*e.g.* some best guess descriptions from Google Image Search describe visual objects).

5.5 Case Studies

It is also instructive to examine individual users and actual posts to better understand the effectiveness of our proposed filtered contextual text. To this end, we examine a few users whose recommendations have a large performance gain when using CITING. In Figure 9, we show such a typical user (refer as *User 1*) and four of her retweets in test set that are

Figure 9: Four image tweets from *User 1*'s retweets in test set benefit from our contextual text.

Figure 10: Five image tweets from *User 2*'s retweets in test set benefit from our contextual text.

enriched by our contextual text. As a consequence, the average recommendation precision of our approach (0.592) significantly outperforms the approach of using visual objects (0.226) and using post's text (0.443). In an even more successful case, 9 out of 10 retweets (we show 5 in Figure 10) for *User 2* obtained contextual text from our approach. The average precision is boosted from 0.423 (using visual objects) and 0.319 (using post's text) to 0.728 (our approach).

Taking a closer look at the these image tweets, we find a few of them trigger multiple context mining channels. Some have both embedded URL and overlaid text in image (see Figure 10: the top leftmost and the bottom rightmost). A further investigation shows the external web pages redirected by embedded URLs contain richer and more relevant information than the overlaid text. This validates our text fusion strategy which assigns a higher priority to text from embedded URL than OCR. Another image tweet (Figure 9, top leftmost) has both overlaid text and search result from Google Image. However, the search result only indicates the image is a quote, but does not reveal its deep semantics as OCR text does. In this case, OCR text is more reliable than search result, validating our text fusion strategy 2.

6. CONCLUSION

Compared to the traditional vision research on stock photo images, we have shown that social media images are more semantic but diverse, which need to be understood within their context of mention. To complement the visual features, we propose a CITING framework that mines both the intrinsic and extrinsic contexts of image tweets. To demonstrate the effectiveness, we focus on the task of personalized image tweet recommendation, developing a feature-aware recommendation system that encodes the contexts as part of user interest modelling. Extensive experiments verify the effectiveness of our proposed CITING method in context mining, significantly boosting recommendation performance.

We have done an analysis of the coverage and efficacy of acquiring the textual context of social media images, but there is still much that can be improved here. To spur additional research on social media images, we have released the code of our feature-aware MF model, our large image tweets dataset, as well as our annotated corpus of 500 sample images with their manually-recognized text[10]. In particular, future work can adapt OCR to better acquire text within the images, as current OCR fares poorly on meme-style images and graphics. Additionally, we plan to examine whether other types of features (*e.g.*, geo-location or publisher) would result in even better user modelling.

Acknowledgments

This research is supported by the Singapore National Research Foundation under its International Research Centre. We also would like to thank Yongfeng Zhang and Hanwang Zhang for their help and discussions.

7. REFERENCES

[1] O. Alonso, C. C. Marshall, and M. Najork. Are Some Tweets More Interesting Than Others? #HardQuestion. In *Proc. of HCIR*, 2013.

[2] J. Bian, Y. Yang, and T.-S. Chua. Multimedia Summarization for Trending Topics in Microblogs. In *Proc. of CIKM*, 2013.

[3] J. Bian, Y. Yang, and T.-S. Chua. Predicting Trending Messages and Diffusion Participants in Microblogging Network. In *Proc. of SIGIR*, 2014.

[4] H. Cai, Y. Yang, X. Li, and Z. Huang. What Are Popular: Exploring Twitter Features for Event Detection, Tracking and Visualization. In *Proc. of MM*, 2015.

[5] V. Campos, A. Salvador, X. Giro-i Nieto, and B. Jou. Diving Deep into Sentiment: Understanding Fine-tuned CNNs for Visual Sentiment Prediction. In *Proc. of ASM*, 2015.

[6] E. F. Can, H. Oktay, and R. Manmatha. Predicting Retweet Count Using Visual Cues. In *Proc. of CIKM*, 2013.

[7] K. Chen, T. Chen, G. Zheng, O. Jin, E. Yao, and Y. Yu. Collaborative Personalized Tweet Recommendation. In *Proc. of SIGIR*, 2012.

[8] T. Chen, D. Lu, M.-Y. Kan, and P. Cui. Understanding and Classifying Image Tweets. In *Proc. of MM*, 2013.

[9] T. Chen, H. M. SalahEldeen, X. He, M.-Y. Kan, and D. Lu. VELDA: Relating an Image Tweet's Text and Images. In *Proc. of AAAI*, 2015.

[10] W. Feng and J. Wang. Retweet or Not?: Personalized Tweet Re-ranking. In *Proc. of WSDM*, 2013.

[11] R. Gemulla, E. Nijkamp, P. J. Haas, and Y. Sismanis. Large-scale Matrix Factorization with Distributed Stochastic Gradient Descent. In *Proc. of SIGKDD*, 2011.

[10] http://wing.comp.nus.edu.sg/downloads/image-tweet-ocr-rec

[12] X. He, T. Chen, M.-Y. Kan, and X. Chen. TriRank: Review-aware Explainable Recommendation by Modeling Aspects. In *Proc. of CIKM*, 2015.

[13] X. He, H. Zhang, and M.-Y. Kan. Fast Matrix Factorization for Online Recommendation with Implicit Feedback. In *Proc. of SIGIR*, 2016.

[14] L. Hong, O. Dan, and B. D. Davison. Predicting Popular Messages in Twitter. In *Proc. of WWW*, 2011.

[15] L. Hong, A. S. Doumith, and B. D. Davison. Co-factorization Machines: Modeling User Interests and Predicting Individual Decisions in Twitter. In *Proc. of WSDM*, 2013.

[16] K. Ishiguro, A. Kimura, and K. Takeuchi. Towards Automatic Image Understanding and Mining via Social Curation. In *Proc. of ICDM*, 2012.

[17] Y. Jia, E. Shelhamer, J. Donahue, S. Karayev, J. Long, R. Girshick, S. Guadarrama, and T. Darrell. Caffe: Convolutional Architecture for Fast Feature Embedding. In *Proc. of MM*, 2014.

[18] C. Kohlschütter, P. Fankhauser, and W. Nejdl. Boilerplate Detection Using Shallow Text Features. In *Proc. of WSDM*, 2010.

[19] Y. Koren, R. Bell, and C. Volinsky. Matrix Factorization Techniques for Recommender Systems. *Computer*, 42(8):30–37, 2009.

[20] H. Kwak, C. Lee, H. Park, and S. Moon. What is Twitter, a Social Network or a News Media? In *Proc. of WWW*, 2010.

[21] D. Laniado and P. Mika. Making Sense of Twitter. In *Proc. of ISWC*, 2010.

[22] N. Naveed, T. Gottron, J. Kunegis, and A. C. Alhadi. Bad News Travel Fast: A Content-based Analysis of Interestingness on Twitter. In *Proc. of WebSci*, 2011.

[23] S. Petrovic, M. Osborne, and V. Lavrenko. RT to Win! Predicting Message Propagation in Twitter. In *Proc. of ICWSM*, 2011.

[24] S. Rendle. Factorization Machines. In *Proc. of ICDM*, 2010.

[25] S. Rendle, C. Freudenthaler, Z. Gantner, and L. Schmidt-Thieme. BPR: Bayesian Personalized Ranking from Implicit Feedback. In *Proc. of UAI*, 2009.

[26] M. Schinas, S. Papadopoulos, Y. Kompatsiaris, and P. A. Mitkas. Visual Event Summarization on Social Media Using Topic Modelling and Graph-based Ranking Algorithms. In *Proc. of ICMR*, 2015.

[27] C. Szegedy, W. Liu, Y. Jia, P. Sermanet, S. Reed, D. Anguelov, D. Erhan, V. Vanhoucke, and A. Rabinovich. Going Deeper with Convolutions. In *Proc. of CVPR*, 2015.

[28] I. Uysal and W. B. Croft. User Oriented Tweet Ranking: A Filtering Approach to Microblogs. In *Proc. of CIKM*, 2011.

[29] A. Wang, T. Chen, and M.-Y. Kan. Re-tweeting from a Linguistic Perspective. In *Proc. of LSM*, 2012.

[30] Z. Wang, P. Cui, L. Xie, H. Chen, W. Zhu, and S. Yang. Analyzing Social Media via Event Facets. In *Proc. of MM*, 2012.

[31] Z. Wang, P. Cui, L. Xie, W. Zhu, Y. Rui, and S. Yang. Bilateral Correspondence Model for Words-and-Pictures Association in Multimedia-Rich Microblogs. *ACM TOMM*, 10(4):34:1–34:21, 2014.

[32] R. Yan, M. Lapata, and X. Li. Tweet Recommendation with Graph Co-ranking. In *Proc. of ACL*, 2012.

[33] T. R. Zaman, R. Herbrich, J. V. Gael, and D. Stern. Predicting Information Spreading in Twitter. In *Computational Social Science and the Wisdom of Crowds Workshop*, 2010.

[34] H. Zhang, G. Kim, and E. P. Xing. Dynamic Topic Modeling for Monitoring Market Competition from Online Text and Image Data. In *Proc. of KDD*, 2015.

[35] H. Zhang, X. Shang, H. Luan, M. Wang, and T.-S. Chua. Learning from Collective Intelligence: Feature Learning Using Social Images and Tags. *ACM TOMM*, 2016.

Semantic Image Profiling for Historic Events: Linking Images to Phrases

Jia Chen[1], Qin Jin[2]*, Yifan Xiong[2]
[1]School of Computer Science, Carneige Mellon University
jiac@cs.cmu.edu
[2]School of information, Renmin University of China
{qjin, xiongyf}@ruc.edu.cn

ABSTRACT

Automatically generating image profiles for historic events is desired for history knowledge preservation and curation. However, a simple profile with groups of related images lacks explicit semantic information, such as which images correspond to which aspects of the event. In this paper, we propose to add explicit semantic information to image profiling by linking images in the profile with related phrases in the event description. We measure the relevance of an image-phrase pair via a real-valued matching score. We exploit instance-wise ranking loss function to learn the matching score and we deal with two challenges: 1) how to automatically generate labeled positive data: we leverage out-of-domain labeled datasets to generate pseudo positive in-domain labels and propose a new algorithm (WIL4PPL) to robustly learn the model from the noisy pseudo positive labels; 2) how to automatically generate negative data: we propose a negative set generation algorithm to guide the model in learning which phrases and images to distinguish. We compare our model to three baselines and conduct detailed analysis and case studies to verify the quality of learnt semantic information. The extensive experiment results show the effectiveness of our proposed algorithms which significantly outperform the baselines.

Keywords

Historic Events; Image Profiling; Image-Phrase Linking

1. INTRODUCTION

Knowledge of history is precious and is recorded in both text and image media. There are many organized text resources for historic events online but relatively few organized image resources. To fill the gap, in [2] we proposed to automatically construct image profiles for historic events on the fly. The input of the task is one sentence event description containing 4Ws and the output is relevant image groups covering different aspects of the event.

(a) image grouping in work[2]

(b) image and phrase links

Figure 1: Illustration of linking images and phrases to enhance the semantic of image profiling for historic events

In work[2] we group images according to genre and visual content as shown in Figure 1(a). The genre groups include document/map, painting and photo. The visual content groups are consistent not only on visual appearance but also on semantic meaning. Both types of groups are useful in organizing the image profiles for the historic events. But such group based image profiles lack explicit semantic information. The genre grouping only focuses on genre, which does not carry explicit semantic information. The semantic information provided by content groups is implicit. That is, users have to figure out the meaning of each content group by themselves.

In this paper, we propose to improve image profiling by

*Qin Jin is the corresponding author

MM '16, October 15-19, 2016, Amsterdam, Netherlands

DOI: http://dx.doi.org/10.1145/2964284.2964306

adding explicit semantic information automatically. To be specific, we add explicit semantic information by linking images to the corresponding noun phrases in the event description automatically. Figure 1 illustrates the links for related image-phrase pairs, contrasted with the grouping image profile proposed in [2]. Users can easily get the correspondence between images and text descriptions. For example, we see that the portrait photos are linked to phrase "Lieutenant Colonel Willima Ranklin Smith" and the plane images are linked to "B-25 Mitchell bomber". We also see that not all images needs to be linked to certain phrase in the event description, e.g. the news paper report photo. These images are relevant to the event but not relevant to any particular phrase. This suggests that image-phrase links and image groups complement each other for a better organized image profiling.

The automatic linking problem is a special version of general image annotation problem. It's specialized in the following two aspects. First, it targets on specific noun phrase (usually entities) rather than general words. Second, the event context is given, i.e. the event sentence and related images. Linking with specific noun phrase is annotation on a much finer scale, which is far more difficult than general words if the event context information is not given. But in our case, we have event context, which provides strong prior knowledge and narrows down the candidate scope.

Instead of directly formalize automatic linking as a classification problem, we model it as a real score and binarize the output by thresholding. To be specific, we compute a real-valued matching score between the image and the phrase. Under such formalization, we could exploit rank loss function to learn the matching score, which is shown to be more robust than $0-1$ loss function on relevance modeling tasks[17].

To learn the matching score through rank loss, we need both labeled positive data and automatically generated negative data. However, it is challenging to obtain both data in historic event domain.

Labeled positive data challenge: manual labeling the relevance of image-phrase pairs for historic events requires very strong background knowledge. The cost of collecting such labels is much higher than selecting a familiar object or scene concept for an image. We propose to leverage out-of-domain labeled dataset to automatically generate pseudo positive in-domain labels. However, the generated pseudo positive labels are not perfect. We use weighted instance learning to tackle the issue.

Negative pair generation challenge: there are two kinds of negative pairs for a positive image-phrase pair (i, w): the first kind of pairs share the same image i but with different phrase w and the second kind of pairs share the same phrase w but with different image i. These two kinds are symmetric and let's consider the first kind for the ease of explanation. Constructing a negative pair by simply picking a phrase that is different from the phrase in the groundtruth pair won't work in historic event domain since we may pick a phrase that is semantically similar to the phrase in the groundtruth. For example, the phrase "aircraft carrier USS Enterprise" is semantically similar to "destroyers USS Maddox". When we link images to phrases, we only consider candidate phrases within the same event. Thus we don't need to distinguish between these two phrases since they rarely appear in the text description of the same event. Such case exists widely in historic event domain. We design a negative pair generation algorithm that generates the proper negative pairs to train the model.

Up to now, we are still vague about the relevance of image-phrase pair. The noun phrase could describe a concrete object such as "B-25 bomber". In this case, it is relevant with an image of B-25. The noun phrase could also describe a very abstract concept such as "world record". Together with an image of an athlete breaking the world record, this image-phrase pair could also be considered as relevant. It is quite challenging to give a clear and general definition on the relevance of image-phrase pair. We therefore derive a case-based definition for image-phrase pair relevance. Under each case, we give a separate definition of relevance so that the groundtruth labeling used in evaluation is both consistent and reproducible.

We make the following contributions:

1. we add explicit semantic information to the image profiling by linking images with phrases.
2. we give a definition of relevance on image-phrase pairs which not only covers the diverse cases in historic event domain but also can be directly transformed to practical reproducible labeling guidance.
3. we propose to automatically generate pseudo positive in-domain data from out-of-domain datasets and leverage these pseudo data to learn the parameters.
4. we propose a negative pair generation algorithm to guide the model to learn what to distinguish in historic event domain.

The remainder of the paper is organized as follows. Section 2 presents related work. Section 3 introduces the definition of image-phrase relevance for historic events. Section 4 formalizes the image-phrase relevance problem as a problem of learning matching score with pseudo positive labels. Section 5 presents the solution to the problem. Section 6 evaluates the quality of image-phrase links and provides some detailed experiment analysis and section 7 draws some conclusions.

2. BACKGROUND AND RELATED WORK

Art, culture and history related multimedia data have received more attentions from the research community[13] [11][8][2][3] in recent years. Authors in work[13] collect an image dataset of artworks exhibited in the Rijksmuseum in Amsterdam and define challenges for visual classification and content-based retrieval of artistic content. Their focus is on collecting a public artwork dataset and designing challenging tasks that could become useful tools for museums. Authors in work[11] design a tool named eHeritage, including a creator module and a manipulator module, to preserve the precious traditional heritage Chinese shadow puppetry. Their focus is on building multimedia tool to help users generating multimedia data and animation in their user cases. Authors in work[8] propose a new language-dependent method for automatic discovery of adjective-noun structures and apply the pipeline on a social multimedia platform for creation of a large-scale multilingual visual sentiment concept ontology. Their focus includes not only collecting a public cross-lingual dataset for research community but also designing multimedia tools to help analyzing cultural difference of visual sentiments. In work[2], we propose to automatically construct an image profile given a one sentence description of the historic event so that a multimedia history event dataset could be automatically collected to preserve precious history knowledge.

All these works share two key elements: multimedia dataset and multimedia tool. These two key elements are interdependent. On the one hand, datasets in these domains are extremely valuable and precious to collect. Once provided a dataset of descent scale, researchers can train models that could finally be transformed to useful tools. On the other hand, once a multimedia extraction tool is built, it can be used to ease the manual labor effort in collecting multimedia data for art/culture/history preservation. This work shares these two key elements with all the above works. Our task is to link images with phrases to enhance the semantic information in image profiling of historic events, which could be finally transformed to a useful multimedia tool for history knowledge preservation. To build such a tool, we need labeled in-domain data to train the model. However, the cost of labeling image-phrase relevance in historic event domain is so high that training model after collecting enough labeled data is not a reasonable choice. We propose to automatically generate pseudo in-domain positive labels from out-of-domain datasets and design an algorithm WIL4PPL to learn the model from these noisy positive labels. Such interdependency between data and tools widely exists in multimedia problems of art, culture and history domain and our solution can be applicable to these problems.

There have been many research works[1][4][19][6] on the image-word relevance problem in the form of image annotation. It is modeled as a matching problem. Authors in work[4] leverage machine translation technique to learn the matching between image and words. Authors in work[1] propose a graphical model to learn the matching between image and words. Authors in work[19] propose a multimodal embedding space to learn the matching between image and words. Authors in work[6] learn embedding space upon deep learning features of images and words. We also model the image-phrase linking problem as a matching problem. Different from these works, we don't have in-domain labeled training data and have to leverage pseudo positive labels based on out-of-domain dataset to train the model, which is very challenging. Our focus is on leveraging the noisy pseudo positive labels to train a matching model.

3. LINKING AN IMAGE TO A PHRASE

3.1 Preliminaries on image profiling task

In the historic event image profiling task[2], the input is a text description of an event e and a set of candidate images $\mathbf{I}_e$. The text description is usually composed of only one sentence. From the sentence, the phrase set $\mathbf{W}_e$ is extracted using standard NLP techniques[12]. Phrases vary from a celebrity name (e.g. "Queen Elizabeth II") to a mountain name (e.g. "Mount Everest"), from detailed description (e.g. "the ten second barrier") to general event name (e.g. "Montgomery Bus Boycott"), from nouns (e.g. "volcano") to verbs (e.g. "erupt"). The content of images varies from object to scene. This indicates that even within each modality (text or image), its type already varies. When considering relevance on the joint modality, for example linking images to texts, the situation becomes much more complex due to combination explosion. Furthermore, it is possible that some images may be irrelevant to any particular phrase in the event description while some images may be relevant to several phrases in the event description. Thus we need to give a clear definition of relevance between an image and a phrase before we try to formulate the problem.

Table 1: Two archetypes of relevance between an image and a phrase: the phrase is underlined in the event description

event description	image
United States President Lyndon B. Johnson proclaims his "Great Society" during his State of the Union address.	
Jim Hines of the USA becomes the first man ever to break the ten second barrier in the 100 metres Olympic final at Mexico City with a time of 9.95 sec. He would be the only man to do so until 1983.	

3.2 Definition of relevance between an image and a phrase

Consider the following two archetypes in Table 1. In the first archetype, the image shows a person standing in the front and the phrase is actually the name of the person in the image. This image-phrase pair is obviously relevant since the phrase describes the object in the image. In the second archetype, the image shows runners at the finish line and the phrase is abstract but contains important background information. This image-phrase pair is also relevant since the phrase could be used to caption this image in a news report. These are the two major archetypes of image-phrase relevance. On the text side, it covers concrete nouns and abstract nouns. On the image side, it has no restriction on image content.

We give the following definitions of image-phrase relevance archetypes:

content relevant an image-phrase pair is content relevant if the phrase is a noun phrase about concrete object or scene and the image contains the concrete object or scene.

background relevant an image-phrase pair is background relevant if the phrase is a meaningful abstract noun phrase in the event description that can be used to caption the image.

irrelevant the rest cases are considered as irrelevant.

4. PROBLEM FORMULATION

Given event e's image set $\mathbf{I}_e$ and phrase set $\mathbf{W}_e$, our problem is to classify an image-phrase pair (i, w) as a relevant pair or not, where $i \in \mathbf{I}_e$ and $w \in \mathbf{W}_e$. Instead of directly modeling relevance as binary 0-1 value, we propose to model the relevance of image-phrase pair (i, w) as a real valued matching score and thresholding it to get the binary classification output. To be specific, we measure the matching score between an image i and a phrase w by $s_{iw} = \mathbf{f}(i)^T\mathbf{M}\mathbf{f}(w)$, where $\mathbf{M}$ is a matching matrix, $\mathbf{f}(i)$ is the feature vector of image i and $\mathbf{f}(w)$ is the feature vector of word w. If the training data is not sufficient, we could mitigate the over-fitting problem by adding regularization on matching matrix $\mathbf{M}$'s rank r. To be specific, we add the regularization by decomposing $\mathbf{M}$ to $\mathbf{U}\mathbf{V}^T$, where the second dimension of $\mathbf{U}$ and $\mathbf{V}$ is r. Then, we learn $\mathbf{U}$ and $\mathbf{V}$ instead of $\mathbf{M}$.

4.1 Instance-wise ranking loss function

For a groundtruth image-phrase pair (i, w), the matching score s_{iw} should be higher than the matching score between the same image i and an unrelated phrase w' with a margin Δ. Similarly, it should also be higher than the matching score between the same phrase w_i and an unrelated image i' with a margin Δ. Such relation is summarized in the following equations:

$$s_{iw} - s_{iw'} \geq \Delta \tag{1}$$

$$s_{iw} - s_{i'w} \geq \Delta \tag{2}$$

Based on such relation, we introduce instance-wise ranking image loss $L_{iw}^{image}(i, w)$ and instance-wise ranking phrase loss $L_{iw}^{word}(i, w)$ for each groundtruth pair (i, w).

$$L_{iw}^{image}(\mathbf{M}) = \sum_{i' \in \overline{\mathbf{I}}_w} max(0, \Delta - s_{iw} + s_{i'w}) \tag{3}$$

$$L_{iw}^{word}(\mathbf{M}) = \sum_{w' \in \overline{\mathbf{W}}_i} max(0, \Delta - s_{iw} + s_{iw'}) \tag{4}$$

where $\overline{\mathbf{I}}_w$ denotes the negative image set of phrase w and $\overline{\mathbf{W}}_i$ denotes the negative phrase set of image i. Note that an image $i' \neq i$ doesn't mean that it is a negative image of phrase w. The same holds to image i when $w' \neq w$. Thus we have the following relations:

$$\overline{\mathbf{I}}_w \subseteq \mathbf{I} \setminus i \tag{5}$$

$$\overline{\mathbf{W}}_i \subseteq \mathbf{W} \setminus w \tag{6}$$

We leave the construction of $\overline{\mathbf{I}}_w$ and $\overline{\mathbf{W}}_i$ for a positive instance (i, w) to the solution section.

4.2 Weighted instance loss function for pseudo positive labels

As our task is to extract semantic links in historic event domain from scratch, we don't have any available in-domain labels yet. Manually labeling the historic event domain images requires volunteers with sufficient background knowledge. Such precious manual labeling is not scalable to collect enough data labels. Thus, we leverage the automatically generated pseudo positive labels to learn the matching score. We leave the details of the pseudo label generation to the solution section. A major issue of the automatically generated pseudo positive labels is that their confidence varies a lot. If we just preserve the top high confidence positive labels, the scale of positive data is not large enough to cover different image-phrase pairs. If we include all the pseudo positive labels and treat them equally, the training data will be very noisy. To tackle this issue, we propose to use weighted instance loss function on the pseudo positive labels:

Table 2: Notations

$\mathbf{I}$	image set
$\mathbf{W}$	phrase set
$\mathbf{I}_e$	image set of event e
$\mathbf{W}_e$	phrase set of event e
$\overline{\mathbf{I}}_w$	negative image set of word w
$\overline{\mathbf{W}}_i$	negative word set of image i
$\mathbf{C}$	out-of-domain concept set
$\mathbf{T}$	all-domain text set
i	image index
w	phrase index
e	event index
c	concept index
t	text index
$\mathbf{f}(c), \mathbf{f}(w), \mathbf{f}(t)$	feature vector of concept c, phrase w and text t
$\mathbf{f}(i)$	feature vector of image i
$\mathbf{M}$	matching matrix between image feature and phrase feature, which has a low dimension decomposition: $\mathbf{M} = \mathbf{U}\mathbf{V}^T$

$$L^{image}(\mathbf{M}; \alpha) = \sum_{iw} \alpha_{iw} L_{iw}^{image}(\mathbf{M}) \tag{7}$$

$$L^{word}(\mathbf{M}; \alpha) = \sum_{iw} \alpha_{iw} L_{iw}^{word}(\mathbf{M}) \tag{8}$$

where α_{iw} is the confidence score associated with the psuedo positive instance (i, w). We get the final loss function by convex combination of $L^{image}(i, w)$ and $L^{word}(i, w)$:

$$L(\mathbf{M}; \alpha, \theta) = \theta L^{image}(\mathbf{M}; \alpha) + (1 - \theta) L^{word}(\mathbf{M}; \alpha) \tag{9}$$

This loss function can be minimized through standard stochastic gradient descent (SGD). The notations are summarized in Table 2.

5. SOLUTION

Our solution consists of three components: pseudo positive label generation, negative set generation and weighted instance learning.

5.1 Pseudo positive label generation

To generate pseudo positive labels for the historic event domain, we leverage out-of-domain labeled datasets to train and predict without additional manual labeling effort involved. Though we don't have an identical labeled dataset that covers both image ($\mathbf{I}$) and text modalities ($\mathbf{C}$) in the historic event domain, we have various public datasets that cover different modalities of different domains. For example we have image-text modality datasets that cover image in similar domains $\mathbf{I}$ but text in other different domains $\mathbf{C}$ such as ImageNet [16] and SUN [20]. They could be used to estimate the probability $p(c|i)$. We also have pure text modality datasets covering almost all domains $\mathbf{T}$, such as google news [14] which could be leveraged to estimate the probability $p(w|c)$. By properly arranging the domain sequence of public labeled datasets, we get the following Markov chain

$\mathbf{I} \rightarrow \mathbf{C} \rightarrow \mathbf{W}$:

$$p(w|i) = \sum_c p(w|c)p(c|i) \quad (10)$$

Here $p(c|i)$ is concept c's conditional probability on the given image i and $p(w|c)$ is phrase w's conditional probability on the given concept c. This Markov chain first generates out-of-domain concepts based on the given images, and then generates the in-domain phrase based on the out-of-domain concepts. Based on eq (10), we generate pseudo phrase labels for images by:

$$\hat{w} = arg\max_w p(w|i) \quad (11)$$

First, we select the suitable datasets for each edge in the Markov chain. For the $\mathbf{I} \rightarrow \mathbf{C}$ edge, we need datasets that cover most image domains. The major content of historic images is object and scene. For object content, ImageNet[16] is one of the most comprehensive public datasets. And for scene content, SUN[20] is one of the most comprehensive public datasets. The text of both datasets comes from WordNet [15], whose majorities are concept words from dictionary. The text modality domain is very different from history event domain, whose majorities are proper nouns. By utilizing pre-trained classifiers on these two image to text datasets, we are able to predict out-of-domain object and scene concepts $\mathbf{C}$ from images. For the $\mathbf{C} \rightarrow \mathbf{W}$ edge, we leverage a pure text dataset, google news [14]. It covers most of the words in almost all text domains $\mathbf{T}$. For phrases in $\mathbf{T}/(\mathbf{C} \cup \mathbf{W})$, we cover them by word composition from $\mathbf{T}$.

To estimate $p(c|i)$, we use the softmax output of the trained image concept classifier:

$$p(c|i) = softmax(\alpha_c^T \mathbf{f}(i)) \quad (12)$$

where α is the weight of the last full connect layer of the concept classifier.

To estimate $p(w|c)$, we learn vector representation of phrases from google news. We don't directly estimate $p(w|c)$ from this corpus because many phrases in the historic events are compound phrases such as "the United States Navy aircraft carrier USS Enterprise", which is a composite of "the United States Navy", "aircraft carrier", "USS Enterprise". There's no direct correpondence in the google news and we need to compound them from google news. Vector representation offers us the flexibility to composite new phrases from learned words. The vector representation is learned by maximizing the probability of the next word t given the previous words t':

$$p(t|t') = softmax(\mathbf{f}(t)^T \mathbf{f}(t')) \quad (13)$$

Once the vector representation of $\mathbf{T}$ is learned, we get the vector representation of a phrase in $\mathbf{W}$ by composition:

$$\mathbf{f}(w) = \sum_{t \in w} \mathbf{f}(t) \quad (14)$$

Given eq (14) and eq (13), we calculate $p(w|c)$ by:

$$p(w|c) = softmax(\mathbf{f}(w)^T \mathbf{f}(c)) \quad (15)$$

$$= \frac{exp(\mathbf{f}(w)^T \mathbf{f}(c))}{\sum_{w'} exp(\mathbf{f}(w')^T \mathbf{f}(c))} \quad (16)$$

Instead of enumerating the condition probabilities of the entire phrase set w, which could be extremely large, we restrict to calculate the condition probability only on the phrase set within event e of the image i for both eq (10) and (15). It is possible that phrases from other events are suitable for the image, but neglecting such phrases has neglectable impact on the recall of pseudo positive labels. In summary, a pseudo positive label is generated by:

$$\tilde{p}(w|c) = \frac{exp(\mathbf{f}(w)^T \mathbf{f}(c))}{\sum_{w' \in \mathbf{W}_e} exp(\mathbf{f}(w')^T \mathbf{f}(c))} \quad (17)$$

$$\tilde{p}(w|i) = \sum_c \tilde{p}(w|c)p(c|i) \quad (18)$$

$$\hat{w} = arg \max_{w \in \mathbf{W}_e} \tilde{p}(w|i) \quad (19)$$

By setting $\alpha_{wi} = \tilde{p}(w|i)$, we get the confidence score associated with the pseudo positive label.

5.2 Negative set generation

We construct negative phrase set $\overline{\mathbf{W}}_i$ for image i of positive image-phrase pair (i, w) by excluding phrases w' that are similar to w. It is possible that some of these w' are hard negatives. But we don't need to introduce such hard negatives into the negative set since in the image profiling task, the possible phrase candidates are limited within an event. For example, we don't need to distinguish between "aircraft carrier USS Enterprise" and "destroyers USS Maddox" as they rarely appear in the same event. If we include such phrase w' in the $\overline{\mathbf{W}}_i$, the learning process has to optimize the parameter by distinguishing s_{iw} away from $s_{iw'}$ according to ranking word loss L_{iw}^{word}, which leads to contradictory condition. The same holds for negative image set $\overline{\mathbf{I}}_w$ for phrase w. We construct it by excluding images that are similar to i.

Now the negative set generation problem is transformed to the similar image/phrase searching problem. That is, we search similar images for each image.and similar phrases for each phrase in the positive (image, phrase) set. We can approximate all these search operations by one clustering operation if we consider points in the same cluster are similar. When new positive pseudo labels are added, we could update the negative set by just assigning the image and phrase in the new pseudo label to the current image cluster and phrase cluster. We select affinity propagation clustering[5] to control the consistency of points within each cluster through the preference value.

5.3 Weighted instance learning

With the pseudo positive labels and negative set generation, we learn the parameters by mini-batch stochastic gradient descent. In each mini-batch, a record is a quadruple (i, w, i', w'), where i, w are the image and word in the positive image-phrase pair (i, w), $i' \in \overline{\mathbf{I}}_w$ and $w' \in \overline{\mathbf{W}}_i$. That is, each quadruple corresponds to one positive pair sample (i, w) and two negative pair samples, (i', w) and (i, w'). In each epoch, we traverse all positive pair samples in a shuffled order and the negative pairs are uniformly sampled with replacement from the generated negative set. That is, the model is fed with different negative pairs in each epoch but the same positive pairs in each epoch. Thus, the epoch number is proportional to the negative to postive ratio. The entire algorithm is summarized in Algorithm 1. Note that $\mathbf{U}$ and $\mathbf{V}$ are updated by weighted combination of gradients from each record. The weights correspond to the confidences of positive pseudo labels.

Algorithm 1: weighted instance learning for pseudo positive labels

input : negative to positive ratio r_{np}, rank r of the matching matrix, learning rate μ
output: $\mathbf{U}, \mathbf{V}$
initilize $\mathbf{U}, \mathbf{V}$ from random distribution or from a pretrained matching model;
for $e \leftarrow$ **to** $\frac{r_{np}}{2}$ **do**
  sample negative pair $(i', w), (i, w')$ for each positive (i, w);
  foreach *mini-batch* $\mathbf{B}$*, where* $b \in \mathbf{B}$ *are indices of postive pair labels* **do**
    $\mathbf{U} \leftarrow \mathbf{U} + \mu \sum_{b \in \mathbf{B}} \alpha_b \frac{\partial L}{\partial \mathbf{U}}$;
    $\mathbf{V} \leftarrow \mathbf{U} + \mu \sum_{b \in \mathbf{B}} \alpha_b \frac{\partial L}{\partial \mathbf{V}}$

6. EXPERIMENT

This section is organized as follows. First we describe the dataset, groundtruth collection, evaluation metric and baselines. Then we evaluate the quality of our models on both content relevance and background relevance, analyze the quality of pseudo positive labels and the impact of negative set construction. We move on to do case studies on the generated image-phrase links and present a distribution of the links on phrase generality and visual semantics. Finally we discuss the difficulty of manual labeling in historic event domain.

6.1 Dataset

The image profiling historic event (IPHE) dataset in work[2] spans from 1816 to 2004 and contains 615 historic events with 17,504 images and 1,890 phrases. The scale of the dataset is relatively small which limits the number and diversity of potential image-phrase links. Thus, the dataset needs to be expanded for investigating the image-phrase linking task and for making evaluation more stable. The IPHE dataset is collected by parsing historic events from Wikipedia articles. We follow the same approach. The difference lies in the article selection strategy. IPHE selects articles that are related to locations from a predefined landmark list. We select articles by enumerating the months and years in the same history timespan of IPHE. Our strategy exploits the resource of a historic event list page for each month and year from Wikipedia. Many items in the event list have links to event article pages as well. Our strategy can expand the scale of the dataset by an order of magnitude.

The expanded dataset, called expanded IPHE, contains 3,226 historic events with 185,173 images and 16,596 phrases. A comparison between IPHE and expanded IPHE is summarized in Table 3. We also show the distribution of the events by year in Figure 2. We see that there are three peaks and one plateau in the timespan, corresponding to four wars in the history: American Civil War (1861-1865), World War I (1914-1918), World War II (1939-1945) and Cold War (1947-1991). This shows that our expanded IPHE dataset covers major historic events.

6.2 Groundtruth collection, evaluation metric and baselines

Groundtruth collection: To label the groundtruth for relevant image-phrase pairs, we transform the definition in section 3 to a guideline for manual labeling as shown in Table 4. It involves two checks before assigning a label. The first check is on the type of noun-phrase: whether it's a concrete object/scene or an abstract phrase? This check guides the worker to one of lines 2 or 7. The worker needs to have a second check on image content together with the phrase. The criteria of the second check are different in these two cases.

With this guidance, we invite 10 volunteers to label the relevance on randomly sampled 1,000 image-phrase pairs. On average it takes a volunteer worker around 30 seconds to label one image-phrase pair. As a compromise to the high cost of manual labeling, we assign one volunteer worker rather than three volunteer workers to each pair. This set of 1,000 image-phrase pairs constitutes our test set. The pseudo positive labels used to train our model are generated

Table 3: Comparison of the dataset scale

	♯ events	♯ phrases	♯ images
IPHE dataset	615	1,890	17,504
expanded IPHE dataset	3,226	16,596	185,173

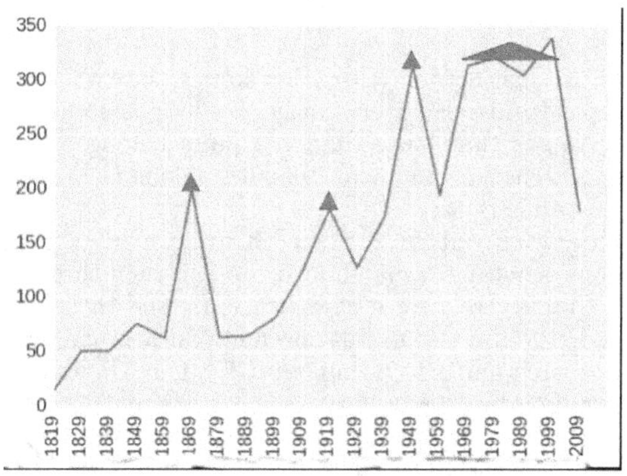

Figure 2: Event distribution on year: the three peaks and one plateau in the dataset correspond to American Civil War (1861-1865), World War I (1914-1918), World War II (1939-1945) and Cold War (1947-1991)

Table 4: Guidance for manual labeling based on the relevance definition

1:	check noun phrase type
2:	`if` the phrase is a concrete noun phrase of object or scene
3:	`if` the image contains the object or scene
4:	label *content relevant*
5:	`else`
6:	label *irrelevant*
7:	`if` the phrase is a meaningful abstract noun phrase
8:	`if` the phrase can caption the image
9:	label *background relevant*
10:	`else`
11:	label *irrelevant*

Table 5: Distribution of relevance archetypes in the historic event image profiling dataset

content relevant	345
background relevant	250
irrelevant	405

outside the test set. The distribution of the two relevance archetypes in historic event image profiling is shown in Table 5. We see that more than 1/3 pairs belong to content relevance archetype and near 1/3 pairs belong to background relevance archetype.

Evaluation metric: For each image-phrase pair, our algorithm generates a matching score and then thresholds it to get a binary relevance classification. The threshold can be tuned. We use two evaluation metrics: average precision (AP) and area under ROC curve(AUC). For AP, we evaluate the corresponding precision at each threshold value t and summarize them by averaging. It focuses on precision. For AUC, we plot the ROC curve by true positive rate tpr and false positive rate fpr at each threshold and calculate the area under the ROC curve. It reflects the probability that a relevant positive image-phrase pair will be ranked higher than an irrelevant image-phrase pair.

$$p(t) = \frac{|\{wi|s_{wi} > t\} \cap grountruth|}{|\{wi|s_{wi} > t\}|} \tag{20}$$

$$AP = \bar{p(t)} \tag{21}$$

$$AUC = \int tpr(t)fpr(t)'\mathrm{d}t \tag{22}$$

Baselines: We introduce three baselines. 1) *pseudo positive label generation algorithm (PPLG)*: it is described in section 5.1. In this baseline, we train models by out-of-domain data. To be specific, VGG16[18] is exploited to predict $p(c|i)$ and public pretrained model from [14] is used to predict $(w|c)$. 2) DeViSE[6]: it learns an embedding model which scales to new concepts and vocabularies. There is no public trained DeViSE model available. We reimplement it on joint dataset of Imagenet[16] and SUN[20][1]. 3) finetuned DeViSE: we directly finetune the above DeViSE model using top 1000 confident pseudo positive labels and set the negative word set to $\mathbf{W} \setminus w$.

6.3 Evaluation on quality of image-phrase links

We compare three models based on our algorithm of weighted instance learning for pseudo positive labels (WIL4PPL) by setting the hyper-parameter θ (see equation (9)) to $0, 0.5, 1$ respectively. When $\theta = 0$, we only use the ranking word loss L^{word} to train our model. When $\theta = 1$, we only use the ranking image loss L^{image} to train our model. Better value of θ could be found by tuning on a validation set. But considering that manual labeling cost in historic event domain is extremely high, we choose to use the whole labeled set as test set to get a stable evaluation result. To train WIL4PPL, we initialize the parameter $\mathbf{U}$ and $\mathbf{V}$ from the pre-trained DeViSE model (our second baseline). The learning rate μ is set to 0.001 and the epoch number is set to 10, which is equivalent to $20 : 1$ negative to positive ratio. We set the regularization rank to 300 and the margin Δ to 0.1.

[1]We use $1,000$ objects concepts in ILSVRC2012 from imagenet and 205 scene concepts from SUN

6.3.1 *Comparison on overall relevance*

We compare our method to the three baselines on overall relevance, mixing content relevance and background relevance together. As shown in Table 6, we see that our best model (WIL4PPL($\theta = 1$)) achieves the best performance on both AP (0.661) and AUC (0.666). On AUC metric, our best model achieves significant improvement, 7.4% boosting over PPLG and 3.4% boosting over DeViSE. All the three WIL4PPL models outperform all the baselines.

The inferior performance of PPLG baseline shows that the generated pseudo positive labels are noisy. Comparing WIL4PPL to PPLG shows that our model robustly learns from the noisy pseudo positive labels. On the contrast, the finetuned DeViSE baseline performs much worse than original DeViSE on both metrics. This shows that directly exploiting pseudo labeled positive data and vanilla negative set construction may hamper the original model. WIL4PPL($\theta =$ 0) performs much better than finetuned DeViSE, 2.5% better on AP and 1.8% better on AUC. Contrasting WIL4PPL($\theta =$ 0) with the finetuned DeViSE, we find that they have similar loss functions, ranking word loss, except that WIL4PPL($\theta =$ 0)'s loss function is weighted on the noisy pseudo positive instances. The negative set construction is also different. It shows that careful negative set construction with weighted instance loss function helps to improve the model using the pseudo positive labels.

6.3.2 *Comparison on content relevance and background relevance separately*

To study what is learned by WIL4PPL, we compare our method to baselines on each relevance archetype separately in Table 7 and Table 8. Comparing the performance on content relevance (Table 7) to that on background relevance (Table 8), we see two consistent trends:

1. all methods perform much better on content relevance than background relevance. Our explanation is that background relevance is more abstract and difficult to be captured by models. We have found that volunteer workers are more likely to disagree on background relevance than on content relevance, sometimes due to the lack of background history knowledge.
2. the improvement on AUC metric of all the WIL4PPL models over pretrained baselines (PPLG and DeViSE) are far more significant on background relevance than on content relevance. This suggests that pretrained models handle the content relevance very well and our models manage to learn the background relevance given the pseudo positive labels.

The performance change of finetuned DeViSE across content relevance and background relevance is not only interesting but also inspiring. Compared to DeViSE, the performance of finetuned DeViSE drops significantly on content relevance but increases quite a lot on background relevance. At first glance, we attribute it to overfitting as we only use top confident pseudo labels to finetune DeViSE. But this is definitely not the only reason. We further look at the pseudo positive labels and find that most of them are related to concrete relevance. This is justified by comparing PPLG's performance on content relevance to background relevance in Table 7 and 8. Recall that finetuned DeViSE uses a vanilla negative set construction. In such construction, the learning process needs to distinguish scores between two semantically similar words such as "aircraft carrier USS

Table 6: Comparison with baselines on overall relevance: numbers in the bracket show the improvement over the best baseline (PPLG, DeViSE, finetuned DeViSE)

	AP	AUC
PPLG	0.642	0.592
DeViSE	0.646	0.632
finetuned DeViSE	0.623	0.616
WIL4PPL($\theta = 0$)	0.648(+0.2%)	0.634(+0.2%)
WIL4PPL($\theta = 0.5$)	0.649(+0.3%)	0.639(+0.7%)
WIL4PPL($\theta = 1$)	**0.661**(+1.5%)	**0.666**(+3.4%)

Table 7: Comparison with baselines on content relevance: numbers in the bracket show the improvement over the best baseline (PPLG, DeViSE, finetuned DeViSE)

	AP	AUC
PPLG	0.576	0.628
DeViSE	0.569	0.654
finetuned DeViSE	0.534	0.623
WIL4PPL($\theta = 0$)	0.572(−0.4%)	0.658(+0.4%)
WIL4PPL($\theta = 0.5$)	0.576(0.0%)	0.668(+1.4%)
WIL4PPL($\theta = 1$)	**0.586**(+0.1%)	**0.682**(+2.8%)

Enterprise" and "destroyers USS Maddox". And such case is very common in the historic event domain dataset. Therefore, it indicates that negative set construction is very important for the relevance classification task. We can further improve our model's performance via improving negative set construction algorithm.

6.3.3 *Comparison of three WIL4PPL models*

In Table 7 and 8, three WIL4PPL models show consistent performance trend on all metrics: WIL4PPL($\theta = 1$) > WIL4PPL($\theta = 0.5$) > WIL4PPL($\theta = 0$). In these three WIL4PPL models, the weights of pseudo positive labels are the same in their loss functions. So the pseudo positive labels have the same impact on all the models. At first glance, we would attribute the difference to the weightings of ranking image loss and ranking word loss. But combination of ranking image loss and ranking word loss has also been successfully exploited in several works[10][9]. It is unusual that model WIL4PPL($\theta = 0.5$) works consistently worse than WI4PPL($\theta = 1$). We attribute this to the imperfect word negative set construction. Recall that on the word side, we cluster words based on features learned from text corpus only. Words that correspond to the same visual content may not be in the same cluster as they are clustered based on their textual meaning. This leads to that the learning process has to distinguish the score between words that share similar visual content. There is no such problem in the image negative set construction. Again, this indicates that negative set construction is very important and we have the potential to improve our model performance further by improving negative set construction in the future work.

6.4 Analysis on the Generated Image-Phrase Links

We set the threshold at $fpr = 0.1, tpr = 0.2$ to generate image-phrase links. Altogether 59,653 image-phrase links

Table 8: Comparison with baselines on background relevance: numbers in the bracket show the improvement over the based pretrained baseline (PPLG and DeViSE)

	AP	AUC
PPLG	0.273	0.494
DeViSE	0.308	0.587
finetuned DeViSE	0.323	0.621
WIL4PPL($\theta = 0$)	0.308(+0.0%)	0.621(+3.4%)
WIL4PPL($\theta = 0.5$)	0.304(−0.4%)	0.638(+5.1%)
WIL4PPL($\theta = 1$)	**0.313**(+0.5%)	**0.643**(+5.6%)

are generated automatically. We first study some cases of the links. Then we automatically categorize phrases to four different categories and list the distribution of the generated links under these four categories.

Case study: Table 9 shows eight image-phrase links generated by our model. The first row shows four content relevant links and the second row shows four background relevant links. For content relevant links, our model could match images to very specific phrase such as celebrity name, ship serial name, place name within an event. For background relevant links, our model outputs meaningful links that are educational to users without enough background knowledge.

Category study: we categorize the phrases from two dimensions. Each dimension contains two categories and we get a 2×2 table for phrase categorization. The first dimension is the generality of a phrase. It includes two categories: common noun phrase and proper noun phrase. This could be automatically categorized based on whether there is a capital letter in the phrase. The second dimension is the visual semantic of a phrase. It includes two categories: object and scene. We consider the concepts from ImageNet dataset as object concepts and concepts from SUN dataset as scene concepts. We calculate cosine similarity between feature vectors of noun phrases and these concepts. If the similarity between the phrase and any object concept is greater than 0.4, we categorize it as object semantic. The same holds for categorization of scene semantic. Note that it is possible that a phrase can be categorized to both object semantic and scene semantic. As shown in Table 10, the proper noun phrase occupies roughly 1/3 of the generated links, which indicates that these links provide rich event-specific semantic information. The object noun phrase occupies roughly 3/4 of the generated links, which indicates that these links contain rich specific image information.

Table 10: Pair Distribution in Our Dataset

	common noun	proper noun
object	32,650	12,846
scene	9,641	4,516

6.5 Discussion on difficulty of manual labeling

Recall that we invite 10 volunteer workers to label the image-phrase pair and each image-phrase pair is labeled by one volunteer worker. We randomly select some labeled pairs in the test set and randomly distribute them to several volunteer workers who didn't label them in the first round.

Table 9: **Case Study on the generated image-phrase links: the first rows shows four content relevant links and the second rows shows four background relevant links.**

<table>
<tr><td>
The United States Navy aircraft carrier USS Enterprise</td><td>
longest bridge</td><td>
New York Highlander Jack Chesbro</td><td>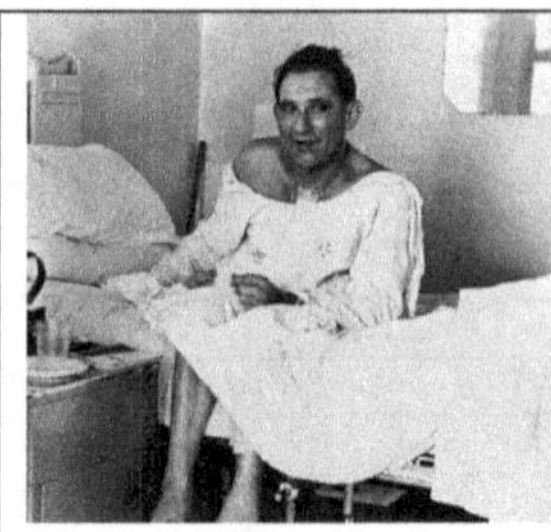
Groote Schuur Hospital</td></tr>
<tr><td>
the Montgomery Bus Boycott</td><td>
the San Francisco Gold Rush</td><td>

the world record</td><td>
World War II Guadalcanal Campaign</td></tr>
</table>

On such pairs, we collect more than one labels from different volunteer workers. We study such pairs by face-to-face interviewing the volunteer workers for the reason of their choice. Table 11 show two typical cases.

In the first case, vol.2 and vol.5 make the "background relevant" choice while vol.1 makes the "irrelevant" choice. After interviewing, we find out that vol.2 and vol.5 looked at the image carefully and read the text on the memorial while vol.1 just glanced at the image and failed to connect the memorial to World War II. In the second case, vol.2, vol.5, vol.7, vol.9 choose "irrelevant" while volunteer 6 chooses "content relevant". We ask vol.6 why she chooses content relevant and she tells that there is a white shoe in the center of the image though it is so easy to miss because it is mixed up with the background.

What are the volunteer workers doing in the average 30 seconds labeling progress? Sometimes they need to search on the web to get the background knowledge of the phrase especially for the proper noun phrases. Sometimes, they have to look at the images very carefully to recognize the linkage between image detail and the phrase. It is much more painful than just to label a general concept. Thus, we choose to learn with pseudo positive labels rather than to wait until enough clean labels are collected.

Table 11: Illustratinon of difficulty of Manual labeling: the first row shows the phrase, the second row shows the image and the third row shows the manual label result.

<table>
<tr><td>World War II</td><td>his shoe</td></tr>
<tr><td>
</td><td></td></tr>
<tr><td>vol.1 (irrelevant), vol.2 (background relevant),vol.5 (background relevant)</td><td>vol.2 (irrelevant), vol.5 (irrelevant), vol.6 (content relevant), vol.7 (irrelevant), vol.9 (irrelevant)</td></tr>
</table>

7. CONCLUSION

In this paper, we propose to improve image profiling for historic events by adding explicit semantic information, linking images to the corresponding noun phrases in the event description, so that users can easily understand the correspondence between images and text descriptions. To achieve this goal, we need to judge whether an image and a phrase is related. Such judgement is made by calculating the relevance of an image-phrase pair via a real-valued matching score and then comparing it to a threshold. The relevance of an image-phrase pair can be quite diverse. We therefore derive a case-based definition of image-phrase pair relevance. Under each case, we give a separate definition of relevance that could be used to make reproducible judgement of relevance. We exploit instance-wise ranking loss function to learn the matching score between an image-phrase pair, which is shown to be more robust then 0-1 loss function on relevance modeling tasks. We deal with two challenges in this learning task: 1) how to automatically generate labeled positive data: we leverage out-of-domain labeled dataset to generate pseudo positive labels and propose a new algorithm (WIL4PPL) that can robustly learn the model from the noisy pseudo positive labels; 2) how to automatically generate negative data: we propose a negative set generation algorithm to automatically generate more proper negative data for model training. We compare our proposed algorithm to three baselines. We evaluate the quality of learnt semantic information - the linkage between related images and phrases - via detailed analysis and case studies. Comprehensive experiments show that our proposed algorithm outperforms the baselines significantly. In the future work, we will further improve the quality of semantic information in image profiling, for example, utilizing self-paced learning [7] for adjusting instance weights in the learning process and improving negative set generation for model training.

8. ACKNOWLEDGMENTS

We thank NVIDIA Corporation for their donation of GPUs. This research was supported by the Fundamental Research Funds for the Central Universities and the Research Funds of Renmin University of China (No. 14XNLQ01) and the Beijing Natural Science Foundation (No. 4142029). This research was also supported in part by the National Science Foundation (NSF) under grant number IIS-1251187. Any opinions, findings, and conclusions or recommendations expressed in this material are those of the authors and do not necessarily reflect the views of the funding agencies.

9. REFERENCES

[1] K. Barnard, P. Duygulu, D. A. Forsyth, N. de Freitas, D. M. Blei, and M. I. Jordan. Matching words and pictures. *Journal of Machine Learning Research*, 3:1107–1135, 2003.

[2] J. Chen, Q. Jin, Y. Yu, and A. G. Hauptmann. Image profiling for history events on the fly. In *Proceedings of the 23rd Annual ACM Conference on Multimedia Conference, MM '15, Brisbane, Australia, October 26 - 30, 2015*, pages 291–300, 2015.

[3] J. Chen, Q. Jin, W. Zhang, S. Bao, Z. Su, and Y. Yu. Tell me what happened here in history. In *ACM Multimedia Conference, MM '13, Barcelona, Spain, October 21-25, 2013*, pages 467–468, 2013.

[4] P. Duygulu, K. Barnard, J. F. G. de Freitas, and D. A. Forsyth. Object recognition as machine translation: Learning a lexicon for a fixed image vocabulary. In *Computer Vision - ECCV 2002, 7th European Conference on Computer Vision, Copenhagen, Denmark, May 28-31, 2002, Proceedings, Part IV*, pages 97–112, 2002.

[5] B. J. Frey and D. Dueck. Clustering by passing messages between data points. *Science*, 315:972–976, 2007.

[6] A. Frome, G. S. Corrado, J. Shlens, S. Bengio, J. Dean, M. Ranzato, and T. Mikolov. Devise: A deep visual-semantic embedding model. In *Advances in Neural Information Processing Systems 26: 27th Annual Conference on Neural Information Processing Systems 2013. Proceedings of a meeting held December 5-8, 2013, Lake Tahoe, Nevada, United States.*, pages 2121–2129, 2013.

[7] L. Jiang, D. Meng, S. Yu, Z. Lan, S. Shan, and A. G. Hauptmann. Self-paced learning with diversity. In *Advances in Neural Information Processing Systems 27: Annual Conference on Neural Information Processing Systems 2014, December 8-13 2014, Montreal, Quebec, Canada*, pages 2078–2086, 2014.

[8] B. Jou, T. Chen, N. Pappas, M. Redi, M. Topkara, and S. Chang. Visual affect around the world: A large-scale multilingual visual sentiment ontology. In *Proceedings of the 23rd Annual ACM Conference on Multimedia Conference, MM '15, Brisbane, Australia, October 26 - 30, 2015*, pages 159–168, 2015.

[9] A. Karpathy, A. Joulin, and F. Li. Deep fragment embeddings for bidirectional image sentence mapping. In *Advances in Neural Information Processing Systems 27: Annual Conference on Neural Information Processing Systems 2014, December 8-13 2014, Montreal, Quebec, Canada*, pages 1889–1897, 2014.

[10] R. Kiros, R. Salakhutdinov, and R. S. Zemel. Unifying visual-semantic embeddings with multimodal neural language models. *CoRR*, abs/1411.2539, 2014.

[11] M. Lin, Z. Hu, S. Liu, M. Wang, R. Hong, and S. Yan. eheritage of shadow puppetry: creation and manipulation. In *ACM Multimedia Conference, MM '13, Barcelona, Spain, October 21-25, 2013*, pages 183–192, 2013.

[12] C. D. Manning and H. Schütze. *Foundations of Statistical Natural Language Processing*. MIT Press, Cambridge, MA, USA, 1999.

[13] T. Mensink and J. van Gemert. The rijksmuseum challenge: Museum-centered visual recognition. 2014.

[14] T. Mikolov, I. Sutskever, K. Chen, G. S. Corrado, and J. Dean. Distributed representations of words and phrases and their compositionality. In *Advances in Neural Information Processing Systems 26: 27th Annual Conference on Neural Information Processing Systems 2013. Proceedings of a meeting held December 5-8, 2013, Lake Tahoe, Nevada, United States.*, pages 3111–3119, 2013.

[15] G. A. Miller. Wordnet: A lexical database for english. *Commun. ACM*, 38(11):39–41, Nov. 1995.

[16] O. Russakovsky, J. Deng, H. Su, J. Krause, S. Satheesh, S. Ma, Z. Huang, A. Karpathy, A. Khosla, M. Bernstein, A. C. Berg, and L. Fei-Fei. ImageNet Large Scale Visual Recognition Challenge. *International Journal of Computer Vision (IJCV)*, 115(3):211–252, 2015.

[17] F. Schroff, D. Kalenichenko, and J. Philbin. Facenet: A unified embedding for face recognition and clustering. In *IEEE Conference on Computer Vision and Pattern Recognition, CVPR 2015, Boston, MA, USA, June 7-12, 2015*, pages 815–823, 2015.

[18] K. Simonyan and A. Zisserman. Very deep convolutional networks for large-scale image recognition. *CoRR*, abs/1409.1556, 2014.

[19] J. Weston, S. Bengio, and N. Usunier. Large scale image annotation: learning to rank with joint word-image embeddings. *Machine Learning*, 81(1):21–35, 2010.

[20] J. Xiao, J. Hays, K. A. Ehinger, A. Oliva, and A. Torralba. SUN database: Large-scale scene recognition from abbey to zoo. In *The Twenty-Third IEEE Conference on Computer Vision and Pattern Recognition, CVPR 2010, San Francisco, CA, USA, 13-18 June 2010*, pages 3485–3492, 2010.

Audio Event Detection using Weakly Labeled Data

Anurag Kumar
Language Technologies Institute
Carnegie Mellon University
Pittsburgh, USA
alnu@andrew.cmu.edu

Bhiksha Raj
Language Technologies Institute
Carnegie Mellon University
Pittsburgh, USA
bhiksha@cs.cmu.edu

ABSTRACT

Acoustic event detection is essential for content analysis and description of multimedia recordings. The majority of current literature on the topic learns the detectors through fully-supervised techniques employing *strongly* labeled data. However, the labels available for majority of multimedia data are generally weak and do not provide sufficient detail for such methods to be employed. In this paper we propose a framework for learning acoustic event detectors using only weakly labeled data. We first show that audio event detection using weak labels can be formulated as an Multiple Instance Learning problem. We then suggest two frameworks for solving multiple-instance learning, one based on support vector machines, and the other on neural networks. The proposed methods can help in removing the time consuming and expensive process of manually annotating data to facilitate fully supervised learning. Moreover, it can not only detect events in a recording but can also provide temporal locations of events in the recording. This helps in obtaining a complete description of the recording and is notable since temporal information was never known in the first place in weakly labeled data.

Keywords

Audio Event Detection; Audio Content Analysis; Multiple Instance Learning; Temporal Localization

1. INTRODUCTION

The amount of consumer-generated multimedia data on the internet has grown almost exponentially in recent times. One popular multimedia upload site, YouTube, reported about a year ago that 300 hours of multimedia recordings are uploaded on it every *minute* [2]. There are several such sites on the internet today, each of which attracts similarly large amounts of data. The recordings are largely unannotated; descriptions if any are limited to simple high-level metadata such as the author, or a brief legend indicating the overall content. Often the legends themselves are cryptic and uninformative to the uninformed, *e.g.* "My favorite clip".

MM '16, October 15 - 19, 2016, Amsterdam, Netherlands

ISBN 978-1-4503-3603-1/16/10...$15.00

DOI: http://dx.doi.org/10.1145/2964284.2964310

In order to be able to organize, categorize, summarize and index these recordings such that they can be retrieved through meaningful queries, one requires analysis of their *content*. Given the rather spotty nature of the metadata, the description of the content must usually be automatically derived. This naturally requires automatic identification of the *objects* and *events* that occur in the recording. Multimedia recordings have both video and audio components. Often, the sounds in the recordings carry information that the video itself may not. Thus, not only the *visual* objects in the recordings be automatically detected, it is also important to detect the sounds that occur in them.

Automatic sound event detection also finds application in other scenarios, such as monitoring traffic for sounds of accidents or impact, surveillance, where one may "listen" for sounds of gunshots [31], screams [25] etc., which might indicate unusual noteworthy activity. It is also useful in cases such as wildlife monitoring [8], context recognition [13] and several health and life style monitoring system.

In all cases, the detectors themselves must be "trained" from examples of the sound to be detected. In general for learning such detectors, one requires annotated data, where the segments of audio containing the desired event are clearly indicated (as well as data in which the events are distinctly *not* present). We will refer to this type of labeling as strongly labeled data. This is fundamentally limiting, since such well-annotated data are generally scarce.

A solution to the scarcity is to use the consumer-produced videos themselves to train the detectors. This immediately raises several challenges, however. Firstly, of course, the recording conditions, styles, and sophistication vary greatly among such recordings, resulting in large within-category variations between different instances of events, making the fundamental learning problem challenging. Much more important however, is the nature of annotations, if any, that they may carry. As mentioned earlier, the vast majority of consumer-produced videos carry little or no content annotation (which is what necessitates the development of automated concept detectors in the first place). Nevertheless, a significant number of these recordings *do* carry some weak information about their content, in the form of title, tags, etc. By "weak" annotation, we mean that while they may provide information about the presence or absence of particular events in the video, they will not provide additional details such as the number of times these events occur, the precise times in the recording where they occur, or the duration of the events. These additional details are required to localize the events in the recordings in order to train detectors using conventional methods. Weak labels can be automatically inferred from metadata (tags, titles etc.) associated with recording. Hence, these weak labels must be used to train the detectors.

Conventional methods for learning classifiers for event detection generally assume the availability of datasets that contain sufficient information to isolate the segments of the recordings where the target class occurs in order to learn their characteristics. For the other kind of datasets for which only weak labels are present (like those available on internet) most methods rely on manually annotating the available data with the boundaries of events, to facilitate learning event detectors. But creating such annotations is a time-consuming and expensive procedure. Supervised learning hence becomes a difficult task.

In this paper we take the view that it must be possible to learn event detectors from the weakly labeled data itself without requiring the additional effort of detailed annotation. Recordings that have been tagged as containing the event will have regions which are consistent with one another because they contain the event, but are not consistent with any region of recordings that are not similarly tagged. Event-carrying segments can be identified and event detectors trained by keying in on this consistency.

We embody this principle into an algorithmic framework which falls under the general rubric of *multiple-instance learning*. Multiple-instance learning is a generalized form of supervised learning in which labels for individual instances are not known; instead labels are available for a collection of instances, or "bag" as it is usually called within this setup. Although multiple-instance learning approaches have previously been employed for learning event detectors from weakly labeled data, most prior work in this area has focused on visual event recognition. The problem of learning to detect *acoustic* events from weakly labeled data has received very little attention.

We propose a successful framework for acoustic event detection based on the multiple instance learning methodology. In our setup, an audio recording is considered as a bag and segments of the recording are considered as instances within the bag. Besides achieving the goal of learning acoustic event detectors using weakly labeled data; as an added benefit, we are also able to assign temporal locations to occurrences of events in the test data.

The rest of the paper is arranged as follows: in Section 2 we give an overview of related work, in Section 3 we formulate the problem and in Section 4 we describe the proposed approach. In Section 5 we describe our experimental setup and results and we conclude in Section 6.

2. RELATED WORK

The problem of multimedia content analysis has received significant attention in the past decade. Although much of the reported work relates to image- or video-based information extraction, audio-based information extraction has also been explored. These audio-based information extraction methods in general involve detection of different kinds of acoustic events such as clapping, cheering, gunshots *etc.* in audio components of multimedia recordings. A nice survey on audio event detection challenges, related work, and the state of art can be found in [30]. A brief summary of some audio event detection work is provided here.

Possibly the most popular application so far of sound-event detection has been for surveillance [31] [25] [9]. Audio-event detection has also found its way into consumer devices, particularly for automatic indexing of multimedia recordings of games [16]. The wider setting of detecting sound events in more generic real-world recordings has been restricted in terms of the "vocabulary" of sound events considered. This is mainly due to the absence of large-vocabulary open source datasets meant for audio event detection research. The authors of [40] model various sound events with Gaussian-mixture models in order to detect them in real-world recordings. The approach followed in [40] is similar to the GMM-HMM architecture used for automatic speech recognition. A simple yet effect approach converts signals into "bags of audio words" – population-count histograms – by clustering feature vectors derived from the signal to a known codebook. Classification is now performed using these bags of words as feature vectors. This approach too has been successfully applied to the problems of detecting events in audio [24] as well as for multimodal approaches to event detection [36] and [33]. It is a general framework for obtaining a fixed length representations for audio clips and can be done on a variety of low-level audio features such as MFCCs [24], autoencoder based features [3] and normalized spectral features [21] to name a few. An alternate approach to obtaining bags of words is used in [18] – sound recordings are first decomposed into sequence of basic sound units called "Acoustic Unit Descriptors" (AUDS), which are themselves learned in an unsupervised manner. Bags of words are then obtained as bags of AUDs. The actual classification may be performed through classifiers such as SVM or random forests [18]. Deep neural network based approaches have also been proposed for audio event detection [15][17] [5].

In every one of these cases, the detectors and classifiers that are used to detect the sound events are trained in a supervised manner. Each classifier/detector is trained using several clearly-demarcated instances of the type of sound event it must detect, in addition to several "negative" instances – instances of audio segments that do not contain the event. Obtaining data of these kinds clearly requires human annotation, and can be a time-consuming and expensive process.

Our focus in this paper is to learn detectors from *weak* annotations – annotations which only indicate the *presence* of sound events in recordings, without additional detail about the number of instances, their location in the recording, etc. Such annotations are, in general, easily available and easy to generate if not available.

In comparison to supervised techniques, there has been relatively little work on learning to detect events in multimedia using weakly labeled data. Even here, the majority of published work focuses on detecting events based on *visual* content of the data [12] [38] [37]. In the case of *audio*, however, literature on learning generic sound event detectors from weakly labeled data is almost negligible. Some audio-related works include music genre classification using semi-supervised approach [22] [29]. Two other audio related works are [26] and [8] where the authors try to exploit weak labels in bird-song and bird-species classification.

In our work we perform audio event detection (AED) using weakly-labeled data by formulating it as a *multiple instance learning* (MIL) problem. MIL is a learning methodology which relies on the labels of an *ensemble* of instances, rather than labels of individual instances. Several well known learning methods such as Support Vector Machines (SVMs)[4], K-NNs [34] have been modified to learn in this paradigm.

3. AED USING WEAKLY LABELED DATA

The problem of audio event *detection* is that of detecting the occurrences of events (*e.g clapping, barking or cheering*) in a given audio recording. In order to be able to do so, we require *models* for these events which can be used to detect their occurrence. Training such models, in turn, requires training instances of these sounds. Such instances may be presented either as explicit recordings of these sounds, or as segments from longer audio recordings within which they occur. Our objective is to train the models, instead, using *weakly-labeled data* which comprise recordings in which only the presence or absence of these events is identified, without indicating the exact location of the event or even the number of times it has occurred.

Let $R = \{R_i : i = 1 \text{ to } N_R\}$ be the collection of audio recordings and $E = \{E_i : i = 1 \text{ to } N_E\}$ be the set of events for which detection models must be built using R.

For each R_i a certain subset of events from E are known to be present (weak-labels). For example, the information might say that R_i contains events E_1, E_3 and E_6. It is also possible that the subset of E present in R_i is empty, meaning that no event from E is present in R_i.

Clearly, to train a detector for an event E_i one cannot simply use all recordings that are marked as containing E_i, since a significant portion of the marked recordings might also contain other events. Moreover, since the start and end times of the occurrences of event E_i in the recordings are not known, it is impossible to extract out the specific segment of the audio that contains the event for further use in supervised learning. Conventional supervised learning is thus not possible. How do we then use these weak labels for learning detectors for the events? We answer the question in the next Section.

4. PROPOSED FRAMEWORK

Our formulation of event detection using weak labels of the kind described above is based on *Multiple-Instance Learning* [10] which is a generalized version of supervised learning in which labels are available for a collection of instances. We propose that audio event detection using weak labels is essentially an MIL problem and in general any suitable MIL algorithm can be used.

4.1 Multiple Instance Learning

The term Multiple Instance Learning was first developed by Dietterich *et al.* in 1997 for drug activity detection [10]. MIL is described in terms of *bags*; a *bag* is simply a collection of instances. Labels are attached to the bags, rather than to the individual instances within them. A *positive* bag is one which has at least one positive instance (an instance from the target class to be classified). A *negative* bag contains negative instances only. A negative bag is thus pure whereas a positive bag is impure. This generates an asymmetry from a learning perspective as all instances in a *negative bag* can be uniquely assigned a negative label whereas for a *positive bag* this cannot be done; an instance in a *positive bag* may either be positive or negative.

Thus, it is the *bag-label* pairs, rather than instance-label pairs, which form the training data from which a classifier which classifies individual instances must be learned.

We represent the bag-label pairs as (B_i, Y_i). Here B_i is the ith bag and contains instances x_{ij} where $j = 1 \text{ to } n_i$ and n_i is the total number of instances in the bag, *i.e.* $B_i = \{x_{ij} : j = 1 \cdots n_i\}$. $Y_i \in \{-1, 1\}$ is the label for bag B_i. $Y_i = 1$ implies a positive bag and $Y_i = -1$ implies a negative bag. We might alternatively represent negative labels by 0 at some place for convenience (in Section 4.3). Let the total number of bags be indicated by N. One can attempt to infer labels of individual instances x_{ij} in the bag from the bag label. The label y_{ij} for instances in bag B_i can be stated as:

$$Y_i = -1 \Rightarrow y_{ij} = -1 \;\forall\; x_{ij} \in B_i, \quad (1)$$

$$Y_i = 1 \Rightarrow y_{ij} = 1 \;\text{ for at least one }\; x_{ij} \in B_i \quad (2)$$

This relation between Y_i and y_{ij} is simply

$$Y_i = \max_j \{y_{ij}\}. \quad (3)$$

The problem now is to learn a classification model C so that given a new bag $\hat{B}_n$ it can predict the label $\hat{Y}_n$ for $\hat{B}_n$. Several methods have been proposed to solve the MIL problem such as Learning Axis-Parallel Concepts [10], Diverse Density[23], Citation-KNN[34], mi-SVM and MI-SVM [4]. In this work we work with two frameworks: (1) mi-SVM which modifies support vector machines for the MIL setting and, (2) neural networks for solving MIL problems

4.2 MIL for SVM (mi-SVM)

In [4] Andrews *et al.* proposed two methods for multiple-instance learning of Support Vector Machines. The first, called *mi-SVM*, operates at the instance level and maximizes the margin of individual instances from a linear discriminant. The second, referred to as *MI-SVM* maximizes the margin of bags of instances, rather than individual instances. In this work we use mi-SVM.

To understand mi-SVM, we first note that the relation between bag label Y_i and instance labels y_{ij} can also be represented in the form of linear constraints.

$$\sum_{j=1}^{n_i} \frac{y_{ij}+1}{2} \geq 1 \;\forall\; i \;s.t\; Y_i = 1, \;;\; y_{ij} = -1 \forall\; i \;s.t\; Y_i = -1$$

The instance labels in mi-SVM are treated as unobserved integer variables subject to the constraints defined above. As in conventional training of SVMs, where we must estimate the parameters of a linear (or kernelized) discriminant function such that the *margin* of training instances from the discriminant function is maximized, here too we must maximize the margin. However, since the instance labels are unknown, we modify the objective: the goal now is to maximize a *soft margin* over both the decision function and the hidden integer variables, namely the unknown labels of instances. Optimization of the generalized soft margin is thus

$$\min_{y_{ij}, \mathbf{w}, b, \xi} \frac{1}{2}||w||^2 + C \sum_{ij} \xi_{ij} \quad (4)$$

such that

$$\forall i, j \;:\; y_{ij}(\langle \mathbf{w}, \mathbf{x}_{ij} \rangle + b) \geq 1 - \xi_{ij} \quad (5)$$

$$\xi_{ij} \geq 0 \;; y_{ij} \;\in\; \{-1, 1\} \;; y_{ij} = -1 \forall\; i \;s.t\; Y_i = -1 \quad (6)$$

$$\sum_{j=1}^{n_i} \frac{y_{ij}+1}{2} \geq 1 \;\forall\; i \;s.t\; Y_i = 1 \quad (7)$$

Algorithm 1 mi-SVM Algorithm

procedure LEARNING SVM IN MIL SETTING(B_i, Y_i) // Input training bags and labels

//Initialization Step

$y_{ij} = Y_i$ for all j in Bag B_i

repeat

compute SVM solution $\mathbf{w}$, b with imputed labels

for all bag B_i s.t $Y_i = 1$ **do**

compute $f_{ij} = (\langle \mathbf{w}, \mathbf{x}_{ij} \rangle + b) \ \forall \ x_{ij}$ in B_i

$y_{ij} = sgn(f_{ij}) \ \forall \ j$ in bag B_i s.t $Y_i = 1$

if $(\sum_{j=1}^{n_i} \frac{y_{ij}+1}{2} == 0)$ **then**

compute $j^* = \arg\max_j (f_{ij})$

set y_{ij^*}=1

end if

end for

until imputed labels no longer change

end procedure

In equation 4 the labels y_{ij} of instances belonging to positive bags are unknown integer variables. As a result both, the optimal labeling of these instances as well as the optimal hyperplane $(\mathbf{w}, b)$, must be computed. The separating hyperplane must be such that there is at least one pattern from every positive bag in the positive half space and all patterns belonging to negative bags are in the negative half space.

The above formulation is, however, a difficult mixed integer problem to solve. Andrews *et al.* [4] proposed an optimization heuristic to solve this integer problem. The main idea behind the heuristic is that for given integer variables *i.e.* fixed labels, it can be solved exactly through usual quadratic programming. The solution thus is a two step iterative process:

- *Step 1:* Given the integer variables (fixed labels), solve the standard SVM.
- *Step 2:* Given the SVM solution, impute the integer label variables for the positive bags.

The labels of instances in the positive bags are all initialized as positive and are updated as described above. The instances in negative bags are obviously labeled negative and remain so through out the procedure. The two steps are iterated until no changes in labels occur. The overall mi-SVM is shown in Algorithm 1. If it happens during an iteration that all instances in a positive bag are labeled as negative, then the one with the maximum value for discriminant function is assigned a positive label. This process is repeated until no change in imputed labels is observed.

4.3 MIL of Neural Networks (BP-MIL)

Neural networks have become increasingly popular for classification tasks [28] [20]. The conventional approach to training neural networks is to provide instance-specific labels for a collection of training instances. Training is performed by updating network weights to minimize the average divergence between the actual network output in response to these training instances and a desired output, typically some representation of their assigned labels [27][35].

In the MIL setting, where only bag-level labels are provided for the training data, this procedure must be appropriately modified. In order to do so, we must modify the manner in which the divergence to be minimized is computed to utilize only bag-level labels. For this, we employ an adaptation of neural networks for multiple instance learning (BP-MIL) proposed in [39].

Let o_{ij} represent the output of the network in response to input x_{ij}, the jth instance in B_i, the ith bag of training instances. We define the *bag-level* divergence for bag B_i as

$$E_i = \frac{1}{2}\left(\max_{1 \le j \le n_i} (o_{ij}) - d_i\right)^2 \tag{8}$$

where d_i, the desired output of the network in response to the set of instances from B_i, is simply set to Y_i, the label assigned to B_i. Thus for positive bags $d_i = 1$, whereas for negative bags $d_i = 0$. The central idea behind the bag-level divergence of Equation 8 is to refer to any bag using the instance which produces the maximal output. This was proposed by Dooly *et al.* in [11] where they showed that irrespective of the number of instances (positive or negative) in a bag, the bag can be fully described by the instance with maximal output.

The bag-level divergence of Equation 8 may be understood by noting that the term "$\max_j o_{ij}$" in it effectively represents the *bag-level output* of the network, and that Equation 8 simply computes the divergence of the bag-level output with respect to the bag-level label of Equation 3.

The ideal output of the network in response to any negative instance is 0, whereas for a positive instance it is 1. For *negative* bags, Equation 8 characterizes the *worst-case* divergence of all instances in the bag from this ideal output. Minimizing this effectively ensures that the response of the network to *all* instances from the bag is forced towards 0. In the ideal case, the system will output 0 in response to all inputs in the bag, and the divergence E_i will go to 0.

For *positive* bags, on the other hand, Equation 8 computes the *best-case* divergence of the instances of the bag from the ideal output of 1. Minimizing this ensures that the response of the network to *at least* one of the instances from the bag is forced towards 1. In the ideal case, one or more of the inputs in the bag will produce an output of 1 and the divergence E_i will go to zero.

The *overall* divergence on the training set is obtained by summing the divergences of all the bags in the set:

$$E = \sum_{i=1}^{N} E_i = \sum_{i=1}^{N} \frac{1}{2}\left(\max_{1 \le j \le n_i} o_{ij} - d_i\right)^2 \tag{9}$$

The parameters of the network are trained using conventional backpropagation, with the difference that we now compute gradients of the divergence given in Equation 9, and that entire bags of data must be processed prior to updating network parameters. During training once all instances in a bag have been fed forward through the network, the weight update for the bag is done with respect to the instance in the bag for which the output was maximum. The process is continued until the overall divergence falls below a desired tolerance.

Prediction using a trained network can now be done instance-wise as in done in classical feed-forward neural networks. Bag labels, if required, can be predicted based on the label obtained for the maximal-scoring instance in the bag.

4.4 MIL for AED using weakly labeled data

In our setting for training audio-event detectors from weakly labeled data, we only have labels informing us whether a recording contains a given event or not. In order to apply the MIL framework to this scenario, we must first represent the weakly labeled recordings in R in terms of bag-label representations.

To convert recording R_i to a bag, it is segmented into a number of short audio segments. Adjacent segments may overlap by design. Let the segments derived from R_i be $[I_{R_i1}\, I_{R_i2} ... I_{R_iK}]$. Each of these smaller segments is now treated as an individual instance within the bag R_i. Formally a bag R_i is thus $R_i = \{I_{R_i1}, I_{R_i2}, ...I_{R_iK}\}$ where K depends upon the duration of recording R_i, the length of the individual segments and the overlap between adjacent segments.

If the weak labels for R_i mark an event as being present in R_i, then it will be present in at least one of the instances within it. Hence, R_i will be a positive bag for the instance. On the other hand, if an event is marked as not being present in a recording, then clearly *none* of the segments(instances) from the recording will be positive for that event, and hence overall that recording is a negative bag for the event. Hence, the weak labels for all the recordings can directly provide bag-label representations needed in MIL. The MIL approaches can now be used to learn a model which can predict the presence or absence of an event in each recording, and even identify the locations of the events within the recordings.

4.5 Temporal Localization of Events

The MIL frameworks we use in this work learn from bag-level labels; but once learning is complete, they can classify individual instances. In the context of audio analysis, this implies that not only can we detect the presence of an event in a test recording (bag) but also in individual segments of the test recording. Formally, if R_x is a test recording, which we may more explicitly represent as $R_x(t)$ where "t" indexes time, the individual segments in the recording, $I_{R_x1}, I_{R_x2}, ...I_{R_xK}$, are given by $I_{R_xk} = R_x(t), \;\; (k-1)l^{'} \leq t < (k-1)l^{'} + l$, where l is the length of the segment in seconds and $l^{'}$ denotes the amount by which a segment window is shifted with respect to the previous segment. In the special case of non-overlapping segments $l^{'} = l$. If an event E_i is detected in segment I_{R_xk} it means this event can be localized to the time segment $\left((k-1)l^{'},\ (k-1)*l^{'}+l\right)$ in the recording R_x. Hence, the framework can generate information about the temporal location of events. Hence, we are able to obtain a complete description of the recording in terms of audio events. This is a unique form of AED learning since the descriptive form of labeling was never present in the training data in the first place.

4.6 GMM based features for audio segments

Before we can apply the MIL framework, each segment of audio must first be converted to an appropriate feature representation. We use Mel-frequency cepstral coefficient (MFCC) vectors to obtain low-level feature representations for audio segments. However, direct characterization of audio as sequences of MFCC vectors tends to be ineffective for the purposes of audio classification [40]; other secondary representations derived from these are required. As described in Section 2, one simple and yet very successful approach is the Bag of Audio Words feature representation, which quantizes the individual MFCC vectors into a set of codewords, and represents segments of audio as histograms over these codewords.

However, while the bag of words representation has been found to be very effective for classification of long segments of audio, for shorter duration segments such as those in our case, they present several problems. Bag of words representations effectively characterize the *distribution* of the MFCC vectors in the segment. However, because of the inherent quantization they lose much of the detail of this distribution, which is required for fine-level analysis, such as in the detection of sound events, particularly when the classifiers must be learned from weak labels. While the loss of resolution may be partially resolved by increasing the size of the codebook used for quantization, this can lead to generation of sparse histograms for short audio segments, with large cross-instance variation in the derived features.

In [19] it was demonstrated that for short audio segments characterization of the audio using a Gaussian Mixture Model (GMM) can provide robust representations for performance of audio event detection. They suggested Gaussian Mixture based characterization of audio events is a combination of two features: the first, which we represent as $\vec{F}$, is similar to bag-of-words characterizations such as [32], and the second, which we represent as $\vec{M}$ is a characterization of the modes of the distribution of vectors in the segment.

As a first step to obtaining the $\vec{F}$ and $\vec{M}$ feature vectors for the audio segments, we train a *universal* Gaussian mixture model (GMM) on MFCC vectors from a large and diverse collection of audio recordings. This background GMM is used to extract the $\vec{F}$ and $\vec{M}$ features. In the following, we will represent this universal GMM as $\mathcal{G} = \{w_k, N(x; \lambda_k)\}$, where w_k is the *a priori* probability or mixture weight of the kth Gaussian in the mixture, $N(.)$ represents a Gaussian, and λ_k collectively represents the set of mean and covariance parameters of the kth Gaussian.

4.6.1 $\vec{F}$ Features

For each audio segment we have a sequence of D-dimensional MFCCs vectors denoted by $\vec{x_t}$ where $t = 1 \; to \; T$. T is the total number of MFCC vectors for the given segment. For each component k of the background GMM we compute

$$Pr(k|\vec{x_t}) = \frac{w_k N(\vec{x_t}; \lambda_k)}{\sum\limits_{j=1}^{G} w_j N(\vec{x_t}; \lambda_j)}, \tag{10}$$

$$F(k) = \frac{1}{T} \sum_{i=1}^{T} Pr(k|\vec{x_t}) \tag{11}$$

The $\vec{F}$ feature vectors are $\vec{F} = [F(1), F(2), \cdots, F(G)]^{\top}$. Thus, $\vec{F}$ is G-dimensional vector representing a normalized *soft-count* histogram of the MFCC vectors in the recording. It captures how the MFCC vectors are distributed across components of $\mathcal{G}$. It is a variant of bag of audio word features where soft assignment is used in place of hard quantization.

4.6.2 $\vec{M}$ Features

A more detailed characterization can be obtained by actually representing the distribution of the feature vectors in the segment. To do so, we train a separate GMM for each audio segment by adapting the universal GMM $\mathcal{G}$ to the collection of MFCC vectors in the segment. The means of the universal GMM are adapted to each training segment using the maximum *a posteriori* (MAP) criterion as described in [6]. This is done as follows for k^{th} component of the mixture

$$n_k = \sum_{t=1}^{T} Pr(k|\vec{x_t}), \tag{12}$$

$$E_k(\vec{x}) = \frac{1}{n_k} \sum_{t=1}^{T} Pr(k|\vec{x_t})\vec{x_t} \tag{13}$$

Finally the updated means are computed as

$$\hat{\vec{\mu_k}} = \frac{n_k}{n_k + r} E_k(\vec{x}) + \frac{r}{n_k + r} \vec{\mu_k} \tag{14}$$

where $\vec{\mu_k}$ is the mean vector of kth Gaussian and r is a relevance factor. The means of all components are then appended to form the $G \times D$ vector $\vec{M}$ as $\vec{M} = [\vec{\mu_1}^\top, \vec{\mu_2}^\top, \cdots \vec{\mu_G}^\top]^\top$. The above two features are unsupervised methods of characterizing the statistical structure of an audio segment. $\vec{F}$ is the coarser representation, but can however be robustly estimated. $\vec{M}$ is more detailed, though it is also more easily affected by inter-instance variability. Together, they give us a robust representation of both the coarse and fine structure of the signals in short audio segments. In our experiments we have used $\vec{F}$ both in combination with $\vec{M}$, and as a standalone feature.

Once we have a robust set of features for representing events in short audio segments we can extract features for each audio segment (instances) of a recording (bag). Thus a recording(bag) $R_i = \{I_{R_i1}, I_{R_i2}, ...I_{R_iK}\}$ in feature space becomes $R_i = \{\vec{x}_{R_i1}; \vec{x}_{R_i2}; ....\vec{x}_{R_iK}\}$ where $\vec{x}_{R_ij}$ are either the $\vec{F}$ features alone or the concatenated $\vec{F}$ and $\vec{M}$ vectors. The bags are then fed into the the MIL frameworks BP-MIL or mi-SVM for learning event detector models.

5. EXPERIMENTS AND RESULTS

We evaluated the proposed MIL framework on a portion of the TRECVID-MED 2011 database [1]. The videos in this dataset are meant for multimedia event detection and belong to broad categories such "Changing a vehicle tire", "Attempting a board trick", "feeding an animal", *etc* which are not particularly suitable for audio event detection study. Hence we work with more meaningful acoustic events such as *clapping, cheering* etc. A subset of the MED dataset is thus annotated with 10 such events. To be able to compare performance with the fully supervised case and to compute performance metrics for temporal localization of events, our annotations include actual locations and duration of occurrences of these events. However, only the information regarding the presence or absence of these sounds is used in our MIL based framework.

A total 457 recordings (bags) are used in the experiments. This is over 22 hours of audio data. We henceforth refer to this set of recordings as the "dataset". The length of each recording in the dataset varies from a few seconds to several minutes with an average length of about 2.9 minutes. This implies that the number of instances in each bag also has a wide range.

Ideally, the length of each segment should be properly set keeping in mind the expected duration of event. However, we observed that segment length decided by heuristics work

Table 1: Number of Positive Bags for each event

Events	Number of Bags
Cheering	171
Children's Voices	33
Clanking	13
Clapping	102
Drums	25
Engine Noise	80
Hammering	17
Laughing	116
Marching Band	24
Scraping	30

well. Since the median length of the chosen sound events was less than 1 second, we will report results for all our results on segment length fixed to 1 seconds. The segments overlap by 50%. This results in well over 150,000 total instances. The names of the 10 events and the total number of positive bags for each events are given in Table 1. It is worth noting that some of the recordings in the dataset do not contain any of the 10 events; also a recording might be a positive bag for more than 1 event. Hence, the sum total of numbers in Table 1 is different from the total number of recordings in the dataset. As is clear from our proposed framework our goal is detection of audio events in recordings. Hence, the training data for the binary classifiers for each event have positive bags equal to the number shown in Table 1, while the rest of the recordings in the dataset are negative bags for that event. The dataset is partitioned into 4 sets. Three of the sets were used to train the models, which were then tested on the fourth set. This was done in all four ways meaning each set becomes a test set. This gives us results on the whole dataset. Hence, all results reported here are on the entire dataset.

All recordings were parameterized into sequences of 21-dimensional Mel Frequency Cepstrum Coefficient (MFCC) vectors. MFCC vectors were computed over analysis frames of 20ms, with an overlap of 50%(10ms) between adjacent frames. The $\vec{F}$ and $\vec{M}$ features were derived from these sequences of MFCC vectors. We trained two background GMMs with 64 and 128 Gaussian components respectively. The number of Gaussian component in the features is represented as subscript in the feature such as $\vec{F}_{64}$, $\vec{M}_{64}$.

ROC curves are used to analyze the performance. "Area Under ROC curve" (AUC) [7] is a well known metric used to characterize ROC curves. AUC is used to compare results in different cases. Higher AUC values indicate better detection performance. We first show results for detection of events at recording (bag) level using miSVM and BPMIL in Section 5.1 and 5.2 respectively. The instance level results for temporal localization of events are provided in Section 5.3.

5.1 miSVM Results

For the miSVM framework linear SVMs are used in all experiments. We use LIBLINEAR [14] in our implementation of the miSVM framework. The slack parameter C in the SVM formulation is obtained by 4 fold-cross validation over the training set. A comprehensive analysis through comparison of results in different cases is provided. The mean AUC over all events is shown in the last row of each table.

Table 2: AUC comparison with supervised SVM

Events	AUC ($miSVM$)	AUC ($supSVM$)
Cheering	0.632	0.682
Children's Voices	0.678	0.668
Clanking	0.714	0.727
Clapping	0.646	0.697
Drums	0.60	0.640
Engine Noise	0.623	0.671
Hammering	0.557	0.568
Laughing	0.527	0.741
Marching Band	0.551	0.558
Scraping	0.723	0.850
Mean	**0.625**	**0.680**

Table 3: AUC for different number of components in GMM (miSVM)

Events	AUC ($\vec{F}_{64}$)	AUC ($\vec{F}_{128}$)
Cheering	0.632	0.638
Children's Voices	0.678	0.633
Clanking	0.714	0.744
Clapping	0.646	0.667
Drums	0.60	0.636
Engine Noise	0.623	0.642
Hammering	0.557	0.587
Laughing	0.527	0.540
Marching Band	0.551	0.554
Scraping	0.723	0.735
Mean	**0.625**	**0.637**

5.1.1 Comparison with supervised SVM

We start by showing comparison of our proposed framework with fully supervised AED where strong labels are available. For supervised learning the time stamps in the annotations are used to obtain pure examples of each event, following which an SVM is trained using feature representations of these examples. Table 2 shows this comparison. Comparison is shown for $\vec{F}_{64}$ features. In Table 2 "$supSVM$" refers to supervised SVM. As is expected, supervised SVMs perform better than $miSVM$. However, there are several events for which the performance obtained with weak labels is comparable to that obtained with strong labels. Although the performance of supervised SVMs can potentially be improved by obtaining more strongly labeled examples for each event, Table 2 illustrates that $miSVM$ too can achieve fairly decent performance using only weak labels.

5.1.2 Number of Gaussian Components

Table 3 shows AUC results for $\vec{F}_{64}$ and $\vec{F}_{128}$ features. It can be noted that there are several events for which increasing the number of Gaussians leads to about $2-4\%$ absolute improvement in AUC values. At the same time there are events such as *Cheering* and *Marching Band* where this improvement is not observed, or the performance goes down as in *Children's Voices*. A performance drop of about 4% is observed in this case. The optimal cluster size is known to be event specific in AED, and this holds for MIL-based audio event detection as well.

5.1.3 Adding $\vec{M}$ Features

We now observe the effect of adding the $\vec{M}$ features to the system, along with $\vec{F}$. Table 4 shows a comparison of AUC values when only $\vec{F}$ is used and when it is combined with $\vec{M}$ features. The results shown are obtained with 64 Gaussian components in the GMM. It can be observed that adding $\vec{M}$ features obtained by *maximum a posteriori* adaptation leads to remarkable improvement of results for almost all events. Events for which $\vec{F}$ features alone results in very poor performance such as *Hammering*, *Laughing* and *Marching Band* benefit significantly from the $\vec{M}$ features. Absolute improvements of 10.3%, 11.4% and 19.4% respectively are observed for these three events. For other events too absolute improvements in the range of $2.1\% - 14.5\%$ can be noted. The only exception is *Engine Noise* for which the *soft-count* $\vec{F}$ seems to be better. It is likely that although we observe improvements in miSVM, the actually improvements may be classifier dependent.

Table 4: Effect of $\vec{M}$ features addition (miSVM)

Events	AUC ($\vec{F}_{64}$)	AUC ($[\vec{F}_{64}, \vec{M}_{64}]$)
Cheering	0.632	0.668
Children's Voices	0.678	0.723
Clanking	0.714	0.859
Clapping	0.646	0.680
Drums	0.60	0.639
Engine Noise	0.623	0.575
Hammering	0.557	0.660
Laughing	0.527	0.641
Marching Band	0.551	0.745
Scraping	0.723	0.744
Mean	**0.625**	**0.693**

Table 5: Overall Results with miSVM

Events	AUC	Events	AUC
Cheering	0.668	Engine Noise	0.642
Children's Voices	0.730	Hammering	0.660
Clanking	0.859	Laughing	0.685
Clapping	0.680	Marching Band	0.745
Drums	0.639	Scraping	0.744
Mean		**0.704**	

5.1.4 Overall Results

The overall AUC results across all experiments using miSVM is shown in Table 5. This is the best result across different feature representations for audio segments. The corresponding ROC curves are in Figure 1. Events such as *Clanking*, *Children's's Voices*, *Scraping* and *Marching Band* are easier to detect compared to other events such as *Drums*. The mean AUC over all events is 0.704 which validates the success of our proposed framework.

5.2 BP-MIL Results

For the BP-MIL neural network three parameters must be defined, namely, number of hidden layers, the number of nodes in each hidden layer (n_{no}) and learning rate(η). We used a network with one hidden layer in all experiments. The network is trained for a total of 60 epochs. The learning rate is either fixed at 0.1 throughout training or 0.1 for the first 30 epochs and then reduced in each epoch till it reaches 0.01. Larger values of n_{no} are used for larger dimensionality of input features. For $\vec{F}_{64}$ and $\vec{F}_{128}$ features 3 different values of n_{no} are used. These are 16, 50 and 100 for $\vec{F}_{64}$ and 50, 100 and 150 for $\vec{F}_{128}$. When both $\vec{F}$ and $\vec{M}$ are used, the values of n_{no} used in the experiments are 256 and

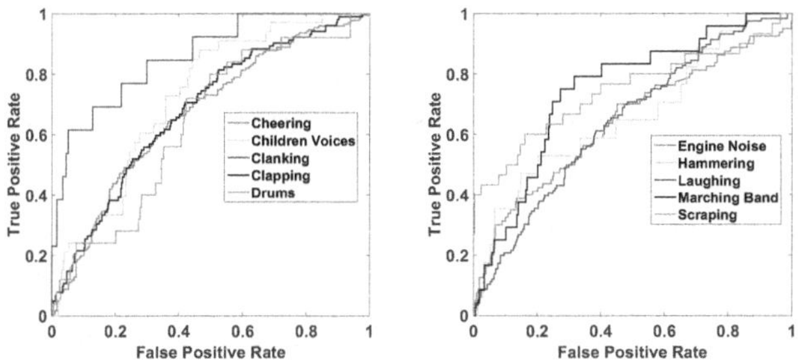

Figure 1: ROC Curves for different events using miSVM framework (Best Viewed in Color)

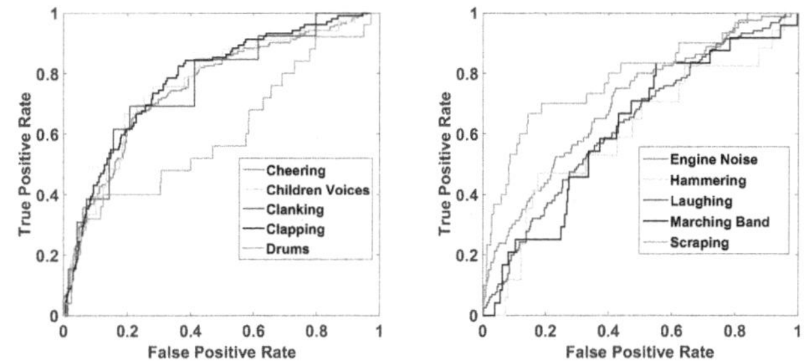

Figure 2: ROC Curves for different events using BP-MIL framework (Best Viewed in Color)

Table 6: Overall Results with BP-MIL

Events	AUC	Events	AUC
Cheering	0.759	Engine Noise	0.698
Children's Voices	0.767	Hammering	0.603
Clanking	0.764	Laughing	0.632
Clapping	0.781	Marching Band	0.618
Drums	0.601	Scraping	0.785
Mean		**0.701**	

512. Training neural networks in general requires exhaustive tuning of parameters to get good results. Although results presented here show reasonable performance for the BP-MIL framework, we believe that better results can be obtained by more aggressive parameter tuning. In fact parameter tuning may give better insight into the BP-MIL framework.

We present only the best results across the different settings. Before looking into these results, we make note of the fact that for BP-MIL adding $\vec{M}$ features in general leads to poorer performance. Some improvement is observed only for *Marching Band* and *Drums*. One possible reason for this might be the substantial increase in total number of weight parameters with the addition of $\vec{M}$ features. As the network size increases by a considerable amount due to increase in input feature size, a substantial increase in training data is expected for learning the model. However, in the present case, the size of our data remains unchanged; this might be one of the reasons for the poor performance for BP-MIL on the addition of M features. It is possible that with a larger dataset M features may be beneficial in the neural network setting as well. Standalone $\vec{F}$ work well for BP-MIL. Table 6 shows overall results for BP-MIL framework. The corresponding ROC curves are shown in Figure 2. If we compare these results with miSVM approach we can observe that events such as *Scraping*, *Clanking* and *Children's Voices* are easier to detect in this case as well. Events such as *Drums* and *Hammering* are harder to detect using BP-MIL as well. The mean AUC remains almost same as miSVM, however, one can note a significant difference with respect to miSVM for several events. An analysis on a larger vocabulary of events might help differentiate the two approaches more clearly.

5.3 Temporal Localization of Events

We now show the performance of the MIL based framework on temporal localization of audio events. To evaluate the performance on this task we need the ground truth labels of all instances in all bags. The instances in the bags have been obtained through uniform segmentation in our work. Each instance is a one second window segment of the recording which is moved in an overlapping manner to segment the recording. However, the annotations providing time stamps of events in the recording does not adhere to this uniform segmentation. Thus an event might start and end within a segment and it can also start or end at any point in the segment. Hence, assigning ground truth labels of instances for a valid analysis is not straightforward. We use a simple heuristic to obtain ground truth labels. As described in Section 4.5 each segment represents a specific time duration of the recording. Looking into the actual annotations available, if an event can be marked to be present in at least 50% of the total length of the segment we call the ground truth label of that segment as positive; otherwise it is negative.

Table 7: AUC for temporal localization of events

Events	AUC (miSVM)	AUC (BP-MIL)
Cheering	0.588	0.669
Children's Voices	0.665	0.705
Clanking	0.925	0.645
Clapping	0.585	0.626
Drums	0.680	0.628
Engine Noise	0.603	0.652
Hammering	0.542	0.572
Laughing	0.548	0.581
Marching Band	0.758	0.701
Scraping	0.684	0.724
Mean	**0.658**	**0.650**

Once the ground truth labels with respect to an event have been obtained for all instances over all bags, we can analyze the performance in the usual fashion. We again present ROC curves and use AUC as the metric characterizing these curves. The best AUC values across all experiments for temporal localization using both *miSVM* and *BP-MIL* are shown in Table 7. The corresponding ROC curves are shown in Figure 3. The figures in the upper row are for *miSVM* and the figures in the bottom row are for BP-MIL. Compared to bag-level results, about 5% drop in mean AUC is observed for both cases. For some events such as *Hammering* and *Laughing* the performance is poor for both frameworks. For others reasonable performance is obtained. Although these numbers are not exceptionally high, they are still significant since no temporal information was used during the training stage. Overall, AUC results validate that our proposed framework can work for temporal localization as well.

6. DISCUSSIONS AND CONCLUSION

A framework for learning acoustic event detectors from weakly labeled data has been presented in this paper. The

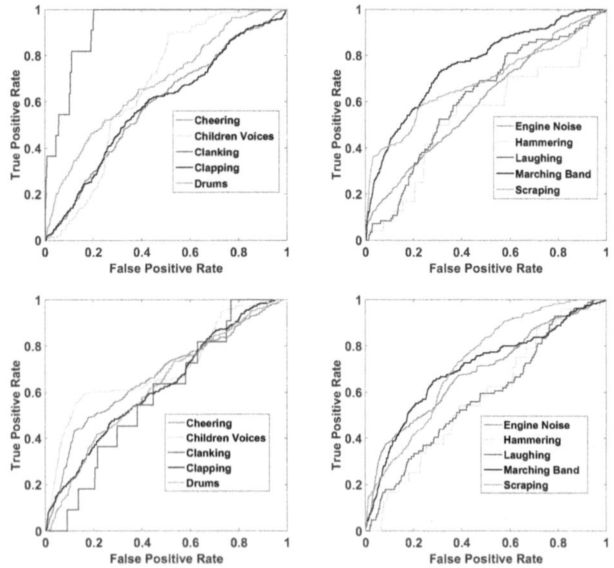

Figure 3: ROC Curves for Temporal Localization (Top-miSVM, Bottom - BP-MIL)

learned detectors can both detect and temporally localize events in a recording. We show that we achieve reasonable performance for both tasks. Specifically, events such as *Clanking*, *Scraping*, and *Children's Voices* are easy to detect using both SVM and neural network approaches. On the other hand events such as Drums, Hammering and Laughing are hard to detect using both methods. Large-scale implementation of both methods on a larger number of events might be able to give a better insights for both methods. The overall performance of both methods is similar. Given the limited amount of training data, a mean AUC of around 0.7 demonstrates the success of the proposed approach. Larger datasets are expected to result in better performance for both cases.

An important factor in this framework is the representation used to characterize the audio segments, *i.e.* the instances in the bags. We employed Gaussian mixture based features ($\vec{F}$ and $\vec{M}$). We do not necessarily claim that these are the best features for audio event classification; nonetheless they have been shown effective for AED in short audio segments [19]. Other features may be expected to result in improved overall MIL performance.

The success of our method is an important step towards reducing the dependence on strongly labeled data for learning audio event detectors. It shows the pathway to utilize the vast amount of multimedia data available on the web for audio event detection. The weak labels for web multimedia (audio) data can be inferred automatically from associated metadata which can then be directly used in the proposed framework. An interesting and extremely useful product of our proposed framework is the ability to temporally locate events in the recording. This is significant since this information was not present in the original data in the first place. Moreover, the predicted instance level labels can be further used in an active learning framework to improve performance.

A number of factors still need to be investigated to create a state-of-art acoustic event detection mechanism in which learning is done using weakly labeled data. We need to consider a large set of events for a more comprehensive view of our framework. Moreover, investigations are required into more effective multiple instance learning methods which can help improve the overall performance and scalability of framework. Multimedia event detection requires detection of higher concepts. In the current work we focused on detecting finer events and their detection can be used for detecting higher concepts. Higher-level concepts in turn may be used to guide MIL. All of these are directions of currently ongoing and future work.

7. REFERENCES

[1] Multimedia event detection. http://www.nist.gov/itl/iad/mig/med11.cfm.

[2] Youtube statistics. http://www.youtube.com/yt/press/statistics.html.

[3] E. Amid, A. Mesaros, K. J. Palomaki, J. Laaksonen, and M. Kurimo. Unsupervised feature extraction for multimedia event detection and ranking using audio content. In *Acoustics, Speech and Signal Processing (ICASSP), 2014 IEEE International Conference on*, pages 5939–5943. IEEE, 2014.

[4] S. Andrews, I. Tsochantaridis, and T. Hofmann. Support vector machines for multiple-instance learning. *Advances in neural information processing systems*, 15:561–568, 2002.

[5] K. Ashraf, B. Elizalde, F. Iandola, M. Moskewicz, J. Bernd, G. Friedland, and K. Keutzer. Audio-based multimedia event detection with DNNs and sparse sampling. In *Proceedings of the 5th ACM on International Conference on Multimedia Retrieval*, pages 611–614. ACM, 2015.

[6] F. Bimbot, J.-F. Bonastre, C. Fredouille, G. Gravier, I. Magrin-Chagnolleau, S. Meignier, T. Merlin, J. Ortega-García, D. Petrovska-Delacrétaz, and D. A. Reynolds. A tutorial on text-independent speaker verification. *EURASIP journal on applied signal processing*, 2004:430–451, 2004.

[7] A. P. Bradley. The use of the area under the roc curve in the evaluation of machine learning algorithms. *Pattern recognition*, 30(7):1145–1159, 1997.

[8] F. Briggs, B. Lakshminarayanan, L. Neal, X. Z. Fern, R. Raich, S. J. Hadley, A. S. Hadley, and M. G. Betts. Acoustic classification of multiple simultaneous bird species: A multi-instance multi-label approach. *The Journal of the Acoustical Society of America*, 131(6):4640–4650, 2012.

[9] M. Cristani, M. Bicego, and V. Murino. Audio-visual event recognition in surveillance video sequences. *Multimedia, IEEE Transactions on*, 9(2):257–267, 2007.

[10] T. G. Dietterich, R. H. Lathrop, and T. Lozano-Pérez. Solving the multiple instance problem with axis-parallel rectangles. *Artificial Intelligence*, 89(1):31–71, 1997.

[11] D. R. Dooly, Q. Zhang, S. A. Goldman, and R. A. Amar. Multiple instance learning of real valued data. *The Journal of Machine Learning Research*, 3:651–678, 2003.

[12] L. Duan, D. Xu, I. W.-H. Tsang, and J. Luo. Visual event recognition in videos by learning from web data.

Pattern Analysis and Machine Intelligence, IEEE Transactions on, 34(9):1667–1680, 2012.

[13] A. J. Eronen, V. T. Peltonen, J. T. Tuomi, A. P. Klapuri, S. Fagerlund, T. Sorsa, G. Lorho, and J. Huopaniemi. Audio-based context recognition. *Audio, Speech, and Language Processing, IEEE Transactions on*, 14(1):321–329, 2006.

[14] R.-E. Fan, K.-W. Chang, C.-J. Hsieh, X.-R. Wang, and C.-J. Lin. Liblinear: A library for large linear classification. *The Journal of Machine Learning Research*, 9:1871–1874, 2008.

[15] O. Gencoglu, T. Virtanen, and H. Huttunen. Recognition of acoustic events using deep neural networks. In *Signal Processing Conference (EUSIPCO), 2014 Proceedings of the 22nd European*, pages 506–510. IEEE, 2014.

[16] Q. Huang and S. Cox. Hierarchical language modeling for audio events detection in a sports game. In *Acoustics Speech and Signal Processing (ICASSP), 2010 IEEE International Conference on*, pages 2286–2289. IEEE, 2010.

[17] Z. Kons and O. Toledo-Ronen. Audio event classification using deep neural networks. In *INTERSPEECH*, pages 1482–1486, 2013.

[18] A. Kumar, P. Dighe, R. Singh, S. Chaudhuri, and B. Raj. Audio event detection from acoustic unit occurrence patterns. In *Acoustics, Speech and Signal Processing (ICASSP), 2012 IEEE International Conference on*, pages 489–492. IEEE, 2012.

[19] A. Kumar, R. M. Hegde, R. Singh, and B. Raj. Event detection in short duration audio using gaussian mixture model and random forest classifier. In *21st European Signal Processing Conference 2013 (EUSIPCO 2013)*, Marrakech, Morocco, Sept. 2013.

[20] Y. LeCun, Y. Bengio, and G. Hinton. Deep learning. *Nature*, 521(7553):436–444, 2015.

[21] X. Lu, Y. Tsao, S. Matsuda, and C. Hori. Sparse representation based on a bag of spectral exemplars for acoustic event detection. In *Acoustics, Speech and Signal Processing (ICASSP), 2014 IEEE International Conference on*, pages 6255–6259. IEEE, 2014.

[22] M. I. Mandel and D. P. Ellis. Multiple-instance learning for music information retrieval. In *ISMIR 2008: Proceedings of the 9th International Conference of Music Information Retrieval*, pages 577–582. Drexel University, 2008.

[23] O. Maron and T. Lozano-Pérez. A framework for multiple-instance learning. *Advances in neural information processing systems*, pages 570–576, 1998.

[24] S. Pancoast and M. Akbacak. Bag-of-audio-words approach for multimedia event classification. In *Proc. of Interspeech*, 2012.

[25] A. Pikrakis, T. Giannakopoulos, and S. Theodoridis. Gunshot detection in audio streams from movies by means of dynamic programming and bayesian networks. In *Acoustics, Speech and Signal Processing, 2008. ICASSP 2008. IEEE International Conference on*, pages 21–24. IEEE, 2008.

[26] J. F. Ruiz-Muñoz, M. Orozco-Alzate, and G. Castellanos-Dominguez. Multiple instance learning-based birdsong classification using unsupervised recording segmentation. In *Proceedings of the 24th International Conference on Artificial Intelligence*, pages 2632–2638. AAAI Press, 2015.

[27] D. E. Rumelhart, G. E. Hinton, and R. J. Williams. Learning representations by back-propagating errors. *Cognitive modeling*, 5:3, 1988.

[28] J. Schmidhuber. Deep learning in neural networks: An overview. *Neural Networks*, 61:85–117, 2015.

[29] Y. Song and C. Zhang. Content-based information fusion for semi-supervised music genre classification. *Multimedia, IEEE Transactions on*, 10(1):145–152, 2008.

[30] D. Stowell, D. Giannoulis, E. Benetos, M. Lagrange, and M. Plumbley. Detection and classification of acoustic scenes and events. *Multimedia, IEEE Transactions on*, PP, 2015.

[31] G. Valenzise, L. Gerosa, M. Tagliasacchi, F. Antonacci, and A. Sarti. Scream and gunshot detection and localization for audio-surveillance systems. In *Advanced Video and Signal Based Surveillance, 2007. AVSS 2007. IEEE Conference on*, pages 21–26. IEEE, 2007.

[32] J. C. Van Gemert, C. J. Veenman, A. W. Smeulders, and J.-M. Geusebroek. Visual word ambiguity. *Pattern Analysis and Machine Intelligence, IEEE Transactions on*, 32(7):1271–1283, 2010.

[33] F. Wang, Z. Sun, Y.-G. Jiang, and C.-W. Ngo. Video event detection using motion relativity and feature selection. *Multimedia, IEEE Transactions on*, 16(5):1303–1315, 2014.

[34] J. Wang and J.-D. Zucker. Solving the multiple-instance problem: A lazy learning approach. In *Proceedings of the Seventeenth International Conference on Machine Learning*, ICML '00, pages 1119–1126, San Francisco, CA, USA, 2000. Morgan Kaufmann Publishers Inc.

[35] P. J. Werbos. Applications of advances in nonlinear sensitivity analysis. In *System modeling and optimization*, pages 762–770. Springer, 1982.

[36] G. Ye, I. Jhuo, D. Liu, Y.-G. Jiang, D. Lee, S.-F. Chang, et al. Joint audio-visual bi-modal codewords for video event detection. In *Proceedings of the 2nd ACM International Conference on Multimedia Retrieval*, page 39. ACM, 2012.

[37] T. Zhang, C. Xu, G. Zhu, S. Liu, and H. Lu. A generic framework for event detection in various video domains. In *Proceedings of the international conference on Multimedia*, pages 103–112. ACM, 2010.

[38] T. Zhang, C. Xu, G. Zhu, S. Liu, and H. Lu. A generic framework for video annotation via semi-supervised learning. *Multimedia, IEEE Transactions on*, 14(4):1206–1219, 2012.

[39] Z.-H. Zhou and M.-L. Zhang. Neural networks for multi-instance learning. In *Proceedings of the International Conference on Intelligent Information Technology, Beijing, China*, pages 455–459, 2002.

[40] X. Zhuang, X. Zhou, M. A. Hasegawa-Johnson, and T. S. Huang. Real-world acoustic event detection. *Pattern Recognition Letters*, 31(12):1543–1551, 2010.

Event Localization in Music Auto-tagging

Jen-Yu Liu[1,2], Yi-Hsuan Yang[2]
[1]Electrical Engineering Department, National Taiwan University, Taiwan
[2]Research Center for IT Innovation, Academia Sinica, Taiwan
{ciaua, yang}@citi.sinica.edu.tw

ABSTRACT

In music auto-tagging, people develop models to automatically label a music clip with attributes such as instruments, styles or acoustic properties. Many of these tags are actually descriptors of local events in a music clip, rather than a holistic description of the whole clip. Localizing such tags in time can potentially innovate the way people retrieve and interact with music, but little work has been done to date due to the scarcity of labeled data with granularity specific enough to the frame level. Most labeled data for training a learning-based model for music auto-tagging are in the clip level, providing no cues when and how long these attributes appear in a music clip. To bridge this gap, we propose in this paper a convolutional neural network (CNN) architecture that is able to make accurate frame-level predictions of tags in unseen music clips by using only clip-level annotations in the training phase. Our approach is motivated by recent advances in computer vision for localizing visual objects, but we propose new designs of the CNN architecture to account for the temporal information of music and the variable duration of such local tags in time. We report extensive experiments to gain insights into the problem of event localization in music, and validate through experiments the effectiveness of the proposed approach. In addition to quantitative evaluations, we also present qualitative analyses showing the model can indeed learn certain characteristics of music tags.

1. INTRODUCTION

The problem of event or object localization arises in many areas of information processing. In speech recognition, the temporal correspondence between the spoken and the recognized words is required [1,2,14,17]. In visual object recognition, people want to know not only whether an object (e.g., a cat) is present in an image, but also where the object really is within the image [11,13,28,29,33].

The localization problem also exists in music auto-tagging, whose goal is to automatically label a music clip with attributes such as instruments, genres/styles or acoustic properties [7,8,15,35]. Although people tend to describe such attributes simply as *tags*, we can also view them as descriptors of music *events*. For example, an instrument tag "guitar" can be thought of as "the presence of guitar." A genre tag such as "Jazz" is usually used to describe a whole piece of music, but it can also be rephrased as "having a Jazz flavor" which describes parts of the piece. From this point of view, a tag should be associated with starting points and ending points in a music piece, if the tag applies to multiple parts of the piece. Localizing the music events is beneficial for many tasks in music information retrieval. For example, a user would not know there are Jazz elements in parts of a music piece, if the piece is only globally labeled as being "Pop." In music search, a user may look for short segments of music pieces featuring certain attributes, such as "metal screaming vocal," "a saxophone solo" or "outside improvisation." If several instruments are used in a music piece, localizing the instruments in time gives us a better understanding of the overall structure and organization of the piece.

Music event localization, however, is seldom addressed in the literature, mainly due to the scarcity of labeled data. In speech recognition, localization is achieved by collecting frame-level annotation and training prediction models directly in the frame level [14,17]. In visual object recognition, manual annotation of the so-called bounding boxes around the objects of interest is usually needed for training a model for localization [11]. Although music event localization may sound similar to these two tasks, labeling music events by hand is arguably more difficult. For example, while speech data usually have only one active speaker at a time [12], it is typical to have multiple instruments, vocals, or styles in music, rendering it a multi-label problem [21]. As opposed to image, labeling music requires certain level of domain expertise. Localizing events in a time stream is also more labor-intense and time-consuming. In consequence, it is not surprising that most datasets available for music auto-tagging contain only clip-level annotations [21,35].

In light of these observations, we propose in this paper a novel approach that conquers the scarcity of labeled data for music event localization by using only clip-level annotation of tags in the training phase. Our contribution is threefold. First, to the best of our knowledge, this work represents one of the first attempts that systematically investigate the localization problem in music auto-tagging. In addition to building a machine learning model that is able to make both *clip-level* and *frame-level* prediction of tag occurrence, we also present a series of experiments to gain insights into is-

MM '16, October 15-19, 2016, Amsterdam, Netherlands

DOI: http://dx.doi.org/10.1145/2964284.2964292

sues specific to the frame-level prediction task, namely music event localization. In general, "event localization" is about locating the start and end time of an event, whereas "frame-level tagging/prediction" is about predicting the labels at frame level. In this paper, we achieve event localization by frame-level prediction, and we will use them interchangeably because we can derive the other if we have one.

Second, by extending a recent convolutional neural network (CNN)-based approach to visual object recognition [28], we develop a new CNN model for predicting and localizing music events in unseen music by training on only clip-level data. Our model is designed to account for the variable duration of music events and the temporal information of music. This is done by adding an *accumulation* layer that uses a Gaussian filter of tag-dependent length for assembling local information, and by feeding multi-scale audio features to CNN. Different from existing CNN models for musical feature extraction [7,8], our model can deal with music of arbitrary length. The code is available online[1].

Third, as no evaluation framework has been proposed for music event localization trained with clip-level annotations, we are also motivated to propose such a framework to facilitate objective evaluation of the prediction result. We argue that existing *multi-track* music datasets originally intended for studying musical source separation or transcription problems can be nicely used to evaluate frame-level prediction of instrument tags, and demonstrate such an evaluation by using the music auto-tagging dataset MagnaTagATune [21] and a recently proposed multi-track dataset called MedleyDB [5]. We also present visualization of some prediction results, which can be used to subjectively evaluate the performance for both instrument and non-instrument tags.

The paper is organized as follows. We survey key related work in Section 2 and present the proposed method in Section 3. We then describe the datasets used in our evaluation in Section 4 and the evaluation result in Sections 5 and 6. Section 7 discusses and concludes the paper.

2. RELATED WORK

A considerable amount of work has been made for music auto-tagging, mostly focusing on only clip-level prediction (i.e., whether a tag can be applied to a music piece) [7–9, 15, 16, 27, 35, 36]. Although audio features are usually extracted in the frame level, the objective of learning is to make clip-level prediction. In recent years, deep neural network architectures have been found superior to competing machine learning models for music auto-tagging [7, 8, 18]. For example, Dieleman *et al.* have shown the effectiveness of CNN in learning features for music auto-tagging [8]. However, this CNN model can neither deal with music of arbitrary length nor perform frame-level prediction.

Some studies investigate audio auto-tagging with finer granularity. Essid *et al.* apply hierarchical clustering for frame-level instrument recognition with temporal annotations of instrument occurrences [10]. Mandel *et al.* study the tag relationships inside a track and between tags with 10-second clips [22–24]. Frame-level prediction on music auto-tagging was discussed by Wang *et al.* [37]. Parascandolo *et al.* conducts polyphonic sound event detection with recurrent neural networks [30]. The main difference between our methods and those in these studies is that our method can predict at a temporal granularity finer than the granularity of the training data.

Labeling the bounding boxes of objects in an image requires more labors than annotating the presence of objects does. Therefore, visual object localization with only image-level annotations has attracted increasing attentions in recent years [13, 28, 29, 33].

These approaches are sometimes referred to as *weakly supervised learning* [29]. Among the prior arts, our approach is closest to the model proposed by Oquab *et al.* [28], a multi-instance learning variant and also based on CNN. A key idea proposed in this work is to use the so-called *full convolutions* (see Section 3 for details), so that the model can process images of arbitrary size. In this way, they can resize an input image arbitrarily in a multi-scale manner to locate a visual object. Being inspired by this approach, our model has two distinct features. First, we adopt a different way to achieve multi-scale learning, as music cannot be easily "resized" as images. Second, we use a dedicated layer to deal with the temporal dimension in music, which is absent in images.

Visual event or action detection in videos, which also have a temporal dimension, has also been studied [19,34,38]. Similar to music event detection, this problem requires weakly-supervised learning because the annotation is at the video clip level. However, little work, if any, has been proposed to address localization problem for visual events in videos.

3. MODEL

Our goal is to develop a model that fulfills the following requirements: 1) can give accurate frame-level prediction in the test phase, given only clip-level annotations in the training phase; 2) can handle music pieces of arbitrary length; 3) can capture the temporal characteristics of music events; and 4) can employ multi-scale features as the input.

We propose to achieve this by using a CNN-based architecture for its well-demonstrated effectiveness in various classification tasks in speech recognition [2], computer vision [20], and also music information retrieval [8]. Moreover, neural networks are modular so it is easy for us to add or change components to attain different goals.

The first requirement is met by assuming that the clip-level prediction is aggregated from *segment-level* predictions, and that accordingly frame-level predictions can be recovered from the segment-level predictions. Here, a segment is considered as a continuous subset of a music piece that spans a number of frames.

The ability to handle music pieces of arbitrary length is realized by implementing the CNN as a *fully convolutional* network, where all the layers are convolutional [28]. That is to say, the so-called *fully connected* layers commonly used in CNNs are replaced by convolution layers with window size being 1. This structure has been used in the computer vision community to process images of arbitrary size [28, 31], but it has not been used in music audio before.

The third requirement is important because the *noticeable duration* of music events may be event-dependent. For example, if a guitar sound only lasts for a very short period of time, it can be either inaudible to human ears or too short to be considered as being present. Henceforth, we may not want to annotate the music piece with the tag "guitar." Furthermore, when there is a music event, its typical duration also depends on the nature of the event. For example, instrumental events may be shorter than genre-related events.

[1]https://github.com/ciaua/clip2frame

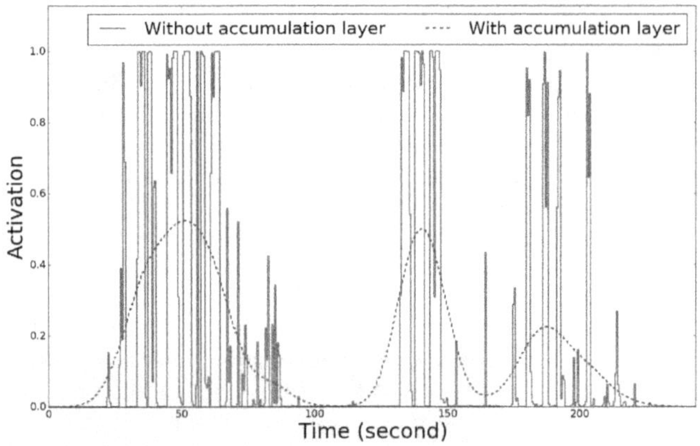

Figure 1: Expected effect of the accumulation layer.

To account for these considerations, we propose to add an *accumulation* layer before the output layer. The role of the accumulation layer is to summarize the predictions made from the previous layer over time, as illustrated in Figure 1. While the typical CNN architecture can already capture the temporal context of the input features by using convolutions, the accumulation layer is needed to capture the contextual information of music events at the decision-level.

In this paper, we realize the accumulation layer by a Gaussian filter. The shape of the Gaussian is controlled by its standard deviation σ, which is a parameter to be learned for different events in the training phase. We expect that the model will learn different σs for different events. An alternative method is to use the so-called *recurrent* layers for decision-level accumulation. Although the recurrent layers can capture contextual information in a more complex way, this complexity comes at a price of increased computational cost. We therefore leave it as a possible future work.

Finally, extracting audio features of different scales is also important in music audio processing, as demonstrated by Dieleman *et al.* [7] in the context of music auto-tagging. We attain this requirement by using multiple stacks of convolution layers to deal with audio features of different resolutions, and later on combining them by concatenation. Different resolutions of audio features are obtained by using the log-scale mel-spectrogram with different window sizes in short-time Fourier Transform (STFT).

The general structure of the proposed network is depicted in Figure 2. According to our design, the proposed model can make both clip-level and frame-level predictions. We provide the details in what follows.

3.1 Clip-level Prediction

As Figure 2 shows, the input layer consists of log mel-spectrogram with N different STFT window sizes [7]. As these are frame-level features computed over time, we refer to a log mel-spectrogram computed with a given window size as a *feature map*. Then, each feature map is processed by its own stack of alternating convolutions and max poolings, referred to altogether as the *early convolution* layers. Max pooling is applied only along the time axis (but not the frequency axis) for every S frames, which is referred to as the *stride size*. All stacks of early convolution layers in our CNN structure have the same number of layers. The outputs of the last early convolution layers are concatenated together

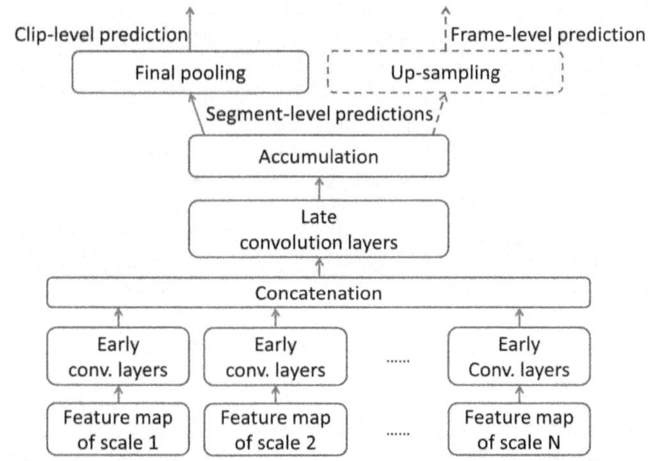

Figure 2: The proposed CNN architecture. Given a trained network for clip-level prediction (the blue one), we replace the final pooling layer by an up-sampling layer for frame-level prediction (the red component).

into one feature map, which aggregates information from different scales. This united feature map is fed into another stack of convolutions, referred to as the *late convolution* layers. The late convolution layers use only convolutions with no strides (i.e., $S = 1$) and no max poolings. They provide the function of fully connected layers commonly used in conventional CNNs and have the benefit of efficiently scanning through a time sequence of arbitrary length. The output of the last late convolution layer is then processed by a Gaussian filter across time to create the *segment-level* predictions. A segment would contain multiple frames, because of the previous max pooling layers. If the σ in the Gaussian is trainable in the training phase, we call it "adaptive Gaussian filter"; otherwise, we call it "fixed Gaussian filter." Finally, the segment-level predictions are pooled over time with the *final pooling* layer to become one clip-level prediction.

To facilitate our discussion later, we define the notion of *total stride size* as the product of all the stride sizes in a stack of early convolution layers. It can be shown that the number of frames covered by a segment in our model equals the total stride size.

3.2 Frame-level model

Given a trained network for clip-level prediction, we modify only the last layer to make it possible to make frame-level predictions, as illustrated also in Figure 2. Therefore, as there are no trainable parameters in the last layers, the parameters of all layers are shared among the networks for making clip- and frame-level predictions.

Specifically, the aforementioned final pooling layer is now replaced by a *up-sampling* layer to recover frame-level predictions from segment-level predictions. We investigate two methods of up-sampling in this paper. The first method is *upscaling*, which simply repeats the segment-level predictions locally such that the final output has the same number of frames as the input. For example, suppose there are two early convolution layers and each of them has stride size 2. The total stride size is then 4. Accordingly, the output, say [0, 1, 0], of the accumulation layer has to be repeated 4 times, that is, [0, 0, 0, 0, 1, 1, 1, 1, 0, 0, 0, 0].

The second method is *patching*, which has been used in related work in computer vision [25,32,33]. Assuming that the total stride size is 4, two temporally neighboring points in the segment-level result can be seen as being 4-frame apart. To fill the values in between, we can simply shift the audio input 4 times and feed each of them to the CNN network. This might be more accurate than the upscaling method, but obviously it is computationally much more expensive.

3.2.1 Thresholding

An important issue not depicted in Figure 2 is the necessity to apply a thresholding on the frame-level predictions to get binary decisions. This is because the output of CNNs lies in the range between 0 and 1 but we may need binary decisions to evaluate the prediction accuracy. As the optimal threshold values may be tag-dependent, we empirically tune the values in the following brute-force way by using validation data (see Section 4.3). First, we divide the output range [0, 1] into K threshold candidates, namely $\{0, 1/K, 2/K, ..., (K-1)/K\}$. For each music event, the F1 scores (i.e., the harmonic mean of precision and recall rates) of frame-level prediction scores are computed with respect to all the threshold candidates, and the candidate with the highest F1 score is selected.

4. DATA

We use two datasets: MagnaTagATune for clip-level training, and MedleyDB for frame-level evaluation.

MagnaTagATune is a music dataset containing clip-level tag annotations [21]. The clips in the dataset were annotated by collecting, through playing a game, human evaluations of music tags that are generated by algorithm. It includes 25,863 29-second clips, annotated with 188 tags. The tags includes instruments such as "guitar" and "flute," genres such as "Jazz" and "new age," tempo such as "slow" and "fast," and acoustic properties such as "silence" and "noise."

MedleyDB is a multi-track instrument dataset [5]. It has instrument and F0 annotations at frame level, so it can be used for research of melody extraction and source separation. It includes 122 multi-track clips and totally 81 instrument tags. The timestamps of instrument activations are provided in terms of starting and ending points, from which we can derive frame-level annotations. In this paper, the multiple tracks of a clip are merged into one channel.

As there are no music auto-tagging dataset that contains frame-level annotations, we found that a multi-track instrument dataset like MedleyDB is especially suitable for evaluating the performance of music event localization. Common music auto-tagging datasets also contain a rich number of instrument tags. In our case, MagnaTagATune and MedleyDB have 46 tags in common. In addition, the multi-track audio of instruments in MedleyDB is also in line with the multi-label nature of music auto-tagging. Therefore, we propose to use MedleyDB for evaluating frame-level result.

To ensure that the data are reasonably rich for both the training phase with MagnaTagATune and the evaluation phase with MedleyDB, we choose the top 9 common instrument tags in our frame-level evaluation. These 9 tags are "drum set," "electric bass," "piano," "male singer," "clean electric guitar," "synthesizer," "vocalists," "female singer," and "acoustic guitar."

4.1 Data processing

The audio feature used in our model is 128-D log mel-spectrogram, which has been used by [7,8,15]. All features are standardized by removing mean and divided by standard deviation derived from training set. We extract features with a Python library Librosa [26] with 16k sampling rate and hop size 512.

In processing MagnaTagATune, we follow [7,8] to use the first 12 sub-folders for training, the 13th sub-folder for validation and the 14th to 16th sub-folders for test. The training set is used to train the CNN models, the validation set to select the best parameters during training (see Section 5 for more information), and the test set to evaluate clip-level result. The union of training and validation sets is used to derive the frame-level thresholds.

In processing MedleyDB, we randomly divide the dataset into validation and test sets of roughly the same number of artists and the same number of clips. The artists in the validation set and the test set have no overlaps. There are 24 artists and 53 clips in validation set, and 25 artists and 55 clips in test set. The validation set is used to derive the frame-level thresholds and the test set is used to evaluate frame-level performance. Please note that MedleyDB is not used at all in training the proposed model, either for clip- or frame-level prediction.

5. EVALUATION

The models are implemented with Lasagne[2] and Theano [3,4]. The models are always trained with 188 output units, which is the total number of tags in MagnaTagATune. The predictions of top 50 tags and 9 instrument tags reported below are directly from the 188-dimensional output. The CNNs are trained using back-propagation with binary cross-entropy as the loss function, 0.5 dropout rate, and 0.01 learning rate. Each early convolution layer consists of 32 filters, each of length 8. The late convolution includes three layers with 512, 512, and 188 filters, where 188 is the number of tags. The filter length and stride size of late convolutions are 1. The size of max pooling after a convolution layer equals the stride size of the convolution layer. We follows [8] to do convolution only along the temporal axis. The accumulation layer is also implemented with convolution whose initial weights form a centered Gaussian distribution. In order to keep the models with different total stride sizes to "see" temporal information of the same duration, the σs of Gaussian are initialized such that $TotalStride \times \sigma = 256$ (in frames). A model is trained with 200 epochs. The parameters from the epoch yielding the best performance on validation set is used as the final parameters for the model.

Because we train the models on MagnaTagATune and evaluate on MedleyDB, we compare the performance using thresholds derived from MagnaTagATune or from MedleyDB in the way described in Section 3.2.1. The [0, 1] range is divided into $K = 1,000$ threshold candidates. Note that, in order to keep the assumption that we have only clip-level information, we divide the MedleyDB clips into smaller clips of 320 frames and aggregate the frame-level annotations into clip-level annotations and use them to derive the thresholds.

Due to the space limit, some details of the model implementation are omitted. Please see the documentation of our codes for the details.

[2]https://lasagne.readthedocs.org/en/latest/

Table 1: Best performance for the clip level and frame level. The baseline in frame-level performance is derived by simply predicting all frames as positive (i.e. all ones).

(a) Frame-level performance, comparing two ways of up-sampling.

	Precision		Recall		F1	
Up-sampling	Micro	Macro	Micro	Macro	Micro	Macro
Upscaling	0.561	0.539	0.846	0.791	0.675	0.633
Patching	0.560	0.538	0.847	0.793	0.674	0.633
Baseline	0.350	0.350	1.000	1.000	0.519	0.495

(b) Clip-level performance for the top 50 tags and all tags.

	Average AUC		MAP	
Top N tags	Per-class	Per-clip	Per-class	Per-clip
50	0.896	0.932	0.406	0.680
188 (All)	0.880	0.952	0.183	0.592

We will first present the best performance of clip-level and frame-level prediction in Section 5.2. The discussions in the subsequent subsections will use variants of the model with the best frame-level performance by changing the parameters or the type of a layer. These variants help us gain insights into the properties of the frame-level model.

5.1 Metrics for Objective Evaluation

For evaluating clip-level result, average area under ROC curve (AUC) and mean average precision (MAP) are used. ROC curve is formed by connecting the points (true negative, true positive) from varied thresholds. Two type of variants are provided: 1) per-class, computing AUC or AP in a tag class first and then taking average over clips, and 2) per-clip, computing AUC or AP in a clip and then taking average over all tags.

For evaluating frame-level result, we show F1 score. In this paper, the frame-level predictions of one tag in all test data are concatenated into one vector first for computing the measure scores. We use two ways to aggregate the measures from different tags. Micro F1 computes a precision score and a recall score globally from all tags and then computes F1 score, while macro F1 computes F1 score for each tag first and then takes average over all tags.

5.2 Best Performance

The best performance for the frame level is achieved by a model with an adaptive Gaussian filter, two early convolution layers of stride size 4 and a final mean pooling. The thresholds are derived from MedleyDB. As Table 1a shows, using upscaling and using patching for up-sampling have little difference. As patching is computationally more demanding, we will report only the results using upscaling in the following experiments.

The best performance for the clip level with top 50 tags, on the other hand, is achieved by a model which has a fixed Gaussian filter, one early convolution layer of stride size 4 and a final max pooling. The average AUC achieved by this model is 0.896, which is comparable to the multi-scale model proposed by [7], which achieving 0.898 average AUC. We also list the result using all 188 tags in Table 1b. The clip-level observations with 50 top tags also generally hold with 188 top tags. For space limit, we will report only the results with 50 top tags regarding clip-level hereafter.

5.3 Effect of Thresholds

As the first investigation, we compare the thresholds for frame-level predictions derived from either MagnaTagATune or MedleyDB. The results are shown in Table 2. The thresholds from MedleyDB yield better recall scores and accordingly F1 scores than those from MagnaTagATune. This indicates that we still need some data in the target domain for deriving thresholds in order for this transfer learning scheme to work. In the following experiments, the reported frame-level predictions are derived with MedleyDB thresholds.

5.4 Effect of Accumulation

In this set of experiments, we compare the effect of accumulation layer. It is either no accumulation, fixed Gaussian filter, or adaptive Gaussian filter. The performance is shown in Table 3. Most of the models with accumulation outperform the one without accumulation in the same category significantly (one-tailed t-test on macro F1 with 0.05 significance level). We first notice that the clip-level performance without accumulation is comparable or even better than the performance with Gaussian filters. However, the frame-level performance without Gaussian filters is worse than those with Gaussian filters. The performance is even worse than the baseline in Table 1a in some case.

None of adaptive Gaussian and fixed Gaussian has clear advantage over the other. As our focus in this paper is frame-level prediction and the adaptive Gaussian yields the best frame-level performance, we will focus on the performance of adaptive Gaussian in the remaining discussion.

To visually see the effect of accumulation, we show in Figure 3 the output of four models: adaptive Gaussian filter with total stride 256, adaptive Gaussian filter with total stride 2, no accumulation with total stride 256, and no accumulation with total stride 2. When no accumulation is applied, the model with small total stride has rapid changes in amplitude and loses continuity of the prediction. In contrast, when Gaussian filters are used, the predictions are smooth with either big or small total stride.

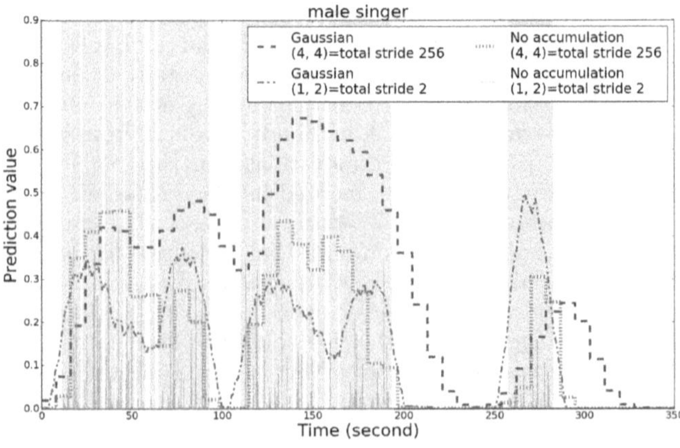

Figure 3: Smoothing effect of accumulation layers for a music piece from MedlyDB. We show the frame-level predictions of four models with final max-pooling. The micro F1 scores achieved by the four settings (Gaussian, stride 2), (Gaussian, stride 256), (No accumulation, stride 2) and (No accumulation, stride 256) are 0.658, 0.601, 0.158, and 0.601, respectively. This is the music piece entitled Alexander-Ross_GoodbyeBolero in the MedlyDB dataset.

Table 2: Effect of thresholds for frame-level predictions. Thresholds are derived either from MedleyDB or MagnaTagATune. "Early conv." refers to the number of layers in early convolutions.

Final pooling	Early conv.	Threshold source	Precision		Rrecall		F1	
			Micro	Macro	Micro	Macro	Micro	Macro
Max	2	MedleyDB	0.530	0.523	0.830	0.806	**0.647**	**0.617**
		MagnaTagATune	0.554	0.506	0.150	0.215	0.236	0.241
	3	MedleyDB	0.462	0.447	0.916	0.883	**0.614**	**0.578**
		MagnaTagATune	0.546	0.566	0.182	0.245	0.273	0.261
Mean	2	MedleyDB	0.561	0.539	0.846	0.791	**0.675**	**0.633**
		MagnaTagATune	0.606	0.489	0.221	0.273	0.324	0.300
	3	MedleyDB	0.498	0.474	0.888	0.844	**0.638**	**0.594**
		MagnaTagATune	0.530	0.540	0.183	0.244	0.273	0.258

Table 3: Accumulation layers. The models either use no accumulation, use accumulation with Gaussian of fixed σs, or use accumulation with Gaussian of adaptive σs. 50 classes for clip-level and 9 classes for frame-level

Final pooling	Early conv.	Accum. (Gaussian)	Frame level F1		Clip level Average AUC	
			Per-class	Per-clip	Micro	Macro
Max	2	None	0.401	0.313	0.878	0.922
		Fixed	**0.654**	0.606	**0.891**	0.928
		Adaptive	0.647	**0.617**	**0.891**	**0.931**
	3	None	0.601	0.525	0.885	0.925
		Fixed	**0.648**	**0.621**	0.886	0.926
		Adaptive	0.614	0.578	**0.894**	**0.930**
Mean	2	None	0.557	0.509	0.893	0.931
		Fixed	0.595	0.558	**0.894**	**0.932**
		Adaptive	**0.675**	**0.633**	0.893	0.931
	3	None	0.591	0.533	**0.896**	0.930
		Fixed	**0.651**	**0.606**	0.894	**0.931**
		Adaptive	0.638	0.594	0.891	0.929

Table 4: Effect of multi-scale inputs. Inputs of 1 scale, 3 scales, or 6 scales are experimented.

Early conv.	# of inputs	F1		Average AUC	
		Micro	Macro	Per-class	Per-clip
2	1	0.605	0.585	0.882	0.921
	3	0.628	0.608	0.892	0.930
	6	**0.675**	**0.633**	**0.893**	**0.931**
3	1	0.628	0.585	0.884	0.922
	3	**0.642**	**0.606**	**0.892**	0.928
	6	0.638	0.594	0.891	**0.929**

5.5 Effect of Multi-scale Input

We compare the performance of input of one scale (window size=1024), inputs of 3 scales (window sizes={1024, 4096, 16384}), and inputs of 6 scales (window sizes={512, 1024, 2048, 4096, 8192, 16384}). We can see in Table 4 that the multi-scale inputs yield better results than input of a single scale. 6 scales yield the best results at either clip-level or frame-level, so we will use 6 scales in all the remaining experiments. We only show the results with adaptive Gaussian in Table 4 due to space limit, but the pattern also holds with fixed Gaussian.

5.6 Resolution and Performance Trade-off

The issue of trade-off between clip-level performance and frame-level performance with CNNs is known in other fields. It has been pointed out [1] that "the pooling and sampling may affect label localization through time because it decreases time resolution for higher CNN layers" in the context of speech recognition. It also happens in visual object recognition [6]: "There is a natural trade-off between classification accuracy and localization accuracy with convolutional networks: Deeper models with multiple max-pooling layers have proven most successful in classification tasks, however their increased invariance and large receptive fields make the problem of inferring position from the scores at their top output levels more."

We can also see this effect in music auto-tagging from our experiments. By controlling the number of early convolution layers, we also control the total stride size, which determines the resolution of the output. We can see a pattern in Table 5. When we use Gaussian for the accumulation layer, the clip-level performance improves as the total stride size increase while the frame-level performance gets worse. On the other hand, when we do not use accumulation, the performance of both clip-level and frame-level get worse as the total stride increases. The pattern of the performance without Gaussian follows our observation in the Section 5.4 that frame-level predictions would be more difficult without accumulation.

5.7 Effect of Final Pooling Functions

We tested two pooling functions for the final layer, mean-pooling and max-pooling. From Table 5, there is no obvious advantage over the other using max and mean pooling. However, in principle, max pooling should be used if the training data have different durations to have comparable outputs.

5.8 Learned Parameters of Gaussian Filters

We show in Figure 4 the standard deviation σs of the Gaussian filters for the top 50 popular classes. The parameters shown here are taken from the model with the best frame-level performance, the one presented in Section 5.2. The x-axis is the number of training samples in the training data, and the y-axis is the learned σs. The first thing we notice visually is a downward trend as the number of training data increases. Indeed, the Pearson's correlation coefficient between σs and the number of training data is -0.442, so they are moderately linearly correlated. The linear regression line is also shown in Figure 4 with green dashed line.

Even though they are linearly correlated to some degree, the number of training data is not the only factor affecting

Table 5: Effect of different total stride sizes. The total stride is related the resolution of the CNN. The larger the total stride, the worse the output resolution. We control the total stride by controlling the number of early convolutional layers.

Accumulation	Final pooling	(stride, # of early conv layers)	total stride	F1 Micro	F1 Macro	Average AUC Per-class	Average AUC Per-clip
None	Max	(4, 1)	4	0.189	0.141	0.872	0.915
		(4, 2)	16	0.401	0.313	0.878	0.922
		(4, 3)	64	**0.601**	0.525	**0.885**	**0.925**
		(4, 4)	256	**0.601**	**0.554**	0.885	0.923
	Mean	(4, 1)	4	0.488	0.463	0.886	0.926
		(4, 2)	16	0.557	0.509	0.893	**0.931**
		(4, 3)	64	0.591	0.533	**0.896**	0.930
		(4, 4)	256	**0.614**	**0.562**	0.889	0.926
Adaptive Gaussian	Max	(4, 1)	4	**0.658**	**0.637**	0.887	0.926
		(4, 2)	16	0.647	0.617	0.891	**0.931**
		(4, 3)	64	0.614	0.578	**0.894**	0.930
		(4, 4)	256	0.601	0.541	0.889	0.926
	Mean	(4, 1)	4	0.650	0.628	0.885	0.925
		(4, 2)	16	**0.675**	**0.633**	**0.893**	**0.931**
		(4, 3)	64	0.638	0.594	0.891	0.929
		(4, 4)	256	0.600	0.540	0.891	0.926

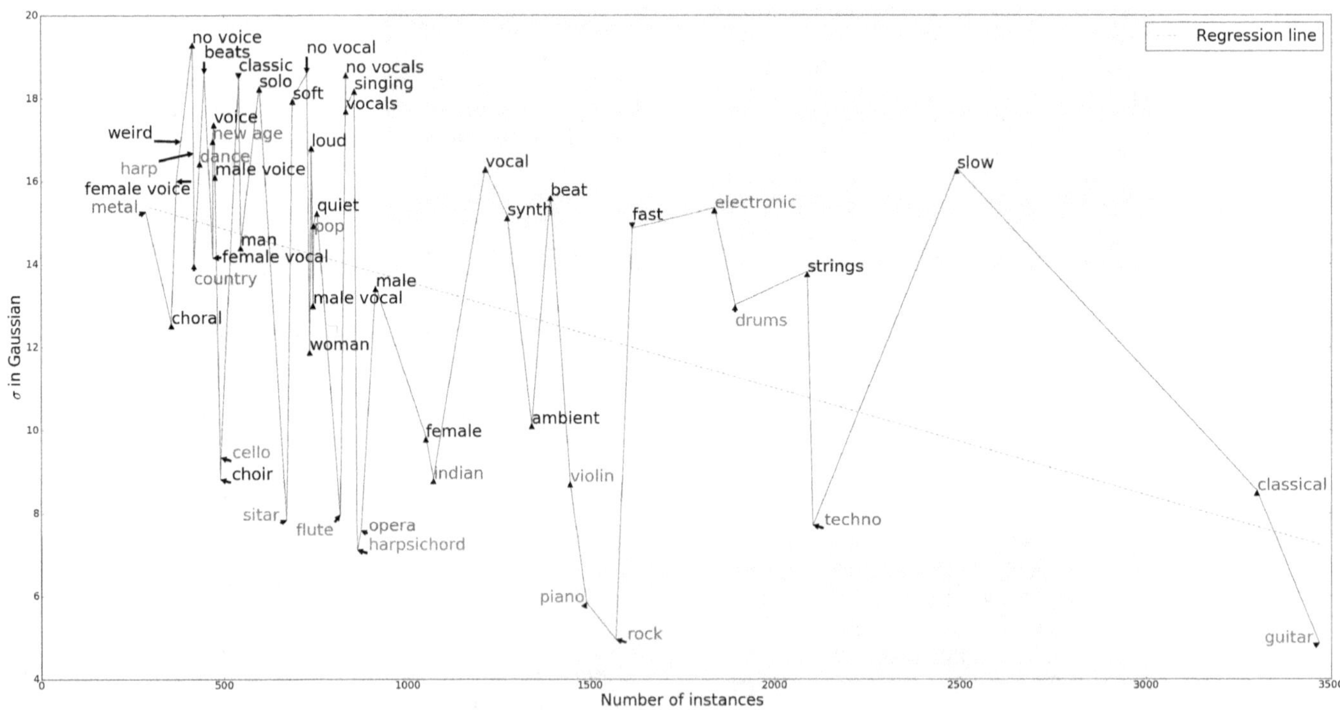

Figure 4: The standard deviation σ in Gaussian filter. x-axis is the number of instances in the training data, and y-axis is the quantity of σ of the classes after training. Instrument tags are in red color, and genre tags are in purple. The green dashed line is the linear regression line of the points on the image.

σs. The labels in red color are instruments, and the labels in purple color are genres. We can see that the σs of instruments are in general smaller than the σs of genres. This verifies our intuition that the instruments require smaller durations of time for recognition while genres are more complex so require larger durations for recognition. We can also see that the tempo-related tags, "fast" and "slow," and the negation tags, "no vocal" and "no vocals," have larger σs, which makes sense because recognition of tempo and determining the non-existence of properties requires longer duration.

Another thing one may wonder is whether these learned parameters could be somewhat random. We observed that the learned parameters from models with varied total stride sizes show similar patterns. To see this quantitatively, we compute the Pearson's correlation coefficient between σs of the top 50 tags from different models. First, the correlation coefficients between σs from the best model and σs from its counterparts of (stride size, # of early conv. layers)=(4, 1), (4, 3), and (4, 4) are 0.990, 0.957, and 0.924, respectively. Second, the correlation coefficient between σs from the best

Table 6: The performance of models trained directly with frame-level annotations. The number under "late layers" represents the number of units used in a layer. If two numbers are present, there are two layers.

Frame model	Precision		Recall		F1	
late layers	Micro	Macro	Micro	Macro	Micro	Macro
128	0.572	0.481	0.627	0.549	0.598	0.471
512	0.565	0.485	0.632	0.548	0.597	0.469
128, 128	0.571	0.480	0.617	0.540	0.593	0.468
512, 512	0.560	0.478	0.634	0.555	0.595	0.471

model and σs from its counterpart using max as final pooling is 0.958. The σs are highly correlated between different models. This result together with the observation from last paragraph suggests that the patterns are not random.

5.9 Comparing with Frame-to-Frame training

We compare our model with a model trained directly with frame-level annotations from MedleyDB. We build neural networks (CNN with pooling_window=1) to conduct frame-to-frame training. We further separate 80% of clips from the validation set in MedleyDB as the training set. The results are shown in Table 6. Our proposed model significantly outperforms these frame-to-frame models (one-tailed t-test on macro F1 with 0.05 significance level).

There are several possible reasons for this counter-intuitive result. First, frame-to-frame training is itself a complex research problem, the models tested here might not be optimal and might not be the best structure. Second, despite of the large number of frames for training, the number of unique clips in the training set is small. In the training set, the number of clips in each class is from 5 to 24 (13 clips per class in average). Furthermore, we have divided the MedleyDB data in a more strict way such that the artists in the training set and the artists in the test set do not overlapping. Therefore, the networks do not see enough data for generalization. In contrast, in MagnaTagATune, the number of clips in each class is from 37 to 1,892 (779 clips per class in average). This conjecture is also supported by the observation that there is a big gap between the validation loss and training loss (training loss is much smaller than validation loss) during the training phase even though we have used dropout and used smaller hidden layers.

This indicates that the clip-to-frame training scheme we propose could be a more realistic solution to this problem.

6. VISUALIZATION OF THE FRAME-LEVEL PREDICTIONS

In this section, we visualize the frame-level predictions from the best frame-level model to subjectively evaluate the frame-level prediction. We show examples from the test data of the two datasets. The pre-accumulation layer in the figures refers to the layer right before the accumulation layer.

6.1 MedleyDB

Examples are shown in Figure 5. The examples in Figure 5a and 5b have good frame-level predictions and the threshold cuts at roughly the right place. The pre-accumulation output in Figure 5c looks reasonable, but the threshold cuts at a wrong place. The Figure 5d example has totally wrong frame-level prediction visually. By listening to the audio, we realize that the activated parts predicted by our model are in fact also electric guitar but are distorted electric guitar, not clean electric guitar. In MagnaTagATune, there is "electric guitar" tag but there is no distinction between distorted and clean electric guitar. We have used the output dimension of "electric guitar" in MagnaTagATune for evaluating frame-level "clean electric guitar" in MedleyDB. In MagnaTagATune, there might be less clean electric guitar and more distorted electric guitar, so the model does not recognize the sound of clean electric guitar.

6.2 MagnaTagATune

We show one example from MagnaTagATune test data in Figure 6. Figure 6a is the predictions derived from the accumulation layer, and Figure 6b is the predictions from the pre-accumulation layer. By listening to the original clip, we can know that there is a man talking from 0 to 4 seconds, and then drums appear. Electrical guitar starts from 8 seconds and the drums continue. At this point, it starts to sound like a rock song. That is why we see the pattern in the figure. Even though "rock" is a genre tag which is usually annotated on the whole clip, we can also consider it as a music event that only exists in some parts of the music.

7. DISCUSSION AND CONCLUSION

In this paper, we have proposed a model that can make frame-level predictions with only clip-level annotations in the training phase. The result demonstrates that this weakly-supervised learning approach for music event localization is possible, and it achieves 0.675 micro F1 score evaluated on MedleyDB. We found that the accumulation layer implemented with Gaussian filter can help improve the frame-level prediction and it also captures the characteristics of the music events.

The initial σs may require more experimentation in the future. Observing the downward trend with the number of training data in Figure 4, it is possible that the initial σs are too large. If the initial is too small or too large, it is difficult for classes with fewer data to learn good σs.

The number and diversity of the training dataset is an important issue. We have argued in Section 5.9 that the frame-to-frame training might not yield better result than our approach because the training data used by the frame-to-frame training is not diverse enough. In addition, we also observed in Section 6.1 that the training data are also not diverse enough to include different types of electric guitar sounds even with our approach. This indicates that it is necessary to collect more diverse data in order to further improve the frame-level performance.

8. REFERENCES

[1] O. Abdel-Hamid, L. Deng, and D. Yu. Exploring convolutional neural network structures and optimization techniques for speech recognition. In *Proc. INTERSPEECH*, pages 3366–3370, 2013.

[2] O. Abdel-Hamid, A. r. Mohamed, H. Jiang, L. Deng, G. Penn, and D. Yu. Convolutional neural networks for speech recognition. *IEEE/ACM TASLP*, 22(10):1533–1545, Oct 2014.

[3] F. Bastien, P. Lamblin, R. Pascanu, J. Bergstra, I. J. Goodfellow, A. Bergeron, N. Bouchard, and Y. Bengio. Theano: new features and speed

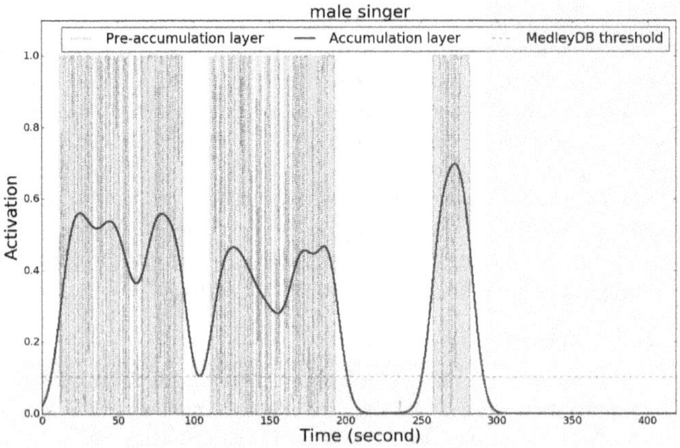

(a) Good. "male singer" from AlexanderRoss_GoodbyeBolero

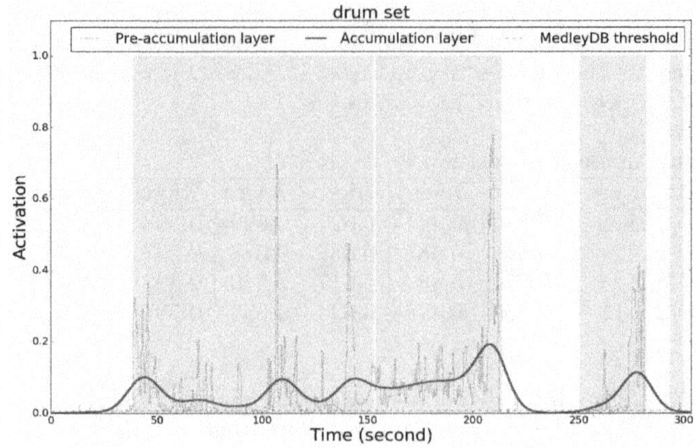

(b) Good. "drum set" from TheScarletBrand_LesFleursDuMal

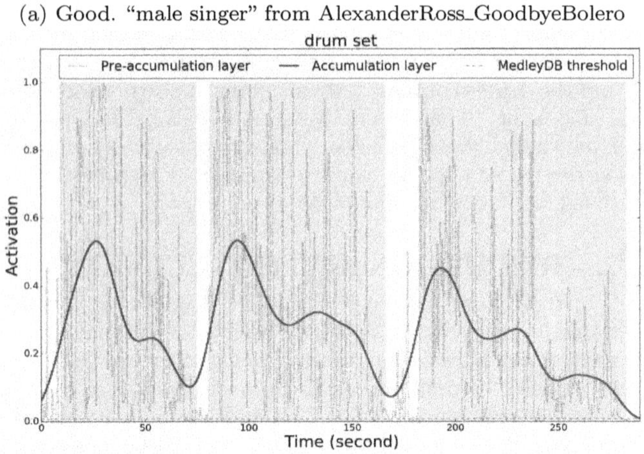

(c) Bad. "drum set" from StevenClark_Bounty

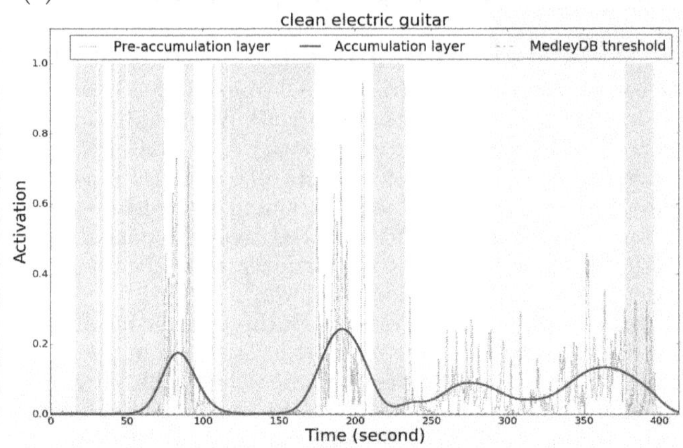

(d) Bad. "clean electric guitar" from Meaxic_YouListen

Figure 5: Visualization of frame-level predictions on MedleyDB test data. Two examples of good frame-level predictions and two of bad frame-level predictions are shown.

improvements. Deep Learning and Unsupervised Feature Learning NIPS 2012 Workshop, 2012.

[4] J. Bergstra, O. Breuleux, F. Bastien, P. Lamblin, R. Pascanu, G. Desjardins, J. Turian, D. Warde-Farley, and Y. Bengio. Theano: a CPU and GPU math expression compiler. In *Proc. the Python for Scientific Computing Conference (SciPy)*, June 2010. http://deeplearning.net/software/theano/.

[5] R. M. Bittner, J. Salamon, M. Tierney, M. Mauch, C. Cannam, and J. P. Bello. Medleydb: A multitrack dataset for annotation-intensive mir research. In *Proc. ISMIR*, pages 155–160, 2014. http://medleydb.weebly.com.

[6] L.-C. Chen, G. Papandreou, I. Kokkinos, K. Murphy, and A. L. Yuille. Semantic image segmentation with deep convolutional nets and fully connected crfs. *arXiv preprint arXiv:1412.7062*, 2014.

[7] S. Dieleman and B. Schrauwen. Multiscale approaches to music audio feature learning. In *Proc. ISMIR*, pages 116–121, 2013.

[8] S. Dieleman and B. Schrauwen. End-to-end learning for music audio. In *Proc. ICASSP*, pages 6964–6968, May 2014.

[9] D. Eck, P. Lamere, S. Green, and T. Bertin-Mahieux. Automatic generation of social tags for music recommendation. In *Proc. NIPS*, pages 1–8, 2007.

[10] S. Essid, G. Richard, and B. David. Instrument recognition in polyphonic music based on automatic taxonomies. *IEEE TASLP*, 14(1):68–80, jan 2006.

[11] P. F. Felzenszwalb, R. B. Girshick, D. McAllester, and D. Ramanan. Object detection with discriminatively trained part-based models. *IEEE TPAMI*, 32(9):1627–1645, 2010.

[12] J. S. Garofolo, L. F. Lamel, W. M. Fisher, J. G. Fiscus, and D. S. Pallett. Darpa timit acoustic phonetic continuous speech corpus. 1993. *US Dept. of Commerce, NIST, Gaithersburg, USA.*

[13] R. Girshick, J. Donahue, T. Darrell, and J. Malik. Rich feature hierarchies for accurate object detection and semantic segmentation. In *Proc. CVPR*, pages 580–587, 2014.

[14] A. Graves. *Supervised Sequence Labelling with Recurrent Neural Networks*, volume 385 of *Studies in Computational Intelligence*. Springer, 2012.

[15] P. Hamel, S. Lemieux, Y. Bengio, and D. Eck. Temporal pooling and multiscale learning for automatic annotation and ranking of music audio. In *Proc. ISMIR*, pages 729–734, 2011.

[16] M. Henaff, K. Jarrett, K. Kavukcuoglu, and

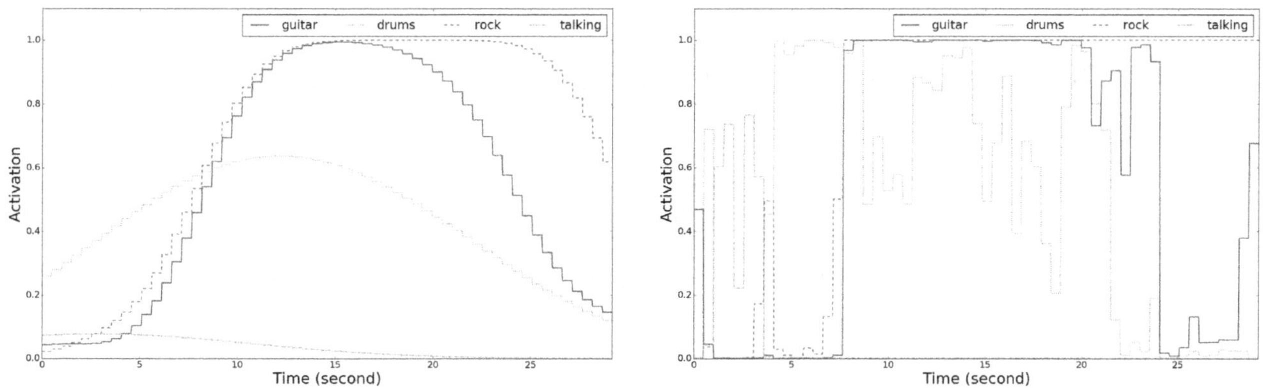

(a) Accumulation

(b) Pre-accumulation

Figure 6: Visualization of frame-level predictions on MagnaTagATune test data. They show predictions of four tags annotated on the clip. The outputs from accumulation layer and from pre-accumulation layer are shown. Both of them are from the same model. Title: jackalopes-jacksploitation-04-kentucky_applejack-0-29.

Y. LeCun. Unsupervised learning of sparse features for scalable audio classification. In *Proc. ISMIR*, pages 681–686, 2011.

[17] G. Hinton, L. Deng, D. Yu, G. E. Dahl, A.-r. Mohamed, N. Jaitly, A. Senior, V. Vanhoucke, P. Nguyen, T. N. Sainath, et al. Deep neural networks for acoustic modeling in speech recognition: The shared views of four research groups. *IEEE Signal Processing Magazine*, 29(6):82–97, 2012.

[18] E. J. Humphrey, J. P. Bello, and Y. LeCun. Moving beyond feature design: Deep architectures and automatic feature learning in music informatics. In *Proc. ISMIR*, pages 403–408, 2012.

[19] A. Karpathy, G. Toderici, S. Shetty, T. Leung, R. Sukthankar, and L. Fei-Fei. Large-scale video classification with convolutional neural networks. In *Proc. CVPR*, 2014.

[20] A. Krizhevsky, I. Sutskever, and G. E. Hinton. Imagenet classification with deep convolutional neural networks. In *Proc. NIPS*, pages 1097–1105, 2012.

[21] E. Law, K. West, M. I. Mandel, M. Bay, and J. S. Downie. Evaluation of algorithms using games: The case of music tagging. In *Proc. ISMIR*, 2009. http://mirg.city.ac.uk/codeapps/the-magnatagatune-dataset.

[22] M. Mandel, D. Eck, and Y. Bengio. Learning tags that vary within a song. *Proc. ISMIR*, pages 399–404, 2010.

[23] M. I. Mandel and D. P. Ellis. A Web-Based Game for Collecting Music Metadata. *Journal of New Music Research*, 37(2):151–165, 2008.

[24] M. I. Mandel, R. Pascanu, D. Eck, Y. Bengio, L. M. Aiello, R. Schifanella, and F. Menczer. Contextual tag inference. *ACM TOMCCAP*, 7S(1):1–18, oct 2011.

[25] J. Masci, A. Giusti, D. Ciresan, G. Fricout, and J. Schmidhuber. A fast learning algorithm for image segmentation with max-pooling convolutional networks. In *Proc. ICIP*, pages 2713–2717, 2013.

[26] B. McFee, M. McVicar, C. Raffel, D. Liang, O. Nieto, E. Battenberg, J. Moore, D. Ellis, R. Yamamoto, R. Bittner, D. Repetto, P. Viktorin, J. F. Santos, and A. Holovaty. librosa: 0.4.1, Oct. 2015.

[27] J. Nam, J. Herrera, M. Slaney, and J. O. Smith. Learning sparse feature representations for music annotation and retrieval. In *Proc. ISMIR*, pages 565–570, 2012.

[28] M. Oquab, L. Bottou, I. Laptev, and J. Sivic. Is object localization for free?-weakly-supervised learning with convolutional neural networks. In *Proc. CVPR*, pages 685–694, 2015.

[29] G. Papandreou, L.-C. Chen, K. P. Murphy, and A. L. Yuille. Weakly-and semi-supervised learning of a deep convolutional network for semantic image segmentation. In *Proc. ICCV*, pages 1742–1750, 2015.

[30] G. Parascandolo, H. Huttunen, and T. Virtanen. Recurrent Neural Networks for Polyphonic Sound Event Detection In Real Life Recordings. In *Proc. ICASSP*, 2016.

[31] D. Pathak, E. Shelhamer, J. Long, and T. Darrell. Fully convolutional multi-class multiple instance learning. *arXiv preprint arXiv:1412.7144*, 2014.

[32] P. O. Pinheiro and R. Collobert. Recurrent convolutional neural networks for scene labeling. In *Proc. ICML*, pages 82–90, 2014.

[33] P. O. Pinheiro and R. Collobert. From image-level to pixel-level labeling with convolutional networks. In *Proc. CVPR*, pages 1713–1721, 2015.

[34] K. Simonyan and A. Zisserman. Two-stream convolutional networks for action recognition in videos. In *Proc. NIPS*, pages 568–576. 2014.

[35] D. Tingle, Y. E. Kim, and D. Turnbull. Exploring automatic music annotation with acoustically-objective tags. In *Proc. ICMR*, pages 55–61, 2010.

[36] D. Turnbull, L. Barrington, D. Torres, and G. Lanckriet. Semantic annotation and retrieval of music and sound effects. *IEEE TASLP*, 16(2):467–476, feb 2008.

[37] S.-Y. Wang, J.-C. W. Y.-H. Yang, and H.-M. Wang. Towards time-varying music auto-tagging based on cal500 expansion. In *Proc. ICME*, pages 1–6, 2014.

[38] Z. Xu, Y. Yang, and A. G. Hauptmann. A discriminative cnn video representation for event detection. In *Proc. CVPR*, 2015.

Face Recognition via Active Annotation and Learning

Hao Ye[1]*, Weiyuan Shao[1]*, Hong Wang[1]*, Jianqi Ma[2],
Li Wang[2], Yingbin Zheng[1]†, Xiangyang Xue[2]
[1]Shanghai Advanced Research Institute, Chinese Academy of Sciences, Shanghai, China
[2]School of Computer Science, Fudan University, Shanghai, China

ABSTRACT

In this paper, we introduce an active annotation and learning framework for the face recognition task. Starting with an initial label deficient face image training set, we iteratively train a deep neural network and use this model to choose the examples for further manual annotation. We follow the active learning strategy and derive the Value of Information criterion to actively select candidate annotation images. During these iterations, the deep neural network is incrementally updated. Experimental results conducted on LFW benchmark and MS-Celeb-1M challenge demonstrate the effectiveness of our proposed framework.

Keywords

Face recognition; active image annotation; deep learning; MSR image recognition challenge

1. INTRODUCTION

With the development of deep learning approaches, face recognition system based on neural networks achieve great improvement on performance as well as the recognition robustness. According to recent progress of deep network applications on computer vision tasks, deeper networks can boost the performance [1, 20, 23, 6]. In order to avoid overfitting, larger amount of training images are usually needed. Moreover, precise annotations of the training images can carry more supervised information and benefit the results of deep networks. Particularly for face recognition tasks, information such as face localization, landmark points, and pose may influence the detection and recognition performance. Therefore, constructing a large-scale fine-annotated face dataset and building face models upon it become very important steps towards a successful face recognition system.

*These authors contributed equally to this work.
†Corresponding author. E-mail: zhengyb@sari.ac.cn

MM '16, October 15-19, 2016, Amsterdam, Netherlands

 ISBN 978-1-4503-3603-1/16/10...$15.00
DOI: http://dx.doi.org/10.1145/2964284.2984059

Recently, many public datasets for face recognition are released and promote a significant amount of progress for face detection and recognition tasks. For instance, the CASIA-WebFace dataset [26] contains more than 400,000 images and 10,000 celebrities, VGG Face dataset [16] is with 2.6 million images and 2,600 celebrities, and MS-Celeb-1M dataset [5] has more than 10 million images and 100,000 celebrities. These datasets were collected from the search engines such as Bing and Google. Due to the massive quantities, the images are usually without further filtering and preprocessing. The influence of these insufficient preprocessing includes two aspects. Firstly, the noisy dataset with incorrect annotations and low quality images may imperil the correctness of model training and reduce the accuracy for recognition. On the other hand, multimodal information such as landmark points and regions are proved to be an important cue [3]; however, the public datasets lack of these kind of annotations.

Manually annotation of a large dataset with detail information such as celebrity label, face location, landmark points and other attributes are infeasible. Various data augmentation approaches are designed to enrich the information and overcome the deficiency of annotated data. [15] employed 3-D alignments to get images with extra face pose and landmark points information. However, it is difficult to extend the celebrity popularity, which leads to the lack of diversity of training samples. Another strategy is to combine several small or partial annotated datasets through multi-task strategy to simulate the larger dataset (e.g. [27]). Although it can alleviate the shortage of data and annotation, this method lacks flexibility to adapt itself to new dataset since each task is designed based on specific dataset.

In this paper, we propose an active annotation and learning framework to handle the training of face recognition models on large-scale dataset with noisy data and insufficient annotations. We design an active sampling strategy and employ the iterative training methods to update the face model. The advantages of active annotation system are in two folds. First, the framework is effective and efficient in sampling hard negative examples which saves costs of annotation. Comparing with the large amount of entire dataset, we only annotate a small subset of the whole dataset and the recognition system can also achieve high performance. Second, the framework is quite flexible - not only new images but also new attributes can be annotated, as the framework is incremental and new annotation tasks can be added at the end of each iteration. The experimental results on face

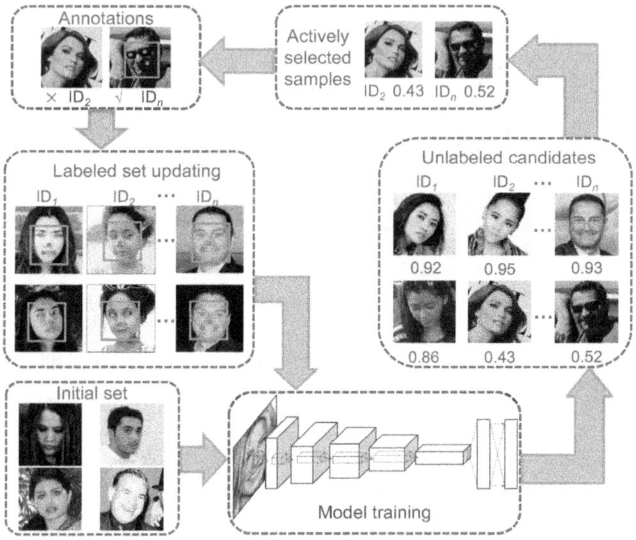

Figure 1: Our face annotation and recognition framework.

recognition benchmarks demonstrate the effectiveness and applicability of our framework.

The remainder of this paper is organized as follows. Section 2 reviews the related work on task of image annotation and face recognition. Section 3 describes our proposed framework. In Section 4, we demonstrate the quantitative study on two face recognition benchmarks. And finally, we conclude our work in Section 5.

2. RELATED WORKS

Constructing a large-scale face dataset requires a lot of time and efforts. Google has built a massive dataset which includes 200 million face identities and 800 million image faces [18], but it is a private dataset. [26] proposed a semi-automatical way to collect 494,414 face images from internet and build the CASIA-WebFace dataset. [12] released the MegaFace dataset, which includes 1 million images and 690,000 identities. Very recently, Microsoft Research provided a face dataset involving 100,000 identities and 10 million images, which is the largest open face dataset to the best of our knowledge [5].

Active learning has gained attention in the field of large-scale image annotation. [7] employed the multi-label active learning engine to automatically select and manually annotate a set of unlabeled sample-label pairs, and then the classifier is updated by taking these newly annotated pairs. [17] integrated machine and human as a loop for object detection annotation and validated on ILSVRC 2014 detection task empirically. [2] proposed an active learning algorithm to measure the sample uncertainty where the density and diversity of the sample were determined simultaneously. [21] introduced a criterion that propagates the human correlation on selected samples over a gradually-augmented graph. [19] used an automatic selection method to automatically choose a small number of hard negative examples which made the training effective and efficient.

3. FRAMEWORK

We now elaborate the construction of our framework, which consists of initial model training, active sampling, and iterative model training. Figure 1 illustrates the architecture of the framework and the details of each phase will be described in the following subsections.

Figure 2: Examples of the noisy images. Left: low resolution; Middle: blur; Right: animation.

3.1 Data Preprocessing

Before we dive into the framework, a data preprocessing step is applied on the original dataset. As the amount of face image increases, some noisy images are inevitably mixed in the dataset, such as low-resolution images, blur images and animation images; examples of these images are illustrated in Figure 2. Although the deep network model has the ability of fault tolerance to a certain extent, the accuracy of the recognition system is affected by these noisy data. Thus, filtering the noisy data out of dataset is necessary and considered as the preprocessing step. Therefore we implement noisy detection tools based on OpenCV [9] to detect these kinds of noisy images.

3.2 Initial Model Training

Our face recognition pipeline includes face detection and landmark point localization, face alignment and transformations, and recognition based on deep network. Considering our main purpose is to inspect the effectiveness of active annotation scheme on recognition, we take the off-the-shelf toolkit dlib [13] for face detection and landmark point localization, as most existing face datasets lack such annotations. Images with detected faces are considered as the initial model training set.

We perform the alignment and transformation operations when corresponding facial landmark points in each face are obtained. Considering the time complexity, we select in-plane 2D alignment method which only use 5 landmark points (i.e., nose, left eye, right eye, left mouth, and right mouth) to align the face image. Then we align and transform the faces based on the landmark points to weaken the influence from the pose variation and augment the versatility of faces.

The deep network architecture of face recognition model is shown in Figure 3. The input of the network is $X=\{(x_1,y_1), (x_2,y_2), ..., (x_n, y_n)\}$, where x_i is the face image after align transformation and y_i is the corresponding identity. We follow the network architecture of lighted CNN [25], which consists of 9 convolutional layers (conv) and 2 fully connected layers (fc). Maxout [4] is used as the active function, and cross entropy loss as the supervisory signal.

3.3 Active Sampling

With the trained deep models, the next step is to actively sample images for annotation. The goal of active sampling is to minimize human interventions. We extend the value of information (VOI) strategy proposed in [11] and derived a value function to choose the instance for annotation.

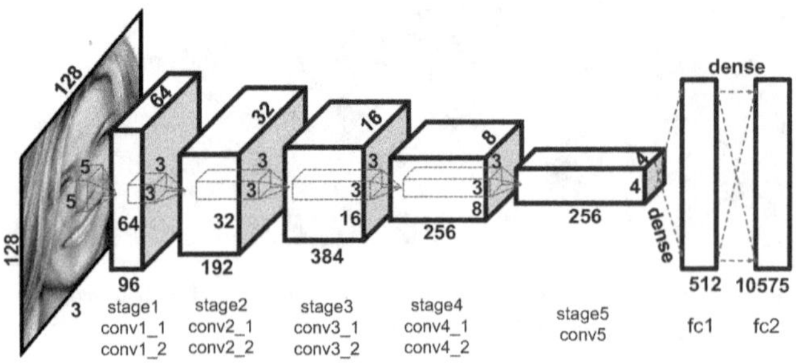

Figure 3: Network design for face recognition.

Each dataset image is with an initial identity, as all of them are gathered from the web using the identity name as keyword. If the image is classified into the same identity, we consider it as a positive instance; otherwise it is negative. The dataset includes unlabeled set X_U and labeled set X_L; both of them are composed of positive instances X_p and negative instances X_n. The risk associated with misclassifying a positive example as negative is denoted by r_p, and r_n for misclassifying a negative. The risk associated with the annotated examples is:

$$Risk(X_L) = \sum_{x_i \in X_p} r_p(1 - p(x_i)) + \sum_{x_i \in X_n} r_n p(x_i), \quad (1)$$

where $p(x)$ denotes the probability of positive prediction, here we use the softmax of the confidence from the network. The corresponding risk for unlabeled examples is:

$$\begin{aligned} Risk(X_U) = \sum_{x_i \in X_U} & [r_p(1 - p(x_i)\Pr(y_i|x_i) \\ & + r_n p(x_i)(1 - \Pr(y_i|x_i))], \end{aligned} \quad (2)$$

where y_i is the true identity label. We approximate the probability as $\Pr(y_i|x_i) \approx p(x_i)$ which lead to a simplifier equation:

$$Risk(X_U) = \sum_{x_i \in X_U} (r_p + r_u)(1 - p(x_i))p(x_i) \quad (3)$$

The total cost associate with the data is the total risk in addition with the cost of annotation,

$$T(X_L, X_U) = Risk(X_L) + Risk(X_U) + \mathcal{C}(X_p) + \mathcal{C}(X_n), \quad (4)$$

where $\mathcal{C}$ is the cost of obtaining the annotations. We ignored $\mathcal{C}$ in our experiments under the assumption that the cost of obtaining annotations for each example is the same. The expected risk of candidate samples for annotation can be calculated by:

$$\begin{aligned} VOI(S) &= T(X_L, X_U) - T(X_L \cup S, X_U \setminus S) \\ &= Risk(X_L) + Risk(X_U) \\ &\quad - (Risk(X_L \cup S) + Risk(X_U \setminus S)) \end{aligned} \quad (5)$$

where S denotes the candidate sampling examples for manual annotation. According the above strategy, the high value indicates large gains and thus our strategy is to choose candidates S with highest VOI for labeling.

3.4 Iterative Training Scheme

The samples selected are then used for the manual annotation; the annotation of both bounding box and 5 landmark points are required. If the annotator confirms an image without its original identity, this image will be removed from the updating set, meanwhile, the positive images with their manually annotation are added into the updating dataset. The deep network is incrementally updated, using the fine-tuning strategy. With the precision level of the annotation, the number of active sampling is gradually decreasing whereas the recognition becomes more robust and accurate. We stop the iterative training when the VOI of the unlabeled images are below a threshold and thus no new samples are selected.

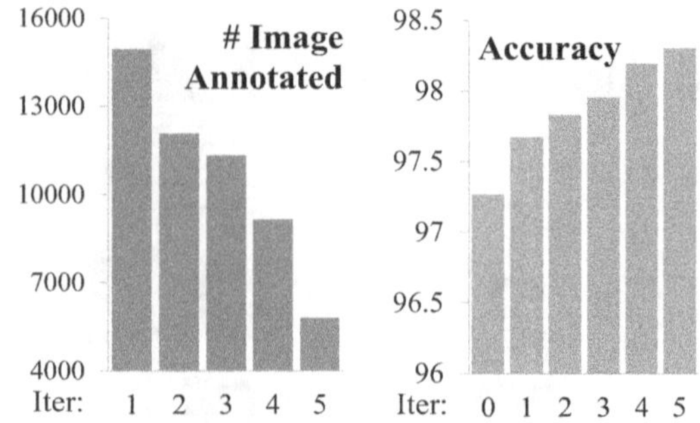

Figure 4: Active sampling image number and performance of LFW after each iteration.

Approach	#Nets	Accuracy
WebFace [26]	1	97.73%
Lightened CNN [25]	1	98.13%
Face Search [24]	7	98.23%
MM-DFR-JB [3]	1	98.43%
Ours	1	98.30%

Table 1: Comparison with previous works using CASIA-WebFace for training.

3.5 Application of Face Models

At any stage of our framework, the deep network can be applied for the face recognition task. As mentioned in previous works (e.g. [22]), if the network can discriminate large number of individuals, the feature from the fully connected layer is a good representation in face recognition task. For an input image, after face detection and alignment, a 512-dimensional deep feature from the response of fc1 is extracted and used as the representation. Finally, we use cosine distance as the similarity metric on the representation and k-Nearest Neighbor classifier for face recognition.

4. EVALUATION

Our framework is based on the annotation and training of the CASIA-WebFace dataset [26]. It contains about 494,414 images with 10,575 individuals, and is a large public available face recognition dataset. The deep network is trained on Caffe [10] and the initial network is trained on an NVIDIA GTX Titan X GPU for about 60 hours.

4.1 LFW

We first evaluate our method in the Labeled Faces in the Wild (LFW) benchmark [8], which is the most popular benchmark for face recognition task. The dataset contains 13,233 face images with 5,749 individuals, and our ex-

(a) Random set (b) Hard set

Figure 5: Examples of dry run images in MS-Celeb-1M.

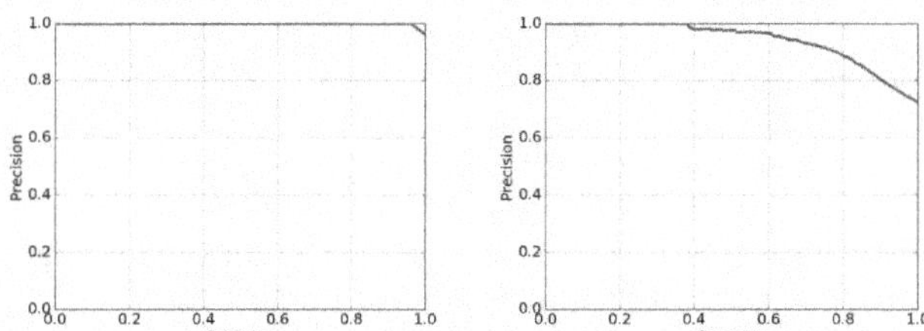

(a) Random set (b) Hard set

Figure 6: The Precision-Coverage curve of our system for the dry run.

periments follow the unrestricted settings which allow using external data in the training period.

In order to test the effectiveness of active sampling, the deep models after each iteration are saved and the corresponding features of the LFW images are extracted and used for the benchmark. Figure 4 illustrates the number of active sampling images from CASIA-WebFace and accuracy of LFW after each iteration. Comparing with the image number of the whole CASIA-WebFace dataset, only about 10% of them are actively sampled for annotation. We also notice that the sampling images in each iteration reduce, while the performance of our deep model improves sustainingly. Table 1 compares our method with previous approaches which are also trained using CASIA-WebFace. The performance of our model reaches the same magnitude of these methods.

4.2 MS-Celeb-1M

We also participate in MSR Image Recognition 2016 Challenge[1]. MS-Celeb-1M [5] is a large scale real world face image dataset to public, encouraging researchers to develop the best face recognition techniques to recognize one million people entities identified from Freebase. In its V1.0 version, the dataset contains 10 million celebrity face images for the top 100,000 celebrities, which can be used to train and evaluate both face identification and verification algorithms. And the dataset provides approximately 100 images for each celebrity, resulting in about 10 million web images. Current dataset only covers 75% of celebrities, which implies that the upper bound of recognition recall rate cannot exceed 75%.

The measurement set samples 1000 celebrities from the 1 million set, which indicates that the remaining 25% celebrities may also appear. To match with real scenarios, the evaluation system will measure the recognition recall at a given precision 95%. For N images in the measurement set, if an algorithm recognizes M images, among which C images are correct, the precision and coverage will be calculated as: $Precision = \frac{C}{M}$, $Coverage = \frac{M}{N}$.

[1]https://www.microsoft.com/en-us/research/project/ms-celeb-1m-challenge-recognizing-one-million-celebrities-real-world/

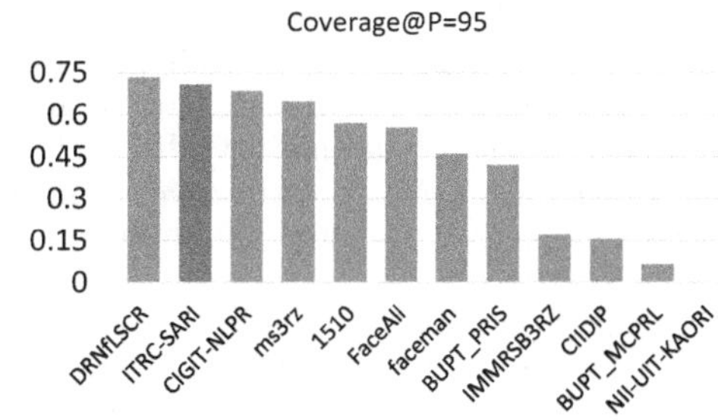

Figure 7: The evaluation performance of our system in MS-Celeb-1M benchmark.

There are two tracks in the Challenge: Random set and Hard set; examples of both sets are shown in Figure 5. the face images in Hard set are with big variations, while the test images in random set are randomly selected and highly likely to be covered by the MS-Celeb-1M training data. Figure 6 is the Precision-Coverage curve of our face model on the dry run. Our approach perform better on Random set, as many faces in Hard set (e.g. profile images) cannot be detected using dlib detector [13] and thus failed to return results.

We also compare our model with other teams on Random set and Figure illustrates the comparison. Our model reaches the coverage 70.7% when Precision=95% and ranks $2rd$ in the Random set competition. Note that during the training phase of the evaluation, we don't use the MS-Celeb-1M training data; the same pipeline and model as LFW are employed. We believe that the performance of our model can be improved after the applying of active framework on MS-Celeb-1M, and we would like to examine in the future.

5. CONCLUSION

In this paper, we have introduced a human-in-the-loop framework for face recognition. After training a deep network from initial face dataset and applying the feature from the network, all the face images have a confidence for its associated celebrity label. The VOI strategy is employed to actively select images and these images are illustrated to the annotator. After each batch of request, the deep network is incrementally updated. The whole framework runs iteratively, and the deep model can be used for the face recognition task at any stage. Experimental comparisons with previous works on LFW and MS-Celeb-1M show the effectiveness of proposed active annotation and learning framework on face recognition task.

Our future work will test our framework on the larger dataset, i.e. the training dataset of MS-Celeb-1M Challenge; we would like to further analysis the relation between the face recognition performance and the manual annotation effort. Another potential direction may be replace our current face detector with state-of-the-art face detection methods such as cascaded CNN [14] and build an end-to-end active and learning system base on deep networks.

Acknowledgment

This work was supported in part by grants from Natural Science Foundation of China (No. 61572138) and Science and Technology Commission of Shanghai Municipality (No. 16511104802).

6. REFERENCES

[1] K. Chatfield, K. Simonyan, A. Vedaldi, and A. Zisserman. Return of the devil in the details: Delving deep into convolutional nets. In *BMVC*, 2014.

[2] M. Chatterjee and A. Leuski. An active learning based approach for effective video annotation and retrieval. *NIPS*, 2015.

[3] C. Ding and D. Tao. Robust face recognition via multimodal deep face representation. *IEEE Transaction on Multimedia*, 17(11):2049–2058, 2015.

[4] I. J. Goodfellow, D. Warde-farley, M. Mirza, A. Courville, and Y. Bengio. Maxout networks. In *ICML*, 2013.

[5] Y. Guo, L. Zhang, Y. Hu, X. He, and J. Gao. Ms-celeb-1m: A dataset and benchmark for large scale face recognition. In *ECCV*, 2016.

[6] K. He, X. Zhang, S. Ren, and J. Sun. Deep residual learning for image recognition. In *CVPR*, 2016.

[7] X.-S. Hua and G.-J. Qi. Online multi-label active annotation: Towards large-scale content-based video search. In *ACM Multimedia*, pages 141–150, 2008.

[8] G. B. Huang, M. Ramesh, T. Berg, and E. Learned-Miller. Labeled faces in the wild: A database for studying face recognition in unconstrained environments. Technical report, Technical Report 07-49, University of Massachusetts, Amherst, 2007.

[9] Itseez. Open source computer vision library. https://github.com/itseez/opencv, 2015.

[10] Y. Jia, E. Shelhamer, J. Donahue, S. Karayev, J. Long, R. Girshick, S. Guadarrama, and T. Darrell. Caffe: Convolutional architecture for fast feature embedding. In *ACM Multimedia*, pages 675–678, 2014.

[11] A. Kapoor, E. Horvitz, and S. Basu. Selective supervision: Guiding supervised learning with decision-theoretic active learning. In *IJCAI*, 2007.

[12] I. Kemelmacher-Shlizerman, S. M. Seitz, D. Miller, and E. Brossard. The megaface benchmark: 1 million faces for recognition at scale. In *CVPR*, 2016.

[13] D. E. King. Dlib-ml: A machine learning toolkit. *Journal of Machine Learning Research*, 10:1755–1758, 2009.

[14] H. Li, Z. Lin, X. Shen, J. Brandt, and G. Hua. A convolutional neural network cascade for face detection. In *CVPR*, pages 5325–5334, 2015.

[15] I. Masi, A. T. Tran, J. T. Leksut, T. Hassner, and G. Medioni. Do we really need to collect millions of faces for effective face recognition? *arXiv preprint arXiv:1603.07057*, 2016.

[16] O. M. Parkhi, A. Vedaldi, and A. Zisserman. Deep face recognition. In *BMVC*, 2015.

[17] O. Russakovsky, L.-J. Li, and L. Fei-Fei. Best of both worlds: Human-machine collaboration for object annotation. In *CVPR*, 2015.

[18] F. Schroff, D. Kalenichenko, and J. Philbin. Facenet: A unified embedding for face recognition and clustering. In *CVPR*, pages 815–823, 2015.

[19] A. Shrivastava, A. Gupta, and R. Girshick. Training region-based object detectors with online hard example mining. In *CVPR*, 2016.

[20] K. Simonyan and A. Zisserman. Very deep convolutional networks for large-scale image recognition. In *ICLR*, 2015.

[21] H. Su, Z. Yin, T. Kanade, and S. Huh. Active sample selection and correction propagation on a gradually-augmented graph. In *CVPR*, 2015.

[22] Y. Sun, X. Wang, and X. Tang. Deep learning face representation from predicting 10,000 classes. In *CVPR*, pages 1891–1898, 2014.

[23] C. Szegedy, W. Liu, Y. Jia, P. Sermanet, S. Reed, D. Anguelov, D. Erhan, V. Vanhoucke, and A. Rabinovich. Going deeper with convolutions. In *CVPR*, 2015.

[24] D. Wang, C. Otto, and A. K. Jain. Face search at scale: 80 million gallery. *arXiv preprint arXiv:1507.07242*, 2015.

[25] X. Wu, R. He, and Z. Sun. A lightened cnn for deep face representation. *arXiv preprint arXiv:1511.02683*, 2015.

[26] D. Yi, Z. Lei, S. Liao, and S. Z. Li. Learning face representation from scratch. *arXiv preprint arXiv:1411.7923*, 2014.

[27] K. Zhang, Z. Zhang, Z. Li, and Y. Qiao. Joint face detection and alignment using multi-task cascaded convolutional networks. *arXiv preprint arXiv:1604.02878*, 2016.

Deep Convolutional Neural Network with Independent Softmax for Large Scale Face Recognition

Yue Wu[†], Jun Li[†], Yu Kong[†], Yun Fu[†‡]
[†]Department of Electrical & Computer Engineering, Northeastern University, Boston, USA
[‡]College of Computer & Information Science, Northeastern University, Boston, USA
{yuewu, yukong, yunfu}@ece.neu.edu, junl.mldl@gmail.com

ABSTRACT

In this paper, we present our solution to the MS-Celeb-1M Challenge. This challenge aims to recognize 100k celebrities at the same time. The huge number of celebrities is the bottleneck for training a deep convolutional neural network of which the output is equal to the number of celebrities. To solve this problem, an independent softmax model is proposed to split the single classifier into several small classifiers. Meanwhile, the training data are split into several partitions. This decomposes the large scale training procedure into several medium training procedures which can be solved separately. Besides, a large model is also trained and a simple strategy is introduced to merge the two models. Extensive experiments on the MSR-Celeb-1M dataset demonstrate the superiority of the proposed method. Our solution ranks the first and second in two tracks of the final evaluation.

Keywords

Convolutional Neural Network; Face Recognition; Independent Softmax

1. INTRODUCTION

Large scale image classification [14] has made a series of breakthroughs led by Deep Convolutional Neural Network(CNN) [9, 10]. Many other computer vision problems benefit from the deep models of CNN, such as face verification [17, 15], object detection [3, 13] and object segmentation[11]. However, by introducing the MS-Celeb-1M [5], this large scale dataset brings new challenges in image classification task. First, up to 100k classes and 10M images are considerably larger than previous publicly available datasets [14, 17, 19, 21, 8]. Second, the provided training set only covers 75% of classes in their measurement set. These challenges come up with two interesting problems: 1) *how to build a system to classify 100k classes in a short time given such large scale data?* 2) *what will happen if the model does not see the class during training?*

MM '16, October 15-19, 2016, Amsterdam, Netherlands

DOI: http://dx.doi.org/10.1145/2964284.2984060

Recently, to solve the large scale text classification problem, Yu *et al.* proposed a generic empirical risk minimization (ERM) model [20], and Rai *et al.* employed a Bayesian multi-label learning via positive labels (BMLPL) model [12]. However, the inference of BMLPL is expensive with increasing the number of labels, and ERM is difficult to extend to more large scale labels as it contains the low-rank regularization. These methods focus on text data. In image classification with CNN, it's easy to think of making the number of neurons in the last layer of a CNN directly equal to the number of classes. But as mentioned by [1], many technical challenges exist in training such kind of big model, such as the storage and seeking of massive data, GPU memory, synchronization between GPUs. These problems may increase the training time drastically. Moreover, the gradient-based optimization [4] of CNN models with a large number of output neurons has not been deeply studied. The convergence of the model is also unclear. Thus, it is difficult for training a large model that directly handles all classes at the same time.

Meanwhile, a straight answer of the second problem is that the model will return the most similar class as the result. In face recognition, this means that the classifier will find the most look like person from all people in training. But how confident the classifier will be? Taken the binary classification as an example, how could we know if a distractor sample does not belong to both two classes? The answer is we can't. But if the classifier gives a fifty-fifty prediction, it has a bigger chance to be a distractor than a sample which has 99% probability to be one class. Extended to the multi-classes problem, if the classifier give all predictions of one sample the same probability $1/N$ where N is the number of classes, this sample has a bigger chance to be a distractor. This gives us an insight that top-1 probability of one sample for multi-classes classification can also be viewed as an indicator of the confidence that this sample belongs to these classes. The higher the probability is, the more confident this sample is in, vice versa.

In this paper, we address the large scale images classification problem by introducing an ***independent softmax*** model. Instead of directly training a classifier to predict all classes at the same time, we train several independent networks with each a softmax function to predict probabilities for a part of classes. By doing this, the large number of classes and images are split into several small groups. The scale of classification problem for each group is reduced and can be solved using some well-established techniques (*e.g.* Torch [2]). This model is based on one proposition that if a classifier does not contain one class, the prediction for images of that class will give lower score than the classifier which contains. As a special case, if all classifiers don't contain that class, all of them will make relative lower predictions compared with classes they have.

We present comprehensive experiments on MS-Celeb-1M [5] to evaluate our method. We show that the large scale classification problem can decomposed into several small classification problems using the independent softmax model. On the MS-Celeb-1M challenge, we obtain excellent results by the independent softmax model. Our final solution has 73.4% and 48.6% coverage@P=95%, which rank the first in random set and second in hard set, respectively. Moreover, when using precision equal to 99%, we rank first in both random set with 52.5% coverage and hard set with 33.6% coverage.

2. METHODS

In this section, we will describe the details of our method to the classification with 100k classes. We first review the softmax model. Then we introduce the independent softmax model. A fusion of the two models is employed to get the final result.

2.1 Softmax Model (SM)

The softmax function can be expressed as

$$f(x_i) = \frac{e^{x_i}}{\sum_{j=1}^{N} e^{x_j}}, \tag{1}$$

where x_i is the i-th dimension output, N is the number of dimension which is usually equal to the number of classes. We can treat $f(x_i)$ as the probability of the i-th class. When making a prediction, a sample is assigned the class which has the largest probability, *i.e.*,

$$F(x_i) = \max_{i \in [1,N]} f(x_i). \tag{2}$$

Softmax function encounters the training problem when the number of class N is large. First, the huge parameters in the last layer not only make the forward-backward propagation slow but also make the synchronization difficult when using multiple GPUs. In practice, we find that to finish a standard 90 epochs training on the whole MS-Celeb-1M dataset, this model may need 4 months using two Titan X GPUs. Second, the convergence is also not guaranteed. In the beginning, we try to optimize the weights from random initialization. But the training loss doesn't decrease after one epoch. Thus we pre-train a model with about 10,000 classes and fine-tune it in the whole dataset. However, before the final evaluation, only 3 epochs are finished. From this we can observe that the large number of classes and images make the training difficult.

2.2 Independent Softmax Model (ISM)

To tackle the the large scale classes problem, we introduce a hypothesis, which is described as

Hypothesis: *a sample has the same probability to be any class in a softmax model if it does not belong to the classes for training.*

More precisely, the prediction of class i for a sample that is not in N classes can be written as

$$F(x_i) = \frac{1}{N}. \tag{3}$$

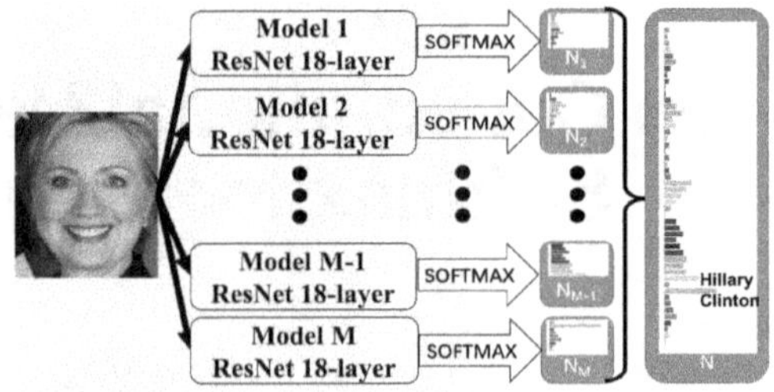

Figure 1: Independent softmax model

In other words, all classes has the same probability to be the final prediction of a sample from an unseen class. However, the probabilities for all classes cannot be the same in real world. This comes from the fact that there should always exist some class that is more similar to that sample than other classes. Instead, the key proposition of that hypothesis we utilized in ISM is

Proposition: *if a classifier does not contain one class, the prediction for images of that class will get lower score than the classifier which contains.*

Mathematically, this can be formalized as

$$F(x_{i_p}) < F(x_{i_q}), \tag{4}$$

where $p \neq q$ and $p, q \in [1, M]$. The q-th fold contains the ground-truth class i_q while the p-th fold doesn't. This proposition is validated by experiments in section 3.3 with a detailed discussion.

In our independent softmax model, the N classes are split into M folds. The k-th fold contains N_k classes, which means $N = \sum_{k=1}^{M} N_k$. Based on Eq 4, the prediction for one sample can be written as

$$\begin{aligned} \max_{k \in [1,M]} F(x_{i_k}) &= \max_{k \in [1,M]} \max_{i_k \in [1,N_k]} f(x_{i_k}) \\ &= \max_{k \in [1,M], i_k \in [1,N_k]} \frac{e^{x_{i_k}}}{\sum_{j=1}^{N_k} e^{x_j}}. \end{aligned} \tag{5}$$

According to Eq 5, probabilities for all classes are first calculated in each fold. Then the class which has the largest probability is chosen as the final prediction, which is shown in Figure 1. Different from SM, ISM separates the large number of classes into several small group of classes. This results in a partition of classes. The training images are also split according to the partition of classes. For each fold of data, it is still a classification problem. The training for them can be distributed into different machines. Moreover, due to the partition, the scale of data and classes is not that large anymore. The convergence is guaranteed according to the previous knowledge and the training time for each model is also acceptable.

2.3 Fusion of SM and ISM

To fuse the two models, we first use a nonlinear mapping to map the two scores in the same scale. After mapping, the two scores can be compared directly. To learn the mapping function, we randomly sampled 10,000 images from the validation set to make predictions using two models. Afterwards, the images that have the correct results from both two models are selected, witch results in 4,660 images. Figure 2 illustrates these scores after sorting. We can observe that the output of the two models varies in different scale. This happens because the two models are trained in different ways and data. In Figure 3, the scores from model SM and

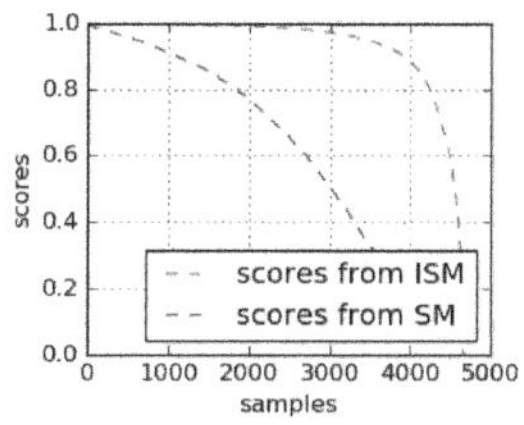

Figure 2: Scores from two models.

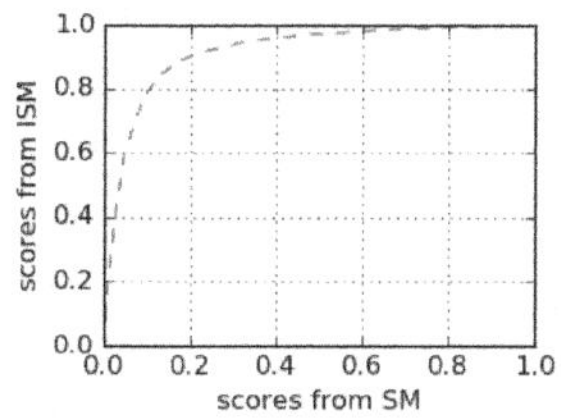

Figure 3: Non-linear mapping curve.

ISM are taken as the x-axis and y-axis, respectively. This is the curve which will be used to map the scores generated by model SM to model ISM.

Function tanh and sigmoid are first used to fit that curve independently but show bad results. Finally, a linear combination of function tanh and sigmoid is utilized. The fitted function is as following

$$s_2^1 = a/(1 + e^{-b \times s_2}) + c \times \tanh(d \times s_2), \tag{6}$$

where s_2 is the score of model A, s_2^1 is the mapped score and a, b, c, d are 0.3, 4.25, 0.7, 13.44, respectively.

The fusion algorithm is described in Algorithm 1. Our intuition is to utilize the good performance of model SM at Coverage@P=99% , which means when model SM gives a high score, it is very likely to be correct. Thus if the score of model SM is higher than a predefined threshold θ, we will use this score as the final result. The θ is set to 0.95 empirically. More details can be found in section 3.3.

Algorithm 1 Two models fusion

```
procedure FUSION(Model SM score s1, Model ISM score s2, threshold θ)
    Compute the mapped score s2^1 via Eq. 6
    if s2^1 > θ then
        Use s2^1 as the final result
    else
        Use s1 as the final result
```

3. EXPERIMENTS

In this section, we first review the dataset and evaluation metric. Then we go through the implementation details and the experiment results.

3.1 Dataset and Evaluation Metric

We evaluate our method on the MS-Celeb-1M dataset [5] that contains 99,892 classes. The models are trained on the provided 8.46 million images and evaluated on a development set with 1k images. We also obtain a final result on 50k test images, reported by the challenge organizer. It is notable that the training set only cover about 75% of classes in the measurement set, which means the upper bound of recognition recall is 75%. Besides, two different kinds of data are utilized for development and testing. The first kind of data have big variations and are harder, which are referred as dev1. The other kind of data are randomly selected and are easier, which are referred as dev2. We evaluate the recognition coverage at both precision 95% and 99%, which are defined as

$$\begin{aligned} \text{precision} &= c/m, \\ \text{coverage} &= m/n, \end{aligned} \tag{7}$$

where for n images in the measurement set, c images are correct among the recognized m images.

3.2 Implementation Details

To train and validate classification models, the 8.46 million images are first randomly split into a training set and a validation set. For each class, 90% of its images are for training and the rest 10% are for validation.

ISM. The dataset is further partitioned into 5 folds manually. We split the dataset by alphabetical order. The details of each fold is in Table 1. The 18-layer model from Deep Residual Network [6] are employed for the classification of each fold. A torch implement [2] is utilized. We replace the last layer with a new layer which has the corresponding classes number. Five 18-layer models are trained for five folds independently. For each model, The batch size is set to 128. The initial learning rate is set to 0.1. Each model is trained for 90 epochs. The learning rate decreases by 10 times every 30 epoch. The training takes about 7 GB GPU memory. These models are trained on a Titan X or a K40c or 2 GTX 970. Each model needs about one week to finish training.

Table 1: Dataset Partition Information

Fold	Classes	Train Images	Val Images
1	10,001	760,656	89,461
2	23,000	1,743,649	205,377
3	23,000	1,740,138	204,921
4	23,000	1,742,208	205,092
5	20,890	1,578,945	185,807

SM. For the softmax model, it is also a 18-layer Deep Residual Network model trained on the whole dataset. It has 99,892 output which each one is corresponding to one class. This model utilizes the fold 1 model as pre-trained weights and then is fine-tuned on the whole dataset. It is trained on 2 titan X with a batch size 256. It takes total 16 GB GPU memory. The training of this model is very slow. Before the challenge final evaluation, we can only train the model for 3 epochs. The first two epochs are with learning rate 0.01 and the third epoch uses 0.001.

3.3 Experiment Results

The proposition is validated in the beginning. Then we show the results of ISM, SM and Fusion of the two models. Final evaluation results are also given.

Proposition Validation. We take the model trained from the second fold to validate the Equation 4. In the 1k development images, classes of 198 images belong to the second fold. In Figure 4, scores of these images from the second model are marked as scores from "in". Scores of the rest 802 images from the second model are marked as scores from "out". The percentage of samples are taken as the x-axis and scores are used as the y-axis. From Figure 4, we can

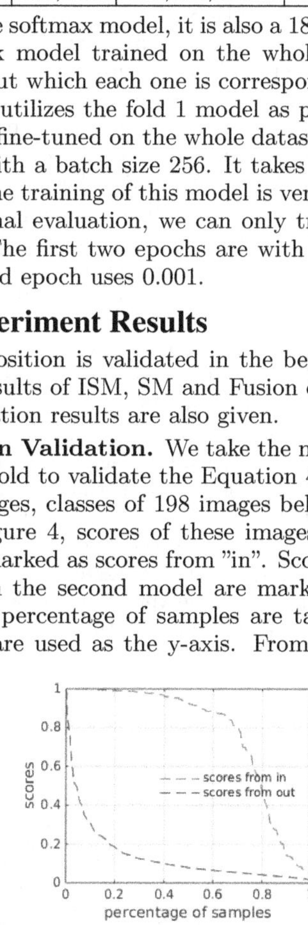

Figure 4: Results of model ISM from 'in' and 'out' data.

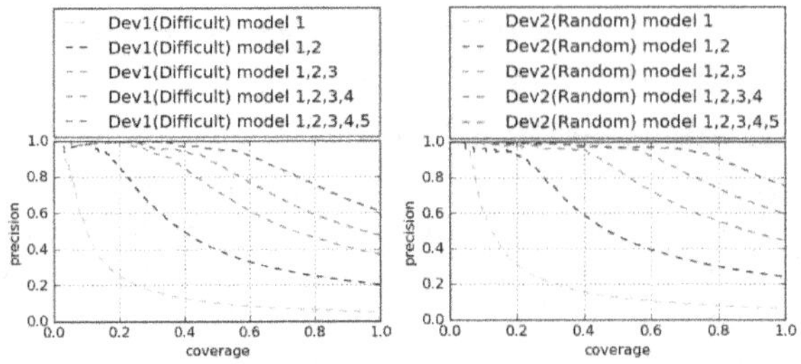

Figure 5: Results of ISM with different number of small models

Table 2: Results of ISM with different number of small models

Model	Coverage@P=95%		Coverage@P=99%	
	dev1	dev2	dev1	dev2
1	3.0	5.8	3.0	4.4
1,2	13.4	17.0	3.0	4.4
1,2,3	28.4	40.6	21.2	9.80
1,2,3,4	37.4	56.4	24.8	29.4
1,2,3,4,5	49.6	71.0	32.8	24.2

observe that 70% of the "in" images have higher scores than 0.8. Meanwhile, about only 1% of "out" images get higher scores than 0.8. This demonstrates that a softmax classifier will give lower scores to the images which classes are not in its training set, but give higher scores to the images which classes are in. Thus, the proposition is reasonable.

ISM. First we evaluate the performance of model ISM. Five independent models are utilized. When predicting, we vary the number of models from one to five which are corresponding to the fold number in Table 1. Results are shown in Figure 5 and Table 2. We can observe that when more models are added, the better the results are. This is because when more models are added, more classes are covered. It is also consistent with that more data lead to higher performance. However, when the model 5 is added, the coverage with precision 99% of dev2 decreases from 29.4% to 24.2%. This makes no sense because the 24.2% is even lower than 32.8% of dev1 which is obvious harder. We believe this is due to the limited samples of the development set. Similar phenomena are also shown in the fusion of two models.

Multi-scale Testing. Usually, in convolutional neural network, multi-scale testing [7, 16, 18], *i.e.*, ten crops or dense crops, gives better results. But since the final evaluation is tested online. we can not afford aggressive cropping approaches. Besides, We also observe that the faces are almost in the center of aligned images. Thus, we do evaluation on the original center-crop, two-crop and ten-crop [9]. Two-crop which takes the center crop of the original and flipped image are a simple version of ten-crop. The results are shown in Figure 6 and Table 3. We can observe

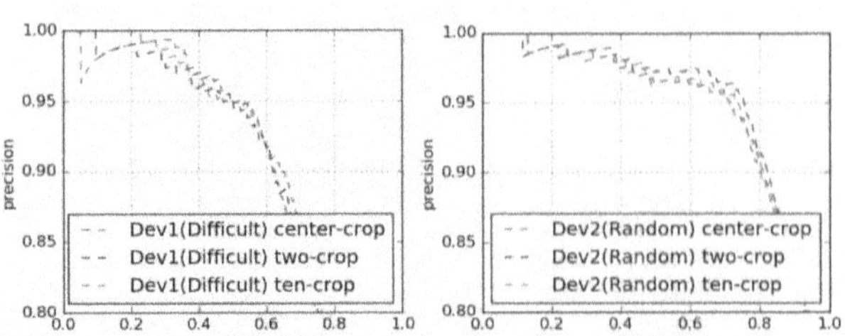

Figure 6: Results of model ISM with different testing views

Table 3: Results of model ISM with different testing views

Model	Coverage@P=95%		Coverage@P=99%	
	dev1	dev2	dev1	dev2
Center-crop	49.6	71.0	32.8	24.2
Two-crop	50.0	75.2	21.6	22.0
Ten-crop	53.2	73.6	27.4	24.6

that when using precision 95%, two-crop and ten-crop has similar performance but are both better than center-crop. Considering the speed issue, our final submission is based on two-crop.

SM. Similar results are also observed from model SM, which are not shown due to the limit space.

Fusion. Results for fusion of SM and ISM are illustrated in Figure 7 and Table 4. We find the model SM is better than model ISM when the precision is high. But the precision of SM drops faster than ISM with the increase of coverage. Fusion of SM and ISM achieve better performance than both SM and ISM except the coverage with precision 99%.

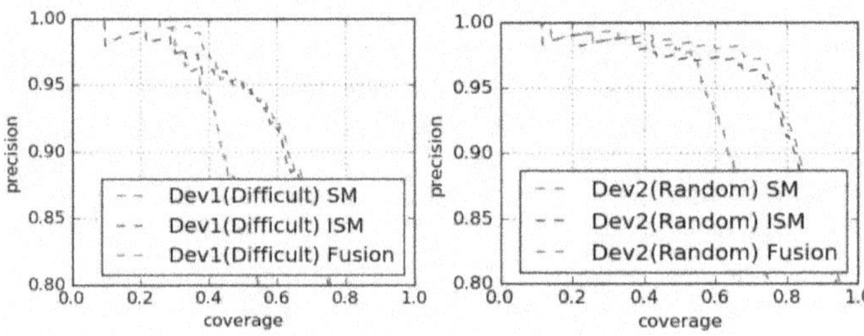

Figure 7: Fusion of SM and ISM

Table 4: Fusion of SM and ISM

Model	Coverage@P=95%		Coverage@P=99%	
	dev1	dev2	dev1	dev2
ISM	50.0	75.2	21.6	22.0
SM	37.6	57.0	29.4	42.4
Fusion	50.2	76.6	34.6	25.6

Final Evaluation. The final result on the final 5k test images are in Table 5. We can see that the at 95%, the results are similar to the results on development set except the coverage with precision 99% of dev2. This demonstrates that small development set makes that result unstable.

Table 5: Results on the final testing set

Model	Coverage@P=95%		Coverage@P=99%	
	dev1	dev2	dev1	dev2
Test	48.6	73.4	33.6	52.5

4. CONCLUSIONS

In this paper, we proposed an independent softmax model to solve the large scale face recognition problem. The model partitions the large scale classification problem into several small classification problems, which can be distributed and easily solved. The good performance in MS-Celeb-1M challenge 2016 demonstrates the superiority of our method. In the future, we plan to investigate the relationship between different models under the independent softmax model.

5. ACKNOWLEDGMENTS

This work is supported in part by the NSF CNS award 1314484, ONR award N00014-12-1-1028, ONR Young Investigator Award N00014-14-1-0484, and U.S. Army Research Office Young Investigator Award W911NF-14-1-0218.

6. REFERENCES

[1] http://mxnet.readthedocs.io/en/latest/tutorials/imagenet_full.html.

[2] https://github.com/facebook/fb.resnet.torch/.

[3] R. Girshick, J. Donahue, T. Darrell, and J. Malik. Rich feature hierarchies for accurate object detection and semantic segmentation. In *Proceedings of the IEEE conference on computer vision and pattern recognition*, pages 580–587, 2014.

[4] X. Glorot and Y. Bengio. Understanding the difficulty of training deep feedforward neural networks.

[5] Y. Guo, L. Zhang, Y. Hu, X. He, and J. Gao. Ms-celeb-1m: A dataset and benchmark for large-scale face recognition. *arXiv preprint arXiv:1607.08221*, 2016.

[6] K. He, X. Zhang, S. Ren, and J. Sun. Deep residual learning for image recognition. *arXiv preprint arXiv:1512.03385*, 2015.

[7] A. G. Howard. Some improvements on deep convolutional neural network based image classification. *arXiv preprint arXiv:1312.5402*, 2013.

[8] A. Karpathy, G. Toderici, S. Shetty, T. Leung, R. Sukthankar, and L. Fei-Fei. Large-scale video classification with convolutional neural networks. In *Proceedings of the IEEE conference on Computer Vision and Pattern Recognition*, pages 1725–1732, 2014.

[9] A. Krizhevsky, I. Sutskever, and G. E. Hinton. Imagenet classification with deep convolutional neural networks. In *Advances in neural information processing systems*, pages 1097–1105, 2012.

[10] Y. LeCun, B. Boser, J. S. Denker, D. Henderson, R. E. Howard, W. Hubbard, and L. D. Jackel. Backpropagation applied to handwritten zip code recognition. *Neural computation*, 1(4):541–551, 1989.

[11] J. Long, E. Shelhamer, and T. Darrell. Fully convolutional networks for semantic segmentation. In *Proceedings of the IEEE Conference on Computer Vision and Pattern Recognition*, pages 3431–3440, 2015.

[12] P. Rai, C. Hu, R. Henao, and L. Carin. Large-scale bayesian multi-label learning via topic-based label embeddings. In *Proceedings of the Neural Info. Processing Systems*, 2015.

[13] S. Ren, K. He, R. Girshick, and J. Sun. Faster r-cnn: Towards real-time object detection with region proposal networks. In *Advances in neural information processing systems*, pages 91–99, 2015.

[14] O. Russakovsky, J. Deng, H. Su, J. Krause, S. Satheesh, S. Ma, Z. Huang, A. Karpathy, A. Khosla, M. Bernstein, et al. Imagenet large scale visual recognition challenge. *International Journal of Computer Vision*, 115(3):211–252, 2015.

[15] F. Schroff, D. Kalenichenko, and J. Philbin. Facenet: A unified embedding for face recognition and clustering. In *Proceedings of the IEEE Conference on Computer Vision and Pattern Recognition*, pages 815–823, 2015.

[16] K. Simonyan and A. Zisserman. Very deep convolutional networks for large-scale image recognition. In *International Conference on Learning Representations*, 2015.

[17] Y. Sun, X. Wang, and X. Tang. Deep learning face representation from predicting 10,000 classes. In *Proceedings of the IEEE Conference on Computer Vision and Pattern Recognition*, pages 1891–1898, 2014.

[18] C. Szegedy, W. Liu, Y. Jia, P. Sermanet, S. Reed, D. Anguelov, D. Erhan, V. Vanhoucke, and A. Rabinovich. Going deeper with convolutions. In *Proceedings of the IEEE Conference on Computer Vision and Pattern Recognition*, pages 1–9, 2015.

[19] D. Yi, Z. Lei, S. Liao, and S. Z. Li. Learning face representation from scratch. *arXiv preprint arXiv:1411.7923*, 2014.

[20] H. Yu, P. Jain, P. Kar, and I. Dhillon. Large-scale multi-label learning with missing labels. In *Proceedings of the Int'l Conf. Machine Learning*, 2014.

[21] B. Zhou, A. Lapedriza, J. Xiao, A. Torralba, and A. Oliva. Learning deep features for scene recognition using places database. In *Advances in neural information processing systems*, pages 487–495, 2014.

Robust Face Recognition with Deep Multi-View Representation Learning

Jianshu Li [1,3]
jianshu@u.nus.edu

Jian Zhao [2]
zhaojian90@u.nus.edu

Fang Zhao [2]
elezhf@nus.edu.sg

Hao Liu [4,2]
hfut.haoliu@gmail.com

Jing Li [1]
etta090807@gmail.com

Shengmei Shen [5]
shengmei.shen@sg.panasonic.com

Jiashi Feng [2]
elefjia@nus.edu.sg

Terence Sim [1]
tsim@comp.nus.edu.sg

[1] School of Computing, National University of Singapore, Singapore
[2] Department of Electrical and Computer Engineering, National University of Singapore, Singapore
[3] SAP Research and Innovation Singapore, SAP Asia Pte Ltd
[4] School of Computer and Information, Hefei University of Technology, Hefei, Anhui China
[5] Core Technology Group, Panasonic R&D Center Singapore

ABSTRACT

This paper describes our proposed method targeting at the MSR Image Recognition Challenge MS-Celeb-1M. The challenge is to recognize *one million* celebrities from their face images captured in the real world. The challenge provides a large scale dataset crawled from the Web, which contains a large number of celebrities with many images for each subject. Given a new testing image, the challenge requires an identify for the image and the corresponding confidence score. To complete the challenge, we propose a two-stage approach consisting of data cleaning and multi-view deep representation learning. The data cleaning can effectively reduce the noise level of training data and thus improves the performance of deep learning based face recognition models. The multi-view representation learning enables the learned face representations to be more specific and discriminative. Thus the difficulties of recognizing faces out of a huge number of subjects are substantially relieved. Our proposed method achieves a coverage of 46.1% at 95% precision on the random set and a coverage of 33.0% at 95% precision on the hard set of this challenge.

Keywords

Face Recognition; Deep Learning; Multi-view Feature Representation; Model Ensemble

1. INTRODUCTION AND OVERVIEW

Recently many deep learning based face recognition techniques have been developed and achieved remarkable performance in various application scenarios, such as DeepFace [9], FaceNet [5] and DeepID [7]. However, most of the existing face recognition techniques do not consider how to disambiguate the identity of a person. Another issue significantly hindering the development of face recognition techniques is that publicly available face datasets are usually far smaller than being sufficient to build real face recognition systems. To address these issues, the MSR Image Recognition Challenge introduces a knowledge base where each face is linked to a unique entity key and provides a large scale face dataset (MsCeleb), which contains about 100,000 celebrities with about 100 images for each subject.

To address the face identification task proposed in the challenge, we propose a two-stage method to learn robust and disambiguated human face representations for effectively recognizing human faces at large scale. The first stage is to clean the noisy data in the provided training set. Since the provided training dataset is crawled from the Internet without manually checking, there are a certain percentage of data which are actually noisy. For example, some of the faces are given wrong labels and some images even do not contain faces. To clean the noise, we first train a deep neural network on an existing large scale face dataset using a classification loss. We use the model pre-trained on the clean dataset to extract features for face images from MsCeleb. The activations from the penultimate layer are adopted as the feature representations of images from the MsCeleb dataset. Then for each subject, we apply an outlier detection method to remove the noisy images for the subject. Built on the cleaned dataset, the second stage of our proposed method is multi-view deep representation learning. To capture the intrinsic diversity of MsCeleb and enhance the generalization performance of face recognition models, we use multiple deep models with various architectures and loss functions to learn the representations of faces. These models provide distinct features to better characterize the data distribution jointly from different "views". Thus, representing a face from different views could effectively decrease the subject ambiguity and enhance recognition performance for an extremely large number of subjects. Then a separate classifier, whose in-

MM '16, October 15-19, 2016, Amsterdam, Netherlands

DOI: http://dx.doi.org/10.1145/2964284.2984061

put is the combined features from multiple deep models, is trained to perform multi-view feature fusion and classification. The overall structure is shown in Figure 1. The two-stage method is proved to be effective at learning robust representation from the noisy training data in the challenge.

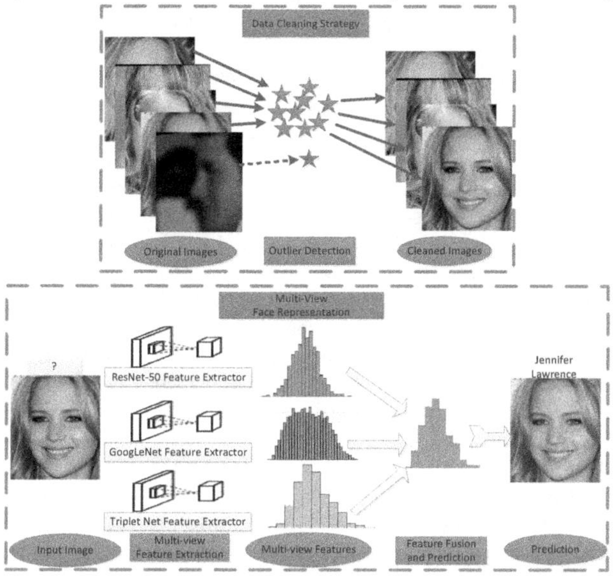

Figure 1: Overall structure of the proposed solution to the challenge: Data Cleaning Strategy and Multi-view Face Representation.

2. THE PROPOSED METHOD

2.1 Noisy Data Cleaning

Real world data are usually noisy, especially those crawled from the Internet. Automatic data cleaning is thus necessary for training machine learning models to better extract useful knowledge from the data. Bearing this in mind, in this face recognition challenge, we observe that the provided dataset is obtained by leveraging the public search engines. Therefore, a certain proportion of noisy data is inevitable and will hurt the performance of face recognition models trained on this dataset. It is clear that manual removal of the noise in the training data is almost impossible with affordable time cost.

Therefore, in our proposed method, automatic noisy cleaning is considered to be very important. We solve the problem of noisy data cleaning through outlier detection. Here, an outlier face image may be the one with an incorrect subject label or the one containing no faces. Firstly we transform the raw images to a high-level representative feature space, where outlier detection is more reliable and easier. In particular, we propose to adopt the activations from certain layers in a pre-trained Convolutional Neural Network (CNN) as the new representations. Then distances between the feature vectors of images for the same subject are calculated. Based on the distances, the feature vectors are clustered and outliers with abnormal distance with others can be detected.

One way to model the distance used in the outlier detection is to use Gaussian Mixture Model (GMM). Theoretically with GMM, we are able to get multiple cluster centers to model the intra-class variations, such as age, pose, illumination *etc.* Then the probability of each feature vector on the trained GMM model can be used as the distance metric to perform outlier detection. Some robustified variants of GMM [4] can also be used to eliminate the effect of outliers when learning the GMM model. Due to highly elevated time cost of the GMM training procedure, we simply use one cluster in the challenge as a practical solution, which is a special case of GMM with one Gaussian center. With only one cluster, we can easily find the cluster center of all feature vectors corresponding to one subject. The cluster center is treated as a reference point, and Euclidean distance of each feature vector of the subject to the center is calculated. Based on the distances, the outlier detection algorithm based on Thompson Tau method [1] is used to remove a fix proportion of the feature vectors as outliers. The above procedure is applied independently to the images of all the subjects in the training set.

2.2 Multi-View Deep Representation Learning

How to learn feature representations of the noisy data that are discriminative for a huge number of subjects (the number is 100,000 in this challenge) is a really challenging task, as the feature dimensions may be far smaller than the number of subjects and are ambiguous in representing the subjects. For the toy example in Figure 2, five classes lie in a two-dimensional space. It is hard to discriminate all the classes from a single direction of view. When combining information from multiple views, *e.g.*, from both x and y axes, it is easier to decide the decision boundaries of all the classes.

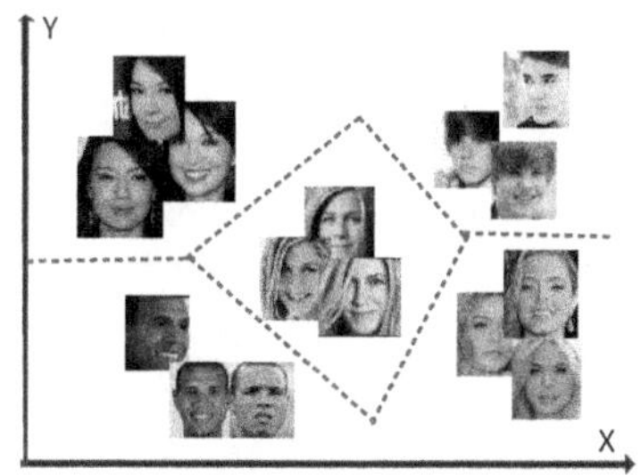

Figure 2: Illustration of benefits of multi-view classification.

We here leverage deep convolutional neural networks, which have been successfully applied to many domains, to learn deep face representations. In particular, we focus on learning the representations from different views in order to enhance the discriminative ability of the learned representations. In order to better characterize the face data distribution from different "views", we employ deep networks with various structures and loss functions to extract data representation from different perspectives. We now proceed to explain the details.

Firstly, two different network structures, Residual Net [2] and GoogLeNet [8] are used. Residual Net has the advantage of training substantially deep networks easily. We utilize the power of residual nets to build deep models and apply them to the large scale face recognition task. With the help of the residual structure, we train a deep model with 50 layers for the face recognition challenge. GoogLeNet is an efficient and successful deep model for computer vision related tasks. Through careful crafted design, GoogLeNet increases the depth and width of the network while keeping the computational budget constant with the Inception modules. Here we adopt it for this face recognition challenge.

Furthermore, two different loss functions, *i.e.*, cross entropy classification loss and triplet loss [5], are used. Cross entropy classification loss directly distinguishes all the classes and focuses on learning the global feature which can give the best decision boundary to differentiate all the classes. The cross entropy loss is defined as

$$\mathcal{L}_{ce} = -\frac{1}{N}\sum_{i}^{N}\left[p_i \log \hat{p}_i + (1-p_i)\log(1-\hat{p}_i)\right],$$

where N is the number of all the images in the training set, p_i is the ground truth label for the i-th image and $\hat{p}_i$ is the corresponding predicted probability.

Triplet loss function aims to generate discriminative feature representation by properly increasing the similarity and difference of positive and negative pairs in each triplet. A triplet of sample images refers to a tuple of three sample images denoted as I, I^+ and I^-, which correspond to the anchor sample, the positive sample and the negative sample respectively. Here I and I^+ come from the same class (positive pair), while I and I^- are from different classes (negative pair). When extracting features from the image triplet, the truly matched images are supposed to be closer than the mismatched images. More specifically, we denote $\mathbf{H}$ as the extracted feature from image I. Then within a triplet of $\langle \mathbf{H}, \mathbf{H}^+, \mathbf{H}^- \rangle$, the feature of the positive sample $\mathbf{H}^+$ should be more similar to the reference sample $\mathbf{H}$ than the feature of the negative sample $\mathbf{H}^-$:

$$\left\|\mathbf{H}-\mathbf{H}^+\right\|_2^2 + \alpha < \left\|\mathbf{H}-\mathbf{H}^-\right\|_2^2.$$

Here α is an additionally introduced margin that is introduced to enhance the discriminative ability of learned features between positive and negative pairs. Therefore, for N triplets, the loss function to minimize is:

$$\mathcal{L}_{tri} = \frac{1}{N}\sum_{i}^{N}\left[\left\|\mathbf{H}_i-\mathbf{H}_i^+\right\|_2^2 - \left\|\mathbf{H}_i-\mathbf{H}_i^-\right\|_2^2 + \alpha\right]_+,$$

where $[\cdot]_+$ truncates the involved variable at zero.

To fuse the multi-view feature representations, we project the features from every model into a common D-dimensional feature space via function $f_i : \mathbb{R}^{d_i} \rightarrow \mathbb{R}^D$ with parameter w_i. A classifier f_c parametrized by w_c takes as input the fused feature in the common feature space and predicts the target label l. The loss function for the fusion process is written as

$$\mathcal{L}_{fusion} = \mathcal{L}_{ce}\left(f_c(\sum_i f_i(x_i)), l\right) + \sum_i \lambda_i R(w_i) + \lambda_c R(w_c),$$

where index i runs over all the base models, R is the regularizer on parameters and λs are the corresponding weights of the regularizers. By minimizing the loss function, the parameters for feature fusion w_i and classification w_c can be learnt jointly.

To summarize, we train the base deep models with three different network architectures for the face recognition challenge. The first one is a ResNet-50 net with the cross entropy loss, the second one is GoogLeNet with the cross entropy loss, and the third one is ResNet-18 with the triplet loss. After training the base models, we use them to extract feature representations of face images. For each image, we pass it through all the base networks and use the activations from penultimate layers of the base networks as high-level representations of the image. Finally we use a two-layer MultiLayer Perceptron (MLP) for feature fusion and classification.

3. IMPLEMENTATION DETAILS

3.1 Data Cleaning

In order to get the high-level representation of the face images facilitating data cleaning, we use CASIA-WebFace [10] to train a ResNet-50 model with classification loss. The activations from its penultimate layer are used as the feature representations of the images. CASIA-WebFace is a large scale clean face dataset containing $10,575$ subjects and $494,414$ images, thus it is good for learning the intended high-level face representation. We use Residual Net with 50 layers as the deep CNN model, with the final layer being a $10,575$ way classification layer with cross entropy loss. The ResNet-50 model is trained from scratch with a batch size of 8. The initial learning rate is set as 0.1, and is then reduced to 0.01 and 0.001 along the training process. We train the model for about 100 epochs for each learning rate step.

The trained model is used to extract data representation for further cleaning. For all the aligned face images in the MsCeleb dataset, we use the pre-trained ResNet-50 to extract their feature vectors. Then for all the feature vectors corresponding to one person, we calculate the median of all these vectors as the cluster center and Euclidean distance of each feature vector to the center. Based on the distances, we remove 10% of the feature vectors as outliers.

With this method, 10% of the training data are removed, resulting in a cleaner dataset. Some of the discarded data are visualized in Figure 3. We can see that the outlier removal algorithm can discover and remove some of the noise in the dataset. The discovered noise contains non-face objects, faces with opposite genders and faces with very low resolution. There are some failure cases, where the correct face belonging to the same celebrity in that class is removed by mistake. The effect of the data cleaning method is twofold. Firstly it reduces the complexity of the training data so that the feature learning becomes easier. Secondly it also removes some of the challenging faces in the dataset, which might also affect the performance negatively. The effect of the data cleaning method is demonstrated in the experiment section.

Figure 3: Correctly and wrongly detected outliers. For each celebrity, the first three images are references and the last image is the detected outlier. For Jennifer Lawrence, Adam Rickitt and Breck Eisner, the outliers are correctly identified. For Dimitra Arliss, the outlier is actually a challenging sample.

3.2 Base Model Feature Learning

3.2.1 ResNet-50

The first network for feature learning is the ResNet-50. We continue fine-tuning the network pre-trained on CASIA-WebFace with the cleaned data from MsCeleb dataset. The network structure is the same as the pre-trained model, except that the final 10,575 way classification layer is replaced by a 76,674 way classification layer. The initial learning rate for the network is 0.001, except for the newly added last layer, which is 10 times larger. With a batch size of 8, the ResNet-50 model is trained at the initial learning rate until convergence. Then the training process is repeated at a learning rate of 0.0001.

3.2.2 GoogLeNet

The second network for feature learning is GoogLeNet. This model is trained on the Labelled Faces in the Wild (LFW) [3] dataset. We continue fine-tuning the network pre-trained on LFW with the cleaned data from MsCeleb dataset. The last layer of this network is modified the same way as ResNet-50, and a similar training schedule is used to fine-tune GoogLeNet.

3.2.3 TripletNet

The third network for feature learning is TripletNet, which is a ResNet-18 with triplet loss. The base Residual net with 18 layers is trained with CASIA-WebFace [10]. Then we use on-line triplet selection strategy to select triplets within each mini-batch. The on-line triplets selection approach selects triplets that are active and can contribute to improving the model within a mini-batch, so it is of higher efficiency and lower resource consumption. Specifically, instead of picking the hard positive, we adopt all positive pairs and randomly sampled negative samples added to each mini-batch. In practice, we find that using all positive pairs makes the model more stable and converge faster than selectively using hard positive pairs in a mini-batch. The TripletNet is trained with a batch size of 140 and a learning rate of 0.001 until convergence.

3.3 Feature Fusion

The dimension of the common feature space is set as 2,048. The feature fusion and classification task is modeled by a two-layer MLP with 2,048 hidden neurons. The MLP first reduces the dimension of the concatenated feature vector to 2,048. Then the final layer performs a 76,674 way classification based on the dimension reduced features. Dropout [6] is used between the two layers with a dropout rate of 0.5 to alleviate over-fitting.

4. EXPERIMENTS

The testing data are not provided, so we use the data from the dry run as the validation set. The validation set has two subsets, Dev1 and Dev2, each of which contains 500 images and ground truth labels. We test the performance of the baseline models as well as the ensemble model on the validation set.

4.1 Experiment with Data Cleaning

Our proposed data cleaning technique helps to clean the noisy data, which also filters out some challenging data. In this section, we conduct experiments to show the effectiveness of data cleaning. Two versions of ResNet-50 model are trained, one is trained on the original (and also noisy) data and the other on the data after applying the proposed data cleaning algorithm in Section 3.1. We train both models with an equal number of epochs and test them on the validation set. The coverages at 95% precision (C@95%P) and 99% precision (C@99%P) are shown in Table 1. From the table we can see that data cleaning can help increase the coverage at lower precision value, but will slightly hurt the performance at higher precision. This demonstrates the necessaries of achieving good trade off between the removal of noise and removal of hard positive samples. On one hand, as the noisy data are removed and the classification task of the data becomes easier. Thus the coverage is higher at lower precision. But on the other hand some of the challenging data, which help train a better face recognition model, are also removed and the valuable information is lost. So the performance at higher precision is compromised.

Table 1: Coverage of the models trained on original data and cleaned data respectively. A higher number indicates a better result. The results clearly demonstrate the effects of data cleaning (see more dicussions in the text).

Dev1	C@95%P	C@99%P
ResNet-50 on Original data	8.6%	7.0%
ResNet-50 on Cleaned data	13.0%	6.6%
Dev2	**C@95%P**	**C@99%P**
ResNet-50 on Original data	17.2%	4.2%
ResNet-50 on Cleaned data	26.4%	1.4%

4.2 Model Averaging v.s. Feature Fusion

Based on the base models, we have several ways of combining the models. One method is to simply averaging the scores from different models. Another method is to use the proposed feature fusion and classification modelling. We test both methods with our base models on the validation set. The base models used in this experiment are the same as the two ResNet-50 models used in Section 4.1. The results are shown in Table 2. Based on the experimental result, we can see our proposed feature fusion and classification method outperforms simply averaging the results.

Table 2: Effects of different model ensemble methods.

Dev1	C@95%P	C@99%P
Average	20.4%	17.4%
Ensemble	33.6%	22.6%
Dev2	**C@95%P**	**C@99%P**
Average	29.8%	0.8%
Ensemble	46.0%	0.8%

4.3 Performance of Each Base Model

For ResNet-50 and GoogLeNet, the final layers are classification layers and they will naturally produce a probability distribution over all the 76,674 given subjects in the training set. We sort the predicted probability and pick the top 5 subjects with their corresponding probability as the identification output. For the TripletNet, direct prediction is not possible as it only learns the relative distance between face images of different subjects. So we use the trained network to extract the features of all the images in the training set as gallery features, and extract the features of all the images in the validation set as the probe features. Then for each validation image, we use its corresponding probe feature to search through the gallery and returns the 5 nearest feature vectors in the gallery as the identification result. The confidence scores of the returned nearest neighbours are the reciprocal of the distance between the probe feature and the gallery feature. The coverages at 95% and 99% precision, together with the top 5 and top 1 accuracies of the three base models on Dev1 and Dev2 are reported in Table 3. Dash symbol indicates that the certain precision in not achieved. The TripletNet is not advantageous in terms of coverages at 95% and 99% precision, as the confidence score is the reciprocal of the distance, which might be very similar in the high dimensional feature space. We include this model for the final ensemble as the top 1 and top 5 accuracies are reasonably good, which indicates the learnt feature from this model is still valuable for our final multi-view model.

Table 3: Performance on Base Models.

Dev1	C@95%P	C@99%P	Top 5	Top 1
ResNet-50	13.0%	6.6%	35.8%	29.2%
GoogLeNet	9.0%	2.8%	37.2%	27.8%
TripletNet	—	—	32.4%	22.6%
Dev2	**C@95%P**	**C@99%P**	**Top 5**	**Top 1**
ResNet-50	26.4%	1.4%	44.8%	39.6%
GoogLeNet	16.2%	12.8%	47.6%	38.2%
TripletNet	0.6%	0.6%	53.8%	48.0%

4.4 Ensemble of Multi-View Models

The final model ensemble involves four models: ResNet-50, GoogLeNet and TripletNet trained on the filtered data, and ResNet-50 trained on the original data. The results are in Table 4 [1]. The corresponding ROC curves of the multi-view ensemble model on Dev1 and Dev2, showing the precision versus coverage, are plotted in Figure 4. Our final model achieves a coverage of 46.1% at 95% precision on the random set and a coverage of 33.0% at 95% precision on the hard set. Due to the use of various deep CNN models with different loss functions, the proposed multi-view model ensemble is effective even at a higher precision. Our model achieves a coverage of 33.9% at 99% precision on the random set and a coverage of 21.1% at 99% precision on the hard set, ranking the fourth and the second place among all the participating teams.

Table 4: Performance of Multi-view Ensemble.

Dev1	C@95%P	C@99%P	Top 5	Top 1
Average	28.4%	20.6%	45.6%	38.4%
Multi-view	40.8%	28.0%	51.0%	46.0%
Dev2	**C@95%P**	**C@99%P**	**Top 5**	**Top 1**
Average	42.6%	2.8%	54.2%	49.4%
Multi-view	50.6%	21.8%	56.2%	52.6%

5. CONCLUSION

In this paper, we introduced our multi-view learning solution for MSR Image Recognition Challenge MS-Celeb-1M. We presented a data cleaning technique to reduce the influence of noisy data, and a multi-view deep representation learning strategy to combine deep networks of diverse structures and loss functions. The experimental results on the provided large-scale face dataset demonstrate the effectiveness of our proposed two-stage approach for the face recognition challenge.

[1]Note that the model we use for this result is different from the model we use during the dry run.

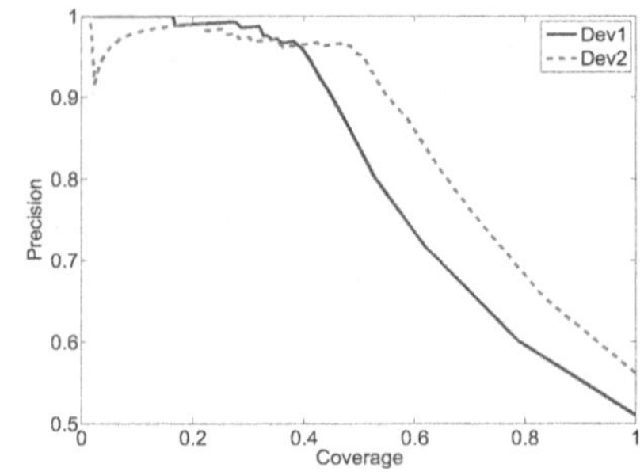

Figure 4: Precision-Coverage Curve of Multi-view Ensemble on the Validation Set.

6. REFERENCES

[1] J. M. Cimbala. Outliers. Technical report, Penn State University, September 2011.

[2] K. He, X. Zhang, S. Ren, and J. Sun. Deep residual learning for image recognition. *arXiv preprint arXiv:1512.03385*, 2015.

[3] G. B. Huang, M. Ramesh, T. Berg, and E. Learned-Miller. Labeled faces in the wild: A database for studying face recognition in unconstrained environments. Technical Report 07-49, University of Massachusetts, Amherst, October 2007.

[4] A. Lucas, R. Van Dijk, and T. Kloek. Outlier robust gmm estimation of leverage determinants in linear dynamic panel data models. *Available at SSRN 20611*, 1997.

[5] F. Schroff, D. Kalenichenko, and J. Philbin. Facenet: A unified embedding for face recognition and clustering. In *Proceedings of the IEEE Conference on Computer Vision and Pattern Recognition*, pages 815–823, 2015.

[6] N. Srivastava, G. E. Hinton, A. Krizhevsky, I. Sutskever, and R. Salakhutdinov. Dropout: a simple way to prevent neural networks from overfitting. *Journal of Machine Learning Research*, 15(1):1929–1958, 2014.

[7] Y. Sun, D. Liang, X. Wang, and X. Tang. Deepid3: Face recognition with very deep neural networks. *arXiv preprint arXiv:1502.00873*, 2015.

[8] C. Szegedy, W. Liu, Y. Jia, P. Sermanet, S. Reed, D. Anguelov, D. Erhan, V. Vanhoucke, and A. Rabinovich. Going deeper with convolutions. In *Proceedings of the IEEE Conference on Computer Vision and Pattern Recognition*, pages 1–9, 2015.

[9] Y. Taigman, M. Yang, M. Ranzato, and L. Wolf. Deepface: Closing the gap to human-level performance in face verification. In *Proceedings of the IEEE Conference on Computer Vision and Pattern Recognition*, pages 1701–1708, 2014.

[10] D. Yi, Z. Lei, S. Liao, and S. Z. Li. Learning face representation from scratch. *arXiv preprint arXiv:1411.7923*, 2014.

Frame- and Segment-Level Features and Candidate Pool Evaluation for Video Caption Generation

Rakshith Shetty
Dept. of Computer Science
Aalto University, Espoo, Finland
rakshith.shetty@aalto.fi

Jorma Laaksonen
Dept. of Computer Science
Aalto University, Espoo, Finland
jorma.laaksonen@aalto.fi

ABSTRACT

We present our submission to the Microsoft Video to Language Challenge of generating short captions describing videos in the challenge dataset. Our model is based on the encoder–decoder pipeline, popular in image and video captioning systems. We propose to utilize two different kinds of video features, one to capture the video content in terms of objects and attributes, and the other to capture the motion and action information. Using these diverse features we train models specializing in two separate input sub-domains. We then train an evaluator model which is used to pick the best caption from the pool of candidates generated by these domain expert models. We argue that this approach is better suited for the current video captioning task, compared to using a single model, due to the diversity in the dataset.

Efficacy of our method is proven by the fact that it was rated best in MSR Video to Language Challenge, as per human evaluation. Additionally, we were ranked second in the automatic evaluation metrics based table.

1. INTRODUCTION

The problem of describing videos using natural language has garnered a lot of interest after the great progress recently made in image captioning. This development has been partly driven also by the availability of large datasets of images and videos with human-annotated captions describing them. The M-VAD [5] and MPII-MD [10] datasets used in the first Large Scale Movie Description Challenge suffered from having only one reference caption for each video. Multiple reference captions improve the language models learned and also lead to better automatic evaluation as shown in [12]. The Microsoft Video to Language dataset (MSR-VTT) [17] addresses this by providing 20 captions for each video.

A popular recipe for solving the visual captioning problem has been to use an encoder–decoder model [14, 13]. The encoder produces a feature vector representation of the input, which the decoder, usually a Long-Short Term Memory (LSTM) network, takes as input and generates a caption.

MM '16, October 15-19, 2016, Amsterdam, Netherlands

DOI: http://dx.doi.org/10.1145/2964284.2984062

Unlike in the case of images, where the convolutional neural network (CNN) image features have become the *de facto* standard features for many image understanding related tasks, no single video feature extraction method has achieved the best performance across tasks and datasets. Dense trajectories [15] and Improved dense trajectories [16] have been popular hand-crafted video feature extractors in action recognition. Following the success of deep CNNs on static images, there have been attempts with 3-D CNNs which operate directly on video segments [4, 11]. However, these models need a lot of training data and are usually pre-trained on some large dataset, e.g. the Sports-1M data.

The task of caption generation also requires us to describe the objects seen in the video and their attributes, in addition to recognizing actions. This can be solved by extracting features from individual frames [13] or keyframes [8] using CNNs pre-trained on the ImageNet dataset.

In this work we explore both problems, video feature extraction and visual content description, for the task of automatic video captioning. We experiment with methods which treat videos as bags of images and with methods mainly focusing on capturing the motion information present in videos. We also study how to combine these features and present an effective method to ensemble multiple caption generators trained on different video features.

2. DATASET

The MSR-VTT dataset consists of 10000 video clips with 20 human-annotated captions for each of them. Each video belongs to one of 20 categories including *music*, *gaming*, *sports*, *news*, etc. The dataset is split into training (6513 clips), validation (497 clips) and test (2990 clips) sets. The training set videos are between 10 to 30 seconds long, with most of them less than 20 seconds in duration.

The reference captions come from a vocabulary of ~30k words, which we have filtered down to ~8k after removing words occurring fewer than 5 times. Although the number of video clips in the dataset is relatively small compared to M-VAD [5] and MPII-MD [10], the dataset is attractive due to the diversity of its videos and due to the larger number of reference captions per video.

Any video captioning algorithm applied to this dataset needs to handle very diverse video styles, eg. video game play footage, news and interviews. Action recognition based features will suffer with videos with lots of cuts and scene changes. Conversely, with frame-based features, the system will fail to identify fine-grained differences in diverse action-oriented categories like sports or cooking. Thus our approach is to use multiple captioning models, each trained on different types of features, and an evaluator network to pick the final caption among the candidates.

3. OUR METHOD

3.1 Overview

We use the standard encoder–decoder framework for our video caption generator. This framework has been widely used in the literature for machine translation and image [14] and video [8, 6] captioning. The encoder stage consists of various feature extraction modules which encode the input video into a vectorial form. The decoder is the language model that generates a caption using these feature vectors.

We also utilize an additional model, an evaluator network which takes as its inputs a generated caption and a video feature, and computes a score measuring how well these two match. This evaluator is used to build an ensemble of multiple caption generator models trained on different features.

3.2 Feature Extraction

We use two different paradigms for video feature extraction. The first one is to treat the video as just a sequence of 2-D static images and use CNNs trained on ImageNet [1] to extract static image features from these frames. The second approach is to treat the video as 3-D data, consisting of a sequence of video segments, and use methods which also consider the variations along the time dimension for feature extraction. In both the above methods, pooling methods are used to combine multiple frame/segment-level features into one video-level feature vector.

3.2.1 Frame-Level Feature Extraction

We use the GoogLeNet [9] model trained on ImageNet for extracting frame-level features. For efficiency, we only extract these features from one frame every second.

In the GoogLeNet we have used the *5th Inception module*, having the dimensionality of 1024. We augment these features with the reverse spatial pyramid pooling proposed in [2] with two scale levels. The second level consists of a 3×3 grid with overlaps and horizontal flipping, resulting in a total of 26 regions, on the scale of two. The activations of the regions are then pooled using diverse combinations of average and maximum pooling. Finally, the activations of the different scales are concatenated resulting in 2048-dimensional features. By using the varying combinations of pooling techniques, we have obtained three somewhat different feature sets from the same network.

We use the mean pooling to fuse the multiple frame-level features extracted from one video into a single vector.

3.2.2 Video Segment Feature Extraction

For extracting segment-based features we have used two different algorithms, namely dense trajectories [15, 16] and 3-D CNN network based C3D features [11].

We have used both the standard [15] and the improved versions [16] of the dense trajectory features. For both versions, the trajectories and their descriptors (HOG, HOF, MBHx and MBHy as described in [15]) are first extracted for the entire video. All of these five features are separately encoded into a fixed-size vector using bag-of-features encoding with a codebook of 1000 vectors. Each codebook is obtained using k-means clustering on 250k random trajectory samples from the training set. Finally, concatenating the vector encodings of each of the descriptors we get a video feature vector of 5000 dimensions.

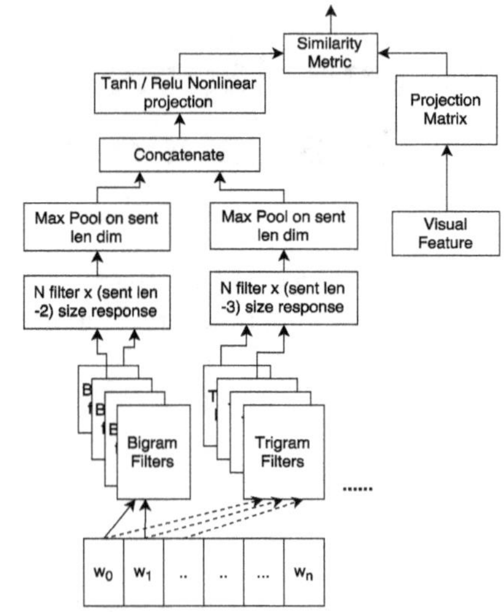

Figure 1: CNN-based evaluator network to compute the similarity between a video and a caption.

As an alternative, we also extract video-segment features with the deep 3-D convolutional model, C3D [11], pre-trained on the Sports-1M dataset. The features are extracted for every 16 frames from the *fc7* layer of the network and mean pooled to get a 4096-dimensional feature vector representation of the video.

We also utilize the video category information available for all videos in all splits of the dataset. This is input to the language model as a one-hot vector of 20 dimensions.

3.3 Language Model

We use the LSTM network based language model and training procedures widely used in visual captioning [14] with some tweaks. Firstly, we train deeper LSTM networks with residual connections between the layers. This is similar to the residual connections introduced in [3] for CNNs. In our case, the output of the lower LSTM layer is added to the output of the above layer with residual connections.

We also allow the language model to use two separate input features, one to initialize the network and the other one to persist throughout the caption generation process as shown in [8]. Thus our language model can be trained using two different feature inputs, *init* and *persist*, fed through separate channels. We utilize this architecture to train many different language models by using the diverse feature pairs from the ones described in Section 3.2.

3.4 Evaluator Network

Using the different video feature combinations we have, we can train diverse caption generator models. Examining the captions generated by them for a set of videos, we find that each model tends to generate the best captions for different videos. If we can reliably evaluate the suitability of a caption for a given video, we can pick out the best candidate and achieve better results than with any single model.

We implement this by training a new *evaluator network* whose task is to pick out the best candidate from the can-

Table 1: Performance of various features and network depths on the validation set of MSR-VTT

#	init	persist	depth	perplex	BLEU-4	METEOR	CIDEr	ROUGE-L
1	dt	gCNN+20Categ	1	27.31	0.396	0.268	0.438	0.588
2	dt	gCNN+20Categ	2	27.73	0.409	0.268	0.433	0.598
3	dt	gCNN+20Categ	3	28.44	0.370	0.262	0.397	0.575
4	idt	gCNN+20Categ	2	28.13	0.398	0.268	0.432	0.587
5	dt	c3dfc7	2	29.58	0.369	0.268	0.413	0.577
6	*CNN evaluator based ensemble of best 4 models*				**0.411**	**0.277**	**0.464**	**0.596**

didate set, given an input video. The model takes as input one video feature and one input sentence and computes a similarity metric between them. The evaluator is trained discriminatively, in contrast to the language models which have been trained generatively. Thus, it learns to focus on semantically interesting phrases without having to learn the details needed to generate a syntactically correct sentence.

Figure 1 shows the block diagram of our evaluator. It consists of a CNN sentence encoder network which takes a sequence of word vectors as input and learns a fixed-size vector embedding of the sentence. The model also has a projection matrix which maps the video feature to the same space as the sentence embedding. We then use the cosine distance to score the similarity between the two embeddings.

The evaluator model is trained to maximize the score assigned to matching caption–video pairs, while minimizing the score assigned to random negative caption–video pairs. We sample up to 50 negative captions per video from the ground truth captions of other videos. The trained evaluator is used to rerank captions from multiple generator models, trained on different feature combinations and architectures, to pick the best matching candidate.

4. EXPERIMENTS AND RESULTS

All LSTM layers in the language models we train have 512 hidden units, but we vary the number of layers as shown in Table 1. We train the language models on the entire training set of the MSR-VTT dataset using stochastic gradient descent with the RMSProp algorithm and dropout regularization. The errors are backpropagated to all the language model parameters and word embedding matrices, but the feature extraction models are kept constant.

In all our experiments we use beam search to generate sentences from a trained model. After experimenting with different beam sizes, we found that the beam size of $b = 5$ works adequately across all our models.

4.1 Validation Set Results

In order to measure the performance differences due to the different feature combinations and architectural changes, we use the validation set of the MSR-VTT dataset which contains 497 videos. Performance is measured quantitatively using the standard automatic evaluation metrics, namely METEOR, CIDEr, ROUGE-L and BLEU.

Table 1 shows the results on the validation set. The columns *init* and *persist* indicate the features used for those input channels, respectively, in the language model. The column *depth* is the number of layers in the language model and *perplex* is the perplexity measure on the validation set.

Models #1, #2 and #3 all use the dense trajectory (dt) features as *init* input and the mean pooled frame-level GoogLeNet features concatenated with the video category vector (gCNN+20Categ) as the *persist* input. They vary in the number of layers in the language model. Comparing their performances we see that the 2-layer model outperforms the single layered model by a small margin, while the 3-layer version is the inferior one.

Model #4 is similar to #2, but uses the improved dense trajectories (idt) as the *init* input instead. Model #5 differs from #2 by the fact that it uses mean pooled 3-D convolutional features as the *persist* input. We see that both #4 and #5 are competitive, but slightly worse than our best single model, #2. Upon qualitatively analyzing the model outputs, we see that each of them performs well on different kinds of videos. For example, model #5, which only uses input features trained for action recognition, does well in videos involving a lot of motion, but suffers in recognizing the overall scenery of the video. Conversely, model #2 trained on frame-level features does better in recognizing objects and scenes, but makes mistakes with the sequence of their appearance, possibly due to the pooling operation. This fact can be observed in examples in Figure 2. Model #5 produces a better caption on the video in the first column, while #2 does better on the video in the second column.

To get maximum utility out of these diverse models, we use the CNN evaluator network to pick the best candidate from the pool of captions generated by our top four models, #1, #2, #4 and #5. The evaluator is trained using the gCNN+20Categ as the video feature. It is shown as model #6 in Table 1. We can see that the CNN evaluator significantly outperforms, in all the four metrics, every model it picks its candidates from. Figure 2 shows an example in the third column where the CNN evaluator picks a better caption than the one generated by our best single model.

4.2 Challenge Results

Since the CNN evaluator model performed the best on the validation set, we submitted that result in the MSR-VTT Challenge. Our submission appears on the leaderboard as *Aalto*. The submissions were evaluated on the blind test set using the above automatic metrics. The results are shown in Table 2a. Our submission was ranked overall second considering the average ranking across the metrics.

The submissions were also subject to human evaluation as the automatic metrics are known to deviate from human judgements in case of both image [7] and video [6] data. The human evaluation was based on three criteria: Coherence (C1), Relevance (C2) and Helpfulness for the blind (C3). Table 2b presents the results of the human evaluation. As per human judgement, our submission was ranked the first among the 22 entries in the challenge.

Comparing the automatic metric and human evaluation based leaderboards we see that the disagreement between the two is relatively minor, with most teams in the top 10

#6: a man is running in a gym
#2: a man is running
#5: a man is playing basketball

#6: a person is playing with a rubix cube
#2: a man is holding a phone
#5: a person is playing with a rubix cube

#6: cartoon characters are interacting
#2: a person is playing a video game
#5: a group of people are talking

Figure 2: Sample captions generated for some test set videos by our models.

Table 2: Top 5 teams as per metrics and human evaluations on the test set

Team	BLEU-4	METEOR	CIDEr	ROUGE-L
v2t_navigator	**0.408**	**0.282**	0.448	**0.609**
Aalto	0.398	0.269	0.457	0.598
VideoLAB	0.391	0.277	0.441	0.606
ruc-uva	0.387	0.269	**0.459**	0.587
Fudan-ILC	0.387	0.268	0.419	0.595

(a) Automatic metric-based evaluation

Team	C1	C2	C3
Aalto	**3.263**	3.104	**3.244**
v2t_navigator	3.261	3.091	3.154
VideoLAB	3.237	**3.109**	3.143
Fudan-ILC	3.185	2.999	2.979
ruc-uva	3.225	2.997	2.933

(b) Human evaluation

changing their ranking by only one position. This can most likely be attributed to having a large number of 20 reference captions per video for the automatic evaluation.

5. CONCLUSIONS

We have presented our video captioning model which shared the first position in the MSR Video to Language Challenge. Our architecture consists of multiple caption generator models, based on the encoder–decoder framework and trained on different video features, and an evaluator model trained to pick the best candidate from the ensemble. We argue that this model is well-suited for the MSR-VTT dataset which contains diverse types of videos. Corroborating our claims, our model topped the human evaluation based leaderboard and finished as second in the automatic metric based leaderboard in the challenge.

6. ACKNOWLEDGMENTS

This work was funded by the grant 251170 of the Academy of Finland and calculations performed with resources of the Aalto University School of Science “Science-IT” project.

7. REFERENCES

[1] J. Deng, W. Dong, R. Socher, L.-J. Li, K. Li, and L. Fei-Fei. ImageNet: A Large-Scale Hierarchical Image Database. In *CVPR*, 2009.

[2] Y. Gong, L. Wang, R. Guo, and S. Lazebnik. Multi-scale orderless pooling of deep convolutional activation features. arXiv.org:1403.1840, 2014.

[3] K. He, X. Zhang, S. Ren, and J. Sun. Deep residual learning for image recognition. *arXiv*, abs/1512.03385, 2015.

[4] A. Karpathy, G. Toderici, S. Shetty, T. Leung, R. Sukthankar, and L. Fei-Fei. Large-scale video classification with convolutional neural networks. In *CVPR*, 2014.

[5] A. Rohrbach, M. Rohrbach, N. Tandon, and B. Schiele. A dataset for movie description. In *CVPR*, 2015.

[6] A. Rohrbach, A. Torabi, M. Rohrbach, N. Tandon, C. J. Pal, H. Larochelle, A. C. Courville, and B. Schiele. Movie description. *arXiv*, abs/1605.03705, 2016.

[7] Y. C. M. Ruggero, Ronchi, and T.-Y. Lin. Microsoft COCO 1st captioning challenge. http://lsun.cs.princeton.edu/slides/caption_open.pdf, 2016 (accessed July 1, 2016).

[8] R. Shetty and J. Laaksonen. Video captioning with recurrent networks based on frame-and video-level features and visual content classification. *ICCV Workshop on LSMDC*, arXiv abs/1512.02949, 2015.

[9] C. Szegedy, W. Liu, Y. Jia, P. Sermanet, S. Reed, D. Anguelov, D. Erhan, V. Vanhoucke, and A. Rabinovich. Going deeper with convolutions. *arXiv*, abs/1409.4842, 2014.

[10] A. Torabi, P. Chris, L. Hugo, and C. Aaron. Using descriptive video services to create a large data source for video annotation research. *arXiv*, abs/1503.01070, 2015.

[11] D. Tran, L. D. Bourdev, R. Fergus, L. Torresani, and M. Paluri. C3D: generic features for video analysis. *arXiv*, abs/1412.0767, 2014.

[12] R. Vedantam, C. Lawrence Zitnick, and D. Parikh. Cider: Consensus-based image description evaluation. In *CVPR*, June 2015.

[13] S. Venugopalan, M. Rohrbach, J. Donahue, R. Mooney, T. Darrell, and K. Saenko. Sequence to sequence-video to text. In *CVPR*, 2015.

[14] O. Vinyals, A. Toshev, S. Bengio, and D. Erhan. Show and tell: A neural image caption generator. In *CVPR*, 2015.

[15] H. Wang, A. Kläser, C. Schmid, and C. Liu. Action recognition by dense trajectories. In *CVPR*, 2011.

[16] H. Wang and C. Schmid. Action recognition with improved trajectories. In *ICCV*, 2013.

[17] J. Xu, T. Mei, T. Yao, and Y. Rui. MSR-VTT: A large video description dataset for bridging video and language. In *CVPR*, 2016.

Contextual Enrichment of Remote-Sensed Events with Social Media Streams

Benjamin Bischke Damian Borth Christian Schulze Andreas Dengel
German Research Center for Artificial Intelligence (DFKI)
D-67663 Kaiserslautern, Germany
{benjamin.bischke, damian.borth, christian.schulze, andreas.dengel}@dfki.de

ABSTRACT

The availability of satellite images for academic or commercial purpose is increasing rapidly due to efforts made by governmental agencies (NASA, ESA) to publish such data openly or commercial startups (PlanetLabs) to provide real-time satellite data. Beyond many commercial application, satellite data is helpful to create situation awareness in disaster recovery and emergency situations such as wildfires, earthquakes, or flooding. To fully utilize such data sources, we present a scalable system for the contextual enrichment of satellite images by crawling and analyzing multimedia content from social media. This information stream can provide vital information from the ground and help to complement remote sensing in situations. We use Twitter as main data source and analyze its textual, visual, temporal, geographical and social dimensions. Visualizations show different aspects of the event allowing high-level comprehension and provide deeper insights into the event as complemented by social media.

Keywords

Social Multimedia;Remote Sensing;Satellite Images

1. INTRODUCTION

We present a solution for the ACM Multimedia 2016 Grand Challenge on the task 'Sky and the Social Eye: Enriching Remote-Sensed Events'. The goal of this challenge is to augment events that can be detected in satellite images with multimedia content from social media streams.

Our system consists of (1) a data crawler, (2) an analysis component and (3) a browser with interactive visualizations. In order to contextualize an event with social media content, users specify a set of keywords and a date range. The crawler requests Twitter's Historical-Powertrack (HPT)API and retrieves all tweets with the corresponding keywords and date range. The system performs an automatic multimedia content analysis and provides visualizations showing the aggregated contextual facets of the event. We establish the link from satellite images to event summarization by considering the temporal and spatial dimension. The low temporal resolution of satellite images is augmented with a continuous timeseries of user activities in social media streams. Thereby, big changes in satellite images can be directly mapped to spikes in user activities and online discourse of the event. Extracted locations from social media are used for collecting satellite images and for linking them to user generated content such as images of the event.

Our solution addresses the evaluation criteria *Interestingness* and *quality of demonstration* by considering multimodality of multimedia content in combination with visualizations that emphasize the contextual facets of an event. The focus of our contextual augmentation is determined by textual, visual, temporal, geographical, social dimensions. Our goal is to tell the broader story of an event by providing a summarization with multiple views of the event.

Scalability and *Technical contribution* are addressed by presenting an architecture that is capable of analyzing tweets at large-scale. Our analysis component relies on a distributed task queue, which allows to scale horizontally, as tasks can be analyzed in parallel on multiple compute nodes. We further suggest a solution for Near-Duplicate Detecion of images in social media streams using features from Convolutional Neural Networks (CNN's).

The remainder of this paper is structured as follows. Section 2 covers related work and in Section 3 details of our system are presented. Section 4 describes the user interface and results while Section 5 concludes the paper.

2. RELATED WORK

Social Media Streams have emerged as a popular medium for collaborative information sharing thus representing valuable information sources for new applications. Researchers leveraged social media content for public opinion mining [18], [11], [6], for monitoring and prediction of infectious disease outbreaks [15], [16], for coordination of rescue efforts after disasters [7], [13], [10] as well as for analyzing the social reflection of the society [9]. Closest to our work is the investigation in the interaction of social media with events caused by natural disasters for situational awareness. The goal of such systems [24] [14] is to provide users a big picture of an event in a way that rescuer can asses the situation and act accordingly. [24] uses a data capturing component for accessing Twitter APIs and applies burst detection, online clustering for topic discovery and classification for impact assessment on these tweets. [14] monitors tweets and to detect a target event and find the center of the event loca-

MM '16, October 15-19, 2016, Amsterdam, Netherlands
© 2016 ACM. ISBN 978-1-4503-3603-1/16/10. . . $15.00
DOI: http://dx.doi.org/10.1145/2964284.2984063

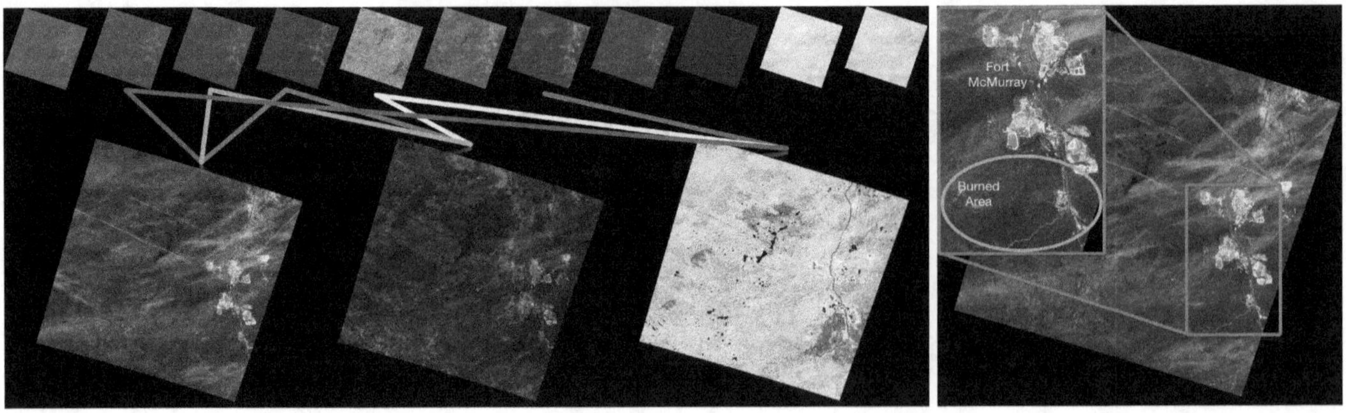

Figure 1: Left: This figure shows the eleven original bands of the Landsat 8 satellite and three generated images after combining bands. Left bottom shows an RGB-Image using Bands 4-3-2. Middle bottom: False-Color Image emphasizing the vegetation in red color using Bands 5-4-3. Right bottom: False-Color Image showing fire burn scars in red color using Bands 7-5-2. Right: This visualization shows an computed RGB-Satellite-Image of Fort McMurray. The brownish color illustrates burned forest scars after the Wildfire in May 2016.

tion. Tweets are classified based on keywords and passed to a probabilistic spatiotemporal model which estimates the location of target event with an particle filter. [1] considers only planned events (such as concerts, sports or political events) and suggests strategies to query and identify related content across social media sites.

While these systems put a strong focus on event detection using methods of burst detection, anomaly detection and unsupervised clustering using text or images, our solution can be understood as a targeted search approach for social media. Given a set of keywords for an event, our system crawls multimedia content and enriches it with multiple contextual aspects. Our motivation is to provide the big picture of an event going beyond a textual or visual event summarization utilizing independent signals in a multimodal fashion [23].

3. SATELLITE IMAGE PROCESSING

NASA's Landsat 8[1] is an American Earth observation satellite which senses the entire earth in 16 days capturing scenes with an approximate size of 170 km north-south by 183 km east-west. The Landsat 8 satellite scans the earth's surface with multiple remote sensors providing 11 bands of spectral images. To construct images from these spectral bands, the following steps are executed:

3.1 Satellite Image Collection

In a first step our system fetches the freely available Landsat 8 images from Amazon S3. In order to download images of a specific location, it is necessary to determine the correct scene's path and row of the satellite. We used the *Landsat8 Metadata API*[2] which provides the mapping from geolocation to scene-id. Our system collects image scenes in two ways: (1) by manually specifying the location and (2) by using extracted locations from social media. Potential positions of an event can be automatically identified by leveraging frequently mentioned location names in text messages and incorporating GPS-annotations of tweets.

[1]http://landsat.usgs.gov/landsat8.php

[2]https://github.com/developmentseed/landsat-api

3.2 Satellite Image Composition

Landsat 8 images consist of nine spectral bands (with different wavelength such as blue, green, red, near infrared(NIR) and short-wave infrared (SWIR)) as well as two thermal infrared bands. Insights of an scene can be extracted by combining different bands into one image. Within this work we computed an RBG color image and two False-Color Images. False-Color images incorporate not the usual Red, Green, Blue colors, but further information (such as NIR or SWIR) into the RGB-channels allowing to focus on different aspects of the scene. We computed two False-Color Images emphasizing the vegetation health and wildfire scars of the scene.

4. SOCIAL MEDIA PROCESSING

The proposed social media processing pipeline can be split into two major processing steps:

1. The social media data crawler gathers all tweets for an related event by requesting public and historical search API of Twitter. The downloaded tweets are bundled into packages and passed to the analysis component.
2. The social media analysis component is divided into multiple tasks, which are queued by the asynchronous task queue Celery. Celery is based on the distributed message passing system RabbitMQ and allows to distribute and analyze the tasks among multiple compute nodes. Analysis results are stored into a MongoDB.

4.1 Social Media Data-Crawler

We use Twitter as a primary data source for analyzing multimedia content. [11] reported that user activities such as online posts and comments are often triggered by specific events, making Twitter an important medium for information spreading. In addition to text messages, tweets contain rich metadata, such as timestamps, geolocations, hyper-links to webpages, news articles and images. This metadata is valuable for a multimodal analysis and for bootstrapping further multimedia content from social media.

Within the scope of this paper, our crawler gathered tweets by requesting Twitter's Historical PowerTrack-API. HPT allows to collect on historical tweets from the past, by specifying filter-rules such as keywords, date-ranges or geospatial searches. We use Twitter's Public-API for realtime events, as the returned tweets are limited to the last seven days.

4.2 Social Media Analysis

After downloading all tweets for one event the analysis is applied in four steps: (1) Metadata-Analysis, (2) Text-Analysis, (3) Image-Analysis and (4) Aggregation.

Metadata Analysis.

The goal of this processing step is to collect all metadata associated with the tweet including the resolution of URLs within the tweet and its linked media content (i.e. images, news). Since locally or globally discussed events are recognized by leveraging GPS-annotations of tweets this information provides a fundamental link to the geo-location for satellite imagery. Geo-locations are mapped to countries and binned into a projected hexagonal grid of the world. Our system creates a timeline by extracting tweet creation timestamps. For scalability reasons, we reduce the range of possible timestamps by means of discretization of the timestamps to the nearest four hours of every day. Influential users in social media applications are determined by multiple aspects, such as the Klout-Score. A Klout-Score represents the social online influence of users based on social media analysis. The score considers the user's network, the generated content and interactions of other users with that content. In addition, we rank users according to the retweet and favourite count of their published tweets. A high retweet or favorite count indicates that the tweet reached many users in the network, thus having some degree of influence on other users. The system identifies URLs in tweets, follows the links and downloads the corresponding resources. Unique hyper-links mentioned in multiple tweets are downloaded only once. Duplicated Web-Resources having different URLs are recognized in the following analysis steps.

Text Analysis.

The following steps are applied on the text messages of tweets: Twitter users have the option to tag their tweets with so-called hashtags. Hastags can be understood as a meta-label, describing an topic or aspect of the event with one word or few words. We extract the most common hashtags in all tweets as they represent a special collaborative form of topic summarization from users. We perform a Sentiment-Analysis on the twitter messages. The analysis is based on the popular linguistics based sentiment model SentiStrength [20], which is optimized on short social web texts. SentiStrength provides a positive and a negative sentiment score in range of -4 to +4. To decide whether an event is globally or more locally discussed, we apply in addition to geographical augmentation a language detection. Tweets from HPT are already partially annotated from Twitter with languages. On the remaining messages we apply Bloomberg's language tool NLP<GO>. Tweet-messages are ranked by retweet and favourite counts. These top tweets have been shared or liked by many users of the social network, thus being an important and influential representation of the topic.

Image Analysis.

Images liked within tweets are analyzed with respect to the following aspects: Since user generated content is often very noisy [22], we first apply a image filtering to remove

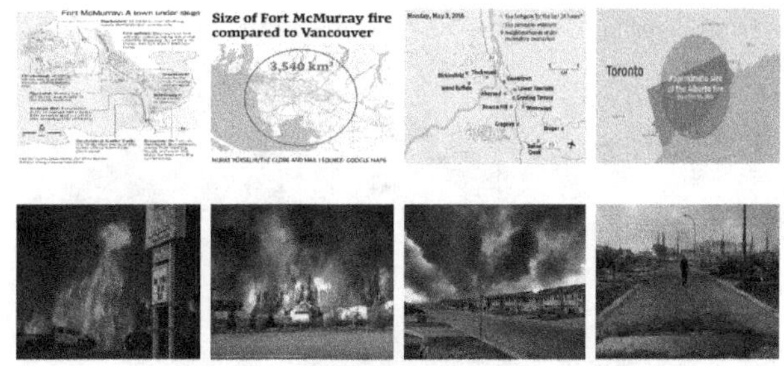

Figure 2: Most frequently shared images on Twitter for the event 'Wildfire Fort McMurray' in Canada. Top: Filtered images classified as synthetically generated. Bottom: Images classified as natural.

synthetic images such as logos, maps, cartoons which appear often but to not directly show evidence of the observed event. We first generated a dataset by crawling 5.716 synthetic images using web search and randomly sampling the same number of images from the YFCC100M dataset [21]. We used 70% of the dataset for training a linear Support Vector Machine with the representation of the fc6 layer of AlexNet [8]. Testing on the remaining images, we achieved an classification accuracy of 98,6%. Compared to the approach proposed in [12] we accomplish a 2% improvement.

Events with a global impact i.e. with high attention in news and social media have often a set of iconic images that stay in the head of the society. Our goal is to find the most popular ones that are strongly associated with the event in social media. A first approach for this is the selection of images with the most frequent hyper-links in the tweet corpus. However, we observed that popular images are often copied on different servers and thereby getting a new URL. Additional image manipulations such as cropping, scaling and different JPEQ-Quality levels applied on the images make a duplicate detection purely based on image pixels infeasible. We solve this problem by using a high-level representation of the image content and searching for every image for its near duplicates. Our detection algorithm extracts the representation of the fc6 feature layer of the 16 layered CNN VGG-Net from [17] for every image in filtered image set. To detect near duplicates the most similar images are retrieved using the cosine distance. Images above a empirically determined threshold are considered as near duplicates and are together with the searched image removed from image set. The approach is iteratively applied on the remaining images.

We tested features from multiple layers (fc6, fc7, pool5) of state-of-the-art CNN's (AlexNet[8], ResNet [5], VGG-Net[17], and GoogLeNet [19]) for our near duplicate detection approach. Our evaluation is based on the INRIA CopyDays dataset[4] which contains 157 original images and includes three transformations (1) 16% resizing of the image surface plus different JPEQ-Quality compressions (2) cropping of the image surface between 5% to 80% as well as (3) strong transformations such as print, scan and perspective effects. While for the former two transformations nine near duplicate images are generated, the latter one has only 223 images. For an overall evaluation, we therefore only used cropping and JPEQ-Compression transformations. By comparing Mean Average Precision of the top nine images, the fc6-feature of VGG-S-Net delivered the best result.

In order to perform visual sentiment analysis on the fil-

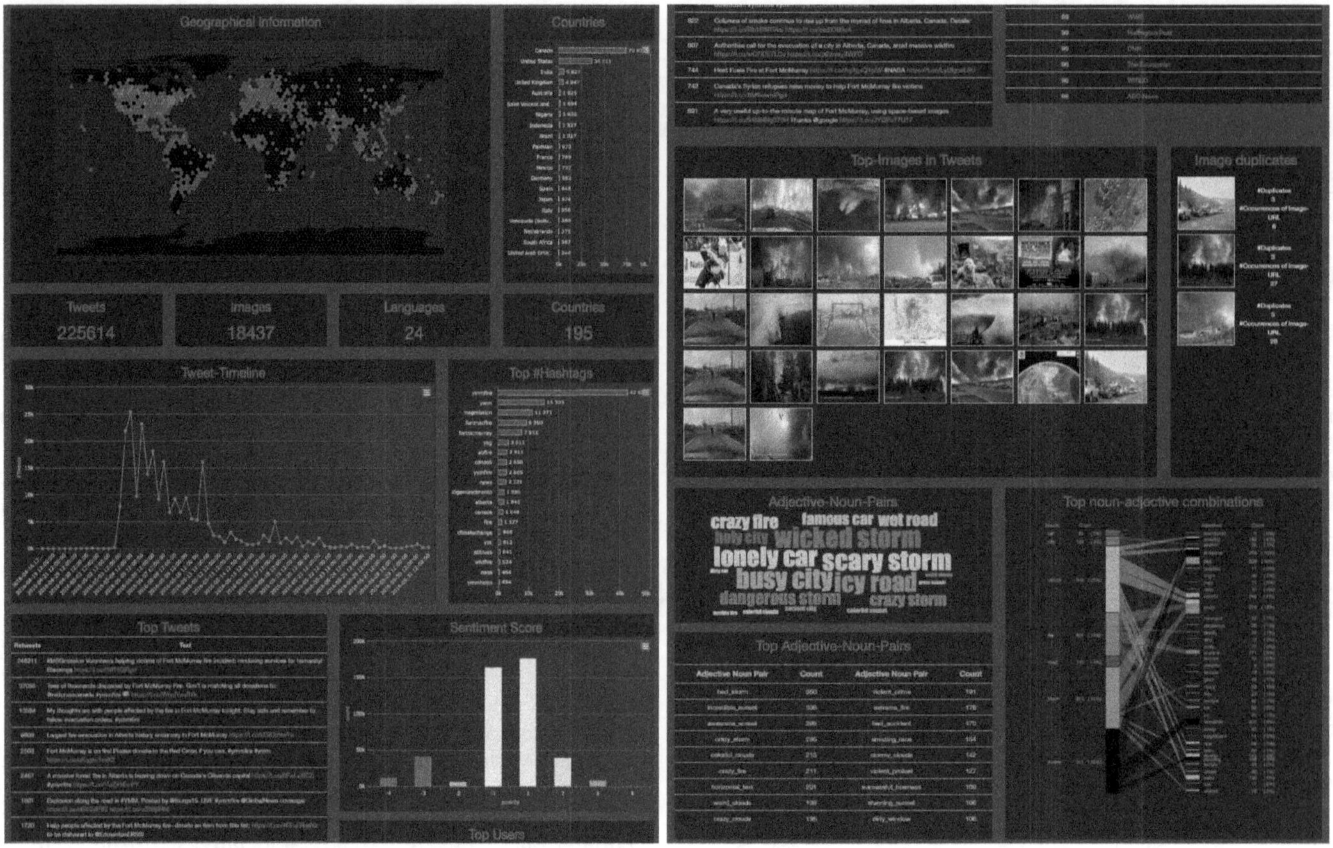

Figure 3: This visualizations shows two sections of our browser. Left: Geographical and temporal activities from social media as well as most influential tweets are visualized for the Wildfire in Fort McMurray are visualized. Left: Most popular images contained in tweets, together with the extracted Adjective-Noun Pairs and near duplicates are visualized. Bottom right shows all combinations of nouns and adjectives on all images

tered images from social media, we apply the concept classifier tool: DeepSentiBank [3]. DeepSentiBank is a fine-tuned Convolutional Neural Network (CNN), that is based on the Visual Sentiment Ontology (VSO) [2]. The VSO consists of 3244 Adjective-Noun-Pairs (ANPs), the classifier is trained on a subset of the VSO with 2089 ANPs. We apply DeepSentiBank on each image and select the top ten ANPs with the highest probability.

Temporal Aggregation.

We aggregate the analysis results from the previous steps for each day which is then aggregated over the entire period. Here, we use the top ranked results of each day as aggregation function for the entire observation period. This allows the system to perform analysis on subsets of days within the observation period.

User Interface.

We developed an online available browser[3] with a suite of visualizations for interacting and exploring the extracted information for an event. Our browser has a entry page which shows all analyzed events and links to the event-specific summary. Visualizations on that website provide an overview of the topic and the contextualized content from social media. Geo-tagged images are visualized on the collected satellite images. Fig. 3 illustrates the geographical, textual and visual extracted and enriched aspects of the example event of the Wildfire in the Fort McMurray, in May 2016.

5. CONCLUSIONS

We presented a scalable system for the contextual enrichment of satellite images by crawling and analyzing multimedia content from social media. We use Twitter as main data source for collecting data and bootstrapping further multimedia content such as images. The focus of our the social media analysis is determined by textual, visual, temporal, geographical and social dimensions. Visualizations show different aspects of the event, allow high-level comprehension and provide deeper insights into the contextualized event from a social media perspective.

6. ACKNOWLEDGMENTS

This work was partially funded by the BMBF project Multimedia Opinion Mining under (MOM: 01WI15002).

[3]http://mom.dfki.de/demos/deep_eye/

7. REFERENCES

[1] H. Becker, D. Iter, M. Naaman, and L. Gravano. Identifying content for planned events across social media sites. In *Proceedings of the Fifth ACM International Conference on Web Search and Data Mining*, WSDM '12, pages 533–542, New York, NY, USA, 2012. ACM.

[2] D. Borth, R. Ji, T. Chen, T. Breuel, and S.-F. Chang. Large-scale visual sentiment ontology and detectors using adjective noun pairs. In *Proceedings of the 21st ACM international conference on Multimedia*, pages 223–232. ACM, 2013.

[3] T. Chen, D. Borth, T. Darrell, and S. Chang. Deepsentibank: Visual sentiment concept classification with deep convolutional neural networks. *CoRR*, abs/1410.8586, 2014.

[4] M. Douze, H. Jégou, H. Sandhawalia, L. Amsaleg, and C. Schmid. Evaluation of gist descriptors for web-scale image search. In *Proceedings of the ACM International Conference on Image and Video Retrieval*, page 19. ACM, 2009.

[5] K. He, X. Zhang, S. Ren, and J. Sun. Deep residual learning for image recognition. *arXiv preprint arXiv:1512.03385*, 2015.

[6] W. He, S. Zha, and L. Li. Social media competitive analysis and text mining: A case study in the pizza industry. *International Journal of Information Management*, 33(3):464–472, 2013.

[7] M. E. Keim and E. Noji. Emergent use of social media: a new age of opportunity for disaster resilience. *American journal of disaster medicine*, 6(1):47–54, 2010.

[8] A. Krizhevsky, I. Sutskever, and G. E. Hinton. Imagenet classification with deep convolutional neural networks. In F. Pereira, C. J. C. Burges, L. Bottou, and K. Q. Weinberger, editors, *Advances in Neural Information Processing Systems 25*, pages 1097–1105. Curran Associates, Inc., 2012.

[9] D. Lazer, A. S. Pentland, L. Adamic, S. Aral, A. L. Barabasi, D. Brewer, N. Christakis, N. Contractor, J. Fowler, M. Gutmann, et al. Life in the network: the coming age of computational social science. *Science (New York, NY)*, 323(5915):721, 2009.

[10] B. R. Lindsay. Social media and disasters: Current uses, future options, and policy considerations, 2011.

[11] D. Maynard, K. Bontcheva, and D. Rout. Challenges in developing opinion mining tools for social media. *Proceedings of the@ NLP can u tag# usergeneratedcontent*, pages 15–22, 2012.

[12] P. J. McParlane, A. J. McMinn, and J. M. Jose. Picture the scene...;: Visually summarising social media events. In *Proceedings of the 23rd ACM International Conference on Conference on Information and Knowledge Management*, pages 1459–1468. ACM, 2014.

[13] L. Palen. Online social media in crisis events. *Educause Quarterly*, 31(3):76–78, 2008.

[14] T. Sakaki, M. Okazaki, and Y. Matsuo. Earthquake shakes twitter users: Real-time event detection by social sensors. In *Proceedings of the 19th International Conference on World Wide Web*, WWW '10, pages 851–860, New York, NY, USA, 2010. ACM.

[15] J. Sarasohn-Kahn. The wisdom of patients: Health care meets online social media, 2008.

[16] C. W. Schmidt. Using social media to predict and track disease outbreaks. *Environmental health perspectives*, 120(1):A31, 2012.

[17] K. Simonyan and A. Zisserman. Very deep convolutional networks for large-scale image recognition. *arXiv preprint arXiv:1409.1556*, 2014.

[18] P. Sobkowicz, M. Kaschesky, and G. Bouchard. Opinion mining in social media: Modeling, simulating, and forecasting political opinions in the web. *Government Information Quarterly*, 29(4):470–479, 2012.

[19] C. Szegedy, W. Liu, Y. Jia, P. Sermanet, S. Reed, D. Anguelov, D. Erhan, V. Vanhoucke, and A. Rabinovich. Going deeper with convolutions. In *Proceedings of the IEEE Conference on Computer Vision and Pattern Recognition*, pages 1–9, 2015.

[20] M. Thelwall, K. Buckley, G. Paltoglou, D. Cai, and A. Kappas. Sentiment strength detection in short informal text. *Journal of the American Society for Information Science and Technology*, 61(12):2544–2558, 2010.

[21] B. Thomee, D. A. Shamma, G. Friedland, B. Elizalde, K. Ni, D. Poland, D. Borth, and L.-J. Li. Yfcc100m: The new data in multimedia research. *Commun. ACM*, 59(2):64–73, Jan. 2016.

[22] A. Ulges, D. Borth, and T. M. Breuel. Visual concept learning from weakly labeled web videos. In *Video Search and Mining*, pages 203–232. Springer, 2010.

[23] A. Ulges, C. Schulze, D. Borth, and A. Stahl. Pornography detection in video benefits (a lot) from a multi-modal approach. In *Proceedings of the 2012 ACM international workshop on Audio and multimedia methods for large-scale video analysis*, pages 21–26. ACM, 2012.

[24] J. Yin, A. Lampert, M. Cameron, B. Robinson, and R. Power. Using social media to enhance emergency situation awareness. *IEEE Intelligent Systems*, 27(6):52–59, 2012.

Early Embedding and Late Reranking for Video Captioning

Jianfeng Dong[†] Xirong Li[‡*] Weiyu Lan[‡] Yujia Huo[‡] Cees G. M. Snoek[§]
[†]College of Computer Science and Technology, Zhejiang University
[‡]Key Lab of Data Engineering and Knowledge Engineering, Renmin University of China
[§]Intelligent Systems Lab Amsterdam, University of Amsterdam

ABSTRACT

This paper describes our solution for the MSR Video to Language Challenge. We start from the popular ConvNet + LSTM model, which we extend with two novel modules. One is *early embedding*, which enriches the current low-level input to LSTM by tag embeddings. The other is *late reranking*, for re-scoring generated sentences in terms of their relevance to a specific video. The modules are inspired by recent works on image captioning, repurposed and redesigned for video. As experiments on the MSR-VTT validation set show, the joint use of these two modules add a clear improvement over a non-trivial ConvNet + LSTM baseline under four performance metrics. The viability of the proposed solution is further confirmed by the blind test by the organizers. Our system is ranked at the 4th place in terms of overall performance, while scoring the best CIDEr-D, which measures the human-likeness of generated captions.

Keywords

Video captioning; MSR Video to Language Challenge; Tag embedding; Sentence reranking

1. INTRODUCTION

The goal of this paper is to automatically assign a caption to a web video, such as 'A teenage couple perform in an amateur musical' or 'Cars racing on a road surrounded by lots of people'. State-of-the-art approaches rely on a deep convolutional network with a recurrent neural network [13,15], and emphasize on innovating inside the network architecture [9,16]. We focus on enhancing video captioning, without the need to change internal structures of the networks.

We are inspired by [2]. The authors employ a bi-modal semantic embedding model to project image and text into a common subspace, wherein image-text similarity is computed and later used for sentence reranking to refine captions for images. We also learn from [4], which annotates a test image with Flickr tags by neighbor voting [5], and reranks sentences generated by an LSTM according to their match with the tags. We adopt the two ideas, but repurpose and redesign the captioning architecture for video.

Contributions of this work are as follows. We answer the MSR Video to Language Challenge by proposing an *Early Embedding* and *Late Reranking* solution. Given the importance of the initial input to LSTM, early embedding is introduced to enrich the network input by tag embeddings, based on a novel re-use of video tagging results. Late reranking is to promote relevant captions by re-scoring a list of candidate sentences. Extensive experiments on the MSR-VTT-10k validation set shows that our solution brings clear improvements to a ConvNet + LSTM baseline under varied metrics including BLEU4, METEOR, CIDEr-D and ROUGE-L. The effectiveness is also verified by the blind test conducted by the organizers.

2. PROPOSED SOLUTION

Our solution is inspired by the popular ConvNet + LSTM architecture [14]. We introduce two new modules, i.e., early embedding and late reranking, designed to enhance the input and the output of the underlying sentence generation model. The proposed solution is illustrated in Fig. 1. Our system is able to cope with novel sentence generation models as long as they accept a real-valued feature vector as input and produce a number of sentences.

2.1 Video Representation

Following the common practice of applying pre-trained ConvNets for video content analysis [7,9,15], we extract ConvNet features for a given video clip. Frames are uniformly sampled from the clip with an interval of 10 frames. A video level representation is obtained by mean pooling on ConvNet features extracted from the frames. Concerning the choice of the ConvNet, we employ Googlenet-bu4k, a variant of Googlenet [10] trained by Mettes *et al.* [7] using a bottom-up reorganization of the ImageNet hierarchy. Our experiments confirm that this model, though originally aiming for video event recognition, is better than its standard counterpart for video captioning as well. The pool5 layer after ReLU is used, resulting in a feature vector of 1,024 dimensions. Observing the increasing popularity of 3-D ConvNets (C3D) for video captioning [9,15], we have also experimented with a C3D model trained by Tran *et al.* on one million sports videos [11]. Though being longer (4,096-dim), the C3D feature is inferior to the Googlenet-bu4k feature according to our experiments. Moreover, in

*Corresponding author (xirong@ruc.edu.cn)

MM '16, October 15 - 19, 2016, Amsterdam, Netherlands

ISBN 978-1-4503-3603-1/16/10...$15.00

DOI: http://dx.doi.org/10.1145/2964284.2984064

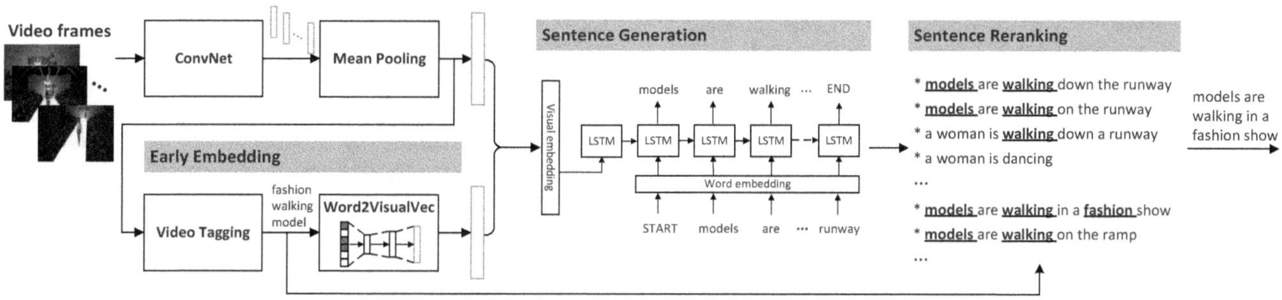

Figure 1: Proposed video captioning system. Given a test video, we extract a video-level ConvNet feature, which is concatenated with a tag embedding by the *Early Embedding* module. The enriched input is fed into the *Sentence Generation* module, which outputs a list of 20 sentences. By *reranking* these sentences either by tag matching or video-text similarity, our system chooses the top ranked sentence as the final video caption.

contrast to previous works [9, 15], the concatenation of the two features does not yield any improvement. Hence, we rely on the Googlenet-bu4k feature as the visual input to the sentence generation module.

2.2 Early Embedding

Instead of directly feeding the visual feature to the sentence generation module as done in previous works, we enrich the input using tags detected to be relevant with respect to the given video. Next, we describe how the tags are predicted, and consequently two strategies for tag embedding.

2.2.1 Video Tagging

Tags are predicted through multiple channels. First, since we have employed two ConvNets, it is natural to leverage their semantic output, i.e., a set of 4k ImageNet labels predicted by Googlenet-bu4k and a set of 487 sport-related concepts from C3D. The 4k labels are down-sampled from the complete ImageNet dataset by using a bottom-up reorganization of the ImageNet hierarchy, excluding over-specific classes and classes with few images and thus making the final classes have balanced positive images [7]. Besides, we train linear SVM classifiers on the public FCVID dataset [3], giving us a video tagging system that predicts 237 video categories. Notice that these three concept sets were constructed independently in advance to this challenge. In order to predict tags more relevant to the challenge, we further exploit the MSR-VTT training set [15] by the neighbor voting algorithm [5]. Despite its simplicity, this algorithm remains on par with more complex alternatives [6]. Given a test video, ten nearest neighbor videos are retrieved from the training set, and tags with the highest occurrence in captions of the neighbors are selected.

Although the C3D feature is less effective than the Googlenet-bu4k feature, it appears to better capture strong motion-related patterns, say in sports. Hence, we employ both features for neighbor voting. This results in tags predicted by five channels, summarized as

1. A pretrained Googlenet-bu4k [7], predicting 4,437 ImageNet classes;
2. A pretrained C3D [11], predicting 487 sport-related concepts;
3. Linear SVMs trained by us on FCVID using the Googlenet-bu4k feature, predicting 237 video categories;
4. Neighbor voting with the MSR-VTT training set as the source set and the Googlenet-bu4k feature for similarity computation;
5. Neighbor voting with the MSR-VTT training set as the source set but using the C3D feature instead.

We fuse the multiple tagging results by majority voting, empirically preserving the top three tags for the subsequent tag embedding.

2.2.2 Tag Embedding

For deriving a vectorized representation from the predicted tags, Bag-of-Words (BoW) is a straightforward choice. We construct the BoW vocabulary by sorting tags in descending order in terms of their frequency in the training set and preserve the top 1,024 tags, a number equaling to the size of the Googlenet-bu4k feature. Entries of the BoW vector are zero except for those dimensions corresponding to the predicted tags.

As BoW is known to have difficulties in describing inter-tag relationships, we further consider a deeper tag embedding using a very recent Word2VisualVec model [1], which is capable of predicting visual ConvNet features from text. Word2VisualVec adds a multi-layer perceptron on top of Word2Vec [8], with the network optimized such that the output of an input sentence is close to the ConvNet feature of an image the sentence is describing. Hence, Word2VisualVec captures visual and semantic similarities. We empirically choose a three layer structure of 500-100-1024 for predicting Googlenet-bu4k features and 500-1000-2000-4096 for predicting C3D features. By default the model embeds tags into the Googlenet-bu4k feature space for its good performance, unless stated otherwise.

Given either BoW or Word2VisualVec embedding, the tag vector is concatenated with the Googlenet-bu4k feature extracted from the video, and fed into the sentence generation module described next.

2.3 Sentence Generation

We train the image captioning model of Vinyals *et al.* [14] for sentence generation. At the heart of the model is an LSTM network which generates a sentence given the visual input, with the goal of maximizing the sentence's posterior probability. Let θ be the network parameters. The probability is expressed as $p(S|x;\theta)$, where x is the video feature, S is a sentence of n words, $S = \{w_1, ..., w_n\}$. Applying the chain rule together with a log function, the probability is computed via

$$\log p(S|x;\theta) = \sum_{t=0}^{n+1} \log p(w_t|x, w_0, ..., w_{t-1};\theta), \quad (1)$$

where w_0 = START and w_{n+1} = END are two special tokens indicting the beginning and the end of the sentence. Conditional probabilities in Eq. 1 are computed in a greedy manner, based on the current chosen word and the LSTM memory. The size of the memory cell in LSTM is empirically set to 512. Beam search is applied to generate a list of 20 sentences most likely to describe the test video.

Next, we aim to improve the quality of video captioning by sentence reranking.

2.4 Late Reranking

We are inspired by concept-based [4] and semantic embedding based [2] sentence ranking, but we repurpose and redesign them for video.

For concept-based sentence reranking, instead of averaging over tags as described in [4], we use the sum function to favor sentences that maximize the matches. For instance, given prediction 'dog' (0.6) and 'playing' (0.3), we prefer 'a dog is playing' to 'a dog is running on grass'. Given the predicted tag set P, the matched score of a sentence S is computed as

$$TagMatch(S;P) = \sum_{w \in P \cap S} score(w), \quad (2)$$

where $score(w)$ is the tag relevance score provided by the video tagging system described in Section 2.2. As our experiments show, using sum instead of averaging gives a clear boost to the performance.

For semantic embedding based sentence reranking, we reuse the previously trained Word2VisualVec to project each sentence into the same visual feature space as the video. Consequently, we compute the video-text relevance score in terms of the cosine similarity between the corresponding ConvNet features.

The sentences are reranked in descending order either by the TagMatch scores or by the cross-media scores, and the top positioned one is chosen as the final video caption.

3. EVALUATION

3.1 Experimental Setup

Datasets. Our video captioning system is trained using the MSR-VTT-10K [15] training set, which consists of 6,513 video clips. Each clip is associated with 20 English sentences generated by crowd sourcing and one of 20 high-level YouTube categories such as "music", "people"and "gaming". The system and its various settings are evaluated using the MSR-VTT-10K validation set of 497 video clips.

Performance metric. Following the evaluation protocol, we report BLEU@4, METEOR, CIDEr-D and ROUGE-L. CIDEr-D is specifically designed to measure the extent to which automatically generated sentences appearing to be written by humans [12], while the other three metrics are originally meant for evaluating machine translation. Averaged value of these metrics is used for overall comparison in the Challenge.

3.2 Experiments

Our baseline is a standard ConvNet + LSTM architecture, without early embedding and late reranking. It scores BLEU4 of 37.9, METEOR of 25.0, CIDEr-D of 35.7 and ROUGE-L of 57.0 on the validation set, see Table 1. In order to investigate the effect of early embedding, late reranking and their joint use on the performance, we incrementally add and evaluate the individual components with varied settings. This results in fifteen runs in total.

Early Embedding. For the ease of comparison, the runs have been sorted in descending order according to average value of the four metrics. As we see from Table 1, the runs with early embedding only, i.e., #2, #6, #7 and #8, are ranked ahead of the baseline, showing the effectiveness of early embedding. Given the same tagging result, either from KNN or from MajorityVote, Word2VisualVec gives comparable or better performance than BoW.

Late Reranking. We compare the four runs using late reranking alone, i.e., #3, #11, #13 and #15, against the baseline. The fact that two runs are positioned after the baseline suggests that the reranking module needs to be designed more carefully. Compared to the baseline, CIDEr-D and METEOR of run#13 in fact increase from 35.7 to 38.1 and from 25.0 to 25.9, respectively. Nonetheless, there is a significant drop on BLEU4, from 37.9 to 31.5. This is probably because BLEU4 (and similarly ROUGE-L) relies on precise matches between n-grams, while such an order is discarded in the Word2VisualVec embedding. Interestingly, video-text similarity computed in the C3D feature space outperforms the baseline, with its BLEU4 remaining lower. The result suggests that utilizing a visual feature different from the feature that is already used for sentence generation is more effective for sentence reranking. TagMatch is the most effective implementation of the reranking module.

Early Embedding and Late Reranking. As Table 1 shows, the runs that jointly use early embedding and late reranking beat the baseline except for run#14 which uses the less effective TagMatch-mean strategy. The best solution is to perform video tagging by MajorityVote, encode the predicted tags via Word2VisualVec, and later rerank the sentences by TagMatch.

Blind test result. For blind test on the test set, we are allowed to submit three runs at the maximum. Their configurations correspond to run #1, #2 and #6 in Table 1. An overview of their performance on the test set is presented in Table 2. Performance rank is consistent with the validation set, showing that our solution generalizes to previously unseen data. Some video tagging and captioning results are given in Table 3. Our system scores the best CIDEr-D.

4. CONCLUSIONS

Experiments on the MSR-VTT validation set and the blind test on the test set support conclusions as follows. The proposed early embedding and late reranking solution can effectively improve the state-of-the-art ConvNet + LSTM method for video captioning. We demonstrate a successful re-use of image classification results from ConvNets for refining video captions, even though they were not meant for this purpose. Our recommendation is to perform video tagging by MajorityVote, encode the predicted tags via Word2VisualVec, and later rerank the sentences by TagMatch.

Table 1: Performance of our solution with varied settings on the validation set, sorted by averaged value of the four metrics in descending order. BoW means representing predicted tags by bag-of-words, while Word2VisualVec is to encode these tags using Word2VisualVec. TagMatch-mean denotes the strategy described in [4].

Run	Module Configuration		Performance Metrics			
	Early Embedding	*Late Reranking*	*BLEU4*	*METEOR*	*CIDEr-D*	*ROUGE-L*
1	MajorityVote + Word2VisualVec	TagMatch	39.4	**27.5**	**48.0**	**60.0**
2	MajorityVote + Word2VisualVec	–	**40.5**	26.0	44.1	58.7
3	–	TagMatch	38.4	27.0	44.1	59.1
4	KNN + BoW	TagMatch	37.0	26.5	45.2	58.3
5	MajorityVote + Bow	TagMatch	37.9	26.4	44.4	58.1
6	KNN + Word2VisualVec	–	40.3	25.4	40.6	57.8
7	KNN + BoW	–	38.6	25.5	41.3	58.7
8	MajorityVote + BoW	–	39.0	25.2	41.5	58.0
9	MajorityVote + Word2VisualVec	video-text similarity (C3D)	34.9	26.4	41.1	57.0
10	MajorityVote + Word2VisualVec	video-text similarity	33.8	26.4	40.9	56.7
11	–	video-text similarity (C3D)	33.9	26.2	40.1	56.5
baseline	–	–	37.9	25.0	35.7	57.0
13	–	video-text similarity	31.5	25.9	38.1	55.4
14	MajorityVote + Word2VisualVec	TagMatch-mean	32.5	23.8	37.2	55.0
15	–	TagMatch-mean	31.6	23.4	31.0	54.0

Table 2: Performance on the test set. The top rows correspond to the top three performers.

Official rank	Submission	BLEU4	METEOR	CIDEr-D	ROUGE-L
1	v2t_navigator	**40.8**	**28.2**	44.8	**60.9**
2	Aalto	39.8	26.9	45.7	59.8
3	VideoLAB	39.1	27.7	44.1	60.6
	This work:				
4	*run#1*	38.7	26.9	**45.9**	58.7
–	*run#2*	39.2	25.4	41.0	58.3
–	*run#6*	39.3	24.7	39.6	57.6

Table 3: Examples showing good (top four rows) and bad (bottom two rows) video tags and captions.

Test video	Tagging	Captioning
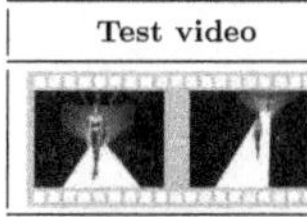	fashion, walking, model	**baseline:** a woman is dancing **run2:** models are walking down the runway **run1:** models are walking in a fashion show
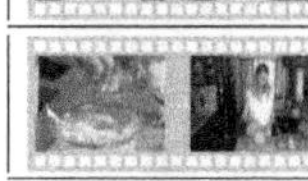	woman, kitchen, cooking	**baseline:** a woman is cooking **run2:** a woman is cooking **run1:** a woman is cooking in a kitchen
	cat, baby, dog	**baseline:** a man and a woman are eating food **run2:** a baby is playing with a cat **run1:** a baby is playing with a cat
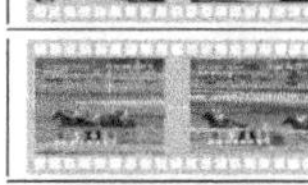	horse, racing, man	**baseline:** gameplay footage of someone playing a game **run2:** people are riding horses **run1:** people are racing horses in a race
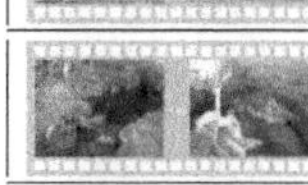	water, people, walking	**baseline:** person is recording the beautiful waterfalls **run2:** a person is explaining something **run1:** there is a man is walking in the water
	girl, singing, show	**baseline:** a woman is singing **run2:** a boy is singing **run1:** a girl is singing

Acknowledgments

This work was supported by the Fundamental Research Funds for the Central Universities and the Research Funds of Renmin University of China (No. 14XNLQ01), Natural Science Foundation of China (No. 61303184), and Social Science Foundation of China (No. 12&ZD141).

5. REFERENCES

[1] J. Dong, X. Li, and C. Snoek. Word2VisualVec: Cross-media retrieval by visual feature prediction. *CoRR*, abs/1604.06838, 2016.

[2] H. Fang, S. Gupta, F. Iandola, R. K. Srivastava, L. Deng, P. Dollár, J. Gao, X. He, M. Mitchell, J. C. Platt, et al. From captions to visual concepts and back. In *CVPR*, 2015.

[3] Y.-G. Jiang, Z. Wu, J. Wang, X. Xue, and S.-F. Chang. Exploiting feature and class relationships in video categorization with regularized deep neural networks. *CoRR*, abs/1502.07209, 2015.

[4] X. Li and Q. Jin. Improving image captioning by

concept-based sentence reranking. In *PCM*, 2016.

[5] X. Li, C. Snoek, and M. Worring. Learning social tag relevance by neighbor voting. *IEEE Trans. Multimedia*, 11(7):1310–1322, 2009.

[6] X. Li, T. Uricchio, L. Ballan, M. Bertini, C. Snoek, and A. D. Bimbo. Socializing the semantic gap: A comparative survey on image tag assignment, refinement, and retrieval. *ACM Computing Surveys*, 49(1):14:1–14:39, 2016.

[7] P. Mettes, D. Koelma, and C. Snoek. The ImageNet shuffle: Reorganized pre-training for video event detection. In *ICMR*, 2016.

[8] T. Mikolov, K. Chen, G. Corrado, and J. Dean. Efficient estimation of word representations in vector space. In *ICLR*, 2013.

[9] Y. Pan, T. Mei, T. Yao, H. Li, and Y. Rui. Jointly modeling embedding and translation to bridge video and language. In *CVPR*, 2016.

[10] C. Szegedy, W. Liu, Y. Jia, P. Sermanet, S. Reed, D. Anguelov, D. Erhan, V. Vanhoucke, and A. Rabinovich. Going deeper with convolutions. In *CVPR*, 2015.

[11] D. Tran, L. Bourdev, R. Fergus, L. Torresani, and M. Paluri. Learning spatiotemporal features with 3d convolutional networks. In *ICCV*, 2015.

[12] R. Vedantam, C. L. Zitnick, and D. Parikh. Cider: Consensus-based image description evaluation. In *CVPR*, 2015.

[13] S. Venugopalan, M. Rohrbach, J. Donahue, R. Mooney, T. Darrell, and K. Saenko. Sequence to sequence-video to text. In *ICCV*, 2015.

[14] O. Vinyals, A. Toshev, S. Bengio, and D. Erhan. Show and tell: A neural image caption generator. In *CVPR*, 2015.

[15] J. Xu, T. Mei, T. Yao, and Y. Rui. MSR-VTT: A large video description dataset for bridging video and language. In *CVPR*, 2016.

[16] H. Yu, J. Wang, Z. Huang, Y. Yang, and W. Xu. Video paragraph captioning using hierarchical recurrent neural networks. In *CVPR*, 2016.

Describing Videos using Multi-modal Fusion

Qin Jin†, Jia Chen♮, Shizhe Chen†, Yifan Xiong†, Alexander Hauptmann♮
†School of Information, Renmin University of China, China
{qjin, cszhe1, xiongyf}@ruc.edu.cn
♮Language Technologies Institute, Carnegie Mellon University, USA
{jiac, alex}@cs.cmu.edu

ABSTRACT

Describing videos with natural language is one of the ultimate goals of video understanding. Video records multi-modal information including image, motion, aural, speech and so on. MSR Video to Language Challenge provides a good chance to study multi-modality fusion in caption task. In this paper, we propose the multi-modal fusion encoder and integrate it with text sequence decoder into an end-to-end video caption framework. Features from visual, aural, speech and meta modalities are fused together to represent the video contents. Long Short-Term Memory Recurrent Neural Networks (LSTM-RNNs) are then used as the decoder to generate natural language sentences. Experimental results show the effectiveness of multi-modal fusion encoder trained in the end-to-end framework, which achieved top performance in both common metrics evaluation and human evaluation.

Keywords

video description generation; multi-modal fusion; end-to-end framework

1. INTRODUCTION

It is an intriguing challenge to automatically describe videos containing complex and diverse contents with natural language sentences. It has a wide range of applications such as assisting blind people or improving search quality for online videos. Inspired by the recent success of image captioning [1, 2], where natural language sentences are generated to describe image content, researchers have been paying more attention to the generation of video captions.

Different from image caption, generating video descriptions encounters two additional challenges: Firstly, video contains temporal information. Semantic concepts involved in the video may evolve over time. Secondly, video consists of multi-modalities. Besides visual information, videos also contain other contents such as aural and speech modalities, which provide additional information. The diversity of groundtruth captions also reflects information from multiple modalities.

Many research efforts have been made to address the first aforementioned challenge in video description generation. Venugopalan et al. [3] use the LSTM to encode the frames in the video to a fixed length vector and learn the encoder in the end-to-end framework. Yao et al. [4] exploit the local temporal structure underlying the video. They use the spatio-temporal convolution neural network (3-D CNN) as action features to encode local temporal structure and temporal attention mechanism based on soft-alignment method to exploit global temporal structure. Pan et al. [5] use a hierarchical recurrent encoder to encode frames in the video to a fixed length and learn the encoder in the end-to-end framework. There are relatively few works focusing on the second challenge of the multi-modality issue. Jin et al. [6] investigate to combine acoustic and visual information at the video representation level to generate video descriptions and achieve significant improvement over visual-only baseline.

As the decoder of the video caption generation, LSTM is widely used in previous works [3, 4, 5, 6, 7]. Pan et al. [7] improve the optimization goal for the decoder. The coherence loss is to locally maximize the next word given previous words and visual content and the relevance loss aims to enforce the relationship between the semantic of the sentence and visual content by creating a visual-semantic embedding space. They joint optimize the two losses in a unified model. Yu et al. [8] exploit a hierarchical-RNN framework including a sentence generator and a paragraph generator as the decoder. The framework models inter-sentence dependency which enables it to generate a paragraph for a long video.

In this paper, we tackle the video description generation problem in the context of MSR Video to Language Challenge. We mainly focus on utilizing multi-modal features from visual, audio, speech and meta-data information to improve the description performance. We propose a multi-modal fusion encoder and combine it with the text sequence decoder in an end-to-end framework. We address the following two questions in the challenge:
1. How much performance gain can additional modalities bring to visual-only systems?
2. What specific categories can benefit from different modalities?
We examine these questions empirically by evaluating our framework on different feature combinations. Experimental results show that combining multi-modal cues can significantly improve the description performance and generate more semantically accurate and comprehensive sentences.

MM '16, October 15-19, 2016, Amsterdam, Netherlands
© 2016 ACM. ISBN 978-1-4503-3603-1/16/10...$15.00
DOI: http://dx.doi.org/10.1145/2964284.2984065

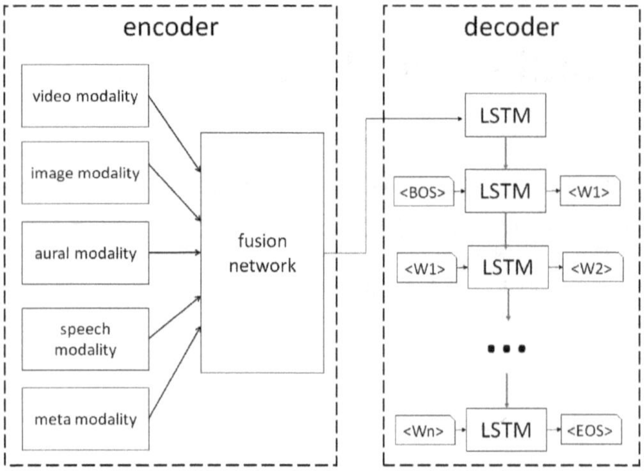

Figure 1: The key components of our system

Our system is the winner in the common metrics evaluation and ranks the second place in the human evaluation.

The rest of the paper is organized as follows: Section 2 describes our solutions for the video to text challenge. Section 3 presents the experiments on the challenge dataset. Section 4 draws the conclusions and future work.

2. PROPOSED SOLUTION

Our solution is based on the typical encoder-decoder framework of video caption task. We design a multi-modal fusion encoder and use the vanilla RNN decoder in our solution. The multi-modal fusion encoder encodes multi-modal features to a fixed length output vector. The initial hidden state of the vanilla RNN decoder is set to be the output of multi-modal fusion encoder and the initial word is set to be <BOS>. The dimension of multi-modal fusion encoder output is aligned to the dimension of decoder hidden state. An illustration of our proposed system is shown in Figure 1.

2.1 Multi-modal Features

We list all the modalities that are used in our solution, including image, video, aural, speech and meta-data. Different modalities cover different information in the video, corresponding to different parts in the video caption.

Image modality feature: The image modality reflects the static content of videos. DCNN is the state-of-the-art model in many visual tasks such as object detection, scene recognition etc. In this task, we use the fc7 layer of VGG-19 [9] pre-trained on ImageNet to extract image features every 16 frames. We perform mean pooling to get the final video-level feature.

Video modality feature: The video modality captures the temporal and motion content. We extract the fc6 layer of C3D [10] and Improved Dense Trajectory (iDT) [11]. Both of them are the state-of-the-art video features. The C3D model is pre-trained on the Sports-1M dataset. We segment the video to non-overlap shots of 16 frames length. The C3D feature is extracted on each shot and we apply mean pooling to aggregate them into one vector for a video. iDT feature is aggregated by fisher vector and we use kernel PCA to reduce dimensionality.

Aural modality feature: Aural modality is complementary to visual modalities, which is especially useful to distinguish different scene events. We extract the Mel-frequency Cepstral Coefficients (MFCCs) [12] over short-time window of 25ms with 10ms shift. We use two encoding strategies to aggregate MFCC frames into one video-level feature vector: Bag-of-Audio-Words (BoAW) [13] and Fisher Vector (FV) [14].

Speech modality feature: Speech modality provides semantic topics and details for what happened in the video. We use the IBM Watson API to extract the transcription of each video. To be specific, the speech modality feature is composed of two parts. The first part is the length of speech content. The length of speech content is usually long in a video about people talking while the length of speech content is usually short in a video about people exercising. We quantize the length of transcriptions into several bins and represent it as the one-hot vector. Another feature is related to the semantic meaning of the content. For example, "news" is a typical word in the outdoor reporters' videos and "car" often appears when people introduce their cars. We use word2vec pretrained on Google News Dataset[15] to generate a codebook with 100 codewords by clustering all the word vectors from training transcriptions. Each cluster represents a topic. Finally we form a bag-of-topics feature representation based on the codebook for each video.

Meta modality feature: Meta-data such as category provides a strong prior information about video content. It is also useful for dynamically weighting other modalities. For example, speech modality plays an important role in the howto category while video modality plays an important role in the sports category. For each video, we encode the category label in a one-hot feature vector.

2.2 Multimodal Fusion Encoder and Text Sequence Decoder

The multi-modal feature encoder is formed as a multi-layer feed-forward network. In the competition we only explore the network structure of one full connect layer without activation function. Other network structures are worth exploring and may bring additional performance boost.

For text sequence decoder, we use the vanilla LSTM [16] which is able to learn complex long-range dependences. The memory cell of LSTM encodes the history information up to the current time step and update with the current input under the control of three gates. The recurrences for the LSTM are defined as:

$$i_t = \sigma(W_{xi}x_t + W_{hi}h_{t-1}) \quad (1)$$

$$f_t = \sigma(W_{xf}x_t + W_{hf}h_{t-1}) \quad (2)$$

$$o_t = \sigma(W_{xo}x_t + W_{ho}h_{t-1}) \quad (3)$$

$$c_t = f_t \odot c_{t-1} + i_t \odot \phi(W_{xc}x_t + W_{hc}h_{t-1}) \quad (4)$$

$$h_t = o_t \odot c_t \quad (5)$$

where i, f, o, c, W represent the input gate, forget gate, output gate, memory cell and weight matrix respectively. σ and ϕ is the sigmoid and hyperbolic tangent function. $\odot$ is the element-wise product.

We learn the encoder and decoder jointly in the end-to-end framework. In training, the groundtruth word is used as the input of each time step for text sequence decoder. In testing, the estimated output word is feed to the next step input for text sequence decoder.

Table 1: Performance of Multi-Modality Fusion

modality	model	BLEU@4	METEOR	ROUGE	CIDEr
video	c3d	36.94	27.27	58.40	41.85
	c3d+iDT	34.96	26.59	57.58	36.51
video+aural	c3d+mfccbow	39.80	27.89	60.02	41.07
	c3d+mfccfv	40.07	27.76	60.02	39.60
	c3d+mfccbow+mfccfv	41.32	28.21	60.45	43.66
video+aural+image	c3d+mfccbow+mfccfv+vgg19	41.81	28.67	60.41	43.35
video+aural+speech	c3d+mfccbow+mfccfv+asr	40.55	27.98	60.10	42.28
video+aural+meta	c3d+mfccbow+mfccfv+category	43.70	28.95	61.35	45.74

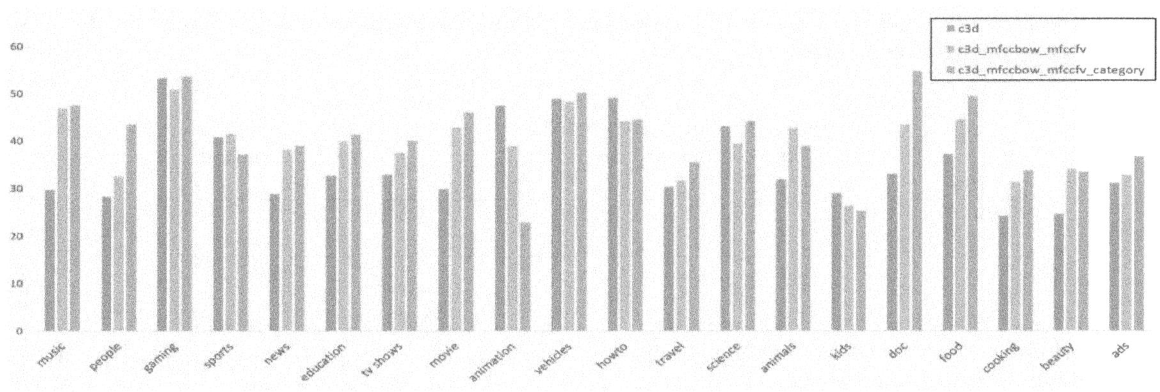

Figure 2: BLEU@4 Performance Comparison among Multi-modal Fusion

3. EXPERIMENTS

3.1 Experimental Setup

The challenge dataset is the MSR-VTT corpus [17], which is composed of 10,000 clips from 20 categories. Each video clip is annotated with 20 sentences by different workers in Amazon Mechanical Turk. In the challenge, we are provided with 6513 training videos and 497 videos for tuning parameters. Following standard data split, we randomly select 200 videos out of the 6513 videos for local validation and report experiment results on the 497 videos as local test set. That is, we use 6313 videos for training, 200 videos for local validation and 497 videos for local test. We evaluate the results comprehensively on all major metrics, including BLEU [18], METEOR [19], ROUGE-L [20] and CIDEr [21].

3.2 Implementation Details

We preserve words which appear more than three times, resulting in a vocabulary size of 10,866. We add begin-of-sentence tag <BOS> and end-of-sentence tag <EOS> to our vocabulary. The max generated caption length is set to 30. For videos without soundtrack or speech transcripts, we simply pad zeros as the audio features or speech features. The dimensionality of the fusion network output, word vector and the size of hidden layer of LSTM are all set to 512 empirically. We apply dropout with rate of 0.5 on the input and output of LSTM to prevent overfitting and use ADAM algorithm to minimize the log-likelihood loss with learning rate of 1×10^{-4}. Beam search with beam width of 5 is used to generate sentences during test process.

3.3 Overall Evaluation of Multi-modal Fusion

To study multi-modality fusion, we start with video modality feature `c3d`, which achieves a decent performance as shown in Table 1. Combining state-of-the-art video feature `iDT` doesn't improve the performance. Then we add aural modality feature `mfccbow` and `mfccfv`. Adding `mfccbow` alone improves the performance by 2.94% on BLEU@4 and 0.62% on METEOR. Adding `mfccfv` alone also improves the performance by 3.07% on BLEU4 and 0.49% on METEOR. Adding `mfccbow` and `mfccbow` together further improves the performance on all metrics consistently. It indicates that the two aural modality features, `mfccbow` and `mfccfv` are complementary.

With video and aural modality fusion `c3d+mfccfv+mfccbow`, we reach the performance plateau. It is very difficult to improve the performance by simply adding more modality features such as image modality feature `vgg19` or speech modality feature `asr` as shown in Table 1. However, adding meta modality feature `category` overcomes the performance plateau by a significant improvement on all metrics, 2.68% on BLEU@4, 0.74% on METEOR, 0.9% on ROUGE, 2.08% on CIDEr. There are two potential reasons for such significant boost. First, the model learns to use `category` to limit the sentence space in generation. Second, the model learns to dynamically weight multi-modal features with `category` as different modalities excel at different categories on caption task. It is intriguing to distinguish between these two potential reasons and we will investigate it in our future work.

3.4 Detailed Study of Multi-modal Fusion

We further conduct category-wise evaluation on multimodal fusion performance. As shown in Figure 2, adding aural modality significantly improves the performance in categories such as music and movie, but deteriorates the per-

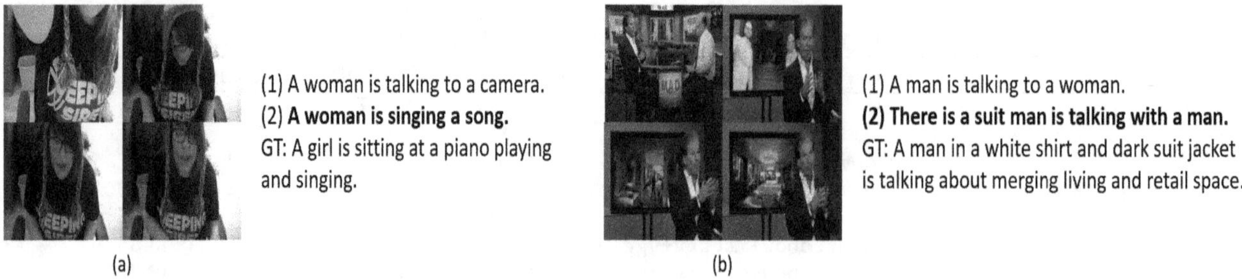

Figure 3: Examples of sentence generation results from different modalities and groundtruth. (1) c3d, (2) c3d+mfccbow+mfccfv. GT is a randomly selected groundtruth human description. Sentences in bold highlight the best generated sentences.

Table 2: Performance on Challenge Test Set

	common metrics evaluation				human evaluation		
run	BLEU@4	METEOR	ROUGE	CIDEr	C1	C2	C3
run1(p)	0.408	0.282	0.448	0.609	3.261	3.091	3.154
run2	0.426	0.288	0.467	0.617	-	-	-

formance in animation. For some categories like animation, video modality performs best. It seems that audio modality brings little information to these categories. Furthermore, adding meta modality `category` consistently improves the performance on most categories.

We present some examples of generated sentences from `c3d` model and `c3d+mfccfv+mfccbow` model in Figure 3. In Figure 3(a), audio modality helps to distinguish talking and singing successfully especially when the behaviour is not obvious from visual information. Figure 3(b) shows that acoustic information helps to identify the gender of the speaker.

3.5 Performance on Test Set

The performance on the challenge test set is presented in Table 2. For human evaluation, the subset of testing sentences generated from the primary run is scored according to C1 (coherence), C2 (relevance) and C3 (helpful for blind) on a scale of 1-5. The generated sentences in our primary run are selected from the `c3d`, `c3d+mfccbow+mfccfv`, `c3d+mfccbow+mfccfv+asr`, `c3d+mfccbow+mfccfv+category` systems by category according to their categories performance on the validation set. The results in the second run are simply generated from the `c3d+mfccbow+mfccfv+category` system.

The primary run might overfit the validation set so do not generalize well on the test set. The multi-modal fusion system alone achieves the best performance in the challenge.

4. CONCLUSION AND FUTURE WORK

This paper proposes a multi-modal fusion encoder to fuse image, video, aural, speech and meta modalities. We integrate the multi-modal fusion encoder with the text sequence decoder in an end-to-end framerwork to generate video descriptions. Adding audio and meta modalities can significantly improve the overall performance of the visual modality description system. In the future, we will explore different structure of the fusion network to improve the performance. We will also explore adding attention to expose each modality feature directly to the text sequence decoder for dynamic fusion in each prediction step.

5. ACKNOWLEDGMENTS

This work is supported by National Key Research and Development Plan under Grant No. 2016YFB1001202.

6. REFERENCES

[1] Oriol Vinyals, Alexander Toshev, Samy Bengio, and Dumitru Erhan. Show and tell: A neural image caption generator. In *Proceedings of the IEEE Conference on Computer Vision and Pattern Recognition*, pages 3156–3164, 2015.

[2] Kelvin Xu, Jimmy Ba, Ryan Kiros, Kyunghyun Cho, Aaron C. Courville, Ruslan Salakhutdinov, Richard S. Zemel, and Yoshua Bengio. Show, attend and tell: Neural image caption generation with visual attention. In *Proceedings of the 32nd International Conference on Machine Learning, ICML 2015, Lille, France, 6-11 July 2015*, pages 2048–2057, 2015.

[3] Subhashini Venugopalan, Marcus Rohrbach, Jeffrey Donahue, Raymond J. Mooney, Trevor Darrell, and Kate Saenko. Sequence to sequence - video to text. In *2015 IEEE International Conference on Computer Vision, ICCV 2015, Santiago, Chile, December 7-13, 2015*, pages 4534–4542, 2015.

[4] Li Yao, Atousa Torabi, Kyunghyun Cho, Nicolas Ballas, Christopher J. Pal, Hugo Larochelle, and Aaron C. Courville. Describing videos by exploiting temporal structure. In *2015 IEEE International Conference on Computer Vision, ICCV 2015, Santiago, Chile, December 7-13, 2015*, pages 4507–4515, 2015.

[5] Pingbo Pan, Zhongwen Xu, Yi Yang, Fei Wu, and Yueting Zhuang. Hierarchical recurrent neural encoder for video representation with application to captioning. *CoRR*, abs/1511.03476, 2015.

[6] Qin Jin and Junwei Liang. Video description generation using audio and visual cues. In *Proceedings of the 2016 ACM on International Conference on Multimedia Retrieval*, pages 239–242. ACM, 2016.

[7] Yingwei Pan, Tao Mei, Ting Yao, Houqiang Li, and

Yong Rui. Jointly modeling embedding and translation to bridge video and language. *CoRR*, abs/1505.01861, 2015.

[8] Haonan Yu, Jiang Wang, Zhiheng Huang, Yi Yang, and Wei Xu. Video paragraph captioning using hierarchical recurrent neural networks. *CoRR*, abs/1510.07712, 2015.

[9] K. Simonyan and A. Zisserman. Very deep convolutional networks for large-scale image recognition. *CoRR*, abs/1409.1556, 2014.

[10] Du Tran, Lubomir Bourdev, Rob Fergus, Lorenzo Torresani, and Manohar Paluri. C3d: generic features for video analysis. *CoRR, abs/1412.0767*, 2:7, 2014.

[11] Heng Wang and Cordelia Schmid. Action recognition with improved trajectories. In *Proceedings of the IEEE International Conference on Computer Vision*, pages 3551–3558, 2013.

[12] Steven Davis and Paul Mermelstein. Comparison of parametric representations for monosyllabic word recognition in continuously spoken sentences. *IEEE transactions on acoustics, speech, and signal processing*, 28(4):357–366, 1980.

[13] Stephanie Pancoast and Murat Akbacak. Softening quantization in bag-of-audio-words. In *2014 IEEE International Conference on Acoustics, Speech and Signal Processing (ICASSP)*, pages 1370–1374. IEEE, 2014.

[14] Jorge Sánchez, Florent Perronnin, Thomas Mensink, and Jakob Verbeek. Image classification with the fisher vector: Theory and practice. *International journal of computer vision*, 105(3):222–245, 2013.

[15] Tomas Mikolov, Ilya Sutskever, Kai Chen, Greg S Corrado, and Jeff Dean. Distributed representations of words and phrases and their compositionality. In *Advances in neural information processing systems*, pages 3111–3119, 2013.

[16] Sepp Hochreiter and Jürgen Schmidhuber. Long short-term memory. *Neural computation*, 9(8):1735–1780, 1997.

[17] Jun Xu, Tao Mei, Ting Yao, and Yong Rui. Msr-vtt: A large video description dataset for bridging video and language. In *Conference on Computer Vision and Pattern Recognition (CVPR)*, 2016.

[18] Kishore Papineni, Salim Roukos, Todd Ward, and Wei-Jing Zhu. Bleu: a method for automatic evaluation of machine translation. In *Proceedings of the 40th annual meeting on association for computational linguistics*, pages 311–318. Association for Computational Linguistics, 2002.

[19] Michael Denkowski and Alon Lavie. Meteor universal: Language specific translation evaluation for any target language. In *In Proceedings of the Ninth Workshop on Statistical Machine Translation*. Citeseer, 2014.

[20] Chin-Yew Lin. Rouge: A package for automatic evaluation of summaries. In *Text summarization branches out: Proceedings of the ACL-04 workshop*, volume 8. Barcelona, Spain, 2004.

[21] Ramakrishna Vedantam, C Lawrence Zitnick, and Devi Parikh. Cider: Consensus-based image description evaluation. In *Proceedings of the IEEE Conference on Computer Vision and Pattern Recognition*, pages 4566–4575, 2015.

Multimodal Video Description

Vasili Ramanishka
UMass Lowell
vramanis@cs.uml.edu

Abir Das
UMass Lowell
adas@cs.uml.edu

Dong Huk Park
UC Berkeley
dong.huk.park@berkeley.edu

Subhashini Venugopalan
University of Texas Austin
vsubhashini@utexas.edu

Lisa Anne Hendricks
UC Berkeley
lisa_anne@berkeley.edu

Marcus Rohrbach
UC Berkeley
rohrbach@berkeley.edu

Kate Saenko
UMass Lowell
saenko@cs.uml.edu

ABSTRACT

Real-world web videos often contain cues to supplement visual information for generating natural language descriptions. In this paper we propose a sequence-to-sequence model which explores such auxiliary information. In particular, audio and the topic of the video are used in addition to the visual information in a multimodal framework to generate coherent descriptions of videos "in the wild". In contrast to current encoder-decoder based models which exploit visual information only during the encoding stage, our model fuses multiple sources of information judiciously, showing improvement over using the different modalities separately. We based our multimodal video description network on the state-of-the-art sequence to sequence video to text (S2VT) [26] model and extended it to take advantage of multiple modalities. Extensive experiments on the challenging MSR-VTT dataset are carried out to show the superior performance of the proposed approach on natural videos found in the web.

1. INTRODUCTION

Understanding a visual scene and expressing it in terms of natural language descriptions has drawn considerable interest from both computer vision and natural language processing communities. Early works on visual description have mostly focused on describing still images [6, 14, 15, 28]. Early efforts to generate automated video descriptions were based on a two stage pipeline which first identifies the semantic visual concepts and then stitches them in a "subject, verb, object" template [5, 8, 13, 22]. Though a template based approach separates the concept identification and description generation tasks, such templates are insufficient in modeling the richness of the language as generally found in human generated descriptions of videos or scenes.

Our model is based on the S2VT [26] model for generating natural language descriptions from videos. S2VT is an encoder-decoder based framework which maps a sequence of frames to a sequence of words. For an input sequence of video frames, the encoder first converts the video frames into a sequence of high-level feature descriptors and then encodes them into a sequence of hidden state vectors using a Long Short Term Memory (LSTM) network [11]. Once all frames are encoded, the decoder generates a sentence by first using the final encoded state as the input to the decoder and then by feeding back the generated words at each step to the decoder LSTM until the sentence is complete.

An encoder-decoder framework allows both the input and the output to be of variable length and has shown prominence in a related task - machine translation [2, 21]. However, machine translation tasks need not consider input and output from different modalities as they only deal with text. S2VT does handle two different modalities with the input being a sequence of frames and the output being sequence of words, but it is limited in the sense that both the input and the output, individually, explore information from single a modality only. Specifically, the input modality is visual while the output modality is textual.

With an eye to explore additional information that is often available with the web videos, such as audio and broad topic (category) of the videos, we have extended the S2VT framework to a multimodal video description framework denoted as the "*MMVD*". This framework supplements the visual information with audio and textual features (derived from the video category information). Such input from three different modalities (visual, audio and textual) enables the generated description to be nearly as complex and rich as human generated descriptions are. In addition, we show that employing a committee of models where each model is an expert in describing videos from a specific category is advantageous than a single model trying to describe videos from multiple categories. We have also simplified the S2VT model by using a single layer LSTM for both encoding and decoding.

The performance of the proposed approach is validated using a publicly available benchmark dataset (MSR-VTT [27]) of web videos which comes with several challenges including diverse content and diverse as well as noisy descriptions.

MM '16, October 15–19, 2016, Amsterdam, The Netherlands.

DOI: http://dx.doi.org/10.1145/2964284.2984066

2. APPROACH

As our model builds on the S2VT model [26], we first describe this model briefly and then describe our approach.

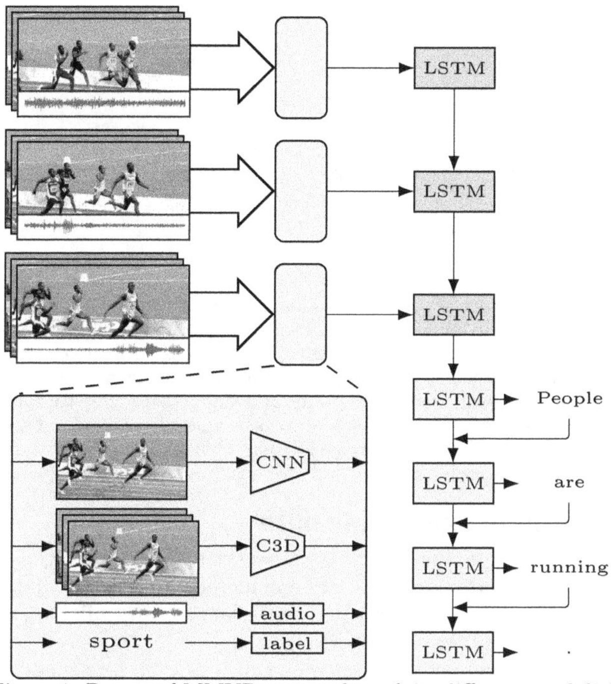

Figure 1: Proposed MMVD approach exploits different modalities of the video, which are first encoded using an LSTM, and then decoded to predict a sentence description. To truly understand the video we propose to rely on static frame features, 3D temporal features across frames, audio, and the video domain or category.

2.1 S2VT video description framework

The S2VT model reads a sequence of input frames $(x_1, x_2, ..., x_n)$, encodes each frame to a fixed dimensional vector representation, and then decodes this vector to a sequence of output words $(y_1, y_2, ..., y_m)$. S2VT uses LSTM [11] units for modeling long-range temporal dependencies in sequences. LSTMs encode the input sequence in their hidden representations (h_n) and then decode the output sequence from this representation. In the encoding phase, an LSTM computes a sequence of hidden states $(h_1, h_2, ..., h_n)$ from the input sequence $(x_1, x_2, ..., x_n)$. During decoding, the model defines the joint probability over the output sequence $(y_1, y_2, ..., y_m)$ as a product of the conditionals as $\prod_{t=1}^{m} p(y_t|h_{n+t-1}, y_{t-1})$, where the conditional probability of each output word y_t is obtained by a *softmax* over all the words in the vocabulary. The model is trained end-to-end using standard backpropagation techniques where the following log-likelihood of the predicted words is maximized for the model parameters θ, where θ denotes all trainable weights and biases.

$$\theta^* = \arg\max_{\theta} \sum_{t=1}^{m} \log p(y_t|h_{n+t-1}, y_{t-1}; \theta) \quad (1)$$

After encoding the frames, the <BOS> (beginning-of-sentence) tag is fed to the LSTM while an <EOS> (end-of-sentence) tag terminates each sentence. During decoding at training time, the input to the LSTM is the embedded representations of the ground truth words while at test time, the word with the maximum probability after the softmax is input to the LSTM until <EOS> token is emitted.

2.2 MMVD model

Our approach MMVD (Multimodal Video Description) extends S2VT [26] to exploit additional multimodal features and is implemented in TensorFlow [1]. Additionally, instead of using a stack of two LSTM layers like S2VT, we use a single layer of LSTMs which not only simplifies the model but also reduces the memory requirement considerably, thus allowing us to incorporate many additional features. A schematic of the MMVD model is shown in Fig. 1.

2.2.1 *Multimodal input features*

Specifically, MMVD incorporates the following features from different modalities to generate the descriptor for the sequence of input frames from each video.

Object recognition features: The deep CNN models applied to image classification and detection tasks (ImageNet) provide a strong visual representation of objects and scenes depicted in the video frames. We used the state-of-the-art ResNet [9] (winner of ILSVRC 2015) features which uses special skip connections and features a heavy use of batch normalization. Transferring knowledge from convnets pre-trained on 1.2M+ images with 1000 category labels helps create open ended descriptions of videos in the wild with large vocabularies. We use 2048 dimensional features from the global average pooling (pool5) layer after the last convoluational layer of ResNet.

Action recognition features: Though ResNet CNN features efficiently capture different visual concepts in static frames, they lack dynamic features that can capture movement/motion in videos. A simple yet effective approach to learn temporal dynamics in videos was proposed by extending a 2-D convnet to a deep 3-D convolutional network (C3D) [23]. Unlike S2VT where optical flow features are used to model motion patterns of activity, the use of C3D features in MMVD allows it to learn relevant motion information from videos in an end-to-end fashion. In our experiments, C3D features from the fc-6 layer of the model pre-trained on Sport1M [12] were used.

Video category information: In our ablation studies, we show that the category or domain of a video (*e.g.*, sports, cooking, music *etc.*) carries a lot of information for generating a proper description of the video. As shown in section 3.3, the background knowledge about the videos in form of their category information helps to discern between videos which have only fine-grained visual differences. We use the category labels supplied with the MSR-VTT video clips as an additional feature descriptor and show that the video domain information can be an useful resource for natural language video description.

Audio features: Although audio tracks associated with the web videos can be useful for generating descriptions of such videos, this information has, traditionally, not been used to effect. Towards this objective, we used the popular audio feature - Mel Frequency Cepstral Coefficients which have been used widely in various audio processing tasks such as automatic speech recognition, music transcription, and environment classification [4, 10, 17]. Feature extraction was performed with *pyAudioAnalysis* [7] for evenly sampled 1 second audio segments aligned with corresponding video frames sampled for object recognition features. Actual audio descriptors were represented by average value and standard deviation of 34 audio features (including 13 MFCCs).

We embed the features from various modalities to a lower dimensional space, where the parameters of the embedding are learned jointly with the description task. Then we concatenate the different embedded features for every time step to create a single feature vector as input to the LSTM.

We also trained models specifically for each video category. For this, a base model is trained on the whole training data by using the combined features as described above. Then the different "*expert*" models are obtained by finetuning the base model with paired video-caption data from specific categories only. During inference every "*expert*" is used to produce descriptions for the corresponding category (the category is provided with the video at test time).

2.2.2 *Model details*

Our model starts by sampling 26 uniformly spaced frames from each video clip. The ResNet and C3D features features are extracted from these 26 frames as the anchor frames. Similarly, audio features are also extracted from one second clips starting with these anchor frames. For category label features, we used one-hot representations of the possible 20 category labels. Though S2VT allows variable length input, to reduce computation we experimented with a fixed number of frames sampled uniformly. The performance difference turned out to be negligible with significantly lower computation overhead.

The increase in the number of input modalities comes with the cost of increased memory and computational requirements as the total dimensionality of the input to the system increases with the number of different features. As a result, we reduce the dimensionality of each feature by passing them through embedding layers (trainable fully connected layers with no activation function). The embedded features are concatenated and passed in as input to the LSTM. The encoder and decoder LSTMs share the same weights. No preprocessing of the text data was done. We used a vocabulary of size 23,667 (of which 13,627 tokens have 2 or more occurrences). The LSTM hidden state size was 512. To avoid overfitting, we apply dropout with a rate of 0.5, which has been shown to be beneficial in video description [20]. The model was optimized by the Adam optimizer with initial learning rate of 5×10^{-4} in batches of size 100.

Some of the hyperparameters are motivated by the properties of the MSR-VTT dataset with a goal to simplify the final model. For example, the strategy to sample 26 uniformly spaced frames was chosen as this number made sure that events in videos from the dataset are not underrepresented by the sampling strategy.

3. EXPERIMENTS

In this section we first describe the dataset and discuss its challenges. Then we detail the evaluation protocol and analyze the experimental evaluation.

3.1 Dataset

In this work, we train and evaluate our models on the MSR-VTT dataset [27]. MSR-VTT is a large-scale dataset collected for the task of describing videos with natural language. The dataset provides 41.2 hours of web videos as 10,000 clips covering diverse visual contents in 20 broad categories or domains. Each clip is annotated with 20 natural language descriptions produced by AMT workers. In addition to "in the wild" nature of the videos, an interesting characteristic of this dataset is the presence of audio. The audio information is complimentary to the visual features and our method takes advantage of it as the human annotators also based their descriptions not only on the video but also on the accompanying sound.

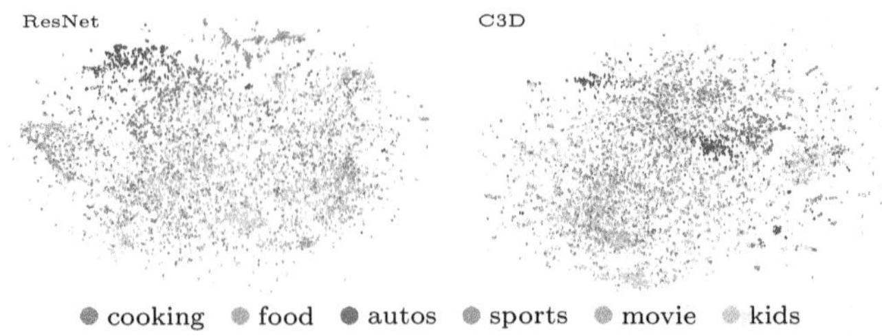

Figure 2: Feature embedding visualizations of visual descriptors on MSR-VTT using t-SNE. It should be noted that semantically close categories like 'food/drinks' and 'cooking' form a common cluster while generic category like 'movie' has large diversity. Each clip is visualized as a point and clips belonging to same category have same color. While for semantically different categories the visual features may be efficient they may not be efficient in generating specific descriptions for visually similar categories.

3.2 Challenges of the data

During our experiments we observed several additional challenges in the dataset. These include noisy text data, high variation in video and sentence length, unavailable audio streams *etc.* as described next.

- Though the total vocabulary size of all the sentences in the training split is 23,667, a total of 10,040 words appear only once. In addition, a comparison with the 400K length vocabulary (based on Wikipedia 2014 + Gigaword 5) used for training a Glove [19] embedding, revealed that 836 words out of 23,667 words are out of vocabulary yet they appear in the dataset multiple times (at least twice). These primarily contain misspelled words like 'backetball' or 'peson'. Such noisy captions add to the challenge of learning a good language model for this dataset.
- As described in section 2.2.1 and as will be shown later, audio features are useful in generating descriptions for "in the wild" videos. However, around 12.5 % of the videos in this dataset do not contain audio and the absence of this useful information makes the task more challenging.
- We also noticed that 95% of the sentences are shorter than 17 tokens (or words) and 95% of video clips in dataset are shorter that 26 seconds. Such clip duration is another motivation to choose 26 anchor frames for each video as this makes sure that the majority of the videos are not under-represented as a result of sampling.
- We also studied the semantic separability of the video clips using the visual descriptors (ResNet and C3D). Fig. 2 visualizes the feature embedding on training and validation clips. We extracted both features from the 26 frames for all training and validation clips. From each clip, the features are mean-pooled across the frames and are projected on 2-dimensional space using t-SNE [24]. The generally intermingled clusters indicate the diversity between the clips along with strong intra category variation. Fig. 2 shows that these visual descriptors may not be a good candidate for describing semantically similar categories of videos (*e.g.*, 'food' and 'cooking') or a generic category like 'movie'. In such cases, audio or topic information of the video become handy to get human like descriptions.

3.3 Results and discussion

We experimented with different modalities individually and with several combinations of them. Table 1 provides the performance of the model on the MSR-VTT validation data

RN:	A man is driving a car	A woman is putting makeup on her face
RN+categories:	A man is driving a car	A girl is applying makeup
RN+all:	A cartoon character is flying a helicopter	A woman is talking about a product
Committee:	A person is playing a video game	A woman is showing how to apply makeup

Figure 3: Examples of sentences produced by the proposed ResNet, ResNet+categories, ResNet+all modalities, and the Committee of experts models. Each video clip is represented by four frames with category label shown in top-left.

after training on the training split. Quantitave evaluation of the model is done using 4 different metrics - BLEU@4 [18], METEOR [3], CIDEr [25] and ROUGE-L [16]. We adopted an early stopping criterion and stopped the training when the model starts to overfit (roughly 10 epochs for all the different trials). The best model was chosen by first normalizing all 4 scores on validation data and then selecting the model which gives the highest sum of scores.

The first two rows in the table show that the model performance is pretty low when only category or audio information is used. This is reasonable as the description is generated without using any visual information. The next two rows show the performance of the model with visual feature descriptors. These two features give a significant boost in terms of all 4 metrics. However, the slightly better performance of ResNet descriptors compared to the C3D can possibly be attributed to greater depth and use of skip connections in state-of-the-art ResNet. Moreover, the data on which the two feature descriptors were pretrained are significantly different. The ImageNet data (in case of ResNet) comes with images from more than 1000 diverse categories while the Sport1M data (in case of C3D) contains sports related videos only, resulting in ResNet serving as a better descriptor for "in the wild" videos seen in MSR-VTT.

The next 3 rows show the performance when the respective features are added in order. Thus '+C3D' implies the use of both ResNet and C3D features. Similarly, '+categories' means the use of three features (ResNet, C3D and category information) simultaneously and so on. We see that the use of C3D features and category information does not change the performance much in terms of BLEU@4, METEOR or ROUGE-L. However, the CIDEr score gets continually improved with the addition of these features. While METEOR compares exact token matches, stemmed tokens, paraphrase matches and WordNet synonyms based semantic matches, BLEU@4 tries to give more weight to human-like grammatically correct sentences. On the other hand, CIDEr measures similarity of a generated sentence to reference sentences by counting TF-IDF weighted common n-grams. Consequently, this metric rewards sentences for generating n-grams of uncommon words and is a good fit for measuring the quality of the generated sentences where a diverse set of reference sentences for the videos are available as is the case with MSR-VTT. The performance is boosted in terms of all the metrics by the incorporation of audio

Table 1: Performance comparison for various feature descriptors on the validation set. +C3D, +categories, +audio were added in this order to ResNet model. Thus +audio line shows results for all modalities. "Committee" refers to the "committee of experts".

Descriptors	BLEU@4	METEOR	CIDEr	ROUGE-L
categories	0.298	0.228	0.236	0.548
audio	0.301	0.222	0.184	0.544
C3D	0.374	0.264	0.389	0.594
ResNet	0.389	0.269	0.400	0.605
+C3D	0.385	0.267	0.411	0.601
+categories	0.381	0.270	0.418	0.597
+audio	0.395	0.277	0.442	0.610
committee	0.407	0.286	0.465	0.610

features signifying the importance of these features in generating natural language descriptions for web videos.

The last row shows the performance of the "*committee of experts*" where "+audio" was taken as the base model on which the experts were trained. It gives a significant improvement in terms of almost all metrics (except ROUGE-L for which it stays the same). A possible reason for this boost is the fact that the experts learn to produce better sentences specific to different categories when they are fine tuned with paired video-caption data specific to a video category.

Fig. 3 shows descriptions generated by MMVD on sample test videos from MSR-VTT using 4 different combinations of modalities. It can be seen that the use of all modalities helps to produce more accurate sentences, *e.g.*, it can identify that the left video is about a cartoon character. "Committee of experts" can even tell that the video is a result of a person playing a video game. Similarly, for the video on the right, "committee" can correctly identify that it is a "how to" video.

We used the following ablation experiment to estimate the human level performance on this dataset. We removed one random ground truth sentence from every annotated video and treated these sentences as a human generated description for each video. The remaining 19 sentences for each video were treated as the ground truth descriptions with which the BLEU@4 and METEOR score were calculated. This naive approach gave us a METEOR score of 0.3 and a BLEU@4 score of 0.36 as an estimate of the human performance on MSR-VTT dataset. From this study and from the results shown in Table 1, it can be seen that our approach outperforms humans in terms of BLUE@4 score and gets close to human level performance in terms of METEOR. Additional results, analysis and code are available in https://github.com/VisionLearningGroup/MMVD

4. CONCLUSION

This paper proposes a MultiModal approach to Video Description (MMVD). Our MMVD model exploits information from several diverse modalities to generate natural language description of web videos using a recurrent encoder-decoder framework. In particular, we have shown that the use of audio information and the topic of a video can supplement the visual features significantly for this task. Despite its conceptual simplicity, our model achieves state-of-the-art performance on the difficult MSR-VTT dataset which comes with challenges both in audio-visual and language domain. The future directions of our research will be to explore different fusion strategies including speech recognition on audio tracks for better video description.

Acknowledgments This work was supported by DARPA under AFRL grant FA8750-13-2-0026 and a Google Faculty Research Award.

5. REFERENCES

[1] M. Abadi, A. Agarwal, P. Barham, E. Brevdo, Z. Chen, C. Citro, G. S. Corrado, A. Davis, J. Dean, M. Devin, et al. TensorFlow: Large-Scale Machine Learning on Heterogeneous Distributed Systems. *arXiv preprint arXiv:1603.04467*, 2016.

[2] D. Bahdanau, K. Cho, and Y. Bengio. Neural Machine Translation by Jointly Learning to Align and Translate. In *International Conference on Learning Representations*, 2015.

[3] S. Banerjee and A. Lavie. METEOR: An Automatic Metric for MT Evaluation with Improved Correlation with Human Judgments. In *Association for Computational Linguistics Workshop*, 2005.

[4] F. Beritelli and R. Grasso. A Pattern Recognition System for Environmental Sound Classification based on MFCCs and Neural Networks. In *IEEE International Conference on Signal Processing and Communication Systems*, pages 1–4, 2008.

[5] P. Das, C. Xu, R. F. Doell, and J. J. Corso. A Thousand Frames in Just a Few Words: Lingual Description of Videos through Latent Topics and Sparse Object Stitching. In *IEEE Conference on Computer Vision and Pattern Recognition*, 2013.

[6] A. Farhadi, M. Hejrati, M. A. Sadeghi, P. Young, C. Rashtchian, J. Hockenmaier, and D. Forsyth. Every Picture Tells a Story: Generating Sentences from Images. In *European Conference on Computer Vision*, 2010.

[7] T. Giannakopoulos. pyaudioanalysis: An open-source python library for audio signal analysis. *PLoS ONE*, 10(12):1–17, 12 2015.

[8] S. Guadarrama, N. Krishnamoorthy, G. Malkarnenkar, S. Venugopalan, R. Mooney, T. Darrell, and K. Saenko. Youtube2text: Recognizing and Describing Arbitrary Activities Using Semantic Hierarchies and Zero-shot Recognition. In *IEEE International Conference on Computer Vision*, 2013.

[9] K. He, X. Zhang, S. Ren, and J. Sun. Deep Residual Learning for Image Recognition. In *IEEE Conference on Computer Vision and Pattern Recognition*, 2016.

[10] G. Hinton, L. Deng, D. Yu, G. Dahl, A. rahman Mohamed, N. Jaitly, A. Senior, V. Vanhoucke, P. Nguyen, T. Sainath, and B. Kingsbury. Deep Neural Networks for Acoustic Modeling in Speech Recognition. *IEEE Signal Processing Magazine*, 29(6):82–97, 2012.

[11] S. Hochreiter and J. Schmidhuber. Long Short-Term Memory. *Neural Computation*, 9(8):1735–1780, 11 1997.

[12] A. Karpathy, G. Toderici, S. Shetty, T. Leung, R. Sukthankar, and L. Fei-Fei. Large-scale Video Classification with Convolutional Neural Networks. In *IEEE Conference on Computer Vision and Pattern Recognition*, June 2014.

[13] N. Krishnamoorthy, G. Malkarnenkar, R. J. Mooney, K. Saenko, and S. Guadarrama. Generating Natural-Language Video Descriptions Using Text-Mined Knowledge. In *AAAI Conference on Artificial Intelligence*, 2013.

[14] G. Kulkarni, V. Premraj, S. Dhar, S. Li, Y. Choi, A. C. Berg, and T. L. Berg. Baby talk: Understanding and Generating Simple Image Descriptions. In *IEEE Conference on Computer Vision and Pattern Recognition*, 2011.

[15] S. Li, G. Kulkarni, T. L. Berg, A. C. Berg, and Y. Choi. Composing Simple Image Descriptions using Web-scale n-grams. In *Conference on Computational Natural Language Learning*, 2011.

[16] C.-Y. Lin. Rouge: A Package for Automatic Evaluation of Summaries. In *Association for Computational Linguistics Workshop*, volume 8, 2004.

[17] B. Logan. Mel Frequency Cepstral Coefficients for Music Modeling. In *International Symposium on Music Information Retrieval*, 2000.

[18] K. Papineni, S. Roukos, T. Ward, and W.-J. Zhu. BLEU: a Method for Automatic Evaluation of Machine Translation. In *Association for Computational Linguistics*, pages 311–318, 2002.

[19] J. Pennington, R. Socher, and C. D. Manning. Glove: Global Vectors for Word Representation. In *Conference on Empirical Methods in Natural Language Processing*, 2014.

[20] A. Rohrbach, M. Rohrbach, and B. Schiele. The Long-Short Story of Movie Description. In *German Conference on Pattern Recognition*, 2015.

[21] I. Sutskever, O. Vinyals, and Q. V. Le. Sequence to sequence learning with neural networks. In *Advances in Neural Information Processing Systems*. 2014.

[22] J. Thomason, S. Venugopalan, S. Guadarrama, K. Saenko, and R. J. Mooney. Integrating Language and Vision to Generate Natural Language Descriptions of Videos in the Wild. In *International Conference on Computational Linguistics*, 2014.

[23] D. Tran, L. Bourdev, R. Fergus, L. Torresani, and M. Paluri. Learning Spatiotemporal Features with 3D Convolutional Networks. In *IEEE International Conference on Computer Vision*, 2015.

[24] L. van der Maaten and G. Hinton. Visualizing Data using t-SNE. *Journal of Machine Learning Research*, 9:2579–2605, 2008.

[25] R. Vedantam, L. C. Zitnick, and D. Parikh. Cider: Consensus-based Image Description Evaluation. In *IEEE Conference on Computer Vision and Pattern Recognition*, 2015.

[26] S. Venugopalan, M. Rohrbach, J. Donahue, R. Mooney, T. Darrell, and K. Saenko. Sequence to Sequence - Video to Text. In *IEEE International Conference on Computer Vision*, 2015.

[27] J. Xu, T. Mei, T. Yao, and Y. Rui. MSR-VTT: A Large Video Description Dataset for Bridging Video and Language. In *IEEE Conference on Computer Vision and Pattern Recognition*, 2016.

[28] B. Z. Yao, X. Yang, L. Lin, M. W. Lee, and S.-C. Zhu. I2t: Image Parsing to Text Description. *Proceedings of the IEEE*, 98(8):1485–1508, 2010.

Tracking Natural Events through Social Media and Computer Vision

Jingya Wang Mohammed Korayem* Saúl Blanco David J. Crandall
School of Informatics and Computing
Indiana University
Bloomington, IN
{wang203,mkorayem,sblancor,djcran}@indiana.edu

ABSTRACT

Accurate, efficient, global observation of natural events is important for ecologists, meteorologists, governments, and the public. Satellites are effective but limited by their perspective and by atmospheric conditions. Public images on photo-sharing websites could provide crowd-sourced ground data to complement satellites, since photos contain evidence of the state of the natural world. In this work, we test the ability of computer vision to observe natural events in millions of geo-tagged Flickr photos, over nine years and an entire continent. We use satellites as (noisy) ground truth to train two types of classifiers, one that estimates if a Flickr photo has evidence of an event, and one that aggregates these estimates to produce an observation for given times and places. We present a web tool for visualizing the satellite and photo observations, allowing scientists to explore this novel combination of data sources.

Keywords

Computer vision; social media; event detection; ecology

1. INTRODUCTION

Monitoring the state of the natural world over time and space is crucial for a variety of scientific fields. Satellites can observe at a large scale but only for phenomena that can be seen from far above, and are affected by clouds and atmospheric conditions. Even a seemingly simple task such as monitoring global ground snow cover is difficult. The MODIS instruments on NASA's Terra satellite, for instance, do not produce useful observations for regions obscured by clouds (e.g., ironically, during snow storms!) and can be misled by materials like sand [23]: is the "snow" on that tropical island a freak event, or a noisy observation?

Ground stations can of course verify and fill in missing data, but they are expensive to install in remote areas. Citizen science [1, 2] uses the public to contribute observations, but requires clever design and significant incentives to derive accurate data from untrained observers. A potentially rich alternative is to mine public social media for evidence of natural events, in effect turning billions of users into citizen scientists without any explicit effort on their part. This idea is motivated by the growing body of work that mines social media to predict and observe properties of the world, including stock markets [3], elections [27], tourism [26], and so on.

Most work has used textual data like Twitter feeds, but social images are potentially a richer source of information. Everyday consumer photos often include incidental evidence about the natural world, e.g., a family portrait might show flowering plants in the background. In addition, unlike textual data, photos record visual documentation that can be analyzed and inspected; the danger of text analysis and importance of validation were recently illustrated by Google Flu Trends, which showed initial promise in tracking the spread of influenza from web search queries [7] but later proved largely inaccurate [15]. However, mining useful semantic information from unstructured image collections is a significant challenge.

In this paper, we test the feasibility of using noisy image collections to observe nature, using modern deep learning-based computer vision to recognize visual content automatically. As a case study, we investigate two particular phenomena: continental-scale snowfall and vegetation coverage. Although not as dramatic as events like earthquakes or tsunamis, these are nonetheless important properties of the environment that are key indicators of climate change, for instance. From a practical perspective, they also are relatively easy to recognize, occur frequently in social images, and have (noisy) satellite ground truth available to let us test at a large scale (over an entire continent, daily, for nine years) instead of just on occasional occurrences. This last property lets us measure statistically meaningful results on how a system may perform in practice, and this insight could be applied to other events in the future.

We first collect millions of geo-tagged, timestamped, public photos from Flickr, and daily snow and weekly vegetation satellite maps for North America. By cross referencing the photo geo-tags and timestamps with the maps, we automatically label each image with whether or not it was taken in a place with actual snow or green vegetation. We then train state-of-the-art Convolutional Neural Networks and Support Vector Machines to recognize these phenomena in individual images. Of course, these classifiers are imperfect, in part because social image data is noisy with inaccurate timestamps and geo-tags, and the satellite data is also incomplete. We thus train an additional classifier that aggregates evidence from multiple images taken at a given time and place, yielding more accurate observations. We evaluate at a large scale, training and testing on millions of Flickr images and quantitatively evaluating the performance at hundreds of thousands of places and times. Finally, we present a tool to visualize the combination of satellite and social photo-derived observations. The tool is general and can be applied to a wide range of phenomena with minimal additional effort.

*MK is now with CareerBuilder, LLC.

MM '16, October 15-19, 2016, Amsterdam, Netherlands
© 2016 ACM. ISBN 978-1-4503-3603-1/16/10... $15.00
DOI: http://dx.doi.org/10.1145/2964284.2984067

2. RELATED WORK

Automatically crowd-sourcing data from public social media has been investigated for a variety of applications, from predicting election outcomes [27], to quantifying tourism patterns [18,26], to predicting the stock market [3], to estimating land use [24]. The vast majority of this work is based on textual analysis, even for photo collections [24, 26, 27]. For example, Zhang et al. [28] analyze Flickr photos to estimate ecological phenomena (including snow) but using text tags, which (as they point out) is limited by how accurately and precisely photographers tag photos. We explore the more difficult but potentially more accurate approach of using visual analysis to extract semantics.

A few papers have applied computer vision to recognize environmental properties in images. Most of these use video (e.g. from static webcams) so that changes over time can be easily detected. For example, Laffont et al. [13] investigate detecting transient attributes of scenes over time, Glasner et al. [8] predict temperature, Murdock et al. [20, 21] estimate cloud cover, Li et al. [19] estimate smog, and Fedorov et al. [5, 6] detect snow on mountain peaks. Compared to webcams, public photos give greater coverage: whenever a user uploads a photo to Flickr, they are contributing a potentially useful observation about the world at that time and place. Most work with photos has only estimated static properties of places like land use [17] and demographics [16, 29], and typically over limited spatial areas, in contrast to estimating time-varying events on a daily basis on a continental scale as we do.

The closest paper to our work is Wang et al. [25], which like us tries to recognize snowfall in images. Their results were quite preliminary, however, and used simple visual features like color histograms. Here we apply cutting-edge deep learning classifiers, and evaluate at a large scale with millions of images at thousands of times and places. Our web-based tool also allows users to navigate and visualize the results, not only letting people validate data from the satellite and the photos and vice-versa, but also giving greater insight into the situations in which crowd-sourced observation of the natural world is likely to succeed and when it is likely to fail.

3. OUR APPROACH

A major goal in this paper is to investigate the extent to which modern image classification could be used to accurately predict environmental conditions at a given time and place, given a collection of social images taken then and there. We investigate two specific types of conditions: (1) whether there was snow on the ground, and (2) whether there was green vegetation. Both of these properties change over time and over geospatial location on Earth. To do this we require two key steps: deciding whether or not there is evidence of snow or greenery in an individual image, and then integrating this (very noisy) evidence across multiple images to estimate the actual real-world natural state at that time and place.

Data. We collected images geo-tagged in North America and time-stamped between 2007–2015 using Flickr's public API (similar to [4]). We removed photos with inaccurate geo-tags (thresholding at 12 on Flickr's GPS precision score) and suspicious timestamps (e.g. time taken after time uploaded), yielding 77.6 million images. We otherwise did not filter images in any way, so our set includes much noisy and confusing image content (e.g. indoor images). Throughout our experiments, we used the 2007–2010 data for training and reserved 2011–2015 as a separate test set.

For the ground truth for training and testing, we used public data from NASA's Terra satellite [9, 14, 23], which gives daily snow and bi-weekly vegetation cover maps gridded into $0.05^\circ \times 0.05^\circ$ latitude-longitude bins (roughly 5km$\times$5km at the middle latitudes). Unfortunately, this data is neither complete nor fully accurate, primarily because many satellites cannot make accurate observations through clouds. For each day and each bin (which we call a "day-geobin"), the satellite data records the percentage of the bin that was visible, the percentage of the visible area that was covered by snow or greenery, and confidence scores. To identify day-geobins with reliable ground truth, we excluded low-confidence bins, computed a probability as a function of the snow (or greenery) and visibility percentages, and labeled those below 0.15 as non-snow (or greenery) day-geobins, and over 0.85 as snow (or greenery) day-geobins. (This is similar to what was done in [28] except that they coarsened to 1° bins, and used unspecified separate thresholds on visibility and coverage). The remaining day-geobins were ignored.

Image classification. We take a machine learning approach to image classification. In training, we consult the satellite data to find all day-geobins where there is a high confidence of the event occurring or not occurring, and label all these images as positive or negative exemplars, respectively. The disadvantage to this approach is that it is very noisy: many images are taken indoors and have no evidence of the natural world, for instance, and many images have incorrect geo-tags and timestamps. The advantage is that it permits cheap, scalable training with little human effort.

We consider two types of features: text tags and visual content. For text tags, we built a vocabulary consisting of the 1,000 most frequent tags in the training set and represented each image as a 1000-d binary vector indicating presence or absence of each tag. We then trained a linear Support Vector Machine [11] to predict whether or not the tags have evidence of the event. For visual features, we learned a model using Convolutional Neural Networks (CNNs), which are the state-of-the-art in image classification [12]. We used the AlexNet network architecture and the Caffe open-source software framework [10], and followed the popular procedure of initializing CNN weights based on a network trained on ImageNet, and then fine-tuning using our training set [22].

Aggregating evidence. The classifications on individual images are not perfect, and mislabeled geo-tags and time-stamps would yield misleading evidence even if they were. To mitigate this, we combine classification results from multiple images taken at the same time and place, taking into account the image classifier's confidence. In particular, for each day-geobin, we build a histogram of quantized confidence scores, recording how many of the photos were classified as snow and non-snow (or green/non-green) at 20 quantized confidence levels. While this improves results compared to considering single images, it suffers from the problem that users with many photos have a disproportionate influence. We thus build a histogram over *users* instead of *photos*, so that each of the 20 histogram bins counts how many users took at least one photo at that confidence level. We then trained an SVM to estimate environmental state from these histograms.

4. EXPERIMENTAL RESULTS

To evaluate the potential of user-contributed social photographs for estimating properties of the natural world, we trained classifiers using data from North America for the years 2007–2010. The training data consisted of any photos taken in any day-geobin in which the probability of the event according to the satellite was below 15% or above 85%, calculated as described above. To make results more easily interpretable and to prevent problems with unbalanced classes, we randomly sampled from the larger class to yield a roughly equal number of positive and negative exemplars for each event. For snow, there were 626,522 such photos taken by 49,462 distinct users in 87,586 distinct day-geobins; for vegetation, there were 645,694 photos by 35,510 users in 84,921 day-geobins. We

Figure 1: Classification results on random images from times and places where satellites reported snow (top), no snow (second row), high vegetation (third row) and low vegetation coverage (bottom). Images are ordered according to the classifier's confidence, from highly certain of absence (left), to uncertainty either way (middle), to highly certain of presence (right). *Faces obscured for privacy.*

tested using data from 2011–2015, again balancing the classes, for a total of 577,186 test images for snow and 769,992 for vegetation.

Individual image classifier. We first tested accuracy on the individual image classification problem. This task is extremely difficult, even for a human, because many images are taken inside or otherwise do not have useful information about the natural world, and many images have incorrect timestamps or geo-tags. The tag features achieve 63.0% accuracy for snow and 67.5% for vegetation, compared to random baselines of 50.0%. Among the vocabulary of 1,000 tags, the SVM found that *snow*, *snowshoeing*, *blizzard*, *ski*, and *sledding* were most positively correlated with snow, while *july*, *florida*, *sandiego*, *baseball*, and *bikes* were most negatively correlated; for vegetation, top positive tags were *ferns*, *redwoods*, *fawn*, *woods*, and *forest*, and top negative tags were *lasvegas*, *newmexico*, *skyscraper*, *tucson*, and *desert*. Although these tags are intuitive, they also reveal a problem with tag-based features: the classifier can easily learn biases in the data. For instance, while the tag *snow* may be a strong indicator of a snowy scene, the tag *july* is simply exploiting the bias that relatively few places in North America have snow in summer. This bias means that the classifier is unlikely to detect a highly unusual event (e.g., unprecedented summer blizzard), reminiscent of the problems discovered with Google Flu [15]. Also, tag-based analysis places the classifier at the mercy of the quality and completeness of user-supplied tags.

Visual features, in contrast, are always present and less ambiguous. We saw this reflected in the results, where visual features performed at 69.2% accuracy for snow and 80.5% for vegetation. A visualization of some sample visual classification results along with the classifier's confidences are shown in Figure 1 (see caption for details). We see that the classifier can generally separate snow images from non-snow images, although some scenes such as beaches (second row, eighth column) are similar enough to snow to cause confusion. The two most extreme "errors" (first row first column, and second row last column) illustrate cases where the CNN actually classified the image correctly; here either the satellite data was erroneous or the photo geotags or timestamps were incorrect.

Day-geobin classifier. Having classified individual images, we next test performance of these estimates in accurately classifying individual day-geobins (e.g. deciding if there was snow on the ground on a given day and place). Our accuracy on this task for snow was about 60.8% for textual features alone, 69.3% for visual features, and 71.7% for the combination of visual features and textual features (in which we combined the two 20-d feature vectors to learn a single SVM on a 40-d feature space), compared to 50.0% random baseline; for vegetation, accuracies were 71.3% for tags, 79.4% for visual features, and 81.9% for the combination.

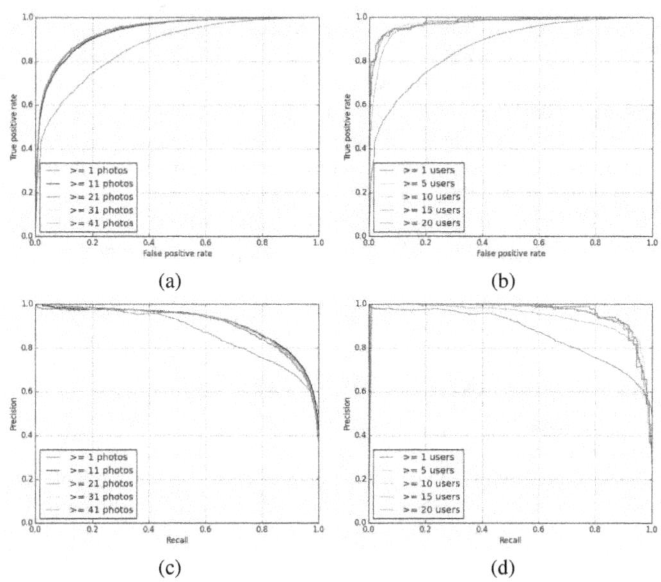

Figure 2: Performance on estimating snow presence for about 98,000 North American day-geobins from 2011–2015, in terms of *(top)* ROC and *(bottom)* Precision-Recall, as a function of number of *(left)* photos and *(right)* distinct users per bin.

We have observed that most incorrectly detected day-geobins occur in places with very few observed photos contributed by few users (and often only a single photo), since in this scenario the classifier is basing its entire decision on very little evidence. Figures 2(a) and (b) plot ROC curves for snow as a function of the number of photos and number of distinct users in each day-geobin; vegetation curves are not shown due to space constraints, but the trend is similar. Accuracy increases when more than one photo is

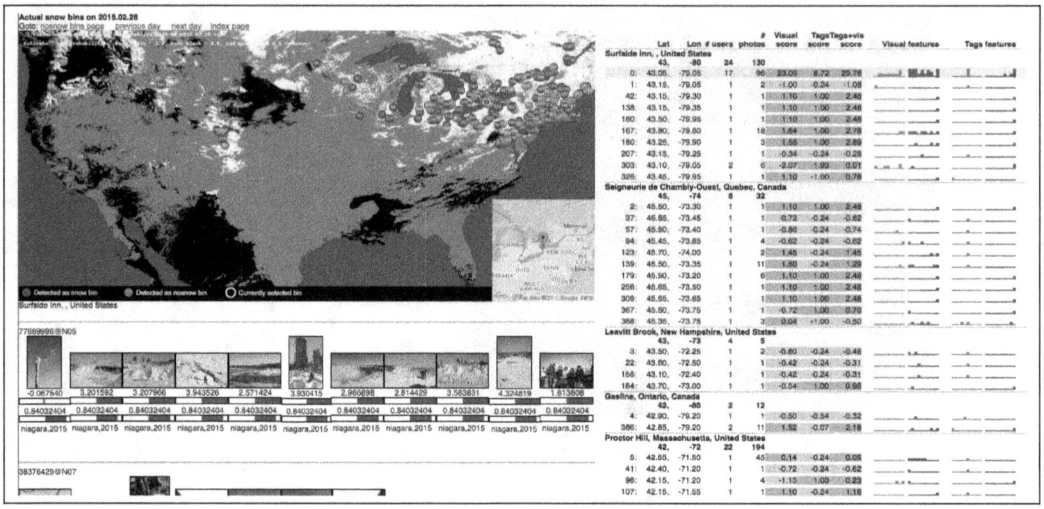

Figure 3: Screenshot of visualization tool, for snow coverage on February 28, 2015.

available, reaching about 85% for 40 photos (and eventually saturating at about 90% for 500 photos). Increasing the number of distinct users improves accuracy more dramatically, up to nearly 95% for 10 users and saturating at about 99% for 50 users. Presumably this boost is because evidence across multiple users is approximately conditionally independent given the event, as opposed to photos from any single photographer which are highly correlated. In many applications, it may be more important for scientists to retrieve places and times when specific events occurred, as opposed to accurately classifying at every place and time. Figures 2(c) and (d) shows precision-recall curves that adopt this retrieval view. At 60% recall, precision nears 90% even for day-geobins with single users, and reaches 99% for 20 users.

5. A VISUALIZATION TOOL

The quantitative results in the last section suggest that social media data could provide useful evidence about nature, but gave little insight into when the analysis would succeed or fail. We have developed a web-based tool that allows users to explore and compare satellite and social media data. Figure 3 shows a screenshot of the tool, visualizing snow coverage on one particular day. We briefly describe the main features here; please check our project website for more detailed information.[1] The map shows the satellite snow coverage, where black, gray, and white indicate no-snow, uncertain (cloud cover) and snow regions, respectively. Blue and red dots on the map indicate locations where the automatic photo-based classifier agrees and disagrees with the satellite, respectively, and the right panel of the interface lists details of these bins including position and output of the automatic day-geobin classifiers. Users can click on any geobin of interest to see photos taken at that time and place (lower left), organized by distinct user, and the visualization also shows the classification results estimated for each image. Clicking a photo shows it in detail, including text tags, geo-tags, timestamps, and other metadata. (In accordance with the Flickr Terms of Service, the images are not stored locally and clicking images leads to the photo page on Flickr.)

Although development of the tool is ongoing and we have not yet conducted a formal user study to test the tool with real users, we have informally found several interesting examples of use cases:

1. **Verifying suspicious satellite observations:** The satellite reported snow in West Virginia in Aug. 2012, but the classifier disagreed, and manual inspection of the photos taken there shows no evidence of snowfall.

2. **Complementing missing satellite data:** The satellite shows little evidence of a Jan. 2015 snowstorm in the northeast because of clouds, whereas the automatic classifier and Flickr photos confirm widespread snow coverage. The photo classifier also flags snow coverage near Blacksburg, VA on March 28, 2015, while the satellite does not; the images show a trace amount of snow that likely were not significant enough to be visible to the satellite.

3. **Debugging classification errors:** The classifier detected snow near Roanoke, VA on Jan. 1, 2014 while the satellite did not; multiple indoor scenes with white walls were incorrectly classified as containing snow. Meanwhile it also flags snow near Eugene, OR on the same day, because of photos of a distant snowy mountain peak that is in an adjacent geospatial bin.

6. CONCLUSION

We presented a technique and visualization tool for combining automatic image analysis of public Flickr photos with satellite maps for tracking natural events. We considered snow and vegetation as test cases, since continental-scale daily coverage data over nearly a decade is publicly available for these events, but the automatic classification techniques and visualization tools are general enough to be applied to a wider range of events. In ongoing work we are applying it to wildfires, flooding, and flowering of particular flower species, for example. We hope our work inspires further interest in using social photo collections and computer vision as a novel source for environmental data.

7. ACKNOWLEDGMENTS

This work was supported in part by the National Science Foundation through CAREER grant IIS-1253549 and the IU Data-to-Insight Center, and used compute facilities donated by NVidia. We thank Dennis Chen and Alex Seewald for assisting with initial data collection and system configuration.

[1]http://vision.soic.indiana.edu/snowexplorer/

8. REFERENCES

[1] Lost ladybug project. http://www.lostladybug.org.

[2] Project BudBurst. http://budburst.org/.

[3] J. Bollen, H. Mao, and X.-J. Zeng. Twitter mood predicts the stock market. *Journal of Computational Science*, 2(1):1–8, 2011.

[4] D. J. Crandall, L. Backstrom, D. Huttenlocher, and J. Kleinberg. Mapping the world's photos. In *International Conference on World Wide Web*, pages 761–770, 2009.

[5] R. Fedorov, P. Fraternali, C. Pasini, and M. Tagliasacchi. SnowWatch: snow monitoring through acquisition and analysis of user-generated content. *arXiv:1507.08958*, 2015.

[6] R. Fedorov, P. Fraternali, and M. Tagliasacchi. Snow phenomena modeling through online public media. In *IEEE International Conference on Image Processing*, pages 2174–2176, 2014.

[7] J. Ginsberg, M. Mohebbi, R. Patel, L. Brammer, M. Smolinski, and L. Brilliant. Detecting influenza epidemics using search engine query data. *Nature*, 457:1012–1014, 2009.

[8] D. Glasner, P. Fua, T. Zickler, and L. Zelnik-Manor. Hot or not: Exploring correlations between appearance and temperature. In *IEEE International Conference on Computer Vision*, pages 3997–4005, 2015.

[9] D. K. Hall, G. A. Riggs, and V. V. Salomonson. MODIS/Terra Snow Cover Daily L3 Global 0.05Deg CMG V004. Boulder, CO, USA: National Snow and Ice Data Center, 2011, updated daily.

[10] Y. Jia, E. Shelhamer, J. Donahue, S. Karayev, J. Long, R. Girshick, S. Guadarrama, and T. Darrell. Caffe: Convolutional architecture for fast feature embedding. In *ACM International Conference on Multimedia*, pages 675–678. ACM, 2014.

[11] T. Joachims. Making large-scale SVM learning practical. In B. Schölkopf, C. J. C. Burges, and A. J. Smola, editors, *Advances in kernel methods – support vector learning*. MIT Press, 1999.

[12] A. Krizhevsky, I. Sutskever, and G. E. Hinton. Imagenet classification with deep convolutional neural networks. In *Advances in Neural Information Processing Systems*, pages 1097–1105, 2012.

[13] P.-Y. Laffont, Z. Ren, X. Tao, C. Qian, and J. Hays. Transient attributes for high-level understanding and editing of outdoor scenes. *ACM Transactions on Graphics (TOG)*, 33(4):149, 2014.

[14] Land Processes Distributed Active Archive Center. MODIS/Terra Vegetation Indices 16-Day L3 Global 0.05Deg CMG V005. Sioux Falls, SD: U.S. Geological Survey, 2011.

[15] D. Lazer, R. Kennedy, G. King, and A. Vespignani. The parable of Google Flu: traps in big data analysis. *Science*, 343(14 March), 2014.

[16] S. Lee, H. Zhang, and D. Crandall. Predicting geo-informative attributes in large-scale image collections using convolutional neural networks. In *IEEE Winter Conference on Applications of Computer Vision*, 2015.

[17] D. Leung and S. Newsam. Proximate Sensing: Inferring What-Is-Where From Georeferenced Photo Collections. In *IEEE Conference on Computer Vision and Pattern Recognition*, 2010.

[18] N. Levin, S. Kark, and D. Crandall. Where have all the people gone? Enhancing global conservation using night lights and social media. *Ecological Applications*, 25(8):2153–2167, December 2015.

[19] Y. Li, J. Huang, and J. Luo. Using user generated online photos to estimate and monitor air pollution in major cities. In *ACM International Conference on Internet Multimedia Computing and Service*, 2015.

[20] C. Murdock, N. Jacobs, and R. Pless. Webcam2satellite: Estimating cloud maps from webcam imagery. In *IEEE Winter Conference on Applications of Computer Vision*, pages 214–221, 2013.

[21] C. Murdock, N. Jacobs, and R. Pless. Building dynamic cloud maps from the ground up. In *IEEE International Conference on Computer Vision*, pages 684–692, 2015.

[22] M. Oquab, L. Bottou, I. Laptev, and J. Sivic. Learning and transferring mid-level image representations using convolutional neural networks. In *CVPR*, 2014.

[23] G. Riggs, H. D., and Salomonson. MODIS Snow Products User Guide. http://modis-snow-ice.gsfc.nasa.gov/uploads/sug_c5.pdf.

[24] M. Šećerov. Analysis of Panoramio photo tags in order to extract land use information. Master's thesis, Universidade Nova de Lisboa, 2015.

[25] J. Wang, M. Korayem, and D. Crandall. Observing the natural world with Flickr. In *IEEE International Conference on Computer Vision Workshops*, pages 452–459, 2013.

[26] S. A. Wood, A. D. Guerry, J. M. Silver, and M. Lacayo. Using social media to quantify nature-based tourism and recreation. *Scientific Reports*, 3, 2013.

[27] Q. You, L. Cao, Y. Cong, X. Zhang, and J. Luo. A multifaceted approach to social multimedia-based prediction of elections. *IEEE Transactions on Multimedia*, 17(12):2271–2280, 2015.

[28] H. Zhang, M. Korayem, D. Crandall, and G. LeBuhn. Mining Photo-sharing Websites to Study Ecological Phenomena. In *International Conference on World Wide Web*, pages 749–758, 2012.

[29] B. Zhou, L. Liu, A. Oliva, and A. Torralba. Recognizing city identity via attribute analysis of geo-tagged images. In *European Conference on Computer Vision*, pages 519–534, 2014.

ConTagNet: Exploiting User Context for Image Tag Recommendation

Yogesh Singh Rawat
School of Computing
National University of Singapore
yogesh@comp.nus.edu.sg

Mohan S Kankanhalli
School of Computing
National University of Singapore
mohan@comp.nus.edu.sg

ABSTRACT

In recent years, deep convolutional neural networks have shown great success in single-label image classification. However, images usually have multiple labels associated with them which may correspond to different objects or actions present in the image. In addition, a user assigns tags to a photo not merely based on the visual content but also the context in which the photo has been captured. Inspired by this, we propose a deep neural network which can predict multiple tags for an image based on the content as well as the context in which the image is captured. The proposed model can be trained end-to-end and solves a multi-label classification problem. We evaluate the model on a dataset of 1,965,232 images which is drawn from the YFCC100M dataset provided by the organizers of Yahoo-Flickr Grand Challenge. We observe a significant improvement in the prediction accuracy after integrating user-context and the proposed model performs very well in the Grand Challenge.

CCS Concepts

•**Information systems** → *Multimedia information systems;*

Keywords

Convolutional Neural Networks; Multi-label Image Tagging; User Context

1. INTRODUCTION

The model presented in this paper is our solution to the ACM Multimedia 2016 Grand Challenge on user tag and caption prediction presented by Yahoo-Flickr. We mainly focus on the user tag prediction task in this work and its extension to caption prediction task is discussed as a future work. We solved the user tag prediction problem as a multi-label classification and proposed a convolutional deep neural network which integrates both the image pixel values and context in a unified framework for predicting a list of user tags.

Social media users like to assign tags to the captured images before sharing with others. One of the biggest advantages of adding tags to photographs is that it makes them searchable and easily discoverable by other users. To help users annotate their photos, researchers have developed visual recognition algorithms which can recommend tags

MM '16, October 15-19, 2016, Amsterdam, Netherlands

DOI: http://dx.doi.org/10.1145/2964284.2984068

(a) **id**: 2714476432 sky, **sunrise**, sunshine

(b) **id**: 5988428428 canoe,orange, **sunset**,water

(c) **id**: 3528351944 ancient,art,statue, **sunrise**,temple,valley

Figure 1: Sample images from YFCC100M dataset [25] along with photo identifier and associated tags assigned by the users. Each photo has been assigned with multiple tags and it can be observed that the visual content of the images is not sufficient to predict the tags. Images in (a) and (b) have similar visual content, however, (a) is captured at sunrise and (b) has been captured at sunset. In addition, image (c) has been assigned 'sunrise' as a tag, which is difficult to predict using visual content of the image.

based on the visual content of the image. Deep convolutional neural networks (CNNs) have shown a great progress in visual recognition tasks in recent years [15, 21, 24]. The existing methods are mainly focused on datasets, such as ImageNet [4], that were manually annotated for single-label classification. Also, the different categories are defined by researchers and not by users, which means they are not necessarily relevant for tag recommendation.

An image can have multiple annotations based on its visual content, interactions between objects present and many other factors. Motivated by this, researchers have shown interest in multi-label image classification task where an image can be annotated with multiple tags [18, 10, 29, 16, 27]. A basic approach to solving multi-label classification problem is to train independent single-label classifiers for each of the label [10]. However, when trained independently, the dependency knowledge between the various labels corresponding to an image is lost. The co-occurrence dependency between labels has also been utilized by earlier works to improve the annotation performance [31, 27].

We further observe that a user assigns tags to a captured image based on not only the image content but also his or her current context, such as time and location. In addition, context can also help in improving the visual recognition task. For example, sunset and sunrise photographs may have similar visual content (Figure 1), however, with available time context, it becomes simpler to identify the correct annotation. In addition, an appropriate tag for an image does not always have to be about the image visual content, it can also be related to the current user context (Figure 1c). Therefore, apart from image content, user context also plays an important role in the recommendation of image tags. Inspired by this, we propose to explore the role of context in multiple-label user-tag prediction using a deep neural network.

In this work, we propose a unified CNN-NN framework to integrate context with image content for multi-label tag prediction. The framework of the proposed model is shown in Figure 2. In comparison with state-of-the-art multi-label tag prediction methods, the

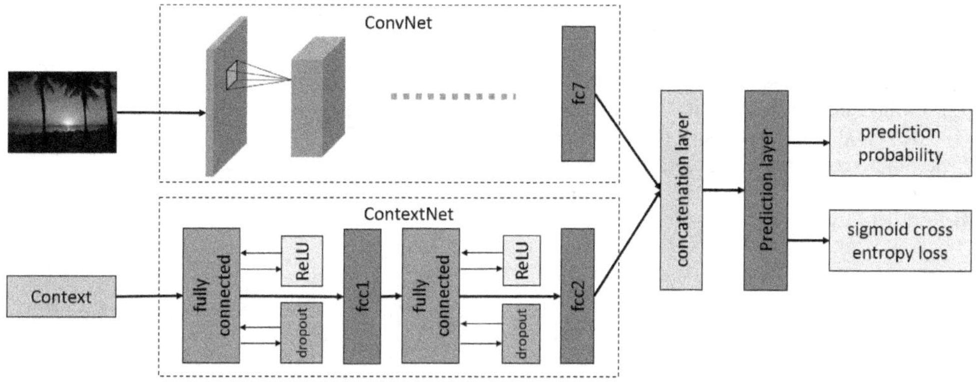

Figure 2: Overview of the proposed model. An input image is passed through a CNN (ConvNet) component of the network which has been adopted from AlexNet [15]. The associated context of the image is processed through a parallel NN (ContextNet). The output of ConvNet (fc7 layer) and ContextNet (fcc2 layer) are merged together and passed to the prediction layer for multi-label prediction. The proposed model can be trained end-to-end using gradient descent optimization.

proposed framework has the following advantages. First of all, it incorporates the context information associated with the image for tag prediction. Secondly, it integrates the user context with image content in a unified way and the complete model can be trained end-to-end. And finally, the model is trained on a large set of user defined tags (1540) which is much bigger as compared to other publicly available datasets for multi-label classification [3, 5, 17]. We evaluate the proposed framework on a dataset exclusively drawn from YFCC100M provided by Yahoo-Flickr [25]. The experimental evaluation shows that integrating context significantly improves the tag prediction accuracy.

The rest of the paper is organized as follows. First of all, we will discuss the related work in section 2. In section 3 we will discuss the proposed method followed by experimental results in section 4. Finally, we will conclude this paper with a conclusion and future research direction in section 5.

2. RELATED WORK

In past few years, image classification has made a significant progress due to development in deep convolutional neural networks [15] and availability of large-scale labeled datasets such as ImageNet [4]. Apart from single-label classification multi-label classification is also making progress because of available datasets, such as NUS-WIDE [3], VOC PASCAL [5] and Microsoft COCO [17]. Some of the attempts to solve multi-label classification task using deep learning include works which treat each label independently and ignore any correlation between corresponding labels [8, 28]. Gong et al. [8] investigated several ranking-based loss functions for CNN and proposed weighted approximated-ranking loss for multi-label annotation. Wei et al. [28] proposed Hypothesis-CNN-Pooling (HCP) where outputs from multiple hypotheses are aggregated using max pooling.

To address the above-mentioned limitation, researchers have proposed joint modeling of image and label embedding. Weston et al. [30] learn a joint representation of images and annotations that optimize top-of-the-list ranking. Similarly, Frome et al. [6] proposed a model for visual-semantic embedding to identify visual objects using both pixel values as well as image semantics. In [9], Gong et al. employ canonical correlation analysis (CCA) to map visual features and labels to the same latent space and incorporate a third view to capture high-level image semantics. These methods effectively capture the semantic relation between tags and image content, however, they ignore the co-occurrence relation between multiple tags.

The label co-occurrence dependency has also been studied by researchers for multi-label classification task [7, 20, 11, 31, 16]. In [7] Ghamrawi et al. proposed conditional random field (CRF) classification models for multi-label classification that parameterize label co-occurrences. Read et al. [20] utilize classifier chains method to model the label correlations for multi-label classification. Guo et al. [11] proposed a graphical model to represent dependencies between multiple labels. In a more recent study [27], Wang et al. proposed a deep convolutional neural network combined with the recurrent neural network (CNN-RNN) to model the dependencies between labels for multi-label classification.

Apart from tag prediction, captioning of an image has also made significant progress in recent years [1, 19, 2, 26]. In one of the recent work [14] Justin et al. proposed a model to localize as well as describe regions of an image. These existing methods for tag and caption prediction make use of the content of the image while ignoring the context in which the image was captured. Although, the works in [23] and [13] have explored the role of context in tag prediction, the methods are focused on single label prediction [23] and used relatively smaller dataset (NUS-WIDE) with lab curated small set of labels [13]. In this work, we explore the role of context for user tag prediction on a much bigger real-world dataset (YFCC100M) with a large number of user tags. We propose the use of a unified network for joint modeling of context along with image content and corresponding labels and demonstrate that context plays an important role in how a user assigns tags to their images.

3. PROPOSED METHOD

3.1 Model

We propose a novel context-aware CNN-NN framework for multi-label classification problem. The network consists of two components, CNN part, and NN part. The CNN part extracts visual information from image pixels and the NN part models the user-context. We adopted AlexNet [15] for convolutional part of the network and integrated the fully-connected (fc7) layer with the ContextNet for performing multi-label classification. An overview of the proposed model is shown in Figure 2.

The YFCC100M dataset [25] provides associated meta-data for each of the images which include time of capture and the geo-location where the image was captured. We utilize this meta information to represent user-context which indicates where and when the corresponding image was captured. We form a 6-dimensional feature vector using geo-coordinates (latitude with a range of -90.0 to 90.0 and longitude with a range of -180 to 180) and time (time in minutes with a range of 0 to 1439, weekday with a range 0-6, month with a range 1-12 and day with a range 1-31). The training data was preprocessed to ensure zero mean and unit variance before feeding into the network. The same scaling was performed on the test and validation set before predicting image tags.

The standardized context descriptor is fed into a 2-layered neural network with fully connected layers. We employ rectified linear units

(ReLU) ($f(x) = max(0, x)$) as activation functions for these layers and each of the layer comprises of 512 neurons. The output of this network (fcc2) is integrated with the last layer of the convolutional network (fc7) to perform multi-label classification. The output of the convolutional network (fc7) and context network (fcc2) are concatenated together and the label scores are computed using a fully connected layer. Finally, softmax normalization is performed on the scores to predict the label probability.

3.2 Training

The first 7 layers of the CNN module [15] in our network are pre-trained on ImageNet 2012 classification challenge dataset [4] using Caffe deep learning framework [12]. We learn the parameters for rest of the layers (while fine-tuning the pre-trained CNN parameters) by optimizing the sigmoid cross-entropy loss for the final layer of the network on a subset of YFCC100M [25] training dataset. A label corresponding to an image i is represented as a 1540-dimensional vector p_i, where each element of p_i indicates the presence or absence of the corresponding tag.

$$p_i = (x_1, x_2, ..., x_{1540}), x_i \in [0, 1] \quad (1)$$

With sigmoid cross-entropy loss, the network is trained by optimizing the following loss objective,

$$L_e = -\frac{1}{N}\sum_{i=1}^{N}[p_i log(\hat{p}_i) + (1 - p_i) log(1 - \hat{p}_i)] \quad (2)$$

where, $\hat{p}_i$ is obtained by applying sigmoid function ($f(x) = \frac{1}{1+e^{-x}}$) to each output (label scores) of the final layer of the network.

We employ stochastic gradient descent for optimizing the loss objective for the network. In our experiments, we use a dropout rate of 0.5 for all the projection layers to avoid over-fitting [22]. The momentum (μ) for the update in gradient descent was set to 0.9, the factor for dropping the learning rate (γ) was set to 0.1 and the weight decay was set to 0.0005 for regularization. We employ a global learning rate (α) of 0.001 for the pre-trained layers and a learning rate of 0.01 for the new layers for a faster learning. Both the learning rates are dropped by a factor of γ after every 100K iterations with a batch size of 64 (3.2 epochs with $\sim$ 2M images).

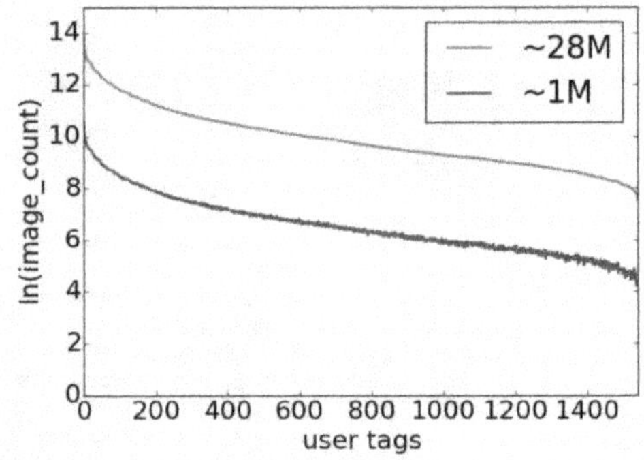

Dataset	Max	Min	Mean
~28M	1017156	1881	40628
~1M	36554	67	1445
Top frequently used tags	travel, nature, wedding, vacation, beach, people, art, architecture, summer, party		

Table 1: Distribution of the number of images for the master tag list in ~28M dataset and a randomly sampled ~1M dataset. The plot shows the natural log of number-of-images per user tag against the tag list sorted in decreasing order. In the table, we have the maximum, minimum and average number of photos per tag. The last row shows the top most tags present in the dataset.

fog,mist,**morning**,rural, wide+angle	sea,silhouette,sky, **sunset**,twilight
sunrise,landscape,**morning**, clouds,sky	**sunset**,sea,sky, travel,clouds
panorama,landscape,lake, nature,panoramic	**sunset**,**sunrise**,sea, ocean,clouds

Table 3: Images from validation set with actual and predicted tags using context-free (third row) and context-aware model (second row) along with the ground truth (first row).

4. EXPERIMENTS

We perform our experiments on a dataset provided by the organizers of the Grand Challenge which is exclusively drawn from Yahoo-Flickr Creative Commons 100M (YFCC100M) [25]. We trained two separate models, one without context and the other integrated with context. We compared these two models for exploring the role of context in user tag prediction. We have also compared our results with other participants in the Grand Challenge. The evaluation demonstrates that the proposed context-aware model outperforms other methods in all the evaluation metrics.

4.1 Dataset

One of the major benefits of YFCC100M dataset is its volume and associated meta information available with the images along with the pixel values. For the tag prediction task, we were provided with a list 1540 tags which were extracted from YFCC100M dataset after some preprocessing by the organizers. The complete dataset was split into train and test set based on the Flickr user identifier (NSID). Only those images with at least one tag present in the master list of 1540 tags were selected for the training set. The training data contains a total of 28,157,620 images and the test set provided for evaluation consists of 46,700 images.

We divided this training dataset of around 28 million images into smaller batches of 1 million images. The order of the images was randomly shuffled before creating the batches. Out of these 29 batches we use 2 random batches with around ~2M images for training our model. The last batch of around 157K images was used as a validation set.

4.2 Evaluation Metric

The proposed method is evaluated based on precision, recall and accuracy measures for the predicted tags on the validation set as well as on the test set provide by the organizers. We predict top-k tags for each of the test images and compared with the ground truth. The precision@k is computed as the proportion of top k generated tags that appear in the user tags, recall@k is computed as the proportion of the user tags that appear in the top k generated tags, and accuracy@k is computed as 1 if at least one of the top k generated tags is present in the user tags and 0 otherwise.

4.3 Results and Analysis

We evaluate both context-free and context-aware model on the test set provided by the organizers for comparison. A detailed comparison is shown in Table 4. The context-free model when trained on ~2M images achieved an accuracy of 0.65, precision of 0.21 and a recall of 0.18 for k=5. The context-aware model, on the other hand, achieved an increased accuracy of 0.71, precision of 0.25 and a recall of 0.20.

We also evaluated the proposed model on a validation set drawn from the training data. The validation set has a total of 157620 im-

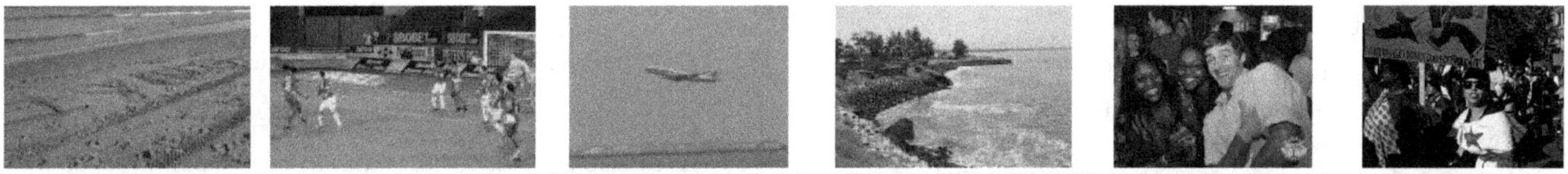

beach,ocean,sand, sun,vacation	club,football,soccer, stadium,wales	aircraft,airplane,airport, aviation,city,travel	beach,fort,lighthouse, seaside,travel,water	bar,club,food, fun,party	demonstration,march, protest,street
beach,sand,ocean, water,shore	football,wales,soccer, stadium,sport	airplane,plane, aircraft,jet,aviation	beach,water,travel, vacation,nature	bar,party,club, nightlife,fun	protest,black+and+white, demonstration,people,rally

Table 2: Images from validation set with actual (first row) and predicted tags (second row) using context-aware model.

Method	Precision@5	Recall@5	Accuracy@5
Baseline1	0.04	0.03	0.18
Baseline2	0.24	**0.20**	**0.72**
SB	0.23	0.19	0.69
P-CF	0.21	0.18	0.65
P-CA	**0.25**	**0.20**	0.71

Table 4: Comparison of evaluation results on test set provided by the organizers. Baseline1 is obtained by assigning the overall most frequent tags to every photo. Baseline2 is a convolutional neural network which is trained on around 5M images from the training dataset. SB is the second best results obtained by other participants in the Grand Challenge. P-CF (context-free) is our proposed method without context when trained for ~2M images (approximately 7 % os the training set) and P-CA is the proposed context-aware model trained on ~2M images.

K	Precision@k		Recall@k		Accuracy@k	
	P-CF	P-CA	P-CF	P-CA	P-CF	P-CA
1	0.39	0.43	0.05	0.07	0.39	0.43
3	0.32	0.35	0.12	0.16	0.60	0.65
5	0.28	0.31	0.18	0.23	0.69	0.73
10	0.22	0.23	0.27	0.33	0.79	0.83

Table 5: Evaluation results on the validation set as described in section 4.1 for different values of k obtained using proposed context-free (P-CF) and context-aware (P-CA) model.

ages and as per the organizer's guidelines, images with at least 5 tags were selected for testing. Based on this, we have a total of 14337 images for evaluation. We computed precision@k, recall@k and accuracy@k for k=(1,3,5,10). The results are shown in table 5. We observe that the context-aware model performs better than the context-free model for all values of k. Table 2 and table 3 shows some of the sample results obtained using the proposed method. We can observe that the tags predicted using context-aware model are more meaningful as compared to the context-free model (table 3).

We computed per-tag precision/recall scores for the images in the validation set. Figure 4 shows the scores corresponding to the top-predicted tags based on their F1 score. We can observe that for most of the tags the context-aware model perform better than the context-free model. We also observe that the context-aware model does not improve the scores for all the tags equivalently. To analyze this further, we plot the cumulative prediction/recall (@5) curve for the top predicted tags arranged in decreasing order of precision. We observe that the cumulative gain in precision and recall curves for context-aware model crosses with the context-free model showing that the gain in precision and recall is not consistent across various tags. We plan to explore the context-awareness of tags in our future work.

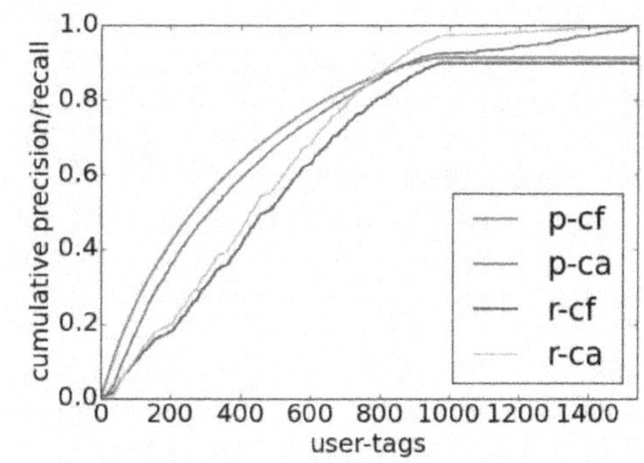

Figure 3: Plot to demonstrate that integrating context has varying effect on the prediction accuracy for different user-tags. (p-cf: cumulative precision for context-free, p-ca: cumulative precision for context-aware, r-cf: cumulative recall for context-free and, r-ca: cumulative recall for context-aware)

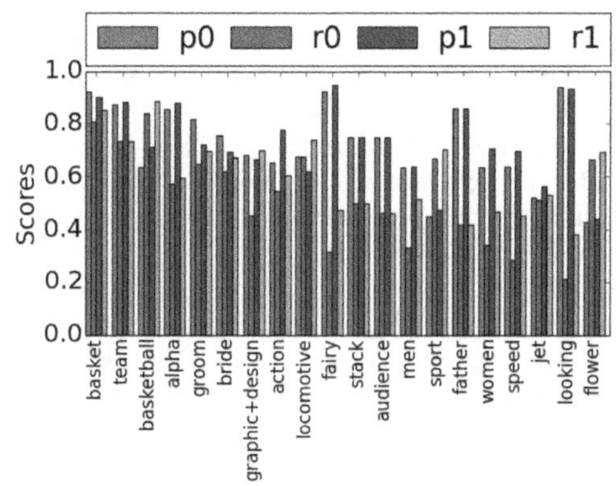

Figure 4: Precision@5 and recall@5 scores for the top predicted user-tags. (p0/r0: precision/recall without context and p1/r1: precision/recall with context.)

5. CONCLUSION AND FUTURE WORK

In this work, we proposed a context-aware model which can predict multiple tags for an image which can be recommended to a user. The network can be trained end-to-end for the image content as well as the context in which the image was captured. We adopted the AlexNet convolutional model [15] for image content and combine it with another network for context to perform multi-label classification. The experimental results showed that integrating context significantly improves the tag prediction.

In the current research, we focused on exploring the role of context in image tagging and showed that the context can be an important factor in predicting how user tags their images. In future work, we will explore the role of user-context in image captioning as context also plays an important role in how user caption their images. We plan to integrate the proposed context-aware network with recurrent neural networks which are known to perform well for caption prediction tasks [14]. In addition, we also plan to explore the role of user-context in understanding the correlation between multiple tags assigned to an image by the user.

6. ACKNOWLEDGMENTS

This research is supported by the National Research Foundation, Prime Minister's Office, Singapore under its International Research Centre in Singapore Funding Initiative.

7. REFERENCES

[1] X. Chen, H. Fang, T. Lin, R. Vedantam, S. Gupta, P. Dollár, and C. L. Zitnick. Microsoft COCO captions: Data collection and evaluation server. *CoRR*, abs/1504.00325, 2015.

[2] X. Chen and C. L. Zitnick. Learning a recurrent visual representation for image caption generation. *arXiv preprint arXiv:1411.5654*, 2014.

[3] T.-S. Chua, J. Tang, R. Hong, H. Li, Z. Luo, and Y. Zheng. Nus-wide: a real-world web image database from national university of singapore. In *Proceedings of the ACM international conference on image and video retrieval*, page 48. ACM, 2009.

[4] J. Deng, W. Dong, R. Socher, L.-J. Li, K. Li, and L. Fei-Fei. Imagenet: A large-scale hierarchical image database. In *Computer Vision and Pattern Recognition, 2009. CVPR 2009. IEEE Conference on*, pages 248–255. IEEE, 2009.

[5] M. Everingham, L. Van Gool, C. K. Williams, J. Winn, and A. Zisserman. The pascal visual object classes (voc) challenge. *International journal of computer vision*, 88(2):303–338, 2010.

[6] A. Frome, G. S. Corrado, J. Shlens, S. Bengio, J. Dean, T. Mikolov, et al. Devise: A deep visual-semantic embedding model. In *Advances in neural information processing systems*, pages 2121–2129, 2013.

[7] N. Ghamrawi and A. McCallum. Collective multi-label classification. In *Proceedings of the 14th ACM international conference on Information and knowledge management*, pages 195–200. ACM, 2005.

[8] Y. Gong, Y. Jia, T. Leung, A. Toshev, and S. Ioffe. Deep convolutional ranking for multilabel image annotation. *arXiv preprint arXiv:1312.4894*, 2013.

[9] Y. Gong, Q. Ke, M. Isard, and S. Lazebnik. A multi-view embedding space for modeling internet images, tags, and their semantics. *International journal of computer vision*, 106(2):210–233, 2014.

[10] M. Guillaumin, T. Mensink, J. Verbeek, and C. Schmid. Tagprop: Discriminative metric learning in nearest neighbor models for image auto-annotation. In *2009 IEEE 12th International Conference on Computer Vision*, pages 309–316, Sept 2009.

[11] Y. Guo and S. Gu. Multi-label classification using conditional dependency networks. In *IJCAI Proceedings-International Joint Conference on Artificial Intelligence*, volume 22, page 1300, 2011.

[12] Y. Jia, E. Shelhamer, J. Donahue, S. Karayev, J. Long, R. Girshick, S. Guadarrama, and T. Darrell. Caffe: Convolutional architecture for fast feature embedding. *arXiv preprint arXiv:1408.5093*, 2014.

[13] J. Johnson, L. Ballan, and L. Fei-Fei. Love thy neighbors: Image annotation by exploiting image metadata. In *Proceedings of the IEEE International Conference on Computer Vision*, pages 4624–4632, 2015.

[14] J. Johnson, A. Karpathy, and L. Fei-Fei. Densecap: Fully convolutional localization networks for dense captioning. In *Proceedings of the IEEE Conference on Computer Vision and Pattern Recognition*, 2016.

[15] A. Krizhevsky, I. Sutskever, and G. E. Hinton. Imagenet classification with deep convolutional neural networks. In *Advances in neural information processing systems*, pages 1097–1105, 2012.

[16] X. Li, F. Zhao, and Y. Guo. Multi-label image classification with a probabilistic label enhancement model. *Proc. Uncertainty in Artificial Intell*, 2014.

[17] T.-Y. Lin, M. Maire, S. Belongie, J. Hays, P. Perona, D. Ramanan, P. Dollár, and C. L. Zitnick. Microsoft coco: Common objects in context. In *European Conference on Computer Vision*, pages 740–755. Springer, 2014.

[18] A. Makadia, V. Pavlovic, and S. Kumar. A new baseline for image annotation. In *Proceedings of the 10th European Conference on Computer Vision: Part III*, ECCV '08, pages 316–329, Berlin, Heidelberg, 2008. Springer-Verlag.

[19] J. Mao, W. Xu, Y. Yang, J. Wang, and A. L. Yuille. Explain images with multimodal recurrent neural networks. *arXiv preprint arXiv:1410.1090*, 2014.

[20] J. Read, B. Pfahringer, G. Holmes, and E. Frank. Classifier chains for multi-label classification. *Machine learning*, 85(3):333–359, 2011.

[21] K. Simonyan and A. Zisserman. Very deep convolutional networks for large-scale image recognition. *arXiv preprint arXiv:1409.1556*, 2014.

[22] N. Srivastava, G. E. Hinton, A. Krizhevsky, I. Sutskever, and R. Salakhutdinov. Dropout: a simple way to prevent neural networks from overfitting. *Journal of Machine Learning Research*, 15(1):1929–1958, 2014.

[23] Y.-C. Su, T.-H. Chiu, G.-L. Wu, C.-Y. Yeh, F. Wu, and W. Hsu. Flickr-tag prediction using multi-modal fusion and meta information. In *Proceedings of the 21st ACM international conference on Multimedia*, pages 353–356. ACM, 2013.

[24] C. Szegedy, W. Liu, Y. Jia, P. Sermanet, S. Reed, D. Anguelov, D. Erhan, V. Vanhoucke, and A. Rabinovich. Going deeper with convolutions. In *Proceedings of the IEEE Conference on Computer Vision and Pattern Recognition*, pages 1–9, 2015.

[25] B. Thomee, D. A. Shamma, G. Friedland, B. Elizalde, K. Ni, D. Poland, D. Borth, and L.-J. Li. Yfcc100m: The new data in multimedia research. *Commun. ACM*, 59(2):64–73, Jan. 2016.

[26] O. Vinyals, A. Toshev, S. Bengio, and D. Erhan. Show and tell: A neural image caption generator. In *Proceedings of the IEEE Conference on Computer Vision and Pattern Recognition*, pages 3156–3164, 2015.

[27] J. Wang, Y. Yang, J. Mao, Z. Huang, C. Huang, and W. Xu. Cnn-rnn: A unified framework for multi-label image classification. *arXiv preprint arXiv:1604.04573*, 2016.

[28] Y. Wei, W. Xia, J. Huang, B. Ni, J. Dong, Y. Zhao, and S. Yan. Cnn: Single-label to multi-label. *arXiv preprint arXiv:1406.5726*, 2014.

[29] J. Weston, S. Bengio, and N. Usunier. Large scale image annotation: learning to rank with joint word-image embeddings. *Machine Learning*, 81(1):21–35, 2010.

[30] J. Weston, S. Bengio, and N. Usunier. Wsabie: scaling up to large vocabulary image annotation. In *Proceedings of the Twenty-Second international joint conference on Artificial Intelligence-Volume Volume Three*, pages 2764–2770. AAAI Press, 2011.

[31] X. Xue, W. Zhang, J. Zhang, B. Wu, J. Fan, and Y. Lu. Correlative multi-label multi-instance image annotation. In *2011 International Conference on Computer Vision*, pages 651–658. IEEE, 2011.

Image Captioning with both Object and Scene Information

Xiangyang Li, Xinhang Song, Luis Herranz, Yaohui Zhu, Shuqiang Jiang
Key Laboratory of Intelligent Information Processing of Chinese Academy of Sciences (CAS)
Institute of Computer Technology, CAS, Beijing, 100190, China
{xiangyang.li, xinhang.song, luis.herranz, yaohui.zhu}@vipl.ict.ac.cn;
sqjiang@ict.ac.cn

ABSTRACT

Recently, automatic generation of image captions has attracted great interest not only because of its extensive applications but also because it connects computer vision and natural language processing. By combining convolutional neural networks (CNNs), which learn visual representations from images, and recurrent neural networks (RNNs), which translate the learned features into text sequences, the content of a image can be transformed into linguistic sequences. Existing approaches typically focus on visual features extracted form an object-oriented CNN (train on ImageNet) and then decode them into natural language. In this paper, we propose a novel model using not only object-related, but also scene-related information extracted from the images. To make full use of both object and scene information, we first combine object information and scene information (extracted from a scene-oriented CNN), and then using as inputs to RNNs. Both types of information provide complementary aspects that help in generating a more complete description of the image. Qualitative and quantitative evaluation results validate the effectiveness of our method.

CCS Concepts

•**Computing methodologies → Natural language generation; Computer vision; Image representations;**

Keywords

Image Caption; Long Short-Term Memory; Convolutional Neural Network; Scene and Object

1. INTRODUCTION

Being able to automatically describe the content of an image, a problem known as image captioning, is becoming an important task in the field of artificial intelligence. The task is interesting not only because it has many applications, such as navigation for the blind, human-machine interaction and image retrieval systems to organize and locate images by the form of verbal communication, but also because it is a core problem connecting computer vision and natural language processing. Compared with conventional tasks in the computer vision community such as image classification, object detection, or attribute prediction, generating a meaningful natural language description of an image needs a more sophisticated and holistic understanding of the image. The description not only should describe the objects appearing in the image, but also should depict their spatial configurations, attributes, interactions with other objects, as well as the activities involved in.

Image captioning models take an image as input and output a sequence text that describes its content. The methods of solving this task can be divided into two categories. The first category is based on retrieval [8, 12]. These approaches first find the closest matching images with captions, and then simply transfer these descriptions to the query image. They depend on the training data too much, so it is hard to add or remove some words for a particular image. The

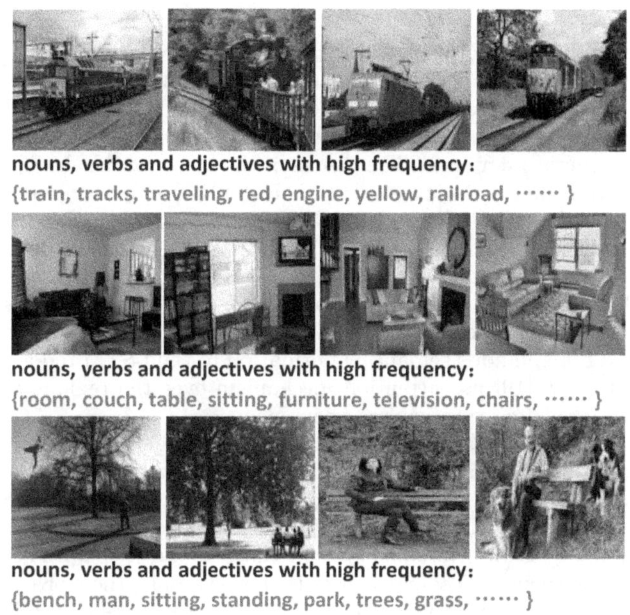

Figure 1: Illustration of the relationship between object information and scene information. The scene categories from top to bottom are railway, bedroom and park respectively.

MM '16, October 15-19, 2016, Amsterdam, Netherlands

DOI: http://dx.doi.org/10.1145/2964284.2984069

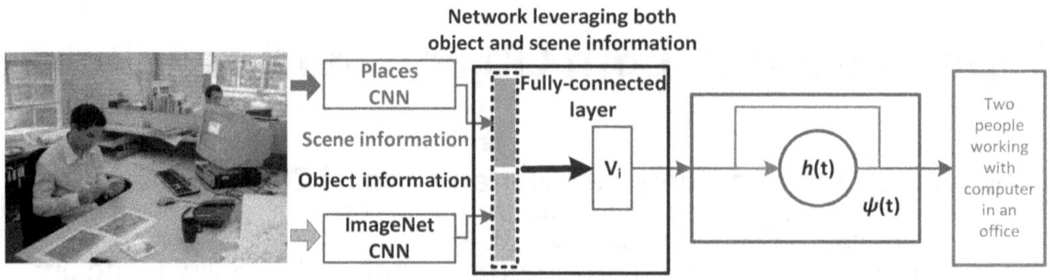

Figure 2: Illustration of the framework. We first use networks pre-trained on ImageNet and Places to extract object information and scene information of the image. And then we train a network to leverage both of the information. The learned feature V_i is used to generate image descriotion.

second category is generating new captions. Some work generates descriptions based on fixed sentence template [2, 9]. They first detect elements such as attributes, objects and actions in the image, and then fill the template with them to generate sentence. The results of these approaches have a fixed format and are less natural. Recently, many researches have adopted CNNs and RNNs to this task [7, 11, 18, 6, 5, 4]. Karpathy *et al.* [7] and Mao *et al.* [18, 11] use a deep CNN to extract visual feature, which is put into a RNN as the initial start word to generate image description. Vinyals *et al.* [18] propose to use LSTM [3]. Jia *et al.* [4] propose gLSTM and adds semantic information to the LSTM model. Xu *et al.* [19] use attention mechanism over the regions of the input image to generate sentence.

However, considering these approaches of generating new captions for images, they just focus on visual features extracted form an object-oriented CNN and then decode them into natural language. Intuitively, the scene information of an image is an invaluable context that can affect the prediction of sequential semantic words. For example, the word of *train* seems unlikely to appear in the *bedroom* scene, while the word of *television* is more likely to appear in the *bedroom* scene than in the *park* scene, as shown in Figure 1.

In this paper, we propose a novel model for image captioning not just using object information, but also using scene information of the images. Similar to Rohrbach's work [14] which learns different oriented classifiers such as verbs, objects and places for movie description, we use CNNs pretrained in ImageNet [15] and Places [20] to extract viusal features. As ImageNet CNN is object-oriented, and Places CNN is scene-oriented, features extracted with different networks contain different information. We include a fully-connected layer to combine object and scene information in visual space, and then feed the RNN units with the enhanced features, as demonstrated in Figure 2. Experimental results demonstrate that the object information and scene information are complementary, and the combination of them can be helpful to improve the performance. Jun *et al.* [6] use scene information from the corpus to factor the LSTM units, while we explicitly use scene information from the images.

The rest of the paper is organized as follow: In section 2, we introduce the framework of our method. In Section 3, we evaluate our method and report the experimental results. Finally, Section 4 gives a summary of this paper.

2. PROPOSED METHOD

In this paper, we proposed a framework to describe the content of an image with both object and scene information. The proposed system is illustrated in in Figure 2. Firstly, networks pre-trained on object-oriented and scene-oriented datasets are used to extract the visual features of the images. And then, a network is trained to leverage both object and scene information. Finally, the enhanced features are put into the RNN units to predict sequential text.

2.1 Object and Scene

Currently, most image captioning approaches [18, 11, 19] only use the CNN pretrained with ImageNet, which focus on the object rather than scene images, to extract visual features. However, the image caption task is not only about the description of particular objects, but is the description of the whole images. While, the scene information can be regarded as the background knowledge and context of the objects contained in the images. Thus, including the scene information into the framework is helpful to generate more complementary and accurate descriptions.

In our framework, we also extract visual features with the CNN pretrained using Places dataset (referred to Places CNN) [20], which is a large scale dataset consisting of 205 scenes. Using Places CNN to extract visual features can be regarded as embedding the scene information into the visual feature, which has never been considered in the previous image captioning approaches.

2.2 Visual Combination

Instead of simple concatenation, we combine the visual features embedded with object and scene information by including another hidden layer in the RNN architecture, which is connected to the both visual features. The connection parameters between input visual features and the hidden layer are learned during the training of the RNN. Thus, the output of the hidden layer can be regarded as the selection among the two input visual features, with the supervision of ground truth sentences during the RNN training.

2.3 Image Captioning

Like most of previous work, our image captioning method follows an encoder-decoder pipeline. The encoder transfers an visual representation into a feature space, and the decoder further converts the feature to a sentence. In our encoding process, CNNs trained on ImageNet and Places are utilized for feature extraction. Then the RNN model is adopted in our decoding process to generate sentence descriptions for images. The core of RNN model is Long Short-Term Memory (LSTM) [3], which has shown state-of-the-art performance on sequence tasks. The memory cell and gates in a LSTM block are defined as follows:

$$i_t = \sigma(W_{ix}x_t + W_{im}m_{t-1})$$
$$f_t = \sigma(W_{fx}x_t + W_{fm}m_{t-1})$$
$$o_t = \sigma(W_{ox}x_t + W_{om}m_{t-1})$$
$$c_t = f_t \odot c_{t-1} + i_t \odot h(W_{cx}x_t + W_{cm}m_{t-1})$$
$$m_t = o_t \odot c_t$$

where $\odot$ represents the elements-wise multiplication, and $\sigma(\cdot)$ represents the sigmoid function and $h(\cdot)$ represents the hyperbolic tangent function. At given time t, LSTM receives different kinds of inputs: current input x_t, the previous hidden state m_{t-1} and the previous memory cell state c_{t-1}. During training, the goal is to maximize the log-likelihood of correct translations given the sentence in the source language. When using this principle to image description generation, the aim is to maximize the log-likehood of the image caption given an image, that is :

$$arg\ \max_{\theta} \sum_{i} log\ p(s^i_{1:L^i}|x_i, \theta)$$

where x^i denotes an image, $s^i_{1:L^i}$ denotes a sequence of words in a sentence of length L^i and θ denotes the parameters of the model.

3. EXPERIMENTAL RESULTS

3.1 Datasets and Settings

We perform experiments on the the popular large scale *MS COCO* dataset [10]. It is composed of 82,783 images for training and 40,504 images for validation, while each images accompanied with 5 reference sentences annotated by humans. In order to compare the proposed method with previous work, we use the splits used by Karpathy [7], that is, all 82,783 images from the training set for training, and 5,000 images for both validation and testing.

We also perform experiments on the the Caption Prediction Challenge dataset (CPC), which is exclusively drawn from the Yahoo-Flickr Creative Commons 100M (YFCC100M) dataset [17]. It is composed of 1,287,522 images in the training set and 36,884 images in the test set. To train our image caption model, we select 253,890 for training and 30,000 images for validation in the 1,287,522 images.

We use the last fully-connected layer of VGG-16 [16] as the visual features. In order to embed the object and scene information, two CNNs are pre-trained on ImageNet and Places datasets. For *MS COCO*, we remove the words that occurs less than 5 times in the training set, resulting a dictionary of size 8498. As CPC covering a much broader domain, we set the threshold as 2, resulting 14067 words. For the model with both object and scene information, the parameters of the fully-connected layer and the LSTM units are jointly trained from scratch. In our experiments, we set both the size of the fully-connected layer and the size of the hidden units in LSTM models as 512.

3.2 Quantitative Evaluation Results

Although it is sometimes not clear whether a description should be deemed successful or not given an image, previous work has proposed several evaluation metrics The most commonly used metric so far in the image description literature is the BLEU score [13], which evaluates a candidate sentence by measuring the fraction of n-grams that appear in a set of references. So we evaluate our method with the BLEU score. As BLEU is critical to favor short sentences,

Table 1: Performance on MS COCO (%).

Models	B-1	B-2	B-3	B-4	METEOR
Karpathy[7]	62.5	45.0	32.1	23.0	19.5
Vinyals[18]	66.6	46.1	32.9	24.6	-
SF-GREEDY[6]	67.8	49.4	34.8	24.2	21.8
C_O	64.5	45.8	32.1	22.7	20.6
C_S	60.5	41.3	28.1	19.5	18.8
C_OS	**68.1**	**50.6**	**36.8**	**26.8**	**22.8**

Table 2: Results on the validation set of CPC (%).

Models	B-1	B-2	B-3	B-4	METEOR
C_O	10.2	4.3	2.6	1.8	3.1
C_S	9.8	4.0	2.4	1.6	3.0
C_OS	**10.7**	**4.6**	**2.9**	**2.2**	**3.2**

METEOR [1] can avoid this weakness by evaluating a generated sentence by computing a score based on word level matches between the generation and a reference and returning the maximum score over a set of related references. In this paper, beside BLEU, we also use METEOR.

Table 1 shows the performance on MS COCO dataset. C_O indicates the baseline method that generates image description just with object information. For fair comparison, the performance of the method that generates image description just with scene information, referred as C_S, is also evaluated. C_OS is the proposed method which leverages both object and scene information. As image captioning need to describe a image as complete as possible, object information contains more details than scene information, so the performance of C_O surpasses C_S. While, scene information contains the contextual relations between objects, so C_S still has a decent performance. C_OS has the best performance as it contains both object and scene information. Experiments results demonstrate that object information and scene information are complementary, and the combination of them can be helpful to improve the performance. Table 2 shows the performance on the validation set of the Caption Prediction Challenge dataset (CPC). It also demonstrates that the combination of object and scene information can get better performance. The performance of C_OS on the test set of CPC is 9.0%.

3.3 Qualitative Analysis

We hypothesize that object information and scene information are complementary for image captions generation. The results shown in Figure 3 verify this hypothesis. As object information often focuses on particular parts of images and has more details of visual attributes, the generated captions highlight the elements such as people, animal, or related activities. While for scene information, it is more sensitive to the contextual relations between objects and spatial structures, the generated captions highlight more holistic elements. For example, the caption of the image in the first column in Figure 3 (a) generated from object information highlights the girl, while the caption generated from scene information just indicates that it is a kitchen. All the experimental results demonstrate that the combination of object and scene information can improve the performance.

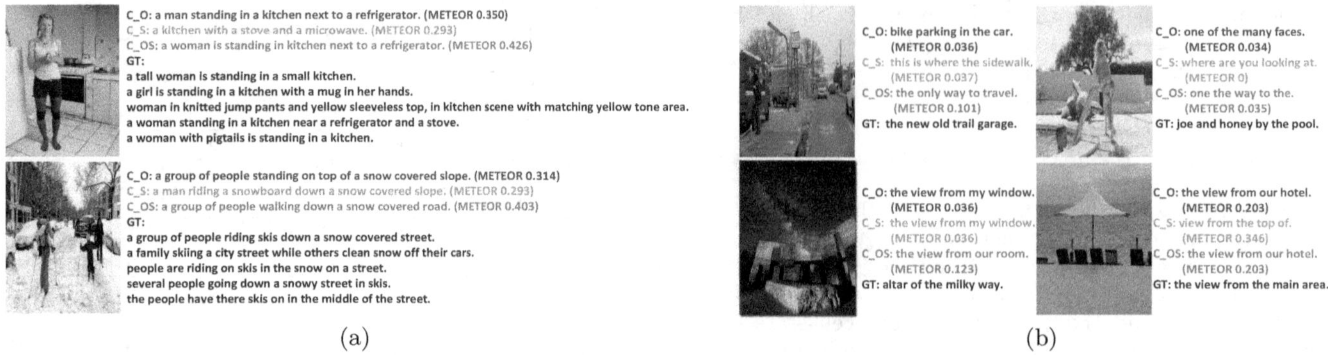

Figure 3: Image descriptions generated with different kinds of information on MS COCO (a) and CPC (b). The METEOR score of each generated sentence is evaluated over the ground truth sentences.

4. CONCLUSION

We have presented a framework to combine both object and scene information to generate the image captions. Both information are embedded in the visual features extracted from the convolutional neural networks pre-trained with ImageNet and Places datasets. And we combine them by include a hidden layer during the recurrent neural network training, which is connected to both input visual features. The experimental results show that including the scene information can get higher performance than only using the object information.

5. ACKNOWLEDGEMENTS

This work is supported in part by the National Basic Research 973 Program of China under Grant No. 2012CB316400, the National Natural Science Foundation of China under Grant Nos. 61532018, 61322212 and 61550110505, the National High Technology Research and Development 863 Program of China under Grant No. 2014AA015202. This work is also funded by Beijing Science And Technology Project under Grant No. D161100001816001 and Lenovo Outstanding Young Scientists Program (LOYS).

6. REFERENCES

[1] M. Denkowski and A. Lavie. Meteor universal: Language specific translation evaluation for any target language. In *EACL 2014 Workshop on Statistical Machine Translation*, 2014.

[2] A. Farhadi, M. Hejrati, M. A. Sadeghi, P. Young, C. Rashtchian, J. Hockenmaier, and D. Forsyth. Every picture tells a story: Generating sentences from images. In *ECCV*, 2010.

[3] S. Hochreiter and J. Schmidhuber. Long short-term memory. *Neural Computation*, 9(8):1735 – 1780, 1997.

[4] X. Ji, E. gavves, B. Fernando, and T. Tuytelaars. Guiding Long-Short Term Memoty for image caption genaration. In *ICCV*, 2015.

[5] J. Johnson, A. Karpathy, and L. Fei-Fei. DenseCap: Fully convolutional localization networks for dense captioning. In *CVPR*, 2016.

[6] J. Jun, K. Fu, R. Cui, F. Sha, and C. Zhang. Aligning where to see and what to tell: image aption with region-based attention and scene factorization. In *arXiv:1506.06272*, 2015.

[7] A. Karpathy and L. Fei-Fei. Deep visual-semantic alignments for generating image descriptions. In *CVPR*, 2015.

[8] P. Kuznetsova, V. Ordonez, A. Berg, T. Berg, and Y. Choi. Generalizing image captions for image-text parallel corpus. In *ACL*, 2013.

[9] R. Lebret, P. Pinheiro, and R. Collobert. Pharse-based image captioning. In *ICCV*, 2015.

[10] T. Lin, M. Maire, S. Belongie, L. Bourdev, R. Girshick, J. Hays, P. Perona, D. ramanan, C. Zitnick, and P. Dollar. Microsoft COCO: Common object in context. In *ECCV*, 2014.

[11] J. Mao, W. Xu, Y. Yang, J. Wang, Z. Huang, and A. Yuille. Deep captioning with multimodal recurrent neural networks (M-RNN). In *ICLR*, 2015.

[12] R. Mason and E. Charniak. Nonparametric method for data-driven image captioning. In *ACL*, 2014.

[13] K. Papineni, S. Roukos, T. Ward, and W.J. Zhu. Bleu: A method for automatic evaluation of machine translation. In *ACL*, 2002.

[14] A. Rohrbach, M. Rohrbach, and B. Schiele. The long-short story of movie description. In *GCPR*, 2015.

[15] O. Russakovsky, J. Deng, H. Su, J. Krause, S. Satheesh, S. Ma, Z. Huang, A. Karpathy, A. Khosla, M. Bernstein, A. C. Berg, and L. Fei-Fei. Imagenet large scale visual recognition challenge. *International Journal of Computer Vision*, 115(3):211 – 252, 2015.

[16] K. Simonyan and A. Zisserman. Very deep convolutional networks for large-scale image recognition. In *ICLR*, 2015.

[17] B. Thomee, D. A. Shamma, G. Friedland, B. Elizalde, K. Ni, D. Poland, D. Borth, and L. Li. YFCC100M: The new data in multimedia research. *Communications of the ACM*, 59(2):64–73, 2016.

[18] O. Vinyals, A. Toshev, S. Bengio, and D. Erhan. Show and Tell: a neural image caption generator. In *CVPR*, 2015.

[19] K. Xu, J. Ba, R. Kiros, K. Cho, A. Courville, R. Salakhutdinov, R. Zemel, and Y. Bengio. Show, Attend and Tell: Neural image caption generation with visual attention. In *ICML*, 2015.

[20] B. Zhou, A. Lapedriza, J. Xiao, A. Torralba, and A. Oliva. Learning deep features for scene recognition using places database. In *NIPS*, 2014.

Generating Affective Captions using Concept And Syntax Transition Networks

Tushar Karayil*
University of Kaiserslautern
Kaiserslautern, Germany.
tushar.karayil@dfki.de

Philipp Blandfort*
University of Kaiserslautern
Kaiserslautern, Germany.
philipp.blandfort@dfki.de

Damian Borth
German Research Center for Artificial Intelligence (DFKI)
Kaiserslautern, Germany.
damian.borth@dfki.de

Andreas Dengel
University of Kaiserslautern
German Research Center for Artificial Intelligence (DFKI)
Kaiserslautern, Germany.
andreas.dengel@dfki.de

ABSTRACT

The area of image captioning i.e. the automatic generation of short textual descriptions of images has experienced much progress recently. However, image captioning approaches often only focus on describing the content of the image without any emotional or sentimental dimension which is common in human captions. This paper presents an approach for image captioning designed specifically to incorporate emotions and feelings into the caption generation process. The presented approach consists of a Deep Convolutional Neural Network (CNN) for detecting Adjective Noun Pairs in the image and a graphical network architecture called "Concept And Syntax Transition (CAST)" network for generating sentences from these detected concepts.

Keywords

Image Captioning, Sentence Generation, Auto Caption, Sentiment, Emotion

1. INTRODUCTION

With its exponential growth in the last two decades, the Internet has become a major source of information exchange across the world. Powered by new technologies and increased computational resources, web sites have become more visual and animated. Moreover, the world wide web is flooded with new images everyday, e.g. Instagram has reported an average of 80 million[1] photo uploads a day. Most of these images come with titles which can be generic (e.g. IMG_123), descriptive or give additional information that can not be directly seen in the image but can be used in an multimodal retrieval setup [17].

Recently, there have been significant advances in generating descriptive image captions ([9],[10],[11]) with focus on generating *factual* descriptive image captions. Available datasets like Microsoft-COCO [4] provide a rich textual description of images. In contrast, large real-world datasets such as "Yahoo Flickr Creative Commom 100 Million" (YFCC100M [15]) display a huge variety of captioning styles but these titles can only be considered to be weak labels (cf. [16]): Here, captions can be descriptive, emotional or mention information that is not visible in the image.

Humans often tend to associate a sentiment with an image and express that in the caption [19]. One such method is by using a emoji[2]. In addition, a richer use of text would be another way to express the associated sentiment with the caption.

It was shown by [2] that adjectives can add an emotional component to nouns and the resulting Adjective Noun Pairs (ANP) can express the visual contents in the image. Hence we assume that incorporating adjectives into machine generated captions is one feasible way of adding an emotional component to the caption.

To this end, we describe a model that is capable of generating subjective image captions and thereby going beyond factual image descriptions. We train and test our model on the YFCC100M dataset in the context of the caption prediction task of the *ACM Multimedia 2016 Grand Challenge.*

2. RELATED WORK

The available methods in linking images to text can be classified broadly into three categories.

The first set of methods is used to detect a triplet (eg. <*object,action,scene*>) of scene elements in the image and convert them into sentences. Triplets provide a holistic idea of what is most important in the image and they are combined using various techniques to generate captions. [5], [10] use this approach and a template based system to generate

*Equal contribution from both authors

[1]https://www.instagram.com/press/

[2]http://instagram-engineering.tumblr.com/post/117889701472/emojineering-part-1-machine-learning-for-emoji

MM '16, October 15-19, 2016, Amsterdam, Netherlands

DOI: http://dx.doi.org/10.1145/2964284.2984070

the sentences after identifying the objects. Although, template based approaches generate a correct description, they cannot create a novel or unique caption as they are bound by the structure of the template used.

The second set of methods bring the images and sentences into a single multi dimensional space by converting each of them into vectors. Thereafter a set of distance measures are used to find the closest matching description of a given image ([6], [14]). [14] uses neural networks to map images and sentences into the same vector space. The main disadvantage here is that images which resemble each other closely in color space need not be semantically related. Therefore the generated captions can be completely unrelated to the given image.

The third set of methods which have shown the most promising results use a combination of Deep Convolutional Neural Networks (DCNN) for feature extraction and a Recurrent Neural Networks (RNN) on top of it for text generation from the extracted features ([18], [12]).

To the best of our knowledge, *SentiCap* [12] is the only neural network based approach for image captioning that deliberately incorporates sentiment into the produced captions. However, this approach relies on ground truth captions with known sentiment values which are not part of the Grand Challenge training data. Moreover, we doubt that using the captions they used would give good results in our case since the style of these captions is quite different from typical YFCC100M captions.

The strong dependency on the training data of RNN based models might in general be problematic when working with YFCC100M data because of the variety of caption types. Since such models are typically trained in an end-to-end fashion resulting issues can be extremely hard to fix.

In order to avoid these problems, we use an existing visual concept detector and generate captions from the extracted concepts with the CAST network architecture instead of RNN. This combination is quite robust and you can follow and influence all the steps from detected concepts to final sentence, giving you much more control and allowing for easier future changes of the architecture.

3. PRESENTED APPROACH

The presented system follows a pipeline approach consisting of the following steps:

1. **Visual concept extraction**: Extract subjective visual concepts from the given image.
2. **CAST network**: Generate ranked sentences from the detected concepts.
3. **Templates**: In case the network can not build any sentence from the given concepts we use a template-based back-up approach to create sentences.

3.1 Data Preparation

The data for the ACM Multimedia Grand Challenge 2016 was provided in the following format:

- Training: 1287522 train images from the YFCC100M dataset with captions that contain at least one word from English Dictionary. It is known that such images are weakly labeled[16]. In addition to the image identifier, the user identifier is also provided.
- Testing: 36884 test images with image-id and user-id

3.2 Visual Concept Extraction

To generate human-like captions, the first step is to capture emotional and visual contents from the image. The work published in [2] introduced Adjective Noun Pair (ANP) concepts able to describe images beyond visual content (e.g. "dog") by capturing positive or negative polarity (e.g. "cute dog" or "scary dog"). This pairing of adjectives and nouns does also provide an insight into the general emotion associated with an analyzed image.

The DCNN *DeepSentiBank* [3] was trained to detect 2089 such ANPs (with 231 distinct adjectives and 424 nouns).

3.3 Concept And Syntax Transition (CAST) Network

The CAST network is a multi-directed graph where each node in the network represents a concept (i.e. noun, adjective, verb or adverb) connected to other concepts. It is generated in the following steps:

1. **Nodes**: For each content word with occurrence count greater than 40 in the training titles, we create a node. This leads to a vocabulary of over 21000 words. Additionally, we add a START and an END node.
2. **Similarity edges**: The vocabulary of *DeepSentiBank* is quite small if we want to generate different styles of sentences. In order to effectively increase the vocabulary size we train a word2vec [13] model on all training sentences. word2vec maps words to a vector space of a given dimension (200 in our case) where words that are used in similar contexts are mapped to vectors that are close together in the target space. Under the assumption that semantically similar words are used similarly, this makes it possible to compute semantic distances between words. For each node we add similarity edges to all nodes that have a word2vec similarity above some fixed threshold. This accounts for the possibility of replacing words by semantically similar words in the sentence generation process.
3. **Syntax edges**: For each sentence in the training titles we check how content words are connected. For each such connection that does not use another content word, a directed edge is created between the corresponding concept nodes. The connecting string (usually consisting of propositions, articles, etc.) is used as edge label and the total number of connection occurrences is annotated as edge weight. These edges contain information about the syntax of the language and are used to connect different concepts.

The whole graph generation was done in less than 40h and the model can be used without any further training. Generating a sentence from a set of concepts is reduced to the problem of finding a path from the start to the end node through a set of activated nodes. We compute a list of such paths in a heuristic way. For each path a score is then computed by summing up the normalized weights of the included edges. Finally, the paths are ranked by these scores and the path with highest score is converted to a sentence in a straight-forward way, where similarity edges

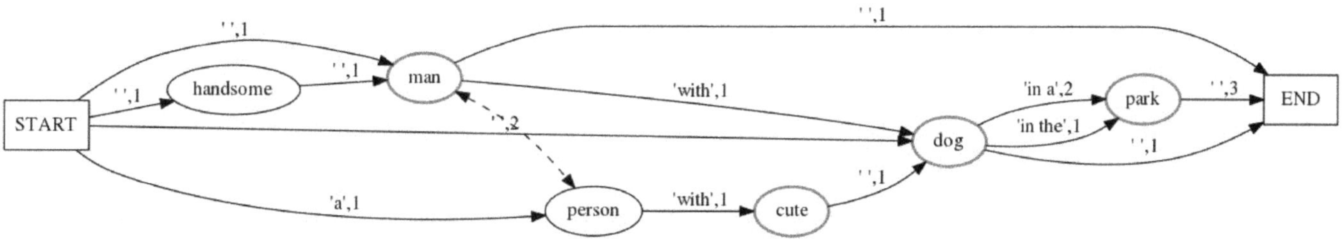

Figure 1: Example of a CAST network generated from the titles "handsome man", "a person with cute dog", "dog in a park", "dog in the park" and "man with dog in a park". The dashed line indicates a similarity edge (and is in this toy example not generated from the given sentences). If the red nodes denote the activated concepts, the resulting sentence would be "person with cute dog in a park". (Substituting "man" by "person" because a similarity edge was traversed.)

are used to substitute words.[3] An illustration of a simple CAST network can be found in Figure 1.

In general, CAST networks provide a new possibility for the challenging task of generating sentences from an arbitrary set of words. By using word similarity in the sentence generation process, they display a high degree of creativity, effectively extending the vocabulary. They do all this in a simple and transparent way which makes it easy to find the source of mistakes, allowing for systematic improvements or customization of the system in the future.

3.4 Template-based Approach

The idea of this approach is to use different templates of the kind "HUMAN with PROPERTY doing VERB on EVENT in LOCATION" to form sentences from a set of visual concepts that have been tagged by according category and are detected in the image.

For this we need:

- **Category tags**: We manually assigned category tags (e.g. "HUMAN" or "LOCATION") to all nouns that occur in any ANPs.
- **Templates**: A few (5) templates based on these category tags were created manually. From that we automatically generated different template variations by removing parts of the template. (E.g. the variations of the above template would include "HUMAN doing VERB in LOCATION" and "HUMAN with PROPERTY on EVENT in LOCATION".)

Sentences are now generated in the following steps:

1. **Input**: Given ANP scores from *DeepSentiBank*, we consider all ANPs that have a score above a fixed threshold to create sentences from all suitable template variations where every category tag is substituted by an ANP of that category. (If no score exceeds the threshold we take the ANP with highest confidence and return it as caption.)
2. **Ranking**: For each resulting sentence we first compute the mean m and the sum s over the *DeepSentiBank* scores of all ANPs that are present in the sentence. The weighted sum $0.3 \cdot m + 0.5 \cdot s$ is then used as final score for the ranking.[4]
3. **Output**: The sentence with the highest score is given as caption.

4. RESULTS AND ANALYSIS

CAST achieved a BLEU score of **0.04** at the leaderboard evaluation. (For the template-based approach the score was 0.02.)

Automatic evaluation of generated captions against the ground truth is a challenging task. One of the main reasons for this difficulty is that two captions which are syntactically different can mean the same thing. For example, an image of a rose could be captioned with "a rose" or "cute and pretty flower". Although both of these captions suit the image, from a machine's point of view they are completely different. Moreover, the scores are affected by the length of the generated captions. A low score might partly be due to the difference in caption length distributions of the generated captions in comparison to the ground truth data. By comparing the corresponding caption length histograms we found that in our case there is indeed a clear discrepancy. These histograms are shown in Figure 2.

The aforementioned points show that metrics like BLEU might fail to capture the correctness of the generated captions. With the absence of metrics addressing these issues, researchers [12, 8] have resorted to human evaluation of the generated captions.

To prove this point further, we calculated the FC7 vectors (last fully connected layer of DeepSentiBank [3]) for 300000 images from the training set and the whole test set. For each FC7 vector of a test image we found the nearest FC7 vector in the train set (using Euclidean distance) and output the title of the corresponding training image as the caption for the test image. As expected, this baseline method gave a higher score of **0.06**. Even though this method gave us a better score, we found that the generated sentences were less related to the images than captions created with CAST networks.

The generated captions from CAST often read naturally and conveyed emotions. Figure 3 shows a small selection of titles generated by our method in comparison to captions created with the Nearest Neighbour baseline approach. In order to get further insights into the emotional aspects of the

[3]Due to the graph size a full search is not feasible and hence it might happen that no path is found in which case the template-based approach serves as back-up method.

[4]Suitable multipliers were determined empirically.

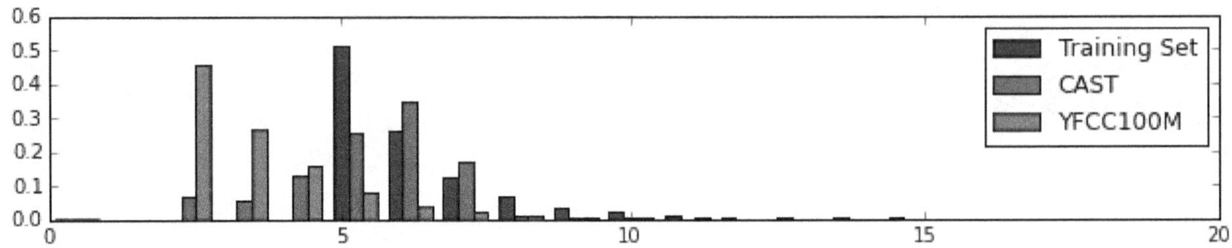

Figure 2: Normalized histograms of the caption lengths over three sets of captions: The ACMMM Grand Challenge 2016 training data ("Training Set"), CAST and a selection of 9 Million YFCC100M english titles obtained by simple filtering as described in [1]. (The filtered YFCC100M titles were included to get a rough estimate of the general distribution of user provided captions.)

Source	#Captions	Absolute Sentiment
CAST	36884	0.3
Training Set	1200000	0.14
MS-COCO	203450	0.07

Table 1: Average absolute sentiment value of captions from different sources. The ACMMM Grand Challenge 2016 training data ("Training Set") which is taken from the YFCC100M displays a higher degree of sentiment than MS-COCO captions. CAST captions have an even higher absolute sentiment value which is twice that of the training set.

captions, we used VADER sentiment analysis tools [7] to calculate the average absolute sentiment value of the captions generated by CAST, the Grand Challenge training data and the MS-COCO dataset. It can be seen in Table 1 that by the usage of ANPs together with CAST a significant amount of sentiment could be added to the captions.

5. CONCLUSIONS

We presented an approach of combining the top Adjective Noun Pairs detected in an image with a graphical model to form captions that are not only descriptive but also carry subjective meaning. We also pointed out limitations of evaluation metrics like BLEU for captions by showing how baseline methods like Nearest Neighbours with FC7 can yield higher BLEU score even without generating any novel sentences.

To improve the existing model further and to get the caption quality closer to human levels we are planning to extend our work by incorporating additional ranking mechanisms and concept detectors.

6. ACKNOWLEDGMENTS

This work was partially funded by the BMBF project Multimedia Opinion Mining (MOM: 01WI15002). The second author would like to thank the Center for Cognitive Science (Kaiserslautern) for financial support.

Figure 3: Example results of our approach for images of the test dataset. The captions from CAST network are marked with "C" and the captions retrieved by FC7 nearest neighbours are marked with "N".

7. REFERENCES

[1] P. Blandfort, T. Karayil, D. Borth, and A. Dengel. Introducing concept and syntax transition networks for image captioning. In *Proceedings of the 2016 ACM on International Conference on Multimedia Retrieval*, pages 385–388. ACM, 2016.

[2] D. Borth, R. Ji, T. Chen, T. Breuel, and S.-F. Chang. Large-scale Visual Sentiment Ontology and Detectors Using Adjective Noun Pairs. In *ACM Int. Conf. on Multimedia (ACM MM)*, 2013.

[3] T. Chen, D. Borth, T. Darrell, and S.-F. Chang. Deepsentibank: Visual sentiment concept classification with deep convolutional neural networks. *arXiv preprint arXiv:1410.8586*, 2014.

[4] X. Chen, H. Fang, T. Lin, R. Vedantam, S. Gupta, P. Dollár, and C. L. Zitnick. Microsoft COCO captions: Data collection and evaluation server. *arXiv:1504.00325*, 2015.

[5] A. Farhadi, M. Hejrati, M. A. Sadeghi, P. Young, C. Rashtchian, J. Hockenmaier, and D. Forsyth. Every picture tells a story: Generating sentences from images. In *Computer Vision–ECCV 2010*, pages 15–29. Springer, 2010.

[6] M. Hodosh, P. Young, and J. Hockenmaier. Framing image description as a ranking task: Data, models and evaluation metrics. *Journal of Artificial Intelligence Research*, pages 853–899, 2013.

[7] C. Hutto and E. Gilbert. Vader: A parsimonious rule-based model for sentiment analysis of social media text, 2014.

[8] J. Johnson, A. Karpathy, and L. Fei-Fei. Densecap: Fully convolutional localization networks for dense captioning. *arXiv preprint arXiv:1511.07571*, 2015.

[9] A. Karpathy and L. Fei-Fei. Deep visual-semantic alignments for generating image descriptions. In *Proceedings of the IEEE Conference on Computer Vision and Pattern Recognition*, pages 3128–3137, 2015.

[10] S. Li, G. Kulkarni, T. L. Berg, A. C. Berg, and Y. Choi. Composing simple image descriptions using web-scale n-grams. In *Proceedings of the Fifteenth Conference on Computational Natural Language Learning*, pages 220–228. Association for Computational Linguistics, 2011.

[11] J. Mao, W. Xu, Y. Yang, J. Wang, and A. L. Yuille. Explain images with multimodal recurrent neural networks. *arXiv preprint arXiv:1410.1090*, 2014.

[12] A. Mathews, L. Xie, and X. He. SentiCap: generating image descriptions with sentiments. In *The Thirtieth AAAI Conference on Artificial Intelligence (AAAI-16)*, Phoenix, USA, feb 2016.

[13] T. Mikolov, I. Sutskever, K. Chen, G. Corrado, and J. Dean. Distributed representations of words and phrases and their compositionality. *CoRR*, abs/1310.4546, 2013.

[14] R. Socher, A. Karpathy, Q. V. Le, C. D. Manning, and A. Y. Ng. Grounded compositional semantics for finding and describing images with sentences. *Transactions of the Association for Computational Linguistics*, 2:207–218, 2014.

[15] B. Thomee, B. Elizalde, D. A. Shamma, K. Ni, G. Friedland, D. Poland, D. Borth, and L.-J. Li. Yfcc100m: The new data in multimedia research. *Communications of the ACM*, 59(2):64–73, 2016.

[16] A. Ulges, D. Borth, and T. M. Breuel. Visual concept learning from weakly labeled web videos. In *Video Search and Mining*, pages 203–232. Springer, 2010.

[17] A. Ulges, C. Schulze, D. Borth, and A. Stahl. Pornography detection in video benefits (a lot) from a multi-modal approach. In *Proceedings of the 2012 ACM international workshop on Audio and multimedia methods for large-scale video analysis*, pages 21–26. ACM, 2012.

[18] O. Vinyals, A. Toshev, S. Bengio, and D. Erhan. Show and tell: A neural image caption generator. *arXiv preprint arXiv:1411.4555*, 2014.

[19] R. B. Zajonc. Feeling and thinking: Preferences need no inferences. *American psychologist*, 35(2):151, 1980.

Visual Analytics for Multimedia: Challenges and Opportunities

Jarke J. van Wijk
Eindhoven University of Technology
The Netherlands
j.j.v.wijk@tue.nl

Abstract

Understanding huge multimedia collections is a big challenge. Given a set of hundreds of thousands or millions of images, how to understand its contents and how to find images that are relevant for the task at hand? The use of a tight integration of automated methods, visualization and interaction, known as visual analytics, is probably the only way to go, combining the strengths of man and machine. An overview of trends in data visualization and visual analytics is given, and examples of recent work in multimedia analytics are presented. Exploiting meta-data, using interaction with relatively simple visual representations, and alignment with the work flow of users are promising routes, but scalability and evaluation are still challenging issues.

Author Keywords: Visual analytics; multimedia analytics; data visualization; interactive image classification

Short Bio

Jarke J. (Jack) van Wijk is full professor in visualization at the Department of Mathematics and Computer Science of Eindhoven University of Technology (TU/e). He received a MSc degree in industrial design engineering in 1982 and a PhD degree in computer science in 1986, both from Delft University of Technology. He has worked for ten years at the Netherlands Energy Research Foundation ECN. He joined Eindhoven University of Technology in 1998, where he became a full professor of visualization in 2001. His main research interests are information visualization and visual analytics, with a focus on the development of new methods for the interactive exploration of large data-sets. The work of his group has led to two start-up companies: MagnaView BV and SynerScope BV. He has (co-)authored more than 150 papers in visualization and computer graphics and received six best paper awards. He received the IEEE Visualization Technical Achievement Award in 2007 and the Eurographics 2013 Outstanding Technical Contributions Award.

MM'16, October 15–19, 2016, Amsterdam, The Netherlands.
ACM ISBN 978-1-4503-3603-1/16/10.
DOI: http://dx.doi.org/10.1145/2964284.2984750

V3I-STAL: Visual Vehicle-to-Vehicle Interaction via Simultaneous Tracking and Localization

Xiaobai Liu
Department of Computer Science
San Diego State University (SDSU), San Diego, CA
xiaobai.liu@mail.sdsu.edu

ABSTRACT

This paper investigates a visual interaction system for vehicle-to-vehicle (V2V) platform, called V3I. Our system employs common visual cameras that are mounted on connected vehicles to perceive the existence of isolated vehicles in the same roadway, and provides human drivers with imagery situational awareness. This allows effective interactions between vehicles even with a low permeation rate of V2V devices. The underlying research problem for V3I includes two aspects: i) tracking isolated vehicles of interest over time through local cameras; ii) at each time-step fusing the results of local visual perceptions to obtain a global location map that involves both isolated and connected vehicles. In this paper, we introduce a unified probabilistic approach to solve the above two problems, i.e., tracking and localization, in a joint fashion. Our approach will explore both the visual features of individual vehicles in images and the pair-wise spatial relationships between vehicles. We develop a fast Markov Chain Monte Carlo (MCMC) algorithm to search the joint solution space efficiently, which enables real-time application. To evaluate the performance of the proposed approach, we collect and annotate a set of video sequences captured with a group of vehicle-resident cameras. Extensive experiments with comparisons clearly demonstrate that the proposed V3I approach can precisely recover the dynamic location map of the surrounding and thus enable direct visual interactions between vehicles .

1. INTRODUCTION

Motivation Vehicle-to-vehicle (V2V) [53] communication platform can exchange GPS positions, speed, intents and other traffic data between nearby connected vehicles and has shown great promises in avoiding traffic crashes, preventing injuries, and reducing traffic congestions. In the last decade, V2V reached a level of maturity, insofar as vehicle-resident wireless hard-wares have undergone multiple generations to achieve their implementations [50]. However, it is still challenging to deploy V2V system in practice, because V2V-equipped vehicles need to share roads with isolated (non-connected) vehicles which will be dominant in amount for a long period.

MM '16, October 15-19, 2016, Amsterdam, Netherlands

 ISBN 978-1-4503-3603-1/16/10. . . $15.00

DOI: http://dx.doi.org/10.1145/2964284.2964285

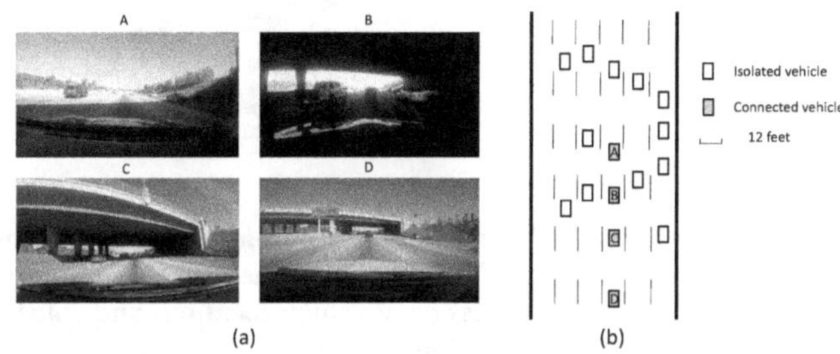

Figure 1: Visual Vehicle-to-Vehicle Interaction (V3I). (a) Inputs: four video frames captured by cameras on the connected vehicles; (b) the fused map of both isolated and connected vehicles. The relative positions of isolated vehicles are automatically estimated. (The road map is used for illustration purpose).

To obtain the traffic data of the isolated vehicles that share the same roadway, an effective and affordable method is to enhance connected vehicles with cameras. Then the isolated vehicles can be perceived and networked with the connected vehicles so as to form a dynamic vehicle network. The human drivers of connected vehicles, for example, are able to access extended range of traffic situations and are notified of potential traffic collisions. This visual system is called *Visual Vehicle-to-Vehicle Interaction* or *V3I*. Our system can work with low penetration rate of connected vehicles and thus allow the smooth transitioning to the next intelligent transportation system.

The key research question of V3I is how to detect, track and localize vehicles that appear in the field of views (FOVs) of the connected vehicles (through cameras). It involves both local visual perceptions and global visual data fusion across the networked cameras. Figure 1 illustrates four FOVs in (a) and the fused map in (b). The main technical difficulties are sourced from the fact that all cameras are moving at relatively high speeds (60-85 miles per hour). In particular, the following issues are ubiquitous in a V3I system.i) While the V3I involves a series of visual perceptions, e.g. detection, tracking, localization, it is crucial to to process all visual inputs with real-time efficiency to allow time-critical warnings or reactions; ii) The localization component is highly ambiguous since it is actually solving regression of high dimension data (video sequence); iii) Since the V2V network is dynamic, there are frequent changes over the spatial configurations of vehicles.

Objectives In this work, we are interested in developing an efficient and scalable V3I system that can extract time-critical, precise, and reliable traffic data with extended range from monocular video sequences. At each time-step, our goal is to construct a dynamic map that includes accurate 3D positions of the nearby vehicles that are either connected or isolated. We will update the map adaptively

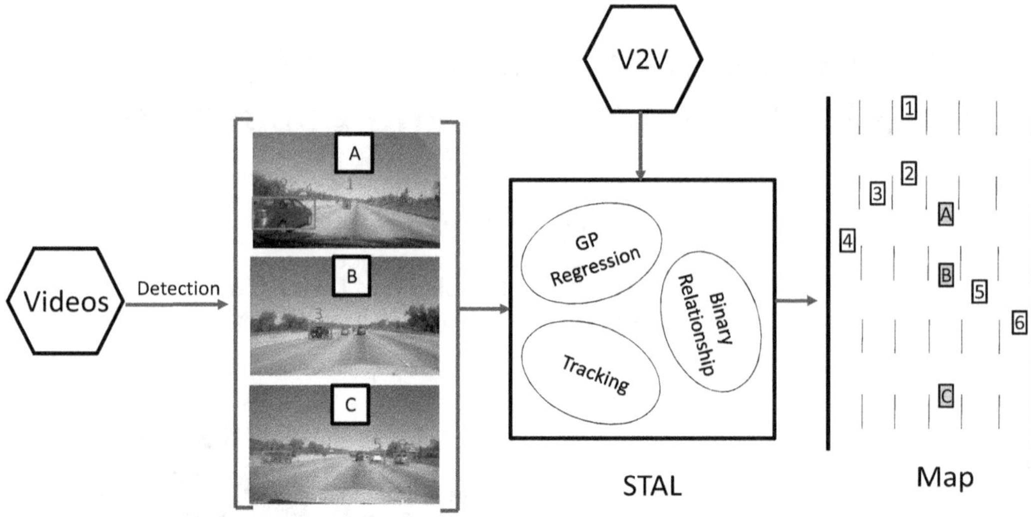

Figure 2: Flowchart of the proposed approach. *Videos*: monocular video sequences captured from multiple connected vehicles; *V2V*: vehicle to vehicle traffic data; *STAL*: the proposed simultaneous tracking and localization method that jointly formulates three components: tracking, regression of vehicle locations and consistencies of a set of between-vehicle spatial relationships; *Map*: location map that includes vehicle positions at every time-step.

over time and use it as an imagery digitalization of the surrounding traffic conditions. The map would be propagated to connected vehicles in the proximity and used as an interaction medium.

The V3I system involves two basic vision tasks: tracking vehicles over time in individual cameras and localizing them in a global 3D map. These two sub-tasks are coupled and mutually beneficial, and should be formulated and solved jointly.

Overview We introduce a unified probabilistic approach for simultaneous tracking and localization (STAL) of vehicles in V3I system. Our approach will exploit both visual information extracted in individual cameras, including lanes, vehicles, etc., and V2V traffic data, e.g. GPS positions. Since none of these observations are reliable nor accurate, it is crucial to perform reasoning while keeping uncertainties to avoid pre-mature decision making.

One of the major components of our approach is to predict the 3D relative locations of isolated vehicles detected in monocular videos. A traditional solution [49] [20] is to calibrate camera parameters and reconstruct 3d position of vehicles based on camera geometry. However, such analytic methods will not work well for V3I system where both cameras and vehicles of interests are moving at relatively high speeds. In this work, we study a calibration-free solution, motivated with the fact that an experienced human driver can roughly estimate the relative distance between a nearby vehicle and the host vehicle. We cast the localization task as a supervised regression problem, which aims to learn to map the visual features of the vehicle images to the 3D locations. In particular, we first collect a set of monocular video sequences and manually annotate the locations of individual isolated vehicles with an interactive annotation toolkit. The annotations are not given in absolute 3D coordinates but only reflect how close the isolated vehicles locates to the host vehicles. At each time-point, we collect the short sequence of video frames in prior as a training sample. Every sample is provided with a continuous label indicative of relative distance. With these training data, we develop a Gaussian Process model [26] [32] with a novel time-series kernel to solve the regression problem. In comparisons to the other discriminative methods, e.g., support vector regression [41], Gaussian Process (GP) models are probabilistic and enjoy the benefits common to all kernel-based models.

Another major component of our approach is a general Bayesian formulation of a set of pair-wise spatial relationships between vehicles. It includes, e.g., left-right (i.e., a vehicle locates on the left to the another one), front-back (i.e., a vehicle locates in front of the other one), or further-closer (depth to the cameras). These spatial relationships are used to test the current solution hypothesis: whether the relationships hold in the estimated location map. The proposed formula is characterized with two folds. First, expressing spatial relationships between vehicles in binary form, instead of in relative coordinates, enables robust measurement from noisy data. Second, although a single relationship carries weak information, there are multiple (hundreds of) relationships even for a short sequence of video frames.

The proposed probabilistic approach will optimize both **discrete variables**, e.g. trajectory identity (ID) of vehicle boxes, and **continuous variables**, e.g., 3D locations, and the optimal solution lies on a joint solution space. While it is in general intractable [46], Markov Chain Monte Carlo (MCMC) method can be used to search the solution space by simulating a Markov Chain walking toward the target distribution. It is a true approximation scheme for the optimal: when run with unlimited resources, it converges to the optimal solution eventually. However, the conventional MCMC algorithms are restricted to their slow mixing rate, which prevents their applications in real-time systems. In this work, we develop a fast MCMC algorithm that can efficiently sample the joint solution space with rapid mixing rate. The key technical contributions are two dynamics. i) Dynamic-I: in the continuous space, we utilize the gradient information of the proposal energy functions to make proposals that are distant from the current solution but are still accepted with high probabilities. ii) Dynamic-II: in the discrete space, we construct multiple adjacent graphs to represent the trajectory solutions and cast tracking as graph coloring problem. At each step we select a cluster of graph nodes, instead of a single node, and change its color to reconfigure the present solution. The two dynamics are alternatively performed following the Metropolis Hasting algorithm [46] to guarantee convergence.

Contributions The three contributions of this paper are (i) a novel V3I problem that have potentials in enhancing the next generation transportation system; (ii) a probabilistic formulation for V3I that integrates both the outputs of a supervised regression model and a large collection of pair-wise binary spatial relationships between vehicles, and (3) a hybrid MCMC optimization algorithm that makes distant proposals in the joint solution space. The proposed approach can generate accurate location maps for both isolated and connected vehicles through common visual sensors, and provide an affordable way for vehicle to vehicle interaction.

2. RELATIONSHIPS TO PREVIOUS WORKS

While V2V techniques have been studied extensively [53, 50], to our best knowledge, V3I is the first system that aims to provide human drivers with imagery situational awareness. The proposed approach is motivated with four research directions in multimedia understanding and computer vision.

Vehicle Detection in images has been extensively studied in the last decade [57]. These detectors can be roughly divided into two categories. The first category tries to combine hand-crafted features, e.g. SIFT [29], HOG [10] [5], and various machine learning algorithms, e.g., boosting [47], SVM [10], decision trees [8]. The other category [23] [18] aims to automatically learn features from images using deep neural network and achieves impressive results fueled by the availability of large-scale image datasets [9] [23]. A recent seminal work is the region-based Convolution Neural Network (R-CNN) [14]. A large variants of R-CNN are proposed to improve convergences [13] or enable end-to-end learning (i.e., getting rid of the post-progressing step) [35]. In this work, we will utilize the R-CNN technique to our real-time system for detecting vehicles of interest in video sequences.

Visual object tracking is a long-standing problem [40] in computer vision. Recently the tracking-by-detection framework [17] has achieved impressive results mostly due to the advances in object detections [11, 35], as aforementioned. Another major stream is to cast visual tracking as data association problem in the Bayesian framework [7]. In particular, Oh et al. proposed a Markov Chain Monte Carlo Data Association (MCMCDA) algorithm, and showed that it clearly outperforms the alternative Bayesian treatments, e.g., joint probabilistic data association (JPDA) [36, 37], multiple hypothesis tracking (MHT) [34], etc. Khan et al. [22] integrated the MCMC sampling within the particle filer tracking framework. Yu et al. [54] utilized the single site sampler for associating foreground blobs to trajectories. Liu et al. [30] introduced a spatial-temporal graph to cast tracking as a graph coloring problem and solve it using MCMC algorithm. These algorithms enjoy the advantages of the Monte Carlo search, e.g., avoiding pre-mature decisions while solving the optimal solution. However, they are restricted to the high computational complexity and can not be applied over real-time systems. In this work, we introduce a few improvements over the MCMC algorithm, including making distant proposals in both continuous and discrete spaces, exploiting the deepest gradient directions and moment information, and casting tracking in the cluster sampling framework. We will demonstrate that, with these modifications, it is feasible for MCMC algorithm to achieve real-time performance.

Joint Recognition and Reconstruction has been investigated for various computer vision problems, including simultaneous localization and mapping (SLAM) [49, 20], image labeling and scene reconstruction [25] [31], object recognition and reconstruction [15], room layout partition and object modeling [16, 39], tracking and camera calibration [24] [55], video reconstruction [45]. In this work, we follow the same methodology but focus on simultaneous tracking and mapping of vehicles of interest, which has not been studied. Fusing visual data on the V2V platform is a new research direction that enables interactions between connected vehicles.

Gaussian Process or GP provides a non-parametric framework for deriving regression or classification with explicit uncertainty models. As a probabilistic generative method, GP requires much less training samples to achieve the same level of performance as the other discriminative models [47, 56]. Although the standard GP suffers from high computational complexity $O(N^3)$ where N is the number of training samples, it is possible to largely reduce the computational cost by imposing sparsity over the training samples [42, 32], e.g., learning a small number of pseudo-input samples [43] [44], or using a sparse subset of the training samples [26, 42]. In computer vision, Kapoor et al. [19] applied GP method for image categorization with human-in-the-loop and achieved impressive results. For all these GP algorithms, the central modeling choice is the specification of a kernel. In this work, we use GP to predict the 3D locations of vehicles and integrate the probabilistic outputs of GP with a unified probabilistic formula. As a technical contribution, we introduce a time-series kernel to explore both appearance and temporal cues in the GP formula, which is a novel concept in this direction.

3. OUR APPROACH

In this section, we introduce our V3I-STAL approach, starting with an introduction of the whole pipeline. Then, we will specify a probabilistic formula.

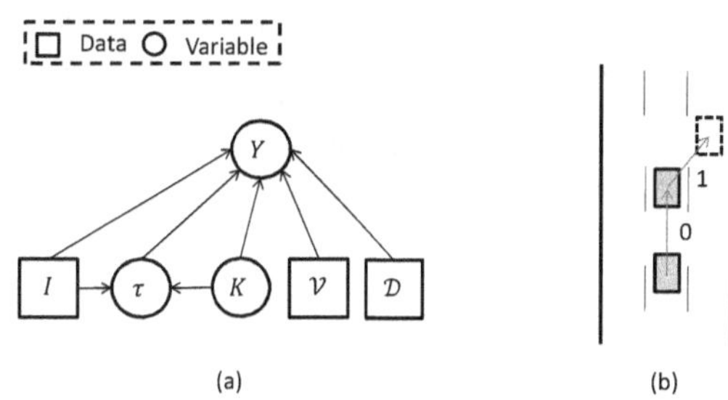

Figure 3: (a) Graphical model of the proposed probabilistic method. (b) state change of a vehicle: staying on the same lane, 0, or changing lane, 1.

3.1 Overview of Our Approach

We consider a set of time-synchronized video sequences that are captured by multiple cameras on a group of connected vehicles in the proximity. Our goal is to track and localize isolated vehicles in videos and generate a global location map at each time-step. We refer this task to *simultaneous tracking and localization* or *STAL*. The cameras on connected vehicles are dynamically networked through V2V protocols and thus form a dynamic ad-hoc camera network. The field of views (FOVs) of cameras might overlap with each other at a certain time and might become disjoint over time.

Figure 2 illustrates the flowchart of the proposed V3I-STAL approach. We utilize the sliding window strategy [30] to deal with streaming video sequences. For the present time window, we start with detecting vehicles and lanes for every monocular video. The detection results along with the status of connected vehicles (e.g., speed, locations) are used as inputs for a probabilistic approach, which aims to solve tracking and localization jointly. The outcome of our STAL approach is a scene map that includes the relative coordinates of both isolated and connected vehicles.

Relative World Coordinate We define a relative coordinate system to facilitate the derivation of our approach. We take one of the connected vehicles as reference and consider its location as the origin, i.e., (0, 0). For any other vehicle in the proximity, its coordinate (y_1, y_2) is defined as: i) $y_1 \in [..., -2, -1, 0, 1, 2, ...]$ indicates the relative lane to the origin where 0 means the same lane with the reference vehicle, -1 means the left lane, and +1 the right lane); ii) $y_2\ in[1, 2, 3, 4, ...]$ which indicates the relative distance projected on the lane direction (larger number indicates being further). In the rest of this paper, 3D vehicle locations are defined in this relative coordinate system unless otherwise specified.

3.2 Probabilistic Formula

We first introduce the notations used in this paper. Let T denote the size of the time-window, or the number of video frames. Let M denote the number of cameras, I^m the m-th video sequence. Let $I = [I^{[1..M]}]$. Let $\mathcal{C}$ denote the pair-wise relationships between vehicles (introduced later), let $\mathcal{D}$ denote the extra training data, $\mathcal{V}$ denote the traffic status of connected vehicles. Let $\mathcal{O} = [\mathcal{I}, \mathcal{C}, \mathcal{D}, \mathcal{V}]$ pool over all the inputs of our approach.

For each camera m, let x^m_{kt} denote the 2D bounding box of the k-th isolated vehicle at the time t. The corresponding 2D trajectory is denoted as $\tau^m_k = [x^m_{kt}]$.Let $\tau = [\tau^m_k]$ pool all the 2D trajectories, $k \in [0..K^m], m \in [1..M]$, where K^m indicates the total number of trajectories to solve in the mth video. τ^m_0 denotes the collection of bounding boxes not assigned to any trajectory. We denote the 3D location of the k-th isolated vehicle at time t by Q^m_{kt}. Let $Q^m_k = [Q^m_{kt}]$ denote the k-th trajectory, $Q = [Q^m_k]$ pool all the 3D trajectories of isolated vehicles. Let R^m_t denote the 3D location of the m-th connected vehicle and $R = [R^m_t]$. Let $Y = \{Q, R\}$. Note that the 2D locations of connected vehicles are fixed (the bottom-central point) throughout the video sequences. Thus, we can describe the solution of STAL as the following representation,

$$W = (K^m, \tau, Y) \tag{1}$$

where

$$\tau = [\tau^m_0, \tau^m_k], \tau^m_k = [x^m_{kt}], \tag{2}$$
$$Y = \{Q, R\}, Q = [Q^m_k], Q^m_k = [Q^m_{kt}] \tag{3}$$
$$R = [R^m], R^m = [R^m_t] \tag{4}$$
$$m \in [1..M], k \in [0..K^m] \tag{5}$$

According to Bayes' rule, we can solve the optimal representation as maximizing a posterior, that is,

$$W^* = \arg\max_W p(W|\mathcal{O}) \tag{6}$$

where the posterior model $p(W|\mathcal{O})$ can be factorized as the product of three probability distributions

$$p(W|\mathcal{O}) \propto \prod_m \Big[p(K^m) \prod_k p(\tau^m_k|K^m, \mathcal{O})\Big] p(Y|\tau, K, \mathcal{O}) \tag{7}$$

The first term $p(K^m) \propto \exp(-K^m)$ is used to encourage the number of trajectories to be small, resulting in a compact representation. The second probability $p(\tau^m_k|K^m, \mathcal{O})$ defines the distribution over 2D trajectories conditioning on the inputs. The third term $p(Y|\tau, K, \mathcal{O})$ defines the distribution over 3D trajectories, which can be further factorized to be the product of three probabilistic models,

$$p(Y|\tau, K, \mathcal{O}) \propto p(Q|\mathcal{D}, \tau, K, \mathcal{I}) p(R|\mathcal{V}, \tau, K, \mathcal{I}) p(Y|\mathcal{C}, \tau, K, \mathcal{I}) \tag{8}$$

The first two terms are distributions over 3D locations of isolated and connected vehicles, respectively. The third term is defined over the pair-wise spatial relationships between vehicles.

Figure 3 (a) illustrates the graphical dependences of the above variables. In the rest of this section, we will elaborate the above probabilistic models .

3.2.1 Probabilistic Model for 2D trajectories

The distribution $p(\tau^m_k|K^m, \mathcal{O})$ is defined over the 2D trajectories, which can be further factorized as

$$p(\tau^m_k|K^m, \mathcal{O}) \propto p(\tau^m_k|K^m) p(I^m|\tau^m_k) \tag{9}$$

where $p(\tau^m_k|K^m)$ is the prior term and $p(I|\tau^m_k)$ is the likelihood term.

Prior In this work, we identify two states of a moving vehicle at each time-step: staying on the same lane as the previous time or not. We will introduce a simple method in Section 4 to detect the state of changing lane. Let $\omega(\tau^m_k, t)$ returns 0 if the vehicle stays on the same lane at time t; otherwise 1. Fig. 3 (b) illustrates the state change. Then, we employ a simple Ising/Potts model [6] to penalize discontinuity of states, i.e.,

$$p(\tau^m_k) \propto \exp\left[-\beta \sum_t \mathbf{1}\Big(\omega(\tau^m_k, t) \neq \omega(\tau^m_k, t-1)\Big)\right] \tag{10}$$

where β is a constant and $\mathbf{1}(\cdot)$ is an indicator function. Eq. (10) is used to constraint the number of times a vehicle change its lane during driving.

Likelihood The likelihood term $p(I|\tau^m_k)$ defines the probability of the observations given the 2D trajectories, which can be factorized as

$$p(I^m|\tau^m_k) = \prod_{x^m_{kt} \in \tau^m_k} \frac{p^f(x^m_{kt})}{p^b(x^m_{kt})} \cdot p^a(x^m_{kt}, x^m_{k,t-1}) \tag{11}$$

where $p^f(\cdot)$ and $p^b(\cdot)$ are foreground and background probabilities, respectively. The first term measures the ratio of the foreground distribution over the background distribution, which can be analogous to a probabilistic foreground/background classifier. We use the detection scores to approximate this ratio, as introduced in Section 4. The second term is defined over the appearance divergence between bounding boxes of the same trajectory. We have, $p^a(x^m_{kt}, x^m_{k,t-1}) \propto \exp\big(-\mathcal{L}(f^m_{kt}, f^m_{k,t-1})\big)$ where f are the visual features extracted from the vehicle boxes, and $\mathcal{L}(\cdot)$ returns the Euclidean distance of two feature vectors. We will introduce the visual features to use in Section 4.

The probability for 2D trajectories are separately defined for individual cameras. While our models follow the previous stochastic data association framework, e.g. [33] [30], we specify a new type of prior model and will solve the discrete variables τ^m_k by maximizing a unified posterior $p(W|I)$, instead of $p(\tau^m_k|K^m, \mathcal{O})$.

3.2.2 Probabilistic Model for Localizing Isolated Vehicles

The probabilistic model $p(Y|\mathcal{D}, \tau, K, \mathcal{I})$ is used to specify the mappings between visual features and 3D locations of vehicles. In other words, given visual features of a vehicle, we aim to predict its relative distance from the camera. This is feasible since the visual features of a vehicle vary while locating at different distances and angles w.r.t. the camera. Such coherences have been modeled by Wu et al. [51] with an image scaling theory, e.g., a distant vehicle will appear with less sketch/boundary features in comparisons to a nearby vehicle.

We formalize the localization problem in the Gaussian process framework. We collect a training dataset where every sample consists of a short sequence of vehicle boxes, e.g. 30-50 frames. For every vehicle in videos, we annotate its location in the relative world coordinate (as aforementioned) considering the camera position as the origin. We use multiple vehicle boxes, instead of a single box, to construct one training sample for two reasons. First, it is technically critical to obtain motion features to estimate depth from a single camera [38]. Second, extracting multiple observations enables robust regression against noises and other variances (lighting changes etc.).

In the following we first introduce our Gaussian Process model and then define a time-series kernel.

Gaussian Regression Process Suppose we have a training dataset $\mathcal{D} = \{(x_i, y_i), i = 1, ..., n\}$, where x denotes a training sample, i.e., a sequence of detected boxes, and y denotes 3D locations of vehicles, with slightly notation abused. The column vectors for all n samples are aggregated in the design matrix X, and the outputs are collected in the output matrix Y, so we can write $\mathcal{D} = (X, Y)$.

GP model is to learn a latent function $h(x_i)$ that maps the input x_i to the output value. The observed value y_i is different from the function value $h(x_i)$ by additive noises, which is assumed to follows an I.I.D. Gaussian distribution with zero mean and variance σ^2, $\epsilon \sim \mathcal{N}(0, \sigma^2)$. GP model will put a zero mean Gaussian process prior on the latent function $h(\cdot)$:

$$h|X \sim \mathcal{N}(0, K_N) \tag{12}$$

where the covariance matrix K_N is constructed from a kernel function, i.e., $K_N(i, j) = K(x_i, x_j)$. The kernel function $K()$ depends on a small number of parameters θ, e.g., kernel width, to control the smoothness properties. In GP, we also assume a Gaussian likelihood model:

$$Y|h \sim \mathcal{N}(f, \sigma^2 \mathbf{I}) \tag{13}$$

where **I** is an integer matrix. Integrating out h in Eq. (13), we can obtain the marginal likelihood,

$$Y|X, \theta \sim \mathcal{N}(0, K_N + \sigma^2 \mathbf{I}) \tag{14}$$

which is used to train the GP model by finding a maximum w.r.t. the kernel parameters θ, e.g.,σ^2.

With a new input point x_*, prediction is made by conditioning on the observed data y_* and the learned hyper-parameter θ. The distribution of the output value y_* at the new point is then:

$$y_*|x_*, \mathcal{D}, \theta \sim \mathcal{N}(\mu, \Sigma) \tag{15}$$

with,

$$\mu = K_*^T (K_N + \sigma^2 \mathbf{I})^{-1} y^*; \tag{16}$$

$$\Sigma = K_{**} - K_*^T (K_N + \sigma^2 \mathbf{I})^{-1} K_* + \sigma^2; \tag{17}$$

where $K_*(i) = K(x_*, x_i)$ is a column vector and $K_{**} = K(x_*, x_*)$.

To define $p(Q|\mathcal{D}, \tau, K, I)$, for every time t of a trajectory, we extract the trajectory segment from the time $t - \delta t$ to $t + \delta t$ as a testing sample, where δt is a small number. Then, we can apply the Eq. (15) to define the probabilistic model for 3D localization,

$$p(Q|\mathcal{D}, \tau, K, \mathcal{I}) \propto \prod_m \left[\frac{1}{|\tau_k^m|} \prod_{x_* \in \tau_k^m} p(Q_{kt}^m | x_*, \mathcal{D}, \theta) \right] \tag{18}$$

where $|\tau_k^m|$ denote the length of the trajectory τ_k^m.

As is clear from the definition in Eq (15), the standard GP is a non-parametric model and all the training samples are explicitly required at test time in order to construct the predictive distribution. It is infeasible to apply GP while the number of training samples is large. In this work, we use the method by Snelson et al. [43] [44], which tried to learn a small number (10-20) of pseudo training samples by minimizing the likelihood function Eq. (14).

Time-series Kernel The key problem left so far is how to define the kernel function $K(x_i, x_j)$ where x_i and x_j are two sequences of vehicle boxes in images.

We define the kernel function $K(x_i, x_j)$ as the product of two kernel distances in terms of both appearance and time. For a training sample x_i, let t_i denote a time-stamp , and f_{it} denote the corresponding visual feature of the vehicle box at time t_i. The time-series kernel is defined as,

$$K(x_i, x_j) = \frac{1}{|x_i| \cdot |x_j|} \sum_{(f_{it}, t_i) \in x_i} \sum_{(f_{jt}, t_j) \in x_j} \phi(f_{it}, f_{jt}) \varphi(t_i, t_j) \tag{19}$$

where $\phi()$ and $\varphi()$ are two squared exponential kernels

$$\varphi(t_i, t_j) = \kappa \exp(-\frac{(t_i - t_j)^2}{2\sigma_t^2}) \tag{20}$$

κ and σ_t are two kernel parameters in θ which can be learned by maximizing the marginal likelihood (14). The above time series kernel acts like a sequential convolution filter and takes both appearance and time proximities into consideration. We will specify the visual features in Section 4.

3.2.3 *Probabilistic Model For Localizing Connected Vehicles*

With V2V traffic data, we can obtain the absolute position of every connected vehicle. However, V2V locations are noisy and only sparsely available (per a few seconds). Therefore, instead of using the raw V2V positions, we aim to solve the location of connected vehicles in the relative world coordinate. In particular, we use the V2V data to measure the spatial displacement between two connected vehicles and enforce the same displacements between the relative locations to solve. We define the probabilistic model over V2V data as ,

$$p(R|\mathcal{V}, \tau, K, \mathcal{I}) \propto \exp\{-\frac{2}{M(M-1)} \sum_{m \neq n} \mathcal{L}(R_t^m - R_t^n, V_{mnt})\} \tag{21}$$

where V_{mnt} is the displacement between the vehicles m and n at time t, $\mathcal{L}(\cdot, \cdot)$returns the Euclidean distance between two vectors. It is worthy noting that, although the relative world coordinates can be scaled up to the world coordinate after calibrating cameras, in V3I, we only care about the relative 3D positions between vehicles.

3.2.4 *Probabilistic Model For Spatial Relationships*

We use a set of spatial relationships to describe the relative locations of vehicles at the time t:

- Left-right, denoted as $(m, i, j, t) \in \mathcal{L}$ where the vehicle i locates on the left of the vehicle j, both of which appear in the camera m;
- front-back, denoted as $(m, i, j, t) \in \mathcal{F}$ where the vehicle i locates in front of the vehicle j ;
- further-closer, denoted as $(m, i, j, t) \in \mathcal{A}$ where the isolated vehicle i is closer to the camera than the vehicle j, and
- equal position, denoted as $(m, n, i, j, t) \in \mathcal{E}$ where the vehicle i in camera m appear in the camera n with index j, and the two vehicles should have the same 3D locations.

Among these relationships, the former three are extracted from a single camera while the last one is from across cameras. These binary information, although not accurate, can provide discriminative constraints over the desired 3D vehicle locations.

We collect these pair-wise relationships from the results of vehicle detection and cross-view matching. Taking further-closer for instance, we can simply compare the size of two detected boxes to determine which one is further to the camera. Expressing the relationships in binary form enable the feasibility of a simple threshold based method. We denote all the relationships by $\mathcal{C} = \mathcal{L} \cup \mathcal{F} \cup \mathcal{A} \cup \mathcal{E}$. For each relationship $C_k \in \mathcal{C}$, we check if it still holds by the current estimation of 3D trajectories Y, which is straightforward since the moving direction is available as well. We denote the validity by $\mathcal{H}(Y, C_k)$ which returns 0 if the relationship holds; 1 otherwise. Thus, the likelihood model conditioning on C is defined as,

$$p(Y|\mathcal{C}, \tau, K, \mathcal{I}) \propto \exp\{-\gamma \sum_{C_k \in C} \mathcal{H}(Y, C_k)\} \tag{22}$$

where γ is a constant parameter. This model $p(Y|C, \tau, K, I)$ is maximized while all the relationships in C hold in Y.

4. INFERENCE

In this section, we first introduce the proposed inference algorithm and then elaborate the implementations of our V3I system.

4.1 Hybrid Monte Carlo for V3I-STAL

Given multiple monocular video sequences and V2V traffic data, our inference algorithm aims to find the optimal solution W by maximizing a posterior $p(W|I)$. This is an intractable problem [46]. As an approximate optimization technique, Markov Chain Monte Carlo (MCMC) algorithm [46, 33, 30] can search the solution space by simulating a Marko Chain. However, existing MCMC methods are restricted to two aspects: i) the mixing rate is slow particularly for the joint solution space which is the case in this work; and ii) the search usually got stuck in local minimal without proper parameter setting in practice.

To address the above issues, we develop a hybrid Monte Carlo algorithm that can search over the joint solution space efficiently. Our algorithm starts with an initial solution of W that could be greedily or randomly obtained. Then, we design a set of dynamics to reconfigure the current solution which simulates a Markov Chain walking toward the target posterior distribution $p(W|\mathcal{O})$. The dynamics are either jump moves, e.g. creating a new trajectory, or diffusion moves, e.g. adding a bounding box into an existing trajectory. These stochastic dynamics are paired with each other to make the solution changes reversible to guarantee convergence to $p(W|I)$. Formally, a dynamic is proposed to drive the solution state from W to W', which is accepted with the probability in the Metropolis-hasting form [46]: $\min(1, \frac{p(W'|\mathcal{O})q(W \to W')}{p(W|\mathcal{O})q(W' \to W)})$, where $q(W \to W')$ is the proposal probability.

Algorithm 1 summarizes the proposed inference algorithm. In this work, we use two dynamics, including a dynamic in the discrete space and a dynamic in the continuous space.

Dynamic-I: Cluster Sampling for 2D tracking This dynamic is used to add, remove or change existing 2D trajectories observed by individual cameras, i.e., τ. We unify all these operations through a cluster sampling procedure with a adjacent graph. Figure 4 illustrates four such graphs where the y-direction indicates the time-step. We detect a set of vehicle boxes, illustrated as blobs, in every frame and use these boxes as graph nodes to construct the adjacent graph. A graph node is only linked to the spatially coherent nodes in the consecutive frames. With these adjacent graphs, the goal of this dynamic is to color these graph nodes such that nodes belonging to the same trajectory have the same color.

We develop a cluster sampling method following the previous Sweden-Wang Cut algorithm [46, 6], including three major steps. First, for every edge $e =< i, j >$, we compute a local probability, denoted as q_e, to indicate how likely the two linked nodes belong to the same trajectory and thus should be assigned with the same color. We set the edge probability using the feature similarity,

$$q_e = \exp\{-\mathcal{L}(f_i, f_j)\} \tag{23}$$

where f_i and f_j are feature vectors of the two bounding boxes. We normalize q_e so that $\sum_{e=<i,\cdot>} q_e = 1$ where $< i, \cdot >$ represents all edges that links the node i to the next frame. Second, we turn off edges at random according to q_e which leads to a set of connected components (CCPs) of graph nodes. Last, we choose one of the CCPs and assign its nodes to a new color, which results in three atomic changes, as Fig. 4 illustrates, i) birth of a new trajectory: $A \to C$; ii) Merge, $C \to A$; iii) Switch: $A \to B$ or $B \to D$.

The proposal probability for the Dynamic I is calculated as $q(W \to W') = \prod_{e \in Cut} q_e$ where Cut denotes the edges that are turned off around the selected CCP.

At each iteration step, the Dynamic I will flip the colors of a cluster of nodes, instead of a single node, like the traditional single-site sampler, e.g. Gibbs [46]. Similar idea has been used for image segmentation [46] and 3D scene reconstruction [30].

Dynamic-II: Hamiltonian dynamics For 3D localization We develop a proposal-making scheme for the continuous parts of W, i.e., the 3D trajectories Y, with the Hamiltonian Dynamics [4] [1].

Hamiltonian Dynamics can be used to draw random samples from a probability distribution with continuous variables for which direct sampling is difficult. The key is to define a Hamiltonian function in terms of the target distribution from and a kinetic energy term parameterized with auxiliary Momentum variables. Then, we can alternate simple updates for those momentum variables with Metropolis updates. A state proposed in this way can be distant from the current state but have a high probability of acceptance. In comparisons to the random-walk proposal schemes [46] that explore the state space slowly, Hamiltonian Dynamics can converge a lot faster to the target distribution.

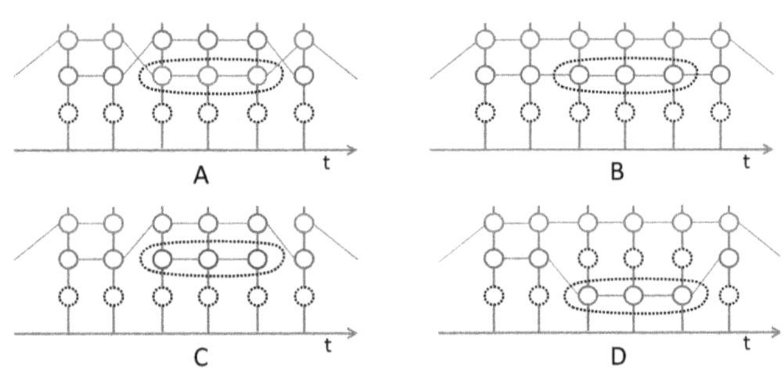

Figure 4: Four atomic states of the discrete tracking solution. There are three atomic changes, i) birth of a new trajectory: $A \to C$; ii) Merge, $C \to A$; iii) Switch: $A \to B$ or $B \to D$. Dotted circles indicate the selected CCPs.

In this work, we aim to sample a joint distribution and use the Hamiltonian dynamics to make proposals in the continuous space. Formally, let $E(Y) = -\log P(W|\mathcal{O})$ denote the target energy function, i.e., the negative log-probability. Consider Y as a position at the energy landscape, g as the momentum at a time t. Sampling Y is equal to moving Y through the energy landscape with a varying moment g. The energy $H(Y, g)$ at a time-step is a combination of the energy $E(Y)$ and the kinetic energy $K(g)$, i.e. $H(Y, g) = E(Y) + K(g)$. We set $K(g) = g^T g/2$ as conventional.

Algorithm 1 Inference .

Input: M monocular video sequences; V2V data
Output: 2D and 3D trajectories of vehicles;
Initialize the solution representation W;
Iterate until convergence,

- Randomly select one of the two dynamics;
- Make proposals accordingly to reconfigure the current solution;
- Accept the change with a probability

The partial derivatives of $H(Y, g)$ determine how Y and g change over time, according to the Hamilton's equations [1]:

$$\frac{\partial Y}{\partial t} = \frac{\partial K(g)}{\partial g} = g, \tag{24}$$

$$\frac{\partial g}{\partial t} = -\frac{\partial E(Y)}{\partial Y} \tag{25}$$

Starting with initial state at time t=0, we can iteratively compute the states of Y and the moment g at each time t, following the Euler's method:

$$Y^{t+1} = Y^t + \alpha g^t \tag{26}$$

$$g^{t+1} = g^t - \alpha \frac{\partial E(Y)}{\partial Y} \tag{27}$$

where α is a constant.

The proposal probability for the Hamiltonian Dynamic is defined over the energy changes after L times updates. Let (Y, g) denote the initial state, (Y^*, g^*) the updated states after L times, we have

$$q(W \to W') = \frac{1}{\mathcal{Z}} \exp\left[H(Y, g) - H(Y^*, g^*)\right] \tag{28}$$

where $\mathcal{Z}$ is a normalization constant . It is worthy noting that we set the evolution times L to be a small number, which allows the other dynamics in our inference algorithm to be done more often to help preserve the detail-balance of the sampling process.

Figure 5: Exemplar results of lane detections. We detected both straight lanes (red) and curved lanes (blue).

4.2 Implementation

Visual Features Instead of using traditional descriptors (e.g. SIFT, HOG) to represent the visual appearances of vehicle images, we employ the powerful Deep Convolution Neural Network (CNN) [23]. With a set of training images of vehicles, we fine tune the CaffeNet [18], which consists of 5 convolutional layers, 2 max-pooling layers, 3 fully-connected layers and a final 1000-dimensional output. The negative training samples are randomly cropped from the video frames in our dataset .

Given an image of vehicle as input, we forward-pass it through the learned DCNN and take the 1000-dimensional output as our appearance descriptor, i.e. f, which is used to define the kernel function $\phi()$ and the edge probability q_e. These descriptors have been proved to function like the Texton filter responses [18] yet with more capabilities of dealing with variances.

Detection of Vehicles and Lanes To detect vehicles in video sequences, we utilize the Region-based Convolutional Neural Network (R-CNN) [14], which includes two steps: making vehicle proposals and classifying proposals. In implementation, we use the Fast R-CNN framework by Girshick [13] that jointly performs proposal classification and bounding box regression by optimizing a multi-task loss function. We use the soft-max functions in the last layer. We use mini-batches of sample size 128. We follow the sampling strategy in the original article. To deal with scale issues, we compute image pyramids which basically augment the training data. This is feasible since our training dataset is relatively small (about 2000 vehicle images). We use the network parameters pre-trained on the VOC 2012 dataset [18] and fine tune it on our training dataset with the same multi-task loss function. The fine-tuning step is very important because that, in V3I system, the camera setting (viewpoints, heights) are completely different from that in the VOC 2012 dataset. Among all the steps of RCNN detector, the bottleneck is the number of region proposals generated for every video frame, which is 64 by default. To accelerate the process, for each vehicle tracked, we predict its position in the new video frames according to its current position and moving speed (in images). We sample a few proposal around the predicted position only. We found that this simple trick can largely reduce the number of proposals while keeping the same detection performance.

In addition, we develop a lane detection algorithm that can process video frames at real-time speed. It includes three major steps: filtering image with Derivative of Gaussian (DOG), Line/Spline Fitting with RANSAC method and Post-processing for lane linking. These algorithms are quite standard and have been discussed in previous efforts, e.g. [2]. We didn't use the top-view of the road [2] because it involves additional computations yet bring minimal gains in our case. Figure. 5 illustrates the two results of lane detection. We will use the estimated lane information to determine if a vehicle stays on the same way over time, as is used in Eq. (10).

Constructing Pair-wise Constraints Given two bounding boxes of vehicles detected in the same video frame, we construct the three pair-wise relationship sets $\mathcal{L}, \mathcal{F}, \mathcal{A}$ as follows. First, we simple compare their horizontal image coordinates to determine which one is on the left hand side. Second, the front-back relationships are derived from the comparisons of their vertical image coordinates. This is feasible because of the cameras are facing forward and moving in parallel directions. Third, we assume the vehicle with larger size box is closer to the camera. Since the above three relationships are all expressed in binary form, instead of relative values (like [10]), they can be robustly extracted even with a simple threshold method.

To obtain the relationships set $\mathcal{E}$, we need to identify the vehicles across cameras. This correspondence problem is traditionally solved with the standard stereo algorithms, e.g. extracting interest points first and applying RANSAC to estimate transform parameters [29]. These algorithms, however, do not work well in V3I, because the viewpoint changes are too big due to the wide baselines between cameras, as is illustrated in Fig. 1. Instead, we utilize a two-step cascade method for detecting such relationships across two cameras. In the first step, given the position of the two connected vehicles, we match the detected lanes across cameras and consider vehicles in different views sharing the same lane as a candidate match. In the second step, we extract the CNN features of each box, calculate their Euclidean distance and prune the candidate matches if their visual distance is beyond than a threshold. We compute pyramid representations for each vehicle image to deal with the viewpoint variances. This simple threshold-based method works well in practice because: i) the lane information from both V2V data and lane detectors can largely narrow the search space; ii) the relationships are used as a soft constraints which means that error predictions will not dominate the final results.

The above relationships, once detected, are used to define the posterior distribution $p(W|I)$. In particular, given 3D trajectories W in the present iteration, we need to verify if every single relationship in C holds or not, i.e. the value of $\mathcal{H}(Y, C_k)$ in Eq. (22). For the relationships $\mathcal{L}, \mathcal{F}, \mathcal{A}$, we can obtain the moving directions of the involved vehicles from the 3D trajectories which make the testing straightforward. For the relationships $\mathcal{L}$, we simply check if the two vehicles have the same 3D locations in Y. Note that a short period of video frames will have hundreds of such relationships which makes this term fairly robust against errors and noises.

Stream Video Parsing The proposed STAL algorithm works on a batch of video sequences and we extend it to deal with streaming videos with the sliding window strategy [30]. At each time t, we take as inputs the video frames during $t - \delta w$ to $t + \delta w$ where $2\delta w$ is the window size, and slide the window with a step (e.g. 25 frames) to get the another window. For each window, we run the Algorithm 1 and initialize the solution using the results over the previous window. In particular, we assume the number of trajectories K^m remains the same, and match every existing trajectory to the frames of the new window with the aforementioned cascade matching algorithm. The matched boxes are added into the existing trajectories. In this way, we obtain a good initialization that is close to the optimal solution. Afterwards, we refine the current solution with the two dynamics. This sliding window method can largely reduce the computational cost while achieving the same level of performance.

5. EXPERIMENTS

Dataset To evaluate the proposed V3I approach, we collect a video dataset that includes four groups of video sequences. Each group consists of 4 time-synchronized video sequences captured by 4 cameras on connected vehicles. Figure 6 illustrates the driving route while shooting the group-1, where the star indicates the starting point. Figures 1 and 2 show video frames from the group-1 and group-2, respectively. These vehicles were running on a freeway at about 60 miles per hour. Each video lasts 10-20 minutes. Since the videos are captured during the peak traffic hours in the morning, there are continuous stream of isolated vehicles appearing in the videos. These video sequences are with many challenges, e.g., lighting changes, motion blur, and work as a challenging benchmark for evaluating V3I algorithms.

We develop an interactive toolkit to manually annotate the 2D and 3D vehicle trajectories for all the 4 groups of video sequences. We use the relative world coordinates. A major feature of the toolkit is that it can interpolate trajectories between the annotated frames in both 2D images and 3D map so that the user does not need to annotate every single frame. A similar system was developed by Vondrick et al. [48], which focused on obtaining 2D trajectories. We also annotate the locations of connected vehicles in videos and use the annotations as V2V data, i.e., $\mathcal{V}$. It takes about 3 hours for a user to annotate a video sequence of 20 minutes that includes hundreds of vehicles.

We divide each video sequence into two even parts and use them for training and testing purposes, respectively.

Learning and Parameters To obtain the hyper-parameters of the time-series kernel $K(\cdot)$, we optimize the marginal likelihood function (14) using the alternate gradient descent algorithm. Following [44], we revise Eq. (14) to learn a few pseudo-inputs to reduce complexity. We set the number of pseudo-inputs to be 20.

The implementation of Algorithm 1 can be found in Section. 4. We use the maximal likelihood method (MLE) [46] to estimate the model parameters in $p(W|I)$, including λ, β, and $\mathcal{Z}$, and fix them throughout the experiments. We set the size of the sliding window to be 60 frames, and sliding step to be 10 frames. The parameters for the vehicle detectors and lane detectors remains the same as in their respective articles.

Figure 6: Driving routine of the video sequences in group-1. Blue star indicates the starting point.

Variants of Our Approach and Baselines We implement three variants of the proposed approach to analyze the benefits of individual components. i) STAL-1, that optimizes the probability models for 2D trajectories and uses Dynamic-I for inference. This is an advanced version of the MCMCDA [33] algorithm. ii) STAL-2: that implements Algorithm 1 without the pair-wise spatial relationship $\mathcal{C}$. We simply set the the probability $p(Y|\mathcal{C}, \tau, K, I)$ to be a constant. iii) STAL-3, that is a full implementation of Algorithm 1.

We compare the proposed approach with 4 recent state-of-the-art trackers: 1) Geiger et al. [12], that follows the track-by-detection pipeline and uses the Kalman Filtering algorithm; 2) Lenz et al. [27], a min-cost flow tracking algorithm; 3) Xiang et al. [52] that tracks objects with multiple Gaussian Decision Processes. 4) Andriyenko et al. [3] that proposed a discrete-continuous optimization for 2D tracking. We use the source codes provided by the authors and properly train their models on our dataset according to their descriptions.

We implement baseline methods for localization as follows. First, we apply each of the above baseline trackers and STAL-1 on the input videos to get 2D trajectories, i.e., τ. Then, with fixed τ, we run the Algorithm 1 with the Dynamic-II only. This leads to five baseline algorithms that solve tracking and localization in turn.

Metrics For *tracking*, we employ the widely used CLEAR met-

Sequences (#vehicles)	Method	MOTA(%)	MOTP(%)	MT(%)	PT(%)	ML(%)	IDSW	FRAG
Group 1 (335)	STAL-3	**67.15**	**71.23**	**47.59**	**78.67**	**8.92**	**181**	**190**
	STAL-2	63.27	68.32	45.32	73.56	9.34	210	205
	STAL-1	56.15	60.94	39.29	67.21	11.52	235	316
	Geiger et al. [12]	59.34	63.34	42.36	69.34	13.46	432	275
	Lenz et al. [27]	60.21	61.12	39.15	68.98	11.97	614	243
	Xiang et al. [52]	58.76	63.27	36.27	64.32	19.24	543	259
	Andriyenko et al. [3]	48.13	56.32	35.37	45.61	20.34	781	345
Group 2 (362)	STAL-3	**62.94**	**67.83**	**46.27**	**68.31**	**10.21**	**276**	**215**
	STAL-2	58.17	61.09	38.49	62.75	13.45	324	229
	STAL-1	55.64	54.36	37.23	58.16	15.18	350	417
	Geiger et al. [12]	56.72	55.68	40.34	57.32	16.29	613	439
	Lenz et al. [27]	54.21	57.13	39.51	60.31	14.53	581	352
	Xiang et al. [52]	53.76	56.19	38.14	61.29	17.59	462	533
	Andriyenko et al. [3]	45.36	48.32	27.89	52.34	21.69	684	726
Group 3 (274)	STAL-3	**52.16**	**62.84**	**47.68**	**73.14**	**12.37**	**324**	**236**
	STAL-2	48.56	59.12	42.75	68.75	14.35	392	397
	STAL-1	43.29	53.87	40.50	64.21	18.57	421	531
	Geiger et al. [12]	47.19	55.12	41.29	63.59	15.66	382	689
	Lenz et al. [27]	46.36	57.27	43.57	65.82	16.14	475	725
	Xiang et al. [52]	42.19	58.34	45.38	61.32	16.34	419	963
	Andriyenko et al. [3]	37.35	49.25	36.21	58.35	21.34	531	1236
Group 4 (281)	STAL-3	**65.72**	**73.59**	**52.76**	**75.96**	**8.16**	**289**	**210**
	STAL-2	61.78	67.31	51.34	68.34	9.34	395	256
	STAL-1	53.29	62.15	46.12	66.72	11.63	441	443
	Geiger et al. [12]	59.42	64.37	48.52	62.36	9.47	476	369
	Lenz et al. [27]	58.51	65.92	50.36	67.82	12.24	497	479
	Xiang et al. [52]	54.97	59.46	49.21	63.49	13.43	531	412
	Andriyenko et al. [3]	49.23	45.29	45.97	52.75	16.53	724	567

Table 1: Results of tracking. STAL-1, STAL-2, STAL-3 are three implementations of the proposed approach. For every group of sequences, The total number of objects are listed in the first column. See text for detailed explanations.

Table 2: Results of 3D localizations (average errors in meters).

Methods	Group-1	Group-2	Group-3	Group-4
STAL-3	**1.24**	**1.72**	**2.03**	**1.16**
STAL-2	1.56	2.14	2.56	1.56
STAL-1	2.03	3.25	2.97	2.79
Geiger et al. [12]	2.34	2.76	2.67	2.53
Lenz et al. [27]	2.21	2.85	2.86	2.13
Xiang et al. [52]	2.17	3.02	3.10	2.24
Andriyenko et al. [3]	3.16	3.75	2.85	3.17
GP	3.67	3.46	3.21	3.24
SVR [41]	5.32	6.32	4.31	5.29

rics [21]: Tracking Accuracy (MOTA) and Tracking Precision (MOTP) to measure three kinds of errors in tracking: false positives, false negatives and identity switches. We also report the percentages of *mostly tracked* (MT), *partly tracked* (PT) and *mostly lost* (ML) groundtruth (referring to [28]), as well as the numbers of identity switches (IDSW) and fragments (FRAG). Hit/miss for the assignment of tracking output to groundtruth is set to a threshold of Intersection over Union (IoU) ratio 50%. For *localization*, we calculate the average localization errors: the Euclidean distances between the estimated coordinates and groundtruth coordinates. We calculate localization errors in meters facilitate interpretation. Note that we only count the mostly tracked vehicles, i.e. the ratio of groundtruth trajectories that are covered by a track hypothesis for at least 80% of their respective life space.

Efficiency Our approach is implemented in MATLAB and runs on a desktop with Intel I7 3.0GHz CPU, 32GB memory and Nvidia K40 GPU. Given 4 sequences of 1080P, the runtime on average is 15-20 fps for object detection, 1000-1500fps for pre-processing, and $10-20$ fps for running the hybrid Monte Carlo method. Overall, the proposed algorithm obtains $10-12$ fps, which is dependent on the vehicle density of the sequence. With proper code migration and optimization, e.g., batch processing, our algorithm can achieve real-time processing.

Results Table 1 reports the tracking results of the various methods. Results over individual groups of videos are listed separately. From the results, we can obtain the following observations. First, the proposed joint tracking and localization methods, i.e., STAL-3 and STAL-2, outperformed the other baseline trackers, which demonstrates the superiority of the proposed joint framework. Second, the comparisons between STAL-3 and STAL-2 further suggest that it is beneficial to include the pair-wise spatial relationships between vehicles. In Figures 1 and 2, we plot the generated scene maps for the group-1 and group-2, respectively.

Table 2 reports the localization results over individual groups of videos. Among these methods, STAL-3 and STAL-2 can directly output 3D locations. The other methods solve tracking and localization in a subsequent fashion. All methods are able to access the V2V traffic data and integrate the outputs of Gaussian Regression Process (GP). We include the results of GP for comparisons as well. We also report the regression results by applying the SVR method over the data $\mathcal{D}$. From the table, we can observe that STAL-3 achieved the minimal localization error. While all the methods can certainly improve the GP results, it is evident that jointly formulating the tracking and localization can generate better localization result, which is consistent with our observations on tracking results.

6. CONCLUSIONS

This paper studies a novel data fusion problem, visual vehicle-to-vehicle interaction (V3I). We developed a unified probabilistic approach to simultaneously track and localize isolated vehicles through cameras on connected vehicles. Our formula integrates a Gaussian Regression Process with time-series kernel, and a set of pair-wise binary relationships in the Bayesian Framework. For inference, we introduced a fast Hybrid Monte Carlo algorithm to efficiently search the joint solution space. Extensive experiments with component analysis clearly demonstrated the effectiveness of the proposal approach.

7. ACKNOWLEDGMENT

The data used in this work was collected and annotated by the Computer Vision Lab at San Diego State University (SDSU). The author would like to thank Dr. Xianfeng Yang (SDSU) for his insightful discussions and suggestions. The original idea of this work was initialized and discussed when the author was traveling in Boston with his friends: Yibiao Zhao (MIT), Yixin Zhu (UCLA) and Tianmin Shu (UCLA).

8. REFERENCES

[1] A. Almeida. Hamiltonian systems: Chaos and quantization. *Cambridge monographs on mathematical physics*, 1992.

[2] M. Aly. Real time detection of lane markers in urban streets. In *IEEE Intelligent Vehicles Symposium*, 2008.

[3] A. Andriyenko and K. Schindler. Discrete-continuous optimization for multi-target tracking. In *Proc. CVPR*, 2012.

[4] M. Audin and D. Babbitt. Hamiltonian systems and their integrability. *American Mathmatical Society*, 2008.

[5] H. Azizpour and I. Laptev. Object detection using strongly supervised deformable part models. In *ECCV*, 2012.

[6] A. Barbu and S. Zhu. Generalizing swendsen-wang to sampling arbitrary posterior probabilities. *IEEE Trans. PAMI*, 27(8):1239–1253, 2007.

[7] J. Berclaz, F. Fleuret, E. Turetken, and P. Fua. multiple object tracking using k-shortest paths optimization. *IEEE Trans. PAMI*, 33(9):1806–1819, 2011.

[8] A. Criminisi, J. Shotton, and E. Konukoglu. Decision forests: A unified framework for classification, regression, density estimation, manifold learning and semi-supervised learning. *Foundations and Trends in Computer Graphics and Vision*, 7(2):81–227, 2012.

[9] M. Everingham, S. Eslami, L. V. Gool, C. Williams, J. Winn, and A. Zisserman. The pascal visual object classes challenge: A retrospective. *IJCV*, 111(1):98–136, 2015.

[10] P. Felzenszwalb, R. Girshick, D. McAllester, and D. Ramanan. Object detection with discriminatively trained part-based models. *IEEE Trans. PAMI*, 32(9):1627–1645, 2010.

[11] P. Felzenszwalb, R. B. Girshick, D. McAllester, and D. Ramanan. Object detection with discriminatively trained part based models. *IEEE Trans. PAMI*, 32(9):1627–1645, 2010.

[12] A. Geiger, M. Lauer, C. Wojek, C. Stiller, and R. Urtasun. 3d traffic scene understanding from movable platforms. *IEEE Trans. PAMI*, 2014.

[13] R. Girshick. Fast r-cnn. In *CVPR*, 2015.

[14] R. Girshick, J. Donahue, T. Darrell, and J. Malik. Rich feature hierarchies for accurate object detection and semantic segmentation. In *CVPR*, 2014.

[15] C. Haene, N. Savinov, and M. Pollefeys. Class specific 3d object shape priors using surface normals. In *CVPR*, 2014.

[16] M. Hejrati and D. Ramanan. Analysis by synthesis: Object recognition by object reconstruction. In *CVPR*, 2014.

[17] C. Huang, Y. Li, and R. Nevatia. Multiple target tracking by learning-based hierarchical association of detection responses. *IEEE Trans. PAMI*, 35(4):898–910, 2013.

[18] Y. Jia, E. Shelhamer, J. Donahue, S. Karayev, J. Long, R. Girshick, S. Guadarrama, and T. Darrell. Caffe: Convolutional architecture for fast feature embedding authors. In *Proc. ACM Multimedia*, 2014.

[19] A. Kapoor, K. Grauman, R. Urtasun, and T. Darrell. Gaussian processes for object categorization. *IJCV*, 2009.

[20] N. Karlsson, E. Bernardo, J. Ostrowski, L. Goncalves, P. Pirjanian, and M. Munich. The vslam algorithm for robust localization and mapping. In *ICRA*, 2005.

[21] R. Kasturi, D. Goldgof, P. Soundararajan, V. Manohar, J. Garofolo, R. Bowers, M. Boonstra, V. Korzhova, and j.. Zhang. Framework for performance evaluation of face, text, and vehicle detection and tracking in video: Data, metrics, and protocol. *IEEE Trans. PAMI*, 31(2):319–336, 2009.

[22] S. Khan and M. Shah. A multiview approach to tracking people in crowded scenes using a planar homography constraint. In *Proc. ECCV*, 2006.

[23] A. Krizhevsky, I. Sutskever, and G. Hinton. Imagenet classification with deep convolutional neural networks. In *Proc. NIPS*, 2012.

[24] A. Kundu, Y. Li, F. Daellert, F. Li, and J. Rehg. Joint semantic segmentation and 3d reconstruction from monocular video. In *ECCV*, 2014.

[25] L. Ladicky, J. Shi, and M. Pollefeys. Pulling things out of perspective. In *CVPR*, 2014.

[26] N. Lawrence, M. Seeger, and R. Herbrich. Fast sparse gaussian process methods: the informative vector machine. In *NIPS*, 2003.

[27] P. Lenz, A. Geiger, and R. Urtasun. Followme: Efficient online min-cost flow tracking with bounded memory and computation. In *ICCV*, 2015.

[28] Y. Li, C. Huang, and R. Nevatia. Learning to associate: Hybridboosted multi-target tracker for crowded scene. In *Proc. CVPR*, 2009.

[29] C. Liu, J. Yuen, A. Torralba, J. Sivic, and W. Freeman. Sift flow: Dense correspondence across different scenes. In *Proc. ECCV*, 2008.

[30] X. Liu, L. Lin, and H. Jin. Contextualized trajectory parsing via spatio-temporal graph. *IEEE Trans. PAMI*, 35(12):3010–3024, 2013.

[31] X. Liu, Y. Zhao, and S. Zhu. Single-view 3d scene parsing by attributed grammar. In *CVPR*, 2014.

[32] L. C. o and M. Opper. Sparse online gaussian processes. *Neural Computation*, (14):641–668, 2002.

[33] S. Oh, S. Russell, and S. Sastry. Markov chain monte carlo data association for multi-target tracking. *IEEE Trans. PAMI*, 54(3):481–498, 2009.

[34] D. Reid. An algorithm for tracking multiple targets. *IEEE Trans. Automatic Control*, 24(6):843–854, 1979.

[35] S. Ren, K. He, R. Girshick, and J. Sun. Faster r-cnn: Towards real-time object detection with region proposal networks. In *Proc. NIPS*, 2015.

[36] J. Roecker. A class of near optimal jpda algorithms. *IEEE Trans.Aerosp. Electron. Syst.*, 30(2):504–510, 1994.

[37] J. Roecker and G. Phillis. Suboptimal joint probabilistic data association. *IEEE Trans. Aerosp. Electron. Syst.*, 29(2):510–517, 1993.

[38] R. Salas-Moreno, R. Newcombe, H. Strasdat, P. Kelly, and A. Davison. Slam++: Simultaneous localisation and mapping at the level of objects. In *Proc. CVPR*, 2013.

[39] A. Schwing, S. Fidler, M. Pollefeys, and R. Urtasun. Box in the box: Joint 3d layout and object reasoning from single images. In *ICCV*, 2013.

[40] A. Smeulders, D. Chu, R. Cucchiara, S. Calderara, A. Dehghan, and M. Shah. Visual tracking: An experimental survey. *IEEE Trans. PAMI*, 36(7):1442–1468, 2014.

[41] A. Smola and V. Vapnik. Support vector regression machines. In *NIPS*, 1997.

[42] A. J. Smola and P. Bartlett. Sparse greedy gaussian process regression. In *NIPS*, 2001.

[43] E. Snelson and Z. Ghahramani. Sparse gaussian processes using pseudo-inputs. In *NIPS*, 2006.

[44] E. Snelson and Z. Ghahramani. Variable noise and dimensionality reduction for sparse gaussian processes. In *UAI*, 2006.

[45] S. Song and M. Chandraker. Robust scale estimation in real-time monocular sfm for autonomous driving. In *CVPR*, 2014.

[46] Z. Tu and S. Zhu. Image segmentation by data-driven markov chain monte carlo. *IEEE Trans. PAMI*, 24(5):657–673, 2002.

[47] P. A. Viola, J. C. Platt, and C. Zhang. Multiple instance boosting for object detection. In *NIPS*, 2006.

[48] C. Vondrick, D. Patterson, and D. Ramanan. Efficiently scaling up crowdsourced video annotation. *IJCV*, 2012.

[49] C.-C. Wang. Simultaneous localization and mapping with detection and tracking of moving objects. In *ICRA*, 2002.

[50] T. Willke, P. Tientrakool, and N. Maxemchuk. A survey of inter-vehicle communication protocols and their applications. *IEEE Communications Surveys*, 2009.

[51] Y. Wu, S. Zhu, and C. Guo. From information scaling of natural images to regimes of statistical models. *Quarterly of Applied Mathematics*, 66(1):81–122, 2008.

[52] Y. Xiang, A. Alahi, and S. Savarese. Learning to track: Online multi- object tracking by decision making. In *ICCV*, 2015.

[53] X. Yang, L. Liu, N. Vaidya, and F. Zhao. A vehicle-to-vehicle communication protocol for cooperative collision warning. In *MOBIQUITOUS*, 2004.

[54] Q. Yu, G. Medioni, and I. Cohen. Multiple target tracking using spatio-temporal markov chain monte carlo data association. In *Proc. CVPR*, 2007.

[55] H. Zhang, A. Geiger, and R. Urtasun. Understanding high-level semantics by modeling traffic patterns. In *ICCV*, 2013.

[56] S. Zhang, X. Yu, Y. Sui, S. Zhao, and L. Zhang. object tracking with multi-view support vector machines. *IEEE Trans. MM*, 17(3):265–278, 2015.

[57] X. Zhang, Y.-H. Yang, Z. Han, H. Wang, and C. Gao. Object class detection: A survey. *ACM Comput. Surv.*, 46(1), 2013.

Are Safer Looking Neighborhoods More Lively? A Multimodal Investigation into Urban Life

Marco De Nadai
FBK and University of Trento
Trento, Italy
denadai@fbk.eu

Radu L. Vieriu
University of Trento
Trento, Italy
radulaurentiu.vieriu@unitn.it

Gloria Zen
University of Trento
Trento, Italy
gloria.zen@unitn.it

Stefan Dragicevic
TIM and University of Trento
Trento, Italy
stefan.dragicevic@unitn.it

Nikhil Naik
MIT Media Lab
Cambridge, MA
naik@mit.edu

Michele Caraviello
TIM
Trento, Italy
michele.caraviello@telecomitalia.it

Cesar A. Hidalgo
MIT Media Lab
Cambridge, MA
hidalgo@mit.edu

Nicu Sebe
University of Trento
Trento, Italy
sebe@disi.unitn.it

Bruno Lepri
FBK
Trento, Italy
lepri@fbk.eu

ABSTRACT

Policy makers, urban planners, architects, sociologists, and economists are interested in creating urban areas that are both lively and safe. But are the safety and liveliness of neighborhoods independent characteristics? Or are they just two sides of the same coin? In a world where people avoid unsafe looking places, neighborhoods that look unsafe will be less lively, and will fail to harness the natural surveillance of human activity. But in a world where the preference for safe looking neighborhoods is small, the connection between the perception of safety and liveliness will be either weak or nonexistent. In this paper we explore the connection between the levels of activity and the perception of safety of neighborhoods in two major Italian cities by combining mobile phone data (as a proxy for activity or liveliness) with scores of perceived safety estimated using a Convolutional Neural Network trained on a dataset of Google Street View images scored using a crowdsourced visual perception survey. We find that: (i) safer looking neighborhoods are more active than what is expected from their population density, employee density, and distance to the city centre; and (ii) that the correlation between appearance of safety and activity is positive, strong, and significant, for females and people over 50, but negative for people under 30, suggesting that the behavioral impact of perception depends on the demographic of the population. Finally, we use occlusion techniques to identify the urban features that contribute to the appearance of safety, finding that greenery and street facing windows contribute to a positive appearance of safety (in agreement with Oscar Newman's defensible space theory). These results suggest that urban appearance modulates levels of human activity and, consequently, a neighborhood's rate of natural surveillance.

MM '16, October 15 - 19, 2016, Amsterdam, Netherlands

ISBN 978-1-4503-3603-1/16/10...$15.00

DOI: http://dx.doi.org/10.1145/2964284.2964312

1. INTRODUCTION

Does a neighborhood's appearance of safety affect how active it is? For decades scholars from a variety of disciplines, but mainly from urban planning, have been exploring the potential connection between a neighborhood's appearance of safety and its levels of human activity.

The modern literature connecting safety, liveliness, and architecture, can be traced back to Jane Jacobs' seminal 1961 book: *The Death and Life of Great American Cities* [22]. In there, Jacobs introduced the eyes-on-the-street, or natural surveillance hypothesis [5], which suggests that citizens can maintain the safety of their neighborhoods naturally through continued surveillance. For natural surveillance to take place, however, Jacobs argued that neighborhoods needed to have certain physical qualities, such as well lit streets and buildings with street facing windows.

Jacobs' idea that the physical quality of a neighborhood can enhance its safety was later expanded by Oscar Newman's *defensible space theory* [39]. Defensible space theory expands on the idea of natural surveillance by suggesting that neighbors will be more likely to protect an area when there are clear physical demarcations separating what is considered public and private property [23, 39]. Examples of architectural markers of defensible space are archways in the entrance of building complexes, or staircases in the entrance of townhouses. These archways and staircases do not only serve an aesthetic purpose, but also, signal the boundary between a city's public space and the private and semi-private spaces that neighbors are expected to watch and defend.

Here, we strengthen the link between Jacobs' and Newman's theories by asking whether safer looking neighborhoods are more likely to experience more human activity–and hence, experience more natural surveillance. We explore this connection, by combining computer vision methods, that can be used to measure the physical characteristics of neighborhoods [34, 44, 45, 43], with mobile phone data, which has become a common proxy for human activity [8, 11, 18, 20, 30], for two Italian cities (Rome and Milan). The combination of computer vision and mobile phone data helps us test whether safer looking neighborhoods are more active, and therefore, if neighborhoods that look physically safer could be experiencing more natural surveillance.

Our data provides support for a connection between appearance and activity. Using spatially filtered multivariate regressions we find that neighborhoods that are perceived as safer are more active than what is expected from their population density, the density of employees, and their distance to the city center. Also, we find that the perception of safety appears to modulate the relative population of females and adults, with unsafer looking neighborhoods experiencing a lower number of female and people over 50 than safer looking neighborhoods. Conversely, we find that younger populations are disproportionately more active in unsafe looking neighborhoods. Finally, we use occlusion techniques to identify the areas of an image that trigger a positive or negative evaluation of safety in the Artificial Neural Network, finding that greenery and street facing windows tend to be associated with higher levels of safety, as suggested by Oscar Newman's defensible space theory. These observational results strongly suggest–but don't causally prove–that the appearance of neighborhoods has an effect on their levels of human activity, and potentially, on a neighborhood's level of natural surveillance.

2. RELATED WORK

The connection between urban perception and human activity speaks primarily to two streams of literature. The first one is the stream of literature focused on the environmental factors contributing to crime, which has a long tradition in criminology and urban sociology. While our paper does not focus on crime per se, the connection between the physical appearance of neighborhoods and natural surveillance suggested by Jacobs and Newman makes our results relevant to that stream of literature [22, 23, 39]. The second one is the stream of literature using surveys, and more recently, computer vision methods to quantify people's perception of urban environments [35, 37, 45].

2.1 Neighborhood appearance and crime

Beyond Jacob's and Newman's theories, the most widely known theory suggesting a connection between urban perception and crime is the *broken windows theory* (BWT) of Wilson and Kelling [26, 55]. The BWT is the hypothesis that urban incivilities, such as broken windows and litter, promote criminal activity. The classical mechanism used to justify the theory says that urban incivilities signal lawlessness, and may cause the offenders of small incivilities to scale their criminal behavior to more predatory forms of crime if they are not reigned in. The policy implications of the BWT, however, vary from community policing—the promotion of ties between police officers and their communities—to zero-tolerance polices, which promote cracking down on all minor offences to deter more serious forms of crime.

Evidence in favor of the broken windows theory has been presented by Kelling and Coles [26], who looked at data and stories from New York to Seattle to argue that community policing is an effective way to deter more serious forms of crime. Kelling and Sousa [27] provide additional evidence by using an extensive dataset on crime, demographics, and economic data from New York City. More recently, Corman and Mocan [3] used New York City data on the policing of misdemeanors (as a proxy for broken windows policing), and on robbery, car theft, and grand larceny, to provide evidence in support of broken windows policing.

The broken windows theory is also supported by a few field experiments, such as those conducted by Keizer *et al.* in The Netherlands [25]. In six experiments, Keizer *et al.* intervened environments by spraying graffiti on walls, or leaving supermarket carts unattended and studied the behavior of subjects, in both the presence and absence of disorder, to see when people broke norms (such as littering). Their data showed a significant increase in people's norm breaking behavior when they were in the presence of disorder.

But not all of the evidence collected to test the BWT, and its policy implications, is favorable to it [13]. In a 2006 paper, Bernard Harcourt re-analyzed the data presented by Kelling and Sousa [27] and found no evidence of the effectiveness of the broken windows policing [14]. More recently, Harcourt and Ludwig used a dataset of more than fifty thousand marijuana related arrests to provide evidence that community policing is not only ineffective, but that it also unfairly targets minorities [15].

Moreover, the BWT has been criticized by work showing that the social and ethnic context of a neighborhood may matter more than urban disorder. In Sampson *et al.* [48] and Sampson and Raudenbush [46, 47], community data from Chicago was used to argue that racial and economic context were more predictive of disorderly behavior than physical disorder. To help bridge their results with the literature, Sampson and Raudenbush [46] proposed an alternative interpretation of the theory, where both neighborhood disorder and crime, are manifestations of a lack of informal forms of control within disengaged and distrusting communities. The reframed theory, therefore, interprets the link between disorder and crime as a manifestation of the lack of informal forms of social control and organization.

2.2 The social and computational image of the city

The second literature our paper speaks to is the literature measuring urban perception and understand its social and economic implications. The original literature on this topic can be traced back to seminal work by the urbanist Kevin Lynch [31], who interviewed people in Boston, Jersey City, and Los Angeles, to understand the large scale image of cities that people made in their heads. This work on a city's imageability was later continued by social psychologists like Stanley Milgram [33], and by urbanists like Jack Nasar [37, 38], who created evaluative maps of cities, also using survey methods.

More recently, however, this literature started leveraging crowdsourcing [45] and computer vision methods [35, 43] to improve the scale, precision, and resolution of the evaluative maps created.

On the data collection side of this literature, Salesses *et al.* [45] created a large crowdsourced visual perception survey to measure people's perception of streetscapes, and to create comparable evaluative maps for New York, Boston, Linz, and Salzburg, which they also used to measure the segregation and inequality of experiences in these cities, and to show that violent crime correlates with the variance of appearence of safety in an area.

These new sources of crowd-sourced data gave rise to studies looking to understand the features of an image that explain how streetscapes are perceived. On a recent study, Quercia *et al.* [44] investigated which visual aspects of London neighborhoods make them appear beautiful, quiet and/or happy. A related study by Porzi *et al.* [43] identified the visual elements that contributed to an image's perceived level of safety.

But to scale the study of urban perception to multiple cities, and to high spatial resolutions, researchers begun developing computer vision methods to score millions of images [35]. These computer vision approaches build on research predicting human perception from visual data [12, 21, 49] and on research analyzing visual streetscapes for city understanding [1, 2, 6, 10, 28, 57]. The latter of these two lines of research has been fueled by the widespread availability of geolocated image data, such as Google Street View maps or city snapshots publicly shared on social networks (e.g. Flickr, Instagram) [1, 51, 57]. Using geotagged image data Doersch *et al.* [6] showed that geographically representative visual elements, like architecture styles, can be automatically discovered from Street View Imagery. In a dynamic study, Naik *et al.* [34] used computer vision and images from different time periods to measure urban change, and to study the factors that contribute to neighborhood improvement. Computer vision methods have also been used to show that a city's visual attributes work as proxy of social and economic characteristics, such as crime rates and proximity to local businesses [2, 28], or census characteristics, such as income and inequality [36].

This new wave of research has benefited from advances in deep learning, which have been used not only to measure appearance, but also for place recognition. Zhou *et al.* [57] introduced Places205 Dataset, a large data collection gathering more than 7 million labeled pictures of scenes. They achieve state-of-the-art classification results by training deep Convolutional Neural Networks (CNNs). More recently, Arandjelović *et al.* [1] introduce NetVLAD, a modified CNN architecture able to address large scale visual place recognition. In this work, we build on top of recent work in place recognition [1, 57] to fine-tune a deep CNN architecture and show experimentally that under scarce training data, sample augmenting helps achieve state-of-the-art results on safety prediction from streescape images.

3. DATASETS

Next, we describe the datasets used to estimate urban appearance, and human activity.

3.1 Urban appearance data

We use urban appearance data from the Place Pulse dataset[1]. Place Pulse is a large, crowdsourcing project on human perception of cities. The data collection is designed as an online game, where participants are shown two images of streetscapes and are asked to choose one image in response to an evaluative question such as: Which place looks safer? Or: Which place looks more lively? A score is later computed for each image using the TrueSkill [16] algorithm.

Place Pulse begun as Place Pulse 1.0 (PP1), which scored 4,109 images from two US cities (New York City and Boston) and two European cities (Linz and Salzburg), and was launched publicly in 2011. PP1 scored images across three evaluative dimensions: *Safety*, *Upper-Class* and *Unique*.

The current version of Place Pulse (Place Pulse 2.0), launched publicly in July 2013, extended the data collection effort to 56 cities from all continents (except Antartica) and to six evaluative questions: *Safety*, *Wealthy*, *Boring*, *Lively*, *Depressing* and *Beautiful*. For more details, please see Dubey *et al.* [7]

Here we use data from the Place Pulse 2.0 dataset for Milan and Rome (PP2-I). The data includes 3,897 images that received about 25,000 evaluations for their perception of safety[2] - corresponding to an average of 7.6 clicks per image.

3.2 Mobile phone activity data

To proxy human activity we use mobile phone billing and operation data. The data records the time of communication, and the radio base station that handled it, for various types of communication (e.g. incoming calls, Internet, outgoing SMS). The natural coarsening of this data are grid cells with an area that is proportional to the underlying coverage area of the radio base stations. The cell size is $\sim 300 \times 300$ m in the city centre of Milan and it increases up to $\sim 2,300 \times 2,300$ m in the peripheral part of the cities, where few customers are served per unit of area. For each grid cell, we count the number of people who made or received a call on an hourly basis, broken down by gender (number of males/females) and age.

Call records were provided by Telecom Italia Mobile (TIM), which is the largest mobile operator in Italy with a market share of 34%[3]. Our data are aggregated every 60 minutes, and includes both TIM customers and roaming customers in Milan and Rome, and covers the time ranging from February to June 2015.

We note that our data cannot distinguish between pedestrians and people using their phones in their homes, so our measures of activity proxy the number of TIM customers in an area, but not necessarily in the street.

4. METHODOLOGY

This paper focuses on investigating the relationship between the appearance of safety and the activity or liveliness of neighborhoods in Rome and Milan. To achieve this goal we estimate the appearance of safety for different districts of the city by spatially aggregating the safety scores obtained from the images within these areas, and then, observe people's activity using mobile phone data. To achieve enough coverage, we densify our maps by collecting additional images and scoring them using computer vision. Finally, we spatially aggregate scores including census tracts for the 2011 Italian census. In the reminder of this section we explain the methodology used to score images and to measure activity.

4.1 Measures of Urban Appearance

4.1.1 Safety Perception from Visual Data

We use deep Convolutional Neural Networks (CNNs) as our model for predicting safety perception from streetscape

[1]http://pulse.media.mit.edu

[2]We include in this sum only pairwise comparisons involving either two Italian cities or one Italian vs one non-Italian city

[3]http://bit.ly/1LtNrFY

imagery. We base this choice on the recent success of CNNs in various computer vision problems (especially object classification, object detection and scene recognition [29, 40, 50]). We show that fine-tuning a CNN on predicting the level of safety along with data augmentation leads to improved performance when compared to recent work on the same task [35, 41].

Since we have a limited amount of training data (*i.e.* a sample of a few thousands), we retrain CNNs trained on related domains (e.g. images captured in urban environments that are likely to show similar visual content). In particular, we fine-tune the well known AlexNet CNN [29], trained on Places205 Dataset [57], also known as *Places205-AlexNet.* This model was trained on 205 categories of scenes (many of which capture different areas from cities such as office buildings, churches, residential neighborhoods, shops, etc.) summing up around 2.5 million images. By retraining a CNN previously trained in a similar domain we transfer some of the knowledge contained in this network. In our case, we find that the resulting network can accurately predict the appearance of safety, as we show in the validation section (see section 4.1.2).

To increase the generalization ability of the trained CNN, we adopt data augmentation by cropping all the images used during training and testing. We find this particularly suitable for our scenario where no constraints regarding image alignment are imposed. Specifically, for every image in the training set, we generate n crops by randomly assigning values to the coordinates of the top left and bottom right cutting points, respectively. We control the size of the crops by bounding the coordinates of the cutting points to ranges proportional with the image size. Formally, given an image I of size $W \times H \times 3$, we generate points $P_1(x_1, y_1)$ and $P_2(x_2, y_2)$ such that the quantities: $x_1/W, y_1/H, 1-x_2/W$ and $1-y_2/H$ are bounded by k_1 and k_2, respectively. We empirically set k_1 to 0.05, k_2 to 0.2 and n to 30 in all our experiments. Additional constraints to control diversity of the crops could be implemented, such as monitoring the *intersection over the reunion (IoU)* between pairs of crops and/or original image. During testing, we average all predictions belonging to the crops of the same test sample. The safety scores obtained at image level are then aggregated into city's districts.

Part of the standard pre-processing steps, all the images are subject to scaling to 227×227 pixels and mean image subtraction. The task is modeled as a regression problem, where the goal is to minimize the l_2 loss between the sample labels and the model predictions. As labels, we refer to the Trueskill scores computed in [35], also used in [41]. We fine-tune with *Caffe* [24] for 10,000 iterations using a base learning rate of $1e^{-4}$. We note no further decrease in the training loss beyond this limit.

4.1.2 Validation of computer vision models

We validate the fine-tuned CNN on the two US cities from PP1 (New York and Boston), following training and evaluation protocols from [35] and [41], respectively. In the first case, we perform a 5-fold cross-validation on the 2920 US images and report the average R^2 measure, after scaling all the scores to the interval [0, 10]. We obtain an average R^2 of 62.2% a 9.5% relative improvement over the best result reported in [35] and 4.8% over the case of not using data augmentation during testing. In the second case, the source (train) and target (test) domains are populated by alternating US cities (e.g. NY - Boston, NY - NY, Boston - Boston, Boston - NY). As performance measure, the authors report Pearson correlation between the predicted regression values and the label scores. Table 1 shows the comparison results, where we consistently outperform [41] in all four combinations. We also observe how the difficulty of the task (for different pairs) modulates the predicting performance of both sets of models in the same way (e.g. training and testing on Boston seems to be the easiest for both our models and the ones from [41]).

Model type	Best from [41]	Our result
NY - NY	0.687	0.718
Boston - Boston	0.718	0.744
NY - Boston	0.701	0.734
Boston - NY	0.636	0.693

Table 1: Performance on the estimated level of safety (comparison with [41]). For all cases, we report Pearson correlations with $p < 0.001$.

4.1.3 Densification of Appearance data using Computer Vision

Since the distribution of the annotated images from PP2-I is sparse, on average 6.7 images/km^2, we retrieve additional images for the cities of Rome and Milan by densely sampling geo-referenced images from Google Street View. Data densification for the analysis of urban landscape has been used in previous works for generating high resolution maps of city perception [35, 41]. First, we generate a grid of points inside the area we want to cover. The granularity we choose is 100 points/km^2. To better represent the safety perception of the location, we retrieve four images from each location, which have 90 degrees horizontal field of view and different headings (north, east, south and west). By doing this we cover 360 degrees from each location, thus getting less biased safety perception of an area by averaging predicted safety scores of these four images. We developed the script which iterates through all the points and used Google Street View API to obtain four images for each location. The script discards locations where no images are available. Using this method we obtained 83,203 images for Rome and 74,815 images for Milan.

4.1.4 Validation of Densification

Table 2 reports the performances on predicting safety perception for the city of Rome and Milan. We evaluate the correlation between the aggregated original scores and (i) the predictions over the images from PP2-I and (ii) the predictions over the images from the densified dataset. In general, a slight decrease in performance is observed in the second case. We can attribute this loss in performance to the fact that images from PP2-I were retrieved in 2010, thus a variation in the urban appearance may have occurred within this time lapse. For example, the Expo Milano 2015 - a Universal Exposition - was held from May to October 2015, and Milan underwent a profound (visual) change in its northwest area to prepare for this event.

Predicting safety on Milan and Rome: We are interested in finding a good candidate model for labeling the densely sampled Street View images from Milan and Rome. We experimented with several model choices (including train-

City	PP2-I	Densified
Milan	0.621	0.488
Rome	0.635	0.548

Table 2: Performance on the estimated safety perception level for each city. All values are statistically significant, with p < 0.001.

ing on PP2-I) and discovered that, surprisingly, using PP1 for training yields the best correlation value for the two Italian cities. We attribute this result to the much inferior average number of votes per image (around 7.6 for PP2-I, compared to around 90 for PP1). For the rest of the experiments, we use only the model trained on PP1 for safety prediction. In Figure 1 we visually report the spatial distribution of the safety prediction for Milan and Rome.

4.2 Metrics for Urban Liveliness or Activity

Next, we define the metrics we use as proxies for an area's level of activity, or liveliness. Here we study only in urban areas where more than 50% of the surface is not composed by farmlands or forests. We measure activity for four populations, all people, females, people younger than 30, and people older than 50.

Formally, we measure the density of all people in district i as:

$$R_p(i, 24h) = \frac{|people_{i,24h}|}{area_i} \tag{1}$$

Next, we measure the fraction of females in a district i as:

$$R_f(i, 24h) = \frac{|females_{i,24h}|}{|people_{i,24h}|} \tag{2}$$

Additionally, we measure the population of people below 30 and above 50 as:

$$R_{<30}(i, 24h) = \frac{|people(<30)_{i,24h}|}{|people_{i,24h}|} \tag{3}$$

$$R_{>50}(i, 24h) = \frac{|people(>50)_{i,24h}|}{|people_{i,24h}|} \tag{4}$$

.

4.3 Spatial Regression

We test the connection between urban appearance of safety and activity using spatially corrected Ordinary Least Squares (OLS) regressions. Since we are dealing with spatial variables, OLS residuals are assumed not to be spatially auto-correlated; otherwise the regression model is said to be misspecified. Thus, we use the Griffith filtering [53] which extracts a set of orthogonal and uncorrelated eigenvectors from the expression:

$$(I - \frac{11^T}{n})W(I - \frac{11^T}{n}) \tag{5}$$

derived from the spatial auto-correlation Moran's I numerator, where I is a $(n \times n)$ identity matrix, 1 is a $n \times 1$ vector containing only 1's and W is a $(n \times n)$ spatial weight matrix based on topological adjacency, so-called Queen criterion: if two areas share a boundary or a vertex, the entity of the spatial weight matrix is coded as 1, and otherwise, 0. The eigenvectors obtained can be employed in a multivariate regression to account for spatial auto-correlation. However, it is clear that employing all n eigenvectors in a regression framework is not desirable for reasons of model parsimony. Thus, a subset of eigenvectors are selected in a step-wise fashion so as to minimize the sequential residual spatial correlation (Moran's I) values [53]. The final subset of candidate eigenvectors represents the *spatial filter* for the variable analysed. Before applying the regression model, the data were Z-score scaled.

5. RESULTS

After describing our methods to measure urban appearance and neighborhood activity we test whether the appearance of safety and the activity of neighborhoods is correlated. To test for this correlation we merge our data with information from the Italian census so we can control for other sources that intuitively correlate with neighborhood activity: population density (residential), density of employment (which should also proxy pedestrian density during the day), distance to city centre, and a deprivation index (to control for poverty in the neighborhood).

We begin by looking simply at the correlation between the number of people per unit of area observed in our mobile phone dataset and the appearance of safety in a neighborhood while controlling for population density, employee density, deprivation, and distance to centre.

Table 3 shows the result of a spatially corrected multivariate regression with the number of people per unit of area measured using the density of all people as the dependent variable. Not surprisingly, the strongest correlate of the number of people present per unit of area is employee density, and the number of people per unit area decreases with distance to the center. Yet, despite the strong effect of the other control variables, the appearance of safety is significantly and positively correlated with the number of people present in a neighborhood per unit area.

Presence of people (1)[1]	
Population density[1]	0.155**
Employees density[1]	0.328**
Deprivation	-0.022
Distance centre	-0.257**
Safety appearence	0.105**
Spatial Eigenvectors	11
Adj-R^2	0.91
Moran's I (p-value)	0.07 (0.08)

[1] log transformed variable.

Table 3: OLS regression model between presence of people and safety perception. The β coefficients are reported in the table. *p < 0.01, **p < 0.001.

Next, we look at the fraction of females present in an area. Looking at the population of females separately is motivated by empirical research showing that women are twice as likely as men to report feeling unsafe [54], even though they have a much smaller risk of being victimized [42, 52]. This suggest that the presence of women in a neighborhood should be more strongly affected by its appearance of safety than the presence of men. In fact, Felson and Clarke [9] suggest that a high ratio of women in the street is a positive sign towards urban safety, as they act as "crime detractors," in agreement

Figure 1: Spatial distribution of perceived safety in each district of Rome and Milan.

with Jacobs' natural surveillance hypothesis. These theories would suggest that the ratio of females is lower in places perceived as unsafe.

Table 4 looks at the ratio of females in the population observed in our cell phone data as the dependent variable, finding that the appearance of safety is highly significant and positive. In fact, the coefficient is roughly twice that observed for the general population.

Presence of women (2)	
% of women (residents)[s]	0.001
Deprivation	-0.005
Distance centre	-0.003
Safety perception	0.020**
Spatial Eigenvectors	12
Adj-R^2	0.65
Moran's I (p-value)	0.06 (0.11)

[s] cube-root transformed variable.

Table 4: OLS regression model between presence of women and safety perception. The β coefficients are reported in the table. *p $<$ 0.01, **p $<$ 0.001.

We also look at the proportion of people younger than 30 and older than 50 in an area. According to Felson and Clarke [9], a younger population is a predictor of criminal incidents in an area, as they show a higher aggression potential compared to older populations. Nevertheless, younger people, especially men, show less fear of crime [19, 32].

Table 5 looks at the ratio of people younger than 30 in the population observed in our cell phone data as the dependent variable. The variable which contributes the most to the correlation is the distance from the city centre, followed by appearance of safety which is highly significant and negative. Contrarily, when we look at the ratio of people older than 50 (Table 6), we find that the appearance of safety is highly significant and positive. This is in agreement with the theory, showing that older people are more likely to be present in places that appear safe.

Presence of people younger than 30 (3)[1]	
% of younger residents[1]	-0.001
Deprivation	0.032**
Distance centre	-0.150**
Safety perception	-0.048**
Spatial Eigenvectors	16
Adj-R^2	0.66
Moran's I (p-value)	0.07 (0.09)

[1] log transformed variable.

Table 5: OLS regression model between presence of younger people and safety perception. The β coefficients are reported in the table. *p $<$ 0.01, **p $<$ 0.001.

Presence of elderly people (4)	
% of elderly residents[s]	0.006**
Deprivation	-0.006**
Distance centre	0.006**
Safety perception	0.017**
Spatial Eigenvectors	14
Adj-R^2	0.64
Moran's I (p-value)	0.07 (0.09)

[s] cube-root transformed variable.

Table 6: OLS regression model between presence of elderly people and safety perception. The β coefficients are reported in the table. *p $<$ 0.01, **p $<$ 0.001.

5.1 Visual Attributes Determining Safety

Finally, we explore the visual attributes of the images that contribute positively, or negatively, to their appearance of safety. To identify these attributes we set up an occlusion sensitivity experiment. In this experiment, inspired by [56], we randomly generate occluding patches in images and replace them with the average pixel value. For every such altered

Figure 2: (Top) Sample images associated to a (left) low and (right) high level of safety and corresponding activation masks: highlighted areas correspond to the ones that mostly contribute to the perception of (center) unsafety and (bottom) safety.

image, we monitor the effect at the output of the predictor (did the image score higher or lower in its appearance of safety). This allows us to identify patches in an image that contribute positively or negatively to their appearance of safety.

Figure 2 shows some examples, with the original image on the (top row), followed by the areas that contribute to a low appearance of safety (middle row) and a high appearance of safety (bottom row). The images are sorted from an overall low appearance of safety to a high one. The examples, while illustrative instead of comprehensive, show that street facing windows and greenery tend to to contribute positively to an streetscapes appearance of safety. The positive effect of street facing windows is in agreement with the natural surveillance hypothesis of Jane Jacobs.

6. CONCLUSION

In this paper we explored the question: "*Are safer looking neighborhoods more lively?*" in the context of two Italian cities: Milan and Rome. Our findings suggest that perceived safety modulates the active population in an area, with effects that depend on age and gender. The overall effect of the appearance of safety in activity appears to be positive, even after controlling for population, employment density, and distance to the city center. Yet, the effect does not appear to be universal, and depends on the demographic with the population, with females and people older than 50 appearing to have a stronger preference for the appearance of safety.

Our results, however, do not provide a causal explanation of the observed effects. For instance, our data cannot distinguish between the hypotheses that people over than 50 prefer safer looking places, or that they modify their homes and shops to make the places they live and work at look safer. Nevertheless, they provide preliminary evidence suggesting a connection between the appearance of safety and levels of human activity that is strong enough to manifest itself at the city scale.

These methods, which could be readily applied to other cities if the data were available, can help improve modern efforts to use computational methods for urban recommendations. Some recent literature has focused on developing algorithms to recommend places for new business by using data on the presence of amenities in neighborhoods [17] and other urban features [4].

7. ACKNOWLEDGMENTS

Most of the computation of this article was done using free software and we are indebted to the developers and maintainers of the following packages: python, pandas, scikits.statsmodels, pysal to mention only a few.

8. REFERENCES

[1] R. Arandjelović, P. Gronat, A. Torii, T. Pajdla, and J. Sivic. NetVLAD: CNN architecture for weakly supervised place recognition. *arXiv preprint arXiv:1511.07247*, 2015.

[2] S. M. Arietta, A. A. Efros, R. Ramamoorthi, and M. Agrawala. City forensics: Using visual elements to predict non-visual city attributes. *IEEE TVCG*, 20(12):2624–2633, 2014.

[3] H. Corman and N. Mocan. Carrots, sticks, and broken windows. *Journal of Law and Economics*, 48(1):235–266, 2005.

[4] M. De Nadai, J. Staiano, R. Larcher, N. Sebe, D. Quercia, and B. Lepri. The Death and Life of Great Italian Cities: A Mobile Phone Data Perspective. In *ACM WWW*, 2016.

[5] H. Doeksen. Reducing crime and the fear of crime by reclaiming New Zealand's suburban street. *Landscape and urban planning*, 39(2):243–252, 1997.

[6] C. Doersch, S. Singh, A. Gupta, J. Sivic, and A. A. Efros. What makes Paris look like Paris? *Communications of the ACM*, 58(12):103–110, 2015.

[7] A. Dubey, N. Naik, D. Parikh, R. Raskar, and C. A. Hidalgo. Deep learning the city: Quantifying urban perception at a global scale. *ECCV*, 2016.

[8] N. Eagle, M. Macy, and R. Claxton. Network diversity

and economic development. *Science*, 328(5981):1029–1031, 2010.

[9] M. Felson and R. V. Clarke. Opportunity makes the thief. *Police research series, paper*, 98, 1998.

[10] E. L. Glaeser, S. D. Kominers, M. Luca, and N. Naik. Big data and big cities: The promises and limitations of improved measures of urban life. Working Paper 21778, National Bureau of Economic Research, 2015.

[11] M. Gonzalez, C. Hidalgo, and L. Barabasi. Understanding individual mobility patterns. *Nature*, 453(7196):779–782, 2008.

[12] H. Grabner, F. Nater, M. Druey, and L. Van Gool. Visual interestingness in image sequences. In *ACM Multimedia*, 2013.

[13] B. E. Harcourt. *Illusion of order: The false promise of broken windows policing*. Harvard University Press, 2009.

[14] B. E. Harcourt and J. Ludwig. Broken windows: New evidence from new york city and a five-city social experiment. *The University of Chicago Law Review*, pages 271–320, 2006.

[15] B. E. Harcourt and J. Ludwig. Reefer madness: Broken windows policing and misdemeanor marijuana arrests in new york city, 1989-2000. *Criminology and Public Policy*, 2007.

[16] R. Herbrich, T. Minka, and T. Graepel. Trueskill^{TM}: A Bayesian skill rating system. In *NIPS*, 2006.

[17] C. A. Hidalgo and E. E. Castañer. Do we need another coffee house? The amenity space and the evolution of neighborhoods. *arXiv preprint arXiv:1509.02868*, 2015.

[18] C. A. Hidalgo and C. Rodriguez-Sickert. The dynamics of a mobile phone network. *Physica A: Statistical Mechanics and its Applications*, 387(12):3017–3024, 2008.

[19] W. Hollway and T. Jefferson. The risk society in an age of anxiety: situating fear of crime. *British journal of sociology*, pages 255–266, 1997.

[20] S. Isaacman, R. Becker, R. Cáceres, S. Kobourov, J. Rowland, and A. Varshavsky. A tale of two cities. In *ACM HotMobile*, pages 19–24, 2010.

[21] P. Isola, D. Parikh, A. Torralba, and A. Oliva. Understanding the intrinsic memorability of images. In *NIPS*, 2011.

[22] J. Jacobs. *The death and life of American cities.* Random House, 1961.

[23] J. M. Jacobs and L. Lees. Defensible space on the move: revisiting the urban geography of alice coleman. In *International Journal of Urban and Regional Research 37.5 (2013): 1559-1583*, 2013.

[24] Y. Jia, E. Shelhamer, J. Donahue, S. Karayev, J. Long, R. Girshick, S. Guadarrama, and T. Darrell. Caffe: Convolutional Architecture for Fast Feature Embedding. *arXiv preprint arXiv:1408.5093*, 2014.

[25] K. Keizer, S. Lindenberg, and L. Steg. The spreading of disorder. *Science*, 322(5908):1681–1685, 2008.

[26] G. L. Kelling and C. M. Coles. *Fixing broken windows: Restoring order and reducing crime in our communities.* Simon and Schuster, 1997.

[27] G. L. Kelling and W. H. Sousa. *Do Police Matter?: An Analysis of the Impact of New York City's Police Reforms.* CCI Center for Civic Innovation at the Manhattan Institute, 2001.

[28] A. Khosla, B. An, J. J. Lim, and A. Torralba. Looking beyond the visible scene. In *CVPR*, 2014.

[29] A. Krizhevsky, I. Sutskever, and G. E. Hinton. Imagenet classification with deep convolutional neural networks. In *NIPS*, 2012.

[30] M. Lenormand, M. Picornell, O. G. Cantú-Ros, T. Louail, R. Herranz, M. Barthelemy, E. Frías-Martínez, M. San Miguel, and J. J. Ramasco. Comparing and modelling land use organization in cities. *Royal Society Open Science*, 2(12), 2015.

[31] K. Lynch. *The image of the city*, volume 11. MIT press, 1960.

[32] W. Mark. Fear of victimization: Why are women and the elderly more afraid? *Social science quarterly*, 65(3):681, 1984.

[33] S. Milgram. The experience of living in cities. *Science*, 167(3924):1461, 1970.

[34] N. Naik, S. D. Kominers, R. Raskar, E. L. Glaeser, and C. A. Hidalgo. Do people shape cities, or do cities shape people? The co-evolution of physical, social, and economic change in five major US cities. Technical report, National Bureau of Economic Research, 2015.

[35] N. Naik, J. Philipoom, R. Raskar, and C. Hidalgo. Streetscore–predicting the perceived safety of one million streetscapes. In *CVPRW*, 2014.

[36] N. Naik, R. Raskar, and C. A. Hidalgo. Cities are physical too: Using computer vision to measure the quality and impact of urban appearance. *The American Economic Review*, 106(5):128–132, 2016.

[37] J. L. Nasar. *The evaluative image of the city.* Sage Publications Thousand Oaks, CA, 1998.

[38] J. L. Nasar, B. Fisher, and M. Grannis. Proximate physical cues to fear of crime. *Landscape and urban planning*, 26(1):161–178, 1993.

[39] O. Newman. *Defensible space.* Macmillan New York, 1972.

[40] M. Oquab, L. Bottou, I. Laptev, and J. Sivic. Learning and transferring mid-level image representations using convolutional neural networks. In *CVPR*, 2014.

[41] V. Ordonez and T. L. Berg. Learning high-level judgments of urban perception. In *ECCV*, 2014.

[42] C. Pantazis. 'Fear of Crime', Vulnerability and Poverty. *British journal of criminology*, 40(3):414–436, 2000.

[43] L. Porzi, S. Rota Bulò, B. Lepri, and E. Ricci. Predicting and Understanding Urban Perception with Convolutional Neural Networks. In *ACM Multimedia*, 2015.

[44] D. Quercia, N. K. O'Hare, and H. Cramer. Aesthetic capital: what makes London look beautiful, quiet, and happy? In *ACM CSCW*, 2014.

[45] P. Salesses, K. Schechtner, and C. A. Hidalgo. The collaborative image of the city: mapping the inequality of urban perception. *PloS one*, 8(7):e68400, 2013.

[46] R. J. Sampson and S. W. Raudenbush. *Disorder in urban neighborhoods: Does it lead to crime.* US Department of Justice, Office of Justice Programs, National Institute of Justice, 2001.

[47] R. J. Sampson and S. W. Raudenbush. Seeing disorder: Neighborhood stigma and the social construction of

"broken windows". *Social psychology quarterly*, 67(4):319–342, 2004.

[48] R. J. Sampson, S. W. Raudenbush, and F. Earls. Neighborhoods and violent crime: A multilevel study of collective efficacy. *Science*, 277(5328):918–924, 1997.

[49] A. Sartori, V. Yanulevskaya, A. A. Salah, J. Uijlings, E. Bruni, and N. Sebe. Affective analysis of professional and amateur abstract paintings using statistical analysis and art theory. *ACM TiiS*, 5(2):8, 2015.

[50] K. Simonyan and A. Zisserman. Very deep convolutional networks for large-scale image recognition. *arXiv preprint arXiv:1409.1556*, 2014.

[51] J. Sivic and A. A. Efros. Urban-Scale Quantitative Visual Analysis. *Smart Cities*, page 43, 2014.

[52] R. B. Taylor and M. Hale. Testing alternative models of fear of crime. *The Journal of Criminal Law and Criminology (1973-)*, 77(1):151–189, 1986.

[53] M. Tiefelsdorf and D. A. Griffith. Semiparametric filtering of spatial autocorrelation: the eigenvector approach. *Environment and Planning A*, 39(5):1193–1221, 2007.

[54] G. R. Wekerle and C. Whitzman. *Safe cities: Guidelines for planning, design, and management.* Van Nostrand Reinhold Company, 1995.

[55] J. Q. Wilson and G. L. Kelling. Broken windows. *Critical issues in policing: Contemporary readings*, pages 395–407, 1982.

[56] M. D. Zeiler and R. Fergus. Visualizing and understanding convolutional networks. In *ECCV*, 2014.

[57] B. Zhou, A. Lapedriza, J. Xiao, A. Torralba, and A. Oliva. Learning deep features for scene recognition using places database. In *NIPS*, 2014.

Detecting Sarcasm in Multimodal Social Platforms

Rossano Schifanella
University of Turin
Corso Svizzera 185
10149, Turin, Italy
schifane@di.unito.it

Paloma de Juan
Yahoo
229 West 43rd Street
New York, NY 10036
pdjuan@yahoo-inc.com

Joel Tetreault
Yahoo
229 West 43rd Street
New York, NY 10036
tetreaul@gmail.com

Liangliang Cao
Yahoo
229 West 43rd Street
New York, NY 10036
liangliang@yahoo-inc.com

ABSTRACT

Sarcasm is a peculiar form of sentiment expression, where the surface sentiment differs from the implied sentiment. The detection of sarcasm in social media platforms has been applied in the past mainly to textual utterances where lexical indicators (such as interjections and intensifiers), linguistic markers, and contextual information (such as user profiles, or past conversations) were used to detect the sarcastic tone. However, modern social media platforms allow to create multimodal messages where audiovisual content is integrated with the text, making the analysis of a mode in isolation partial. In our work, we first study the relationship between the textual and visual aspects in multimodal posts from three major social media platforms, i.e., Instagram, Tumblr and Twitter, and we run a crowdsourcing task to quantify the extent to which images are perceived as necessary by human annotators. Moreover, we propose two different computational frameworks to detect sarcasm that integrate the textual and visual modalities. The first approach exploits visual semantics trained on an external dataset, and concatenates the semantics features with state-of-the-art textual features. The second method adapts a visual neural network initialized with parameters trained on ImageNet to multimodal sarcastic posts. Results show the positive effect of combining modalities for the detection of sarcasm across platforms and methods.

Keywords

Sarcasm; Social Media; Multimodal; Deep Learning; NLP

1. INTRODUCTION

Sarcasm is a peculiar form of sentiment expression where the surface sentiment differs from the implied sentiment.

MM '16, October 15 - 19, 2016, Amsterdam, Netherlands

ISBN 978-1-4503-3603-1/16/10... $15.00

DOI: http://dx.doi.org/10.1145/2964284.2964321

In a rubbish city with rubbish weather
#Liverpool #nofilter

Figure 1: Example of an Instagram post where the image is needed to detect the sarcasm. The observation "rubbish weather" can only been interpreted correctly by *looking* at the picture. Same holds for "rubbish city."

Merriam-Webster[1] defines sarcasm as *"the use of words that mean the opposite of what you really want to say especially in order to insult someone, to show irritation, or to be funny."* Sarcasm is a common phenomenon in social media platforms, and the automatic detection of the implied meaning of a post is a crucial task for a wide range of applications where it is important to assess the speaker's real opinion, e.g., product reviews, forums, or sentiment analysis tools.

Most approaches to sarcasm detection to date have treated the task primarily as a text categorization problem, relying on the insight that sarcastic utterances often contain lexical indicators (such as interjections and intensifiers) and other linguistic markers (such as nonveridicality and hyperbole) that signal the sarcasm. In modern online platforms, hashtags and emojis are common mechanisms to reveal the speaker's true sentiment. These purely text-based

[1] http://www.merriam-webster.com/dictionary/sarcasm

approaches have been shown to be fairly accurate across different domains [6, 13, 30, 9, 29].

However, in many occasions this text-only approach fails when contextual knowledge is needed to decode the sarcastic tone. For example, in Figure 1, "rubbish weather" is the opposite of what the image represents (i.e., beautiful weather). Without this image, the text could be interpreted as a negative comment about the weather in Liverpool. Recently, several approaches [2, 27, 17, 19, 37] have integrated contextual cues (e.g., the author's profile, author's past posts and conversations) with the in-post text, showing consistent improvements when detecting sarcasm.

Previous approaches have failed to consider the media linked to the posts as a possible source of contextual information. Tweets, for example, can have audiovisual content attached to the text. Multimodality is the combination of modes of communication (i.e., text, images, animations, sounds, etc.) with the purpose to deliver a message to a particular audience, and it is present in all major social media platforms.

In this work, we leverage the contextual information carried by visuals to decode the sarcastic tone of multimodal posts. Specifically, we consider two types of visual features with different model fusion methods for sarcasm detection. The first approach exploits visual semantics trained on an external dataset, and concatenates the semantics features with state-of-the-art text features. The second method adapts a visual neural network initialized with parameters trained on ImageNet to multimodal (text+image) sarcastic posts. In both methods, we find that visual features boost the performance of the textual models.

We summarize our main contributions as follows:

- We study the interplay between textual and visual content in sarcastic multimodal posts for three main social media platforms, i.e., Instagram, Tumblr and Twitter, and discuss a categorization of the role of images in sarcastic posts.
- We quantitatively show the contribution of visuals in detecting sarcasm through human labeling. This data will be shared with the research community.
- We are the first to propose and empirically evaluate two alternative frameworks for sarcasm detection that use both textual and visual features. We show an improvement in performance over textual baselines across platforms and methods.

We first discuss related work in Section 2. We then describe our data in Section 3, and introduce a categorization of the different roles images can play in a sarcastic post in Section 4. In the same section, we describe how we collect human judgments to build a gold set, and analyze the distribution of posts with respect to the proposed categories. Section 5 describes the details of the two methods for sarcasm detection, and Section 6 presents the experiments carried out to evaluate the frameworks, and their results. Finally, Section 7 concludes the paper, and points to future work.

2. RELATED WORK

Sarcasm as linguistic phenomenon. While the use of irony and sarcasm is well studied from its linguistic and psychological aspects [12], automatic recognition of sarcasm has become a widely researched subject in recent years due to its practical implications in social media platforms. Starting from foundational work by Tepperman et al. [32] which uses prosodic, spectral (average pitch, pitch slope), and contextual (laughter or response to questions) cues to automatically detect sarcasm in a spoken dialogue, initial approaches mainly addressed linguistic and sentiment features to classify sarcastic utterances. Davidov et al. [6] proposed a semi-supervised approach to classify tweets and Amazon products reviews with the use of syntactic and pattern-based features. Tsur et al. [34] focus on product reviews and try to identify sarcastic sentences looking at the patterns of high-frequency and content words. González-Ibáñez et al. [13] study the role of lexical (unigrams and dictionary-based) and pragmatic features such as the presence of positive and negative emoticons and the presence of replies in tweets. Riloff et al. [30] present a bootstrapping algorithm that automatically learns lists of positive sentiment phrases and negative situation phrases from sarcastic tweets. They show that identifying contrasting contexts yields improved recall for sarcasm recognition. More recently, Ghosh et al. [9] propose a reframing of sarcasm detection as a type of word sense disambiguation problem: given an utterance and a target word, identify whether the sense of the target word is literal or sarcastic.

Sarcasm as contextual phenomenon. Recently it has been observed that sarcasm requires some shared knowledge between the speaker and the audience; it is a profoundly contextual phenomenon [2]. Bamman et al. [2] use information about the authors, their relationship to the audience and the immediate communicative context to improve prediction accuracy. Rajadesingan et al. [27] adopt psychological and behavioral studies on when, why, and how sarcasm is expressed in communicative acts to develop a behavioral model and a set of computational features that merge user's current and past tweets as historical context. Joshi et al. [17] propose a framework based on the linguistic theory of context incongruity and introduce inter-sentential incongruity for sarcasm detection by considering the previous post in the discussion thread. Khattri et al. [19] present a quantitative evidence that historical tweets by an author can provide additional context for sarcasm detection. They exploit the author's past sentiment on the entities in a tweet to detect the sarcastic intent. Wang at al. [37] focus on message-level sarcasm detection on Twitter using a context-based model that leverages conversations, such as chains of tweets. They introduce a complex classification model that works over an entire tweet sequence and not on one tweet at a time. On the same direction, our work is based on the integration between linguistic and contextual features extracted from the analysis of visuals embedded in multimodal posts.

Sarcasm beyond text. Modern social media platforms allow to create multimodal forms of communication where audiovisual content integrates the textual utterance. Previous work [35] studied how different types of visuals are used in relation to irony in written discourse, and which pictorial elements contribute to the identification of verbal irony. Most scholars who looked at the relationship between verbal irony and images limited themselves to studying visual markers [1]. Usually a visual marker is either used to illustrate the literal meaning, or it may also exhibit incongruence with the literal evaluation of an ironic utterance (incongruence between the literal and intended evaluation). Following Kennedy [11], the image itself is usually consid-

Platform	Text	Images
IG	Optional (up to 2,200 chars)	1
TU (photo)	Optional	1-10
TU (text)	Required	0 or more
TW	Required (up to 140 chars)	0 or more

Table 1: Text and image limitations.

Platform	#Posts	w/Text	w/Images	w/Both
IG	517,229	99.74%	100%	99.74%
TU	63,067	94.22%	45.99%	40.22%
TW	20,629	100%	7.56%	7.56%

Table 2: Presence of textual and visual components.

ered not ironic; however, it may sometimes be important in deciding whether a verbal utterance is ironic or not. According to Verstraten [36], two types of elements play a role in the process of meaning-giving in the visual domain of static images. These include the *mise en scène* and *cinematographic* techniques. The mise en scène is concerned with the question of who and/or what is shown, cinematography deals with the question of how something is shown. Despite the similarities in the intent, our work shows few novel points: first of all, we analyze a large sample of non-curated posts from three different social media platforms, while past work focuses mainly on curated content like advertisements, cartoons, or art. Moreover, to the best of our knowledge, we propose the first computational model that incorporates computer vision techniques to the automatic sarcasm detection pipeline.

Making sense of images. Recently, a number of research studies were devoted to combine visual and textual information, motivated by the progress of deep learning. Some approaches [21, 8] pursue a joint space for visual and semantic embedding, others consider how to generate captions to match the image content [24, 23], or how to capture the sentiment conveyed by an image [4, 38]. The most similar approach to our work is that of [31] which investigates the fusion of textual and image information to understand metaphors. A key aspect of our work is that it captures the relation between the visual and the textual dimensions as a whole, e.g., the utterance is not a mere description of an image, while in previous studies text is generally adopted to depict or model the content of an image.

3. DATA

To investigate the role images play in sarcasm detection, we collect data from three major social platforms that allow to post both text and images, namely Instagram (IG), Tumblr (TU) and Twitter (TW), using their available public APIs. Each of these platforms is originally meant for different purposes regarding the type of media to be shared. Whereas Instagram is an image-centric platform, Twitter is a microblogging network. Tumblr allows users to post different types of content, including "text" or "photo". Regardless of the post type, images (one or more) can be added to textual posts, and captions can be included in photo posts. The text and image restrictions and limitations for each platform are presented in Table 1.

The three platforms allow users to use hashtags to annotate the content, by embedding them in the text (Instagram, Twitter), or by adding them through a separate field (Tumblr). To collect positive (i.e., sarcastic) examples, we follow a hashtag-based approach by retrieving posts that include the tag *sarcasm* or *sarcastic*. This is a technique extensively used to collect sarcastic examples [9]. Additionally, and for all platforms, we filter out posts that are not in English, and remove retweets (Twitter) and reblogs (Tumblr) to keep the original content only and avoid duplicates.

Table 2 shows the distribution of posts with text, image(s), or both for each of the three platforms. Instagram is the platform where the the textual and visual modalities are most used in conjunction; in fact, almost the totality of posts have a caption accompanying the image. In contrast, less than 8% of the posts on Twitter contain images. Among the 63K Tumblr posts, 56.96% are of type "text", and 43.04% are of type "photo". This means that most of the photo posts contain also text (similar to Instagram, but without the limitation on the number of images), but very few of the text posts contain images (similar to Twitter, but without the character limitation).

Filtering the data.

To clean up the data and build our final dataset we apply a series of four filters commonly used in literature [13, 6, 27]. First, we discard posts that do no contain any images, or whose images are no longer available by the time we collect the data; we then discard posts that contain mentions (@username) or external links (i.e., URLs that do not contain the platform name, or "t.co" or "twimg.com", in the case of Twitter), as additional information (e.g., conversational history, news story) could be required to understand the context of the message. We also discard posts where *sarcasm* or *sarcastic* is a regular word (not a hashtag), or a hashtag that is part of a sentence (i.e., if it is followed by any regular words), as we are not interested in messages that explicitly address sarcasm (e.g., "I speak fluent sarcasm."). Finally, we discard posts that might contain memes or *ecards* (e.g., tag set contains *someecards*), and posts whose text contains less than four regular words.

Final dataset. We randomly sample 10,000 posts from each platform to build our final dataset. Given the limitations of its public API, and the fact that less than 8% of the sarcastic posts have both text and images, only 2,005 were available for Twitter. We further clean up the data by removing internal links and the tags that we used to collect the samples (*sarcasm* and *sarcastic*). These posts are composed of two main aspects: a *textual* and a *visual* component. When we speak about the textual component, we are referring not only to the regular words that form the message, but also to *emojis* and *hashtags* that might be part of that message. These three elements (words, emojis and hashtags) are crucial for the interpretation of the post: while regular words are generally used to present the literal meaning, emojis and hashtags are commonly used to reveal the speaker's intended sentiment [16], or to share contextual cues with the audience to help decode the sarcasm.

Table 3 shows the average number of regular words, emojis and tags (after having removed *sarcasm/sarcastic*) per post. Due to its tight character limitation (which also accounts for the hashtags), Twitter is the platform with the shortest text and the lowest number of tags per post. While

Platform	#Words	#Emojis	#Tags
IG	10.77	0.37	7.44
TU	24.75	0.21	7.00
TW	9.45	0.29	1.96

Table 3: Average number of words, emojis and tags.

Tumblr posts are the longest, the average number of tags is similar to that of Instagram, which has in turn the highest tag-to-word ratio. Indeed, Instagram users seem to express heavily through hashtags, especially compared to Twitter users, whose posts have a similar average word count. Both platforms also have a similar emoji-to-word ratio, which is much lower on Tumblr. The fact that there is a character limitation for both Instagram and Twitter might justify the usage of emojis, which are compact representations of concepts and reactions that would be much more verbose if expressed in words.

Finally, we collect 10,000 negative examples from each platform (2,005 from Twitter, to keep the dataset balanced) by randomly sampling posts that do **not** contain *sarcasm* or *sarcastic* in either the text or the tag set. These negative posts are subject to the same processing described above, when applicable. To verify that there are no relevant topical differences between the positive and the negative sets that could correlate with the presence/absence of sarcastic cues, we manually examined a sample of positive and negative posts from each platform. We did not observe such differences; however, we did find some recurring topics in the positive set, such as weather, food, fashion, etc., but these topics were also found in the negative set, only along with non-sarcastic observations (e.g., a picture of a greasy slice of pizza would be captioned as "healthy" in the positive set, but as "unhealthy" in the negative set). This might indicate that the range of topics in the positive set is more limited, but there is a clear overlap with those in the negative set.

4. CHARACTERIZING THE ROLE OF IMAGES IN SARCASTIC POSTS

As presented in Section 1, there are two main elements to a sarcastic utterance: the *context* and the *meaning* or *sentiment*. Detecting sarcasm—at a human level—involves evaluating to what extent the intended meaning corresponds to a declared or expected response. If this literal meaning does not agree with the one implied, the utterance will be perceived as sarcastic. In the following sections, we will analyze what role text (i.e., words, emojis and tags) and images play in the conception of sarcasm.

4.1 Defining a Categorization

To understand what role images play with respect to these two elements, three of the authors independently annotate a set of 100 randomly sampled positive posts from each platform. The question we are looking to answer is: *Is the image **necessary** to find the post sarcastic?* To answer that, we first identify the posts whose sarcastic nature can be positively determined by just looking at the text. This text, as explained in Section 3, can include words, emojis and tags. In many examples, emojis reveal the intended sentiment (in contrast to the literal sentiment presented in the regular text). Hashtags are generally useful to provide context, but can also be used to expose the sentiment. Regardless of whether the sarcastic tone is clear from the text or not, the image can still provide useful clues to understand the intended meaning. The posts where the intended meaning can **not** be inferred from the text alone are precisely what we are looking for. In these cases, the image turns out to be necessary to interpret the post, providing a depiction of the context, or visual clues to unravel the implied sentiment.

Does the **IMAGE** help?	Is the **TEXT** enough? Yes	Is the **TEXT** enough? No
Yes	The text is clearly sarcastic; the image provides additional cues for better interpretability and engagement.	Both are needed to interpret the post. The clues to understand the intended meaning can be textual or visual.
No	The text is clearly sarcastic; the image does not provide any added value.	Post is **not** sarcastic.

Table 4: Roles of text and image in sarcastic posts.

Table 4 summarizes the four possible roles of text and image. We will refer to the category that represents the combination of the two cases to the left as `Text Only`, as the text from the posts belonging to it should be enough to understand the implied sarcasm. Figures 2(a) and 2(b) are instances of this category. The posts from the top-left case represent a subset of this category, where the image is somewhat redundant, but could replace or augment some of the textual clues. For instance, the image in Figure 2(b) would have been necessary if the tags *snow* and *winter* were not part of the text. In this case, also the emojis reveal the implied sentiment, which makes it unnecessary to infer that snow on a spring day is not "beautiful" or "nice", and that people are not supposed to wear shorts in such weather.

The top right case corresponds to the category that we will call `Text+Image`, where both modalities are required to understand the intended meaning. Figure 2(c) belongs to this category: the image depicts the context that the text refers to. Rather than a sentiment, the text presents an observation ("crowds of people") that is the opposite of what is shown in the picture (the room is empty). It is worth noting that, regardless of the category, many times the image itself contains text. In this case, the motivation to use an image instead of plain text is generally to provide additional information about the context of this text (e.g., a chat conversation, a screenshot, a street sign, and so on). Figure 2(a) is an example of this case.

4.2 Building a Ground Truth for Sarcasm

The data collection process described in Section 3 relies on the ability of the authors to self-annotate their posts as sarcastic using hashtags. Training a sarcasm detector on noisy data is a commonly used approach in literature, especially when that data comes from social media platforms. However, what the audience perceives as sarcastic is not always aligned with the actual intention of the speakers. Our goal is to create a curated dataset of multimodal posts whose sarcastic nature has been agreed on by both the author and the readers, and where both the textual and visual components are required to decode the sarcastic tone. To do that,

(a) (b) (c)

Figure 2: Examples of sarcastic posts.

we use CrowdFlower,[2] a large crowdsourcing platform that distributes small, discrete tasks to online contributors. The two goals of this annotation task are: 1) characterize the distribution of posts with respect to the categories defined in Section 4.1, and evaluate the impact of visuals as a source for context for humans; and 2) identify truly sarcastic posts by validating the authors' choice to tag them as such.

Task interface and setup. We focus only on the two main categories of interest, `Text Only` and `Text+Image`, and create two independent tasks. In the first task, only the text (including the tags and emojis) is shown to the annotator, along with the question "Is this text sarcastic?". The goal is to identify which posts belong to the `Text Only` category, i.e., posts where the textual component is enough to decode the sarcasm, and the image has a complementary role. We select 1,000 positive posts for this task, using the filters defined in Section 3. These posts are randomly sampled from the original sources, with no overlap with the dataset presented in that Section. We collect 5 annotations for each post, where the answer to the question can be "Yes" (text is sarcastic), "No" (text is **not** sarcastic) or "I don't know".

For the second experiment, we take only those posts that have been marked as non-sarcastic by the majority of the annotators on the first task (i.e., we discard the posts that belong to the `Text Only` category). Now we present both the textual and visual components, with the question "Is this post sarcastic?", and the same possible answers as before. Again, we collect 5 annotations per post.

The reason we run two independent experiments is to keep the tasks as simple as possible, and to guarantee that the judgment of the annotators is not affected by the knowledge that some information is missing. On the first task, annotators are not aware that the posts originally had one or more images, and are asked to judge them under that impression (same as a text-only based detector would do). If we did a two-step experiment instead, annotators would learn about the missing image(s) after having annotated the very first post, which would invite them to answer "I don't know" based on that indication. We run these experiments for both Instagram and Tumblr. Given the limited amount of data that we were able to collect for Twitter, and the fact that only a small percentage of the posts are actually multimodal, we do not build a gold set for this platform.

Quality control and inter-rater agreement. *Test Questions* (also called *Gold Standard* in CrowdFlower jargon) are curated job units that are used to test and track the contributor's performance and filter out bots or unreliable contributors. To access the task, workers are first asked to correctly annotate a set of *Test Questions* in an initial *Quiz Mode* screen, and their performance is tracked throughout the experiment with *Test Questions* randomly inserted in every task, disguised as normal units.

Judgments from contributors whose accuracy on the *Test Questions* is less than 78% are discarded and marked as not trusted.

Task	Matching%		Fleiss' κ	
	IG	TU	IG	TU
`Text Only (task 1)`	80.36	76.11	0.38	0.28
`Text+Image (task 2)`	74.65	86.40	0.21	0.23

Table 5: Inter-rater agreement.

To assess the quality of the collected data, we measure the level of agreement between annotators (see Table 5). *Matching%* is the percentage of matching judgments per object. For both experiments, the agreement is solid, with an average value around of 80%. However, the ratio of matching votes does not capture entirely the extent to which agreement emerges. We therefore compute the standard *Fleiss' κ*, a statistical measure for assessing the reliability of the agreement between a fixed number of raters. Consistently, the *Fleiss' κ* shows a Fair level [22] of agreement where, as expected, the second experiment reaches a lower agreement due to its intrinsic subjectivity and difficulty, even for human annotators [3].

Results. Table 6 shows the distribution of the 1,000 posts with respect to the categories described in Section 4.1. For over 60% of the posts (62.20% for Instagram, 76.40% for Tumblr) the text alone (task 1) is **not** enough to determine whether they are sarcastic or not. However, when those posts are shown with their visual component (task 2), more than half (60.13% for Instagram, 58.25% for Tumblr) are actually annotated as sarcastic, i.e., these posts were **mis-**

[2]http://www.crowdflower.com

Category	IG	TU
Not sarcastic	24.8%	31.9%
Text Only	37.8%	23.6%
Text+Image	**37.4%**	**44.5%**
D-80	19.1%	19.7%
D-100	8.6%	14.1%

Table 6: Percentage of posts in each category. The D-80 and D-100 subclasses refer to, respectively, posts where at least 80% or the totality of the annotators agree on the sarcastic nature of the post.

classified as non-sarcastic by the annotators on the first task, so the contribution of the image is crucial. It is interesting to note that a non-negligible fraction of the data (24.80% for Instagram, 31.90% for Tumblr) was not perceived as sarcastic by the majority of the annotators, which highlights the existing gap between the authors' interpretation of sarcasm and that of the readers, and the amount of noise we can expect in the dataset. In summary, the majority of the annotators found that both the text and the image are necessary to correctly evaluate the tone of the post in more than one third of the examples (37.40% for Instagram, 44.50% for Tumblr). Among these, 51.07% of the Instagram posts and 44.27% of the Tumblr posts were agreed to be sarcastic by at least 80% of the annotators (D-80), and 22.99% (IG) and 31.69% (TU) were unanimously declared sarcastic (D-100).

5. AUTOMATED METHODS FOR SARCASM DETECTION

We investigate two automatic methods for multimodal sarcasm detection. The first, a linear Support Vector Machine (SVM) approach, has been commonly used in prior work, though this prior work has relied on features extracted mainly from the text of the post (or set of posts). In our proposal, we combine a number of NLP features with visual features extracted from the image. The second approach relies on deep learning to fuse a deep network based representation of the image with unigrams as textual input. For both of these approaches, we evaluate the individual contributions of the respective textual and visual features, along with their fusion, in Section 6.

5.1 SVM Approach

For all experiments within this approach, we train a binary classification model using the sklearn toolkit[3] with its default settings.[4]

NLP Features. Our goal here is to replicate the prior art in developing a strong baseline composed of NLP features from which to investigate the impact that images have in detecting sarcasm. We adopt features commonly found in the literature: lexical features which measure aspects of word usage and frequency, features which measure the sentiment and subjectivity of the post, and word sequences (n-grams). We also make use of word embeddings, which has seen limited application to this task, save for a few works, such as [10], but has been used as a strong baseline in the sister task of sentiment analysis [7]. Finally, we select some of our best performing features and create a combination feature class. A description of each class is listed below:

- **lexical**: average word length, average word log-frequency according to the Google 1TB N-gram corpus,[5] number of contractions in sentence, average formality score as computed in [26].
- **subjectivity**: subjectivity and sentiment scores as computed by the TextBlob module,[6] number of passive constructions, number of hedge words, number of first person pronouns, number of third person pronouns.
- **n-grams**: unigrams and bigrams represented as one-hot features.
- **word2vec**: average of word vectors using pre-trained word2vec embeddings [25]. OOV words are skipped.
- **combination**: n-grams, word2vec and readability features (these include length of post in words and characters, as well as the Flesch-Kincaid Grade level score [20]).

Text is tokenized using nltk.[7] In addition, we treat hashtags in Instagram and Twitter, and tags in Tumblr, as well as emojis, as part of the text on which the features are derived from.

Visual Semantics Features (VSF). A key module to detect sarcasm is to understand the semantics in images. We employ the visual semantics models from Yahoo Flickr Creative Commons 100M (YFCC100M) [33], which include a diverse collection of complex real-world scenes, ranging from 200,000 street-life-blogged photos by photographer Andy Nystrom to snapshots of daily life, holidays, and events. Specifically, the semantics models were built with an off-the-shelf deep convolutional neural network using the Caffe framework [14], and the penultimate layer of the convolutional neural network output as the image-feature representation for training classifiers for 1,570 concepts which are popular in YFCC100M. Each concept classifier is a binary support vector machine, for which positive examples were manually labeled based on targeted search/group results, while the negatives drew negative examples from a general pool. The classifiers cover a diverse collection of visual semantics in social media, such as people, animals, objects, foods, architecture, and scenery, and will provide a good representation of image contents. Examples of concepts include terms such as "head", "nsfw", "outside", and "monochrome". In our experiments, we use the output of the content classifiers as one-hot features for the SVM regression model. Essentially, if a concept is detected, no matter what its associated confidence score, we treat it as a one-hot feature.

Multimodal Fusion. We concatenate the textual and visual features into a long vector, and once again use the linear SVM to train the fusion model. Previous research suggests that linear SVMs are fit for text classification [15], and our experiments find that linear SVM works very robustly to combine different kinds of features.

[3]http://scikit-learn.org/

[4]We acknowledge that performance could be improved by experimenting with different parameters and kernels, however, our focus is not on optimizing for the best sarcasm detection system, but rather to construct a framework with which to show that visual features can complement textual features.

[5]https://catalog.ldc.upenn.edu/LDC2006T13

[6]https://textblob.readthedocs.org/en/dev/

[7]http://www.nltk.org/

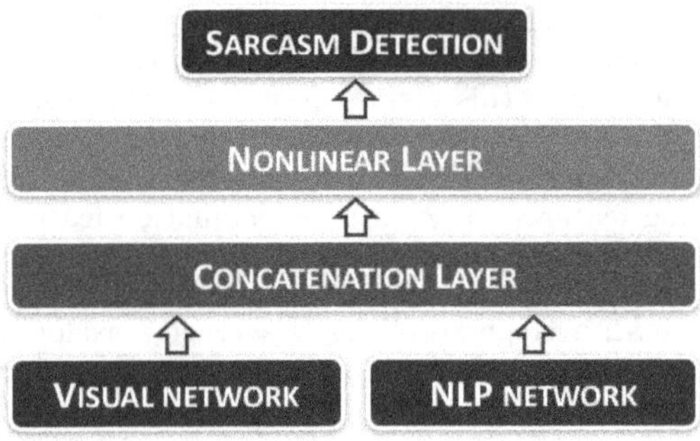

Figure 3: Network structure of our model. The visual network in the figure is initialized with the model weights in [5] trained on ImageNet.

5.2 Deep Learning Approach

Adapted Visual Representation (AVR). The visual semantics classifiers described in the previous section are limited by a fixed vocabulary. To get a stronger visual representation, we follow the work in [28] and [18] that adopt a deep neural network. We borrow a model trained on ImageNet exactly from [5], which is based on roughly one million images annotated with 1,000 object classes. There are originally seven layers in the model, but we remove the last layer of 1,000 neurons which correspond to the objects in ImageNet. The second to last layer has 4,096 neurons, which we will use to fine-tune with sarcastic and non-sarcastic data.

Textual Features. If we were to use all the NLP features in Section 5.1, our deep learning framework would quickly overfit given the limited size of the training set. As a consequence, a subset of the textual features were used in this fusion method. The NLP network is a two two layer perceptron based on unigrams only. The size of the first layer of the NLP network is the size of the unigram vocabulary for every platform. We employ a hidden layer in the NLP network with 512 hidden neurons, which is comparable with the number of neurons in the AVR.

Multimodal Fusion via Deep Network Adaptation. Figure 3 illustrates the neural network adaptation framework. We initialize a network with fixed image filters from the ImageNet model and random weights in other layers, and adapt it to our data. This adaption framework works with the deep CNN trained on ImageNet. The concatenation layer has 4,608 neurons. We use the rectify function as the activation function on all the nonlinear layers except for the last layer, which uses softmax over the two classes (sarcastic vs. non-sarcastic). Since in practice it is hard to find the global minimum in a deep neural network, we use Nesterov Stochastic Gradient Decent with a small random batch (size = 128). We finish training after 30 epochs.

6. EVALUATION

We evaluate our two methods under the same conditions, and with two different evaluation settings. For the first evaluation, models are developed on the data as described in Section 3, where we train on 50% of the data and evaluate on the remaining 50%. Please recall that the three data sets are evenly split between sarcastic and non-sarcastic posts, with the Instagram and Tumblr data sets containing a total of 20K posts each, and Twitter totaling 4,050 posts. We call this the **Silver Evaluation**, since the data is dependent on the authors correctly labeling their posts as sarcastic. As we saw in Table 6, 24.8% and 31.8% of Instagram and Tumblr posts marked by the authors as sarcastic are actually not sarcastic. For both the SVM and deep learning methods, we show results for *Text-Only*, *Image-Only* and the fusion of both modalities.

Next, we evaluate the respective Instagram and Tumblr models on the crowd-curated data sets in Section 4.2 (henceforth **Gold Evaluation**). Unlike the evaluation on the silver sets, the models are tested on re-judged data, and thus are of much higher quality, though there are fewer examples.

We use accuracy as our evaluation metric, and the baseline accuracy is 50% since all sets are evenly split.

6.1 Fusion with SVM

6.1.1 Evaluation on Silver Set

Feature Set	IG	TU	TW
lexical	56.7	54.3	57.8
subjectivity	61.7	59.9	58.3
1,2-grams	80.7	80.0	78.6
word2vec	74.9	73.6	75.3
combination	81.4	80.9	**80.5**
VSF only	68.8	65.7	61.7
n-gram + VSF	81.7	80.6	79.0
combination + VSF	**82.3**	**81.0**	80.0

Table 7: Silver Set evaluation using SVM fusion.

We first evaluate the contribution of the individual NLP features from Section 5.1 on the three data sets, as shown in the first main block in Table 7. The top individual feature is n-gram (1- and 2-grams), roughly performing at close to 80% accuracy across all data sets. In fact, even though we use three disparate data sets, the performance figures for each feature are consistently the same as the the ranking of the features. This may suggest that users do not alter the way they use sarcasm across platforms, though the best way of testing this hypothesis would be to investigate whether models trained on one platform, e.g., Twitter, can approximate the performance found on the other platforms, e.g., Instagram, when models are trained on native data. Finally, merging several of the feature classes into one (*combination*) yields the best performance, exceeding 80% for all data sets.

Using only the visual semantics features (VSF) yields an accuracy around 65% across the data sets. This is more than 15 points lower than the best NLP models; however, we were surprised that such a simple feature class actually outperformed the lexical and subjectivity features, both of which have been used in prior NLP work for the sarcasm detection task.

Finally, we combine the visual semantics features with the two best performing NLP features, i.e., n-grams and the combination feature class (last two rows of Table 7). For all the three data sets, the model with n-grams + VFS outperformed the model solely trained on n-grams by a small margin. However, it was not better than using the combination features. When combining the visual features with the combination features, we achieve the highest performance in Instagram (82.3%) and Tumblr (81.0%). In Twitter, the fusion produces the second highest performance (80.0%) to the 80.5% yielded by combination features only. These results show that including simple, noisy image-related features can improve sarcasm detection, albeit by a small margin.

6.1.2 Evaluation on Gold Set

Next, we investigate how well our models perform on the curated gold sets in Instagram and Tumblr. For the sake of simplicity, we focus our NLP evaluation on just the two top performing feature classes: n-grams and combination.

Feature Set	D-50 N=374	D-80 N=191	D-100 N=86
1,2-grams	81.7	81.9	80.2
combination	81.7	82.5	80.2
VSF only	75.7	72.8	68.0
1,2-grams + VSF	**86.6**	**87.7**	**83.7**
comb. + VSF	84.8	85.3	80.8

Table 8: SVM evaluation on Instagram Gold Sets.

Feature Set	D-50 N=445	D-80 N=197	D-100 N=141
1,2-grams	88.3	84.8	84.0
combination	**88.8**	86.0	84.4
VSF only	70.7	73.1	73.8
1,2-grams + VSF	88.5	**87.8**	**89.7**
comb. + VSF	88.0	87.1	**89.7**

Table 9: SVM evaluation on Tumblr Gold Sets.

Table 8 shows the results for the different modalities in Instagram. For the NLP features, the combination and n-gram are tied for the 50% and 100% agreement conditions (D-50 and D-100), while combination narrowly outperforms its counterpart in the 80% condition (D-80). As in the previous silver results, using the VSF only causes a loss in performance of nearly 15 points. The best results come from fusing n-grams with VSF, yielding a performance improvement of about 5% on all three agreement levels. Interestingly, while combination + VSF was generally the best feature in the silver evaluation, it is the second best here.

The Gold Tumblr results in Table 9 show a similar pattern with Table 8: the combination features outperform the n-gram features by a small margin across all three agreement levels, and only using VSF results in a performance loss of around 15 points accuracy compared to combination. We see the best performance when fusing the NLP and VSF features. At the 80% agreement level, n-gram + VSF yields a performance of 87.8%, which outperforms the best non-fusion performance by 1.8 points (86.0%). At the 100% agreement level, both fusion sets perform at 89.7%, a 5% point improvement. However, at the lower agreement rate (50%), the best performing fusion method just narrowly misses the combination method (88.5% to 88.8%).

The main message from both the silver and gold evaluations is that incorporating simple features which describe the image in a very traditional framework can improve performance. In general, the best performance comes not from fusing VSF with combination features, but rather with n-grams. We speculate that this may be due to the mismatch between the silver and gold sets. We do note that in some cases the performance improvement was small or non-existent. This is partially due to the noisiness of the data, the high baseline set by the NLP features, and also the accuracy of the VSF features, which can be viewed as hypotheses of what the classifier believes is present in the photo, even if weakly present.

6.2 Fusion with Deep Network Adaptation

Next, we evaluate our deep learning approach on our silver and gold sets. We additionally evaluate the model with image (AVR) and text (unigram) features only, for which the concatenation layer (see Figure 3) still exists but has no effect with single modality input. The three models use the same learning rates.

6.2.1 Evaluation on Silver Set

Feature Set	IG	TU	TW
1-grams	71.0	65.3	54.1
AVR only	73.8	69.2	68.7
1-grams + AVR	**74.2**	**70.9**	**69.7**

Table 10: Silver Set evaluation using DNA fusion.

Table 10 shows the the evaluation on the silver set. It is easy to see that fusing the textual and image signals together provides the best performance across all three sets, ranging from 74.2% in Instagram to 69.7% in Twitter. That confirms our hypothesis that the visual aspect plays a role in the detection of sarcasm.

Another interesting phenomenon is that the image-only network outperforms the visual semantics features consistently in all three platforms: 73.8% vs. 68.8% in Instagram, 69.2% vs. 65.7% in Tumblr, and 68.7% vs. 61.7% in Twitter. This suggests that the adapted deep CNN better captures the diversity of sarcastic images. On the other hand, our text-based network is worse than the text models using SVM. The reason is mainly because our text network does not use bigrams or higher dimensional features. Since the visual semantics features are not fine-tuned, the simpler fusion by SVM method does not overfit the training set. As a result, all state-of-the-art NLP features described in Section 5.1 can be used in this model.

Among the three platforms, the performance in Twitter is lower than in the other two. We believe that this is mainly due to the small amount of training data (2,000 posts), which is an issue for deep learning. Also, given that Twitter is mostly a textual platform (especially compared to the more image-centric Instagram and Tumblr), the weaker textual baseline seems to fail to capture the nuances of sarcasm used in this platform.

6.2.2 Evaluation on Gold Set

Feature Set	D-50 N=374	D-80 N=191	D-100 N=86
1-grams	69.7	67.7	63.1
AVR only	77.0	74.6	74.8
1-grams + AVR	**77.8**	**78.4**	**77.6**

Table 11: DNA evaluation on Instagram Gold Sets.

Our gold results show a similar pattern. In the Tumblr set, the fusion of text and image yields the best performance

Feature Set	D-50 N=445	D-80 N=197	D-100 N=141
1-grams	68.4	65.8	64.6
AVR only	75.8	74.6	**75.5**
1-grams + AVR	**77.6**	**75.6**	74.7

Table 12: DNA evaluation on Tumblr Gold Sets.

over D-50 and D-80, but is narrowly behind just using the image on D-100. In the Instagram set, the fusion of text and images yields the best performance in all three platforms. Since the text feature is limited, the performance of deep network adaptation is not as competitive as the SVM based fusion method. However, we think the performance of deep neural network adaption will be improved with more training examples.

7. CONCLUSIONS

To the best of our knowledge, this work represents the first empirical investigation on the impact of images for sarcasm detection in social media. In particular, we first investigate the role of images, and quantitatively show that humans use visuals as situational context to decode the sarcastic tone of a post. The collected and annotated data will be shared with the research community. Second, we show that automatic methods for sarcasm detection can be improved by taking visual information into account. Finally, while most previous work has focused on the study of textual utterances on Twitter, our research shows breadth by tackling two other popular social media platforms: Instagram and Tumblr.

We propose two types of multimodal fusion frameworks to integrate the visual and textual components, and we evaluate them across three social media platforms with heterogeneous characteristics. With the use of visual semantics features, we observe an improved performance for the noisy dataset in the case of Instagram (the most image-centric platform), while the impact of images in Tumblr and Twitter was not perceived as relevant. We argue that this behavior is due to their text-centric nature. In the case of curated data though, we observe higher predictive accuracy across all the platforms, and across almost all of the agreement levels, which suggests that the visual component plays an important role when human judgments are involved.

By using deep network adaptation, we show a consistent increment in performance across the three platforms. Also in this case, Instagram was the platform that reached the highest accuracy. We have pointed out the weak performance of the textual features used in the deep learning approach. The challenges that prevent us from using more advanced textual features (such as those used in the SVM model) are two-fold: 1) given the limited size of the training set, the network adaptation method suffers from overfitting; adding new features does not help when the fusion network can get almost perfect accuracy on the training set; and 2) a higher dimensionality brings difficulties for a fast neural network training due to the limitations of the GPU memory. Collecting more training data should, at the very least, address the overfitting issue.

Images can be thought of as another form of contextual clue, much like the role of previous tweets by a user or the overall sarcasm levels of a discussion thus far. In our future work, we wish to build a model which integrates all these contextual clues within our framework to assess which ones have the largest impact per platform. We are also interested in including visual sentiment frameworks in the evaluation of the sarcastic tone.

8. ACKNOWLEDGMENTS

This work is partially supported by the project "ExceptionOWL: Nonmonotonic Extensions of Description Logics and OWL for defeasible inheritance with exceptions", Progetti di Ateneo Università degli Studi di Torino and Compagnia di San Paolo, call 2014, line "Excellent (young) PI".

9. REFERENCES

[1] S. Attardo, J. Eisterhold, J. Hay, and I. Poggi. Multimodal markers of irony and sarcasm. *Humor-international Journal of Humor Research*, 16:243–260, 2003.

[2] D. Bamman and N. A. Smith. Contextualized sarcasm detection on twitter. In M. Cha, C. Mascolo, and C. Sandvig, editors, *Proc. of the Ninth Int. Conference on Web and Social Media, ICWSM*, pages 574–577. AAAI Press, 2015.

[3] F. Barbieri, H. Saggion, and F. Ronzano. Modelling sarcasm in twitter, a novel approach. In *Proc. of the Workshop on Computational Approaches to Subjectivity, Sentiment and Social Media Analysis*, pages 50–58, Baltimore, Maryland, June 2014. Association for Computational Linguistics.

[4] D. Borth, T. Chen, R. Ji, and S.-F. Chang. Sentibank: Large-scale ontology and classifiers for detecting sentiment and emotions in visual content. In *Proc. of the ACM Int. Conference on Multimedia*, MM '13, pages 459–460, New York, NY, USA, 2013. ACM.

[5] K. Chatfield, K. Simonyan, A. Vedaldi, and A. Zisserman. Return of the devil in the details: delving deep into convolutional nets. In *BMVC*, 2014.

[6] D. Davidov, O. Tsur, and A. Rappoport. Semi-supervised recognition of sarcastic sentences in twitter and amazon. In *Proc. of the Conference on Computational Natural Language Learning*, CoNLL '10, pages 107–116, Stroudsburg, PA, USA, 2010. Association for Computational Linguistics.

[7] M. Faruqui and C. Dyer. Non-distributional word vector representations. In *Proc. of the Annual Meeting of the Association for Computational Linguistics (ACL)*, volume 2, pages 464–469, Beijing, China, July 2015. Association for Computational Linguistics.

[8] A. Frome, G. Corrado, J. Shlens, S. Bengio, J. Dean, M. Ranzato, and T. Mikolov. Devise: A deep visual-semantic embedding model. In *Advances In Neural Information Processing Systems, NIPS*, 2013.

[9] D. Ghosh, W. Guo, and S. Muresan. Sarcastic or not: Word embeddings to predict the literal or sarcastic meaning of words. In L. Màrquez, C. Callison-Burch, J. Su, D. Pighin, and Y. Marton, editors, *EMNLP*, pages 1003–1012. The Association for Computational Linguistics, 2015.

[10] D. Ghosh, W. Guo, and S. Muresan. Sarcastic or not: Word embeddings to predict the literal or sarcastic meaning of words. In *Proc. of the Conference on Empirical Methods in Natural Language Processing*, pages 1003–1012, Lisbon, Portugal, September 2015. Association for Computational Linguistics.

[11] R. Gibbs. *The Cambridge Handbook of Metaphor and Thought.* Cambridge Handbooks in Psychology. Cambridge University Press, 2008.

[12] R. Gibbs and H. Colston. *Irony in Language and Thought: A Cognitive Science Reader.* Lawrence Erlbaum Associates, 2007.

[13] R. González-Ibáñez, S. Muresan, and N. Wacholder. Identifying sarcasm in twitter: A closer look. In *Proc. of the Annual Meeting of the Association for Computational Linguistics (ACL)*, volume 2 of *IILT '11*, pages 581–586, Stroudsburg, PA, USA, 2011. Association for Computational Linguistics.

[14] Y. Jia, E. Shelhamer, J. Donahue, S. Karayev, J. Long, R. Girshick, S. Guadarrama, and T. Darrell. Caffe: Convolutional architecture for fast feature embedding. *arXiv preprint arXiv:1408.5093*, 2014.

[15] T. Joachims. Text categorization with suport vector machines: Learning with many relevant features. In *Proceedings of the 10th European Conference on Machine Learning*, ECML '98, pages 137–142, London, UK, UK, 1998. Springer-Verlag.

[16] A. Joshi, P. Bhattacharyya, and M. J. Carman. Automatic sarcasm detection: A survey. *CoRR*, abs/1602.03426, 2016.

[17] A. Joshi, V. Sharma, and P. Bhattacharyya. Harnessing context incongruity for sarcasm detection. In *Proc. of the Annual Meeting of the Association for Computational Linguistics (ACL)*, volume 2, pages 757–762. The Association for Computer Linguistics, 2015.

[18] S. Karayev, A. Hertzmann, H. Winnemoeller, A. Agarwala, and T. Darrell. Recognizing image style. *BMVC*, 2014.

[19] A. Khattri, A. Joshi, P. Bhattacharyya, and M. Carman. Your sentiment precedes you: Using an author's historical tweets to predict sarcasm. In *Proc. of the Workshop on Computational Approaches to Subjectivity, Sentiment and Social Media Analysis*, pages 25–30, Lisboa, Portugal, September 2015. Association for Computational Linguistics.

[20] J. P. Kincaid, R. P. Fishburne Jr., R. L. Rogers, and B. S. Chissom. Derivation of new readability formulas (automated readability index, fog count and Flesch reading ease formula) for navy enlisted personnel. Technical report, DTIC Document, 1975.

[21] R. Kiros, R. Salakhutdinov, and R. S. Zemel. Unifying visual-semantic embeddings with multimodal neural language models. *CoRR*, abs/1411.2539, 2014.

[22] J. R. Landis and G. G. Koch. The measurement of observer agreement for categorical data. *Biometrics*, 33(1), 1977.

[23] L. Ma, Z. Lu, L. Shang, and H. Li. Multimodal convolutional neural networks for matching image and sentence. *CoRR*, abs/1504.06063, 2015.

[24] J. Mao, W. Xu, Y. Yang, J. Wang, and A. L. Yuille. Deep captioning with multimodal recurrent neural networks (m-rnn). *CoRR*, abs/1412.6632, 2014.

[25] T. Mikolov, I. Sutskever, K. Chen, G. S. Corrado, and J. Dean. Distributed representations of words and phrases and their compositionality. In *Advances in neural information processing systems*, pages 3111–3119, 2013.

[26] E. Pavlick and A. Nenkova. Inducing lexical style properties for paraphrase and genre differentiation. In *Proc. of the Conference of the North American Chapter of the Association for Computational Linguistics: Human Language Technologies*, pages 218–224, Denver, Colorado, May–June 2015. Association for Computational Linguistics.

[27] A. Rajadesingan, R. Zafarani, and H. Liu. Sarcasm detection on twitter: A behavioral modeling approach. In *Proc. of the ACM Int. Conference on Web Search and Data Mining*, WSDM '15, pages 97–106, New York, NY, USA, 2015. ACM.

[28] A. S. Razavian, H. Azizpour, J. Sullivan, and S. Carlsson. CNN features off-the-shelf: an astounding baseline for recognition. *CVPR DeepVision workshop*, 2014.

[29] A. Reyes, P. Rosso, and T. Veale. A multidimensional approach for detecting irony in twitter. *Lang. Resour. Eval.*, 47(1):239–268, Mar. 2013.

[30] E. Riloff, A. Qadir, P. Surve, L. D. Silva, N. Gilbert, and R. Huang. Sarcasm as contrast between a positive sentiment and negative situation. In *EMNLP*, pages 704–714. ACL, 2013.

[31] E. Shutova, D. Kiela, and J. Maillard. Black holes and white rabbits: Metaphor identification with visual features. In *Proc. of the 2016 Conference of the North American Chapter of the Association for Computational Linguistics: Human Language Technologies*, pages 160–170, San Diego, California, June 2016. Association for Computational Linguistics.

[32] J. Tepperman, D. Traum, and S. S. Narayanan. "yeah right": Sarcasm recognition for spoken dialogue systems. In *Proc. of InterSpeech*, pages 1838–1841, Pittsburgh, PA, Sept. 2006.

[33] B. Thomee, B. Elizalde, D. A. Shamma, K. Ni, G. Friedland, D. Poland, D. Borth, and L.-J. Li. Yfcc100m: The new data in multimedia research. *Communications of the ACM*, 59(2):64–73, 2016.

[34] O. Tsur, D. Davidov, and A. Rappoport. Semi-Supervised Recognition of Sarcastic Sentences in Online Product Reviews. In M. Hearst, W. Cohen, and S. Gosling, editors, *Proc. of the Int. Conference on Weblogs and Social Media (ICWSM-2010)*. The AAAI Press, Menlo Park, California, 2010.

[35] T. Veale, K. Feyaerts, and C. Forceville. *Creativity and the Agile Mind: A Multi-Disciplinary Study of a Multi-Faceted Phenomenon.* Applications of Cognitive Linguistics [ACL]. De Gruyter, 2013.

[36] P. Verstraten. *Film Narratology : film narratives his primary focus, while noting.* University of Toronto Press, 2006.

[37] Z. Wang, Z. Wu, R. Wang, and Y. Ren. Twitter sarcasm detection exploiting a context-based model. In J. Wang, W. Cellary, D. Wang, H. Wang, S. Chen, T. Li, and Y. Zhang, editors, *Web Information Systems Engineering - WISE 2015 - 16th Int. Conference, Miami, FL, USA, November 1-3, 2015, Proc., Part I*, volume 9418 of *Lecture Notes in Computer Science*, pages 77–91. Springer, 2015.

[38] Q. You, J. Luo, H. Jin, and J. Yang. Robust Image Sentiment Analysis using Progressively Trained and Domain Transferred Deep Networks. In *AAAI Conference on Artificial Intelligence (AAAI)*, 2015.

User Redirection and Direct Haptics in Virtual Environments

Cristiano Carvalheiro, Rui Nóbrega, Hugo da Silva, Rui Rodrigues
FEUP, Faculdade de Engenharia da Universidade do Porto
INESC TEC, Instituto de Engenharia de Sistemas e Computadores, Tecnologia e Ciência
{ ei10041, ruinobrega, hmgcms, rui.rodrigues }@fe.up.pt

ABSTRACT

This paper proposes a haptic interaction system for Virtual Reality (VR) based on a combination of tracking devices for hands and objects and a real-to-virtual mapping system for user redirection. In our solution the user receives haptic stimuli by manipulating real objects mapped to virtual objects. This solution departs from systems that rely on haptic devices (e.g., haptic gloves) as interfaces for the user to interact with objects in the Virtual Environment (VE). As such, the proposed solution makes use of direct haptics (touching) and redirection techniques to guide the user through the virtual environment. Using the mapping framework, when the user touches a virtual object in the VE, he will simultaneously be physically touching the equivalent real object. A relevant feature of the framework is the possibility to define a warped mapping between the real and virtual worlds, such that the relation between the user and the virtual space can be different from the one between the user and the real space. This is particularly useful when the application requires the emulation of large virtual spaces but the physical space available is more confined. To achieve this, both the user's hands and the objects are tracked. In the presented prototype we use a head-mounted depth sensor (i.e., Leap Motion) and a depth-sensing camera (i.e., Kinect). To assess the feasibility of this solution, a functional prototype and a room setup with core functionality were implemented. The test sessions with users evaluated the mapping accuracy, the user execution time and the awareness of the user regarding the warped space when performing tasks with redirection. The results gathered indicate that the solution can be used to provide direct haptic feedback in VR applications and for warping space perception within certain limits.

Keywords

Virtual Reality; Haptic Interaction; Direct Haptics

MM '16, October 15–19, 2016, Amsterdam, Netherlands.
© 2016 ACM. ISBN 978-1-4503-3603-1/16/10...$15.00
DOI: http://dx.doi.org/10.1145/2964284.2964293

1. INTRODUCTION

VR applications are currently present in a variety of fields, being the virtual experience a core concept common to those applications. Even if this virtual experience has evolved significantly in the near past [33], there is still a need for more immersive and interactive systems.

To increase the sense of presence the VR experience has to try to provide feedback for the majority of the human senses. Current technologies and devices that support the visual and auditory senses in VR are relatively well developed. However, devices that support feedback to other relevant senses – taste, smell and touch – are in their infancy.

Adding support for haptic feedback can enhance the sense of presence in a VE [7]. In fact, without haptic feedback it is difficult to interact accurately with objects, as the user can neither feel the objects nor the movement restrictions that they impose [17].

In the last decades, there have been attempts to solve this problem based on devices that recreate the sense of touch or restrict the user movement – active haptics. Most of these devices are VR gloves or tables that provide haptic feedback. However, most of these solutions end up being somewhat limited, expensive or complex [28].

Thus, we identified two problems: the lack of a robust and transparent solution to allow the user of a VR system to feel real objects when virtual objects are touched in the VE, while maintaining the feeling of presence; and the need for cost-effective and less limited alternative to current solutions that usually do not provide haptic feedback close to the real haptic experience (i.e., VR gloves).

To reduce these problems, we propose to use real objects to provide haptic feedback to the users – passive haptics. Passive haptics can increase the user's sense of presence as well as his spatial memory of the VE [7]. Thus, redirecting the user to real objects that are mapped to virtual ones in a way that when the user touches a virtual object, he touches simultaneously the equivalent real one, may be a solution to transparently provide haptic feedback which is closer to a real-world touching experience.

Other techniques such as Redirected Walking [22] and Redirected Touching [12] can also be implemented, adding the possibility to construct large VEs when the real spatial availability is relatively small. Therefore, it can be a significant advantage in a variety of fields that make use of VR applications.

Letting users interact with real objects directly with their hands – direct haptics [10] (sometimes, referred in the same context, as passive haptics) – to provide haptic feedback in VR experiences can make these experiences even more immersive and increase the sense of presence of users during a VR experience. In this paper, we present a solution to support direct haptic feedback in VEs with the possibility of changing the VE dimensions to a different scale while using Redirected Touching.

In section 2 we present the related work that serves as basis for the developed solution. The solution is described in section 3 along with the implemented prototype. The experimental setup of the tests performed to evaluate this functional prototype is presented in section 4 and the results gathered are discussed in section 5. Finally, conclusions are discussed in section 6.

2. RELATED WORK

2.1 Haptic Interaction in Virtual Reality

The study of the interaction between humans and computers has gained more relevance in recent years. The recent technological advancements and development of new devices has encouraged different ways of thinking about interaction design [21].

The limitations of common 2D input devices, such as the mouse, pose major challenges when working in most 3D applications. For this reason, significant research efforts have been applied to the design and analysis of input devices for providing input in 3D applications. In particular, input devices for two-handed interaction in immersive VEs have been extensively researched, leading to emerging technologies that enable haptic interaction and feedback in those VEs [6, 3].

These devices intend to mimic the tactile and force feedback that exist in the real world by means of different mechanisms. Most of the haptic interfaces use electrical actuators to provide the sense of touch to the user. In force feedback interfaces, there is also a need of support for resistance or constraint of user actions [4, 6].

In spite of the progress achieved so far, the integration of haptic feedback into VEs faces several challenges and limitations. Further improvements in range, resolution and frequency bandwidth both in terms of forces and displacements are needed to match the performance of human users and their level of interaction with real environment [4, 28, 27, 20]. In addition, haptic devices remain the most difficult and costly to build, slowing the research and development in this field [8].

Current haptic interfaces only can provide stimuli that approximate our interactions with real environments. Although it can be enough to provide a relatively realistic feeling, it only can be achieved because we keep multiple clues consistent in the VE [27]. At the same time, the way human perception and performance works is not as well understood as other relevant areas [28].

2.2 Redirection Techniques in Virtual Reality

A crucial problem in VEs is the development of natural mechanisms for exploring virtual spaces. According to Slater et al. [26] the use of the user's body, with real proprioceptive sensations, is correlated to a significant increase in the sense of presence felt during the experience [26, 32].

Walking inside a VE enhances the sense of presence and naturalness, while also improving task performance [5]. However, in most situations the freedom of walking is restricted by physical barriers, as the space available can be small or inconsistent with the virtual space. Therefore, problems with the setup of large VEs arise, raising concerns related to user safety [5].

In his work, Berthoz [1] states that perceptual visual clues often dominate over proprioceptive and vestibular clues, when the senses disagree. Researchers also found that users tend to compensate these inconsistencies with their body, making possible the redirection of the user's path in the real world so that it diverges from his virtual path without him knowing [22]. Razzaque, S. et al demonstrated a technique called Redirected Walking where the users could walk through very large VEs while physically constrained to a smaller space in the real world [22]. Exploiting the limits of the human perception of visual, proprioceptive and vestibular clues the technique introduces a rotational distortion to the virtual scene that varies with the position, orientation, linear velocity and angular velocity in the real environment [22].

Further research introduced distortion in translational and curvature movements to achieve a higher efficiency in using the real spatial availability [19, 30]. In addition, studies [18, 29] have been developed that analyze the user sensitivity to redirection and estimate detection thresholds. These studies also suggest that the user is more sensible to rotational distortions when in motion.

More generally applicable algorithms to redirect throughout the VE while walking towards objects or evading obstacles have also been researched [14, 29, 31]. Furthermore, other studies integrated direct haptic feedback with VEs where redirected walking was applied, exploring the redirection of users to real objects that are modelled in the VE [14, 29].

Just like walking, research shows that using real objects to provide haptic feedback to the user can significantly enhance the sense of presence in a virtual experience [7].

A single real object can be used to provide feedback for multiple virtual objects as they might be replicated or positioned in different locations [11]. However, research has shown that it is possible to deceive the user into perceiving that he is touching a virtual object that has small differences relatively to the real one [11, 23].

Kohli, et al performed a study where the users would perceive small amounts of distortion modelled in a virtual table when touching a flat table in the real world. The study reported that in similar a way, small distortions could be introduced in the virtual objects relatively to the real objects and use the latter as source of haptic feedback without the user's perception [11].

Further research by the same authors suggests that the virtual space can be warped in such a way that it is possible to remap the correspondences between the real and virtual objects. In other words, the virtual space can be deformed in relation to the real space, and by maintaining all the perceptual clues consistent the user will perform the given tasks without perceiving the deformation or losing his sense of presence [13, 12].

Results of the analysis of training, adaptation and task performance indicate that after adaptation the users can perform tasks in a warped space as well as in an unwarped one [15, 16].

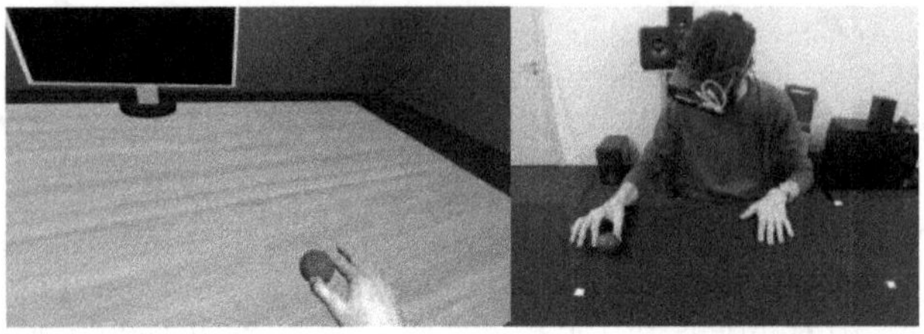

Figure 1: A user receiving haptic feedback directly from a sphere (right) coherent with what he sees in the VE (left).

3. DIRECT HAPTICS FRAMEWORK

Minding that direct haptics can significantly enhance virtual experiences we propose that rather than resorting to devices that try to recreate or simulate the sense of touch, direct haptics should be used or, in other words, the haptic feedback should be delivered to the user from real objects when he touches the equivalent ones in the VE with his hands [7]. This behavior is illustrated in Figure 1. When the user reaches for the object in the VE (left image), he will have been guided by the system so that his hand in the real world is also touching the real object (right image), thus getting haptic feedback directly from the real object, while visualizing the virtual one.

Considering a VE that is a 1-to-1 mapping of a real environment – in which a user can touch the real objects – this should suffice to attend the need of transparently providing haptic feedback to the user from real objects.

However, there are situations where it is not possible to have a 1-to-1 mapping between real and virtual objects because the available real space does not meet the necessary requirements. Hence, the VE that the user sees through the Head Mounted Display (HMD) does not necessarily have the same configuration as the real environment surrounding him. As an example, the virtual world can be larger or smaller than the real world. In this situation there is a need for reorientation of the user relative to the real objects that he intends to touch.

Considering that it is possible to exploit the dominance of visual clues over proprioceptive clues to redirect the real path of the user when walking through the environment [22], in the same way, it should be possible to redirect the user to objects that are in relatively different positions between real and VEs, without him perceiving that he (or the object) is being manipulated [12]. As such, it should be possible to warp the virtual space in order to place virtual objects in a different spatial distribution than the real spatial distribution [13, 12]. This way, the user is led to perceive a larger or smaller freedom of movement in the virtual space even if this is not the case for the real space.

3.1 Architecture Overview

As previously stated, the solution integrates direct haptics, meaning that it does not make use of a haptic device capable of haptic rendering to provide feedback to the users. Thus, our solution has a *Hand Tracking Module* (HTM), an *Object Tracking Module* (OTM) and a *Redirection Module* (RM) as well as a *Hand Tracking Device* (HTD) and an *Object Tracking Device* (OTD). For a better understanding on how these fit together in a working VR system, a diagram of the architecture is presented in Figure 2.

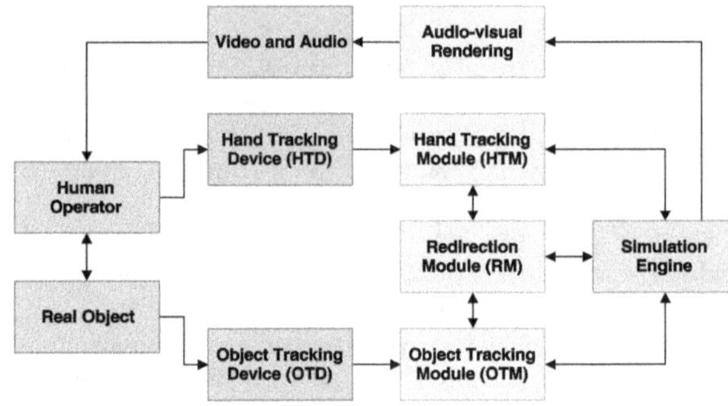

Figure 2: High level architecture of the solution.

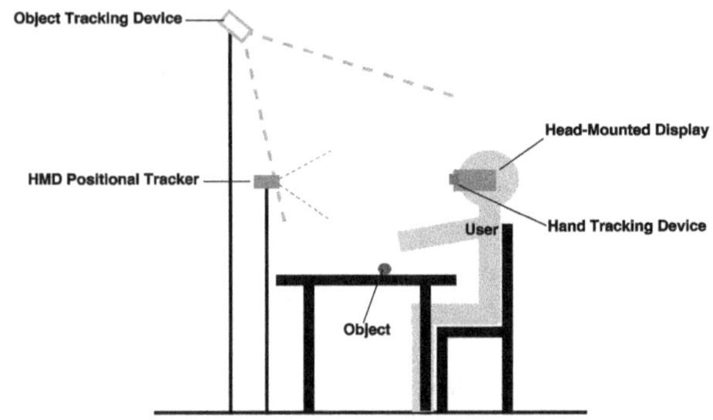

Figure 3: A visual diagram of the experimental setup used.

Throughout the entire experience, the user interacts and receives haptic feedback directly from real objects while visual and audio feedback is computer generated. As can be seen, the *HTD* and *OTD* feed data to the *HTM* and *OTM* respectively. Both modules process the input and trigger the changes in the entities that they detect and track. When the user interacts with an object in the real world, the virtual hand interacts with the virtual objects in the VE. The *RM* holds the distortion data defined for a given VE for a correct redirection of the user (See section 3.2) and provides both virtual hands and objects with the distortion offsets of their positions accordingly to that pattern.

These main modules of the framework are controlled by the *Simulation Engine* in order to adjust the necessary properties, so that the desired behavior of the system is achieved. Details regarding the remaining modules, as well as the possibility of using a single device for object and hand tracking, are outside of the scope of this paper, and hence will not be discussed.

Figure 3 shows a visual diagram of the setup as used throughout the development and testing of the current prototype.

3.2 Redirection

The purpose of the *Redirection* Module is to change the user's hands and virtual objects' positions according to a distortion pattern defined for the VE. By distortion pattern, we mean the mapping between the real world space and the virtual world space. Figure 4 illustrates an exam-

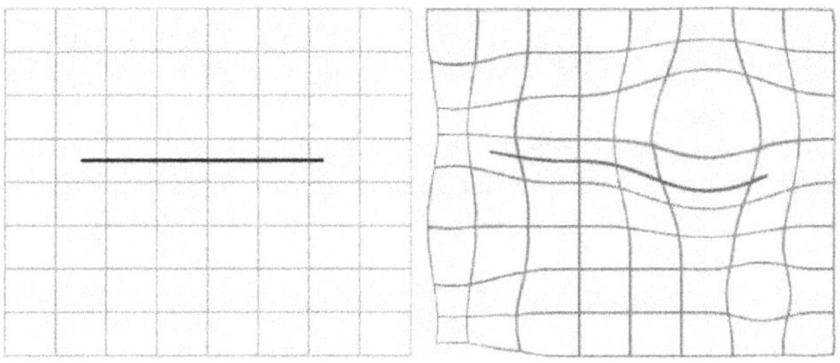

Figure 4: Example of mapping for a non-linear two-dimensional distortion pattern.

ple of mapping according to a non-linear two-dimensional distortion pattern, which can be seen as the correspondence between two polygonal meshes.

The green mesh has no distortion since it represents the real world space and each 2D coordinate in the mesh corresponds to a 3D coordinate in a plane in the real world. In a similar way, every 2D coordinate on the red mesh, maps to a 3D coordinate in the virtual world.

The positions of user's hands or objects delivered by the HTM and OTM (see Sections 3.4 and 3.3) is represented by the black line in the green mesh. The new position that the user will see in the VE should be the corresponding 2D coordinate of the red mesh, represented by the blue line.

The previous explanation considers a 2D distortion pattern, however it is also possible to have 1D and 3D distortions patterns. While a 1D distortion pattern could be, for example, a distortion applied only in the Z axis, a 3D distortion pattern should be a volumetric pattern.

The output positions of this Module are the virtual offset positions that the user will see in the VE. It is important to note that only one pattern can exist at a time in the VE, as redirection for user's hands and all objects has to be coherent. In other words, the same pattern ensures that when the user approaches an object to grab it, his hand and the object will suffer the same distortion.

3.2.1 Implementation

In the current system, only 2D distortion patterns were implemented. Both linear and non-linear patterns were implemented, although only the linear distortion patterns were evaluated.

The linear pattern was defined by a distortion value for each dimension. The default distortion value is 1, which translates to no distortion. A value less than 1 mean less movement of the virtual hands and objects compared to the real world, while a value greater than 1 results in the opposite. For example, a pattern with a distortion value of 1.1 means that the user will see his hands or the objects 10% farther than their real position, and the further they are, the faster they move as the distortion will give higher offsets.

The non-linear pattern was implemented as a two dimensional array of points defining a mesh of quads, with a given number of divisions and pattern size on each axis. Figure 5 illustrates this implementation where the undistorted green mesh represents the world space, and the warped red mesh represents the distortion pattern in the VE.

3.2.2 Distortion Calculation

The RM provides offset positions for the virtual hands

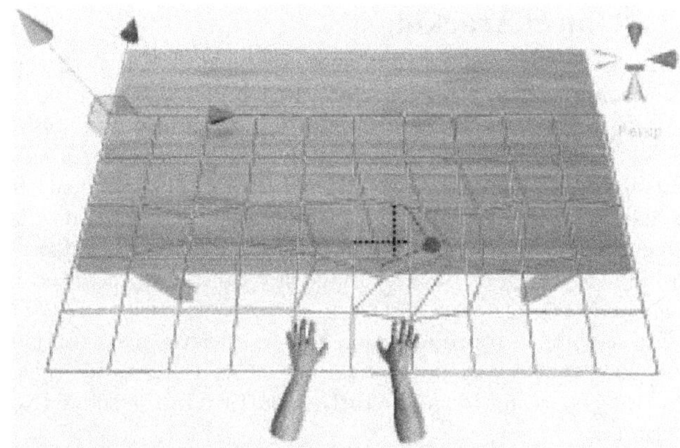

Figure 5: Redirection implementation overview (Similar colors as in Figure 4). The dashed black line represents the interpolation in the green mesh while the dashed blue line is in the red mesh.

and object. As such, the calculation of a distortion offset of a hand or object is always done in relation to the pattern's root position.

The offset position $O(P_{(x,z)})$ in a linear distortion pattern is given by Equation 1, where $P_{(x,z)}$ is the position of the object, $R_{(x,z)}$ is the root position of the pattern and $D_{(x,z)}$ the value of the distortion to be applied.

$$O(P_{(x,z)}) = P_{(x,z)} - (R_{(x,z)} + (P_{(x,z)} - R_{(x,z)}D_{(x,z)})) \quad (1)$$

On the other hand, the offset position in a non-linear pattern is more complex to calculate. The algorithm to calculate the offset position of a hand or object is presented in Algorithm 1.

Algorithm 1: Offset calculation of non-linear 2D Pattern.

Data: $O_{(x,z)}$, $P_{(x,z)}$, M
Result: R, the offset to apply to the object's position
begin
- $D \longleftarrow O - P$ *//offset*;
- $Q_{(i,j)} \longleftarrow$ *index of quad undistorted pattern (D)*;
- $B_{(x,y)} \longleftarrow$ *get position of the ball in the quad (D)*;
- $A[4] \longleftarrow$ *get points in the distortion pattern M (Q,B)*;
- $I \longleftarrow$ *calculate interpolation(A)*;
- **return** *O - (P + I)*;

The algorithm begins by calculating the offset position of the object in relation to the distortion pattern. Then it finds the quad in which the object is located, by calculating the index of the upper left point in the two-dimensional array, and calculates the middle position between the unwarped quad points in each dimension (Figure 5, black dashed line). With this information, we can get the four equivalent points in the warped quad by interpolation, as well as calculate the intersection between the lines that those points define (Figure 5, blue dashed line).

Finally, the offset position of the object is given by subtracting the result of the interaction – in relation to the pattern's position – from the object's position.

3.3 Object Tracking

The purpose of the *OTM*, is to ensure an accurate representation of the real objects – which the user is able to interact with – inside the VE. As such, it should be capable of: recognizing the real environment and performing a calibration step, so that the position, rotation and scale of the objects in the real world space is coherent with the one displayed in the VE; detecting and tracking the real objects and provide the relevant data so that they can be represented in the VE.

For a correct representation of the virtual position this module interacts with the RM in order to get the offset position according to the distortion pattern in the scene (See Section 3.2).

3.3.1 Implementation

For the current prototype a Kinect v2 camera was used as tracking device with the objective of interacting with a spherical object. This spherical object was made of styrofoam painted with two layers of ink: a first layer of black to minimize the infrared reflectiveness of the material in order to minimize negative effects on the accuracy of the Leap Motion controller (that is used for hand tracking); and a second layer of a dark red color so that the sphere can be detected with the Kinect RGB sensor. The spherical object used was chosen due to the fact that rotation tracking is not necessary and the haptic feedback it provides is virtually the same, regardless of position, orientation or type of interaction.

The Module is responsible for updating the transform of the object according to the data received from the Kinect. The images retrieved from the sensor are processed to detect the sphere's position and using its SDK it is possible to get 3D coordinates for the virtual world. The detection algorithm is based on the segmentation of the color data and tracking is done via kernel search.

As the Kinect Sensor's refresh rate is limited and the position should be updated every frame, dead reckoning was implemented to solve this issue. In addition, when the user interacts with the sphere, the position of the hand is given by the HTM instead of the OTM.

In addition, a timeout mechanism was implemented so that when the sphere's detection fails, the dead reckoning mechanism continues to work until five new frames arrive from Kinect Sensor, before the object being destroyed.

3.3.2 Calibration

For a correct positioning of the objects, the precise position and orientation of the Kinect sensor must be determined to update the OTM transform. To this end, four white markers were placed on the table of the setup (See Figure 6, right). It is important to note that the detection of markers was done through several frames in order to cope with noise and random detection errors.

3.4 Hand Tracking

The purpose of the *HTM* is to ensure an accurate representation of the user's hands inside the VE. As such, it is responsible for conducting an accurate detection and tracking of the user's hands and their articulations position, rotation and scale. For a correct representation of the virtual position this module interacts with the RM in order to get the offset position according to the distortion pattern in the scene (See Section 3.2). In addition, this Module is responsible for the detection of the interaction with objects by analysing the hand's pose.

Since the haptic feedback is delivered directly from real objects – upon contact with them in the VE – there is no need for the HTM to have haptic rendering capabilities.

3.4.1 Implementation

To implement the hand tracking in the functional prototype built, a Leap Motion controller mounted on the HMD was used, making use of its SDK capabilities to detect and track the user's hands. The results in the prototype rendered credible hands with occasional misdetections from the sensor.

Disturbance factors include the fact that the maximum recommended distance to work with the controller is twenty–five centimeters and the users were working at least thirty centimeters away. In addition, external sources of infrared light have a major negative impact on the tracking mechanism of the controller. With the need of enough visible light so the objects can be detected using the Kinect RGB sensor and the Kinect infrared sensors working at the same time, we had two additional sources of infrared light that were affecting the controller capabilities. In addition, despite attempts to minimize the infrared reflectiveness of the sphere's material, it also affected the accuracy of the controller.

Given this limitation, the implementation of filters was required. The filters implemented were based on the velocity of changes of the hand and its fingers. Therefore, if the velocity of the changes in the hand was too high, its update was canceled. A similar approach was taken for the fingers. The filtering of some impossible positions was also applied, fixing problems like a hand rotated backwards.

In this iteration of development, only the detection of a pinch interaction was implemented via a state machine. The state machine has two states: *PINCHED*, when the distance between thumb and index fingertips is less than a *pinchThreshold* and the distance between the *pinchPosition* – position between both fingertips – and the sphere is less than a *distanceThreshold*; and *RELEASED* if the conditions are not met. As only analysing the fingertips and distance is somewhat limited when occlusions occur, other assumption had to be made. When the sphere's vertical position is slightly above the table – not resting on the surface – it is assumed that the user is interacting with it.

Actions only take place on state transitioning and, as such, when the sphere is pinched the Module starts updating the sphere's position. In addition, it communicates with the OTM to halt its update of the sphere's transform and disable both collision detection and physics. When the sphere is released, the opposite happens. It should also be stated that an interpolation of the sphere's position is performed when it is pinched, in order to provide a seamless transition.

3.4.2 Calibration

The calibration of the Leap Motion Controller is done via an external tool. However, at the beginning of the system's execution, small errors in the gyroscope of the HMD could arise. These errors were, for example, rotations in one of the axis that were not coherent with the rotation of the user's head, causing a disparity between the real and virtual rotations. As the Leap Motion was mounted on the HMD, the rotation disparity caused an incoherent relation between the

Figure 6: Overview of the hardware setup of the testing environment.

position of the real and virtual user's hands. In order to correct this issue, the inverse amount of the rotation disparity was introduced in the HMD virtual object when the user was facing forward, correcting the disparity.

3.5 System Calibration

Given that the two tracking controllers presented some degree of inaccuracy, additional mechanisms for calibrating the system were implemented, hoping to decrease the negative impact of that imprecision in the experience. The mechanisms were controlled via a simple state machine.

The main steps of the whole system calibration were: 1) Detection of the user's body by the Kinect Sensor, required for starting the calibration; 2) Execution of the calibration routines described in Sections 3.3.2 and 3.4.2; 3) Calibration of the OTM scale, calculated by measuring the difference of distances between the hand's positions detected with Leap Motion Controller and the Kinect Sensor; 4) Alignment of the tracking modules, with information of hand's positions from the Leap Motion and Kinect Sensor, as well as the position of the sphere. 5) HTM vertical calibration, required because the Leap Motion Controller exhibited a cumulative error in vertical tracking, so an additional vertical translation to the camera was performed.

Steps 2 to 5 were performed throughout a series of image frames to cope with noise and random detection errors. In addition, in step 3 and 4 the users were asked to pick up the sphere and hold it between the hands so the alignment could be performed (See Figure 6, right). In step 5 the users were asked to rest their hands on the table.

4. EXPERIMENTAL SETUP

The hardware setup of the prototype can be seen in Figure 6. The images illustrate several details such as: 1) *Oculus Rift DK2*, the HMD used for providing visual feedback from the VE to the user; 2) *DK2 Positional Tracker*, used in the detection of the user's head position and rotation for coherent visual rendering of the VE; 3) *Leap Motion Controller*, the HTD used for user's hands detection and tracking in order to consistently represent their pose in the VE. This device is mounted on the HMD; 4) *Kinect Sensor*, the OTD used for object detection and tracking in order to consistently represent the object in the VE, and for user's body tracking in order to better calibrate the system; 5) *Sphere*, which is the real object that the user will interact with and the source of haptic feedback; 6) *Space calibration markers*, used for calibration of the OTM so that the virtual representation of the sphere is consistent with the real one (See Section 3.3.2).

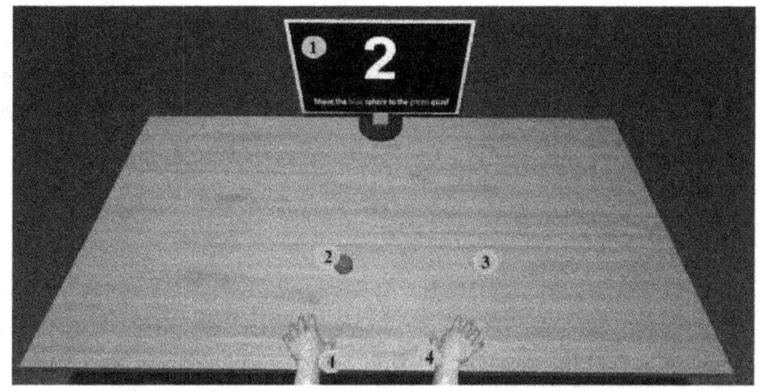

Figure 7: Overview of the VE scene as seen by the users and where they performed the tasks.

Figure 7 presents a view of the virtual scene designed in Unity 3D to test the functional prototype. The virtual scene is a room with a table in the center. The four remaining elements of the virtual scene are: 1) *Interface Area*, where the test number and instructions to perform the task are displayed; 2) *Virtual Sphere*, the virtual model of the sphere that the user will interact with; 3) *Goal*, the goal of a task is represented by the green cube, which accordingly to the task type, the user should touch or move the sphere into; 4) *Virtual hands*, the 3D models of the user's hands – provided by Leap Motion's Unity integration package.

4.1 Evaluation

In order to test the experimental setup several testing sessions were organized. Each user testing session had two actors: The *facilitator*, conducting the user through the test, giving him instructions and taking notes on his performance and feedback; The *user*, the test subject who actually performs the tasks and provides both oral and written feedback.

Despite being a VR prototype where the user is immersed in a VE, the audio output was carried through speakers so that the two actors could easily communicate with each other.

Each session took 15 to 25 minutes. At the beginning, a brief explanation of the purpose and format of the session took place. The experiment had two main phases:

First Phase – Blind Test: the user performs the tasks described next in Section 4.3 only knowing details about the tasks but not details about the system or how it works, thus, being unaware that the VE exhibits distortion during the experiment;

Second Phase – Aware Test: similar to the first phase. However, before this phase the *facilitator* gives more details about the experiment and how the user's perception is manipulated. In addition, the *facilitator* asks the user for feedback – at each test with a different distortion value – namely if he can identify and classify the manipulation. The manipulation can be classified as slow, normal or fast, resembling the velocity of the virtual user's hand regarding what he thinks that the real velocity is.

Finally, after the experiment the user fills a questionnaire with questions that allow assessing the simulator sickness score [9], the user's profile and how he felt using the system during both first and second phases. The reason to this being done at the end of the experiment was to avoid distracting the user and affecting the results.

4.2 Users Profile

A total of 40 users participated in the testing sessions from which resulted 38 valid samples. The goal was to have a diversified set of users. As such, there was no prior selection and all the users volunteered to participate in the experiment.

Our set of users was composed of 33 male subjects and 5 female subjects, of which 28 are aged between seventeen to twenty-four and 10 between twenty-five and forty. In addition, 12 subjects had previous experience with VR applications, while only 6 did not play games regularly.

4.3 Tasks

During the first and second phases of each session, the user was first asked to perform the necessary steps for the system calibration (See Section 3.5) after which they would start to perform a set of tasks. The functional prototype included two types of interaction techniques: **Touch** with the index's fingertip on a goal, and pick up a sphere and **Move** it towards a goal.

A description of the experiment execution flow (equal on each phase) that the user had to perform is now presented: **1)** First **Touch** interaction technique was tested with every distortion level (explained next) and only then the **Move** interaction was tested; **2)** For each interaction technique, there were **six** sets of tests at different distortions, always in the same sequence for each user; **3)** For each distortion level there were **two** tasks to be performed. The first task's T_r goal is to the right of the user and the second to the left, T_l; **4)** The position of these goals was procedurally generated, being different from task to task within a threshold; **5)** A task is considered finished when either the user touches the goal or the sphere is near the goal for an uninterrupted period of two seconds. The goal then disappears and a beep sound is triggered which is audible by the user; **6)** When every two tasks at a distortion level are completed, the test system advances to the next distortion level.

Besides tests with no distortion, there were four distortion levels selected to be integrated in the testing sessions: -20%, -10%, +10% and +20%. The no distortion was repeated twice in the 6 tests mentioned before. These distortion levels were selected by taking into account the feedback from preliminary test sessions. A negative level of distortion represents a linear distortion pattern were the virtual mapping of the user's hands and sphere was reduced by the percentage of the level (See Section 3.2.1). For positive levels the opposite applies. Despite of the implementation of non-linear 2D distortion patterns, these tests only evaluated linear 2D distortions with the same distortion level in both dimensions.

It is important to notice that there were different sequences of distortion levels for each user, enumerated from U to Z and a counterbalanced order designed in a Latin Square Design [25] fashion. The reason for this choice was the need to avoid biased results that could have arisen if all the users experimented the same sequence of distortion levels.

4.4 Performance Metrics

Given the implementation of the functional prototype and the testing setup presented, the following performance metrics to evaluate the solution were defined: **Accuracy error in task execution**, measured as the average horizontal distance between the index fingertip or sphere and the task's goal, in centimeters; **Execution time of the task**, the time that the user took to complete a given task, in seconds, which provided insights on whether the user has an adaptation phase to the distortion; **Detection of the distortion**, which shows if the user detected that the VE was exhibiting different distortions during the first phase, and if he was able to correctly classify those distortions during the second phase; *Simulator Sickness Score*, and sub scores that provided insights on how the system is prone to induce simulator sickness symptoms, and how these affect other performance metrics of the system. These were gathered through the Simulator Sickness Questionnaire (SSQ) [9].

The discussion of the obtained results also considered the interference in the following external factors: **System calibration**, which introduces some disparity between the real and virtual world mapping that affects the ability of the user to pinch the sphere correctly and execute the tasks with precision; **User's spatial awareness**, which is different from user to user and can affect performance and their distortion detection thresholds. Due to time constraints, this factor was not measured.

5. RESULTS

The results of the average accuracy can be seen in Table 1. The table presents the results for all tests (with all users and tasks). The Filtered@75 is the subset of samples that does not include the worst quartile of tests. The goal was to remove most of the experiments that were affected by miscalibration of the system.

Regarding the accuracy of the tasks, the system achieved an average accuracy error of 7 millimeters. Although it cannot be said that users can perform tasks as well in distorted environments as in undistorted environments, – complying with previous studies [15, 16] – the results seem to indicate that there is no significant degradation in accuracy.

As expected, the Move interaction results in less accuracy as the users have less control over the sphere's position (See Figure 9). Some users reported problems with the pinch gesture when they tried to pick up the sphere (introduced by the Leap Motion's accuracy problems). In addition, it appears that the users adapted to the system as the accuracy achieved is better in the second phase of the experience.

As can be seen in Figure 8, the average execution time of each task shows that, as expected, the Move interaction technique tested is more time-consuming than the simpler Touch interaction. In addition, both interaction techniques exhibited an adaptation phase that was noticeable but that requires further studies for generalization. This adaptation phase seems to be related to the learning of the system and understanding of the interaction technique. An adaptation phase to the distortion was also registered as shown in Fig-

Table 1: Results of the Mean accuracy error and Standard Deviation (SD) for all samples (All@100) and the filtered set of samples (Filtered@75).

		-20%	-10%	0%	+10%	+20%
All@100	**Mean**	0.92	0.93	0.93	0.94	0.95
	SD	0.58	0.60	0.60	0.61	0.64
Filtered@75	**Mean**	0.70	0.70	0.70	0.71	0.69
	SD	0.39	0.41	0.40	0.41	0.41

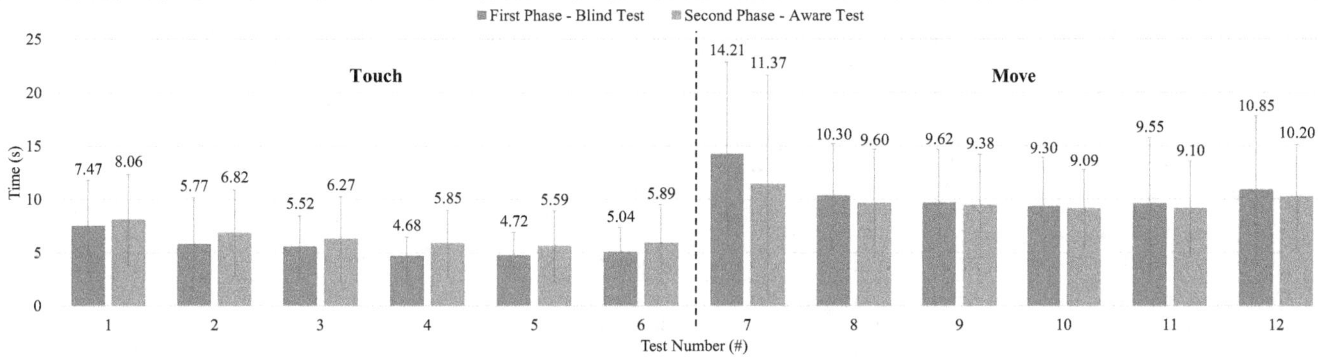

Figure 8: Results gathered on average task execution time per test number for both phases.

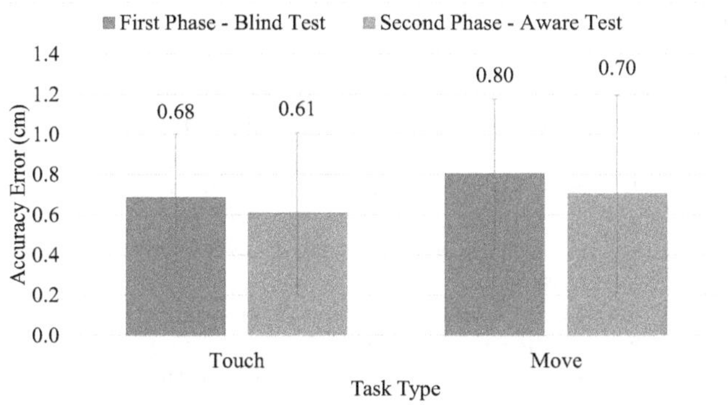

Figure 9: Results gathered on how distortion levels affects the accuracy. The values represent the average accuracy error for all samples at each distortion level and also removing the samples with poor calibration.

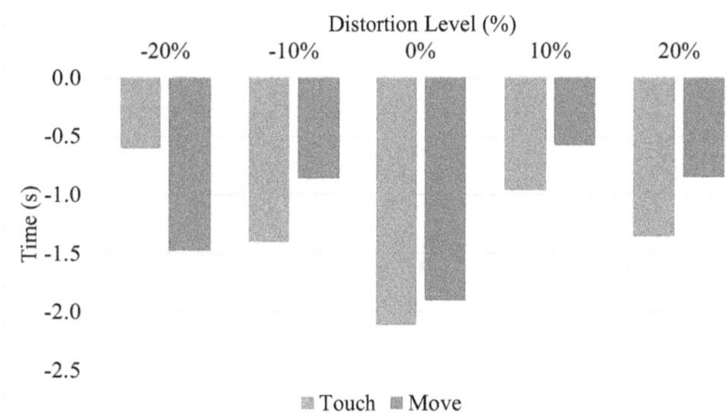

Figure 10: Results gathered on the average execution time difference between the first (T_r) and second (T_l) tasks of a given distortion level for both task types.

ure 10. Since the average difference of times between the first (T_r) and second (T_l) tasks is negative for all distortion levels on both tasks types, it appears that the users adapt to the distortion of the environment, yet more tasks in a given distortion should be performed for a stronger conclusion.

The users took more time performing the touch task during the second phase of the experience because the *facilitator* asked them to classify the distortion level and they took their time to figure it out, as seen in Figure 8. They took less time for the Move task which may have been caused by the adaptation to the system.

Only seven users were able to detect the distortion in both phases of the experiment. Another seven users did not detect distortions at all in either phase. The remaining users only perceived the manipulation in the second phase, when the *facilitator* explicitly asked to pay attention to it.

However, the detection of distortions by the users in the second phase did not mean that they were able to classify them right. Regarding classification precision, as can be seen in Figure 11, naturally, higher distortion levels are correctly detected and identified with more assertiveness. In addition, it can be seen that users are less sensitive to negative distortion levels and thus not detecting those as frequently as the positive ones.

Analysing the answers from users through the final questionnaire (See Table 2), it seems that they felt more impact of calibration errors during the second phase, which does not corroborate what the logs, annotations and remaining results present. One of the causes can be the prolonged exposure to the system that makes the users prone to more easily detect errors. Another may have been the fact that the questionnaire was filled for both phases at the end – which may have led to user misunderstanding of the purpose of the questionnaire.

The results obtained from the SSQ showed that the system does not induce more sickness than the systems used in other recent studies [2]. No user felt the need to interrupt the experiment, although four of them alleged being slightly disturbed after the experiment. This might be caused by the repeating change in distortion pattern. As such, further research on the correlation of the simulator sickness symptoms, the application of distortion to the VE and continuous change of that distortion is recommended in order to confirm how it affects the experience of the user. Even so, the results showed that the simulation sickness does not affect other performance metrics.

The overall performance of the system reported by the users was satisfactory. Although Leap Motion controller tracking and calibration errors seemed to affect almost all experiences, the fact that all the users finished all the tasks shows that, with better calibration mechanisms, the results

Table 2: Results gathered through the final questionnaire were users classified in a Likert-style scale from 1 to 7 different aspect of the experiment. The results presented are for both First (Blind Test) and Second (Aware Test) phases.

Question	Phase	Median	Low. Quart.	Up. Quart.	Mean
a) Noticed disparity between the movement of hands and what saw in the VE.	First	3	-1	+1	3.1
	Second	4	-1	+1	3.9
b) Felt that the disparity prevented him from performing the tasks normally.	First	2	-1	+1.75	2.4
	Second	2	0	+2	2.6
c) Felt that the movements of his hands were consistent with what I saw in the VE.	First	5	-1	+1	4.9
	Second	4.5	-1.5	+1.25	4.5
d) When trying to touch the sphere, its position was coherent with the one seen in the VE.	First	5	-2	+1	4.4
	Second	4.5	-1.5	+1.5	4.2
e) Sometimes he perceived a movement of the hands in the VE different from expected.	First	3	-2	+2	+3.2
	Second	5	-1.75	+1	4.5

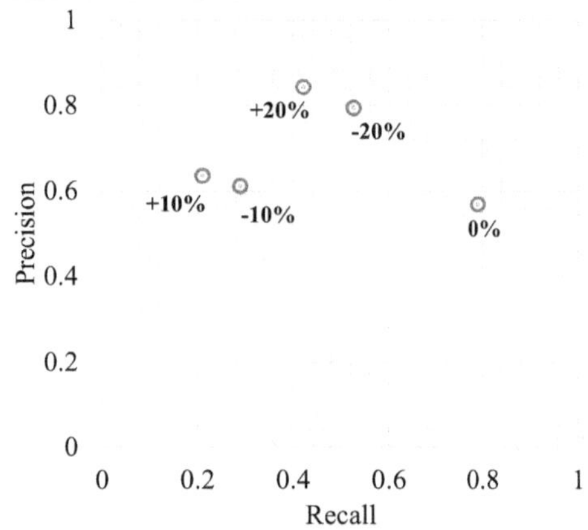

Figure 11: Results gathered on the average precision and recall of distortion classification for all users during second phase of the experience.

could be improved. Nonetheless, these errors were frequently pointed by the users as a major issue in the experience. Most of the users said that the system is intuitive, presents a reliable source of haptic feedback, the real sphere position was where they expected it to be and they could pick it up easily.

6. CONCLUSIONS

The main contribution of this work is the design, implementation and evaluation of a system for direct haptic feedback in VR systems, which led to the development of a prototype with the potential to improve VR experiences. This prototype is part of the MASSIVE [24] project which aims to explore multi-sensorial immersion.

This paper presents a solution for providing feedback directly from real objects in VEs in a transparent way, as direct haptics can increase the user's sense of presence [7].

The main problem identified was the lack of a solution that provides the user of a VR system with the possibility to directly feel real objects without losing the sense of presence; and the lack of alternatives to haptic devices that face significant limitations.

In our solution the user receives haptic feedback directly from real objects when interacting with them in the VE. Therefore, in the VE, the user is redirected for the objects he intends to touch, unaware of the fact that mapping between real and VEs may exhibit a certain amount of distortion.

A functional prototype was implemented to test the initial hypothesis and testing sessions with 40 users were conducted to evaluate this prototype.

The results presented in section 5 show that the system performs as expected, with the user receiving the desired haptic feedback. In addition, they suggest that there may be an adaption of the user to the distortion, nonetheless they perform as well in a distorted VE as in an undistorted one.

The users reported a good experience using the system and no significant simulator sickness symptoms were reported. We can conclude that in hand reaching tasks, a distortion of up to 20% in the mapping between the real and visual clues provided in a VE does not induce significant changes in performance nor simulation sickness. Even so, future work will be done in this prototype in order to improve the solution and the results.

7. ACKNOWLEDGMENTS

This work has been financed by FourEyes, "TEC4Growth - Pervasive Intelligence, Enhancers and Proofs of Concept with Industrial Impact/NORTE-01-0145-FEDER-000020", financed by the North Portugal Regional Operational Programme (NORTE 2020), under the PORTUGAL 2020 Partnership Agreement, and through the European Regional Development Fund (ERDF). The authors would also like to acknowledge the support in terms of infrastructures and technologies from the "MASSIVE – Multimodal Acknowledgeable multiSenSorial Immersive Virtual Enviroments" project (REC I/EEI-SII/0360/2012 - COMPETE, QREN and FEDER).

8. REFERENCES

[1] A. Berthoz. *The brain's sense of movement.* Harvard University Press, 2002.

[2] S. Bouchard, G. Robillard, and P. Renaud. Revising the factor structure of the simulator sickness questionnaire. *Annual Review of CyberTherapy and Telemedicine*, 5:128–137, 2007.

[3] D. A. Bowman. *Interaction techniques for common tasks in immersive virtual environments.* PhD thesis, Citeseer, 1999.

[4] G. C. Burdea. Haptics issues in virtual environments. In *Computer Graphics International, 2000. Proceedings*, pages 295–302. IEEE, 2000.

[5] G. Cirio, P. Vangorp, E. Chapoulie, M. Marchal, A. Lécuyer, and G. Drettakis. Walking in a cube: Novel metaphors for safely navigating large virtual environments in restricted real workspaces. *IEEE Transactions on Visualization and Computer Graphics*, 18(4):546–554, 2012.

[6] V. Hayward, O. R. Astley, M. Cruz-Hernandez, D. Grant, and G. Robles-De-La-Torre. Haptic interfaces and devices. *Sensor Review*, 24(1):16–29, 2004.

[7] B. E. Insko. *Passive haptics significantly enhances virtual environments*. PhD thesis, University of North Carolina at Chapel Hill, 2001.

[8] F. Karray, M. Alemzadeh, J. A. Saleh, and M. N. Arab. Human-computer interaction: Overview on state of the art. *International Journal on Smart Sensing and Intelligent Systems*, 1:137–159, 2008.

[9] R. S. Kennedy, N. E. Lane, K. S. Berbaum, and M. G. Lilienthal. Simulator sickness questionnaire: An enhanced method for quantifying simulator sickness. *The international journal of aviation psychology*, 3(3):203–220, 1993.

[10] T. A. Kern. *Engineering haptic devices: a beginner's guide for engineers*. Springer Science & Business Media, 2009.

[11] L. Kohli. Exploiting perceptual illusions to enhance passive haptics. In *IEEE VR Workshop on Perceptual Illusions in Virtual Environments*, pages 22–24. Citeseer, 2009.

[12] L. Kohli. Redirected touching: Warping space to remap passive haptics. In *3D User Interfaces (3DUI), 2010 IEEE Symposium on*, pages 129–130. IEEE, 2010.

[13] L. Kohli. Warping virtual space for low-cost haptic feedback. In *Proceedings of the ACM SIGGRAPH Symposium on Interactive 3D Graphics and Games*, pages 195–195. ACM, 2013.

[14] L. Kohli, E. Burns, D. Miller, and H. Fuchs. Combining passive haptics with redirected walking. In *Proceedings of the 2005 international conference on Augmented tele-existence*, pages 253–254. ACM, 2005.

[15] L. Kohli, M. C. Whitton, and F. P. Brooks. Redirected touching: The effect of warping space on task performance. In *3D User Interfaces (3DUI), 2012 IEEE Symposium on*, pages 105–112. IEEE, 2012.

[16] L. Kohli, M. C. Whitton, and F. P. Brooks. Redirected touching: training and adaptation in warped virtual spaces. In *3D User Interfaces (3DUI), 2013 IEEE Symposium on*, pages 79–86. IEEE, 2013.

[17] M. R. Mine, F. P. Brooks Jr, and C. H. Sequin. Moving objects in space: exploiting proprioception in virtual-environment interaction. In *Proceedings of the 24th annual conference on Computer graphics and interactive techniques*, pages 19–26. ACM Press/Addison-Wesley Publishing Co., 1997.

[18] C. Neth, J. Souman, D. Engel, U. Kloos, H. Bülthoff, and B. Mohler. Velocity-dependent curvature gain and avatar use for redirected walking. In *2010 Joint Virtual Reality Conference of EuroVR-EGVE-VEC (JVRC 2010)*, volume 12, 2010.

[19] C. T. Neth, J. L. Souman, D. Engel, U. Kloos, H. H. Bülthoff, and B. J. Mohler. Velocity-dependent dynamic curvature gain for redirected walking. *Visualization and Computer Graphics, IEEE Transactions on*, 18(7):1041–1052, 2012.

[20] R. Nóbrega and N. Correia. Interactive 3d content insertion in images for multimedia applications. *Multimedia Tools and Applications*, pages 1–35, 2015.

[21] J. Preece, H. Sharp, and Y. Rogers. *Interaction Design-beyond human-computer interaction*. John Wiley & Sons, 2015.

[22] S. Razzaque, Z. Kohn, and M. C. Whitton. Redirected walking. In *Proceedings of EUROGRAPHICS*, volume 9, pages 105–106, 2001.

[23] I. Rock and J. Victor. Vision and touch: An experimentally created conflict between the two senses. *Science*, 143(3606):594–596, 1964.

[24] R. Rodrigues, E. Magalhães, H. da Silva, M. Bessa, A. Coelho, and A. Sousa. Modelo de descrição de experiências multissensoriais multiutilizador. In *Proceedings of the 2015 Encontro Português de Computação Gráfica e Interação*, EPCGI '15, 2015.

[25] D. J. Saville and G. R. Wood. Latin square design. In *Statistical Methods: The Geometric Approach*, pages 340–353. Springer, 1991.

[26] M. Slater, J. McCarthy, and F. Maringelli. The influence of body movement on subjective presence in virtual environments. *Human Factors: The Journal of the Human Factors and Ergonomics Society*, 40(3):469–477, 1998.

[27] M. A. Srinivasan. What is haptics? *Laboratory for Human and Machine Haptics: The Touch Lab, Massachusetts Institute of Technology*, 1995.

[28] M. A. Srinivasan and C. Basdogan. Haptics in virtual environments: Taxonomy, research status, and challenges. *Computers & Graphics*, 21(4):393–404, 1997.

[29] F. Steinicke, G. Bruder, L. Kohli, J. Jerald, and K. Hinrichs. Taxonomy and implementation of redirection techniques for ubiquitous passive haptic feedback. In *Cyberworlds, 2008 International Conference on*, pages 217–223. IEEE, 2008.

[30] F. Steinicke, G. Bruder, T. Ropinski, and K. Hinrichs. Moving towards generally applicable redirected walking. In *Proceedings of the Virtual Reality International Conference (VRIC)*, pages 15–24, 2008.

[31] E. Suma, Z. Lipps, S. Finkelstein, D. M. Krum, M. Bolas, et al. Impossible spaces: Maximizing natural walking in virtual environments with self-overlapping architecture. *Visualization and Computer Graphics, IEEE Transactions on*, 18(4):555–564, 2012.

[32] M. Usoh, K. Arthur, M. C. Whitton, R. Bastos, A. Steed, M. Slater, and F. P. Brooks Jr. Walking walking-in-place flying, in virtual environments. In *Proc. of the 26th annual conference on Computer graphics and interactive techniques*, pages 359–364. ACM Addison-Wesley Publishing Co., 1999.

[33] N.-N. Zhou and Y.-L. Deng. Virtual reality: A state-of-the-art survey. *International Journal of Automation and Computing*, 6(4):319–325, 2009.

LightNet: A Versatile, Standalone Matlab-based Environment for Deep Learning

[Simplify Deep Learning in Hundreds of Lines of Code]

Chengxi Ye, Chen Zhao*, Yezhou Yang, Cornelia Fermüller and Yiannis Aloimonos
Computer Science Department, University of Maryland
College Park, MD, USA.
cxy@umiacs.umd.edu, chenzhao@umd.edu, yzyang@umiacs.umd.edu, cornelia@umiacs.umd.edu, yiannis@umiacs.umd.edu

ABSTRACT

LightNet is a **lightweight**, **versatile**, **purely Matlab-based** deep learning framework. The idea underlying its design is to provide an easy-to-understand, easy-to-use and efficient computational platform for deep learning research. The implemented framework supports major deep learning architectures such as Multilayer Perceptron Networks (MLP), Convolutional Neural Networks (CNN) and Recurrent Neural Networks (RNN). The framework also supports both CPU and GPU computation, and the switch between them is straightforward. Different applications in computer vision, natural language processing and robotics are demonstrated as experiments.

Availability: the source code and data is available at: https://github.com/yechengxi/LightNet

Keywords

Computer vision; natural language processing; image understanding; machine learning; deep learning; convolutional neural networks; multilayer perceptrons; recurrent neural networks; reinforcement learning

1. INTRODUCTION

Deep neural networks [8] have given rise to major advancements in many problems of machine intelligence. Most current implementations of neural network models primarily emphasize efficiency. These pipelines (Table 1) can consist of a quarter to half a million lines of code and often involve multiple programming languages [5, 13, 2]. It requires extensive efforts to thoroughly understand and modify the models. A straightforward and self-explanatory deep learning framework is highly anticipated to accelerate the understanding and application of deep neural network models.

We present LightNet, a **lightweight**, **versatile**, **purely Matlab-based** implementation of modern deep neural network models. Succinct and efficient Matlab programming techniques have been used to implement all the computational modules. Many popular types of neural networks, such as multilayer perceptrons, convolutional neural networks, and recurrent neural networks are implemented in LightNet, together with several variations of stochastic gradient descent (SDG) based optimization algorithms.

Table 1: Deep Neural Network Packages

Framework	Language	Native Models	Lines of Code
Caffe	C++	CNN	74,903
Theano	Python, C	MLP/CNN/RNN	148,817
Torch	Lua, C	MLP/CNN/RNN	458,650
TensorFlow	C++	MLP/CNN/RNN	335,669
Matconvnet	Matlab, C	CNN	43,087
LightNet	Matlab	MLP/CNN/RNN	951 (1,762)*

* Lines of code in the core modules and in the whole package.

Since LightNet is implemented **solely** with Matlab, the major computations are vectorized and implemented in **hundreds** of lines of code, orders of magnitude more succinct than existing pipelines. All fundamental operations can be easily customized, only basic knowledge of Matlab programming is required. Mathematically oriented researchers can focus on the mathematical modeling part rather than the engineering part. Application oriented users can easily understand and modify any part of the framework to develop new network architectures and adapt them to new applications. Aside from its simplicity, LightNet has the following features: 1. LightNet contains the most modern network architectures. 2. Applications in computer vision, natural language processing and reinforcement learning are demonstrated. 3. LightNet provides a comprehensive collection of optimization algorithms. 4. LightNet supports straightforward switching between CPU and GPU computing. 5. Fast Fourier transforms are used to efficiently compute convolutions, and thus large convolution kernels are supported. 6. LightNet automates hyper-parameter tuning with a novel Selective-SGD algorithm.

2. USING THE PACKAGE

An example of using LightNet can be found in (Fig. 1): a simple template is provided to start the training process. The user is required to fill in some critical training parameters, such as the number of training epochs, or the training method. A Selective-SGD algorithm is provided to facilitate the selection of an optimal learning rate. The learning rate is

MM '16 October 15-19, 2016, Amsterdam, Netherlands

ACM ISBN 978-1-4503-3603-1/16/10.
DOI: http://dx.doi.org/10.1145/2964284.2973791

```
n_epoch=20; %training epochs
dataset_name='mnist'; %dataset name
network_name='cnn'; %network name
use_gpu=1; %use gpu or not

%function handle to prepare your data
PrepareDataFunc=@PrepareData_MNIST_CNN;
%function handle to initialize the network
NetInit=@net_init_cnn_mnist;

%automatically select learning rates
use_selective_sgd=1;
%select a new learning rate every n epochs
ssgd_search_freq=10;
learning_method=@sgd; %training method: @sgd

%sgd parameter
%(unnecessary if selective-sgd is used)
%sgd_lr=5e-2;

Main_Template(); %call training template
```

Figure 1: A basic example, which shows how to train a CNN on the MNIST dataset with LightNet.

selected automatically, and can optionally be adjusted during the training. The framework supports both GPU and CPU computation, through the *opts.use_gpu* option. Two additional functions are provided to prepare the training data and initialize the network structure. Every experiment in this paper can reproduced by running the related script file. More details can be found on the project webpage.

3. BUILDING BLOCKS

The primary computational module includes a feed forward process and a backward/back propagation process. The feed forward process evaluates the model, and the back propagation reports the network gradients. Stochastic gradient descent based algorithms are used to optimize the model parameters.

3.1 Core Computational Modules

LightNet allows us to focus on the mathematical modeling of the network, rather than low-level engineering details. To make this paper self-contained, we explain the main computational modules of LightNet. All networks (and related experiments) in this paper are built with these modules. The notations below are chosen for simplicity. Readers can easily extend the derivations to the mini-batch setting.

3.1.1 Linear Perceptron Layer

A linear perceptron layer can be expressed as: $y = Wx+b$. Here, x denotes the input data of size $input\_dim \times 1$, W denotes the weight matrix of size $output\_dim \times input\_dim$, b is a bias vector of size $output\_dim \times 1$, and y denotes the linear layer output of size $output\_dim \times 1$.

The mapping from the input of the linear perceptron to the final network output can be expressed as: $z = f(y) = f(Wx+b)$, where f is a non-linear function that represents the network's computation in the deeper layers, and z is the network output, which is usually a loss value.

The backward process calculates the derivative $\frac{\partial z}{\partial x}$, which is the derivative passing to the shallower layers, and $\frac{\partial z}{\partial W}$, $\frac{\partial z}{\partial b}$, which are the gradients that guide the gradient descent process.

$$\frac{\partial z}{\partial x} = \frac{\partial z}{\partial y} \cdot \frac{\partial y}{\partial x} = f'(y)^T \cdot W \tag{1}$$

$$\frac{\partial z}{\partial W} = \frac{\partial z}{\partial y} \cdot \frac{\partial y}{\partial W} = f'(y) \cdot x^T \tag{2}$$

$$\frac{\partial z}{\partial b} = \frac{\partial z}{\partial y} \cdot \frac{\partial y}{\partial b} = f'(y) \tag{3}$$

The module adopts extensively optimized Matlab matrix operations to calculate the matrix-vector products.

3.1.2 Convolutional Layer

A convolutional layer maps N_{map_in} input feature maps to N_{map_out} output feature maps with a multidimensional filter bank k_{io}. Each input feature map x_i is convolved with the corresponding filter bank k_{io}. The convolution results are summed, and a bias value b_o is added, to generate the o-th output map: $y_o = \sum_{1\leq i\leq N_{map\_in}} k_{io} * x_i + b_o$. To allow using large convolution kernels, fast Fourier transforms (FFT) are used for computing convolutions (and correlations). According to the convolution theorem [10], convolution in the spatial domain is equivalent to point-wise multiplication in the frequency domain. Therefore, $k_i * x_i$ can be calculated using the Fourier transform as: $k_i * x_i = \mathcal{F}^{-1}\{\mathcal{F}\{k_i\} \cdot \mathcal{F}\{x_i\}\}$. Here, $\mathcal{F}$ denotes the Fourier transform and $\cdot$ denotes the point-wise multiplication operation. The convolution layer supports both padding and striding.

The mapping from the o-th output feature map to the network output can be expressed as: $z = f(y_o)$. Here f is the non-linear mapping from the o-th output feature map y_o to the final network output. As before (in Sec. 3.1.1), $\frac{\partial z}{\partial x_i}$, $\frac{\partial z}{\partial k_i}$, and $\frac{\partial z}{\partial b_o}$ need to be calculated in the backward process, as follows:

$$\frac{\partial z}{\partial x_i} = \frac{\partial z}{\partial y_o} \cdot \frac{\partial y_o}{\partial x_i} = f'(y_o) \star k_i, \tag{4}$$

where $\star$ denotes the correlation operation. Denoting the complex conjugate as $conj$, this correlation is calculated in the frequency domain using the Fourier transform as: $x \star k = \mathcal{F}^{-1}\{\mathcal{F}\{x\} \cdot conj(\mathcal{F}\{k\})\}$.

$$\frac{\partial z}{\partial k^*_{io}} = \frac{\partial z}{\partial y_o} \cdot \frac{\partial y_o}{\partial k^*_{io}} = f'(y_o) \star x_i, \tag{5}$$

where k^* represents the flipped kernel k. Thus, the gradient $\frac{\partial z}{\partial k_{io}}$ is calculated by flipping the correlation output. Finally,

$$\frac{\partial z}{\partial b_o} = \frac{\partial z}{\partial y_o} \cdot \frac{\partial y_o}{\partial b_o} = 1^T \cdot vec(f'(y_o)) \tag{6}$$

In words, the gradient $\frac{\partial z}{\partial b_o}$ can be calculated by point-wise summation of the values in $f'(y_o)$.

3.1.3 Max-pooling Layer

The max pooling layer calculates the largest element in $P_r \times P_c$ windows, with stride size $S_r \times S_c$. A customized *im2col_ln* function is implemented to convert the stridden pooling patches into column vectors, to vectorize the pooling computation in Matlab. The built-in max function is called on these column vectors to return the pooling result and the indices of these maximum values. Then, the indices in the original batched data are recovered accordingly. Also, zero padding can be applied to the input data.

Without the loss of generality, the mapping from the max-pooling layer input to the final network output can be expressed as: $z = f(y) = f(Sx)$, where S is a selection matrix, and x is a column vector which denotes the input data in this layer.

In the backward process, $\frac{\partial z}{\partial x}$ is calculated and passed to the shallower layers: $\frac{\partial z}{\partial x} = \frac{\partial z}{\partial y} \cdot S = f'(y)^T S$.

When the pooling range is less than or equal to the stride size, $\frac{\partial z}{\partial x}$ can be calculated with simple matrix indexing techniques in Matlab. Specifically, an empty tensor $dzdx$ of the same size with the input data is created. $dzdx(from) = dzdy$, where $from$ is the pooling indices, and $dzdy$ is a tensor recording the pooling results. When the pooling range is larger than the stride size, each entry in x can be pooled multiple times, and the back propagation gradients need to be accumulated for each of these multiple-pooled entries. In this case, the $\frac{\partial z}{\partial x}$ is calculated using the Matlab function: $accumarray()$.

3.1.4 *Rectified Linear Unit*

The rectified linear unit ($ReLU$) is implemented as a major non-linear mapping function, some other functions including $sigmoid$ and $tanh$ are omitted from the discussion here. The $ReLU$ function is the identity function if the input is larger than 0 and outputs 0 otherwise: $y = relu(x) = x \cdot ind(x > 0)$. In the backward process, the gradient is passed to the shallower layer if the input data is non-negative. Otherwise, the gradient is ignored.

3.2 Loss function

Usually, a loss function is connected to the outputs of the deepest core computation module. Currently, LightNet supports the softmax log-loss function for classification tasks.

3.3 Optimization Algorithms

Stochastic gradient descent (SGD) algorithm based optimization algorithms are the primary tools to train deep neural networks. The standard SGD algorithm and several of its popular variants such as Adagrad [3], RMSProp [12] and Adam [6] are also implemented for deep learning research. It is worth mentioning that we implement a novel Selective-SGD algorithm to facilitate the selection of hyper-parameters, especially the learning rate. This algorithm selects the most efficient learning rate by running the SGD process for a few iterations using each learning rate from a discrete candidate set. During the middle of the neural net training, the Selective-SGD algorithm can also be applied to select different learning rates to accelerate the energy decay.

4. EXPERIMENTS

4.1 Multilayer Perceptron Network

A multilayer perceptron network is constructed to test the performance of LightNet on MNIST data [9]. The network takes 28×28 inputs from the MNIST image dataset and has 128 nodes respectively in the next two layers. The 128-dimensional features are then connected to 10 nodes to calculate the softmax output. See Fig. 2 for the experiment results.

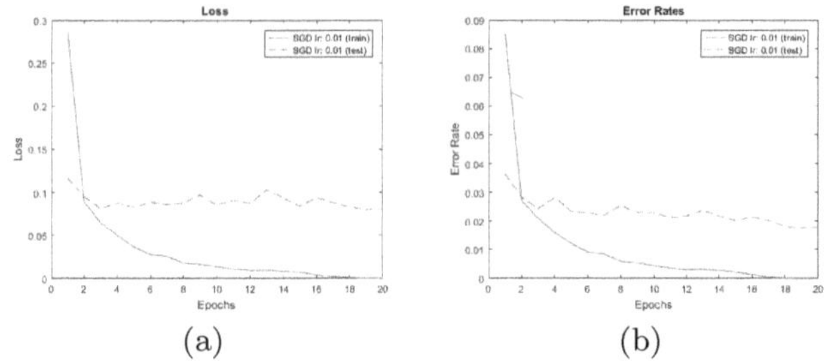

Figure 2: Loss and error rates during training and testing phases using LightNet on the MNIST dataset.

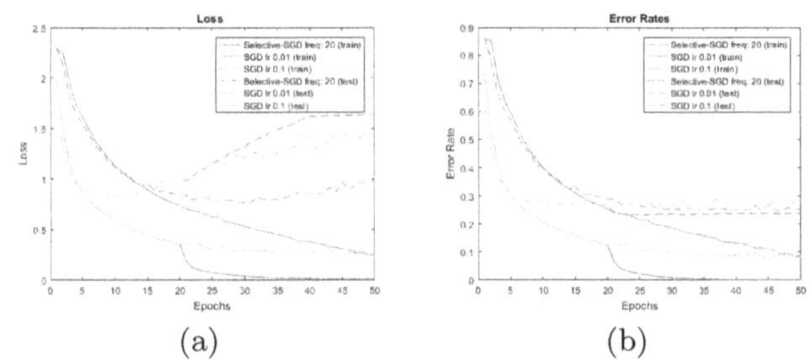

Figure 3: Loss and error rates of training and testing with LightNet on the CIFAR-10 dataset.

4.2 Convolutional Neural Network

LightNet supports using state-of-the-art convolutional network models pretrained on the ImageNet dataset. It also supports training novel network models from scratch. A convolutional network with 4 convolution layers is constructed to test the performance of LightNet on CIFAR-10 data [7]. There are $32, 32, 64, 64$ convolution kernels of size 5×5 in the first three layers, the last layer has kernel size 4×4. $relu$ functions are applied after each convolution layer as the non-linear mapping function. LightNet automatically selects and adjusts the learning rate and can achieve state-of-the-art accuracy with this architecture. Selective-SGD leads to better accuracy compared with standard SGD with a fixed learning rate. Most importantly, using Selective-SGD avoids manual tuning of the learning rate. See Fig. 3 for the experiment results. The computations are carried out on a desktop computer with an Intel i5 6600K CPU and a Nvidia Titan X GPU with 12GB memory. The current version of LightNet can process 750 images per second with this network structure on the GPU, around $5\times$ faster than using CPU.

4.3 LSTM Network

The Long Short Term Memory (LSTM) [4] is a popular recurrent neural network model. Because of LightNet's versatility, the LSTM network can be implemented in the LightNet package as a particular application. Notably, the core computational modules in LightNet are used to perform time domain forward process and back propagation for LSTM.

The forward process in an LSTM model can be formulated as:

$$i_t = sigmoid(W_{ih}h_{t-1} + W_{ix}x_t + b_i), \qquad (7)$$

$$o_t = sigmoid(W_{oh}h_{t-1} + W_{ox}x_t + b_o), \quad (8)$$

$$f_t = sigmoid(W_{fh}h_{t-1} + W_{fx}x_t + b_f), \quad (9)$$

$$g_t = tanh(W_{gh}h_{t-1} + W_{gx}x_t + b_g), \quad (10)$$

$$c_t = f_t \odot c_{t-1} + i_t \odot g_t, h_t = o_t \odot tanh(c_t), \quad (11)$$

$$z_t = f(h_t), z = \sum_{t=1}^{T} z_t. \quad (12)$$

Where $i_t/o_t/f_t$ denotes the response of the input/output/forget gate at time t. g_t denotes the distorted input to the memory cell at time t. c_t denotes the content of the memory cell at time t. h_t denotes the hidden node value. f maps the hidden nodes to the network loss z_t at time t. The full network loss is calculated by summing the loss at each individual time frame in Eq. 12.

To optimize the LSTM model, back propagation through time is implemented and the most critical value to calculate in LSTM is: $\frac{\partial z}{\partial c_s} = \sum_{t=s}^{T} \frac{\partial z_t}{\partial c_s}$.

A critical iterative property is adopted to calculate the above value:

$$\frac{\partial z}{\partial c_{s-1}} = \frac{\partial z}{\partial c_s}\frac{\partial c_s}{\partial c_{s-1}} + \frac{\partial z_{s-1}}{\partial c_{s-1}}. \quad (13)$$

A few other gradients can be calculated through the chain rule using the above calculation output:

$$\frac{\partial z_t}{\partial o_t} = \frac{\partial z_t}{\partial h_t}\frac{\partial h_t}{\partial o_t}, \frac{\partial z}{\partial \{i,f,g\}_t} = \frac{\partial z}{\partial c_t}\frac{\partial c_t}{\partial \{i,f,g\}_t}. \quad (14)$$

The LSTM network is tested on a character language modeling task. The dataset consists of 20,000 sentences selected from works of Shakespeare. Each sentence is broken into 67 characters (and punctuation marks), and the LSTM model is deployed to predict the next character based on the characters before. 30 hidden nodes are used in the network model and RMSProp is used for the training. After 10 epochs, the prediction accuracy of the next character is improved to 70%.

4.4 Q-Network

As an application in reinforcement learning, We created a Q-Network [11] with the MLP network. The Q-Network is then applied to the classic Cart-Pole problem [1]. The dynamics of the Cart-Pole system can be learned with a two-layer network in hundreds of iterations. One iteration of the update process of the Q-Network is:

$$\begin{aligned} Q_{new}(state_{old}, act) &= reward + \gamma Q_{current}(state_{new}, act_{best}) \\ &= reward + \gamma max_a Q_{current}(state_{new}, a) \\ &= reward + \gamma V(state_{new}). \quad (15) \end{aligned}$$

The *action* is randomly selected with probability *epsilon*, otherwise the *action* leading to the highest score is selected. The desired network output Q_{new} is calculated using the observed reward and the discounted value $\gamma V(state_{new})$ of the resulting state, predicted by the current network through Eq. 15.

By using a least squared loss function:

$$\begin{aligned} z &= (y - Q_{current}(state_{old}, act))^2 \\ &= (Q_{new}(state_{old}, act) - Q_{current}(state_{old}, act))^2, \quad (16) \end{aligned}$$

the Q-Network can be optimized using the gradient:

$$\frac{\partial z}{\partial \theta} = \frac{\partial z}{\partial Q_{current}}\frac{\partial Q_{current}}{\partial \theta}. \quad (17)$$

Here θ denotes the parameters in the Q-Network.

5. CONCLUSION

LightNet provides an easy-to-expand ecosystem for the understanding and development of deep neural network models. Thanks to its user-friendly Matlab based environment, the whole computational process can be easily tracked and visualized. This set of the main features can provide unique convenience to the deep learning research community.

6. ACKNOWLEDGEMENTS

This work was funded by the support of the National Science Foundation under grant SMA 1540917 and grant CNS 1544797, and by DARPA through U.S. Army grant W911NF-14-1-0384.

7. REFERENCES

[1] Barto, A. G., Sutton, R. S., and Anderson, C. W. Neuronlike adaptive elements that can solve difficult learning control problems. *Systems, Man and Cybernetics, IEEE Transactions on, 5* (1983), 834–846.

[2] Bastien, F., Lamblin, P., Pascanu, R., Bergstra, J., Goodfellow, I., Bergeron, A., Bouchard, N., Warde-Farley, D., and Bengio, Y. Theano: new features and speed improvements. *arXiv preprint arXiv:1211.5590* (2012).

[3] Duchi, J., Hazan, E., and Singer, Y. Adaptive subgradient methods for online learning and stochastic optimization. *The Journal of Machine Learning Research 12* (2011), 2121–2159.

[4] Hochreiter, S., and Schmidhuber, J. Long short-term memory. *Neural computation 9*, 8 (1997), 1735–1780.

[5] Jia, Y., Shelhamer, E., Donahue, J., Karayev, S., Long, J., Girshick, R., Guadarrama, S., and Darrell, T. Caffe: Convolutional architecture for fast feature embedding. In *Proceedings of the ACM International Conference on Multimedia* (2014), ACM, pp. 675–678.

[6] Kingma, D., and Ba, J. Adam: A method for stochastic optimization. *arXiv preprint arXiv:1412.6980* (2014).

[7] Krizhevsky, A., and Hinton, G. Learning multiple layers of features from tiny images, 2009.

[8] Krizhevsky, A., Sutskever, I., and Hinton, G. E. Imagenet classification with deep convolutional neural networks. In *Advances in neural information processing systems* (2012), pp. 1097–1105.

[9] LeCun, Y., Bottou, L., Bengio, Y., and Haffner, P. Gradient-based learning applied to document recognition. *Proceedings of the IEEE 86*, 11 (1998), 2278–2324.

[10] Mallat, S. *A wavelet tour of signal processing: the sparse way.* Academic press, 2008.

[11] Mnih, V., Kavukcuoglu, K., Silver, D., Rusu, A. A., Veness, J., Bellemare, M. G., Graves, A., Riedmiller, M., Fidjeland, A. K., Ostrovski, G., et al. Human-level control through deep reinforcement learning. *Nature 518*, 7540 (2015), 529–533.

[12] Tieleman, T., and Hinton, G. Lecture 6.5-rmsprop: Divide the gradient by a running average of its recent magnitude. *COURSERA: Neural Networks for Machine Learning 4* (2012), 2.

[13] Vedaldi, A., and Lenc, K. Matconvnet: Convolutional neural networks for matlab. In *Proceedings of the 23rd Annual ACM Conference on Multimedia Conference* (2015), ACM, pp. 689–692.

Morph: A Fast and Scalable Cloud Transcoding System

Guanyu Gao
School of Computer Science and Engineering
Nanyang Technological University
ggao001@ntu.edu.sg

Yonggang Wen
School of Computer Science and Engineering
Nanyang Technological University
ygwen@ntu.edu.sg

ABSTRACT

Morph is an open source cloud transcoding system. It can leverage the scalability of the cloud infrastructure to encode and transcode video contents in fast speed, and dynamically provision the resources in cloud to accommodate the workload. The system is composed of a master node that performs the video file segmentation, concentration, and task scheduling operations; and multiple worker nodes that perform the transcoding for video blocks. Morph can transcode the video blocks of a video file on multiple workers in parallel to achieve fast speed, and automatically manage the data transfers and communications between the master node and the worker nodes. The worker nodes can join into or leave the transcoding cluster at any time for dynamic resource provisioning. The system is very modular, and all of the algorithms can be easily modified or replaced. We release the source code of Morph under MIT License, hoping that it can be shared among various research communities.

Keywords

Video transcoding; cloud computing; distributed system; task scheduling; resource provisioning;

1. INTRODUCTION

Video transcoding is a popular solution for content adaptation [8]. It is commonly used in adaptive bitrate (ABR) streaming to encode video contents into multiple representations in different bitrates and resolutions. Particularly, with the rapid growth of mobile devices and global mobile data traffic, transcoding has become a must for content adaptation to ensure that the source content can be viewed on any device and in any network conditions. However, transcoding is a complicated signal conversion procedure [8], which consumes massive computing resource and incurs excessive processing delays. Moreover, the traditional in-house transcoding methods, which maintain a fixed number of servers, typically need to over-provision the computing resource by at least 30% to meet the peak workload [4]. This creates a resource wastage when the workload is low.

A new trend for transcoding is to adopt the cloud infrastructure to provide transcoding as a cloud service. Specifically, the cloud transcoding system can use many VM instances or Containers to transcode the video contents in parallel to achieve fast speed. Meanwhile, by leveraging the elasticity of the cloud infrastructure, the system can dynamically provision the resource to adapt to the workload, avoiding excessive processing delays or resource wastage.

Seeking to address the transcoding demand for the fast growing volume of video contents, many online cloud transcoding services have emerged in recent years. Bitcodin [3, 7] is capable of encoding up to 100x faster than real time. Amazon Elastic Transcoder is designed to be scalable and cost-effective for developers to transcode the video files [1]. Zencoder can encode high-definition (HD) quality video faster than real time. The content delivery network service provider Akamai also launched cloud-based transcoding service Sola Vision for adaptive media delivery [2]. Encoding.com can automatically scale the computing resource to achieve a level of computation efficiency. For managing the multiple versions of the video content in ABR cost-efficiently, we implemented the video content management system in our previous work [6] for reducing the operational cost.

Many commercial cloud transcoding services are available online, however, we observe there is still a lack of mature open source software projects for cloud transcoding. This paper presents the design and implementation of our cloud video transcoding system Morph, which is a well documented open source project. We believe it can be used in the research area of transcoding, distributed system, task scheduling, resource provisioning, etc. The system is reliable even under heavy workload, and we provide multiple types of service interfaces so that it can be easily deployed in a production environment. We release the source code of Morph on Github under MIT License. We are still developing new features for Morph, and we welcome suggestion and contribution from communities. The source code and documentation are available at the following links:

Source Code: https://github.com/cap-ntu/Morph
Project Page: http://morph.aidynamic.com/

2. FEATURES

Morph can transcode the video files in fast speed; schedule the tasks according to their Qos profiles; and dynamically

MM '16, October 15-19, 2016, Amsterdam, Netherlands
© 2016 ACM. ISBN 978-1-4503-3603-1/16/10...$15.00
DOI: http://dx.doi.org/10.1145/2964284.2973792

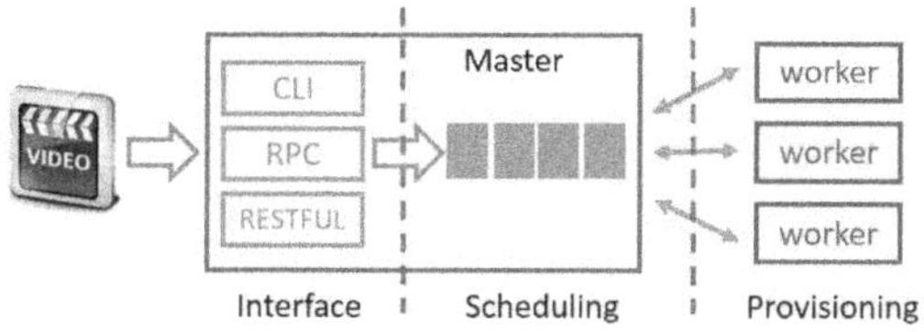

Figure 1: System architecture.

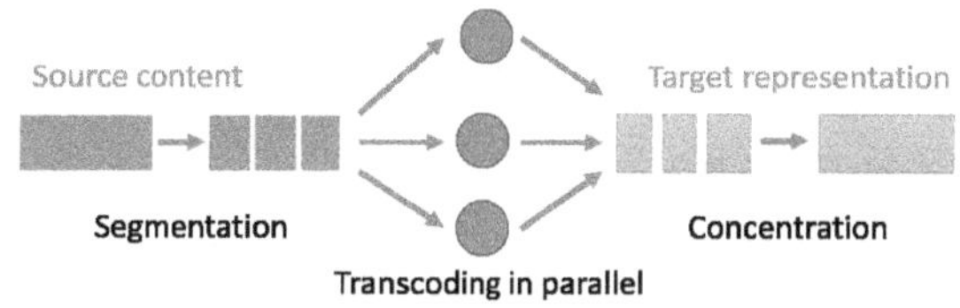

Figure 2: Workflow for a transcoding task.

provision the computing resource to accommodate the workload. Specifically, it has the following main features:

Block level parallelism: Each video file is segmented into many equal-size video blocks, and the video blocks can be transcoded on multiple workers in parallel. Compared with the file level parallelism, this can greatly improve the transcoding speed for the large video files if the number of available transcoding workers in the system is large.

Scheduling to meet QoS requirements: The video contents may have different QoS requirements for transcoding. We implement many scheduling algorithms in our system for meeting the QoS profiles of the transcoding tasks. It is easy to modify or extend the scheduling algorithms in our system.

Elasticity for resource provisioning: The master node of Morph can work with an arbitrary number of transcoding workers. The workers can dynamically joint in or leave the cluster to accommodate the time-varying workload. The system can activate more workers when the transcoding workload is high, and turn off some workers when the workload decreases to achieve dynamic resource provisioning.

3. DESIGN

We first present the architecture of Morph, and then we introduce the workflow for fulfilling transcoding requests.

3.1 Architecture

We illustrate the system architecture of Morph in Fig. 1. The system is composed of the following layers:

Interface layer: It interacts with the users for processing the transcoding requests and preprocessing the video contents. The system provides three types of service interfaces, namely, command line interface (CLI), remote procedure call (RPC), and Restful API. The users can submit the transcoding tasks and query the transcoding progress via the service interfaces. For each of the user submitted transcoding tasks, it will estimate the required computing time for the task and segment the video files into video blocks for transcoding in parallel on the workers.

Scheduling layer: The user submitted transcoding tasks will be put into the scheduling queue. The task scheduler sequences the pending tasks in the queue according to the scheduling policy and the QoS profiles of the tasks. Whenever the master node receives a transcoding request from the worker, the task scheduler will select a video block from the pending tasks for dispatching by applying the scheduling policy. The transcoded video blocks on the worker will be sent back to the master for video concentration.

Provisioning layer: It manages the transcoding workers for dynamic resource provisioning. Our system can adopt the virtual machines (e.g., KVM) or containers (e.g., Docker) for resource virtualization. Each VM instance or container runs a worker. The worker will request a video block from the master node whenever it is idle. The worker will transcode the video block into the target representations, which will be sent back to the master node.

3.2 Workflow

We illustrate the workflow for transcoding a video content in Fig. 2. The user submit a transcoding task by uploading a video file and specifying the transcoding parameters. The video content will be segmented into independent video blocks according to the group of pictures (GOP) structure. The video block information of the task will be then put into the scheduling queue. When an idle worker requests a video block from the master node, the scheduler determines which video block in the scheduling queue will be selected for dispatching by applying the scheduling policy. The worker will transcode the video block into the target representation, and then send back the target representation to the master node. Because the system may have many available workers, the video blocks in the scheduling queue can be requested and transcoded by the workers in parallel. The master node continuously checks the transcoding status of the video blocks of each task. If all the video blocks of a task have been successfully completed, the master node will concentrate the video blocks into one video file. Then, the transcoding task is finished and the target representations of the video content are ready to be downloaded by the users.

4. IMPLEMENTATION

In this section, we present the system implementation. The main components of the system are illustrated in Fig. 3. The components of the interface, segmenter, scheduler, data transfer, and concentrater, are implemented as independent threads in the master node. Each worker is an independent progress running on a VM instance or container. The resource controller is an independent progress for managing the status of the workers. We adopt the FFmpeg for the transcoding operations. We discuss the details of the implementation for each part in the following subsections.

4.1 Interface

We provide three types of interfaces for the users to access the transcoding service, namely, CLI, RPC, and Restful API. When the user submits a task, the system will return a key. The user can use the key for querying the transcoding progress of the task. We adopt the SimpleXMLRPCServer for implementing the XML-RPC servers in Python.

4.2 Segmenter

The video segmenter determines the duration of each video block when segmenting the video files. The video block duration impacts the transcoding performance of the system. Specifically, if the duration of each video block is short, a video file is to be segmented into more blocks, and it would incur more communication overhead among the master and

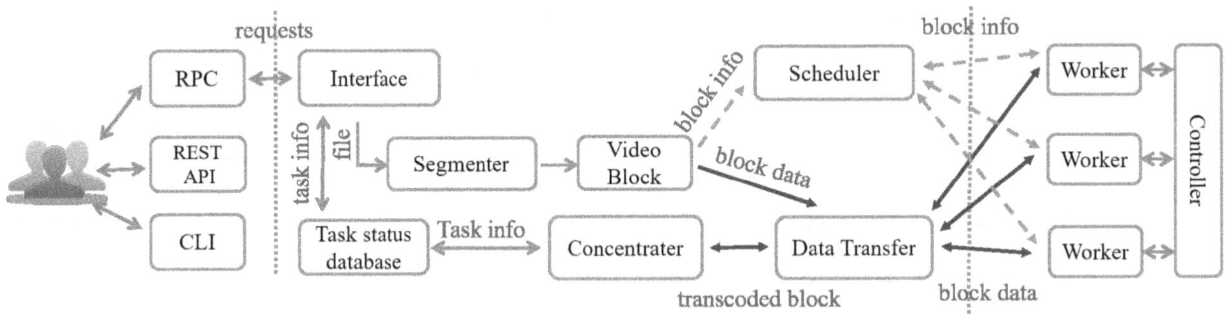

Figure 3: The system implementation of Morph.

the workers. On the other hand, if the duration of each video block is very long, a video file is to be segmented into fewer blocks, it cannot take the advantage of the large number of workers for parallel transcoding the video file. Our system provides the two following methods for determining the duration of the video block for a task:

1) *Predefined*: The system can read a predefined value from the configuration file when starting. With this method, the video blocks of all tasks have the same duration.

2) *Dynamically determined*: The duration of a video block for a specified task can be determined on the fly when segmenting the video file by applying a segmentation algorithm.

4.3 Scheduler

The system maintains a queue for the pending transcoding tasks, and the scheduler sequences the tasks in the queue periodically according to the scheduling algorithms. The scheduling algorithms are implemented as an independent module in the source file of 'algorithms/scheduling.py'. Each scheduling algorithm is implemented as a function. It is easy to modify or extend the scheduling algorithms without affecting the other modules of the system. We have implemented the following scheduling algorithms in the system: 1) *FIFO*: First In First Out. 2) *LIFO*: Last In First Out. 3) *EDF*: Earliest Deadline First. 4) *HPF*: Highest Priority First. 5) *HVS*: Highest Value First. The scheduling algorithms affect the QoS of the transcoding service. The system operator can set the scheduling algorithm in the configuration file based on the QoS considerations of the service. For instance, one can set sch_alg = 'hpf' in configuration for scheduling the tasks with the highest priority first.

4.4 Transfer

The data transfer interacts with the workers to send the video blocks and receive the transcoded video blocks from the workers. The video block data will be packed with the transcoding parameters and MD5 checksum of the data, and then sent to the worker for transcoding. The format for packing and unpacking the video block data is defined in the file 'common.py'. The data transfer uses multithreading mechanism for sending and receiving the data, and it can communicate with multiple workers at the same time.

4.5 Worker

The worker requests the video block for transcoding from the master whenever it is idle. After receiving the video block data from the master, it will check the validity of the data and transcode it into the target representations. If the transcoding for the video block is finished successfully, it will pack the video data with the transcoding information and send it to the master. Otherwise, it will notify the master of the failure of the task.

4.6 Concentrater

The concentrater is implemented as a thread for checking and updating the status of each transcoding task. If all the video blocks of a task have been transcoded successfully, it will concentrate the video blocks of the task into one video file and update the status of the task as success. If any video block of a task is transcoded unsuccessful, it will update the status of the task as fail.

4.7 Controller

The controller determines which worker should be activated. It reads the pending tasks information from the system database for calculating the workload, and makes the control decisions by applying the provisioning policy. In our implementation, the control of the status of the workers is independent of starting or stopping the VMs or Containers. We create a field for each worker in the database to represent the status of the workers, where 1 represents active and 0 represents sleep. The controller updates the values according to the control decisions. The worker determines its own working status by accessing the value of this field. The API for starting or stopping a VM or container depends on the specific resource virtualization software. Each software provides its own version of interfaces (e.g., the remote API for Docker). We did not cover the control for the VM and Container in our implementation due to the dependence on the API interface of the specific virtualization software.

5. DEPLOYMENT

In this section, we present the system deployment in the real environment. We also discuss the potential system bottleneck in large scale deployments and the possible solutions.

5.1 Software Stack

We illustrate the software stack of Morph in Fig. 4. The master and worker depend on ffmpeg for video transcoding. Therefore, each VM or Container that runs the master or worker needs to install ffmpeg. We adopt MySQL database for storing the task information. The master, workers, and controller should all can connect to the MySQL server for accessing the information. If one needs to use the Restful API to access, the Apache HTTP webserver should be installed and configured for processing the HTTP requests.

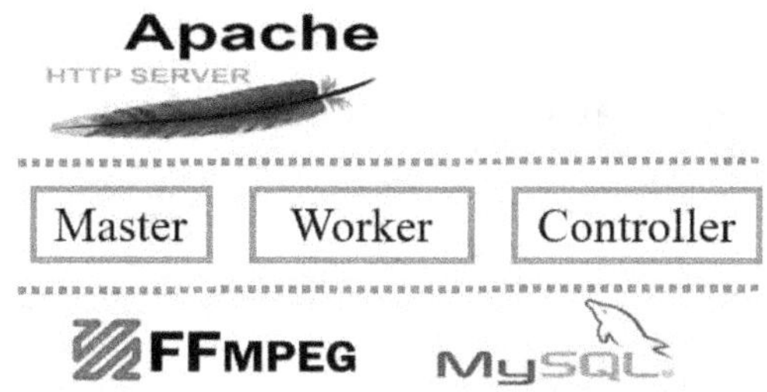

Figure 4: The software stack of Morph.

5.2 Potential Bottleneck

We design and implement the system in a simple and reliable way, however, it still have some potential performance bottleneck. The main performance bottleneck is from the master node, which is a single point of failure. One concern is that the master node will have more overhead for transferring and processing the video data with more active workers in a cluster. However, the video data transferring and processing (segmentation and concentration) time in the master node is relatively small compared with the transcoding time in the worker node. In our experiment, the workload of the master node is very small when the system has 30 active workers that work at the full capacity. If the number of provisioned workers in the system is very large, the performance bottleneck of the master node will become significant. Another concern is that the single point failure of the master node will make the transcoding service unavailable, while the system reliability is critical for the online service.

One effective solution for the above discussed problems is to introduce a load balancer into the system, as illustrated in Fig. 5. A load balancer has daemon processes and can recover itself from failure very fast if it collapses on its own. We can divide the system into smaller groups, and each group consists of a master node and many workers. Normally, the balancer balances the workload among the groups. If the balancer detects the failure of one master node, it will direct the transcoding requests to the other active groups until the broken-down master node recovers.

6. PERFORMANCE

Testbed: The duration of the test video file is 138 minutes. The resolution is 1920x1080, and the bitrate is 2399 kb/s. The video data is encoded in H.264, and the audio data is encoded in AAC. The CPU frequency is 2.10GHz. The master node is allocated with 8 CPU cores, and the memory size is 8GB. The worker node is allocated with 4 CPU cores, and the memory size is 2GB. We use the Docker to build the cloud platform. The video block duration is 2 minutes. The target resolution of the transcoding is 480x360. *Transcoding time:* We measure the transcoding time using Morph with different number of active workers, and compare it with the standalone FFmpeg method. The transcoding time and the speedup ratio compared with the standalone FFmpeg method are illustrate in Table 1. The transcoding time for using a standalone FFmpeg on a single server is 1775 seconds. With one active worker, the transcoding time for Morph is 1843 seconds, larger than the standalone ffmpeg method. The overhead comes from the video segmentation, transmission, and concentration operations. Specifically, the video segmentation time is 46 seconds, and the video block concentration time is 13 seconds. With more active workers, the transcoding time for Morph decreases, because it can transcode the video blocks in parallel with more workers.

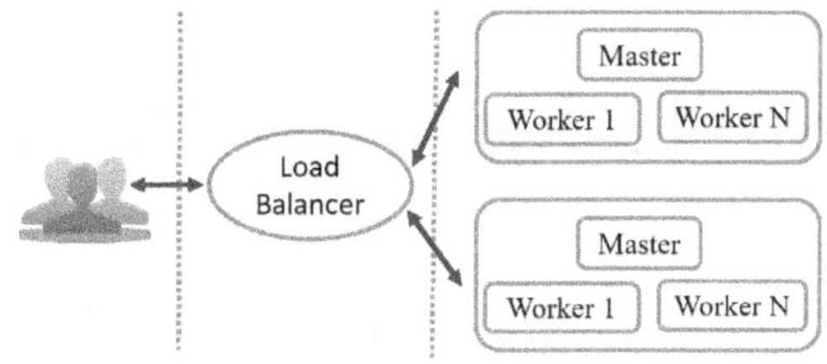

Figure 5: Load balancing for large scale deployment.

Table 1: Transcoding time comparison

Worker Num	FFmpeg	1	5	10	20	30
Time (s)	1775	1843	605	369	213	181
Speed-up (x)	1	0.96	2.9	4.8	8.3	9.8

Task scheduling and resource provisioning: We have also designed some task scheduling and resource provisioning algorithms based on Morph, and evaluated the performances in our previously work [5].

7. CONCLUSION

This paper presents the design and implementation of our open source cloud transcoding system Morph. We aim to design a cloud transcoding system that can achieve fast transcoding speed and elastic system scaling. The system is useful for the research and system development in the field of video transcoding, distributed system, task scheduling, and resource provisioning. The project is open sourced and well documented. In the future, we will continue to maintain and develop new features and functions to extend the system. We hope it can be easy for the researcher to verify the algorithms on it, and we also expect that it can be used as an efficient software for transcoding in a cloud environment.

8. REFERENCES

[1] http://aws.amazon.com/elastictranscoder/.
[2] http://www.beet.tv/2012/09/akamaicloud.html.
[3] Bitcodin. https://www.bitmovin.com/encoding/.
[4] J. Careless. Cloud video encoding: When to go online and when to stay in-house. *Streaming Media*, 2012.
[5] G. Gao, Y. Wen, and C. Westphal. Resource provisioning and profit maximization for transcoding in information centric networking. Infocom Workshop on Muisc, 2016, http://arxiv.org/abs/1605.05758.
[6] G. Gao, Y. Wen, W. Zhang, and H. Hu. Cost-efficient and qos-aware content management in media cloud: Implementation and evaluation. In *IEEE International Conference on Communications (ICC)*. IEEE, 2015.
[7] C. Timmerer, D. Weinberger, M. Smole, R. Grandl, C. Müller, and S. Lederer. Cloud-based transcoding and adaptive video streaming-as-a-service. *E-letter.*
[8] A. Vetro, C. Christopoulos, and H. Sun. Video transcoding architectures and techniques: an overview. *Signal Processing Magazine, IEEE*, 20(2):18–29, 2003.

Smart Beholder: An Extensible Smart Lens Platform

Chun-Ying Huang[1], Ching-Ling Fan[2], Chih-Fan Hsu[3], Hsin-Yu Chang[2], Tsung-Han Tsai[3], Kuan-Ta Chen[3], and Cheng-Hsin Hsu[2]

[1]Department of Computer Science, National Chiao Tung University
[2]Department of Computer Science, National Tsing Hua University
[3]Institute of Information Science, Academia Sinica

ABSTRACT

Smart Lenses refer to detachable, orientable and zoomable lenses that stream live videos over wireless networks to heterogeneous computing devices, including tablets and smartphones. Various novel applications are made possible by smart lenses, including mobile photography, smart surveillance cameras, and Unmanned Aerial Vehicle (UAV) cameras. However, to our best knowledge, existing smart lenses are closed and proprietary, and thus we initiate an open-source project called Smart Beholder for end-to-end solutions of smart lenses. The code and documents of Smart Beholder can be found at our website http://www.smartbeholder.org. Our Smart Beholder platform are useful to researchers for fast prototyping, developers for rapid development, and amateurs for hobbies. We have implemented Smart Beholder server (camera) using a popular embedded Linux platform, called Raspberry Pi. We have also realized Smart Beholder client (controller) on various OS's, including Android. Our experimental results show the practicality and efficiency of our proposed Smart Beholder: we outperform commercial products in the market in terms of both objective and subjective metrics. We believe the release of Smart Beholder will stimulate future studies on novel multimedia applications enabled by smart lenses.

Keywords: Streaming; wireless networks; camera; optimization; smartphones; mobile devices; quality of experience

1. INTRODUCTION

Miniature sensors and actuators are getting increasingly popular, and users expect to access intelligent information gathering systems, such as *smart lenses*, from their tablets, smartphones, and smart watches. Smart lenses refer to detachable, orientable, and zoomable lenses that stream live videos to heterogeneous computing devices over wireless networks. Users exercise these computing devices to control smart lenses for: (i) adjusting various settings, such as orientation and optical/digital zoom, (ii) previewing the current view, and (iii) capturing photos or videos. Through the separation of optical lenses and computing devices, smart lenses offer higher flexibility and enable novel multimedia applications that were not possible before. These applications include, but are not limited to:

- **Mobile photography.** Although smartphones are widely used by casual photographers, smartphone cameras often adopt small sensors without optical zoom supports due to limited spaces. This in turn leads to inferior photo/video quality and limited camera features [1]. In contrast, regular digital cameras give users full control over aperture, white balance, shutter speed, and so on. Smart lenses [2,5,13] are not limited by the small form factor of smartphones, and may provide similar features/quality as digital cameras.
- **Smart surveillance cameras.** Governments and organizations, such as police departments, may deploy surveillance cameras for real-time, high-quality, and interactive photo/video gathering, so as to improve urban safety, such as identifying fights, riots, protests, demonstrations, fires, chemical leaks, and stampedes. Amateurs may also deploy surveillance cameras at home [11], e.g., to check on their pets when traveling.
- **UAV (Unmanned Aerial Vehicle) cameras.** Increasingly more hobbyists and journalists adopt UAVs to capture aerial photos/videos, which are made possible because of UAVs' 3D mobility. Several UAV manufacturers [4,14], provide different mounts to turn smart lenses [5,7] and thermal imaging cameras [6], into UAV cameras.

Optimizing smart lenses for good user experience in these and future applications is not an easy task, because smart lenses are connected to computing devices via wireless networks, which are vulnerable to interference, channel fading, and shadowing. In addition, users have two expectations: (i) low interaction delay and (ii) high graphics quality, which are inherently contradicting to each other. Last, smart lenses are typically implemented on resource-scarce embedded systems, which further complicate the design, development, and implementation of smart lenses for diverse applications. Fortunately, researchers and developers have plenty of ideas on addressing these challenges. However, existing smart lenses products [2, 5, 7, 11, 13] are closed and proprietary, preventing researchers and developers from fast prototyping so as to validate their ideas.

To resolve the problem, we present *Smart Beholder*, which is an open-source end-to-end platform for smart lenses. The

MM '16, October 15-19, 2016, Amsterdam, Netherlands
© 2016 ACM. ISBN 978-1-4503-3603-1/16/10...$15.00
DOI: http://dx.doi.org/10.1145/2964284.2973793

Figure 1: Sample usage scenarios of Smart Beholder.

code and documents of Smart Beholder are publicly available at http://www.smartbeholder.org, and detailed system designs are given in Huang et al. [8]. Figure 1 shows typical usage scenarios of Smart Beholder, which consists of a server and a client. Smart Beholder server is an embedded system equipped with a lens and a wireless interface, while Smart Beholder client runs on a computing devices such as a tablet or a smartphone. The server captures views and streams them in real-time to the client via wireless networks. Smart Beholder is designed with three goals: (i) cost effectiveness, (ii) low interaction latency, and (iii) high preview quality. These goals are achieved by: (i) choosing a just-powerful-enough embedded system (Raspberry Pi [12]), (ii) minimizing latency in all software components, and (iii) dynamically adapting the video coding parameters.

2. SYSTEM DESIGN

Figure 2 gives the high-level design of Smart Beholder. The server consists of network interface and video streamer. The network interface includes: (i) AP (Access point) service that allows clients to connect to the server, and (ii) the DHCP server that assigns clients IP addresses. The networks between Smart Beholder server and client can be single-hop WiFi networks (e.g., for mobile photography and UAV cameras) or multi-hop wired and wireless networks (e.g., for smart surveillance cameras). The video streamer captures videos using camera capturer, encodes videos using encoder module, and streams videos to the clients through the RTSP (Real-Time Streaming Protocol)/RTP (Real-Time Protocol) server. The Smart Beholder client consists of UI (User Interface) and video streamer. The UI renders received videos via viewfinder and takes user inputs using camera controller. The user inputs are interpreted as user commands and transferred from controller client to controller server. The user commands may include taking photos, recording videos, and configuring effect settings, such as white balancing, exposure, and sensitivity. In addition, the RTSP/RTP client periodically measures the available bandwidth and sends the results to server for dynamic parameter selections of preview videos.

3. INTENDED AUDIENCE

Smart Beholder is designed for three kinds of intended audience. First, researchers may use Smart Beholder platform to analyze and evaluate their new ideas without implementing everything from scratch. That is, Smart Beholder enables fast prototyping on smart lens based applications for academic exploration. Second, developers may use Smart Beholder to develop new products with high-quality user experience. The developers only need to adjust some parameters and add/delete components to improve the performance or offer new functionalities. This promotes rapid development of smart lens based applications. Third, amateurs may also build our platform and customize it for fun. This may encourage them to try innovative smart lens based applications. Smart Beholder works for researchers, developers, and amateurs because it is extensible, portable, configurable, and open. We envision that the release of Smart Beholder will stimulate more projects on new smart lens based applications. For example, in Section 8, we demonstrate how to use Smart Beholder to build a panoramic camera.

4. SOURCE TREE STRUCTURE

Smart Beholder is released with two types of software packs: `all-in-one` and pre-compiled binary packs. In addition, the source codes are available on our project website at http://www.smartbeholder.org. The `all-in-one` pack includes Smart Beholder source codes, third-party library source code, pre-compiled binaries, while a pre-compiled binary pack includes only binaries for running the software on Raspberry Pi [12]. Users may extend Smart Beholder to support other hardware platforms running embedded Linux. There are five subdirectories in the `all-in-one` pack; their descriptions are given in the following.

- `bin/`: Pre-compiled run-time files, including the executables, modules, and configurations. The current pre-compiled files are built on Raspbian Linux.
- `codes/`: Source codes for Smart Beholder, which is divided into three parts: libcore, module, and server.
- `deps.posix/`: Dependencies for POSIX platforms, including libraries and headers. Smart Beholder currently supports Raspberry Pi, which runs a POSIX-compatible Linux. This subdirectory is empty by default, as the files in this subdirectory are built from the sources in `deps.src`.
- `deps.src/`: Source files of the dependent third-party packages. You will need these files to build dependencies for POSIX platforms.
- `scripts/`: Sample setup scripts, e.g., to turn a Raspberry Pi into a WiFi AP.

5. COMPILATION AND SETUP

Smart Beholder can be installed by uncompressing the software packs, with or without the source codes. If `all-in-one` software pack is downloaded, the complete Smart Beholder system can be compiled from scratch. Smart Beholder is a platform dependent software, and the compilation and setup instructions are written for Raspberry Pi [12].

Users attach an official camera module to a Raspberry Pi, and install Raspbian Wheezy Linux To build Smart Beholder, users first make sure that `g++`, `pkg-config`, `libX11`, `libXext`, `libXtst`, `libfreetype6`, `libgl1-mesa`, `libglu1-mesa`, `libpulse`, `libasound2`, `libmp3lame`, `libopus`, `libogg`, `libvorbis`, `libtheora`, `libvpx`, `libx264`, and `libxvidcore` are installed. Users must install both binaries and development files for the above packages. Next, the following instructions are recommended:

1. Edit the `env-setup` script and point `GADEPS` to the absolute path of `beholder/deps.posix/`.
2. Load environment variables from `env-setup` by using `.` or `source` commands.

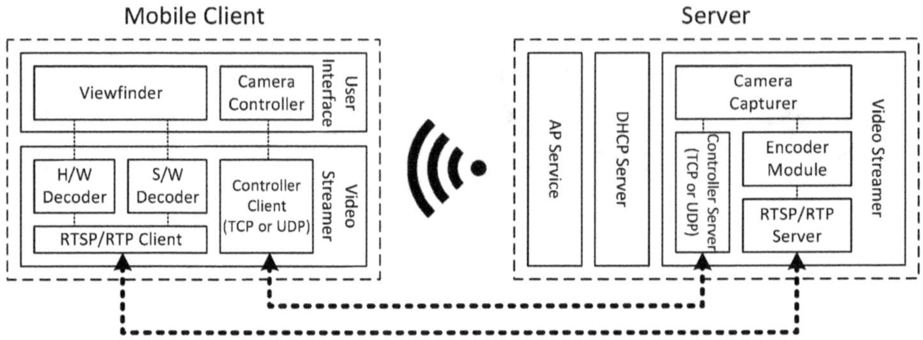

Figure 2: The design of Smart Beholder.

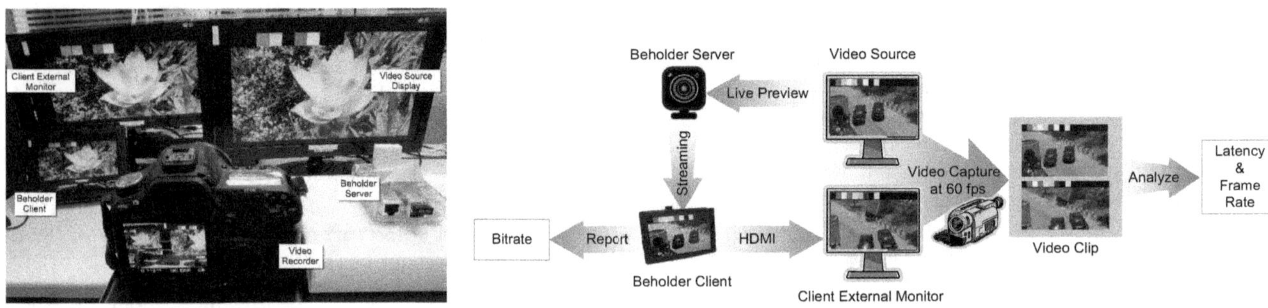

(a) (b)

Figure 3: Experimental setup: (a) testbed and (b) procedure.

3. Build dependencies using `make -f Makefile.raspbian` under `deps.src/`. All third-party libraries will be then installed in `deps.posix/`.
4. Build Smart Beholder using `make all` under `codes/`.
5. Install Smart Beholder using `make install` under `codes/`. All binaries and configurations will be copied to `bin/`.

Users next configure Raspberry Pi into a WiFi AP using `hostapd` and `dhcpd` tools. Users may modify our sample configurations `scripts/hostapd.conf` and `scripts/dhcpd.conf` for this purpose. However, `hostapd` does not work with all wireless modules. In particular, a Linux wireless driver must support `nl80211` interface to work properly with `hostapd`, and thus users have to carefully choose WiFi adaptors.

6. EXECUTION GUIDE

This section explains how to run Smart Beholder server and client. Before running binaries, please ensure that the full path to `deps.posix/lib` has been added to the system-wide `ld.so` search path. Smart Beholder can be launched using the following command: `server-rpi config/server.rpi.conf`. If a Raspberry Pi is configured as an AP using our `hostapd.conf` and `dhcpd.conf`, a wireless device can associate to the AP's SSID `smartb` using password `smartbeholder`. On a PC or a Mac client, please use the following command: `client config/client.abs.conf rtsp://192.168.11.254:8554/beholder` to connect to Smart Beholder. On an Android device, the client can connect to `rtsp://192.168.11.254:8554/beholder`. Alternatively, users can use an RTSP video player to connect to the same URL to watch the live video captured by Smart Beholder. By default, Smart Beholder uses TCP port 8554 for RTSP streams and TCP/UDP port 8555 for control messages. Once connected, a client can send a mouse click or screen touch event to Smart Beholder for taking a camera shot. The captured photos are by default stored in `/tmp` directory. The photo directory can be changed using the `photo_dir` option in Smart Beholder server configuration.

7. PERFORMANCE EVALUATIONS

We conduct real experiments to evaluate and compare our proposed Smart Beholder against two products: Altek Cubic [2] and SONY QX100 [5]. In our experiments, we consider the following performance metrics: bitrate, latency, frame rate, and preview quality in MOS (Mean Opinion Score). Figure 3(a) shows our testbed setup. The video source is played on the right monitor, which is captured by the Smart Beholder server. The server then streams the preview video to the client running on the tablet on the left via a WiFi network. The tablet is connected to an external monitor, and we use a Canon EOS 600D camera to capture the two monitors at 60 fps (frame-per-second), and report the objective experiments results (see Figure 3(b)). For subjective evaluations, we recruit 52 subjects and perform 117 sessions that totaled 14,410 comparison rounds.

Sample experiment results are given in Figure 4 due to the space limitations. Figure 4(a) shows that the bitrate of Smart Beholder is 3 Mbps, which is half of other commercial products. Figures 4(c) and 4(b) reveal that the Smart Beholder achieves slightly higher frame rate as well as has higher interactivity since the latency of Smart Beholder is

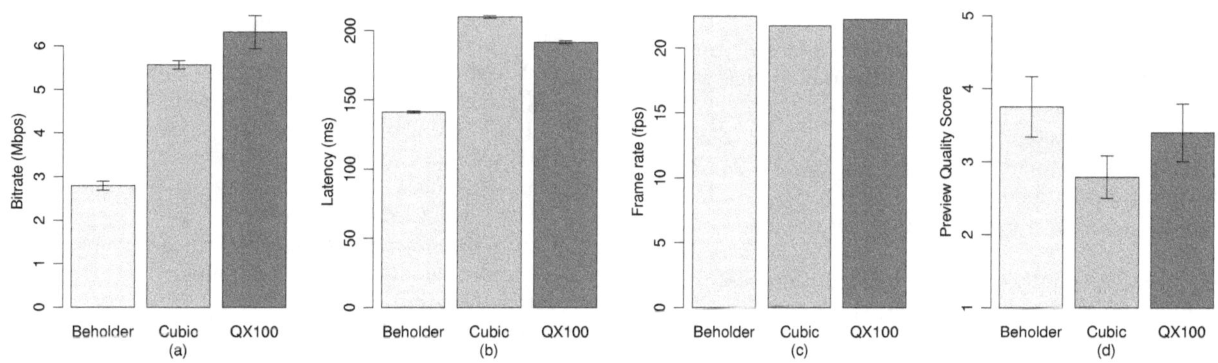

Figure 4: Sample performance comparisons among smart lenses: (a) bitrate, (b) latency, (c) frame rate, and (d) preview quality.

lower than that of others by at least 50 ms. The subjective evaluations of Smart Beholder on the preview quality also achieve higher scores than others as reported in Figure 4(d). In summary, our proposed Smart Beholder achieves higher preview quality without incurring network overhead. More details are provided in Huang et al. [8].

8. PANORAMIC SMART LENS: A USE CASE OF SMART BEHOLDER

There are increasingly more novel cameras in the market, such as panoramic [16] or 360° [9, 15] cameras. We build a panoramic smart lens using Smart Beholder, which works as follows. It continuously captures multiple images with multiple cameras pointing at different orientations, stitches these images, and then passes the resulting images to the encoder module. In this way, users see panoramic video on their Android devices.

In particular, we equip Raspberry Pi board with a multi-camera adapter board [10], which supports up to 4 cameras. While streaming, we program the GPIO pins to switch among cameras for images from different cameras, in a round-robin fashion. The resulting videos are then stitched using OpenCV [3] running on the Raspberry Pi. The resulting videos are then handled by a software-based video source. This video source iteratively feeds a sequence stitched images into a ring-buffer based pipe, which is shared with the encoder module. The encoder module then reads each frame from the pipe, performs the encoding task, and sends the encoded frames to a client via the RTSP and RTP protocols. The encoder module is put into sleep if no frame is available in the pipe, and is waked up right after a frame is pushed into the pipe. The video source and the encoder module are launched in different threads and the use of pipe increases the parallelism of the running threads.

Because Smart Beholder is designed and realized with high extensibility in mind, implementing the panoramic video source module (`vsource-stimage`) becomes relatively easy. In fact, we have only created 3 files with about 500 non-comment lines, before getting a working panoramic camera, which is illustrated in Figure 5.

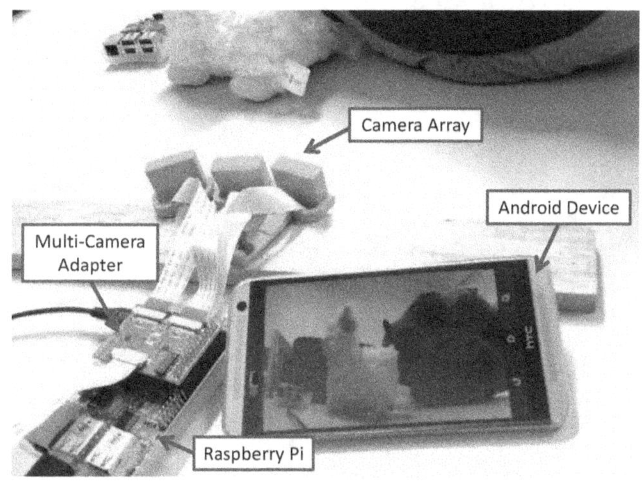

Figure 5: Our panoramic smart lens built on Smart Beholder.

9. CONCLUSION

We presented Smart Beholder, an open-source smart lens platform, which is available at http://www.smartbeholder.org. Smart Beholder enables various new multimedia applications, such as mobile photography, smart surveillance cameras, and UAV cameras. We designed Smart Beholder for three goals: (i) cost effectiveness, (ii) low interaction latency, and (iii) high preview quality. Our evaluations reveal that Smart Beholder indeed achieves the three goals by: (i) using a just-powerful-enough embedded system, (ii) reducing latency in individual software components, and (iii) adapting video coding parameters based on measured wireless network conditions. Smart Beholder can be leveraged by researchers for fast prototyping, developers for rapid development, and amateurs for fun. We envision that the release of Smart Beholder will stimulate more projects related to smart lenses and result in many new smart lens based applications. For example, we used panoramic camera as a sample application to demonstrate that Smart Beholder is highly extensible.

10. ACKNOWLEDGEMENTS

This work was partially supported by the Ministry of Science and Technology of Taiwan under the grants: 103-2221-E-001-023-MY2, 103-2221-E-009-230-MY2, 102-2221-E-007-062-MY3.

11. REFERENCES

[1] 5 areas where cameras still beat smartphones if you want great photo quality. http://tinyurl.com/n8f5w8d.

[2] Altek Cubic: Perfect to selfies. http://www.altek.com.tw/cubic/.

[3] G. Bradski. The OpenCV Library. *Dr. Dobb's Journal of Software Tools*, 2000.

[4] Dragonfly innovative uav aircraft & aerial video systems. http://www.draganfly.com/industrial/products.php.

[5] DSC-QX100 lens-style camera with 1.0-type sensor. http://www.sony.co.uk/electronics/cyber-shot-compact-cameras/dsc-qx100.

[6] FLIR Thermal Imaging. http://www.flir.co.uk/cs/display/?id=41702.

[7] GoPro 3+ high-performance life capture. http://shop.gopro.com/cameras/hero3plus-silver/CHDHN-302-master.html.

[8] C. Huang, C. Hsu, T. Tsai, C. Fan, C. Hsu, and K. Chen. Smart beholder: An open-source smart lens for mobile photography. In *Proc. of ACM Multimedia'15*, Brisbane, Australia, 2015.

[9] LUNA 360 Camera - luna 360 vr camera. http://luna.camera.

[10] Multi Camera Adapter Module for Raspberry Pi. http://www.arducam.com/multi-camera-adapter-module-raspberry-pi.

[11] Petcube remote wireless pet camera. https://petcube.com/.

[12] Raspberry Pi. http://www.raspberrypi.org/.

[13] RE Camera a remarkable little camera. http://www.htc.com/us/re/re-camera/.

[14] Skybotix uav navigation solutions. http://www.skybotix.com/.

[15] The Bublcam - experience true 360 spherical technology. https://www.bublcam.com/.

[16] V360 - capture everything the way you play in full 360. http://www.vsnmobil.com/products/v360.

A Platform for Building New Human-Computer Interface Systems that Support Online Automatic Recognition of Audio-Gestural Commands*

Nikolaos Kardaris
nick.kardaris@gmail.com

Isidoros Rodomagoulakis
irodoma@cs.ntua.gr

Vassilis Pitsikalis
vpitsik@cs.ntua.gr

Antonis Arvanitakis
antonisar@gmail.com

Petros Maragos
maragos@cs.ntua.gr

School of Electrical and Computer Engineering
National Technical University of Athens, 15773 Greece

ABSTRACT

We introduce a new framework to build human-computer interfaces that provide online automatic audio-gestural command recognition. The overall system allows the construction of a multimodal interface that recognizes user input expressed naturally as audio commands and manual gestures, captured by sensors such as Kinect. It includes a component for acquiring multimodal user data which is used as input to a module responsible for training audio-gestural models. These models are employed by the automatic recognition component, which supports online recognition of audiovisual modalities. The overall framework is exemplified by a working system use case. This demonstrates the potential of the overall software platform, which can be employed to build other new human-computer interaction systems. Moreover, users may populate libraries of models and/or data that can be shared in the network. In this way users may reuse or extend existing systems.

1. INTRODUCTION

Gestures and speech are the natural way, we humans, communicate. Inspired by this, research in human-computer interaction (HCI) and interfaces is continuously evolving to incorporate natural human communication features, which are more intuitive, perceptive and familiar [16]. Interfaces may incorporate audio/visual information via gesture, speech recognition and natural language processing, as well as physical information and haptics [13]. At the same time scientific and technological advances in speech, vision and machine learning along with sensors such as Kinect, natural interfaces such as Apple's Siri and datasets of challenging recognition tasks e.g. [23, 10, 12], signify the emerging trend of machine learning applied on natural multimodal HCI. Apart from commercial systems, we observe a steady effort since [18, 24] e.g. a crisis management system of [8], that continues to our days [15, 20, 14, 25] e.g. on natural gesture interaction [27], and multimodal recognition challenges [9, 11, 17].

Next, we present not only a software for multimodal automatic recognition. We rather introduce a complete framework for constructing new human-computer interfaces from scratch, that work online and support automatic speech/gesture recognition. To our knowledge, there is no such platform, that allows building complete task-specific multimodal recognition systems with natural interaction. Moreover we also prompt the users to upload, share and reuse the building blocks and developed models. The core software component (Sec. 2.3) performs automatic recognition of audio phrases and hand gestures from video/audio streams coming from common or depth cameras (e.g. Kinect) and microphones. It fuses recognition results from the two modalities to enhance performance. Audio-visual processing is carried out in an online fashion with real-time performance. This can be employed for multimodal audio-gestural recognition out of the box, since we provide pre-trained models for a specific task, as a use case. Particularly, our use case concerns human-robot interaction via a set of commands that are mapped to audio phrases and gestures. In addition, we provide a pipeline of components whereby users may construct new multimodal recognition systems. It includes software components for data acquisition and audio-visual training (Sec. 2.1, 2.2). The newly constructed interface system may contain new sets of concepts based on another dataset, and may employ alternative sub-components to the ones we already include; e.g. one may incorporate a different feature extraction method. Moreover, we present an actual working example. For this, we briefly show results in two alternative datasets that correspond to a specific task (Sec. 3) on which we have built our use case, evaluating the system's performance. In previous work [22, 21, 17, 19] one may find details on the datasets, acquisition and the related scientific concepts.

*For further information and source code visit `http://robotics.ntua.gr/software/building-interfaces-multimodal-interaction`.

MM '16, October 15–19, 2016, Amsterdam, Netherlands

DOI: http://dx.doi.org/10.1145/2964284.2973794

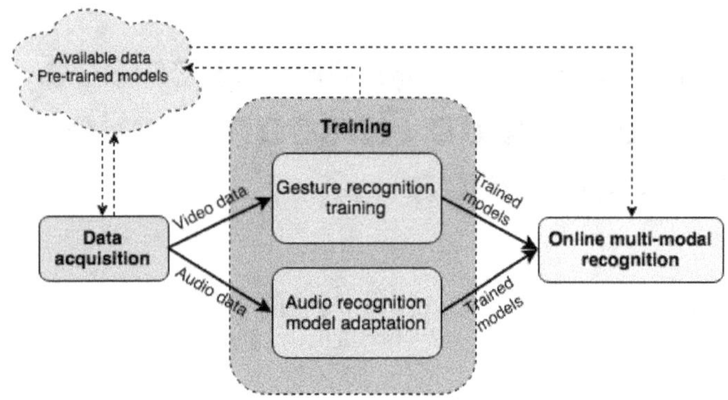

Figure 1: Conceptual block diagram of our overall framework. The three components included are: audio-visual data acquisition, training and online recognition of audio-gestural commands.

2. OVERALL SYSTEM DESCRIPTION

The overall framework is based on the *Robot Operating System* (ROS) and comprises three individual components depicted in Fig. 1, that allow users to implement their own audio-gestural interface. The data acquisition system (Sec. 2.1) assists and guides task-specific audio and video recordings. The acquired data may be employed as input to the training component (Sec. 2.2) to build audio and visual gesture models. Trained models can be used for online multi-modal recognition (Sec. 2.3). Recognition output may be directly used or further processed in multiple ways according to the developer's needs. The overall pipeline provides the software tools to develop custom user interfaces that enable them to interact with a system in new natural ways.

2.1 Multimodal data acquisition component

The data acquisition component provides the functionality of acquiring audio/video data for training and developing task-specific models and recognizers. The component has a remotely controlled GUI that assists a) the supervisor to guide the subject and annotate on-the-fly the temporal boundaries of the recorded audio-gestural commands and b) the subject to perform the audio/gestural commands by appropriate video prompts shown on the screen. The web interface allows parameterisation of the recordings and data organisation. The recorded data are streamed from the sensors to specific ROS data streams (topics) and finally stored as ROS-bag files along with the accompanying annotations. Both the annotation file format and the input data streams are customizable.

2.2 Multimodal training components

2.2.1 Training for audio commands' recognition

This component implements acoustic model adaptation leveraging off-the-shelf tools such as HTK [28, 2] allowing the developer to use other speech processing and modeling tools as well. The basic function is to adapt a set of pretrained subword HMMs to the conditions of the targeted environment and potentially to the voice of a specific user when building systems with user profiles. The developer can find publicly available training recipes and resources [7] for a variety of languages and recognition engines. Adaptation can be realized on a small dataset of transcribed utterances recorded in the targeted environment which can be easily acquired by using the proposed interface. The recorded ROS-bags and annotations are converted to HTK format and then provided to the HTK binary "HERest" for MLLR adaptation.

2.2.2 Training for gesture commands' recognition

The system for training on the visual gesture data follows a pipeline often employed in the field of action recognition. The main steps include feature extraction, feature encoding and Support Vector Machine (SVM) training. We employ the popular Dense Trajectory features with the MBH descriptor [26]. Features are encoded with Bag-of-Visual-Words using a visual codebook of $K = 4000$ centres constructed with K-means. Encoded features are used to train one-versus-all SVM classifiers with the χ^2 kernel. The output of the training phase includes the codebook, encoded features, a kernel normalization factor and SVM models and is used at runtime for testing.

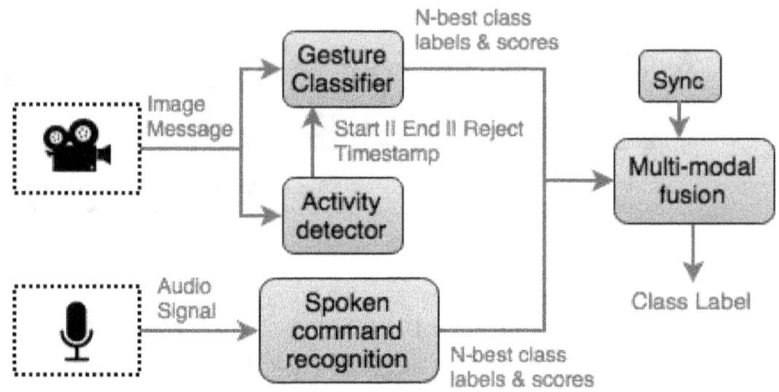

Figure 2: Multimodal command recognition system overview.

2.3 Online recognition component

2.3.1 Interprocess communication

The on-line recognition system relies on ROS to provide the main software layer for interprocess communication. Components are implemented as *ROS nodes*; communication, synchronization and data exchange is accomplished by *message passing*. In addition, input data from sensors are acquired at runtime as ROS message streams.

Our overall system comprises two separate sub-systems: (a) The spoken command recognizer, is a single node (*SPK node*) that performs always-listening speech recognition of specific user-defined command phrases that accompany the gestures. (b) The gesture recognizer consists of two nodes: the activity detector (*AD node*) that performs temporal localization of segments that contain visual activity and the gesture classifier (*GC node*) that assigns each detected activity segment to one of the pre-defined classes. The output from both sub-systems are combined at the *Fusion node* producing a single result. These interconnections between the ROS nodes are illustrated in Fig. 2. Synchronization issues are handled by an auxiliary node, which receives the final recognized command. All nodes are automatically launched by a single ROS launch file (Listing 1).

```
<launch>
  <!-- launch Kinect -->
  <include file="$(find openni_launch)/launch/
      openni.launch" />
  <!-- load configuration -->
  <rosparam command="load" file="$(find cvsp_hri)/
      config/gestures.yaml" />
  <rosparam command="load" file="$(find cvsp_hri)/
      config/fusion.yaml" />
  <!-- launch ROS nodes-->
  <node name="GC_node" pkg="cvsp_hri" type="
      DenseTrack" output="screen" required="true"/
      >
  <node name="AC_node" pkg="cvsp_hri" type="
      activity_detection.py" output="screen"
      required="true"/>
  <node name="audio_feedback" pkg="cvsp_hri" type=
      "soundplay.py" output="screen" required="
      true"/>
  <node name="SPK_node" pkg="cvsp_hri" type="scr.
      py" output="screen" required="true"/>
  <node name="sync" pkg="cvsp_hri" type="clock.py"
       output="screen" required="true"/>
  <node name="fusion_node" pkg="cvsp_hri" type="
      audioGestCmdRec.py" output="screen" required
      ="true"/>
</launch>
```

Listing 1: ROS launch file used to start separate nodes of the online multimodal recognition system.

2.3.2 *Audio commands' recognition*

The SPK node is designed to detect and recognize the commands provided by the user freely, at any time, among other speech and non-speech events possibly affected by environmental noise and reverberation. We enhance robustness through a) denoising of the far-field signals, b) adaptation of the acoustic models, and c) combined command detection/recognition by performing traditional ASR in overlapping windows with rejection mechanisms of non-speech and generic speech segments.

As depicted in Fig. 3, a sliding window of 2.5 *sec* duration slides every 0.6 *sec* in which we enforce recognition of one of the pre-defined command sentences against other phrases of various lengths included in the employed finite state grammar to catch any speech or non-speech cases different than the expected commands. Moreover, rejection of background events is feasible by thresholding their low-likelihoods. For robustness, the node outputs a recognition result only in case the same result is found in two successive overlapping windows.

The node is implemented as a multithreaded Python class with separate threads dedicated to recording and recognition. The recording thread streams multichannel audio from the audio card to an allocated buffer in memory where the signals are accessed,segmented and processed by the recognition thread. Processing includes delay-and-sum beamforming for denoising with the implemented *dsb* class and extraction of standard MFCCs-plus-derivatives features utilizing HTK's "HCopy". Finally, N-Best, grammar-based recognition is realized with "HVite".

2.3.3 *Gesture commands' recognition*

The AD node processes the RGB stream in a frame-by-frame basis and determines whether there is any visual activity in the scene, based on an activity "score", whose value is thresholded. When a transition from non-activity (activity) to activity (non-activity) is detected, a `START` (`END`) signal is sent to the GC node, along with the timestamp

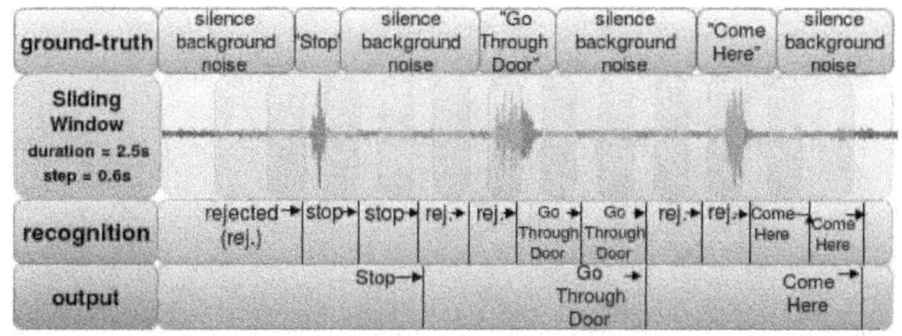

Figure 3: SPK node timeline: Sliding window based spoken command processing and recognition.

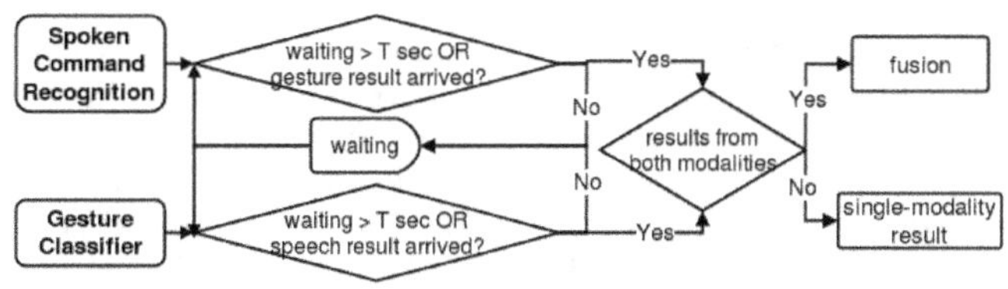

Figure 4: Fusion node: Handling and synchronizing outputs from the individual recognizers. If outputs from both modalities are available they are fused to form a single recognition result.

of the corresponding frame. Small segments of activity are rejected (a `REJECT` signal instead of an `END` signal is sent to the GC node) to ensure that small spontaneous movements of the user are not processed.

The Gesture Classifier node processes video segments and assigns them to one of the pre-defined categories. The classification pipeline includes feature extraction, feature encoding and SVM classification. The segments' temporal boundaries are indicated by the AD node as described previously. In particular, the GC node caches input frames from the camera. When a `START` signal is received, feature extraction begins immediately, starting from the indicated timestamp, until an `END` signal is received. Subsequently, features are extracted from the remaining frames of the activity segment, the classification pipeline continues and the result is broadcast to the Fusion node.

2.3.4 *Multimodal post-processing and fusion*

We combine the individual multi-class results using a late fusion scheme that encodes inter-modality agreement described simply with the following ranking rule: "if the best speech recognition hypothesis is among the 2-best gesture hypotheses, then it is announced as the multi-modal result". We found it quite effective and fast among other approaches like the N-best hypothesis rescoring we have proposed in [22]. Nevertheless, the developer is allowed to incorporate any other rules and fusion schemes.

The implemented Fusion node of Fig. 4 receives the N-best results announced by the individual recognizers. It checks for available results every 0.5 *secs* by receiving periodically messages from the clock node Sync in order to synchronize the recognizers. A waiting period T is also defined, during which the node waits to combine the incoming messages. If this period expires, it is assumed that one modality either was not activated by the user, or failed to detect the given input. In such cases, the node announces single-modality results.

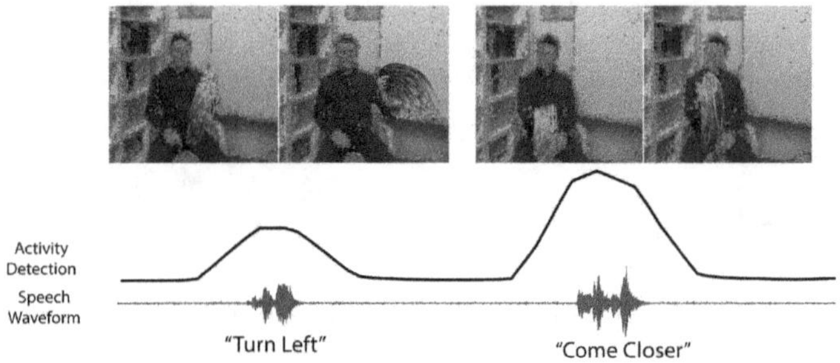

Figure 5: Multimodal command recognition example. The user gestures and utters audio commands. Activity segments are detected by the AD node based on an "activity" score (second row). These are processed by the GC node (top row; dense trajectories superimposed to RGB frames). The third row depicts the respective audio waveforms.

3. CASE STUDY: AN HRI SYSTEM

Based on the above described software platform, we provide a specific audio-gestural interface. This is a working human-robot interaction (HRI) system developed with the presented platform in the context of the MOBOT project [4]. This application concerns elderly people communicating with a robotic platform in order to get assistance. Our audio-gestural vocabulary includes 19 verbal commands along with the corresponding gestures for concepts like "Come here", "Help me", "I want to stand up" etc. The robot reacts either providing audio responses or moving in order to assist the elderly user. The system was trained on the data acquired in [21] using the acquisition system described briefly in Sec. 2.1. To reduce the total processing time we downsample RGB frames both in space and time by a factor of 2. This results to an average processing rate of 20 fps. The SPK node supports close to real time spoken command recognition in German, English, and Greek. Figure 5 illustrates visual processing aspects of online recognition.

Our online recognition system is tested on MOBOT-6a task [22] and is currently being evaluated on the multimodal gesture dataset acquired in [21]. All experiments are carried out with the leave-one-out scheme, i.e. testing on one subject, while the rest of the subjects are used for training; this is repeated for all subjects. We report average recognition accuracy across all subjects.

The MOBOT-6a includes 8 different gestural and German verbal commands performed by 8 elderly subjects. These are developed to accommodate their communication with the robotic platform. Patients are sitting in front of the rollator, placed at a distance of 2.5 meters. Each command is performed $3-6$ times by each patient. We obtained 84.13%, 56.98%, and 90.15% accuracy for the audio, visual modality, and their fusion respectively. The dataset described in [21] includes 13 subjects performing the 19 gestural and Greek audio commands $4-5$ times under different settings, e.g. sitting, standing, with viewpoint change. Preliminary evaluation yields 66.15% and 82.46% accuracy for the audio and visual modality respectively. Note that the designed Greek verbal commands were not as discriminative as the German ones, yielding lower results.

3.1 Practical issues and dependencies

Other employed software: Our training and recognition components have been developed mainly in Python and C. In addidion, we use publicly available 3rd party software. Specifically, spoken command recognition is based on the HTK 3.4 toolkit [2] which can be downloaded upon registration. Regarding the gesture recognizer: a) dense trajectories [26] are extracted using an custom version of the publicly available code [1], b) optical flow for activity detection is estimated by using the openCV library [5], c) the VLFeat library [6] is utilized for encoding and other operations and finally d) SVM training and classification is based on LIBSVM [3].

Sensors: We have successfully tested our system with a linear 8-channel MEMS array and a Kinect camera, though conventional microphones and cameras supported by Linux have been tested and can be used as well. Note that distant speech recognition performance depends on the quality of the audio signals and our system takes advantage of the configuration of a microphone array's channels internally. Nevertheless, the user is free to use any external or built-in microphone.

3.2 Building new interfaces and models

Apart from reusing the provided models to perform online audio-gestural command recognition and mapping the recognition results to specific user or system defined actions, the overall framework allows the design and implementation of various multimodal audio-gestural automatic recognition interfaces. This is accomplished by setting basic parameters such as the task, the concepts, and other configuration variables or metadata information. Guided by the acquisition software one may record data with multiple subjects performing gestures and uttering audio prompts according to the task definition. The training pipeline is responsible to produce the appropriate models using the acquired data, or reusing models which can be found on the web. Finally, given the available or new models built from scratch, the online system is ready to be used.

4. CONCLUSIONS

We presented a complete software platform for the development of multimodal interface systems that offer audio-gestural commands' automatic recognition. We also briefly describe a specific system that has been constructed as a use case, tested and employed for human-robot interaction. Moreover, we have provided experimental evidence on the performance of the employed methods. These are only instances related to the current use case and users may employ other algorithms for the included components. Considering the emergent fields of human-computer interaction and multimodal human action, gesture, speech recognition we think that the introduced software platform, as well as the sharing and reusability of data/models opens new perspectives for human-computer natural interaction.

5. ACKNOWLEDGMENTS

This research work was supported by the EU under the projects MOBOT with grant FP7-ICT-2011.2.1-600796 and I-SUPPORT with grant H2020-643666.

6. REFERENCES

[1] Dense trajectories. https://lear.inrialpes.fr/people/wang/dense_trajectories. Accessed: 20/5/2016.

[2] Htk. http://htk.eng.cam.ac.uk/. Accessed: 20/5/2016.

[3] libsvm. https://www.csie.ntu.edu.tw/ cjlin/libsvm/. Accessed: 20/5/2016.

[4] MOBOT project. http://www.mobot-project.eu/.

[5] Open cv. http://opencv.org/. Accessed: 20/5/2016.

[6] Vlfeat. http://www.vlfeat.org/. Accessed: 20/5/2016.

[7] Voxforge. http://www.voxforge.org/. Accessed: 20/5/2016.

[8] P. Agrawal, I. Rauschert, K. Inochanon, L. Bolelli, S. Fuhrmann, I. Brewer, G. Cai, A. MacEachren, and R. Sharma. Multimodal interface platform for geographical information systems (geomip) in crisis management. In *Proceedings of the 6th international conference on Multimodal interfaces*, pages 339–340. ACM, 2004.

[9] I. Bayer and T. Silbermann. A multi modal approach to gesture recognition from audio and video data. In *Proceedings of the 15th ACM on International conference on multimodal interaction*, pages 461–466. ACM, 2013.

[10] C. Chen, R. Jafari, and N. Kehtarnavaz. Utd-mhad: a multimodal dataset for human action recognition utilizing a depth camera and a wearable inertial sensor. In *Image Processing (ICIP), 2015 IEEE International Conference on*, pages 168–172. IEEE, 2015.

[11] S. Escalera, J. Gonzàlez, X. Baró, M. Reyes, I. Guyon, V. Athitsos, H. Escalante, L. Sigal, A. Argyros, C. Sminchisescu, R. Bowden, and S. Sclaroff. Chalearn multi-modal gesture recognition 2013: grand challenge and workshop summary. ACM, 2013.

[12] S. Escalera, J. Gonzàlez, X. Baró, M. Reyes, O. Lopes, I. Guyon, V. Athitsos, and H. Escalante. Multi-modal gesture recognition challenge 2013: Dataset and results. In *Proc. of the 15th ACM on Int'l Conf. on Multimodal Interaction*, pages 445–452. ACM, 2013.

[13] M. A. Goodrich and A. C. Schultz. Human-robot interaction: a survey. *Foundations and trends in human-computer interaction*, 1(3):203–275, 2007.

[14] F. Grani, D. Overholt, C. Erkut, S. Gelineck, G. Triantafyllidis, R. Nordahl, and S. Serafin. Spatial sound and multimodal interaction in immersive environments. In *Proceedings of the Audio Mostly 2015 on Interaction With Sound*, page 17. ACM, 2015.

[15] J. Hare, M. Karam, P. Lewis, et al. igesture: A platform for investigating multimodal, multimedia gesture-based interactions. 2005.

[16] A. Jaimes and N. Sebe. Multimodal human–computer interaction: A survey. *Computer vision and image understanding*, 108(1):116–134, 2007.

[17] G. Pavlakos, S. Theodorakis, V. Pitsikalis, S. Katsamanis, and P. Maragos. Kinect-based multimodal gesture recognition using a two-pass fusion scheme. pages 1495–1499, 2014.

[18] A. Pirhonen, S. Brewster, and C. Holguin. Gestural and audio metaphors as a means of control for mobile devices. In *Proceedings of the SIGCHI conference on Human factors in computing systems*, pages 291–298. ACM, 2002.

[19] V. Pitsikalis, S. Katsamanis, S. Theodorakis, and P. Maragos. Multimodal gesture recognition via multiple hypotheses rescoring. 16:255–284, 2015.

[20] O. Portillo-Rodriguez, O. O. Sandoval-Gonzalez, E. Ruffaldi, R. Leonardi, C. A. Avizzano, and M. Bergamasco. Real-time gesture recognition, evaluation and feed-forward correction of a multimodal tai-chi platform. In *Haptic and Audio Interaction Design*, pages 30–39. Springer, 2008.

[21] I. Rodomagoulakis, N. Kardaris, V. Pitsikalis, A. Arvanitakis, and P. Maragos. A multimedia gesture dataset for human-robot communication: Acquisition, tools and recognition results. In *IEEE International Conference on Image Processing (ICIP-16), to appear*, sep 2016.

[22] I. Rodomagoulakis, N. Kardaris, V. Pitsikalis, E. Mavroudi, A. Katsamanis, A. Tsiami, and P. Maragos. Multimodal human action recognition in assistive human-robot interaction. In *Proc. IEEE Conference on Acoustics, Speech and Signal Processing (ICASSP-16)*, mar 2016.

[23] S. Ruffieux, D. Lalanne, E. Mugellini, and O. A. Khaled. A survey of datasets for human gesture recognition. In *Human-Computer Interaction. Advanced Interaction Modalities and Techniques*, pages 337–348. Springer, 2014.

[24] R. Stiefelhagen, C. Fügen, P. Gieselmann, H. Holzapfel, K. Nickel, and A. Waibel. Natural human-robot interaction using speech, head pose and gestures. In *Intelligent Robots and Systems, 2004.(IROS 2004). Proceedings. 2004 IEEE/RSJ International Conference on*, volume 3, pages 2422–2427. IEEE, 2004.

[25] H. A. Vasquez, H. S. Vargas, and L. E. Sucar. Using gestures to interact with a service robot using kinect 2. *Advances in Pattern Recognition*, page 85, 2015.

[26] H. Wang, A. Kläser, C. Schmid, and C. L. Liu. Action recognition by dense trajectories. In *Proc. IEEE Conference on Computer Vision and Pattern Recognition (CVPR 2011)*, pages 3169–3176, June 2011.

[27] Y. Yin and R. W. Davis. Real-time continuous gesture recognition for natural human-computer interaction. In *Visual Languages and Human-Centric Computing (VL/HCC), 2014 IEEE Symposium on*, pages 113–120. IEEE, 2014.

[28] S. J. Young et al. *The HTK Book, version 3.4*. Cambridge University Engineering Department, 2006.

madmom: a new Python Audio and Music Signal Processing Library

Sebastian Böck†, Filip Korzeniowski†, Jan Schlüter‡, Florian Krebs†, Gerhard Widmer†‡
† Department of Computational Perception, Johannes Kepler University Linz, Austria
‡ Austrian Research Institute for Artificial Intelligence (OFAI), Vienna, Austria

ABSTRACT

In this paper, we present *madmom*, an open-source audio processing and music information retrieval (MIR) library written in Python. *madmom* features a concise, *NumPy*-compatible, object oriented design with simple calling conventions and sensible default values for all parameters, which facilitates fast prototyping of MIR applications. Prototypes can be seamlessly converted into callable processing pipelines through *madmom*'s concept of *Processors*, callable objects that run transparently on multiple cores. *Processors* can also be serialised, saved, and re-run to allow results to be easily reproduced anywhere.

Apart from low-level audio processing, *madmom* puts emphasis on musically meaningful high-level features. Many of these incorporate machine learning techniques and *madmom* provides a module that implements some methods commonly used in MIR such as hidden Markov models and neural networks. Additionally, *madmom* comes with several state-of-the-art MIR algorithms for onset detection, beat, downbeat and meter tracking, tempo estimation, and chord recognition. These can easily be incorporated into bigger MIR systems or run as stand-alone programs.

Keywords

Music Information Retrieval, Audio Analysis, Signal Processing, Machine Learning, Python, Open Source

1. INTRODUCTION

Music information retrieval (MIR) has become an emerging research area over the last 15 years. Especially audio-based MIR has become more and more important, since the amount of available audio data in the last years exploded beyond being manageable manually.

Most state-of-the-art audio-based MIR algorithms consist of two components: first, low-level features are extracted from the audio signal (*feature extraction* stage), and then the features are analysed (*feature analysis* stage) to retrieve the desired information. Most current MIR systems incorporate machine learning algorithms in the feature analysis stage, with neural networks currently being the most popular and successful ones [2, 3, 11, 19, 20].

Numerous software libraries have been proposed over the years to facilitate research and development of applications in MIR. Some libraries concentrate on low-level feature extraction from audio signals, such as *Marsyas* [21], *YAAFE* [16] and *openSMILE* [9]. Others also include higher level feature extraction such as onset and beat detection as for example in the *MIRtoolbox* [15], *Essentia* [6] and *LibROSA* [17]. However, to our knowledge, there exist no library that also includes machine learning components (except *Marsyas* [21], which contains two classifiers), although machine learning components are crucial in current MIR applications.

Therefore, we propose *madmom*, a library that incorporates low-level feature extraction *and* high-level feature analysis based on machine learning methods. This allows the construction of the full processing chain within a single software framework, making it possible to build standalone programs without any dependency on other machine learning frameworks. Moreover, *madmom* comes with several state-of-the-art systems including their trained models, for example for onset detection [8, 19, 20], tempo estimation [3], beat [2, 11] and downbeat tracking [4, 14], and chord recognition [12, 13].

madmom is written in Python, which has become the language of choice for scientific computing for many people due to its free availability and its simplicity of use. The code is released under BSD license and pre-trained models are released under the CC BY-NC-SA 4.0 license.

1.1 Design and Functionality

1.1.1 Object-oriented programming

madmom follows an object-oriented programming (OOP) approach. We encapsulate everything in objects that are often designed as subclasses of *NumPy*'s *ndarray*, offering all array handling routines inherited from *NumPy* [22] with additional functionality. This compactly bundles data and meta-data (e.g. a *Spectrogram* and its *frame rate*) and simplifies meta-data handling for the user.

1.1.2 Rapid prototyping

madmom aims at minimising the turnaround time from a research idea to a software prototype. Thus, object instantiation is made as simple as possible: e.g., a *Spectrogram* object can be instantiated with a single line of code by only providing the path to an audio file. *madmom* automatically creates all objects in between using sensible default values.

MM '16, October 15 - 19, 2016, Amsterdam, Netherlands

ISBN 978-1-4503-3603-1/16/10...$15.00

DOI: http://dx.doi.org/10.1145/2964284.2973795

1.1.3 Simple conversion into runnable programs

Once an audio processing algorithm is prototyped, the complete workflow should be easily transformable into a runnable standalone program with a consistent calling interface. This is implemented using *madmom*'s concept of *Processors*.

1.1.4 Machine learning integration

We aim at a seamless integration of machine learning methods without the need of any third party modules. We limit ourselves to testing capabilities (applying pre-trained models), since it is impossible to keep up with newly emerging training methods in the various machine learning domains. Models that have been trained in an external library should be easily be convertible to an internal *madmom* model format.

1.1.5 State-of-the-art features

Many existing libraries provide a huge variety of low-level features, but few musically meaningful high-level features. *madmom* tries to close this gap by offering high-quality state-of-the-art feature extractors for onsets, beats, downbeats, chords, tempo, etc.

1.1.6 Reproducible research

In order to foster reproducible research, we want to be able to save and load the specific settings used to obtain the results for a certain experiment. In *madmom* this is implemented using Python's own *pickle* functionality which allows to save an entire processing chain (including all settings) to a file.

1.1.7 Few dependencies

madmom is built on top of three excellent and wide-spread libraries: *NumPy* [22] provides all the array handling subroutines for *madmom*'s *data classes*. *SciPy* [10] provides optimised routines for the fast Fourier transform (FFT), linear algebra operations and sparse matrix representations. Finally, *Cython* [1] is used to speed up time critical parts of the library by automatically generating C code from a Python-like syntax and then compiling and linking it into extensions which can be transparently used from within Python. These libraries are the only installation and runtime dependencies of *madmom* besides the *Python* standard library itself, supported in version 2.7 as well as 3.3 and newer.

1.1.8 Multi-core capability

We designed *madmom* to be able to exploit the multi-core capabilities of modern computer architectures, by providing functionality to run several programs or *Processors* in parallel.

1.1.9 Extensive documentation

All source code files contain thorough documentation following the *NumPy* format. The complete API reference, instruction on how to build and install the library, as well as interactive *Jupyter* [18] notebooks can be found online at `http://madmom.readthedocs.io`. The documentation is built automatically with *Sphinx*[1].

1.1.10 Open development process

We follow an open development process and the source code and documentation of our project is publicly available on GitHub: `http://github.com/CPJKU/madmom`. To maintain high code quality, we use continuous integration testing via TravisCI[2], code quality tests via QuantifiedCode[3], and test coverage via Coveralls[4].

2. LIBRARY DESCRIPTION

In this section, we will describe the overall architecture of *madmom*, its packages as well as the provided standalone programs.

madmom's main API is composed of classes, but much of the functionality is implemented as functions (in turn used internally by the classes). This way, *madmom* offers the 'best of both worlds': concise interfaces exposed through classes, and detailed access to functionality through functions. In general, the classes can be split in two different types: the so called *data classes* and *processor classes*.

Data classes represent data entities such as audio signals or spectrograms. They are implemented as subclasses of *NumPy*'s *ndarray*, and thus offer all array handling routines inherited directly from *NumPy* (e.g., transposing or saving the data to file in either binary or human readable format). These classes are enriched by additional attributes and expose additional functionality via methods.

Processor classes exclusively store information on how to process data, i.e. how to transform one data class into another (e.g., from an (audio-)*Signal* into a *Spectrogram*). In order to build chains of transformations, each data class has its corresponding processor class, which implements this transformation. This enables a simple and fast conversion of algorithm prototypes to callable processing pipelines.

2.1 Packages

The library is split into several packages, grouped by functionality. For a detailed description including examples of usage please refer to the library's documentation.

2.1.1 madmom.audio

The *madmom.audio* package includes basic audio signal processing and "low-level" functionality.

The *Signal* and *FramedSignal* classes are used to load an audio signal and split it into (overlapping) frames. Following *madmom*'s automatic instantiation approach, both classes can be instantiated from any object up the instantiation hierarchy – including a simple file name. *madmom* supports almost a wide range of audio and video formats – provided *ffmpeg*[5] is installed – and transparently converts sample rates and number of channels if needed.

Signal is a subclass of *ndarray* with additional attributes like *sample rate* or *number of channels*. *FramedSignal* supports float hop sizes, making it possible to build systems with an arbitrary frame rate – independently of the signal's sample rate – and ensures that all frames are temporally aligned, even if computed with different frame sizes.

The *ShortTimeFourierTransform* and *Spectrogram* classes represent the complex valued STFT and magnitudes respectively. They are the key classes for spectral audio analysis and provide windowing, automatic circular shifting (for correct phase) and zero-padding. Both are independent of the

[1] `http://www.sphinx-doc.org`

[2] `http://www.travis-ci.org`

[3] `http://www.quantifiedcode.com`

[4] `http://www.coveralls.io`

[5] `http://www.ffmpeg.org`

data type (integer or float) of the underlying *Signal*, resulting in spectrograms of the same value range. A *Spectrogram* can be filtered with a *Filterbank* (e.g., Mel, Bark, logarithmic), which in turn can be parametrised to reduce the dimensionality or transform the spectrogram into a logarithmically spaced pitch representation closely following the auditory model of the human ear. *madmom* also provides standard *MFCC* and *Chroma* features.

Listing 1 shows an example of how a standard spectral flux onset detection function can be prototyped with *madmom* in a few lines of code.

```
from madmom.audio import (Spectrogram,
                          SpectrogramDifference)

# compute spectral flux
spec = Spectrogram('sample.wav')
diff = SpectrogramDifference(spec,
                             positive_diffs=True)
sf = np.mean(diff, axis=1)
```

Listing 1: Rapid prototyping of the spectral flux onset detection function using *madmom*'s data classes.

2.1.2 madmom.processors

Processors are one of the fundamental building blocks of *madmom*. Each *Processor* accepts a number of processing parameters and must provide a *process* method, which takes the data to be processed as its only argument and defines the processing functionality of the *Processor*. An *OutputProcessor* extends this scheme by accepting a second argument which defines the output and can thus be used to write the output of an algorithm to a file. All *Processors* are callable, making it easy to use them interchangeably with normal functions. Furthermore, the *Processor* class provides methods for saving and loading any *Processor* to a file – including all parameters – using Python's own *pickle* library. This facilitates the reproducibility of an experiment.

Multiple *Processors* can be combined into a processing chain using either a *SequentialProcessor* or a *ParallelProcessor*, which execute the chain sequentially or in parallel, using multiple CPU cores if available.

```
from madmom.audio import (
    SpectrogramProcessor,
    SpectrogramDifferenceProcessor)
from madmom.processors import SequentialProcessor
from functools import partial

# define spectral flux processing chain
spec = SpectrogramProcessor()
diff = SpectrogramDifferenceProcessor(
    positive_diffs=True)
mean = partial(np.mean, axis=1)
# wrap everything in a SequentialProcessor
sf_proc = SequentialProcessor([spec, diff, mean])

# process an audio file by calling the processor
sf = sf_proc('sample.wav')
```

Listing 2: Spectral flux onset detection implemented as a callable *Processor*.

Listing 2 shows the conversion of the prototyped algorithm in Listing 1 into a callable *Processor* by simply replacing the used *data classes* with their respective *processor classes* and wrapping them into a *SequentialProcessor*.

2.1.3 madmom.features

The *madmom.features* package includes "high-level" functionality which are related to certain MIR tasks, such as onset detection or beat tracking. *madmom*'s focus is on providing musically meaningful and descriptive features rather than a vast number of low to mid-level features. At the time of writing, *madmom* contains state-of-the-art features for onset detection, beat and downbeat tracking, rhythm pattern analysis, tempo estimation and chord recognition.

All features are implemented as *Processors* without a corresponding *data class*. Users can thus use the provided functionality and build algorithms on top of these features. For most of the features, *madmom* also provides stand-alone programs with a consistent calling interface to process audio files (see Section 2.2).

```
from madmom.features.beats import (
    RNNBeatProcessor, DBNBeatTrackingProcessor)
from madmom.processors import SequentialProcessor

# define beat tracking processor
rnn = RNNBeatProcessor()
dbn = DBNBeatTrackingProcessor(
    min_bpm=50, max_bpm=200)
tracker = SequentialProcessor([rnn, dbn])

# track the beats by calling the processor
beats = tracker('sample.wav')
```

Listing 3: Beat tracking with a recurrent neural network (RNN) and dynamic Bayesian network (DBN) in *madmom* using provided *Processors*.

2.1.4 madmom.evaluation

All features come with code for evaluation. The implemented metrics are those commonly found in the literature of the respective field.

2.1.5 madmom.ml

Most of today's top performing music analysis algorithms incorporate machine learning, with neural networks being the most universal and successful ones at the moment. *madmom* includes Python implementations of commonly used machine learning techniques, namely *Gaussian Mixture Models*, *Hidden Markov Models*, linear-chain *Conditional Random Fields*, and different types of *neural networks*, including feed forward, convolutional, batch normalisation, and recurrent layers, various activation functions and special purpose *long short-term memory* and gated recurrent units.

madmom provides functionality to use these techniques without any dependencies on third-party modules, but does not contain training algorithms. This decision was made on purpose since the library's main focus is on applying machine learning techniques to MIR, rather than providing an extensive set of learning techniques. However, trained models can be easily converted to be compatible with *madmom*, since neural network layers usually are simply defined as a set of weights, biases and an activation function they apply to the input data. Listing 4 shows the code necessary to convert a simple neural network trained using the *Lasagne* library [7].

```
import lasagne
from madmom import ml

# ... here comes the Lasagne training code
# 'net' is the Lasagne network handle
p = lasagne.layers.get_all_param_values(net)
# create a NeuralNetwork in madmom
nn = ml.nn.NeuralNetwork([
    ml.nn.layers.FeedForwardLayer(
        p[0], p[1], ml.nn.activations.relu),
    ml.nn.layers.FeedForwardLayer(
        p[2], p[3], ml.nn.activations.relu),
    ml.nn.layers.FeedForwardLayer(
        p[4], p[5], ml.nn.activations.relu),
    ml.nn.FeedForwardLayer(
        p[6], p[7], ml.nn.activations.sigmoid)
])
# save the network (can be used as a processor)
nn.dump('neural_net.pkl')
```

Listing 4: Converting a deep neural network with three hidden layers from *Lasagne* to *madmom*.

2.1.6 madmom.models

madmom comes with a set of pre-trained models which are distributed under a Creative Commons attribution non-commercial share-alike license, i.e. they can be freely used for research purposes as long as derivative works are distributed under the same license. *madmom* uses the exact same mechanism to save and load the models it uses for *Processors* to be pickled.

2.2 Standalone Programs

madmom comes with a set of standalone programs, covering many areas of MIR. Table 1 lists selected programs included in the library with the performance achieved at the annual *Music Information Retrieval Evaluation eXchange* (MIREX)[6], where MIR algorithms are compared on test datasets. We aggregated the results of all years (2006-2016), i.e. a rank 1 means that the algorithm is the best performing one of all submissions from 2006 until present. The outstanding results in Table 1 highlight the state-of-the-art features *madmom* provides.

Table 1: Ranks of the programs included in *madmom* for the MIREX evaluations, results aggregated over all years (2006-2016).

Program	Task	Year	Rank
CNNOnsetDetector [19]	onset	2016	1
OnsetDetector [8]	onset	2013	2
BeatTracker [5]	beat MCK	2015	1
DBNBeatTracker [2]	beat SMC	2015	1
CRFBeatDetector [11]	beat MAZ	2015	1
DBNDownBeatTracker [4]	downbeat	2016	1
TempoDetector [3]	tempo	2015	1
CNNChordRecognition [13]	chord	2016	1

[6] http://www.music-ir.org/mirex/wiki/

These programs are simple wrappers around the functionality provided by the *madmom.features* package, and provide a simple and easy to use command line interface. They are implemented as *Processors* and can operate either in *single* or *batch* mode, processing single or multiple input files, respectively. Additionally all programs can be *pickled*, serialising all parameters in a way that the program can be executed later on with the exact same settings.

Listing 5 shows the beat tracking algorithm of Listing 3 converted into a runnable program. The usage of an *IOProcessor* instead of a *SequentialProcessor* enables the program to output the detected beats into a file or to **STDOUT**. **io_arguments** provides all the handling needed for the different operation modes.

```
#!/usr/bin/env python

from madmom.processors import (
    IOProcessor, io_arguments)
from madmom.features.beats import (
    RNNBeatProcessor, DBNBeatTrackingProcessor)
from madmom.utils import write_events
from argparse import ArgumentParser

if __name__ == '__main__':
    # define parser
    p = ArgumentParser()
    # add I/O related arguments and define
    # single/batch/pickle processing mode
    io_arguments(p, output_suffix='.beats.txt')
    # parse arguments
    args = p.parse_args()
    # define beat tracking processor
    rnn = RNNBeatProcessor()
    dbn = DBNBeatTrackingProcessor()
    out = write_events
    # wrap as IOProcessor
    processor = IOProcessor([rnn, dbn], out)
    # call the processor in single/batch/pickle
    # mode defined by 'args.func'
    args.func(processor, **vars(args))
```

Listing 5: Beat tracking algorithm of Listing 3 converted into a runnable program.

3. CONCLUSION

This paper gave a short introduction to *madmom*, its design principles and library structure. Up-to-date information on functionality can be found in the project's online documentation at https://madmom.readthedocs.io and source code repository at https://github.com/CPJKU/madmom.

Future work aims at including a streaming mode, i.e. providing online real-time processing of audio signals in a memory efficient way instead of processing whole audio files at a time. In addition, we will gradually extend the set of features and algorithms, as well as add tools to automatically convert models that have been trained with machine learning libraries.

4. ACKNOWLEDGMENTS

This work is supported by the European Union Seventh Framework Programme FP7 / 2007-2013 through the GiantSteps project (grant agreement no. 610591) and the Austrian Science Fund (FWF) project Z159.

5. REFERENCES

[1] S. Behnel, R. Bradshaw, C. Citro, L. Dalcin, D. Seljebotn, and K. Smith. Cython: The Best of Both Worlds. *Computing in Science Engineering*, 13(2), 2011.

[2] S. Böck, F. Krebs, and G. Widmer. A Multi-model Approach to Beat Tracking considering Heterogeneous Music Styles. In *Proc. of the 15th Int. Society for Music Information Retrieval Conf. (ISMIR)*, 2014.

[3] S. Böck, F. Krebs, and G. Widmer. Accurate Tempo Estimation based on Recurrent Neural Networks and Resonating Comb Filters. In *Proc. of the 16th Int. Society for Music Information Retrieval Conf. (ISMIR)*, 2015.

[4] S. Böck, F. Krebs, and G. Widmer. Joint Beat and Downbeat Tracking with Recurrent Neural Networks. In *Proc. of the 17th Int. Society for Music Information Retrieval Conf. (ISMIR)*, 2016.

[5] S. Böck and M. Schedl. Enhanced Beat Tracking with Context-Aware Neural Networks. In *Proc. of the 14th Int. Conf. on Digital Audio Effects (DAFx)*, 2011.

[6] D. Bogdanov, N. Wack, E. Gómez, S. Gulati, P. Herrera, O. Mayor, G. Roma, J. Salamon, J. Zapata, and X. Serra. Essentia: an open source library for sound and music analysis. In *In Proc. of ACM Multimedia*, 2013.

[7] S. Dieleman, J. Schlüter, C. Raffel, E. Olson, S. K. Sønderby, D. Nouri, E. Battenberg, A. van den Oord, et al. Lasagne: First release., 2015.

[8] F. Eyben, S. Böck, B. Schuller, and A. Graves. Universal Onset Detection with Bidirectional Long Short-Term Memory Neural Networks. In *Proc. of the 11th Int. Society for Music Information Retrieval Conf. (ISMIR)*, 2010.

[9] F. Eyben, F. Weninger, F. Gross, and B. Schuller. Recent Developments in openSMILE, the Munich Open-Source Multimedia Feature Extractor. In *In Proc. of ACM Multimedia*, Barcelona, Spain, 2013.

[10] E. Jones, T. Oliphant, P. Peterson, et al. SciPy: Open source scientific tools for Python, 2001–. [Online; accessed 2016-05-20].

[11] F. Korzeniowski, S. Böck, and G. Widmer. Probabilistic Extraction of Beat Positions from a Beat Activation Function. In *Proc. of the 15th Int. Society for Music Information Retrieval Conf. (ISMIR)*, 2014.

[12] F. Korzeniowski and G. Widmer. Feature learning for chord recognition: The deep chroma extractor. In *Proc. of the 17th Int. Society for Music Information Retrieval Conf. (ISMIR)*, 2016.

[13] F. Korzeniowski and G. Widmer. A fully convolutional deep auditory model for musical chord recognition. In *Proc. of the IEEE Int. Workshop on Machine Learning for Signal Processing (MLSP)*, 2016.

[14] F. Krebs, S. Böck, and G. Widmer. Rhythmic Pattern Modeling for Beat and Downbeat Tracking in Musical Audio. In *Proc. of the 14th Int. Society for Music Information Retrieval Conf. (ISMIR)*, 2013.

[15] O. Lartillot and P. Toiviainen. A Matlab toolbox for musical feature extraction from audio. In *Proc. of the 10th Int. Conf. on Digital Audio Effects (DAFx)*, 2007.

[16] B. Mathieu, S. Essid, T. Fillon, and J. Prado. YAAFE, an easy to use and efficient audio feature extraction software. In *Proc. of the 11th Int. Society for Music Information Retrieval Conf. (ISMIR)*, 2010.

[17] B. McFee, C. Raffel, D. Liang, D. Ellis, M. McVicar, E. Battenberg, and O. Nieto. librosa: Audio and Music Signal Analysis in Python. In *Proc. of the 14th Python in Science Conf. (SCIPY)*, 2015.

[18] F. Pérez and B. E. Granger. IPython: A System for Interactive Scientific Computing. *Computing in Science Engineering*, 9(3), 2007.

[19] J. Schlüter and S. Böck. Musical Onset Detection with Convolutional Neural Networks. In *Proceedings of the 6th International Workshop on Machine Learning and Music*, Prague, Czech Republic, 2013.

[20] J. Schlüter and S. Böck. Improved musical onset detection with convolutional neural networks. In *Proc. of the 39th Int. Conf. on Acoustics, Speech and Signal Processing (ICASSP)*, 2014.

[21] G. Tzanetakis and P. Cook. MARSYAS: a framework for audio analysis. *Organised Sound*, 4, 2000.

[22] S. van der Walt, S. C. Colbert, and G. Varoquaux. The NumPy Array: A Structure for Efficient Numerical Computation. *Computing in Science Engineering*, 13(2), 2011.

Kvazaar: Open-Source HEVC/H.265 Encoder

Marko Viitanen, Ari Koivula, Ari Lemmetti, Arttu Ylä-Outinen, Jarno Vanne, Timo D. Hämäläinen
Department of Pervasive Computing
Tampere University of Technology, Finland

{marko.viitanen, ari.koivula, ari.lemmetti, arttu.yla-outinen, jarno.vanne, timo.d.hamalainen}@tut.fi

ABSTRACT

Kvazaar is an academic software video encoder for the emerging High Efficiency Video Coding (HEVC/H.265) standard. It provides students, academic professionals, and industry experts a free, cross-platform HEVC encoder for x86, x64, PowerPC, and ARM processors on Windows, Linux, and Mac. Kvazaar is being developed from scratch in C and optimized in Assembly under the LGPLv2.1 license. The development is being coordinated by Ultra Video Group at Tampere University of Technology (TUT) and the implementation work is carried out by an active community on GitHub. Developer friendly source code of Kvazaar makes joining easy for new developers. Currently, Kvazaar includes all essential coding tools of HEVC and its modular source code facilitates parallelization on multi and manycore processors as well as algorithm acceleration on hardware. Kvazaar is able to attain real-time HEVC coding speed up to 4K video on an Intel 14-core Xeon processor. Kvazaar is also supported by FFmpeg and Libav. These de-facto standard multimedia frameworks boost Kvazaar popularity and enable its joint usage with other well-known multimedia processing tools. Nowadays, Kvazaar is an integral part of teaching at TUT and it has got a key role in three Eureka Celtic-Plus projects in the fields of 4K TV broadcasting, virtual advertising, Video on Demand, and video surveillance.

Keywords

Open source; Video coding; Video encoder; High Efficiency Video Coding (HEVC); Kvazaar HEVC encoder

1. INTRODUCTION

Video traffic is reported to reach 80-90% of all global consumer Internet traffic by 2019 [1]. This is due to rapid proliferation of video applications together with universal expectations of better-quality video content and immersive user experience. The holistic growth of video inevitably sparks a need for better compression.

The latest international video coding standard, *High Efficiency Video Coding* (*HEVC/H.265*) [2], [3] is developed to address the increasing transmission and storage requirements of video. HEVC reduces the bit rate by almost 40% over the preceding state-of-the-art standard AVC [4] for the same objective quality but at about 40% encoding complexity overhead. Therefore, implementing a powerful HEVC encoder with a reasonable coding speed, cost, and power budget requires an efficient encoder implementation.

In software encoders, HEVC complexity can be primarily tackled by two techniques: multithreading through data-level parallelism and *single instruction multiple data* (*SIMD*) optimizations. Further speedup and lower power dissipation can be obtained by offloading the compute-intensive coding tools to hardware accelerators or implementing the entire encoder on hardware.

Currently, there exist a couple of open-source HEVC encoders [5]-[9]. The summary of these projects is given in Table 1. *HEVC reference encoder* (*HM*) [5] supports all HEVC coding tools and is able to achieve high coding efficiency. However, it is slow and single threaded, as it is targeted for research and conformance testing rather than practical encoding. The commercially funded x265 [6] is probably the most well-known practical open-source HEVC encoder at the moment. It is based on the C++ source code of HM which has been enhanced by extensive assembly optimizations, multithreading, and techniques from the open-source x264 encoder [10]. HomerHEVC [7] and f265 [8] are less feature complete encoders and both of them have only a single active developer.

Kvazaar [9] is an academic cross-platform HEVC encoder coordinated by Ultra Video Group [11] at *Tampere University of technology* (*TUT*). The development of Kvazaar was started by us in a private academic project in May 2012. The source code of Kvazaar was published on GitHub under GPLv2 in Jan 2014 and relicensed as LGPLv2 in Feb 2015. The latest version of its source code and issue tracker can be found on GitHub [9]. Kvazaar allows participation without any copyright transfers contrary to x265, f265, and HomerHEVC that require signing a *contributor licence agreement* (*CLA*) before accepting code into the project.

This paper gives an overview of Kvazaar including its main features, high-level functionality, and target applications. It serves as a Kvazaar synopsis for software programmers, video coding experts, and end-users in academia and industry.

2. OVERVIEW OF KVAZAAR

The development of Kvazaar was started from scratch in C while using HM as a clarification of the standard text and as a source of fundamental HEVC algorithms. Currently, Kvazaar supports HEVC Main, Main Still Picture, and Main 10 profiles for 8-bit 4:2:0 progressive video.

MM '16, October 15 - 19, 2016, Amsterdam, Netherlands

ACM 978-1-4503-3603-1/16/10…$15.00
DOI: http://dx.doi.org/10.1145/2964284.2973796

Table 1. Open-source HEVC encoders

Feature	HM [5]	x265 [6]	HomerHEVC [7]	f265 [8]	Kvazaar
License	BSD	GPL2 / Commercial	LGPLv2.1	BSD	LGPLv2.1
Coordinator	JCT-VC	MulticoreWare	Juan Casal	Vantrix	TUT
Contribution	Free	With CLA	With CLA	With CLA	Free
Core language	C++	C++	C	C	C
Lines of C/C++	56k	51k	21k	23k	22k
Lines of assembly	0	149k	0	4k	2k
% of comments	14 %	7 %	13 %	25 %	22 %
Contributors	133	102	2	3	15
Commits	4879	11458	243	67	2068
Last commit	Active	Active	2/2016	9/2014	Active

The main development goals of Kvazaar are: 1) Coding efficiency close to HM; 2) Easy portability to various platforms; 3) Real-time coding speed; 4) Optimized computation and memory resources; and 5) Well-documented source code. A priority list for these objectives is specified by a target application since working simultaneously for all of them needs compromises. In practice, predefined presets are used to facilitate selecting different speed and quality settings for Kvazaar.

2.1 Usage

Kvazaar accepts uncompressed video in YUV 4:2:0 format and outputs HEVC bitstream. It comes with own *command line interface* (*CLI*) that is documented in the readme file. Alternatively, Kvazaar can be compiled as a library for embedding into other applications. The C-language interface is defined in kvazaar.h and is also used by the Kvazaar CLI. So far, support for using Kvazaar as a library has been included into FFmpeg and Libav multimedia frameworks.

Kvazaar supports ten presets: *ultrafast*, *superfast*, *veryfast*, *faster*, *fast*, *medium*, *slow*, *slower*, *veryslow*, and *placebo*. The naming convention follows that of x264. The fastest preset, *ultrafast*, is targeted for low-cost real-time coding. It reduces encoding complexity by supporting the most essential coding tools only. On the other hand, the most computation-intensive preset, *placebo*, enables every available tool. It is mainly recommended for testing and offline coding for the best possible quality. In practise, *veryslow* preset tends to be a better selection for high-quality coding due to better balance between quality and speed. Other presets are defined to fit between these two ends with respect to coding speed.

2.2 Software Architecture

Figure 1 depicts the high-level architecture of Kvazaar. Each module is implemented using one or more compilation units as described in the readme file and Doxygen documentation.

The entry point for users is either *Kvazaar CLI* or the library *libkvazaar* that is used by 3rd party software such as FFmpeg and Libav. The core of Kvazaar is an *Encoder* module which controls the state of the encoder and implements the interfaces for libkvazaar. Efficient *Threading* module is crucial for Kvazaar. The implementation is a thread queue built on top of Posix threads. On Windows, Pthreads-w32 is used to provide native threading.

Compression, *Reconstruction*, and *HEVC bitstream* modules implement the HEVC coding tools that handle compression and output standard-compliant bitstream, while *Strategies* module provides platform-specific optimized implementations via dynamic dispatch. An optional *Visualization* module provides a graphical presentation of the state of the currently encoded pictures.

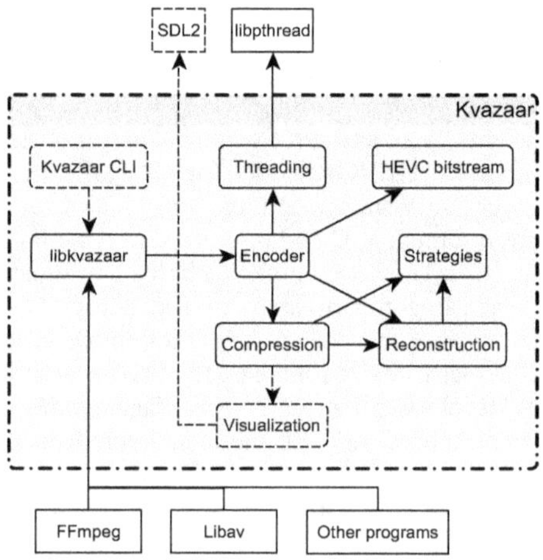

Figure 1. Module structure of Kvazaar.

2.3 Implementation

Kvazaar has three types of threads: an input-thread for reading the uncompressed images, worker threads for conducting the actual encoding, and the main thread for the remaining tasks. After receiving the input picture, the main thread assigns it to a picture level encoding.

Table 2 lists the essential coding parameters and coding tools of Kvazaar. The supported HEVC coding configurations are *all-intra* (*AI*), *random access* (*RA*), and *low-delay P* (*LP*). Kvazaar encodes pictures at the granularity of a *coding tree block* (*CTB*) of 64 × 64 pixels, according to the block diagram depicted in Figure 2. CTBs can be optionally divided into four equal-sized square *coding blocks* (*CBs*) and the division can be recursively continued until the minimum size of CBs is reached. The final quadtree structure is selected based on coding cost using a depth-first search with an early termination condition.

Within each CB, a *rate-distortion optimized* (*RDO*) prediction mode search is performed. Kvazaar offers all 35 *intra prediction* (*IP*) modes for choosing an *intra mode* (P_{intra}) and all square, *symmetric* (*SMP*), and *asymmetric* (*AMP*) motion partition modes for choosing an *inter mode* (P_{inter}). The motion parameters (MV, idx) are obtained through *motion estimation* (*ME*) that refers to previously coded pictures. ME includes *integer ME* (*IME*) stage and optional *fractional ME* (*FME*) stage that interpolates values between the pixels. *Motion compensation* (*MC*) produces P_{inter} by using motion parameters to access pixels from a *decoded picture buffer* (*DPB*) which contains the previously reconstructed *reference pictures* (D_{ref}).

After choosing a prediction mode for the CB, the *difference* (*D*) between the original picture and prediction is transformed (*T*)

Table 2. Coding parameters of Kvazaar

Feature	Kvazaar HEVC encoder
Profile	Main, Main Still Picture, Main 10
Internal bit depth	8 (10 if enabled when compiling)
Color format	4:2:0
Coding modes	Intra, Inter, Skip, Merge
Slice Types	I, P, B
Coding Configurations	AI, RA, LP
Coding Blocks	64×64, 32×32, 16×16, 8×8
Intra Prediction modes	DC, planar, 33 angular
Intra Prediction Blocks	32×32, 16×16, 8×8, 4×4
Inter Prediction Blocks	64×64, 32×32, 16×16, 8×8, 4×4, AMP, SMP
Transform Blocks	32×32, 16×16, 8×8, 4×4
Transform	Integer DCT (Integer DST for luma 4×4)
4x4 transform skip	Enabled
Transform split	64×64
Parallelization	Tiles, Wavefront, Picture-level
Rate Control	Available
RDO	Partial (includes RDOQ)

with *Discrete Cosine/Sine Transforms* (*DCT/DST*) to *transform domain coefficients* (*TCOEFFs*) and quantized (*Q*). It is possible to use *RDO quantization* (*RDOQ*) and sign hiding at this stage. After *inverse quantization* (Q^{-1}) and inverse *transformation* (T^{-1}), *loop filtering* (*LF*) is applied to the reconstructed pixels (D_{Rec}) stored in *coded picture buffer* (*CPB*). Deblocking is done after the CTU is finished, but *sample adaptive offset* (*SAO*) is only applied for a single row of CTUs at a time. The loop filtered pixels are stored in a DPB which is implemented as a single reference counted pixel buffer that can be read from the other picture-level encoders, even before the encoding is finished. All syntax elements are converted into a standard compliant HEVC bitstream by *entropy coding* (*EC*).

2.4 Parallelization

For parallel encoding, Kvazaar offers three schemes: 1) tiles; 2) *Wavefront Parallel Processing* (*WPP*); and 3) picture-level parallel processing. WPP and tiles divide a picture into multiple partitions that can be processed in parallel.

All these schemes have been implemented using a dynamic task graph and a thread pool, where the workers in the pool perform the tasks with no unmet dependencies. This scheme is illustrated with pictures of size 3×3 CTUs in Figure 3 where black arrows show the direction of dataflow and grey arrows depict a possible dependency graph. The input thread reads the uncompressed video and stores it in the buffer. The main thread creates new frame encoders and the task graphs required to encode the frame correctly. The workers in the thread queue perform encoding. The size of the work unit is a single CTB/LF. The main thread collects the resulting bitstreams and outputs the compressed video.

Experiments with Intel 8-core i7 [12] and 61-core Xeon Phi [13] processors show that Kvazaar scales almost linearly to the number of cores in the processor.

2.5 Optimizations

Kvazaar is compatible with x86, x64, PowerPC, and ARM processors on Windows, Linux, and Mac. It uses a dynamic dispatch mechanism for SIMD-optimized functions, i.e., the function is chosen based on instruction sets supported by the processor. Optimizations exist for SSE2, SSE4.1, AVX, AVX2, and AltiVec, but the majority of them are for AVX2. Most of the optimized functions are implemented in C using intrinsics, but a few assembly versions are also maintained in order to have an infrastructure for contributors using assembly directly.

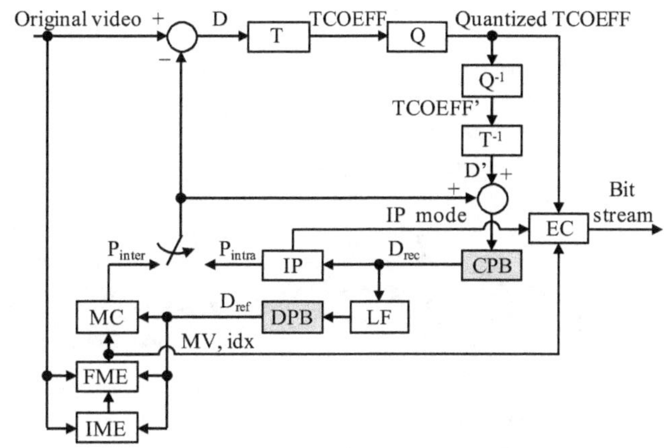

Figure 2. Block diagram of HEVC encoding in Kvazaar.

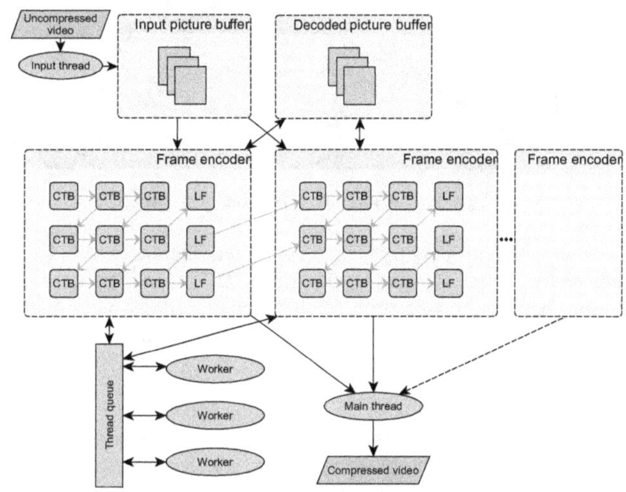

Figure 3. Diagram of Kvazaar parallelization architecture.

The cumulative speedup from the optimizations for the whole encoder is around 2.0× for all-intra coding, which is enough to encode Full HD resolution in real time on Intel 8-core i7 processor [14]. Kvazaar is also able to attain real-time HEVC coding speed up to 4K resolution on Intel 14-core Xeon processor.

Hardware-oriented source code eases acceleration of Kvazaar, e.g., on *field-programmable gate array* (*FPGA*) through high-level synthesis [15].

3. VISUALIZATION TOOL

The analysis of HEVC block structures and coding mode decisions is an integral part of the encoder development. However, the needed analysis tools are usually meant for offline use. In Kvazaar, a tool for visualizing the encoding process is integrated into the encoder. This allows real-time debugging of the encoding, which is more informative than the offline analysis since the information used for coding decisions is also available.

The visualizer is built using *Simple DirectMedia Layer* (*SDL*) multi-platform graphics library version 2. Illustrated components are 1) block partitioning; 2) intra prediction; 3) inter prediction; and 4) block reconstruction [16]. Figure 4 depicts two snapshots of the visualization. The block reconstruction is used as the background layer and the other layers can be toggled on and off. This way, Kvazaar developers can focus on visualization elements of particular interest.

Figure 4. Kvazaar visualizer output.

Multi-threaded processing is also visualized, including WPP, tiles, and picture-level parallel processing. The block borders and motion between consecutive pictures are marked with distinct colors to make identification of the individual pictures easier.

4. USE IN EDUCATION

Kvazaar is used as an exercise application for teaching embedded system development in the system design course at TUT. The exercise work is to implement a live streaming Kvazaar on a *System-on-Chip FPGA* (*SoC-FPGA*) which consists of a dual-core ARM processor, programmable logic, Full HD camera, and gigabit Ethernet. The design tasks include Kvazaar source code profiling for identifying the critical functions for FPGA acceleration and implementing the respective hardware/software partitioning to meet the performance goals. Deploying research results immediately into teaching resembles the development work in a company due to which the student feedback of the course has been very positive.

5. CONCLUSION AND FUTURE WORK

This paper presented a cross-platform academic Kvazaar encoder for the newest international video coding standard HEVC. Kvazaar is already included in the popular FFmpeg and Libav multimedia frameworks, deployed in teaching at TUT, and selected as a core component in three European multinational R&D projects where Kvazaar is being used in application development for 4K TV broadcasting, virtual advertising, Video on Demand, video surveillance, and video conferencing.

In the future, the objective is to make Kvazaar a leading open-source HEVC encoder globally in terms of performance, versatility, portability, and popularity among end-users and developers in the open-source community. HEVC Format Range Extensions will be added in the portfolio of Kvazaar coding tools to enable: 1) Format range extensions up to 12-bit 4:4:4 8K@120 fps Super Hi-Vision video; 2) Scalable HEVC coding to guarantee video streaming in resource-constrained environments; and 3) Multiview/3D coding to produce 3D, free viewpoint, and 360-degree panoramic videos. Foreseen future applications include virtual/augmented reality, free-viewpoint TV, telerobotics, telemedicine, and self-driving vehicles.

6. ACKNOWLEDGMENTS

This work was supported in part by the three European Celtic-Plus Projects: 4KREPROSYS, H2B2VS, and VIRTUOSE and by the Academy of Finland, decision no 301820. The authors would also like to thank all contributors of Kvazaar open-source project [9].

7. REFERENCES

[1] Cisco, *Cisco Visual Networking Index: Forecast and Methodology*, 2014-2019, May 2015.

[2] *High Efficiency Video Coding*, document ITU-T Rec. H.265 and ISO/IEC 23008-2 (HEVC), ITU-T and ISO/IEC, Apr. 2013.

[3] G. J. Sullivan, J. R. Ohm, W. J. Han, and T. Wiegand, "Overview of the High Efficiency Video Coding (HEVC) standard," *IEEE Trans. Circuits Syst. Video Technol.*, vol. 22, no. 12, Dec. 2012, pp. 1649-1668.

[4] *Advanced Video Coding for Generic Audiovisual Services*, document ITU-T Rec. H.264 and ISO/IEC 14496-10 (AVC), ITU-T and ISO/IEC, Mar. 2009.

[5] *Joint Collaborative Team on Video Coding Reference Software, ver. HM 16.0* [Online]. Available: http://hevc.hhi.fraunhofer.de/

[6] *x265* [Online]. Available: http://x265.org/

[7] *HomerHEVC encoder* [Online]. Available: https://github.com/jcasal-homer/HomerHEVC

[8] *f265* [Online]. Available: http://f265.org/

[9] *Kvazaar HEVC encoder* [Online]. Available: https://github.com/ultravideo/kvazaar

[10] *x264* [Online]. Available: http://www.videolan.org/developers/x264.html

[11] *Ultra video group* [Online]. Available: http://ultravideo.cs.tut.fi/

[12] A. Koivula, M. Viitanen, J. Vanne, T. D. Hämäläinen, and L. Fasnacht, "Parallelization of Kvazaar HEVC intra encoder for multi-core processors," *in Proc. IEEE Workshop Signal Process. Syst.*, Hangzhou, China, Oct. 2015.

[13] A. Koivula, M. Viitanen, A. Lemmetti, J. Vanne, and T. D. Hämäläinen, "Performance evaluation of Kvazaar HEVC intra encoder on Xeon Phi many-core processor," *in Proc. IEEE Global Conf. Signal Information Process.,* Orlando, Florida, USA, Dec. 2015.

[14] A. Lemmetti, A. Koivula, M. Viitanen, J. Vanne, and T. D. Hämäläinen, "AVX2–Optimized Kvazaar HEVC Intra Encoder," *Accepted to IEEE Int. Conf. Image Processing*, Phoenix, Arizona, USA, Sept. 2016.

[15] P. Sjövall, J. Virtanen, J. Vanne, and T. D. Hämäläinen, "High-level synthesis design flow for HEVC intra encoder on SoC-FPGA," *in Proc. Euromicro Symp. Digit. Syst. Des.*, Funchal, Madeira, Portugal, Aug. 2015.

[16] M. Viitanen, A. Koivula, J. Vanne, and T. D. Hämäläinen, "Live Demonstration: Run-time Visualization of Kvazaar HEVC Intra Encoder," *in Proc. IEEE Int. Symp. Circuits Syst.*, Montreal, Canada, May 2016.

vitrivr – A Flexible Retrieval Stack Supporting Multiple Query Modes for Searching in Multimedia Collections

Luca Rossetto Ivan Giangreco Claudiu Tănase Heiko Schuldt
Department of Mathematics and Computer Science
University of Basel, Switzerland
{luca.rossetto | ivan.giangreco | c.tanase | heiko.schuldt}@unibas.ch

ABSTRACT

vitrivr is an open source full-stack content-based multimedia retrieval system with focus on video. Unlike the majority of the existing multimedia search solutions, vitrivr is not limited to searching in metadata, but also provides content-based search and thus offers a large variety of different query modes which can be seamlessly combined: Query by sketch, which allows the user to draw a sketch of a query image and/or sketch motion paths, Query by example, keyword search, and relevance feedback. The vitrivr architecture is self-contained and addresses all aspects of multimedia search, from offline feature extraction, database management to frontend user interaction. The system is composed of three modules: a web-based frontend which allows the user to input the query (e.g., add a sketch) and browse the retrieved results (vitrivr-ui), a database system designed for interactive search in large-scale multimedia collections (ADAM), and a retrieval engine that handles feature extraction and feature-based retrieval (Cineast). The vitrivr source is available on GitHub under the MIT open source (and similar) licenses and is currently undergoing several upgrades as part of the Google Summer of Code 2016.

Keywords

Content-based multimedia retrieval; multimedia search

1. INTRODUCTION

The continuous increase of multimedia content on the Internet requires new ways of storing, organizing, and searching within collections of photos or videos. Especially for searching in large multimedia collections, a one-size-fits-all approach which relies on just one query paradigm is no longer sufficient as user intentions in different applications tend to be very diverse. However, most currently available multimedia search solutions mainly focus on tag-based keyword searches.

Multimedia information retrieval (MMIR) is an ever growing field in research concerned with the extraction of semantic information from large collections of multimedia content. MMIR has enormous potential for application in search engines, yet current commercial search engines are essentially metadata retrievers that do not consider the visual content and are vulnerable to tag abuse or copyright infringement. We consider visual information and sketching valuable ways of describing video content that are currently only slightly scientifically understood and completely absent from the software landscape.

MM '16, October 15 - 19, 2016, Amsterdam, Netherlands

ISBN 978-1-4503-3603-1/16/10. . . $15.00
DOI: http://dx.doi.org/10.1145/2964284.2973797

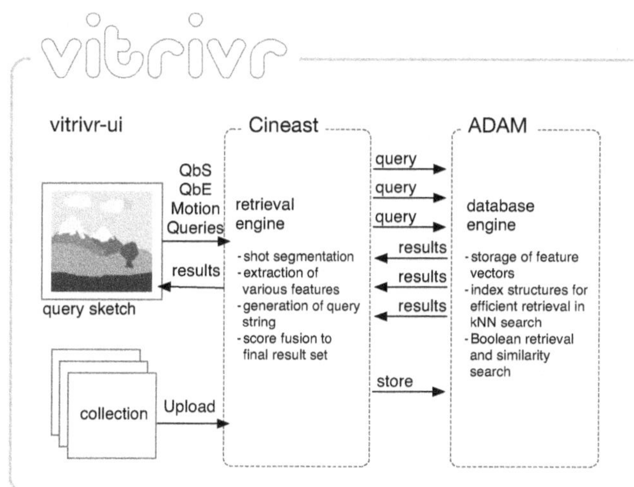

Figure 1: Architecture of vitrivr

Compared to content-based image retrieval (CBIR) which has recently gained widespread popular awareness thanks to initiatives like Google Brain[1] or the ImageNet challenge[2], content-based video retrieval (CBVR) has so far attracted only relatively little scientific support. The state-of-the-art in video retrieval research has been, with a few exceptions, reduced to CBIR through the use of keyframing. This fact is also reflected in the open source community: according to Wikipedia[3] there are at least 10 open source CBIR engines, but there is no open source CBVR system we are aware of. Motion is an important mode in video content which is considerably more challenging to exploit than images. In particular, sketching for motion has remained a research-only question limited to small video datasets [5].

[1]https://research.google.com/teams/brain/
[2]http://image-net.org/challenges/LSVRC/
[3]https://en.wikipedia.org/wiki/List_of_CBIR_engines

The vitrivr stack is an open source search system that supports scalable Query by sketch, in the form of color or motion sketches, over video collections spanning hundreds of hours of content. vitrivr is available for download from https://vitrivr.org.

The remainder of the paper is structured as follows: in Section 2, we briefly summarize the functionality of vitrivr. The complete vitrivr architecture is presented in Section 3, the query modes are described in Section 4, and Section 5 lists the features used. Section 6 briefly surveys related work. Information on how to download and deploy the vitrivr stack are given in Section 7. Section 8 concludes.

2. MAIN FUNCTIONALITY

The vitrivr stack is a content-based multimedia retrieval engine with focus on video. Its modular architecture makes it however easy to process different types of media as well. The main capabilities of the vitrivr stack not found in this combination in other retrieval systems are:

- Content-based retrieval in multimedia documents
- Multiple complementary query modes
- Distributable across multiple machines
- Scalable to large multimedia collections

3. THE VITRIVR STACK

The vitrivr stack is comprised of three main components: the feature database ADAM [3], the retrieval engine Cineast [8], and the browser-based vitrivr frontend. Figure 1 summarizes the architecture of vitrivr discussed in the following in more detail.

3.1 ADAM

ADAM is a database system that is able to store and retrieve multimedia objects by seamlessly combining aspects from databases and information retrieval. ADAM applies both the relational database model and the vector space model. The latter considers multimedia objects as vectors in a high-dimensional feature space and defines the similarity between two objects by the distance in the spanned space. For structured data, ADAM queries can use Boolean filter predicates and make use of traditional database B-tree index structures; for ranking the elements of a collection according to a similarity score, a similarity retrieval can be performed using the Vector Approximation-File (VA-File) [11].

ADAM is implemented in PostgreSQL 9.3. We have extended PostgreSQL to support the storage of feature vector data using a new data type. Furthermore, we have added the VA-File as a new index structure to PostgreSQL and we have adapted the query execution to support Boolean retrieval and nearest neighbor retrieval at the same time and in combination.

ADAM is able to scale to multimedia collections of multiple million objects with still performing well below a few seconds: In our evaluation with 14 million feature vectors each having 144 dimensions, ADAM returns results on average in 0.55 seconds for the 100 most similar objects [3].

3.2 Cineast

Cineast is a content-based retrieval engine which forms the main query processing component of the vitrivr stack. Its primary focus is on video retrieval, but its modular architecture allows for easy extensions towards other types of multimedia such as images or audio. Cineast is implemented in Java and supports multiple query modes [7] such as *Query by Example* (QbS), *Query by Sketch* (QbS) which includes not only color but also motion sketches and *Relevance Feedback* (RF). Section 4 offers more details on these query modes. Cineast provides a simple networked JSON API which can be used to query the system.

Cineast can logically be divided into two parts, one being concerned with feature extraction from multimedia documents and the population of the metadata storage system (*offline phase*) while the other takes care of interpreting user queries and retrieving relevant documents (*online phase*). Both phases use a very similar software architecture employing a multitude of independent feature modules in parallel. A feature module is a self contained unit responsible for extracting feature vectors from multimedia and query documents and comparing such vectors. An overview of available modules is given in Section 5.

Given a query and a connection to the ADAM database system, each module is capable of producing a list of scored documents which are similar to the query by the metric employed by the module. These lists of scored documents resulting from the feature modules are combined by the retrieval runtime using a late-fusion approach. Additional details on this method are provided in [8].

3.3 Frontend

The vitrivr frontend is browser-based and thus offers a high degree of flexibility and customization. A web server is used to provide the static content such as multimedia files and the components of the UI itself while also serving as a proxy (implemented in PHP) between the UI and Cineast.

Queries are specified using one or multiple canvases which can be used to either sketch a query or use an existing input image which can be added via drag and drop. Imported images can also be modified using the sketching tools to closer approximate or further refine a query.

The frontend uses Oboe.js[4] to stream query results. This enables the system to start displaying partial results while the retrieval backend is still processing the query. Whenever new results are ready, the result display is updated and the results are re-ranked dynamically. The user has the possibility to influence the ranking by adjusting the weights for different measures of similarity. Changing these weights, even after a query has been processed, changes the order of the displayed results accordingly.

Putting the frontend in a browser enables access from a wider range of devices and also facilitates scaling, storage and retrieval across multiple servers or deployment in the cloud.

4. USAGE & QUERY MODES

4.1 Offline mode

The feature extraction process enables vitrivr to make a document searchable. This process is time consuming and hence performed offline. To perform the extraction task, the Cineast command line interface can be used. Using the `extract` command followed by a folder path, Cineast will

[4]http://oboejs.com

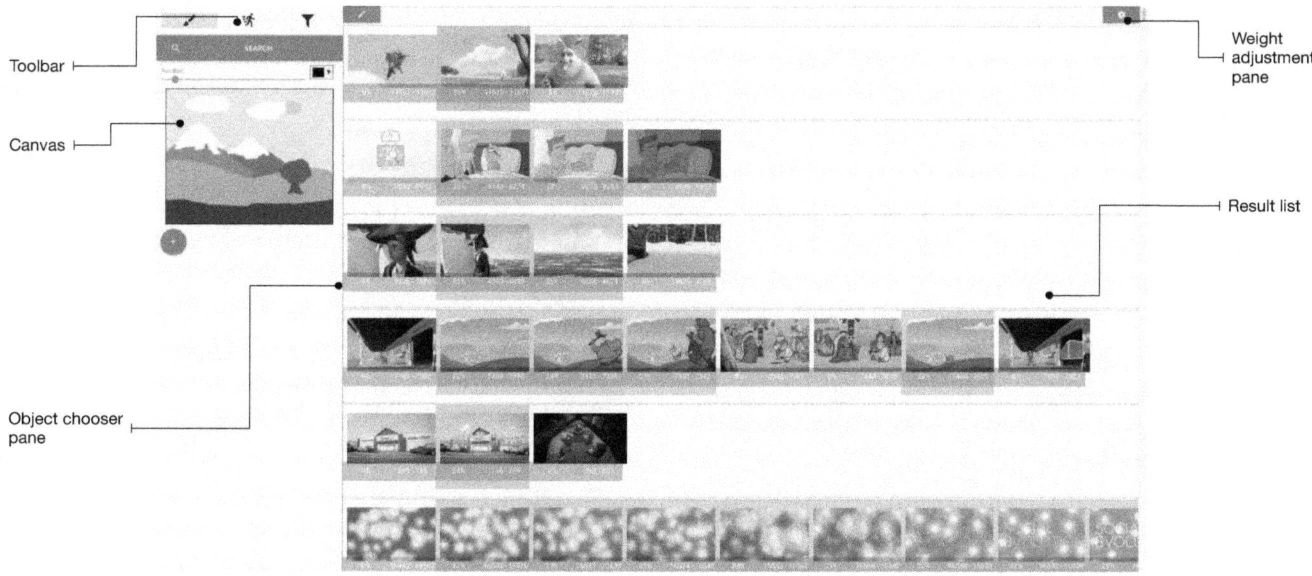

Figure 2: Screenshot of the vitrivrUI.

extract features from the video file within the folder as well as any available subtitle files. For larger collections, it is also possible to add custom extraction logic which directly invokes the internal routines. More flexible extraction via the API will be provided in the future.

4.2 Online mode

Once deployed on a multimedia collection, the frontend (see Figure 2) serves as querying and result display interface. The user can specify a query by sketching with colors or drawing motion paths (QbS) and she can re-use a result as a query (QbE) or import a frame into the drawing area. Furthermore, using the buttons, she can provide feedback on the retrieved results and refine the query. The interaction modes are detailed below.

Query by Sketch is the main interaction mode with the vitrivr system. In this mode the query is represented by a drawing, created by using the sketching tools present in the UI and/or dragging one of the results into the sketching area. The system retrieves shots that visually match the closest with the query. As the query is passed to Cineast, feature extractors process the query image and obtain query feature vectors. Each vector queries for k nearest neighbors in ADAM, which thanks to its indexes speeds up this operation. Returned results and their distances are aggregated using a 2-step hierarchical score fusion leading to the final list of results presented to the user.

Query by Example retrieves shots from the collection similar to a specific shot, which the user can select from the results list. QbE also makes use of the indexing mechanisms of ADAM for retrieving near neighbors and is faster than QbS since it bypasses feature extraction.

Relevance Feedback enables more complex result filtering by allowing several shots in the results list to be marked as *relevant* or *non-relevant*. The system retrieves results that are simultaneously similar to the relevant shots and dissimilar with the non-relevant ones.

5. FEATURES

This section provides a brief overview of the feature modules currently[5] available in the Cineast retrieval engine.

Global Features

- Average / Median color
- Dominant shot colors
- Color Histogram

Regional color features

- Color moments: channel-wise statistical moments over regional partitions (uniform grid, angular radial partitioning) of an aggregation over all frames of a shot
- Registered color grid: grid of quantized colors registered during retrieval
- Color Layout Descriptor
- Color element grids: grids containing partial color information in various representation (average saturation, variance of hue, etc.)
- Subdivided color histogram: color histograms of image partitions

Regional edge features

- Partitioned edge image: regional ratios of edge- and non-edge pixels
- Edge Histogram Descriptor
- Dominant edge grid: regional dominant edge direction quantised into 5 categories.

Motion features

- Directional motion histograms: regional normalised histograms of motion quantized into 8 directions.
- Regional motion sums: regional sums of the lengths of all motion vectors.

[5] as of Q2 2016

6. RELATED WORK

MMIR has been an active research topic for decades. The influential paper by Flickner et. al. on the QBIC system [2] demonstrated the feasibility of image retrieval with shape, texture and sketch. However, it was only years later (around 2002) when the first open source fully integrated CBIR systems like imgSeek[6] came along.

For CVBR, ongoing benchmarks such as TRECVID [6] focus on very large scale video datasets an mostly deal with non-interactive retrieval. A common approach involves keyframing video shots, which reduces the problem to CBIR, thus throwing away all motion information. On the side of interactive video search, some research prototypes offer query by sketch capabilities, but this approach is far from mainstream [10]. Aside from vitrivr, none of these research prototypes nor the very few published systems that support motion sketch-based video retrieval [1, 5] have evolved into open source software.

7. DOWNLOAD AND DEPLOYMENT

The vitrivr stack can be downloaded from our project website https://vitrivr.org. To facilitate the deployment, we offer a docker[7] image containing an ADAM database prepopulated with features from a video collection comprised of creative commons videos [9] together with the relevant thumbnails.

To run the vitrivr stack, the following components have to be present on a system:

- Docker (unless the database is installed natively)
- Java 8
- a PHP-capable web server

8. FUTURE WORK

Future work is planned in all three areas covered by the vitrivr stack, i.e., at the frontend, query processing, and data storage layer.

ADAM We are currently in the process of migrating the vitrivr stack from ADAM to its successor, called ADAM_{pro} [4], in order to improve the scalability to even larger multimedia collections and to ensure flexibility in the retrieval plans. ADAM_{pro} is a new storage system capable of storing and efficiently retrieving feature data of arbitrary dimensionality as well as structured metadata. It supports a large variety of index structures (VA-File, Locality-Sensitive Hashing, Spectral Hashing, etc.) and allows a flexible combination of multiple indexes and data sources.

Cineast currently focuses mainly on video. We plan to change this by adding additional feature modules for visual, auditory and spatio-temporal modalities. Additionally, a distributed extraction system is currently being developed which will facilitate feature extraction on large collections across many machines.

Frontend The vitrivr frontend will be extended by a natural-language interface as well as additional query modes for speech and sound. Additional functionality is also planned to facilitate exploratory searches.

[6]http://server.imgseek.net

[7]https://www.docker.com

9. ACKNOWLEDGMENTS

This work was partly supported by the Swiss National Science Foundation (SNSF), project IMOTION (contract no. 20CH21_151571).

10. REFERENCES

[1] S.-F. Chang, W. Chen, and H. Sundaram. VideoQ: A Fully Automated Video Retrieval System Using Motion Sketches. In *Proc. Int. Workshop on Applications of Computer Vision, WACV 1998*, pages 270–271, 1998.

[2] M. Flickner, H. Sawhney, W. Niblack, J. Ashley, Q. Huang, B. Dom, M. Gorkani, J. Hafner, D. Lee, D. Petkovic, et al. Query by Image and Video Content: The QBIC system. *IEEE Computer*, 28(9):23–32, 1995.

[3] I. Giangreco, I. Al Kabary, and H. Schuldt. ADAM — A Database and Information Retrieval System for Big Multimedia Collections. In *Proc. Int. Congress on Big Data (BigData Congress)*, pages 406–413, Anchorage, USA, 2014.

[4] I. Giangreco and H. Schuldt. ADAM_{pro}: Database Support for Big Multimedia Retrieval. *Datenbank-Spektrum*, 16(1):17–26, 2016.

[5] R. Hu, S. James, T. Wang, and J. Collomosse. Markov Random Fields for Sketch based Video Retrieval. In *Proc. Int. Conf. on Multimedia Retrieval, ICMR 2013*, pages 279–286, 2013.

[6] P. Over, G. Awad, M. Michel, J. Fiscus, W. Kraaij, A. F. Smeaton, G. Quéenot, and R. Ordelman. TRECVID 2015 – An Overview of the Goals, Tasks, Data, Evaluation Mechanisms and Metrics. In *Proc. of TRECVID 2015*. NIST, USA, 2015.

[7] L. Rossetto, I. Giangreco, S. Heller, C. Tănase, and H. Schuldt. Searching in Video Collections Using Sketches and Sample Images–The Cineast System. In *International Conference on MultiMedia Modelling, MMM 2016*, pages 336–341, Miami, USA, 2016.

[8] L. Rossetto, I. Giangreco, and H. Schuldt. Cineast: A Multi-Feature Sketch-based Video Retrieval Engine. In *Proc. Int. Symposium on Multimedia, ISM 2014*, pages 18–23, Taichung, China, 2014.

[9] L. Rossetto, I. Giangreco, and H. Schuldt. OSVC — Open Short Video Collection 1.0. Technical report, (CS-2015-002), University of Basel, 2015.

[10] K. Schoeffmann, M. A. Hudelist, and J. Huber. Video Interaction Tools: A Survey of Recent Work. *ACM Computing Surveys (CSUR)*, 48(1):14, 2015.

[11] R. Weber, H.-J. Schek, and S. Blott. A Quantitative Analysis and Performance Study for Similarity-Search Methods in High-Dimensional Spaces. In *Proc. Int. Conf. on Very Large Data Bases, VLDB 1998*, pages 194–205, New York, USA, 1998.

Kurento: the WebRTC Modular Media Server

Luis López
Universidad Rey Juan Carlos
Camino del Molino S/N
28943 Fuenlabrada (Spain)
luis.lopez@urjc.es

Miguel París
Universidad Rey Juan Carlos
Camino del Molino S/N
28943 Fuenlabrada (Spain)
miguel.paris@urjc.es

Santiago Carot
Universidad Rey Juan Carlos
Camino del Molino S/N
28943 Fuenlabrada (Spain)
santiago.carot@urjc.es

Boni García
Universidad Rey Juan Carlos
Camino del Molino S/N
28943 Fuenlabrada (Spain)
boni.garcia@urjc.es

Micael Gallego
Universidad Rey Juan Carlos
Camino del Molino S/N
28943 Fuenlabrada (Spain)
micael.gallego@urjc.es

Francisco Gortázar
Universidad Rey Juan Carlos
Camino del Molino S/N
28943 Fuenlabrada (Spain)
francisco.gortazar@urjc.es

Raul Benítez
Universidad Rey Juan Carlos
Camino del Molino S/N
28943 Fuenlabrada (Spain)
raul.benitez.mejias@urjc.es

Jose A. Santos
Naevatec
C/ Chile 10, Of. 8
Las Rozas de Madrid (Spain)
jcaden@naevatec.com

David Fernández
Naevatec
C/ Chile 10, Of. 8
Las Rozas de Madrid (Spain)
dfernandez@naevatec.com

Radu Tom Vlad
Naevatec
C/ Chile 10, Of. 8
Las Rozas de Madrid (Spain)
rvlad@naevatec.com

Iván Gracia
Naevatec
C/ Chile 10, Of. 8
Las Rozas de Madrid (Spain)
igracia@naevatec.com

Francisco Javier Lopez
Naevatec
C/ Chile 10, Of. 8
Las Rozas de Madrid (Spain)
fjlopez@naevatec.com

ABSTRACT

In this paper we introduce Kurento Media Server: an open source WebRTC Media Server providing a toolbox of capabilities which include group communications, recording, routing, transcoding and mixing. Kurento supports a large number of media protocols such as WebRTC, plain RTP, RTSP or HTTP and bunch of codecs including VP8, VP9, H.264, H.263, OPUS, Speex, PCM or AMR. Kurento Media Server is based on a modular architecture, which makes it possible for developers to extend and customize its native capabilities with advanced media processing features such as computer vision, augmented reality or speech analysis. Kurento is ideal for WWW developers who find natural programming with its Java and JavaScript APIs following the traditional three tiered WWW development model.

Keywords

Media Server; Real-Time Multimedia, WebRTC; Modularity; Recording, Computer Vision, Augmented Reality

MM '16, October 15-19, 2016, Amsterdam, Netherlands
© 2016 ACM. ISBN 978-1-4503-3603-1/16/10…$15.00
DOI: http://dx.doi.org/10.1145/2964284.2973798

1. INTRODUCTION

WebRTC [1] is the umbrella term for a number of emerging technologies and APIs having the ambition of bringing Real-Time Communications (RTC) to the WWW. Although still in its infancy, WebRTC is one of the technological initiatives getting most worldwide attention. WebRTC standardization bodies are investing huge efforts on addressing most of the problems of creating client-side WebRTC implementations for the WWW [1]. Thanks to this, both Chrome and Firefox browsers support it. This means that, at the time of this writing, around 2 billion devices enjoy built-in WebRTC capabilities. This number is expected to grow during the next few years as other browsers, including Edge and Safari are creating their WebRTC implementations.

Originally, most WebRTC applications were based on peer-to-peer communication models. However, the use of WebRTC media servers and infrastructures for making richer applications is becoming common practice. For example, WebRTC media gateways are typical on services requiring protocol or format adaptations (as happens when integrating WebRTC with IMS), Multi Point Control Units (MCUs) are often used to support group communications, recording media servers are helpful when one needs to persist WebRTC calls, etc.

In this paper, we concentrate on that infrastructure side of the problem. For this, we present Kurento [2]: a WebRTC media server and a set of client APIs making simple the development of advanced video applications for WWW and smartphone platforms. Kurento features include group communications, transcoding, recording, mixing, broadcasting and routing of audiovisual flows. Kurento also provides advanced media processing capabilities such as computer vision, or augmented reality. Kurento modular architecture makes simple the integration of third party media processing algorithms (i.e. speech recognition, sentiment analysis, face recognition, etc.), which can be seamlessly used by application developers as the rest of Kurento built-in features through a coherent and unified API. This is possible thanks to an automatic media transcodification capability that works among a wide spectrum of codecs including VP8, H.264, H.263, AMR, OPUS, Speex, G.711, etc.

Kurento's core element is Kurento Media Server (KMS), responsible for media transmission, processing, transcoding and recording. It is implemented in low level technologies based on GStreamer to optimize resource consumption, but with the mediation of an abstraction layer that makes it possible a friendlier development experience for developers.

Kurento is open source, released under the terms of the Apache version 2.0 license. Its source code is hosted on GitHub [3]. If you want to put your hands on it quickly, the best way is to install the Kurento Media Server and to take a look to our documentation [4] that includes tutorials and guides.

2. EVOLVING WEBRTC MEDIA SERVERS

As stated above, some WebRTC applications are peer-to-peer, so that browsers can directly communicate without the mediation of any kind of infrastructure. This is enough for creating basic applications but features such as group communications, media stream recording, media broadcasting or media transcoding are difficult to implement on top of it. For this reason, most interesting applications require using a media server.

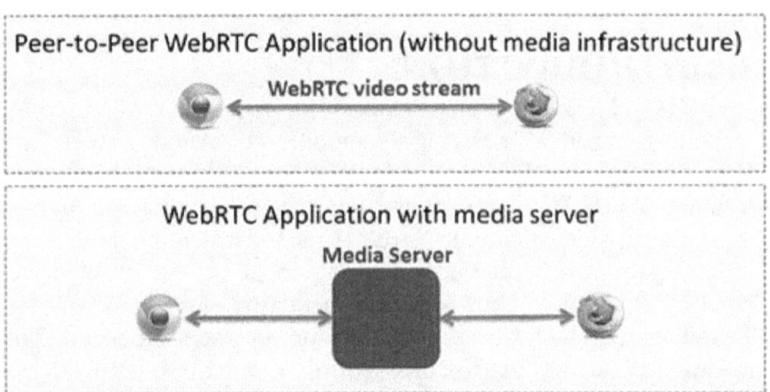

Figure 1. WebRTC applications may have a peer-to-peer architecture (top) in which clients communicate directly without the mediation of any media infrastructure. They may also be based on a media server architecture, in which case the media infrastructure acts as a media middleware that can manage, archive and process the media.

As illustrated on Figure 1, a WebRTC media server is just a kind of "multimedia middleware" (it is in the middle of the communicating peers) where media traffic pass through when moving from source to destination. As shown on Figure 2, common media servers are capable of providing just three types of features. The first is transcoding, so that the media server solves interoperability problems. The second is group communications (distributing the media stream that one source peer generates among several receivers) through mixing (transforming several incoming stream into one single composite stream) or routing models. Third, archiving through recording (storing in a persistent way the media exchanged among peers) and playing (recovering a previously recorded clip).

Current state-of-the-art WebRTC media servers are typically monolithic pieces of technology that cannot be evolved beyond the above three mentioned capabilities. However, there are many interesting additional things we can do with real-time media. Why don't enriching it using augmented reality? Why don't analyzing it using computer vision? Why can't we blend, replicate or add special effects to the media as it is travelling? These kinds of capabilities might provide differentiation and added value to applications in many scenarios such as e-Health, e-Learning, security, entertainment, games or advertising just to cite a few. For example, we may wish to blur faces on videoconferences where participants want to maintain anonymity, we may also wish to replace backgrounds or adding costumes on a videoconference so that participants feel "inside" a virtual world. We can also detect and track user's movements in front of their web-cam for creating interactive WebRTC (Kinect-like) games, or we can use it for reporting incidents (e.g. specific faces, violence, crowds) detected at security video streams.

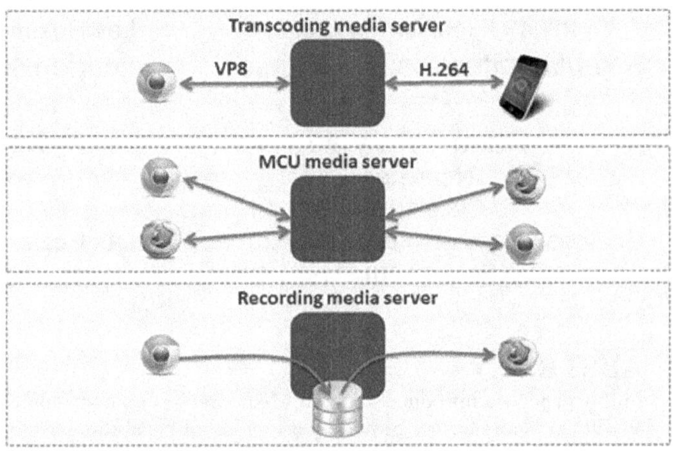

Figure 2. Current state-of-the-art media servers just provide three types of capabilities: (1) transcoding, (2) group communications and (3) archiving.

Based on these ideas, we have created Kurento Media Server as an evolution of current state-of-the-art technologies by providing a modular architecture where further capabilities can be plugged as modules. This idea is illustrated on Figure 3. This architecture complies with the 5 main characteristics of modularity:

- Isolation: Whatever happens inside a module is not affecting other modules.
- Abstraction: The internal complexities of a module are hidden to developers through an interface.
- Composability: The capabilities of modules can be combined or aggregated by applications, so that modules are interconnected building blocks that developers may use without restriction.
- Reusability: If a module is implementing a given capability, an application should be able to use it.
- Extensibility: If there is no module implementing a driven capability, it should be possible to plug a new module providing it.

As a result, Kurento Media Server behaves as a complete media middleware that developers can leverage for creating WebRTC applications combining real-time media communications and advanced media processing. There are other open source WebRTC media servers available that include Jitsi, Janus, Medooze and Licode. Kurento is quite unique, as the following comparisons illustrate:

- Jitsi (https://jitsi.org/) is an open source videoconferencing application that is based on a SFU (Selective Forwarding Unit) architecture enforced by a video router component called Jitsi Videobridge. However, Jitsi Videobridge is not modular and its SFU capability cannot be extended nor combined with other types of media processing modules in a seamless way. Due to this, extending Jitsi or developing applications based on Jitsi beyond the plain room videoconferencing model is quite complex.
- Janus (https://janus.conf.meetecho.com/) is a general purpose WebRTC gateway released under the GPL license based on a modular architecture. Janus philosophy is similar to the one of Kurento, but the Janus modular system lacks many of the nice modularity properties of Kurento. For example, Janus modules are not composable and their modules cannot be interconnected seamlessly. In addition, the number of modules that Kurento exposes is significantly higher.
- Medooze (http://www.medooze.com/) is a multiparty videoconferencing service based on a MMM (Media Mixer Mixing) MCU. Medozee is not modular and cannot provide easily other types of group communication models such as SFU nor any kind of media processing modules.
- Licode (http://lynckia.com/licode/) is a videoconferencing application very similar to Jitsi as it is based on SFU models. As Jitsi, it is not modular and cannot be extended seamlessly with further composable capabilities.

As a result, we can conclude that Kurento Media Server implements a novel modularity concept in the area of Open Source Software real-time multimedia media servers and that its properties and features are quite unique and adapt to the needs of developers requiring a really modular WebRTC infrastructure.

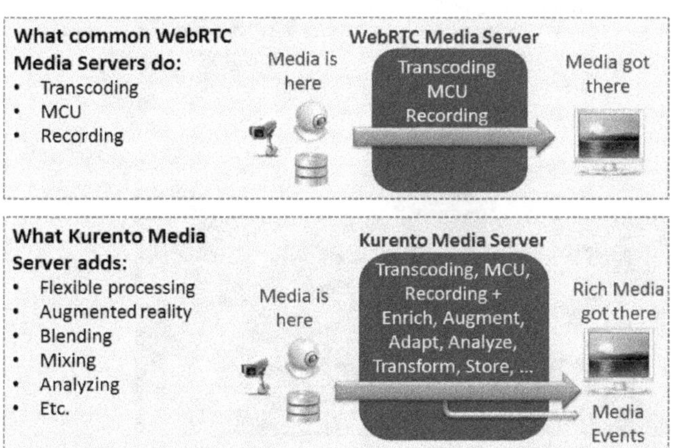

Figure 3. Kurento Media Server evolves current state-of-the-art on the WebRTC media server arena by introducing a modular architecture where arbitrary media processing capabilities can be plugged by developers. This makes possible to extend the typical features provided by common WebRTC media servers with advanced capabilities including computer vision, augmented reality, computer generated imagery, etc.

3. KURENTO CLIENT AND PROTOCOL

Kurento Media Server capabilities are exposed by the Kurento API to application developers. This API is implemented by means of libraries called Kurento Clients. Kurento offers two clients out of the box for Java and JavaScript. If you have another favorite language, you can still use Kurento using directly the Kurento Protocol. This protocol allows to control Kurento Media Server and it is based on Internet standards such as WebSocket and JSON-RPC. As shown on Figure 4, you can use the Kurento Client in three scenarios:

- Using the Kurento JavaScript Client directly in a compliant WebRTC browser
- Using the Kurento Java Client in a Java EE Application Server
- Using the Kurento JavaScript Client in a Node.js server

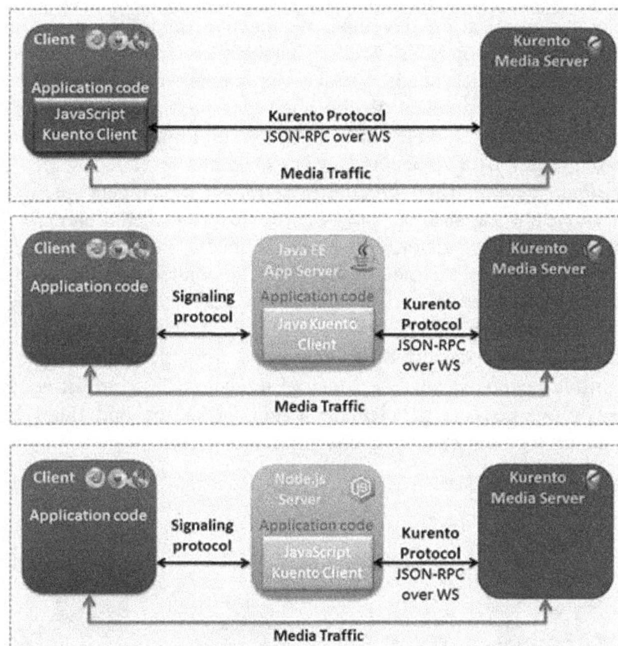

Figure 4. Kurento Media Server exposes its capabilities through a protocol, that we call Kurento Protocol, which is based on JSON-RPC over WebSockets. Client applications can directly use this protocol for consuming Kurento Media Server capabilities. However, for convenience, we also provide programming-language dependent SDKs that enable to access the protocol capabilities in a simpler and direct way. At the time of this writing, there are two Kurento Client SDKs: the Kurento Java Client and the Kurento JavaScript client.

Kurento Client APIs are based on the concept of *Media Element*. A Media Element is a Kurento module that holds a specific media capability. For example, the media element called `WebRtcEndpoint` holds the capability of sending and receiving WebRTC media streams, the media element called `RecorderEndpoint` has the capability of recording into the file system any media streams it receives, the `FaceOverlayFilter` detects faces on the exchanged video streams and adds a specific overlaid image on top of them, etc. Kurento exposes a rich toolbox of media elements as part of its APIs based on the following classification:

- We call *endpoint* to any media element with the capability of communicating media with the external world. `WebRtcEndpoint`, `RecorderEndpoint`, `PlayerEndpoint` or `RtpEndpoint` are some examples of endpoints.
- We call *filter* to any media element with the capability of processing media. `FaceOverlayFilter`, `ImageOverlayFilter`, `PointerDetectionFilter` or `CrowdDetectionFilter` are just examples of filters.
- We call *hub* to the media elements that make possible group communications: `Composite` and `Dispatcher` are examples of hubs

4. CREATING KURENTO APPLICATIONS

From the application developer perspective, and thanks to our composability properties, Media Elements are like Lego pieces: the developer just needs to take the elements needed for an application and connect them following the desired topology. Some of the available elements are shown on Figure 5. In Kurento jargon, a graph of connected media elements is called a *Media Pipeline*. Hence, when creating a pipeline, developers need to determine the capabilities they want to use (the media elements) and the topology determining which media elements provide media to which other media elements (the connectivity). Remark that a media pipeline does not need to be really as "pipeline" (i.e. a sequence of media elements) but can follow any arbitrary topology. The connectivity is controlled through the `connect` primitive, exposed on all Media Elements. This primitive is always invoked in the element acting as source and takes as argument the sink following this scheme:

```
sourceMediaElement.connect(sinkMediaElement)
```

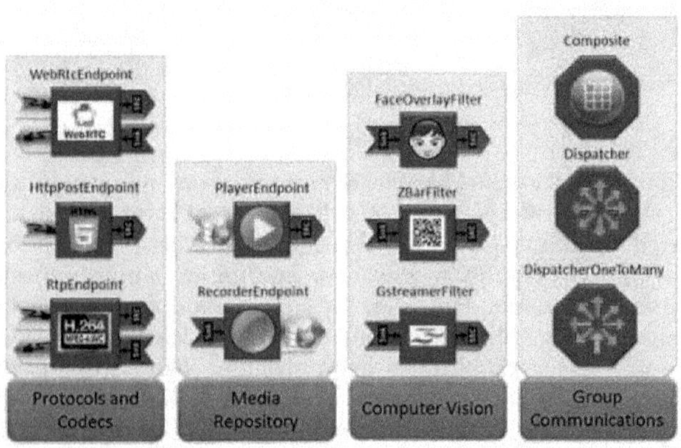

Figure 5. From the perspective of developers, creating applications with Kurento is like playing with a Lego game. Kurento exposes as building blocks its modules, that are called media elements, and developers just need to instantiate and interconnect them following the patterns they like.

For example, if you want to create an application recording WebRTC streams into the file system, you'll need two media elements: `WebRtcEndpoint` and `RecorderEndpoint`. When a client connects to the application, you will need to instantiate these media elements making the stream received by the `WebRtcEndpoint` (which is capable of receiving WebRTC streams) to be fed to the `RecorderEndpoint` (which is capable of recording media streams into the file system). Finally, you will need to connect them, as shown in Figure 6, so that the stream received by the former is fed into the later:

```
webRtcEndpoint.connect(recorderEndpoint)
```

To simplify the handling of WebRTC streams in the client-side, Kurento provides a utility called `WebRtcPeer`. Nevertheless, the standard WebRTC API (`getUserMedia`, `RTCPeerConnection`, and so on) can also be used to communicate with `WebRtcEndpoints`.

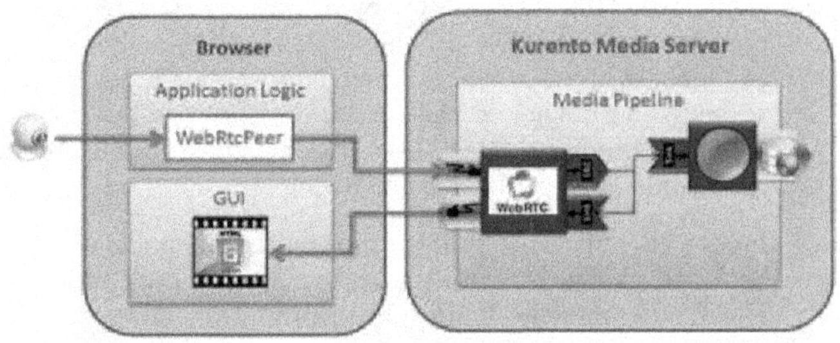

Figure 6. Illustration of a Kurento application comprising a media pipeline with two elements: a WebRtcEndpoint and a RecorderEndpoint. Based on the media pipeline topology, we can understand that this application receives a WebRTC stream from the browser, records it into the file system and gives back the stream to the browser.

5. KURENTO MEDIA SERVER CAPABILITIES

Kurento Media Server provides a very detailed documentation [4] with information on how to install and use its capabilities. The following paragraphs introduce some of them.

5.1 Group communications

Group communications are supported in Kurento through SFU and MMM models. Developers can obtain the SFU model just by interconnecting their `WebRtcEndpoints` at wish. For leveraging MMM capabilities the Composite media element must be used. A complete demo of a video conferencing application using the SFU model can be seen in [6]. A snapshot of such application working is depicted on Figure 7.

Figure 7. Snapshot of the Kurento room videoconferencing application that has been created using a Kurento SFU.

5.2 Recording and playing

Recording and playing are enforced by the `RecorderEndpoint` and `PlayerEndpoint` media elements. You just need to connect your source/sinks to these elements to have your streams recorded/played. You can see a see demo of these capabilities in [8].

5.3 WebRTC stats and monitoring

Kurento Media Server exposes a monitoring API enabling the runtime inspection of pipelines and media elements. In addition, the `WebRtcEndpoint` exposes an API enabling developers to collect WebRTC Quality of Service metrics in agreement with the WebRTC Stats W3C draft. A demo of this is available in [10].

5.4 DataChannels and multisensory multimedia

Kurento fully supports multisensory media streams meaning that any stream can be composed by video, audio and data tracks. The WebRtcEndpoint has support for WebRTC DataChannels so that any data received through them is fed to the data track of the corresponding media stream. This enables to create applications [9] transforming cameras into sensors or leveraging sensor data for processing and managing audio and video information.

5.5 Media filters for augmented reality

Kurento provides augmented reality filters supporting both marker and markerless augmented reality based on planar or 3D models. You can see these filters in action at different demos [11, 12]. Figure 8 shows a snapshot of one of those demos.

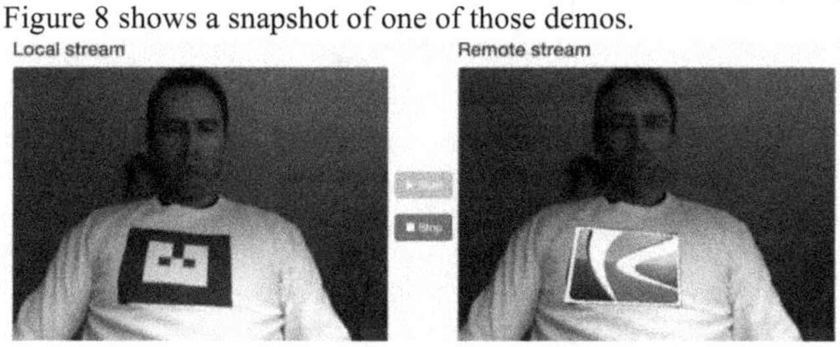

Figure 8. Snapshot of a Kurento demo illustrating the use of marker Augmented Reality filters on a WebRTC service.

5.6 Computer vision filters

Currently, there are more than 15 computer-vision based filters implementing features such as face detection, movement detection, virtual fence and crowd detection. You can see some demos for them in [13, 14]. Figure 9 shows a snapshot of a computer vision filter providing a crowd detector capability.

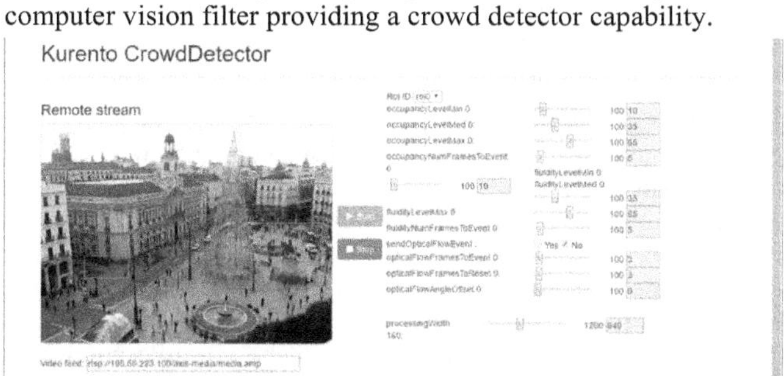

Figure 9. Snapshot of a Kurento WebRTC application leveraging a crowd-detection filter for a smart-city scenario.

5.7 Mixers supporting alpha blending

Kurento also provides modules suitable for alpha mixing. These can be combined with other types of filters for enabling automatic video production as illustrated in [15]. In Figure 10 you can see a snapshot of an application combining face detection with alpha blending for providing such type of feature.

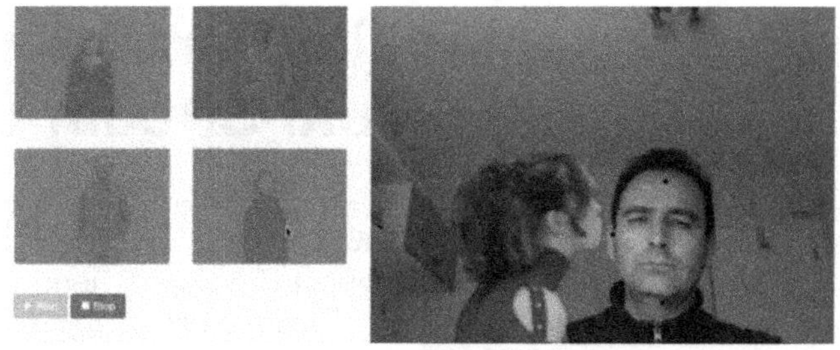

Figure 10. Snapshot of a Kurento WebRTC application combining face detection with alpha mixing for

6. CONCLUSION

Kurento is an open source WebRTC media server that makes possible for developers to create advanced media processing applications basing on the concept of media pipeline. Pipelines are created by interconnecting modules that are called media elements. This type of modularity is a novelty in the area of real-time-multimedia media servers. Through different examples, we illustrate that this model can be useful for creating a wide spectrum of media applications and services combining WebRTC with advanced media processing features in diverse areas including augmented reality, computer vision, smart cities, advanced videoconferencing and more.

7. ACKNOWLEDGMENTS

This work has been supported by the European Commission under projects FI-WARE (FP7-2011-ICT-FI GA-285248), FI-CORE (FP7-2013-ICT-FI GA-632893), and NUBOMEDIA (FP7-ICT-2013-1.6, GA-610576); by Spanish Ministerio de Educación under project Reactive Media (TIN2013-41819-R); and by the Regional Government of Madrid (CM) under project Cloud4BigData (S2013/ICE-2894) co-funded by FSE & FEDER.

8. REFERENCES

[1] S. Loreto, and S.P. Romano, "Real-Time Communications in the Web: Issues, Achievements, and Ongoing Standardization Efforts." IEEE Internet Computing, vol. 16, no. 5, 2012, pp. 68-73.

[2] https://www.kurento.org

[3] https://github.com/kurento

[4] http://www.kurento.org/documentation

[5] http://doc-kurento.readthedocs.io/en/stable/tutorials.html

[6] https://www.youtube.com/watch?v=hkT8fLROdwo

[7] https://www.youtube.com/watch?v=-QTMXqw6r6E

[8] https://www.youtube.com/watch?v=rDd2NjFXcS0

[9] https://www.youtube.com/watch?v=2WZQjfkpwLk

[10] https://www.youtube.com/watch?v=vxDgp-fOO_s

[11] https://www.youtube.com/watch?v=JlRg4PzeRKQ

[12] https://www.youtube.com/watch?v=Bp6FFYPBfnc

[13] https://www.youtube.com/watch?v=c1abmB6AB5o

[14] https://www.youtube.com/watch?v=9ztT5p8s5Co

[15] https://www.youtube.com/watch?v=WRmzzblZGDo

Modular Parallelization Framework for Multi-Stream Video Processing

Tim Lenertz
Université Libre de Bruxelles, LISA department
Avenue Franklin D. Roosevelt 50
1050 Brussels, Belgium
+32 2 650 30 82
tim.lenertz@ulb.ac.be

Gauthier Lafruit
Université Libre de Bruxelles, LISA department
Avenue Franklin D. Roosevelt 50
1050 Brussels, Belgium
+32 2 650 30 89
gauthier.lafruit@ulb.ac.be

SUBMITTED to ACM MULTIMEDIA 2016 OPEN SOURCE SOFTWARE COMPETITION

ABSTRACT
A flow-based software framework specialized for 3D and video is presented, which in particular handles automatic parallelization of multi-stream video processing. The workflow is decomposed into a set of filter units which become nodes in a graph. Execution with support for time windows on node inputs is automatically handled by the framework, as well as low-level manipulation of multi-dimensional data.

Keywords
video; view synthesis; FTV; parallelization; multi-stream; 3D

1. INTRODUCTION
In video and image processing, algorithms are often developed in an ad hoc manner. An existing solution is used as test bed, and incremental improvements are made to it in order to improve the visual quality of the output.

This is for instance the case in the MPEG-FTV (free viewpoint TV) standardization activities [5], where the goal is to synthesize virtual-viewpoint images of a scene that is captured by multiple real cameras, and possibly depth sensors which output point cloud data.

Such an exploratory development approach often lacks a software architecture and eventually causes maintenance problems. To remedy this problem, we propose a neat software framework providing a generic implementation of elements common to FTV-related algorithms, including a data flow structure into which *filter* modules that process video frames are inserted. A major feature is the support for automatic parallelization of the workflow, and output-driven partial activation of multi-stream input.

Figure 1 shows an example of such a flow graph for FTV which will be further elaborated in section 4. The diamond-shaped nodes are filters implemented as independent modules. Also shown are thumbnails of image frames passing through the graph.

MM '16, October 15-19, 2016, Amsterdam, Netherlands
© 2016 ACM. ISBN 978-1-4503-3603-1/16/10…$15.00
DOI: http://dx.doi.org/10.1145/2964284.2973799

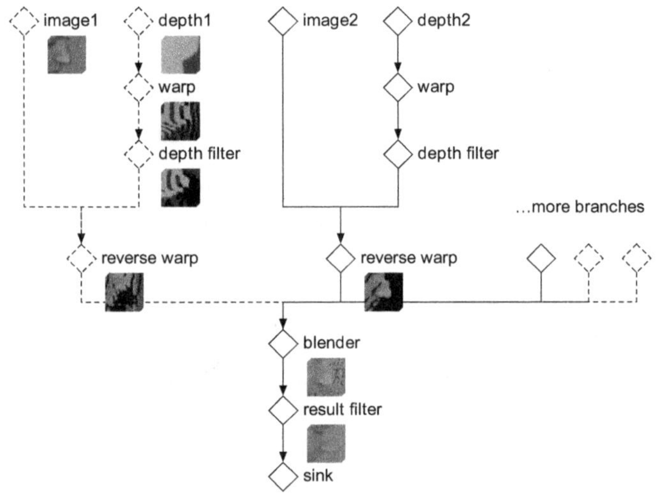

Figure 1. Example flow graph of FTV virtual view synthesis with multiple input streams

2. GOALS
One aim in the design of the framework is to clearly separate incrementally developed *experimental* code, and the *definite* code of the generic, reusable framework components.

It should also be *modular*, in the sense that external code, which does not reference any of the framework functionality, can easily be fitted into a plug-in and used as a node in the flow graph.

The framework remains as versatile as possible, and provides a greatest common denominator of the functionality required for multi-stream FTV applications. For instance, *filter* nodes may have many inputs which get dynamically activated or deactivated, and may receive bidirectional time windows of their inputs. For example the "blender" node in Figure 1 activates its input branches in function of a virtual camera position that varies in time. The flow graph framework should be versatile enough to make it possible for complex algorithms to be decomposed and remodeled into this structure.

Parallelization is handled by the framework itself, both on an *inner* (code used by the filters) and *outer* (coordination of nodes) level.

Also, the framework is written in modern C++, using techniques like RAII[1] and static polymorphism, and is extensively tested.

[1] Resource acquisition is initialization

3. FEATURES

The framework is currently built following a bottom-up approach with the goal of getting the required components to eventually develop FTV view synthesis. It consists of low-level *core* components for multi-dimensional data manipulation and queuing, the *flow graph system* which is built on top of this, and additionally a *media toolkit*, which is a loose collection of useful components for 3D and video applications.

3.1 N-d array

The data processed in DIBR[2] and 3D point cloud algorithms often has the form of *n*-dimensional homogeneous arrays, whereby types can be scalars, vectors or tuples and may be null-able. For instance, a masked image is a 2D array of null-able RGB 3-vectors, and a point cloud is a 1D array of XYZRGB tuples.

A strided *n*-d array type is therefore provided at the core level of the framework, with the basic functionality like slicing, sectioning and iteration.

Copy-less type casts make it possible to pass for example an `ndarray<1,xyzrgb>` object to a function which expects an `ndarray<1,xyz>`, or possibly an `ndarray<2,float>`, without copying data or breaking the encapsulation, or unnecessarily templatizing the function.

A wrapper `masked_elem<T>` adds a binary mask flag that makes the type null-able, and it can also be cast away similarly. Having this support at the core level removes difficulties in application code caused by differing conventions for marking null values, e.g. separate binary mask images or special "background color" values.

Type erasure of lower dimensions is also supported. For instance components which work on full video frames may safely receive video data in the form of an `ndarray<1,frame>` instead of `ndarray<3,rgb>`. Code complexity is reduced, but the framework still assures type safety and proper memory alignment.

3.2 Queues

On top of the type-erased `ndarrays`, FIFO ring buffer classes are implemented. Features include absolute time indices on frames, and dual-thread support (one reader and one writer) with mutual waiting for readable/writable frames and deadlock prevention. These rings allow to access past and future frames for temporal processing in the flow graph, cf. next section.

Two variants exist, a *seekable* ring buffer where the reader may seek to another absolute time in the stream and the writer responds accordingly, and a *non-seekable* ring buffer where the stream duration does not need to be known at construction and the writer marks the end after it has written the last frame.

The circular buffer wrap-around is implemented using the operating system's virtual memory mapping functionality. This way, no special handling is required for views that cross the buffer's boundary.

The flow graph system makes use of these classes to implement the data flow with both seekable files, as well as non-seekable real-time sources.

[2] Depth image-based rendering

3.3 Flow graph

The flow graph is the tree structure through which frames of the processed media stream flow. All data in the flow graph has an *n*-d array format, described by a dimension, element type, and frame shape[3]. Nodes in the graph perform a concrete frame-wise media processing step.

The flow graph always contains exactly one *sink* node, and one or multiple *source* nodes. Frames are recursively *pulled* from the sink, back through the preceding nodes, up to the sources. Nodes may have more than one input. Currently, nodes always have one output, and inputs are connected to outputs of other nodes in a one-by-one manner. The graph can have no loops.

Each node is associated to a *filter* which does the concrete frame processing and may be implemented as a module external to the framework.

3.3.1 Features

Input and output ports of nodes can each have different formats. Time is represented as an integral index value. The nodes operate frame-wise and invariably write one frame to their output at each step.

Nodes can receive a *bidirectional time window* on their inputs: on construction, the node specifies, for each input, the number of past and future frames that it needs to receive, in addition to the current frame. The system ensures that nodes receive this time window for each frame. It gets truncated only near the beginning and end of the stream. Previous frames are retained, and no unnecessary copies are made. This allows, for example, the implementation of a node which applies an image kernel filter over both time and space, on a 3D *n*-d array.

Nodes may *activate* and *deactivate* their inputs at runtime. No frames are pulled from graph branches connected to deactivated inputs. When an input is reactivated after having been deactivated (e.g. a change of virtual view position, modifying the processing flow), the intermediary frames are skipped. If the source node at the end of the branch is seekable, a *seek* request gets propagated towards it, and intermediary frames are never loaded or processed. With this it is possible to implement nodes with a large number of inputs, out of which only a small number are active at a time.

Finally, inter-node parallelism is supported with *asynchronous nodes*. These nodes have the same features as *synchronous nodes*, but instead of processing frames when pulled from the output, they run a separate thread and independently process frames in advance. Pull requests wait until the requested frames become available. For example, while the sink is processing frame t, a preceding asynchronous node may be processing frame $t + k$ at the same time. The maximal number of frames an asynchronous node may be in advance of the frame pulled from its output is called its *prefetch duration* and can also be configured at runtime. Any *filter* can be run on a synchronous or asynchronous node, and this can be specified at runtime.

[3] e.g. for 2D images, its width and height

3.4 Media toolkit

Currently the media toolkit mainly consists of an encapsulation of extrinsic and intrinsic camera matrices that are often used in FTV and point cloud applications. In a *space object* hierarchy 3D objects have poses relative to each other, and classes for pin-hole camera models are implemented. Several depth projection conventions are implemented, providing direct support for different depth image formats, and for *OpenGL* integration.

Also included are an interface to *OpenCV* for image processing tasks, generic *n*-dimensional kernel filter functions, and point cloud support. The next section describes a concrete example of some of its functions used in a multi-stream FTV application.

4. DEMONSTRATION PROGRAM

As stated in the introduction, the goal of free-viewpoint video (FTV) is to synthesize virtual-viewpoint images of a scene that is captured by multiple real cameras and possibly depth sensors. This typically involves a reconstruction step where scene geometry is estimated from the captured images, followed by a view synthesis step which generates the virtual view.

Numerous approaches to this have been developed [3][7], and a call for evidence for new FTV technologies was recently published by MPEG, end of 2015 [5]. MPEG uses the programs DERS[4] and VSRS[5] as reference software to evaluate the results of candidate algorithms proposed by MPEG committee members. They use an algorithm based on stereo matching and image warping.

A small demonstration program was written using the framework which generates a video with a moving virtual camera based on the *Poznan Blocks* sequence [4] (see Figure 2). The input data consists of 9 fixed position camera feeds, along with depth sensor data. These depth images are of low quality and have blurred edges and other artifacts.

The algorithm replicates the one employed by VSRS in its most basic form, except that now more than two input views are taken. A more advanced version of VSRS was also implemented within the framework. Here, the flow graph system is used for automatically activating or deactivating the contributing or idle nodes. The goal of the demonstration program is not to reach high-quality output (much better FTV results exist already), but to have a program which is written from scratch and uses almost all of the framework's features, for validation.

Figure 2. Demonstration program output

[4] Depth Estimation Reference Software [5]

[5] View Synthesis Reference Software

4.1 Algorithm

Figure 1 shown earlier depicts the flow graph and the filters that this demonstration program consists of. The *main* function of the program only constructs and runs the graph. All of the concrete processing steps are implemented as filter modules. Note that the "blender" node has 9 inputs; only two of the branches are shown on the figure.

4.1.1 Method

In two camera images depicting the same scene from different viewpoints, 2D points from one *source* image can be mapped to points from the other *destination* image, knowing its depth in either image, and the homography matrix. The process of copying each pixel in an image into its corresponding location on a new destination image is called *image warping*, and is an elementary method for view synthesis.

The algorithm first warps the input depth image into the virtual camera view. The resulting depth image (see Figure 3) contains virtual shadows for regions occluded from the original viewpoint, and small holes due to the limited resolution of the input images. The depth image is refined using a kernel filter. Then a *reverse warping* is performed to transform the input image into the virtual camera view, using the new *destination* depth image. (Figure 3)

The resulting images for each input view depict the scene from the same viewpoint, but have different occlusions. The three whose original camera positions are closest to the virtual camera are picked out and blended together.

The final image is again refined using a 3D kernel filter over an image and time window. It removes flickering pixels for example.

4.1.2 Implementation

The different steps are performed by connected nodes in a flow graph. Holes in the transformed images and depth maps are represented using the `masked_elem` wrapper. The 4×4 homographic matrices used for warping are obtained using the camera model classes from the media toolkit, and also include the depth reprojection. No low level matrix operations are performed by the filter code.

The "blender" node activates at each frame 3 of its 9 inputs, and deactivates the others. When – due to a new virtual viewpoint position – an input is reactivated after having been inactive, the branches need to jump to the new time index. This *seek* operation is implicitly propagated through the branch, up to the source nodes which then change the file position. Intermediary frames are never loaded or processed by the "warp" or "depth filter" nodes.

The "reverse warp" nodes are set to be *asynchronous*. Thanks to this, the program gets automatically parallelized into 4 threads, with three separate threads for the branches connected to the active blender inputs. The point of synchronization of two threads is restricted to the ring buffer between two nodes. This improves runtime on multiprocessor systems, as shown in the next section.

Figure 3. Image after reverse warping \ after depth warping

5. BENCHMARK

In order to measure the performance gains reached with the parallelization, we compared the processing durations and CPU usage of the demonstration program without parallelization (Figure 4) and with the 4-thread configuration described before (Figure 5).

The X-axis represents real time in seconds. The black curve (with the markers) is the real time between subsequent frames arriving at the sink. The blue curve indicates the CPU usage of the program at that time. An 8-core machine is used, and a value of 800% means that all cores are fully used. The full stream consists of 200 frames.

With parallelization, the total time it takes to process the streams is lowered from 170 seconds to 65 seconds.

CPU usage averages at around 350%, for the 4 threads. The spike at the beginning occurs because the "blender" deactivates its input branches only when it starts processing the first frame. Without parallelization, only one CPU core is used at 100%.

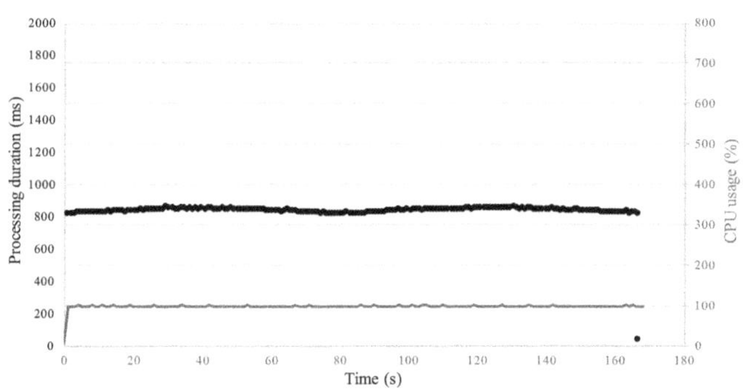

Figure 4. Sequential processing times and CPU usage

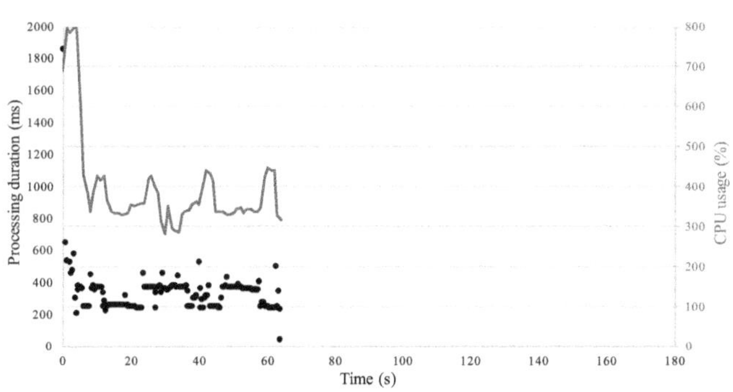

Figure 5. Parallelized processing times and CPU usage

6. FURTHER DEVELOPMENT

More functionality is being added in the current and future versions of the flow graph system. In the most recent version, it is possible to connect inputs from different filters to the output of one same filter. So the graph is no longer necessarily a tree with one-to-one connections. This required fundamental changes in the framework:

Firstly, a distinction is now made between the *filter graph* that is set up by the application, and the internal *node graph* which handles the actual data flow. It is automatically created by the system and can differ from the filter graph. For one-to-many connections, *multiplex nodes* are inserted. They handle the consequent time synchronization issues automatically, without needing to copy frames or process them multiple times. With this it is for instance possible to reuse frames at different stages in the flow graph. All functionalities, such as seeking or asynchronous nodes, remain available.

Possible features for future revisions are support for filters with multiple outputs, more parallelization options (such as processing frames of the same filter in parallel), real-time support, and more.

7. USAGE

The current version of the framework is available for download at http://timlenertz.github.io/mf/. The site also contains source code documentation, the test sequence, build and usage instructions.

The framework currently only supports Linux and Darwin (OS X). Some low-level components (virtual memory mapping, thread synchronization) depend on the operating system and are only implemented for these targets. A compiler with full support for C++14 is required. The framework is developed and tested on *LLVM/Clang* 3.8. Standard GNU *Makefiles* are used for building.

8. SIMILAR SYSTEMS

RabbitFire [6] is a comparable parallelization framework targeted towards image and video processing. It reaches very high efficiency by using lockless thread synchronization, and supports intra-node parallelism and input time windows. However, filters can only be placed in a serial pipeline, and there is no support for a graph structure. It also runs only on Windows.

Intel Thread Building Blocks [2] is a more general-purpose solution for data flow graphs. It is based on a notion of message passing instead of a stream of frames, making it less useful for the workflow used here.

GStreamer [1] is an open-source modular data-flow system with heterogeneous media formats. It is mostly intended for conversion and playback of different video and audio formats, and not specific for frame-wise processing.

9. CONCLUSION

A C++ software framework specialized for multi-stream FTV was presented. It handles low-level data manipulation and implements a high-level data flow structure, providing support for application modules that concentrate on the specific image processing. In particular, multi-stream input, parallelization, time windows and implicit seek operations are supported. Its main advantage against similar systems is its targeted development towards FTV applications.

10. ACKNOWLEDGEMENT

This work was supported by Innoviris, the Brussels Institute for Research and Innovation – Belgium, under contract number 2015-DS-39c, financing the 3DLicorneA project.

11. REFERENCES

[1] GStreamer Team. GStreamer. https://gstreamer.freedesktop.org

[2] Intel®. Thread Building Blocks. https://www.threadingbuildingblocks.org

[3] Lee, C., Tabatabai A. and Tashiro K. 2015. Free viewpoint video (FVV) survey and future research direction. *APSIPA Transactions on Signal and Information Processing.* 15, 4 (Oct 2015).

[4] Domański, M., Dziembowski, A., Kuehn, A., Kurc, M., Łuczak, A., Mieloch, D., Siast, J., Stankiewicz, O., Wegner,

K. Poznan Blocks - a multiview video test sequence and camera parameters for Free Viewpoint Television. *ISO/IEC JTC1/SC29/WG11 MPEG 2014/M32243*. San Jose, USA, (Jan 2014)

[5] MPEG. Call for Evidence of Free-Viewpoint Television: Super-Multiview and Free Navigation – update. *ISO, Coding of Moving Pictures and Audio. N15733*. (Oct 2015) http://mpeg.chiariglione.org/standards/exploration/free-viewpoint-television-ftv/call-evidence-free-viewpoint-television-super-0

[6] NEXTWave Technologies SPRL. RabbitFire™. http://www.nextwave-techs.com/rabbitfire.html

[7] Smolic, A. 2011. 3D video and free viewpoint video - From capture to display. *Pattern Recognition*. 44 (2011), 1958-1968

OpenVQ - A Video Quality Assessment Toolkit

Kristian Skarseth[1], Henrik Bjørlo[2], Pål Halvorsen[3,4], Michael Riegler[3,4], Carsten Griwodz[3,4]
[1]LABO Mixed Realities, Norway [2]Sopra Steria, Norway
[3]Simula Research Laboratory, Norway [4]University of Oslo, Norway
skarseth@mixedrealities.no, henrbjor@ifi.uio.no, {paalh, michael, griff}@simula.no

ABSTRACT

This paper presents an open source video quality assessment tool called OpenVQ and OPVQ, an objective quality metric based on work of the Video Quality Experts Group. It was primarily developed to satisfy the need of the community for a freely accessible and easy-to-use quality assessment tool, which would remove the need for using throughly outdated methods that is still prevalent because only those are easily available.

OpenVQ is implemented as a toolbox of full-reference quality assessment methods, which can be extended with improved methods in the future. The primary method provided by OpenVQ at this time is OPVQ, the Open Perceptual Video Quality metric. It is very much inspired by the formal model of ITU-T Rec. J.247 Annex B, however with many modifications to deal with errors and inconsistencies in formulas and pseudo code, and restrictions to avoid violating known patents. OPVQ has been validated with several IRRCyN datasets and was found to yield results similar to those reported in ITU.T J.247.

OpenVQ implements also PSNR (Peak signal-to-noise-ratio), because it is in high demand in spite of its bad performance, and SSIM (Structural similarity index), an image quality metric that is known to perform quite well in many cases.

1. INTRODUCTION

Researchers working with video must frequently assess the visual quality of the video that they have processed. Performing large-scale subjective studies under controlled conditions is currently the only way to achieve truly valid answers concerning the quality of the video as perceived by humans. Doing this is, however, rarely affordable.

It is much more desirable to compare original and processed video objectively, using deterministic mathematical operations, preferably a metric, which can express distance and thereby also order. What remains elusive is how such a metric is related to the human perception of video quality when watching the video, i.e., which Quality of Experience [7] is achieved. Its performance is defined by its ability to accurately predict quality ratings given by human test subjects.

The prevalent metric in research articles is PSNR (peak signal-to-noise ratio), which is a pixel-by-pixel mean square error (MSE) between an original and a compressed video. The limited precision in using PSNR for estimating video quality as a human perceives it has been shown time and again [13, 1]. Efforts to create objective metrics for digital video that correlate better with subjective assessments have been made since the early days of digital transmission [14, 2]. The Alliance for Telecommunications Industry Solutions (ATIS) performed the first large scale validation test of such metrics in 1994–95, and since the late 1990s the Video Quality Experts Group (VQEG) has performed several similar tests resulting in various standards [8].

MM '16 October 15-19, 2016, Amsterdam, Netherlands

ACM ISBN 978-1-4503-3603-1/16/10.
DOI: http://dx.doi.org/10.1145/2964284.2973800

2. THE TOOL

OpenVQ can be used to implement a variety of full-reference objective quality estimation algorithms, and provides unified base classes, I/O functions and statistical functions. The 3 existing metrics have also been structured in a modular manner to allow the re-use of algorithms like spatial alignment in future algorithms. Currently, the central algorithm of OpenVQ is OPVQ, but it also supports the PSNR and SSIM algorithms. With OPVQ, we attempt to provide an independent and free implementation of the ITU.T standard for full-reference objective video quality assessment, J.247. Within the constraints discussed in Sections 2.2 and 2.3, we have achieved this goal.

2.1 Algorithm selection

Choosing the algorithm that we would implement was not a straight-forward decision. The OPVQ algorithm is inspired by ITU-T J.247 Annex B [4], which appears to be a description of PEVQ (Perceptual evaluation of video quality). J.247 is supposed to be more up-to-date than J.144 [3], which targeted MPEG-1 and H.263-encoded videos. Software for J.144 Annex C (VQM) is freely available as Matlab code[1], and sometimes used for video quality assessment.

J.247 was the result of a competition initiated by VQEG, which should identify the most promising objective quality metric for MPEG-2- and H.264-encoded videos with resolutions up to VGA. Several competitors are included in the standard, with Annex B yielding the lowest average error rate with respect to subjective assessments, while Annex C

[1]http://www.its.bldrdoc.gov/resources/video-quality-research/software.aspx

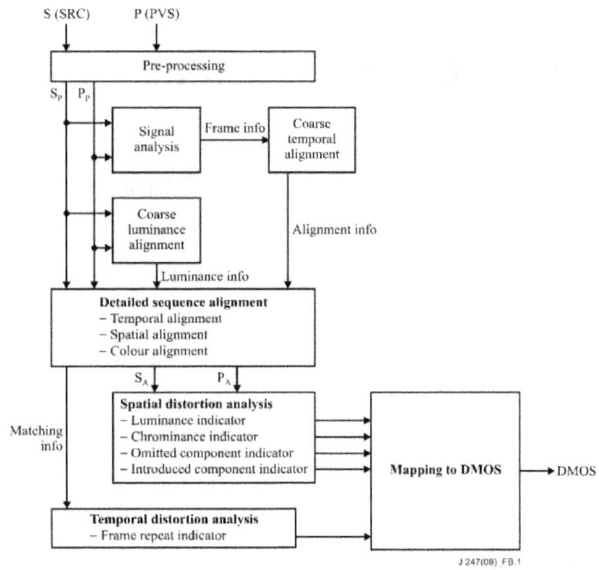

Figure 1: Overview of the PEVQ model (from J.247 [4])

yielded the best average difference from subjective assessments.

J.341 [5] is supposed to be more up-to-date again than J.247, targeting H.264-encoded videos of resolution up to HD. J.341 reports the results for a single contender.

Obviously, we intended to provide a more recent objective quality metric than J.144, which already exists. J.341 would be desirable for two reasons. First, because it has been validated for HD videos, and second, because the dataset including subjective assessment scores that was used in its evaluation has been released to the public. The major problem with implementing J.341 is that large parts of the standard itself are formulated as simplified C++ code. A direct implementation of the standard would, consequently, result in a violation of copyright.

This problem did not exist for J.247, because the contenders were in this standard described in a mix of pseudo code and formulas. A major problem with an independent implementation of J.247 is that the dataset used for its assessment has not been released to the public. Still, we chose J.247 Annex B as the basis for OPVQ.

2.2 Constraints

We studied J.247 Annex B, which comprises a series of steps that are best illustrated by Figure 1. In trying to understand whether we would be able to publish our work as source code, we tried to identify patents that the code could violate, and found a series of patents held by Opticom related to the temporal alignment of video sequences (in particular US Patents 8,228,385 [6] and 9,037,435 [11]).

These seem to affect the use of any implementation of J.247 Annex B that includes the coarse and detailed temporal alignments steps. To provide a free objective quality assessment tool, we could either design our own temporal alignment mechanism or leave temporal alignment out all together. We removed this part from our implementation, and discuss the impact of this decision.

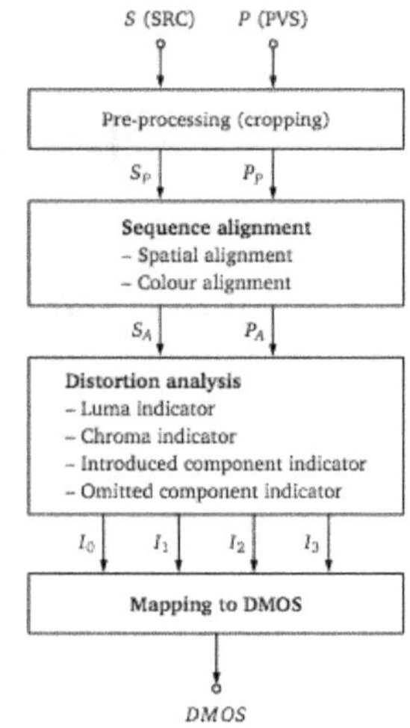

Figure 2: OPVQ model

J.247 aims at quality assessment of sequences with "transmission errors with packet loss" and "temporal errors (pausing with skipping) of maximum 2 seconds". Clearly, the situation will occur in every setting that makes use of UDP-based streaming, and occurs also in HTTP adaptive streaming when a buffer under-run occurs.

We find, however, that a playback device is fully aware of the difference between the progression of its own playback clock and the clock of video stream itself, because the latter is carried in timestamps of the transport stream. The majority of research testbeds will not require a blind analysis of independently captured and decoded original and modified video. They will have the temporal alignment information directly available, and have access to the compensation decisions made by the decoder. The resulting, simplified, structure is shown in Figure 2. Still, by making this decision, OPVQ departs from J.247 Annex B in a major way.

2.3 Further modifications

In analyzing the formulas in J.247 Annex B, we deviated further from the standard. The spatial alignment step was simplified without any change in semantics.

The clipping of ranges for the Luma indicator in distortion analysis is incorrect in the standard, because clipping occurs far outside the possible value range. However, it cannot be discarded because it reflects the strength of an impact that incorrect edges have on human perception. The impact is clearly capped at a maximum disturbance, after which a stronger color difference does no longer matter. Figure 3 illustrates this point. We could only repair the problems with a best-guess decision.

The Chroma indicator has a similar problem, but there are also indices referring to Luma and Chroma planes in the original and modified images that appeared unreasonable. We modified the indices to copy the behaviour of the Luma indicator, and added a buest guess in edginess as before.

In the Omitted Component indicator, we found a negation of differences that appeared unreasonable, whereas it was missing in the Introduced Component indicator. We chose to remove the negation.

Finally, J.247 Annex B defines a table of mapping coefficients to create an overall DMOS from the various indicators. We found it curious that some of these indicators improve the resulting DMOS value when a disturbance increases between original and modified image. All other parameters remaining equal, this can obviously yield valid results, as illustrated in Figure 2.3, but this is not generally true.

We decided therefore to restrict the coefficient for each indicator to the sensible range, so that more disturbance would also reduce DMOS, and to create a new table of coefficients based on the freely available IRCCyN [9] datasets.

Figure 3: More pronounced error, but equal disturbance

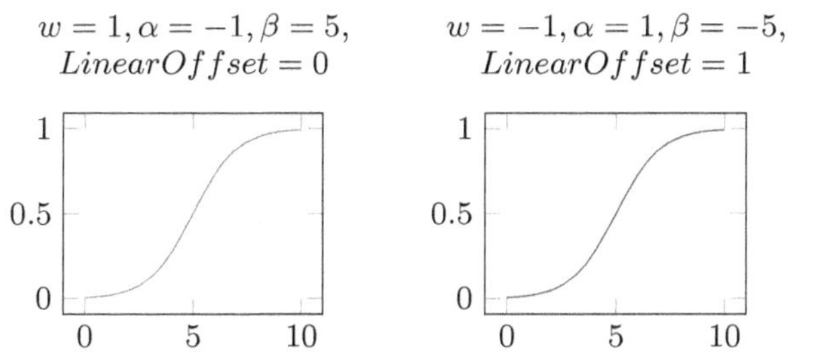

Figure 4: Equal curves with different parameters

The final DMOS score is defined as in the J.247 Annex B:

$$Score = \epsilon + \sum_{i=0}^{3} \frac{\omega[i]}{1 + e^{\alpha[i] I_{lim}[i] + \beta[i]}} \qquad \begin{matrix} \alpha, \omega \in \mathbb{R}_{>0} \\ \beta, \epsilon \in \mathbb{R} \end{matrix} \tag{1}$$

$$DMOS_P = \begin{cases} 1 & if \text{Score} < 1 \\ 5 & if \text{Score} > 5 \\ Score & otherwise \end{cases} \tag{2}$$

where each index i refers to one of the 4 main indicators. The final result is a value between 1 and 5, where 1 represents the lowest and 5 the highest quality.

3. PERFORMANCE EVALUATION AND COMMAND LINE EXAMPLES

The OpenVQ software is meant for video quality evaluations in general. The primary goal of this software is to implement a video quality metric that performs significantly better than PSNR.

3.1 OPVQ Evaluation

One of the goals of OPVQ is to provide a video quality assessment metric that performs significantly better than PSNR. We therefore ran tests on multiple datasets to compare PSNR and OPVQ using various IRCCyN [9] and ETFOS [10] datasets. In summary, our experimental results show a clear difference in performance in all configurations, and strongly indicate that OPVQ significantly outperforms PSNR [12]. However, since the amount of subjective test data available is small, we encourage further validation of the metrics performance using new datasets.

To investigate if OPVQ performs significantly better than PSNR, we calculated PSNR ratings for the applicable datasets, and used cubic polynomial fitting to best fit the scores to the subjective scale of each dataset. We used our own implementation of PSNR with spatial alignment enabled to ensure optimal conditions for PSNR. We also calculated the final performance evaluation data for OPVQ with cubic polynomial fitting, using unaltered PEVQ coefficients as well as optimized coefficients using both schemes described in more detail in [12].

The results in table 1 show a clear difference in performance between PSNR and OPVQ in all configurations, and strongly indicate that we have achieved our goal of implementing a video quality metric that significantly outperforms PSNR. An interesting observation is that the best performance for OPVQ after polynomial fitting is achieved when using the unaltered PEVQ coefficients — if only slightly better than with trained coefficients. The coefficients from the PEVQ description are not logically sound for some indicators, as they reward increase in amount of errors with higher contribution to the final score. Because of this, and the fact that the difference recorded is only minimal, our recommendation is to use optimised coefficients adhering to the constraints defined for OPVQ.

As we have not had access to any software or hardware that computes PEVQ scores, and the dataset that was used for the analysis in J.247 is unavailable, we do not have the means to investigate the subsequent goal of keeping OPVQ's performance on par with PEVQ. The performance data we could produce shows correlation and error values for the IRCCyN and ETFOS datasets that are close to the values reported in J.247. However, since these results are not produced using the same dataset, this is at most a hint that performances are comparable.

	Dataset					
	AVC/SVC	*Infl.cont.*	*QP0 QP1 (A)*	*QP0 QP1 (B)*	*EVVQ*	Average
OPVQ w/coeffs unaltered from PEVQ						
Pearson R	**0.943**	**0.907**	**0.872**	0.873	**0.890**	**0.897**
RMS error	**0.201**	**0.454**	**0.567**	0.578	**0.283**	**0.416**
Outlier ratio	**0.000**	**0.521**	0.643	0.665	**0.078**	**0.381**
OPVQ w/coeffs optimised using all other datasets						
Pearson R	**0.943**	**0.907**	0.869	0.871	**0.890**	0.896
RMS error	**0.201**	**0.454**	0.574	0.583	**0.283**	0.419
Outlier ratio	**0.000**	0.529	0.649	0.677	**0.078**	0.386
OPVQ w/coeffs optimised using datasets of same test methodology						
Pearson R	**0.943**	**0.907**	0.867	0.871	0.886	0.895
RMS error	**0.201**	**0.454**	0.576	0.583	0.288	0.420
Outlier ratio	**0.000**	0.525	0.655	0.671	0.111	0.392
PEVQ as reported in J.247 – not tested with the same data						
Pearson R	-	-	-	-	-	0.825
RMS error	-	-	-	-	-	0.571
Outlier ratio	-	-	-	-	-	0.502

Table 1: Overall performance evaluation after cubic fitting (best results in bold)

The evaluation shows that for the subjective data available to us and within an expected range of quality degradations, OPVQ performs significantly better than PSNR. Because the amount of subjective test data available is small, we encourage further validation of the metrics performance using other datasets. We have not been able to conclusively compare the performance of OPVQ with PEVQ.

3.2 Command Line Examples

In order to use the program, OpenVQ provides a simple command line interface. Running the program with `-help` or without any arguments displays the help screen. First,

```
openvq [global options] \
command [command specific options]
```

shows the overall command format where *[global options]* are `-help` and `-log-level`, *command* is video quality metric to use (`opvq`, `psnr` or `ssim`) and particular *[command specific options]* are options for the individual quality evaluations like frame number limits (`-max-frames`), path to source (original) and processed video files (`-src` and `-pvs`), number of threads to use (`-num_threads`), etc.

The OPVQ algorithm may be used like this:

```
openvq opvq -src src01.avi -pvs pvs01.avi
```

Here, the quality of the processed video file *pvs01.avi* will be evaluated compared to the original source video *src01.avi*, and a final *opvq* score between 1 and 5 is returned. Replacing the command *opvq* with psnr or ssim gives similar quality evaluations using the respective metrics.

4. INSTALLATION AND LICENSE

OpenVQ is meant as a tool for researchers. It is licensed under the terms of the GNU Affero General Public License (AGPL) version 3, as published by the Free Software Foundation. The decision to use AGPL was made to ensure that OpenVQ can fulfill its intended role in the research community, while avoiding use in a commercial service. The primary dependencies of OpenVQ are OpenCV (3-clause BSD), Libav (LGPL v2.1) and Boost (Boost license).

OpenVQ is distributed as a CMake project. For UNIX systems, CMake can be invoked from the command line. If no other project type is specified, CMake will generate a Makefile that can be invoked with Make. If no errors are reported, OpenVQ was built successfully and is ready to be installed into the system path. The install command may have to be invoked with sudo, depending on the user's privileges and the permissions of the install prefix.

We have tested our software on *Linux*, *Mac OS X* and *Windows*. The following instructions are meant for Ubuntu Linux:

- Clone the *OpenVQ* source code from https://bitbucket.org/mpg_code/openvq.
- Install the pre-requisites that are listed on the repository web page. You can also find them in the cloned repository in `README.md`.
- Use CMake and Make to compile the source code. The installation directory is chosen at this time, with a default installation in `/usr/local`.
- Optionally install the program `openvq` after compilation.
- Provide the program with an original video using `-src` and a processed video using `-pvs` and an algorithm to run. It will output the final score, which is algorithm-dependent.

5. RELATED WORK

PSNR is frequently used because freely available quality estimation tools are not discovered, although they do exist. Beyond PSNR and SSIM, NTIA VQM was mentioned in Section 1, the free version of MSU VQMT[1] provides MSU's own metrics, MMSPG VQMT[2] provides a Visual Information Fidelity (VIFp), while LIVE MOVIE[3] makes use of motion trajectories in its quality assessment. The machine-learning based VMAF Development Kit (VDK)[4] is provided by Netflix and based on their own (partly public) datasets. The VQEG Joint Effort Group (JEG)[5] has been established to collect implementations of separately developed metrics, but has not released code yet.

1 http://compression.ru/video/quality_measure/index_en.html
2 http://mmspg.epfl.ch/vqmt
3 http://live.ece.utexas.edu/research/Quality/movie.html
4 http://techblog.netflix.com/2016/06/toward-practical-perceptual-video.html
5 http://vqegjeg.intec.ugent.be/wiki/index.php/Main_Page

6. CONCLUSION

The video quality is highly important for the users' perceived experience of the video service. However, it has for a long time been discussed how to evaluate the quality. The OpenVQ open source software provides a general tool to easily calculate objective metrics for video quality evaluation in general. It provides algorithms for PSNR and SSIM, but also the new full reference objective video quality assessment metric OPVQ, which is an independent implementation of the ITU.T Rec. J.247 for a full-reference objective quality metric.

We are searching for freely available datasets to determine a parameter set that applies to HD and higher resolutions videos. We are also planning to create and assess a spin-off from OPVQ by integrating considerations that are found in standards J.341 and J.343.

7. REFERENCES

[1] Q. Huynh-Thu and M. Ghanbari. Scope of validity of PSNR in image/video quality assessment. *Electronics Letters*, 44(13):800–801, 2008.

[2] ITU-R. Methods for objective picture quality assessment in relation to impairments from digital coding of television signals. Technical report, ITU, 1992.

[3] ITU-T. J.144 : Objective perceptual video quality measurement techniques for digital cable television in the presence of a full reference, 2004.

[4] ITU-T. J.247: Objective perceptual multimedia video quality measurement in the presence of a full reference, 2008.

[5] ITU-T. J.341: Objective perceptual multimedia video quality measurement of HDTV for digital cable television in the presence of a full reference, 2011.

[6] M. Keyhl, C. Schmidmer, and R. Bitto. Apparatus for determining information in order to temporally align two information signals, July 2012. US Patent 8,228,385.

[7] F. Kuipers, R. Kooij, D. De Vleeschauwer, and K. Brunnström. Techniques for Measuring Quality of Experience. In *Proc. of WWIC*, 2010.

[8] M. Pinson, N. Staelens, and A. Webster. The history of video quality model validation. In *Proc. of IEEE MMSP*, 2013.

[9] Y. Pitrey, M. Barkowsky, P. L. Callet, and R. Pepion. Subjective quality assessment of MPEG-4 Scalable Video Coding in a mobile scenario. In *Proc. of EUVIP*, 2010.

[10] S. Rimac-Drlje, M. Vranješ, and D. Žagar. Foveated mean squared error—a novel video quality metric. *Multimedia Tools and Applications*, 49(3):425–445, 2010.

[11] C. Schmidmer, R. Bitto, and M. Keyhl. Device and method for determining a sample rate difference, May 19 2015. US Patent 9,037,435.

[12] K. Skarseth and H. Bjørlo. OPVQ and OpenVQ – Creating free software tools for video quality assessment. Master's thesis, Department of Informatics, University of Oslo, Norway, 2015.

[13] S. Winkler and P. Mohandas. The Evolution of Video Quality Measurement: From PSNR to Hybrid Metrics. *IEEE Trans. on Broadcasting*, 54(3):660–668, 2008.

[14] S. Wolf. NTIA Report 90-264: Features for Automated Quality Assessment of Digitally Transmitted Video. Technical report, National Telecommunications and Information Administration, 1990.

CNNdroid: GPU-Accelerated Execution of Trained Deep Convolutional Neural Networks on Android

Seyyed Salar Latifi Oskouei, Hossein Golestani, Matin Hashemi*
Sharif University of Technology
salarlatifi@ee.sharif.edu, hossein_golestani@ee.sharif.edu, matin@sharif.edu
Soheil Ghiasi
University of California, Davis
ghiasi@ucdavis.edu

ABSTRACT

Many mobile applications running on smartphones and wearable devices would potentially benefit from the accuracy and scalability of deep CNN-based machine learning algorithms. However, performance and energy consumption limitations make the execution of such computationally intensive algorithms on mobile devices prohibitive. We present a GPU-accelerated library, dubbed CNNdroid [1], for execution of trained deep CNNs on Android-based mobile devices. Empirical evaluations show that CNNdroid achieves up to 60X speedup and 130X energy saving on current mobile devices. The CNNdroid open source library is available for download at https://github.com/ENCP/CNNdroid

Keywords

Deep Learning, Deep Convolutional Neural Network (CNN), Mobile GPU, Performance Optimization, Low Energy Consumption, Open Source Software, Android, RenderScript

1. INTRODUCTION

Mobile platforms such as smartphones, wearable devices, tiny autonomous robots and IoT devices have been increasingly finding their way into many areas (Figure 1). Numerous applications, such as speech recognition and image recognition [2], would potentially benefit from local execution of accurate machine learning algorithms on mobile devices. Local execution allows data to stay on the mobile device and hence avoids latency issues of cloud-assisted processing.

Deep CNNs can achieve state-of-the-art results in terms of both prediction accuracy and scalability. However, they are highly computationally intensive, and hence, not practical on current mobile devices without acceleration.

*Contact author: Matin Hashemi, matin@sharif.edu

MM '16, October 15 - 19, 2016, Amsterdam, Netherlands

ISBN 978-1-4503-3603-1/16/10...$15.00
DOI: http://dx.doi.org/10.1145/2964284.2973801

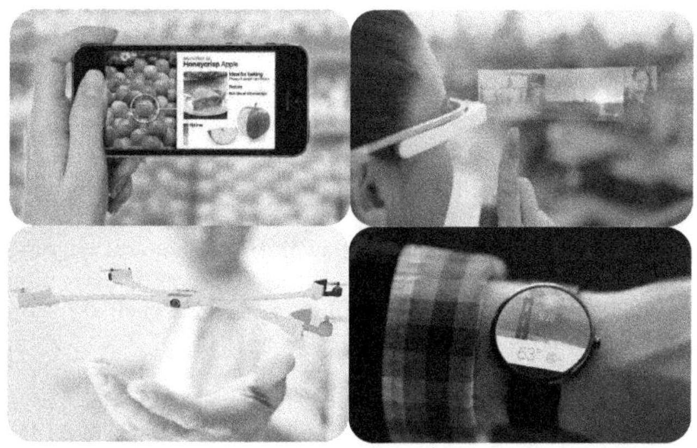

Figure 1: Example applications of deep CNNs in mobile systems. Image credits: IBM Research, Guardianlv, Nixie, Android Wear.

Many hardware-based solutions have been proposed for acceleration of deep CNNs [3, 4]. IBM has also introduced a neuromorphic CMOS chip for execution of learning applications on smartphones and IoT devices [5]. While promising, such solutions are still in early stages of development and not available on current mobile devices.

As opposed to hardware-based engines, GPU already exists in many current mobile devices and can be programmed completely in software. Therefore, parallel processing capabilities of mobile GPUs can be exploited to accelerate deep CNN computations on *current* mobile devices.

On server and desktop platforms, there exists many GPU-accelerated deep CNN libraries [6, 7, 8, 9, 10, 11, 12]. However, because of architecture differences (Section 2.1), mere porting of such libraries to mobile platforms yields sub-optimal performance or is impossible in some cases (Section 2.2).

On mobile platforms, to the best of our knowledge, such GPU-accelerated libraries are not available. The few existing mobile libraries for CNN computations [13, 14, 15, 16] are limited to the processing power of multi-core mobile CPUs (Section 2.3).

We present an open source GPU-accelerated library, dubbed CNNdroid, which is specifically designed and optimized for execution of trained deep CNNs on Android-based mobile devices. The main highlights of CNNdroid are as follows.

1. Support for nearly all CNN layer types (Section 3.1).
2. Compatible with CNN models trained by common desktop/server libraries, namely, Caffe [6], Torch [7] and Theano [8] (Section 3.2).
3. Easy to configure and integrate into any Android app without additional software requirements (Section 3.3).
4. User-specified maximum memory usage (Section 3.4).
5. GPU or CPU acceleration of supported CNN layers (Section 3.5).
6. Automatic tuning of performance (Section 3.6).
7. Up to 60X speedup and up to 130X energy saving on current mobile devices (Section 4).

2. BACKGROUND AND RELATED WORK

2.1 Comparing Mobile and Desktop GPUs

A modern graphics processing unit (GPU), in addition to computer graphics, can be programmed for general purpose computations as well. While desktop GPUs have long been programmable, major mobile chip manufacturers have recently made the GPU hardware available for general purpose computations. Due to strict area and power constraints, mobile GPUs have important differences with their desktop counterparts.

A modern mobile GPU is typically composed of several programmable parallel computing units called Shader Cores (SC). Every shader core is composed of several parallel ALUs. For example, Samsung Exynos 5433 chip is composed of ARM A53/A57 CPU and Mali T-760 GPU (Figure 2). Each SC in T-760 GPU has two 128-bit ALUs in VLIW format. Each 128-bit ALU is capable of performing SIMD operations, i.e., two 64-bit, four 32-bit or eight 16-bit operations in parallel [17]. In comparison with desktop GPUs, the above parallel ALU architecture relies more on software and compiler than dynamic hardware scheduler in efficient execution of parallel threads.

More importantly, fast shared memory in thread blocks which are present in desktop GPUs and widely employed in many CUDA-based desktop libraries are not available in mobile GPUs.

There are some differences on the software side as well. For example in RenderScript, Android's parallel computing platform [18], thread synchronization is not available. In addition, there must be a one-to-one correspondence between parallel threads and the data items inside one of the memory buffers that parallel threads work on.

2.2 Comparing CNNdroid with Desktop Libraries

On server and desktop platforms, there exists many libraries such as Caffe [6], Torch [7], Theano [8], TensorFlow [9], cuDNN [10], cuda-convnet [11], and Velesnet [12], which employ GPU-based parallel processing for acceleration of deep CNN computations. However, the acceleration methodologies and parallel algorithms of such libraries could not be directly utilized in mobile platforms due to the existing hardware and software differences.

For example in Caffe [6], the convolution operation is unrolled and converted to matrix multiplication, which requires considerable amount of memory and therefore is not suitable for mobile devices with small cache and memory sizes. As another example, the parallel algorithm in Theano [8] is similar to CNNdroid but without efficient use of SIMD units in mobile GPUs. Refer to Section 3.5 for details.

More importantly, desktop libraries take advantage of thread management facilities provided by desktop GPUs and CUDA framework, such as fast shared memory and thread synchronization, which are not available in mobile GPUs and RenderScript.

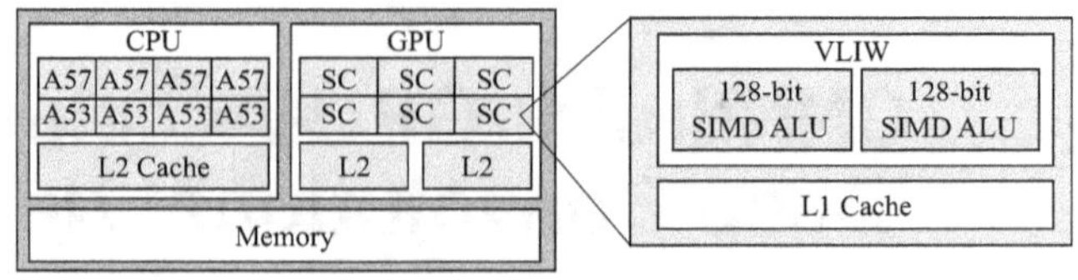

Figure 2: Example: Exynos 5433 mobile processor with ARM A53 / A57 CPU and Mali T-760 GPU (SC: Shader Core, VLIW: Very Long Instruction Word, SIMD: Single Instruction Multiple Data).

2.3 Comparing CNNdroid with Mobile Libraries

On mobile platforms, to the best of our knowledge, only few deep CNN libraries exist [13, 14, 15, 16]. All such libraries, including Caffe Mobile [13] and Torch Mobile [14], are limited to the processing power of multi-core mobile CPUs, while CNNdroid efficiently employs both GPU and CPU (Section 3.5).

In addition, CNNdroid is compatible with CNN models trained by Caffe [6], Torch [7] and Theano [8], which facilitates the process of porting the trained models to mobile devices (Section 3.2).

The existing libraries require installation of Android NDK alongside Android SDK, while in CNNdroid, only Android SDK is required.

3. CNNDROID LIBRARY

3.1 CNN Layer Types

CNNdroid library supports nearly all common types of CNN layers, namely, convolution, max/mean pooling, fully connected, rectified linear unit, local response normalization and softmax. Detailed description of every layer type and its corresponding parameters are available in the library documentations [1]. Other new layers may be added as well, due to the open source nature of the library.

3.2 Model Preparation

Model Conversion Scripts: Figure 3 shows an overview of the steps involved in deploying trained CNN models on mobile devices. CNNdroid library provides a set of scripts which take the models trained by common desktop/server libraries, namely, Caffe [6], Torch [7] and Theano [8], as input and convert them into CNNdroid format. Therefore, the models which are trained by these libraries can be executed by CNNdroid library on mobile devices.

It is possible to write similar scripts for other libraries as well. CNNdroid uses MessagePack serialization format [19] for storing layer parameters in the trained model. Detailed procedure is presented in the library documentations [1].

NetFile: The developer needs to prepare a *.txt* file, called *NetFile*, similar to the *.prototxt* file in Caffe [6]. The *NetFile* specifies layer setup of the trained model, i.e., order of the CNN layers along with their configurations, e.g., padding and stride values of convolution layers. Figure 4 presents an example. Detailed instructions for preparing the *NetFile* as well as a few examples are included in the library documentations [1].

The *NetFile* also specifies three configuration parameters (Figure 4), namely, **allocated_ram** which specifies the maximum amount of memory that CNNdroid engine is allowed to allocate at runtime (Section 3.4), **execution_mode** which selects between sequential or parallel execution modes of the library (Section 3.5), and **auto_tuning** which specifies whether or not auto-tuning is turned on (Section 3.6).

3.3 Model Execution

Once the trained model and its corresponding *NetFile* are both uploaded to mobile device (Figure 3), the model can be executed in the target Android application in a few simple steps as described below (Figure 5).

The first step is to include the provided CNNdroid library files. Note that CNNdroid library is self-sufficient and does not require installation of third-party libraries. In addition, it does not require installation of Android NDK alongside Android SDK.

Next, **RenderScript** and **CNNdroid** objects are constructed (Figure 5, steps 2 and 3). The CNNdroid constructor takes the provided *NetFile* as input and automatically creates the corresponding objects for the network layers.

Finally, **compute** function of the constructed **CNNdroid** object is called, which automatically executes the trained model on either a single image or a batch of images.

3.4 Memory Allocation

The trained CNN model, which is uploaded to SD card of the mobile device, contains layer parameters in form of matrices. Inside the **compute** function (Figure 5, step 5), and before execution of every layer, the corresponding matrices are automatically loaded from SD card into RAM, which incurs an overhead.

In order to reduce this overhead, CNNdroid selects certain layers and keeps their data in RAM, while other layers are allocated and de-allocated every time. The selection procedure is automatically done in **CNNdroid** constructor (Figure 5, step 3). Starting from the largest layer, as many layers as possible are selected, till the sum of their memory sizes reaches the maximum developer-specified amount, i.e., the **allocated_ram** parameter in the *NetFile*.

Note that the **allocated_ram** parameter cannot be arbitrarily large due to practical limitations. For example, Android 5 limits the memory usage of every app to 512MB.

3.5 Acceleration Methods

Different methods are employed in acceleration of different layers in CNNdroid. Convolution and fully connected layers, which are data-parallel and normally more compute intensive, are accelerated on the mobile GPU using RenderScript framework.

A considerable portion of these two layers can be expressed as dot products. In specific, in the convolution layer, kernels get convoluted with the input frames, and in the fully connected layer, the computation can be expressed as a ma-

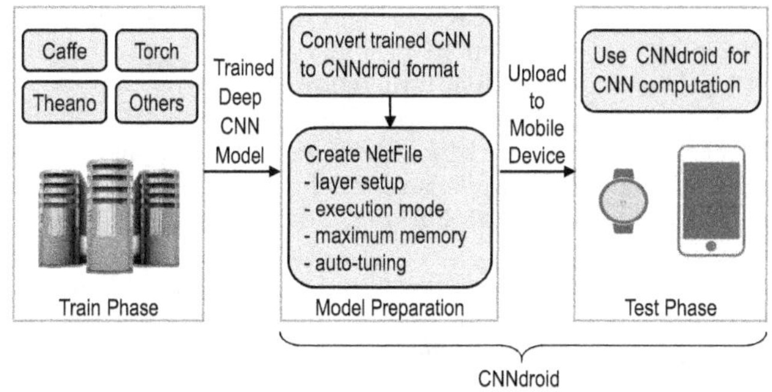

Figure 3: Overview of CNNdroid's model deployment procedure.

```
root_directory: "/sdcard/AlexNet/"
allocated_ram: 50
execution_mode: "parallel"
auto_tuning: "on"
layer {
 type: "Convolution"
 name: "conv1"
 parameters_file: "param_conv1.msg"
 pad: 0
 stride: 4
 group: 1
}
layer {
 type: "ReLU"
 name: "ReLU1"
}
layer {
 type: "LRN"
 name: "norm1"
 local_size: 5
 alpha: 0.0001
 beta: 0.75
 norm_region: "across_channels"
}
layer {
 type: "Pooling"
 name: "pool1"
 pool: "max"
 kernel_size: 3
 pad: 0
 stride: 2
}
```

Figure 4: Example NetFile showing three layers of AlexNet [20], along with **allocated_ram**, **execution_mode** and **auto_tuning** parameters.

```
// 1) Import CNNdroid library
import network.CNNdroid;

 ...

// 2) Construct Renderscript object
RenderScript myRenderScript = RenderScript.create(this);

// 3) Provide NetFile and construct CNNdroid object
String NetFile = "/sdcard/AlexNet/AlexNet_NetFile.txt";
CNNdroid myCNN = new CNNdroid(myRenderScript, NetFile);

// 4) Prepare your input, which can be
//    a single image or a batch of images
float[][][]  inputSingle = loadSingleInput();
float[][][][] inputBatch = loadBatchInput();

// 5) Call 'compute' function for CNN execution
//    and receive the result as an object
Object output = myCNN.compute(inputBatch);
```

Figure 5: Simple steps involved in using CNNdroid for execution of trained deep CNN models on Android apps. Refer to the library documentation for up-to-date details and sample projects [1].

trix to vector multiplication. The dot products are more efficiently calculated on SIMD units of the target mobile GPU. Therefore, we divide the computation in many vector operations and use the pre-defined *dot* function of the RenderScript framework. In other words, we explicitly express this level of parallelism in software, and as opposed to CUDA-based desktop libraries, do not leave it to GPU's hardware scheduler.

Comparing with convolution and fully connected layers, other layers are relatively less compute intensive and not efficient on mobile GPU. Therefore, they are accelerated on multi-core mobile CPU via multi-threading. Since ReLU layer usually appears after a convolution or fully connected layer, it is embedded into its previous layer in order to increase the performance in cases where multiple images are fed to the CNNdroid engine.

In addition to above parallel implementations, CNNdroid also includes sequential (single-thread) implementations of all layers. The execution will be sequential or parallel depending on the `execution_mode` parameter specified in the *NetFile* (Figure 4).

3.6 Auto-Tuning

In order to reach better performance across different Android based mobile devices, our GPU-accelerated parallel algorithms are developed with tuning parameters which select the amount of work assigned to parallel GPU threads and the amount of work assigned to SIMD ALUs in execution of every GPU thread. The tuning parameters basically determine the granularity of parallelism.

If turned on in the *NetFile* (Figure 4), the auto-tuner is automatically executed when the Android app is launched for the first time. It executes the CNN model for a number of predefined scenarios on the mobile device, measures their runtime and saves the optimum tuning parameters for future executions. As a result, the first launch of the application takes much longer time. For the purpose of clear and fair comparisons, auto-tuning is turned off in our experiments in Section 4.

4. EMPIRICAL EVALUATION

CNNdroid is empirically evaluated on two mobile devices, namely, Samsung Galaxy Note 4 and HTC One M9. We employ three well-known benchmark CNNs, namely, LeNet network for MNIST dataset [21], Alex Krizhevsky's network for CIFAR-10 (Alex's CIFAR-10) [22] and Alex Krizhevsky's network for ImageNet 2012 dataset (AlexNet) [20].

Layer setup of the benchmark CNNs are shown in Figure 6. We also measured the storage and memory requirement of the benchmark CNNs when ported to CNNdroid format. The results are reported in Figure 7.

We execute forward paths of the benchmark CNNs on the mobile devices and measure their accuracy, runtime and energy consumption. All benchmarks accept batches of 16 images as input in our experiments. Before running every experiment, mobile devices are fully charged and put into airplane mode and minimum screen brightness. The measurements reported below are only for CNN execution and not for loading the network parameters from SD card, because in our benchmarks network parameters are loaded only once in the beginning but CNN execution is performed on every input image.

Layer	LeNet	Alex's CIFAR-10	AlexNet
1	Conv	Conv	Conv+ReLU
2	Pooling	Pooling+ReLU	LRN
3	Conv	Conv+ReLU	Pooling
4	Pooling	Pooling	Conv+ReLU
5	FC+ReLU	Conv+ReLU	LRN
6	FC	Pooling	Pooling
7	-	FC	Conv+ReLU
8	-	FC	Conv+ReLU
9	-	-	Conv+ReLU
10	-	-	Pooling
11	-	-	FC+ReLU
12	-	-	FC+ReLU
13	-	-	FC

Figure 6: Layer setup of benchmark CNNs.

	SD Card Storage (MB)	RAM (MB)
LeNet	2	~10
Alex's CIFAR-10	0.7	~20
AlexNet	290	~300

Figure 7: Storage and memory requirements of benchmark CNNs when ported to CNNdroid format.

4.1 Accuracy

In order to measure CNNdroid accuracy, output of the last network layer in both CNNdroid and Caffe are compared for the same input. The resulting mean square error is in the order of 10^{-12}, which means there is no meaningful difference and CNNdroid is correctly implemented.

4.2 Performance

Figure 8.a shows the total measured runtime for CPU-only sequential CNN implementation as well as the speedup gained by GPU acceleration. The reported values are the average of ten executions.

Note that real-time performance is achieved on mobile devices in LeNet and Alex's CIFAR-10 benchmarks. For instance on the HTC One M9 device, the accelerated implementation achieved 60.2 and 32.2 frames per second for LeNet and Alex's CIFAR-10 benchmarks, respectively.

We also measured runtime of the heaviest convolution layer in order to observe direct impact of the GPU-based acceleration (Figure 8.b). The highest achieved speedup is 63.4X for AlexNet benchmark on Galaxy Note 4 device with Mali-T760 GPU. This GPU has 6 shader cores, each with two 128-bit ALUs. Since all elements of the matrices in our CNN model are 32-bit floating point values, a maximum of $6 \times 2 \times \frac{128}{32} = 48$ operations may run in parallel. In other words, the maximum theoretically achievable speedup is 48X. Therefore, the measured 63.4X speedup most probably comes from other factors such as software language performance of RenderScript(c99) over Java or cache effects.

Note that the benchmark CNNs in our experiments accept batches of 16 images as input, and the runtime values reported in Figure 8 are per image. It is recommended to process a batch of input images rather than a single image to get higher performance in CNNdroid.

As for the performance comparison of our mobile devices, we see that the overall speedup in AlexNet, which is a large network, is approximately 30% higher on Galaxy Note 4 compared with HTC One M9. This can be either the result of lower GPU frequency of HTC One M9 or its aggressive throttling policy in order to prevent overheating issues in long runtimes.

(a)		Sequential Runtime (ms)	Accelerated Runtime (ms)	Speedup Rate
Samsung Galaxy Note 4	LeNet	62	12.8	4.84
	Alex's CIFAR-10	313	25.3	12.37
	AlexNet	20767	481.7	43.11
HTC One M9	LeNet	81	16.6	4.88
	Alex's CIFAR-10	326	31	10.51
	AlexNet	21382	709	30.16

(b)		Sequential Runtime (ms)	Accelerated Runtime (ms)	Speedup Rate
Samsung Galaxy Note 4	LeNet	44	1.8	24.44
	Alex's CIFAR-10	162	7.5	21.6
	AlexNet	5876	92.6	63.45
HTC One M9	LeNet	62	4.3	14.42
	Alex's CIFAR-10	168	8.7	19.31
	AlexNet	5828	152	38.34

Figure 8: Average runtime of (a) the entire CNN and (b) the heaviest convolution layer, per image in a batch of 16 images, and the corresponding speedup rate.

4.3 Energy Consumption

We measured power and energy consumption per image for AlexNet benchmark on HTC One M9 by employing "Qualcomm Trepn Profiler" application [23].

The GPU accelerated execution consumes around 523 mW power and 0.4 J energy while the CPU-only sequential execution consumes 2338 mW power and 51.6 J energy. As a result, the GPU accelerated execution consumes $51.6 \div 0.4 =$ 129X less battery energy.

It should be noted that we observed about 20% variability in our measurements which is expected since Trepn Profiler provides a software-only method for measuring energy consumption of a single app.

5. CONCLUSIONS

We introduced CNNdroid, an open source GPU accelerated deep CNN library for Android-based mobile devices. Empirical evaluations demonstrated up to 60X speedup and up to 130X energy saving. The source code, documentation and sample projects are published online [1].

6. REFERENCES

[1] CNNdroid open source GPU-accelerated library. https://github.com/ENCP/CNNdroid.

[2] Inchul Song, Hyun-Jun Kim, and Paul Barom Jeon. Deep learning for real-time robust facial expression recognition on a smartphone. In *IEEE International Conference on Consumer Electronics*, pages 564–567, Jan 2014.

[3] Yu-Hsin Chen, Tushar Krishna, Joel Emer, and Vivienne Sze. 14.5 eyeriss: an energy-efficient reconfigurable accelerator for deep convolutional neural networks. In *IEEE International Solid-State Circuits Conference*, pages 262–263, Jan 2016.

[4] Mohammad Motamedi, Philipp Gysel, Venkatesh Akella, and Soheil Ghiasi. Design space exploration of fpga-based deep convolutional neural networks. In *Asia and South Pacific Design Automation Conference*, pages 575–580, Jan 2016.

[5] Paul A Merolla, John V Arthur, Rodrigo Alvarez-Icaza, Andrew S Cassidy, Jun Sawada, Filipp Akopyan, Bryan L Jackson, Nabil Imam, Chen Guo, Yutaka Nakamura, Bernard Brezzo, Ivan Vo, Steven K Esser, Rathinakumar Appuswamy, Brian Taba, Arnon Amir, Myron D Flickner, William P Risk, Rajit Manohar, and Dharmendra S Modha. A million spiking-neuron integrated circuit with a scalable communication network and interface. *Science*, 345(6197):668–673, 2014.

[6] Yangqing Jia, Evan Shelhamer, Jeff Donahue, Sergey Karayev, Jonathan Long, Ross Girshick, Sergio Guadarrama, and Trevor Darrell. Caffe: Convolutional architecture for fast feature embedding. *arXiv preprint arXiv:1408.5093*, 2014.

[7] Torch. http://torch.ch/. Accessed 2016-08-01.

[8] James Bergstra, Olivier Breuleux, Frédéric Bastien, Pascal Lamblin, Razvan Pascanu, Guillaume Desjardins, Joseph Turian, David Warde-Farley, and Yoshua Bengio. Theano: a CPU and GPU math expression compiler. In *Proceedings of the Python for Scientific Computing Conference*, 2010.

[9] TensorFlow. https://www.tensorflow.org. Accessed 2016-08-01.

[10] Nvidia cuDNN. https://developer.nvidia.com/cudnn. Accessed 2016-08-01.

[11] cuda-convent. https://code.google.com/p/cuda-convnet/. Accessed 2016-08-01.

[12] Velesnet. https://velesnet.ml/. Accessed 2016-08-01.

[13] Caffe Android Library. https://github.com/sh1r0/caffe-android-lib. Accessed 2016-08-01.

[14] Torch-7 for Android. https://github.com/soumith/torch-android. Accessed 2016-08-01.

[15] A convolutional neural network for the Android phone. https://github.com/radiodee1/awesome-cnn-android-python. Accessed 2016-08-01.

[16] Facial attractiveness prediction on Android. https://github.com/eldog/fmobile. Accessed 2016-08-01.

[17] ARM. Mali-T600 Series GPU OpenCL, Version 1.1.0, Developer Guide. Accessed 2016-08-01.

[18] Android RenderScript Developers Guide. http://developer.android.com/guide/topics/renderscript/compute.html. Accessed 2016-08-01.

[19] Messagepack. http://msgpack.org/index.html.

[20] Alex Krizhevsky, Ilya Sutskever, and Geoffrey E. Hinton. Imagenet classification with deep convolutional neural networks. In *Advances in Neural Information Processing Systems*, 2012.

[21] Y. Lecun, L. Bottou, Y. Bengio, and P. Haffner. Gradient-based learning applied to document recognition. *Proceedings of the IEEE*, 86(11):2278–2324, Nov 1998.

[22] Alex Krizhevsky. Learning multiple layers of features from tiny images. Technical report, University of Toronto, 2009.

[23] Trepn power profiler. https://developer.qualcomm.com/software/trepn-power-profiler.

Tamp: A Library for Compact Deep Neural Networks with Structured Matrices

Bingchen Gong*
Zhejiang University
gbc@zju.edu.cn

Brendan Jou, Felix Yu, Shih-Fu Chang
Columbia University
{bjou,yuxinnan,sfchang}@ee.columbia.edu

ABSTRACT

We introduce **Tamp**, an open source C++ library for reducing the space and time costs of deep neural network models. In particular, **Tamp** implements several recent works which use structured matrices to replace unstructured matrices which are often bottlenecks in neural networks. **Tamp** is also designed to serve as a unified development platform with several supported optimization back-ends and abstracted data types. This paper introduces the design and API and also demonstrates the effectiveness with experiments on public datasets.

1. INTRODUCTION

Deep neural networks have achieved outstanding performances in many fields over the past several years. However, training and inference of most neural networks often have high computational costs preventing many popular neural network architectures, particularly those for visual recognition, from being deployed on-board in resource-limited devices such as mobile phones, low cost robots and other embedded devices. One major bottleneck comes from the fully-connected layers which compute the matrix vector product followed by an element-wise activation function: $\phi(\mathbf{Cx})$. For a layer with a k-dimension input and n-dimension output, the linear transformation matrix has nk parameters and usually costs nk operations to compute.

One family of promising methods for reducing the memory and time costs of fully connected layers is to impose structure on the matrices used in these networks [1, 7, 10, 11]. By replacing unstructured dense matrices with *structured matrices* the number of network parameters can be dramatically reduced, with very modest accuracy loss. For example, by imposing the [1] structure on the AlexNet architecture [5], one can get 4,000× space saving and 1.38× speedup with a less than a 2% cost to accuracy on ILSVRC2012 [9]. The intuition behind the "compressibility" of these networks is that there exist redundancies in the dense matrices. However, many of these proposed approaches are based on closed-source implementations or are reported on different software architectures. This makes real-world application and benchmarking across such methods difficult.

In this open source submission, we introduce **Tamp**[1], an open-sourced C++ library providing a unified platform to develop, benchmark and deploy structured matrices in deep neural networks. The library supports using two popular frameworks, Caffe [3] and TensorFlow [2], as back-ends.

2. STRUCTURED TRANSFORMS

We briefly summarize several different structures in **Tamp**. Note that the projection matrix is restricted to be square by some of these methods, requiring pre or post-processing for input or output vectors.

Circulant [1, 11]. Given an n-dimensional real-valued vector $\mathbf{v}$ as the first column vector of it, a corresponding circulant matrix $\mathbf{C} \in \mathbb{R}^{n \times n}$ has the structure:

$$\mathbf{C} = \mathrm{circ}(\mathbf{v}) = \begin{bmatrix} v_0 & v_{n-1} & \dots & v_2 & v_1 \\ v_1 & v_0 & v_{n-1} & & v_2 \\ \vdots & v_1 & v_0 & \ddots & \vdots \\ v_{n-2} & & \ddots & \ddots & v_{n-1} \\ v_{n-1} & v_{n-2} & \dots & v_1 & v_0 \end{bmatrix}. \quad (1)$$

With a circulant matrix as the matrix of parameters in a fully-connected layer, for an input data vector $\mathbf{x}$, the layer output $\phi(\mathbf{Cx})$ can be calculated efficiently using the Fast Fourier Transform (FFT):

$$\phi(\mathbf{Cx}) = \phi(\mathbf{ifft}(\mathbf{fft}(\mathbf{v}) \circ \mathbf{fft}(\mathbf{x}))), \quad (2)$$

where **fft** and **ifft** denote FFT and inverse FFT, respectively; $\circ$ corresponds to Hadmard (elementwise) product between two vectors. This FFT equivalence allows us to compute circulant projections in $\mathcal{O}(n \log n)$ time $\mathcal{O}(n)$ space. In practice, a random sign flipping diagonal matrix $\mathbf{D}$ is added between $\mathbf{C}$ and $\mathbf{x}$ to improve the capacity of the model [1].

Toeplitz-like [11]. A Toeplitz-like matrix is composed by f-circulant matrix, a generalization of circulant matrices defined by a real-valued scalar f:

$$\mathbf{Z}_f(\mathbf{v})_{i,j} = \begin{cases} \mathrm{circ}(\mathbf{v})_{i,j} * f & : i < j \\ \mathrm{circ}(\mathbf{v})_{i,j} & : i \geq j \end{cases} \quad (3)$$

*This work was done in part while the first author was an undergraduate visiting researcher at Columbia University's Digital Video & Multimedia Lab.

[1] https://github.com/ColumbiaDVMM/Tamp

MM '16, October 15 - 19, 2016, Amsterdam, Netherlands

ISBN 978-1-4503-3603-1/16/10...$15.00

DOI: http://dx.doi.org/10.1145/2964284.2973802

Method	Complexity	Method	Complexity
Unstructured	$\mathcal{O}(nk)$	Low Rank [10]	$\mathcal{O}(r(n+k))$
Circulant [1]	$\mathcal{O}(n \log n)$	Toeplitz [11]	$\mathcal{O}(n \log n)$
Skew-circulant [11]	$\mathcal{O}(n \log n)$	ACDC [7]	$\mathcal{O}(n \log n)$

Table 1: Summary of Computational Complexities of Several Structured Matrix Transforms.

When f is 1, the f-circulant matrix is the same as a circulant matrix and when f is -1, it is a skew-circulant matrix. Order-r Toeplitz-like matrices then are all $n \times n$ matrices which can be composed by two f-circulant matrices [11] as:

$$\mathbf{C}_r(\mathbf{G}, \mathbf{H}) = \sum_{i=1}^{r} \mathbf{Z}_1(\mathbf{g}_i)\mathbf{Z}_{-1}(\mathbf{h}_i), \qquad (4)$$

where $\mathbf{G} = [g_1 \dots g_r]$, $\mathbf{H} = [h_1 \dots h_r] \in \mathbb{R}^{n \times r}$. For most space complexity saving, order-1 Toeplitz-like matrices are used in this initial release. Similar to circulant matrices, FFTs can be used to speed up computation.

Low Rank [10]. For a matrix in the form of $\mathbf{C} \in \mathbb{R}^{n \times k}$ whose rank is r, there exist two matrices $\mathbf{A} \in \mathbb{R}^{n \times r}$ and $\mathbf{B} \in \mathbb{R}^{r \times k}$ such that $\mathbf{C} = \mathbf{AB}$. By this factorization, the number of parameters reduces from nk to $r(n+k)$, and the time complexity reduces from nk to $r(n+k)$. It is also shown recently that tensor factorization, a generalization of low-rank factorization, can also be used in compressing neural networks [8].

ACDC [7]. With $\mathbf{A} = [a_1 \dots a_r]$, $\mathbf{D} = [d_1 \dots d_r] \in \mathbb{C}^{n \times r}$ to scale the signal in the original domain and the Fourier domain respectively [7], an order-r AFDF transformation replaces linear projection in neural networks as

$$\mathbf{AFDF}_r(\mathbf{x}) = \mathbf{x}^T [\prod_{i=1}^{r} \text{diag}(\mathbf{a}_i)\mathcal{F}\text{diag}(\mathbf{d}_i)\mathcal{F}^{-1}]$$

where $\mathcal{F}$ denotes the FFT matrix, so $\mathcal{F}\mathbf{x}$ and $\mathcal{F}^{-1}\mathbf{x}$ correspond to $\mathbf{fft}(\mathbf{x})$ and $\mathbf{ifft}(\mathbf{x})$. AFDF can be viewed as a further generalization of circulant structures. ACDC is the real-valued version of AFDF, where the Fourier transform is replaced by the Discrete Cosine Transformation (DCT) [7].

3. LIBRARY FEATURES

3.1 Interfaces & Tools

Tamp is a C++ library for implementing, benchmarking and easy execution of structured transforms in deep neural networks. It provides convenient interfaces via C++ template classes, abstracts device/host memory management, and BLAS and FFT library.

To create a new structured matrix model in **Tamp**, develop a subclass of the `ProcessorBase` class and override forward/backward calculation functions like below.

The `Forward` function computes the feedforward stage of the structured matrix model, and the `Backward` function computes gradients of the model. These two functions can be overloaded to add support for different acceleration architectures, e.g. GPUs or coprocessors.

An `Environment` struct is passed to the constructor containing model parameters such as the output dimensions and whether to include a random sign flipping diagonal matrix **D**. To summarize, the following steps are necessary to develop a new structured matrix model with **Tamp**:

```
class Processor : ProcessorBase
{
  Processor(Environment* env) :
    ProcessorBase(env) {}
  void Forward(
    ExecutiveCore* core,
    const ProcessorTape* atape)
  { /* Forward calculation */ }
  void Backward(
    ExecutiveCore* core,
    const ProcessorTape* atape,
    const ProcessorTape* btape)
  { /* Gradient calculations */ }
  void Shape(
     ExecutiveCore* core,
     ProcessorTape* atape)
  { /* Set output size */ }
};
```

- Override `Forward` and `Backward` calculation methods.
- Override the `Shape` method. This method is called each time before forward calculation to set the output size and allocate the proper buffer size.

The following additional steps are optional for developers to provide additional acceleration support like on GPUs:

- Implement a constructor to set the inner class status.
- Overload `Forward` and `Backward` calculation methods to support acceleration.

3.2 Data Type Abstraction

Although not required, inheriting from `ProcessorBase` by a template class is preferred since **Tamp** is designed for different data types. Using templates, a `Processor` can be registered as:

```
template <typename T>
class Processor : ProcessorBase
{
  /* Functions to override */
}
INSTALL_PROCESSOR(float, Processor<float>)
INSTALL_PROCESSOR(double, Processor<double>)
```

Most of the classes and math functions in **Tamp** are implemented as templates. One of them, `TypedData<T>`, class template abstracts data management. `TypedData<T>` is a pure virtual class that inherits from `BufferedData` and uses backend-specific implementations such as `TypedDataTensor<T>` and `TypeDataCaffe<T>`.

3.3 Context Management

Because of the multi-threaded nature of TensorFlow [2], member functions of `ProcessorBase` may be called concurrently, necessitating context management. **Tamp** provides a class `ExecutiveCore` as an interface for current execution context and uses the `ProcessorTape` class to record data. Although Caffe [3] will not call instances concurrently, similar context management is provided for coherence.

Through the `ProcessorTape` and `ExecutiveCore` classes, developers can allocate memory buffers and limit their access within context to avoid the use of mutexes.

```
void Forward(
  ExecutiveCore* core,
  const ProcessorTape* atape)
{
  const TypedData<float>& input =
      atape->input[0]->typed<float>();
  TypedData<float>& output =
      atape->output[0]->typed<float>();
  ...
  auto conv_buffer =
    core->allocateBuffer<float>({3,3});
  ...
}
```

3.4 Math Library

By using standard C pointers for data I/O interface, libraries are kept lightweight and easy to use in **Tamp**. Most functions use a CBLAS back-end and a small subset of FFT operations require libfftw3. For efficient CPU operations, we use various libraries like ATLAS/FFTW/MKL/etc, while for GPU, we use NVIDIA's cuBLAS and cuFFT along with CUDA. Also noteworthy, in Caffe [3], their portable header `math_functions` conveniently makes all math function templates type independent.

3.5 Backend Differences

Tamp currently integrates both TensorFlow [2] and Caffe [3], and so any structured matrix models implemented in **Tamp** can be run with a TensorFlow or Caffe back-end. Although we have abstracted most of the back-end interfacing to developers, some nuanced differences exist when using each of these back-ends due to their inherent differences.

TensorFlow [2]. A model is defined via two "operators" in TensorFlow, a forward and backward operator. The backward operator is bound to a forward operator through a Python wrapper using a `RegisterGradients` decorator [2]. Technically, developers can override the forward method, then implement backward code in Python and register them manually; however, doing so prevents the model from being compatible with Caffe [3].

```
# Python definition of network: Circulant section
weights = _variable_
biases = _variable_
circulant = struct.circulant(pool, weights) + biases
```

Calling the structured model like a normal TensorFlow operation from this point on will then work normally.

Caffe [3]. In Caffe, a structured matrix model corresponds to a single layer, and can be defined for example as:

```
layer {
  name: "circulant"
  type: "CirculantProjection"
  bottom: "pool"
  top: "circulant"
}
```

In Caffe, biases are implemented within layers, thus they can not be added outside the model. **Tamp** provides a trivial biases which can be added to model automatically.

Along with the **Tamp** library, we release two basic structure implementation: Circulant and Skew-circulant. These two models can be used directly or can be combined to form more complex structures, like Toeplitz-like matrices [11].

4. BENCHMARKS & PERFORMANCE

We used **Tamp** to implement multiple structured matrices and benchmarked them using both Caffe [3] and TensorFlow [2] on MNIST, CIFAR10 and ILSVRC2010. The experiments were run on a Intel(R) Xeon(R) CPU E5-2609 @ 2.40GHz.

MNIST. The MNIST handwritten digits dataset contains 60K/10K 28×28 greyscale train/test examples. We trained the convolutional neural network LeNet [6] here, replacing the second-to-last fully-connected layer with structured matrices. Results are given in Table 2.

		Caffe [3]		TensorFlow [2]	
Method	**#Params**	**Acc**	**Speed**	**Acc**	**Speed**
Unstructured	250,000	99.07	798	99.20	131
Circulant [1]	500	98.84	797	99.00	138
Skew-circulant [11]	500	98.75	703	98.90	130

Table 2: *Tamp* Accuracy ("Acc" in %) and Speed (examples/sec) Benchmarks on MNIST.

CIFAR10. In the CIFAR10 dataset, there are 50K/10K 32×32 color train/test examples from ten classes [4]. We trained a CIFAR10-CNN network on CIFAR10 [4], where we replaced the only fully-connected layer with structured transforms. Our CIFAR10 results are shown in Table 3. Note that the structured matrices should often be used to structure intermediate fully-connected layers not the last fully-connected layer providing classification output. In the case of CIFAR10-CNN, however, we found that introducing structure in the last layer also leads to minimal compromise on accuracy.

		Caffe [3]		TensorFlow [2]	
Method	**#Params**	**Acc**	**Speed**	**Acc**	**Speed**
Unstructured	10,240	82.53	1111	86.00	621
Circulant [1]	1,024	80.35	1176	83.70	680
Skew-circulant [11]	1,024	79.77	1136	81.20	671
Low Rank [10]	6,144	71.82	1153	78.70	690
Toeplitz [11]	2,048	81.03	1142	81.40	643
ACDC [7]	2,048	81.08	1153	81.50	658

Table 3: *Tamp* Accuracy (%) and Speed (examples/sec) on CIFAR10. Number of parameters is also shown for one fully-connected layer.

ILSVRC. We trained AlexNet [5] on ILSVRC2010 [9]. Our results show a ~90% reduction in the memory requirement of AlexNet using a circulant structure in exchange for ~2% increase in top-1 and top-5 error rate. Here, we replaced the two fully-connected layers before the last fully-connected layer containing 4096 output units with circulant transforms. Results are shown below in Table 4.

	Top-5 Err	**Top-1 Err**	**Memory**
Unstructured	17.1%	42.8%	233.2 MB
Circulant [1]	19.4%	44.1%	20.5 MB

Table 4: *Tamp* Benchmarks of Circulant Structures [1] in AlexNet [5] on ILSVRC10 [9].

5. CONCLUSIONS

We introduces a C++ library **Tamp** as a unified platform for constructing structured matrices to replace dense linear transformation operations in neural networks. Developers can easily utilize either Caffe [3] or TensorFlow [2] deep network back-end to develop, benchmark and deploy compressed networks. As part of the initial release, we provide implementations of several structured matrices including circulant, low rank, Toeplitz-like matrices and the ACDC transform. **Tamp** uses templates to implement data abstraction and type independent math operations, and also provides context management to support concurrent computing. In particular, our experiments on MNIST, CIFAR10 and ILSVRC verify the claims of structured matrices in neural networks for reducing the number of parameters with modest cost to accuracy compared to unstructured transforms. We believe that our work will enable repeatable research and enable neural network applications with limited resource.

6. REFERENCES

[1] Y. Cheng, F. X. Yu, R. S. Feris, S. Kumar, A. Choudhary, and S.-F. Chang. An exploration of parameter redundancy in deep networks with circulant projections. In *ICCV*, 2015.

[2] Google, Inc. TensorFlow: Large-scale machine learning on heterogeneous systems, 2015. http://tensorflow.org.

[3] Y. Jia, E. Shelhamer, J. Donahue, S. Karayev, J. Long, R. Girshick, S. Guadarrama, and T. Darrell. Caffe: Convolutional architecture for fast feature embedding. In *ACM Multimedia*, OSSC, 2014.

[4] A. Krizhevsky. Learning multiple layers of features from tiny images. Master's thesis, University of Toronto, 2009.

[5] A. Krizhevsky, I. Sutskever, and G. E. Hinton. ImageNet classification with deep convolutional neural networks. In *NIPS*, 2012.

[6] Y. LeCun, L. Bottou, Y. Bengio, and P. Haffner. Gradient-based learning applied to document recognition. *Proc. of the IEEE*, 86(11), 1998.

[7] M. Moczulski, M. Denil, J. Appleyard, and N. de Freitas. ACDC: A structured efficient linear layer. In *ICLR*, 2016.

[8] A. Novikov, D. Podoprikhin, A. Osokin, and D. Vetrov. Tensorizing neural networks. In *NIPS*, 2015.

[9] O. Russakovsky, J. Deng, H. Su, J. Krause, S. Satheesh, S. Ma, Z. Huang, A. Karpathy, A. Khosla, M. Bernstein, A. C. Berg, and L. Fei-Fei. ImageNet Large Scale Visual Recognition Challenge. *arXiv:1409.0575*, 2014.

[10] T. N. Sainath, B. Kingsbury, V. Sindhwani, E. Arisoy, and B. Ramabhadran. Low-rank matrix factorization for deep neural network training with high-dimensional output targets. In *ICASSP*, 2013.

[11] V. Sindhwani, T. N. Sainath, and S. Kumar. Structured transforms for small-footprint deep learning. In *NIPS*, 2015.

Barrista – Caffe Well-Served

Christoph Lassner[1,3]
classner@tue.mpg.de

Daniel Kappler[2]
dkappler@tue.mpg.de

Martin Kiefel[1,3]
mkiefel@tue.mpg.de

Peter Gehler[1,3]
pgehler@tue.mpg.de

Bernstein Center for
Comp. Neuroscience[1]
Otfried-Müller-Str. 25
Tübingen, Germany

MPI for Intelligent Systems,
Autonomous Motion Dep.[2]
Paul-Ehrlich-Str. 15
Tübingen, Germany

MPI for Intelligent Systems,
Perceiving Systems Dep.[3]
Spemannstr. 41
Tübingen, Germany

SUBMITTED to ACM MULTIMEDIA 2016 OPEN SOURCE SOFTWARE COMPETITION

ABSTRACT

The caffe framework is one of the leading deep learning toolboxes in the machine learning and computer vision community. While it offers efficiency and configurability, it falls short of a full interface to Python. With increasingly involved procedures for training deep networks and reaching depths of hundreds of layers, creating configuration files and keeping them consistent becomes an error prone process.

We introduce the barrista framework, offering full, pythonic control over caffe. It separates responsibilities and offers code to solve frequently occurring tasks for pre-processing, training and model inspection. It is compatible to all caffe versions since mid 2015 and can import and export .prototxt files.

Examples are included, e.g., a deep residual network implemented in only 172 lines (for arbitrary depths), comparing to 2320 lines in the official implementation for the equivalent model.

Categories and Subject Descriptors

I.5.1 [**Pattern Recognition**]: Applications—*Computer Vision*; D.2.2 [**Software Engineering**]: Design Tools and Techniques—*Software libraries*; I.5.1 [**Pattern Recognition**]: Models—*Neural Nets*

Keywords

Open Source; Computer Vision; Machine Learning; Neural Networks; Deep learning; caffe

MM '16, October 15 - 19, 2016, Amsterdam, Netherlands

ISBN 978-1-4503-3603-1/16/10. . . $15.00

DOI: http://dx.doi.org/10.1145/2964284.2973803

1. INTRODUCTION

Deep learning is one of the biggest success cases of machine learning in the last years. For problems like image classifications, previously considered one of the most challenging problems, deep learning has led to solutions that surpassed human performance. The tremendous commercial and academic success spurred development of several software packages. For the computer vision community, the *caffe* [7] framework is popular and frequently used. It is well-tested with many custom layer implementations and published models.

caffe does provide Python bindings for the core features, however the main workflow relies on *Google protocol buffers*[1] (which we will abbreviate to 'protobuf') for configuration, network design and serialization. This has been a pragmatic solution for network layouts so far, but new, increasingly complex, training strategies and networks with multiple hundreds of layers [4, 5] push this architecture to its limits.

We present the *barrista* framework, which provides a more powerful, programmatic interface, and propose solutions and insights that may be of general interest. Furthermore, we strongly advocate the concept of callbacks (which we refer to as 'monitors' throughout the paper, due to the *monitor* software design pattern). We use monitors as an easy-to-write and easy-to-combine tool to create data loaders, pre-processing, hyperparameter modification, logging, post-processing and visualization.

The features of *barrista* can be summarized as follows:

- The *barrista* framework provides full Python access to all *caffe* functionalities. Multi-GPU training is not yet available, but in the final development stage. Networks can be programmatically created and edited in a convenient way.
- Protobuf object introspection is at the core of the *barrista* library. It enables almost automatic parsing of the basic *caffe* interface and guarantees full compatibility and consistency with the used version of *caffe*. This includes custom-written layers and their parameters, which need to be referenced just by their name. All layer implementation is then inferred automatically.
- We maintain full compatibility with *caffe* models. By using the internal protobuf representation, it is possible to load and save all models and prototxt files *caffe* can read and write.

[1] https://developers.google.com/protocol-buffers/

- *barrista* provides a *monitor* interface with many existing monitors for pre-processing, post-processing, data augmentation, visualization, training and model inspection. Many of them can be executed in parallel to the network forward and backward pass to make the execution efficient.
- This provides a principled separation of responsibilities for steps such as data-preparation, data-feedback (i.e., incorporating training results to influence further training for, e.g., active learning) and visualization.

2. RELATED WORK

A full overview of deep learning software is out of the scope of this paper. We restrict the discussion to the most prominent frameworks and interface packages targeting the Python language.

The ***Theano*** package [11] with its three interface add-ons *Lasagne* [3], *Keras*[2] and *blocks* [13] is similar to *caffe* and *barrista*. *Theano* is a more general machine learning software compared to *caffe*. Therefore, the wrappers are convenient for the specific use case of deep learning. Whereas *Lasagne* keeps a focus on being a lightweight and close wrapper around *Theano*, *Keras* aims for more generality and offers a backend for *Tensorflow* [1] as well, which will be discussed in the next paragraph. ***Keras*** includes a convenient fitting method, but does not separate responsibilities as clearly as the framework we propose. It offers the possibility to use callbacks, but these can not influence the training or the provided data as deeply as *barrista* and are not executed in parallel. ***Lasagne*** is a lightweight wrapper that focuses solely on Theano's deep learning components. It requires the user to implement a training loop including preprocessing and monitoring. ***blocks*** is very similar to *barrista* in its aims and offers a callback concept with its *Extensions*.

Tensorflow [1] is Google's open source deep learning framework and subject to rapid changes. This framework may emerge as a successor to *caffe*. Currently (v0.9), does not offer high level training and pre-processing routines. There is a thriving and competitive infrastructure ecosystem growing around it with no mature and clearly leading framework yet.

Mxnet [2] provides APIs for several languages, including Python. It offers high-level training methods and two separate concepts for callbacks. Plain callbacks do not have access to the network's gradient in contrast to a specific monitor object. However, only one such object can be used for training. Both callback types are not executed in parallel and can not be used for data-preprocessing.

Chainer [12] fully leverages the Python software stack and is designed for easy modification. This does not extend over the course of training methods, probably because it is relatively easy to implement these methods. However, reimplementation leads to creating the same pre-processing and optimization code repeatedly, which is what we address with our callback stack.

Neon[3] relies on the Python stack with the focus on runtime. It provides a comprehensive callback system, but not for parallel execution. While *Neon* is fast, its commercial distribution model offers parts as premium content. With open source alternatives available, this software has not found widespread use in the research community.

[2]http://keras.io/

[3]https://github.com/NervanaSystems/neon

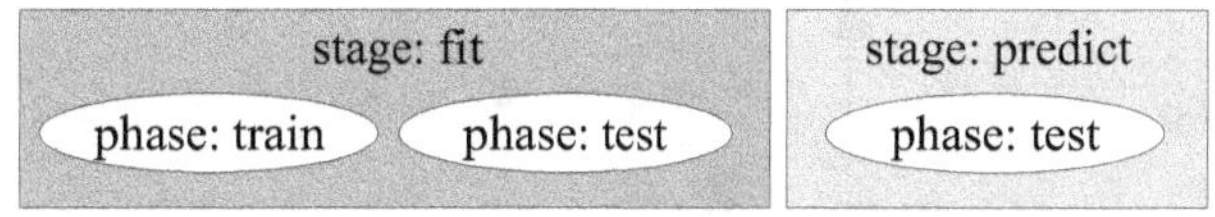

Figure 1: Usage of stages and phases by the 'Net' object. If available, the 'predict' stage is used automatically by the 'predict' function.

3. CONCEPTS AND DESIGN

3.1 Separation of responsibilities

One of the core ideas of the library design is the separation of responsibilities:

The user is responsible for preparing the data. This action is highly dataset specific and can hardly be generalized.

The library offers data augmentation, solver setup, logging, training and prediction. Data augmentation methods (like rotation, flipping) can be shared across learning tasks, therefore this responsibility can be moved to the deep learning library.

We believe that a library should solve repetitive tasks for the user out-of-the-box, but remain configurable. As in the popular *scikit-learn*[4] package, *barrista* offers many default options with sensible values that can be overridden. For example, input data can be passed as a list to the 'fit' or 'predict' methods of a model, but if the data does not fit into memory, it is straightforward to extend the *CyclingDataMonitor* to process a dataset chunkwise.

3.2 Representation

The description of a network is captured in a *NetSpecification* object. It can be programmatically constructed, altered, converted to and from a protobuf, the lingua franca for *caffe*. It describes a network layout in all possible stages and phases and is independent of a trained model.

To use a network model, its description can be instantiated to obtain a *Net* object. A *Net* has parameters and can be fitted to data or used to make predictions. If the network description includes a distinction between the 'fit' and 'predict' phases, then the corresponding architectures are automatically generated and used (see Fig. 1).

In contrast to other frameworks, the *Solver* is represented as a stateful entity, which reflects the underlying *caffe* structure for optimization methods such as Adam [8]. Furthermore, this has the advantage that the object can be serialized correctly. All solvers implemented in *caffe* are encapsulated with parameter checks.

3.3 Monitoring

We propose a powerful monitoring system with nearly full control over the training process. Our experience is that this offers an easy way to experiment with different training strategies. The monitors can access and modify both, the network and solver. Monitors for data loading and augmentation can be combined arbitrarily, to quickly adapt to the specific training needs without having to rewrite and test the code.

[4]http://scikit-learn.org

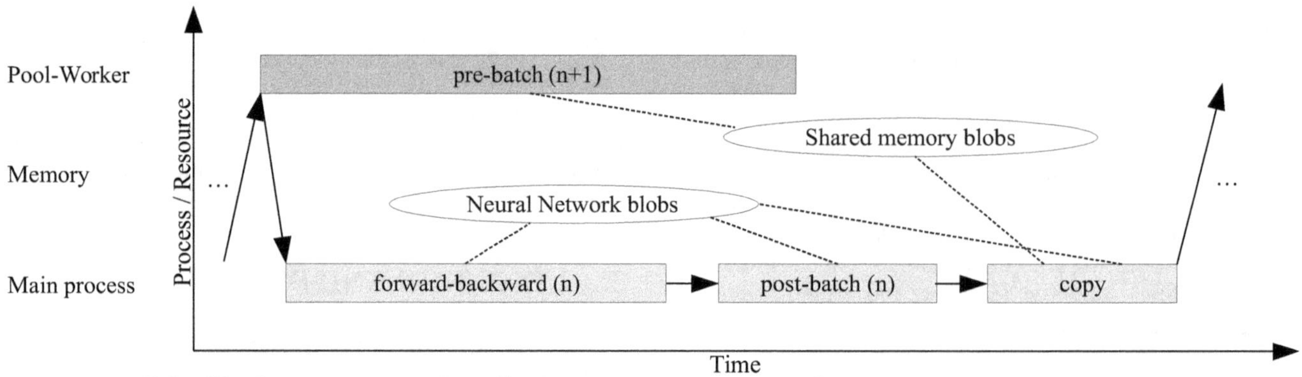

Figure 2: Parallel callback processing pipeline. Solid arrows indicate control flow, dashed lines resource access. The duration of the 'forward-backward' and 'pre-batch' operation strongly depends on network layout/pre-processing steps, hence the length of the boxes is not necessarily proportional to execution time. Memory is only allocated once at the beginning of training and does not change over time (the blobs have limited extent only for easier visualization).

4. IMPLEMENTATION

4.1 Protobuf object introspection

Python offers full object introspection abilities: all properties can be queried and their name and type examined. We use this feature to analyze the *caffe*-generated protobuf object. Exploiting the knowledge about *caffe*'s naming convention, we can infer significant parts of the interface automatically.

This allows us to work with upstream and custom defined layers. The only additional information which must be provided is the relationship between a layer and its parameters, since this is not encoded in the protobuf specification. It is sufficient to specify layer and parameter names, the rest is inferred from *barrista*.

With this architecture, we are able to elegantly avoid the maintenance overhead for wrapping an evolving library. Additionally, we keep the additional effort for new layer definitions as low as possible. In the core *caffe* library, adding new layers requires changes in several places.

4.2 Monitor implementation

We use an inheritance-based Signal/Slot design pattern implementation to create the monitors. This makes (1) creation of new signals as well as (2) creation of new monitors easy and preserves simplicity and separation of the code. The monitors receive their parameters solely through a dictionary. This keeps the interface flexible and extensible and enables state modification.

4.3 Parallel monitor execution

True parallel threaded execution in one process is inherently difficult in Python due to the global interpreter lock. However, data loading can be time-consuming and slow down the training. The *caffe* data loading facilities can be used like any other layer, additionally we provide parallel data layers that are executed in a true parallel context. To make this functionality available on all platforms, we rely on the Python *multiprocessing* module to create an additional worker process. To avoid interprocess communication overhead, we use shared memory with locks for data transfer. Any monitor implementing the *ParallelDataMonitor* interface will be executed in parallel, which is useful for expensive pre-processing tasks. A control flow visualization is given in Fig. 2.

Exploiting Python's duck typing, we create a dummy *Net* object that implements the basic interface of the *Net* with its memory pointing to shared memory with the main process. Thus, the data monitors executed in parallel can be used unchanged for serial execution, e.g., for debugging. After parallel execution, the main process copies the shared memory to the original *Net* object, an operation that usually takes less than 1ms.

4.4 Visualization

With visualization monitors it is possible to create plots in regular intervals and create movies of filter evolution. We include a basic set of monitors. This includes (1) activation, (2) gradient histogram, (3) gradient magnitude and (4) loss visualization; all of which allow to keep a close view of the network during training to diagnose obstacles for the optimizer, e.g., vanishing gradients in very deep architectures [14]. Adding more involved visualizations such as the 'guided backprop' visualization [10] can easily be integrated using a monitor.

4.5 Examples

We include three self-contained examples with the library: an overview over the most important functions, the classical MNIST training example with a three layer CNN, and an implementation of a state-of-the art residual network for CIFAR10 [9, 4]. The latter two are complete setups that can directly be adapted for new training scenarios. The folders come with 'data.py', 'train.py', 'test.py', 'visualize.py' and a model folder with the proposed model file. All the files are executable and highlight one aspect of the setup.

4.6 Quality assurance

To provide high quality code, we follow best practices. With a public CI server that checks primary (tests) and secondary (style) quality of the code, we assure that the library is usable and bugs are detected before a code release.

Monitoring the test coverage at the same time (currently more than 94% for the non-user-interface functions of the library; the UI can not be tested on the headless CI server), we make sure that no important parts remain untested. All parts of the library are covered with documentation. Python 3 compatibility is implemented, but is currently not maintainable due to the lacking compatibility of the core *caffe* framework.

(a) (b) (c) (d)

Figure 3: Example visualizations. **(a)** Human pose estimation and semantic segmentation, **(b)** intrinsic image reflection component, **(c)** bilateral feature space with x, y, r, g, b features of an image [6] (non-standard caffe layer), **(d)** activations from the last layer of a deep residual network on CIFAR10 [9] using visualization monitors during training.

5. USAGE SCENARIOS

The library wraps the entire *caffe* functionality, currently with the exception of multi-GPU support (which can be added by a minimal C++ patch to *caffe*). *barrista* can be used for all applications of *caffe*. We used it successfully for several applications: human pose estimation, semantic segmentation, image filtering, image classification, character recognition, material classification, intrinsic image decomposition as well as robotic grasp pose prediction. Some example visualizations are shown in Fig. 3. With this wide array of applications, we are confident that *barrista* can deliver a high level of convenience for a large user base.

LSTM support in *caffe* is currently under development and discussion. It is likely to be integrated in the main framework. Since the underlying representation remains tied to protobuf, only minimal changes should be required to make these features available in *barrista*.

6. AVAILABILITY AND CONCLUSION

The source code is available under the MIT license from Github at https://github.com/classner/barrista. It is currently necessary to apply a C++ patch to *caffe* to make *barrista* work. A pull request for the required changes to the master branch of *caffe* is pending (#3629). The change is of general interest, and once accepted we will make *barrista* available as a PyPi project. In the meantime we provide a patched *caffe* version as a submodule of the project.

barrista is highly flexible and aims to bridge the gap between performance, convenience and continuity. We are confident that it prove useful in many applications and contribute to an easier usage of *caffe* by reducing development time for both, beginners and experts of deep learning.

We thank Yangqing Jia and the BVLC vision group for creating and maintaining *caffe*.

7. REFERENCES

[1] M. Abadi, A. Agarwal, P. Barham, E. Brevdo, Z. Chen, C. Citro, G. S. Corrado, A. Davis, J. Dean, M. Devin, S. Ghemawat, I. Goodfellow, A. Harp, G. Irving, M. Isard, Y. Jia, R. Jozefowicz, L. Kaiser, M. Kudlur, J. Levenberg, D. Mané, R. Monga, S. Moore, D. Murray, C. Olah, M. Schuster, J. Shlens, B. Steiner, I. Sutskever, K. Talwar, P. Tucker, V. Vanhoucke, V. Vasudevan, F. Viégas, O. Vinyals, P. Warden, M. Wattenberg, M. Wicke, Y. Yu, and X. Zheng. TensorFlow: Large-scale machine learning on heterogeneous systems. http://tensorflow.org/, 2015.

[2] T. Chen, M. Li, Y. Li, M. Lin, N. Wang, M. Wang, T. Xiao, B. Xu, C. Zhang, and Z. Zhang. Mxnet: A flexible and efficient machine learning library for heterogeneous distributed systems. http://mxnet.rtfd.org, 2015.

[3] S. Dieleman, J. Schlüter, C. Raffel, E. Olson, S. K. Sønderby, D. Nouri, D. Maturana, M. Thoma, E. Battenberg, J. Kelly, J. D. Fauw, M. Heilman, diogo149, B. McFee, H. Weideman, takacsg84, peterderivaz, Jon, instagibbs, K. Rasul, CongLiu, Britefury, and J. Degrave. Lasagne: First release. http://dx.doi.org/10.5281/zenodo.27878, 2015.

[4] K. He, X. Zhang, S. Ren, and J. Sun. Deep residual learning for image recognition. In *CVPR*, 2016.

[5] K. He, X. Zhang, S. Ren, and J. Sun. Identity mappings in deep residual networks. *arXiv preprint arXiv:1603.05027*, 2016.

[6] V. Jampani, M. Kiefel, and P. V. Gehler. Learning sparse high dimensional filters: Image filtering, dense crfs and bilateral neural networks. In *CVPR*, 2016.

[7] Y. Jia, E. Shelhamer, J. Donahue, S. Karayev, J. Long, R. Girshick, S. Guadarrama, and T. Darrell. Caffe: Convolutional architecture for fast feature embedding. *arXiv preprint arXiv:1408.5093*, 2014.

[8] D. P. Kingma and J. Ba. Adam: A method for stochastic optimization. *arXiv preprint arXiv:1312.6980*, abs/1412.6980, 2014.

[9] A. Krizhevsky. Learning Multiple Layers of Features from Tiny Images. Master's thesis.

[10] J. T. Springenberg, A. Dosovitskiy, T. Brox, and M. A. Riedmiller. Striving for simplicity: The all convolutional net. *arXiv preprint arXiv:1412.6806*, abs/1412.6806, 2014.

[11] Theano Development Team. Theano: A Python framework for fast computation of mathematical expressions. *arXiv preprint arXiv:1605.02688*, 2016.

[12] S. Tokui, K. Oono, S. Hido, and J. Clayton. Chainer: a next-generation open source framework for deep learning. In *Proc. of the Workshop on Machine Learning Systems (LearningSys) of NIPS*, 2015.

[13] B. van Merriënboer, D. Bahdanau, V. Dumoulin, D. Serdyuk, D. Warde-Farley, J. Chorowski, and Y. Bengio. Blocks and fuel: Frameworks for deep learning. *arXiv preprint arXiv:1506.00619*, 2015.

[14] S.-E. Wei, V. Ramakrishna, T. Kanade, and Y. Sheikh. Convolutional pose machines. In *CVPR*, 2016.

Pyo, the Python DSP toolbox

Olivier Bélanger
Faculty of Music, University of Montreal
200 rue Vincent d'Indy
Montréal, Québec, Canada
olivier.belanger@umontreal.ca

SOFTWARE SUBMITTED TO ACM MULTIMEDIA 2016 OPEN SOURCE SOFTWARE COMPETITION.

The software presented in this article is free of charge and open-source.

Please visit http://ajaxsoundstudio.com/software/pyo/ or the github repository at https://github.com/belangeo/pyo for source code, downloads, documentation and other resources.

ABSTRACT

This paper introduces *pyo*, a python module dedicated to the digital processing of sound. This audio engine distinguishes itself from other alternatives by being natively integrated to a common general programming language. This integration allows incorporating audio processes quickly to other programming tasks, like mathematical computations, network communications or graphical interface programming. We will expose the main features of the library as well as the different contexts of use where pyo can be of a great benefit to composers and audio software developers.

Keywords

Python, Digital Signal Processing, Audio Programming

1. INTRODUCTION

Over the years, several ways and means were developed to facilitate audio programming. Max Mathews's MUSIC-N[1] series and Barry Vercoe's Csound[5] program used the instrument/score paradigm to allow the user to create synthesizers or processing instruments in one file and specify the events controlling the notes and parameters over time into another file. Perhaps more intuitive for musicians, the patching paradigm implemented in Pure Data[4] lets the user connect objects in processing chains to generate both sound and control structures. SuperCollider[2], developed by James McCartney in 1996, uses an object-oriented programming language to allow dynamic real-time audio synthesis and algorithmic composition.

All these tools perform well for a wide variety of tasks in music composition, audio synthesis, signal analysis and live digital signal processing. So, what was the motivation for the development of an entirely new audio engine? The common thing to all these tools is the specialized language they each use to perform audio programming tasks. If one wishes to develop an audio platform answering to needs for general programming tasks, such as accessing databases, creating a custom graphical user interface or analyzing the content of a text file, these languages fall short as they were not designed to efficiently perform these kinds of tasks. They were purpose-built to perform audio signal processing. Of course, there are ways to communicate between these programs and more general programming languages, such as Python. It can be done either via an application programming interface (API) or with a communication protocol like Open Sound Control (OSC), but this can lead to several programming problems and force the developer to deal with two different environments at the same time.

The development of pyo as a Python module was motivated by the need to provide a complete audio programming toolkit for a general programming language. Pyo is a Python module where the logic and API are written in pure Python while all the signal processing parts are written in C. The communication between the two layers is entirely done with the Python C-API. This integration to a popular language allows the user to concentrate all his efforts on the development of audio algorithms, without the need to learn a whole new programming language. The program benefits from the power and speed of an extended audio toolkit and from the syntax and versatility of a mature programming language that is widely used.

This article is divided into three parts. First, we will introduce the programming environment we propose to make the sound. In the second part, we will explore the possible applications with pyo and to whom this module can be useful. Finally, we will explain the main features of the library and illustrate them with simple code examples.

2. PROGRAMMING ENVIRONMENT

Python is a cross-platform, open-source, dynamic programming language used in a wide variety of application domains. His clear and readable syntax makes it a perfect choice to learn to program. Python offers an intuitive object orientation that is very suitable for signal processing design

[1]https://en.wikipedia.org/wiki/MUSIC-N

MM '16, October 15 - 19, 2016, Amsterdam, Netherlands

ISBN 978-1-4503-3603-1/16/10...$15.00

DOI: http://dx.doi.org/10.1145/2964284.2973804

and algorithmic composition. One can use Python to build sophisticated software or simply as a scripting language for light duty tasks. An active community of developers regularly updates the source code and provides new versions. It is well documented and offers extensive standard libraries and third party modules for virtually any purpose. Because it allows programmers to write efficient code very quickly, it's one of the best choices to start writing audio programs.

Pyo is a Python module written in C to help digital signal processing script creation. It is entirely integrated, which means the audio engine has no need for an API or protocol like OSC to communicate with the language. It contains classes for a wide variety of signal processing types. With pyo, users can include signal processing chains directly in Python scripts or projects and manipulate them in real time through the interpreter. Tools in the pyo module offer primitives like arithmetic operations on an audio signal, basic signal processing (filters, delays, oscillators, etc.) and complex algorithms to create sound granulation or other creative audio manipulations. pyo supports the OSC protocol (Open Sound Control), to ease communications between programs and includes a full implementation of the MIDI protocol for generating sound events and controlling process parameters. pyo allows the creation of sophisticated signal processing chains with all the benefits of a mature and widely used general programming language.

One significant constraint in audio programming is that the program must run for an extended period. While most programs can just quit in a friendly way after the execution of each line of code, an audio performance must compute samples as long as they are needed. The Python interpreter (the engine evaluating the commands) can be invoked directly in a terminal window and used to create an audio processing loop. It will stay active until the user explicitly asks to terminate. The interpreter is very useful for live coding or for experimenting with some small functions. However, most of the time, it will be easier to call a graphical user interface which will keep the interpreter alive as long as a window is shown on the screen. Pyo provides such interfaces for the audio server and also for object's display and control.

3. APPLICATIONS

Pyo is well suited for any tasks that involve sound and programming. One of its primary purposes is for music creation and algorithmic composition. One can use pyo to process audio inputs and control effect parameters while performing on stage. Another way of composing with pyo is to take advantage of python's algorithmic capabilities to create complex control structures for a synthesis engine. We have created a web radio continuously processing and playing such algorithmic compositions from whoever wants its tune to be played. The radio can be listened to at http://radiopyo.acaia.ca/.

As part of a larger programming eco-system, pyo can easily be integrated into the engine of a music software. Here are some softwares where pyo provides the audio services:

- **Cecilia5**, a digital signal processing toolbox. http://ajaxsoundstudio.com/software/cecilia/
- **Soundgrain**, a granular sound synthesis interface. http://ajaxsoundstudio.com/software/soundgrain/
- **PsychoPy**, psychology and psychophysic experiments. http://www.psychopy.org/

The distribution of pyo comes with E-Pyo, a simple but powerful text editor offering live coding facilities such as a background audio server and shortcuts to increase the coding speed. It's especially useful for quickly exploring new processing techniques.

Pyo also offers a simple C-API that allow embedding a Python interpreter in another application written in C/C++. There are examples in the sources showing pyo embedded inside OpenFrameworks, PureData and in a Juce audio plugin.

4. INTENDED AUDIENCE

The intended audience of a python module like pyo is vast. Any music composer who wants to build its tools or to explore with sound can make a good use of pyo. Because there is libraries for almost any programming task in python, software developers from a variety of backgrounds can benefit from pyo if they need to include an audio part in their projects. Since 2010, I use pyo in my university classes to teach digital signal processing theory and practice and to introduce musicians to audio programming. The combination Python and pyo offers a very gentle learning curve and one or two semesters are usually enough for students to produce original and exciting work. In conjunction with scientific modules like numpy or music21, pyo should be in the toolbox of any electronic music teacher or researcher.

5. MAIN FEATURES

5.1 The audio engine

Pyo uses a callback function to allow real-time audio processing without blocking the main thread. In blocking mode, the user could not enter new commands from the interpreter or a graphical interface could not be refreshed until the process exit. This function is part of the Server object and is called by the audio driver, in a high priority thread, every time a new block of samples is needed. Audio and MIDI configurations can be modified at the Server's initialization if, for example, the default sound card or the default MIDI interface are not the ones needed by the user. We specify the sampling rate and the size of each block of samples as arguments to the Server. Another role of the Server is to manage the connections between pyo objects and the order in which they will be computed. The callback function will ask all registered objects, in the order they were created by the program, for a new block of samples unless the objects tree is explicitly modified during the execution. To be properly registered, the first thing an audio object did at its creation, is to look for the current server in the program memory. As a consequence, a server must be present and booted before creating any audio object. The following sequence of instructions create, initialize and start an audio server:

```
>>> from pyo import *
>>> # Create a stereo server
>>> s = Server(sr=48000, nchnls=2, buffersize=64)
>>> # Set the audio and MIDI devices
>>> s.setInOutDevice(2)
>>> s.setMidiInputDevice(1)
>>> # Boot the server
>>> s.boot()
>>> # Now we can create a processing chain...
>>> s.start() # Start the audio callback loop
```

5.2 Everything is computed at audio rate

One significant difference between pyo and older audio engines is the removal of the control rate. The control rate is a second rate, slower than the audio rate, used to compute variations over time for some parameters of the generators or the effect processors. The control rate is cheaper to process, as it computes only a single floating-point value instead of a block of samples, and therefore uses fewer CPU resources. The cost for this gain in CPU is that the control rate can causes artifacts, like zipper noise, in the sound when values are changing too fast. With computers growing more powerful, the need for saving CPU resources is less significant, and the audio quality can be prioritized at a reasonable cost. Within pyo, every object generates an audio signal, and almost all parameters accept audio as a control signal. This flexibility allows a broad range of modulations without having to care about audio degradation by a downsampled signal given as a modulator of a parameter such as a filter's frequency. In the example below, an oscillator modulates the center frequency of a bandpass filter to create a kind of FM (*frequency modulation*) effect on the microphone input:

```
>>> from pyo import *
>>> s = Server().boot()
>>> src = Input()
>>> mod = Sine(freq=500, mul=250, add=500)
>>> filter = ButBP(src, freq=mod, q=5).out()
>>> s.start()
```

5.3 Sample-accurate timing

One of the benefits of the fact that everything is an audio signal is the trigger framework, with which it is possible to create sample-accurate timing structure. A trigger is a signal with a value of one, surrounded by zeros. All trigger generators, such as a metronome or a step sequencer, are sampled at the audio rate, allowing the most precise possible timing. A lot of objects in the library are configured to respond to this kind of signal, so, one could create a tempo-style control structure with the guarantee of the best timing accuracy. The following piece of code generates a polyphonic melody with an exponential envelope and a square wave:

```
>>> from pyo import *
>>> s = Server().boot()
>>> wav = SquareTable()
>>> env = ExpTable([(0,0), (64,1), (8191,0)])
>>> met = Metro(time=.125, poly=8).play()
>>> amp = TrigEnv(met, table=env, dur=1, mul=.1)
>>> mid = TrigRandInt(met, max=12, add=48)
>>> hz = Snap(mid, [0,2,3,5,7,8,10], scale=1)
>>> out = Osc(table=wav, freq=hz, mul=amp).out()
>>> s.start()
```

5.4 List expansion

A powerful property, called "multichannel expansion," introduced in the textual synthesis language SuperCollider uses an array to duplicate processes on a single line of code [3]. If we give an array of frequencies to a resonator, it will create as many resonators as there are values in the array. Pyo uses the python's list type to implement a similar duplication of object's processing. Almost all parameters accept a list as an argument, creating as many audio streams as necessary to process all values in the list. A stream is a monophonic audio signal container, and a pyo object can manage any number of these streams. One can create two hundred oscillators in one line by giving a list of two hundred values to the frequency parameter of a Sine object. A pyo object is also considered as a list by Python, which means that if an object receives another pyo object in one of its parameters, the receiver will generate the same number of streams, each one with its audio variation. This system is very expressive and allows to create highly flexible and compact scripts. The next example generates a chorus of N oscillators with random frequencies, phases, and amplitudes.

```
>>> from pyo import *
>>> from random import random, uniform
>>> s = Server().boot()
>>> N = 200
>>> freqs = [uniform(100, 900) for i in range(N)]
>>> phases = [random() for i in range(N)]
>>> amps = [uniform(.001, .02) for i in range(N)]
>>> oscs = Sine(freqs, phases, amps).out()
>>> s.start()
```

5.5 Multichannel environment

Pyo can be turned into a multichannel environment, instead of stereo, simply by giving the desired number of channels as an argument to the Server object. When a pyo object is asked to send its audio streams to the sound card, the default behavior is to alternate its streams over the available channels cyclically. This behavior can be overridden in many ways, either with random functions, or by specifying the exact output for each stream managed by the object, or with the available panning functionalities of the library. The panning objects take the number of channels as an argument, allowing one to switch quickly between a stereo and a multichannel workstation.

```
>>> from pyo import *
>>> CHNLS = 8
>>> s = Server(nchnls=CHNLS).boot()
>>> n = Noise(.5)
>>> lfo = Sine(.1, mul=0.5, add=0.5)
>>> pan = Pan(n, outs=CHNLS, pan=lfo).out()
>>> s.start()
```

5.6 Arithmetic with audio objects

Pyo objects also override the basic math operators ($*$, $/$, $+$, $-$, $**$, $\%$), meaning you can do arithmetic involving audio objects. When math operations contain pyo objects, a new audio object, called Dummy, is automatically created to hold the result of the computation. The action leaves the original object untouched. This behavior can be very useful as a single audio object can be multiplied by a list of floats to return a list of similar, but slightly different, audio objects. Arithmetic operations can involve only audio objects or both audio objects and floats.

In a similar way, conditional operators ($<$, $<=$, $>$, $>=$, $==$, $!=$) are overridden in pyo objects to return an audio stream containing zeros and ones, depending on the result of the comparison.

The next sample illustrates some arithmetics with audio objects by creating a complex tone with the summation of three sine waves. The frequency of each oscillator is a harmonic of a given fundamental with an independent jitter and a common vibrato.

```
>>> from pyo import *
>>> s = Server().boot()
>>> f = 100
>>> vib = Sine(5, mul=0.02, add=1)
>>> jit = Randi(min=0.99, max=1.01, freq=[1,2,3])
>>> a1 = Sine(freq=f * vib * jit[0], mul=0.5)
>>> a2 = Sine(freq=f * 2 * vib * jit[1], mul=0.3)
>>> a3 = Sine(freq=f * 3 * vib * jit[2], mul=0.1)
>>> total = (a1 + a2 + a3).out()
>>> s.start()
```

5.7 MIDI and OSC support

Music is all about instrument and control. In this regards, pyo offers a complete support for MIDI and OSC[6] (*Open Sound Control*) communication. These two protocols are widely used and incorporated into many commercial and custom musical interfaces. It is a very efficient way to modify and generate sound events in real-time. Here is the bare minimum to play notes in pyo with a MIDI keyboard:

```
>>> from pyo import *
>>> s = Server()
>>> s.setMidiInputDevice(99) # open all devices!
>>> s.boot()
>>> note = Notein(poly=10, scale=1)
>>> amp = MidiAdsr(note['velocity'], mul=0.2)
>>> osc = RCOsc(freq=note['pitch'], mul=amp)
>>> out = osc.mix(2).out()
>>> s.start()
```

5.8 Other features

After several years of development of pyo, it is now a DSP toolkit pretty complete. In addition to essential processes like soundfile players, filters, wave shapers, oscillators, random generators, reverbs, etc., there is an all set of objects to do spectral transformations with the phase vocoder technique[1]. Scientists and psychoacoustics will find analysis tools to retrieve and display sound characteristics such as fundamental frequency, spectrum envelope, amplitude envelope, brightness and spectral center of gravity. Pyo also has many built-in operators to create and manipulate tables or matrices and much more. See the documentation for the detail about the hundreds of objects in the library.

6. CONCLUSION

In this article we have introduced a new audio engine that, developed as a Python module, is part of a larger programming environment than the sound itself. It is a dedicated module amongst thousands of other specialized modules. We have also demonstrated that this integration to a general and common language can be of a great benefit. There is no need to learn a new syntax and new paradigms before starting to make sound with code; we just need to write programs in a familiar language. Crunching numbers to store in an audio table can be easily done with the numpy module. Creating audio software with a sophisticated graphical user interface become an easy task because there is already plenty of GUI modules available. Python is very powerful when comes the time to develop algorithms and pyo now provides a complete and high quality DSP toolbox to produce sound within Python.

7. REFERENCES

[1] R. Boulanger and V. Lazzarini. *The audio programming book*. MIT Press, Cambridge, Massachussets, 2010.

[2] J. McCartney. Supercollider: a new real time synthesis language. In *ICMC'96 Conference Proceedings*, pages 257–258. International Computer Music Association, 1996.

[3] J. McCartney. Continued evolution of the supercollider real time environment. In *ICMC'98 Conference Proceedings*, pages 133–136. International Computer Music Association, 1998.

[4] M. Puckette. Pure data: another integrated computer music environment. In *Conference Proceedings*, pages 37–41. Second Intercollege Computer Music Concerts, 1996.

[5] B. Vercoe and D. Ellis. Real-time csound: Software synthesis with sensing and control. In *ICMC'90 Conference Proceedings*, pages 209–211. International Computer Music Association, 1990.

[6] M. Wright, A. Freed, and AliMomeni. Opensound control: State of the art. In *NIME'03 Conference Proceedings*. Conference on New Interfaces for Musical Expression, 2003.

SenseCap: Synchronized Data Collection with Microsoft Kinect2 and LeapMotion

Julian F. P. Kooij
Pattern Recognition & Bioinformatics Group
Delft University of Technology
Mekelweg 2, 2628 CD
Delft, The Netherlands
Division of Image Processing
Leiden University Medical Center
Albinusdreef 2, 2333 ZA
Leiden, The Netherlands
J.F.P.Kooij@tudelft.nl

SUBMITTED to ACM MULTIMEDIA 2016 OPEN SOURCE SOFTWARE COMPETITION

ABSTRACT

We present a new recording tool to capture synchronized video and skeletal data streams from cheap sensors such as the Microsoft Kinect2, and LeapMotion. While other recording tools act as virtual playback devices for testing on-line real-time applications, we target multi-media data collection for off-line processing. Images are encoded in common video formats, and skeletal data as flat text tables. This approach enables long duration recordings (e.g. over 30 minutes), and supports post-hoc mapping of the Kinect2 depth video to the color space if needed. By using common file formats, the data can be played back and analyzed on any other computer, without requiring sensor specific SDKs to be installed. The project is released under a 3-clause BSD license, and consists of an extensible C++11 framework, with support for the official Microsoft Kinect 2 and LeapMotion APIs to record, a command-line interface, and a Matlab GUI to initiate, inspect, and load Kinect2 recordings.

Keywords

Multi-media data collection, RGB+D, skeletal tracking, Kinect2

1. INTRODUCTION

In recent years, various cheap sensors have reached the consumer marker which provide multi-media data for a myriad of multi-media and computer vision applications. Examples include the LeapMotion, and the Microsoft Kinect2, the successor of the original Microsoft Kinect. The Kinect2 contains two calibrated cameras, one time-of-flight for 512×424 16-bit depth images, and a HD 1920×1080 RGB camera, and the LeapMotion has two 640×240 infrared cameras. In addition, both sensors deliver estimated skeletal data using an embedded tracking module, namely up to 6 full body skeletons for Kinect2 [8] (each body having 25 3D joints), and 2 hands for LeapMotion [10] (each hand having 20 3D joints). Use cases of such data include scene reconstruction [3], semantic labeling [9], and skeletal tracking for Human Computer Interaction [1, 2, 5], and RGB+D motion analysis [4].

These sensors have traditionally been used for real-time and interactive applications, requiring on-line processing of the selected streams. This workflow is even facilitated by official tools such as KinectStudio (see Section 2). On the other hand, for researchers wishing to perform *off-line* processing of one or more streams, and who need to create datasets with long recordings, there is surprisingly no straightforward solution. Our sensor capturing project, *SenseCap*[1], was designed to fill this gap (e.g. it was successfully used in [4]). It provides an extensible C++11 framework, a command-line tool for standard recording/playback tasks, and a Matlab GUI to initiate recording with the Kinect2 (through the command-line tool) and load the data for inspection. The data is stored in common file formats, such as AVI for video streams, and text tables for skeletal poses. The benefits of data collection with this approach are:

1. It enables proof-of-concept applications that cannot process all data streams on-line. In contrast, real-time processing of the Kinect2 HD color video must at most take 33ms per frame (30 Hz), on average.

2. Data collected on one machine can be loaded and played back on another machine using either our tool (compiled without sensor specific APIs), or in any other processing environment that can load video and text tables, e.g. Matlab, python.

3. Video comprises the largest amount of the recorded data on disk. Using FFmpeg for video compression, our tool can record long sessions at a good quality/disk space trade-off. For color video we use lossy compression, as is common in datasets with large amounts of images or video [6, 7], but depth is stored (near)lossless.

4. Synchronous recording is not limited to a single sensor per PC. Our system cal also simultaneously capture the complementary skeletal data from both the Kinect

[1]Public repository at https://bitbucket.org/jkooij/sensecap

MM '16, October 15 - 19, 2016, Amsterdam, Netherlands

ISBN 978-1-4503-3603-1/16/10...$15.00

DOI: http://dx.doi.org/10.1145/2964284.2973805

2 and the LeapMotion (spatial calibration or alignment of multiple sensors is outside the scope of this project).

In the remainder of this paper, Section 2 will first discuss related work. Section 3 describes how our setup records video and skeletal data on disk, and how to use recorded depth data of the Kinect2 for post-hoc image space mapping. We then discuss in Section 4 the extensible Object-Oriented C++11 framework to encapsulate the sensor and FFmpeg APIs. Next, Section 5 describes the provided a command-line and Matlab user interfaces to the framework. We end with conclusions and future improvements in Section 6.

2. RELATED TOOLS AND FRAMEWORKS

There are various general purpose coding environments that handle streaming data. The Robot Operating System (ROS)[2] is open source and general purpose, but also Linux specific. Unity[3] is another proprietary platform that is supported by many sensor manufacturers, but its focus is on visually rich interactive environments. National Instruments' LabView[4] is popular for real-time signal processing applications, but is proprietary. Mathworks Matlab does not currently provide out-of-the-box support for the Kinect2, though recently mex wrappers have been developed for the low-level API [5]. Each of these environments is very flexible, but none provides a ready solution for low-latency data collection; One would still need to develop the actual application that combines all components (sensors, video encoders) within the environment.

The official Kinect2 SDK[6] only supports Windows, but includes KinectStudio, a desktop GUI to view and synchronously record all the streams. KinectStudio stores all recorded streams in a single file of a proprietary format, with no control over quality versus disk space. The file can later only be opened in KinectStudio for playback as a virtual Kinect2 device. There is no way to export individual streams into common data formats.

The OpenKinect community created an open source driver (libfreenect) for the original Kinect, and recently also the libfreenect2[7] driver for the Kinect2. The libfreenect project also included Fakenect[8], which served a similar purpose as KinectStudio to record and playback streams as a virtual device. Unfortunately, fakenect has not been updated to the Kinect2, and does not by itself encode video streams for data collection. MSOpenTech developed the Kinect Common Bridge (KCB), later also ported to the Kinect2 (KCBv2)[9], which is a C++ wrapper to provide a managed API on-top of the low-level API provided by the SDK.

On the LeapMotion side there is a similar situation, with an official SDK and binary closed-source drivers for Windows, MacOS and Linux, and a community built open source alternative, OpenLeap[10].

[2]http://www.ros.org/
[3]https://unity3d.com/
[4]http://www.ni.com/labview/
[5]https://github.com/jrterven/Kin2
[6]https://developer.microsoft.com/en-us/windows/kinect/develop
[7]https://github.com/OpenKinect/libfreenect2
[8]https://openkinect.org/wiki/Fakenect
[9]github.com/MSOpenTech/KinectCommonBridge/tree/2.0
[10]http://openleap.org/

3. DATA FORMATS ON DISK

SenseCap stores different streams from a sensor as distinct files within a target directory. Skeletal data is stored in a Space Separated Value (SSV) text files, each line containing a timestamp, skeleton id, and then a fixed number of joint values. For the Kinect's skeleton, this means $2+25\times 8 = 202$ values per line, as we store for each joint its 3D position, 4D orientation quaternion, and a tracking state integer (i.e. is the joint seen or not). A file containing LeapMotion hand skeletons contains $2+20\times 6+3 = 125$ values per line, representing each joint with two 3D vectors, and also storing per hand a tracking state, confidence, and left/right indicator.

As stated before, the video streams are stored on disk by encoding the frames through the FFmpeg library. Which codecs are available depends on how FFmpeg is built, but we consider here H.264 which we found to give good encoding quality. Different video streams can have different encoding options to trade-off between the video quality and its size on disk. Still, we have to take into account several issues when recording video data.

First, most video codecs have limited capabilities to store custom timestamps per frame, let alone easily retrieve them in Matlab or python. To ensure that each video frame contains a timestamps at the desired numerical precision and in an easily accessible manner, we simply write the timestamps to an additional text file per video file.

Second, the Kinect2 API natively supports mapping the depth image space onto the color image space, and vice versa. This pixel to pixel mapping needs to be recomputed per frame using the actual depth image, as the disparity between both cameras depends on the distance of the objects to the sensor. Since different use cases may require different mappings, and because applying the mappings is processing intensive (increasing the risk of frame skips) and requires significant additional disk space, our tools provide an optional post-processing step to only map the recorded depth to the color space if needed (Note: the Kinect2 sensor *must* be connected for this step). Therefore, the depth video should be stored with (near)lossless compression and avoid interpolation artifacts around object edges. Common video codecs are designed for YUV color or gray-scale images, and while encoder settings can be tuned to lossless encoding (e.g. by setting quantization parameter `qp=0` in H.264), the required YUV 4:2:0 image layout only preserves the 8-bit intensity channel at full resolution, Our solution thus reduces the 16-bit value to an 8-bit value for fixed depth-range of 0-4 meter, i.e. with a depth resolution of $4000/256 \approx 16mm$. The impact on the resulting depth-to-image mapping is minimal.

We compare our tool to KinectStudio on a Dell Precision T3610 workstation running Windows 8.1. A recording of 30 seconds with KinectStudio (depth, color, body foreground masks and skeletal data) results in a file of ~ 4.5 Gb, while our tool stores the same streams in a total of $\sim$ 185 Mb (132 Mb for color video, 40 Mb for depth video). Post-hoc mapping of the lossless depth video to the color image space results in a high-quality video at the full 1920×1080 resolution, taking an additional $\sim$ 175 Mb.

4. FRAMEWORK SETUP

The command-line utility (Section 5.1) is created on top of an Object-Oriented library written in C++11, which consists of various modules to encapsulate the distinct APIs of

FFmpeg 3.0.0x	LGPL 2.1/GPL
OpenCV 3.1	3-clause BSD license
Boost 1.57+[11]	Boost software license
GLFW 3.1[12]	zlib/libpng license
recommended	
LeapMotion SDK 2.1+	proprietary
Kinect for Windows SDK 2.0	proprietary
Kinect Common Bridge v2	Apache 2.0

Table 1: Library dependencies, and their licenses.

the sensors, FFmpeg encoders/decoders, and simple UI elements. This modular setup also enables custom configurations, and addition of new modules to support novel sensor APIs or novel functionalities (e.g. networking).

Between these modules data is exchanged in common data structures that are independent of any sensor's API. All images are internally represented by OpenCV `cv::Mat` instances, and the library defines its own structs for skeletal data to avoid API header dependencies. For instance, the Kinect2 capturing module is responsible for converting the APIs data representations to the library's common formats. The modules that load or save video/skeletal data to disk, or visualize them on screen also use the common formats, hence playback in our framework is even possible if no sensor SDK is present.

The class hierarchy ensures that each module has methods to setup and release resources in a synchronized manner. Run-time execution therefore exists of several *stages*, namely (1) to start background threads, (2) to acquire sensors and files, (3) to perform the main loops, (4) to release the sensors and files, and (5) join all threads. The main thread is responsible for executing each stage in order. It requests each module to execute the target stage, and blocks until all modules are finished with the stage before moving to the next one. To 'glue' the components together we use simple callback functions that are iteratively called by a special execution module during the main loop (stage 3). Such callback functions can be conveniently defined using C++11 lambda syntax to describe simple data exchange or processing tasks, e.g. grab a video frame from a sensor and send it to video writer instance, using the modules' thread-safe methods.

Our project currently targets the official LeapMotion and Kinect2 drivers, which are only available on Windows 8+, and was tested with Visual Studio 2013. Doxygen is used to generate API documentation, and CMAKE as a flexible open source build-system to discover the installed SDKs, and generate appropriate Visual Studio solution files. These tools are cross-platform, and our framework code is in principle also platform independent through the Boost library. All additional dependencies are listed in Table 1. The KCBv2 is only needed when using the Kinect2 SDK.

5. USER INTERFACES

There are two user interfaces provided with the framework, namely a command-line utility, and a Matlab based GUI that uses the command-line utility to interface with the Kinect2. Both are discussed next.

5.1 The command-line utility

The `sensecap` command-line utility implements various common data collection tasks using the presented framework, such as recording data with the Kinect2, post-processing to map the depth image to the color space (see Figure 1), recording with the LeapMotion, and even recording both sensors together (see Figure 2). Its only GUI elements are simple windows to visualize the streams.

The `sensecap` tools provides two interaction modes. By default, it displays a simple menu in the shell and lets the user select which functionality to execute. After execution finishes, the menu is displayed again to allow the user to playback or convert the recording immediately after, for instance. Alternatively, each functionality can be started directly using the `--option` command-line switch to avoid the interactive menu. This approach makes it easy to initiate data collection from other applications with a system call invoking `sensecap`, as is done in the Matlab GUI.

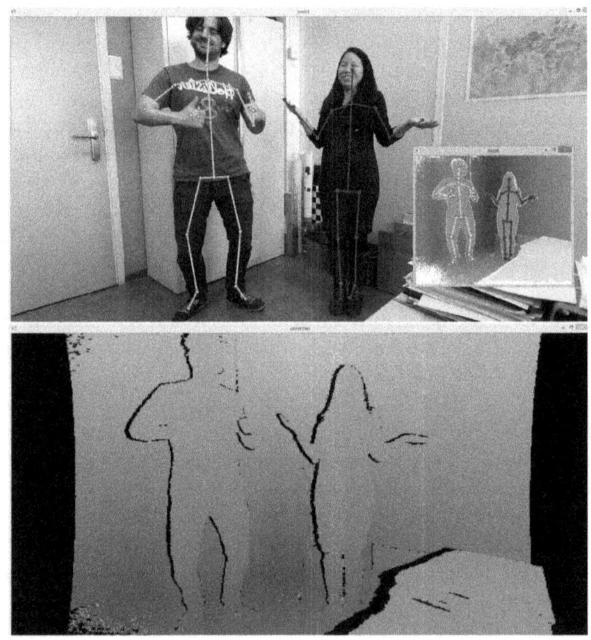

Figure 1: (Top) `sensecap` shows captured data in simple windows. (Bottom) Post-hoc depth-to-color mapping creates HD video of the recorded depth.

5.2 The Matlab GUI

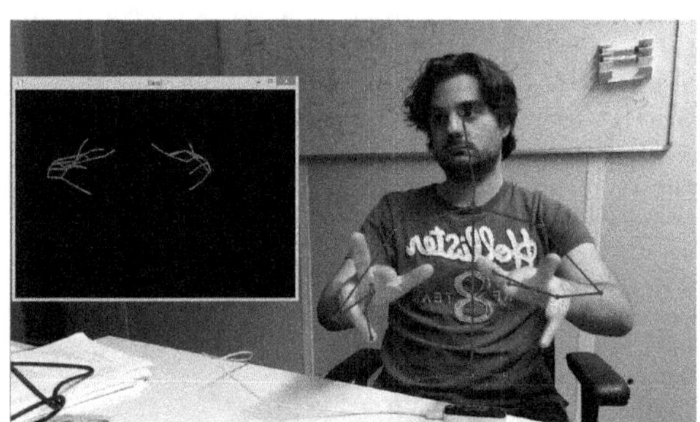

Figure 2: Synchronized recording with Kinect2 and LeapMotion for complementary skeletal tracking.

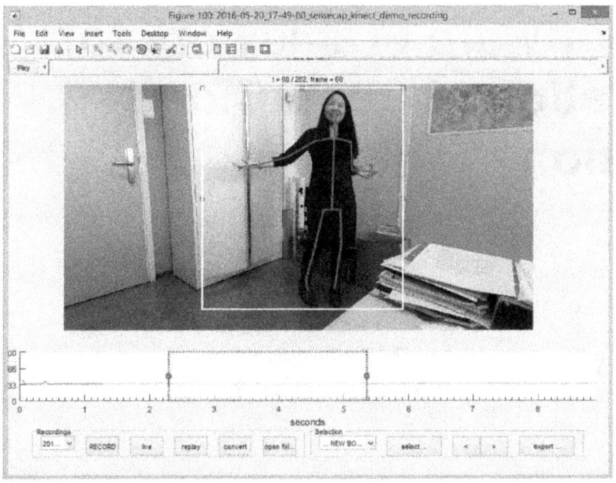

Figure 3: The Matlab GUI enables to start, convert, and inspect Kinect2 recordings using `sensecap`, and load the results in Matlab as regular datatypes.

The Matlab GUI uses the `sensecap` utility to initiate new recordings for the Kinect 2, perform post-hoc mapping, inspect stored recordings, and annotate spatio-temporal regions (the LeapMotion is not supported yet). It maintains base directory where it searches for and stores new recordings as sub-directories. Each sub-directory is automatically named after the start date and time by the GUI.

As the screenshot in Figure 3 shows, the GUI fits in a single Matlab figure, and draws at the center the color video and tracked skeletons. At the top is a playback toolbar (playback in Matlab is however slow, the *replay* button below starts `sensecap` for real-time playback), and a frame count. The bottom contains of a timeline axis where the temporal difference between subsequent color frames (in red) and skeletal frames (in green) is shown. If there are no frame skips, these graphs should be at 33 (ms). Below the graphs are a drop-down menu to select a recording, and buttons to start a new recording, compute the post-hoc depth mapping, or view the current streams. For simple annotations of spatio-temporal regions, another button allows the user to draw a rectangle in the image plane and in the timeline axis. These annotations can be bookmarked to easily retrieve them later, or load the particular space-time slice from a Matlab script.

6. CONCLUSIONS AND FUTURE WORK

The SenseCap software package for multi-modal data collection offers several advantages over existing approaches supporting the Microsoft Kinect2 and the LeapMotion. For instance, the data is stored in readily accessible file formats (AVI video, plain text, etc.) to allow off-line processing in many environments. Standard video encoders are used for low-latency, efficient disk storage, and to record depth as accurately as possible. This enables long recordings, and optional Kinect2 depth-to-color mapping in a post-processing step. Futhermore, the code is written as a modular C++11 framework, and the accompanying executable provides basic capturing and playback functionality. The Matlab GUI can be used to initiate and inspect data collection with the Kinect2. More information on the framework and interfaces can be found in the documentation.

An important improvement would be to increase cross-platform support, especially by using the open source drivers such as libfreenect2 and OpenLeap. Note that the selected core dependencies (OpenCV, Boost, etc.) are already platform independent. CMAKE files still have to be adjusted. Another future goal is to add networking support, e.g. to record sensor streams obtained at one ore more remote PCs using our framework, and to support more sensors such as the Intel RealSense.

Acknowledgments

This work is part of the research programme Technology in Motion (TIM [628.004.001]), financed by the Netherlands Organisation for Scientific Research (NWO). We thank Niels Dekker for helping to test and debug early versions of the software, and Hayley Hung for helping create example data.

7. REFERENCES

[1] Z. Cheng, L. Qin, Y. Ye, Q. Huang, and Q. Tian. Human daily action analysis with multi-view and color-depth data. In *Computer Vision–ECCV 2012. Workshops and Demonstrations*, pages 52–61. Springer, 2012.

[2] J. Han, L. Shao, D. Xu, and J. Shotton. Enhanced computer vision with microsoft kinect sensor: A review. *Cybernetics, IEEE Transactions on*, 43(5):1318–1334, 2013.

[3] S. Izadi et al. Kinectfusion: real-time 3d reconstruction and interaction using a moving depth camera. In *Proceedings of the 24th annual ACM symposium on User interface software and technology*, pages 559–568. ACM, 2011.

[4] J. F. P. Kooij and J. C. van Gemert. Depth-aware motion magnification. In *European Conference on Computer Vision (ECCV), 2016*. Springer, (to appear).

[5] G. Marin, F. Dominio, and P. Zanuttigh. Hand gesture recognition with leap motion and kinect devices. In *Image Processing (ICIP), 2014 IEEE International Conference on*, pages 1565–1569. IEEE, 2014.

[6] A. Prest, C. Leistner, J. Civera, C. Schmid, and V. Ferrari. Learning object class detectors from weakly annotated video. In *Computer Vision and Pattern Recognition (CVPR), 2012 IEEE Conference on*, pages 3282–3289. IEEE, 2012.

[7] O. Russakovsky, J. Deng, H. Su, J. Krause, S. Satheesh, S. Ma, Z. Huang, A. Karpathy, A. Khosla, M. Bernstein, et al. Imagenet large scale visual recognition challenge. *International Journal of Computer Vision*, 115(3):211–252, 2015.

[8] J. Shotton, T. Sharp, A. Kipman, A. Fitzgibbon, M. Finocchio, A. Blake, M. Cook, and R. Moore. Real-time human pose recognition in parts from single depth images. *Communications of the ACM*, 56(1):116–124, 2013.

[9] S. Song, S. P. Lichtenberg, and J. Xiao. Sun rgb-d: A rgb-d scene understanding benchmark suite. In *Proceedings of the IEEE Conference on Computer Vision and Pattern Recognition*, pages 567–576, 2015.

[10] F. Weichert, D. Bachmann, B. Rudak, and D. Fisseler. Analysis of the accuracy and robustness of the leap motion controller. *Sensors*, 13(5):6380–6393, 2013.

MP3DG-PCC, Open Source Software Framework for Implementation and Evaluation of Point Cloud Compression

Rufael Mekuria
CWI
SciencePark 123
1098 XG Amsterdam
r.n.mekuria@cwi.nl

Pablo Cesar
CWI
SciencePark 123
1098 XG Amsterdam
p.s.cesar@cwi.nl

ABSTRACT
We present MP3DG-PCC, an open source framework for design, implementation and evaluation of point cloud compression algorithms. The framework includes objective quality metrics, lossy and lossless anchor codecs, and a test bench for consistent comparative evaluation. The framework and proposed methodology is in use for the development of an international point cloud compression standard in MPEG. In addition, the library is integrated with the popular point cloud library, making a large number of point cloud processing available and aligning the work with the broader open source community.

Categories and Subject Descriptors
H.5.1 [**Multimedia Information Systems**]: Compression, Evaluation, 3D Virtual Reality, Point Cloud Compression

Keywords: Compression, Benchmarking, Software

1. INTRODUCTION
More 3D Point Cloud data are becoming available from 3D scanning and reconstruction. These data are useful in a large range of applications such as virtual and augmented reality, 3D imaging, and 3D simultaneous localization and mapping (SLAM). Typical 3D point cloud scans contain thousands up to millions of points and are sometimes acquired at fast rates (10-30 fps using current Time-of-Flight and LiDaR scanners). Therefore, to support efficient storage and exchange of such data, efficient compression becomes critical. This is of interest of both the research community, the open source community and standardization organizations such as MPEG and JPEG that develop standards for adaption in large scale consumer electronics. Both consortia are in the process of developing standards for static and dynamic point cloud compression, to address the large amounts of data becoming available from 3D scanners.

MM '16, October 15 - 19, 2016, Amsterdam, Netherlands

ACM 978-1-4503-3603-1/16/10…$15.00
DOI: http://dx.doi.org/10.1145/2964284.2973806

Compression of point clouds has received quite some attention from the 3D Graphics research community. Much emphasis has been on compression of the geometry positions representing a point sampled surface and/or respective attributes such as colors. This research establishes some fundamental ideas for point cloud compression. However, it fails to address many of the current requirements for point cloud compression for 3D scanning/imaging in emerging VR applications. Some of these insufficiently addressed requirements are as follows.

Lossy/lossless coding of attribute data (colors, properties) is important, but it has received little attention. Often methods optimized for geometry are applied, but this is not optimal for coding attributes such as colors and/or surface properties.

Time-varying point cloud compression is important, as scans are often acquired at a fast rate. In this case exploiting inter frame redundancy can be exploited, but this is still an unexplored topic.

Real-time compression and *parallelization* are important in many emerging consumer and professionally oriented applications (virtual reality, 3D tele-immersive communication, simultaneous mapping and localization (SLAM) for robotics etc.). Most work in the literature does not support real-time and parallel coding well.

We expect that it will take multiple cycles to develop and fine tune compression techniques that address each of these requirements sufficiently well. To align such cycles, common datasets, assessment criteria and methodology are useful. For point cloud compression such a common framework is currently lacking. In this work we present MP3DG-PCC an open source framework based on common methodology, assessment criteria and datasets enabling future work on point cloud compression with a common assessment methodology. In addition, it contains an anchor codec that already addresses some of the requirements and can be developed towards a sophisticated and standardized solution (i.e. real-time inter-predictive and lossy attributes coding).

These contributions will benefit researchers that are developing codecs in open source communities and/or standardization organizations, or in industry. In addition, it will also be useful for researchers working on complex multimedia systems that want to readily integrate the anchor codecs in larger AR/VR systems.

The package is available in the MPEG software repository and the trunk version is aligned with the open source version available in an open source GitHub repository (https://github.com/RufaelDev/pcc-mp3dg). The build process uses cross platform make (CMake). The software can both be used for evaluating compression of point cloud datasets and for further development and evaluation of the codec anchor.

This paper is structured as follows. Section 2 presents an overview of Point Cloud Compression. Section 3 presents the MP3DG PCC software in detail. Section 4 concludes the work and highlights its usefulness.

2. POINT CLOUD COMPRESSION

Point cloud compression deals with compression of points and their attributes located in the 3D space. Many of the compression methods proposed in the literature utilize the octree structure to organize the unstructured data. The octree provides a sparse and easily serializable representation of the point cloud and enables many levels of detail. With emerging applications areas such as 3D Tele-immersive communications and 3D printing additional requirements need to be addressed. For example, in [1] we describe the design implementation and evaluation of a point cloud codec for 3D tele-immersive real-time conferencing addressing lossy color coding, inter predictive coding and real-time encoding.

To support consistent evaluation for coding with these additional requirements, we introduce MP3DG-PCC, a framework for quality assessment and benchmarking of PCC. This framework will enable more consistent quality evaluations and codec development. Before we continue we detail some of the requirements for point cloud compression that need to be taken into account in its evaluation.

Scalable coding: Progressive, or coding with many levels of detail has been considered in the literature [2]. For emerging applications scalable with few levels of detail but low complexity for encoding and decoding are desirable.

Real-time coding and parallelization is needed in many applications, while a real-time PCC codec was proposed, there is still much work to be done enabling good parallelization

Lossy geometry coding is desirable for point clouds with millions of points that need to be stored with a small number of bytes.

Lossy Color Attributes coding the coding of attributes associated to geometry points needs more attention. More efficient techniques for lossy attributes coding such as in [3] are needed.

Lossless Coding is important in many applications such as computer aided design, medical and so on

Multi-view coding sometimes directional information is important and needs to be incorporated in the codec. Depending on the angle of inspection point properties (colors), might be different.

Material properties and generic attribute coding 3D reconstruction, sometimes provides detected material properties and/or generic attributes. These may be beneficial for rendering and or further processing and should also be stored efficiently

Inter-predictive coding clouds are often captured at a fast rate, inter-predictive coding still needs attention.

The MP3DG-PCC open source framework enables assessment and codec development based on these requirements. The specific **contributions** of this framework are the following:

- Quality metrics for point cloud geometry and color attributes analogous to Peak Signal to Noise Ratio (PSNR)
- A test bench including file loaders and evaluation routines with easy configuration enabling automatic benchmarking
- Point Cloud pre-processing (outlier removal, octree bounding box normalization) ensuring consistent evaluation
- Commonly available datasets based on data reconstructed with Microsoft Kinect 1, Kinect 2 and other devices.
- A time varying PCC anchor codec. Support for benchmarking time varying point cloud compression.
- A real-time, parallelized, anchor PCC codec. Support for benchmarking real-time performance and parallelization of point cloud codecs.
- A lossy attribute coding anchor codec. Support for benchmarking lossy color attribute coding

While the presented software framework can be used in different contexts, its primary aim is to support the development of a point cloud compression in the Moving Picture Experts Group (MPEG). The Moving Picture experts group has completed the exploration on point cloud compression defining requirements [4], use cases [5] test datasets [6] and evaluation criteria [7]. Based on these a draft call for proposals was released in June 2016 [7]. The documents are available to the public on the MPEG webpage of the June 2016 meeting [8] and provide a good overview of the scope and methodology of this activity.

3. BENCHMARKING PLATFORM

3.1 MP3DG-PCC overview & config

The benchmarking platform software contains three major components that can be located in separate folders in the C++ software source code. It contains a quality metric in the folder quality for performing a PSNR like quality assessment of the point cloud (both attribute and geometry, see [1] for more details on the metric). The anchor codec contains time varying (inter-predictive) and lossy color coding techniques. It can be found in cloud_codec_v2. The benchmarking platform (including preprocessing and file loaders) can be found in compression_eval. Compression_eval compiles to an executable to run the test bench. The test bench parameters can be configured through parameter_config.txt. When the test bench is ran, an input folder containing all point clouds in the .ply format can be given as an input argument. The flow of the test bench is illustrated in Figure 1. All clouds are loaded into memory, optionally fused (if clouds from different angles have been recorded, i.e. view selective clouds). In the next step bounding box, normalization and outlier filtering is performed to enable normalized inputs to the codec (normalize all points to the 0-1 scale, such that rms distances can be consistently evaluated). Next, all codec configurations are traversed and outputs are written to a .csv file. The quality scores include bit rates (for geometry, attribute), encoding/decoding time, and quality (based on a PSNR like metric adapted for point clouds see [1]).

The flow of compression_eval is illustrated in Figure 1 and Table 1 outlines the different components in the software. The source code is embedded in the version 1.7.2 of the point cloud library, and will soon be ported to the latest version.

The test bench can be configured using the parameter_config.txt file. This file contains all options for running the test bench using anchor codecs. The option octree bit-settings and color bit-settings can be used to control the number of octree levels. The color coding types can be set to 0,1,2 which correspond to DPCM, JPEG based (grid), and jpeg based lines. Table 1 Components in the software these modes map the depth first scan of the octree to an image grid for further compression. The enh_bit_settings can be used to set the bits in the enhancement layer (beyond the octree). We found that the octree compression only works well upto a certain level of detail, after which another mode of compression is preferable. This mode is in the enhancement layer. The option keep_centroid can be used to also code the centroid in the leaf node, enabling smoother low res representations. The bounding box expand factor can be set, which slightly enlarges the octree bounding box to enable inter predictions (consistent bounding box frames). The output .csv file containing all results can be set. Then, optionally decoded .ply files can be written. With do_delta_frame coding inter-predictive coding in the anchor can be enabled. The pframe_quality_log sets the output csv for inter-predictively encoded frames. For inter predictive coding the macroblock size for inter prediction in the anchor can be set in macroblock size. The option test bbalign can be used to test the effectiveness of the boundingbox alignment only in a single test run. The code_color_offset can be used to code color offsets in the anchor codec in inter-predicted frames. The options related to the radius outlier filter enable pre-filtering of the point clouds to avoid outliers that disturb the octree based coding mechanism. The parameter_config.txt can be located at the location of the binary or one level beneath.

Table 1 Component in framework for PCC

Quality	Quality metric
Compression_eval	Test bench
Cloud_codec_v2	Anchor PCC Codec

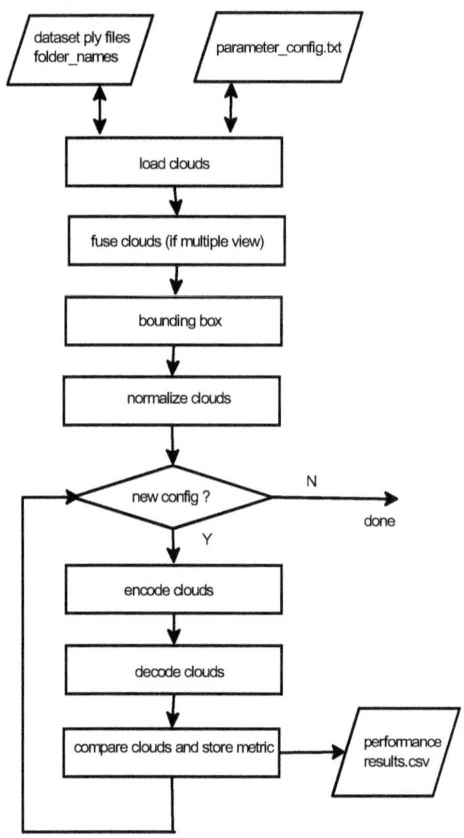

Figure 1 Compression eval testbench

Figure 2 Some examples of .ply testdata available for benchmarking

Table 2 settings for codec (parameter_config.txt)

#configuration file for testing the color encoding
octree_bit_settings=9
color_bit_settings=8
color_coding_types= 0 # color coding types 0=dpcm 1=grid 2=lines
enh_bit_settings = 0
keep_centroid=0 # option for keeping centroid instead of voxel centers only
bb_expand_factor=0.20# expansion factor used to keep bounding box constant over time
output_csv_file=intra_frame_quality_11_DPCM.csv
write_output_ply=1
do_delta_frame_coding=1
icp_on_original=0
pframe_quality_log=predictive_quality_11_DPCM.csv
macroblocksize=16
testbbalign=0
code_color_off=0
radius_outlier_filter=0
radius_size=0.1
jpeg_value=75
omp_cores=0
scalable=0

3.2 Datasets

Test datasets from 4 CERTH/ITI [1] based on [10] and Queen Mary University captured with Kinect 1 and Kinect 2 are available online, and form cultural heritage (reconstruction from multiple images) [2]. Screenshots of the data are shown in Figure 2. In addition in [7] additional datasets have been proposed such as from Microsoft Research.

3.3 Anchor Codec

The open source framework includes an anchor codec. It is based on octree, inter prediction and lossy color coding by mapping to an image grid. This codec is described in detail in [1], in addition the codec described in using octree and DPCM for color coding can be used as an anchor [11]. Improvements in each of the blocks can be tested using the test bench can be easily evaluation. This

[1] http://vcl.iti.gr/reconstruction/

[2] http://wg11.sc29.org/content//MPEG-04/Part16 Animation_Framework_eXtension_(AFX)/3DGraphics/pointCloud

enables collaborative improvements of the test model. For more information on the anchor codec we refer to [1].

3.4 Dependencies and installation guidelines

The package shares dependencies with the point cloud library [12] and can be build in similar fashion. Additionally, the anchor coding uses the JPEG codec using the libJPEGTurbo library which should also be installed. The framework does depend on boost, Flann, and Eigen, but not on QT, VTK etc. The package can be build on platforms such as Linux, windows and Mac. The build system uses CMake build scripts and can be build using the CMake configuration and generation GUI.

4. Discussion and Conclusion

This work presented a full benchmarking platform for point cloud compression algorithms including an improved anchor codec and PCC quality metrics. This framework addresses the need in the industry for improved compression and consistent evaluation of point cloud compression. The code is based on the popular point cloud library which is used as a defacto standard for point cloud processing in academia and industry and written in standard C++. We further discuss two use cases of this work on point cloud compression. The first is in the development of international and de-facto standards for point cloud compression. The second is the direct application in the development of AR/VR and other advanced 3D Multimedia Systems.

International Standardization of point cloud compression is still in an early stage. The Moving picture experts group (MPEG) consortium, has developed many industry standards for compression of visual media in the past. The rise in 3D point cloud data made it of increasing interest to MPEG. The development of an MPEG PCC standard will enable more requirements to be addressed and a wider range of experts on media coding to contribute to the codec, compared to previous work on PCC. In addition, it can enable fast industry adoption. The MPEG consortium will further develop this standard in the coming years. The MPEG group on 3D Graphics initiated this work. The currently presented test bench serves as a starting point for the standardization process. The trunk version of the MPEG source is aligned with the open source version available in a GitHub repository (https://github.com/RufaelDev/pcc-mp3dg).

Close to MPEG, the Joint Picture Experts Group (JPEG), known for developing compression for still image coding, included the possibility of point cloud compression in its emerging JPEG PLENO standard[3]. This software might also be of use there, but this standard addresses slightly different use cases targeting compression of data coming from plenoptic cameras. Still this work might also benefit work in JPEG PLENO.

Secondly, this framework can benefit the multimedia research community at large such as in the development of point cloud streaming protocols and advanced systems. An example of a point cloud streaming in mixed reality was developed in earlier work as can be shown in Figure 3. In this Figure, a captured 3D point cloud is transmitted to a remote site, and rendered in a 3D virtual world, enabling a mixed reality tele-immersive experience. In this framework, users could navigate remotely as a realistic representation of themselves. Further, 3D point clouds may be used as a more generic 3D Video format, in this case HTTP based streaming of this kind of data will becoming a hot research topic. The anchor codec developed in this framework can be an excellent starting point to start an investigation of adaptive streaming of point clouds over HTTP or other protocols.

Figure 3 Point Cloud rendering in a virtual environment

5. REFERENCES

[1] R.N. Mekuria K. Blom, P. Cesar, "Design, Implementation and Evaluation of a Point Cloud Codec for 3D Tele-immersive Video," *IEEE Transactions on Circuits and Systems for Video Technology*, september 2016.

[2] Y. Huang, J. Peng, C. Kuo, C. Gopi , "A generic scheme for progressive point cloud coding," *IEEE Transactions on Visualization and Computer Graphics*, vol. 14, no. 2, pp. 440-453, 2008.

[3] C. Zhang , D. Florencio, C.Loop, "Point cloud attribute compression with graph transform" in *IEEE ICIP*, Paris, France, 2014, pp. 2066-2070.

[4] MPEG "N16330 Requirements for Point Cloud Compression" ISO/IEC JTC1 SC29 WG11 Geneva, June 2016

[5] MPEG "N16331 Use Cases for Point Cloud Compression" ISO/IEC JTC1 SC29 WG11 Geneva, June 2016

[6] MPEG "N16332 Evaluation Criterion for Point Cloud Compression" ISO/IEC JTC1 SC29 WG11 Geneva, June 2016

[7] MPEG "N16333 Draft Dataset for Point Cloud Compression", ISO/IEC JTC1 SC29 WG11 Geneva, June 2016

[8] MPEG "N16334 Draft Call for Proposals for Point Cloud ISO/IEC JTC1 SC29 WG11 Compression", Geneva, June 2016

[9] "MPEG 115" http://mpeg.chiariglione.org/meetings/115 accessed 1/8/2016

[10] D. Alexiadis, D. Zarpalas, P. Daras , "Real-Time, full 3D Reconstruction of moving foreground objects from multiple consumer depth cameras," *IEEE Transactions on Multimedia*, vol. 15, no. 2, pp. 339-358, Februari 2013.

[11] J. Kammerl. , N. Blodow, R.B. Rusu, S. Gedikli, and E. Steinbach M Beetz, "Real-time compression of point cloud streams," in *Robotics and Automation (ICRA), 2012 IEEE International Conference on , pp.778,785, 14-18 May*, 2012.

[12] Rusu, R.B. "3D is here: Point Cloud Library," in *Robotics and Automation (ICRA), 2011 IEEE International Conference on*, Shanghai, 2011.

[3] https://jpeg.org/items/20150320_pleno_summary.html

Human Pose Estimation from Depth Images via Inference Embedded Multi-task Learning

Keze Wang[1,2], Shengfu Zhai[1,2], Hui Cheng[1,2]*, Xiaodan Liang[1,2], Liang Lin[1,2]
[1]Sun Yat-Sen University, Guangzhou, China
[2]Collaborative Innovation Center of High Performance Computing,
National University of Defense Technology, Changsha 410073, China

ABSTRACT

Human pose estimation (i.e., locating the body parts / joints of a person) is a fundamental problem in human-computer interaction and multimedia applications. Significant progress has been made based on the development of depth sensors, i.e., accessible human pose prediction from still depth images [32]. However, most of the existing approaches to this problem involve several components/models that are independently designed and optimized, leading to suboptimal performances. In this paper, we propose a novel inference-embedded multi-task learning framework for predicting human pose from still depth images, which is implemented with a deep architecture of neural networks. Specifically, we handle two cascaded tasks: i) generating the heat (confidence) maps of body parts via a fully convolutional network (FCN); ii) seeking the optimal configuration of body parts based on the detected body part proposals via an inference built-in MatchNet [10], which measures the appearance and geometric kinematic compatibility of body parts and embodies the dynamic programming inference as an extra network layer. These two tasks are jointly optimized. Our extensive experiments show that the proposed deep model significantly improves the accuracy of human pose estimation over other several state-of-the-art methods or SDKs. We also release a large-scale dataset for comparison, which includes 100K depth images under challenging scenarios.

Keywords

human pose estimation, deep learning, multi-task learning

*The corresponding author is Hui Cheng (Email: chengh9@mail.sysu.edu.cn). This work was supported in part by Guangdong Natural Science Foundation under Grant S2013050014548 and 2014A030313201, in part by State Key Development Program under Grant No 2016YFB1001000, and in part by the Fundamental Research Funds for the Central Universities. This work was also supported by Special Program for Applied Research on Super Computation of the NSFC-Guangdong Joint Fund (the second phase).

MM '16, October 15-19, 2016, Amsterdam, Netherlands
© 2016 ACM. ISBN 978-1-4503-3603-1/16/10... $15.00
DOI: http://dx.doi.org/10.1145/2964284.2964322

1. INTRODUCTION

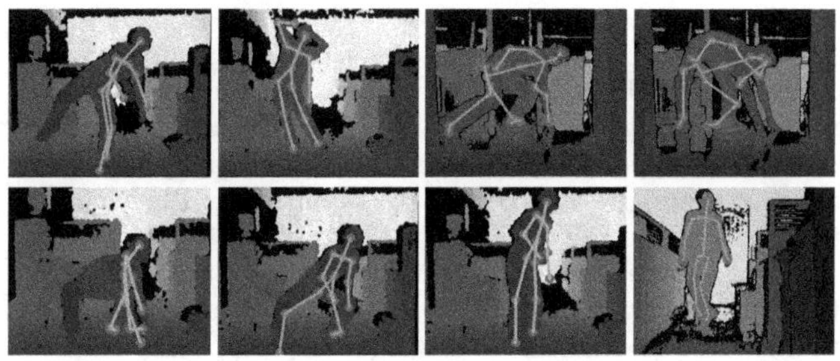

Figure 1: Several failure examples generated by the latest version of Microsoft Kinect SDK in dealing with human pose estimation from depth data under challenging cases (e.g., unusual poses and self-occlusions).

Accurately locating the body parts/joints of a person (also referd as human pose estimation) is a widely studied problem in the research of multimedia. With the advent of cheap depth sensors like the structured-light scanner and ToF (Time of Flight) camera, the great performances have been achieved by the methods taking advantage of the depth data. For example, an approach based on decision forests has been proposed by researchers from Microsoft [31], which classifies depth pixels corresponding to different parts of human body. This approach has been extended by Shotton et al. [32] by employing the regression forest. As a result, a great number of intelligent systems such as robotics and digital entertainments have been benefited a lot.

However, there are several difficulties under complex circumstances (e.g., the failure examples shown in Fig. 1):

1. *Unusual poses/views.* The user may appear in diverse views or poses in real applications, while current solvers (e.g., the latest version of Microsoft Kinect SDK) often fail in handling exceptional and unusual cases. This limits the applications to subtle human-computer interaction, to some extent.

2. *Self-occlusions.* The depth data captured from one single sensor inevitably contains much occlusions of the body parts, especially in playing complex gestures. The state-of-the-art performances are still far away from being satisfying.

The bottleneck of solving the above mentioned issues for further improving the accuracy performance is the fact that

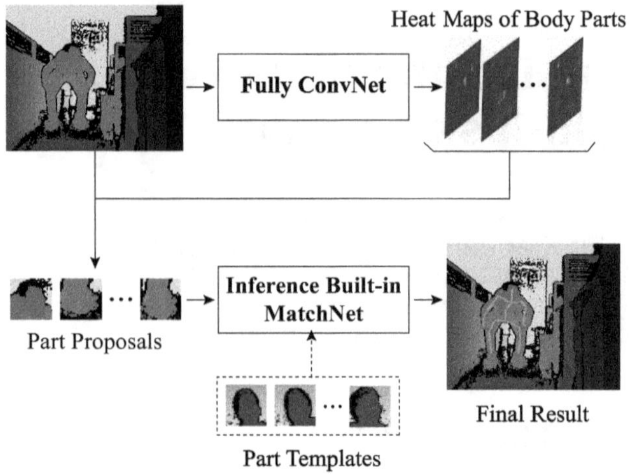

Figure 2: Our framework subsequently performs two cascaded tasks. The first task predicts the heat maps of all body parts with a fully convolutional neural network. Thus the candidate proposals for all parts can be conveniently obtained. The second task infers the best configurations of body parts with a novel inference built-in MatchNet structure. This tailored MatchNet provides the appearance and geometric compatibility of body parts between the part proposals and part templates. The dynamic programming inference is naturally embedded into the network learning to generate final pose estimation results.

most of the traditional methods rely on handcrafted feature representations and carefully tuned constraints for modeling human body structures. And these methods usually involve several components/models that are independently designed and optimized. Recently proposed deep convolutional neural network (CNN) models have made incredible progress on image classification [16, 45], object recognition [16, 7, 43, 50, 19], human activity recognition [44, 25], person re-indentification [24, 42, 41], scene labeling [47, 18, 27, 30, 23] and other vision problems. Improved performances are also achieved by the deep learning approaches [15, 38] on estimating human poses from RGB images. For example, Tompson et al. [38] proposed to impose a random field model upon CNNs for joint training and demonstrated the promising human pose estimation results on color data. However, directly applying these methods to the depth data is unfeasible due to the different challenges and requirements between the pose estimation tasks via color and depth data. Specifically, the depth images usually include sensor noises and preserve very coarse appearance details. Though this limits the human body part detection, the extra depth information can provide stronger contexts and skeletons for modeling human body structures and eliminating the effect of unrelated background clutters. Hence, we aim to develop a specialized neural network model that jointly incorporates the feature learning and the affinity constraints of body parts into a unified learning framework for the pose estimation from the depth data.

In this work, we propose a novel deep Inference-Embedded Multi-Task learning framework to estimate the human pose from still depth images. Specifically, our framework includes two networks for solving the two cascaded tasks, i.e., generating the heat (confidence) maps of body parts and further predicting body joints based on the generated body part proposals, respectively. Fig. 2 illustrates the overview architecture of our deep multi-task learning framework, in which these two tasks are conducted in the progressive coarse-to-fine manner and jointly optimized for pursuing higher pose estimation performance.

The first task is performed by utilizing a fully convolutional network (FCN) [27], which generates heat maps for indicating the coarse locations of human body parts. The FCN enables regressing pixel-wise confidence maps of the body parts in depth images without the parameter-redundant fully-connected layers. With these maps, we can detect a batch of candidate patches (proposals) of human body parts for the subsequent task.

Due to the low resolutions and discontinuities of depth images, the generated body part proposals may include many false positives. To overcome this issue in the second task, we develop an inference built-in MatchNet, which incorporates the feed-forward inference step into the deep architecture for seeking the optimal configuration of body joints. The original version of MatchNet [10] was proposed to jointly learn the patch-based features and distance metric. Here we adapt it for the following goals: i) measuring the unary appearance compatibility of the body part proposals with the standard part templates, and ii) measuring the geometric consistency of two body parts in the 3-D coordinate. We represent the human pose via a kinematic tree-based structure. (See Fig. 1 for clarification)

Moreover, we treat the Dynamic Programming inference as an extra neural layer, which is built upon the neural layers to generate best part configurations based on calculated appearance and geometric compatibility. Given all the optimized parameters, the dynamic programming inference computes the optimal configuration from the leaf nodes (e.g., feet and hand nodes) of the proposed kinematic tree-based structure to the root node (say head nodes).

The two tasks in our learning framework are cascaded yet complementary to each other. The employed FCN is able to coarsely localize the candidate part proposals in a real-time speed. Then, the inference built-in MatchNet employs a more complex and deeper architecture to improve the final pose estimation accuracy from a global perspective. Therefore, jointly optimizing the two cascaded networks can benefit both accuracy and efficiency. Another advantage of our framework is the natural embedding of inference, that is, the heavy computational demand can be counter-balanced in a parallel manner by using Graphic Processing Unit (GPU).

The main **contributions** of this work are summarized as follows. First, we propose a task-driven deep learning model achieving a new state-of-the-art performance in predicting human body joints from still depth images. Our extensive experiments and comparisons with the existing approaches demonstrate the effectiveness and efficiency of our model. Second, the integration of dynamic programming inference with deep neural networks is original in the literature to the best of our knowledge. At last, we release a large-scale dataset of depth images for human pose estimation, which includes 100K depth images with various challenges.

The remainder of the paper is organized as follows. Sect. 2 presents a review of related works. Then we present our inference embedded multi-task learning model in Sect. 3, fol-

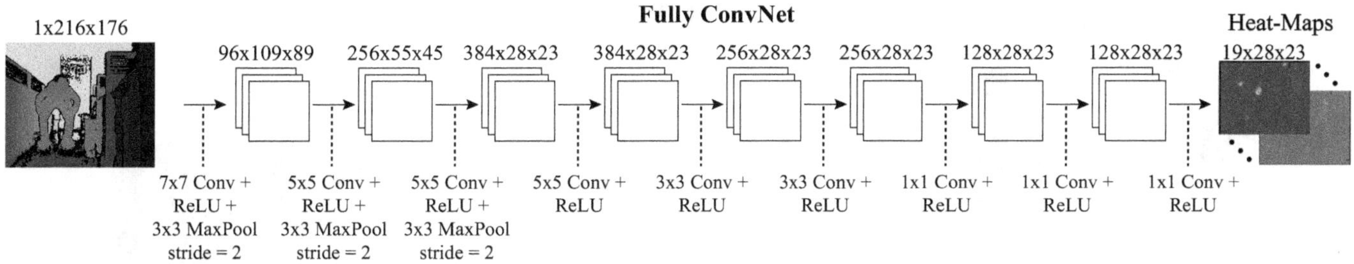

Figure 3: The architecture of the proposed fully convolutional network for the part proposal generation.

lowed by the multi-task learning procedure of our model in Sect. 4. The experimental results, comparisons and component analysis are exhibited in Sect. 5. Sect. 6 gives a conclusion of this paper.

2. RELATED WORK

Estimating the human pose from unconstrained color data is an important but challenging problem. Many approaches have been recently developed [29, 28, 13, 9, 46, 11, 22, 21, 20, 40]. Mori et al. [28] introduced an edge-based histogram, named "shape-context", to represent exemplar 2D views of the human body in a variety of different configurations and viewpoints with respect to the camera. Grauman et al. [9] introduced silhouette shape features to infer 3D structure parameters using a probabilistic multi-view shape model. More recently, Pictorial Structures [6, 4] and Deformable Part Models [3, 17, 26] were proposed and have achieved tractable and practical performance on handling large variances of the body parts. As a result, large amounts of related models have been subsequently developed. Yang et al. [48] proposed to capture orientation, co-occurrence and spatial relations with a mixture of templates for each body part. In order to introduce richer high-level spatial relationships, Tian et al. [36] presented a hierarchical spatial model that can capture an exponential number of poses with a compact mixture representation on each part. Kiefel et al [15] presented a binary conditional random field model to detect human body parts of articulated people in a single color image.

As for estimating human pose from depth data, several approaches [31, 8, 34, 32, 33, 14, 35, 2] have also been proposed. Shotton et al. [31] employed a random forest classifier to perform per-pixel classification of parts, and clustered these pixels for each part to localize the joints. Girshick et al. [8] developed an approach for general-activity human pose estimation from depth images by building upon Hough forests. Shotton et al. [32] further made an extension by adopting the regression forest to directly regress the positions of body joints with the use of a large, realistic and highly varied synthetic set of training images. Jung et al. [14] proposed a highly efficient approach, which applies a supervised gradient descent and MCMC like random sampler in the form of Markov random walks beyond the pixel-wise classification. All these approaches suffer from the fact that they use hand crafted features such as HoG features, edges, contours, and color histograms.

Recently, deep convolutional neural networks (CNNs) [16] with sufficient training data have achieved remarkable success in computer vision. Several approaches have been proposed to employ CNNs to learn feature representation for human pose estimation. Toshev et al. [39] formulated the pose estimation as a deep CNN based regression problem towards body joints. Tompson et al. [38] proposed a novel hybrid architecture that consists of a convolutional neural network and a Markov Random Field for human pose estimation in the color monocular images. In [37], Tompson further proposed an efficient 'position refinement' model that is trained to estimate the joint offset location within a small region of the image. Chen et al. [1] presented a deep graph model, which exploits deep CNNs to learn conditional probability for the presence of parts and their spatial relationships within these parts.

3. INFERENCE EMBEDDED MULTI-TASK LEARNING

In this section, we present our inference embedded multi-task learning framework. Our model first generates the heat (confidence) maps of body parts via a fully convolutional network, and further predicts body joints based on the generated body part proposals via the introduced inference built-in MatchNet.

3.1 Fully Convolutional Network

Motivated by the recent methods [38, 39], we regard the body part proposal generation as a problem of deep convolutional neural network regression. As shown in Fig. 3, given an input depth image, our model produces a dense heat map output for each body part via a fully convolutional network (FCN), which is stacked by nine convolutional layers. Though a little deeper than [39] in the architecture, this FCN has smaller computation demands due to the small number and size of our used filters, i.e., much fewer network parameters. The output of FCN, called heat map, denotes a per-pixel likelihood for K human body parts. We regard the coordinates of maximum value of the predicted heat-map (x_k^*, y_k^*) as the center position of the k-th body part, $k = [1, ..., K]$.

$$(x_k^*, y_k^*) = \max_{x_k, y_k} z(k|I; \theta_c) \tag{1}$$

where θ_c denotes the network parameters, $z(k|I; \theta_c)$ denotes the output heat map of the k-th body part for the input depth image I. Note that, since the neighboring pixels of the predicted heat-map also have similar heat values, only considering the maximum value may not achieve high accuracy for subtle localization of body parts. Based on this observation, we generate the predictions within the observation window (say 17×17) of the maximum value's position to increase the number of candidate body part proposals.

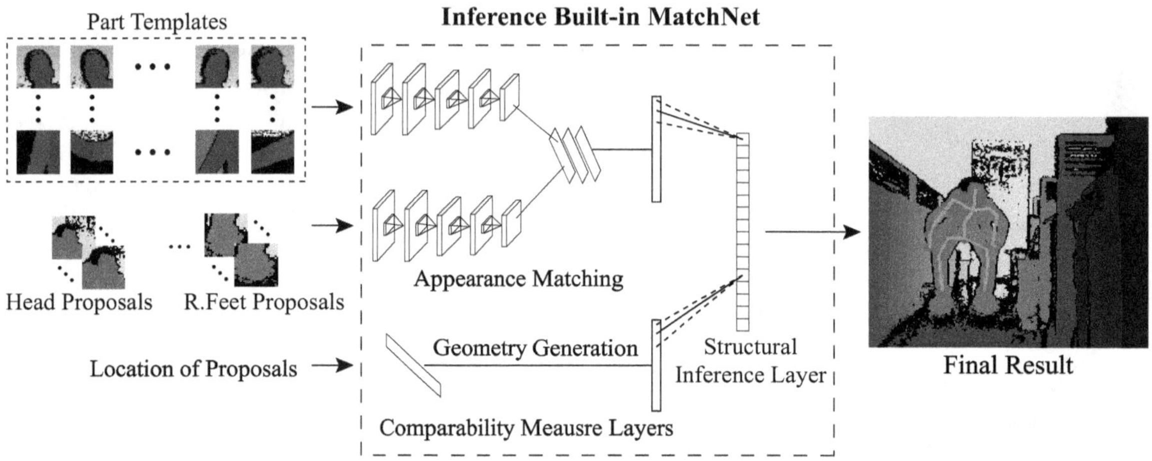

Figure 4: The illustration of the inference built-in MatchNet for a fast part configuration inference.

To express a body part proposal for the k-th body part, we specify the body part proposal $\mathbf{b}_i^k{=}[x_i, y_i, w_i, h_i, k]$, where (x_i, y_i) denotes the center coordinates of the body part proposal $\mathbf{b}_i^k$, w_i and h_i denotes the width and height of $\mathbf{b}_i^k$, respectively. Note that, since our final goal is the human pose estimation, w_i and h_i are not necessary to be very accurate, thus they are pre-defined and fixed as 10 pixels' distance between opposing joints on the human torso in our implementation.

3.2 Inference Built-in MatchNet

Our approach represents the human pose with a 3D kinematic K-node tree structure $\mathcal{G}{=}\{\mathcal{V}, \mathcal{E}\}$, where the node set $\mathcal{V}$ ($K{=}|\mathcal{V}|$) denotes the positions of body-joints/parts of the human pose, and the edge set $\mathcal{E}$ specifies the relationships of these body-joints/parts (see Fig. 4). Given the candidates for the k-th and m-th body part in the depth image I, we define the 3D spatial relationship between the i-th and j-th body part proposals as $R(\mathbf{b}_i^k, \mathbf{b}_j^m|I)$. Considering the local appearance compatibility of each body part and global contextual relationships between body parts, the score function F of our model is defined as the sum of unary and pairwise terms according to the proposed kinematic tree structure:

$$F(\hat{g}|I) = \sum_{k=1}^{K} U(\mathbf{b}_i^k|I) + \sum_{m\in\Omega_k} R(\mathbf{b}_i^k, \mathbf{b}_j^m|I), \tag{2}$$

where $i, j \in \{1, ..., n\}$ and n is the total number of the body part proposals, I denotes the input depth image with K body parts inside, the unary term $U(\mathbf{b}_i^k|I)$ gives local evidence for the body part k to lie at the center of the i-th body part proposal. The pairwise term $R(\mathbf{b}_i^k, \mathbf{b}_j^m|I)$ captures the geometric compatibility of the k-th and m-th body parts, where m belongs to k's neighboring body part set Ω_k. $\hat{g}$ is the hidden variable in our model to configure the body part proposals for the final human pose estimation.

Unary Terms: The unary terms $\{U(\mathbf{b}_i^k|I)\}_{k=1}^K$ are defined based on the local body part proposal $\mathbf{b}_i^k$. Inspired by the recent deep patch-based matching technique [10], we learn to extract features from body part proposals to calculate the appearance similarity. In our model, the appearance potential for the i-th body part proposal is measured according to the level of similarity between the extracted features of the proposal $\mathbf{b}_i^k$ and the ones of the standard k-th body part templates, i.e., the similarity between input proposals $\mathbf{b}_i^k$ and the part template set $\mathbf{B}_*^k = \{\mathbf{b}_t^k\}_{t=1}^T$. To handle unusual poses/views, diverse templates for each body part are off-line learned via K-means clustering to represent various possible appearance/orientation of human poses. Specifically, the appearance potential score for the body part proposal $\mathbf{b}_i$ being the i-th body part is defined as:

$$\begin{aligned} U(\mathbf{b}_i^k|I) =& \omega_k \cdot \phi(\mathbf{b}_i^k, \mathbf{B}_*^k|I; \theta_u^k) \\ =& \omega_k \cdot \sum_{t=1}^{T} \phi(\mathbf{b}_i^k, \mathbf{b}_t^k|I; \theta_u^k), \end{aligned} \tag{3}$$

where $\phi(\cdot, \cdot|\cdot; \theta_u^k)$ is the appearance score term for being the k-th body part with the parameters θ_u^k.

Pairwise Terms: Besides matching the generated part proposal with part templates via the appearance similarity, we consider the geometry relationships among different human body parts, and define the pairwise terms accroding to the 3D kinematic constraint. Specifically, the constraints for the neighboring body parts are represented by the spatial deformation [3] of the 3D geometric layout. The pairwise terms are:

$$R(\mathbf{b}_i^k, \mathbf{b}_j^m|I) = \Gamma_{km}\psi(\mathbf{b}_i^k, \mathbf{b}_j^m), \tag{4}$$

where $\psi(\mathbf{b}_i^k, \mathbf{b}_j^m)$ denotes the 3D displacement vector, i.e., $[dx, dx^2, dy, dy^2, dz, dz^2]^T$ of the body part proposal $\mathbf{b}_j^m$ relative to $\mathbf{b}_i^k$, Γ_{km} corresponds to the spatial deformation parameter, which indicates the contextual 3D spatial relations between the k-th and m-th body parts.

Inference built-in MatchNet In our approach, the inference procedure is to predict body joints based on currently generated part proposals $\mathbf{B} = [..., \mathbf{b}_i^k, ...]$ by taking the appearance and geometric compatibility into account. The proposed inference built-in MatchNet integrates three components into a unified network architecture: i) Appearance matching to obtain appearance evidence (unary terms); ii) Geometry generating to calculate the 3D kinematic constraint (pairwise terms); iii) Structural inference to maximize the score function F as:

$$\max_{\hat{g}} \mathbf{w} \cdot F(\hat{g}|I), \tag{5}$$

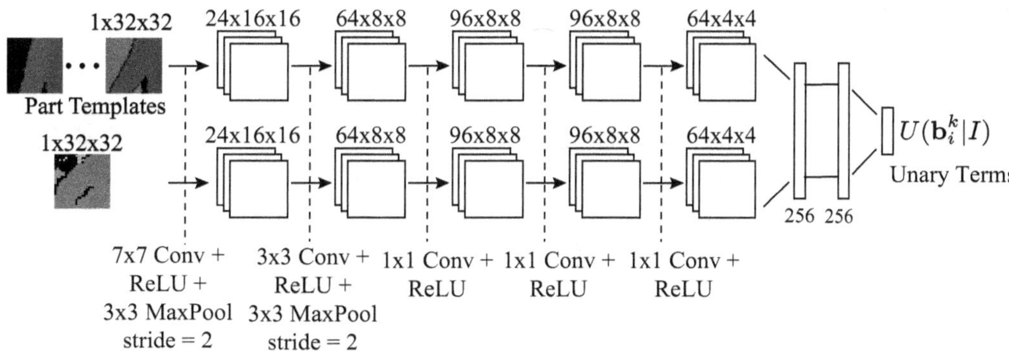

Figure 5: The architecture of the appearance matching component.

where $\mathbf{w}$ denotes all the parameters of the inference built-in MatchNet for simplicity, i.e., $\mathbf{w}= \{\Gamma_{km}, \omega_k\}_{k=1,m=1}^{K}$.

4. MULTI-TASK LEARNING

Since our model includes two types of networks for human pose estimation, the network structure and parameters are optimized in a multi-task learning way. Let $\mathcal{D} = \{(I_1, g_1), ..., (I_l, g_l), ..., (I_N, g_N)\}$, be a set of training samples, where g_l denotes the annotated pose configuration for the K body parts of the depth image I_l. In the following section, we will present the details of how our model learns to generate the part proposal $\mathbf{b}_i^k$ and search for optimal configuration $\hat{g}_l$ from the candidate body part proposals under 3D kinematic constraint for the final pose estimation.

Fully Convolutional Network: We employ the widely used batch Stochastic Gradient Descent (SGD) algorithm to train this network. Specifically, given the input depth image I_l, we employ the Mean Squared Error (MSE) criterion to minimize the distance between the predicted output $z(k|I_l;\theta_c)$ and the ground truth heat-map $H(g_k|I_l)$ as [37], where $H(g_k|I_l)$ is a 2D Gaussian with a small variance and mean centered at the ground truth joint locations:

$$\min_{\theta_c} \sum_{l=1}^{N} \sum_{k=1}^{K} \|z(k|I_l;\theta_c) - H(g_k|I_l)\|_2^2. \tag{6}$$

Inference built-in MatchNet: During training the fully convolutional network, the inference built-in MatchNet is optimized simultaneously. As illustrated in Fig. 4, there are two different types of layers in our model: the comparability measure layers and structural inference layer.

Comparability Measure Layers: The goal of these layers is to measure the appearance similarity between ground truth body parts and candidate body part proposals, which are generated by the fully convolutional network. Motivated by recent deep patch matching technique [10], we employ a two-tower like neural network to jointly train the feature extraction and metric learning layer in a supervised setting (See Fig. 5). The network parameters is also optimized by using SGD with the cross-entropy error:

$$\begin{aligned} E = -\frac{1}{N \cdot T} \sum_{l=1}^{N} \sum_{t=1}^{T} & \mathrm{y}_i \log\left(\phi(\mathbf{b}_i^k, \mathbf{b}_t^k|I_l;\theta_u^k)\right) \\ & +(1-\mathrm{y}_i)\log\left(1-\phi(\mathbf{b}_i^k, \mathbf{b}_t^k|I_l;\theta_u^k)\right) \end{aligned} \tag{7}$$

where $\mathbf{b}_t^k$ is one of the body part templates for the k-th body part, and is obtained by clustering all the ground truth body part regions into T centers via the K-means algorithm directly on the raw depth pixel. y_i is the 0/1 label for the input proposal pair $\{\mathbf{b}_i^k, \mathbf{b}_t^k\}$ (1 indicates match, i.e., the Intersection of Unit (IoU) between the predicted $\mathbf{b}_i^k$ and ground truth $\mathbf{b}_t^k$ is larger than 0.5). $\phi(\mathbf{b}_i^k, \mathbf{b}_t^k|I;\theta_u^k)$ is the output activation value of two-tower structure network, which represents the probability for being a matched pair. θ_u^k is the network parameter to be optimized for the k-th body part.

Structural Inference Layer: In our method, the configuration of body part proposals $\mathbf{B}$ for the depth image I_l is determined by the latent variable $\hat{g}_l$. The MSE function $h(\hat{g}_l, g_l)$ is used to minimize the distance between the predicted body part location of the configuration $\hat{g}_l$ and the ground truth configuration of g_l. To simplify, $h(\hat{g}_l, g_l)$ is binarized according to the empirical threshold variable τ as follows:

$$h(\hat{g}_l, g_i) = \begin{cases} 0, & \mathrm{MSE}(\hat{g}_l, g_l) \le \tau \\ 1, & \text{otherwise.} \end{cases} \tag{8}$$

where $\mathrm{MSE}(\hat{g}_l, g_l)$ denotes the average MSE error between the predict configurations $\hat{g}_l$ and the ground truth configuration g_l.

During the training phase, we optimize this layer by a latent learning method extended from the CCCP framework [49] in a dynamic manner. The learning objective of this layer is to learn the parameter set $\mathbf{w}$ as described in Sect. 3.2, which can be formulated as follows:

$$\begin{aligned} & \min_{\mathbf{w}} \frac{1}{2}\|\mathbf{w}\|_2^2 + C\sum_{l=1}^{N} \max_{\hat{g}_l}(\mathbf{w} \cdot F(\hat{g}_l|I_l) - h(\hat{g}_l, g_l) \\ & \quad - \max_{\hat{g}_l}(\mathbf{w} \cdot F(g_l|I_l)) \\ & = \frac{1}{2}\|\mathbf{w}\|_2^2 + C\sum_{l=1}^{N} \max_{\hat{g}_l}(\mathbf{w} \cdot F(\hat{g}_l|I_l) - h(\hat{g}_l, g_l) \\ & \quad - C\sum_{l=1}^{N} \max_{\hat{g}_l}(\mathbf{w} \cdot F(g_l|I_l)) \\ & = f_1(\mathbf{w}) - f_2(\mathbf{w}) \end{aligned} \tag{9}$$

where $\mathbf{w} = \{\omega_k, \Gamma_{km}\}_{k=1,m=1}^{K}$, and C is a penalty parameter set empirically. Following the CCCP framework, we convert the function into a convex and concave form as $f_1(\mathbf{w}) - f_2(\mathbf{w})$, where $f_1(\mathbf{w})$ represents the first two terms,

Algorithm 1

Input: Training samples $(I_1, g_1), (I_2, g_2), ..., (I_N, g_N)$
Output: The parameters of our model $\{\theta_c, \theta_u \mathbf{w}\}$
Initialization:

Initialize FCN's parameters θ_c, the inference built-in MatchNet's network parameter θ_u and structural inference parameters $\mathbf{w}$.

repeat

1: Optimize the fully convolutional network via Eqn. (6) and generate candidate body part proposals $\mathbf{B}$;
2: Given $\mathbf{B}$, optimize the network parameter θ_u via Eqn. (7), and calculate the unary and pairwise terms;
3: Given the unary and pairwise terms, optimize structural inference parameters $\mathbf{w}$ via Eqn. (9);

until The optimization function Eqn. (2) converges

Figure 6: Human pose examples from the K2HGD dataset. The ground truth body parts are illustrated in red and connected in white.

and $f_2(\mathbf{w})$ the last term. This leads to an iterative learning algorithm that alternates between estimating model parameters and the hidden variables. This type of learning problem is known as a structural SVM, and there are many solvers as the cutting plane solver [5] and SGD based solver [3].

The entire algorithm for multi-task learning can be summarized into Algorithm 1.

5. EXPERIMENTS

In this section, we compare our model with several state-of-the-art methods and SDKs, and justify the effectiveness of each component.

5.1 Dataset and Parameter Setting

Dataset. We evaluate the human pose estimation performance of our inference-embedded multi-task learning framework on our Kinect2 Human Gesture Dataset (K2HGD)[1], which includes about 100K depth images with various human poses under challenging scenarios. As illustrated in Fig. 6, this dataset consists of 19 body joints of 30 subjects under ten different challenging scenes. The subject is asked to perform both normal daily poses and unusal poses. The human body joints are defined as follows: *Head, Neck, UpperSpine, MiddleSpine, DownSpine, RightShoulder, RightElbow, RightWrist, RightHand, LeftShoulder, LeftElbow, LeftWrist, LeftHand, RightHip, RightKnee, RightFoot, LeftHip, LeftKnee, LeftFoot.* The ground truth body joints are firstly estimated via the Kinect SDK, and further refined by active users.

[1]http://vision.sysu.edu.cn/projects/k2hpd

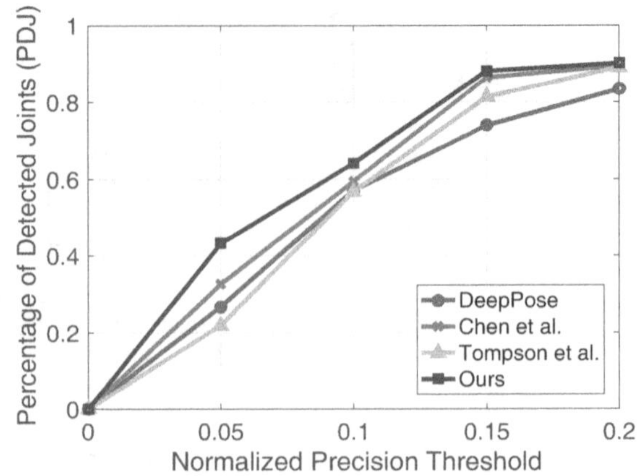

Figure 7: Performance comparison with three state-of-the-art methods on PDJ curves of average body parts on the K2HGD dataset.

Method	DeepPose [39]	Chen et al. [1]	Tompson et al. [37]	Ours
PDJ (0.05)	26.8%	32.6%	21.9%	**43.2%**
PDJ (0.10)	57.1%	59.5%	56.8%	**64.1%**
PDJ (0.15)	73.9%	86.5%	81.3%	**88.1%**
PDJ (0.20)	83.4%	89.5%	89.0%	**91.0%**
Average	60.3%	67.0%	62.3%	**71.6%**

Table 1: Detailed comparison of the estimation accuracy on the K2HGD dataset. The entries with the best precision values for each row are bold-faced.

Compared Methods. On the K2HGD dataset, we make a quantitative comparison with three deep state-of-the-art methods: DeepPose [39], Tompson et al. [37] and Chen et al. [1]. We adopt their public implementations. Due to commercial reasons, the widely used OpenNI SDK and Microsoft SDK are not supported to estimate human pose in given still depth images. Hence, we conduct a qualitative comparison with them.

Metric. To measure the accuracy of predicting human body joints, we employ the popular Percent of Detected Joints (PDJ) metric as the evaluation criterion. This metric considers a body joint is correctly estimated only if the distance between the predicted and the true joint position is within a certain fraction of the torso diameter. Given different normalized precision threshold (i.e., normalized distance to the ground truth body part), the estimation accuracy is obtained under different degrees of overall localization precision.

Experimental Details. In all experiments, 60K still depth images are used for training while the rest 40K used for testing. We set the parameters $\{n, \tau, K, C, T\} = \{$ 289, 0.2, 19, 0.001, 10$\}$. The patch size of each part is set to 32×32. Our model is implemented on Caffe library [12]. All of our experiments are carried out on an intel 3.4 GHz and a NVIDIA GTX-980Ti GPU. In order to reduce overfitting, we

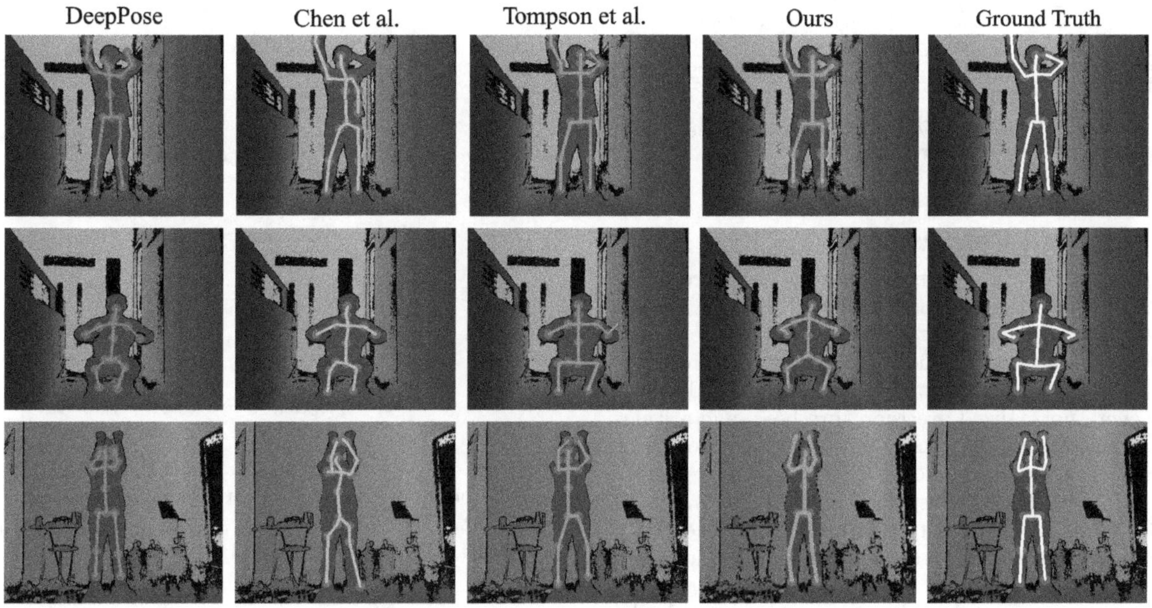

Figure 8: Qualitative comparison with the existing state-of-the-art methods. The estimation is perfromed on the whole depth image. We have cropped some irrelevant background for better viewing.

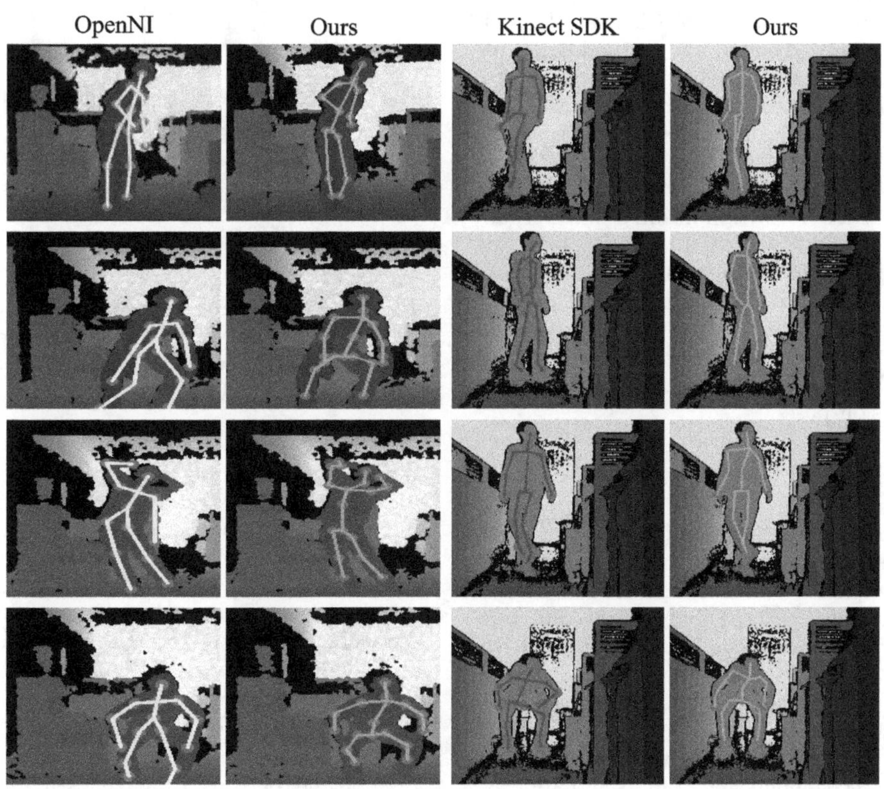

Figure 9: Qualitative comparison with OpenNI and Kinect SDK. The results of OpenNI are in yellow lines. The results of Kinect SDK are in blue lines. The results of our method are in green lines.

employ the common cropping and horizontal-flipping strategy to augment the training data. In this way, spatial relationships between body parts and their neighbors can be increased. The learning rate for the fully convolutional networks is 0.01 while the momentum is 0.9, the weight decay is 0.0005 and the batch size is 20. The number of body parts K is set as 19 and 289 candidate proposals for each body part are generated. For the inference built-in MatchNet, the learning rate is 0.1 while the momentum is 0.9, the weight decay is 0.0005 and the batch size is 20.

Method	DeepPose [39]	Chen et al. [1]	Tompson et al. [37]	Ours
Time	0.02	7.6	0.2	0.04

Table 2: Comparison of the average running time (seconds per image) on the K2HGD dataset.

5.2 Results and Comparisons

Quantitative Comparison. The quantitative comparison results is demonstrated in Fig. 7 and Tab. 1. Fig. 7 shows the PDJ curves of ours model over the other three compared state-of-the-art methods. As one can see that, our approach consistently outperforms all the compared methods under every normalized precision threshold, and are significantly superior to others under the requirement of strict estimation accuracy, i.e., the normalized precision threshold ranges from 0 to 0.1. As illustrated in Tab. 1, our model achieves 11.3%, 4.6%, 9.3% better accuracy than DeepPose, the method of Chen et al. and Tompson et al. in average, respectively.

To justify the effectiveness of the proposed inference built-in strategy, we further quantitatively analyze time efficiency of our method and all compared approaches on the K2HGD dataset. As demonstrated in the Tab. 2, our method runs 190x and 5x faster than the approach of Chen et al. and Tompson et al., respectively. Though our method contains the time-consuming inference step as Chen et al. and Tompson et al., inference in our method is embedded in the forward process of networks. Hence, our method is much faster. Since DeepPose directly regresses all body parts in a holistic manner from the depth image, our method is 2x slower than it. However, our performance is significantly better than DeepPose.

Qualitative Comparison. Fig. 8 and Fig. 9 demonstrate the qualitative comparison of our method, OpenNI, latest Kinect SDK and three existing state-of-the-art methods. As one can see from Fig. 9 and Fig. 8, our method achieves more robust and accurate performance for predict unusual and self-occlusion poses.

5.3 Empirical Analysis

To perform a component analysis of our method, we conduct the following experiment to validate the contributions of different parts of the proposed framework. To justify the effectiveness of the proposed inference built-in MatchNet, we directly use the output, i.e., heat map, of the full convolutional network (FCN) inside our method to estimate human pose. This variant version of our method represents the pure performance of the FCN, and is denoted as "FCN"; we also use the output of appearance matching component to predict human pose. This variant version of our method represents the combination of FCN and appearance evidence via the standard MatchNet, and is denoted as "FCN+MatchNet". We compare it with our method both in average PDJ curves of body parts (See Fig. 10) and average PDJ estimation accuracy for each body part. (See Fig. 11).

Fig. 10 demonstrates that there lies a significant performance gap between our method and FCN. This validates the superiority of our proposed inference built-in MatchNet. As one can see from Fig. 10, "FCN+MatchNet" performs consistently better than FCN. This justifies the contribution of the appearance matching (unary term) inside our model. Moreover, we can also show the effectiveness of the 3D kinematic constraint (pairwise term) for the result that our method also outperforms FCN+MatchNet.

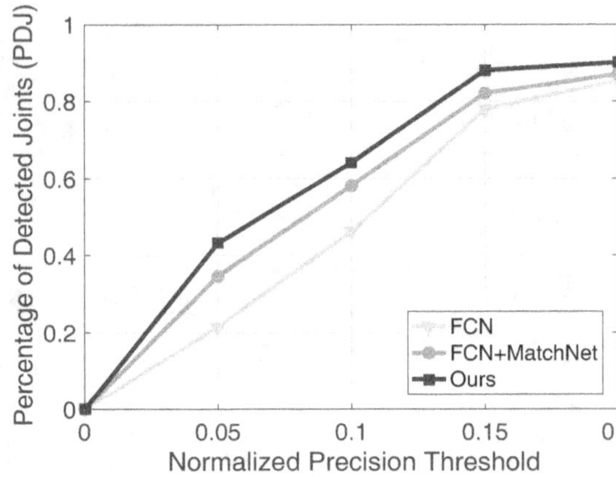

Figure 10: Component analysis for the contribution of different network in our model on the K2HGD dataset. The PDJ curves imply the average pose estimation accuracy of all body parts.

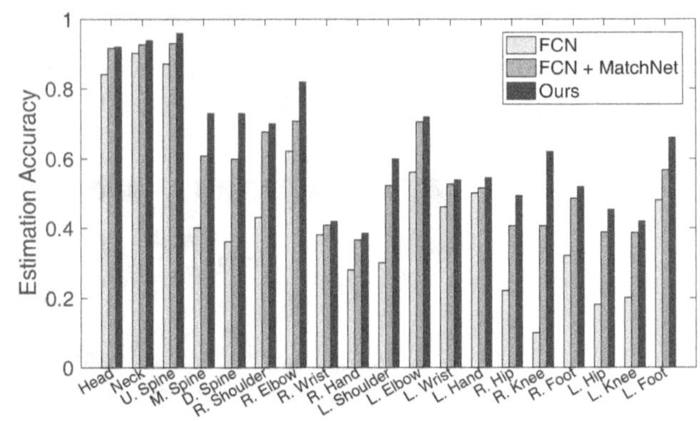

Figure 11: Component analysis for the contribution of different network in our model on the K2HGD dataset. The average PDJ accuracy for each body part is reported.

To explore the detailed improvement of our model's component, we report the PDJ for each body part in the Fig. 11, which also shows that the proposed inference MatchNet effectively improve the estimation accuracy, especially for {*Elbow, Shoulder, Knee, Foot*} body parts.

5.4 Limitations

The proposed framework may fail to estimate the poses of multiple persons from the still depth image. As the employed fully convolutional network can only output 19 heat maps for the body parts of a single person, our model may generate unsatisfying estimations due to the confusion body parts caused by multiple persons. Another limitation stems from our assumption, i.e., most of main body parts (e.g., torso, shoulder and spin) should be visible from depth data. Based on this assumption, we propose the above mentioned 3D kinematic constraint for the final pose estimation. Hence, our model may not work well when all main body parts are severely occluded.

6. CONCLUSION

We proposed a novel deep inference-embedded multi-task learning framework for predicting human pose from depth data. In this framework, two cascaded tasks were jointly optimized: i) detecting a batch of proposals of body parts via a fully convolutional network (FCN); ii) searching for the optimal configuration of body parts based on the body part proposals via a fast inference step (i.e., dynamic programming), which operates with a inference built-in MatchNet to incorporate the single term of appearance cost and the pairwise 3D kinematic constraint. We believe that it is general to be extended into other similar tasks such as object parsing. Extensive experiments validated the effectiveness of the proposed framework. In the future, we will try to support the pose estimation for multiple persons from depth data.

7. ACKNOWLEDGMENTS

We would like to thank Huitian Zheng and Dengke Dong for their preliminary contributions on this project. We gratefully acknowledge the support of NVIDIA Corporation with the donation of the GPU used for this research.

8. REFERENCES

[1] X. Chen and A. L. Yuille. Articulated pose estimation by a graphical model with image dependent pairwise relations. In *Advances in Neural Information Processing Systems (NIPS)*, pages 1736–1744, 2014.

[2] X. Chu, W. Ouyang, H. Li, and X. Wang. Structured feature learning for pose estimation. In *Proc. of IEEE Conference on Computer Vision and Pattern Recognition (CVPR)*, 2016.

[3] P. F. Felzenszwalb, R. B. Girshick, D. McAllester, and D. Ramanan. Object detection with discriminatively trained part-based models. *IEEE Transactions on Pattern Analysis and Machine Intelligence (TPAMI)*, 32(9):1627–1645, 2010.

[4] P. F. Felzenszwalb and D. P. Huttenlocher. Efficient matching of pictorial structures. In *Proc. of IEEE Conference on Computer Vision and Pattern Recognition (CVPR)*, pages 66–73, 2000.

[5] T. Finley and T. Joachims. Training structural svms when exact inference is intractable. In *Proceedings of the International Conference on Machine Learning (ICML)*, pages 304–311, 2008.

[6] M. A. Fischler and R. A. Elschlager. The representation and matching of pictorial structures. *IEEE Transactions on Computers*, C-22(1):67–92, 1973.

[7] R. Girshick, J. Donahue, T. Darrell, and J. Malik. Rich feature hierarchies for accurate object detection and semantic segmentation. In *Proc. of IEEE Conference on Computer Vision and Pattern Recognition (CVPR)*, 2014.

[8] R. Girshick, J. Shotton, P. Kohli, A. Criminisi, and A. Fitzgibbon. Efficient regression of general-activity human poses from depth images. In *Proc. of IEEE International Conference on Computer Vision (ICCV)*, pages 415–422, 2011.

[9] K. Grauman, G. Shakhnarovich, and T. Darrell. Inferring 3d structure with a statistical image-based shape model. In *Proc. of IEEE International Conference on Computer Vision (ICCV)*, 2003.

[10] X. Han, T. Leung, Y. Jia, R. Sukthankar, and A. C. Berg. Matchnet: Unifying feature and metric learning for patch-based matching. In *Proc. of IEEE Conference on Computer Vision and Pattern Recognition (CVPR)*, pages 3279–3286, 2015.

[11] C. Hong, J. Yu, D. Tao, and M. Wang. Multimodal deep autoencoder for human pose recovery. *IEEE Transactions on Image Processing (TIP)*, 2016.

[12] Y. Jia, E. Shelhamer, J. Donahue, S. Karayev, J. Long, R. Girshick, S. Guadarrama, and T. Darrell. Caffe: Convolutional architecture for fast feature embedding. *arXiv preprint arXiv:1408.5093*, 2014.

[13] S. Johnson and M. Everingham. Learning effective human pose estimation from inaccurate annotation. In *Proc. of IEEE Conference on Computer Vision and Pattern Recognition (CVPR)*, pages 1465–1472, 2011.

[14] H. Y. Jung, S. Lee, Y. S. Heo, and I. D. Yun. Random tree walk toward instantaneous 3d human pose estimation. In *Proc. of IEEE Conference on Computer Vision and Pattern Recognition (CVPR)*, pages 2467–2474, 2015.

[15] M. Kiefel and P. V. Gehler. Human pose estimation with fields of parts. In *Proc. of European Conference on Computer Vision (ECCV)*, 2014.

[16] A. Krizhevsky, I. Sutskever, and G. E. Hinton. Imagenet classification with deep convolutional neural networks. In *Advances in neural information processing systems (NIPS)*, 2012.

[17] X. Liang, L. Lin, and L. Cao. Learning latent spatio-temporal compositional model for human action recognition. In *Proceedings of the ACM International Conference on Multimedia (ACM MM)*, pages 263–272, 2013.

[18] X. Liang, S. Liu, X. Shen, J. Yang, L. Liu, L. Lin, and S. Yan. Deep human parsing with active template regression. *IEEE Transactions on Pattern Analysis and Machine Intelligence (T-PAMI)*, 37(12):2402–2414, 2015.

[19] X. Liang, S. Liu, Y. Wei, L. Liu, L. Lin, and S. Yan. Towards computational baby learning: A weakly-supervised approach for object detection. In *Proc. of IEEE International Conference on Computer Vision (ICCV)*, 2015.

[20] X. Liang, X. Shen, D. Xiang, J. Feng, L. Lin, and S. Yan. Semantic object parsing with local-global long short-term memory. In *Proc. of IEEE Conference on Computer Vision and Pattern Recognition (CVPR)*, 2016.

[21] X. Liang, C. Xu, X. Shen, J. Yang, S. Liu, J. Tang, L. Lin*, and S. Yan. Human parsing with contextualized convolutional neural network. In *Proc. of IEEE International Conference on Computer Vision (ICCV)*, 2015.

[22] Z. Liang, X. Wang, R. Huang, and L. Lin. An expressive deep model for parsing human action from a single image. In *Proc. of IEEE International Conference on Multimedia and Expo (ICME)*, 2014.

[23] L. Lin, G. Wang, R. Zhang, R. Zhang, X. Liang, and W. Zuo. Deep structured scene parsing by learning with image descriptions. In *Proc. of IEEE Conference on Computer Vision and Pattern Recognition (CVPR)*, 2016.

[24] L. Lin, G. Wang, W. Zuo, X. Feng, and L. Zhang. Cross-domain visual matching via generalized similarity measure and feature learning. *IEEE Transctions on Pattern Analysis and Machine Intelligence (T-PAMI)*, 2016.

[25] L. Lin, K. Wang, W. Zuo, M. Wang, J. Luo, and L. Zhang. A deep structured model with radius-margin bound for 3d human activity recognition. *International Journal of Computer Vision (IJCV)*, 118(2):256–273, 2016.

[26] L. Lin, X. Wang, W. Yang, and J. H. Lai. Discriminatively trained and-or graph models for object shape detection. *IEEE Transactions on Pattern Analysis and Machine Intelligence (TPAMI)*, 37(5):959–972, 2015.

[27] J. Long, E. Shelhamer, and T. Darrell. Fully convolutional networks for semantic segmentation. In *Proc. of IEEE Conference on Computer Vision and Pattern Recognition (CVPR)*, 2015.

[28] G. Mori and J. Malik. Estimating human body configurations using shape context matching, 2002.

[29] J. O'Rourke and N. I. Badler. Model-based image analysis of human motion using constraint propagation. *IEEE Transactions on Pattern Analysis and Machine Intelligence (TPAMI)*, 1980.

[30] Z. Peng, R. Zhang, X. Liang, X. Liu, and L. Lin. Geometric scene parsing with hierarchical lstm. In *Proc. of International Joint Conference on Artificial Intelligence (IJCAI)*, 2016.

[31] J. Shotton, A. Fitzgibbon, M. Cook, T. Sharp, M. Finocchio, R. Moore, A. Kipman, and A. Blake. Real-time human pose recognition in parts from single depth images. In *Proc. of IEEE Conference on Computer Vision and Pattern Recognition (CVPR)*, pages 1297–1304, 2011.

[32] J. Shotton, R. Girshick, A. Fitzgibbon, T. Sharp, M. Cook, M. Finocchio, R. Moore, P. Kohli, A. Criminisi, A. Kipman, and A. Blake. Efficient human pose estimation from single depth images. *IEEE Transactions on Pattern Analysis and Machine Intelligence (TPAMI)*, 35(12):2821–2840, 2013.

[33] J. Shotton, T. Sharp, A. Kipman, A. Fitzgibbon, M. Finocchio, A. Blake, M. Cook, and R. Moore. Real-time human pose recognition in parts from single depth images. *Commun. ACM*, 56(1):116–124, 2013.

[34] M. Sun, P. Kohli, and J. Shotton. Conditional regression forests for human pose estimation. In *Proc. of IEEE Conference on Computer Vision and Pattern Recognition (CVPR)*, pages 3394–3401, 2012.

[35] B. Tekin, A. Rozantsev, V. Lepetit, and P. Fua. Direct prediction of 3d body poses from motion compensated sequences. In *Proc. of IEEE Conference on Computer Vision and Pattern Recognition (CVPR)*, 2016.

[36] O. Tian, C. L. Zitnick, and S. G. Narasimhan. Exploring the spatial hierarchy of mixture models for human pose estimation. In *Proc. of European Conference on Computer Vision (ECCV)*, 2012.

[37] J. Tompson, R. Goroshin, A. Jain, Y. LeCun, and C. Bregler. Efficient object localization using convolutional networks. In *Proc. of IEEE Conference on Computer Vision and Pattern Recognition (CVPR)*, pages 648–656, 2015.

[38] J. Tompson, A. Jain, Y. Lecun, and C. Bregler. Joint training of a convolutional network and a graphical model for human pose estimation. In *Advances in Neural Information Processing Systems (NIPS)*, pages 1799–1807, 2014.

[39] A. Toshev and C. Szegedy. Deeppose: Human pose estimation via deep neural networks. In *Proc. of IEEE Conference on Computer Vision and Pattern Recognition (CVPR)*, pages 1653–1660, 2014.

[40] C. Wang, Y. Wang, Z. Lin, A. L. Yuille, and W. Gao. Robust estimation of 3d human poses from a single image. In *Proc. of IEEE Conference on Computer Vision and Pattern Recognition (CVPR)*, pages 2369–2376, 2014.

[41] F. Wang, W. Zuo, L. Lin, D. Zhang, and L. Zhang. Joint learning of single-image and cross-image representations for person re-identification. In *Proc. of IEEE Conference on Computer Vision and Pattern Recognition (CVPR)*, 2016.

[42] G. Wang, L. Lin, S. Ding, Y. Li, and Q. Wang. Dari: Distance metric and representation integration for person verification. In *Proc. of AAAI Conference on Artificial Intelligence (AAAI)*, 2016.

[43] K. Wang, L. Lin, W. Zuo, S. Gu, and L. Zhang. Dictionary pair classifier driven convolutional neural networksfor object detection. In *Proc. of IEEE Conference on Computer Vision and Pattern Recognition (CVPR)*, 2016.

[44] K. Wang, X. Wang, L. Lin, M. Wang, and W. Zuo. 3d human activity recognition with reconfigurable convolutional neural networks. In *Proceedings of the ACM International Conference on Multimedia (ACM MM)*, pages 97–106, 2014.

[45] K. Wang, D. Zhang, Y. Li, R. Zhang, and L. Lin. Cost-effective active learning for deep image classification. *IEEE Transactions on Circuits and Systems for Video Technology (TCVST)*, 2016.

[46] M. Wang, X. Liu, and X. Wu. Visual classification by l1-hypergraph modeling. *IEEE Transactions on Knowledge and Data Engineering*, 27(9):2564–2574, 2015.

[47] W. Y. P. L. J. H. Xiaodan Liang, Liang Lin and S. Yan. Clothes co-parsing via joint image segmentation and labeling with application to clothing retrieval. *IEEE Transactions on Multimedia (T-MM)*, 18(6):1175–1186, 2016.

[48] Y. Yang and D. Ramanan. Articulated human detection with flexible mixtures of parts. *IEEE Transactions on Pattern Analysis and Machine Intelligence (TPAMI)*, 35(12):2878–2890, 2013.

[49] A. L. Yuille and A. Rangarajan. The concave-convex procedure (cccp). In *Advances in Neural Information Processing Systems (NIPS)*, 2002.

[50] R. Zhang, L. Lin, R. Zhang, W. Zuo, and L. Zhang. Bit-scalable deep hashing with regularized similarity learning for image retrieval and person re-identification. *IEEE Transactions on Image Processing (T-IP)*, 24(12):4766–4779, 2015.

Cross-batch Reference Learning for Deep Classification and Retrieval

Huei-Fang Yang
Res. Center for IT Innovation
Academia Sinica, Taiwan
hfyang@citi.sinica.edu.tw

Kevin Lin
Inst. of Information Science
Academia Sinica, Taiwan
kevinlin311.tw@iis.sinica.edu.tw

Chu-Song Chen
Inst. of Information Science
Academia Sinica, Taiwan
song@iis.sinica.edu.tw

ABSTRACT

Learning feature representations for image retrieval is essential to multimedia search and mining applications. Recently, deep convolutional networks (CNNs) have gained much attention due to their impressive performance on object detection and image classification, and the feature representations learned from a large-scale generic dataset (e.g., ImageNet) can be transferred to or fine-tuned on the datasets of other domains. However, when the feature representations learned with a deep CNN are applied to image retrieval, the performance is still not as good as they are used for classification, which restricts their applicability to relevant image search. To ensure the retrieval capability of the learned feature space, we introduce a new idea called *cross-batch reference* (CBR) to enhance the stochastic-gradient-descent (SGD) training of CNNs. In each iteration of our training process, the network adjustment relies not only on the training samples in a single batch, but also on the information passed by the samples in the other batches. This inter-batches communication mechanism is formulated as a cross-batch retrieval process based on the *mean average precision* (MAP) criterion, where the relevant and irrelevant samples are encouraged to be placed on top and rear of the retrieval list, respectively. The learned feature space is not only discriminative to different classes, but the samples that are relevant to each other or of the same class are also enforced to be centralized. To maximize the cross-batch MAP, we design a loss function that is an approximated lower bound of the MAP on the feature layer of the network, which is differentiable and easier for optimization. By combining the intra-batch classification and inter-batch cross-reference losses, the learned features are effective for both classification and retrieval tasks. Experimental results on various benchmarks demonstrate the effectiveness of our approach.

Keywords

Image retrieval; image classification; CNN

MM '16, October 15–19, 2016, Amsterdam, The Netherlands

DOI: http://dx.doi.org/10.1145/2964284.2964324

1. INTRODUCTION

Learning effective feature representations plays a key role in content-based image retrieval (CBIR). When good features are employed, a retrieval algorithm would place images of similar content to a query at the front of a ranked list and those dissimilar (i.e., irrelevant) at the rear. In the past decade, features such as SIFT [22], Fisher vector (FV) [27, 28], and bag-of-words (BoW) were popular descriptors used in the retrieval systems. Recently, deep convolutional neural networks (CNNs) have re-emerged and advanced the performance of various visual recognition tasks, e.g., image classification, and they are capable of learning discriminative features directly from raw data. It is also suggested that CNN features trained on a large, diverse dataset (e.g., ImageNet [34]) can be transferred to other recognition tasks such as scene recognition [5] and object detection [8, 25]. In addition, the deep descriptors have been adopted for image retrieval [2, 3, 11, 46, 26] and have shown improved accuracy.

Despite better performance, most current retrieval approaches simply treat CNN representations learned from a classification task as off-the-shelf features and do not take full advantage of the CNN's ability to evolve its parameters into a feature space more suited to retrieval. This could hamper the retrieval performance because the features learned for classification may not be optimal for retrieval. In this paper, we consider the problem of learning feature representations favorable for retrieval in deep CNNs and introduce a new scheme to enhance the network training.

Our inspiration comes from the learning algorithm, stochastic gradient descent (SGD), that is widely employed for network training. In SGD, the gradient direction is computed over only the training samples in a mini-batch at each iteration. Hence, unlike gradient descent, SGD does not ensure convergence to a local minimum of the loss function. Even so, it enhances the chance of jumping out poor local minima through randomness, and could reach a better minimum in the optimization process. Performing optimization within a mini-batch also fulfills the physical requirement as most GPUs have limited on-board memory — the batch size should meet the memory constraint to avoid swapping, or the learning process will be intolerably slow. However, in batch-based learning, the network parameters are tuned via minimizing a loss function formed by the training samples in a batch only. When the number of training samples becomes large, the batch size appears relatively small; thus samples in a batch cannot reflect the main portion (nor even a small but significant part) of the data distribution.

To address the data scarcity problem in a mini-batch, we

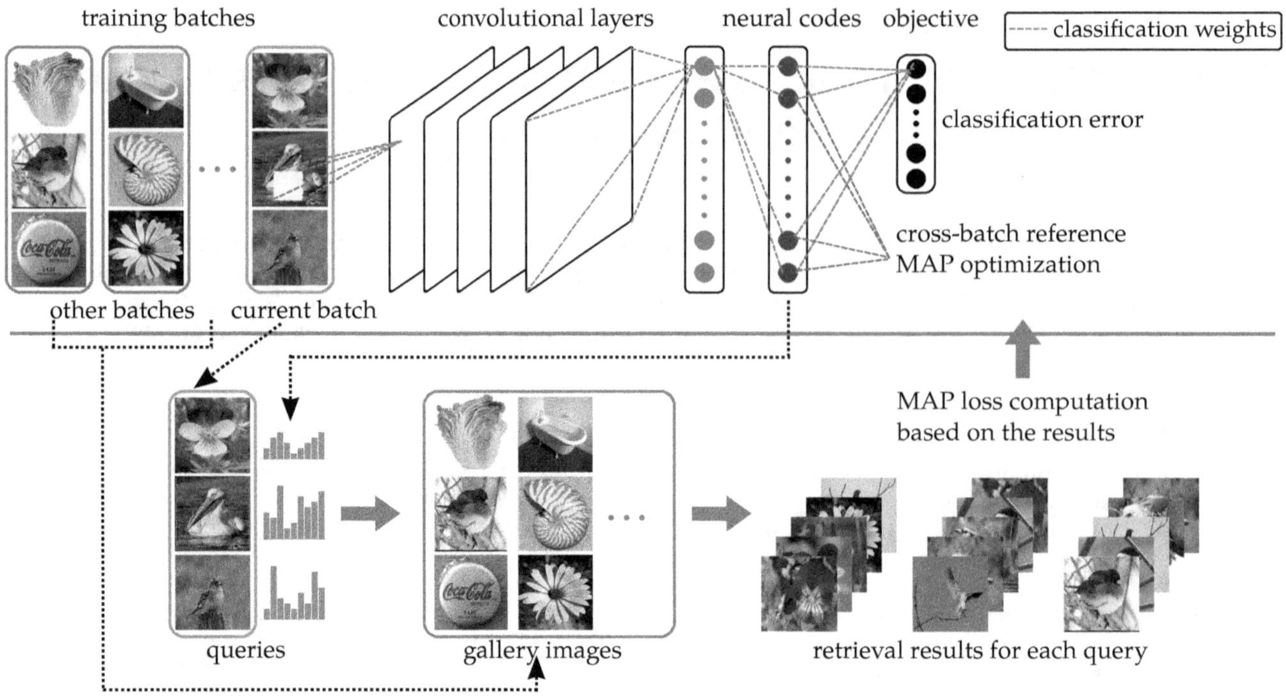

Figure 1: An overview of our method that combines the cross-batch reference (CBR) MAP optimization and the intra-batch classification loss. For the samples in a current batch, we use the neural codes as feature representations and perform retrieval in a cross-batch manner, where the gallery is composed of training samples in other batches. Our network can learn representations effective for retrieval if only the MAP criterion is employed; learn features effective for classification and retrieval when trained with both criteria.

introduce a new idea called *cross-batch reference* (CBR) to facilitate the learning of a feature space for retrieval. As its name suggests, the CBR employs information between mini-batches to enhance the SGD learning. At each iteration, the network parameters are adjusted based not only on the samples in a single batch but also on those distributed in others. This inter-batch communication is inspired by the nature of the retrieval process. The retrieval task aims at returning a ranked list of images, sorted by their relevance to a *query* from a *gallery*. Analogously, we treat the samples in the current batch (with respect to the current iteration) as the query and those in the remaining batches as the gallery. When the returned ranked lists are good, the *mean average precision* (MAP), a criterion that measures the goodness of a retrieval algorithm, should be as high as possible; that is, our network training involves optimizing the MAP criterion through cross-batch retrieval for learning a feature space in which the relevance between samples are well maintained. To our best knowledge, this is the first time that inter-batch information is integrated with deep CNN learning. Figure 1 gives an overview of our CBR learning method.

Direct maximization of the cross-batch MAP with SGD is computationally demanding because the discrete form of MAP is non-differentiable. A possible remedy is to smooth the MAP function to estimate its partial derivatives [19, 36]. However, the associated gradient computation is rather complicated. We instead introduce an approximated lower bound of MAP, which can be understood as the ratio of a weighted sum of affinities of relevant samples to the total affinity. Such a lower bound also simplifies the gradient computation. Maximizing this lower bound will make the relevant samples centralized (i.e., of high affinity) and keep the irrelevant ones apart (i.e., of low affinity) in the feature space, essentially following the distance-metric learning principle [42]. Moreover, when trained with the intra-batch classification loss and the cross-batch reference MAP loss, the network seeks feature representations effective for both image classification and retrieval tasks.

To sum up, our contributions are as follows: (1) We propose a novel learning idea, cross-batch reference learning, to enhance a network's capability of learning discriminative features for image retrieval. The employment of inter-batch communication facilitates optimizing the MAP loss; (2) We derive an approximate lower bound for the MAP loss that is difficult to optimize directly; the proposed bound is differentiable and easy to implement. Our proposed approach is versatile and can handle datasets with different levels of annotations. When only information of sample relevance is available, our network is capable of learning feature representations with merely the MAP criterion. When rich annotations such class labels are provided, our network learns discriminative descriptors effective for classification and retrieval with a learning objective that combines the classification loss and the MAP loss.

2. RELATED WORK AND BACKGROUND

The review focuses only on the work related to ours: deep learning for image retrieval and MAP maximization.

Deep Learning for Image Retrieval. Recent deep CNNs have shown their powerfulness on image classification and object detection. The seminal work AlexNet in [18] demonstrates that deep CNNs can achieve more favorable performance on large-scale image classification than conventional approaches. Following this direction, several advanced (and usually deeper) CNNs have been proposed, such as NIN [21], GoogleNet [39], VGG [38], ResNet [12], and so on. These networks provide strong tools to learn image representations in an end-to-end manner directly from the raw images.

The recent pioneer work in [18] also reveals that deep CNN can be applied not only to image classification but also image retrieval. The outputs of the deepest layer right before the classification layer of the network trained on a large-scale labelled dataset can be used as feature representations for image retrieval as well. Later, the work in [3] reports that such CNN features perform competitively on several standard retrieval benchmarks; in addition, by combining with PCA, the compressed compact representations can give good results too [3]. Apart from simply re-using the CNN features, domain-specific fine-tuning provides a way to obtain deep representations more favorable for retrieval. This can be achieved by fine-tuning the network on a dataset [3] related to the retrieval task or re-fining the network with a similarity learning objective on a target domain [41].

Though providing high-level visual content of an image, global CNN representations lack geometric invariance [11]. Hence, recent work has proposed methods for improvements. For example, the works in [11, 26, 31] extract and combine the activations of local patches at multiple scales for image retrieval. The approaches in [2, 23] aggregate the activations from the convolutional layers that carry information about local image regions better than fully connected layers. The works in object detection also focus on finding the local regions containing the objects of interest. For example, the approach of RCNN [9] demonstrates that the deep CNNs pre-trained for image classification can be used for object localization through fine-tuning and region proposals' identification on other datasets. Faster RCNN [33] shows that the region-proposal step of RCNN can be absorbed in the deep network, resulting in more effective and faster training processes for local object detection.

In this paper, we follow the idea of fine-tuning a pre-trained network to the retrieval task in the other domain. We use the entire image as the training samples without fully exploiting the patches or region proposals that could find more critical contents for image retrieval. Instead, our focus is on training the network with a MAP criterion and seeking to find a feature space optimal for retrieval through the new idea of CBR learning. Such a training criterion for feature learning has not been explored before in deep learning. The CBR learning also makes our work distinct from [43] that tackles the multimodal similarity learning problem by deep learning but with handcrafted features.

MAP Optimization. Performance evaluation criterion is a core part of many information retrieval problems, such as recommendation, web search, and online advertising. Our work is most germane to the recent research that aims to learn a model that optimizes the retrieval performance measures employed to evaluate the systems. Commonly used metrics include Discounted Cumulative Gain (DCG), Normalized Discounted Cumulative Gain (NDCG) [4, 49], ROCArea [36], and MAP. We focus on optimizing MAP because it is a popular criterion used to measure the performance of image retrieval approaches [10, 30, 50].

Optimization based on the performance measures directly is also referred to as the figure-of-merit learning [7]. However, directly optimizing objective functions composed of evaluation criteria is intractable due to the non-smoothness. Hence, in practice, some work has proposed to optimize a smoothed version of retrieval performance measure [16, 40]. For MAP maximization, sigmoid functions are used to approximate the ranks in the average precision (AP) computation in [19, 48], and hence a smoothed MAP can be optimized directly. Others have approached the problem alternatively by optimizing a continuous and differentiable bound of the losses defined on the evaluation measures, for instance, SVM^{map} [48] and AdaRank [47].

Unlike prior work, our MAP optimization is not restricted to be realized based on the samples only in a single batch like [19]. Inspired by the idea of cross-batch retrieval, we exploit inter-batch communication during network training to enhance the performance. Moreover, we introduce an approximate and differentiable bound that can be interpreted from the viewpoint of distance-metric learning; it is easily implementable by using current deep CNN packages.

3. METHOD

Our aim is to learn features effective for image classification and retrieval. The learning objective is given as:

$$\arg\min_{W} \quad \alpha E_{\text{class}}(W, W_c) - \beta E_{\text{map}}(W), \tag{1}$$

where $E_{\text{class}}(W, W_c)$ is the classification loss defined over samples in a batch, E_{map} is the cross-batch MAP loss we wish to maximize, α and β are parameters weighting the importance of each term, and W and W_c denote the network parameters that will be explained below.

This formulation lies in the multi-task learning paradigm, in which multiple related tasks are learned jointly by using shared representations. However, our approach differs from [6, 37] that use parallel networks to take multiple sources of inputs. The cross-batch reference helps learn a better feature space for image retrieval in addition to classification.

3.1 Preliminary

In a deep CNN, given an input sample, any intermediate layer can be employed to extract the features for the sample. Without loss of generality, we consider the case that the deepest layer right before the final classification layer is used for feature extraction, as illustrated in Figure 1.[1] The extracted feature representation is often referred to as the neural code of that sample.

Consider a sample x whose neural code is represented by $y = f(x; W)$, with $f(\cdot, \cdot)$ the deep feature extractor and W the network parameters controlling the outputs of the feature layer. When the data is of supervision labels, a classification layer is often added immediately after the feature extraction layer, which classifies the feature vector y by a discriminating function $h(y, W_c)$ learned by the network, where W_c denotes the parameters of the final classification layer.

In network training, the entire network parameters W and W_c are learned to correctly classify samples according to their class labels. The learned feature representation function $f(\cdot, W)$ is useful for various tasks. For example, it can be employed to extract features for new samples in the same or other related domains [5]. It can also be used in a transfer-learning manner that the parameters W are fine-tuned for

[1]Our approach can also be used when an intermediate layer or a combination of layers are used to acquire the feature representations.

Table 1: Listing of notations.

Notation	Definition
X	set of n training samples
x_i	the ith training sample
X_c	training samples in the current batch
x	a sample in the current batch X_c
D	training samples with X_c excluded
D_x	x's relevant samples in D
$\text{rank}_S(x_i)$	rank of x_i in set S, where S is D or D_x
W	set of network parameters
$f(x;W)$	neural codes (i.e., deep features) of x
$\text{sim}(x,x_i;W)$	similarity of x and x_i based on features depending on W
$d_i(x;W)$	dissimilarity between x and x_i
$AP(x)$	average precision of the returned list given query x
$MAP(X_c)$	mean average precision of query samples in X_c
$g(\cdot)$	a monotonically increasing function
σ_{x_i}	the weight for x_i
$\text{smax}(\cdot)$	the softmax function

the datasets of other domains, and then classification or retrieval are performed in the new domain [35, 41]. However, the classification-driven learning framework depicted above tends to learn features that are more favorable to classification but not retrieval. It is because that the classification goal forces the samples of different classes to be separated on different sides in the feature space, but does not enforce the relevant (and/or same-class) samples to be close to each other in the feature space. One such feature space thus performs worse when employed for relevant sample retrieval.

In classification-driven learning, the supervision (or driving goal) is set in the classification layer, and thus the feature layer is loosely controlled. A possible remedy to enhance the retrieval capability of the learned feature space is to set the goal directly on the feature layer. A question thus arises. How to set the goals in the feature layer? An intuitive idea is to use the mean feature of the relevant samples as the learning goal. By doing so, relevant images will be close to each other and form a group in the feature space. But, where can we obtain features that are representative enough for being used as the learning goals? Because all retrieval criteria require a gallery for the performance assessment, we propose to use the samples in the other batches as the gallery for deriving a practically useful goal to facilitate the learning of deep CNNs via SGD.

3.2 Cross-batch Retrieval Learning

To begin, we list the notations in Table 1. Let $X = \{x_i | i = 1 \cdots n\}$ be the set of training samples. It is divided into m disjoint batches, $X = X_1 \cup X_2 \cup \cdots \cup X_m$, for learning the network parameters with SGD. Each batch has l samples and $n = ml$. We use " $\sim$ " to represent the relevance of two samples. That is, $x_i \sim x_j$ means x_i is a relevant sample of x_j, and $x_i \nsim x_j$ means that they are irrelevant. Whether two samples are relevant depends on the settings of the datasets adopted. For some datasets, x_i and x_j are relevant if they share a common class label, whereas for others, x_i and x_j are relevant if they are near duplicates of similar visual contents.

To train a neural network by SGD (i.e., finding W), each iteration uses only the current batch for the objective function optimization. We extend SGD training with inter-batch association as follows. Consider an ongoing iteration. Our idea is to employ every sample in the current batch as a query to retrieve the samples in the remaining batches, so that cross reference between the present and the other batches is established. More specifically, for every training sample x in the current batch (say, X_c), the average precision (AP) is calculated for x; then the MAP is computed as the mean of the l APs obtained from the current batch, and a high MAP is desirable. In the following, we first investigate the analytic form of AP and then conduct a distance-metric learning criterion for MAP maximization.

Analytic Form of Average Precision (AP): AP is a retrieval criterion measuring whether relevant samples are placed at the top of an ordered list, in which images are ranked in a descending order based on their relevance to a query. For a query x and a gallery set D consisting of the training samples with those in the current batch excluded, $D = X \backslash X_c$, the AP of the returned list is

$$AP(x) = \frac{1}{|D_x|} \sum_{x_i \in D_x} \frac{\text{rank}_{D_x}(x_i)}{\text{rank}_D(x_i)}, \tag{2}$$

where $D_x = \{x_i \in D | x_i \sim x\}$ is the subset of x's relevant samples in D, $|D_x|$ is the cardinality of D_x (i.e., the number of x's relevant samples), and $\text{rank}_D(x_i)$ and $\text{rank}_{D_x}(x_i)$ are the ranks of x_i in the sets D and D_x, respectively.

To determine the rank of an element in a list, we need to evaluate the relevance between two images. We consider using the similarity of the features of two images in the feature space as a relevance indicator. Specifically, the similarity $\text{sim}(x, x_i; W)$ of images x and x_i is defined as the inner product of their respective features in our current study,[2]

$$\text{sim}(x, x_i; W) = f^T(x;W) f(x_i;W) = y^T y_i. \tag{3}$$

With the similarity defined above, one can easily compute the dissimilarity between two images as

$$d_i(x;W) = -\text{sim}(x, x_i; W).$$

Without loss of generality, we will use $d_i(x)$ to simplify the notation in what follows.

Given the dissimilarity measure, the rank of x_i in the sorted list of D_x can be written as the following closed-form equation,

$$\text{rank}_{D_x}(x_i) = \sum_{x_j \in D_x} I(d_i(x) - d_j(x)), \tag{4}$$

where $I(\cdot) = 1$ if the argument is greater than zero, and $I(\cdot) = 0$ otherwise. Similarly, the rank of a relevant sample x_i in the sorted list of D is obtained by

$$\text{rank}_D(x_i) = \sum_{x_k \in D} I(d_i(x) - d_k(x)). \tag{5}$$

The analytic form of AP is then obtained by substituting Eqs. (4), (5) into (2). The MAP is obtained by averaging

[2]Other similarity measures can be used in our framework as well. The inner product is used here because it can result in the soft-max functions easily realized by the powerful and currently popular deep CNN package, CAFFE [15].

the APs of query samples in the current batch X_c,

$$MAP(X_c) = \frac{1}{l}\sum_{x\in X_c}\frac{1}{|D_x|}\sum_{x_i\sim x}\frac{rank_{D_x}(x_i)}{rank_D(x_i)}, \qquad (6)$$

with $x_i \sim x$ an equivalent representation of $x_i \in D_x$.

Lower Bound of Average Precision (LAP): Direct maximization of the MAP is difficult because of the discrete form in the AP computation of Eq. (2). Some approaches [19] approximate the function $I(\cdot)$ with the sigmoid function to smooth the MAP. However, the resultant objective is fairly complex with nested sums of fractions.

We instead maximize a lower bound of $AP(x)$, which is more tractable and can be linked to distance-metric learning with an insightful interpretation. The lower bound, denoted as $LAP(x)$, is given as

$$\begin{aligned} LAP(x) &= \frac{1}{l|D_x|}\frac{\sum_{x_i\sim x} e^{-d_i(x)} g(\mathrm{rank}_{D_x}(x_i))}{\sum_{x_k\in D} e^{-d_k(x)}} \\ &= \frac{1}{l|D_x|}\frac{\sum_{x_i\sim x} e^{-d_i(x)} g(\mathrm{rank}_{D_x}(x_i))}{\sum_{x_k\sim x} e^{-d_k(x)} + \sum_{x_k\nsim x} e^{-d_k(x)}}, \end{aligned} \qquad (7)$$

where $g(\cdot)$ is a monotonically increasing function satisfying $g(z) \le z$, $z \in N^+$ (e.g., $g(x) = \sqrt{x}$). The proof of that $LAP(\cdot)$ is lower bound of $AP(\cdot)$ can be found in Appendix.

It is worth noting that the lower bound $LAP(x)$ is correlated to distance metric learning in a way that the term $e^{-d_i(x)}$ can be referred to as the *affinity* between x and x_i. With this in mind, we can further express the meaning of the lower bound as:

- The numerator of Eq. (7) is a weighted sum of the affinities between the query sample x and its relevant samples, each weighted by a monotonically increasing function $g(\mathrm{rank}_{D_x}(x_i))$ with respect to the rank of x_i in the retrieved relevant list.

- Similarly, the denominator of Eq. (7) is the sum of the affinities between the query sample x and all samples in the gallery D; it is also equivalent to the total affinity of both relevant and irrelevant samples.

When the weights $g(\mathrm{rank}_{D_x}(x_i))$ are set to 1 for all relevant samples, Eq. (7) becomes a common distance metric learning criterion. Maximizing Eq. (7) is then equivalent to maximizing the sum of affinities of the relevant samples over the sum of affinities of all samples. Hence, the relevant samples' total affinity is desired to be high, whereas the irrelevant samples' total affinity is expected to be low. A better distance-metric space is thus learned for the discrimination of the relevant and irrelevant samples. It enforces the relevant samples to be ranked on top of the retrieval list as their distances to the query are smaller.

Moreover, in the formulation of Eq. (2), the relevant samples placed on rear of a list gets larger weights, $g(\mathrm{rank}_{D_x}(x_i))$. Thus, lower-ranked relevant samples are assigned with higher penalties in the optimization, which coincides with the rational of enhancing the AP.

Finally, by replacing $-d_i(x)$ with $\mathrm{sim}(x, x_i)$ and overlooking the constant l, our MAP maximization turns into maximizing a loss formed by the lower bound of AP as:

$$\begin{aligned} &\arg\max_W \quad E_{\mathrm{map}}(W) \\ &= \sum_{x\in X_c}\frac{1}{|D_x|}\frac{\sum_{x_i\in D_x} e^{\mathrm{sim}(x,x_i;W)} g(\mathrm{rank}_{D_x}(x_i), W)}{\sum_{x_k\in D} e^{\mathrm{sim}(x,x_k;W)}}, \end{aligned} \qquad (8)$$

where X_c is the current batch and $D = X\backslash X_c$ is the set of the other batches.

3.3 Cross-batch Reference (CBR) Learning

An issue worthy of note lies in the computation of neural codes for gallery images. To optimize $E_{\mathrm{map}}(W)$ of Eq. (8), one has to compute the similarity between the neural codes of x and x_k, i.e., $\mathrm{sim}(x, x_k; W) = f^T(x_k; W)f(x; W)$. It thus requires the neural code $f(x_k; W)$ available for the sample x_k in other batches ($D = X\backslash X_c$). In an ideal setting, to keep neural codes up-to-date, the codes of all samples are to be updated once the network learning takes place. This would result in very complex partial derivatives with respect to W as well as slow computation that is infeasible in practice.

To address this issue, we relax the objective $E_{\mathrm{map}}(W)$ by keeping fixing the neural codes of x_k, denoted as y_k, when the current batch is employed in the optimization process. By doing so, the similarity between x and x_k in the feature space becomes $y_k^T f(x; W)$, and Eq. (8) can be re-written as

$$E_{\mathrm{map}}(W) = \sum_{x\in X_c}\frac{\sum_{x_i\sim x}\sigma_{x_i} e^{y_i^T f(x;W)}}{\sum_{x_k\in D} e^{y_k^T f(x;W)}}, \qquad (9)$$

where $\sigma_{x_i} = \frac{g(\mathrm{rank}_{D_x}(x_i))}{|D_x|}$. Because the codes y_i have been fixed, $\mathrm{rank}_{D_x}(x_i)$ can be initially determined by sorting the relevant samples in the gallery according to their similarities to the query x. The weight σ_{x_i} thus becomes a constant when the current batch is used for the optimization. Here, we choose $g(\cdot) = \sqrt{(\cdot)}$ to moderately increase the penalties of the samples that are relevant to x but ranked lower.

To set the target codes y_i for the gallery samples, two strategies could be adopted. One is to use the most recently updated codes when previous batches are used for training. The other is to update the codes for all samples every r batches. Currently, we choose the later in the implementation. The setting of r is dataset-dependent, typically $r = \eta m$ (where $\eta = 32$) in our experiments, with m the number of total batches. During learning, we update the target code twice, which amounts to $96m$ (including a step to learn features for better initialization) training batches for datasets with class labels and $64m$ for those without class labels.

To further simplify the implementation, we assign samples relevant to each other a representative code which is the average of their neural codes in the code-updating step. Consider a sample x in the current batch and its relevant samples $x_i \sim x$ in the other batches. When the codes $f(x_i; W)$ are re-computed via the updated parameters W in every r batches, we use the mean $y_i = \frac{1}{|D_x|}\sum_{x_i\sim x} f(x_i; W)$ as the target code for all x_i that are the relevant samples of x. This step further alleviates the computational burden because y_i are fixed for all $x_i \sim x$, and thus the term $e^{y_i^T f(x,W)}$ needs to be computed only once for each sample x in the current batch. Though the ranks of x's relevant samples are tie in this setting, lower ranked relevant samples will still get the same but a higher penalty weight. Consider that we wish to make relevant samples close; it implies that their neural codes should be as similar as possible and relevant samples would form a cluster in the feature space.

With this simplification, we do not have to exactly implement cross-batch retrieval that would be time consuming, but reduce it to a simpler setting of cross-batch *reference* (CBR) learning—the target codes are summarized (by averaging) from the other batches and provide the driving force for the feature-representation learning. Though a relaxation is adopted, as having been explained, the criterion is for distance-metric learning and is positive for increasing the AP; hence, it still benefits the separation of relevant/irrelevant samples and AP enhancement.

We implement our approach using the CAFFE [15] package. To realize the MAP maximization of Eq. (9), by letting $y = f(x; W)$ and

$$\text{smax}(y, y_i) = \frac{e^{y^T y_i}}{\sum_{x_k \in D} e^{y^T y_k}},$$

where smax(·) is the softmax function, we obtain Eq. (9) as

$$E_{\text{map}}(W) = \sum_{x \in X_c} \sum_{x_i \sim x} \sigma_{x_i} \text{smax}(y, y_i). \qquad (10)$$

Hence, for each sample x in the batch X_c, its E_{map} is formed by a linear combination of $|D_x|$ softmax functions. The MAP maximization can thus be easily realized via using the built-in softmax layer in CAFFE. More precisely, as each term $\sigma_{x_i}\text{smax}(y, y_i)$ is upper-bounded by σ_{x_i} (because softmax is upper-bounded by 1), maximizing E_{map} is equivalent to minimizing the difference between the outputs and the upper-bounds. We set the desired output of $\sum \sigma_{x_i}\text{smax}(y, y_i)$ as $\sum \sigma_{x_i}$ in our implementation for the MAP maximization in CAFFE. Algorithm 1 outlines our CBR learning.

Our network training is performed by using a machine with NVIDIA GTX Titan X GPU with 12 GB memory. When training with only the retrieval criterion, we add a CBR layer on top of the feature-extraction layer in CAFFE and set $\alpha = 0$; when training with both classification and retrieval criteria, we further add a standard classification layer in CAFFE and set both α and β as 1 in Eq. (1).

4. EXPERIMENTS

We start with experimental settings and then introduce the benchmarks. We present the results and performance comparison with the state-of-the-arts.

4.1 Experimental Settings

To explore the applicability of our method to different networks, we choose AlexNet [18] and VGG16 [38] as our network models. AlexNet is composed of 5 convolutional layers, followed by 2 fully connected layers and one classification layer; VGG16 is a deeper network with 13 convolutional layers, followed by 2 fully connected layers and one classification layer. In both networks, the dimension of the last fully connected layer is 4096, which is relatively high to be deployed in large-scale search. We hence add a new layer composed of 512 nodes right after the 4096-D layer and use it as the feature representation layer in our approach.

An important issue in the evaluation is determining the relevance between samples. For datasets annotated with class labels, following the common practice [44], we consider two images relevant if they share the same class label. For those lack of class labels, the relevance between images are derived from the ground-truth retrieval lists. Images in the same retrieval list are deemed relevant.

To train the network, we initialize its weights with the ones pre-trained on ImageNet and then fine-tune the features on the new domain with the MAP criterion with or without the classification loss.

Algorithm 1: Cross-batch Reference Learning (and Intra-batch Classification)

Input: Training samples divided into m batches, $X = X_1 \cup X_2 \cup ... \cup X_m$
Output: A set of non-linear projection parameters W
Step 1 (Initialization):
Fine-tune the network with only classification for better target codes if class labels are available;
Step 2 (Optimization):
iter = 0;
while *iter < max_iter* **do**
  if *iter is a multiple of* ηm **then**
    Extract neural codes of samples in other batches and compute the target codes;
  Compute the MAP loss of the current batch w.r.t to the target codes using Eq. (10);
  Update the network parameters W based on the MAP loss with back-propagation;
return W;

Table 2: Statistics of the datasets used.

Dataset	# Labels	# Gallery Images	# Queries
CIFAR-10	10	50,000	10,000
Flower-17	17	680	340
SUN397	397	100,754	8,000
Oxford	—	5,062	55
Paris	—	6,412	55

4.2 Datasets

We conduct experiments on datasets of diverse types to show the efficacy of our approach on image retrieval. The considered ones are with or without class labels; the images types include tiny objects of CIFAR-10, flowers of Flower-17, and scenes of SUN397, Oxford, and Paris. In addition, the data sizes range from small ($<$ 1K) to large ($>$ 100K); the number of class labels also varies greatly (from 10 to 397) when class labels are available. We elaborate on each dataset below.

CIFAR-10 [17] contains 60,000 32 $\times$ 32 color images categorized into 10 classes. The class labels are mutually exclusive, and thus each class has 6,000 images. The entire dataset is partitioned into two non-overlapping sets: a training set with 50,000 images and a test set with 10,000 images.
Flower-17 [24] contains 1,360 images in 17 categories, with 80 images per category. The dataset is split into the training (40 images per class), validation (20 images per class), and test (20 images per class) sets. In the experiments, we use only training and test sets.

Figure 2: Samples images from the CIFAR-10, Flower-17, SUN397, Oxford, and Paris datasets.

SUN397 [45] is a large scene dataset composed of 108,754 images in 397 categories. The number of images varies across categories, with each category containing at least 100 images. Following the settings in [20], we randomly select 8,000 images to form the query set for testing and use the remaining 100,754 as training samples.
Oxford [29] is a standard benchmark for instance-level image retrieval. It consists of 5,062 images corresponding to 11 Oxford landmarks. A set of 55 queries (5 per landmark) are used to evaluate the retrieval performance.
Paris [30] is another dataset for instance-level retrieval. It contains 6,412 images of Paris landmarks (e.g., Eiffel Tower, Notre Dame, and Louvre) collected from flickr. Same as the Oxford, the retrieval performance is assessed on 55 queries.

Information about the used datasets is shown in Table 2 and some samples images in Figure 2.

4.3 Results on CIFAR-10

CIFAR-10 is a labeled dataset and we thus train our network with a combination of the classification and CBR layers, or with only the CBR layer for retrieval. As a first experiment, we use a classic model, AlexNet, and compare our approach with two settings using the same network. One is the 4096-D features of AlexNet trained on ImageNet as signatures without fine-tunning. The other is the 4096-D AlexNet features fine-tuned on CIFAR-10.

Though recent studies [12, 21, 18, 31] have shown that the rich features of deep neural networks trained on large-scale datasets demonstrate outstanding performance on image classification, they are unfavourable for image retrieval as can be seen in Table 3. Fine-tuning boosts the performance by a significant margin, from a 39.66% MAP to 81.16%. Our method combining CBR and classification layers (named as CrossMAP + Class) further promotes the MAP to as high as 87.36%. These results suggest that the networks trained with the classification and MAP losses learn a feature space where relevant samples are centralized and irrelevant ones are apart. The classification accuracy of our CrossMAP+Class, 87.98%, is slightly worse than that obtained by using fine-tuned AlexNet, 89.56%. It reveals that our method considerably increases the retrieval performance with a little sacrifice of the classification performance.

We also train the network on CIFAR-10 by using only the CBR loss in our method, and report the retrieval performance in Table 3. Our method with the CBR layer only (CrossMAP) attains retrieval performance comparable to the network trained with two criteria. This indicates that our cross-batch reference MAP learning itself is effective for learning effective feature representations for retrieval.

4.4 Results on Flower-17

Our method is general and can be integrated with others networks. In this experiment, we present the results with a more recent model, VGG16, in addition to AlexNet. We train the network with a combination of classification and CBR layers by using our method.

Table 3: Performance of different methods on CIFAR-10. Acc. and MAP denote classification accuracy and mean average precision, respectively.

Method	Dim.	Acc.(%)	MAP(%)
AlexNet	4096	—	39.66
AlexNet, fine-tuned	4096	89.56	81.16
Ours, CrossMAP	512	—	88.40
Ours, CrossMAP+Class	512	88.75	87.36

Table 4: Performance of different approaches on Flower-17. Acc. and MAP denote classification accuracy and mean average precision, respectively.

Method	Dim.	Acc.(%)	MAP(%)
AlexNet, fine-tuned	4096	80.29	59.11
VGG16, fine-tuned	4096	89.11	71.25
Ours, AlexNet	512	83.82	86.44
Ours, VGG16	512	86.76	87.72

Table 4 compares our approach to those based on fine-tuned AlexNet and VGG16 features. Our approach has an advantage over the others in terms of the MAP. It is worth noting that our approach with the CBR layer to enhance the retrieval ability leads to 27.33% and 16.47% MAP points improvement compared to the fine-tuned AlexNet and VGG16, respectively. These results indicate that our network not only learns a feature space with great discrimination to flower categories but also forces features of relevant samples to be close to each other in the feature space. One may note that our approach performs more favorably when integrated with VGG16 than AlexNet. Hence, we opt for VGG16 as the network model for the rest experiments.

Figure 3 shows the top 8 retrieved images from the Flower-17 dataset with our learned compact 512-D neural codes and the 4096-D features of AlexNet. Our method is able to make neural codes of relevant images close even when they are in different viewpoints and sizes. In contrast, relevant samples are less centralized in the fine-tuned 4096-D feature space; the returned list contains many false positives.

4.5 Results on Paris

The Paris dataset contains landmark images, which greatly differ from the object images in ImageNet. Directly initializing the network with the pre-trained weights on ImageNet

Figure 3: Top 8 ranked returned images of using different feature representations on a sample query of the Flower-17. Images with red border are false positives. Upper row: ours. Lower row: AlexNet fine-tuned.

Table 5: Retrieval comparison of different methods on Paris. MAP denotes mean average precision.

Method	MAP(%)
BOW-200k-D [13]	59.11
Ng et al. [23]	69.40
CNN-aug-ss [31]	79.50
Multi-resolution-ss [32]	85.30
ReDSL.FC1 [41]	94.74
Ours	95.88

may not provide a good starting point for network training. As suggested in [3], we re-train the network on the Landmarks dataset with class label supervision for learning a feature space suited to building categorization. We then follow the settings in [41] and fine-tune the network with only the CBR layer because Paris provides no class labels. Also note that the Paris dataset does not specifically define the query and gallery images, i.e., a query image can also be a gallery image for the other queries. For a fair comparison, all query images are not used in network training.

Table 5 shows the comparison of our approach with VGG16 to other state-of-the-art retrieval methods, including those using traditional descriptors (BOW [13]), and CNN-based methods (ReDSL [41], Multi-resolution-ss [31], Ng et al. [23]). Our approach performs more favorably against the other approaches. We owe this to the reason that cross-batch reference learning can enhance the network with the ability of encouraging relevant samples to have similar neural codes, coinciding with the observations made on CIFAR-10 and Flower-17. Figure 4 shows the top returned images of our method for a sample query.

4.6 Results on Oxford

The Oxford dataset is similar to Paris and so we adopt the same training procedure in learning image representations. That is, we train VGG16 with the CBR layer only.

However, images in this dataset vary greatly in the viewpoints and scales. To tackle this problem, we employ the spatial search suggested in [31] in the testing stage. The spatial search extracts descriptors for local patches at multiple scales. The distance between a local query patch and a gallery image is defined as the maximum among the inner products of the query and gallery patches pairs. Then, the mean inner product of all query patches to the gallery is used as the relevance distance for retrieval.

Table 6 compares our method with state-of-the-arts. Our method with VGG16 achieves a MAP of 68.33%, comparable to several approaches but worse than ReDSL.FC1 [41] and [32]. This could be because CNN-aug-ss adopts a series of post-processing, including L2 normalization and power transform to enhance the features, and ReDSL.FC1 and [32] employ high-dimensional features, for example, 4K-D and 10K-D, respectively. By contrast, our descriptors are of only 512-D, which are more compact and suitable for large-scale search. The bottom row of Figure 4 shows the top returned images of our method for a sample Oxford query.

We notice that our approach performs better on Paris than Oxford. The reason could be that the number of relevant images for the same object in Paris is much greater than that in Oxford: On average, Paris has 162.8 relevant images per object while Oxford has only 51.6. To verify this hypothesis, we augment the number of relevant images for an object in Oxford. In specific, in addition to the full-sized image, we add 4 patches of size covering 1/4 of the image and 9 patches of size covering 1/3 of the image. Doing so makes the number of relevant images 14x larger than the original setting. Table 6 shows that data augmentation boosts the performance to 77.95% MAP on Oxford, indicating that our approach would perform better on the datasets with sufficient amount of relevant images.

Like Paris, the Oxford dataset has no classification labels for training. It thus demonstrates again that our method can be flexibly used for the problems containing either classification labels or relevance ground truths, or both.

4.7 Results on SUN397

Finally, we evaluate our method on SUN397 that is of a larger scale and has diverse class labels. We train the VGG16 with the classification and the CBR criteria, and present the results in Table 7. Our approach enhances the retrieval performance and leads to 17.81% MAP points improvement when compared to the fine-tuned VGG16 features, demonstrating that our approach can handle images with numerous classes and is scalable to larger datasets.

Figure 5 shows the top returned images using our learned descriptors and the VGG16 fine-tuned ones. As can be seen, our approach retrieves images that are not only visually similar but also have the same label with the query. On the other hand, the returned images of the VGG16 features contain visually similar images in wrong categories.

5. CONCLUSIONS AND FUTURE WORK

We have presented a novel learning idea, cross-batch ref-

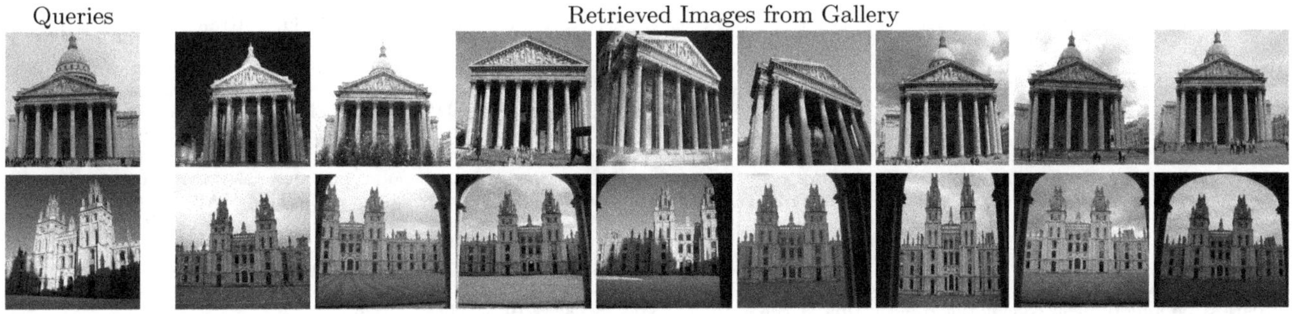

Figure 4: Query images and their corresponding top 8 ranked images retrieved from the Paris and Oxford datasets. Upper row: Paris. Lower row: Oxford.

Figure 5: Top 8 ranked returned images of using different feature representations on a sample query of the SUN397. Images with red border are false positives. Upper row: ours. Lower row: VGG16 fine-tuned.

Table 6: Retrieval comparison of different methods on Oxford. MAP denotes mean average precision.

Method	MAP(%)
BOW-200k-D [13]	36.40
Multi-resolution-ss (256-D) [32]	53.30
VLAD + adapt + innorm [1]	55.55
Deep convolutional + Max pooling [32]	53.30
Deep fully connected + fine-tuning [3]	55.70
Sum pooling [2]	58.90
Ng et al. [23]	64.90
T-embedding [14]	67.60
CNN-aug-ss [31]	68.00
ReDSL.FC1 (4K-D) [41]	78.34
Multi-resolution-ss (10K-D) [32]	84.40
Ours	68.33
Ours w/ data augmentation	77.95

erence learning, to enhance a network with abilities to learn features effective for classification and retrieval. Our idea employs inter-batches communication mechanism based on the MAP criterion, where the relevant and irrelevant samples are encouraged to be placed on top and rear of the retrieval list, respectively. To maximize the cross-batch MAP, we design a loss function that is a lower bound of the MAP on the feature layer of the network.We then reduce the approach to an inter-batch target-codes driven one that is efficiently implementable on the publicly available CNN package, CAFFE. Experiments on several benchmarks show that our approach constantly increases the retrieval performance and meanwhile provides promising classification accuracy.

Future work includes improving the target code updates stage during network learning. We consider more frequent code updates without re-computations could be a promising way for performance improvement. Another direction is to learn binary-valued codes, which facilitate fast image search in large-scale datasets.

Table 7: Performance comparison of different methods on SUN397. Acc. and MAP denote classification accuracy and mean average precision, respectively.

Method	Dim.	Acc.(%)	MAP(%)
FastH-N [20], bits	1024	—	18.40
VGG16, fine-tuned	4096	60.78	42.55
Ours, VGG16	512	57.06	60.36

6. REFERENCES

[1] R. Arandjelovic and A. Zisserman. All about vlad. In *Proc. CVPR*, pages 1578–1585, 2013.

[2] A. Babenko and V. S. Lempitsky. Aggregating deep convolutional features for image retrieval. In *Proc. ICCV*, pages 1269–1277, 2015.

[3] A. Babenko, A. Slesarev, A. Chigorin, and V. S. Lempitsky. Neural codes for image retrieval. In *Proc. ECCV*, pages 584–599, 2014.

[4] C. J. C. Burges, R. Ragno, and Q. V. Le. Learning to rank with nonsmooth cost functions. In *Proc. NIPS*, pages 193–200, 2006.

[5] J. Donahue, Y. Jia, O. Vinyals, J. Hoffman, N. Zhang, E. Tzeng, and T. Darrell. DeCAF: A deep convolutional activation feature for generic visual recognition. In *Proc. ICML*, pages 647–655, 2014.

[6] X. Fan, K. Zheng, Y. Lin, and S. Wang. Combining local appearance and holistic view: Dual-source deep neural networks for human pose estimation. In *Proc. CVPR*, pages 1347–1355, 2015.

[7] S. Gao, W. Wu, C.-H. Lee, and T.-S. Chua. A maximal figure-of-merit learning approach to text categorization. In

Proc. ACM SIGIR, pages 174–181, 2003.

[8] R. Girshick, J. Donahue, T. Darrell, and J. Malik. Region-based convolutional networks for accurate object detection and segmentation. *IEEE Trans. Pattern Anal. Mach. Intell.*, 38(1):142–158, 2016.

[9] R. B. Girshick, J. Donahue, T. Darrell, and J. Malik. Rich feature hierarchies for accurate object detection and semantic segmentation. In *Proc. CVPR*, pages 580–587, 2014.

[10] Y. Gong, S. Lazebnik, A. Gordo, and F. Perronnin. Iterative quantization: A procrustean approach to learning binary codes for large-scale image retrieval. *IEEE Trans. Pattern Anal. Mach. Intell.*, 35(12):2916–2929, 2013.

[11] Y. Gong, L. Wang, R. Guo, and S. Lazebnik. Multi-scale orderless pooling of deep convolutional activation features. In *Proc. ECCV*, pages 392–407, 2014.

[12] K. He, X. Zhang, S. Ren, and J. Sun. Deep residual learning for image recognition. In *Proc. CVPR*, 2016.

[13] H. Jégou, F. Perronnin, M. Douze, J. Sanchez, P. Perez, and C. Schmid. Aggregating local image descriptors into compact codes. *IEEE Trans. Pattern Anal. Mach. Intell.*, 34(9):1704–1716, 2012.

[14] H. Jégou and A. Zisserman. Triangulation embedding and democratic aggregation for image search. In *Proc. CVPR*, pages 3310–3317, 2014.

[15] Y. Jia, E. Shelhamer, J. Donahue, S. Karayev, J. Long, R. B. Girshick, S. Guadarrama, and T. Darrell. Caffe: Convolutional architecture for fast feature embedding. In *Proc. ACM MM*, pages 675–678, 2014.

[16] I. Kim and C. Lee. An efficient gradient-based approach to optimizing average precision through maximal figure-of-merit learning. *Signal Processing Systems*, 74(3):285–295, 2014.

[17] A. Krizhevsky. Learning multiple layers of features from tiny images. *Computer Science Department, University of Toronto, Tech. Report*, 2009.

[18] A. Krizhevsky, I. Sutskever, and G. E. Hinton. ImageNet classification with deep convolutional neural networks. In *Proc. NIPS*, pages 1106–1114, 2012.

[19] K. Li, Z. Huang, Y. Cheng, and C. Lee. A maximal figure-of-merit learning approach to maximizing mean average precision with deep neural network based classifiers. In *Proc. ICASSP*, pages 4503–4507, 2014.

[20] G. Lin, C. Shen, Q. Shi, A. van den Hengel, and D. Suter. Fast supervised hashing with decision trees for high-dimensional data. In *Proc. CVPR*, pages 1971–1978, 2014.

[21] M. Lin, Q. Chen, and S. Yan. Network in network. In *Proc. ICLR*, 2014.

[22] D. G. Lowe. Distinctive image features from scale-invariant keypoints. *Int'l J. Computer Vision*, 60(2):91–110, 2004.

[23] J. Y. Ng, F. Yang, and L. S. Davis. Exploiting local features from deep networks for image retrieval. In *Proc. CVPR Workshops*, pages 53–61, 2015.

[24] M.-E. Nilsback and A. Zisserman. A visual vocabulary for flower classification. In *Proc. CVPR*, pages 1447–1454, 2006.

[25] M. Oquab, L. Bottou, I. Laptev, and J. Sivic. Learning and transferring mid-level image representations using convolutional neural networks. In *Proc. CVPR*, pages 1717–1724, 2014.

[26] M. Paulin, M. Douze, Z. Harchaoui, J. Mairal, F. Perronnin, and C. Schmid. Local convolutional features with unsupervised training for image retrieval. In *Proc. ICCV*, pages 91–99, 2015.

[27] F. Perronnin and C. R. Dance. Fisher kernels on visual vocabularies for image categorization. In *Proc. CVPR*, 2007.

[28] F. Perronnin, J. Sánchez, and T. Mensink. Improving the Fisher kernel for large-scale image classification. In *Proc. ECCV*, pages 143–156, 2010.

[29] J. Philbin, O. Chum, M. Isard, J. Sivic, and A. Zisserman. Object retrieval with large vocabularies and fast spatial matching. In *Proc. CVPR*, 2007.

[30] J. Philbin, O. Chum, M. Isard, J. Sivic, and A. Zisserman. Lost in quantization: Improving particular object retrieval in large scale image databases. In *Proc. CVPR*, 2008.

[31] A. S. Razavian, H. Azizpour, J. Sullivan, and S. Carlsson. CNN features off-the-shelf: An astounding baseline for recognition. In *Proc. CVPR Workshops on DeepVision*, 2014.

[32] A. S. Razavian, J. Sullivan, A. Maki, and S. Carlsson. A baseline for visual instance retrieval with deep convolutional networks. *arXiv preprint arXiv:1412.6574*, 2014.

[33] S. Ren, K. He, R. Girshick, and J. Sun. Faster r-cnn: Towards real-time object detection with region proposal networks. In *Proc. NIPS*, pages 91–99, 2015.

[34] O. Russakovsky, J. Deng, H. Su, J. Krause, S. Satheesh, S. Ma, Z. Huang, A. Karpathy, A. Khosla, M. Bernstein, A. C. Berg, and L. Fei-Fei. ImageNet Large Scale Visual Recognition Challenge. *Int'l J. Computer Visionl*, pages 1–42, 2015.

[35] P. Sermanet, D. Eigen, X. Zhang, M. Mathieu, R. Fergus, and Y. LeCun. Overfeat: Integrated recognition, localization and detection using convolutional networks. In *Proc. ICLR*, 2014.

[36] Y. Shi, A. Karatzoglou, L. Baltrunas, M. Larson, A. Hanjalic, and N. Oliver. TFMAP: optimizing MAP for top-n context-aware recommendation. In *Proc. SIGIR*, pages 155–164, 2012.

[37] K. Simonyan and A. Zisserman. Two-stream convolutional networks for action recognition in videos. In *Proc. NIPS*, pages 568–576, 2014.

[38] K. Simonyan and A. Zisserman. Very deep convolutional networks for large-scale image recognition. In *Proc. ICLR*, 2015.

[39] C. Szegedy, W. Liu, Y. Jia, P. Sermanet, S. Reed, D. Anguelov, D. Erhan, V. Vanhoucke, and A. Rabinovich. Going deeper with convolutions. In *Proc. CVPR*, pages 1–9, 2015.

[40] M. J. Taylor, J. Guiver, S. Robertson, and T. Minka. Softrank: optimizing non-smooth rank metrics. In *Proc. WSDM*, pages 77–86, 2008.

[41] J. Wan, D. Wang, S. C. Hoi, P. Wu, J. Zhu, Y. Zhang, and J. Li. Deep learning for content-based image retrieval: A comprehensive study. In *Proc. ACM MM*, pages 157–166, 2014.

[42] K. Q. Weinberger and L. K. Saul. Distance metric learning for large margin nearest neighbor classification. *Journal of Machine Learning Research*, 10:207–244, 2009.

[43] P. Wu, S. C. H. Hoi, H. Xia, P. Zhao, D. Wang, and C. Miao. Online multimodal deep similarity learning with application to image retrieval. In *Proc. ACM MM*, pages 153–162, 2013.

[44] R. Xia, Y. Pan, H. Lai, C. Liu, and S. Yan. Supervised hashing for image retreieval via image representation learning. In *Proc. AAAI*, pages 2156–2162, 2014.

[45] J. Xiao, J. Hays, K. A. Ehinger, A. Oliva, and A. Torralba. SUN database: Large-scale scene recognition from abbey to zoo. In *Proc. CVPR*, pages 3485–3492, 2010.

[46] L. Xie, R. Hong, B. Zhang, and Q. Tian. Image classification and retrieval are ONE. In *Proc. ICMR*, pages 3–10, 2015.

[47] J. Xu and H. Li. Adarank: A boosting algorithm for information retrieval. In *Proc. SIGIR*, pages 391–398, 2007.

[48] Y. Yue, T. Finley, F. Radlinski, and T. Joachims. A support vector method for optimizing average precision. In *Proc. SIGIR*, pages 271–278, 2007.

[49] F. Zhao, Y. Huang, L. Wang, and T. Tan. Deep semantic ranking based hashash for multi-label image retreieval. In *Proc. CVPR*, pages 1556–1564, 2015.

[50] Y. Zhen and D.-Y. Yeung. A probabilistic model for multimodal hash function learning. In *Proc. ACM SIGKDD*, pages 940–948, 2012.

APPENDIX

Following the definition $g(z) \leq z$ for $z \in N^+$, we have

$$AP(x)l|D_x| = \sum_{x_i \sim x} \frac{rank_{D_x}(x_i)}{rank_D(x_i)} \geq \sum_{x_i \sim x} \frac{g(rank_{D_x}(x_i))}{\sum_{x_k \in D} I(d_i(x) - d_k(x))}.$$

Because $I(z) \leq e^z$ for $z \in R$ (empirical loss is bounded by the exponential loss), it yields

$$\sum_{x_i \sim x} \frac{g(rank_{D_x}(x_i))}{\sum_{x_k \in D} I(d_i(x) - d_k(x))} \geq \sum_{x_i \sim x} \frac{g(rank_{D_x}(x_i))}{\sum_{x_k \in D} e^{d_i(x) - d_k(x)}}$$

$$= \sum_{x_i \sim x} \frac{g(rank_{D_x}(x_i))}{e^{d_i(x)} \sum_{x_k \in D} e^{-d_k(x)}} = \frac{\sum_{x_i \sim x} e^{-d_i(x)} g(rank_{D_x}(x_i))}{\sum_{x_k \in D} e^{-d_k(x)}}$$

$$= LAP(x)l|D_x|,$$

Hence, $LAP(x) \leq AP(x)$, i.e., (2) is a lower bound of (1).

Binary Optimized Hashing

Qi Dai[1], Jianguo Li[2], Jingdong Wang[3], Yu-Gang Jiang[1]
[1]School of Computer Science, Shanghai Key Lab of Intelligent Information Processing, Fudan University, Shanghai, China
[2]Intel Labs China, Beijing, China
[3]Microsoft Research Asia, Beijing, China
{daiqi, ygj}@fudan.edu.cn, jianguo.li@intel.com, jingdw@microsoft.com

ABSTRACT

This paper studies the problem of learning to hash, which is essentially a mixed integer optimization problem, containing both the binary hash code output and the (continuous) parameters forming the hash functions. Different from existing relaxation methods in hashing, which have no theoretical guarantees for the error bound of the relaxations, we propose *binary optimized hashing* (BOH), in which we prove that if the loss function is Lipschitz continuous, the binary optimization problem can be relaxed to a bound-constrained continuous optimization problem. Then we introduce a surrogate objective function, which only depends on unbinarized hash functions and does not need the slack variables transforming unbinarized hash functions to discrete functions, to approximate the relaxed objective function. We show that the approximation error is bounded and the bound is small when the problem is optimized. We apply the proposed approach to learn hash codes from either handcraft feature inputs or raw image inputs. Extensive experiments are carried out on three benchmarks, demonstrating that our approach outperforms state-of-the-arts with a significant margin on search accuracies.

CCS Concepts

•**Computing methodologies** → **Visual content-based indexing and retrieval; Image representations;** *Neural networks;*

Keywords

Hashing; Binary Optimized Hashing; Image Retrieval; CNN

1. INTRODUCTION

Hashing has been attracting broad attention due to the explosive growth of various kinds of data like documents, images and videos. It aims at encoding input data to a set of compact binary codes, while preserving some notion of similarity of the original data in the Hamming space. With the compact hash codes, one can easily realize highly efficient search applications with the Hamming distance under significant lower storage cost.

The early exploration on hashing began with the well-known locality sensitive hashing (LSH) [4], which imposes random projection on data to generate hash codes. LSH is a data-independent hashing method, so that its results are usually not satisfying. Realizing the limitation of the data-independent hashing methods, many recent hashing techniques try to exploit various machine learning paradigms to learn effective hash functions from a given dataset, ranging from unsupervised to supervised or even semi-supervised settings [32, 31]. Recently, as deep learning has demonstrated strong results on many visual recognition tasks [11], several researches also proposed to learn hash codes from input images in an end-to-end manner with deep learning [34, 15], which led to significant improvements over traditional handcraft feature based hashing methods. All these data-dependent methods are generally called learning to hash.

Learning to hash is essentially a mixed integer nonlinear optimization problem with binary code outputs and continuous parameters for hash functions. The problem is difficult to be solved directly due to its NP-hard nature. Various relaxations have been introduced, such as (1) continuous relaxation which discards the sign function and discrete constraints to solve one continuous problem and then thresholds the continuous outputs to produce hash codes; (2) two-step schemes which inference hash-bit first and train hash functions with given hash-bits [18, 17, 27]. Although some methods in this category were claimed to be optimal with the relaxed objective functions, there are no theoretical guarantees for the error-bound of the relaxations.

Inspired by the works on discrete optimization [3, 22], this paper proposes an optimal hashing method, namely *binary optimized hashing* (BOH). We relax the binary variable to a bounded continuous variable, and show that the binary program is equivalent to a bound-constrained continuous optimization problem with an additional penalty function if the objective function satisfies certain conditions. We further introduce a surrogate objective function with respect to unbinarize hash functions only, to approximate the relaxed problem. We show that the approximation error is bounded and the bound is small when the problem is optimized. We apply the proposed approach to learn hash codes directly from either handcraft feature inputs or raw image inputs in a unified learning paradigm.

Extensive experiments show that coupling with neural networks, BOH can achieve superior performance over the

MM '16, October 15-19, 2016, Amsterdam, Netherlands
© 2016 ACM. ISBN 978-1-4503-3603-1/16/10...$15.00
DOI: http://dx.doi.org/10.1145/2964284.2964331

state-of-the-art methods. In details, coupling with multi-layer perceptron (MLP), BOH gives superior results over compared methods for handcraft feature inputs; while coupling with convolutional neural networks (CNN), BOH outperforms all state-of-the-arts with a significant margin for raw image inputs. The main contributions of this paper are summarized as below:

(1) We relax the binary optimization problem to a bound-constrained continuous optimization problem. We further prove that the two problems are equivalent if the loss functions satisfy certain conditions. Hence we derive a surrogate objective function with respect only to hash functions, so that we can learn hash codes in a unified framework.

(2) We prove the feasibility of using two popular loss functions: triplet ranking loss and contrastive loss. We apply BOH to learn hash codes from both the handcraft feature inputs and raw image inputs.

(3) We demonstrate superior performance of the proposed approach on popular benchmarks. Our approach outperforms state-of-the-art approaches on both handcraft feature inputs and raw image inputs with clear margins.

This paper is organized as follows. We introduce related works in Section 2 and present details of the BOH in Section 3. Section 4 discusses experimental settings and results. Conclusions are drawn in Section 5.

2. RELATED WORKS

In this section we discuss related works in the following three aspects.

Learning to hash can be roughly divided into the following three categories: unsupervised, supervised and semi-supervised. Unsupervised methods try to preserve the inherent properties within data. Such properties include data distributions (e.g., spectral hashing [33], kernelized locality sensitive hashing [13, 14]), manifold structures (e.g., graph hashing [21]) and various similarities in feature space (e.g., angular quantization hashing [5], spherical hashing [8]). Although unsupervised hashing methods work well to preserve distance/similarity in the feature space, many applications also require to preserve semantical similarity in the Hamming space. For this purpose, various supervised hashing methods are proposed, ranging from metric learning to kernel learning (e.g., LDAHash [29], supervised hash with kernels [20], Hamming distance metric learning [24], supervised discrete hashing [27]). In addition, as it is very expensive to annotate large-scale datasets, it is practically needed to learn hash codes with both labeled and unlabeled data (e.g., semi-supervised hashing [30]).

Deep learning based hashing has recently shown very strong performance improvements over the shallow learning counterparts. Semantic Hashing [26] employs a two-stage learning (pretraining and fine-tuning) on deep generative models to abstract input documents to several bits. Deep hashing [2] seeks multiple hierarchical non-linear transformations to learn hash codes. Besides, convolutional neural networks (CNN) provides a way to learn hash codes from raw input in an end-to-end way. Specially, deep semantic ranking hashing [35] presents a new ranking loss, preserving the similarity relationships between multi-label images. Convolutional neural network hashing [34] also uses a two-step learning framework. The first stage performs semantic similarity matrix factorization to obtain hash codes, and the second stage trains a CNN network to obtain hash functions from raw image inputs. Deep neural network hashing [15] uses triplet ranking loss to model the similarity relations between images. A divide-and-encode module is employed to map the image features to approximate hash codes.

Different relaxations are implicitly or explicitly employed in learning to hash due to the NP-hard nature of the mixed integer optimization problem. Most aforementioned methods discard the discrete constraints to solve one continuous problem, and then threshold the continuous outputs to be binary codes. This simplifies the optimization greatly, but usually yields low-quality approximated solutions. Recently, some novel relaxations are proposed. The two-step schemes first produce binary codes with some discrete optimization such as binary quadratic optimization [18], graph cuts [17], semantic matrix factorization [34], discrete cyclic coordinate descent [27], etc. After that, certain learning techniques are employed to learn the hash functions with the desired hash codes. Iterative multi-step schemes are also proposed to optimize binary codes and hash functions alternatively [19, 27].

3. BINARY OPTIMIZED HASHING

The purpose of learning-to-hash is to seek a set of hash functions $H(\boldsymbol{x}) = \{h_1(\boldsymbol{x}), h_2(\boldsymbol{x}), ..., h_d(\boldsymbol{x})\}$, which map the feature $\boldsymbol{x}$ to the Hamming space $\{0,1\}^d$, obtaining a sequence of binary codes $\boldsymbol{b} = H(\boldsymbol{x})$, so that the similarity in the Hamming space, defined from the Hamming distance $\|\boldsymbol{b}_i - \boldsymbol{b}_j\|_1$, is able to preserve some notion of similarity evaluated in the original feature space. In general, the objective function can be written as follows,

$$\begin{aligned} \min \quad & L(\boldsymbol{b}_1, \boldsymbol{b}_2, \cdots, \boldsymbol{b}_N) \\ s.t. \quad & \boldsymbol{b}_i \in \{0,1\}^d \\ & \boldsymbol{b}_i = H(\boldsymbol{x}_i), i = 1, 2, \cdots N, \end{aligned} \tag{1}$$

where N is the number of training samples. Usually the loss function $L(\cdot)$ is defined as the sum of loss functions over cliques $\mathcal{C} = \{c\}$ with c being a set of points, $L(\boldsymbol{b}_1, \boldsymbol{b}_2, \cdots, \boldsymbol{b}_N) = \sum_{c \in \mathcal{C}} \ell(\boldsymbol{b}_{i_1}, \ldots, \boldsymbol{b}_{i_{|c|}})$, $(i_1, \ldots, i_{|c|}) = c)$. There are various forms to formulate the loss function. In this paper, we will study two widely-used forms: triplet ranking loss, in which c is a triplet (i, j, k) and contrastive loss where c is a point pair (i, j).

The problem (1) is a mixed-integer optimization problem. Due to its NP-hard nature, the problem is solved with various relaxations, such as continuous relaxation, two-step schemes, and iteratively multi-step schemes as mentioned in related works. Our solution starts from relaxing the binary variable into a bounded continuous variable and introducing a penalty function. We first only consider the binary variables in the problem (1) and show that the 0-1 program is equivalent to a continuous optimization problem if the objective function $L(\cdot)$ satisfies certain condition. Then we take into consideration the hash function and relax the whole problem into a continuous problem, which subsequently is transformed to a surrogate objective function with respect to only the hash functions.

3.1 Equivalent Continuous Problem

Let us consider the following generic 0-1 program,

$$\begin{aligned} \min \;\; & f(\boldsymbol{y}) \\ s.t. \;\; & \boldsymbol{y} \in \{0,1\}^d, \end{aligned} \tag{2}$$

and a transformed optimization problem,

$$\begin{aligned} \min \;\; & f(\boldsymbol{y}) + \lambda\phi(\boldsymbol{y}) \\ s.t. \;\; & \boldsymbol{y} \in [0,1]^d, \end{aligned} \tag{3}$$

where $\phi(\boldsymbol{y}) : \mathbb{R}^d \to \mathbb{R}$ to $f(\boldsymbol{y})$ is a penalty term and λ is the penalty coefficient. It is shown in [3, 22] that under certain conditions, the above two problems are equivalent.

Lemma 1: *Let $\|\cdot\|$ be a suitably chosen norm. Suppose the following hypotheses hold:*

a) $f(\boldsymbol{y})$ is bounded when $\boldsymbol{y} \in [0,1]^k$, and there exists an open set $A \supset \{0,1\}^d$ and real number $\alpha, \eta > 0$, such that $\forall \boldsymbol{y}_1, \boldsymbol{y}_2 \in A$, $f(\cdot)$ satisfies the following Hölder condition:

$$|f(\boldsymbol{y}_1) - f(\boldsymbol{y}_2)| \leqslant \eta\|\boldsymbol{y}_1 - \boldsymbol{y}_2\|^\alpha. \tag{4}$$

b) It is possible to find $\phi : \mathbb{R}^d \to \mathbb{R}$, such that:

(1) ϕ is continuous on $[0,1]^d$;

(2) $\phi(\boldsymbol{y}) = 0, \forall \boldsymbol{y} \in \{0,1\}^k$; and $\phi(\boldsymbol{y}) > 0, \forall \boldsymbol{y} \in (0,1)^k$

(3) $\forall \boldsymbol{z} \in \{0,1\}^k$, there exists a neighborhood $S(\boldsymbol{z})$ of $\boldsymbol{z}$, and a real $\epsilon(\boldsymbol{z}) > 0$, such that:

$$\phi(\boldsymbol{y}) \geqslant \epsilon(\boldsymbol{z})\|\boldsymbol{y} - \boldsymbol{z}\|^\alpha, \forall \boldsymbol{y} \in S(\boldsymbol{z}) \cap (0,1)^k. \tag{5}$$

Then, a real value λ_0 exists, such that $\forall \lambda > \lambda_0$, the two problems (2) and (3) are equivalent.

When $\alpha = 1$, the condition (a) is also called *Lipschitz condition*, and $f(\cdot)$ is called *Lipschitz continuous.*

Lemma 2: *If $f_1(\cdot)$ and $f_2(\cdot)$ are* Lipschitz continuous, *then $f_1(\cdot) + f_2(\cdot)$ is also* Lipschitz continuous.

In [22], the equivalence between (2) and (3) has been proved for various forms of function ϕ. This paper considers a simple penalty form

$$\phi(\boldsymbol{y}) = \boldsymbol{y}^T(\boldsymbol{e} - \boldsymbol{y}), \tag{6}$$

where $\boldsymbol{e} = [1, 1, \ldots, 1]^T$. This leads to the following equivalent problem,

$$\begin{aligned} \min \;\; & f(\boldsymbol{y}) + \lambda\boldsymbol{y}^T(\boldsymbol{e} - \boldsymbol{y}) \\ s.t. \;\; & \boldsymbol{y} \in [0,1]^d \end{aligned} \tag{7}$$

Lemma 3: *Let f satisfy condition (a) of **Lemma 1** with $\alpha = 1$, i.e. $f(\boldsymbol{y})$ is bounded when $\boldsymbol{y} \in [0,1]^d$ and also Lipschitz continuous on an open set $A \supset \{0,1\}^d$. Then, there exists $\lambda_0 \in \mathbb{R}$ such that for every $\lambda \geq \lambda_0$ problems (2) and (7) are equivalent.*

We take two popular loss functions, triplet ranking loss [15, 16, 24] and contrastive loss as examples, and show that they are *Lipschitz continuous* below.

3.1.1 *Triplet Ranking Loss is Lipschitz Continuous*

The triplet loss function is given as

$$\begin{aligned} f(\boldsymbol{y}) &= \ell(\boldsymbol{b}_i, \boldsymbol{b}_j, \boldsymbol{b}_k) \\ &= \max(0, 1 - (\|\boldsymbol{b}_i - \boldsymbol{b}_k\|_2^2 - \|\boldsymbol{b}_i - \boldsymbol{b}_j\|_2^2)), \end{aligned} \tag{8}$$

where (i,k) is a similar pair and (i,j) is a dissimilar pair and $\boldsymbol{y} = [\boldsymbol{b}_i^T, \boldsymbol{b}_j^T, \boldsymbol{b}_k^T]^T$. In the following, we show that $f(\boldsymbol{y})$ is Lipschitz continuous, from which the overall objective function, the summation of Lipschitz continuous functions, $L(\boldsymbol{b}_1, \boldsymbol{b}_2, \cdots, \boldsymbol{b}_N) = \sum_{(i,j,k)\in\mathcal{C}} \ell(\boldsymbol{b}_i, \boldsymbol{b}_j, \boldsymbol{b}_k)$ is obviously Lipschitz continuous according to **Lemma 2**.

Lemma 4: *Any continuously differentiable function is locally Lipschitz continuous.*

Lemma 5: *If $f_1(\cdot)$ and $f_2(\cdot)$ are Lipschitz continuous, then $\max(f_1(\cdot), f_2(\cdot))$ is also Lipschitz continuous.*

Theorem 1: *The triplet ranking loss function (8) is* Lipschitz continuous.

Proof: It is obvious that $0 \leqslant f(\boldsymbol{y}) \leqslant d^2 + 1$, i.e., $f(\cdot)$ is bounded.

For the *Lipschitz condition* on an open set A, we separate the max function to two functions $g(\boldsymbol{y})$ and $k(\boldsymbol{y})$, where $g(\boldsymbol{y}) = 0$, and $k(\boldsymbol{y}) = 1 - (\|\boldsymbol{b}_i - \boldsymbol{b}_k\|_2^2 - \|\boldsymbol{b}_i - \boldsymbol{b}_j\|_2^2)$.

Suppose the open set A to be $(-1,2)^k$ $(k = 3d)$. It is obvious that function $k(\boldsymbol{y})$ is continuously differentiable on A. According to **Lemma 4**, $k(\boldsymbol{y})$ is *Lipschitz continuous* on A. On the other side, function $g(\boldsymbol{y})$ is a constant function, indicating that $g(\boldsymbol{y})$ is also *Lipschitz continuous* on A. Then two functions are both *Lipschitz continuous.*

According to **Lemma 5**, $\max(g(\boldsymbol{y}), k(\boldsymbol{y}))$ is *Lipschitz continuous.* This completes the proof.

3.1.2 *Contrastive Loss is Lipschitz Continuous*

Contrastive loss [7] is widely used for metric learning with only pairwise constraints. Suppose we have a pair of images $(\mathcal{I}, \mathcal{I}_c)$, and $(\boldsymbol{b}, \boldsymbol{b}_c)$ are the corresponding hash codes. $\boldsymbol{y} = [\boldsymbol{b}; \boldsymbol{b}_c]$. The contrastive loss function f is defined as:

$$f(\boldsymbol{y}) = l_c\|\boldsymbol{b} - \boldsymbol{b}_c\|_2^2 + (1 - l_c)\max(0, m - \|\boldsymbol{b} - \boldsymbol{b}_c\|_2^2) \tag{9}$$

where $l_c = 1$ indicates $\mathcal{I}$ and $\mathcal{I}_c$ are similar, otherwise 0. This loss function is indeed similar to LDAHash [29].

Theorem 2: *The contrastive loss function (9) is* Lipschitz continuous.

Proof: According to **Lemma 4** and previous proof, we can easily prove the two parts $u(\boldsymbol{y}) = l_c\|\boldsymbol{b} - \boldsymbol{b}_c\|_2^2$ and $v(\boldsymbol{y}) = (1 - l_c)\max(0, m - \|\boldsymbol{b} - \boldsymbol{b}_c\|_2^2)$ are *Lipschitz continuous* on the open set $A = (-1,2)^k$ separately.

According to **Lemma 2**, the linear combination of $u(\boldsymbol{y})$ and $v(\boldsymbol{y})$ is also *Lipschitz continuous.* This completes the proof.

3.2 Surrogate Objective Function

We derive hash function $h(\boldsymbol{x}) \in \{0,1\}$ from its unbinarized version $\tilde{h}(\boldsymbol{x})$, ($\tilde{h}(\boldsymbol{x}) \in [0,1]$ in this paper): $h(\boldsymbol{x}) = \tilde{h}(\boldsymbol{x}) + \epsilon$, where $|\epsilon| = \min(\tilde{h}(\boldsymbol{x}), 1 - \tilde{h}(\boldsymbol{x}))$. The hash function optimization is equivalent to the quantization loss problem,

$$\begin{aligned} \min \;\; & \|h(\boldsymbol{x}) - \tilde{h}(\boldsymbol{x})\|_2^2 \\ s.t. \;\; & h(\boldsymbol{x}) \in \{0,1\}. \end{aligned} \tag{10}$$

Considering the hash function as a constraint of the problem (1) and combining the optimization problem (10) into (1), we have

$$\begin{aligned} \min \;\; & L(\boldsymbol{b}_1, \cdots, \boldsymbol{b}_N) + \rho\sum_{i=1}^{N}\|\boldsymbol{b}_i - \tilde{H}(\boldsymbol{x}_i)\|_2^2 \\ s.t. \;\; & \boldsymbol{b}_i \in \{0,1\}^d, i = 1, 2, \cdots N, \end{aligned} \tag{11}$$

where $\tilde{H}(\boldsymbol{x}_i) = [\tilde{h}_1(\boldsymbol{x}_i), \tilde{h}_2(\boldsymbol{x}_i), \ldots, \tilde{h}_d(\boldsymbol{x}_i)]$. It can be proved that a real value ρ_0 exists, such that $\rho > \rho_0$, the problems (11) and (1) are equivalent.

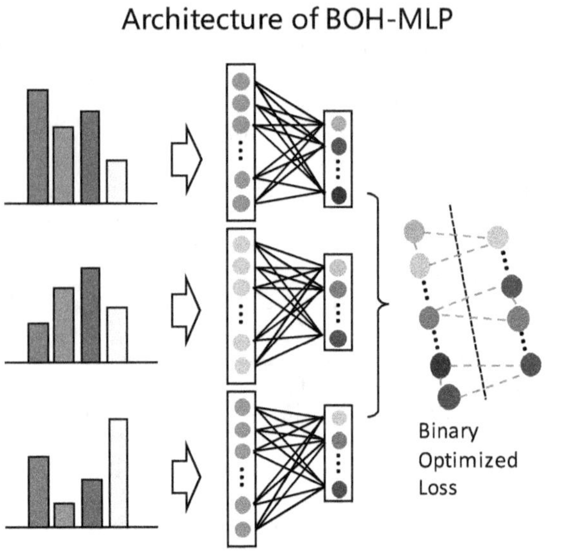

Figure 1: Architecture of BOH-MLP, in which we adopt MLP as hash functions, and use triplet ranking loss for training, with handcraft features as inputs.

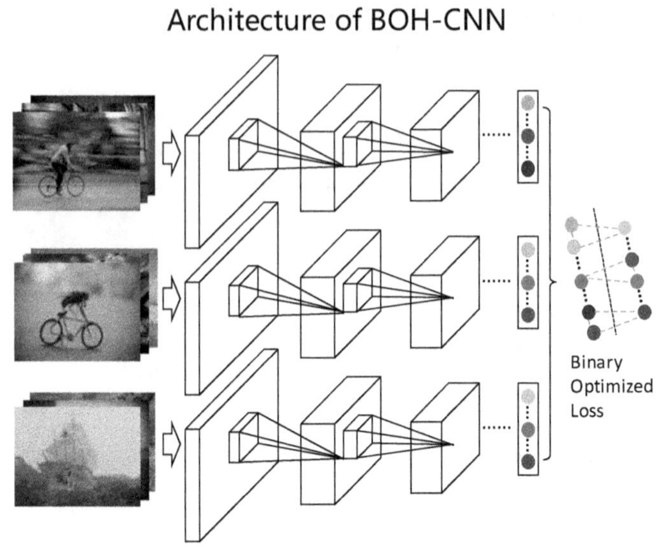

Figure 2: Architecture of BOH-CNN, in which we adopt CNN as hash functions. Similar to Figure 1, triplet ranking loss is used here, but with raw image inputs.

It is obvious that $\sum_{i=1}^{N} \|\boldsymbol{b}_i - \tilde{H}(\boldsymbol{x}_i)\|_2^2$ is Lipschitz continuous. We have shown $L(\cdot)$ is Lipschitz continuous. Therefore, problem (11) is relaxed to the following equivalent problem:

$$\begin{aligned} \min \quad & L(\tilde{\boldsymbol{b}}_1 + \boldsymbol{\epsilon}_1, \cdots, \tilde{\boldsymbol{b}}_N + \boldsymbol{\epsilon}_N) + \rho \sum_{i=1}^{N} \|\boldsymbol{\epsilon}_i\|_2^2 \\ & + \lambda \sum_{i=1}^{N} \phi(\tilde{\boldsymbol{b}}_i + \boldsymbol{\epsilon}_i) \\ s.t. \quad & \tilde{\boldsymbol{b}}_i + \boldsymbol{\epsilon}_i \in [0,1]^d, i = 1, 2, \cdots N, \end{aligned} \tag{12}$$

where $\tilde{\boldsymbol{b}}_i = \tilde{H}(\boldsymbol{x}_i)$, $\boldsymbol{\epsilon}_i = H(\boldsymbol{x}_i) - \tilde{H}(\boldsymbol{x}_i) = \boldsymbol{b}_i - \tilde{\boldsymbol{b}}_i$ and $\phi(\cdot)$ follows Equation (6).

Suppose $F(\tilde{\boldsymbol{b}}_1, \cdots, \tilde{\boldsymbol{b}}_N) = L(\tilde{\boldsymbol{b}}_1, \cdots, \tilde{\boldsymbol{b}}_N) + \lambda \sum_{i=1}^{N} \phi(\tilde{\boldsymbol{b}}_i)$. As both $L(\cdot)$ and $\phi(\cdot)$ are Lipschitz continuous, according to **Lemma 1**, we have

$$\begin{aligned} & |F(\boldsymbol{b}_1, \cdots, \boldsymbol{b}_N) - F(\tilde{\boldsymbol{b}}_1, \cdots, \tilde{\boldsymbol{b}}_N)| \\ = & |F(\tilde{\boldsymbol{b}}_1 + \boldsymbol{\epsilon}_1, \cdots, \tilde{\boldsymbol{b}}_N + \boldsymbol{\epsilon}_N) - F(\tilde{\boldsymbol{b}}_1, \cdots, \tilde{\boldsymbol{b}}_N)| \\ \leqslant & \eta \sum_{i=1}^{N} \|\boldsymbol{\epsilon}_i\|^1. \end{aligned} \tag{13}$$

This means the approximation error $|F(\boldsymbol{B}) - F(\tilde{\boldsymbol{B}})|$ is bounded, where $\boldsymbol{B} = [\boldsymbol{b}_1, \ldots, \boldsymbol{b}_N]$. Therefore, we could transform problem (12) to an approximate problem

$$\begin{aligned} \min \quad & L(\tilde{\boldsymbol{b}}_1, \cdots, \tilde{\boldsymbol{b}}_N) + \rho \sum_{i=1}^{N} \|\boldsymbol{\epsilon}_i\|_2^2 + \lambda \sum_{i=1}^{N} \phi(\tilde{\boldsymbol{b}}_i) \\ s.t. \quad & \tilde{\boldsymbol{b}}_i \in [0,1]^d, i = 1, 2, \cdots N. \end{aligned} \tag{14}$$

which can be approximately optimized with two subsequent problems. First, we optimize unbinarized hash codes $\tilde{\boldsymbol{b}}_i$ with

$$\begin{aligned} \min \quad & L(\tilde{\boldsymbol{b}}_1, \cdots, \tilde{\boldsymbol{b}}_N) + \lambda \sum_{i=1}^{N} \phi(\tilde{\boldsymbol{b}}_i), \\ s.t. \quad & \tilde{\boldsymbol{b}}_i \in [0,1]^d. \end{aligned} \tag{15}$$

Then we optimize $\boldsymbol{\epsilon}_i$ with

$$\begin{aligned} \min \quad & \rho \sum_{i=1}^{N} \|\boldsymbol{\epsilon}_i\|_2^2 \\ s.t. \quad & \tilde{\boldsymbol{b}}_i + \boldsymbol{\epsilon}_i \in \{0,1\}^d, i = 1, 2, \cdots N. \end{aligned} \tag{16}$$

The second sub-problem is very simple with solution $\epsilon_{ij} = -\tilde{b}_{ij}$ if $\tilde{b}_{ij} \leq 0.5$ and otherwise $\epsilon_{ij} = 1 - \tilde{b}_{ij}$, from which we can easily obtain the binarized hash codes $\boldsymbol{b}_i$. Equation (13) proves that $\tilde{\boldsymbol{b}}_i$ is a good approximation of $\boldsymbol{b}_i$ with bounded error. Along with the optimization, $\tilde{\boldsymbol{b}}_i$ becomes closer and closer to $\boldsymbol{b}_i$. We will verify this point in experiments (ref. Section 4.2.3).

Considering the second term in the final objective function (15), we have (drop the subscript i for clarity)

$$\begin{aligned} \phi(\tilde{\boldsymbol{b}}) & = \tilde{\boldsymbol{b}}^T (1 - \tilde{\boldsymbol{b}}) \\ & \geqslant (\min(\tilde{\boldsymbol{b}}, 1 - \tilde{\boldsymbol{b}}))^2 \\ & = \|\boldsymbol{\epsilon}\|_2^2, \end{aligned} \tag{17}$$

which indicates that $\|\boldsymbol{\epsilon}\|_2^2$ is small when $\tilde{\boldsymbol{B}}$ reaches the optimal solution of the problem (15) and we choose an unbinarized hash fucntion whose range is $[0,1]$ implying ϵ is small. This means that the error bound in Equation (13) is small. In other words, the solution of the problem (14) is an accurate approximation of that of the problem (12).

Finally, the surrogate objective function of learning the hash functions is rewritten as follow,

$$\begin{aligned} \min \quad & L(\tilde{H}(\boldsymbol{x})) + \lambda \tilde{H}(\boldsymbol{x})^T (\boldsymbol{e} - \tilde{H}(\boldsymbol{x})), \\ s.t. \quad & \tilde{H}(\boldsymbol{x}) \in [0,1]^d. \end{aligned} \tag{18}$$

3.3 Model Details

3.3.1 Hash Functions

We formulate the unbinarized hash function $\tilde{b} = \tilde{h}(\boldsymbol{x})$ using a neural network with the output based on a sigmoid

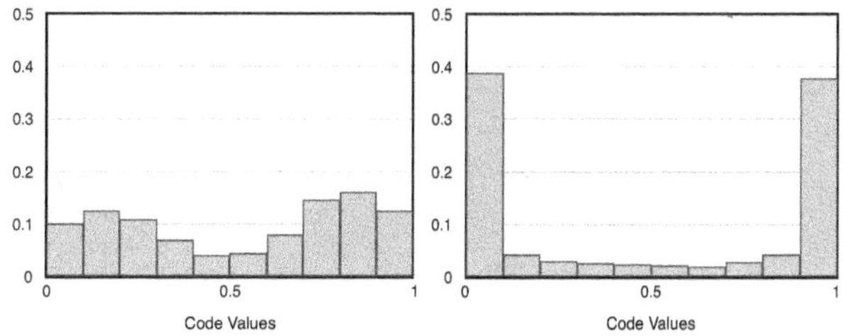

Figure 3: Histogram of output values by CNN trained with only the triplet ranking loss and the unified BOH loss. The vertical axis represents the frequency ratio of samples falling to certain intervals in the range [0,1]. Left: triplet ranking loss. Right: unified BOH loss.

Table 1: Result comparison on the effectiveness of the unified BOH loss, using 48 bits output and triplet ranking loss. The table above shows the results of mAP, and the table below shows the results of P@R⩽2.

Method	mAP		
	CIFAR-10	SVHN	NUS-WIDE
MLP	0.400	0.799	0.602
MLP+Regularization	0.352	0.800	0.603
BOH-MLP	0.420	0.818	0.623
CNN	0.627	0.914	0.831
CNN+Regularization	0.521	0.908	0.801
BOH-CNN	0.657	0.927	0.855

Method	P@R⩽2		
	CIFAR-10	SVHN	NUS-WIDE
MLP	0.421	0.774	0.600
MLP+Regularization	0.424	0.795	0.601
BOH-MLP	0.434	0.823	0.615
CNN	0.563	0.918	0.796
CNN+Regularization	0.220	0.710	0.327
BOH-CNN	0.666	0.924	0.839

function $s(t) = \frac{1}{1+e^{-t}}$ $(\in [0,1])$, which ensures that the error bound given in the Equation (13) is not large, as well as that the output satisfies the border constraint $[0,1]$. The input of the neural network could be either handcraft features or raw images, which leads to different architectures.

For the handcraft feature inputs, we take multi-layer perceptron (MLP) as hash functions, denoted as BOH-MLP. Figure 1 illustrates an architecture example with triplet ranking BOH loss. The inputs of BOH-MLP are dimension-fixed handcraft feature vectors, followed by several fully-connection (FC) layers, where the last FC layer is of size d, indicating the number of output hash bits. A sigmoid layer is connected to the last FC layer, ensuring the output values are in the range $[0,1]$.

For the raw image inputs, we take CNN as hash functions, and learn hash codes in an end-to-end manner, denoted as BOH-CNN. Figure 2 illustrates an architecture example also with triplet ranking BOH loss. We do not train CNN hash functions from scratch, but take parameters from the pre-trained CNN models (i.e. on ImageNet etc), and fine-tune the network parameters with stochastic gradient descent (SGD).

As it is trivial to get gradient from triplet ranking loss and contrastive loss, we omit the derivations here.

Table 2: The mAP (table above) and P@R⩽2 (table below) of BOH with contrastive loss (contra. in short) and triplet ranking loss, using 48 bits output.

Method	mAP		
	CIFAR-10	SVHN	NUS-WIDE
BOH-MLP Contra.	0.383	0.799	0.599
BOH-MLP Triplet	0.420	0.818	0.623
BOH-CNN Contra.	0.608	0.892	0.651
BOH-CNN Triplet	0.657	0.927	0.855

Method	P@R⩽2		
	CIFAR-10	SVHN	NUS-WIDE
BOH-MLP Contra.	0.422	0.779	0.591
BOH-MLP Triplet	0.434	0.823	0.615
BOH-CNN Contra.	0.370	0.893	0.349
BOH-CNN Triplet	0.666	0.924	0.839

3.3.2 Additional Regularization Term

In addition to the aforementioned two kinds of losses, we introduce one regularization term

$$\psi(\boldsymbol{y}) = \|\boldsymbol{b} + \boldsymbol{b}^- - \boldsymbol{e}\|_2^2, \tag{19}$$

where $\boldsymbol{y} = [\boldsymbol{b}; \boldsymbol{b}^-]$, $\boldsymbol{b}$ and $\boldsymbol{b}^-$ are hash codes of dissimilar images, and $\boldsymbol{e}$ is a vector with all elements being 1. The motivation behind this term is that dissimilar images should have opposite hash codes, i.e., they should have a larger Hamming distance.

It is easy to prove that $\psi(\boldsymbol{y})$ is Lipschitz continuous. We therefore define a unified loss by combining triplet ranking loss or contrastive loss $f(\cdot)$ with the regularization term

$$f(\boldsymbol{y}) + \lambda \boldsymbol{y}^T(\boldsymbol{e} - \boldsymbol{y}) + \beta\psi(\boldsymbol{y}), \tag{20}$$

where β is a hyper parameter, which controls the strength of regularization.

According to **Lemma 2**, the unified BOH loss is also Lipschitz continuous. We optimize problem (18) with this unified loss function.

3.3.3 Complexity Analysis

The training complexity of BOH-MLP is the same as MLP based hashing method, such as HDML [24]. Besides, BOH-CNN also has the same training complexity as the CNN baseline like DNNH [15]. For the testing part, the computation complexity of two-layer BOH-MLP is $O((d_i + d_o) \times d_h)$, while d_i, d_h and d_o are the dimension of input features, hidden neuron node size, and number of output hash bits. The testing complexity of BOH-CNN depends on the CNN structure used. However, it is generally with same order as DNNH [15].

4. EXPERIMENTS

4.1 Datasets and Experimental Settings

We conduct comprehensive experiments on three datasets, CIFAR-10 [10], SVHN [23] and NUS-WIDE [1], and compare our proposed method with several state-of-the-art hashing methods.

CIFAR-10 consists of 60K images of size 32×32, which are categorized into 10 classes, with 6K images per class. Each image has a unique label. We follow the settings of [34, 15], if there are no additional explanations. 1K images

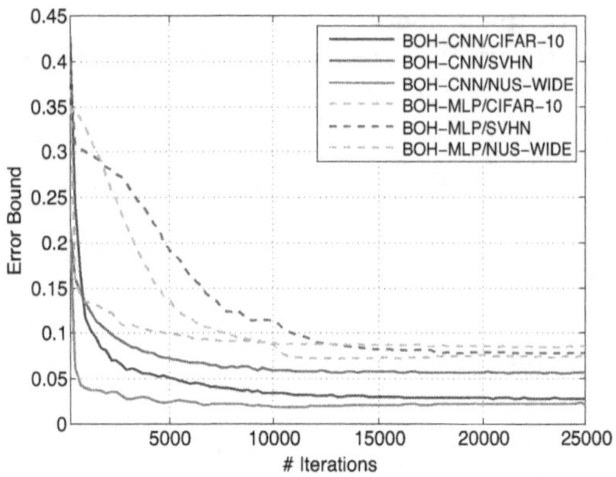

Figure 4: Average error bound vs. number of iterations. Here the triplet ranking loss function is used, with 48 bits hash codes.

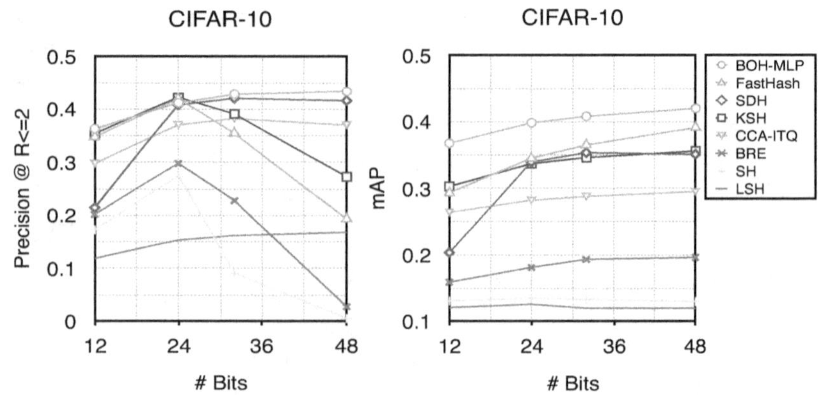

Figure 5: The mAP (right) and P@R⩽2 (left) of the compared methods on CIFAR-10 with the number of hash bits ranging from 12 to 48. The number of used training samples is 5,000.

(100 images per class) are randomly sampled to form the test query set. For the unsupervised methods, the training set contains the rest 59K images, while for the supervised methods, we randomly sample 5K images (500 images per class) for training. One exception is that in Sec. 4.3, we add one more additional training setting.

SVHN is a real-world image dataset which contains over 600K small 32×32 digits images. These images are split into three subset, named train set, test set and extra set. Following the settings in [15], we randomly select 1K images (100 images per class) from the whole set as test queries. For the unsupervised methods, rest of the images form the training set, while for the supervised methods, we randomly sample 5K images (500 images per class) for training. When testing, we use all the remaining images (over 600K) as query database.

NUS-WIDE contains about 270K Flickr images associated with 81 tags. Unlike CIFAR-10 and SVHN, each image in NUS-WIDE may have multiple tags. We follow the settings of [21, 15]. We only use 21 most frequent tags, where each tag has at least 5K images. We randomly sample 2,100 images (100 images per tag) to form the test query set. For the unsupervised methods, all the remaining images are used as training data. For the supervised methods, we randomly sample 10,500 images (500 per tag) for training.

For BOH-MLP, we use 512-dimensional GIST feature [25] for CIFAR-10/SVHN, and the provided 500-dimensional bag-of-words feature for NUS-WIDE. We design BOH-MLP with two hidden FC layers for all our experiments. The number of hidden neurons are 250 and 100 for the two layers, respectively. For BOH-CNN, we use raw image inputs directly. Different network structures are used for different datasets. For NUS-WIDE and CIFAR-10, we take the VGG-16 model [28] as our network structure. For SVHN, a smaller network structure is used, which contains three convolutional layers and two FC layers. The optimal values for hyper parameters β and λ in Equation (20) are determined on the training set in a cross-validation manner. Both BOH-MLP and BOH-CNN are implemented using Caffe [9].

We adopt the following four widely used metrics to evaluate the results: (1) mean average precision (mAP), (2) mean precision within Hamming radius 2 (in short P@R⩽2), (3) precision-recall curves, and (4) precision of top returned neighbors. In particular, on NUS-WIDE, we compute the mAP on top-5000 returned results. For P@R⩽2, if a query has no neighbors within radius 2, we treat the query with zero precision.

4.2 Design Evaluations

In this section we evaluate several design factors which affect the performance of our method.

4.2.1 *Effectiveness of the Unified BOH Loss*

One may be interested in knowing how much the unified BOH loss can contribute to the performance. To answer this question, we carry out experiments for the triplet ranking loss with the following three kinds of settings: 1) MLP or CNN trained with triplet ranking loss; 2) MLP or CNN trained with triplet ranking loss plus the regularization term from Equation 19; 3) MLP or CNN trained with the unified BOH loss (triplet ranking loss under BOH relaxation) from Equation 20. We set the number of hash bits $d = 48$.

Table 1 lists the comparison results. On CIFAR-10, the unified BOH loss reaches 2% and 3% gains on mAP with MLP and CNN hash function respectively. On SVHN, the performance gains are 1.9% and 1.3% for MLP and CNN respectively. And on NUS-WIDE, 2.1% and 2.4% improvements are observed. This shows that the improvements are consistently large over both CNN (strong) and MLP (weak) baseline. It is interesting to note that pure MLP or CNN with regularization term even yields noticeable accuracy drops to the counter part with the same settings. For instance, the mAP drops 5% and 10% on CIFAR-10 from the model trained with triplet ranking loss only. In terms of P@R⩽2 metric, the accuracy drops are even larger. This is due to the fact that MLP or CNN training with triplet loss does not guarantee optimal hash value outputs. We further present a visual illustration in Figure 3, which shows the histogram distribution of the hash values by CNN trained with triplet loss and unified BOH loss. It is obvious that BOH produces values mostly closer to 0 and 1, indicating the optimization nature of the method.

The results indicate that merely using regularization term does not bring performance improvement. On the contrary, it even hurts the performance seriously. Therefore, we conclude that the unified BOH loss as a whole is the most effective way for learning hash codes.

Table 3: The mAP (table above) and P@R⩽2 (table below) of HDML and BOH-HDML, with 48 bits output.

Method	mAP		
	CIFAR-10	SVHN	NUS-WIDE
HDML	0.273	0.679	0.544
BOH-HDML	0.306	0.714	0.582

Method	P@R⩽2		
	CIFAR-10	SVHN	NUS-WIDE
HDML	0.348	0.798	0.523
BOH-HDML	0.369	0.807	0.575

4.2.2 Triplet Ranking Loss vs. Contrastive Loss

In this experiment, we compare the performance of triplet ranking loss and contrastive loss under the unified BOH framework. Both BOH-MLP and BOH-CNN are evaluated, with the number of output hash bits $d = 48$.

Table 2 lists the comparison results on the three datasets. It shows that triplet ranking loss performs much better than contrastive loss on all metrics for these datasets. Specially, triplet ranking loss yields 1.9∼20.4% performance gain over contrastive loss on the mAP metric. For the P@R⩽2 metric on CNN based solutions, the differences are 29.6%, 49% and 3.5% on CIFAR-10, NUS-WIDE and SVHN respectively, where the results are much lower on the former two datasets. The reasons are two-fold. First, contrastive loss yields quite a few query cases that have no returned results within Hamming distance radius 2, and we treat these as zero precision so the P@R⩽2 accuracy is much lower. Second, the triplet ranking loss is naturally good for ranking so it has better top-ranked retrieval results. Based on these results, we use the triplet ranking loss in the following studies.

4.2.3 Convergence of BOH

It has been shown in Sec. 3.2 that we get an approximate problem (14) by optimizing the surrogate objective function. The approximation error is bounded by $\|\boldsymbol{\epsilon}\|^1$, as in (13). The optimization will yield the approximation error converged to a small value. In order to verify such approximation, we evaluate the error bound in this experiment.

Figure 4 illustrates the average error bound vs. number of iterations. Suppose the hash code is d bits, the average error bound is defined as $\|\boldsymbol{\epsilon}\|^1/d$ over all evaluating samples. We use triplet ranking loss here, and set the number of hash bits $d = 48$. We compute the average error bound every 250 iterations. It could be observed that the average error bound decreases gradually when training is performed. The error bound becomes stable and keeps at a low value after certain number of iterations, revealing that the obtained solution is very close to the optimal binarized solution. Besides, it also demonstrates that BOH-CNN could achieve much lower error bound than BOH-MLP.

4.2.4 Generalization to Existing Hashing Methods

The proposed BOH loss is fairly generic. It could be applied to some existing hashing methods, especially for those with triplet ranking loss. Here, we consider extending our BOH loss to HDML [24], which defines the loss as

$$L(\boldsymbol{w}) = \sum l_{triplet}(\boldsymbol{b}(\boldsymbol{x};\boldsymbol{w}), \boldsymbol{b}(\boldsymbol{x}^+;\boldsymbol{w}), \boldsymbol{b}(\boldsymbol{x}^-;\boldsymbol{w})) + \frac{\lambda}{2}\|\boldsymbol{w}\|_2^2,$$

where $\{\boldsymbol{x}^+, \boldsymbol{x}, \boldsymbol{x}^-\}$ is a triplet, $\boldsymbol{b}(\boldsymbol{x};\boldsymbol{w})$ is the hash function with parameter $\boldsymbol{w}$, and $l_{triplet}(\cdot)$ is triplet ranking loss. HDML adopts perceptrons as hash functions, and optimizes it with triplet ranking loss plus one matrix norm regularization term. In this study, we replace the regularized triplet ranking loss with the proposed BOH loss, and use one-layer perceptron with sigmoid activation as hash functions. We evaluate the performance on three datasets with 48 hash bits. The results are shown in Table 3. It could be observed that we gain substantial improvement with BOH loss, which demonstrates the generalization capability of the proposed method.

Table 4: mAP and P@R⩽2 of various methods on CIFAR-10 with 48 bits codes. The "# training" column indicates the number of training samples used.

Method	# training	mAP	P@R⩽2
LSH	5000	0.120	0.168
SH	5000	0.130	0.017
BRE	5000	0.196	0.028
CCA-ITQ	5000	0.295	0.370
KSH	5000	0.356	0.273
FastHash	5000	0.391	0.194
SDH	5000	0.351	0.416
BOH-MLP	5000	**0.420**	**0.434**
FastHash	59000	0.581	0.162
SDH	59000	0.509	0.529
BOH-MLP	59000	**0.626**	**0.598**

4.3 Result Comparison on Handcraft Features

We first compare BOH-MLP with existing state-of-the-art methods, including LSH [4], SH [33], BRE [12], CCA-ITQ [6], KSH [20], FastHash [17] and SDH [27]. We conduct experiments on CIFAR-10. Besides the regular 5K training samples, we also use one additional 59K training samples for SDH, FastHash and the proposed BOH-MLP. Note that for fair comparison, we use handcraft features as inputs for all the methods.

Table 4 shows the mAP and P@R⩽2 results with 48 bits output. We see that BOH-MLP achieves promising results on both training settings. For instance, when the number of training samples is 5K, the mAP of BOH-MLP exceeds FastHash by 2.9% and SDH by 6.9%. In addition, it is not surprising that when we use more training samples (59K), the performance of all the methods becomes better. In particular, BOH-MLP achieves the best performance on mAP (0.626) and P@R⩽2 (0.598), with improvements of 20.6% and 16.4% respectively over 5K training set. FastHash also achieves substantial improvement on mAP (19% improvement). However, its performance on P@R⩽2 is very poor (0.162). The poor P@R⩽2 of FastHash is consistent with the observations in [27]. Besides, SDH obtains approximately 16% improvement on mAP and 11% improvement on P@R⩽2. Moreover, by observing Table 1 and 4 (5K training samples), we can see that MLP achieves similar performance to FastHash (40% vs. 39.1%). The high-bar baseline of MLP (without BOH loss) is majorly due to the triplet ranking loss we used. However, when BOH loss is applied, the BOH-MLP achieves even better performance (42%). This improvement is substantial and verifies the superiority of the proposed method.

Figure 5 further shows the performance over different output hash bits. BOH-MLP shows stable improvements on

Figure 6: Top returned neighbors of BOH-CNN, FastHash, SDH and KSH, with 48 bits on NUS-WIDE. The images surrounded by red bounding boxes are negative neighbors.

Table 5: The mAP of BOH and state-of-the-art methods on CIFAR-10 and NUS-WIDE. For NUS-WIDE, we compute mAP on top-5000 returned samples. To ensure a fair comparison, we use 5K training samples for CIFAR-10.

Method	CIFAR-10				SVHN				NUS-WIDE			
	12 bits	24 bits	32 bits	48 bits	12 bits	24 bits	32 bits	48 bits	12 bits	24 bits	32 bits	48 bits
LSH [4]	0.121	0.126	0.120	0.120	0.110	0.122	0.120	0.128	0.403	0.421	0.426	0.441
SH [33]	0.131	0.135	0.133	0.130	0.140	0.138	0.141	0.140	0.433	0.426	0.426	0.423
BRE [12]	0.159	0.181	0.193	0.196	0.165	0.206	0.230	0.237	0.485	0.525	0.530	0.544
CCA-ITQ [6]	0.264	0.282	0.288	0.295	0.428	0.488	0.489	0.509	0.435	0.435	0.435	0.435
KSH [20]	0.303	0.337	0.346	0.356	0.469	0.539	0.563	0.581	0.556	0.572	0.581	0.588
SDH [27]	0.203	0.340	0.354	0.351	0.317	0.746	0.761	0.781	0.530	0.546	0.536	0.582
FastHash [17]	0.293	0.345	0.365	0.391	0.689	0.768	0.783	0.802	0.496	0.568	0.596	0.613
BOH-MLP	**0.367**	**0.398**	**0.408**	**0.420**	**0.791**	**0.803**	**0.806**	**0.818**	**0.574**	**0.605**	**0.613**	**0.623**
CNNH [34]	0.465	0.521	0.521	0.532	0.897	0.903	0.904	0.896	0.623	0.630	0.629	0.625
DNNH [15]	0.552	0.566	0.558	0.581	0.899	0.914	0.925	0.923	0.674	0.697	0.713	0.715
BOH-CNN	**0.620**	**0.633**	**0.644**	**0.657**	**0.904**	**0.923**	**0.926**	**0.927**	**0.786**	**0.834**	**0.837**	**0.855**

both mAP metric and P@R⩽2 metric, while some other methods even show accuracy drops on the P@R⩽2 metric when the number of output bits surpass a threshold.

4.4 Result Comparison on Raw Image Inputs

We then compare BOH to state-of-the-art methods on raw image inputs, which are usually based on end-to-end deep learning framework. The compared methods are CNNH [34] and DNNH [15].

Table 5 shows the comparison results of mAP on the three datasets. The bottom part of the table lists the results with raw image inputs, while the top part of the table still keeps some results with the handcraft features. The results clearly show the power of end-to-end deep learning over shallow learning. Figure 7 further illustrates P@R⩽2 over different hash bits, precision-recall curve and precision of top returned images at 48 bits. Besides, Figure 6 shows some retrieval results of several methods, with 48 bits on NUS-WIDE.

Our method produces very promising results. Compared with the deep learning based method DNNH, BOH-CNN achieves a fairly significant improvement. For instance, BOH-CNN gains an increase of 7.6%, 0.4% and 14% in terms of mAP at 48-bit outputs on CIFAR-10, SVHN and NUS-WIDE, respectively. Note that DNNH is also based on triplet ranking loss under the same CNN framework. As CNN does not explicitly generate binary codes, DNNH then presents a divide-and-encode module to approximate hash codes from the CNN outputs. The approximation is much weaker than our theoretical guaranteed solution, which is the reason that it produces much worse results.

5. CONCLUSION

This paper proposes *binary optimized hashing* (BOH), in which we prove that if the loss function is Lipschitz continuous, the mixed integral hashing learning problem can be relaxed to a bound-constrained continuous optimization problem. We introduce a surrogate objective function to approximate the relaxed objective function. We show that the

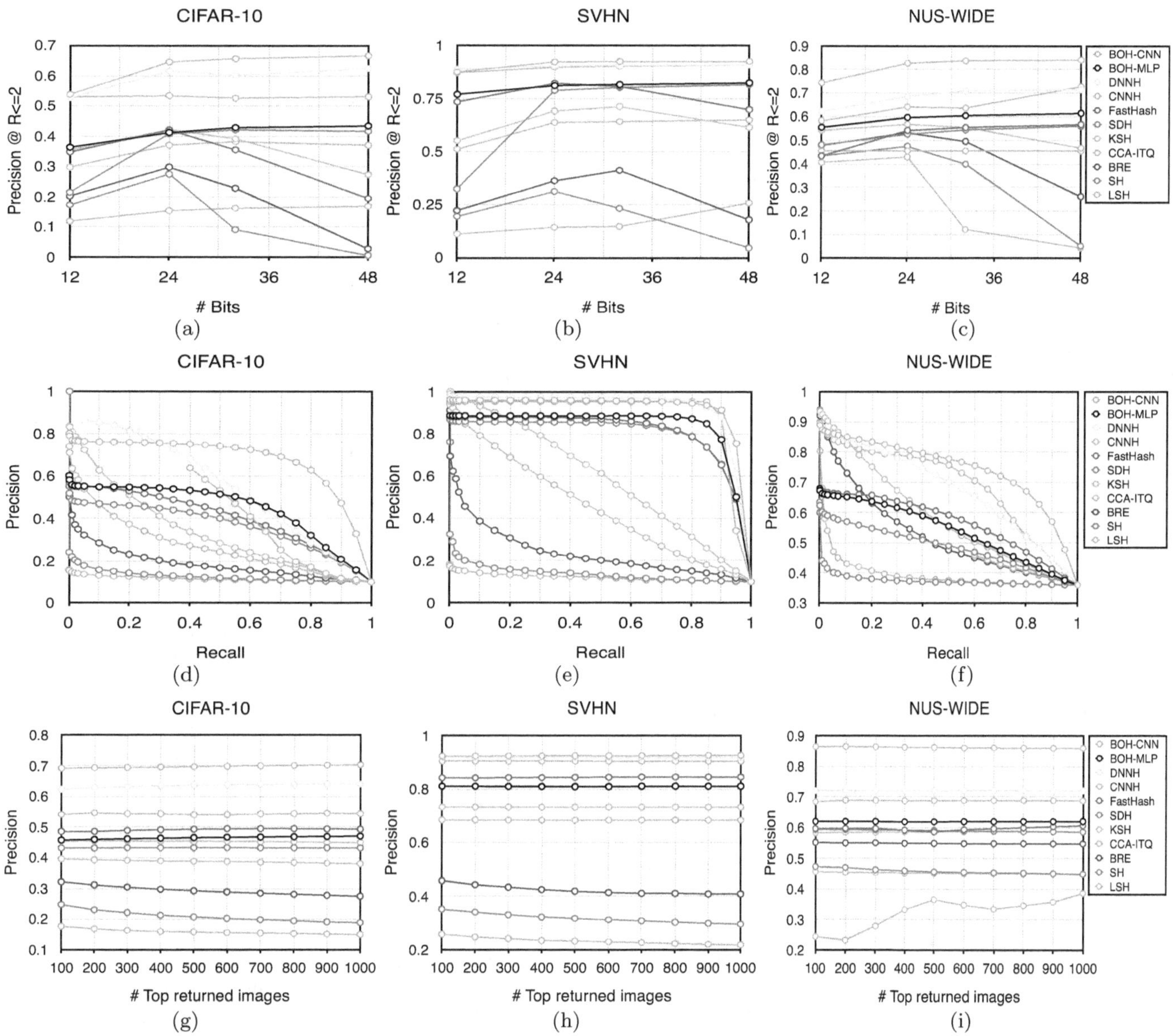

Figure 7: First row: P@R⩽2 over different numbers of bits. Second row: precision-recall curves with 48 bits. Third row: precision of top returned images. First column: on CIFAR-10. Second column: on SVHN. Third column: on NUS-WIDE.

approximation error is bounded, and bound is small when the problem is optimized.

The proposed approach is applied to learn hash codes from either handcraft feature inputs or raw image inputs in an end-to-end manner. Experiments are carried out on three benchmarks, which clearly demonstrate that our approach outperforms the state-of-the-arts (both traditional hashing techniques and deep learning based hashing techniques) with a significant margin on search accuracies. Future works are on the extension of the proposed BOH framework to other loss functions and different learning to hash problems like unsupervised hashing.

Acknowledgments

This work was supported by China's National 863 Program (#2014AA015101) and a grant from NSF China (#U1509206).

6. REFERENCES

[1] T.-S. Chua, J. Tang, R. Hong, H. Li, Z. Luo, and Y. Zheng. Nus-wide: a real-world web image database from national university of singapore. In *CIVR*, 2009.

[2] V. Erin Liong, J. Lu, G. Wang, P. Moulin, and J. Zhou. Deep hashing for compact binary codes learning. In *CVPR*, 2015.

[3] F. Giannessi and F. Tardella. Connections between nonlinear programming and discrete optimization. In *Handbook of Combinatorial Optimization*. Springer, 1999.

[4] A. Gionis, P. Indyk, R. Motwani, et al. Similarity search in high dimensions via hashing. In *VLDB*, 1999.

[5] Y. Gong, S. Kumar, V. Verma, and S. Lazebnik. Angular quantization-based binary codes for fast similarity search. In *NIPS*, 2012.

[6] Y. Gong and S. Lazebnik. Iterative quantization: A procrustean approach to learning binary codes. In *CVPR*, 2011.

[7] R. Hadsell, S. Chopra, and Y. LeCun. Dimensionality reduction by learning an invariant mapping. In *CVPR*, 2006.

[8] J.-P. Heo, Y. Lee, J. He, S.-F. Chang, and S.-E. Yoon. Spherical hashing. In *CVPR*. IEEE, 2012.

[9] Y. Jia, E. Shelhamer, J. Donahue, S. Karayev, J. Long, R. Girshick, S. Guadarrama, and T. Darrell. Caffe: Convolutional architecture for fast feature embedding. *arXiv preprint arXiv:1408.5093*, 2014.

[10] A. Krizhevsky and G. Hinton. Learning multiple layers of features from tiny images, 2009.

[11] A. Krizhevsky, I. Sutskever, and G. E. Hinton. Imagenet classification with deep convolutional neural networks. In *NIPS*, 2012.

[12] B. Kulis and T. Darrell. Learning to hash with binary reconstructive embeddings. In *NIPS*, 2009.

[13] B. Kulis and K. Grauman. Kernelized locality-sensitive hashing for scalable image search. In *ICCV*, 2009.

[14] B. Kulis and K. Grauman. Kernelized locality-sensitive hashing. *TPAMI*, 2012.

[15] H. Lai, Y. Pan, Y. Liu, and S. Yan. Simultaneous feature learning and hash coding with deep neural networks. In *CVPR*, 2015.

[16] X. Li, G. Lin, C. Shen, A. Hengel, and A. Dick. Learning hash functions using column generation. In *ICML*, 2013.

[17] G. Lin, C. Shen, Q. Shi, A. Hengel, and D. Suter. Fast supervised hashing with decision trees for high-dimensional data. In *CVPR*, pages 1963–1970, 2014.

[18] G. Lin, C. Shen, D. Suter, and A. Hengel. A general two-step approach to learning-based hashing. In *ICCV*, pages 2552–2559, 2013.

[19] W. Liu, C. Mu, S. Kumar, and S.-F. Chang. Discrete graph hashing. In *NIPS*, pages 3419–3427, 2014.

[20] W. Liu, J. Wang, R. Ji, Y.-G. Jiang, and S.-F. Chang. Supervised hashing with kernels. In *CVPR*, 2012.

[21] W. Liu, J. Wang, S. Kumar, and S.-F. Chang. Hashing with graphs. In *ICML*, 2011.

[22] S. Lucidi and F. Rinaldi. Exact penalty functions for nonlinear integer programming problems. *Journal of optimization theory and applications*, 2010.

[23] Y. Netzer, T. Wang, A. Coates, A. Bissacco, B. Wu, and A. Y. Ng. Reading digits in natural images with unsupervised feature learning. In *NIPS workshop on deep learning and unsupervised feature learning*, volume 2011, 2011.

[24] M. Norouzi, D. M. Blei, and R. R. Salakhutdinov. Hamming distance metric learning. In *NIPS*, 2012.

[25] A. Oliva and A. Torralba. Modeling the shape of the scene: A holistic representation of the spatial envelope. *IJCV*, 2001.

[26] R. Salakhutdinov and G. Hinton. Semantic hashing. *International Journal of Approximate Reasoning*, 50(7):969–978, 2009.

[27] F. Shen, C. Shen, W. Liu, and H. T. Shen. Supervised discrete hashing. In *CVPR*, 2015.

[28] K. Simonyan and A. Zisserman. Very deep convolutional networks for large-scale image recognition. *CoRR*, abs/1409.1556, 2014.

[29] C. Strecha, A. M. Bronstein, M. M. Bronstein, and P. Fua. Ldahash: Improved matching with smaller descriptors. *IEEE TPAMI*, 2012.

[30] J. Wang, S. Kumar, and S.-F. Chang. Semi-supervised hashing for large-scale search. *TPAMI*, 2012.

[31] J. Wang, W. Liu, S. Kumar, and S.-F. Chang. Learning to hash for indexing big data - a survey. *Proceeding of The IEEE*, 2016.

[32] J. Wang, H. T. Shen, J. Song, and J. Ji. Hashing for similarity search: A survey. *CoRR*, abs/1408.2927, 2014.

[33] Y. Weiss, A. Torralba, and R. Fergus. Spectral hashing. In *NIPS*, 2009.

[34] R. Xia, Y. Pan, H. Lai, C. Liu, and S. Yan. Supervised hashing for image retrieval via image representation learning. In *AAAI*, 2014.

[35] F. Zhao, Y. Huang, L. Wang, and T. Tan. Deep semantic ranking based hashing for multi-label image retrieval. In *CVPR*, 2015.

Linear Distance Preserving Pseudo-Supervised and Unsupervised Hashing

Min Wang†, Wengang Zhou†, Qi Tian‡, Zhengjun Zha†, Houqiang Li†
† CAS Key Laboratory of Technology in Geo-spatial Information Processing and Application System, University of Science and Technology of China
‡ Computer Science Department, University of Texas at San Antonio
wm123@mail.ustc.edu.cn, {zhwg, zhazj, lihq}@ustc.edu.cn, qitian@cs.utsa.edu

ABSTRACT

With the advantage in compact representation and efficient comparison, binary hashing has been extensively investigated for approximate nearest neighbor search. In this paper, we propose a novel and general hashing framework, which simultaneously considers a new linear pair-wise distance preserving objective and point-wise constraint. The direct distance preserving objective aims to keep the linear relationships between the Euclidean distance and the Hamming distance of data points. Based on different point-wise constraints, we propose two methods to instantiate this framework. The first one is a pseudo-supervised hashing method, which uses existing unsupervised hashing methods to generate binary codes as pseudo-supervised information. The second one is an unsupervised hashing method, in which quantization loss is considered. We validate our framework on two large-scale datasets. The experiments demonstrate that our pseudo-supervised method achieves consistent improvement for the state-of-the-art unsupervised hashing methods, while our unsupervised method outperforms the state-of-the-art methods.

Keywords

Distance preserving hashing; approximate nearest neighbor search; learning to hash

1. INTRODUCTION

Approximate nearest neighbors (ANN) search is a fundamental research problem in computer vision and multimedia fields. Given a query sample, ANN search aims to identify those nearest data points with high probability from a large corpus with a sub-linear, or even constant time complexity. To solve this problem efficiently, lots of methods have been proposed, such as tree-based approaches [1] and hashing algorithms [31, 2, 30, 17, 32, 29, 33, 22]. With the advantage in compact representation and efficient comparison, binary hashing techniques have become more and more popular.

MM '16, October 15-19, 2016, Amsterdam, Netherlands

DOI: http://dx.doi.org/10.1145/2964284.2964334

Existing binary hashing methods can be classified into two categories: data-independent and data-dependent methods according to whether the training data is involved. As the representative data-independent methods, Locality Sensitive Hashing (LSH) [4] and its variants [12, 10] have been widely explored. On the other hand, lots of research efforts are devoted to data-dependent methods to learn more compact hash codes with the training dataset. The data-dependent methods can be divided into three categories according to whether they use labels or class information: unsupervised methods [5, 23, 7, 18, 6, 9, 34], semi-supervised methods [20], and supervised methods [11, 14, 16, 26]. Although in most literature, supervised and semi-supervised methods are demonstrated with much better performance than unsupervised ones, it is a non-trivial issue to assume the availability of labels or class information for training data in many scenarios. In this paper, we only focus on unsupervised binary hashing.

The fundamental of unsupervised hashing is to achieve distance preservation across the original data space and Hamming space, which intuitively results in a pair-wise constraint. Some hashing methods implicitly achieve distance preserving with point-wise constraints, which explore the intrinsic properties of expected binary codes (such as balance and independence) or the data distribution information. For instance, Iterative Quantization (ITQ) [5] learns an orthogonal rotation matrix by minimizing the quantization loss while mapping the data generated by PCA projections to binary codes. It realizes the independence properties of binary codes by the orthogonal basis vectors of PCA. Spherical Hashing (SpH) [7] exploits hypersphere-based hashing function maps spatially coherent data points to similar binary codes. SpH aims to preserve the balance and independence properties of binary code. Although these unsupervised methods achieve promising performance, improvement can be expected by further imposing the additional explicit distance-preserving constraint.

On the other hand, deep-learning based hashing methods become more and more popular. Many supervised hashing methods [13, 24, 28, 27] adopt the deep neural networks or deep convolutional neural networks to generate hash code, which fully explore the pair-wise or triplet-wise constraints denoted by the class labels. But for unsupervised hashing, the methods based on deep neural networks [19, 15, 3] only involve the point-wise constraints, due to the lack of labels or class information. For instance, in [15], a novel neural network is developed to seek multiple hierarchical non-linear transformations to learn binary codes to preserve the non-

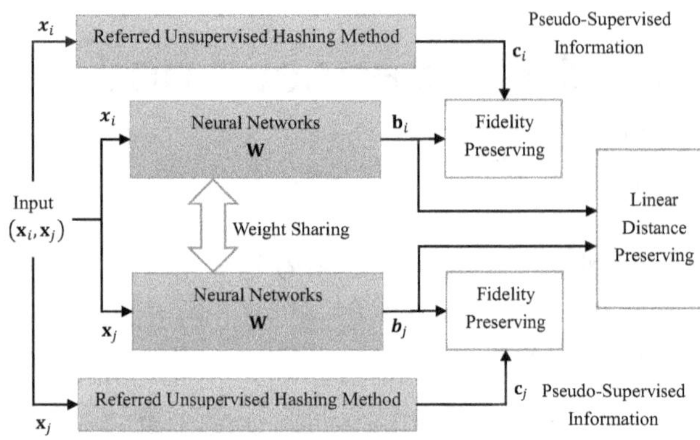

Figure 1: The basic idea of our pseudo-supervised hashing method. The input of the dual neural networks is a pair of data points, $\mathbf{x}_i$ and $\mathbf{x}_j$. $\mathbf{c}_i$ and $\mathbf{c}_j$ are the binary codes generated by the referred unsupervised hashing method, which are used as the pseudo-supervised information for training the dual neural networks in the Fidelity Preserving term. The binarized outputs of the dual neural networks are $\mathbf{b}_i$ and $\mathbf{b}_j$. We use the Hamming distance $h_{i,j}$ between $\mathbf{b}_i$ and $\mathbf{b}_j$ in the Linear Distance Preserving term to train our dual neural networks.

linear relationship of samples. The model in [15] is learnt by minimizing the quantization loss between the original real-valued feature descriptor and the learnt binary code, which is typically a point-wise constraint. Since the point-wise constraint is not essential to ensure the distance-preserving fundamental of unsupervised hashing, the unsupervised methods based on neural networks [19, 15, 3] usually do not achieve much better performance than the classical methods.

In this paper, we propose a novel and general framework which involves a new pair-wise linear distance preserving objective and point-wise constraint. In this framework, our distance preserving objective aims to preserve the linear transformation between the Euclidean distance and the Hamming distance for pairs of data. Based on different point-wise constraints, we propose two methods to instantiate the framework. The first one is a pseudo-supervised hashing method, in which we generate the pseudo-supervised information by an existing unsupervised hashing method. The motivation of this method is to apply pair-wise distance preserving objective based on neural networks to improve the performances of the referred unsupervised hashing methods. We preserve the new distance preserving objective, and simultaneously keep the fidelity of the selected unsupervised hashing method in this method. This method is solved by dual neural networks. The basic idea of this method is shown in Fig. 1. Note that the pseudo-supervised method is a general boosting method, which can be applied to existing unsupervised hashing methods. The second one is an unsupervised hashing method, in which we minimize the quantization loss between the projected data and the binarized data. By fully exploring pair-wise and point-wise constraints at the same time, our unsupervised hashing method demonstrates excellent performance.

There are three main contributions in this paper:

- A novel and general linear distance preserving hashing framework is proposed, in which a new pair-wise linear distance preserving objective and point-wise constraint are considered simultaneously.
- The framework is instantiated by a pseudo-supervised hashing method, which provides a general paradigm to boost existing unsupervised hashing methods. The experiments on two large-scale datasets validate that our pseudo-supervised method improves the performances of existing state-of-the-art methods largely.
- A new unsupervised hashing method is developed to instantiate the framework, which simultaneously preserve the pairwise distance-preserving objective and the point-wise constraint. The experiments prove that our unsupervised method outperforms the state-of-the-art unsupervised hashing methods.

The rest of this paper is organized as follow. We first review the related work with our approach in Section 2. Then in Section 3, we present the proposed hashing framework, and its two instantiations, *i.e.*, pseudo-supervised method and unsupervised hashing method. After that, the experiments are shown in Section 4. Finally we make a conclusion in Section 5.

2. RELATED WORK

In this section, we review the related work from two aspects: unsupervised binary hashing methods, and the use of deep learning techniques in hashing.

Unsupervised hashing methods learn hash functions with training data points without any label or class information. The fundamental of unsupervised hashing methods is distance preservation across the original space and the Hamming space. K-means Hashing (KMH) [6] simultaneously performs k-means clustering and learns the binary indices of the quantized cells. The Euclidean distance between data points is implicitly approximated by the Hamming distance between the binary indices of the corresponding cells. Spectral Hashing (SH) [23] formulates the hash function learning problem as a particular form of graph partition to seek a binary code with balanced and uncorrelated bits. Minimal Loss Hashing (MLH) [18] adopts a pairwise hinge-like loss function and minimizes its upper bound to learn binary codes. Order Preserving Hashing (OPH) [21] learns hash functions by maximizing the alignment between the similarity orders computed from the original space and the ones in the Hamming space. Topology Preserving Hashing (TPH) [25] aims at preserving the neighbor rankings of data points in Hamming space. Binary Reconstructive Embedding (BRE) [11] utilizes pairwise relations between samples and minimizes the squared error between the original normalized Euclidean distance and the normalized Hamming distance. In our approach, we generalize the distance preserving constraint with a linear transformation and optimize it in a different way.

Nowadays, deep learning becomes more and more popular. Many supervised hashing methods are involved with deep learning techniques. [24] proposes a supervised hashing method based on convolutional neural networks, which automatically learns a good image representation tailored to hashing as well as a set of hash functions. [13] proposes a deep architecture for supervised hashing, in which images are mapped into binary codes via carefully designed deep neural networks. The model in [13] considers a triplet ranking loss denoted by the image labels. [28] proposes a deep semantic ranking based method for hashing function learning to handle multi-level semantic similarity between multi-label images. [27] proposes a supervised learning framework to generate compact and bit-scalable hashing code directly from raw images. The model in [27] maximizes the margin between the matched pairs and the mismatched pairs in the Hamming space.

On the other hand, most existing unsupervised hashing methods based on deep learning techniques learn to generate binary codes by exploring the data distribution or the intrinsic properties of expected binary codes. To our best knowledge, there is no work explicitly exploring distance preserving constraint with neural networks for unsupervised binary hashing, which is probably due to the lack of labels or class information. Semantic hashing [19] is a pioneering work using deep learning techniques for hashing. They apply the stacked Restricted Boltzmann Machine (RBM) to learn compact binary codes for visual search. [3] also uses a point-wise objective function. It focuses on the binary auto-encoder model, which seeks to reconstruct a data point from binary code produced by the hash functions. Compared with these unsupervised methods, our pseudo-supervised method uses dual neural networks to realize linear distance projection relationship and simultaneously keep original hashing functions learnt by existing hashing methods, which involves pairwise constraint and adheres to the distance-preserving goal of hashing.

3. OUR APPROACH

In this section, we first give some notations to facilitate the following discussion in Section 3.1. Then, we discuss our linear distance preserving objective and the corresponding general hashing framework in Section 3.2 and 3.3. After that, we discuss two instantiations of our hashing framework in Section 3.4 and 3.5, respectively.

3.1 Notations

Given a dataset $\mathbf{X} \in \mathbb{R}^{n\times D}$, each row of $\mathbf{X}$ is a high dimensional data vector $\mathbf{x}_i \in \mathbb{R}^D$. The Euclidean distance between the original data vector $\mathbf{x}_i$ and $\mathbf{x}_j$ is computed by $L2$-norm, $d(\mathbf{x}_i,\mathbf{x}_j) = \|\mathbf{x}_i - \mathbf{x}_j\|_2$, and we denote it as $d_{i,j}$ for conciseness.

Using binary hashing, each original high dimensional data vector $\mathbf{x}_i$ is mapped to a low dimensional binary vector $\mathbf{b}_i \in \mathbb{H}^L$ (usually, $L << D$). The resulted binary vectors significantly reduce the memory cost and the distance in Hamming space (*i.e.*, Hamming distance) can be efficiently computed by modern CPUs. The Hamming distance $h(\mathbf{b}_i, \mathbf{b}_j)$ between the corresponding binary vector $\mathbf{b}_i$ and $\mathbf{b}_j$ is denoted as $h_{i,j}$ for conciseness.

The usual paradigm of binary hashing is to first map each data point into a low dimensional space, then quantize the mapped data point to a binary vector. Usually the mapping function is supposed to be a linear form. Let $\mathbf{W} = [\mathbf{w}_1, \mathbf{w}_2, \ldots, \mathbf{w}_L] \in \mathbb{R}^{D\times L}$ be the learned projection matrix, then the mapping of $\mathbf{X}$ can be obtained as $\mathbf{U} = \mathbf{XW}$, which is further binarized to obtain the binary codes as follows:

$$\mathbf{B} = (sgn(\mathbf{U}) + 1)/2 = (sgn(\mathbf{XW}) + 1)/2, \tag{1}$$

where $sgn(\cdot)$ is an element-wise sign function.

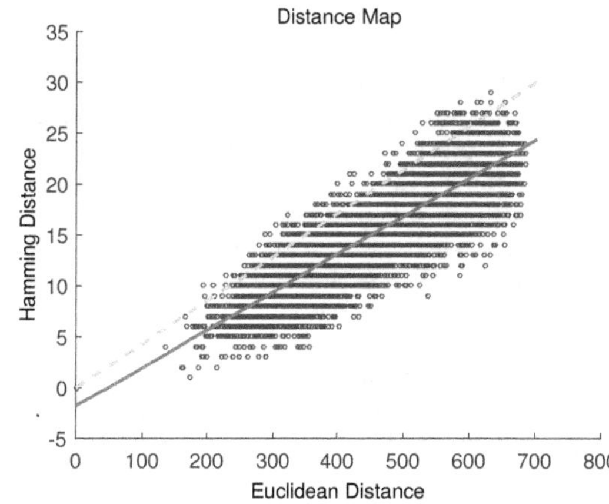

Figure 2: Distance map between Hamming distance and Euclidean distance of pairs. The Hamming distance of a pair of data points is computed from the corresponding binary codes generated by ITQ[5]. Each blue point denotes the Euclidean distance and the corresponding Hamming distance of a pair of data points. The green dash line is adopted in BRE [11]. The red line is generated by our method, which fits the distribution of the distance map.

3.2 Linear Distance Preserving Objective

The main methodology of unsupervised hashing methods is distance-preserving across the original Euclidean space and Hamming space, *i.e.*, $h_{i,j} \propto d_{i,j}$. To utilize the distance-preserving constraint in our framework, we propose a new distance preserving objective, in which we keep the linear projection relationship of the two distances between pairwise data points. The objective can be achieved by minimizing the following function:

$$\Phi(\mathbf{W}, a, b) = \|\mathbf{H} - a\mathbf{E} - b\|_F^2, \tag{2}$$

where $\|\cdot\|_F$ denotes Frobenius norm, a and b[1] are the parameters of linear distance transformation, which define the red line in Fig. 2 for intuitive, and implicitly impact the selection of the projection matrix $\mathbf{W}$. $\mathbf{E}$ and $\mathbf{H} \in \mathbb{R}^{n\times p}$, where p denotes the number of pairs for each data point. The element $\mathrm{E}(i,j)$ in $\mathbf{E}$ denotes the $L2$ distance between $\mathbf{x}_i$ and $\mathbf{x}_j$ in the Euclidean space, *i.e.*, $d_{i,j}$, while the element $\mathrm{H}(i,j)$ in $\mathbf{H}$ denotes the Hamming distance between the corresponding binary code $\mathbf{b}_i$ and $\mathbf{b}_j$ in the Hamming space, *i.e.*, $h_{i,j}$. To facilitate the solution, the Hamming distance between the binary code $\mathbf{b}_i$ and $\mathbf{b}_j$ can be described as

$$\mathrm{H}(i,j) = L - \mathbf{b}_i^T\mathbf{b}_j - (\mathbf{1}_{L\times 1} - \mathbf{b}_i)^{\mathrm{T}}(\mathbf{1}_{L\times 1} - \mathbf{b}_j). \tag{3}$$

We give a visual illustration for this distance preserving goal in Fig. 2. We randomly select 10,000 pairs of data points from ANN_SIFT1M dataset [8] and compute their Euclidean distances. Then we generate their corresponding binary codes in Hamming space by ITQ [5] with code length equal to 32 bits, and compute the Hamming distance between the binary codes of these pairs. Each pair of data

[1] a, b are scalars, the multiplication between a and $\mathbf{E}$ is element-wise multiplication between a and each element of $\mathbf{E}$, and the subtraction to b is also element-wise, we omit the $\mathbf{1}$ matrix for conciseness.

points is painted by a blue marker in Fig. 2. The red linear line is generated by Least Square method applied on those distance pairs. All those data pairs distribute in a long strip area, which locates around the red line. We can intuitively find that if the strip area shrinks towards the red linear line, *i.e.*, becomes thinner, the distance preserving performance of the hash functions will be better. The shrink manipulation makes the pairs with the same Euclidean distance have more similar Hamming distances, which implicitly realizes the distance-preserving objective.

Similar to our approach, BRE [11] imposes distance preserving constraint by minimizing the deviation between the normalized Hamming distance and the normalized Euclidean distance. It can be regarded as a special case of our method, when $a = L/e_{max}, b = 0$ (e_{max} is the maximum of the Euclidean distance). The BRE method chooses the diagonal of the coordinate area as the supervisor of distance map, as the green dash line in Fig. 2. We can intuitively find the diagonal line is not essentially the best choice for the real data distribution, which makes the strip area shrink slow and degrades the performance.

3.3 Linear Distance Preserving Framework

In our framework, we randomly select N_p pairs of data, and save their indices into $\mathbf{P} = \left[\mathbf{p}_1^T, \mathbf{p}_2^T, \ldots, \mathbf{p}_{N_p}^T\right]^T \in \mathbb{R}^{N_p \times 2}$, where each row $\mathbf{p}_i \in \mathbb{R}^{1\times 2}$ denotes the indices of a pair of data points. Then we can compute the $L2$ distance $\mathbf{d}$ for these pairs. Noted that the $\mathbf{d} \in \mathbb{R}^{N_p \times 1}$ here is a vector, which can be seen as the vector form of the matrix $\mathbf{E}$ in Eq. (2). To make our description clear, we rewrite two vector forms of the indices $\mathbf{P}$ as $\tilde{\mathbf{P}} = [\mathbf{p}_1(1), \mathbf{p}_2(1), \ldots, \mathbf{p}_{N_p}(1), \mathbf{p}_1(2), \mathbf{p}_2(2), \ldots, \mathbf{p}_{N_p}(2)]^T$ and $\hat{\mathbf{P}} = [\mathbf{p}_1(2), \mathbf{p}_2(2), \ldots, \mathbf{p}_{N_p}(2), \mathbf{p}_1(1), \mathbf{p}_2(1), \ldots, \mathbf{p}_{N_p}(1)]^T$. We use these indices to reorganize our training data matrix $\mathbf{X}$ as $\tilde{\mathbf{X}} = \mathbf{X}(\tilde{\mathbf{P}}) \in \mathbb{R}^{2N_p \times D}$, in which each row $\tilde{\mathbf{x}}_i$ of $\tilde{\mathbf{X}}$ is $\mathbf{x}_{\tilde{\mathbf{P}}_i}$. Similarly, $\hat{\mathbf{X}} = \mathbf{X}(\hat{\mathbf{P}})$, in which each row $\hat{\mathbf{x}}_i$ of $\hat{\mathbf{X}}$ is $\mathbf{x}_{\hat{\mathbf{P}}_i}$. In our optimization, we replace the sign function with sigmoid function, *i.e.*, the projected data $\mathbf{U} = sigmoid(\mathbf{XW}) \in \mathbb{R}^{n\times L}$, and the binary codes $\mathbf{B} = round(\mathbf{U})$. We reorganize $\mathbf{U}$ as $\tilde{\mathbf{U}} = \mathbf{U}(\tilde{\mathbf{P}}) \in \mathbb{R}^{2N_p\times L}$, and $\hat{\mathbf{U}} = \mathbf{U}(\hat{\mathbf{P}})$. And we can compute Hamming distance $\mathbf{h}$ for all the pairs as Eq. (3).

Our linear distance preserving framework simultaneously considers the pairwise linear distance preserving objective, point-wise constraint, and orthogonal projection constraint. The whole optimization function of the proposed framework can be devised as follows:

$$\min_{\mathbf{W},a,b} \frac{\lambda}{N_p}\|\mathbf{h} - a\mathbf{d} - b\|_2^2 + \frac{\alpha}{N_p}\left\|\tilde{\mathbf{U}} - \mathbf{C}\right\|_F^2 + \beta\|\mathbf{W}^T\mathbf{W} - \mathbf{I}\|_F^2, \tag{4}$$

where the first term focuses on linear distance preserving, which can be seen as the vector form of Eq. (2), and the third term imposes the orthogonality constraint between projection vectors to achieve the bit independence. The second term is a point-wise constraint, and $\mathbf{C}$ can be interpreted in different ways, which leads to different instantiations. When $\mathbf{C}$ is obtained by a certain existing binary hashing method, we can obtain a pseudo-supervised hashing scheme, which can be realized with dual neural networks, as discussed in the following Section 3.4. On the other hand, we can also regard $\mathbf{C}$ as a constant matrix and derive a new unsupervised hashing scheme, which will be discussed in Section 3.5.

3.4 Linear Distance Preserving Pseudo Supervised Hashing

Since the existing unsupervised hashing methods have fully explore the data distribution or the intrinsic properties of expected binary codes, which helps learn good hashing function. We instantiate the proposed framework by a pseudo-supervised hashing method, which can boost the performance of existing unsupervised hashing methods by further imposing the pairwise distance preserving objective. In this implementation, we first select an existing unsupervised hashing method to generate binary codes $\mathbf{C}$ as pseudo-supervised information. The supervised binary codes $\mathbf{C}$ are also reorganized as $\tilde{\mathbf{C}} = \mathbf{C}(\tilde{\mathbf{P}}) \in \mathbb{H}^{2N_p\times L}$. This method preserves the linear distance transformation relationships, and simultaneously keeps the hashing functions learnt by original unsupervised hashing methods. It merges the pseudo-supervised information into our framework as follows:

$$\min_{\mathbf{W},a,b} \frac{\lambda}{N_p}\|\mathbf{h} - a\mathbf{d} - b\|_2^2 + \frac{\alpha}{N_p}\left\|\tilde{\mathbf{U}} - \tilde{\mathbf{C}}\right\|_F^2 + \beta\|\mathbf{W}^T\mathbf{W} - \mathbf{I}\|_F^2, \tag{5}$$

where the second part of this objective aims to preserve the fidelity of the involved unsupervised method. This part can make the binarized output of our method similar with the output of the original unsupervised hashing method, which preserves the projections of the referred unsupervised hashing functions. Here to solve the whole objective function with pairwise distance-preserving constraint, we propose a new learning algorithm based on dual neural networks. We use neural networks here with the motivation of the fact that neural networks can imitate the transformations of any complexity. The two neural networks share the same structure, parameters, and weight matrices, but are fed with different input samples, as shown in Fig. 1.

It is difficult to simultaneously optimize the Eq. (5) with respect to $\mathbf{W}, a$, and b. To address this difficulty, we propose an alternative scheme. First, we fix $\mathbf{W}$, and optimize the objective function with respect to a and b. Then we fix a and b, and optimize the objective function with respect to $\mathbf{W}$. The above two steps are repeated until we achieve a convergence. In the following, we discuss the learning process in details.

3.4.1 a, b-step

With $\mathbf{W}$ fixed, the optimization on the objective function in Eq. (5) becomes

$$\min_{a,b} \|\mathbf{h} - a\mathbf{d} - b\|_2^2. \tag{6}$$

This is a Linear Regression problem, which can be directly solved by Least Square method.

3.4.2 $\mathbf{W}$-step

With a and b fixed, the optimization in Eq. (5) degenerates to

$$\min_{\mathbf{W}} \frac{\lambda}{N_p}\|\mathbf{h} - a\mathbf{d} - b\|_2^2 + \frac{\alpha}{N_p}\left\|\tilde{\mathbf{U}} - \tilde{\mathbf{C}}\right\|_F^2 + \beta\|\mathbf{W}^T\mathbf{W} - \mathbf{I}\|_F^2. \tag{7}$$

In our optimization, we use the Back Propagation to learn the weight matrices of neural networks. We only need to compute the gradient of the objective function with respect to the weight matrix of output layer, which is denoted by $\mathbf{W}$ for simplicity.

To compute the gradient of the output layer, we expand the Eq. (7) as follows:

$$J(\mathbf{W}) = \frac{1}{N_p}\sum_i \Big\{\lambda\,(h_i - ad_i - b)^2 + \alpha\|\mathbf{u}_{\mathbf{p}_i(1)} - \mathbf{c}_{\mathbf{p}_i(1)}\|_2^2 + \alpha\|\mathbf{u}_{\mathbf{p}_i(2)} - \mathbf{c}_{\mathbf{p}_i(2)}\|_2^2\Big\} + \beta\|\mathbf{W}^T\mathbf{W} - \mathbf{I}\|_F^2. \quad (8)$$

According to the above objective function and the chain rule in computing derivatives, we can compute the gradient of the objective function as follows:

$$\frac{\partial J}{\partial \mathbf{W}} = \frac{2}{N_p}\sum_i \Big\{\lambda\,(h_i - ad_i - b)\Big(\frac{\partial h_i}{\partial \mathbf{b}_{\mathbf{p}_i(1)}}\cdot\frac{\partial \mathbf{b}_{\mathbf{p}_i(1)}}{\partial \mathbf{W}} + \frac{\partial h_i}{\partial \mathbf{b}_{\mathbf{p}_i(2)}}\cdot\frac{\partial \mathbf{b}_{\mathbf{p}_i(2)}}{\partial \mathbf{W}}\Big) + \alpha\big(\mathbf{u}_{\mathbf{p}_i(1)} - \mathbf{c}_{\mathbf{p}_i(1)}\big)\frac{\partial \mathbf{u}_{\mathbf{p}_i(1)}}{\partial \mathbf{W}} + \alpha\big(\mathbf{u}_{\mathbf{p}_i(2)} - \mathbf{c}_{\mathbf{p}_i(2)}\big)\frac{\partial \mathbf{u}_{\mathbf{p}_i(2)}}{\partial \mathbf{W}}\Big\} + 2\beta\mathbf{W}\left(\mathbf{W}^T\mathbf{W} - \mathbf{I}\right), \quad (9)$$

where

$$\frac{\partial h_i}{\partial \mathbf{b}_{\mathbf{p}_i(1)}} = (\mathbf{1} - 2\mathbf{b}_{\mathbf{p}_i(2)}),\ \frac{\partial h_i}{\partial \mathbf{b}_{\mathbf{p}_i(2)}} = (\mathbf{1} - 2\mathbf{b}_{\mathbf{p}_i(1)}). \quad (10)$$

For the $\frac{\partial \mathbf{b}_{\mathbf{p}_i(1)}}{\partial \mathbf{W}}$ and $\frac{\partial \mathbf{b}_{\mathbf{p}_i(2)}}{\partial \mathbf{W}}$ in Eq. (9), we can not compute them directly because $\mathbf{b}_{\mathbf{p}_i(1)}$ and $\mathbf{b}_{\mathbf{p}_i(2)}$ are not continuous. We use the sigmoid function instead of the binarized function. In other words, we use the $\frac{\partial \mathbf{u}_{\mathbf{p}_i(1)}}{\partial \mathbf{W}}$ instead of $\frac{\partial \mathbf{b}_{\mathbf{p}_i(1)}}{\partial \mathbf{W}}$, and $\frac{\partial \mathbf{u}_{\mathbf{p}_i(2)}}{\partial \mathbf{W}}$ instead of $\frac{\partial \mathbf{b}_{\mathbf{p}_i(2)}}{\partial \mathbf{W}}$. The terms $\frac{\partial \mathbf{u}_{\mathbf{p}_i(1)}}{\partial \mathbf{W}}$ and $\frac{\partial \mathbf{u}_{\mathbf{p}_i(2)}}{\partial \mathbf{W}}$ are computed as the classical neural networks do. Compared with classical neural networks, we can find the dual neural networks have different coefficients for each $\frac{\partial \mathbf{u}}{\partial \mathbf{W}}$.

In the experiments, we use the original unsupervised hashing method to pretrain the neural networks. The objective function used in the pretraining is the same as the second term in Eq. (5). The binary codes generated by the original unsupervised hashing method are used as supervised information in the pretraining. Since the two neural networks in the dual neural networks share the same parameters, we initialize them with the same pretrained neural networks.

Note that after each iteration, we use one neural network from the dual neural networks as the hash projection functions, and generate a new supervised matrix instead of the old $\mathbf{C}$. Since after the updating process for $\mathbf{W}$ converges, the binary codes generated by our hash functions are expected to compute new parameters of linear distance transformation. The new parameters are expected to be better than the old ones to fit the distance distribution. The learning algorithm is summarized in Algorithm 1.

Algorithm 1 The pseudo-supervised boosting method

Input:
Training data matrix $\mathbf{X}$, the number of training pairs N_p, the required length L of binary code, and the pseudo-supervised binary codes $\mathbf{C}$ generated by one unsupervised hashing method.

Output:
One trained neural network $\mathbf{W}$.

Initialization:
  Randomly select N_p training pairs $\mathbf{P}$;
  Pretrain one neural network;
  Initialize the dual neural networks with the pretrained neural network.
Generate $\tilde{\mathbf{P}}$ and $\hat{\mathbf{P}}$.
Compute the $L2$ distance $\mathbf{d}$ for all the pairs.
Repeat:
  Input $\mathbf{X}$, compute the output of neural networks $\mathbf{U}$, $\mathbf{B} = \mathit{round}(\mathbf{U})$, $\tilde{\mathbf{C}} = \mathbf{C}(\tilde{\mathbf{P}})$.
  Compute the Hamming distance $\mathbf{h}$ for all the pairs.
  Compute a, b in Eq. (6) using Least Squared method.
  Repeat:
    Input $\mathbf{X}$, compute the output of neural networks $\mathbf{U}$, $\mathbf{B} = \mathit{round}(\mathbf{U})$, $\tilde{\mathbf{U}} = \mathbf{U}(\tilde{\mathbf{P}})$, $\hat{\mathbf{U}} = \mathbf{U}(\hat{\mathbf{P}})$.
    Compute the Hamming distance $\mathbf{h}$ for all the pairs.
    Compute the gradient of output layer as Eq. (9).
    Update the weight matrices of dual neural networks by Back Propagation.
  until convergence
  Generate new pseudo-supervised binary codes $\mathbf{C}$ by one trained neural network.
until convergence

3.5 Linear Distance Preserving Unsupervised Hashing

In this section, we describe a simple instantiation of our proposed linear distance preserving hashing framework, in which the quantization loss is considered as most unsupervised hashing methods do. This leads to an unsupervised hashing method, we denote it as Linear Distance Transformation Hashing (LDTH). The final objective of our LDTH method is described as follows:

$$\min_{\mathbf{W},a,b}\frac{\lambda}{N_p}\|\mathbf{h} - a\mathbf{d} - b\|_2^2 - \frac{\alpha}{N_p}\|\tilde{\mathbf{U}} - 0.5\|_F^2 + \beta\|\mathbf{W}^T\mathbf{W} - \mathbf{I}\|_F^2, \quad (11)$$

where λ, α, and β are set as constants, and N_p denotes the number of all involved training pairs. Maximizing the second term in the above function is equivalent to minimize the quantization loss[2].

Similar with the optimization scheme discussed in Section 3.4, we alternatively optimize Eq. (11) over $\mathbf{W}$ and a, b. We first fix $\mathbf{W}$ and optimize with respect to a and b. This step is the same as the solution of Eq.(6) discussed in Section 3.4.1. After that, we fix a and b, and optimize with respect to $\mathbf{W}$. The only difference between Eq. (5) and Eq. (11) is the second part of the two objective functions. The second part of Eq. (11) focuses on the quantization loss, while the second part in Eq. (5) imposes the fidelity constraints of the referred unsupervised hashing method. This step is a little different from the solution described in Section 3.4.2. In the following, we describe the learning process with respect to $\mathbf{W}$ in detail.

[2] 0.5 is a scalar, the subtraction to 0.5 is an element-wise manipulation, *i.e.*, each element of $\tilde{\mathbf{U}}$ subtracts 0.5. We omit the full-one matrix $\mathbf{1}$ for conciseness.

With a and b fixed, the optimization in Eq. (11) becomes

$$\min_{\mathbf{W}} \frac{\lambda}{N_p}\|\mathbf{h} - a\mathbf{d} - b\|_2^2 - \frac{\alpha}{N_p}\|\tilde{\mathbf{U}} - 0.5\|_F^2 + \beta\|\mathbf{W}^T\mathbf{W} - \mathbf{I}\|_F^2. \quad (12)$$

We use Gradient Descent algorithm to solve the above optimization problem. To compute the gradient, we first expand the above function as follows:

$$J(\mathbf{W}) = \frac{1}{N_p}\sum_i \Big\{\lambda\left(h_i - ad_i - b\right)^2 - \alpha\|\mathbf{u}_{\mathbf{p}_i(1)} - 0.5\|_2^2 - \alpha\|\mathbf{u}_{\mathbf{p}_i(2)} - 0.5\|_2^2\Big\} + \beta\|\mathbf{W}^T\mathbf{W} - \mathbf{I}\|_F^2. \quad (13)$$

According to the Eq. (13) and the chain rule in computing derivatives, we can compute the gradient of the objective function as follows

$$\frac{\partial J}{\partial \mathbf{W}} = \frac{2}{N_p}\sum_i \Big\{\lambda\left(h_i - ad_i - b\right)\left(\frac{\partial h_i}{\partial \mathbf{b}_{\mathbf{p}_i(1)}}\cdot\frac{\partial \mathbf{b}_{\mathbf{p}_i(1)}}{\partial \mathbf{W}} + \frac{\partial h_i}{\partial \mathbf{b}_{\mathbf{p}_i(2)}}\cdot\frac{\partial \mathbf{b}_{\mathbf{p}_i(2)}}{\partial \mathbf{W}}\right) - \alpha\left(\mathbf{u}_{\mathbf{p}_i(1)} - 0.5\right)\frac{\partial \mathbf{u}_{\mathbf{p}_i(1)}}{\partial \mathbf{W}} - \alpha\left(\mathbf{u}_{\mathbf{p}_i(2)} - 0.5\right)\frac{\partial \mathbf{u}_{\mathbf{p}_i(2)}}{\partial \mathbf{W}}\Big\} + 2\beta\mathbf{W}\left(\mathbf{W}^T\mathbf{W} - \mathbf{I}\right), \quad (14)$$

where $\frac{\partial h_i}{\partial \mathbf{b}_{\mathbf{p}_i(1)}}$ and $\frac{\partial h_i}{\partial \mathbf{b}_{\mathbf{p}_i(2)}}$ share the same forms as in Eq. (10). And we also use the $\frac{\partial \mathbf{u}_{\mathbf{p}_i(1)}}{\partial \mathbf{W}}$ instead of $\frac{\partial \mathbf{b}_{\mathbf{p}_i(1)}}{\partial \mathbf{W}}$, and $\frac{\partial \mathbf{u}_{\mathbf{p}_i(2)}}{\partial \mathbf{W}}$ instead of $\frac{\partial \mathbf{b}_{\mathbf{p}_i(2)}}{\partial \mathbf{W}}$. Then we compute the gradient of the objective function as follows:

$$\frac{\partial J}{\partial \mathbf{W}} = \tilde{\mathbf{X}}^T\left(\left\{\lambda\begin{bmatrix}\mathbf{h} - a\mathbf{d} - b\\ \mathbf{h} - a\mathbf{d} - b\end{bmatrix}\circ\left(1 - 2\hat{\mathbf{B}}\right) - \alpha\left(\tilde{\mathbf{U}} - 0.5\right)\right\}\odot\tilde{\mathbf{U}}\odot\left(1 - \tilde{\mathbf{U}}\right)\right)\frac{2}{N_p} + 2\beta\mathbf{W}\left(\mathbf{W}^T\mathbf{W} - \mathbf{I}\right). \quad (15)$$

where $\odot$ denotes element-wise multiplication, and $\circ$ denotes that each element of the left vector element-wisely multiplies the elements from the same row of the right matrix. After that, we can update the projection matrix as follows

$$\mathbf{W} = \mathbf{W} - \delta\frac{\partial J}{\partial \mathbf{W}}, \quad (16)$$

where δ denotes learning rate, and we empirically set $\delta = 0.8$ in all the experiments. At the beginning of our learning algorithm, we initialize $\mathbf{W}$ as a randomized orthogonal matrix. We repeat this gradient-descent algorithm until the objective function in Eq. (12) converges. The whole learning algorithm is summarized in Algorithm 2.

Although our method can not guarantee to converge to a global minimum, it always leads to a local minimum, which suffices to give a good result. Typically, we show the convergence curve of our cost function in Fig. 3.

4. EXPERIMENTS

4.1 Setup

We evaluate our method on two large-scale datasets: (1) ANN_SIFT1M [8]: this dataset consists of 10,000 query vectors, 1,000,000 base vectors, and 100,000 training vectors, with each vector corresponding to a 128-D SIFT feature.

Algorithm 2 Linear Distance Transformation Hashing

Input:
Training data matrix $\mathbf{X}$, the number of training pairs N_p, the required length L of binary code.
Output:
The projection matrix $\mathbf{W}$.

```
Initialization:
    Randomly select N_p training pairs P,
    generate a randomized orthogonal matrix W.
Generate P~ and P^.
Compute the L2 distance d for all the pairs.
Repeat:
    U = sigmoid(XW), B = round(U).
    Compute the Hamming distance h for all the pairs.
    Compute a, b in Eq. (6) using Least Squared method.
    Repeat:
        U = sigmoid(XW), B = round(U),
        U~ = U(P~), B^ = B(P^).
        Compute the Hamming distance h for all the pairs.
        Compute the gradient of objective function in
        Eq. (12) as Eq. (15).
        Update W = W - δ ∂J/∂W.
    until convergence
until convergence
```

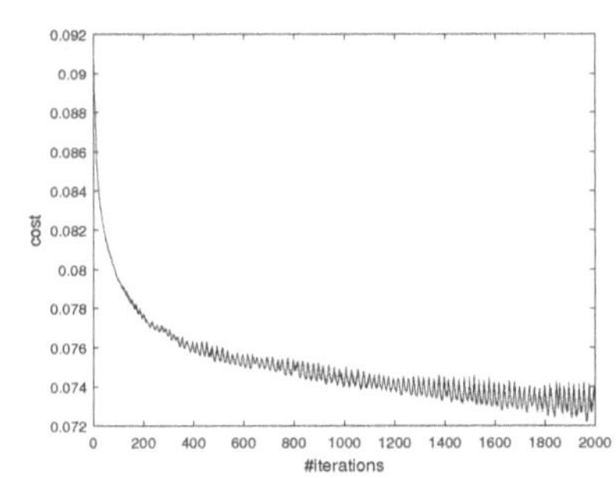

Figure 3: The convergence curve of our cost function.

The groundtruth for each query corresponds to its 100 nearest neighbors ordered by increasing Euclidean distance. (2) ANN_GIST1M [8]: this dataset consists of 1,000 query vectors, 1,000,000 base vectors, and 500,000 training vectors, and each vector is a 960-D GIST feature. The groundtruth for each query contains its 100 nearest neighbors ordered by Euclidean distance in ascending order.

Since our method is unsupervised, we compare it with five representative unsupervised hashing methods, including LSH [4], BRE [11], SpH [7], ITQ [5], and MLH's unsupervised version [18]. In our experiments, we use the implementations of all these five hashing methods released by their authors with the default parameters.

In this paper, we use binary codes to perform approximate nearest neighbor search based on hash code ranking strategy, which sorts the binary codes by increasing Hamming distance. Based on this strategy, we use three evaluation metrics to measure the performance of different methods in this paper:

- Precision@K: it measures the percentage of the true neighbors in the top K retrieved results.

Table 1: Comparison on Precision(%)@500. The bold number indicates the best result under the same bit length setting. The underline text denotes the case that our pseudo-supervised boosting method does not give an improvement over the original algorithm. "Ours" denotes our pseudo-supervised boosting methods on the corresponding unsupervised hashing methods. LDTH denotes the proposed linear distance preserving unsupervised hash method.

Dataset	Code Length	Approaches					
		LSH[4]/Ours	BRE[11]/Ours	MLH[18]/Ours	SpH[7]/Ours	ITQ[5]/Ours	**LDTH**
ANN_SIFT1M	16	0.94/1.12	0.83/1.69	0.71/0.84	1.38/1.51	1.32/**2.30**	1.66
	32	2.52/2.95	2.20/4.27	2.63/2.73	3.65/3.93	3.54/**5.09**	4.12
	64	5.23/6.20	4.45/7.15	5.84/6.39	7.06/7.51	7.03/**7.71**	7.46
	128	9.30/10.21	7.70/8.62	8.64/9.12	10.63/**11.42**	10.82/10.78	11.22
ANN_GIST1M	16	0.32/0.69	0.86/0.99	0.65/0.92	0.76/0.91	1.09/**1.24**	1.23
	32	0.76/1.35	1.85/1.95	1.38/2.00	1.87/1.91	2.22/2.37	**2.45**
	64	1.61/2.79	3.06/3.05	2.74/**3.75**	3.51/3.55	3.37/3.55	3.74
	128	3.25/4.63	4.62/4.76	4.07/5.36	5.39/**5.49**	4.40/5.46	5.18

- Recall@K: it counts the percentage of true neighbors among all the ground-truth in the retrieved K samples.
- mAP (mean Average Precision): it is obtained by computing the area under the Precision-Recall curve.

4.2 Evaluation for the Pseudo-Supervised Hashing

In this section, we focus on evaluating the results of our pseudo-supervised hashing method on different hashing methods on different datasets. We use the dual neural networks to solve our boosting objective. There are two neural networks sharing the same structure and weight matrices. Considering the computational complexity issue, we adopt a neural network with three layers, including one input layer, one hidden layer, and one output layer. In terms of the activation functions, we select the tanh function for the hidden layer, and sigmoid function for the output layer. The number of units in hidden layer is simply set as the number of units in the input layer, and the number of units in the output layer is equal to the code length of objective binary codes. The parameters are set as $\alpha = 0.05$, $\beta = 5 \times 10^{-5}$, and $\lambda = 1/2L$ in all the experiments, where L denotes the code length. And for each dataset, we randomly select 20,000 training samples from the training datasets, and the total number of pairs N_p is 200,000. We alternatively optimize the a, b-step and $\mathbf{W}$-step until convergence. In the alternating update for $\mathbf{W}$, we train the neural networks for 10 epoches with the batch size equal to 500.

Fig. 4, and Fig. 5 show the recall of original unsupervised hashing methods and our corresponding pseudo-supervised boosting method on the ANN_SIFT1M dataset with the code length equal to 16 and 32 bits. Comparing with the original methods, our boosting methods consistently make considerable improvements. Fig. 6, and Fig. 7 show the recall comparisons between the five methods and our corresponding boosting methods on ANN_GIST1M dataset with the code length equal to 16 and 32 bits. Note that on each dataset we only show the results with two settings of code length, the comparisons with other code lengths are similar. We present the precision comparisons on different datasets with more settings of code lengths over all the five unsupervised hashing methods in Table 1. The mAP comparisons on different datasets are shown in Table 2. In sum, our boosting method consistently improves the performances of the five unsupervised hashing methods on different datasets under all code lengths.

4.3 Evaluation for LDTH

We report the results of our proposed LDTH method on different datasets. All the data points used in our method are pre-processed by PCA (Principal Components Analysis), which makes the pairwise dimensions in one data point uncorrelated. This helps to produce an efficient code, as justified in [5]. In all the experiments for each dataset, we randomly select 20,000 training samples from the training datasets, and randomly select two data points from the training samples as a pair. The total number of pairs N_p is 200,000. And we set α and β as 5×10^{-7}, and set λ as $1/2L$ in the experiments. We alternatively optimize the a, b-step and $\mathbf{W}$-step until convergence. In the alternating update for $\mathbf{W}$, we iteratively run the Gradient-Descent algorithm for 10 times before the update of a and b.

Fig. 8 shows the Recall@K on ANN_SIFT1M under different bit length settings. And Fig. 9 shows the Recall@K on ANN_GIST1M under different bit length settings. We evaluate the precision@500 of different methods under different code length settings in Table 1. The mAP comparison is shown in Table 2. From all the comparisons, we can see that our LDTH method outperforms the state-of-the-art methods, if not, gives comparable results.

4.4 Complexity and Time Cost

In this section, we make an analysis on the complexity of our pseudo-supervised hashing method and the proposed unsupervised LDTH method. The main time cost of our method lies in the $\mathbf{W}$-step, *i.e.*, computing the gradient of objective function with respect to $\mathbf{W}$. The computational complexity of computing gradient in LDTH is $O(N_pL^2+L^3)$. The pseudo-supervised boosting method will be a little slower than LDTH, because it has a more complex networks structure, which gives a large constant factor to the computational complexity. Finally, we test the computational time of the proposed LDTH and boosting methods, and compare them with the baseline unsupervised hashing methods. Our PC is configured with dual-core 2.00 GHz

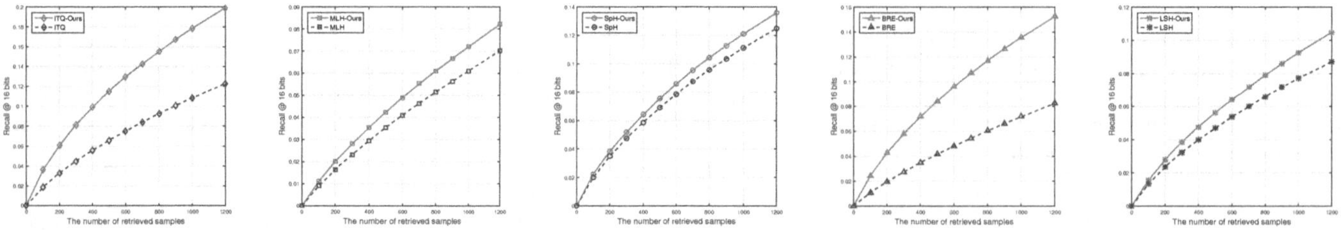

Figure 4: Recall@K comparisons on ANN_SIFT1M between the original unsupervised hashing methods and our corresponding pseudo-supervised boosting methods. Code length: 16

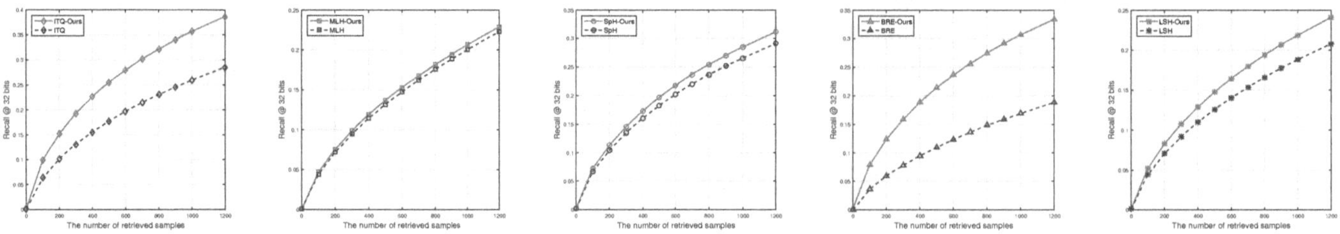

Figure 5: Recall@K comparisons on ANN_SIFT1M between the original unsupervised hashing methods and our corresponding pseudo-supervised boosting methods. Code length: 32

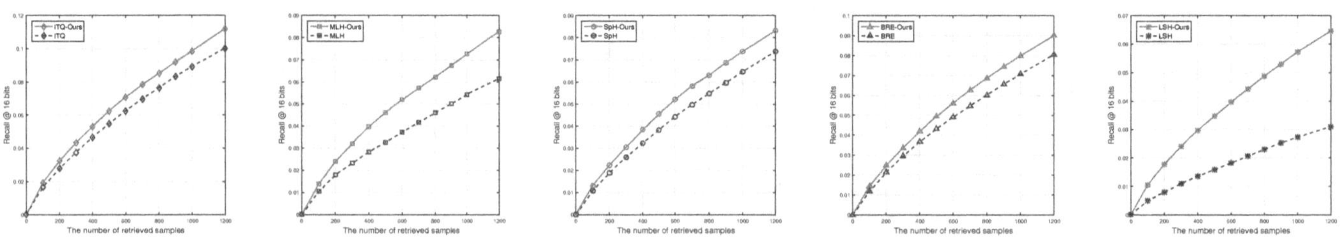

Figure 6: Recall@K comparisons on ANN_GIST1M between the original unsupervised hashing methods and our corresponding pseudo-supervised boosting methods. Code length: 16

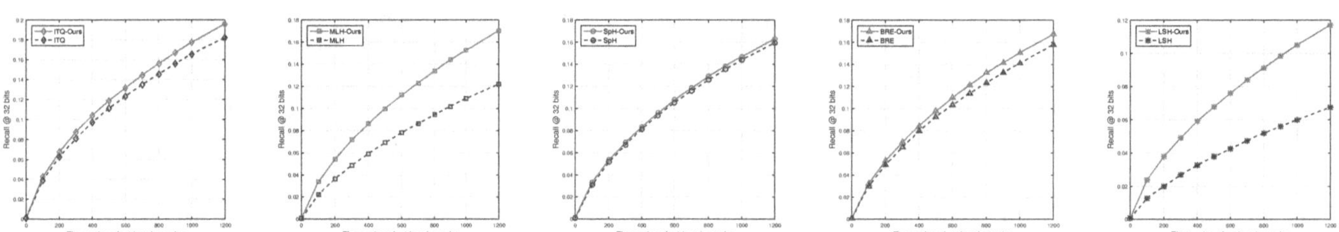

Figure 7: Recall@K comparisons on ANN_GIST1M between the original unsupervised hashing methods and our corresponding pseudo-supervised boosting methods. Code length: 32

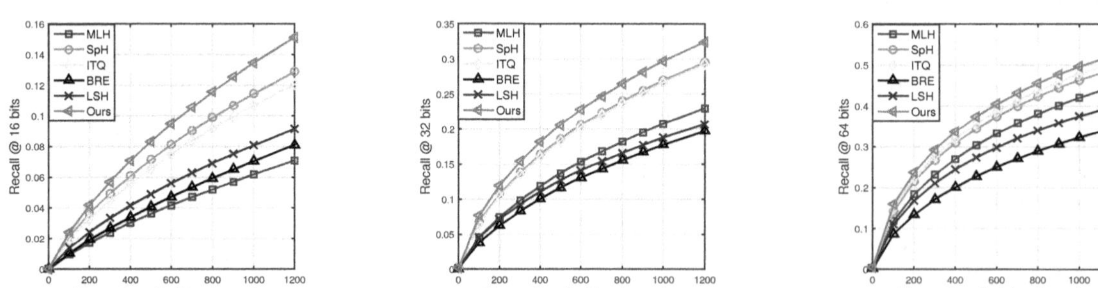

Figure 8: Recall@K comparisons between our LDTH method and the comparison methods on ANN_SIFT1M. The code length of the three figures (from left to right) is 16, 32, and 64, respectively.

Table 2: Comparison on mAP(%). The bold number indicates the best result under the same bit length setting. The underline text denotes the case that our pseudo-supervised boosting method does not give an improvement over the original algorithm. "Ours" denotes our pseudo-supervised boosting methods on the corresponding unsupervised hashing methods. LDTH denotes the proposed linear distance preserving unsupervised hash method.

Dataset	Code Length	Approaches					
		LSH[4]/Ours	BRE[11]/Ours	MLH[18]/Ours	SpH[7]/Ours	ITQ[5]/Ours	**LDTH**
ANN_SIFT1M	16	0.56/0.70	0.57/1.09	0.48/0.56	0.84/0.98	0.93/**1.62**	1.13
	32	2.12/2.55	1.75/4.18	2.17/2.33	3.37/3.75	3.31/**5.52**	4.07
	64	6.29/7.92	4.71/9.73	6.88/7.92	9.47/10.38	9.34/**11.29**	10.53
	128	15.71/18.26	11.11/13.11	12.94/14.19	19.42/**21.74**	19.91/19.68	21.40
ANN_GIST1M	16	0.18/0.38	0.43/0.52	0.38/0.53	0.41/0.49	0.64/**0.75**	0.74
	32	0.56/1.11	1.26/1.40	0.92/1.46	1.34/1.44	1.77/1.96	**2.03**
	64	1.38/2.54	2.75/2.77	2.45/3.68	3.43/3.51	3.39/3.57	**3.86**
	128	3.51/5.29	5.18/5.28	4.35/6.23	6.45/6.49	5.53/**6.56**	6.30

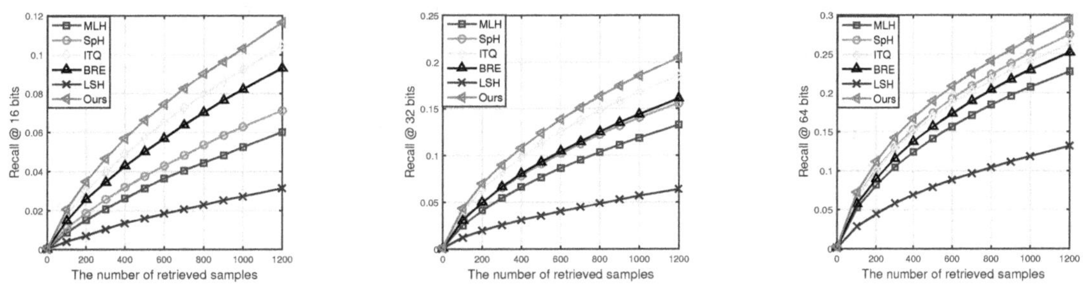

Figure 9: Recall@K comparisons between our LDTH method and the comparison methods on ANN_GIST1M. The code length of the three figures (from left to right) is 16, 32, and 64, respectively.

CPU. Table 3 shows the training and testing time of different hashing methods on ANN_GIST1M dataset with the code length equal to 32 bits. The training time of boosting method does not comprise the training time of the original hashing method. We see that training time of LDTH method is similar with the baseline hashing methods, and that of our boosting method is a little higher than our unsupervised hashing method because of the more complex network structure. The test time of our methods is comparable to those previous methods.

Table 3: Computational time of different hashing methods on ANN_GIST1M dataset. LDTH denotes the proposed linear distance-preserving unsupervised hash method. "boosting" denotes our linear distance preserving pseudo-supervised hashing method.

Method	Training(seconds)	Testing(seconds)
LSH[4]	0.002	26.584
BRE[11]	498.001	43.690
MLH[18]	255.325	30.772
SpH[7]	4.901	45.207
ITQ[5]	1.284	29.249
LDTH	56.120	26.459
boosting	106.726	28.289

5. CONCLUSIONS AND DISCUSSIONS

In this paper, we propose a general unsupervised hashing framework which simultaneously applies pairwise distance-preserving objective and point-wise constraint. Our pairwise linear distance preserving objective aims at keeping the linear projection relationships between the Euclidean distance in the original space and the Hamming distance in the binary space. This direct distance-preserving objective makes our method fully cohere with the fundamental of binary hashing. We give two instantiations of this framework. The first one is a pseudo-supervised hashing method, which aims to use the pseudo-supervised information generated by a selected hashing method to improve the performance of the selected unsupervised hashing method. It provides a general paradigm to boost existing unsupervised hashing methods. The second one is an unsupervised hashing method, which considers the quantization loss into the framework. Fully considering the pair-wise and point-wise constraints in the same framework makes our unsupervised hashing method achieve promising performance. The experiments on two large-scale datasets demonstrate that our pseudo-supervised method makes an obvious improvement for five unsupervised hashing methods, while our LDTH method outperforms the state-of-the-art unsupervised hashing methods.

In our future work, we will extend our framework with different distance-preserving constraints, such as high-order distance relationships and triplet-wise constraints. Besides, we will also explore the potential of our framework to boost supervised hashing methods, in which deeper neural networks or convolutional neural networks may be involved.

6. ACKNOWLEDGEMENTS

This work is supported in part by the 973 Program under Contract 2015CB351803, the National Natural Science Foundation of China under Contract 61390514, 61325009, 61472378, 61429201 and 61472392, the Natural Science Foundation of Anhui Province under Contract 1508085MF109, and the Fundamental Research Funds for the Central Universities. It is also supported in part to Dr. Qi Tian by the ARO grant W911NF-15-1-0290, and Faculty Research Gift Awards by NEC Laboratories of America and Blippar.

7. REFERENCES

[1] J. L. Bentley. Multidimensional binary search trees used for associative searching. *Communications of the ACM*, 18(9):509–517, 1975.

[2] L. Cao, Z. Li, Y. Mu, and S.-F. Chang. Submodular video hashing: a unified framework towards video pooling and indexing. In *ACM Multimedia*, pages 299–308, 2012.

[3] M. A. Carreira-Perpinán and R. Raziperchikolaei. Hashing with binary autoencoders. In *CVPR*, 2015.

[4] A. Gionis, P. Indyk, and R. M. others. Similarity search in high dimensions via hashing. In *VLDB*, volume 99, pages 518–529, 1999.

[5] Y. Gong and S. Lazebnik. Iterative quantization: A procrustean approach to learning binary codes. In *CVPR*, pages 817–824, 2011.

[6] K. He, F. Wen, and J. Sun. K-means hashing: An affinity-preserving quantization method for learning binary compact codes. In *CVPR*, pages 2938–2945, 2013.

[7] J. Heo, Y. Lee, J. He, S. Chang, and S. Yoon. Spherical hashing. In *CVPR*, pages 2957–2964, 2012.

[8] H. Jegou, M. Douze, and C. Schmid. Product quantization for nearest neighbor search. *IEEE TPAMI*, 33(1):117–128, 2011.

[9] T. Ji, X. Liu, C. Deng, L. Huang, and B. Lang. Query-adaptive hash code ranking for fast nearest neighbor search. In *ACM Multimedia*, pages 1005–1008, 2014.

[10] A. Joly and O. Buisson. A posteriori multi-probe locality sensitive hashing. In *ACM Multimedia*, pages 209–218, 2008.

[11] B. Kulis and T. Darrell. Learning to hash with binary reconstructive embeddings. In *NIPS*, pages 1042–1050, 2009.

[12] B. Kulis and K. Grauman. Kernelized locality-sensitive hashing. *IEEE TPAMI*, 34(6):1092–1104, 2012.

[13] H. Lai, Y. Pan, Y. Liu, and S. Yan. Simultaneous feature learning and hash coding with deep neural networks. In *CVPR*, pages 3270–3278, 2015.

[14] R.-S. Lin, D. A. Ross, and J. Yagnik. Spec hashing: Similarity preserving algorithm for entropy-based coding. In *CVPR*, pages 848–854, 2010.

[15] V. E. Liong, J. Lu, G. Wang, P. Moulin, and J. Zhou. Deep hashing for compact binary codes learning. In *CVPR*, 2015.

[16] W. Liu, J. Wang, R. Ji, Y.-G. Jiang, and S.-F. Chang. Supervised hashing with kernels. In *CVPR*, pages 2074–2081, 2012.

[17] Z. Liu, H. Li, W. Zhou, R. Zhao, and Q. Tian. Contextual hashing for large-scale image search. *IEEE TIP*, 23(4):1606–1614, 2014.

[18] M. Norouzi and D. M. Blei. Minimal loss hashing for compact binary codes. In *ICML*, pages 353–360, 2011.

[19] R. Salakhutdinov and G. Hinton. Semantic hashing. *International Journal of Approximate Reasoning*, 50(7):969–978, 2009.

[20] J. Wang, S. Kumar, and S. Chang. Semi-supervised hashing for large-scale search. *IEEE TPAMI*, 34(12):2393–2406, 2012.

[21] J. Wang, J. Wang, N. Yu, and S. Li. Order preserving hashing for approximate nearest neighbor search. In *ACM Multimedia*, pages 133–142, 2013.

[22] M. Wang, W. Li, D. Liu, B. Ni, J. Shen, and S. Yan. Facilitating image search with a scalable and compact semantic mapping. *IEEE Transactions on Cybernetics*, 45(8):1561–1574, 2015.

[23] Y. Weiss, A. Torralba, and R. Fergus. Spectral hashing. In *NIPS*, pages 1753–1760, 2009.

[24] R. Xia, Y. Pan, H. Lai, C. Liu, and S. Yan. Supervised hashing for image retrieval via image representation learning. In *AAAI*, volume 1, page 2, 2014.

[25] L. Zhang, Y. Zhang, J. Tang, X. Gu, J. Li, and Q. Tian. Topology preserving hashing for similarity search. In *ACM Multimedia*, pages 123–132, 2013.

[26] P. Zhang, W. Zhang, W.-J. Li, and M. Guo. Supervised hashing with latent factor models. In *ACM SIGIR Conference on Research and Development in Information Retrieval*, pages 173–182, 2014.

[27] R. Zhang, L. Lin, R. Zhang, W. Zuo, and L. Zhang. Bit-scalable deep hashing with regularized similarity learning for image retrieval and person re-identification. *IEEE TIP*, 24(12):4766–4779, 2015.

[28] F. Zhao, Y. Huang, L. Wang, and T. Tan. Deep semantic ranking based hashing for multi-label image retrieval. In *CVPR*, pages 1556–1564, 2015.

[29] W. Zhou, H. Li, R. Hong, Y. Lu, and Q. Tian. Bsift: toward data-independent codebook for large scale image search. *IEEE TIP*, 24(3):967–979, 2015.

[30] W. Zhou, Y. Lu, H. Li, Y. Song, and Q. Tian. Spatial coding for large scale partial-duplicate web image search. In *ACM Multimedia*, pages 511–520, 2010.

[31] W. Zhou, Y. Lu, H. Li, and Q. Tian. Scalar quantization for large scale image search. In *ACM Multimedia*, pages 169–178, 2012.

[32] W. Zhou, M. Yang, H. Li, X. Wang, Y. Lin, and Q. Tian. Towards codebook-free: Scalable cascaded hashing for mobile image search. *IEEE TMM*, 16(3):601–611, 2014.

[33] W. Zhou, M. Yang, X. Wang, H. Li, Y. Lin, and Q. Tian. Scalable feature matching by dual cascaded scalar quantization for image retrieval. *IEEE TPAMI*, 38(1):159–171, 2016.

[34] X. Zhu, L. Zhang, and Z. Huang. A sparse embedding and least variance encoding approach to hashing. *IEEE TIP*, 23(9):3737–3750, 2014.

A Pragmatically Designed Adaptive and Web-compliant Object-based Video Streaming Methodology

Implementation and Subjective Evaluation

Maarten Wijnants Gustavo Rovelo Peter Quax Wim Lamotte
Hasselt University – tUL – iMinds
Expertise Centre for Digital Media
Wetenschapspark 2, 3590 Diepenbeek, Belgium
firstname.lastname@uhasselt.be

ABSTRACT

The bulk of contemporary online video traffic is encoded in a traditional manner, hereby neglecting most, if not all, of the semantics of the underlying visual scene. One essential piece of semantic information in the context of video streaming is awareness of the objects that jointly constitute the scene. A canonical example of a benefit associated with such object awareness is the ability to subdivide a video fragment in respectively a background and one or more foreground objects. This paper reports on a pragmatically designed video streaming approach that exploits object-related knowledge in order to improve the real-time adaptability of video streaming sessions (manifested in the form of increased granularity in terms of streaming quality control). The proposed approach is completely compliant with present-day video codecs and HTTP Adaptive Streaming schemes, most notably H.264 and MPEG-DASH. Findings from subjecting the proposed video streaming technique to a comparative subjective evaluation suggest that scenarios exist where the presented approach holds the capacity to improve on traditional streaming in terms of user-perceived video quality.

Keywords

H.264; MPEG-DASH; MPEG-4; WebGL; object-based video

1. INTRODUCTION

Traditional video compression and streaming solutions are (largely) semantics-agnostic. For example, the majority of contemporary mainstream video codecs apply so-called *pixel-* or *frame-based* (de)compression. This implies that the encoder takes integral video frames as input and, via specific Rate-Distortion (RD) optimizations, divides the target encoding bitrate over the constituting frames and then over the constituting pixels of each frame. This happens without underlying knowledge of the individual objects that appear in the scene. The term "object" in this regard must be interpreted broadly, as it can refer to any entity that is distinguishable from the background (e.g., actors, salient props, and so on). Having access to object-related metadata paves the way for implementing a range of coding and streaming optimizations. One prime example that will be exclusively focused on in this paper is the additional versatility that it introduces in the streaming process. Being aware of the scene composition allows for deliberately distributing the bitrate budget over respectively the background and the foreground object(s). When starting our research, we hypothesized that, if executed properly, such an approach might benefit the perceptual quality of streamed video.

The MPEG Working Group recognized the potential coding benefits that are associated with object-based video compression as early as 1999, when they released their MPEG-4 specification with explicit support for the coding of video objects, both natural and synthetic [6, 13]. In particular, the MPEG-4 bitstream syntax encompasses so-called Video Object (VO) constructs and BIFS directives to represent (arbitrarily shaped) objects that are discernible in the video scene and to describe the scene composition, respectively. For each VO in a scene, the bitstream will carry separately encoded shape and texture information. Unfortunately, the object-based video part of the standard has witnessed very limited adoption in practice. We argue that this lack of adoption can be attributed to the disruptive nature of the proposed approach. The MPEG-4 VO standard breaks the traditional video processing workflow, at both encoding and decoding side, primarily due to the inclusion of the shape information in the encoded bitstream. As such, we believe that it suffered from poor hardware support and from the (costly) necessity to develop specialized software. Unsurprisingly, non-standardized object-based video coding solutions like the one proposed by Hakeem et al. [4] have seen even lower practical uptake.

In contrast, this article proposes an object-aware video streaming solution that is fully compliant not only with traditional video compression and streaming paradigms but also with prevailing Web standards. In particular, in this paper, our solution is shown to be compatible with H.264, arguably one of the most popular contemporary frame-based video codecs, and with MPEG-DASH (Dynamic Adaptive Streaming over HTTP), the de facto present-day streaming standard on the Web [7]. Although not yet confirmed experimentally, we are confident that the proposed approach could readily be incorporated in alternative compression and streaming setups as well. Seamless integration in existing workflows implies intrinsic inheritance of their advantages. As an example, the proposed solution fully pre-

MM '16, October 15–19, 2016, Amsterdam, The Netherlands.

DOI: http://dx.doi.org/10.1145/2964284.2964300

serves the server-side scalability, adaptive streaming and CDN compatibility benefits that are associated with MPEG-DASH.

Besides unambiguously establishing the technical and practical viability of the proposed object-based streaming approach in a Web browser context, this article will share, as an equally important research contribution, insights accumulated from a subjective video assessment test. This subjective evaluation was implemented as a comparative study, in which participants were asked to express their preference when presented with video sequences streamed using either the proposed object-based or a traditional approach (under identical bitrate limitations).

Although the proposed object-based streaming methodology is compatible (both theoretically and practically) with arbitrary video genres, we believe it to be especially well suited for those video scenarios in which one or more foreground objects substantially outweigh the scene background in terms of perceptual relevance to the viewer. Video conferencing, talk shows and interviews, and presentations (e.g., a news broadcast) are all prime examples of use cases belonging to the video streaming market niche that we will concentrate on in this manuscript.

In summary, the strengths of the proposed approach, either in relation to object-based MPEG-4 or in general, are the following: (i) the option to adaptively and independently stream the constituting entities of a video scene (e.g., background versus foreground objects), (ii) the portability benefits that are afforded by the Web-based implementation at client side, and (iii) the pragmatic nature of our solution that stems from its ability to exploit commodity video codecs (popularly implemented in both soft- and hardware) which, among other benefits, maximizes the range of supported playback devices.

2. CONCEPT AND METHODOLOGY

2.1 Object Segmentation

A fundamental prerequisite of any object-based streaming implementation is knowledge about the composition of the to-be-streamed video scene. To be able to distinguish between respectively background and foreground objects, for example, detailed information about the spatial location of these objects in the video clip over time is needed.

The problem of acquiring metadata pertaining to the location of in-scene video objects can be addressed in multiple ways. The results reported on in this article were obtained by manually segmenting the objects of interest from (the background of) the video scene as part of an offline pre-processing effort. Off-the-shelf products and software exist to facilitate this task. We found the rotoscoping tool of the Adobe After Effects software [1] to serve our object segmentation needs quite nicely. That being said, we are well aware that a more automated object segmentation scheme would be needed to render our approach economically viable and also to enable live streaming scenarios. Several unsupervised video segmentation algorithms are described in the academic literature that show promise in this regard (e.g., [12]).

The object segmentation task produces as output a number of distinct video signals, each depicting either a specific constituting video object or the residual background. All of these video fragments have the same spatiotemporal resolution as the original input (i.e., the unprocessed video). The video fragments for the objects hold the pixel data for that object over time, on a frame-by-frame basis, with the remainder of the pixels in each frame being set to a predefined color. For the video conveying the scene background, that same pixel color is used to fill up the holes caused by "cutting out" the foreground objects. All the content items that were prepared for the research described in this article use pure green (i.e., RGB (0, 255, 0)) as color value to represent pixels that have been segmented away. This is illustrated in Figure 1.

Figure 1: Segmented video scene involving a background and one single foreground object.

2.2 Encoding and Streaming Preparation

Each of the video fragments that emerge from the object segmentation operation is frame-based encoded in multiple qualities (see also Section 4.3). Then, conform to the general MPEG-DASH methodology, the resulting quality versions of both the isolated objects and the residual background are temporally divided in successive chunks and described by means of dedicated Media Presentation Description (MPD) manifests.

2.3 Distribution

The MPDs as well as MPEG-DASH video data that result from the encoding step are published simply by hosting them on an off-the-shelf Web server and are delivered to the client over HTTP in a pull-based manner. In line with the MPEG-DASH design philosophy, the client hereby retains total freedom to on-the-fly adapt, for example driven by prevailing network conditions, the quality in which the residual background as well as each of the isolated video objects is streamed during the media presentation. As the distribution task of the proposed methodology does not deviate from traditional MPEG-DASH streaming, neither conceptually nor technologically, it will not be elaborated on.

What is of interest in terms of content transport though, is the observation that the availability of dedicated video data for respectively the background and the constituting objects of a scene greatly extends the flexibility with which the streaming session can be implemented. In particular, it introduces an additional degree of freedom in terms of quality scalability by enabling the client to trade off the background for the foreground object(s) in terms of allocated streaming bitrate. This bitrate balancing effort could be settled depending on, for example, the relative contribution of the involved video streams to the user-perceived quality of the overall video scene.

2.4 Rendering and Playback

To be able to stream a video scene in the proposed methodology, the client first needs to fetch the MPDs that are associated with respectively the scene background and the foreground object(s). These manifest files inform the client about the different qualities in which background and foreground object(s) are available, as well as about their associated bitrate requirements. From this point on, the client possesses all necessary information to enable the flexible implementation of the back- versus foreground streaming process discussed in Section 2.3.

Irrespective of the quality in which the constituent background and foreground object(s) are streamed, these video sources need to be combined somehow to recreate the original video scene. This *recompositing* operation is realized by resorting to the *chroma keying* paradigm. Intuitively speaking, this implies that pixels carrying the predefined (opaque) chroma value denoting an "empty" patch in the video fragment (see Section 2.1) are first made fully transparent, after which the different sources are stacked on top of each other in the appropriate order, on a frame-by-frame basis. When done correctly, the resulting video and the original, unprocessed video will depict exactly the same visual scene, yet the former will not necessarily exhibit the latter's largely uniform distribution of visual quality over respectively background and foreground object(s).

3. RELATED WORK

The reader is reminded that the work presented in this article does not aim to develop a new object-based video coding solution, but rather to re-use mainstream video coding approaches to realize, in a pragmatic and standards-compliant fashion, the proposed object-based streaming methodology. As such, we will not dwell on the low-level technicalities of object-based video codecs. Instead, the related work discussion will focus on the high-level mindset behind object-based video streaming, while also touching on the topic of object-based video playback control and on complementary video streaming optimizations.

3.1 Object-based Video Coding & Streaming

Wuenschmann et al. have compared the data rate requirements of H.264 frame-based versus MPEG-4 object-based coding of a scene consisting exclusively of rotating (synthetic) cubes [20]. It is concluded that object-based schemes hold the potential to surpass frame-based codecs with respect to coding efficiency, especially as the complexity of the to-be-coded video scene rises.

Vetro and Sun have proposed a method to model the RD characteristics of a lossy shape coding scheme [16]. Combined with existing texture-centric RD models, the proposed work enables joint rate control of respectively the texture and shape data of an MPEG-4 Video Object.

Vetro et al. have also discussed the additional degrees of freedom that object-based coding injects in (MPEG-4-powered) video transcoding frameworks [17]. The presented results highlight the increased adaptation flexibility that is unlocked by relying on object-based video compression (e.g., which objects need to be included in the transcoded result, and at what quality). Furthermore, potential RD gains by reducing the temporal resolution of individual Video Objects are demonstrated. However, it is also shown that combining objects with varying temporal resolutions in a single video scene might introduce composition issues.

A high-level discussion of the benefits that are associated with the object prioritization options inherent to an adaptive object-based streaming system is given by Goor and Murphy [3]. In particular, a system is envisioned that apportions resources (e.g., network bandwidth) among the constituent objects of a video scene proportionally to their relative priority or perceptual significance. Unfortunately, a concrete implementation of the weighted resource distribution concept is lacking, as are experimental or perceptual results.

Finally, an interesting application of the object-based streaming concept to the domain of Intelligent Transportation Systems is given by Hsiao et al. [5]. The described distributed system at capture side isolates vehicles in car traffic footage, compresses the resulting assets as well as the background using MPEG-4 object-based coding (hereby favoring the foreground objects in terms of assigned bitrate), and then transmits the encoded bitstream to a remote traffic monitoring module. This module in turn recomposes the streamed scene to implement traffic event detection and analysis, hereby benefiting from the high(er) visual quality of the vehicles compared to the scene background.

3.2 Object-based Video Playback

A number of comparable approaches are described in the academic literature that focus on object-mediated video browsing. Notable examples of such approaches are *Trailblazing* [9] and the scheme proposed by Nguyen et al. [10]. In essence, these approaches enable viewers to control the playback of a video clip via direct manipulation of the objects that it embeds. The direct manipulation in this case takes the form of spatially dragging an object along its movement trajectory in the video scene. During such dragging operations, the playback leaps to exactly that temporal instant in the video timeline when the manipulated object occupies the specified spatial position in the video scene.

While these approaches are concerned with video playback control rather than video streaming, there nonetheless exists a substantial conceptual match with the proposed methodology. In particular, they both fundamentally revolve around exploiting awareness of the composition of the video scene and, more precisely, of the objects that are featured in it.

3.3 Video Streaming Optimization

One specific way to look at the work presented in this article is in its capacity of a video streaming optimization. In this context, it is important to emphasize that the proposed methodology is applicable not only to traditional video formats (which is the focus in this paper) but also to panoramic or even 360 degree video. In fact, the frames depicted in Figure 1 are part of an equirectangularly projected 360 degree video capture. Given the extended spatial reach of panoramic footage, it could make sense to extract meaningful objects from the scene, disseminate those in full fidelity, and apply quality degradation to the residual background so as to reduce the streaming bandwidth requirements while still maintaining an acceptable video quality at receiver side.

An important research track in the area of panoramic video streaming is the *spatial tiling* concept (see, for example, [14]). The rationale of this concept consists of spatially segmenting the video footage into patches (typically rectangularly shaped) which can then be independently streamed. As such, it becomes feasible to assign variable bandwidth budgets to individual tiles depending on, for instance, the saliency of the video substance they contain [2]. The proposed methodology and the tiled streaming concept are complementary rather than mutually exclusive. Indeed, spatial tiling could be exploited to optimize the streaming of the background of an object-based scene [19]. Please also note that both approaches preserve compatibility with the adaptive streaming provisions offered by MPEG-DASH.

An alternative approach towards video streaming optimization is taken by the Scalable Video Coding (SVC) paradigm that enables the perceptual quality of a video sequence to be upgraded by adaptively streaming and applying so-called enhancement layers [15]. As is the case with spatial tiling, the proposed methodology and SVC are compatible, in the sense that the

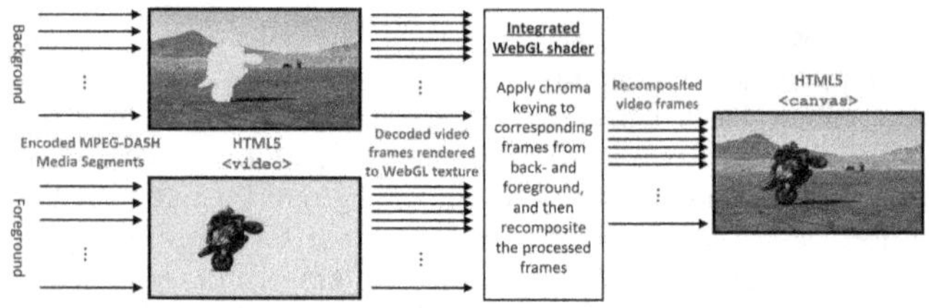

Figure 2: Chroma keying and scene recompositing.

latter could be applied to scalably distribute the background and/or constituting objects of an object-segmented scene.

4. IMPLEMENTATION

This section will focus exclusively on the implementation of the final part of the proposed methodology, namely the client-side rendering and playback of received footage in a Web browser context (see Section 2.4). The preceding steps in our end-to-end streaming pipeline are deliberately intended to reuse existing workflows and hence do not require specialized implementations.

4.1 Overview

The proposed object-based video streaming methodology is implemented as a fully standards-compliant Web application, with all of the client-side logic being handled in JavaScript. The MPDs describing the constituent entities of the to-be-streamed scene (i.e., background as well as isolated video objects) are fetched via AJAX, as is their video contents (packaged in the form of MPEG-DASH Media Segments). The client maintains a dedicated `HTMLVideoElement` per scene entity, which is fed with downloaded Media Segments via the W3C Media Source Extensions (MSE) specification [18]. Recall from Section 2.4 and Figure 1 that the resulting videos are not suitable for direct playback, as they still need to be composited together after first having been subjected to chroma keying processing. Abstractly speaking, the chroma keying processing task makes transparent those pixels in the decoded video frames that do not carry meaningful color data for the entity at hand, while the compositing task rebuilds the original video scene by superimposing the processed frames over each other in depth descending order. The outcome of the compositing task is rendered in an output `HTMLCanvasElement` for presentation to the user.

4.2 Chroma Keying

The chroma keying and scene compositing operations that form the cornerstone of our client-side methodology have been jointly implemented as an integrated WebGL shader (see Figure 2). In fact, two alternative fragment shader implementations have been developed to fulfill this compound task. Both expect to receive WebGL textures depicting temporally corresponding frames from the scene's composing entities as input and produce as output a single frame depicting the recomposited scene.

4.2.1 Classic Chroma Keying

The first WebGL fragment shader performs chroma keying in a classical manner. The shader iterates over all contributing entities in the scene (starting from the background and then continuing in depth descending order), extracts the color of the indexed pixel in the entity's video frame, applies the chroma keying operation on it, and then performs alpha blending with the previous composition state. The chroma keying operation itself first calculates the Euclidian distance between respectively the color of the indexed pixel and the color value that is used to represent transparency in the encoded video frame. The calculated Euclidian distance is then transformed into an alpha amount based on a lower and upper tolerance value (see Listing 1).

```
1  // vec4 pixClr = color of indexed pixel, int d = Euclidian distance,
2  // int x = dominant RGB channel of chroma value denoting transparency
3
4  if (d > tola) { d = 1.0; }
5  else if (tolb < d) {
6    // Reduce color intensity of chroma key value
7    pixClr[x] = pixClr[x] - min((1.0-d), (15.0/255.0));
8    // Map ]tolb,tola] interval to ]0,1] alpha value
9    d = (d-tolb)*(1.0/(tola-tolb));
10 } else { d = 0.0; }
11
12 pixClr[3] = d; // set pixel's alpha value
```

Listing 1: Classic chroma keying implementation.

4.2.2 Alpha Mask Optimization

The second chroma keying implementation combines the video object representation method described in Section 2.1 with an alpha mask as a complementary means to convey pixel opacity information. The alpha mask is baked into the video data that results from the object segmentation operation, in a top-bottom composition (see Figure 3). As such, video frames in the alpha mask approach exhibit twice the vertical resolution compared to those employed in the classic chroma keying implementation.

Implementation-wise, each decoded video frame (carrying at the same time image data and associated alpha mask) is rendered to a single texture, with separate texture coordinates being applied in the WebGL fragment shader to discriminate between the two conceptual data sources it encapsulates. The pixel color that is extracted from the lower part of the texture (any channel in the RGB color space will do as they will always hold equivalent values) is applied as the alpha channel of the corresponding pixel in the upper part of the texture. The scene compositing implementation is equivalent to the one described in Section 4.2.1.

4.2.3 Color Contamination Issues

The chroma keying module of our client-side implementation operates on video data that has undergone lossy (de)compression. This seemingly trivial observation can have substantial implications on the achievable perceptual accuracy of the (color-driven) chroma keying process. In particular, the lossy coding might cause imperfect preservation of the color information that is carried in the video. In the context of the proposed methodology, this color corruption issue manifests itself most relevantly in the form of potential "color bleeding" artifacts introduced at object segmentation edges. At such edges, there must ideally be a hard transition from the chroma keying color to (the color of) either the in-video object or the residual background. The lossy (de)compression however might cause this color boundary to fade (see the magnified area in the bottommost picture in Figure 1), which in turn complicates the chroma keying processing. In practice, the color contamination can cause segmented video objects to be surrounded with a uniformly colored contour in the recomposited scene (with the color of the contour corresponding with the applied chroma keying value). An illustration of this effect is given in the middlemost frame in Figure 5.

Both chroma keying implementations have been optimized to attenuate the perceptual impact of the color corruption issue. In the classic chroma keying solution, the WebGL shader reduces, for each semi-transparent pixel in the processed image, the magnitude of the dominant RGB channel of the chroma keying color (see Listing 1, line 7). While this introduces (modest) color deformation in the processed image, it also smoothens the colored

Figure 3: Video object representation plus alpha mask.

contour. On the other hand, in the alpha mask approach, the values read from the mask are discretely clamped to denote either full transparency or full opacity (as the lossy compression might cause black-versus-white boundaries in the alpha mask to be transformed into a grayish color). This optimization however cannot amend the color bleeding that occurs in the video object representation itself. A rather pragmatic solution to cope with the latter problem consists of combining an alpha mask that tightly fits the video object in the scene with video data in which the object boundaries have been shifted a few pixels outwards (see the magnified area in the object representation in Figure 3). This approach produces a spatial buffer area to absorb the color spill, with this buffer area subsequently being trimmed away by the closely fitting alpha mask.

4.3 Quality Adaptation Considerations

In theory, arbitrary types of quality adaptation can be applied to the video fragments that result from the object segmentation step in the proposed methodology. In effect, both spatial and temporal resolution modifications are theoretically supported, as is alteration of the Quantization Parameter (which intrinsically influences video output quality). In practice however, mixing video fragments that exhibit heterogeneous spatial or temporal fidelities holds the risk of introducing visual inconsistencies in the recomposited scene. In particular, spatial downsampling inherently hurts the accuracy of the carried color information, which in turn could cause alignment issues to arise. As an example, the surface area of a segmented object as encoded in respectively a downsized residual background and its full resolution video object representation might not match spatially. On the other hand, as has already been established by Vetro et al. [17], temporal resolution variation among video fragments contributing to a single scene might lead to the introduction of spatial patches in the recomposed frames for which no color data is available, this way effectively creating transparent "holes". Such a scenario arises, for example, when a high-framerate foreground object has changed its position in the scene, while its associated low-framerate residual background did not update yet.

4.4 Limitations Imposed By Web Browser

The client-side implementation is intended to be executed in a Web browser environment. There exist important hiatuses in the multimedia support offered by the targeted execution context, which considerably complicated our implementation and limits its achievable level of perceptual performance. First of all, the media APIs exposed by contemporary Web browsers prevent frame-accurate video seeking. This restriction forced us to read the constituting frames of a video while its playback is ongoing, via a timer-based approach (with the timeout period set according to the frame rate of the involved video). As the precision of JavaScript timers is known to be rather coarse, it is not guaranteed that every single input frame actually finds its way to the chroma keying module (or, conversely, that the chroma keying module never operates on duplicate frames). Secondly, even though media synchronization provisions are stipulated in the HTML5 standard, to date none of the mainstream Web browsers implement them. Our client-side methodology requires the video playback of the contributing entities in an object-based scene to be in sync, as the chroma keying and compositing operations need to be supplied with temporally matching frames from all involved entities for the recomposited result to be visually correct. To circumvent this functional deficiency, we resorted to a manual synchronization implementation in JavaScript which entails starting the playback of the involved videos in immediate succession and re-syncing them as soon as their playback time starts to diverge too heavily. While this heuristic approach works fine most of the time, it does not warrant frame-precise inter-video synchronization. To the best of our knowledge, exact video sync is (for the time being) impossible to achieve in plain JavaScript. Please note that this observation also substantiates our design decision in the alpha mask implementation to combine the object representation with its associated alpha mask in an integrated video stream instead of packaging both separately.

5. EVALUATION SETUP

Both an objective and subjective evaluation has been conducted with the goal of perceptually comparing the two object-based video streaming implementations described in Section 4.2, not only mutually but also with respect to traditional video streaming. This section will describe the evaluation setup.

5.1 Content Sample

The evaluation featured three distinct video fragments. Two of these fragments (i.e., clips "captain" and "concert") were taken from the *IRCCyN IVC 1080i* video quality database [11], while the third video (called "NTIA poolhall") was fetched from the *Consumer Digital Video Library* (http://www.cdvl.org/). All involved videos have a Full HD spatial resolution, have a playback duration between 8 and 10 seconds, are free of shot transitions (e.g., scene cuts), and were collected in raw YUV422 format. If present, the video fragments' audio track was dropped.

Content-wise, the three clips are quite similar, in that they all depict scenes featuring a human actor in front of a rather trivial background. In particular, the captain clip shows a man looking through a spyglass in front of an artificial fountain, the concert clip portrays musical performer Jean-Michel Jarre walking around on a stage and talking in his microphone, while the poolhall scene depicts a talking person seated in a restaurant. The first two video fragments did not undergo any content-related editing, whereas the last clip was converted into a single shot video fragment by removing the trailing scene of the pool table. The captain and poolhall clips were recorded with a statically positioned and oriented camera, while in the concert fragment the movement of the performer was tracked by rotating a fixed camera. Representative frame excerpts from the content sample are shown in Figure 4. We hypothesized that

Figure 4: Representative frames taken from respectively the captain, concert and poolhall videos.

Table 1: Back- versus foreground bitrate, in kbps.

	Captain		Concert		Poolhall	
Low	200	400	200	500	350	750
Medium	300	700	400	850	450	1450
High	800	1200	800	1300	450	1950

the three considered videos could match well with the proposed object-based streaming approach, as we expected prospective viewers to focus their attention primarily on the foreground actor and much less on the (somewhat irrelevant) background (cf. the targeted video use cases mentioned in Section 1).

The spatial perceptual information (SI) and temporal perceptual information (TI) figures (as defined by Recommendation ITU-T P.910 [8]) of the content sample are as follows: the captain, concert and poolhall videos have a SI value of 33.15, 45.86 and 57.96, respectively, while their TI values respectively equal 20.35, 24.94 and 32.26. Intuitively speaking, these SI and TI measures quantify the intra-frame visual complexity and the amount of inter-frame motion, respectively. Whereas the items in our content set are conceptually and content-wise largely analogous, they nonetheless span a rather large area in the SI and TI continua (which range from 0 to infinity). We would have preferred to include videos with more comparable SI and TI values in our evaluation, yet this was found to be irreconcilable with the other requirements that we put forward for our content sample (i.e., the videos had to be available in uncompressed form and in addition had to depict conceptually largely similar content).

5.2 Content Preparation

For each item in the content sample, 3 discrete bitrate levels were determined (which will be abstractly denoted with the terms low, medium and high) so that each bitrate transition resulted in a clearly discernible quality difference as ascertained by an independent video quality expert. Then, via a manual and offline object segmentation step, the prominent actor in each of the three video clips was converted into a video object, with the remainder of the video scene being classified as belonging to the background. The three established bitrate amounts were finally distributed over respectively the scene background and the segmented foreground object for each of the processed videos (again in close consultation with the video quality expert). As can be read from Table 1, this was always done in such a way that the foreground object was allotted considerably more encoding bitrate compared to the background. The bitrate budget divisions as listed in Table 1 were enforced for both chroma keying implementations.

The practical considerations enumerated in Section 4.3 had two tangible implications on the content preparation. First of all, it was decided not to apply any temporal resolution scaling to the object-based video footage. This concretely implies that, for each of the three videos, the framerate of respectively the scene background and its associated foreground object always equaled the temporal resolution of the unprocessed video. Secondly, although compositing footage with varying spatial resolution might introduce object alignment issues, the consulted video expert nonetheless recommended to factor in spatial resolution manipulation in the evaluation. Therefore, whereas the foreground objects were always streamed in the original (i.e., Full HD) resolution, the scene backgrounds were spatially downgraded to a 1280x720 resolution (except for the concert background in the high bitrate setting, which the video expert preferred to stream in the original resolution, partly because the foreground object in this clip is spatially considerably smaller compared to the two other clips). To intrinsically mask any resulting perceptual errors, the scene background was in the evaluation always streamed integrally, without the foreground being "cut out" from it. This decision undoubtedly impaired the overall visual quality of the background (i.e., there is a bitrate cost associated with encoding the presence of the foreground object as opposed to a uniformly colored area), yet this penalty was deemed to be outweighed by the fact that it enabled the exploitation of spatial resolution as an additional degree of streaming freedom in the evaluation.

The content preparation actions described thus far yielded a total of 6 video clips: the unprocessed material (which immediately also served as background in the object-based footage) as well as the segmented foreground of three distinct videos. These were all VBR (Variable BitRate) encoded using the H.264 Main profile according to the target bitrates listed in Table 1. Please note that the bitrate sum of each back- and foreground pair in Table 1 served as target encoding bitrate for the corresponding non-object-based video. The resulting videos were next temporally divided into 2 second long MPEG-DASH Media Segments. Then, the object-based material was streamed via the proposed methodology and processed at client side using the two chroma keying implementations described in Section 4.2. The resulting output was screengrabbed (by periodically reading the raw pixel data of recomposited frames from the WebGL frame buffer) and subsequently losslessly encoded (Quantization Parameter value of 0) using the H.264 High profile. Although the non-object-based video footage could in theory have been evaluated directly, it nonetheless underwent the same processing (by treating it as an object-based scene consisting of only a single video object), just to exclude the impact of any perceptual effect introduced by the applied screen grabbing technique from the quality comparison results.

In summary, the content preparation finally amounted to 27 video clips (3 video fragments streamed in 3 different bitrates and in either a traditional or object-based fashion, with two chroma

Figure 5: Quality comparison: traditional (top) vs classic chroma keying (middle) vs alpha mask (bottom).

keying implementations being available for the latter streaming technique). Figure 5 displays a corresponding frame from the captain sequence when streamed using the three investigated techniques in the medium bitrate setting. Although complicated by the limited size of the images in print (please consult the paper's supplemental material for a veracious comparison), one should be able to discern that the detail and general quality of the background in the middle and bottom frame is lower compared to that in the traditional streaming snapshot. In contrast, the traditional approach is seen to perceptually suffer from a less sharp representation of the foreground actor, most notably his face. The color contamination issues described previously in Section 4.2.3 are noticeable in the middle image in Figure 5, especially around the person's hat in the right-hand side of the frame, whereas it does not appear in the object-based streaming implementation that applies the alpha mask optimization.

5.3 Subjective Assessment Methodology

The subjective part of our evaluation was implemented as a user study in which the Pair Comparison (PC) method as defined in Recommendation ITU-T P.910 [8] was applied. In the PC method, users are requested to mutually compare two video stimuli presented as a pair. The primary motivation for resorting to this evaluation technique is its high discriminatory power. As the user-perceptible visual differences that exist between the three tested streaming approaches were anticipated to be potentially small, Pair Comparison was deemed an excellent assessment method to quantify these differences. As a subordinate motivation, the PC mechanism involves a simple cognitive task that does not require specific knowledge or expertise from the assessor.

The subjective video quality assessment study logically encompassed three consecutive phases. In the first phase, some demographic information was collected by requesting the participant to fill in a short survey inquiring (primarily) about his or her video consumption habits. Then, the participant was handed written instructions about the test procedure. After verbally addressing any potential questions the participant had about the test procedure, he or she was then asked to complete a training session consisting of 5 representative test conditions (i.e., 5 video pairs exhibiting quality differences comparable to those appearing in the actual test later on). The objective of this trial run was three-fold: (i) familiarize the assessor with the test procedure in general and the employed rating scale in particular, (ii) counter potential learning effects, and (iii) stabilize the observer's opinion with respect to the range of quality differences that items in a pair might exhibit. The video content that featured in the practice session was not re-used in the actual test and the outcome of the session was discarded.

Once the training session was completed, the researcher left the room and the second phase of the user study commenced, which involved the participant conducting the actual experiment. Here, the participant was asked to assess a total of 57 pairs. For each of the three videos and predefined bitrate levels, the three investigated streaming techniques were paired in both the possible orders, this way giving rise to 54 pairs. Three control conditions, each consisting of two (arbitrarily chosen) identical video fragments, were randomly interspersed among these 54 meaningful pairs. The constituting items of a pair were always presented sequentially on the screen, with a fixed 2 second time interval being enforced between the two (during which the screen turned gray). After the presentation of the second item in each pair, the assessor was asked to grade the statement "I prefer the second video over the first" on a 5-point Likert scale ranging from "strongly disagree" to "strongly agree", with the middlemost value representing a neutral opinion. After the assessment of the 19th as well as the 38th pair, the participant was given the opportunity to relax (for as long as he or she saw fit) before continuing with the experiment. The pair presentation order was counterbalanced across test subjects (generalized Latin square experimental design) to minimize the impact of fatigue and other confounding factors on the aggregated set of observations.

While the participant was performing the actual PC test, the researcher observed his or her progress in real-time via an IP camera feed. As soon as the final pair had been rated, the researcher rejoined the participant in the study room to implement the third and final phase in the study consisting of a structured post-experiment interview. During the interview, the three tested streaming techniques were explained to the participant and then discussed. In its totality, a test session on average lasted approximately 1 hour, distributed nearly linearly over the three consecutive phases.

5.3.1 Apparatus and Setup

The user study was carried out in a dedicated room in our research institute. The apparatus of the study consisted of a desktop PC running Windows 8.1, a 22" Full HD Samsung SyncMaster S22B300 monitor, and the Tobii EyeX optical gaze tracker (http://www.tobii.com/xperience/). The Pair Comparison test was implemented as a Web application. The desktop PC ran an Apache HTTP server to locally host this Web application as well as the 27 prepared video stimuli (see Section 5.2). The test application was executed in a commodity Web browser (i.e., Google Chrome version 48.0.2564.116 m) that was set to full screen mode. The brightness and contrast settings of the employed monitor were calibrated using the Windows "Display Color Calibration" tool.

5.3.2 Participants

A total of 18 users (4 female) participated in the subjective evaluation. All but two participants were between 20 and 30 years old, with the two outliers being older. All participants were either colleagues or university students. The subjects were screened for (corrected-to-)normal visual acuity and for absence of color vision deficiencies. The former test was implemented with a Snellen eye chart, the latter by resorting to Ishihara colored plates. On average, participants indicated to watch about 11 hours of video per week, with a PC being the most frequently used video consumption device, followed at considerable distance by smartphones and TV sets; tablets were found not to be a popular video consumption context in our population.

6. RESULTS

6.1 Objective Video Quality Assessment

The perceptual fidelity of the 27 content configurations (see Section 5.2) was objectively assessed by comparing their quality against that of their respective source signal (i.e., the unprocessed video on which the object segmentation was applied) using the PSNR and Structural Similarity (SSIM) metrics. The results are listed in Table 2. The PSNR and SSIM value spaces respectively equal $[0, +\infty[$ and $[-1,1]$, with higher values denoting better video quality. Please note that the reported objective figures were generated using a specialized Web implementation that overcomes the sync problems described in Section 4.4 by operating on decomposed frame sequences instead of video input. Contrary to video input, image-based input does allow tightly synchronized playback of the constituting entities of an object-based scene in the Web browser. Such frame-accurate entity playback sync is a prerequisite to enable objective frame-by-frame comparison with the source signal.

Table 2 reveals that the employed objective metrics found the tested video streaming techniques to be roughly comparable in terms of produced visual quality for the considered content sample. Therefore, the objective results will not be elaborated on.

6.2 Statistical Analysis of Subjective Data

A statistical analysis of the subjective results was conducted to ascertain whether the factors content (i.e., video fragment), bitrate and presentation order (i.e., when comparing streaming techniques A and B, did the participant first see them in either the AB or BA order) had a significant effect on the variable under investigation, in casu participants' preference with regard to the three compared streaming techniques. In the remainder of this subsection, we will denote the involved streaming schemes using the terms *traditional* (TR), (classic) *chroma keying* (CK) and *alpha mask* (AM).

Please recall that the evaluation adhered to a within-subjects experimental design (every participant assessed each of the 57 pairs) in which the presentation order of the factor combinations was randomized. After removing the results pertaining to the three control conditions (see Section 5.3) from the data set, the remainder of the recorded preference ratings was divided into three disjoint collections depending on the two video streaming techniques they applied to. The contents of the resulting groups was then halved by dropping the ratings that users expressed when comparing the streaming techniques in inverse presentation order (for any given video content and bitrate). In effect, the data resulting from reversing the presentation order was solely used as a reliability metric in the statistical analysis (see Section 6.3). Finally, for the three result groups separately, either the repeated measures ANOVA method or the Kruskal-Wallis non-parametric test was applied depending on whether Bartlett's test revealed a violation of the homogeneity of variances. If the ANOVA revealed a factor to have a statistically significant effect on the evaluation variable, a pairwise t-Test with Bonferroni corrections was applied as a post hoc method.

Concerning the alpha mask versus traditional streaming comparison results, the ANOVA did not show a significant main effect of any of the factors on users' preference for either of the two involved streaming techniques. For the comparison of the chroma keying versus the traditional approach, the ANOVA revealed a significant main effect of the bitrate factor on streaming technique preference ($F(2,153)=3.75$, $p=2.56e^{-2}$). However, the post hoc analysis did not show any significant differences among the three different bitrate levels. In the remaining result cluster (i.e., alpha mask versus chroma keying), the ANOVA detected a significant main effect of the content factor on streaming technique preference ($F(2,153)=21.78$, $p=6.15e^{-8}$). The post hoc analysis did show statistically significant differences between respectively the captain and poolhall videos ($p=3.2e^{-8}$) and the concert and poolhall videos ($p=9.9e^{-4}$). No statistically significant effect of the technique presentation order was discovered for any of the technique comparisons, nor were significant interactions among the three considered factors.

Figure 6 summarizes the results of participants' streaming technique preferences, accumulated across the three considered bitrate levels. In these plots, again only those ratings are retained that users expressed in the original (instead of in the inverse) streaming technique presentation order. The bar charts cardinally plot the number of times participants preferred one or the other paired streaming technique, without taking the amplitude of their preference into account. For each streaming technique combination and tested video clip, the number of neutral responses issued by assessors can be calculated by subtracting the number of votes jointly received by the two techniques from the aggregated number of comparisons, being 54. For example, for the alpha mask versus chroma keying comparison with the captain clip, a total of 28 neutral responses were registered. The numbers that are printed on top of the individual bars express the mean and standard deviation of users' comparison ratings when preference amplitude is taken into account (using numerical values 1 and 2 to respectively denote "(dis)agree" and "strongly (dis)agree" responses). Although we believe these results to be valuable, the reader is reminded that their statistical relevance was found to be limited.

6.3 Reliability of the Subjective Results

As a data reliability measure, the PC test included three hidden control conditions (in which identical videos were compared), while assessors also needed to grade all of the streaming technique comparison pairs twice, in alternative presentation orders.

Table 2: Objective video quality assessment results. Each table cell first lists the PSNR and then the SSIM value.

	Captain			Concert			Poolhall		
	TR	CK	AM	TR	CK	AM	TR	CK	AM
Low	31.223998	29.763731	29.651776	30.827201	27.220299	27.140646	37.110095	33.663130	33.704654
	0.856273	0.855087	0.851589	0.810569	0.780561	0.777704	0.946131	0.926638	0.927252
Medium	32.980461	31.224099	31.202164	33.431212	31.080416	31.050734	38.415972	34.142184	34.253600
	0.873295	0.865927	0.864808	0.837656	0.818014	0.816874	0.955235	0.933228	0.934946
High	35.116511	33.813269	33.843309	34.832957	32.246662	32.261694	38.876903	34.172041	34.295821
	0.896118	0.885625	0.885589	0.851363	0.829584	0.829355	0.958167	0.934060	0.935986

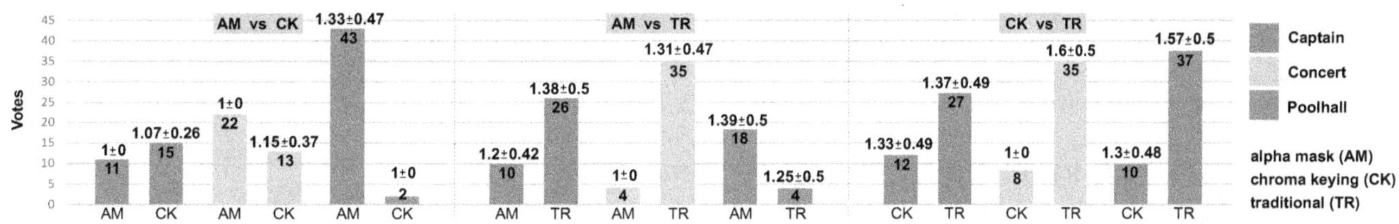

Figure 6: Absolute preference numbers for each of the streaming technique comparisons and tested video clips.

Analysis of the control condition data revealed that only once a strong preference for one of the compared videos was expressed by a test subject, whereas more than half of the grades (correctly) corresponded with a neutral opinion (i.e., 29 out of the total 54). We numerically encoded users' preference ratings for the control conditions as follows: 0 for neutral responses, 1 for (dis)agree preferences, and 2 for the strongly (dis)agree options. Using this coding scheme, the average preference value turned out to be 0.48±0.53. Please remark that in an ideal scenario, both values would be 0 (denoting neutrality). Concerning the results pertaining to the presentation order permuting, the analysis revealed little to no intra-subject variation. In absolute figures, in 204 out of the total 486 cases, participants expressed perfectly consistent preference ratings when comparing the same two streaming techniques in the two alternative presentation orders. In 121 of the residual 282 cases, participants maintained their preference yet with a different magnitude, whereas the remaining 161 cases yielded inconsistent ratings. By discretely mapping the numerical interval [-2,2] to the 5-point preference scale, the average rating difference for the 486 cases was found to equal -0.16±1.19. Again, the closer these values are to 0, the better.

6.4 Discussion

The statistical analysis of the subjective assessment findings did not turn out to be especially favorable to the proposed object-based streaming technique. However, we believe that this result needs to be put into proper perspective by also considering the outcome of the post-experiment interviews and participants' recorded gaze information.

As part of the post-experiment interview phase, we informed about the criteria participants applied when comparing the investigated video streaming techniques. It turned out that, even though we explicitly asked assessors to express their *preference* per paired streaming techniques (without explicitly mentioning the term *video quality* in this context), participants nearly unanimously interpreted their role in the experiment to primarily be that of a video quality assessor. In particular, many participants indicated that they actively searched for visual artifacts in the compared videos and, if present, were typically inclined to favor the video showing the least amount of artifacts. Recognized types of artifacts included general video blockiness or pixelation, the presence of contours surrounding segmented objects, and (overly noticeable) quality differences between back- and foreground. It is apparent that the application of such evaluation criteria hurt the appreciation of the tested object-based video sequences. Some participants explicitly mentioned that their appreciation of the object-based approach would likely be different if they would simply be watching videos at home at their leisure.

Participants' just described active scanning behavior (in search of visual artifacts) is objectively confirmed by the gaze tracking data. In particular, whereas many users initially tended to focus on the foreground objects, their attention was found to diverge to increasingly also include the scene backgrounds as the experiment progressed. This behavior of course unarguably defies the tested object-based streaming premise (i.e., shift bitrate allocation from back- to foreground, as this is the part of the video the viewer will most likely concentrate on). Besides artifact scanning, the observed gaze evolution can partly also be attributed to the large number of repetitions of the same 3 video clips (albeit in different bitrates or using different streaming techniques).

Many test users also indicated that, during the test, they had often tended to prefer the traditional streaming approach because it yielded the familiar scenario in which visual quality is rather uniformly distributed among back- and foreground. However, when we explained the rationale behind the investigated object-based approach, all 18 participants unanimously were found to be receptive to the idea. This is evidenced by the fact that nearly every test subject was able to independently devise at least one use case in which the proposed methodology could prosper. Some notable examples of imagined use cases were the streaming of a fashion show (with the models wearing the showcased clothes acting as foreground objects), video conferencing, task-centric or educational video applications (e.g., surgery training), and discourse scenarios (e.g., a human news presenter).

Finally, some participants remarked that the object-based streaming approach could have benefited from the inclusion of audio in the experiment. Especially for the concert video in the content sample, they thought that the presence of an accompanying audio track would have caused their attention to intrinsically be pulled more towards the foreground object.

6.5 Broader Implications

The subjective evaluation has revealed two broader video research implications. First of all, the contour artifact turned out to be either very annoying or very distracting (or both) for nearly all of the 18 test participants. The classic chroma keying implementation considerably suffered from the presence of such artifacts, which we consider to be a determining factor for its slightly lower subjective appreciation compared to the alternative alpha mask implementation (although the difference was not found to be statistically relevant). We argue that the negative impact of the contour artifact on the viewing experience is likely to be extrapolatable to video streaming applications in general. Secondly, the quality differences as applied between respectively the back- and foreground in the evaluated object-based content sample were also classified by many test participants as being an undesirable video artifact. Quantifying the acceptable amount of quality variation among back- and foreground therefore represents an essential avenue for follow-up research.

7. CONCLUSIONS & FUTURE RESEARCH

This article has proposed and subjectively evaluated an object-based video streaming methodology that maintains full compatibility with contemporary frame-based video coding and HTTP Adaptive Streaming workflows. Statistically speaking, no decisive preference difference has been found to exist between respectively the proposed methodology and classical video streaming for the tested content sample. However, we believe that the reported subjective results correspond with the worst-case scenario (from our methodology's perspective), given the high amount of content repetition in the evaluation (causing assessors' attention to diverge to the background of the tested scenes), the lack of sound output, and the finding that participants overreacted to the presence of "artifacts" in the compared videos (although we really asked them to intuitively express their preference). This observation, combined with structurally elicited test participant feedback, causes us to conclude that the proposed methodology nonetheless holds the potential to outperform traditional streaming with respect to perceptual appreciation, at least in the targeted specialized video use cases involving salient foreground objects and plain backgrounds.

The work presented in this article has only scratched the tip of the iceberg with regard to pragmatic object-based video streaming. First of all, the reported experimental results exclusively concern simple video scenes consisting of a background and a single object of interest. Although it has already been empirically established that the proposed methodology is able to cope with the presence of multiple video objects in a single scene, such scenarios introduce complications which require further investigation. Secondly, given the detrimental effect of visual artifacts like object contours on user-perceived quality, integrating inpainting algorithms or other error concealment techniques in the proposed methodology seems advocated. Third, although not reported earlier in the article due to space constraints, the proposed methodology suffers from suboptimal performance on handheld devices like tablets. We therefore plan to conduct a workload analysis to amend computational bottlenecks. The final and probably most ambitious future research topic involves the design of an automated solution (e.g., based on emperically established heuristics) to optimally distribute the available streaming bandwidth over the constituting entities in an object-based video scene.

8. ACKNOWLEDGMENTS

The research leading to these results has received funding from the European Union's Seventh Framework Programme (FP7/2007-2013) under grant agreement nr 610370, ICoSOLE ("Immersive Coverage of Spatially Outspread Live Events", http://www.icosole.eu).

9. REFERENCES

[1] Adobe After Effects CC tutorials. Use the Roto Brush. Online, https://helpx.adobe.com/after-effects/how-to/aftereffects-roto-brush-cc.html, 2016.

[2] P. R. Alface, J.-F. Macq, F. Lee, and W. Bailer. Adaptive coding of high-resolution panoramic video using visual saliency. In *Proceedings of the 1st International Workshop on Interactive Content Consumption at EuroITV 2013*, June 2013.

[3] S. A. Goor and L. Murphy. An adaptive MPEG-4 streaming system based on object prioritisation. In *Proceedings of Irish Signals and Systems Conference*, July 2003.

[4] A. Hakeem, K. Shafique, and M. Shah. An object-based video coding framework for video sequences obtained from static cameras. In *Proceedings of ACM MULTIMEDIA '05*, pages 608–617, New York, NY, USA, 2005. ACM.

[5] M.-H. Hsiao, H.-P. Kuo, H.-C. Wu, Y.-K. Chen, and S.-Y. Lee. Object-based video streaming technique with application to intelligent transportation systems. In *IEEE International Conference on Networking, Sensing and Control*, volume 1, pages 315–320, March 2004.

[6] ISO/IEC 14496-2:1999. Information technology – Coding of audio-visual objects – Part 2: Visual, 1999.

[7] ISO/IEC 23009-1. Information technology – Dynamic adaptive streaming over HTTP (DASH) – Part 1: Media presentation description and segment formats, 2014.

[8] ITU-T P.910. Subjective video quality assessment methods for multimedia applications, April 2008.

[9] D. Kimber, T. Dunnigan, A. Girgensohn, F. Shipman, T. Turner, and T. Yang. Trailblazing: Video playback control by direct object manipulation. In *2007 IEEE International Conference on Multimedia and Expo*, pages 1015–1018, July 2007.

[10] C. Nguyen, Y. Niu, and F. Liu. Direct manipulation video navigation in 3D. In *Proceedings of the SIGCHI Conference on Human Factors in Computing Systems*, CHI '13, pages 1169–1172, New York, NY, USA, 2013. ACM.

[11] S. Péchard, R. Pépion, and P. L. Callet. Suitable methodology in subjective video quality assessment: A resolution dependent paradigm. In *International Workshop on Image Media Quality and its Applications*, IMQA2008, Kyoto, Japan, September 2008.

[12] S. Poullot and S. Satoh. VabCut: A video extension of GrabCut for unsupervised video foreground object segmentation. In *2014 International Conference on Computer Vision Theory and Applications*, volume 2, pages 362–371, January 2014.

[13] A. Puri and A. Eleftheriadis. MPEG-4: An object-based multimedia coding standard supporting mobile applications. *Mobile Networks and Applications*, 3(1):5–32, June 1998.

[14] P. Quax, P. Issaris, W. Vanmontfort, and W. Lamotte. Evaluation of distribution of panoramic video sequences in the eXplorative Television project. In *22nd International Workshop on Network and Operating System Support for Digital Audio and Video*, NOSSDAV '12, pages 45–50, New York, NY, USA, 2012. ACM.

[15] H. Schwarz, D. Marpe, and T. Wiegand. Overview of the Scalable Video Coding extension of the H.264/AVC standard. *IEEE Transactions on Circuits and Systems for Video Technology*, 17(9):1103–1120, September 2007.

[16] A. Vetro and H. Sun. An overview of MPEG-4 object-based encoding algorithms. In *International Conference on Information Technology: Coding and Computing*, pages 366–369, April 2001.

[17] A. Vetro, H. Sun, and Y. Wang. Object-based transcoding for adaptable video content delivery. *IEEE Transactions on Circuits and Systems for Video Technology*, 11(3):387–401, March 2001.

[18] W3C Candidate Recommendation. Media Source Extensions. Online, https://www.w3.org/TR/media-source/, November 2015.

[19] H. Wang, V.-T. Nguyen, W. T. Ooi, and M. C. Chan. Mixing tile resolutions in tiled video: A perceptual quality assessment. In *24th International Workshop on Network and Operating System Support on Digital Audio and Video*, NOSSDAV '14, pages 25–30, New York, NY, USA, 2014. ACM.

[20] J. Wuenschmann, T. Roll, C. Feller, and A. Rothermel. Analysis and improvements to the object based video encoder MPEG 4 part 25. In *2011 IEEE International Conference on Consumer Electronics - Berlin*, pages 115–119, September 2011.

A Perceptual Quality Metric for Videos Distorted by Spatially Correlated Noise

Chao Chen
Google Inc.
1600 Amphitheatre Parkway
Mountain View, California
chaochen@google.com

Mohammad Izadi
Google Inc.
1600 Amphitheatre Parkway
Mountain View, California
izadi@google.com

Anil Kokaram
Google Inc.
1600 Amphitheatre Parkway
Mountain View, California
anilkokaram@google.com

ABSTRACT

Assessing the perceptual quality of videos is critical for monitoring and optimizing video processing pipelines. In this paper, we focus on predicting the perceptual quality of videos distorted by noise. Existing video quality metrics are tuned for "white", i.e., spatially uncorrelated noise. However, white noise is very rare in real videos. Based on our analysis of the noise correlation patterns in a broad and comprehensive video set, we build a video database that simulates the commonly encountered noise characteristics. Using the database, we develop a perceptual quality assessment algorithm that explicitly incorporates the noise correlations. Experimental results show that, for videos with spatially correlated noises, the proposed algorithm presents high accuracy in predicting perceptual qualities.

Keywords

Subjective Video Quality, Video Quality Assessment, No-reference Quality Metric, Noise, Power Spectrum Density

1. INTRODUCTION

During video acquisition, compression and communication, various types of distortion may be introduced. Among them, noise is typically introduced in the acquisition process, and it may propagate throughout the video processing and communication pipeline. Accurately predicting the impact of noise on perceptual quality helps in optimizing the overall efficiency of video services. For example, using the estimated noise level, we may be able to predict the likelihood of severe blocking in a subsequent transcoding operation[1]. We can then select a suitable pre-processor to reduce the knock-on effects both on bitrate and quality.

The best way of assessing video quality is to collect human scores by conducting subjective tests. However, human studies are labor intensive and not applicable to real-time applications. It is, therefore, appealing to devise an algorithm that can accurately predict perceptual quality. Perceptual image and video quality assessment have been extensively studied, and several high-performance metrics have been invented. For image quality assessment, SSIM (Structural SIMilarity index [29]) achieves very high correlation with perception and has been widely used due to its low complexity. For video quality assessment, MOVIE (MOtion-based Video Integrity Evaluation index [24]) and STMAD (Spatial-Temporal Most Apparent Distortion [28]) report the best accuracy.

A common drawback of these high-performance metrics is that they need a pristine reference of the video clip under test. In practice, for instance in quality assessment of YouTube uploads, such a reference is unavailable. This limitation motivated research on no-reference image/video quality metrics. One approach to this problem is to measure the "unnaturalness" of a picture or a video. It has been found that certain statistics of a pristine image/video follow certain models[27] [34]. Quality can then be evaluated by measuring the deviation of these statistics from the models. The image quality metrics proposed by [16], [18], [26] and video quality metrics proposed by [23] and [33] follow this methodology. Another method of no-reference quality prediction is based on the free-energy principle in brain science [9]. In this theory, when a visual signal is perceived, the human brain tries to infer the signal using an internal generative model. The free energy of this inference process, i.e., the discrepancy between the visual signal and the inference of the internal generative model thus can be used to quantify the level of distortion. The algorithms proposed in [15] and [32] follow this method to predict image quality.

Besides the aforementioned general-purpose quality metrics, several algorithms are specifically designed for noise [14, 30, 31]. These algorithms, along with the general-purpose algorithms are designed or tuned for predicting the videos distorted by white noise. However, the noise on neighboring pixels is typically correlated. As demonstrated in [25], the demosaicing operation in video acquisition is performed over neighboring pixels and thus introduces correlation. We verified this in the videos uploaded to YouTube and found that the noise all presents some degree of correlations (see section 2.1 for more details).

In this paper, we propose a no-reference video quality metric for realistic noise. To this end, we first analyzed the noise correlation patterns on a vast and comprehensive video set. Using the typical noise correlation patterns we found in the video set, we construct a video database that simulates the commonly encountered noise. A series of subjective tests are then performed to evaluate the perceptual quality of the noisy videos in the database. Then, we develop a perceptual

MM '16, October 15-19, 2016, Amsterdam, Netherlands
© 2016 ACM. ISBN 978-1-4503-3603-1/16/10...$15.00
DOI: http://dx.doi.org/10.1145/2964284.2964302

quality metric that explicitly incorporates noise correlation patterns in quality assessment. Experimental results show that the proposed algorithm can accurately predict the perceptual quality of noisy videos.

The rest of the paper is organized as follows: section 2 describes the construction of our quality database for practical noisy videos. Section 3 details the proposed quality metric. Section 4 shows the performance of the proposed metric. The paper is concluded in section 5

2. CONSTRUCTING THE DATABASE

Since the number of sample videos in a subjective test session is limited, they should be carefully selected to represent noise patterns observed in practice. We analyzed the noise structure of a large set of consumer generated videos. Based on the distribution of the noise structures, we created a series of test videos that are representative. The perceptual quality of the videos is then assessed in a series of subjective tests for the development of our quality prediction algorithm.

2.1 Realistic Noise Analysis

Every type of video capture pipeline may present different noise statistics. Hence, there exist many different noise structures in practical videos. YouTube is a video-sharing platform with an enormous amount of consumer-generated video contents. We collect 46,000 videos uploaded to YouTube to analyze their noise patterns. These videos are selected such that

- they represent varying contents e.g. sports, movies, nature, music video, etc.
- they are captured with over 200 different types of cameras or device models.
- they represent varying resolutions including 360p, 720p, 1080p, 2K and 4K.
- their length is longer than 30 seconds to focus on contents that have a chance of being watched.

We analyze the noise patterns of the video collection with a 2D auto-regressive (AR) model. This model has been widely used to analyze noise structure and synthesize film grain [8, 6]. Denoting by $\mathsf{N}(x,y)$ the synthesised noise at position (x,y), the AR model is:

$$\mathsf{N}(x,y) = \sum_{(i,j)\in\mathcal{S}_\Delta} w_{i,j}.\mathsf{N}(x+i,y+j) + \mathsf{G}^\sigma(x,y), \quad (1)$$

where $\mathsf{G}^\sigma(x,y) \sim \mathcal{N}(0,\sigma^2)$ is a Gaussian random variable with zero mean and variance σ^2. The set $\mathcal{S}_\Delta$ is the square neighborhood of $(0,0)$ with size $(2\Delta+1)\times(2\Delta+1)$. The noise at a pixel (x,y) is modeled as the sum of a white noise sample and a weighted sum of the noise in its neighborhood. The weight assigned to the pixel at $(x+i,y+j)$ is the model parameter $w_{i,j}$. Note that this is a prediction equation and so $w_{i,j} = 0$ for the pixels succeeding to the center pixel in raster-scan order. In the following we denote by $\boldsymbol{w}$ the vector of weight parameters, i.e., $\boldsymbol{w} = (w_{i,j} : \forall(i,j) \in \mathcal{S}_\Delta)^\mathsf{T}$. The parameter σ^2 characterizes the power of noise. For a fixed $\boldsymbol{w}$, larger σ^2 leads to larger noise power.

To analyze the structure of the noise in a video sequence we employ aspects of the noise estimation method proposed in [13]. That method estimates the Power Spectral Density [20] of the noise in texture-less areas of video frames. This idea has been used in well-known post-production toolkits e.g. NUKE and Neat Video. The rationale of this method is that the noise is easier to separate in flat regions of a frame. The method first searches for flat patches from all the frames in a video and then applies hyper-planes to approximate the true values of the patches. The approximation error on the patch is considered as the noise. We applied this method on our video collections and fit the AR model to the separated noise to obtain minimum mean square error estimations for the model parameters $\boldsymbol{w}$ and σ. From this analysis, we have the following observations:

1. An AR model with $\Delta = 4$ is sufficient to model the noise in all the 46000 clips ($\Delta > 4$ did not improve the fitting error significantly compared to $\Delta = 4$). This implies that the noise at two pixels separated by a distance of > 4 is uncorrelated in a typical video. In the following analysis, we use $\Delta = 4$.

2. The histogram of $||\boldsymbol{w}||_2$ estimated on the video collection is shown in Figure 1. According to (1), $\boldsymbol{w}$ reflects the correlation among neighboring pixels. As $||\boldsymbol{w}||_2^2$ decreases to zero, the noise $\mathsf{N}(x,y)$ converges to white noise $\mathsf{G}(x,y)$. It is shown in the figure that a large fraction of videos in our collection has non-zero $||\boldsymbol{w}||_2^2$. This observation suggests that the noise in real videos is not white in general.

3. We note that the estimation of the model parameter $\hat{\boldsymbol{w}}$ and $\hat{\sigma}$ may be inaccurate. For videos with textures, the noise separation method may confuse the texture with noise and overestimate the correlation. Therefore, we cannot directly use the noise pattern obtained from the video collection to synthesize the noise for our subjective test.

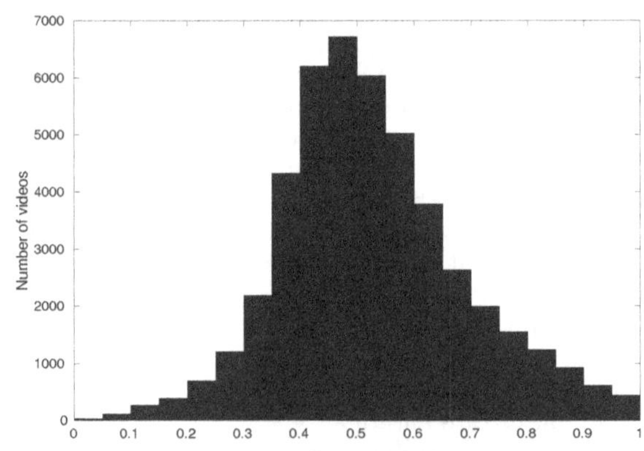

Figure 1: The histogram of $||\hat{\boldsymbol{w}}||_2^2$ estimated on a video collection of 46000 videos.

For $\Delta = 4$, the number of non-zero weights $w_{i,j}$ of our AR model is $((2\Delta+1)^2-1)/2 = 40$. To find out the most typical noise pattern, we may perform a Principal Component Analysis (PCA) on all the $\hat{\boldsymbol{w}}$ in the 40-dimensional space and use the eigenvectors as typical noise patterns for noise synthesis. However, as discussed above, the estimated $\hat{\boldsymbol{w}}$ may contain outliers, and PCA is not robust for the analysis of data with outliers [3].

To rule out poorly estimated vectors $\boldsymbol{w}$, we applied K-means clustering [2] to cluster the estimated vectors into K groups. We vary the number of groups K from 3 to 15 and, for a given K, calculate the mean vector of each group as $\{\bar{\boldsymbol{w}}_\ell^{\mathrm{K}} : 1 \le \ell \le \mathrm{K}\}$. Thus we obtain the least correlated and most correlated noise parameter as

$$\bar{\boldsymbol{w}}_{\min}^{\mathrm{K}} = \arg\min_{\bar{\boldsymbol{w}}_\ell^{\mathrm{K}}} ||\bar{\boldsymbol{w}}_\ell^{\mathrm{K}}||_2, \tag{2}$$

and

$$\bar{\boldsymbol{w}}_{\max}^{\mathrm{K}} = \arg\max_{\bar{\boldsymbol{w}}_\ell^{\mathrm{K}}} ||\bar{\boldsymbol{w}}_\ell^{\mathrm{K}}||_2, \tag{3}$$

We observed that both $\bar{\boldsymbol{w}}_{\min}^{\mathrm{K}}$ and $\bar{\boldsymbol{w}}_{\min}^{\mathrm{K}}$ is not changing further as we increase K over 10. Therefore, we fix K = 10 and define a linear interpolation function between $\bar{\boldsymbol{w}}_{\min}^{10}$ and $\bar{\boldsymbol{w}}_{\max}^{10}$ as:

$$\mathbf{w}(\alpha) = \bar{\boldsymbol{w}}_{\min}^{10} + \alpha \left(\bar{\boldsymbol{w}}_{\max}^{10} - \bar{\boldsymbol{w}}_{\min}^{10}\right). \tag{4}$$

For any $\alpha \in (0, 1)$, $\mathbf{w}(\alpha)$ gives a noise pattern with intermediate correlation level between $\bar{\boldsymbol{w}}_{\min}^{10}$ and $\bar{\boldsymbol{w}}_{\max}^{10}$. To verify that this interpolation yields points close to the 10 clusters, we computed the mean distance of $\bar{\boldsymbol{w}}_\ell^{10}$s (excluding $\bar{\boldsymbol{w}}_{\min}^{10}$ and $\bar{\boldsymbol{w}}_{\max}^{10}$) from the interpolating line, normalized by the length between $\bar{\boldsymbol{w}}_{\min}^{10}$ and $\bar{\boldsymbol{w}}_{\max}^{10}$. The normalized mean distance of 0.11 indicates that the line is fairly close to the cluster centers. We also project all $\bar{\boldsymbol{w}}_\ell^{10}$s on the interpolating line and compute the distance between every two neighboring projected points on that line. The standard deviation of the gaps is around 0.08 of the length, which implies $\bar{\boldsymbol{w}}_\ell^{10}$s are reasonably scattered along the line. In sum, the noise patterns given by (4) provides a reasonable approximation for realistic noise patterns.

2.2 Test Clip Generation

The visual quality of a clip depends both on the level of noise and the spatio-temporal characteristics of the video. Therefore, we need to include videos that represent a broad spectrum of spatial and temporal complexities in our test. A simple way to evaluate the spatial/temporal complexity is to measure the average size of their I frames and P frames. However, videos with large I frames tend to have large P frames because high spatial complexity also gives rise to more prediction residuals in motion compensation. To decouple the correlation between I frame size and P frame size, we normalize the size of P frame by the I frame size and use $\frac{\text{P frame size}}{\text{I frame size}}$ as the indicator for the temporal complexity. We selected 3226 video clips with 4K resolutions from YouTube such that their encoding bit rates are all higher than 100 Mbps, hence ensuring that they contain minimal noise at source. We then encoded them using the H.264 encoder with FFmpeg. To make the frame size a better indicator for spatial-temporal complexity, we apply a constant quantization parameter of 28 to all videos. The distribution of spatial-temporal features is shown in Fig. 2. It is seen that the values of the I frame sizes and the normalized P frame sizes are scattered widely and loosely coupled.

We partition the space of I frame size and normalized P frame size using the percentile of their marginal distributions, respectively. In particular, we calculated the 33% and 66% percentile of the marginal distribution of I frame size and the 50% percentile of the normalized P frame size, respectively. Then we partition the space of spatial-temporal complexity using these percentiles into six regions as shown in Figure 2. In each region, we selected 20 videos that are closest to the centroid of the region (shown by the $\triangledown$ markers in Figure 2). We manually reviewed each of these 20 clips and selected one video that was free from noise and other artifacts such as out-of-focus and over-exposure (shown by $\triangle$ markers in Figure 2). The chosen videos are shown to be close to the centroid of the respective regions and thus are representative of a wide range of spatial-temporal complexity. From each video, we extract a 10-second clip and resize the video from 4K to 1080p resolution using Ffmpeg's scaling filter. The scaled videos are saved as Y'UV raw videos without further compression. The scaling is necessary because we would like to show two video clips side by side on our 4K display. A brief description of the selected clips are given in Table. 1.

Table 1: A brief description of the video clips in our database.

Name	Description
beach	shot from a airplane, beach landscape.
goose	still camera, gooses in front of a lake.
singer	handhold camera, a singer in a concert.
snow	still camera, snow storm over a forest.
sony	still camera, a SONY smartphone.
talkingman	handhold camera, a man is talking.

We then employ the AR model (1) to synthesize noise. We considered 3 models, $\mathbf{w}(0)$, $\mathbf{w}(0.5)$ and $\mathbf{w}(1)$, where $\mathbf{w}(\cdot)$ is defined in (4). The noise synthesized using the three parameters thus present low, medium, and high noise correlations, respectively. For each noise pattern, we select 4 different σ to create 4 test clips with different noise strength. We manually checked the 4 clips to make sure their perceptual quality is visually distinguishable and covers a wide range. In total, we created $3 \times 4 = 12$ distorted versions for each video. Because the duration of a test session is limited to be less than 30 minutes, 9 randomly sampled examples from each set of 12 clips were used for our subjective test [12]. Thus, we used $6 \times 9 = 54$ clips in total.

2.3 Subjective Experiment

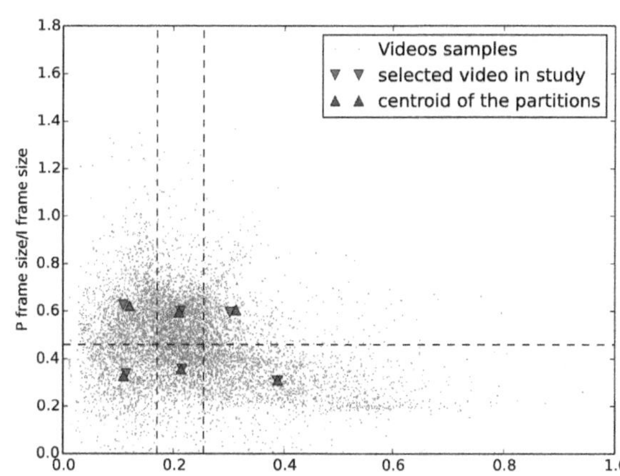

Figure 2: The joint distribution of I frame size and $\frac{\text{P frame size}}{\text{I frame size}}$ of 3226 high quality 4K videos uploaded to YouTube.

We conducted a Double Stimulus Continuous Quality Scale (DSCQS) subjective test following the ITU guidelines [12]. We use a 55 inch Samsung TV for our test, and the participants sit 2.0 m away from the screen. The screen of the 3840 x 2160 display was equally split into two parts. The original video and the noisy video were synchronously played in the two parts such that the subjects could view and compare the two clips easily. There were 28 subjects involved in the test. After each pair of clips had been played, the subject was asked to grade the test video using the original video as a reference.

Fig. 3 shows the Mean Opinion Scores (MOS) obtained from the subjective test versus the power of the synthesized noise in each test video. It can be seen that the MOS obtained in our tests covers a wide range of values. The plot also demonstrates that, as the power of noise increases, the perceptual quality tend to decrease. However, the noise power itself cannot provide a good prediction for MOS. The rank-order correlation between noise power and MOS is only 0.755. That is because the visibility of noise depends on the video contents. The MOS of the videos with dark scenes such as 'talkingman' is lower than videos with brighter contents such as 'snow'. The videos with complex textures or motions such as 'beach' and 'goose' shows better MOS than other videos.

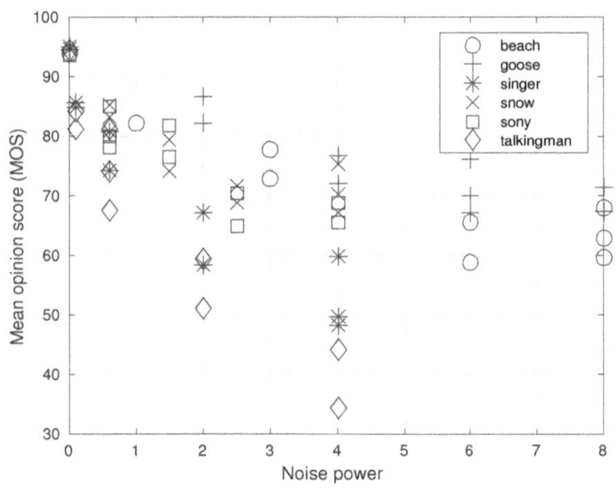

Figure 3: The Mean Opinion Scores of the test videos.

We also analyzed the relation between noise correlation and MOS. The average MOS for the test clips distorted by noise of low, medium, and high correlation are 76.11, 70.88, and 68.7, respectively. It seems videos with highly correlated noise tend to have worse quality.

In sum, the perceptual quality of noisy video depends not only on noise power but also on video contents and the structure of noise. In the next section, we present a no-reference quality metric that can accurately predict perceptual qualities based on the noise pattern and video characteristics.

3. PERCEPTUAL QUALITY METRIC

The flow chart of the proposed no-reference perceptual quality assessment algorithm is shown in Fig. 4. The noise is first estimated from an input video using the method proposed in [13]. Then, the Power Spectral Densities (PSD) of the noise and the input video are estimated in the frequency domain, respectively (module ① and ② in Fig. 4). For a given frequency channel, the ratio between the PSD of the noise and that of the input video (biased by a regularizing constant α) are considered as the noise features of that frequency channel (module ③). These features are further adjusted according to the brightness of the video to incorporate contrast sensitivity (module ④). A visual importance pooling method is applied to the adjusted features to estimate the visibility of noise in each frequency (module ⑤). The final quality metric is then calculated by summing the estimated visibility over the frequencies that show high correlation with subjective quality (module ⑥). Details follow.

3.1 Noise Feature Extraction

We denote by $\{\mathrm{v}(x,y,t) : 0 \le x < W, 0 \le y < H, t \in \mathbb{N}^+\}$ a noisy video signal with resolution $W \times H$. To analyze the local characteristics of the video, we partition the video frames into $B \times B$ non-overlapping blocks and denote by $\{\mathrm{v}^{p,q}(x,y,t) = \mathrm{v}(Bp+x, Bq+y, t) : 0 \le x, y < B\}$ be the (p,q)'th block of a frame.

We model $\mathrm{v}^{p,q}(x,y,t)$ as the sum of a noise-free video block $\mathrm{u}^{p,q}(x,y,t)$ and a noise signal $\mathrm{n}(x,y,t)$, i.e.,

$$\mathrm{v}^{p,q}(x,y,t) = \mathrm{u}^{p,q}(x,y,t) + \mathrm{n}^{p,q}(x,y,t), \tag{5}$$

where $\mathrm{n}^{p,q}(x,y,t)$ is a realization of a zero-mean random variable $\mathsf{N}(x,y)$.

As shown in [4, 7, 19], the visual cortex of human brain decomposes the received visual signal into different orientations and frequencies. In fact, as shown in [10, 24], an overcomplete wavelet transform can be used to imitate such behavior and extract spatial-temporal features for visual quality assessment. In this paper, we approximate the frequency decomposition in visual cortex using the 3D Discrete Fourier Transform (3D-DFT) and propose to use the ratio of power spectrum density (PSD) of $\mathrm{n}^{p,q}(\cdot)$ and $\mathrm{v}^{p,q}(\cdot)$ as the noise feature.

For a discrete video signal $\{\mathrm{f}(x,y,t) : 0 \le x, y < B, 0 \le t < T\}$, its 3D-DFT is given by

$$\hat{\mathrm{f}}(\ell_x,\ell_y,\ell_t) = \sum_{t=0}^{T-1} \omega_T^{\ell_t t} \left(\sum_{y=0}^{B-1} \omega_B^{\ell_y y} \left(\sum_{x=0}^{B-1} \mathrm{f}(x,y,t)\omega_B^{\ell_x x} \right) \right).$$

Here, $\omega_B = \exp(-2\pi \mathrm{i}/B)$ and $\omega_T = \exp(-2\pi \mathrm{i}/T)$ are spatial and temporal discrete Fourier basis, respectively. The PSD of $\mathrm{f}(x,y,t)$ [1] is defined by

$$\mathrm{S_{ff}}(\ell_x,\ell_y,\ell_t) = |\hat{\mathrm{f}}(\ell_x,\ell_y,\ell_t)|^2. \tag{6}$$

PSD captures the signal energy corresponding to spatial frequency $(2\pi\ell_x/B, 2\pi\ell_y/B)$ and temporal frequency $2\pi\ell_t/T$. We define the following distortion feature:

$$\mathrm{r}(\ell_x,\ell_y,\ell_t) = \frac{\mathrm{S_{nn}}(\ell_x,\ell_y,\ell_t)}{\mathrm{S_{vv}}(\ell_x,\ell_y,\ell_t) + \alpha}, \tag{7}$$

where $\mathrm{S_{nn}}$ and $\mathrm{S_{vv}}$ are the PSDs for noise $\mathrm{n}(x,y,t)$ and video signal $\mathrm{v}(x,y,t)$, respectively. The constant α is employed to stabilize potential numerical errors. The feature $\mathrm{r}(\ell_x,\ell_y,\ell_t)$ therefore gives the relative noise strength at a given spatial-temporal frequency.

[1] Strictly speaking, $\mathrm{S_{ff}}$ should be called periodgram.

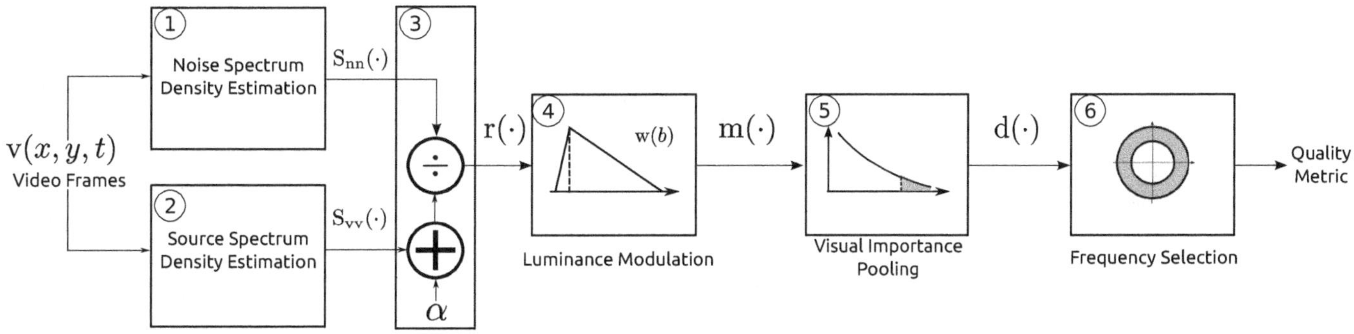

Figure 4: The flow chart of the proposed noisy video quality metric.

Another motivation for using $r(\cdot)$ as the distortion feature is that it captures the correlation pattern of noise. In fact, it can be shown that the PSD of a signal equals to the Fourier transform of its auto-correlation function. The correlation pattern of noise is captured by S_{nn} and thus by $r(\cdot)$.

In our implementation, following the parameters used in [13], we fix the blocksize to be $B = 32$ and the temporal length to be $T = 3$. For each block in a video frame, we concatenate the block with the two co-located blocks in the adjacent frames to form a 3-D array, i.e., $\{v^{p,q}(x,y,t-1), v^{p,q}(x,y,t), v^{p,q}(x,y,t+1) : 0 \leq x, y < 32\}$. Then the 3D-FFT is applied to the array to obtain $\{S_{vv}^{p,q,t}(\ell_x, \ell_y, \ell_t) : 0 \leq \ell_x, \ell_y < 32, 0 \leq \ell_t < 3\}$. The noise PSD $S_{nn}(\ell_x, \ell_y, \ell_t)$ are estimated with the method proposed in [13]. Then, using (7), we get the distortion features $\{r^{p,q,t}(\ell_x, \ell_y, \ell_t) : 0 \leq \ell_x, \ell_y < 32, 0 \leq \ell_t < 3\}$, which is a $32 \times 32 \times 3$ array. The stabilizing constant α is fixed to be 0.3.

3.2 Visibility Modulation

The visibility of noise depends on the background luminance. As shown in [5, 10], in the dark regions of a video, the noise is much less visible than in the regions of mid-grey brightness. On the other hand, for regions of higher than mid-grey luminance, the noise visibility decreases with luminance, which follows Weber's law. To incorporate the impact of luminance, we modulate the distortion feature $r^{p,q,t}(\cdot)$ by a function of local luminance. Assuming the luminance of pixels are normalized to $[0, 1]$, we define the following function that approximately maps brightness to noise visibility:

$$w(b) = \begin{cases} b/\beta & 0 \leq b \leq \beta, \\ 1 - (b - \beta)/(1 - \beta) & \beta < b \leq 1. \end{cases} \tag{8}$$

It is a piecewise linear function which connects points $(0, 0)$, $(\beta, 1)$, and $(1, 0)$. The function $w(b)$ is defined so as to capture the relationship between error visibility threshold and background luminance given by [5]. The parameter β is set to 0.15 to approximate the luminance under which the noise is most visible. Letting $b^{p,q,t} = \sum_{x,y} v(x, y, t)/B^2$ be the average luminance of the (p, q)'th block, the visibility modulated noise feature of the block is given by

$$m^{p,q,t}(\ell_x, \ell_y, \ell_t) = r^{p,q,t}(\ell_x, \ell_y, \ell_t)\, w\left(b^{p,q,t}\right). \tag{9}$$

We show an example of the effect of this visibility modulation effect in Fig. 5. Although equal amount of noise is added everywhere in the frame shown in Fig. 5(a), the noise in the dark region is not quite visible. Fig. 5(b) shows that the perceptual noise level is overestimated by $r(\ell_x, \ell_y, \ell_t)$ in

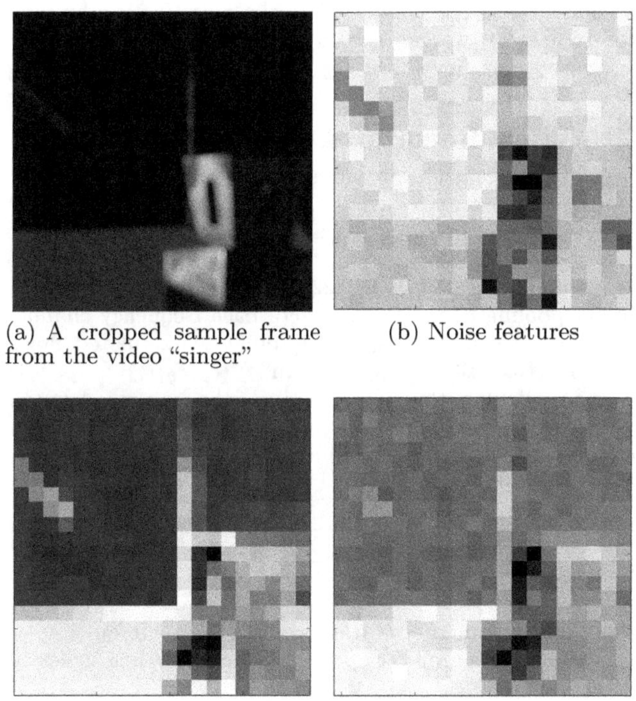

(a) A cropped sample frame from the video "singer" (b) Noise features (c) Visibility modulation factors (d) Visibility modulated noise features

Figure 5: (a) A cropped sample frame from the test clip "singer". (b) The average noise feature $\frac{1}{B^2T}\sum_{\ell_x,\ell_y,\ell_t} r(\ell_x, \ell_y, \ell_t)$ for all the 32×32 blocks; (c) The average visibility modulation factor $\frac{1}{B^2T}\sum_{\ell_x,\ell_y,\ell_t} w(\ell_x, \ell_y, \ell_t)$ for all blocks; (d) The average modulated noise feature $\frac{1}{B^2T}\sum_{\ell_x,\ell_y,\ell_t} m(\ell_x, \ell_y, \ell_t)$ for all blocks. Brighter color indicate larger value.

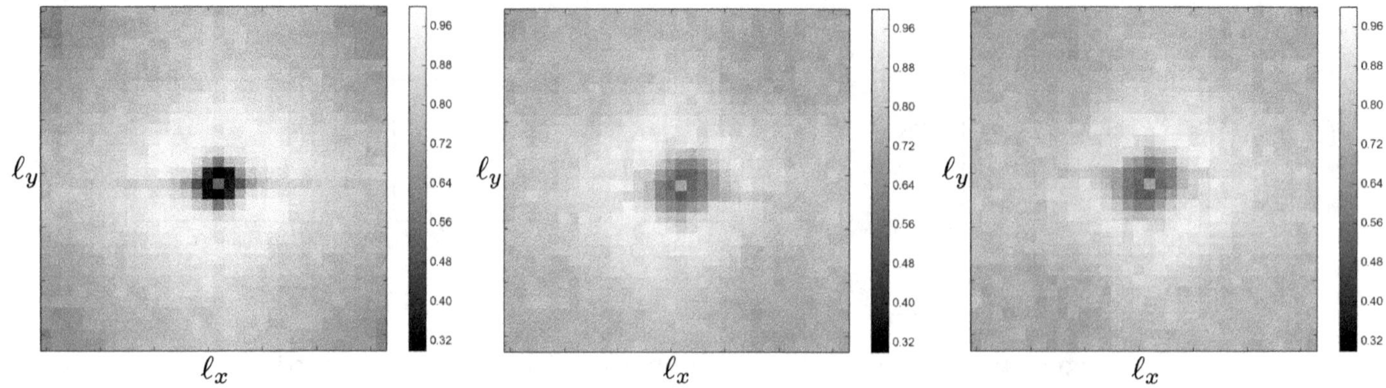

(a) $\ell_t = 0$ (b) $\ell_t = 1$ (c) $\ell_t = 2$

Figure 6: The absolute value of the rank-order correlation coefficient between $\mathrm{d}(\ell_x, \ell_y, \ell_t)$ with the MOS obtained from the subjective test. The coefficients are rearranged such that $\ell_x = 0, \ell_y = 0$ is located at the center of image.

the dark regions. By modulating the noise feature by $\mathrm{w}(\cdot)$ (see Fig. 5(c)), we can obtain a better estimation for the perceptual noise level (see Fig. 5(d)).

3.3 Visual Importance Pooling

In [17, 21], it has been recognized that the worst part of a video tends to attract more attention of the viewers and thus dominates the overall quality of the video. This fact has been exploited by a variety of visual importance pooling algorithms such as [17] and [22]. In our work, we applied a similar pooling method as [17]. For each frequency channel (ℓ_x, ℓ_y, ℓ_z), we first group the luminance modulated noise feature across all blocks, i.e., $\{\mathrm{m}^{p,q,t}(\ell_x, \ell_y, \ell_t) : \forall p, \forall q\}$. Then we calculate the p% percentile of the features, denoted by $\mathrm{k}^t(\ell_x, \ell_y, \ell_t)$. Finally, we obtain the average distortion score for frequency (ℓ_x, ℓ_y, ℓ_z) as

$$\mathrm{d}(\ell_x, \ell_y, \ell_t) = \frac{1}{\mathrm{F}} \sum_{t=1}^{\mathrm{F}} \mathrm{k}^t(\ell_x, \ell_y, \ell_t). \tag{10}$$

where F is the number of frames of the video. In our implementation, the parameter p for percentile pooling is set to 80%.

3.4 Frequency Selection

The final step of our algorithm is to combine the distortion scores $\mathrm{d}(\cdot)$ for different spatial-temporal frequencies to predict MOS. For all the test clips in our subjective test, we calculated their distortion scores $\mathrm{d}(\ell_x, \ell_y, \ell_t)$ for each frequency and then computed its rank-order correlation coefficients with the MOS obtained in our subjective test. The results are shown in Fig 6. It shows that for each temporal frequency ℓ_t, the correlation coefficients are roughly concentric around the frequency $\ell_x = 0, \ell_y = 0$. In other words, the level of correlation mainly depends on the radial frequency $\ell_r = \sqrt{\ell_x^2 + \ell_y^2}$. At medium radial frequency, $\mathrm{d}(\ell_x, \ell_y, \ell_t)$ achieves very strong correlation with MOS (more than 0.9).

Based on the above observations, we use the sum of distortion scores on selected frequencies to predict the perceptual quality. The overall distortion metric is given by:

$$\mathrm{D} = \sum_{t=0}^{T} \sum_{\ell_x=0}^{B} \sum_{\ell_y=0}^{B} \mathrm{d}(\ell_x, \ell_y, \ell_t) \mathrm{I}^{\ell_t}(\ell_x, \ell_y), \tag{11}$$

where $\mathrm{I}^{\ell_t}(\ell_x, \ell_y)$ is a binary frequency selection function. Because $\mathrm{d}(\ell_x, \ell_y, \ell_t)$ achieves maximum correlation with perceptual quality at medium radial frequencies, we use a simple "band-pass" frequency selection function as follows:

$$\mathrm{I}^{\ell_t}(\ell_x, \ell_y) = \begin{cases} 1 & \Psi_{\ell_t} \le \sqrt{\ell_x^2 + \ell_y^2} \le \Phi_{\ell_t}, \\ 0 & \text{otherwise}, \end{cases} \tag{12}$$

where the parameters Ψ_{ℓ_t} and Φ_{ℓ_t} defines the pass-band for the ℓ_t'th temporal frequency plane. In our implementation, we choose $\Psi_0 = \Psi_1 = \Psi_2 = 4$, $\Phi_0 = 8$, and $\Phi_1 = \Phi_2 = 6$. These parameters are optimized using out database.

4. PERFORMANCE EVALUATION

We evaluated the proposed metric on the videos tested in our subjective test. We employ a simple linear model to map our quality metric D to the MOS. The fitted model is

$$\hat{\mathrm{MOS}}(D) = -429.7171D + 90.9003.$$

Our metric gives accurate predictions for perceptual quality. The linear correlation coefficient and the rank order correlation coefficient between the predicted MOS and the MOS is 0.9490 and 0.9518, respectively.

We also compared the performance of our metric with several widely used video quality metrics, including PSNR, SSIM, VQM, and STMAD. The comparison is based on three measurements: 1) rank order correlation coefficients (SROCC); 2) linear correlation coefficients (LCC) and variance of residuals (VoR) between predicted MOS and the empirical MOS. For each metric, we employ the following monotonic logistic regression model recommended by ITU in [11]:

$$\mathrm{MOS}^{\mathrm{pred}} = \frac{a_1 - a_0}{1 + \left(\frac{M + a_4}{a_2}\right)^{a_3}} + a_0, \tag{13}$$

where M is the score given by a video quality metric and $\mathrm{MOS}^{\mathrm{pred}}$ is the MOS predicted by the quality metric. The

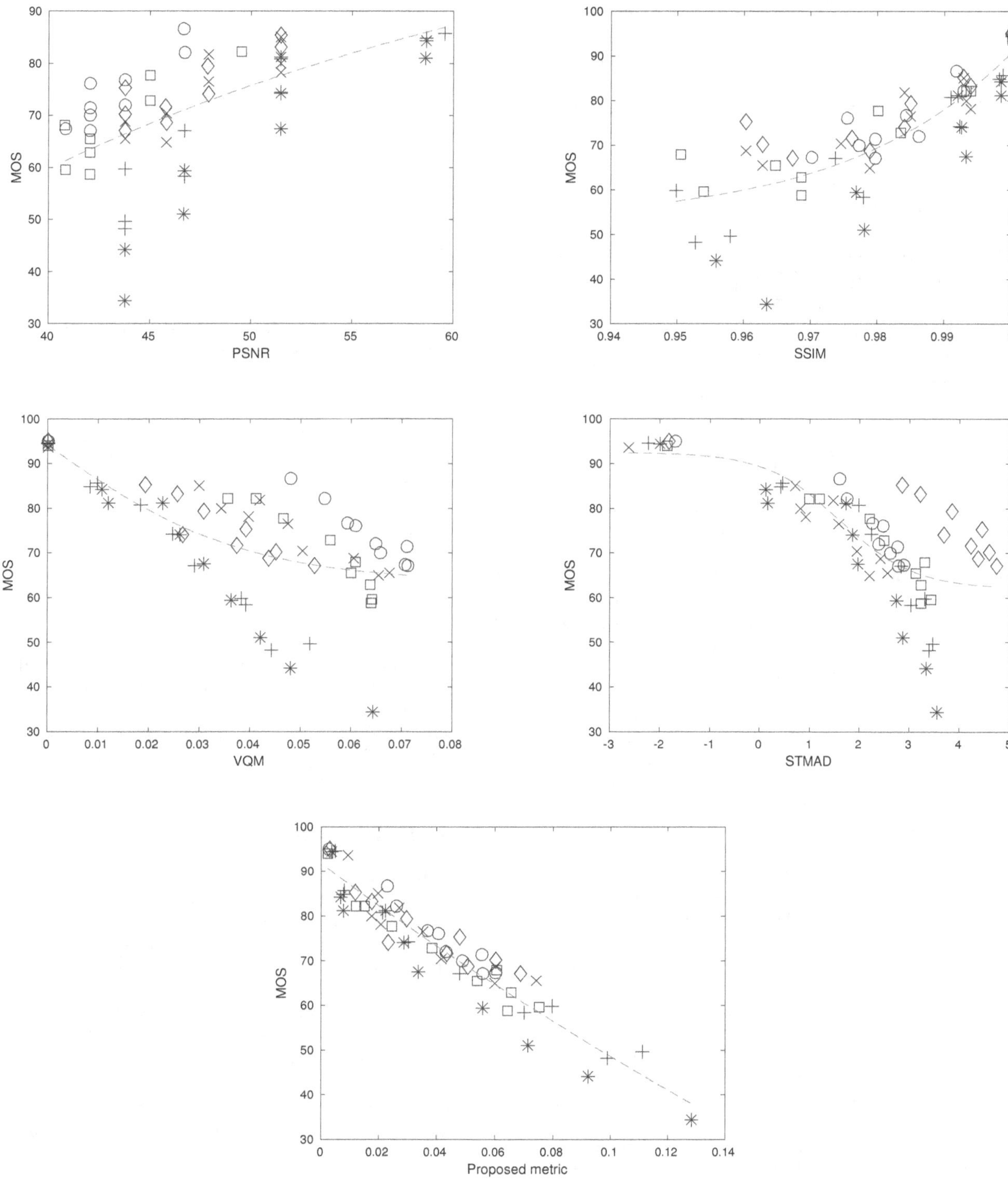

Figure 7: The regression results of PSNR, SSIM, VQM, STMAD, and the proposed noise metrics. The dashed lines show the fitted sigmoid model (13) for each metric. Different markers represents different video content. ○: 'goose', +: 'singer', ∗: 'talkingman', ×: 'sony', □: 'beach', ◇: 'snow'.

Table 2: Performance comparison with other full-reference quality metrics.

Quality Metrics	SROCC	LCC	VoR
Proposed	**0.9518**	**0.9497**	**16.4933**
PSNR	0.6382	0.5838	86.4300
SSIM	0.8560	0.8287	52.7269
VQM	0.6707	0.6917	87.7917
STMAD	0.7412	0.7533	72.8135

Table 3: Performance of the proposed metric on the testing sets when 60% of the video database is used for training.

Quality Metrics	SROCC	LCC	VoR
Proposed	**0.9417**	**0.9545**	**16.8952**
PSNR	0.7019	0.6549	86.6038
SSIM	0.8390	0.8103	65.0248
VQM	0.7450	0.7108	89.3259
STMAD	0.7100	0.7236	87.9041

function parameters $a_0 \cdots a_4$ are obtained by minimizing the mean square error of MOS^{pred}. The results are shown in Fig. 7. The SROCC, LCC, and VoR of all the metrics are summarized in Table 2. The proposed algorithm outperforms all the other quality metrics in all the performance measurements. Note that PSNR, SSIM, VQM and STMAD all need to have access to the original noise-free video, which is typically unavailable for video sharing services such as YouTube. The proposed metric does not need the original video and is thus more appealing for consumer generated video contents.

The parameters of our algorithm such as the numerical stabilizing constant α, visual importance pooling parameter p and frequency selection parameters Φ, Ψ are tuned on our video database. To check if the database is large enough for training the algorithm parameters, we conducted cross-validations on our database. Each time, we partition our database into a training set and a test set. We tune the parameters of our algorithm on the training set and evaluate the VoR on the test set. We vary the size of the training sets from 20% to 90% of the whole database. For a given training set size, cross-validations are repeated on 1000 random training/test set partitions and the average VoR is then calculated and shown in Fig. 8. It shows that the VoR decreases quickly as the size of training set increases. When the size of training set covers more than 60% of the database, the average VoR does not decrease further. In other words, using 60% of our database is enough for tuning the parameters of our model and the model parameter trained on our database is reliable.

To further verify out algorithm, we applied the algorithm to 1% of the videos uploaded to YouTube. From these videos, we randomly select 7 videos such that their MOS predicted by the proposed algorithm is around 30, 40, ..., 90, respectively. We found that their perceptual quality agree well with the predicted MOS.

5. CONCLUSIONS AND FUTURE WORK

In this paper, we proposed a no-reference quality assessment algorithm for video distorted by noise. The algorithm captures the correlation structure of noise by using an estimated PSD. It also incorporated the impact of luminance and visual importance on the noise visibility in its design. The algorithm is trained and validated on a new database of noisy videos that simulates the typical noise patterns encountered in consumer-generated video content. The proposed algorithm can achieve up to 0.95 linear correlation with the MOS obtained from subjective studies, outperforming several high-performance video quality metrics.

The database we used for developing our metric only involves the videos distorted by noise. In practice, videos could be distorted by different types of artifacts in the same time. In the future, we plan to combine our noise metric with other artifacts detectors to predict the quality of videos suffering from multiple types of distortions.

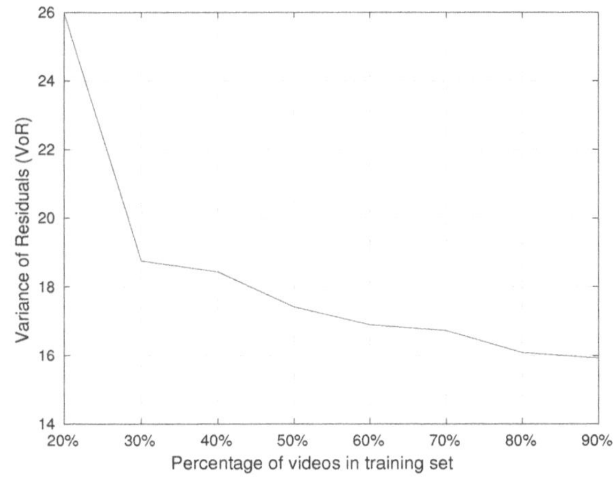

Figure 8: The variation of residuals (VoR) on the test set versus the size of the training set in cross validations.

6. REFERENCES

[1] O. K. Al-Shaykh and R. M. Mersereau. Restoration of lossy compressed noisy images. *IEEE Transactions on Image Processing*, 8(10):1348–1360, Oct 1999.

[2] D. Arthur and S. Vassilvitskii. k-means++: The advantages of careful seeding. In *ACM-SIAM symposium on Discrete algorithms*, pages 1027–1035. Society for Industrial and Applied Mathematics, 2007.

[3] C. M. Bishop. *Pattern Recognition and Machine Learning*. Springer-Verlag Inc., Secaucus, NJ, USA, 2006.

[4] A. C. Bovik. Automatic prediction of perceptual image and video quality. *Proceedings of the IEEE*, 101(9):2008–2024, Sept 2013.

[5] C.-H. Chou and Y.-C. Li. A perceptually tuned subband image coder based on the measure of just-noticeable-distortion profile. *IEEE Transactions on Circuits and Systems for Video Technology*, 5(6):467–476, Dec 1995.

[6] W. Collis, S. Robinson, and P. White. Synthesising film grain. In *European Conference on Visual Media Production*, pages 231–234, 2004.

[7] J. G. Daugman. Uncertainty relation for resolution in space, spatial frequency, and orientation optimized by two-dimensional visual cortical filters. *Journal of the Optical Society of America A*, 2:1160–1169, July 1985.

[8] A. De Stefano, B. Collis, and P. White. Synthesising and reducing film grain. *Journal of Visual Communication and Image Representation*, 17(1):163–182, 2006.

[9] K. Friston. The free-energy principle: a unified brain theory? *Nature Reviews Neuroscience*, 11:127–138, February 2010.

[10] B. Girod. The information theoretical significance of spatial and temporal masking in video signals. In *Proc. SPIE Human Vision, Visual Processing, and Digital Display*, pages 178–189, 1989.

[11] ITU. Objective perceptual assessment of video quality: Full reference television. https://www.itu.int/ITU-T/studygroups/com09/docs/tutorial_opavc.pdf, 2004.

[12] ITU-R Recommendation BT.500-13. Methodology for the subjective assessment of the quality of television pictures. http://www.itu.int/dms_pubrec/itu-r/rec/bt/R-REC-BT.500-13-201201-I!!PDF-E.pdf, Jan. 2012.

[13] A. Kokaram, D. Kelly, H. Denman, and A. Crawford. Measuring noise correlation for improved video denoising. In *IEEE International Conference on Image Processing (ICIP)*, Sept 2012.

[14] C. L. Lim and R. Paramesran. Blind image quality assessment for color images with additive gaussian white noise using standard deviation. In *International Symposium on Intelligent Signal Processing and Communication Systems (ISPACS)*, pages 039–041, Dec 2014.

[15] M. Liu, G. Zhai, Z. Zhang, Y. Sun, K. Gu, and X. Yang. Blind image quality assessment for noise. In *IEEE International Symposium on Broadband Multimedia Systems and Broadcasting (BMSB)*, pages 1–5, June 2014.

[16] A. Mittal, M. A. Saad, and A. C. Bovik. A completely blind video integrity oracle. *IEEE Transactions on Image Processing*, 25(1):289–300, Jan 2016.

[17] A. K. Moorthy and A. C. Bovik. Visual importance pooling for image quality assessment. *IEEE Journal of Selected Topics in Signal Processing*, 3(2):193–201, April 2009.

[18] A. K. Moorthy and A. C. Bovik. Blind image quality assessment: From natural scene statistics to perceptual quality. *IEEE Transactions on Image Processing*, 20(12):3350–3364, Dec 2011.

[19] B. A. Olshausen and D. J. Field. How close are we to understanding v1? *Neural Computation*, 17(8):1665–1699, 2005.

[20] A. V. Oppenheim, R. W. Schafer, and J. R. Buck. *Discrete-time Signal Processing (2Nd Ed.)*. Prentice-Hall, Inc., Upper Saddle River, NJ, USA, 1999.

[21] J. Park, K. Seshadrinathan, S. Lee, and A. C. Bovik. Video quality pooling adaptive to perceptual distortion severity. *IEEE Transactions on Image Processing*, 22(2):610–620, Feb 2013.

[22] M. H. Pinson and S. Wolf. A new standardized method for objectively measuring video quality. *IEEE Transactions on Broadcasting*, 50(3):312–322, Sept 2004.

[23] M. A. Saad, A. C. Bovik, and C. Charrier. Blind image quality assessment: A natural scene statistics approach in the DCT domain. *IEEE Transactions on Image Processing*, 21(8):3339–3352, Aug 2012.

[24] K. Seshadrinathan and A. C. Bovik. Motion tuned spatio-temporal quality assessment of natural videos. *IEEE Transactions on Image Processing*, 19(2):335–350, Feb 2010.

[25] T. Seybold, C. Keimel, M. Knopp, and W. Stechele. Towards an evaluation of denoising algorithms with respect to realistic camera noise. In *IEEE International Symposium on Multimedia (ISM)*, pages 203–210, Dec 2013.

[26] J. Shen, Q. Li, and G. Erlebacher. Hybrid no-feference natural image quality assessment of noisy, blurry, JPEG2000, and JPEG images. *IEEE Transactions on Image Processing*, 20(8):2089–2098, Aug 2011.

[27] A. Srivastava, A. Lee, E. Simoncelli, and S.-C. Zhu. On advances in statistical modeling of natural images. *Journal of Mathematical Imaging and Vision*, 18(1):17–33, 2003.

[28] P. V. Vu, C. T. Vu, and D. M. Chandler. A spatiotemporal most-apparent-distortion model for video quality assessment. In *IEEE International Conference on Image Processing (ICIP)*, pages 2505–2508, Sept 2011.

[29] Z. Wang, A. C. Bovik, H. R. Sheikh, and E. P. Simoncelli. Image quality assessment: from error visibility to structural similarity. *IEEE Transactions on Image Processing*, 13(4):600–612, April 2004.

[30] G. Zhai, A. Kaup, J. Wang, and X. Yang. A dual-model approach to blind quality assessment of noisy images. In *Picture Coding Symposium (PCS)*, pages 29–32, Dec 2013.

[31] G. Zhai and X. Wu. Noise estimation using statistics of natural images. In *IEEE International Conference on Image Processing (ICIP)*, pages 1857–1860, Sept 2011.

[32] G. Zhai, X. Wu, X. Yang, W. Lin, and W. Zhang. A psychovisual quality metric in free-energy principle. *IEEE Transactions on Image Processing*, 21(1):41–52, Jan 2012.

[33] K. Zhu, C. Li, V. Asari, and D. Saupe. No-reference video quality assessment based on artifact measurement and statistical analysis. *IEEE Transactions on Circuits and Systems for Video Technology*, 25(4):533–546, April 2015.

[34] D. Zoran and Y. Weiss. Scale invariance and noise in natural images. In *IEEE International Conference on Computer Vision*, pages 2209–2216, Sept 2009.

Zero-Shot Hashing via Transferring Supervised Knowledge

Yang Yang[†], Yadan Luo[†], Weilun Chen[†], Fumin Shen[†], Jie Shao[†], Heng Tao Shen[§,†]
[†]University of Electronic Science and Technology of China, Chengdu, China
[§]The University of Queensland, Brisbane, Australia
{dlyyang, lyadanluol, chenweilunster, fumin.shen}@gmail.com
shaojie@uestc.edu.cn, shenht@itee.uq.edu.au

ABSTRACT

Hashing has shown its efficiency and effectiveness in facilitating large-scale multimedia applications. Supervised knowledge (*e.g.*, semantic labels or pair-wise relationship) associated to data is capable of significantly improving the quality of hash codes and hash functions. However, confronted with the rapid growth of newly-emerging concepts and multimedia data on the Web, existing supervised hashing approaches may easily suffer from the scarcity and validity of supervised information due to the expensive cost of manual labelling. In this paper, we propose a novel hashing scheme, termed *zero-shot hashing* (ZSH), which compresses images of "unseen" categories to binary codes with hash functions learned from limited training data of "seen" categories. Specifically, we project independent data labels (*i.e.*, 0/1-form label vectors) into semantic embedding space, where semantic relationships among all the labels can be precisely characterized and thus seen supervised knowledge can be transferred to unseen classes. Moreover, in order to cope with the semantic shift problem, we rotate the embedded space to more suitably align the embedded semantics with the low-level visual feature space, thereby alleviating the influence of semantic gap. In the meantime, to exert positive effects on learning high-quality hash functions, we further propose to preserve local structural property and discrete nature in binary codes. Besides, we develop an efficient alternating algorithm to solve the ZSH model. Extensive experiments conducted on various real-life datasets show the superior zero-shot image retrieval performance of ZSH as compared to several state-of-the-art hashing methods.

Keywords

zero-shot hashing; discrete hashing; supervised knowledge transfer; semantic alignment

1. INTRODUCTION

Hashing is a powerful indexing technique for enabling efficient retrieval on large-scale multimedia data, such as image [22, 33] and video [1]. Specifically, in order to achieve shorter response time and less computational cost, hashing encodes high-dimensional data into compact binary codes (*i.e.*, 0 or 1) substantially. In this way,

MM '16, October 15-19, 2016, Amsterdam, Netherlands
© 2016 ACM. ISBN 978-1-4503-3603-1/16/10...$15.00
DOI: http://dx.doi.org/10.1145/2964284.2964319

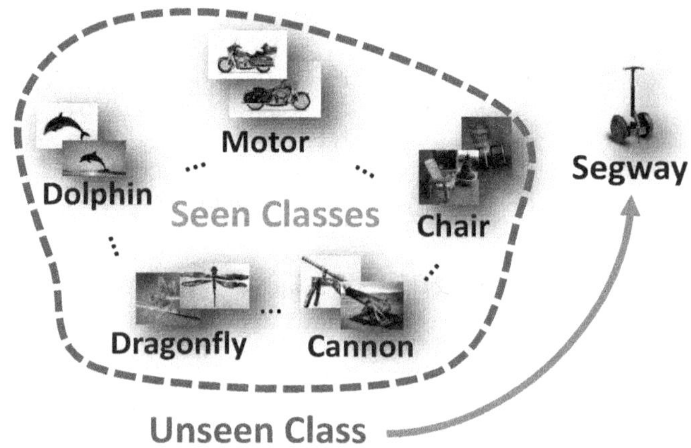

Figure 1: An illustration of newly-emerging concepts and images unseen to the existing learning systems.

data can be compactly stored and Hamming distances can be efficiently calculated with bit-wise XOR operations. Because of its impressive capacity of dealing with "curse of dimensionality" problem, hashing has been extensively employed in various real-world applications, ranging from multimedia indexing [8] to multimedia event detection [20].

There are mainly two branches of hashing, *i.e.*, data-independent hashing and data-dependent hashing. For data-independent hashing, such as Locality Sensitive Hashing [6], no prior knowledge (*e.g.*, supervised information) about data is available, and hash functions are randomly generated. Nonetheless, huge storage and computational overhead might be cost since more than $1,000$ bits are usually required to achieve acceptable performance. To address this problem, research directions turn to data-dependent hashing, which leverages information inside data itself. Roughly, data-dependant hashing can be divided into two categories: unsupervised hashing (*e.g.*, Iterative Quantization [7], Order Preserving Hashing [26] and Robust Discrete Spectral Hashing [32]), and supervised hashing (*e.g.*, Supervised Hashing with Kernels [16], Weakly-supervised Hashing [34] and Supervised Discrete Hashing [22]). In general, supervised hashing usually achieves better performance than unsupervised ones because supervised information (*e.g.*, semantic labels and/or pair-wise data relationship) can help to better explore intrinsic data property, thereby generating superior hash codes and hash functions.

Along with the explosive growth of Web data, traditional supervised hashing methods have been facing an enormous challenge, *i.e.*, the generation of reliable supervised knowledge cannot catch up with the rapid increasing speed of newly-emerging semantic concepts and multimedia data. In other words, due to the expensive cost of manual labelling (time-consuming and labor-intensive), sufficient labelled training data is usually not timely available for learning new hash functions that can accurately encode data of new concepts. As illustrated in Figure 1, within the "seen" zone, where images are attached with known categories, existing supervised hashing algorithms may perform well because they are fed with correct guidance. However, outside the seen area, supervised hashing algorithms may easily fail to generalize to data of new categories that they never observe, *e.g.*, *segway*, a two-wheeled, self-balancing, battery-powered electric vehicle. Moreover, most of current approaches use supervised information in the form of either 0/1 semantic labels or pair-wise data relationship for guiding the learning process, which implies that precious correlation among label semantics are inevitably ignored. One straightforward consequence of the semantic independency is that each category can neither learn from other relevant categories nor distribute its own supervised knowledge to other seen classes and/or even those unseen ones.

The aforementioned disadvantages motivate us to consider if we can encode images of "unseen" categories into binary codes with hash functions learned from limited training samples of "seen" categories? The key challenge of achieving this goal is how to set up a tunnel to transfer supervised knowledge between "seen" and "unseen" categories. In recent years, zero-shot learning (ZSL) [2, 12, 21, 24] has been widely recognized as a way to deal with this problem. The ZSL paradigm aims to learn a general mapping from the feature space to a high-level semantic space, which helps to avoid rebuilding models for unseen categories with extra manually labelled data. ZSL is mostly achieved by using class-attribute descriptors to bridge the semantic gap between low-level features and high-level semantics, where new categories are thus learned using only the relationship between attributes and categories. However, most of existing attribute based ZSL methods still suffer from: (1) erroneous guidance derived from imprecise or incomplete human-labelled attributes [10], which is usually due to the lack of expertise or mislabeling by annotators, etc.; (2) diminishing of discrimination for pre-defined attributes when facing domain shift [14, 19].

Recently, mining other auxiliary datasets has been shown to be helpful to tackle the zero-shot learning problem. For instance, with a huge corpus such as Wikipedia, one can obtain word embeddings that capture distributional similarity in the text corpus [25], such that similar words can be located in similar place. During the learning phase, visual modality can be grounded by the word vectors, and such knowledge can thus be transferred into the learned model. Inspired by this, many approaches choose to utilize auxiliary modalities to address the zero-shot problem. Socher et al. [24] used word embedding as supervision in order to detect novel categories and perform classification accordingly. Frome et al. [5] adopted a similar manner, which connects raw features and word embedding space using the dot-product similarity and hinge rank loss.

As aforementioned, with the explosion of the newly-emerging concepts and multimedia data, we are in urgent demand of a reliable and flexible hash function that can be adopted to hash images of unseen categories. However, in the hashing domain, the zero-shot problem has been rarely studied. In this work, we propose a novel hashing scheme, termed *zero-shot hashing* (ZSH). Inspired by the superior capacity of the word embedding for capturing the semantic correlations among concepts, we map mutually independent labels into a semantic-rich space, where supervised knowledge of both seen and unseen labels can be completely shared. This strategy helps to encode images of unseen categories without any assistance of visual observation in those unknown classes. Besides, even though we cannot retrieve images of exactly the same category, semantically related objects can be returned. Moreover, we recognize the problem of semantic shift caused by off-the-shelf embedding. The embedded space is then rotated to make the hash functions more generalized to images of unseen categories. To further improve the quality of hash functions, we also preserve local structural property and discrete nature in binary codes. We summarize our main contributions as below:

- We address the problem of employing limited training data of seen categories to learn reliable hash functions for transforming images of unseen categories into binary codes. We propose a novel zero-shot hashing scheme, which bridges gaps between originally independent labels through a semantic embedding space. To the best of our knowledge, this is one of the first works that study the problem of hashing data from newly-emerging concepts with limited seen supervised knowledge.

- We devise an effective strategy for transferring available supervised knowledge from seen classes to unseen classes. In particular, we project labels into a word embedding space, where semantic correlations among labels can be quantitatively measured and captured. In this way, unseen labels can leverage the well-established mapping from its semantically close seen categories. For instance, *segway* may learn from *bicycle* and *automobile*.

- Since the initial semantic embedding is from an off-the-shelf word embedding space, which may bring in potential semantic shift between categories and the original visual feature. To alleviate the influence, we propose to further rotate the embedding space to better fit the underlying feature characteristics, thereby narrowing down the semantic gap effectively.

- In order to generate more reliable hash functions, we propose to improve the intermediate binary codes by exploring underlying data properties. Concretely, we impose discrete constraints on binary codes during the learning process as well as preserve data local structure, *i.e.*, if two datums share similar representations in the original space, they are supposed to be close to each other in the learned Hamming space.

The rest of this paper is organized as follows. In Section 2, we briefly review some related work on zero-shot learning and hashing. In Section 3, we elaborate our proposed ZSH, together with an efficient optimization method and the corresponding algorithm analysis. Extensive experimental results on various different datasets are reported and analyzed in Section 4, followed by the conclusion of this work in Section 5.

2. RELATED WORK

In this section, we briefly review some related works on zero-shot learning and hashing, and discuss the relationship between our proposed approach and existing solutions.

2.1 Zero-Shot Learning

Learning with no data, *a.k.a.*, zero-shot learning, has been proved to be an effective direction to tackle the increasing difficulty posed by insufficient training samples. A promising strategy for solving this problem is to utilize an intermediate semantic layer to represent an image. Specifically, with visual attributes or other semantic abundant descriptors, a novel image can thus be defined as

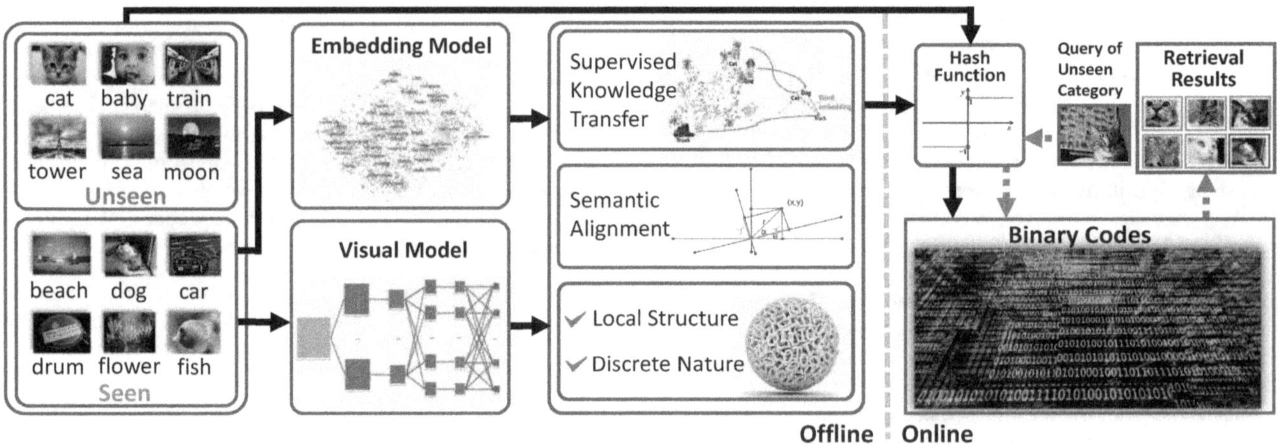

Figure 2: The overall architecture of the proposed zero-shot hashing framework.

the relationship between category and intermediate representation. Farhadi *et al.* [4] proposed to classify unseen objects by describing them with visual attributes. The work in [15] studies the problem of zero-shot learning for facilitating new tasks, which has also proven to be useful when predicting categories not shown in the training dataset. Recently, learning for classifying novel images with auxiliary knowledge (*e.g.*, leveraging textual relationship in a large corpus) has been shown to be powerful for zero-shot tasks. By exploring the correlations among semantic concepts, the label of any unseen data can be reasonably inferred. Socher *et al.* proposed a cross-modal transfer method for zero-shot learning [24], which uses word embedding to detect unseen classes. The work in [5] also adopts the similar scheme as [24]; but the difference is that a new language model and a different loss function is employed to connect two modalities. However, all above methods are only evaluated in classification or recognition scenario. To our best knowledge, our proposed ZSH is one of the first works that focus on handling the large-scale high-dimensional visual indexing problem in zero-shot scenario, *i.e.*, hashing novel images that are not observed by existing learning systems. By adopting a natural language model [9], we can precisely capture the correlations between different concepts, and thus hash unseen images into correct spots in Hamming space.

2.2 Hashing

In this part, we briefly review fast search with binary codes using hashing techniques. Similarity search is a challenge of pursuing data points of smallest distance in a large scale database. One of the easiest hashing schemes is dubbed Local Sensitive Hashing [6], which designs hashing function with no prior knowledge of the data distribution. However, such hashing methods require significantly large code length to achieve acceptable performance, which may cause unnecessary overheads in a database. To address this problem, learning-based hashing comes as a trend. Unsupervised hashing methods mine the statistic distributional information in the data, generating an optimized hashing function to preserve certain data properties in the original space. Classical algorithms (*e.g.*, Spectral Hashing (SH) [27]) learns binary codes which preserve local structural information in the data. Shen *et al.* proposed Inductive Manifold Hashing (IMH) [23], which adopts manifold learning techniques to better model the intrinsic structure embedded in the feature space. In [7], Gong et al. devised an effective approach, termed Iterative Quantization, focusing on minimizing quantization error during unsupervised training. Note that a real-world database is commonly described by multiple modalities/resources, such as visual features or textual information. In [36, 29], they utilized information of at least two different resources to achieve promising performance in cross-media search. Since the unsupervised way is guided with little human-level knowledge, supervised hashing has been proposed to use guiding information to learn binary codes. Hashing techniques in this category have been emerging continuously in recent years, and representative methods include Kernel Supervise Hashing (KSH) [16], Minimal Loss Hashing (MLH) [18], Supervise Discrete Hashing (SDH) [22], Latent Factor Hashing (LFH) [35] and Column Sampling Based Discrete Supervised Hashing (COSDISH) [11], etc. Recently, with the success of deep learning, hashing using CNN has also shown the promising performance [31].

Admittedly, hashing algorithms have provided a possible solution for tackling the "curse of dimensionality" problem. When no training samples of certain "unseen" categories are provided, all above hashing methods may easily fail to generalize to the new data, limiting the hashing capability in the "seen" area where each category possesses some training images. Besides, as the database evolves all the time, re-training hashing function frequently is expensive, thereby leading to impractical usage in large dynamic real-world databases. Based on the above analysis, a hashing method that can perform well on unseen data draws a strong need.

3. ZERO-SHOT HASHING

In this section, we elaborate our zero-shot hashing (ZSH). We firstly present a formal definition of hashing in zero-shot scenario, and then depict the details of ZSH, including a brief introduction of overall framework, transferring supervised knowledge, semantic alignment as well as hashing model. Finally, we introduce the optimization process and algorithm analysis.

3.1 Problem Definition

Suppose we are given n training images $X = [x_1, x_2, \ldots, x_n] \in \mathbb{R}^{d\times n}$ labeled with a seen concept set $\mathcal{C}$, where $x_i \in \mathbb{R}^{d\times 1}, i = 1, 2, \ldots, n$ and d is the dimensionality of visual feature space. Denote $Y = [y_1, y_2, \ldots, y_n] \in \{0,1\}^{c\times n}$ is the binary label matrix, where $y_i \in \{0,1\}^{c\times 1}$ is the label vector of the i-th sample x_i and c is the number of seen classes in $\mathcal{C}$. Different from conventional supervised hashing scenario, where both testing data and training data are associated with the same concept set, *i.e.*, $\mathcal{C}$, we intend to cope with the situation where testing data and training data share no common concepts. In other words, testing data (denoted as $X^{(u)}$) belongs to an "unseen" category set $\mathcal{C}^{(u)}$, *i.e.*, $\mathcal{C}^{(u)} \cap \mathcal{C} = \emptyset$. Using only the training images X where no training samples of the "unseen" categories in $\mathcal{C}^{(u)}$ are available, we aim to learn a hash function $f : \mathbb{R}^{d\times 1} \mapsto \{-1, 1\}^{l\times 1}$, which can map images belonging to both $\mathcal{C}^{(u)}$ and $\mathcal{C}$ from original visual feature space to l-bit binary codes. The learned hash function f not only guarantees that the binary codes of semantically relevant objects have short Hamming distances, but also generalizes well to the testing data belonging to the unseen categories.

3.2 Overall Framework

The flowchart of our overall framework is illustrated in Figure 2. As we can see, there are two stages: the offline phase and the online phase. In the offline phase, suppose only images of a limited number of categories are visible to our system. We firstly extract visual features of the training images through a convolutional neural network. At the same time, we use an off-the-shelf NLP model to transform seen labels into a semantic-rich embedding space, where each label is represented by a real-valued vector. With the embedded semantics, the relationships among both seen and unseen categories can be well captured and characterized. Instead of $0/1$-form label vector, ZSH supervises the learning of hash functions with the embedded semantic vectors to transfer supervised knowledge. We further rotate the off-the-shelf embedding space to better align with the low-level visual feature space. Meanwhile, ZSH preserves local structural information and discrete nature of the intermediate binary codes to improve hash functions. Finally, we use the learned hash functions to transform all the images in the database into binary codes for subsequent retrieval. In the online phase, when a new query image of any unseen category arrives, we encode the new image into binary code following the same mapping and retrieve images that are close to this query in the Hamming space.

3.3 Transferring Supervised Knowledge

In general, most of existing supervised hashing algorithms may retrieve relevant results of queries in the seen categories since there are supervised information for understanding the queries. Nevertheless, when the hashing systems have no knowledge of certain unseen classes, query images from these classes will be probably be misunderstood, thereby leading to inaccurate search. One of the main causes is that the supervised information is in the form of $0/1$-form label vectors or pair-wise data relationship, which implicitly makes labels independent to each other and omits the inherent correlation among their high-level semantics (*e.g., cat* is as different from *truck* as from *dog*). As illustrated in Figure 3, using independent labels, each object will be mapped to an independent vertex of a hypercube, and the distance between any two categories will be the same. In order to address such disadvantage, we propose to connect label semantics by taking advantage of the superior ability endowed by neural language processing techniques. Specifically, as illustrated in Figure 3, we map independent labels into a word embedding space, where semantic correlations among labels can be quantitatively measured and captured. Therefore, unseen labels can leverage the well-established mapping from its semantically close seen categories. For example, in the embedding space, *cat* and *dog* will be close to each other. Hence even the hashing systems may never observe any *cat* images, they can still gain some useful clues from the supervised knowledge of *dog*. We adopt the language model [9] pre-trained using free Wikipedia text. This model leverages not only local information but also global document context, thereby achieving superior performance over other competitive ap-

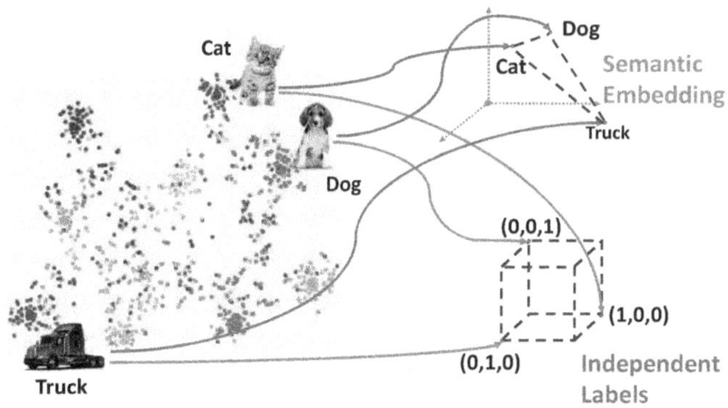

Figure 3: An illustration of independent $0/1$-form labels v.s. word embedding.

proaches. Every category is embedded into a 50-d word vector[1]. In the subsequent part, we consistently represent the label matrix Y with the embedded label matrix instead of the original 0/1 label matrix, and c is the dimensionality of the embedding space.

3.4 Semantic Alignment

Note that the transformed supervised knowledge from the off-the-shelf embedding space may potentially deviate from the underlying semantics of the image data due to the problems of domain difference, semantic shift, semasiological variation, etc. This will inevitably jeopardize the whole learning process in our proposed model. In order to prevent this issue, we propose to a semantic alignment strategy, which actively aligns the initial embedding space with the distributional properties of low-level visual feature. In particular, we seek for certain transformation $R \in \mathbb{R}^{50\times c}$ matrix with orthogonal constraint $R^T R = I_c$ to rotate the embedding space to $R^T Y$, where I_c is an identity matrix of size $c \times c$. Recall that our goal is to use the amendatory supervised knowledge to guide the learning of high-quality hash codes and hash functions, therefore, we minimize the following error:

$$\left\| R^T Y - W^T B \right\|_F^2, \tag{1}$$

which $W \in \mathbb{R}^{l\times c}$ is the mapping matrix from binary codes to the supervised information. $B = [b_1, b_2, \cdots, b_n] \in \{-1, 1\}^{l\times n}$ denotes the binary codes of X, where $b_i \in \{-1, 1\}^{l\times 1}$ is the binary codes of the i-th sample x_i. l is the code length. The above transformation of semantics can help to effectively narrow down the semantic gap between binary codes and the supervised knowledge.

3.5 Hashing Model

For convenience, we firstly recap some previous settings here. Suppose we have n training samples $X = [x_1, x_2, \cdots, x_n] \in \mathbb{R}^{d\times n}$. For brevity, we denote the corresponding embedded label knowledge as $Y = [y_1, y_2, \cdots, y_n] \in \mathbb{R}^{c\times n}$. Our ultimate target is to learn a set of hash functions from "seen" training data X supervised by Y, enabling generating high-quality binary codes for data of "unseen" categories. Meanwhile, the quality of hash functions may heavily rely on the reliability of the intermediate binary codes of training data. In other words, the model is supposed to simultaneously well control both hash functions and hash codes. To achieve the above goals, we propose the following model:

[1]In practice, we find that by setting word vector to unit length, retrieval performance can be augmented with no distortion of the cosine similarities. Thus, we empirically normalize word vector to be unit length.

$$\min_{f,W,B,R} \left\|R^TY - W^TB\right\|_F^2 + \lambda\|W\|_F^2 + \alpha\|f(X) - B\|_F^2$$
$$+ \beta\Omega(f) + \gamma\sum_{i=1}^{n}\sum_{j=1}^{n} S_{ij}\|f(x_i) - f(x_j)\|_F^2 \quad (2)$$
$$\text{s.t. } B \in \{-1,1\}^{l\times n} \wedge R^TR = I_c,$$

where $R \in \mathbb{R}^{c\times c}$ is the semantic rotation matrix. $W \in \mathbb{R}^{l\times c}$ is the mapping matrix. $B \in \{-1,1\}^{l\times n}$ denotes the binary codes. $\|\cdot\|_F$ denotes the Frobenius norm of a matrix. $\lambda > 0, \alpha > 0, \beta > 0$ and $\gamma > 0$ are balancing parameters. $f : \mathbb{R}^{m\times 1} \to \mathbb{R}^{l\times 1}$ define a hash function from a non-linear embedded feature space to the desired Hamming space:

$$f(x) = P^T\phi(x), \quad (3)$$

where $f(X) = [f(x_1), f(x_2), \ldots, f(x_n)]$. $P \in \mathbb{R}^{m\times l}$ is the transformation matrix. $\Omega(f) = \|P\|_F^2$ is a regularizer P. Following the successful practice for learning hash functions in [16], we employ kernel mapping to handle the potential problem of linear inseparability:

$$\phi(x) = \left[\exp(-\frac{\|x-a_1\|^2}{\delta}), \ldots, \exp(-\frac{\|x-a_m\|^2}{\delta})\right]^T, \quad (4)$$

where $\{a_i\}|_{i=1}^m$ are m anchors randomly sampled from X and δ is the bandwidth parameter.

Note that we keep the discrete constraint on the variable B to prevent information loss of binary codes to the greatest extent. The term $\gamma\sum_{i=1}^n\sum_{j=1}^n S_{ij}\|f(x_i) - f(x_j)\|_F^2$ in Eq. (2) preserves local structural information of training data, *i.e.*, if two samples are similar in the original feature space, then they are enforced to share similar binary codes in the Hamming space. Here, S_{ij} is the similarity of x_i and x_j in the original visual feature space.

In the next part, we introduce an efficient algorithm to optimize our zero-shot hashing model.

3.6 Optimization

We first rewrite the model in matrix form as follows:

$$\min_{P,W,B,R} \left\|R^TY - W^TB\right\|_F^2 + \lambda\|W\|_F^2 + \alpha\left\|P^T\phi(X) - B\right\|_F^2$$
$$+ \beta\|P\|_F^2 + \gamma Tr(P^T\phi(X)L\phi(X)^TP)$$
$$\text{s.t. } B \in \{-1,1\}^{l\times n} \wedge R^TR = I_c, \quad (5)$$

where $\phi(X) = [\phi(x_1), \phi(x_2), \ldots, \phi(x_n)]$. $Tr(\cdot)$ is the trace of a matrix. The Laplacian matrix L is computed as:

$$L = D - S, \quad (6)$$

where D is a diagonal matrix with its i-th diagonal element computed as $D_{ii} = \sum_{j=1}^n S_{ij}$ and $S = \{S_{ij}\}|_{i,j=1,2,\ldots,n}$ is the similarity matrix of X.

Next, we present an algorithm to optimize the model in Eq. (5) by alternatingly updating P, W, B, R.

3.6.1 Update P

Fixing all variables except for P, we get the quadratic problem as:

$$\min_P \alpha\|P^T\phi(X) - B\|_F^2 + \beta\|P\|_F^2 + \gamma Tr(P^T\phi(X)L\phi(X)^TP). \quad (7)$$

By setting its derivative with respect to P to 0, we have the following solution:

$$P = \left(\phi(X)\phi(X)^T + \frac{\beta}{\alpha}I_m + \frac{\gamma}{\alpha}\phi(X)L\phi(X)^T\right)^{-1}\phi(X)B^T, \quad (8)$$

where I_m is an identity matrix of size $m \times m$.

3.6.2 Update B

In this step, we fix all other variables and learn binary codes B with discrete constraint. The objective function can be reduced to

$$\min_B \left\|R^TY - W^TB\right\|_F^2 + \alpha\left\|P^T\phi(X) - B\right\|_F^2$$
$$\text{s.t. } B \in \{-1,1\}^{l\times n}. \quad (9)$$

The above formulation can be further written as

$$\min_B \left\|W^TB\right\|_F^2 - 2Tr(B^TH)$$
$$\text{s.t. } B \in \{-1,1\}^{l\times n}, \quad (10)$$

where $H = WR^TY + \alpha P^T\phi(X)$.

Inspired by [30], we apply the *discrete coordinate descent (DCC)* algorithm to solve the problem (10). Let $B = [q_1^T, q_2^T, \ldots, q_l^T]$, $H = [h_1^T, h_2^T, \cdots, h_l^T]$ and $W = [u_1^T, u_2^T, \cdots, u_l^T]$, where q_i^T, h_i^T and u_i^T are the i-th row of B, H and W, respectively. Furthermore, for convenience, we denote

$$\begin{cases} B_{\neg i} = [q_1{}^T, \ldots, q_{i-1}{}^T, q_{i+1}{}^T, \ldots, q_l{}^T], \\ H_{\neg i} = [h_1{}^T, \ldots, h_{i-1}{}^T, h_{i+1}{}^T, \ldots, h_l{}^T], \\ W_{\neg i} = [u_1{}^T, \ldots, u_{i-1}{}^T, u_{i+1}{}^T, \ldots, u_l{}^T]. \end{cases} \quad (11)$$

Then, we can have

$$\begin{aligned}\left\|W^TB\right\|_F^2 &= Tr(B^TWW^TB) \\ &= const + \|q_iu_i^T\|_F^2 + 2u_i^TW_{\neg i}^TB_{\neg i}q_i \\ &= const + 2u_i^TW_{\neg i}^TB_{\neg i}q_i.\end{aligned} \quad (12)$$

Here, $\|q_iu_i^T\|^2 = Tr(u_iq_i^Tq_iw_i^T) = const$. Following the same rule, we also have the following conclusion

$$Tr(B^TH) = const + h_i^Tq_i. \quad (13)$$

The sub-problem can be transformed to

$$\min_{q_i} (u_i^TW_{\neg i}^TB_{\neg i} - h_i)q_i$$
$$\text{s.t. } h_i \in \{-1,1\}^{n\times 1}. \quad (14)$$

The optimal solution of above equation is

$$q_i = \text{sgn}(h_i - B_{\neg i}^TW_{\neg i}u_i), \quad (15)$$

where sgn$(\cdot)$ is the sign function. We can see that each bit of the desired binary code B can be learned based on other $l-1$ bits. Thus, we can use cyclic coordinate descent approach to generate the optimal codes until the entire procedure converges.

3.6.3 Update R

With B, W, P fixed, we then have

$$\min_R \left\|R^TY - W^TB\right\|_F^2$$
$$\text{s.t. } R^TR = I_c, \quad (16)$$

which can efficiently solved by the algorithm in [28].

3.6.4 *Update W*

By fixing P, B, R, we arrive at a classic ridge regression problem:

$$\min_{W} \left\| R^T Y - W^T B \right\|_F^2 + \lambda \|W\|_F^2. \tag{17}$$

The above equation has a closed-form solution:

$$W = (BB^T + \lambda I_l)^{-1} BY^T R, \tag{18}$$

where I_l is a diagonal matrix of size $l \times l$.

By iteratively updating P, W, B, R until convergence, we can arrive at an optima. The overall algorithm is summarised in Algorithm 1.

Algorithm 1 Algorithm for optimizing Zero-Shot Hashing

Input: Training data X and the embedded label matrix Y;
Output: Binary codes B, rotation matrix R, hash function P and mapping matrix W;

```
1: Randomly initialize B, P and W;
2: Randomly initialize R to be orthogonal;
3: Map X to φ(X) using m anchors randomly selected from X;
4: Construct Laplacian matrix L;
5: repeat
6:     Update P according to Eq. (8);
7:     Update B iteratively by using the solution of (15);
8:     Update R by solving the problem in Eq. (16);
9:     Update W according to Eq. (18);
10: until there is no change to P, W, B, R
11: return P, W, B, R;
```

3.7 Algorithm Analysis

In this section, we analyze the convergence and time complexity of our algorithm.

3.7.1 *Convergence Study*

As shown in Algorithm 1, in each iteration, the updates of all variables make the value of the objective function decreased. We also conducted empirical study on the convergence property using ImageNet [3]. Specifically, we trained our zero-shot hashing model with $30,000$ seen images randomly sampled from the ImageNet dataset, with label embedding as supervised information. We selected $1,000$ anchors and set the code length to 64. As Figure 4 shows, our algorithm starts with cost function value at roughly $30,000$, but descends dramatically within only 10 iterations, and reaches a stable local minima at the 20-th iteration. This phenomenon clearly indicates the efficiency of our algorithm.

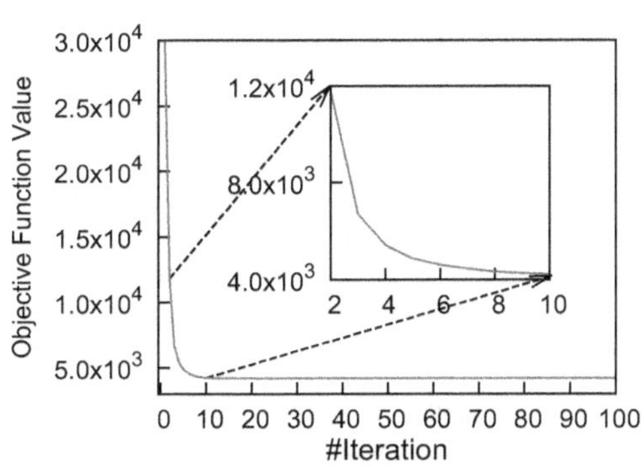

Figure 4: Convergence study on ImageNet.

3.7.2 *Computational Complexity*

In each iteration (line 6-9), the time cost is analyzed as follows. The computation of P in Eq. (8) is $O(m^2n+nml+m^3)$. The DCC algorithm for updating B costs $O(cl^2+l^2n)$. As to the optimization of the sub-problem in Eq. (16), the time cost is $O(c^3)$. Finally, the computational cost of updating W is $O(l^2n+lnc+lc^2+l^3)$. Given that $m \ll n$, $l \ll n$, $c \ll n$ and our algorithm converges within a few iterations (less than 10), the overall time cost of our algorithm is $O(n)$. It is worth noting that the dominant operation of our algorithm is matrix multiplication, which can be greatly speeded up by using parallel and/or distributed algorithms.

4. EXPERIMENT

4.1 Experimental Settings

In our experiments, we employ three real-life image datasets, including CIFAR-10[2], ImageNet[3] and MIRFlickr[4].

CIFAR-10 consists of $60,000$ images which are manually labelled with 10 classes including *airplane, automobile, bird, cat, deer, dog, frog, horse, ship, truck*, with $6,000$ samples in each class. The classes are completely mutually exclusive, *i.e.*, no overlap between classes (*e.g.*, automobiles and trucks).

ImageNet is an image dataset organized according to the WordNet [17] hierarchy. The subset of ImageNet for the Large Scale Visual Recognition Challenge 2012 (ILSVRC2012) is used for our experiments, consisting of over 1.2 million Web images, manually labeled with $1,000$ object categories.

MIRFlickr comprises $25,000$ images collected from the social photography site Flickr through its public API. Firstly introduced in 2008, this dataset is wildly used in multimedia research. MIRFlickr is a multi-label dataset with every image associating with 24 popular tags such as *sky*, *river*, etc.

For all image data, we adopted the winning model for the 1000-class ImageNet Large Scale Visual Recognition Challenge 2012 [13] to extract the fully connected layer fc-7 as visual feature.

Various metrics are employed for measuring performance of different evaluation tasks. For image retrieval, we used the two traditional metrics *i.e.*, Precision and Mean Average Precision (MAP). MAP focuses on the ranking of retrieval results and we reported the results over the top $5,000$ retrieved samples. Precision mainly concentrates on the retrieval accuracy and we reported the results with Hamming radius $r \leq 2$.

We compared our proposed ZSH with four state-of-the-art supervised hashing approaches, including COSDISH [11], SDH [22], KSH [16] and LFH [35]. For all anchor-based algorithms, we randomly sampled $1,000$ anchors from the training dataset. Furthermore, we compared to one of the most representative unsupervised hashing method, *i.e.*, Inductive Hashing on Manifolds (IMH) [23].

For all comparing approaches, we followed their suggested parameter settings. For ZSH, we empirically set α to 10^{-5} and γ to 10^{-6}. For regularization parameters λ and β, we set them to 10^{-2} and 10^{-4}, respectively. The number of iterations is set to 10. We define the similarity matrix S as follows:

$$S_{ij} = \begin{cases} \exp(-\frac{\|x_i - x_j\|}{2\sigma^2}), & \text{if } x_i \in \mathcal{N}_k(x_j) \text{ or } x_i \in \mathcal{N}_k(x_j) \\ 0, & \text{otherwise}, \end{cases}$$

---

[2]https://www.cs.toronto.edu/ kriz/cifar.html
[3]http://image-net.org/
[4]http://press.liacs.nl/mirflickr/

where $\mathcal{N}_k(\cdot)$ is the function of searching k nearest neighbors. In our experiment, we set $\sigma = 1$.

4.2 Results on CIFAR-10

4.2.1 *Overall Comparison of Zero-Shot Image Retrieval*

To evaluate the efficacy of retrieving images in unseen categories, we split CIFAR-10 into a "seen" training set and an "unseen" testing set. In particular, we selected *truck* as unseen testing category and left the rest 9 categories as seen training set. For all comparing algorithms, we randomly sampled $10,000$ images for learning hash functions. For testing purpose, we randomly selected $1,000$ images from the unseen category as query images, and the remaining $5,000$ test images together with the $54,000$ images of seen categories are combined to form the retrieval database.

The performance of all comparing approaches *w.r.t.* different codes lengths (*i.e.*, $\{16, 32, 64, 96, 128\}$) is illustrated in Figure 5. As we can see, the proposed ZSH outperforms all the other hashing algorithms in terms of MAP at all code lengths. As to Precision, ZSH still shows superior image retrieval performance in most cases. The underlying principle is that our method not only utilizes inherent semantic relationship among labels to transfer supervised knowledge, but also preserves discrete and structural properties of data in the learning of hash codes and hash functions. An interesting observation is that the performance of IMH, which is an unsupervised method, gains competitive even better retrieval results in terms of Precision as compared to some supervised methods such as KSH, SDH. While unsupervised methods encode images solely with the distributional properties in the feature space, the supervised ones may be misled by independent semantic labels in the learning processing.

Besides, MAP increases rapidly for all methods when code length varies from 16 to 64, and then reaches a slow-growth stage from 64 bits to 128 bits. When code length is short, more codes are required to guarantee the descriptive and discriminative power. However, after encoding space is large enough (*e.g.* 64 bits), with the expression ability saturated, providing more bits cannot significantly improve the performance. As to Precision, hashing performance significantly deteriorates as code length is larger than 64. Recall that our searching radius is empirically set to 2, forming a hyperball of radius 2 in Hamming space. When the code length increases from 16 to 64, significant improvement in retrieval ability counteracts the searching difficulty. However, as Hamming space becomes larger, searching difficulty grows linearly, thereby degrading the Precision performance. Therefore, as a trade-off between efficiency and effectiveness, an eclectic code length should be chosen.

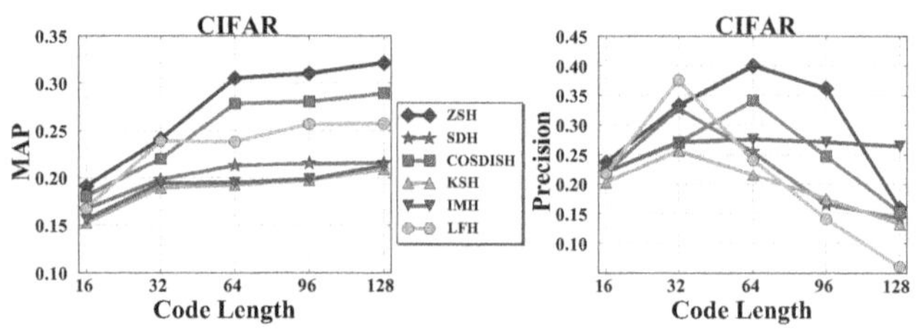

Figure 5: Performance (MAP and Precision) of different comparing methods on zero-shot image retrieval over CIFAR-10 dataset.

4.2.2 *Effect of Different Unseen Category*

In this experiment, we aim to evaluate the performance of zero-shot image retrieval on different unseen categories. The experimental settings are the same as that in the previous subsection. Figure 6 illustrates the MAP and Precision performance of ZSH using each individual label as unseen testing data.

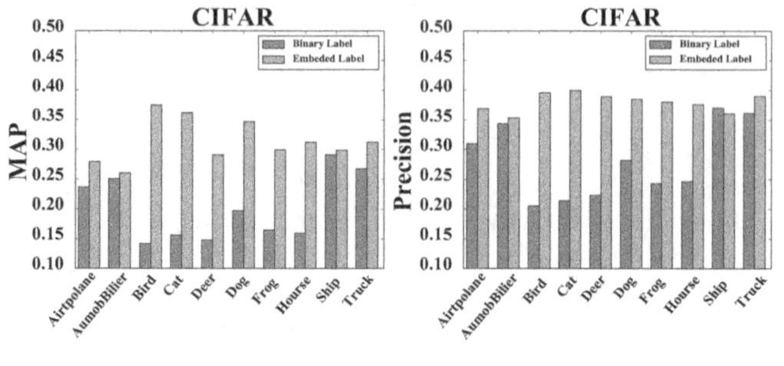

Figure 6: Performance (Precision and MAP) of zero-shot image retrieval for each individual unseen category on CIFAR-10 dataset.

We can observe that zero-shot image retrieval performance varies from one class to another, reaching peak at *bird* and bottom at *automobile*. Intuitively, if an unseen class is semantically closer to other seen categories, more relevant supervised knowledge can be transferred from word embedding space for boosting the retrieval performance. To dig deeper about the reason behind the fluctuation of performance on different unseen objects, we computed the average cosine similarity between each unseen category and other seen categories, and list the corresponding MAP in Table 1.

Category	Average Cosine Similarity	MAP
airplane	0.2191	0.2791
automobile	0.1567	0.2603
bird	0.3565	0.3751
cat	0.3661	0.3621
deer	0.2981	0.2912
dog	0.3826	0.3467
frog	0.3485	0.2991
horse	0.3015	0.3125
ship	0.1663	0.2987
truck	0.3358	0.3120

Table 1: Average cosine similarity of each category and all other categories, together the corresponding MAP performance.

We observe that the MAP performance is positively related to the average cosine similarity. For instance, those of larger cosine similarity (*e.g., dog, cat*) performs relatively well, while those of smaller similarity (*e.g., airplane, automobile*) gain relatively poor performance. This observation implies that in order to achieve satisfactory retrieval results, unseen classes should have sufficient correlation with seen ones.

As we can see in Figure 6, we also compare the effects of embedded labels and binary labels. The performance of embedded labels is obviously better than that of binary labels. The underlying reason is that the embedding space can help to capture the relationship between seen and unseen categories for transferring supervised knowledge. In contrast, binary labels neglect semantic correlations, thereby leading to irregular fluctuations of retrieval performance.

4.2.3 *Effect of Seen Category Ratio*

In this experiment, we evaluate the performance of our proposed ZSH *w.r.t.* different numbers of seen categories. Specifically, we varied the ratio of seen categories in the training set from 0.1 to 0.9. For each ratio, we randomly sampled $10,000$ images from the

Figure 7: A demonstration of the zero-shot image retrieval exemplars using different comparing hashing algorithms on CIFAR-10, where top 15 retrieval images are reported. Pictures with green bounding box indicate the correct results while those with red outlines indicate failure results. As can be seen, our proposed ZSH method returns the largest number of correct retrieved results with query from unseen category, followed by COSDISH which returns four correct samples.

seen categories for training. Further, we randomly selected $1,000$ images from the unseen set as queries to search in the remaining $59,000$ images. Note that when the ratio of seen categories decreases to 0.1, we use all $6,000$ datums of that class as training set.

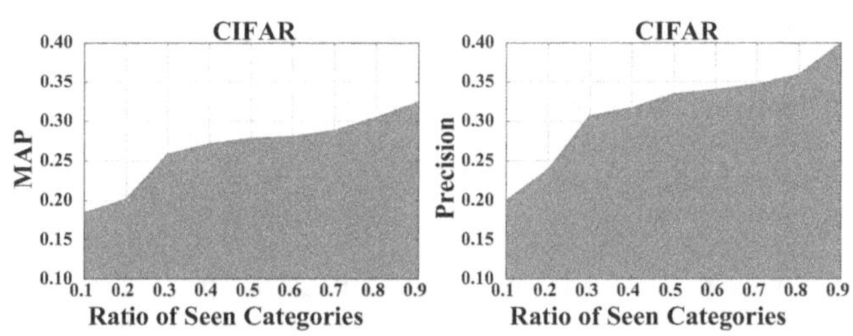

Figure 8: Effects of different ratios of seen categories on CIFAR-10 dataset.

We report the experimental results in Figure 8, from which we have the following observations: (1) The performance of both MAP and Precision boosts as the ratio of the seen categories grows; (2) As the ratio increases from 0.1 to 0.3, we see a dramatic leap of the retrieval performance, followed by a relatively slight performance improvement from 0.3 to 0.9. We analyze that by observing more "seen" categories, we have higher possibility to find relevant supervision for the unseen class, which guides to learn better intermediate hash codes, thereby simultaneously improving the quality of hash functions.

4.2.4 *Effect of Training Size*

This part of experiment mainly focuses on evaluating the effect of training size on the searching quality of ZSH. For simplicity, we chose Precision as evaluation metric and selected *truck* as the unseen object and varied the size of training data in the range of $\{1000, 2000, \ldots, 10000, 20000, \ldots, 50000\}$.

The experimental results are demonstrated in Figure 9. As we can see, when the size increases from $1,000$ to $10,000$, we observe a rapid rise of the Precision performance. Nonetheless, when fed with more training data, ZSH does not gain noticeable performance boost. For the balance of training efficiency and effectiveness, in the rest experiments, we consistently set the training size to $10,000$.

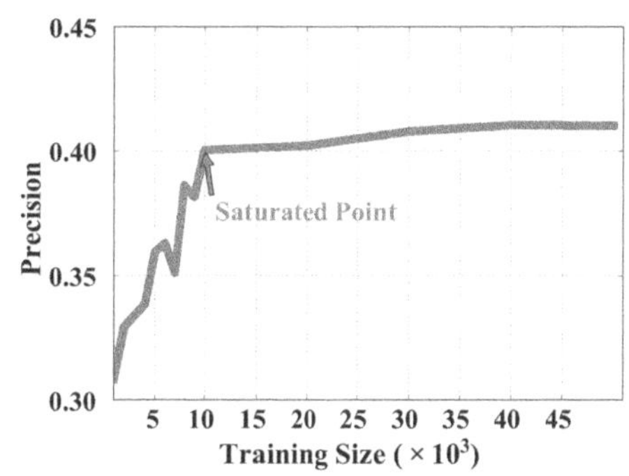

Figure 9: Effects of training size on Precision performance over CIFAR-10 dataset.

4.3 Results on ImageNet

4.3.1 *Overall Comparison of Zero-Shot Image Retrieval*

In this part, we evaluate our proposed ZSH on zero-shot image retrieval as compared to other state-of-the-art methods using the Large Scale Visual Recognition Challenge 2012 (ILSVRC2012) dataset. Recall that the ILSVRC2012 dataset contains more than 1.2 million images tagged with $1,000$ synsets without any overlap. For evaluation purpose, we randomly chose 100 categories which have corresponding word embedding learned from Wikipedia text corpus. This gives us a set of roughly $130,000$ images. We split the data into a training set (90 seen categories) and a testing set (10 unseen categories). For all comparing algorithms, we randomly selected $10,000$ images of seen categories for training. As to image queries, we randomly sampled $1,000$ images from the unseen categories. We used the learned hash function to encode all the remaining images to form the retrieval database.

The performance of our proposed ZSH and other four state-of-the-art supervised hashing methods with different code lengths are reported in Figure 10. As we can see, ZSH consistently outperforms all other competitors in most cases. As code length varies from 16 to 128, we can observe the similar variation tendency of performance on ImageNet to that on CIFAR-10. This phenomenon again implies that we should choose a trade-off code length to guarantee the retrieval performance.

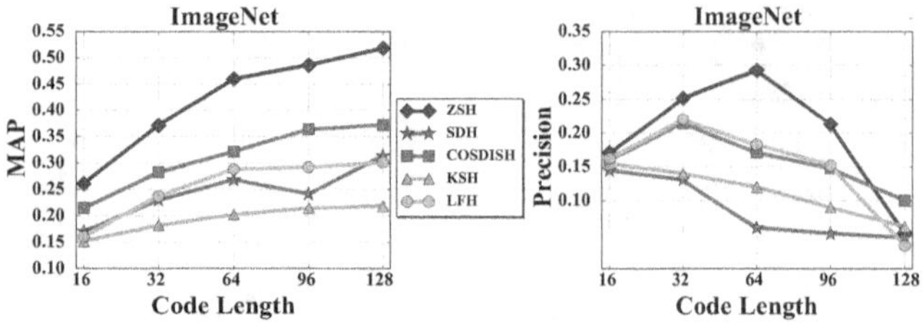

Figure 10: Performance (MAP and Precision) of different comparing methods on zero-shot image retrieval over ImageNet dataset.

4.3.2 *Image Retrieval in Related Categories*

In zero-shot image retrieval scenario, we expect that even though we fail to retrieve relevant images of the same category, we can still obtain semantically related images. For instance, if the query image describes a *cat*, we may prefer to retrieve images of *dog* rather than images of *car*. Our proposed ZSH utilizes semantic embedding to set up connections between semantically similar labels in the embedded space. In this way, the supervised knowledge of seen categories can be transferred into the learning of hash functions, which can effectively encode images of unseen categories.

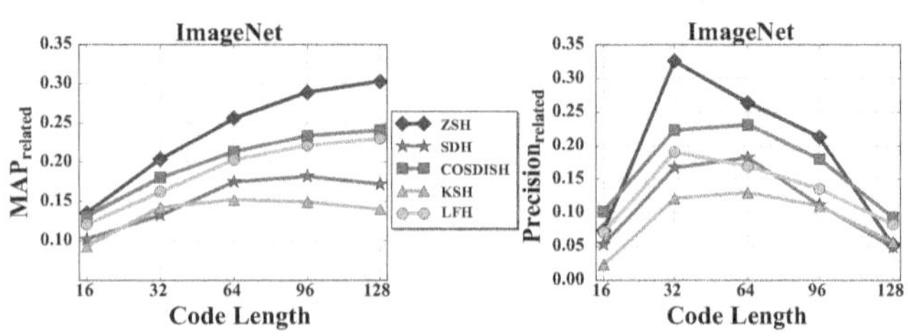

Figure 11: Comparison of ZSH and other hashing approaches on the capability of retrieving semantically similar images from related categories.

Since we need to search more related categories, all remaining images of both seen and unseen categories are used to form retrieval database. All the other settings are the same as that in Section 4.3.1. In order to evaluate the performance of retrieving related categories, we use two modified metrics, named $\text{MAP}_{related}$ and $\text{Precision}_{related}$, which are defined as

$$\text{MAP}_{related} = \sum_{i=1}^{K} \frac{\text{AP}_{related}@i}{K}, \tag{19}$$

$$\text{Precision}_{related} = \frac{n_{related}}{n_{retrieved}}, \tag{20}$$

where $\text{MAP}_{related}$ is calculated based on the top K retrieved results, $\text{AP}_{related}@i$ is the average precision based on the related results, calculated by

$$\text{AP}_{related}@i = \frac{n_{related}^{(i)}}{i}, \tag{21}$$

where $n_{related}^{(i)}$ is the number of related images in top i retrieved results. $n_{related}$ and $n_{retrieved}$ are the related retrieval under Hamming radius 2 and total examples retrieved under Hamming radius 2, respectively. Using WordNet [17], which is a lexical database for the English language, we define query A and retrieved object B are related if: 1) A and B are not of the same category; and 2) A can reach B on WordNet within 5 hops.

In practice, we set $K = 5,000$. Figure 11 shows the experimental results. We can see that in terms of $\text{MAP}_{related}$, our method always outperforms other methods at every code length. When we look at $\text{Precision}_{related}$, our proposed ZSH achieves 0.3262, 0.2636, 0.2129 at 32 bits, 64 bits and 96 bits, respectively, which significantly outperforms the second best method. This observation indicates that ZSH is capable of detecting the semantically similar images from the most related categories.

4.4 Results on MIRFlickr

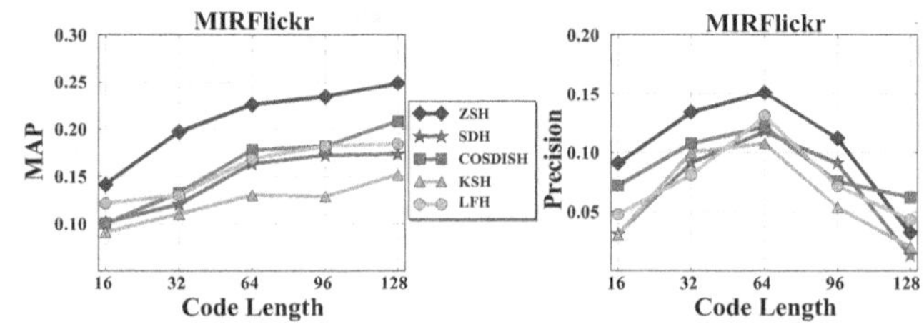

Figure 12: Performance (MAP and Precision) of different comparing methods on zero-shot image retrieval over MIRFlickr dataset.

In real-world images, especially in user-generated photos, there often exists multiple tags in each individual picture. To further examine the practical efficacy of our proposed ZSH, we conducted an extra experiment on a real-life multi-label dataset, *i.e.*, MIRFlickr, which contains $25,000$ images downloaded from the social photography site Flickr. Each image is associated with 24 tags. In multi-label image dataset, different categories share overlapping images, which makes it difficult to divide the dataset into training set and testing set. Therefore, we employed ImageNet as an auxiliary dataset to train our hash functions and evaluated the zero-shot image retrieval performance on MIRFlickr. Specifically, from the ILSVRC2012 dataset we selected 100 categories which does not overlap with the 24 tags in MIRFlickr. For fair comparison, all hashing approaches used $10,000$ randomly sampled images for training. After the hash function was learned, we directly applied them to transform the MIRFlickr images into binary codes. We then sampled $1,000$ datums as query images and searched relevant results in the remaining $24,000$ images. We regarded the retrieval images sharing at least two tags with the query as the true neighbors, and computed MAP on the top $5,000$ retrieved results and Precision under Hamming distance 2. Figure 12 illustrates the results of our ZSH and other comparing algorithms on MIRFlickr. In the left sub-figure, we can see that with different code lengths, our ZSH can consistently achieve the best MAP performance among all the comparing algorithms. As the code length increases, the MAP performance of each algorithm keeps increasing, reaching 0.2488 at 128 bits, which outperforms the second best hashing method COSDISH by 19% at the same length. In terms of Precision, ZSH exceeds all other methods in most cases. Similar to that of CIFAR-10 and ImageNet, we can see a variation pattern with an increasing trend from 16 to 64 and a performance drop from 64 to 128. The promising performance on MIRFlickr demonstrates the potential of ZSH in indexing and searching real-life image data.

5. CONCLUSION

With the explosion of newly-emerging concepts and multimedia data on the Web, it is impossible to supply existing supervised hashing methods with sufficient labeled data in time. In this paper, we studied the problem of how to map images of unseen categories using hash functions learned from limited seen classes. We proposed a novel hashing scheme, termed *zero-shot hashing* (ZSH), which is capable of transmitting supervised knowledge from seen categories to unseen categories. Independent 0/1-form labels were projected into an off-the-shelf embedding space with abundant semantics, where label semantic correlations can be fully characterized and quantified. Considering the issues of domain difference and semantic shift, we further narrowed down the gap between binary codes and high-level semantics by a semantic alignment operation. Specifically, we intentionally rotated the embedding space to adjust the supervised knowledge more suitable for learning high-quality hash codes. Besides, we also preserved local structural property and discrete nature of hash codes in the ZSH model. An efficient algorithm was designed to optimize the model in an alternating manner and the empirical study showed the convergency and efficiency. We evaluated our proposed ZSH hashing approach on three real-world image datasets, including CIFAR-10, ImageNet and MIRFlickr. The experimental results demonstrated the superiority of ZSH as compared to several state-of-the-art hashing approaches on zero-shot image retrieval task.

In the future, we plan to enhance the exploration of label semantic correlations by integrating knowledge from multiple sources, including textual corpus and visual clues. We expect this will compensate the incomplete representation of each individual modality, thereby solving the problem of domain difference and semantic shift fundamentally.

6. ACKNOWLEDGMENTS

This work was supported in part by the National Natural Science Foundation of China under Project 61572108 and Project 61502081, the National Thousand-Young-Talents Program of China, and the Fundamental Research Funds for the Central Universities under Project ZYGX2014Z007 and Project ZYGX2015J055.

7. REFERENCES

[1] L. Cao, Z. Li, Y. Mu, and S.-F. Chang. Submodular video hashing: a unified framework towards video pooling and indexing. In *ACM Multimedia*, 2012.

[2] G. Castañón, Y. Chen, Z. Zhang, and V. Saligrama. Efficient activity retrieval through semantic graph queries. In *ACM Multimedia*, 2015.

[3] J. Deng, W. Dong, R. Socher, L.-J. Li, K. Li, and L. Fei-Fei. Imagenet: A large-scale hierarchical image database. In *IEEE CVPR*, 2009.

[4] A. Farhadi, I. Endres, D. Hoiem, and D. Forsyth. Describing objects by their attributes. In *IEEE CVPR*, 2009.

[5] A. Frome, G. S. Corrado, J. Shlens, S. Bengio, J. Dean, T. Mikolov, et al. Devise: A deep visual-semantic embedding model. In *NIPS*, 2013.

[6] A. Gionis, P. Indyk, R. Motwani, et al. Similarity search in high dimensions via hashing. In *VLDB*, 1999.

[7] Y. Gong and S. Lazebnik. Iterative quantization: A procrustean approach to learning binary codes. In *IEEE CVPR*, 2011.

[8] Y. Hu, Z. Jin, H. Ren, D. Cai, and X. He. Iterative multi-view hashing for cross media indexing. In *ACM Multimedia*, 2014.

[9] E. H. Huang, R. Socher, C. D. Manning, and A. Y. Ng. Improving word representations via global context and multiple word prototypes. In *ACL*, 2012.

[10] D. Jayaraman and K. Grauman. Zero-shot recognition with unreliable attributes. In *NIPS*, 2014.

[11] W.-C. Kang, W.-J. Li, and Z.-H. Zhou. Column sampling based discrete supervised hashing. In *AAAI*, 2016.

[12] P. Kankuekul, A. Kawewong, S. Tangruamsub, and O. Hasegawa. Online incremental attribute-based zero-shot learning. In *IEEE CVPR*, 2012.

[13] A. Krizhevsky, I. Sutskever, and G. E. Hinton. Imagenet classification with deep convolutional neural networks. In *NIPS*, 2012.

[14] C. H. Lampert, H. Nickisch, and S. Harmeling. Attribute-based classification for zero-shot visual object categorization. *IEEE TPAMI*, 2014.

[15] H. Larochelle, D. Erhan, and Y. Bengio. Zero-data learning of new tasks. In *AAAI*, 2008.

[16] W. Liu, J. Wang, R. Ji, Y.-G. Jiang, and S.-F. Chang. Supervised hashing with kernels. In *IEEE CVPR*, 2012.

[17] G. A. Miller. Wordnet: a lexical database for english. *Communications of the ACM*, 1995.

[18] M. Norouzi and D. J. Fleet. Minimal loss hashing for compact binary codes. *ICML*, 2011.

[19] D. Parikh and K. Grauman. Relative attributes. In *IEEE ICCV*, 2011.

[20] S. Petrović, M. Osborne, and V. Lavrenko. Streaming first story detection with application to twitter. In *ACL*, 2010.

[21] B. Romera-Paredes and P. Torr. An embarrassingly simple approach to zero-shot learning. In *ICML*, 2015.

[22] F. Shen, C. Shen, W. Liu, and H. Tao Shen. Supervised discrete hashing. In *IEEE CVPR*, 2015.

[23] F. Shen, C. Shen, Q. Shi, A. Hengel, and Z. Tang. Inductive hashing on manifolds. In *IEEE CVPR*, 2013.

[24] R. Socher, M. Ganjoo, C. D. Manning, and A. Ng. Zero-shot learning through cross-modal transfer. In *NIPS*, 2013.

[25] J. Turian, L. Ratinov, and Y. Bengio. Word representations: a simple and general method for semi-supervised learning. In *ACL*, 2010.

[26] J. Wang, J. Wang, N. Yu, and S. Li. Order preserving hashing for approximate nearest neighbor search. In *ACM Multimedia*, 2013.

[27] Y. Weiss, A. Torralba, and R. Fergus. Spectral hashing. In *NIPS*, 2009.

[28] Z. Wen and W. Yin. A feasible method for optimization with orthogonality constraints. *Mathematical Programming*, 2013.

[29] F. Wu, Z. Yu, Y. Yang, S. Tang, Y. Zhang, and Y. Zhuang. Sparse multi-modal hashing. *IEEE TMM*, 2014.

[30] T. T. Wu and K. Lange. Coordinate descent algorithms for lasso penalized regression. *The Annals of Applied Statistics*, 2008.

[31] R. Xia, Y. Pan, H. Lai, C. Liu, and S. Yan. Supervised hashing for image retrieval via image representation learning. In *AAAI*, 2014.

[32] Y. Yang, F. Shen, H. T. Shen, H. Li, and X. Li. Robust discrete spectral hashing for large-scale image semantic indexing. *IEEE TBD*, 2015.

[33] Y. Yang, H. Zhang, M. Zhang, F. Shen, and X. Li. Visual coding in a semantic hierarchy. In *ACM Multimedia*, 2015.

[34] H. Zhang, N. Zhao, X. Shang, H. Luan, and T. seng Chua. Discrete image hashing using large weakly annotated photo collections. In *AAAI*, 2016.

[35] P. Zhang, W. Zhang, W.-J. Li, and M. Guo. Supervised hashing with latent factor models. In *ACM SIGIR*, 2014.

[36] X. Zhu, Z. Huang, H. T. Shen, and X. Zhao. Linear cross-modal hashing for efficient multimedia search. In *ACM Multimedia*, 2013.

SDNDASH: Improving QoE of HTTP Adaptive Streaming Using Software Defined Networking

Abdelhak Bentaleb
School of Computing, National University of Singapore
Singapore
bentaleb@comp.nus.edu.sg

Ali C. Begen
Ozyegin University
& Networked Media, Inc.
Istanbul, Turkey
ali.begen@ozyegin.edu.tr

Roger Zimmermann
National University of Singapore
& FX Palo Alto Laboratory
Singapore & USA
rogerz@comp.nus.edu.sg

ABSTRACT

HTTP adaptive streaming (HAS) is being adopted with increasing frequency and becoming the de-facto standard for video streaming. However, the client-driven, on-off adaptation behavior of HAS results in uneven bandwidth competition and this is exacerbated when a large number of clients share the same bottleneck network link and compete for the available bandwidth. With HAS each client independently strives to maximize its individual share of the available bandwidth, which leads to bandwidth competition and a decrease in end-user quality of experience (QoE). The competition causes scalability issues, which are quality instability, unfair bandwidth sharing and network resource underutilization. We propose a new software defined networking (SDN) based dynamic resource allocation and management architecture for HAS systems, which aims to alleviate these scalability issues and improve the per-client QoE. Our architecture manages and allocates the network resources dynamically for each client based on its expected QoE. Experimental results show that the proposed architecture significantly enhances scalability by improving per-client QoE by at least 30% and supporting up to 80% more clients with the same QoE compared to the conventional schemes.

CCS Concepts

•Information systems → Multimedia streaming; **•Networks → Network resources allocation;**

Keywords

QoE; DASH; Bitrate adaptation logic; Scalability issues; SDN; OpenFlow; Convex optimization; MPC.

1. INTRODUCTION

In recent years, a new paradigm of Internet video streaming called HTTP adaptive streaming (HAS) has emerged and quickly become the main method for streaming. Cisco is estimating that by 2019 video traffic will account for approximately 80% of the total transmitted Internet data volume [8]. As a consequence, network operators are looking for novel ways to better utilize their network capacities. While several non-interoperable commercial HAS systems are available from various vendors, the Motion Picture Experts Group (MPEG) in conjunction with the 3rd Generation Partnership Project (3GPP) developed a standardized solution termed *Dynamic Adaptive Streaming over HTTP* (DASH) [22] in 2012. A number of solutions have emerged based on this standard, where the source video is segmented into short duration chunks of 2–10 seconds, each of which is encoded at several different bitrate levels and resolutions. Then the generated chunks are stored on a server from which the clients fetch them. During playback each client uses its bitrate adaptation logic to dynamically fetch the chunk encoded at the optimal bitrate level based on metrics such as the average throughput and the buffer occupancy.

In DASH, the bitrate adaptation logic is integrated into the client and unspecified in the standard. However, a completely client-side adaptation may be sub-optimal in large systems and recently Seufert *et al.* [20] showed that utilizing some centralized management can enhance the overall video quality, while improving the quality of experience (QoE) among competing DASH clients in a shared network environment. Hence, for large-scale deployments it is important to design a robust DASH scheme that provides scalability when a multitude of clients compete for the available bandwidth, while at the same time ensuring high QoE and increased system performance. A robust DASH scheme should strive for the following main properties: *Quality stability, fairness* and *high utilization.*

In a shared network environment, a purely client-driven scheme has at least two drawbacks. First, inaccurate available bandwidth estimations may result in frequent quality and bitrate oscillations. This leads to sub-optimal bitrate decisions that degrade clients' QoE [2]. Second, service differentiations (*e.g.*, gold, silver and bronze clients) and management policies cannot be assured on the delivered quality [11]. An earlier measurement study [1] has indicated that the above listed properties are violated by most of the widely used commercial video streaming solutions when a large set of clients compete for the available bandwidth. The issue arises when purely client-driven bitrate adaption logic algorithms are working independently without any coordination. Recently, a new architecture for communication networks termed *Software Defined Networks*

MM '16, October 15-19, 2016, Amsterdam, Netherlands
© 2016 ACM. ISBN 978-1-4503-3603-1/16/10...$15.00
DOI: http://dx.doi.org/10.1145/2964284.2964332

(SDN) [21] has emerged, with the goal to manage networks more flexibly and programmatically. The main purpose of SDN is to decouple the packet forwarding process from the network control, which is centralized in a programmable controller. SDN promotes migration of network functions from dedicated hardware to virtual machines running on shared commodity hardware. This is also referred to as *Network Function Virtualization* (NFV).

To address the fundamental scalability limitations we propose an SDN-based dynamic resource allocation and management architecture for DASH systems that aims to maximize per-client QoE, whilst taking into account different clients' needs (*e.g.*, buffer sizes, display resolutions and quality requirements, etc.) and network requirements (*e.g.*, available bandwidth, latency, etc.). The main contribution of our architecture is that it is able to scale to a large number of DASH clients while maximizing the per-client QoE in a fair manner, and improving the per-client network resource allocation, provisioning and monitoring. To achieve this, our architecture leverages SDN to include an external application that communicates with the controller to select for each client the optimal quality and bitrate level for the next chunks to maximize per-client QoE. To the best of our knowledge, no current work exists that proposed such a complete end-to-end architecture to address DASH scalability in the context of a shared network. Experimental results confirm that our architecture outperforms existing state-of-the-art bitrate adaptation algorithms.

The rest of this paper is organized as follows. Section 2 surveys recent related bitrate adaptation algorithms. Section 3 describes our proposed SDN-based dynamic resource allocation and management architecture for DASH systems and Section 4 presents our architecture components. A performance evaluation and comparison is presented in Section 5. Finally, Section 6 concludes the paper and outlines future directions.

2. RELATED WORK

Several HAS bitrate adaptation logic algorithms (also called ABR algorithms) and heuristics have been published in the literature. We present a set of the most recent algorithms that address some of the scalability issues.

Huang *et al.* [7] proposed a class of buffer-based rate selection algorithms, termed BBA, that are based only on the current playback buffer occupancy as bitrate selection heuristic and not on any bandwidth estimation. BBA aims to achieve two goals. First, it tries to maximize the average video quality by selecting the highest bitrate level that the network can support. Second, it avoids unnecessary re-buffering events caused by buffer starvation. However, this scheme exhibits many limitations such as decreasing the QoE in the case of long-term bandwidth variations and slow bandwidth fluctuation detection.

Jiang *et al.* [9] proposed a general bitrate adaptation framework called FESTIVE that consists of a set of methods that strive to achieve a trade-off between video stability, fairness and efficiency. A stateful bitrate selection heuristic is used to compensate for the biased interaction between the bitrate and the estimated bandwidth, as well as to trade-off between stability and efficiency using a delayed update approach. However, the method may manifest instability when the number of clients increases, likely due to a bandwidth overestimation effect. Furthermore, it is not very responsive to bandwidth fluctuations, which may lead to a large buffer undershoot. It has difficulty to ensure bandwidth fairness between competing DASH clients efficiently in a distributed shared network environment.

Georgopoulos *et al.* [6] proposed an SDN-assisted QoE Fairness Framework, called QFF, which seeks to optimize the QoE by ensuring video quality fairness among multiple heterogeneous competing DASH clients. To this end, QFF takes into account two main constraints, namely the devices' resolutions and current network requirements. The proposed framework components connect to the SDN controller and leverage OpenFlow [15] capabilities to satisfy QoE optimization and fairness. However, the QoE model (utility function) considers only the device resolution and currently available bandwidth and not the current buffer occupancy. Thus, the client may be subject to buffer starvation, reducing end-user QoE. Further, the proposed framework cannot support a large number of clients, as it generates a lot of overhead that can negatively affect the performance of the whole system.

The authors of QDASH [17] designed a QoE-aware system as a proxy between the clients and the streaming server. The aim is to avoid video quality oscillations by ensuring a gradual change in bitrate levels by introducing an intermediate level into the bitrate switching process (in between quality changes) instead of suddenly switching up/down to the target bitrate level. However, QDASH generates significant network overhead especially with a large number of clients.

Thomas *et al.* [23] were motivated by the fact that client-driven rate adaptation provides less control for the network and service providers, *e.g.*, precluding service differentiation. Thus, they proposed the Server and Network-assisted DASH (SAND) architecture. SAND introduces a centralized control component that offers asynchronous network-to-client and network-to-network communication. It receives QoE metrics from the clients and returns network feedback measurements, which are used by clients heuristically in their adaptation logics.

3. SDNDASH ARCHITECTURE

We propose a novel SDN-based dynamic resource allocation and management architecture for both DASH systems and DASH-like approaches including Apple HLS. It leverages an SDN conceptual design [17] and has the capabilities to dynamically monitor and allocate network resources and to maximize QoE for each client, while avoiding scalability issues among a large number of competing clients in a shared network environment. Our design supports various client-driven bitrate adaptation logic algorithms by optimally limiting the possible set of selectable bitrate levels and qualities for each client and offering them as recommendations. Subsequently the client uses its corresponding recommendation as an upper bound together with its buffer level during the bitrate selection process. This strategy enables the clients to react quickly to sudden bandwidth variations and maximize their QoE. Furthermore, our architecture supports heterogeneous clients (*e.g.*, smartphones, tablets, connected TVs, etc.), as it optimizes the per-client QoE while reaching the maximum fairness level in terms of optimized QoE. Furthermore, our method avoids sub-optimal, purely client-driven network resource management and bitrate level decisions, where the available bandwidth is randomly distributed among the competing clients. Our method is not restricted to the equal sharing of network resources between the clients. Simple network management mechanisms do not take into account any criterion such as device characteristics (heterogeneity), QoE, buffer occupancy, etc., for allocation, thus leading to scalability issues while reducing per-client and overall QoE. For example, a large-screen connected TV client may obtain a lower QoE compared to a a small-screen smartphone client. Such issues lower user satisfaction, in contrast to our novel SDN-based architecture (SDNDASH), which can easily account for such heterogeneous factors.

As illustrated in Figure 1, our architecture consists of **three layers**, namely application, control and network layers (planes), and **six entities** within those layers: DASH server, DASH clients, external SDN-based application, RYU SDN controller [19], internal SDN-based application and forwarding devices. Each layer contains a set of core entities that are described at the high level as follows.

3.1 Application Layer

This layer defines a set of services for end users that ensure an effective network management, programming and communication. It contains three core elements:

A) DASH Server: Represents an HTTP server that stores the media chunks of each video content and the corresponding manifest (MPD) files. We added a simple XML file called *chunk quality file* to list chunks with their perceptual quality, which is measured based on the SSIMPlus index [18] objective metric. In our experiments we performed offline quality measurements for the videos in a DASH dataset [4] to produce the chunk quality file, which is stored at the DASH server together with the MPD. We use SSIMPlus to represent the quality because in practice the correspondence between bitrate and perceptual quality is not only non-linear and but variable over time (for details see Section 4.1 and Begen *et al.*. [12]).

B) DASH Clients: We use the DASH reference video player dash.js as the DASH client. To support our architecture, we integrated three additional classes into the bitrate adaptation algorithm of dash.js, namely:

1. *Communication Interface*: A new client HTTP-based communication interface, which allows dash.js clients [5] to interact with our external SDN-based application.
2. *Distributed QoE Optimizer*: It allows the dash.js bitrate adaptation logic to use the optimal recommendation values (optimal bitrate level and quality) as an upper-bound together with the buffer level in its decisions.
3. *File Logger*: Periodically records state variables of dash.js clients including: buffer size, QoE, chunk RTT delays, bitrate switches, stalls, etc.

C) External SDN-Based Resource Management Application: This is implemented outside of the SDN RYU controller and responsible for QoE-optimization, resource allocation and monitoring. Our external SDN-based application implements **six modules** (1-6) and **three components** (i-iii) as described in Figure 1:

1. *Packet monitoring engine* monitors and inspects packets from different entities of our architecture (*e.g.*, get the MPD file from the DASH server). Thereafter, it parses and classifies the inspected data and offers them to different modules. Our packet monitoring uses a packet sampling approach to differentiate between the cross and DASH traffic, thus dynamically estimating the required throughput for each. Hence, our optimizer can work with only the DASH traffic fraction of the bandwidth to produce the optimal quality assignment for each client.
2. *Management module* is the main manager of the components, collecting the required input data from various modules and then offering them to components. It also receives the output data from different components for plotting and visualization purposes.
3. *Per-client QoE measurement* measures and estimates the QoE of each DASH client. Thereafter, it records the per-client QoE in a specific table called *QoE table.*
4. *MAP tables* defines three kinds of mapping tables including *bitrate level ↔ device resolution, bitrate level ↔ chunk perceptual quality,* and *device name ↔ device capabilities.*
5. *Bandwidth estimator* uses the PANDA algorithm [13] to estimate the available bandwidth accurately. PANDA was proposed to avoid the root cause that triggers bitrate oscillations.
6. *Log and network/server statistics* records all logging files and statistics (*e.g.*, per-client QoE, client information, optimal per-client bitrate level and quality recommendations) periodically. These data are then plotted and visualized.

i. *Specification component* offers three main functionalities. At each step, it first generates a specific data structure that describes the current per-client QoE requirements as a QoE policy, as shown in Figure 2. Second, it maximizes per-client QoE (based on Eq. 10) and outputs the optimal per-client bitrate level and quality for the next chunks to be downloaded. Finally, it manages and stores the per-client optimized QoE, and then passes these outputs to the *communication component* for plotting and visualization.

ii. *Abstraction programming component* is responsible for formulating the per-client network resource requirements (QoS) based on the optimal per-client QoE resulting from the *specification component.* To achieve this goal, it offers two main functionalities. First, it implements an exponential mapping function (Eq. 1) that allows for the correlation between the optimized QoE metric and QoS metric.

$$\begin{cases} QoS = K \times \{(W \times BW)\} \\ QoE = \alpha \times e^{-\beta \times QoS} + \gamma, \end{cases} \tag{1}$$

where BW is the bandwidth, K is a constant access network factor (depending on the type of network, wired or wireless), W is a weight factor, which defines the relative importance degree of QoS metric based on application type (*e.g.*, DASH video streaming bandwidth metric is the most important). α, β are network layer parameters, which are defined based on the QoS service differentiation (gold, sliver and bronze clients). γ is a video codec parameter. Eq. 1 is obtained from the mapping model proposed by Fiedle *et al.* [14]. Second, the *abstraction programming component* generates a specific data structure that describes each per-client QoS requirement as a QoS policy, as shown in Figure 2. These QoS policies are sent to the internal SDN-based application for QoS provisioning.

iii. *Communication component* ensures the interaction between different entities of the application layer. For

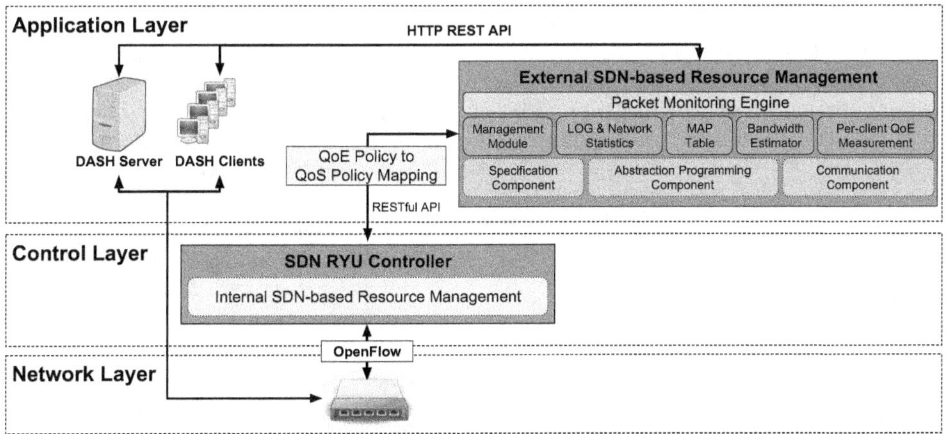

Figure 1: Our proposed SDN-based architecture.

example, it sends the per-client optimal bitrate levels and quality recommendations to the corresponding client. Further, it provides a communication interface between the application layer and control layer (Restful API). For instance, it sends the per-client QoS policy messages to the internal SDN-based application.

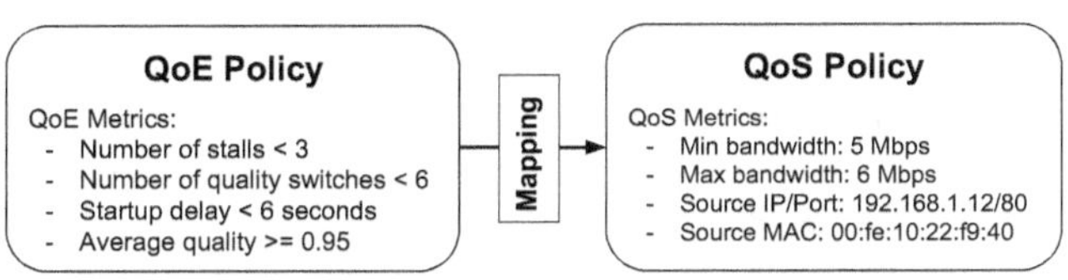

Figure 2: QoE and QoS policies example.

3.2 Control Layer

The control layer represents the central element in the network that has the ability to manage and control network infrastructure and network resources. Further, it defines two communication interfaces to simplify resource abstraction and data exchange between layers (Northbound interface), and also network device programming (Southbound interface). It consists of an SDN controller and an internal SDN-based resource management application.

D) RYU SDN Controller: This represents the control plane of our architecture. It is a central entity that manages flow control to enable intelligent network management. We select and integrate the RYU framework [19] within our architecture as an SDN controller. Therefore, the RYU controller receives per-client QoS policy messages coming from the external SDN-based application for network resource provisioning. The SDN-controller then passes these messages to the internal SDN-based application to configure, allocate, provision, and monitor the network resources for each client accordingly.

E) Internal SDN-Based Resource Management Application: This is implemented inside the SDN RYU controller and responsible for resource allocation, monitoring and QoS provisioning. Upon receiving the QoS policy that contains the per-client bandwidth allocation of each client, it constructs an OpenFlow based messages (*e.g.*, Multipart Request, Flow Mod: OFPFC_ADD)[1] for each QoS policy in order to interact with forwarding devices using OpenFlow. Thus, the internal application dynamically allocates and provisions bandwidth for each DASH client based on per-client QoS policy sent by the external SDN-based application. Further, it monitors per-client resource allocation based on QoS policy timeout until its corresponding timeout becomes zero, where it generates a Flow Mod OpenFlow message (OFPFC_DELETE) that orders forwarding devices to delete the flow from their tables (flow tables and meter tables). Otherwise, it modifies the flow in order to satisfy the new client QoS requirements using a Flow Mod OpenFlow message (OFPFC_MODIFY).

3.3 Network Layer

The network layer represents the infrastructure that is responsible for data forwarding and carrying user traffic.

F) Forwarding Devices: The forwarding devices include switches and routers that support OpenFlow v1.3 and meter table installations such as: CPqD switch[2]. These devices forward data traffic based on the forwarding control policies that are established by the SDN RYU controller, and per-flow rate (QoS provisioning) based on the QoS policy OpenFlow messages coming from the internal SDN-based application. Further, they delete, modify and add flows based on different control policies.

4. ARCHITECTURE DESIGN

To simplify the design of our architecture, we divide the solution into five steps, which are detailed as follows:

4.1 Chunk Quality Measurement

The DASH client in our architecture uses both the chunk bitrate level and perceptual quality during the bitrate adaptation process. This allows us to alleviate many number of quality oscillations, thus, we can ensure consistency in video quality [12]. Hence, the main purposes of this step are summarized as follows: To *(a)* confirm that there is non-linear correlation between chunk perceptual quality and its bitrate level, *(b)* find a relationship (non-linear mapping function) between chunk bitrate levels and qualities, and *(c)* create chunk qualities manifest file.

To achieve the goals above, we perform an objective video quality measurement on two reference source video files with different resolutions. One is animation video called *Big*

[1]https://www.opennetworking.org/openflow

[2]http://cpqd.github.io/ofsoftswitch13/

Buck Bunny and the second is a documentary film called *Of Forests And Men* [4]. We select these two videos because they are widely used by researchers in the field of DASH and are of different genres (animation vs. documentary). This measurement is conducted using an objective video quality assessment model, namely the Structural Similarity Index Plus (SSIMPlus) index [18]. SSIMPlus provides an accurate estimation of the video perceptual quality mimicking the human visual system, video content features including resolution, temporal and spatial complexity, device screen options like size and brightness.

We downloaded the original YUV video files of Big Buck Bunny[3] and Of Forests And Men[4] in various resolutions, while we acquired the processed video files with the same resolutions and various bitrate levels as shown in Table 1 from the DASH dataset [4]. These resolutions fit capabilities of most devices such as smartphones, tablets and connected TVs. In presenting our results, we performed 11 objective tests for each video and computed the averages.

Table 1: Resolutions and bitrates (Kbps).

Resolution	Big Buck Bunny	Of Forests And Men
360p	50, 100, 150, 200, 250, 300, 400, 500	100, 150, 200, 250, 300, 400
480p	600, 700	500, 600, 700
720p	900, 1200, 1500, 2000	800, 1000, 1300, 1500, 1800, 2100, 2500, 3200, 3700
1080p	2100, 2400, 2900, 3300, 3600, 3900	/

The results of our objective quality measurements are shown in Figure 3. The scatter plot shows the mapping of bitrate levels to SSIMplus (top plot) and Big Buck Bunny's per-chunk quality (bottom plot). From the results we see that the correlation between bitrate level and video quality is not linear, although the quality gradually increases as the bitrate increases. Finally, chunk quality is different from one video to another.

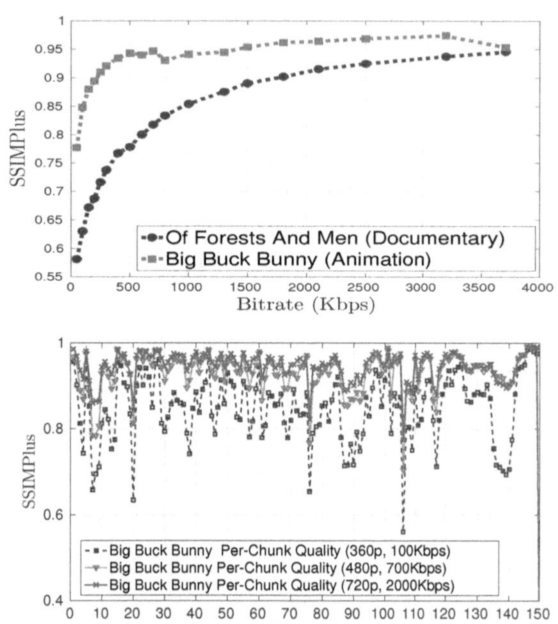

Figure 3: SSIMPlus objective quality measurement.

[3] http://media.xiph.org/video/derf/

[4] http://www.offorestsandmen.org/en/film-en

4.2 QoE Metrics

In this step, we present a set of QoE metrics that are used to calculate the user satisfaction. Inspired by Seufert *et al.* [20], our QoE model utilizes the most influential metrics on end-user satisfaction including: startup delay, number of stalls, average video quality and number of video quality switches.

- *Chunk Quality* (Q_{i,l_i}): Assume a video stream that includes N chunks and each chunk is encoded with L bitrate levels, with l representing a specific bitrate level. At each step i, the quality of chunk i which is encoded at l_i is defined as:

$$Q_{i,l_i} = SSIMPlus_{i,l_i} \tag{2}$$

where $SSIMPlus_{i,l}$ represents the quality value of chunk i at level l. $SSIMPlus_{i,L_{max}}$ denotes the quality of the chunk i with the highest bitrate level L_{max}.

- *Startup Delay* (D_s): This represents the delay between the request of the first chunk and its rendering onset. An efficient video streaming system must achieve a startup time less than the maximum buffer occupancy ($buff_{max}$).

$$D_s << buff_{max} \tag{3}$$

- *Number of Stalls* (S_{nbr}): Video stalls occur when the client buffer is empty. In other words, if the playback buffer size reaches its minimum threshold $buff_{min}$ and the current chunk i has not been downloaded yet, there will be a stall. The total number of stalls can be calculated as:

$$S_{nbr} = \frac{1}{N}\sum_{i=1}^{N} S_i \quad \text{if } 0 \leq buff_i < buff_{min} \tag{4}$$

where, $buff_i$ is current buffer level in seconds, and S_i is 0 or 1.

- *Average Video Quality* (TQ_{avg}): This represents the total average quality of the downloaded chunks, which can be calculated as:

$$TQ_{avg} = \frac{1}{N}\sum_{i=1..N}^{l=1..L} Q_{i,l} \tag{5}$$

- *Video Quality Switches* (SQ_{avg}): This represents the total quality differences between successively downloaded chunks[5]. It is defined as:

$$SQ_{avg} = \frac{1}{N-1}\sum_{i=1}^{N-1} |Q_{i+1,l_{i+1}} - Q_{i,l_i}| \tag{6}$$

Finally, we define the QoE as a weighted function of the above four metrics as:

$$QoE_i = \alpha TQ_{avg} - \beta SQ_{avg} - \gamma S_t - \delta D_t \tag{7}$$

where $\alpha, \beta, \gamma, \delta$ are non-negative weighting factors. Such factors are selected based on [9] and our own experiments (many tests were performed for value tuning, and we selected trade-off values of 0.25 for each factor).

4.3 Objective Function

At each step, our architecture aims to optimize the global and per-client QoE over all DASH clients during an active

[5] This metric helps SDNDASH maintain a consistent quality.

video playback session, while ensuring a fair bandwidth allocation based on the QoE. For that purpose, we formulate our problem as a linear convex optimization problem. Our convex optimization framework is flexible enough to accommodate a set of dynamic constraints including:

- *Buffer Occupancy Level:* The selected bitrate level and quality must not be affecting the buffer occupancy. For that reason, we define two buffer thresholds $buff_{min}$ and $buff_{max}$. At each step i, the buffer level must be between these two thresholds $buff_{min} < buff_i < buff_{max}$ in order to avoid stalls.
- *Available Bandwidth (BW_e):* The selected bitrate must not exceed the current available bandwidth.
- *Content Type Constraint* (CT): The selected chunk quality must fit the content type.
- *Device Capabilities* (DC): The decision of bitrate level and quality must fit the device capabilities.

A network topology is represented by a directed or undirected graph $G = (V, E)$, depending on the nature of the links, where V represents the set of nodes and E is the set of links between the nodes. The network topology consists of a set of V nodes including: DASH clients $C \subset V$, DASH server $s \in V$, external SDN-based application $a \in V$, SDN controller with internal SDN-based application $b \in V$ and forwarding devices $F \subset V$. These nodes are connected by a set of links E, where each node $v_x \in V$ has at least one link $e_{xy} \in E$ connecting to another node $v_y \in V$, where $x, y = 1, 2, ..., |V|$. A set of DASH clients C share the available bandwidth of capacity BW_{all} of the last mile M (a shared network environment). Periodically at each step i, the SDN-based external application a estimates the available bandwidth BW_e, maximizing the per-client QoE $MAX(QoE_{i,c_n})$ with $c_n \in C$ (representing a client) by finding the optimal bitrate level l_{i,c_n} and quality $Q_{i,l_{i,c_n}}$ for the next chunk to be downloaded, and allocates the suitable amount of bandwidth BW_{alloc_i,c_n} from BW_e that fits $MAX(QoE_{i,c_n})$. Obviously, the total bandwidth allocated to all clients should not exceed the total capacity on the bottleneck link BW_{all}:

$$\sum_{n=1}^{C} BW_{alloc_i,c_n} \leq BW_{all}, \forall i \text{ (during all steps i)}. \quad (8)$$

We assume that the internal SDN-based application can provision and update network resources per client periodically at each time slot Δt (from one step till the next step).

The DASH server s, has a set of video contents R. Each video $r \in R$ consists of T seconds of media and is divided into a set of fixed small chunks, and the total number is denoted as N. Each chunk has a duration of τ seconds with $N = \frac{T}{\tau}$ and is associated with a set of B representations (bitrate levels and their qualities), for which every representation $\rho \in P$ has a bitrate $l_\rho \in L$ and quality $q_\rho \in Q$, where L and Q are bitrate level list and perceptual qualities, respectively. At each step i, for each client $c_n \in C$, the set of available chunks with their bitrate level list L and their corresponding perceptual qualities Q_L (SSIMPlus) is presented in manifest files (MPD and quality list) as:

$$\begin{cases} L_{i,c_n} = \{l_{i,c_n}^1, l_{i,c_n}^2, ..., l_{i,c_n}^k ...., l_{i,c_n}^N\} \\ Q_{i,c_n} = \{q_{i,c_n}^1, q_{i,c_n}^2, ..., q_{i,c_n}^k ...., q_{i,c_n}^N\}. \end{cases} \quad (9)$$

Our *QoE Optimizer* solves the objective function by finding for each client $c_n \in C$ the optimal bitrate level $l_{i,c_n}^k \in L$ and its corresponding quality $q_{i,c_n}^k \in Q$ that maximize c_n's QoE (see Eq. 7) based on the available bandwidth, buffer occupancy, video content type and device capabilities constraints. We note that, $q_{i,c_n}(.)$ represents the non-linear mapping function for chunk i in the c_n DASH client. Hence, $q_{i,c_n}(l_{i,c_n})$ denotes the bitrate level with its corresponding quality.

At each step i, and for each client $c_n \in C$ our objective function with its constraints can be expressed formally as:

$$\begin{cases} \text{Find} & q_{i,c_n}(l_{i,c_n}), \text{ where:} \\ \max & QoE_{i,c_n} \\ \text{s.t.} & l_{i,c_n} \leq BW_{i,e}, \forall i, \forall c_n \\ & \sum_{n=1}^{C} BW_{alloc_i,c_n} < BW_{all}, \forall i \\ & buff_{min,c_n} \leq buff_{i,c_n} \leq buff_{max,c_n}, \forall i, \forall c_n \\ & MAP(q_{i,c_n}(l_{i,c_n}), CT_{c_n}), CT \in MAP\ tables, \forall i, \forall c_n \\ & MAP(q_{i,c_n}(l_{i,c_n}), DC_{c_n}), DC \in MAP\ tables, \forall i, \forall c_n. \end{cases} \quad (10)$$

4.4 Solution

The objective function (Eq. 10) can be solved using an online linear convex optimal control, termed online MPC (Model Predictive Control) [3]. The total complexity of our solution is independent of the total number of clients C, since the effect of more frequent updates balances out the effect of shorter horizon within each step. At each step i, and for each DASH client $c_n \in C$, our *QoE Optimizer* uses online MPC (see Algorithm 1) to find the optimal $q_{i,c_n}(l_{i,c_n})$ for the next chunk to be downloaded that can maximize the QoE of c_n. Then, the optimal values are mapped into QoS metric (bandwidth) and sent to our internal SDN-based application for QoS provisioning.

Algorithm 1 Simple optimization problem solution.

procedure –Online MPC dynamic programming
    Input:
    $N, i, buff_{min,c_n}, buff_{max,c_n}, BW_{all}, BW_{i,e}, CTc_n, DCc_n$
    Output:
    $q_{i,c_n}(l_{i,c_n}), \forall c_n$
    for (each step i = 1,2,....,N) **do**
        for (each client c_n, n = 1,2,....,C) **do**
            for (L_{i,c_n} **and** $Qi, c_n, \forall c_n$) **do**
                $q_{i,c_n}(l_{i,c_n})$ = Find-MAX($Q_{i,c_n}(L_{i,c_n})$)
                if ($l_{i,c_n} \leq BW_{i,e}$ **and** $\sum_{n=1}^{C} BW_{alloc_i,c_n} <$
                BW_{all} **and** $buff_{min,c_n} \leq buff_{i,c_n} \leq$
                $buff_{max,c_n}$ **and** $MAP(q_{i,c_n}(l_{i,c_n}), CT_{c_n})$
                and $MAP(q_{i,c_n}(l_{i,c_n}), DC_{c_n}), \forall c_n$) **then**
                    Return($q_{i,c_n}(l_{i,c_n}), \forall c_n, \forall(step\ \ i+1)$)
                    $Lookup_{store}(buff_{i,c_n}, BW_{i,e}, CTc_n, DCc_n,$
                    $q_{i,c_n}(l_{i,c_n}), c_n, \forall c_n)$
                else
                    Remove($q_{i,c_n}(l_{i,c_n})$)
                    Go to (8)
                end if
            end for
        end for
    end for
end procedure

4.5 dash.js Client Integration

At each step, the online MPC dynamic program (Algorithm 1) computes the optimal bitrate level and its quality for each client. The results are sent to the SDN controller for QoS provisioning and each corresponding client for bitrate adaptation process. To enable this, we modified the original bitrate adaptation logic algorithm of dash.js [5]. The modifications are denoted by the dashed grey boxes in Figure 4.

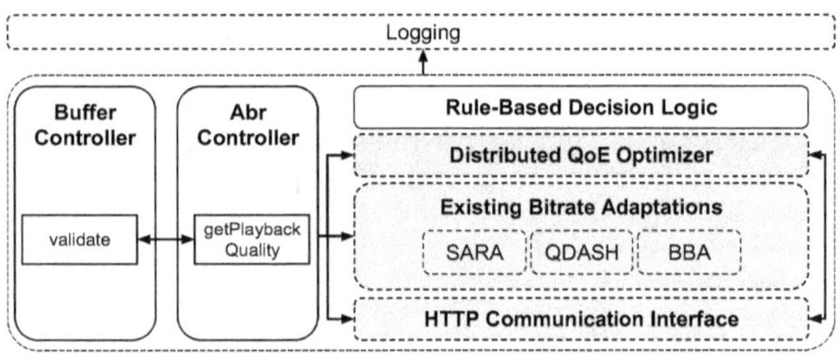

Figure 4: dash.js modifications shown in grey.

5. PERFORMANCE EVALUATION

To evaluate the performance of our architecture and modified client (**SDNdash.js**), we carried out a set of VoD streaming experiments using 50 clients and 100 Mbps total network bandwidth over a complete video streaming system as illustrated in Figure 5. Six test scenarios with different client numbers and bandwidths were also performed. Due to space limit, we show only one test with 50 clients. To simplify the maximization problem, we used the same device capabilities (connected TV) and content type (animation) in our experiments. Our evaluation system is a hybrid combination between a real system and an emulated virtualization system (DASH clients and OpenFlow switches are created using Mininet [16]). We compare the performance of our architecture SDNdash.js against three bitrate adaptation logic heuristics found in literature QDASH [17], BBA [7] and SARA [10] (We use these colors for all comparison results), where we implemented them as a class in the bitrate adaptation logic module (see Figure 4) within the newest dash.js (stable master branch v2.0 release) [5]. Further, we compare **SDNdash.js** with conventional bitrate adaptation heuristic of dash.js [5] that combines buffer level with chunk downloading-based available bandwidth and equal bandwidth allocation algorithm during bitrate decision process. These comparisons are conducted using three scalability metrics, namely video stability, fairness and utilization.

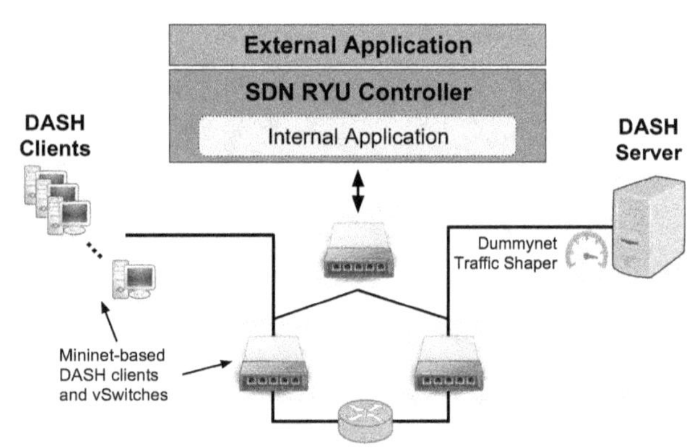

Figure 5: Network topology for the evaluation.

5.1 Network Topology

Figure 5 shows our network topology, which consists of dash.js clients, DASH server, SDN RYU controller with our resource management internal application, the SDN-based external application and three CPqD vSwitches. We also throttle the bandwidth to *100 Mbps* using *Dummynet* in order to emulate a shared network environment scenario.

5.2 Input and Constant Parameters

- **Bandwidth Estimator:** Table 2 shows the parameters used in our bandwidth estimator module, which are set according to the default values in PANDA.

Table 2: Bandwidth estimator parameters.

Parameter	N	κ	ω	β	τ	$buff_{min}$	$buff_{max}$
Value	150 steps	0.14	0.3	0.2	4 seconds	8 seconds	35 seconds

- **QoE, QoS and Optimizer:** All input parameters used by our QoE, QoS and optimizer modules are selected based on suggestions from [20] and [14].
- **MPD File:** We used the Big Buck Bunny video [4], which is $T = 600$ seconds long and consists of $N = 150$ chunks (150 downloading steps), where each chunk has a duration of $\tau = 4$ seconds. This video is encoded using H.264 format at 20 different bitrate levels.
- **Various Bitrate Adaptation Logic Heuristics:** For a fair comparison, we used the same input parameters suggested by the respective authors.
- **Normalized QoE:** Our QoE model outputs a value between 0 and 1. We define a normalized QoE (N-QoE) to represent a user's satisfaction MOS (1 to 5) and report the normalized values in Table 3.

Table 3: Normalized QoE.

QoE	N-QoE	Quality
$0.8 \leq value \leq 1$	between 4 and 5	Excellent
$0.6 \leq value < 0.8$	between 3 and 4	Good
$0.4 \leq value < 0.6$	between 2 and 3	Fair
$0.2 \leq value < 0.4$	between 1 and 2	Poor
$0 \leq value < 0.2$	between 0 and 1	Bad

5.3 Results, Discussion and Analysis

We evaluate the effectiveness of our proposed method by comparing the average results over all clients in video stability, fairness and utilization.

5.3.1 Video Stability

We evaluate the video stability in terms of bitrate level switches, stalls and perceptual quality oscillations. Figures 6a and 6b depict video stability of all competing DASH clients. We can see that our architecture accommodates all its **SDNdash.js** clients by achieving the best video stability compared to other heuristics (see Table 4). This is because **SDNdash.js** clients switch between adjacent bitrate levels smoothly while maintaining a high average bitrate level as much as possible, where the overall average bitrate level of all clients ranges from 1,473 Kbps to 2,087 Kbps (Figure 6a). Moreover, it minimizes the total number of bitrate level switches and stalls as well, and the result is five switches with zero stalls (see Table 4). This is due to the fact that **SDNdash.js** provides an accurate available bandwidth estimation, which eventually leads to a suitable per-client

Table 4: Video stability.

	AVG Bitrate Level (Kbps)	AVG # of Bitrate Switches	AVG # of Stalls	AVG Quality (SSIMPlus)	AVG Quality Variance	AVG # of Oscillations
SDNdash.js	**1,473 to 2,087**	**3%**	**0%**	**0.957 to 0.967**	**0.01**	**7**
QDASH	45 to 2,944	98%	8%	0.92 to 0.967	0.047	52
BBA	45 to 2,089	26%	4%	0.93 to 0.967	0.037	22
SARA	45 to 3,936	46%	6%	0.93 to 0.967	0.037	83
dash.js	45 to 3,936	16%	7%	0.77 to 0.973	0.203	38

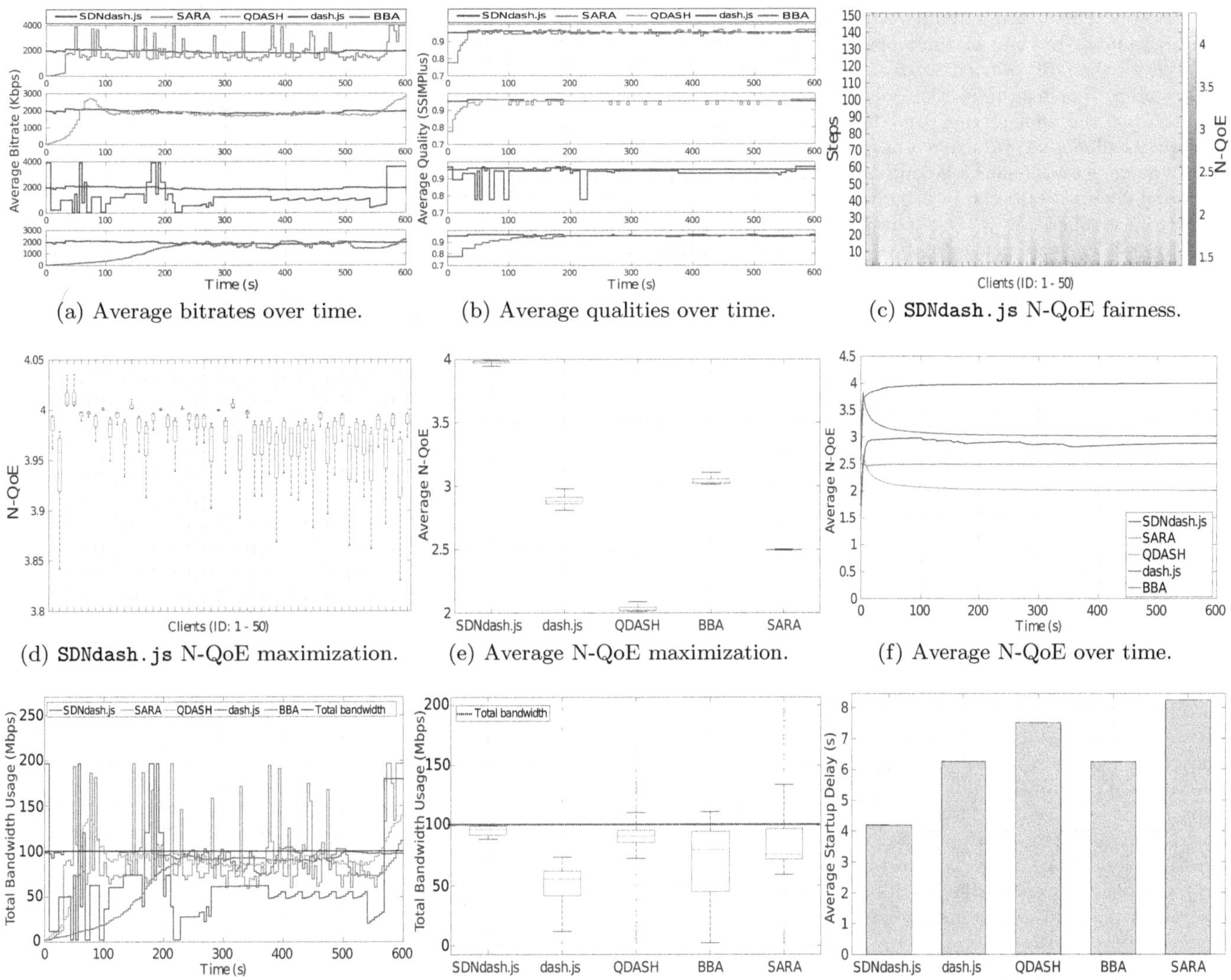

(a) Average bitrates over time. (b) Average qualities over time. (c) **SDNdash.js** N-QoE fairness.

(d) **SDNdash.js** N-QoE maximization. (e) Average N-QoE maximization. (f) Average N-QoE over time.

(g) Bandwidth utilization. (h) Bandwidth utilization variation. (i) Average startup delays.

Figure 6: Experimental results of stability, fairness and utilization for 50 clients and 100 Mbps total system bandwidth.

bitrate level and quality decision and network resource allocation at each step, thus increasing per-client QoE.

Our main results for video stability are summarized in Table 4, where:

- *AVG Bitrate Level* and *AVG Quality* are the average range of the selected bitrate and selected quality across 50 clients, respectively,
- *AVG Number of Bitrate Switches* and *AVG Number of Stalls* are the percentile average of number of bitrate switches and number of stalls across 50 clients, respectively, and
- *AVG Number of Oscillations* is the total average number of quality (SSIMPlus) switches across 50 clients during the video streaming session.

5.3.2 *Fairness and QoE*

This part analyzes the fairness in terms of QoE and end-user satisfaction level (QoE). Figure 6c depicts the heat-map of N-QoE distribution of each **SDNdash.js** client. As can be seen, the QoE is generally distributed fairly between the competing DASH clients (orange color). This confirms that our architecture provides QoE fairness between competing clients and eliminates the unfairness problem compared to purely client-driven heuristics QDASH, BBA, SARA and dash.js as shown in Figure 6e. We anticipated these results because **SDNdash.js** uses the SDN-based application to provide a fairness in terms of QoE to all clients, where they ensure: (1) optimal bitrate level and quality decisions that maximize per-client QoE at each step (2) dynamic network resource allocation based on optimal decisions that maximize end-user QoE in a fair manner across all clients.

Figure 6e shows a boxplot of N-QoE maximization variation (from low to high) of each `SDNdash.js` client during the DASH video steaming session. The minimum value of whisker (dashed line) represents the first QoE value at the start of the playback, the red line is the median of all QoE values of each client, the maximal value of whisker is the last QoE value at the end of video playback. Hence, Figure 6d illustrates the QoE of each `SDNdash.js` client maximized at every step. For example, the QoE of client 1 increases from 3.87 at the video start to 3.94 at the video end. Furthermore, `SDNdash.js` achieves a higher performance in terms of average per-client QoE compared to QDASH, BBA, SARA and dash.js. This can be seen from Figures 6e and 6f, where QoE in `SDNdash.js` is maximized at each step: it starts from 3 at step 1 (t = 4s) to reach approximately the maximum value of 4 at step 30 (t = 120s). Figure 6i also shows that `SDNdash.js` delivers a lower average startup delay compared to other clients.

5.3.3 *Utilization*

Figure 6g shows the total bandwidth usage over time. `SDNdash.js` has the best bandwidth utilization without any violation[6]. Our *bandwidth estimator* module can accurately estimate the available bandwidth, and subsequently, the SDN-based external application chooses the optimal bitrate level and quality at each step that can maximize the end-user QoE without violating available bandwidth and/or affecting other clients' QoE. Furthermore, Figure 6h shows the total bandwidth utilization by DASH clients. We can see that `SDNdash.js` achieves around 95% without any violation from the total available bandwidth of *100 Mbps* compared to QDASH: 80% with significant violations, BBA: 77% with minor violations, SARA: 94% with significant violations and dash.js: 50% with minor violations. The bandwidth utilization in QDASH, SARA and dash.js fluctuates significantly with many violations during the video streaming session. This is because of the incorrect bitrate level decisions that are made due to the overestimation of the available bandwidth per client. This eventually leads to congestion as illustrated in Figure 6g, thus, increasing stalls, bitrate switches, etc., which produces a low per-client QoE.

5.4 Summary of Results

Note, in the list items below, the four consecutive numbers represent results for QDASH, BBA, SARA and dash.js, in that order:

- `SDNdash.js` achieves the highest video stability with 40%, 20%, 60% and 30% improvement.
- `SDNdash.js` achieves 87%, 16%, 45%, and 22% less bitrate switches.
- `SDNdash.js` outperforms existing algorithms in terms of high and consistent quality by 42%, 7%, 41% and 24% among all clients.
- `SDNdash.js` improves the QoE of DASH clients by 35%, 25%, 30% and 28% over other heuristics.
- `SDNdash.js` outperforms QDASH, BBA, SARA and dash.js in terms of fairness by 40%, 25%, 30% and 35%, respectively.
- `SDNdash.js` improves utilization by 12%, 13%, 5% and 52%.

5.5 Interesting Real-World Cases

We present two interesting issues in real-world cases and discuss potential future research directions.

5.5.1 *Arbitrary Arrival/Departure Times*

A user can join and leave the network at different times. This case represents one of the main real-world cases that we are interested in. For each bitrate adaptation heuristics implemented within dash.js player (`SDNdash.js`, QDASH, BBA, SARA and original dash.js), we performed a new test with five clients sharing a 10 Mbps bottleneck link (We used the same parameters as in the previous experiment). Each client arrives 60 seconds after the previous one (ΔT = 60 s). Table 5 highlights the performance of each client. `SDNdash.js` is more stable in terms of bitrate level and video quality than other algorithms, and achieves a high QoE at each step. Moreover, `SDNdash.js` improves the bandwidth utilization by approximately 30%.

5.5.2 *Heterogeneous System*

With the diversity of device capabilities nowadays, we expect that there will be heterogeneity in DASH clients: smartphones, tablets and connected TVs. In our experimental scenarios we considered a homogeneous device population. One interesting question is how our architecture behaves with heterogeneous clients. In Section 3, we designed our architecture to handle both homogeneous and heterogeneous systems. So far, we did just preliminary experiments to study the interaction and behavior between multiple heterogeneous clients with different device capabilities and communication technologies (wired, WiFi, LTE). The early results are encouraging, though we consider this topic an interesting problem to solve in a future study.

6. CONCLUSIONS

In HAS, scalability issues arise when a set of multiple clients compete for the available bandwidth in a shared network environment. These problems are growing as the number of clients is increasing in the last mile network, and thus, resulting in an unsatisfactory end-user experience. In this paper, we proposed a new SDN-based resource allocation and management architecture for DASH systems, called SDNDASH. SDNDASH equally applies to other DASH-like approaches including Apple HLS. It leverages the flexibility, capabilities and features of SDN in the dynamic rapid/simple network level infrastructure management. Therefore, SDN enables our architecture to create an efficient and smart adaptive video streaming network. The experimental results demonstrate that our implementation (`SDNdash.js`) provides a good network stability with optimized end-user QoE across all the clients in a shared network environment. As part of our future work, we plan to evaluate our architecture using a large scale SDN-based testbed like FELIX[7], to test various

[6]Bandwidth violation occurs when the total of the bitrates selected by all clients is greater than the total available bandwidth.

[7]http://www.ict-felix.eu/

Table 5: BL, QT, N-QoE and total bandwidth of `SDNdash.js` clients.

	Bitrate Level (Kbps)			Quality (SSIMPlus)			N-QoE (Maximum = 5)			Total Bandwidth Usage (Kbps)
	MIN	MAX	MED	MIN	MAX	MED	MIN	MAX	MED	
Client 1	2,089	3,936	2,409	0.964	0.967	0.964	4.5	4.9	4.8	MIN = 80% MAX = 100% MED= 95%
Client 2	2,089	2,944	2,409	0.964	0.965	0.964	3.8	4.7	4.5	
Client 3	1,473	2,409	2,089	0.945	0.964	0.964	3.9	4.85	4.7	
Client 4	1,473	2,944	2,089	0.945	0.967	0.964	3.9	4.65	4.45	
Client 5	1,009	3,639	2,089	0.93	0.967	0.964	3.93	4.69	4.5	

heterogeneous scenarios with multiple SDN controllers and various clients, and to execute trace-driven emulations with both Mininet [16] and ns-3[8] for various network conditions and types including wireless scenarios.

Acknowledgements

This research has been supported by Singapore's Ministry of Education (MOE) Academic Research Fund Tier 1, grant number T1 251RES1415.

7. REFERENCES

[1] S. Akhshabi, L. Anantakrishnan, A. C. Begen, and C. Dovrolis. What Happens when HTTP Adaptive Streaming Players Compete for Bandwidth? In *Proceedings of the 22nd international workshop on Network and Operating System Support for Digital Audio and Video*, pages 9–14, 2012.

[2] S. Akhshabi, S. Narayanaswamy, A. C. Begen, and C. Dovrolis. An Experimental Evaluation of Rate-daptive Video Players over HTTP. *Signal Processing: Image Communication*, 27(4):271–287, 2012.

[3] E. F. Camacho and C. B. Alba. *Model Predictive Control.* Springer Science & Business Media, 2013.

[4] DASH External Dataset. http://www-itec.uni-klu.ac.at/ftp/datasets/DASHDataset2014/.

[5] DASH Industry Forum. http://www.dashif.org/.

[6] P. Georgopoulos, Y. Elkhatib, M. Broadbent, M. Mu, and N. Race. Towards Network-wide QoE Fairness using Openflow-assisted Adaptive Video Streaming. In *Proceedings of the 2013 ACM SIGCOMM workshop on Future human-centric multimedia networking*, pages 15–20, 2013.

[7] T.-Y. Huang, R. Johari, N. McKeown, M. Trunnell, and M. Watson. Using The Buffer to Avoid Rebuffers: Evidence From a large Video Streaming Service. *arXiv preprint arXiv:1401.2209*, 2014.

[8] C. V. N. Index. The Zettabyte Era–Trends and Analysis. *Cisco white paper*, 2014.

[9] J. Jiang, V. Sekar, and H. Zhang. Improving Fairness, Efficiency, and Stability in HTTP-based Adaptive Video Streaming with Festive. In *Proceedings of the ACM 8th international conference on Emerging networking experiments and technologies*, pages 97–108, 2012.

[10] P. Juluri, V. Tamarapalli, and D. Medhi. SARA: Segment Aware Rate Adaptation Algorithm for Dynamic Adaptive Streaming over HTTP. In *Communication Workshop (ICCW), 2015 IEEE International Conference on*, pages 1765–1770, 2015.

[11] V. Krishnamoorthi, N. Carlsson, D. Eager, A. Mahanti, and N. Shahmehri. Helping Hand or Hidden Hurdle: Proxy-assisted Http-based Adaptive Streaming Performance. In *Modeling, Analysis & Simulation of Computer and Telecommunication Systems (MASCOTS), 2013 IEEE 21st International Symposium on*, pages 182–191, 2013.

[12] Z. Li, A. C. Begen, J. Gahm, Y. Shan, B. Osler, and D. Oran. Streaming Video over HTTP With Consistent Quality. In *Proceedings of the 5th ACM Multimedia Systems Conference*, pages 248–258, 2014.

[13] Z. Li, X. Zhu, J. Gahm, R. Pan, H. Hu, A. Begen, and D. Oran. Probe and Adapt: Rate Adaptation for HTTP Video Streaming at Scale. *Selected Areas in Communications, IEEE Journal on*, 32(4):719–733, 2014.

[14] F. Markus, H. Tobias, and P. Tran-Gia. A Generic Quantitative Relationship between Quality of Experience and Quality of Service. *IEEE Network Magazine*, 2010.

[15] N. McKeown, T. Anderson, H. Balakrishnan, G. Parulkar, L. Peterson, J. Rexford, S. Shenker, and J. Turner. OpenFlow: Enabling Innovation in Campus Networks. *ACM SIGCOMM Computer Communication Review*, 38(2):69–74, 2008.

[16] Mininet. http://mininet.org/.

[17] R. K. P. Mok, X. Luo, E. W. W. Chan, and R. K. C. Chang. QDASH: A QoE-aware DASH System. In *Proceedings of the 3rd Multimedia Systems Conference*, MMSys '12, pages 11–22, New York, NY, USA, 2012.

[18] A. Rehman, K. Zeng, and Z. Wang. Display Device-adapted Video Quality-of-experience Assessment. In *IS&T/SPIE Electronic Imaging*, pages 939406–939406. International Society for Optics and Photonics, 2015.

[19] RYU SDN Framework. http://osrg.github.io/ryu/.

[20] M. Seufert, S. Egger, M. Slanina, T. Zinner, T. Hobfeld, and P. Tran-Gia. A Survey on Quality of Experience of HTTP Adaptive Streaming. *Communications Surveys & Tutorials, IEEE*, 17(1):469–492, 2015.

[21] Software Defined Networking (SDN). https://www.opennetworking.org/.

[22] T. Stockhammer. Dynamic Adaptive Streaming over HTTP–: Standards and Design Principles. In *Proceedings of the second annual ACM conference on Multimedia systems*, pages 133–144, 2011.

[23] E. Thomas, M. van Deventer, T. Stockhammer, A. C. Begen, and J. Famaey. *Enhancing MPEG DASH Performance via Server and Network Assistance.* Stevenhage: IET, 2015.

[8]https://www.nsnam.org/

Query Adaptive Instance Search using Object Sketches

Sreyasee Das Bhattacharjee[1], Junsong Yuan[1], Weixiang Hong[1], Xiang Ruan[2]
[1] School of Electrical and Electronics Engineering, Nanyang Technological University, Singapore
[2] Tiwaki Co. Ltd. Japan
dbhattacharjee, jsyuan, wxhong@ntu.edu.sg, ruanxiang@tiwaki.com

ABSTRACT

Sketch-based object search is a challenging problem mainly due to two difficulties: (1) how to match the binary sketch query with the colorful image, and (2) how to locate the small object in a big image with the sketch query. To address the above challenges, we propose to leverage object proposals for object search and localization. However, instead of purely relying on sketch features, e.g., Sketch-a-Net, to locate the candidate object proposals, we propose to fully utilize the appearance information to resolve the ambiguities among object proposals and refine the search results. Our proposed query adaptive search is formulated as a sub-graph selection problem, which can be solved by maximum flow algorithm. By performing query expansion using a smaller set of more salient matches as the query representatives, it can accurately locate the small target objects in cluttered background or densely drawn deformation intensive cartoon (Manga like) images. Our query adaptive sketch based object search on benchmark datasets exhibits superior performance when compared with existing methods, which validates the advantages of utilizing both the shape and appearance features for sketch-based search.

Categories and Subject Descriptors

H.4 [**Information Systems Applications**]: Miscellaneous; D.2.8 [**Image Processing, Computer Vision**]: [Scene Analysis, object recognition]

Keywords

Mobile Visual Search, Sketch-Based Object Recognition, Localization, Graph-based Search

1. INTRODUCTION

Given a query image, the goal of the object instance search is to retrieve and localize all similar objects in the database images. With the ever increasing amount of image and video data through Flickr, Facebook etc., an effective object instance search can support automatic annotation of multimedia contents and help content-based retrieval. Considering precise image example sufficing the user specification may not be always handy, sketch can be an alternative solution to initialize the search. Although the hand drawn sketch may not be precise, if drawn with care, it can still provide sufficient amount of object details to achieve an effective instance search [1, 2, 3, 4]. Despite previous work of sketch-based image retrieval, still there are two challenges to apply it for object instance search. First of all, it is a difficult problem to match a sketch which largely abstracts the object from an original image that exhibits much richer set of information. For example, if a user is looking for some 'pyramid' images, only drawing a 'triangle' is not sufficiently discriminative to uniquely resemble the pyramids. Thus it is important to fully utilize the original image information. Second, for object instance search, it is a non-trivial problem to accurately match and locate the small objects of interest in a big image of cluttered background. Such a localization problem is not fully explored in the previous works of sketch based image retrieval.

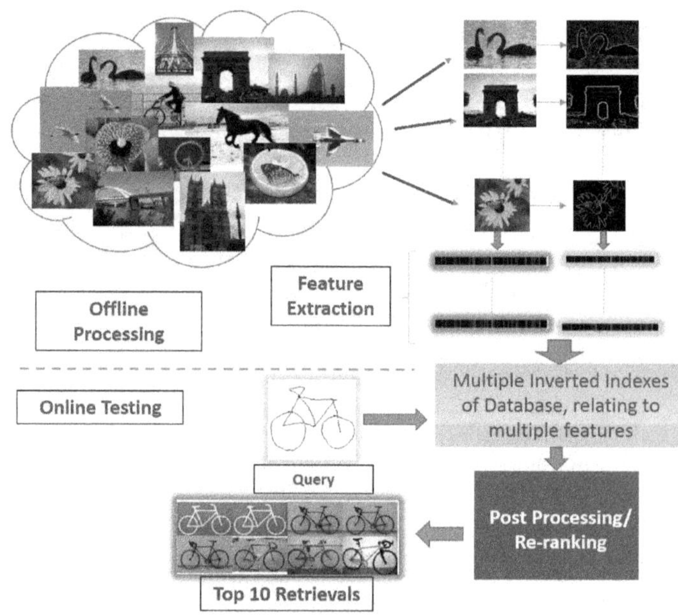

Figure 1: The outline of the Sketch-based Image Retrieval system.

To address the above two challenges, we propose a novel graph-based optimization framework to enable query adaptive object instance search using sketches. To match the sketch with the RGB image, we leverage recent deep learning feature such as Sketch-a-Net [5] to provide robust matching. However, considering the quality of the sketch provided by a random user may not be satisfactory, instead of purely relying on the sketch features, we also

MM '16, October 15-19, 2016, Amsterdam, Netherlands

DOI: http://dx.doi.org/10.1145/2964284.2964317

explore the appearance features among images in the database to improve the search quality.

The entire process proposed in this work can be illustrated in Fig. 1. To find the object instance, each database image is represented by a collection of object proposals, which are then matched with the query sketch. After extracting the edge maps, Sketch-a-Net model is used to extract shape features while Convolution Neural Networks (CNN) applies to the original image to extract the appearance features. Our proposed query adaptive search is then formulated as a graph selection problem. Each object proposal corresponds to a graph node with its prior weight depending on the shape matching quality with the query sketch. The edges among the proposals, however, depend on the similarities of both the sketch and appearance features. A joint optimization is performed via maximum flow to select the subset of object proposals that are similar to the query in terms of their sketches, and also mutually similar to each other in terms of both sketches and appearances. The finally selected object proposals then can well capture all the object instances at different images.

An extensive evaluation is performed on multiple benchmark datasets including Flickr15K [6], a subset of Flickr3M [7] called FlickrLarge, and eBDtheque Comic collection [8]. The superior performance compared with existing methods validates the advantages of our query adaptive object instance search, which can be summarized as follows:

- Even with a simple sketch, by exploring the appearance similarities among the object proposals in the database, it still can obtain satisfactory search results by simultaneously performing query expansion and outlier elimination via graph selection. Thanks to object proposals, it can also accurately locate the object instance in the cluttered background.
- Our graph selection formulation seamlessly fuses deep sketch and appearance features to achieve robust object instance search. As a generic formulation, it can be easily extended to other object search problems, e.g., comic character retrievals as shown in our experiments.

The rest of the paper is organized as follows: Section 2 briefly describes some related works. The detailed description of the proposed search approach is given in Section 3. Section 4 presents the experimental results. Finally the conclusion is in Section 5.

2. RELATED WORK

Our work is related to the problem of Sketch Based Image Retrieval (SBIR) , which uses only a single hand drawn sketch without having used any additional information such as text keywords, user-click etc.. Based on the underlying features in use, the entire spectrum of SBIR methods can be partitioned into two categories: methods using (1) global descriptors and (2) local descriptors.

Global descriptors have been very handy in the traditional SBIR methods. For example, Park et al. [9] use frequency histogram of the edge orientations or Chalechale et al. [2] use a histogram representing the distribution of edge pixels as the descriptors. Bimbo & Pala [10] propose Elastic contours to define a parametric curve that is deformed appropriately to fit with the object boundary. Similarity invariant Zarnike moments [11] have also been used for matching sketches to the image. Cao et al. [12] propose Edgel index, an indexing scheme using a Chamfer Distance based descriptors for such purpose. Contour consistency filtering is performed using Shape Context descriptor. Cao et al. [1] propose SYM-FISH which incorporates the symmetry information into the shape context descriptor. However, such global descriptors [11, 13] are not very suitable for this task as they are more sensitive to deformation, occlusion and transformations etc. and thus not suitable for many generic real life problem scenario.

In order to address these, various sophisticated local descriptors have been proposed in the recent literature. Hu et al. [6, 14] use a gradient field (GF) image to represent the sketches, which is then used to compute a multi-scale HoG descriptor in a BoF model. Some other variants of HoG descriptors [15, 16] have also been proposed for the retrieval problem scenario. Wang et al. [7] treat the query and the edgemap as a collection of edge-segments. Histogram of Line Relationship (HLR) descriptor captures the relations between these line segments within the descriptor.

While the majority of these literatures relies on hand crafted feature, they remain effective for the near-planer objects with limited view angle variations, so that sufficient correspondences can be established between query and the database entries. As mentioned earlier that the database images typically contain a single dominating object capturing a significant portion of it. Therefore, precise localization is not a big concern in such cases. However, in a real-life image, objects of interest may also be small occupying only a small portion of the entire image content. Therefore, an accurate localization is still a critical issue to address in a generic scenario.

This motivates us to design a framework which is equally adept at tracing small objects in a database image. In order to evaluate, we therefore test the proposed algorithm for searching a specific comic character in a comic album database, where the characters are typically hand-drawn and very much sketch like. In fact, a larger range of deformation along with a dense placement of the sequential story snapshots observed in the instances make the problem even more challenging. Matsui et al. [17, 18] capture the local spatial information by defining a histogram of edge orientation for a local area. While some commercial products like search engines have already attempted to address this problem, their solution heavily relies on the text based query related information provided by the user, the scope of the search process is therefore pretty limited.

By using multiple automatically generated deep learnt features, specialized in capturing shape and appearance information within a single framework, enables the proposed method to handle various issues faced by the typical global and local features used in the community. While most of the recent search methods have their main focus on retrieval than localization (specifically for small objects) except some [19, 6, 14, 17], the proposed search strategy shows an equal expertize in retrieval and localization simultaneously. A handful of top-ranked Edgebox generated proposals identified as the candidate object regions are then investigated thoroughly by the proposed search methodology for attaining an impressive matching and localization performance.

3. PROPOSED APPROACH

Given an image database $\mathcal{D}_{img} = \{\mathcal{I}_i\}_{i\in 1,..,M}$, the ultimate task in this paper is to identify the subset $\{\mathcal{I}_g\}$ of images containing the similar instances as the object of interest whose single hand-drawn sketch Q is provided as query. This also involves localizing the object's position within each gray level (or color) database image $\mathcal{I}_g$. In order to achieve this goal, the first task is to identify a set of interest candidate regions called 'proposals', at which the probability of an object's presence is high.

3.1 Image Representation and Query Matching

EdgeBox by Zitnick & Dollar [20] is used to pick out a smaller set of candidate object regions in an image. Due to its sole dependence on the sparse yet informative edge-based representation,

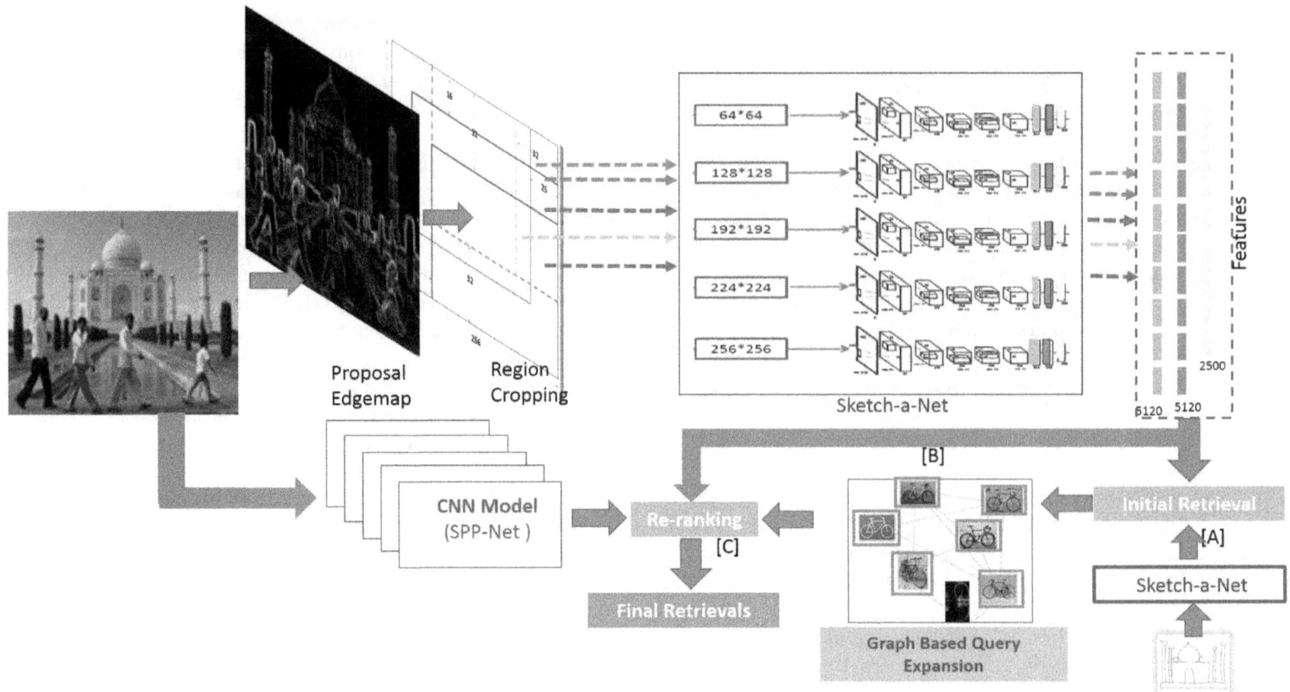

Figure 2: The Overview of the Proposed SBIR framework. Nodes highlighted with 'green' rectangles in the 'Graph Based Query Expansion' stage represents the selected nodes by our method.The steps A, B and C are the online parts of the framework, while the others can be made offline.

EdgeBox is simultaneously efficient and more accurate in spotting a smaller set of image interest regions. Given each such region identified using a bounding box, the associated 'objectness measure' quantifies its likelihood to contain an object.

Each image in the database is presented as a pool of N object proposals, $\mathcal{I} = \{P_j\}_{j=1}^{N}$, where each proposal P_j is represented by a high dimensional feature vector $\mathbf{p}_j \in \mathbb{R}^n$, e.g., Sketch-a-Net features. The whole image dataset is thus presented as a big pool of object proposals $\mathcal{D} = \{\mathcal{I}_i\}_{i=1}^{M} = \{P_j\}_{j=1}^{M \times N}$. Given a query object sketch Q represented by $\mathbf{q} \in \mathbb{R}^n$, our goal is to rank the proposals in the database $\mathcal{D}$ such that the higher ranked proposals can find the similar object instances. In this work, the automatically learnt DNN features obtained from various layers of Sketch-a-Net model are used as the proposal descriptors. and the L2 distance is used to compute the dissimilarity between two object regions represented by $\mathbf{p}_i, \mathbf{p}_j$, i.e. $d(\mathbf{p}_i, \mathbf{p}_j) = \|\mathbf{p}_i - \mathbf{p}_j\|$.

Given the matching scores of object proposals in $\mathcal{D}$, the dissimilarity score between query Q and any image $\mathcal{I}$ is defined in terms of its best matched proposal score : $d(Q, \mathcal{I}) = \underset{P_j \in \mathcal{I}}{min}[d(\mathbf{q}, \mathbf{p}_j)]$.

3.2 Initial Retrieval using Sketch-a-Net

The deep neural network (DNN), Sketch-a-Net [5] learnt on the TU-Berlin sketch dataset [15], is used to represent the edgemap of each database proposal (resized to a pre-defined size) in terms of a multi dimensional feature $\mathbf{p}$. Sketch-a-Net has five convolution layers each with rectifier (ReLU) units and the first, second and fifth layers followed by max pooling. Then added three Fully Connected Layer (FC) with a dropout regularization applied to each of the first two. For more details on the architecture, we refer the interested readers to [5]. We have used three kinds of Sketch-a-Net features for representation: the 512 dimensional outputs of first (and second) fully connected layers, called L6 (and L7) obtained after dropout regularization and the 250 dimensional output of the third fully connected layer called L8. More details on their individual performances will be discussed in section 4.

As shown in the region cropping of Figure 2, 5 sub-regions are cropped from a resized proposal. Given a database proposal, the entire set of 10 d dimensional descriptors representing its 5 cropped regions (and their corresponding horizontally flipped versions) are concatenated together to obtain its $(10 \times d)$ dimensional Sketch-a-Net representative $\mathbf{p}$. In addition to the better representation scheme, another advantage of using Sketch-a-Net feature is that it can process the variability of the structural abstraction automatically with an ensemble of multi-scale model. Each module in the 5 network ensemble independently learns a model by backdrops at varying coarseness by blurring (down-sampling and up-sampling) the original image to different degrees.

3.3 Re-ranking

Give a query Q, we first find the initial retrieval set is denoted as $\mathcal{N}_Q$. While Sketch-a-Net generated features work well compared to other state-of-the-art shape descriptors, due to the lack of an equivalent amount of information, it is unfair to expect a performance competitive to the typical deep features designed for gray (or color) images. Now it is important to note that, not all of these $\hat{K}$ retrievals are actually similar to Q. Moreover, although Q provides only a sketch based query information, an efficiently chosen subset of $\mathcal{N}_Q$ consisting of a smaller collection of some more reliable matches, can actually serve as an expanded representation for Q. Therefore, it is important to choose the subset E_Q $(\subset \mathcal{N}_Q)$, which can serve as the effective representatives for Q. In fact if properly chosen, E_Q can provide a more insightful and complete representation (in terms of both its structure and gray/color level appearances) for Q. In contrast to the common practice [21] of choosing just a collection of handful few of top retrievals as the expanded query representation, we propose a graph based re-ranking scheme to obtain a set of more reliable entries in E_Q.

In order to capture the sufficient appearance information within the descriptor, the first step is to obtain the effective representation schemes for the database proposals.

3.3.1 Extracting Appearance Features

In the re-ranking phase, two types of appearance features are used : (1) Gabor Descriptor, (2) CNN learnt feature. While, Gabor descriptor is efficient to handle the local object structural details under varying conditions, CNN features are specialized to capture the high level semantic information. Using both these complementary features within an unified framework ensures an improved performance.

Gabor Descriptor: Each proposal in $\mathcal{D}$ is represented using their corresponding Gabor filter based response in the spatial domain. Due to its invariance to similarity transformation and various lighting conditions [22], Gabor filter is found to be advantageous for our purpose. In the spatial domain, the two dimensional Gabor filter is a Gaussian kernel function modulated by a complex sinusoid and computed as:

$$G(x,y) = \frac{f^2}{\pi\gamma\eta}exp(-\frac{x_0^2+\gamma^2y_0^2}{2\sigma^2})exp(j2\pi x_0+\phi) \quad (1)$$

where $x_0 = xcos(\theta)+ysin(\theta)$ and $y_0 = -xsin(\theta)+ycos(\theta)$. f represents the sinusoid frequency, θ is the orientation, ϕ is the phase offset, σ the standard deviation and finally γ is the spatial aspect ratio which specifies the ellipticity of the support of the Gabor function. Forty Gabor filters are employed at five scales and eight uniformly sampled orientation angles. Each proposal is resized to a size 120×120 and represented in terms of a $120 \times 120 \times 8 \times 5 = 576000$ dimensional descriptor. As the image pixels in a very closeby neighborhood are usually very highly correlated, each feature map is down-sampled by a factor of 8 and the resulting reduced sized proposal representative ($\mathbf{g}_i$) has a size of $\frac{576000}{(8\times 8)} = 9000$, which are then normalized to zero mean and unit variance.

CNN Features: Convolution Neural Network (CNN) activations are used to represent each proposal in the database. Each proposal captures some dominant object region in an image. A CNN-based feature descriptor therefore represents a very generic object level representation for the underlying image. The 4096 dimensional SPP-net [23] activation ($\mathbf{c}_j$), which is an aggregated descriptor obtained from the collection of deep features (generated using a fast model by Zeiler and Fergus [24]) is used to represent each proposal in $\mathcal{D}$.

3.3.2 Query Expansion via Graph Based Reranking

Given a query Q, the set of initial top-K retrieved proposals $\mathcal{N}_K \subset \mathcal{N}_Q$ can now be represented in terms of a query adaptive graph $G_Q = (\mathcal{V}_Q, E_Q, W_Q)$, where each $v \in \mathcal{V}_Q$ represents one proposal in $\mathcal{N}_K$. Given a pair of nodes $v_i, v_j \in \mathcal{V}_Q$, there is a connecting edge between them, if and only if the corresponding proposals (represented by v_i and v_j respectively) are the K-reciprocal neighbors to each other, i.e. $|\mathcal{N}_K^i \cap \mathcal{N}_K^j| \neq 0$ and $\mathcal{N}_K^i$ represents the set of top-K retrievals using P_i (represented by v_i) as query. In order to compute the reciprocal neighbors, the proposals P_i and P_j (representing $v_i, v_j \in \mathcal{V}_Q$) in $\mathcal{N}_K$ are represented in terms of their corresponding SPP-features $\mathbf{c}_i$ and $\mathbf{c}_j$. The required pairwise appearance dissimilarity between two proposals is computed using L2 distance. Each edge-weight between $v_i, v_j \in \mathcal{V}_Q$ is computed as:

$$W_Q(v_j, v_i) = \begin{cases} sim(\mathbf{p}_j,\mathbf{p}_i)sim(\mathbf{c}_j,\mathbf{c}_i) & |\mathcal{N}_K^i \cap \mathcal{N}_K^j| \neq 0 \\ 0 & \text{otherwise} \end{cases} \quad (2)$$

where $\mathbf{p}_i$ and $\mathbf{c}_i$ respectively represent the Skatch-a-Net and SPP-feature of a proposal represented by v_i in G_Q, $sim(,)$ computes the cosine similarity between two vectors.

Each node $v_i \in \mathcal{N}_K$ represents one of the top-K retrieved database proposals P_i using Q as a query and is tagged with a utility measure. This represents the similarity extent of P_i with Q and defined as:

$$U_i^Q = sim(\mathbf{q}, \mathbf{p}_i) \quad (3)$$

here $\mathbf{q}$ and $\mathbf{p}_i$ respectively represent the Skatch-a-Net feature of the query Q and a proposal $P_i \in \mathcal{N}_K$.

Given this G_Q, we propose to use a graph based re ranking scheme that can select a maximal subset of the pairwise similar proposals through graph regularization using an objective function [25], defined as follows:

$$\underset{\mathbf{b}\in\{0,1\}^K}{\arg\max} \left[\mathbf{U}_Q^T\mathbf{b} - \lambda\mathbf{b}^T L_Q\mathbf{b} - \eta||\mathbf{b}||_0\right] \quad (4)$$

where $\mathbf{U}_Q = [U_1^Q, ..., U_K^Q]^T \in \mathbb{R}^K$, $L_Q = D - W_Q$ and $D \in \mathbb{R}^{K\times K}$ a diagonal matrix with $D(i,i)$ representing the degree of the node i in G_Q and $\mathbf{b} \in \{0,1\}^K$ is an indicator vector specifying the inclusion/exclusion of a node in the resulting subgraph.

The first term $\mathbf{U}_Q^T\mathbf{b}$ of Eq. (4) aims at maximizing the cumulative similarity score of the selected subgraph to the query. Given the structure of the Laplacian L_Q, the focus of the second term $\mathbf{b}^T L_\mathbf{q}\mathbf{b}$ is on minimizing the outliers by emphasizing more on the edge connections with higher weights, while at the same time attempting to eliminate the nodes with larger degrees. Thus, the system is designed to reject those generic images having similarity to many others. Parameter λ controls the effect of this connectivity constraint. Finally the third term $||\mathbf{b}||_0$ acts as a regularizing factor that ensures a certain amount of sparsity of $\mathbf{b}$. η controls the effect of sparsity. In order to obtain an optimized solution of Eqn. (4), it is possible to represent both the terms in the equation in terms of the cut functions. In our implementation, we use the Boykov Kolmogorov algorithm [26] for this purpose. With an order $O(K^2en)$, where e represents the number of edges in the graph and n is the size of the minimum cut, this effectively serves our purpose. The resulting maximum flow identifies a small number of graph nodes, maximally similar within themselves, which are then re-ranked based on their assignment scores to obtain a salient expanded query representation for Q, denoted as E_Q, with a size constraint $|E_Q| < k$. Typically, k is small compared to K, e.g. $\frac{k}{K} = 0.2$.

3.4 Matching with Fusion

Given the query Q and $\mathcal{N}_Q$ as the initial set of its top retrievals, E_Q is used as an expanded representation for Q and its resulting matching cost with $P_i \in \mathcal{N}_{\hat{K}}$ is defined as:

$$d_{rank}(Q, P_i) = w_i d(\mathbf{q}, \mathbf{p_i})[\min_{j\in E_Q}[d(\mathbf{c}_j, \mathbf{c}_i)] \quad (5)$$

where $w_i = \frac{1-s(\mathbf{g},\mathbf{g}_i)}{2}$, $\mathbf{g}$ and $\mathbf{q}$ respectively represent the Gabor feature and Skatch-a-Net feature of Q, $\mathbf{c}_i$ represents the 4096 dimensional SPP feature of P_i and $d(,)$ computes the L2 distance between two vectors and thus w_i works only as a weighting factor

Figure 3: Given the sketch query in the left, top-10 image level retrievals using the proposed framework are shown in the right. For the second comic query, edge map of the query is extracted to be used as an input to the system.

(lying in the range $[0, 1]$) in the function above. Based on the user requirement, one can choose to omit the Gabor similarity component in the Eqn. (5) above and use $w_i = 1$. In section 4, we will discuss more on this.

The entire set of proposals in $\mathcal{N}_Q$ is reranked using $d_{rank}(,)$ to obtain the final search result. Some example localization results are shown in Figure 3.

4. EXPERIMENT

The proposed Sketch Based Image Retrieval (SBIR) framework is used for mainly two types of search related tasks: (1) given only its rough user-drawn sketch as a query, search for an object's instances in the real life gray/color images and (2) comic character retrieval, where given a single image of the query comic character, the task is to count/localize the same character within the entire comic album. While SBIR is difficult due to the huge difference in the content of the database image and the query, the challenge for the comic character search is attributed to the fact that the instances of a comic character are often small in the very densely drawn comic pages. Moreover, they are mostly hand drawn, having a wider range of shape and appearance deformation compared to the objects seen in a real-life image. A successful evaluation for these two tasks on the varied datasets therefore experimentally proves the generalization capability of the proposed SBIR framework.

Dataset and their Accuracy Measures: SBIR being a relatively new problem, there are comparatively lesser number of benchmark results available for any dataset used in the community. The proposed SBIR method in this paper, is evaluated in three different datasets containing images of a wide range of objects with diverse structural characteristics: Flickr15K [6], a subset of Flickr3M [7] called FlickrLarge and eBDtheque Comic collection [8].

Flickr15K [6] is a large-scale dataset containing around $15k$ photographs sampled from Flickr under Creative Commons license. It consists of a set of 330 sketch queries drawn by 10 random users. The collection of sketch queries are partitioned into 33 shape categories like "circular", "heartshape", etc. The database images are taken from 60 semantics categories (e.g., "pyramid", "bicycle", etc.). A query can represent objects from multiple semantic categories, for example, the "circular" shape belongs to three different semntic categories ("moon", "fire-balloon", and "london-eye") of database images. Following the standard protocol, we use mean Average Precision (mAP) as a metric for evaluation.

FlickrLarge is a subset of the original Flickr3M [7], which is a very recent dataset containing objects from 80 different categories with 20 object images per category and 3M distracters. Five sketches per category, with a total of 400 object drawings are used as the queries for experiments. Due to resource constraints, we have used a subset of the dataset, which consists of the 1600 object images and 200K distractors and thus the entire dataset contains a total $201,600$ images. The mAP scores computed over all the sketch queries are used for evaluation.

In order to evaluate the performance for the task of comic character retrieval, eBDtheque [8] dataset is used in the experiments. eBDtheque [8] is a corpus of 100 pages (72 of which are colored) of comic pages from 25 different albums, Franco-Belgian, American comics and Mangas. Important to note that, except Rigaud et al. [27], this dataset is popularly used for evaluating the task of comic document analysis, where the goal is to extract panels, balloons, tails, texts, comic characters etc. In contrast, we use this dataset to assess the localization performance of the proposed framework. Following [27], Object level precision, recall measures are used for the evaluation purpose. Given a query object image, the set of top-100 retrievals are treated as the system output. A matched proposal is considered as correctly detected, if it overlaps with the query's ground truth. Recall (R) computes the number of correctly detected object divided by the number of objects to detect. Precision (P) measures the number of correctly detected objects divided by the number of detected objects. In our experiments, we use the top-100 retrieved proposals as the system output and compute precision/recall measure on this set.

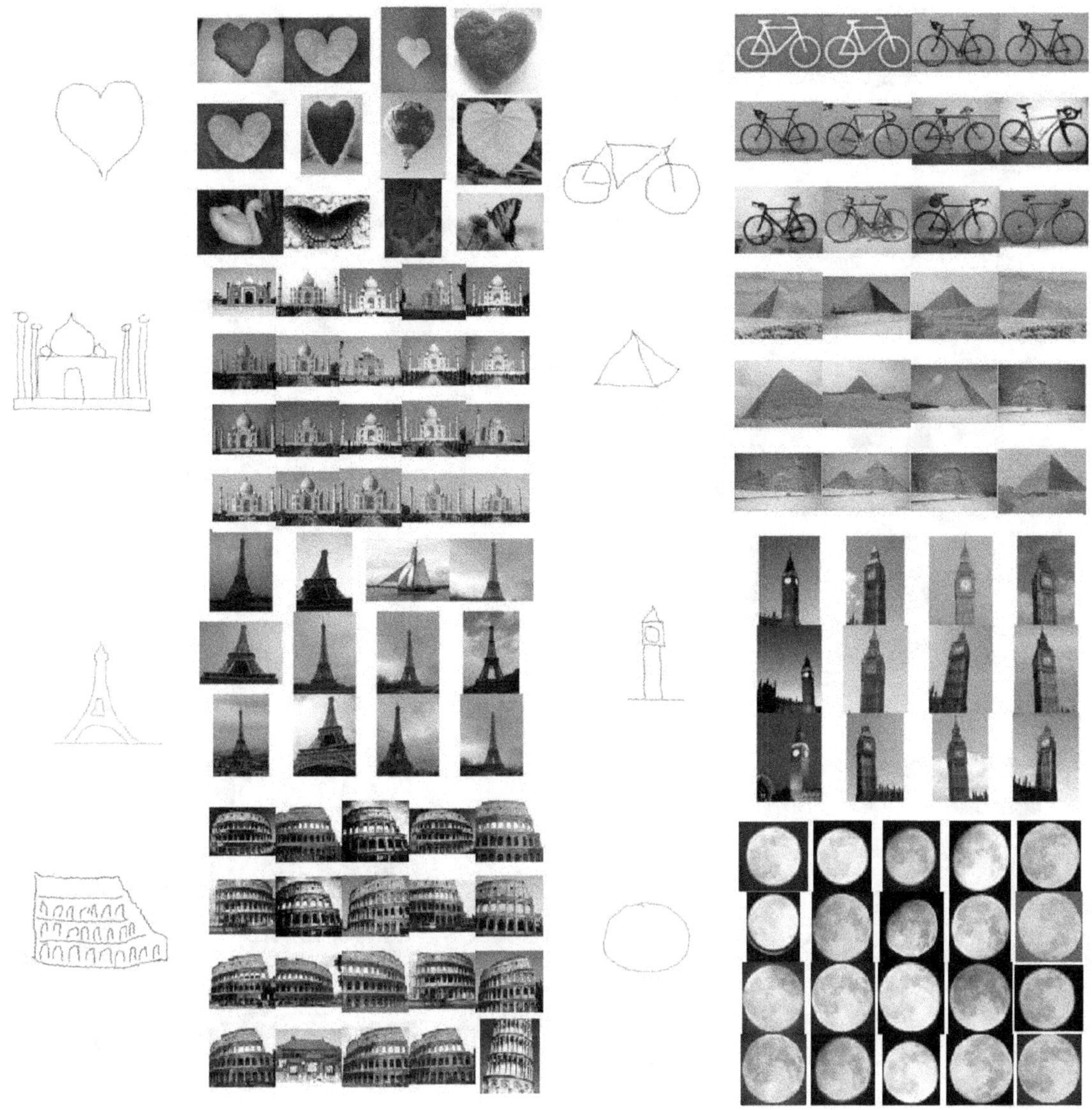

Figure 4: Some example proposal retrieval results from the Flickr15K dataset [6].

4.1 Evaluating for the SBIR task in the natural images

Flickr15K and FlickrLarge datasets are used for this part of the experiments. Since these databases are larger and the image backgrounds are cluttered, 100 top-ranked EdgeBox proposals are extracted from each image in the Flickr15K dataset. The object backgrounds being relatively cleaner, for FlickrLarge we have chosen top -20 proposals per image. For all the proposals extracted from the entire collection of images are re-sized to 256×256. Figure 4 and 5 show some visual results of the top-20 retrievals obtained by the proposed SBIR framework. Typically the retrieved objects are small in a given database image. Therefore, in order for clarity in visualization, we have chosen to display the proposal level retrievals in the figures. As shown in Figure 3, the proposed search process actually identifies these retrieved proposals as a subregion of the image, whose locations are known a-priory.

Comparative Evaluation of the Sketch-a-Net Features: Three kinds of Sketch-a-Net deep features have been used for the experiments: 5120 dimensional L6 layer activation output (**f6**), 5120 dimensional L7 layer activation output (**f7**) and 2500 dimensional L8 layer activation output (**f8**). Table 1 shows their comparative performance in the Flickr15K and FlickrLarge dataset. The mAP scores reported in the table are calculated from the collection of initial retrievals, obtained after step [A] in the figure 2. As seen in the table 1, the 5120 dimensional **f6** and **f7** are found to be more effective as the descriptors compared to the more compact 2500 dimensional **f8**.

Table 1: Performance of the various Sketch-a-Net features using mAP scores.

Features \ Dataset	Flickr15K	FlickrLarge
f6 (5120 dim. L6 layer output)	0.27	0.29
f7 (5120 dim. L7 layer output)	0.25	0.30
f8 (2500 dim. L8 layer output)	0.23	0.25

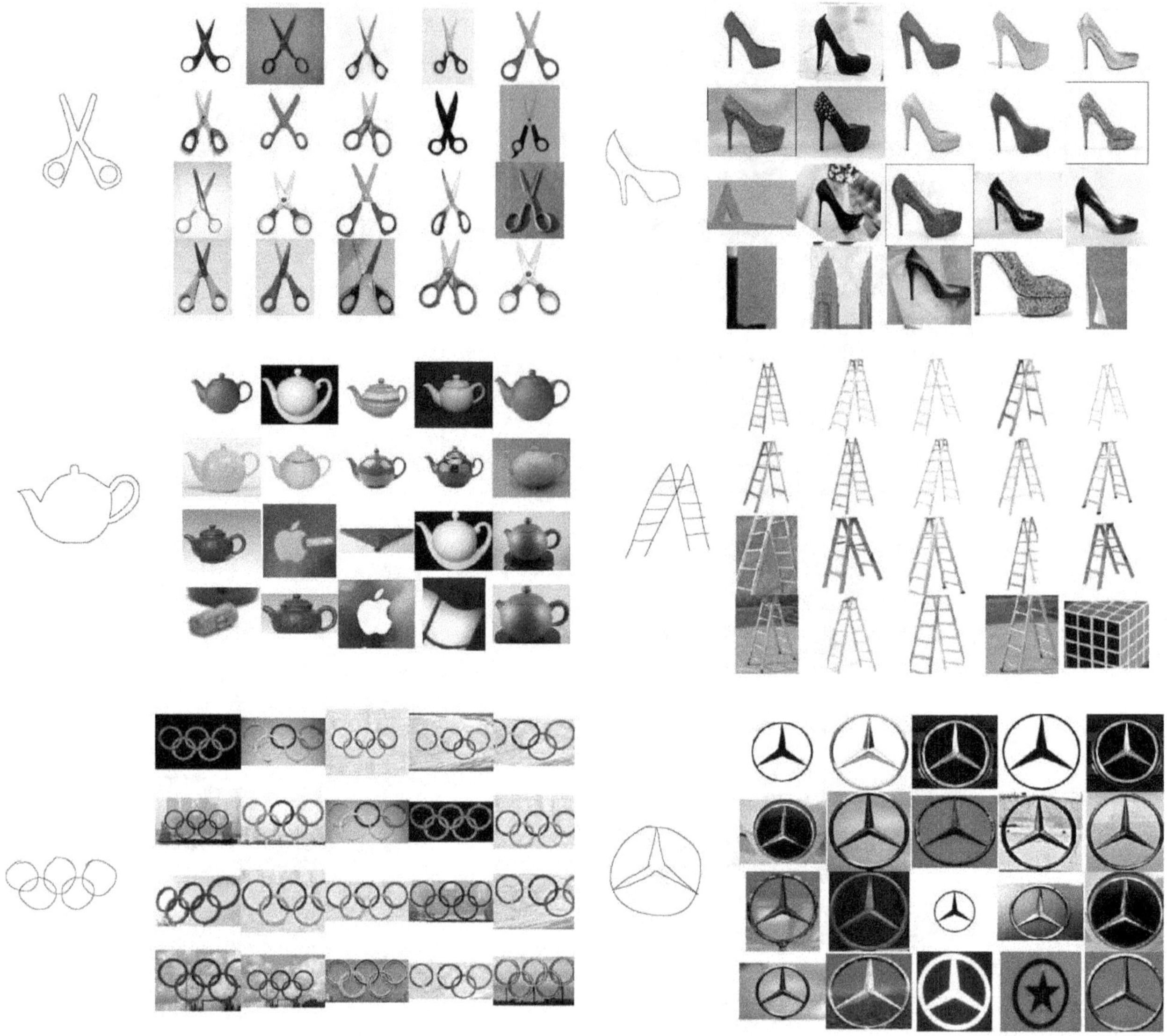

Figure 5: Some example proposal retrieval results from the FlickrLarge dataset.

Effect of Reranking: Table 2 shows the performance improvement contributed by the proposed graph based reranking in both Flickr15K and FlickrLarge dataset. It is important to note that, unlike Average Query Expansion [21] where all the top-20 retrievals are used as a representative of the query, the proposed graph based selection process aims to shortlist only those reliable matches, which are highly probable to contain the true instances of the object whose sketch is actually provided as the query. In our experiments we select the top-K (K=100) initial retrievals to further explore their mutual similarity within the proposed graph-based method and identify a smaller subset of at the most k matches ($k = 20$) , which act as the expanded representation of the query. We have used the **f7** feature as the descriptors for this set of experiments. As can be observed from the table that the proposed graph based reranking scheme contributes of around 6% gain in mAP performance score on average. The Gabor descriptors help to improve the performance a little.

Table 2: Effect of Reranking using **f6** as the proposal descriptors. The performance is evaluated using the mAP scores.

Dataset / Mathod	Flickr15K	FlickrLarge
Initial Retrieval	0.27	0.30
Initial retrieval + Reranking (using $w_i = 1$ in Eqn. 5)	0.319	0.418
Initial retrieval + Reranking (Eqn. 5)	0.323	0.431

Comparative Study: Table 3 reports the performance achieved by the proposed framework on the Flickr15K dataset. As seen in the table, GF-HoG [6] descriptor reports a better performance compared to other five representative features, namely shape context, structure tensor, HoG, self similarity and SIFT. Recently, Wang et al. [7] propose a new line segment-based descriptor named histogram of line relationship (HLR) which treats sketches and extracted edges of photo-realistic images as a series of piece-wise line segments and captures the relationship between them. While

Table 3: Performance of the proposed framework Vs Other State-of-the-art methods on the Flickr15K dataset using mAP measure. * marked methods are learning based.

Methods	mAP
Bag of Features [28]	0.131
SIFT [29]	0.091
Self Similarity [30]	0.096
Shape Context [31]	0.081
Structure Tensor [32]	0.080
HoG [33]	0.109
GF-HoG [6]	0.139
PH-HoG [34]	0.20
HLR descriptor [7]	0.171
Color Gradient [35]	0.19
HELO [36]	0.0967
S-HELO [37]	0.1236
RST S-HELO [38]*	0.2002
Learnt Key Shapes [39]*	0.245
Spatial Pyramid Pooling Deep Feature [23]	0.0472
Object level Sketch-a-Net descriptor + Reranking	**0.323**

HLR descriptor [7] outperforms GF-HoG by showing about 4% improvement on its resulting mAP score, PH-HoG [34], a variant of HoG further improves the performance. HELO (histogram of edge local orientations) and its multiple variants have also been proposed to improve the scenario. In order to achieve a better system, Saavedra & Barrios [39] relies on learning a set of key shapes through an intensive offline processing phase and we report their result in the table for completion purpose, such supervised methods are not directly comparable to our unsupervised scenario. Spatial Pyramid Pooling Deep Feature [23] is not found effective for this purpose. Thus, the detailed comparative evaluation of the proposed Sketch-a-Net based SBIR framework shows a promising insight against some of the established literatures [28, 6, 7, 39, 34, 35, 37] using a set of hand crafted features. The object level Sketch-a-Net offers a reliable description scheme, by showing a dominating performance over other state-of-the-art methods.

4.2 Evaluating for the Comic Character Retrieval

In this section, the proposed method is evaluated on the comic album dataset eBDtheque [8]. Some visual results are shown in Figure 6(a) and (b).

Experimental Setup: In these experiments the users were shown the pages from a whole album. Each of them was asked to choose a page at random and identify his/her query region (or object of interest) with a bounding box cropping. The user expertise was expected to be standard, typically having no specialized knowledge of the specific research domain, e.g. the University administrative stuffs. For each participating user, this process of query collection was iterated multiple times to select only one randomly chosen instance of all the prominent queries in a given comic album. Total 39 queries were used for evaluation process.

The proposed framework was evaluated on 41 comic pages from 10 different albums of eBDtheque representing 26 comic characters appearing more than 400 times in total. In order to evaluate the Sketch-a-Net object descriptor, we report the performances at 3 levels, e.g. the retrieval performance of the $\mathbf{f}8$, $\mathbf{f}7$ and finally the performance of the full system. Table 4 compares the details of our experimental findings against Rigaud et al. [27] treated as the baseline. In an ideal case, we expect a higher precision at a higher recall. As can be seen from the table that the $\mathbf{f}8$ Sketch-a-Net descriptor achieves the precision/recall scores $62.76/85.83$, which is like gaining around 17% in precision at the cost of just 3% drop in the recall, as compared to $45.79/88.37$ obtained by Rigaud et al. [27]. Compared to $\mathbf{f}8$, $\mathbf{f}7$ improves both the precision and recall scores on average. Finally, using $\mathbf{f}7$ as the feature, the entire proposed framework is able to attain an impressive $82.21/97.02$ precision/recall scores averaged over all the 7 albums. Important to note that the proposed sketch based retrieval framework remains pretty effective also for those albums where the color information are minimum and color based feature descriptors proposed by Rigaud et al. [27] will not be applicable.

5. CONCLUSION

This paper addresses the problem of sketch (or sketch like object) based object search in a real life scenario. A multi-stage graph based matching strategy using both shape (Sketch-a-Net) and appearance information (CNN) extracted by its deep descriptors, can ensure a more impressive retrieval and object localization performance while still remaining discriminative to the outliers. Object Regions identified by 'proposals' are leveraged to localize small objects occupying only a small fraction of an image. Unlike popular methods exploring a coarse image-level pairwise similarity, the search is designed to exploit the similarity measures at the proposal level for a salient localization performance. Its generalization ability to deal with both the clutter intensive gray level as well as the deformation intensive sketch-like comic images within a single framework is promising. Further extensions may include its application to object instance search in video inputs.

6. ACKNOWLEDGMENTS

This research is supported in part by Singapore Ministry of Education Academic Research Fund Tier 2 MOE2015-T2-2-114 and was carried out at the Rapid-Rich Object Search (ROSE) Lab in the Nanyang Technological University, Singapore. The ROSE Lab is supported by the National Research Foundation, Singapore, under its Interactive Digital Media (IDM) Strategic Research Programme.

7. REFERENCES

[1] X. Cao, H. Zhang, S. Liu, X. Guo, and L. Lin, "Sym-fish: A symmetry-aware flip invariant sketch histogram shape descriptor," in *Proceedings of the International Conference on Computer Vision*, 2013.

[2] A. Chalechale, G. Naghdy, and A. Mertins, "Sketch-based image matching using angular partitioning," *IEEE Transactions on Systems, Man, and Cybernetics - Part A: Systems and Humans*, vol. 35, no. 1, pp. 28–41, 2004.

[3] T. Furuya and R. Ohbuchi, "Visual saliency weighting and cross-domain manifold ranking for sketch-based image retrieval," in *Proceedings of the International Conference on MultiMedia Modeling - Volume 8325*, 2014.

[4] J. M. Saavedra and B. Bustos, "Sketch-based image retrieval using keyshapes," *Multimedia Tools Appl.*, vol. 73, no. 3, pp. 2033–2062, 2014.

[5] Q. Yu, Y. Yang, Y. Song, T. Xiang, and T. M. Hospedales, "Sketch-a-net that beats humans," in *British Machine Vision Conference*, 2015.

[6] R. Hu and J. Collomosse, "A performance evaluation of gradient field hog descriptor for sketch based image retrieval," *Comput. Vis. Image Underst.*, vol. 117, no. 7, 2013.

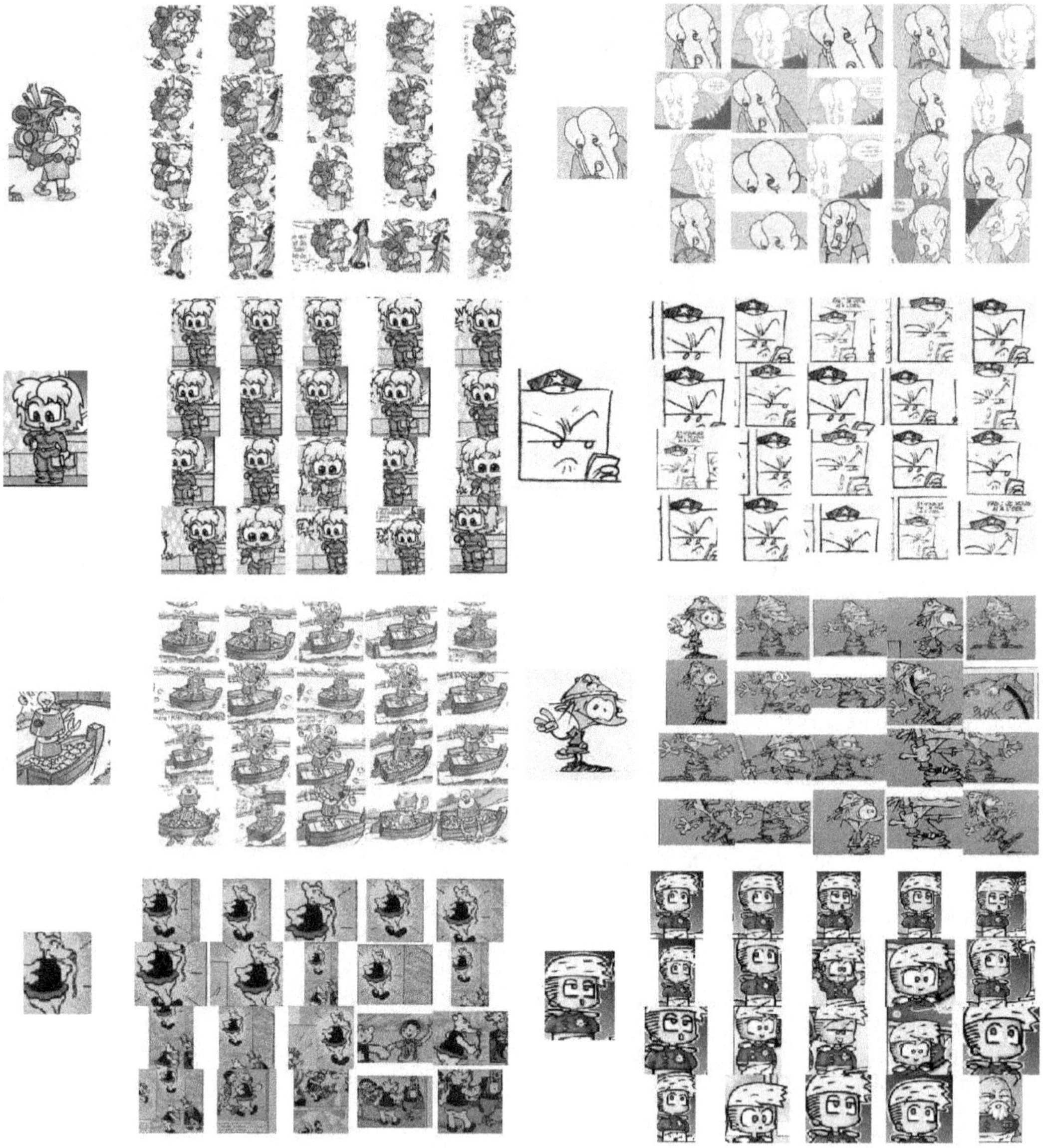

Figure 6: Some example proposal retrieval results from the eBDtheque dataset [8] . To evaluate the proposed SBIR, only the edge maps of all the queries are used as an input to the system.

[7] S. Wang, J. Zhang, T. X. Han, and Z. Miao, "Sketch-based image retrieval through hypothesis-driven object boundary selection with HLR descriptor," *IEEE Transactions on Multimedia*, vol. 17, no. 7, pp. 1045–1057, 2015.

[8] C. Guérin, C. Rigaud, A. Mercier, F. Ammar-Boudjelal, K. Bertet, A. Bouju, J.-C. Burie, G. Louis, J.-M. Ogier, and A. Revel, "ebdtheque: a representative database of comics," in *Proceedings of the International Conference on Document Analysis and Recognition (ICDAR)*, 2013.

[9] D. K. Park, Y. S. Jeon, and C. S. Won, "Efficient use of local edge histogram descriptor," in *Proceedings of the 2000 ACM Workshops on Multimedia*, 2000.

[10] A. D. Bimbo and P. Pala, "Visual image retrieval by elastic matching of user sketches," *IEEE Transactions on Pattern Analysis and Machine Intelligence*, vol. 19, no. 2, pp. 121–132, 1997.

[11] A. Khotanzad and Y. H. Hong, "Invariant image recognition by zernike moments," *IEEE Transactions on Pattern Analysis and Machine Intelligence*, vol. 12, pp. 489–497, May 1990.

[12] Y. Cao, C. Wang, L. Zhang, and L. Zhang, "Edgel index for large-scale sketch-based image search," in *Proceedings of the Computer Vision and Pattern Recognition*, 2011.

[13] S. Belongie, J. Malik, and J. Puzicha, "Shape matching and object recognition using shape contexts," *IEEE Transactions on Pattern Analysis and Machine Intelligence*, vol. 24, no. 4, pp. 509–522, 2002.

[14] R. Hu, M. Barnard, and J. Collomosse, "Gradient field descriptor for sketch based retrieval and localization," in *IEEE Conference on Image Processing*, 2010.

[15] M. Eitz, J. Hays, and M. Alexa, "How do humans sketch objects?," *ACM Trans. Graph. (Proc. SIGGRAPH)*, vol. 31, no. 4, pp. 44:1–44:10, 2012.

[16] Y.-L. Lin, C.-Y. Huang, H.-J. Wang, and W. Hsu, "3d sub-query expansion for improving sketch-based multi-view

Table 4: Performance of the proposed framework Vs baseline reported by Rigaud et al. [27] on the eBDTheque dataset using Precision/Recall as the accuracy measures. The asterisk (*) marked albums are not very rich in color and the results in these albums are not reported by Rigaud et al. [27].

Comic Album (No. of Pages/No. of Char. used for exp.)	Rigaud et al.[27]	Sketch-a-Net (**f**8)	Sketch-a-Net (**f**7)	Full System using **f**7
MIDAM GAMEOVER (10/2)	40.9/92.05	75.0/100.0	71.0/100.0	87.0/100.0
CYB COSMOZONE (5/4)	48.07/97.77	53.33/89.33	56.33/96.0	73.0/100.0
CYB MAGICIENLOOSE (1/1)	85.7/85.7	84/100	86/100	92/100
CYB MOUETTEMAN (4/2)	51.4/75.0	61.5/86.5	69.0/86.5	93.5/92.5
LAMISSEB LESNOEILS1 (5/2)	20.0/85.9	63.0/95.0	67.0/95.0	74.0/95.0
TRONDHEIM LES TROIS CHEMINS 005 (2/4)	31.25/91.28	75.0/75.0	73.5/72.5	90.0/100
MIDAM KIDPADDLE7 (2/2)	43.25/90.9	27.5/54.99	27.5/54.99	66.0/91.67
7 Album Average	45.79/88.37	**62.76**/85.83	**64.33**/86.42	**82.21**/**97.02**
SAINTOGAN_PROSPER_ET_LE_MONSTRE_MARIN* (5/5)	-	42.0/100	38.0/80.0	65.0/93.25
ROUDIER_LESTERRESCREUSEES* (4/2)	-	41.0/61.43	40.0/65.0	63.0/85.71
CYB_TRAFFIC* (3/2)	-	51.5/70.0	57.0/73.33	73.5/73.33
10 Album Average	-	**57.38**/82.87	**58.23**/82.33	**77.69**/**93.14**

image retrieval," in *Proceedings of the International Conference on Computer Vision*, 2013.

[17] Y. Matsui, K. Aizawa, and Y. Jing, "Sketch2manga: Sketch-based manga retrieval," in *IEEE Conference on Image Processing*, pp. 3097–3101, 2014.

[18] K. Levi and Y. Weiss, "Learning object detection from a small number of examples: the importance of good features," in *Proceedings of the Computer Vision and Pattern Recognition*, 2004.

[19] T. Chen, M.-M. Cheng, P. Tan, A. Shamir, and S.-M. Hu, "Sketch2photo: Internet image montage," *ACM Trans. Graph.*, vol. 28, no. 5, pp. 124:1–124:10, 2009.

[20] C. L. Zitnick and P. Dollár, "Edge boxes: Locating object proposals from edges," in *Proceedings of the European Conference on Computer Vision*, 2014.

[21] J. Philbin, O. Chum, M. Isard, J. Sivic, and A. Zisserman, "Object retrieval with large vocabularies and fast spatial matching," in *Proceedings of the Computer Vision and Pattern Recognition*, 2007.

[22] J.-K. Kamarainen, V. Kyrki, and H. KaÌĹlviaÌĹinen, "Invariance properties of gabor filter-based features-overview and applications," *Image Processing, IEEE Transactions on*, vol. 15, no. 5, pp. 1088–1099, 2006.

[23] K. He, X. Zhang, S. Ren, and J. Sun, "Spatial pyramid pooling in deep convolutional networks for visual recognition," *IEEE Transactions on Pattern Analysis and Machine Intelligence*, vol. 37, no. 9, pp. 1904–1916, 2015.

[24] M. D. Zeiler and R. Fergus, "Visualizing and understanding convolutional networks," in *Proceedings of the European Conference on Computer Vision*, 2014.

[25] S. D. Bhattacharjee, J. Yuan, Y. P. Tan, and L. Y. Duan, "Query-adaptive small object search using object proposals and shape-aware descriptors," *IEEE Transactions on Multimedia*, vol. 18, no. 4, pp. 726–737, 2016.

[26] Y. Boykov and V. Kolmogorov, "An experimental comparison of min-cut/max-flow algorithms for energy minimization in vision," *IEEE Transactions on Pattern Analysis and Machine Intelligence*, vol. 26, pp. 359–374, 2001.

[27] C. Rigaud, J.-C. Burie, J.-M. Ogier, and D. Karatzas, "Color descriptor for content-based drawing retrieval," in *IAPR International Workshop on Document Analysis Systems (DAS)*, 2014.

[28] M. Eitz, K. Hildebrand, T. Boubekeur, and M. Alexa, "Sketch-based image retrieval: Benchmark and bag-of-features descriptors," *IEEE Transactions on Visualization and Computer Graphics*, vol. 17, no. 11, pp. 1624–1636, 2011.

[29] D. G. Lowe, "Distinctive image features from scale-invariant keypoints," *International Journal of Computer Vision*, vol. 60, pp. 91–110, 2004.

[30] E. Shechtman and M. Irani, "Matching local self-similarities across images and videos," in *Proceedings of the Computer Vision and Pattern Recognition*, 2007.

[31] S. Belongie, J. Malik, and J. Puzicha, "Shape matching and object recognition using shape contexts," *IEEE Transactions on Pattern Analysis and Machine Intelligence*, vol. 24, pp. 509–522, Apr. 2002.

[32] M. Eitz, K. Hildebrand, T. Boubekeur, and M. Alexa, "A descriptor for large scale image retrieval based on sketched feature lines," in *Proceedings of the Eurographics Symposium on Sketch-Based Interfaces and Modeling*, 2009.

[33] N. Dalal and B. Triggs, "Histograms of oriented gradients for human detection," in *Proceedings of the Computer Vision and Pattern Recognition*, 2005.

[34] K. Bozas and E. Izquierdo, "Horizontal flip-invariant sketch recognition via local patch hashing," in *Proc. of the Int. Conf. on Acoustics Speech and Signal Processing*, pp. 1146–1150, 2015.

[35] T. Bui and J. Collomosse, "Scalable sketch-based image retrieval using color gradient features," in *The IEEE International Conference on Computer Vision (ICCV) Workshops*, 2015.

[36] J. M. Saavedra and B. Bustos, "An improved histogram of edge local orientations for sketch-based image retrieval," in *Proceedings of the DAGM Conference on Pattern Recognition*, 2010.

[37] J. M. Saavedra, "Sketch based image retrieval using a soft computation of the histogram of edge local orientations (S-HELO)," in *IEEE Conference on Image Processing*, 2014.

[38] J. M. Saavedra, "Rst-shelo: sketch-based image retrieval using sketch tokens and square root normalization," *Multimedia Tools and Applications*, pp. 1–21, 2015.

[39] J. M. Saavedra and J. M. Barrios, "Sketch based image retrieval using learned keyshapes (lks)," in *British Machine Vision Conference*, 2015.

Key Color Generation for Affective Multimedia Production: An Initial Method and Its Application

EunJin Kim
Department of Industrial Design, KAIST
291 Daehak-ro, Yuseong-gu
Daejeon 34141, Republic of Korea
82-42-350-4523
kejkim8@kaist.ac.kr

Hyeon-Jeong Suk
Department of Industrial Design, KAIST
291 Daehak-ro, Yuseong-gu
Daejeon 34141, Republic of Korea
82-42-350-4523
color@kaist.ac.kr

ABSTRACT

In this paper, we introduce a method that generates a key color to construct an aesthetic and affective harmony with visual content. Given an image and an affective term, our method creates a key color by combining a dominant hue of the image and a unique tone associated with the affective word. To match each affective term with a specific tone, we collected color themes from a crowd-sourced database and identified the most popular tone of color themes that are relevant to each affective term. The results of a user test showed that the method generates satisfactory key colors as much as designers do. Finally, as a prospective application, we employed our method to a promotional video editing prototype. Our method automatically generates a key color based on a frame of an input video and apply the color to a shape that delivers a promotional message. A second user study verifies that the video editing prototype with our method can effectively deliver the desired affective state with a satisfactory quality.

Keywords

color selection; key color generation; color perception; affective multimedia production

1. INTRODUCTION

Color is one of the most important factors that have a strong influence on human perception. A wide range of aesthetic and affective responses can be elicited by either one or more colors. The aesthetic and affective meanings of color have been investigated in many fields and such studies have expanded our understandings of color perception. In the practice of media production, however, colors are rarely utilized solitarily. Instead of being isolated, colors are often accompanied with various visual content including images, videos and infographics. We can easily find such combinations of colors and visual content on book covers, commercial film, websites, and a variety of user interfaces (Figure 1).

MM '16, October 15-19, 2016, Amsterdam, Netherlands
© 2016 ACM. ISBN 978-1-4503-3603-1/16/10…$15.00
DOI: http://dx.doi.org/10.1145/2964284.

Figure 1. Colors with accompanying visual contents

In these cases, the harmonization of colors and visual content plays a pivotal role in delivering informative and persuasive content. Accordingly, in the process of multimedia production, it is important to select a suitable color that can enhance the aesthetic and affective quality of accompanying content.

However, little is known about the aesthetic harmonization between colors and visual content and how such combinations evoke affective responses. Lacking useful knowledge and methods, designers often resolve the color selection problems by expert intuition and/or repetitive trials during the multimedia production process. Understanding the color selection process of designers is intriguing and also valuable to make use of procedural knowledge produced by designers. Furthermore, due to the emergence of automatic design, the color selection has become the task of automatic design systems beyond the task of designers. The change raises a new issue about the extent of a computational method emulates the capability of expert designers.

In this regard, we made a novel attempt to understand the aesthetic and affective association between colors and visual content in the context of multimedia production. In more detail, the goal of this study is to understand how designers select colors in consideration of the given visual contents and to develop a key color generation method that is applicable to the automatic design system. We focused on the strategies that designers employ and tried to reflect the strategies on the method we developed. Hence, the major contribution of this study does not lie upon the maturity and/or complexity of the developed method. It rather has a strength on its methodological novelty and how such a new approach brings promising advantages in affective multimedia production.

The study consists of three research activities: (1) investigating the color selection process of designers; (2) developing a key color generation method that suggests a color in relation to aesthetic and affective quality of multimedia content; (3) testing the method in the practice of media production. For prior two research activities, the main interest of investigations was image data, which is one of the most prevalent visual contents in multimedia. The key color generation method was developed in consideration of aesthetic and affective quality of color-image combinations. Then, the method was verified in a wider context through the last research activity that utilized videos.

In the following sections, we firstly overview the related research and present the process and results of research activities involved in this study. For the first research activity, we conducted an experiment with 10 designers to understand their color selection process. Based on the findings from designers, we built a structure of a key color generation method and refined its detail by utilizing a crowd-sourced database. A user test was carried out to examine the performance of the method by comparing its results against those of designers. Finally, we embedded our method in an automatic video editing system, and examined the performance of the method in a wider context of multimedia production.

2. RELATED WORK

Aiming at developing a key color generation method that enhances the aesthetic and affective quality of visual content, we reviewed previous studies in relation to any of these factors: color perception, color emotion, and color semantics of images. Based on these studies, we were able to identify three main contexts for our research: 1) the effects of color on emotion, 2) principles and tools to construct harmonious color combinations, and 3) method to extract colors from images.

2.1 Color Emotion

The choice of color has a complex but strong relationship with the aesthetic and affective experience of design. Hence, the perception of color and color combinations has attracted interests of many researchers. For instance, Adams and Osgood [1, 26] revealed the cross-cultural universality of affective feelings about colors. They associated colors with perceptual dimensions such as evaluation, activity, and potency. According to their study, red is active and strong, while gray is passive, bad and weak. Wright and Rainwater [41] suggested six connotative factors including happiness, showiness, forcefulness, warmth, elegance and calmness. These six factors were the most susceptible to the changes in saturation, and the least influenced by the hue. Similarly, the study of Valdez and Mehrabian [38] reported that saturation and brightness evidenced the strong and consistent effects on emotions.

Since color is rarely perceived in isolation, there have been many investigations on color combinations as well. Ou and Luo [27, 28] developed a three-dimensional color-emotion space with axes of color activity, color weight and color heat. By applying the same space to single colors and color combinations, they confirmed that emotion induced by combination of two colors can be predicted by the mean of single color emotions. Kobayashi [11, 12] examined the meaning of color and color combinations, and he developed the Color Image Scale. The scale correlated single colors, 3-color themes and 180 affective keywords together on the image scale map and provided the relationship between affective keywords and colors.

These studies have contributed to the understanding of emotional aspects of colors and have been utilized prominently in various applications [32, 34, 40]. However, these findings have not yet been examined in the presence of other visual content, which is more prevalent cases in multimedia practice. To our best knowledge, this study is the first to understand the perception of colors with accompanying visual content as an extension of previous color-emotion studies.

2.2 Color Harmony

In addition to the perception of color combinations, many early studies concentrated on identifying principles of harmonious color combinations. Like Goethe [5], Munsell [23] viewed balance as a key to creating harmonious color combinations. Based on the Munsell color system, various color harmony principles were suggested and a quantitative measure developed by Moon and Spencer [19] was one of them. Itten [10] designed a new color wheel of twelve hues and introduced relative positioning of hues that would harmonize together. A more recent study of Ou and Luo [28] also emphasized the great influence of hue on color harmony.

Given the principles and theories of these studies, a variety of tools have been developed to assist color selection of both experts and novices. Hu et al. [7] presented a tool that helps users to interactively explore and generate color schemes based on color harmony principles. Moretti [21, 22] developed 'color harmonizer' that automates the generation of harmonious color schemes and demonstrated its application in GUI design. Meier et al. [18] introduced a toolset, Interactive Palette Tools, that enables browsing, breeding and displaying of color palettes.

Although these tools and methods have provided easier ways of tailoring colors, their applications have mainly focused on suggesting harmonious color combinations, instead of constructing a harmony between the color and visual content. Since visual content such as images and videos comprises more complex and contextual features than a single color, multifaceted approaches should be devised in order to construct reliable harmony principles and materialize the principles in automatic multimedia production. As an attempt to do so, we believe that this study can contribute to creating aesthetic and affective multimedia works by investigating the association of colors and visual content and developing a computational method to generate a key color.

2.3 Color Extraction from Images

In the image processing field, extracting representative colors from images has long been an interest of several researchers. The purpose of color extraction was widely distributed over image abstraction [13], image indexing [34], color transfer [2, 24] and creating color schemes for design [6]. The methods also varied from clustering algorithms [8, 36], histogram thresholding [33, 37] and even to computational learning algorithms [14]. As shown in their purpose and application, however, these studies rarely considered the color as a design component that can contribute to the process of creating multimedia works. Although there has been an attempt to utilize the perspective of art students in extracting color themes [14], the outcomes have yet to be applied to multimedia production in order to enhance the affective quality. In this regard, our study has a unique standpoint that views color as a component of multimedia outcomes.

Moreover, we tried to reflect the procedural knowledge of designers in developing the key color generation method. Most of color extraction studies have examined colors that have already extracted by human [14, 15], instead of investigating the process that people extract a color from an image. In contrast, our approach to develop a computational method considered findings from both process and outcomes of designers.

3. ANALYSIS OF COLOR SELECTION PROCESS

We conducted experiments with 10 designers to understand their creative color selection process. We analyzed the qualitative data from verbal protocols and quantitatively investigated the colors generated by designers.

3.1 Methodology

3.1.1 Participants

We recruited ten designers who majored in graphic or industrial design (4 females and 6 males). Three of them had three, four, and eight years of professional experiences, respectively, and the others are currently enrolled in a graduate school of industrial design. The participants' mean age was 28.0, ranging from 25 to 33.

3.1.2 Stimuli: Images and Keywords

As stated before, image data was chosen among various types of visual content due to its commonality with other visual contents and popularity in media. For the experiment, 30 images of 1000 pixels by 1000 pixels were prepared. The selected images were pictures of various topics including people, objects, animals, plants and landscapes. We also prepared four affective terms such as excited, afraid, depressed and relaxed in order to present them as target emotions of final designs. As shown in the Figure 2, each corresponds to one of the four quadrants of the emotion space derived from PAD theory [31, 38], which are characterized by the pleasure state (horizontally) and the arousal state (vertically). Since these four emotions are primary and discrete to each other, we've thought that they could be a good anchor point to expand our finding into more variations. This experimental design allowed us to investigate how designers express an emotion with a variety of visual content, and how a key color can be determined differently depending on target emotions.

3.1.3 Procedure

The experiment was conducted individually in an isolated room that disguised as an office environment with a desk, a chair and a desktop computer. When the experiment began, one of the 30 images was randomly presented with an affective keyword. The designers were instructed to decide a key color that is harmonious with a given image and expresses the emotion described by the affective word. As shown in Figure 3, they applied the selected color to a rectangle of 1000 pixels wide and 350 pixels tall positioned below the image by using Adobe Photoshop® CS6. The color-selection task was described as a part of designing a book cover or a poster. By specifying the design context, we've tried to help participants perform the task with confidence in its purpose and applications.

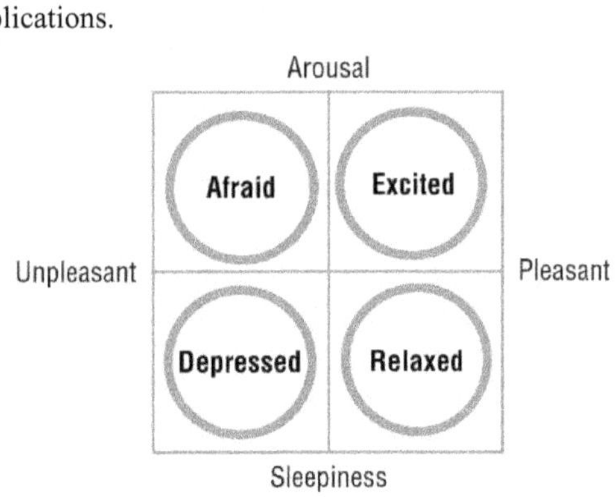

Figure 2. Four emotions defined by PAD theory

Figure 3. Key color selection task presented to designers

Throughout the experiment, each designer received 30 images and selected four colors for each image to deliver four affective keywords. Consequently, we obtained 120 color-image combinations from each designer. When finished, we made a retrospective interview to retrieve the latent thoughts and criteria that designers employed during the color selection process. While reviewing their design outcomes one by one, designers were asked to retrace their preceding design process and to report what they were thinking as they create colors based on perceived images and affective terms.

3.1.4 Data Analysis

Through the experiments, we obtained verbal protocols and colors selected by designers. After analyzing the verbal protocols using an open-coding, we interwove the findings with the quantitative analysis of colors to validate and confirm the results from the protocols. As a result of an integrated analysis, we identified a general procedure of designers to select key colors and noted how emotion and image affect the selection of colors. Since the aim of this analysis was understanding the general color selection process of designers, main findings are presented in the following section instead of reporting the specific results.

3.2 Characterizing Color Selection Process

3.2.1 Representative Color of a Given Image

Designers firstly explored existing colors of a given image in order to find a good starting point. They were often interested in a dominant color that represents a relatively large area of the image. Dominant colors were preferred since they could provide a robust harmony between a color and the image. For instance, the left two picture of Figure 4 are images dominated by a narrow range of hue. The colors selected by participants tended to follow the dominant hue of the given image. Contrary to the consideration of dominance, participants also interested at salient colors that are much more distinctive and noticeable than the rest. The right two images of Figure 4 are examples that few salient regions had a strong influence on participants' color selection. In general, participants investigated a better representative while exploring in between dominance and salience.

Figure 4. Images and related key colors by participants

3.2.2 *Tone Guided by Emotions*

Once they finished selecting a starting color from an image, designers proceeded to elaborate their selection in a more detail. They often explored contiguous colors with minor changes in hue and tone. In relation to color elaboration, we found repetitive and explicit mentions regarding the association of emotion and color tone. Four participants recognized the association by themselves and explicitly mentioned about it. Other designers did not elicited it into verbal expression, but showed a strong congruence in selecting tones of colors.

The congruence was also supported by the quantitative analysis of designers' colors as well. In Figure 5, the saturation and brightness values of designers' key colors are plotted across the four emotion words. Although the given images were distributed in a wide range of brightness and saturation, the key colors showed a coherent pattern for each emotion. Vivid colors with higher brightness were preferred for vigorous emotion. Pale colors were frequently chosen to deliver relaxed emotion, while dark-grayish colors were selected to express sad emotion. This results indicate that designers tend to articulate the tone of color in consideration of emotions rather than the image itself.

In summary, designers began their color selection process by picking a representative color of a given image. Once a satisfactory color was identified, designers proceeded to polish the color by applying minor changes to its hue and tone. In particular, the tone of the color was mainly refined and finally confirmed according to the target emotion. Such tendency of designers seems to align with the findings of previous color studies that showed emotional responses to colors are varied more by the tone rather than the hue [4, 28, 35, 38].

4. KEY COLOR GENERATION METHOD

Based on the insights from the designers, we formulated the framework of a key color generation method. Similar to the general color selection process of designers, our method involves two steps that consist of *hue-extraction* and *tone-match*. Figure 6 illustrates the framework of the method with an image and four emotional keywords that were utilized in the designers' experiment.

The latent principle of the framework corresponds to the earlier color studies. Itten [10] and Ou and Luo [28] argued that hue is the most important factor to construct a harmony among colors. In our method, the key color inherited hue from the color semantics of an image. By synchronizing the hue of a key color with a given image, we expect an aesthetic harmony between the image and the key color. Contrary to the hue, the brightness and saturation values are totally independent from an image. The tone is defined according to the target emotion by referring to color-emotion scales. We viewed the tone as a tuner of the emotional aspect of a key color, and this conforms to the findings of previous color-emotion studies that have revealed the major influence of tone upon the emotion [28, 35, 38].

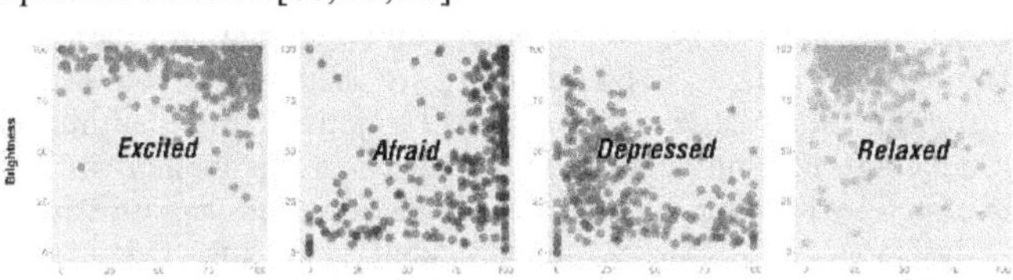

Figure 5. Saturation (x-axis) and brightness (y-axis) of designers' key colors for each emotion

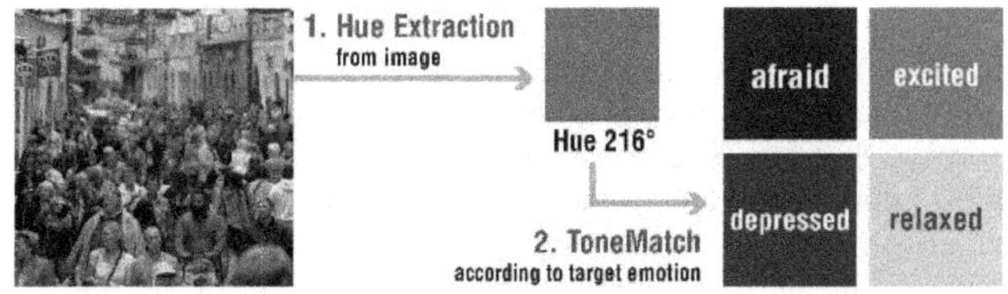

Figure 6. Framework of key color generation method

The novelty of our method is the articulation of the tone of a key color exclusively depending on the affective term given by a user. Most of previous color extraction studies have aimed at *extracting* colors from color features of a given images. Hence, regardless of their diversity in methods and results, the range of extracted colors were constrained within the color features of the image. In contrast, our method *generates* a novel color that may not belong to a given image by separating the tone of a key color from the image.

4.1 Hue-extraction from an Image

The aim of this step is to extract a hue that is perceptually dominant within an image. Since the method is an initial attempt to embody the strategies of designers, we devised a K-means clustering for simplicity rather than fine methods suggested by previous studies [2, 14, 15]. Through iterative simulations, we decided to form 10 clusters using the normalized HSB values of image pixels. We extracted a hue value from the center of the largest cluster, and used it as the hue of a key color to be suggested for the given image.

4.2 Tone-match

In order to complete a key color, the hue extracted from an image was matched to a specific tone composed of brightness and saturation values. The core of the tone-match step is manifestation of the affective characteristic by matching a certain tone with a specific emotion. To identify an appropriate tone for a given affective term, we utilized color themes from Adobe Color CC® (Adobe Kuler), a well-known crowd-sourced color database. The platform enables users to create, rate and modify the themes with five colors. Over 45,000 themes have been created on this platform and each theme has a name and a rating score by users. Its richness has provided a reliable resource to infer color emotion in several studies [15, 39, 40]. Like these studies, we've tried to derive a solid and latest knowledge about color emotion by associating color features and the name of each theme.

Figure 7 demonstrates the process of matching a tone with a certain affective term. To define the tone for affective term 'excited', up to 40 color themes were crawled from the searching results in order of their ratings. Since each color theme has five colors, a total of 200 colors is obtained. Each color mapped on the saturation-brightness matrix according to its values.

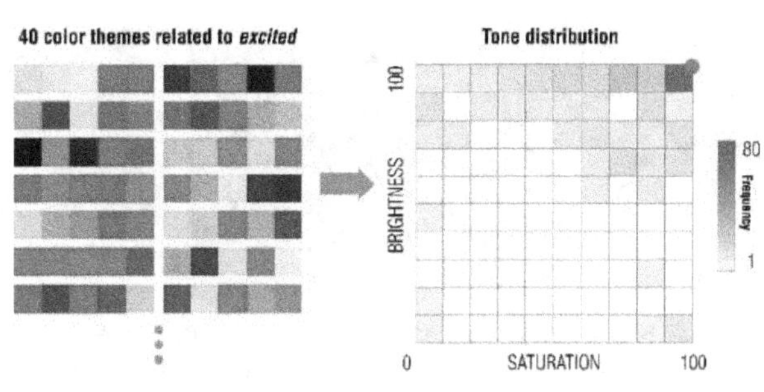

Figure 7. Identifying tone for *excited* key colors

Then, we quantized the matrix into 10 by 10 cells and counted the frequency of colors belong to each cell. By utilizing the histogram of saturation and brightness, we've tried to avoid the limitation of average that can be compromised by outliers. We identified the most popular tone range among 100 cells, and defined the tone of an affective term as the highest saturation and brightness value of the cell. In the case of *excited*, the tone range with the highest frequency was saturation 90~100% and brightness 90~100%. Among 200 colors, 76 colors were located in the cell. As a result, the tone of *excited* was defined as the combination of 100% saturation and 100% brightness.

By combining the hue extracted from an image and the tone defined by color themes from Adobe Color CC®, a key color is generated. In Figure 8, examples of key colors with four affective terms are presented. Since the hue of a key color is inherited from the given image, all key colors have the same hue but are differentiated by the tones matched with affective terms.

4.3 User Test 1: Verification of Our Method

Based on the developed method, a user test was conducted. The goal of the first user test was to assess the performance of our method in comparison with the designers' selection. Since our method is composed of two separate steps, we evaluated the key color generation method in two aspects. In more details, the performance of hue-extraction step was assessed by rating the aesthetic harmony between a color and an image, and the performance of tone-match step was assessed by rating the affective quality of each color-image combination.

4.3.1 Stimuli and Procedure

As stimuli for the test, we used 30 images from the previous designers' workshop and prepared six variations of key colors for each of the images. Five of the variations were made by five experienced designers and the sixth one was generated by our method. Moreover, an image-color combination had one of the four affective terms – excited, afraid, depressed and relaxed – as the theme. As a result, we had a total of 120 image-color combination sets for the experiment.

A total of 30 subjects (15 male, 15 female) participated in the test and exposed to the 120 sets. When one set is displayed, the subjects rated each of the six variations in terms of aesthetic harmony and affective quality using a 7-point-Likert scale.

4.3.2 Results

The average ratings on designers' key colors and our method are presented in Table 1. A repeated measures one-way ANOVA was conducted twice to compare the aesthetic harmony and overall affective quality of key colors generated by designers and our method. In addition, a one-way ANOVA was performed four times in order to compare the affective quality of key colors for each of four affective terms.

Figure 8. Key colors generated by our method: hue extracted from image and tone matched according to emotion

Key color generator	Mean(SD) 1: very poor ~ 7: excellent	
	5 designers	**our method**
Aesthetic quality	4.17 (1.61)	3.63 (1.55)
Affective quality	4.27 (1.54)	4.56 (1.45)
excited	4.28 (1.54)	4.73 (1.49)
afraid	3.88 (1.58)	3.66 (1.37)
depressed	4.52 (1.55)	4.85 (1.15)
relaxed	4.40 (1.41)	5.00 (1.39)

Table 1. Average ratings on 120 image-color combinations created by five designers and by our method (N = 30)

For the ratings on **aesthetic harmony**, there was a significant difference among key colors generated by designers and by our method ($F(5,7194) = 70.68$, $p < .05$). The post hoc comparison with Tukey's HSD indicated that the ratings on colors by our method were significantly lower ($M = 3.63$, $SD = 1.55$) than the ones on colors by four designers. Only one designer showed a nonsignificant difference with our method in the perspective of aesthetic harmony.

In the case of **overall affective quality**, key colors by our method have received the highest mean ratings and the ratings were significantly higher ($M = 4.56$, $SD = 1.45$) than colors by four designers ($F(5,7194) = 13.88$, $p < .05$). We also performed a one-way ANOVA test and post hoc test for each emotion. The results confirmed significant differences in six variations for all four affective terms. In cases of *excited* and *relaxed*, our method received the highest mean score, and significantly better than four designers ($p < .01$ with Bonferroni correction). Our method also received significantly better score for *depressed* key colors than three designers ($p < .01$). In the case of *afraid* state, there were no significant differences among our method and four designers ($p < .01$). Only one designers showed a significant better performance than our method ($p < .01$).

With regard to the aesthetic quality, the designers' choices were more appreciated than the colors generated by our method. In the present study, we devised a simple K-means clustering to extract the most dominant hue of an image. Although the method provided us simple and acceptable solutions, it does not consider the spatial information and saliency of each pixel that have been highlighted in designers' color selection process. A more elaborated method will be explored further using a knowledge base of computer vision studies. In particular, studies related to saliency [9, 16] and human perception [14] could be employed in the process of improving hue-extraction algorithm.

In the case of affective quality, our method has a strength in expressing desired affective states in comparison with designers. It indicates that exclusive engagement of tone and affective term could have a practical benefits and potential. Compared to previous color extraction methods, our method can generated a wider range of colors by assigning a tone regardless of the color features of images. This could provide more creative and insightful alternatives for color selection of multimedia production. For future study, an extension of this method will be explored by refining the tone identification process and utilizing a wider range of resources. In particular, prior knowledge upon color emotion could be used in order to process and filter possible noise of crowd-sourced data [12, 30].

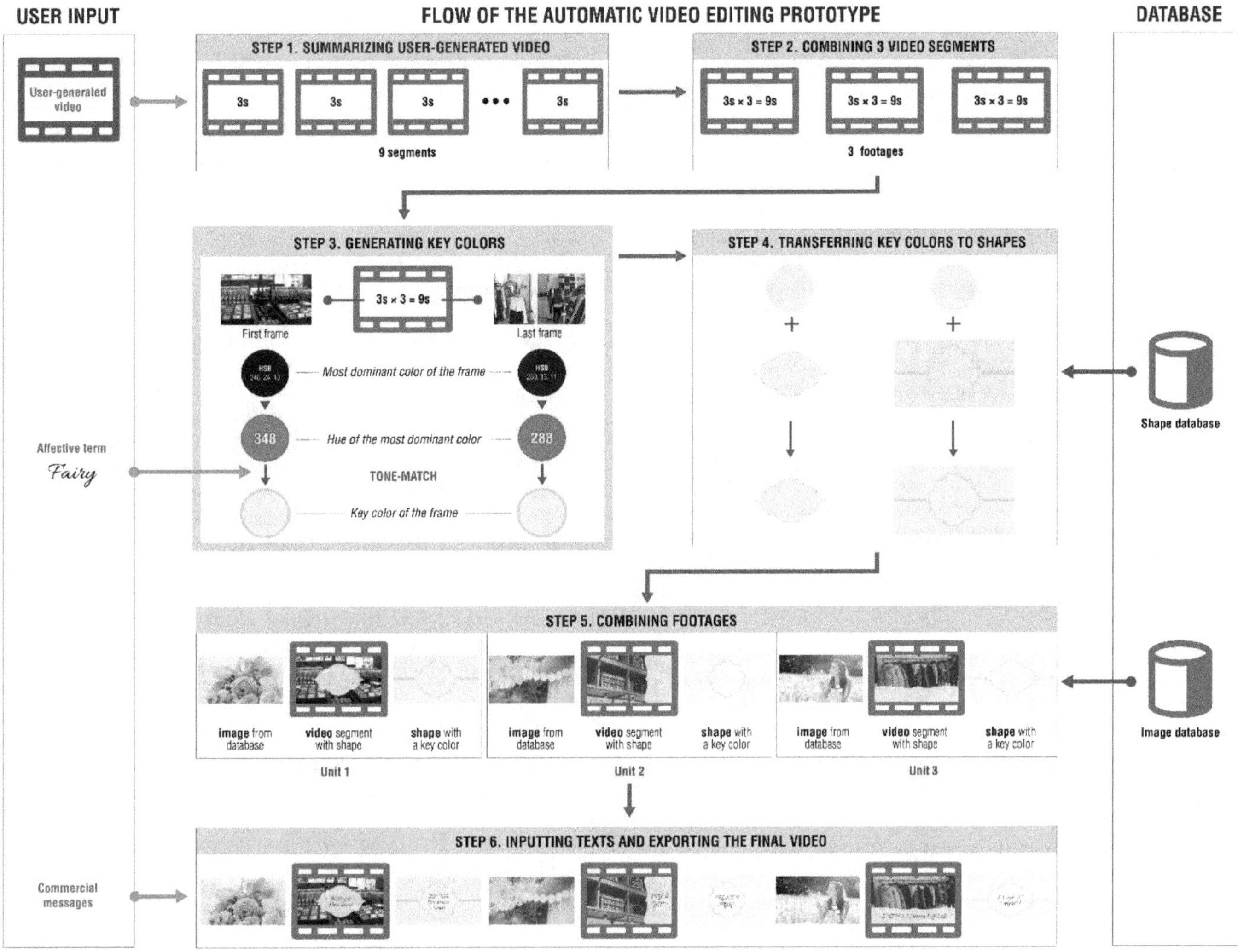

Figure 9. Overview of the automatic video editing prototype

5. APPLICATION POTENTIAL

As a prospective application, we adopted our key color generation method into a prototype of an automatic video editing system. The system aims at creating a commercial film or a promotional video for local retail stores, which are mainly operated by individual owners. Unlike stores from franchised chains, it is difficult for local retail store owners to manage and update their promotional materials continuously. The video editing prototype allows users to quickly make a promotional video of their retail stores with a video taken by themselves and a keyword of an affective style they want to express.

Among various application alternatives, we have chosen this video editing prototype for three reasons. First, a video can be viewed as a series of images. In this manner, video is a type of media that an image-based method can be easily extended. Second, the quality of user-generated videos are poor in general. Hence, the performance of our method in enhancing the aesthetic quality of multimedia outcomes can be examined effectively. At last, unlike home videos, commercial films usually have target emotions or styles to express. In this sense, we thought that it is an appropriate application to verify the affective tone-match of our method.

5.1 Overview of the Video Editing System

Figure 9 illustrates the overall flow of the automatic video editing system. It has two pre-constructed databases; one is a shape database of various graphical elements and the other is an image database regarding diverse themes. And three types of algorithms or computational methods are embedded as core functions of the system; the first one is a video summarization algorithm, the second one is a key color generation method and the last is a set of motion graphic algorithms to combine multiple footages. In this paper, we will only discuss the role and advantages of the key color generation method, where the main focus of this study is laid on.

By utilizing the two databases and three algorithms, the prototype generates a video from three types of user input including a user-generated video, an affective term and commercial messages to be presented in the final video. In step 1, the system summarizes the user-generated video into nine segments of three seconds long. Previous studies about the qualities of videos have suggested that the shot length is one of the most crucial aspect that enables people to distinguish the work of professionals and amateurs [3, 25]. Majority of professional video shots are shorter than 6 seconds, and shot of 3~4 second length were appeared most frequently [25]. Base on this finding, we decided to summarize a user-generated video into multiple segments of 3 second footage. Then, three segments are combined into a footage of 9 seconds in step 2. This process enables us to construct longer video footages while improving the perceived quality.

The step 3 is the core part that our key color generation method contributes. The system captured the first and the last frame from each of 9s footages. For each frame, our method generates a key color through extracting the most dominant hue of the frame and matching the tone defined by the affective term. Since two key colors are generated for a footage, total six key colors are generated during this process. In step 4, the system retrieves three partial elements and three full elements from the shape database, and change the color of each shape into a key color. For each footage, a key color from the first frame is transferred to a partial element and the one from the last frame is used for a full element. The shape database was constructed by three industrial designers, and the system randomly retrieves six among approximately 100 shapes.

In step 5, the system combines all footages including images from the database, video footages and shapes with full element. As shown in the Figure 9, each video footage constructs a unit with a preceding image and a followed full shape. The partial element is overlaid on the video with 10% reduced opacity. Finally, in step 6, a commercial film is created by entering the commercial messages that a user want to deliver. A motion graphic algorithm plays a pivotal role in these step 5 and 6 to combine each footage into a smooth narrative.

The system involves a variety of techniques, algorithms and decision making protocols that did not fully described in this paper. The details of them are beyond the scope of this paper. Instead, we tried to provide a brief but holistic view in order to locate our method in the overall system.

5.2 User Test 2: Investigating Benefits of Key Color Generation Method in Video Editing

A user test was carried out in order to examine the benefits of the key color generation method within the automatic video editing system. The study was composed of two experiments. For the first experiment, we focused on assessing the overall performance of the system in comparison with other automatic video editing systems. The aesthetic benefits of our method was examined in this experiment. The second experiment measured the extent to which our method delivers the desired affective state. Both experiments conducted in a room with a 40inch display and a supplementary 27inch display (Figure 10). In total, 30 subjects (15 male, 15 female) participated in both experiments, and they were 21.33(± 3.20) old in average. None of them have participated in the first user test.

Figure 10. Display setting of the experiment 1

Table 2. Pairs of retail-affective term for experiment 1

Retail	Affective term	Retail	Affective term
Fashion	Feminine	Restaurant	Fresh
Leisure	Noble	Performance	Provocative
Medical	Modern	Education	Cheerful
Living	Tranquil		

5.2.1 Experiment 1: Assessing Overall Quality

To assess the overall performance of the system, we searched for comparable services or systems that help users to create a video with few steps. As a result, we identified three alternative systems. The first one is *magisto*, an automatic online video editor that turns videos and images into an edited film. Although the solution of *magisto* does not perfectly fit to the commercial film, it was selected due to its popularity with more than 70M users. The second one is *Shakr*, which provides hundreds of video design templates specialized in a business purpose. Up to our best knowledge, *Shakr* showed the highest similarity with our system in the aspects of considering target emotions for a promotional purpose. The last one is *MagicInfo*, a bundle software of a digital signage display manufactured and sold by a well-known global company. Unlike prior two systems, it offers a set of images that represents diverse retails. Using these images, user can create a promotional video without taking any footage by themselves.

5.2.1.1 Stimuli

Utilizing these three systems and ours, we prepared four variations of commercial films for each of seven retails. Table 2 shows the seven pairs of a retail and a target affective state. We used the same images, user-generated videos and commercial messages for a retail. However, commercial messages were not included in *magisto,* and videos were not utilized for *MagicInfo* due to their functional limitation.

5.2.1.2 Procedure

Each participant saw one of the commercial films presented in a 40inch display. For each retail, four variations of commercial films were presented in a random order. A supplementary 27inch display was used to play four variations together in a screen (Figure 10). After watching four variations, participants asked to rank them in four aspects; aesthetic quality, attention capturing, message deliverability and preference as a commercial film. We've devised these four criteria based on several studies that have investigated the quality and effectiveness of advertisements with diverse perspectives [17, 20, 29].

5.2.1.3 Results and Discussions

The ranking data of each evaluation criteria was analyzed with a Friedman test and multiple Wilcoxon signed rank tests for post hoc analysis. Table 3 summarizes the results of analysis.

For **aesthetic quality**, a Friedman test showed a significant difference among four types of commercial films ($\chi^2(3) = 106.68$, $p < .05$). Wilcoxon signed rank tests showed that *Shakr* ranked as significant better than our system ($Z = 2.50$, $p < .05$). There was a significant difference between ours and *MagicInfo* ($Z = 6.69$, $p < .05$), while there was no significant difference between ours and *magisto*. There was a statistically significant difference in **attention capturing** among four variations (χ^2 (3)= 150.15, $p < .05$). Our system received significantly better ranks compared to the second ranked *Shakr* ($Z = 3.50$, $p < .05$).

Table 3. Comparison of four video editing systems. Asterisks* indicate ties.

	Ours	*Shakr*	*magisto*	*Magic-Info*
Aesthetic quality	**2nd rank***	1st rank	2nd rank*	4th rank
Attention capturing	**1st rank**	2nd rank	3rd rank	4th rank
Message deliverability	**1st rank**	2nd rank	4th rank	3rd rank
Preference	**1st rank***	1st rank*	4th rank	3rd rank

For **message deliverability**, a Friedman test showed a significant difference (χ^2 (3) = 273.41, p <.05). Our system ranked significantly better than any other services, especially in comparison with the second ranked *Shakr* (Z = 5.50, p <.05). Finally, for the **preference as a commercial film**, a significant difference was confirmed (χ^2 (3) = 121.96, p <.05). Our system ranked significantly better than *MagicInfo* (Z = 6.65, p <.05), but was not significantly different with *Shakr*.

In general, the performance of our system and *Shakr* were quite comparable, while *Shakr* has a competency in aesthetics and ours has strengths in message deliverability and promotional preference. Although it is hard to discriminate the effect of the key color generation method in the entire system, key colors may have a strong influence on the aesthetic quality and attention capturing rather than the message deliverability. In this regard, it seems like that the key color generation method requires an improvement in constructing an aesthetic harmony with a given visual content. This implication also resonates with the results of the method verification presented in section 4.3.2. For further investigation, we will explore established knowledge in computer vision, image processing and color theory, and will refine our key color generation method by adopting relevant methods.

5.2.2 *Experiment 2: Assessing Affective Quality*
The goal of the second experiment was to assess the performance of the video editing prototype in delivering a desired affective state. As shown in the Table 4, seven retails were targeted same as the first experiment and three different affective terms were tested for each retail. Accordingly, a total of 21 films was prepared using the video editing prototype. Figure 11 shows the exemplar scenes of fashion retail films. Although each film has used the same user-generated videos, key colors with different tones provide distinctive and satisfactory visuals for all three cases.

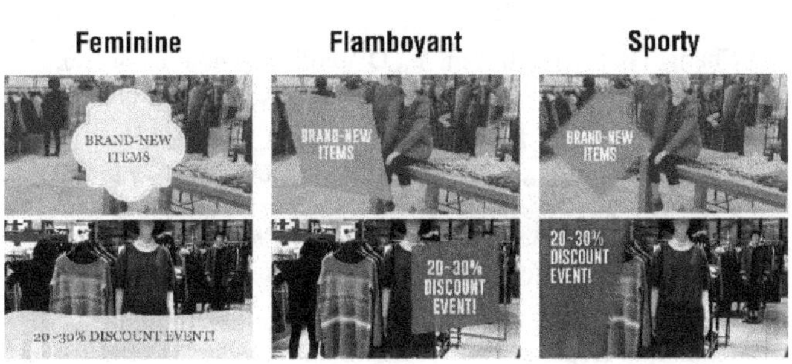

Figure 11. Example scenes from fashion retail films

Table 4. Pairs of retail-affective term for experiment 2. Highlighted cell indicates films that have expressed the target emotion successfully according to the assessment results.

Retail	Affective term		
Fashion	Feminine	Flamboyant	Sporty
Leisure	Enjoyable	Noble	Natural
Medical	Gentle	Trustworthy	*Modern*
Living	Classic	Dynamic	Tranquil
Restaurant	Traditional	*Modern*	Fresh
Performance	Elegant	Fiery	Progressive
Education	Cheerful	Free	Intellectual

5.2.2.1 *Procedure*
Each participant watched one of the 21 commercial films and asked to mark 2 ~ 4 keywords that describe the affective state or the style of the film. For each film, we provided a list of eight affective terms including a term that the film originally targeted. The affective terms were derived from the word set of Color Image Scale developed by Kobayashi [12]. This process was repeated for all 21 films.

5.2.2.2 *Results and Discussions*
We compared the participants' selection with the affective terms which were targeted originally. Among 630 trials (30 participant × 21 films), 553 were correct matches with the target emotions, that indicate 87.78% of agreement. We analyzed the responses for individual films as well. The frequency of selected words was calculated in order to identify the most frequently chosen word for each film. The results showed that 15 films successfully delivered the target emotion as the most appealed one. These films are highlighted in Table 4. In cases of four films, the target term was ranked as the second, and the remaining two films were better described by two other terms than the original one.

According to the results, it seems like that the prototype performs well in creating commercial films to deliver a desired emotion in general. However, the detailed analysis shows a possibility of confusions and misleading about the affective state the film wants to express. In particular, two films – *sporty* in fashion retail, *trustworthy* in medical retail – were not successful enough to deliver the target emotion.

There could be several reasons for this. First, certain contents may have a higher variability due to the subjectivity of people's perception on films and interpretation of keywords. In the perspective of key color generation, it implies a limitation of tone-match process. The method now uses colors crawled from Adobe Color CC®, and the collected dataset reflects the characteristics of a given affective term, but does not the context of retails. Hence, the tone of a key color defined by the dataset may not suitable to the context of a specific retail. In fact, the affective state *modern* was fully expressed in medical retail while it was not fully delivered in restaurant retail (Table 4). In addition, the amount of colors we used was quite limited and they were constrained in the Adobe Color CC® database. To improve the performance of tone-match process, more diverse data sources can be incorporated. We believe a context-specific tone match with a larger database might suggest a more persuasive tone of a key color.

6. DISCUSSIONS AND FUTURE WORK

We constructed an initial version of a key color generation method in order to create aesthetic and affective harmony between color and visual content. Two successive user tests revealed limitations of our method that should be resolved in the advanced study. The issues are summarized below for each step of the method individually. Not only the limitations, but we were also able to identify its potential in the practice of multimedia production. By addressing practical advantages we've brought, we locate our study in the growing body of knowledge in the multimedia discipline.

6.1 Improving Hue-Extraction Method

In computer vision and image processing discipline, a variety of color extraction algorithms have been developed and verified. By utilizing established knowledge of the field, we will fully considered the various color features that images possess. In addition to color features, contextual information will be considered in the future study. We noticed that similar colors can evoke distant feelings depending on the objects that each color represents. For instance, yellow from fruits was regarded as warm and tender, while the yellow from a New York taxi was rarely associated with warm and tender images. By incorporating the meanings and contexts of a given content, hue-extraction method could be strengthen in order to produce persuasive results for various contents. In addition, other types of images such as drawings and illustrations could be used for further investigation.

6.2 Elaborating Tone-match Method

For each keyword, the current method utilizes 200 colors from the searching results of Adobe Color CC® database. Although we selected these colors based on their ratings in the most recent database, there are several pitfalls that should be handled in the future study. First of all, 200 colors may not be enough to gratify the comprehensive needs and wants of users considering the diversity of colors and emotions that people pursue. Increasing the number of colors used can be a possible solution, but it also increases the amount of possible noises that crowd-sourced data innately has. Especially the data from Adobe Color CC® has possibilities of an internal dissonance, since there could be a discrepancy between the emotion of a color theme and the one of an individual color belongs to the theme. In order to maximize the benefits of a crowd-sourced data, we will firstly filter the database by employing acknowledged color emotion theories and increase the number of colors that to be used for the tone-match step. In addition, real-time data crawling could leverage the advantages of a crowd-sourced database, which is susceptible to changes and adjustments. Moreover, each affective term can be interpreted differently depending on the contexts, retails and events the term is used for. Context-specific color searching process can enhance the congruency between desired emotion and retrieved colors.

6.3 Implications on Multimedia Production

Contrary to previous color extraction studies, our key color generation method can generate colors beyond the color features of a given images due to the tone-match. This feature makes our method novel and be capable of generating creative color solutions. We believe that this feature could bring not only a wider range of alternatives but also unexpected insights to designers in the multimedia discipline. Our key color generation method also showed a possible extensibility across content types. Although it has developed based on image database, it generates acceptable solutions with videos. This implies the compatibility of a key color generation method with various visual contents. As a starting point, we hope that this paper inspires localized works in diverse multimedia domains to fully enjoy the aesthetic and affective effects of colors. Lastly, a versatility of crowd-sourced data was introduced in multimedia production. The tone-match algorithm highly depends on the external databases constructed by crowds. By employing the knowledge of crowd-sourced data, the method has a dynamic and evolving properties that respond to the situations, trends and even to target users. For future investigation, utilization of social data can be a possible direction to suggest a customized solution for each user.

7. CONCLUSIONS

In this study, we proposed a key color generation method to construct an aesthetic and affective harmony between color and visual content. Inspired from the color selection process of designers, our method is composed of two steps including *hue-extraction* and *tone-match*. With a given image and an affective term, a key color was generated by combining a dominant hue of an image and a specific tone defined by the affective term. To identify the most dominant hue of an image, K-means clustering was devised due to its simplicity that supports a quick and easy embodiment of the initial concept of *hue-extraction* method. The second step *tone-match* defines saturation and brightness values of the dominant hue by identifying the prevalent tone of colors among color themes related to a specific emotion. A crowd-sourced database was utilized in this step, which comprises approximately 45,000 color themes with respective names that describe characteristics of each theme. Since a key color has a tone independent of a given image, the key color by our method possesses an eccentric but creative feature beyond the color features of the image. This specificity differentiates our method with previous studies related to color extraction.

The key color generation method was examined through two user tests. The prior test aimed at comparing the performance of our method with the ability of designers. The later one weighed our method in a more complex situation – video editing tasks – against existing video editing tools. The results of both tests indicated that our method is good at generating affective key colors while aesthetic performance is needed to be refined further. As the first attempt to bring the strategy of designers into a computational method, we believe that this study can broaden the design space in multimedia production by promoting creative and affective color usages.

8. REFERENCES

[1] Adams, F. M., and Osgood, C. E. 1973. A cross-cultural study of the affective meanings of color. *Journal of cross-cultural psychology.* 4, 2, 135-156.

[2] Chang, H., Fried, O., Liu, Y., DiVerdi, S., and Finkelstein, A. 2015. Palette-based photo recoloring. *ACM Transactions on Graphics (TOG).* 34, 4, 139.

[3] Choi, J.-H., and Lee, J.-S. (2015. *Automated Video Editing for Aesthetic Quality Improvement.* Paper presented at the Proceedings of the 23rd Annual ACM Conference on Multimedia Conference.

[4] Gao, X. P., and Xin, J. H. 2006. Investigation of human's emotional responses on colors. *Color Research & Application.* 31, 5, 411-417.

[5] Goethe, J. v. W. 1971. *Goethe's Color Theory* (Matthei, R., Trans.). New York. Van Nostrand Reinhold.

[6] Hsiao, S. W., and Tsai, C. J. 2014. Transforming the natural colors of an image into product design: A computer-aided color planning system based on fuzzy pattern recognition. *Color Research & Application.*

[7] Hu, G., Pan, Z., Zhang, M., Chen, D., Yang, W., and Chen, J. 2014. An interactive method for generating harmonious color schemes. *Color Research & Application.* 39, 1, 70-78.

[8] Hu, Y.-C., and Lee, M.-G. 2007. K-means-based color palette design scheme with the use of stable flags. *Journal of Electronic Imaging.* 16, 3, 033003.

[9] Huang, C., Liu, Q., and Yu, S. 2011. Regions of interest extraction from color image based on visual saliency. *The Journal of Supercomputing.* 58, 1, 20-33.

[10] Itten, J. 1961. *The Art of Color; The Subjective Experience and Objective Rationale of Color* (Hagen, E.V., Trans.). New York. Ernst Van Hagen.

[11] Kobayashi, S. 1981. The aim and method of the color image scale. *Color Research & Application.* 6, 2, 93-107.

[12] Kobayashi, S. 1991. *Color image scale.* Kodansha Amer Incorporated.

[13] Kyprianidis, J. E., and Döllner, J. (2008. *Image Abstraction by Structure Adaptive Filtering.* Paper presented at the TPCG.

[14] Lin, S., and Hanrahan, P. (2013. *Modeling how people extract color themes from images.* Paper presented at the SIGCHI Conference on Human Factors in Computing Systems.

[15] Liu, S., and Luo, H. 2015. Hierarchical emotional color theme extraction. *Color Research & Application.*

[16] Liu, Z., Le Meur, O., Luo, S., and Shen, L. 2013. Saliency detection using regional histograms. *Optics letters.* 38, 5, 700-702.

[17] Ma, Z., Qing, L., Miao, J., and Chen, X. (2009. *Advertisement evaluation using visual saliency based on foveated image.* Paper presented at the Multimedia and Expo, 2009. ICME 2009. IEEE International Conference on.

[18] Meier, B. J., Spalter, A. M., and Karelitz, D. B. 2004. Interactive color palette tools. *Computer Graphics and Applications, IEEE.* 24, 3, 64-72.

[19] Moon, P., and Spencer, D. E. 1944. Aesthetic measure applied to color harmony. *JOSA.* 34, 4, 234-242.

[20] Moorthy, A. K., Obrador, P., and Oliver, N. 2010. *Towards computational models of the visual aesthetic appeal of consumer videos.* Computer Vision–ECCV 2010. Springer. 1-14.

[21] Moretti, G., Lyons, P., and Marsland, S. 2013. Computational production of colour harmony. Part 1: A prototype colour harmonization tool. *Color Research & Application.* 38, 3, 203-217.

[22] Moretti, G., Marsland, S., and Lyons, P. 2013. Computational production of colour harmony. Part 2: Experimental evaluation of a tool for gui colour scheme creation. *Color Research & Application.* 38, 3, 218-228.

[23] Munsell, A. H., and Birren, F. 1969. *A grammar of color.* Van Nostrand Reinhold.

[24] Nagai, Y., Uchida, Y., Myodo, E., and Sakazawa, S. (2013. *A color transformation method based on color theme that takes constraints on color ratio and spatial coherence into consideration.* Paper presented at the 2013 IEEE International Conference on Image Processing (ICIP).

[25] Niu, Y., and Liu, F. 2012. What makes a professional video? a computational aesthetics approach. *Circuits and Systems for Video Technology, IEEE Transactions on.* 22, 7, 1037-1049.

[26] Osgood, C. E., Suci, G. J., and Tannenbaum, P. H. 1957. *The measurement of meaning.* Urbana, USA. University of Illinois Press.

[27] Ou, L. C., Luo, M. R., Woodcock, A., and Wright, A. 2004. A study of colour emotion and colour preference. Part I: Colour emotions for single colours. *Color Research & Application.* 29, 3, 232-240.

[28] Ou, L. C., Luo, M. R., Woodcock, A., and Wright, A. 2004. A study of colour emotion and colour preference. part II: colour emotions for two-colour combinations. *Color Research & Application.* 29, 4, 292-298.

[29] Pawlowski, D. R., Badzinski, D. M., and Mitchell, N. 1998. Effects of metaphors on children's comprehension and perception of print advertisements. *Journal of Advertising.* 27, 2, 83-98.

[30] Plutchik, R. 1980. *Emotion: A psychoevolutionary synthesis.* Harpercollins College Division.

[31] Russell, J. A. 1980. A circumplex model of affect. *Journal of personality and social psychology.* 39, 6, 1161.

[32] Shin, Y., and Kim, E. Y. (2010. *Affective prediction in photographic images using probabilistic affective model.* Paper presented at the ACM International Conference on Image and Video Retrieval.

[33] Siang Tan, K., and Mat Isa, N. A. 2011. Color image segmentation using histogram thresholding–Fuzzy C-means hybrid approach. *Pattern Recognition.* 44, 1, 1-15.

[34] Solli, M., and Lenz, R. (2010. *Color semantics for image indexing.* Paper presented at the Conference on Colour in Graphics, Imaging, and Vision.

[35] Suk, H. J., and Irtel, H. 2010. Emotional response to color across media. *Color Research & Application.* 35, 1, 64-77.

[36] Sulaiman, S. N., and Isa, N. A. M. 2010. Adaptive fuzzy-K-means clustering algorithm for image segmentation. *IEEE Transactions on Consumer Electronics.* 56, 4, 2661-2668.

[37] Sural, S., Qian, G., and Pramanik, S. (2002. *Segmentation and histogram generation using the HSV color space for image retrieval.* Paper presented at the 2002 IEEE International Conference on Image Processing (ICIP).

[38] Valdez, P., and Mehrabian, A. 1994. Effects of color on emotions. *Journal of Experimental Psychology: General.* 123, 4, 394.

[39] Wang, B., Yu, Y., Wong, T.-T., Chen, C., and Xu, Y.-Q. (2010. *Data-driven image color theme enhancement.* Paper presented at the ACM Transactions on Graphics (TOG).

[40] Wang, X., Jia, J., and Cai, L. 2013. Affective image adjustment with a single word. *The Visual Computer.* 29, 11, 1121-1133.

[41] Wright, B., and Rainwater, L. 1962. The meanings of color. *The Journal of General Psychology.* 67, 1, 89-99.

Academic Coupled Dictionary Learning for Sketch-based Image Retrieval

Dan Xu[♯], Xavier Alameda-Pineda[♯], Jingkuan Song[♯], Elisa Ricci[‡], Nicu Sebe[♯]
[♯]Department of Information Engineering and Computer Science, University of Trento, Trento, Italy
[‡]Fondazione Bruno Kessler (FBK), Trento, Italy and University of Perugia, Perugia, Italy
{dan.xu, xavier.alamedapineda, jingkuan.song, niculae.sebe}@unitn.it,elisa.ricci@fbk.eu

ABSTRACT

In the last few years, the *query-by-visual-example* paradigm gained popularity, specially for content based retrieval systems. As sketches represent a natural way of expressing a synthetic query, recent research efforts focused on developing algorithmic solutions to address the sketch-based image retrieval (SBIR) problem. Within this context, we propose a novel approach for SBIR that, unlike previous methods, is able to exploit the visual complexity inherently present in sketches and images. We introduce academic learning, a paradigm in which the sample learning order is constructed both from the data, as in self-paced learning, and from partial curricula. We propose an instantiation of this paradigm within the framework of coupled dictionary learning to address the SBIR task. We also present an efficient algorithm to learn the dictionaries and the codes, and to pace the learning combining the reconstruction error, the prior knowledge suggested by the partial curricula and the cross-domain code coherence. In order to evaluate the proposed approach, we report an extensive experimental validation showing that the proposed method outperforms the state-of-the-art in coupled dictionary learning and in SBIR on three different publicly available datasets.

CCS Concepts

•Information systems → Retrieval models and ranking; Image search; •Computing methodologies → Machine learning;

Keywords

Sketch-based image retrieval; self-paced and curriculum learning; dictionary learning

1. INTRODUCTION

Favored by the widespread diffusion of consumer touchscreen devices, recently sketch-based image retrieval became popular as an effective means of querying large image databases. Most prior works on SBIR [12, 8, 27, 28, 9, 29] focused on designing robust feature representations, common for both sketches and images, to allow a direct matching. Typically such approaches involve three steps: (i) extract edges from images so to approximate the sketch, (ii) compute a bag-of-words representation [9] of the sketches and of the resulting edge maps and (iii) finally query by matching the sketch to the edge maps in the common feature space. The major issue with this strategy is that the features are not learned to satisfy the final objective, *i.e.*, robust matching, but hand-crafted in advance under the hypothesis that the statistical distributions of the extracted image edges and the sketch edges are the same. In addition, such strategy must use the same features for both image and sketch modalities, while intuitively different features could better represent different modalities. It is thus unsurprising that more recent studies proposed learning methods able to deal with different feature representations, thus partially addressing the limitations of the classical strategy. A series of approaches based on dictionary learning (DL) [19] was proven especially useful for learning coupled sparse representations [42, 36, 13] from data coming from different modalities.

In parallel, curriculum learning (CL) [3] and self-paced learning (SPL) [18] strategies, have proven to be advantageous for various tasks in computer vision and multimedia, such as object tracking [32], event detection [16] or multimedia search [15]. Both CL and SPL work by constructing a sample learning order that depends on the inherent data complexity, such as to increase the chances of the learner to avoid local minima. Intuitively, SBIR would also benefit from such strategies, since the visual complexity across samples varies significantly. Indeed, natural images are characterized by cluttered backgrounds and objects-of-interest captured at different scales or various poses. Similarly, the visual complexity of sketches drawn by expert/non-expert shows notorious variations. Both CL

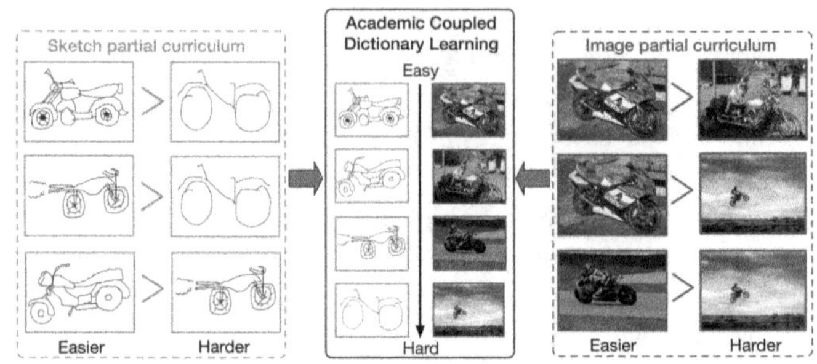

Figure 1: In real SBIR scenarios, humans can easily assess which of the images or sketches in a pair is easier to learn from, while providing a full order of the image/sketch set is chimeric. Academic coupled dictionary learning combines the flexibility of partial modality-specific curricula with the power of self-paced learning strategies to automatically construct a full sample learning order that evolves over time until all training samples are used to build a dictionary-based representation.

MM '16, October 15-19, 2016, Amsterdam, Netherlands

DOI: http://dx.doi.org/10.1145/2964284.2964329

and SPL aim to provide a sample learning order in which the easiest samples are presented first. However, while in CL the order is provided by an expert, in SPL the algorithm extracts the order from the data points typically based on the representation power of the model being learned. Recently, Jiang *et al.* [17] demonstrated the advantages of combining CL and SPL within the framework of dictionary learning. The authors model the given curriculum as a sort of a prior for the pacing variable. However, there are two main limitations in this approach. Firstly, data are assumed to come only from a single domain, and hence the method is not specifically designed for multimedia tasks such as SBIR. Secondly and more important, a full curriculum (*i.e.*, complete order) must be specified. This limits the applicability of the method to small-medium scale problems, since the curriculum is usually designed by humans. Moreover, in many tasks (*e.g.*, SBIR), assessing the easiness of each sample (*e.g.*, image or sketch) may not be straightforward, and thus full curricula are naturally inappropriate. Finally, full curriculum strategies are not appropriate either for continuously growing datasets, since each sample must be included into the full order and this process can be tedious and highly time-consuming.

To tackle the aforementioned issues, in this paper we present a novel learning paradigm and propose an instantiation within the framework of dictionary learning so to address the SBIR task. In academia, the students learn from different sources (textbooks, courses, on-line, etc) and, more importantly, no single full curriculum is available, but many different partial curricula (one per source). Indeed, the learning order suggested by the professor will be different from the order in which a textbook presents the concepts. In our model, instructors provide prior knowledge in the form of a partial order of samples, while leaving students the freedom to decide the full curriculum according to their learning pace. We formalize this intuition and introduce academic learning, where different partial curricula influence the learning pace (see Figure 1). More precisely, we address the SBIR task with an instantiation of academic learning within the framework of coupled dictionary learning, leading to *academic coupled dictionary learning* (ACDL). Intuitively, our method learns a pair of image- and sketch-specific dictionaries, together with the sparse codes, enforcing the similarity between the codes of corresponding sketches and images. At each iteration, the representation power of the learned dictionaries, the code correspondence and the partial modality-specific curricula determine which samples to learn from. We extensively evaluate ACDL on three publicly available datasets, demonstrating improved retrieval performance with respect to previous cross-domain dictionary learning methods and state-of-the art SBIR approaches.

To summarize, the main contributions of this paper are: (i) We introduce the academic learning paradigm, so to effectively merge the self-pacing philosophy with modality-specific partial curricula and propose an instantiation within the framework of coupled dictionary learning, leading to ACDL so as to address the SBIR task; (ii) We derive an efficient algorithm to learn the modality-specific dictionaries and codes, assessing the learning pace from the dictionary representation power, the code correspondence and the a priori partial order from the curricula; (iii) We report an extensive experimental evaluation proving that ACDL outperforms previous coupled dictionary learning methods and other state-of-the-art SBIR approaches in three different publicly available datasets.

2. RELATED WORK

In this section we describe related work on (i) the addressed task, SBIR, (ii) the ground learning framework, cross-domain DL and (iii) the closest learning paradigms to academic learning: SPL and curriculum learning.

2.1 Sketch-based image retrieval

Early works on SBIR attempted to use generic descriptors, *i.e.*, features not designed for this application. Both global (*e.g.*, distribution of edge pixels [6], elastic contours [4]) and local (*e.g.*, SIFT [9]) feature representations were investigated. More recently, SBIR methods focused on designing *ad hoc* descriptors, *i.e.*, features able to properly describe sketches, which are sparse images containing strokes. For instance, Hu *et al.* [12] presented gradient field images and used them in combination with a bag-of-words approach for retrieving images from sketches. They also performed an extensive evaluation of these descriptors on a large dataset, named the Flickr15k dataset. Saavendra *et al.* [28] proposed a modified version of the HOG descriptor, called histogram of edge local orientations, to explicitly tackle the problem of sparsity arising when traditional HOG descriptors are applied to sketches. In [27] mid-level patterns called learned keyshapes were introduced for representing sketches. Sun *et al.* [31] described a large scale SBIR system based on features derived from edge pixels and Chamfer matching. Shape words features for SBIR were introduced in [38]. Lin *et al.* [22] proposed the 3D sub-query expansion approach: to improve the retrieval performance, 2D sketches are first converted into a 3D sketch model, which is then used to generate multi-view sketches acting as expanded sub-queries. Qi *et al.* [26] introduced a perceptual grouping framework to organize image edges into a meaningful structure and used it for generating human-like sketches useful for SBIR. Fine-grained SBIR was tackled in [21], where the emphasis is on modeling fine-grained characteristics of sketches to retrieve specific images within object categories, as opposite to traditional SBIR focusing on retrieving images of the same class. Cao *et al.* [5] introduced MindFinder, an interactive sketch-based image search engine where multimodal queries (sketch+text) are used for retrieval. A sketch-based system for manga image retrieval was described in [24]. However, none of these works proposed a cross-domain DL approach for SBIR.

2.2 Cross-domain dictionary learning

Dictionary learning approaches [19] have become popular in computer vision and multimedia, as they were shown to be effective in many tasks, such as image denoising [23] and video event detection [41]. When data from multiple domains are available, traditional DL approaches have been extended to benefit from the wealth of multimodal information. Yang *et al.* [42] proposed to learn a set of source-specific dictionaries from samples corresponding to different domains in a coupled fashion and applied it to image super-resolution. In [36] a semi-coupled DL scheme was introduced, where source-specific dictionaries were learned together with a mapping function which describes the intrinsic relationship between domains. Similarly, Huang and Wang [13] proposed a framework to simultaneously learn a pair of domain-specific dictionaries and the associated representations. Coupled DL approaches have been tested on the SBIR task both in [36] and [13]. Similarly, DL has been employed for other related tasks, *i.e.*, sketch-based 3D object retrieval [43] or sketch recognition [11]. However, none of these works considers the sample easiness while learning, *i.e.*, apply a SPL or a curriculum learning strategy, in order to construct robust representations.

2.3 Self-paced and curriculum learning

Self-paced [18] and curriculum [3] learning originate from the idea that models must be learned in an incremental fashion, using the easy samples before the difficult ones. Due to their generality, these techniques have been considered in a broad spectrum of learning algorithms, including matrix factorization [45, 17], clus-

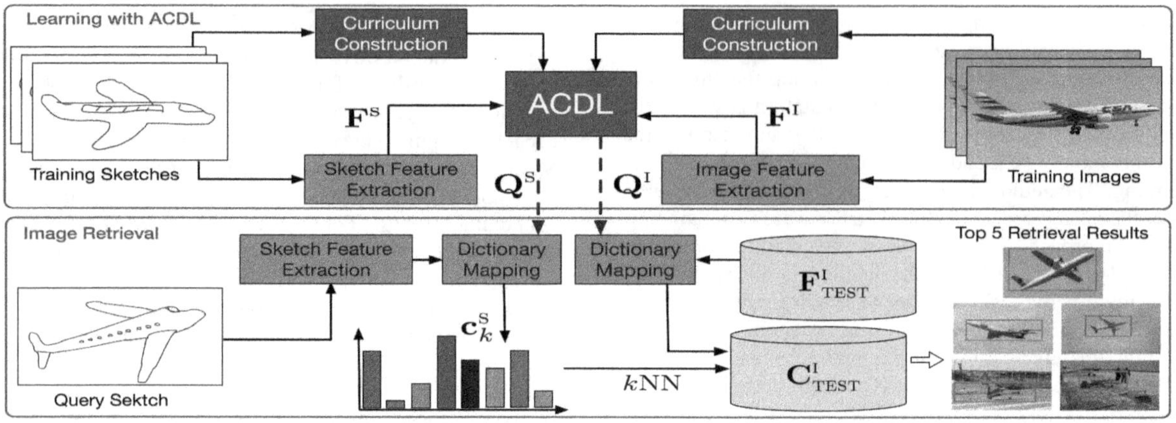

Figure 2: Overview of the proposed ACDL framework for sketch-based image retrieval.

tering [39], multi-task [25] and dictionary learning [34]. In the area of multimedia they have proved successful in many applications such as media retrieval [15] and event detection [16].

Among previous works, the two studies essentially related to this paper are [34] and [17]. While Tang *et al.* [34] proposed a SPL strategy in the context of dictionary learning, Jiang *et al.* [17] introduced the first hybrid full curriculum and SPL approach. However, none of them is able to handle data arising from multiple domains. Our approach does not only overcome this issue, but more importantly, is naturally able to incorporate domain specific partial curricula, thus benefiting from the wealth of information present in both domains. Moreover, opposite to [17] where the need to account for the difficulty of each training sample greatly limits the scalability of the method, in ACDL the adoption of partial curricula permits to tackle large scale problems.

3. ACADEMIC COUPLED DICTIONARY LEARNING FOR SBIR

As discussed in Section 1, in this paper we introduce the academic learning paradigm and instantiate it within the framework of coupled DL so to address SBIR. The proposed approach is articulated in two phases (see Figure 2). In the learning phase, the features extracted from the given set of images and corresponding sketches are fed into the ACDL method that learns the image and sketch-specific dictionaries together with the associated codes, taking into account the modality-specific partial curricula. At retrieval time, the representation of a sketch is computed by projecting its feature vector to the learned code. Image retrieval is performed by searching for the closet image code (in the Euclidean sense) to the given sketch code. In the following we present the proposed ACDL method (Section 3.1), its solver (Section 3.2), along with the technique we use for generating curricula (Section 3.3).

3.1 Academic Coupled Dictionary Learning

Let us assume the existence of K sketches and denote the features extracted from the k-th sketch as $\mathbf{f}_k^{\mathrm{S}} \in \mathbb{R}^{d_{\mathrm{S}}}$. Similarly, we assume the existence of L images and denote the features extracted from the l-th image as $\mathbf{f}_l^{\mathrm{I}} \in \mathbb{R}^{d_{\mathrm{I}}}$. We also assume two N-word dictionaries, one per modality: $\mathbf{Q}^{\mathrm{S}} = [\mathbf{q}_n^{\mathrm{S}}]_{n=1}^{N} \in \mathbb{R}^{d_{\mathrm{S}} \times N}$ and $\mathbf{Q}^{\mathrm{I}} = [\mathbf{q}_n^{\mathrm{I}}]_{n=1}^{N} \in \mathbb{R}^{d_{\mathrm{I}} \times N}$. Each sketch (resp. image) corresponds to a sparse code $\mathbf{c}_k^{\mathrm{S}} \in \mathbb{R}^{N}$ (resp. $\mathbf{c}_l^{\mathrm{I}} \in \mathbb{R}^{N}$). We also define $\mathbf{F}^{\mathrm{S}} = [\mathbf{f}_1^{\mathrm{S}}, \ldots, \mathbf{f}_K^{\mathrm{S}}] \in \mathbb{R}^{d_{\mathrm{S}} \times K}$ as the matrix of all sketch features, and $\mathbf{F}^{\mathrm{I}}$, $\mathbf{C}^{\mathrm{S}}$ and $\mathbf{C}^{\mathrm{I}}$ analogously. Given the feature matrices $\mathbf{F}^{\mathrm{S}}$ and $\mathbf{F}^{\mathrm{I}}$, we propose to compute the associated dictionaries and codes by minimizing the following dictionary representation (DR) loss:

$$\begin{aligned} \min_{\mathbf{Q}^{\mathrm{S}},\mathbf{Q}^{\mathrm{I}},\mathbf{C}^{\mathrm{S}},\mathbf{C}^{\mathrm{I}}} \ell_{\mathrm{DR}} = \quad & \|\mathbf{F}^{\mathrm{S}} - \mathbf{Q}^{\mathrm{S}}\mathbf{C}^{\mathrm{S}}\|_{\mathcal{F}}^2 + \|\mathbf{F}^{\mathrm{I}} - \mathbf{Q}^{\mathrm{I}}\mathbf{C}^{\mathrm{I}}\|_{\mathcal{F}}^2 \\ & + \alpha\left(\|\mathbf{C}^{\mathrm{S}}\|_1 + \|\mathbf{C}^{\mathrm{I}}\|_1\right), \\ \text{s.t.} \quad & \|\mathbf{q}_n^{\mathrm{S}}\|, \|\mathbf{q}_n^{\mathrm{I}}\| \leq 1 \quad \forall n, \end{aligned} \tag{1}$$

where $\alpha \geq 0$ is a regularization parameter and $\|\cdot\|_{\mathcal{F}}$ denotes the Frobenius norm. The constraints remove any scale ambiguities due to the matrix products $\mathbf{Q}^{\mathrm{S}}\mathbf{C}^{\mathrm{S}}$ and $\mathbf{Q}^{\mathrm{I}}\mathbf{C}^{\mathrm{I}}$, while the regularization terms induce sparsity in the learned codes.

We also assume a relational link between sketches and images in the training set. Ideally, each sketch corresponds to at least an image (*e.g.*, for sketch to photo face recognition [37] in the context of security and biometrics applications). Alternatively, the association among sketches and images is derived from image class information [12]. Generally speaking, in this paper we consider both intra-modality and cross-modality relationships, modeled by a non-negative weight matrix $\mathbf{W} \in \mathbb{R}^{+(K+L)\times(K+L)}$. Intuitively, the larger w_{pq} is, the stronger the relationship between the p-th and q-th codes is. Importantly, when $1 \leq p,q \leq K$ (respectively, $K < p,q \leq K+L$), w_{pq} relates two sketches (respectively, two images) creating an intra-modality link, otherwise w_{pq} relates a sketch and an image (cross-modality link). Interpreting $\mathbf{W}$ as the weight matrix of a graph and denoting the associated Laplacian matrix[1] by $\mathbf{L}$, the code-coupling (CC) loss is defined as:

$$\ell_{\mathrm{CC}} = \beta\,\mathrm{Tr}\left(\mathbf{C}^{\mathrm{J}}\mathbf{L}\mathbf{C}^{\mathrm{J}\top}\right) = \frac{1}{2}\beta \sum_{p,q=1}^{K+L} w_{pq}\|\mathbf{c}_p^{\mathrm{J}} - \mathbf{c}_q^{\mathrm{J}}\|^2, \tag{2}$$

where $\mathbf{C}^{\mathrm{J}} = [\mathbf{c}_p^{\mathrm{J}}]_{p=1}^{K+L} = [\mathbf{C}^{\mathrm{S}}\,\mathbf{C}^{\mathrm{I}}] \in \mathbb{R}^{N\times(K+L)}$ is the joint code matrix, and $\beta \geq 0$ is a regularization parameter controlling the importance of the relational knowledge.

As already mentioned in the introduction, and inspired by previous works [18, 16], we embrace the philosophy of SP learning in which there is a pacing binary variable $v_k^{\mathrm{S}} \in \{0,1\}$ (respectively $v_l^{\mathrm{I}} \in \{0,1\}$) associated to sketch k (respectively to image l), indicating whether the observation (sketch or image) has to be used for learning or not. Importantly, v_k^{S} and v_l^{I} are not fixed and evolve during the training phase. Additionally, we relax the binary condition and v_k^{S} and v_l^{I} become real numbers $v_k^{\mathrm{S}}, v_l^{\mathrm{I}} \in [0,1]$ since this strategy has proven to be successful in several applications [45, 17]. By defining $\mathbf{V}^{\mathrm{S}} = \mathrm{diag}_k(v_k^{\mathrm{S}}) \in \mathbb{R}^{K\times K}$ as a diagonal matrix with entries $v_1^{\mathrm{S}}, \ldots, v_K^{\mathrm{S}}$, $\mathbf{V}^{\mathrm{I}}$ analogously to $\mathbf{V}^{\mathrm{S}}$, and $\mathbf{V}^{\mathrm{J}} = \mathrm{diag}(\mathbf{V}^{\mathrm{S}}, \mathbf{V}^{\mathrm{I}})$,

[1]The Laplacian matrix of a graph with weight matrix $\mathbf{W}$ is defined as $\mathbf{L} = \mathbf{D} - \mathbf{W}$, where $\mathbf{D}$ is a diagonal matrix with $d_{pp} = \sum_q w_{pq}$.

we rewrite ℓ_{DR} and ℓ_{CC}:

$$\ell_{\text{DR}}(\mathbf{Q}^{\text{S}}, \mathbf{Q}^{\text{I}}, \mathbf{C}^{\text{J}}, \mathbf{V}^{\text{J}}) := \|(\mathbf{F}^{\text{S}} - \mathbf{Q}^{\text{S}}\mathbf{C}^{\text{S}})\mathbf{V}^{\text{S}}\|_{\mathcal{F}}^2 + \|(\mathbf{F}^{\text{I}} - \mathbf{Q}^{\text{I}}\mathbf{C}^{\text{I}})\mathbf{V}^{\text{I}}\|_{\mathcal{F}}^2 + \alpha\left(\|\mathbf{C}^{\text{S}}\|_1 + \|\mathbf{C}^{\text{I}}\|_1\right), \quad (3)$$

$$\ell_{\text{CC}}(\mathbf{C}^{\text{J}}, \mathbf{V}^{\text{J}}) := \beta \operatorname{Tr}\left(\mathbf{C}^{\text{J}}\mathbf{V}^{\text{J}}\mathbf{L}\mathbf{V}^{\text{J}\top}\mathbf{C}^{\text{J}\top}\right). \quad (4)$$

Classically, and in order to avoid trivial solutions (*i.e.*, all v's set to zero) a self-paced regularizer is used:

$$r_{\text{SP}}(\mathbf{V}^{\text{J}}) = \nu\left(\frac{1}{2}\sum_{k=1}^{K}\gamma(v_k^{\text{S}}) + \frac{1}{2}\sum_{l=1}^{L}\gamma(v_l^{\text{I}})\right) \quad (5)$$

where $\gamma(v) = v^2 - 2v$, as in [45], and $\nu \geq 0$ is the self-paced parameter that increases at each iteration as in traditional SPL methods [18]. By further considering the code-coupling loss and the self-paced regularizer, the optimization problem (1) rewrites:

$$\begin{aligned}\min_{\mathbf{Q}^{\text{S}},\mathbf{Q}^{\text{I}},\mathbf{C}^{\text{J}},\mathbf{V}^{\text{J}}} \quad & \ell_{\text{DR}}(\mathbf{Q}^{\text{S}}, \mathbf{Q}^{\text{I}}, \mathbf{C}^{\text{J}}, \mathbf{V}^{\text{J}}) + \ell_{\text{CC}}(\mathbf{C}^{\text{J}}, \mathbf{V}^{\text{J}}) - r_{\text{SP}}(\mathbf{V}^{\text{J}}) \\ \text{s.t.} \quad & \|\mathbf{q}_n^{\text{S}}\|, \|\mathbf{q}_n^{\text{I}}\| \leq 1 \quad \forall n, \\ & 0 \leq v_k^{\text{S}}, v_l^{\text{I}} \leq 1 \quad \forall k, l\end{aligned}$$

The major methodological contribution of our work is to include per-modality partial curricula into the framework of DL with relational knowledge and to study its behavior within the SPL strategy already discussed. Subsequently, we assume the existence of two per-modality sets of constraints $\mathcal{C}^{\text{S}}$ and $\mathcal{C}^{\text{I}}$. Each element of the sets consists of an index pair meaning that if $(k, k') \in \mathcal{C}^{\text{S}}$, then $v_k^{\text{S}} < v_{k'}^{\text{S}}$ and learning should be performed considering a priori $\mathbf{f}_{k'}^{\text{S}}$ before $\mathbf{f}_k^{\text{S}}$, as it corresponds to an easier sample. Depending on the way the curricula are constructed $\mathcal{C}^{\text{S}}$ could contain incompatibilities, for instance, $\{(k, k'), (k', k''), (k'', k)\} \subset \mathcal{C}^{\text{S}}$. In addition, the cross-modal terms could also induce incompatibilities between the two modalities. Therefore, it is desirable to relax the constraints using a set of slack variables $\xi_{kk'}^{\text{S}}$ and $\xi_{ll'}^{\text{I}}$. In all, the optimization problem for *academic coupled dictionary learning* writes:

$$\begin{aligned}\min_{\mathbf{Q}^{\text{S}},\mathbf{Q}^{\text{I}},\mathbf{C}^{\text{J}},\mathbf{V}^{\text{J}},\boldsymbol{\xi}^{\text{J}}} \quad & \ell_{\text{DR}}(\mathbf{Q}^{\text{S}}, \mathbf{Q}^{\text{I}}, \mathbf{C}^{\text{J}}, \mathbf{V}^{\text{J}}) + \ell_{\text{CC}}(\mathbf{C}^{\text{J}}, \mathbf{V}^{\text{J}}) \\ & - r_{\text{SP}}(\mathbf{V}^{\text{J}}) + r_{\text{PC}}(\boldsymbol{\xi}^{\text{J}}) \qquad (6) \\ \text{s.t.} \quad & \|\mathbf{q}_n^{\text{S}}\|, \|\mathbf{q}_n^{\text{I}}\| \leq 1 \quad \forall n, \\ & 0 \leq v_k^{\text{S}}, v_l^{\text{I}} \leq 1 \quad \forall k, l \\ & v_k^{\text{S}} - v_{k'}^{\text{S}} < \xi_{kk'}^{\text{S}}, \ \xi_{kk'}^{\text{S}} \geq 0, \ \forall (k, k') \in \mathcal{C}^{\text{S}} \\ & v_l^{\text{I}} - v_{l'}^{\text{I}} < \xi_{ll'}^{\text{I}}, \ \xi_{ll'}^{\text{I}} \geq 0, \ \forall (l, l') \in \mathcal{C}^{\text{I}},\end{aligned}$$

where $\boldsymbol{\xi}^{\text{J}} = [[\xi_{kk'}^{\text{S}}]_{(k,k')\in\mathcal{C}^{\text{S}}} [\xi_{ll'}^{\text{I}}]_{(l,l')\in\mathcal{C}^{\text{I}}}]$ is the vector of all slack variables and r_{PC} is the partial curricula regularizer regulated by the parameter $\gamma \geq 0$ and defined as:

$$r_{\text{PC}}(\boldsymbol{\xi}^{\text{J}}) = \gamma\left(\sum_{(k,k')\in\mathcal{C}^{\text{S}}} \xi_{kk'}^{\text{S}} + \sum_{(l,l')\in\mathcal{C}^{\text{I}}} \xi_{ll'}^{\text{I}}\right). \quad (7)$$

The algorithm we propose to solve (6) is outlined in Algorithm 1 and detailed in the following section.

3.2 Solving ACDL

The ACDL optimization problem is not jointly convex in all variables. However, efficient alternate optimization techniques can solve it since it is convex on $\{\mathbf{Q}^{\text{S}}, \mathbf{Q}^{\text{I}}\}$, $\{\mathbf{C}^{\text{J}}\}$ and $\{\mathbf{V}^{\text{J}}, \boldsymbol{\xi}^{\text{J}}\}$ when the other two sets of variables are fixed.

Algorithm 1 ACDL optimisation procedure.

Input: $\mathbf{F}^{\text{S}}$, $\mathbf{F}^{\text{I}}$ and the parameters α, β, γ.

Initialize $\mathbf{Q}^{\text{S}}$, $\mathbf{C}^{\text{S}}$, $\mathbf{Q}^{\text{I}}$, $\mathbf{C}^{\text{I}}$ as described in Section 4.
repeat
  Update $\mathbf{V}^{\text{J}}$ and $\boldsymbol{\xi}^{\text{J}}$ following (12);
  Update $\mathbf{C}^{\text{S}}$, $\mathbf{C}^{\text{I}}$ with (10);
  Update $\mathbf{Q}^{\text{S}}$, $\mathbf{Q}^{\text{I}}$ by solving (8);
  Increase ν so to enlarge the training set;
until All the training data points are selected.

Output: $\mathbf{Q}^{\text{S}}$, $\mathbf{C}^{\text{S}}$, $\mathbf{Q}^{\text{I}}$, $\mathbf{C}^{\text{I}}$.

Solve for $\mathbf{Q}^{\text{S}}$ and $\mathbf{Q}^{\text{I}}$. Fixing $\mathbf{C}^{\text{J}}$, $\mathbf{V}^{\text{J}}$ and $\boldsymbol{\xi}^{\text{J}}$, the optimization problem for $\mathbf{Q}^{\text{S}}$ (analogously for $\mathbf{Q}^{\text{I}}$) writes:

$$\min_{\mathbf{Q}^{\text{S}}} \left\|(\mathbf{F}^{\text{S}} - \mathbf{Q}^{\text{S}}\mathbf{C}^{\text{S}})\mathbf{V}^{\text{S}}\right\|_2^2 \quad \text{s.t.} \quad \left\|\mathbf{q}_k^{\text{S}}\right\| \leq 1. \quad (8)$$

This problem is a Quadratically Constrained Quadratic Program (QCQP) that can be solved using gradient descent with e.g. Lagrangian duality [19].

Solve for $\mathbf{C}^{\text{J}}$. By fixing $\mathbf{Q}^{\text{S}}$, $\mathbf{Q}^{\text{I}}$, $\mathbf{V}^{\text{J}}$ and $\boldsymbol{\xi}^{\text{J}}$ the optimization function for the codes can be rewritten as:

$$f(\mathbf{C}^{\text{J}}) = \left\|\left(\mathbf{F}^{\text{S}} - \mathbf{Q}^{\text{S}}\mathbf{C}^{\text{S}}\right)\mathbf{V}^{\text{S}}\right\|_{\mathcal{F}}^2 + \left\|\left(\mathbf{F}^{\text{I}} - \mathbf{Q}^{\text{I}}\mathbf{C}^{\text{I}}\right)\mathbf{V}^{\text{I}}\right\|_{\mathcal{F}}^2 + \alpha\left\|\mathbf{C}^{\text{J}}\right\|_1 + \beta \operatorname{Tr}\left(\mathbf{C}^{\text{J}}\mathbf{V}^{\text{J}}\mathbf{L}\mathbf{V}^{\text{J}\top}\mathbf{C}^{\text{J}\top}\right). \quad (9)$$

According to FISTA [2], f can be viewed as a proximal regularization problem, solved using the following recursion (over r):

$$\mathbf{C}_r^{\text{J}} = \operatorname*{argmin}_{\mathbf{C}^{\text{J}}}\left\{\frac{\|\mathbf{C}^{\text{J}} - \mathbf{C}_{r-1}^{\text{J}} + t_r \nabla f(\mathbf{C}_{r-1}^{\text{J}})\|_{\mathcal{F}}^2}{2t_r} + \alpha\left\|\mathbf{C}^{\text{J}}\right\|_1\right\}, \quad (10)$$

where $t_r > 0$ is the step size and $\nabla f(\mathbf{C}^{\text{J}}) = [\nabla f(\mathbf{C}^{\text{S}}) \ \nabla f(\mathbf{C}^{\text{I}})]$ is the concatenation of the two gradients defined as:

$$\nabla f(\mathbf{C}^{\text{S}}) = 2\mathbf{Q}^{\text{S}\top}(\mathbf{Q}^{\text{S}}\mathbf{C}^{\text{S}} - \mathbf{F}^{\text{S}})(\mathbf{V}^{\text{S}})^2 + 2\beta\left(\mathbf{C}^{\text{S}}\mathbf{V}^{\text{S}}\mathbf{L}^{\text{S}} + \mathbf{C}^{\text{I}}\mathbf{V}^{\text{I}}\mathbf{L}^{\text{IS}}\right)\mathbf{V}^{\text{S}}, \quad (11)$$

where the sublaplacian matrices are taken from the Laplacian matrix as $\mathbf{L} = [\mathbf{L}^{\text{S}}\,\mathbf{L}^{\text{SI}}; \mathbf{L}^{\text{IS}}\,\mathbf{L}^{\text{I}}]$. The second gradient, $\nabla f(\mathbf{C}^{\text{I}})$ is defined analogously to $\nabla f(\mathbf{C}^{\text{S}})$. Moreover, (10) is a standard LASSO problem whose optimal solution can be found using the feature-sign search algorithm in [19].

Solve for $\mathbf{V}^{\text{J}}$ and $\boldsymbol{\xi}^{\text{J}}$. By fixing the dictionaries $\mathbf{Q}^{\text{S}}$, $\mathbf{Q}^{\text{I}}$ and the codes $\mathbf{C}^{\text{J}}$, we can rewrite the joint optimization problem with respect to $\mathbf{V}^{\text{J}}$ and $\boldsymbol{\xi}^{\text{J}}$ as a quadratic programming problem with a set of linear inequality constraints. Denoting the optimization variable as $\mathbf{y} = [[v_k^{\text{S}}]_k [v_l^{\text{I}}]_l [\xi_{kk'}^{\text{S}}]_{kk'} [\xi_{ll'}^{\text{I}}]_{ll'}] \in \mathbb{R}^{K+L+C^{\text{S}}+C^{\text{I}}}$, the problem writes:

$$\begin{aligned}\min_{\mathbf{y}} \quad & \mathbf{y}^\top\mathbf{R}\mathbf{y} + \mathbf{b}^\top\mathbf{y} \\ \text{s.t.} \quad & \mathbf{G}\mathbf{y} \leq \mathbf{h},\end{aligned} \quad (12)$$

where the values of $\mathbf{R}$, $\mathbf{b}$, $\mathbf{G}$ and $\mathbf{h}$ are defined in the following. $\mathbf{R}$ is a $(K+L+C^{\text{S}}+C^{\text{I}}) \times (K+L+C^{\text{S}}+C^{\text{I}})$ matrix with all zeros except for the first $(K+L) \times (K+L)$ block. More precisely:

$$R_{pq} = \begin{cases} \|\mathbf{f}_p^{\text{S}} - \mathbf{Q}^{\text{S}}\mathbf{c}_p^{\text{S}}\|^2 - \nu/2 & q = p \leq K \\ \|\mathbf{f}_{p-K}^{\text{I}} - \mathbf{Q}^{\text{I}}\mathbf{c}_{p-K}^{\text{I}}\|^2 - \nu/2 & K < q = p \leq L + K \\ \beta w_{pq}\|\mathbf{c}_p^{\text{J}} - \mathbf{c}_q^{\text{J}}\|^2 & 1 \leq p \neq q \leq K + L \\ 0 & \text{otherwise} \end{cases}$$

and $\mathbf{b} = [\nu\mathbf{1}_{K+L}^\top \ \gamma\mathbf{1}_{C^{\text{S}}+C^{\text{I}}}^\top]^\top$, where $\mathbf{1}_K$ is a $K \times 1$ vector filled with ones. $\mathbf{G}$ and $\mathbf{h}$ represent the inequality and bound constraints in (6) and their derivation is straightforward. Since there are $2(K+L+C^{s}+C^{l})$ constraints, $\mathbf{G} \in \mathbb{R}^{2(K+L+C^{s}+C^{l})\times(K+L+C^{s}+C^{l})}$ and $\mathbf{h} \in \mathbb{R}^{2(K+L)+C^{s}+C^{l}}$.

3.3 Laplacian and Curricula Construction

In this section we describe how we construct the modality-specific curricula and the Laplacian matrix representing the relational knowledge. However, it is worth noting that ACDL is a general framework and other design choices are possible. We build both the curricula and the Laplacian in the training set from the sketch and image features and a group association, that could arise from the class membership or from unsupervised clustering. In our experiments, we also devised a protocol to construct a curriculum for sketches from human manual annotations.

3.3.1 Laplacian construction

To build the Laplacian matrix (computed from the weights w_{pq}), the intra-modality relationships are defined using the Gaussian kernel and the inter-modality with group association, as in [44]:

$$w_{pq} = \begin{cases} e^{-\|\mathbf{f}^{s}_{p}-\mathbf{f}^{s}_{q}\|_2^2/2\sigma^2}, & p,q \leq K \\ e^{-\|\mathbf{f}^{l}_{p-K}-\mathbf{f}^{l}_{q-K}\|_2^2/2\sigma^2}, & K < p,q \\ 1, & \begin{matrix} p \leq K < q \text{ and } p \sim q \\ q \leq K < p \text{ and } q \sim p \end{matrix} \\ 0, & \text{otherwise,} \end{cases} \tag{13}$$

where σ is the Gaussian kernel parameter fixed to 1 with no significant performance variation around this value. The symbol $\sim$ indicates samples belonging to the same cluster/class.

3.3.2 Curriculum construction

Regarding the curricula construction, as stated above, a fundamental aspect of the the proposed ACDL framework is the possibility to handle partial curricula. Previous CL or hybrid CL-SPL methods [3, 17] instead assume that a full curriculum, *i.e.* a complete order of samples, is provided. This is a strong assumption that may not be satisfied in real-world large-scale tasks. On the one hand, even if automatic measures of the easiness of an image [20] have been developed, these metrics are accurate up to some extent and therefore deriving a full ranking from these measures may be inappropriate. On the other hand, manually annotating the entire set of images represents a huge human workload, highly demanding for medium-scale problems and chimeric for large-scale datasets. In addition, if the multimedia dataset is gathered incrementally, the cost of updating the curriculum grows with the size of the dataset.

The partial curricula for the image domain is obtained by means of an automated procedure based on previous studies [20, 1]. Intuitively, easy images are those containing non-occluded high-resolution objects in low-cluttered background. Previous works [20] proposed to define the easiness of an image from the "objectness" measures [1]. In the same line of though, we compute the easiness measure as the median of the 30 highest "objectness" scores among a set of 1,000 window proposals. This procedure approximates the easiness of a training image. Notice that, two images with largely different scores are likely to correspond to samples with different easiness. On the contrary, if the scores are similar, imposing that the image with the lowest score is the easiest in the pair may induce some errors. The constraint associated to an image pair is included in $\mathcal{C}^{l}$ only if the difference of their associated scores exceeds a certain threshold δ^{l} (*i.e.* if one of the images in the pair is significantly easier than the other).

Contrary to the image domain, there is no widely-accepted procedure to define the easiness of a sketch. Therefore, we consider two methods for constructing the partial curriculum in the sketch

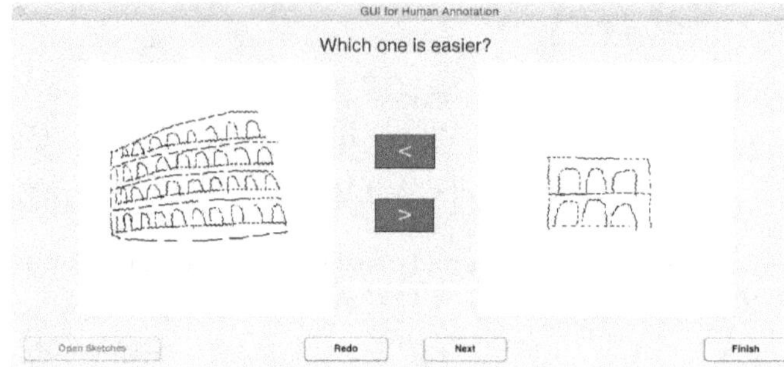

Figure 3: The graphical interface used for annotation. Easy sketches are those with more details and easy images are those with non-occluded high-resolution objects in low-cluttered background.

domain. First, an automatic method that follows again the philosophy of [1]. Given a sketch, we randomly sample 100 windows at different scales and positions. For each window we compute the "edgeness" score, representing the edge density within the window as proposed in [1]. Intuitively, the edgeness should implement the rationale that easy sketches are those with more details. As previously done for images, the constraint associated to a pair of sketches is included into $\mathcal{C}^{s}$ only if their measure of edgeness differs by at least δ^{s}. Second, a semi-automatic strategy for building the partial curricula of the sketches by including human annotators in the loop. A naive retrieval method based on SHOG features [9] generates potential constraints (pairs of sketches). In details, we pair each sketch with the closest among the cluster/class. The human annotator is then queried which sketch is easier to learn from. Ten PhD students (6 male, 4 female) of age 24.3 ± 1.4 (mean, standard deviation) performed the annotation after being instructed that "easy" sketches meant sketches with more details. Importantly, since ACDL is specifically designed to handle partial curricula, annotators had the possibility to "skip" sketch pairs if they were unable to decide. A simple GUI (Fig.3) was developed for annotation.

4. EXPERIMENTS

To evaluate the effectiveness of our approach, we conduct extensive experiments on three publicly available datasets: the CUHK Face Sketch (CUFS) [37], the Flickr15k [12] and the Queen-Mary SBIR [21]. In our experiments, the dictionaries of ACDL were initialized with joint DL [42] when both features have the same dimension and with modality-independent DL otherwise.

4.1 Experiments on CUFS

The CUFS dataset is a very popular benchmark for sketch-to-face-photo recognition. CUFS contains sketch-photo image pairs of 188 CUHK students. The recognition task is to identify the face photo corresponding to a given sketch. We evaluate the performance of ACDL on CUFS and compare it to other cross-domain retrieval methods and previous coupled DL approaches.

4.1.1 Settings

In our experiments, 88 sketch-photo image pairs are randomly selected for training the model, and the remaining 100 pairs are used for testing, as in [33]. To facilitate comparison with previous works [42, 13], we use raw pixels as features. We compare the proposed ACDL method to seven baseline methods: canonical correlation analysis (CCA), partial least squares (PLS) [30], bilinear model (Bil) [35], semi-coupled dictionary learning (SCDL) [36], joint dictionary learning (JDL) [42] and coupled dictionary learn-

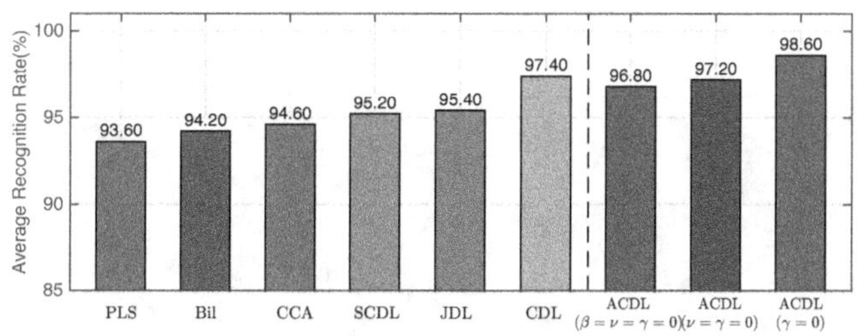

Figure 4: Average recognition rate for all methods on CUFS.

ing (CDL) [13]. For the bilinear model, we used 70 PLS bases and 50 eigenvectors (see [30]). ACDL, SCDL, JDL and CDL are all DL-based approaches and we set the dictionary size to 50. In all cases, the recognition is performed using the nearest neighbor on the newly learned sparse representation as in [30, 13]. For ACDL, we explicitly evaluate the importance of the relational knowledge (β) and of self-pacing (ν). Instead, as both images and sketches are quite homogeneous (*i.e.*, sketches were drawn by experts, faces in images are centered and equally illuminated), we did not use any curriculum ($\gamma = 0$), The parameters α, β were set by cross-validation to 1 and 5, respectively.

4.1.2 Results

Figure 4 reports average recognition results over five trials. ACDL($\gamma = 0$) achieves the best average recognition rate: 98.6%. Remarkably, ACDL($\gamma = 0$) outperforms CDL, which is the best of the DL-based approaches. Importantly, we notice that the effect of the relational knowledge is crucial in the performance of the overall method (CDL also uses relational knowledge). Among the compared methods, SCDL, JDL and CDL are the strongest competitors, achieving 95.2%, 95.4% and 97.4% recognition rate respectively. This means that DL for cross-modal retrieval is an effective strategy. We also remark that ACDL($\gamma = 0$) outperforms the other two versions of ACDL, suggesting that the relational knowledge within the SP learning framework is beneficial for accurate retrieval.

4.2 Experiments on Flickr15K

Flickr15k dataset is a widely used dataset for SBIR, containing around 14,660 images collected from Flickr and 330 free-hand sketches drawn by 10 non-expert sketchers. All samples are classified into 33 categories with a manual annotation for each sample. As this dataset does not provide a training set, to evaluate our approach, we partition the dataset into a training set with randomly chosen 40% samples and a test set with the remaining samples.[2]

4.2.1 Settings

We compare the retrieval performance of ACDL against several state of the art SBIR baselines, including SHOG [9] and SIFT, SSIM, GFHOG tested in [12], Structure Tensor [8], Learned Key Shapes (LKS) [27] and PerceptualEdge [26]. The first five baselines extract low-level features (SHOG, SIFT, SSIM, GFHOG and StructureTensor) over Canny edge maps (for images) and sketched images, and then use a bag-of-words (BOW) approach to obtain both image and sketch representations. LKS learns mid-level sketch patterns named keyshapes. The learned keyshapes are used to construct image and sketch descriptors. PerceptualEdge uses an edge grouping framework to create synthesized sketches from images. The retrieval is performed by querying the synthesized sketches instead of the images directly. For LKS and PerceptualEdge, we use the original codes provided by the authors with the same parameter setting described in the associated papers, and we reimplemented other baselines whose codes are not publicly available. All the methods are evaluated on the same test set for a fair comparison.

[2]Due to the random training/test splitting, performance may differ from results reported in previous studies. Our experimental protocol will be made publicly available.

Table 1: Flickr15K dataset: comparison of different methods.

Methods	mAP
StructureTensor [8]	0.0801
SIFT [12]	0.0967
SSIM [12]	0.1068
SHOG [9]	0.1152
GFHOG [12]	0.1245
LKS [27]	0.1640
PerceptualEdge [26]	0.1741
$\text{ACDL}_{\text{GFHOG}}$	0.1675
ACDL_{LKS} ($\gamma = \nu = 0$)	0.2278
ACDL_{LKS}	0.2495
$\text{ACDL}_{\text{CNN+LKS}}$	0.2656

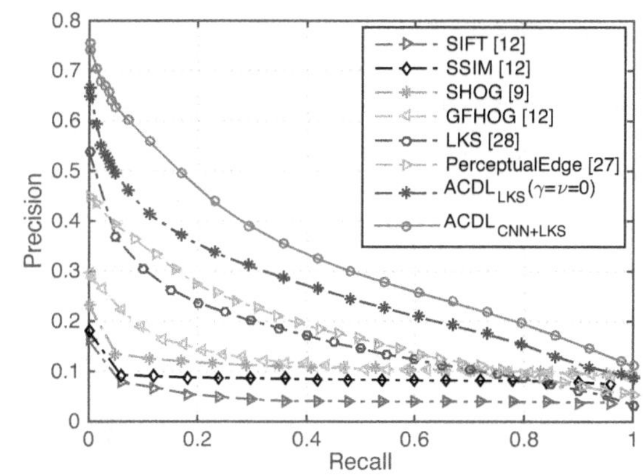

Figure 5: Precision recall curves of the different methods on Flirckr15K dataset.

We evaluate the proposed ACDL with different settings, including (i) $\text{ACDL}_{\text{GFHOG}}$: ACDL using GFHOG features for both image and sketch domains; (ii) ACDL_{LKS}, ($\gamma = \nu = 0$): ACDL without the curricula and self-pacing, using LKS features for both image and sketch domains; (iii) ACDL_{LKS}: ACDL using LKS features for both image and sketch domains; (iv) $\text{ACDL}_{\text{CNN+LKS}}$: ACDL using CNN features for image domain (*i.e.*, features extracted from the sixth layer of the Caffe reference network trained on ImageNet [14]) and LKS features for sketch domain. The sketch curriculum, when used, is constructed using 60% of human annotations, since we did not observe any significant differences between the automatic and the manual procedures (see Section 4.4). For all ACDL methods, we set α, β, γ with cross-validation and $N = 1000$.

4.2.2 Results

The quantitative SBIR performance comparison is shown in Table 1, reporting the mean average precision (mAP), and in Figure 5, depicting the precision-recall (PR) curve. We observe that $\text{ACDL}_{\text{CNN+LKS}}$ obtains the best mAP of 0.2656, which corresponds to a significant performance increase (7.13 points improvement) with respect to the best state-of-the-art method (0.1741 of PerceptualEdge [26]). The advantage of the academic learning paradigm and its instantiation under the framework of dictionary

Figure 6: Top 5 retrieval results with sample query sketches in the Flickr15K dataset. Red boxes show false positive retrievals.

Table 2: Benchmark on the Queen-Mary SBIR dataset.

Methods	mAP
SIFT [12]	0.0685
SSIM [12]	0.0745
SP-SHOG [8]	0.0804
SP-GFHOG [12]	0.0858
LKS [27]	0.1182
PerceptualEdge [26]	0.1246
ACDL_{LKS} ($\gamma = \nu = 0$)	0.1265
ACDL_{LKS}	0.1467
$\text{ACDL}_{\text{CNN+LKS}}$	0.1598

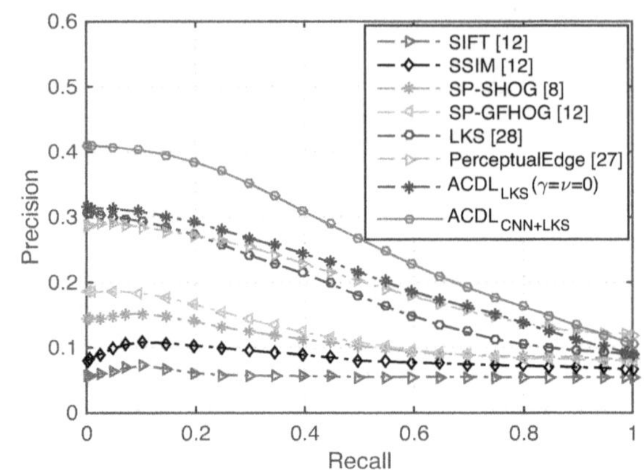

Figure 7: Precision recall curves of the different methods on Queen-Mary SBIR dataset.

learning is clear and independent of the features used. Indeed, $\text{ACDL}_{\text{GFHOG}}$ and ACDL_{LKS} compares favorably to GFHOG [12] and to LKS [27], with 4.3 points and 7.61 points improvement, respectively. Similarly, the clear performance gap when ACDL_{LKS} is compared to the ACDL_{LKS}, ($\gamma = \nu = 0$), demonstrates the usefulness of the combination of a variable pacing rate under the prior knowledge of multiple partial curricula. The fact that the best performance is obtained with $\text{ACDL}_{\text{CNN+LKS}}$ confirms our original intuition that different features can represent better the two different modalities. Finally, Figure 6 shows some qualitative results (top-five retrieved images) associated with the proposed method.

4.3 Experiments on Queen-Mary SBIR

The Queen-Mary SBIR dataset [21] contains 1,120 sketches and 7,267 images, built by intersecting 14 common categories from the Eitz 20,000 sketch dataset [7] and the PASCAL VOC dataset [10]. In this dataset, cluttered background conditions and significant scale variations greatly increase the complexity of the retrieval task. We use the given training and test set. While this dataset was conceived for fine-grained SBIR, since our task is category-level SBIR, we only use image-level category annotations.

4.3.1 Settings

We compare our approach to SIFT [12], SSIM [12], SP-SHOG [21], SP-GFHOG [12], LKS [27], PerceptualEdge [26]. SP-HOG and SP-GFHOG use a spatial pyramid model on SHOG and GFHOG features respectively to construct a new representation. The QueenMary SBIR dataset is designed for complex SBIR task, therefore we do not consider the weakest baselines (*i.e.*, StructureTensor) evaluated on Flickr15k dataset, and use SP-SHOG and SP-GFHOG instead of SHOG and GFHOG, as it has been demonstrated that the spatial pyramid model is able to obtain more robust image representations than BOW. We evaluate the proposed ACDL using the settings described in Section 4.2, *i.e.* ACDL_{LKS} ($\gamma = \nu = 0$), ACDL_{LKS} and $\text{ACDL}_{\text{CNN+LKS}}$, and the strategy for constructing the curricula. We set $N = 1000$ and cross-validate for the other parameters.

4.3.2 Results

From Table 2, we observe that the mAP of $\text{ACDL}_{\text{CNN+LKS}}$ is 0.1598, *i.e.*, 3.52 points better than the best of all the baselines, which is not a trivial improvement on this challenging dataset. $\text{ACDL}_{\text{CNN+LKS}}$ also outperforms ACDL_{LKS}, clearly demonstrating the effectiveness of using different descriptors for sketches and images in SBIR. We also believe that LKS features are not robust enough to represent objects with various poses and cluttered backgrounds, as in Queen-Mary SBIR dataset. ACDL_{LKS} obtains a clear improvement over ACDL_{LKS}, ($\mu = \gamma = 0$), further verifying the usefulness of the proposed learning scheme. Figure 7 depicts the PR curves of the different methods, confirming the findings so far. Additionally, Figure 8 shows the retrieval performance for each category-level task. We observe that for most of the classes (except for Airplane and Bicycle), $\text{ACDL}_{\text{CNN+LKS}}$ significantly outperforms all the baseline methods. Finally, Figure 9 reports the top 5 retrieval results of $\text{ACDL}_{\text{CNN+LKS}}$ for six sample query sketches.

4.4 In-depth analysis of ACDL

Finally, we provide some additional results and an empirical analysis (on the Flickr15k dataset) of the proposed approach regarding several aspects.

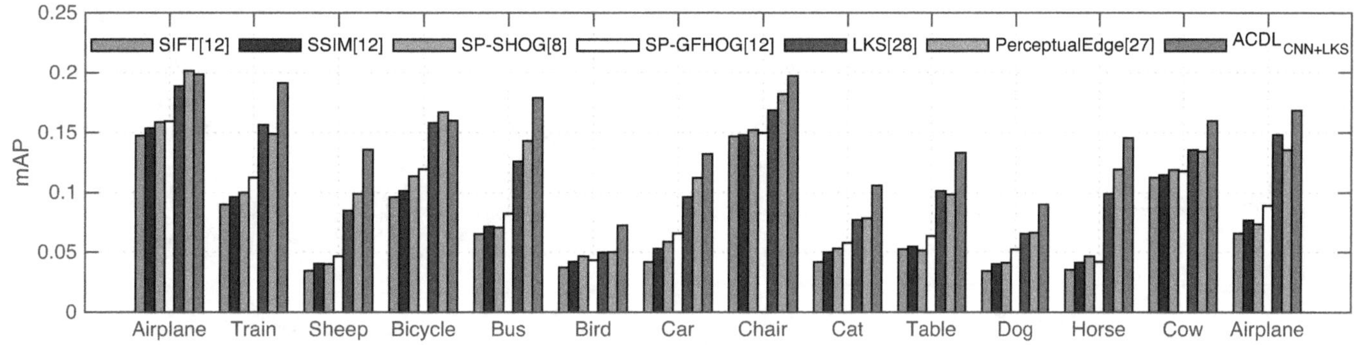

Figure 8: Retrieval performance comparison for each category on Queen-Mary SBIR dataset.

Figure 9: Top 5 retrieved images (2nd to 6th columns) using the query sketch samples (1st column) in the QueenMary SBIR dataset. Red boxes show false positive retrievals.

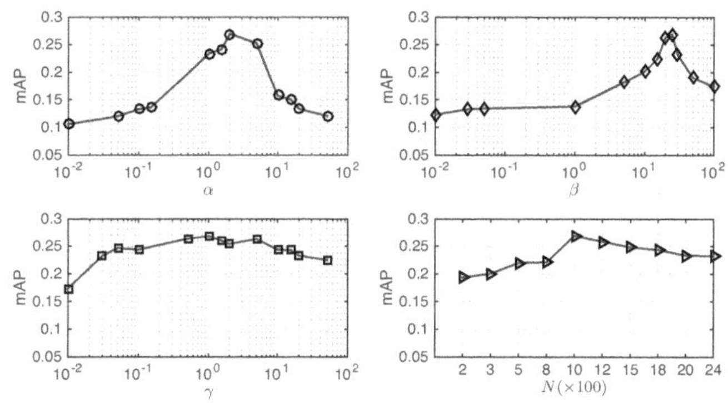

Figure 10: Empirical analysis of the model parameters: α, β, γ and the dictionary size N.

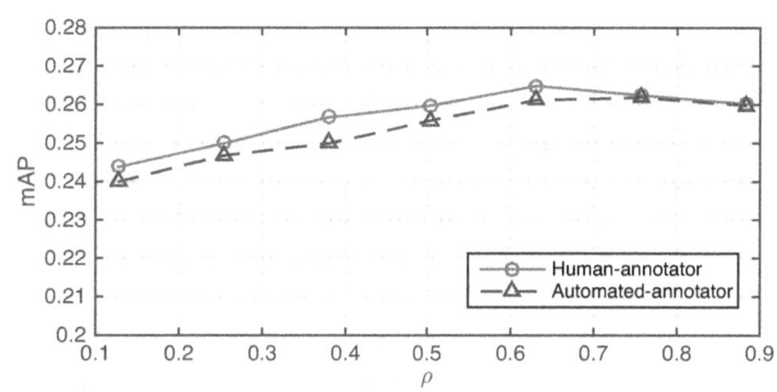

Figure 11: Performance of the automated and human-annotated sketch partial curricula.

4.4.1 *Sensitivity analysis*

In order to assess the influence of the different model parameters on ACDL retrieval performance, we report a sensitivity analysis around the working point. Figure 10 shows the mAP as a function of α, β, γ, N. The analysis on α, β and γ is in the range $[10^{-2}, 10^{2}]$, on N in the range $[200, 2400]$. The plots clearly show that, while the method is sensitive to α and β, its performance does not change drastically with a wide range of γ and N. The sensitivity on β was already found in the experiments on CUFS and by previous researchers [13].

4.4.2 *Analysis of curriculum construction*

In our approach, the human and the automated annotator can both be employed to construct the partial curricula. To investigate the difference in terms of the final retrieval performance, we plot the mAP as a function of ρ, the proportion of constraints used for the sketch curriculum relative to the number of possible constraints. The proportion of image constraints was set to 10% of all possible constraints. Figure 11 shows these two plots. While the human annotations build a more useful partial curricula, the differences when compared with the automated curricula constructions are tiny. Interestingly, the excess of constraints leads to a slight decrease in performance, which is an experimental finding that supports the use of partial curricula for SBIR.

4.4.3 *Convergence analysis*

Figure 12 plots the objective function value as a function of the iteration index for the proposed learning models ACDL and ACDL ($\gamma = \nu = 0$) for one of our experiments. These results clearly demonstrate the convergence of the proposed iterative optimization procedure. ACDL and ACDL ($\gamma = \nu = 0$) attain a stable solution within less than 40 iterations and 30 iterations respectively, proving the efficiency of the algorithm proposed to solve the ACDL optimization problem. It is worth noting that ACDL reaches a much lower local minima than ACDL ($\gamma = \nu = 0$) (6.8×10^4 vs. 1.98×10^5), verifying the beneficial effect of the proposed partial curriculum and self-paced learning scheme.

4.4.4 *Computational analysis*

To perform an empirical analysis of the computational overhead, we ran experiments on a PC with a quad core (2.1 GHz) CPU, 64GB RAM and an Nvidia Tesla K40 GPU. The proposed SBIR approach is implemented mostly in Matlab, and partially in C++

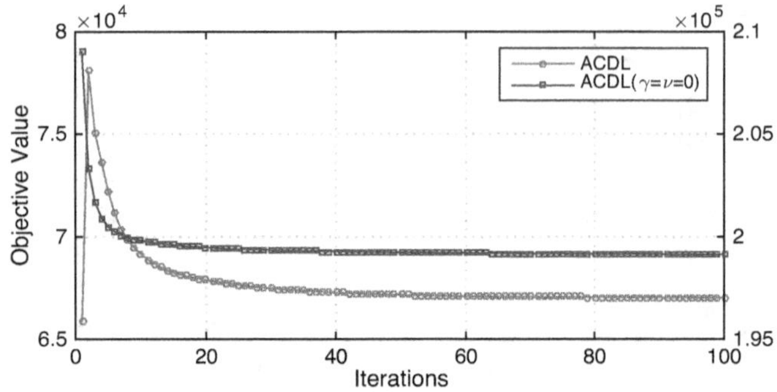

Figure 12: Convergence in terms of objective value: the left and right y axes show ACDL and ACDL($\gamma = \nu = 0$), respectively.

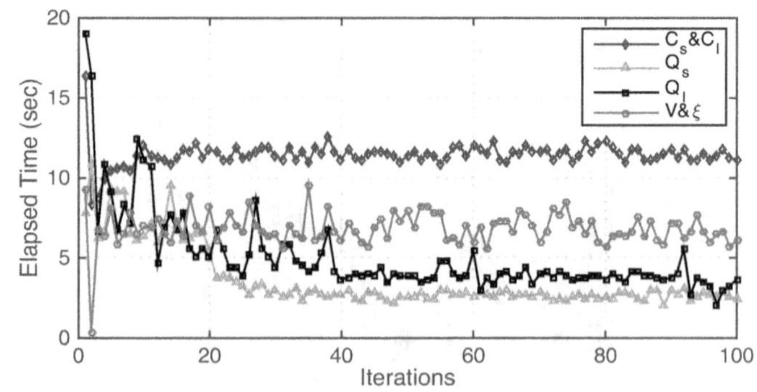

Figure 13: The elapsed time of updating four different components of each iteration in an ACDL training.

Table 3: Computational cost of the different training steps.

Phase	Component	Time overhead
Feature extraction	CNN (for images)	0.04 sec/sample
	LKS (for sketches)	1.1 sec/sample
Training	Curriculum Construction	8 min
	ACDL	27 min
	ACDL($\nu = \gamma = 0$)	21 min

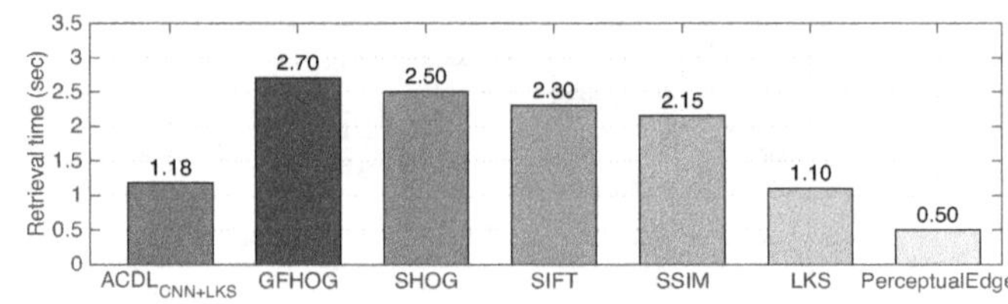

Figure 14: Comparison of average retrieval time.

(the most computationally expensive components). For LKS features [27], we use a C++ implementation, and wrap it to be called from Matlab. For CNN image features, the Caffe reference network pre-trained on ImageNet [14] is used to extract features from the sixth layer. In the following, we conduct the analysis from the off-line training phase and the on-line retrieval phase respectively.

Off-line retrieval time

The training phase of our method mainly contains three steps: (i) feature extraction, (ii) curriculum construction and (iii) ACDL optimization. Table 3 reports computational times of different components of the method. For the feature extraction, we consider CNN features from the image domain, which cost 0.04 seconds per image sample. The CNN image features are extracted with the GPU. LKS is used to extract features from the sketch domain, and obtains a speed of 1.1 seconds per sketch sample. The automated curriculum construction takes around 8 minutes, and training ACDL and ACDL ($\nu = \gamma = 0$) with 50 iterations cost 27 and 21 minutes, respectively.

Figure 13 shows elapsed times of updating $\mathbf{Q}_I$, $\mathbf{Q}_S$, $\mathbf{C}_I$ & $\mathbf{C}_S$ and $\mathbf{V}$ & ξ of each iteration within the model training. The input for ACDL is CNN features (for images) and LKS features (for sketches). 4833 and 132 are the number of training image and sketch samples, respectively. For curricula, we use the same strategy as in Section 4.2 (10% of image constraints and 60% of sketch constraints) as at this ratio the retrieval performance and the computational overhead reach good balance. The average elapsed times of these four components within the first 50 iterations are 6.5, 4.8, 12.1, 6.9 seconds, respectively. Updating $\mathbf{V}$ & ξ occupies only around 20% of the entire training time, demonstrating the reasonable computational efficiency of the proposed ACDL scheme.

On-line retrieval time

Online retrieval efficiency is a very important performance index for SBIR, especially for large-scale retrieval scenarios. We compare the online retrieval time of our method with the state-of-the-art, and the results are shown in Figure 14. Our method (here we consider $\text{ACDL}_{\text{CNN+LKS}}$) contains three steps for the retrieval: (i) feature extraction from a query sketch sample using LKS, (ii) dictionary mapping to obtain a new feature representation and (iii) query the image features database with k-NN. The last two steps are very fast, and the feature extraction using LKS takes around 1 second. The average retrieval time for each query sample is around 1.18 seconds. PerceptualEdge method achieves the best retrieval speed, as it uses only two steps namely the HOG feature extraction and direct matching. The retrieval speed of ours is comparable to the LKS method, and almost 2 times faster than GFHOG, SHOG, SIFT and SSIM, which first extract features, and then construct bag-of-words features and finally perform the retrieval. The reason is that the step of constructing the bag-of-words features is more time consuming than the dictionary mapping step.

5. CONCLUSIONS

In this paper we introduce academic coupled dictionary learning (ACDL) to tackle the SBIR task. In our approach the learning pace is determined from the reconstruction error, the cross-modal code coherence and the prior knowledge suggested by the modality-specific partial curricula. Importantly, the proposed framework naturally handles different descriptors for the sketch and the image domains. Therefore, domain-specific discriminative feature representations (*e.g.*, CNN features for images) are considered, overcoming the limitations of previous works. Extensive evaluations on three publicly available datasets show that ACDL outperforms state-of-the-art approaches for SBIR. Since the method is able to learn from a small training subset and handle partial curricula, the proposed method is applicable on very large-scale datasets. Future works include investigating cross-domain deep architectures [40] able to incorporate prior information from the partial curricula.

6. ACKNOWLEDGMENTS

This research has been partially supported by the EU projet xLiMe.

7. REFERENCES

[1] B. Alexe, T. Deselaers, and V. Ferrari. Measuring the objectness of image windows. *IEEE Trans. on PAMI*, 34(11):2189–2202, 2012.

[2] A. Beck and M. Teboulle. A fast iterative shrinkage-thresholding algorithm for linear inverse problems. *SIAM J. Imag. Sciences*, 2(1):183–202, 2009.

[3] Y. Bengio, J. Louradour, R. Collobert, and J. Weston. Curriculum learning. In *ICML*, 2009.

[4] A. D. Bimbo and P. Pala. Visual image retrieval by elastic matching of user sketches. *IEEE Trans. on PAMI*, 19(2):121–132, 1997.

[5] Y. Cao, H. Wang, C. Wang, Z. Li, L. Zhang, and L. Zhang. Mindfinder: interactive sketch-based image search on millions of images. In *ACM Multimedia*, 2010.

[6] A. Chalechale, G. Naghdy, and A. Mertins. Sketch-based image matching using angular partitioning. *IEEE Trans. on Systems, Man, and Cybernetics*, 35(1):28–41, 2005.

[7] M. Eitz, J. Hays, and M. Alexa. How do humans sketch objects? *ACM Trans. on Graphics*, 31(4):44, 2012.

[8] M. Eitz, K. Hildebrand, T. Boubekeur, and M. Alexa. An evaluation of descriptors for large-scale image retrieval from sketched feature lines. *Computers & Graphics*, 34(5):482–498, 2010.

[9] M. Eitz, K. Hildebrand, T. Boubekeur, and M. Alexa. Sketch-based image retrieval: Benchmark and bag-of-features descriptors *IEEE Trans. on Visualization and Computer Graphics*, 17(11):1624–1636, 2011.

[10] M. Everingham, L. Van Gool, C. K. Williams, J. Winn, and A. Zisserman. The pascal visual object classes (VOC) challenge. *IJCV*, 88(2):303–338, 2010.

[11] J. Guo, C. Wang, and H. Chao. Building effective representations for sketch recognition. In *AAAI*, 2015.

[12] R. Hu and J. Collomosse. A performance evaluation of gradient field hog descriptor for sketch based image retrieval. *CVIU*, 117(7):790–806, 2013.

[13] D.-A. Huang and Y.-C. F. Wang. Coupled dictionary and feature space learning with applications to cross-domain image synthesis and recognition. In *ICCV*, 2013.

[14] Y. Jia. Caffe: An open source convolutional architecture for fast feature embedding, 2013.

[15] L. Jiang, D. Meng, T. Mitamura, and A. G. Hauptmann. Easy samples first: Self-paced reranking for zero-example multimedia search. In *ACM Multimedia*, 2014.

[16] L. Jiang, D. Meng, S.-I. Yu, Z. Lan, S. Shan, and A. Hauptmann Self-paced learning with diversity. In *NIPS*, 2014.

[17] L. Jiang, D. Meng, Q. Zhao, S. Shan, and A. G. Hauptmann. Self-paced curriculum learning. In *AAAI*, 2015.

[18] M. P. Kumar, B. Packer, and D. Koller. Self-paced learning for latent variable models. In *NIPS*, 2010.

[19] H. Lee, A. Battle, R. Raina, and A. Y. Ng. Efficient sparse coding algorithms. In *NIPS*, 2006.

[20] Y. J. Lee and K. Grauman. Learning the easy things first: Self-paced visual category discovery. In *CVPR*, 2011.

[21] Y. Li, T. M. Hospedales, Y.-Z. Song, and S. Gong. Fine-grained sketch-based image retrieval by matching deformable part models. In *BMVC*, 2014.

[22] Y.-L. Lin, C.-Y. Huang, H.-J. Wang, and W.-C. Hsu. 3d sub-query expansion for improving sketch-based multi-view image retrieval. In *ICCV*, 2013.

[23] J. Mairal, F. Bach, J. Ponce, G. Sapiro, and A. Zisserman. Non-local sparse models for image restoration. In *ICCV*, 2009.

[24] Y. Matsui. Challenge for manga processing: Sketch-based manga retrieval. In *ACM Multimedia*, 2015.

[25] A. Pentina, V. Sharmanska, and C. H. Lampert. Curriculum learning of multiple tasks. *CVPR*, 2015.

[26] Y. Qi, Y.-Z. Song, T. Xiang, H. Zhang, T. Hospedales, Y. Li, and J. Guo. Making better use of edges via perceptual grouping. In *CVPR*, 2015.

[27] J. M. Saavedra, J. M. Barrios, and S. Orand. Sketch based image retrieval using learned keyshapes (LKS). In *BMVC*, 2015.

[28] J. M. Saavedra and B. Bustos. An improved histogram of edge local orientations for sketch-based image retrieval. In *Pattern Recognition*, pages 432–441. Springer, 2010.

[29] J. M. Saavedra and B. Bustos. Sketch-based image retrieval using keyshapes. *Multimedia Tools and Applications*, 73(3):2033–2062, 2014.

[30] A. Sharma and D. W. Jacobs. Bypassing synthesis: Pls for face recognition with pose, low-resolution and sketch. In *CVPR*, 2011.

[31] X. Sun, C. Wang, C. Xu, and L. Zhang. Indexing billions of images for sketch-based retrieval. In *ACM Multimedia*, 2013.

[32] J. S. Supancic and D. Ramanan. Self-paced learning for long-term tracking. In *CVPR*, 2013.

[33] X. Tang and X. Wang. Face sketch recognition. *IEEE Trans. Cir. Sys. Video Tech.*, 14(1):50–57, 2004.

[34] Y. Tang, Y.-B. Yang, and Y. Gao. Self-paced dictionary learning for image classification. In *ACM Multimedia*, 2012.

[35] J. B. Tenenbaum and W. T. Freeman. Separating style and content with bilinear models. *Neural Computation*, 12(6):1247–1283, 2000.

[36] S. Wang, L. Zhang, Y. Liang, and Q. Pan. Semi-coupled dictionary learning with applications to image super-resolution and photo-sketch synthesis. In *CVPR*, 2012.

[37] X. Wang and X. Tang. Face photo-sketch synthesis and recognition. *IEEE Trans. on PAMI*, 31(11):1955–1967, 2009.

[38] C. Xiao, C. Wang, L. Zhang, and L. Zhang. Sketch-based image retrieval via shape words. In *ACM ICMR*, 2015.

[39] C. Xu, D. Tao, and C. Xu. Multi-view self-paced learning for clustering. In *IJCAI*, 2015.

[40] D. Xu, E. Ricci, Y. Yan, J. Song, and N. Sebe. Learning deep representations of appearance and motion for anomalous event detection. In *BMVC*, 2015.

[41] Y. Yan, Y. Yang, H. Shen, D. Meng, G. Liu, A. Hauptmann, and N. Sebe. Complex event detection via event oriented dictionary learning. In *AAAI*, 2015.

[42] J. Yang, J. Wright, T. S. Huang, and Y. Ma. Image super-resolution via sparse representation. *IEEE Trans. on Image Processing*, 19(11):2861–2873, 2010.

[43] S. M. Yoon, G.-J. Yoon, and T. Schreck. User-drawn sketch-based 3d object retrievalusing sparse coding. *Multimedia Tools App.*, 74(13):4707–4722, 2015.

[44] X. Zhai, Y. Peng, and J. Xiao. Heterogeneous metric learning with joint graph regularization for cross-media retrieval. In *AAAI*, 2013.

[45] Q. Zhao, D. Meng, L. Jiang, Q. Xie, Z. Xu, and A. G. Hauptmann. Self-paced learning for matrix factorization. In *AAAI*, 2015.

Time Matters: Multi-scale Temporalization of Social Media Popularity

Bo Wu[1,2], Wen-Huang Cheng[3], Yongdong Zhang[1], Tao Mei[4]
[1]Key Laboratory of Intelligent Information Processing,
Institute of Computing Technology, Chinese Academy of Sciences, China
[2]University of Chinese Academy of Sciences, China
[3]Research Center for Information Technology Innovation, Academia Sinica, Taiwan
[4]Microsoft Research, China
{wubo, zhyd}@ict.ac.cn; whcheng@citi.sinica.edu.tw; tmei@microsoft.com

ABSTRACT

The evolution of social media popularity exhibits rich temporality, i.e., popularities change over time at various levels of temporal granularity. This is influenced by temporal variations of public attentions or user activities. For example, popularity patterns of street snap on Flickr are observed to depict distinctive fashion styles at specific time scales, such as season-based periodic fluctuations for Trench Coat or one-off peak in days for Evening Dress. However, this fact is often overlooked by existing research of popularity modeling. We present the first study to incorporate multiple time-scale dynamics into predicting online popularity. We propose a novel computational framework in the paper, named Multi-scale Temporalization, for estimating popularity based on multi-scale decomposition and structural reconstruction in a tensor space of user, post, and time by joint low-rank constraints. By considering the noise caused by context inconsistency, we design a data rearrangement step based on context aggregation as preprocessing to enhance contextual relevance of neighboring data in the tensor space. As a result, our approach can leverage multiple levels of temporal characteristics and reduce the noise of data decomposition to improve modeling effectiveness. We evaluate our approach on two large-scale Flickr image datasets with over 1.8 million photos in total, for the task of popularity prediction. The results show that our approach significantly outperforms state-of-the-art popularity prediction techniques, with a relative improvement of 10.9%–47.5% in terms of prediction accuracy.

Keywords

Social media popularity; multi-scale temporal modeling; tensor decomposition and reconstruction; popularity prediction

MM '16, October 15-19, 2016, Amsterdam, Netherlands
© 2016 ACM. ISBN 978-1-4503-3603-1/16/10...$15.00
DOI: http://dx.doi.org/10.1145/2964284.2964335

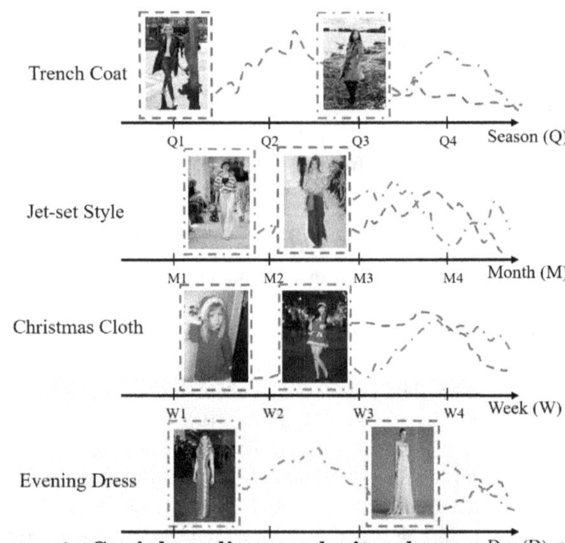

Figure 1: Social media popularity changes over time and often exhibits varying temporality across different time scales. Clothing fashion, as a typical example, gives a vivid expression of the temporal characteristics for social media popularity. The life spans of four particular fashions are observed to be diversified from few days (e.g., evening dress), specific weeks (e.g., Christmas cloth), several months (e.g., Jet-set style), to certain seasons (e.g., trench coat). Each dashed curved line after an image represents the life cycle of popularity of the corresponding clothes.

1. INTRODUCTION

Social media has changed the way human interact and has connected billions of users worldwide with friends and family through online content posting. Meanwhile, a plethora of information is generated for competing their attention, e.g., 1.3 million pieces of content are shared on Facebook every single minute [1]. Only few posts have the opportunity to become popular while most are ignored over time [2, 3]. Thus, modeling the popularity evolution and predicting the individual popularity (the popularity of a specific post or item) are very active fields of social media research and can lead to a number of applications, such as content recommendation [4, 5], advertisement placement [6], information retrieval [7, 8] and online media caching services [9].

The existing studies of exploiting temporal information for popularity modeling can be grouped into two main categories. The first category builds popularity models to discover general patterns for temporal trends in popularity data [10, 11, 12, 13, 14, 15]. The statistics are typically computed over the entire popularity data, such that specific characteristic needed for individual popularity prediction is often lost. The second category is to estimate the individual popularity of online content by temporal factors or variables with intrinsic time information [3, 6, 16, 17, 18]. Characteristics of time-dependent factors are explicitly incorporated into prediction, and most of the recent researches in this field fall into this category.

Popularities are mirror of society, reflecting shifts in people's preferences in the context of social alteration. Taking clothing fashion as an illustration, images or videos about trendy dresses naturally receive much more attention than out-of-date clothes on social media [19, 20]. Also, a fashion can have a short or long life cycle. For example, as shown in Figure 1, certain types of clothing fashion tend to last for a period that is as short as only few days to weeks, while others will decline slowly or even turn into what is known as a timeless classics. These observations reveal an essential characteristic of popularities, i.e., popularities not only change over time but also operate across a range of different time scales. Recently, several researchers also found similar phenomena on different social platforms influenced by various temporal factors [21, 3], such as user habits, timely events, headline news, and popular products. The underlying momentum is related to temporal variations in the life spams of human activities and preferences. However, to the best of our knowledge, little work has been done to leverage multi-scale temporal dynamics for popularity prediction.

In this paper, therefore, we propose to understand popularity dynamics from a multiple time-scale perspective, named *Multi-scale Temporalization* (MT), which is a structured modeling for popularity dynamics into multiple levels of time scale. As shown in Figure 2, it is distinctive from the conventional paradigm that considers all the popularity data as a whole popularity tensor [3, 22, 23]. We attempt to explore them by considering multi-scale effects together over time, simultaneously in multiple time scales. As preprocessing, we design a data rearrangement step to enhance contextual relevance of neighboring data for reducing the noise caused by context inconsistency. Then we propose a multi-scale tensor decomposition with considering temporal information and context information in three-dimensional data space of popularity (formed by the user, post, and time dimensions). Finally, we perform reconstruction through minimizing a joint low-rank constraint for predicting online popularity. Therefore, our approach can leverage multiple levels of temporal characteristics and reduce data noise to improve the prediction effectiveness.

In the experiments, we demonstrate the effectiveness of the proposed framework through experiments with two large-scale Flickr datasets for the task of popularity prediction. One of the datasets is from VSO [24] and the other is crawled from Flickr, with over 1.8 million photos in total. The results show that our approach significantly outperforms state-of-the-art popularity prediction techniques, with a relative improvement of averagely 10.9%–47.5% in prediction accuracy. Moreover, the proposed framework is novel and can be readily extended to other content domains and application scenarios with the analysis of various evolutionary dynamics.

The main contributions of this study are: (i) we address popularity prediction within the multiple time-scale perspective; (ii) we propose a framework MT to predict online popularity based on decomposition via joint low-rank constraints; (iii) we also propose a data rearrangement strategy based on the aggregation of context information for reducing the noise caused by context inconsistency; (iv) we evaluate our approach on large scale datasets and achieve a significant outperformance over the state-of-the-art methods.

The rest of the paper is organized as follows. Related approaches of temporal modeling for popularity are discussed in Section 2. We propose the multi-scale temporalization model in Section 3. In Section 4, we report experimental evaluations of the proposed approach and comparisons with state-of-the-art algorithms. Finally, the conclusions and future work are presented in Section 5.

2. RELATED WORK

The temporal information modeling for popularity dynamics on social media has received much research attention recently. Existing works can be concluded into two main paradigms.

The first paradigm focuses on exploring the patterns of evolving trend for popularity variations [10, 11, 14, 13]. Throughout the early years, Szabo and Huberman attempted to analyze online popularity trend growth with pattern characteristics [12]. Mathioudakis and Koudas detected popularity trends by bursty key words in Twitter [13]. Yang and Leskovec found the cluster centroids of patterns associated with overall items and how the content's popularity grows and fades over time [14]. Roy *et al.* proposed a novel transfer learning framework to grasp sudden popularity trend bursts with temporal knowledge from social streams [11]. Kong *et al.* explored the problems of real-time prediction of bursting hashtags. Although these works exploited general comprehension on the variance mechanisms of popularity evolution, most of them are designed for general popularity or a group of items online [10]. These models have limited effectiveness on predicting the individual popularity in social media.

The other paradigm is modeling the individual popularity by temporal factors or variables with intrinsic time information [3, 16, 17, 18], while researchers notice that temporal information is useful cues to predict individual popularity on social media in recent years [3, 6, 18]. Wu *et al.* proposed to predict popularity in social media by unfolding its contextual dynamics and incorporated temporal context into the prediction [3]. Zhao *et al.* combined human reaction time and post infectiousness to build the theory of self-exciting point processes [18]. Shen *et al.* proposed a reinforced Poisson process to model explicitly the dynamic popularity of individual items based on the arrival time of attention [16]. He *et al.* used comments as a time-aware bipartite graph for estimating the popularity of item [17]. Although these models succeed in using temporal information, the essential multi-scale characteristic of popularity dynamics is lacking of investigation.

Therefore, how to incorporate multiple time-scales information into the study of popularity prediction in social media is still an open research issue. This motivated us to design the proposed framework of temporal modeling.

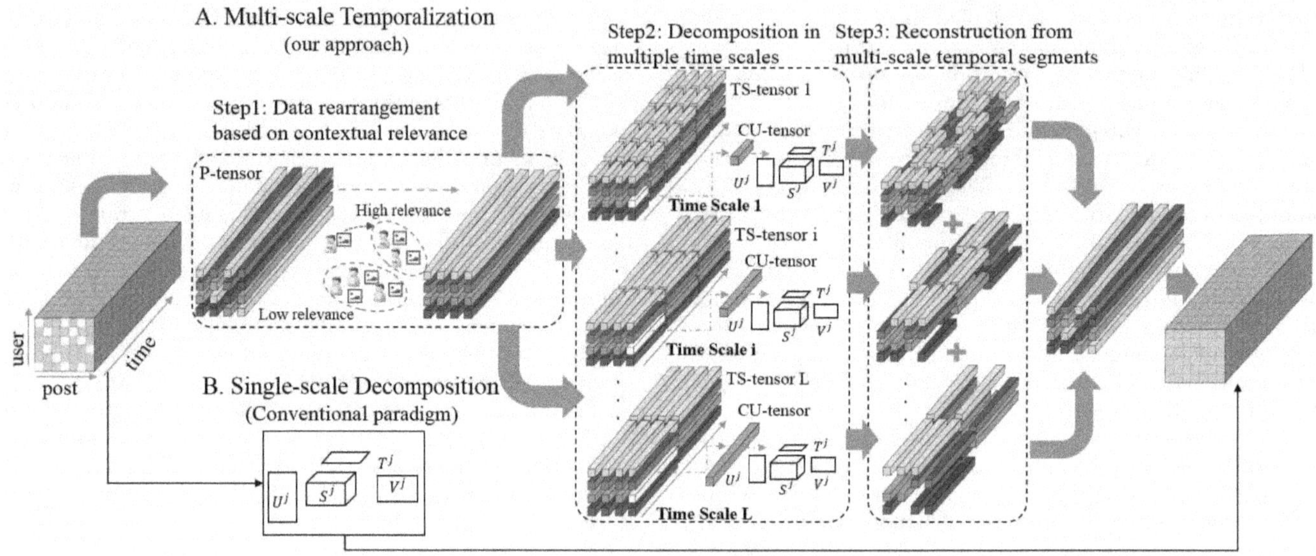

Figure 2: An overview of our proposed Multi-scale Temporalization (MT). In the first step, we proposed a data rearrangement step to re-organize data locations in tensor space with considering the corresponding contextual factors. Then we model temporal dynamics of popularity by multi-scale decomposition structures. Finally, we predict popularity with join low-rank constraints based on multi-level reconstruction.

3. MULTI-SCALE TEMPORALIZATION MODELING

3.1 Framework Overview

In this section, we introduce the proposed multi-scale temporalization modeling for popularity dynamics. First, we formally define the problem of popularity prediction. Without loss of generality, we take photo posts on social media as our initial research focus.

Problem Formulation **(Popularity Prediction)**: Given a group of users U and a collection of photo posts V, the popularity of photos can be recorded as the collection S. Since the generation of popularity on social media is a collaborative process [3], an individual popularity (the popularity of a specific post or item) s corresponds to a sharing behavior that can be described by a three-dimensional tuple $\langle u, v, t\rangle$ denoting that a user u shared a new photo v at time t. A mathematical representation of the popularity data is defined as a three-dimensional data matrix, called popularity tensor $\mathbf{R}$, with the user dimension, photo dimension, and time dimension. The popularity prediction problem can thus be formulated as predicting unobserved popularity entries (with sharing behaviors that are unknown or not happened yet) in the tensor R based on other observed data (entries with known popularities).

In Figure 2, we illustrate the proposed framework of multi-scale temporalization for popularity dynamics. Unlike traditional methods, our temporalization is a novel technique to unfold the temporal dynamics of popularity over time at multiple time scales, which includes three main analysis steps: (1) data rearrangement based on contextual relevance, (2) decomposition in multiple time scales, and (3) reconstruction from multi-scale temporal segments. Firstly, since the popularity data with similar contexts (e.g., users with similar profiles or photos with similar contents) tend to gain similar levels of popularity on social media [4], we group the popularity data with high contextual relevance to be in close proximity, cf. Section 3.2. Next, we perform multi-scale tensor decomposition to derive an approximate representation of the popularity data at different time scales. For each time scale (e.g., a scale of day, week, or month), the corresponding scale tensor is divided into a sequence of temporal segments with multiple time-scale representations, cf. Section 3.3. Finally, we perform a joint optimization strategy to combine a set of the temporal segments from all the time scales to best approximate the rearranged popularity tensor, where joint low-rank constraints are applied, cf. Section 3.4. As a consequence, estimates of the unobserved values in the popularity tensor can be effectively obtained.

3.2 Data Rearrangement based on Contextual Relevance

The popularity of a post is context-aware signal, which is highly correlated with certain post contexts, e.g., who shared the post, what the post is about, etc. As suggested by the previous findings [22, 25, 26], the posts with relevant contexts tend to gain similar popularity [4, 27, 28]. In the paper, our purpose is to partition a popularity tensor as a disjoint collection of smaller tensors, and predict new popularity in popularity tensor via pattern reconstruction on these tensors. However, uncovering patterns of the popularity data is difficult because the noise caused by context inconsistency (such as contextual differences in user factors or content factors) behind the temporal variation would result in analysis challenges. That is, if two neighboring data regions are contextually correlated, there would exist context-related noise in the popularity tensor prediction. Hence we hope popularity data in neighboring regions would have high correlation of the contextual information, such that each smaller tensor can help construct a "compact" representation for the corresponding popularity data in prediction.

Therefore, we propose a approach of contextual data rear-

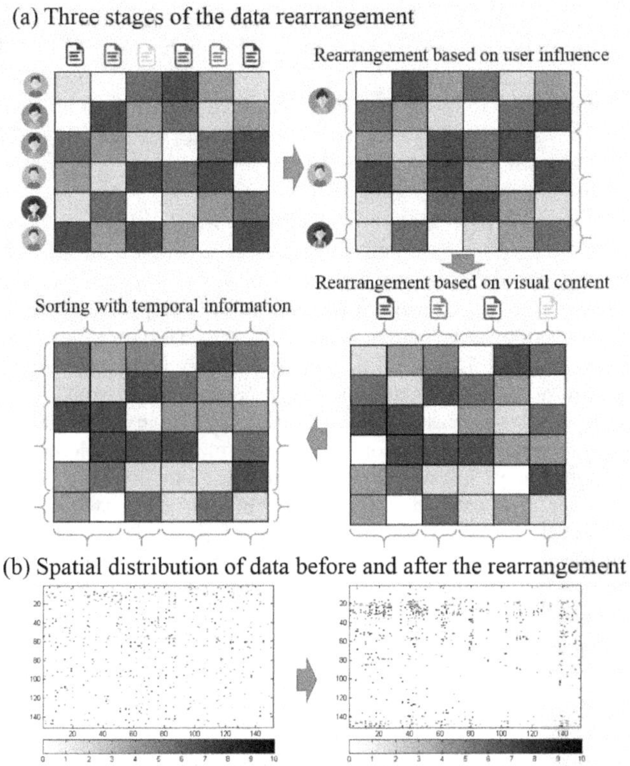

Figure 3: (a)The three main steps of the data rearrangement. (b) After the rearrangement is applied, neighboring data have higher contextual relevance.

rangement for the challenge in popularity temporalization. Most of previous works apply sorting-based methods to perform element-wise rearrangement in a matrix, but the high correlation of neighboring local data might not be guaranteed if multiple dimensions (e.g., user, photo, etc.) are involved in the sorting process. As inspired by [29], we group the given tensor data in the multi-dimensional feature space without enforcing to sort the data. The proposed data rearrangement can help us to obtain the data units with multi-dimensional contextual consistency for more effective CU-tensor decomposition.

To extract the contextual information of individual popularities, contextual features are built from three main perspectives: user influence, visual content, and post metadata.

User Influence. User influence reflects the personal reputation on social media, and the user features we adopted include: mean number of views, photo count, number of contacts, average number of members in a user's groups, and having a Pro Flickr account or not.

Visual Content. To describe photo content, we extract both low-level and object-level vision features. Low-level vision features are adopted to measure the color distribution and image local structures, including color patch descriptors [30], Local Binary Pattern (LBP) descriptors, and locality-constrained gradient descriptors [2, 31]. For object-level vision features, we use deep learning features by convolutional neural networks (CNNs) with the DeCAF method [32] to determine object categories in photos, resulting in 4,096 feature dimensions.

Post Information. Post information can be directly extracted from the metadata of photo files [25], containing the sharing time, the number of image tags, the length of the post title, and the length of post descriptions.

After the above context factors being extracted, the popularity tensor is rearranged in a three-step manner. Since the user influence has been shown to be a dominant factor in photo popularity prediction [3, 25, 26], the popularity data are first grouped along the user dimension by the k-means algorithm [33] based on the user influence features. Note that the exact spatial order of either the groups or the data inside a group is not important because the purpose of our grouping here is to place "similar" data as close as possible but not to rank the data. As the second step, another grouping is performed along the post dimension based on the features of both the visual content and the post information (excluding the sharing time). Finally, for each data group (on the post dimension) of a specific user, we sort the data inside the group by the sharing time (from the post information) as a refinement step, cf. Figure 3.

3.3 Decomposition in Multiple Time Scales

We try to predict the popularity by the joint approximation with considering multiple time scales together. To capture the local dynamics of popularity over time, the proposed multiple time-scale decomposition operates by decomposing a popularity tensor (P-tensor) into a number of time-scale tensors (TS-tensors) each composed of a set of compositional unit tensors (CU-tensors), as detailed below. Conceptually, we attempt to break down the popularity variation into multiple levels of detail for constructing an accurate representation of popularity for popularity prediction.

Let $T = \{T_i\}_{i=1}^{L}$ denotes a set of adopted time scales. Given a popularity tensor $\mathbf{R}$ associated with a collection of users U and a collection of photo posts V, the multiple time-scale decomposition can be expressed as the sum of L components with each corresponding to an adopted time scale:

$$\mathbf{R} = \sum_{i=1}^{L} \mathbf{R_i}, \tag{1}$$

where $\mathbf{R_i}$ is the same size of $\mathbf{R}$ and called a TS-tensor of $\mathbf{R}$ in the T_i time scale. Since data with high contextual relevance are rearranged to be spatially close in $\mathbf{R}$ (cf. Section 3.2), each TS-tensor can be further partitioned into smaller pieces called CU-tensors as the unit of analysis, in order to take benefit of the data homogeneity for decomposition. That is, each CU-tensor in $\mathbf{R_i}$ has the dimensions of $m_j \times n_j \times t_j$, where the time dimension t_j is a base-2 or base-e number related to the time scale of $\mathbf{R_i}$ as discussed in the experiments. Then the user dimension m_j and the post dimension n_j are set to be the same order of magnitude as t_j. Note that m_j (or n_j) needs to be larger than the smallest group size of users (or posts) as obtained in the data rearrangement.

The exact locations of CU-tensors in $\mathbf{R_i}$ can thus be indexed by a location set $M = \{M_j\}_{j=1}^{J_i}$ where J_i is the total number of CU-tensors in $\mathbf{R_i}$. Thus $\mathbf{R_i}$ can be formulated as a summation of the CU-tensors by defining a reshaping transformation below.

Definition 1. **(CU-tensor Transformation)** Given an TS-tensor $\mathbf{R_i}$, the CU-tensor transformation is defined as an operation O_i for converting one of $\mathbf{R_i}$'s CU-tensors, $\mathbf{R_i}^j$, $j = 1, ..., J_i$, into a zero tensor of the same size as $\mathbf{R_i}$ with only values of $\mathbf{R_i}^j$ in the corresponding location M_j, such that $\mathbf{R_i} = \sum_{j=1}^{J_i} O_i(M_j, \mathbf{R_i}^j)$.

Therefore, the multiple time-scale decomposition of an original P-tensor can be simplified into a series of smaller-scale decompositions performed on the CU-tensors. In this paper, we applied the Singular Value Decomposition (SVD) [34, 35] as our decomposition tool. The expression of $\mathbf{R}$ can be thus changed to:

$$\mathbf{R} = \sum_{i=1}^{L}\sum_{j=1}^{J_i} O_i(M_j, \mathbf{S_i}^j \times \mathbf{U_i}^j \times \mathbf{V_i}^j \times \mathbf{T_i}^j), \qquad (2)$$

where $\mathbf{S_i}^j \times \mathbf{U_i}^j \times \mathbf{V_i}^j \times \mathbf{T_i}^j$ is the factorization of $\mathbf{R_i}^j$.

3.4 Reconstruction from Multi-scale Temporal Segments

In the previous section, we introduced the multi-scale decomposition process of temporalization for a P-tensor. The P-tensor can be further formed by a series of CU-tensor decompositions at multiple time scales. Since an individual popularity is related with a complex interplay among the contextual factors, where there often exists a high level of noise in the popularity data, making it a non-trivial task to conduct the popularity prediction [11, 16]. Therefore, it is always a challenge about how to reduce the noise during recovering the P-tensor from multi-scale temporal segments.

For this challenge in the P-tensor reconstruction, we propose to apply joint low-rank constraints to reduce the noise level by minimizing the ranks of CU-tensors. More specifically, since the data rearrangement step (as proposed in Section 3.2) has aggregated the P-tensor entries with high contextual relevance in the data space, each CU-tensor has high contextual relevance among the data entries and the rank of the CU-tensor tends to be low. Therefore, we create joint low-rank constraints on CU-tensors instead of minimizing the gradients of the original objective function directly. Thus the optimization is formulated as:

$$\begin{aligned} &\min_{\mathbf{R_1},\ldots,\mathbf{R_L}} \sum_{i=1}^{L}\sum_{j=1}^{J_i} rank(\mathbf{R_i}^j) \\ &\text{subject to} \quad \mathbf{R} = \sum_{i=1}^{L} \mathbf{R_i}. \end{aligned} \qquad (3)$$

Especially, if the rank of a decomposed $\mathbf{R}_i^j$ is zero (calculated by SVD computation), we will ignore it for P-tensor reconstruction, which means the joint low-rank constraints will select the CU-tensors with a non-zero rank only in every optimization steps.

Since the minimization for the summation of rank constraints is a non-convex problem, we are unable to get an effective solution by optimizing it directly. Hence we convert the problem to a convex optimization problem by nuclear norm relaxation, which is inspired by the similar techniques applied in low-rank matrix completion [36]. Specifically, we construct the nuclear norm $||\cdot||_{nuc}$ to calculate the sum of singular values of overall elements of a CU-tensor $\mathbf{R_i^j}$, which is a minimization constraint of convex envelope of its rank. Meanwhile we have the nuclear norm $||\cdot||^{(i)}$ for each TS-tensor $\mathbf{R_i}$:

$$||\cdot||^{(i)} = \sum_{j=1}^{J_i} ||O_j(\cdot)||_{nuc}. \qquad (4)$$

Then we incorporate the regularization term $||\mathbf{Z_i}||^{(i)}$ to obtain an equivalent relaxation formulation of our problem with two optimization objectives: a) the indicator constraint $\mathbb{1}\{\cdot\}$ for recovering $\mathbf{R}$ based on multiple time-scale information components (CU-tensors), and b) the summation of regularization terms $\sum_{i=1}^{L} \lambda_i ||\mathbf{Z_i}||^{(i)}$ as a nuclear norm objective for optimization on joint rank constraints. The final objective function to estimate the partially known P-tensor $\mathbf{R}$ is formulated by:

$$\begin{aligned} &\min_{\mathbf{R_i},\mathbf{Z_i}} \mathbb{1}\{\mathbf{R} = \sum_{i=1}^{L} \mathbf{R_i}\} + \sum_{i=1}^{L} \lambda_i ||\mathbf{Z_i}||^{(i)} \\ &\text{subject to} \quad \mathbf{R}_i = \mathbf{Z_i}, \end{aligned} \qquad (5)$$

where the regularization parameter λ_i is to adjust the weight of proximal regularizations $||\mathbf{Z_i}||^{(i)}$. Note that, we compute parameters as $\lambda_i = \sqrt{m_i} + \sqrt{n_i}$ in our experiments inspired by similar parameter estimation of the previous work [37].

Since Alternating Direction Method of Multipliers (ADMM) is a powerful algorithm for convex optimization problems [38], we apply it on solving our optimization. The solution of the function is based on the joint optimization of two objectives and the iterative computation of $\mathbf{R_i}$ and $\mathbf{Z_i}$. At each iteration of the reconstruction of P-tensor $\mathbf{R}$, we need to estimate TS-tensors $\mathbf{R_i}$ at first with the following alternative updating steps:

$$\mathbf{R_i} \leftarrow (\mathbf{Z_i} + \tfrac{1}{L}(\mathbf{R} - \sum_{i=1}^{L} \mathbf{Z_i})), \qquad (6)$$

$$\mathbf{Z_i} \leftarrow SVD_{\lambda_i}(\mathbf{R_i}). \qquad (7)$$

$SVD_{\lambda_i}(\cdot)$ is the abbreviation of SVD method with the mentioned regularization parameters λ_i for updating $\mathbf{Z_i}$. SVD_{λ_i} is a proximal constraint function of the regularization summation term, we define $SVD_{\lambda_i}(R_i) = Umax(\Sigma - \lambda_i, 0)T^{\mathrm{T}}$.

After updating all TS-tensors in each iteration, we identify them by estimating the individual correlation between the updated versions and the corresponding training data in P-tensor. By this step, we select the components with a positive correlation for the next iteration of P-tensor estimation. The algorithm of our method is the combination of alternative updating processes in each iteration, as summarized in Algorithm 1.

Algorithm 1 The Algorithm of Multi-scale Temporalization

Require: estimated tensor: $\mathbf{R}$; maximal interaction: n;

Initial $\mathbf{R_0}$ and $\mathbf{Z_0}$ randomly on three-dimensional space with temporal information;
repeat
  repeat
    Optimization update steps:

$$\mathbf{R_i} \leftarrow (\mathbf{Z_i} + \tfrac{1}{L}(\mathbf{R} - \sum_{i=1}^{L} \mathbf{Z_i}))$$
$$\mathbf{Z_i} \leftarrow SVD_{\lambda_i}(\mathbf{R_i})$$

    Update $\mathbf{R_i}$ and $\mathbf{Z_i}$ followed by Alternating Direction Method of Multipliers
  until each TS-tensor $\mathbf{R_i}$ has been estimated
  Select $\mathbf{R_i}$ by correlation computation
  Compute results of objective function:

$$\mathbf{R} = \sum_{i=1}^{L}\sum_{j=1}^{J_i} O_i(M_j, \mathbf{S_i}^j \times \mathbf{U_i}^j \times \mathbf{V_i}^j \times \mathbf{T_i}^j)$$

until procedure convergence or the number of interactions is over n

3.5 Popularity Formulation

The popularity of a shared post is related to the interaction behaviors of user preference in social media. For example, tweets popularity can be represented by "retweeted count" on Twitter, and video popularity is "visiting count" on YouTube. On Flickr, when browsing a personal photo stream or image search results, users can view details of a photo content with its metadata through clicking photo thumbnails. In our prediction, we use "viewing count" to describe the photo popularity, since it is a significant indicator of public preference of a new photo.

To alleviate the large variation (i.e. the number of views of different photos varies largely from zero to millions), we apply the log-normalization approach [2] on the popularity formulation. As a result, the log-normalized popularity of a photo can be defined as

$$s = \log_2 \frac{r}{d} + 1, \tag{8}$$

where r is the original view count of each published photo, and d is the number of days since the photo was shared.

4. EXPERIMENTS

In this section, we report three groups of experiments: (1) we compare our proposed method and state-of-the-art algorithms for popularity prediction on over 1.8 million photos from Flickr, and our method is shown to be more effective on popularity prediction, (2) we perform further experiments to validate our algorithmic choices, e.g., the proposed time scales are effective to decompose popularity dynamics of social media photos, (3) we demonstrate the temporal prediction ability of our approach for popularity prediction and showcase some sample results.

4.1 Datasets

For validating our proposed approach on real-world data, we collected over 1.8 million photos from over 70K users in total for two large-scale photo collections: the photo-mix dataset and the user-album dataset. These settings represent two different scenarios in social media platform.

Photo-mix Dataset (PmD): We use the Visual Sentiment Ontology (VSO) dataset [24] consisting of approximately 1.2M images from over 70K users. Each user has five published photos at least. This setting often occurs on image retrieval or photo streams where people can browse various kinds of photos. We put all the images of these users together and performed popularity prediction on the full data.

User-album Dataset (UaD): We collected 600K photos from the personal albums of 400 different users, and organized the photos into training data and testing data randomly. This setting is built for the scenario of finding interesting photographers by published albums. The prediction for the dataset tends to use more photos for each user than PmD.

For providing results on both of "big data" and "small data", we selected photos to get smaller subsets from PmD and UaD in number of photos, i.e., 400K from VSO_CC dataset (a set of Flickr images with Creative Common (CC) licenses of VSO), 800K from VSO_full (a set of images associated with the full VSO) and 300K from UaD (this set include half images of UaD), respectively.

4.2 Evaluation Metric

To evaluate performances of comparisons, we use the median Spearman Ranking Correlation with 10 fold cross-validation in our following experiments. The correlation is used to identify and test the strength of a relationship between a predicted popularity set $\hat{P}$ and the actual popularity set P. Supposing the size of test sample set is k, the calculation of spearman ranking correlation r_s can be expressed as:

$$r_s = \frac{1}{k-1} \sum_{i=1}^{k} \left(\frac{P_i - \bar{P}}{\sigma_P} \right) \left(\frac{\hat{P}_i - \bar{\hat{P}}}{\sigma_{\hat{P}}} \right), \tag{9}$$

where $\bar{P}$ and σ_P are the mean and the variance of the corresponding popularity set.

4.3 Baselines

Baseline for Comparing Methods: In order to compare with state-of-the-art models, we implemented the following approaches which can be applied into popularity prediction problem as different baselines.

Baseline 1: **Average Views (AV).** Since similar photos tend to obtain similar popularity, the popularity of testing photos can be estimated by the average views of its top five similar photos from training data. The popularity s_j can be formulated by $\frac{1}{k} \sum_{n=1}^{k} s_n$,where k is the number of similar photos, s_n is the popularity of each similar photo with v_j. If the number of similar photos is over five, we rank them by the posting time and select the most recent photos.

Baseline 2: **Logistic Regression (LR) [12].** From the early research, Szabo *et al.* used Linear Regression (LR) in predicting popularity of online content, and it is a important work on popularity prediction tasks as baseline model. The multiple factors are organized as feature vectors in using this model.

Baseline 3: **Support Vector Regression (SVR) [2].** Khosla *et al.* used Support Vector Regression (SVR) in prediction and incorporated user cues and photo content as feature vectors. A linear kernel is used in the SVR.

Baseline 4: **Bipartite Graph (BG) [17].** Bipartite Graph model is widely used in popularity prediction and ranking. Suppose $G = (< U \cup V >, E)$ is a bipartite graph, where the set U and set V represent users and items respectively, and edges E are posting behaviors. We use a regularization term $R(f)$ as

$$R(f) = \frac{1}{2} \sum_{j=1}^{n} \sum_{i=1}^{m} \omega_{ij} \left(\frac{f(u_i)}{\sqrt{d_i^u}} - \frac{f(v_j)}{\sqrt{d_j^v}} \right), \tag{10}$$

where w_{ij} is defined by the posting behaviors between users and items. d_i^u and d_j^v are the weighted degrees of photo v_j and user u_i for normalization, respectively.

Baseline 5: **Temporal Matrix Factorization (TMF) [23].** The decomposition of a whole tensor on large data is not practical because large data is often too sparse to find an optimal solution. Hence we adopted a temporal modeling approach to incorporate temporal extension [39] into a practical Non-negative Matrix Factorization [23] for prediction as one baseline. We combine the user-item interaction ($\mathbf{B}_u(t)$), temporal terms ($\mathbf{B}_i(t)$) and regular terms in the optimiza-

Table 1: Prediction performances on PmD and UaD datasets (metric: Spearman Ranking Correlation).

Method	400K PmD	800K PmD	300K UaD	600K UaD
AV	0.0419	0.0785	0.1043	0.2022
LR [12]	0.2805	0.3026	0.5582	0.6359
SVR [2]	0.2627	0.2725	0.4415	0.6273
BG [17]	0.2385	0.2573	0.2851	0.5465
TMF [23]	0.2186	0.2839	0.4352	0.5795
MT (ours)	**0.2916**	**0.3264**	**0.5972**	**0.6574**

tion objective:

$$\arg\min_{\mathbf{U},\mathbf{V}} \|\mathbf{R} - \mathbf{B}_u(t) - \mathbf{B}_i(t) - \mathbf{U}\mathbf{V}\|_F^2 + \lambda_U\|\mathbf{U}\|^2 + \lambda_{\mathbf{V}}\|\mathbf{V}\|^2. \tag{11}$$

Note that, we use the intrinsic time series as the temporal feature in the feature vectors for LR, SVR, BG and TMF.

Baseline for the Effectiveness Evaluation of Time Scales: Currently, we adopt three time scales in our approach, including a week of year, a month of year, and a season of year. In order to validate the use of the adopted time scales and get more insights into our approach on the prediction effectiveness while different time scales are applied, we add some specific time scales in the experiments, including 2, 3, and 5 days, and 4, 5, and 6 months. For abbreviation, the three adopted time scales are altogether called GT (general time scales). The specific day and month scales are called DST (day specific time scales) and MST (month specific time scales), respectively. Three baselines are then created below and evaluated on 100K UaD.

Baseline 6: **GT-GT$_i$.** We evaluate the individual contribution of each time scale in GT by removing a time scale from GT one at a time.

Baseline 7: **GT-DST$_i$.** We extend the GT by adding a time scale from DST one at a time.

Baseline 8: **GT-MST$_i$.** We extend the GT by adding a time scale from MST one at a time.

4.4 The Comparison of Prediction Methods

In Table 1, we give the prediction performance of our approach and the comparing methods. In each column of the table, our approach achieves the best performances. Especially in 800K PmD and 300K UaD, the relative improvements of our approach over the best baseline model LR is about 7.9% and 6.9%. Unlike TMF, which is also a temporal model based on matrix decomposition technique, our method considers multiple time-scale structure of popularity dynamics and even achieves a better relative increase about 13.4%–37.2%. That suggests the decomposition with multiple time scales is more adequate for utilizing temporal information. Besides, the models of LR and SVR generally outperform the temporal model TMF. It might imply if the temporal information is not well utilized, the resultant performance can be even worse than the scenario when temporal information is excluded. Meanwhile, Average Views is the worst and its best correlation is only about 0.2, it ignores abundant contextual data of popularity and results in limited prediction.

From the comparison with the different methods, the correlation of experiments on large dataset of PmD or UaD tends to obtain a better performance. This is consistent with the intuition that the prediction performance depends heavily on the numbers of data, and "big data" provides better prediction ability. Moreover, Table 1 shows that the performances of prediction on UaD can be as high as up to 0.6574, which are higher than on PmD. This indicates that the prediction on less photos per user (photo-mix application) is more difficult even on a large dataset (the most performances are about 0.3 even on 800K photos).

Overall our approach achieves the best performance and gives more relative rank correlation than the other four comparing methods (excluding AV) in a relative improvement of 20.3%–109.5% (with BG), 15.0%–37.2% (with TMF), 4.8%–35.3% (with SVR) and 3.4%–7.9% (with LR). The average improvement of our approach over the four methods is thus from 10.9%–47.5%. It suggests that the temporalization technique are more effective on the prediction task.

Table 2: Prediction Performances of predicting popularity based on GT without GT$_i$ (metric: Spearman Ranking Correlation).

Settings	GT-GT$_{week}$	GT-GT$_{month}$	GT-GT$_{season}$	GT
r_s	0.3176	0.3578	0.1759	**0.5342**

Table 3: Prediction performances of GT by incorporating DST or MST (metric: Spearman Ranking Correlation).

GT+DST$_i$	Performance	GT+MST$_i$	Performance
2(D)	0.4485	4(M)	**0.5208**
3(D)	**0.4845**	5(M)	0.5142
5(D)	0.4688	6(M)	0.4553

4.5 Evaluation of Time Scales for Popularity Prediction

The results of using our predefined time-scales are shown in the right column of Table 2, where the highest ranking correlation is 0.5342 when using all GT in multi-scale decomposition. It indicates that using suggested general time scales is effective in unfolding temporal dynamics of popularity on social media. Furthermore, the other "leave-one-out" results are to validate the importance of each time scale. The result with the absence of season time scale achieves the lowest ranking correlation. That means the season-level time scale is more crucial than the others for photo popularity prediction. From the observation on the overall result, all the leave-one-out results are lower than using all the time scales in GT, implying that all the currently adopted time scales are important.

Next, we analyze the improvements of performance in terms of DST and MST, respectively. Compared with the performance of GT in Table 2, the performances in Table 3 drop down by 1.3%–8.5%. Also, we found that MST prediction using the same data performs more accurately than using the DST (Table 3). This finding illustrates that the monthly temporalization of photo popularity dynamics on Flickr are more effective than day based analysis.

4.6 Sample Results

The purpose of this experiment is to observe the time-sensitive characteristic of our model by predicting the average ranking correlation of different photo categories. Sample photos with the associated image category tags are illustrated in Figure 4. It can be found that our model does per-

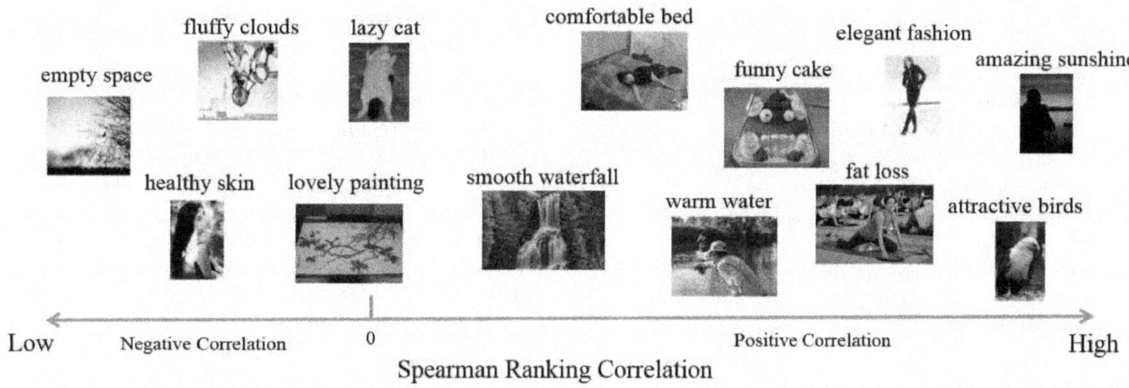

Figure 4: Sample photos with annotated image tags. In comparison to state-of-the-art methods, our approach takes into account both multi-scale temporal and contextual information. Accordingly, we can obtain higher correlation not only on the photos with clear temporal characteristic (e.g. "amazing sunshine" photos) but also on other common photos (e.g. "attractive birds" photos).

form better for photos with time-related tags (e.g., "amazing sunshine") than those with general tags (e.g., "healthy skin"). According to the results, our model have good prediction performance on time-related photos, such as those tagged with "amazing sunshine", "fat loss" or "elegant fashion" (the performance on several photos is even as high as up to over than 0.6 in prediction). The content of these photos are related with temporal natural evolution, user activity or public preference [40]. Besides, the popularity of those with general category tags in the left part of Figure 4 are difficult to predict, such as "empty space", "fluffy clouds" etc. We found that three observations may lead to the results. Firstly, the popularity of photos are varying without obvious patterns even on content, such as "empty space" and "healthy skin" in Figure 4. That means the image tags are limited representations on abstract categories of photos. The second one is that some photos are blurred. This is also an unavoidable challenge not only to our model but also to others. Furthermore, several categories of photos like "lazy cat" or "lovely painting" have no obvious temporal patterns or even without explicit semantics for comprehension. This is a limitation of our model but might be improved in future works by incorporating into the text description content.

5. CONCLUSIONS AND FUTURE WORK

In this paper, we have presented a general framework named Multi-scale Temporalization for modeling dynamic popularity in social media from multiple time scale view. Specially, we propose a structured decomposition model at different time-scales instead of computation on whole popularity tensor directly with only intrinsic time information. The experimental results showed that our approach outperform the state-of-the-art methods, with a relative improvement of averagely 10.9%–47.5% of our approach, which demonstrates the effectiveness on predicting power.

There are several possible directions for future investigation on temporal popularity prediction. One is to exploit new clustering strategies for capturing contextual relevance in data rearrangement with temporal factors. Another open question would be discovering prospective strategies for popularity in evolving systems. Furthermore, to unfold evolving popularity online content for detecting or predicting the user activity or influence is also essential for exploring social signal in social media.

6. ACKNOWLEDGEMENTS

This work is supported by National High Technology Research and Development Program of China (2014AA015202), National Nature Science Foundation of China (61525206, 61571424, 61428207) and Beijing Advanced Innovation Center for Imaging Technology (BAICIT-2016009).

7. REFERENCES

[1] J. Bagadiya. 125 amazing social media statistics you should know in 2016. https://socialpilot.co/blog/125-amazing-social-media-statistics-know-2016/. [Online].

[2] A. Khosla, A. Das Sarma, and R. Hamid. What makes an imag e popular? In *Proc. of WWW*, 2014.

[3] B. Wu, T. Mei, W.-H. Cheng, and Y. Zhang. Unfolding temporal dynamics: Predicting social media popularity using multi-scale temporal decomposition. In *Proc. of AAAI*, 2016.

[4] P. J. McParlane, Y. Moshfeghi, and J. M. Jose. Nobody comes here anymore, it's too crowded; predicting image popularity on flickr. In *Proc. of ICMR*, 2014.

[5] H.-Y. Chi, C.-C. Chen, W.-H. Cheng, and M.-S. Chen. Ubishop: Commercial item recommendation using visual part-based object representation. *Multimedia Tools and Applications*, pages 1–23, 2015.

[6] C. Li, Y. Lu, Q. Mei, D. Wang, and S. Pandey. Click-through prediction for advertising in twitter timeline. In *Proc. of KDD*, 2015.

[7] C.-C. Wu, T. Mei, W. H. Hsu, and Y. Rui. Learning to personalize trending image search suggestion. In *Proc. of SIGIR*, 2014.

[8] T.-H. Tsai, W.-H. Cheng, and Y.-H. Hsieh. Dynamic social network for narrative video analysis. In *Proc. of ACM MM*, 2011.

[9] Z. Wang, W. Zhu, X. Chen, L. Sun, J. Liu, M. Chen, P. Cui, and S. Yang. Propagation-based social-aware multimedia content distribution. *ACM Transactions*

on Multimedia Computing, Communications, and Applications (TOMM), 9(1s):52, 2013.

[10] S. Kong, Q. Mei, L. Feng, F. Ye, and Z. Zhao. Predicting bursts and popularity of hashtags in real-time. In *Proc. of SIGIR*, 2014.

[11] S. D. Roy, T. Mei, W. Zeng, and S. Li. Towards cross-domain learning for social video popularity prediction. *IEEE Transactions on multimedia*, 15(6):1255–1267, 2013.

[12] G. Szabo and B. A. Huberman. Predicting the popularity of online content. *Communications of the ACM*, 53(8):80–88, 2010.

[13] M. Mathioudakis and N. Koudas. Twittermonitor, trend detection over the twitter stream. In *Proc. of SIGMOD*, 2010.

[14] J. Yang and J. Leskovec. Patterns of temporal variation in online media. In *Proc. of WSDM*, 2011.

[15] J. Zhuang, T. Mei, S. C. Hoi, X.-S. Hua, and S. Li. Modeling social strength in social media community via kernel-based learning. In *Proc. of ACM MM*, 2011.

[16] H.-W. Shen, D. Wang, C. Song, and A.-L. Barabási. Modeling and predicting popularity dynamics via reinforced poisson processes. In *Proc. of AAAI*, 2014.

[17] X. He, M. Gao, M.-Y. Kan, Y. Liu, and K. Sugiyama. Predicting the popularity of web 2.0 items based on user comments? In *Proc. of SIGIR*, 2014.

[18] Q. Zhao, M. A. Erdogdu, H. Y. He, A. Rajaraman, and J. Leskovec. Seismic, a self-exciting point process model for predicting tweet popularity. In *Proc. of KDD*, 2015.

[19] S. C. Hidayati, K.-L. Hua, W.-H. Cheng, and S.-W. Sun. What are the fashion trends in new york. In *Proc. of ACM MM*, 2014.

[20] S. C. Hidayati, W.-H. Cheng, and K.-L. Hua. Clothing genre classification by exploiting the style elements. In *Proc. of ACM MM*, 2012.

[21] S. M. Preum, J. A. Stankovic, and Y. Qi. Maper: A multi-scale adaptive personalized model for temporal human behavior prediction. In *Proc. of ICKM*, 2015.

[22] S. Cappallo, T. Mensink, and C. G. Snoek. Latent factors of visual popularity prediction. In *Proc. of ICMR*, 2015.

[23] D. Kong, C. Ding, and H. Huang. Robust nonnegative matrix factorization using l21-norm. In *Proc. of CIKM*, pages 673–682, 2011.

[24] D. Borth, R. Ji, T. Chen, T. Breuel, and S.-F. Chang. Large-scale visual sentiment ontology and detectors using adjective noun pairs. In *Proc. of ACM MM*, 2013.

[25] F. Gelli, T. Uricchio, M. Bertini, A. Del Bimbo, and S.-F. Chang. Image popularity prediction in social media using sentiment and context features. In *Proc. of ACM MM*, 2015.

[26] E. Denton, J. Weston, M. Paluri, L. Bourdev, and R. Fergus. User conditional hashtag prediction for images. In *Proc. of KDD*, 2015.

[27] M. Jiang, P. Cui, F. Wang, W. Zhu, and S. Yang. Scalable recommendation with social contextual. information. *IEEE Transactions on Knowledge and Data Engineering*, 26(11):2789–2802, 2014.

[28] Z. Jin, J. Cao, Y. Zhang, and J. Luo. News verification by exploiting conflicting social viewpoints in microblogs. In *Proc. of AAAI*, 2016.

[29] C. Gu, J. J. Lim, P. Arbeláez, and J. Malik. Recognition using regions. In *Proc. of CVPR*, 2009.

[30] R. Khan, J. Van de Weijer, F. Shahbaz Khan, D. Muselet, C. Ducottet, and C. Barat. Discriminative color descriptors. In *Proc. of CVPR*, 2013.

[31] N. Dalal and B. Triggs. Histograms of oriented gradients for human detection. In *Proc. of CVPR*, pages 886–893, 2005.

[32] J. Donahue, Y. Jia, O. Vinyals, J. Hoffman, N. Zhang, E. Tzeng, and T. Darrell. Decaf: A deep convolutional activation feature for generic visual recognition. In *Proc. of ICML*, pages 647–655, 2014.

[33] K. Wagstaff, C. Cardie, S. Rogers, S. Schrödl, et al. Constrained k-means clustering with background knowledge. In *Proc. of ICML*, 2001.

[34] J. Chen and Y. Saad. On the tensor svd and the optimal low rank orthogonal approximation of tensors. *Journal on Matrix Analysis and Applications*, 30(4):1709–1734, 2009.

[35] B. Gu, V. S. Sheng, K. Y. Tay, W. Romano, and S. Li. Incremental support vector learning for ordinal regression. *IEEE Transactions on Neural networks and learning systems*, 26(7):1403–1416, 2015.

[36] V. Koltchinskii, K. Lounici, and A. B. Tsybakov. Nuclear-norm penalization and optimal rates for noisy low-rank matrix completion. *The Annals of Statistics*, pages 2302–2329, 2011.

[37] A. S. Bandeira and R. van Handel. Sharp nonasymptotic bounds on the norm of random matrices with independent entries. *arXiv preprint arXiv:1408.6185*, 2014.

[38] S. Boyd, N. Parikh, E. Chu, B. Peleato, and J. Eckstein. Distributed optimization and statistical learning via the alternating direction method of multipliers. *Foundations and Trends in Machine Learning*, 3(1):1–122, 2011.

[39] Y. Koren. Collaborative filtering with temporal dynamics. *Communications of the ACM*, 26(11):2789–2802, 2010.

[40] C. Gan, N. Wang, Y. Yang, D.-Y. Yeung, and A. G. Hauptmann. Devnet: A deep event network for multimedia event detection and evidence recounting. In *Proc. of CVPR*, 2015.

Transform-Invariant Convolutional Neural Networks for Image Classification and Search

Xu Shen
CAS Key Laboratory of Technology in Geo-spatial Information Processing and Application System
University of Science and Technology of China
Hefei, Anhui, China 230027
shenxu@mail.ustc.edu.cn

Xinmei Tian
CAS Key Laboratory of Technology in Geo-spatial Information Processing and Application System
University of Science and Technology of China
Hefei, Anhui, China 230027
xinmei@ustc.edu.cn

Anfeng He
CAS Key Laboratory of Technology in Geo-spatial Information Processing and Application System
University of Science and Technology of China
Hefei, Anhui, China 230027
heanfeng@mail.ustc.edu.cn

Shaoyan Sun
CAS Key Laboratory of Technology in Geo-spatial Information Processing and Application System
University of Science and Technology of China
Hefei, Anhui, China 230027
sunshy@mail.ustc.edu.cn

Dacheng Tao
Centre for Quantum Computation & Intelligent Systems and the Faculty of Engineering and Information Technology
University of Technology, Sydney
Ultimo, NSW 2007, Australia
dacheng.tao@uts.edu.au

ABSTRACT

Convolutional neural networks (CNNs) have achieved state-of-the-art results on many visual recognition tasks. However, current CNN models still exhibit a poor ability to be invariant to spatial transformations of images. Intuitively, with sufficient layers and parameters, hierarchical combinations of convolution (matrix multiplication and non-linear activation) and pooling operations should be able to learn a robust mapping from transformed input images to transform-invariant representations. In this paper, we propose randomly transforming (rotation, scale, and translation) feature maps of CNNs during the training stage. This prevents complex dependencies of specific rotation, scale, and translation levels of training images in CNN models. Rather, each convolutional kernel learns to detect a feature that is generally helpful for producing the transform-invariant answer given the combinatorially large variety of transform levels of its input feature maps. In this way, we do not require any extra training supervision or modification to the optimization process and training images. We show that random transformation provides significant improvements of CNNs on many benchmark tasks, including small-scale image recognition, large-scale image recognition, and image retrieval.

MM'16, October 15–19, 2016, Amsterdam, The Netherlands.

DOI: http://dx.doi.org/10.1145/264284.2964316

Keywords

Convolutional Neural Networks; transform invariance.

1. INTRODUCTION

In recent years, computer vision has been significantly advanced by the adoption of convolutional neural networks (C-NNs). We are currently witnessing many CNN-based models achieving state-of-the-art results in many vision tasks, including image recognition [35, 32, 17, 8, 36], semantic segmentation [14], image captioning [19, 4, 5], image retrieval [40, 41, 39], action recognition [11, 31], video concept learning [7, 9] and video captioning [38, 28].

The local transform-invariant property of CNNs lies in the combination of local receptive fields with shared weights and pooling. Because distortions or shifts of the input can cause the positions of salient features to vary, local receptive fields with shared weights are able to detect invariant elementary features despite changes in the positions of salient features [24]. Moreover, average-pooling or max-pooling reduces the resolution of the feature maps in each layer, which reduces the sensitivity of the output to small local shifts and distortions. However, due to the typically small local spatial support for pooling (e.g., 2×2 pixels) and convolution (e.g., 9×9 kernel size), large global invariance is only possible for a very deep hierarchy of pooling and convolutions, and the intermediate feature maps in CNNs are not invariant to large transformations of the input data [25]. This limitation of C-NNs results from the poor capacity of pooling and the convolution mechanism in learning global transform-invariant representations (Fig. 1).

In this work, we introduce a random transformation module of feature maps that can be included in any layer in a CNN. Intuitively, with sufficient layers and parameter-

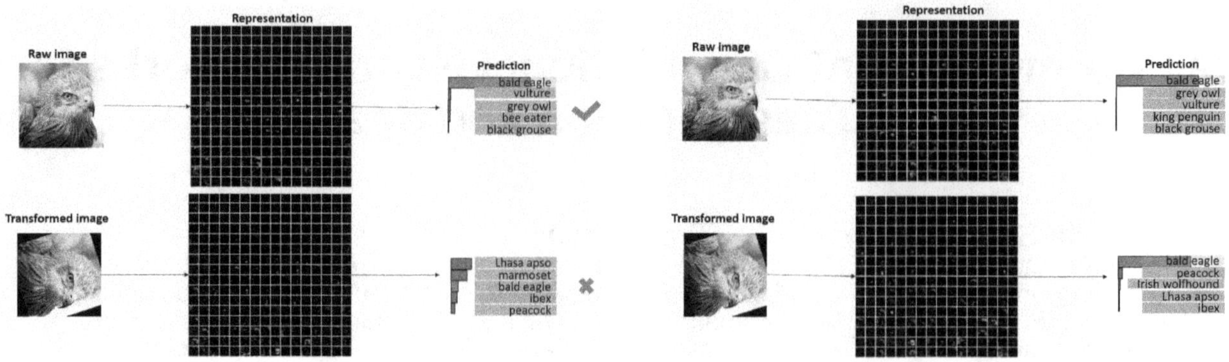

(a) CNN (b) Transform Invariant CNN

Figure 1: Limitation of current CNN models. The length of the horizontal bars is proportional to the probability assigned to the labels by the model, and pink indicates ground truth. Transform of input image causes the CNN to produce an incorrect prediction (a). Additionally, the representations ($256 \times 14 \times 14$ conv5 feature maps of AlexNet [21]) are quite different, while the representation and prediction of our transform-invariant CNN (same architecture as [21]) is more consistent (b).

s, hierarchical combinations of convolution (matrix multiplication and non-linear activation) and pooling operations should have sufficient complexity to learn a robust mapping from input images with any transform to transform-invariant representations. All we need is to introduce a global way to push the CNN to learn with little dependency on the transform of input images. Our method is inspired by the success of dropout [27]. In dropout, each hidden unit is randomly omitted from the network with a probability (e.g., 0.5) on each presentation of each training case. Therefore, a hidden unit cannot rely on other hidden units being present. In this way, each neuron learns to detect a independent feature that is generally robust for producing the correct answer with little dependency on the variety of internal contexts in the same layer. Similarly, randomly transforming (rotation, scale, and translation) feature maps of CNNs during the training stage prevents complex dependencies of specific rotation, scale, and translation levels of training images in CNN models. Rather, each convolutional kernel learns to detect a feature that is generally helpful for producing the transform-invariant answer given the combinatorially large variety of transform levels of its input feature maps.

In contrast to pooling layers, in which receptive fields are fixed and local, the random transformation is performed on the entire feature map (non-locally) and can include any transformation, including scaling, rotation, and translation. This guides the CNN to learn global transformation-invariant representations from raw input images. Notably, CNNs with random transformation layers can be trained with standard back-propagation, allowing for end-to-end training of the models in which they are injected. In addition, we do not require any extra training supervision or modification of the optimization process or any transform of training images.

The main contributions of this work are as follows. (i) We propose a very simple approach to train robust transform-invariant convolutional neural networks. (ii) Because our model does not possess any extra parameters or extra feature extraction modules, it can be used to replace traditional CNNs in any CNN-based model. Therefore, this is a general approach for improving the performance of CNN-based models in any vision task. (iii) The validity of our method confirms that CNNs still have the potential to model a more robust mapping from transform-variant images to transform-invariant representations; we just need to push them to do so.

The remainder of this paper is structured as follows. Related works of transform-invariant CNNs are discussed in Section 2. The architecture and learning procedure of the proposed transform-invariant CNNs are described in Section 3. Extensive evaluations compared with the state-of-the-art and comprehensive analysis of the proposed approach are reported in Section 4. Conclusions are presented in Section 5.

2. RELATED WORK

The equivalence and invariance of CNN representations to input image transformations were investigated in [34, 3, 10]. Specifically, Cohen and Welling [3] showed that the linear transform of a good visual representation was equivalent to a combination of the elementary irreducible representations by using the theory of group representations. Lenc and and Vedaldi [25] estimated the linear relationships between representations of the original and transformed images. Gens and Domingos [10] proposed a generalization of CNN that forms feature maps over arbitrary symmetry groups based on the theory of symmetry groups in [34], resulting in feature maps that were more invariant to symmetry groups. Bruna and Mallat [2] proposed a wavelet scattering network to compute a translation-invariant image representation. Local linear transformations were adopted in feature learning algorithms in [33] for the purpose of transformation-invariant feature learning.

Many recent works have focused on introducing transformation invariance in deep learning architectures explicitly. For unsupervised feature learning, Sohn and Lee [33] presented a transform-invariant restricted Boltzmann machine that compactly represented data by its weights and their transformations, which achieved invariance of the feature representation via probabilistic max pooling. Each hidden unit was augmented with a latent transformation assignment variable that described the selection of the transformed view of the weights associated with the unit in [20]. In these two works, the transformed filters were only applied at the center of the largest receptive field size. In tied convolutional neural works [23], invariances were learned explicitly by square-root pooling hidden units that were computed by partially un-tied weights. Here, additional learned parameters were needed when un-tying weights. Alvarez *et al.* [1] learned each ConvNet over multiple scales independently without weight sharing and fused the outputs of these ConvNets. Sermanet and LeCun [30] utilized multi-scale CNN features by feeding the outputs of all the convolutional layers to the classifier. In these two models, multiple-scale information was captured from different levels or models of the hierarchy, but scale invariance was not encoded in the features learned at a layer because each layer is only applied to the original scale. In [6], the raw input image was transformed through a Laplacian pyramid. Each scale was fed into a 3-stage convolutional network, which produces a set of feature maps with different scales disjointly. Then, the outputs of all scales were aligned by up-sampling and concatenated. However, concatenating multi-scale outputs to extract scale-independent features involves extra convolution models and extra parameters, thereby increasing the complexity of the models and the computational cost.

The latest two works on incorporating transform invariance in CNNs are described in [18, 15]. In [18], feature maps in CNNs were scaled to multiple levels, and the same kernel was convolved across the input in each scale. Then, the responses of the convolution in each scale were normalized and pooled at each spatial location to obtain a locally scale-invariant representation. In this model, only limited scales were considered, and extra modules were needed in the feature extraction process. To address different transformation types in input images, [15] proposed inserting a spatial transformer module between CNN layers, which explicitly transformed the input image into the proper appearance and fed that transformed input into CNN model. In this work, invariance comes from the extra transformation module, while invariance of the CNN itself is not improved.

In conclusion, all the aforementioned related works improve the transform invariance of deep learning models by adding *extra feature extraction modules*, *more learnable parameters* or *extra transformations on input images*, which makes trained CNN models problem dependent and not easy to be generalized to other datasets. In contrast, in this paper, we propose a very simple random transform operation on feature maps during the training of CNN models. Intrinsic transform invariance of the current CNN model is obtained by pushing the model to learn more robust parameters from raw input images only. No extra feature extraction modules or more learnable parameters are required. Therefore, it is very easy to apply the trained transform-invariant CNN model to any vision task because we only need to replace current CNN parameters by this trained model.

3. TRANSFORM-INVARIANT CONVOLUTIONAL NEURAL NETWORKS

3.1 Convolutional Neural Networks

Convolutional neural networks (CNNs) are a supervised feed-forward multi-layer architecture in which each layer learns a representation by applying feature detectors to previous feature maps. The outputs of the final layer are fed into a classifier or regressor with a target cost function such that the network can be trained to solve supervised tasks. The entire network is learned through stochastic gradient descent with gradients obtained by back-propagation [24]. In general, a layer in a CNN consists of local patch-based linear feature extraction and non-linear activation, occasionally followed by spatial pooling or normalization.

The core concept of CNNs is a combination of local receptive fields, shared weights, and spatial pooling. Each unit in a layer receives inputs from a set of units located in a small neighborhood in the previous layer. This idea of connecting units to local receptive fields is inspired by Wiesel's discovery of locally sensitive and orientation-selective neurons in the visual system of cats [24]. The output of convolving an input layer with one kernel is called a *feature map*. Because elementary feature detectors (convolutional weights) that are useful on one part of the image should also be useful across the entire image, units in the same feature map share the same set of weights at multiple locations. This is a good way to reduce the number of trainable parameters and ensure some local shift and distortion invariance. Pooling is a simple way to reduce the spatial resolution of the feature map and also reduces the sensitivity of convolution outputs to shifts and distortions.

In the forward pass of a CNN, each output feature map is computed by convolving input feature maps with kernel weights and then activated by a non-linear activation function:

$$x_j^l = f((W_j^l * x^{l-1}) + b_j^l) \tag{1}$$

where $*$ is the convolution operator, x^{l-1} is the input feature maps from the previous layer, and f is a non-linear function. W_j^l and b_j^l are the trainable weights and bias of jth output feature map x_j^l.

3.2 Transformation of an Image

The basic 2D transformation of an image consists of 3 types: *translation*, *rotation*, and *scale* [29]. The locations of pixels in an image before transformation and after transformation are denoted as (x, y) and (x', y'), respectively. Translation is calculated by:

$$(x', y', 1) = (x, y, 1)\begin{bmatrix} 1 & 0 & 0 \\ 0 & 1 & 0 \\ d_x & d_y & 1 \end{bmatrix} \tag{2}$$

where d_x and d_y are the numbers of translated pixels in the x and y axes, respectively.

Scale is computed by:

$$(x', y', 1) = (x, y, 1)\begin{bmatrix} s_x & 0 & 0 \\ 0 & s_y & 0 \\ 0 & 0 & 1 \end{bmatrix} \tag{3}$$

where s_x and s_y are the scale factors in the x and y axes, respectively.

Rotation is computed by:

$$(x', y', 1) = (x, y, 1)\begin{bmatrix} cos\theta & sin\theta & 0 \\ -sin\theta & cos\theta & 0 \\ 0 & 0 & 1 \end{bmatrix} \tag{4}$$

where θ is the rotation angle ranging from $-180°$ to $180°$.

When translation, scale, and rotation are applied to an

image simultaneously, the output can be computed as:

$$(x', y', 1) = (x, y, 1)\begin{bmatrix} cos\theta & sin\theta & 0 \\ -sin\theta & cos\theta & 0 \\ 0 & 0 & 1 \end{bmatrix} \begin{bmatrix} s_x & 0 & 0 \\ 0 & s_y & 0 \\ 0 & 0 & 1 \end{bmatrix} \begin{bmatrix} 1 & 0 & 0 \\ 0 & 1 & 0 \\ d_x & d_y & 1 \end{bmatrix} \quad (5)$$

3.3 Transform-Invariant Convolutional Neural Networks

Weight sharing makes CNN capable of detecting features regardless of their spatial locations in the input feature maps. Pooling reduces the sensitivity of CNN to local shifts and distortions in input images. However, when faced with global transformations of input images, the performance of CNNs is significantly decreased. In this section, we describe our transform-invariant CNN (TICNN). By introducing random transformations (scale, rotation, and translation) of feature maps in the CNN model, convolutional kernels are trained to be invariant to these transformations. Fig. 2 presents a side-by-side comparison of the overall structure of these two CNN layers.

One perspective to interpret TICNN is to compare it with dropout [27]. Dropout attempts to introduce a neuron-level randomness to deep models; in this way, the dependency of the feature detector on the existence of neurons in the same layer is reduced. TICNN attempts to incorporate a feature map (concept)-level randomness in CNN models, which can reduce the dependence of feature detectors in the current layer on the transform level of previous feature maps (appearance).

From the perspective of transformation, Jaderberg *et al.* [15] proposed transforming the input into a proper and easy-to-recognize appearance. TICNN forces the architecture to learn a more robust model for all possible transformations, and the intrinsic transform invariance of the architecture is improved.

From the perspective of data augmentation, training data augmentation and multi-scale model augmentation [18, 6] only provide the model with limited transform levels of input images or feature maps. While in TICNN, as training proceeds, the model will learn almost all transformation levels of inputs randomly. Therefore, TICNN should be more robust when input images are transformed.

Considering the spatial range of transformation invariance, pooling can only address a local invariance for shifts and distortions (e.g., 3×3 pixels). Our TICNN paves the way for global invariance of transformations in CNN models.

3.3.1 Forward Propagation

Our goal is to push each feature detector to learn a feature that is generally helpful for producing the transform-invariant answer given a large variety of transform levels of its input feature maps. To accomplish this goal, before being convolved by the convolutional kernels/filters, the input feature maps are first scaled, rotated and translated via a random sampled scale factor, rotation angle and translate proportion. To keep the size of feature maps unchanged, the transformed feature maps are either cropped or padded with 0s to be properly convolved.

Specifically, let $\mathcal{T}$ be a linear image transform operator that applies random spatial transformations to an input x. The output feature map y is computed as:

$$\hat{x} = \mathcal{T}(x) \quad (6)$$

$$y = f((W * \hat{x}) + b) \quad (7)$$

Here, the 3×3 transformation matrix $\mathcal{T}$ is randomly sampled as follows:

$$\mathcal{T} = \begin{bmatrix} cos\theta & sin\theta & 0 \\ -sin\theta & cos\theta & 0 \\ 0 & 0 & 1 \end{bmatrix} \begin{bmatrix} s_x & 0 & 0 \\ 0 & s_y & 0 \\ 0 & 0 & 1 \end{bmatrix} \begin{bmatrix} 1 & 0 & 0 \\ 0 & 1 & 0 \\ d_x & d_y & 1 \end{bmatrix} \quad (8)$$

where $\theta \sim \mathcal{N}(\mu_\theta, \sigma_\theta^2)$, $s_x, s_y \sim \mathcal{N}(\mu_s, \sigma_s^2)$, and $d_x, d_y \sim \mathcal{N}(\mu_d, \sigma_d^2)$. In the presence of each training image, $\{\theta$, s_x, s_y, d_x, and $d_y\}$ are randomly sampled.

3.3.2 Back-Propagation

Because the transform-invariant convolution layer consists of only linear operations, its gradients can be computed by a simple modification of the back-propagation algorithm. For each transformation, the error signal is propagated through the bilinear coefficients used to compute the transformation.

Let x^{l-1} denote the vectorized input of layer l of length m ($m = hwc$ for a h by w by c image). If the dimensionality of the transformed output is n, the transformation $\mathcal{T}$ of input x^{l-1} can be computed via Tx^{l-1}, where T is an $n \times m$ interpolation coefficient matrix. Specifically, each row of T has 4 non-zero coefficients with bilinear interpolation. By encoding kernel weights W as a Toeplitz matrix, the convolution operation can be expressed as:

$$z^l = toep(W)(Tx^{l-1}) + b^l \quad (9)$$

$$x^l = f(z^l) \quad (10)$$

where f is a non-linear function and b^l is the bias.

Then, the error propagated from the previous layer δ^{l+1} to the current layer δ^l can be computed by:

$$\delta^l = T^\top toep(W)^\top f'(z^l) \odot \delta^{l+1} \quad (11)$$

3.3.3 Testing

Because our model does not introduce any extra parameters or feature extraction modules, we only need to replace parameters in the CNN model with parameters trained by our model. The test architectures and all other settings are identical.

4. EXPERIMENTS

In this section, we evaluate our proposed transform-invariant CNN on several supervised learning tasks. First, to compare our model with state-of-the-art methods, we conduct experiments on the distorted versions of the MNIST handwriting dataset as in [18, 15]. The results in Section 4.1 show that TICNN is capable of achieving comparable or better classification performance with only raw input images and without adding any extra feature extraction modules or learnable parameters. Second, to test the improvement of TICNN on CNN for large-scale real-world image recognition tasks, we compare our model with AlexNet [21] on the ImageNet-2012

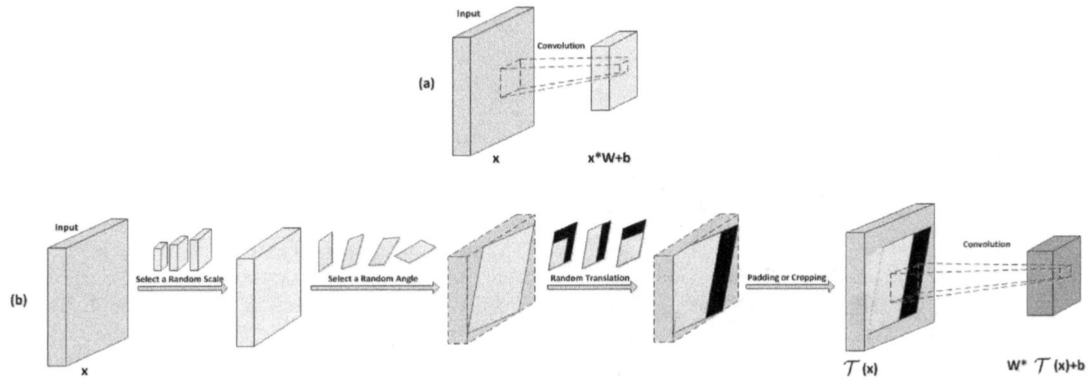

Figure 2: Detailed comparison of the structure of (a) convolution layer and the proposed (b) *transform-invariant* convolution layer. In (b), after convolving the inputs with the kernel, the output feature maps are transformed by a random rotation angle, scale factor, and translation proportion. Then, the randomly transformed feature maps are fed into the next layer.

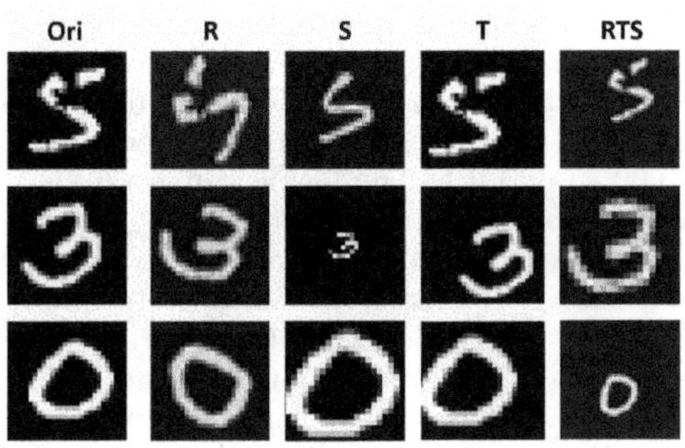

Figure 3: Examples of distorted MNIST dataset. Ori: raw images. R: rotated images. S: scaled images. T: translated images. RTS: images with scale, rotation and translation.

Method	R	S	T	RST
FCN	2.1	2.8	2.9	5.2
CNN	1.2	1.4	1.3	0.8
ST-CNN[15]	**0.8**	0.9	0.8	**0.6**
SI-CNN[18]	-	1.0	-	-
TI-CNN(ours)	**0.8**	**0.8**	**0.7**	**0.6**

Table 1: Classification error on the transformed MNIST dataset. The different distorted MNIST datasets are R: rotation, S: scale, T: translation, and RST: rotation-scale-translation. All models have the same number of parameters and use the same basic architectures.

dataset in Section 4.2. The results demonstrate that, with little degradation on the performance of classifying original test images, random transform can be applied to any layer in the CNN model and is able to consistently improve the performance on transformed images significantly. Finally, to evaluate the generalization ability of the TICNN model on other vision tasks with real-world transformations of images, we apply our model to solve the image retrieval task on the UK-Bench [26] dataset in Section 4.3. The improvement of retrieval performance reveals that the TICNN model has a good generalization ability and is better at solving real-world transformation varieties. We implement our method using the open source Caffe framework [16]. Our code and model will be available online.

4.1 MNIST

In this section, we use the MNIST handwriting dataset to evaluate all deep models. In particular, different neural networks are trained to classify MNIST data that have been transformed in various ways, including rotation (R), scale (S), translation (T), and rotation-scale-translation (RTS). The rotated dataset was generated from rotating MNIST digits with a random angle sampled from a uniform distribution $U[-90°, 90°]$. The scaled dataset was generated by scaling the digits randomly with a scale factor sampled from $U[0.7, 1.2]$. The translated dataset was generated from randomly locating the 28×28 digit in a 42×42 canvas. The rotated-translated-scaled dataset (RTS) was generated by randomly rotating the digit by $-45°$ to $-45°$, randomly scaling the digit by a factor ranging from [0.7, 1.2] and placing the digit at a location in a 42×42 image randomly, all with a uniform distribution. Some example images are presented in Fig. 3.

Following [15], all networks use the ReLU activation function and softmax classifiers. All CNN networks have a 9×9 convolutional layer (stride 1, no padding), a 2×2 max-pooling layer with stride 2, a subsequent 7×7 convolutional layer (stride 1, no padding), and another 2×2 max-pooling layer with stride 2 before the final classification layer. All CNN networks have 64 filters per layer. For the method in [18], convolution layers are replaced by scale-invariant layers using six scales from 0.6 to 2 at a scale step of $2^{1/3} = 1.26$. The spatial transformer module is placed at the beginning of the network [15]. In our random transform-invariant C-NN, the random transformation of the feature map module is applied to the second convolution layer, and *our model is only trained on the raw input images.* The rotation angle is sampled from $\mathcal{N}(0, 30^2)$, the scale factor is sampled from $\mathcal{N}(1, 0.15^2)$, and the translation proportion is sampled from $\mathcal{N}(0, 0.2^2)$.

All networks were trained with SGD for 150000 iterations, 256 batch size, 0.01 base learning rate, no weight decay,

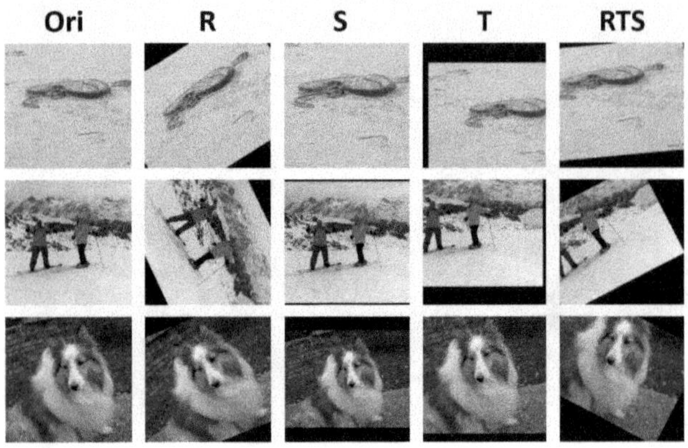

Figure 4: Distorted images in ImageNet. Ori: raw images. R: rotated images. S: scaled images. T: translated images. RTS: images with scale, rotation and translation.

and no dropout. The learning rate was reduced by a factor of 0.1 every 50000 iterations. The weights were initialized randomly, and all networks shared the same random seed.

The experimental results are summarized in Table 1. Please notice that we do not report the best result of ST-CNN [15], which was trained with a more narrow class of transformations selected manually (affine transformations).In our method, we did not optimize with respected to transformation classes. Therefore we compare with the most general ST-CNN defined for a class of projection transformations as in [22]. This table shows that our model achieves better performance on scale and translation and comparable performance on rotation and rotation-scale-translation. Because our model does not require any extra learnable parameters, feature extraction modules, or transformations on training images, the comparable performance still reflects the superiority of TICNN. In addition, the experimental results also indicate that the combination of convolution and pooling modules have some limitations on learning the invariance of rotation. Placing extra transformation modules at the beginning of the CNN is a more powerful way to compensate for this limitation.

4.2 ILSVRC-2012

The ILSVRC-2012 dataset was used for ILSVRC 2012 – 2014 challenges. This dataset includes images of 1000 classes, and it is split into three subsets: training (1.3M images), validation (50K images), and testing (100K images with held-out class labels). The classification performance is evaluated using two measures: the top-1 and top-5 errors. The former is a multi-class classification error. The latter is the main evaluation criterion used in ILSVRC and is defined as the proportion of images whose ground-truth category is not in the top-5 predicted categories. We use this dataset to test the performance of our model on large-scale image recognition tasks.

CNN models are trained on raw images and tested on both raw and transformed images. For all transform types, specific transformations are applied to the original images. Then, the transformed images are rescaled to have a 256 smallest image side. Finally, the center 224×224 crop is used for the test. The rotated (R) dataset was generated by randomly rotating the original images from $-45°$ to $45°$ with a uniform distribution. The scaled dataset (S) was generated by scaling the original images randomly in $U[0.7, 1.5]$. The translated dataset (T) was generated by randomly shifting the image by a proportion of $U[-0.2, 0.2]$. For the rotation-scale-translation (RTS) dataset, all the aforementioned transformations were applied. Some examples of transformed images are presented in Fig. 4.

The architecture of our CNN model is the same as that of AlexNet [21]. This model consists of 5 convolution layers and 2 fully connected layers. The first convolution layer contains 96 kernels of size $11 \times 11 \times 3$. The second convolution layer contains 256 kernels of size $5 \times 5 \times 48$. The third convolutional layer contains 384 kernels of size $3 \times 3 \times 256$. The fourth convolutional layer contains 384 kernels of size $3 \times 3 \times 192$, and the fifth convolutional layer contains 256 kernels of size $3 \times 3 \times 192$. The fully connected layers have 4096 neurons each. Please refer to [21] for more details.

The model is trained for 450,000 iterations. We use a base learning rate of 0.01 and decay it by 0.1 every 100,000 iterations. We use a momentum of 0.9, weight decay of 0.0005, and a weight clip of 35. The convolutional kernel weights and bias are initialized by $\mathcal{N}(0, 0.01^2)$ and 0.1, respectively. The weights and bias of fully connected layers are initialized by $\mathcal{N}(0, 0.005^2)$ and 0.1. The bias learning rate is set to be $2\times$ the learning rate for the weights.

To investigate the influence of a random transformation module on the CNN model, we apply it to different convolution layers. The experimental results are summarized in Table 2 (test on raw validation set) and Table 3 (test on transformed validation set). Some key insights obtained from the results are listed as follows:

- In general, when random transforms are applied to feature maps of higher layers in the CNN model, the recognition performance on both the original dataset and transformed dataset tends to be better. A possible explanation for this result is that representations extracted by lower layers are elementary features; they are related to a very precise location and have a very high resolution. Feature maps with higher resolution will be considerably more sensitive to transformations and noise, and location changes in lower-level feature maps could lead to a significant change in their visual pattern. Therefore, when a random transform is applied to feature maps of lower layers, it could be very difficult for the model to infer the original image content. Consequently, the useful information that the model can efficiently learn from each sample is reduced.

- By incorporating a random transformation, the model can still obtain comparable or even better performance than the CNN model on raw test images; this phenomenon shows that this randomness can prevent overfitting. Notably, the performance on transformed images is significantly improved on all transformation types (rotation, translation, scale, and rotation-translation-scale), indicating that TICNN improves the generalization ability of the CNN model on transformation variances.

- Applying our random transform module on the image data layer is identical to unlimited data augmentation. Models with random transformations on the

Model	R	T	S	RTS
CNN+Data Augmentation	56.3/79.7	56.3/79.4	55.6/78.9	56.6/79.8
TI-Conv1	55.0/78.4	56.6/79.7	56.2/79.1	56.5/79.4
TI-Conv2	56.1/79.3	56.5/79.7	56.2/79.3	56.6/79.7
TI-Conv3	56.7/79.6	56.9/79.9	56.4/79.4	57.0/80.0
TI-Conv4	57.1/80.1	57.2/80.1	56.7/79.5	56.9/79.9
TI-Conv5	57.1/80.2	**57.6/80.5**	57.0/80.0	57.1/80.0
TI-Conv1,2,5	57.2/80.2	57.5/80.4	57.1/80.2	57.2/80.3
SI-CNN	57.3/80.3			
CNN	57.1/80.2			

Table 2: Classification accuracy on the ILSVRC-2012 validation set (raw). TI-Conv$i$ indicates that we apply random transformations on the feature maps of layer i. R, T, S, and RTS represent rotation, translation, scale, and rotation-scale-translation, respectively.

Model	R	T	S	RTS
CNN+Data Augmentation	36.5/58.3	50.0/73.9	54.0/77.6	36.0/58.2
TI-Conv1	35.7/57.9	50.5/74.4	54.0/77.5	35.6/58.0
TI-Conv2	36.1/58.2	49.9/74.0	53.9/77.5	35.5/57.8
TI-Conv3	36.8/58.9	50.0/74.2	54.6/77.9	36.3/58.9
TI-Conv4	37.2/59.5	50.3/74.3	54.5/77.7	36.2/58.9
TI-Conv5	37.1/59.2	50.1/74.6	54.7/78.0	36.0/58.7
TI-Conv1,2,5	**37.3/60.2**	**51.3/75.4**	**55.0/78.5**	**37.5/60.5**
SI-CNN	-	-	53.8/77.3	-
CNN	36.6/57.7	46.5/70.8	53.3/76.9	33.3/55.2

Table 3: Classification accuracy on the transformed ILSVRC-2012 validation set. TI-Conv$i$ indicates that we apply random transformations on the feature maps of layer i. R, T, S and RTS represent rotation, translation, scale, and rotation-translation-scale, respectively.

image data layer are worse than models with random transformations on the convolutional layer, revealing that TICNN model is better than simple image data augmentation.

- Comparing Table 2 with Table 3, we can observe that the performance of CNN models significantly decreases when faced with transformations. The combination of convolution operations and pooling operations shows limited capacity for transform invariance. We need to add more powerful modules into current CNNs in the future.

Effect on Feature Detectors. We evaluate the transform invariance achieved by our model using the invariance measure proposed in [12]. In this approach, a neuron is considered to be firing when its response is above a certain threshold t_i. Each t_i is chosen to satisfy the condition that $G(i) = \sum |h_i(x) > t_i|/N$ is greater than 0.01, where N is the number of inputs. Then *local firing rate* $L(i)$ is computed as the proportion of transformed inputs that a neuron fires to. To ensure that a neuron is selective and with a high local firing rate (invariance to the set of the transformed inputs), the invariance score of a neuron is computed by the ratio of its invariance to selectivity, i.e., $L(i)/G(i)$. We report the average of the top 20% highest scoring neurons ($p = 0.2$) as in [18]. Please refer to [12] for more details.

Here, we construct the transformed dataset by applying rotation ($[-45°, 45°]$ with step size 9°), scale ($[0.7, 1.5]$ with step size 0.08) and translation ($[-0.2, 0.2]$ with step size 0.04) on the 50,000 validation images of ImageNet-2012. Fig. 5 shows the invariance scores of CNN (AlexNet) and

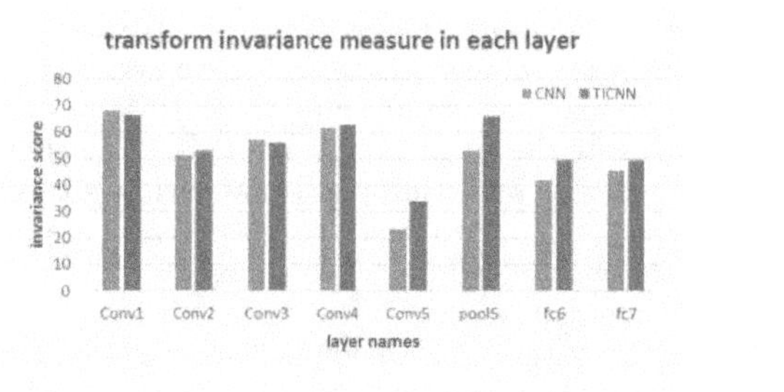

Figure 5: Transform invariance measure (the larger the better).

TICNN (TI-Conv1,2,5) measured at the end of each layer. We can observe that by applying random transformation on feature maps during training, TICNN produces features that are more transform invariant than those from CNN models.

Some Examples. Figure 6 shows some test cases in which CNN is unable to predict correct labels for the input images while TICNN generates true predictions. They demonstrate that TICNN is more robust than the CNN model.

4.3 UK-Bench

We also evaluate our TICNN model on the popular image retrieval benchmark dataset UK-Bench [26]. This dataset includes 2550 groups of images, each containing 4 relevant samples about one certain object or scene from different

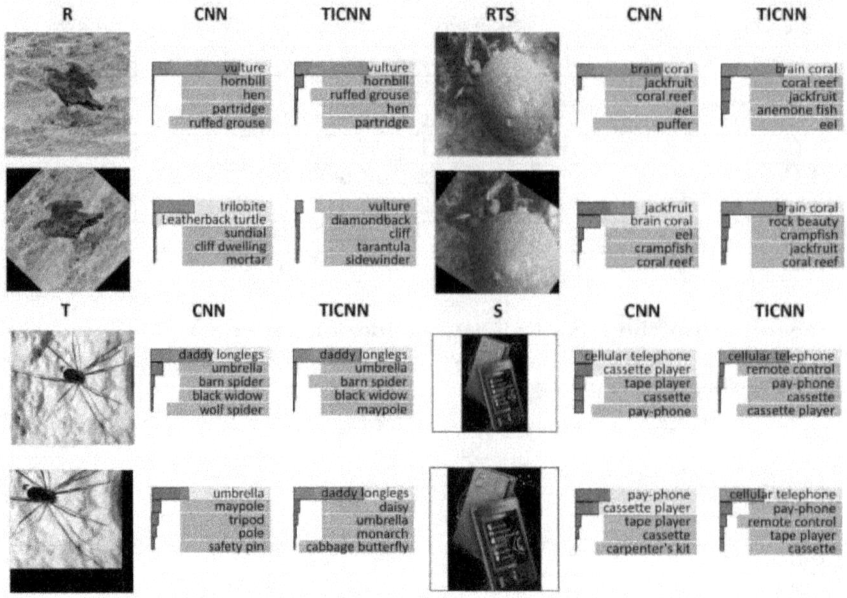

Figure 6: Some ImageNet test cases with the 5 most probable labels as predicted by AlexNet and our model. The length of the horizontal bars is proportional to the probability assigned to the labels by the model. Pink indicates ground-truth. The transformations applied to input images are rotation (R), scale (S), translation (T), and rotation-scale-translation (RTS).

viewpoints. Each of the total 10200 images is used as one query to perform image retrieval targeting at finding all its 3 counterparts. We choose UK-Bench because the viewpoint variation in the dataset is very common. Although many of the variation types are beyond the three types of geometry transformations that we attempt to address in this paper, we demonstrate the effectiveness of TICNN for solving many severe rotation, translation and scale variance cases in image retrieval tasks. To test the CNNs in a dataset with larger scale, we also add the $1M$ images in MIR Flickr [13] as negative examples.

For feature extraction, we follow the practice proposed in [37] to feed each image into the TICNN and CNN models, and we perform average pooling on the last pooling layer to obtain a compact feature representation. Specifically, we apply the AlexNet architecture for the baseline CNN model and the TICNN model, of which the fifth pooling layer generates a $13 \times 13 \times 256$ shape response map. We obtain the average values for each of the 256 channels and obtain a 256-dimensional feature for every image. Subsequently, we compute the root value of each dimension and perform $L2$ normalization.

To perform image retrieval in UK-Bench, the Euclidean distances of the query image with respect to all 10200 database images are computed and sorted. Images with the smallest distances are returned as top ranked images. The NS-Score (average top four accuracy) is used to evaluate the performance, and a score of 4.0 means that all the relevant images are successfully retrieved in the top four results.

In the evaluation, we compare our TI-Conv1,2,5 model with the AlexNet model trained on ImageNet. As shown in Table 4, TICNN achieves a considerable performance improvement. After carefully analyzing the retrieved results, we find that our model successfully solves multiple transformation cases in the retrieval task. In Fig. 7, we illustrate six positive cases in which TICNN outperforms the baseline in Figs. 7(a)-7(f), and we also provide two negative cases in Fig. 7(g)-7(h).

Model	UK-Bench	UK-Bench+MIRFlickr
TICNN (R)	**3.572**	**3.483**
TICNN (T)	3.536	3.452
TICNN (S)	3.551	3.461
TICNN (RTS)	3.561	3.479
CNN	3.518	3.350
SIFT	3.350	3.295

Table 4: Performance of the TICNN and CNN models on the UK-Bench retrieval dataset. TICNN has the same architecture as AlexNet. R, T, S and RTS represent ration, translation, scale, and rotation-translation-scale, respectively.

As shown in Fig. 7(a), the CNN model only retrieves one relevant image, while TICNN retrieves another one as shown in the bottom row. The additionally returned database image has an obvious scale transformation with respect to the query, and it is successfully retrieved as the most similar one in the database by our model. As shown in Fig. 7(b) and Fig. 7(c), our model also performs better for rotation variance than CNN. In Fig. 7(d) and Fig. 7(e), the objects (the road sign and basketball) appear in different scales and different spatial locations, which impacts the performance of CNN but is well handled by TICNN.

Regarding the failure cases of TICNN shown in Fig. 7(g), our model returns a false positive sample as shown in the third column of the bottom row. We observe that this false

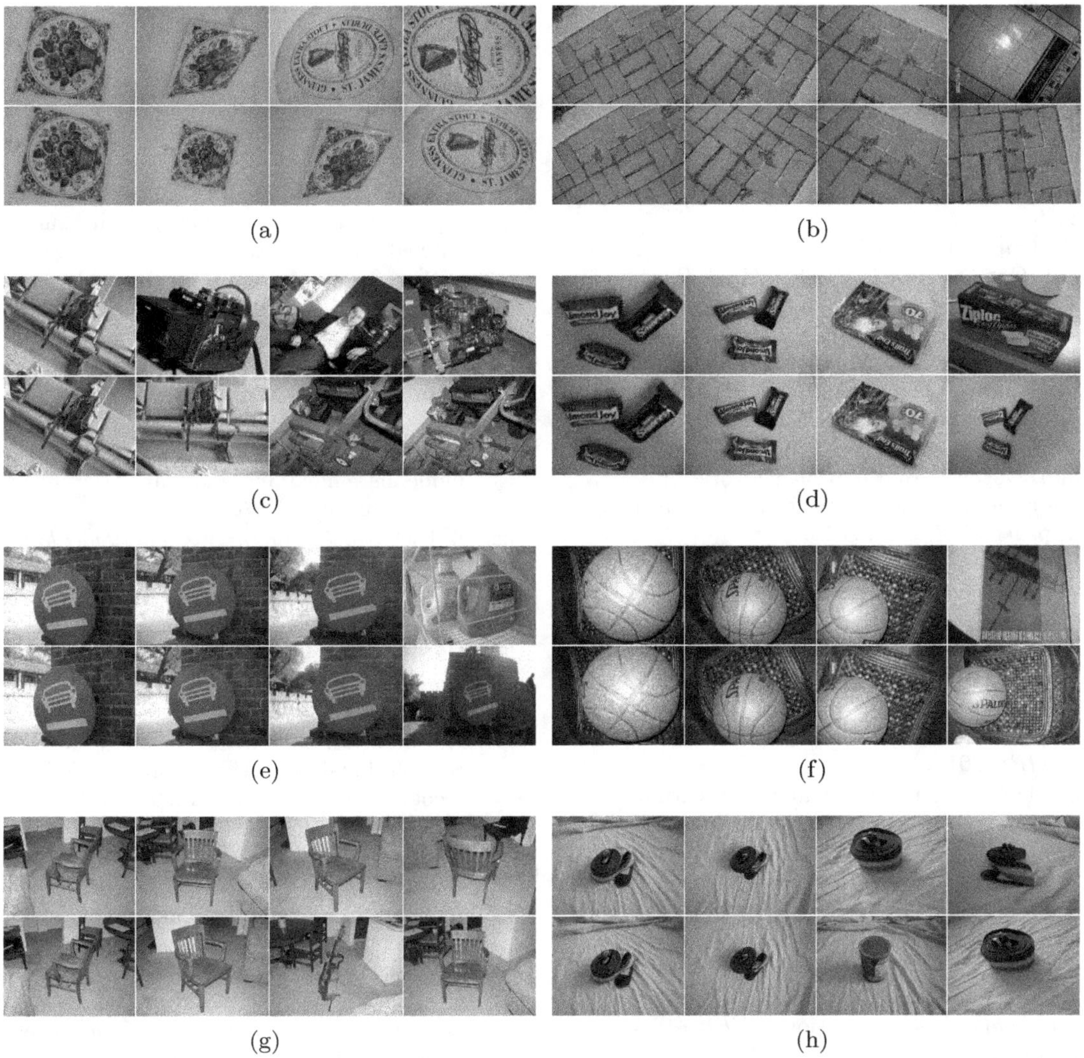

Figure 7: Top 4 retrieval results on the UK-Bench dataset with the CNN and TICNN models. In each group, the results of the CNN model and TICNN model are given in the top and bottom row, respectively. The results in (a)-(f) are positive cases, whereas (g)-(h) show two failure cases.

positive image also contains a chair like the query, but it appears in different scales and locations, which leads to a false match. Some other failure cases are similar to that in Fig. 7(h), where a large 3D viewpoint variance occurs, which is impossible to be produced in our training phase.

5. CONCLUSIONS

In this paper, we introduce a very simple and effective approach to improve the transform invariance of CNN models. By randomly transforming the feature maps of CNN layers during training, the dependency of the specific transform level of the input is reduced. Our architecture is different from that of previous approaches because we improve the invariance of deep learning models without adding any extra feature extraction modules, any learnable parameters or any transformations on the training dataset. Therefore, the transform invariances of current CNN models are very easy to be improved by just replacing their corresponding weights with our trained model. Experiments show that our model outperforms CNN models in both image recognition and image retrieval tasks.

Acknowledgments This work is supported by NSFC under the contracts No.61572451 and No.61390514, the 973 project under the contract No.2015CB351803, the Youth Innovation Promotion Association CAS CX2100060016, Fok Ying Tung Education Foundation, Australian Research Council Projects: DP-140102164, FT-130101457, and LE140100061.

6. REFERENCES

[1] J. M. Alvarez, Y. LeCun, T. Gevers, and A. M. Lopez. Semantic road segmentation via multi-scale ensembles of learned features. *ECCV Workshop on Computer Vision in Vehicle Technology: From Earth to Mars*, 2012.

[2] J. Bruna and S. Mallat. Invariant scattering convolution networks. *IEEE Trans. Pattern Anal. Mach. Intell.*, 35:1872–1886, 2013.

[3] T. S. Cohen and M. Welling. Transformation properties of learned visual representations. *ICLR*, 2015.

[4] J. Donahue, L. A. Hendricks, S. Guadarrama, M. Rohrbach, S. Venugopalan, K. Saenko, and T. Darrell. Long-term recurrent convolutional networks for visual recognition and description. *CVPR*, 2015.

[5] H. Fang, S. Gupta, F. Iandola, R. Srivastava, L. Deng, P. Dollar, J. Gao, X. He, M. Mitchell, J. C. Platt, L. Zitnick, and G. Zweig. From captions to visual concepts and back. *CVPR*, 2015.

[6] C. Farabet, C. Couprie, L. Najman, , and Y. LeCun. Learning hierarchical features for scene labeling. *IEEE Trans. Pattern Anal. Mach. Intell*, 2013.

[7] C. Gan, N. Wang, Y. Yang, D.-Y. Yeung, and A. G. Hauptmann. Devnet: A deep event network for multimedia event detection and evidence recounting. In *CVPR*, pages 2568–2577, 2015.

[8] C. Gan, T. Yang, and B. Gong. Learning attributes equals multi-source domain generalization. *CVPR*, 2016.

[9] C. Gan, T. Yao, K. Yang, Y. Yang, and T. Mei. You lead, we exceed: Labor-free video concept learning by jointly exploiting web videos and images. *CVPR*, 2016.

[10] R. Gens and P. M. Domingos. Deep symmetry networks. *NIPS*, 2014.

[11] R. G. Georgia Gkioxari and J. Malik. Contextual action recognition with r*cnn. *ICCV*, 2015.

[12] I. J. Goodfellow, Q. V. Le, A. M. Saxe, H. Lee, and A. Y. Ng. Measuring invariances in deep networks. *NIPS*, 2009.

[13] M. J. Huiskes and M. S. Lew. The mir flickr retrieval evaluation. In *MIR*. ACM, 2008.

[14] E. S. J. Long and T. Darrell. Fully convolutional networks for semantic segmentation. *CVPR*, 2015.

[15] M. Jaderberg, K. Simonyan, A. Zisserman, and K. Kavukcuoglu. Spatial transformer networks. *NIPS*, 2015.

[16] Y. Jia, E. Shelhamer, J. Donahue, S. Karayev, J. Long, R. Girshick, S. Guadarrama, and T. Darrell. Caffe: Convolutional architecture for fast feature embedding. *arXiv preprint arXiv:1408.5093*, 2014.

[17] S. R. Kaiming He, Xiangyu Zhang and J. Sun. Deep residual learning for image recognition. *CVPR*, 2016.

[18] A. Kanazawa and A. Sharma. Locally scale-invariant convolutional neural networks. *NIPS*, 2014.

[19] A. Karpathy and L. Fei-Fei. Deep visual-semantic alignments for generating image description. *CVPR*, 2015.

[20] J. J. Kivinen and C. K. I. Williams. Transformation equivariant boltzmann machines. In *Artificial Neural Networks and Machine Learning*, pages 1–9, 2011.

[21] A. Krizhevsky, I. Sutskever, and G. E. Hinton. Imagenet classification with deep convolutional neural networks. *NIPS*, pages 1097–1105, 2012.

[22] D. Laptev, N. Savinov, J. M. Buhmann, and M. Pollefeys. Ti-pooling: transformation-invariant pooling for feature learning in convolutional neural networks. In *CVPR*, 2016.

[23] Q. V. Le, J. Ngiam, Z. Chen, D. J. hao Chia, P. W. Koh, and A. Y. Ng. Tiled convolutional neural networks. *NIPS*, 2010.

[24] Y. Lecun, L. Bottou, Y. Bengio, and P. Haffner. Gradient-based learning applied to document recognition. In *Proceedings of the IEEE*, pages 2278–2324, 1998.

[25] K. Lenc and A. Vedaldi. Understanding image representations by measuring their equivariance and equivalence. *CVPR*, 2015.

[26] D. Nister and H. Stewenius. Scalable recognition with a vocabulary tree. In *CVPR*, pages 2161–2168, 2006.

[27] S. Nitish, H. Geoffrey, K. Alex, S. Ilya, and S. Ruslan. Dropout: A simple way to prevent neural networks from overfitting. *Journal of Machine Learning Research*, pages 1929–1958, 2014.

[28] Y. Pan, T. Mei, T. Yao, H. Li, and Y. Rui. Joint modeling embedding and translation to bridge video and language. *CVPR*, 2016.

[29] S. Richard. *Computer Vision: Algorithms and Applications*. 2010.

[30] P. Sermanet and Y. LeCun. Traffic sign recognition with multi-scale convolutional networks. *IJCNN*, 2011.

[31] K. Simonyan and A. Zisserman. Two-stream convolutional networks for action recognition in videos. *NIPS*, 2014.

[32] K. Simonyan and A. Zisserman. Very deep convolutional networks for large-scale image recognition. *CoRR*, abs/1409.1556, 2014.

[33] K. Sohn and H. Lee. Learning invariant representations with local transformations. In *ICML*, 2012.

[34] K. Sohn and H. Lee. Understanding image representations by measuring their equivariance and equivalence. *CVPR*, 2015.

[35] C. Szegedy, W. Liu, Y. Jia, P. Sermanet, S. Reed, D. Anguelov, D. Erhan, V. Vanhoucke, and A. Rabinovich. Going deeper with convolution. *CVPR*, 2015.

[36] Z. Wang, J. Yang, H. Jin, E. Shechtman, A. Agarwala, J. Brandt, and T. S. Huang. Deepfont: Identify your font from an image. In *ACM MM , 2015*, pages 451–459, 2015.

[37] L. Xie, L. Zheng, J. Wang, A. Yuille, and Q. Tian. Interactive: Inter-layer activeness propagation. In *CVPR*, 2016.

[38] L. Yao, A. Torabi, K. Cho, N. Ballas, C. Pal, H. Larochelle, and A. Courville. Describing videos by exploiting temporal structure. *ICCV*, 2015.

[39] L. Zheng, S. Wang, Z. Liu, and Q. Tian. Packing and padding: Coupled multi-index for accurate image retrieval. In *CVPR*, pages 1939–1946, 2014.

[40] L. Zheng, S. Wang, L. Tian, F. He, Z. Liu, and Q. Tian. Query-adaptive late fusion for image search and person re-identification. In *CVPR*, pages 1741–1750, 2015.

[41] L. Zheng, S. Wang, J. Wang, and Q. Tian. Accurate image search with multi-scale contextual evidences. *International Journal of Computer Vision*, pages 1–13, 2016.

PL-ranking: A Novel Ranking Method for Cross-Modal Retrieval

Liang Zhang[1,3], Bingpeng Ma[1,2,3]*, Guorong Li[1,3], Qingming Huang[1,2,3], Qi Tian[4]
[1] University of Chinese Academy of Sciences, China
[2] Key Lab of Intell. Info. Process., Inst. of Comput. Tech., CAS, China
[3] Key Laboratory of Big Data Mining and Knowledge Management, CAS, China
[4] Department of Computer Science, University of Texas at San Antonio, TX, 78249, USA
zhangliang14@mails.ucas.ac.cn {bpma, liguorong, qmhuang}@ucas.ac.cn
qitian@cs.utsa.edu

ABSTRACT

This paper proposes a novel method for cross-modal retrieval named **P**airwise-**L**istwise **ranking** (PL-ranking) based on the low-rank optimization framework. Motivated by the fact that optimizing the top of ranking is more applicable in practice, we focus on improving the precision at the top of ranked list for a given sample and learning a low-dimensional common subspace for multi-modal data. Concretely, there are three constraints in PL-ranking. First, we use a pairwise ranking loss constraint to optimize the top of ranking. Then, considering that the pairwise ranking loss constraint ignores class information, we further adopt a listwise constraint to minimize the intra-neighbors variance and maximize the inter-neighbors separability. By this way, class information is preserved while the number of iterations is reduced. Finally, low-rank based regularization is applied to exploit the correlations between features and labels so that the relevance between the different modalities can be enhanced after mapping them into the common subspace. We design an efficient low-rank stochastic subgradient descent method to solve the proposed optimization problem. The experimental results show that the average MAP scores of PL-ranking are improved 5.1%, 9.2%, 4.7% and 4.8% than those of the state-of-the-art methods on the Wiki, Flickr, Pascal and NUS-WIDE datasets, respectively.

Keywords

Multi-modal analysis; Cross-modal retrieval; Subspace learning; Learning to rank

1. INTRODUCTION

With the rapid growth of multi-modal data, including image, text, video and audio, cross-modal retrieval has been widely studied in recent years [7, 9, 13, 15, 17, 18, 20, 21, 22, 26, 27]. The key problem for cross-modal matching is how to push relevant samples from another modality appearing at the top of the ranked list when we give a query sample from one modality. This motivates that the techniques of the learning to rank have become increasingly popular, which can exploit the correlation shared by different modalities. These methods optimize the top of ranking by maximizing a criterion (*e.g.*, MAP or NDCG) related to the ultimate retrieval performance.

The most successful ranking method in cross-modal retrieval may be bi-directional cross-media semantic representation model (Bi-CMSRM), which optimizes ranking performance directly [27]. Bi-CMSRM is based on the structural SVM and optimized by using the 1-Slack cutting plane algorithm, and it has shown good performance in cross-modal retrieval. However, despite using an efficient convex method to solve the dual problem,Bi-CMSRM has shown the weaknesses on the scalability to large, high-dimensional dataset [16]. Besides, Bi-CMSRM only focuses on learning optimal mappings but ignores the structure of mappings such that it can not further exploit the label relevance between the different modalities.

In this paper, we propose an efficient ranking method for cross-modal retrieval named PL-ranking. PL-ranking integrates the weighted approximate rank pairwise (WARP) loss[1], listwise loss[2] and low-rank constraint into a generic minimization formulation, and then is optimized by extending the recently proposed FAST-SSGD [8]. By this way, PL-ranking not only optimizes the top of ranking, but also effectively captures the label correlations as well as scales to high-dimensional and large datasets. Thus, we can effectively retrieve relevant samples by searching in a small neighborhood of the query sample. Specifically, there are three important components contained in PL-ranking.

We first extend WARP to bi-directional WARP (bWARP) such that the learned model can be applied to image-query-texts and text-query-images simultaneously. Since both the directions of retrieval are optimized in the training period, bWARP ensures that the different modalities are projected

*Corresponding author.

MM '16, October 15-19, 2016, Amsterdam, Netherlands
© 2016 ACM. ISBN 978-1-4503-3603-1/16/10... $15.00
DOI: http://dx.doi.org/10.1145/2964284.2964336

[1]The pairwise ranking method takes the sample pairs as the training instances and formulates the ranking as a task of learning a classification or regression model from the collection of the pairwise instances of samples.

[2]The listwise information reflects the class relation of multiple samples, *e.g.*, intra-class and inter-class relations.

into the same semantic space such that the generalization performance is improved. What's more, by assigning the larger values for the first few larger losses, bWARP guarantees that the relevant samples appear at the top of the ranked list for the two directions of retrieval.

Furthermore, we adopt a listwise constraint for preserving the class information and reducing the iteration number of optimization. WARP uses the pairwise ranking loss to approximate the total ranking loss, and the paired samples are obtained by a random sampling trick. This will lose the class information due to the randomness in sampling. By calculating the nearest intra-neighbors and inter-neighbors in each sampling, the listwise constraint preserves the class information. Considering that the class information is beneficial to the retrieval task, the performance of PL-ranking can be improved. Besides, compared with WARP, the iteration number can be reduced because more positive samples and violators[3] are found in each iteration.

In Fig.1, we provide a simple matching illustration of pairwise ranking method and the proposed PL-ranking. The yellow circle represents an image query $\mathbf{x}$, and the red square represents $\mathbf{x}$'s first violator from the text modality. The yellow squares represent $\mathbf{x}$'s six-nearest intra-neighbors from the text modality, and the other squares represent $\mathbf{x}$'s nearest inter-neighbors. Fig.1(b) shows the matching result of pairwise ranking method [10]. Since the image query $\mathbf{x}$ and its violator $\mathbf{y}_1$ are used to optimize the pairwise ranking loss, they can be separated as far as possible. However, this method ignores the class information, so the nearest intra-neighbors $\mathbf{y}_2$ and $\mathbf{y}_3$ still have the large separation with the image query $\mathbf{x}$ while the distance among the different classes like $\mathbf{y}_2$ and $\mathbf{y}_4$ can not be enlarged. As shown in Fig.1(c), PL-ranking also enlarges the margin between the image query $\mathbf{x}$ and its violator $\mathbf{y}_1$ by using the pairwise ranking constraint. Moreover, the margin between the different classes can be enlarged since the listwise constraint minimizes the variance between $\mathbf{x}$ and its five nearest intra-neighbors and maximizes the separability between $\mathbf{x}$ and the other four nearest inter-neighbors.

To effectively exploit the semantic information embedded in the high-dimensional feature space, we further adopt a nuclear norm based the regularization to learn the low-rank mapping matrices. The low-rank based regularization of the mappings can effectively exploit the correlations between labels and features because the label/feature relevance vectors can be explicitly described via the left/right singular vectors of the mapping [11]. Then the relevance between the heterogeneous features can be enhanced in the low-dimensional subspace. Besides, the low-rank constraint also enhances the mappings' scalability to the high-dimensional data.

Finally, a novel low-rank optimization framework is designed to efficiently solve the complex minimization problem. PL-ranking is optimized by extending FAST-SSGD [8]. FAST-SSGD combines the low-rank stochastic subgradients with the efficient incremental SVD so that the number of iterations is greatly reduced. Extensive experiments have been performed on four public datasets, Wiki[20], Flickr[2], Pascal VOC 2007 [4] and NUS-WIDE [2]. Experimental results show that PL-ranking outperforms several state-of-the-art methods.

[3]Violator denotes the first negative sample which is more relevant than the positive sample in the sampling stage.

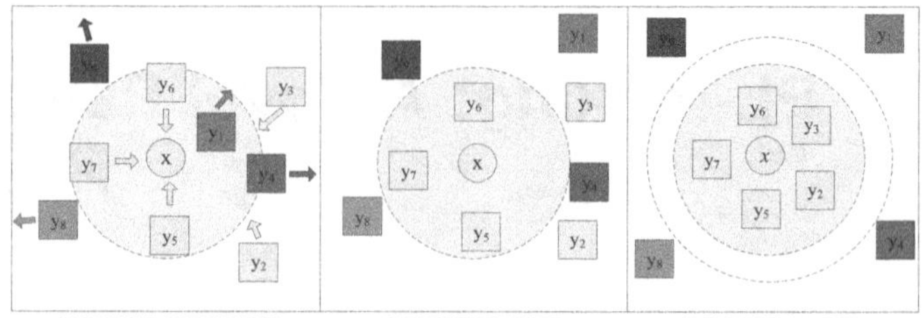

Figure 1: A simple illustration of the common subspace learnt by pairwise ranking method and the proposed PL-ranking. Shapes represent modalities. The same color indicates relevant samples. The circle represents an image query, and squares denote the retrieved text documents. The different shapes with the yellow color belong to same semantic class, and the squares with other colors (*e.g.*, green and purple) represent the text documents from the other classes. The red square represents the first violator found in the sampling stage.

2. RELATED WORK

Since the problem of cross-modal retrieval is considered as an important component in some real applications, extensive research have been proposed to learn a common subspace for image and text modalities in the recent past.

One popular direction of methods obtain the common subspace by learning the maximal correlations among different modalities [5, 9, 12, 17, 18, 19, 20, 21]. The most classic method is canonical correlation analysis (CCA) [9], which learns paired linear transformations to maximize the correlations between two modalities. As a supervised extension of CCA, generalized multiview analysis (GMA) [21] solves a joint, relaxed quadratic constrained program over the different feature spaces to obtain a single subspace.

An alternative direction of methods learn the common subspace by manifold learning [14, 15, 25]. The manifold learning methods project the different modalities into a common manifold by learning their underlying manifold representation due to that high dimensional data may embed in a lower dimensional intrinsic space. Mao *et al.*[15] project the relevance between two different modalities into a latent semantic space during the process of manifold alignment.

Different from the aforementioned categories of approaches which do not maximize a criterion related to the ultimate retrieval performance, another direction of methods use the technique of learning to rank [1, 6, 24, 27, 28] for learning the common subspace. These methods obtain the common subspace by the large margin learning with certain ranking criteria. Passive-aggressive model for image retrieval (PAMIR) [6] learns a discriminative retrieval model by using certain ranking criterion. Different from the uni-directional ranking method like PAMIR, Wu *et al.*[27] propose a general cross-modal ranking algorithm Bi-CMSRM, which obtains a latent space embedding via learning the structural large margin to optimize the bi-directional listwise ranking loss.

In this paper, we propose a novel ranking method, which integrates pairwise ranking loss, listwise loss and low-rank constraint into a generic minimization formulation. The proposed method jointly optimizes the ultimate retrieval performance directly and scales to large, high-dimensional dataset.

3. PAIRWISE-LISTWISE RANKING

In this section, we first present our proposed framework of PL-ranking for cross-modal problem and then introduce an efficient method to solve the optimization. Lastly, we provide the convergence analysis.

3.1 Formulation of PL-ranking

Based on the idea of latent space embedding, we focus on learning two linear mappings $\mathbf{U}$ and $\mathbf{V}$. They can map the image and text modalities into a common subspace, in which the samples from the different modalities are much closer to each other within the same class while the samples from the different classes are separated as far as possible.

We are given a training set of s paired samples, with s images from $\mathbf{X}$ and s texts from $\mathbf{Y}$. It is assumed that m and n are the dimension of image and text samples, respectively. Then the correlation between an image $\mathbf{x} \in \mathbb{R}^m$ and a text $\mathbf{y} \in \mathbb{R}^n$ can be measured by a linear mapping function as:

$$f(\cdot) = (\mathbf{U}^T\mathbf{x})^T(\mathbf{V}^T\mathbf{y}), \tag{1}$$

where T denotes the transpose of a matrix or vector, $\mathbf{U} \in \mathbb{R}^{m\times c}$ is the linear mapping matrix which maps the image $\mathbf{x}$ from the image space into the common subspace, and $\mathbf{V} \in \mathbb{R}^{n\times c}$ is the mapping which maps text $\mathbf{y}$ from the text space into the common subspace. c is the dimensionality of the common subspace. It is to be noted that c is equal to the rank of $\mathbf{U}$ and $\mathbf{V}$. In the following, $f_{\mathbf{x}}(\mathbf{y})$ measures the correlation between an image query $\mathbf{x}$ and its retrieved text $\mathbf{y}$, and $f_{\mathbf{y}}(\mathbf{x})$ measures the correlation between a text query $\mathbf{y}$ and its retrieved image $\mathbf{x}$.

To learn the optimal mappings, we formulate our objective function by integrating the pairwise ranking loss, listwise loss and nuclear based regularization into a generic minimization problem as follows:

$$\min_{\mathbf{U}\succeq 0,\mathbf{V}\succeq 0} L(\mathbf{U},\mathbf{V}) + \lambda\Psi(\mathbf{U},\mathbf{V}) + \gamma\Omega(\mathbf{U},\mathbf{V}), \tag{2}$$

where $L(\mathbf{U},\mathbf{V})$ is the sum of the pairwise losses, which adopts a sampling trick to optimize the top of ranking; $\Psi(\mathbf{U},\mathbf{V})$ is the sum of the listwise losses, which is applied to preserve the class information by constraining the nearest intra-neighbors and nearest inter-neighbors; $\Omega(\mathbf{U},\mathbf{V})$ is a low-rank constraint, which is used to enforce the relevance of mapped data by exploring the low-dimensional subspace structures embedded in data. $\lambda > 0$ and $\gamma > 0$ are the trade-off parameters to balance the weights of the different constraints. Since the left/right singular vectors of the larger singular values are more effective than those of the small values on strengthening the label correlation and feature correlation, we set $\mathbf{U} \succeq 0$ and $\mathbf{V} \succeq 0$ to ensure the non-negative singular values.

Pairwise ranking loss constraint: Recently, the ranking based methods obtain the good performance in information retrieval [3, 10, 23]. These methods validate that the top of ranking can be obtained by giving the bigger weights to the larger losses. Especially, Ordered Weighted Pairwise Classification (OWPC) [23] is proposed to optimize a few larger loss functions for ranking. To make the training time efficient, WARP [10] adopts a novel sampling trick to approximate the ranking loss of OWPC.

Motivated by the fact that the top of ranking is more applicable in practice, we first focus on improving the precision of the top of ranked list for a given sample. Similar to WARP, we use the pairwise ranking loss to ensure that the relevant samples appear at the top of ranked list. However, since cross-modal retrieval includes image-query-texts and text-query-images, it is imperative to design a single learned model which can be applied to two directions of retrieval at the same time. Thus, we extend WARP to bWARP for ensuring that image and text modalities are projected into the same semantic space. In this paper, we define the bi-directional pairwise ranking loss as:

$$L(\mathbf{U},\mathbf{V}) = \sum_{\mathbf{x}\in\mathbf{X}} L(\mathbf{x},\mathbf{Y};\mathbf{U},\mathbf{V}) + \sum_{\mathbf{y}\in\mathbf{Y}} L(\mathbf{y},\mathbf{X};\mathbf{U},\mathbf{V}), \tag{3}$$

where $(\mathbf{x},\mathbf{y})$ is a sample pair from two different modalities, and they belong to the same class. $L(\mathbf{x},\mathbf{Y};\mathbf{U},\mathbf{V})$ denotes the ranking texts from an image query $\mathbf{x}$, and $L(\mathbf{y},\mathbf{X};\mathbf{U},\mathbf{V})$ denotes the ranking images from a text query $\mathbf{y}$.

For each sample $\mathbf{x}$, $L(\mathbf{x},\mathbf{Y};\mathbf{U},\mathbf{V})$ is defined as the sum of the WARP losses:

$$L(\mathbf{x},\mathbf{Y};\mathbf{U},\mathbf{V}) = \sum_{\mathbf{x}\in\mathbf{X},\mathbf{y}^+\in\mathbf{Y}_x^+} E[\mathcal{L}(\lfloor\frac{s-1}{s_{\mathbf{x}}}\rfloor) \times [g_{\mathbf{x}}(\mathbf{y})]_+, \tag{4}$$

where $g_{\mathbf{x}}(\mathbf{y})=1 + f_{\mathbf{x}}(\bar{\mathbf{y}}^-) - f_{\mathbf{x}}(\mathbf{y}^+)$; $\mathbf{Y}_{\mathbf{x}}^+$ and $\mathbf{Y}_{\mathbf{x}}^-$ denote the relevant and irrelevant text sets of the image query $\mathbf{x}$, respectively; $E[\cdot]$ denotes the mathematical expectation; $\lfloor\cdot\rfloor$ denotes the floor function and $[\cdot]_+ := \max(0,\cdot)$; s_x is the number of sampling that we obtain the first negative sample $\bar{\mathbf{y}}^- \in \mathbf{Y}_{\mathbf{x}}^-$ which satisfies $1 + f_{\mathbf{x}}(\bar{\mathbf{y}}^-) > f_{\mathbf{x}}(\mathbf{y}^+)$, and $\bar{\mathbf{y}}^-$ denotes a violator for the given pair $(\mathbf{x},\mathbf{y}^+)$; $1 + f_{\mathbf{x}}(\bar{\mathbf{y}}^-) > f_{\mathbf{x}}(\mathbf{y}^+)$ is used to penalize the negative samples so that the margin between the positive and negative samples is larger than 1; $\mathcal{L}(\cdot) : \mathbb{Z}^+ \to \mathbb{R}^+$ is the mapping function that transforms the rank (denotes the order relation) into a loss:

$$\mathcal{L}(k) = \sum_{i=1}^{k} \alpha_i, \alpha_1 > \alpha_2 \cdots \geq 0, \tag{5}$$

where α_i is set to $1/i$, which has shown the good MAP and precision-at-k performance in image retrieval [3] and image annotation [10]. More details about the WARP loss can be found in [10].

Similarly, $\mathbf{X}_{\mathbf{y}}^+$ and $\mathbf{X}_{\mathbf{y}}^-$ represent the relevant and irrelevant image sets of the text query $\mathbf{y}$, respectively. The pairwise ranking loss for the text query $\mathbf{y}$ is defined as:

$$L(\mathbf{y},\mathbf{X};\mathbf{U},\mathbf{V}) = \sum_{\mathbf{y}\in\mathbf{Y},\mathbf{x}^+\in\mathbf{X}_{\mathbf{y}}^+} E[\mathcal{L}(\lfloor\frac{s-1}{s_{\mathbf{y}}}\rfloor) \times [g_{\mathbf{y}}(\mathbf{x})]_+, \tag{6}$$

where $g_{\mathbf{y}}(\mathbf{x})=1 + f_{\mathbf{y}}(\bar{\mathbf{x}}^-) - f_{\mathbf{y}}(\mathbf{x}^+)$.

Listwise loss constraint: The WARP-based methods have some problems in practice by using the pairwise ranking loss to approximate the total ranking loss. First, some rare occurrence queries may not be sampled in the large training set due to the randomness in the limited iterations. Thus, it is hard to enhance the semantic information of these queries. Second, in each sampling stage, one positive sample only finds 1-nearest inter-neighbor, and then the ranking loss is approximated by the loss of the paired samples. Since query samples have a lot of nearest inter-neighbors in a large dataset, it may need more iterations to converge.

To alleviate these problems, we use a listwise loss to improve the performance of pairwise ranking loss. Generally speaking, the listwise information represents the correlation of intra-class and inter-class. We can use the class information to minimize the variance of the samples within the same semantic class and maximize the separability of the samples from the different classes. In PL-ranking, the bi-directional listwise constraint is defined as:

$$\Psi(\mathbf{U},\mathbf{V}) = \sum_{\mathbf{x}\in\mathbf{X}} \Psi(\mathbf{x},\mathbf{Y};\mathbf{U},\mathbf{V}) + \sum_{\mathbf{y}\in\mathbf{Y}} \Psi(\mathbf{y},\mathbf{X};\mathbf{U},\mathbf{V}), \quad (7)$$

where $\Psi(\mathbf{x},\mathbf{Y};\mathbf{U},\mathbf{V})$ is used to enhance the listwise correlation between the image query $\mathbf{x}$ and a text training set, and it is computed as follows:

$$\Psi(\mathbf{x},\mathbf{Y};\mathbf{U},\mathbf{V}) = \sum_{\mathbf{y}^-\in\mathbf{Y}_{\mathbf{x}}^{\text{inter}}} f_{\mathbf{x}}(\mathbf{y}^-) - \sum_{\mathbf{y}^+\in\mathbf{Y}_{\mathbf{x}}^{\text{intra}}} f_{\mathbf{x}}(\mathbf{y}^+), \quad (8)$$

where $\mathbf{Y}_{\mathbf{x}}^{\text{intra}} \in \mathbf{Y}_{\mathbf{x}}^{+}$ and $\mathbf{Y}_{\mathbf{x}}^{\text{inter}} \in \mathbf{Y}_{\mathbf{x}}^{-}$ represent the k_1 nearest intra-neighbors and k_2 nearest inter-neighbors of $\mathbf{x}$, respectively. We calculate the nearest neighbors by k-nearest-neighbor which is performed after mapping features into the common subspace. Since the dimension of this subspace is very low, PL-ranking is still efficient when it handles the high-dimensional features.

Similarly, $\Psi(\mathbf{y},\mathbf{X};\mathbf{U},\mathbf{V})$ enhances the correlation between a text query $\mathbf{y}$ and an image training set and is defined as:

$$\Psi(\mathbf{y},\mathbf{X};\mathbf{U},\mathbf{V}) = \sum_{\mathbf{x}^-\in\mathbf{X}_{\mathbf{y}}^{\text{inter}}} f_{\mathbf{y}}(\mathbf{x}^-) - \sum_{\mathbf{x}^+\in\mathbf{X}_{\mathbf{y}}^{\text{intra}}} f_{\mathbf{y}}(\mathbf{x}^+). \quad (9)$$

In the listwise loss, the usage of k_1 nearest intra-neighbors and k_2 nearest inter-neighbors can overcome the above problems of the WARP-based methods. First, the queries can find more relevant samples and irrelevant samples in each sampling. Some rare occurrence samples can increase the semantic information by building the semantic relation with other sampled data. Second, the iterations are reduced since a sample can find more positive samples and violators in each iteration.

Low-rank constraint: In cross-modal retrieval, the multi-modal data are usually represented as the high-dimensional vectors. Since the intrinsic dimensionality of a semantic space is usually much lower than that of original feature space, we use the low-rank constraint to exploit the low-dimensional subspace structures embedded in data. In PL-ranking, the low-rank constraint is defined as:

$$\Omega(\mathbf{U},\mathbf{V}) = \|\mathbf{U}\|_* + \|\mathbf{V}\|_*, \quad (10)$$

where $\|\mathbf{U}\|_*$ and $\|\mathbf{V}\|_*$ denote the nuclear norm based regularization. This regularization has been successfully applied to various applications such as multi-label learning [11] and cross-modal matching [26].

Based on singular value decomposition, a low-dimensional mapping matrix can be represented as the product of the left/right singular vectors. The left/right singular vectors of the mapping explicitly describe the label/feature relevance vectors, so the low-rank based regularization can effectively exploit label and feature correlations. For example, the linear mapping $\mathbf{U}$ can be characterized as:

$$\mathbf{U}^T = \sum_{i=1}^{r} \mathbf{M}_i(U)\mathbf{\Sigma}_i(U)\mathbf{N}_i^T(U), \quad (11)$$

where $r = \min\{m, c\}$, $\mathbf{M}_i(U) \in \mathbb{R}^{c\times r}$ and $\mathbf{N}_i(U) \in \mathbb{R}^{m\times r}$ are left/right singular vectors of $\mathbf{U}$, $\mathbf{\Sigma}_i(U)$ is the i-th singular value of $\mathbf{U}$ and all the singular values are real and non-negative. Assuming $\mathbf{\Sigma}_1(U) \geq \mathbf{\Sigma}_2(U) \geq \cdots \mathbf{\Sigma}_r(U)$, we can measure the complexity of $\mathbf{U}$ by summing its singular values, *i.e.*, how many singular values of $\mathbf{U}$ or singular vectors $\mathbf{M}_i(U)$ and $\mathbf{N}_i(U)$ we should keep. When we keep the largest r' singular values of $\mathbf{U}$, the rank of $\mathbf{U}$ is equal to r'. In this paper, we adopt the nuclear norm regularization to measure the complexity of $\mathbf{U}$:

$$\|\mathbf{U}\|_* = \sum_{i=1}^{r} \mathbf{\Sigma}_i(U). \quad (12)$$

Moreover, each image sample $\mathbf{x}_i$ can be mapped based on the minimization of nuclear norm:

$$\mathbf{U}^T\mathbf{x}_i = \sum_{j=1}^{r'} \mathbf{\Sigma}_j(U)[\mathbf{N}_j^T(U)\mathbf{x}_i]\mathbf{M}_j(U). \quad (13)$$

We note that the resulting vector is a linear combination of label-relevance vectors: $\mathbf{M}_1(U), \mathbf{M}_2(U), \cdots, \mathbf{M}_{r'}(U)$, so it is relevant to the label space. Therefore, the label relevance can be exploited by optimizing these label-relevance vectors. The feature correlations can be reflected by the mapped feature value $\mathbf{N}_j^T(U)\mathbf{x}_i$ which is determined by r' feature-relevance vectors $\{\mathbf{N}_j(U)\}_{j=1}^{r'}$. By using these label-relevance and feature-relevance vectors, both the feature correlations and label correlations can be exploited.

Similarly, each text sample $\mathbf{y}_i$ can also be mapped as a linear combination. Then, minimizing the pairwise ranking loss, listwise loss and low-rank constraint can learn two sets of label-relevance vectors: $\{\mathbf{M}_j(U)\}_{j=1}^{r'}$ and $\{\mathbf{M}_j(V)\}_{j=1}^{r'}$, and feature-relevance vectors $\{\mathbf{N}_j(U)\}_{j=1}^{r'}$ and $\{\mathbf{N}_j(V)\}_{j=1}^{r'}$. Based on these vectors, mapped samples from the different modalities are close to each other within the same class and far away between different classes.

3.2 Optimization via bFAST-SSGD

It is difficult to optimize the objective function in Eq. (2) directly due to that as a matrix function, the nuclear norm is not differentiable.

The recently proposed FAST-SSGD method [8] combines the low-rank stochastic subgradients with the incremental SVD. FAST-SSGD maintains a low-rank factorization in each iteration, and it makes the objective function more easily convergent. Since only one matrix variable is optimized in [8], we extend FAST-SSGD to the bi-variable FAST-SSGD (bFAST-SSGD). bFAST-SSGD can simultaneously learn two optimal low-rank mappings $\mathbf{U}$ and $\mathbf{V}$. Furthermore, we set $\|\mathbf{U}\|_* = \|\mathbf{V}\|_*$ to enforce the interaction of $\mathbf{U}$ and $\mathbf{V}$, by which the number of iterations will be greatly reduced.

In Algo. 1, we show the optimization procedure for learning $\mathbf{U}$ and $\mathbf{V}$. First, $\mathbf{U}$ and $\mathbf{V}$ are initialized with a normal distribution with mean zero and standard deviation one. Then, given the current $\mathbf{U}^{(t)}$ and $\mathbf{V}^{(t)}$, the optimization is conducted as follows:

(1) We sample a paired samples $(\mathbf{x}, \mathbf{y})$ randomly, and conduct the bi-directional sampling to obtain $(\mathbf{x}, \mathbf{y}^+, \bar{\mathbf{y}}^-, s_{\mathbf{x}})$ and $(\mathbf{y}, \mathbf{x}^+, \bar{\mathbf{x}}^-, s_{\mathbf{y}})$;

(2) We calculate the subgradients $\mathbf{G}_U^{(t)}$ and $\mathbf{G}_V^{(t)}$ for $\mathbf{U}$ and $\mathbf{V}$;

(3) We set the step size $\eta_Z^{(t)}$ (Z denotes U or V) to ensure the convergence in $O(c/r)$ iterations:

$$\eta_Z^{(t)} = \beta \frac{\sqrt{r}\Delta_Z}{\sqrt{c}(G_Z + \gamma\sqrt{c})}, \quad (14)$$

Algorithm 1 PL-ranking

Input: $\mathbf{U}^{(t)} \in \mathbb{R}^{m\times c^{(t)}}$, $\mathbf{V}^{(t)} \in \mathbb{R}^{n\times c^{(t)}}$, image data matrix $\mathbf{X} \in \mathbb{R}^{m\times M}$, text data matrix $\mathbf{Y} \in \mathbb{R}^{n\times M}$

Output: Optimal $\mathbf{U}$ and $\mathbf{V}$

repeat
  Pick a pair of labeled samples $(\mathbf{x}, \mathbf{y})$ randomly
  Draw $\mathbf{y}^+$ from $\mathbf{Y}_\mathbf{x}^+$; $s_\mathbf{x} \leftarrow 0$;
  Calculate the nearest intra-neighbors $\mathbf{Y}_\mathbf{x}^{\text{intra}} \in \mathbf{Y}_\mathbf{x}^+$ and inter-neighbors $\mathbf{Y}_\mathbf{x}^{\text{inter}} \in \mathbf{Y}_\mathbf{x}^-$
  Draw $\mathbf{x}^+$ from $\mathbf{X}_\mathbf{y}^+$; $s_\mathbf{y} \leftarrow 0$;
  Calculate the nearest intra-neighbors $\mathbf{X}_\mathbf{y}^{\text{intra}} \in \mathbf{X}_\mathbf{y}^+$ and inter-neighbors $\mathbf{X}_\mathbf{y}^{\text{inter}} \in \mathbf{X}_\mathbf{y}^-$
  repeat
    Sample $\mathbf{y}^-$ from $\mathbf{Y}_\mathbf{x}^-$
  until $1 + f_\mathbf{x}(\bar{\mathbf{y}}^-) > f_\mathbf{x}(\mathbf{y}^+)$ or $s_\mathbf{x} > |\mathbf{Y}_\mathbf{x}^-|$
  repeat
    Sample $\mathbf{x}^-$ from $\mathbf{X}_\mathbf{y}^-$
  until $1 + f_\mathbf{y}(\bar{\mathbf{x}}^-) > f_\mathbf{y}(\mathbf{x}^+)$ or $s_\mathbf{y} > |\mathbf{X}_\mathbf{y}^-|$
  if $1 + f_\mathbf{x}(\bar{\mathbf{y}}^-) > f_\mathbf{x}(\mathbf{y}^+)$ or $1 + f_\mathbf{y}(\bar{\mathbf{x}}^-) > f_\mathbf{y}(\mathbf{x}^+)$ **then**
    bFAST-SSGD:
    1). Generate a probing matrix $\mathbf{P}^{(t)} \in c^{(t)} \times r^{(t)}$
    2). $\mathbf{U}^{(t+1)} \leftarrow$ FAST-SSGD$(\mathbf{U}^{(t)}, \mathbf{P}^{(t)}, \mathbf{G}_U^{(t)}, \eta_U^{(t)})$
    3). $\mathbf{V}^{(t+1)} \leftarrow$ FAST-SSGD$(\mathbf{V}^{(t)}, \mathbf{P}^{(t)}, \mathbf{G}_V^{(t)}, \eta_V^{(t)})$
    4). Ensure $\|\mathbf{U}^{(t+1)}\|_* = \|\mathbf{V}^{(t+1)}\|_*$
    end bFAST-SSGD
  else
    continue
  end if
until validation performance does not improve or max iterations exceeded

where $\beta > 0$, Δ_Z and G_Z denote the upper bounds of $\|\mathbf{Z}\|_F$ and $\|\mathbf{G}_Z^{(t)}\|_F$.

(4) $\mathbf{U}^{(t+1)}$ and $\mathbf{V}^{(t+1)}$ are obtained via Algo. 2.

In Algo. 1, $\mathbf{P} \in \mathbb{R}^{c\times r}$ is a probing matrix and $E[\mathbf{P}\mathbf{P}^T] = \mathbf{I}_{c\times c}$, where $r \le c$ is the adjustable parameter, and $\mathbf{I}_{c\times c}$ is the identity matrix. By the linearity of the expectation, for any subgradient $\mathbf{G}^{(t)}$, we have $E[\mathbf{G}^{(t)}\mathbf{P}\mathbf{P}^T] = \mathbf{G}^{(t)}E[\mathbf{P}\mathbf{P}^T] = \mathbf{G}^{(t)}$. Thus, $\mathbf{G}^{(t)}\mathbf{P}\mathbf{P}^T$ can be used as an unbiased estimator of $\mathbf{G}^{(t)}$. Since $\mathbf{G}^{(t)}\mathbf{P}\mathbf{P}^T$ has the rank at most r, this estimator is a low-rank unbiased estimator, by which $\mathbf{U}$ and $\mathbf{V}$ are guaranteed as the low-rank mappings in each iteration.

To effectively learn the label-relevance and feature-relevance vectors, we set $\|\mathbf{U}\|_* = \|\mathbf{V}\|_*$ after each iteration, which we briefly reason below. From Eq. (13), we conclude:

$$\begin{aligned} \mathbf{U}^T\mathbf{x}_i &= \sum_{j=1}^{r'} \mathbf{\Sigma}_j(U)[\mathbf{N}_j^T(U)\mathbf{x}_i]\mathbf{M}_j(U) \\ \mathbf{V}^T\mathbf{y}_i &= \sum_{j=1}^{r'} \mathbf{\Sigma}_j(V)[\mathbf{N}_j^T(V)\mathbf{y}_i]\mathbf{M}_j(V) \end{aligned} . \tag{15}$$

It is obvious that the singular values are the coefficients of the above linear combinations. We hope to learn the optimal singular vectors $\mathbf{M}(U)$, $\mathbf{N}(U)$, $\mathbf{M}(V)$ and $\mathbf{N}(V)$ such that the correlations between two modalities can be exploited. If $\sum_{j=1}^{r'} \mathbf{\Sigma}_j(U)$ is equal to $\sum_{j=1}^{r'} \mathbf{\Sigma}_j(V)$, we can truly optimize these singular vectors, otherwise the correlations may be resulted from these singular values rather than the optimal label-relevance and feature-relevance vectors. Besides, $\|\mathbf{U}\|_* = \|\mathbf{V}\|_*$ can construct certain relations between two mappings to some extent.

Algorithm 2 FAST-SSGD

Input: $\mathbf{Z}^{(t)}$, $\mathbf{P}^{(t)}$, $\mathbf{G}_Z^{(t)}$, $\eta_Z^{(t)} > 0$

SVD computation: $\mathbf{Z}^{(t)} = \mathbf{M}^{(t)}(Z)\mathbf{\Sigma}^{(t)}(Z)(\mathbf{N}^{(t)}(Z))^T$
$\mathbf{S}^{(t)} \leftarrow \mathbf{G}_Z^{(t)}\mathbf{Y}^{(t)}$
$\hat{\mathbf{M}}^{(t+1)} \leftarrow [\mathbf{M}^{(t)}(Z)\mathbf{\Sigma}^{(t)}(Z) \;\; \mathbf{S}^{(t)}]$
$\hat{\mathbf{N}}^{(t+1)} \leftarrow [\mathbf{N}^{(t)}(Z) \;\; -\eta_Z^{(t)}\mathbf{P}^{(t)}]$
Factorize:$\hat{\mathbf{M}}^{(t+1)} = \mathbf{Q}_M\mathbf{R}_M$
Factorize:$\hat{\mathbf{N}}^{(t+1)} = \mathbf{Q}_N\mathbf{R}_N$
$\mathbf{D} \leftarrow \mathbf{R}_M\mathbf{R}_N^T$
SVD computation: $\mathbf{D} = \mathbf{M}(D)\mathbf{\Sigma}^{(t+1)}(D)\mathbf{N}^T(D)$
$\mathbf{M}^{(t+1)}(Z) \leftarrow \mathbf{Q}_M\mathbf{M}(D)$, $\mathbf{N}^{(t+1)}(Z) \leftarrow \mathbf{Q}_N\mathbf{N}(D)$
$\mathbf{Z}^{(t+1)} \leftarrow \mathbf{M}^{(t+1)}(Z)\mathbf{\Sigma}^{(t+1)}(D)\mathbf{N}^{(t+1)}(Z)$
return $\mathbf{Z}^{(t+1)}$

Thus, in bFAST-SSGD, $\mathbf{U}$ and $\mathbf{V}$ are forced to be multiplied by a constant respectively to ensure $\|\mathbf{U}\|_* = \|\mathbf{V}\|_*$ after each subgradient descent. Suppose after the t-th iteration, we obtain $\mathbf{U}^{(t)} = \mathbf{M}^{(t)}(U)\mathbf{\Sigma}^{(t)}(U)\mathbf{N}^{(t)}(U)$, $\mathbf{V}^{(t)} = \mathbf{M}^{(t)}(V)\mathbf{\Sigma}^{(t)}(V)\mathbf{N}^{(t)}(V)$. Then the update is defined as:

$$\begin{aligned} \mathbf{U}^{(t)} &= \alpha(\mathbf{U}^{(t)}./\text{Tr}(\mathbf{\Sigma}^{(t)}(U))) \\ \mathbf{V}^{(t)} &= \alpha(\mathbf{V}^{(t)}./\text{Tr}(\mathbf{\Sigma}^{(t)}(V))) \end{aligned} , \tag{16}$$

where $\alpha = \sqrt{\text{Tr}(\mathbf{\Sigma}^{(t)}(U)) \times \text{Tr}(\mathbf{\Sigma}^{(t)}(V))}$.

The computational complexity of PL-ranking scales as $O(d(c^{(t)}+r^{(t)})^2)$ for each iteration [8], where $d = \max(m, n)$. Since $c^{(t)}$ is far smaller than m and n, PL-ranking results in large computational savings on learning $\mathbf{U}$ and $\mathbf{V}$. Generally, the current metric learning approaches usually scale as $O(d^2)$ or $O(d^3)$. The complete derivation of PL-ranking is given in the supplementary material.

3.3 Convergence analysis

In this section, we present the convergence analysis of the proposed framework. We prove that Algo. 1 will monotonically decrease the objective function in Eq. (2).

According to the definition of the objective function, the pairwise ranking loss has the following equation:

$$\begin{aligned} & L(\mathbf{U}^{(t+1)}, \mathbf{V}^{(t+1)}) - L(\mathbf{U}^{(t)}, \mathbf{V}^{(t)}) = \\ & \{L(\mathbf{U}^{(t+1)}, \mathbf{V}^{(t+1)}) - L(\mathbf{U}^{(t)}, \mathbf{V}^{(t+1)})\} + . \\ & \{L(\mathbf{U}^{(t)}, \mathbf{V}^{(t+1)}) - L(\mathbf{U}^{(t)}, \mathbf{V}^{(t)})\} \end{aligned} \tag{17}$$

The two terms at the right side of Eq. (17) are less than or equal to zero. Taking one sampling as example, we have:

$$\begin{aligned} & L(\mathbf{x}, \mathbf{Y}, \mathbf{U}^{(t+1)}, \mathbf{V}^{(t+1)}) - L(\mathbf{x}, \mathbf{Y}, \mathbf{U}^{(t)}, \mathbf{V}^{(t+1)}) \\ & = -\mathbf{x}^T\mathbf{G}^{(t)}(U)\mathbf{V}^{(t+1)^T}(\bar{\mathbf{y}}^- - \mathbf{y}^+) \le 0 \end{aligned} , \tag{18}$$

since $\mathbf{x}^T\mathbf{G}_U^{(t)}\mathbf{V}^{(t+1)^T}\bar{\mathbf{y}}^-$ is greater than $\mathbf{x}^T\mathbf{G}_U^{(t)}\mathbf{V}^{(t+1)^T}\mathbf{y}^+$ before convergence, the above inequality is satisfied.

Similarly, both the listwise loss and the low-rank constraint also satisfy this property. Therefore, the overall objective function will monotonically decrease after each iteration and can converge to a global optimum eventually.

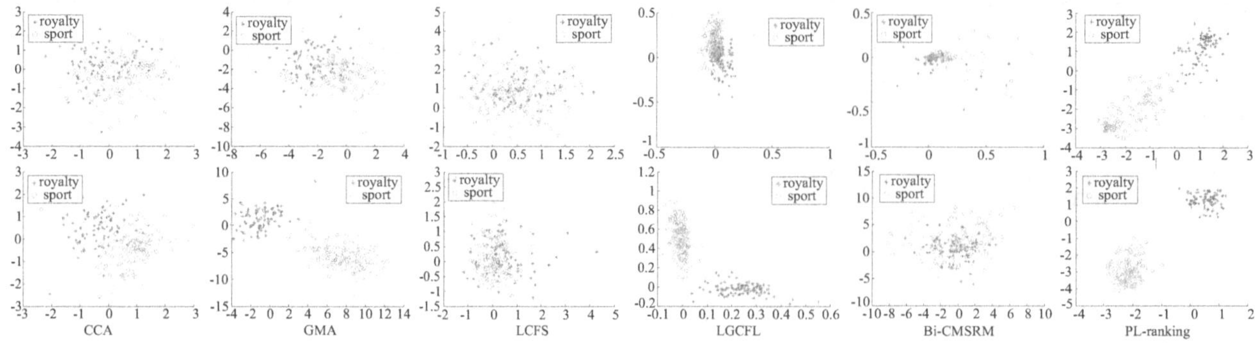

Figure 2: Low-dimensional mapping of images and texts from 'royalty' and 'sport' classes of Wiki. The top row shows the mapping for image modality, and the bottom shows the mapping for text modality.

4. EXPERIMENTS

In this section, we present the experimental results of PL-ranking and the other methods for image-text retrieval, *i.e.*, image-query-texts and text-query-images. We evaluate and compare different methods on four public datasets-Wiki [20], Flickr [2], Pascal VOC 2007 [4] and NUS-WIDE [2]. There are many distinct properties of these datasets. The text modality of the four datasets are article, sentences and tags, respectively. The size of these datasets ranges from 2k to 26k and the number of the classes ranges from 10 to 20.

4.1 Experiment settings

The proposed PL-ranking is compared with several related methods, such as CCA [9], GMA [21], LCFS [26], Bi-CMSRM [27] and LGCFL [13]. Both CCA and PL-ranking focus on learning a latent space. Comparing with CCA aims to test PL-ranking's ability to learn a useful latent space. PL-ranking is a supervised learning method like GMA. The comparison between PL-ranking and GMA can validate the effectiveness of PL-ranking on exploiting the label information. LCFS also uses the nuclear norm as the low-rank constraint. This comparison can test PL-ranking's ability to learn the low-rank mappings. We further highlight the advantages of low-rank optimization based ranking method by comparing PL-ranking with Bi-CMSRM. LGCFL uses the valuable class information to learn the consistent features and achieves the state-of-the-art performance. Additionally, since the listwise loss and nuclear norm constraints are used to improve the performance of the pairwise ranking in PL-ranking, we simplify PL-ranking as PL-ranking$_p$ to validate their impacts on the performance. In other words, PL-ranking$_p$ only uses the pairwise ranking loss constraint.

For the evaluation, we use mean average precision (MAP) [20] as the performance measure. MAP@R measures MAP at fixed number of the retrieved samples, and we set $R = 10$ for the top 10 retrieved samples and $R = all$ for all the samples. Besides, we also display the precision-recall curve [20] for all methods to pictorially demonstrate performance.

Since CCA and GMA just focus on the common subspace learning, principal component analysis (PCA) is performed on the original features before learning the latent space. By this way, the redundant information of the original features is greatly reduced. For the compared methods, we use the parameters' optimal settings tuned by a parameter validation process except for the specified values. PL-ranking uses the following parameter setting: $\lambda = 0.001$, $\gamma = 0.1$, $\beta = 0.01$, $k_1 = 20$, $k_2 = 200$, in all experiments. Specially, we set r to c to avoid an additional tunable parameter. For fair comparison, we conduct experiments 10 times by randomly selecting training/validating/testing combinations, and compare the average performance for all methods.

4.2 Results on mappings

In this section, we show the data distribution after the low-dimensional mapping. To demonstrate this, we construct a toy dataset using the 'royalty' and 'sport' classes of the Wiki dataset. The texts are represented as 5,000-dimensional Bag-of-Words (BoW) features, and images use the 1,000-dimensional Bag-of-Visual-Words (BoVW) features. For both modalities, the first and second most correlated components of the different methods are shown in Fig. 2. The red color represents the data distribution of the 'royalty' class, and green color represents the 'sport' class. From this figure, we can see that PL-ranking can unit the same-class samples and separates the different classes for both directions of retrieval, but the second best results (GMA and LGCFL) only unit the same-class samples and separate the different classes for text query. Furthermore, both image and text distributions of PL-ranking are in the same coordinate range, while the other methods' coordinate ranges are quite different. These results validate that PL-ranking is able to map the different features into a discriminative subspace such that the low-dimensional representations are enforced with the high correlation.

4.3 Results on Wiki

The Wiki dataset [20] is generated from Wikipedia's "featured articles". It consists of 2,866 image-text pairs with 10 semantic categories. For the texts, we extract the 5,000-dimensional features using the BoW representations with the TF-IDF weighting scheme. For the images, we use the 1,000-dimensional BoVW features. We randomly choose 1,500 pairs of the data for training, 500 pairs for validating and 866 pairs for testing. In Table 1, we report the MAP scores for image query, text query and their average. From this table, we draw the following conclusions:

First, compared to PL-ranking$_p$, PL-ranking gains significant improvements. For example, under R=*all*, the MAP scores of PL-ranking$_p$ are 0.1715, 0.2042 and 0.1879 for text query, image query and their average, respectively, while PL-ranking achieves 0.2221, 0.2625 and 0.2423, respectively. The improvements are 29.50%, 28.55% and 28.95%, respec-

Table 1: The performance comparison in terms of MAP@R on Wiki dataset.

Methods \ Tasks	$R=10$			$R=all$		
	Text query	Image query	Average	Text query	Image query	Average
CCA	0.3081	0.2425	0.2753	0.1415	0.1595	0.1505
GMA	0.3805	0.2284	0.3045	0.1726	0.2305	0.2016
LCFS	0.4632	0.2637	0.3635	0.1917	0.2481	0.2199
LGCFL	0.4472	0.2849	0.3661	0.2156	0.2615	0.2386
Bi-CMSRM	0.4599	0.2732	0.3666	0.2123	0.2528	0.2326
PL-ranking$_p$	0.3840	0.2487	0.3164	0.1715	0.2042	0.1879
PL-ranking	**0.4823**	**0.2882**	**0.3853**	**0.2221**	**0.2625**	**0.2423**

Table 2: The performance comparison in terms of MAP@R on Flickr dataset.

Methods \ Tasks	$R=10$			$R=all$		
	Text query	Image query	Average	Text query	Image query	Average
CCA	0.3106	0.2000	0.2553	0.1438	0.1455	0.1447
GMA	0.4437	0.2951	0.3694	0.1884	0.2657	0.2271
LCFS	0.4797	0.2600	0.3699	0.1868	0.2103	0.1986
LGCFL	0.4734	0.3028	0.3881	0.2234	0.2767	0.2501
Bi-CMSRM	0.4209	0.2774	0.3492	0.2040	0.2791	0.2416
PL-ranking$_p$	0.4255	0.3101	0.3678	0.1856	0.2156	0.2006
PL-ranking	**0.5376**	**0.3098**	**0.4237**	**0.2323**	**0.2851**	**0.2587**

Table 3: The performance comparison in terms of MAP@all on Pascal and NUS-WIDE datasets.

Tasks \ Methods		CCA	GMA	LCFS	LGCFL	Bi-CMSRM	PL-ranking
Pascal	Image query	0.163	0.308	0.344	0.401	0.292	**0.418**
	Text query	0.150	0.244	0.267	0.320	0.204	**0.338**
	Average	0.157	0.276	0.306	0.361	0.248	**0.378**
NUS-WIDE	Image query	0.248	0.374	0.413	0.424	0.338	**0.443**
	Text query	0.201	0.241	0.274	0.307	0.217	**0.323**
	Average	0.225	0.308	0.344	0.366	0.278	**0.383**

tively. Since PL-ranking adds the listwise loss and nuclear norm constraints on PL-ranking$_p$, the superior performance of PL-ranking indicates that the combination of the listwise loss and nuclear norm can improve the performance of the pairwise ranking. Besides, we also do experiments to validate that the nuclear norm is superior to F-norm. The MAP scores of image query and text query are 0.2198 and 0.1929 in R=all, and 0.2316 and 0.4237 in R=10 by adopting F-norm. This is mainly because F-norm leads to high-rank gradient such that the mappings' structures are destroyed. Thus, its generalization performance cannot be ensured.

Second, the MAP scores of PL-ranking outperform those of Bi-CMSRM on both retrieval tasks. The MAP scores of Bi-CMSRM are 0.2123 and 0.2528 under R=all. Though Bi-CMSRM and PL-ranking are both the ranking-based methods, Bi-CMSRM only optimizes the listwise ranking loss by learning the structural large margin. But PL-ranking integrates the pairwise ranking loss, the listwise loss and nuclear norm constraints. The advantage of PL-ranking demonstrates that it is reasonable to use the pairwise ranking loss and low-rank constraints for ranking.

Third, the performance of PL-ranking is also better than that of LCFS. The MAP scores of LCFS are 0.1917 and 0.2481 for text query and image query when under R=all. Although the nuclear norm is also adopted to optimize the low-rank mappings, LCFS mainly focuses on preserving the correlations between the paired samples. In PL-ranking, the pairwise ranking loss and listwise loss are also adopted except for the nuclear norm. The improvement of PL-ranking indicates that PL-ranking can improve the precision at the top of ranked list by using the pairwise ranking loss, and the listwise loss can preserve the class information.

Finally, the improvement of PL-ranking under R=10 is as significant as that under R=all,. For example, compared with Bi-CMSRM, the average MAP of PL-ranking improves about 4.17% under R=all and 5.1% under R=10. These results show that PL-ranking optimizes the top of ranking, which has the practical significance since the relevant samples are pushed at the top of ranked list.

Fig. 3(a) and 3(b) show the precision-recall curves of the different methods on the Wiki dataset. We select 3 maximum curves to make the clear presentation. For two retrieval tasks, PL-ranking achieves the higher precision than the other methods at the low levels of recall, which demonstrate that the top of ranking is optimized in PL-ranking. We also see that LGCFL achieves lower precision at low levels of recall in image query. LGCFL learns coupled mappings by optimizing the labeling approximation error between the given data and labels. Since the class labels apply more directly to texts than images, the image query is more likely to mismatch. As a result, the relevant samples may be pushed in the front of the ranked list but not the top of ranked list.

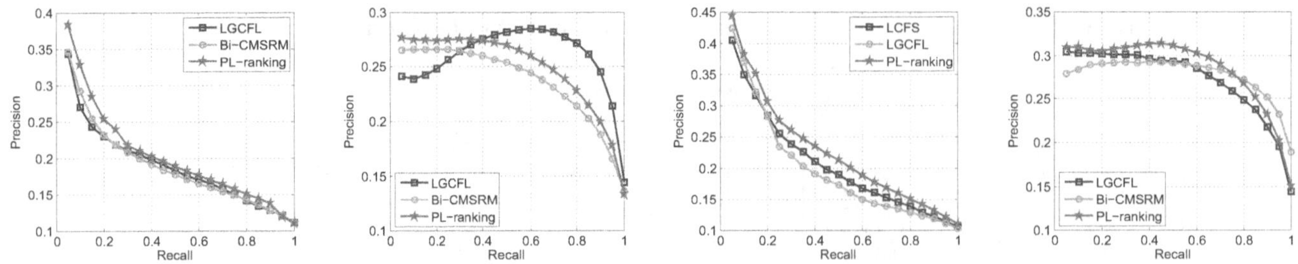

(a) Wiki Text Query (b) Wiki Image Query (c) Flickr Text Query (d) Flickr Image Query

Figure 3: Precision-Recall curves on Wiki and Flickr datasets.

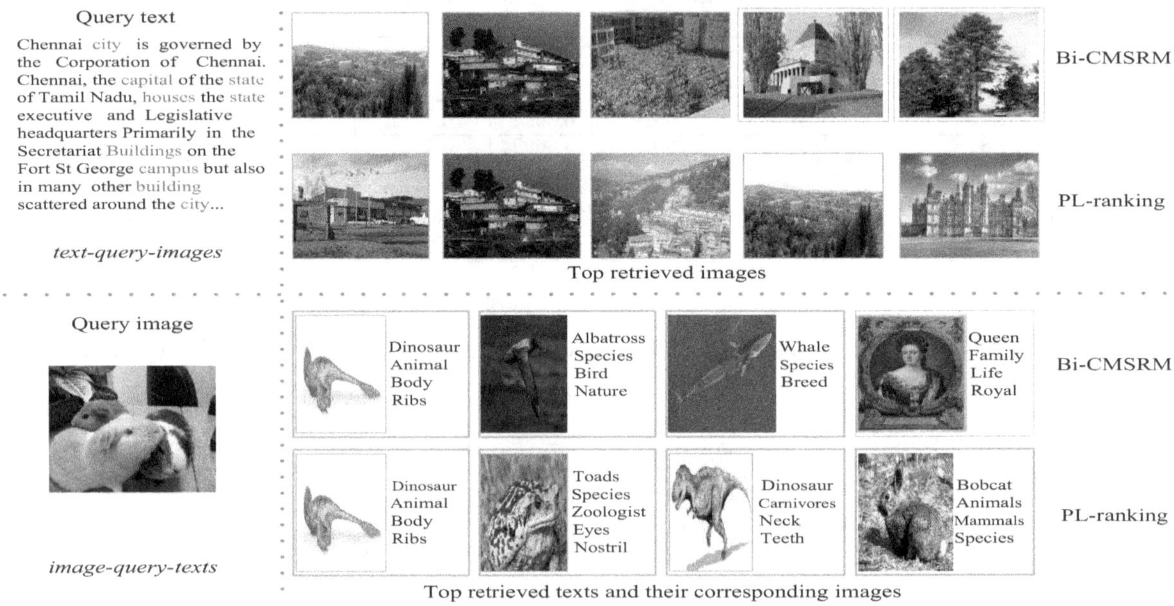

Figure 4: Two examples of text-query-images and image-query-texts on Wiki dataset. For each example, we show the query and its corresponding top retrieved samples by PL-ranking and Bi-CMSRM. In top half figure, we give a text about "city", "building" and etc; and a "Guinea pigs" image belonging to the "biology" class is given in bottom half figure. The incorrect retrieved samples are shown in the red frame.

We demonstrate two examples of retrieved results on two directional retrieval in Fig. 4. In this paper, the retrieved sample is relevant to the query if they belong to the same semantic class. Based on the intuitive judgement, we can observe that the top retrieved samples of PL-ranking are clearly relevant while Bi-CMSRM produces some irrelevant samples for both examples. It is encouraging that the proposed method retrieves more relevant results comparing with Bi-CMSRM.

4.4 Results on Flickr

The Flickr dataset is a subset selected from NUS [2]. It consists of 5,730 paired samples that belong to the 10 largest classes (concepts) with each pair having a unique class label (concept). Images are represented by 500-dimensional BoVW based on the SIFT descriptors, and texts are represented by the index vectors of the most frequent 1,000 tags. We randomly choose 75% of the data for training, 10% for validating, and the remaining 15% for testing.

The MAP scores and precision-recall curves of the different methods on the Flickr dataset are shown in Table 2 as well as Fig. 3(c) and 3(d). From Table 2, we conclude that PL-ranking achieves the average MAP scores of 0.2587 and 0.4237 under $R = all$ and $R = 10$ respectively, which are about 3.4% and 9.2 % higher than the second best results (0.2501 and 0.3881 for LGCFL). These results validate that PL-ranking can achieve the best results on Flickr dataset, and the analysis on the Wiki dataset is reasonable.

4.5 Results on Pascal and NUS-WIDE

To validate the generalization performance of PL-ranking, we also do experiments on Pascal [4] and NUS-WIDE [2].

The Pascal dataset consists of 5,011/4,952(testing/training) images-tag pairs, which belongs to 20 semantic classes. We only select the single-labeled data, which results in 2,808 training and 2,841 texting data. We use the publicly available 512-dimensional GIST features for images. For texts, we use the 399-dimensional word frequency features. The NUS-WIDE dataset consists of 15,628/10,437 (training/testing) image-tag pairs. This dataset is pruned from the original

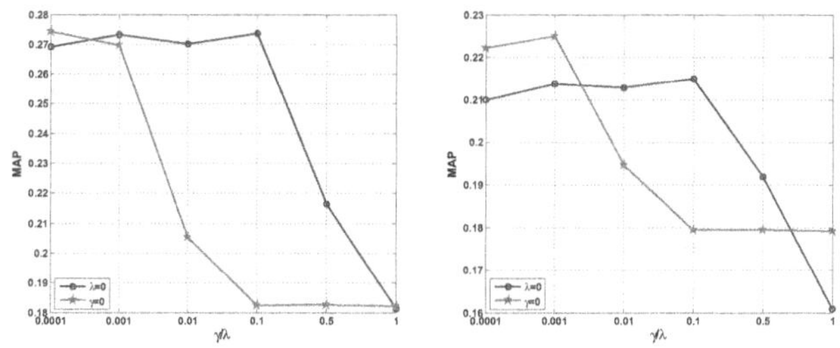

(a) Image Query (b) Text Query

Figure 5: Sensitivity test of λ and γ on Flickr dataset. For the curve of $\lambda = 0$, x-axis means that γ varies from 0.0001 to 1. x-axis means that λ varies from 0.0001 to 1 for the curve of $\gamma = 0$.

train-test split of the NUS dataset by keeping the pairs which belongs to the 10 largest classes. Each image-tag pair belongs to a unique class. Each text is represented by a 1000 dimensional word frequency vector based tag features while each image is represented as a 500 dimensional SIFT feature.

The MAP scores on the two datasets are reported in Table 3. The average MAP scores of PL-ranking on Pascal and NUS-WIDE are 0.378 and 0.383, which are about 4.7% and 4.8% higher than the second best results (0.361 and 0.366 for LGCFL). It is to note that image features of Pascal is different from other datasets, and the sample size of NUS-WIDE is greater than other datasets. The superior results show that PL-ranking can effectively handle the various features and the large-scale dataset.

4.6 Parameter sensitivity analysis

There are mainly three parameters in PL-ranking: λ, γ and c. On the Flickr dataset, we conduct the empirical analysis on the parameter sensitivity to show how to select the values for them.

First, Fig. 5 shows the MAP scores on both retrieval tasks in order to explore the contribution of each constraint. $\lambda = 0$ means that the listwise loss constraint is removed from PL-ranking. In this case, we observe that the performance is stable when γ varies from 10^{-4} to 10^{-1} on both directional retrieval, and both maximum values are achieved at 10^{-1}. This figure also shows the MAP scores by varying λ when γ is fixed with 0, which means that the low-rank constraint is removed. From the figure, we can know that PL-ranking obtains the highest MAP score at 10^{-3}. Thus, λ is set to 10^{-3}, and γ is set to 10^{-1} in all experiments.

Then, we repeat the experiments with the different iterations. The MAP scores of PL-ranking under the different iterations are shown in Fig. 6. From the figure, we know that for different ranks, MAP scores are improved with the increase of the iterations when the number of iterations is smaller than 15,000. But they are near to the constant after about 15,000 iterations. This experiment validates that PL-ranking can achieve the stable performance on the different ranks. In our experiment, we find 1.189 seconds are needed for each iteration in MATLAB R2013a, and our hardware configuration comprises a 3.6-GHz CPU and a 16GB RAM.

In Fig. 6, we also show the MAP scores of PL-ranking when λ is set to 0, which means that the listwise loss is removed from PL-ranking. From the figure, we observe that

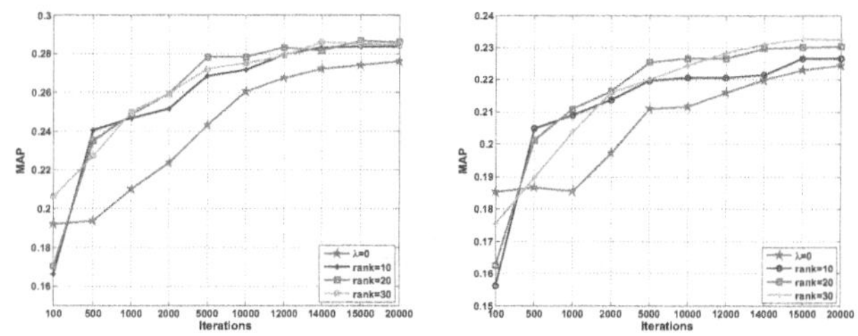

(a) Image Query (b) Text Query

Figure 6: The MAP scores of PL-ranking with the different iterations on Flickr dataset.

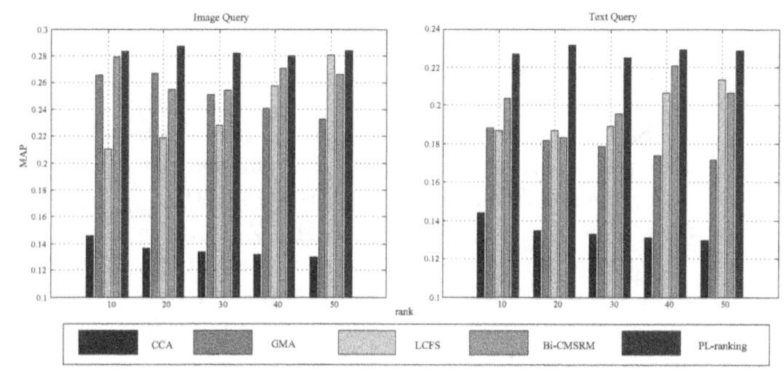

Figure 7: Performance of all methods with different ranks on Flickr dataset.

the MAP scores are still increasing after 15,000 iterations. But for PL-ranking, the MAP scores are near to the constant after 15,000 iterations. The iterations of PL-ranking are greatly reduced by using the listwise loss. This phenomenon validates that the listwise loss can reduce the iterations via preserving the class information in each iteration.

Furthermore, we show the MAP scores of the different methods on two retrieval tasks with varying ranks (*i.e.*, the dimensionality of the latent space) in Fig. 7. From the figure, we know that compared with other methods, the performance of PL-ranking is stable with the variation of ranks. These results show that the dimension of the latent space has little influence on the performance of PL-ranking.

Finally, we report the MAP scores without the bi-directional constraint. When we only perform the image-query-texts retrieval, the MAP scores of image query and text query are 0.2041 and 0.1694 on Wiki, and 0.2117 and 0.1904 on Flickr. In the other directional retrieval, the MAP scores of image query and text query are 0.1829 and 0.1583 on Wiki, and 0.2186 and 0.1852 on Flickr. These results demonstrate that putting the optimization of two directions of retrieval together can further improve the retrieval performance.

5. CONCLUSION

This paper proposes a novel ranking method named PL-ranking for cross-modal retrieval based on the low-rank optimization framework. In PL-ranking, the pairwise constraint ensures that the relevant samples appear at the top of ranked list. The listwise constraint enhances the separability among the different classes by minimizing the nearest intra-neighbors variance and maximizing the nearest inter-neighbors separability for each sample. The low-rank constraint reveals the latent semantic information. Experimental results on four public cross-modal datasets have shown that the proposed method improves at least 4.7% than that of the state-of-the-art method. Our future work will focus on making our method more efficient and online, so that it can be applied to deal with more practical problems.

6. ACKNOWLEDGMENTS

This work was supported in part by National Basic Research Program of China (973 Program): 2012CB316400 and 2015CB351802, Natural Science Foundation of China (NSFC): 61332016, 61303153, 61572465 and 61429201. This work was supported in part to Dr. Qi Tian by ARO grants W911NF-15-1-0290 and Faculty Research Gift Awards by NEC Laboratories of America and Blippar.

7. REFERENCES

[1] B. Bai, J. Weston, D. Grangier, R. Collobert, K. Sadamsda, Y. Qi, O. Chapelle, and K. Weinberger. Learning to rank with (a lot of) word features. *Information Retrieval*, 13(3):291–314, 2010.

[2] T. Chua, J. Tang, R. Hong, H. Li, Z. Luo, and Y. Zheng. Nus-wide: A real-world web image database from national university of singapore. In *ACM International Conference on Image and Video Retrieval*, 2009.

[3] L. Daryl and L. Gert. Efficient learning of mahalanobis metrics for ranking. In *International Conference on Machine Learning*, 2014.

[4] M. Everingham, V. Gool, C. Williams, J. Winn, and A. Zisserman. The pascal visual object classes (voc) challenge. *International Journal of Computer Vision*, 2010.

[5] Y. Gong, Q. Ke, M. Isard, and S. Lazebnik. A multi-view embedding space for modeling internet images, tags, and their semantics. *International Journal of Computer Vision*, 106(2):210–233, 2014.

[6] D. Grangier and S. Bengio. A discriminative kernel-based approach to rank images from text queries. *IEEE Transactions on Pattern Analysis and Machine Intelligence*, 30(8):1371–1384, 2008.

[7] A. Habibian, T. Mensink, and C. Snoek. Videostory: A new multimedia embedding for few-example recognition and translation of events. In *ACM International Conference on MultiMedia*, 2014.

[8] A. Haim, K. Satyen, P. Shiva, and S. Vikas. Efficient and practical stochastic subgradient descent for nuclear norm regularization. In *International Conference on Machine Learning*, 2012.

[9] D. Hardoon, S. Szedmark, and J. Shawe-Taylor. Canonical correlation analysis: An overview with application to learning methods. *Neural Computation*, 16(12):2639–2664, 2004.

[10] W. Jason, B. Samy, and U. Nicolas. Large scale image annotation: learning to rank with joint word-image embeddings. *Machine Learning*, 81:21–35, 2010.

[11] L. Jing, L. Yang, and J. Yu. Semi-supervised low-rank mapping learning for multi-label classification. In *IEEE Conference on Computer Vision and Pattern Recognition*, 2015.

[12] M. Kan, S. Shan, H. Zhang, S. Lao, and X. Chen. Multi-view discriminant analysis. In *European Conference on Computer Vision*, 2012.

[13] C. Kang, S. Xiang, S. Liao, C. Xu, and C. Pan. Learning consistent feature representation for cross-modal multimedia retrieval. *IEEE Transactions on Multimedia*, 17(3):370–381, 2015.

[14] V. Mahadevan, C. Wong, J. Pereira, T. Liu, N. Vasconcelos, and L. Saul. Maximum covariance unfolding: Manifold learning for bimodal data. In *Advances in Neural Information Processing Systems*, 2011.

[15] X. Mao, B. Lin, D. Cai, X. He, and J. Pei. Parallel field alignment for cross media retrieval. In *ACM International Conference on MultiMedia*, 2013.

[16] B. McFee and G. Lanckriet. Metric learning to rank. In *International Conference on Machine Learning*, 2010.

[17] J. Pereira, E. Coviello, G. Doyle, N. Rasiwasia, G. Lanckriet, R. Levy, and N. Vasconcelos. On the role of correlation and abstraction in cross-modal multimedia retrieval. *IEEE Transactions on Pattern Analysis and Machine Intelligence*, 36(3):521–535, 2014.

[18] V. Ranjan, N. Rasiwasia, and C. Jawahar. Multi-label cross-modal retrieval. In *IEEE International Conference on Computer Vision*, 2015.

[19] N. Rasiwasia, D. Mahajan, V. Mahadevan, and G. Aggarwal. Cluster canonical correlation analysis. In *International Conference on Artificial Intelligence and Statistics*, 2014.

[20] N. Rasiwasia, J. Pereira, E. Coviello, G. Doyle, G. Lanckriet, R. Levy, and N. Vasconcelos. A new approach to crossmodal multimedia retrieval. In *ACM International Conference on MultiMedia*, 2010.

[21] A. Sharma, A. Kumar, D. Hal, and D. Jacobs. Generalized multiview analysis: A discriminative latent space. In *IEEE Conference on Computer Vision and Pattern Recognition*, 2012.

[22] G. Song, S. Wang, Q. Huang, and Q. Tian. Similarity gaussian process latent variable model for multi-modal data analysis. In *IEEE International Conference on Computer Vision*, 2015.

[23] N. Usunier, D. Buffoni, and P. Gallinari. Ranking with ordered weighted pairwise classification. In *International Conference on Machine Learning*, 2009.

[24] Y. Verma and C. Jawahar. Im2text and text2im: Associating images and texts for cross-modal retrieval. In *British Machine Vision Conference*, 2014.

[25] C. Wang and S. Mahadevan. Heterogeneous domain adaptation using manifold alignment. In *International Joint Conference on Artificial Intelligence*, 2011.

[26] K. Wang, R. He, W. Wang, L. Wang, and T. Tan. Learning coupled feature spaces for cross-modal matching. In *IEEE International Conference on Computer Vision*, 2013.

[27] F. Wu, X. Lu, Z. Zhang, S. Yan, Y. Rui, and Y. Zhuang. Cross-media semantic representation via bi-directional learning to rank. In *ACM International Conference on MultiMedia*, 2013.

[28] Y. Yang, D. Xu, F. Nie, J. Luo, and Y. Zhuang. Ranking with local regression and global alignment for cross media retrieval. In *ACM International Conference on MultiMedia*, 2009.

Video eCommerce: Towards Online Video Advertising

Zhi-Qi Cheng[1,2]*, Yang Liu[2], Xiao Wu[1,#], Xian-Sheng Hua[2,#]
[1]School of Information Science and Technology, Southwest Jiaotong University, Chengdu, China
[2]Alibaba Group, Hangzhou, China
zhiqicheng@gmail.com; wuxiaohk@swjtu.edu.cn; {panjun.ly, xiansheng.hxs}@alibaba-inc.com

ABSTRACT

The prevalence of online videos provides an opportunity for e-commerce companies to exhibit their product ads in videos by recommendation. In this paper, we propose an advertising system named *Video eCommerce* to exhibit appropriate product ads to particular users at proper time stamps of videos, which takes into account video semantics, user shopping preference and viewing behavior feedback by a two-level strategy. At the first level, Co-Relation Regression (CRR) model is novelly proposed to construct the semantic association between keyframes and products. Heterogeneous information network (HIN) is adopted to build the user shopping preference from two different e-commerce platforms, Tmall and MagicBox, which alleviates the problems of data sparsity and cold start. In addition, Video Scene Importance Model (VSIM) utilizes the viewing behavior of users to embed ads at the most attractive position within the video stream. At the second level, taking the results of CRR, HIN and VSIM as the input, Heterogeneous Relation Matrix Factorization (HRMF) is applied for product advertising. Extensive evaluation on a variety of online videos from Tmall MagicBox demonstrates that *Video eCommerce* achieves promising performance, which significantly outperforms the state-of-the-art advertising methods.

Keywords

Online Advertising; E-commerce; Video Analysis

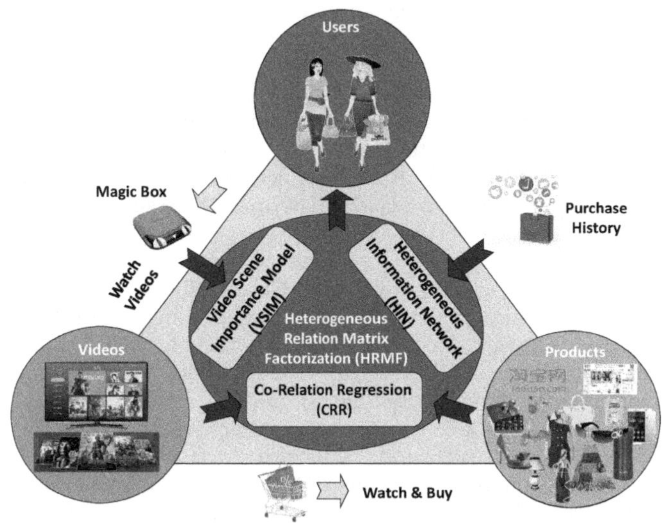

Figure 1: The architecture of Video eCommerce. The associations between videos and products, users and products, as well as users and videos are modeled by Co-Relation Regression (CRR), Heterogeneous Information Network (HIN), and Video Scene Importance Model (VSIM), respectively. With these three components, the personalized video advertising is achieved under Heterogeneous Relation Matrix Factorization (HRMF).

1. INTRODUCTION

The online video streaming service business shows the vast market potential. It is forecasted that the online video market in China will post total revenue worth US$ 14.67 billion by 2018, up from 3.75 billion in 2014. In addition, it is reported that the online spending in China will reach one trillion dollars by 2019[1]. The combination of e-commerce platforms and video content providers is inevitable and mutually beneficial, since e-commerce platforms expose their products to videos to increase Gross Merchandise Volume(GMV), and video content providers look forward to traffic monetizing by product exhibition. Unfortunately, video content based product exhibition is still one of the most under-utilized e-commerce strategies, which has an extraordinarily positive impact on consumers.

Traditional personalized product recommendation systems [7, 10, 31] can match consumers with appropriate products by analyzing the user behavior history and video textual tags. Previous browsing and shopping histories may indicate the level of satisfaction with particular products, providing cues for their interests and tastes, which is very useful to enhance user's shopping experience and satisfaction. E-

*This work is done while Zhi-Qi Cheng was an intern at Alibaba Group. # indicates corresponding authors.

[1]https://techcrunch.com/2015/02/04/china-1trillion-ecommerce

MM '16, October 15-19, 2016, Amsterdam, Netherlands.

ISBN 978-1-4503-3603-1/16/10...$15.00
DOI: http://dx.doi.org/10.1145/2964284.2964326

commerce companies like Amazon.com and video content providers such as Netflix have made the recommended systems salient parts of their websites. However, few works pay attention to the online video advertising with the combination of recommendation and video content analysis.

Existing video advertising and recommendation methods also encounter several challenges, although visual information has been taken into account. First, recommendation results for most advertising systems are only from searching visually similar products by object detection and image classification [15]. Unfortunately, the category number of pre-trained detectors and classifiers is limited, which results in the poor product coverage. Second, the diversity and abundance of products in e-commerce platforms lead to the association between users and product ads extremely sparse. Especially, since the purchase records of products exhibited on videos are pretty limited, current recommendation systems are always suffered from typical problems, such as cold-start, data sparsity and so on. Third, without considering user preference, state-of-the-art systems recommend the same product ads to all users, which are non-personalized. Fourth, few works have paid attention to the insert positions of product ads to attract users.

In this paper, a novel personalized product advertising system is proposed to recommend product ads to users of Tmall MagicBox. The videos are provided by set-top box, Tmall MagicBox. It is an integrated household digital entertainment system designed by Alibaba, which offers a wide variety of content, including movies, TV series, entertainment programs, documentaries, kids' programs, games and e-commerce. It has over 8,000 movies, 2,600 TV series, 2,100 entertainment programs, and 25,000 educational programs. The products are from Alibaba B2C and C2C online retail platforms, Taobao.com and Tmall.com. The number of products is approximately one billion. In addition, the user preference comes from two different domains, Tmall and Tmall MagicBox. The goal of this work is to transfer shopping behavior of users from e-commerce websites to online video advertising. The architecture of Video eCommerce is illustrated in Figure 1. The associations between videos and products, users and products, as well as users and videos are modeled by Co-Relation Regression (CRR), Heterogeneous Information Network (HIN), and Video Scene Importance Model (VSIM), respectively. With these three components, the personalized video advertising is achieved under Heterogeneous Relation Matrix Factorization (HRMF). To the best of our knowledge, this is the first video e-commerce system has been running on online dataset and comprehensively taking into account the relationships among users, videos and products. Its target is to recommend appropriate product ads to particular customers at proper time stamps, when users are watching movies or TV series. The contributions of this work are as follows:

- Co-relation Regression (CRR) is proposed to model the association between video keyframes and products, by exploiting vast amount of hidden linkages within keyframes, products, and co-relation of keyframes and products.

- Heterogeneous Information Network (HIN) is applied to build the relationship between users and products. Cross-domain user preference is propagated along different meta-paths in HIN to generate latent features for users and products. Therefore, HIN is able to alleviate the problems of data sparsity and cold-start.

- Video Scene Importance Model (VSIM) is proposed to leverage user click-through data and a voting approach is used to automatically adjust the importance of video scenes. In this way, user click-through can be tracked and ads will be embedded at the most attractive positions within the video stream.

- Heterogeneous Relation Matrix Factorization (HRMF) is presented to take the outputs of CRR, HIN and VSIM as the input and mine the relationship among users, keyframes and products. It determines the insert positions in videos of product ads according to user-keyframe relationship, and enables the personalized advertising based on user-product relationship.

This paper is organized as follows. Section 2 gives a brief overview of related work. Section 3 introduces the framework of the proposed advertising system and the preprocessing. Section 4 elaborates the association modeling, including CRR, HIN and VSIM. Heterogeneous Relation Matrix Factorization is presented in Section 5. Experimental results and performance comparison are described in Section 6. Finally, this paper is concluded with a summary.

2. RELATED WORK

This work is closely related to online advertising and product recommendation, which will be briefly reviewed in this section.

2.1 Online Advertising

In the last two decades, there has been substantial volume of works done on online advertising. According to the order of evolution, it can be divided into: (a) content agnostic advertising (random placing advertisements), (b) contextual advertising (placing relevant advertisements based on keywords) [15, 16], and more recently (c) semantic advertising (placing advertisements based on the semantic analysis of the text) [20].

The main objectives of the online advertising are in revenue management through ad allocation. Text-based contextual advertising methods are popular, e.g. Google's AdSense, whose ad allocation ways are optimized by using linear programming [2, 24] or dynamic programming [1, 9, 17]. Although contextual advertising is popular in text-based advertising, contextual multimedia advertising is developed slowly. The trend of online multimedia advertising is summarized and a broad survey on the methodologies for advertising is conducted in [13]. In online image advertising, a contextual advertising system called ImageSense is studied in [14, 16], which can automatically associate relevant ads with an image in the non-intrusive areas. Meanwhile, in online video advertising, a VideoSense system is introduced in [15] which aims to embed more contextually relevant ads at less intrusive positions within the video stream. More recently, the linear in-stream ad allocation problem in an online video is studied in [8] through a dynamic programming approach that accounts for ad prices, ad quality, and externalities from other advertisements. Unfortunately, existing online multimedia advertising algorithms do not consider the personalized user preference.

2.2 Product Recommendation

Recommender systems have been extensively studied in the past decade, and been applied to many successful online services, such as product recommendation at Amazon, movie recommendation at Netflix, video recommendation at Hulu, and music recommendation at Pandora. It has drawn much attention in computer vision, data mining, information retrieval and multimedia communities. Methods based on collaborative filtering [3, 6, 10, 22] have been actively studied recently, which represent the user-item rating matrix with low dimensional latent vectors. A REgularized DualfActor Regression (REDAR) method based on collaborative filtering is proposed in [3], in which social attributes and content attributes are flexibly combined. Although collaborative filtering achieves a huge success, there are two main drawbacks: data sparsity and cold-start. Recently, a large number of works address these two problems directly or indirectly by incorporating additional information, such as social data [11], user feedback [18] and latent factor models [30].

Since the relationship between products is an essential factor for recommendation task, some works try to supply good shopping experience for users by considering product relationship. A novel problem called the bundle recommendation problem is introduced in [32], which takes into account of the dependency of items in the same set. A method is developed in [12] to infer networks of substitutable and complementary products. It is formulated as a supervised link prediction task, where the semantics of substitutes and complements can be learned from data associated with products.

There are also some works for recommendation task based on other factors, such as time, price and so on. The conception of life stage is introduced into product recommendation [7]. The current life-stage of a user is first predicted and corresponding products are then recommended. A stock aware recommender system [31] is developed for Tmall to select recommended items based on both the user preference and the inventory size of items. Although extensive research has been conducted for recommended systems, for video advertising, froementioned research mainly considers the relationship between users and products, the semantics of product and video are totally ignored, which motivates this work.

3. FRAMEWORK AND PREPROCESSING

3.1 Framework

The framework of the proposed online video advertising system, *Video eCommerce*, is illustrated in Figure 2. Preprocessing is first conducted. After video structure analysis, a video is represented as a set of keyframes. Object detection and scene classification are applied on keyframes to obtain the visual-terms (category tags). Different relationships among keyframes, visual-terms, products, product-terms (product textual tags) form five initial association matrices, which are exploited for Co-Relation Regression (CRR). The semantic association between keyframes and products is constructed by CRR. To alleviate the problem of data sparsity and mine user behavior, cross-domain purchase histories from MagicBox and Tmall are integrated to infer user shopping preference, which is modeled with Heterogenous Information Network (HIN). Video Scene Importance Model (VSIM) is integrated to determine the product insertion

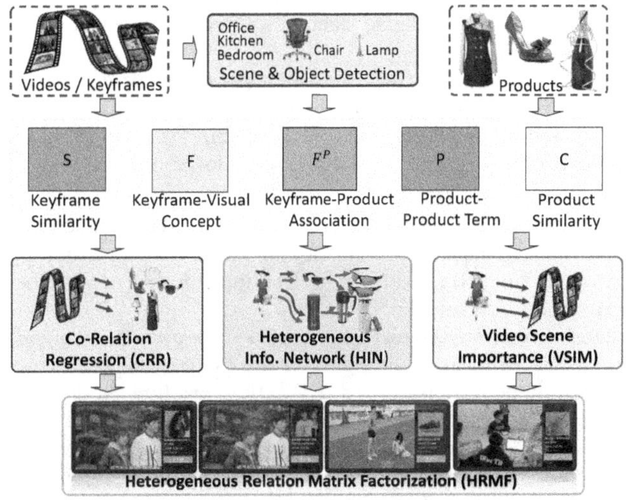

Figure 2: Framework of the proposed *Video eCommerce* advertising system.

position. HRMF is novelly proposed to integrate keyframe-product association, user-product interest relationship and video scene importance to recommend appropriate product ads to users, which is modeled as an optimization problem.

3.2 Object Detection and Scene Classification

After shot boundary detection and keyframe extraction [26], each video is represented as a set of keyframes. A large scale detection network based on deep convolutional models, LSDA framework [5], is adopted to detect objects in keyframes. We fine-tune the layers of 1-7 using our labeled data with bounding box annotation. Totally, the object detection supports 170 object categories that are commonly occurred in videos and have the vast market potentials, such as clothes, furniture, electrical appliances, and so on.

GoogleNet [23] deep convolutional network is applied for scene classification. To accelerate the training process, the size of input images is reduced to 128x128 and small network architecture is used. The stride of conv1 layer is enlarged from 2 to 4, and the kernel number of conv2 layer is reduced from 192 to 96. For remaining Inception layers, the kernel number is set as the half of its original number. Similar to the categories of object detection, the scene categories are determined based on the advertising potentials and appearance frequency in videos, such as office, meeting room, playground, and so on. Totally, 49 scenes are recognized in our work.

3.3 Association Matrix Initialization

The initial association matrices are computed with the assistance of scene classification, object detection and similarity measurement among different components, which are defined as follows:

Modeling the relations between keyframes and visual-concepts (F matrix) The visual-concepts refer to the category labels of object detection and scene classification. The relationship between keyframe f_i and visual-concept t_j is measured based on the $tf - idf$ weight, which is defined as follows:

$$F_{ij} = tf_{ij} \cdot idf_j$$

where tf_{ij} is the term frequency of concept t_j in keyframe

f_i, and idf_j is the inverse document frequency for concept t_j across all keyframes.

Modeling the relations between products and product-terms (P matrix) The product-terms denote the textual description of products. The relationship between product p_i and product-term t_j is defined as follows:

$$P_{ij} = tf_{ij} \cdot idf_j$$

where tf_{ij} is the term frequency of term t_j in product p_i, and idf_j is the inverse document frequency for term t_j across all products.

Modeling of relations between keyframes and products (F^P matrix) The relationship matrix of keyframes and products is denoted as F^P. If a product p_j is relevant to a detected object in keyframe f_i, F^P_{ij} is equal to 1. Otherwise, it is 0. For an object detected in a keyframe, the detected object region is treated as the query example and searched to find visually similar products in database. Meanwhile, products are also searched with text search engine in Tmall using the text label of the object category. These results are further fused as the final relevant products by linear fusion.

Modeling the relations between keyframes (S matrix) The keyframe similarity matrix is denoted as S, in which each item is a linear fusion of visual (V_{ij}) and textual (T_{ij}) similarity between two keyframes.

$$S_{i,j} = e^{-(\alpha V_{ij} + (1-\alpha) T_{ij})}$$

Each keyframe is represented as a 4,096 dimensional CNN feature, and cosine similarity is used to measure their visual similarity V_{ij}. The tf-idf vector in F is adopted to calculate their textual similarity T_{ij} using cosine distance.

Modeling the relations between products (C matrix) Similarly, the product relevance matrix C is a linear fusion of visual and textual similarity between two products, which is the same as S.

4. ASSOCIATION MODELING

The associations between videos and products, users and products, as well as users and videos are modeled by Co-Relation Regression (CRR), Heterogeneous Information Network (HIN), and Video Scene Importance Model (VSIM), respectively, which will be elaborated as following subsections.

4.1 Co-Relation Regression

In order to model the association between keyframes and products, we consider the following two relations from the viewpoints of video semantics and product description, respectively. The relation of video semantics is defined as $E_1 = F^P P$, which assumes that similar keyframes should be mapped to the same product-terms. At the same time, the relation of product description $E_2 = (F^P)^T F$ is also defined, which assumes that similar products should be mapped to the same visual concepts too. With these two co-relations, we have the following three intuitions:

- The co-relations from E_1 and E_2 should be consistent with the initial relations between keyframes and products i.e. F^P.
- If two keyframes have high similarity in S, the association in E_1 should be mapped to the same product-terms.

Algorithm 1 Co-Relation Regression (CRR)

Input: F^P, S, C, F, P, $t_k^{E_1}$, $t_k^{E_2}$, γ_1, γ_2, γ_3.
Output: $\hat{E}_1$, $\hat{E}_2$

Initialize: $E_1^0 = F^P P$, $E_2^0 = (F^P)^T F$;
for $k = 1 \to n$ **do**
  Calculate $\frac{\partial f_1^k}{\partial E_1}, \frac{\partial f_1^k}{\partial E_2}, \frac{\partial f_2^k}{\partial E_1}, \frac{\partial f_3^k}{\partial E_2}, \frac{\partial g^k}{\partial E_1}$ and $\frac{\partial g^k}{\partial E_2}$
  $\bigtriangledown F_{E_1}(E_1, E_2) = \frac{\partial f_1^k}{\partial E_1} + \gamma_1 \frac{\partial f_2^k}{\partial E_1} + \gamma_3 \frac{\partial g^k}{\partial E_1}$
  $\bigtriangledown F_{E_2}(E_1, E_2) = \frac{\partial f_1^k}{\partial E_2} + \gamma_2 \frac{\partial f_3^k}{\partial E_2} + \gamma_3 \frac{\partial g^k}{\partial E_2}$
  $E_1^{(k+1)} = E_1^k + t_{k+1}^{E_1} \bigtriangledown F_{E_1}(E_1, E_2)$
  $E_2^{(k+1)} = E_2^k + t_{k+1}^{E_2} \bigtriangledown F_{E_2}(E_1, E_2)$
end for
return $\hat{E}_1$, $\hat{E}_2$

- Meanwhile, if two products have high similarity in C, the association in E_2 should be mapped to the same visual concepts.

The issue of keyframe and product association is modeled as an optimization problem. According to these intuitions, an objective function is proposed to solve these two targeting matrices E_1 and E_2. Our target is to minimize the cost function:

$$\begin{aligned} \min_{E_1, E_2} & (\left\| \left(\alpha E_1 P^T + (1-\alpha) F E_2^T\right) - F^P \right\|_F^2 \\ & + \gamma_1 \left\| E_1 E_1^T - S \right\|_F^2 + \gamma_2 \left\| E_2 E_2^T - C \right\|_F^2 \\ & + \gamma_3 (\|E_1\|_F^2 + \|E_2\|_F^2)) \end{aligned} \tag{1}$$

To simplify the description, we get:

- $f_1(E_1, E_2) = \left\| (\alpha E_1 P^T + (1-\alpha) F E_2^T) - F^P \right\|_F^2$ means that the recommended products should not deviate much from the objects detected from the keyframes.
- $f_2(E_1) = \left\| E_1 E_1^T - S \right\|_F^2$ denotes that the recommended products should be similar if two keyframes are semantically similar.
- $f_3(E_2) = \left\| E_2 E_2^T - C \right\|_F^2$ means that two related products should be recommended to the same keyframes.
- $g(E_1, E_2) = \|E_1\|_F^2 + \|E_2\|_F^2$ is a regularization term for smoothing.

where $\alpha \in [0, 1]$ is a weighting factor to control the contribution of keyframes and products, and $\gamma_1, \gamma_2, \gamma_3$ are non-negative parameters less than 1, which control the weights of each constraint.

In order to minimize the cost function, we differentiate $f(E_1, E_2)$ with regard to E_1 and E_2 at each iteration, respectively. The following iterative formulas are proposed for the optimization problem.

$$\frac{\partial f_1}{\partial E_1} = 2\alpha(\alpha E_1 P^T + (1-\alpha) F E_2^T - F^P) P$$

$$\frac{\partial f_1}{\partial E_2} = 2(1-\alpha)((\alpha E_1 P^T + (1-\alpha) F E_2^T - F^P)^T) F$$

$$\frac{\partial f_2}{\partial E_1} = 4(E_1 E_1^T - S) E_1$$

$$\frac{\partial f_3}{\partial E_2} = 4(E_2 E_2^T - C) E_2$$

$$\frac{\partial g}{\partial E_1} = 2\gamma_3 E_1$$

$$\frac{\partial g}{\partial E_2} = 2\gamma_3 E_2$$

The optimization is summarized as an iterative algorithm, which is introduced in Algorithm 1. E_1 and E_2 are updated at each iteration until the function is converged. The results of E_1 and E_2, denoted as $\hat{E_1}$ and $\hat{E_2}$, respectively, are adopted to estimate the keyframe-product correlation by:

$$F^p = \alpha \hat{E_1} P^T + (1-\alpha) F \hat{E_2^T}$$

Time complexity analysis. The time complexity of CRR is determined by the matrix calculation and the number of iterations, which is $O(N_I(N_K+N_P)^2)$, where N_I, N_K, N_P are the numbers of iterations, keyframes and products, respectively.

4.2 Cross-domain User Preference Diffusion

In this section, we will introduce the modeling of user preference, in which user-product association is constructed through meth-paths under the framework of Heterogeneous Information Network (HIN) [28]. The *Video eCommerce* system can be regarded as a HIN, which contains different types of relationships among users and products, as shown in Figure 3. In HIN, two entities (such as, users, videos or products) can be connected via different paths (relations). These paths may contain different entity types and relationship types in inconsistent orders and with various lengths. The meta-path [22] is adopted to describe path types. Previous studies suggest that meta-paths can be used to facilitate entity similarity and proximity measurement [22, 28].

Meta-Path: A meta-path $MP = A_0 \overset{R_1}{\rightarrow} A_1 \overset{R_2}{\rightarrow} ... \overset{R_k}{\rightarrow} A_k$ is a path in a network schema $G_T = (A, R)$, which defines a new composite relation $R_1 \times R_2 \times ... \times R_k$ between type A_0 and A_k, where $A_i \in A$ and $R_i \in R$ for $i = 0, ...k$. $A_0 = sub(R_1) = sub(MP)$, $A_k = obj(R_k) = obj(MP)$ and $A_i = obj(R_i) = sub(R_{i+1})$ for $i = 1, ..., k-1$, where $sub(\cdot)$ defines the subject of certain relationship, and $obj(\cdot)$ defines the object. In our HIN (as showed in Figure 3), the subject of our $MP_1 \sim MP_4$ is users, and the object is products.

Now the cross-domain user preference can be diffused by a couple of meta-paths. The intuition is that if a user purchased a product from Tmall.com directly or through MagicBox, the user and the product will be linked. Meanwhile, other products that are semantically relevant to the purchased product, can be treated as substitutes or alternative ones. The user will be treated as having a hidden relationship with these products. The four meta-paths showed in Figure 3 are listed as follows.

1. $MP_1 : user \overset{purchase}{\rightarrow} product$
2. $MP_2 : user \overset{purchase}{\rightarrow} product \overset{similar}{\rightarrow} product$
3. $MP_3 : user \overset{view\&buy}{\rightarrow} video \overset{contain}{\rightarrow} keyframe \overset{contain}{\rightarrow} object \overset{associate}{\rightarrow} product$
4. $MP_4 : user \overset{view\&buy}{\rightarrow} video \overset{contain}{\rightarrow} keyframe \overset{contain}{\rightarrow} object \overset{associate}{\rightarrow} product \overset{similar}{\rightarrow} product$

in which the observed user-product preference can be directly obtained from meta-paths of MP_1 and MP_3, the potential reference can be induced from meta-paths of MP_2 and MP_4.

The user preference diffusion score between user s and product t along the k_{th} meta-path is calculated as follows:

$$R_k(s,t) = \frac{2 * C(s,t)}{C(s,:) + C(:,t)}$$

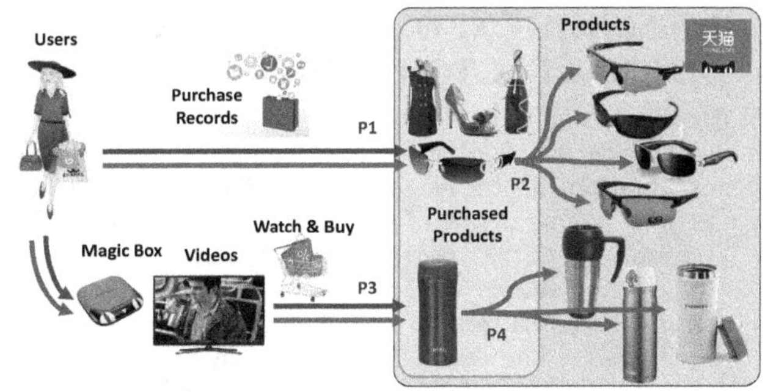

Figure 3: Four meta-paths for cross-domain user preference diffusion between users and products.

where $C(s,t)$ is the number of meta-path instances between s and t. $C(s,:)$ denotes the path count starting with s; and $C(:,t)$ denotes the path count ending with t.

4.3 Video Scene Importance Model

In this section, we will introduce the modeling of video scene importance. As video is a time evolving sequence with diverse contents, users may have different degrees of interest on different parts of the video. The recommended products should be inserted to the keyframes where viewers will stay for a longer time. Therefore, the keyframe is defined as the basic unit of video segment.

In order to obtain the matrix of video scene importance, U^F, we leverage user click-through (user browsing behaviors on a video sequence) to obtain the video scene importance weight. The weight of video scene importance $U^f_{i,j}$ is the importance degree of user u_i to keyframe f_j which is extracted from video shots, where $j = \{1, ..., |D|\}$ and $|D|$ is the number of keyframes in a video. If a user fast-forwards or fast-backwards a scene (i.e., keyframe), he/she may not be interested in this scene, then the weight $U^f_{i,j}$ for keyframe f_j should be decreased. If a user seeks a specific keyframe or to replay a scene, he/she may have strong interest on the content of this scene, then the weight $U^f_{i,j}$ should be increased. Based on these observations, we record the user browsing behaviors and classify the behaviors into four categories. The weight $U^f_{i,j}$ is then dynamically adjusted by a voting-based approach.

The weight $U^{f(t+1)}_{i,j}$ for keyframe f_j at the $t+1$ iteration depends on that in previous step $U^{f(t)}_{i,j}$. It will be added a weight of 0.5 (pause and then browse), 1.0 (seek or replay) and -0.5 (fast browse or skip), respectively, according to user behavior. Please note that $U^{f(t)}_{i,j}$ is normalized to [0, 1] by

$$U^{f(t)}_{i,j} = \frac{U^{f(t)}_{i,j} - U^{f(t)}_{min}}{U^{f(t)}_{max} - U^{f(t)}_{min}}$$

where $U^{f(t)}_{max}$ and $U^{f(t)}_{min}$ denote the maximum and minimum of $U^{f(t)}_{i,j}$ in the t_{th} iteration, respectively. When a viewer watches the video which contains keyframe f_j more than once, $U^{f(t)}_{i,j}$ directly indicates the video scene importance for user u_i.

For a new viewer who has not seen the video before, based on the assumption that watching behavior of reviewers is approximately homophily [4], we use the average of all users who have seen the video before to initialize its weight.

5. HETEROGENEOUS RELATION MATRIX FACTORIZATION

With the association modeling presented in last section, the personalized video advertising is achieved under Heterogeneous Relation Matrix Factorization (HRMF). Three target matrices can be defined for aforementioned three models. The first target matrix is user-keyframe preference matrix $\hat{U}_f$, which denotes the interests between viewers and keyframes. It is utilized to find the best insert position of product ads. The second one is keyframe-product association matrix $\hat{F}_p$, referring to the association between keyframes and products, which combines user preference and video semantics. The third one is meta-path weigh matrix W, denoting the importance of user-product interaction under certain meta-path semantics. It is used to fuse cross-domain user preference elegantly.

The personalized product advertising is converted to an optimization problem. The first term of the model incorporates the collaborative filtering component, which keeps the recommended product results closer to the observed user-product interactions. The second and third items consider the video scene importance and the association between keyframes and products, respectively. The fourth term of the model is the user-product relationship from the cross-domain user preference diffusion method. The last one is the smoothing term. It is defined as follows:

$$J = \min_{\hat{U^f},\hat{F^p},W} \Big(\sum_{i=0}^{N_U}\sum_{j=0}^{N_K}(\hat{U_i^f}\hat{F_j^p} - R_{i,j})^2 + \alpha\sum_{i=0}^{N_U}\|(\hat{U_i^f} - U_i^f)\|_F^2 + \beta\sum_{j=0}^{N_K}\|\hat{F_j^p} - F_j^p\|_F^2 + \mu\sum_{k=0}^{N_M} W_k \sum_{i=0}^{N_U}\sum_{j=0}^{N_K}(\hat{U_i^f}\hat{F_j^p} - R_{i,j}^k)^2 + \lambda(\|\hat{U^f}\|_F^2 + \|\hat{F^p}\|_F^2 + \|W\|_F^2)\Big) \quad (2)$$

These symbols have the same meanings as introduced in previous sections. N_U, N_K, N_M are the number of users, keyframes and meta-paths, respectively. $R_{i,j}$ is the purchase records that user i purchased product j in Tmall MagicBox. α and β are parameters capturing the importance of video scene and video semantics, respectively, which will be discussed in the experimental part. Similar to [19], the logistic function $f(x) = 1/(1 + exp(-x))$ is used to normalize the values in U^f, F^p and $R_{i,j}^k$ within the range of $[0, 1]$.

The learning of HRMF is implemented in a two-step iteration approach, where the preference matrix of viewers to keyframes $\hat{U^f}$, the keyframe-product association matrix $\hat{F^p}$ and the weight matrix for meta-paths W will be mutually enhanced. In the first step, the weight matrix W is fixed and the optimal $\hat{U^f}$ and $\hat{F^p}$ are learnt. In the second step, $\hat{U^f}$ and $\hat{F^p}$ are fixed, and the optimal weight matrix W is learnt. The optimization is summarized as an iterative algorithm, which is introduced in Algorithm 2.

Step 1: Optimize $\hat{U^f}$ and $\hat{F^p}$ given W: When W is fixed, the model becomes a traditional collaborative filtering method. Therefore, similar to [27], Stochastic Gradient Descent (SGD) is adopted to solve this problem.

Step 2: Optimize W given $\hat{U^f}$ and $\hat{F^p}$: When $\hat{U^f}$ and $\hat{F^p}$ are fixed, it only includes $\hat{U^f}$, and $\hat{F^p}$ can be discarded. The objective function is reduced to:

Algorithm 2 Heterogeneous Relation Matrix Factorization (HRMF)

Input: F^p of CRR, R^k of HIN, U^F of VSIM, $R_{i,j}$ of Tmall MagicBox, and learning rate $\alpha^s \in (0, 1)$.
Output: $\hat{R}$

Initialize $\hat{U^f}$, $\hat{F^p}$, W randomly;
while $\hat{U^f}$, $\hat{F^p}$ are not converged **do**
  for each observed user-product pair $(i, j) \in R$ **do**
    Calculate $\frac{\partial J}{\partial \hat{U_i^f}}, \frac{\partial J}{\partial \hat{V_j^p}}$,
    $\hat{U_i^f} \leftarrow \hat{U_i^f} - \alpha^s \frac{\partial J}{\partial \hat{U_i^f}}$
    $\hat{V_j^p} \leftarrow \hat{V_j^p} - \alpha^s \frac{\partial J}{\partial \hat{V_j^p}}$,
  end for
  while W is not converged **do**
    Calculate $\frac{\partial J_1}{\partial W_k}$,
    $W_i \leftarrow W_i - \alpha^s \frac{\partial J_1}{\partial W_k}$,
  end while
end while
return The predicted ratings $\hat{R} = \hat{U^f}\hat{F^p}$.

$$J_1 = \mu\sum_{k=0}^{N_M} W_k \sum_{i=0}^{N_U}\sum_{j=0}^{N_K}(\hat{U_i^f}\hat{F_j^p} - R_{i,j}^k)^2 + \lambda(\|W\|_F^2)$$

We can see that J_1 becomes a linear model for each W_k. Therefore, Stochastic Gradient Descent is also used to obtain W.

$$\frac{1}{2}\frac{\partial J}{\partial \hat{U_i^f}} = \sum_{i=0}^{N_U}\hat{U_i^f}(\hat{U_i^f}\hat{F_j^p} - R_{i,j}) + \alpha\sum_{i=0}^{N_U}(\hat{U_i^f} - U_i^f) + \mu\sum_{k=0}^{N_M}\sum_{i=0}^{N_U}\hat{U_i^f}(\hat{U_i^f}\hat{F_j^p} - R_{i,j}^k) + \sum_{i=0}^{N_U}(\hat{U_i^f})$$

$$\frac{1}{2}\frac{\partial J}{\partial \hat{V_j^p}} = \sum_{j=0}^{N_K}\hat{V_j^p}(\hat{U_i^f}\hat{F_j^p} - R_{i,j}) + \beta\sum_{j=0}^{N_K}(\hat{V_j^p} - V_j^p) + \mu\sum_{k=0}^{N_M}\sum_{j=0}^{N_K}\hat{V_i^f}(\hat{U_i^f}\hat{F_j^p} - R_{i,j}^k) + \sum_{j=0}^{N_K}(\hat{V_j^p})$$

$$\frac{1}{2}\frac{\partial J_1}{\partial W_k} = \lambda W_k + \mu\sum_{i=0}^{N_U}\sum_{j=0}^{N_K}(\hat{U_i^f}\hat{F_j^p} - R_{i,j})^2$$

After minimizing this model, $\hat{U^f}$, $\hat{F^p}$, and W can be obtained. The predicted ratings can be obtained as $\hat{R} = \hat{U^f}\hat{F^p}$. In practice, the recommended insert positions should meet the uniform distribution. Assume that there are M insert positions, the video will be divided into M equal portions. For a user u_i, according to the maximun $\hat{R_{i,j}}$, the product p_j will be recommended at the keyframe which is indicated by maximum $\hat{U_i^f}$ in each portion.

Time complexity analysis. The time complexity of computing the gradients of U, F and W is $O(N_I N_U)$, $O(N_I N_U)$ and $O(N_I N_U N_P)$, respectively. N_I, N_K, N_P and N_U are the number of iterations, keyframes, products and users, respectively. Therefore, the upper bound of the complexity of Alg. 2 is $O(N_I N_U N_P)$

6. EXPERIMENTS

In this section, we evaluate the effect of individual component for the performance of *Video eCommerce*, and compare it with state-of-the-art approaches. We study this problem empirically by conducting a live controlled experiment with real customers in a real industrial setting.

Figure 4: The personalized product advertising examples recommended by *Video eCommerce* for different users. The top of the figure (with blue border) shows a complete advertising procedure.

6.1 Experimental Design

To eliminate the bias from user sampling, we select at least 400 users having purchase records from every video. Several statistical tests, including t-test and Chi-square test, are conducted to keep the consistency between the selected users and whole customer database, based on six variables: 1) age; 2) gender; 3) number of orders; 4) number of purchased items at different domains; 5) money spent on the Website; 6) year of subscription. We measure the distributions of each variable between the selected users and the customer database, and update the selected users until there is no any statistically significant difference on similarities. Each performance metric is then averaged across customers instead of using the absolute values for every video.

To evaluate the performance, we select the latest released 235 videos and their associated information as our dataset, which consists of 25 movies, 4 TV series (157 videos) and 53 variety shows. Totally, there are 47,768 users, 235 videos, 52,405 keyframes, 288,200 products, 219 visual concepts and 10,932 product terms.

6.2 Evaluation Criteria

Video eCommerce is an online system, we focus on business related performance matrices. A complete advertising procedure is illustrated on the top of Figure 4 (with blue border). From left to right, when a user views a video, the *Video eCommerce* will pop up an ads on bottom right corner of the screen. If a user is interested in this product ads, he/she may click ads. By viewing the details, if the user is really interested in it, he/she may favorite it. At this point, the business-related crucial performance measures are defined as follows:

- **Page View Click Ratio (PVC)**: It refers to the ratio of product ads which are clicked to all product ads that are popped up.
- **Unique Visitor Click Ratio (UVC)**: It is the ratio of the unique individuals who click product ads to total individuals who view product ads, regardless how many product ads they click.
- **Page View Favorite Ratio (PVF)**: It denotes the ratio of product ads which are favorited to all product ads that are clicked.
- **Unique Visitor Favorite Ratio (UVF)**: It refers to the ratio of unique individuals who favorite products to total individuals who click product ads, regardless how many products they favorite.

6.3 Performance Comparison of CRR Model

In this subsection, we evaluate the impact of CRR to the *Video eCommerce* system.

6.3.1 Baselines

To evaluate the performance, we compare the proposed method with three baseline methods (Search_T, Search_V and Search_T+V) and four variants of CRR. The results of these methods are treated as the input of HRMF model to evaluate the overall performance. Search_T, Search_V and Search_T+V represent that only textual features (the tags of object and scene detection), only visual features (CNN features of detected objects), and their combinations are used to retrieve the similar products, respectively. Meanwhile, to evaluate the effects of different components of CRR, four variants of CRR are also tested. CRR-KA and CRR-PA refer to CRR with keyframe relation and product relation is considered, when α is set to 1 and 0 in Eqn. 1, respectively. CRR-KR and CRR-PR refer to CRR with regularizer of keyframes and products when γ_1 or γ_2 is set to 0 in Eqn. 1, respectively.

6.3.2 Experiment Results

The performance comparison of CRR model according to different categories is shown in Figure 5. Generally, the performance of Search_T is poor, since products with the same text words are too monotonous, so that recommendation purely based on text cannot meet the requirements of users. When users are attracted by a video, visually similar products are more accepted for users. Therefore, Search_V association has a better performance than Search_T. The combination of textual and visual features improves the performance, since users will meet a lot of bizarre ads when sys-

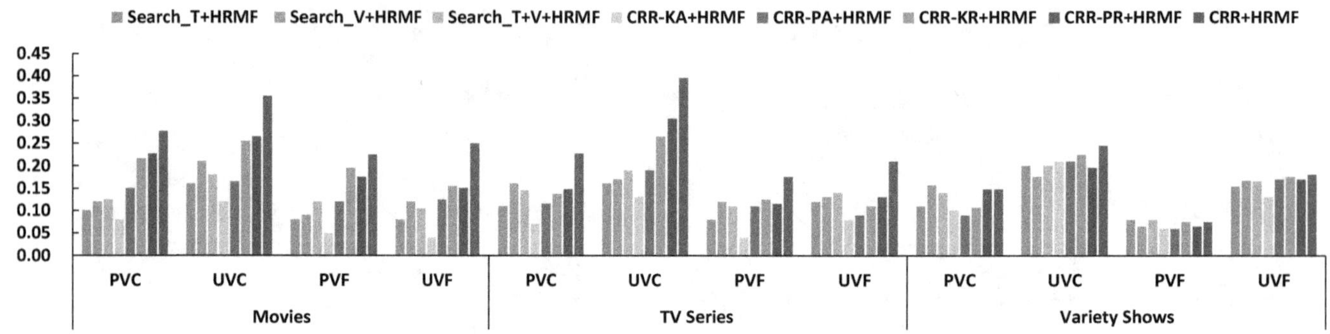

Figure 5: Performance comparison for CRR model.

Table 1: Performance comparison for HIN and VSIM models

Approach	Movies				TV Series				Variety Shows			
	PVC	UVC	PVF	UVF	PVC	UVC	PVF	UVF	PVC	UVC	PVF	UVF
Tmall	0.18	0.20	0.16	0.14	0.18	0.25	0.16	0.12	0.13	0.19	**0.08**	0.13
MagicBox	0.16	0.16	0.13	0.13	0.12	0.20	0.10	0.10	0.11	0.16	0.06	0.10
HIN-Equal	0.22	0.26	0.20	0.16	0.16	0.29	0.15	0.13	0.15	0.23	**0.08**	**0.18**
HIN-Random	0.22	0.27	0.18	0.16	0.16	0.32	0.13	0.13	0.14	0.19	0.07	0.17
HIN	**0.28**	**0.36**	**0.23**	**0.25**	**0.23**	**0.40**	**0.18**	**0.21**	0.15	**0.25**	**0.08**	**0.18**
VSIM-Un	0.16	0.17	0.16	0.14	0.13	0.21	0.13	0.11	0.13	0.21	0.06	0.17
VSIM-Random	0.24	0.26	0.16	0.16	0.16	0.28	0.14	0.14	**0.16**	0.20	**0.08**	0.17
VSIM	**0.28**	**0.36**	**0.23**	**0.25**	**0.23**	**0.40**	**0.18**	**0.21**	0.15	**0.25**	**0.08**	**0.18**

tem only relies on the visual information. And because users have dissimilar viewing habits for different video categories, which contain completely diverse semantic information, the performance for different categories are inconsistent. Furthermore, most of variety show videos in our dataset are talk show, which contain little semantic information, so the improvement for variety shows is minor.

CRR-KA has the worst performance than CRR-PA, since the semantic of video is more important than product when the user is concentrate on videos. All regularizers imposed to the main regression term play important roles in CRR model. Comparatively, the keyframe regularizer (CRR-KR) is more helpful than the product regularizer (CRR-PR). It indicates that video semantics are more useful than the relationship between products for *Video eCommerce*. Finally, it is easy to find that CRR model well addresses the association between keyframes and products, which achieves the best performance.

6.4 Performance Comparison of HIN Model

To evaluate the performance of the proposed HIN model, in this subsection, we analyze the impact of cross-domain user shopping preference.

6.4.1 Baselines

We compare the proposed method with single-domain baselines Tmall and MagicBox. That is, only MP1 and MP2 meta-paths are used for Tmall, while MP3 and MP4 meta-paths are deployed for MagicBox. In addition, we also evaluate the performance of different weighs for meta-paths. HIN-Equal and HIN-Random mean that weights for each selected meta-path are equal and randomly selected, respectively. For HIN, the weights (learned by HRMF) of four meta-paths are assigned as 0.40, 0.24, 0.21 and 0.15, respectively.

6.4.2 Experiment Results

The performance comparison is listed in Table 1. We can see that the performance using Tmall purchase history has better performance than MagicBox. This is because the number of purchase records from MagicBox is much sparser than Tmall, since MagicBox is still a newborn product. In this situation, the user preference induced from Tmall is very meaningful. Furthermore, HIN has better performance than HIN-Equal and HIN-Random. This is because our HRMF model can automatically learn regression weights, and do not need to set parameters in advance. HIN model not only integrates clues from Tmall and MagicBox, but also learns suitable weights to integrate user performance, which outperforms the single-domain methods and other HIN variants.

6.5 Performance Comparison of VSIM Model

In this subsection, the impact of video scene importance is conducted.

6.5.1 Baselines

To evaluate the impact of the proposed VSIM model, we compare it with two variants of VSIM, VSIM-Un and VSIM-Random, which mean that video scene importance is not considered, and it is randomly selected, respectively.

6.5.2 Experiment Results

The experimental results are reported in Table 1. We can see that the performance of VSIM-Un is poor, when video scene importance is ignored. VSIM and VSIM-Random have conspicuously better performance than VSIM-Un. It means that user attention based on video scene importance can be rationally used to improve the performance. VSIM model outperforms VSIM-Random, indicating that VSIM model can choose suitable video scene weights to insert advertisement.

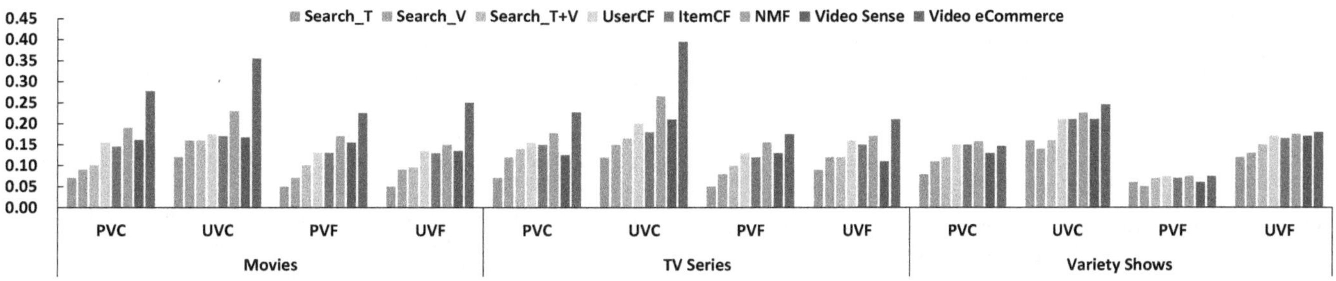

Figure 6: Performance comparison of the state-of-the-art methods

6.6 Performance Comparison With State-of-the-art Approaches

In this subsection, we will compare the performance of *Video eCommerce* with state-of-the-art approaches.

6.6.1 Baselines

To verify the performance, we compare our system with non-personalized methods, such as retrieval-based methods (Search_T, Search_V and Search_T+V) and VideoSense [15]. Here, Search_T, Search_V and Search_T+V are different from Sec. 6.3 where HRMF is not applied. We also compare it with three commonly used recommender systems, UserCF [25], ItemCF [21], and NMF [29]. UserCF [25] and ItemCF [21] are the most popular user-based and item-based collaborative filtering approaches, respectively. NMF [29] is a non-negative matrix factorization method. For these recommender approaches, the results from CRR are used to associate videos to corresponding products.

6.6.2 Experiment Results

The performance comparison is shown in Figure 6. Generally, the personalized recommender systems have much better performance than non-personalized ones, such as traditional retrieval-based methods. This is because the click and favorite behaviors of users are more related to their personalized interests. For classic recommendation methods, NMF performs much better than UserCF and ItemCF, since it has better performance in approximating the user-product interactions. People may have an impulse to buy semantically related products, so VideoSense has better performance than traditional retrieval-based methods. Video eCommerce combines video semantics and user preference, which performs better than VideoSense. Compared with these personalized recommendation, Video eCommerce achieves the best performance across all measures and obtains approximately 25% improvement in terms of PVC compared to the best baseline NMF. Furthermore, the experiments demonstrate that video content (semantics, scene, and association rule) and cross-domain user shopping preference have direct effects on the performance of video recommendation. The proposed *Video eCommerce* is an effective recommendation system, which can recommend appropriate products by simultaneously considering product property, video semantics and user's shopping preference. It can meet user's requirement and bring significant value for e-commerce websites.

6.6.3 Advertising Examples

Video eCommerce can recommend different products to various users according to their preference, even if they are watching the same keyframe. As a user has no obvious shopping preference, visually similar products will be advertised. As shown in the bottom of Figure 4, when a user has a clear preference (e.g., she likes jeans), a jeans is recommended. What's more, Video eCommerce also considers video semantics. A coffee cup and Nike running shoe are advertised according to video semantics, in which these two objects are not detected in the keyframes.

6.7 Parameter Study

There are four parameters in CRR and four parameters in HRMF. For the parameter setting, grid search is used to obtain the optimal parameters. To verify the importance of co-relation, we test the performance of α from 0 to 1 with the step size of 0.1. In our application, the best result is achieved when $\alpha = 0.6$. As the value of α is too small, the largest performance degradation is occurred, referring to CRR-KA in Figure 5. When it is too large, the result will not be good enough, as CRR-PA in Figure 5.

In HRMF, to verify the contextual and video scene constraint, we test the performance of α and β from 0 to 20 with the step size of 0.1. In our application, the best result is achieved when $\alpha = 10$ and $\beta = 4$. When the values of α and β are too small, the largest degree of performance degradation is occurred. From the experimental experience, μ is an important parameter, which directly affects the performance of our algorithm. When R is sparse, a larger μ can improve the recommendation results, because more information can be added to the training process. On the other hand, when R is not sparse, a larger μ will bias the recommendation results. Therefore, the value of μ depends on how sparse R is. In this sense, we can use the proportion of non-zero elements in matrix R to calculate μ. In our application, the best result is achieved when $\mu = 0.75$.

7. CONCLUSIONS

In this paper, an innovative system, *Video eCommerce*, is presented for online video advertising, which is able to exhibit appropriate product ads to particular users according to video content. Co-Relation Regression, Heterogeneous Information Network, Video Scene Importance are proposed to effectively model the associations among users, videos and products, which ensure the product diversity, alleviate the problems of data-sparsity and cold-start, and portray the importance of video content. Finally Heterogeneous Relation Matrix Factorization is applied for product recommendation. Extensive experiments have been conducted over a large-scale of online video dataset and promising results have been achieved in crucial business-related performance measures, which outperforms state-of-the-art approaches. To the best of our knowledge, this is one of the first video e-commerce systems have been running online comprehensively taking into account the relationships among users, videos and products. In the future, we will explore large scale online advertising and conduct real-time update for new objects, so that the whole framework can be efficiently performed in real time.

8. ACKNOWLEDGMENTS

This work was supported in part by the National Natural Science Foundation of China (Grant No. 61373121), Program for Sichuan Provincial Science Fund for Distinguished Young Scholars (Grant No. 13QNJJ0149), and Graduate Innovation Fund of Southwest Jiaotong University (Grant No. YC201504110).

9. REFERENCES

[1] G. Aggarwal, J. Feldman, S. Muthukrishnan, and M. Pál. Sponsored search auctions with markovian users. In *Internet and Network Economics*, pages 621–628. 2008.

[2] D. M. Chickering and D. Heckerman. Targeted advertising on the web with inventory management. *Interfaces*, 33(5):71–77, 2003.

[3] P. Cui, Z. Wang, and Z. Su. What videos are similar with you?: Learning a common attributed representation for video recommendation. In *ACM MM*, pages 597–606, 2014.

[4] K. Eyal and A. M. Rubin. Viewer aggression and homophily, identification, and parasocial relationships with television characters. *Journal of Broadcasting & Electronic Media*, 47(1):77–98, 2003.

[5] J. Hoffman, S. Guadarrama, E. S. Tzeng, R. Hu, J. Donahue, R. Girshick, T. Darrell, and K. Saenko. Lsda: Large scale detection through adaptation. In *NIPS*, pages 3536–3544, 2014.

[6] S. Isaacman, S. Ioannidis, A. Chaintreau, and M. Martonosi. Distributed rating prediction in user generated content streams. In *RecSys*, pages 69–76, 2011.

[7] P. Jiang, Y. Zhu, Y. Zhang, and Q. Yuan. Life-stage prediction for product recommendation in e-commerce. In *KDD*, pages 1879–1888, 2015.

[8] W. Kar, V. Swaminathan, and P. Albuquerque. Selection and ordering of linear online video ads. In *RecSys*, pages 203–210, 2015.

[9] D. Kempe and M. Mahdian. A cascade model for externalities in sponsored search. In *Internet and Network Economics*, pages 585–596. 2008.

[10] Y. Koren, R. M. Bell, and C. Volinsky. Matrix factorization techniques for recommender systems. *IEEE Computer*, 42(8):30–37, 2009.

[11] H. Ma. On measuring social friend interest similarities in recommender systems. In *SIGIR*, pages 465–474, 2014.

[12] J. J. McAuley, R. Pandey, and J. Leskovec. Inferring networks of substitutable and complementary products. In *KDD*, pages 785–794, 2015.

[13] T. Mei and X.-S. Hua. Contextual internet multimedia advertising. *Proceedings of the IEEE*, 98(8):1416–1433, 2010.

[14] T. Mei, X.-S. Hua, and S. Li. Contextual in-image advertising. In *ACM MM*, pages 439–448, 2008.

[15] T. Mei, X.-S. Hua, and S. Li. Videosense: A contextual in-video advertising system. *Circuits and Systems for Video Technology, IEEE Transactions on*, 19(12):1866–1879, 2009.

[16] T. Mei, L. Li, X.-S. Hua, and S. Li. Imagesense: towards contextual image advertising. *ACM TOMM*, 8(1):6, 2012.

[17] G. Roels and K. Fridgeirsdottir. Dynamic revenue management for online display advertising. *Journal of Revenue & Pricing Management*, 8(5):452–466, 2009.

[18] I. Ronen, I. Guy, E. Kravi, and M. Barnea. Recommending social media content to community owners. In *SIGIR*, pages 243–252, 2014.

[19] R. Salakhutdinov and A. Mnih. Probabilistic matrix factorization. In *NIPS*, pages 1257–1264, 2007.

[20] S. Sarawagi. Information extraction. *Foundations and trends in databases*, 1(3):261–377, 2008.

[21] B. Sarwar, G. Karypis, J. Konstan, and J. Riedl. Item-based collaborative filtering recommendation algorithms. In *WWW*, pages 285–295, 2001.

[22] Y. Sun, J. Han, X. Yan, P. S. Yu, and T. Wu. Pathsim: Meta path-based top-k similarity search in heterogeneous information networks. *PVLDB*, 4(11):992–1003, 2011.

[23] C. Szegedy, W. Liu, Y. Jia, P. Sermanet, S. Reed, D. Anguelov, D. Erhan, V. Vanhoucke, and A. Rabinovich. Going deeper with convolutions. *arXiv:1409.4842*, 2014.

[24] J. Turner, A. Scheller-Wolf, and S. Tayur. Or practice-scheduling of dynamic in-game advertising. *Operations research*, 59(1):1–16, 2011.

[25] J. Wang, A. P. De Vries, and M. J. T. Reinders. Unifying user-based and item-based collaborative filtering approaches by similarity fusion. In *SIGIR*, pages 501–508, 2006.

[26] X. Wu, A. G. Hauptmann, and C.-W. Ngo. Practical elimination of near-duplicates from web video search. In *ACM MM*, pages 218–227, 2007.

[27] B. Yang, Y. Lei, D. Liu, and J. Liu. Social collaborative filtering by trust. In *AAAI*, pages 2747–2753, 2013.

[28] X. Yu, X. Ren, Y. Sun, Q. Gu, B. Sturt, U. Khandelwal, B. Norick, and J. Han. Personalized entity recommendation: A heterogeneous information network approach. In *WSDM*, pages 283–292, 2014.

[29] S. Zhang, W. Wang, J. Ford, and F. Makedon. Learning from incomplete ratings using non-negative matrix factorization. In *SDM*, volume 6, pages 548–552, 2006.

[30] Y. Zhang, M. Zhang, Y. Zhang, G. Lai, Y. Liu, H. Zhang, and S. Ma. Daily-aware personalized recommendation based on feature-level time series analysis. In *WWW*, pages 1373–1383, 2015.

[31] W. Zhong, R. Jin, C. Yang, X. Yan, Q. Zhang, and Q. Li. Stock constrained recommendation in tmall. In *KDD*, pages 2287–2296, 2015.

[32] T. Zhu, P. Harrington, J. Li, and L. Tang. Bundle recommendation in ecommerce. In *SIGIR*, pages 657–666, 2014.

Affective Contextual Mobile Recommender System

Chao Wu[1], Jia Jia[1], Wenwu Zhu[1], Xu Chen[2], Bowen Yang[1], Yaoxue Zhang[1,3]
[1]Department of Computer Science and Technology, TNList, Tsinghua University, China
[2]Institute of Computer Science, University of Göttingen, Germany
[3]School of Information Science and Engineering, Central South University, China
cwu12@mails.tsinghua.edu.cn, zyx@csu.edu.cn

ABSTRACT

Exponential growth of media consumption in online social networks demands effective recommendation to improve the quality of experience especially for on-the-go mobile users. By means of large-scale trace-driven measurements over mobile Twitter traces from users, we reveal the significance of affective features in shaping users' social media behaviors. Existing recommender systems however, rarely support this psychological effect in real-life. To capture this effect, in this paper we propose KALEIDO, a real mobile system to achieve an affect-aware learning-based social media recommendation. Specifically, we design a machine learning mechanism to infer the affective feature within media contents. Furthermore, a cluster-based latent bias model is provided for jointly training the affect, behavior and social contexts. Our comprehensive experiments on Android prototype expose a superior prediction accuracy of 82%, with more than 20% accuracy improvement over existing mobile recommender systems. Moreover, by enabling users to offload their machine learning procedures to the deployed edge-cloud testbed, our system achieves speed-up of a factor of 1,000 against the local data training execution on smartphones.

Keywords

Recommender system; affective computing; mobile application; social networks

1. INTRODUCTION

The mass-adoption of mobile social networking services and the wide integration of sharing media content on popular mobile applications have paved the way for quantitative research efforts tackling the relations between content and virality [1]. Very recently, a novel kind of user experience is working its way through the online space, i.e., designed to take the affective pulses appeared in online social network (OSN) usage, such interface supports people to explicitly bridge their emotional states with OSN information subscription [2].

To capture users' attention, many tweets in OSNs nowadays are usually published with affective media content [3].

MM '16, October 15-19, 2016, Amsterdam, Netherlands
© 2016 ACM. ISBN 978-1-4503-3603-1/16/10...$15.00
DOI: http://dx.doi.org/10.1145/2964284.2964327

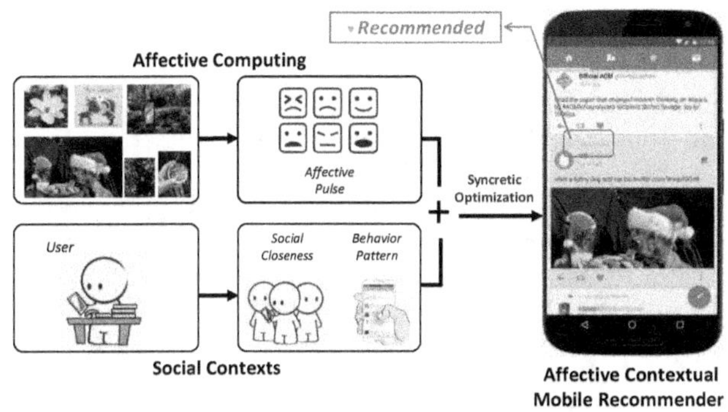

Figure 1: Conceptual Kaleido diagram.

In real-life usage, due to the *affective pulse* [4], i.e., the first feeling when accessing an object, triggers the mind 3,000x faster than rational thoughts, many users sensibly make a quick decision whether to subscribe a media tweet by such affective pulse (e.g., happiness, sadness, or disgust) [5]. This actually opens up a new venue to integrate the affective feature for future media recommender system design. Indeed, by means of large-scale data-driven measurements in our early stage work, we reveal that 60% user clicks are motivated by media contents, among which, more than 76% are triggered with explicitly affective pulses (§2.2). Moreover, with further affect-aware measurement in our established system, users are benefited with 82% accuracy to subscribe the right tweets (§5.3). Therefore, it is highly promising to rethink the social media recommender mechanism by jointly considering users' affective pulses as well as traditional features.

Existing recommender systems, however, provide recommendations largely based on users' content preference, using content- [6], demographic- [7], knowledge- [8], or utility- [9] based methods. To boost the prediction accuracy, recent studies [10] and [11] proposed methods which input the user's OSN usage pattern into a linear regression for prediction. To further improve social media propagation or streaming delivery, some researchers try to use both user preference and network context to determine the appropriate presentation method [12]. However, we have yet to see an approach that shifts mobile social media recommendation from the above approaches to a scheme that jointly tackles user's feeling, which plays a critical role in media content consumption in OSNs, behavior pattern (i.e., user preference, content attributes, media formats, time, and network) and social closeness (i.e., social interaction strength).

To fill this void, in this paper we propose a real system *Kaleido*, which jointly utilizes the unique visual features (to capture user's affective pulse), mobile behavior patterns and social friendship closeness, in OSNs for mobile media rec-

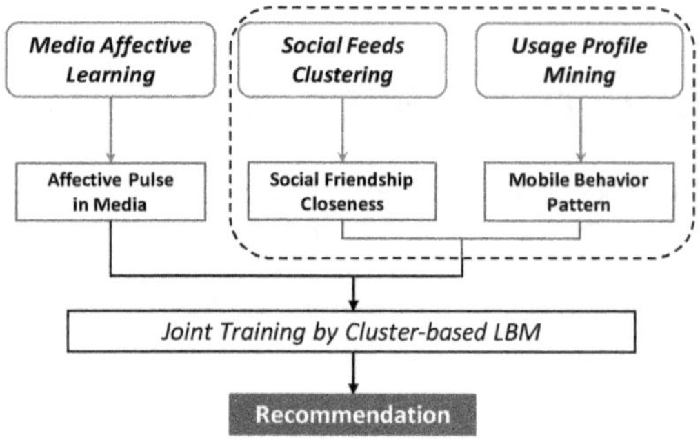

Figure 2: Framework of Kaleido system.

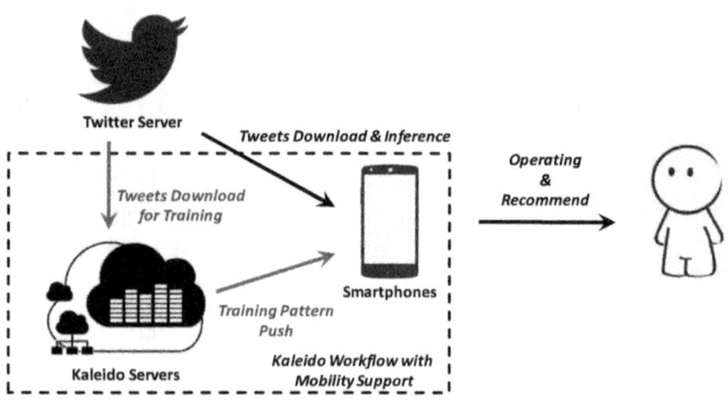

Figure 3: Logical workflow of Kaleido.

ommendation. Let us consider the case of Figure 1 where, by integrating Kaleido into a third-party Twitter app, i.e., Twidere [13], the user's social media experience is benefited from her habits along both affective (i.e., happiness) and social closeness (i.e., keep eyes on the sender) directions. To this end, we propose a learning-based scheme to infer affective pulses from media files. On this basis, we combine the affective feature with user behavior pattern and social friendship to further predict users' potential interests in media usage. Moreover, we employ such inference and network environment (e.g., WiFi available or not), to execute the whole prediction.

Specifically, to better understand affective pulses in social media, we employ a learning-based affective computing mechanism and a Flickr image dataset with well-known ground-truths, which has been manual tagged with affective tags by prior work [14], to infer the probability distribution of the affective pulse. In particular, as visually presented in Figure 7, we input the affective pulse as a 6-dimension feature to the recommender algorithm. On the other hand, through early stage measurements, we observe that the social friendship (i.e., the social interaction strength among users in OSN) has a critical impact on the user's tweet click behavior. Then we conduct the social friendship clustering to classify a user's social friends into different groups with different levels of importance. On this basis, we next design a cluster-based Latent Bias Model (LBM) to predict user's likelihood of media click with considering all the above contexts as well as different network and time contexts. Last, by integrating Kaleido into Twidere, an Android Twitter app which has 500,000 downloads on Google Play, we collect user traces from a demographical composition of 16,952 people who consented to report usage data to us. This also enables us to conduct a data-driven measurement and design and realistic experiments to evaluate the performance of Kaleido's mobility support (§5.3). In addition, by collecting system logs from our edge-cloud servers, we reveal the effect of Kaleido testbed (§5.2).

We summarize the major contributions and vantage points of this paper as:

- We collect a large set of real-life mobile traces from 16,952 participants, and reveal the significance and importance of affective feature in social media usage. To our best knowledge, we are the first to employ the affective context in such recommender system.

- We propose a learning-based model to infer affective pulses in media files with 75% accuracy. Furthermore, we design a cluster-based LBM for jointly training affect, behavior, and social contextual features. Through data-driven experiments, we illustrate that it achieves a prediction accuracy of 82%, which outperforms baselines using the same training features.

- We deploy a worldwide edge-cloud testbed for real-life Twidere users by enabling them to offload machine learning procedures with a speed-up of 1,000x factor over the local execution. Our Android prototype consumes user with a low cost of cellular data and energy, which is a significant improvement against the benchmark approaches.

We shall emphasize the feasibility of using Twidere and Android smartphone as a study case. Nevertheless, the proposed methedologies are applicable to most mobile apps and OS platforms.

2. KALEIDO: THE FRAMEWORK AND SYSTEM DESIGN

Kaleido provides a real system which consists of an edge-cloud testbed as well as a mobile framework. We start with a brief review of Kaleido system (§2.1), and close the section with describing the key measurements that relate to inspire Kaleido's design details (§2.2).

To keep the illustration concrete, we assume for now that all servers use a learning-based algorithm to identify affective pulses in media; we relax that assumption in the next section. We defer a discussion of the overall algorithm within Kaleido until §4.

2.1 System Overview

Conceptual Framework: To better present the logic, Figure 2 introduces the framework of Kaleido from a high level. By learning affective pulses, social closeness, and behavior pattern, Kaleido enables users with media recommendation during their operating process. More specifically, when a fresh media content arrives, Kaleido is triggered to take the relevant features of the media context (user behavior, affect, and social friendship) as input to the trained cluster-based LBM, to identify the likelihood of user actions ahead of time. We will elaborate how the proposed cluster-based LBM jointly train the features in §4.3.

Mobility Support: Figure 3 depicts how Kaleido mobile framework works in a user-centric manner (i.e., implemented on a user's mobile device), and collects social feeds when accessing new media content with Twitter app. Specifically, it offloads user's machine learning procedure to cloud servers and pushes the training patterns to smartphones asynchronously. Also note that these traces are retrieved using

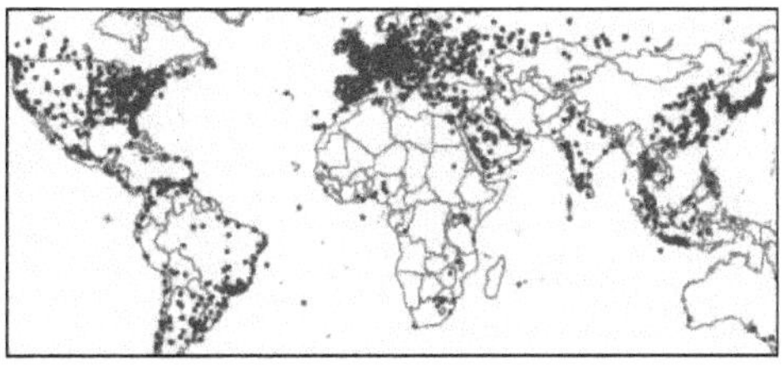

Figure 4: Kaleido users' demographic composition.

Table 1: Description of collected user profiles.

Contents	Collected traces
Tweets	time, sender, receivers
Media files	URL link, sender, receivers
User behaviors	publish, like, retweet, mention
App usage	launch time, close time, present time
Feature training	start time, end time
User request	DNS resolution, HTTP metadata

the Twitter REST APIs [15] in the servers in according to collected user traces. Furthermore, by pushing the training pattern to smartphone, Kaleido executes the inference locally and rapidly. Finally, it highlights the recommended tweets for user in according to the inference results (e.g., see Figure 1).

System Infrastructure: Similar to existing techniques, Kaleido employs an edge-cloud architecture for building a testbed to process users' machine learning offloading. Specifically, such architecture supports the time-varying bandwidth and storage allocations requested by different regions. By collecting system logs from early stage deployed servers, we further setup the hardware configuration as illustrated in Table 4. We further discuss the efficiency of such infrastructure in §5.2.

Caching Policy: Since the traces are cached temporarily, to ensure privacy, text content in tweets is not recorded and all personal fields are anonymized in advance. In addition, the cached data is uploaded to the cloud server only for further analysis when the smartphone is charging and connected to WiFi. To accelerate the process, Kaleido offloads the machine learning procedure to the testbed whose deployment information are shown in Table 4. Furthermore, the learned patterns are stored on the device to enable real-time inference by Kaleido.

Network Congestion: To relief the network congestion caused by the offloading procedure, in this paper, end-user's processing is delivered to the topological nearest server by leveraging her DNS resolution, as we elaborate on in §5.1.

2.2 Measurements in Early Stage Work

To capture the effect of affective pulse in recommending social media, we conduct data-driven measurements in early stage work.

Specifically, inspired by a very recent study [14], in this paper, we adopt 6 basic affects in describing human emotional state [16], i.e., *happiness*, *surprise*, *anger*, *disgust*, *fear* and *sadness*, to investigate the forming of users' affective pulses. Furthermore, for evaluating the effectiveness of affective learning in §3, we use a well known dataset from Flickr which covers more than 1 million image traces that

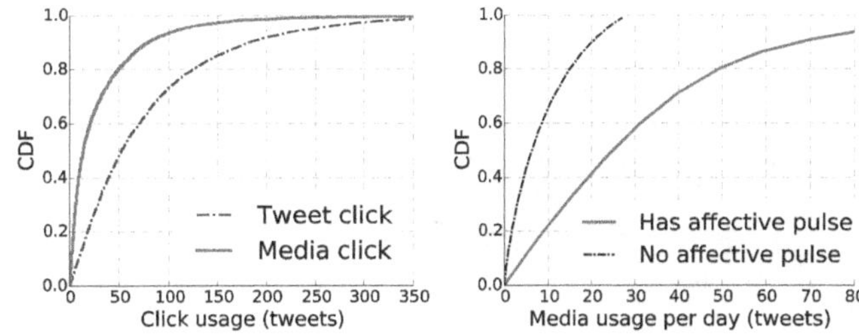

(a) Daily tweets usage (b) Affect-motivated usage

Figure 5: 16,952 users' app usage across 7 months.

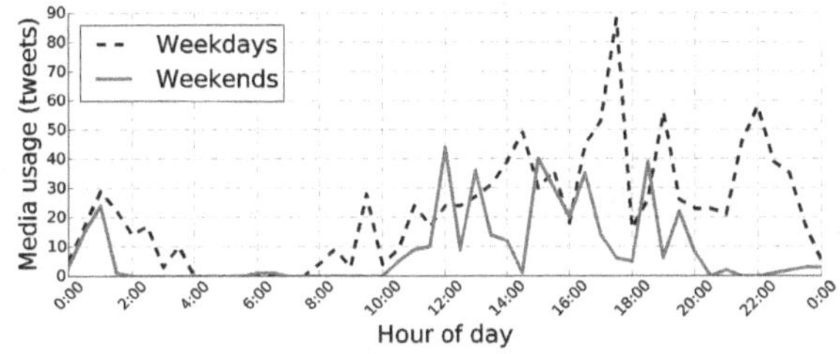

Figure 6: A user's media usage across hour of day.

published by 4,725 users and has been manual tagged with the affective labels by prior work [14]. To further investigate users' media behaivor in mobile environment, during the whole early stage, i.e., from March to October 2015, as Figure 4 illustrates, we also have collected data traces from more than 16,952 Twidere [13] users [1] from all over the world with a diverse demographic composition. Because, although Twitter's contents are publicly available, information about when, how, and where they access these social streams are not available in particular in the mobile environment. As the aim is to enable Kaleido system by identifying the affective pulse within media tweets that the user is most interested in, a set of tweet attributes are collected as well. Twidere tracks the user social behaviors (e.g., retweet, like, or mention) of the individual tweets. The source of a tweet is also recorded by identifying whether the tweet is obtained from a direct friend or propagated through friends of others' friends. In addition, with the consent from the user, Twidere enables us to keep track of the user's activity events when reading the tweets (watching, clicking, or commenting along the timeline). The collected trace items are shown in Table 1. Moreover, in this paper, we deploy the Kaleido geographical servers by referring to user composition provided by Figure 4.

The users clicked more than 900 million referred tweets in total. Specifically, as Figure 5 illustrates, on average, a user refreshes 536 tweets a day but only clicked 15% of them. We further observe that more than 60% of the clicked tweets contain media files. Moreover, by referring to the affective learning in §3, we find that more than 76% media have explicitly affective pulses. Note that we infer whether a media file owns an explicitly affect, which shapes the affective pulse, by comparing with the corresponding probability with

[1] Twidere discloses the usage statistics on installation or update. Users are able to opt in or not. There are 43% active users grant us permissions, which indicates user privacy-awareness and the effectiveness of the privacy disclosure. Data are collected in an anonymous style. Also note that the social graphs and tweets are publicly available.

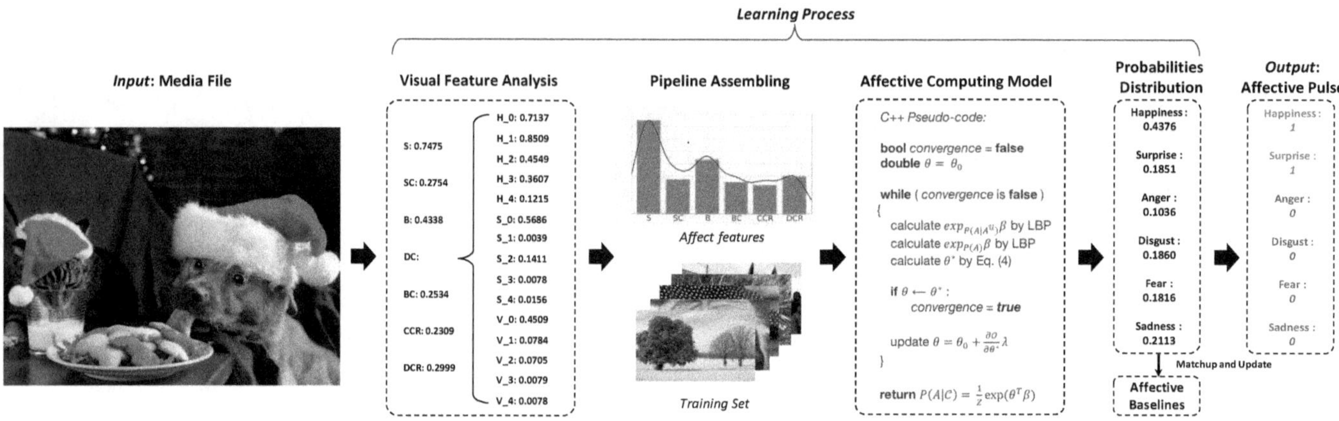

Figure 7: Flowchart of learning affective pulse from a media. We first extract the values of 7 visual features respectively. By training with the Flickr dataset, it learns the probabilities of 6 affects with the loopy belief propagation (LBP) [17] algorithm. Last, we regularize each $P(a|\mathcal{C})$ (where $a \in \mathcal{A}$) with comparing its probability with corresponding baseline.

a set of trained baseline thresholds [2] in §3. Figure 6 illustrates that users are time-sensitive, e.g., on weekdays, the user tends to use the app more frequently in the nighttime especially in the midnight, while use the app sporadicly in the daytime. It motivates us to analyze user behavior pattern by taking time feature in accounts. The volume and diversity of data also reflects the real-life behavior of the participant users, which is crucial for understanding and recommending media in mobile social application network traffic, and significant in evaluating the system in a data-driven scheme.

3. LEARNING AFFECTIVE PULSE FROM MEDIA CONTENT

In this section, we introduce a learning-based affective computing mechanism by which we identify the affective pulse in a media file.

As aforementioned in §1, the forming of *affective pulse*, e.g., probability distribution of the 6 affects in an object, is complicated. To proceed, we employ a machine learning process. Specifically, we denote the space of affective pulse as $\mathcal{A}$ ={*Happiness, Surprise, Anger, Disgust, Fear, Sadness*}. As different people might have distinct affect even when accessing the same media [3], in our learning algorithm, we adopt the approach provided by [3], i.e., we denote every affect as a linguistic label for the matchup in the learning process. To proceed, we further denote the affect $a \in \mathcal{A}$ expressed by a media file. Inspired by [14], we use visual variables to capture the affect expressed by the media file. We characterize each affect by training with 7 visual features, i.e., saturation (SR), saturation contrast (SRC), brightness (B), bright contrast (BRC), 5 dominant HSV colors (DC), cool color ratio (CCR), and dull color ratio (DCR). Thus, we have feature set $\mathcal{U} = \{SR, SRC, B, BRC, DC, CCR, DCR\}$. For each media $c \in \mathcal{C}$, we have the ground truth $a_c \in \{1, 0\}$ such that $a_c = 1$ ($a_c = 0$) means that whether the media file c has the specific affective feature $a \in \mathcal{A}$ (e.g., happiness) or not. Then we have:

$$f(u_c, a_c) = \frac{1}{z_\theta} \exp\{\theta^T u_c\} \tag{1}$$

where u_c are the mentioned visual features, a_c is the affect express by the media file c, θ is a vector of real valued parameters, and z_θ is a normalization term to avoid the potential over-fittings. On this basis, the probability distribution P of the affect a in the media files $c \in \mathcal{C}$ can be formulated as:

$$P(A|\mathcal{C}) = \frac{1}{Z} \prod_{\mathcal{C}} f(u_c, a_c) = \frac{1}{Z} \exp\{\theta^T \beta\} \tag{2}$$

where $Z = z_\theta$ is the normalization term, β is the aggregation of factor function.

Furthermore, by taking all the affects $a \in \mathcal{A}$ in account, the objective function can be derived as:

$$\begin{aligned} \mathcal{O} &= \log P(A|\mathcal{C}) = \log \sum_{A|A^{\mathcal{U}}} \exp\{\theta^T \beta\} - \log Z \\ &= \log \sum_{A|A^{\mathcal{U}}} \exp\{\theta^T \beta\} - \log \sum_{A} \exp\{\theta^T \beta\} \end{aligned} \tag{3}$$

In addition, the gradient of θ can be represented as:

$$\begin{aligned} \frac{\partial \mathcal{O}}{\partial \theta} &= \frac{\partial (\log \sum_{A|A^{\mathcal{U}}} \exp\{\theta^T \beta\} - \log \sum_{A} \exp\{\theta^A \beta\})}{\partial \theta} \\ &= (\exp_{P(A|A^{\mathcal{U}})} - \exp_{P(A)})\beta \end{aligned} \tag{4}$$

Note that the algorithm updates the parameters by $\theta = \theta_0 + \frac{\partial \mathcal{O}}{\partial \theta} \lambda$. Where λ is a regularization parameter to be manually tuned.

Visual Illustration: After illustrating the affective learning model, Figure 7 visually illustrates how each visual feature u_c contributes to the proposed mechanism [4]. We take a snapshot of the Christmas cat & dog as a study case, it results in a set of probabilities of {0.43, 0.18, 0.10, 0.18, 0.18, 0.21}. By filtering the insignificant affective features via

[2]In our measurements, the baseline set inclines to {0.24, 0.14, 0.63, 0.19, 0.33, 0.49}. However, it changes with different OSN cases.

[3]Note that since the volume of video sharing in Twitter is rare. Thus, unless otherwise specified, we mainly focus on inferring affective pulses of images.

[4]Note that the DC feature consists of a 15-dimension HSV martix. Due to space limit, we omit the details of DC feature in Figure 7's pipeline assembling illustration, and interested readers can refer to [18].

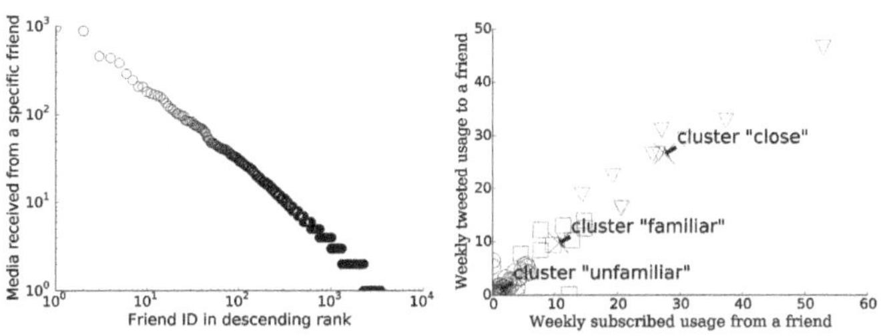

(a) Her social media usage (b) Her friendship clustering

Figure 8: Statistics of a user's social interaction frequency and friendship clustering with 1 year usage.

Table 2: Media click probability (%) by measuring different features of 16,952 users across one year.

		close	familiar	unfamiliar
Totality	*Media click*	51.33	28.39	13.67
Time Features	*Weekdays*	56.38	32.63	13.06
	Weekends	36.94	19.30	11.75
Interaction Features	*Mentioned by*	28.57	17.72	10.81
	Liked by	43.66	27.92	14.58
	Retweeted by	38.10	27.69	9.60
	Replied by	51.82	28.85	13.42

comparing with the baselines (as illustrated in §2.2), it reports that the happiness and surprise features are significant and hence have value 1 while the rest affective features are with value 0. Finally, we obtain the affective pulse of {1, 1, 0, 0, 0, 0} as the input affective feature to the recommender model later.

In addition, through training with 80,000 affect-aware images that manual tagged by [14], we further evaluate the accuracy of our learning algorithm. We observe that our model achieves an average prediction accuracy of 0.75, which significantly beyonds the benchmarks in identifying the probability distribution of each affect $a \in \mathcal{A}$ in a specific media. On the other hand, we also discuss the significance and importance of adopting affective pulse in recommending media in §6.

4. JOINT RECOMMENDATION WITH AFFECTS AND SOCIAL CONTEXTS

In this section, we first conduct a data-driven analysis on user's mobile behavior and social interactions. Then we reveal their impact on the user's media click actions. On this basis, we last introduce how Kaleido jointly train the affective features with this two features for a socially-driven affect-aware media recommendation.

4.1 Behavior Pattern Analysis

In OSNs, the generation and propagation of a media content is simple: any user who generates or re-shares it will become a new host of the media content. Users can fetch these contents from their direct friends in the social network. Intuitively, the social relationships and interactions among a user and her friends have a significant impact on the twittering behaviors. A user might treat different friends differently, and interact with some close friends frequently, while having little contact or response with some unfamiliar friends on Twitter [19].

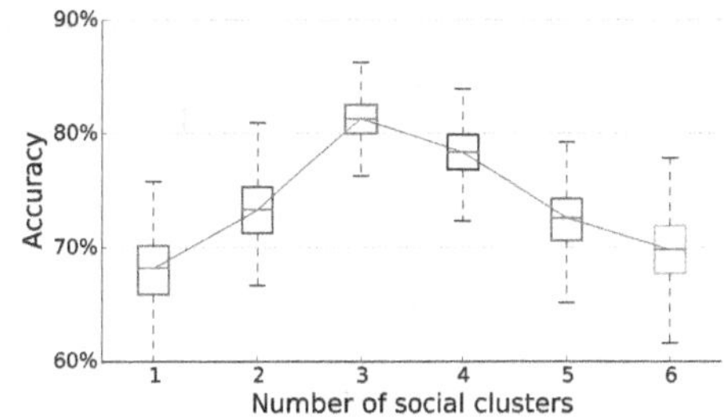

Figure 9: Accuracy variation of different social cluster number by referring to all users' usage.

As mentioned in §2.2, user's media click actions enjoy characteristics of high selectiveness and time sensitivity. With this insight, in Figure 8a, we plot the number of one real-life user's clicked tweets with media content (i.e., media tweets) from her friends (i.e., social neighbors) on Twitter in the log-log scale. We rank the set of friends in descending order according to the number of tweets sent by them. We observe a strong power law phenomenon, i.e., almost 70% of the tweets are from only a few friends (less than 10%), and most other friends have little contribution. This demonstrates that friendship (or social interaction strength) plays a critical role on shaping her usage behavior on Twitter.

4.2 Social Friendship Closeness

With this insight, we further quantify the impact of social friendship on the user's media tweet click behaviors. To proceed, we first carry out the social friendship clustering. The intuition is that in reality a user typically has very close relationships with a small set of people (e.g., close friends), and is familiar with a group of people (e.g., colleagues). For many other people, the user would have little contact with them. With this observation, we conduct the friendship clustering using the commonly-adopted an unsupervised machine learning with K-Means algorithm [20]. As illustrated in Figure 8b, we utilize the number of tweets subscribed from a specific friend and the number of tweets published by the user to that friend as the features, and cluster the set of her friends into three types: close friends (i.e., cluster "close"), familiar friends (i.e., cluster "familiar"), and acquaintances with infrequent contacts (i.e., cluster "unfamiliar").

After the social friendship clustering, we then explore the impact of friendship on users' media click behavior when accessing the media tweets. Table 2 measures all users' average media click probability under different feature scenarios. In total, we observe that users click the media file with a probability of 0.42 (0.28, 0.13), when the media is sent by a close (familiar, unfamiliar) friend, respectively. This again confirms that social friendship has a significant impact on user's media click behavior. As another example, for the interaction feature, if the media tweet has been replied or mentioned by a close friend, then user would click the media file with a probability gap of 0.17.

Effectiveness of $K = 3$ Social Clustering: Figure 9 visually confirms that $K = 3$ achieves a good balance and the best prediction accuracy with a performance gap of 0.13. In addition, it comforts a fact in our daily life observation that people tend to classify their friends into three types: close friends, familiar friends, and acquaintances.

4.3 Training with Affect for Recommendation

After illustrating mobile behavior pattern and social friendship closeness, we now introduce the machine learning principle in our system by jointly identifying the set of important training features to build up the learning model.

Training Context Features: As mentioned above, we found that three types of context features are critical: affective pulse in media, behavior pattern, and social closeness. Furthermore, we use these three features as the input to our proposed cluster-based machine learning algorithm. For the behavior feature, whenever the user would click a media depends on her regular usage behavior. For the affective feature, what she prefers to click is mainly influenced by each affect that reflect from the media content. For the social feature, the host (close, familiar or unfamiliar friend) of receiving media file is decisive. In the following, we denote the number of these training features as F, and their set as $\mathcal{F}$.

Cluster-Based Latent Bias Model: We propose the learning model which is based on the Latent Bias Model (LBM) introduced in [21] that aims to utilize proper bias terms to capture the importance of different features for prediction. Here we extend the standard LBM to our case with social friendship clustering, and develop the cluster-based LBM approach for a data-driven learning scheme.

Specifically, we define $b_{f,a,k}$ as the cluster-based bias term to stand for the case that a media is sent by a friend in the friendship cluster k, express affects $a_i \in \mathcal{A}$, and contains the feature f. Moreover, for a given media content c, we first introduce an indicator function $I^c_{f,a,k} \in \{0,1\}$ such that $I^c_{f,a,k} = 1$ if the media c is sent by a friend in the friendship cluster $k \in \mathcal{K}$ with affect $a \in \mathcal{A}$ and contains the feature $f \in \mathcal{F}$. Then, we define the user action score for the media c as follows:

$$\gamma_c = \alpha + b_0 + \sum_{f\in\mathcal{F}}\sum_{a\in\mathcal{A}}\sum_{k\in\mathcal{K}} b_{f,a,k} I^c_{f,a,k} \tag{5}$$

α is the user's average click rate across all historical media content usage, and b_0 is the overall bias for the user. In general, a higher user action score γ_c implies a higher probability that the user will click the media content c.

Then, the critical task is to train the cluster-based LBM, i.e., to learn the proper bias terms in Equation 5 in order to well capture a user's media click actions. Suppose that the set of historical user data traces (historical media usage set of the user) is denoted as $\mathcal{C}$. For each media $c \in \mathcal{C}$, we have the ground truth $y_c \in \{1, -1\}$ such that $y_c = 1$ ($y_c = -1$) means that the user clicks (open) the media file c in tweet of arrival. To quantify the discrepancy between the prediction based on the media click score γ_c and the desired ground-truth output y_c, we adopt the widely-used logistic loss measure

$$\mathcal{L}(\gamma_c, y_c) = \log[1 + \exp(-\gamma_c y_c)]. \tag{6}$$

Thus, we learn proper bias terms to minimize the total loss across over the historical data trace $\mathcal{C}$, i.e., $\sum_{c\in\mathcal{C}} \mathcal{L}(\gamma_c, y_c)$. Following common practice in machine learning, in order to avoid overfitting, we also impose L_2 regulation into minimization. That is, we minimize the following objective function:

$$\mathcal{O} = \sum_{c\in\mathcal{C}} \mathcal{L}(\gamma_c, y_c) + \lambda \left(||b_0||^2 + \sum_{f\in\mathcal{F}}\sum_{a\in\mathcal{A}}\sum_{k\in\mathcal{K}} ||b_{f,a,k}||^2 \right), \tag{7}$$

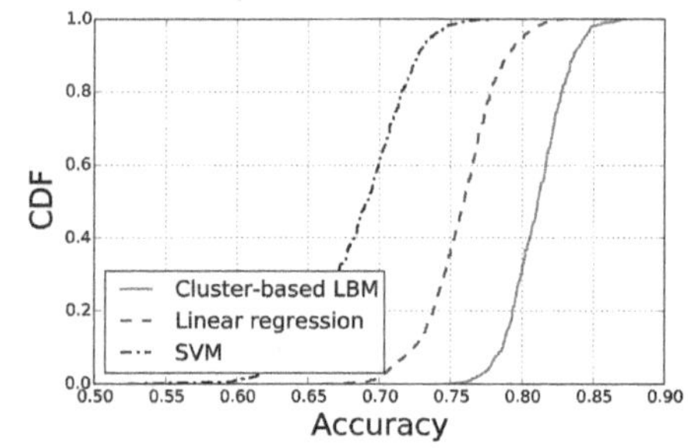

Figure 10: Accuracy of three baseline algorithms.

Table 3: Summarization of Figure 10.

Algorithm	Balanced accuracy	Best accuracy	Worst accuracy
Cluster-based LBM	0.82	0.87	0.73
Linear regression	0.71	0.82	0.65
SVM	0.68	0.77	0.52

where λ is the regularization parameter to be manually tuned.

Since the function in Equation 7 is convex, we can apply the first-order condition and derive the gradients as

$$\frac{\partial\mathcal{O}}{\partial b_0} = -\sum_{c\in\mathcal{C}} \left(\frac{\exp(\gamma_c y_c)}{1+\exp(\gamma_c y_c)} \right) y_c + 2\lambda b_0, \tag{8}$$

$$\frac{\partial\mathcal{O}}{\partial b_{f,a,k}} = -\sum_{c\in\mathcal{C}} \left(\frac{\exp(\gamma_c y_c)}{1+\exp(\gamma_c y_c)} \right) y_c I^c_{f,a,k} + 2\lambda b_{f,a,k} \tag{9}$$

Similar to many machine learning studies, we can adopt the Stochastic Gradient Descent (SGD) method [22], to learn optimal bias terms. The key idea is to utilize the data samples to iteratively update the gradient as follows:

$$b^{t+1}_* = b^t_* - \epsilon_t \frac{\partial\mathcal{O}}{\partial b^t_*}, \tag{10}$$

where b^t_* denotes a given bias term at the t-th iteration and $0 < \epsilon_t < 1$ is the smoothing factor for updating. As shown in [22], the SGD method converges to the optimal learning point provided a sufficiently small ϵ_t.

After learning, when a fresh tweet with media c arrives, we predict a user's click likelihood using the loss measure in (6). Specifically, we predict that a user will click the media file if $y_c = 1$ has a lower risk, i.e., $\mathcal{L}(\gamma_c, y_c = 1) < \mathcal{L}(\gamma_c, y_c = -1)$. In this case, the media is clicked by the user and otherwise in reverse.

Model Baselines: We last evaluate the performance of the proposed cluster-based LBM algorithm by referring to all the participants' usages. Figure 10 depicts the cumulative probability distribution (CDF) of the prediction accuracy for all tested tweets. As mentioned above, when the friendship cluster number $K = 3$, it achieves the best performance with an average prediction accuracy of 0.82. As baselines, we also evaluate the prediction process with linear regression (LR) in [11] and SVM. Jointed with Table 3, Figure 10 evaluates all baselines' performance that LR approach can mostly achieve an average prediction accuracy of 0.71, which outperforms SVM approach by 3%, but be inferior to the cluster-based LBM by 11%. This demonstrates the efficiency of the cluster-based LBM. The gain of cluster-based LBM stems from the fact that the defined cluster-based bias

Table 4: Details of network topology, geographic distribution and configuration of Kaleido testbed.

Region	Location	Carrier and OS	Bandwidth	Service	Configuration (CPU, Memory, Storage)
US	Los Angeles	Vultr (Debian 8.0)	10Mb	Server-load Balancing	2.4GHz single-core, 768MB, 20GB
	San Mateo	Aliyun (Debian 7.5)	5MB	Caching, Content Services	2.3GHz dual-core, 2GB, 1TB
Europe	Frankfurt	Vultr (Debian 8.0)	10Mb	Server-load Balancing	2.4GHz single-core, 768MB, 15GB
Asia	Tokyo	Vultr (Ubuntu 14.04)	10Mb	Server-load Balancing	2.4GHz single-core, 512MB, 20GB
	Shanghai	Tencent (CentOS 7)	5MB	Caching, Content Services	2.6GHz quad-core, 12GB, 1TB
	Beijing	Tsinghua (Debian 8.0)	1MB	Caching	2.2GHz octa-core, 128GB, 6TB

terms can well capture the impact of affective feature on user's media click, we elaborate it in §6.

5. EXPERIMENTS

In this section, we conduct the trace-driven evaluation over the testbed and Android smartphones to investigate the performance of Kaleido.

5.1 Implementations

To evaluate the performance of Kaleido system, we deploy a worldwide network testbed to undertake users' machine learning procedure. Table 4 summarizes the network topology, geographic distribution and configuration of our testbed. Specifically, there are 3 categories of service for the deployed servers, i.e., server-load balancing (as a streaming server), caching (as a data center), and content service (as a computing center).

Moreover, to illustrate the effect of performance of the provided mobile framework, we also run a trace-driven evaluation for the 16,952 users that each of them keeps active for a long and consecutive period of at least 3 months with detailed trace records. The emulator runs on a Google Nexus 6, Nexus 5 and Samsung Galaxy S4 smartphone, respectively, that with access to both China Mobile TDD LTE network as well as a campus WiFi network. The emulator reads and replays the usage events collected from real-life users, including connecting to or disconnecting from WiFi networks, accessing Twitter, and reacting its media files.

5.2 Testbed Measurements

The testbed serves a diverse workload spanning massive machine learning procedure: friendship clustering, training, media content downloading, content caching, and other miscellaneous process. We use the latest 3 months' (from December 2015 to March 2016) user request logs and UNIX round robin database (RRD) logs collected from 6 vantage servers, i.e., 2 in US, 1 in Europe and 3 in Asia, to measure the performance of our deployed testbed. To this end, we leverage the Metalink standard [23], which is an XML-based download description format that provides the metadata of the content [5]. Metalink-enabled HTTP clients and proxies understand the relevant HTTP headers (e.g., to verify the authenticity and integrity of the data, discover faster mirrors, etc.), while legacy clients simply ignore them. In addition, the RRD log reports the system load, network bandwidth and stock prices with a constant disk footprint.

Table 5 summarizes that the balance and costs of Kaleido edge-cloud infrastructure. Specifically, we recorded that the most heavy system load appeared in the machine learning process server (with an average usage of 21.4%) while the most bandwidth consuming was the server-load balancing (with an average usage of 0.2MBps) [6]. In addition, the latency for all the Kaleido edge servers are less than 670ms which again comforts the factuality of our testbed.

Table 5: Testbed performance across 3 months.

Service	Latency (ms)	Bandwidth usage (%)	System load (%)
Service	170	4.7	21.4
Caching	211	3	7.3
Server-load	670	14.4	5.7

5.3 Benchmarks

After the testbed efficiency has been discussed, we next evaluate the performance of Kaleido mobile framework running on the smartphones in against with existing representative recommendation algorithms. As illustrated in Figure 10 the cluster-based LBM algorithm in Kaleido is very efficient, and achieves the average prediction accuracy of 0.82. Upon comparison, the linear regression (LR) algorithm using tweet training features can only achieve the average prediction accuracy of 0.73. In the following, we also compare different recommendation algorithms given as: In the following, we further consider the three recommendation approaches as performance benchmarks in this paper as:

- *Kaleido approach*: We implement the recommender system by running the proposed cluster-based LBM with affective context, user behavior contexts, and social contexts.

- *Content-based approach*: We implement the recommender system with content training features in [6].

- *Social contextual approach*: We replace the content features with social information contexts in [12].

Specifically, we evaluate the performance of Kaleido recommender system, by considering different users, i.e., top 5% users (the most 750 active users who refresh 1,301 tweets and consume 40 media tweets per day on average), top 30% users (users that daily refresh 780 tweets and consume 22 media tweets), and top 60% users (users that daily refresh 429 tweets and consume 11 media tweets). For the evaluation of each approach, the same user trace are replayed, and

[5]E.g., see http://releases.ubuntu.com/releases/15.10/ubuntu-15.10-desktop-i386.metalink.

[6]Note that this low average bandwidth consumption is due to the training procedure for all users are sporadicly triggered when each smartphone is in charge and WiFi available and after a time slot of one day from the last calling. In addition, user profiles are usually no more than 200KB.

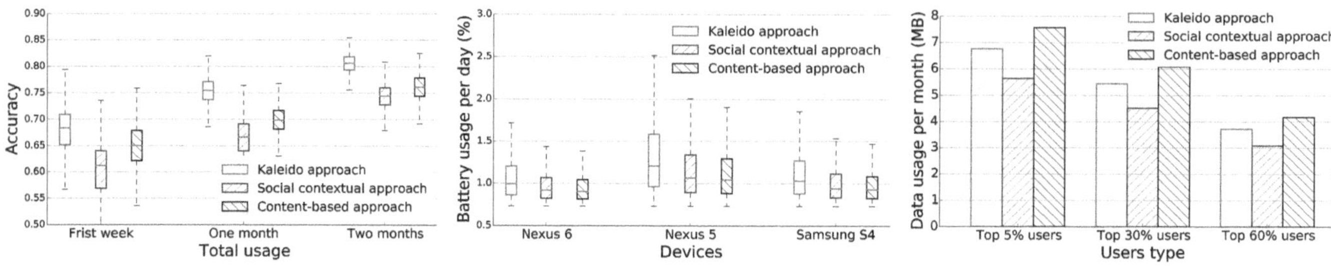

(a) Accuracy growth across time (b) Battery overhead for using Kaleido (c) Data usage for using Kaleido

Figure 11: Benchmarks across accuracy growth, daily battery overhead and monthly cellular data cost.

media files are obtained by using the WebView component provided by the Android framework. To embrace stable data and battery consumption results, we evaluate this two items by training with each user's first 2 month trace and using at least another 2 month traces for testing.

Accuracy Growth: We first compare different approaches' accuracy growth with time. As illustrated in Figure 11a, our algorithm tends to be stale after one month's usage. We see that Kaleido approach climbs from 0.67 to 0.82 when after 2 months' use. Upon comparison, content-based (social contextual) approach starts with lower accuracy of 0.62 (0.65) and reaches to a balanced accuracy of 0.74 (0.76). This is due to the fact that affective feature plays a significant role in learning users' media click (we shall discuss it in §6). This demonstrates the efficiency of the proposed Kaleido approach in media recommendation.

Data and Battery Overheads: We next compare different recommendation approaches in terms of cellular data consumption of Twidere app (which includes the cellular traffic overhead by both Kaleido and on-demand contexts fetching by the user), and battery consumption of the app per day (i.e., the percentage of the fully-charged battery capacity). The results are shown in Figure 11c and Figure 11b respectively. We observe, take the top 5% users for instance, that Kaleido uses 6.8MB cellular traffic per month and about 1.4% battery usage per day on average. On the other hand, the content-based (social contextual) approach costs users with 7.5MB (5.8MB) cellular traffic per month and 1.1% (1.2%) battery usage per day on average.

Moreover, evaluations in Figure 11 also illustrate Kaleido outperforms existing approaches in all kinds of usage cases.

6. DISCUSSIONS

Does Affective Pulse Really Matter? Kaleido, as mentioned above, is the first step towards an affective media recommender system. Performance of the proposed algorithm in this paper demonstrates that Kaleido is promising when integrating the affective feature with user behavior and social friendship contexts. However, we have yet known how critical the affective feature plays. To understand it, in Figure 12, we compare the accuracies of all the mentioned algorithms in §4.3 (with the same user group) by removing the affective feature, i.e., we only put the behavior and social contexts into the training model. Similar to the prediction evaluation above, we adopt the $K = 3$ social clustering as the study case. We observe that the LBM enjoys a positive impact with affective feature and achieves an average prediction accuracy of 0.71, which has 11% performance

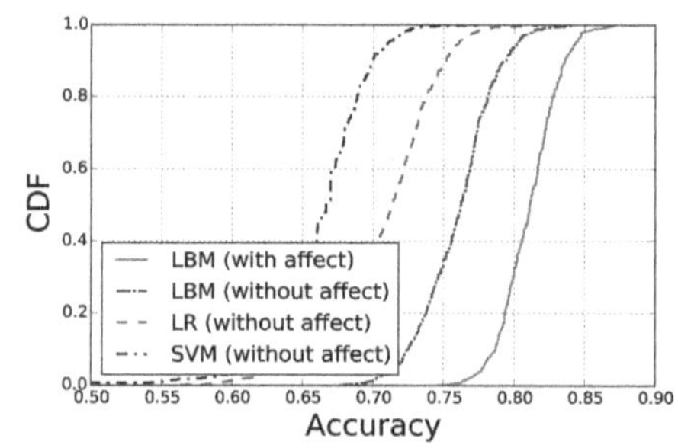

Figure 12: Evaluation of no affective feature in cluster-based LBM (11% degradation), LR (3% degradation), and SVM (2% degradation).

degradation with respect to the standard algorithm. Upon comparison, the LR (SVM) algorithm achieves an accuracy of 0.68 (0.66), with a slightly small performance degradation of 0.03 (0.02). This again demonstrates the uniqueness and significance of Kaleido approach in exploiting the affective feature for efficient media recommendation.

Why Training on Cloud? One key component of Kaleido is to implement the cluster-based LBM algorithm for the data training (i.e., learning the optimal bias terms from the user data traces). Intuitively, there are two data processing approaches: 1) processing on local device, i.e., we conduct the data training procedure on user's smartphone locally. 2) processing on cloud, i.e., we offload the data training to the cloud server is to leverage the strong parallel computing power to speed up the data training. To investigate the characteristics, in Figure 13, we emulate the average time overhead of these two data processing approaches with the top 60% active users, by setting different size of user trace in the learning algorithm, with considering the network connection latency we measured in Table 5. We find that the cloud approach can significantly decrease the daily time overhead for data processing, by a factor of 1,000. We further compare the monthly data consumption for training on cloud for different users respectively. We compare that this procedure consumes user largely 2.5MB [7] data per month, which confirms that the effectiveness of training on cloud. Note that since the user's behavior tends to be stable, to further save both cellular data and energy usage, we can aggregate the training data for a longer while (e.g., one week) but not everyday any more, and carry out data training weekly by

[7]Kaleido consumes additional 4.5MB/month since additional data/information download is needed for the testing.

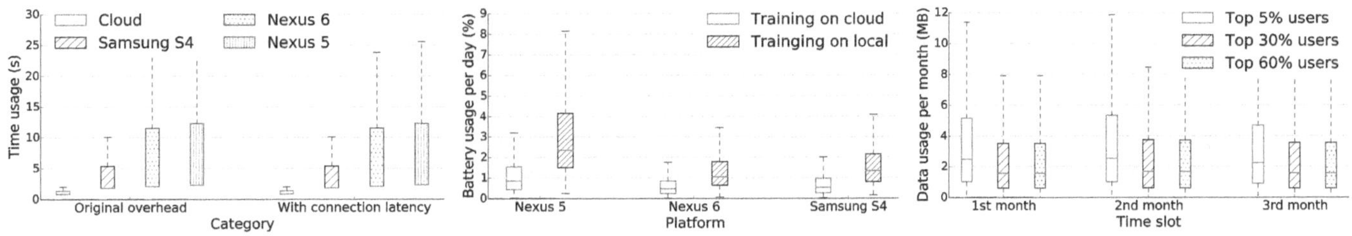

(a) Daily training time consumption (b) Daily battery overhead for training (c) Monthly data cost for training

Figure 13: Overhead with different training schemes for the machine learning procedure in Kaleido.

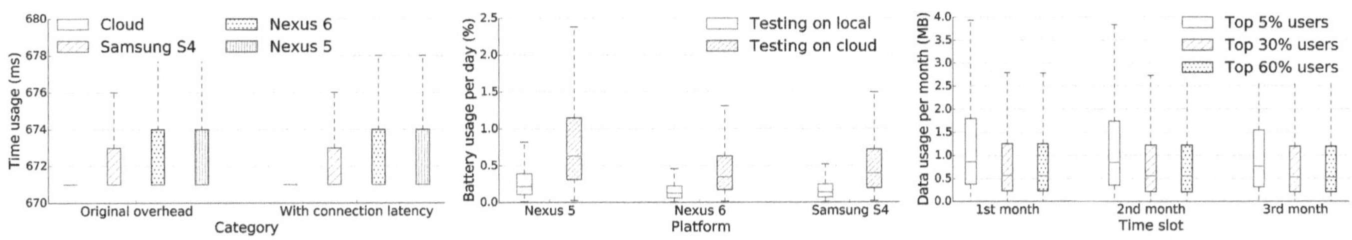

(a) Daily testing time consumption (b) Daily battery cost for testing (c) Monthly data consumption for testing

Figure 14: Daily costs with different testing schemes for Kaleido.

offloading the training to the cloud only when the user is on WiFi while charging.

Why Testing on Local? Furthermore, we also evaluate the testing schemes based on above approaches. The results are shown in Figure 14. We observe that the cloud approach consumes more energy (0.5% of total battery usage per day), leading to additional cellular data usage (0.9MB per month). In addition, since the cloud approach requires network connection, it brings a latency of 670ms each time, daily time overhead for testing all the tweets on local ties to the cloud approach. Thus, the local testing approach is more preferable. The reason is that, different from the training process that is computation-intensive, the testing procedure is data-centric and offloading to the cloud would incur higher delay and energy overhead for data exchange between the cloud and the device.

7. RELATED WORK

In this section, we review three directions of prior research directly related to our work. Specifically, we highlight the key differences of Kaleido against them respectively.

Media-based Affective Computing: Although many recent studies, e.g., [24], keep on emphasizing the significance of affective media computing, but their approaches are still highly subjective and difficult to embrace quantitative measurements [25]. A recent study [14] focus on training data and models for identifying the emotional influence, based on the ground-truth affects that are manually labeled in order to guarantee the prediction accuracy. However, it also brings a challenge to efficiently process massive images in OSNs [14]. Along a different line, motivated by the insight that user behavior, social friendship and media affect play critical roles on user's emotion-triggered action in OSNs, in this paper, we propose a novel learning-based mechanism to intelligently deal with media recommender system which support the affective-aware recommendation.

Recommendation Techniques: There are two prevalent schemes for building recommender systems, i.e., content-based (CB) [11] and collaborative filtering (CF) [26]. The CB method is on a basis of recommending items, e.g., images or videos, that are similar to those in which users are interested in according to the historical feeds. The CF approach, on the other hand, recommends items to the user based on other individuals with similar preferences or tastes. Many recent studies, such as [12, 27], are built on both CB and CF systems, usually by rating a set of items. To avoid this extra burden on the user, leveraging implicit interest indicators [28], such as the purchase history, views, clicks, or queries, has recently become more popular in recommender systems. Motivated by the insight that time, social, and network context play critical roles on users' media click behavior, in this paper we propose a novel recommendation system based on the generalized cluster-based bias model.

Mobile OSN Studies: To analyze social behaviors of mobile Twitter users, [29] identifies people using microblogging to talk about their daily activities and to seek or share information as well as analyzing the user intentions associated at a community level, showing how users with similar intentions connect with each other. In addition, a number of recent studies, such as [30, 31], address the problem of computing influence in Twitter-like networks and finding leaders whose tweets are influential. Our work does not aim at finding users who are influential directly. Instead, we exploit that different social friends have different impact on a user's activation on media usage or propogation. [32] proposes a tree-based algorithm to mine user-friend graphs to discover strong friends of a user. In contrast to our work, [32] does not consider how to utilize the social friendship structure to facilitate the information and content sharing among users, in particular, under a rich communication environment.

8. CONCLUSION

We have presented Kaleido, a system for smart OSN media recommendation on smartphones. Building upon our cluster-based machine learning mechanism, Kaleido automatically learns relationships among various content and context impacts. Experiments with real Twitter traces from 16,952 people and an Android prototype show that Kaleido can achieve superior performance of a significant media recommendation accuracy while with minor additional data or energy consumption. Moreover, our design enables offloading of machine learning procedures to a cloud server, and achieves a speed-up of up to about 1,000 over local execution on smartphones. For future work, we will consider extending our system with a comprehensive implementation to support more media formats, e.g., video.

9. ACKNOWLEDGMENTS

We thank the Multimedia reviewers for the helpful comments on this paper, Ningyuan Li, Liyuan Wang, Boya Wu, Hangcheng Zhao, Taoran Tang and Yaohua Pu for preliminaries. We also thank all the data providers for their contributions on this paper. This work is supported by Tsinghua University Initiative Scientific Research Program, National Key Research and Development Plan (2016YFB1001200), National Basic Research Program (973 Program) of China (2012CB316401), and National Natural, and Science Foundation of China (61370023).

10. REFERENCES

[1] Arjan Geven, Manfred Tscheligi, and Lucas Noldus. Measuring mobile emotions: Measuring the impossible? In *MobileHCI*, page 109. ACM, 2009.

[2] Marco Guerini and Jacopo Staiano. Deep feelings: A massive cross-lingual study on the relation between emotions and virality. In *WWW*, pages 299–305. ACM, 2015.

[3] Jie Tang et al. Quantitative study of individual emotional states in social networks. *Affective Computing, IEEE Transactions on*, 3(2):132–144, 2012.

[4] Rosalind W Picard and Roalind Picard. *Affective computing*, volume 252. MIT press Cambridge, 1997.

[5] Lisa Sayegh et al. Managerial decision-making under crisis: The role of emotion in an intuitive decision process. *Human Resource Management Review*, 14(2):179–199, 2004.

[6] Nikolaos Georgis et al. System and method of selective media content access through a recommednation engine, August 17 2007. US Patent App. 11/840,814.

[7] Elizabeth A Vandewater et al. Digital childhood: electronic media and technology use among infants, toddlers, and preschoolers. *Pediatrics*, 119(5):e1006–e1015, 2007.

[8] Börkur Sigurbjörnsson and Roelof Van Zwol. Flickr tag recommendation based on collective knowledge. In *WWW*, pages 327–336. ACM, 2008.

[9] Martin Prangl et al. A framework for utility-based multimedia adaptation. *Circuits and Systems for Video Technology, IEEE Transactions on*, 17(6):719–728, 2007.

[10] Moon-Hee Park et al. Location-based recommendation system using bayesian user's preference model in mobile devices. In *Ubiquitous Intelligence and Computing*, pages 1130–1139. Springer, 2007.

[11] Michael J Pazzani and Daniel Billsus. Content-based recommendation systems. In *The adaptive web*, pages 325–341. Springer, 2007.

[12] Meng Jiang et al. Social contextual recommendation. In *CIKM*, pages 45–54. ACM, 2012.

[13] Twidere-twitter client. http://twidere.mariotaku.org.

[14] Xiaohui Wang et al. Modeling emotion influence in image social networks. *Affective Computing, IEEE Transactions on*, 6(3):286–297, 2015.

[15] Twitter rest apis. https://dev.twitter.com/rest/public.

[16] Paul Ekman. An argument for basic emotions. *Cognition & emotion*, 6(3-4):169–200, 1992.

[17] Kevin P Murphy, Yair Weiss, and Michael I Jordan. Loopy belief propagation for approximate inference: An empirical study. In *Uncertainty in artificial intelligence*, pages 467–475. Morgan Kaufmann Publishers Inc., 1999.

[18] Costantino Grana et al. Enhancing hsv histograms with achromatic points detection for video retrieval. In *CIVR*, pages 302–308. ACM, 2007.

[19] Mark EJ Newman. Modularity and community structure in networks. *Proceedings of the National Academy of Sciences*, 103(23):8577–8582, 2006.

[20] Paul S Bradley and Usama M Fayyad. Refining initial points for k-means clustering. In *ICML*, volume 98, pages 91–99. Citeseer, 1998.

[21] Liangjie Hong et al. Learning to rank social update streams. In *SIGIR*, pages 651–660. ACM, 2012.

[22] Léon Bottou. Stochastic gradient descent tricks. In *Neural Networks: Tricks of the Trade*, pages 421–436. Springer, 2012.

[23] Anthony Bryan et al. Metalink/http: Mirrors and hashes. Technical report, 2011.

[24] Bing Li et al. Context-aware affective images classification based on bilayer sparse representation. In *MM*, pages 721–724. ACM, 2012.

[25] Marco Cristani et al. Unveiling the multimedia unconscious: Implicit cognitive processes and multimedia content analysis. In *MM*, pages 213–222. ACM, 2013.

[26] David Goldberg et al. Using collaborative filtering to weave an information tapestry. *Communications of the ACM*, 35(12):61–70, 1992.

[27] Ido Guy et al. Social media recommendation based on people and tags. In *SIGIR*, pages 194–201. ACM, 2010.

[28] Mark Claypool et al. Implicit interest indicators. In *IUI*, pages 33–40. ACM, 2001.

[29] Akshay Java et al. Why we twitter: understanding microblogging usage and communities. In *SNA-KDD*, pages 56–65. ACM, 2007.

[30] Meeyoung Cha et al. Measuring user influence in twitter: The million follower fallacy. *ICWSM*, 10(10-17):30, 2010.

[31] Chao Wu et al. Spice: Socially-driven learning-based mobile media prefetching. In *INFOCOM*. IEEE, 2016.

[32] Juan J Cameron et al. Finding strong groups of friends among friends in social networks. In *DASC*, pages 824–831. IEEE, 2011.

Predicting Personalized Emotion Perceptions of Social Images

Sicheng Zhao[†‡], Hongxun Yao[†*], Yue Gao[‡], Rongrong Ji[♯], Wenlong Xie[†], Xiaolei Jiang[†], Tat-Seng Chua[§]
[†]School of Computer Science and Technology, Harbin Institute of Technology, China.
[‡]School of Software, TNLIST, KLISS, Tsinghua University, China.
[♯]School of Information Science and Engineering, Xiamen University, China.
[§]School of Computing, National University of Singapore, Singapore.
[*]Corresponding author. schzhao@gmail.com; {h.yao, wlxie, xljiang}@hit.edu.cn; gaoyue@tsinghua.edu.cn; rrji@xmu.edu.cn; dcscts@nus.edu.sg

ABSTRACT

Images can convey rich semantics and induce various emotions to viewers. Most existing works on affective image analysis focused on predicting the dominant emotions for the majority of viewers. However, such dominant emotion is often insufficient in real-world applications, as the emotions that are induced by an image are highly subjective and different with respect to different viewers. In this paper, we propose to predict the personalized emotion perceptions of images for each individual viewer. Different types of factors that may affect personalized image emotion perceptions, including visual content, social context, temporal evolution, and location influence, are jointly investigated. Rolling multi-task hypergraph learning is presented to consistently combine these factors and a learning algorithm is designed for automatic optimization. For evaluation, we set up a large scale image emotion dataset from Flickr, named Image-Emotion-Social-Net, on both dimensional and categorical emotion representations with over 1 million images and about 8,000 users. Experiments conducted on this dataset demonstrate that the proposed method can achieve significant performance gains on personalized emotion classification, as compared to several state-of-the-art approaches.

1. INTRODUCTION

With the rapid development of digital photography technology and wide-spread popularity of social networks, people have become used to sharing their lives and expressing their opinions using images and videos together with text. The explosively growing volume of online social data have greatly motivated and promoted the research on large-scale multimedia analysis. As what people feel may directly determine their decision making, the understanding of these data at the emotional level is of great importance, which can benefit social communication and enable wide applications [4, 48], ranging from marketing [11] to political voting forecasts [34].

Despite the promising progress of textual sentiment analysis [23], emotion analysis of social images remains an open problem [52].

MM '16, October 15–19, 2016, Amsterdam, The Netherlands.

DOI: http://dx.doi.org/10.1145/2964284.2964289

(a)

Title: Light in Darkness
Tags: london, stormy, dramatic weather, ...
Description: ...there was a break in the clouds such that a strip of the far bank and bridge were lit up while the sky behind remained somewhat foreboding. I thought it made for a pretty intense scene....

(b)

Expected emotion:
Emotion category: fear
Sentiment: negative
Valence: 4.1956
Arousal: 4.4989
Dominance: 4.8378

(c)

Comments to this image from different viewers	Personalized emotion labels
Wow, that is fantastic...it looks so incredible, like a painting...slightly unreal. That sky is amazing.	Emotion: awe, Sentiment: positive V: 7.121 A: 4.479 D: 6.635
Yup a fave for me as well. Exciting drama at its best.	Emotion: excitement, Sentiment: positive V: 7.950 A: 6.950 D: 7.210
Hey, it really frightened me! My little daughter just looked scared.	Emotion: fear, Sentiment: negative V: 2.625 A: 5.805 D: 3.625

(d)

Figure 1: Illustration of personalized image emotion perceptions in social networks. (a) The uploaded image to Flickr. (b) The title, tags and description given by the uploader to the image. (c) The expected emotion labels that we assign to the uploader using the keywords in (b) in red with both categorical and dimensional representations. (d) The comments to this image from different viewers and the personalized emotion labels that we obtain using the keywords in red. We can find that the emotions perceived by the viewers are truly subjective.

The main challenges that limit the development of image emotion analysis lie in the so-called affective gap, as well as the subjective evaluation [12, 48]. Trying to find features that can express emotions better to bridge the affective gap, previous works mainly focused on predicting the dominant emotions for the majority of viewers, without considering the subjective evaluation. However, predicting personalized emotion is usually more practical, as the emotions that are induced in viewers by an image are highly subjective and different, due to the influence of social, educational and cultural backgrounds [17, 25, 49, 50], as shown in Figure 1. Under such a circumstance, traditional dominant emotion based methods may not work well for personalized emotion prediction [41]. So far, little progress has been made on predicting personalized emotion perceptions (termed PEP), mainly due to two key challenges:

The Lack of Benchmarks. To the best of our knowledge, there is no public dataset on PEP of images, though a few works have been done on emotion or sentiment analysis of social multimedia data [16, 32, 41, 2, 42, 43, 4]. To avoid the tedious manual labeling of large scale social images, existing works on emotion analysis mainly used two methods to obtain the emotion labels based on different emotion representation models. First, from the dimensional emotion perspective, traditional lexicon-based methods are used to find out the polarity values of the comments with a predefined word dictionary. Yang *et al.* [41, 42] adopted this method for Chinese microblog analysis with emotions represented by one dimension. However, they just classified the emotions into two discrete categories by taking threshold of the continuous polarities. No large scale dataset on social image emotions using dimensional representation based on English dictionary has been released. Second, from the categorical emotion perspective, keywords or synonyms based retrieval of specified emotions are used. The works in [16, 32, 2, 43] adopted this strategy. The emotion categories used for classification are ad hoc and arbitrary with categories numbers ranging from six to tens [21, 25]. Besides, the numbers of positive and negative emotions are unbalanced [32, 43].

Multi-factor influence. Besides the visual content of images, there are many other factors that may influence the personalized perception of image emotions. Personal interest may directly influence the emotion perceptions [31]. Viewers' emotions are often temporally influenced by their recent past emotions [7]. In social networks, the emotions are widely influenced by the social connections. Whitfield [39] showed that how happy you are is influenced by your social links to people even you've never heard of and never met. How a viewer's emotion is influenced by their friends on social networks is quantitatively studied in [32, 43]. The locations of social images, if known, can also be used for visual data analysis [8]. How to consistently and effectively combine these factors in a unified framework for robust personalized emotion analysis is a challenging problem.

In this paper, we make the first attempt in predicting PEP of social images to tackle the two challenges above. For the first challenge, we set up a large scale image dataset of personalized emotions, named Image-Emotion-Social-Net (IESN), which are represented by both dimensional and categorical emotion models. We use 8 categories as the categorical emotion states which are defined in a rigorous psychological study [22], including *anger*, *disgust*, *fear*, *sadness* as negative emotions, and *amusement*, *awe*, *contentment*, *excitement* as positive emotions. Tens of keywords for each emotion category are used to search the titles, tags and descriptions of images or the comments to the images to obtain the personalized emotion labels. Then we computed the average value of valence, arousal and dominance (VAD) for dimensional emotion space using recently published VAD norms of 13,915 English lemmas [38]. Besides, we give the sentiment category (positive or negative).

For the second challenge, we take different types of factors into account, including visual content, social context, temporal evolution and location influence. We propose a rolling multi-task hypergraph learning (RMTHG) to formalize the personalized emotion perception prediction problem by modelling these various factors. Experiments are conducted on our collected IESN dataset and the results demonstrate that by incorporating the various factors, the proposed model can significantly improve the prediction performance compared with the state-of-the-art approaches. Please note that in this paper we do not clearly distinguish expressed, perceived and induced emotions as in music [18]. We use "perceive (perception)" and "induce (induction)" from the perspective of emotion subjects, such as "User A perceives fear from image B" and "Image B induces fear in user A".

The contributions of this paper are three-fold:

1. We propose to distinguish personalized emotions from traditional dominant emotions. What's more, we also consider different types of factors, including visual content, social context, temporal evolution and location influence.
2. We present a compound vertex hypergraph to model all the different factors in a consistent and expandable way. To enable efficient inference in this framework, we devise a rolling multi-task hypergraph learning algorithm, which can simultaneously predict individual emotions of different users.
3. We set up a large scale personalized emotion dataset of social images from Flickr with over 1 million images and 1.4 million labels for about 8,000 users. The dataset, containing images, metadata, social connections and personalized emotions, will be released along with this work.

The rest of this paper is organized as follows. Section 2 introduces related work of image emotion and sentiment analysis, social media analysis and (hyper)graph based learning. Section 3 introduces the constructed Image-Emotion-Social-Net dataset. Section 4 gives an overview of the proposed method. Hypergraph construction and rolling multi-task hypergraph learning are described in Section 5 and Section 6, respectively. Experimental evaluation and analysis are presented in Section 7, followed by conclusion and future work in Section 8.

2. RELATED WORK

Image emotion and sentiment analysis. Some research efforts have been dedicated to improving the accuracy of image emotion prediction. Related works can be divided into different types, according to the adopted emotion models, the required tasks, the extracted features and the models used.

There are two kinds of emotion representation models: categorical emotion states (CES) and dimensional emotion space (DES). CES methods model emotions as one of a few basic categories[1] [37, 21, 44, 20, 19, 32, 16, 51, 43], while DES methods employ 3-D or 2-D space to represent emotions, such as valence-arousal-dominance [29], natural-temporal-energetic [1] and valence-arousal [12, 33, 20, 48]. Accordingly, related works on image emotion analysis can be classified into three different tasks: affective image classification [19, 2, 21, 44, 32, 43, 20, 16, 41, 42, 48], regression [20, 48] and retrieval [37, 52]. We model image emotions using both representation models.

From a feature's view point, different levels of visual features are extracted for image emotion analysis. Low level holistic image features including Wiccest features and Gabor features are extracted to classify image emotions in [44]. Lu *et al.* [20] investigated the computability of emotion through *shape* features. Machajdik *et al.* [21] extracted features inspired from psychology and art theory, including *color*, *texture* as low level features, *composition* as mid level features while *face* and *skin* as high level features. Zhao *et al.* [48] proposed to extract mid level principles-of-art based emotion features, which are demonstrated to be more interpretable by humans and have stronger link to emotions than the elements-of-art based ones. Yuan *et al.* [46] used mid level scene attributes for binary sentiment classification. Image based global sparse representation and region based local sparse representation are proposed to define the similarities of a test image and all training images [19]. Visual sentiment ontology and detectors are proposed to detect high level adjective noun pairs (ANP) based on large-scale social multimedia data [2]. Similarly, Chen *et al.* [4] used object based methods to detect ANP. We extract features of different levels and investigate the performance on personalized emotion prediction.

The commonly used models are based on machine learning methods, such as Naive Bayes [21], SVM or SVR [20, 48], sparse learn-

[1]Specifically, image emotion is often called image sentiment for binary classification (positive or negative) [30, 46, 2, 4, 45].

ing [19] and multi-graph learning [52]. These methods may perform well for traditional affective image classification, regression or retrieval, but they are difficult to incorporate different factors, such as social connections, temporal evolution, *etc.* We attempt to combine different kinds of factors with visual content to predict personalized image emotions.

Social media analysis. The extremely large volume of data in social networks have motivated various research topics related to multimedia, computer vision and data mining, such as brand data gathering [8], outbreak prediction [6], social event detection [27, 10], online collaborative learning [47] and emotion related analysis [30, 16, 32, 2, 41, 5, 43, 42, 4]. Among all these works, the emotion related analysis is similar to our work. Jia *et al.* [16] simply used the uploaded time of images and the ID of image owner as social features, while no social features are used in [30, 2, 4]. The social connections between different users are modelled [32, 41, 43, 42]. The works in [32, 43] used social connections to model emotion influence of one user to another. Yang *et al.* [42] utilized social factors together with visual and textual ones to discover representative images for social events. Social connections are used for predicting emotions for individuals [41], which is similar to our work. But they just simply classified the sentiments of Chinese microblogs and did not consider the temporal influence of emotions.

(Hyper)graph based learning. As the structure of graph model is similar to that of social networks, it is widely used for social media analysis [32, 41, 42]. Factor graph model is used to analyze individual emotional states in [32]. Social influence and user interest are modelled by a hybrid graph [41]. Emotionally similar images were retrieved via multi-graph learning [52] which was firstly used in video retrieval [36]. Compared with conventional graph, hypergraph can reflect the higher order information [53, 3, 9] and is widely used in music recommendation [3], 3D object retrieval [9], image retrieval [14] and brand data gathering [8]. In this paper, we present rolling multi-task hypergraph learning to model the various factors that may contribute to personalized emotion perception.

3. IMAGE-EMOTION-SOCIAL-NET

In this section, we introduce the dataset (Image-Emotion-Social-Net, IESN[2]) on emotions of social images, including the construction process, the statistics and the challenging tasks.

3.1 Dataset Construction

We downloaded 21,066,920 images from Flickr with 2,060,357 users belonging to 264,683 groups. Each image is associated with the metadata, such as the title, tags, taken time and location if available. Each user is associated with the personal information, the contact list and the group list they joined in. As how to measure emotions is still far from consensus in research community [28], we defined emotions using both categorical and dimensional representations. For CES, we used the 8 categories rigorously defined in psychology [22], including 4 negative and 4 positive emotions. To get the ground truth labels, we adopted keywords based searching strategy as in [43, 2, 16]. Tens of keywords for each emotion category are obtained from a public synonym searching site[3] and are manually verified, with examples shown in Table 1. Expected emotions of the image uploaders are firstly considered. The keywords are searched from the title, tags and descriptions given by the uploaders. The emotion category with the most frequent keywords is set as the ground truth of expected emotions from the uploaders.

[2]https://sites.google.com/site/schzhao/

[3]http://www.thesaurus.com/browse/synonym/

Table 1: The keyword examples of each emotion category. '#' indicates the total keyword numbers.

Emotion	#	Keyword examples
amusement	24	amused, amusement, cheer, delight, funny, pleasing
anger	79	angry, annoyed, enraged, hateful, offended, provoked
awe	36	amazing, astonishment, awesome, impressive, wonderful
contentment	28	comfortable, fulfilled, gladness, happy, pleasure, satisfied
disgust	35	detestation, disgusted, nauseous, queasy, revolt, weary
excitement	49	adventure, enthusiastic, inspired, stimulation, thrilled
fear	71	afraid, frightened, nightmare, horror, scared, timorous
sadness	72	bereaved, heartbroken, pessimistic, sadness, unhappy

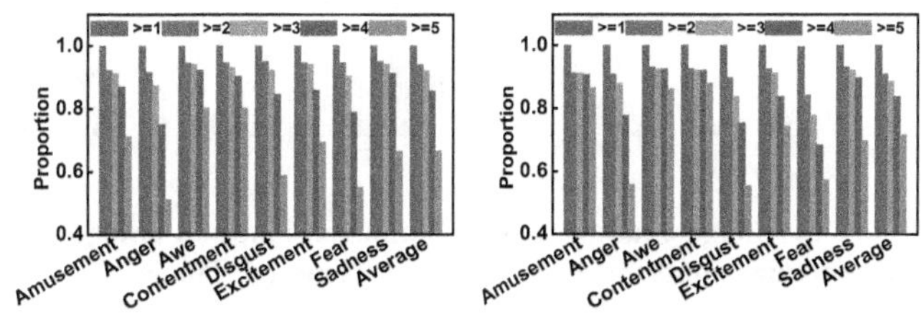

(a) Expected emotion (b) Personalized emotion

Figure 2: Dataset validation results. $>= n$ means $\geq n$ Yes's.

As we are focusing on PEP, we then searched from all the comments of related images to get the personalized emotion labels of each viewer. We removed the images if the searched title, tags or descriptions contain negation adjacent and prior to the target keywords, such as "I am not happy". Similarly, we also removed the comments with negation adjacent and prior to the target keywords. Note that the labels of an image for a specific user are allowed to have different emotion categories (such as fear, disgust) but must have only one sentiment (positive or negative). Then we computed the average value of valence, arousal and dominance as ground truth for dimensional emotion representation based on recently published VAD norms of 13,915 English lemmas [38]. Besides, we also gave the sentiment categories (positive or negative). We combined the expected emotions and actual emotions of all involved images for each user. This process resulted in a dataset containing 1,012,901 images uploaded by 11,347 users; and 1,060,636 comments on these images commented by 106,688 users. We chose 7,723 active users with more than 50 involved images. Finally we obtained 1,434,080 emotion labels of three types, including 8 emotion categories, 2 sentiment categories and continuous VAD values. Note that all the involved images of one user are labelled with sentiment categories and VAD values, while a tiny proportion of them are not assigned with the emotion categories if no keyword is found.

If one user is the uploader of an image, then the emotion of the metadata text (title, tags and descriptions) is the personalized emotion of this user, which is also the expected emotion that is expected to induce in other viewers by this user. If one user is a viewer of an image, then the emotion of the comment is the personalized emotion of this user.

3.2 Dataset Validation

To validate the quality of the dataset, we did a crowdsourcing experiment on discrete emotions. For each emotion category, we randomly selected 200 images with associated titles, tags and descriptions for expected emotions, and 200 comments with corresponding images for personalized emotions. 5 graduate students (3 males, 2 females) were invited to judge whether the text was used to express the assigned emotions of related images. To facilitate this judgement, they were asked simple question like "*Do you think*

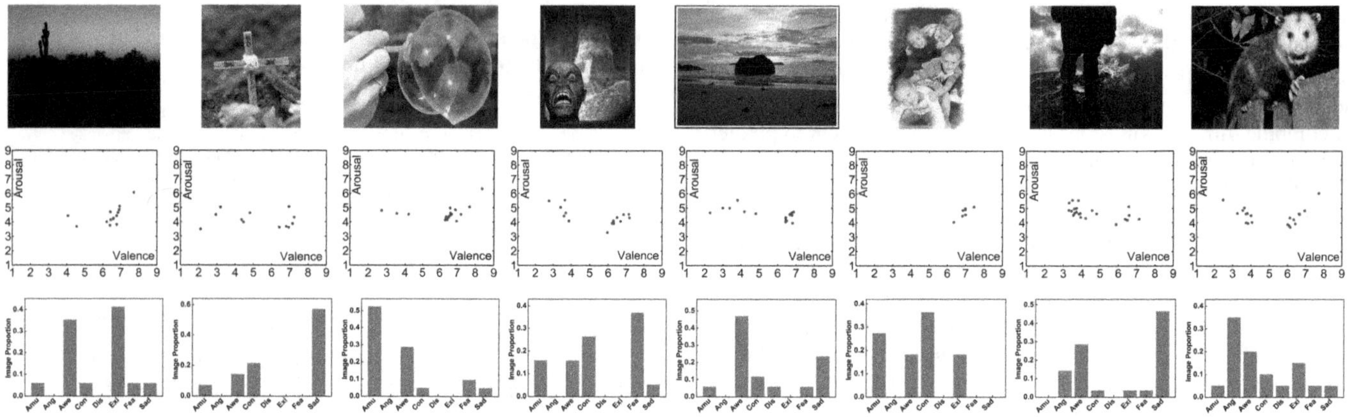

Figure 3: Image examples of personalized emotion categories in the IESN dataset. From top to bottom are: original images, VA emotion labels and the distribution of 8 emotion labels.

Table 2: Image numbers of categorical emotions.

amusement	awe	contentment	excitement	positive
270,748	328,303	181,431	115,065	1,016,186
anger	disgust	fear	sadness	negative
29,844	20,962	55,802	57,476	362,400

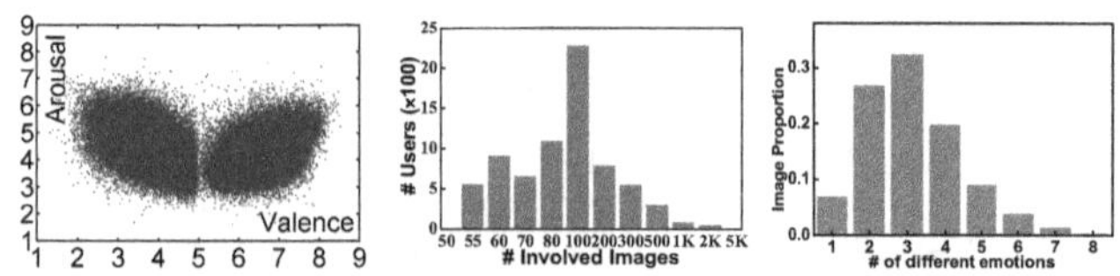

(a) VAD distribution (b) User distribution (c) Emotion number

Figure 4: Statistical distributions of dataset.

that the text is used to express excitement for this image?", and they just needed to choose YES or NO. Each image was judged by all the 5 annotators. The result is shown in Figure 2. We can find that for both expected and personalized emotions, on average more than 88% of emotion labels receive at least 3 Yeses, which verifies the quality of the constructed dataset. In such cases, the expected emotion labels are 3.5% more accurately assigned than personalized emotions. To assess the inter-rater agreement, we also calculate the Fleiss' kappa[4] of the 5 annotators. The average Fleiss' kappa (the standard deviation) for the 8 emotion categories of expected emotions and personalized emotions are 0.2297 (0.0748) and 0.3224 (0.1411), respectively.

3.3 Statistics of Dataset

The distribution of images per emotion category is shown in Table 2, where the first four columns represent the number of images in each of the 8 emotions; while the last column is the number of images with binary sentiments. We can find that the number of negative emotions is relatively small. The distribution of valence, arousal (without showing dominance here) is illustrated in Figure 4(a), which looks like a petal or heart, similar to the emotion space in [13]. The user distribution based on the involved images is shown in Figure 4(b). The distribution of emotion numbers for the images with more than 20 labels each is shown in Figure 4(c). Some image examples with assigned emotions in both CES and DES forms are given in Figure 3. We can find that the emotion perceptions of different users are truly subjective and personalized.

[4]https://en.wikipedia.org/wiki/Fleiss%27_kappa

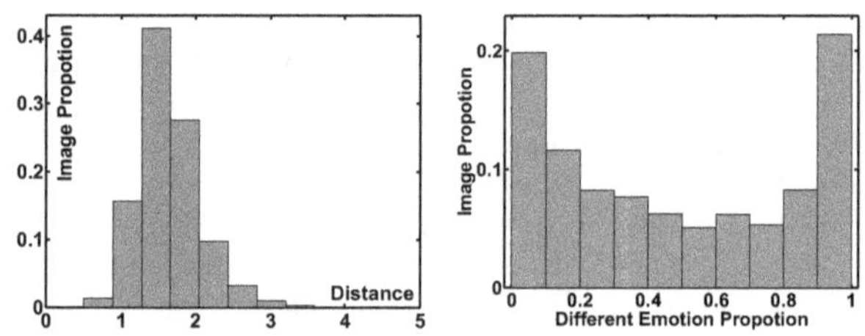

(a) VA distance (b) CES proportion

Figure 5: The relation between expected vs personalized emotions of the images with more than 20 emotion labels on both DES and CES representations.

We also analyze the relation between the expected and personalized emotions. For each of the images with more than 20 labels, we compute the Euclidean distances between personalized emotions and expected emotion in VA space, and average all the distances. The histogram of the average VA distance is shown in Figure 5(a). For CES, we count the proportion of personalized emotions that are different from expected emotion for each image. The histogram of different emotion proportions is illustrated in Figure 5(b). It is clear that there exists great inconsistency between expected and personalized emotions.

The average and standard deviation of friend numbers among the 8k users are 45.7 and 21.4, respectively. Besides, users can be correlated by joining the same groups. So there exist rich social connections in the dataset. The time of the collected dataset ranges from Oct. 5, 2012 to Mar. 29, 2013, lasting about 6 months.

3.4 Challenging Tasks

The challenging tasks that can be performed by researchers on this dataset include, but are not limited to, the followings:

1. Image-centric emotion analysis. For each image, we can predict the dominant emotion category like the traditional affective image classification. Besides, we can also predict the emotion distribution of each image, taking the normalized emotion proportion as the ground truth.

2. User-centric emotion prediction. For each user, we can predict their personalized emotion perception of some specific images. The above two tasks can be extended to regression and retrieval tasks, all of which can be done using visual, social, temporal and the combination of all features.

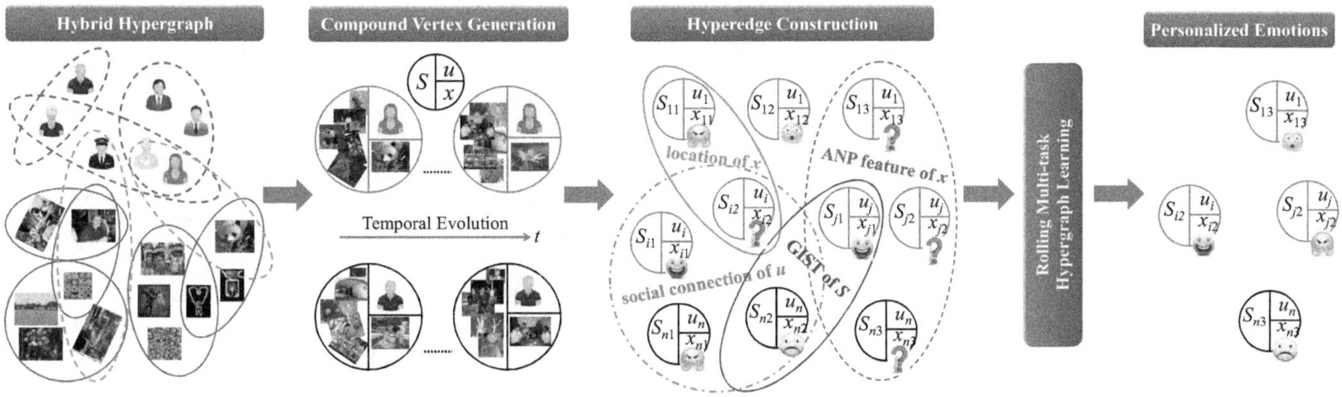

Figure 6: The framework of the proposed method for personalized image emotion prediction.

3. Emotion related data mining and applications. This dataset contains visual and social information to support research on emotion influence mining, social advertising, affective image retrieval and affective recommender systems, *etc.*

For different tasks, the roles of expected and personalized emotions are different. For image-centric expected emotion analysis, only the expected emotions can be used. For image-centric dominant emotion analysis or emotion distribution analysis, the expected emotions can be viewed as one type of personalized emotions. For user-centric emotion prediction, the expected emotions can also be viewed as one type of personalized emotions, but only for the uploaders of the related images. In this paper, we focus on the second task, trying to combine social, temporal and other factors with traditional visual features to predict PEP for each viewer.

4. OVERVIEW

Our goal is to predict the emotions of a specified user after viewing an image, associated with online social networks. Different types of factors can influence the emotion perception and can be exploited for emotion prediction. The following factors are hypothesized to contribute to emotion perceptions:

Visual Content. The visual content of an image can directly influence the emotion perception of viewers. Different from traditional image emotion prediction, both the images viewed in the recent past and the current image are taken into account in our system. This point is also mentioned in the factor of temporal evolution. The visual descriptors used in this paper include low, middle, and high level features.

Social Context. One viewer's emotion may be easily and largely affected by the social environment that they live in, e.g. their friends, so social context is highly helpful to make our prediction more accurate. Specifically, we consider the following social contexts: whether two users are in common interest groups, have common contact lists and the similarity of comments to same images.

Temporal Evolution. One viewer's emotional variation within a short time is not so obvious, i.e., the current emotion is not independent on the recent past emotion, so temporal evolution gives additional information with respect to emotion prediction. Our system can take the recent past emotion into consideration.

Location Influence. Where and when a picture is taken is another factor which may contribute to emotional variation. One example is that photographs taken in entertainment venues usually lead people to feel happy. We encapsulate location information (if available) in our framework to improve the prediction performance.

We present rolling multi-task hypergraph learning to jointly combine these factors. Formally, a user u_i in social networks observes an image x_{it} at time t, and their perceived emotion after viewing the image is y_{it}. Before viewing x_{it}, the user u_i may have seen many other images. Among these images we select the recent past ones, which we believe to affect the current emotion. These selected images comprise a set S_i. The emotional social network is formalized as a hybrid hypergraph $\mathcal{G} = \langle\{\mathcal{U}, \mathcal{X}, \mathcal{S}\}, \mathcal{E}, \mathbf{W}\rangle$. Each vertex $v = (u, x, S)$ in vertex set $\mathcal{V} = \{\mathcal{U}, \mathcal{X}, \mathcal{S}\}$ is a compound triple (u, x, S), where u represents user, x and S are the current image and the recent past images, which are named as 'Target Image' and 'History Image Set', respectively. It should be noted that in this triple, both x and S are viewed by user u. $\mathcal{E}$ is the hyperedge set. Each hyperedge e of $\mathcal{E}$ represents a link between two or more vertices based on one component of the triple and is assigned with a weight $w(e)$. $\mathbf{W}$ is the diagonal matrix of the edge weights.

Mathematically, the task of personalized emotion prediction is to find the appropriate mapping

$$f : (\mathcal{G}, y_{i1}, ..., y_{i(t-1)}) \rightarrow y_{it}, \tag{1}$$

for each user u_i.

The framework of the proposed method is shown in Figure 6. First, we generate the compound triple vertex for each viewer based on the time of related images which they uploaded or commented. Second, the hypergraphs are constructed for each component of the triple based on different factors. Finally, we obtain the personalized emotion prediction results after the rolling learning of the multi-task hypergraphs.

5. HYPERGRAPH CONSTRUCTION

As stated in Section 4, a vertex of the proposed RMTHG is a compound one, which consists of three components. It should be emphasized that the images in such a vertex is a general concept, which not only refers to the pixel array itself, but also includes some additional information associated with the image, such as location, time, and emotional labels (if any) with respect to the specified user. For conventional emotion prediction, a vertex containing a pixel array is sufficient. In contrast, the compound vertex formulation enables our system to model all the four kinds of factors in Section 3: visual descriptors both in the target image and history image set can be extracted to represent visual content; user relationship can be exploited from the user component to take social context into consideration; past emotion can be inferred from history image set to reveal temporal evolution; location influence is embedded in the associated information with target image and his-

(a) Visual content (b) Location influence

Figure 7: Illustration of target image centric hyperedge construction.

tory image set. Consequently, such a vertex generation mechanism is flexible and extensible.

In our hypergraph framework, hyperedges are used to indicate some types of similarity among vertices, meaning that vertices sharing a common hyperedge tend to have similar emotions. Based on the vertex components, we construct different types of hyperedges, including target image centric, history image set centric, and user centric hyperedges.

5.1 Target Image Centric Hyperedges

5.1.1 Visual Content

As demonstrated in [52], the features that determine the emotions of an image are different for various kinds of images. Similar to [52], we extract commonly used visual features of different levels, including low-level GIST and elements-of-art [21], mid-level attributes [24] and principles-of-art [48], and high-level adjective noun pairs (ANPs) [2] and facial expressions [40]. See [52] for detail. The six sets of extracted visual features are abbreviated as GIST, Elements, Attributes, Principles, ANP and Expressions with dimension 512, 48, 102, 165, 1200 and 8, respectively. Given two triple vertices $v_{it_1} = (u_i, x_{it_1}, S_{it_1})$ and $v_{jt_2} = (u_j, x_{jt_2}, S_{jt_2})$, where x_{it_1} and x_{jt_2} also represent related visual features, the visual similarity based on target image (T) is computed by

$$s_V^T(v_{it_1}, v_{jt_2}) = \exp\left(-\frac{d(v_{it_1}, v_{jt_2})}{\sigma}\right), \tag{2}$$

where $d(.,.)$ is a specified distance function, σ is set as the average distance of the distance matrix of all images. Here the Euclidean distance is used for $d(.,.)$. We can construct 6 kinds of hyperedges based on different visual features. Figure 7(a) illustrates the construction procedure of visual content based hyperedges.

5.1.2 Location Influence

Besides the image itself, there are often other metadata of social images, such as the time taken, the location, *etc.* We consider the location influence here, as the images taken around the similar place within a short time tend to describe similar events and express similar emotions. The geographical similarity between v_{it_1} and v_{jt_2} with locations $l(x_{it_1}) = (lat_{it_1}, lon_{it_1})$ and $l(x_{jt_2}) = (lat_{jt_2}, lon_{jt_2})$ (if available) is measured by the Harversion formula [27]. Figure 7(b) illustrates the construction procedure of location based hyperedges.

5.2 History Image Set Centric Hyperedges

Similar to target images, we can construct hyperedges for the history image sets based on the visual features and known locations. Besides, the emotion labels of the history image sets are known. So we can also construct hyperedges based on this information by using the normalized emotion distribution to explore the temporal influence of emotions.

As each history image set is composed of different numbers of sequential images, we use dynamic time warping (DTW) [26] to measure the distance between two history image sets. For pairwise images from two history image sets, the Euclidean distance is used to measure the visual distance and the visual similarity can be obtained using Eq. (2). Pairwise location similarity is computed by the Harversion formula. Similar to Plutchik's wheel [15], pairwise emotion distance is defined as 1+"the number of steps required to reach one emotion from another on by Mikels' wheel (see Figure 8))". Pairwise emotion similarity is defined as the reciprocal of pairwise emotion distance. Finally, we can obtain the visual similarity $s_V^H(v_{it_1}, v_{jt_2})$, location similarity $s_L^H(v_{it_1}, v_{jt_2})$ and emotion similarity $s_E^H(v_{it_1}, v_{jt_2})$ for two history image sets.

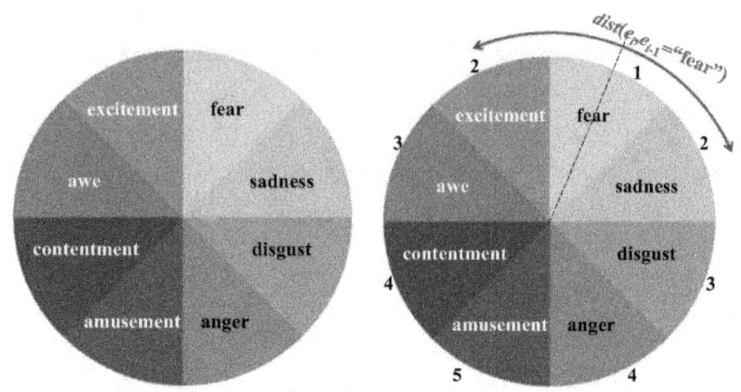

(a) Mikels' wheel (b) Mikels' emotion distance

Figure 8: Mikels' emotion wheel.

5.3 User Centric Hyperedges

In social networks, the emotions perceived by one user can be easily influenced by their friends. In our dataset, there are various kinds of social connections. The social similarity between two users (U) v_{it_1} and v_{jt_2} is measured by

$$s_S^U(v_{it_1}, v_{jt_2}) = \begin{cases} 1, & \text{if } u_i = u_j, \\ \max\{g_S + c_S + f_S, 1\}, & otherwise, \end{cases} \tag{3}$$

where $g_S(u_i, u_j)$ is defined as the ratio between the common groups that both users join, and the groups that either of them joins,

$$g_S(u_i, u_j) = \frac{|g(u_i) \bigcap g(u_j)|}{|g(u_i) \bigcup g(u_j)|}, \tag{4}$$

where $g(u_i)$ is the group set that u_i joins, $|.|$ is the element number of a set. Similar to g_S, $c_S(u_i, u_j)$ is defined as the ratio between the common contact lists that both users follow, and the contact lists that either of them follows. $f_S(u_i, u_j)$ is the average BoW similarity of comments to the same images

$$f_S(u_i, u_j) = \frac{1}{M}\sum_{k=1}^{M} s(BoW_k^i, BoW_k^j), \tag{5}$$

where M is the number of images that both users comment on, BoW_k^i is the BoW feature of the kth comment from user u_i, $s(.,.)$ is the cosine function that computes the similarity of two BoW features.

6. ROLLING MULTI-TASK HYPERGRAPH LEARNING

Given the emotional hybrid hypergraph $\mathcal{G} = \langle\{\mathcal{U}, \mathcal{X}, \mathcal{S}\}, \mathcal{E}, \mathbf{W}\rangle$, we obtain the incidence matrix $\mathbf{H}$ by computing each entry as,

$$h(v, e) = \begin{cases} 1, & \text{if } v \in e, \\ 0, & \text{if } v \notin e. \end{cases} \tag{6}$$

Algorithm 1: Learning procedure for RMTHG

Input: Error threshold ε, regularization λ, max-epochs K, training labels $\mathbf{Y}$

Output: Predicted emotion labels $\hat{\mathbf{E}}$

Initialization: $\hat{\mathbf{E}}^{(0)} \leftarrow \mathbf{0}$; Construct hypergraph $\mathcal{G}^{(0)} = \langle\{\mathcal{U}, \mathcal{X}, \mathcal{S}\}, \mathcal{E}^{(0)}, \mathbf{W}^{(0)}\rangle$;

for $k \leftarrow 1$ *to* K **do**

  Compute $\mathbf{H}^{(k-1)}, \mathbf{D}_e^{(k-1)}, \mathbf{D}_v^{(k-1)}$ from $\mathcal{G}^{(k-1)}$;

  Compute $\Delta^{(k-1)}$ by Eq.(12) using $\mathbf{H}^{(k-1)}, \mathbf{D}_e^{(k-1)}, \mathbf{D}_v^{(k-1)}$;

  $\mathbf{R}^{(k)} \leftarrow (\mathbf{I} + \frac{1}{\lambda}\Delta^{(k-1)})^{-1}\mathbf{Y}$;

  $\hat{\mathbf{E}}^{(k)} \leftarrow F(\mathbf{R}^{(k)})$;

  if $||\hat{\mathbf{E}}^{(k)} - \hat{\mathbf{E}}^{(k-1)}||_2 < \varepsilon$ **then**

    break;

  end

  Update the hypergraph $\mathcal{G}^{(k)} = \langle\{\mathcal{U}, \mathcal{X}, \mathcal{S}\}, \mathcal{E}^{(k)}, \mathbf{W}^{(k)}\rangle$ based on the emotions of history image set $s^H_{\hat{\mathbf{E}}^{(k)}}$;

end

return $\hat{\mathbf{E}}^{(k)}$.

The vertex degree of vertex $v \in \mathcal{V}$ and the edge degree of hyperedge $e \in \mathcal{E}$ are defined as $d(v) = \sum_{e \in \mathcal{E}} w(e)h(v,e)$ and $\delta(e) = \sum_{v \in \mathcal{V}} h(v,e)$. According to $d(v)$ and $\delta(e)$, we define two diagonal matrices $\mathbf{D}_v$ and $\mathbf{D}_e$ as $\mathbf{D}_v(i,i) = d(v_i)$ and $\mathbf{D}_e(i,i) = \delta(e_i)$.

Given N users $u_1, \ldots, u_N$ and the related images, our objective is to explore the correlation among all involved images and the user relations. Suppose the training vertices and the training labels are $\{(u_1, x_{1j}, S_{1j})\}_{j=1}^{m_1}, \cdots, \{(u_N, x_{Nj}, S_{Nj})\}_{j=1}^{m_N}$, and $\mathbf{Y}_1 = [y_{11}, \cdots, y_{1m_1}]^{\mathrm{T}}, \ldots, \mathbf{Y}_N = [y_{N1}, \cdots, y_{Nm_N}]^{\mathrm{T}}$, and the to-be-estimated relevance values of all images related to the specified users are $\mathbf{R}_1 = [R_{11}, \cdots, R_{1m_1}]^{\mathrm{T}}, \ldots R_N = [R_{N1}, \cdots, \mathbf{R}_{Nm_N}]^{\mathrm{T}}$. We denote $\mathbf{Y}$ and $\mathbf{R}$ as

$$\mathbf{Y} = [\mathbf{Y}_1^{\mathrm{T}}, \cdots, \mathbf{Y}_N^{\mathrm{T}}]^{\mathrm{T}}, \mathbf{R} = [\mathbf{R}_1^{\mathrm{T}}, \cdots, \mathbf{R}_N^{\mathrm{T}}]^{\mathrm{T}}. \quad (7)$$

The proposed rolling multi-task learning can be conducted as a semi-supervised learning to minimize the empirical loss and the regularizer on the hypergraph structure simultaneously by

$$\arg\min_{\mathbf{R}}\{\Gamma + \lambda\Psi\}, \quad (8)$$

where λ is a trade-off parameter, Γ is the empirical loss defined by

$$\Gamma = ||\mathbf{R} - \mathbf{Y}||^2, \quad (9)$$

and Ψ is the regularizer on the hypergraph structure defined by

$$\Psi = \frac{1}{2}\sum_{e \in \mathcal{E}}\sum_{\mu,\nu \in \mathcal{V}} \frac{w(e)h(\mu,e)h(\nu,e)}{\delta(e)}\left(\frac{\mathbf{R}(\mu)}{\sqrt{\mathbf{D}_v(\mu,\mu)}} - \frac{\mathbf{R}(\nu)}{\sqrt{\mathbf{D}_v(\nu,\nu)}}\right)^2$$
$$= \mathbf{R}^{\mathrm{T}}(\mathbf{I} - \mathbf{D}_v^{-1/2}\mathbf{H}\mathbf{W}\mathbf{D}_e^{-1}\mathbf{H}^{\mathrm{T}}\mathbf{D}_v^{-1/2})\mathbf{R}. \quad (10)$$

By setting the derivative of Eq. (8) with respect to $\mathbf{R}$ to zero, we can derive the solution for the objective function Eq. (8)

$$\mathbf{R} = (\mathbf{I} + \frac{1}{\lambda}\Delta)^{-1}\mathbf{Y}, \quad (11)$$

where Δ is the hypergraph Laplacian [53, 9], defined as

$$\Delta = \mathbf{I} - \mathbf{D}_v^{-1/2}\mathbf{H}\mathbf{W}\mathbf{D}_e^{-1}\mathbf{H}^{\mathrm{T}}\mathbf{D}_v^{-1/2}. \quad (12)$$

By using the relevance scores in $\mathbf{R}$, we can rank the related images for each user. The top results with high relevance scores are assigned with related emotion category. Suppose the predicted results of the test images are $\hat{\mathbf{E}} = F(\mathbf{R})$ based on relevance score threshold function F, which is simply 'of top M results' [9, 8], where M is selected by the average F1. We can then iteratively update Eq. (11) until convergence, as shown in Algorithm 1. We call this method rolling multi-task hypgergraph learning, because it simultaneously classifies the emotions of a specified category for N users in a hypergraph framework and the learning process is iteratively updated.

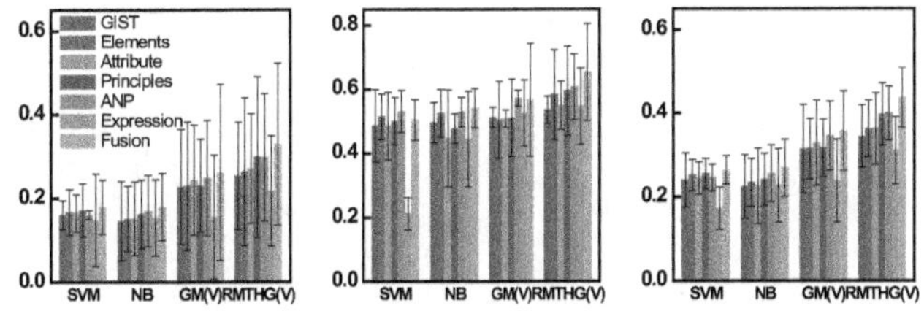

(a) Precision (b) Recall (c) F1

Figure 9: The average performance on different visual features of different methods for emotion classification.

7. EXPERIMENTS

To evaluate the effectiveness of the proposed RMTHG method for personalized image emotion prediction, we carried out emotion classification experiments on the IESN dataset. We also designed one novel application using the predicted emotions.

7.1 Experimental Settings

As users upload or comment on images in chronological order and the perceived emotions can be influenced temporally, we split the dataset into a training set and a test set based on the uploading time and the commenting time of related images. The first set covering 50% of images of each viewer is used for training and the rest is used for test. As there are about 8,000 users in the dataset, we randomly split them into 80 groups to facilitate fast computation and save memory. Each time we conduct experiments on one group and eventually we computed the average performance and the standard deviation of all experiments.

For emotion classification, we used three state-of-the-art classifiers as baselines: (1) Naive Bayes (NB), (2) Support Vector Machine (SVM) with RBF kernel, which are commonly used for traditional affective image classification in [21] and [20, 48], respectively, and (3) Graph Model (GM), which is used for personalized emotion prediction [41]. In GM, the social factors in [41] and our visual features are combined.

For emotion regression, we tested the performances of Support Vector Regression (SVR) as in [20, 48] and multiple linear regression (MLR). It is difficult for these methods to model features like social context, so we just used visual features. Different kernels were tested for emotion regression using SVR. How to effectively combine the different factors for emotion analysis in a regression framework remains our future work.

We used precision, recall and F1[5] as measurements to evaluate the emotion classification results, and mean squared error (MSE)[6] for emotion regression. All the four measurements range from 0 to 1. Higher values of precision, recall and F1 represent better performances for emotion classification, while lower MSE indicates better performance for emotion regression.

[5] http://en.wikipedia.org/wiki/Information_retrieval

[6] http://en.wikipedia.org/wiki/Mean_squared_error

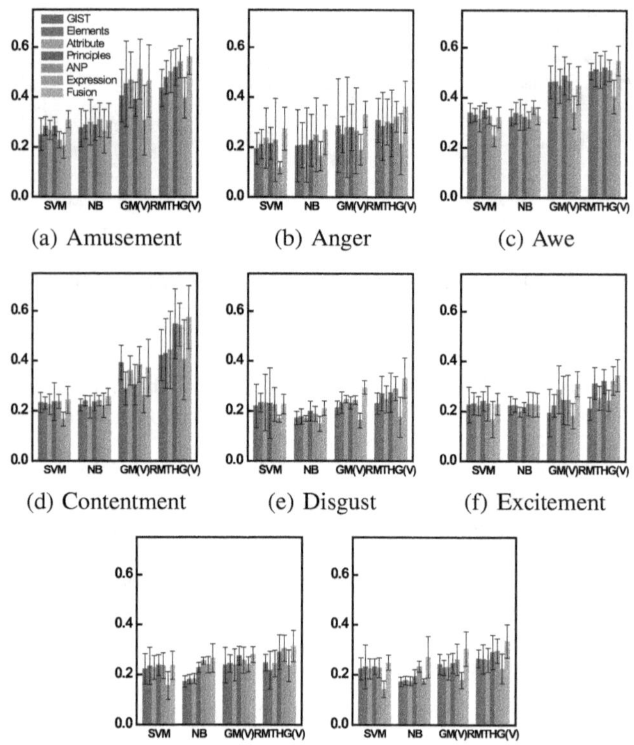

(a) Amusement (b) Anger (c) Awe
(d) Contentment (e) Disgust (f) Excitement
(g) Fear (h) Sadness

Figure 10: Performance comparison on F1 of 8 emotions using all the 4 methods and 7 kinds of features.

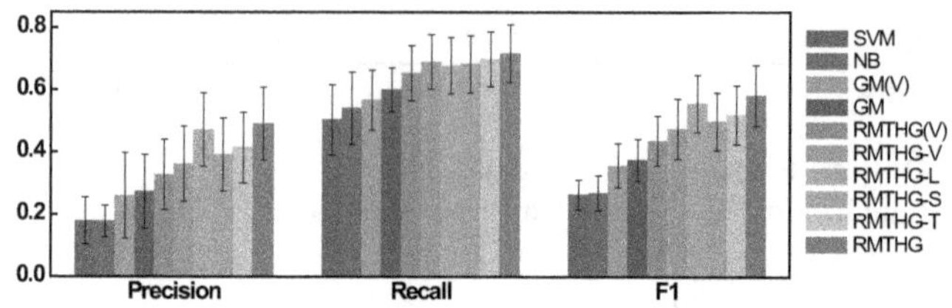

Figure 11: The average influence of different factors in the proposed method for emotion classification.

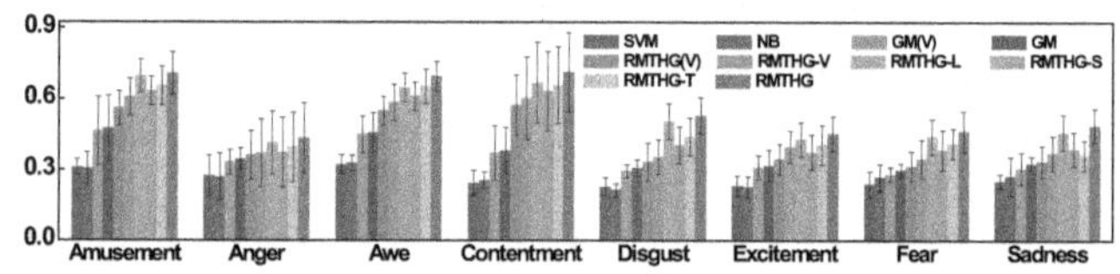

Figure 12: The influence of different factors in the proposed method on F1 of 8 emotions.

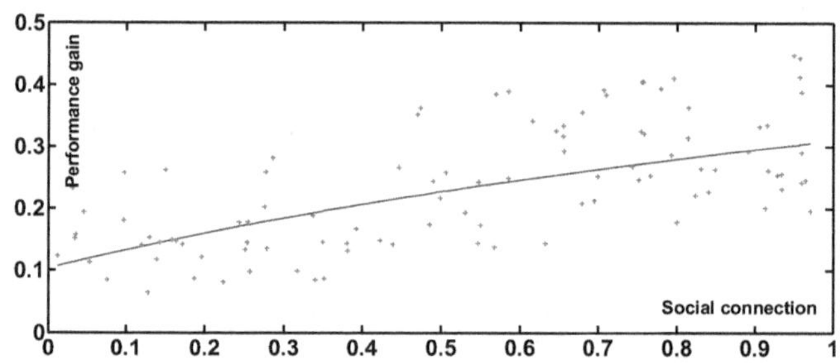

Figure 13: The performance improvement of social connection.

7.2 Personalized Emotion Classification

7.2.1 On Visual Features

First, we conducted experiments to compare the performance of different visual features for personalized emotion classification; and used SVM and NB as baselines. For comparison, we used a simple version of GM and RMTHG that consider only visual features, abbreviated as GM(V) and RMTHG(V). The average performances on emotion classification using different visual features and learning models are given in Figure 9. The performances of F1 for every emotion category are shown in Figure 10.

From the results, we can observe that: (1) generally, the fusion of different kinds of visual features outperforms the use of only single feature, possibly because it can utilize the advantages from different aspects; (2) the proposed hypergraph learning method greatly outperforms the baselines on almost all features; (3) for the 8 emotion categories, the most discriminative features are different; but overall the high-level and mid-level features have stronger discriminability than low-level ones, which is consistent with the conclusions in [52]; (4) the positive emotions are more accurately modelled than the negative ones by almost all the four methods; and (5) the overall precision, recall and F1 are still very low, indicating that only using visual features to classify personalized image emotions is not sufficient.

7.2.2 On Different Factors

Besides, we evaluated the influence of different factors in the proposed method. We computed the performance of the proposed method without visual content (RMTHG-V), without social context (RMTHG-S), without temporal evolution (RMTHG-T), and without location influence (RMTHG-L). RMTHG-T means that the history image sets of all vertices are empty. Here all the visual features are considered. Figure 11 shows the average performance on emotion classification, while Figure 12 presents the F1 performance for every emotion category. We can observe that: (1) by incorporating the various factors, the classification performance is greatly improved; compared to RMTHG(V), the improvement of RMTHG on precision, recall and F1 are 49.4%, 9.5% and 33.2%, respectively, which indicates that the social emotions are jointly affected by these factors; (2) for the GM method, the combination of the social factors in [41] can improve the performance, though the improvement is not that significant; and (3) the contributions of these factors to emotion perceptions are different; on average, the discriminability order of these factors is visual content > social context > temporal evolution > location influence.

7.2.3 Case Studies

Here we show some interesting cases to demonstrate the effectiveness of the proposed method. By leveraging the statistics on the performance improvement and different factor influences, we have the following discoveries.

The performance improvement in the prediction of negative emotions is higher than positive ones. Comparing the prediction results of RMTHG(V) and RMTHG in Figure 12, we can observe that when taking temporal evolution, social context and location influence into account, the performance of negative emotion classification improves more significantly than position ones. This observation means that these factors play a more important role in personalized perception of negative emotions, which indicates that the influence of negative emotions is likely to be stronger than pos-

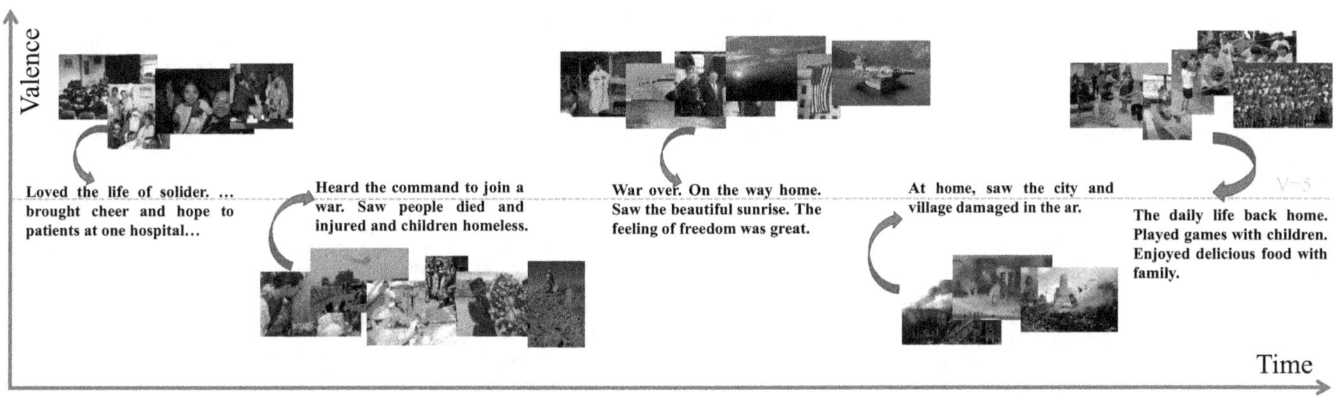

Figure 14: Emotion based image storyline for User A.

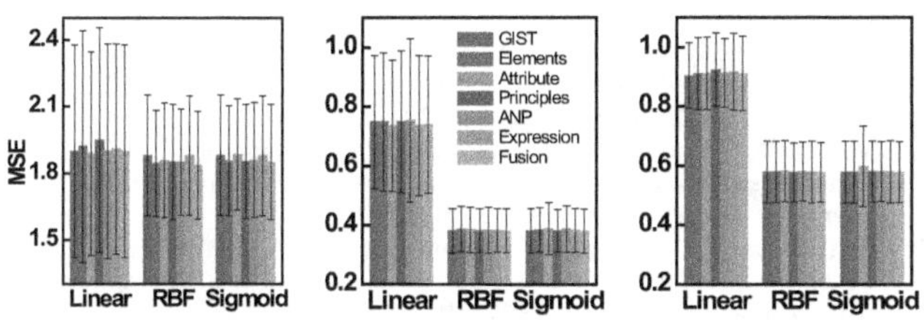

(a) Valence (b) Arousal (c) Dominance

Figure 15: Personalized emotion regression results.

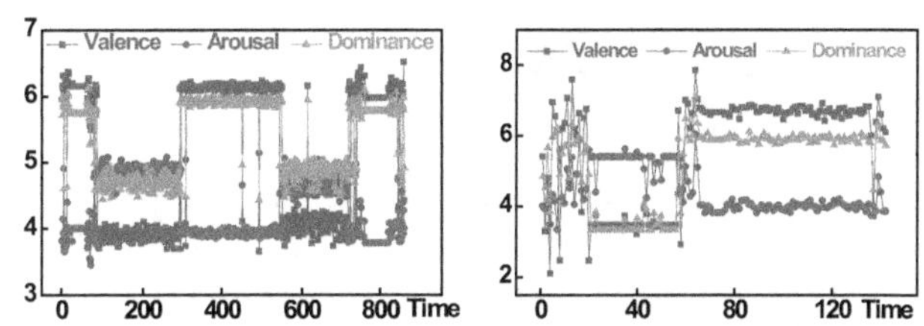

(a) User A (b) User B

Figure 16: Personalized affective curves.

itive ones. Similar conclusion can be obtained when comparing GM(V) and GM.

Sadness is one special category that the influence of temporal evolution is larger than social context. From Figure 12, it is easy to see that the performance gain of social context is larger than temporal evolution for all the 4 positive emotions and the 3 negative emotions of anger, disgust and fear, while it is the opposite for sadness emotion. This is probably because sadness tends to be a long lasting emotion [35]. So sadness requires one to make meaning of the event and cope with the new situation which takes time, while fear, disgust or awe following event offset often lacks purpose [35].

Stronger social connections tend to have more influences on performance improvement. We randomly selected 100 users from the dataset and collected the images they uploaded or commented together with various metadata. For each of the 100 users, we first obtained the average social similarity in the constructed hypergraph and then computed the performance gains with the help of social context. The relation is depicted in Figure 13. It seems that with the increase of social connections, the overall trend of performance gains is growing, which indicates that stronger social connections correlate with higher performance gains. This fact also demonstrates the basic hypothesis of social context's contribution to emotion perceptions.

7.3 Personalized Emotion Regression

MLR performs the worst with MSE much greater than 10, which indicates that the linear regression is not appropriate for emotion regression. The results of average MSE on valence, arousal and dominance using SVR are shown in Figure 15. It is clear that valence is regressed the worst, while arousal and dominance are relatively better predicted. SVR performs much better than MLR, which demonstrates its effectiveness on emotion regression. Besides, the RBF kernel works slightly better than Sigmoid kernel.

7.4 Application: Affective Curve Visualization

Given a specified user, we can predict the personalized emotion perceptions of the current image based on the proposed method, which simultaneously considers various factors, including visual content, social context, temporal evolution and location influence. We can then draw an affective curve for each user to learn about the process of their emotion changes. We use VAD models to represent both different dimensions of emotions for better visualization. By adding related images to the affective curve, we can clearly understand what emotion is perceived by the specified user and what kind of image causes this perception. Besides, by comparing the affective curves, we can also analyze whether this emotion is influenced by their friends and to what extent this emotion is influenced. Figure 16 shows two examples of visualized affective curves. We can observe that the perceived emotions of both users are relatively stable within a short time, which corroborates the hypothesis that the perceived emotions are temporally evolved. In such cases, we can construct emotion based image storyline for these users and concentrate on the turning point images to understand what causes each variation in emotion. Figure 14 shows the image storyline of User A together with the turning point images and corresponding behaviors. For clarity, we just use valence to represent the pleasantness of emotions. From this figure, we can clearly see the emotional status change of a solider before, in and after war.

8. CONCLUSION AND FUTURE WORK

In this paper, we proposed to predict personalized perceptions of image emotions by incorporating various factors (social context, temporal evolution, and location influence) with visual content. Rolling multi-task hypergraph learning was presented to jointly combine these factors. A large-scale personalized emotion dataset of social images was constructed and some baselines were provided. Experimental results on personalized emotion classification demonstrated that the performance of the proposed method is superior over the state-of-the-art approaches. The predicted personalized emotions can be used to develop various applications, such as affective curve visualization.

For further studies, we will try to model the different emotions in a multi-task learning framework to explore the emotion relations. Modelling social connections of users dynamically and considering interest prior by mining related personal profile may improve the performance of emotion prediction. How to extend the proposed method for personalized emotion regression is also worth studying.

9. ACKNOWLEDGMENTS

This work was supported by the National Natural Science Foundation of China (No. 61472103, 61402388, 61422210, 61373076) and Key Program (No. 61133003), and partially supported by the Singapore National Research Foundation under its International Research Centre @ Singapore Funding Initiative and administered by the IDM Programme Office.

10. REFERENCES

[1] S. Benini, L. Canini, and R. Leonardi. A connotative space for supporting movie affective recommendation. *IEEE Transactions on Multimedia*, 13(6):1356–1370, 2011.

[2] D. Borth, R. Ji, T. Chen, T. Breuel, and S.-F. Chang. Large-scale visual sentiment ontology and detectors using adjective noun pairs. In *ACM MM*, pages 223–232, 2013.

[3] J. Bu, S. Tan, C. Chen, C. Wang, H. Wu, L. Zhang, and X. He. Music recommendation by unified hypergraph: combining social media information and music content. In *ACM MM*, pages 391–400, 2010.

[4] T. Chen, F. X. Yu, J. Chen, Y. Cui, Y.-Y. Chen, and S.-F. Chang. Object-based visual sentiment concept analysis and application. In *ACM MM*, pages 367–376, 2014.

[5] Y.-Y. Chen, T. Chen, W. H. Hsu, H.-Y. M. Liao, and S.-F. Chang. Predicting viewer affective comments based on image content in social media. In *ICMR*, page 233, 2014.

[6] P. Cui, S. Jin, L. Yu, F. Wang, W. Zhu, and S. Yang. Cascading outbreak prediction in networks: a data-driven approach. In *SIGKDD*, pages 901–909, 2013.

[7] N. H. Frijda. *The emotions*. Cambridge University Press, 1986.

[8] Y. Gao, F. Wang, H. Luan, and T.-S. Chua. Brand data gathering from live social media streams. In *ICMR*, page 169, 2014.

[9] Y. Gao, M. Wang, D. Tao, R. Ji, and Q. Dai. 3-d object retrieval and recognition with hypergraph analysis. *IEEE Transactions on Image Processing*, 21(9):4290–4303, 2012.

[10] Y. Gao, S. Zhao, Y. Yang, and T.-S. Chua. Multimedia social event detection in microblog. In *MMM*, pages 269–281, 2015.

[11] K. A. Goyal and A. Sadasivam. A critical analysis of rational & emotional approaches in car selling. *International Journal of Business Research and Management*, 1(2):59–63, 2010.

[12] A. Hanjalic. Extracting moods from pictures and sounds: Towards truly personalized tv. *IEEE Signal Processing Magazine*, 23(2):90–100, 2006.

[13] A. Hanjalic and L.-Q. Xu. Affective video content representation and modeling. *IEEE Transactions on Multimedia*, 7(1):143–154, 2005.

[14] Y. Huang, Q. Liu, S. Zhang, and D. Metaxas. Image retrieval via probabilistic hypergraph ranking. In *CVPR*, pages 3376–3383, 2010.

[15] G. Irie, T. Satou, A. Kojima, T. Yamasaki, and K. Aizawa. Affective audio-visual words and latent topic driving model for realizing movie affective scene classification. *IEEE Transactions on Multimedia*, 12(6):523–535, 2010.

[16] J. Jia, S. Wu, X. Wang, P. Hu, L. Cai, and J. Tang. Can we understand van gogh's mood? learning to infer affects from images in social networks. In *ACM MM*, pages 857–860, 2012.

[17] D. Joshi, R. Datta, E. Fedorovskaya, Q. Luong, J. Z. Wang, J. Li, and J. Luo. Aesthetics and emotions in images. *IEEE Signal Processing Magazine*, 28(5):94–115, 2011.

[18] P. N. Juslin and P. Laukka. Expression, perception, and induction of musical emotions: A review and a questionnaire study of everyday listening. *Journal of New Music Research*, 33(3):217–238, 2004.

[19] B. Li, W. Xiong, W. Hu, and X. Ding. Context-aware affective images classification based on bilayer sparse representation. In *ACM MM*, pages 721–724, 2012.

[20] X. Lu, P. Suryanarayan, R. B. Adams Jr, J. Li, M. G. Newman, and J. Z. Wang. On shape and the computability of emotions. In *ACM MM*, pages 229–238, 2012.

[21] J. Machajdik and A. Hanbury. Affective image classification using features inspired by psychology and art theory. In *ACM MM*, pages 83–92, 2010.

[22] J. A. Mikels, B. L. Fredrickson, G. R. Larkin, C. M. Lindberg, S. J. Maglio, and P. A. Reuter-Lorenz. Emotional category data on images from the international affective picture system. *Behavior Research Methods*, 37(4):626–630, 2005.

[23] B. Pang and L. Lee. Opinion mining and sentiment analysis. *Information Retrieval*, 2(1-2):1–135, 2008.

[24] G. Patterson and J. Hays. Sun attribute database: Discovering, annotating, and recognizing scene attributes. In *CVPR*, pages 2751–2758, 2012.

[25] K.-C. Peng, A. Sadovnik, A. Gallagher, and T. Chen. A mixed bag of emotions: Model, predict, and transfer emotion distributions. In *CVPR*, pages 860–868, 2015.

[26] T. M. Rath and R. Manmatha. Word image matching using dynamic time warping. In *CVPR*, pages 521–527, 2003.

[27] T. Reuter, P. Cimiano, L. Drumond, K. Buza, and L. Schmidt-Thieme. Scalable event-based clustering of social media via record linkage techniques. In *ICWSM*, 2011.

[28] K. R. Scherer. What are emotions? and how can they be measured? *Social Science Information*, 44(4):695–729, 2005.

[29] H. Schlosberg. Three dimensions of emotion. *Psychological Review*, 61(2):81, 1954.

[30] S. Siersdorfer, E. Minack, F. Deng, and J. Hare. Analyzing and predicting sentiment of images on the social web. In *ACM MM*, pages 715–718, 2010.

[31] R. C. Solomon. *The passions: Emotions and the meaning of life*. Hackett Publishing, 1993.

[32] J. Tang, Y. Zhang, J. Sun, J. Rao, W. Yu, Y. Chen, and A. C. M. Fong. Quantitative study of individual emotional states in social networks. *IEEE Transactions on Affective Computing*, 3(2):132–144, 2012.

[33] M. Tkalčič, U. Burnik, and A. Košir. Using affective parameters in a content-based recommender system for images. *User Modeling and User-Adapted Interaction*, 20(4):279–311, 2010.

[34] A. Tumasjan, T. O. Sprenger, P. G. Sandner, and I. M. Welpe. Predicting elections with twitter: What 140 characters reveal about political sentiment. In *ICWSM*, volume 10, pages 178–185, 2010.

[35] P. Verduyn and S. Lavrijsen. Which emotions last longest and why: The role of event importance and rumination. *Motivation and Emotion*, 39(1):119–127, 2015.

[36] M. Wang, X.-S. Hua, R. Hong, J. Tang, G.-J. Qi, and Y. Song. Unified video annotation via multigraph learning. *IEEE Transactions on Circuits and Systems for Video Technology*, 19(5):733–746, 2009.

[37] W.-n. Wang, Y.-l. Yu, and S.-m. Jiang. Image retrieval by emotional semantics: A study of emotional space and feature extraction. In *IEEE SMC*, pages 3534–3539, 2006.

[38] A. B. Warriner, V. Kuperman, and M. Brysbaert. Norms of valence, arousal, and dominance for 13,915 english lemmas. *Behavior Research Methods*, 45(4):1191–1207, 2013.

[39] J. Whitfield. The secret of happiness: grinning on the internet. *Nature*, 26, 2008.

[40] P. Yang, Q. Liu, and D. N. Metaxas. Exploring facial expressions with compositional features. In *CVPR*, pages 2638–2644, 2010.

[41] Y. Yang, P. Cui, W. Zhu, and S. Yang. User interest and social influence based emotion prediction for individuals. In *ACM MM*, pages 785–788, 2013.

[42] Y. Yang, P. Cui, W. Zhu, H. V. Zhao, Y. Shi, and S. Yang. Emotionally representative image discovery for social events. In *ICMR*, page 177, 2014.

[43] Y. Yang, J. Jia, S. Zhang, B. Wu, Q. Chen, J. Li, C. Xing, and J. Tang. How do your friends on social media disclose your emotions? In *AAAI*, pages 306–312, 2014.

[44] V. Yanulevskaya, J. Van Gemert, K. Roth, A.-K. Herbold, N. Sebe, and J.-M. Geusebroek. Emotional valence categorization using holistic image features. In *ICIP*, pages 101–104, 2008.

[45] Q. You, J. Luo, H. Jin, and J. Yang. Robust image sentiment analysis using progressively trained and domain transferred deep networks. In *AAAI*, pages 381–388, 2015.

[46] J. Yuan, S. Mcdonough, Q. You, and J. Luo. Sentribute: image sentiment analysis from a mid-level perspective. In *WISDOM*, page 10, 2013.

[47] H. Zhang, X. Shang, W. Yang, H. Xu, H. Luan, and T.-S. Chua. Online collaborative learning for open-vocabulary visual classifiers. In *CVPR*, pages 2809–2817, 2016.

[48] S. Zhao, Y. Gao, X. Jiang, H. Yao, T.-S. Chua, and X. Sun. Exploring principles-of-art features for image emotion recognition. In *ACM MM*, pages 47–56, 2014.

[49] S. Zhao, H. Yao, and X. Jiang. Predicting continuous probability distribution of image emotions in valence-arousal space. In *ACM MM*, pages 879–882, 2015.

[50] S. Zhao, H. Yao, X. Jiang, and X. Sun. Predicting discrete probability distribution of image emotions. In *ICIP*, pages 2459–2463, 2015.

[51] S. Zhao, H. Yao, and X. Sun. Video classification and recommendation based on affective analysis of viewers. *Neurocomputing*, 119:101–110, 2013.

[52] S. Zhao, H. Yao, Y. Yang, and Y. Zhang. Affective image retrieval via multi-graph learning. In *ACM MM*, pages 1025–1028, 2014.

[53] D. Zhou, J. Huang, and B. Schölkopf. Learning with hypergraphs: Clustering, classification, and embedding. In *NIPS*, pages 1601–1608, 2006.

StressClick: Sensing Stress from Gaze-Click Patterns

Michael Xuelin Huang, Jiajia Li, Grace Ngai, Hong Va Leong
CHI Lab, Department of Computing
Hong Kong Polytechnic University
Hong Kong, China
{csxhuang,csjjli,csgngai,cshleong}@comp.polyu.edu.hk

ABSTRACT
Stress sensing is valuable in many applications, including online learning crowdsourcing and other daily human-computer interactions. Traditional affective computing techniques investigate affect inference based on different individual modalities, such as facial expression, vocal tones, and physiological signals or the aggregation of signals of these independent modalities, without explicitly exploiting their inter-connections. In contrast, this paper focuses on exploring the impact of mental stress on the coordination between two human nervous systems, the somatic and autonomic nervous systems. Specifically, we present the analysis of the subtle but indicative pattern of human gaze behaviors surrounding a mouse-click event, i.e. the *gaze-click pattern*. Our evaluation shows that mental stress affects the gaze-click pattern, and this influence has largely been ignored in previous work. This paper, therefore, further proposes a non-intrusive approach to inferring human stress level based on the gaze-click pattern, using only data collected from the common computer webcam and mouse. We conducted a human study on solving math questions under different stress levels to explore the validity of stress recognition based on this coordination pattern. Experimental results show the effectiveness of our technique and the generalizability of the proposed features for user-independent modeling. Our results suggest that it may be possible to detect stress non-intrusively in the wild, without the need for specialized equipment.

General Terms
Experimentation, Human Factors.

Keywords
Gaze-click pattern; stress detection; cross-modal feature.

1. INTRODUCTION
Mental stress occurs when the cognitive load of a task exceeds the cognitive capacity of the person performing it [22]. There is growing recognition that advances in technology and society have led to new challenges and pressures, which in turn have increased the level of mental stress experienced in daily life [32]. This stress has been linked to numerous physical and mental problems [2], including agitation, anxiety, cardiovascular diseases, diabetes, and even cancer. Thus, there is growing awareness of the importance of regulating and intervening acute and chronic stress [32]. This suggests a pressing need for non-intrusive and automated techniques that monitor stress levels continuously and implicitly, thereby enhancing early self-awareness of mental stress.

In spite of the clinical success of stress understanding through self-report and questionnaires [7], these methods are intrusive and subjective. Conventional objective techniques that measure stress rely on physiological signals, such as galvanic skin response, pupil dilation and heart rate variability [26][27][35][37]. However, the relationship between physiological signals and human mental states can be influenced by multiple variables, including stimulus specificity, individual specificity, or even initial mental/physical state [3]. In addition, the intrusiveness and special equipment that would be required by these approaches discourage the wide use of physiology-based stress detection *in-situ*.

Non-intrusive stress detection has also been explored. Visual cues such as facial expression [11] and body movement [1], and audio information such as vocal tone [25], have been investigated for stress inference. However, these signals are sensitive to noise and are highly person-dependent. In addition, given the subtleness of stress displays in the visual and audio channels, the indicative signals can be easily overwhelmed by environmental variability.

An alternative approach for stress detection uses information from daily input devices, *i.e.* keyboard and mouse [4][34][36]. There has been some effort into combining these daily interactional cues with visual features [23] and other contextual information, such as weather and personality [5]. The non-intrusiveness of these techniques makes it possible to perform stress monitoring in normal computer use environment.

However, to the best of our knowledge, most approaches in multimodal stress detection perform a simple combination of the modalities. Some concatenate features from different modalities into one feature vector for modeling, or train a predictive model for each modality and aggregate the predictions for the final decision. There is little work that explicitly considers the temporal interconnection between different modalities.

Psychophysiological studies show that the central nervous system controls the human gaze and the somatic nervous system controls the mouse-click behavior. These nervous systems are directly or indirectly associated with the autonomic nervous system that controls the release of stress hormones [32]. Studies have also shown that mental stress impacts muscular tension [26][35][37]. Therefore, we hypothesize that stress similarly affects the gaze-click pattern. This paper then proposes to discover cross-modal features that describe the coordination between eye gaze behavior and mouse-click in human-computer interaction contexts.

In previous work, Huang et al. [19] has been successful in using webcam signals to identify the moment of gaze and click alignment. Therefore, we postulate that informative gaze-click behaviors can also be extracted from webcam signals and adopted to infer stress level. If this is successful, it ensures the applicability of our work as a non-intrusive mode of data collection that is invisible to the

MM '16, October 15-19, 2016, Amsterdam, Netherlands.
© 2016 ACM. ISBN 978-1-4503-3603-1/16/10…$15.00.
DOI: http://dx.doi.org/10.1145/2964284.2964318

user, and which does not rely on any gaze point estimation or special equipment.

The contribution of this paper is twofold:

- We present an in-depth behavior analysis that corroborates our hypothesis that stress affects the gaze-click pattern. This impact of stress has been neglected in previous gaze-cursor studies, and may be able to explain the conflicting results from prior human subject empirical studies.
- We develop cross-modal features that describe the gaze-click pattern and exploit them for stress detection in a non-intrusive manner. This approach is promising for automated stress detection in the wild.

2. RELATED WORK

Affective computing has attracted considerable attention recently. This section starts with an overview of automated stress recognition techniques, followed by recent research efforts on non-intrusive stress detection in daily computer interaction scenarios. We then discuss the cross-modal features and gaze-hand coordination studies that motivate this research work.

2.1 Automated Stress Detection

Prior research has investigated automated stress detection based on different modalities, such as visual, audio, and physiological signals. Dinges et al. [11] explored facial stress monitoring for astronauts based on face tracking. Aigrain et al. [1] explored the combination of facial expression and body posture to infer stress. Lu et al. [25] leveraged voice in real-life conversation to detect stress. Although facial expression and speech analysis are two prevalent modalities for automated affect detection in the field of affective computing [41], these approaches are susceptible to variabilities and not always applicable. For instance, facial affect detection is easily affected by pose variation and environmental illumination. Accurate speech analysis depends on the sound quality, which is not always available in real-use environments, and on contexts in which the person is speaking.

Healey and Picard [14] used multiple channels of physiological signals to detect stress of drivers, including electrocardiogram, electromyogram, skin conductance, and respiration. However, the reliable measurement of physiological signals relies on specialized devices. In addition, physiological sensing devices normally require sensors to be attached to the human body, which in real-use is prone to various artifacts, such as pressure or touch condition, among others, which are described in recent surveys on stress detection [2][32].

2.2 Stress Detection from Daily Human-Computer Interactions

Studies of psychological and ergonomic research have explored the impact of stress on human behaviors and reactions during human-computer interaction. Hernandez et al. [15] used special pressure-sensitive equipment to investigate the keyboard and mouse usage behaviors under different stressed conditions. They affirm that people in stress tend to have an increased typing force and mouse handling contact. Lundberg et al. [26] point out that mental stress increases the muscular tension given different stressors. Wahlstrom et al. [37] studied the psychological effect of mental stress on mouse usage. They confirm that time pressure increases the subjects' psychological and physiological reactions, and this effect results in high tensions in neck, shoulder and arm muscles. Visser et al. [35] also showed that mental pressure has substantial effects on muscular tension, notably on the wrist muscle, which increases mouse grip- and click- forces, and affects the mouse-targeting tempo.

Given the strong association between mental stress and muscular system, researchers have sought to estimate the level of stress in an automated and non-intrusive manner. Sun et al. [34] suggest that stress can be measured by the "stiffness" of mouse movement trajectory. In this sense, the manifestation of stress can be estimated by the parameters of a mass-spring-damper model that matches the mouse movement.

Keystroke behaviors have also been explored for affect recognition. Epp et al. [12] identified multiple emotional states from typing rhythms of single keystrokes, digraphs, and trigraphs. Bixler and D'Mello [4] analyzed the keystroke dynamics in conjunction with the self-reported task appraisal and user traits to infer the level of engagement and boredom. Vizer et al. [36] investigated stress detection through keystroke timing, frequency and linguistic features. These non-intrusive approaches make it possible to do universally accessible, long-term monitoring of stress in the wild. However, these approaches consider the impact of stress on a single modality (keypress or mouse usage) alone.

2.3 Multimodal and Cross-Modal Stress Detection

Multimodal approaches have been deployed for affect recognition. Koldijk et al. [21] developed a dataset of desktop usage scenarios for stress analysis. Subjects were asked to perform typical knowledge-based tasks (e.g. writing reports) and multimodal signals were collected, including facial expression, body posture, keystroke and mouse dynamics, heart rate and skin conductance. Bogomolov et al. [5] explored stress detection on the smart phone platform, by conjunctively considering the smart phone activities, weather, and personal trait. Their results show the advantage of a model that uses all multimodal information, compared to those of using a single or even pairwise modalities.

In affective computing, feature- and decision- level fusion are frequently employed in multimodal recognition systems [2][41]. Feature-level fusion concatenates features from multimodalities and feeds them into a classifier. Liao et al. [23] combined the visual and physiological features in a Dynamic Bayesian Network for stress detection. Decision-level fusion models unimodal cues independently and then aggregates their results. For example, Celiktutan and Gunes [8] applied Bidirectional Long Short-Term Memory Networks to aggregate the predictions of individual classifiers that use visual and audio features, respectively. However, the vast majority of prior multimodal techniques perform information fusion between multimodal signals within the same temporal sampling period and seldom consider features from different modalities across multiple time frames, or explicitly develop features that describe such temporal relationships between different modalities. In other words, there is little work that investigates the coordination between modalities. Our method, in contrast, focuses on cross-modal features for stress inference. Our specific concern is the gaze behaviors surrounding every mouse-click event.

2.4 Gaze-Hand Coordination

Gaze-hand coordination is important for daily human-computer interaction. This generally includes gaze-type and gaze-cursor coordination. Inhoff and Gordon [20] reported that gaze is most likely to be 4 characters to the right of the last typed character during copy typing. However, this span can vary across different factors, such as typing task and skill. Xu et al. [40] proposed to use keypress location with interface component information and mouse trajectory for gaze estimation.

Gaze-cursor coordination is a perennially popular topic of study, especially for web browsing behaviors. Chen et al. [10] suggest that there is a strong correlation between gaze and saccade-like mouse movement. Rodden et al. [29] demonstrated a strong correlation in gaze-cursor alignment during active mouse usages, such as using the cursor as a reading aid (in both horizontal and vertical directions) and to mark particular results. Although a prevalent belief suggests that "gaze is well approximated by cursor", this has been shown to not always be the case [16]. Huang et al. [17] found that correlation does exist between gaze and cursor position, but with substantial variation across contexts and target types. Smucker et al. [33] reported that gaze-cursor coordination is weak and it varies across search topics. Huang et al. [18] discovered that the alignment between gaze and interaction (cursor or caret) varies from individuals and activities in daily interactions. Similarly, Liebling et al. [24] showed that gaze-cursor coordination contains complex and nuanced characteristics in real-life scenarios.

These conflicting views suggest that some important hidden factors may have been overlooked in previous research on gaze-cursor pattern analysis. Despite the fact that both gaze and cursor information can be non-intrusively accessed in common computer setups, and the plethora of studies on this topic, no prior work has explored the impact of stress on gaze-click behavior.

3. CONSTRUCTING A GAZE-CLICK DATASET

The first task in our study is to build a dataset that reliably captures human interactive behavior in stress and non-stress conditions under conditions that are comparable. Stress may well interleave with interest, attention and workload. It is difficult to fully separate or clearly define such mental state(s), due to the complexity of human affect. Since we intend to investigate the relation between gaze-click pattern and stress, our experiment will have to be designed to eliminate other possible biases.

Prior studies show that recursive mental math calculation [1][26][34][36] and time pressure [21][37] are effective in inducing cognitive stress. We therefore select a math calculation task for evaluation.

Figure 1 shows the experimental interface. Two automatically-generated math expressions are displayed. The subject is asked to calculate the result of these two expressions, and determine which (if either) is greater. Pressing the "show" button displays the answer buttons (">", "=" and "<"), which are randomly positioned each time a new question is generated. This additional step ensures that the subject's gaze and mouse movement will start from the "show" button and move towards one of the answer buttons. To investigate the influence of the click target attributes, the answer buttons can be varied (diameter: 70, 120 pixels) as well as their distances to the "show" button (450, 700 pixels) between different experiment sessions.

An image of the subject's face and eyes is captured by a normal webcam placed on the top center of the monitor. The relevant gaze information will be extracted from this video feed. Huang et al. [18] show that the temporal variation of gaze behavior with respect to interaction target usually occurs within a second of the interaction event. We therefore logged the gaze data in the 2 seconds preceding and 1 second after a click on the answer buttons for analysis.

Our dataset will use math as a common stressor, but we need to vary the stress level. This is done by varying the difficulty of the math expressions. Our experiment looks at two distinct states: calm and stress. The calm session involves twenty 1-digit addition and subtraction questions. This is adjusted to 2-digit math for the stress session. To ensure the difficulty of the task, the numeric difference between the results of the two expressions is constrained to be no more than 10. To further induce stress, a countdown time bar is added to the bottom of the interface during the stress sessions. If the subject fails to answer within the allotted time, the interface advances automatically to the next question.

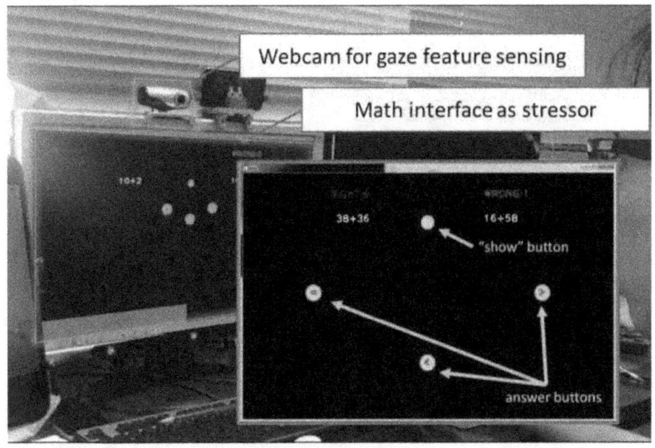

Figure 1. Experiment environment. A common webcam is used to sense the eye features. The math interface serving as the stressor is displayed in maximized mode.

To allow for differences in math aptitude and to familiarize subjects with the interface, the experiment starts with a short calibration session. Subjects are asked to complete a number of 2-digit questions as quickly as they can. The time spent on each question is recorded. The mean plus 2 standard deviations of the time taken to finish a question is taken as the time constraint for the stress induction session. Assuming that speed can be well approximated by a Gaussian distribution, this ensures that all subjects should have just enough time to finish most of the questions while still ensuring a somewhat stressful experience.

Since human subjects are prone to fatigue and boredom, it is also necessary to control the subjects' attention/engagement by constraining the length of the experiment. We keep the questions at a constant difficulty and the sessions are short. Analysis of the data does not exhibit a peak-end effect. To consider the impact from Fitts's law, the design of our experiment involves three factors (stress level, size and distance of the click target), with two levels for each factor. Our experiment therefore contains 2×2×2 sessions, each of which has a different factor combination. There are 25 questions per session, and the subject is asked to report his/her level of stress on a 9-point scale at the end of each session. The score>=5 were annotated as "stress" and the rest as "calm".

Finally, we need to ensure that each set of experiments starts from a common base point with respect to stress level. Therefore, at the beginning of the experiment, and after each session of 25 questions, the subject is asked to take a break (~10min) to calm down before beginning the next session (~2min).

We recruited 20 subjects (13 males, aged 20-33) for our study. A standard off-the-shelf webcam is used to capture the visual signal (resolution 640×480; 30fps) and a 22" monitor at 1680×1050 resolution displays the math interface in full screen mode. Removing the questions that the subjects fail to answer (<5%) in time gives us a total of 3818 click points over all subjects.

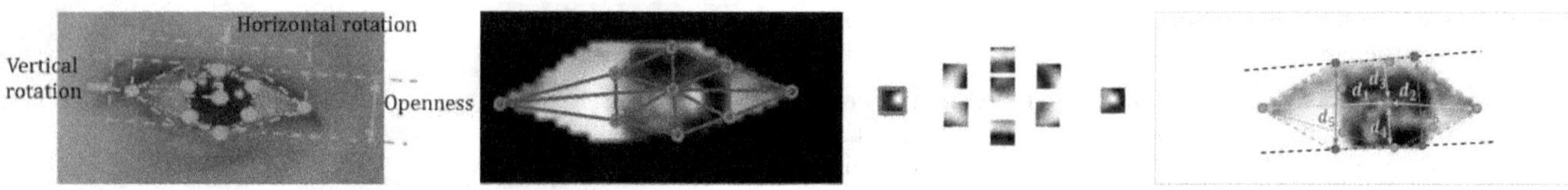

(a) (b) (c) (d)

Figure 2. (a) Illustration of the eye features: openness, horizontal and vertical rotation. The eye-tracking model tracks eye landmarks in green, and the face-tracking model tracks the landmarks in red. Both models track the two corner points; (b) Eye landmark annotation of an eye image; (c) The patch models of the corresponding eye landmarks; (d) A masked eye image. The eye features are measured by the geometry of the facial and eye landmarks in the eye image.

Inspecting the data, we note that the self-reported stress level (on a 9-point scale) has a marked difference between the 1-digit section (M=2.10, SD=1.09) and the 2-digit section (M=7.28, SD=0.94). This difference confirms that the experiments are successful at inducing stress during the appropriate sessions.

4. EXTRACTING GAZE-CLICK PATTERN

Our method uses a standard webcam to capture video of the user's head and shoulders. To ensure that we can accurately deduce the gaze behavior of the subject from this video, we use two tracking models to identify the face and eye landmarks from the frames of the video stream, respectively. These landmarks are then piped as input to a two-layer feature extraction mechanism. The first layer continuously extracts six *eye features* from the changes of the eye-related landmarks. The second layer is triggered by each mouse-click event, whereupon it extracts eight *gaze-click features* based on the eye feature signals in the 3-second time window surrounding the click.

4.1 Extracting Six Eye Features

This section introduces the six eye features that describe the essential eye geometry of each frame, including the openness, horizontal and vertical rotation of both eyes (see Figure 2-a).

These eye features are measured according to the facial and eye landmarks. To obtain accurate locations of the facial landmarks, we employ the Supervised Descent Method (SDM) [39] to track 48 facial landmarks. Since the SDM model tracks landmarks based on both textures of the landmarks' local patches and their geometry inter-dependency, it performs robustly against illumination influences and gives reliable landmarks that describes the eye contour (see the red landmarks in Figure 2-a).

In order to obtain an accurate description of eye geometry, it is crucial that the pupil center be properly located. However, in unconstrained situations, the appearance information of the eye region often has no clear cue of the pupil center. Additionally, we observe that in real-use scenarios, low video resolution and reflections on glasses and cornea usually makes the region of the pupil and its periphery unobservable. As a result, simple techniques based on image texture or edge often fail to reliably track the pupil center.

To mitigate the localization issues caused by the unconstrained environment and noisy images with low resolution, we use eye geometry to estimate the pupil center. The general idea is to track landmarks with good salient features on the iris contour and eye lid corners, and deduce the pupil center locations based on their geometric interdependency. We therefore apply eye CLMs [31] to track the eye landmarks, including the pupil center. Unlike the 28-landmark model in [38], our eye models use only 9 landmarks, as shown in Figure 2-b. Given the low resolution and blurred image in real-use, we believe only those fiducial points with the most salient features can facilitate tracking. Besides, reducing the number of tracking landmarks can decrease the model complexity, which is highly favorable for real-time systems.

We manually annotated 3000 eye images from 5 people (not from the StressClick subjects), and used this data to train the eye tracking model. The resulting patch models are shown in Figure 2-c. It is surprising that the pupil center patch learnt from our annotated data shows edge-like pattern, which may be caused by reflections. This supports our hypothesis that additional landmarks inside the iris region may not help the reliable tracking.

Table 1. Description and mental state implication of gaze-click patterns extracted from the eye features and used in this work. All features are calculated relative to a given mouse click.

Index	Feature description	Mental state implication
g_1	Existence of a fixation in the 0.5s period preceding a click	Level of visual attention to click target
g_2	Duration of the fixation corresponding to a click	
g_3	Reaction Latency – duration of time in which eye remains fixated after the corresponding mouse click	Reaction latency of moving to the next task
g_4	Click Latency – duration of time between gaze moving away from target and corresponding mouse click	"Hastiness" of the user in locating the next target.
g_5	Max gaze velocity between the fixation corresponding to the mouse click and the fixation before it.	"Hastiness" of the user in locating the current target
g_6	Duration between the fixation corresponding to the mouse click and the fixation before it.	
g_7	Max gaze velocity between the fixation corresponding to the mouse click and the fixation after it.	"Hastiness" of the user in locating the next target.
g_8	Duration between the fixation corresponding to the mouse click and the fixation before it.	

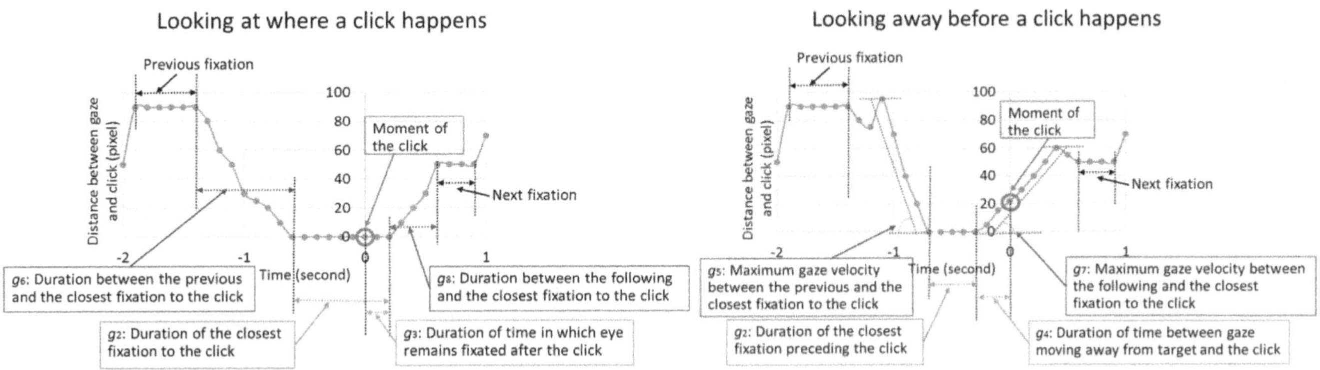

Figure 3. Illustrations of the features that describe the gaze-click pattern. The x-axis indicates the time relative to the click event. The y-axis indicates the difference between eye gaze and click position. (Left) The user is looking at the click location at the moment of the click, and (right) he/she has looked away before the click happens.

To validate the eye tracking state, we apply a robust but rough tracking model that uses the integral image [28] to approximate the pupil center from the eye image, with the assumption that the darkest rectangular area is the iris. If the CLM estimation is too distant (>half of the distance between the upper and lower eyelids) from the integral image approximation, we assume that the CLM tracking has failed and we redetect the eye for tracking.

Based on the landmarks identified from the face and the eye trackers, we extract eye features $\boldsymbol{e}_r, \boldsymbol{e}_l$ from the right and left eye respectively. Each $\boldsymbol{e}$ is calculated according to the eye landmark distances shown in Figure 2-d:

$$\boldsymbol{e} = \langle \alpha(d_5 + d_6), \frac{d_1}{d_1 + d_2}, \frac{d_3}{d_3 + d_4} \rangle \qquad (1)$$

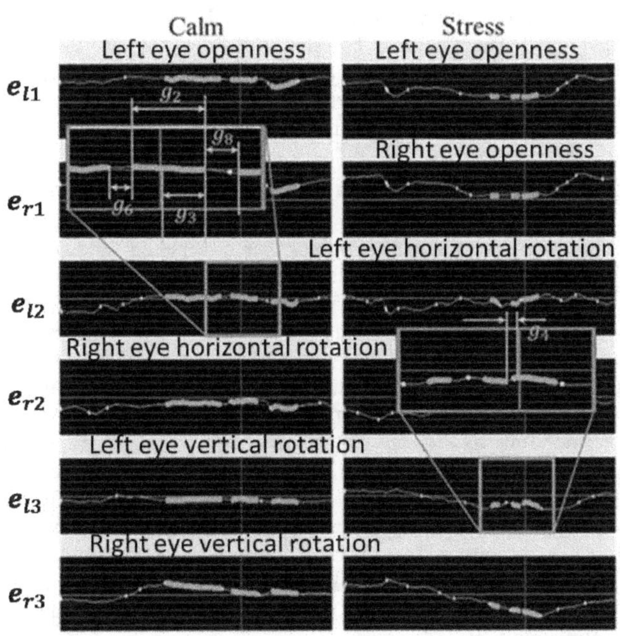

Figure 4. Example eye features from the 3-second window surrounding a mouse click during calm (left) and stressed (right) conditions. The red vertical line indicates the moment of the click, the 3 fixations nearest to the click are highlighted in pink.

where α is a constant scale factor that bounds the value of the eye openness feature range within [0,1).

4.2 Identifying Eight Gaze-Click Features

To understand the gaze movement pattern, which can be indicative of mental stress and in the meanwhile observable from the webcam signal, we propose eight potentially useful gaze-click features. These features describe the type, duration and velocity of the gaze movements within a *gaze-click window* 2 seconds preceding and 1 second after a click event.

We calculate the gaze-click features based on the temporal changes of the eye features $\boldsymbol{e}_r$ and $\boldsymbol{e}_l$ within the gaze-click window. The gaze-click features are all defined with respect to a mouse click and describe the gaze pattern preceding (g_4, g_5, g_6), during (g_1, g_2), and after (g_3, g_7, g_8) the click event. Table 1 shows the description of each gaze-click feature and the implied mental state.

Figure 3 illustrates the gaze-click features describing temporal durations within the 3-second window surrounding a mouse click. The x-axis indicates the time prior to (negative) and after (positive) the mouse click. The y-axis indicates the distance between the actual gaze point and the location of the click. A distance of zero indicates overlap between the eye gaze point and the click location. Similarly, a positive distance means a fixation somewhere else. Since most of our features investigate the fixations and non-fixations surrounding a click, it is worth noting that in the absolute majority (95%) of the cases in our dataset, there is indeed a fixation during (Figure 3, left) or shortly preceding a click (Figure 3, right).

Figure 4 shows some annotated examples of gaze-click patterns under both calm and stressed conditions. Some of the gaze-click pattern features are magnified for illustration (in blue frames). It is interesting to note that under stressed conditions, the user's gaze often shifts away from the fixation point *before* he/she clicks on it ("stressed" column, e.g. Figure 4, 5th row). To accommodate this phenomena, we define the fixation corresponding to a click as the fixation that starts at least 80ms (a minimal fixation duration [13]) before the click occurs. Only in cases where such a fixation does not exist is the corresponding fixation defined as the closest fixation immediately preceding the click.

To compensate for visual noise in the raw eye signals (i.e. sequences of eye features) and the uneven sampling rate, we first resample the eye feature temporal sequences by interpolating them to 100Hz. We then apply band-pass filtering to remove the

Table 2. Correlations between the gaze-click features and the stress level, click distance, and target size.

	g_1	g_2	g_3	g_4	g_5	g_6	g_7	g_8
Calm/Stress	-0.04	-0.35	-0.26	0.09	0.16	0.14	0.03	0.04
Click distance	-0.06	-0.05	-0.05	0.12	0.04	0.05	0.03	0.08
Click target size	0.01	-0.06	-0.03	-0.01	0.09	0.03	0.03	0.01

unnatural high frequency noise. The filtered signal of the *i-th* eye feature is calculated as

$$\hat{f}_i = \mathcal{F}^{-1}[\mathcal{F}(f_i) * \Omega(\omega)] \quad (2)$$

where $\mathcal{F}$ and $\mathcal{F}^{-1}$ indicate the one-dimensional forward and inverse Discrete Fourier transform, respectively, and the filter

$$\Omega(\omega) = \begin{cases} 1, & \omega \leq \omega_h \\ 0, & otherwise \end{cases} \quad (3)$$

where ω_h (=2.5Hz as in [19]) is the cutoff frequency. Given the eye feature signal $\boldsymbol{F} \in \Re^{m \times n}$, where m(=300) is the number of data points in a 3-second gaze-click window and n(=6) the number of eye-related features, we identify the fixation periods using the dispersion-based approach [30]. All the signals in a fixation period (FP) (>80ms) should be subject to the condition:

$$\max(\hat{f}_i^{FP}) - \min(\hat{f}_i^{FP}) < \xi \quad (4)$$

where $\hat{f}_i^{FP}$ represents the *i-th* eye feature in a fixation period and ξ is the fixation threshold.

To quantify the degree of "hastiness" on the part of the user, we calculate the maximum *gaze velocity* between two fixations as the sum of the maximum slope of each eye signal during the non-fixation period (NFP):

$$\beta \sum_{i=1}^{n} (\max(\hat{f}_i^{NFP}) - \min(\hat{f}_i^{NFP}))/\Delta t_i \quad (5)$$

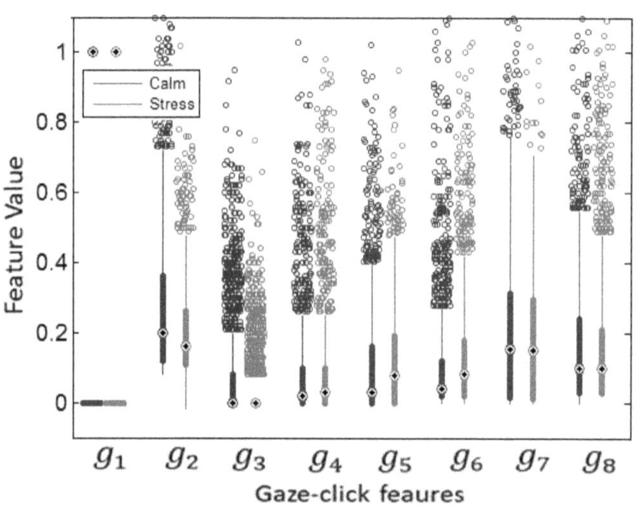

Figure 5. Box plot of the gaze-click features under the calm and stressed conditions. The central mark is the median, the thick bar covers the 25th and 75th percentiles and the thin line extends to the most extreme data points not considered outliers, and outliers are plotted individually in circles.

where Δt_i is the time elapsed between two data points at the maximum and minimum moments. β is a constant scale factor which normalizes the value of this velocity feature such that it lies within [0,1) and is comparable with the gaze-click features depicting temporal duration.

5. EXPERIMENTAL EVALUATION

5.1 Understanding Gaze-Click Behavior under Calm and Stressed Conditions

Replacing the calm and stress labels with numeric "0" and "1" to represent the stress level, allows us to calculate the correlation between the gaze-click features and the experiment independent factors. Table 2 gives the correlations between the gaze-click features and the stress level, click distance (between "show" and "answer" buttons) and target size (i.e. "answer" button diameter).

It is not difficult to see that the gaze-click features basically have no clear correlation with the click target distance and size. It therefore indicates that the on-screen distance between the locations of the cursor and the click target does not have a significant impact on the gaze movement behaviors surrounding a mouse-click. Nor does the size of the click target. However, it is interesting that two gaze-click features, the closest fixation duration preceding/during a click and the reaction latency after a click, show fair correlation with calm/stress, compared to click distance and target size. The negative correlation values suggest that long fixation duration and reaction latency associate more strongly with the calm state than stress state, which appears to make sense because subjects who are not under stress may operate less hastily and more slowly.

Figure 5 compares the overall values of individual gaze-click feature under calm (blue) and stressed (red) conditions. The dotted circles mark the median, the thick bar covers the 25th and 75th percentiles, the thin line extends to the most extreme data points not considered outliers (defined as values >*q3*+1.5(*q3*-*q1*) or <*q1*-1.5(*q3*-*q1*), where *q1* and *q3* are the 25th and 75th percentiles), and outliers are plotted individually in circles. It is not difficult to see that some gaze-click features differ considerably between calm and stress conditions. For example, the average duration of the corresponding fixation, g_2, in stress (M=0.20) is 30.3% shorter than that of in calm contexts (M=0.29). Similarly, the reaction latency, g_3, in stress (M=0.04) is 46.7% lower than that of in calm (M=0.07). In contrast, the click latency g_4 (calm M=0.08; stress M=0.11), velocity g_5 (calm M=0.10; stress M=0.12) and duration g_6 (calm M=0.11; stress M=0.14) of the preceding non-fixation period in stress are 31.4%, 14.5% and 21.1% higher than those of in calm conditions.

Intuitively, these differences make sense. It is highly likely that subjects would fixate longer (g_2, g_3) on the target when calm than when stressed. Likewise it is common that stress may induce people to move their gaze away (g_4) from the target, scan more hastily and at higher speed (g_5) and scan, rather than read, more often (g_6).

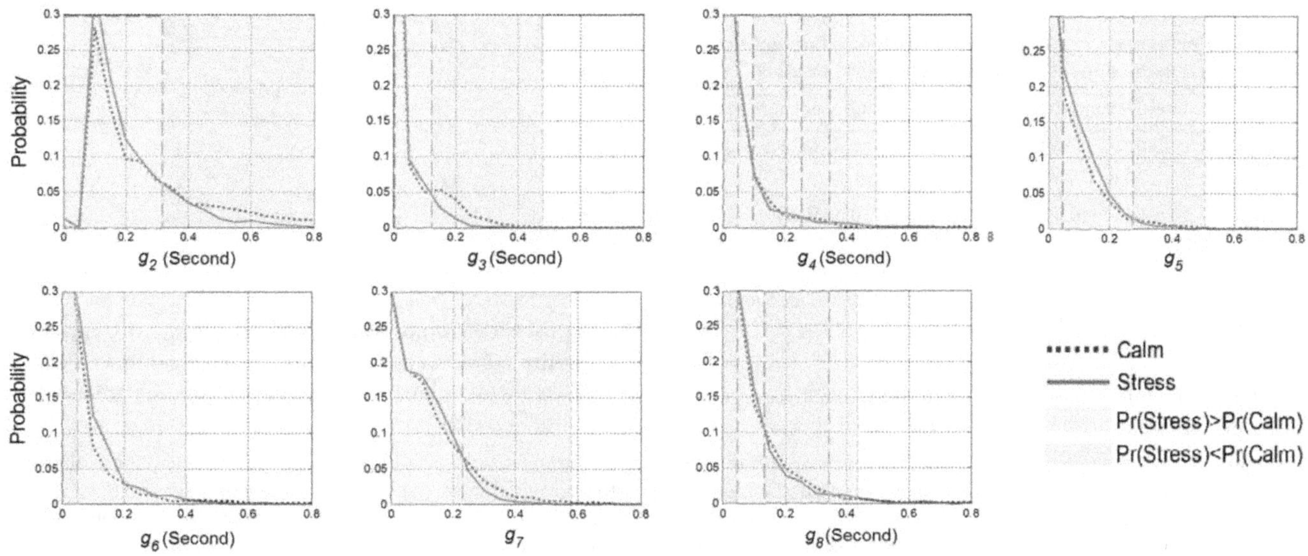

Figure 6. Conditional probability mass function of the gaze-click features. The red line indicates stress, and the blue dotted line indicates the calm condition. Light red shadow denotes the stress probability is higher than that of calm, and the light blue shadow shows that calm probability is higher than that of stress. Some gaze-click features (g_2, g_3, g_5, g_6, g_7) present clear pattern under different stress levels, while others' patterns (g_4, g_8) are rather ambiguous in term of conditional probability distribution.

To further explore the probability distribution behind the overall differences, we present the conditional probability mass functions (pmf) of each gaze-click feature given both calm and stress mental conditions in Figure 6. For the time-related features (g_2, g_3, g_4, g_6, g_8), each point on the curve represents the probability of feature values in the corresponding 50ms bin; with respect to the velocity-related features (g_5, g_7), each bin represents an incremental value of 0.05. The red line indicates the probability of stress and the blue dotted line indicates calm. For a clear demonstration, where the probability of stress is higher than that of calm, i.e. $\text{Pr(Stress)} > \text{Pr(Calm)}$, we annotate the region in light red, and light blue for the converse situation, i.e. $\text{Pr(Stress)} < \text{Pr(Calm)}$. We observe that an absolute majority of probabilities drop to zero when the value of the feature goes over 0.8. Therefore, we show feature distributions in the value range (x-axis) of [0,0.8]. Similarly, for display purposes, we show the probability range (y-axis) of [0,0.3]. It should be noted that we follow the definition in [13] that a fixation should last at least 80ms, so the figure of g_2 has no value for durations shorter than this threshold.

We have not shown g_1 in the figure, since it is a binary feature, and the probability difference of a closely preceding fixation in calm (95.2%) and stress (96.6%) is marginal. Encouragingly, most of the gaze-click features (g_2, g_3, g_5, g_6, g_7) present clear patterns under different stress levels. In other words, the relationship between the value of these features and stress level are relatively stable and consistent. However, other features' (g_4, g_8) relations with mental stress are vague. As their values increase, the higher probability switches back and forth between stress and calm.

Generally speaking, the data indicates that the gaze behaviors surrounding a mouse-click event show a certain degree of connection with the changes of mental stress. Although the connection appears slightly ambiguous between an individual gaze-click feature and the human stress level, it can be indicative for discriminating stress and calm given a proper model exploring the relation with multiple features.

5.2 Evaluating Stress Detection at Individual Click-Level

To model stress from the eight gaze-click features, we adopt the random forest algorithm [6], which is an ensemble learning method that has been shown to achieve good performance in various applications. The parameters are empirically determined based on grid searches using 10-fold cross-validation on the training set. Our final model contains 75 trees with max depth truncated to 4, and each tree employs 3 features for random selection.

In order to fully investigate the generalizability of the proposed features, we present the results of both within-subjects and between-subjects studies. For the within-subjects evaluation, we build a user-dependent model for each individual subject and use 10-fold cross-validation for evaluation. The final performance is the average performance across all folds. The between-subjects study employs leave-one-subject-out cross-validation, testing on each subject in turn. For reference, we provide the baseline performance given by a naïve classifier that predicts the majority class in the training set.

Table 3 summarizes the performance comparisons of both user-dependent and independent models to the baselines. Weighted average of correctly classified rate (CCR), F1-measure, and area under the receiver operating characteristic curve (AUC) across subjects are used as performance metrics. The comparison shows that our models significantly outperform the naïve classifiers. The user-dependent model (F1=0.66), as expected, outperforms the user-independent model (F1=0.60). This makes sense, as the user-independent model needs to accommodate differences between individuals, which generally can be difficult. Our technique gives

Table 3. Performance comparison of click-level detection between user- dependent and independent models

	User-Dependent Model	User-Independent Model
CCR	65.72 (51.05)	60.27 (51.1)
F1	0.66 (0.36)	0.60 (0.35)
AUC	0.70 (0.5)	0.63 (0.5)

Numbers in parentheses denote the baseline performances. The performance is the weighted average results across different subjects, whose values may have slight difference from the average, due to the differences of data amount of subjects.

satisfactory results despite being agnostic to the click target size and distance and inferring based on only individual clicks.

For a thorough understanding of the model performance on every individual, Figure 7 presents the CCR comparison across subjects. Performances of the user-dependent model is marked in green and user-independent model in orange. The subject IDs are ranked in ascending order by the performance of the user-independent model. Although the user-independent model (M=60.2, SD=5.6) has a modest 4.8% reduction in performance on average compared to its counterpart (M=65.0, SD=9.2), it is encouraging that it performs more stably with a smaller standard deviation. In addition, the user-independent model actually succeeds in outperforming the user-dependent model in a quarter of our cases (5 out of 20 subjects). This result suggests the generalizability of our proposed gaze-click features - in other words, these features are general enough to adapt to different individuals.

5.3 Evaluating Stress Detection at Session-Level

Normally, people would stay in a similar mental state during the period of conducting a task. Inferring stress from the behaviors surrounding only one click may be influenced by the randomness of human behaviors. Given the success of stress detection based on the gaze-click pattern of individual mouse event, we believe it makes sense to consider the sequential mouse-click events for stress detection.

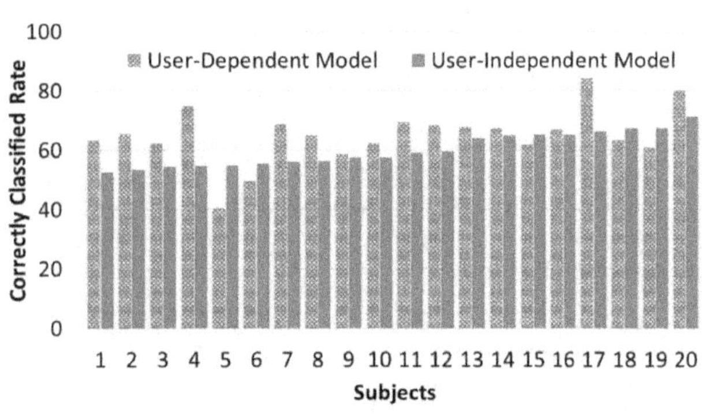

Figure 7. Classifying stress at individual click-level with user-dependent and independent models. User-dependent evaluation uses 10-fold cross-validation on individual subject's data and averages over all folds. User-independent evaluation reports results on leave-one-subject-out cross-validation. The subject IDs are ranked by the ascendant performance of the user-independent model.

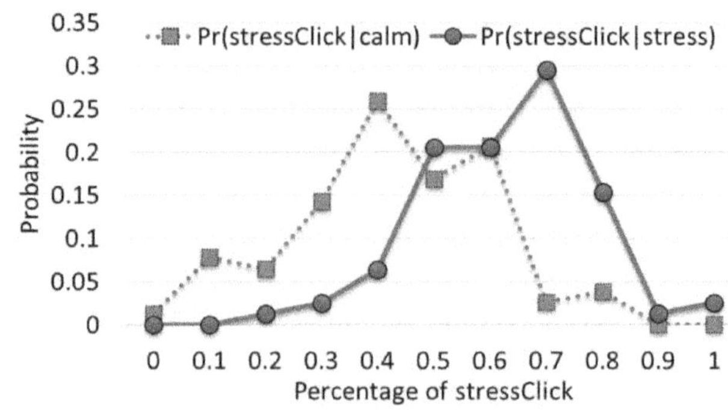

Figure 8. Conditional probability functions of StressClick given the subject is in calm and stressed conditions. People in stress tend to have a higher percentage of StressClick.

We define the mouse-click whose gaze-click pattern leads to a stress prediction by the click-level classifier (i.e. random forest) as *StressClick*. Figure 8 presents the conditional probability of the percentage of StressClick in the stress and calm sessions.

It is not difficult to see that the conditional probability of StressClick in the stress session peaks at 0.7, which means there is a clear chance that StressClick occupies the dominant percentage of clicks in a session. In contrast, conditional probability of StressClick in the calm sessions is likely to be lower than in stress. This means that the percentage of StressClick events can be useful for session-level stress detection.

We introduce a 2nd-layer classifier to recognize stress given the click-level predictions. We construct 3 features for the 2nd-layer classifier: (1) number of StressClicks, (2) number of clicks being considered, and (3) the ratio of StressClicks to the total number of clicks. The rationale of the first feature is that it may take a certain number of StressClicks to confirm a reliable stress prediction. The third feature, a seemingly redundant description of the first two, explicitly instructs the classifier to apply the ratio of StressClick for a time period. Given the simplicity of the 2nd-layer features, a logistic classifier [9] is used for stress detection from multiple clicks.

Table 4 summarizes the performances of the user- dependent and independent models for the session-level prediction. It is very encouraging that the session-level user-independent model (F1=0.79) outperforms the user-dependent model (F1=0.74), given enough click data. Furthermore, as expected, session-level user-dependent and independent models outperform their click-level counterparts, with 8.31% and 20.23% CCR improvements, respectively. The F1-measure of the user-independent model also improves by around 0.2 from 0.6 to 0.79. This also supports the validity of the ratio feature.

Figure 9 further shows the performance on individual subjects. The session-level user-independent model (M=79.4, SD=16.9)

Table 4. Performance comparison of session-level detection between user- dependent and independent models

	User-Dependent Model	User-Independent Model
CCR	74.0 (49.35)	80.5 (50.0)
F1	0.74 (0.33)	0.79 (0.33)
AUC	0.73 (0.5)	0.89 (0.5)

Numbers in parentheses denote the baseline performances.

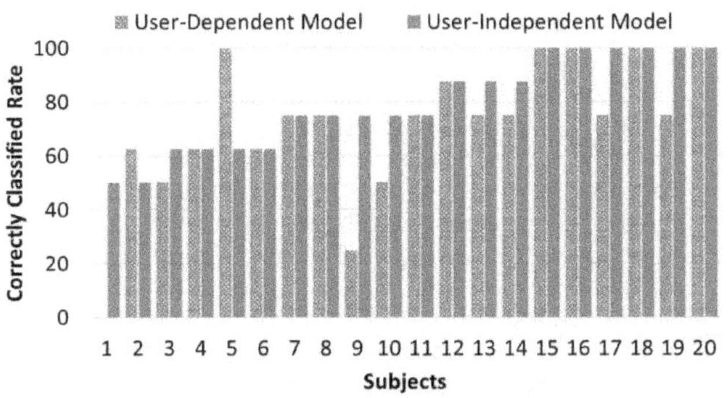

Figure 9. Classifying stress at session-level with user-dependent and independent models. The subject IDs are ranked in ascending performance of user-independent model.

outperforms the user-dependent model (M=71.3, SD=25.3) in both overall accuracy and stability (with smaller SD). This is probably because there is not sufficient data to build an accurate user-dependent model at the session level. However, when more training data is available, the session-level user-independent model performs quite well. It achieves over 80% accuracy on 45% of our subjects.

Comparing to previous state-of-the-art work that uses off-the-shelf devices for non-intrusive stress detection, Sun et al [34] reports 71% accuracy based on 30 samples of mouse movements in the user-dependent evaluation. Our method compares favorably with theirs, and maintains this performance even in the user-independent paradigm.

6. CONCLUSIONS

This paper presents a technique that aims to non-intrusively detect user stress through the gaze-click pattern. Using a series of multi-user experiments, we empirically demonstrate the impact of stress on the gaze-click pattern, which has been largely ignored in previous work. We also propose the cross-modal gaze-click features for stress recognition and investigate their effectiveness in both user- dependent and independent studies. Our results show that not only is it feasible to detect user stress through non-intrusively collected data, but also that our proposed features are generalizable across different users.

Given that our method does not rely on gaze point estimation, we believe that this is a significant contribution to affective computing and human computer interaction, as it establishes a novel and reliable cross-modal approach to detect stress in the non-intrusive manner and thus can be used in the wild.

It is not difficult to see that our technique can also be applied in conjunction with mouse stiffness modeling [34] or take into consideration multiple clicks or click-trajectory history to facilitate stress classification. Our future work will therefore investigate more sophisticated multimodal signals with which to reinforce the stress-sensing model.

7. ACKNOWLEDGMENTS

We sincerely thank the anonymous reviewers for their time and effort of reviewing this paper. This work is supported by grants PolyU 5222/13E from HK Research Grants Council, and PolyU 152126/14E from Hong Kong Polytechnic University.

8. REFERENCES

[1] Aigrain, J., Dubuisson, S., Detyniecki, M. and Chetouani, M. 2015. Person-specific behavioural features for automatic stress detection. *IEEE International Conference and Workshops on Automatic Face and Gesture Recognition* (2015).

[2] Alberdi, A., Aztiria, A. and Basarab, A. 2016. Towards an automatic early stress recognition system for office environments based on multimodal measurements : A review. *Journal of Biomedical Informatics*. 59,(2016),49–75.

[3] Andreassi, J.L. 2006. *Psychophysiology: Human Behavior and Physiological Response*. Psychology Press.

[4] Bixler, R. and D'Mello, S. 2013. Detecting boredom and engagement during writing with keystroke analysis, task appraisals, and stable traits. *Proceedings of the 2013 international conference on Intelligent user interfaces - IUI '13* (New York, New York, USA, 2013), 225.

[5] Bogomolov, A., Lepri, B., Ferron, M., Pianesi, F. and Pentland, A. (Sandy) 2014. Daily Stress Recognition from Mobile Phone Data, Weather Conditions and Individual Traits. *Proceedings of the ACM International Conference on Multimedia - MM '14* (2014), 477–486.

[6] Breiman, L. 2001. Random forests. *Machine Learning*. 45, (2001), 5–32.

[7] Bryant, R.A., Moulds, M.L. and Guthrie, R.M. 2000. Acute Stress Disorder Scale: a self-report measure of acute stress disorder. *Psychological assessment*. 12, (2000), 61–68.

[8] Celiktutan, O. and Gunes, H. 2016. Automatic Prediction of Impressions in Time and across Varying Context: Personality, Attractiveness and Likeability. *IEEE Transactions on Affective Computing*. (2016), 1–1.

[9] Le Cessie, S. and van Houwelingen, J.C. 1992. Ridge Estimators in Logistic Regression. *Applied Statistics*. 41, 1 (1992), 191–201.

[10] Chen, M.C., Anderson, J.R. and Sohn, M.H. 2001. What can a mouse cursor tell us more? *CHI '01 extended abstracts on Human factors in computing systems - CHI '01* (New York, New York, USA, 2001), 281.

[11] Dinges, D.F., Venkataraman, S., McGlinchey, E.L. and Metaxas, D.N. 2007. Monitoring of facial stress during space flight: Optical computer recognition combining discriminative and generative methods. *Acta Astronautica*. 60, (2007), 341–350.

[12] Epp, C., Lippold, M. and Mandryk, R.L. 2011. Identifying emotional states using keystroke dynamics. *Proceedings of the 2011 annual conference on Human factors in computing systems - CHI '11*. (2011), 715.

[13] Hansen, D.W. and Ji, Q. 2010. In the eye of the beholder: a survey of models for eyes and gaze. *IEEE transactions on pattern analysis and machine intelligence*. 32, 3 (Mar. 2010), 478–500.

[14] Healey, J.A. and Picard, R.W. 2005. Detecting stress during real-world driving tasks using physiological sensors. *IEEE Transactions on Intelligent Transportation Systems*. 6, (2005), 156–166.

[15] Hernandez, J., Paredes, P., Roseway, A. and Czerwinski, M. 2014. Under pressure: Sensing Stress of Computer Users. *Proceedings of the 32nd annual ACM conference on Human factors in computing systems - CHI '14* (2014), 51–60.

[16] Huang, J., White, R. and Buscher, G. 2012. User see, user point: gaze and cursor alignment in web search. *Proceedings of the 2012 ACM annual conference on Human Factors in Computing Systems - CHI '12* (New York, New York, USA, 2012), 1341.

[17] Huang, J., White, R.W. and Dumais, S. 2011. No clicks, no problem: using cursor movements to understand and improve search. *Proceedings of the 2011 annual conference on Human factors in computing systems - CHI '11* (New York, New York, USA, 2011), 1225.

[18] Huang, M.X., Kwok, T.C.K., Ngai, G., Chan, C.F.S. and Leong, H.V. 2016. Building a Personalized, Auto-Calibrating Eye Tracker from User Interactions. *Proceedings of the Thirty-third Annual SIGCHI Conference on Human Factors in Computing Systems (CHI 2016)* (2016).

[19] Huang, M.X., Kwok, T.C.K., Ngai, G., Leong, H.V. and Chan, C.F.S. 2014. Building a Self-Learning Eye Gaze Model from User Interaction Data. *ACM Multimedia* (2014).

[20] Inhoff, A.W. and Gordon, A.M. 1997. Eye Movements and Eye-Hand Coordination During Typing. *Current Directions in Psychological Science*. 6, (1997), 153–157.

[21] Koldijk, S., Sappelli, M., Verberne, S., Neerincx, M.A. and Kraaij, W. 2014. The SWELL Knowledge Work Dataset for Stress and User Modeling Research. *Proceedings of the 16th International Conference on Multimodal Interaction* (2014), 291–298.

[22] Lazarus, R.S. 1966. *Psychological stress and the coping process*. McGraw-Hill.

[23] Liao, W., Zhang, W., Zhu, Z. and Ji, Q. 2005. A Real-Time Human Stress Monitoring System Using Dynamic Bayesian Network. *2005 IEEE Computer Society Conference on Computer Vision and Pattern Recognition (CVPR'05) - Workshops*. 3, (2005), 70–70.

[24] Liebling, D.J. and Dumais, S.T. 2014. Gaze and mouse coordination in everyday work. *Proceedings of the 2014 ACM International Joint Conference on Pervasive and Ubiquitous Computing Adjunct Publication - UbiComp '14 Adjunct* (2014), 1141–1150.

[25] Lu, H., Frauendorfer, D., Rabbi, M., Mast, M.S., Chittaranjan, G.T., Campbell, A.T., Gatica-Perez, D. and Choudhury, T. 2012. StressSense. *Proceedings of the 2012 ACM Conference on Ubiquitous Computing - UbiComp '12* (2012), 351.

[26] Lundberg, U., Kadefors, R., Melin, B., Palmerud, G., Hassmen, P., Engstrom, M. and Dohns, I.E. 1994. Psychophysiological stress and EMG activity of the trapezius muscle. *International journal of behavioral medicine*. 1, (1994), 354–370.

[27] Lyu, Y., Luo, X., Zhou, J., Yu, C., Miao, C., Wang, T., Shi, Y. and Kameyama, K. 2015. Measuring Photoplethysmogram-Based Stress-Induced Vascular Response Index to Assess Cognitive Load and Stress. *Proceedings of the 33rd Annual ACM Conference on Human Factors in Computing Systems - CHI '15* (2015), 857–866.

[28] Paul Viola, M.J. 2001. Robust Real-time Object Detection. *International Journal of Computer Vision*. (2001).

[29] Rodden, K., Fu, X., Aula, A. and Spiro, I. 2008. Eye-mouse coordination patterns on web search results pages. *Proceeding of the twenty-sixth annual CHI conference extended abstracts on Human factors in computing systems - CHI '08* (New York, New York, USA, 2008), 2997.

[30] Salvucci, D.D., Salvucci, D.D., Goldberg, J.H. and Goldberg, J.H. 2000. Identifying Fixations and Saccades in Eye-Tracking Protocols. *Proceedings of the Eye Tracking Research and Applications Symposium*. (2000), 71–78.

[31] Saragih, J.M., Lucey, S. and Cohn, J.F. 2009. Face alignment through subspace constrained mean-shifts. *2009 IEEE 12th International Conference on Computer Vision* (Sep. 2009), 1034–1041.

[32] Sharma, N. and Gedeon, T. 2012. Objective measures, sensors and computational techniques for stress recognition and classification: A survey. *Computer Methods and Programs in Biomedicine*. 108, (2012), 1287–1301.

[33] Smucker, M.D., Guo, X.S. and Toulis, A. 2014. Mouse movement during relevance judging: implications for determining user attention. *Proceedings of the 37th international ACM SIGIR conference on Research & development in information retrieval* (2014), 979–982.

[34] Sun, D., Paredes, P. and Canny, J. 2014. MouStress: Detecting Stress from Mouse Motion. *Proceedings of the 32nd annual ACM conference on Human factors in computing systems - CHI '14* (2014), 61–70.

[35] Visser, B., De Looze, M., De Graaff, M. and Van Dieën, J. 2004. Effects of precision demands and mental pressure on muscle activation and hand forces in computer mouse tasks. *Ergonomics*. 47, (2004), 202–217.

[36] Vizer, L.M., Zhou, L. and Sears, A. 2009. Automated stress detection using keystroke and linguistic features: An exploratory study. *International Journal of Human Computer Studies*. 67, (2009), 870–886.

[37] Wahlstrom, J., Hagberg, M., Johnson, P.W., Svensson, J. and Rempel, D. 2002. Influence of time pressure and verbal provocation on physiological and psychological reactions during work with a computer mouse. *European Journal of Applied Physiology*. 87, (2002), 257–263.

[38] Wood, E., Baltrusaitis, T., Zhang, X., Sugano, Y., Robinson, P. and Bulling, A. 2015. Rendering of Eyes for Eye-Shape Registration and Gaze Estimation. *IEEE International Conference on Computer Vision (ICCV)* (2015), 3756–3764.

[39] Xiong, X. and De la Torre, F. 2013. Supervised Descent Method and Its Applications to Face Alignment. *2013 IEEE Conference on Computer Vision and Pattern Recognition* (Jun. 2013), 532–539.

[40] Xu, P., Sugano, Y. and Bulling, A. 2016. Spatio-Temporal Modeling and Prediction of Visual Attention in Graphical User Interfaces. *Proceedings of the 2016 ACM annual conference on Human Factors in Computing Systems - CHI '16* (San Jose, CA, USA, 2016).

[41] Zeng, Z., Pantic, M., Roisman, G.I. and Huang, T.S. 2009. A survey of affect recognition methods: audio, visual, and spontaneous expressions. *IEEE transactions on pattern analysis and machine intelligence*. 31, 1 (Jan. 2009), 39–58.

Ensemble of Sparse Cross-Modal Metrics for Heterogeneous Face Recognition

Jing Huo[†], Yang Gao[†], Yinghuan Shi[†], Wanqi Yang[‡,†], Hujun Yin[§]
[†]State Key Laboratory for Novel Software Technology, Nanjing University, China
[‡]School of Computer Science and Technology, Nanjing Normal University, China
[§]School of Electrical and Electronic Engineering, The University of Manchester, UK
huojing1989@gmail.com, gaoy@nju.edu.cn, syh@nju.edu.cn
nju.yangwanqi@gmail.com, hujun.yin@manchester.ac.uk

ABSTRACT

Heterogeneous face recognition aims to identify or verify person identity by matching facial images of different modalities. In practice, it is known that its performance is highly influenced by modality inconsistency, appearance occlusions, illumination variations and expressions. In this paper, a new method named as ensemble of sparse cross-modal metrics is proposed for tackling these challenging issues. In particular, a weak sparse cross-modal metric learning method is firstly developed to measure distances between samples of two modalities. It learns to adjust rank-one cross-modal metrics to satisfy two sets of triplet based cross-modal distance constraints in a compact form. Meanwhile, a group based feature selection is performed to enforce that features in the same position of two modalities are selected simultaneously. By neglecting features that attribute to "noise" in the face regions (eye glasses, expressions and so on), the performance of learned weak metrics can be markedly improved. Finally, an ensemble framework is incorporated to combine the results of differently learned sparse metrics into a strong one. Extensive experiments on various face datasets demonstrate the benefit of such feature selection especially when heavy occlusions exist. The proposed ensemble metric learning has been shown superiority over several state-of-the-art methods in heterogeneous face recognition.

Keywords

Multi-modal learning; metric learning; feature selection; ensemble learning; heterogeneous face recognition

1. INTRODUCTION

Face recognition has been extensively researched over the past few decades and satisfactory performances have been achieved mostly under controlled environments. In practical situations, the problem often becomes heterogeneous where faces are of different modalities and performance degrades considerably. This is mainly caused by drastic appearance variations between face images of different modalities. There are several studies in heterogeneous face recognition in the literature such as matching sketches to photos, low resolution images to high resolution videos, visible light to near infrared images. Such situations are commonly encountered in multimedia applications. A general face recognition process often has two stages. The first is feature extraction and the second is learning a similarity measurement to measure similarities between the face features. Therefore, there are mainly two ways to alleviate modality variations for robust cross-modal face matching. One is to extract modality invariant face features and the other is to design cross-modal similarity measurements. This work focuses on the second one.

For learning a similarity measurement, metric learning is widely used [3]. However the currently widely used metric learning methods are Mahalanobis distance based. The main disadvantage when applied to cross-modal face recognition is that it is not able to remove modality variations, which influence recognition performance the most. Although there exist cross-modal metric learning methods [26], there are still serious issues to be addressed. One is that not all the face features are informative when faces are occluded or influenced by expressions or illumination variations. Thus it is beneficial to perform feature selection. The existing sparse Mahalanobis metric learning methods [35] are able to do feature selection, but it is hard to interpret which features are more important from the parameters learned. Besides, for face recognition, as features are extracted on local patches, it is beneficial to take the implicit spatial information of features into consideration with feature selection.

We therefore propose to learn a cross-modal metric that is able to remove modality variations and persist the ability of informative feature selection. Different with most sparse metric learning methods, the proposed method also has good interpretability. A simple cross-modal metric is firstly defined with two sets of parameters. They can be interpreted as two projection vectors to project face features of two different modalities into a common subspace and the distance is measured in the new subspace. Learning such a cross-modal metric is efficient as it has much fewer parameters compared with metrics parameterized by matrices. The goal of metric learning is to adjust the metric to satisfy two sets of triplet based cross-modal distance constraints. Each triplet includes a sample of one modality and a pair of samples from the other modality with one being the same label and the other of different label. From the triplet, one same labeled and one differently labeled cross-modal sample pairs can be constructed. The goal is to make the distances of the same labeled pairs smaller than that of the differently labeled pairs. Besides, another characteristic of the cross-modal metric is that it is learned by incorporating group based feature selection. Two kinds of

MM '16, October 15-19, 2016, Amsterdam, Netherlands

DOI: http://dx.doi.org/10.1145/2964284.2964311

groups are defined. One is single feature based group that takes two elements respectively from two projection vectors in the same position. The other is patch based group and is defined as two sets of elements from the two projection vectors corresponding to features extracted from patches of the same position. By using group based feature selection, relations of features of two modalities are incorporated. Such a learned metric is named as sparse cross-modal metric (SPAC). Once learned, a SPAC selects a set of features to measure the distances between samples.

Since one SPAC has few parameters, it may not fit well for samples of all kinds of variations. A simple idea is to learn groups of SPACs that are able to deal with different kinds of variations and are complementary. Therefore, an ensemble scheme is further applied. A set of SPACs are learned on differently weighted triplets with different variations. Once a SPAC is learned, the weights of triplets are reassigned according to whether the constraint encoded in a triplet is met by the previously learned SPACs. The learned SPACs are therefore complementary. Each SPAC is also assigned a weight when the outputs of all the SPACs are combined to make the final decision. The reweighting and combining scheme of the Adaboost framework [28] is used to learn SPACs and combine them into a strong metric. The ensemble framework of SPACs is termed as ESPAC.

2. RELATED WORK

Three related topics are reviewed, heterogeneous face recognition, single-modal metric learning and cross-modal metric learning.

2.1 Heterogeneous Face Recognition

Methods for solving heterogeneous face recognition problems can be categorized into three categories. The first category is the synthesis based methods which map data of one modality into another by synthetic methods. Related work includes synthesizing sketches from photos and then comparing synthesized images with sketches drawn by artists [31, 36]. One drawback of this kind of methods is that different synthetic methods have to be used if the modalities change.

The second category is modality invariant feature extraction based methods. In [34], Gabor features together with restricted boltzmann machines were used to learn shared representations. Jin *et al.* [12] proposed to learn a set of image filters to reduce the appearance differences of cross-modality images by maximizing inter-class variations and minimizing intra-class variations.

The last is the common subspace based methods [20, 22, 13] and the proposed method belong to this kind. Data of different modalities are mapped into a new, common subspace, so that data of different modalities become comparable. In [22], a common discriminant feature extraction (CDFE) was proposed to learn a common subspace for samples of two modalities to attain both intra-class compactness and the inter-class dispersion. In [20], Lei *et al.* proposed a spectral regression based method (CSR) to learn a discriminative subspace. The objective is similar to linear discriminant analysis (LDA) [2]. These methods all learn common subspaces to remove modality variations. However, none of them have considered the cases where there are also occlusions, expressions and illumination changes, which widely exist in real-world heterogeneous face data.

2.2 Single-modal Metric Learning

Metric learning for single modal data has been extensively studied over the past decade. The existing approaches can be mainly grouped into two categories; Mahalanobis metric and bilinear metric based. A comprehensive review can be found in [3]. We herein mainly review related work regarding ensemble based metric learning and sparse metric learning. For ensemble based methods, Shen *et al.* proposed a PSDBoost method [30] to learn a positive semidefinite (PSD) matrix by column generation for Mahalanobis metrics. The method was later extended into a more efficient version in [29]. The main idea of the method is that a PSD matrix, the parameter of Mahalanobis based metric, can be decomposed into a linear combination of trace-one rank-one matrices. Therefore, rank-one PSD matrices parameterized weak metrics are learned sequentially. In [4], Bi *et al.* proposed to learn Mahalanobis metrics in an Adaboost manner. The same decomposition property of PSD matrix [30] was used and weak metrics were also parameterized by rank-one PSD matrices. Another boosting framework was proposed in [33] for combining weak metrics with binary outputs. These existing ensemble based metric learning methods are designed for single modal data.

For sparse metric learning, there have been several attempts to learn sparse low-rank metric matrices [35]. Such settings are related to finding low dimensional subspaces instead of finding informative features. For finding informative features and feature relationships, Liu *et al.* [23] proposed to learn a sparse bilinear similarity function by decomposing the PSD matrix as a combination of rank-one sparse PSD matrices. The rank-one sparse PSD matrices were defined with certain structures with only four non-zero elements related to a pair of features. Such rank-one matrices were greedily added to the final similarity function during learning. In [1], a PSD matrix was decomposed into a diagonal matrix and a set of all-zeros diagonal matrices with only one row and one column have non-zero elements. The learning procedure lead to many of the all-zeros diagonal matrices to zeros and the final combined matrix is thus sparse. Our proposed feature selection scheme differs from these methods in that sparsity is forced not on the metric matrix but on projection vectors. As the projection vectors directly relate to the weights of features, the proposed feature selection scheme thus has better interpretability on which features being more important. Besides, the proposed feature selection scheme differs from these methods in that feature selection is done jointly with the modality relations of features and the structures of face features considered.

2.3 Cross-modal Metric Learning

With the development of multi-modal data, there has been an increase in the study of cross-modal metric learning. Mignon *et al.* [26] proposed a common subspace based cross-modal metric learning method to satisfy both the pairwise similar/dissimilar cross-modal distance constraints. In [38], Zhou *et al.* proposed to incorporate both homogeneous local information and heterogeneous constraints into a whole framework to learn a cross-modal metric by using an extension of locally linear embedding (LLE). A low-rank bilinear cross-modal similarity method is proposed in [14]. Our method differs with these methods in several aspects. One is the distance constraints used. These methods use pairwise cross-modal distance constraints, while triplet based distance constraints are used in our proposed methods. The second is that the proposed metric is learned in a boosting manner with each weak metric focusing on different groups of features thus eliminating noise features for different groups of inseparable triplets.

3. FRAMEWORK OF ESPAC

Fig. 1 shows the framework of the proposed method. In the training stage, face alignment and face feature extraction are firstly performed on the training face images. Local feature extraction

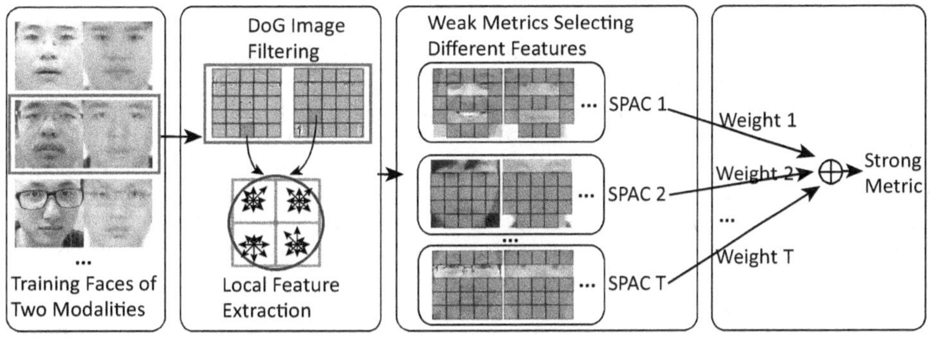

Figure 1: Framework of ESPAC. Local based feature extraction is firstly performed on given training data. Then a set of SPACs together with their weights are learned using an ensemble learning framework with each focusing on different features to measure cross-modal distances. The final output of ESPAC is the sum of weighted outputs of all the learned SPACs.

method is adopted. For faces of different modalities, same feature extraction process is applied. The extracted face features can be highly influenced by modality differences.

Then a set of weak sparse cross-modal metrics (SPACs) are learned. There are several properties of the learned SPACs. 1) The cross-modal metric is able to remove modality variations in the extracted features. 2) Each SPAC is learned with the weights of triplet based constraints differently so that the cross-modal metrics are complementary. The reweighting scheme of the Adaboost framework is used to assign different weights to different triplets. Bisection method is used to find the weight of a SPAC (or the contribution of a SPAC) to the final strong metric by minimizing the training error of the final strong metric. 3) For different appearance variations existing in different triplets, a group based feature selection scheme is used while learning SPACs. Two kinds of group based feature selection methods are proposed. In the first setting, two features of two modalities at the same position are simultaneously selected. In the second setting, features extracted in the patches of same position of two modalities are forced to be selected together. We prove that the two feature selection schemes achieve better results compared with no feature selection based one. Specifically, the second one can highly improve recognition performances in high occlusion cases.

In the testing stage, the same feature extraction process is applied. The outputs of all the learned sparse cross-modal metrics are weighted and combined to make the final prediction.

4. LOCAL FACE FEATURE EXTRACTION

For face normalization, faces are firstly rotated so that two eyes are located on a horizontal line, and then resized to make the distances between two pupils of 75 pixels. A face region of 160×160 is cropped out, with the eye central to the region's upper edge by 35 pixels and to the region's left edge by 80 pixels.

The second step adopted is image filtering techniques (difference of gaussian, DoG) to help compensate illumination variations and also to reduce the variations caused by modality difference [16].

The last step is to extract features of these filtered face images. Each face image is firstly partitioned into patches. As is shown in Fig. 2, the face image is partitioned into 5×5 patches, with each patch of size 32×32. In the experiments, different partition configurations are tested. The 160×160 face images are also partitioned into 3×3, 4×4, 5×5, 6×6 and 7×7. For some partition settings, patches may be of different size, but the difference is only one pixel in row size or column size. In the final experiments, we used the setting of partition images into 6×6 which produces relative good performance. After partition, local feature extraction methods are then used to extract features on each patch, in our case, scale-invariant feature transform (SIFT) [9] is adopted following an empirical comparison with other features. By concatenating all the local features into a whole vector, the final face feature is obtained. In the final feature vector, the features therefore have implicit spatial positions and patch-based structures.

5. PROBLEM FORMULATION OF SPAC

5.1 Notations

Suppose the training face image sets of two modalities are denoted as $\mathcal{X} = \{(\ _i, l_i^x)|i = 1, 2, ..., N_x\}$ and $\mathcal{Y} = \{(\ _i, l_i^y)|i = 1, 2, ..., N_y\}$, where $\ _i \in \mathbb{R}^{d_x}$ is the ith training sample of the first modality of dimension d_x and $\ _i \in \mathbb{R}^{d_y}$ is the ith training sample of the second modality of dimension d_y. In our case, as same feature extraction process is applied to both modalities, $d_x = d_y$. Suppose there are n different persons within the training set. $l_i^x \in \{1, 2, ..., n\}$ is the label of the sample $\ _i$ and $l_i^y \in \{1, 2, ..., n\}$ is the label of the sample $\ _i$. N_x and N_y are sample sizes of two modalities respectively.

To learn a metric on the given training datasets, a set of distance constraints should be constructed. Relative distance constraints encoded in triplets are used in the proposed method. Different with metric learning for single modality dataset, there are two kinds of triples for datasets of two modalities. One is of the form $(\ _i, \ _j, \ _k)$, with $l_i^x = l_j^y$ and $l_i^x \neq l_k^y$. The constraint is to force $d(\ _i, \ _j) < d(\ _i, \ _k)$. It can be constructed by setting every sample of the first modality as a focal sample. Then the second sample and the third sample are selected from samples of the second modality with the second one of the same label and the third one of different label. Another type of triplet is of the form $(\ _i, \ _j, \ _k)$ with $l_i^y = l_j^x$ and $l_i^y \neq l_k^x$. And it can be constructed similarly by setting the focal sample of the second modality. Suppose two sets of triplets $\mathcal{T}_1 = \{(\ _i, \ _j, \ _k)|l_i^x = l_j^y, l_i^x \neq l_k^y\}$ and $\mathcal{T}_2 = \{(\ _i, \ _j, \ _k)|l_i^y = l_j^x, l_i^y \neq l_k^x\}$ are constructed. The goal is to learn a cross-modal metric which meets the constraints defined in the two sets of triplets.

5.2 Sparse Cross-Modal Metric Learning

Suppose $\ \in \mathbb{R}^{d_x}$ and $\ \in \mathbb{R}^{d_y}$ are the face features of two modalities. The cross-modal metric is defined as:

$$d(\ ,\ ) = [f(\ ) - g(\ )]^2. \quad (1)$$

In case where both $f(\ )$ and $g(\ )$ are linear functions, they can be defined as $f(\ ) = \ ^{\top}_{x}$ and $g(\ ) = \ ^{\top}_{y}$. $_{x} \in \mathbb{R}^{d_x}$ and $_{y} \in \mathbb{R}^{d_y}$ are parameters. Such a metric can be seen as projecting samples into a one dimensional common subspace and then measuring their Euclidean distance. As the number of parameters is small, such metric is weak. The ultimate goal of the proposed method is to combine a set of these weak metrics into a strong one. The ensemble scheme will be illustrated later. We firstly present how to learn a weak sparse metric.

As being mentioned previously, the goal is to learn week metrics that satisfy the two sets of triplet based constraints. For the first set of triplets, the goal is to maximize the value of $d(\ _{i},\ _{k}) - d(\ _{i},\ _{j})$, which can be represented as:

$$\rho_r = d(\ _{i},\ _{k}) - d(\ _{i},\ _{j}) = (\ ^{\top}\ ^{d}_{r})^2 - (\ ^{\top}\ ^{s}_{r})^2, \quad (2)$$

where $\ = [\ _{x};\ _{y}] \in \mathbb{R}^{d_x+d_y}$ is the concatenation of the two parameters and r is the index of the triplet in $\mathcal{T}_1$. $^{s}_{r} = [\ _{i}; -\ _{j}] \in \mathbb{R}^{d_x+d_y}$ is formed by concatenating the same labeled sample pair of the rth triplet into one. $^{d}_{r} = [\ _{i}; -\ _{k}] \in \mathbb{R}^{d_x+d_y}$ is formed using the differently labeled sample pair. Similarly, for triplets in the second set, $d(\ _{k},\ _{i}) - d(\ _{j},\ _{i}) = (\ ^{\top}\ ^{d}_{r})^2 - (\ ^{\top}\ ^{s}_{r})^2$ can be represented in the same form, with $^{s}_{r} = [\ _{j}; -\ _{i}]$ and $^{d}_{r} = [\ _{k}; -\ _{i}]$. By using the above formulation and combining the two sets into one, the loss of a weak metric on the defined triplets can be represented as:

$$J = \sum_{r=1}^{|\mathcal{T}_1|+|\mathcal{T}_2|} \ell(\rho_r), \quad (3)$$

where $\ell(a)$ is a convex loss function which is selected as exponential loss $\exp(-a)$.

In weak cross-modal metric learning, merely minimizing the loss defined in Eq. (3) will suffer from server overfitting problem and regularization terms need to be added. In practice, the final objective of the no feature selection based weak cross-modal metric learning is defined as minimizing the following function:

$$\min_{\mathbf{w}} \sum_{r=1}^{|\mathcal{T}_1|+|\mathcal{T}_2|} \ell(\rho_r) + \tau \sum_{k=1}^{|\mathcal{S}|} \delta_k + \frac{\eta}{2}\ ^{\top} L\ + \frac{\lambda}{2} \|\ \|^2, \quad (4)$$

where τ, η and λ are regularization parameters. is constrained to be unit vector.

The first term in Eq. (4) is to minimize the loss defined in Eq. (3). The second term is a regularization term to control the distances of same labeled cross-modal pairs to be small, with $\mathcal{S} = \{(\ _{i},\ _{j}) | l^{x}_{i} = l^{y}_{j}\}$ the set of same labeled cross-modal sample pairs. $\delta_k = (\ ^{\top}\ _{k})^2$ is the distance of the kth same labeled cross-modal sample pair, $_{k} = [\ _{i}; -\ _{j}] \in \mathbb{R}^{d_x+d_y}$ is the concatenation of the kth same labeled cross-modal pair in set $\mathcal{S}$. Thus $\sum_{k=1}^{|\mathcal{S}|} \delta_k$ is the sum of all the same labeled cross-modal sample distances. This regularization term is used; because during the learning to force the distances of differently labeled pairs to be larger than the distances of the same labeled pairs, the distances of both the same labeled pairs and the differently labeled pairs may increase together, leading to poor generalization ability. The third term in Eq. (4) is also a regularization term. $L = D - S$ is a Laplacian matrix, with $S = \begin{bmatrix} & I \\ I & \end{bmatrix}$, $\ \in \mathbb{R}^{d \times d}$ is a zero matrix and $I \in \mathbb{R}^{d \times d}$ is an identity matrix, where d equals to d_x or d_y. D is a diagonal matrix whose elements are column sums of S. This term is equivalent to $\|\ _{x} -\ _{y}\|_2^2$ and the objective is to penalize $_{x}$ and $_{y}$ from differing too much. This is based on the prior knowledge that face features at the same position of two modalities are correlated, so the parameters of $_{x}$ and $_{y}$ at the same position should also be correlated. The last regularization term is related to control the l_2 norm of to avoid overfitting.

Group based Feature Selections. By using non-sparse projection vectors $_{x}$ and $_{y}$, all the extracted face features of two modalities are used for measuring distances. However, due to expression differences, high occlusions and face images captured under different illumination environments, not all patches of face images are useful for identifying the identities of face images. For cross modal face matching, once a feature in the first modality is selected, the corresponding feature of the same position of the second modality should also be selected. Therefore, group based feature selection is incorporated to select face features that are useful for distinguishing persons' identities. As the values in $_{x}$ and $_{y}$ indicate the importance of face features, group sparsity is forced on $_{x}$ and $_{y}$ to perform feature selection. Two schemes are proposed. An illustration is shown in Fig. 2. The first one is single feature based groups. In this case, a group contains two elements of with one element corresponds to $_{x}$ and the other corresponds to $_{y}$. Use $G_i = \{G^{x}_{i}, G^{y}_{i}\}, i = 1, 2, ..., d$ to denote the set of indices within corresponding to the ith features of two modalities. Therefore, there is a total number of d single feature based groups. In the second case, as for faces of heavy occlusions or with expression changes, some patches of the face images are completely unusable. We therefore propose patch based groups. The ith group is defined as the elements of both $_{x}$ and $_{y}$ corresponding to the features of the ith patch. $G_i = \{G^{x}_{i}, G^{y}_{i}\}, i = 1, 2, ..., p$ is used interchangeably to denote the set of indices within which correspond to features of ith patches of two modalities. p is the total number of patches. With such a definition, the learned cross-modal metric uses the features selected from either the same positions or the same face regions of two cross-modal face images, leading to the following final objective function to learn a SPAC:

$$\begin{aligned} \min_{\mathbf{w}} & \sum_{r=1}^{|\mathcal{T}_1|+|\mathcal{T}_2|} \ell(\rho_r) + \gamma \sum_{i=1}^{N_G} \|\ _{G_i}\|^2 \\ & + \tau \sum_{k=1}^{|\mathcal{S}|} \delta_k + \frac{\eta}{2}\ ^{\top} L\ + \frac{\lambda}{2} \|\ \|^2, \end{aligned} \quad (5)$$

where γ is a balance parameter and N_G is the number of groups which equals to either d or p. The objective function defined in Eq. (5) balances satisfying distance constraints and group based feature selection. Once a SPAC is learned, it selects a few face features or face regions for measuring cross-modal distances.

5.3 Optimization

As there is a group sparsity term in Eq. (5), alternating direction method of multipliers (ADMM) [5] is used to efficiently minimize the objective function. We firstly transform the minimization problem of Eq. (5) into an equivalent form:

$$\min_{\mathbf{w},\mathbf{v}} F(\ ) + H(\ ) \quad \text{s.t.} \quad\ =\ , \quad (6)$$

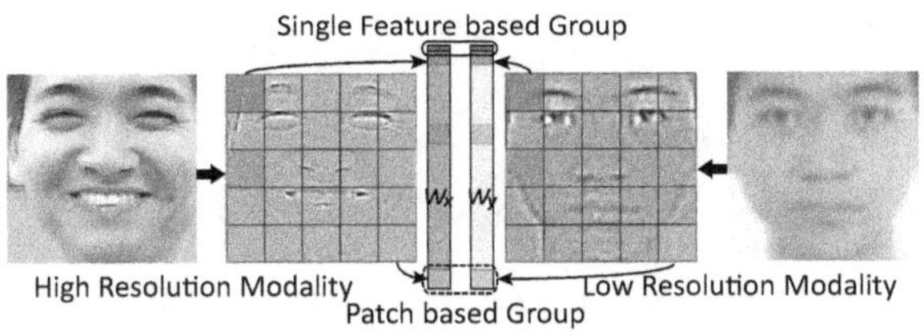

Figure 2: Illustration of two kinds of groups. A single feature based group contains two elements with one from $_x$ and one from $_y$ which are of the same position. Patch based group is defined as two groups of elements of $_x$ and $_y$ corresponding to features of two modalities extracted in patches of same position.

where

$$F(\ ) = \sum_{r=1}^{|\mathcal{T}_1|+|\mathcal{T}_2|} \ell(\rho_r) + \tau \sum_{k=1}^{|\mathcal{S}|} \delta_k + \frac{\eta}{2}\ {}^{\top} L\ + \frac{\lambda}{2} \|\ \|^2$$

$$H(\ ) = \gamma \sum_{i=1}^{p} \|\ _{G_i}\|^2.$$

The augmented Lagrangian for Eq. (6) is:

$$\mathcal{L}_\varrho = F(\ ) + H(\ ) + \nu^{\top}(\ -\ ) + \frac{\varrho}{2}\|\ -\ \|^2, \quad (7)$$

where ϱ is a scale parameter and ν is the lagrange multiplier. The ADMM optimization procedure for the above problem is therefore as follows:

$$\begin{aligned} {}^{k+1} &:= \arg\min_{\mathbf{w}} F(\ ) + \frac{\varrho}{2}\|\ -\ ^{k} +\ ^{k}\|^2 \\ {}^{k+1}_{G_i} &:= S_{\frac{\gamma}{\varrho}}(\ ^{k+1}_{G_i} +\ ^{k}_{G_i}) \\ {}^{k+1} &:=\ ^{k} +\ ^{k+1} -\ ^{k+1}, \end{aligned} \quad (8)$$

where $= \frac{1}{\varrho}\nu$. S_κ is a vector soft thresholding operator which is defined in [5]. For the first minimization problem to find optimal , a solution is to use the gradient descent. However, as the gradient calculation of the term $\sum_{r=1}^{|\mathcal{T}_1|+|\mathcal{T}_2|} \ell(\rho_r)$ with respect to is very time consuming. A modified scheme proposed in [25] is adopted. Then, the gradient term is of the form $\begin{bmatrix} \mathbf{X}\ \ \mathbf{X}^T & \mathbf{X}\ \ ^T \\ \ ^T\mathbf{X}^T & \ ^T \end{bmatrix}$, where $\mathbf{X} \in \mathbb{R}^{d_x \times N_x}$ and $\in \mathbb{R}^{d_y \times N_y}$ are matrices of samples of two modalities. By first calculating , and , the gradient can be efficiently updated. A summary of the algorithm is given in Algorithm 1.

Algorithm 1 ADMM for Learning Sparse Cross-Modal Metric (SPAC)

1: Two sets of constructed triplets $\mathcal{T}_1$ and $\mathcal{T}_2$.
2: Initialize ^{1}, ^{1} and ^{1}.
3: Initialize $k = 1$.
4: **while** not converged **do**
5: $\quad ^{k+1} := \arg\min_{\mathbf{w}} F(\ ) + \frac{\varrho}{2}\|\ -\ ^{k} +\ ^{k}\|^2$.
6: $\quad ^{k+1}_{G_i} := S_{\frac{\gamma}{\varrho}}(\ ^{k+1}_{G_i} +\ ^{k}_{G_i})$.
7: $\quad ^{k+1} :=\ ^{k} +\ ^{k+1} -\ ^{k+1}$.
8: $\quad k = k + 1$.
9: **end while**
10: Output .

6. ENSEMBLE OF SPACS

An ensemble framework is used to further combine a set of weak SPACs into a strong one. Suppose the final strong metric is represented as $D(\ ,\ ) = \sum_{t=1}^{T} \alpha_t d_t(\ ,\ )$, where α_t is the coefficient of the tth SPAC. Then the subtraction of the distances of a same labeled pair and a differently labeled pair measured by the strong metric is $D(\ _i,\ _k) - D(\ _i,\ _j) = \sum_{t=1}^{T} \alpha_t \rho_r^t$, where $\rho_r^t = d_t(\ _i,\ _k) - d_t(\ _i,\ _j)$. Therefore the objective of the final strong metric is to minimize the following loss:

$$J = \sum_{r=1}^{|\mathcal{T}_1|+|\mathcal{T}_2|} \left[s_r \ell\left(\sum_{t=1}^{T} \alpha_t \rho_r^t \right) \right], \quad (9)$$

where s is a distribution over the two sets of triplets. s_r is the weight of the rth triplet and is initialized as $1/(|\mathcal{T}_1| + |\mathcal{T}_2|)$. The ensemble scheme is summarized in Algorithm 2.

Theorem 1. *With Z_t defined in step 7 of Algorithm 2, the following equation holds for the initial distribution s:*

$$J = \sum_{r=1}^{|\mathcal{T}_1|+|\mathcal{T}_2|} \left[s_r \exp\left(-\sum_{t=1}^{T} \alpha_t \rho_r^t \right) \right] = \prod_{t=1}^{T} Z_t.$$

Proof: According to the definition of distribution:

$$s_r^{T+1} = \frac{s_r \exp(-\sum_{t=1}^{T} \alpha_t \rho_r^t)}{\prod_{t=1}^{T} Z_t}.$$

Therefore

$$\begin{aligned} J &= \sum_{r=1}^{|\mathcal{T}_1|+|\mathcal{T}_2|} \left[s_r \exp\left(-\sum_{t=1}^{T} \alpha_t \rho_r^t \right) \right] \\ &= \sum_{r=1}^{|\mathcal{T}_1|+|\mathcal{T}_2|} s_r^{T+1} \prod_{t=1}^{T} Z_t \\ &= \prod_{t=1}^{T} Z_t. \end{aligned}$$

Therefore, minimizing J is equivalent to minimizing Z_t at each iteration. The step 5 in Algorithm 1 for learning a SPAC is therefore changed slightly in the ESPAC framework. The first term in SPAC's objective function Eq. (5) is changed to Z_t, a weighted loss, so as to meet the objective of ESPAC. This leads to $F(\ )$ in Eq. (6) becoming the following form:

$$F(\ ) = \sum_{r=1}^{|\mathcal{T}_1|+|\mathcal{T}_2|} s_r \ell(\rho_r) + \tau \sum_{k=1}^{|\mathcal{S}|} \delta_k + \frac{\eta}{2}\ {}^{\top} L\ + \frac{\lambda}{2}\|\ \|^2. \quad (10)$$

However the optimization procedure of Algorithm 1 remains unchanged. The only change is $F(\ )$ in step 5 of Algorithm 1 is changed to Eq. (10) and it can be optimized in the same way.

The weight of a weak metric α_t (step 6 of Algorithm 2) is calculated by taking the derivative of Z_t with respect to α_t and using bisection search for the value that meets $\frac{\partial Z_t}{\partial \alpha_t} = 0$.

7. EXPERIMENTAL RESULTS

Experimental results on four face recognition datasets are presented. The AR dataset [24] was used for an illustration of the effect of patch-based feature selection. As AR is a single modal dataset, comparisons of recognition performance with two single-modal boosting based metric learning methods are also given. The other three datasets are cross-modal based. The first is

Algorithm 2 Ensemble of Sparse Cross-Modal Metrics (ESPAC)

Construct two sets of triplets $\mathcal{T}_1$ and $\mathcal{T}_2$.
Initialize $s_r^1 = 1/(|\mathcal{T}_1| + |\mathcal{T}_2|), r = 1, 2, ..., |\mathcal{T}_1| + |\mathcal{T}_2|$.
Initialize $t = 1$.
while not converged **do**
  Train a weak metric $d_t(\ , \ )$ using distribution s^t by Algorithm 1.
  Choose the weight of the weak metric α_t using bisection.
  Update the distribution using:

$$s_r^{t+1} = \frac{s_r^t \exp\left(-\alpha_t \rho_r^t\right)}{Z_t}$$

  where $Z_t = \sum_{r=1}^{|\mathcal{T}_1|+|\mathcal{T}_2|} s_r^t \exp\left(-\alpha_t \rho_r^t\right)$ is a normalization factor such that s^{t+1} is a distribution.
  $t = t + 1$.
end while
Output $D(\ , \ ) = \sum_t \alpha_t d_t(\ , \ )$.

a newly collected Chinese resident identity card face dataset (NJU-ID) which was used for evaluating the performance of matching high resolution faces to low resolution faces. CUHK face sketch FERET (CUFSF) dataset [31, 37] was also used to evaluate the performance of recognizing sketches from photos. Whilst the CASIA NIR-VIS 2.0 dataset [21] was evaluated for matching visible light images (VIS) to near infrared images (NIR).

7.1 Datasets and Evaluation Protocols

AR Dataset: The AR dataset consists of over 4000 facial images with different variations, including facial expressions, illumination and occlusion by sunglasses or scarf. Two subsets of the dataset with occlusion variations of sunglasses and scarf were used in experiments, denoted as AR-Sunglasses and AR-Scarf in the following experiments. In total, the two subsets are from 111 subjects with each having 4 images, two are frontal images with no other variations and the two images are from two sessions. The other two are face images with occlusions of sunglasses or scarf. Example images are given in Fig. 3. For result reporting, both AR-Scarf and AR-Sunglasses were randomly divided into four parts for ten times. Each time, three parts were used for training and the remaining part for testing.

NJU-ID Dataset: The NJU-ID dataset contains images of 256 persons. For each person, there are one low resolution NJU-ID card image and fifty images collected from a high resolution digital camera. Only randomly chosen one of the fifty high resolution images was used in the experiment (Available from: http://cs.nju.edu.cn/rl/Data.html). The resident identity card image is of resolution 102×126 and the high resolution image is of resolution 640×480. Exemplar pairs from the dataset are shown in Fig. 7. To report results on this dataset, we randomly divided the dataset into 10 folds according to identity information and 10-fold cross-validation was used.

CUHK Face Sketch FERET Dataset (CUFSF): The CUFSF dataset was used for photo to sketch face recognition. It includes 1194 persons from the FERET dataset [27]. Samples are shown in Fig. 8. For each person, there are one photo and one sketch drawn by an artist after viewing the photo. To evaluate on this dataset, we randomly split the dataset into two parts for ten times and each time the first part was used for training and the other part was used for testing.

The CASIA NIR-VIS 2.0 Dataset: The CASIA NIR-VIS 2.0 dataset was used for evaluating the VIS-NIR face recognition. Example images in Fig. 9. It contains 725 subjects. We followed the same evaluation protocol on this dataset by [21]. The dataset was divided into two views. View 1 was used for parameter tuning and view 2 for reporting results.

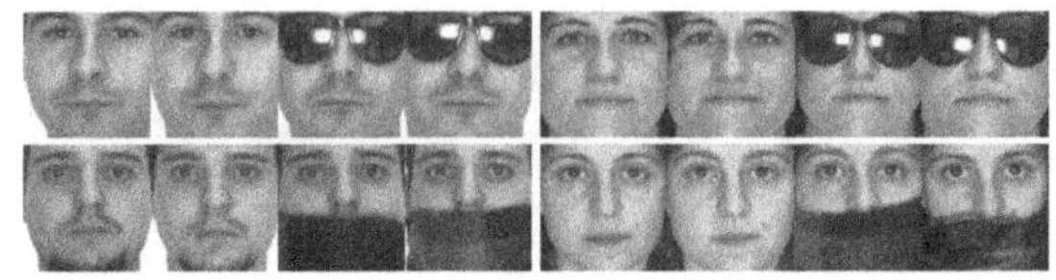

Figure 3: Examples of aligned face images of AR-Sunglasses and AR-Scarf. The first row are face images of AR-Sunglasses of two persons with each having four images. The second row are from AR-Scarf.

On all the four datasets, the feature extraction method described in Section 4 was applied. To maintain a processable number of features for our method and the compared methods, all the extracted local features were applied with principal component analysis (PCA) [2] locally with the features of a patch of dimension 15. When applying PCA locally, the first three components of PCA were removed.

Verification rates with equal error rates (EER) denoted as (VR-EER) and verification rates with false positive rates (FPR) equal to 0.1% denoted as (VR-FPR0.1%) are reported and we also provide the value of area under the receiver operating characteristic (AUC). Rank-1 recognition rates on NJU-ID, CUFSF and CASIA NIR-VIS 2.0 are also reported. To report rank-1 on NJU-ID dataset, high resolution face images in the test folds are registered as gallery images and low resolution images as probe images. On CUFSF dataset, photos are gallery images and sketches are probe images. On CASIA NIR-VIS 2.0, visible light images are registered as gallery images and near-infrared images are used as probe images.

7.2 Parameter Settings

There are a few parameters to tune in the proposed methods. The parameters of τ and η were tuned by setting γ and ϱ to zero without the sparse feature selection term. They were tuned separately; when tuning τ, η was set to zero and vise versa. After tuning τ and η, γ and ϱ were tuned together, with τ and η setting to the best parameters on each dataset. For tuning parameters, on AR and CUFSF, a separate split of data was used different from the ten partitions for results reporting. On NJU-ID dataset, a separate cross validation was used. On CASIA, the parameters were tuned on View 1 as required by the evaluation protocol.

Other parameters include the numbers of triplets used for training. In all the experiments, triplets were constructed by finding focal samples' intra-personal and inter-personal k-nearest neighbors. AR is a single modal dataset. On AR, intra-personal nearest neighbors denoted as $K1$ was set to 3 as there are four images per person. Inter-personal nearest neighbors denoted as $K2$, set to 100. On both NJU-ID and CUFSF, $K1$ was set to 1. $K2$ was set to 100 for NJU-ID dataset and 150 for CUFSF dataset. The setting of $K2$ on these three datasets were tuned. On CASIA NIR-VIS 2.0 dataset, both $K1$ and $K2$ were set to 10. Generally, larger $K1$ and $K2$ can lead to better results but it is not always the case as the results may become saturated. The settings on CASIA NIR-VIR 2.0 dataset need to balance between the performance and training time.

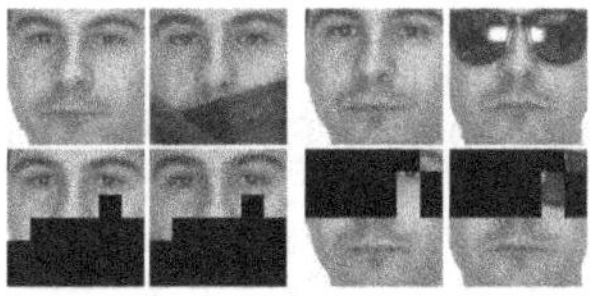

Figure 4: The first row shows example training images. In the second row, black patches on images correlate to zeros in the parameters of $_x$ and $_y$ of the weak learners. The two weak metrics successfully identify the occluded structures of faces.

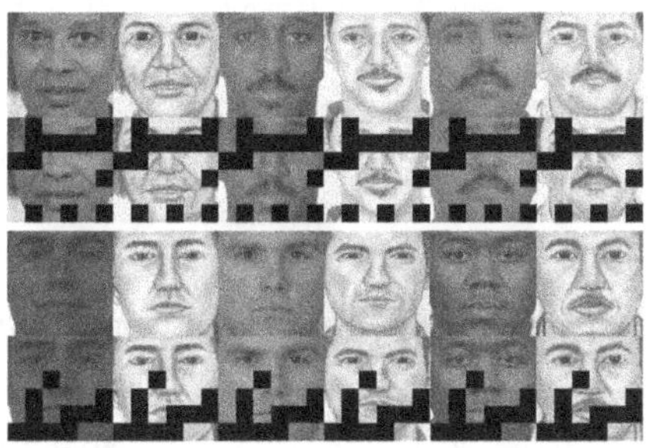

Figure 5: Results of patch based feature selection of the first two weak metrics on CUFSF dataset.

7.3 Visualization of Sparse Structures of Learned Weak Metrics

Fig. 4 shows the visualization results of the sparse structures of the patch-based weak metrics on AR-Sunglasses and AR-Scarf. The first row shows example training images. In the second row, the black patches correspond to zero values of the first learned weak metrics on two datasets. From the left four images in Fig. 4, the first weak metric on AR-Scarf does not use the lower parts of the face images for measuring distances as the lower parts are occluded. Same results are observed on AR-Sunglasses.

In Fig. 5, sparse structures of the first two weak metrics on CUFSF dataset are given. In the first row, the first three face pairs are those with the largest distances by using the first weak metric. In the second row, corresponding sparse structure of the first weak metric is given. The first weak metric does not use the features corresponding to eyes and jaws. By carefully observing the faces of this dataset, eye regions are less informative in distinguish person identities possibly because humans' eyes are hard to capture in sketches (Note that we have manually remove all the samples with eyeglasses in this experiment). For the jaws, as can be seen in the first three face pairs, since our alignment procedure is done by setting eyes in the same position, due to the error estimation of the ratio of faces' heights and widths, the faces in the sketches are shorter than their corresponding faces in photos, leading to misalignment in the jaw part. The third row also shows three face pairs with the largest distances by using the second weak metric. The forth row shows the structure of the second weak metric. The second weak metric does not use most of the jaw part. This is because the first weak learner is not sufficient to handle those images that have misalignment problems. The first and second weak learners are complementary as they use different face regions for measuring distances and the resulting same labeled pairs with large distances are different.

7.4 Influences of Different Number of Weak Metrics

Fig. 6 shows the influences of different number of weak metrics

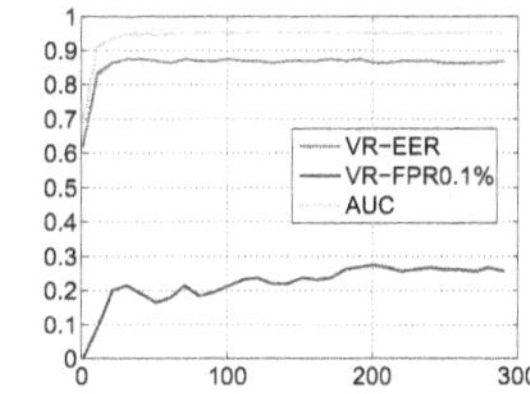

(a) BoostMetric

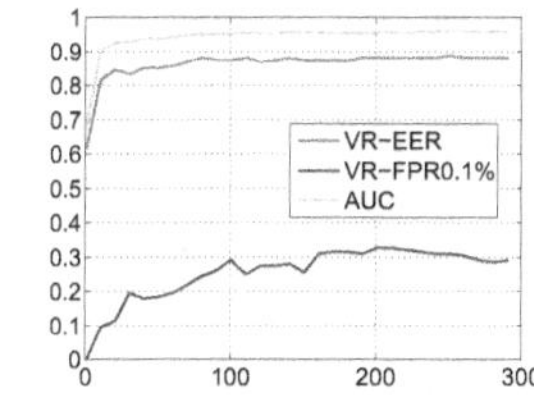

(b) AdaboostMetric

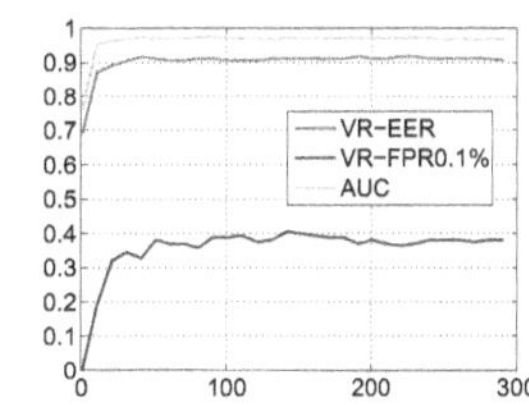

(c) ESPAC-S

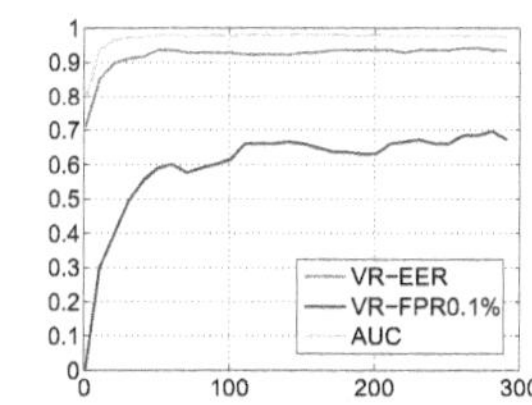

(d) ESPAC-PS

Figure 6: Influence of different number of weak metrics on AR-Scarf.

Table 1: Comparison with other boosting based metric learning methods on AR-Sunglasses dataset.

Methods	VR-EER(%)	VR-FPR0.1%(%)	AUC
BoostMetric	79.9 ± 1.7	18.0 ± 3.5	0.885
AdaboostMetric	80.2 ± 1.7	18.2 ± 3.4	0.884
ESPAC-NS	81.7 ± 2.0	18.0 ± 6.5	0.896
ESPAC-S	81.5 ± 2.2	18.1 ± 5.4	0.898
ESPAC-PS	$. \pm .$	$. \pm .$	.

on AR-Scarf and also comparative convergence results with BoostMetric [29] and AdaboostMetric [4]. In the following, ESPAC-NS denotes the proposed method with no feature selection. ESPAC-S is the proposed method with single-feature based group selection and ESPAC-PS uses the patch-based feature selection. As can be seen, the proposed methods, ESPAC-S and ESPAC-PS can obtain similar convergence results compared with BoostMetric and AdaboostMetric while achieving better results. Both ESPAC-S and ESPAC-PS converged with about 100 weak metrics. In the following, for reporting results, on all the four datasets, we used 150 weak metrics.

Table 2: Comparison with other boosting based metric learning methods on AR-Scarf dataset.

Methods	VR-EER(%)	VR-FPR0.1%(%)	AUC
MetricBoost	89.1 ± 1.3	34.8 ± 3.8	0.961
AdaboostMetric	89.2 ± 1.1	32.4 ± 3.6	0.960
ESPAC-NS	90.7 ± 1.2	40.6 ± 4.3	0.969
ESPAC-S	92.0 ± 0.9	45.3 ± 5.0	0.974
ESPAC-PS	$. \pm .$	$. \pm .$	.

7.5 Results on AR Dataset

Table 1 and Table 2 present results on AR-Sunglasses and AR-Scarf. The proposed methods have been compared with two boosting based metric learning methods. The code of BoostMetric [29] was provided by the authors. AdaboostMetric [4] was implemented by ourselves. The parameters of the two methods were tuned to their optimal. The best results were achieved by ESPAC-PS, followed by ESPAC-S. All three versions of the proposed method performed better than BoostMetric and

AdaboostMetric, except for VR-FPR0.1% on AR-Sunglasses, with the results of ESPAC-NS and ESPAC-S similar to those of BoostMetric and AdaboostMetric. ESPAC-PS improves the results to a large extent. This is mainly because that the face data of this dataset is under heavy occlusion and ESPAC-PS can successfully identify such occluded sparse structures.

7.6 Results on NJU-ID Dataset

Table 3 presents results on NJU-ID dataset. The proposed method has been compared with a set of state-of-the-art methods for face recognition. The parameters of the compared methods were adjusted to their optimal. In the table, the first six compared methods are single-modal based, including PCA [2], LDA [2], kernel principal component analysis (KPCA) [15], kernel discriminant analysis (KDA) [6], neighbourhood components analysis (NCA) [10] and large margin nearest neighbor (LMNN) [32]. Among them, PCA, LDA and KPCA are relatively worse than the other three. This is mainly that because PCA and KPCA are unsupervised. The performance of LDA is also unsatisfactory, as there are only two images per person. This leads to the within-class scatter matrix of LDA becomes singular and the performance degrades. The following six methods are multi-modal based, including CSR [20], kernel coupled spectral regression (KCSR) [20], canonical correlation analysis (CCA) [11], kernel canonical correlation analysis (KCCA) [18], CDFE [22] and multi-view discriminant analysis(MvDA) [13]. CSR, KCSR, CDFE and MvDA are widely used for multi-modal face recognition. Among all the compared methods, ESPAC-PS is the best with respect to all the evaluation protocols. Among the proposed three versions of our methods, ESPCA-NS is the worst. On NJU-ID dataset, as the face data has many other variations besides modality variation, this proves that by using feature selection together with the proposed boosting based cross-modal metric learning, the performances can be improved. The proposed methods are able to capture the variations in the extracted face features and neglect these noisy features.

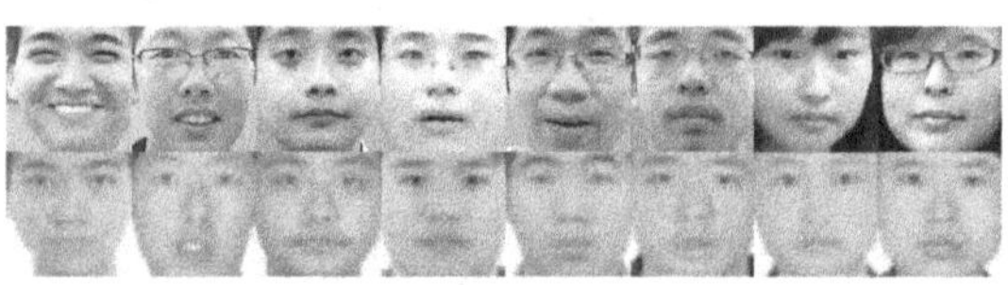

Figure 7: Examples of aligned face images. The first row are samples of high resolution and the second row are corresponding samples of low resolution.

7.7 Results on CUFSF Dataset

Table 4 presents the recognition results on CUFSF dataset. The six single-modal methods and six multi-modal methods are also compared. Compared with these state-of-the-art methods, the proposed ESPAC-PS is the best among three of all the evaluation protocols (though for rank-1, CSR achieved similar performance). Among the six single-modal methods, the best results were achieved by KDA. The results of KDA are comparable with our methods. As KDA is a non-linear method, this may illustrate that the data distribution has non-linear properties, while the proposed method is linear-based. It is likely that extending our method to non-linear based by design non-linear weak metrics can further improve the recognition results.

Figure 8: Examples of aligned face images. The first row are samples of photos and the second row are corresponding s-ketches.

Table 3: Comparison with other methods on NJU-ID dataset.

Methods	VR-EER(%)	VR-FPR0.1%(%)	Rank-1(%)	AUC
PCA	63.6 ± 5.2	8.2 ± 7.3	13.3 ± 6.5	0.688
LDA	59.7 ± 5.3	8.1 ± 8.7	10.9 ± 8.1	0.637
KPCA	64.0 ± 4.8	8.2 ± 6.8	14.0 ± 5.8	0.687
KDA	67.6 ± 4.7	11.7 ± 8.8	18.3 ± 8.4	0.723
LMNN	69.9 ± 3.9	13.4 ± 11.2	20.3 ± 6.4	0.737
NCA	65.6 ± 3.3	9.4 ± 6.8	15.6 ± 6.2	0.715
CSR	67.2 ± 3.9	11.2 ± 11.1	18.6 ± 8.2	0.730
KCSR	68.3 ± 4.2	16.5 ± 11.1	19.4 ± 9.4	0.727
CCA	62.5 ± 4.5	5.1 ± 5.8	10.5 ± 5.8	0.638
KCCA	62.1 ± 3.6	7.0 ± 8.6	10.6 ± 5.0	0.632
CDFE	58.2 ± 5.1	2.3 ± 2.6	6.2 ± 3.6	0.588
MvDA	62.1 ± 4.3	4.3 ± 5.6	10.2 ± 4.3	0.628
ESPAC-NS	65.0 ± 7.5	14.8 ± 6.0	19.7 ± 5.1	0.738
ESPAC-S	69.2 ± 6.9	16.6 ± 8.6	20.4 ± 5.5	0.747
ESPAC-PS	. ± .	. ± .	. ± .	.

Table 4: Comparison with other methods on CUFSF dataset.

Methods	VR-EER(%)	VR-FPR0.1%(%)	Rank-1(%)	AUC
PCA	85.6 ± 5.2	23.9 ± 7.3	37.9 ± 6.5	0.937
LDA	79.0 ± 5.3	20.2 ± 8.7	21.4 ± 8.1	0.874
KPCA	85.6 ± 4.8	23.8 ± 6.8	37.9 ± 5.8	0.937
KDA	93.9 ± 4.7	41.1 ± 8.8	53.2 ± 8.4	0.985
LMNN	93.2 ± 3.9	35.4 ± 11.2	49.2 ± 6.4	0.982
NCA	92.8 ± 3.3	31.8 ± 6.8	42.5 ± 6.2	0.979
CSR	92.8 ± 3.9	44.9 ± 11.1	. ± .	0.980
KCSR	93.7 ± 4.2	16.4 ± 11.1	45.1 ± 9.4	0.983
CCA	91.6 ± 4.5	17.5 ± 5.8	35.5 ± 5.8	0.973
KCCA	93.1 ± 3.6	14.0 ± 8.6	35.6 ± 5.0	0.980
CDFE	89.7 ± 5.1	17.6 ± 2.6	24.4 ± 3.6	0.960
MvDA	80.2 ± 4.3	7.3 ± 5.6	9.7 ± 4.3	0.884
ESPAC-NS	94.0 ± 3.8	43.4 ± 2.8	52.2 ± 5.5	0.987
ESPAC-S	94.2 ± 3.4	44.6 ± 3.8	53.3 ± 2.0	0.987
ESPAC-PS	. ± .	. ± .	53.7 ± 2.2	.

7.8 Results on CASIA NIR-VIS 2.0 Dataset

On CASIA NIR-VIS 2.0 dataset, results of the proposed methods and state-of-the-art methods are given in Table 5. Note that results of NCA is not given as the computational cost of NCA is too heavy on this dataset. The compared methods were all adjusted to their optimal. On this dataset, ESPAC-S and ESPAC-PS achieved the best AUC result. ESPAC-PS is best for the VR-EER performance measure. Among the three versions of the proposed methods, the improvement of ESPAC-S and ESPAC-PS over ESPAC-NS is relatively small. As this dataset is collected under near controlled environment, the only variations are eyeglasses and a few expression changes which are of a small portion. Another observation is that our methods are worse than LDA and CSR with respect to VR-FPR0.1% and Rank-1. This is due to that our methods use part of all the triplets constructed on this dataset. For low rank-1 rate, it means for some samples, their intra-personal distances are still larger than one of their inter-personal distances. As in ESPAC, triplets are all pre-constructed and kept fixed during optimization. Although

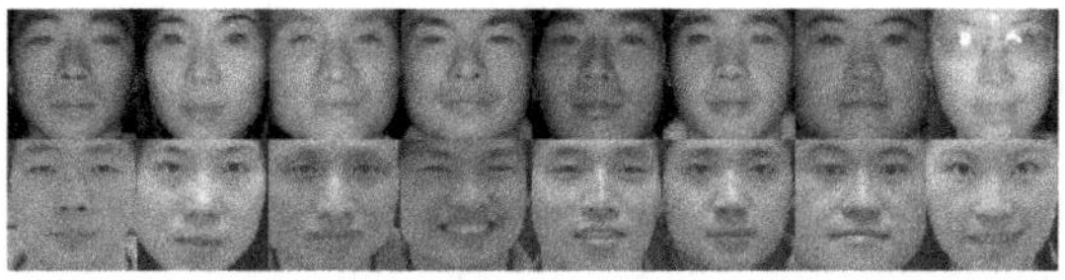

Figure 9: Examples of aligned faces in CASIA NIR-VIS 2.0 dataset.

Table 5: Comparison with other methods on CASIA NIR-VIS 2.0 dataset.

Methods	VR-EER(%)	VR-FPR0.1%(%)	Rank-1(%)	AUC
PCA	83.1 ± 0.5	20.8 ± 1.7	38.6 ± 1.0	0.909
LDA	88.6 ± 0.6	$. \pm .$	$. \pm .$	0.954
KPCA	82.2 ± 0.5	17.6 ± 1.5	34.0 ± 1.1	0.902
KDA	90.2 ± 0.4	31.6 ± 3.1	50.7 ± 1.6	0.963
LMNN	87.3 ± 0.6	27.1 ± 1.8	41.7 ± 0.8	0.946
CSR	89.3 ± 0.6	44.2 ± 1.4	55.6 ± 0.7	0.957
KCSR	90.1 ± 0.5	27.2 ± 3.3	49.6 ± 0.9	0.962
CCA	84.0 ± 0.5	23.7 ± 1.1	30.2 ± 1.0	0.917
KCCA	82.5 ± 0.4	20.6 ± 1.3	25.8 ± 1.1	0.905
CDFE	76.7 ± 0.3	1.9 ± 0.2	19.4 ± 1.2	0.832
MvDA	84.1 ± 0.4	16.2 ± 1.7	29.5 ± 1.4	0.918
ESPAC-NS	90.3 ± 0.5	33.6 ± 1.3	45.1 ± 1.6	0.972
ESPAC-S	90.8 ± 0.5	35.0 ± 1.4	46.6 ± 1.7	.
ESPAC-PS	$. \pm .$	34.8 ± 1.2	46.5 ± 1.5	.

ESPAC can learn well on the given sets of triplets, there are still unseen triplets that the learned ESPAC not perform well. A solution is to perform ESPAC multiple passes to further enhance the performances, as is also suggested by [32, 29].

7.9 Comparison of Training Time

A comparison of training time on AR-Scarf is given in Table 6. The two compared methods, BoostMetric and AdaboostMetric, also use triplets for training. Implementation of BoostMetric was provided by its authors. AdaboostMetric was implemented by strictly following its paper. The experiments were conducted on the same computer under exactly the same setting. The training time of each of the methods is related to the number of triplets used. For 5 different numbers of triplets constructed, the training times (in seconds) are given in Table 6. The complexity of BoostMetric per iteration mainly relies on the number of triplets ($O(N \times S \times D)$, N the number of samples, S the number of same class neighbors, D the number of different classes neighbors). AdaboostMetric decomposes triplets into pairs ($O(N \times (S + D))$) and is more efficient. The implementation of the proposed methods uses a modification of the scheme in the work of McFee and Lanckriet [25], which is neither triplet nor pair based. ESPAC-NS with this scheme is very efficient. While ESPAC-S and ESPAC-PS use ADMM to learn SPAC which takes hundreds of iterations to converge, the training processes are longer. However, with this scheme, the training time increases little with the triplets' number increases.

Table 6: Comparison of training time (in seconds).

Methods	9960	19920	29880	39840	49800
MetricBoost	924	1863	2724	3926	5040
AdaboostMetric	573	987	1412	1839	2203
ESPAC-NS	61	69	75	82	91
ESPAC-S	2237	2364	2513	2647	2773
ESPAC-PS	2434	2626	2768	2776	2898

7.10 Interpretations and Some Possible Extensions

Relationship with face attribute learning. In [17], the authors proposed to learn semantic face features to describe face attributes. The proposed SPAC also can be seen as learning a classifier but with the objective of separating pairs of samples encoded in triplets. SPAC automatically determines the best regions for separating the current inseparable groups of triplets. From Fig. 4 and Fig. 5, the learned SPAC also have some implicit semantic meanings such as misaligned jaw on CUFSF dataset or occluded eye areas on AR dataset. In this way, the proposed method is related to automatic face semantic feature learning, without the need of labeling attributes and manually determine attribute related face regions for training. As the method in [17] used non-linear SVM for training, this further provides us insight to make SPAC non-linear in our future work.

Relationship with Mahalanobis metric learning. As the proposed method is also applicable for single-modal metric learning. Compared with Mahalanobis metric learning, it is easy to see that Mahalanobis metric tries to separate samples in the space of ${}_i - {}_j$, while the cross-modal metric is using the space of $[{}_i; -{}_j]$. As has been discussed in [7], the former space may reduce data separability and our formulation is a more generalized one. We have partly proved this on AR dataset that our method even the non-sparse based version is either better or comparable to BoostMetric and AdaboostMetric. So it is worth trying to test it on more single-modal based datasets.

Extend to other feature extraction frameworks. In Section 4, we have introduced the local face feature extraction method used in this paper. It is clear that combinations with other facial landmark features and features at multiple scales [8] are also possible. In this way, the proposed method will be able to find more informative face landmarks for recognition. Combining with the convolutional neural networks (CNN) [19] is also an interesting new line of research as the features of CNN have invariant spatial properties.

8. CONCLUSION

In this paper, an ensemble of sparse cross-modal metric learning method is proposed for heterogeneous face recognition. A set of sparse cross-modal weak metrics are learned to remove modality variations. In addition, feature selection is performed to remove noisy features relating to the variations such as, occlusions, expressions and illumination changes. Each learned weak metric selects a few face features or a few face regions for measuring distances between samples. Although one weak cross-modal metric is not able to handle all the variations, by using an Adaboost framework to reassign weights based on triplets, the finally learned weak metrics become complementary. All the weak metrics are combined into a strong one which is able to deal with various variations. State-of-the-art performances on three heterogeneous face recognition datasets are achieved. On the AR dataset, we have shown that the proposed methods can improve the recognition results by a large extent for faces with heavy occlusions.

There are a few future directions of this work. One is to extend the linear weak metrics to non-linear ones which may further improve face recognition performances. Another is that multi-pass ensembles can be further tested. Besides, as the framework is fairly flexible, combination with other face feature extraction framework such as face landmark indexed features, can also be tested to find which face landmarks convey more information for face matching.

Acknowledgement

The work is supported by the National Science Foundation of China (Nos. 61432008, 61305068, 61321491), the Graduate Research Innovation Program of Jiangsu, China (KYLX_0047) and the Collaborative Innovation Center of Novel Software Technology and Industrialization. J. Huo is also supported by a scholarship from the China Scholarship Council as a one-year visiting student at the University of Manchester.

9. REFERENCES

[1] Y. Atzmon, U. Shalit, and G. Chechik. Learning sparse metrics, one feature at a time. In *Proc. 1st Workshop on Feature Extraction Modern Questions and Challenges*, pages 30–48, 2015.

[2] P. N. Belhumeur, J. P. Hespanha, and D. J. Kriegman. Eigenfaces vs. fisherfaces: Recognition using class specific linear projection. *TPAMI*, 19(7):711–720, 1997.

[3] A. Bellet, A. Habrard, and M. Sebban. Metric learning. *Synthesis Lectures on Artificial Intelligence and Machine Learning*, 9(1):1–151, 2015.

[4] J. Bi, D. Wu, L. Lu, M. Liu, Y. Tao, and M. Wolf. Adaboost on low-rank psd matrices for metric learning. In *CVPR*, pages 2617–2624, 2011.

[5] S. Boyd, N. Parikh, E. Chu, B. Peleato, and J. Eckstein. Distributed optimization and statistical learning via the alternating direction method of multipliers. *Foundations and Trends in Machine Learning*, 3(1):1–122, 2011.

[6] D. Cai, X. He, and J. Han. Speed up kernel discriminant analysis. *VLDB J.*, 20(1):21–33, 2011.

[7] D. Chen, X. Cao, L. Wang, F. Wen, and J. Sun. Bayesian face revisited: A joint formulation. In *ECCV*, pages 566–579. 2012.

[8] D. Chen, X. Cao, F. Wen, and J. Sun. Blessing of dimensionality: High-dimensional feature and its efficient compression for face verification. In *CVPR*, pages 3025–3032, 2013.

[9] C. Geng and X. Jiang. Face recognition using sift features. In *ICIP*, pages 3313–3316, 2009.

[10] J. Goldberger, S. Roweis, G. Hinton, and R. Salakhutdinov. Neighbourhood components analysis. In *NIPS*, pages 513–520, 2004.

[11] H. Hotelling. Relations between two sets of variates. *Biometrika*, pages 321–377, 1936.

[12] Y. Jin, J. Lu, and Q. Ruan. Coupled discriminative feature learning for heterogeneous face recognition. *TIFS*, 10(3):640–652, 2015.

[13] M. Kan, S. Shan, H. Zhang, S. Lao, and X. Chen. Multi-view discriminant analysis. In *ECCV*, pages 808–821. 2012.

[14] C. Kang, S. Liao, Y. He, J. Wang, W. Niu, S. Xiang, and C. Pan. Cross-modal similarity learning: A low rank bilinear formulation. In *CIKM*, pages 1251–1260, 2015.

[15] K. I. Kim, K. Jung, and H. J. Kim. Face recognition using kernel principal component analysis. *IEEE Signal Process. Lett.*, 9(2):40–42, 2002.

[16] B. F. Klare and A. K. Jain. Heterogeneous face recognition using kernel prototype similarities. *TPAMI*, 35(6):1410–1422, 2013.

[17] N. Kumar, A. C. Berg, P. N. Belhumeur, and S. K. Nayar. Attribute and simile classifiers for face verification. In *ICCV*, pages 365–372, 2009.

[18] P. L. Lai and C. Fyfe. Kernel and nonlinear canonical correlation analysis. *IJNS*, 10(05):365–377, 2000.

[19] Y. LeCun and Y. Bengio. Convolutional networks for images, speech, and time series. *The handbook of brain theory and neural networks*, pages 255–258, 1998.

[20] Z. Lei and S. Z. Li. Coupled spectral regression for matching heterogeneous faces. In *CVPR*, pages 1123–1128, 200.

[21] S. Li, D. Yi, Z. Lei, and S. Liao. The casia nir-vis 2.0 face database. In *CVPR Workshops*, pages 348–353, 2013.

[22] D. Lin and X. Tang. Inter-modality face recognition. In *ECCV*, pages 13–26. 2006.

[23] K. Liu, A. Bellet, and F. Sha. Similarity learning for high-dimensional sparse data. In *AISTATS*, pages 653–662, 2015.

[24] A. M. Martinez. The ar face database. *CVC Technical Report*, 24, 1998.

[25] B. McFee and G. R. Lanckriet. Metric learning to rank. In *ICML*, pages 775–782, 2010.

[26] A. Mignon and F. Jurie. Cmml: a new metric learning approach for cross modal matching. In *ACCV*, pages 1–14, 2012.

[27] P. J. Phillips, H. Moon, S. A. Rizvi, and P. J. Rauss. The feret evaluation methodology for face-recognition algorithms. *TPAMI*, 22(10):1090–1104, 2000.

[28] R. E. Schapire and Y. Singer. Improved boosting algorithms using confidence-rated predictions. *Mach. Learn.*, 37(3):297–336, 1999.

[29] C. Shen, J. Kim, L. Wang, and A. Van Den Hengel. Positive semidefinite metric learning using boosting-like algorithms. *JMLR*, 13(1):1007–1036, 2012.

[30] C. Shen, A. Welsh, and L. Wang. Psdboost: Matrix-generation linear programming for positive semidefinite matrices learning. In *NIPS*, pages 1473–1480, 2009.

[31] X. Wang and X. Tang. Face photo-sketch synthesis and recognition. *TPAMI*, 31(11):1955–1967, 2009.

[32] K. Q. Weinberger and L. K. Saul. Distance metric learning for large margin nearest neighbor classification. *JMLR*, 10:207–244, 2009.

[33] L. Yang, R. Jin, L. Mummert, R. Sukthankar, A. Goode, B. Zheng, S. C. Hoi, and M. Satyanarayanan. A boosting framework for visuality-preserving distance metric learning and its application to medical image retrieval. *TPAMI*, 32(1):30–44, 2010.

[34] D. Yi, Z. Lei, and S. Z. Li. Shared representation learning for heterogenous face recognition. In *FG*, volume 1, pages 1–7, 2015.

[35] Y. Ying, K. Huang, and C. Campbell. Sparse metric learning via smooth optimization. In *NIPS*, pages 2214–2222, 2009.

[36] W. Zhang, X. Wang, and X. Tang. Lighting and pose robust face sketch synthesis. In *ECCV*, pages 420–433. 2010.

[37] W. Zhang, X. Wang, and X. Tang. Coupled information-theoretic encoding for face photo-sketch recognition. In *CVPR*, pages 513–520, 2011.

[38] P. Zhou, L. Du, M. Fan, and Y.-D. Shen. An lle based heterogeneous metric learning for cross-media retrieval. In *SDM*, pages 64–72, 2015.

Shorter-is-Better: Venue Category Estimation from Micro-Video

Jianglong Zhang[†,‡,*], Liqiang Nie[§,‡], Xiang Wang[‡], Xiangnan He[‡], Xianglin Huang[†], Tat-Seng Chua[‡]
[†] Faculty of Science and Technolgy, Communication University of China, Beijing, China
[‡] School of Computing, National University of Singapore, Singapore
[§] Department of Computer Science and Technology, Shandong University, Shandong, China
{ajiang.zh, nieliqiang, xiangwang.nus, xiangnanhe, exl.huang}@gmail.com, dcscts@nus.edu.sg

ABSTRACT

According to our statistics on over 2 million micro-videos, only 1.22% of them are associated with venue information, which greatly hinders the location-oriented applications and personalized services. To alleviate this problem, we aim to label the bite-sized video clips with venue categories. It is, however, nontrivial due to three reasons: 1) no available benchmark dataset; 2) insufficient information, low quality, and information loss; and 3) complex relatedness among venue categories. Towards this end, we propose a scheme comprising of two components. In particular, we first crawl a representative set of micro-videos from Vine and extract a rich set of features from textual, visual and acoustic modalities. We then, in the second component, build a tree-guided multi-task multi-modal learning model to estimate the venue category for each unseen micro-video. This model is able to jointly learn a common space from multi-modalities and leverage the predefined Foursquare hierarchical structure to regularize the relatedness among venue categories. Extensive experiments have well-validated our model. As a side research contribution, we have released our data, codes and involved parameters.

Keywords

Micro-Video Analysis; Multi-Modal Multi-Task Learning; Venue Category Estimation.

1. INTRODUCTION

The popularity of the traditional online video sharing platforms, like Youtube[1], has changed everything about the Internet [39, 18]. Servers like Youtube have enabled users to capture high-quality and long videos, upload and share them socially with everyone. But the late 2012 has seen a dramatic shift in the way Internet users digest videos: micro-videos spread rapidly across various online flagship platforms, such as Viddy[2], Vine[3], Instagram[4] and Snapchat[5]. Considering Vine as an example, as of December 2015, it has experienced an exponential explosion in its user and video base, reaching approximately 200 million active users monthly and 1.5 billion video loops daily[6]. One reason that such bite-sized videos are gaining popularity is because users can conveniently shoot and instantly share videos via their smartphones without the need for professional camera work, editing, and, therefore, significant budgets. Besides, it takes seconds rather than minutes or even hours to view. The micro-video trends confirms this saying: "every good comes in small packages".

In addition to their value in brevity, authenticity and low cost, micro-video platforms have started encouraging users to associate spatial contexts (venues) to videos. The venue information is usually selected manually by the user relying on a GPS enabled device, and each venue is automatically aligned with a venue category via the Foursquare API[7]. This new feature benefits multifaceted aspects: 1) Footprints recording. It facilitates users to vividly archive where they were and what they did. 2) Personalized applications. Such people-centric location data enables precise personalized services, such as suggesting local restaurants, alerting regional weather, and spreading business information to nearby customers. And 3) other location-based services. Location information is helpful for the inference of users' interests, the improvement of activity prediction, and the simplification of landmark-oriented video search. Despite its significance, users of micro-video platforms have been slow to adopt this geospatial feature: in a random sample over 2 million Vine videos, we found that only 1.22% of the videos are associated with venue information. It is thus highly desired to infer the missing geographic cues.

As a preliminary research, we aim to first infer the venue categories from micro-videos, rather than the exact venues. This task is, however, non-trivial due to the following challenges: 1) **Insufficient information**. The most prominent attribute of micro-video platforms is that they are thriving heavily in the realm of shortness and instant. For example, Vine allows users to upload about

*Jianglong Zhang is a visiting student of National University of Singapore, supervised by Dr. Liqiang Nie and Prof. Tat-Seng Chua.
[1]https://www.youtube.com.

[2]http://www.fullscreen.com/.
[3]https://vine.co/.
[4]https://www.instagram.com/.
[5]https://www.snapchat.com/.
[6]http://tinyurl.com/zttwt6u.
[7]https://github.com/mLewisLogic/foursquare.
[9]https://developer.foursquare.com/categorytree.

MM '16, October 15-19, 2016, Amsterdam, Netherlands

DOI: http://dx.doi.org/10.1145/2964284.2964307

Figure 1: The hierarchical structure of the venue categories. We only illustrate part of the structure due to the limited space. The entire tree can be viewed here[9].

six-second videos online; Snapchat offers its users the option to create 10-second micro-videos; and Viddy limits the length of its upload videos to 30 seconds. Persuasively, short length makes video production and broadcasting easily, downloading timely, and playing fluently on portable devices. However, in contrast to the traditional long videos, the visual information conveyed by micro-videos is somehow inadequate and it is thus unable to provide rich contexts for effective similarity measurement. Besides, as aforementioned, only around 1.22% of videos have venue labels, which brings in a challenge for training data collection. 2) **Low quality**. Most portable devices have nothing to offer for video stabilization. Some videos can thus be shaky or bumpy, which greatly hinders the visual expression. Furthermore, the audio track that comes along with the video, can be in different types of distortion and noise, such as buzzing, hums, hisses, and whistling, which is probably caused by the poor microphones or complex surrounding environments. 3) **Information loss**. Apart from acoustic and visual modalities, micro-videos are, more often than not, uploaded with textual descriptions, which express some useful cues that may be not available in the other two modalities. However, the textual information may be not well correlated with visual and acoustic cues. Moreover, according to our statistics upon 276,624 Vine videos, more than 11.4% of them do not have such texts, probably the results of users' casual habits. This serious information missing problem greatly reduces the usability of textual modality. And 4) **hierarchical structure**. The venues of micro-videos are organized into hundreds of categories, which are not independent but hierarchically correlated. Part of this structure is shown in Figure 1. How to explore such structure to guide the venue category estimation is largely untapped.

To address the aforementioned challenges, we propose a scheme consisting of two components, as illustrated in Figure 2. In the first component, we work towards data preparation. In particular, we first collect a representative set of micro-videos with their associated venue IDs and map these venue IDs to venue categories via Foursquare API. We then extract discriminant features from the textual, visual and acoustic modalities of each video, respectively. In a sense, appropriate fusion of multi-modal features are able to comprehensively and complementarily represent micro-videos, which somehow alleviates the data insufficiency and is robust to the low quality of some modalities. Thereafter, we complete the missing modalities for some videos via matrix factorization techniques, which well solves the information loss problem. The second component aims to label micro-videos with venue categories. Towards this end, we present a TRee-guided mUlti-task Multi-modal leArNiNg model, **TRUMANN** for short. This model intelligently learns a common feature space from multi-modal heterogeneous spaces and utilizes the learned common space to represent each micro-video. Meanwhile, the **TRUMANN** treats each venue category as a task and leverages the pre-defined hierarchical structure of venue categories to regularize the relatedness among tasks via a novel group lasso. These two objectives are accomplished within a unified framework. As a byproduct, the tree-guided group lasso is capable of learning task-sharing and task-specific features. Extensive experiments on our collected real-world dataset have demonstrated the advantages of our model.

The main contributions are in threefold:

1. As far as we know, this is the first work on venue category estimation for micro-videos. We conducted an in-depth analysis of the challenges of this research problem.
2. We proposed a novel tree-guided multi-task multi-modal learning approach. This approach is able to jointly fuse multi-modal information, capture the task relatedness constrained by a pre-defined tree structure.
3. We built a large-scale micro-video datasets. Meanwhile, we have released our data, codes, and involved parameter settings to facilitate the research communities[10].

The remainder of the paper is organized as follows. Section 2 reviews the related work. Section 3 and 4 detail our data preparation and our proposed **TRUMANN** model, respectively. Experimental settings and results are reported in Section 5, followed by the conclusion and future work in Section 6.

2. RELATED WORK

Our work is related to a broad spectrum of multimedia location estimation, and multi-modal multi-task learning.

2.1 Multimedia Venue Estimation

Nowadays, it has become convenient to capture images and videos on the mobile end and associate them with GPS tags. Such a hybrid data structure can benefit a wide variety of potential multimedia applications, such as location recognition [19], landmark search [6], augmented reality[4], and commercial recommendations [44]. It hence has attracted great attention from the multimedia community. Generally speaking, prior efforts can be divided into two

[10]http://acmmm16.wix.com/mm16.

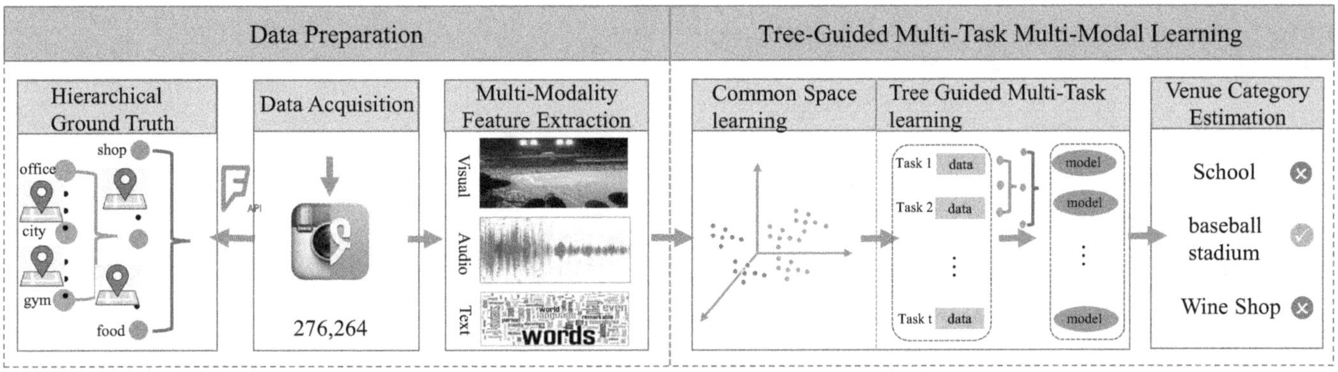

Figure 2: Graphical representation of our framework.

categories: mono-modal venue estimation [4, 6] and multi-modal venue estimation [19, 13, 8]. Approaches in the former category extract a rich set of visual features from images and leverage the visual features to train either shallow or deep models to estimate the venues of the given images. As reported in [19], the landmark identification [6] and scene classification [4] of images are the key factors to recognize the venues. The basic philosophy behind these approaches is that certain visual features in images correlate strongly with certain geographies even if the relationship is not strong enough to specifically pinpoint a location coordinate. Beyond the mono-modal venue estimation which only takes the visual information into consideration, multi-modal venue estimation works by inferring the geo-coordinates of the recording places of the given videos by fusing the textual metadata and visual or acoustic cues [12, 8]. Friendland et al. [12] determined the geo-coordinates of the Flickr videos based on both textual metadata and visual cues. Audio tracks from the Placing Task 2011 dataset videos were also used to train a location estimation models and it achieved reasonable performance [27]. The main idea is that the integration of multiple modalities can lead to better results, and it is consistent to the old saying "two heads are better than one". However, multi-modal venue estimation is still at its infant stage, and more efforts should be dedicated to improve this line of research.

Noticeably, the venue granularity of the targeted multimedia entities in the aforementioned literature varies significantly. Roughly, the spatial resolutions are in three-levels: city-level [19, 13], within-city-level [35, 6, 28] and close-to-exact GPS level [12]. City-level and within-city-level location estimation can be applied to multimedia organization [9], location visualization [6], and image classification [37]. However, their granularities are large, which may be not suitable for some application scenarios, such as business venue discovery [5]. The granularity of close-to-exact GPS level is finer; nevertheless, it is hard to estimate the precise coordinates, especially for the indoor cases. For example, it is challenging to distinguish an office on the third floor and a coffee shop on the second floor within the same building, since the GPS is not available indoors.

Our work differs the above methods from the following two aspects: 1) We focus on the estimation of venue category which is neither city-level nor the precise location. This is because, venue category is more abstract concept than single venue name, which can help many applications for personalized and location-based services/marketing [5]. And 2) micro-videos are the medium between images and traditional long videos, which pose tough challenges.

2.2 Multi-Modal Multi-Task Learning

Venue category estimation of micro-videos exhibits dual-heterogeneities. In particular, a single learning task have features from multiple modalities and multiple learning tasks could be related to each other via their commonalities [41]. In the light of this, our proposed **TRUMANN** falls into the community of multi-view multi-task learning.

The literature on the multi-task problem with multi-modal data is relatively sparse. He et al.[20] proposed a graph-based iterative framework for multi-view multi-task learning (**IteM^2**) and applied it to text classification. However, it can only deal with problems with non-negative feature values. In addition, it is a transductive model. Hence it is unable to generate predictive models for independent and unseen testing samples. To address the intrinsic limitations of transductive models, Zhang et al.[47] proposed an inductive multi-view multi-task learning model (**regMVMT**). **regMVMT** penalizes the disagreement of models learned from different sources over the unlabeled samples. However, without prior knowledge, simply restricting all the tasks to be similar is inappropriate. As an extension of **regMVMT**, an inductive convex shared structure learning algorithm for multi-view multi-task problem (**CSL-MTMV**) was developed in [23]. Compared to **regMVMT**, **CSL-MTMV** considers the shared predictive structure among multiple tasks.

However, none of the methods mentioned above can be applied to venue category estimation directly. This is due to the following reasons: 1) **IteM^2**, **regMVMT** and **CSL-MTMV** are all binary classification models, of which the extension to multi-class or regression problem is nontrivial, especially when the number of classes is large; and 2) the tasks in venue category prediction are pre-defined as a hierarchical structure.

3. DATA PREPARATION

In this section, we detail the data preparation, containing dataset collection, feature extraction and missing data completion.

3.1 Dataset and Ground Truth Construction

We crawled the micro-videos from Vine through its public API[11]. In particular, we first manually chose a small set

[11] https://github.com/davoclavo/vinepy.

Table 1: Number of micro-videos in each of the top ten layer categories.

Top-layer Category	Num.	Top-layer Category	Num.
Outdoors & Recreation	93,196	Shop & Service	10,976
Arts & Entertainment	88,393	Residence	8,867
Travel & Transport	24,916	Nightlife Spot	8,021
Professional & Other	18,700	Food	6,484
College & Education	12,595	Event	1,047

Table 2: Leaf categories with the most and the least of micro-videos.

Leaf Category with the Most Videos	Num.	Leaf Category with the Least Videos	Num.
City	30,803	Bakery	53
Theme Park	16,383	Volcano	51
Neighborhood	15,002	Medical	51
Other Outdoors	10,035	Classroom	51
Park	10,035	Toy & Games	50

of active users from Vine as our seed users. We then adopted the breadth-first strategy to expand our user sets via gathering their followers. We terminated our expansion after three layers. For each collected user, we crawled his/her published videos, video descriptions and venue information if available. In such way, we harvested 2 million micro-videos. Thereinto, only about 24,000 micro-videos contain Foursquare check-in information. After removing the duplicate venue IDs, we further expanded our video set by crawling all videos in each venue ID with the help of vinepy API. This eventually yielded a dataset of 276,264 videos distributed in 442 Foursquare venue categories. Each venue ID was mapped to a venue category via the Foursquare API, which serves as the ground truth. As shown in Figure3, 99.8% of videos are shorter than 7 seconds.

Foursquare organizes its venue categories into a four-layer hierarchical structure[12], with 341, 312 and 52 leaf nodes in the second-layer, third-layer and fourth-layer, respectively. The top-layer of this structure contains ten non-leaf nodes (coarse venue categories). To visualize the coverage and representativeness of our collected micro-videos, we plotted and compared the distribution curves over the number of leaf categories between our dataset and the original structure, as shown in Figure 4. It is worth mentioning that, the number of leaf categories distributed in Foursquare is extremely unbalanced. For instance, the 'Food' category has 253 leaf nodes; while the 'Residence' only contains five leaf nodes. Accordingly, the distribution of our crawled videos over the top-layer categories also shows such unbalance, as displays in Table 1.

On the other hand, we observed that some leaf categories contain only a small number of micro-videos. For instance, 'Bank/Financial' only consists of 3 samples in our dataset, which is hard to train a robust classifier. We hence removed the leaf categories with less than 50 micro-videos. At last, we obtained 270,145 micro-videos distributed in 188 Foursquare leaf categories. Table 2 lists the top five leaf categories with the most and the least micro-videos, respectively.

3.2 Feature Extraction

We extracted a rich set of features from visual, acoustic and textual modalities, respectively.

[12]https://developer.foursquare.com/categorytree.

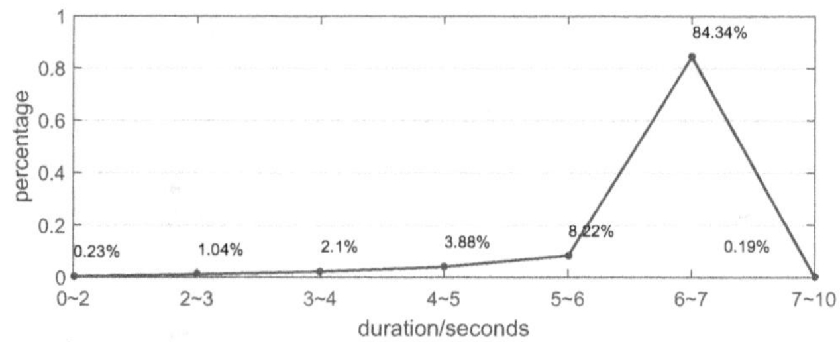

Figure 3: Duration distribution in our dataset.

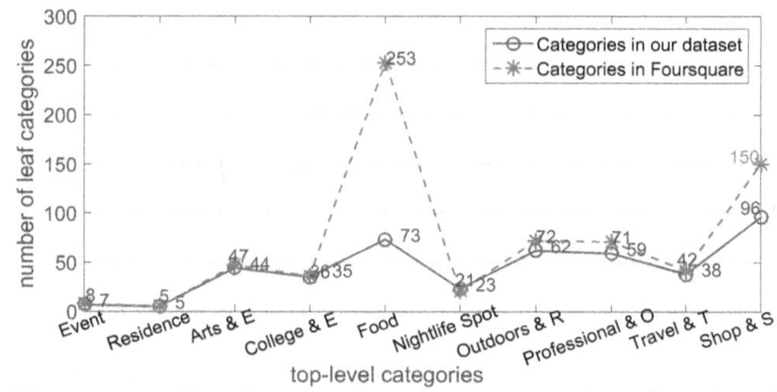

Figure 4: Top-level venue category distribution in terms of the number of their leaf nodes.

3.2.1 *Features in Visual Modality*

Scenes or visual concepts conveyed by the visual modality are intuitive signals of the venue category. For instance, dishes, drinks, waiter and tables are the main elements of restaurants. This motivates us to extract high-level semantics from the visual modality to represent the micro-videos. Deep convolutional neural networks (CNNs) have been established as a powerful model to capture the visual concepts of images [45, 43]. We employed the AlexNet [26] model to extract the visual features through the publicly available Caffe [22]. The model was pre-trained on a set of 1.2 million clean images of ILSVRC-2012[13] and it hence provides a robust initialization for recognizing semantics. Before feature extraction, we first extracted the key frames from each micro-video by using OPENCV[14], and then employed the AlexNet to get CNN features of each frame. Following that, we took the mean pooling strategy over all the key frames of one video, and generated a single 4,096 dimensional vector for each micro-video.

3.2.2 *Features in Acoustic Modality*

The audio clips embedded in the micro-videos contain useful cues or hints about the places. For example, within the clothing stores, audio clips capture employees answering customers questions as to clothing sizes or colors, and welcoming them to the store. Considering the nightclub as another example, the audio clips can reflect the mixed noise but young sounds. The acoustic information is especially useful for the cases where the visual features are too diverse or cannot carry satisfied information. To extract the acoustic features, we first separated audio tracks from micro-videos with the help of FFmpeg[15]. Hereafter, the audio tracks were transformed into a uniform format: 22,050Hz, 16bits, mono-channel and pulse-code modulation signals.

[13]http://www.image-net.org/challenges/LSVRC/2012/.

[14]http://opencv.org/.

[15]https://www.ffmpeg.org/.

Table 3: **List of the 10 representative hashtags and their frequencies in our dataset.**

ID	Hashtag	Num	ID	Hashtag	Num
1	NYC	1688	6	Paris	352
2	LosAngles	715	7	Food	345
3	Beach	694	8	Hollywood	335
4	Chicago	467	9	London	323
5	Travel	436	10	Disney	309

We then performed a spectrogram with a 46ms window and 50% overlap via librosa[16]. After getting the shallow representation of each audio track with 512 dimensional features, we adopted theano [2] to learn the deep learning features. In particular, the stack Denosing AutoEncoder (DAE) [38], which has been successful applied in speech recognition and speaker recognition [48, 11], was employed to extract acoustic features. The DAE was pre-trained on an external Vine micro-videos, which contains 120,000 samples. The deep model contains three hidden layers, with 500, 400, and 300 nodes on each layer. We ultimately obtained 200 dimensional acoustic features for each micro-video.

3.2.3 Features in Textual Modality

The textual descriptions of micro-videos, including user generated text and hashtags, can provide strong cues for micro-video venue estimation. For instance, this description *"Vining the #beach while tanning the thighs on a glorious Anzac Day"* clearly indicates that the venue category is beach. According to our statistics, 27.7% of our collected 276,264 micro-videos have hashtags, and the total number of hashtags is 253,474. Table 3 lists ten representative hashtags with their frequencies. It can be seen that, these hashtags are strongly related to venue categories. These textual data are, however, very sparse and lack of sufficient contexts. Therefore, the traditional approaches such as topic-level features [3] or n-grams may be unsuitable in such scenario. Instead, we utilized the Paragraph Vector method [33], which has been found to be effective to alleviate the semantic problems of word sparseness [14]. In particular, we first eliminated the non-English characters, followed by removing the stop words. We then employed Sentence2Vector tool[17] to extract the textual features. We finally extracted 100 dimensional features for each micro-video description.

Apart from the deep learning features mentioned above, we also extracted some traditional features such as color histogram and Mel-frequency spectrogram (MFS) to enrich the feature set, which are summarized in Table 4.

3.3 Missing Data Completion

We observed that the acoustic and textual modalities are missing in some micro-videos. More precisely, there are 169 and 24,707 micro-videos with missing acoustic and textual modality, respectively. Information missing is harmful for most machine learning performance [10, 46], including the models for venue category estimation. To alleviate such problem, we cast the data completion task as a matrix factorization problem [50]. In particular, we first concatenated the features from three modalities in order, which naturally constructed an original matrix. We then applied the matrix factorization technique to factorize this original matrix into two latent matrices with 100 latent features, such that the empirical errors between the production of these two latent matrices and the original matrix are as small as possible. The entries in the two latent matrices are inferred by the observed values in the original matrix only, and over-fitting is avoided through a regularized model.

[16]https://github.com/bmcfee/librosa.

[17]https://github.com/klb3713/sentence2vec.

Table 4: Feature summarization of three modalities.

Modality	Extracted features
Visual	4,096-D CNN, 96-D color histogram
Acoustic	200-D DAE, 256-D MFS
Textual	100-D paragraph vector

4. OUR TRUMANN MODEL

4.1 Notations and Assumptions

We first declare some notations. In particular, we use bold capital letters (e.g., $\mathbf{X}$) and bold lowercase letters (e.g., $\mathbf{x}$) to denote matrices and vectors, respectively. We employ non-bold letters (e.g., x) to represent scalars, and Greek letters (e.g., β) as parameters. We denote the Frobenius norm and the group lasso (i.e., $\ell_{2,1}$-norm) matrix $\mathbf{X}$ as $\|\mathbf{X}\|_F$ and $\|\mathbf{X}\|_{2,1}$, respectively. Moreover, let X_{ij} denote the entry in row i and column j. If not clarified, all vectors are in column forms.

Suppose we have a set of N micro-video samples. Each has S modalities and is associated with one of T venue categories. In this work, we treat each venue category as a task. We utilize $\mathbf{X}^s = [\mathbf{x}_1^s, \mathbf{x}_2^s, \ldots, \mathbf{x}_N^s]^T \in \mathbb{R}^{N \times D^s}$ to denote the representation of N samples with a D^s dimensional feature space from the s-th modality, and utilize $\mathbf{Y} = [\mathbf{y}_1, \mathbf{y}_2, \ldots, \mathbf{y}_N]^T \in \mathbb{R}^{N \times T}$ to denote the labels of the N samples over the T pre-defined tasks $\{t_1, t_2, \ldots, t_T\}$. Our objective is to jointly learn the mapping matrix $\mathbf{A}^s$ from the individual space $\mathbf{X}^s$ to the common space $\mathbf{B} \in \mathbb{R}^{N \times K}$, and learn the optimal coefficient matrix $\mathbf{W} = [\mathbf{w}_1, \mathbf{w}_2, \ldots, \mathbf{w_T}] \in \mathbb{R}^{K \times T}$. Based on $\mathbf{A}^s$ and $\mathbf{W}$ we are able to estimate the venue categories for the unseen videos.

To intuitively demonstrate our proposed model, we introduce TWO assumptions first:

1. We assume that there exists a common discriminative space for micro-videos, originating from their multi-modalities. Micro-videos can be comprehensively described in this common space and the venue categories are more distinguishable in this space. The space over each individual modality can be mathematically mapped to the common space with a small difference.

2. The tasks (venue categories) are organized into a tree structure. We assume that such structure encodes the relatedness among tasks and leveraging this prior knowledge is able to boost the learning performance.

To consider the aforementioned assumptions simultaneously, we devise a tree-guided multi-task multi-modal learning method, which will be detailed in a stepwise way.

4.2 Common Space Learning

Common space learning [42, 16] over multiple modalities or views has been well studied. Theoretically, it can capture the intrinsic and latent structure of data, which preserveps information from multiple modalities [29, 40]. It is thus able to alleviate the fusion and disagreement problems of the classification tasks over multiple modalities [16, 30]. Based upon our first assumption, we propose a joint optimization framework which minimizes the reconstruction errors over multiple modalities of the data, and avoids overfitting using Frobenius norm on the transformation matrices. It is formally defined as,

$$\min_{\mathbf{A}^s,\mathbf{B}} \frac{\lambda_1}{2}\sum_{s=1}^{S}\|\mathbf{X}^s\mathbf{A}^s - \mathbf{B}\|_F^2 + \frac{\lambda_2}{2}\sum_{s=1}^{S}\|\mathbf{A}^s\|_F^2, \quad (1)$$

where $\mathbf{B} \in \mathbb{R}^{N\times K}$ is the representation matrix in the common space learned from all modalities, and K is the latent feature dimension. $\mathbf{A}^s \in \mathbb{R}^{D^s\times K}$ is the transformation matrix from the original feature space over the s-th modality to the common space; and λ_1 and λ_2 are nonnegative tradeoff parameters.

4.3 Tree-guided Multi-task Learning

Although the existing multi-task learning methods, such as graph-regularized [49] and clustering-based [21], achieve sound theoretical underpinnings and great practical success, the tree-guided method [25] is more suitable and feasible for our problem. This is because the relatedness between the venue categories are naturally organized into a hierarchical tree structure by experts from Foursquare. As Figure1 shows, the relatedness among different tasks can be characterized by a tree τ with a set of nodes $\mathcal{V}$, where the leaf nodes and internal nodes represent tasks and groups of the tasks, respectively. Intuitively, each node $v \in \mathcal{V}$ of the tree can be associated with a corresponding group $\mathcal{G}_v = \{t_i\}$, which consists of all the leaf nodes t_i belonging to the subtree rooted at the node v. To capture the strength of relatedness among tasks within the same group $\mathcal{G}_v$, we assign a weight e_v to node v according to an affinity function, which will be detailed in the next subsection. Moreover, the higher level the internal node locates at, the weaker relatedness it controls, and hence the smaller weight it obtains. Therefore, we can formulate such tree-guided multi-task learning as follows,

$$\min_{\mathbf{W},\mathbf{B}} \Gamma = \frac{1}{2}\|\mathbf{Y} - \mathbf{B}\mathbf{W}\|_F^2 + \frac{\lambda_3}{2}\sum_{v\in\mathcal{V}} e_v\|\mathbf{W}_{\mathcal{G}_v}\|_{2,1}, \quad (2)$$

where $\mathbf{W}_{\mathcal{G}_v} = \{\mathbf{w}_i : t_i \in \mathcal{G}_v\} \in \mathbb{R}^{K\times|\mathcal{G}_v|}$ is the coefficient matrix of all the leaf nodes rooted at v, where each column vector is selected from $\mathbf{W}$ according to the members within the task group $\mathcal{G}_v$; $\|\mathbf{W}_{\mathcal{G}_v}\|_{2,1} = \sum_{k=1}^{K}\sqrt{\sum_{t_i\in\mathcal{G}_v} w_{ki}^2}$ is the $\ell_{2,1}$-norm regularization (i.e., group lasso) which is capable of selecting features based on their strengths over the selected tasks within the group $\mathcal{G}_v$, and in this way, we can simultaneously learn the task-sharing features and task-specific features. Lastly, the nonnegative parameter λ_3 regulates the sparsity of the solution regarding $\mathbf{W}$. By integrating the common space learning function in Eqn.(1) and the tree-guided multi-task learning framework in Eqn.(2), we reach the final objective function as follows,

Algorithm 1 optimization of **TRUMANN** model

Input: $\mathbf{X}^s$, $\mathbf{Y}$, λ_1, λ_2, λ_3, $\mathbf{e}$, $\mathcal{V}$,
K: dimension of the desired common space.
Output: $\mathbf{A}^s$, $\mathbf{B}$, $\mathbf{W}$.
Initialize $\mathbf{A}^s$, $\mathbf{B}$, $\mathbf{W}$ and $\mathbf{Q}$
while not converge **do**
  Fixing $\mathbf{B}$ and $\mathbf{W}$, update $\mathbf{A}^s$ according to
  $\mathbf{A}^s \leftarrow (\lambda_1\mathbf{X}^{sT}\mathbf{X}^s + \lambda_2\mathbf{I})^{-1}(\lambda_1\mathbf{X}^s\mathbf{B})$.
  Fixing $\mathbf{A}$ and $\mathbf{W}$, update $\mathbf{B}$ according to
  $\mathbf{B} \leftarrow (\mathbf{Y}\mathbf{W}^T + \lambda_1\sum_{s=1}^{S}\mathbf{X}^s\mathbf{A}^s)(\lambda_1 S\mathbf{I} + \mathbf{W}\mathbf{W}^T)^{-1}$
  while not converge **do**
    Fixing $\mathbf{W}$, update $q_{k,v}$ according to
    $q_{k,v} \leftarrow \frac{e_v\|\mathbf{W}_{\mathcal{G}_v}^k\|}{\sum_{k=1}^{K}\sum_{v\in\mathcal{V}} e_v\|\mathbf{W}_{\mathcal{G}_v}^k\|}$
    Updating $\mathbf{Q}^t$ according to
    $\mathbf{Q}^t \leftarrow \sum_{v\in\mathcal{V}}\frac{e_v^2}{q_{k,v}}$
    Fixing $\mathbf{A}$, $\mathbf{Q}^t$ and $\mathbf{B}$, update $\mathbf{w}^t$ according to
    $\mathbf{w}^t \leftarrow (\mathbf{B}^T\mathbf{B} + \lambda_3\sum_{t=1}^{T}\mathbf{Q}^t)^{-1}\mathbf{B}^T\mathbf{y}^t$
  end while
end while

$$\min_{\mathbf{W},\mathbf{B},\mathbf{A}^s} \Gamma = \frac{1}{2}\|\mathbf{Y} - \mathbf{B}\mathbf{W}\|_F^2 + \frac{\lambda_1}{2}\sum_{s=1}^{S}\|\mathbf{X}^s\mathbf{A}^s - \mathbf{B}\|_F^2 + \frac{\lambda_2}{2}\sum_{s=1}^{S}\|\mathbf{A}^s\|_F^2 + \frac{\lambda_3}{2}\sum_{v\in\mathcal{V}} e_v\|\mathbf{W}_{\mathcal{G}_v}\|_{2,1}. \quad (3)$$

4.4 Optimization

We adopt the alternating optimization strategy to solve the three variables $\mathbf{A}^s$, $\mathbf{B}$ and $\mathbf{W}$ in Eqn.(3). To be more specific, we optimize one variable while fixing the others in each iteration. We keep this iterative procedure until the objective function converges.

4.4.1 *Computing $\mathbf{A}_s$ with $\mathbf{B}$ and $\mathbf{W}$ fixed*

We first fix $\mathbf{B}$ and $\mathbf{W}$, and take derivative of Γ with respect to $\mathbf{A}^s$. We have,

$$\frac{\partial\Gamma}{\partial\mathbf{A}^s} = \lambda_1(\mathbf{X}^s\mathbf{A}^s - \mathbf{B})\mathbf{X}^s + \lambda_2\mathbf{A}^s. \quad (4)$$

By setting Eqn.(4) to zero, it can be derived that,

$$\mathbf{A}^s = (\lambda_1\mathbf{X}^{sT}\mathbf{X}^s + \lambda_2\mathbf{I})^{-1}(\lambda_1\mathbf{X}^{sT}\mathbf{B}), \quad (5)$$

where $\mathbf{I} \in \mathbb{R}^{D^s\times D^s}$ is an identity matrix. The first term in Eqn.(5) can be easily proven to be positive definite and hence invertible according to the definition of positive-definite matrix.

4.4.2 *Computing $\mathbf{B}$ with $\mathbf{A}^s$ and $\mathbf{W}$ fixed*

With $\mathbf{A}^s$ and $\mathbf{W}$ fixed, we compute the derivative of Γ regarding $\mathbf{B}$ as follows,

$$\frac{\partial\Gamma}{\partial\mathbf{B}} = \lambda_1\sum_{s=1}^{S}(\mathbf{B} - \mathbf{X}^s\mathbf{A}^s) + (\mathbf{B}\mathbf{W}\mathbf{W}^T - \mathbf{Y}\mathbf{W}^T). \quad (6)$$

By setting Eqn.(6) to zero, we have,

$$\mathbf{B} = (\mathbf{Y}\mathbf{W}^T + \lambda_1\sum_{s=1}^{S}\mathbf{X}^s\mathbf{A}^s)(\lambda_1 S\mathbf{I} + \mathbf{W}\mathbf{W}^T)^{-1}, \quad (7)$$

where $(\lambda_1 S\mathbf{I}+\mathbf{W}\mathbf{W}^T)$ can be easily proven to be invertible according to the definition of positive-definite matrix.

4.4.3 Computing $\mathbf{W}$ *with* $\mathbf{A}^s$ *and* $\mathbf{B}$ *fixed*

Considering that the last term in Eqn.(3) is not differentiable, we use an equivalent formulation of it, which has been proven by [1], to facilitate the optimization as follows,

$$\frac{\lambda_3}{2}(\sum_{v\in\mathcal{V}} \|\mathbf{W}_{\mathcal{G}_v}\|)^2. \quad (8)$$

Still, it is intractable. We thus further resort to another variational formulation of Eqn.(8). According to the Cauchy-Schwarz inequality, given an arbitrary vector $\mathbf{b}\in\mathbb{R}^M$ such that $\mathbf{b}\neq\mathbf{0}$, we have,

$$\sum_{i=1}^{M}|b_i| = \sum_{i=1}^{M}\theta_i^{\frac{1}{2}}\theta_i^{-\frac{1}{2}}|b_i| \le (\sum_{i=1}^{M}\theta_i)^{\frac{1}{2}}(\sum_{i=1}^{M}\theta_i^{-1}b_i^2)^{\frac{1}{2}} \le (\sum_{i=1}^{M}\theta_i^{-1}b_i^2)^{\frac{1}{2}}, \quad (9)$$

where θ_i's are the introduced variables that should satisfy $\sum_{i=1}^{M}\theta_i = 1$, $\theta_i > 0$ and the equality holds for $\theta_i = |b_i|/\|\mathbf{b}\|_1$. Based on this preliminary, we can derive the following inequality,

$$(\sum_{v\in\mathcal{V}} e_v\|\mathbf{W}_{\mathcal{G}_v}\|)^2 \le \sum_{k=1}^{K}\sum_{v\in\mathcal{V}}\frac{e_v^2\|\mathbf{w}_{\mathcal{G}_v}^k\|_2^2}{q_{k,v}}, \quad (10)$$

where $\sum_k\sum_v q_{k,v}=1$, $q_{k,v}\ge 0$, $\forall k,v$; $\mathbf{w}_{\mathcal{G}_v}^k$ denotes the k-th row vector of the group matrix $\mathbf{W}_{\mathcal{G}_v}$. It worth noting that the equality holds when

$$q_{k,v} = \frac{e_v\|\mathbf{w}_{\mathcal{G}_v}^k\|_2^2}{\sum_{k=1}^{K}\sum_{v\in\mathcal{V}} e_v\|\mathbf{w}_{\mathcal{G}_v}^k\|_2^2}. \quad (11)$$

Thus far, we have theoretically derived that minimizing Γ with respect to $\mathbf{W}$ is equivalent to minimizing the following convex objective function,

$$\min_{\mathbf{W},q_{k,v}} \frac{1}{2}\|\mathbf{Y}-\mathbf{B}\mathbf{W}\|_F^2 + \frac{\lambda_1}{2}\sum_{s=1}^{S}\|\mathbf{X}^s\mathbf{A}^s-\mathbf{B}\|_F^2 + \frac{\lambda_2}{2}\sum_{s=1}^{S}\|\mathbf{A}^s\|_F^2 + \frac{\lambda_3}{2}\sum_{k=1}^{K}\sum_{v\in\mathcal{V}}\frac{\|e_v\mathbf{w}_{\mathcal{G}_v}^k\|^2}{q_{k,v}}. \quad (12)$$

To facilitate the computation of the derivative of objective function Γ with respect to $\mathbf{w}_t$ for the t-th task, we define a diagonal matrix $\mathbf{Q}^t\in\mathbb{R}^{K\times K}$ with the diagonal entry as follows,

$${Q^t}_{kk} = \sum_{\{v\in\mathcal{V},|t\in v\}}\frac{e_v^2}{q_{k,v}}. \quad (13)$$

We ultimately have the following objective function,

$$\min_{\mathbf{W},\mathbf{Q}} \frac{1}{2}\sum_{t=1}^{T}\|\mathbf{y}_t-\mathbf{B}\mathbf{w}_t\|_F^2 + \frac{\lambda_1}{2}\sum_{s=1}^{S}\|\mathbf{X}^s\mathbf{A}^s-\mathbf{B}\|_F^2 + \frac{\lambda_2}{2}\sum_{s=1}^{S}\|\mathbf{A}^s\|_F^2 + \frac{\lambda_3}{2}\sum_{t=1}^{T}\mathbf{w}_t^T\mathbf{Q}^t\mathbf{w}_t. \quad (14)$$

The alternative optimization strategy is also applicable here. By fixing $\mathbf{Q}^t$, taking derivative of the above formulation regarding $\mathbf{w}_t$, and setting it to zero, we reach,

$$\mathbf{w_t} = (\mathbf{B}^T\mathbf{B}+\lambda_3\mathbf{Q}^t)^{-1}(\mathbf{B}^T\mathbf{y_t}). \quad (15)$$

Once we obtain all the $\mathbf{w}_t$, we can easily compute $\mathbf{Q}^t$ based on Eqn.(11)

4.5 Task Relatedness Estimation

According to our assumption, the hierarchical tree structure of venue categories plays a pivotal role to boost the learning performance in our model. Hence, the key issue is how to precisely characterize and model the task relatedness in the tree, namely, how to estimate the reasonable weight e_v for each node v in the tree appropriately. Although the existing tree-guided multi-task learning approaches [36, 17] have addressed this issue by exploring the geometric structure, they do not consider the semantic relatedness among tasks. To remedy this problem, we aim to model the intrinsic task relatedness based on the feature space. Towards this goal, we introduce the affinity measurement of the node group proposed in [31]. A high affinity value e_v of the node group $\mathcal{G}_v$ indicates the dense connections and compact relations among the leaf nodes within the given group. We hence can employ the affinity measurement to characterize the task relatedness in the tree.

To facilitate the affinity measurement of each node group $\mathcal{G}_v$, we need to obtain the pairwise similarity between all leaf nodes. For simplicity, we utilize the adjacency matrix $\mathbf{S}\in\mathbb{R}^{T\times T}$ to denote the pairwise similarity matrix and the entry S_{ij} to capture the non-negative relatedness between the i-th and j-th leaf nodes, which can be formulated as,

$$S_{ij} = \exp\left(-\frac{\|\bar{\mathbf{x}}_\mathbf{i}-\bar{\mathbf{x}}_\mathbf{j}\|^2}{\theta^2}\right), \quad (16)$$

where $\bar{\mathbf{x}}_\mathbf{i}$ represents the mean feature vector of the samples belonging to the i-th venue category which can be extracted from the training dataset; θ is radius parameter that is simply set as the median of the Euclidean distances of all node pairs.

For ease of formulation and inspired by the work in [31], we define a scaled assignment vector $\mathbf{u}_v\in\mathbb{R}^T$ for each node of the tree over all the T leaf nodes which can be stated as,

$$u_{vt} = \begin{cases}\frac{1}{\sqrt{|\mathcal{G}_v|}}, & \text{if} \quad t\in\mathcal{G}_v \\ 0, & \text{otherwise}\end{cases}. \quad (17)$$

Based on the scaled assignment $\mathbf{u}_v$ and the pairwise similarity matrix $\mathbf{S}$, we can further formulate the affinity e_v for the node v as follows,

$$e_v = \mathbf{u}_v^T\mathbf{S}\mathbf{u}_v. \quad (18)$$

Since the characteristics of the affinity definition, the value of the e_v are limited within the range of [0, 1]. More importantly, such affinity measurement can guarantee that higher nodes correspond to weaker relatedness, and vice versa.

4.6 Complexity Analysis

In order to analyze the complexity of our proposed **TRUMANN** model, we have to estimate the time complexity for constructing $\mathbf{A}$, $\mathbf{B}$ and $\mathbf{W}$ as defined in Eqn.(5), Eqn.(7) and Eqn.(15). The computational complexity of the training process is $O(M\times(O_1+O_2+O_3))$, where O_1, O_2 and O_3 respectively equal to $((D^s)^2N +$

$(D^s)^3 + (D^s)^2K)S$, $(NK^2 + NDKS + K^3 + K^2T)$ and $(2NK^2 + K^3)T$. Thereinto, M is the iteration times of the alternative optimization, which is a small value less than 10 in our above analysis. N, T, S, K and D respectively refer to the number of micro-videos, venue categories, modalities, latent dimension and the total feature dimensions over all the modalities. Usually, we consider only a few number of modalities. S is hence very small. In our experimental settings, K and T are in the order of a few hundreds. Meanwhile, the number of feature dimension is about 5,000. Therefore, D^2 is greater than K^2T. In the light of this, we can reduce the time complexity to be ND^2, which is faster than **SVM**, in terms of $O(N^3)$.

5. EXPERIMENTS

All the experiments were conducted over a server equipped with Inter(R) Core(TM) CPU i7-4790 at 3.6GHz on 32Gb RAM, 8 cores and 64-bit Windows 10 operation system.

5.1 Experimental Settings

To thoroughly measure our model and the baselines, we employed multiple metrics, namely, macro-F1 and micro-F1[15]. The averaging macro-$F1$ gives equal weight to each class-label in the averaging process; whereas the averaging micro-$F1$ gives equal weight to all instances in the averaging process. Both macro-$F1$ and micro-$F1$ metrics reach their best value at 1 and worst score at 0.

The experimental results reported in this paper were based on 10-fold cross-validation. In particular, the stratified cross-validation [34] was adopted to ensure all categories contain approximately the same percentage between training and testing samples. In each round of the 10-fold cross-validation, we split our dataset into three chunks: 80% of the micro-videos (i.e., 194,505 videos) were used for training, 10% (i.e., 24,313 videos) were used for validation, and the rest (i.e., 24,313 videos) were held-out for testing. The training set was used to adjust the parameters, while the validation set was used to avoid overfitting, i.e., verifying that any performance increase over the training dataset actually yields an accuracy increase over a dataset that has not been shown to the model before. The testing set was used only for testing the final solution to confirm the actual predictive power of our model with optimal parameters. Grid search was employed to select the optimal parameters with small but adaptive step size.

5.2 Performance Comparison among Models

We carried out experiments to compare the overall effectiveness of our proposed **TURMANN** model with several state-of-the-art baselines:

- **SRMTL**: The Sparse Graph Regularization Multi-Task Learning method can capture the relationship between task pairs and further impose a sparse graph regularization scheme to enforce the related pairs close to each other [32].
- **regMVMT**: This semi-supervised inductive multi-view multi-task learning model considers information from multiple views and learns multiple related tasks simultaneously [47]. Besides, we also compared our model with the variant of **regMVMT** method, dubbed **regMVMT+**. **regMVMT+** can achieve better performance by modeling the non-uniformly related tasks.

Table 5: Performance comparison between our model and the baselines on the venue category estimation. (p-value*: p-value over micro-F1.)

Models	Macro-$F1$	Micro-$F1$	p-value*
SRMTL	2.61±0.19%	15.71±0.21%	1.1e-3
regMVMT	4.33±0.41%	17.16±0.28%	7.0e-3
regMVMT+	4.53±0.31%	18.35±0.13%	9.1e-3
MvDA+RMTL	2.46±0.18%	17.28±1.67%	1.0e-3
TRUMANN-	3.75±0.17%	24.01±0.35%	1.0e-2
TRUMANN	**5.21±0.29%**	**25.27±0.17%**	-

- **MvDA+RMTL**: This baseline is the combination of Multi-view Discriminant Analysis [24] and Robust Multi-Task Learning [7]. In particular, **MvDA** seeks for a single discriminant common space for multiple views by jointly learning multiple view-specific linear transforms. Meanwhile, the **RMTL** is able to capture the task relationships using a low-rank structure via group-sparse lasso.
- **TURMANN-**: This baseline is the variant of our proposed model by setting all e_v in Eqn.(3) to be 1. In other words, this baseline does not incorporate the knowledge of the pre-defined hierarchical structure.

The comparative results are summarized in Table 5. From this table, we have the following observations: 1) **TRUMANN** achieves better performance, as compared to other multi-task learning approaches, such as **SRMTL**. This is because, the **SRMTL** cannot capture the prior knowledge of task relatedness in terms of tree structure. On the other hand, it reflects that micro-videos are more separable in the learnt common space. 2) Multi-modal multi-task models, such as **regMVMT** and **TRUMANN** remarkably outperform pure multi-task learning models, such as **SRMTL**. This again demonstrates that the relatedness among multi-modalities can boost the learning performance. 3) The joint learning of multi-modal multi-task models, including **regMVMT** and **TRUMANN**, shows their superiors to the sequential learning of multi-view multi-task model, **MvDA+RMTL**. This tells us that multi-modal learning and multi-task learning can mutually reinforce each other. 4) We can see that **TRUMANN** outperforms **TRUMANN-**. This demonstrate the usefulness of the pre-defined hierarchical structure, and reveals the necessity of tree-guided multi-task learning. And 5) we conducted the analysis of variance (known as ANOVA) micro-$F1$. In particular, we performed paired t-test between our model and each of the competitors over 10-fold cross validation. We found that all the p-value are substantially smaller than 0.05, which shows that the improvements of our proposed model are statistically significant.

5.3 Representativeness of Modalities

We also studied the effectiveness of different modality combination. Table 6 shows the results. From this table, we observed that: 1) The visual modality is the most discriminant one among visual, textual and acoustic modalities. This is because, the visual modality contains more location-specific information than acoustic and textual modality. On the other hand, it signals that the CNN features are capable of capturing the prominent visual characteristics of venue categories. 2) The acoustic modality provide important cues for venue categories as compared to the textual modality across micro-$F1$ and

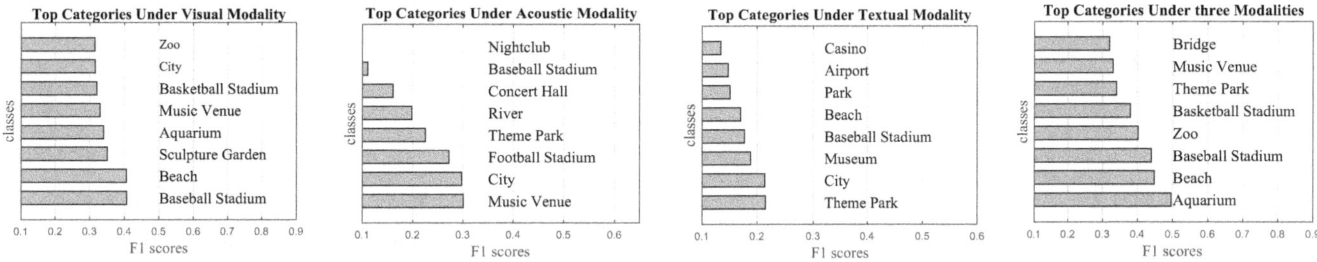

(a) Visual Modality (b) Acoustic Modality (c) Textual Modality (d) Modality Combination

Figure 5: Categories with best classification performance under visual, acoustic, textual modality and their combination, respectively.

macro-$F1$ metrics. But only given the acoustic modality, it is hard to estimate the venue categories for most of the videos, while the combination of visual and acoustic modality get an improvement than visual modality. 3) Textual modality is the least descriptive for venue category estimation. This is due to that the textual descriptions are noisy, missing, sparse, and even irrelevant to the venue categories. And 4) the more modalities we incorporate, the better performance we can achieve. This implies that the information of one modality is insufficient and multi-modalities is complementary to each other rather than mutually conflicting. This is a consensus to the old saying "two heads are better than one".

5.4 Case Studies

In Figure 5, we respectively list the top eight categories with best performance in only visual modality, acoustic modality, textual modality, and their combination. From this figure, we have the following observations: 1) For visual modality, our model achieves stable and satisfactory performance on many venue categories, especially on those with discrimiant visual characteristic, such as the micro-videos related to 'Zoo' and 'Beach'. 2) Regarding the acoustic modality, our model performs better on those with regular sounds or noisy noise, such as, 'Music Venue' and 'Concert Hall', which have discriminate acoustic signals as compared to other venue categories. 3) When it comes to the textual modality, we found that the top eight best performing categories are with high frequencies in micro-video descriptions. For instance, the terms of 'Park' and 'Beach' occur 2,992 and 3,882 times in our dataset, respectively. It is worth noting that not all the textual descriptions are correlated with the actual venue category, which in fact decreases the performance. For example, the textual description of one micro-video is *'I love my city'*. Nevertheless, its venue category is 'Park'. And 4) unsurprisingly, we obtained a significant improvement for 'Aquarium' category, which is hard to recognize with only one modality. Moreover, compared to the performance over visual modality, the 'Basketball Stadium' and 'Zoo' categories are also improved about 8% in micro $F1$. Besides, the more training samples one venue category contains, the higher probability of this category will yield, such as 'Theme Park' and 'City'.

5.5 Parameter Tuning and Sensitivity

We have four key parameters as shown in Eqn.(3): K, λ_1, λ_2 and λ_3. The optimal values of these parameters were carefully tuned with 10-fold cross-validation in the

Table 6: Representativeness of different modalities. (p-value*: p-value over micro-F1.)

Modality	Macro-$F1$	Micro-$F1$	p-value*
Visual	4.49±0.09%	22.56±0.10%	2.3e-2
Acoustic	2.79±0.01%	16.25±0.46%	2.9e-4
Textual	1.44±0.29%	12.36±0.38%	5.4e-4
Acoustic+textual	2.87±0.16%	16.86±0.06%	6.4e-3
Visual+acoustic	4.61±0.08%	23.85±0.20%	1.8e-2
Visual+textual	4.52±0.11%	23.54±0.17%	1.1e-2
All	**5.21±0.29%**	**25.27±0.17%**	-

training data. In particular, for each of the 10-fold, we chose the optimal parameters by grid search with a small but adaptive step size. Our parameters were searched in the range of [50, 500], [0.01,1], [0,1] and [0,1], respectively. The parameters corresponding to the best micro $F1$-score were used to report the final results. For other competitors, the procedures to tune the parameters are analogous to the ensure fair comparison.

Take the parameter tuning in one of the 10-fold as an example. We observed that our model reached the optimal performance when K=200, $\lambda_1 = 0.7$, $\lambda_2 = 0.4$ and $\lambda_3 = 0.3$. We then investigated the sensitivity our model to these parameters by varying one and fixing the others. Figure 6 illustrates the performance of our model with respect to K, λ_1, λ_2 and λ_3. We can see that: 1) When fixing λ_1, λ_2, λ_3 and tuning K, the micro $F1$ score value increases first and then reaches the peak value at K=200. And 2) the micro $F1$ score value changes in a small range, when varying λ_1, λ_2 and λ_3 from 0 to 1. The slight change demonstrates that our model is non-sensitive to parameters.

At last, we recorded the value of micro $F1$ along with the iteration time using the optimal parameter settings. Figure7 shows the convergence process with respect to the number of iterations. From this figure, it can be seen that our algorithm can converge very fast.

6. CONCLUSION AND FUTURE WORK

In this paper, we present a novel tree-guided multi-task multi-modal learning method to label the bite-sized video clips with venue categories. This model is capable of learning a common feature space from multiple and heterogonous modalities, which preserves the information of each modality via disagreement penalty. In this common space, the venue categories of micro-videos are more distinguishable. Meanwhile, the proposed method intelligently leverages the pre-defined Foursquare hierarchical structure to regularize the relatedness among venue categories. We seamlessly integrate the common space learning and multi-task

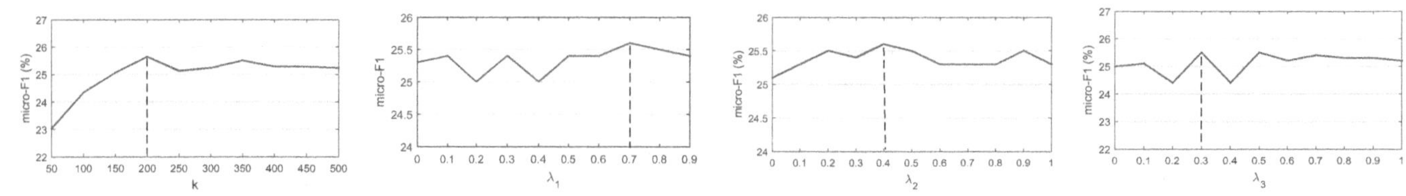

(a) parameter k (b) parameter λ_1 (c) parameter λ_2 (d) parameter λ_3

Figure 6: Performance of TRUMANN with regards to varying parameters.

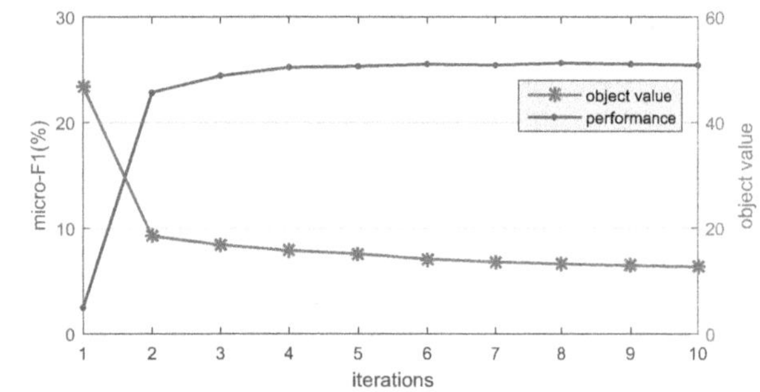

Figure 7: Performance of TRUMANN with the iteration times

classification into a unified model. To validate our model, we crawl a representative set of micro-videos from Vine and extract a rich set of features from textual, visual and acoustic modalities. Based upon the extensive experiments on this dataset, we have shown that our model is superior to several state-of-the-art baselines.

In the future, we plan to study the relatedness among multiple modalities, such as conflict, complementary and consistent relatedness, to boost the learning performance.

7. ACKNOWLEDGMENTS

This work is supported by National Key Technology Research and Development Program of the Ministry of Science and Technology of China (No.2012BAH17B02), CUC Engineering Project (No.3132014XNG1429), and China Scholarship Council (CSC). It is also supported by Singapore National Research Foundation under its International Research Centre @ Singapore Funding Initiative and administered by the IDM Programme Office.

8. REFERENCES

[1] F. R. Bach. Consistency of the group lasso and multiple kernel learning. *JMLR*, 9(Jun):1179–1225, 2008.

[2] F. Bastien, P. Lamblin, R. Pascanu, J. Bergstra, I. Goodfellow, A. Bergeron, D. Warde-Farley, and Y. Bengio. Theano: new features and speed improvements. *arXiv preprint arXiv:1211.5590*, 2012.

[3] D. M. Blei, A. Y. Ng, and M. I. Jordan. Latent dirichlet allocation. *JMLR*, 3:993–1022, 2003.

[4] S. Cao and N. Snavely. Graph-based discriminative learning for location recognition. In *IEEE CVPR*, pages 700–707, 2013.

[5] B.-C. Chen, Y.-Y. Chen, F. Chen, and D. Joshi. Business-aware visual concept discovery from social media for multimodal business venue recognition. In *AAAI*, pages 61–68, 2016.

[6] D. M. Chen, G. Baatz, K. Köser, S. S. Tsai, R. Vedantham, T. Pylvä, K. Roimela, X. Chen, J. Bach, M. Pollefeys, et al. City-scale landmark identification on mobile devices. In *IEEE CVPR*, pages 737–744, 2011.

[7] J. Chen, J. Zhou, and J. Ye. Integrating low-rank and group-sparse structures for robust multi-task learning. In *ACM KDD*, pages 42–50, 2011.

[8] J. Choi, G. Friedland, V. Ekambaram, and K. Ramchandran. Multimodal location estimation of consumer media: Dealing with sparse training data. In *IEEE ICME*, pages 43–48, 2012.

[9] D. J. Crandall, L. Backstrom, D. Huttenlocher, and J. Kleinberg. Mapping the world's photos. In *ACM WWW*, pages 761–770, 2009.

[10] P. Cui, Z. Wang, and Z. Su. What videos are similar with you?: Learning a common attributed representation for video recommendation. In *ACM MM*, pages 597–606, 2014.

[11] X. Feng, Y. Zhang, and J. Glass. Speech feature denoising and dereverberation via deep autoencoders for noisy reverberant speech recognition. In *IEEE ICASSP*, pages 1759–1763, 2014.

[12] G. Friedland, J. Choi, H. Lei, and A. Janin. Multimodal location estimation on flickr videos. In *ACM SIGMM*, pages 23–28, 2011.

[13] G. Friedland, O. Vinyals, and T. Darrell. Multimodal location estimation. In *ACM MM*, pages 1245–1252, 2010.

[14] D. Ganguly, D. Roy, M. Mitra, and G. J. Jones. Word embedding based generalized language model for information retrieval. In *ACM SIGIR*, pages 795–798, 2015.

[15] S. Gopal and Y. Yang. Recursive regularization for large-scale classification with hierarchical and graphical dependencies. In *ACM KDD*, pages 257–265, 2013.

[16] Y. Guo. Convex subspace representation learning from multi-view data. In *AAAI*, pages 2–9, 2013.

[17] L. Han and Y. Zhang. Learning tree structure in multi-task learning. In *ACM KDD*, pages 397–406, 2015.

[18] Z. Hanwang, W. Meng, H. Richang, N. Liqiang, and C. Tat-Seng. Play and rewind: Optimizing binary representations of videos by self-supervised temporal hashing. In *ACM MM*, October 2016.

[19] J. Hays and A. A. Efros. Im2gps: estimating geographic information from a single image. In *IEEE CVPR*, pages 1–8, 2008.

[20] J. He and R. Lawrence. A graph-based framework for multi-task multi-view learning. In *ICML*, pages 25–32, 2011.

[21] L. Jacob, J.-p. Vert, and F. R. Bach. Clustered multi-task learning: A convex formulation. In *NIPS*, pages 745–752, 2009.

[22] Y. Jia, E. Shelhamer, J. Donahue, S. Karayev, J. Long, R. Girshick, S. Guadarrama, and T. Darrell. Caffe: Convolutional architecture for fast feature embedding. In *ACM MM*, pages 675–678, 2014.

[23] X. Jin, F. Zhuang, S. Wang, Q. He, and Z. Shi. Shared structure learning for multiple tasks with multiple views. In *MLKDD*, pages 353–368, 2013.

[24] M. Kan, S. Shan, H. Zhang, S. Lao, and X. Chen. Multi-view discriminant analysis. *IEEE TPAMI*, 38(1):188–194, 2016.

[25] S. Kim and E. P. Xing. Tree-guided group lasso for multi-task regression with structured sparsity. In *ICML*, pages 1–8, 2010.

[26] A. Krizhevsky, I. Sutskever, and G. E. Hinton. Imagenet classification with deep convolutional neural networks. In *NIPS*, pages 1097–1105, 2012.

[27] H. Lei, J. Choi, and G. Friedland. Multimodal city-verification on flickr videos using acoustic and textual features. In *IEEE ICASSP*, pages 2273–2276, 2012.

[28] T.-Y. Lin, Y. Cui, S. Belongie, and J. Hays. Learning deep representations for ground-to-aerial geolocalization. In *IEEE CVPR*, pages 5007–5015, 2015.

[29] A. Liu, W. Nie, Y. Gao, and Y. Su. Multi-modal clique-graph matching for view-based 3d model retrieval. *IEEE TIP*, 25(5):2103–2116, 2016.

[30] A. Liu, Z. Wang, W. Nie, and Y. Su. Graph-based characteristic view set extraction and matching for 3d model retrieval. *Inf. Sci.*, 320:429–442, 2015.

[31] H. Liu, X. Yang, L. J. Latecki, and S. Yan. Dense neighborhoods on affinity graph. *IJCV*, 98(1):65–82, 2012.

[32] J. Liu, S. Ji, and J. Ye. Multi-task feature learning via efficient l2, 1-norm minimization. In *UAI*, pages 339–348, 2009.

[33] T. Mikolov, I. Sutskever, K. Chen, G. S. Corrado, and J. Dean. Distributed representations of words and phrases and their compositionality. In *NIPS*, pages 3111–3119, 2013.

[34] F. Pedregosa, G. Varoquaux, A. Gramfort, V. Michel, B. Thirion, O. Grisel, M. Blondel, P. Prettenhofer, R. Weiss, V. Dubourg, et al. Scikit-learn: Machine learning in python. *JMLR*, 12:2825–2830, 2011.

[35] G. Schindler, M. Brown, and R. Szeliski. City-scale location recognition. In *IEEE CVPR*, pages 1–7, 2007.

[36] X. Song, L. Nie, L. Zhang, M. Liu, and T.-S. Chua. Interest inference via structure-constrained multi-source multi-task learning. In *AAAI*, pages 2371–2377, 2015.

[37] K. Tang, M. Paluri, L. Fei-Fei, R. Fergus, and L. Bourdev. Improving image classification with location context. In *IEEE CVPR*, pages 1008–1016, 2015.

[38] P. Vincent, H. Larochelle, I. Lajoie, Y. Bengio, and P.-A. Manzagol. Stacked denoising autoencoders: Learning useful representations in a deep network with a local denoising criterion. *JMLR*, 11:3371–3408, 2010.

[39] M. Wang, X.-S. Hua, R. Hong, J. Tang, G.-J. Qi, and Y. Song. Unified video annotation via multigraph learning. *IEEE TCSVT*, 19(5):733–746, 2009.

[40] M. Wang, H. Li, D. Tao, K. Lu, and X. Wu. Multimodal graph-based reranking for web image search. *IEEE TIP*, 21(11):4649–4661, 2012.

[41] M. Wang, X. Liu, and X. Wu. Visual classification by-hypergraph modeling. *IEEE TKDE*, 27(9):2564–2574, 2015.

[42] M. White, X. Zhang, D. Schuurmans, and Y.-l. Yu. Convex multi-view subspace learning. In *NIPS*, pages 1673–1681, 2012.

[43] Z. Xu, Y. Yang, and A. G. Hauptmann. A discriminative cnn video representation for event detection. In *IEEE CVPR*, pages 1798–1807, 2015.

[44] M. Ye, P. Yin, and W.-C. Lee. Location recommendation for location-based social networks. In *ACM AGIS*, pages 458–461, 2010.

[45] J. Yue-Hei Ng, M. Hausknecht, S. Vijayanarasimhan, O. Vinyals, R. Monga, and G. Toderici. Beyond short snippets: Deep networks for video classification. In *IEEE CVPR*, pages 4694–4702, 2015.

[46] H. Zhang, X. Shang, W. Yang, H. Xu, H. Luan, and T.-S. Chua. Online collaborative learning for open-vocabulary visual classifiers. In *IEEE CVPR*, June 2016.

[47] J. Zhang and J. Huan. Inductive multi-task learning with multiple view data. In *ACM KDD*, pages 543–551, 2012.

[48] Z. Zhang, L. Wang, A. Kai, T. Yamada, W. Li, and M. Iwahashi. Deep neural network-based bottleneck feature and denoising autoencoder-based dereverberation for distant-talking speaker identification. *EURASIP*, 2015(1):1–13, 2015.

[49] J. Zhou, J. Chen, and J. Ye. Malsar: Multi-task learning via structural regularization. In *Arizona State University*, pages 1–50, 2011.

[50] Y. Zhou, D. Wilkinson, R. Schreiber, and R. Pan. Large-scale parallel collaborative filtering for the netflix prize. In *AAIM*, pages 337–348, 2008.

Multimodal-based Multimedia Analysis, Retrieval, and Services in Support of Social Media Applications

Rajiv Ratn Shah
School of Computing, National University of Singapore, Singapore
rajiv@comp.nus.edu.sg

ABSTRACT

The rapid growth in the amount of user-generated content (UGCs) online necessitates for social media companies to automatically extract knowledge structures (concepts) from user-generated images (UGIs) and user-generated videos (UGVs) to provide diverse multimedia-related services. For instance, recommending preference-aware multimedia content, the understanding of semantics and sentics from UGCs, and automatically computing tag relevance for UGIs are benefited from knowledge structures extracted from multiple modalities. Since contextual information captured by modern devices in conjunction with a media item greatly helps in its understanding, we leverage both multimedia content and contextual information (*e.g.*, spatial and temporal metadata) to address above-mentioned social media problems in our doctoral research. We present our approaches, results, and works in progress on these problems.

Keywords

Multimodal analysis; UGCs; Social media applications

1. INTRODUCTION AND MOTIVATION

Due to advancements in technologies, capturing UGCs anytime and anywhere, and then instantly sharing them on social media platforms has become a very popular activity. This activity attracts social media companies to provide diverse multimedia-related services leveraging multimedia content. However, providing such services are very challenging because it is difficult to capture semantics and sentics from a large collection of real-world UGIs and UGVs. Since multimodal information augments knowledge bases by inferring semantics and sentics from unstructured multimedia content and contextual information [23], it is beneficial in several significant multimedia-related applications such as tag ranking for social media photos [28], automatic lecture video segmentations [26, 27], adaptive news video uploading [24], SMS-based FAQ retrieval systems [32, 33]. We leverage multimodal information in first answering automatic soundtrack recommendation for user-generated videos (UGVs) [30, 31]. Next, we deal with the semantics understanding of UGIs and automatically generate a multimedia summary for a given event in real-time [25]. Finally, in our works in progress, we focus on sentics understanding and computing tag relevance for UGCs [29].

Since many outdoor UGVs consist of ambient background noise, it necessitates replacing the noise with matching soundtracks that matches with scenes, locations, and users' preferences. However, manually generating soundtracks for a UGV is tedious and time-consuming. Thus, we present a fast and effective heuristic ranking approach based on heterogeneous late fusion by jointly considering three aspects: venue categories, visual scenes, and listening histories of users. First, we predict scene moods for the UGV. Next, we perform heuristic rankings to fuse the predicted confidence scores of multiple models. Finally, we customize the video soundtrack recommendation functionality to make it compatible with mobile devices. Additionally, we consider areas where UGIs are exploited to provide services.

We present the EventBuilder[1] system that deals with the semantics understanding of user-generated images (UGIs) aggregated in social media sharing platforms and automatically generates a multimedia summary for a given event. It has three novel characteristics: (i) leveraging Wikipedia as event background knowledge to obtain additional contextual information about the input event during event detection, (ii) visualizing an interesting event on a Google Maps in real-time with a diverse set of social media activities, and (iii) solving an optimization problem to produce text summaries for the event. Subsequently, we present the EventSensor system that aims to address the sentics understanding of UGCs and produces a multimedia summary for a given mood. It extracts concepts and mood tags from the visual content and textual metadata of UGCs and exploits them in supporting several significant multimedia-related services such as a musical multimedia summary. Finally, we present a tag ranking system which computes tag relevance for UGIs based on voting from neighbors derived leveraging the three proposed high-level features. It is very helpful in the analysis, search, and retrieval of UGCs on social media.

In this doctoral research, we aim to exploit the multimodal information of UGCs in the support of the above-mentioned problems. Figure 1 shows an overview of our approach that leverage contextual information (*e.g.*, temporal, spatial, and sensor data) in conjunction with captured multimedia content in our solutions. Moreover, we also exploit knowledge bases in the semantics and sentics understanding of UGCs.

MM '16, October 15-19, 2016, Amsterdam, Netherlands

© 2016 ACM. ISBN 978-1-4503-3603-1/16/10...$15.00

DOI: http://dx.doi.org/10.1145/2964284.2971471

[1]eventbuilder.geovid.org

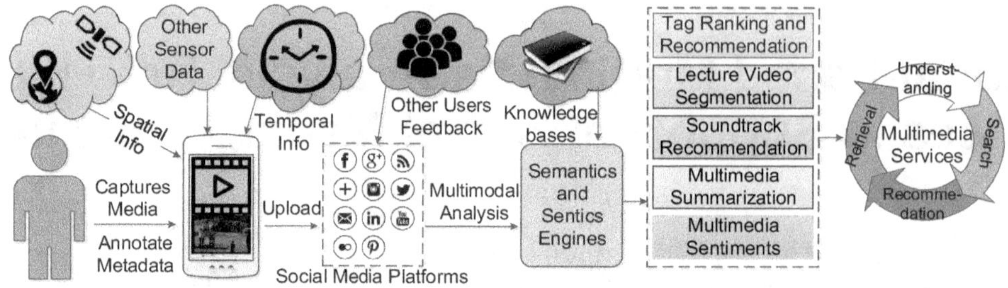

Figure 1: Overview of our approaches in this doctoral research studies.

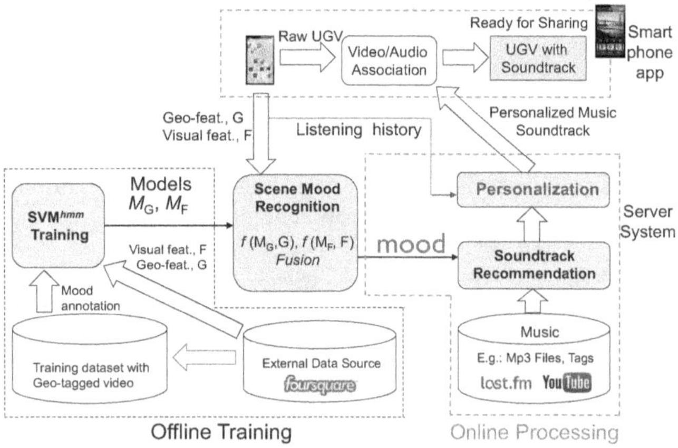

Figure 2: System overview of soundtrack recommendations for UGVs with ADVISOR [30].

2. STATE OF THE ART

Earlier works [11,34,37] recognize emotions from videos but the field of soundtrack recommendation for UGVs [9,39] is largely unexplored. Our ADVISOR system [30] to recommend a matching soundtrack to a UGV is inspired by prior works [7,16,38]. It performs heterogeneous late fusion to recognize moods and retrieve a ranked list of songs using a heuristic approach for sensor-annotated videos (UGVs). Moreover, significant prior works [8,10,17,18,40] in the area of event modeling, understanding, detection, and summarization from multimedia, inspired us to leverage multimodal information and knowledge bases in an effective event detection and summarization from UGIs [25]. Earlier works [13,35] added soundtracks to the slideshow of photos. Moreover, notable contributions [3,4,6,19,21,22] in the area of sentiment analysis motivated us to exploit multimodal information in the sentics understanding of UGIs. Furthermore, regarding computing tag relevance for photos, Liu *et al.* [15] and Li *et al.* [14] proposed methods based on random walk and neighbor voting, respectively. However, they computed neighbors using costly low-level visual features.

3. PROPOSED APPROACH

In this doctoral research we focus on the following three objectives. In our first objective (**OBJ-1**), our goal is to recommend soundtracks for outdoor UGVs that correlates preference-aware activities from different behavioral signals of individual users (*e.g.*, online listening activities and physical activities). Furthermore, in our second objective (**OBJ-2**), we address the problem of semantics and sentics understanding of UGCs. Finally, in our third objective (**OBJ-3**), we focus on computing the tag relevance of UGIs.

OBJ-1. Figure 2 shows the architecture of our proposed music video generation system, called ADVISOR [30]. It consists of two parts: an offline training and an online processing component. The online processing is further divided into two modules: a smartphone app and a server backend system. This app allows users to capture sensor-annotated videos. Geographic contextual information (*i.e.*, geo-categories such as *Park* and *Lake* derived from Foursquare [2]) for a UGV serves as an important dimension to represent valuable semantics information while its video frame content is often used in scene understanding. During offline processing, models M_G and M_F are trained by exploiting geo- and visual features (G and F) to predict geo- and visual aware mood tags (C_G and C_F), respectively, using a SVM^{hmm} technique from a dataset with geo-tagged videos. Next C_G and C_F are fused, and mood tags with high likelihoods are regarded as scene moods C_1 of the UGV. Then, songs matching the scene moods are recommended. Among them, the songs matching a user's listening history are considered as user preference-aware songs.

We proposed a heuristic music retrieval method to recommend a list of songs for input scene moods. We calculate the total score of each song based on the likelihood of predicted mood tags for a UGV and then retrieve a ranked list of soundtracks. Further, our system extracts audio features including MFCC and pitch from a user's frequently listened audio tracks. We re-rank the retrieved list by correlating it with the computed audio features, and then recommending a list of user preference-aware songs. Next, the soundtrack selection component automatically chooses the most appropriately matching song from this list and attaches it as the soundtrack to the UGV (see Figure 3). We leverage soundtracks of Hollywood movies to select an appropriate UGV soundtrack since such music is generated by professionals and ensures a good harmony with the movie content. We learn from experiences of such experts using their *professional soundtracks* of Hollywood movies through a SVM^{hmm} learning model M. We construct this model based on heterogeneous late fusion of SVM^{hmm} models constructed from visual features such as a color histogram and audio features such as MFCC, mel-spectrum, and pitch. The soundtrack selection process consists of two components. First a music video generation model that maps visual features F and audio features A of the UGV with a soundtrack S_t, to mood tags C_2 based on the late fusion of F and A. Second, a soundtrack selection component that attaches S_t to the UGV if C_2 is similar to C_1 (predicted based on G and F).

OBJ-2. Figure 4 shows the architecture of EventBuilder which detects events by computing the relevance score $u(p, e)$ of a UGI p for a given event e. It is computed by combining confidence scores from different modalities as follows: $u(p, e) = w_1\ \xi + w_2\ \lambda + w_3\ \gamma + w_4\ \mu + w_5\ \rho$, where $w_{i\,i=1}^{\,5}$ are weights for different modalities such that $\sum_{i=1}^{5} w_i = 1$, and ξ, λ, γ, μ, and ρ are similarity functions for the given

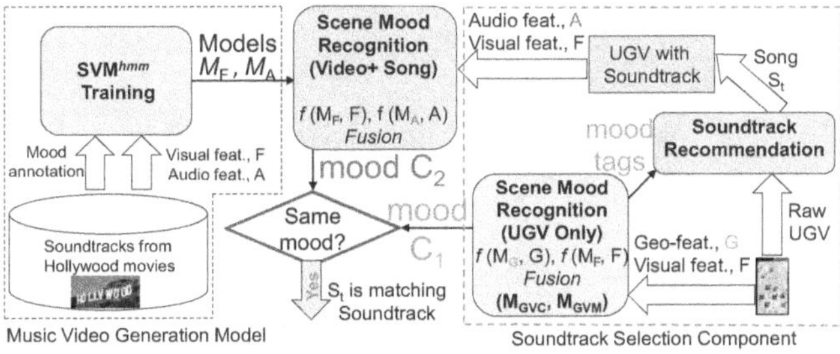

Figure 3: Soundtrack selection process in [30].

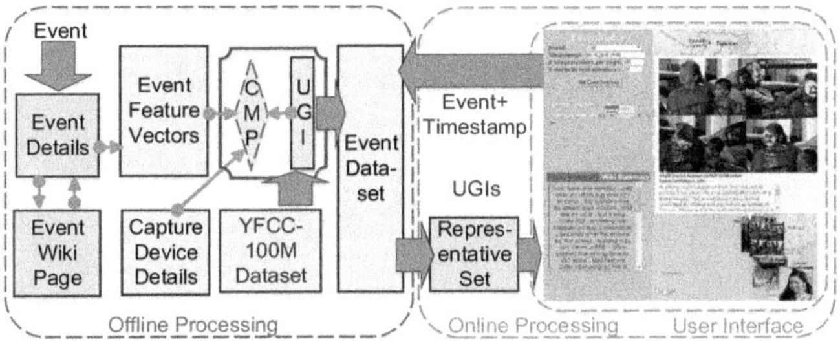

Figure 4: System framework of EventBuilder [25].

p and e with respect to event name, temporal information, spatial information, keywords, and camera model, respectively, as described in [25]. EventBuilder also produces text summaries from UGIs and the Wikipedia article of e. First, it determines important *concepts* (*e.g.*, *kid-play-holi* for the event named *Holi*) from available texts. Next, it solves an optimization problem by selecting the minimal number of sentences which cover the maximal number of *concepts*.

Figure 5 depicts the architecture of the EventSensor system consisting of two components: (i) a client which accepts a user's inputs such as a mood tag, an event name, and a timestamp, and (ii) a backend server which contains semantics and sentics engines. EventSensor leverages the semantics engine (EventBuilder) to obtain the representative set of UGIs R for a given event and timestamp. Subsequently, it uses its sentics engine to generate a mood-based event summarization. It attaches soundtracks to the slideshow of UGIs in R. The soundtracks are selected corresponding to the most frequent mood tags of the UGIs derived from the sentics engine in EventSensor.

Figure 6 shows the system framework of the sentics engine which leverages multimodal information to perform sentiments analysis. Specifically, we exploit concepts (knowledge structures) from the visual content and textual metadata of UGCs. We extract visual concepts for each multimedia item and compute concepts from the textual metadata of multimedia content using the semantic parser API [20]. Next we fuse the extracted visual and textual concepts. After determining the fused concepts C for the multimedia content, we compute the corresponding SenticNet-3 [5] concepts C_P since they bridge the conceptual and affective gap and contain sentics information. Finally, we compute a six-dimensional mood vector M_P of p by combining mood vectors of all concepts in C_P using an arithmetic mean. Experimental results indicate that the arithmetic mean of different mood vectors for concepts performs better than their geometric and harmonic means. Semantics and sentics information computed in earlier steps are very useful in providing different multimedia-related services to users. For instance

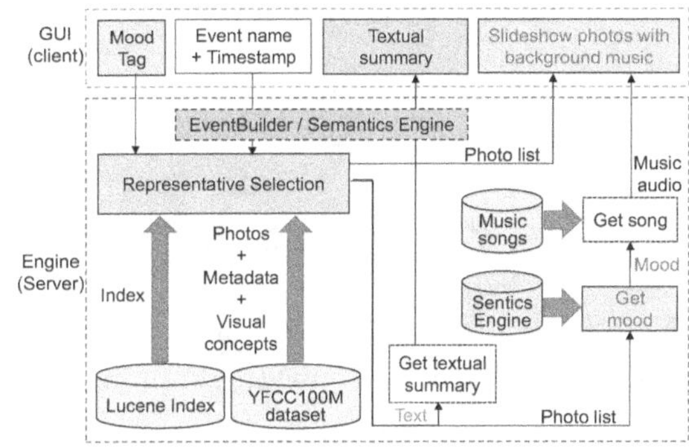

Figure 5: System framework of EventSensor [29].

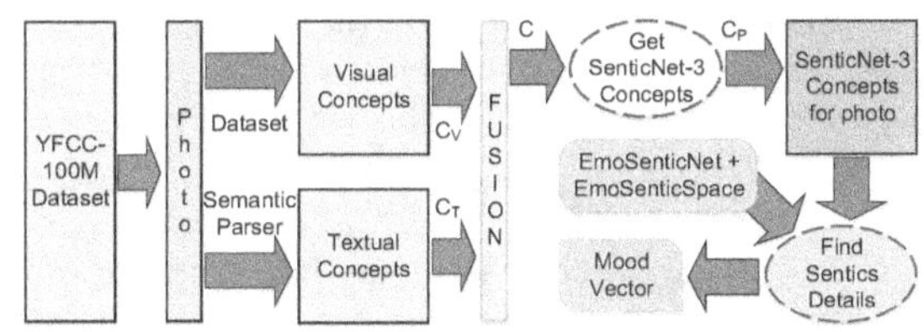

Figure 6: System framework of sentics engine [29].

we provide multimedia summaries from UGIs aggregated on social media such as Flickr. Once the affective information of UGCs is known, it can be used to provide different services related with affect. For instance, we can query Last.fm to retrieve songs for the determined mood tags and enable users to obtain a musical multimedia summary.

OBJ-3. Figure 7 shows the system framework of our tag ranking system based on neighbor voting. We propose three novel high-level features based on geo, visual, and textual content to compute neighbors of UGIs. Initial results indicate that the proposed features complement each others in computing tag relevance. We compute the weights for different modalities based on their recall scores, *i.e.*, the proportion of a seed UGI's tag covered by different modalities, and perform their late fusion to compute tag relevance.

We leverage the Foursquare API to map the GPS location of a UGI to geo concepts (*e.g.*, cafe, hotel, and office). Next, we treat each geo concept as a word and exploit the bag-of-words model [12] on a set of 1194 different geo concepts to create feature vectors. Similarly, we construct 1732-dimensional feature vectors corresponding to visual concepts (*e.g.*, nature, building, and art) present in the YFCC100M dataset [36]. Finally, to construct feature vectors from the textual metadata, we extract semantics concepts from the title, description, and tags of UGIs using the semantic parser provided by Poria *et al.* [20]. Next, we leverage SenticNet-3 knowledge base to construct an unified vector space, which is a publicly available resource for concept-level sentiment analysis [5] and consists of 30,000 common and common-sense concepts such as *food* and *accomplish_goal*. With the bag-of-words model, we construct 13727-dimensional feature vectors from textual metadata. After computing feature vectors for different modalities, we compute their k nearest neighbors using the cosine similarity metric.

After computing neighbors for a seed UGI p, we compute the relevance score of the seed UGI's tag as follows:

$$s(t,p) = \sum_{i=1}^{m} w_i \, (v_i(t,p) - prior(t,k)) \qquad (1)$$

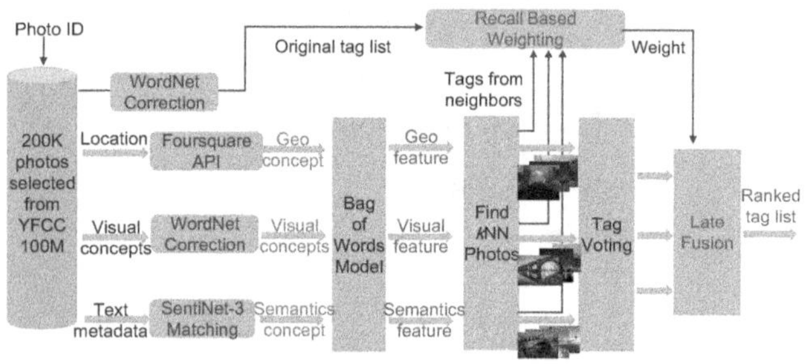

Figure 7: Architecture of our tag ranking system [28].

where m is the number of modalities, w_i is weight for different modalities such that $\sum_{i=1}^{m} w_i = 1$, $s(t,p)$ is the tag t's final relevance score, and $v_i(t,p)$ is the vote count from the k nearest neighbors derived for the ith modality. $prior(t,k)$ indicates the prior frequency of the tag t.

$$prior(t,k) = k\frac{M_t}{N} \quad (2)$$

where N and M_t are a total number UGIs and the number of UGIs tagged with t, respectively, in experimental dataset. For fast processing, we perform Apache Lucene [1] indexing of tags and UGIs. Finally, we rank the tags $t_1, t_2, ..., t_n$ based on their relevance score as follows:

$$rank(s(t_1,p), s(t_2,p), ..., s(t_n,p)). \quad (3)$$

4. RESULTS

To evaluate **OBJ-1** we used 402 soundtracks D_1 from Hollywood movies, 1213 sensor-annotated videos D_2, 729 songs D_3 from ISMIR, and 20 most frequent mood tags from Last.fm. To investigate scene moods prediction accuracy for UGVs, we randomly divided D_2 into training and testing datasets. After 10-fold cross validation, our experiments confirm that the model based on late fusion of geo- and visual features outperforms the models when they are trained with geo- and visual features alone. Moreover, to investigate the accuracy of soundtrack selection process, we randomly divided D_1 into a training and a testing dataset with a 80:20 ratio, and performed 5-fold cross validation experiments to calculate the scene moods prediction accuracy of M for UGVs in the test dataset. We predict the scene mood C_2 of a UGV from D_2 with a recommended soundtrack S_t using M, and compared with C_1. If both C_1 and C_2 are similar then we treat S_t as matching soundtrack since the prediction accuracy of C_1 is high. In this way we achieved the accuracy of 70.0% for 80 UGVs from D_2, which is comparable to the mood prediction accuracy of 68.8% for 80 soundtrack videos from D_1 (see [30] for detailed results).

We evaluate our event detection system [25] in **OBJ-2**, on the YFCC100M dataset [36] with 100 million photos and videos. We performed an extensive user study on results derived from baseline and EventBuilder. A photo consists the name of a given event in its metadata is considered as a result from the baseline. We randomly selected four photos each for the seven events used in EventBuilder [25] and asked 63 users to evaluatef the results by selecting photos which are relevant to the input events. We accepted 52 responses which fulfilled the annotation consistency criteria. Moreover, we also created ground truths for the results leveraging their content and contextual information. We compared responses of users with ground truths based on two metrics (i) precision, recall, and F measure, and (ii) cosine similar-

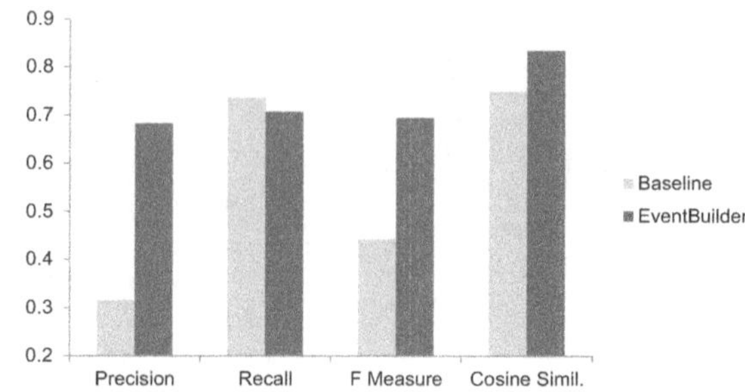

Figure 8: Results for event detection from 52 users, where x- and y-axis indicate evaluation metrics and scores between 0 to 1, respectively [29].

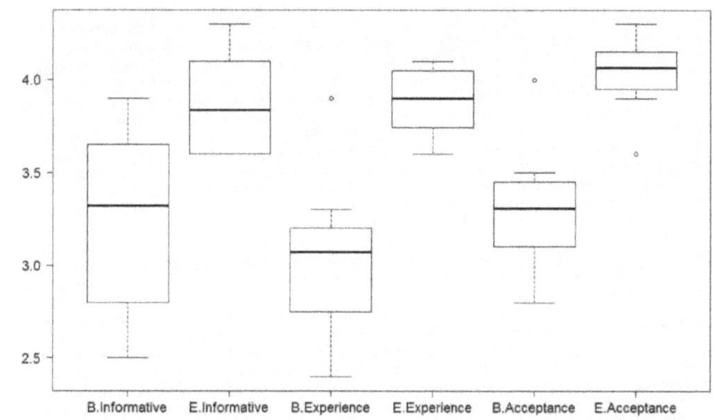

Figure 9: Boxplot for the informative, experience, and acceptance ratings of text summaries, where prefix *B* and *E* in x-axis indicate baseline and EventBuilder, respectively. In y-axis ratings range from 1 (low satisfaction) to 5 (high satisfaction) [29].

ity. Figure 8 confirms that EventBuilder outperforms the proposed baseline in event detection.

Next, we asked ten evaluators to assess produced text summaries by providing scores from 1 to 5, with a higher score indicating better satisfaction, based on the following three perspectives [25]: (i) informativeness, (ii) experience, and (iii) acceptance. We asked users to rate both the Flickr summary (baseline) which is derived from descriptions of UGIs and the Wikipedia summary which is derived from Wikipedia articles of events. Experimental results in Figure 9 indicate that users generally think that the Wikipedia summary is more informative than the baseline and can help them to obtain a quick overview of the events. However, the Flickr summary is also very helpful since they give an overview about what users thinks about the events.

5. CONCLUSIONS

This doctoral research studied the following three problems: (i) soundtracks recommendation for outdoor UGVs, (ii) semantics and sentics understanding of UGIs, and (iii) computing tag relevance for UGIs. We perform multimodal analysis and exploit knowledge bases to solve above problems. Experimental results confirm that they augment semantics and sentics understanding from multimedia content.

ACKNOWLEDGMENTS

This research was supported in part by Singapore's Ministry of Education (MOE) Academic Research Fund Tier 1, grant number T1 251RES1415.

6. REFERENCES

[1] Apache Lucene. https://lucene.apache.org/core/, April 2016. Java API: Last Accessed April, 2016.

[2] FourSquare. https://developer.foursquare.com/, March 2016. API: Last Accessed March, 2016.

[3] B. Agarwal, S. Poria, N. Mittal, A. Gelbukh, and A. Hussain. Concept-level Sentiment Analysis with Dependency-based Semantic Parsing: A Novel Approach. *In Springer Cognitive Computation*, pages 1–13, 2015.

[4] E. Cambria, J. Fu, F. Bisio, and S. Poria. AffectiveSpace 2: Enabling Affective Intuition for Concept-level Sentiment Analysis. In *AAAI Conference on Artificial Intelligence*, pages 508–514, 2015.

[5] E. Cambria, D. Olsher, and D. Rajagopal. SenticNet 3: A Common and Common-sense Knowledge Base for Cognition-driven Sentiment Analysis. In *AAAI Conference on Artificial Intelligence*, pages 1515–1521, 2014.

[6] E. Cambria, S. Poria, F. Bisio, R. Bajpai, and I. Chaturvedi. The CLSA Model: A Novel Framework for Concept-Level Sentiment Analysis. In *Springer Computational Linguistics and Intelligent Text Processing*, pages 3–22. 2015.

[7] B. Chen, J. Wang, Q. Huang, and T. Mei. Personalized Video Recommendation through Tripartite Graph Propagation. In *ACM MM*, pages 1133–1136, 2012.

[8] J. Choi, E. Kim, M. Larson, G. Friedland, and A. Hanjalic. Evento 360: Social Event Discovery from Web-scale Multimedia Collection. In *ACM MM*, pages 193–196, 2015.

[9] M. Cristani, A. Pesarin, C. Drioli, V. Murino, A. Rodà, M. Grapulin, and N. Sebe. Toward an Automatically Generated Soundtrack from Low-level Cross-modal Correlations for Automotive Scenarios. In *ACM MM*, pages 551–560, 2010.

[10] M. Del Fabro, A. Sobe, and L. Böszörmenyi. Summarization of Real-life Events based on Community-contributed Content. In *MMEDIA*, pages 119–126, 2012.

[11] A. Hanjalic and L.-Q. Xu. Affective Video Content Representation and Modeling. *In IEEE Transactions on Multimedia*, 7(1):143–154, 2005.

[12] Y. Ko. A Study of Term Weighting Schemes using Class Information for Text Classification. In *ACM SIGIR*, pages 1029–1030, 2012.

[13] C. T. Li and M. K. Shan. Emotion-based Impressionism Slideshow with Automatic Music Accompaniment. In *ACM MM*, pages 839–842, 2007.

[14] X. Li, C. G. Snoek, and M. Worring. Learning Social Tag Relevance by Neighbor Voting. *In IEEE Transactions on Multimedia*, 11(7):1310–1322, 2009.

[15] D. Liu, X.-S. Hua, L. Yang, M. Wang, and H.-J. Zhang. Tag Ranking. In *ACM WWW*, pages 351–360, 2009.

[16] L. Lu, H. You, and H. Zhang. A New Approach to Query by Humming in Music Retrieval. In *IEEE ICME*, pages 22–25, 2001.

[17] V. Mezaris, A. Scherp, R. Jain, and M. S. Kankanhalli. Real-life Events in Multimedia: Detection, Representation, Retrieval, and Applications. *In Springer MTAP*, 70(1):1–6, 2014.

[18] P. Pakray, S. Pal, S. Poria, S. Bandyopadhyay, and A. Gelbukh. JU_CSE_TAC: Textual Entailment Eecognition System at TAC RTE-6. In *System Report, TAC RTE Notebook*, 2010.

[19] S. Poria, B. Agarwal, A. Gelbukh, A. Hussain, and N. Howard. Dependency-based Semantic Parsing for Concept-level Text Analysis. In *Springer Computational Linguistics and Intelligent Text Processing*, pages 113–127. 2014.

[20] S. Poria, E. Cambria, A. Gelbukh, F. Bisio, and A. Hussain. Sentiment Data Flow Analysis by Means of Dynamic Linguistic Patterns. *In IEEE Computational Intelligence Magazine*, 10(4):26–36, 2015.

[21] S. Poria, E. Cambria, A. Hussain, and G.-B. Huang. Towards an Intelligent Framework for Multimodal Affective Data Analysis. *Elsevier Neural Networks*, 63:104–116, 2015.

[22] S. Poria, E. Cambria, G. Winterstein, and G.-B. Huang. Sentic Patterns: Dependency-based Rules for Concept-level Sentiment Analysis. *In Elsevier Knowledge-Based Systems*, 69:45–63, 2014.

[23] R. R. Shah. Multimodal Analysis of User-Generated Content in Support of Social Media Applications. In *ACM ICMR*, pages 423–426, 2016.

[24] R. R. Shah, M. Hefeeda, R. Zimmermann, K. Harras, C.-H. Hsu, and Y. Yu. NEWSMAN: Uploading Videos over Adaptive Middleboxes to News Servers in Weak Network Infrastructures. In *Springer MMM*, pages 100–113, 2016.

[25] R. R. Shah, A. D. Shaikh, Y. Yu, W. Geng, R. Zimmermann, and G. Wu. EventBuilder: Real-time Multimedia Event Summarization by Visualizing Social Media. In *ACM MM*, pages 185–188, 2015.

[26] R. R. Shah, Y. Yu, A. D. Shaikh, S. Tang, and R. Zimmermann. ATLAS: Automatic Temporal Segmentation and Annotation of Lecture Videos Based on Modelling Transition Time. In *ACM MM*, pages 209–212, 2014.

[27] R. R. Shah, Y. Yu, A. D. Shaikh, and R. Zimmermann. TRACE: A Linguistic-based Approach for Automatic Lecture Video Segmentation Leveraging Wikipedia Texts. In *IEEE ISM*, pages 217–220, 2015.

[28] R. R. Shah, Y. Yu, S. Tang, S. Satoh, A. Verma, and R. Zimmermann. Concept-Level Multimodal Ranking of Flickr Photo Tags via Recall Based Weighting. In *MMCommons Workshop at ACM MM*, 2016.

[29] R. R. Shah, Y. Yu, A. Verma, S. Tang, A. D. Shaikh, and R. Zimmermann. Leveraging Multimodal Information for Event Summarization and Concept-level Sentiment Analysis. *In Elsevier KBS*, pages 1–8, 2016.

[30] R. R. Shah, Y. Yu, and R. Zimmermann. ADVISOR: Personalized Video Soundtrack Recommendation by Late Fusion with Heuristic Rankings. In *ACM MM*, pages 607–616, 2014.

[31] R. R. Shah, Y. Yu, and R. Zimmermann. User Preference-Aware Music Video Generation Based on Modeling Scene Moods. In *ACM MMSys*, pages 156–159, 2014.

[32] A. D. Shaikh, M. Jain, M. Rawat, R. R. Shah, and M. Kumar. Improving Accuracy of SMS Based FAQ Retrieval System. In *Springer FIRE*, pages 142–156. 2013.

[33] A. D. Shaikh, R. R. Shah, and R. Shaikh. SMS based FAQ Retrieval for Hindi, English and Malayalam. In *ACM FIRE*, page 9, 2013.

[34] M. Soleymani, J. J. M. Kierkels, G. Chanel, and T. Pun. A Bayesian Framework for Video Affective Representation. In *IEEE ACII*, pages 1–7, 2009.

[35] A. Stupar and S. Michel. Picasso: Automated Soundtrack Suggestion for Multi-modal Data. In *ACM CIKM*, pages 2589–2592, 2011.

[36] B. Thomee, B. Elizalde, D. A. Shamma, K. Ni, G. Friedland, D. Poland, D. Borth, and L.-J. Li. YFCC100M: The New Data in Multimedia Research. *In Communications of the ACM*, 59(2):64–73, 2016.

[37] H. L. Wang and L. F. Cheong. Affective Understanding in Film. *In IEEE TCSVT*, 16(6):689–704, 2006.

[38] G. Ye, D. Liu, I.-H. Jhuo, and S.-F. Chang. Robust Late Fusion with Rank Minimization. In *IEEE CVPR*, pages 3021–3028, 2012.

[39] Y. Yu, Z. Shen, and R. Zimmermann. Automatic Music Soundtrack Generation for Outdoor Videos from Contextual Sensor Information. In *ACM MM*, pages 1377–1378, 2012.

[40] M. Zaharieva, M. Zeppelzauer, and C. Breiteneder. Automated Social Event Detection in Large Photo Collections. In *ACM ICMR*, pages 167–174, 2013.

Geospatial Multimedia Data for Situation Recognition

Mengfan Tang
Department of Computer Science
University of California, Irvine
mengfant@uci.edu

ABSTRACT

Many emerging problems increasingly rely on integrating complex heterogeneous sensor streams, ranging from photos, texts, environmental data streams and other participating human sensors. The diversity of data types from disparate sensors poses a major challenge in data aggregation and assimilation. EventShop was originally designed for situation recognition using diverse data sources. We propose and develop new interpolation and prediction models on top of EventShop, allowing for effective ingesting and combining appropriate data streams to improve data quality and predict specific situations. We also incorporate data from participatory sensing into the system. The synergy of data gives powerful insight into better understanding of evolving situations, in which participatory sensing is integrated with the surrounding environment. Furthermore, the enhanced system is used for two real-world problems: asthma risk management and smart city.

Keywords

geospatial data, situation recognition, interpolation, prediction

1. INTRODUCTION

To understand constantly evolving situations, data is collected from disparate sensors, social media, Internet-of-Things, and from people using effective participatory sensing. The heterogeneous nature of sensing is essential to capture different attributes at a point in physical space and time. Using this data, it is important to detect and predict evolving situations using adaptable models and take corrective actions promptly.

To build a platform for situation modeling and recognition, the EventShop project was started [20]. This framework allows for ingestion of different data streams and converts them to a unifying space, time, and thematic (STT) representation [19]. Using different spatio-temporal operators, disparate data streams with different themes can be combined to generate new spatio-temporal themes of interest in a given application. Pattern recognition operators can detect and recognize different situations allowing for appropriate actions to be taken.

Current EventShop was designed with an 'always-on' stream of data in mind. Its ability is limited when used with data stores. Stored historic data in real time cyber physical systems may be used in important tasks like spatial interpolation, prediction, and system modeling. This is an important area lacking in the current framework. This dissertation is enhancing EventShop performance using stored data, and processing these heterogeneous data. The current setup favors data input in grid or raster form. However, much data is created and collected in different forms and in different spatial, temporal, and symbolic granularities. Many data sources use socio-political concepts and relationships in production and representation of data. In this case, most computations of input as well as output are performed in grid format. This introduces many computational as well as result quality related issues. We are also working on making this part computationally efficient. In addition to integrating data sources from different sources, operators for handling missing values is crucial in data processing. It's more challenging to deal with it with diverse data sources, in terms of granularity, coverage, availability and reliability. Moreover, prediction is needed. Recognition of situations in real-time is good, but it is much better if they can be predicted. For several cases, even a very small notice can enable a timely response, and hence change the outcome. Application of predictive analytics in any system will increase its applicability.

To sum up, this thesis builds on EventShop. We identify opportunities to greatly extend the scope and abilities of EventShop and propose new components and operators to achieve that. In particular, we develop new approaches and collect various data sources to address the following specific issues and deal directly with data quality and data analysis.

- Statistical spatio-temporal interpolation approaches are developed to increase the availability of sensory data across space and time.
- Situation prediction allows for time to take appropriate actions in managing complex emergency situations. By identifying relevant data across domains and utilizing a unified representation, we propose more accurate predictions of a given situation.
- Developed methodologies and collected data are applied to solve real problems in two emerging applications: smart city and asthma risk management.

MM '16, October 15-19, 2016, Amsterdam, Netherlands

DOI: http://dx.doi.org/10.1145/2964284.2971472

2. MOTIVATION

We focus on two data categories, persistent location sensor data and citizen contributed data. Persistent location sensors are relatively fixed at some locations, monitoring and measuring some variables from environment. Air quality sensors are placed to collect meteorological data and air pollution data commonly used for weather prediction and air pollution situation detection. Environment dynamics can be analyzed by using this data. Data generated from persistent location sensors usually has data-missing and sparsity problems. Reliance on these measurements not only restricts the geographical region of situation recognition, but can also result in spatial uncertainty. Consequently, there is a great demand for spatial interpolation with additional information to increase the availability of these data across space and time. One of the existing challenges is to combine data sources that arise from different spatial resolutions. For example, one data stream is provided as grid cells, while other data streams are only available at point locations. This challenge motives us to develop multiscale statistical approaches.

Participatory citizen sensing and crowdsourcing are increasingly playing more important roles in understanding current trends and evolving situations. Citizen contributed data comes as mobile streams. Mobile devices carried by people are becoming the source of this data. The act of leveraging a human mobility enabled sensing of the environment is referred to as 'Participatory Sensing'. The accuracy of situation detection depends on the quality of data. However, Micro-blogs from systems like Twitter are very noisy and subjective [18]. Most applications may benefit from objective and factual citizen contributed data. Waze is an application on phones that uses GPS data and Micro-reports, and provides actionable guidance to its users. We are motivated to explore use of **multimedia micro-reports** as compared to **micro-blogs** for radical improvement in the quality of participatory sensing data.

3. STATE OF THE ART

For persistent location data, in geographic information system, interpolation can be used to estimate elevation, chemical dispersion, and other spatially related phenomena. Its formulation can typically base on geostatistical concepts, locality (nearest neighbor), smoothness (splines), or ad hoc functions. However, different methods can produce quite different interpolated results [13]. Therefore, a comprehensive understanding of the phenomenon is required in finding suitable interpolation methods for GIS applications. Many spatial interpolation methods have been developed to predict unknown values at the unsampled point from the known values of the (nearby) sampled points. Spatial interpolation models track back to Kriging, a Gaussian model that is widely used in geospatial analysis to interpolate values in a random field. Multitask Gaussian process [4], which assumes a Gaussian prior over latent functions to directly induce correlations between tasks. All available data is jointly modeled in a spatial process [6], but auxiliary data may dominate the interpolation results. Average weighted auxiliary data methods [3, 16] are used to model the output smoothly, resulting in a better interpolation, especially when predicting observations geographically far away from others. Multiscale spatial process proposed in [15] models the bias of each data source, for multiple auxiliary data. However, these approaches suffer from scalability problem which hinders their application to large-scale problem.

Among diverse citizen contributed data, photo and video are the biggest data source. Every minute, millions of photo and videos are uploaded by people to social media. More and more photo and video data has geo-tag information. Geo-tagged Flickr data has been used to explore users' trajectories, interest, and participated events [1, 10]. Structuring these geo-tagged photo and video data for analysis is challenging because of different levels of understanding, such as concepts, topics, semantics. To analyze the data, there have been a great of efforts to perform automatic semantic classification of media contents into a number of predefined concepts [9, 14]. However, how to effectively utilize concepts for situation detection and trend analysis is still a challenging problem.

In [20, 25, 23], persistent location sensor data such as air pollution data and pollen data are combined with citizen contributed Twitter data, to study the situation of asthma risk. The accuracy of situation detection depends on the quality of data. However, Micro-blogs from systems like Twitter are very noisy and subjective. Applications can benefit from objective and factual citizen contributed data, such as multimedia micro-reports.

4. PROPOSED APPROACHES

EventShop [17] is an open source project, which has been developed as a framework to allow accepting diverse data streams, provides appropriate mappings to index and integrate all spatio-temporal heterogeneous data streams into a common representation, and then assimilate these data into evolving situations. It provides a generic infrastructure for a large number of domain experts and application developers to experiment with and analyze heterogeneous spatio-temporal data streams about real-world objects and events with the aim of recognizing situations and defining actions such as personalized alerts. Situations, on EventShop, can vary from daily or routine situations such as a traffic jam, to unusual situations such as an Ebola outbreak. Data can be streamed from a very diverse set of sources, like social media, sensor networks, distributed cameras, and knowledge bases such as census and maps. The Action Control Unit allows an application developer or domain expert to visualize the detected situations, and perform specified actions in response.

Three new components are adding into EventShop: persistent location sensor data interpolation, concept detection for citizen contributed data, and situation recognition and prediction.

4.1 Persistent Location Sensor Data Interpolation

A new interpolation model is proposed, which performs interpolation and data integration at the same time by space alignment. Given a set of auxiliary data, correlated across different domains, this model attempts to place the correlated data in a manifold space, and allows effective associations between auxiliary data and observations at multiple resolutions. By incorporating adaptive multiscale features of observed covariance into the interpolation, this model is able to improve results on geospatial interpolation tasks.

In addition, we develop new scalable optimization methods for larger scale data sets. To further reduce the computational cost caused by the so called 'Big n' problem, these methods take advantage of spatial information in optimization as well as existing techniques such as such as covariance tapering, statistical methods numerical likelihood approximation,low rank approximation of covariance matrix.

4.2 Concept Detection for Citizen Contributed Data

More and more photos are coming with geo information. An important characteristic of these geo-tagged photo data is its space-time nature. For example, when a public event occurs, people take photos related to the event, which enables detection of event occurrence promptly, simply by observing the photo. With information of space and time, the objective and factual nature of photo and video makes them the best resources of Multimedia Micro-reports. On Feb. 4 2016, UC Irvine issued an emergency alert to the UCI community about fire reported on campus, Langson Library and Gateway Study Center. Before we received alerts from emails and text messages, many photos and short videos had been posted in WeChat. These photos were perfect compelling and objective micro-reports of the evolving situation. We investigate the real-time interaction of events, and develop algorithms to treat photos as micro-reports to understand evolving situations.

One of the major efforts in recent years is automatic semantic classification of media contents into a number of predefined concepts [5]. These concepts and their relations are defined in an ontology from the results of user studies or data mining techniques applied to media contents. The evaluations of concept detection involves a large number of training and testing data. Machine learning models are trained and then used to classify testing data to each concept. Developed in video and image analysis, such as Caffe [8], Theano[2], Cuda-convnet [11], and have been available as open source. We will use results from these concept detector frameworks to provide informative and objective micro-reports along with their location and time. Thus, EventShop can convert photo and video to STT data and use them as powerful data streams for situation recognition.

4.3 Situation Recognition and Prediction

Situation recognition based on the latest observations alone could be too late for taking appropriate actions for critical events. Accurate prediction of situations can allow for time to take appropriate actions by connecting people to the resources they need, especially in life threatening situations. Typically, predictions in specific fields are derived from numerical models and data, limited to the field. By utilizing large scale data integration, machine learning models can be used in conjunction with the scientific theory based models, to obtain more accurate predictions.

Common methods for time series prediction are regressive based models [7]. Multivariate spatio-temporal autoregressive models take into account both spatial and temporal correlations but require estimation of a large number of parameters. In order to reduce the number of estimated parameters, we develop new models which consider the spatial and temporal correlation in neighbors. The time series models are further extended to tensor time series model incorporating spatio-temporal correlation. Those models can manifest hidden, evolving trends in the multidimensional data by preserving the sensor structure. We aim to implement these machine learning models in EventShop with a built-in ability to cope with SST data.

5. APPLICATION

Many emerging applications increasingly rely on assimilating heterogeneous data streams to solve problems in physical and social situations. We believe that our framework will be useful in many applications. Here, we use two motivating examples in our research: smart cities and asthma management.

Smart cities address many aspects of living, such as identifying functional regions [26], smart driving directions [27], detection of anomalies in road traffic flows [12], real-time air pollution [28]. These studies try to use several data to sense and understand the city dynamics. However, there's no framework to integrate disparate data for effective strategies design for improving city lives. Equipped with the components proposed here, the proposed framework will be a key for broad applications using diverse data sources in a smart city.

Any given air quality index forecast is a communication of the health risk to the public via various media sources (i.e. internet, TV, radio). Asthma patients take it as a guidance to outdoor activities. Many studies [21, 22] based on large environmental databases have been performed on the association between air quality measures and asthma. The use of many large environmental databases contributes to the asthma related research and health advice. EventShop will not only collect large environmental databases but also account for other potential confounding factors such as wind velocity, traffic, and personal life style. Our group is also developing an asthma mobile application, collecting data streams from the users such as motion tracking, location tracking, activity level, personal calendar and asthma symptoms for asthma patients. This can provide a precise recommendation for each individual patient. An asthma risk alert will be sent to patients for prevention of asthma attacks.

To evaluate the integration of EventShop framework, We have been building an Event Warehouse at UC Irvine for harvesting, storing, and analyzing data coming from large scale heterogeneous sensors. Specifically, for persistent location sensors, air pollution data, traffic sensor data and camera data, satellite image data are automatically collected; for citizen contributed data, Flickr, Instgram and so on, will be stored. They will both be pre-processed in Event Warehouse. Quantitative evaluation improvements in situation recognition and prediction will be verified by comparing to other state-of-the-art methods.

6. RESULTS

To improve the data coverage of persistent location data, we develop data interpolation framework on top of EventShop. The framework is validated using PM2.5 interpolation task. In our study [24], we identified three effective data sources which are shown in Table 1. Traffic data, PM2.5 physical model numerical outputs and satellite MODIS AOD data are in different formats and resolutions, however, are efficiently combined in EventShop to generate features in frequency domain, then the features are used in a Spatial Gaussian Process model, which achieves more comprehensive (covering wider range) and accurate interpolation results.

The results are particularly significantly improved around

Table 1: Data sources for PM2.5 concentration analysis with diverse spatial and temporal granularities.

Theme	Data Source	Temporal Resolution	Spatial Resolution
PM2.5 Concentration	US EPA Air Quality System	hourly	isolated points
PM2.5 Estimation	Community Modeling & Analysis System	daily	12 km × 12 km grid
Aerosol Concentration	MODIS Aerosol Optical Depth	aperiodic	10 km × 10 km grid
Traffic Flow	Caltrans Performance Measurement System	5 mins	isolated points

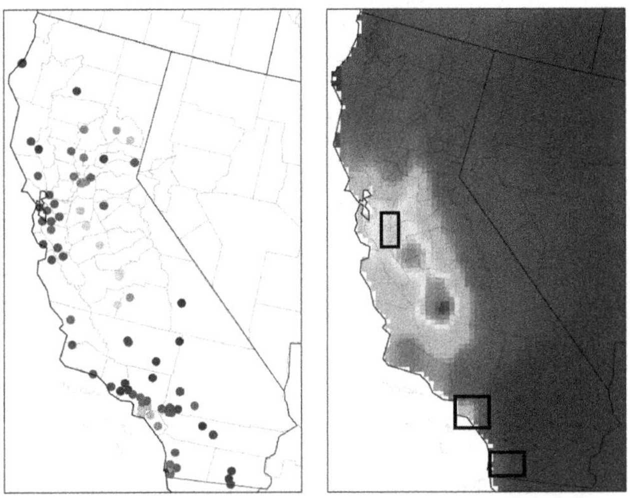

(a) Station Measurements (b) Gaussian Process

Figure 1: (a) PM2.5 monitoring stations in California (b) Prediction results using Spatial Gaussian Process on available auxiliary data sources.

Los Angeles, Orange County, San Diego, Ventura County, Sacramento, and San Joaquin Area, where our values are closer to the observed station values, than Community Modeling & Analysis System physical model outputs. The errors are reduced by more than 10%. In particular, these areas are some of the most populated areas of the state and account for around half of California's population.

At the application level, we use interpolated PM2.5 values from the operator for the asthma risk management application on EventShop to analyze the asthma risk situation across California. The asthma risk model further aggregates data from three sources: pollen level[1], air quality index[2], and PM2.5. It then classifies the result into three risk categories: low (green), medium (yellow) and high (red). The screen-shots of the risk map from EventShop are shown in Figure 2. We compare the risk indications of the two models to the number of asthma related hospitalizations per 10,000 people, in the year 2008, at the county level[3]. To measure the improvement, we calculate the correlation of our risk values with the hospitalizations data. The model using the developed operator improves significantly over previous EventShop.

[1]Pollen Concentrations: http://pollen.com
[2]AirNow: http://airnow.gov
[3]Data from http://californiabreathing.org

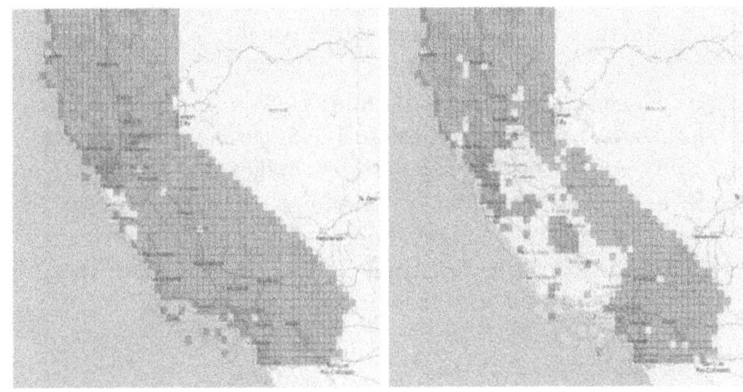

(a) Earlier EventShop (b) After interpolation

Figure 2: Asthma risk situations across California detected by EventShop

7. WORK IN PROGRESS

First, We have started building spatial prediction approaches with new operators in EventShop. Collaborating with Washington DC Sustainabilty Initiatives to build a smart city applications for trash level prediction and trash pickup route recommendation, we will explore spatio-temporal prediction analytics, and combine them with real-time states of objects. For example, for each upcoming event in the city, we can model the potential volume in a trash bin that will be generated for that event based on its past history and its location. We will create a spatio-temporal model of the trash bin state using a spatio-temporal kernel density estimation. By combining this trash prediction model with the actual current trash situation, we can weight the spatial kernel of the historical data for the current predictive task for more accurate trash prediction in the near future. This information will significantly help city planners to make better decisions from increasing number of trash bins to rerouting trash pickup routes.

8. FUTURE WORK AND CONCLUSION

Previous work establishes a basis for improving persistent location sensor data quality and contributes to asthma risk application. The next project phase will incorporate photographs as objective and informative micro-reports from citizen sensors. Using advances in deep learning, photos become a powerful information stream for detecting evolving situations. The synergy of physical sensor data and citizen contributed data will give powerful insight into the understanding of evolving situations, in which participatory sensing is integrated with the surrounding environment. We will identify relevant data across domains and propose more accurate prediction models. Eventually, we will apply the framework for applications in smart city.

9. REFERENCES

[1] G. Andrienko, N. Andrienko, P. Bak, S. Kisilevich, and D. Keim. Analysis of community-contributed space-and time-referenced data.

[2] F. Bastien, P. Lamblin, R. Pascanu, J. Bergstra, I. Goodfellow, A. Bergeron, N. Bouchard, D. Warde-Farley, and Y. Bengio. Theano: new features and speed improvements. *arXiv preprint arXiv:1211.5590*, 2012.

[3] V. J. Berrocal, A. E. Gelfand, and D. M. Holland. A spatio-temporal downscaler for output from numerical models. *J. AGR. BIOL. ENVIR. ST.*, 15(2).

[4] E. V. Bonilla, K. M. Chai, and C. Williams. Multi-task gaussian process prediction. In *Advances in neural information processing systems*, pages 153–160, 2007.

[5] S.-F. Chang, D. Ellis, W. Jiang, K. Lee, A. Yanagawa, A. C. Loui, and J. Luo. Large-scale multimodal semantic concept detection for consumer video. In *Proceedings of the international workshop on Workshop on multimedia information retrieval*, pages 255–264. ACM, 2007.

[6] M. Fuentes and A. E. Raftery. Model evaluation and spatial interpolation by bayesian combination of observations with outputs from numerical models. *Biometrics*, 61(1).

[7] J. D. Hamilton. *Time series analysis*, volume 2. Princeton university press Princeton, 1994.

[8] Y. Jia, E. Shelhamer, J. Donahue, S. Karayev, J. Long, R. B. Girshick, S. Guadarrama, and T. Darrell. Caffe: Convolutional architecture for fast feature embedding. In *ACM Multimedia*, volume 2, page 4, 2014.

[9] Y.-G. Jiang, G. Ye, S.-F. Chang, D. Ellis, and A. C. Loui. Consumer video understanding: A benchmark database and an evaluation of human and machine performance. In *ICMR*, page 29. ACM, 2011.

[10] S. Kisilevich, M. Krstajic, D. Keim, N. Andrienko, and G. Andrienko. Event-based analysis of people's activities and behavior using flickr and panoramio geotagged photo collections. In *ICIV*, pages 289–296. IEEE, 2010.

[11] A. Krizhevsky, I. Sutskever, and G. E. Hinton. Imagenet classification with deep convolutional neural networks. In *NIPS*, pages 1097–1105, 2012.

[12] W. Liu, Y. Zheng, S. Chawla, J. Yuan, and X. Xing. Discovering spatio-temporal causal interactions in traffic data streams. In *KDD*, pages 1010–1018. ACM, 2011.

[13] L. Mitas and H. Mitasova. *Spatial interpolation.* Wiley, 1999.

[14] M. Naphade, J. R. Smith, J. Tesic, S.-F. Chang, W. Hsu, A. L. Kennedy, A. Hauptmann, and J. Curtis. Large-scale concept ontology for multimedia. *MultiMedia, IEEE*, 13(3):86–91, 2006.

[15] H. Nguyen, N. Cressie, and A. Braverman. Spatial statistical data fusion for remote sensing applications. *J. AM. STAT. ASSOC.*, 107(499).

[16] C. J. Paciorek. Combining spatial information sources while accounting for systematic errors in proxies. *J. R. STAT. SOC.*, 61(3).

[17] S. Pongpaichet, V. K. Singh, M. Gao, and R. Jain. EventShop: Recognizing Situations in Web Data Streams. In *WWW*, pages 1359–1368. ACM, 2013.

[18] S. Ponpaichet, M. Tang, and R. Jain. Using photos as micro-reports of events. In *ICMR*. ACM, 2016.

[19] S. Ponpaichet, M. Tang, L. Jalali, and R. Jain. Observing real-world phenomena through eventweb over space, time and theme. In *2nd International Workshop on Building Web Observatories, ACM Web Science 2014*, 2014.

[20] V. K. Singh and R. Jain. *Situation Recognition using EventShop.* Springer; Auflage: 1st ed. 2016, 2016.

[21] D. A. Stern, W. J. Morgan, M. Halonen, A. L. Wright, and F. D. Martinez. Wheezing and bronchial hyper-responsiveness in early childhood as predictors of newly diagnosed asthma in early adulthood: a longitudinal birth-cohort study. *The Lancet*, 372(9643):1058–1064, Sept. 2008.

[22] D. M. Stieb, R. T. Burnett, M. Smith-Doiron, O. Brion, H. H. Shin, and V. Economou. A New Multipollutant, No-Threshold Air Quality Health Index Based on Short-Term Associations Observed in Daily Time-Series Analyses. *Journal of the Air & Waste Management Association*, Jan. 2012.

[23] M. Tang, P. Agrawal, and R. Jain. Habits vs environment: What really causes asthma? In *Proceedings of the ACM Web Science Conference*, page 30. ACM, 2015.

[24] M. Tang, P. Agrawal, S. Pongpaichet, and R. Jain. Geospatial interpolation analytics for data streams in eventshop. In *ICME*, pages 1–6. IEEE, 2015.

[25] M. Tang, P. Agrawal, S. Pongpaichet, and R. Jain. A graph based multimodal geospatial interpolation framework. In *ICME*. IEEE, 2016.

[26] J. Yuan, Y. Zheng, and X. Xie. Discovering regions of different functions in a city using human mobility and pois. In *KDD*, pages 186–194. ACM, 2012.

[27] J. Yuan, Y. Zheng, C. Zhang, W. Xie, X. Xie, G. Sun, and Y. Huang. T-drive: driving directions based on taxi trajectories. In *ACM SIGSPATIAL*, pages 99–108. ACM, 2010.

[28] Y. Zheng, F. Liu, and H. Hsieh. U-air: When urban air quality inference meets big data. In *KDD*, pages 1436–1444, 2013.

Image Emotion Computing

Sicheng Zhao
School of Computer Science and Technology
Harbin Institute of Technology, Harbin, China
schzhao@gmail.com

ABSTRACT

Images can convey rich semantics and induce strong emotions in viewers. My research aims to predict image emotions from different aspects with respect to two main challenges: affective gap and subjective evaluation. To bridge the affective gap, we extract emotion features based on principles-of-art to recognize image-centric dominant emotions. As the emotions that are induced in viewers by an image are highly subjective and different, we propose to predict user-centric personalized emotion perceptions for each viewer and image-centric emotion probability distribution for each image. To tackle the subjective evaluation issue, we set up a large scale image emotion dataset from Flickr, named Image-Emotion-Social-Net, on both dimensional and categorical emotion representations with over 1 million images and about 8,000 users. Different types of factors may influence personalized image emotion perceptions, including visual content, social context, temporal evolution and location influence. We make an initial attempt to jointly combine them by the proposed rolling multi-task hypergraph learning. Both discrete and continuous emotion distributions are modelled via shared sparse learning. Further, several potential applications based on image emotions are designed and implemented.

Keywords

Image emotion; principles-of-art; personalized perceptions; emotion distribution; hypergraph learning; sparse learning

1. INTRODUCTION

The explosively growing volume of multimedia content results in great demand of processing and understanding the visual content of images and videos. Compared to low-level visual features, humans are able to perceive and understand images and videos only at high level semantics, including cognitive level and affective level [9]. Most previous works on image content analysis focus on understanding the cognitive aspects of images, namely describing the actual content, such as object detection and recognition. However, with the increasing use of digital photography technology by the public and the high requirement for image emotion representation, the analysis of image content at the highest semantic level, i.e. the affective level, is becoming increasingly urgent.

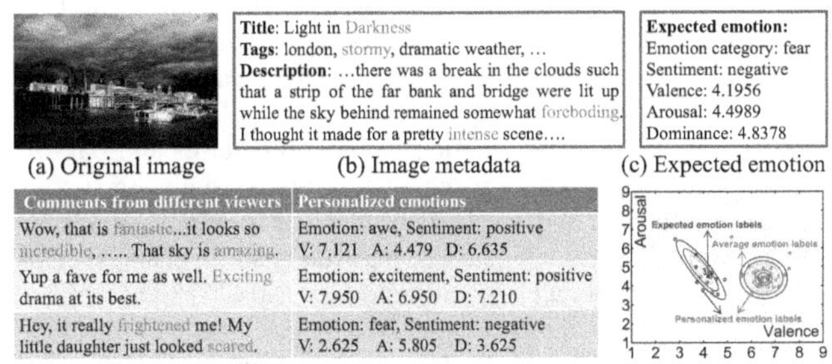

(a) Original image (b) Image metadata (c) Expected emotion

(d) Personalized emotion labels (e) Emotion distribution

Figure 1: Illustration of image emotion prediction from different aspects. The expected emotions in (c) and the personalized emotions in (d) are assigned using the keywords in red based on the metadata (b) from the uploader and the comments from different viewers. (e) shows the differences of expected, personalized and average emotions, while the contour lines are the estimated emotion distributions by the expectation maximization (EM) algorithm based on Gaussian mixture models (GMM).

The research of my PhD thesis focuses on the analysis of image content at the affective level, abbreviated as image emotion computing (IEC), which aims to understand the emotional reactions of users after viewing give images. Emotions are generally represented by two typical models: categorical emotion states (CES) and dimensional emotion space (DES) [35]. Accordingly, there are three different tasks traditionally performed on IEC: affective image classification [32, 16, 14, 11, 15, 1, 35, 2], regression [15, 35] and retrieval [26, 43]. Affective image classification and regression try to assign one of a few predefined emotion categories and the average dimension values to the give image respectively, while affective image retrieval aims to retrieve images with similar emotions to the given image. The state-of-the-art methods on the three above tasks are mainly image-centric.

The development of IEC is greatly limited by two main challenges. One is the affective gap, which can be defined as "the lack of coincidence between the measurable signal properties, commonly referred to as features, and the expected affective state in which the user is brought by perceiving the signal" [8]. The other is the subjectivity of image emotion perceptions and evaluations, which can be considered as the fact that "due to the influence of cultural backgrounds, educational status and social context, the emotions that are induced in different viewers by an image are highly subjective and different" [12].

We work on the aforementioned challenges of IEC and try to

MM '16, October 15–19, 2016, Amsterdam, The Netherlands.

DOI: http://dx.doi.org/10.1145/2964284.2971473

answer the following questions during the PhD study: (1) Compared to the widely used low-level features, can we find some higher level features that are more interpretable and have stronger link to emotions? (2) Are the emotions that are induced in viewers by an image subjective and different? If they are, how can we tackle the user-centric emotion prediction? (3) For image-centric emotion computing, can we predict the emotion distribution instead of the dominant emotion category or dimension values?

2. STATE OF THE ART

Traditional IEC. Existing works mainly focused on finding features that can express emotions better to bridge the affective gap. Holistic features including Wiccest features and Gabor features were extracted to classify image emotions in [32]. Machajdik *et al.* [16] extracted features inspired from psychology and art theory, such as *color*, *texture* and *composition*. Lu *et al.* [15] investigated the computability of emotion through *shape* features. Solli and Lenz [22] classified emotions using emotion-histogram features and bag-of-emotion features derived for patches surrounding each interest point. Yuan *et al.* [33] used mid-level scene attributes for binary sentiment classification. The trained datasets are usually small-scale, such as IAPS [13, 18], Abstract [16], ArtPhoto [16] and GAPED [4].

The commonly used models are based on machine learning methods. Naive Bayes [16], SVM [15] and sparse learning [14] are used for affective image classification. SVR is adopted as the learning model for affective image regression [15] and retrieval [26].

Social media based IEC. Compared with traditional IEC, the social media based IEC can provide large volume data and social features [5, 34], which can be modelled to tackle the subjective evaluation issue. Jia *et al.* [11] simply used the uploaded time of images and the ID of image owner as social features, which were modelled by factor graph learning for affective image classification. Visual sentiment ontology and detectors are proposed to detect high-level adjective noun pairs based on social media data [1, 2], without using social features (similar to [21]). The social connections between different users are modelled [23, 28, 30, 29]. The works in [23, 30] used social connections to model emotion influence of one user to another. Social factors together with visual and textual ones were utilized to discover representative images for social events [29]. Yang *et al.* [28] used social influences by hybrid graph learning to predict emotions for individuals [28], but they just simply classified the sentiments of Chinese microblogs and did not consider the temporal influence of emotions.

From emotion representation models' view point, all the above IEC works are based on either CES or DES. 3-D valence-arousal-dominance (VAD) space [13], 2-D valence-arousal (VA) space [15] and 3-D activity-weight-heat factors [22] are employed as DES models, while the rest works consider emotions to be one of a few basic categories, including binary sentiments.

Note that affective content analysis has also been widely studied in text [19], speech [17], music [31] and videos [41, 40, 39, 25].

3. RESEARCH OVERVIEW

This PhD thesis proposes to study different aspects of IEC. The overview of the proposed research is shown in Figure 2. Similar to [9], image emotions are classified into expected emotions and actual (personalized) emotions. As expected emotions are difficult to obtain in practice, dominant emotions are used as alternatives.

For image-centric dominant emotions, the main challenge is affective gap. Low-level features extracted for emotion recognition are mostly based on the elements-of-art (EAEF), which are the building blocks or ingredients used by artists to create an artwork [10], including *color*, *texture*, etc. However, the link of EAEF to emotions is weak and EAEF are not interpretable by humans [10, 16]. For the first research question, we propose to extract emotion features based on principles-of-art (PAEF) to recognize image-centric dominant emotions (Section 4.1).

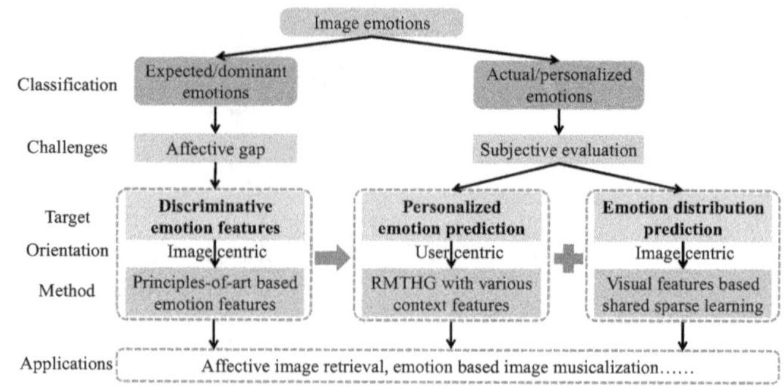

Figure 2: Overview of the proposed research on IEC.

For personalized emotions, the main challenge is the subjectiveness of emotion perceptions. Besides the qualitative study [12, 20], we quantitatively show that the induced emotions in different viewers by an image are highly subjective and different, as shown in Figure 1 (b) (c) (d). For the second research question, we set up a large scale dataset from Flickr, named Image-Emotion-Social-Net, to predict personalized emotion perceptions for each viewer. In such cases, the emotion prediction tasks become user-centric. Rolling multi-task hypergraph learning is presented to jointly combine different types of factors that may influence personalized image emotion perceptions (Section 4.2).

By the statistical analysis on the images viewed by a large population, we observe that though subjective and different, the personalized emotion perceptions follow certain distributions (see Figure 1 (e)). For the third research question, we propose to predict the image-centric emotion distribution instead of a single dominant emotion for an image, which reveals the difference of emotional reactions between users. Generally, the distribution prediction task can be formalized as a regression problem. For different emotion representation models, the distribution prediction varies slightly. For CES, the task aims to predict the discrete probability of different emotion categories, the sum of which equals to 1. For DES, the task usually transfers to predict the parameters of specified continuous probability distribution. Shared sparse learning is presented to predict both distributions (Section 4.3).

Further, we design and implement several applications based on image emotions, such as affective image retrieval and emotion based image musicalization (Section 4.4).

4. METHODOLOGY

To address the challenges in the introduction, we conducted a number of studies on image-centric and user-centric IEC. The thorough discussions of these directions, detailed methods and experimental results are provided in [35, 38, 37, 43, 42].

4.1 Principles-of-Art Based Emotion Features

The rules, tools or guidelines of arranging and orchestrating the elements-of-art in an artwork are known as the principles-of-art, which consider various artistic aspects, including *balance* (*symmetry*), *emphasis* (*contrast*), *harmony* (*unity*), *variety*, *gradation*, *movement*, *rhythm*, and *proportion* [3, 10]. We systematically study and formalize the former 6 artistic principles, without considering *rhythm* and *proportion*, as they are ambiguously defined. For each principle, we explain the concepts and meanings, under the art theory in [3, 10], and translate these concepts into mathematical formulae for quantization measurement.

Take *emphasis* for example. *Emphasis*, also known as *contrast*, is used to stress the difference of certain elements. It can be accomplished by using sudden and abrupt changes in elements, which is usually used to direct and focus viewers' attention to the most important area or centers of interests of a design. We adopt Itten's color contrasts and the rate of focused attention (RFA) to measure *emphasis*. Please refer to [35] for more details.

4.2 Personalized Emotion Prediction

4.2.1 The Image-Emotion-Social-Net Dataset

As there is no public dataset on personalized emotion prediction, we set up a large-scale dataset, named Image-Emotion-Social-Net dataset, with images downloaded from Flickr. To get the personalized emotion labels, firstly we use traditional lexicon-based methods to obtain the text segmentation results of the title, tags and descriptions from uploaders for expected emotions and the comments from viewers for actual emotions. For CES, we use eight categories rigorously defined in psychology [18]. To obtain the labels, we adopt synonym based searching strategy as in [1, 11]. Tens of synonyms for each emotion category are obtained from a public synonym searching site (www.thesaurus.com/browse/synonym) and are manually verified. The emotion category with the most frequent synonyms is set as the ground truth. Note that we remove the images if related text contains negation near the target synonyms, such as "I am not happy". For DES, we compute the average value of valence, arousal and dominance of the segmentation results as ground truth based on recently published VAD norms of 13,915 English lemmas [27]. After refinement, we obtain 1,434,080 emotion labels on 1,012,901 images uploaded by 11,347 users and commented by 106,688 users.

4.2.2 Rolling Multi-Task Hypergraph Learning

Our goal is to predict the perceived emotions of a specified user after viewing an image, associated with online social networks. Intuitively, four types of factors can influence the emotion perception and can be exploited for emotion prediction: visual content, social context, temporal evolution, and location influence.

We present rolling multi-task hypergraph learning (RMTHG) to jointly combine these factors. Formally, a user u_i in social networks observes an image x_{it} at time t, and her perceived emotion after viewing the image is y_{it}. Before viewing x_{it}, the user u_i may have seen many other images. Among them we select the recent past ones, which are believed to influence the current emotion. These selected images comprise a set S_i. The emotional social network is formalized as a hybrid hypergraph $\mathcal{G} = \langle\{\mathcal{U}, \mathcal{X}, \mathcal{S}\}, \mathcal{E}, \mathbf{W}\rangle$. Each vertex $v = (u, x, S)$ in vertex set $\mathcal{V} = \{\mathcal{U}, \mathcal{X}, \mathcal{S}\}$ is a compound triple (u, x, S), where u represents user, x and S are the current image and the recent past images viewed by u, which are named as 'Target Image' and 'History Image Set', respectively. Each hyperedge e of $\mathcal{E}$ represents a link between two vertices based on one component of the triple and is assigned with a weight $w(e)$. $\mathbf{W}$ is the diagonal matrix of the edge weights.

The compound vertex formulation enables our system to model all the four kinds of factors: visual descriptors both in the target image and history image set can be extracted to represent visual content; user relationship can be exploited from the user component to take social context into consideration; past emotion can be inferred from history image set to reveal temporal evolution; location influence is embedded in the associated information with target image and history image set. Consequently, we can construct hyperedges based on each element of the compound vertices.

Given N users $u_1, \ldots, u_N$ and related images, our objective is to explore the correlation among all involved images and the user relations. Suppose the training vertices are $\{(u_1, x_{1j}, S_{1j})\}_{j=1}^{m_1}, \cdots,$ $\{(u_N, x_{Nj}, S_{Nj})\}_{j=1}^{m_N}$, the training labels are $\mathbf{Y}_1 = [y_{11}, \cdots, y_{1m_1}]^{\mathrm{T}}$, $\ldots, \mathbf{Y}_N = [y_{N1}, \cdots, y_{Nm_N}]^{\mathrm{T}}$, the to-be-estimated relevance values of all images related to specified users are $\mathbf{R}_1 = [R_{11}, \cdots, R_{1m_1}]^{\mathrm{T}}$, $\ldots, R_N = [R_{N1}, \cdots, \mathbf{R}_{Nm_N}]^{\mathrm{T}}$. We denote $\mathbf{Y}$ and $\mathbf{R}$ as

$$\mathbf{Y} = [\mathbf{Y}_1^{\mathrm{T}}, \cdots, \mathbf{Y}_N^{\mathrm{T}}]^{\mathrm{T}}, \mathbf{R} = [\mathbf{R}_1^{\mathrm{T}}, \cdots, \mathbf{R}_N^{\mathrm{T}}]^{\mathrm{T}}. \tag{1}$$

The proposed rolling multi-task learning can be conducted as a semi-supervised learning to minimize the empirical loss and the regularizer on the hypergraph structure simultaneously by

$$\arg\min_{\mathbf{R}}\{\Gamma + \lambda\Psi\}, \tag{2}$$

where λ is a trade-off parameter, $\Gamma = ||\mathbf{R} - \mathbf{Y}||^2$ is the empirical loss and $\Psi = \mathbf{R}^{\mathrm{T}}(\mathbf{I} - \mathbf{D}_v^{-1/2}\mathbf{H}\mathbf{W}\mathbf{D}_e^{-1}\mathbf{H}^{\mathrm{T}}\mathbf{D}_v^{-1/2})\mathbf{R}$ is the regularizer on the hypergraph structure. Here $\mathbf{H}$ is the incidence matrix $\mathbf{D}_v$ and $\mathbf{D}_e$ are two diagonal matrices with the diagonal elements denoting the vertex degree and the edge degree.

Now we can use standard hypergraph learning methods [44, 6, 5, 7] to solve Eq. (2). Please refer to [36] for detail of personalized emotion perception prediction.

4.3 Emotion Distribution Prediction

There are two types of probability distribution: discrete and continuous, corresponding to CES and DES. For discrete probability distribution, the goal is to predict the discrete probability of different emotion categories, the sum of which equals to 1 [38].

For continuous probability distribution, we should firstly decide the form of distribution, such as Gaussian distribution and exponential distribution. From the statistics analysis with one example in Figure 1 (e), we observe that (1) the perceived dimensional emotions follow certain distributions, which can be clearly grouped into two clusters, corresponding to the positive and negative sentiments; (2) the VA emotion labels can be well modeled by a mixture of two bidimensional Gaussian distributions. Based on these observations, we define the distribution of VA emotion labels as a GMM by $p(\mathbf{x}; \boldsymbol{\theta}) = \sum_{l=1}^{L} \pi_l \mathcal{N}(\mathbf{x}|\boldsymbol{\mu}_l, \boldsymbol{\Sigma}_l)$, where $\mathbf{x} = (v, a)$ is pair-wise VA emotion labels, $\boldsymbol{\mu}_l$ and $\boldsymbol{\Sigma}_l$ are the mean vector and covariance matrix of the lth Gaussian component, while π_l is the mixing coefficient, which satisfies $\pi_l \geq 0$ and $\sum_{l=1}^{L} \pi_l = 1$. In this paper, $L = 2, \boldsymbol{\theta} = (\boldsymbol{\mu}_1, \boldsymbol{\Sigma}_1, \boldsymbol{\mu}_2, \boldsymbol{\Sigma}_2, \pi_1, \pi_2)$. The problem of continuous distribution prediction turns to predict the parameters $\boldsymbol{\theta}$.

We present shared sparse learning to predict both distributions and provide several baselines. Please refer to [38, 37] for detail.

4.4 Emotion Based Applications

The first application is affective image retrieval, which aims to retrieve images with similar emotions to the given image. We propose to use multi-graph learning as a feature fusion method to efficiently explore the complementation of different features [43], including low-level GIST and elements-of-art, mid-level attributes and principles-of-art, and high-level ANPs and expressions. Please refer to [43] for details.

The second application is emotion based image musicalization, which aims to make images vivid when people are watching them. The music with approximate emotions to the image emotions is selected to musicalize these images. Please refer to [42] for details.

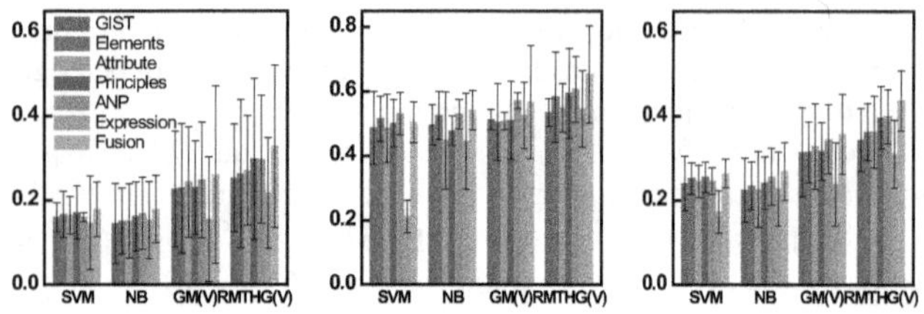

(a) Precision (b) Recall (c) F1

Figure 3: Performance comparison on different visual features of different methods for emotion classification.

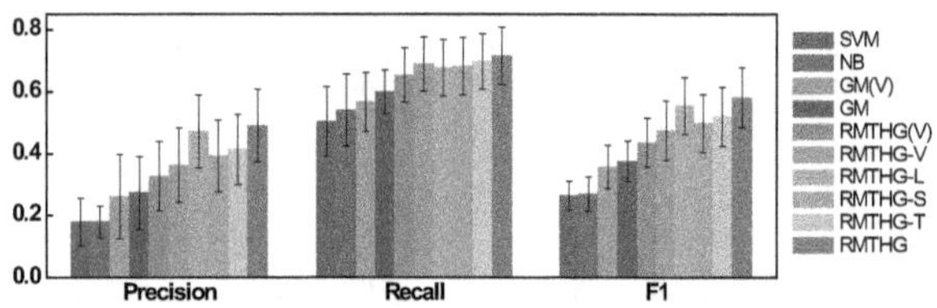

Figure 4: Influences of different factors in the proposed method for emotion classification.

5. EXPERIMENTS

To evaluate the effectiveness of the proposed PAEF features, we conduct experiments on affective image classification results on the IAPSa [18], Abstract [16] and ArtPhoto [16] datasets and affective image regression results on the IAPS dataset [13]. Overall, the principles-of-art based emotion features obtain about 5% improvement on classification accuracy and 0.2 decrease in mean squared error [35]. The detailed results on discrete and continuous emotion distribution prediction, multi-graph learning based affective image retrieval and emotion based image musicalization can be referred in [38], [37], [43] and [42], respectively.

Now we report the experimental results of our ongoing work personalized emotion classification. We use precision, recall and F1-Measure[1] to evaluate the performance of different methods. The first involved 50% images of each viewer are used for training and the rest are used for test. We randomly split the about 8,000 into 80 groups to facilitate fast computation and save memory. Each time we conduct experiments on one group and eventually we computed the average performance and the standard deviation of all experiments. Three state-of-the-art classifiers as adopted as baselines: Naive Bayes (NB) [16], Support Vector Machine (SVM) [15, 35] with RBF kernel and Graph Model (GM) [28], in which the social factors in [28] and our visual features are combined.

The initial average performances of precision, recall and F1 using different visual features [43] and learning models are shown in Figure 3. Note that a simple version of GM and RMTHG that consider only visual features, abbreviated as GM(V) and RMTHG(V), are used for comparison. From the results, we can find that: (1) generally, the fusion of different kinds of features outperforms single feature based method, possibly because it can utilize the advantages from different aspects; (2) the proposed RMTHG method greatly outperforms the baselines on almost all features.

We also evaluate the influence of different factors in the proposed method. We computed the performance of the proposed method without visual content (RMTHG-V), without social context (RMTHG-S), without temporal evolution (RMTHG-T), and without location influence (RMTHG-L). RMTHG-T means that the history image sets of all vertices are empty. Here all the visual features are considered. Figure 4 shows the average performance on emotion classification, while Figure 5 presents the performances on F1 of every emotion category. We can observe that: (1) by incorporating the various factors, the classification performance is greatly improved, which indicates that the social emotions are jointly affected by these factors; (2) for the GM method, the combination of the social factors in [28] can improve the performance, though the improvement is not that significant; and (3) the contributions of these factors to emotion perceptions are different; on average, the discriminability order of these factors is visual content > social context > temporal evolution > location influence.

[1]http://en.wikipedia.org/wiki/Information_retrieval

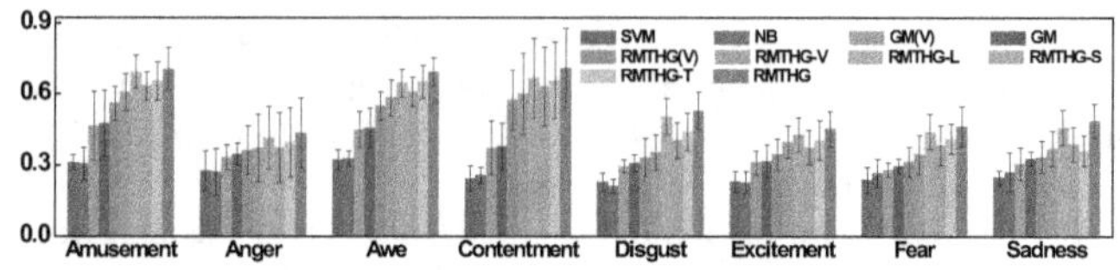

Figure 5: The influence of different factors in the proposed method on F1 of 8 emotions.

Some interesting cases are shown to demonstrate the effectiveness of the proposed method. (1) *The performance improvement in the prediction of negative emotions is higher than positive ones.* This observation can be obtained by comparing the prediction results of RMTHG(V) and RMTHG in Figure 5, which means that these factors play a more important role in personalized perception of negative emotions. (2) *Sadness is one special category that the influence of temporal evolution is larger than social context.* From Figure 5, it is clear that the performance gain of social context is larger than temporal evolution for all emotions except sadness. This is probably because that sadness tends to be a long lasting emotion [24].

6. CONCLUSION AND FUTURE WORK

In this paper, we studied a fundamental research problem of affective computing in visual contents from different aspects. For image-centric IEC, we firstly proposed to extract principles-of-art based emotion features to recognize the dominant emotions. And then we proposed to predict the discrete and continuous probability distributions of image emotions via shared sparse learning. For user-centric IEC, we presented rolling multi-task hypergraph learning to jointly combine various factors for personalized emotion perception prediction. The extensive experiments demonstrated that the proposed methods outperform the state-of-the-art approaches for different IEC tasks.

There are several research issues to de discussed and addressed in our study. For **principles-of-art based emotion features**, the issue is how to quantize the principles using more effective measurements and improve the efficiency for real time implementation. For **personalized emotion prediction**, the first work is to combine different context features with deep learning features; the second work is to select appropriate machine learning methods that might be used for personalized dimensional emotion regression by exploring different kinds of factors. For **emotion distribution prediction**, the first issue is how to combine other factors with visual features; the second issue is how to try unsupervised learning methods to automatically mine the emotional structures in large volume of data. For **emotion based applications**, we plan to modify the images without changing the high level content to transfer the original induced emotions. Which existing methods that can modify the low level features, such as color and texture, should be chosen remains to be discussed.

7. ACKNOWLEDGMENTS

This work was supported by the National Natural Science Foundation of China (No. 61472103) and Key Program (No. 61133003).

8. REFERENCES

[1] D. Borth, R. Ji, T. Chen, T. Breuel, and S.-F. Chang. Large-scale visual sentiment ontology and detectors using adjective noun pairs. In *ACM International Conference on Multimedia*, pages 223–232, 2013.

[2] T. Chen, F. X. Yu, J. Chen, Y. Cui, Y.-Y. Chen, and S.-F. Chang. Object-based visual sentiment concept analysis and application. In *ACM International Conference on Multimedia*, pages 367–376, 2014.

[3] R. G. Collingwood. *The principles of art*, volume 62. Oxford University Press, USA, 1958.

[4] E. S. Dan-Glauser and K. R. Scherer. The geneva affective picture database (gaped): a new 730-picture database focusing on valence and normative significance. *Behavior Research Methods*, 43(2):468–477, 2011.

[5] Y. Gao, F. Wang, H. Luan, and T.-S. Chua. Brand data gathering from live social media streams. In *ACM International Conference on Multimedia Retrieval*, page 169, 2014.

[6] Y. Gao, M. Wang, D. Tao, R. Ji, and Q. Dai. 3-d object retrieval and recognition with hypergraph analysis. *IEEE Transactions on Image Processing*, 21(9):4290–4303, 2012.

[7] Y. Gao, S. Zhao, Y. Yang, and T.-S. Chua. Multimedia social event detection in microblog. In *International Conference on Multimedia Modeling*, pages 269–281, 2015.

[8] A. Hanjalic. Extracting moods from pictures and sounds: Towards truly personalized tv. *IEEE Signal Processing Magazine*, 23(2):90–100, 2006.

[9] A. Hanjalic and L.-Q. Xu. Affective video content representation and modeling. *IEEE Transactions on Multimedia*, 7(1):143–154, 2005.

[10] J. Hobbs, R. Salome, and K. Vieth. *The visual experience*. Davis Publications, 1995.

[11] J. Jia, S. Wu, X. Wang, P. Hu, L. Cai, and J. Tang. Can we understand van gogh's mood? learning to infer affects from images in social networks. In *ACM International Conference on Multimedia*, pages 857–860, 2012.

[12] D. Joshi, R. Datta, E. Fedorovskaya, Q.-T. Luong, J. Z. Wang, J. Li, and J. Luo. Aesthetics and emotions in images. *IEEE Signal Processing Magazine*, 28(5):94–115, 2011.

[13] P. Lang, M. Bradley, B. Cuthbert, et al. *International affective picture system (IAPS): Affective ratings of pictures and instruction manual.* NIMH, Center for the Study of Emotion & Attention, 2005.

[14] B. Li, W. Xiong, W. Hu, and X. Ding. Context-aware affective images classification based on bilayer sparse representation. In *ACM International Conference on Multimedia*, pages 721–724, 2012.

[15] X. Lu, P. Suryanarayan, R. B. Adams Jr, J. Li, M. G. Newman, and J. Z. Wang. On shape and the computability of emotions. In *ACM International Conference on Multimedia*, pages 229–238, 2012.

[16] J. Machajdik and A. Hanbury. Affective image classification using features inspired by psychology and art theory. In *ACM International Conference on Multimedia*, pages 83–92, 2010.

[17] Q. Mao, M. Dong, Z. Huang, and Y. Zhan. Learning salient features for speech emotion recognition using convolutional neural networks. *IEEE Transactions on Multimedia*, 16(8):2203–2213, 2014.

[18] J. A. Mikels, B. L. Fredrickson, G. R. Larkin, C. M. Lindberg, S. J. Maglio, and P. A. Reuter-Lorenz. Emotional category data on images from the international affective picture system. *Behavior Research Methods*, 37(4):626–630, 2005.

[19] B. Pang and L. Lee. Opinion mining and sentiment analysis. *Information Retrieval*, 2(1-2):1–135, 2008.

[20] K.-C. Peng, A. Sadovnik, A. Gallagher, and T. Chen. A mixed bag of emotions: Model, predict, and transfer emotion distributions. In *IEEE Conference on Computer Vision and Pattern Recognition*, pages 860–868, 2015.

[21] S. Siersdorfer, E. Minack, F. Deng, and J. Hare. Analyzing and predicting sentiment of images on the social web. In *ACM International Conference on Multimedia*, pages 715–718, 2010.

[22] M. Solli and R. Lenz. Color based bags-of-emotions. In *Computer Analysis of Images and Patterns*, pages 573–580, 2009.

[23] J. Tang, Y. Zhang, J. Sun, J. Rao, W. Yu, Y. Chen, and A. C. M. Fong. Quantitative study of individual emotional states in social networks. *IEEE Transactions on Affective Computing*, 3(2):132–144, 2012.

[24] P. Verduyn and S. Lavrijsen. Which emotions last longest and why: The role of event importance and rumination. *Motivation and Emotion*, 39(1):119–127, 2015.

[25] S. Wang and Q. Ji. Video affective content analysis: a survey of state of the art methods. *IEEE Transactions on Affective Computing*, 6(4):410–430, 2015.

[26] W.-n. Wang, Y.-l. Yu, and S.-m. Jiang. Image retrieval by emotional semantics: A study of emotional space and feature extraction. In *IEEE International Conference on Systems, Man and Cybernetics*, pages 3534–3539, 2006.

[27] A. B. Warriner, V. Kuperman, and M. Brysbaert. Norms of valence, arousal, and dominance for 13,915 english lemmas. *Behavior research methods*, 45(4):1191–1207, 2013.

[28] Y. Yang, P. Cui, W. Zhu, and S. Yang. User interest and social influence based emotion prediction for individuals. In *ACM International Conference on Multimedia*, pages 785–788, 2013.

[29] Y. Yang, P. Cui, W. Zhu, H. V. Zhao, Y. Shi, and S. Yang. Emotionally representative image discovery for social events. In *ACM International Conference on Multimedia Retrieval*, page 177, 2014.

[30] Y. Yang, J. Jia, S. Zhang, B. Wu, Q. Chen, J. Li, C. Xing, and J. Tang. How do your friends on social media disclose your emotions? In *AAAI Conference on Artificial Intelligence*, pages 306–312, 2014.

[31] Y.-H. Yang and H. H. Chen. Machine recognition of music emotion: A review. *ACM Transactions on Intelligent Systems and Technology*, 3(3):40, 2012.

[32] V. Yanulevskaya, J. Van Gemert, K. Roth, A.-K. Herbold, N. Sebe, and J.-M. Geusebroek. Emotional valence categorization using holistic image features. In *IEEE International Conference on Image Processing*, pages 101–104, 2008.

[33] J. Yuan, S. Mcdonough, Q. You, and J. Luo. Sentribute: image sentiment analysis from a mid-level perspective. In *ACM International Workshop on Issues of Sentiment Discovery and Opinion Mining*, page 10, 2013.

[34] H. Zhang, X. Shang, H. Luan, M. Wang, and T.-S. Chua. Learning from collective intelligence: Feature learning using social images and tags. *ACM Transactions on Multimedia Computing, Communications and Applications*, 2016.

[35] S. Zhao, Y. Gao, X. Jiang, H. Yao, T.-S. Chua, and X. Sun. Exploring principles-of-art features for image emotion recognition. In *ACM International Conference on Multimedia*, pages 47–56, 2014.

[36] S. Zhao, H. Yao, Y. Gao, R. Ji, W. Xie, X. Jiang, and T.-S. Chua. Predicting personalized emotion perceptions of social images. In *ACM International Conference on Multimedia*, 2016.

[37] S. Zhao, H. Yao, and X. Jiang. Predicting continuous probability distribution of image emotions in valence-arousal space. In *ACM International Conference on Multimedia*, pages 879–882, 2015.

[38] S. Zhao, H. Yao, X. Jiang, and X. Sun. Predicting discrete probability distribution of image emotions. In *IEEE International Conference on Image Processing*, pages 2459–2463, 2015.

[39] S. Zhao, H. Yao, and X. Sun. Video classification and recommendation based on affective analysis of viewers. *Neurocomputing*, 119:101–110, 2013.

[40] S. Zhao, H. Yao, X. Sun, X. Jiang, and P. Xu. Flexible presentation of videos based on affective content analysis. In *International Conference on Multimedia Modeling*, pages 368–379. 2013.

[41] S. Zhao, H. Yao, X. Sun, P. Xu, X. Liu, and R. Ji. Video indexing and recommendation based on affective analysis of viewers. In *ACM International Conference on Multimedia*, pages 1473–1476, 2011.

[42] S. Zhao, H. Yao, F. Wang, X. Jiang, and W. Zhang. Emotion based image musicalization. In *IEEE International Conference on Multimedia & Expo Workshops*, pages 1–6, 2014.

[43] S. Zhao, H. Yao, Y. Yang, and Y. Zhang. Affective image retrieval via multi-graph learning. In *ACM International Conference on Multimedia*, pages 1025–1028, 2014.

[44] D. Zhou, J. Huang, and B. Schölkopf. Learning with hypergraphs: Clustering, classification, and embedding. In *Advances in Neural Information Processing Systems*, pages 1601–1608, 2006.

First Person View Video Summarization Subject to the User Needs

Ana Garcia del Molino
Institute for Infocomm Research (A*STAR) and
Nanyang Technological University, Singapore
stugdma@i2r.a-star.edu.sg

ABSTRACT

Our life is becoming heavily documented and expressed on the digital substrate. This booming flow of consumer video has lead to an increasing demand of multimedia analysis tools to organize and summarize those visual memories. Due to the personal nature of such videos, though, the summarization needs to be adapted to the user needs and preferences. Yet, most summarization systems rely solely on pre-defined criteria, e.g. story-coherence or interestingness pre-trained classifiers. I propose a system which is capable of finding relevant digital memories to a given semantic query, and then summarize them on a customized manner. The proposed framework includes a wide set of tools to match a user's needs, from retrieval using multimodal queries to summarization striving to his/her preferences, both provided passively and actively. Preliminary results show the high potential of such a framework, with over 70% retrieval accuracy. More importantly, as seen from the user study, the summaries generated achieve an unprecedented compromise between usability and quality.

Keywords

Video Summarization; Wearable and Consumer Videos; First Person View; Episodic Memory Retrieval; User's Preferences

1. INTRODUCTION

Do you usually record videos of your life (*e.g.* holidays, celebrations) with the intention of sharing part of those events with friends and family? How do you edit the videos to mine said moments? What if there was a tool to ease such tedious process?

The accessibility of affordable wearable cameras in the market, as well as the high specifications of current smartphone cameras, has allowed us to record any single moment of our lives, most of it from a First Person View (FPV) perspective. As a result, our phones, computers and social media are filled with videos we may never revisit nor share. Thus, the addressed multimedia situation calls for semi-automatic tools to organize and edit consumer videos.

As these videos are fundamentally personal, and generally displayed to small audiences, adapting the summary to specific user's preferences is desirable. On the one hand, the inherent characteristics of FPV videos can be used to our advantage to get the wearer's patterns of attention and behavior. On the other, interaction with the viewer can allow for a better user experience through customization.

I propose a framework to browse and summarize our digital memories according to the user's needs. Taking an automatically generated summary (section 3.1), there are different ways we can customize it (section 3.2). Firstly, the user may provide a query to extract segments of interest by discarding all other segments that do not match (section 3.2.1). Secondly, the user may set some interest preferences, *i.e.* conditions to be preferably met (section 3.2.2). In addition, the user may further refine the generated output online, to bring it closer to what he/she wants (section 3.2.3).

Preliminary results based on a FPV dataset have shown the potential of the proposed framework. The retrieval system (section 4.1) provides an accuracy above 70% for videos never seen, and a 100% when the query shot was taken just before or after one of the stored videos. As for active summarization (section 4.2), the conducted user study proves a higher level of satisfaction of the proposed methodology compared to other automatic baselines.

2. RELATED WORK

This section presents the current state of the art for wearable video summarization, with an emphasis on the few customized approaches.

The organization and summarization of our digital memories has been addressed in different ways since lifelogging (the practice of continuously capturing and recording images and videos of one's life) was first introduced. Whereas some researchers target the management of such large amounts of data by providing indexing and retrieval systems [2, 18, 19, 22], others try to summarize the content of the videos or image sets, so that the user can appreciate the overall meaning and experience of the recorded memory in a much shorter time [1, 5, 6, 10–13, 21, 23, 26].

When summarizing, the output may either be a set of key frames or pictures, *i.e.* storyboards, or a concatenation of key subshots, *i.e.* dynamic video skiming. Thus, the process generally requires two steps: video segmentation into subshots or picture clusters (section 2.1), and then selection of the most relevant subshots or pictures (section 2.2).

MM '16, October 15-19, 2016, Amsterdam, Netherlands
© 2016 ACM. ISBN 978-1-4503-3603-1/16/10...$15.00
DOI: http://dx.doi.org/10.1145/2964284.2971474

2.1 Segmentation

Whereas traditional segmentation approaches typically try to identify the shot boundaries comparing consecutive frames, or even using the frames' time-stamp [15], this methodology cannot be directly applied over FPV or consumer wearable video, since such videos generally consist of long shots with smooth transitions between consecutive events.

The most frequently used features for wearable video clustering or segmentation are **color** [1, 10, 11, 13] and **motion** cues such as optical flow and blurriness [1, 5, 13, 21]. Motion features are usually used to segment according to the wearer's activity or attitude patterns [5, 21]. When combined, color can be used to smooth the motion-based classification [1] or to identify similar events separated in time [13].

2.2 Selection

Once the video is segmented, the next natural step is to select the most appropriate parts for the summary. New techniques have been explored lately for FPV videos, as presented in [4]. Dictionaries [26], machine learning pre-trained detectors [12], or combinations of objectives (minimizing energy functions [11] or maximizing objective functions [6, 13, 21, 23]) have been used to select the relevant segments. Such objectives are related to video coherence (such as diversity of events and temporal uniformity), visual pleasantness, and inherent importance of the segment.

Since I find personalization to be a needed step into the summarization process, I want to improve the importance estimation. In the current state of the art, however, importance is frequently inferred from impersonal cues such as saliency and people and object interaction (direct scoring from the observables [5], or machine learning estimation [6, 10, 11, 13]). Only a few works customize the importance estimation for each specific viewer (the user to watch the generated summary) or for the wearer (the person recording the original video).

Customization: Some works propose personalized systems that can retrieve subshots using a query based on text [21, 22, 24] or a set of video segments that match the user's preferences [7, 20]. However, even though retrieval can be used to provide personalized summaries, its use as a tool for summarization is not well explored yet. In [21], the wearer's attention patterns (such as time spent at a certain place, or interacting with a certain item or person) are also used to summarize the video. Other works use physiological measurements such as gaze [23] and EEG signals [1] to detect the wearer's interest.

Another strand of methods asses each segment's interest from the users's behaviour while watching that video [16], or similar ones [14, 25]. However, wearable videos are of unconstrained nature and, as such, previous behaviour patterns may not be applicable, relying on the watching of the full video, and the inherent time consumption.

3. CUSTOMIZED FPV SUMMARIZATION

To fill the need for a user-driven memory organization and summarization, the proposed framework combines a wide range of tools to meet the user requirements.

Such a framework provides a customized summary with as little effort as possible from the user side. The summary is generated automatically (section 3.1), using preferences obtained both passively (pre-given constraints) and actively (on-line modifications of the generated summary), as presented in section 3.2.

3.1 Summarization Process

A probabilistic approach based on a Conditional Random Fields (CRFs) [9] is used to infer the most likely summary. The CRF models the video creating a very intuitive representation of the semantic connections among segments. Minimizing the energy function of such CRF encourages the selection of the segments that will most likely meet the summary requirements.

Let $\mathbf{s} = \{s_i\}$ be the set of random binary variables that represent the summary of the video by indicating whether a segment (or subshot) of the video appears in the summary or not. The energy function of the CRF is defined as

$$E_{\boldsymbol{\theta}}(\mathbf{s}) = \lambda \sum_i \underbrace{\phi_u(s_i)}_{\text{unary}} + \sum_{ij} \underbrace{\phi_p(s_i, s_j)}_{\text{pairwise}}. \tag{1}$$

The unary potentials, $\{\phi_u(x_i)\}$, encourage selecting segments matching the given requirements and are defined as

$$\phi_u(s_i) = \begin{cases} Q_i & \text{if } s_i = 1 \\ L & \text{if } s_i = 0 \end{cases}, \tag{2}$$

in which Q_i is a function related to the requirements and L is a constant offset to control the summary length, such that decreasing L (where $L > 0$) generates longer outputs.

The pairwise potentials, $\{\phi_p(s_i, s_j)\}$, are defined between each pair of segments. Similar to most methods in the literature, they enforce selecting representative segments with diverse content. To determine such diversity, each segment is described using the available neural network models (the last layer from AlexNet [8]) trained in Places dataset [27] and ImageNet [17]. The distance between the segments' descriptors, $\mathbf{d}(\boldsymbol{\psi}_i, \boldsymbol{\psi}_j)$, is used to weight the pairwise potential,

$$\phi_p(x_i, x_j) = -\exp\left(-d(\boldsymbol{\psi}_i, \boldsymbol{\psi}_j)\right)\phi'_p(s_i, s_j), \tag{3}$$

where

$$\phi'_p(s_i, s_j) = \begin{cases} \alpha L & \text{if } s_i = s_j = 0 \\ \beta L & \text{if } s_i = s_j = 1 \\ \gamma & \text{if } s_i \neq s_j \end{cases} \tag{4}$$

To enforce semantic diversity in the summary while encouraging the exclusion of most segments, the parameters are initially set to be $\alpha = 5$, $\beta = -1$ and $\gamma = 1$ for all $\{i, j\}$. The initial value of the weight λ is empirically set to -0.2.

3.2 Obtaining the User Preferences

To customize the summary, the proposed system is able to retrieve a specific memory given a text, image or video query (section 3.2.1); summarize stored videos according to certain requirements (section 3.2.2); and actively modify the generated summary by interacting in the summarization process (section 3.2.3).

3.2.1 Passive Customization: Retrieval of Events

If the user only wants to summarize the parts of the video corresponding to a given query, the summarization can be initiated as a retrieval problem. All non-matching segments shall be assumed as not wanted, and thus the unary potentials $\{\phi_u(s_i)\}$ are modified accordingly to strongly discourage such segments, *i.e.* Q_i takes an extremely low value.

Retrieval tool: Given a query video, image or text, the proposed system searches the memories (raw FPV videos) stored in the database and retrieves the most similar memories in the form of small subshots [3].

Each frame i (both for the videos in the database and the query) is described using a set of semi-automatic tags, $\mathbf{x}_i \in \mathbf{X}$, including objects, places, activity, location, day and time, illumination, people, and motion. Given a frame m in query video q, the similarity sim to frame n in video v is defined as the number of shared tags between both frames:

$$sim(q_m, v_n) = \#\{x_{q_m} \cap x_{v_n}\} \quad (5)$$

The closest match in the database DB to query q is thus the video segment $\mathbf{s} = \{\mathbf{v}_{i \in \mathbf{n}}\}$ whose frames have the highest similarity value with the query:

$$match(q, DB) = \underset{v,\mathbf{n}}{\text{argmax}} \sum_{m \in \mathbf{q}} sim(q_m, v_n) \quad (6)$$

3.2.2 *Passive Customization: Personal Interests*

When the user has specific interests to be input as initial requirements (*e.g.* he/she wants to see a certain person, object or place), these can be added to the system. To encourage choosing segments matching any of the given preferences, the initial value of such segments' unaries for $\mathbf{s}_i = 1$, Q_i, is increased.

Let the user preferences be a subset of the existing tags in video v, $\mathbf{x}_u \in \mathbf{X_v}$. Q_i is a representation of to which extent the segment matches the user interests, *i.e.* a similarity measure between each segment's tags $\mathbf{x}_i$ and the given requirements $\mathbf{x}_u$.

3.2.3 *Active Customization*

Initially, the values of the parameters of the CRF (λ, L, Q_i, α_{ij}, β_{ij} and γ_{ij}) are $\boldsymbol{\theta}_1$, which are estimated from the input video in an automatic way, as presented above. These parameters, however, can be modified to infer the user's preferences. To do so in an on-line fashion, Active Video Summarization (AVS) is proposed.

AVS interacts with the user by asking specific questions about segments of the video. It shows one selected segment, and asks the following two binary questions: *Do you recommend this segment to be in the summary?*, and *Do you want to include or exclude similar segments?* Additionally, the user can decide at any time to go through the segments in the summary, and give such feedback about them. Although AVS is not limited to these two questions, they are effective in practice, and they serve as a proof of concept. Note that the original video is not shown to the user, as the summary and the segments shown during the interaction provide an accurate idea of the content of the video in much less time.

Thus, AVS can be divided into two inference problems: *(i)* infer the customized summary (as described in section 3.1), and *(ii)* infer the next question to ask. The same CRF used to infer the summary is used to estimate the next question to ask.

Once the initial summary $\mathbf{s}^\star_{\boldsymbol{\theta}_1}$ is generated (with or without customization), it is shown to the user. The algorithm selects a segment to question, and the parameters' values are updated, $\boldsymbol{\theta}_2$, to match the user's answer. Thus, after the t-th answer, the parameters' values are $\boldsymbol{\theta}_{t+1}$. The potentials are updated by modifying the unaries according to the answer to the 1st question, and the pairwise for the 2nd. The length is adjusted last.

Act.		Length	Description	Queries
#1		56'	Lunch at the office	II
#2		13'	Dinner on holidays	I
#3		56'	Dinner with friends	I
#4		30'	Sunset at the beach	II
#5		15'	*Afterwork* drinks	II
#6		45'	Hanging out with friends	II
#7		15'	Excursion / visiting	II
#8		16'	Traveling on motorbike	I
#9		134'	Train commuting	II
#10		15'	Bike commuting	I
#11		45'	Watching football	I
#12		15'	Friends playing tennis	I
#13		30'	Bowling	0
#14		45'	Cooking	I
#15		11'	Cooking with friends	I
Total:	15 activities	~540'	38 recording sessions	19

Table 1: List of activities in the database. Each query and video in the database is mapped to one of the 15 activities.

	All queries	Matching queries
1st memory:	74%	100%
1st or 2nd memory:	89%	100%

Table 2: Evaluation of the Retrieval System. The accuracy for all queries and the queries with a perfect match in the database are evaluated separately.

When deciding which segment to question next, AVS ranks all possible segments with a score, and asks for the one with the highest rank. The score is based on a reward function that evaluates the change produced in the summary given the answer of the user, *i.e.* it compares $\mathbf{s}^\star_{\boldsymbol{\theta}_{t+1}}$ to $\mathbf{s}^\star_{\boldsymbol{\theta}_t}$, to choose the segment which may lead to the greatest difference.

4. RESULTS

Experiments have been conducted for two modules of the framework: the retrieval tool, and AVS for a customized summary. Customization given the user interests is yet to be tested. This section details the conducted experiments and obtained results.

4.1 Retrieval of Similar Events

To test the performance of the presented system, a set of videos were recorded using a Google Glass. More than 500 minutes from 38 different recording sessions were stored in the system to build the database. Additionally, 19 short videos (at most 1 minute long) were selected as queries. For 7 of those queries, another video segment from the same recording session exists in the database. Each query has been mapped to the closest video in the database, if there is a perfect match, or set of videos according to a semantic clustering, as summarized in Table 1.

The results shown in Table 2 prove the high potential of the system, also to be used standalone. For the 7 queries with perfect existing match, an accuracy of 100% is achieved. When evaluating the whole set of queries, the retrieval accuracy is of 74%, or 89% if also considering the 2nd closest memory.

Much worse	Worse	Similar	Better	Much better
0%	16.8%	16.8%	41.6%	24.8%

Table 3: Comparison of the usability of Active Summary against the random baseline: Percentage of answers to the question "How would you rate the ease to find the ideal summary compared to the previous (random) method?".

Active	Random	Manual
5.89 ± 3.85	7.26 ± 5.39	21.66 ± 6.59

Table 4: Time (minutes) to generate the summary.

4.2 Active Customization

AVS has been evaluated on a user study comparing it to these baselines:

– **Manual:** Manual annotation of the 10 seconds that better represent the video.

– **Uniform:** Summary from uniformly sampled segments.

– **Non-customized:** Summary created by our algorithm at iteration zero, before interacting with the user, *i.e.* $\mathbf{x}^{\star}_{\theta_1}$.

– **Random Questions:** Interactive summarization with random selection of the question, instead of AVS.

12 independent subjects were asked to summarize 3 videos they had never seen before both with AVS and with the *random question* baseline. The subjects were not aware whether they were using AVS or the *random* baseline, by randomly changing the order of the algorithms in each video.

To evaluate the question inference of AVS, the users were asked to rate the usability of one approach against the other at the end of the experiment. This comparison is reported in Table 3, and in Table 4 the time spent to create each summary. These results demonstrate the usefulness of estimating the next questions to ask, as opposing to selecting *random* segments. Moreover, in Table 4 we can also see that the users are 4 times faster in creating the summary with AVS than with the *manual* baseline. This is a significant improvement of the usability of the *manual annotation*, since, as shown next, the quality of AVS is competitive with the quality of the *manual annotation*.

Four days after the usability experiment, a test was conducted to compare the quality of the summaries generated with all the different baselines and AVS. For the three videos the subject had summarized, all the different summaries were showed, including the ones that the subject did. Then, the subject assessed the quality of the summaries. The responses are reported in Figure 1. AVS is preferred over all methods but the manual annotation.

5. CONCLUSIONS AND FUTURE DIRECTIONS

The analysis conducted in this paper shows that customizing a summary for FPV videos in a fast and interactive way is possible, although challenging.

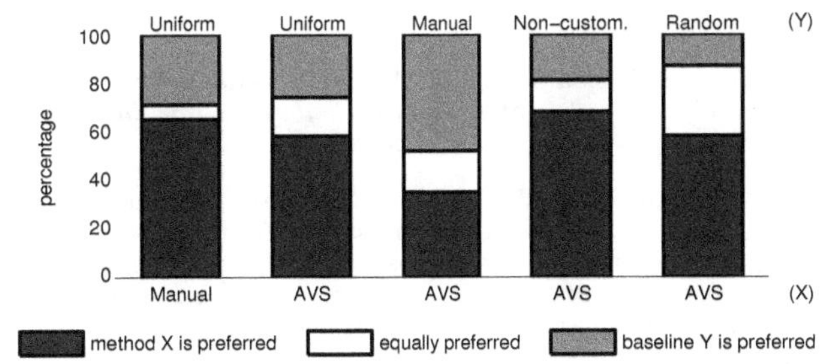

Figure 1: Percentage of subjects who preferred each summary versus another.

From the results above, we can observe that uniform sampling is still a fair solution for consumer video summarization (as opposed to other FPV such as instructional videos), obtaining more than a 20% preference over manual annotation of a 3rd person. This proves the challenging nature of such videos. Moreover, the personal essence of the summary makes its evaluation difficult, since ground truth may not be useful to test them. As I see it, the challenge of consumer video summarization is to obtain the best compromise between time consumption and improvement over a uniform summary. Therefore, modifying such summary to meet the user needs and expectations must be the objective.

On-line customization improves the user experience and satisfaction of the summary. Although the manually annotated summaries are generally reported better than AVS, users stated that the compromise time-quality made AVS better than visualizing the full video to select the important parts. Therefore, the proposed framework can be of great assistance to all those users editing their holiday or celebration videos at home.

To improve the current framework, the following research directions will be further explored:

- Mining of past events or collective memories to enrich the generated summary. Videos similar to the one being summarized will be found using the retrieval tool presented in section 3.2.1, and showed to the user in case he or she wants to include parts of such videos.

- Considering the wearer attention, along with emotion inferred from the recording, to depict the most meaningful events.

- Adaptation of the algorithms to be used in other fields, *e.g.* interactive editing of pictures.

Finally, a Web Interface where the user can upload a video to have it summarized should be implemented. Such service can be of great use for the user community, providing fast personalized summarizations. Moreover, having this tool on-line will allow me to obtain feedback from the users to improve the framework, understand how it is being used, include additional questions, and foresee further needs.

Acknowledgments

This work was partially supported by the Singapore International Graduate Award (SINGA), and the Obra Social "La Caixa" and Casa Asia Fellowship.

References

[1] K. Aizawa, K. Ishijima, and M. Shiina. Summarizing wearable video. In *International Conference on Image Processing*, volume 3, pages 398–401. IEEE, 2001.

[2] V. Chandrasekhar, W. Min, X. Li, C. Tan, B. Mandal, L. Li, and J. H. Lim. Efficient retrieval from large-scale egocentric visual data using a sparse graph representation. In *Proceedings of the IEEE Conference on Computer Vision and Pattern Recognition Workshops*, pages 527–534, 2014.

[3] A. G. del Molino, B. Mandal, L. Li, and J. H. Lim. Organizing and retrieving episodic memories from first person view. In *International Conference on Multimedia and Expo Workshops*, pages 1–6. IEEE, 2015.

[4] A. G. del Molino, C. Tan, J. H. Lim, and A. H. Tan. Summarization of egocentric videos: A comprehensive survey. *submitted for publication on THMS*, 2016.

[5] M. Gygli, H. Grabner, H. Riemenschneider, and L. Van Gool. Creating summaries from user videos. In *Computer Vision–ECCV*, pages 505–520. Springer, 2014.

[6] M. Gygli, H. Grabner, and L. Van Gool. Video summarization by learning submodular mixtures of objectives. In *Proceedings of the IEEE Conference on Computer Vision and Pattern Recognition*, pages 3090–3098, 2015.

[7] B. Han, J. Hamm, and J. Sim. Personalized video summarization with human in the loop. In *Applications of Computer Vision (WACV), 2011 IEEE Workshop on*, pages 51–57. IEEE, 2011.

[8] A. Krizhevsky, I. Sutskever, and G. E. Hinton. Imagenet classification with deep convolutional neural networks. In *Advances in neural information processing systems*, pages 1097–1105, 2012.

[9] J. Lafferty, A. McCallum, and F. C. Pereira. Conditional random fields: Probabilistic models for segmenting and labeling sequence data. In *ICML*, 2001.

[10] Y. J. Lee, J. Ghosh, and K. Grauman. Discovering important people and objects for egocentric video summarization. In *Computer Vision and Pattern Recognition*, volume 2, page 6, 2012.

[11] Y. J. Lee and K. Grauman. Predicting important objects for egocentric video summarization. *International Journal of Computer Vision*, pages 1–18, 2015.

[12] Y.-L. Lin, V. Morariu, and W. Hsu. Summarizing while recording: Context-based highlight detection for egocentric videos. In *Proceedings of the IEEE International Conference on Computer Vision Workshops*, pages 51–59, 2015.

[13] Z. Lu and K. Grauman. Story-driven summarization for egocentric video. In *Computer Vision and Pattern Recognition*, pages 2714–2721. IEEE, 2013.

[14] K. Masumitsu and T. Echigo. Video summarization using reinforcement learning in eigenspace. In *Image Processing, 2000. Proceedings. 2000 International Conference on*, volume 2, pages 267–270. IEEE, 2000.

[15] A. G. Money and H. Agius. Video summarisation: A conceptual framework and survey of the state of the art. *Journal of Visual Communication and Image Representation*, 19(2):121–143, 2008.

[16] W.-T. Peng, W.-T. Chu, C.-H. Chang, C.-N. Chou, W.-J. Huang, W.-Y. Chang, and Y.-P. Hung. Editing by viewing: automatic home video summarization by viewing behavior analysis. *Multimedia, IEEE Transactions on*, 13(3):539–550, 2011.

[17] O. Russakovsky, J. Deng, H. Su, J. Krause, S. Satheesh, S. Ma, Z. Huang, A. Karpathy, A. Khosla, M. Bernstein, et al. Imagenet large scale visual recognition challenge. *International Journal of Computer Vision*, 115(3):211–252, 2015.

[18] Y. Sawahata and K. Aizawa. Wearable imaging system for summarizing personal experiences. In *International Conference on Multimedia and Expo*, page 45. IEEE, 2003.

[19] D. Tancharoen, T. Yamasaki, and K. Aizawa. Practical experience recording and indexing of life log video. In *Proceedings of the 2nd ACM workshop on Continuous archival and retrieval of personal experiences*, pages 61–66. ACM, 2005.

[20] B. L. Tseng and J. R. Smith. Hierarchical video summarization based on context clustering. In *ITCom 2003*, pages 14–25. International Society for Optics and Photonics, 2003.

[21] P. Varini, G. Serra, and R. Cucchiara. Egocentric video summarization of cultural tour based on user preferences. In *Proceedings of the 23rd Annual ACM Conference on Multimedia Conference*, pages 931–934. ACM, 2015.

[22] B. Xiong, G. Kim, and L. Sigal. Storyline representation of egocentric videos with an applications to story-based search. In *Proceedings of the IEEE International Conference on Computer Vision*, pages 4525–4533, 2015.

[23] J. Xu, L. Mukherjee, Y. Li, J. Warner, J. M. Rehg, and V. Singh. Gaze-enabled egocentric video summarization via constrained submodular maximization. In *Proceedings of the IEEE Conference on Computer Vision and Pattern Recognition*, pages 2235–2244, 2015.

[24] H. Yang, L. Chaisorn, Y. Zhao, S.-Y. Neo, and T.-S. Chua. Videoqa: question answering on news video. In *Proceedings of the eleventh ACM international conference on Multimedia*, pages 632–641. ACM, 2003.

[25] A. Yoshitaka and K. Sawada. Personalized video summarization based on behavior of viewer. In *Signal Image Technology and Internet Based Systems (SITIS), 2012 Eighth International Conference on*, pages 661–667. IEEE, 2012.

[26] B. Zhao and E. Xing. Quasi real-time summarization for consumer videos. In *Proceedings of the IEEE Conference on Computer Vision and Pattern Recognition*, pages 2513–2520, 2014.

[27] B. Zhou, A. Lapedriza, J. Xiao, A. Torralba, and A. Oliva. Learning deep features for scene recognition using places database. In *Advances in Neural Information Processing Systems*, pages 487–495, 2014.

Sentiment and Emotion Analysis for Social Multimedia: Methodologies and Applications

Quanzeng You
Department of Computer Science, University of Rochester
Rochester NY, USA 14623
qyou@cs.rochester.edu

ABSTRACT

Online social networks have attracted the attention from both the academia and real world. In particular, the rich multimedia information accumulated in recent years provides an easy and convenient way for more active communication between people. This offers an opportunity to research people's behaviors and activities based on those multimedia content. One emerging area is driven by the fact that these massive multimedia data contain people's daily sentiments and opinions. However, existing sentiment analysis typically focuses on textual information regardless of the visual content, which may be as informative in expressing people's sentiments and opinions. In this research, we attempt to analyze the online sentiment changes of social media users using both the textual and visual content. Nowadays, social media networks such as Twitter have become major platforms of information exchange and communication between users, with tweets as the common information carrier. As an old saying has it, an image is worth a thousand words. The image tweet is a great example of multimodal sentiment. In this research, we focus on sentiment analysis based on visual and multimedia information analysis. We will review the state-of-the-art in this topic. Several of our projects related to this research area will also be discussed. Experimental results are included to demonstrate and summarize our contributions.

Keywords

Visual Sentiment Analysis; Joint Sentiment Analysis; Multimodal

1. INTRODUCTION

Online social networks are providing more and more convenient services to their users. Today, social networks have grown to be one of the most important sources for people to acquire information on all aspects of their lives. Meanwhile, every online social network user is a contributor to such large amounts of information. Online users love to share their experiences and to express their opinions on virtually all events and subjects.

Among the large amount of online user generated data, we are particularly interested in people's opinions or sentiments towards specific topics and events. There have been studies on using online users' sentiments to predict box-office revenues for movies, political elections and economic indicators. These results have suggested that online users' opinions or sentiments are closely correlated with our real-world activities. All of these results hinge on accurate estimation of people's sentiments according to their online generated content. Currently all of these studies only rely on sentiment analysis from textual content. However, multimedia content, including images and videos, has become prevalent over all online social networks. Indeed, online social network providers are competing with each other by providing easier access to their increasingly powerful and diverse services.

A picture is worth a thousand words. People with different backgrounds can easily understand the main content of an image or video. Apart from the large amount of easily available visual content, today's computational infrastructure is also much cheaper and more powerful to make the analysis of computationally intensive visual content analysis feasible. In this era of big data, it has been shown that the integration of visual content can provide us more reliable or complementary online social signals [12, 38].

On the other hand, images and text always come in pairs, which is becoming increasingly prevalent in online social networks. Intuitively, we can alleviate the discussed challenges in visual sentiment analysis by the integration of textual knowledge, which has been well studied.

To the best of our knowledge, little attention has been paid to the sentiment analysis of visual content as well as multi-modality sentiment analysis. Only a few recent works attempted to predict visual sentiment using features from images [26, 4, 3, 38] and videos [25]. Visual sentiment analysis is extremely challenging, as image sentiment involves a much higher level of abstraction and subjectivity in the human recognition process [13], on top of a wide variety of visual recognition tasks including object, scene, action and event recognition. However, Convolutional Neural Networks [19, 8, 16] have been proved to be very powerful in solving computer vision related tasks. In addition, the successes of deep learning make the understanding and jointly modeling of vision and language content feasible. In the context of deep learning, many related publications have proposed novel models that address image and text simultaneously. Starting with matching images with word-level concepts [9] and recently onto sentence-level descriptions [15, 27, 21, 22, 14], deep neural networks exhibit significant performance improvements on these tasks. These models have inspired the idea of joint feature learning [29], semantic transfer [9] and design of margin ranking loss [34].

Inspired by the recent advancement in deep learning, we are particularly interested in utilizing it to solve the challenging social multimedia sentiment analysis. To that end, we address in this thesis proposal the following challenges: 1) how to learn with large

MM '16, October 15-19, 2016, Amsterdam, Netherlands
© 2016 ACM. ISBN 978-1-4503-3603-1/16/10...$15.00
DOI: http://dx.doi.org/10.1145/2964284.2971475

scale weakly labeled training data, 2) how to generalize and extend the learned model across domains, 3) we propose novel multi-modality models, which can integrate different modality features for sentiment analysis, and 4) we demonstrate a recently collected visual emotion dataset, which is publicly available for research purpose.

2. RELATED WORK

In this section, we review literature closely related to our study on social multimedia sentiment analysis.

2.1 Single modality sentiment analysis

For sentiment analysis of online user generated textual content, dictionaries based approaches [2, 10] have been widely used due to its efficiency and simplicity. Very recently, distributed representation of words started to attract research attention due to its ability in learning robust features for words [24]. Le and Mikolov [18] further proposed an approach to learn distributed representation for documents. They applied their document representations to sentiment analysis and achieve the best performance over existing competing algorithms.

There are also several recent works on visual sentiment analysis. Siersdorfer et al. [26] is a machine learning algorithm to predict the sentiment of images using pixel-level features. Motivated by the fact that sentiment involves high-level abstraction, which may be easier to explain by objects or attributes in images, both [3] and [38] propose to employ visual entities or attributes as features for visual sentiment analysis. In [3], 1200 adjective noun pairs (ANP), which may correspond to different levels of different emotions, are extracted. These ANPs are used as queries to crawl images from Flickr. Next, pixel-level features of images in each ANP are employed to train 1200 ANP detectors. The responses of these 1200 classifiers can then be considered as mid-level features for visual sentiment analysis. The work in [38] employed a similar mechanism of using scene attributes.

2.2 Joint visual and textual analysis

Computer vision and natural language processing are important application domains of machine learning. Recently, deep learning has made significant advances in tasks related to both vision and language [17]. Consequently, the task of higher-level semantic understanding, such as machine translation [1], image aesthetic analysis [20], and visual sentiment analysis [5, 35] have become tractable. A more interesting and challenging task is to bridge the semantic gap between vision and language, and thus help solve more challenging problems.

Notably, automatic image captioning is widely studied [7, 32, 14], which more intimately connects visual content and language semantics. In general, these models handle two primary tasks: 1) how to represent image and text, and 2) how to learn the model on top of visual and textual features. Indeed, Convolutional Neural Networks (CNNs) [17] become the common approaches for extracting visual features. Meanwhile, multimodal semantic mapping following a pairwise ranking loss is widely adopted for optimizing joint visual and textual models. Different approaches, including sequential [22, 14] and tree-structured models [27, 21], are selected to encode the text, among which Recurrent Neural Networks [30] and Recursive Neural Networks [28] are particularly popular. However, there are only a few publications on analyzing sentiment using both text and images, which are prevalent in user generated content. Both [33] and [6] employed both text and images for sentiment analysis, where late fusion is employed to combine the prediction results of using n-gram textual features and mid-level visual features [3].

Inspired by these studies on learning joint visual and textual models. In this proposal, we are going to present two of our projects on using deep learning for joint visual-textual sentiment analysis.

3. APPROACHES

In this section, we describe our proposed models for visual sentiment analysis as well as joint visual-textual sentiment analysis. The proposed models intend to solve the discussed challenges in social multimedia sentiment analysis.

3.1 Visual sentiment analysis with progressive CNN

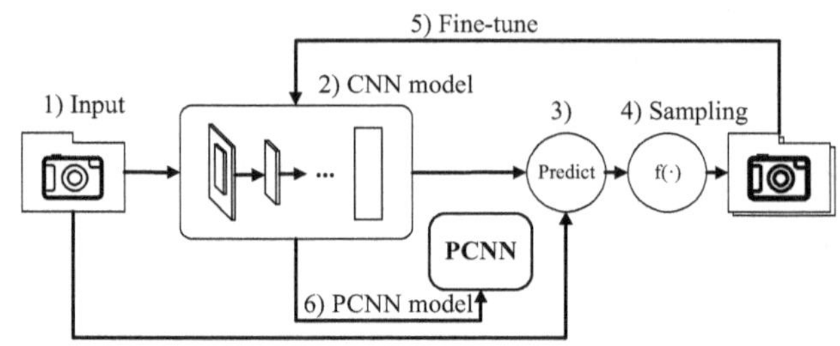

Figure 1: Progressive CNN (PCNN) for visual sentiment analysis.

To train a convolutional neural network, we need a large amount of high-quality labeled images. However, in visual sentiment analysis, this could be too challenging. It is difficult to collect such a large and high quality image database. Part of the reason can be attributed to the challenging nature of the task, which may lead inconsistent opinions for different people. Thus, we work on weakly labeled images. This can lead to the possibility that the neural network can get stuck in a bad local optimum. This may lead to poor generalizability of the trained neural network. But, the neural network is still able to correctly classify a large proportion of the training instances. Therefore, our idea is to progressively select a subset of the training instances to reduce the impact of noisy training instances. Figure 1 shows the overall flow of the proposed progressive CNN (PCNN). We first train a CNN on Flickr images. Next, we select training samples according to the prediction score of the trained model on the training data itself. Instead of training from the beginning, we further fine-tune the trained model using these newly selected, and potentially cleaner training instances. This fine-tuned model will be our final model for visual sentiment analysis.

In particular, we employ a probabilistic sampling algorithm to select the new training subset. Let $s_i = (s_{i1}, s_{i2})$ be the prediction sentiment scores for the two classes of instance i. We choose to remove the training instance i with probability p_i given by Eqn.(1).

$$p_i = \max\left(0, 2 - \exp(|s_{i1} - s_{i2}|)\right) \quad (1)$$

When the difference between the predicted sentiment scores of one training instance are large enough, this training instance will be kept in the training set. Otherwise, the smaller the difference between the predicted sentiment scores become, the larger the probability of this instance being removed from the training set.

3.2 Joint visual-textual sentiment analysis

In this section, we present two of our proposed models on joint visual-textual sentiment analysis. Cross-modality consistent regression focuses on enforcing task consistency between textual and visual modalities. The second one focus on learning semantic mappings for visual and textual data.

3.2.1 Cross-modality consistent regression (CCR)

Our main idea is that the penalties between the predicted label distributions of different modality features need to be taken into consideration. To measure the penalty between any two different predicted label distributions, we employ KL divergence. We define $D(p \parallel q)$ as the sum of KL divergence between two probability distributions p and q.

The objective function is formulated in Eqn. (2). We denote by x_i^m (for $m \in \{1, \cdots, M\}$) the m-th modality features of the i-th instance and by x_i^c the concatenated features from all the M modality features of the i-th instance. $\Theta = \{\theta^c, \theta^1, \cdots, \theta^M\}$ are the parameters that needs to be learned.

$$\min_{\Theta} \sum_i (D(y_i \parallel p_{\theta^c}(x_i^c)) + \sum_{m=1}^{M} \gamma_m D(p_{\theta^c}(x_i^c) \parallel p_{\theta^m}(x_i^m))) \tag{2}$$

Let $p_\theta(x_i)$ be the prediction function for the label distribution of x_i given the parameter vector θ. We use softmax function to evaluate the probability distribution.

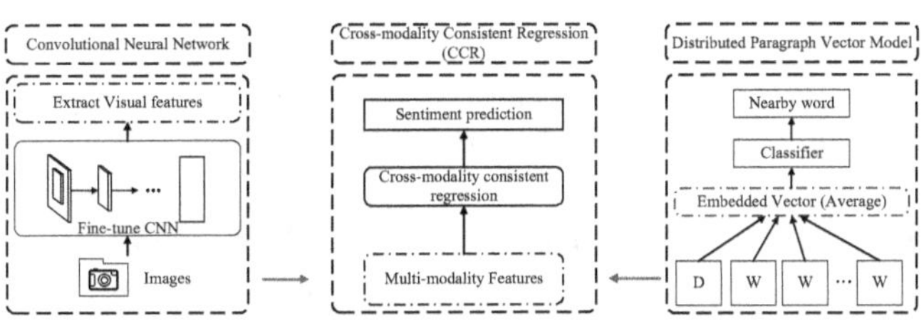

Figure 2: The framework for multi-modality sentiment analysis. *Left:* We fine-tune a CNN visual sentiment analysis model. *Right:* We train a distributed paragraph vector model to learn textual features. *Middle:* The proposed CCR is trained on the visual and textual features.

The first component of the objective function is the consistency constraint between the ground-truth label and the predicted label distribution using concatenated features. The last component considers the predicted distribution consistency between each single modality features and the concatenated features. In this way, we hope that knowledge is propagated to each other to improve the overall performance of the system.

There are two groups of parameters in our model, namely θ^c and $\{\theta^1, \theta^2, \cdots, \theta^M\}$. In our implementation, we learn those two groups of parameters iteratively. Specifically, in each iteration, the learning algorithm will try to update the two groups of parameters sequentially. Since, we built a large data set for our experiments, we employ mini-batch L-BFGS to learn the parameters[1].

3.2.2 Tree-structured LSTM for sentiment analysis

Different from CCR, which focuses on the output of the classifiers, we propose another framework trying to integrate their semantic content. In particular, we utilize tree-structured LSTM (T-LSTM), which is built on top of textual semantic parsing trees [31, 39]. Both of current studies build T-LSTM on text (single modality). We will generalize it to multimodality scenario where a pair of sentence and image (t^m, v^m) are taken into account jointly. We take the hidden state at the root node of the T-LSTM as the representation for the sentence and image pair. Next, this representation can be supplied as input to build a softmax classifier for sentiment analysis.

To learn and establish the joint representation $h[t^m, v^m]$ of a given pair of sentence and image (t^m, v^m), we focus on the leaf nodes, which directly accept textual words and visual representations as inputs. In particular, we want the *leaf* nodes of T-LSTM to jointly accept both individual words and image regions and produce its output based on both inputs. Eventually, the root node of the parsing tree will learn a joint embedding by receiving both the visual and the textual information propagated structurally from the *leaf* nodes. In such a way, we are able to integrate the visual information into the tree-structures. We use a bilinear attention model as the joint module to learn the alignments and produce the outputs of leaf nodes simultaneously.

Semantic Embedding Learning Inspired by the recent successes of deep visual-textual semantic embedding learning [14, 15, 21], we incorporate the semantic learning task to pilot the learning of attention model. Let (t^m,v^m) be a sentence and image pair, and v^n (randomly picked from the training set) be a contrasting image of t^m. We then use the previously introduced T-LSTM model with the bilinear attention mechanism to encode both (t^m,v^m) and (t^m,v^n). Next, the pairwise margin ranking function is optimized to learn the semantic embedding:

$$L'(t^m, v^m, v^n) = \max(0, \mu - g(h[t^m, v^m]) + g(h[t^m, v^n])) \tag{3}$$

where $g(\cdot)$ learns the embedding score given the hidden features $h[t^m, v^m]$ and $h[t^m, v^n]$ from T-LSTM. This objective function tries to make sure that the score defined by $g(\cdot)$ is at least greater than μ for correct pair (t^m, v^m) compared to the contrastive pair (t^m, v^n).

Similar to [21], we use a multi-layer perception (MLP) to learn the score of each sentence and image pair given their hidden state. In particular, we define $g(\cdot)$ as follows:

$$g(h_i) = W_2^e(\delta(W_1^e h_i)) \tag{4}$$

where W_2^e and W_1^e are the parameters of the MLP and $\delta(\cdot)$ is the activation function for the hidden state.

Multi-task Learning for Joint Sentiment Analysis Our model can be trained by a simultaneous optimization of both the sentiment analysis and the embedding tasks. Figure 3 shows the overall structure of the proposed model with the two tasks. The semantic embedding learning task is implemented using a Siamese network, where the parameters of T-LSTM (W_1 in Figure 3) and the parameters of the scoring MLP (W_2 in Figure 3) are shared. The loss of one training image-sentence pair is the summation of the sentiment classifier loss and the margin ranking loss (Eq.(3)). For each training pair (t^m, v^m), we randomly choose one image v^n to make a contrasting pair (t^m, v^n), which is also given as the input to the semantic embedding module. We use a mini-batch gradient descent algorithm with an adaptive learning rate to optimize the loss functions.

4. EXPERIMENTAL RESULTS

For visual sentiment analysis, we mainly focus on Visual Sentiment Ontology[2] dataset. In addition, we build several datasets for joint visual-textual sentiment analysis. Two of them are crawled from Flickr and Getty Images individually. They are weakly la-

[1]When the whole data set can fit into the machine's memory, it is also possible to employ full-batch L-BFGS.

[2]http://visual-sentiment-ontology.appspot.com

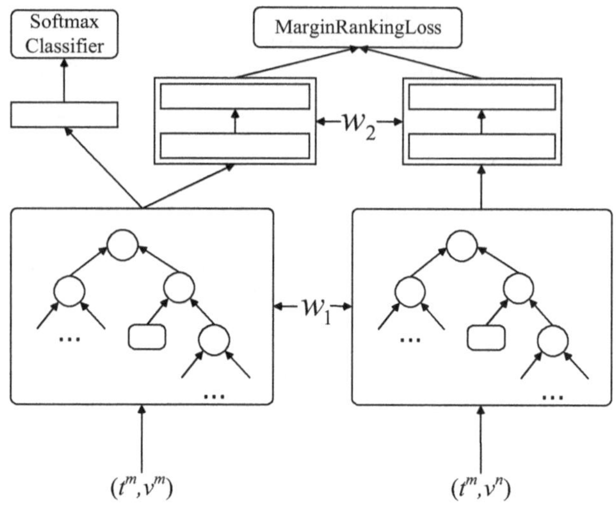

Figure 3: A multi-task learning framework for jointly training the sentiment classifier as well as the semantic embedding. (t^m, v^m) is the correct sentence and image pair and v^n is a randomly picked image from the training set.

belled. The third one is labelled by Amazon Mechanical Turks. Details on the dataests can be found in our work [37].

4.1 Performance analysis

Visual sentiment analysis Table 1 shows the performance of both CNN and PCNN on the 10% randomly chosen testing data. PCNN outperformed CNN in terms of *Precision*, *Recall*, *F1* and *Accuracy*. Both algorithms show better performance than results using lower-level and mid-level features (for more results see [35]).

Joint visual-textual sentiment analysis We compare the two proposed joint models for sentiment analysis. The results of the following baselines are also reported and analyzed. We also compare with these baselines: 1) single visual model, 2) single textual model, 3) early fusion and 4) late fusion. Due to the limit of space, we only compare the performance on the Twitter testing dataset for different algorithms. Table 2 summarizes the results. Both CCR and T-LSTM have improved the performance for joint sentiment analysis. The authors [37] have indicated that they collect the weak or noisy sentiment labels of the image tweets by analyzing the Tweets text only using a rule-based classifier VADER [11]. It is possible to generate overlap information with the parsing trees, which may explain the significant performance improvements of T-LSTM over previous models on this dataset.

Table 1: Performance on the Testing Dataset by CNN and PCNN.

Algorithm	Precision	Recall	F1	Accuracy
CNN	0.714	0.729	0.722	0.718
PCNN	**0.759**	**0.826**	**0.791**	**0.781**

4.2 Qualitative analysis of the results

Figure 4 shows two positive and negative examples for T-LSTM Attention. This indicates that the auxiliary embedding learning task helps the model to align words and image regions. Furthermore, the sentiment analysis task allows the attention mechanism to focus more on sentiment related regions. For instance, positive words *love* in Figure 4(a) and *sad* in Figure 4(b) of the negative example.

Table 2: Results of different T-LSTM variants and previously reported results on the Twitter testing dataset.

Model	Precision	Recall	F1	Accuracy
Textual	0.746	0.693	0.727	0.722
Visual	0.584	0.561	0.573	0.553
Early Fusion	0.730	0.744	0.737	0.717
Late Fusion	0.634	0.610	0.622	0.604
CCR	0.831	0.805	0.818	0.809
T-LSTM Embedding	**0.958**	**0.977**	**0.967**	**0.964**

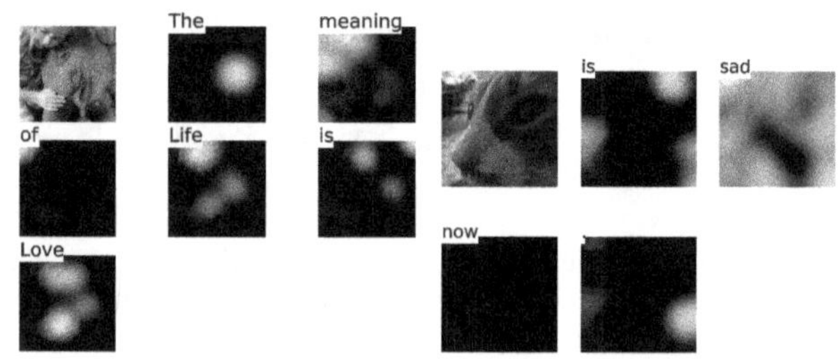

(a) T-LSTM Attention (b) T-LSTM Attention

Figure 4: Visualization of *attention* on two examples with positive sentiment (left) and negative sentiment (right).

5. CONCLUSIONS AND FUTURE WORK

Social multimedia sentiment analysis is a challenging and interesting problem. In this thesis proposal, we adopt deep learning to solve this problem. We have designed a new architecture, as well as new training strategies to overcome the noisy nature of the large-scale training samples. We also present two frameworks for joint visual-textual sentiment analysis. Both of which are trying to integrate textual and visual information into a unified model. The experimental results suggest that convolutional neural networks that are properly trained can outperform both classifiers that use predefined low-level features or mid-level visual attributes for the highly challenging problem of visual sentiment analysis. Meanwhile, experimental results have demonstrated that the proposed joint models have significantly improved the performance of joint textual-visual sentiment analysis on several datasets. We hope our sentiment analysis results can encourage further research on online user generated content.

Future work We think there are several topics to explore to further promote the performance of machines on this task: 1) Localized visual sentiment. A more interesting task is to automatically identify the local regions of an image, which is mostly close to visual sentiment. 2) Fine-grained sentiment. We have been focusing on a binary classification. The next step would be analyzing the fine-grained sentiments. We have release a dataset on this topic [36]. 3) Sentiment for bridging visual-textual gap. We believe that the understanding of visual and textual sentiment will lead to better visual-textual semantics, which is helpful for tasks such as image captioning [23].

6. REFERENCES

[1] D. Bahdanau, K. Cho, and Y. Bengio. Neural machine translation by jointly learning to align and translate. In *ICLR 2015*, 2014.

[2] J. Bollen, H. Mao, and A. Pepe. Modeling public mood and emotion: Twitter sentiment and socio-economic phenomena. In *ICWSM*, 2011.

[3] D. Borth, T. Chen, R. Ji, and S.-F. Chang. Sentibank: large-scale ontology and classifiers for detecting sentiment and emotions in visual content. In *ACM MM*, pages 459–460. ACM, 2013.

[4] D. Borth, R. Ji, T. Chen, T. Breuel, and S.-F. Chang. Large-scale visual sentiment ontology and detectors using adjective noun pairs. In *ACM MM*, pages 223–232. ACM, 2013.

[5] D. Borth, R. Ji, T. Chen, T. M. Breuel, and S. Chang. Large-scale visual sentiment ontology and detectors using adjective noun pairs. In *ACM MM*, pages 223–232, 2013.

[6] D. Cao, R. Ji, D. Lin, and S. Li. A cross-media public sentiment analysis system for microblog. *Multimedia Systems*, pages 1–8, 2014.

[7] X. Chen and C. Lawrence Zitnick. Mind's eye: A recurrent visual representation for image caption generation. In *CVPR*, June 2015.

[8] D. C. Cireşan, U. Meier, J. Masci, L. M. Gambardella, and J. Schmidhuber. Flexible, high performance convolutional neural networks for image classification. In *IJCAI*, pages 1237–1242, 2011.

[9] A. Frome, G. S. Corrado, J. Shlens, S. Bengio, J. Dean, M. Ranzato, and T. Mikolov. Devise: A deep visual-semantic embedding model. In *Advances in Neural Information Processing Systems (NIPS)*, pages 2121–2129, 2013.

[10] X. Hu, J. Tang, H. Gao, and H. Liu. Unsupervised sentiment analysis with emotional signals. In *WWW*, pages 607–618, 2013.

[11] C. J. Hutto and E. Gilbert. VADER: A parsimonious rule-based model for sentiment analysis of social media text. In *ICWSM*, 2014.

[12] X. Jin, A. Gallagher, L. Cao, J. Luo, and J. Han. The wisdom of social multimedia: using flickr for prediction and forecast. In *ACM MM*, pages 1235–1244. ACM, 2010.

[13] D. Joshi, R. Datta, E. Fedorovskaya, Q.-T. Luong, J. Z. Wang, J. Li, and J. Luo. Aesthetics and emotions in images. *IEEE Signal Processing Magazine*, 28(5):94–115, 2011.

[14] A. Karpathy and F. Li. Deep visual-semantic alignments for generating image descriptions. In *CVPR*, pages 3128–3137, 2015.

[15] R. Kiros, R. Salakhutdinov, and R. S. Zemel. Unifying visual-semantic embeddings with multimodal neural language models. *CoRR*, abs/1411.2539, 2014.

[16] A. Krizhevsky, I. Sutskever, and G. E. Hinton. Imagenet classification with deep convolutional neural networks. In *NIPS*, volume 1, page 4, 2012.

[17] A. Krizhevsky, I. Sutskever, and G. E. Hinton. Imagenet classification with deep convolutional neural networks. In *Advances in Neural Information Processing Systems (NIPS)*, pages 1106–1114, 2012.

[18] Q. Le and T. Mikolov. Distributed representations of sentences and documents. In *ICML*, 2014.

[19] Y. LeCun, L. Bottou, Y. Bengio, and P. Haffner. Gradient-based learning applied to document recognition. *Proceedings of the IEEE*, 86(11):2278–2324, 1998.

[20] X. Lu, Z. Lin, H. Jin, J. Yang, and J. Z. Wang. Rapid: Rating pictorial aesthetics using deep learning. In *ACM MM*, pages 457–466. ACM, 2014.

[21] L. Ma, Z. Lu, L. Shang, and H. Li. Multimodal convolutional neural networks for matching image and sentence. In *The IEEE International Conference on Computer Vision (ICCV)*, December 2015.

[22] J. Mao, W. Xu, Y. Yang, J. Wang, Z. Huang, and A. Yuille. Deep captioning with multimodal recurrent neural networks (m-rnn). *ICLR*, 2015.

[23] A. P. Mathews, L. Xie, and X. He. Senticap: Generating image descriptions with sentiments. In *AAAI*, pages 3574–3580, 2016.

[24] T. Mikolov, I. Sutskever, K. Chen, G. S. Corrado, and J. Dean. Distributed representations of words and phrases and their compositionality. In *NIPS*, pages 3111–3119, 2013.

[25] L.-P. Morency, R. Mihalcea, and P. Doshi. Towards multimodal sentiment analysis: Harvesting opinions from the web. In *ICMI*, pages 169–176, 2011.

[26] S. Siersdorfer, E. Minack, F. Deng, and J. Hare. Analyzing and predicting sentiment of images on the social web. In *ACM MM*, pages 715–718. ACM, 2010.

[27] R. Socher, A. Karpathy, Q. V. Le, C. D. Manning, and A. Y. Ng. Grounded compositional semantics for finding and describing images with sentences. *TACL*, 2:207–218, 2014.

[28] R. Socher, C. C. Lin, A. Y. Ng, and C. D. Manning. Parsing natural scenes and natural language with recursive neural networks. In *ICML*, pages 129–136, 2011.

[29] N. Srivastava and R. Salakhutdinov. Multimodal learning with deep boltzmann machines. *Journal of Machine Learning Research*, 15(1):2949–2980, 2014.

[30] I. Sutskever. *Training recurrent neural networks*. PhD thesis, University of Toronto, 2013.

[31] K. S. Tai, R. Socher, and C. D. Manning. Improved semantic representations from tree-structured long short-term memory networks. In *ACL*, pages 1556–1566, July 2015.

[32] O. Vinyals, A. Toshev, S. Bengio, and D. Erhan. Show and tell: A neural image caption generator. In *CVPR*, June 2015.

[33] M. Wang, D. Cao, L. Li, S. Li, and R. Ji. Microblog sentiment analysis based on cross-media bag-of-words model. In *ICIMCS*, pages 76:76–76:80. ACM, 2014.

[34] J. Weston, S. Bengio, and N. Usunier. WSABIE: scaling up to large vocabulary image annotation. In *IJCAI*, pages 2764–2770, 2011.

[35] Q. You, J. Luo, H. Jin, and J. Yang. Robust image sentiment analysis using progressively trained and domain transferred deep networks. In *AAAI*, pages 381–388, 2015.

[36] Q. You, J. Luo, H. Jin, and J. Yang. Building a large scale dataset for image emotion recognition: The fine print and the benchmark. In *AAAI*, pages 308–314, 2016.

[37] Q. You, J. Luo, H. Jin, and J. Yang. Cross-modality consistent regression for joint visual-textual sentiment analysis of social multimedia. In *WSDM*, pages 13–22, 2016.

[38] J. Yuan, S. Mcdonough, Q. You, and J. Luo. Sentribute: image sentiment analysis from a mid-level perspective. In *Proceedings of the Second International Workshop on Issues of Sentiment Discovery and Opinion Mining*, page 10. ACM, 2013.

[39] X. Zhu, P. Sobhani, and H. Guo. Long short-term memory over recursive structures. In *Proceedings of the 32nd International Conference on Machine Learning (ICML)*, pages 1604–1612, 2015.

n-Dimensional Display Interface

Charles D. Estes
University of North Carolina at Chapel Hill
Brooks Computer Science Building, CB 3175
Chapel Hill, NC 27599-3175 USA
cdestes@cs.unc.edu

ABSTRACT

The n-Dimensional Display Interface is a display abstraction conceived from first principles with the intention of replacing the framebuffer as a new "narrow waist" for modern display pipelines.

Keywords

Display interface, framebuffer, scalable display

1. INTRODUCTION

Modern display use cases are dramatically pushing the limits of data transmission requiring higher channel capacity to meet their needs.[1] The growing trend of televisions with UltraHD spatial resolutions brings steep requirements. HDMI 1.4 [2] allows for 4096x2160 at 30 Hz with 48 bits/pixel requiring an uncompressed channel capacity of 12.15 Gbps. Emerging 8K use cases at higher 60 Hz refresh rates will then increase that by nearly an order of magnitude. Refresh rates likely will not stop at 60 Hz either, as many common LCD display panels can already refresh at 240 Hz. HDMI 1.4a [3] additionally handles 3D video at current HD standards while doubling the video output due to the need of producing two stereoscopic images for every frame.

The digital display standards are still keeping pace with these more traditional use cases, but the signaling requirements for the cables and connectors is getting increasingly restrictive. Furthermore, they are all intended for scenarios where the rendering device is connected to the display within the same room. Both remote displays such as VNC [4] and small wireless devices do not have the luxury of such high channel capacities and of a guaranteed quality of service. WirelessHD is addressing UltraHD video at 240 Hz with 48 bits/pixel, but only over special wireless video area networks (WVAN).[5] The Wi-Fi Alliance released a display specification over Wi-Fi along with its Miracast device specification that allow the streaming of high definition content of Wi-Fi networks.[6] Less traditional use cases such as remote displays and massive display walls often require novel solutions beyond the current standards.[7][8][9][10][11]

MM '16, October 15-19, 2016, Amsterdam, Netherlands

DOI: http://dx.doi.org/10.1145/2964284.2971476

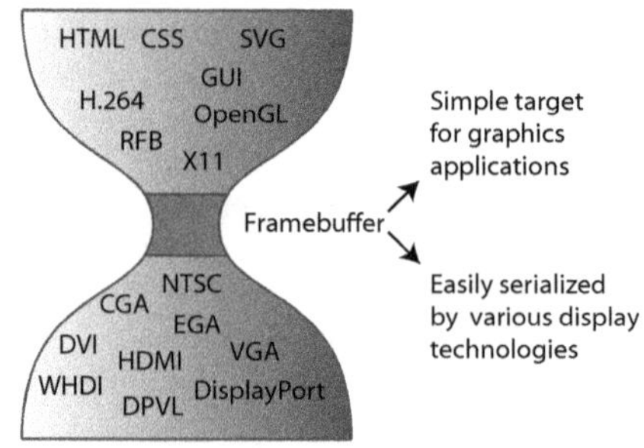

Figure 1: The framebuffer has served as a narrow waist for the display pipeline.

For the earliest computer display systems, the display interface was carefully designed based both on display and the attached host system. Such systems required a discrete *display generator* to drive the electronics of the display and a *display processor* to translate input form the host system for the display generator. Early work to optimize these display processors made tradeoffs between memory, channel capacity, and physical connections to the display. These custom solutions offered little re-use as their designs were just trips around the *wheel of reincarnation*.[12] With the emergence of CRT displays, a new more obvious display interface abstraction took shape, figuratively stopping the wheel.[13] The framebuffer served as a "narrow waist" for the display pipeline as computer graphics on the host system rapidly advanced independently of the signaling standards on the display side (figure 1). By all accounts, the framebuffer has been a great success. Modern displays have digital transmission standards that send compressed data, but nearly all of them still scan the contents of a framebuffer at a fixed refresh rate.

My research seeks to define a new, more flexible narrow waist, just above the framebuffer in terms of complexity. The concept was first introduced at NOSSDAV and later refined in a full conference paper at MMSYS.[14][15] The second phase of research published at ACMMM involved extensions for blending that allowed me to use a novel approach to video rendering on an nDDI display.[16] I am entering into the third phase of my research. With several promising directions available, I hope to use the Doctoral Symposium to collaborate and narrow my focus.

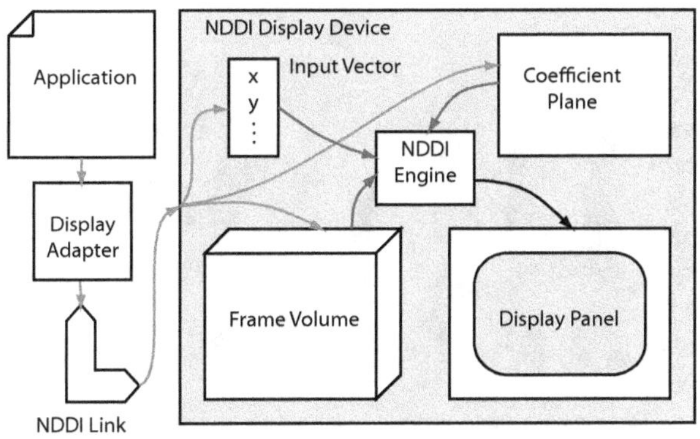

Figure 2: NDDI concept diagram.

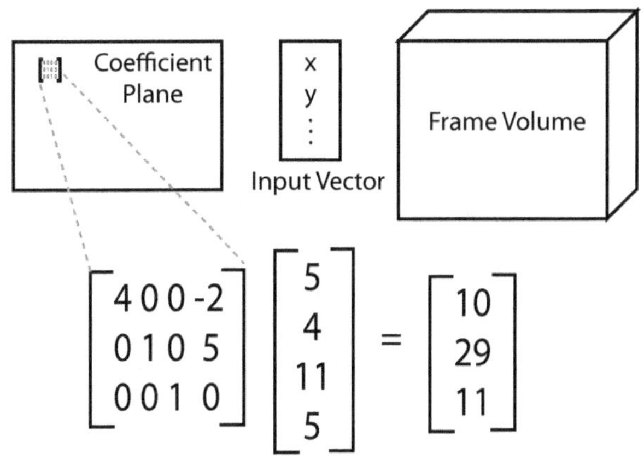

Figure 3: Example matrix multiplication for pixel mapping.

2. N-DIMENSIONAL DISPLAY INTERFACE

The *n-Dimensional Display Interface* is a new abstraction from first principles. My goal for the research is to define a new, future-proof abstraction that is:

- **Framebuffer Compatible** for simple applications
- **Data-Driven** avoiding any use of stateful logic
- **Progressively Beneficial** per application needs
- **Highly Parallel** allowing for ideal scalability
- **Asynchronous** avoiding timing constraints

nDDI defines an abstraction just above the framebuffer in terms of complexity making it trivially compatible framebuffer. The primary strength of the interface is a highly flexible addressing scheme; reducing the transmission cost of both pixel data and the addressing information. This is accomplished by creating a large pixel store on the display itself, called the *frame volume* (figure 2). The frame volume can be configured by the driving application to any dimensionality using n-tuples to address pixels, pixel strips, planes, and n-volumes. This allows for efficient fill commands and quick remapping of display pixel values to newly arrived pixels or existing values in the frame volume. The highly parallel mapping operations occur within the *nddi engine* at each pixel site and are controlled by *coefficient matrices* at each display location within the *coefficient plane*. The entire operation is driven by the *input vector*. The length of the vector is configured by the application. The minimal length is two, where the x and y values are driven by the nDDI engine and any additional values are driven by the application. The mapping operation consists of a simple matrix multiplication which multiplies the input vector by the coefficient matrix for each location (x, y) where the x and y values of the input vector are inherently set to the same location (figure 3).

For basic framebuffer compatibility, an application can configure the frame volume in two dimensions and set the input vector to a length of two. Configuring those parameters will determine the size of each coefficient matrix, 2×2 in this case. The application would initialize those coefficient matrices to an identity matrix and then simply write to the frame volume as if it were a framebuffer at a refresh rate of 60 Hz. Configuring an nDDI display in more sophisticated ways can achieve a reduction in channel capacity.

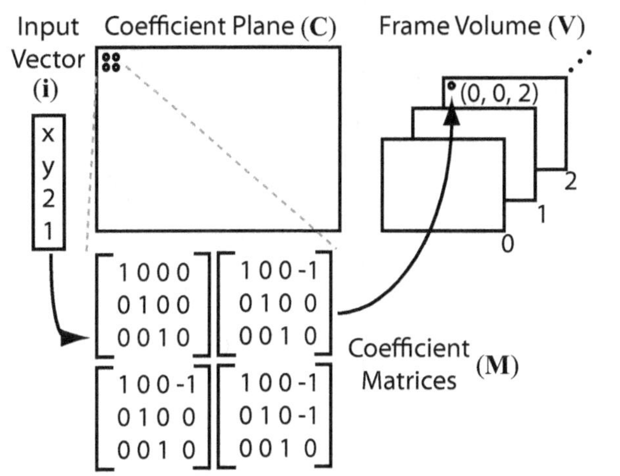

Figure 4: Example NDDI Configuration for simple video player with 4x scaling.

In the case of a video player, the application can configure the frame volume in three dimensions with x and y dimensions matching the video source and then some number of frames in the z dimension for buffering (figure 4). Frames are buffered into the frame volume, and the frames are advanced using the z value in the input vector. The physical display can be larger that the video source, and so the coefficient matrices are configured as simple affine transforms that map a source pixel from the video to multiple pixels on the display.

3. DRIVING AN NDDI DISPLAY

My initial experiments sought to configure an nDDI display in novel ways to provide transmission savings while still not utilizing any application level semantics. These *Pixel Bridge* experiments simply looked at each frame of an input video source and drove the display according to one of three different modes.

- **Framebuffer** - Configured as a 2D framebuffer
- **Flat Tiled** - Configured as a 2D, tiled framebuffer
- **Cached Tiled** - Configured as a cache of tiles

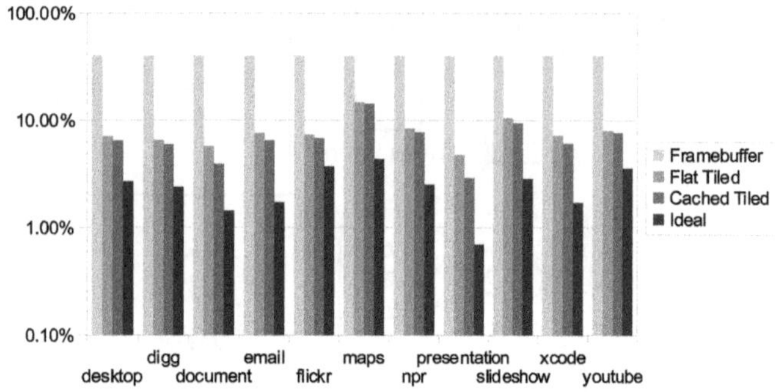

Figure 5: Results for large recordings.

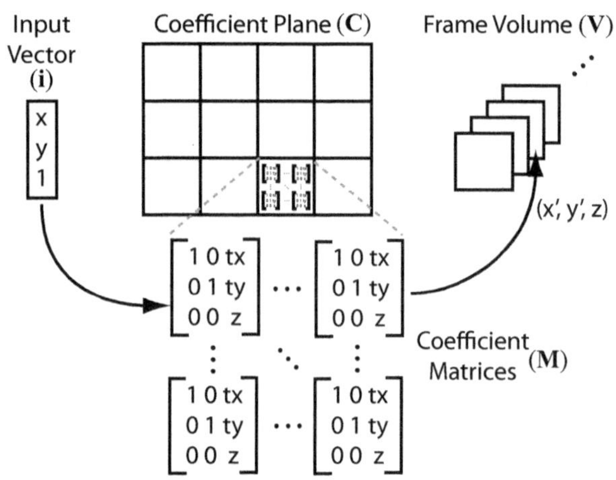

Figure 6: Cached tiler nDDI configuration.

The source videos were recorded video sessions and full motion video clips. The results for the recorded compute sessions are shown (figure 5) as a percentage ratio of the pixels sent for each mode compared to that of 60 Hz signal. Framebuffer Mode produced a basic 40% rate because it is only updating the display at 24 fps vs. 60 Hz. Flat Tiled produced a significant reduction at well under 10%. Cached Tiled mode configured the frame volume as a deep cache of tiles (figure 6) and produced a moderate improvement. All of the results were compared against a Perfect mode which was achieved simply by calculating the data needed to update changed pixels without considering any addressing information.

3.1 Video

For full motion video, my previous Pixel Bridge tiling modes did not fare well. For video, I introduced a DCT tiled mode that leveraged the semantics of video codecs to render the output video as a weighted blending of pre-rendered 8×8 DCT basis functions.[17] To achieve this blending, I experimented with three different blending modes and finally settled on coefficient plane based blending. I extended the single coefficient plane to 64 coefficient planes and added a 3-channel scaler alongside each of the coefficient matrices. Blending in this manner works by performing all 64 mappings for a pixel location, multiplying each pixel channel by the associated scaler, summing each channel, and then dividing by a configured max scaler value.

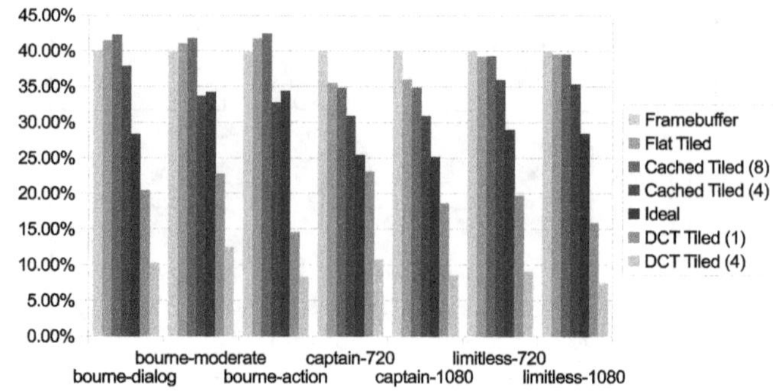

Figure 7: Revised video results with new DCT tiler.

For the DCT tiled mode, the 64 pre-rendered 8×8 basis functions were rendered into the frame volume. Then for each frame, only the significant DC and AC coefficients were transmitted. The results show a significant savings (figure 7). The previous cached tiler did not perform well even when using a lossy matching scheme (Cached Tiled 4). DCT tiled outperformed perfect with a very strong PSNR ($\sim$ 40) at the highest quality levels (DCT Tiled 1,4).

4. THE NEXT PHASE

I have conducted some preliminary investigations into the possible areas of research below. I strongly hope to use this forum of the Doctoral Symposium to collaborate with multimedia experts and researchers to narrow my focus and pave the final path to my dissertation.

- **Advanced nDDI Video** - I introduced a trivial prediction-residual decoder for the DCT tiler. I feel better rate control and a new approach to caching predictions will deliver even strong results.
- **Mixed Multimedia Blending** - Coefficient plane blending is well suited for simple blending use cases. I plan to add support for a per-pixel alpha channel in the frame volume. Extending coefficient plane blending in this way remains highly parallel and provides additional flexibility in terms of use cases supported: masks, compositing, anti-aliasing, font smoothing, etc.
- **Display Wall Simulation** - Display walls are a strong motivation behind the new nDDI abstraction, and I intend to simulate a massive display wall using an nDDI Link that will support multiple clients streaming content to the single nDDI display.
- **Memory Modeling and Simulation** - Extending the architecture to support multiple coefficient planes dramatically increased the memory requirements for the nDDI display, however the access patterns are all very regular and the memory can be localized to each pixel. On the other hand, the frame volume access patterns are much more dynamic. I hope to model them further and to work out a practical and novel caching scheme.

5. REFERENCES

[1] Benjamin Watson and David Luebke. The Ultimate Display: Where Will All the Pixels Come From? *Computer*, 38(8):54–61, aug 2005.

[2] High-definition multimedia interface specification version 1.4. HDMI Founders, June 2009.

[3] High-definition multimedia interface specification version 1.4a extraction of 3d portion. HDMI Founders, March 2010.

[4] T Richardson, Q Stafford-Fraser, K R Wood, and A Hopper. Virtual network computing. *IEEE Internet Computing*, 2(1):33–38, 1998.

[5] Wirelesshd specification version 1.1 overview, May 2010.

[6] Wi-Fi Alliance. Best Practices Document for Wi-Fi CERTIFIED Miracast ł Devices version 1.0, 2014.

[7] Greg Humphreys, Mike Houston, Ren Ng, Randall Frank, Sean Ahern, Peter D. Kirchner, and James T. Klosowski. Chromium: a stream-processing framework for interactive rendering on clusters. In *Proceedings of the 29th annual conference on Computer graphics and interactive techniques - SIGGRAPH '02*, SIGGRAPH '02, page 693, New York, New York, USA, 2002. ACM Press.

[8] Nirnimesh, P. Harish, and P.J. Narayanan. Garuda: A Scalable Tiled Display Wall Using Commodity PCs. *Visualization and Computer Graphics, IEEE Transactions on*, 13(5):864 – 877, 2007.

[9] R. Singh, L. Renambot, A. Johnson, and J. Leigh. TeraVision: a distributed, scalable, high resolution graphics streaming system. In *IEEE International Conference on Cluster Computing (IEEE Cat. No.04EX935)*, pages 391–400. IEEE, 2004.

[10] Byungil Jeong, Luc Renambot, Ratko Jagodic, Rajvikram Singh, Julieta Aguilera, Andrew Johnson, and Jason Leigh. High-Performance Dynamic Graphics Streaming for Scalable Adaptive Graphics Environment. In *ACM/IEEE SC 2006 Conference (SC'06)*, pages 24–24. IEEE, nov 2006.

[11] Jianli Luo, Kaihuai Qin, Yanxia Zhou, Miao Mao, and Ruirui Li. GPU rendering for tiled multi-projector autostereoscopic display based on chromium. In *Visual Computer*, volume 26, pages 457–465, 2010.

[12] T. H. Myer and I. E. Sutherland. On the design of display processors, 1968.

[13] Robert L. Myers. *Display Interfaces: Fundamentals and Standards.* Series in Display Technology. Wiley, 2003.

[14] Charles D Estes and Ketan Mayer-Patel. Moving beyond the framebuffer. *Proceedings of the 21st international workshop on Network and operating systems support for digital audio and video - NOSSDAV '11*, page 93, 2011.

[15] Charles D Estes and Ketan Mayer-Patel. The n-Dimensional Display Interface A More Elastic Narrow Waist for the Display Pipeline. In *MMSYS*, 2012.

[16] Charles D Estes and Ketan Mayer-Patel. Video Killed The Data Store Extending the n-Dimensional Display Interface for Full Screen Video. In *ACM Multimedia*, Brisbane, Australia, 2015.

[17] McMillan, L. (Sun Microsystems Inc., Research Triangle Park, NC, USA) and L. Westover. A forward-mapping realization of the inverse discrete cosine transform. In *Data Compression Conference*, pages 219 – 228, Snowbird, UT, USA, 1992.

[18] Vesa digital packet video link standard: Version 1. Video Electronics Standards Association, April 2004.

[19] Mitsubishi electric diamond vision is dallas cowboys' choice for new stadium. Press Release, April 2008. http://www.businesswire.com/news/home/20080416005327/en.

[20] Ibm introduces world's highest-resolution computer monitor. Press Release, June 2001. http://www-03.ibm.com/press/us/en/pressrelease/1180.wss.

[21] The insane hardware driving the world's biggest led billboard. website. http://gizmodo.com/#!5096475/the-insane-hardware-driving-the-worlds-biggest-led-billboard.

[22] New displayport 1.4 standard can drive 8k monitors over a usb type-c cable. website. http://arstechnica.com/gadgets/2016/03/new-displayport-1-4-standard-can-drive-8k-monitors-over-a-usb-type-c-cable/.

[23] Robert W Scheifler and Jim Gettys. The x window system. *ACM Trans Graph*, 5(2):79–109, 1986.

[24] Tristan Richardson, Frazer Bennett, Glenford Mapp, and Andy Hopper. A ubiquitous, personalized computing environment for all: Teleporting in an X Window System Environment. *IEEE Personal Communications*, 1(3):6–12, 1994.

[25] Kenneth (IBM T.J. Watson Research Center Ocheltree, Steven (IBM T.J. Watson Research Center Millman, David (Teradici Corporation) Hobbs, Jason (Columbia University) Nieh, and Ricardo (Columbia University) Baratto. Net2Display: A Proposed VESA Standard for Remoting Displays and I/O Devices over Networks. In *ADEAC*, 2006.

[26] F. Jutand, Z.J. Mou, and N. Demassieux. DCT architectures for HDTV. *1991., IEEE International Sympoisum on Circuits and Systems*, pages 196–199, 1991.

[27] Henry Fuchs. Distributing a Visible Surface Algorithm Over Multiple Processors. In *Proceedings of the 1977 annual conference on - ACM '77*, pages 449–451, 1977.

[28] Henry Fuchs, Jack Goldfeather, Jeff P Hultquist, Susan Spach, John D Austin, Frederick P Brooks Jr., John G Eyles, and John Poulton. Fast Spheres, Shadows, Textures, Transparencies, and Image Enhancements in Pixel-planes. *SIGGRAPH Comput. Graph.*, 19(3):111–120, July 1985.

[29] Steven Molnar, John Eyles, and John Poulton. PixelFlow: high-speed rendering using image composition. In *Proceedings of the 19th annual conference on Computer graphics and interactive techniques - SIGGRAPH '92*, SIGGRAPH '92, pages 231–240, New York, New York, USA, 1992. ACM Press.

[30] Turner Whitted, Jim Kajiya, Erik Ruf, and Ray Bittner. Embedded Function Composition. In *Proceedings of the Conference on High Performance Graphics 2009*, HPG '09, pages 47–50, New York, NY, USA, 2009. ACM.

Multi-Modal Learning: Study on A Large-Scale Micro-Video Data Collection

Jingyuan Chen
School of Computing
National University of Singapore, Singapore
jingyuanchen91@gmail.com

ABSTRACT

Micro-video sharing social services, as a new phenomenon in social media, enable users to share micro-videos and thus gain increasing enthusiasm among people. One distinct characteristic of micro-videos is the multi-modality, as these videos always have visual signals, audio tracks, textual descriptions as well as social clues. Such multi-modality data makes it possible to obtain a comprehensive understanding of videos and hence provides new opportunities for researchers. However, limited efforts thus far have been dedicated to this new emerging user-generated contents (UGCs) due to the lack of large-scale benchmark dataset. Towards this end, in this paper, we construct a large-scale micro-video dataset, which can support many research domains, such as popularity prediction and venue estimation. Based upon this dataset, we conduct an initial study in popularity prediction of micro-videos. Finally, we identify our future work.

Keywords

Micro-Videos; Popularity Prediction; Venue Estimation; Multi-Modal Learning

1. INTRODUCTION

The last couple of years have witnessed the unprecedented growth of smart mobile devices, enabling users to record life stories vividly with short videos and then instantly upload them to social media websites, such as Snapchat, Vine and Instagram[1]. Since micro-videos are usually short in length, they need little bandwidth and hence gain tremendous user enthusiasm [2]. Micro-videos represent a new form of UGCs, which can be viewed, discussed and even reposted by users once they are uploaded; this leads to their rapid rise. It is reported that Vine hit 1.5 billion daily loops in 2015[2]

[1]https://snapchat.com, https://vine.co, https://instagram.com.

[2]http://blog.vine.co.

MM '16, October 15-19, 2016, Amsterdam, Netherlands

DOI: http://dx.doi.org/10.1145/2964284.2971477

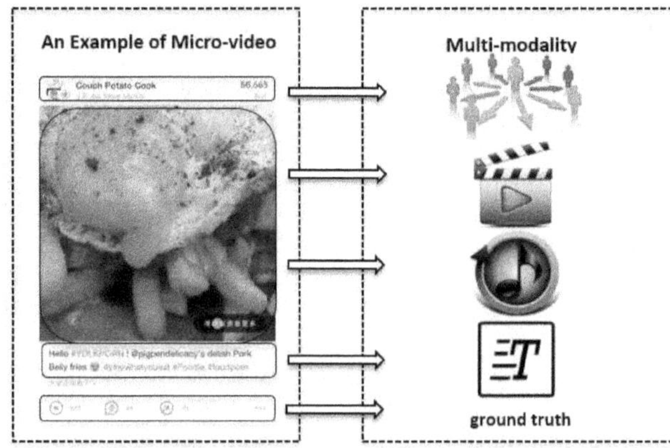

Figure 1: Illustration of the multi-modality micro-videos.

and Snapchat hit 7 billion daily video views in 2016[3]. As a video messaging platform, it is hard to crawl micro-videos from Snapchat. Hence, we focus on Vine here, which can be gathered more easily for research.

In a sense, micro-videos have the following distinct characteristics: 1) Short Length. Most micro-video services set limits, usually around 10 seconds, on the length of the micro-videos uploaded. 2) Timely transmission. As micro-videos need less bandwidth, they are always easy to be uploaded timely via mobile devices and widely viewed and spreaded by users. 3) Multi-modality. Apart from visual and acoustic information, micro-videos are always associated with social clues and rich textual data, such as the video descriptions and user comments, as shown in Figure 1. 4) Low quality. Due to certain external factors, such as camera shakes and lighting condition, some modalities of micro-videos, such as visual or acoustic contents, may be of poor quality.

The brief nature of micro-videos allows us to study acoustic-visual as well as textual information at a fine-grained level, which enables us to comprehensively understand the contents of micro-videos. However, challenges coexist with the opportunities:

- **Insufficient information.** Due to the short-length nature of micro-videos, each modality can only provide limited information, the so-called modality limitation. Fortunately, micro-videos always involve multiple modalities, namely, social, visual, acoustic and textual modalities. In a sense, these modalities are co-related

[3]http://goo.gl/YYnBbd.

rather than independent and essentially characterize the same micro-videos. Therefore, the major challenge lies in how to effectively fuse heterogeneous multiple modalities.

- **Low quality.** Due to certain external factors, some modality of the micro-videos may be of poor quality. Hence, learning directly from the original feature spaces of modalities, which was adopted by most multi-modal learning methods may be imprecise. Consequently, to improve the learning performance, how to compensate the noisy modality with reliable ones poses a crucial challenge for us.

- **Benchmark dataset.** Another challenge we are facing is the lack of benchmark dataset to support our research. As far as we know, the only available micro-video dataset [12] does not contain the important textual and social modalities, which makes it less comprehensive and unsuitable for our research. It is thus necessary to build a comprehensive micro-video dataset and further extract a rich set of discriminant features to enhance the learning performance.

To address these challenges, we introduce a large-scale benchmark dataset[4] of user generated micro-videos. It is able to serve as a standard dataset to facilitate various applications, such as video popularity prediction [5] and venue estimation [3]. To the best of our knowledge, our dataset is the largest real-world micro-video dataset comprising of 579,506 videos, among which 276,264 videos have venue category tags, which is crawled from a prominent video-sharing social website—Vine.

Based upon the constructed dataset, we plan to focus on two research directions, video popularity prediction and venue estimation. In this paper, we present a novel **T**ransductive **M**ulti-mod**AL** **L**earning approach, TMALL for short, to predict the popularity of micro-videos. For venue estimation, which aims to infer the venue categories from micro-videos, we will introduce it in future work.

2. RELATED WORK

There is not much work on micro-video analysis. Redi et al. [12] address the problem of automatic detection of creative micro-videos, by studying a number of new and existing computational features. Sano et al. [14] explore the problem of loop micro-video (that are designed to be played in a continuous six-second loop) detection. Nguyen et al. [10] focus on analyzing general properties of micro-videos, with the explicit goal of constructing a benchmark dataset for hashtag prediction.

Due to the enormous commercial potential, popularity prediction of UGCs has attracted great attention from both the industry and academia. Hong et al. [4] explored the popularity prediction of tweets, which is measured by the number of future retweets, by introducing a rich set of features, such as topological features, temporal features and meta features. Beyond the text popularity prediction, McParlane et al. [9] focused on the popularity of images. They extracted some sophisticated features and cast the task of image popularity prediction as a problem of binary

[4]The dataset can be accessible via http://acmmm2016.wix.com/micro-videos.

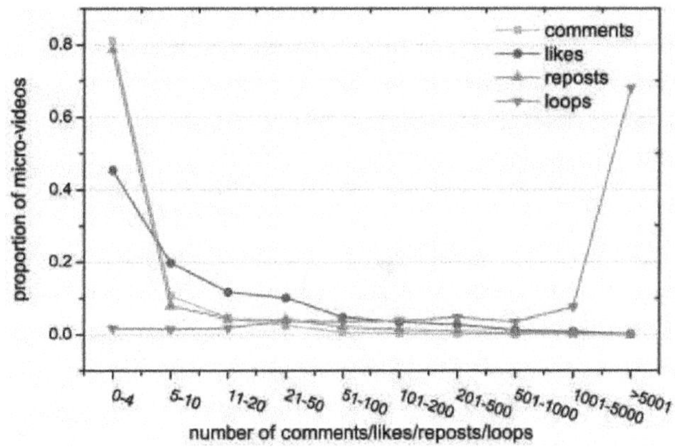

Figure 2: Distribution of the number of comments, likes, reposts and loops of micro-videos in our dataset.

classification, where the given image would be classified as popular or not. Later, Cappallo et al. [1] proposed a latent ranking method for the image popularity prediction solely based on the visual content. The proposed method was evaluated on several image datasets collected from micro-blogging and photo-sharing websites. Although huge success has been achieved by these approaches, limited efforts have thus far been dedicated to the problem of video popularity prediction, where multiple modalities coexist. Noting this gap, Trzcinski et al. [16] shifted from images to videos, and studied the problem of video popularity prediction utilizing both the visual cues and the early popularity pattern of the video once it is released. However, this approach suffered from two limitations. First, the proposed approach can only work on videos that have been published over a certain period. Second, the authors only used the traditional machine learning method, which failed to make full use of the relationship among modalities. As a complement, we aim to timely predict the popularity of a given micro-video even before it get published by proposing a novel multi-modal learning scheme.

3. DATA COLLECTION

3.1 Crawling Strategy

In particular, we first randomly selected 10 active Vine users from Rankzoo[5] as seed users. We then adopted the breadth-first crawling strategy to expand the seed users by crawling their followers. Considering that these seed users may have millions of followers, we practically only retained the first 1,000 come across followers for each seed user to improve the crawling efficiency. After three layers of crawling, we harvested a densely connected user set consisting of 98,166 users as well as 120,324 following relationships among users. For each user, his/her brief profile was also crawled. Besides, we also collected the timeline[6] of each user between July 1st and October 1st, 2015. Finally, we obtained 1.6 million video postings, including a total number of 303,242 unique micro-videos. Each micro-video is related to four popularity-related

[5]https://rankzoo.com.

[6]The micro-video posting history, including the repostings from others.

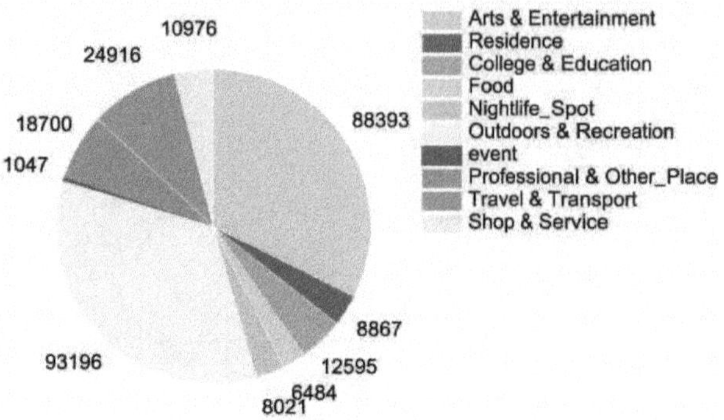

Figure 3: Illustration of location category distribution of our dataset.

indicators, namely, the number of comments, the number of likes, the number of reposts and the number of loops, which could be used as ground truth for popularity prediction.

Among the 1.6 million postings, only about 24,000 micro-videos contain Foursquare check-in information. After removing the duplicate venue IDs, we further expanded our video set by crawling all videos in each venue ID. This eventually yielded a dataset of 276,264 videos distributed in 442 Foursquare venue categories. Each venue ID was mapped to a venue category via the Foursquare API, which could serve as the ground truth.

3.2 Dataset Statistics

Finally, we collected a multi-modal dataset including 579,506 videos with popularity scores, among which 276,264 videos have venue category tags. Figure 2 illustrates the proportion of micro-videos regarding each of the four popularity indicators in our dataset. Foursquare organizes its venue categories into a four-layer hierarchical structure[7], with 10 non-leaf nodes (coarse venue categories) in the top-layer. Figure 3 shows the distribution of the 276,264 videos among the 10 top-level categories.

4. FEATURE EXTRACTION

It is apparent that both the publisher influence and content influence contribute to the popularity of UGCs. In particular, we characterized the publisher influence via the social modality, and the content influence via visual, acoustic and textual modalities. For content influence, we first examined the popular micro-videos in our dataset and propose three common characteristics of online micro-videos. For each characteristic, we then explained the insights, and transformed it into a set of features for video representation. Finally, we developed a rich set of popularity-oriented features from each modality.

Universal Appeal. The subjects of widely popular micro-videos cannot be something that can only be appreciated by a small group of people. Therefore, the topics and objects contained in micro-videos should be something common so that to be interpreted the same way across people and cultures. To capture this characteristic, we extracted Sentence2Vector feature from the textual modality and deep object feature from the visual one.

[7]https://developer.foursquare.com/categorytree.

Table 1: List of computed features (social/visual/acoustic/textual) in the dataset.

Modality	Features
Social Modality	Follower/Followee Count, Loop Count, Post Count, Twitter Verification
Visual Modality	50-D Color Histogram, 1,000-D CNN feature, 2,089-D SentiBank Feature 149-D Aesthetic Feature
Acoustic Modality	MFCC [8], Audio-Six
Textual Features	100-D Sentence2Vector[8], Textual Sentiment [7]

Emotional Content. People are naturally drawn to things that arouse their emotions. Micro-videos showing funny animals or lovely babies make people feel urge to share them to express the same emotions. As a result, micro-videos that are highly emotional are more likely to be shared. Therefore, we extracted textual sentiment, visual sentiment features for each video as well as several acoustic features, which is widely used in emotion recognition in music [17].

High Quality and Aesthetic Design. When people share information on social networks, people are actually showing a little piece of themselves to their audience. Therefore, high quality and aesthetic design of the content, which could reflect the taste of people, is another important characteristic of popular micro-videos. Color histogram, aesthetic feature and visual quality feature were thus extracted to encode such characteristic. In addition, the acoustic features we extracted are frequently used in music modeling, which could help to detect music in the audio track of micro-videos [8].

Based on these observations, we developed a rich set of popularity-oriented features from each modality, summarized in Table 1.

5. METHODOLOGY

Without loss of generality, suppose we have N labeled samples and M unlabeled samples with $K \geqslant 2$ modalities. It is worth noting that the unlabeled samples also serve as testing samples. Z_k stands for the number of features generated from the k-th modality. Then the k-th modality can be represented as $\mathbf{X_k} \in \mathbb{R}^{(N+M)\times Z_k}$. The popularity of all the videos are denoted by $\mathbf{y} = \{y_1, y_2, \cdots, y_N\}^T \in \mathbb{R}^N$. Let $\mathbf{f} = \{f_1, f_2, \cdots, f_N, f_{N+1}, f_{N+2}, \cdots, f_{N+M}\}^T \in \mathbb{R}^{N+M}$ stand for the predicted results regarding popularity for all samples, including the labeled and unlabeled ones. We aim to jointly learn the common space $\mathbf{X_0} \in \mathbb{R}^{(N+M)\times Z_0}$ shared by multiple modalities and the popularity for the M unlabeled micro-videos.

Our proposed model targets at reasoning from observed training micro-videos to testing ones. Such prediction belongs to transductive learning, in which both labeled samples as well as unlabeled samples are available for training. It hence obtains better performance. In contrast, inductive model is reasoning from observed training cases to general rules, which are then applied to the test cases.

5.1 Problem Formulation

It is apparent that different modalities may contribute distinctive and complementary information about micro-videos. For example, textual modality gives us hints about the topics of the given micro-video; acoustic and visual modalities may respectively convey location and situation of micro-videos, and user modality demonstrates the influence of the micro-video publisher. These clues jointly contribute to the popularity of a micro-video. Obviously, due to the noise and information insufficiency of each modality, it may be suboptimal to conduct learning directly from each single modality separately. In contrast, we assume that there exists an optimal latent space, in which micro-videos can be better described. Moreover, the optimal latent space should maintain the original intrinsic characteristics conveyed by multi-modalities of the given micro-videos. Therefore, we penalize the disagreement of the normalized Laplacian matrix between the latent space and each modality. In particular, we formalize this assumption as follows. Let $\mathbf{S}_k \in \mathbb{R}^{(N+M)\times(N+M)}$ be the similarity matrix[9], which is computed by the Gaussian similarity function as follows,

$$S_k(i,j) = \begin{cases} exp\Big(-\frac{\left\|\mathbf{x}_k^i - \mathbf{x}_k^j\right\|^2}{2\sigma_k^2}\Big) & , \text{ if } i \neq j; \\ 0 & , \text{ if } i = j. \end{cases} \tag{1}$$

where $\mathbf{x}_k^i$ and $\mathbf{x}_k^j$ are the micro-video pairs in the k-th modality space. Thereinto, the radius parameter σ_k is simply set as the median of the Euclidean distances over all video pairs in the k-th modality. We then derive the corresponding normalized Laplacian matrix as follows,

$$\mathbf{L}(\mathbf{S_k}) = \mathbf{I} - \mathbf{D}_k^{-\frac{1}{2}}\mathbf{S}_k\mathbf{D}_k^{-\frac{1}{2}}, \tag{2}$$

where $\mathbf{I}$ is a $(N+M)\times(N+M)$ identity matrix and $\mathbf{D}_k \in \mathbb{R}^{(N+M)\times(N+M)}$ is the diagonal degree matrix, whose (u,u)-th entry is the sum of the u-th row of $\mathbf{S}_k$. Since $S_k(i,j) > 0$, we can derive that $tr(\mathbf{L}(\mathbf{S_k})) > 0$. We thus can formulate the disagreement penalty between the latent space and the original modalities as,

$$\sum_{k=1}^{K} \| \frac{1}{tr(\mathbf{L}(\mathbf{S_0}))}\mathbf{L}(\mathbf{S_0}) - \frac{1}{tr(\mathbf{L}(\mathbf{S_k}))}\mathbf{L}(\mathbf{S_k}) \|_F^2, \tag{3}$$

where $tr(\mathbf{A})$ is the trace of matrix $\mathbf{A}$ and $\|\cdot\|_F$ denotes the Frobenius norm of matrix. In addition, considering that similar micro-videos attempt to have similar popularity in the latent common space, we adopt the following regularizer,

$$\frac{1}{2}\sum_{m=1}^{N+M}\sum_{n=1}^{N+M}\Big(\frac{f(\mathbf{x}_0^m)}{\sqrt{D_0(\mathbf{x}_0^m)}} - \frac{f(\mathbf{x}_0^n)}{\sqrt{D_0(\mathbf{x}_0^n)}}\Big)^2 S_0(m,n)$$
$$= \mathbf{f}^T\mathbf{L}(\mathbf{S_0})\mathbf{f}. \tag{4}$$

Based upon these formulations, we can define the loss function that measures the empirical error on the training samples. As reported in [11], the squared loss usually yields good performance as other complex ones. We thus adopt the squared loss in our algorithm for simplicity and efficiency. In particular, since we do not have the labels for testing samples, we only consider the squared loss regarding the N unlabeled samples to guarantee the learning performance. We ultimately reach our objective function as,

[9]To facilitate the illustration, k ranges from 0 to K.

Table 2: Performance comparison between our proposed TMALL model and several state-of-the-art baselines in terms of nMSE.

Methods	nMSE	p-value
Early Fusion	59.931 ± 41.09	9.91E-04
Late Fusion	8.461 ± 5.34	3.25E-03
regMVMT[18]	1.058 ± 0.05	1.88E-03
MSNL[15]	1.098 ± 0.13	1.42E-02
MvDA[6]	0.982 ± 7.00E-03	9.91E-04
TMALL	0.979 ± 9.42E-03	–

$$\min_{\mathbf{f},\mathbf{L}(\mathbf{S_0})} \sum_{i=1}^{N}(y_i - f_i)^2 + \mu\mathbf{f}^T\mathbf{L}(\mathbf{S_0})\mathbf{f}$$
$$+\lambda\sum_{k=1}^{K} \| \frac{1}{tr(\mathbf{L}(\mathbf{S_0}))}\mathbf{L}(\mathbf{S_0}) - \frac{1}{tr(\mathbf{L}(\mathbf{S_k}))}\mathbf{L}(\mathbf{S_k}) \|_F^2, \tag{5}$$

where λ and μ are both nonnegative regularization parameters. To be more specific, λ penalizes the disagreement among the latent space and modalities, and μ encourages that similar popularity will be assigned to similar micro-videos.

6. EXPERIMENT

To demonstrate the effectiveness of our proposed TMALL model, we carried out experiments with several state-of-the-art multi-view learning approaches. Table 2 shows the performance comparison among different models.

From this table, we have the following observations: 1) TMALL outperforms the Early_Fusion and Late_Fusion. Regarding the Early_Fusion, features extracted from various sources may not fall into the same semantic space. Simply appending all features actually brings in a certain amount of noise and ambiguity. Besides, Early_Fusion may lead to the curse of dimensionality since the final feature vector would be of very high dimension. For the Late_Fusion, the fused result however might not be reasonably accurate due to two reasons. First, a single modality might not be sufficiently descriptive to represent the complex semantics of the videos. Separate results would be thus suboptimal and the integration may not result in a desired outcome. Second, it is labor-intensive to tune the fusion weights for different modalities. Even worse, the optimal parameters for one application cannot be directly applied to another one. 2) TMALL achieves better performance, as compared with regMVMT and MSNL. This could be explained that linking different modalities via a unified latent space is better than imposing disagreement penalty directly over original spaces. 3) The less satisfactory performance of MvDA indicates that it is necessary to explore the consistency among different modalities when building the latent space. And 4) as compared to the multi-view learning baselines, such as regMVMT, MSNL, and MvDA, our model stably demonstrates its advantage. This signals that the proposed transductive models can achieve higher performance than inductive models under the same experimental settings. This can be explained by the fact that TMALL leverages the knowledge of testing samples.

7. CONCLUSION AND FUTURE WORK

This work has presented a micro-video dataset, consisting of 579,506 videos, among which 276,264 videos have venue category tags. Based on this dataset, we present a novel transductive multi-modal learning method, dubbed as TMALL, to predict the popularity of micro-videos. In particular, TMALL works by learning an optimal latent common space from multi-modality of the given micro-videos, in which the popularity of micro-videos are much more distinguishable. It is worth mentioning that our released dataset is applicable to verify many other research problems, such as venue estimation and video summarization.

In future, we mainly focus on the following two research directions.

Recent studies have shown that bursty/sudden rise of video popularity cannot be accounted by video domain features alone [13]. Therefore, we plan to utilize knowledge from social streams (e.g., Twitter) to grasp sudden popularity bursts in online social network, which allows us to model the social prominence of video content and improve popularity predictions in the video domain. In addition, some micro-videos on Vine are categorized by their uploaders into the respective channels, such as news, art and music. According to our statistics, both the venue category and the general category (channel) information have a correlation with the popularity of micro-videos. Future work will include both location context and category information in the cross-domain popularity prediction model.

We also focus on developing a cross-domain micro-video venue estimation framework, which aims to transfer the knowledge from external sources, such as existing image dataset with venue categories or user uploaded images on Foursquare, to boost the venue estimation performance on user-generated micro-videos.

8. ACKNOWLEDGMENTS

This research is supported by the National Research Foundation, Prime Minister's Office, Singapore under its IRC@SG Funding Initiative.

9. REFERENCES

[1] S. Cappallo, T. Mensink, and C. G. M. Snoek. Latent factors of visual popularity prediction. In *Proceedings of the 5th ACM on International Conference on Multimedia Retrieval*, pages 195–202. ACM, 2015.

[2] J. Chen, X. Song, L. Nie, X. Wang, H. Zhang, and T. Chua. Micro tells macro: predicting the popularity of micro-videos via a transductive model. In *Proceedings of the 24th Annual ACM Conference on Multimedia*. ACM, 2016.

[3] G. Friedland, O. Vinyals, and T. Darrell. Multimodal location estimation. In *Proceedings of the 18th Annual ACM Conference on Multimedia*, pages 1245–1252. ACM, 2010.

[4] L. Hong, O. Dan, and B. D. Davison. Predicting popular messages in twitter. In *Proceedings of the 20th ACM International Conference on World Wide Web*, pages 57–58. ACM, 2011.

[5] L. Jiang, Y. Miao, Y. Yang, Z. Lan, and A. G. Hauptmann. Viral video style: A closer look at viral videos on youtube. In *Proceedings of the 4th ACM on International Conference on Multimedia Retrieval*, page 193. ACM, 2014.

[6] M. Kan, S. Shan, H. Zhang, S. Lao, and X. Chen. Multi-view discriminant analysis. *IEEE Transactions on Pattern Analysis and Machine Intelligence*, 38(1):188–194, 2016.

[7] A. Khosla, A. D. Sarma, and R. Hamid. What makes an image popular? In *Proceedings of the 23rd ACM International Conference on World Wide Web*, pages 867–876, 2014.

[8] Z. Li, J. Wang, J. Cai, Z. Duan, H. Wang, and Y. Wang. Non-reference audio quality assessment for online live music recordings. In *Proceedings of the 21st Annual ACM Conference on Multimedia*, pages 63–72. ACM, 2013.

[9] P. J. McParlane, Y. Moshfeghi, and J. M. Jose. "nobody comes here anymore, it's too crowded"; predicting image popularity on flickr. In *Proceedings of the 4th ACM International Conference on Multimedia Retrieval*, page 385. ACM, 2014.

[10] P. X. Nguyen, G. Rogez, C. C. Fowlkes, and D. Ramanan. The open world of micro-videos. *CoRR*, abs/1603.09439, 2016.

[11] L. Nie, L. Zhang, Y. Yang, M. Wang, R. Hong, and T.-S. Chua. Beyond doctors: future health prediction from multimedia and multimodal observations. In *Proceedings of the 23rd Annual ACM Conference on Multimedia Conference*, pages 591–600. ACM, 2015.

[12] M. Redi, N. O'Hare, R. Schifanella, M. Trevisiol, and A. Jaimes. 6 seconds of sound and vision: Creativity in micro-videos. In *2014 IEEE Conference on Computer Vision and Pattern Recognition*, pages 4272–4279. IEEE, 2014.

[13] S. D. Roy, T. Mei, W. Zeng, and S. Li. Towards cross-domain learning for social video popularity prediction. *IEEE Transactions on Multimedia*, 15(6):1255–1267, 2013.

[14] S. Sano, T. Yamasaki, and K. Aizawa. Degree of loop assessment in microvideo. In *Proceedings of the 2014 IEEE International Conference on Image Processing*, pages 5182–5186. IEEE, 2014.

[15] X. Song, L. Nie, L. Zhang, M. Akbari, and T. Chua. Multiple social network learning and its application in volunteerism tendency prediction. In *Proceedings of the 38th International ACM SIGIR Conference on Research and Development in Information Retrieval*, pages 213–222, 2015.

[16] T. Trzcinski and P. Rokita. Predicting popularity of online videos using support vector regression. *CoRR*, abs/1510.06223, 2015.

[17] B. Wu, E. Zhong, A. Horner, and Q. Yang. Music emotion recognition by multi-label multi-layer multi-instance multi-view learning. In *Proceedings of the 22nd Annual ACM Conference on Multimedia*, pages 117–126. ACM, 2014.

[18] J. Zhang and J. Huan. Inductive multi-task learning with multiple view data. In *The 18th ACM SIGKDD International Conference on Knowledge Discovery and Data Mining*, pages 543–551. ACM, 2012.

Weakly-Supervised Recognition, Localization, and Explanation of Visual Entities

Pascal Mettes

University of Amsterdam

ABSTRACT

To learn from visual collections, manual annotations are required. Humans however can no longer keep up with providing strong and time consuming annotations on the ever increasing wealth of visual data. As a result, approaches are required that can learn from fast and weak forms of annotations in visual data. This doctorial symposium summarizes my ongoing PhD dissertation on how to utilize weakly-supervised annotations to recognize, localize, and explain visual entities in images and videos. In this context, visual entities denote objects, scenes, and actions (in images), and actions and events (in videos). The summary is performed through four publications. For each publication, we discuss the current state-of-the-art, as well as our proposed novelties and performed experiments. The end of the summary discusses several possibilities to extend the dissertation.

CCS Concepts

•Information systems → Multimedia and multimodal retrieval; •Computing methodologies → Computer vision;

Keywords

weakly-supervised recognition; event detection; action localization; image categorization

1. BAG-OF-FRAGMENTS

The first publication, *Bag-of-Fragments: Selecting and Encoding Video Fragments for Event Detection and Recounting*, was presented at ICMR 2015 [15]. This work aims to detect events in videos, such as Birthday Party or Board trick. A second goal is to explain why a video is relevant by recounting which visual concepts occur in the video.

A wide range of works have proposed video representations for event detection based on low-level features that describe local spatial and motion information [5, 9, 27]. These representations however lack semantic interpretation for event recounting. Several recent works therefore perform event detection by aggregating concept scores over the whole video [10, 12, 13]. Global aggregation of detector scores poses two problems to event detection and recounting. First, event videos are a complex interplay of various sub-events with a varying degree of relevance [1] which are blended into a single representation. Second, in a global aggregation, the event recounting is unable to state where in the video relevant concepts occur.

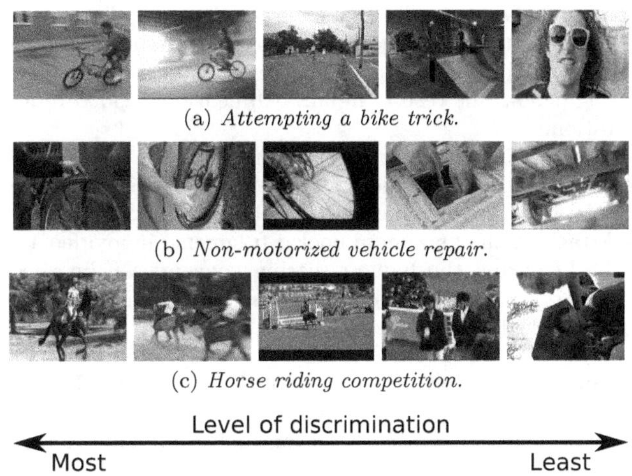

(a) *Attempting a bike trick.*

(b) *Non-motorized vehicle repair.*

(c) *Horse riding competition.*

Figure 1: **Bag-of-fragments** (publication 1) is a video representation that selects and encodes the most discriminative fragments for event detection and recounting. The figure shows the middle frame of five fragments for three events, ordered by level of discrimination. The most discriminative fragments are exemplary for the event and will be included in the bag-of-fragments, while the more ambiguous and less discriminative fragments are ignored.

Contributions. Rather than performing global concept aggregation, this work proposes to encode a video using fragments, dubbed *bag-of-fragments.* These fragments form discriminative sub-events to represent a complex event. Examples of fragments for three events, ranked from most to least discriminative, are shown in Figure 1. Representing a video based on discriminative fragments both captures sub-events within videos and can localize where in the video relevant concepts occur.

Typically, event videos are weakly-supervised, i.e. only global video labels are provided. Given the lack of annotation on fragment level, this work is tasked with learning

MM '16, October 15-19, 2016, Amsterdam, Netherlands

© 2016 ACM. ISBN 978-1-4503-3603-1/16/10...$15.00

DOI: http://dx.doi.org/10.1145/2964284.2971479

a bag-of-fragments automatically from training videos. The bag-of-fragments are computed in three steps. 1) Each video is split into a concise set of fragments. The search space of all possible fragments in a video is vast, so this work proposes to hierarchically cluster video frames into fragments. This approach captures all temporal scales of a video using a limited set of fragments. 2) The most discriminative fragments are selected from training videos. From a set of training videos for an event, all fragments are extracted and a classifier is trained for each fragment. The classifiers are pooled over the fragments over all positive and negative training videos of the event. The idea here is to select those fragments that best rank the positive videos over the negative videos using the pooled scores. 3) Each video is encoded into a bag-of-fragments. The classifiers of the most discriminative fragments are pooled over the fragments of each video and the maximum pooled score is retained as a feature. For N fragments, this results in an N-dimensional video representation.

The fragment-based representation allows for event detection by training a classifier on the representations and using the classifier to rank unseen test videos. Furthermore, by backtracking the maximum pooled fragments in a video and by backtracking the highest scoring concepts within these fragments, it is possible to provide semantic explanation of highly ranked test videos.

Experiments. The effectiveness of the proposed video representation is evaluated through several experiments. Here, the experiments regarding the event detection and event recounting are highlighted.

The video event detection performance is evaluated on the TRECVID 2013 dataset, which contains 20 events and 100 positive examples per event. Using a representation from 2,000 discriminative fragments per event results in a mean Average Precision of 27.6%. This is a direct improvement over a global aggregation of the same frame representations, which yields a mean Average Precision of 23.2%. More interestingly, fusing both approaches results in a significant boost to 37.3%. It is concluded from this experiment that bag-of-fragments is both a competitive and complementary video representation.

Event recounting, explaining event detection results semantically, is evaluated qualitatively. Using multiple examples, it is shown that the proposed approach is able to provide which visual concepts are relevant and also where in the video the concepts are present.

2. THE IMAGENET SHUFFLE

The second publication, *The ImageNet Shuffle: Reorganized Pre-training for Video Event Detection*, was presented at ICMR 2016 [14]. Where the bag-of-fragments, described in the previous section, focuses on improving video representations given frame representations, this work focuses on improving the frame representations themselves. This is performed with deep convolutional neural networks for video frames.

Leading approaches [7, 18, 28] attack this problem by learning frame representations from deep neural networks. Such deep networks are pre-trained on a collection of 1,000 image categories from the ImageNet dataset [3], as specified by the Large Scale Visual Recognition Challenge [20]. Pre-training on large-scale image collections results in robust frame representations for event detection. The complete ImageNet dataset however consists of 21,814 classes and 14 million images organized in a tree hierarchy. This means that current approaches only utilize a subset of the large-scale image dataset for pre-training deep networks.

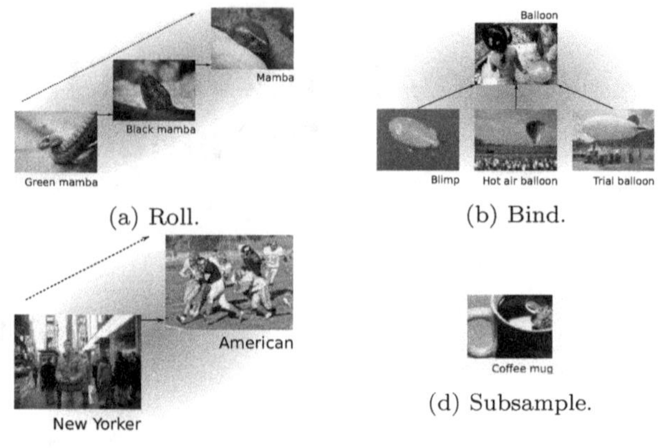

(a) Roll. (b) Bind. (c) Promote. (d) Subsample.

Figure 2: **The ImageNet Shuffle** (publication 2) introduces two protocols to reorganize the ImageNet dataset using its own hierarchy for pre-training deep networks. This figure shows an example of the four operations applied in the bottom-up reorganization.

Contributions. This work presents an empirical investigation on the effect of using the full ImageNet dataset for event detection in web videos. Two problems are identified when trying to pre-train a deep network on the complete ImageNet hierarchy. First, there is an imbalance in the number of examples for each class. For example, the class Yorkshire Terrier contains 3,072 images, whereas 296 other classes contain just a single image. Second, some classes seem over-specific for event detection in web videos. The complete ImageNet dataset is therefore deemed weakly-supervised to pre-train for event detection, in that care has not been taken to yield a balanced and general image collection. As a result, it seems suboptimal to directly pre-train a deep network on all 21,814 classes.

Two protocols are introduced to reorganize the complete ImageNet hierarchy to be able to pre-train deep networks. The reorganizations tackle the image imbalance and over-specific class problems. For the first protocol, bottom-up reorganization, four operations are introduced to merge classes from the bottom of the hierarchy towards the higher layers. The operations, highlighted in Figure 2, are: *Roll*: Move up classes with a single parent-child link. *Bind*: Merge a small subtree where the individual classes only have a few image examples. *Promote*: Merge small classes to their parent. *Subsample*: Subsample over-represented classes. Applying these operations to the ImageNet dataset results in a balanced and generalized class hierarchy fit for pre-training.

The second protocol, top-down reorganization, conversely investigates a breath-first search approach. Starting from the top of the hierarchy and moving down, classes with enough examples are added until a desired amount of classes is reached.

Experiments. Experimental evaluation is performed on

the TRECVID 2013 and 2015 datasets. Experiments on the TRECVID 2013 dataset show that:

- Pre-training on the reorganized ImageNet hierarchies improves significantly over standard pre-training (5 to 11% absolute improvement in mean Average Precision using 100 video examples per event during training, 5-12% absolute improvement using 10 video examples per event during training).
- Fusing the two pre-training protocols further improves results, i.e. the two approaches contain complementary information.
- The representations from deep networks improve over well-known visual, motion, and audio video representations.

The pre-trained deep networks have furthermore been employed on the TRECVID 2015 event detection benchmark, resulting in top performance on all example-based event detection tasks [22]. This result further signifies the effectiveness of pre-training deep networks on reorganized ImageNet hierarchies for event detection.

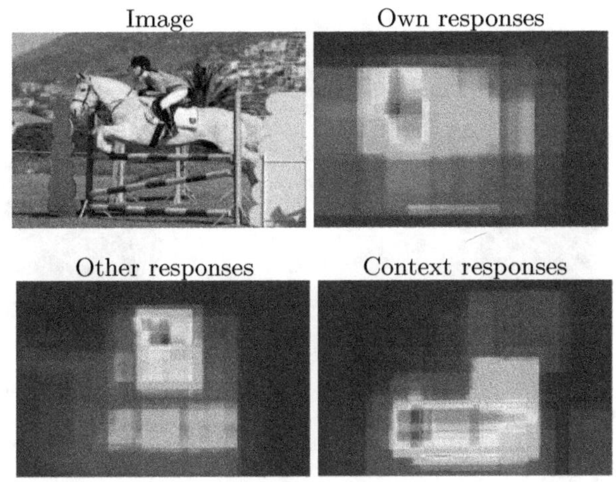

Figure 3: **No Spare Parts** (publication 3) establishes three part types relevant for image categorization and aims to jointly select and share these part types for image categorization.

3. NO SPARE PARTS

The third publication, *No Spare Parts: Sharing Part Detectors for Image Categorization*, will be published in the journal CVIU [16]. While the two publications discussed so far have focused on detection and temporal location in videos, this work aims for detection and spatial location in images. Different from event detection, where each event is processed separately, image categorization is typically performed for multiple classes at the same time.

A common image categorization pipeline is related to the bag-of-fragments approach, in that each image split into parts, the most discriminative parts are selected for each class, and the discriminative parts are used as image representation. Current approaches however perform this pipeline for each class separately [2, 4, 8, 19]. By treating each class separately, these approaches do not share common parts across classes. Furthermore, part selection is performed independently from the global image representation - typically from deep networks - with which they are fused [4, 8].

Contributions. This work makes three contributions to part-based image categorization using only weakly-supervised global image labels:

1. Three part types relevant for image categorization are established, which are all naturally shared between categories when learning a part-representation for image categorization. The part types are *Own* (the same class), *Other* (other classes), and *Context* (background) parts. Figure 3 shows the importance of each part type, as all types provide different information relevant for image categorization. The Figure furthermore shows that plotting top scoring part scores provide spatial information about what makes an image category discriminative, without no spatial annotations have been provided.
2. An algorithm is presented for part selection, sharing, and image categorization based on boosting. It embeds all three part types, without the need for explicit part type definition.
3. A shared fusion technique, called *bootstrap fusion*, for combining part-based models with global image representations.

By identifying the three part types and by jointly optimizing the part selection, part sharing, and image categorization, we arrive at a more discriminative and more compact part-based image representation.

Experiments. The experimental evaluation is performed on four image datasets consisting of objects, scenes, actions, and fine-grained bird classes. In the first experiment, we evaluate relevance of each of the three parts types. The results show that on average, all three part types improve results and are complementary to each other. Naturally, *Own* parts are most relevant. Surprisingly, this part type is not always most relevant. For example for the object Sofa, it is more relevant to have parts of dogs and cats, than to have parts of sofa itself, as sofas are typically photographed with animals resting on them.

In subsequent experiments, it is shown that the introduced algorithms improve over separately optimized alternatives on all datasets for several limits on the number of parts selected in the image representations. State-of-the-art results are achieved when applying the proposed bootstrap fusion between the part-based and global image representation, further improving over the very deep convolutional neural networks of [21, 24]. These results indicates the importance of optimizing for all three part types and the importance of sharing parts for image categorization.

4. SPOT ON

The fourth publication, *Spot On: Action Localization from Point Supervision*, will be presented at ECCV 2016 [17]. This work aims to detect and localize actions in both space and time in videos. Given a video, the goal is to state which action occurs and to yield a bounding box around each frame in which the action occurs, called a tube.

Starting from a sliding window legacy [25], the common approach these days is to generate tube proposals at test time, encode each of them with a feature embedding, and

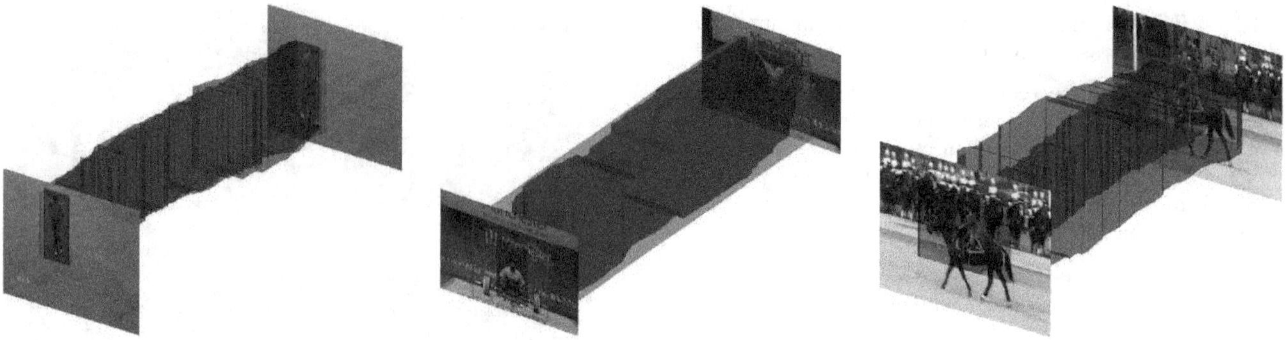

(a) *Walking.* (b) *Lifting.* (c) *Riding horse.*

Figure 4: **Spot on** (publication 4) challenges the need for box annotations to train action localization classifiers. Rather than using boxes (red), point annotations are used to mine the most suitable proposals for training the classifiers (blue).

select the most relevant one, e.g., [6, 29, 26, 23]. All these works, be it sliding windows or tube proposals, assume that a carefully annotated training set with boxes per frame is available a priori. Such strong supervision is tremendously expensive and cumbersome for human annotators. As such, current action localization dataset are sparse and contain a small amount of videos.

Contributions. This paper challenges the need for bounding box annotations for action localization. An algorithm is proposed that leverages proposals at training time, with a minimum amount of supervision, to speedup action location annotation. Rather than annotating boxes, we propose to annotate actions in video with points on a sparse subset of frames only. Overall, the following contributions are reported:

1. This work proposes to train action localization classifiers using spatio-temporal proposals as positive examples, rather than ground truth tubes. While common in object detection, such an approach is as of yet unconventional in action localization. In fact, it will be shown that using proposals does not lead to a decrease in action localization accuracy.

2. A Multiple Instance Learning algorithm is introduced that is able to mine a proposal with a good spatio-temporal fit to the action of interest by including point supervision. It extends the traditional MIL's objective with an overlap measure that takes into account the affinity between proposals and points.

3. With the aid of the proposal mining algorithm, the complete Hollywood2 dataset by Marszałek et al. [11] is supplemented with action location annotations resulting in *Hollywood2Tubes*, which will be made publicly available.

Experiments. The effectiveness of point annotation for action localization is evaluated through four experiments. In the first experiment, it is shown that using the proposals discovered by the proposed proposal mining to train classifiers is equally effective as using strong box annotations. In the second experiment, it is shown that not all frames need to be annotated with a point. A reduction of up to 90% (i.e. annotating every 10th frame) provides enough supervision for effective action localization. The third experiment evaluates the localization performance on the newly introduced *Hollywood2Tubes* dataset. The fourth experiment compares the approach of this work to the current state-of-the-art, where it outperforms other weakly-supervised approaches and is even competitive to strongly supervised results.

Figure 4 provides three qualitative examples of training videos with strong annotations (red) and mined proposals (blue). With the proposed approach, the strong box annotations are no longer required; using point supervision, proposals can be mined that yield equally strong localization performance.

5. CONCLUSIONS

The goal of my PhD dissertation is to leverage weakly-supervised annotations to recognize, localize, and explain visual entities in images and videos. The highlighted publications aim to leverage weak supervision to reason in the temporal, spatial, and spatio-temporal domains. The current publications offer several opportunities for future work. These opportunities include combining the pre-trained deep networks from The ImageNet Shuffle to improve the Bag-of-Fragments video representation. Furthermore, the notion of point supervision in the spatio-temporal domain (publication 4) can be extended to other domains or multimedia problems.

Acknowledgements

This research is supported by the STW STORY project.

6. REFERENCES

[1] S. Bhattacharya, F. X. Yu, and S.-F. Chang. Minimally needed evidence for complex event recognition in unconstrained videos. In *ICMR*, 2014.

[2] L. Bossard, M. Guillaumin, and L. Van Gool. Food-101–mining discriminative components with random forests. In *ECCV*, 2014.

[3] J. Deng, W. Dong, R. Socher, L.-J. Li, K. Li, and L. Fei-Fei. ImageNet: A large-scale hierarchical image database. In *CVPR*, 2009.

[4] C. Doersch, A. Gupta, and A. A. Efros. Mid-level visual element discovery as discriminative mode seeking. In *NIPS*, 2013.

[5] I. Everts, J. C. van Gemert, and T. Gevers. Evaluation of color spatio-temporal interest points for human action recognition. *TIP*, 23(4), 2014.

[6] M. Jain, J. Van Gemert, H. Jégou, P. Bouthemy, and C. G. M. Snoek. Action localization with tubelets from motion. In *CVPR*, 2014.

[7] L. Jiang, S.-I. Yu, D. Meng, Y. Yang, T. Mitamura, and A. G. Hauptmann. Fast and accurate content-based semantic search in 100m internet videos. In *MM*, 2015.

[8] M. Juneja, A. Vedaldi, C. V. Jawahar, and A. Zisserman. Blocks that shout: Distinctive parts for scene classification. In *CVPR*, 2013.

[9] I. Laptev, M. Marszalek, C. Schmid, and B. Rozenfeld. Learning realistic human actions from movies. In *CVPR*, 2008.

[10] J. Liu, Q. Yu, O. Javed, S. Ali, A. Tamrakar, A. Divakaran, H. Cheng, and H. Sawhney. Video event recognition using concept attributes. In *WACV*, 2013.

[11] M. Marszałek, I. Laptev, and C. Schmid. Actions in context. In *CVPR*, 2009.

[12] M. Mazloom, A. Habibian, and C. G. M. Snoek. Querying for video events by semantic signatures from few examples. In *ACM MM*, 2013.

[13] M. Merler, B. Huang, L. Xie, G. Hua, and A. Natsev. Semantic model vectors for complex video event recognition. *TMM*, 14(1), 2012.

[14] P. Mettes, D. C. Koelma, and C. G. M. Snoek. The imagenet shuffle: Reorganized pre-training for video event detection. *ICMR*, 2016.

[15] P. Mettes, J. C. van Gemert, S. Cappallo, T. Mensink, and C. G. M. Snoek. Bag-of-fragments: Selecting and encoding video fragments for event detection and recounting. In *ICMR*, 2015.

[16] P. Mettes, J. C. van Gemert, and C. G. M. Snoek. No spare parts: Sharing part detectors for image categorization. *CVIU*, 2016.

[17] P. Mettes, J. C. van Gemert, and C. G. M. Snoek. Spot on: Action localization from pointly-supervised proposals. *ECCV*, 2016.

[18] M. Nagel, T. Mensink, and C. G. M. Snoek. Event fisher vectors: Robust encoding visual diversity of visual streams. In *BMVC*, 2015.

[19] S. N. Parizi, A. Vedaldi, A. Zisserman, and P. Felzenszwalb. Automatic discovery and optimization of parts for image classification. *ICLR*, 2015.

[20] O. Russakovsky, J. Deng, H. Su, J. Krause, S. Satheesh, S. Ma, Z. Huang, A. Karpathy, A. Khosla, M. Bernstein, et al. Imagenet large scale visual recognition challenge. *IJCV*, 115(3):211–252, 2015.

[21] K. Simonyan and A. Zisserman. Very deep convolutional networks for large-scale image recognition. In *ICLR*, 2015.

[22] C. G. M. Snoek, S. Cappallo, D. Fontijne, D. Julian, D. C. Koelma, P. Mettes, K. E. A. Sande, A. Sarah, H. Stokman, and R. B. Towal. Qualcomm research and University of Amsterdam at trecvid 2015: Recognizing concepts, objects, and events in video. *TRECVID workshop*, 2015.

[23] K. Soomro, H. Idrees, and M. Shah. Action localization in videos through context walk. In *ICCV*, 2015.

[24] C. Szegedy, W. Liu, Y. Jia, P. Sermanet, S. Reed, D. Anguelov, D. Erhan, V. Vanhoucke, and A. Rabinovich. Going deeper with convolutions. In *CVPR*, 2015.

[25] Y. Tian, R. Sukthankar, and M. Shah. Spatiotemporal deformable part models for action detection. In *CVPR*, 2013.

[26] J. C. van Gemert, M. Jain, E. Gati, and C. G. M. Snoek. APT: Action localization proposals from dense trajectories. In *BMVC*, 2015.

[27] H. Wang and C. Schmid. Action recognition with improved trajectories. In *ICCV*, 2013.

[28] Z. Xu, Y. Yang, and A. G. Hauptmann. A discriminative cnn video representation for event detection. *CVPR*, 2015.

[29] G. Yu and J. Yuan. Fast action proposals for human action detection and search. In *CVPR*, 2015.

Zero-Example Multimedia Event Detection and Recounting with Unsupervised Evidence Localization

Yi-Jie Lu
Department of Computer Science, City University of Hong Kong
yijie.lu@my.cityu.edu.hk

ABSTRACT

Retrieval of a complex multimedia event has long been regarded as a challenging task. Multimedia event recounting, other than event detection, focuses on providing comprehensible evidence which justifies a detection result. Recounting enables "video skimming", which not only enhances video exploration, but also makes human-in-the-loop possible for improving the detection result. Most existing systems treat event recounting as a disjoint post-processing step over the result of event detection. Unlike these systems, this doctoral research aims to provide an in-depth understanding of how recounting, i.e., evidence localization, helps in event detection in the first place. It can potentially benefit the overall design of an efficient event detection system with or without human-in-the-loop. More importantly, we propose a framework for detecting and recounting everyday events without any needs of training examples. The system only takes a text description of an event as input, then performs evidence localization, event detection and recounting in a large, unlabelled video corpus. The goal of the system is to take advantage of event recounting which eventually improves zero-example event detection. We present preliminary results and work in progress.

Keywords

Multimedia Event Detection; Video Search; Zero Example; Event Recounting

1. INTRODUCTION

The exponential growth of web videos in the past decade has posed significant needs in developing broad video understanding techniques for content indexing and searching. Multimedia event detection is one of the challenging task intended for understanding high-level content in videos, which is typically characterized by objects, actions, activities, scenes, and the complex interactions between them [14]. Techniques for recognizing a complex multimedia event have been developing for years, and due to its difficulty, still attracting a lot of attention among researchers [25]. While event detection focuses on retrieval of videos that contain relevant event, event recounting complements event detection by providing comprehensible evidence that justifies a detection result. For example, what confides a video clip belonging to the event of "changing a car tyre"? One may expect appearances of a car, a zoomed-in shot of a tyre, and a lug wrench. However, any single appearance of such evidence does not necessarily justify the video clip. *Key evidence* such as an action of a person removing an old tyre with a wrench is crucial to discriminate a true positive. Notwithstanding the difference of importance, the evidence provides an explanation for a detection result, which can be used to enhance user experience for video browsing.

Most existing works treat event recounting as a disjoint post-processing step on top of the event detection result [16, 29]. Widely-used approaches in event detection such as average and max pooling take all sampled frames of a video into account [18, 19]. But the content relevant to an event in a video is usually scattered along the timeline [33]. Collecting information from all the frames would inevitably bring noise into the video representation. Therefore, we think that event recounting should benefit event detection in the first place by localizing key evidence in videos, thus forming a purified video representation. Although several works have already explored either ranking the importance of temporal regions [33], or jointly optimizing both detection and recounting [3], they need training examples to discover the discriminative evidence. In contrast, we conduct study under the zero-example scenario, which does not use training examples. We propose zero-example event detection with unsupervised evidence localization that helps improve the detection accuracy.

On the other hand, although there are known studies which automatically discover discriminative evidence given training examples, few provide insights on how evidence can help human make decisions. We stress the benefit of involving human-in-the-loop especially for zero-example event detection because it is an applicable way to quickly distinguish the *near-miss* videos – videos of a different event that are visually similar to the query event. Figure 1 illustrates examples of near-miss videos. We find near-miss videos widely exist in everyday events, but are difficult to be discriminated by a machine learner. While it is still possible to learn a specialized classifier to distinguish them, the fine details that can distinguish a near-miss video are trivial to learn and are not generalizable across events, not to mention it requires extensive human labeling to identify the near-miss

MM'16 October 15–19, 2016, Amsterdam, The Netherlands
© 2016 ACM ISBN 978-1-4503-3603-1/16/10 ...$15.00
DOI: http://dx.doi.org/10.1145/2964284.2971480

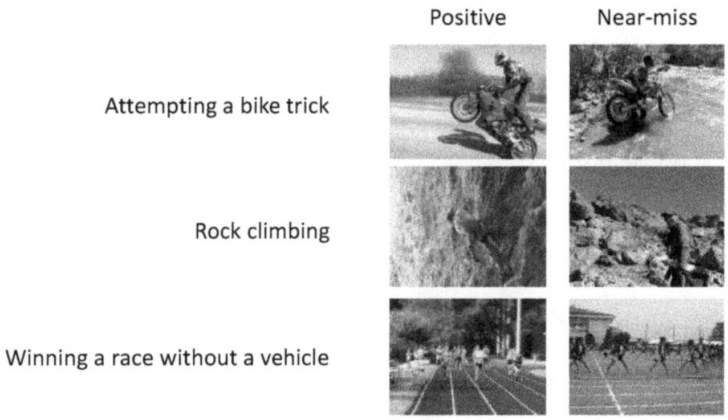

Figure 1: Examples of near-miss videos in different events. The near misses from top to bottom are: carrying a motorbike across the river, trekking over a rock hill, and doing setting-up exercise on the field.

videos. This problem becomes more crucial in zero-example scenario because a zero-example event detection system has to leverage a general knowledge base to relate textual information to visual information. Obviously, it is not feasible to prepare a knowledge base recognizing fine details that can distinguish the near-miss videos before hand. However, a human can identify decades of near-miss videos in a second as long as the evidence presented is sufficient for a human to make a decision. This renders the value of studying a better evidence presentation which eases human's judgement.

This doctoral research aims to have two outputs: First, an in-depth understanding of event recounting, both for how evidence localization can directly improve event detection performance, and for how evidence presentation can help a human make quick judgements. Second, an overall zero-example detection framework that can incorporate the benefit of event recounting with or without human-in-the-loop. The rest of the paper is organized as follows: Related work and contributions regarding the state of the art is discussed in the next section. Section 3 presents an overview of the proposed framework and approaches. Section 4 discusses the preliminary results and ongoing work.

2. STATE OF THE ART

Multimedia event detection usually needs training examples. Event detectors are trained by low-level features [7, 24, 30] or semantic features [9, 10, 26] that are directly extracted from training videos. *Zero-example* multimedia event detection (0Ex) is an emerging topic yet to be explored. In contrast to zero-shot learning which focuses on the recognition of images with unseen labels, 0Ex emphasizes the use of general and external knowledge for textual-to-visual relation. A decent 0Ex system usually consists of a semantic concept library as knowledge base, and a good search module that handles video ranking given a collection of concepts. A few pilot studies were proposed very recently [4, 31]. These works built a small concept library, typically hundreds of concepts, for textual-to-visual relation. More recent work starts to resort to a larger concept library. Ye et al. [32] collected a dataset with 500 events in which more than 4,000 concepts were hierarchically organized. Singh et al. [27] automatically discovered salient visual concepts by web search according to the text query. In event search phase, Habibian et al. [8] indexed concepts with AND/OR constraints. Chang et al. [2] proposed a rank aggregation framework that addressed the incomparable scales of scores when merging concepts from different feature spaces. Jiang et al. studied pseudo relevance feedback [12] and self-paced reranking [11] that further improved the performance by reranking. Jiang et al. [13] also systematically investigated 0Ex problem. This state-of-the-art work explored the contribution of multiple features including thousands of concepts, as well as the performance of several search models.

The primary concern of multimedia event recounting is the localization of key evidence that can discriminate an event. A related topic in recent research trends is semantic pooling [33], which suggests to only pool the evidential parts that are semantically important to an event query [20, 33]. The idea is based on the underlying assumption that important evidence is sparsely scattered in a video's timeline, thus aggregating all keyframes like average pooling [18, 19] would collect a bunch of junk information. Yu et al. [33] learned the concept importance of a small concept set and pooled the low-level features according to the importance of their related concepts. Mettes et al. [20] clustered the keyframes into fragment proposals and learned the importance of each proposal. Lately, more complex work tends to optimize the event detection by jointly discovering the evidence, given that a good recounting should assist detection in the first place [3, 28], rather than only interpret a detection result [6]. On the other hand, Bhattacharya et al. [1] conducted a user study and found that a human can recognize most events by only looking into very few sample segments of a video. Inspired by this finding, we develop unsupervised evidence localization which takes query words to locate key evidence in a video. We perform event detection merely on the evidence in order to improve the detection performance.

Our contributions relative to the state of the art are two-fold:

- We propose unsupervised evidence localization under the framework of zero-example event detection, which is different from previous work that utilizes training examples. The evidence localization serves to improve event detection accuracy in the first place, rather than only explain the detection result.
- We provide insights on event recounting aiming to find a better evidence presentation that eases human's judgement.

3. PROPOSED APPROACH

Figure 2 illustrates the overall zero-example framework. The system only takes a text event query as input, then retrieves and recounts videos in a large, unlabelled video corpus. The core of the framework is a large concept bank containing concept detectors of objects, scenes, actions, and activities. The semantic concepts in the concept bank provide essential prior knowledge for text-to-visual relation.

In the offline phase, all frames of videos are uniformly extracted from the video corpus, and are represented by a concept-based representation in which each dimension represents the likelihood of presence of a particular concept. In the online phase, given an event query, e.g. "cleaning an appliance" with detailed text explanation, the noun and verb phrases are first extracted as tokens by an NLP parser. Then these tokens are mapped to an internal query representation called *semantic query* by concept matching. In

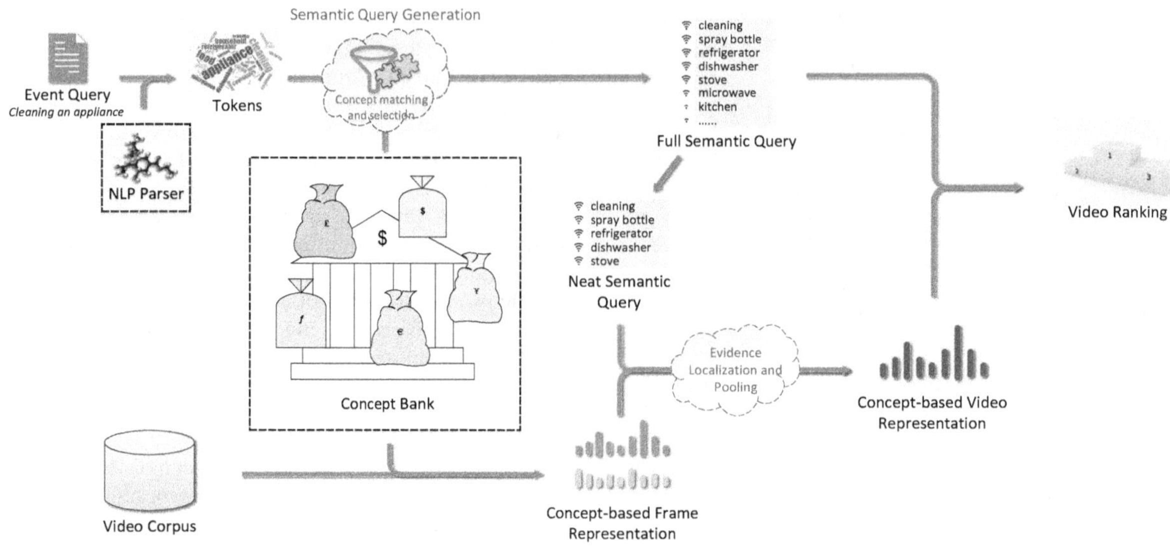

Figure 2: The overall framework for zero-example event detection with unsupervised evidence localization.

this way, the query is converted to the concept-based representation as well. Having the semantic query, we seek to derive a *neat semantic query* which only retains the most important relevant concepts. This neat semantic query is used for evidence localization in all videos, and then pooling over the evidence, thus forming a neat concept-based video representation. Finally, event search is performed having all the concept-based representations of both queries and videos.

There are two cruxes in this framework that have a large impact on the event detection performance. The first crux is the concept matching and selection in semantic query generation. We have conducted extensive study on how to pick up concepts in the concept bank for query representation [23, 17]. This includes various similarity measurements, such as TFIDF, WordNet [22] and Word2Vec [21]. Basically, the performance of TFIDF and Word2Vec similarities fall in the same scale. WordNet barely works in zero-shot event detection. We also find the selection of a few relevant concepts crucial to event detection performance [17]. The second crux is the representation of video by evidence. It includes an objective goal which aims to improve the detection accuracy and a subjective goal which aims to promote a better evidence presentation for human judgments. As this is an on-going study, we elaborate these two goals in the following sections.

3.1 Unsupervised evidence localization

Unsupervised evidence localization is intended to improve the performance of zero-example event detection. The localization process basically takes the neat semantic query as input and ranks the frames of a video according to their similarities to the query. The adjacent keyframes can be agglomerated to a shot if they are of similar importance. Then video representation is formed by average pooling over the evidence (keyframes or shots that are of top importance). Our preliminary study suggests that only three pieces of evidence are sufficient for a video representation that generates good performance (Table 1). This new representation has a notable benefit: It is robust to noisy concepts when using the full semantic query to perform the video search, which is the final step in Figure 2. In addition, this representation is not sensitive to the choice of the neat semantic query: We find the performance is relatively the same if simply choosing the top 2 to 16 concepts in the full semantic query as the neat semantic query.

We also study various methods for evidence localization. A typical variation is to cluster the frames of a video before hand, and rank the clusters by importance rather than rank the frames. Bisecting K-means is used to track each split of the clustering for analysis. We include the preliminary results in the experiment section, but the specific settings for clustering and pooling are not discussed in this paper.

3.2 Event recounting

Event recounting aims to provide a user with better understanding that can justify an event detection result. As discussed in Section 1, considering human-in-the-loop is an efficient way to address the near-miss problem. The key criterions to be considered here are the importance of evidence and user experience. Specifically, how fast a user can declare that a video is relevant by reading the presented evidence? General speaking, the goal is to display the minimal amount of evidence in the shortest possible time. To optimize both criterions, we will consider three aspects of information: (1) *concept-to-event relevancy* which prioritizes the importance of concepts to events, (2) *evidence diversity* which avoids redundancy by suggesting evidences of diverse content, and (3) *the shorter the better* which recommends only thumbnails that are just sufficient and necessary to evidence the presence of event. We will conduct user studies and design appropriate optimization algorithms on top of the evidence localization module that can integrate different criterions for event recounting.

4. EXPERIMENTS AND DISCUSSIONS

The experiments are conducted on the TRECVID Multimedia Event Detection (MED) datasets. We use the event kits that contain 20 event queries from E021 to E040. The

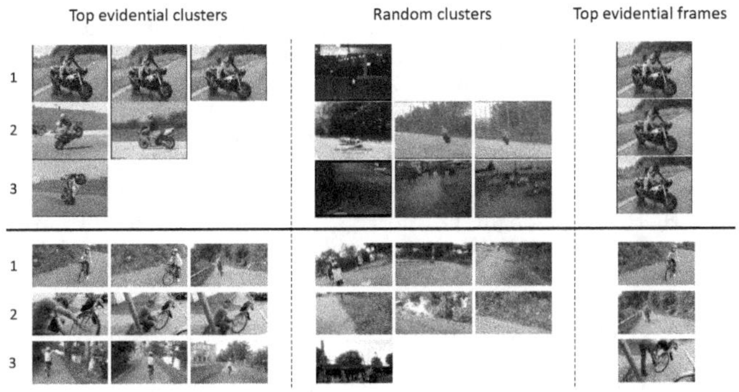

Figure 3: Visual examples of three evidential pooling methods for the event "attempting a bike trick". Two videos are listed: The one on the top is a true positive; bottom a false positive. Three pieces of evidence are presented for each video and for each method. Note that for clustering method, as the size of a cluster is varied, we present at most three frames for a cluster.

test set, named MED14Test, includes around 25,000 testing videos with no textual metadata. The performance is evaluated by the standard metric Mean Average Precision (MAP).

For preliminary experiments, we build a concept bank containing a total of 2,048 semantic concepts with varied granularity. They are sourced from off-the-shelf datasets with concept types covering most common objects, scenes, and actions. The four datasets are *ImageNet* 1000 concepts [5], *SIN* 346 concepts [34], *Places* 205 concepts [35] and *Research Collection* 497 concepts [23]. Except *ImageNet*, all the datasets are individually fine-tuned with AlexNet DCNN structure [15] on their own data. The concept responses are extracted for each frame uniformly sampled from a test video at the pace of two seconds one frame. The responses among different datasets are concatenated, forming a 2,048 dimensional feature vector. The individual performance of each dataset on MED14Test was reported in [17].

4.1 Obtained Results

Other than the results we previously reported [23, 17], the new results are mostly from the portion of the system discussed in Section 3.1. Table 1 summarizes the performance of various evidence localization settings. The best method is the video representation with only three evidential clusters, which improves average pooling by 88%. Surprisingly, the much simpler and time-efficient method using three evidential keyframes/shots without clustering can already achieve the MAP of 0.094. Meanwhile, we use the same number of random selected clusters as counterpart. The performance difference between evidential clusters and random selected clusters justifies the benefit of evidence localization. Figure 3 shows insights of three typical methods, which somewhat explains the result in Table 1. The key information for a human to justify a video is easily spotted in evidential clusters, while random clusters usually lie in segments not helpful to make a judgement. Evidential frames, on the other hand, may need more focus for a judge to make a decision than evidential clusters. It also has more tendencies to neglect key evidence due to imperfection of evidence localization.

The state of the art for automatic zero-example event detection has the MAP of 0.115 [13]. But different from our preliminary experiment settings, they used almost twice as many concepts, including event-level concept detectors such as Sports-1M. Sports-1M was proved to have significant contribution to the performance. However, due to the lacking of frame-level concept responses, we haven't yet included any event-level detectors into our concept pool for preliminary comparisons.

Video Representation Method	*MAP*
3 evidential clusters	0.0979
3 evidential keyframes/shots	0.0936
10 evidential clusters	0.0900
10 evidential keyframes/shots	0.0879
Average pooling	0.0522
10 random clusters	0.0488
Max pooling	0.0485
3 random clusters	0.0461

Table 1: Performance summarization of different video representation methods on MED14Test.

4.2 Work in Progress

Currently, we primarily focus on the research described in Section 3.2, that is to promote a better evidence presentation for involving human in the loop. This will include extensive user studies. We have already found that, although clustering does not significantly improve the detection performance, presenting the evidence in clusters can reduce both human's judgement time and judgement error. This is because clustering can help organize duplicate evidence, thus increasing the evidence diversity. We are still trying more ways of evidence presentation and comparing human's experience between the different ways.

Acknowledgement

This work was supported in part by the National Natural Science Foundation of China (No. 61272290), and the National Hi-Tech Research and Development Program (863 Program) of China under Grant 2014AA015102.

5. REFERENCES

[1] S. Bhattacharya, F. X. Yu, and S.-F. Chang. Minimally needed evidence for complex event recognition in unconstrained videos. In *ACM ICMR*, pages 105–112, 2014.

[2] X. Chang, Y. Yang, A. G. Hauptmann, E. P. Xing, and Y.-L. Yu. Semantic concept discovery for large-scale zero-shot event detection. In *IJCAI*, 2015.

[3] X. Chang, Y.-L. Yu, Y. Yang, and A. G. Hauptmann. Searching persuasively: Joint event detection and evidence recounting with limited supervision. In *ACM MM*, pages 581–590. ACM, 2015.

[4] J. Dalton, J. Allan, and P. Mirajkar. Zero-shot video retrieval using content and concepts. In *CIKM*, pages 1857–1860. ACM, 2013.

[5] J. Deng, W. Dong, R. Socher, L.-J. Li, K. Li, and L. Fei-Fei. ImageNet: A Large-Scale Hierarchical Image Database. In *CVPR*, 2009.

[6] N. Gkalelis, V. Mezaris, I. Kompatsiaris, and T. Stathaki. Video event recounting using mixture subclass discriminant analysis. In *ICIP*, pages 4372–4376, Sept 2013.

[7] A. Habibian, T. Mensink, and C. G. Snoek. Videostory: A new multimedia embedding for few-example recognition and translation of events. In *ACM MM*, pages 17–26, 2014.

[8] A. Habibian, T. Mensink, and C. G. M. Snoek. Composite concept discovery for zero-shot video event detection. In *ACM ICMR*, pages 17–24, 2014.

[9] A. Habibian, K. E. van de Sande, and C. G. Snoek. Recommendations for video event recognition using concept vocabularies. In *ACM ICMR*, pages 89–96, 2013.

[10] L. Jiang, A. G. Hauptmann, and G. Xiang. Leveraging high-level and low-level features for multimedia event detection. In *ACM MM*, pages 449–458, 2012.

[11] L. Jiang, D. Meng, T. Mitamura, and A. G. Hauptmann. Easy samples first: Self-paced reranking for zero-example multimedia search. In *ACM MM*, pages 547–556, 2014.

[12] L. Jiang, T. Mitamura, S.-I. Yu, and A. G. Hauptmann. Zero-example event search using multimodal pseudo relevance feedback. In *ACM ICMR*, pages 297–304, 2014.

[13] L. Jiang, S.-I. Yu, D. Meng, T. Mitamura, and A. G. Hauptmann. Bridging the ultimate semantic gap: A semantic search engine for internet videos. In *ACM ICMR*, pages 27–34, 2015.

[14] Y.-G. Jiang, S. Bhattacharya, S.-F. Chang, and M. Shah. High-level event recognition in unconstrained videos. *International Journal of Multimedia Information Retrieval*, 2(2):73–101, 2013.

[15] A. Krizhevsky, I. Sutskever, and G. E. Hinton. Imagenet classification with deep convolutional neural networks. In F. Pereira, C. Burges, L. Bottou, and K. Weinberger, editors, *Advances in Neural Information Processing Systems 25*, pages 1097–1105. Curran Associates, Inc., 2012.

[16] K.-T. Lai, D. Liu, M.-S. Chen, and S.-F. Chang. Recognizing complex events in videos by learning key static-dynamic evidences. In *ECCV*, pages 675–688. Springer, 2014.

[17] Y.-J. Lu, H. Zhang, M. de Boer, and C.-W. Ngo. Event detection with zero example: Select the right and suppress the wrong concepts. In *ACM ICMR*, 2016.

[18] M. Mazloom, A. Habibian, and C. G. Snoek. Querying for video events by semantic signatures from few examples. In *ACM MM*, pages 609–612, 2013.

[19] M. Merler, B. Huang, L. Xie, G. Hua, and A. Natsev. Semantic model vectors for complex video event recognition. *IEEE Transactions on Multimedia*, 14(1):88–101, Feb 2012.

[20] P. Mettes, J. C. van Gemert, S. Cappallo, T. Mensink, and C. G. Snoek. Bag-of-fragments: Selecting and encoding video fragments for event detection and recounting. In *ACM ICMR*, pages 427–434, 2015.

[21] T. Mikolov, I. Sutskever, K. Chen, G. S. Corrado, and J. Dean. Distributed representations of words and phrases and their compositionality. In *NIPS*, pages 3111–3119, 2013.

[22] G. A. Miller. Wordnet: A lexical database for english. *Commun. ACM*, 38(11):39–41, Nov. 1995.

[23] C.-W. Ngo, Y.-J. Lu, H. Zhang, T. Yao, C.-C. Tan, and L. Pang. VIREO-TNO @ TRECVID 2014: Multimedia event detection and recounting (MED and MER). In *NIST TRECVID Workshop*, 2014.

[24] S. Oh, S. Mccloskey, I. Kim, A. Vahdat, K. J. Cannons, H. Hajimirsadeghi, G. Mori, A. G. Perera, M. Pandey, and J. J. Corso. Multimedia event detection with multimodal feature fusion and temporal concept localization. *Mach. Vision Appl.*, 25(1):49–69, Jan. 2014.

[25] P. Over, G. Awad, M. Michel, J. Fiscus, W. Kraaij, A. F. Smeaton, G. Queenot, and R. Ordelman. TRECVID 2015 – an overview of the goals, tasks, data, evaluation mechanisms and metrics. In *Proceedings of TRECVID 2015*. NIST, USA, 2015.

[26] B. Safadi, M. Sahuguet, and B. Huet. When textual and visual information join forces for multimedia retrieval. In *ACM ICMR*, pages 265–272, 2014.

[27] B. Singh, X. Han, Z. Wu, V. I. Morariu, and L. S. Davis. Selecting relevant web trained concepts for automated event retrieval. In *ICCV*, pages 4561–4569, Dec 2015.

[28] C. Sun and R. Nevatia. Discover: Discovering important segments for classification of video events and recounting. In *CVPR*, pages 2569–2576, June 2014.

[29] C.-Y. Tsai, M. L. Alexander, N. Okwara, and J. R. Kender. Highly efficient multimedia event recounting from user semantic preferences. In *ACM ICMR*, pages 419:419–419:422. ACM, 2014.

[30] F. Wang, Z. Sun, Y.-G. Jiang, and C.-W. Ngo. Video event detection using motion relativity and feature selection. *IEEE Transactions on Multimedia*, 16(5):1303–1315, Aug 2014.

[31] S. Wu, S. Bondugula, F. Luisier, X. Zhuang, and P. Natarajan. Zero-shot event detection using multi-modal fusion of weakly supervised concepts. In *CVPR*, pages 2665–2672, June 2014.

[32] G. Ye, Y. Li, H. Xu, D. Liu, and S.-F. Chang. Eventnet: A large scale structured concept library for complex event detection in video. In *ACM MM*, pages 471–480. ACM, 2015.

[33] Q. Yu, J. Liu, H. Cheng, A. Divakaran, and H. Sawhney. Semantic pooling for complex event detection. In *ACM MM*, pages 733–736, 2013.

[34] W. Zhang, H. Zhang, T. Yao, Y. Lu, J. Chen, and C.-W. Ngo. VIREO @ TRECVID 2014: instance search and semantic indexing. In *NIST TRECVID Workshop*, 2014.

[35] B. Zhou, A. Lapedriza, J. Xiao, A. Torralba, and A. Oliva. Learning deep features for scene recognition using places database. In *NIPS*, pages 487–495, 2014.

Emerging Topics in Learning from Noisy and Missing Data

Xavier Alameda-Pineda
University of Trento
Trento, Italy
xavier.alamedapineda@unitn.it

Timothy M. Hospedales
Queen Mary University
London, UK
t.hospedales@qmul.ac.uk

Elisa Ricci
FBK / Univ. of Perugia
Trento, Italy / Perugia, Italy
eliricci@fbk.eu

Nicu Sebe
University of Trento
Trento, Italy
sebe@disi.unitn.it

Xiaogang Wang
The Chinese University of Hong Kong
Hong Kong, China
xgwang@ee.cuhk.edu.hk

ABSTRACT

While vital for handling most multimedia and computer vision problems, collecting large scale fully annotated datasets is a resource-consuming, often unaffordable task. Indeed, on the one hand datasets need to be large and variate enough so that learning strategies can successfully exploit the variability inherently present in real data, but on the other hand they should be small enough so that they can be fully annotated at a reasonable cost. With the overwhelming success of (deep) learning methods, the traditional problem of balancing between dataset dimensions and resources needed for annotations became a full-fledged dilemma. In this context, methodological approaches able to deal with partially described data sets represent a one-of-a-kind opportunity to find the right balance between data variability and resource-consumption in annotation. These include methods able to deal with noisy, weak or partial annotations. In this tutorial we will present several recent methodologies addressing different visual tasks under the assumption of noisy, weakly annotated data sets.

Keywords

Noisy and missing data; Low rank models; Zero-shot learning; Deep learning

1. COURSE DESCRIPTION

In the last decades the bond between machine learning, computer vision and multimedia has strengthened and a large variety of powerful learning frameworks have emerged for the automatic analysis of visual data. Earlier works addressed visual tasks considering the ideal condition in which features were complete and labels were available for all training samples. The research community soon realized that acquiring fully described data sets for certain tasks was resource-consuming, and often not affordable. Exemplar tasks are classification of web images, social signal processing in unrestricted environments, face analysis in the wild or the recognition of subjective properties of images and videos. In the last few years, the success of data-hungry deep architectures has made this problem even more evident. Indeed, data sets need to be large and variate enough so that neural network-based learning strategies can successfully exploit the variability inherently present in real data, and small enough so that they can be fully annotated at a reasonable cost. In this context, methodological approaches able to deal with noisy, weak or partial annotations are of particular interest.

In this tutorial we will present several recent methodologies addressing different visual tasks under the assumption of noisy, weakly annotated data sets. Special emphasis will be given to methods based on deep architectures for unsupervised domain adaptation [6, 5], low-rank modeling for learning in transductive settings and zero-shot learning [3]. We will show how these approaches exhibit excellent performance in crucial tasks such as pedestrian detection or fine-grained visual recognition. Furthermore, we will discuss emerging application domains which are of great interest to the multimedia community and where handling noisy or missing information is essential. For instance, we will present recent works on multimodal complex scene analysis using wearable sensors [2], on the estimation of physiological signals from face videos in realistic conditions [4], and on the recognition of emotions elicited from abstract paintings [1].

1.1 Outline

The total duration of the tutorial is 3 hours. The topics to be covered (including estimated duration of each topic) are:

- Introduction: challenges in learning from noisy and missing data (30 min)
- Robust low-Rank modeling and transductive learning in emerging application domains (60 min)
- Zero-shot learning (45 min)
- Unsupervised domain adaptation in deep neural architectures (45 min)

MM '16 October 15-19, 2016, Amsterdam, Netherlands

ACM ISBN 978-1-4503-3603-1/16/10.

DOI: http://dx.doi.org/10.1145/2964284.2986910

2. TARGET AUDIENCE

The intended audience (intermediate/advanced level) is (i) researchers interested in vision and multimedia applications necessitating robust learning approaches and (ii) researchers interested in sparse modelling and deep learning in scarcely labeled setting. Slides of the presentations and code associated to the main algorithms presented in the course will be distributed to the audience.

3. RELATED TUTORIALS

This tutorial will provide an overview of very recent methodologies for addressing an increasingly pressing need in multimedia and computer vision: the possibility to learn robust models from noisy and partially annotated datasets.

This one-of-a-kind course (recent tutorials do not specifically focus on this topic) will be of great interest for the research community, both from the methodological and from the application perspective. Specifically, this tutorial will introduce several algorithms for handling noisy, partially annotated data, focusing on recent learning paradigms, such as low rank modelling, deep learning and domain adaptation. The methodologies that will be presented in this short course (e.g. zero-shot learning, deep domain adaptation and matrix completion) have not been considered in previous tutorials. Furthermore, we will discuss emerging application scenarios which benefit from the proposed techniques and are of great interest for the multimedia community, given recent related tutorials in the areas of social signal processing and human-centric visual content analysis:

- Emotional and Social Signals for Multimedia Research (ACM MM 2015),
- Human-centric images and videos analysis (ACM MM 2015),
- Social Multimedia Computing: A User-centric Perspective (ICME 2015).

4. BIOGRAPHIES

Xavier Alameda-Pineda received his PhD from INRIA and University of Grenoble in 2013. He was a post-doctoral researcher at CNRS/GIPSA-Lab. Currently he holds a research fellowship at the University of Trento, in the Deep Relational Group, working on signal processing and machine learning for scene and behavior understanding using multimodal data. He is the IEEE WASPAA 2015 best student paper award winner and the ACM Multimedia 2015 best paper prize winner.

Timothy Hospedales is a Senior Lecturer (associate professor) at Queen Mary University of London. He leads the Applied Machine Learning lab at QMUL, studying applications of weakly supervised, transfer and cross-modal learning within computer vision and multimedia. He was area chair of WACV 2016 and BMVC 2015 best paper prize winner.

Elisa Ricci is a researcher at FBK and an assistant professor at the University of Perugia. She received her PhD from the University of Perugia in 2008. She has been a post-doctoral researcher at Idiap and FBK, Trento and a visiting researcher at the University of Bristol. Her research interests are directed along developing machine learning algorithms for video scene analysis, human behavior understanding and multimedia content analysis. She is area chair of ACM MM 2016 and of ECCV 2016.

Nicu Sebe is a full professor in the University of Trento, Italy, where he is leading the research in the areas of multimedia information retrieval and human behavior understanding. He was a General Co-Chair of FG 2008 and ACM MM 2013, and a program chair of CIVR 2007 and 2010, and ACM MM 2007 and 2011. He is a program chair of ECCV 2016 and ICCV 2017. He is a senior member of IEEE and ACM and a fellow of IAPR.

Xiaogang Wang received the PhD degree in Computer Science from Massachusetts Institute of Technology in 2009. He is an associate professor in the Department of Electronic Engineering at the Chinese University of Hong Kong. He received the Outstanding Young Researcher in Automatic Human Behavior Analysis Award in 2011, HK RGC Early Career Award in 2012, and Young Researcher Award of the Chinese University of Hong Kong. He was the area chair of ICCV 2011, ICCV 2015, ECCV 2014, 2016 and ACCV 2014. His research interests include computer vision, deep learning, crowd video surveillance, object detection, and face recognition.

5. REFERENCES

[1] X. Alameda-Pineda, E. Ricci, Y. Yan, and N. Sebe. Recognizing emotions from abstract paintings using non-linear matrix completion. In *Proceedings of the IEEE Conference on Computer Vision and Pattern Recognition*, pages 5240–5248, Las Vegas, USA, 2016.

[2] X. Alameda-Pineda, Y. Yan, E. Ricci, O. Lanz, and N. Sebe. Analyzing free-standing conversational groups: a multimodal approach. In *Proceedings of the 23rd ACM international conference on Multimedia*, pages 5–14, Brisbane, Australia, 2015.

[3] Y. Fu, T. M. Hospedales, T. Xiang, and S. Gong. Transductive multi-view zero-shot learning. *IEEE Transactions on Pattern Analysis and Machine Intelligence*, 37(11):2332–2345, 2015.

[4] S. Tulyakov, X. Alameda-Pineda, E. Ricci, L. Yin, J. F. Cohn, and N. Sebe. Self-adaptive matrix completion for heart rate estimation from face videos under realistic conditions. In *Proceedings of the IEEE Conference on Computer Vision and Pattern Recognition*, pages 2396–2404, Las Vegas, USA, 2016.

[5] T. Xiao, T. Xia, Y. Yang, C. Huang, and X. Wang. Learning from massive noisy labeled data for image classification. In *Proceedings of the IEEE Conference on Computer Vision and Pattern Recognition*, pages 2691–2699, Boston, USA, 2015.

[6] X. Zeng, W. Ouyang, M. Wang, and X. Wang. Deep learning of scene-specific classifier for pedestrian detection. In *European Conference on Computer Vision*, pages 472–487, Zurich, Switzerland, 2014.

The Lifecycle of Geotagged Multimedia Data

Rossano Schifanella
University of Turin
Turin, Italy
schifane@di.unito.it

Bart Thomée
Yahoo Labs
San Francisco, CA, USA
bthomee@yahoo-inc.com

ABSTRACT

The world is a big place. At any given instant something is happening somewhere, but even when nothing is going on people still find ways to generate multimedia data, ranging from social media posts, to photos and videos. A substantial number of these media objects is associated with a location, and in an increasingly mobile and connected world (both in terms of people and devices), this number is only bound to get larger. Yet, in the multimedia literature we observe that many researchers often unwittingly treat the geospatial dimension as if it were a regular feature dimension, despite it requiring special attention. In order to avoid pitfalls and to steer clear of erroneous conclusions, this tutorial aims to teach researchers and students how geotagged multimedia data differs from regular data and to educate them on best practices when dealing with such data. We will cover the lifecycle of geotagged data in multimedia research, where the topics range from how this kind of data is *represented*, *processed*, *analyzed*, and *visualized*. The tutorial requires both passive and active involvement, where we not only present the material, but the attendees also get the opportunity to interact with it using a variety of open source data and tools that we have prepared using a virtual machine.

Keywords

Geospatial, geotagged, multimedia data.

1. OUTLINE

The tutorial is organized in 4 modules that cover the main phases of the lifecycle of geotagged multimedia data in research. Each module will be about 60 minutes long with each unit divided in 45 minutes of frontal lecture and 15 minutes of interactive session where the participants will play with the data and the tools introduced in the module to solve a real problem.

Module 1: Represent *Instructed by Bart Thomee.* We present common ways of representing geographic data, from simple coordinates to polygons with holes, and using different data formats. We discuss different world models and how to perform projections of data that are represented using different coordinate reference systems. A hands-on session will let the attendees play with real geotagged data to get familiar with a number of data representations and projections, and will let them solve a problem by combining geographic data from multiple sources.

Module 2: Process *Instructed by Rossano Schifanella.* We cover techniques for determining the distance between geographic coordinates, computing areas of and overlaps between polygons, and how the data representation influences which techniques should (not) be used. We discuss different strategies for efficiently storing, reading and querying geotagged data, such as indexes, as well as for efficiently processing the data. We will let the attendees experience all these facets of processing geotagged data themselves.

Module 3: Analyze *Instructed by Bart Thomee.* We cover a variety of techniques the attendees can use to derive actionable insights from geotagged multimedia data. We present methods like clustering and density estimation, and applications like predicting locations and recommending activities. We show how geotagged data differs from traditional data and often requires special considerations in order to obtain reliable output.

Module 4: Visualize *Instructed by Rossano Schifanella.* The world is not flat, so visualizing geographic data is not straightforward. We present the attendees several tools that can assist them to better understand the data. A hands-on session will let them understand how to effectively use the right tool at the right time to maximize the knowledge they can extract from the data.

In the field of GIS research there have been several conferences and tutorials covering a wide range of topics, e.g. related tutorials held at GeoInfo 2015[1]. There are also initiatives related to the use of a specific technology or set of tools to mine spatial data, e.g. tutorials held at PyData 2015[2]. In contrast with these initiatives, the main objective of this tutorial is to arm attendees with both theoretical and practical knowledge about the whole process of making sense of geospatial data, rather than focusing on specific technologies and tools. The tutorial aims to provide a broad vision of all the processes and technologies available to researchers,

MM '16 October 15-19, 2016, Amsterdam, Netherlands

ACM ISBN 978-1-4503-3603-1/16/10.

DOI: http://dx.doi.org/10.1145/2964284.2986911

[1]http://www.geoinfo.utm.my/jointgeoinfo2015/tutorial.html

[2]http://nyc2015.pydata.org/schedule/presentation/7/

and our tutorial centers on the basics of geospatial understanding to convey best practices when dealing with such data. In addition, we center on how geospatial data is different from other kinds of data, and therefore requires special considerations when representing, processing, analyzing and visualizing.

2. AUDIENCE

This introductory tutorial targets all researchers and students that want to learn more about how to properly work with geotagged multimedia data. It provides information to get complete novices started, while at the same time do not shy away from presenting advanced representation, processing and visualization techniques for those interested in a deeper understanding of geographic data. Due to the broad scope and our primary focus on the basics and best practices of working with geospatial data, the tutorial could be potentially appealing also for the *European Conference on Computer Vision* (ECCV) audience that will be held in conjunction with *ACM Multimedia*.

3. MATERIAL

The tutorial material is published on the tutorial website[3] at least one week before the event to give time to the attendees to explore the material needed to successfully complete the interactive sessions assignments in advance. The tutorial web site constains a general description of the topics covered and for each module it makes available:

- Slides presented by the tutor during the lecture.
- Links to external material referred to in the slides.
- Development environment used in the interactive session.

The tutorial web site provides a detailed how-to for setting up the development environment. To minimize the attendees effort and have a homogeneous platform for each participant we will make a virtual machine available that provides all the tools, libraries, code, examples, exercises, and data in an easy-to-install cross-platform package. For last minute registrants we will have the virtual machine stored on a portable hard disk for them to copy onto their own laptops. Our tutorial does not require internet connectivity, but can benefit from it when available.

4. BIOGRAPHIES

Rossano Schifanella is an Assistant Professor in Computer Science at the University of Turin, Italy, where he is a member of the Applied Research on Computational Complex Systems group. He is a former visiting scientist at Yahoo Labs and at the Center for Complex Networks and Systems Research at the Indiana University where he was applying computational methods to model social behavior in online platforms. His research embraces the creative energy of a range of disciplines across technology, computational social science, data visualization, and urban informatics. He is passionate about building new mapping tools that capture the sensorial layers of a city [1, 2], and designing computational frameworks to model aesthetics [4], creativity [3], and figurative language in multimedia platforms.

[3]http://www.di.unito.it/~schifane/geocycle-acmmm16/

Bart Thomee is a Senior Research Scientist at Flickr/Yahoo Labs in San Francisco, CA, USA. His research focuses on the visual and spatiotemporal dimensions of media, in order to better understand how people experience and explore the world and how to better assist them with doing so [5, 6, 7]. He led the development of the YFCC100M [8] dataset released in 2014, and previously was part of the efforts leading to the creation of both MIRFLICKR datasets. He has furthermore been part of the organization of the ImageCLEF photo annotation tasks 2012–2013, the MediaEval placing tasks 2013–2016, and the ACM MM Yahoo-Flickr Grand Challenges 2015–2016. In addition, he has served on the program committees of, amongst others, ACM MM, ICMR, SIGIR, ICWSM and ECIR. Last year, he was part of the Steering Committee of the Multimedia COMMONS workshop at ACM MM and will co-chair the workshop this year; he also co-organized last year's TAIA workshop at SIGIR.

5. REFERENCES

[1] D. Quercia, R. Schifanella, and L. Aiello. The shortest path to happiness: Recommending beautiful, quiet, and happy routes in the city. In *Proceedings of the ACM Conference on Hypertext and Social Media*, pages 116–125, 2014.

[2] D. Quercia, R. Schifanella, L. Aiello, and K. McLean. Smelly maps: The digital life of urban smellscapes. In *Proceedings of the AAAI International Conference on Weblogs and Social Media*, 2015.

[3] M. Redi, N. O'Hare, R. Schifanella, M. Trevisiol, and A. Jaimes. 6 seconds of sound and vision: Creativity in micro-videos. In *Proceedings of the IEEE Conference on Computer Vision and Pattern Recognition*, pages 4272–4279, 2014.

[4] R. Schifanella, M. Redi, and L. Aiello. An image is worth more than a thousand favorites: Surfacing the hidden beauty of flickr pictures. In *Proceedings of the AAAI International Conference on Web and Social Media*, 2015.

[5] B. Thomee, I. Arapakis, and D. Shamma. Finding social points of interest from georeferenced and oriented online photographs. *ACM Transactions on Multimedia Computing, Communications, and Applications*, 12(2):36, 2016.

[6] B. Thomee and G. De Francisci Morales. Automatic discovery of global and local equivalence relationships in labeled geo-spatial data. In *Proceedings of the ACM International Conference on Hypertext and Social Media*, pages 158–168, 2014.

[7] B. Thomee and A. Rae. Uncovering locally characterizing regions within geotagged data. In *Proceedings of the IW3C2 International Conference on World Wide Web*, pages 1285–1296, 2013.

[8] B. Thomee, D. Shamma, G. Friedland, B. Elizalde, K. Ni, D. Poland, D. Borth, and L. Li. YFCC100M: The new data in multimedia research. *Communications of the ACM*, 59(2):64–73, 2016.

Technology & Art in Stimulating Creative Placemaking in Public-Use Spaces

Wendy Ann Mansilla
wendy.mansilla@ntnu.no

Andrew Perkis
andrew@iet.ntnu.no

Norwegian University of Science and Technology
Department of Electronics and Telecommunications
7491 Trondheim, Norway

ABSTRACT

In this tutorial we are going to elaborate on how technology and art can contribute in stimulating creative placemaking in public-use spaces. This presentation will highlight the authors approach and several other past and potential approaches that embrace on technology and connectivity to refocus on a creative function in public spaces that aims to move away from traditional planning and textbook concepts. Our approach, which is demonstrated by our design and implementation of a multi-use public space called "*Adressaparken*" is aimed to create a space towards greater flexibility, changeability, and appreciation for the public`s contribution.

The presenters will also identify key lessons learned in the design and implementation of a technology re-usable public space. Potential variables needed to address the challenges in the integration and evaluation of digital public art installations will also be elaborated. By surveying past and present exhibited contributions and the presenters' own contributions in a public realm, this tutorial will offer guidance to artists, designers, researchers and practitioners on how they can successfully blend in to this interdisciplinary area of research.

Keywords

Technology and Art; Design; Public Space, Collaboration; Pokémon Go game, Creative Placemaking.

1. MOTIVATION

In the last decades, several scholars argued that public spaces are moving away from its intended use and function leading to the so-called "*decline of the city*". Along with the increasing interaction between digital and physical space, the evolution of technology is changing urban landscapes and public's behavior towards it. Richard Sennet [9] discusses the concept of the "*theatrum mundi*" (the theater of the world), a place of performance for strangers, where he attempted to convey the "*union of aesthetics and social reality*". Sennett contrasted the life of the 18th-century *theatrum mundi* to that of the 19th century self-absorption, of little interest in the world beyond our own lives - the "*me generation*". Sennett argues that public relations in the 18th century were more "*theatricality*" of the public than "*representation*" of self, which Sennett sees as more conducive to public life than of present times.

Furthermore, Sennett argued that there has emerged what he called the "*intimate society*", in which individuals confuse public affairs as something personal, and social matters are regarded only as opportunities for self-disclosure. As he himself puts it, "*The self no longer concerns man as actor or man as maker; it is a self composed of intentions and possibilities. Intimate society has entirely reversed* [Henry] *Fielding's dictum that praise or censure should apply to actions rather than actors; now what matters is not what you have done but how you feel about it. [10]*"

Sennett`s thesis can make us ponder if public life left no place for us to take part in the physical realm other than our own. John Hanke, founder of the augmented reality-meets-GPS game *Pokémon Go* offers an alternative observation, he said that when players were asked about the *Pokémon Go* game, "*Why are you playing this game? Why are you doing this? Is it weird that people are out in the middle of the night?" The response is, "It's amazing, it changed my life. I've met so many new people; I'm seeing the world in a completely different way. I'm walking three miles a day and I was housebound and watching TV all day before I started playing this game*" [7].

The growing use of *Pokémon Go*, which launched last July 6, 2016, has resulted to a positive effect on public space use and awareness. The so-called self-absorbed and introverted public is now starting to socialize with stranger while exploring unfamiliar places.

In public art as well as in gaming, the persistence of the "decline of the city" led to the increasing need for collaborative thinking, discovery process, and action. To address this phenomenon collaborators coined the terms "*creative placemaking*" [5] and "*hackable citymaking*" [11]. These terms demand that in order for a public space to be considered as a place for participation, creative practitioners, such as enthusiasts, designers, artists, architects, and urban planners must function in this environment as more than simple creators, but rather as creative collaborators.

To promote creative placemaking (or hackable citymaking) and to acknowledge the need for multi-use infrastructures to facilitate evolving individual`s needs, we have designed a public space called "*Adressaparken*" [8]. *Adressaparken* is located in the heart of Trondheim City, Norway adjacent to the main office of the regional newspaper. It was built to provide a technological

MM'16, October 15–19, 2016, Amsterdam, The Netherlands.
ACM ISBN 978-1-4503-3603-1/16/10.
DOI: http://dx.doi.org/10.1145/2964284.2986912

infrastructure for digital public art and technology installations, multimedia exhibitions, and various gaming platforms. Throughout this tutorial the presenters will use the lessons learned from *Adressaparken* to bring the participants in this course closer to understanding what a technologically enhanced public-use space is.

2. TUTORIAL OVERVIEW

This half-day tutorial is broken down into the following topics and activities:

1. *Introduction (40 minutes):* Technology and other new forms of aesthetics are changing expectations and needs of individuals in a public sphere (e.g. [2] [4] [6]). But exactly how a technology such as *Pokémon Go* game or how an artwork such as Rafael Lozano-Hemmer`s "*Pulse Park*" [3] is encouraging people to engage with public spaces has become a major topic of discussion. This tutorial will look upon the meteoric success of the *Pokémon Go* game and other digital public installations to think creatively about how we can use digital technologies to enable interactions and narratives in real places such as *Adressaparken.*

   Like any gaming environment, *Pokémon Go`s* popularity will eventually reach its peak and decline, but what lasting lessons can we learn from it? In the same way, the lessons learned and challenges from hosting and implementing several public art installations at *Adressaparken* will be explored.

   Furthermore, this tutorial will outline and discuss potential new fields of research and practices in a technologically enhanced public sphere.

2. *Digital Art and Gaming Project showcases (20 minutes):* Several art and gaming contribution will be highlighted to explore and discuss the technology, tools and interactions employed to design and produce engaging public art and gaming works.

3. *Designing Interactive Experience for creative placemaking (20 minutes):* This tutorial has prepared a modified version of the *Hackable Cities* toolkit [1] to fit into the *Adressaparken*`s infrastructure and environment. The modified step-by-step *Hackable Cities* toolkit will be presented to help the participants better understand how interactive experiences can be designed and implemented for creative placemaking.

4. *Designing and Implementing Adressaparken (40 minutes):* The presenters' process of designing the infrastructure will be shown and the technology enabler and tools in the *Adressaparken* will be highlighted.

5. *Pitch your own Public Art/Gaming Project with us! (30 - 40 minutes):* Participants in this tutorial will be requested to form a group. The presenters will ask the participants to take the role of a team that have been granted an access to *Adressaparken* for an art installation or a gaming project. Based on the description of *Adressaparken`s* multi-use technology and infrastructure, participants will be asked to generate a concept or an idea of a project that can promote creative citymaking practices in *Adressaparken.* The team with the best concept gets a chance to use *Adressaparken.*

6. *Open Discussion:* The floor will be opened for discussions and question. Collaboration possibilities or interested parties who would like to use *Adressaparken* to create their own projects are invited in this section.

3. MATERIALS

Selected materials including the outcome of the *"Pitch your own Public Art/Gaming Project" section in this tutorial* will be available at https:*//www.ntnu.edu/thepark/.*

4. REFERENCES

[1] Bilak M., et al. (2014). Hackable Cities: A toolkit for re-imagining your neighborhood. Retrieved from: *https://issuu.com/pgildner/docs/hackable-cities-pages* [Accessed 1st August 2016].

[2] de Souza e Silva A., Frith J. (2012). *Mobile Interfaces in Public Spaces: Locational Privacy, Control, and Urban Sociability.* New York: Routledge.

[3] Hemmer L. (2008). Pulse Park. Retrieved from: *http://www.lozano-hemmer.com/pulse_park.php* [Accessed 1st August 2016].

[4] Hampton, K.N., Sessions Goulet, L., Albanesius, G. (2014). Change in the social life of urban public spaces: The rise of mobile phones and women, and the decline of aloneness over 30 years. *Urban Studies*, pp. 1-16.

[5] Kent F., Nikitin C. (2011). Collaborative placemaking: good public art depends on good public spaces. *Public Art Review*, (45).

[6] Mansilla, W. A. (2013). *Quality of Aesthetic Experience and Implicit Modulating Factors.* Ph.D. Thesis. University of Science and Technology: Norway.

[7] Peckham M. (2016). Meet the Mastermind Behind This Summer's Pokémon Craze. Retrieved from: *Time.com/4404282/pokemon-go-john-hanke/* [Accessed 3rd August 2016].

[8] Perkis A., (2015). Adressaparken. Retrieved from: *https://www.ntnu.edu/thepark/* [Accessed 7th August 2016].

[9] Sennet, R. (1977). *The Fall of the Public Man.* New York: Knopf.

[10] Sennet, R (2016). The intimate lives of others. Retrieved from: *http://www.spiked-online.com/spiked-review/article/the-intimate-lives-of-others/17977#.V7J43o4tyr0* [Accessed 7th August 2016].

[11] The Hackable City Research (2012). Retrieved from: *http://thehackablecity.nl/* [Accessed 3rd August 2016].

Situation Recognition from Multimodal Data

Vivek K. Singh
Rutgers University
New Brunswick, NJ, USA
v.singh@rutgers.edu

Siripen Pongpaichet
University of California, Irvine
Irvine, CA, USA
spongpai@ics.uci.edu

Ramesh Jain
University of California, Irvine
Irvine, CA, USA
jain@ics.uci.edu

Keywords

Events; Situation Recognition; Concept Detection; Event Detection; Multimedia Data Fusion

1 EXTENDED ABSTRACT

Situation recognition is the problem of deriving actionable insights from heterogeneous, real-time, big multimedia data to benefit human lives and resources in different applications. This tutorial will discuss the recent developments towards converting multitudes of data streams including weather patterns, stock prices, social media, traffic information, and disease incidents into actionable insights.

For multiple decades, multimedia researchers have been building approaches like entity resolution, object detection, and scene recognition, to understand different aspects of the observed world. Unlike the past though, now we do not need to undertake sense-making based on data coming from a single media element, modality, time-frame, or location of media capture. Real world phenomena are now being observed by multiple media streams, each complementing the other in terms of data characteristics, observed features, perspectives, and vantage points. Each of these multimedia streams can now be assumed to be available in real-time and increasingly larger portion of these come inscribed with space and time semantics. The number of such media elements available (e.g. tweets, Flickr posts, sensor updates) is already in the order of trillions, and computing resources required for analyzing them are becoming increasingly available. We expect these trends to continue and one of the biggest challenges in multimedia computing in the near term to be that of concept recognition from such multimodal data. As shown in Figure 1, the challenges in situation recognition are fundamentally different from those in object or event recognition. They involve dealing with multiple media, each capturing real world phenomena from multiple vantage locations spread over time.

Detecting situations in time to take appropriate actions for saving lives and resources can transform multiple aspects of human life including health, natural disaster, traffic, economy, social reforms, business decisions and so on. Examples of such relevant situations include beautiful-days/ hurricanes/ wildfires, traffic (jams/ smooth/ normal), economic-recessions/ booms, block-busters, droughts/ great-monsoons, seasons (early-fall/ fall/ late-fall), demonstrations/ celebrations, social uprisings/ happiness-index, flash-mobs, flocking and so on.

MM '16 October 15-19, 2016, Amsterdam, Netherlands

ACM ISBN 978-1-4503-3603-1/16/10.
DOI: http://dx.doi.org/10.1145/2964284.2986913

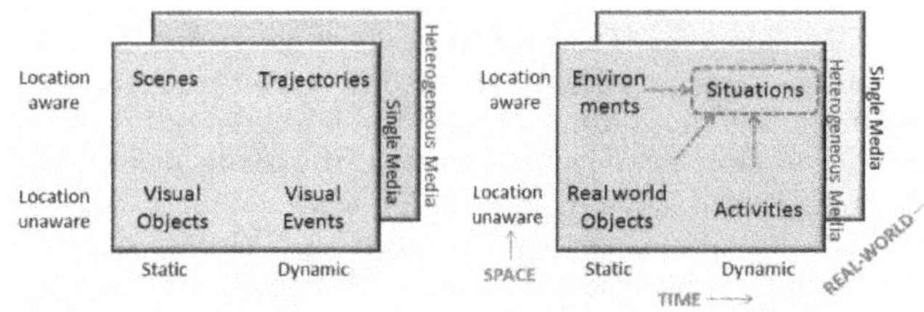

Figure 1: Different types of concepts can be detected in different data availability settings. Single media, such as images, results in concepts more in images than in the real world, but using different media it is possible to detect concepts in the real world.

This tutorial will provide the audience with a thorough theoretical will bring together the work by multiple scholars working in the area of situation recognition both within and outside the multimedia research community. The attendees would be introduced to the different interpretations of situations across multiple fields, and how it builds upon and extends the efforts on object detection, event detection, scene recognition and so on. The tutorial will provide a review of recent efforts within the multimedia community towards detecting real-time situations, and the attendees will be introduced to multiple practical situation recognition approaches and applications. Specific attention will be paid to discussing the relevant open research challenges for the community to extensively advance the state of the art in situation recognition.

Learning objectives: At the end of the tutorial the attendees should be able to

1. Describe the problem of situation recognition and how it is different from object detection, event recognition, scene understanding etc.
2. Outline the different interpretations of situations across different fields e.g. multimedia, ubiquitous computing, robotics, aviation etc.
3. Articulate a computational definition for the concept of "situation" and the problem of situation recognition.
4. Identify the important categories of operators needed for the task of situation recognition.
5. Relate to the practical experience of creating at least one practical situation recognition application using an open-source situation recognition toolkit.
6. Articulate the emerging trends in situation-based computing and identify the open challenges in the field of situation recognition.

2 MODULES OF THE TUTORIAL

1) Concept recognition from Multimedia data

As shown in Figure 1, ***Situation recognition*** builds on and extends object recognition, scene recognition, activity and event recognition, and complex event processing. It pushes the envelope beyond detecting ***intra-media concepts*** (i.e. those which manifest themselves, and can be detected within a single media object e.g. a tree, or a chair in an image), to define and making quick progress on detecting ***real-world concepts*** (i.e. those which occur in real world, are constantly evolving, and inherently manifest themselves over heterogeneous multimedia streams from numerous sources). As a simple example, we may now look beyond the problem of creating a *tree* detector and/or testing it over Millions of Flickr images; to that of using a stream of Billions of such images and other available data to detect seasonal patterns, plant disease spreads, deforestation trends, or global warming. These are the problems which could not be tackled earlier because of the lack of data and computational resources; but those are no longer the bottlenecks.

2) Situation recognition across multiple domains There has been a large amount of work done in the areas like ubiquitous/pervasive computing building automation, mobile application software, aviation/air traffic control, robotics, industrial control, military command and control, surveillance, linguistics, stock market databases, multimodal presentation, about situation modeling, situation awareness, situation calculus, situation control, and situation semantics (*c.f.* [5, 2]). The interpretation of *situation* however is different across different areas and even across different works within the same area. Multiple such interpretations will be discussed and the differences as well as the commonalities in these interpretations will be identified.

3) Situation recognition
To combine heterogeneous real-time data streams into actionable situations, one may focus on the spatio-temporal commonality across streams to integrate them. A recent approach proposed in the multimedia community focuses on using a simple unified representation (called Emage, *E*vent-based-i*mage*, as shown in Figure 2), that indexes and organizes all data into a common representation. Similarly, for going from individual data nuggets (micro-events) to macro-situations it uses a set of generic spatio-temporal analysis operators [3, 4]. Other researchers have identified variants of this representation called *Cmages* (*C*oncept-based-i*mages*) to allow for concept-based-images that can be created using heterogeneous data and allow for information fusion and situation recognition [6]. Yet other set of researchers have defined a *FraPPE* (*Fra*me, *P*ixel, *P*eople, *E*vents) ontology for combining heterogeneous spatio-temporal data into actionable insights [1]. A common thread in all these approaches is the unified representation of heterogeneous data as pixels and defining analytics operators on them. The salient points of these approaches and the application of the defined operators for situation recognition will be discussed.

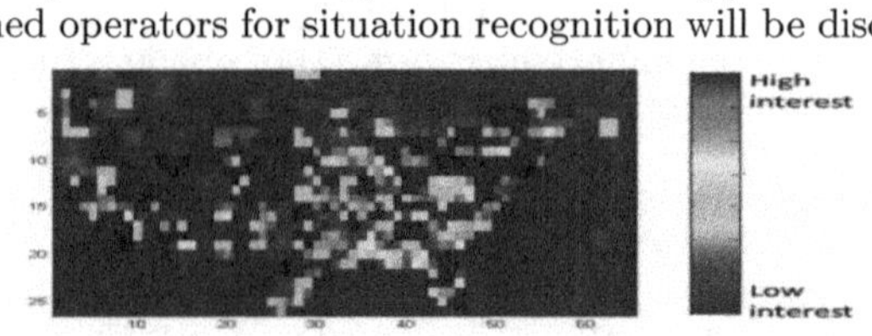

Figure 2: An Emage showing user interest across mainland USA in terms of number of tweets containing the term 'iPhone' on 11th June 2009

4) Designing situation based applications
Participants will be exposed to multiple platforms that support integration of heterogeneous multimedia data for situation recognition. The open-source framework of EventShop focuses on declarative operators that work on top of the Emage representation [3]. The FraPPE model works on an ontology model and employ a human in the loop to undertake Visual Analytics [1]. The tutorial will discuss multiple examples, and the participants will get hands-on experience with creating one practical application - asthma risk score for any location.

5) Future trends and open problems
There exist multiple open problems in situation recognition. These include issues of scalability, network based models for situations, data discovery, dealing with data uncertainty, and spatio-tempoal concept detection. Consequently there lie tremendous opportunities in leveraging and repurposing multimedia processing techniques (e.g. convolution, vector representation, optical flow) for analysis of spatio-temporal gridded data and spatio-temporal situation recognition. Further, newer trends in computational crowd-sourcing and human-in-the-loop methods for multimedia processing tasks can be used for distributed multimedia data generation and processing. This tutorial will encourage multimedia researchers to tackle these problems.

3 IMPORTANCE AND RELEVANCE TO MULTIMEDIA RESEARCH COMMUNITY

Multimedia research community is particularly well positioned to take on the challenge of situation recognition. First, the community's core competence lies in handling heterogeneous media (audio, video, text, phone logs, microblogs, sensors etc.). Equally importantly, it is the only research community which has studied concept detection across both time (event detection), and space (like spatial organization of pixels in images). The tools for raster image processing translate directly onto spatial data layouts and notions of neighborhood, regions, boundaries, and motion vectors translate seamlessly across to spatio-temporal analysis. Recognizing situations in the right place at the right moment to take appropriate actions can save lives and resources in various aspects of human life. For instance, approximately 250,000 people die prematurely each year from asthma attacks, and almost all of these deaths are avoidable. Asthma patients can be notified to avoid the places that can cause their asthma attacks when they are in critical situation. Similar applications of situation recognition lie in areas including emergency evacuations, business analytics, and epidemic detection.

4 REFERENCES

[1] M. Balduini, E. Della Valle, M. Azzi, R. Larcher, F. Antonelli, and P. Ciuccarelli. Citysensing: visual story telling of city-scale events by fusing social media streams and call data records captured at places and events. *IEEE MultiMedia*, 22(3), 2015.

[2] C. Dousson, P. Gaborit, and M. Ghallab. Situation recognition: representation and algorithms. In *IJCAI*, volume 93, pages 166–172, 1993.

[3] V. K. Singh, M. Gao, and R. Jain. Social pixels: genesis and evaluation. In *Proc. Int. Conf. on Multimedia*, pages 481–490. ACM, 2010.

[4] V. K. Singh, M. Gao, and R. Jain. Situation recognition: an evolving problem for heterogeneous dynamic big multimedia data. In *Proc. Int. Conf. on Multimedia*, pages 1209–1218. ACM, 2012.

[5] V. K. Singh and R. Jain. *Situation Recognition using EventShop*. Springer; Auflage: 1st ed. 2016, 2016.

[6] Y. Wang and M. S. Kankanhalli. Tweeting cameras for event detection. In *Proc. Int. Conf. on World Wide Web*, pages 1231–1241. ACM, 2015.

Social and Affective Robotics Tutorial

Maja Pantic[1,2], Vanessa Evers[2], Marc Deisenroth[1], Luis Merino[3] and Bjoern Schuller[4,1]
[1]Imperial College London, Exhibition Road, London SW7 2AZ, UK
[2]University of Twente, Drienerlolaan 5, 7522 NB Enschede, Netherlands
[3]Pablo de Olavide University, 41013 Sevilla, Spain
[4]University of Passau, Innstrasse 43, 94032 Passau, Germany
m.pantic@imperial.ac.uk; v.evers@utwente.nl; m.deisenroth@imperial.ac.uk; lmercab@upo.es; bs@fim.uni-passau.de

ABSTRACT
Social and Affective Robotics is a growing multidisciplinary field encompassing computer science, engineering, psychology, education, and many other disciplines. It explores how social and affective factors influence interactions between humans and robots, and how affect and social signals can be sensed and integrated into the design, implementation, and evaluation of robots. With talks by renowned researchers in this area, Social and Affective Robotics Tutorial will help both new and experienced researchers to identify trends, concepts, methodologies and applications in this field, identified as a technological megatrend driving the fourth industrial revolution.

CCS Concepts
• Computing methodologies ⊙ Artificial Intelligence
• Computing methodologies ⊙ Machine Learning • Human-centered computing.

Keywords
Affective computing, Social robotics, Machine Learning, Signal Processing, Robotic Planning.

1. INTRODUCTION
Until recently, the use of robots was confined to tightly controlled tasks in specific industries such as automotive. Today, however, robots are increasingly used across all sectors and for a wide range of tasks from precision manufacturing to nursing. Rapid progress in robotics makes naturalistic interaction between humans and machines an everyday reality. Advances in sensors, computer vision, audio processing, and machine learning, are enabling robots to understand their environment and their users better and, in turn, to become more adaptive and flexible, responding better and engaging in a broader variety of tasks such as household chores, tourists guiding, education, autism research, healthcare, etc. As robots become capable of sensing and responding to the context in which they (and their human users) operate, the next generation of robots emerges, where the emphasis will be on human-machine collaboration. Collaborative Robotics are a technological megatrend expected to reach its tipping point – the moment when it hits mainstream society – in the next ten years [1], shaping our AI-empowered future and robot-aided personal ecosystem. Social and Affective Robotics Tutorial will identify concepts, methodologies, and trends in this burgeoning field and explore some of the ethical and psychological questions raised by human-machine relations.

The tutorial is divided into seven main parts: five talks on the main aspects of Affective and Social Robotics including sensing affect and social signals, machine learning, and socially-adaptive navigation and planning, an interactive demo session exhibiting a number of socially-aware and affective robots, and a panel discussion revolving around technological, ethical, and psychological questions raised by this robotic technology driving the fourth industrial revolution.

MM'16, October 15–19, 2016, Amsterdam, The Netherlands.
ACM ISBN 978-1-4503-3603-1/16/10.
DOI: http://dx.doi.org/10.1145/2964284.2986914

2. TALKS
2.1 The Rise of Social Robotics
Robotics and AI are expected to leave factory floors and to co-inhabit our homes, our schools, our hospitals and our streets. These environments are social and if the technology put in these environments isn't socially intelligent, it is likely that it will not be accepted by human users. The talk by Prof. Vanessa Evers explains the core idea behind making machines socially intelligent – that sentient beings need social referencing to learn – and identifies technical challenges that need to be addressed in order to realize the full potential of this technology.

2.2 Robot Social Navigation
Robots acting among humans require social awareness when performing their tasks. This has to be considered in each step, from high-level planning and supervision, to motion planning and execution. The talk by Dr. Luis Merino identifies different techniques employed for robot social navigation, including techniques for human-aware motion planning, learning users' navigation intention models and social cost functions from observations, planning based on the learned models, and how all these different techniques can be combined to achieve social navigation.

2.3 Machine Learning for Robotics
One of the fundamental challenges in fully autonomous robots is learning from data directly. This requires data-driven statistical methods for modeling, predicting, and decision making, while taking uncertainty into account, e.g., due to measurement noise, sparse data, or stochasticity in the environment. A practical challenge that comes with autonomous robots is that learning needs to be efficient – performing millions of experiments with robots is time consuming and wears out the hardware. The talk by Dr. Marc Deisenroth identifies practical algorithms for data-efficient learning in robotics and discusses further challenges and opportunities in the field.

2.4 Visual Affect & Social Signals Sensing

While the physiognomy (and the dynamics) of the face serves to identify other members of our species, facial behavior is our preeminent means to communicating affective and social signals. The talk by Prof. Maja Pantic summarizes a number of aspects of the human face and facial behavior and how they can be automatically sensed and analyzed by computers. Past research in the field and how far are we from enabling robots to identify and verify human users and sense and recognize human facial expressions and behavior are discussed in greater detail.

2.5 Auditory Affect & Social Signals Sensing

Speech processing technology is the crux to making human-robot interaction more intuitive, more efficient, and more naturalistic. To reach this goal, rich speaker traits and personal states, carried by the tone of the voice and the spoken words, must be reliably identified by machines. The talk by Prof. Bjoern Schuller explains novel holistic and time-evolving techniques for multi-task and weakly supervised learning of universal speaker characteristics, which have been considered only in isolation so far. The talk will also discuss overcoming today's sparseness of annotated realistic speech data by large-scale speech and meta-data mining from public sources (e.g., social media, crowd-sourcing for labelling and quality control, and shared semi-automatic annotation).

3. DEMOS

Attendees will be able to take part in an interactive exhibition were the Tutorial organizers showcase examples of the Social and Affective robotics technology in action.

3.1 FROG Robot

Imagine the local Zoo guide or the info kiosk in Disneyland being replaced by an attentive robot. This is exactly what FROG Robot is! There are two FROG robots, the red one and the green one. The red one is the info bot and messenger between buildings at the University of Twente, Netherlands. The green one is tourist guide bot at Royal Alcazar in Seveille, Spain. FROG is pretty much autonomous – it spots and approached people, shows them around based on its automatic estimation of their interest level, and then moves on to the next group. The red FROG will be shown in Amsterdam in October 2016. For a video of FROG see: https://www.facebook.com/FrogEU/videos/1515431328741253/.

3.2 TERESA Robot

TERESA is a tele-presence robot built upon the commercially available Giraff robot, which consists of a video screen attached to a base with wheels. The robot is controlled by a user at a remote location, whose face is displayed on the robot's video screen. The robot has a camera, microphone and a speaker to enable video conferencing. The user remotely interacts with people by guiding a remotely located robot, allowing the user to be more physically present than with standard teleconferencing. TERESA is socially intelligent in that it navigates semi-autonomously among groups of people, maintains face-to-face contact during conversations, and displays appropriate body-pose behavior. For a video synopsis see: https://www.youtube.com/watch?v=eaDYa6TIMQM. For more info see: http://teresaproject.eu

3.3 "Mimic Me" with NAO Robot

"Mimic-Me" is an interactive game played with the NAO robot. It is designed to engage both typically developing and autistic children, to raise their interest in information and communication technologies (ICT), and in the later case, to help autistic kids to practice the recognition and display of facial expressions of emotions. The game involves the robot 'mimicking' the player's expression using a combination of body gestures and audio cues. The robot interacts with players in a naturalistic way by automatically recognizing their speech, head movements, and facial expressions [2]. The "Mimic-Me" game is implemented as a modular, loosely coupled, software system using the HCI^2 Framework [3]. As a result, the system and its modules can be easily reused, or extended, for the purposes of other studies on human-robot interactions. For a video synopsis of "Mimic-Me" game see: http://www.youtube.com/watch?v=i49KUjFz-nM. For video synopsis of the performed facial expression tracking, see: https://www.facebook.com/maja.pantic.758/videos/vb.100003177678822/773346092781306/?type=2. For info on human-robot interaction studies with autistic children, see: http://de-enigma.eu.

4. PANEL DISCUSSION

Social and Affective Robots and the future Collaborative Robots are set to transform many services we use each day and to co-inhabit our personal ecosystems, but what exactly does this mean? In future, humanoid robots could improve security, healthcare, education, and revolutionize industry. But despite its reach, this powerful technology raises many questions. Would we consult an AI-driven robot doctor with a perfect or near-perfect diagnostic success rate or stick with the human GP who has known us for years? If our own behavior in any context becomes predictable by robot (or AI), how much personal freedom would we have or feel that we have to deviate from the prediction? How do we maintain our individuality, the very source of our diversity, in the digital age? Our panel of speakers will discuss these and other related issues raised by this powerful technology driving the fourth industrial revolution.

5. ACKNOWLEDGMENTS

This work has been funded by the European Community 7th Framework Programme [FP7/2007-2013] under grant agreement no. 611153 (TERESA) and the European Community Horizon 2020 Programme [H2020] under grant agreement no. 688835 (De-Enigma). Previous work on the topic was also funded in part by the European Community 7th Framework Programme [FP7/2007-2013] under grant agreement no. 288235 (FROG).

6. REFERENCES

[1] Schwab, K. 2016. *The Fourth Industrial Revolution.* World Economic Forum Press, Geneva, Switzerland.

[2] Shen, J., Rudovic, O., Cheng, S., and Pantic, M. 2015. Sentiment Apprehension in Human-Robot Interaction with NAO. *IEEE Proc. Int'l Conf. Affective Computing and Intelligent Interaction.* 1st International Workshop on Automatic Sentiment Analysis in the Wild (WASA'15). DOI=10.1109/ACII.2015.7344676.

[3] Shen, J., and Pantic, M. 2013. HCI^2 Framework: A Software Framework for Multimodal Human-Computer Interaction Systems. IEEE Trans. Cybernetics, 43, 6 (Dec. 2013), 1593-1606. DOI=10.1109/TCYB.2013.2271563.

Multimedia Privacy

[ACM MM 2016 Tutorial]

Gerald Friedland
Department of EECS
University of California,
Berkeley, CA, USA
fractor@eecs.berkeley.edu

Symeon Papadopoulos
Information Technologies
Institute
CERTH, Thessaloniki, Greece
papadop@iti.gr

Julia Bernd
International Computer
Science Institute
Berkeley, CA, USA
jbernd@icsi.berkeley.edu

Yiannis Kompatsiaris
Information Technologies
Institute
CERTH, Thessaloniki, Greece
ikom@iti.gr

ABSTRACT

This tutorial brings together a number of recent advances at the nexus of multimedia analysis, online privacy, and social media mining. Our goal is to offer a multidisciplinary view of the emerging field of Multimedia Privacy: the study of privacy issues arising in the context of multimedia sharing in online platforms, and the pursuit of new approaches to mitigating those issues within multimedia computer science.

CCS Concepts

•Networks → Network privacy and anonymity; •Social and professional topics → Privacy policies;

Keywords

Multimedia; Privacy; Social Media

1. MOTIVATION

The growth of online multimedia, especially due to social networking sites such as Facebook and YouTube, combines with advances in multimedia retrieval (geo-tagging, web search, face recognition, speaker verification, location estimation, etc.) to provide novel opportunities for the malicious and unethical use of multimedia. Multimedia analytics have always had the potential to be a powerful privacy threat, but in isolation or at small scale, that threat has been reasonably contained. However, when analysis systems are linked together and used on an Internet scale, the threat can be enormous and pervasive. Many in the multimedia-analysis community therefore believe that we have an obligation to understand and attempt to mitigate these risks.

Engineering and computer science curricula usually include an abundance of material on multimedia retrieval methods that rely on analysis of the underlying content, but only rarely do they talk about the negative impacts of these technologies. Privacy research per se often focuses more on securing vs. co-opting communication channels—encryption, steganography, and the like—than on content privacy. Though there is a growing community of concern around content privacy, non-specialists may view it as "out of scope" for both education/training and for research and development. Because of this gap in education and organizational culture, many multimedia researchers lack knowledge about how to react to concerns and mitigate potential privacy risks.

In the drive to make the next big advance, it can be easy to say, "We'll deal with privacy and ethics later—right now we need to focus on making it work." But the truth is that it can be quite difficult to "add on" privacy when a system or technique has already developed momentum—even when the researchers and developers have the time and will to do it. For example, if privacy and security had been more of a concern in the earliest stages of developing the Internet, many current issues, such as spam, phishing email, and man-in-the-middle attacks, would probably be much less of a problem.

At the same time, some solutions to security and privacy concerns are quite simple, following a limited set of basic principles that are fairly well-known in the privacy and security communities—but less so in multimedia. If these guidelines are followed in the early stages, developers and researchers can avoid creating larger problems down the line.

2. OBJECTIVES

The Multimedia Privacy tutorial will introduce interested multimedia researchers, engineers, and students to a multidisciplinary perspective on privacy. The tutorial will provide a vivid overview, with many examples based on material developed for the CS10 "Beauty and Joy of Computing" course at UC Berkeley, for the NSF-sponsored Teaching Privacy project (http://teachingprivacy.org), and for the EC-funded USEMP project (User Empowerment for enhanced online

MM '16 October 15-19, 2016, Amsterdam, Netherlands

ACM ISBN 978-1-4503-3603-1/16/10.

DOI: http://dx.doi.org/10.1145/2964284.2986915

management, http://www.usemp-project.eu/). These materials are based in turn on current research from top-notch privacy, multimedia, and security groups and conferences.

Using real-world examples and their consequences, the tutorial will focus on threats related to multimedia retrieval in the context of modern social networking structures. While it will cover a number of technical parameters that should be considered, the tutorial's main thread of argument is that user awareness and empowerment are two crucial requirements for improving privacy management through the design of multimedia sharing and social networking applications.

3. OUTLINE

Who's concerned about multimedia privacy and why:

- Privacy perception as a function of age, technical awareness, and cultural background
- Social vs. institutional privacy
- Legal frameworks and ethical standpoints in the U.S. and the EU
- Crime potentially enabled by multimedia: cyberstalking, cybercasing, identity theft, etc.
- Non-criminal consequences of privacy leaks

The state of the art in multimedia and privacy:

- Geotagging and its implications for privacy
- Multimedia retrieval and its implications for privacy (location estimation, activity detection, etc.)
- Matching users across accounts with multimedia content analysis
- Facebook & LinkedIn vs. physical-world social networking

Mitigation strategies and tools:

- Attack and defense model and taxonomy
- Personalizing privacy via settings and via inference
- Scoring and visualizing personal information disclosure
- Potential techniques for built-in identity obfuscation
- User education: ten principles for social media privacy

Conclusions:

- Possible implications for research, education, industry
- Opportunities for start-ups, new research
- First steps everybody can take right now

4. TUTORS

Dr. Gerald Friedland is a Principal Scientist responsible for Audio and Multimedia Analysis at Lawrence Livermore National Lab and is also teaching as an adjunct professor at the Electrical Engineering and Computer Sciences department of the University of California, Berkeley. He has published more than 200 peer-reviewed articles in conferences, journals, and books. He led the development of the teachingprivacy.org portal and also co-authored a new textbook on multimedia computing together with Dr. Ramesh Jain. He is associate editor for *ACM Transactions on Multimedia* and *IEEE Multimedia Magazine* and regularly reviews for *IEEE Transactions on Acoustics, Speech, and Language Processing*; Springer's *Machine Vision and Application*; and other journals. Among other recognitions, he won the ACM Multimedia Grand Challenge in 2009 and 2016. Dr. Friedland received his doctorate (summa cum laude) and master's degree in computer science from Freie Universitaet Berlin, Germany, in 2002 and 2006, respectively.

Dr. Symeon Papadopoulos received his Diploma degree in Electrical and Computer Engineering from the Aristotle University of Thessaloniki in 2004. In 2006, he received the Professional Doctorate in Engineering (P.D.Eng.) from the Technical University of Eindhoven, the Netherlands. Since 2006, he has been working with the Information Technologies Institute of CERTH. In 2012, he defended his PhD dissertation on the topic of knowledge discovery from large-scale mining of social media content. He has participated in several EU-funded research projects (WeKnowIt, SocialSensor, REVEAL, USEMP) as technical leader, and has co-authored more than 70 publications in refereed journals and conferences. Dr. Papadopoulos successfully led the organization of the Workshop on Social Multimedia and Storytelling in ICMR 2014 and the Workshop on Web Multimedia Verification in ICME 2015, and co-organized the Social News on the Web (SNOW) workshop in the context of WWW 2014 and 2016. In addition, he was one of the organizers of the 10th European Summer School on Information Retrieval (ESSIR 2015).

Julia Bernd is a staff researcher at the International Computer Science Institute in Berkeley, CA. She coordinates the Teaching Privacy project, which aims to educate people about how online sharing works, what the risks are, and what individuals can and can't do to protect themselves. Teaching Privacy, begun by Friedland and others, grew out of research on multimedia privacy and often focuses on multimedia examples (such as geotagging—and content-based location estimation for untagged images and videos). In other words, the goal is to leverage the expertise of multimedia computer scientists to educate the general public, in particular young people, about potential issues arising out of advances in the field. Bernd is a linguist by training (MA, Stanford, 2002), but her recent academic work focuses largely on multimedia corpus development (in the context of the Multimedia Commons) and on developing CS curricula that integrate potential impacts of advances in computing.

Dr. Yiannis Kompatsiaris is a Senior Researcher (Researcher A') with the Information Technologies Institute of CERTH, Thessaloniki, Greece. His research interests include semantic multimedia analysis, indexing and retrieval, social media and big data analysis, knowledge structures, reasoning and personalization for multimedia applications, eHealth, security, and environmental applications. He received his PhD in 3-D model-based image sequence coding from the Aristotle University of Thessaloniki in 2001. He is the co-author of 90 papers in refereed journals, 38 book chapters, 8 patents, and more than 320 papers in international conferences. He has been the co-organizer of numerous international conferences and workshops and has served as a regular reviewer for a number of journals and conferences. He is a Senior Member of IEEE and of ACM.

5. ACKNOWLEDGMENTS

S. Papadopoulos and Y. Kompatsiaris received support from the European Commission-funded USEMP project, contract #611596. J. Bernd and G. Friedland were supported by US National Science Foundation awards #1637601 and #1514509.

AltMM 2016 - 1st International Workshop on Multimedia Alternate Realities

Teresa Chambel
LaSIGE, Faculdade de Ciências, Universidade de Lisboa
1749-16 Lisboa, Portugal
tc@di.fc.ul.pt

Rene Kaiser
Joanneum Research
Steyrergasse 17, Graz, Austria,
rene.kaiser@joanneum.at

Omar Niamut
TNO
Anna van Buerenplein 1, 2595 DA
Den Haag, The Netherlands
omar.niamut@tno.nl

Wei Tsang Ooi
National University of Singapore
13 Computing Drive, Singapore 117417
weitsang@nus.edu.sg

Judith A. Redi
Delft University of Technology
Mekelweg 4, 2628CD Delft, The Netherlands
J.a.redi@tudelft.nl

ABSTRACT

Multimedia experiences allow us to access other worlds, to live other people's stories, to communicate with or experience alternate realities. Different spaces, times or situations can be entered thanks to multimedia contents and systems, which coexist with our current reality, and are sometimes so vivid and engaging that we feel we are living in them. Advances in multimedia are making it possible to create immersive experiences that may involve the user in a different or augmented world, as an alternate reality. AltMM 2016, the 1st International Workshop on Multimedia Alternate Realities at ACM Multimedia, aims at exploring how the synergy between multimedia technologies and effects can foster the creation of alternate realities and make their access an enriching, valuable and real experience. The workshop program will contain a combination of oral and invited keynote presentations, and poster, demo and discussion sessions, altogether enabling interactive scientific sharing and discussion between practitioners and researchers.

CCS Concepts

• Human-centered computing → Interaction paradigms • Human-centered computing → Interaction devices • Information Systems → Multimedia Information Systems → Multimedia content creation.

Keywords

Immersive Media; Interactive Multimedia; Mulsemedia; Multimedia Experience; Alternate Realities;

MM '16, October 15-19, 2016, Amsterdam, Netherlands
ACM 978-1-4503-3603-1/16/10.
http://dx.doi.org/10.1145/2964284.2980531

1. INTRODUCTION

Advances in multimedia technology are transforming the way we experience multimedia content. New devices, transmission paradigms, and content formats are making it possible to create immersive experiences that may involve the user in a different or augmented world, as an alternate reality. Such alternate realities can spring from multiple media, something as simple as a book with a compelling story; a beautiful or impactful picture that the user contemplates, imagining or recalling the reality the picture is portraying or inducing; or a song, so engaging and affectively close that the user accesses another reality only by listening to it. But audiovisual media, and in particular video and animation, in cinema, TV and teleconferencing, and increasingly with multiple devices, have been for long a preferred medium for its dynamics and richness, its ability to show real events and to tell stories, and its potential to engage us perceptually, cognitively and emotionally, while involving both visual and auditory senses. With the increased capabilities to represent, process, interact and communicate with or through media with higher quality in the audiovisual domain, and possibly involving all the other human senses as well, emergent multimedia technology holds the potential to take the experience of alternate realities to a new level. These will be the core themes addressed and discussed at the AltMM 2016 workshop.

2. MULTIMEDIA ALTERNATE REALITIES

Alternate *realness* relates with the feelings of presence, engagement, flow and full immersion in a multimedia experience. This can be achieved, for example, through the production of immersive ultra-high quality and panoramic/360° content, and the consumption of media through immersive devices and environments (e.g. AR/VR, HMD and UHD displays, mulsemedia). But independent of the content format and the device on which it is consumed, content itself has the potential to be engaging and transport the user to an alternate reality. Engaging storytelling based on linear or interactive narratives, but also aesthetic perfection, can capture the users and hold them in a flow related to the media experience. Users might *live the story* in a lean-backward setting or exploit interaction mechanisms to participate, shape and personalize the story and reality actively. The engagement in alternate realities might be particularly strong if the experience is shared with others, through means to

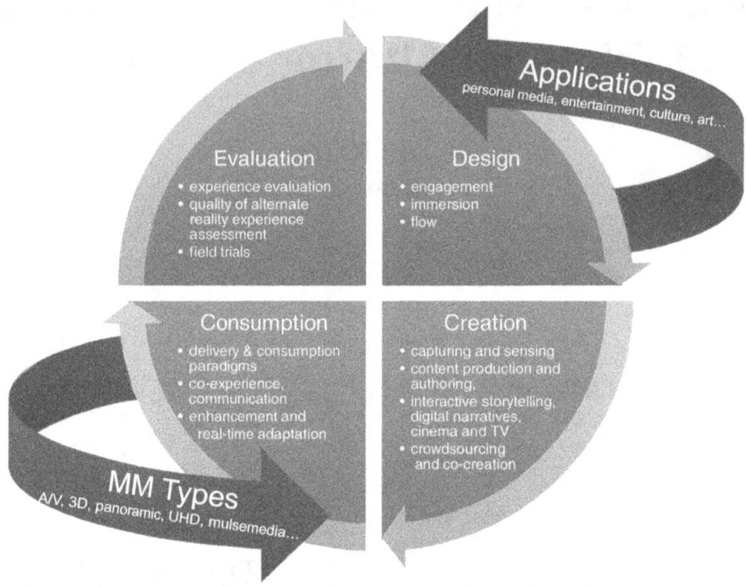

Figure 1. Topics of the First International Workshop on Multimedia Alternate Realities (AltMM'2016)

communicate live, or capture to recount later. The extent to which multimedia content and systems facilitate the access of alternate realities is a measure of their effectiveness. So finally, we must have the means to design and evaluate our experience in alternate realities, with methods and measures to create and assess presence, engagement and full immersion.

The AltMM 2016 workshop explores how the synergy between the aforementioned multimedia technologies and effects can foster the creation of alternate realities and make their access an enriching, valuable and *real* experience. Contributions to the workshop presented multimedia technologies, methods and measurement approaches from the perspective of "enabling other realities". In particular, one or more of the following dimensions were addressed in the contributions to the workshop, when characterizing the type of multimedia alternate realities that they were aiming for:

- **Alternate** - refers to what is alternate about it: different space, time, situation, and so on;
- **Virtual/Augmented** - how far or close to the actual reality content can be experienced, ranging from totally virtual to augmented reality;
- **Real/Fictional** - how real or fictional the content is;
- **Interactive** - the level of interactivity as a means of engagement and immersion;
- **Immersive** - level in perceptual, cognitive and emotional terms, the sense of presence and belonging, the quality of the content and the experience, imagination and engagement;
- **Multisensorial** - the media involved and how much mulsemedia it is, also going beyond audiovisual content to include the five senses;
- **Personal** - adaptation to individual preferences and contexts;
- **Social** - individualized vs shared experiences and communication.

3. TOPICS

AltMM 2016 welcomed contributions with the goals and the perspective of enabling alternate realities experiences as characterized above, through multimedia technologies, and design and evaluation methods for its creation and consumption. This involves the use of different types of media content (audio-visual, haptics, smell, and taste), increased immersion (e.g., 3D, holographic, UHD, ultra-wideview, and stereoscopic audio), new interaction devices, environments, modalities, and formats. Topics addressed creation and consumption of alternate realities, design and evaluation of alternate realities experience and applications, as depicted in Figure 1.

4. PROGRAM

The workshop proposes a program combining oral presentations, an invited keynote presentation, a poster and demo session for interactive presentation, and a fishbowl discussion.

Wijnand IJsselsteijn, Professor at the Eindhoven University of Technology, was invited to deliver the keynote talk on the sense of presence in multimedia alternate realities.

AltMM 2016 received a total of 16 submissions. Of these, 5 were accepted as long papers, corresponding to oral presentations, and 4 were accepted as short papers, to be presented in an interactive poster session along with demos. All papers received at least three double blind reviews, and 3.8 reviews on average. The organizers are grateful to the Program Committee[1] for their efforts in reviewing and for their insightful comments.

5. ACKNOWLEDGMENTS

Teresa Chambel would like to thank the support of the Portuguese Foundation for Science and Technology through LaSIGE Strategic Project, ref. PEst-OE/EEI/UI0408/2014;

[1] http://altmm2016.di.fc.ul.pt/committee.html

Summary for AVEC 2016 – Depression, Mood, and Emotion Recognition Workshop and Challenge

Michel Valstar
University of Nottingham
School of Computer Science

Jonathan Gratch
University of Southern California, ICT

Björn Schuller*
University of Passau
Chair of Complex & Intelligent Systems

Fabien Ringeval
Université Grenoble Alpes
Laboratoire d'Informatique

Roddy Cowie
Queen's University Belfast
Department of Psychology

Maja Pantic†
Imperial College London
Intelligent Behaviour Understanding Group

ABSTRACT

The sixth Audio-Visual Emotion Challenge and workshop AVEC 2016 was held in conjunction ACM Multimedia'16. This year the AVEC series addresses two distinct sub-challenges, multi-modal emotion recognition and audio-visual depression detection. Both sub-challenges are in a way a return to AVEC's past editions: the emotion sub-challenge is based on the same dataset as the one used in AVEC 2015, and depression analysis was previously addressed in AVEC 2013/2014. In this summary, we mainly describe participation and its conditions.

Keywords

Affective Computing; Social Signal Processing; Depression

1. INTRODUCTION

This year's Audio-Visual Emotion Challenge and workshop (AVEC 2016) has been organised in conjunction with the 24th ACM International Conference on Multimedia, held in Amsterdam, The Netherlands, 15 – 19 October 2016.

The AVEC 2016's theme is 'Depression, Mood, and Emotion Recognition' and it is the sixth competition event aimed at comparison of multimedia processing and machine learning methods for automatic audio, visual and audio-visual emotion analysis, with all of the participants competing under strictly the same conditions in this first of its kind series [3, 5, 6, 9, 10]. However, further similar endeavours that have been undertaken since AVEC started in 2011 are to be noted, e. g., [1].

The AVEC 2016 edition features besides true multimodal emotion recognition in its emotion recognition sub-challenge, where besides audio and video participants also have access to physiological data. In addition, we take emotion analysis to a higher-level behaviour understanding by looking at mood disorders, in particular the serious and important problem of automatic detection of depression. Adding objective measures to what is otherwise an entirely subjective process of diagnosing and monitoring depression promises to be an invaluable support to the mental health profession besides the usage in media retrieval systems.

As before, the goal of the Challenge is to provide a common benchmark test set for individual multimodal information processing and to bring together the audio and video emotion recognition communities (extended with the physiological analysis community for the emotion recognition sub-challenge), to compare the relative merits of these approaches to emotion and depression recognition under well-defined and strictly comparable conditions and to establish to what extent fusion of the approaches is possible and beneficial. A second motivation is the need to advance emotion recognition for multimedia retrieval to a level where *behaviomedical* systems [7] are able to deal with large volumes of non-prototypical naturalistic behaviour in reaction to known stimuli, as this is exactly the type of data that diagnostic tools and other applications would have to face in the real world.

We called for participation in two Sub-Challenges: (i) fully-continuous emotion detection from audio, from video, and physiological data or from any combination thereof, and (ii) classification of depression. As benchmarking database an enhanced subset of the AVEC 2015 RECOLA database is used [4]. Emotion needed to be recognised in terms of continuous time, *and* continuous valued dimensional affect in two dimensions: valence and arousal. For depression, the Distress Analysis Interview Corpus - Wizard of Oz (DAIC-WOZ) database was used. This is part of a larger corpus, the Distress Analysis Interview Corpus (DAIC) [2], that contains clinical interviews designed to support the diagnosis of psychological distress conditions such as anxiety, depression, and post-traumatic stress disorder. Depression needed

*The author is further affiliated with Imperial College London, Department of Computing, London, U.K.

†The author is further affiliated with Twente University, EEMCS, Twente, The Netherlands.

AVEC'16, October 16 2016, Amsterdam, Netherlands

ISBN 978-1-4503-4516-3/16/10...$15.00

DOI: http://dx.doi.org/10.1145/2988257.2988258

to be estimated in terms of binary classes depressed/non-depressed, based on a widely accepted clinical self-report questionnaire, PHQ8.

Besides participation in the Challenge we called for papers addressing the overall topics of this workshop, in particular works that address the differences between audio and video processing of emotive data, and the issues concerning combined audio-visual emotion recognition.

In the following sections, we will describe the participation in this year and outline the conditions for participation in particular in the competitive challenge event. We further acknowledge those that helped realise AVEC 2016.

2. CHALLENGE CONDITIONS

A baseline paper explaining the dataset, the challenge evaluation procedure, baseline features and baseline results was made available while the challenge was ongoing [8]. Due to the sensitive nature of the data, a strict registration for access to the challenge data policy was followed. As in previous years, a web-based database was used, however, we required to sign a new end user license agreement and for the depression sub-challenge no raw video was made available, only video features. After downloading the data participants could directly start their own experiments with the train and development sets. Once they found their best method they should write a paper for the Workshop. At the same time they could compute their results per instance of the test set. Participants' results needed to be sent as a single packed file per Sub-Challenge to the organisers by email and scores were returned within 24 hours during typical working days.

Each participant had up to five submission attempts per Sub-Challenge. Badly formatted results were not counted towards one of these five submissions. The organisers provided for each affective dimension the Concordance Correlation Coefficient (CCC), which is used to rank participants on the emotion sub-challenge. For the depression sub-challenge the F1 measure was used to rank participants. The RMS error of the actual PHQ8 scores was provided as well, which could be used by the authors to further discuss their results in the paper accompanying their submission.

3. PARTICIPATION

The call for participation and papers attracted registrations of 56 teams from all over the world. 13 teams submitted results for the Affect recognition Sub-Challenge, and 7 teams submitted results for the Depression recognition Sub-Challenge. Finally, 12 paper submissions were received, which were assigned three reviewers, each, and reviewed independently. AVEC 2016 reviewing was double blind, and acceptance was based on relevance to the workshop, novelty, and technical quality. The programme committee accepted 12 papers in addition to the baseline paper as oral presentation. Again, we hope that these proceedings will serve as a valuable reference for researchers and developers in the area of audio-visual emotion recognition and depression analysis.

Acknowledgments

The challenge in general has been generously supported by the Association for the Advancement of Affective Computing (AAAC). The research leading to these results has received funding from the EC's 7th Framework Programme through the ERC Starting Grant No. 338164 (iHEARu), and the European Union's Horizon 2020 Programme through the Innovative Action No. 645094 (SEWA), and the Research Innovative Action No. 645378 (ARIA-VALUSPA), and No. 688835 (DE-ENIGMA).

4. REFERENCES

[1] A. Dhall, R. Goecke, J. Joshi, M. Wagner, and T. Gedeon. Emotion Recognition In The Wild Challenge 2013. In *Proceedings ICMI*, pages 509–516, Sydney, Australia, December 2013. ACM.

[2] J. Gratch et al. The distress analysis interview corpus of human and computer interviews. In *Proc. of LREC*, pages 3123–3128, Reykjavik, Iceland, May 2014. ELRA.

[3] F. Ringeval, B. Schuller, M. Valstar, S. Jaiswal, E. Marchi, D. Lalanne, R. Cowie, and M. Pantic. Av+ec 2015: The first affect recognition challenge bridging across audio, video, and physiological data. In *Proceedings of the 5th International Workshop on Audio/Visual Emotion Challenge*, pages 3–8. ACM, 2015.

[4] F. Ringeval, A. Sonderegger, J. Sauer, and D. Lalanne. Introducing the RECOLA multimodal corpus of remote collaborative and affective interactions. In *Proc. of EmoSPACE, FG*, Shanghai, China, 2013.

[5] B. Schuller, M. Valstar, F. Eyben, R. Cowie, and M. Pantic. AVEC 2012 – The Continuous Audio/Visual Emotion Challenge. In *Proceedings ICMI*, pages 449–456, Santa Monica, CA, October 2012. ACM.

[6] B. Schuller, M. Valstar, F. Eyben, G. McKeown, R. Cowie, and M. Pantic. AVEC 2011 - The First International Audio/Visual Emotion Challenge. In *Proceedings ACII*, volume II, pages 415–424. Springer, Memphis, TN, October 2011.

[7] M. Valstar. Automatic behaviour understanding in medicine. In *Proceedings of the 2014 Workshop on Roadmapping the Future of Multimodal Interaction Research including Business Opportunities and Challenges*, pages 57–60. ACM, 2014.

[8] M. Valstar, J. Gratch, B. Schuller, F. Ringeval, D. Lalanne, M. Torres Torres, S. Scherer, G. Stratou, R. Cowie, and M. Pantic. Avec 2016 – depression, mood, and emotion recognition workshop and challenge. In *Proc. of AVEC, ACM MM*. ACM, 2016.

[9] M. Valstar, B. Schuller, J. Krajewski, R. Cowie, and M. Pantic. Workshop summary for the 3rd international audio/visual emotion challenge and workshop (AVEC'13). In *Proceedings MM*, pages 1085–1086, Barcelona, Spain, October 2013. ACM.

[10] M. Valstar, B. Schuller, K. Smith, T. Almaev, F. Eyben, J. Krajewski, R. Cowie, and M. Pantic. Avec 2014: 3d dimensional affect and depression recognition challenge. In *Proceedings of the 4th International Workshop on Audio/Visual Emotion Challenge*, pages 3–10. ACM, 2014.

Multimedia COMMONS Workshop 2016 (MMCommons'16)

Datasets, Evaluation, and Reproducibility

Bart Thomee
Yahoo Labs
San Francisco, CA, USA
bthomee@yahoo-inc.com

Damian Borth
German Research Center for Artificial Intelligence (DFKI)
Kaiserslautern, Germany
damian.borth@dfki.de

Julia Bernd
International Computer Science Institute
Berkeley, CA, USA
jbernd@icsi.berkeley.edu

ABSTRACT

Leveraged wisely, new datasets can inspire new multimedia methods and algorithms, as well as catalyze innovations in how their efficacy, efficiency, and generalizability can be evaluated. The availability of very large multimedia datasets like the Yahoo-Flickr Creative Commons 100 Million has offered unique opportunities for advancing the state of the art in multimedia processing, analysis, search, and visualization.

The Multimedia Commons Initiative has been developing a community around the YFCC100M, including associated annotation and evaluation efforts. In addition to research in several multimedia subfields, including computer vision, image processing, and video content analysis, the YFCC100M and Multimedia Commons resources have been used in various competitions and benchmarks, such as the MediaEval Placing Task and the ACM Multimedia Grand Challenge competition. With additional annotation and curation, the data has the potential to enable major leaps forward in research.

As use of the YFCC100M and the Multimedia Commons resources broadens across the multimedia community, the MMCommons'16 workshop offered an opportunity for researchers to share new research results, compare approaches, and coordinate efforts to maximize the scientific benefit of the initiative. In particular, the Multimedia Commons data has the potential to provide both inspiration and concrete resources to pursue some important "meta-research" questions, such as how to measure the scalability, generalizability, and reproducibility of methods across datasets, whether we need to rethink our evaluation paradigms as the field moves in new directions, and how annotation strategies affect the impact of benchmarks and data challenges using that data.

Keywords

multimedia; datasets; annotation; evaluation; retrieval

MM '16 October 15-19, 2016, Amsterdam, Netherlands

ACM ISBN 978-1-4503-3603-1/16/10.

DOI: http://dx.doi.org/10.1145/2964284.2980533

1. MOTIVATION AND GOALS

The Multimedia Commons Initiative has been developing a community around the Yahoo-Flickr Creative Commons 100 Million dataset (YFCC100M[1] [2]), which spans 99.2 million images and 0.8 million videos. Associated annotation and evaluation efforts have prospered during the past two years; the Multimedia Commons initiative is a multi-institute collaboration to compute features, generate annotations, and develop analysis tools, principally for the YFCC100M [1]. These resources have been released into the public domain, hosted via Amazon's Public Data Sets program[2].

The first edition of the MMCommons Workshop, held in 2015, focused on bringing together researchers to discuss the initial endeavors that had been launched since the release of the dataset in 2014, as well as to form priorities and plans for future projects based on community needs and interests. In this second edition of the workshop, with new features generated, annotations collected, expansion packs released, benchmarks held, discoveries made, and papers written, interested researchers came together to consolidate all these accomplishments, and to coordinate efforts that will stimulate new research that is both ground-breaking and reproducible.

The goals of MMCommons '16 included:

- Sharing novel research using the YFCC100M dataset, particularly focusing on solving multimedia problems in ways that were not possible with previous multimedia collections;
- Re-examining the scalability, generalizability, and reproducibility of algorithms and methods, and how we use data challenges and benchmarking tasks to catalyze advances in these areas;
- Exploring how we can best leverage this massive new dataset to update evaluation paradigms and practices, encouraging evaluation that better approximates "in the wild" conditions;
- Discussing priorities, methods, and plans for continuously expanding annotation efforts, based on the needs and research interests of a diverse set of multimedia researchers.

[1] https://bit.ly/yfcc100md
[2] http://www.multimediacommons.org/

2. SCOPE AND THEMES

Massive, open datasets challenge us to ask new questions about the scalability, generalizability, and reproducibility of algorithms that are not conclusively answerable with smaller or more restricted collections. There is broad agreement that one of the most exciting aspects of the YFCC100M is its potential to enable significant changes in how we approach frameworks and best practices for evaluation. The papers and special sessions at MMCommons'16 spoke to these possibilities, bringing in perspectives from researchers working on a variety of tasks, including better understanding, indexing, and searching multimedia content.

Themes that received particular focus included:

- Improving the understanding and representation of multimedia content;
- Leveraging user-supplied metadata to bootstrap analysis and benchmarking;
- Enabling web-scale distributed search and indexing;
- Defining strategies for performance evaluation, with an eye towards the goal of maximizing generalizability.

3. PROGRAM AND PAPER SUMMARY

Submissions to the Multimedia COMMONS Workshop covered major areas of interest for users of the YFCC100M dataset, such as how to derive insights about the dataset's content or structure, comparisons of methods for various recognition and classification tasks, and how to both address and leverage the scale and size of the dataset. The reviewers on the program committee accepted six high-quality papers, which covered into the following areas:

One set of papers provided novel insights about this large-scale dataset, beyond what was given in the original metadata. Insights were derived from either the given metadata or the associated image and video content, and provided context for parts of the dataset such as videos, additional annotations such as language, and refinements and relevance measurements for user-generated metadata (such as tags, titles, and descriptions/captions). Such submissions, and accompanying data releases, provide a valuable foundation for further work around the YFCC100m.

Several of the papers addressed scalability and best practices for processing large amount of data, for example indexing methods or how to utilize processing frameworks such as Spark. Since this dataset is of such large scale, any type of indexing work in combination with features is of use for the community, providing a basis to make use of such tools for further research. In particular, it helps researchers who do not have access to cluster environments to work with this dataset.

Finally, some of the presented papers addressed specific retrieval tasks such as automatic geotagging, including an evaluation of sampling-based benchmarking those tasks. This work links the YFCC100M dataset with challenges such as the MediaEval Placing Task, illustrating the potential of the dataset to support work on established classification tasks beyond the YFCC100M community.

In a complementary segment of the workshop program, participants in one of the ACM Multimedia Grand Challenges, the *Yahoo-Flickr Challenge on User Tag and Caption Prediction*[3], were invited to present their approaches. This challenge focuses on the YFCC100M dataset, and addresses the very exciting area of tag prediction and image captioning. Here the challenge lies in approximating how people annotate photos, for example in predicting what is most notable and what affective evaluation might be communicated.

[3]http://mmcommons.org/tag-caption-prediction-challenge/

The research described in the paper and challenge presentations provided a backdrop for a broader discussion in a panel on "Dataset Bias, Generalizability, and Reproducibility". Researchers who have created or worked intensively with different multimedia datasets discussed how the varying structures and purposes of those datasets has supported – or has limited – the impact of research. This panel, along with the keynote talk, fit with the workshop's special theme of re-examining evaluation paradigms and practices to align with new research agendas and leverage the size and affordances of new datasets.

ACKNOWLEDGMENTS

First of all, we would like to thank all the speakers for providing the content of the program, as well as other enthusiastic participants. In addition, we thank the ACM Multimedia organizers for giving us the opportunity to organize the workshop. Finally, we greatly appreciate the program committee's time and effort in reviewing papers, and the steering committee for helping to shape the workshop.

Steering Committee:

- Gerald Friedland (Lawrence Livermore National Laboratory, International Computer Science Institute, and University of California, Berkeley)
- Martha Larson (Technische Universiteit Delft)
- Doug Poland (Lawrence Livermore National Laboratory)
- Chong-Wah Ngo (VIREO Research Group, City University of Hong Kong)
- David Ayman Shamma (Centrum Wiskunde & Informatica)
- Jaeyoung Choi (International Computer Science Institute and Technische Universiteit Delft)
- Benjamin Elizalde (Carnegie Mellon University)
- Karl Ni (In-Q-Tel)

Technical Program Committee/Reviewers: Elisavet Chatzilari, Fabrizio Falchi, Fernando Fernández Martínez, Bogdan Ionescu, Go Irie, Adam Janin, Yiannis Kompatsiaris, Hervé Le Borgne, Mathias Lux, Henning Müller, Symeon (Akis) Papadopoulos, Roger Pearce.

References

[1] J. Bernd, D. Borth, C. Carrano, J. Choi, B. Elizalde, G. Friedland, L. Gottlieb, K. Ni, R. Pearce, D. Poland, K. Ashraf, D. A. Shamma, and B. Thomee. Kickstarting the Commons: The YFCC100M and the YLI corpora. In *Proceedings of MMCommons '15*, 2015.

[2] B. Thomee, D. A. Shamma, G. Friedland, B. Elizalde, K. Ni, D. Poland, D. Borth, and L.-J. Li. YFCC100M: The new data in multimedia research. *Communications of the ACM*, 59(2):64–73, 2016.

LTA 2016 — The First Workshop on Lifelogging Tools and Applications

Cathal Gurrin
Dublin City University
cathal.gurrin@dcu.ie

Xavier Giro-i-Nieto
Universitat Politecnica de Catalunya
xavier.giro@upc.edu

Petia Radeva, Mariella Dimiccoli
University of Barcelona
petia.ivanova@ub.edu, mariella.dimiccoli@ub.edu

Håvard D. Johansen
University of Tromsø
havard.johansen@uit.no

Hideo Joho
University of Tsukuba
hideo@slis.tsukuba.ac.jp

Vivek K Singh
Rutgers University
vivek.k.singh@rutgers.edu

ABSTRACT

The organisation of personal data is receiving increasing research attention due to the challenges we face in gathering, enriching, searching, and visualising such data. Given the increasing ease with which personal data being gathered by individuals, the concept of a lifelog digital library of rich multimedia and sensory content for every individual is fast becoming a reality. The LTA 2016 workshop aims to bring together academics and practitioners to discuss approaches to lifelog data analytics and applications; and to debate the opportunities and challenges for researchers in this new and challenging area.

CCS Concepts

•**Information systems → Digital libraries and archives; Multimedia information systems;**

Keywords

Personal information management, Lifelogging, Personal digital archives

1. INTRODUCTION

Given the increasing quantities of personal data being gathered by individuals, the concept of a digital library of rich multimedia and sensory content for every individual is fast becoming commonplace. Recent technological advances have introduced new types of personal sensors (e.g., wearable sensors and informational sensors) and devices (e.g., Google Glass or Apple's iWatch), which allow the individual to passively compile vast archives of personal data, commonly referred to as lifelogs [4]. The success of the quantified-self movement [7] is testament to the willingness of individuals to gather archives of such lifelogs, which are unprecedented in terms of volume and variety. Captured over a long period of time, heterogeneous lifelogs can provide a detailed picture of the activities of an individual, with numerous applications in terms of personal data archiving [3], health and wellness [1] and assistive technologies for human memory [2].

Applications of lifelogging ideally require knowledge extraction, search, summarisation, and visualisation tools to support individuals or practitioners to extract value from the data. Therefore it comes as no surprise that lifelogging is receiving increasing attention within the research community and is fast becoming a mainstream research topic in its own right. However, there are significant technical challenges to be solved, arising from the gathering, semantic enrichment, and pervasive accessing of these vast personal data archives. Yet what makes lifelogging unique is that there are many related aspects that need to be considered, such as privacy and data security [5], which has implications for both the individual and society as a whole [6]. Hence, we felt that there was a need for a interdisciplinary workshop in the area of lifelogging.

MM '16 October 15-19, 2016, Amsterdam, Netherlands

ACM ISBN 978-1-4503-3603-1/16/10.

DOI: http://dx.doi.org/10.1145/2964284.2980534

2. AIM OF THE WORKSHOP

The primary aim of the LTA 2016 workshop is to bring together interdisciplinary researchers and practitioners to discuss approaches for, and experiences of lifelog data capture, analytics and applications, as well as identifying opportunities and challenges for researchers in this new and challenging area. The disciplines involved in the workshop are expected to include multimedia analytics, wearable and ubiquitous computing, human computer interaction, information retrieval, cognitive science and healthcare & wellness.

The workshop has been designed to be highly interactive with a range of workshop elements chosen to encourage discussion and cross-fertilisation of research ideas. There will be the typical oral and poster presentations, but there will also be there will be stimulating keynote speakers (academic and practitioner), a boaster/spotlight session and a panel discussion of experts.

3. TOPICS OF INTEREST

We sought full papers (oral session) and short papers (poster session) related to the topics of interest for the workshop, which included, but were not limited to:

- Tools supporting the creation of lifelogs
- Multimedia data analytics and semantic enrichment for lifelog and quantified-self data
- User experience design for accessing lifelogs
- Privacy and data security challenges of lifelogging
- Egocentric vision and first-person camera vision
- Experiences of lifelogging and quantified-self activities
- Social applications and implications of life-logging
- Lifelogging applications in computational social science
- General applications of lifelogging and experiences of same
- Ethical issues arising from lifelogging activities
- Digital preservation and maintenance of lifelogs

4. WORKSHOP PROGRAMME

LTA 2016 is a one-day workshop. After a thorough review process by the programme committee, we have accepted four papers for full oral (and poster) presentation. Five additional papers were accepted to be presented solely in poster format. These papers will be presented in dedicated morning and afternoon sessions. In addition, the workshop will have two keynote speakers: one to open the workshop in the morning, and one in the afternoon. The following speakers are invited:

- Maarten Den Braber (Quantified Self Amsterdam, NL & SingularityU, NL)
- Alisha Williams (University of Utrecht, NL)

To wrap-up the workshop, we are having a panel discussion with a team of expert researchers and practitioners.

5. ORGANISING COMMITTEE

The LTA 2016 workshop was organised by:

- Cathal Gurrin (Insight Centre for Data Analytics & Dublin City University)
- Xavier Giro-i-Nieto (Universitat Politecnica de Catalunya)
- Petia Radeva (University of Barcelona)
- Hideo Joho (University of Tsukuba)
- Håvard Johansen (University of Tromsø, the Arctic University of Norway)
- Vivek K. Singh (Rutgers, the State University of New Jersey)
- Mariella Dimiccoli (Computer Vision Centre, University of Barcelona)

6. PROGRAMME COMMITTEE

We thank the LTA 2016 programme committee for their commitment and time in reviewing the submissions and helping us to create a stimulating workshop schedule. The programme committee members were:

- Jochen Meyer (OFFIS)
- Giuseppe Serra (University of Modena)
- Tom Van Daele (Thomas More University College)
- Jenny Benois-Pineau (University of Bourdeaux)
- Yiannis Kompatsiaris (Center for Research and Technology Hellas)
- Alishia Williams (University of Utrecht)
- Paulina Piasek (Dublin City University)
- David Crandall (Indiana University)
- Kris Kitani (CMU)
- Gregory Rogez (INRIA Rhones-Alpes)
- Alejandro Betancourt (TU Eindhoven)
- Cheston Tan (Institute for Infocomm Research, A*STAR)
- Edison Thomaz (University of Texas at Austin)
- Giovanni Maria Farinella (University of Catania)
- Jiang Zhou (Dublin City University)
- Frank Hopfgartner (Glasgow University)
- Duc Tien Dang Nguyen (University of Trento)
- Wolfgang Hurst (University of Utrecht)
- Mariella Dimiccoli (Computer Vision Centre, University of Barcelona).

7. REFERENCES

[1] M. B. Amin, O. Banos, W. A. Khan, H. S. Muhammad Bilal, J. Gong, D.-M. Bui, S. H. Cho, S. Hussain, T. Ali, U. Akhtar, T. C. Chung, and S. Lee. On curating multimodal sensory data for health and wellness platforms. *Sensors*, 16(7):980, 2016.

[2] G. Browne, E. Berry, N. Kapur, S. Hodges, G. Smyth, P. Watson, and K. Wood. Sensecam improves memory for recent events and quality of life in a patient with memory retrieval difficulties. *Memory*, 19(7):713–722, 2011.

[3] J. Gemmell, G. Bell, R. Lueder, S. Drucker, and C. Wong. Mylifebits: Fulfilling the memex vision. In *Proceedings of the Tenth ACM International Conference on Multimedia*, pages 235–238, New York, NY, USA, 2002. ACM.

[4] C. Gurrin, A. F. Smeaton, and A. R. Doherty. LifeLogging: Personal Big Data. *Foundations and Trends in Information Retrieval*, 8(1):1–125, 2014.

[5] H. Johansen, C. Gurrin, and D. Johansen. Towards consent-based lifelogging in sport analytic. In *MMM 2015, Part II*, number 8936, pages 335–344. Springer, Jan. 2015.

[6] K. O'Hara, M. M. Tuffield, and N. Shadbolt. Lifelogging: Privacy and empowerment with memories for life. *Identity in the Information Society*, 1(1):155–172, December 2008.

[7] M. Swan. The Quantified Self: Fundamental Disruption in Big Data Science and Biological Discovery. *Big Data*, 1(2):85–89, June 2013.

Overview of the ACM MultiMedia 2016 International Workshop on Multimedia Assisted Dietary Management

Stavroula Mougiakakou
University of Bern, Switzerland
stavroula.mougiakakou@artorg.unibe.ch

Giovanni Maria Farinella
University of Catania, Italy
gfarinella@dmi.unict.it

Keiji Yanai
The University of Electro-Communications, Japan
yanai@cs.uec.ac.jp

ABSTRACT
This abstract provides a summary and overview of the 2nd international workshop on multimedia assisted dietary management.

CCS Concepts
- Information systems → Multimedia information systems
- Information systems → Mobile information processing systems
- Applied computing → Health informatics

Keywords
Food recognition; food volume estimation; food detection/segmentation; computer vision; machine learning; semantics; wearable technologies; mobile technologies; nutrient estimation; diet assessment.

1. INTRODUCTION
The prevention of onset and progression of diet-related acute and chronic diseases (e.g. diabetes, obesity, cardiovascular diseases and cancer) requires reliable and intuitive dietary management. The need for accurate, automatic, real-time and personalized dietary advice has been recently complemented by the advances in computer vision and smartphone technologies, permitting the development of the first mobile food multimedia content analysis applications. The proposed solutions rely on the analysis of multimedia content captured by wearable sensors, smartphone cameras, barcode scanners, RFID readers and IR sensors, along with already established nutritional databases and often require some user input. In the field of nutritional management, multimedia not only bridges diverse information and communication technologies, but also computer science with medicine, nutrition and dietetics. This confluence brings new challenges and opportunities on dietary management.

The first published attempts towards multimedia content analysis for dietary management took place in 2008. At that time, only some research groups were working in the field from the USA [1]-[3] and Japan [4], [5]. In Europe, the first (and only) related research project was funded in 2011 under the FP7 framework (GoCARB project) [6]. Since then, the field has attracted increasing interest with at least 30 groups from universities and companies around the world proposing portable systems that aim to help users with every-day diet management. This trend was triggered by the escalating prevalence of diet-related chronic diseases and was supported by the recent advances in computer vision and smartphone technologies. To this end, the European Commission announced several related calls for proposals, as well as a € 1 million prize for a non-invasive portable food scanner within the framework of Horizon 2020. Furthermore, according to market analysis reports [7], nutrition apps will become increasingly popular, personalized and integrated.

MM '16, October 15-19, 2016, Amsterdam, Netherlands
ACM 978-1-4503-3603-1/16/10.
http://dx.doi.org/10.1145/2964284.2980535

Although significant progress has already been made in this newborn field, there are plenty of issues that detain its further development and need to be addressed. A closer collaboration between the involved researchers should be promoted that will result in a strict problem definition, a basic categorization of the proposed approaches as well as a collection of widely accepted datasets and evaluation protocols.

2. AIM OF THE WORKSHOP
The main scope of MADiMa2016 is to bring together researchers from the diverse fields of engineering, computer science and nutrition who investigate the use of information and communication technologies for better monitoring and management of food intake. The combined use of multimedia, machine learning algorithms, ubiquitous computing and mobile technologies permit the development of applications and systems able to monitor the dietary behavior, analyze food intake, identify eating patterns and provide feedback to the user towards healthier nutrition. The researchers will present and demonstrate their latest progress and discuss novel ideas in the field. Besides the technologies used, emphasis will be given to the precise problem definition, the available nutritional databases, the need for benchmarking multimedia databases of packed and unpacked food and the evaluation protocols.

3. TOPICS OF INTEREST
Topics of interest include the following:

- Ubiquitous and mobile computing for dietary assessment
- Computer vision for food detection, segmentation and recognition
- 3D reconstruction for food portion estimation
- Augmented reality for food portion estimation
- Wearable sensors for food intake detection
- Computerized food composition (nutrients, allergens) analysis
- Multimedia technologies for eating monitoring
- Smartphone technologies for dietary behavioral patterns
- Food multimedia databases
- Evaluation protocols of dietary management systems
- Multimedia assisted self-management of health and disease

4. WORKSHOP SUMMARY
The MADiMA2016 workshop attracted in total 14 submissions from America, Europe and Asia. Out of these, 10 papers and two

demo proposals were accepted covering a wide variety of topics related to the theme of the workshop.

Merler et al. in “Snap, eat, repEat: a Food Recognition Engine for Dietary Logging” presented a smartphone-based system to assist users in dietary logging habits, by using food recognition and geolocation information. In “Food Search Based on User Feedback to Assist Image-based Food Recording Systems”, Amano et al. proposed a system that combines image recognition and interactive search in order to record users food intake. Ahmad in the paper entitled “A Mobile Food Record For Integrated Dietary Assessment”, presents a mobile application that connects to an image-based food nutrient database with additional focus given on the user interfaces. Singla et al. with their paper “Food/Non-food Image Classification and Food Categorization using Pre-Trained GoogLeNet Model” they report the results of a series of experiments on food/non-food classification and food recognition using the GoogleNet CNN model. In “An Automatic Calorie Estimation System of Food Images on a Smartphone”, Okamoto et al. propose a novel single-image-based food calorie estimation system which runs on a smartphone as a standalone application without external recognition servers. Ragusa et al. in “Food vs Non-Food Classification” consider the most recent classification approaches employed for food vs non-food classification, and compare them on a publicly available dataset. Hassannejad et al. in “Food Image Recognition with Very Deep Convolutional Networks”, evaluated the effectiveness in classifying food images of a deep-learning approach based on the specifications of Google's image recognition architecture Inception. Shimoda et al. in “Foodness proposal for Webly-supervised food detection” propose a method which generates high “food-ness” regions by using fully convolutional networks-based backward approach with training food images gathered from the Web. In “Performance Evaluation Methods of Computer Vision Systems for Meal Assessment” Anthimopoulos et al. present an overview of the datasets and protocols used for evaluating the computer vision stages of the proposed automatic meal assessment systems. In “Food Image Segmentation for Dietary Assessment” Dehais et al. proposed a method to detect and segment the food of already detected dishes in an image by combining region growing/merging techniques with a deep CNN-based food border detection. Finally, Tanno et al. in “DeepFoodCam: A DCNN-based Real-time Mobile Food Recognition System” and Dehais et al. in “GoCARB: a Smartphone Application for Automatic Assessment of Carbohydrate Intake” provided short presentations of two automatic meal assessment systems that will be demonstrated during the workshop.

5. CONCLUSION

We expect that MADiMa2016 will support the expansion of the researcher’s community working on multimedia assisted dietary management all over the world, and that it will facilitate cross-disciplinary research collaboration towards innovative solutions in the related fields.

6. REFERENCES

[1] Zhu F, Mariappan A, Boushey CJ, Kerr D, Lutes KD, Ebert DS, et al. Technology-assisted dietary assessment. *Proceedings SPIE-The International Society for Optical Engineering*. 2008;6814:1–10.

[2] Mei Chen; Dhingra, K.; Wen Wu; Lei Yang; Sukthankar, R.; Jie Yang, “PFID: Pittsburgh fast-food image dataset,” in *16th IEEE International Conference on Image Processing (ICIP2009)*, pp.289-292, 7-10 Nov. 2009.

[3] Puri M., Zhu Z., Yu Q., Divakaran A., and Sawhney H, “Recognition and volume estimation of food intake using a mobile device,” *Applications of Computer Vision (WACV), 2009 Workshop on*, Snowbird, UT, 2009, pp. 1-8.

[4] Kitamura K., Yamasaki T., Aizawa K., Food log by analyzing food images, *Proceedings of the 16th ACM international conference on Multimedia*, October 26-31, 2008, Vancouver, British Columbia, Canada.

[5] Joutou T. and Yanai K., “A food image recognition system with Multiple Kernel Learning,” *2009 16th IEEE International Conference on Image Processing (ICIP)*, Cairo, 2009, pp. 285-288.

[6] http://gocarb.eu/.

[7] Research2Guidance, *mNutrition: The impact of smartphones on the nutrition industry*, Marker observation, 2014.

Multimedia for Personal Health and Health Care

Susanne Boll
University of Oldenburg, Germany
Susanne.Boll@uol.de

Kiyo Aizawa
The University of Tokyo, Japan
aizawa@hal.k.u-tokyo.ac.jp

Alexia Briasouli
Centre for Research and Technology Hellas, Greece
abria@iti.gr

Cathal Gurrin
Dublin City University, Ireland
cgurrin@computing.dcu.ie

Laleh Jalali
University of California, Irvine, USA
lalehj@ics.uci.edu

Jochen Meyer
OFFIS–Institute for Information Technology, Germany
meyer@offis.de

ABSTRACT

Ever since the emergence of digitization, the term multimedia has been used to represent a combination of different kinds of media types, such images, audio, and videos. As new sensing technologies emerge and are now becoming omnipresent in daily lives, the definition, role and significance of multimedia is changing. Multimedia now represents the means for communicating, cooperating, and also for monitoring numerous aspects of daily life, at various levels of granularity and application, ranging from personal to societal. With this shift, we have since moved from comprehending single media and its state toward comprehending media in terms of its use context.

Multimedia is thus no longer confined to documentation and preservation, entertainment or personal media collections; rather, it has become an integral part of the tools and systems that are providing solutions to today's societal challenges—including challenges related to health care and personal health , aging, education, societal participation, sustainable energy, and intelligent transportation. Multimedia has thus evolved into a core enabler for future interactive and cooperative applications at the heart of society. In this workshop we explore the relevance and contribution of multimedia to health care and personal media.

Keywords

Multimedia; health care; personal health

1. BACKGROUND AND MOTIVATION

Personal health and health care involves some of the state of the art technologies in multimedia. Multimedia technologies related to health and personal health can range from medical imaging to daily life monitoring. Medical imaging itself can range from molecular imaging that visualize biological processes, to x-ray, ultrasound, MRI scans, CAT scans. In recent years, the rapidly increasing use of wearable and environmental sensors is providing a rich source of data describing numerous aspects of a person's daily life, behavior and lifestyle. A great variety of wearable and ambient sensors have been developed and are constantly being improved and incorporated in peoples' daily lives, measuring physiological parameters in a non-intrusive and accurate manner, and producing new types of multimedia.

This data comes in a multitude of formats, targeted at virtually any type of device, thanks to progress in web and mobile technology. Electronic healthcare records (EHRs), incorporating this data, are also adapting, to allow for the inclusion of medical imagery and other multimedia files, enabling the protection of privacy in their storage and transmission, while also allowing their rapid and reliable communication when needed.

Looking back about 10 years, in a research project pursued at Arizona State University, multimedia technology was employed to help people rehabilitate after a stroke[1]. Movements that a person made during a training session after his or her stroke were captured by a real-time motion-capture system and translated into real-time musical feedback. This direct feedback guided the person in training and correcting his or her movements during rehabilitation. Although the technical setup was extremely large at that time, this work demonstrated well how multimedia could help enable interaction, showing its potential for becoming an integral part of larger interactive systems. Another example is the award-winning work from Curtin University in Australia in which researchers employed pervasive multimedia technology and touchpads for autism interventions[2]. The focus for design was driven by the needs of teachers, parents and autistic children altogether. While multimedia is acting as the part of a pervasive stimulus to the child the media moves into the background in itself while facilitating a learning platform that integrates early intervention in the child's daily life. These examples show how multimedia is enabler for visionary applications solving societal challenges of our age. In this workshop we explore the challenges and potentials of multimedia for and in personal health and health care.

2. WORKSHOP GOALS AND PROGRAM

Research in multimedia and health is driven by the current technological advancements in sensors and personalized healthcare, with many healthcare applications addressed by core multimedia research questions, such as monitoring daily life

MM '16, October 15-19, 2016, Amsterdam, The Netherlands.
ACM 978-1-4503-3603-1/16/10.
http://dx.doi.org/10.1145/2964284.2980536

[1] Mixed Reality System for Stroke Rehabilitation. School of Arts, Media and Engineering. Arizona State University. http://ame2.asu.edu/projects/mrrehab/.

[2] TOBY: Early Intervention in Autism through Technologyhttp://tobyplaypad.com/research/

activities, building lifestyle and behavioral profiles, physiological and cognitive multimedia-based monitoring for health status assessment, among others. Applications can be as specific as the recognition of food to estimate its nutritional content, multimodal visualization and correlation of lifestyle parameters to understand conditions such as dementia, or the development of personalized home assistants, to help the elderly in their daily life, as society ages and the care ratio dwindles. There is an increasing number of research work that shows how core multimedia research is became an important enabler for applications with an application and relevance for the societal questions of health.

The special characteristic of the workshop is the joining of a challenging and highly application-oriented domain with more fundamental multimedia research and advances in the related technologies. The workshop is of a very interdisciplinary nature which is reflected by its faceted topics of contributions.

- *Visualization of Complex Health Data on Mobile Devices* by Jochen Meyer and Susanne Boll
- *On the Development of an ASR-based Multimedia Game for Speech Therapy: Preliminary Results* by Mario Ganzeboom, Emre Yilmaz, Catia Cucchiarini and Helmer Strik.
- *Evaluation of A Multi-Tier Heterogeneous Sensors Network for Patient Monitoring The case of a Cardiologic Intensive Care Unit in Benin*
  Thierry Edoh, Athanase Atchome and Bidossessi R. U. Alahassa
- *A Dual Screen Concept for User-Controlled Hypervideo-Based Physiotherapy Training* by Britta Meixner, Christian Handschigl, Stefan John and Michael Granitzer
- *A technology platform for enabling behavioural change as a "PATHway" towards better self-management of CVD* by Kieran Moran, Haolin Wei, David Monaghan, Noel E. O Connor, Catherine Woods, Dimitrios Zarpalas, Anargyros Chatzitofis, Petros Daras, Jens Piesk and Andrew Pomazanskyi
- *Supporting Self-Assembly: The IKEA Effect on Mobile Health Persuasive Technology* by Yunlong Wang, Ulrike Pfeil and Harald Reiterer
- *Multimodal Sensing and Intelligent Fusion for Remote Care and Support* Thanos G. Stavropoulos, Georgios Meditskos, Alexia Briassouli and Ioannis Kompatsiaris
- *Perspectives on tablet-based multimedia interventions for behavioral health: populations, venues, and delivery modalities* by Alexander Bennett, Ian Aronson, Honoria Guarino and Theodore Bania
- *Focus on accessibility: Multimodal healthcare technology for all* by Jobke Wentzel and Thea van der Geest.

The workshop program reflects the interdisciplinary challenges in different fields of personal health and health care. We also expect the workshop to be highly attractive to the European community related to multimedia and health.

3. ORGANIZERS

The workshop will be held the first time. It bases, however, on the research background and experience by the organizers in both multimedia and health. It is also based on previous events which have been organized by the organizers that strongly relate to multimedia and health such as PervasiveHealth 2014, SenseCam Symposium 2010, the ACM MM 2013 Workshop on Multimedia Indexing and Information Retrieval for Healthcare, the Workshop on Cooking and Eating Activities 2015, the ICIP 2015 Special Session On Image/Video Indexing And Retrieval For Healthcare, among others.

The organizers are working in the different fields of multimedia in health such as tracking of nutrition[1], digital interventions for personal health [2], activity recognition in lifelogging [3] using statistical methods, signal processing and computer vision [4], from multimodal heterogeneous data [5] and interpretation for personal health [6].

4. REFERENCES

[1] Kiyoharu Aizawa, Makoto Ogawa: FoodLog: Multimedia Tool for Healthcare Applications. IEEE MultiMedia 22(2): 4-8 (2015)

[2] Jutta Fortmann, Vanessa Cobus, Wilko Heuten, Susanne Boll: WaterJewel: design and evaluation of a bracelet to promote a better drinking behaviour. MUM 2014: 58-67.

[3] Terziyski, Stefan and Albatal, Rami and Gurrin, Cathal (2015) Fast human activity recognition in lifelogging. MultiMedia Modeling, 8936 . pp. 369-379. ISSN 0302-9743

[4] C.F. Crispim-Junior, V. Buso, K. Avgerinakis, G. Meditskos, A. Briassouli, J. Benois-Pineau, I. Kompatsiaris, F. Bremond, "Semantic Event Fusion of Different Visual Modality Concepts for Activity Recognition", Special Issue on Multimodal Human Pose Recovery and Behavior Analysis, IEEE Transactions on Pattern Analysis and Machine Intelligence (TPAMI), accepted for publication, 2016.

[5] Hyungik Oh, Laleh Jalali, Ramesh Jain: An intelligent notification system using context from real-time personal activity monitoring. Multimedia and Expo (ICME'15), pp. 1-6, 2015.

[6] S. Boll, W. Heuten, and J. Meyer, "From tracking to personal health," Interactions, vol. 23, iss. 1, pp. 72-75, 2016.

Vision and Language Integration Meets Multimedia Fusion

Proceedings of ACM Multimedia 2016 Workshop

Marie-Francine Moens
KU Leuven
Heverlee, Belgium
sien.moens@cs.kuleuven.be

Katerina Pastra
CSRI / ILSP / ATHENA
Athens, Greece
kpastra@csri.gr

Kate Saenko
UMass Lowell
Lowell, MA, USA
saenko@cs.uml.edu

Tinne Tuytelaars
KU Leuven
Heverlee, Belgium
tinne.tuytelaars@esat.kuleuven.be

ABSTRACT

Multimodal information fusion both at the signal and the semantics levels is a core part in most multimedia applications, including multimedia indexing, retrieval, summarization and others. Early or late fusion of modality-specific processing results has been addressed in multimedia prototypes since their very early days, through various methodologies including rule-based approaches, information-theoretic models and machine learning. Vision and Language are two of the predominant modalities that are being fused and which have attracted special attention in international challenges with a long history of results, such as TRECVid, ImageClef and others. During the last decade, vision-language semantic integration has attracted attention from traditionally non-interdisciplinary research communities, such as Computer Vision and Natural Language Processing. This is due to the fact that one modality can greatly assist the processing of another providing cues for disambiguation, complementary information and noise/error filtering. The latest boom of deep learning methods has opened up new directions in joint modelling of visual and co-occurring verbal information in multimedia discourse. The workshop on Vision and Language Integration Meets Multimedia Fusion has been held during the workshop weekend of the ACM Multimedia 2016 Conference and the European Conference on Computer Vision (ECCV 2016) on October 16, 2016 in Amsterdam, the Netherlands. The proceedings contain seven selected long papers, which have been orally presented at the workshop, and three abstracts of the invited keynote speeches. The papers and abstracts discuss data collection, representation learning, deep learning approaches, matrix and tensor factorization methods and graph based clustering with regard to the fusion of multimedia data. A variety of applications is presented including image captioning, summarization of news, video hyperlinking, sub-shot segmentation of user generated video, cross-modal classification, cross-modal question-answering, and the detection of misleading metadata of user generated video.

The workshop is organized and supported by the EU COST action iV&L Net, the European Network on Integrating Vision and Language: Combining Computer Vision and Language Processing for Advanced Search, Retrieval, Annotation and Description of Visual Data (IC 1307, 2014-2018).

CCS Concepts

•Information systems → Multimedia and multimodal retrieval; *Web mining;* **•Computing methodologies → Natural language processing; Computer vision;**

Keywords

Cross-modal and multimodal processing of visual and language data

MM '16 October 15-19, 2016, Amsterdam, Netherlands
ACM ISBN 978-1-4503-3603-1/16/10.
DOI: http://dx.doi.org/10.1145/2964284.2980537

Seventh International Workshop on Human Behavior Understanding (HBU 2016)

Mohamed Chetouani
Univ. Pierre et Marie CURIE
CC173-4 Place Jussieu
75005 Paris, France
chetouani@isir.upmc.fr

Jeffrey Cohn
University of Pittsburgh
4327 Sennott Square
Pittsburgh, PA 15260, USA
jeffcohn@pitt.edu

Albert Ali Salah
Boğaziçi University
34342 Bebek
Istanbul, Turkey
salah@boun.edu.tr

ABSTRACT

With advances in pattern recognition and multimedia computing, it becomes possible to analyze human behavior via multimodal sensors at varying time-scales, levels of analysis, and meaning. This ability opens up far-ranging possibilities for multimedia and multimodal interaction. Research has the, potential to endow computers with the capacity to detect and understand people's actions and activities and infer their attitudes, preferences, personality, and social relationships. This workshop brings together researchers in this rapidly emerging area and especially those concerned with behavior analysis and multimedia in children.

Keywords

Human behavior understanding; computer analysis of human behavior

1. INTRODUCTION

The HBU workshops gather researchers dealing with the problem of modeling human behavior under its multiple facets (expression of emotions, display of complex social and relational behaviors, performance of individual or joint actions, etc.). This year, the seventh edition of the workshop was organized with challenges of designing solutions with children in mind, with the cross-pollination of different disciplines, bringing together researchers of multimedia, robotics, HCI, artificial intelligence, pattern recognition, interaction design, ambient intelligence, and psychology. The diversity of human behavior, the richness of multi-modal data that arises from its analysis, and the multitude of applications that demand rapid progress in this area ensure that the HBU Workshops provide a timely and relevant discussion and dissemination platform.

The HBU Workshops are previously organized as satellite to ICPR (Istanbul, Turkey, 2010), AMI (Amsterdam, The Netherlands, 2011), IROS (Vilamoura, Portugal, 2012), ACM Multimedia (Barcelona, Spain, 2013), ECCV (Zurich, Switzerland, 2014) and UBICOMP (Osaka, Japan, 2015) Conferences, with different focus themes.

The focus theme of this year's HBU workshop is **behavior analysis and multimedia for children**. With each passing year, children begin using computers and related devices at younger and younger ages. The initial age of computer usage is steadily getting lower, yet there are many issues open in children's use of computers and multimedia. In order to tailor multimedia applications to children, we need smarter applications that understand and respond to the users' behavior, distinguishing children and adults if necessary. Collecting data from children and working with children in interactive applications call for additional skills and interdisciplinary collaborations. Subsequently, this year's workshop promoted research on automatic analysis of children's behavior.

2. TOPICS

We have solicited papers whose topics would span items from the following topic dimensions, and/or targeting a focus theme challenge:

1. **Human Behavior Analysis Systems**
    - Action and activity recognition
    - Affect analysis
    - Social signal processing
    - Face analysis
    - Gestures and haptic interaction
    - Voice and speech analysis
    - Learning and adaptation
    - Gaze, attention and saliency
2. **Theory and Methodology of Human Interactive Behaviors**
    - Theoretical frameworks of behavior analysis
    - Data collection, annotation, and benchmarking
    - User studies and human factors
    - Interaction design
    - Temporal models
3. **Applications**
    - Education
    - Creativity
    - Visual and digital arts
    - Games and entertainment

MM '16 October 15-19, 2016, Amsterdam, Netherlands

ACM ISBN 978-1-4503-3603-1/16/10.

DOI: http://dx.doi.org/10.1145/2964284.2980538

- Healthcare and well-being
- Robotics

4. **Focus Theme Challenges: Behavior analysis for children**
   - Age estimation
   - Detection of abusive and aggressive behaviors, cyberbullying
   - Inappropriate content detection
   - Privacy and ethics of multimedia access for children
   - Databases collected from children
   - Monitoring children during social interactions
   - Investigations into children's interaction with multimedia content

3. FORMAT AND REVIEWING

The Workshop is organized as a one day, single track event with oral and poster presentations, and a panel discussion on the focus theme, organized by Dr. Rita Cucchiara (Univ. of Modena and Reggio Emilia). We thank Dr. Cucchiara for her continuing contributions to the HBU Workshop.

We have received 17 submissions, of which 10 were accepted for oral presentation in the workshop (the acceptance rate is 58%). Each paper was reviewed by at least two members of the technical program committee. The papers submitted by the co-chairs were handled by other chairs both during reviewing and during decisions. The EasyChair system was used for processing the papers.

4. KEYNOTES

The keynote speakers of the Workshop are Dr. Paul Vogt (Tilburg University), with a talk entitled "Modelling child language acquisition in interaction from corpora" and Dr. Isabela Granic (Radboud University Nijmegen), with a talk on "Bridging developmental science and game design to video games that build emotional resilience". We thank our keynotes for their contributions.

5. TECHNICAL PROGRAM COMMITTEE

We thank our technical program committee for their support:

- Elisabeth André, Univ. Augsburg, DE
- Lisa Anthony, University of Florida, US
- Oya Aran, Idiap Research Institute, CH
- Antonio Camurri, University of Genova, IT
- Marco Cristani, University of Verona, IT
- Abhinav Dhall, University of Canberra, AU
- Hamdi Dibeklioğlu, Delft University of Technology, NL
- Weidong Geng, Zhejiang University, CN
- Hatice Gunes, University of Cambridge, GB
- Sibel Halfon, Bilgi University, TR
- Zakia Hammal, Carnegie Mellon University, US
- Dirk Heylen, University of Twente, NL
- Andri Ioannou, Cyprus University of Technology, CY
- Mohan Kankanhalli, National University of Singapore, SG
- Alexey Karpov, SPIIRAS, RU
- Heysem Kaya, Namık Kemal University, TR
- Cem Keskin, Microsoft Research, US
- Hatice Kose, Istanbul Technical University, TR
- Ben Kröse, University of Amsterdam, NL
- Matei Mancas, University of Mons, BE
- Panos Markopoulos, Eindhoven Univ. of Technology, NL
- Louis-Philippe Morency, Carnegie Mellon University, US
- Florian Mueller, RMIT, AU
- Helio Pedrini, University of Campinas, BR
- Francisco Florez Revuelta, Kingston University, GB
- Stefan Scherer, University of Southern California, USA
- Ben Schouten, Eindhoven Univ. of Technology, NL
- Suleman Shahid, University of Tilburg, NL
- Reiner Wichert, AHS Assisted Home Solutions, DE
- Bian Yang, Norwegian University of Science and Technology, NO

We also thank the following external reviewers for their help: Alp Kındıroğlu, Necati Cihan Camgöz.

6. ACKNOWLEDGMENTS

This workshop is supported by Boğaziçi University project BAP-12060.

Author Index

www.ingramcontent.com/pod-product-compliance
Lightning Source LLC
LaVergne TN
LVHW080102011026
849160LV00013B/1016
* 9 7 8 1 4 5 0 3 4 6 8 7 0 *